Legal Information Buyer's Guide and Reference Manual

2014

by
Kendall F. Svengalis

N. Stonington, Connecticut

Legal Information Buyer's Guide and Reference Manual

Kendall F. Svengalis

New England LawPress
204 Wyassup Road
N. Stonington, CT 06359
Mailing address:
P.O. Box 331
Westerly, RI 02891
Editorial: (860) 535-0362
Orders and Editorial FAX: (860) 535-0378

Cover design and layout by Hillary Talmadge
Cover photo by Ellen Svengalis

Trademarks

ISBN: 978-0-9819995-8-6

CD-ROM: 978-0-9819995-9-3

Printed in the United States of America

Dedicated to the memory of my parents,

Frank Anthony and Alvida Linnea Svengalis,

to whom I owe my love of books;

and to my brother,

Cordell Meredith Svengalis

Preface to the Eighteenth Edition

The Legal Information Buyer's Guide and Reference Manual is an outgrowth of my long-standing interest in legal bibliography and the cost-effective acquisition of legal materials. For twenty-years, acquisitions-related activities occupied a major portion of my work as the Rhode Island State Law Librarian. Now, as an independent author, publisher, and retired adjunct faculty member at the University of Rhode Island's Graduate School of Library and Information Studies, I continue to take an active interest in the affairs of the legal publishing industry and its impact on law libraries and other consumers of legal information. This interest has coincided with the most dramatic developments in the legal publishing industry since the latter part of the 19th century. Between 1985 and 1995, most of my professional activity in this area took the form of articles written for an audience of law librarians frustrated by the high cost of legal publications and the practices of certain publishers. From 1988 to 1994, I edited The CRIV Sheet, the Newsletter of the Committee on Relations with Information Vendors of the American Association of Law Libraries (AALL). During those years, I was uniquely positioned to monitor the practices of legal publishers and to track the developments in the industry as a whole, aided in no small part by my fellow committee members and scores of dedicated law librarians who have shared their knowledge and insights with me. The first edition of the Legal Information Buyer's Guide and Reference Manual appeared just as the shape of legal publishing began to coalesce around three major international corporations.

Over the past twenty-two years, the legal publishing industry has been in an almost constant state of change and upheaval, reflecting global trends toward corporate consolidation, the impact of technology upon the delivery of legal information, and the increased profitability of the legal publishing segment of the economy. While this consolidation has ushered in dramatic and enhanced product developments, it has also brought with it rising costs which have had an adverse effect upon the ability of many law libraries to maintain collection quality. Rapidly escalating prices for legal information have forced may law libraries to re-evaluate their collections and to implement a variety of cost-saving measures as a means of controlling expenditures. While the impact of these developments has been most acute in publicly supported law libraries, it has also forced changes in the buying habits of lawyer-practitioners.

It became clear to me that any serious attempt to create a more hospitable environment for the purchase of legal information would depend upon better-educated consumers. This book remains the first serious attempt to provide consumers with the kind of information needed to make appropriate and cost-effective purchasing decisions and to bring the costs of legal information under control. The book's initial premise remains the same: that there is no one "right way" to buy legal materials and that economic concerns need to be balanced against professional needs. Accordingly, I have attempted to provide consumers with substantive and cost information which can form the basis for appropriate acquisition decisions. In addition, I have provided numerous cost-saving tips and strategies which can be utilized in a variety of circumstances and environments.

I am extremely gratified by the warm and enthusiastic response the publication of this guide has engendered among the legal and law library communities both in the United States and abroad since its first appearance in 1996. In September, 2004, **Legal Information Alert** included the **Legal Information Buyer's Guide & Reference Manual** in its list of the top 20 innovations in the field of legal information over the prior twelve years.

It remains my hope that it will contribute to a more effective and consumer-friendly market for the purchase of legal information.

Acknowledgements

I am deeply grateful to my daughter, Hillary Svengalis Talmadge, who has assumed responsibility for the design and layout of this edition. Her efforts build upon the work of my brother, Cordell Svengalis, who sheparded the book though its first twelve editions. I also wish to thank my wife, Ellen Haffling Svengalis, for her expert editorial assistance in the process of preparing this edition and for her cover photograph and design.

The author also wishes to express his deepest gratitude to the many colleagues in the field of law librarianship who have contributed in various ways to the development of this book over the past twenty years. These include my colleagues in the American Association of Law Libraries (AALL), Law Librarians of New England, the State, Court and County Law Libraries Section of AALL, and the New England Law Library Consortium, whose professional input over the years has been invaluable. I particularly wish to thank the past Chairs and members of the Committee on Relations with Information Vendors (CRIV) with whom I have had the good fortune to work during the six years that I served as editor of the Committee's newsletter, The CRIV Sheet. Their advice and counsel contributed immeasurably to the development of the ideas expressed in this book. I wish to thank Maria Sekula, formerly of the Social Law Library, who first encouraged me to publish on the subject of cost-effective acquisitions.

I am also indebted to the many law librarians across the country who contributed information for the State Legal Publications chapter or who have contributed pricing and supplementation data, including Margaret Ackroyd, Mary Aldridge, Barbara Allen, Anita Anderson, Marvin Anderson, Kay Andrus, Cynthia Aninao, Donald A. Arndt, Paul Axel-Lute, Margaret Maes Axtmann, David P. Bader, Anne Bardolph, Donna Barratt, Marsha Baum, A. Michael Beaird, Sandra A. Beehler, Beth Behrens, Joan Bellistri, Dennis Benamati, Marcie Bierlein, Carol Billings, Richard Boaz, Peter Boll, Sylvia Brown, Kelly Browne, Catherine A. Bruhn, Heather Buckwalter, Colleen Buskirk, Colleen Cable, Jean Callihan, Lois Calvert, Mary Lou Calvin, Francis D. Campbell, Martha Campbell, Barbara Carde, Kathy Carlson, Emily Carr, Georgia Chadwick, Mike Chiorazzi, Christopher Chiofolo, Shelley K. Clement, Wes Cochran, Jane Colwin, Nola Crawford, Joseph Custer, Shirley David, Julie Davis, Tom Davis, Susan Delp, Pam Dempsey, Rita Dermody, Mary Dickson, Austin Doherty, Nancy Downing, Mark Durbin, Charles R. Dyer, Jean Eisenhauer, Marie Emerson, Marie Erickson, Mary Ertl, Teresa Farley, Mary Farner, Kerri Fedale, Cherie Feenker, Cynthia Fellows, Michelle Finerty, Joel Fishman, Catherine Fitz, Kathryn C. Fitzhugh, LeGrande Fletcher, Dennis Fossum, Diane Frake, Ruth Fraley, Kevin Fredette, Anne-Marie Fulfer, Sarah Galligan, Ellen M. Gibson, Christine L. Graesser, Pamela J. Gregory, John Hagemann, Brian Harkins, Gail Hartzell, Janeen Heath, Jill Henderson, Lisa Henry, Ana Hinman, Jean Holcombe, Sally Holterhoff, Byron Hill, Tim Holthoff, Mary Hotchkiss, Sallie M. Howard, Michael Hughes, Anne F. Jennings, Louise Jensen, Mary Kay Jung, Jacqueline J. Jurkins, James Kelly, Kathryn Kerchof, Berry Kern, Thomas Killian, Claire King, Carol Klink, Joan Kohout, Marcia Koslov, Ann S. Koto, Casey Kralik, Marcella Kramer, Kathy Krisciunas, Cindy Landau, Martha Lappe, Brenda Larison, Mary Lu Linnane, Anna Belle Leiserson, Jennifer Lentz, Tim Lewis, Letty Limbach, Ann Long, Terry Long, Mon Yin Lung, Janice Lustiger, Lovisa Lyman, Michael Lynch, Sandy Marz, David S. Matthewson, Constance Matts, Constance E. Matzen, Catherine McGuire, Jennifer McLean, Judy Meadows, Jan Medved, Charlotte Melius, Pamela Melton, Janet Meyer, Lawrence R. Meyer, Laurie Bingham Miller, Mary E. Miller, Mary F. Miller, Michael S. Miller, Jack Montgomery, Suzanne Morrison, James Mumm, Lynn Murray, Rajguru Nalini, Kay E. Newman, Carol Nicholson, Deborah Norwood, Michael O'Brien, Beth Odsen, Kent C. Olson, Susan L. Orchard, Laura Orr, Joyce Pacenza, Suzanne Parent, Judith Parisi, Alison Perry, Laura Pershing, Elizabeth Peterson, Tammi R. Pickering, Joan Pilgrim, Karlye Pillai, Larry Piper, Peter Pogacar, Howard Polansky, Marjorie Price, Nancy Rabasca, Larry Raftery, Lynn Randall, Mary Rice, Rob Richards, Linda Robertson, Terri Ross, Gordon Russell, Kay Schlueter, Dennis Schrader, Mary Searles, Gitelle Seer, Anita Shew, Lynette Simonsen, Karen Smith, Fritz Snyder, Susan Southwick, Candice Spurlin, Louise Stafford, Colleen Stella, Jerry Stephens, Joe K. Stephens, Jonathan C. Stock, Richard Stroup, Bobbie Studwell, Carol Suhre, Kathie J. Sullivan, Melissa Surber, Christine H. Swan, Elizabeth Swan, David M. Turkalo, Reba Turnquist, Richard Vaughan, Donna C. Wair, Bill Walker, Mary Louise Walker, Betty Ward, Lyn Warmath, Victoria Weber, Margaret Webster, Maureen Well, Bill Wells, Michael Whiteman, Marie Wiechman, Mary Lou Wilker, Linda Will, Jane Woldow, the late Bardie Wolfe, Irene Wong, Jacqueline S. Wright, Rene Yucht, Claudia Zaher, and Joyce Ziegler. I remain indebted to Hazel Inglis, formerly Director of the Law Library at the Southern New England School of Law and Librarian at Brown, Rudnick in Providence, who provided invaluable editorial assistance on the first edition.

I also wish to thank Sarah Palmer at the American Bar Association; Marilyn Bromley of BNA; Linda Lev-Dunton of CCH, Andrew Given of PLI, Dee Kitzen at Juris Publishing, Ann Grady of LexisNexis Matthew Bender, and Mike Garner of Wolters Kluwer Law & Business for its kind assistance in providing editorial, pricing and supplementation cost information.

Table of Contents

Preface to 18th Edition iv
Acknowledgements v
Table of Contents vi

PART I: **A General View....1**
Chapter 1. Introduction....3
Chapter 2. A Brief History of Legal Publishing....7
Chapter 3. Taking on the Legal Publishers: the Making of the FTC Guides....21
Chapter 4. Building and Maintaining Your Law Library....25
Chapter 5. Evaluating Legal Materials....33
Chapter 6. The Question of Supplements....37
Chapter 7. Unsolicited Shipments, Telemarketing and Other Practices....45
Chapter 8. Used Law Books: The Economical Alternative....49

PART II: **Categories of Legal Publications....53**
Chapter 9. State Statutes....55
Chapter 10. Federal Statutes....59
Chapter 11. Regulations....63
Chapter 12. Municipal Ordinances....67
Chapter 13. CaseReporters....79
Chapter 14. Annotated Reports....75
Chapter 15. Digests....83
Chapter 16. Citators....89
Chapter 17. Legal Encyclopedias....95
Chapter 18. LooseleafServices....101
Chapter 19. LegalPeriodicals....103
Chapter 20. Legal Newspapers....107
Chapter 21. Legal Newsletters....111
Chapter 22. Legal Reference Titles....113
Chapter 23. Legal Acquisitions Toolbox....135
Chapter 24. Legal Resources on CD-ROM....143
Chapter 25. Computer-Assisted Legal Research....151
Chapter 26. Finding Law on the Internet....169
Chapter 27. Legal Treatises: Administrative Law to Zoning....177
Administrative Law....182
Admiralty and Maritime Law....187
Advertising Law....190
Agency Law....192
Antitrust Law....192
Appellate Practice....202
Arbitration and Alternative Dispute Resolution....209
Arts, Entertainment and Sports Law....216
Automobile Law and Practice....225
Banking and Finance Law....230
Bankruptcy Law....240
Civil Rights....245
Class Actions....250
Commercial Law....253
Computer Law....264
Constitutional Law....270
Construction Law....281
Contract Law....287
Copyright Law....293
Corporations....296
Criminal Law....308
Disabilities Law....327
Education Law....330
Elder Law....337
Environmental Law....345
Equity Jurisprudence....358
Evidence....359

Family Law 370
Federal Practice and Procedure....................381
Gambling Law....................390
Health and Hospital Law....................394
Immigration Law....................405
Indian Law 411
Insurance Law....................415
Judges and Judicial Conduct....................423
Juries and Jury Instructions....................430
Labor and Employment Law....................434
Legal Forms....................456
Legal Profession....................460
Medical Jurisprudence....................494
Military Law and National Security....................501
Municipal Corporations....................512
Natural Resources and Energy Law....................517
Nonprofit Corporations....................521
Partnership....................524
Patents, Trademarks and Intellectual Property....................525
Products Liability.................... 540
Public Utilities.................... 542
Real Property....................546
Religion and the Law....................556
Restatements of the Law....................559
Securities Law....................562
Social Security Law....................570
Statutory Construction....................572
Taxation....................575
Telecommunications Law....................585
Tort Law....................588
Trial Practice....................599
Trusts and Estates....................619
Workers' Compensation Law....................628
Zoning and Planning Law....................631

Chapter 28. **State Legal Publications: A Practitioner's Guide....................637**
Alabama....................637
Alaska....................639
Arizona....................641
Arkansas....................642
California....................644
Colorado....................647
Connecticut....................649
Delaware....................652
District of Columbia....................653
Florida....................655
Georgia....................657
Hawaii....................659
Idaho....................661
Illinois....................662
Indiana....................665
Iowa....................667
Kansas....................669
Kentucky....................670
Louisiana....................672
Maine....................674
Maryland....................675
Massachusetts....................677
Michigan....................680
Minnesota....................682
Mississippi....................684

Missouri ... 686
Montana ... 688
Nebraska ... 689
Nevada ... 691
New Hampshire ... 693
New Jersey ... 694
New Mexico ... 696
New York ... 698
North Carolina ... 701
North Dakota ... 703
Ohio ... 704
Oklahoma ... 706
Oregon ... 708
Pennsylvania ... 710
Rhode Island ... 712
South Carolina ... 714
South Dakota ... 716
Tennessee ... 717
Texas ... 719
Utah ... 721
Vermont ... 723
Virginia ... 724
Washington ... 727
West Virginia ... 729
Wisconsin ... 730
Wyoming ... 732

Appendices ... 735
Appendix A. Leading Legal Publishers: Their History, and Product Lines ... 737
Appendix B. Legal Publishers: Addresses and Contact Numbers ... 761
Appendix C. Used Lawbook Dealers: Addresses and Contact Numbers ... 785
Appendix D. State and Local Legal Newspapers ... 787
Appendix E. Representative Used Lawbook Prices ... 803
Appendix F. AALL Guide to Fair Business Practices for Legal Publishers ... 811
Appendix G. A Selective List of Looseleaf Services ... 819
Appendix H. Costs of Legal Treatises Spreadsheet ... 825
Appendix I. State Statutory Codes by Publisher ... 859
Appendix J. Online Coverage of Appellate Court Decisions ... 861
Appendix K. Cost Saving Tips ... 863
Appendix L. Bibliography ... 867
Index ... 875
About the Author ... 877

Part I
A General View

Chapter 1: Introduction

The worlds of legal information and legal publishing have undergone a dramatic transformation over the past forty years. From an environment dominated by the printed word to one dominated by digital formats and computer-assisted legal research tools, the roles of the publisher and user have undergone a mega-shift. As an attorney, law librarian, or other legal professional, you cannot function without access to accurate and timely legal and general information, whether in the form of statutes, court reports, administrative regulations, municipal ordinances, court rules, forms, legal treatises, encyclopedias, practice books, citator services, law reviews, legal newspapers and newsletters. That information is now being delivered to the end-user primarily in digital form, with the printed formats taking a back seat. Even among the general population, sales of books on Kindle now exceed those in paperback form. Legal researchers do most of their work utilizing comprehensive proprietary online legal databases. The proper representation of your clients in the third millennium requires nothing less. As a legal professional, it is essential that you have a sophisticated understanding of the world of legal information and the legal information resources in your field of specialization, as well as an ability to utilize that information effectively.

We are living in an age dominated by information, otherwise described as a post-industrial age. The United States has been transformed from a nation that manufactures products and goods into a nation that produces, enhances, processes, and sells information. Lawyers and other legal professionals make their living transforming raw information, legal and otherwise, into knowledge and solutions for their clients. The attorney's role in this age of information is dramatically complicated by its sheer volume.

It has been estimated that, in 1900, the entire body of information in the world was doubling every seventy-five years. By 1950, it was doubling every twenty-five years, and by 1980, every five years. A 2010 IBM study projected that, by 2014, the amount of digital information would be doubling every eleven hours. Indeed, as individuals, we are increasingly awash with information and data, making us ever more dependent on tools which can sort and select that which is most useful and desirable. In the legal publishing field, synergies created by the consolidation of the industry have precipitated a heightened level of product development not only illustrated by the dramatic enhancements to Westlaw and LexisNexis, but also by the introduction of a number of competing online legal information providers trying to carve out a niche.

Attorneys have responded to this information explosion by specializing. From the perspective of legal information, an attorney in the 21st century simply cannot practice in more than one major regulatory field and still do justice to his or her clients. For example, simply monitoring environmental regulations on a daily basis is a full time job for an information professional. Legal information vendors have responded to this explosion by developing and marketing more specialized legal reference tools. While legal publishers may still maintain the currency of such broad-based products as Corpus Juris Secundum or American Jurisprudence 2d for their existing customers, such products are increasingly becoming dinosaurs in the this new digital world. Consequently, legal information providers are directing their energies to new product development, toward the specialized legal information products, and the application of sophisticated computer-based technologies to integrated legal information packaging and retrieval.

Transformation of the Legal Publishing Industry

Legal publishing is undoubtedly one of the most dynamic sectors of the American economy, evolving into a multi-billion dollar business that has attracted the interest of leading foreign investors. In the 1980's and early 1990's, as antitrust standards were relaxed, the legal community witnessed a dramatic consolidation of the legal publishing industry. The leading English, Canadian and Dutch conglomerates snapped up one domestic American legal publisher after another. In sharp contrast to 1977, when at least 23 legal publishers of some size and reputation were separately owned (along with scores of smaller ones), the bulk of legal publishing in the new millennium has been brought under three major corporate umbrellas: Thomson Reuters (Canadian-British), Reed-Elsevier (British-Dutch), and Wolters Kluwer (Dutch). Under their new ownership, these consolidated entities have responded to the information revolution by reorganizing product lines, restructuring operations, and developing more sophisticated and integrated means of information retrieval and delivery. In 2010, a new competitor entered the online market—Bloomberg Law, which acquired BNA in 2011.

The most dramatic of these developments took place in 1996 when the Thomson Corporation of Canada purchased the venerable West Publishing Company for $3.425 billion, creating the world's largest legal publishing enterprise that now controls roughly 40% of the domestic market in legal information, as well as a sizable share of the world market. Though the merger of Thomson and West raised a host of antitrust concerns, particularly among law library consumers, the Department of Justice's Antitrust Division allowed the merger to proceed with only minor and inconsequential divestitures. The fruits of the Justice Department's misguided approval of this historic merger are clearly evident thirteen years later. On April 17, 2008, the Thomson Corporation acquired Reuters, a leading network of media, financial and economic services, creating the world's leading source for business and professional information. The Thomson family owns 53 percent of the resulting Thomson Reuters Corporation.

Seeds of Industry Consolidation

The seeds of the present organization of the legal publishing industry were planted in the late 1970s, when the Thomson Corporation of Canada came to appreciate the strategic importance of legal publishing from an investment perspective. High profitability, reliable cash flow from subscription sales, a relatively affluent customer base, and lower risks in product development all contributed to the desirability of acquiring legal publishing entities. What distinguishes this recent wave of mergers and acquisitions, however, from those that preceded them is that these are being played out on a global stage by foreign-owned corporations primarily interested in maximizing their profit potential.

Back in the days when they were the two major competitive forces in the industry, West and Lawyers Cooperative claimed to offer complete systems of legal information--West around its National Reporter and Key Number systems, and Lawyers Cooperative around its Total Client-Service Library. However much they and their customers may have believed their marketing claims, legal information consumers still had to shop elsewhere for a variety of additional products, including citators, looseleaf services, legal treatises, and practice books, as well as legal periodicals, newsletters, and government publications. As the merger frenzy picked up steam in the late 1980s and early 1990s, however, it became obvious to industry analysts that future global competitiveness would require the integration of a full range of legal research products and services under common ownership. This product integration was also converging with the growing power of online research, which was already bringing these products straight to the lawyer's desktop.

Clearly, the acquisition of a major on-line service was to be the sina qua non for any legal publishing enterprise, which hoped to compete successfully in this new world of legal research product integration. Conversely, the lack of a complementary line of analytical and practice products would handicap an online provider whose aim was to compete on this emerging global landscape. A successful legal publisher in this new environment has to be in a position to offer legal information consumers a complete and integrated product line.

The Legal Publishing Mega-Mall

Since the dust settled on this merger frenzy in the late 1990s, the legal publishing industry has become far more clearly defined and highly concentrated. Two major publishing giants—Thomson Reuters and Reed Elsevier--stand like two major anchor stores at opposite ends of the Legal Publishing Mega-Mall. Their two leading legal information companies—Thomson West and LexisNexis—each provide legal information consumers with an integrated product line consisting of a major on-line research service (WestlawNext and LexisNexis), a sophisticated and citator service (KeyCite and Shepard's), a significant line of primary law and a large body of analytical and legal practice products in both print and online. Behind them stand a stable of news, financial, tax, medical, and scientific services.

A third conglomerate, Wolters Kluwer now stands on the second tier, with a solid presence in the field of current awareness and analytical tools. The company is organized into four major divisions: Legal & Regulatory; Tax & Accounting; Health; and Financial & Compliance. The Legal & Regulatory and Tax & Accounting divisions, which serve markets in the United States, Canada and Asia Pacific, are comprised of two major information segments: Wolters Kluwer Tax and Accounting; and Wolters Kluwer Law & Business. In the United States, the leading brands are Wolters Kluwer Law & Business (formerly Aspen Law & Business), CCH (formerly Commerce Clearing House), and Loislaw. Wolters Kluwer's acquisition of Loislaw.com in December 2000 provided it with the base from which to integrate its various product lines into an electronic environment. However, Loislaw is a hardly a competitive threat to either Westlaw or LexisNexis. It commands but a thin slice of the domestic online legal research market, lacks an editorially-enhanced citator service of proven value to the American legal community, has far fewer (but growing) analytical works in its catalog, and is now facing stiff competition from other, sometimes low-cost, CALR providers, including Casemaker, Fastcase, VersusLaw, and Bloomberg Law.

The remainder of the mall is filled with dozens of smaller specialty boutiques, offering everything from inexpensively priced online access to primary law, practice books, subject specific treatises and CD-ROMs (now on their way out), monographs newsletters, and regulatory awareness products. Ironically, Loislaw.com, which once proudly held itself out as an independent and less costly on-line alternative for legal information consumers, found itself a takeover target after its stock price plummeted in 2000. The largest American legal publisher still independent after this thirty-year wave of mergers and acquisitions was, until recently, Bureau of National Affairs (BNA), an employee-owned company headquartered in Arlington, Virginia. In August, 2011, however, it was acquired by Bloomberg, which has been on the lookout for more substantive analytical content to enhance Bloomberg Law. Other niche legal publishers include the American Bar Association, Lawyers & Judges Publishing Company, Law Journal Publishing, James Publishing, Juris Publishing, and the Practising Law Institute. Publishers serving the academic market have substantially expanded their legal offerings, among them Carolina Academic Press, Cambridge University Press, and Oxford Press.

Whither the Consumer?

When the Justice Department approved the merger of Thomson and West in 1996, it sanctioned a legal publishing industry dominated by two major players. The divestiture of a few high profile products and a star pagination licensing provision were supposed to appease opponents of the merger, while preserving Thomson's ability to assemble more content rich computer-based products. Moreover, the Justice Department was convinced that weaknesses in West's star pagination copyright claims together with the momentum of vendor-neutral case citation, were sufficient to protect the public interest. Since 1996, however, it has stood silent while West consumed additional regional or specialty information providers, solidified its hold on the legal information consuming public, and raised prices to such industry-leading levels that the profit margin of its legal division now exceeds 25 per cent.

Benefits of Consolidation

It would be easy to find fault with the concentration of the industry without acknowledging some rather substantial benefits. There is no question that the merger wave has ushered in a heightened level of product development and integration. Both West (Thomson Reuters) and LexisNexis (Reed Elsevier) have successfully integrated multiple product lines in both print and on-line formats. Both Westlaw and LexisNexis have now moved almost exclusively to Web-based search engines and provided their users with a wider variety of primary and secondary materials than previously offered.

Citator "Wars" a Boon to Legal Researchers

What does all this mean for you as a consumer of legal information? Your research options have certainly increased dramatically, thanks to the combined efforts of the modern legal information industry. Research tools exist in a multiplicity of formats, with enhanced indexing and research aids. Computer-assisted legal research (CALR), CD-ROM, and the Internet make the task of locating desired information easier and faster, supplementing the traditional indexing and digesting tools which were fraught with human limitations. Supplementation options have also expanded to provide you with more current and up-to-date information. With this panoply of available research tools, the responsibility now falls upon you to select that complement of materials best suited to your practice needs and financial resources. The drive to the Web has also had a profound impact on the configuration of the typical law firm library which has abandoned its reliance on print tools with their rising and duplicative costs.

Competition between Shepard's and KeyCite, coupled with substantial investments in product development, will guarantee that each of these services will be far better and far less expensive than their ancestors. We have also witnessed acceleration in the development of new treatise titles, both from the major players and smaller niche publishers. Online product catalogs provide consumers with more content and pricing information than ever before, although the availability of historical supplementation cost information long sought by law librarians remains an elusive goal.

The relatively high cost of online legal research has also brought forth marketplace challenges from Casemaker, VersusLaw, Fastcase, and others who are prepared to offer consumers access to desired primary law databases at sharply reduced costs. Responding to these challenges, but also trying to more fully tap the substantial small law office market, Westlaw and LexisNexis now offer a variety of lower cost, fixed-rate plans tailor-made to the needs of small firms.

The Down Side of Concentration

Despite the benefits of consolidation, the legal publishing environment also presents a number of challenges and pitfalls for legal information consumers. Both initial and supplementation costs have continued their upward spiral from some publishers who are much more likely to milk subscription lists to maximize revenues than to cut deals for their best customers. Some legal publishers have creatively engineered the growth of multi-volume sets by increasing their size, and accelerating the revision cycle of bound volumes, including the expansion of tables of cases, indices, and ancillary research aids. The decline in the number of subscribers to print reporters, driven by the rising popularity of online access and by rising costs for office space in major cities, has forced up reporter costs at faster rates than in previous years. Hardcopy reporters, for example, are now routinely being given away by major firms for the cost of postage.

While there are no barriers to entering the legal information marketplace, the near-term prospects for greater price competition are substantially reduced by the current concentration of authors and editorial resources in the hands of the major legal publishers and by the expectation of similar profit margins by potential competitors who are likely to recognize that consumer buying decisions are more commonly based on substantive content than on price. An overriding concern is that smaller legal publishers with an attractive product line will find themselves tempting acquisition targets, as was Loislaw.com.

Using the Legal Information Buyer's Guide

Now in its eighteenth edition, the **Legal Information Buyer's Guide & Reference Manual** was written primarily to address the needs of the solo practitioner and the attorney in the small or medium-sized law firm operating without a law librarian, but will also serve as a valuable resource in a variety of law firm, academic and public libraries. It is based on the assumption that while lawyers are highly educated people, sophisticated in their knowledge of the law, they often lack even the most rudimentary understanding of the ways of legal publishing and the marketing techniques which unnecessarily siphon away their hard-earned dollars.

Several years ago, it was estimated that the average lawyer spends more than $4,000 per year on information, a figure greater than that of any other professional and more than six times that of the average doctor. A major portion of that $4,000 is wasted, either because many of the materials are poorly selected, are never or rarely used, are ill suited to the lawyer's specialty, or are overpriced. I would hazard to say that the average practitioner could reduce his or her expenditures for legal information by 50% without any essential loss of utility or currency. Applied judiciously, the information and strategies presented in this book will save you thousands of dollars in unnecessary expenditures over the course of your legal career.

Most of the advice offered in this book is information known to law librarians for years, but not effectively conveyed by them to the vast majority of practicing lawyers. These lessons have particularly escaped lawyers operating in small firms without trained information specialists. Law librarians have rubbed elbows with legal publishers for years at professional meetings and conferences. One of the messages we have heard repeatedly is that the primary market for legal information consists of lawyers, not law libraries. After all, we are told, there are more than a million lawyers in the United States and no more than 3,000 law libraries. A survey conducted by the American Association of Law Libraries, however, calls this assumption into question. Academic, governmental, corporate and law firm libraries with professional law librarians account for a substantial portion of the more than $5 billion spent annually on legal research materials. Marshaling the power represented by these combined expenditures must be the goal of law librarians in an increasingly concentrated industry. Bringing a heightened sense of consumer awareness to both law librarians and lawyers is the major goal of this book.

This **Buyer's Guide** has many uses: acquisition guide, budgeting tool, bibliography, reference book, directory, and consumer awareness vehicle. Chiefly, it is designed to be used as (1) a manual on the best and most cost-effective means of acquiring legal information, and (2) as a reference guide to specific legal materials. Nearly one-half of the volume (Chapter 27) is dedicated to substantive reviews of legal treatises, CD-ROMs, and other materials in 61 subject specialties. Another major portion (Chapter 28) provides information regarding the primary law sources for each state and the District of Columbia, Internet sites, legal research guides, and leading sources for state specific materials. Nineteen chapters are dedicated to discussions of the major categories of legal materials and the most cost-effective means of acquiring them.

The Appendices include several valuable features, including the history and product lines of the most important legal publishers, a representative sampling of used law book prices (increasingly difficult to measure), a list of toll-free numbers for all major and many minor legal publishers, a spreadsheet of the legal specialty products with prices reviewed in Chapter 27, and a list of essential law library cost-saving tips. I have attempted to selectively enhance the text with a number of cost-saving tips that can be utilized in a variety of law library environments. In response to the Federal Trade Commission's rescission of the **Guides for the Law Book Industry** in January 2000, the American Association of Law Libraries has developed, and approved, a new set of industry standards in its **AALL Guide to Fair Business Practice for Legal Publishers** (3d ed., 2012). These are reprinted in Appendix F.

Ideally, most of chapters 1 to 25 should be read in their entirety. Chapters 27 and 28, which contain information on subject-specific and state-specific legal information sources, should be consulted when your firm or library is contemplating the purchase of materials in those areas. In addition, it is highly recommended that you consult Appendix H which contains a spreadsheet of pricing and supplementation cost data for every supplemented title reviewed in chapter 27. This unique tool will better allow you to compare competing titles in the subject areas in which you are contemplating a purchase and get an immediate handle on the likely supplementation costs going into the future. No other publication on the market provides this critical information to legal information consumers.

Assuming your firm is in the unfortunate position of lacking a professionally trained law librarian, I would also suggest that the appropriate chapters be read by the individual responsible for library maintenance to ensure that your firm maintains control over both acquisitions and the processing of invoices. The primary reason most law firms lack effective control over their libraries and library expenditures is that either there is no supervision over the library or the supervision is not centralized. Therefore, your first task should be to delegate library responsibilities to one person in the firm and ensure that all orders, acquisitions and invoice approvals are channeled through that person. Their first assignment, however, should be to read the appropriate chapters of this book in their entirety so that they can become the gatekeeper protecting the firm from the excesses of the legal publishing industry. In purchasing this book, you have already taken the first major step in gaining control over your legal information costs.

Chapter 2: A Brief History of Legal Publishing

English Roots

The history of Anglo-American legal publishing is nearly as old as the history of printing itself. About 1481, William de Machlinia printed the English Year Books, anonymous collections of court decisions which had existed in manuscript form since the latter part of the 13th century. Shortly thereafter, Guillaume Le Tailleur, of Rouen, working at the behest of publisher Richard Pynson, issued Statham's Abridgment, a work containing summaries of cases from the Year Books organized under broad subject headings. Statham, a Baron of the Exchequer during the reign of Edward IV, prepared summaries of cases which spanned the reigns of Edward I through Henry VI (1272-1471). Though crude by modern standards, Statham's Abridgment was an early forerunner of the present day case digest.

In the period between 1480 and 1516, it is estimated that roughly 125 editions of sixty law books were issued by English presses. These books consisted primarily of case reports and statutes which were usually issued in editions of 500 copies. Other English law books consisted of treatises, legal manuals, formbooks, a legal dictionary, and additional abridgments of cases and statutes. However, most of the early lawbooks were the product of printers who supported themselves by publishing books on a variety of subjects. When the publication of the **Year Books** ceased in 1535, the task of preparing reports of court decisions fell to named reporters, the most famous of which were James Dyer (1513-1582), Edmund Plowden (1550-1580) and Edward Coke (1572-1616). The development of the doctrine of stare decisis owes much to these nominative reporters whose reports recorded the courts' judicial reasoning and use of earlier precedents.

The publication of statutes began in 1485 with the appearance of **Machlinia's Nova Statuta**, a compilation covering the period from 1327. Later compilations, including those published by Thomas Berthelet in 1543 and William Rastell in 1557, brought together all the statutes then in force and reaching as far back as the **Magna Carta**. These statutory compilations, and the session law volumes upon which they were based, constituted a major component of the corpus of legal publishing in England. Legal treatises and commentaries constituted another significant body of legal publications in the 16th through the 18th centuries. These included such works as Ranulf Glanville's **Treatise on the Laws and Customs of England**, Henry de Bracton **Of the Laws and Customs of England**, Thomas Littleton's **Tenures**, Edward Coke's **Institutes of the Laws of England**, and William Blackstone's **Commentaries on the Laws of England** (1765-1769), the last great general legal treatise.

American Legal Publishing

During the American colonial era, the number of domestically produced law books was insignificant in comparison with those works imported from England. Members of the colonial bar were far more likely to have the works of Coke, Bracton and Littleton on their shelves than any American imprint. Other than books of statutes, domestically produced law books were limited chiefly to manuals for justices of the peace. While it came at the end of the colonial era, Blackstone's **Commentaries on the Laws of England** enjoyed considerable popularity on the North American continent where it appeared in numerous domestic editions and later served as the inspiration for James Kent's **Commentaries on the American Law** (1826-30).

With the winning of American independence, a general feeling arose among the legal community that a free people should not be subject to the laws of England. However, not a single volume of court decisions was published in the thirteen colonies or states until the appearance of Ephraim Kirby's **Reports of Cases Adjudged in the Superior Court of the State of Connecticut** from the Year 1785 to May 1888 in the year 1789. Kirby's two volumes of reports were the first building blocks in the development of a permanent body of American common law. The nominative reporters which were published in a number of states in the early years of the republic represented an unsystematic attempt by a number of private individuals to fill this void.

Statutory law fared considerably better during the colonial era. The printing of both session laws and codifications provided an uneven source of commissions for printers during the 17th and 18th centuries. While these volumes lacked the kind of indices and editorial features we have come to expect from modern publishers, they served as reasonably useful reference tools for colonial lawyers. Once independence had been achieved, there was a general sense of obligation among both politicians and printers that newly enacted laws should be made available to the public in a timely fashion. In the American colonies, as in England, however, legal publications were produced by printers who depended upon a variety of commissions and publishing opportunities. It was not until the early 19th century that specialized legal publishers emerged in both England and the United States, including former booksellers like Butterworth, Alexander Maxwell, Stephen Sweet, and Stevens & Sons in England and Stephen Gould (later Banks-Baldwin) in the United States. Little, Brown and Company, a general commercial publisher, also achieved prominence as a leading publisher of legal treatises from the time of its founding in 1837. The 19th century and early 20th centuries witnessed the appearance of other legal publishers who were eventually absorbed by their more powerful competitors or simply went out of business.

The early 19th century also witnessed the rise of official legal publishing by a number of states. "Official" reporters, published under state authority, gradually replaced the nominative reporters which had existed until that time. In most cases, the early nominative reporters were absorbed into the numbering scheme of the official reports. Paralleling this growth in government sanctioned case law reporting was the rise of the statutory codification movement, the growth in the number legal textbooks, and a growing interest in developing finding tools which could assist lawyers in accessing the expanding body of common and statutory law.

The Rise of West Publishing and Lawyers Cooperative

The 19th century's most significant development in the field of legal publishing, however, was the emergence of the West Publishing Company and its comprehensive system of case reporting and digesting. John and Horatio West took advantage of the pressing need among lawyers and judges for the timely and accurate reporting of court decisions. Between 1876 and 1896, West's **National Reporter System** of case reporting and key number system providing subject access to case law were universally embraced by the legal community. West's strong position in the marketplace as a publisher of primary law continued throughout the 20th century as it released a number of annotated statutory codes, including the **United States Code Annotated** in 1927. It also became an important source of legal treatises and law school textbooks, a major legal encyclopedia (**Corpus Juris** and, later, **Corpus Juris Secundum**), state and federal practice books, and legal forms.

West's major competitor, the Lawyers Cooperative Publishing Company, adopted a different philosophy of legal publishing which emphasized the more selective publication of court decisions and the creation of an integrated library of practical legal reference works for the practicing attorney, called the Total Client-Service Library (TCSL). It also went head-to-head with West with its American Jurisprudence legal encyclopedia, **U.S. Supreme Court Reports Lawyers' Edition**, and **United States Supreme Court Digest, Lawyers' Edition**.

Other major legal publishers that emerged in the latter half of the 19th century included the Michie Company (1897), a leading publisher of state statutory codes; the Shepard's Company (1873), the premier case citation service; Matthew Bender and Company (1887), an important publisher of practitioner-oriented legal treatises; and Callaghan and Company (1863), a major source of national practitioner treatises and primary law for several Midwestern states. The Anderson Publishing Company, founded in 1887 and serving the needs of lawyers from Ohio and neighboring states with a line of both state specific and national titles, was acquired by LexisNexis in October, 2002.

Companies founded in the 20th century included Commerce Clearing House (now CCH) (1913), Clark Boardman (1916), Bureau of National Affairs (1933), the Practising Law Institute (1933), Research Institute of America (1935), Warren, Gorham & Lamont (1961), Prentice Hall Law & Business (1973) and John Wiley Law Publications (1983). Emerging initially as used lawbook dealers, the William S. Hein Company, Fred B. Rothman (acquired by Hein in 1998), and the former William W. Gaunt have also served the law library market as publishers of books, microfiche, and CD-ROM, and as subscription agents and legal reprinters.

20th Century Developments

Significant 20th century developments included the publication of the first looseleaf service by Commerce Clearing House in 1913, and the introduction of the pocket part to update **McKinney's Consolidated Laws of New York** by the West Publishing Company in 1916. In the 1960's, microforms were introduced to address the problems presented by burgeoning hardcopy collections and shrinking shelf space.

The 1970s brought with them transformational developments in the field of legal information delivery. In 1973, Mead Data Central introduced LexisNexis, the first computer-assisted legal research system, a development whose influence on the law and the process of legal research has rivaled the appearance of the National Reporter System, and even printing itself Mead's achievement was matched two years later when the West Publishing Company introduced Westlaw. In the late 1980's, the introduction of legal titles on CD-ROM further transformed the nature of legal publishing and the process of legal research.

In the 1990s, the emergence of the World Wide Web, or Internet opened up tremendous potentialities in the worlds of education and commerce. The development of sophisticated search engines and web directories allowed people to more fully tap the resources on the Internet. In 1994, WebCrawler, the first full-text Web search engine was introduced. Lycos, another full-text search engine, was the first to achieve commercial success. During the late 1990s, both Web directories and Web search engines were popular. Yahoo! and Altavista, both founded in 1995, became the respective industry leaders. By August 2001, however, the directory model had begun to give way to search engines such as Google (founded in 1998) which developed more effective techniques for relevancy ranking.

This vast computer network transformed the delivery of legal information from the exclusive province of a few large commercial databases, such as Lexis and Westlaw, with their own proprietary search protocols, into one accessible at multiple levels. The Internet now provides the technology to allow companies large and small to tap its commercial possibilities, although the advantages have chiefly accrued to those large companies that have assembled the largest body of content desired by the professional marketplace.

Thirty Years of Mergers and Acquisitions

Thomson Reuters

Over the past thirty years, the world of legal publishing has been completely transformed by a wave of corporate acquisitions and mergers. While small legal publishers continue to enter the fray, most of the leading legal publishing entities have been acquired by three major international conglomerates. Foremost among these is Thomson Reuters Corporation, of Canada, which acquired Callaghan and Company, Clark Boardman, Warren, Gorham & Lamont, Lawyers Cooperative, Bancroft-Whitney, Research Institute of America, Practitioners Publishing, Counterpoint Publishing, Gale Research, Information Access, Barclays Law Publishers, Carswell (of Canada), the West Publishing Company, Federal Publications, Findlaw, the Harrison Company, Andrews Publications, Elite Information Systems, Glasser Legalworks, Hildebrandt International, Global Securities Information, Quantitative Analytics, Reuters, Deloitte Tax LLP. Legal Research Systems, and the LRP Publications Public Employment and Bankruptcy/Banking Law Groups. West itself had already acquired Banks-Baldwin to go with its earlier purchases of Foundation Press, the American Law Book Company, the Edward Thompson Company, and Boston Law Book, among others.

On June 11, 2002, the Thomson Corp. was listed on the New York Stock Exchange (NYSE), one of the largest companies added to that market that year. The lead underwriters were Merrill Lynch & Co. and Morgan Stanley. In making the decision, Thomson originally intended to raise $1.5 billion, with shares listed on the Toronto Stock Exchange (TSE). The company anticipated raising $500 million from issuing new shares and an additional $1 billion from selling shares held by Woodbridge, Inc., the Thomson family's holding company. Also, in July, 2002, the West Group and Factiva announced an expanded alliance to provided access to global news and business information from Factiva for customers of Westlaw. And with nary a peep from the Justice Department or Federal Trade Commission, West, in 2002, announced its acquisition of the assets of The Harrison Company, a 94-year-old regional legal publisher for the southeastern United States. Integrating Harrison's product line into that of Thomson/West will eliminate one of the few remaining regional competitors to West's industry dominance.

On April 17, 2008, Thomson acquired Reuters, the world's largest multimedia news operation and a major reporting network of financial and economic services, in a $17.2 billion cash and stock deal, thereby creating the world's largest news and data services company. Post-merger, the Woodbridge Company, a holding company for the Thomson family, held 53 per cent of Thomson Reuters. The new Professional Division of Thomson Reuters was organized into the following divisions:

Legal (formerly North American Legal and Legal & Regulatory)
Healthcare
Scientific (formerly Thomson Scientific)
Tax & Accounting (formerly Thomson Tax & Accounting)

The Legal segment of the Professional Division is organized around the following lines of business:

• U.S. Law Firm Solutions includes businesses such as Westlaw, FindLaw and Elite that sell products and services to large, medium and small law firms;

• Corporate, Government & Academic and Risk & Compliance these businesses serve general counsels/corporate legal departments, government customers and law schools as well as support customers' regulatory needs; and

• Global Businesses, including the legal businesses in Latin America, Asia and other countries outside of the United States.

Thomson Reuters, headquartered in New York City, has more than 59,000 employees worldwide and annual revenues of more than $13.6 billion. Reuters, headquartered in London has gross revenues of $2.7 billion and over 16,000 employees representing over 100 nationalities across the globe. On May 15, 2007, Reuters and the Thomson Corporation entered into a definitive agreement under which Reuters agreed to be acquired by Thomson by implementing a dual listed company structure. The agreement was finalized on April 17, 2008. The merger, which was reviewed by both the U.S. Department of Justice and the European Commission, required the divestment of databases responsible for approximately $25 million in revenues, a small fraction of the more than $13 billion of the two company's combined revenues.

In 2013, 91% of Thomson Reuters revenues were derived from electronic, software and services, and only 9% from print offerings. Within its portfolio, software and services tend to be less capital intensive, have high growth rates and yield a higher return on investment than print and CD products. However, print and CD products typically have a higher incremental profit margin than software and services. In the Legal Division, 86% of 2013 revenues were derived from subscription and transaction sales and 14% from print products. Since its introduction in February, 2010, WestlawNext now comprises more than 80% of Westlaw's revenue base, representing more than 50,000 legal organizations. Westlaw Classic will be phased out in 2014. In 2013, revenues of the legal division increased 3%, to $3.351 billion, reflecting an EBITDA of 1.194 billion, and an operating profit of $903 million, down from an EBITDA of 1.246 billion, and an operating profit of $967 million in 2012. In 2013, the Legal segment achieved an underlying operating profit margin of 26.9%, down 7% from the 29.3% achieved in 2012, and the 29.2% in 2011.

According to Thomson Reuters, the results, in part, reflected a continuing decline in U.S. print revenues (6%) attributable to a decline in discretionary spending by law firms as well as a 10% drop in revenues from Latin American business. However, the decline is more accurately attributable to the continuing customer response to double-digit increases in print supplementation costs that are driving customers away from print and towards online offerings, a progression that is entirely a product of the corporation's policies. Law firms have fewer discretionary dollars because abnormally higher cost increases for existing subscriptions shrink the available dollars left over for discretionary spending. The loss of print revenues is, thus, largely self-inflicted, although the pain felt by customers is far more considerable than that felt by Thomson Reuters.

Thomson Reuters also recognizes threats to its continued profitability in the highly competitive legal information environment and the rapidity of technological change. It also recognizes the challenges posed by free or relatively inexpensive information, particularly over the Internet, including some governmental and regulatory agencies providing information at no cost.

In 2013, Thomson Reuters sold West Academic to Eureka Growth Capital of Philadelphia, reflecting a desire to divest itself of a lower-performing division geared to the law student market rather than the practicing attorneys who can afford to pay for their overpriced supplemented publications. West Academic publishers, which include West Academic, Foundation Press, and Gilbert Law Summaries, will publish West hornbooks, nutshells, textbooks, casebooks, study guides and other materials for law students.

As of January 1, 2014, the Thomson Reuters Legal business segment was organized around four key customer segments built around end users: U.S. law firm solutions; corporate and government; academic; and global businesses.

Reed Elsevier

Reed Elsevier, now an English-Dutch conglomerate, had previously acquired Congressional Information Service (1979), R.R. Bowker (1985), University Publications of America (1988), and Martindale-Hubbell (1990). It became a major player in the legal information marketplace with the acquisition of LexisNexis,

Michie, and Butterworths in 1994. It later added Matthew Bender and Shepard's in 1998, CD Law, a minority interest in Web-based rival VersusLaw, and Anderson Publishing in 2002. Times Mirror, a major publisher of newspapers, magazines, and professional publications, had acquired Matthew Bender & Company in 1963, but sold both Matthew Bender and its one-half interest in Shepard's to Reed Elsevier in 1998 for the sum of $1.65 billion. Reed Elsevier also acquired Gould Publishing and Seisint, Inc. in 2004, Weil Publishing in 2005, and Redwood Analytics, and Choice Point in 2008. The $4.1 billion acquisition of Choice Point initially aroused opposition from the Federal Trade Commission on antitrust grounds, but was subsequently approved when Reed Elsevier agreed to sell its U.S. public records business serving the government sector.

Reed Elsevier was formed in 1993 with the merger of Elsevier and Reed International PLC. Headquartered in London and Amsterdam, it now has over 32,000 employees and realized $8.374 billion in revenues in 2013, down from $8.847 billion in 2012, but reflecting an operating profit margin of 29.0%, up from 27.6% in 2012. Reed Elsevier now operates through five major divisions:

Scientific, Technical and Medical
Risk Solutions
Legal
Exhibitions
Business Information

Combined revenues in from LexisNexis Risk Solutions and LexisNexis Legal & Professional were $3.469 billion in 2013, down from $3.844 billion in 2012. These results generally reflect a stabilization of legal industry activity. The adjusted operating profit margin of LexisNexis Legal & Professional division was 15.18% in 2013, based in revenues of $2.174 billion and profits of $330 million.

Revenues from LexisNexis Risk Solutions were 94% from electronic sales and 6% from print; revenues in from LexisNexis Legal & Professional were 76% from electronic sales and 23% from print. Results continue to show strong demand for electronic solutions and weak print sales.

Wolters Kluwer

Wolters Kluwer is a leading global information services and publishing company providing products and services for professionals in the health, tax, accounting, corporate, financial services, legal and regulatory sectors. The company was founded in 1987 when Kluwer Publishers merged with Wolters Samson as a defensive move against an attempted hostile takeover of Kluwer Publishers by Elsevier.

Its entry into the legal information market was initiated in 1994 when Wolters Kluwer acquired Aspen Law & Business. In rapid succession, it acquired Commerce Clearing House in 1995, the Little Brown legal treatise line in 1996, Wiley Law Publications in 1997, and Loislaw.com in December, 2000. In March 2002, it acquired Casenotes, Publishing Company, a leading publisher of study aids for law students. In May, 2002, Wolters Kluwer North America acquired Charles D. Spencer & Associates, a leading provider of print and online pension, benefits, and compensation information. Aspen Publisher's, Inc. acquired Accounting Research Manager (ARM) from Arthur Anderson in September, 2002, and Bowne & Company's securities publishing division in October, 2002.

With headquarters in Amsterdam, Wolters Kluwer had revenues of $4.630 billion in 2012. It employs approximately 19,000 people in 150 countries worldwide and maintains operations across Europe, North America and Asia Pacific. It operates through four major divisions:

Health & Pharma Solutions
Corporate & Financial Services
Tax, Accounting & Legal
Legal, Tax & Regulatory Europe

In 2011, Wolters Kluwer Corporate Legal Services acquired National Registered Agents, Inc., a Princeton, N.J.-based company with a 16-year history of providing registered agent services to small and mid-sized businesses and the legal community that supports them. It has also changed the name of its Aspen Publishers product line to that of Wolters Kluwer Law & Business. The online segment of the business has grown to 74%, with print declining to 26%. The company's overall operating profit margin was approximately 21.5% in 2013.

In the Legal and Regulatory division, revenues were $2.008 billion in 2013, down from $2.061 billion in 2012. Ordinary EBITA were $435 million in 2013, down from $453 million in 2012, reflecting an operating profit margin of 21.66%, down slightly from 21.97% in 2012.

Antitrust Revolution—A Case Study

The acquisition of the West Publishing Company by the Thomson Corporation in 1996 provides an interesting case study in the revolution which overtook the field of antitrust law in the United States in the final decades of the 20th century. In 1995, the West Publishing, the crown jewel of legal publishing, shocked the legal world by announcing that it was putting itself on the auction block. The Thomson Organisation which, in 1994, had lost out to Reed Elsevier in its attempt to purchase LexisNexis, was poised to acquire a company which could provide it with the online database to complement its strong position in the publication of secondary legal materials. With its massive Westlaw database and major presence in the publication of both primary and secondary legal materials, West was exactly what the Thomson Corporation needed to pursue its strategic objectives in the field of professional information.

On February 26, 1996, Thomson announced its plan to purchase West for the sum of $3.425 billion, pending antitrust clearance by the Department of Justice. Industry analysts contended at the time that Thomson paid an excessive price for West, probably $1 billion more than its true worth based on historic sales. The purchase price of $3.425 billion was four times historic sales of $800 million and 16 times its operating profits of slightly more than $215 million. For a business increasing revenue at only 10% per year, such multiples were very steep, it was argued.

They pointed out that Reed not only paid a lower multiple for LexisNexis, but was able to cut its effective purchase price by $300 million by exploiting tax advantages not available to Thomson. And while Reed was able to increase LexisNexis' profit margins from 11 to 16%, the thinking at the time was that Thomson would be unable to improve significantly upon West's healthy 25% profit margins. By 2009, Thomson Reuter's profit margins were more than 32%, but fell to 26.9% in 2013.

Despite some early indications that it was going to force some major concessions from the merging parties, the Department of Justice, on June 19, ultimately accepted a watered-down consent decree which provided almost no relief to consumers troubled by the size and market power of this legal publishing behemoth. Law librarians, in particular, were troubled by the price escalation which followed in the wake of previously acquired Thomson publications, a price escalation which has virtually killed the standing order for secondary materials as a central operating principle in many law libraries. Protests from law librarians, large and small legal publishers, and others were summarily dismissed by attorneys at the Department of Justice's Antitrust Division who solidified their reputation as pusillanimous apologists for pro-monopoly antitrust policy.

The person most responsible for this charade was undoubtedly Anne Bingaman, President Clinton's former head of the Antitrust Division at the Department of Justice, who set the tone for the Division's feeble enforcement of the antitrust laws. Yet, on June 26, 1996 she had the effrontery to issue what can only be characterized as one of the most patently absurd and self-serving press releases in Justice Department history. "This settlement is a victory for all of us," she said. "We are all consumers of legal advice from time to time and as citizens we rely on access to information about our nation's laws." A more apt description of the agreement was made by HyperLaw's President Alan Sugarman whose view of the merger is prominently displayed on HyperLaw's Web Site: "The Department of Justice and the State Attorneys General have served up a glass that is 90% empty, and the 10% in the glass is watered down."

The consent decree specified that Thomson-West divest itself of 51 print titles and Auto-Cite, Lawyers Cooperative's electronic citation verification service. Included among the print titles were **United States Reports, Lawyers' Edition, United States Supreme Court Digest, Lawyers' Edition, United States Code Service, Corbin on Contracts, Appleman's Insurance Law and Practice, Deering's Annotated California Code, Illinois Jurisprudence,** the **Annotated Laws of Massachusetts, Callaghan's Michigan Digest, Michigan Statutes Annotated,** and the **New York Consolidated Laws Service**. Also included were thirty state-specific titles of no real consequence whose presence on the list only served to highlight the weakness of the consent decree. Only six national treatises were included, the greatest indication that the consent decree was a hollow instrument. These six titles, in the subject areas of bankruptcy, contracts, criminal law, federal practice, and insurance law, represent only 1.1% of the 533 treatises selected for inclusion in the first edition of this book. In each of these five subject areas, the West-Thomson percentage of market control ranged between 63% and 73%. Strangely, the Justice Department provided no relief in at least thirteen additional subject areas where Thomson/West had an equal or greater market concentration, including: administrative law (66.66%); admiralty and maritime law (85.71%), arts, entertainment & sports law (71.42%); civil rights (66.66%); constitutional law (83.33%); education law (66.66%); municipal corporations (80%); products liability (66.66%); social security (66.66%); taxation (63.63%); tort law (63.63%); and trusts and estates (66.66%). Prior to the merger, Thomson's overall control of the treatise market amounted to 187, or 35.08%, of the 533 treatises selected for inclusion in the first edition of this book. The purchase of West added another 96 titles, or 18.01% of the market, bringing the total to 283 titles, or 53.09%.

The Antitrust Division's second major error was in permitting Thomson-West to gain control of both systems of legal research: West's Key Number System, and Lawyers Cooperative's Total Client-Service Library System, a system which has now been fully integrated into the West Group product line. The West-Thomson attorneys were able to persuade the ill-prepared Justice Department lawyers that comparing the two systems of legal information was like comparing apples and oranges. In doing so, they not only distorted the fact that both are valid and useful methods of conducting legal research, but succeeded in distancing themselves from years of Lawyers Cooperative's marketing and promotional literature which described the TCSL system as " a comprehensive legal research system" covering "everything from on point cases in both state and federal jurisdictions, to principles of law, statutes, procedure, model forms, trial techniques ... in short, everything you need to handle almost any legal matter."

What can explain the Antitrust Division's inept performance in accepting such a feeble consent decree? As John Morris explains in his excellent overview of the entire matter in the September, 1996 issue of the **American Lawyer** (see "How West Was Won"), the stalemate was broken three days after the Thomson-West lawyers offered to openly license West's star pagination, the page breaks in the West case reporters, to other publishers (albeit at hefty rates certain to deter all but the largest publishers). At that point, the government's lawyers, believing they had forced a major concession from the merging parties, were ready to sign on the dotted line. Only later, after public criticism erupted, did they realize that they had purchased "a pig in a poke." With the very legitimacy of West's claim to copyright in star pagination under heavy fire in the aftermath of the U.S. Supreme Court's Feist decision, which dismissed the "sweat of the brow" theory of copyright protection, the Justice Department's lawyers were thoroughly outmaneuvered in accepting an ultimately worthless concession. Revealingly, West's claims to copyright in its page breaks were simultaneously being challenged in the U.S. District Court for the Southern District of New York in an action brought, and ultimately won, by Matthew Bender and HyperLaw, Inc.

Once the consent decree was fashioned, the merger was allowed to proceed. The only step remaining was for the final imprimatur of the U.S. District Court for the District of Columbia. Judge Paul Friedman, who was assigned to hear the case after the withdrawal of Judge Robert Richey (who, it was pointed out, was a Thomson/West author), held several hearings prior to issuing a 51-page opinion on December 26, 1996. While Judge Friedman was severely constrained in his role by the earlier Microsoft decision which criticized another District court judge for exceeding his authority in rejecting a Justice Department consent decree, he indicated that "Like Judge Martin [Southern

District of New York], this court has serious doubts about the validity of the Eighth Circuit's 1986 opinion in Mead Data in view of the subsequent decision of the Supreme Court in Feist ... and it finds unpersuasive the reasoning in Oasis Publishing." He also indicated that "the court is concerned that including the star pagination license provision in the Final Judgment might be construed as an endorsement of West's dubious copyright claim." He further opined that "the weakness of West's claim and the limited market power of many of those who must pay the license fee, particularly now that the most economically powerful critic of West's position, Thomson, has lost its incentive to contest the claim and joins West in advancing it."

In addressing Judge Friedman's concerns on the pagination issue, Thomson/West proposed free star pagination licenses for small publishers until the legal issue is settled, or until the year 2001. The major publishers, however, defined as those with annual sales of over $25 million, would get no price break on the pagination licenses. Those publishers were identified as LexisNexis, Commerce Clearing House, Matthew Bender, and the Bureau of National Affairs. Hyperlaw, Inc. was granted intervener status for purposes of appeal by Judge Friedman once it was apparent that LexisNexis, having acquired the divested products, was withdrawing its challenge to the merger. Among other issues, Hyperlaw alleged numerous abuses by the Justice Department, particularly its failure to require public disclosure of investigatory files under the terms of the Tunney Act. Among these documents, according to Hyperlaw, was West's 1988 settlement pact with LexisNexis, a secret agreement which Hyperlaw alleges resulted in the total domination of the on-line market by the Westlaw and LexisNexis. Hyperlaw ask that "This court must take notice of the fact, or allow Hyperlaw to place before the Court, the facts of the 1988 fiasco--so that it will not be repeated." "In 1988," Hyperlaw contends, "what is now Thomson/West had their original agreement with what is now LexisNexis/Reed-Elsevier similarly blessed (out of the public eye) by a Minnesota federal district court which permitted them to share the on-line market to the exclusion of all others with respect to star-pagination and the text of legal opinions and statutes."

Reed Elsevier and Wolters Kluwer Acquisitions

The sale of West was not the only significant industry development in 1996. Wolters Kluwer, the Dutch-owned parent of Commerce Clearing House, Aspen Law & Business, and Panel Publishers, acquired the professional publishing business of Little, Brown and Company. The legal, tax and educational divisions of Little, Brown were integrated into Aspen Law & Business operation. In other developments, Times Mirror, the parent of Matthew Bender & Company, entered into a partnership with Reed Elsevier to own and operate Shepard's, the nation's premier legal citation service. The arrangement was initiated with the sale of its Higher Education Group to the McGraw-Hill Companies in exchange for Shepard's and additional undisclosed considerations. Following the completion of this transaction, Times Mirror would contribute 50% of Shepard's to a joint venture with Reed Elsevier, an arrangement which was consummated on November 27, 1996. This partnership is part of a broader strategic alliance between Matthew Bender, Times Mirror's legal publisher, and LexisNexis, a subsidiary of Reed Elsevier. A cross-licensing arrangement between the two companies provides the basis for the availability of Matthew Bender publications online through LexisNexis and the use of the LexisNexis caselaw database on Matthew Bender's print and CD-ROM treatise products. All these transactions represented deliberate strategic positioning in the wake of the competitive challenges posed by the Thomson-West merger.

Merger Frenzy Continues

The continued consolidation of the legal publishing industry in recent years is symptomatic of the rise of the global markets generally. Responding to the end of the cold war and a new era of political stability and expanding capitalism, American and foreign corporations are feeling pressures to create new entities which can effectively compete on a global scale. The record $1 trillion in mergers which took place in 1997 was 50% higher than the value of those achieved in 1996. Moreover, 156 of those mergers involved deals of $1 billion or more, up from 97 in 1996. The number of $1 billion+ mergers rose even more dramatically to 288 in 2000. Not since the turn of the 20th century has the United States witnessed such a wave of mergers involving American corporations, a phenomenon which has affected every segment of the economy, from banking and telecommunications to aerospace and legal publishing.

Robert Pitofsky, chairman of the Federal Trade Commission, indicated in the **New York Times** (January 19, 1998, p.1) that "more and more deals we see really should be judged on a global market scale, not just on national or local markets. Mergers go through now that would have been challenged just 10 years ago because competition now comes from all corners of the world." An understanding of these world-wide developments can, in large measure, explain the rather anemic performance of the U.S. Justice Department's Antitrust Division in the Thomson-West merger, which it approved in 1996. In this environment, the Antitrust Division creates the illusion of conducting serious scrutiny of proposed mergers which it must know it will inevitably approve. However, unless the Antitrust Division demands sufficient concessions from the merging parties, in the form of divestitures, it opens itself up to criticism that those divestitures will reveal, as they have in the Thomson-West merger, serious logical inconsistencies.

In the current legal publishing environment, three major international corporations have dominated the merger wave--Thomson Reuters, Reed Elsevier, and Wolters Kluwer. The activities of these three corporations, each of which possess the financial resources to acquire smaller companies and expand their critical mass, have convinced a number of smaller legal publishers to throw in the towel. In most cases, these smaller companies have been publishers of print legal treatises without the electronic databases of primary law which would allow them to transform their properties into cutting edge products for the practitioner market.

Wiley Law Publications Sold to Wolters Kluwer

On September 3, 1997, Charles Ellis, President and CEO of John Wiley & Sons, Inc., announced that his company had signed a letter of intent to sell its Wiley Law Publications division to Wolters Kluwer, the Dutch publishing giant. Ellis' comments at the time of this announcement are reflective of the pressures faced by small legal publishers generally. "Given recent developments in the U.S. law publishing field," he said, "we came to the conclusion that Wiley could not be a leading contender without substantial further investments." And, in remarks that closely paralleled those of Shepard's McGraw-Hill executives in 1995, he further indicated that "the sale will allow us to concentrate more strongly on our core businesses." Wiley Law Publications, based in Colorado Springs, CO, published approximately 300 legal treatises in the areas of construction law, intellectual property, employment law, medical malpractice, trial practice, and bankruptcy. The Wiley acquisition reflected Wolters Kluwer's strategy of acquiring legal and tax publications in specialized and local markets. Under this new ownership, the titles formerly published by Wiley Law Publications will be merged with those of Aspen Publishers, a division of Wolters Kluwer Law & Business, headquartered in New York City.

LexisNexis Publishing Created

Following its acquisition of the 52 products divested by the Thomson Corporation, Reed Elsevier created a new entity called Lexis Law Publishing which combined the b**ooks and CD-ROMs published under the Michie imprint with the United States Code Service, United States Supreme Court Reporter, Lawyers' Edition**, and the other acquired titles. Currently headquartered in New York City, the LexisNexis Group now provides a premier online legal research service (LexisNexis), annotated code services for 35 states and territories, CD-ROM products for a number of jurisdictions, more than 800 national and state practice publications, and the Shepard's line of citators products. It maintains offices in a number of U.S. cities for separate divisions of its operations, including Albany, NY (LexisNexis Matthew Bender), Dayton Ohio (LexisNexis), Conklin, NY (LexisNexis Matthew Bender), Newark, NJ (LexisNexis Matthew Bender), Charlottesville, VA (LexisNexis Matthew Bender), Colorado Springs (LexisNexis/Shepard's), Bethesda, MD (LexisNexis Academic Library Solutions, and New Providence, NJ (Martindale-Hubbell). While a number of product brand names will continue to exist, a consolidation of marketing and customer service operations has already taken place.

Reed Elsevier - Wolters Kluwer Merger Proposed, and Abandoned

On October 13, 1997, the Anglo-Dutch publisher Reed Elsevier announced a merger with its Dutch competitor, Wolters Kluwer. In 1996, the combined sales of these two international publishing giants were estimated to be in the neighborhood of $6.6 billion. The new entity would have become the world's largest publishing enterprise, with particular strengths in the scientific and professional markets. Under the terms of the merger, Reed shareholders would have commanded a 38.3% share in the new entity, while Elsevier and Wolters Kluwer shareholders would have controlled 34.2% and 27.5% respectively. In the 1997 American legal publishing market, Reed Elsevier and Wolters each commanded sales of $600-$700 million. While the merger would have created the world's largest publishing enterprise, it would have amounted, at the time, to slightly less than the Thomson Corporation's roughly $1.5 billion in sales in the American legal market. Although the merger required scrutiny by authorities at both the Justice Department and the European Union, both of these bodies would have been hard pressed to oppose a merger whose size did not quite approach that of the Thomson-West merger to which the Justice Department has already given its blessing.

Then, on March 9, 1998, industry observers were stunned by the sudden decision by the respective boards of directors of Reed International P.L.C., Elsevier NV and Wolters Kluwer nv to abandon the proposed merger. According to a joint press release, "within the last few days, Wolters Kluwer has made it known to Reed Elsevier that it needed to renegotiate a number of terms of the proposed merger ... as announced on 13 October 1997. This was in the main based on expectations about the conditions which were likely to attach to any clearance by the Regulatory Authorities and the consequent adverse implications for the benefits of the merger for the respective shareholders of all three companies. " Reed International and Elsevier concluded "that to make the significant changes to the merger terms that Wolters Kluwer felt necessary to protect the interests of its shareholders would make the merger unattractive from the standpoint of the Reed International and Elsevier shareholders." The press release concluded that "Reed Elsevier and Wolters Kluwer will continue to pursue their respective core strategies of growth as leading international professional publishers and information providers, through both organic developments and acquisitions."

Times Mirror Sells Matthew Bender to Reed Elsevier

Responding to the rising pressures of operating in global markets, Times Mirror announced on November 24, 1997 that it was commencing a comprehensive review of the strategic position and alternatives of its legal publisher, Matthew Bender & Company, and its medical publisher, Mosby, Inc. Matthew Bender, the nation's premier publisher of secondary legal publications, including such notable legal treatises as **Moore's Federal Practice** and **Collier on Bankruptcy**, was reacting, at least in part, to the October 13, 1997 announcement of the proposed merger between Reed Elsevier and Wolters Kluwer. According to Mark Willes, Times Mirror chairman, president and chief executive officer, "the quickening pace of consolidations in these industries and our normal strategic review process led to this broader scale review." Times Mirror said it would evaluate a variety of alternatives including a sale to a third party, a spin-off to shareholders and swaps for other strategic assets. It retained Goldman, Sachs & Company to assist in this review.

After months of speculation, Times Mirror announced on Monday, April 27 that it had struck a deal to sell its legal publishing holdings to Reed Elsevier Plc. in a deal valued at $1.65 billion. The announcement was not unexpected to those familiar with the world of legal publishing. With annual sales in the $650-$700 million range, Matthew Bender had to have been a tempting target for Reed Elsevier with whom it was already engaged in a number of strategic alliances. Moreover, Reed Elsevier was in a position to take maximum advantage of Bender's rich product line of analytical treatises to bolster its product line and allow it to compete effectively with the product offerings of the Thomson Corporation. Moreover, the breakdown of Reed Elsevier's proposed merger with Wolters Kluwer made its acquisition of Matthew Bender, and its 50% share of Shepard's, even more inevitable. Matching the Matthew Bender product line with the massive LexisNexis database provided Reed Elsevier with the key ingredients fundamental to success in the increasingly global online environment. In 1998, Reed Elsevier acquired CD Law, a Washington state-based CD-ROM and Internet legal information provider, a minority interest in VersusLaw in 1999, and Anderson Publishing in 2002.

Future Appears Uncertain for Consumers of Legal Information

While these mega-mergers appear to make considerable sense from a global business perspective, their impact on consumers of legal information is already being felt, and not always in positive ways. Having already approved the merger of the Thomson Corporation and West Publishing Company, the Justice Department and Federal Trade Commission were hard pressed to prevent additional mergers in the industry. They believed, perhaps correctly, that there were no significant barriers to the entry of new competitors into the marketplace. However, from the consumer's perspective, it must be acknowledged that the likelihood of such competitors emerging is extremely remote, particularly in the short term. In the course of acquiring most legal publishers of any significance and name recognition, Thomson and Reed Elsevier have acquired the product names most likely to attract the interest of prospective authors. Law professors and practitioners are not fully aware of the transformation which has engulfed the industry; and it is highly unlikely that the authors among them will seek out smaller publishers for the purpose of promoting greater competition in the marketplace. Indeed, it is more likely that they will be attracted by the prospect of higher royalty payments offered by publishers who can charge $300 for a single-volume treatise and $200 for an annual pocket part. And should a viable new competitor emerge once the dust has settled on the current wave of acquisitions, there is little to prevent one of the big three, or four if Bloomberg is included, from devouring that entity as well.

From the perspective of the legal information consumer, the future, at least on the cost front, appears relatively bleak. While the Internet offers new opportunities for the exchange of legal information, it is still too limited and diffuse to have much impact upon the world of value-added legal information which will remain under the control of the big three for the foreseeable future.

Capturing the Small Law Office Market

With the saturation of the large law firm market by the two leading providers of online legal research, the focus of marketing efforts has now shifted to law firms of ten lawyers or less where most lawyers practice. While both Westlaw and LexisNexis now provide more economical access to defined bodies of state and federal materials (see Chapter 26), other online providers have mounted challenges to their hegemony in this market. VersusLaw is offering unlimited access to a complete library of state and federal primary law at a cost of only $167.40 per year per password, as well as other attractively priced premium packages of primary law. Casemaker has developed databases for more than 25 individual state bar associations and has now expanded its coverage to all fifty states and the major bodies of federal statutory and case law. Fastcase, a new entrant to this market, represents another low-cost and technologically sophisticated alterative. Loislaw, part of Wolters Kluwer, which for several years raised its per password cost to $3,000, is now priced at $1,512.00 per year (or $1,680.00 when billed monthly).

Dramatic Developments at LexisNexis

The consolidation in the legal publishing industry has precipitated a number of positive developments for users of legal information. Among the most significant of these is the enhanced quality of citator services in the wake of the West Group's challenge to Shepard's former monopoly in the field. West's introduction of KeyCite in 1997 added a dramatic new wrinkle in the time-honored practice of updating the law. This challenge, and the merging of LexisNexis and Shepard's, have provided the ingredients for impressive product enhancements which are now offering consumers the ability to purchase access to either local jurisdictional or full Shepard's at extremely attractive rates.

On another, but related, front, LexisNexis has invested considerable editorial effort in overcoming its long-standing research disadvantage vis-a-vis Westlaw by introducing both the LexisNexis Search Advisor classification system and by adding core terms to all the case law in its database. These core terms provide online researchers with the ability to retrieve cases whether or not the judges authoring the opinions have used them. It provides the added editorial advantages which were formerly the exclusive domain of Westlaw, which could marshal the editorial content of the headnotes and synopses which accompany its print versions of cases. These enhancements by LexisNexis are probably the most significant developments since the introduction of computer-assisted legal research in 1973.

Wolters Kluwer Acquires Loislaw.com

In the most significant industry development of 2000, legal publishing giant Wolters Kluwer acquired Loislaw.com for the sum of $95 million. In acquiring this comprehensive online database of primary law, Wolters Kluwer placed itself in a position to strategically develop and position its other analytical and practice-oriented offerings. This acquisition gave Wolters Kluwer the online legal database it needed if it hoped to compete with Thomson and Reed-Elsevier. However, the current Loislaw pricing structure may handicap its ability to tap the small law office market in the face of mounting challenges from VersusLaw, Casemaker, and Fastcase. Nevertheless, this development reinforces my previous predictions about new and promising legal publishers being bought up by one of the big three. Unfortunately, Wolters Kluwer has made limited efforts in upgrading the functionality and content of the Loislaw to make it a viable competitor to LexisNexis or Westlaw, although its subject specific Treatise Libraries (see Chapter 27) are making a strong effort in that direction.

West Group Acquires Findlaw

At the start of the third millennium the West Group acquired FindLaw, one of the most popular portals for accessing free legal information on the Internet. In a press release issued January 26, 2001, West Group president Michael Wilens promised that FindLaw will continue to operate as an independent subsidiary of the West Group and "everything that exists on FindLaw today - from caselaw to career services and Continuing Legal Education will remain." This acquisition highlighted the degree to which the major legal publishers are poised to exploit all possible avenues for business development and marketing, even to extent of positioning themselves along the highways to free legal content on the Internet. By 2010, however, Wilens' promises had evaporated with Findlaw's removal of links to legal content of rival commercial online providers.

Recent Acquisitions by Thomson Corporation

The Thomson Corporation continued to make strategic acquisitions of companies which can enhance its market positioning and provide additional content and professional services to its customer base. These include Findlaw, acquired in 2001, Legalworks (formerly Glasser Legalworks), a producer of legal and law practice seminars, events and publications, acquired in 2004; and Hildebrandt International, a respected legal management consulting firm. In 2005, Thomson acquired Global Securities, Inc., a leading provider of securities and securities-related information and research services, including LIVEDGAR, a leading online securities research service. In 2006, Thomson acquired the privately held Quantitative Analytics, Inc., a leading provider of financial database integration and analysis solutions. And, as previously discussed, it made the major acquisition of Reuters in 2008. In 2013, it acquired a Practical Law Company, which offers valuable know-how, practical tools and check lists for law firms, the kinds of resources lawyers need in order to get up to speed on a task or move more efficiently to a higher level of thinking that general counsels typically call upon outside counsel for.

Wolters Kluwer Law & Business

On January 17, 2006, Wolters Kluwer announced that it was aligning several of its legal and business compliance product lines under the brand name Wolters Kluwer Law & Business. Included under this new marketing umbrella are Aspen, CCH (law and business compliance products), Kluwer Law International, and Loislaw. By 2011, these individual brand names were subsumed by that of Wolters Kluwer Law & Business. Additional acquisitions by the big three are listed below.

The Shape of the Legal Publishing Industry in the New Millennium

The result of this twenty-five year drive toward consolidation is a legal publishing industry now under the control of three major corporations: (1) the Thomson Financial & Professional Publishing Group (of which the West Group and the RIA Group are the largest divisions); (2) Reed Elsevier; and (3) Wolters Kluwer. These three corporations and the history of their major acquisitions are as follows:

Based on their 2013 annual reports, the Thomson Corporation, Reed Elsevier, and Wolters Kluwer account for over $28 billion in combined international sales across all product lines. Of these three, Thomson was firmly positioned in first place with a 48.20% market share, while Reed Elsevier and Wolters Kluwer accounted for 34.84% and 16.95% of the market respectively. For purposes of comparison, all product segments are included including legal, tax, regulatory, financial, corporate, accounting, scientific, health, and news:

2013 Worldwide Sales of Professional Publishing's Big Three (in billions)

Thomson Reuters	$12.702 billion (48.20%)
Reed Elsevier (LexisNexis)	$9.181 billion (34.84%)
Wolters Kluwer	$4.466 billion (16.95%)
Total	$26.347 billion

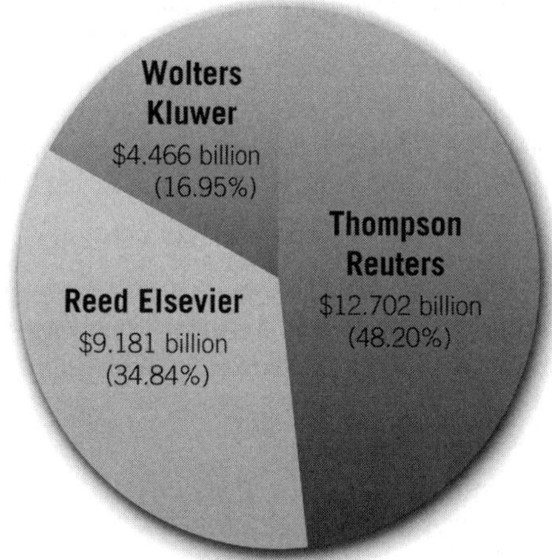

Bloomberg Law

Just when the legal information market appeared to have settled down to a stable triumvirate of major players, a new participant emerged on the scene in the form of Bloomberg Law. Based in New York, **Bloomberg L.P.** had already established itself as a multinational mass media corporation with a one-third share of the $16 billion global financial data market, and an estimated revenue of $7.6 billion in 2011. Bloomberg L.P. was founded in 1981 by Michael Bloomberg with the help of Thomas Secunda, Duncan MacMillan, and Charles Zegar, and a 30% ownership interest by Merrill Lynch. The company provides financial software tools such as analytics and an equity trading platform, data services and news to financial companies and organizations around the world through the Bloomberg Terminal, for which over 300,000 subscribers supply 85% of its revenues. Bloomberg L.P. has grown to include a global news service, including television, radio, the Internet and printed publications.

In 2009, Bloomberg introduced Bloomberg Law, a comprehensive online provider which integrates legal content, company and client information, and proprietary news. In addition to its primary law content, Bloomberg law provides keyword and special content searching, practice centers, litigation and dockets, transactional law resources, companies and markets, legislative and regulatory materials, a legal citator service (BCite), alerts manager, research trail capability, workspaces, and seamless integration of real-time news, company and market information, and legal resources. In 2010, Bloomberg acquired BNA and BNA Books, major publishers of current awareness and analytical products in a variety of legal and regulatory fields, giving it a major substantive content boost. In 2012, the American Association of Law Libraries selected Bloomberg Law as the recipient of the 2012 New Product Award, recognizing "Bloomberg Law's innovation in providing access to legal information." The major question is whether Bloomberg Law can compete on a head-to-head basis with the far better established Westlaw and LexisNexis for s share of the high-end legal information market.

Bloomberg Law is a legal, regulatory, and compliance research platform, offering a suite of news, data and analytics to the legal and compliance community. It can be tailored specifically for the needs of modern professionals, providing resources for legal research, compliance, business development, sector intelligence, and other information needs. Bloomberg Law, which debuted in December, 2009, builds upon Bloomberg L.P., a service that had already established itself as a premier source of proprietary news and financial intelligence. Its chief competitors in the high-end legal research market are Westlaw and LexisNexis. Bloomberg L.P. has expended enormous capital in developing this competitive, high-end legal research service. Thus far, those efforts have not paid off, with Bloomberg Law capturing only 0.7% of the fee-based online market. The New York-based company, that employs more than 15,000 people in over 192 offices around the globe, is the fastest-growing real-time financial information network in the world.

Thomson Reuters

Callaghan & Company (1979)	Clark Boardman (1980)
Warren, Gorham & Lamont (1980)	Lawyers Cooperative (1989)
Research Institute of America (1989)	Maxwell Macmillan (1991)
Counterpoint Publishing (1994)	Information Access (1994)
Information America, Inc. (1994)	Barclays (1995)
Shepard's (treatises only) (1995)	West Publishing Company (1996)
Banks Baldwin (1996)	Foundation Press (1996)
Federal Publications (1998)	Dialog (Info Services Division) (2000)
Findlaw (2001)	Harrison Company (2002)
Andrews Publications (2003)	Elite Information Systems (2003)
Glasser Legalworks (2004)	Hildebrandt International (2005)
Global Securities Information, Inc. (2005)	Quantitative Analytics, Inc. (2006)
Aspatore Books (2007)	Deloitte Tax LLP Prop. Tax Services (2007)
Reuters (2008)	Breakingviews (2009)
Legal Research Systems, Inc. (2010)	Sabrix, Inc. (2009)
LRP Publications Public Employment Group (2011)	Practical Law Company (2013)
LRP Bankruptcy/Banking Products Group (2011)	
FX Alliance Inc. (2012)	
MarkMonitor (2012)	
Dr. Tax (2012)	

Reed Elsevier

Congressional Information Service (1979)	R. R. Bower (1985)
University Publications of America (1988)	Martindale Hubbell (1990)
Butterworths (1994)	Michie (1994)
LexisNexis (1994)	Shepard's (1998)
Matthew Bender & Company (1998)	Mealey's Publications (2000)
Book Publishing Company (2001)	Courtlink (2001)
Anderson Publishing (2002)	Seisint, Inc. (2004)
Gould Publishing (2004)	Weil Publishing (2005)
Redwood Analytics (2008)	ChoicePoint (2008)
Accuity Holdings (2011)	

Wolters Kluwer

Aspen Law & Business (1994)	CCH (1995)
Little, Brown treatises (1996)	Wiley Law Publications (1997)
Loislaw.com (2000)	Bowne Publishing (2002(
Panel Publishers (2002)	Casenotes Publishing Company (2002)
Charles D. Spencer & Associates (2002)	Best Case Solutions, Inc. (2005)
ATX/Kleinrock (2006)	TaxWise Corporation (2006)
TeamMate (2007)	One Legal LLC (2007)
Tax Compliance Software (2010)	Health Language, Inc. (2013)

Other players of significance outside the control of these major corporations include the American Bar Association, Practising Law Institute, Law Journal Press, James Publishing, Lawyers & Judges Publishing, and others.

While these movements of personnel have stimulated a cross-fertilization of ideas and marketing strategies, they have also helped ensure a steady rise in both basic and supplementation costs, as well as the further refinement of practices designed to siphon an ever-increasing flow of dollars from the wallets of lawyers and other consumers of legal information to the publishers' bank accounts. Even without the movement of company personnel, legal publishers are quick to take note of what methods work to enhance sales and profitability.

For example, while 19th century legal publishers were content to issue new editions of legal treatises every six, eight, or ten years, most legal publishers operating in the late 20th century have taken steps to maximize the income which flows from the sale of supplementation to standing order customers. Indeed, the Thomson Reuters' investor financial presentations typically highlight the importance of recurring services revenues in the total revenue stream (87%). Very few will let a year go by without issuing a pocket part or revised volume to one of their serial titles. Double-digit price increases, increases in supplementation frequency, and acceleration of bound volume revisions have all added fuel to the fire of law book price inflation in the current marketplace. All the more reason to jettison print publications and obtain materials as part of a flat-rate online contract.

It should come as no surprise that inflation in the cost of legal publications easily outpaces that of the general economy. Legal publishers benefit from an information asymmetry vis-a-vis their existing and potential customers. Lawyers, for example, are largely a captive market. They require legal publications to carry on their practices, and are generally more affluent than the average consumer. Moreover, they are far less likely to quibble when purchasing a book or other product essential to their work. And once that book is purchased, they are far less likely to question, or even to notice, the continuing cost to which that book will subject them. Quite frankly, many legal publishers think that lawyers are gullible when it comes it buying law books and other forms of legal information. In fact, it is only when a firm hires a professional law librarian that such waste is likely to be controlled. This explains the high prices which the international conglomerates were willing to pay to acquire many of the domestic legal publishing companies in the late 1980's and 1990's. The characteristics of legal publishing which have made it particularly attractive to potential buyers include the following:

(1) Higher profit margins than trade publishing, a fact not fully appreciated until recent years;

(2) Lower risks in product development;

(3) An identifiable audience;

(4) No huge advances to authors;

(5) The ability to test ideas in the marketplace before product development;

(6) More favorable cash flow due to income from subscription sales;

(7) Greater upward flexibility in pricing resulting from the fact that information provided to the professional market is often viewed as absolutely vital to the customer's business.

(8) Costs for legal materials are often paid by the user's employer, i.e. the individual using the legal publishers' products is often not the individual paying the bills.

The dramatic increases in the prices and supplementation costs from some legal publishers are a direct result of policies instituted since their acquisition by the conglomerates. Their ability to continue on this road will largely depend on the passivity of lawyers in the face of such price increases. Law librarians, I am told by one former industry executive, are viewed as the major obstacle to the publishers' ability to roll over the lawyer market. During the period from 1973 to 1996, for example, when the **Consumer Price Index** showed an increase of 253%, the average cost of legal serials rose 495%. According to the **Price Index for Legal Publications** 1996, the mean cost of the average legal serial rose from $50.08 in 1973/74 to $297.89 in 1993/94, a 495% increase.[1] However, as the accompanying table will demonstrate, the most dramatic increase over that time frame took place in the category of legal continuations, which rose an astounding 1006%. In the past four years alone, the prices of legal continuations rose nearly 72%, much of that increase resulting from increased supplementation costs for Thomson-owned publications.[2] In the average law office, better than 95% of the law library expenditures consist of serial publications (as opposed to monographs which are not supplemented), and a high percentage of those serials fall into the category of legal continuations.[3]

Price Index for Legal Publications 2d

After an absence of more than five years, the American Association of Law Libraries released the Price Index for Legal Publications 2d on aallnet. The Price Index was the work of an AALL Advisory Committee and editor which selected titles representing the "broad range of purchasing done by law libraries across the country." Adopting 1998 as its base year, the committee assembled a list of 916 print titles in the following categories: serials (including periodicals), periodicals (excluding periodicals), periodicals (all), periodicals (academic), periodicals (commercial), reporters, citators, digests, codes, legal encyclopedias, looseleaf services, newsletters, and supplemented treatises.

Unlike the former Price Index, the Price Index for Legal Publications 2d adopted a January to December reporting year to reflect the manner in which legal publishers collect supplementation costs. The Committee's first charge was to collect prices for the period 1998-2001. Subsequent year's figures have been published annually in the spring and include data down to the title level. Price Index for Legal Publications 2d made its debut on the Members-Only section of the AALL Web site on December 19, 2002 (aallnet.org).[4]

Price Index for Legal Publications 3d

After a brief life of seven years, the **Price Index for Legal Publications 2d** was abandoned in 2006 in favor of the **Price Index for Legal Publications 3d** which adopted 2005 as a new base year. This move was a direct result of Thomson/ West's chronic refusal to provide supplementation cost data to the AALL Price Index Committee and, ultimately, the unwillingness of the AALL Board to press Thomson/West on the issue. Moreover, the Board determined that, in light of Thomson/West's refusal to cooperate, it would not direct the Committee to continue collecting supplementation cost data from member libraries' financial records and other sources. Moreover, this task had been complicated by the fact that many law libraries are now under Thomson/West Library Management Agreements (LMAs) and no longer have price data for individual titles. Thus, Thomson/West's marketing efforts have largely eroded the ability of the Committee to collect accurate supplementation cost data. Unfortunately, with the West titles temporarily removed, the Index was both methodologically unsound and statistically meaningless.

It was understandable that AALL unveiled the Price Index 3rd with little fanfare. With the West titles removed, the number of indexed titles dropped from 914 to 584 (36% of the total having been eliminated). Among the categories covered by the Index, slightly more than 50%% of the legal serial titles (527 to 260) were dropped, as well as 66% of the legal encyclopedias (9 to 3), 47% of the statutory codes (62 to 33), and, incredibly, 98.4% of the digests (62 to 1). But, perhaps the AALL membership will be comforted by the fact the Committee has focused its remaining scrutiny on the **U.S. Supreme Court Digest**, **Lawyer's Edition**, published by LexisNexis in the absence of 61 Thomson/West digests.

In 2009, West agreed to supply pricing data for the years 2005-2009. Unfortunately, in doing so, it provided new sets costs rather than the supplementation costs that had traditionally been used in the **Price Index**. For full explanation, go to: http://www.aallnet.org/main-menu/Publications/products/pub-price/price-index-2009.html

This error in data reporting skewed the price index for the years involved. For far more accurate West data, consult the **Legal Information Buyer's Guide & Reference Manual**, which has consistently collected supplementation costs (discounted to all subscribers in the case of West) since its inception in 1996. Moreover, the **Buyer's Guide** retains prior years' supplementation costs for most titles, including all treatise titles.

Price Increases of Legal Serial Publications, 1973/74-1995/96

	Legal Periodicals	Looseleaf Services	Court Reporters	Continuations	All Serials
1973/74	$11.95	$181.80	$173.63	$44.07	$50.08
1995/96	$60.50	$970.59	$722.10	$487.55	$297.89
% Increase	406%	434%	316%	1,006%	495%
C.P.I. Jan. 1973	253%	253%	253%	253%	253%

Data from the **Price Index for Legal Publications 2d**, covering the years 1998 to 2004, will remain available on aallnet.org as an archival document, but the two indexes will bear no statistical correlation to one another. Interested readers can visit the aallnet web site to access this index, but it will not, for the reasons stated above, be reproduced here.

AALL Price Index for Legal Publications [4th], 2010-

In 2011, AALL unveiled its 4th price index for legal publications, based on data collected for 2010 and 2011. The new index was developed by the AALL's Price Index for Legal Publications Committee (PILP) following recommendations of the 2011 **Full Report of the Price Index Review Task Force**. The position of editor, which had been created for the **Price Index for Legal Publications 3d**, was restored. The imposition of new data definitions and guidelines in 2010 required that the price index base year be reset to 2010. As with prior indices, the data is reported by publication category (court reporters, digests, supplemented treatises, serials, etc.). With only two years' worth of data reported thus far, the index provides only one year of percentage increase for each of the covered categories. Also, as reported in the introduction, errors in data provided by LexisNexis (now corrected going forward) compromise the accuracy of the index as it applies to categories of publications to which LexisNexis contributed. For further information, visit the Price Index site on the AALL web site: http://www.aallnet.org/main-menu/Publications/products/pub-price/Price-Index-2011.html

An added benefit of the AALL Price Index for Legal Publication web site is the availability of raw data from 1998 to 2011 (with the above caveats), using the AALL Price Index Query.

Serials (Including Periodicals)

Year	Titles	Total Price	Average Price	% change	Consumer Price Index	Price Index change
1998	914	$350,689.56	$383.69	100.00	1.6%	
1999	914	$387,035.33	$423.45	10.36%	110.36	2.7%
2000	914	$408,830.39	$447.30	5.63%	116.58	3.4%
2001	914	$469,972.26	$514.19	14.96%	134.01	1.6%
2002	914	$513,874.35	$562.23	9.34%	146.53	2.4%
2003	914	$532,853.61	$582.99	3.69%	151.94	1.9%
2004	914	$565,473.11	$618.68	6.12%	161.25	3.3%

Library Maintenance Agreements (LMAs)

Indeed, Thomson/West's realization of the problems its pricing policies has created for libraries with large print collections has led to the introduction of Library Maintenance Agreements (LMAs). These multi-year contracts are designed to give customers a single price for combined print and online collections, while, at the same time, providing predictable monthly, or annual, pricing and the potential for cost savings over time. However, Thomson West also views these LMAs as tools to preserve print subscription lists and maximize long-term print revenues in the face of the cancellations, which inevitably result from double-digit supplementation cost increases, which cannot be sustained by most libraries.

Library Maintenance Agreements are available for large and medium-sized law firms, government, and academic law libraries. Eligibility rules exclude partial LMAs and exclusions. Libraries are encouraged to sign three-year contracts, but two-year contracts available for select customers. One-year contracts are not permitted. Contracts typically include confidentiality clauses, which prevent libraries from revealing contractual terms.

Law librarians contemplating signing such Library Maintenance Agreements must, at the very least: (1) refuse to sign any non-competitive provision which prevents the library from disclosing its terms and conditions to other consumers; (2) cancel, in advance, any titles for which standing orders are not desirable in order to exclude them from the LMA, and (3) make a careful comparison between the aggregate subscriber costs of the individual titles falling within the terms of the agreement and the contractual costs under the LMA. Indeed, the longer a library falls under the terms of an LMA, the more divorced it will become from the real costs of the products to which it subscribes, and the true nature of the savings achieved. If you do chose an LMA, the contract should reflect real savings over current expenditures and include only those titles for which the library wishes to remain on standing order. Moreover, future years' percentage increases should not exceed a realistic projection of your library's projected budget increases.

Cost Saving Tip: Although West generally negotiates LMA's with annual percentage increase in the 6-8% range, some libraries have, through skilled and hard-nosed negotiations, been able to secure contacts with annual increases of only 3%. Successes like these come when a library is willing to walk away from the LMA, particularly when West places severe restrictions on the library's ability to reduce its print subscriptions under the new contract. In instances like this, West returned and accepted the library's demands.

Monthly Assured Print Pricing: Adding a new twist to West's attempts to stop the hemorrhaging of its print subscriptions is its **Monthly Assured Print Pricing** (APP). Unlike the LMA described above, the **APP** is a fixed monthly payment plan that attempts to provide predictable pricing down to the individual title level. Customers are given the option of locking in annual supplementation cost increases of 5-6%, depending on whether they elect a two or three-year contract. The alternative for the standing order subscriber is to continue pay the subscriber discounted price for individual items of supplementation as they are issued (generally 80% of the list cost). For example, **American Jurisprudence 2d**, which currently sells for $13,313.00 (exclusive of discount), cost $13,547.00 to supplement in the calendar year 2013 under the traditional pricing scheme. Under the **APP**, however, the first year monthly supplementation cost is $901.00, or $10,812.00 annually. The cost increases in the second and third years, however, are dependent on whether the customer elects a two or three contract. Under the two-year contract, the second year cost increase is 6% in the second year, while under a three-year contract, the cost increase is 5% each in years two and three.

The advantage of **APP** is that it relieves standing order subscribers of the 11-12% increases that have plagued most West titles for many years. However, it also locks those customers into monthly payments that may exceed the actual cost of the supplements in some years. The aim, of course, is to preserve revenue streams in the face of customer cancellations. Whether it is the best interest of the customer will depend on a careful comparison of the **APP** pricing with the actual subscriber cost of supplements outside of the plan, or the far lesser cost of acquiring **Am Jur** on WestlawNext. It is for this reason that the **Legal Information Buyer's Guide** will continue to track traditional subscriber costs of supplementation to provide consumers with a baseline from which to make these comparisons.

Continuing Shift Toward Electronic Access

The shift in consumer preferences toward online and other electronic services has caused print sales to decline in recent years, a movement accelerated by the economic downturn. Thus, these price reductions were attempts to bolster print sales in the face in this phenomenon. In 2013, Professional Division sales of electronic products, software and services accounted for more than 80% of revenues as opposed to less than 20% from print products.

The Future of Legal Publishing

The future of legal publishing is full of promise and pitfalls for both legal publishers and consumers of legal information. Technological advances, including the Internet and CD-ROM, present significant challenges to the established legal publishers who have traditionally relied upon the publication and distribution of primary law, but offer great opportunities to consumers. Significant opportunities exist for online providers who can effectively deliver primary law while undercutting the prices charged by the two major online legal services. As more courts, legislatures, and administrative agencies offer information on the World Wide Web, the role of the traditional primary law publishers will diminish in those instances where value-added content is not important.

The companies in the best position to prosper in the coming years will be those which can make effective use of technology to produce high quality "value-added" analytical materials packaged with the supporting primary law. The online products of LexisNexis/Matthew Bender and Thomson West are excellent examples of this cutting-edge product development. Each company now has a huge online database upon which to draw. In fact, the strategic development between Matthew Bender and LexisNexis is a critical ingredient in the latter's ability to compete with the West and its impressive combination of Westlaw and a majority of the leading secondary materials. There are pitfalls for the consumer in this electronic environment, however. As more attorneys embrace online access, the publishers will be in a better position to dictate the terms under which those materials are acquired and used.

Now in the 21st century, the consumer should demand the following from those legal publishers with whom they do business:

(1) Open and accurate pricing and supplementation cost data for all products, large and small. The Internet provides all publishers with the ability to post current prices, the recent history of supplementation costs (per the AALL Guide to **Fair Business Practices for Legal Publishers**), and standard discounting policies, as readily as it posts bibliographic data. The charade of forcing the customer to contact a sales representative to obtain such basic information is unacceptable. Even when discounts may affect the final sale price, the customer has the right to know the publisher's list price and recent year's supplementation cost history of each item prior to making an informed purchasing decision. West has made considerable progress in this area by allowing customers to determine the fill-up costs for its products on its Web site. However, West and all other legal publishers could significantly improve this situation by providing annual historical supplementation costs for each product in their online catalogs.

(2) The abandonment of non-disclosure provisions in online and Library Maintenance Agreement (LMA) contracts which prevent the customer from revealing the terms of the contract to other parties. Such anti-competitive provisions only serve to keep consumers in the dark and hinder their ability to negotiate for better terms.

(3) The ability of a law firm to purchase the number of user licenses to an online service which its usage requires, not a number dictated by the number of attorneys in the firm. Loislaw was the first online provider to offer this consumer friendly pricing.

(4) Postage costs which more accurately reflect the actual cost of shipping materials rather than some fixed percentage of the materials' cost.

(5) No unsolicited shipments of related materials without the express, written authorization of the customer.

[1]**Statistical Abstract of the United States 1996, p. 482; Monthly Labor Review**, November, 1996, p. 88; Margaret Ames Atman, **Price Index of Legal Publications 1996**, Chicago, American Association of Law Libraries, 1996. The **Price Index** has not been issued since 1996. In July, 1999, AALL President-Elect Margaret Axtmann appointed a Special AALL Committee to investigate and make recommendations regarding the future of the **Price Index**. Those recommendations were submitted to her in November, 1999. In 2000, the AALL Board voted to appoint a Committee and retain economist Mark McCabe of the Georgia Institute of Technology to conduct an Economic Study of Law Book Pricing since 1990.

[2]This was during a period when Matthew Bender supplementation costs were essentially flat due to a price freeze in effect from 1992-1996.

[3]The first three categories of legal serials are largely self-defining; the fourth category, legal continuations, includes all the remaining publications which are supplemented in some form: state and federal codes, digests, **Shepard's** citators, encyclopedias and practice sets, legal treatises, legal forms sets, etc. The supplements may take the form of pocket parts, free-standing supplements, interfiled supplements, or revised and recompiled bound volumes.

[4]**Price Index for Legal Publications 2d**. Chicago: American Association of Law Libraries, 2005. Available on the Members-Only section of AALL Web site (www.aallnet.org)

Chapter 3: Taking on the Legal Publishers

Ever since the days when Hammurabi ordered his Code to be chiseled into stone tablets in ancient Babylon, legal publishers have played a key role in the life of the legal profession. The lawyers of ancient Babylon not only had to suffer the expense of supplementary tablets every time Hammurabi got it into his head to amend the Code, but they had to endure back pain lugging them around from office to courthouse and back again. Legal publishers had not yet heard of papyrus, to say nothing of the cumulative pocket part or computer-assisted legal research.

In the late 19th century, the first organized attempt to deal with the ever-increasing numbers of official reports of court decisions published in the United States occupied the attention of a committee of the American Bar Association. Although much discussion ensued, virtually nothing was accomplished save, perhaps, for a heightened awareness of the problem among some members of the Bar. In retrospect, we would view these concerns as trivial in comparison with the virtual flood of published legal materials which was inundating the average lawyer's office by the 1960's. By this time, however, the excesses of the legal publishing industry came up against a rising consumer consciousness which pervaded the country as a whole.

Raymond Taylor's Salvo at the Legal Publishing Industry

The opening salvo in the movement to defend legal information consumers took the form of an article in the June 1969 issue of the **American Bar Association Journal** entitled "Law book Consumers Need Protection."[1] Its author, Raymond M. Taylor, then Librarian for the North Carolina Supreme Court Library, argued that lawyers were being "victimized" by lawbook publishers and needed to take collective action to eliminate or render unprofitable some of their more undesirable practices. On the surface, Taylor's charges might have provoked a degree of disbelief or amusement among the members of the general public. After all, said Taylor, "one would expect the lawyer to be the consumer best able to protect himself, particularly when the producer against whom he needs protection is the supplier of what probably is the most essential product the lawyer consumes--lawbooks."[2]

Taylor observed, however, that the time of the modern lawyer is simply too valuable to devote much time to a consideration of all those individual tasks which are required to assemble and manage a law library. In an age of specialization, such tasks are often assigned to a new associate or uninterested secretary who neither appreciates the importance of the responsibility he or she has been given nor takes the time to learn something of law library management. The fact that no individual takes personal responsibility for the management of the law library opens the firm to a host of unfair practices by publishers which, Taylor suggested, "are not likely to be detected by other than the most careful purchaser." Despite the radical transformation of the legal publishing industry since 1969, Taylor's fundamental premise that most lawyers don't take responsibility for their legal information purchases remains as true today as when his words were first written, unless, of course, they have hired a librarian to perform this vital function.

Taylor identified eleven of the more "objectionable practices" by which lawyers were being victimized, including:

(1) Putting new titles and new bindings on old books.
In this category, Taylor placed those books marketed both individually and as part of multi-volume sets without notification to the consumer who might unwittingly buy the same volume twice.

(2) Including the same book in two different sets.
As an example of this practice, Taylor cited the issuance of substantially the same looseleaf treatise as both volume 3 of a set on real estate and volume 7 of a set on eminent domain.

(3) Overpricing supplementation.
In this category, Taylor listed the high cost of supplementation to certain looseleaf treatises, some of whose costs were driven up by the issuance of several updates per year.

(4) Using advertising circulars and letters that mislead.
Books advertised as "new" or "revised and enlarged" which were merely updated with a cumulative supplement were placed in this category.

(5) Using unnecessarily expensive bindings and format.
Included in this category, Taylor listed books of limited shelf life (e.g. annual tax volumes included with legal encyclopedia) bound in expensive bindings and books employing large print for the benefit of old lawyers with weak eyes rather than young lawyers with small budgets.

(6) Putting local names on books that are not truly local.
Books in this class included those written for a national or regional audience but marketed as local books to increase their overall sales. Such books may have a few localized amendments or annotations to justify the practice.

(7) Adding remotely related books to established sets to assure their automatic sale.
Taylor termed this practice the "piggyback marketing of books" in order to increase sales of books that might not sell well as individual items, but which will be accepted when linked to the sale of popular and widely distributed sets.

(8) Failing to advertise prices of major items.
Taylor noted that the prices of many higher priced sets were omitted from advertisements and suggested that this could be a convenient means of permitting the publishers to have more than one price for the same item.

(9) Failing to issue supplements for books that otherwise soon will become obsolete.
According to Taylor, some publishers seem unmindful of the custom of providing appropriate supplementation to their books. He suggested that reputable publishers avoid publishing works of authors who consider their responsibility completed when the first edition has been completed. He also criticized publishers who offer one year's free service to new subscribers, but who then fail to issue any supplementation for several years.

(10) Issuing treatises in looseleaf forms.
Taylor took issue with the practice of publishing otherwise reputable treatises in looseleaf format, thus rendering them unsuitable for citation because the material may change from day to day. He suggested that the careful lawyer or judge cites only to permanently bound authorities.

(11) Failing to put correct printing date on reprinted books. This practice results when publishers use original plates or matrices to print new copies of a book as they are needed. For example, a book actually printed and bound in 1964 might indicate that it was printed in 1902. He suggested that the publisher insert the line "Reprinted in 1964 from original plates."

A Call to Action

Taylor called for increased consumer awareness on the part of lawyers to help correct these abuses. He indicated that the prior ineffectiveness of the American Association of Law Libraries was a result of the publishers' recognition that libraries comprised only about 1,000 of the potential 175,000 lawbook customers in the United States.[3] He called for a voluntary code of practices to be followed by lawbook publishers in publishing, titling, binding, supplementing, pricing, advertising, selling, delivering, and collecting payment for publications. He urged combined action on the part of the American Bar Association, the American Association of Law Libraries, and state and local bar associations in pressuring the Federal Trade Commission (FTC) to prescribe appropriate practices to be followed in the publication, advertisement, and sale of lawbooks. He suggested that the FTC might "enter cease and desist orders against publishers who persist in engaging in unfair or undesirable practices."[4]

As a direct consequence of Taylor's article, the FTC, on November 10, 1969, announced that it would conduct an industry-wide investigation to determine whether law book publishers were engaged in unfair or deceptive acts or practices in commerce, in violation of § 5 of the Federal Trade Commission Act.[5] At Taylor's urging, the American Bar Association established a special Subcommittee on Law Book Publishers at its 1970 annual meeting and charged it to investigate and consider questions which have arisen concerning practices in the publication, promotion, and marketing of law books and services" and to recommend means by which the ABA could "provide for the protection of the Bar and the public from undesirable and improper practices." [6]

On January 16, 1970, the Committee on Library Services of the American Bar Foundation issued a statement entitled "Lawyers' Checklist for Buying Law Books," a list of sixteen recommendations for lawyers making lawbook purchasing decisions.[7] The American Association of Law Libraries established a Committee on Relations with Publishers and Dealers headed up by Raymond Taylor and Julius Marke.[8] Also, standards for the advertising of new law publications were approved by AALL on June 15, 1971.[9] Finally, the state bar associations in Michigan and Texas created committees to study the problem.[10]

Genesis of the FTC Guides

The Federal Trade Commission had a choice of three regulatory enforcement mechanisms: (1) cease and desist orders, (2) trade practice rules similar to those concerning the subscription and mail order book publishing industry, and (3) guides, which are not intended to be comprehensive statements of the law, but are intended to provide the business community with the FTC's interpretation of the relevant federal statutes.

By 1973, the FTC was ready to propose a set of Guides as a means of encouraging voluntary compliance. Its underlying assumption was that most business people wanted to do the right thing and conform their behavior to the law. During the comment period, the FTC received over 500 responses to its proposed guides. Finally, on August 8, 1975, the FTC announced the promulgation of 17 voluntary **Guides for the Law Book Industry** which would become effective on April 8, 1976.[11] The FTC **Guides** existed as an industry standard for nearly 24 years, until they were rescinded by the FTC on January 19, 2000. During that time, they were the only **Guides** applicable to any segment of the publishing industry, and one of only a handful of **Guides** applicable to any industry.

The introduction to the **Guides** made it clear that they were not an "all-inclusive list of situations when affirmative disclosures may be required or representations disallowed in the advertising of and representations appearing on industry products." The Guides were intended to insure that a prospective purchaser has "accurate and truthful information readily available" so that the consumer can make an informed decision about whether to purchase. The Guides apply only to "new" material. Material is "new" for only 18 months after it is first distributed. Used or secondhand materials are specifically excluded. While nine of the 17 Guides apply to advertising, they also cover disclosures on the publications themselves, upkeep service, subscription renewal notices, and billing practices.

While the participation of the American Bar Association and other groups in the development of the Guides seemed to portend greater vigilance on the part of the legal community at large, it fell to the American Association of Law Libraries and its Committee on Relations with Publishers and Dealers to provide sustained oversight of the legal publishing industry. This oversight has been exercised chiefly through a complaint investigation process involving the volunteer efforts of law librarians. "Requests for Mediation" received by the Committee are assigned to a member of the Mediation Subcommittee for investigation. Once an investigation into the complaint has been concluded, a summary of the problem, and the publisher or vendor's response, is published in the Committee's newsletter, **The CRIV Sheet.**

This public airing of complaints has, on the whole, had a positive influence upon publishers' practices since it began in 1976, although it certainly has not resolved all matters of dispute. A review of the 132 complaints received by the Committee between 1976 and 1985 revealed that 40 of them cited the Guides and 92 did not.[12] Of those which cited the Guides, the major problems were:

Lack of copyright or publication date on advertising flyers
[Guide 256.1(d)]
(six complaints)

Reprints advertised without notification that they were reprinted materials
[Guide 256.1(e)] (five complaints)

Representations, express or implied, describing a work as "new," "current," or "up-to-date"

[Guide 256.5] (three complaints)

Upkeep service [Guide 256.14] (nine complaints)

Misrepresentations (general) [Guide 256.17] (eight complaints)

The study reached two main conclusions: (1) Most of the problems were due to a failure of communication and not the result of any nefarious intent on the part of the legal publishers, and (2) many of the same problems which gave rise to the Guides were continuing to occur frequently, including advertising flyers without publication or copyright dates, billing for unsolicited materials, and interpretations of "standing order" to include materials which are tangential to a particular set or series.

Have the FTC Guides worked? There is no question that the Guides have exerted a positive influence upon the law book publishing industry, particularly in their dealings with law libraries. Through voluntary compliance, publishers have cleaned up most of the nuisance type violations which plagued the industry in years past. It is much less common in the 1990's to see new titles on old books, the same book in two different sets, misleading advertising circulars, local names on national or regional books, and books without the correct printing or copyright date. In retrospect, there was probably not much money to be made by irritating law book consumers with such practices.

On the other hand, there are a number of practices which persist to this day, several of which are probably too great a source of income for legal publishers to abandon willingly. These include the adding of related books to established sets to ensure their automatic sale, overpricing supplementation, and failing to provide easy access to supplementation cost history, a major consideration in any legal information purchase. of major items. And certainly not all legal publishers persist in these specific violations of the Guides. Some have eliminated the practice of automatically shipping related titles to customers who failed to exercise the negative option by checking the correct box on the order form. Others may have stopped sending related titles to law library customers, but continued to take advantage of unsuspecting lawyer customers.

By 2001, two of Taylor's original complaints continued to plague the lawbook consuming public. These include: overpricing of supplements, the adding of remotely related books to established sets to assure their automatic sale. Of these, only the **Guides** themselves addressed the second. The other complaint--the overpricing of supplements is, unfortunately, outside the pale of legitimate governmental action. Pricing issues are ultimately addressed by the marketplace. About the only thing the FTC Guides could hope to guarantee is that the information regarding supplementation costs is: (1) provided in advertising circulars and (2) is accurate and not misleading. Legal publishers who continue to overprice their supplements will eventually be chastened by the marketplace and an atmosphere of open competition.

As a result of voluntary compliance by lawbook publishers, the FTC Guides have helped eliminate most of the nuisance violations in legal publishing. However, they are not a substitute for consumer education and vigilance. Moreover, a close examination of the Guides (see Appendix F) will reveal that most of them deal with advertising disclosures and representations. They do not protect the consumer from excesses in price or supplementation, except insofar as these excesses violate the Guide regarding upkeep service. The publisher has the right in a free market to charge what the market will bear. Conversely, the consumer has the responsibility to either accept or reject such pricing.

Guide to Fair Business Practices for Legal Publishers

With the rescission of the **Guides for the Law Book Industry** on January 19, 2000, the American Association of Law Libraries appointed a Special Committee on Fair Business Practices to draft standards of practice for both publishers and librarians. After considerable effort on the part of committee members, the **Guide to Fair Business Practices for Legal Publishers** was submitted to and approved by the AALL Board in November, 2002. While these standards of practice have had some degree of success by substituting voluntary industry compliance for government oversight, they have been a failure on the most critical issue—publishers' publication of supplementation cost history.

By the end of 2006, however, it had become clear that the intransigence of Thomson/West on the issue of providing supplementation cost history to consumers was seriously compromising a critical element of the Guide to Fair Business Practices for Legal Publishers and the very viability of the Price Index for Legal Publications which is now in a state of limbo.

In reality, only the rare publisher provides supplementation cost history on its web site, the place from which most legal information consumers now get their pricing information. However, the vast majority of publishers have voluntarily supplied supplementation cost data to AALL's Price Index for Legal Publications 2d, published from 1998 to 2004. The importance of supplying this critical data to consumers was addressed by both the Guides for the Law Book Industry, which specified the prior two years' costs, and Principle 2 (h) (iv) of the new Guide to Fair Business Practices for Legal Publishers, which specified that publishers provide "where possible, historic data on the cost of supplementation for the product." Indeed, it is impossible for any legal information consumer to make an informed judgment without knowledge of a product's supplementation cost history.

In reality, the FTC had neither the staff nor much desire to investigate those who violated the Guides. The FTC staff attorney under whose jurisdiction the Guides fell was responsible for monitoring a host of other industries and, since 1975, had taken little interest in the law book industry. Lawbook consumers will simply have to educate themselves regarding the practices of certain legal publishers and take action when those practices are unacceptable. If supplementation prices are exorbitant, or supplementation too frequent for your needs, you must be prepared to cancel your standing orders or look for a substitute product, if available. If you receive an undesired "related" title, you must be prepared to either keep it as a gift under the provisions of

U.S. Postal law or offer to return it to the publisher. While the FTC Guides for the Law Book Industry were extremely valuable as a model for proper practices, they, and the new Guide to Fair Business Practices for Legal Publishers, are not a substitute for personal responsibility.

Another positive result of vigilance on the part of law librarians and other legal information consumers is the drastic improvement in the availability of pricing information, both through 800 numbers and publishers' Web sites. While some work remains to be done on the supplementation cost front, the situation is light years away from the dark days when the only person who would give you complete pricing information was the local representative on a sales call.

Consumer Advocacy Caucus Formed

One of the most significant developments on the consumer front in many years was the formation of the Consumer Advocacy Caucus under the leadership of Michael Ginsborg and other dedicated law librarians. The caucus took form following an informal gathering of interested law librarians in Philadelphia, in conjunction with the 2011 AALL annual meeting. From a core group of about a dozen law librarians, the caucus has grown to more than 50 members. After considerable preliminary work by interested law librarians, and the circulation of a petition to AALL members that garnered the support of more than 175 law librarians, the following petition was submitted to the AALL Executive Board for its approval:

A Petition Of Undersigned AALL Members To AALL's Executive Board

As AALL members, we petition AALL's Executive Board to approve this statement of purpose for the creation of the AALL Caucus on Consumer Advocacy: "The AALL Caucus on Consumer Advocacy will recommend to AALL that it petition appropriate governmental bodies for specific remedies to anticompetitive and unfair business practices by legal information sellers." We do not consent to any disclosure of our names as signatories. Disclosure could allow legal information sellers to retaliate against us by singling out our employers for less favorable business relations.

On November 5, 2011, the AALL executive board unanimously approved the Consumer Advocacy Caucus's petition for official recognition. The petition was also endorsed by the Private Law Libraries-SIS. This spontaneous movement to take a bolder stand on consumer advocacy was prompted, among things, by: (1) dissatisfaction with the current state of publisher practices; (2) the inadequacy of the current response by the American Association of Law Libraries and its related committees; (3) dissatisfaction with AALL's proposed Antitrust Policy which would have unfairly stifled comment and criticism of publisher practices (including pricing practices); and (4) the need for a more robust mechanism whereby members can petition government bodies for specific remedies for "anticompetitive and unfair business practices by legal information sellers."

Notes:

1. Taylor, Raymond M., "Lawbook Consumers Need Protection," 55 **A.B.A. J.** 553-56 (1969).
2. Id.
3. While the number of library customers has remained fairly constant since 1969, the number of lawyers has risen to a present total of more than 1,000,000.
4. Taylor, supra note 1, at 556.
5. Kempel, Peter M. "New Guides for the Lawbook Industry," 54 **Mich. S.B.J.** 938 (1975).
6. Wright, Edward L., "President's Page," 57 **A.B.A. J.** 197 (1971).
7. "Lawyers' Checklist for Buying Lawbooks," 56 **A.B.A. J.** 272 (1970).
8. Statement by Roy Mersky, panel discussion titled, "Law Publishing Under Attack: A Panel," 64 **Law Libr. J.** 539-45 (1971).
9. Proceedings from the Third Business Session, 64th Annual Meeting, American Association of Law Libraries, June 16, 1971, 64 **Law Libr. J.** 440 (1971).
10. Statement by Roy Mersky, supra note 8, at 541; Kempel, supra note 5, at 939.
11. 40 **Fed. Reg.** 33,436 (1975) codified at 16 **C.F.R.** §§ 256.0-256.17 (1985).
12. Kosek, Reynold and Sue Welch, "Law Librarians as Consumer Advocates - Some Thoughts and Recommendations Based on the FTC Guides for the Law Book Industry," AALL Program, Washington, DC, 1986.

Chapter 4: Building and Maintaining Your Law Library

The acquisition of a law office library is just one of a host of expenditures which will consume the start-up capital of any lawyer going into practice for the first time. Before that first paying client has walked through the door, limited funds are apt to be quickly consumed by rent payments, utilities, office furniture, computers, telephones, secretarial assistance, insurance, professional dues, license fees, advertising, and paper clips. It may be a year, or more, before a law practice begins to turn a profit. Like any business, operating a law office requires that a tight rein on expenditures be maintained until such time as paying clients begin easing the financial strain.

In years past, buying shelving to house a law library was a normal procedure. Today, with the availability of computer-assisted legal research and attractively packaged libraries of primary and secondary materials in an online format, such an expense has become unnecessary. The cost of print reporters, advance sheets, codes, digests, and major reference tools like **American Jurisprudence 2d**, **American Law Reports**, and **Am Jur Pleading & Practice Forms**, to name just a few, has risen so sharply that savvy consumers should avoid them like the plague.

The **Atlantic Reporter 3d** advance sheets, for example, cost just a few hundred dollars back in the mid 1990s. Today, their cost is $2,866.56 per year. That money can be far more effectively utilized to pay for an annual subscription to Primary Law Resources on WestlawNext PRO for a small state like Rhode Island, priced at just $2,724 per year. Similarly, new or recompiled bound volumes to major reference sets can exceed $500 each. A standing order to such sets can soon deplete your bank account before you realize what is happening. Warning:: It's all about the supplementation, which is where legal publishers derive 80-90% of their revenues. Don't ever buy a print set, like **Am Jur 2d**, without first finding out what the supplements cost over the last couple of years. I'm convinced that when you do, you'll opt for a WestlawNext add-on rather than a print subscription.

When shopping for a law office, it is essential to consider its proximity to the nearest court or bar library. Ready access to a publicly accessible law library will pay for itself many times over in the form of reduced travel time and convenient access when essential research must be performed. Particularly in the early years of a practice, the local court or bar library will be an absolutely vital resource. Many larger metropolitan areas also have membership law libraries which, for a relatively modest annual fee, provide access to first-rate collection of legal information in a variety of formats. Alternatively, the lawyer should investigate the possibility of gaining access to the law library of a larger firm in his or her area in exchange for an annual contribution to aid in its maintenance.

As many of the materials in the average law library are rarely or only occasionally used, it makes great sense for one to share this expense with other members of the bar rather than attempting to bear the full expense alone. A shared law library can give the attorney access to a much greater variety of resources than he or she could possibly hope to purchase on his or her own.

Except in the case of the core collection, which will be described below, the attorney must resist the urge to purchase additional materials for his or her own library until every opportunity has been taken to examine, use, or borrow them from the local court or bar library. Law books, online services, and CD-ROM's are simply too expensive to buy on a whim and usually entail significant ongoing supplementation costs. It is essential that law library purchases be made with a fairly well-developed set of priorities in mind. These priorities should be established before the first lawbook salesperson finds his way to the lawyer's office and suggests the purchase of materials which are either inappropriate or beyond the attorney's limited financial resources.

Used lawbooks were once a viable alternative to acquiring whole sets new from the publishers. Today, while used lawbooks are still around, there is no longer an effective marketplace for their acquisition, except in limited instances, such as the monographs that show up on amazon,com. The availability attractively packaged online libraries at reasonable annual subscription rates have largely rendered the used market irrelevant. Indeed, major law firms have been disposing of their major print sets for years to willing takers for just the cost of postage. And with annual upkeep costs for National Reporter System regional reporters ranging from $5,434 to $15,094 per year, it's no wonder. Frankly, it's far less costly to acquire a state primary law package on WestlawNext than it is to maintain a single regional reporter series in hardcopy.

For a further discussion of used law books as an option see Chapter 8 and the representative used lawbook prices in Appendix E.

The Core Collection

A basic working library for the vast majority of law offices should consist of the following:

(1) an annotated state code; (2) state administrative regulations (at least those in your area of specialty); (3) appellate court reports for your state and federal circuit; (4) state and federal court rules (5) a case digest or its equivalent in the form of **editorial enhancements under the West Key Number System**; (6) a national citator service; (7) state practice books in one's area of specialty; (8) a legal dictionary; (9) a local legal newspaper; and (10) a national legal newspaper. The order in which these items are purchased will reflect the importance of primary law to any law practice. The additional tools are necessary to access the primary law and ensure that it is still current. The content of your core collection will depend on a number of factors, including the nature and scope of your practice, the distance to a publicly accessible law library, anticipated frequency of use, and a balancing of print versus electronic resources, among other factors.

The judicious selection of books for a law office library requires that the attorney have a firm understanding of the hierarchy of legal authorities. Ranked in order of importance, this hierarchy includes the following:

1. Constitutional provisions and appellate court decisions interpreting these provisions.
2. Statutory law, administrative regulations, and appellate

court decisions interpreting the statutes.

3. Common law determinations of the chief appellate court.

The attorney's first task in assembling a core collection for his or her law office, then, is to acquire those sources containing the law of these three levels of legal authority, the finding tools necessary to access the applicable constitutional, statutory or common law, and the tools necessary to ensure that those authorities are still valid. In order of importance, the components of this core collection include the following:

The attorney's first task in assembling a core collection for his or her law office, then, is to acquire those sources containing the law of these three levels of legal authority, the finding tools necessary to access the applicable constitutional, statutory or common law, and the tools necessary to ensure that those authorities are still valid. In order of importance, the components of this core collection include the following:

(1) Annotated state code. An annotated code is an absolutely essential first purchase. It contains your state constitution and all statutory enactments of your state legislature. Many state codes also include an advance annotation service providing access to recent cases interpreting particular constitutional and statutory provisions, and an advance legislative service providing access to legislation enacted since the appearance of the current pocket parts. Both advance services are essential for the attorney who wishes to ensure the currency of his or her law office collection.

In addition to its value as a source of constitutional and statutory law for the jurisdiction in which the attorney practices, an annotated code provides other useful editorial features, including brief summaries (annotations) of appellate court decisions which have interpreted particular provisions of the law, historical notes which track the evolution of each statute in the session laws, and, useful references to such relevant secondary sources as **American Law Reports** annotations, and legal encyclopedias, among others. Annotated state codes are updated by means of annual pocket supplements, pamphlet supplements, and periodically revised volumes which incorporate the text of the pocket parts into new bound volumes.

With the availability of packages of state legal materials on WestlawNext and LexisNexis, your annotated state code can be acquired along with other forms of primary law for your state as part of a package. Those with more limited funds can access the unannotated version of their state code on their state legislative web site, on less costly commercial online services (e.g. VersusLaw), or on bar-sponsored services like Casemaker until such time as funds permit purchase of one of the premium commercial packages. Despite its availability in electronic form, the annotated code is still useful in hardcopy, particularly if you are relying upon an electronic source without case annotations and historical notes. CD-ROM, which served as a viable alternative for a time, is rapidly losing favor with users who require more a more up-to-date resource or wish to avoid the dual look-up associated with CD-ROM supplemented with online access. Those who prefer statutory law in print can nevertheless use the online format to locate obscure statutory provisions and then read the text, annotations and historical notes in the hardcopy. For further discussion of state statutes, see Chapter 9.

(2) State code of administrative rules and regulations. As forms of delegated legislation, administrative regulations are a significant source of primary law. These exist in many forms, including print, CD-ROM, on LexisNexis, WestlawNext, a variety of alterative commercial online providers, and, increasingly, on state government web sites. Until recently, the acquisition of a state code of administrative regulations was beyond the means of most small law firms. For example, at $3,604.00, the **Code of Rhode Island Rules**, is nearly four times the cost of the **General Laws of Rhode Island** ($773.00 in-state). In such instances, however, the solo practitioner or small law firm can acquire only those volumes containing the regulations in their area(s) of specialty. WestlawNext PRO or Lexis Advantage libraries for your state, however, will contain this material at no additional cost, along with your state code and court decisions. A growing number of states are making regulations available on state government web states at no cost to the end user. At last count, forty-three had done so. Finally, the cost-conscious attorney should not neglect his or her own local public law library as a source for these materials, or any materials, were are consulted infrequently.

(3) Appellate court reports. Acquisition of the decisions of the state's highest court or courts is another essential purchase for any law office library. Before the introduction computer-assisted legal research (CALR), young lawyers typically acquired these in hardcopy, whether in the form of official state reports, regional off-print volumes or the full regional reporter series. In Massachusetts, for example, the attorney might have acquired the **Massachusetts Reports** (official), **Massachusetts Decisions** (West offprint), or **Northeastern Reporter** (regional reporter). Online offerings have changed all that. For good reason, lawyers now overwhelmingly prefer to acquire their state appellate court decisions In an online format, providing nearly instantaneous access to relevant case law and the ability to search it in ways impossible in a print environment.

And in light of significant increases in the cost of subscribing to West's regional reporters, the acquisition of court decisions in hardcopy has become a costly, unnecessary, and often duplicative, expenditure, particularly for those who are adept at computer-assisted legal research.

Whether the online or CD-ROM product chosen is one sold by West (which includes the ability to search editorial synopses and headnotes), LexisNexis, with its own panoply of editorial enhancements (Search Advisor), or one of several online providers, the decision must only be made after weighing all available options. The factors to be considered include: (1) the range of databases contained in the same package or CD-ROM; (2) historical coverage of case law; (3) editorial features attached to the databases (headnotes, synopses, core terms, etc.); (4) price (5) search engine; (6) hardware requirements (see "A Note of computer configurations" at the end of chapter 24). CALR services typically make court decisions available within days of their release. CD-ROM products containing appellate case law are typically updated on a quarterly basis, but with an online update).

If your state appellate case law is acquired as part of an online subscription (or CD-ROM), it is recommended that you develop some systematic routine of reviewing current appellate decisions from your state in your area(s) of practice which will replace whatever routine you may have performed with the print reporters and advance sheets. This is an essential practice for the any competent and well-prepared attorney. Eliminating a subscription to your regional reporter advance sheets will save you anywhere from $2,401 (New York Supplement 2d) to $2,866.56 per year (**Atlantic Reporter 2d**). Indeed, eliminating the cost of the National Reporter System advance sheets for your region will save you enough money to afford a basic primary law package on WestlawNext. If your state supreme court provides these decisions on its web site, so much the better. Or, perhaps, you are fortunate to be practicing in a state whose bar association is part of the Casemaker Consortium, in which case you will have access to these decisions as a part of your bar membership.

(4) State and federal court rules. For the practicing attorney, ready access to the rules of both state and federal courts in your jurisdiction is an absolute necessity. In most jurisdictions, the court rules are available in an annual paperbound edition of one or two volumes from either West or LexisNexis. These volumes contain the rules of both appellate and trial courts, including rules of the appropriate Federal District Court and Court of Appeals. See Chapter 28: State Legal Publications for references to state court rules (Category #6).

(5) State digest. In the days before LexisNexis, WestlawNext, and CD-ROM, the West digests were the only effective comprehensive tools for locating cases by subject and case name. With electronic access, the researcher can now perform full text searches and link multiple data fields. Is there still a place for the print digest? If expense is a serious consideration, you may wish to forego the purchase of a print digest entirely, particularly if you have access to the West Key Number System through WestlawNext or the LexisNexis Search Advisor, both of which provide the legal researcher with a means of transcending the inherent limitations of full-text searching.

The West digest, whether in print, or in the form of Key Number searching on WestlawNext provides that intellectual filter (the Key Number System) which collects cases by legal issue and groups them for quick perusal. In my view, the hardcopy digest has now been rendered obsolete by West's aggressive price increases which are increasingly driving customers to abandon them in favor of key number access via WestlawNext. Steep increases in the cost of annual pocket supplements and frequently recompiled volumes can cause annual costs of digests to jump significantly, as they have in a number of states in recent years. If you do acquire a used West digest in print, and have a WestlawNext subscription, consider dropping the standing order to the print in favor of updating online.

For LexisNexis subscribers, the Search Advisor feature provides a detailed classification system which combines the editorial subject expertise of Matthew Bender with the vast resources of the Lexis database. Search Advisor is based on a list of 40 broad legal subjects which correspond to established areas of the law and the subject matter covered in the law school curriculum. A researcher can either type in a legal topic and be guided to the appropriate location in the Search Advisor classification system, or click on an appropriate topic and navigate to a subtopic which best encompasses the subject of his inquiry. Once one has identified an appropriate topic, a hidden search, constructed in advance by attorneys on the Search Advisor editorial team, will be run automatically. Search Advisor provides researchers with an excellent alternative to the Key Number searching available from West.

(6) Citator Service. The ultimate embarrassment for the practicing attorney is discovering too late that the law he or she has relied upon as controlling authority has been overturned by the courts or amended by the legislature. The only systematic way of guaranteeing against that possibility is to consult Shepard's Citations, or KeyCite, the West citation service. Shepard's now provides all of its citators in print and online, the CD-ROMs having been discontinued in 2001. The all-inclusive prices of individual state citators are included in Chapter 26: State Publications, and a full discussion of citators is contained in Chapter 16. But print citators are now obsolete, certainly from a cost perspective. Both Shepard's and KeyCite are made available at no additional charge as part of an online jurisdictional package, whether that be Shepard's on LexisNexis or KeyCite on WestlawNext. KeyCite, unlike rival Shepard's Citations, is only available online

(7) State Practice books. These publications run the gamut, from exhaustive sources published by West and Matthew Bender to more superficial state continuing legal education (CLE) publications. State practice sets, like West's **Massachusetts Practice** or Bender's **California Point and Authorities**, provide specific guidance which the practitioner is unlikely to find in books aimed at a national audience. Your library should contain the most important of these practice books in your area(s) of specialty. However, again, these publications should be avoided in print if they can be acquired as part of an enhanced state WestlawNext subscription. Also, be aware that it is not always necessary to purchase a complete practice set. Most publishers will allow you to purchase individual components which reflect those areas in which you practice.

(8) A legal dictionary. Every law office should have at least one annotated legal dictionary. **Black's Law Dictionary** (9th edition/2009), the most widely used of those on the market, includes numerous citations to court decisions and statutes wherein the word has been defined. New editions appear every 10-12 years. Other useful reference tools are listed in Chapter 22: Law-Related Reference Sources.

(9) A local legal newspaper. As a current awareness tool, a local legal newspaper is another must for any practicing attorney. A local legal newspaper provides timely coverage of decisions of trial and appellate courts, administrative agencies, and legislative developments. Coverage also includes legal notices and advertisements, feature articles, and court procedural developments. A local legal newspaper is required reading for any attorney who wishes to keep abreast of current developments, including state appellate court decisions.

(10) National legal newspaper. The attorney who wishes to keep well-informed, should also subscribe to one of the three weekly legal newspapers that are national in scope: **Legal Times, National Law Journal** or **Lawyers Weekly USA**. All include timely coverage of significant decisions of the United States Supreme Court and lower federal courts, as well as selective coverage of state appellate courts. Coverage also extends to legal technology, classifieds, employment opportunities, etc. This is an essential tool for the attorney who wishes to keep on top of national trends and developments. The American Lawyer, a tabloid-sized monthly, provides a more personality-oriented perspective on the law.

Exploring Media Options

Technological advances in the world of legal information have expanded the options available to the consumer and made decision-making a far more complicated process today than it was thirty years ago. Today, the consumer must not only choose from among competing publishers, but from among multiple formats. Information which once existed only in print, may now be available on a commercial online service, on CD-ROM, or a free government Internet site. The CD-ROM offerings which existed just a few year ago are rapidly disappearing from the marketplace.

Flat-Rate Online Legal Research Options

Building a law office library in today's technologically sophisticated world will involve selecting from among several flat-rate online plans offered by WestlawNext, LexisNexis, Bloomberg Law, VersusLaw, Fastcase, and a variety of other online providers. Other computer-assisted legal research services are discussed in chapter 25. The plans offered by WestlawNext and LexisNexis, for example, involve building a package of online resources best suited to a specific jurisdiction and practice. Both begin with a library of state specific materials and can be expanded to include a package consisting of materials for your federal circuit and the United States Supreme Court, as well as a citator service. Using these libraries as a base, you have the option of adding other primary law, including cases. statutes, and regulations, and a variety of secondary sources, including treatises and practice tools. Subject-specific libraries, particularly those offered by WestlawNext and LexisNexis, provide additional options for those who practice in a particular specialty. See Chapter 25: Computer-Assisted Legal Research for additional pricing information, or contact you local sales representative.

The sample CALR options which follow are intended to provide the reader with a basic understanding of some of the most common pricing models. Both WestlawNext and LexisNexis, for example, increase prices incrementally depending upon firm size (called "banded pricing"). The Thomson Reuters web site allows customers to price WestlawNext plans for 1-3 attorneys. Those interested in pricing plans for firms greater than three attorneys are directed to their local sales representative.

Sample Westlaw Fixed Rate Plans (2013)
(Solo Practitioner)

1. Primary Law Resources CA*	$303/mo. or $3,636 /yr.
1. Primary Law Resources CA Plus**	$365/mo. or $4,380/yr.
2. Primary Law Resources OH*	$263/mo. or $3,156/yr.
2. Primary Law Resources OH Plus**	$166/mo. or $3,804/yr.
3. Primary Law Resources RI*	$227/mo. or $2,224/yr.
3. Primary Law Resources RI Plus**	$269/mo. or $3,228/yr.

*State Primary Law Resources on WestlawNext PRO typically include decisions for the state in question, the applicable federal circuit, U.S. Supreme Court, state annotated code, full text of court decisions plus editorial enhancements under the West Key Number System, United States Code Annotated, KeyCite, and more.

**State Primary Resources Plus on WestlawNext PRO typically includes case law for all fifty states, federal case law from the U.S. district courts, Courts of Appeal and U.S. Supreme Court, specialized case law, annotated codes and court rules for all fifty states, federal court rules, subject specific case law, full text of court decisions plus editorial enhancements under the West Key Number System, KeyCite, and more.

Thomson Reuters also offers state Essentials plans with less content than the above plans. A CT Essentials plan, for example, is only $150.00 per month or $1,800.00 per year on a two-year contract. For full details, and special deals, contact your local sales representative.

Popular WestlawNext add-ons
(Solo Practitioner)

Title	WestlawNext Monthly	WestlawNext Annual
American Jurisprudence 2d	$147.00	$1,764.00
Am Jur Legal Forms	$106.00	$1,272.00
Am Jur Pl. & Prac Forms	$106.00	$1,272.00
American Law Reports	$174.00	$2,088.00
Am Jur Trials	$106.00	$1,272.00
Am Jur Proof of Facts	$106.00	$1,272.00
Am Jur Trials & POF	$133.00	$1,596.00
All Am Jur Library*	$236.00	$2,832.00

*Includes **American Jurisprudence 2d, American Law Reports Library** (1st-6th and Fed 1st and 2d), **ALR Index, Am Jur Legal Forms, Am Jur Trials, and Am Jur Proof of Facts**. These list prices, however, can be sharply discounted when added to a state plan and dealing with a sales representative. The **All Am Jur Library** is only $1,996.80 per year when added to a state plan on a one-year contract, or $1,747.00 per year on a two-year contract.

Contrast the cost of these offerings with cost of the equivalent print resources, both annual print set maintenance (2013) and individual volumes:

Title	Annual upkeep	Bound volumes (ea.)
American Jurisprudence 2d	$13,456.00	$539.00
Am Jur Legal Forms	$4,845.00	$468.00
Am Jur Pl. & Prac Forms	$6,347.00	$537.00
American Law Reports	$12,554.00	$404.00
Am Jur Trials	$5,590.00	$556.00
Am Jur Proof of Facts	$6,926.00	$549.00
Am Jur Trials & POF	$13,388.00	n/a
All Am Jur Library	$49,718.00	n/a

As you can readily see, the cost of maintaining print sets has become prohibitively expensive, with the components of the **American Jurisprudence Library** alone costing nearly $50,000 annually in supplementation costs (to say nothing of the initial acquisition costs) (the **Am Jur POF and Trials** combo is excluded from total) versus $2,832 annually for the **All American Jurisprudence 2d Library with ALR on WestlawNext PRO**. If print is on its death bed as a viable consumer option, these figures provide irrefutable proof.

Cost Saving Tip: As an addition to a state jurisdictional package on Westlaw, the All Am Jur Library Is probably the best addition to your online library and the best bargain. But that should not preclude you from negotiating further with your Westlaw representative for a better deal than the published rates.

Sample Lexis Advance Legal Research Plans

Lexis Advantage State Plans fall into three categories: State Primary, Primary Enhanced, and State Enhanced with Full Federal. The following sample states will give you an understanding of how they are priced:

State	Primary Law	Primary Law Enhanced	Enhanced w/ Full Federal
California	$1,200.00	$1,800.00	$2,400.00
Connecticut	$1,200.00	$1,440.00	$1,920.00
Louisiana	$1,200.00	$1,800.00	$2,400.00
Massachusetts	$1,200.00	$1,800.00	$2,400.00
Michigan	$1,200.00	$1,800.00	$2,400.00
New York	$1,500.00	$1,800.00	$2,400.00
S. Carolina	$1,200.00	$1,800.00	$2,400.00

State Primary typically includes state constitution, statutes, court cases, bills, bill tracking, state and federal court rules, and the full Shepard's Citation service.

Primary Enhanced typically includes state constitution, statutes, state regulatory and administrative materials, state court cases, federal court cases from the respective circuit, attorney general opinions, bills, bill tracking, state and federal court rules, 300+ law reviews and journals, and the full Shepard's Citation service.

State Enhanced with Full Federal adds to the above materials the full library of federal cases from all federal courts of appeal, U,S. District Courts, and specialized federal courts.

VersusLaw: 2014 Pricing

Plan Type	Price per password (Large or small state)
Standard Plan (one password required for each attorney in firm) (Federal and state appellate court decisions)	$167.40 per year ($13.95/mo.)
Premium Plan (Standard Plan contents plus state source materials and increased search engine capabilities)	$299.40 per year ($24.95/mo.)
Professional Plan (Premium Plan contents plus federal specialty practice courts, and current versions of the U.S. Code and Code of Federal Regulations)	$479.40 per year ($39.95/mo.)

*A complete description of WestlawNext, LexisNexis and nine other Computer-assisted legal research services follows in Chapter 25.

*A complete description of WestlawNext, LexisNexis and nine other Computer-assisted legal research services follows in Chapter 25.

Sample Lexis Advance Legal Research Plans

The cost to purchase and supplement this core collection obviously varies from state to state; however, the elimination of most costly print publications, including print case reporters, advance sheets, statutes, and digests, and other costly reference sets in favor of an online access will sharply reduce these costs. Law librarians may, justifiably, lament the degree to which current law graduates have largely abandoned the use of print resources in favor of computer-assisted legal research; however, the time has come to concede the reality and tailor our recommendations to an online world.

Consequently, one of the premium online services (WestlawNext or LexisNexis) with its respective citator (KeyCite or Shepard's), is recommended for the active practitioner who routinely performs legal research. These services provide access to your state primary law, including annotated state code, state regulations, a complete archive of state appellate court decisions, and searching capabilities which can replicate some of the features of, if not replace, the traditional print case digest. These recommendations should not preclude the acquisition of some appropriate print resources where funds allow, including a new or, preferably, used state digest, and, perhaps, a back run of print reporters (if you prefer to read cases in print), but are not dependent on them. You must also be prepared for the annual cost of supplementing this core collection.

Primary Law Resources CA Plus with KeyCite, for example, including statutes, state regulations, state and federal court decisions, law reviews, and more, is priced at $4,380 per year for a sole practitioner. Building the core collection around the WestlawNext PRO plan will eliminate a significant portion of the cost formerly incurred when assembling a library more dependent on print materials, including not only print statutes, case reporters, digests, and citators, but such popular reference sets as American Jurisprudence 2d, American Law Reports, Am. Jr. Legal Forms, Am. Jur. Pleading & Practice Forms, Am. Jur. Trials, and Am. Jur. Proof of Facts, among others. All of these are far cheaper to acquire as WestlawNext add-ons than as print resources. A similar core library can be assembled using a LexisNexis Advantage plan as a base. A number of West titles, such as American Jurisprudence 2d and American Law Reports, are licensed for use on LexisNexis.

The sample small state plan below (using Rhode Island as an example), includes some print resources not included in the sample California collection. This is chiefly because the cost of the General Laws of Rhode Island and Rhode Island Digest are significantly less costly than their counterparts for California. Used costs are included in both instances, although the elimination of print materials for California effectively eliminates the differential between the new and used costs. In the case of both states, both the new and used costs of a core collection are about one-third to one-half what they were in previous editions of this work because of the shift from print to online.

Sample Costs of Core Collections

Large State (California)	New	Renewal (2014)
Primary Law Resources CA (Westlaw)	$4,380/yr.	$4,380/yr.
California Rules of Court (West)	$72	$72
Black's Law Dictionary, 9th ed.	$79.95	n/a
Los Angeles Daily Journal	$735	$735
National Law Journal (online)	**$99	$299

Small State (Rhode Island)	New	Used	Renewal (2014)
Lexis Advance Primary Law Enhanced (RI)	$1,440	$1,440*	$1,440
General Laws of Rhode Island	$773	$773*	$550
R.I. Court Rules Annotated	$71	$71*	$71
Rhode Island Digest	$2,929	$600	$1,852
Black's Law Dictionary, 9th ed.	$79.95	$79.95*	0
R.I. Lawyers Weekly	$319	$319*	$319
National Law Journal	$299	$299*	$299

*New price provided because used book option is not applicable or offers negligible cost savings. State regulations and state practice books excluded from the lists because of the variety of options, including acquisition of individual volumes. Note: The above examples eliminate court decisions in print.

Moving Beyond the Core

The following print publications are among the most useful additions to the core collection, all of which are available used. They are all also available as add-ons to a WestlawNext subscription, usually at significant savings over the cost of maintaining them in print. Indeed, the attractive prices to subscribe to these publications on WestlawNext demolishes any justification to maintain these subscriptions in print. For example, a solo practitioner can add **American Jurisprudence 2d** to a basic WestlawNext plan for an additional $1,560.00 per year, a savings of about $11,692 over the cost of maintaining the print subscription. Those who prefer print, but wish to avoid high maintenance costs, can acquire any of these sets used, but then update them with less costly online access (provided you wish to update them at all). The following titles are listed for comparative purposes to allow the prospective customer the substantial differential between subscribing in print and through WestlawNext.

Title	New	Used	Annual Supp. (2013)	On Westlaw*
American Jurisprudence 2d	$14,909	$1,295	$13,456	$1,764*
American Law Repts 3d-6th	$12,719	$1,300	$8,762	$2,088*
American Law Rpts Index	$1,150	$75	$188	n/a
Am. Jur. Legal Forms	$8,499	$800	$4,845	$1,272*
Am. Jur. Pl. & Prac. Forms	$9,639	$600	$6,347	$1,272*
Am. Jur. Trials	$7,304	$600	$5,590	$1,272*
Am. Jur POF [1st] - 3d	$9,697	$1,150	$6,926	$1,272*
Am. Jur. Trials & P.O.F.	***	***	***	$1,596*

*For 1-2 attorneys at the same location

Acquiring and Maintaining a Federal Library

The following federal publications are among the most likely candidates for a federal library. However, the contents of these sets are also available as components of a WestlawNext or LexisNexis subscription. The **United States Code Annotated**, for example, is available as a part of a WestlawNext Pro Plus subscription, as are **Federal Practice & Procedure**, **Federal Procedure/Federal Procedure Forms**, the **Code of Federal Regulations/Federal Register**, and the caselaw reported in the **Supreme Court Reporter**, **Federal Reporter**, and **Federal Supplement 2d**. The **United States Code Service** is available on LexisNexis as part of a State Enhanced MVP Plan. In addition, LexisNexis provides researchers with the option of subscribing to selected databases by the day or week, an ideal solution for the occasional user. Contact your sales representative for further details on specific titles. He or she can offer special package deals for primary law combined with additional reference sets like **American Jurisprudence 2d**.

Title	New	Used*	Annual Supp (2013)
U.S. Code Annotated (West)	$13,532	$1,500	$11,585.00
United States Code Service (Lexis)	$3,338	$495	$3,338.00
Code of Fed. Regulations (G.P.O.)	$1,804	$1,804	$1,804.00
Supreme Court Digest (West)	$3.877	$895	$2,460.00
Supreme Court Reporter (West)	$5,489	$1,700	$106.00
U.S. Sup. Ct. Rpts, L.Ed. 2d (Lexis)	$6,843	$895	$350.00
U.S. Sup. Court Digest, L. Ed. (Lexis)	$3,235	$395	$1,173.00
Federal Practice and Proc. (West)	$4,118	$500	$3,389.00
Federal Reporter 3d (West)	$15,895	$2,500	$10,642.00
Federal Supplement 2d (West)	$26,833	$2,300	$23,542.00

Federal Prac. Digest 4th-5th (West)	$23,742	$595	$22,614.00
Federal Procedure, L. Ed. (West)	$10,381	$350	$7,414.00
Fed. Civil Jud. Proc. & Rules (West)	$139	*$139	$139.00
Fed. Crim. Code & Rules (West)	$146	*$146	$146.00

These sample prices are provided merely to illustrate why hardcopy case reporters and many other publications are no longer a viable options for law firms. The price escalation of print reporters since West's acquisition by the Thomson Corporation in 1996, together with the availability of these decisions on WestlawNext (or any number of other online providers) has rendered the bound volume obsolete as a practical matter. The same hold true with practically any hardcopy volumes that are simultaneously available on WestlawNext. Determining in advance what you wish to accomplish with your library, and what to avoid, will better enable you to select those resources you really need and spare you much unnecessary expense.

Special Alert: West's price increases in 2014 on the initial costs of many of the above sets has ranged from 9% (**Proof of Facts**) to 27% (**Supreme Court Digest**).

While the titles selected for illustrative purposes are generally limited to those of the LexisNexis and West, the author does not mean to suggest that these are the only available alternatives. This is particularly true now that both companies together control 65% of the market for legal information in the United States. For example, the last seventy years of federal appeals court decisions are available on the Internet from VersusLaw at a cost of only $167.40 per year. Furthermore, in most states, attorneys have access to Casemaker, a CALR service made available as a benefit of bar membership (see Appendix I for a complete list of states in which Casemaker is available). The unannotated text of the **United States Code** is also available on CD-ROM from the U.S. Government Printing Office at $30.00, but it is less than current and must be updated online. It is also available at no cost on several public Internet sites, including GPOAccess located at: http://www.gpoaccess.gov

Similarly, the **Code of Federal Regulations** and the **Federal Register** are available online at the Office of the Federal Register at: www.archives.gov/federal-register/index.html.

For libraries, and others, who prefer print, the **Code of Federal Regulations** and the **Federal Register** are available at an annual cost of $1,804.00 and $929.00 respectively.

The reader is also directed to the appropriate chapters of this book for a fuller discussion of the relative merits of various legal publications, federal and state. With this information, you can then select those individual titles most appropriate to your practice, preferences, and financial resources. And don't neglect to take advantage of the sales representatives for WestlawNext and LexisNexis who can present competitive packages of online access designed to meet your specific legal research needs. And don't forget to tell them that you are making a close evaluation of both services.

This chapter has highlighted the major legal publications which the typical law firm is likely to acquire and maintain. In addition to these general publications, your record keeping must include all other specific publications which your practice requires and which you maintain on a regular basis. With a complete inventory of your library and its attendant costs, you will be in a far better position to monitor your level of expenditures and to make those decisions necessary to bring library costs under control.

Chapter 5: Evaluating Legal Materials

In Chapter 4, we examined the many issues which impact the process of assembling and maintaining a law office library. We now turn our attention to those factors which should be considered before you purchase a particular book, set, online or CD-ROM product. There are at least sixteen factors which should be a part of your evaluative process.

Critical Factors in Selecting Legal Information Tools

(1) The reputation of the author. What experience or special knowledge does the author bring to the subject matter? Has he or she published previously in the field or have a national reputation based on years of teaching, practice, or professional association activity? Is the author actually involved in writing the book or has that task been delegated to the publisher's editorial staff. Legal publishers routinely retain the names of famous authors on their books years after those authors have departed for the great law office in the sky. Erastus C. Benedict has been dead for more than 100 years, yet that doesn't stop Matthew Bender & Company from continuing the use of his name to market **Benedict on Admiralty**. If the author's name is merely being used as a front for a book or set prepared by the publisher's editorial staff, you should be apprised of this fact.

A first-rate legal publisher should devote editorial resources to the substantive review of an author's work, yet few publishers do so. Consequently, much depends on the quality of the original author's work. If an author makes a serious substantive error, some legal publishers do not have an editorial mechanism in place to catch it. In recent years, editorial resources devoted to some major legal publications have been cut and pay rates for outside editors reduced in the drive to fatten profit margins. These developments are affecting a number of well-known publications with established reputations. Since many established legal publications are never re-reviewed, their publishers may believe they can live off of their past reputations. In light of these developments, the careful legal researcher must avoid an undue reliance upon the content of secondary sources by consulting primary sources whenever possible.

(2) The reputation of the publisher. In the current world of legal publishing, this factor is closely related to the previous one. A number of legal publishers have established excellent reputations for producing works of high quality and scholarship. An excellent publisher can take a work of modest pretensions and mold it into first-class work of scholarship and legal reference. Whether a book is actually written by the named author or authors, or is largely produced by the publisher's editorial staff, its quality is heavily dependent on the quality control exercised by the publisher to ensure that it meets the highest standards. Of course, a legal publisher can have an excellent editorial reputation, but be found wanting on such criteria as pricing, supplementation, and marketing practices. Be particularly aware of publishers who take advantage of their past reputation, or the reputation of products they have acquired, to put profit ahead of editorial quality.

(3) The place of the book or other product in one's practice. Is the book, CD-ROM, or ebook under consideration essential to your practice, or is it only tangential to the areas in which you generally practice? Will ownership of this title save you time running to the local public law library which may or not have the book on the shelves when you need it? If the item falls in your area of specialty, you owe it yourself and your clients to have it readily available to answer questions as they arise.

(4) The work's organization and scope. Is the title logically arranged and easy to use? Does the coverage match your needs or is it too superficial? Is it an introductory overview of the subject matter or an exhaustive analysis?

(5) Style and readability. Is the text written in a clear and understandable style or is its prose an exercise in academic obfuscation? If in an area outside your area of expertise, is it written in such manner as to be comprehensible to the generalist? Does it include sufficient real-life examples and illustrations to illuminate the text?

(6) Scholarly attributes and reference features. Is the work sufficiently laden with citations to both primary and secondary authorities to support your legal arguments or as an aid to further research. How many of these citations are annotated as an aid to determining if the complete case or citation should be consulted? Does the work cite to cases and statutes from all jurisdictions? Does it cite to the secondary works of a wide range of legal publishers or largely the works from the same publisher? If the title is a part of an integrated legal research "system," like that of the ThomsonWest, which combines the resources of West and many former Lawyer's Cooperative products, do you own or do you plan to purchase other sets in that system? The cross-references to the various sets in this system are an especially valuable research feature.

(7) Supplementation. Supplementation is a critical issue when choosing legal publications, because it is largely profit-driven. Particularly if the field is one subject to frequent change, does the publisher plan to supplement the title in the future? In general, this is a little like asking if water is wet since, as I will explain in Chapter 6, the astute publishers see supplementation as a steady stream of future income. Indeed, in 2013, Thomson Reuters West derived nearly 90% of its revenue from recurring and subscription sales, both print and electronic. There are some publishers, however, who are less aggressive about supplementing their treatises and may issue supplements infrequently, or not at all (many West Hornbooks fall into this category, though now sold off to West Academic Publishing). If you desire to leave the title on a standing order, it is important that the supplementation frequency closely match your actual needs. If not, you will have to take steps to control the level of supplementation to bring it in line with your personal requirements and budget. If you want a treatise with annual supplementation for example, don't buy one which is updated 3-4 times per year with non-cumulative supplements requiring complicated filing.

(8) Format. Is the volume or set in a casebound, looseleaf format, or electronic format? Substantively, this factor should not make much difference. In recent years, however, some publishers have been transforming casebound books or sets into looseleaf sets, presumably to better allow them to replace individual pages or pamphlets, but also, some would argue, to supplement with greater frequency. If this is a print looseleaf format, do you have the clerical resources to handle all the filings? Might an online equivalent be a better alternative?

(9) Is the title or set available in an online format? In an age in which electronic formats are making serious inroads into the sales of hard copy this is a critical question. No longer in their infancy, online access offers all sorts of advantages over hard copy. They provide the user with the ability to search a database for relevant terms with high speed, a vast improvement over the hard copy index or digest. For reasons which I will explain in greater detail in a later chapter, these technologies works best when applied to bodies of material which lack a logical and systematic organization of their own. Thus, large bodies of case law are ideal candidates for an online format because the cases are published randomly as far as their subject matter is concerned. A legal treatise, provided it is systematically and logically organized, can be utilized almost as well, if not better, in hard copy as it can in electronic form.

In recent years, West has made most of its secondary/analytical works available in an online format. With the exception of such large sets as American Jurisprudence 2d, American Law Reports, individual treatises are generally not available as standalone products, but as part of more comprehensive specialized libraries on WestlawNext. They are commonly marketed as a part of a Practitioner Library as an add-on to a WestlawNext subscription. Thus, such works as Norton on Bankruptcy, are available as a part of Westlaw Bankruptcy Practitioner together with Bankruptcy texts and treatises, cases, codes and rules, court documents, judge and attorney profiles, filing software, and other subject specific content. For the specialist, these packages can provide superior research advantages as well as cost savings. A researcher working in one of these specialized libraries can navigate between analytical discussion and primary law.

(10) How does it compare with other works on the same subject? Is the coverage superior to that of its competitor? In this regard, it is important to compare it with a work of similar size and scope--for example, a multi-volume treatise with another work of similar length. Thus, Frumer and Friedman's Products Liability (Matthew Bender) should be compared with the American Law of Products Liability (West), not with Owen, Madden and Davis' three-volume Products Liability (West). Compare the writing style, citations, research aids, organization, cost, and other criteria already discussed. Take a close look at the treatment of a subject you are currently researching.

(11) Initial and supplementation cost. In an era of rapidly escalating prices for law books and their supplements, it is essential that you pay close attention to cost before making a purchase (note that I did not say "investment"). Legal treatise initial and supplementation costs have increased dramatically over the past several years. Single-volume treatises which cost $65.00-$70.00 in the early 1980's now cost $200 to $300, or more. In fact, one major legal publisher recently issued a single-volume treatise priced at $625.00. Annual pocket supplements which averaged $20.00-$25.00 now easily exceed $150.00. This says nothing of the single-volume casebound works which have been expanded into two or three-volume looseleaf works to permit the inclusion of cumulative or interfiled supplements two or three times per year. Thus, after determining the initial cost of a work, the most important question you can ask is how much the supplements have cost in recent years. The now rescinded **FTC Guides for the Law Book Industry** required publishers to inform consumers of supplementation costs for the last two years in order to provide them with some sense of what the future is likely to hold. And the newly approved **AALL Guide to Fair Business Practices for Legal Publishers** (November, 2012), urges publishers to supply "where possible, historic data on the cost of supplementation for the product." Without this information, you may be setting yourself up for a major financial drain over the course of a few years. With the demise of the **FTC Guides for the Law Book Industry** and the failure of legal publishers to make historic supplementation costs readily available to the public, the **Legal Information Buyer's Guide & Reference Manua**l is the only book on the market that has consistently provided this data to legal information consumers.

As an illustration, consider the single-volume treatise **Brady on Bank Checks**, (now published by A.S. Pratt & Sons). Several years ago, it was converted to a subscription service publication at an annual cost of more than $335.00 (it is now $623 per year). However, under its prior owner, Warren, Gorham & Lamont, the customer had the option of purchasing the thrice-yearly supplements only as often as he or she desired. By buying one supplement per year, the customer was able to reduce the annual cost from $210.00 to $70.00. By 2010, the annual subscription cost had risen to $499 per year. Does this mean that the work should not be purchased? No. It simply means that you must take steps to control supplementation to meet the needs of your practice and expense account. In this instance, subscribing every other year will still provide you with annual supplementation, but cut the supplementation cost in half. A similar evaluation of every work in your library will give you a sense of what your library's total supplementation costs are over the course of a year and the steps which can be taken to reduce them.

(12) Is the book for the generalist or the specialist? A brief examination of the treatise or other work under consideration should tell you whether it is designed with the needs of the general practitioner or the specialist in mind. Does the work assume some prior knowledge of the field, or does it cover elementary concepts thoroughly? Does the treatment match your own knowledge of the field? An ideal work will serve the needs of both kinds of users.

(13) What is the date of publication? The work should have been published recently enough to encompass recent important developments in the field. Coverage of current developments may be treated in the supplementation, but this is no substitute for an integrated analysis which incorporates these developments into the body of the text. For example, a work on securities law published before the enactment of the Sarbanes-Oxley Act of 2002, would be clearly inferior on this score to one written after 2002.

(14) Do you have a real or demonstrated need for this work? Many law books are purchased because the publisher's local sales representative or telemarketer made a successful "pitch" to the lawyer or other customer. However, did you really need this work at this particular time or were you merely anticipating its possible future utility? As I have already illustrated, law books and their supplements are simply too expensive to purchase unless one has a present need for them. You must ask yourself: Would I have purchased this title independently of the sales promotion? If the answer is "no," then send the book back for credit. In my view, the good local sales representatives can perform a valuable function by introducing you to new or existing products or by presenting special offers, but he or she should not persuade you to buy something you really don't need or won't use.

This buyer's guide was designed to give you the tools necessary to approach the sales promotion with intelligence and perspective. Telemarketers are another matter. Their entire approach of pitching titles over the phone to lawyers they have never met and whose needs they do not comprehend is a crude method of selling law books. I would recommend refusing their calls. If, on the other hand, you find it difficult to do this, don't buy anything over the phone, even if it is on a 30-day approval. Simply say: "I have a firm policy against buying anything over the phone. If you wish, you may send me a sales flyer of the product for my examination." This approach usually stops the vast majority of telemarketers dead in their tracks. Ideally, the sales representatives should call at your request after you have thoroughly researched the books, sets, or CD-ROM titles in which you are interested. Your local public law library probably has most of these items in its collection. Set aside a few hours to examine titles in which you are interested, or make notes regarding those titles you have used to advantage at your local public law library.

(15) Buy only what you need for your practice. It is not always necessary to buy a complete set of law books when a partial set or volume will suit your needs. For example, if you practice labor law, you may be able to get along with only those volumes of the **United States Code Annotated** or **United States Code Service** containing Title 29. Do you use federal or state regulations? Buy only those volumes of the **Code of Federal Regulations** or your state administrative code covering your area of specialty. Unless you heed this rule, you may find that most of the volumes in the large multi-volume set you have purchased at considerable expense will never be opened. Does a multi-volume treatise you desire include several volumes of appendices containing primary source materials you already own in other forms (e.g. in your **U.S. Code**). Or, can you buy individual chapters of multi-volume works on the publisher's website? Does a treatise include forms on disc or a monthly newsletter or annual handbook which you can do without? Determine exactly what your standing order will contain at point of purchase and take steps to eliminate all those extras which are unnecessary to your practice.

(16) Is the material available on the Internet and is it reliable? In recent years, the Internet has improved dramatically as a medium for delivering legal information. State and federal statutes, regulations, court decisions, administrative rulings and other forms of primary and secondary law are being added to government web sites daily. As your confidence in a particular web site grows, you can allow the availability of information at those sites to influence your buying decisions for materials in other formats. You should be aware, however, that most government sites will not provide complete archives of decisional material. In these and other instances, a commercial Web site may be a better alternative because of the depth of its coverage. For example, the Web site maintained by the State of North Carolina contains North Carolina Supreme Court decisions from February 10, 1997 to date. On the other hand, the commercial Web sites of Westlaw, LexisNexis and Loislaw contain decisions back to 1778. You owe it to yourself to become thoroughly familiar with the Internet and with those governmental and commercial Web sites containing information of particular value to your practice so that you can reduce your library expenses accordingly.

Millions of dollars are wasted annually by lawyers who never take the time to seriously evaluate their libraries or to question the practices to which they are being subjected by some legal publishers. By utilizing these factors in your decision-making process, you will take a major step toward ensuring that your law library properly reflects both your needs and financial resources.

Chapter 6: The Question of Supplements

One of the central issues which must be addressed by anyone who purchases legal information is how to deal with the steady flow of supplementary materials which will inevitably accompany those purchases. In recent years, the vast majority of legal publishers have come to rely heavily upon the automatic sale of supplements to standing order customers as a major source of their revenues. It has been estimated that as much as 89% of the revenues garnered by some legal publishers is derived from the sale of supplementary materials, including pocket parts, releases, revised volumes, periodic CD-ROM updates, or, increasingly, online subscription renewals.

Dealing With the Flow of Supplements

This is a dramatic reversal of the situation that existed earlier in the century when the vast majority of legal treatises were updated chiefly by the issuance of new editions at irregular intervals. Present-day legal publishers, however, have come to the realization that the sale of supplementary materials to the lawyers who constitute the vast majority of their customers is a generally reliable source of additional profits. Since each title in their catalogs represents a potential revenue stream, most legal publishers have a vested interest in ensuring that each title is supplemented annually, if not more frequently. While the average title is updated by an annual pocket part free-standing supplement, or, increasingly, an annual replacement volume, others may be updated as many as three or four times in a single year, and many current awareness looseleaf services are updated weekly.

Gone are the days when the law book consumer could purchase a title, enter a standing order for supplementation, and then sit back and relax. Rapidly escalating prices and aggressive marketing tactics have rendered such an approach obsolete, if not foolhardy. Not only have supplements become more common and frequent, but their costs have reached levels which should make even the most affluent attorney sit up and take notice. While the cost of maintaining a multi-volume treatise may commonly exceed a thousand dollars, the cost of pocket parts to single-volume treatises should also raise eyebrows among the law book consuming public. It was not that long ago that one could purchase the annual pocket to a single-volume treatise for $10.00-$15.00. Today, that cost is likely to be $150.00 - $200.00. It should be a source of considerable concern that the $25.00 you shell out to purchase the latest John Grisham bestseller will buy you only one-seventh of the average pocket part to a single-volume legal treatise. A full set of 125 pocket parts to West's American **Law Reports, 5th** cost $870.00 (list) in 2013 (or $6.96 per volume). The cost of supplementing 125 single-volume treatises, however, may easily exceed $25,000 annually.

Multi-volume treatises have also been subject to significant price increases in recent years. For example, annual supplementation to West's legal encyclopedia **American Jurisprudence 2d** rose from $1,300.00 in 1993 to $13,546.00 in 2013, an increase of 942% in 20 years. In fact, the entire catalog of Thomson West titles has been subject to enormous price and supplementation cost increases since 1996. Indeed, the cost increases are so egregious that it would appear that West's intention in to drive customers away from print and into the arms of Westlaw, not that this is necessarily a bad thing. But it is for those not paying attention and still maintaining print subscriptions.

Many legal publishers, through the development and use of sophisticated market analysis, have been able to probe the limits of consumer resistance. Even some of the more recent entrants to the field of legal publishing have quickly learned from and adopted the supplementation practices of the more aggressive legal publishers. This is not only the result of market research, but also of the continuing flow of legal publishing executives between various companies and the number of mergers and acquisitions which have significantly altered the fabric of the industry since the early 1980's. Put simply, legal publishers have learned what the market will bear and most have taken advantage of that knowledge to maximize profits. By 2011, it has become clear that the vast majority of the most widely-used legal publications are best acquired in an online format, saving not only the initial acquisition cost, but also the more significant cost of supplementation over the long run. A Westlaw subscriber, for example, would be well advised to acquire such titles as **American Jurisprudence 2d**, **American Law Reports**, **Am. Jur. Legal Forms**, **Am. Jur. Trials**, **Proof of Facts,** and others, as Westlaw add-ons and abandon any thought of maintaining them in print.

Lawyers Unwary of Publisher Practices

Law librarians have certainly been the best-equipped of the legal publishers' customers to analyze and weigh the costs, offers and promotions which are the stock-in-trade of the legal publishing business. Unfortunately, the same cannot be said for the lawyers who constitute the vast majority of law book consumers. While knowledgeable in the law, lawyers tend to be rather unsophisticated in their understanding of the legal publishing industry and this makes them easy targets for the more aggressive publishers. They particularly vulnerable to publishers who urge them to maintain or update publications in order to "protect their investment" even when that "investment" has a used market value that is a mere fraction of what they spent on it. Lawyers are also extremely vulnerable to publishers who offer sales on basic sets while downplaying the more significant costs of supplementation where the real money is made.

Lawyers and other purchasers have been gradually trained to anticipate the automatic shipment of supplementary materials to those books and other materials they have consciously purchased for their libraries. In fact, the lax attitude exhibited by many lawyers towards their libraries has emboldened some legal publishers into not only shipping supplements to legal materials consciously purchased, but shipping related titles in the subject area of the original purchase. Every year, millions of dollars worth of law books are acquired unwittingly by attorneys who understand neither the dynamics of the legal publishing business nor the marketing strategies employed by some publishers. If lawyers are spared these publisher excesses, it is generally because they have a law librarian on staff to monitor publisher practices.

About twenty years ago, I was hired as a consultant to a Providence law firm, which sought advice on how to bring its library costs under control. One of the firm's associates, who practiced in the area of construction law, related the story of how he had purchased a single-volume treatise on some specific aspect of construction law from a well-known legal publisher. Two years later, as he explained it, he was the proud owner of twenty-three, single-volume treatises on construction law which had cost his firm over $2,000.00, to say nothing of the annual supplementation bill of more than $1000.00 for all the pocket parts. Sadly, he couldn't even comprehend how this could have happened, as he recalled buying only one book. This scenario has no doubt been repeated time and time again in law firms all across the United States because most law book customers are too wrapped up in the day-to-day practice of law to give much thought to their law libraries and their attendant costs.

Increasingly, however, there are signs that the captive market legal publishers have relied on for the automatic sale of supplementation is beginning to collapse. Legal publishing companies whose market value was heavily dependent on the length of their subscriber lists are beginning to witness a dramatic loss of a once loyal customer base. Turned away by high supplementation costs, the lawyer-customer shows no more loyalty to the company than the company feels toward its customers.

FTC Guides for the Law Book Industry

When the FTC promulgated the **Guides for the Law Book Industry** (16 **CFR** Part 256) in 1975, it directed its attention, in part, to the supplementation practices of legal publishers (see Part 256.14, "Upkeep Service"). The **Guides** clearly distinguished between "Basic Upkeep," which includes "only those parts of upkeep which are absolutely essential and without which a set cannot remain functional (this might include such parts as pocket part supplements, replacement pages, releases and inserts, advance sheets, and replacement, revised, recompiled or split volumes)" and "Additional Upkeep" which includes "additional, companion or related volumes, series or sets, new editions, or any related items."

The FTC **Guides** were promulgated precisely because, among other questionable business practices, certain legal publishers had chosen to broaden the definition of what could be shipped to customers automatically. Common sense dictates that while it may have been proper for publishers to ship customers "basic upkeep" materials to those titles they have consciously purchased, it is inappropriate for them to automatically ship related materials not specifically ordered. For several years, the American Association of Law Libraries, through its Committee on Relations with Information Vendors (CRIV), formerly the Committee on Relations with Publishers and Dealers (CORPUD), led an effort to reform publishers practices in this regard and to clearly distinguish "basic upkeep" from "additional upkeep." While those efforts appear to have achieved some success with regards to law libraries (which employ professional librarians who can act as watchdogs), some publishers continue to ship related titles ("additional upkeep") to lawyers who remain generally uninformed on such matters.

AALL Guide to Fair Business Practices for Legal Publishers

As described in Chapter 3, the Federal Trade Commission rescinded the **Guides for the Law Book Industry** on January 19, 2000. In their place, the American Association of Law Libraries (AALL) created a Special Committee on Fair Business Practices to draft new standards for publishers. Approved by the AALL Board in November, 2002, the **Guide to Fair Business Practices for Legal Publishers** addresses a number of supplementation-related issues (see Appendix F for the full text of the new **Guide**). In November 2012, the third edition of the **Guide** was approved by the AASL Board.

For example under **Principle 2: Disclosure**, the Guide urges publishers to provide information on supplementation costs, including (i) expected extent, content, and format of supplementation, (ii) expected frequency of supplementation or schedule of issues, (iii) whether cost of supplementation is included in the flat rate subscription or separately charged by shipment or some other arrangement, and, most importantly, (iv) where possible, historic data on the cost of supplementation for the product.

While publishers have complied with some of these provisions, few are in compliance with the provision that urges them to supply historic data on the cost of supplementation. Publisher web sites typically provide initial cost information, but rarely provide any historic data on supplementation costs in recent years. The former FTC Guides required publishers to supply the last two year's supplementation costs, and many complied in print advertising literature. With the migration to online catalogs, however, this remains a glaring omission. Without it, consumers lack a critical piece of information upon which to base purchasing decisions.

Since most law firms are simply too small to justify the employment of a law librarian, lawyers generally lack the professional input of those with the specialized knowledge to help steer them around the aggressive sales tactics of some legal publishers. For example, how many lawyers realized that the law book industry was the only segment of the publishing industry which was covered by FTC **Guides** or that the existence of these **Guides** was the direct result of the efforts of a group of lawyers and librarians acting through the American Association of Law Libraries back in the early 1970's?

In many ways, lawyers and law libraries have never been better served by the legal publishing industry. Never before have they witnessed such an array of legal titles, both general and specialized, in such a variety of formats. These publications are far superior in most respects to what existed little more than twenty years ago and are generally superior in coverage, editorial oversight, research aids, paper quality, and binding to their predecessors. Employing sophisticated market research, legal publishers are also far more likely to respond to the needs of the marketplace by introducing new titles and formats in record time. While the number of major legal publishers has been reduced through mergers and acquisitions, competition for business remains keen.

The downside to the current legal publishing environment is that the publishers are far more sophisticated in the means of maximizing profits than were the publishers of an earlier day. The huge sums paid for some legal publishing companies by a few international conglomerates has virtually guaranteed that prices would rise significantly to justify those investments. With few exceptions, the days when publishers could take a casual attitude toward the supplementation of titles in their catalogs are history. The annual pocket part is virtually guaranteed in most instances. In other cases, supplementation to secondary sources may appear two, three or even four times a year. In many cases, there is little editorial justification for such excess, despite the publishers proffered rationalizations.

Supplementation Costs: A Closer Look

Supplementation to print publications may take a variety of forms, including pocket parts, interfiled looseleaf pages, free-standing supplements, special ancillary volumes, new editions, and revised, split or recompiled volumes. The alert consumer must be attuned to the various forms supplementation may take in order to control costs. For example, publishers of many multi-volume sets have become particularly adept at generating a sufficient number of recompiled volumes (i.e. integrating the contents of pocket parts into new bound volumes) every year to drive costs ever upward. With sets such as **American Jurisprudence 2d** or the **Federal Practice Digest 4th**, the West Group is able to generate enough recompiled volumes to almost invariably ensure that total supplementation costs rise year after year. For example, the cost of supplementing **American Jurisprudence 2d** has risen from $1,300.00 in 1993 to $3,325.00 in 2003 and $13,546.00 in 2013. For purposes of illustration, we'll examine 2013 as a test case of how supplementation costs break down:

American Jurisprudence 2d
2013 Supplementation Cost Analysis (list prices)

Recompiled vols. (13 @ $604 ea.)	$7,852.00
Pocket supplements	$3,818.00
2010 General Index pamphlets (7 @ $281 ea.)	$1,967.00
Federal Tax pamphlets (5 @ $552.00 ea.)	$2,760.00
Tables of Laws and Rules	$294.00
General Index pocket part	$243.00
Total list cost	$16,934.00*
Cost to subscribers	$13,547.00*

The total cost of supplementing Am. Jur 2d has risen 942% since 1993. Probably the most egregious of these price increases are the overpriced and largely unnecessary seven Index volumes which rose from $567.00 in 2004 to $1,967.00 (list) in 2013. Recompiled volumes are now priced at $604.00 each (list).

Supplementation costs almost always follow an upward trajectory. With smaller sets, however, it is not always possible for the publisher to recompile volumes at a frequency necessary to guarantee steadily rising costs. For example, all of the West's state digests have undergone extensive recompilation programs in recent years, causing supplementation costs to spike upwards. And even when West is unable to recompile a sufficient number of volumes to push the annual cost higher, it will increase the cost of the pocket part package to make up the difference. One way or the other, the publisher guarantees that your costs will rise inexorably.

Between 1998 and 2001, for example, West recompiled 23 of the 27 volumes now in the **Rhode Island Digest**. During this period the cost of a new set fluctuated from $1,089.00 to $432.00 (interestingly, this was just prior to the initiation of the major compilation program), $903.00 and, currently, $2,929.00. Supplementation cost fell to $450.25 in 2004, but rose to $925.00 in 2005. It was $710.00 in 2009 and $2,315 (list) in 2013, reflecting the cost of pocket parts and more recompiled volumes. Future supplementation costs for these digests reflect the costs of both annual pocket supplements and bound volume recompilations, reflecting the parent corporation's drive for increased revenues. Generally speaking, it should take 10-15 years before pocket parts have grown sufficiently large to justify a new recompilation program, but that doesn't stop the aggressive publisher. While publishers are not going to telegraph their plans to subscribers in advance, the alert consumer should be aware of the dynamics which affect supplementation costs in order that he or she can take the steps necessary to reduce them. Otherwise, you will simply be at the mercy of the publisher's revenue-driven recompilation decisions.

In this world of high priced supplementation, however, there is one publisher whose supplementation practices stand out as the most customer-friendly in the industry: James Publishing. Not only are its high quality practitioner-oriented titles reasonable in price, but its supplementation costs have not increased for years. For example, its highly regarded **How Insurance Companies Settle Cases** has been priced at $99.00 for years and its annual supplementation costs frozen at $59.95 for a similar time.

The question of how to deal with supplementation is one, which can be adequately addressed only by the law librarian or lawyer himself. While the legal researcher is "blessed" with greater supplementation options than ever before, he or she must exercise greater caution to ensure that the options chosen are consistent with legal and editorial necessity and financial resources. While, in the abstract, one can argue that all the books in one's law library should be kept up-to-date through standing orders, it will quickly become apparent that the frequency of supplementation is determined more by profit considerations than editorial necessity.

Steps for dealing with supplementation issues

In the current legal publishing environment, the sophisticated law library user can save much unnecessary expense by taking heed of the following observations and recommendations:

1. Inventory your entire law library at least once a year (twice would be better) and determine the proper level of supplementation for each set or volume you own. Place all titles in a database management program and indicate how frequently you wish to purchase supplementation to each title. For example, it is highly recommended that you establish standing orders for your primary law and citator service. If you have a Westlaw or Lexis subscription, this is not an

issue as the entire package of primary law products for your state, as well your citator service (KeyCite or Shepard's) will be continually updated. You must also establish appropriate supplementation frequencies for your secondary sources. If funds are available, you may wish to maintain standing orders to treatises in your major areas of practice while purchasing current supplements to other secondary works on an as-needed (or "write-for-order") basis. Publishers are generally prepared to provide "Rush" service in such instances through private carriers for a small surcharge. The responsibility of conducting this periodic inventory can be assigned to a new associate or secretary as long as he or she is adequately impressed with the significance of this responsibility. They should read the introductory chapters of this book for starters.

2. A necessary corollary to Step #1 is to determine exactly how much you are actually paying to support your current collection. The total will probably amaze you. It is easy to ignore total supplementation costs when they are growing incrementally. You must remember, however, that practically every new purchase you make adds another layer to your annual expense. After many years, a great deal of this expense becomes sheer waste as you continue to support works, which are little, if ever, consulted. Consider, for example, the legal encyclopedia which you consult infrequently, and then only to use the volumes in your areas of specialty. Don't make the mistake of continuing to supplement a secondary source year-after-year when you no longer have cases in that subject area. Millions of dollars are wasted each year because law firms continue to supplement titles which have lost their usefulness. Law libraries and their supplementation costs can grow out of hand when they are neglected.

3. Clearly distinguish between supplementation to primary works and supplementation to secondary sources. Primary works include statutory codes, case reporters (or their online equivalent), and administrative regulations, to which should be added the finding tools and citators necessary to make proper use of them (including KeyCite or Shepard's Citations and jurisdictional case digests). Current supplementation to these reference sources is a virtual necessity if you wish to avoid the possibility of being sued for malpractice. Supplementation to secondary sources is another story entirely. "Current" supplementation to a legal treatise or practice book may, in some instances, make it more useful; nevertheless, it remains a secondary source whose legal propositions must be supported by the weight of primary authority, whether judicial or legislative. A secondary source should primarily be used to provide an introductory overview of a subject area and to the relevant cases and statutes. They are rarely the last word on a given subject.

4. There is an editorial lag time with all published legal materials. In the case of secondary sources, such as treatises, this lag time can run anywhere from three months to eight months, depending upon whether the publisher is providing in-depth analysis or a series of supplementary case notes. Thus, the legal researcher must be prepared to update his or her research to accommodate this gap in coverage. This may be accomplished by Shepardizing or KeyCiting relevant cases, checking jurisdictional digests and reporter volumes for recent cases, examining annotated state statutes, perusing your local legal newspaper, reading slip opinions from your state's appellate court (or monitoring them online). The chances are great that the standard legal treatise, with its national perspective, will neither cite nor analyze the relevant cases or statutes from your jurisdiction. The danger here is that the researcher will place undue reliance upon the secondary source and fail to perform the additional steps in the research process. Secondary sources cannot, nor should not, do all these things for you. This is where your professional skills as an attorney come into play, following the path only suggested by the secondary sources and discovering the current state of the law. You owe your clients no less.

5. If you decide to drop the standing order to a particular title, you may wish to keep it in the collection for background reference. You are advised, however, to mark the spine "NOT CURRENT" to indicate that it is no longer being supplemented or is being supplemented on an irregular basis. The user can best determine when it has lost its usefulness and should be discarded or replaced by a current edition. One additional observation is in order here. Don't be overly influenced by the publisher's supplementation philosophy, motivated as it is by profit. West publishes many treatises which it does not supplement regularly, yet customers keep them on the shelves because they are "current" as far as that publisher is concerned. Should we be more inclined to discard the more frequently supplemented treatise of another publisher simply because supplements have been issued and we have chosen not to purchase them? I would contend that the core treatise retains residual value for some time after the supplementation has been dropped, particularly if the user is conscious of its limitations and acts accordingly.

6. Publishers' marketing rhetoric notwithstanding, you are not "protecting your investment" by buying supplements year-after-year. In actuality, pocket parts or free-standing supplements are generally cumulative, and the purchaser always has the ability to bring them up-to-date by simply buying the latest year's issues and any intervening revised volumes. High supplementation costs often mean that it is commonly cheaper to purchase an entire new set after a hiatus of several years than to update an existing set (your law book salesperson can be of assistance in making this determination). The purchase of law books is an expense of practicing law, **not** an investment. Most lawyers would be shocked to discover how little their "investment" will bring on the used law book market. This is one good reason why you should almost **never** buy law books new when they are available used--unless, of course, the amount of free supplementation with the new set is large enough.

7. Be sure to inform the publishers with whom you do business exactly what your desires are in relation to the titles you have acquired from them. Do you want your titles on a standing order or on a "write-for-order" basis? Do you wish to receive related titles on approval, or not? Don't allow the publisher to continue sending supplements by default. Institute a check-in system to guarantee that the supplements which arrive at your door are there legitimately. Law office secretaries or mail-room personnel are apt to think that all shipments are legitimate and accept everything. Providing them with a list of active subscriptions is excellent way of keeping things under

control. And, unless your firm is in the habit of lending books to other firms, avoid placing your stamp on new shipments so that they can be returned, if necessary, in a salable condition.

8. Be conscious of the supplementation format of those titles for which you wish to drop the standing order. It is easier to skip several years worth of supplements when they are cumulative. This works whether they are pocket parts or free-standing supplements (such as those from Warren, Gorham & Lamont). Titles with numbered releases are more difficult to contend with because updating a lapsed subscription involves purchasing the same supplements (although on a less timely basis) and contending with all the filings at once. In these instances, it is simpler and less costly to wait several years before purchasing a new copy or until such time as the cost of the new set is less than the cost of the missing updates.

9. If you purchase a set or title on the used law book market, be sure to enter a standing order for supplementation directly with the publisher (assuming it's a title you wish to have on standing order). Also, make sure that the used set contains the current supplement(s). Used law books are generally sold with current supplements and the prices reflect that fact. If the set is not current, you should expect the dealer to adjust the price accordingly (unless, of course, it was advertised as being out-of-date). Some used law book dealers will, as a courtesy, contact the publishers and set up a standing order for you. They may also assist you in obtaining any revised volumes from the publisher.

10. Some publishers make special offers to reinstate lapsed subscriptions on terms which can be particularly advantageous to the law book consumer. These programs may offer, for example, all missing materials at a 50% discount combined with six months free service. The only caveat is that these special promotions are only available sporadically at times determined by the publisher and not necessarily when the customer wants them.

11. The greater availability of much primary law on the Internet adds another dimension to decision-making on matters of supplementation. Statutes, session laws, case reporters, and administrative regulations are increasingly available at no-cost public Internet sites, or at low-cost commercial sites (e.g. VersusLaw). These developments open up new possibilities to the attorney anxious to control supplementation costs. For example, if the primary law for your state is readily available on the Internet, you may wish to forego the purchase of these materials in hardcopy or CD-ROM, or you may wish to purchase the hardcopy only for those areas specific to your practice and use the Internet for those occasional forays into other subject areas. Take every opportunity to familiarize yourself with the Internet resources available for your state and federal circuit and area of specialty and use this knowledge to reduce the unnecessary expenditures for commercial materials.

    Case in point: West's high-priced monthly legislative (or session law) services, which can cost anywhere from $600 to $900, or more, annually. West's **New York Session Law Service**, for example, currently costs $904.56 per year, providing information readily available on the New York state government web site.

12. **Beware of West's Library Maintenance Agreements (LMAs).** These were created by ThomsonWest in response to customer complaints about high maintenance costs for print and online products and in order to inject a degree of predictability into subscription maintenance costs. However, they are also a tool used to increase company revenues by inducing libraries to maintain standing orders to products they might otherwise allow to lapse or re-purchase on a cyclical basis. These multi-year Library Maintenance Agreements also contain non-competitive confidentiality provisions designed to prevent law librarians from sharing their terms and conditions with other customers. Furthermore, ThomsonWest, by a tortured bit of logic, has used the confidential nature of these agreements as justification for its refusal to provide the AALL Price Index Committee with subscriber supplementation cost data. Yet without that data, there is no way in which a library can accurately gauge the degree of savings achieved by the LMA.

    For several years, the refusal of ThomsonWest to supply the Price Index Committee with supplementation cost data effectively emasculated that entire enterprise. The Price Index Committee consequently abandoned its attempts to secure supplementation cost data from Thomson West and dropped all West titles from the Price Index. In 2006, it quietly introduced the **Price Index for Legal Publications 3d**, utilizing 2005 as its new base year and removing 267 Thomson West serial titles, or 49% of the total in that category. It is beyond imagining how any price index which excludes the products of the industry's largest publisher can be taken seriously. Since that time, West has begun supplying supplementation cost data to the Index.

    Law librarians contemplating signing such Library Maintenance Agreements must, at the very least: (1) refuse to sign any provision which prevents them from disclosing its terms and conditions to other consumers; (2) exclude any titles for which standing orders are not desirable, and (3) make a careful comparison between the aggregate subscriber costs of the individual titles falling within the terms of the agreement and the contractual costs under the LMA. Indeed, the longer a library falls under the terms of an LMA, the more divorced it will become from the real costs of the products to which it subscribes, and the true nature of the savings achieved.

13. **West's Monthly Assured Print Pricing (APP) program.** This is the latest wrinkle in West's effort to arrest the hemorrhaging of standing order subscriptions by customers outraged by West's double-digit cost increases. On its face, this program seeks to do for the individual West title what the **Library Maintenance Agreement (LMA)** does for an entire collection. The ostensible goal is to provide lower and more predictable monthly/annual pricing for supplementation. The program is available, however, only to new customers. Customers are required to sign 2-3 year contracts during which time cost increases are limited to five or six percent, the five percent increase being applied in years two and three of a three-year contract, and a six percent increase being applied in year two of a two-year contract (i.e. the longer the contract, the lower the percentage increase). The purchase includes the full complement of volumes of the publication in question, whether a two-volume treatise or thousand volume

set of case reporters. Unlike traditional print supplementation, for which the customer pays by the unit received, the **Monthly Assured Print Pricing** is based on a flat monthly charge.

One problem with the **Monthly Assured Print Pricing (APP)** is in the setting of the initial monthly/annual cost. While in some instances, the initial cost reflects a modest increase over the prior year's subscriber discounted cost, in others it is substantially higher.

Consider the case of **Atlantic Reporter 3d.** In 2013, the annual subscriber cost was $11,704.00. Yet the APP for 2013 was set at $13,956.00 per year, an almost 20% (19.24% to be exact) increase. Granted, the publisher is providing the participant a complete set of books whose cost must be amortized by the APP cost. Nevertheless, any potential savings achieved by holding future cost increases to 5-6% would be completely negated by West's decision to set the initial APP at a substantially higher level. Indeed, my review of initial cost increases in 2011 and supplementation cost increases for the full 2010 calendar year indicate that West has substantially jacked-up both in anticipation of the **Assured Monthly Print Price** (APP) program. Thus, rather than giving a break to standing order subscribers, West is using this program as just another opportunity to reap excessive profits by locking in high supplementation revenue.

Knowing these facts, no rational customer would opt for the APP in lieu of the traditional subscriber discounted pricing which, at least, offers the opportunity to discontinue supplementation when appropriate. Indeed, once a customer is aware of the high and rising costs of West publications, the more inclined he or she should be in exercising extreme caution in buying them in the first place, or, once purchased, keeping them on an extremely short leash.

The other problem with the APP is that, while it may help the publisher reduce standing order cancellations, it may lock customers into annual expenditures they cannot afford. It amounts to a half-hearted, and in some cases, ham-handed, attempt to address a problem driven by the publisher's own excessive price increases over the past decade and a half, and by an industry driven by the profits supplementation provide.
Cost Saving Tip: If you opt for a standing order, be sure to compare the APP with the traditional subscriber costs as provided in this book, or by calling West sales. The APP may not be the best option, and may be a far more costly one.

Conclusion

In summary, there is no reason why you, as a law book consumer, should be a willing captive to the supplementation practices of legal publishers. While publishers are able and willing to supply you with all manner of supplements, there is no reason for you to blindly accept everything they send your way. Taking control over this flood of material will save you and your law firm thousands of dollars annually and many times that over the course of your career. Bringing supplements under firm and conscious control is one of the most important steps you can take to reduce unnecessary law library expenditures.

Obtaining Supplementation Cost Data

One of the advantages of the **Legal Information Buyer's Guide & Reference Manual** is that it assembles a large body of supplementation costs data for all the publications we cover, a benefit provided by no other publication. Obtaining supplementation cost data from publishers varies considerably. Some publishers provide detailed supplementation cost data on their web sites; others provide little or none. The following chart will provide you with guidance on how to obtain supplementation cost data from the web sites of publishers that most commonly issue supplements, or, alternatively, by calling them directly.

Thomson Reuters (West) Legal Solutions
http://legalsolutions.thomsonreuters.com
Thomson Reuters maintains one of the most transparent web sites when it comes to providing detailed supplementation costs. A Search on TR's **Legal Solutions** web site, will provide new set cost, the **Monthly Assured Print Pricing Service** cost for thousands of titles, and allow you to "Select Volumes" to ascertain the cost of individual volumes or components, and the dates of their issuance. While the site does not provide an annual cost of supplementation for individual titles, it does allow you to compute the annual cost by adding up the individual components for a given year. Be aware that the costs provided are retail, rather than subscriber-discounted costs. Subscriber discounted costs generally average 80% of retail for most publications, and 75% of retail for most reporter volumes. The retail costs will only be relevant when the customer is not on standing order. In those rare instances when supplementation costs are not provided, call -1-800-328-4880 and say "Product Information" to be connected to a West sales representative.

LexisNexis Store
http://www.lexisnexis.com/store/us
The LexisNexis Store provides product and pricing information for all products falling under the LexisNexis umbrella, including ALM, A.S. Pratt, Lexis, Mealey's, Matthew Bender, NITA, and Sheshunoff. Once you have done a product search and obtained product and initial pricing, you can obtain the "Estimated annual upkeep," by selecting "Add to cart." While this will not provide you an exact supplementation cost for prior years (as does the West site), it will provide you with a rough idea of projected future supplementation costs. Short of actually making a purchase, this option will also allow you to choose either the Automatic Shipment option or to be notified when an update is available. For further supplementation, call Customer Support at 1-800-9844 and select Option 3.

Wolters Kluwer Law & Business
http://www.aspenpublishers.com
The Wolters Kluwer Law & Business web site provides product and pricing information for hundreds of titles under the Wolters Kluwer corporate umbrella, including Aspen Publishers, CCH, Kluwer Law International and Loislaw.

Product listings will indicate initial cost and date of last supplement, but do not provide the cost of supplementation. For this you will need to call a Customer Care Representative at 1-800-234-1660. Product information for CCH titles, may be obtained at: http://www.cchgroup.com Pricing for major loose-leaf or online services is not available except by being put in contact with the sales representative for your area. In-house Customer Care representatives will not provide that information.

Bloomberg BNA
http://www.bna.com
Bloomberg BNA embraces the BNA and BNA Books products lines. The web site provides access to product information for both product lines, but pricing and supplementation cost information only for the BNA Books products. While the Customer Care Center will assist with product questions for BNA Books titles, all pricing questions regarding pricing for BNA loose-leaf or online services will be referred to the customer's local sales representative.

Juris Publishing
http://www.jurispub.com
Product, initial pricing, and the date of the most recent supplement for all Juris Publishing titles may be obtained on the publisher's web site. Supplementation costs may only be obtained by calling Customer Service at 1-800-887-4064.

Law Journal Press, a division of ALM
http://lawjournalpress.com
Product and pricing information for all Law Journal Press titles may be found on the company's web site. All LJP titles have been, or are in the process of being, converted to annual subscription pricing, an action which has significantly increased their cost of maintenance. Be aware that "subscriptions to books are auto-renewed to avoid disruptions in service. Print editions must be returned within 30 days in resalable condition for refund. For downloadable eBook products, a refund will be granted if the eBook has not been downloaded." Consumers are encouraged to avoid all auto-renew programs in order to keep a handle on subscription costs.

Practising Law Institute
http://www.pli.edu/
The Practising Law Institute publishes a number of supplemented titles. While product, initial pricing, and date of the most recent supplement are provided on their web site, you must call PLI Customer Service at 1-900-260-4754 to obtain the cost of those supplements.

Chapter 7: Unsolicited Shipments, Telemarketing and Other Practices

Legal publishing is a multi-billion dollar business which has, over the past decade, attracted the interest of a number of international conglomerates anxious to tap the rich market represented by the one million members of the legal profession. Legal publishers, like Lawyers Cooperative, which had remained under family ownership for over 100 years, fell before the onslaught of these cash-rich buyers in the late 1980's and early 1990's. The extraordinarily high prices paid for these companies ultimately reflected the value their buyers placed on their subscription lists and the guaranteed cash flow which can be generated from those lists of, largely, professional customers and law libraries.

The potential of companies like the West Publishing and Lawyers Cooperative (both now part of Thomson Reuters) was viewed as significant due to several key factors: (1) lawyers are generally more affluent than most consumers, (2) lawyers require professional reference materials to conduct the practice of law, (3) lawyers generally lack the time or inclination to conduct cost comparisons of legal information products, and (4) the use of automatic shipments, whether legitimate (the standing order) or unsolicited, have generally been a successful means of selling legal reference materials to lawyers. As a consequence of these factors, legal publishers have, to varying degrees, employed a variety of tactics that are unique to the legal market.

Unsolicited Shipments

The most egregious of the tactics employed by certain legal publishers is the use of the unsolicited shipments as a means of generating new sales. In fairness to the legal publishers, it should be stated that there are actually few totally unsolicited shipments of law books. The vast majority of questionable shipments to lawyers and law libraries do have their origin in a legitimate order. The problem arises when some legal publishers take that legitimate order as an open invitation to ship related titles. However, law librarians have universally come to view the shipment of related titles as a violation of United States Postal law under 39 **U.S.C.** § 3009 which states that:

> The mailing of unordered merchandise or of communications prohibited by subsection (c) of this section constitutes an unfair method of competition and an unfair trade practice in violation of section 45(a)(1) of title 15.

The law further states that:

> Any merchandise mailed in violation of subsection (a) of this section, or within the exceptions contained therein, may be treated as a gift by the recipient, who shall have the right to retain, use, discard, or dispose of it in any manner he sees fit without any obligation whatsoever to the sender. All such merchandise shall have attached to it a clear and conspicuous statement informing the recipient that he may treat the merchandise as a gift to him and has the right to retain, use, discard, or dispose of it in any manner he sees fit without any obligation whatsoever to the sender.

A few years ago, a major legal publisher, responding to complaints regarding the automatic shipment of related volumes to subscribers of existing books, wrote a letter to law librarians which explained the practice. In his view, the shipment of related titles was a standard industry practice which offered three benefits to the consumer. He argued that:

1. We are producing quite a few closely related titles, both form books or titles which explore further the subject matter of existing titles. We felt subscribers would want these new titles.

2. Since our costs are lower to automatically send related titles, we were able to offer price reductions of $10-$25.

3. Of course, the standard industry order cards that we use allowed us to send companion or related volumes.

It would be difficult to imagine a more self-serving set of rationalizations for what most consumers would regard as unacceptable business practices. In the first place, most customers do not want or need the volumes being shipped. The lawyers who genuinely desire these related titles are greatly outnumbered by those who are oblivious of what is being done to them. Secondly, the $10.00-$15.00 reduction in the price of the new title is quickly made up in the cost of annual (or semi-annual) supplementation. The discounted book is merely the disguised bait for a future stream of annual supplement-driven charges. Finally, there is no such thing as a standard industry order card. While some publishers' order cards do exhibit similar characteristics (including the negative option to decline related titles), publishers as a group have never developed a standard order card.

As a result of complaints from law librarians, the publisher reprogrammed its subscription fulfillment system "to allow accounts to continue to receive regular updates from our titles, but not to receive any more automatically distributed, related volumes." To take advantage of this new policy, the law librarians were asked to complete and return an enclosed card. Thus, ironically, the publisher was offering to stop a negative option program by requiring the law librarians to exercise a negative option. Unfortunately, while the vast majority of law librarians took advantage of the offer, the practice of sending related volumes continues to this day with unsuspecting lawyers as the chief prey. Like the proverbial bad penny, however, the practice continues to turn up. Recently, this same publisher acquired a family law title from another legal publisher and almost immediately took advantage of that title's standing-order customers by shipping a related family law title. Thus, despite all their efforts, law librarians have still not completely rid themselves of this publisher's practice. And if law librarians have such difficulty stopping such practices, what hope can there be for the lawyer population which is generally oblivious to such goings-on.

Law librarians contend that the shipment of related titles is a practice governed by U.S. Postal law on unsolicited shipments. Furthermore, they argue that the only legitimate shipments are those required to keep the purchased title up-to-date. If a publisher wishes to automatically ship related titles in a subject specific library, for example, he can do so only after securing specific permission from the customer. Shipments which do not observe these rules may be kept as gifts from the publisher (see

39 **U.S.C.S.** §3009(b) (2000)).

The Bureau of Consumer Protection at the FTC, in its "Facts for Consumers," advises consumers that, while they are under no obligation to notify the seller of unordered merchandise, they should write to them by certified mail and state their intention to keep the shipment as a free gift. They suggest that this approach may discourage the seller from sending repeated bills or dunning notices and should help eliminate future unsolicited shipments. Also, should the shipment be the result of an honest shipping error, the customer is advised to give the seller an opportunity to retrieve the item by paying return postage and handling costs within a reasonable amount of time. Some publishers enclose prepaid return labels with each shipment.

In short, don't stand for publishers who insist on shipping you unsolicited, "related" materials. Make sure that each publication you receive is the result of a conscious purchasing decision by you, not an act of omission. And instruct the attorneys and staff in your office to do the same. Shipping related materials may have been a fairly common industry practice at one time, but it was **never** ethical.

Telemarketing

The first rule regarding telephone solicitations is to never buy anything from a telemarketer or show the slightest interest in the product they are selling. Remember that if you respond positively to a pitch from a telemarketer, your name will find its way onto one or more "hot prospect" lists. Succumbing to one telemarketing pitch will only guarantee that you will receive many more such solicitations in the future. One response to intrusive telemarketing calls is to request that your name, or the name of your firm, be taken off the publisher's telemarketing lists. This approach does not always work, however, because publishers routinely buy customer lists from professional marketing firms, and the request may simply result in your name being moved to the cold prospect or optional call list. The attorney can train his secretary or receptionist to recognize such calls and prevent them from reaching his desk in the first place.

Responding to consumer complaints about annoying telephone solicitations, Congress enacted the Telephone Consumers Protection Act in 1991. This act requires that the telemarketer provide the consumer with certain information upon request, including the name, address (not a post office box) and a telephone number of the company, the name of the caller, and the date and time of the call. It also requires that, upon request, the telemarketer agree to add you to his "do-not-call" list, mail you a confirmation of your being added to this list, and agree to send you a copy of his "do-not-call" list policy. The cost of complying with your request is sufficiently great that you can almost be certain that your name will be placed on the do-not-call" list. When you receive the policy and confirmation, you should attach it, together with the postmarked envelope in which it arrived, to the record you made upon the initial call. Then, should the company call again, you will have proof that the law has been violated. If the telemarketer fails to send you the written information you requested, you are entitled to sue in small claims court. Quite simply, you can make it too costly for the telemarketing firm to attempt to call you again.

On Feb. 13, 2003, the Congress passed the Do Not Call Implementation Act, which authorized the FTC to collect fees from sellers and telemarketers to implement and enforce the provisions relating to the do-not-call registry. The bill was signed into law by President Bush on March 11, 2003. Furthermore, on Feb. 20, 2003, the President signed the Omnibus Appropriations Act, which authorizes the FTC to implement and enforce the do-not-call provisions of the Telemarketing Sales Rule. By the end of 2006, more than 65 million telephone numbers had been registered.

Putting an End to Telephone Solicitations

The first rule regarding telephone solicitations is to never buy anything from a telemarketer or show the slightest interest in the product they are selling. Remember that if you respond positively to a pitch from a telemarketer, your name will find its way onto one or more "hot prospect" lists. Succumbing to one telemarketing pitch will only guarantee that you will receive many more such solicitations in the future. One response to intrusive telemarketing calls is to request that your name, or the name of your firm, be taken off the publisher's telemarketing lists. This approach does not always work, however, because publishers routinely buy customer lists from professional marketing firms, and the request may simply result in your name being moved to the cold prospect or optional call list. The attorney can train his secretary or receptionist to recognize such calls and prevent them from reaching his desk in the first place.

Responding to consumer complaints about annoying telephone solicitations, Congress enacted the Telephone Consumers Protection Act in 1991. This act requires that the telemarketer provide the consumer with certain information upon request, including the name, address (not a post office box) and a telephone number of the company, the name of the caller, and the date and time of the call. It also requires that, upon request, the telemarketer agree to add you to his "do-not-call" list, mail you a confirmation of your being added to this list, and agree to send you a copy of his "do-not-call" list policy. The cost of complying with your request is sufficiently great that you can almost be certain that your name will be placed on the do-not-call" list. When you receive the policy and confirmation, you should attach it, together with the postmarked envelope in which it arrived, to the record you made upon the initial call. Then, should the company call again, you will have proof that the law has been violated. If the telemarketer fails to send you the written information you requested, you are entitled to sue in small claims court. Quite simply, you can make it too costly for the telemarketing firm to attempt to call you again.

On Feb. 13, 2003, the Congress passed the Do Not Call Implementation Act, which authorized the FTC to collect fees from sellers and telemarketers to implement and enforce the provisions relating to the do-not-call registry. The bill was signed into law by President Bush on March 11, 2003. Furthermore, on Feb. 20, 2003, the President signed the Omnibus Appropriations Act, which authorizes the FTC to implement and enforce the do-not-call provisions of the Telemarketing Sales Rule. By the end of 2006, more than 65 million telephone numbers had been registered.

Financing Your Purchases

Many legal publishers have taken effective steps to remove the major deterrent to purchasing law books or other legal research materials--their high initial cost. Interest-free terms offer the attorney an attractive way to achieve instant bibliographic gratification by amortizing the expense over time. In truth, the terms are hardly interest-free. The publisher's profit margin more than compensates for the "interest-free" loan which you are receiving.

I have known lawyers whose monthly payments to legal publishers were significantly higher in later months than they were initially because the annual cost of the supplementary materials exceeded the sum of the annual payments. Making the minimum monthly payment is a bad enough idea because it greatly lengthens the time necessary to pay off a loan and significantly increases the interest charges. It is an even worse idea when the cost of the materials being "paid off" keeps rising. Furthermore, there is no advantage to an "interest-free" loan when it is for books you could have purchased second hand at a substantial savings.

I once encountered an attorney in rural Texas whose annual payments to a single legal publisher were around $16,000, even though his gross annual income was less than $40,000 per annum. While he was caught in a trap of the publisher's making, he failed to take the steps necessary to cancel the supplementation and, thus, begin the process of financial recovery. Interestingly, much of that $16,000 he was handing over each year was for supplementation to titles he initially received "FREE" with various purchases. Those "FREE" titles simply produced a future revenue stream for the publisher which helped bury the attorney in debt.

Thoroughly investigate all the available options from all competitors before making a purchase, and then pay cash. If you must talk terms, don't neglect to bargain for the greatest possible discount first. Law book salespersons are a lot like car salespersons. They try their best to get you to focus on the monthly payment rather than the bottom line. If they can get you to focus on the monthly payments, they may cause you to neglect bargaining for the lowest possible price and the biggest discount. If you must buy on terms, arrange to pay off the "loan" in the shortest possible time. If you cannot afford to do this, don't buy. Use your local public law library until you are in a position to pay cash.

Also, be aware that not all legal publishers offer significant discounts. Publishers whose materials fall into the discretionary category are much more likely to discount than publishers of standard primary materials. For example, some publishers offer a discount if payment is made within 30 days, but rarely offer the kind of discounts you are likely to see from Matthew Bender, for example. And while general discount policies are listed in the publishers' catalogs (e.g. quantity discounts), sales representatives may have special promotions or discounts to offer at any given time. It pays to talk to them when you are in the market for legal information.

Thomson West frequently offers "special" promotional discounts of 20% on new set purchases. Standing order customers receive a discount of anywhere from 20-25% on the cost of supplementation, depending on the publication. Given the rising cost of supplementation, however, this is small concession. A single volume of the **Atlantic Reporter 2d**, for example, which listed for $350.00 in 2010, cost $263.50 to the standing order subscriber, a discount of approximately 25%. What West "loses" on the discount, however, it easily makes up on the rapidly escalating subscriber costs which have risen at double-digit rates for nearly 15 years. At the end of 2010, the **Atlantic Reporter 2d** went into its **3d** series, and, true to form, the price was increased to $590.00 per volume ($442.50 to subscribers). a 68% increase.
Finally, there is no substitute for doing your homework before buying lawbooks or other forms of legal information. Take the time to investigate your options before you meet with a sales representative. Otherwise, you will find yourself led down the financial garden path without a knowledge base from which to counter his or her appeals. If you are in a firm, you should appoint a library committee and designate one member of that committee to handle all purchases and negotiations based upon pre-determined needs and financial resources.

The Standing Order

One of the primary reasons why legal publishing has been so successful, and its profit margins so high in comparison with corporations generally, is because of the standing orders from which they garner 80-90% of their revenues. In the hands of certain publishers, the standing is a virtual license to print money. This is because lawyers have been taught to fear the possibility that their research might be out-of-date, that the case upon which they are relying might have been overruled, or, in the case, of a statute, repealed. This blanket fear makes them more likely to accept the standing order as a means of avoiding a charge of malpractice. But, more significantly, it can cause them to fail to distinguish between those publications that should be on standing order and those for which a standing order is really not required, or to consider an online alternative to a print product..

The standing order is generally manifest in the form of ever-rising supplementation costs, I would argue, because publishers know they have you on the hook. These result, for example, in 20% annual increases for National Reporter System, advance sheets, $2,760 for annual American Jurisprudence 2d Tax volumes, $1,967.00 for seven annual American Jurisprudence 2d Index volumes, and $604.00 for individual replacement volumes. Total supplementation costs for individual titles inevitably rise every year because of the ability to generate revised volumes at will and the corporation's revenue targets for individual titles which drive the process. Ironically, the solution to such high costs lies with the very publisher generating them—a WestlawNext add-on for the publications in question.

Finally, there is no substitute for doing your homework before buying lawbooks or other forms of legal information. Take the time to investigate your options before you meet with a sales representative. Otherwise, you will find yourself led down the financial garden path without a knowledge base from which to counter his or her appeals. If you are in a firm, you should appoint a library committee and designate one member of that committee to handle all purchases and negotiations based upon pre-determined needs and financial resources.

Chapter 8: Used Law Books - The Economical Alternative

A number of years ago, a classified ad in the **New Jersey Law Journal** offered for sale complete sets of the **New Jersey Reports** (vols.1-138) and **New Jersey Superior Court Reports** (vols. 1-278). The seller, who likely bought both sets new, was willing to "sacrifice" both for the paltry sum of $15,000 or a "reasonable offer." A leading used law book dealer, based in New Jersey, offered virtually the same volumes for only $3,195.00 What gives here? Was the attorney taken to the proverbial cleaners when he acquired this $15,000.00 library? Is he now hoping to do the same to another unsuspecting buyer?

In the days before online access and high square footage costs for office space drove law firms to discard their print libraries, a newly organized Providence, Rhode Island law firm needed a complete set of the **Federal Reporter 2d** to support its active federal practice. A member of the firm called up the local West sales representative and orders a pristine set in the publisher's shrink-wrap for the sum of $15,000.00. At the time, the same used law book dealer could have supplied a nearly identical run for $3,495.00. The attorney responsible for the purchase learned this too late and offered to slit his wrists. One wag in the firm suggests that he would have had a lot more fun throwing 11,000 one-dollar bills from the roof of their office building.

A lawyer gets a "great deal" on a partial set of **Atlantic 2d** from an attorney closing down his practice. He pays $1,500.00 for volumes 1-400, figuring he will pick up the remaining, at the time, 400-odd volumes at a similar price and complete the set. He soon discovers that no one has a partial set of the recent volumes for sale and that the cost of buying the remaining volumes new from the publisher (West) is prohibitive. He then calls a used law book dealer and discovers that he could have had a nearly complete set of over 800 volumes for less than $1,500.00. After buying the complete used set for $1,500.00, he studiously avoids telling his wife about his $1,500.00 "great deal."

A Massachusetts attorney offers to give away his set of **Massachusetts General Laws Annotated** to an attorney or law firm willing to take over the monthly payments. With used sets available for $895.00, the total of the payments will significantly exceed the set's current used value.

Do you see a pattern here? Sorry to say, but most lawyers have a less than adequate understanding of the value of law books in general and the used law book market in particular. Attorneys who may be the most skilled negotiators and deal makers are often the unwitting victims of poor decision-making when it comes to purchasing law books. As the above examples illustrate, there is probably no other area in which this lack of understanding is more costly than in the area of used law books. This chapter will undoubtedly give you enough information to save you or your firm many thousands of dollars over the course of your legal career.

Sources of used law books

With over 1,000,000 practicing attorneys in the United States and thousands retiring each year, it should come as no surprise that there is a steady flow of used law books turning up on the market. More books are made available when law firms merge and consolidate their individual libraries or replace their hardcopy collections with online access. Naturally, it is not in the interests of the legal publishers to inform lawyers of the used law book option, so their knowledge of used law book dealers is likely to be gleaned from classified ads in legal newspapers or word of mouth from satisfied customers

Hardly an "investment"

One major misconception regarding law books is that they are an "investment." A quick perusal of one of the used law book dealers' catalogs will quickly put this false notion to rest. In fact, the value of law books falls even more rapidly than that of used cars. According to published accounts, the value of the average automobile falls 21% after the first year and another 17% after the second year of ownership. By contrast, it is not uncommon for the value of lawbooks to fall more than 80% as soon as they become the permanent property of the purchaser; in other words, as soon as they can no longer be returned to the publisher for credit. An "investment" generally increases in value or, at least, holds its value in anticipation of future appreciation. Used law books exhibit none of these traits. Trading in law books is akin to buying a stock at the market's peak and then selling it at the depth of a bear market. Yet, how many times have lawyers been urged by legal publishers to buy this or that supplement or revised volume in order to "protect their investment."

The sets comprising West's National Reporter System volumes are a dramatic illustration of these observations. A new set of the **Federal Reporter 2d**, volumes 1-999, plus **Federal Reporter 3d**, volumes 1-737, list for $25,885.00. Several years ago, one of the major used law book dealers, Law Book Exchange, Ltd., offered 1,541 of these volumes for $3,990.00, an 82% reduction from their new cost at the time. A few years ago, a similar complete used set of **Federal Reporters** would have sold for more than $7,000.00. That was before the rapid acceptance of online access stimulated a dramatic sell-off of hard copy volumes. Similarly, the prices of the West Group's highly regarded **American Law Reports** series have dropped dramatically. **ALR 3d**, listing at $2,793.00 and **ALR 4th**, listing at $2,375.00, may now be picked up used for $395.00 and $495.00 respectively. And **ALR Federal** [1st series], which lists for $2,528.00, has seen its used price drop dramatically in recent months to as low as $600.00.

Market for Hardcopy Evaporates in Face of Online Offerings

In general, however, the market for hardcopy reporter series has dried up to the point of near extinction. This has been largely driven by the attractive pricing of online offerings by Westlaw and LexisNexis, as well as other online providers. Quite frankly, so few are the potential buyers and sellers that an active market cannot be said to exist. A potential seller would be extremely fortunate to find a willing buyer; for his hardcopy library. In fact, most hardcopy volumes are now simply given away by law firms for the cost of postage.

As legal publishers have embraced computer-assisted legal research as a means of delivering legal information, the desirability of large hardcopy sets of case reporters, statutes, legal encyclopedias, and other legal reference works has evaporated. The impact of this development has been felt no more dramatically than in the world of used law books. For the attorney anxious to avoid the high costs of new lawbooks, or the costs of online access, used lawbooks can still an attractive alternative, but only if they are obtained at minimal cost and **not updated in the print format.**

Leading used law book dealers

One of the country's leading used lawbook dealers is **The Lawbook Exchange, Ltd.**, a Union, NJ - based concern which handles a wide variety of used lawbooks, including scholarly and antiquarian lawbooks, microfiche, and legal periodicals. It is also a reprinter of classic legal works, a subscription agent, and appraiser. For a number of years, it has published several extremely useful lists of used lawbook prices. In 1996, it made these price lists available on the Internet at: **http://www.lawbookexchange.com** The Lawbook Exchange is now the only concern still engaged in buying and selling used law books to the practitioner market.

Buying and selling your used law books

The obvious lesson from all this turmoil in the used law book market is that it is even more imperative to buy low because you will be selling low--if you can sell at all. This is in the face of law firms giving away their hardcopy collections for the cost of postage. Of course, for the subsequent buyer, the expense of maintaining the set will quickly exceed the cost of the initial purchase (the cost of a bound volume subscription to **Federal Reporter 3d** was $10,642.00 in 2013). A wiser alternative might be to acquire a substantial library in hard copy, but avoid the high maintenance costs by obtaining more recent decisions from an inexpensive online service such as VersusLaw, or as a part of a Westlaw Pro or Lexis Advantage online subscription for your state's legal materials.

Another factor to remember when buying or selling used law books is that a current run of reporters is in much greater demand than an earlier run. A buyer who picks up a partial set consisting of the earlier portion of a set will have great difficulty completing the set unless, fortuitously, he or she is personally able to locate a seller with a complementary series of later volumes. Used law book dealers are much more likely to acquire partial sets of earlier volumes because their acquisitions are generally made after a lawyer's death, law firm breakup, or merger, or because the subscription has been abandoned due to the high cost of current volumes. In many cases, the sets have not been maintained for a number of years prior to their disposal. If the time gap is too great, it may be more economical to purchase a complete (or near-complete) used set than to attempt to fill-in the partial set.

For example, the recipient of a free partial set of the **Atlantic Reporter 2d** from 950 which lacks the last 49 bound volumes (it's now up to 999 volumes and as well as 80 volumes of a 3d series) would—believe or not-- have to pay over $92,248.00 to complete the set with new volumes from the publisher (i.e. $708.00 x 49 = $34,692.00 + $708.00 x 84 = $59,556). This is far more than the $29,514.00 cost of new sets from the publisher. As of 2014, free sets lacking as few as 6 bound volumes would be less economical than a complete used set priced at $3,495.00 (6 x $708.00 = $4,248.00). In fact, given the sharply increased cost of individual "fill-up" volumes, the wise consumer should simply avoid completing the print set with the publisher and obtain more recent decisions as a part of a WestlawNext subscription.

It is imperative that, before acquiring a partial used set of books directly from the seller, you compute the ultimate cost of a complete set by consulting not only with used book dealers but with the publisher as well. There is nothing particularly complicated about this, but you do have to do a bit of homework. Once you have struck a deal, the used law book dealer may offer to set up a continuing subscription to the set you have purchased. If not, it is a simple matter to call in the local publisher's representative and arrange to do that yourself. However, don't expect legal publishers to promote the used law book options.

West, for example, is not in the business of promoting the used trade in its own books. You should not expect their sales representatives to inform you of the superior financial advantages of acquiring their books used. They are not in the used law book business and their employers would seriously frown on their encouraging the trade in used books. You must take this initiative yourself! In any event, the publisher is much more likely to sell you access to case law on Westlaw than in hardcopy.

A word about condition. The vast majority of used law books are in good to very good condition, unless they happen to be ex-library sets or sets from large firms. The chances are small that any of the volumes in a large set will have been handled with sufficient frequency to render them unusable. Nevertheless, it is probably best to buy subject to approval of condition or to request that a few representative volumes be shipped to you for your examination, if visiting the dealer personally is not an option. If you don't wish to contend with another firm's stampings on the volumes (a minor concern in my view), inform the dealer of this condition as well.
Also, some dealers have been known to charge buyers a re-stocking charge if they return or cancel a planned purchase. Don't stand for this. Returns or cancellations are some of the risks of doing business. However, it is reasonable that the customer be expected to pay the cost of shipping a set back to the dealer if your return is not the dealer's fault. After all, the postage or shipping charges on a set of 600 to 1000 volumes is a considerable expense and the dealer should not have to suffer a financial loss because of a mere change of heart on the part of the customer. To avoid such situations, purchasers must make certain that all parties at their end are firmly committed to the purchase.

Best candidates for used purchase

What sets are the best candidates for used purchase? Practically anything which is sold as a set and not as a subscription, although even the latter can be acquired under the right conditions. These sets include court reports, digests, legal encyclopedias, **American Law Reports**, state and federal statutes, legal forms, and legal treatises. Sets which are easily brought up-to-date are much better candidates for the used law book market than sets that require the filing of noncumulative supplements consisting of interfiled pages. It is a simple matter to update a set of **American Law Reports** by buying the latest year's pocket parts, should you choose to do so. For example, none of the bound volumes in **ALR** through **ALR 5th** have ever been replaced or revised (excluding such items as the **ALR 2d** Later Case Service volumes). Sets like **American Jurisprudence 2d** or **American Jurisprudence Legal Forms**, on the other hand, are periodically updated with revised bound volumes which makes the process of updating a lapsed set somewhat more complicated. In such instances, it is best to consult with the publisher's local representative to determine exactly what must be purchased to bring the used set up-to-date.

Your chief consideration is to determine what value the core material in a set of used lawbooks will provide to your practice even if it is not current. For example, a used set of **American Jurisprudence 2d** can be of great value for a basic, introductory discussion of the entire range of legal subjects even if it is not kept up-to-date. Given the high cost of updating the set ($13,547.00 in 2013), the cost-conscious attorney is advised to acquire a used set at the going rate of $1,300.00 and avoid supplementation. That discussion can easily be updated when necessary using standard research tools, including digests, and citators, or in the form of a WestlawNext add-on. Naturally, these considerations will apply far more readily to fields for which the common law is paramount than to those areas subject to frequent statutory and regulatory modification, such as taxation.

While used law book dealers trade in Matthew Bender treatises, for example, they must dispose of these quickly or the supplementation issue becomes more complicated and the values drop dramatically. However, from the customer's perspective, even these "outdated" sets may offer a great opportunity if sold at the right price. If, for example, you are interested in acquiring a set of **Benedict on Admiralty** and don't mind the fact that it is two years out-of-date because the basic discussion and analysis is still sound, you may be able to buy one for as little as $150.00, a dramatic savings over the $6,273.00 cost (2014) of a new set. The sets which once comprised Lawyers Cooperative's Total Client-Service Library system (now folded into the West family of products) are always readily available on the used law book market; however, their very ubiquity may make it difficult to dispose of your own sets when you are ready to sell. Wright and Miller's **Federal Practice and Procedure**, on the other hand, is less easy to come by and commands a somewhat higher re-sale price ($995.00). The prices offered to you by used law book dealers will vary depending upon national market conditions and the supply already in the dealer's inventory.

There are other sets marketed and sold as subscriptions which have little or no used value. In this class are the true looseleaf services such as those published by Commerce Clearing House, Research Institute of America and the Bureau of National Affairs. Since anyone interested in a current awareness service in a regulatory field must have an on-going subscription, there is no advantage to buying a used set as the publisher will supply a complete set to all new subscribers. A somewhat similar principle holds with the **United States Code Servic**e published by Lexis. Since all owners of the **U.S.C.S.** receive a complete set from the publisher when the order is placed and pay periodic charges for upkeep, the value of the used set is negligible. In fact, the only justification for buying the **U.S.C.S.** used is that you have no intention of keeping it current. With such publications, one common strategy is to purchase another used set every three or four years. **The United Stated Code Annotated**, on the other hand, retains a greater value because the owner pays for pocket parts and revised volumes as received once the initial purchase price is paid.

The market for West's ultrafiche has similarly evaporated with the ubiquity of Westlaw contracts. Due to the unique licensing agreements involved, however, there is no market in used CD-ROM products, most of which are on time expiration.

While many law books are available used, there will be many instances in which the purchase of a used set is not a viable option. Some will simply not turn up used with enough frequency to make their purchase convenient. Others are subject to frequent supplementation which heightens the risk of missing critical sections of text. In some instances, the purchase of a used set may not be the most economical move because the publisher provides some level of free service with the new set purchase. Still others are marketed as subscription services, rendering the used set a superfluous commodity. In your areas of specialty, you may prefer, depending upon price, to purchase directly from the publisher and keep a standing order for supplements in place. This still leaves scores of major sets and hundreds of individual titles as viable options for the cost conscious attorney. Given the variety of materials available on the used market, the lawyer should assume that a used set exists until he or she determines otherwise.

When it comes time to sell your law books, you should at least attempt to sell them locally without involving a dealer. If you can locate a ready buyer locally, both you and the buyer can each gain something from the transaction by splitting what would have been the dealer's profit. A little homework on your part and a few phone calls to used law book dealers to determine what they are willing to pay for your books should allow you proceed confidently with a deal satisfactory to both parties. Say, for example, that you have a complete set of Federal Reporter 2d-3d for which you have been offered $1,000.00 by a dealer. Noting the dealer's retail price of $3,990.00, you offer to sell to your own buyer for $2,500.00. You have gained an additional $1,500.00 and your buyer has saved $1,500.00. The used law book dealer will have plenty of other opportunities from attorneys who are not interested in personally selling their own libraries and who would rather cash out quickly, even at a reduced price. It should be noted, however, that a complete sets of Federal Reporter 2d and 3d are not infrequently offered for the cost of postage on law-lib, the law librarians' list-serv.

It is also important for the lawyer to be realistic about the value of his or her law library. I cannot tell you the number of times I have been called by attorneys for quick over-the-phone appraisals of their libraries. In many instances, they have sets which have not been updated in years and are prime candidates for the dumpster. In these instances, I could only offer the consoling news that they have saved thousands of dollars by not buying the supplements all those years, a fact which should more than compensate them for the present lack of marketable value. In such instances, however, I can only speculate regarding the disadvantageous position into which their clients might have been placed as a result of their failure to maintain the currency of their libraries. If annual supplementation costs are high in relation to the cost of the initial set, the used set will lose value rapidly if allowed to lapse. The General Laws of Rhode Island, for example, has virtually no marketable value if allowed to lapse for two years or more, given the fact that the initial cost to in-state attorneys is only $773.00 and the annual supplementation cost roughly $650.00 (2013). This and other sets which have lapsed even longer become far more expensive to update than to completely replace. Facts such as these certainly lead one to the conclusion that law book expenditures should be held to a minimum in light of the low residual values which used law books command.

Amazon.com

While Amazon.com is not a good source for most legal practice materials, it is an excellent source for used (or discounted) legal reference books, law school textbooks, monographs, and histories. In addition to its own mammoth inventory, Amazon.com serves as an intermediary for sellers of new and second-hand books on legal and other topics. Depending on condition, you may be able to acquire a desired reference book or monograph for a fraction of what you would pay for a new copy. The highly regarded **Oxford Companion to American Law**, for example, which lists for $79.95, can be obtained in "like new" condition on Amazon.com for about $.75. There are many similar values on Amazon.com.

Another, less positive, development on Amazon.com, however, is the appearance of some out-of-print titles at outrageous prices. Some associated sellers—not Amazon, mind you—will take advantage of their out-of-print status to offer titles at prices many times what they cost when they were in print. Many of these are ABA monographs, some costing $1000.00 or more for titles that were originally priced at less than $100.00. In cases such as this, the buyer is urged to consult the volume at the nearest law library. This situation can also be addressed by urging the original publisher to issue a new edition, or reprint the original edition.

AddALL

Another outstanding source of inexpensive used books in all subject areas is AddAll.com, a book search and price comparison site allows users to search and compare among more than 40 sites, 20,000 sellers, and millions of books. Users may search by author, title, key word and ISBN.

Sources of Free Law Books

Another major development of interest to the cost-conscious attorney is the increased availability of used lawbooks over the Internet for the cost of postage. As more law libraries and law firms are accessing court decisions on the Internet, they are disposing of their accumulated print reporters, among other print legal materials. The impact of this shift to electronic delivery of legal information and the high cost of office space have produced a glut of used lawbooks on the market. Rather than sell them for a pittance to the used lawbook dealers, who may already be overstocked with such sets, they have chosen to give them to the first party willing to pay the cost of postage or cart them away. Postings on the Law-Lib listserv provide ample evidence of this trend.

Frankly, interest in used lawbooks has waned in recent years in response to the online environment in which most lawyers practice today. The availability of large bodies of caselaw online has replaced law offices filled with bookshelves and casebound reporters. Nevertheless, they can still be a cost-saving alternative, particularly in selective instances in which currency is not critical (e.g. for boiler-plate form language), and books can be acquired at little or no cost.

In any event, the cost conscious attorney should make an effort to get on the mailing lists of used lawbook dealers, or access the used lawbook prices on **The Lawbook Exchange's** web site. A listing of used law book dealers as well as a representative sampling of used law book prices culled from these lists may be found in Appendices C and E. And remember, don't ever buy new until you have thoroughly investigated the used option.

Part II
Categories of Legal Materials

An Essential Acquisition

The young lawyer just opening his or her practice will be besieged with all manner of appeals from legal publishers and their sales representatives to purchase everything from legal encyclopedias and case reporters to treatises and online packages. While over the course of your career, you will undoubtedly acquire many of these items, selectivity needs to be your guiding principle at the start. If you are a bibliophile, your appetite for law books is likely to exceed your financial resources until you have acquired a sufficient number of paying clients. In the meantime, you are advised to use your local court or bar library to best advantage and get a feel for the types of materials you are using in your day-to-day practice. What sets do you use with regularity? Which do you borrow repeatedly? It will become apparent soon enough that the purchase of a few well-selected legal titles for which you are continually running to the library will save you precious time and money.

As you are determining the shape your personal law library is to take, you are on firm ground in purchasing a set of your home state annotated statutes. As a form of primary law, statutes provide the basis for the resolution of most legal issues. Though often neglected in law schools as an object of study and analysis, statutes should be the first resource consulted when you are presented with a legal issue. While research in case law will undoubtedly occupy much of your research time, many of those cases may provide the critical interpretation of a relevant statute. Even areas of the law largely based on the common law may involve statutes governing certain aspects of the law. For example, while tort law is mainly controlled by an imposing body of case law, most states have comparative negligence statutes which govern the assignment of damage awards. Once the existence of a relevant statute is ascertained, you can proceed to the analysis provided by case law and other pertinent forms of authority.

State Codes and Session Laws

A brief word regarding nomenclature. The terms "code," "statutes" and "laws" are often used interchangeably. I prefer the term "code", or perhaps "statutory code" because it designates that publication of the public, general and permanent statutes of a given jurisdiction which are compiled in a systematic subject or topical arrangement. Do not confuse "codes" with "session laws," the generic term applied to those publications containing the annual output of a legislative body.

In some states, both "official" and "unofficial" state codes are available for purchase. Official state codes are published pursuant to government authorization, either by the government itself or by a commercial publisher under contract with the state. Unofficial state codes are published by commercial publishers with or without government authorization. The unofficial codes are no less accurate than the official codes, but may lack the official sanction of the government. The unofficial codes are far more likely to include useful editorial enhancements, however, such as case annotations and cross references.

"The titles of annotated state codes vary from state to state, but usually include the following terms: "Statutes," "Code," "Laws," "Annotated," "General" and "Compiled" which will distinguish them from session laws. Massachusetts, for example, has both the **Annotated Laws of Massachusetts** (LexisNexis) and the **Massachusetts General Laws Annotated** (West). In some cases, the title will be preceded by the name of an earlier compiler which the publisher has retained for sake of marketing or historical continuity (e.g. **McKinney's Consolidated Laws of New York Annotated** (West)).

Session laws, which are usually published annually (the exception being those states whose legislatures meet biennially) always require the designation of the year of the legislative session (e.g. 2012 **Rhode Island Public Laws**). To add further confusion to the matter, some states publish separate, annual volumes of local and private acts. Furthermore, there is no uniformity to the manner in which the various states designate these three types of publications. Thus, the **Massachusetts Acts and Resolves** are that state's general session laws, while the **Rhode Island Acts and Resolves** constitute that state's local and private acts.

Your First Purchase

More than 80% of the attorneys in the United States practice in just one jurisdiction. Thus, assuming you are practicing state rather than federal law, an annotated code for your home state is your obvious first purchase. The legislative history references accompanying each section of the code will list the session laws from which they draw their authority. If the legislative history of the statute is at issue, or if you wish to trace the evolution of given statute, your local court or bar library will contain a complete collection of these volumes. It is not necessary for the practicing attorney to attempt to collect session laws unless he or she enjoys collecting books and filling up shelf space which will be consumed soon enough by more valuable resources. Moreover, most state legislative web sites contain the full text of session laws enacted in recent years.

Your annotated state code will also contain summaries of all the appellate court decisions which have cited each section of the code. A code without annotations is about as useful as a dictionary without definitions, since the bare language of a statute often provides little guidance unless it has been interpreted in light of a specific factual situations. Of course, the text of the laws is, or should be, identical in both the annotated and unannotated versions.

An important distinction needs to be drawn between official and unofficial codes. The former are the more authoritative if a conflict in statutory language arises, while the latter are merely prima facie evidence of the law. However, since in most states only unofficial commercial codes are available, this is not a significant issue. Fortunately, annotated codes exist for all fifty states, most of them published by one of the two major legal publishers: West and LexisNexis. In a few states, lawyers may have a choice of two competing annotated state codes, as well as an official unannotated code, usually published by the state itself. The attorney contemplating the purchase of an annotated state code can visit his or her local law library and examine the competing versions prior to making a decision he or she is going to have to live with, and pay for, for a long time to come.

Unlike lawyers of an earlier era, lawyers in the 21st century have the advantage of having free access to online statutes provided by their state governments. Others have access to state statutes via Casemaker, a national database of legal materials available as a benefit of bar association membership. While these provide an excellent initial source of state statutes, most lawyers will require online access to annotated statutes via one of the two major online services.

Online and CD-ROM Statutes

Statutes, as well as other forms of legal information, have been available online since Lexis introduced its service in 1973, followed by Westlaw in 1975. Beginning with LOIS in the early 1990s, legal publishers have also been marketing state statutes on CD-ROM, although this format is rapidly fading in the marketplace. Statutes are available as a part of state online primary law packages (e.g. **Westlaw PRO** or **LexisNexis**), a development which has significantly improved the accessibility of these primary law sources. The CD-ROM products or online packages also typically contain state appellate court decisions, court rules, and, in some instances, trial court decisions, administrative rules and regulations, and law review articles. While the publishers involved in the online or CD-ROM markets are, generally speaking, the same major players which have for years produced the hard copy statutes, they have been joined by a number of new companies attempting to challenge their preeminent position.

Online Alternatives

Loislaw (formerly CASEBASE), originally produced by Law Office Information Systems (LOIS) of Fort Smith, Arkansas, challenged both the Michie Company (now part of LexisNexis) and the West Publishing Company (now West) in Arkansas, Connecticut, Massachusetts and Rhode Island, before being sold to Lawyers Cooperative Publishing Company (now also part of West) in the early 1990's. Following the expiration of covenants not to compete against its original product line, LOIS developed a new line of state specific CD-ROM products using a 32-bit search engine called PITA. It was also the first commercial legal information provider to offer libraries of primary law over the Internet, as opposed to access via proprietary software (**Westlaw** and **LexisNexis**) through Loislaw.com. Its National Collection now provides the primary law of all state and federal jurisdictions at an annual cost of $1,512.00 per year per password. Loislaw was acquired by Wolters Kluwer in 2000. Its original CD-ROM products have now been replaced by online access.

Other companies, having gained access to public domain statutes and cases, have been carving out niches in the online legal environment historically dominated by the legal publishing giants. These include **Fastcase, VersusLaw,** which offers a complete library of state and federal cases and statutes, and Geronimo Development Corporation which created the **Casefinder** product for Virginia primary law.

Casemaker

A more recent entry into the field is **Casemaker**, a consortium of primary law databases now available to lawyers in more than 28 states. Casemaker, which enters into partnerships with state bar associations, is generally available to attorneys as an expanded benefit of bar membership (and at a cost of less than $20.00 per attorney). Savvy attorneys in Casemaker states are already tapping the online resources of this no-cost CALR service before upgrading to a Westlaw and LexisNexis contract. And those in firms with contracts to one of the two premium CALR services can use Casemaker as a default service to effectively reduce Westlaw or Lexis online charges.

Other online and CD-ROM providers are described more fully in Chapter 25. The astute consumer should make a point of exploring these alternative options which may offer significant cost savings along with greater attention to the research needs of the specific jurisdictions in which they appear.

One of the leading questions which arises when the attorney is considering the purchase of his or her state statutes is whether to buy them in hard copy, as one component of a CALR subscription, or on CD-ROM. In many cases, the financial outlay will preclude the purchase of multiple formats, particularly in large states. One should, of course, compare the cost of all the hardcopy materials involved with the cost of the equivalent online formats, including both the initial outlay and the expected supplementation cost (this assumes that you already have, or are about to acquire, the necessary computer hardware to access the materials online or on CD-ROM).

Most publishers have, of course, taken the cost of the equivalent hardcopy sources into account when pricing their products. Legal publishers have abandoned initial licensing fees which had characterized the sale of these products when they were first introduced and substituted straight annual, quarterly, or monthly subscription charges. These initial licensing fees were a distinct disadvantage to the consumer who may have felt compelled to stay with a particular product because of the substantial initial "investment" involved. Under the straight annual, quarterly, or monthly subscription option, the consumer should have no financial reservations about switching products once the terms of his or her current contract have been satisfied.

Superiority of Online Alternatives

The online or CD-ROM versions of state statutes are demonstrably more powerful research tools since they provide the user with the ability to search for even the most obscure term or expression, buried though it may be in the most unlikely corner of the code and inaccessible through the traditional printed subject index. Of course, it is difficult to curl up with a computer; and the more tradition-bound attorney may find it difficult to dispense with the print version entirely. If there is going to be an area of duplication in your law library, it is more likely to be of your state code in both print and online formats. The print version does give you the added flexibility of being able to carry specific volumes with you to court or home without having to contend with the necessary equipment; although laptops with CD-ROM drives or wireless access have largely eliminated this objection for the technologically savvy.

In the final analysis, the decision will be based on financial considerations, ease of use, and personal taste. A buyer's guide to state publications, contained in Chapter 28, will provide the reader with a state-by-state listing of state codes and their prices to aid in this process. A discussion of computer-assisted legal research options for your state primary law is discussed in chapter 25. Local law libraries may also give you the opportunity to test competing CD-ROM products or CALR services on your own prior to purchase. This will allow you to make a selection free from the biased presentations of the local sales representatives.

In reality, CD-ROM is no longer a viable option for most attorneys. Prices for many products on CD-ROM, to the extent that they still exist, have risen so sharply that the savvy consumer will seek out the online alternative. Consider **West's Oklahoma Digest CD-ROM Edition**, which is now priced at $12,981 annually. Annotated state codes on **LexisNexis** and **Westlaw** provide a superior alternative to print or CD-ROM. LexisNexis offers a special programs for the solo practitioner called **Lexis Total Practice Advantage** which allow unlimited access to the practitioner's home state materials for a fixed cost (see Chapter 25 for details). Westlaw has similar programs called **WestlawNext PRO** and **Westlaw PRO PLUS**. Many unannotated, but fully searchable state codes are also available at no cost on government sponsored Internet sites.

Cost Saving Tip: Save the cost of a print subscription to your annotated state code and its upkeep by subscribing to either a **WestlawNext PRO**, **LexisNexis Total Practice Advantage**, or alternative CALR service plan for you state. In states with large state codes (CA, NY, etc.), your savings on the print code and its maintenance will often exceed the cost of your state online plan. Deering's **California Code Annotated** in print, for example, costs $4,175.00 new, with annual supplementation costs of more than $2,000. An annual subscription to a California basic state primary law package on Lexis Advance, by contrast, is only $1,200.00 annually.

Similarly, West's **Annotated California Code** in print has an initial cost of $10,836.00 and annual supplementation costs of more than $8,000.00. By contrast, a **WestlawNext PRO** subscription to **California Essentials Plus** is only $2,700.00 annually. Not only will the online package provide you with the annotated code for your state, but a collection of other primary law sources as well, including case law. If necessary, you can purchase individual annotated code volumes in print only for the areas in which you practice.

The preceding discussion has been primarily directed to a consideration of state codes. However, if your practice involves a substantial amount of federal law, you will also be faced with purchasing one of two competing federal codes: the **United States Code Annotated** (West) or **United States Code Service** (LexisNexis). Formerly published by the Lawyers Cooperative Publishing Company, **U.S.C.S.** was acquired in 1997 by Reed Elsevier under the terms of the consent decree which was crafted pursuant to the merger of Thomson and West in 1996. Reed Elsevier assigned responsibility for **U.S.C.S.** to **LexisNexis**. The distinctive features and respective prices of these and several unannotated editions will be considered in Chapter 10.

Chapter 10: Federal Statutes

United States Code

Just as state statutes constitute an indispensable acquisition for the vast majority of practicing attorneys, a set of federal statutes is an essential tool for the attorney involved in matters of federal law or practicing before federal agencies. The official publication containing the complete, systematic arrangement of all public, general and permanent federal statutes is entitled the **United States Code**. The present codification of federal law, with its organizational structure and title arrangement, first appeared in 1926, nearly fifty years after the prior codification, the 1878 **Revised Statutes**. The West and Edward Thompson Publishing Companies played a major role in the preparation of this codification, and the West Group continues to assist in the preparation of the subsequent editions.

With the growth of the Internet, obtaining the text of the **United States Code** is becoming easier than ever. The legal researcher now has a variety of options, including print, CD-ROM, commercial online services (LexisNexis, Westlaw, VersusLaw, etc.), and a number of public Internet sites, including GPOAccess. However, the version you select will depend upon a number of factors, including the nature of your practice, the value of case annotations to your research, and the currency of the text itself. The user cannot be cautioned enough about ensuring the currency of the text upon which he may be relying. The fact that a particular version of the **U.S. Code** is in electronic form does not necessarily guarantee that it is more current than print, for example. In fact, one of the risks of using any legal source in electronic form is that it may give the user the illusion of currency. For example, several CD-ROM editions of the **U.S. Code** are current as of January 5, 2009 and must be updated by other means.

The online version is available from the Office of the Law Revision Counsel of the U.S. House of Representatives. Titles 1 through 40 are based on Supplement II of the 2006 edition (January 7, 2011) of the Code. Titles 41 through 50 Appendix, Tables I-VII and the Table of Popular Names are based on Supplement I of the 2006 edition (January 3, 2011) of the Code.

The growth of the Internet has certainly leveled the legal research playing field for both citizen and professional. It is now possible to gain access to the raw text of the **U.S. Code** without the expenditure of hundreds or thousands of dollars for a commercial print publication, CD-ROM, or online service. And this avenue may be adequate for the casual or occasional user, or for the legal professional engaged in preliminary research. But for the serious researcher or legal professional, these sources will soon prove to be inadequate. For these individuals, the case annotations, historical notes, cross-references, and other editorial features provided by the commercial vendors will prove to be invaluable research aids and well worth the additional cost. This chapter will examine the various print and CD-ROM options for the **U.S. Code**. Internet sites are listed in Chapter 25.

Official U.S. Code Site Launched in Beta

On July 27, 2011, the Office of the Law Revision Counsel of the U.S. House of Representatives — the entity responsible for preparing and publishing the official U.S. Code — unveiled a beta version of a new U.S. Code website that features a number of enhancements for searching and working with the nation's governing body of laws.

The most dramatic enhancement in the new site is its search capability that shows results in context, Google style. This enables a much quicker assessment of a result's relevance. If you prefer to see the results listed by citation, you can easily toggle the view. You can also choose to sort results either by relevance or order within the Code. To use the new U.S. Code web site, go to: http://uscodebeta.house.gov/.

United States Code in Print

1. **United States Code (USC)**. Washington, D.C.: U.S. Government Printing Office, 1926, and 1934-date. New edition published every six years. Updated between editions by five annual bound supplements. Current edition: Vols. 1-14 (through Feb. 2014). Titles 1 through 41 are based on the 2012 edition (January 3, 2008) of the Code. Titles 42 through 50 Appendix, Tables I-VI, and the Table of Popular Names are based on Supplement i of the 2006 edition (January 3, 2007) of the Code. **Cost**: Not sold as a complete set; Individual volumes priced at $90.50 - $140.00 each, most commonly available at federal depository libraries. Also available on CD-ROM at cost of $30.00 per year (to January 5, 2009); and at no cost on the Internet at the Office of the Law Revision Counsel's web site: http://uscode.house.gov/search/criteria.shtml (current within 30 days).

The official **United States Code (USC)**, published by the U.S. Government Printing Office, is organized into fifty subject-matter titles which are arranged in a rough alphabetical order. Each of the fifty titles is organized into chapters and sections. Citations to provisions of the **U.S. Code** reference the title and the section numbers and year of publication, e.g. 42 U.S.C. § 1983 (1988). A new edition is published every six years. Between editions, the set is updated with annual bound supplements. More than twenty of the fifty titles have been reenacted into positive law by Congress, meaning that the researcher need not consult the official session laws, called the **Statutes at Large**, to determine the most authoritative form of federal law. For the remaining titles, the language of the **Statutes at Large** is the more authoritative positive law while the language of the **U.S. Code** is prima facie evidence of the law. Only in rare circumstances will this distinction be significant to the practicing attorney.

As we observed with state statutes, federal statutes are issued in both annotated and unannotated versions. While the official **U.S. Code** has its uses, the majority of practicing attorneys who require access to federal statutes use one of the two unofficial annotated codes: the **United States Code Annotated**, published by West, and the **United States Code Service**, published by LEXIS Publishing. These two codes, as their names imply, are enhanced by the fact that they include brief summaries of court decisions which have cited or interpreted each section of the code. Without these annotations, the provisions of the official **U.S. Code** may remain vague and ambiguous, lacking the judicial interpretations which give them life in the context of specific factual situations. Using an unannotated code is a lot like using a dictionary with only words and no definitions.

2. **United States Code Annotated**. St. Paul, MN: West Publishing Co., 1927-date. 378 vols. Subscription includes annual pocket parts, quarterly noncumulative pamphlets, and periodic revised volumes. Monthly updating available through separate **United States Code Congressional and Administrative News (USCCANS)** pamphlets which provide text of new legislation with parallel tables providing citations to Code sections affected. Also available in quarterly CD-ROM format (see description below).
Cost: $13,532.00; supplementation: 1995: $820.00; 1996: $902.00; 1997: $1,591.50; 1998: $1,445.00; 1999: $1,576.50; 2000: $1,627.25; 2001: $1,627.25; 2002: $2,478.25; 2003: $2,871.25; 2004: $3,391.75; 2005: $3,721.00; 2006: $4,206.50; 2007: $3,993.50; 2008: $4,193.00; 2009: $5,919; 2010: 6,812.50; 2011: $7,694.50; 2012: $8,635; 2013: $11,585. Also included as a part of most WestlawNext primary law packages. The cost of a subscription to the U.S. Code Congressional and Administrative News advance sheets: $1,560.90; bound volumes: 2000: $267.50; 2001: $234.00; 2002: $268.00; 2003: $540.00; 2004: $498.00; 2005: $505.00; 2006: $525.00; 2007: $448; 2008: $486.00; 2009: $648.00; 2010: $885.00; 2011: $579; 2012: $840; 2013: to be announced.

West's **United States Code Annotated (U.S.C.A.)** was first published in 1927, shortly after the appearance of the newly organized official U.S. Code. It contains all statutory law of the United States of a general and permanent nature currently in force, including all provisions of the United States Constitution. It presently consists of 307 bound volumes and annual paperbound indexes. While each statutory provision includes historical notes and cross-references to other important research tools, it is the voluminous annotations to court cases which account for its expanded size. The set is updated by means of annual pocket parts, quarterly non-cumulative pamphlets which update the entire set, and the monthly advance pamphlets of West's session law service entitled **U.S. Code Congressional and Administrative News (USCCANS)**.

The text is drawn from the exact language of the official **United States Code**. The set also includes a variety of practical features, including tables, court rules, citations to the **Code of Federal Regulations**, West key numbers, **Corpus Juris Secundum**, and relevant West treatises. Newly revised volumes will also contain references to the former Lawyers Cooperative Library of legal publications, including the **American Law Reports** and **American Jurisprudence 2d**. Bound volumes are revised as the pocket parts become too large to fit comfortably in the backs of the volumes. Access to the set is provided by both general index volumes and indexes to individual titles.

Since the purchase of the West Publishing by the Thomson Corporation in 1996, the editorial content of the United States Code Annotated has been significantly enhanced. Although Thomson West was forced, under the terms of the consent decree approving the sale, to divest itself of United States Code Service, they have incorporate many of its unique features into an enhanced **U.S.C.A.**, including more complete references to the former Lawyers Cooperative's Total Client-Service Library. It is the publisher's stated intention is to provide the researcher with summaries of every relevant case which cites a particular provision of the **United States Code**, a goal which reflects the West Publishing Company's philosophy of comprehensive coverage. This goal is significantly furthered by the fact that West can reuse the thousands of headnotes its editors prepare to accompany decisions appearing in the volumes of the National Reporter System. While West generally succeeds in its goal of providing comprehensive coverage of relevant case law in its annotations, it occasionally omits citations to cases appearing in the competing **United States Code Service**. The significantly greater number of annotations in the **United States Code Annotated** includes many which simply restate prior holdings. Thus while the **United States Code Annotated** will give the researcher far more case annotations, those contained in the **United States Code Service** are more likely, at least in the view of its editors, to be more significant. As a result of the divestiture, **U.S.C.A.** will presumably be even stronger in comparison to **U.S.C.S.**

3. **United States Code Service (U.S.C.S.).** Charlottesville, VA: LexisNexis, 1936-date. 246 vols. Subscription includes annual pocket parts, periodic revised volumes, cumulative quarterly supplements entitled Later Case and Statutory Service, and monthly advance pamphlets containing the text of recently enacted legislation, court rules, executive documents and selected regulations. Also available in CD-ROM format (see description below).
Cost: $3,338.00 per year (or $278.16 per month, minimum 12-month contract) (2012). **Monthly Advance Legislative Service** available for $99.00 per year. The **U.S.C.S.** was divested by the West Group and sold to Reed Elsevier in January, 1997, and is now published and marketed by LexisNexis.

Originally published between 1936 and 1971 by the Bobbs-Merrill Company under the title **Federal Code Annotated**, the code was purchased by the Lawyers Cooperative Publishing Company, assuming its present title as the earlier volumes were replaced. Unlike the **United States Code Annotated, The United States Code Service (U.S.C.S.)** draws its text from the United States Statutes at Large. Not having the ability to reuse headnotes as West does (except in the case of the **U.S. Supreme Court Reports, Lawyers' Edition**), the LEXIS Publishing editors (many of them former Lawyers Cooperative employees) personally examine each case to determine its relevance to the section(s) of the **United States Code**. Annotations to decisions of federal administrative agencies are included as well as those of state and federal courts. The **United States Code Service** will continue to provide references to other former Lawyers Cooperative publications now owned by the West Group, including the **American Law Reports** and **American Jurisprudence 2d**, as well as law review articles, etc.

In January, 1997, **United States Code Service** was sold to Reed Elsevier along with fifty-one other products under the terms of a Department of Justice Consent Decree which approved the merger of Thomson Corporation and West Publishing. LEXIS Publishing, a new publishing entity created by Reed Elsevier, now assumes responsibility for both the print and electronic versions of the **U.S.C.S.**

Annotated United States Codes on CD-ROM

1. **United States Code Annotated.** St. Paul, MN: West. Two discs. Updated regularly. Contains the full text of the **United States Code Annotated**, including the **United States Constitution**, federal court rules, selective federal regulations, General Index and Popular Name Table. Search Engine: PREMISE.
Cost: $4,035.00 per year (single user) (2014). See also WestlawNext.

2. **U.S.C.S. on DVD-ROM**. Albany, NY: LexisNexis. Two discs. Updated quarterly. Contains the full text of the **United States Code Service** in the exact language of the **United Stated Statutes at Large** and annotations to relevant case law as selected by the editors. Search Engine: Folio VIP CD.
Cost: 1st year cost:$1,888; 2d year cost: $1,750.32; 3d year cost: $1,785.33; (single user) (2014).

Unannotated United States Codes on CD-ROM

1. **United States Code.** [official]. Washington, D.C.: U.S. Government Printing Office. One disc. Updated annually. Contains the full text of the official, unannotated United States Code, including popular name table and subject index. This 6th edition of the **U.S. Code on CD-ROM** is the official compilation of all Federal statutes of a general and permanent nature in force on January 5, 2009. Available for DOS and Windows. Search Engine: I-SEARCH. An excellent and inexpensive means of accessing the complete text of the **United States Code**, but without the annotations and editorial enhancements found in the commercial versions. On the downside, the official **U.S. Code** CD-ROM suffers from the time lag characteristic of the print edition.
Cost: $30.00 per year (2014). Also available from Bernan Associates: (800) 274-4447.

Comment: Although the **United States Code** exists in an unannotated edition, the effective legal researcher must have access to an annotated **Code** in order to locate applicable case law, as well as relevant regulations and secondary sources. The choice, then, is between West's **United States Code Annotated** and LEXIS Publishing's **United States Code Service**. Both of these major primary sources have their own unique characteristics. If you prefer a **Code** with significantly more case annotations, as well as references to West key numbers, **Corpus Juris Secundum**, **American Jurisprudence 2d**, and other secondary sources published by West, the **United States Code Annotated** is probably the preferred code. If, on the other hand, you prefer a code containing case annotations carefully selected by editors for their particular relevance you will probably prefer the **United States Code Service**. Prior to the West-Thomson merger in 1996, West and Lawyers Cooperative cited only to their own families of publications as a means of stimulating their sales. In the post-merger era, however, both annotated codes provide cross-references to the practice sets published by the other.

A comparison of the **United States Code Annotated** and **United States Code Service** conducted in 1981 by Jeanne Benioff (2 Legal Reference Services Quarterly pp. 37-53), revealed that the **U.S.C.A.** contained more citations to case law than **U.S.C.S.**, but that the latter contained more varied references to both primary and secondary sources. Her analysis revealed that, although **U.S.C.A.** contained more citations to case law, the **U.S.C.S.** often contained case citations not cited by **U.S.C.A.** In other words, the case citations in **U.S.C.S.** are not merely a sub-set of the case citations found in **U.S.C.A.** In fact, in one instance, 50% of the citations in **U.S.C.S.** were not to be found in **U.S.C.A.** despite its fuller coverage overall.

My more recent examination of both federal code sets uncovered similar findings. Comparing the coverage of 29 **U.S.C.** § 210 revealed the following: **U.S.C.A.** cited 31 cases in the bound volume (1965) and an additional 16 cases in the 1995 pocket part for a total of 47 case citations. It also cited **Corpus Juris Secundum**, **Federal Practice and Procedure**, **West's Federal Forms**, and relevant West digest key numbers. U.S.C.S. on the other hand, cited 10 cases in the bound volume (1992) and no cases in the 1995 pocket part. It also provided cross references to **Federal Procedure**, **Federal Procedural Forms**, **American Jurisprudence 2d**, **Am Jur Trials**, the **ALR** series, and law review articles. Curiously, however, four of the ten cases cited in **U.S.C.S.** were not cited by **U.S.C.A.** Thus, the researcher who wishes to conduct a thorough search will have to use both sets to locate all cited cases.

What does this mean for the prospective purchaser who must choose one of these two annotated codes? From a strictly editorial perspective, the **U.S.C.A.** provides a significantly greater number of case citations because it is able to recycle headnotes from the vast array of West case reporters. Whether these citations are particularly relevant will largely depend on the issue being researched. **U.S.C.S.**, on the other hand, contains citations which are editorially selected because of their particular relevance to the statute and does contain citations which were missed by the editors of **U.S.C.A.** Both sets now provide more citations to administrative agency decisions and federal regulations. In the pre-merger era, both codes almost exclusively cited to their own collateral publications as a means of promoting their sale. Now, look for both publishers to cite to a wider range of these publications—West because it now owns most of the Total Client Service publications, and LexisNexis Publishing out of competitive necessity.

If you are less tied to the purchase of the **United States Code** in hardcopy, the various CD-ROM versions provide a superior alternative to the print editions. The choice of CD-ROM versions of the two codes involves a consideration of the same factors since their editorial content parallels that of the hardcopy. The CD-ROM, however, offers the researcher a vastly more sophisticated search capability which cannot be matched by the traditional printed indices. Be cautious, however, about completely abandoning the hardcopy edition(s) for CD-ROM because computer system failure can leave you without access to the law. It is helpful if you have a local public law library or friendly law firm you can run to in an emergency.

While the CD-ROM versions of the **United States Code** Annotated and **United States Code Service** are comparable in price, additional charges will be required to place them on a local area network (LAN). Networking the CD-ROM may save you significantly if your firm has traditionally purchased several copies of one of the federal codes. You should also investigate those companies which do not charge extra for networking, Finally, you may also wish to consider purchasing individual annotated code volumes covering the specialties of attorneys in specific areas of practice rather than purchasing additional complete sets. Streamlining your collection of federal statutory law in this way can help your firm achieve significant savings in both the short and the long run.

While statutory codes, both federal and state occupy a significant place in the library of the practicing attorney, the resolution of a particular legal issue may rest more squarely on the application and interpretation of administrative rules and regulations promulgated by executive branch agencies. These rules and regulations have been described as subordinate or delegated legislation since they derive their authority from the statutes passed by legislative bodies and signed into law by the executive. Unlike federal or state statutory codes these rules and regulations have received less attention as objects of research and analysis. As administrations employ them to circumvent Congressional intent, or in the absence or Congressional action, their use can also become highly controversial. This chapter will describe the sources of administrative rules and regulations at both the federal and state levels as well as the sources from which they may be obtained.

Federal Regulations

Since the passage of the **Federal Register Act** in 1935, the the publication of federal agency regulations has been a responsibility of the Office of the Federal Register. This Act was a response to the chaotic regulatory environment which had existed since the creation of the Interstate Commerce Commission in 1887, an act which extended the regulatory authority of the federal government, but failed to provide an orderly and systematic mechanism for publishing the regulations of this and other agencies. The issue came to a head in 1934 and 1935 when two cases involving the regulation of the oil industry were argued before the United States Supreme Court. A few days before the case of Panama Refining Company v. Ryan, 293 U.S. 388 (1935) was to be argued before the high court, it was discovered that the regulatory provisions under which the parties had been prosecuted had already been revoked.

The **Federal Register Act** sought to remedy this situation by providing for prompt publication of Presidential proclamations and Executive orders, documents or classes of documents which the President determines to have general applicability and legal effect, documents or classes of documents required by Act of Congress, and every document or order which prescribes a penalty or has general applicability and legal effect. These documents were to be published in the Federal Register, a daily publication which first appeared on March 14, 1936. Publication in the Federal Register has been determined to provide any parties affected by its regulations with constructive notice of its contents.

When Congress passed the Administrative Procedure Act in 1946, it extended to the public the opportunity to participate in the administrative rulemaking process. The Federal Register was expanded to include notices of proposed regulations along with a mechanism by which the public was allowed the opportunity to comment. This "Proposed Rule Making" section first appeared on January 1,1947. Since that time, the coverage of the Federal Register has been further expanded to include the publication of agency organizational descriptions and policy statements as well as meeting notices.

Attorneys who practice in the federal arena are often called upon to monitor the Federal Register on a daily basis for publication of any regulations or other notices which may affect their clients. While there is a variety of specialized publications on the market which publish the text of rules, regulations and notices in specific subject areas, my intention here is to provide information on the Federal Register itself and the Code of Federal Regulations (CFR) which cumulates these regulations on an annual basis. The research process begins by searching the current edition of the CFR before ascertaining whether any recent changes have been published in the daily **Federal Register**.

Federal Register in Print

Federal Register. Washington, DC: Office of the **Federal Register**, 1936-date. Published daily, Monday through Friday. An annual subscription to the Federal Register includes approximately 260 issues annually (one published each business day of the year) together with both monthly and annual indices.
Cost: $929.00 per year plus postage for combined subscription to the **Federal Register, Federal Register Index**, and the **List of Sections Affected** (LSA) (2014).

Weekly Compilation of Presidential Documents.
Washington, DC: National Archives and Records Administration, Office of the Federal Register, 1965-date. Weekly. Available in pamphlet format, 1965-date; and online from 1993-date. Weekly periodical with quarterly, semiannual, and annual indices. Contains Executive Orders, proclamations, transcripts of Presidential news conferences, messages to Congress, public speeches and statements, and other Presidential materials released by the White House. Discontinued on January 29, 2009 and replaced by the online **Daily Compilation of Presidential Documents**: http://www.gpo.gov/fdsys/browse/collection.action?collectionCode=CPD

The **Compilation of Presidential Documents**is composed of the Daily Compilation of Presidential Documents (online) and its predecessor Weekly Compilation of Presidential Documents (print and online).
Cost: Also available free on GPO Access at: http://www.gpo.gov/fdsys/browse/collection.action?collectionCode=CPD

Daily Compilation of Presidential Documents. Washington, DC: National Archives and Records Administration, Office of the Federal Register, 2009-date. Daily. Available online only. Contains Executive Orders, proclamations, transcripts of Presidential news conferences, messages to Congress, public speeches and statements, and other Presidential materials released by the White House. First issued on January 29, 2009.
Cost: free on GPO Access: http://www.gpo.gov/fdsys/browse/collection.action?collectionCode=CPD

Subscriptions or individual issues are available from:

Public Documents Distribution Center
U.S. Government Printing Office
710 N. Capitol Street, NW
Washington, DC 20401
(202) 512-0132
Fax: (202) 512-1355
Bookstore: http://bookstore.gpo.gov/

Federal Register on CD-ROM

RegScan's Federal Register Service. Williamsport, PA: Solutions Software Corp. Available online or on CD-ROM. Twelve monthly HTML based CDs with full text searching capabilities using RegScan's search engine. System requirements: Windows XP or Vista, with CD-ROM drive. Contains the full text of the **Federal Register** generated from the Government Printing Office database. Data is current to the previous month.
Cost: $755.00 per year (2014)..

U.S. Federal Register Archive on CD-ROM. Williamsport, PA: Solutions Software Corp. One disc. Updated annually. HTML based CD-ROM with full text searching capabilities. Search requirements: Windows XP or Vista, with a CD-ROM. Contains the full text of the **Federal Register**.
Cost: archival discs: 2013: $180.00; prior years also available: call for quote: (877-373-4625) (2014).

Federal Register on the Internet

Federal Register Online via GPO Access. The full text of the **Federal Register** for 1994-date is available on the Internet as a service of the U.S. Government Printing Office. Access to the Office of the Federal Register is available at: https://www.federalregister.gov/
This Web site is also accompanied by detailed instructions for searching the database, including the use of Boolean operators, relevance ranking, and sample searches and search techniques. Unlike editorially enhanced products like the **United States Code Annotated**, the **Federal Register**, whether on proprietary CD-ROM or the Internet, contains the same regulatory text obtained from governmental sources.

Federal Register on HeinOnline

HeinOnline contains comprehensive coverage of the **Federal Register** (1936 to date) on its Federal Register Library Module. This module also contains the **Code of Federal Regulations** from 1938 to date, the **United States Government Manuals** from 1935, to date, and the **Weekly Compilation of Presidential Documents** from 1965 to date. Multiple browsing and searching features are available. For pricing options, contact Hein at 1-800-828-7571.

Code of Federal Regulations in Print

Code of Federal Regulations (CFR). Washington, DC: Office of the Federal Register, 1939-date. Published annually on a quarterly schedule (January, April, July and October).
Cost: $1,804.00 annually (2014) (in paper); Individual issues also available. **Lists of Sections Affected**: $35.00 per year. Price list available upon request.

Organization

The **Code of Federal Regulations (CFR)** is organized into fifty titles, thirty-eight of which correspond to the titles of the **United States Code**. Each of these fifty titles is then organized into Parts containing the regulations of a specific agency or topic. Since 1967, the **CFR** has been published in a paperback format with each volume revised annually. Although a quarterly schedule of annual republication has been established, the delay in the appearance of the individual volumes generally means that volumes from at least two different years will be shelved in the same set. The republication schedule is as follows:

Titles 1-16	January 1
Titles 17-27	April 1
Titles 28-41	July 1
Titles 42-50	October 1

The use of a different color for each year, however, allows the user to distinguish the years from each other. Each part of the **CFR** includes an authority note which designates the legislative or executive authority under which the regulation was issued. Also, a source note to each section provides citations to those issues of the **Federal Register** where the regulation and its amendments first appeared. A subscription to the **Code of Federal Regulations** also includes an **Index and Finding Aids** volume.

The **Code of Federal Regulations** can be purchased as a complete subscription to all fifty titles which will be shipped as they are published. If you only need particular issues or titles, you can request a price list from the Government Printing Office and place your order for these using a credit card. Individual titles or issues are not available on subscription, but must be re-ordered annually. The prices for individual issues are somewhat higher than their per-volume price as a part of the entire set. Depending upon the number of volumes you need, it may be more economical to purchase the entire **CFR** from the Government Printing Office than to buy them individually. This gives you the added advantage of receiving them automatically upon publication.

The **Code of Federal Regulations** is also available on CD-ROM from a number of publishers (listed below). The CD-ROM version provides the user with the ability to conduct full-text searching of each word in the **CFR**, a facility not previously available through the hardcopy indices. Prices vary from the more sophisticated products available from the West Group to the more basic versions or individual paper CFR titles.

The **Code of Federal Regulations** is available in print from:
Public Documents Distribution Center
U.S. Government Printing Office
710 N. Capitol Street, NW
Washington, DC 20401
(202) 512-0132
Fax: (202) 512-1355

CAUTION: Depending on the number of individual issues you need, it may be more economical to purchase the complete CFR from the Superintendent of Documents than to purchase a large number of individual issues from either the government or one of the commercial vendors. For example, while the Superintendent of Documents sells the entire paperbound subscription for $1,664.00, the cost of buying all the volumes individually would total more than $4,800.00. However, some companies sell official government publications like the CFR at an even greater markup. One vendor offers individual titles at a total cost of more than $8,000.00. A little comparative shopping may save you hundreds of dollars in unnecessary expense.

Code of Federal Regulations on CD-ROM or Internet

e-CFR/U.S. Federal Register Archive on CD-ROM. Williamsport, PA: Solutions Software Corp., 2001-date. Internet or HTML based CD-ROM with full text searching capabilities. Search requirements: Windows XP or Vista, with a CD-ROM. Contains the full text of the Federal Register. Contains the full text of all 50 titles of the Code of Federal Regulations complete and current through December 31 of each year as well as the complete text of each issue of the Federal Register for that calendar year. Obtained from government sources.
Cost: $230.00 per year (2014) (800) 734-7226.

e-CFRlite [CD-ROM or Internet]. Williamsport, PA: Solutions Software Corp. Two CDs. Updated quarterly. Updated quarterly on CD-ROM or available via internet download. Contains the full text of all fifty titles of the Code of Federal Regulations. Intended as a regulatory compliance tool. Provides up-to-date integration of Federal Register with CFR. System requirements: System capable of running Windows XP or Vista, with a CD-ROM drive. Cost: $299.00; eCFRlite subscription plus Lookout E-Mail Alert Bundle: $474.00 (2014).

LexisNexis CD - Code of Federal Regulations (CD-ROM). LexisNexis, 2001-date.
Cost: 1st year cost: $1,380; 2d year cost: $1,407.00; 3d year cost: $1,435.00 (2013).
The **Code of Federal Regulations** is a codification of the rules published in the Federal Register by the executive department and agencies of the Federal Government. The Code is divided into 50 titles which represent broad areas subject to federal regulation.

West's Code of Federal Regulations on CD-ROM. Eagan, MN: West Group. Two discs. Updated monthly. Contains the full text of the **Code of Federal Regulations** with Hypertext links to **U.S.C.A., Supreme Court Reporter**, **Federal Reporter** and **Federal Supplement**. Available for DOS, Windows, and Macintosh. Search Engine: Premise or LawDesk (Folio). Subscription includes online updating via Westlaw.
Cost: $4,218.00 per year (2013) .

Code of Federal Regulations on the Internet

Code of Federal Regulations Online. The full text of the **Code of Federal Regulations** is available on the Internet as joint project authorized by the publisher, the National Archives and Records Administration's Office of the **Federal Register**, and the Government Printing Office (GPO). It is located at: http://www.gpo.gov/fdsys/browse/collectionCfr.action?collectionCode=CFR

Citators

Shepard's Code of Federal Regulations. Bound volumes: 3
Print cost (all-inclusive): 1st year cost: $2,454.00; 2d year cost: $2,503.00; 3d year cost: $2,553.00; also available online as part of the Full Shepard's Citation Service at an annual cost of $900.00 (2013).

West's Code of Federal Regulations Annotated. Eagan, MN: West, 2006-date. 38 vols. Annual editions.
These volumes contain the complete text of selected titles of the **CFR** current through amendments published in the Federal Register through January 31, 2008. The volumes are annotated with relevant source and authority materials from the **United States Code** and the **Federal Register** as well as citations to relevant law reviews, corollary cross-references to the **United States Code Annotated**®, and full case summaries from all federal courts reported in West's® National Reporter System® including West topic and key numbers. The set is fully indexed. As of February 1, 2014, **West's Code of Federal Regulations Annotated** has been issued for the following titles:

Title 8 (Aliens & Nationality, 2 vols.): $514.00
Title 29 (Labor, 7 vols.): $1,022.00
Title 37 (Patents, Trademarks & Copyright, 2 vols.): $584.00
Title 42 (Chapter IV, Medicare/Medicaid, 4 vols.): $652.00
Title 48 (Fed. Regulations Acquisition System, 4 vols.): $592.00
General Index (4 vols.): $636.00

REGULATIONSPLUS on WestlawNext

RegulationsPlus is a regulation research service that revolutionizes and simplifies the task of finding and analyzing federal regulations. It may be used to locate or validate the status of a relevant **Code of Federal Regulations** (CFR) section, find interpretive cases and administrative options, view Federal Register Summary or archival content. It provides the tools to determine immediately whether or not a regulation is valid, and see how courts and federal agencies have interpreted it. It includes the following content and features:

1.The Online CFR Index. An index of than 1 million references created by West attorney-editors is arranged by topic and linked directly to CFR sections.

2. CFR notes of decisions. More than 600,000 notes of decisions by West attorney-editors which provide outlines and summaries of federal case law, each note of which links to the case and to West key numbers and topics.

3. Links to related code sections. CFR sections are linked to cited sections and subsections of the U.S. Code so you can move effortlessly between the two.

4. KeyCite Alerts of regulatory changes. KeyCite flags alert you when a CFR regulation has changed or is subject to proposed changes, with links to relevant Federal Register sections, so you can effortlessly monitor specific sections and get automatic notification of changes or proposed changes.

5. Agency materials and decisions. From a regulation, you can link to relevant administrative agency manuals, guidelines, bulletins, and decisions from more than 150 agency sources.

6. Historical Federal Register content. Provides summaries from 1981-date for any section you can view, with links to the full text.

7. Prior versions of CFR content. Get quick access to previous CFR versions (back to February 2005), future versions, and renumbered versions so you know how a CFR section appeared at a specific point in time.

8. Federal Agency Tracking Service. Receive notification for specific federal agency actions reported in the Federal Register, along with new agency opinions and decisions.

State Regulations

Although an impressive and systematic regulatory publication apparatus has been established at the federal level, the publication of regulations on the state level developed more slowly. At present, 45 states have published administrative codes, most of which are updated by weekly or monthly registers. By way of contrast, only 14 states had published administrative codes in 1965. Citizens in the other 36 states who desired copies of regulations were forced to contact their respective Secretaries of State with whom regulations had to be filed under their state administrative procedures acts, or contact the agencies themselves. Despite the vast improvement in the publication of state administrative codes and registers, much work remains to be done to improve their organization, indexing, and thoroughness.

Those interested in accessing state regulations are first advised to consult the listings of **Leading Web Sites for State Legal Research** in Chapter 28 of this volume before considering the purchase of a commercial product. Access to your state's regulatory code is becoming a more viable option with the proliferation of state primary law products on CD-ROM or the Internet. What formerly entailed the purchase of a multi-volume print code may now simply involve Internet access of a state government website, or the acquisition of a CALR subscription (e.g. Westlaw, LexisNexis, etc.) or state CD-ROM containing cases, statutes, session laws, and regulations. If state regulations are not available as a part of your CALR subscription or state CD-ROM, investigate the purchase of those volumes of the print administrative code containing regulations relevant to your area(s) of specialty.

State CD-ROM titles are changing rapidly in terms of operation and coverage, some disappearing altogether. The state regulations are now routinely available on a number of commercial online services often contain state regulations, as well as statutes and case law. The wise purchaser will seek out those CALR subscriptions or CD-ROM products with the full range of state primary law over those with more limited coverage.
In April, 2005, LexisNexis acquired the Weil Publishing Company, a leading publishing of state administrative regulations in print and online. As a result of the acquisition, LexisNexis now publishes fifteen administrative codes, fourteen state registers, and fourteen guides (indices) formerly published by Weil.

State Regulations on the Internet

The Internet is rapidly becoming a reliable source for state regulations. State governments providing free access to their state administrative codes now number forty-eight, while other states are expected to mount administrative codes shortly. Forty-0ne state registers are also available on free government Web sites. As the reliability of these state government Web sites grows, the cost-conscious attorney may choose to drop his or her print subscription in favor of electronic access. For those who already subscribe to an online service with comprehensive state primary law, or a comprehensive state CD-ROM product, access to a government Internet site can serve as a convenient back-up or updating medium. Those who wish to determine the availability of state administrative codes on the Internet can visit the **National Association of Secretaries of State** web site: http://www.administrativerules.org/.

The bibliographic details and prices of administrative codes which currently exist on the state level, in hardcopy, CD-ROM, or the Internet may be found in **Chapter 26: State Legal Publications**.

Chapter 12: Municipal Ordinances

While many legal issues are governed by state statutes or regulations, other issues of local significance are addressed by ordinances emanating from governmental units at the city, town or county level. Ordinances are a form of delegated legislation which derive their authority from powers granted to local governments by state legislatures. Matters which are primarily or largely addressed at the local level include education, zoning, housing, social welfare, municipal services, transportation, public safety, and local taxation. Attorneys employed by local governmental units or who represent clients in their dealings with municipal authorities or departments must have some familiarity with the sources of law at the local level.

The primary sources of law at the local level are municipal charters, ordinances, and regulations. Municipal charters are the equivalent of constitutions at the state or federal levels which contain the organic law of a local unit of government. Municipal charters establish the basic organizational structure for the government of a city, town, village or county. For example, they determine if the municipality is a mayor-council, council-manager, or commission form of government. Municipal charters also typically lay out the departmental structure of municipal government, as well as establish separate boards, districts and authorities to oversee the performance of such specific functions as education and housing.

Ordinances are the local equivalent of laws passed by state legislatures or the United States Congress. Passed by city councils or other local governing bodies, ordinances provide the kind of detail necessary for carrying out the broader charge contained in the municipal charter. Local ordinances provide more specific authorization or direction to municipal officers or employees and regulate conduct within the municipality. Ordinances may govern matters ranging from education and zoning to speed limits and public drunkenness. Individual municipal departments and agencies may also promulgate rules and regulations; however, except in the case of a few major cities (New York City being the best example), these are not published in any systematic way and are best obtained directly from the department or agency in question.

Ordinances are the local equivalent of laws passed by state legislatures or the United States Congress. Passed by city councils or other local governing bodies, ordinances provide the kind of detail necessary for carrying out the broader charge contained in the municipal charter. Local ordinances provide more specific authorization or direction to municipal officers or employees and regulate conduct within the municipality. Ordinances may govern matters ranging from education and zoning to speed limits and public drunkenness. Individual municipal departments and agencies may also promulgate rules and regulations; however, except in the case of a few major cities (New York City being the best example), these are not published in any systematic way and are best obtained directly from the department or agency in question.

Codification of Municipal Ordinances

As might be expected from units at the lowest levels of the governmental hierarchy, the publication of local legislation is uneven at best, though the situation has improved markedly with the availability of online municipal codes for many jurisdictions. Some cities and towns have well organized codes of ordinances produced by one of several companies specializing in such publications. These municipal code volumes typically contain the full text of the municipal charter and all current municipal ordinances, including those governing zoning matters. They are typically published in a looseleaf or post-binder format to allow for convenient and regular updating, although, increasingly, many municipal codes have now found their way onto the Internet. Those companies specializing in the publication of municipal ordinances also provide a full range of editorial services to the communities with which they have contracted, including legal drafting, formatting and indexing. They may also publish such items as local building codes or police manuals.

For example, the Municipal Code Corporation (Municode) of Tallahassee, Florida now publishes more than 2,900 codes which are available at no charge on the Internet. Employing a staff of full-time attorneys, it works with communities to review codes and ordinances, analyze ordinances against current state statutes and court decisions, make recommendations to local municipal attorneys, and make suggestions regarding the organization and numbering system for local codes of ordinances. A Sample Ordinance Service provides subscribers with examples of ordinances in codified form so that they can examine how other communities have dealt with similar matters. It employs a style manual to impose a consistent format on all codes, provides historical notes at the end of each section, and includes cross references and state law references for the legal researcher.

Municipal Code Corporation also provides local communities with a looseleaf supplement service to guarantee that codes are kept up-to-date through replacement pages. It also has the capability of providing codes in electronic format with an information retrieval program. Municipalities can elect to receive the supplemented Code more frequently in electronic format than in hardcopy supplements. The search software is available for DOS, Windows and Macintosh. The availability of municipal codes on the Internet in recent years has dramatically enhanced citizen access to local law.

Municipal Code Corporation provides free online access to more than 2,700 codes in fifty states by clicking on a list of municipalities for each state. It is available at: **www.municode.com**. Simply click on the appropriate state and municipality.

There are many smaller communities which lack the financial resources to contract out the publication of their local ordinances. In these instances, local attorneys and citizens must rely on locally produced ordinance books prepared in the offices of the city or town clerk. These often lack the systematic organization, regular supplementation, and more sophisticated editorial features which characterize the professionally produced volumes. They are typically typed by local secretarial staff and hole punched for insertion in three-ringed binders. The Internet, however, now provides such communities with another means of making their ordinances available to the public.

Generally speaking, there is no local equivalent of state or federal session laws. While state law or local charter provisions typically require publication of proposed ordinances in a local newspaper prior to their consideration and enactment, individual, or slip, ordinances usually appear only in typewritten form following passage and prior to their incorporation in the next supplement to the codified ordinances. These slip ordinances are usually available only upon specific request; and the attorney interested in tracking such matters must be particularly alert for pending or recent enactments.

Municipal codes rarely include annotations to case law. Relevant cases can be located by consulting the appropriate West digests and topics, state legal encyclopedias, and local practice guides. The attorney can also consult one of several national treatises in the field of municipal law for access to case law (for reviews of the leading treatises in the field of Municipal Corporations, see Chapter 27). Other sources for locating citations to cases interpreting local ordinances include the state statutory citators published by Shepard's (now owned by Reed Elsevier) or available online. Now, with the availability of computer-assisted legal research services and CD-ROM products containing state case law, key word searches can be conducted to locate cases involving selected local issues involving particular municipalities. Attorneys and others interested in conducting further research into case law interpreting city or town ordinances can also consult:

Ordinance Law Annotations. St. Paul, MN: ThomsonWest, 1969-date. 13 vols. Annual pocket parts.
Cost: $3,443; supplementation: 1996: $324; 1997: $340.20; 1998: $360.50; 1999: $389.50; 2000: $421.00; 2001: $498; 2002: $570; 2003: $738; 2004: $826; 2005: $904.50; 2006: $1,016; 2007: $1,056; 2008: $1,271.50; 2009: $1,434.00; 2010: $1,673; 2011: $1,624; 2012: $1,819; 2013: $2,394; **Monthly Assured Print Price** (APP): $233.00 per mo./$2,796.00 per yr.

Drawing upon the vast Westlaw database, this comprehensive digest consists of annotations to court decisions which have interpreted local ordinances. Annotations are grouped under broad, alphabetically arranged subject headings which are then sub-divided into specific subtopics. The coverage is national in scope, allowing the researcher to locate cases from across the country which have addressed a particular issue. Given its initial and supplementation cost, this is a resource designed for the attorney or law firm specializing in municipal law. Others can consult this research tool in a local public and academic law library.

Organizational Support to Municipalities and Municipal Attorneys

The most important national organization for attorneys or public officials interested in obtaining advice regarding municipal issues or the publication or municipal ordinances is:

International Municipal Lawyers Association (IMLA)
(formerly the National Institute of Municipal Law Officers (NIMLO)
7910 Woodmont Avenue
Suite 1440
Bethesda, MD 20814
(202) 466-5424
FAX: (202) 785-0152
www.imla.org

IMLA publishes a bimonthly magazine entitled **Municipal Attorney** which tracks recent court decisions, local ordinances and federal regulations of interest to local government attorneys. It also publishes the **IMLA Model Ordinance Service**, a comprehensive collection of municipal ordinances and annotations designed to assist local governments and their legal staffs in drafting ordinances which meet local needs and comply with local, state, and federal laws. Regular IMLA members receive a subscription to the **IMLA Model Ordinance Service**, including ordinance installments, as a part of their annual dues. Dues for municipalities range from $375.00 per year for communities of less than 5,000 inhabitants to $6,160.00 per year for communities of more than 800,000. Associate IMLA members may join for $450.00 per year as individuals or $600.00 as law firms (for two members; $60.00 for each additional member). Law professors and judicial personnel may subscribe to the **Municipal Lawyer** and the **IMLA Model Ordinance** Service for $125.00 per year. Libraries may subscribe to Municipal Attorney and the **Ordinance Law Service** for $250.00 for a two-year subscription. Members have online access to a five-year archive of back issues.

American Legal Publishing Co. 432 Walnut Street, Ste. 1200 Cincinnati, OH 45202 (800) 445-5588 www.amlegal.com	**Municipal Code Corp.** 1700 Capital Circle SW Tallahassee, FL 32310 (800) 262-2633 www.municode.com
Code Publishing, Inc. 9410 Roosevelt Way NE Seattle, WA 98115-2844 (800) 551-2633 www.codepublishing.com	**Sterling Codifiers, Inc.** 7600 Mineral Drive Coeur d'Alene, ID 83815 (800) 338-7458 www.sterlingcodifiers.com
Coded Systems Corp. 68 State Highway 71 Spring Lake Heights, NJ 07762 (732) 775-2300 www.codedsystems.com	**General Code Publishers Corp.** 781 Elmgrove Road Rochester, NY 14624-2991 (800) 836-8834 www.generalcode.com

Municipal Code Publishers

The companies which specialize in the publication of municipal ordinances include the following:

Municipal Code Corporation (MCC)

The Municipal Code Corporation (MuniCode) provides a broad range of legal publishing products and services to all its governmental customers . For casual users of our services access to its online library of municipal codes should be sufficient. Details are available at:
http://www.municode.com/Codification.

The attorney interested accessing his or her municipal ordinances should first determine if they available on the Internet from Municipal Code Corporation or another vendor. This will save the expense of a hardcopy code. When in doubt, contact the city or town clerk to determine the publisher and local availability. If your usage is not sufficient to justify the purchase of an office copy, and it is not available online, you may wish to consult the copy at your local public law library. Some law libraries make a point of collecting all the municipal codes for a given state or area. Rhode Island, for example, has a state statute mandating that all cities and towns in the state provide both the State Law Library and State Library with copies of their ordinances and the periodic supplements to them. Now, the ordinances or eighteen Rhode Island cities and towns are available free-of-charge on the Municipal Code Corporation web site. Also, since the supplementation of local ordinances is likely to be irregular (particularly if it is a locally produced volume), the attorney must always contact the city or town clerk to determine the current status of the ordinance or subject matter in question.

Municipal Ordinances on the Web

There are a number of Web sites providing links to hundreds of local municipal codes, including:

Code Publishing, Inc.
http://www.codepublishing.com/
Provides links to over 200 municipal codes from 16 states.

General Code Publishers, Inc.
http://www.codepublishing.com/elibrary.html
Provides access to over 600 municipal codes from 22 states.

Municipal Code Corporation
www.municode.com
The Web site of the leading publisher of municipal codes, with links to more than 2,900 municipal codes.

Sterling Codifiers, Inc.
www.sterlingcodifiers.com/
Its web site provides links to 900 municipal, county and special district governmental codes from

Chapter 13: Case Reporters

For nearly 200 years after the first English settlers set foot on the the North American continent, lawyers and judges relied upon the English common law as precedent in American legal disputes. Despite this heavy reliance upon English case law, few English case reporters found their way into the American law offices or judicial chambers. It was in response to the paucity of published domestic precedent that Connecticut's Ephraim Kirby prepared the first American case reporter volume in 1789. **Kirby's Reports**, a collection of decisions from the Connecticut Superior Court, was the first attempt in a broader movement to create a permanent body of American case law which would suit the unique requirements of citizens of a new nation.

Following Kirby's lead, other reporters prepared collections of appellate court decisions for use by members of the bench and bar. However, these early nominative reports often consisted of the reporters' notes and observations, rather than the actual text of the judges' decisions. They also suffered from a lack of numerical consistency, the volume numbers beginning and ending with the involvement of the individual reporters. Many years later, the courts themselves imposed order on these nominative reporters by renumbering them as state reports in one continuous sequence. Some states never did incorporate these early nominative reports into a uniform numbering scheme. In fact, some states did not even begin publishing decisions of their appellate courts until the middle of the 19th century. Rhode Island, for example, did not issue its first volume of the **Rhode Island Reports** until 1849, although it drew upon cases going back to 1828 to fill its first volume.

The lack of uniformity which existed in the publication of official state reports was not the only deficiency which afflicted American case reporting during much of the 19th century. The delays and inaccuracies which attended many official court reports were serious obstacles to the timely and uniform administration of justice in a rapidly growing and industrialized society. It was in response to this chaotic world of legal publishing that John B. West began publishing decisions of the Minnesota Supreme Court in 1876. His weekly **Syllabi** provided Minnesota attorneys and judges with timely access to selected decisions which would otherwise have taken many months or years to appear in print. In 1879, West combined the decisions of five additional states into what he called the **Northwestern Reporter**. By 1887, he had developed a national system of appellate case reporting which has come to be known as the National Reporter System.

More significantly, the West Publishing Company provided its customers with valuable research aids which permitted effective subject and case name access to all of its published opinions. The West key number system, incorporating the comprehensive classification system of topics and key numbers first appearing in the **United States Digest** (1848) consisted of more than four hundred topics and thousands of subtopics, together with editorially drafted case synopses. These innovations provided legal researchers with their first truly comprehensive system for locating relevant cases from among the thousands published every year. More than 150 years later, in an increasingly computer-driven age, West's National Reporter System and Key Number Digests remain the backbone of American legal publishing.

West has not been content to rest on its laurels. In 1975, it introduced Westlaw, a computerized legal research system which has in many ways supplanted the manual forms of legal research. In recent years, West's dominance in the field of primary law is coming under growing pressure from publishers large and small who have begun tapping the potential of the Internet as a vehicle for disseminating court decisions and other primary and secondary forms of legal information.

Thus, over the span of 225 years (1789 to 2014), American case reporting has seen the successive appearance of nominative reports, official reports, commercial reports, computer-assisted legal research, and CD-ROM. This multiplicity of formats offers the practicing attorney a variety of options from which to choose when setting up or enhancing his or her law office library. This chapter will focus on the alternative formats for case reporters and the relative merits of each.

One consequence of the rapid acceptance of Westlaw, LexisNexis, Casemaker and other online databases as a format for delivering legal information has been the sharp decline in used prices for reporter series in hardcopy. For the attorney who still appreciates reading his law off the printed page, this has been a great boon. Complete sets of the **Atlantic Reporter 2d**, which just a few years ago sold for around $4000, are so ubiquitous that their prices have fallen nearly 40%, to less than $2,200. Others have been obtaining them for the cost of postage. Times have never been better for those acquiring court reports in hardcopy. The cost of current hardcopy volumes, however, continues to rise inexorably. Individual volumes of the **Atlantic Reporter 2d**, for example, now cost $708 each ($532 to subscribers). Moreover, when the per volume costs are increased, they are extended to all volumes in the series.

Bottom Line: The practitioner should avoid print reporters at all costs in favor of some form of online access. This warning is particularly true with regional and federal reporters whose per-volume costs have skyrocketed in recent years.

Official State Reporters

The acquisition of the appellate court decisions for one's own jurisdiction is certainly one of the most important purchases for any practicing attorney. When selecting case reporters in hardcopy, there are three possible options, or a combination of these. The first consists of the official reports published by your appellate court, or courts (if your state also has an intermediate appellate court). While twenty-seven states continue to issue official reports, another twenty-three have discontinued them in favor of a West offprint of the regional reporter or the regional reporter itself. Official state reports, provided they are still being published, have several distinct disadvantages. Many continue to lag behind the reports published commercially by West and are not available for citation until sometime after the regional reporter citation has appeared. And, more significantly, they typically lack the headnotes and other editorial enhancements which make the West reporters and accompanying digests such effective research tools.

With the rapid acceptance of computer-assisted research

and CD-ROM as vehicles for delivering state appellate court decisions, official state reports have experienced significant declines in price. In the period before CD-ROM, official state reports were often difficult to locate on the used lawbook and, when available, commanded prices approaching 50% of the cost of a new set. Today, the seller of older official reports would, in many instances, be lucky to garner 25% of the cost of a new set. For example, potential buyers for the 122-volume set of **Rhode Island Reports** (1828-1980) often had to await the death of an attorney to have the opportunity to acquire a used set for prices ranging from $1,500 to $2,000, a savings of 42-56% off the $3,563.00 cost of a new set from the Secretary of State. With the appearance of these decisions on a host of online databases, demand for the print reports has largely evaporated.

The prices for state reports from official state agencies generally remain fixed, as they must recover the original cost of printing the volumes. Official reports published by contract with commercial publishers may be discounted because the commercial publishers are not under the same cost recovery strictures as state agencies. Volumes 1-100 of the official **New York Court of Appeals Reports, 2d**, for example, have been discounted by the publisher, West, to a level ($1,093) slightly below that of used sets ($1,100). Sadly, most state agencies will probably continue to retain hardcopy volumes in warehouses or sub-basements, unable to price them attractively enough to compete against the alternatives now on the market. For those official state reports available on the used lawbook market, see the entries in **Chapter 26: State Publications**, and contact one of the used lawbook dealers listed in the Appendix C.

West Off-Print Reporters

A better alternative to the official reports are West's state offprint reporters available for more than thirty states, particularly if these can be acquired on the used lawbook market. These volumes can be supplemented by accessing recent decisions on your state court web site. The offprint reporters, such as **Massachusetts Decisions**, also provide a space-saving alternative to the full regional reporter, which is no longer an advisable purchase given their high per volume and advance sheet cost. The cost differential between a subscription to the state offprint and the regional reporter may easily exceed $3,000 annually, particularly if the attorney is from a small state whose decisions are dominated by those of its larger neighbors. While the regional reporter may provide attorneys in small states with convenient access to a wealth of case law not found in a small state, these reporters should only be consulted at law libraries when online access is not available.

West print reporters and advance sheets have increased in cost so dramatically over the past 15 years that they are no longer a cost-effective acquisition. Given the fact that almost all the regional reporter advance sheets are now priced in the $1,600+ per year range, and have been going up at a rate of 20% per year, the cost-conscious attorney should consider dropping them altogether in favor of some form of online access. The prices, both new and used, for state offprint reporters may be found in **Chapter 26: State Publications**.

West Regional Reporters

The most costly alternative to the official state reports is to acquire the full regional reporter of which your state is a part. Unfortunately, the availability of used sets has become more problematic, with fewer used law book dealers having fewer complete sets in inventory. For the patient, acquiring a set for the cost of postage by monitoring the law-lib listserv is a more likely alternative. Purchased new, the second series of the regional reporters list at prices ranging between $10,222 (**California Reporter 3d**) and $20,134 (**South Western Reporter 3d**), although West has of late begun offering discount pricing for complete sets. Despite these discounts, however, the price differential between new and used sets continues to widen. But fundamentally, the age of the print reporter is over, done in by an age of many on-line alternatives and out-of-control print costs.

The following table provides a quick overview of the costs of the various components of the National Reporter System, including the cost of a new set, cost of additional bound volumes in 2013, current cost of an advance sheet subscription, approximate cost of a used set (if available), and the annual cost of a subscription on CD-ROM:

Regional Reporter	List price*	2013 Upkeep	Advance Sheets**	Used***	CD-ROM
Atlantic Reporter 3d	$15,080.00	$11,704.00	$2,866.56	$3,495.00	No new sales
California Reporter 3d	$10,222.00	$7,263.00	$2,700.00	$595.00	No new sales
New York Supplement 2d	$12,968.00	$9,342.00	$2,401.00	$995.00	No new sales
North Eastern Reporter 2d	$15,333.00	$10,117.00	$2,866.56	$1,995.00	No new sales
North Western Reporter 2d	$10,225.00	$6,873.00	$2,808.00	$3,795.00	No new sales
Pacific Reporter 3d	$15,201.00	$11,401.50	$2,866.56	$1,995.00	No new sales
South Eastern Reporter 2d	$10,480.00	$6,877.50	$2,825.00	$1,995.00	No new sales
Southern Reporter 3d	$17,639.00	$12,178.50	$2,866,56	$1,995.00	No new sales
South Western Reporter 3d	$20,134.00	$15,094.50	$2,799.00	$1,495.00	No new sales
Southern Reporter 3d	$12,743.00	$11,492.00	$2,389.00	$1,995.00	No new sales
South Western Reporter 2d	$12,480.00	n/a	n/a	$2,295.00	No new sales
South Western Reporter 3d	$13,982.00	$12,615.00	$2,333.00	$1,495.00	No new sales

*Contact your West sales representative for current prices and applicable discounts, including combination print/CD-ROM discounts. West sales representatives have authority to offer discounts on CD-ROM prices quoted here.
**No charge with bound volume subscription.
***Fluctuation of used prices is a direct result of the limited number of full sets on the market. and the fact that most sets are given away for the cost of postage.

Monthly Assured Print Pricing

In 2010, West instituted a new pricing model to entice new subscribers to subscribe to their print products. Subscribers receive a complete and up-to-date set of the publication in question in exchange for signing a two- or three-year contract that caps future supplementation cost increases at 5% (under a 3-year contract) or 6% (under a two-year contract). The monthly/annual contractual costs are usually higher than the existing subscriber discount because they amortize the cost of the complete set as a part of the two- or three-year contract. In 2013, however, the spread widened even farther. **The Monthly (and Annual) Assured Print Price** of the National Reporter volumes are as follows, followed by the normal annualized subscriber discounted cost for 2013:

Monthly Assured Print Pricing	Monthly	Yearly	Regular Sub. Discount 2013
Atlantic Reporter 3d	$1,163.00	$13,956.00	$11,704.00
California Reporter 3d	$724.00	$8,688.00	$7,263.00
New York Supplement 2d	$921.00	$11,052.00	$9,342.00
North Eastern Reporter 2d	$1,087.00	$13,044.00	$10,117.00
North Western Reporter 2d	$709.00	$8,508.00	$6,873.00
Pacific Reporter 3d	$1,141.00	$13,692.00	$11,401.50
South Eastern Reporter 2d	$846.00	$10,152.00	$6,877.50
Southern Reporter 3d	$1,274.00	$15,288.00	$12,178.50
South Western Reporter 3d	$1,399.00	$16,788.00	$15,094.50

The astronomical cost increases of West's print reporters since their acquisition by Thomson in 1996 have rendered them an unwise purchase in print form. While the acquisition of a print set on the used law book market, or free for the cost of postage, may be justified, the standing order for new volumes cannot be justified under any circumstances. For example, the annual cost of subscribing to the regional reporter would have cost you anywhere between $6,873 (N. W. Reporter 3d) and $15,094.50 (S.W. Reporter 3d) per year in 2013, depending on the region. Under the **Monthly Assured Print Price** model shown above, the annual costs of the regional reporters currently range from $8,508 (Cal. Reporter 2d) to $16,788 (So. Reporter 3d). The premium paid for the **Monthly Assured Print Price** plan may be attributed to the fact that the subscriber receives a complete set of reporters at the outset. In other words, the additional monthly/ annual cost is a way of amortizing the cost of the complete set provided at the initially.

Moreover the cost of individual volumes has risen dramatically in recent years, For example, **Atlantic Reporter 3d** bound volumes were priced at $532.00 to subscribers in 2013 ($708 list). With 22 new volumes being published in that year alone, the cost was $11,704 (i.e. $532 x 22). At those prices, it won't take long for the annual subscription to the regional reporter to cost you far more than your initial expenditure for an entire used set. In fact, you would have to acquire only seven bound volumes of the **Atlantic Reporter 3d** from West for the total cost to exceed the $3,495 you paid for the complete used (assuming they are readily available). If you prefer the broader coverage of the regional reporter, a better alternative is to acquire these decisions online. Whether this is West's intention or not, the rapidly escalating price of regional reporter bound volumes is driving customers away from the print subscription and into the arms of Westlaw, or another online alternative. Moreover, even the cost of advance sheet subscriptions continues to rise at a rate of 20% per year. The cost of the **Atlantic Reporter 2d** advance sheets, for example, rose from $1,382.50 in 2010 to $1,659.00 in 2011, $2,389.00 in 2013, and $2,866,56 in 2014.

In either case, a subscription to the print reporters is not recommended, even if the **Monthly Assured Print Price (APP)** plan provides the subscriber with a means of capping future price increases at the 5-6% level (as opposed to the 11-12% increases to the normal subscriber). And as the evidence clearly reveals, the **APP** costs have risen precipitously as well. Given the declining numbers of print subscribers to print reporters, the **Monthly Assured Print Price** is just a means by which West is attempting to lock in standing order revenues. Moreover, the **APP** is available to new subscribers only, which eliminates most law libraries.

Special alert: The steeply rising cost of bound reporter volumes acquired in a serial fashion from the publisher can no longer be justified by the cost-conscious attorney or law library. The monies spent on one year's worth of bound regional reporter volumes, for example, could be far more effectively spent on a LexisNexis or Westlaw subscription plan providing the full range of primary law for your state and federal circuit. The only bound volumes you should acquire are those you may acquire used or free for the cost of postage. Once acquired, these sets should not be supplemented in print. Current decisions should only be obtained online. In the past few years, even many of the largest and most consequential law school libraries have abandoned subscriptions to the National Reporter System bound volumes and advance sheets in favor of online access via Westlaw.

Primary Law Resources — All (WestlawNext PRO)

Law firms interested in access to state and federal cases, and statutes, from all jurisdictions can subscribe to **Primary Law Resources – All** on WestlawNext PRO at a cost substantially below that which they would have paid for little more than one regional reporter series in print. The above referenced subscription costs only $8,880 per year for a solo practitioner, $11,988 ($5,994 per attorney) for a two-attorney firm, and $14,388 for a three-member firm ($4,796 per attorney). Larger firms qualify for special negotiated pricing.

Pre-National Reporter System Volumes

There are few additional considerations to bear in mind if you are interested in acquiring a complete back run of your state's appellate court decisions. The first series of all the regional reporters are also available from the used lawbook dealers, although usually in a condition which requires greater scrutiny on the part of the purchaser. Also, with the West regional reporters first appearing in the period between 1879 and 1887, there may well be official reports for your state which precede the appearance of the regional reporters. The used lawbook dealers are often prepared to sell these pre-national reporter volumes to those attorneys who wish to acquire a full set of reporters for their jurisdiction. For the average attorney more interested in current decisions, however, this is probably not a pressing concern.

United States Supreme Court

For the attorney who requires ready access to the decisions of the United States Supreme Court, there are three bound reporter series from which to choose, as well as two commercial looseleaf services and a variety of CD-ROM products. Of course, the decisions are also available on Westlaw and LexisNexis and over the Internet. This chapter will focus upon the competing bound reporter series. As in the case of the states, the early decisions of the United States Supreme Court were designated by the names of the individuals who compiled them. These "nominative" reporters were later incorporated into the overall numbering scheme of the **United States Reports** and comprise the first 90 volumes of the official set. These 90 volumes, together with their nominative and **U.S. Reports** citations include the following:

A.J. Dallas	1-4 Dall.	1-4 U.S.
William Cranch	1-9 Cranch	5-13 U.S.
Henry Wheaton	1-12 Wheat	14-25 U.S.
Richard Peters	1-16 Pet	26-41 U.S.
Benjamin Howard	1-24 How	42-65 U.S.
J. S. Black	1-2 Black	66-67 U.S.
John William Wallace	1-23 Wall	69-90 U.S.

Official Reports

United States Reports. Washington, D.C.: U.S. Government Printing Office, 1790-date. 554 vols.; 3-5 volumes published per Term.
Cost: $26,095 (complete reprint price from William Hein Co.); volumes 1-499: $68; vols. 500-545: $80.00; vol. 546: $100.00; 547-551: $80.00; 552: $90.00; 553: $85; 554: $80; used sets available for approx. $5,995. Advance sheet subscription: $92 per term. Also included in the typical WestlawNext primary law package. Current volumes also available from Bernan. Slip opinion subscription: $426 per term (2013 term) (1st class mail). Also available on HeinOnline, and via the U.S. Supreme Court web site (vols. 502-date):
http://www.supremecourt.gov/opinions/opinions.aspx

The official **U.S. Reports** appear first as individual slip opinions, then as advance sheets (called "Preliminary Prints"), and finally as bound volumes. It is only with the official advance sheet that the decisions are citable to volume and page number. Unfortunately, the "preliminary print," as it is called, does not appear until nearly two years after the decision has been announced. Another year passes prior to the appearance of the bound volume. Due to this sluggish publication schedule, and the lack of useful editorial features, attorneys have come to rely on two commercial reporter series for the text of Supreme Court decisions. While the **United States Reports** are found in many law libraries, they are not recommended for the practicing attorney who requires prompt access to citable decisions. The official bound volumes 502 (1991) to date are available on the U.S. Supreme Court web site at: http://www.supremecourtus.gov/opinions/boundvolumes.html The U.S. Supreme Court also provides a fairly comprehensive list of both commercial and non-commercial sources for U.S. Supreme Court decisions on its web site at: http://www.supremecourtus.gov/opinions/obtainopinions.pdf

Lawyers' Edition

United States Supreme Court Reports, Lawyers' Edition. [1st] - **2d**. LexisNexis, 1882-date. 1st series: 100 vols. 2d series: 180 vols. (as of March, 2013). Sold to Reed Elsevier January, 1997 pursuant to the consent decree by which the Department of Justice approved the merger of the Thomson Corporation and West Publishing Company.
Cost: 1st series: $3,750 (promotions may be available); used sets also available for $1,100; 2d series: $6,843 (promotions may be available); supplementation: 2013: $350 (3 vols.); used sets approx. $900. Current volumes priced at $69 each. Advance sheet subscription available for $239 per year. Also available in CD-ROM format (below).

The two series of the **Lawyers' Edition** contain every case decided by the United States Supreme Court since its inception, as well as some early decisions of the Pennsylvania Supreme Court. The first series encompasses volumes 1-351 of the **United States Reports** (1790-1956). The second series includes all decisions decided since 1956. Each decision includes the syllabus prepared by the official reporter, as well as a summary and headnotes written by the Lawyers Cooperative editors. Other unique editorial features of the **Lawyers' Edition** include summaries of the briefs of counsel, references to other Lawyers Cooperative publications in the "Total Client-Service Library" and, in the case of a few important cases, annotations reviewing some of the more significant points of law considered by the court. The headnotes appearing in the **Lawyers' Edition** are reused as digest paragraphs in the **U.S. Lawyers' Edition** Digest. Decisions generally appear in citable advance sheet form within six-eight weeks of their release by the court. They also appear in interim volumes before taking the form of bound volumes. The CD-ROM subscription also includes a subscription to the advance sheets

Supreme Court Reporter

West's Supreme Court Reporter. St. Paul, MN: West, 1882-date. 128 in 204 vols. (as of April, 2014). Subscription includes interim and permanent bound volumes.
Cost: $5,489; used sets available for approx. $1,800. Annual cost of bound volumes (2): $132.75/$177 (subscriber/list); 2012: $106; 2013: $106. Advance sheets alone: $2,210 per year; Monthly Assured Print Price (APP): $125 per mo./$1,500 per yr.

Initiated in 1882, the first volume of West's Supreme Court Reporter encompasses decisions reported in volumes 106-107 of the official United States Reports. There was no attempt by West to duplicate the retrospective coverage of the official and Lawyers Edition volumes. As with other volumes in the National Reporter System, each decision in the Supreme Court Reporter includes a synopsis and headnotes drafted by West editors. These headnotes are reused in West's United States Supreme Court Digest as a means of locating cases by subject matter. By the time the final bound volumes are published, the parallel citations to the United States Reports and Lawyers' Edition are included, as are the page breaks in the official United States Reports.

Comparison

For the practicing attorney, the selection of a bound volume reporter series comes down to a choice between **West's Supreme Court Reporter** and **LexisNexis's Lawyers' Edition**. The **Supreme Court Reporter** has the advantage of being tied into the National Reporter System, employing the topics and key numbers appearing in all West reporters and digests.

The attorney already familiar with the West digest system will be able to use the United States Supreme Court Digest without difficulty. **The Lawyers Edition**, on the other hand, has greater retrospective coverage than the West set, encompassing 92 more years of Supreme Court decisions. However, its topics and subtopics do not, for obvious reasons, correspond to the West system.

A price comparison reveals that used sets of the complete **Lawyers' Edition** [1st] and **2d** may be obtained for approximately $1,800 while complete used sets of **West's Supreme Court Reporter** may be had for approximately $1,675.00. Thus, while the **Lawyers' Edition** is slightly more expensive, it provides 92 years more case law than the West version. The prospective purchaser must decide whether the editorial advantages of the West digest system outweigh the advantages of a set with greater chronological coverage.

Of course, the entire debate is rendered moot by the acquisition of the decisions in an online format. WestlawNext or LexisNexis packages, including state packages, typically include decisions of the U.S. Supreme Court and federal courts. Contact your local sales representatives for details,

Court Decisions in Looseleaf Format

U.S. Law Week. Washington, D.C.: Bureau of National Affairs, 1933-date. 2 vols. Weekly.
Cost: Print: $1,909 per year; Internet: $2,295 per year (1-5 users); print also available at discount to those purchasing the 1-5 user license. Contact publisher for single-user pricing.

This two-volume service provides timely reporting of current United States Supreme Court decisions. Although issues generally appear on a weekly basis, extra issues are released during the term's busy weeks. Releases also include Supreme Court Proceedings containing lists and summaries of newly docketed cases, news developments and reports on oral arguments. The General Law Sections include news and abstracts of decisions from other federal and state courts.

Lower Federal Courts

Federal Reporter [1st] - **3d.** St. Paul, MN: West, 1880-date. 1st series: 300 vols.; 2d series: 999 vols.; 3d series (1993-date): 740 vols. (as of April, 2014); approx. 33 vols. Issued per year.
Cost: 1st series: out-of-print; used sets available for approx. $900; 2d series: $9,990; 3d series: $15,895; annual cost of bound volumes (2013): $10,642 (33 vols.); per volume cost: $322.50/$430 (subscriber/list); advance sheets: $3,105 per year; used sets available for approx. $1,200. Also available on CD-ROM (see below); **Monthly Assured Print Price** (APP): $1,149 per mo./$13,680 per yr.

Federal Appendix. St. Paul, MN: West, 2001-date. 540 vols. (as of April, 2014). Unpublished decisions began appearing in the **Federal Reporter 3d** advance sheets in 2000. Volume one of the Federal Appendix appeared in January, 2001; approx. 48 new volumes issued per year.
Cost: $12,154 (540 vols.) (exclusive of discount); annual cost of bound volumes (2013): $8,742 (47 vols.); per volume cost: $186/$248 (subscriber/list); see **Federal Reporter 3d** advance sheets for current decisions: $3,105 per year; **Monthly Assured Print Price (APP)**: $873 per mo./$10,476 per yr.

Contains decisions of the U.S. Courts of Appeals that have not been selected for publication in the **Federal Reporter 3d** series. Unpublished decisions emerged in 1996 when the U.S. Court of Appeals Judicial Counsel recommended that only cases of "general precedential value" be published. They are chiefly useful to researchers because they often include relevant fact patterns and particular applications of settled law. West suggests that users "consult local rules to determine when and under what circumstances these cases may be cited."

Federal Supplement [1st] - **2d**. St. Paul, MN: West, 1932-date. 1st series: 999 vols.; 2d series: 960 vols. (as of April, 2014); approx. 74 volumes issued per year.
Cost: 1st series: $9,990 (exclusive of discount); 2d series: $33,508; annual cost of bound volumes (2013): $23,542; per volume cost: $322.50/$430 (subscriber/list); used sets available for approx. $2,195. advance sheets: $3,105.00 per year. Also available on CD-ROM (see below); **Monthly Assured Print Price (APP):** $2,237 per mo./$26,844.00 per yr.

Unlike the decisions of the United States Supreme Court and a majority of state supreme courts, the decisions of the lower federal courts do not appear in official reporter series. Bound decisions of the United States Courts of Appeals and United States District Courts are only available in West's **Federal Reporter** and **Federal Supplement**, respectively. At its inception, the **Federal Reporter** contained decisions of both the U.S. Circuit Courts of Appeals and U.S. District Courts. In 1932, the decisions of the U.S. District Courts were spun-off into a new reporter series called the **Federal Supplement**. A law firm which desires hardcopy access to complete runs of both series will require considerable shelf space to house the more the 2,500 volumes in **Federal Reporter 2d - 3d** and **Federal Supplement**.

With used sets readily available on the market, there is no point in throwing away your hard-earned dollars on a new set in the publisher's shrink-wrap. You will note that the cost of maintaining a current subscription will quickly exceed the cost of your used purchase. If you must have bound books, a far better alternative to this expense is to acquire a fairly complete used set, but only maintain currency through an online subscription. This will reduce your annual outlay from approximately $20,000 for both series to the far lower cost of online access to the U.S. District Court and Court of Appeals decisions for your own circuit.

Federal Claims Reporter. St. Paul, MN: West, 1993-date. 113 vols. (as of April, 2014). Biweekly advance sheets; 6-7 bound vols. per year. Continues the **United States Claims Court Reporter** (1982-1992, vols. 1-26). **Federal Claims Reporter** starts with vol. 27.
Cost: $3,325; annual cost of bound volumes (2013): $2,992.25; per vol. cost: $498.75/$665 (subscriber/list); advance sheets: $3,613 per year (bi-monthly); **Monthly Assured Print Price (APP)**: $239 per mo./$2,868 per yr.
Includes the text of cases decided in the United States Court of Federal Appeals and selected decisions of the United States Court of Appeals, Federal Circuit and Supreme Court of the United States in review.

Federal Rules Decisions. St. Paul, MN: West, 1938-date. Monthly. 295 vols. (as of April, 2014); approx. 9 vols. Issued per year. Contain decisions of the federal courts construing the federal rules.
Cost: $3,657; supplementation (2013): $3,287.25; individual vols. $365,25/$487 (subscriber/list); used sets sell for approx. $750; advance sheets: $730; **Monthly Assured Print Price (APP)**: $229.00 per mo./$2,748 per yr.

Federal Court Decisions on CD-ROM, DVD or Online

Supreme Court

The past few years have witnessed a sharp diminution in the number of companies offering federal court decisions on CD-ROM as well as a reduction in the offerings from the two major publishers. Thomson/West is the only company with substantial offerings in this format, but it has now withdrawn some of these products from the market, including those providing federal court of appeals and district court decisions for most of the federal circuits. LexisNexis is no longer making new sales of federal appellate and district court decision in this format. These developments appear to be signaling the end of the CD-ROM era in favor of total online access.

Supreme Court Reporter (West's). Eagan, MN: West, 1789-date. Two discs. Updated regularly. Available for Windows or Macintosh. Search Engine: PREMISE.
Cost: $6,135 per year (2014).
Unlike the coverage of the print product, the **Supreme Court Reporter** on CD-ROM contains case coverage from volume one of the official U.S. Reports to date. One disc replicates the coverage of the **Supreme Court Reporter** volumes, with coverage from 1882 to date. The other disc contains the text of the official **U.S. Reports**, with coverage from 1789 to date.

United States Supreme Court Reports, Lawyers' Edition. [CD-ROM]. Albany, NY: LexisNexis, 1954-date.One disc. Updated quarterly. Available for Windows Folio 3.1.
Contains the full text of all materials in the 100 bound volumes of the first series and 177+ volumes of the second series, including decisions, annotations, and summaries of briefs of counsel.
Cost: 2d Series: $1,757 1st year; $1,629,96 2d year; $1,662.56 3d year (2014). Price includes print advance sheets and binders. See sales representative for special discounts or promotions.

USSC + CD-ROM. Reno, NV: AccessLaw, Inc. One CD-ROM or DVD. Updated semiannually. Available for Windows and Macintosh (with 3rd Party Software).. Search Engine: Folio. (800) 784-7036
Cost: Discontinued following purchase of AccessLaw by CEB (2014).
Contained full text of U.S. Supreme Court decisions from 1792 to date. Includes 27,000 U.S. Supreme Court decisions and 600,000 pages of text. Available on Internet at: **www.accesslawsales.com.**

Lower Federal Courts

Federal Reporter Library, Premise CD-ROM ed.—1880-1979. Eagan, MN: West, 1980-date. 1 CD-ROM. Covers from 1880 to 603 F. 2d. Updated monthly. Available for Windows or Macintosh. Search Engine: PREMISE. Optional online link to WESTLAW. Subscription includes the weekly Federal Reporter advance sheets and online updating via Westlaw.
Cost: $5,685 per year (single user license) (2014).

Federal Reporter Library, Premise CD-ROM ed.—1980-Date. Eagan, MN: West, 1980-date. 6 CD-ROMs. Covers 604 F.2d through 3d series. Updated monthly. Also available for 9th Circuit. Available for Windows or Macintosh. Search Engine: PREMISE. Optional online link to WESTLAW. Subscription includes the weekly Federal Reporter advance sheets and online updating via Westlaw.
Cost: $15,543 per year (single user license) (2014).

Federal Supplement PREMISE CD-ROM ed.—1931-1979. Eagan, MN: West, 1931-1979. 1 CD-ROM. Updated monthly. Available for Windows or Macintosh. Search Engine: PREMISE. Optional online link to WESTLAW. Subscription includes the weekly Federal Supplement advance sheets.
Cost: $5,685 per year (single user license) (2014).

Federal Supplement PREMISE CD-ROM ed.—1980-Date. Eagan, MN: West, 1980-date. 4 CD-ROMs. Updated monthly. Available for Windows or Macintosh. Search Engine: PREMISE. Optional online link to WESTLAW. Subscription includes the weekly Federal Supplement advance sheets.
Cost: $15,543 per year (single user license) (2014).

Federal Rules Decisions on CD-ROM. St. Paul, MN: West Publishing Co., 1939-date. 1 disc. Updated quarterly. Available for Windows or Macintosh. Search Engine: PREMISE. Optional online link to WESTLAW. Subscription includes the weekly Federal Rules Decisions advance sheets.
Cost: $6,672 per year (single user license) (2014).

West's 10th Circuit Reporter Service Premise CD-ROM Ed. Eagan, MN: West. 1 disc per circuit. Updated monthly. Available for Windows or Macintosh. Search Engine: PREMISE. Coverage includes decisions from all district courts within individual circuits taken from volumes 1-60 of the Federal Reporter 2d (1925-1932) and volume 1-date of the Federal Supplement and Federal Supplement 2d, with the exception of the U.S. District Court for the District of Columbia which includes decisions form volume 16-date of the Federal Supplement and the Federal Rules Decisions Includes hypertext links to other cases cited within an opinion, to the United States Code Annotated, and West's Code of Federal Regulations. Optional online link to WESTLAW.
Cost: (only 9th and 10th Circuit still being produced): 9th Circuit: $4,086 per year; 10th Circuit: $4,905; West's Federal District Court Reporter 10th Circuit: $8,337 per year (single user license) (2014).

Court Decisions on the Internet

While the preceding discussion has focused primarily on the purchase of court decisions in print, on CD-ROM, and over the Internet, any legal professional anxious to hold the line on information costs has an obligation to investigate the availability of those decisions on no-cost, public Internet sites. Thus, compiling and bookmarking a list of the public sites most likely to be utilized in your practice should precede your considering the purchase of those decisions for a fee. Bookmarking these most commonly accessed sites using your Internet browser's software is the most effective means of compiling that list.

Depending on the state in which you practice, you will notice, however, that the historical case law coverage will often be less than complete. Most states have chosen to mount decisions prospectively, leaving proprietary sites as the only sources for archives of court decisions. There are exceptions, however. The Oklahoma courts have created a truly impressive Web site containing significant historical coverage of decisions of both the Oklahoma Supreme Court and Court of Appeals. Until other states follow Oklahoma's lead, however, most practitioners will be obtaining more complete archives of court decisions from such proprietary sources as VersusLaw, Westlaw, LexisNexis, Fastcase, Loislaw, or through the through their bar membership connection to Casemaker, Fastcase or some other commercial vendor. For a more complete discussion of these issues, see Chapters 24 and 25 and Appendix I.

Chapter 14: Annotated Reports

The late19th century was a critical era in the history of American legal publishing. It was a time when the commercial potential of legal publishing asserted itself in the marketplace and achieved dominance over the official governmental publication of court decisions. In its early manifestations, two competing philosophies of commercial case reporting emerged. One of these philosophies, represented by the West Publishing Company, championed the comprehensive reporting of court decisions. The competing philosophy, promoted by the Lawyers Cooperative Publishing Company (LCP), advocated the selective reporting of "leading" court decisions to which commentaries, called annotations, were appended. James Briggs, President of Lawyers Cooperative, took a major gamble that lawyers, unable to afford the purchase of comprehensive series of regional reporters, would opt instead to purchase volumes containing leading decisions selected for inclusion by the LCP editors. While both companies have survived, the comprehensive publication philosophy advocated by West eventually established itself as the dominant form of case reporting.

While Lawyers Cooperative may have lost the big battle of publication philosophies, it nevertheless emerged as one of the major forces in American legal publishing. Its success was aided in no small part by the popularity of the annotations it appended to the selective case reports in its **American Law Reports** (**ALR**) series. Today, the annotations published in the six series of **American Law Reports** and the two series of **American Law Reports Federal** represent one of the most useful resources for the legal researcher.

The **American Law Reports** combine the characteristics of the law review article and legal encyclopedia with the case report. The annotations are designed to provide thorough coverage of a narrowly defined legal issue combined with a representative case on that subject. In the beginning, the **American Law Reports** did attempt to publish leading decisions important in their own right. As time passed, however, the leading cases were replaced by decisions which merely illustrated the issue(s) discussed in the annotations. These annotations include citations to case authorities from all available jurisdictions and provide discussion of conflicting decisional outcomes. They also include references to relevant sections of other publications in what is now the West Group's Total Client-Service Library, including **American Jurisprudence 2d**, **Am. Jur. Trials**, **Am. Jur. Proof of Facts**, **Am. Jur. Legal Forms**, and **Am. Jur. Pleading and Practice Forms**. Citations to **ALR** found in a wide range of primary and secondary sources, including state statutory codes, provide researchers with an excellent gateway to begin their analyses of selected legal issues.

American Law Reports in Print

The **American Law Reports** series now consists of the following components and finding tools:

1. **American Law Reports** [1st series]. Rochester, NY: Lawyers Cooperative Publishing Co., 1919-1948. 175 volumes.
Cost: Out-of print, but available used at a cost of approximately $995.00 (see list of used law book dealers in Appendix C). **American Law Reports 1st Blue Books [of Supplemental Decisions]** available from publisher at a cost of $428.00.

2. **American Law Reports 2d**. Rochester, NY: Lawyers Cooperative Publishing Co., 1948-1965. 100 volumes. Updated by **ALR 2d Later Case Service**.
Cost: $695.00; supplementation is in **ALR 2d Later Case Service**. Used sets sell for approximately $295.00. See list of used law book dealers in Appendices.

3. **American Law Reports, 2d Later Case Service**. Rochester, NY: Lawyers Cooperative Publishing Co./West, 1980-date. Covering volumes 1-100 (in 44 books). This is the updating medium for **ALR 2d**. Later series all use pocket parts. Updated by annual pocket parts and periodic revised volumes.
Cost: $3,201; supplementation: 1993: $373; 1994: $442; 1995: $442; 1996: $589; 1997: $544; 1998: $578; 1999: $623; 2000: $667; 2001: $739.50; 2002: $814; 2003: 860; 2004: $829; 2005: $900; 2006: $1,257; 2007: $1,057.50; 2008: $1,176.50; 2009: $1,355; 2010: $1,706.50; 2011: $1,811; 2012: $1,271; 2013: $2,296; individual volumes: $383/$479 (subscriber/list); used sets available for approx. $200; **Monthly Assured Print Price (APP):** $238 per mo./$2,856 per yr.

4. **American Law Reports 3d**. Rochester, NY: Lawyers Cooperative Publishing Co./West, 1965-1980. 100 volumes. Updated by annual pocket parts. Also available on **WestlawNext.**
Cost: $2,793; supplementation: 1994: $311; 1995: $311; 1996: $358; 1997: $378; 1999: $429; 2000: $464; 2001: $522; 2002: $615; 2003: $700; 2004: $750; 2005: $821.25; 2006: $1.030; 2007: $985.00; 2008: $1,074.00; 2009: $1,170; 2010: $1,481; 2011: $1,590; 2012: $1,781; 2013: $1,995; individual volumes: $54 (list); used sets available for $400; **Monthly Assured Print Price (APP):** $208 per mo./$2,496 per yr.

5. **American Law Reports 4th**. Rochester, NY: Lawyers Cooperative Publishing Co./Thomson West, 1980-1991. 90 volumes. Updated by annual pocket parts. [Series was attenuated due to agreement with West Publishing to include references to West digest key numbers in future volumes and the subsequent decision to incorporate these features in a new 5th series]. Also available on **WestlawNext.**
Cost: $2,375; supplementation: 1994: $239; 1995: $239; 1996: $275; 1997 $290; 1998: $307.50; 1999: $333; 2000: $355; 2001: $397; 2002: $465.50; 2003: $530; 2004: $583; 2005: $1,041.50; 2006: $1,050; 2007: $766.50; 2008: $849.00; 2009: $944; 2010: $1,194.50; 2011: $1,282; 2012: $1,436; 2013: $1,652; individual volumes: $54 (list); used sets available for $400.00; **Monthly Assured Print Price (APP):** $172 per mo./$2,064 per yr.

6. **American Law Reports 5th**. Rochester, NY: Lawyers Cooperative Publishing Co./Thomson West, 1991-2005. 125 volumes. Set updated by annual pocket supplements. Set now closed. 6th series started in 2005. Also available on **WestlawNext.**
Cost: $1,674; supplementation: 1994: $609; 1995: $609; 1996: $660; 1997: $744; 1998: $858.50; 1999: $929; 2000: $986; 2001: $1,342.50; 2002: $1,577; 2003: $1,446.50; 2004: $2,080; 2005: $1,041.50; 2006: $1,125; 2007: $1,100.00; 2008: $365.00; 2009: $412; 2010: $834.50; 2011: $555; 2012: $621; 2013: $696; individual volumes: $158 (list); used sets available for $300;

Monthly Assured Print Price (APP): $74 per mo./$888 per yr.

7. **American Law Reports 6th**. Eagan, MN: Thomson West, 2005-date. 92 volumes (as of April, 2014). Updated by annual pocket supplements and 8-10 new volumes per year. Also available on **WestlawNext.**
Cost: $5,877; supplementation: 2005: $1,237.50; 2006: $2,429; 2007: $1,713.50; 2008: $2,211.50; 2009: $2,499; 2010: $3,141.50; 2011: $3,526; 2012: $3,949; 2013: $4,419; individual volumes: $505 (list); **Monthly Assured Print Price (APP):** $357 per mo./$4,284 per yr.

8. **American Law Reports Federal**. Rochester, NY: Lawyers Cooperative Publishing Co./ThomsonWest, 1969-2005. 200 volumes. Annual pocket parts. Also available on **WestlawNext.**
Cost: $2,528; supplementation: 1994: $716.11; 1995: $716.11; 1996: $856; 1997: $963.50; 1998: $1,082; 1999: $1,178.50; 2000: $1,312; 2001: $1,437.25; 2002: $1,498.75; 2003: $1,853; 2004: $2,074; 2005: $1,400.50; 2006: $1,321; 2007: $1,192.00; 2008: $943.00; 2009: $1,069; 2010: $1,341; 2011: $1,439; 2012: $1,611; 2013: $1,806; individual volumes: $166 (list); also available used for approximately $600; **Monthly Assured Print Price (APP):** $153 per mo./$1,836 per yr.

9. **American Law Reports Federal 2d**. Eagan, MN: Thomson West, 2005-date. 82 volumes (as of April, 2014). Annual pocket parts and approx. six new volumes per year. Also available on **WestlawNext.**
Cost: $7,040; supplementation: 2005: $937; 2006: $2,731; 2007: $2,192.50; 2008: $2,057.50; 2009: $2,991; 2010: $3,483.50; 2011: $3,483.50; 2012: $3,900; 2013: $5,125; individual volumes: $523 (list); also available used for approximately $700; **Monthly Assured Print Price (APP):** $428 per mo./$5,112 per yr.

10. **American Law Reports Digest to 3d - 6th and Federal**. Rochester, NY: Lawyers Cooperative Publishing Co./West, 2004-date. 26 volumes. Updated by annual pocket parts and periodic revised volumes.
Cost: $1,214; supplementation: 1994: $414; 1995: $456; 1996: $474; 1997: $120.50; 1998: $155; 1999: $167; 2000: $180; 2001: $199.50; 2002: $219.50; 2003: $250; 2004: $449; 2005: $480; 2006: $102.50; 2007: $157.00; 2008: $238.50; 2009: $268; 2010: $249.50; 2011: $249.50; 2012: $280; 2013: $412; individual volumes: $132 (list); complete set also available used for approx. $100; **Monthly Assured Print Price (APP):** $44 per mo./$528 per yr.

11. **ALR Index to ALR 2d - 6th, Federal & Federal 2d**. St. Paul, MN: West, 2008-date. 10 volumes. Quarterly pocket supplements and periodic revised volumes.
Cost: $1,150; supplementation: 1993: $73; 1994: $92; 1995: $113; 1996: $130; 1997: $63.50; 1998: $73; 1999: new edition: $450; 2000: $150; 2001: $310; 2002: $310; 2003: $195; 2004: $220.50; 2005: $241.50; 2006: $780; 2007: $269.50; 2008: $1,024.28; 2009: $119; 2010: $149.52; 2011: $149.52; 2012: $168; 2013: $188.

Cost-saving Tips: Although the list prices of several **ALR** series have been slashed dramatically in recent years, they may be available on the used law book market at additional savings. The publisher may offer periodic discounts to the various components of **ALR**, but these will never approach the savings which can be achieved by buying them used, or accessing them online. The cost-conscious attorney can achieve additional savings by foregoing the purchase of new bound volumes which add only marginally to the research value of the more than 800 volumes in the existing sets. I would also recommend dropping supplementation to the **ALR Digest** which has less practical use as a finding tool than the **ALR Index to 2d, 3d, 4th, 5th, 6th** and **Federal** and is a largely unnecessary financial drain. **ALR** indexing is uniformly excellent and the annotations feature lists of related annotations, making it difficult to miss annotations relevant to your research project.

Thus, your supplementation cost can be limited to the purchase of the annual pocket parts to **ALR 3d, 4th, 5th and ALR Federal** (or those components contained in your library) and, if necessary, to the **ALR 2d Later Case Service** and **ALR Index to 2d, 3d. 4th, 5th, 6th and Federal**. As a practical working library, the purchase of **ALR 3d, 4th, 5th, 6th** and **Federal** and the Index to these sets should suffice for most attorneys (most of the annotations in **ALR** [1st] and **2d** have been revised in the later series). Supplementation can be purchased less often for even greater savings. Fortunately, since Lawyers Cooperative and, now West) have never issued a revised volume to any of its substantive **ALR** volumes, you are unlikely to incur the additional expense of revised volumes. It has been publisher's approach to update the annotations individually in the volumes of new series, not by revising the volumes in earlier series.

While buying the pocket supplements to the existing **ALR** series can be justified, buying the currently released volumes is not a wise expenditure given the extraordinarily high cost of the individual volumes. At $505 (list) per volume for the **ALR 6th** and $523 (list) for **ALR Federal** volumes, you will be paying top dollar if you acquire them serially from the publisher. For example, even if the price of **ALR Federal** volumes remains fixed at the current price of $523 per volume, you will be spending over $52,300 for 100 volumes. Wait until the set is complete and buy the same volumes new or used for a small fraction of that amount. The **ALR**'s are not like a comprehensive and integrated legal treatise in which all volumes are necessary. The annotations in **ALR** appear randomly. Considering the high cost and marginal utility of additional volumes released in the ongoing series (**ALR 6th** and **ALR Federal**), I would suggest acquiring the sets (with their present number of volumes) on the used law book market and dispensing entirely with a subscription to future volumes. Updating of the volumes you do have can be accomplished by the periodic purchase of current pocket supplements (some of which will, naturally, not have bound volumes into which they can be inserted). Or visit your local public law library to locate relevant **ALR** annotations.

Monthly Assured Print Price (APP)

As a means of enhancing supplementation revenues, West instituted the **Monthly Assured Print Price (APP)** model in 2010. This program, directed to new sales, provides the purchaser with the complete set of volumes and updates for a fixed monthly/annual cost. On average, the annual cost of the APP is slightly higher than the standard subscriber discounted cost.
This is because the APP cost includes not only supplementation but also the amortized cost of the complete set provided at the outset. The advantage of the APP is that it caps annual

supplementation cost increases at 5-6% (depending upon whether the customer elects a two- or three-rear contract), as opposed to the 11-12% annual increases typical of West products. But it is also a means of preserving a revenue stream in the face of possible subscription cancellation. Frankly, the APP is no bargain, particularly for the customer who is smart enough to avoid automatic supplementation to the print ALR sets and does his or her updating using either a WestlawNext subscription, acquires individual ALR annotations on WestlawNext, or pays on a per use basis for access.

American Law Reports on Westlaw

Given the substantial cost of maintaining a complete collection of the **American Law Reports** (3d-6th, Federal, Federal 2d & Digest and Index) in print (over $16,000 in 2013), adding all **ALRs** to a Westlaw subscription can provide significant cost savings. In fact, the cost for a solo practitioner has recently been only $2,088 per year, or about one-eighth the cost of maintaining print subscriptions to **ALR 3d**, **4th**, **5**th, **6th**, **Federal, and Federal 2d, ALR Digest, and ALR Index**. Moreover, through skillful negotiation, you may be able to obtain the **ALR** series at even lower cost as part of an add-on to a WestlawNext PRO subscription. Law firms which still desire the set in print, can acquire the more than 905 volumes used at significant savings, but supplement them through their WestlawNext subscription. The trick is to avoid the continuing cost of subscribing to the volumes in print. Annual pricing for All **ALRs** on WestlawNext is as follows:

1 attorney	$2,088.00 per year
2 attorneys	$2,712.00 per year
3 attorneys	$3,528.00 per year

Moreover, for a few dollars more, the solo practitioner can subscribe to the entire **American Jurisprudence Library** on **WestlawNext,** certainly one of the best bargains going in comparison with the cost of a print subscription.

Title	WestlawNext	WestlawNext
	Monthly	Annual
American Jurisprudence 2d	$147.00	$1,764.00
Am Jur Legal Forms	$106.00	$1,272.00
Am Jur Pl. & Prac Forms	$106.00	$1,272.00
American Law Reports	$174.00	$2,088.00
Am Jur Trials	$106.00	$1,272.00
Am Jur Proof of Facts	$106.00	$1,272.00
Am Jur Trials & POF	$133.00	$1,596.00
All Am Jur Library*	$236.00	$2,832.00

American Law Reports on CD-ROM

American Law Reports on LawDesk [CD-ROM]. Eagan, MN: West Group. One disc. Updated quarterly. Search Engine: Available on Folio or Premise. Contains the full text of **ALR 3d**, **4th**, **5th & 6th**.
Cost: **Discontinued**; was $6,909 per year (single user) in 2013.
Best acquired on WestlawNext.
One of the primary reasons why the prices of used sets of the **American Law Reports** have fallen so dramatically is that the appearance of these volumes online and in the CD-ROM format has stimulated a sell-off of hardcopy sets. **ALR on LawDesk** contains over 13,000 annotations from **ALR 3d**, **4th**, **5th, and 6th**. Considering the high quality of **ALR** indexing, I do not see as great a necessity to have these sets in CD-ROM format as I do primary sources which are organized randomly (e.g. case reporters). Once you have located an annotation in the **ALR Index**, you are more likely to want to read it in printed form than off a computer screen.

American Law Reports Federal, PREMISE CD-ROM Ed. Eagan, MN: West Group. One disc. Updated quarterly. Search Engine: Folio or Premise. This CD-ROM product contains the full text of all the annotations contained in over 200 hard copy volumes of **ALR Federal**.
Cost: Discontinued; was $6,147 per year (single user) in 2013.
Best acquired on WestlawNext.

Cost Saving Alert: Thomson West is gradually abandoning its CD-ROM products and steering customers to its WestlawNext offerings, surely a more cost-effective option for consumers. The print version of the ALR series has been rendered obsolete from a cost perspective by their availability at reasonable cost on WestlawNext. For one-half the cost of one's year's supplementation to just **American Law Reports 6th**, for example, a solo practitioner can have the entire ALR series of WestlawNext and, for a few dollars more, the entire **American Jurisprudence Library** (see also Chapter 25).

American Law Reports Online

The **American Law Reports** are also available on a per use basis on both LexisNexis and Westlaw. From a cost-saving perspective, the occasional **ALR** user may find this mode of access preferable to maintaining the publications in print, CD-ROM, or online. This observation is particularly relevant if you or your firm have a fixed-rate contract and the use of ALR online adds nothing to your marginal cost. If not, accessing **American Law Reports** on a daily or weekly basis on LexisNexis, or acquiring individual annotations on WestlawNext may be a more cost-effective solution for the occasional user.

Chapter 15: Digests

In a legal system based upon the common law, the task of the legal researcher is to locate a prior case from the highest court of the same jurisdiction that deals with the same legal issue and has not been overturned or modified. Locating this "case on point" has become increasingly complicated as the body of American case law has grown to more than six million published rulings to which over 200,000 additional cases are added each year in both print and online. Bringing order to the randomly organized decisions appearing in the various case reporters is a task performed by a number of finding tools, including case digests, annotated reports, computer-assisted legal research (CALR), CD-ROM, and the Internet. This chapter will focus upon the traditional case digest.

To a considerable extent, online services and CD-ROM have replaced the traditional print digest as the preferred case law finding research medium. Twenty years ago, a state digest was among the first purchases made by the young lawyer opening his or her practice. Today, that first purchase is more likely to be a subscription to state primary law on Lexis or Westlaw. The digest, if purchased at all, is likely to be viewed as a supplement to, not a substitute for, online databases and, perhaps, CD-ROM. Nevertheless, the West Key Number System remains an impressive product of human ingenuity which retains its utility after nearly 100 years. Moreover, those attorneys performing Key Number searches on Westlaw or a West CD-ROM product are taking advantage of a research system which has its origins in the print digest.

Despite the growing popularity of computer-assisted legal research (CALR), both in the form of online services and CD-ROM, traditional forms of legal research remain an essential ingredient in the legal research process. Unfortunately, free and relatively unlimited access to Westlaw and LexisNexis at law schools has left many law school graduates with an inadequate understanding of the traditional case finding tools, of which the case digest is the most important. Furthermore, studies of database searching by computer scientists have demonstrated that even experienced users of CALR can have difficulty estimating the comprehensiveness of a given search. Searchers may be able to determine how many of the located documents are relevant to the question at hand, but have little or no idea how many additional relevant documents have not been found. On a deeper level, the reliance on computer-assisted legal research is having a profound impact on the nature of legal research itself. As Barbara Bitliff argues in a compelling article in **Law Library Journal** (Summer, 1996), computer-assisted legal research is transforming the traditional rule-based approach to legal research into a fact-based approach. The computer may be able to retrieve cases with similar fact patterns, but is not very adept at identifying the underlying legal rules which can provide a basis for the resolution of issues. Thus, it is imperative that the legal researcher utilize a variety of finding tools and reference sources as a part of a comprehensive search for relevant case law and the legal rules which undergird those rules. In this context, the case digest, whether in print or on CD-ROM, provides an essential conceptual framework for the subject arrangement of American case law.

This point has been reiterated by Daniel Dabney, a former law librarian who now serves as senior director for Thomson Reuters Global Resources in Zug, Switzerland. He points out in **Law Librarians in the News** (vol. 3, No. 5) that one of the positive features of free-text searching is its ability to circumvent the limitations of a classification system to locate cases with particular fact patterns. However, free-text searching is not particularly good at finding the law using conventional legal concepts. The important task for the legal researcher is choosing either an index-based system (e.g. West Digest, either print or on Westlaw), or a free-text system (e.g. LexisNexis, Westlaw, etc.) depending upon whether legal concepts or facts are being sought.

History

Although the concept of the case digest goes back to late 15th century England (**Statham's Abridgment,** 1488), comprehensive American case digests have only been around since the mid-19th century. The digest system now employed by the West Publishing Company was originally developed by Benjamin Vaughan Abbott and his brother Austin and first published as the **United States Digest** by Little, Brown and Company in 1848. In 1887, West introduced the **American Digest**, consisting of monthly advance pamphlets and an annual bound cumulation, as a direct competitor to the **United States Digest**. Anticipating the futility of competing with West's superior editorial resources, Benjamin Abbott and Little, Brown sold their rights to the **United States Digest** to West in 1889. In 1897, under the editorial leadership of John A. Malloy, West published its **Century Digest,** a comprehensive cumulation of all American cases from 1658 to 1896 which drew upon the earlier work of the Abbotts. The refinement of what became known as West's Key Number system was largely completed by 1906 when the **First Decennial Digest** appeared.

The West Key Number digests are organized into approximately 410 legal topics and each topic into many subtopics called Key Numbers. The Key Numbers have been further subdivided by the use of decimals, and parenthetical numbers. The digest paragraphs which constitute the substance of each West digest are headnotes reused from the many West state and federal reporters. Although the West editors may periodically revise the Key Number arrangement within a given topic, or add a topic, the arrangement is essentially identical to what it was in the **First Decennial Digest**. In addition to the mammoth **American Digest System**, which consists of the **Decennial** and **General Digests**, West has issued digests covering 47 states and the District of Columbia, regional digests covering the Atlantic, North Western, South Eastern, and Pacific regions and those for a variety of federal courts. Through its comprehensive and universal Key Number system, the West Publishing has come to dominate the case digest field in the United States, leaving virtually all imitators in its wake.

West has also refined key number searching on Westlaw by creating a new search tool called KeySearch. Introduced in 2001, KeySearch is an attempt to make the Key Number System less cumbersome by using a classification system that is less finely articulated. Unlike the 100,000 key lines and 400-odd topics in West's Key Number System, Key Search employs about 10,000 lines in 40 broad subject areas, and arranges them in a format that's easier to browse. In a sense, KeySearch is conceptually similar to the Search Advisor feature on Lexis, which employs a more limited number of broad subject categories to organize the body of American caselaw. This is just another indication of how competition between the two major CALR vendors has benefited the end-user. Lexis created Search Advisor to help overcome the competitive disadvantages it confronted with West's Key Number System. But West correctly realized that the complexities of its century-old classification system had limitations of its own which Lexis was exploiting in its development of Search Adviser.

Search Advisor (Lexis-Nexis)

Search Advisor is Lexis' answer to West's Key Number System. Unlike the Key Number System, however, it employs only twenty broad subject areas of the law, each of which is subdivided into numerous subcategories:

Administrative Law	Governments
Admiralty Law	Healthcare Law
Antitrust & Trade Law	Immigration Law
Banking Law	Insurance Law
Bankruptcy Law	International Law
Business & Corporate Entities	International Trade Law
Civil Procedure	Labor & Employment Law
Commercial Law (UCC)	Legal Ethics
Communications Law	Mergers & Acquisitions Law
Constitutional Law	Patent Law
Contracts Law	Pension & Benefits Law
Copyright Law	Public Contracts Law
Criminal Law & Procedure	Public Health & Welfare Law
Cyberlaw	Real Property Law
E-Commerce Law	Securities Law
Energy & Utilities Law	Tax Law
Environmental Law	Torts
Estate, Gift & Trust Law	Trademark Law
Evidence	Transportation Law
Family Law	Workers' Compensation & SSDI

The American Digest System

The **American Digest System** is made up of the **Century Digest** and a series of **Decennial Digests.** It combines all state appellate and federal decisions published by the West in its National Reporter System. The American Digest System with its chronological coverage and used prices includes the following components:

American Digest System	Vols.	Coverage	New	Used
Century Digest	50 vols.	1658-1896	O/P	$695
First Decennial Digest	25 vols.	1896-1906	O/P	$495
Second Decennial Digest	24 vols.	1906-1916	O/P	$495
Third Decennial Digest	28 vols.	1916-1926	O/P	$495
Fourth Decennial Digest	34 vols.	1926-1936	O/P	$495
Fifth Decennial Digest	52 vols.	1936-1946	O/P	$495
Sixth Decennial Digest	36 vols.	1946-1956	O/P	$495
Seventh Decennial Digest	38 vols.	1956-1966	O/P	$595
Eighth Decennial Digest	50 vols.	1966-1976	O/P	$695
Ninth Decennial Digest, Pt. 1	38 vols.	1976-1981	O/P	$595
Ninth Decennial Digest, Pt. 2	48 vols.	1981-1986	O/P	$495
Tenth Decennial Digest, Pt. 1	44 vols.	1986-1991	O/P	$850
Tenth Decennial Digest, Pt. 2	64 vols.	1991-1996	O/P	$1,495
Eleventh Decennial Digest, Pt.1	64 vols.	1996-2001	O/P	n/a
Eleventh Decennial Digest, Pt. 2	62 vols.	2001-2004	O/P	n/a
Eleventh Decennial Digest, Pt. 3	62 vols.	2004-2007	$6,126	n/a
Twelfth Decennial Digest, Pt. 1	56 vols.	2008-2010	$6,854	n/a
Twelfth Decennial Digest, Pt. 2	25 vols.	2010-2014	$6,854	n/a
General Digest 11th	60 vols.	2004-2008	$4,710	n/a
General Digest 12th	50 vols.	2008-2010	$6,026	n/a
General Digest 13th	50 vols.	2010-2013	$6,026	n/a
General Digest 14th	12 vols.	2013-date	$6,975	n/a

Cost: Most components of the **American Digest System** are available used at a fraction of the cost of new sets. The Law Book Exchange of New York, for example, has advertised the **Century Digest** through the **Tenth Decennial**, part 2 (13 digests in all) for a total cost of $4,500.00, more than $25,000.00 below the list price of those which are still in print. Note that with the **Ninth Decennial**, West began dividing the Digests into a Part 1 and a Part 2 to shorten the time necessary to produce a cumulation of the recent **General Digest** volumes. The Eleventh Decennial Digest has now been divided into three parts and Twelfth Decennial, thus far, into two parts.. Approximately fifteen **General Digest** volumes are issued annually a cost of over $7,700. The 70 volumes of the **General Digest 13th** issued between 2010 and 2013 cost more than $17,000 to subscribers acquiring them serially. Twelve volumes of the **General Digest 14th** have now been released at a cost of more than $6,000.

Cost saving alert: Established libraries which still wish to acquire **General Digest** volumes would be wise to consider dropping their subscriptions and instead acquire all the published volumes every two years. At the current price of $515.00 per volume, you can save your institution substantially over that time period.

Comment: In an age of rising print costs, however, the **Decennial** and **General Digests** have become cash-consuming dinosaurs that have been rendered obsolete by WestlawNext, a description that applies to West print reporter series as well. This includes West reporters and digests. Time has simply passed them by. The **Decennial Digests** are now acquired only by major research law libraries interested in such publications for their historical value and to maintain a sense of collection comprehensiveness. They are not recommended for law firms or smaller law libraries, particularly those with Westlaw access. **The American Digest System** represents a major expenditure even when purchased used. Due to its massive size and cost to maintain, it is recommended only for the largest research law libraries with sufficient shelf space to house its more than 500 four-inch thick volumes. For overwhelming majority of practitioners, the **American Digest System** has been rendered obsolete by the computer-assisted legal research, a bygone relic of an earlier era in legal research.

State Digests

West has published digests covering the case law of forty-seven states and the District of Columbia. North Dakota and South Dakota are combined in one digest as are Virginia and West Virginia. Delaware, Nevada, and Utah lack a state digest, with the appellate court decisions from those states covered by their respective regional digest. The West Group gradually released state digests on CD-ROM for all states during the 1990s, but has now withdrawn from production those from a number of smaller states where sales were insufficient to justify their continuance. Nevertheless, the state digest in print still represents a viable purchase option. The print digest provides the user with the ability to easily scan digest summaries under specific Key Numbers and obtain a quick overview of relevant case law. Both the print and CD-ROM formats provide summaries of federal case law arising from that state. The digest, whether in print or on CD-ROM, may also provide full historical coverage not found on Westlaw or LexisNexis.

Cost: The price of West's state digests naturally varies depending upon the size of the state (the prospective purchaser can consult the listings in **Chapter 28: State Publications** for specific costs). Supplementation costs for the West digests, once reasonably modest, have risen significantly in recent years under Thomson ownership, particularly as the editors engage in wholesale revisions of bound volumes. The cost of supplementation usually includes both annual pocket parts and a number of revised or split volumes. On the other hand, more than ten states have two series of digests to encompass the history of case law. New York now has four series to provide full historical coverage of its case law. Maintaining digest coverage in these states will entail a greater financial investment than that incurred for small states. The prospective purchaser should first investigate the possibility of obtaining his or her state digest on the used lawbook market where prices are generally less than half the cost of a new set. Having acquired a set in this fashion, a standing order for upkeep can then be entered directly with the publisher.

Comment: CD-ROM, long described as an interim technology, is finally passing from the scene in favor of WestlawNext access. Those CD-ROM products that hung on until recently had seen their annual subscription costs rise dramatically, leading one to conclude that West was driving customers into the arms of Westlaw. The cost of the **Oklahoma Digest on CD-ROM**, for example, rose from $1,059 per year to $12,981 annually. Alternatively, a key number search on WestlawNext can provide a far less costly way of accessing cases under a particular key number. For further discussion of CD-ROM as an option see **Chapter 24: Legal Resources on CD-ROM**.

Regional Digests

Although the National Reporter System is comprised of seven regional reporters (as well as reporters for New York and California), there are, at present, only four regional digests: **Atlantic Digest**, **North Western Digest**, **Pacific Digest**, **and South Eastern Digest**. Digests for the three remaining regions either never existed (South Western Digest) or were discontinued by West as the market for regional coverage declined for reasons known best to the publisher (**North Eastern Digest** and **Southern Digest**). One can surmise, however, that in the case of the former **North Eastern Digest**, for example, the demand eroded for a digest whose aim was to encompass the case law for five major northern states. The simultaneous existence of individual state digests for these states, each of which probably had sufficient case law to satisfy most users in those states, no doubt rendered the regional coverage unmarketable. The set simply grew too large for its potential audience to justify its continuation.

Of the four remaining regional digests, the **Atlantic**, **North Western**, and **South Eastern** are in two series, with each of the second series beginning in the 1930's. The **Pacific Digest** is now in four series. For the attorney in a small state with an inadequate body of appellate case, the regional digest provides a convenient index to the persuasive case law of neighboring states. Attorneys from a small state like Rhode Island, for example, are often frustrated by the lack of relevant case law in the **Rhode Island Digest**, a situation which can be remedied by access to the **Atlantic Digest**. Similarly, the Idaho attorney can benefit by accessing the **Pacific Digest** which provides appellate case law for fourteen additional states.

Cost: The four regional digests are available used at a fraction of their list price:

West's Atlantic Digest 2d	New Cost	Supp. (2013)	Used
North Western Digest 2d	$15,856.00	$9,808.00	$1,695
West's Pacific Digest 2d (vols. 367-584)	$11,521.00	$7,516.00	$1,895
West's Pacific Digest 2d (vols. 585-date)	$3,531.00	n/a	$695
West's South Eastern Digest 2d	$16,928.00	$9.466.00	$995
West's South Eastern Digest 2d	$14,450.00	$11,076.00	$1,295

Monthly Assured Print Price (APP)

An alternative to the standard discounted subscription to the West's regional digests is the **Monthly Assured Print Price** program which provides a complete set at the outset and then caps future supplementation costs at 5 or 6% depending upon whether the customer elects a two- or three-year contract. This program applies to new subscribers and not to existing law library customers. The following table provides the monthly and annual costs for the four West regional Digests:

Monthly Assured Print Price (APP)	Monthly	Annual (2014)
West's Atlantic Digest 2d	$794.00	$9,528.00
North Western Digest 2d	$668.00	$8,016.00
West's Pacific Digest 2d (vols. 585-date)	$830.00	$9,960.00
West's South Eastern Digest 2d	$679.00	$8,148.00

Comment: These tools are now appropriate only for the large law library with a budget adequate to support their costly maintenance. For all others Westlaw access is the preferred and most effective option or Key Number searching. As in the case of the regional reporter, the decision to purchase the regional digest will largely depend on the frequency with which the case law of foreign jurisdictions is consulted for persuasive authority. The smaller the jurisdiction in which you practice, the more likely you are to require the wider coverage provided by a regional digest. Note that the federal case law found in the state digests is not duplicated in the regional digests. The regional digests are only available in print and not in the CD-ROM format. Avoid the APP program which is chiefly designed to preserve West's print revenues in the face of its substantial price increases.

Federal Court Digests

West also publishes Key Number digests which provide coverage of general and specialized federal courts and subject areas, including the following:

	Coverage	New	Supp. (2013)	Used
U.S. Supreme Court Digest	1754-date	$3,877.00	$2,460.00	$895
Federal Digest	1789-1939	O/P	N/A	$495
Modern Federal Prac. Digest	1939-1961	O/P	N/A	$150
Federal Practice Digest 2d	1961-1975/78	O/P	N/A	$195
Federal Practice Digest 3d	1975-1983/86	O/P	N/A	$595
Federal Practice Digest 4th-5th	1983/86-date	$23,742.00	$22,614.00	$2,495

The **Federal Practice Digest 4th** is now moving into the **Federal Practice Digest 5th**. Given the high cost of maintenance, however, both should now be jettisoned in favor of WestlawNext access to digest coverage of federal court decisions. The question now is how much longer Thomson Reuters will continue to maintain such obsolete research tools in face of the wide popularity of online legal research and steeply rising prices for print.

Monthly Assured Print Price (APP)

Monthly Assured Print Price (APP)	Monthly	Annual (2012)
U.S. Supreme Court Digest	$188.00	$2,256.
Federal Practice Digest 4th	$1,155.00	$13,860.

Cost: Again, you will observe that the federal digests are all available on the used lawbook market at considerable savings. Since there are now five individual Federal digests, however, each covering a different chronological period, you are probably better off purchasing only the most recent series. **The Federal Practice Digest 4th** will provide digest coverage from the early 1980's to date. This choice is based on the premise that most cases cited in federal decisions are ten years old or less. Research into older cases can be conducted at your public law library which will have the four prior federal digests in its collection. In addition, the specialized federal digests discussed in the following section provide specialists with a more economical source of case indexing than that offered by the federal digests.

Specialized Digests

Unlike the state, federal, and regional digests, and the **American Digest System**, the specialized digests are not tied to any specific jurisdiction or level of court. Rather, their coverage is based upon their subject matter. Although West's specialized digests cover only a handful of subject areas, they do offer a cost-effective alternative to attorneys practicing in those fields. An attorney representing school committees, for example, can purchase **West's Education Law Digest** and **West's Education Law Reporter** as an alternative to purchasing whole jurisdictional digests and reporter series.

Cost: Of all the specialized digests published by West, only the **Bankruptcy Digest** and **Education Law Digest** represent a significant expense. The remainder still consist of one or more non-cumulative, paperbound digest volumes, each covering a particular range of specialized reporter volumes. **West's Bankruptcy Digest** is available used at a cost of about $400.00. The **Federal Claims Digest**, on the other hand, consists of only three non-cumulative, paper-bound volumes providing digest coverage for 78 volumes of the **Federal Claims Reporter**.

	Years covered	New	Supp. (2013)	Used
Federal Claims Digest	1983-	$589.08	$419.52	n/a
Federal Immigration Digest	1996-	$215.00	$281.50	n/a
U.S. Merit Sys. Protect Bd. Digest	1985-	$423.00	$229.50	n/a
West's Veterans Appeals Digest	1991-	$176.00	$176.00	n/a
West's Bankruptcy Digest	1979-	$6,170.00	$2,011.00	$495.00
West's Education Law Digest	1984-	$4,673.00	$2,565.00	$249.00
West's Military Justice Digest	1978-	$134.00	$112.00	n/a

Monthly Assured Print Price (APP)

An alternative to the standard discounted subscription to the West's regional digests is the **Monthly Assured Print Price** program which provides a complete set at the outset and then caps future supplementation costs at 5 or 6% depending upon whether the customer elects a two- or three-year contract. This program applies to new subscribers and not to existing law library customers. Be sure to compare the annual cost to the recent history of supplementation costs under the traditional subscription. The higher APP is at least partially a reflection of the amortized cost of the complete set which is provided to new subscribers.

Monthly Assured Print Price (APP)	Monthly	Annual
Federal Claims Digest	$42.00	$504.00
Federal Immigration Digest	$18.00	$216.00

U.S. Merit Sys. Protect Bd. Digest	$28.00	$336.00
West's Veterans Appeals Digest	$14.00	$168.00
West's Bankruptcy Digest	$286.00	$3,432.00
West's Education Law Digest	$334.00	$4,008.00
West's Military Justice Digest	$9.00	$108.00

Non-West Digests

Although the West Publishing Company clearly dominates the field of case digest publishing as a consequence of its comprehensive Key Number System, other digests do exist. These, however, are limited to the case law of specific jurisdictions and lack the transferability of the Key Number System. These digests are published by LexisNexis. The purchaser is probably better off with a West digest because it is based on what should be an already familiar Key Number System. To compete effectively, other digest publishers may offer special deals which could make their digest the more financially attractive option.

United States Supreme Court Digest, Lawyers Edition 2d. Charlottesville, VA: LexisNexis, 1948-date. 43 vols. Annual supplements and periodic revised volumes.
Cost: $3,235; supplementation: 2007: $900; 2008: $1,122; 2009: $1,256; 2010: $1,310; 2011: $1,196; 2012: $1,275.00; 2013; $1,173; used sets: $795. In the past, the set has been supplied free of charge to purchasers of a certain quantity of the **U.S. Supreme Court Reports**, Lawyers' Edition. Contact your LexisNexis sales representative for current special offers.
A worthy alternative to West's **United States Supreme Court Digest**, the **Lawyers' Edition Digest** is organized by topic and numbered subdivision. For obvious reasons, neither the roughly 400 digest topics nor the subdivisions correspond to the Topics and Key Numbers in the West system. As such, this digest stands on its own and subjects located in it cannot be transferred to other jurisdictional or specialized digests. It does have Library References to volumes in what was formerly Lawyers Cooperative's Total Client-Service Library, a useful feature for attorneys who may own other sets in this series. Also, where appropriate, the editors have inserted notations to other Supreme Court decisions which have overruled, distinguished, or disapproved particular holdings, a feature not found in the West digest. On the negative side, the paragraph entries do not cite to prior lower federal court decisions or subsequent history, a feature of West's **U.S. Supreme Court Digest.**

Comment: No indexing tool edited by mere mortals is without blemish, even when those editors are lawyers. Decisions without the appropriate tags (headnotes) are lost to the researcher. This is the value of the online services and CD-ROM products which are not editor dependent and provide the researcher with access to each word of a decision. Nevertheless, the print digest does provide a wider perspective from which to view the vast majority of decisions on a specific legal issue. Unlike West's **U.S. Supreme Court Digest** which must adapt to the national Key Number System, the topics and subdivisions in the **Lawyers Edition Digest** are more specifically tailored to the types of issues arising before U.S. Supreme Court. At the very least, it can serve as a valuable alternative to the West digest.

Conclusion

Your decision to purchase a hardcopy digest for your state will largely depend upon your personal preference for print over online or, to a lesser degree, CD-ROM. I personally find the digest easier and more convenient to use in its print form and as a complement to online searching. Also, West's introduction of its state digests on CD-ROM may be a bit of a redundancy for WestlawNext subscribers since Key Number searching is already available on WestlawNext. What the state digest uniquely provides the researcher is access to the federal case law arising out of that state. Whether you obtain that information on Westlaw, in print, or CD-ROM is largely a matter of personal preference. Our course, if you already have a WestlawNext subscription (providing key number searching), there is no compelling reason to buy it in print or, given its imminent demise, CD-ROM.

Chapter 16: Citators

One of the most important tasks to be performed by the practicing attorney or legal researcher is that of determining if a legal authority cited as controlling in a particular case is still good law. In a common law tradition based upon the doctrine of legal precedent, or stare decisis, courts are generally bound by decisions made in earlier cases when the factual circumstances are substantially the same. This is particularly true in the case of lower courts, which are obliged to follow the precedents established by the appellate courts in their jurisdiction. This is not to say that appellate courts will always uphold previously enunciated legal doctrines. Over time, they may question, criticize, reverse, or overrule earlier precedents. They may distinguish the facts in a current case from those which influenced an earlier decision. On the other hand, and more typically, precedents can grow in authority as subsequent courts follow their reasoning and support their holdings.

Shepard's Citations

The task of tracking the history of such legal authorities as cases, statutes, regulations and ordinances, and determining their current validity, is a critical step in the legal research process. While a number of legal publications function as citators, in the sense that they provide citations to relevant authority, **Shepard's Citations** provide an exhaustive and systematic mechanism for locating not only the history of a case as it has traveled through the court system (or a statute through subsequent amendments by the legislature), but its subsequent treatment by courts in other cases. Cases and statutes are cited in legal treatises, legal encyclopedias, **ALR** annotations, digests, and law review articles. **Shepard's Citations**, however, provides a systematic means of locating all instances in which a particular legal authority has been cited or affected by later action or cited by later courts. Shepard's Citations contains over 140 million citing references to over 6 million state and federal cases. It provides comprehensive coverage of all principal sources of law, including federal and state; U.S. Code and 50 state statutes; Code of Federal Regulations; court rules; constitutional provisions; U.S. patents; more than 700 law reviews and more than 800 Matthew Bender® treatises and publications. A further explanation of the process of "Shepardizing" a legal authority, can be found by reading one of the standard legal research texts, obtaining a complimentary copy of Shepard's pamphlet entitled "How to Shepardize," at: http://www.lexisnexis.com/shepards-citations/printsupport/shepardize_print.pdf or by using the Shepard's online tutorials located at: http://www.lexisnexis.com/en-us/products/shepards.page

Sorting Out the Options

For more than a hundred years, Shepard's Citations existed in only one format--print. With the introduction of computerized legal research, however, Shepard's Citations has been available in a variety of formats, including print, online through Westlaw and LexisNexis, CD-ROM, and a hybrid which combined CD-ROM with an online Daily Update service. Following the expiration of its contract with West on June 30, 1999, however, Shepard's online became available exclusively on LEXIS. CD-ROM, which served for a time as a more effective means of Shepardizing, has now been replaced in favor of Shepard's on LexisNexis. While print Shepard's still exist, they have increasingly given way to the editorial superiority and significantly lower cost of the online format. This transition to the online Shepard's has been propelled by several generations of newly minted lawyers who have come to accept the online format as the preferred means of updating the law. For the legal information consumer currently examining citator options, Shepard's on LexisNexis is now the only viable option and one of the most significant advances in legal information technology. Print Shepard's, while still viable, are, quite frankly, an archaic and far more costly form of Shepardizing. The print pricing provided in this chapter is intended solely for comparative purposes, and to indicate to the consumer how it is no longer a cost effective option.

The New Shepard's

Shepard's Citations is positioned on a sophisticated and multi-featured LexisNexis browser interface located on the Internet at **LexisNexis.com**. This service combines traditional Shepard's editorial expertise with a number of features made possible by computer technology. One of the most important of these features is the merging of all Shepard's information from parallel citations into one search result. Now, it is no longer necessary to check separate online documents if a case is listed in more than one Shepard's citator. The new Shepard's also combines the features previously available in AutoCite and LexCite. Researchers may now obtain analyses of unpublished decisions and law reviews as well as other sources. They may also obtain references to statutes when a case is listed in the annotations of an annotated code, a feature not previously available in a Shepard's Citations list of citing references.

The new Shepard's also gives the researcher the power to limit the citation results from a Restrictions screen. Once a case has been Shepardized, the Restrictions screen gives the researcher the ability to limit the citation list to cases from a given court or a specific West or official headnote. It also combines the power of the old LEXIS Focus feature. With Shepard's, it is now possible to employ the Focus feature with a Shepard's citation list to conduct a new, more focused search using a more select body of cases.

The Shepard's Signal, patterned after similar editorial symbols on KeyCite, gives the researcher an at a glance indication of the precedential status of a case. Shepard's Signal indicators appear at the top of Shepard's results and on LexisNexis case documents. When you're reading a case online, click the Shepard's Signal to Shepardize that decision.

Subscribers to Shepard's on **LexisNexis Advance** also have the ability to retrieve the full text of any authority in the LexisNexis database by citation. One can either type in the citation to a case and view (and print) its full text, or click on any case retrieved as a part of Shepardizing another citation and view the full text. This one feature opens the content of the complete Lexis database to researchers who have a citation to guide them. A LexisNexis Total Practice Advantage subscription includes All Jurisdictional Shepard's at no additional cost.

Special Promotions

As with WestlawNext, **Shepard's Advance** offers many special promotions not revealed on the lexisnexis.com web site. For example, solo practitioners in any jurisdiction may obtain a state enhanced package which includes All Jurisdictional Shepard's at a cost of only $121.00 per month or $1,452.00 per year (regularly $201.00 per month). Please contact your local LexisNexis customer service representative for current promotions and options not provided on the LexisNexis web site.

Essential Acquisition

An essential purchase for any practicing attorney is the **Shepard's Citations** for the jurisdictions in which he or she practices. Given the cost advantages of the online Shepard's, the print should be avoided. If your practice is confined to state courts, the Shepard's Citations for your state will provide you with the means of Shepardizing your state's appellate court decisions, statutory code, constitution, session laws, municipal charters and ordinances, court rules, and jury instructions. State citators have separate sections for Shepardizing appellate court decisions as they appear in official state reports and the West regional reporter volumes (or state off-print reporters which have the same pagination).

While the purchase of Shepard's citators in print is not recommended, this Guide will continue to provide descriptive and cost information for print citators as long as LexisNexis continues to publish them in that format. The acquisition of a complete Shepard's print library for your state or jurisdiction involves the purchase of one or more bound volumes and an on-going subscription to paper supplements which are issued at frequencies which vary from six times per year in smaller states to twice a month in larger states. Over time, the paper issues will be cumulated into supplementary bound volumes; and, at periodic intervals, the existing bound volumes and supplements will be totally recompiled. These total recompilations are produced to reduce the number of separate "look-ups" which must be performed to do a complete job of Shepardizing. Again, the potential purchaser must be aware that the Shepard's online service is a more efficient and less costly option which eliminates the need to acquire an expensive initial collection of bound volumes.

Shepard's Citations Sold to Reed Elsevier

In 1996, the citator division of Shepard's/McGraw-Hill was acquired under the terms of a joint venture between Times Mirror, the former parent company of Matthew Bender, and Reed Elsevier, the parent company of LexisNexis and Lexis Publishing (formerly Michie). This strategic alliance between Matthew Bender and LexisNexis was the catalyst for a number of innovative products, including the availability of subject specific caselaw libraries on Matthew Bender online and CD-ROM products, updating of Matthew Bender treatises through an online connection to LexisNexis, and the effective utilization of **Shepard's Citations** on both LexisNexis and Matthew Bender's online and CD-ROM products. Under its new ownership, Shepard's also introduced "all inclusive subscriptions" for each of its print citator products which provide customers with predictable fixed annual pricing. The adoption of this all-inclusive annual subscription model was Matthew Bender's attempt to extend to Shepard's pricing the same level of predictability it had previously brought to Matthew Bender treatise products in 1992. The all-inclusive subscription includes not only the periodic paper advance sheets, but also any of the irregularly issued bound volume supplements or revisions. On April 27, 1998, Reed Elsevier announced its purchase of Matthew Bender from Times Mirror and, with it, Times Mirror's 50% share in Shepard's, thereby bringing all of Shepard's under the Reed-Elsevier umbrella.

Choosing from Among the Format Options

Once LexisNexis introduced Shepard's on its enhanced, redesigned and multi-featured browser interface, it was the beginning of the end for the print and CD-ROM products, at least for the technological savvy lawyer. Both in terms of functionality and price, Shepard's on **LexisNexis.com** is a vastly superior product to the earlier formats. Nevertheless, Shepard's will continue to maintain the print versions of its citators for the indefinite future to meet the needs of its diverse customer base. Consequently, this chapter will address both formats, even though our clear recommendation is the online version. Not only is the All Jurisdictional online version vastly superior to the print format, but it is priced at a level comparable to the cost of subscribing to just a single state in print.

Assembling the Shepard's Citations Library in Print

To assemble a complete print library of Shepard's Citations for your jurisdiction, it is necessary to acquire one or more bound volumes as well as a subscription to the current supplements. For example, an attorney in Michigan who desires a print subscription will require the **Shepard's Michigan Citations**, which presently consists of 10 bound volumes at a current price of $4,343, and an all-inclusive monthly subscription to the softbound supplements and any bound volume replacements issued during the year at a cost of $2,441 per year for the monthly subscription or $2,741 for the bi-monthly subscription. This all-inclusive subscription program provides an essential element of predictability in the annual cost of maintaining an up-to-date subscription to a specific Shepard's citator product. Shepard's has now converted all of its print subscriptions to this all-inclusive model.

For customers still using the print version of **Shepard's, Shepard's Daily Update**, a service available over the Internet or by telephone, can be used to update the information contained in the most recent print release. While **Shepard's Daily Update** has served as a useful interim technology for the delivery of current citator information, it has been largely replaced by the online Shepard's at **LexisNexis.com/shepards** as the preferred delivery medium.

It should be obvious by now that there is little justification for utilizing Shepard's in print. In fact, the only reason print is discussed at all is because the **Legal Information Buyer's Guide** feels obliged to discuss all existing options available from the publisher which command some level of customer support. As long as the publisher continues to offer both print and online options, we will continue to provide guidance on both formats.

Contacting Shepard's

Shepard's Customer Service Options:	http://www.lexisnexis.com/shepards-citations/printsupport/printfeatures.asp
LexisNexis/Shepard's Product Support Line:	1-800-899-6000
LexisNexis Editorial Support:	1-800-899-6000 & Option 5 or e-mail: helpcite@lexisnexis.com

The research staff at the **Daily Update Desk** will provide updating citations from the Shepard's database. Editorial analysis is available 24-48 hours after opinions are received by Shepard's. Once you have used **Shepard's Citations** on **LexisNexis.com**, you will have difficulty returning to the print products. For speed, ease of use, and printing capability it is far superior to the other formats. In addition, it offers hyperlinks to other relevant cases with a click of your mouse. If you are just establishing your law library, buying the hardcopy is a completely unnecessary expense, particularly when one compares the cost of a complete bound volume collection with the annual cost of an all-jurisdictional subscription to Shepard's.

The print option involves a substantial initial investment which is not required with the online subscription. A solo practitioner in Illinois, for example, would incur an initial expense for print of $8,040.00 and an all-inclusive annual subscription charge of $2,716 (twice-monthly) or $2,430 (monthly), for a total expenditure of $10,756.00 in the first year. On the other hand, the Lexis Advance Legal Research subscriber will obtain the Shepard's at no additional charge, a benefit prompted by West's offer of rival KeyCite with WestlawNext jurisdictional packages. While supplementation to various secondary sources can be allowed to lapse as a cost-saving measure, your citatory service, in whatever format you choose, **must be current at all times**.

Full jurisdictional Shepard's also comes at no extra charge with any Lexis Advance Legal Research State Primary Law package, whether basic or enhanced.

Prices of Federal and National Reporter System Citations

The prices for the **Shepard's United States Citations**, **Shepard's Federal Citations**, and **Shepard's Regional Reporter Citations** follow. Prices for the state citators, whether in hardcopy or CD-ROM, may be found in **Chapter 26: State Publications**. Prices quoted for print are for all-inclusive subscriptions which bear a fixed annual cost for all advance sheets and bound volumes issued in the course of the year (including periodic total recompilations). Further information regarding Shepard's products may be obtained by calling: **(800) 223-1940** or your local LexisNexis representative.

Shepard's United States Citations (**Supreme Court Reporter Cases and Federal Statutes**). Bound volumes: 13
Also available for the **U.S. Reports, L.Ed.** and official **United States Reports**)
Print cost: $25,923 ($9,960 for cases only); all-inclusive advance subscription: $3,600 per year (2x/month).

Shepard's Federal Citations Post 1970 Edition. Bound volumes: 42
Print cost: $21,871; all-inclusive subscription: $4,862 per year (2x/mo.).

Shepard's Atlantic Reporter Citations. Bound volumes: 13
Print cost: $6,331; all-inclusive subscription: $2,396 per year (monthly only).

Shepard's California Reporter Citations. Bound volumes: 5
Print cost: $4,018; all-inclusive subscription: $2,683 per year (monthly only).

Shepard's New York Supplement Citations. Bound volumes: 24
Print cost: $11,779; all-inclusive subscription: $2,335 (1x/mo.); $2,683 (2x/mo.).

Shepard's Northeastern Reporter Citations. Bound volumes: 20
Print cost: $7,305; all-inclusive subscription: $2,665 per year (monthly only).

Shepard's Northwestern Reporter Citations. Bound volumes: 14
Print cost: $4,525; all-inclusive subscription: $2,665 per year (monthly only).

Shepard's Pacific Reporter Citations. Bound volumes: 31
Print cost: $12,272; all-inclusive subscription: $2,665 per year (monthly only).

Shepard's Southeastern Reporter Citations. Bound volumes: 18
Print cost: $8,879; all-inclusive subscription: $2,716 (monthly only).

Shepard's Southern Reporter Citations. Bound volumes: 18
Print cost: $6,154; all-inclusive subscription: $2,665 per year (monthly only).

Shepard's Southwestern Reporter Citations. Bound volumes: 15.
Print cost: $5,144; all-inclusive subscription: $2,665 per year (monthly only).

These figures should demonstrate that print Shepard's have been rendered obsolete by the far superior online product, which is not only has far superior functionality, but is far less expensive.

West's KeyCite

The introduction of West's KeyCite service was another significant development in the world of legal publishing. KeyCite is an integrated caselaw citation service on Westlaw which gives the legal researcher the ability to trace the history of a case, retrieve a list of all cases on Westlaw that cite a case, and selectively track legal issues by using West topics and headnotes. KeyCite was created by employing a combination of artificial intelligence, human editorial input, the vast Westlaw database, and upgraded mainframe computers.

Although KeyCite had been under development for nearly three years, its debut at the American Association of Law Libraries (AALL) Annual Meeting in Baltimore on July 21, 1997 appeared to suggest a special urgency to head-off possible competitive challenges from rival LexisNexis which purchased Shepard's in a strategic partnership with Matthew Bender in 1996. The withdrawal of Shepard's from Westlaw on July 1, 1999 reinforced the strategic importance of this new product to the West Group's product line.

One the most impressive features of KeyCite is its sophisticated integration with the Westlaw and, now, WestlawNext databases and West's patented key number system. KeyCite is accessible through the button palette or pull-down menu on Westlaw.com. The KeyCite function may also be accessed by clicking on the case status flag in the upper left-hand corner of a case you are viewing. KeyCite uses three graphic icons to indicate the current status of a case. A red flag indicates that a case (or at least part of a case) is no longer good law. A yellow flag indicates that the case has some negative history, but has not been reversed or overruled. A blue "H" indicates that there is some other direct history that is not of a negative variety. The absence of a flag or a blue "H" indicates that there is no direct history or negative indirect history for the case.

Once a case is KeyCited, the Citations to the Case window displays all the cases on Westlaw and secondary sources which have cited it. All negative cases are displayed first, followed by a list of all those other cases citing your case. A significant feature of KeyCite is that the cases are categorized according to the depth of treatment they give to your case. This depth of treatment is indicated by the use of one to four stars, with four stars indicting the most extended discussion and one star usually indicating its appearance in a string citation.

Another impressive feature of KeyCite is its effective blending of the citation service with the power of West's key number system. Citing references may be limited to those citing particular West topics and headnotes by clicking on the Limit Citations button when viewing the Citations to the Case window. By clicking the Limit Citations button, the Limit Citations window displays all the headnotes which appear in the cited case. The researcher can then check only those headnotes which specifically impact the legal issues being researched and, by clicking "O.K.," retrieve a list of citations restricted to those citing only the desired headnotes. A further explanation and demonstration of the KeyCite citation service can be found on the Westlaw home page.

The introduction of KeyCite also addresses what had become a confusing panoply of citator services, including Shepard's, Insta-Cite, QuickCite, and Shepard's PreView. Because KeyCite is available the same day a case is posted on Westlaw, it eliminates the four to six week time lag which formerly existed between the appearance of case of Westlaw and its appearance in Shepard's PreView. It also provides the equivalent of the QuickCite function by which Westlaw was used as a citator, but by adding improved features, graphic and otherwise.

The major question on the minds of industry observers, however, is the likely competitive impact upon Shepard's which has been the dominant citator service for more than 135 years. Certainly the seamless integration of KeyCite and Westlaw will give many users the illusion, if not quite the reality, of complete decisional authority verification. In tests, West developers found that KeyCite performed almost flawlessly at catching negative history. It has now achieved full acceptance in the legal community.

KeyCite Pricing

KeyCite All is now part of a basic WestlawNext PRO subscription, priced by jurisdiction. Connecticut attorneys, for example, have the several WestlawNext options available to them. Westlaw Store pricing is as follows. Contact your local sales representatives for current pricing and options.

Connecticut Essentials
$131.00 per month, or $1,572 per year
Connecticut Essentials and Connecticut Practice Series
$150.00 per month or $1,800.00 per year
Primary Law Resources Connecticut Plus All Cases & Statutes
$317.00 per month or $3,804.00 per year

These libraries both include KeyCite All at no additional charge. KeyCite is no longer available as a stand-alone product, but must be paired with a jurisdictional subscription.

Special Promotions

It is always a good idea to speak with your local Westlaw representative to ensure that you getting the best possible value for your money. For example, in April 2013, WestlawNext was offering Primary Law Resources Connecticut on WestlawNext PRO for an annual cost of $3,156 per year. This package includes Connecticut state and federal (2d Circuit) cases, state and federal headnotes, state statutes, the United States Code Annotated, and KeyCite All. Comparable deals were being offered in all jurisdictions (see table in Chapter 25). Contract terms are for a minimum or two and a maximum of three years, after which a renewal at comparable, but slightly higher, terms is predicted. The important thing to remember is that Westlaw representatives are empowered to offered far better deals than published subscription rates would suggest, both for basic jurisdictional packages and for valuable add-ons like the All American Jurisprudence Library (or subsets of same), or specific practice area packages.

Contact your local sales representative for current pricing and other options.

Shepard's and KeyCite—Sorting Out the Rival Claims

The introduction of KeyCite to the legal information marketplace in 1997 has significantly heightened product development and market competition between it and Shepard's. A number of commentators have conducted head-to-head comparisons of the two citator services, including Fred Shapiro, William L. Taylor, Jane W. Morris, and Dan Dabney. Shapiro, the Associate Law Librarian for Public Services at Yale Law School, conducted a comparison of the two citator services for the April, 1998 issue of **Legal Information Alert** by evaluating a 10% sampling of the 4,210 state and federal cases decided in January, 1996 (a total of 421 cases). Among other findings, he concluded that KeyCite retrieved 57% more citations than did Shepard's (1,597 versus 1,017) and that KeyCite provided a total of 619 citations which did not appear in Shepard's. Shepard's, on the other hand, provided a total of 39 citations which did not appear in KeyCite. Of the 619 citations appearing in KeyCite but not in Shepard's,

Shapiro counted 23 cases reported in standard reporters, 41 cases listed in standard reporters in table form, 205 unreported cases, 244 law review articles, 77 **ALR** annotations, 27 Practising Law Institute materials, a **Federal Rules Decisions** article, and a **Education Law Reporter** article. His study goes on to explain the reasons for KeyCite's edge in case citations, much of which he attributes to a difference in scope of coverage. KeyCite, for example, encompasses more than 1 million unreported cases which will generally not be covered by Shepard's.

Shapiro's study is accompanied in this same issue by a thoughtful rebuttal from Shepard's. Among other points, the author(s) of the Shepard's response point out that the Shapiro study compares the number and currency of unanalyzed citing references in KeyCite against the analyzed citing references in Shepard's, that Shepard's is actually more current than KeyCite in providing analyzed citing references about 75% of the time, and that Shepard's historical coverage is far more extensive than that of KeyCite. The rebuttal further points out that Shepard's editors read, editorially verify, and validate all citations, in contrast to KeyCite's computer program which "indiscriminately picks up all references from such [unreported] decisions, regardless of their publication status or usability as precedent." The people at KeyCite point out, however, that all decisions are given the full editorial treatment by lawyer-editors.

One of the challenges of conducting such studies is that the results will be closely scrutinized by the research and development people at both Shepard's and KeyCite. For example, William Taylor's comparison of the two citator services which appeared in **Law Library Journal** (92 **L. Libr. J.** 143, 2000), gives the edge to Shepard's for the comparative speed with which indirect history references are added to its database and, more significantly, for its assignment of negative history tags. This was followed by a rebuttal from Dan Dabney, Senior Director for Research and Development, Legal Product Development at the West Group. On the first point, Dabney explains that, at the time that Taylor was conducting his experiment, West Group's editorial department was experiencing an unusual backlog of cases awaiting full editorial treatment. Since that time, procedures have been implemented to help maintain currency in peak periods. On the issue of assignment of negative history tags, Dabney argues persuasively that it is not possible to make judgments about the assignment of history postings in the two systems unless one makes quality judgments about such postings. He argues that history errors are as likely to be errors of commission as they are to be errors of omission. Thus, if Shepard's included more incorrect negative history references, it would lead to misleading conclusions about the relative accuracy of the two systems. A qualitative evaluation of the negative history postings of the two systems (using Taylor's citation pairs) conducted by research attorneys with the Legal Research Center, an independent legal research company based in Minneapolis, concluded that KeyCite came out ahead in overall accuracy by a slight margin (35 to 32). The chief beneficiary of such comparative evaluations, and the subsequent improvements made by the two services, are the legal researchers who rely upon them. Those legal researchers are far better served than in previous years when only one citator service existed. And while these comparative studies are extraordinarily beneficial, they soon become obsolete as statements of the current relative position of the two services. The final determination of whether Shepard's or KeyCite is the better citation service for ascertaining the validity of case law and other legal authorities will ultimately be made by their respective users. It is clear at this point that the introduction of KeyCite has stimulated a healthy level of competition in the marketplace which can only benefit the consumer and advance the cause of rigorous legal research and that, for all practical purposes, both services provide a sufficiently high level of accuracy to serve the needs of all legal researchers.

Assuming a relative degree of editorial parity, however, the chief comparative advantages of the two citator services are as follows:

Shepard's: The **Full Shepard's Citation Service** is available at no additional charge with any **Lexis Advance Legal Research** package. In fact, the basic primary law packages for every state, which include Shepard's, are sold at a price lower than the cost of Shepard's print alone.

The **Full Shepard's Citation Service** subscription opens the entire Lexis database to those who have a specific citation. Full searching, however, is limited to the jurisdictions included in one's LexisNexis subscription.

KeyCite: Through its integration into Westlaw, KeyCite provides users with instantaneous indication of the value of a given case through the use of its KeyCite Flags (red, yellow and blue). KeyCite also uniquely provides indication of the depth of discussion (or lack thereof) of various cases through the use of depth of treatment stars. Finally, its use of quotation marks indicates exactly where your case has been quoted. Shepard's provides the equivalent of the KeyCite Flags through its classic editorial treatment, and other new depth of treatment indicators. Compared to the days when print Shepard's was the only option, today, both Shepard's and KeyCite are now basic features of any WestlawNext state primary law package, whether basic or enhanced. For further information on KeyCite, go to: **http://info.legalsolutions.thomsonreuters.com/pdf/wln2/L-356347.pdf.**

Chapter 17: Legal Encyclopedias

Among the most popular and ubiquitous reference tools available in law libraries and law offices across the country are legal encyclopedias, both national and state. On the national level, legal encyclopedias are embodied in two massive and ongoing publication projects: **Corpus Juris Secundum (C.J.S.)**, and **American Jurisprudence 2d (Am. Jur. 2d)**, both now published by the West. In one sense, these legal encyclopedias reflect a bold and comprehensive attempt to organize and describe the entire body of American case law. In another sense, however, they are relics of an earlier era in American legal publishing when an effort to summarize all aspects of the common law was still viewed as a realistic goal.

There was a time, earlier in the century, when the courts frequently cited legal encyclopedias as independent sources of legal authority; and the use of these works by lawyers, scholars, and law students was more common. In recent years, the authority of the legal encyclopedia has been eroded by the growth of statutes and regulations as dominant sources of legal doctrine. While some areas of the law are still chiefly embodied common law doctrine, e.g. torts, trusts, and contracts, many others reflect the dynamic interplay of statutes, regulations, cases, and administrative rulings. Imagine, for example, attempting to describe the current state of American environmental law by primarily referencing the common law. In this more complex and dynamic environment, research tools which largely reflect common law doctrines are increasingly limiting and incomplete.

In addition, it has become increasing impossible for encyclopedia editors to draft text which can accurately reflect not only the profusion of American case law, but also the doctrinal variations reflected by the courts of 51 separate jurisdictions. The broad view generated by such an approach is rarely useful in fashioning the legal argument since it allows little room for analysis of the holdings. Yet, such text must necessarily be accompanied by profuse citations to local authorities if it is to retain some level of scholarly respectability and avoid the statement of bland generalities. And while the citations are copious, they often seem to be from every jurisdiction except your own. Moreover, in some instances, the citations do not support the propositions for which they have been cited.

As a consequence of these developments, legal encyclopedias have been transformed from their former status as sources of authoritative statements of law into case-finding tools which can provide a useful introductory overview of the law. In an age of specialization, the legal researcher interested in topical discussion and analysis must examine the specialized subject-matter treatises which combine the various types of primary law, as well as relevant secondary sources, into an integrated whole. This is not to say that legal encyclopedias have lost their usefulness. In the average law office, they often provide the only available introductory coverage of most areas of the law. Think of them as a collection of over 430 subject-matter legal treatises, the overwhelming majority of which the average attorney will never acquire individually. However, they are only one possible resource for the legal researcher who must examine other relevant primary and secondary sources as a part of a thorough research process. Nor should they purchased before one has acquired his or her state reports, statutes, digest, and local practice books.

Corpus Juris Secundum

Corpus Juris Secundum (C.J.S.). St. Paul, MN: West, 1936-date. 164 vols. + 5 index and 11 table of cases vols. Annual pocket supplements and revised volumes.
Cost: $13,521; supplementation: 1996: $856; 1997: $864.50; 1998: $1,262.75; 1999: $1,454; 2000: $1,809.50; 2001: $2,000.50; 2002: $1,254.25; 2003: $3,162; 2004: $3,998.50; 2005: $3,885; 2006: $4,422; 2007: $5,692; 2008: $6.482; 2009: $5,596.00; 2010: $7,288; 2011: $7,288; 2012: $8,104.50; 2013: $9.929. Individual volumes: $367/$459 (subscriber/list); **Monthly Assured Print Pricing:** $817.00 per month or $9,804 per year. Available used for approx. $1,200. Not available on CD-ROM. For Westlaw pricing, see below.
Corpus Juris Secundum (**C.J.S.**), now a product of West, first appeared in 1936 as an imprint of the American Law Book Company, replacing the earlier **Corpus Juris** (1911-1937). It currently consists of 164 bound volumes, five paperbound index volumes and eleven tables of cases volumes which are revised and replaced annually. The publisher's original editorial philosophy stated that **Corpus Juris Secundum** is a "complete statement of the entire body of American law, mainly in the language of the courts, based upon the authority of all the reported cases from 1658 to date." The law is organized into over 430 alphabetically arranged topics, each of which is then subdivided into numerous subheadings reflecting the topic's complexity. Up until 1986, the set also included definitions of important legal terms and maxims. The text is accompanied by profuse citations to case law which, in many cases, dominate the text itself. The set is updated by means of annual pocket supplements and periodic revised volumes.

An analysis of **C.J.S.** conducted in 1980 by Robert Berring and Valerie Wedin (1 **Legal Reference Services Quarterly** 67) pointed out that, at the time, 34, or 23%, of the 148 volumes were copyrighted before 1950 and 48, or 32%, were copyrighted between 1950 and 1960. Thus, 82, or 55% of the 148 bound volumes were copyrighted before 1960. At that time, it appeared that West's commitment to the set was flagging. In the 20 years which have elapsed since their analysis, West has revised more than 100 bound volumes. While the pocket parts can provide citations to recent cases, they cannot substitute for the complete replacement of the base text which may require substantial textual revision rather than only citations to recent case law.

In the mid-1980's, the West editors began dropping older case citations from the revised volumes without alerting subscribers, a practice particularly disturbing to law libraries which may have wished to retain the older volumes in order to preserve a complete collection of case citations. In place of its former subtitle, which declared **C.J.S.** to be a "Complete Restatement of the Entire American Law As Developed by All Reported Cases," the new subtitle indicates that the set is now "A Contemporary Statement of American Law as Derived from Reported Cases and Legislation." In addition to this more limited citation base, the new **C.J.S.** volumes provide some discussion of federal and state statutory law and court decisions interpreting these statutes. These revised volumes could be considered, in the view of some observers, the beginning of a **Corpus Juris Tertium** [3d] in light of their more limited citation base. However, while

West will continue to maintain the set for the benefit of existing subscribers, it is highly unlikely that it will publish a third edition in light of general trends in the field of legal publishing.

Cost Saving Tips: The only cost-effective way of owning **C.J.S.** is as an add-on to a Westlaw subscription. The dramatic rise in the cost of supplementation has rendered the print set an unjustifiable expense. In the 2013 alone, the cost of supplementation rose 22.76% to $9,929.00. In light of these factors, the cost to buy and supplement **Corpus Juris Secundum** is, in my view, too high to justify purchase of a new print set from the publisher. The cost of supplementation has risen sharply over recent years, from $1,254.25 in 2002 to $9,929.00 in 2013, reflecting the publisher's effort to revise volumes with greater frequency. Used sets generally sell for $1100-$1200, a savings of more than $6,000.00 over the cost of a new set (depending on the amount of supplementation included in the purchase price). If the purchaser intends to keep the set current (which I do not recommend), the price differential between buying new and used sets narrows somewhat because of the value of the supplementation included in the new set purchase, but not if you drop supplementation. Actual prices will vary, depending on condition, currency, and the used lawbook dealer's inventory. Sets may be also acquired locally by word of mouth for a somewhat lower price. Additional steps can and should also be taken to reduce the cost of supplementation. These steps may include: (1) eliminating the annual Internal Revenue and General Index and Tables of Case pamphlets from the standing order, (2) buying the pocket parts in alternate years (or less often), or allowing the entire set to lapse for several years. If yours is a specialized practice, you may also wish to consider purchasing only the volumes addressing topics with which you deal. Your decision to update the set after several years will depend on the number of bound volumes which have been revised over the period. Currency should not be a pressing concern with this set, since you should be using it only as an introductory research tool. It will help you locate cases on point and help you frame your initial understanding of the topic, but it should never serve as the last step in your research process.

The introduction of **Monthly Assured Print Pricing (APP)** provides a new wrinkle in the West pricing structure. While it promises more reasonable future annual supplementation cost increases (5-6%, depending on whether a 2 or 3-year contract is selected), it does this on a base inflated substantially over the course of the past 14 years. Also, its intent is to lock the customer into a standing order and guarantee West's revenue stream in the face of rising cancellations of such high priced serial titles. But what happens once the 2-3 year contract has expired? Your renewal will be based on the current APP costs. Evidence of the past year's increase In the APP cost of CJS indicates a 10.55% increase. In other words, while the APP may provide you with some limited protection of double-digit cost increases during the length of the contract, your new contract will reflect the current APP pricing. If one year's increase is 10.55%, one may assume a three-year increase of better than 30%.

To avoid these potentially significant supplementation cost increases, the only way to acquire **Corpus Juris Secundum** in the current publishing environment is to buy it on Westlaw, either individually or as part of a broader Westlaw subscription. A used print set can be acquired, but not supplemented, for those who prefer that format for introductory research.

Corpus Juris Secundum on Westlaw

Corpus Juris Secundum is also available on **WestlawNext**, either individually or as an add-on to a **WestlawNext PRO** subscription. Indeed, the annual cost is substantially less than that of maintaining it in print. At $1,764.00 per year, for example, a solo practitioner would have saved $6,340.50 over the annual print subscription cost in 2013. Moreover, online subscribers also save the entire $7,205 initial cost of the print set, bringing the total net savings in the first year for a solo practitioner to more than $10,000.00. Westlaw's banded pricing schedule in recent years included the following annual subscription charges for CJS:

1 Attorney	$1,764.00
2 Attorneys	$2,304.00
3 Attorneys	$2,988.00

There are significant economies of scale for larger firms which can reduce the per attorney cost to less than $300.00 per attorney.

The above costs can be reduced substantially as a part of negotiations for a package of Westlaw databases, including one's state and relevant federal databases, **American Law Reports, C.J.S. or Am. Jur. 2d, Am. Jur. Proof of Facts, Am. Jur. Trials,** etc. Rather than accept the first proposal, the skillful negotiator will hold out for additional databases, lower annual subscription cost, or some combination of these. Also, bringing LexisNexis into the picture will place additional competitive pressures to bear on the Westlaw sales representative.

American Jurisprudence 2d

American Jurisprudence 2d (**Am. Jur. 2d**). St. Paul, MN: West, 1962-date. 140 vols. Annual pocket supplements and revised volumes. Also available on Westlaw.
Cost: $14,909; supplementation: 1993: $1,300; 1994: $1,516.50; 1995: $1,403; 1996: $1,849; 1997: $1,799; 1998: $2,266.75; 1999: $2,491; 2000: $2,660; 2001: $3,058.75; 2002: $2,925.25; 2003: $3,325; 2004: $4,560.75; 2005: $4,133; 2006: $4,673; 2007: $5,992.50; 2008: $6,456; 2009: $6,337; 2010: $7,106; 2011: $7,956.50 (up 12% from 2010); 2012: $8,938; 2013: $13,547; single volumes are now available even to non-subscribers to the full set at a list of $604 each ($483 to subscribers). **Monthly Assured Print Pricing (APP)**: $901.00 per month/$10,812.00 per year. See sales representative for current promotions and applicable discounts. Used sets sell for approx. $1,300. If you wish to maintain an electronic version of **Am. Jur.2d**, a better alternative would be to add it to your WestlawNext PRO plan at a cost of $147.00 per month or $1,764.00 per year for a solo practitioner. The entire **All American Jurisprudence Library** is priced at only $2,832 per year, but subject to negotiation.

American Jurisprudence 2d, is the major multi-volume legal encyclopedia published by the West (formerly by the Lawyers Cooperative Publishing Company) and the head-to-head competitor to **Corpus Juris Secundum**. It has its origins in two earlier multi-volume reference works: **Ruling Case Law**, a 38-volume set published between 1914 and 1931 and **American Jurisprudence**, a 66-volume set published between 1936 and 1960. Currently, it consists of 143 substantive volumes as well as volumes containing Tables, Statutes, and the General Index.

Like **C.J.S.**, **Am. Jur. 2d** is organized around approximately 430 topics, each of which is broken down into sections. Each topic contains its own index, with coverage more detailed than that offered in the General Index. A New Topic Service binder allows the publisher to introduce new subjects prior to their incorporation into the set itself. Unlike **C.J.S.**, **Am. Jur. 2d** does provide some coverage of statutes, although almost exclusively on the federal level (Federal Taxation being the chief example). More significantly, **Am. Jur. 2d** provides more selective citations to case law than that attempted by **C.J.S.**, this in keeping with the publishing philosophy of its original publisher, Lawyers Cooperative. This selectivity, however, is more than compensated for by the inclusion of citations to other titles in the West's Integrated Legal Research System including the **American Law Reports** series, **Am. Jur. Proof of Facts** and **Am. Jur.** Trials. These titles form parts of an extremely effective interrelated law office library system.

Due to the fact that it was first published in 1962, twenty-six years later than **C.J.S.**, **Am. Jur. 2d** has consistently retained its primacy on the level of currency, although a more conscientious revision program by West has begun to narrow the gap in recent years, a fact correspondingly reflected in the rising cost of supplementation to **C.J.S.** which rose to $9,929.00 in 2013 in comparison to the $13,547.00 cost of supplementation to **Am. Jur. 2d** in the same year.

Despite its obvious advantages on the grounds of currency, **American Jurisprudence 2d** has begun to display some weaknesses which reflect a lack of editorial coherence and other structural flaws. More sections of text are finding their way into the general sections of a particular topic rather than into the specific subsections where they belong. In recent years, fewer lawyer-editors are responsible for a greater number of revised volumes. There are also complaints from some editors that there is no one to exercise effective editorial supervision over their work, i.e. to see the big picture. They suggest that revisers simply don't have the substantive knowledge to correct deficiencies in the work of the authors. Where once the revisers used to flag errors, corrections and questions, now they rarely do so. These observations may partially reflect the limitations and growing irrelevance of such broad-based statements of the law which are being put on automatic pilot by owners who view them as cash cows marketed to an unsuspecting consuming public. In such an environment, it behooves the researcher to use such materials with caution, and to defer to the superiority of the more highly regarded subject-specific treatise with named authors who bear responsibility for their content. As with any secondary source, however, the astute researcher should use **Am. Jur. 2d** as a case finder, rather than as a source of probing scholarly analysis.

Cost Saving Tips: Although **American Jurisprudence** has an edge over **Corpus Juris Secundum** on the level of currency, it, too, can be purchased used. Second-hand sets abound on the used lawbook market and most are in very good to excellent condition. And given the steep rise in supplementation costs in recent years, any promotion the publisher is likely to offer will inevitably turn out to be a bad deal in comparison with the periodic purchase of a current used set. With the annual cost of supplementation running at more than $13,547.00 (2013), the wise consumer will avoid the print supplementation altogether and add **Am Jur. 2d** to his or her WestlawNext subscription for a fraction of the cost, i.e. $1,764.00 per year versus $13,547.00 for the print supplementation. In fact, for $11,783 less than the cost of maintaining the print set, you can have the full Am Jur Library on WestlawNext PRO for only $2,856 per year. Eliminating the initial expenditure for the print set, Westlaw access will save the customer nearly $20,000 in the first year alone.

While one may wish to hear the publisher representative's offer, the recent steep rise in supplementation costs for this set have all but rendered any special promotions of little value to the cost-conscious attorney. A typical promotion may include free pocket parts for two years and free revised volumes for thirty days, which may reduce your supplementation cost slightly in the first two years (it is unlikely that a revised volume will be issued during the thirty days so the offer applies chiefly to the annual pocket parts which are only a fraction of the total supplementation cost). But all this pales next to the savings of a WestlawNext subscription.

If you prefer the print format, the best strategy, however, is to buy a current used set for $1,300, let it remain lapsed indefinitely, and then eventually purchasing another current used set. By doing this, you will save $12,013.00 on the initial purchase ($13,313 - $1,300) and over $30,000.00 in supplementation costs over the three years, for a total savings of over $42,000.00. Over six years, the savings will total more than $78,000.00 (assuming purchase of all supplementary materials). Chances are good that the general overview of the subject being researched will not have changed much over that period and, yet, you will have been able to locate local cases on point which provided you an entry point into your own currently maintained state digest, online service or state online or CD-ROM subscription. Given the high cost of supplementing **Am. Jur. 2d**, your decision to re-purchase a current used set every three years (or at whatever interval with which you feel comfortable), makes very sound financial sense provided you take the necessary steps to update the authorities you find there. Alternatively, you may wish to buy a used set for reading, but only supplement it with an **Am Jur. 2d** on Westlaw add-on subscription:

Buy new with standing order	Buy used, update on Westlaw
New set - $14,909.00	Used set - $1,300.00
Year 1 upkeep - $7,370.00 (no charge for p.p.)	Westlaw add-on - $1,764.00
Year 2 upkeep - $12,306.00 (est.)	Westlaw add-on - $1,764.00
Year 3 upkeep - $13,537.00 (est.)	Westlaw add-on - $1,764.00
Year 4 upkeep - $14,891.00 (est.)	Westlaw add-on - $1,764.00
Year 5 upkeep $16,380.00 (est.)	Westlaw add-on - $1,764.00
Year 6 upkeep $18,018.00 (est.)	Westlaw add-on - $1,764.00

Total cost after 6 years - $97,411.00	after 6 years - $11,884.00
Total est. savings of used set with WestlawNest subscription after 6 years - $85,527.00	

The introduction of Monthly Assured Print Pricing provides a new wrinkle in the West pricing structure. While it promises more reasonable future annual supplementation cost increases (5-6%, depending on whether a 2 or 3-year contract is selected), it does this on a base inflated substantially over the course of the past 14 years. Also, its intent is to lock the customer into a standing order and guarantee West's revenue stream in the face of rising cancellations of such high priced serial titles. In addition, the annual increase in the cost of the APP between 2013 and 2014 was about 12%. Given the likelihood of similar cost increases in the future years, your new contract after 2-3 years will be at a substantially higher cost. Don't ever assume that West is going to do you any favors. Practically every marketing decision they make is designed to inflate their bottom line and extract maximum revenue from each product they sell.

American Jurisprudence 2d on Westlaw

American Jurisprudence 2dis also available as an add-on to a **WestlawNext PRO** subscription. For a solo practitioner, the cost is currently $147.00 per month, or $1,764 per year. For larger firms, comparable savings can be achieved by contacting your sales representative. A law office with 15 attorneys can obtain **Am Jur 2d on WestlawNext** for about $5,000 per year, or $6,000 less than the cost of maintaining one print subscription. This amounts to an annual cost of a little more than $400 per attorney. Moreover, online subscribers also save the entire $13,313.00 cost of the initial print set, bringing the total net savings in the first year for a solo practitioner to nearly $19,000 (i.e. $13,313 + $7,370 = $20,683 - $1,764 = $18,919).

Subscribing to **American Jurisprudence 2d** on Westlaw will save the solo practitioner nearly $84,000.00 (assuming average annual cost increases of 10%) over the cost of a print subscription over a period of six years. And those who prefer the set in print can still purchase a used set for initial research, while using WestlawNext for updating purposes.

As West continues to increase the cost of print supplementation and widen the gap between the cost of maintaining a print set and the same publication on WestlawNext, it inevitably loses print subscribers and drives them into the arms of its WestlawNext service. By utilizing this strategy, it effectively maximizes the power of its superior product offerings to capture an ever larger segment of the online market. Thus, lawyers who desire **Am. Jur. 2d, ALR, Am. Jur Legal Forms, Am Jur. Proof of Facts** and other standard reference tools, and who are aware of the cost savings of obtaining them in the online format, will choose WestlawNext as their basic CALR service.

In 2009, Westlaw's banded pricing included the following annual subscription charges:

1 attorney	$1,764 per year
2 attorneys	$2,304 per year
3 attorneys	$2,988 per year

Subscribing to **American Jurisprudence 2d** on Westlaw will save the solo practitioner over $50,000.00 (given West's average annual cost increases of 11%) over the cost of a print subscription over a period of six years. And those who prefer the set in print can still purchase a used set for initial research, while using Westlaw for updating purposes.

As West continues to increase the cost of print supplementation and widen the gap between the cost of maintaining a print set and the same publication on Westlaw, it inevitably loses print subscribers and drives them into the arms of its Westlaw service. By utilizing this strategy, it effectively maximizes the power of its superior product offerings to capture an ever larger segment of the online market. Thus, lawyers who desire **Am. Jur. 2d**, **ALR**, **Am. Jur Legal Forms**, **Am Jur. Proof of Facts** and other standard reference tools, and who are aware of the cost savings of obtaining them in the online format, will choose Westlaw as their basic CALR service.

American Jurisprudence on CD-ROM

American Jurisprudence 2d [CD-ROM]. Eagan, MN: West. One disc. Updated quarterly.
Available for DOS, Windows, and Macintosh. Search Engine: Folio or Premise
Cost: Discontinued; was $12,879.00 (up 56% from 2011) (single user license) (2013). See sales representative for current promotions and applicable discounts.

Cost Saving Tips: American Jurisprudence 2d in print or on CD-ROM are no longer viable economic options given the high annual subscription costs of these two formats in comparison with Westlaw access. Those who still prefer having a print set on hand should buy a used set, but conduct their updating online. Alternatively, you may wish to simply choose to access **Am.Jur. 2d** on an hourly basis on Westlaw if your usage is infrequent. Do not maintain this expensive print set on your shelves if your use is likely to be infrequent. Given the extraordinarily high cost of supplementation to both print legal encyclopedias, this is one of the most foolhardy library decisions you may ever make. It may have looked good resting on the shelves behind Perry Mason, but it's a guaranteed budget buster today.

State Legal Encyclopedias

In addition to the two major national legal encyclopedias, there are a number of state legal encyclopedias which provide a comprehensive approach to the legal doctrines of their respective jurisdictions. Unlike the national encyclopedias, however, the state works provide greater coverage of state statutes as well as case law. They should be preferred over the national encyclopedias because of their localized coverage and analysis of legal doctrines which are specific to that jurisdiction. Following the mergers of recent years, and their accompanying divestitures, most of the state legal encyclopedias are now published by either LexisNexis or Thomson Reuters (West).

California Jurisprudence 3d (West)	Florida Jurisprudence 2d (West)
Encyclopedia of Georgia Law (West)	Georgia Jurisprudence (West)
Illinois Jurisprudence (LexisNexis)	Illinois Law and Practice (West)
Indiana Law Encyclopedia (West)	Kentucky Jurisprudence (West)
Maryland Law Encyclopedia (West)	Massachusetts Jurisprudence (West)
Callaghan's Michigan Civil Jurisprudence (West)	Michigan Law and Practice (LexisNexis)
New York Jurisprudence 2d (West)	Strong's North Carolina Index 3d (West)
Ohio Jurisprudence 3d (West)	Pennsylvania Law Encyclopedia (LexisNexis)
Summary of Pennsylvania Jurisprudence (West)	South Carolina Jurisprudence (West)
Tennessee Jurisprudence (LexisNexis)	Texas Jurisprudence 3d (West)
Michie's Jurisprudence of Virginia and West Virginia (LexisNexis)	

For further information on these publications see **Chapter 27: State Publications.**

Cost Saving Tips: : As with the national legal encyclopedias, the state encyclopedias are often available on the used lawbook market at substantial savings over the new set. Many are now also available on Westlaw, providing the same cost-saving potential as **Am Jur 2d** or **C.J.S**. Compare all options before making your purchase, including the purchase of a used set which you will not supplement. Contact used law book dealers for information on price and availability.

Chapter 18: Looseleaf Services

One of the ways in which legal publishers have responded to the rising complexity and volatility of the law has been through the development of the commercial looseleaf service. Looseleaf services provide access to a wide variety of primary sources, including court decisions, statutes, regulations, and administrative rulings, and are updated regularly with either current newsletters or interfiled pages. Looseleaf services are particularly useful to the attorney or other subscriber who requires timely access to the latest developments in a particular area of law and who would otherwise have to track these down in a number of separate publications.

Although several looseleaf services appeared early in the century to track the activity of Congress and the United States Supreme Court, the growth in the number and complexity of looseleaf services has paralleled the rise of the modern regulatory state, particularly with the advent of the New Deal in 1933. While looseleafs began as print publications, utilizing ring binders and easily replaced interfiled pages, they have in recent years been largely replaced, for all practical purposes, by online services providing the same content, but in a more easily and quickly updatable format. Currently, the major publishers of looseleaf services in the United States are the Bloomberg BNA, CCH, a Wolters Kluwer business and the RIA (Thomson Reuters).

The Interfiled Looseleaf Service

Looseleaf services generally fall into two different classes: the interfiled service and the newsletter-type service, although some combine the characteristics of both. The interfiled service is characterized by the issuance of periodic packages of new pages, some replacing existing pages and others adding to the existing body of material. The "releases" of new pages are accompanied by a "report letter" which highlights recent developments in the field and provides instructions for the filing of the new pages. Looseleaf services are generally updated weekly, biweekly or monthly in order to keep pace with current developments. In their online format, however, they may be updated on a continuous basis by the publishers. Typical looseleaf services falling into this category are the **Standard Federal Tax Reports** (CCH), the **All States Tax Guide** (RIA), and the **Consumer Credit Guide** (CCH).

The Newsletter-Type Looseleaf Service

The second class of looseleaf services consists of the newsletter-type services. These publications are characterized by large bodies of material which are retained permanently rather than discarded. Current releases typically include a newsletter or current awareness portion of the service which is designed to be read regularly by the subscriber as a means of keeping up-to-date on the latest happenings in the field. Pages containing decisions are meant to be added to existing pages with the ultimate goal of their replacement by bound volumes or removal and placement in transfer binders. Many of the services published by the Bureau of National Affairs are of this variety, including the **Family Law Reporter**, **Occupational Safety & Health Reporter**, and **United States Law Week**. In their online format, these newsletter services are preserved in a permanent archival collection.

The Hybrid Looseleaf Service

Finally, a third category reflects characteristics of both the interfiled and the newsletter-type looseleaf service. These services include sections in which individual pages of new statutes and regulations replace existing pages and other sections containing newsletter-type releases which are retained on a semi-permanent basis. The Bureau of National Affairs' **Labor Relations Reporter**, for example, includes both interfiled pages with current laws and regulations and weekly Analysis/ News & Background Information pamphlets designed to be used as a current awareness tool. These combined characteristics are exemplified in BNA's **Environment Reporter** and **Antitrust & Trade Regulation Resource Center**. Decisional material contained in the **Environment Reporter** and **Labor Relations Reporter** is eventually replaced by permanent bound volumes.

Distinguishing Characteristics

True looseleaf services are distinguished by their goal of providing the user with current materials in the subject field, whether these consist of interfiled pages or newsletter-type releases designed for regular reading or perusal. Current materials are typically stored in three-ringed binders which can easily be opened for updating purposes. They should not be confused with looseleaf treatises which may employ either three-ringed binders of post-binders to permit the insertion of supplementary material. Looseleaf treatises are exactly that--treatises which just happen to be housed in a looseleaf binder. They do not attempt to duplicate the current awareness functions of the looseleaf services, but instead focus on in-depth description and analysis. Part of the confusion may lie with law librarians themselves who have never quite decided whether the distinction should be drawn based on the format (type of binder) or the substantive content.

The most comprehensive and authoritative guide to looseleaf services, Arlene Eis's annual **Legal Looseleafs in Print** (Infosources Publishing), accommodates both views by including both true looseleaf services and looseleaf treatises (see Chapter 22 for a description of this publication).

Purchase Rationale

Based on their frequency of supplementation, it should come as no surprise that looseleaf services are expensive publications to maintain. Annual subscription charges can exceed $10,000.00 to some of the more voluminous services such as BNA's Labor Relations Reporter. Your decision to subscribe to a looseleaf service, whether in a print or online format, must be based on a clear understanding of how frequently you intend to consult it. Obviously, there is little point in subscribing to a publication with weekly, bi-weekly, or continuous updating if you are not going to consult with regularity. If you are not, you will probably be better off utilizing a medium-sized legal treatise with annual supplementation, and relying on your local public law library for looseleaf publications.

Looseleaf Maintenance

In the case of the print looseleaf service, an often overlooked expense is the cost of filing the service over the course of the year. Depending, of course, on the size of the service, filing times can average 15-30 minutes of staff time per week. An office with several looseleaf services must be prepared to devote a certain segment of secretarial or library staff time to the task. Filing times can also exceed the averages if the person performing the filing is subject to frequent interruptions, phone calls, etc. If filings are not kept current, however, there is little justification for maintaining the subscription in your office. Also, a point should be made of impressing upon the individual responsible for the filing the importance of the task. Better yet, arrange to have the publisher's representative meet briefly with the filer for the purpose of explaining the filing process, the importance of accuracy, the function of transfer binders, the routing of the current awareness newsletter, and the toll-free number to call when releases don't arrive on schedule, or in correct sequence. Converting to an online version of the product will, of course, eliminate these maintenance and filing concerns.

Once a subscription is entered and the service is shelved in your office, you must make a concerted effort to monitor its usage. This will give you a better grasp of its continued utility and the information necessary for making an informed decision regarding its possible renewal. You may wish to attach a usage card to the front of each volume which can be checked each time the volume is consulted. Then, when the subscription comes up for renewal, you can count the check marks and use the findings to inform your decision. With the advent of looseleaf services in an online format, such considerations have been rendered obsolete.

How to File Looseleaf Services: A Filing Manual and Reference Handbook

Filing looseleaf services is an important, but often undervalued, function in law firms and law libraries. Yet, the accurate filing of these publications is essential if lawyers are to have accurate and timely access to the current law. Until recently, filers, to the extent that they made a conscious effort to educate themselves regarding looseleaf services and their proper maintenance, had to rely on instructions provided by the looseleaf publishers themselves and in-house filing guides drafted by library staff. We are now fortunate to have a comprehensive guide to looseleaf services which addresses all aspects of their filing and maintenance. Written by Elyse H. Fox of Legal Information Services (see Appendix B for contact information), **How to File Looseleaf Services** is a detailed examination of all types of publications issued in a looseleaf format which provides detailed guidance in all aspects of filing. In Part I, the author discusses the nature and organization of looseleaf services generally, including filing instructions and procedures, shifting among binders, transfer binders, filing problems, and provides some valuable perspectives and suggestions from other looseleaf filers. Part III is devoted to sample filing instructions from sixteen looseleaf publishers, with annotations by the author. Part II is a filer's quiz with answers. **How to File Looseleaf Services** is an excellent resource designed to provide looseleaf filers and their supervisors with a broader perspective on the significance and intricacies of their important task.

Looseleaf Filing Services

While most looseleaf services are filed by library or law office staff, many law firms have contracted with local filing services to perform this function. Most large cities have filing services which can perform this function on a contractual basis, many of them operated by former law librarians who provide a variety of professional library, consultative, and clerical services to law firms without in-house library staff. These include such companies as AccuFile in Boston, McCaughtry & Associates in Connecticut, A Library Service in Van Nuys, Library Management Systems of Troy, Michigan, Law Library Consultants of Minneapolis/St. Paul, California, Taylor and Associates in San Francisco, Metro Library Services of Dallas/Fort Worth, Library Update of Hasbrouck Heights, NJ, Library Services Group of King of Prussia, PA, Balkin Library & Information Services of Rochester, and many others.

Migration to the Internet

Technology has had a major impact upon the market for looseleaf services in recent years. Although sales of these products on CD-ROM were significant for a few years, the majority of new sales are now for the Internet version. Both eliminate the filing headaches formerly associated with the print medium. Furthermore, their full-text searching capabilities make them superior research tools which circumvent all the limitations of manual indexing systems. Both Internet and CD-ROM products are usually priced marginally lower than their print equivalents, but their versatility, ease of use and elimination of laborious filing provide additional values heretofore unavailable to the attorney. The now rapid migration of these fee-based subscriptions to the Internet will help ensure that the user receives information in as timely a manner as possible. Although the term "looseleaf service" is probably inappropriate to the new medium, it will no doubt persist as a term of art.

Used Value of Print Services

Finally, you must be aware that print looseleaf services have no marketable value on the used lawbook market. As subscription publications, looseleafs are almost always acquired by individuals who wish to maintain their currency. As long as this is the case, the marketability of used sets is virtually nonexistent because all new subscribers automatically receive a complete new set upon entering a subscription. The cost of a used set in such circumstances would be completely unnecessary. As the percentage of subscribers to the Internet services grows, however, this will become less and less an issue.

A relatively complete list of looseleaf titles published by the Bloomberg BNA, CCH, and RIA is included in **Appendix G** of this volume. Entries for a number of major looseleaf service services and looseleaf treatises are also included **Chapter 27: Legal Treatises and Other Specialty Materials**.

Chapter 19: Legal Periodicals

An important class of secondary materials for the practicing attorney consists of the legal periodical literature. Legal periodicals perform several important functions. They provide description and analysis of legal issues and developments, ranging from the scholarly to the practical. This literature also provides researchers with cutting-edge analysis prior to its introduction in legal treatises and monographs. Legal periodicals also serve as important sources of citations to primary authority, providing researchers with contextualized access to relevant cases, statutes, and regulations.

Legal periodicals fall into three main classes: academic law reviews, bar association journals, and commercial legal periodicals. Academic law reviews, produced by this country's roughly 180 law schools, constitute one of the primary sources for the scholarly analysis of legal issues. Every accredited law school, and most unaccredited law schools, publish at least one law review. Some of the larger and more prestigious law schools, such as Harvard, publish as many as ten. Bar association journals are published by national, state, and local bar associations as well as associations organized around certain areas of specialization. In addition to news of association activities, these journals provide practical, "how to" articles of value to their membership, the scholarly quality of such which has improved markedly in recent years. Finally, commercial legal periodicals provide subject-specialized analysis, particularly in such areas as corporations, taxation, and banking.

The average practicing attorney is likely to purchase legal periodicals selected from three categories: those published by the law school from which he or she graduated; those published by the bar associations of which he or she is a member; and those periodicals in his or her area(s) of specialty. Academic law reviews are among the better bargains available to the practicing attorney. Published, as they are, by educational institutions, the annual subscription prices rarely exceed $60.00, while the average annual cost is closer to $40.00. While many academic law reviews are general in coverage, a growing number are specialized in focus. This makes many of them inexpensive additions to the library of the lawyer who wishes to keep current in his or her areas of specialization. Examples include the **Stanford Environmental Law Journal** priced at $40.00 per year, and the **Georgetown Immigration Law Journal**, priced at $35.00 per year.

Bar association journals offer another economical source for useful articles at a reasonable price. Generally a benefit of association membership, national, state, and local bar journals provide their readerships with timely information regarding association activities and articles of particular interest to lawyers practicing in those states and localities. American Bar Association membership offers optional membership in more than 30 sections, divisions and forums, each of which publishes journals and newsletters of great value to the specialist. The cost of these sectional memberships ranges from $30.00 to $55.00 a year, a modest expense which, in many instances, provides the member with a journal, newsletter, and notices of specialty books, pamphlets, and audio and videotapes. Members of the Administrative Law and Regulatory Practice section, for example, receive the **Administrative Law Review** (4x/yr.), the **Administrative Law News** (4x/yr.) and notices regarding book and other educational materials published in that field by the ABA.

These sectional memberships are available to members of the parent American Bar Association which, at the present time, has the following sections, divisions, and forums:

ABA Sections	Annual Dues (2014)
Administrative Law And Regulatory Practice	$60.00
Antitrust Law	$60.00
Business Law	$55.00
Criminal Justice	$45.00
Dispute Resolution	$45.00
Environment, Energy and Resources	$75.00
Family Law	$50.00
Health Law	$50.00
Individual Rights and Responsibilities	$45.00
Intellectual Property Law	$75.00
International Law and Practice	$55.00
Labor and Employment Law	$45.00
Law Practice Management	$50.00
Legal Education and Admissions to the Bar	$40.00
Litigation	$60.00
Public Contract Law	$45.00
Public Utility, Communications, and Transport. Law	$60.00
Real Property, Probate, and Trust Law	$55.00
Science and Technology	$50.00
State and Local Government Law	$45.00
Taxation	$60.00
Tort and Insurance Practice	$50.00
ABA Divisions	
General Practice, Solo & Small Practice Division	$45.00
Government and Public Sector Lawyers Division	$40.00
Judicial Division	$30.00
Senior Lawyers Division (age 55 or older)	$50.00
Young Lawyers Division (under age 36)	FREE

ABA Forums: (you must belong to at least one section or division to join a forum)	
Affordable Housing and Community Develop. Law	$50.00
Air and Space Law	$40.00
Communications Law	$55.00
Construction Industry	$50.00
Entertainment and Sports Industries	$50.00
Franchising	$50.00

Further information regarding the American Bar Association, its sections, divisions, and forums can be obtained by calling its Chicago headquarters at (800) 285-2221, or the Web at: http://www.abanet.org/members/join/currentmembers.html.

The American Bar Association is not the only organization to offer publications of value to its members. The American Trial Lawyers Association, the American Bar Foundation, the American Law Institute, and the American Immigration Lawyers Association, among others, provide similar, if less comprehensive, offerings and benefits.

Commercial law journals represent the third and most costly of the options available in legal periodical literature. The majority of the domestic commercial journals, particularly those indexed in H.W. Wilson's **Index to Legal Periodicals**, or the Gale Group's **Current Law Index** (print), and **LegalTrac** (online) are published by about 15 commercial publishers, including some of the major publishers of treatises and other legal reference books. Most are of high quality and written by leading experts in their respective fields. Many of them are also published more frequently than some of the bar association or academic publications. However, some are simply overpriced and should be avoided when possible. The practitioner should also be on the lookout for those commercial law journals which merely reprint articles originally appearing in other journals and law reviews. One such commercial journal, priced at $165.00 for a one year subscription of four issues, consists almost entirely of reprinted articles. As a legal information consumer, you have the right to expect that commercial journals costing more than $100.00 annually will consist almost exclusively of original articles.

For example, it is difficult for a publicly-funded law library to justify spending precious tax dollars on a overpriced title like the **Journal of Criminal Justice** (Pergamon Press Ltd.) at an institutional cost of $1,583.00 a year (personal subscription $308.00) when that same library can purchase thirty or more academic law reviews for the same cost. Law libraries closely monitor their interlibrary loan requests as a means of documenting patterns of periodical usage and will purchase additional titles only if sufficient demand exists for a specific title. In most cases, interlibrary loans will satisfy the occasional need for some of the lesser-used and more expensive journals. For the practitioner, the purchase of individual articles on an as needed basis makes far more sense than maintaining a subscription. In the case of the **Journal of Criminal Justice** cited above, an attorney can purchase an individual article from Reed Elsevier for a cost just $19.95

Similarly, the practicing attorney must determine if he or she reads, or is likely to read, a sufficient number of the articles in the commercial law journals to which he or she subscribes or wishes to subscribe. Studies have shown that most of the articles simply go unread. If that is the case, the attorney would be wiser to locate relevant articles, as needed, through the legal periodical indices (**Index to Legal Periodicals**, **Current Law Index**, or **LegalTrac**) located in the local public law library or available on **LexisNexis**, **Westlaw** or **HeinOnline**, and then obtain them on one of the commercial online databases, or at a local law library, either on the shelves or through the library's interlibrary loan service. Most of these law reviews are also available on both Lexis and Westlaw. Moreover, single issues of commercial law journals containing desired articles can generally be purchased directly from the publisher. Or perhaps your local bar library offers a photocopy or fax service for those periodicals registered with the Copyright Clearance Center.

Publishers of some commercial law journals send sample issues to prospective customers as a means of increasing sales. While these sample issues provide you with an excellent opportunity to evaluate individual titles, they should be compared with the available alternatives both in terms of quality and price. **The Current Law Index** (Gale Cengage Learning located in your local public or academic law library, is one of the best sources for bibliographic information on legal periodical titles. It lists more than 900 law journals together with their publishers' names and addresses and annual subscription costs. Also, be wary of sample issues of the commercial law journals which are followed by renewal invoices, particularly when you have never had an actual subscription requiring renewal. This is simply a clever marketing device based on the premise that you are more likely to renew a subscription that you think you already have than you are to initiate a new subscription. Law librarians have been on to these tactics for years. Don't be fooled.
The publishers accounting for the majority of indexed commercial journals include the following:

Aspen Law & Business	LexisNexis Matthew Bender
Bloomberg BNA	Environmental Law Institute
CCH Inc.	Kluwer Law and Taxation Publishers
Federal Publications Inc.	Pergamon Press Ltd.
Sage Publications Inc.	Thomson Reuters
Wolters Kluwer Law & Business	Warren, Gorham & Lamont

The cost-conscious attorney should take advantage of the subscriptions offered by academic institutions and bar associations before he or she considers subscribing to the more costly commercial journals on the market. You may discover that your needs are adequately addressed by these two categories of publications and that a subscription to one of the commercial journals is unnecessary. If you are tempted to subscribe to one or more of the more costly commercial journals, your comparative analysis will provide you with a better understanding of the available options and their relative costs. But the better option is to simply to obtain individual articles by the least costly means possible, whether through library access, interlibrary loan, or direct purchase from the vendor.

Legal Periodicals Online
Westlaw and Lexis

A significant number of law reviews are now available on both Lexis and Westlaw. Beginning in 1982, both online services began adding the full text of law reviews to their databases. Lexis included the full text of thirty selected law reviews, while Westlaw chose to mount selective articles from a larger number of journals. Since then, both services have increased the number of full text law journals. The Lexis database now includes the full text of more than 400 law reviews and the Westlaw database more than 1000 law reviews and journals (check the services' respective database directories for the chronological coverage of specific journals). Unless you practice in an area with a defined body of specialized law reviews, you will, in most instances, be better off obtaining random articles off one of these online services than attempting to subscribe to them directly. WestlawNext and Lexis Advance state offerings, for example, offer law reviews and journals as a part of their package plans. The CT Enhanced Plan with Full Federal, for example, includes over 300 law review and journals.

Legal Periodicals on the Internet

The legal periodical literature is also becoming increasingly available on the Internet. The recent issues of a number of law reviews are already available online in full text while others are available in abstract form. In other instances, tables of contents and editorial information are provided. One of the pioneers in the effort to bring the law review literature to a wider audience on-line is the University Law Review Project, a joint effort of FindLaw and the Coalition of Online Journals, with assistance from Verity, the Australasian Legal Information Institute, Inherent, the Legal Information Institute at Cornell, Stanford University and many law schools and journals throughout the world. Located on the FindLaw Academic Journal Page, the Project provides an alphabetical list of journals, a list of journals by law school, journals with full text articles on-line, a law review abstracts E-Mail Archive, and the law review Editorial addresses of more than 165 law reviews. It also provides full text searching of law journals and law reviews on the Internet. Its URL is:
http://www.lawreview.org/

FindlawFindlaw also provides a free subscription service to newsletters, including those containing (1) daily summaries of court decisions; (2) weekly summaries of decisions in more than 50 subject areas ranging from Arbitration and Mediation to White Collar Crime; and (3) legal news topics. Its URL is:
http://newsletters.findlaw.com/

Additional Web sites providing links to online law reviews include:

Hieros Gamos. Providing access to hundreds of legal and law related journals, including full-text, abstracts, tables of contents and subscription information. It is located at:
http://www.hg.org/journals.html

Law Journals at Washburn University School of Law in Kansas. A full text search site which lets you examine and search an extensive list of international law reviews and select them individually if you desire. It also includes a number of journals which are not strictly law-related, including the **Chronicle of Higher Education**. Its URL is:
http://www.washlaw.edu/lawjournal/

Michigan Telecommunications and Technology Law Review. Published by the University of Michigan, this electronic journal founded in 1994 was one of the first law journals to "champion the use of interactive media to promote informed discourse about the interrelated legal, social, business and public policy issues raised by emerging technologies. It may be found at:
http://www.mttlr.org/html/home.html

The first law review available electronically was the **Federal Communications Law Journal**, published by the Indiana University School of Law, mounted in 1994. By 1996, such journals as **Villanova Law Review**, **Cornell Law Review** and the **Cardoon Arts and Entertainment Law Journal** have been added to the list.

While the first law reviews on the Internet were essentially print journals provided in electronic form, the second generation of electronic law journals are without a print equivalent. These include the Journal of Online Law published by the William and Mary Law School and the Michigan Telecommunications and Technology Law Review. For a useful history of law reviews available online, see "Last Writes?: Re-assessing the Law Review in the Age of Cyberspace," by Bernard J. Hibbitts of the University of Pittsburgh Law School, and available at:
http://www.uakron.edu/dotAsset/726664.pdf
or through the **University Law Review Project** home page (see above).

Most-Cited Legal Periodicals U.S. and selected non-U.S.

John Doyle of Washington & Lee University Law School Library created a valuable website, now maintained by his colleague, Stephanie Miller, which ranks 1,532 law journals according to the number of times they have been cited in the previous eight years (the survey covers the period 2002-2011). His intent is to provide a record to citations to current scholarship. The study examines academic legal periodicals published in the United States as well as some non-U.S. legal periodicals (usually English language). Thus, the current eight-year time frame eliminates the bias which would favor long published journals. The sources for citation counts are limited to documents in Westlaw's JLR database (primarily U.S. articles) and Westlaw's ALLCASES databases (U.S. state and federal cases). The Combined-Score rankings of the top ten journals, representing each journals impact factor and total citation court, are as follows:

Harvard Law Journal	100
Yale Law Journal	90.2
Columbia Law Review	84.8
Stamford Law Review	77.8
New York University Law Revieq	71.9
California Law Review	70.9
U. Pennsylvania Law Review	66
Texas Law Review	65.5
Virginia Law Review	65.3
U. Chicago Law Review	62.1

Doyle suggests that nothing much should be made of the absolute numbers, but they are useful when comparing journals. Citations-per-article impact factor rankings should be used cautiously as they are biased against journals that publish a larger number of shorter articles, such as book reviews. A valuable selection tool for larger academic and research law libraries.

A further explanation of the website and its features may be found at:
http://lawlib.wlu.edu/LJ/method.asp#citespercost

A recent feature added to this web site is a selection tool which permits a library to cost-effectively select law journals based on a specific budgetary allocation. For example, a $10,000 budget will allow a library to select the 288 most cited law reviews. For example, a $50,000 budget will allow a library top select the 704 most heavily journals. To employ this feature, go to:
http://lawlib.wlu.edu/LJ/selecting.aspx

Another useful feature is the Cites/Cost ranking, which allows a library to determine, on average, how many citations are obtained in relation to a given journal's cost. The Cites/Cost ranking is the average yearly number of cites to the journal divided by the annual US$ cost to U.S. academic libraries. This tool indicates, for example, that, at $120.00 per year, the ABA Journal has a Cites/Cost ratio of 0.71 and should, hypothetically, be priced at $85.20 based on the number of citations provided. Naturally, the ABA Journal, which is devoted largely to news and practice oriented articles, would not be expected to rank high on the Cites/Cost scale. By comparison, the Yale Law Journal, has a Cites/Cost ratio of 14.11, reflecting a high number of cites for its $55.00 annual subscription cost. Following John Doyle's retirement, Law Journals: Submissions and Ranking is being maintained by Stephanie Miller of Washington and Lee University School of Law Library.

HeinOnline

HeinOnline is a fully searchable digital collection of retrospective and current legal journals produced by the Williams S. Hein Company in collaboration with Cornell Information Technologies and the Cornell Law Library. Accessible on the Web, **HeinOnline** currently provides access to more than 100 million pages of image-based text and backfiles of more than 1,800 law and law-related periodicals, most from inception to the most current volume allowed under contract. The journal collection received over 57,000,000 hits and 16,000,000 article requests in 2007, reflecting the profound impact it has had legal periodical research, as most people now begin their research with Hein rather than **Westlaw** or **Lexis**. All content within **HeinOnline** is image-based in PDF format, from inception and fully searchable. It is now the world's largest image-based legal research collection, containing nine centuries of legal history. The law and law-related periodicals now constitute more than 24 million pages, more than 50% of which are now updated issue-by-issue. In October, 2010, it released its Intellectual Property Collection. Hein Online is now available in over 3,200 locations in over 200 countries.

Presently, **HeinOnline** has fifty-two major library collections: the Law Journal Library, American Law Institute Library, Federal Register Library (including the **Federal Register** from 1936-date, and the **CFR** from 1938-1912), English Reports, European Center for Minority Issues, Foreign and International Law Resources Database, Foreign Relations of the United States, International Law Association Reports, Legal Classics (over 3,000 titles), New York Court of Appeals Records and Briefs, Philip C. Jessup Library, Political Science Journals, State Session Laws, Treatises and Agreements Library. U.S. Attorney General Opinions, U.S. Congressional Documents Library, U.S. Federal Agency Library, U.S. Federal Legislative History Library, U.S. Presidential Library, U.S. Statutes at Large, U.S. Supreme Court Library, World Trials Library, and more. The U.S. Supreme Court Library now has full text of the official **United States Reports**, including bound volumes 1-552 (1754-2008), **Preliminary Prints**, and slip opinions. For a complete list of the libraries on HeinOnline, visit:

http://home.heinonline.org/content/list-of-libraries/

Moreover, the Law Journal Library is now being offered in multiple library modules, allowing libraries the opportunity to select the entire collection or one of its subsets, including: American Bar Association Journals, Core U.S./Most Cited U.S. Journals, Criminal Justice, Journals, International and Non-U.S. Journals, Intellectual Property Journals, and Most Cited Law Journals.

While initially developed as a retrospective project, HeinOnline has been able to achieve near-currency for many of the law journals in its collection, including the **Columbia Law Review**, **Cornell Law Review**, **Duke Law Journal**, **Harvard Law Review**, **University of Chicago Law Review**, the **Virginia Law Review**, and over 1,630 more. The law journal collection now comprises more than 41,324 volumes and nearly 26 million pages.

A recent addition to Heinline is **Spinelli's Law Librarian Reference Shelf**, containing over 1,014 reference titles in over 2,625 volumes, including the AALL GD-SIS State Bibliographies, AALL Publication Series, Legal Dictionaries, Serials, Cataloging Publications, Bibliographies, **Bibliography of Early American Law**, the **Legal Information Buyer's Guide & Reference Manual** (1996-2010), the Legal Research Guide Series, Memorials of Law Librarians and more.

HeinOnline provides users with access to high-quality digital images of the original materials and provides them with the ability to search and browse the entire collection of documents. It also unveiled a new user interface providing users with greater flexibility and additional search options.

Designed initially for larger research libraries, HeinOnline has made its archival resources available to the general public and other research organization outside the legal community. Annual subscription charges are based on the size, nature, and scale of the institution. The following factors are used in determining the annual subscription price:

(1) Type of institution (academic law library, law firm library, general college/university library, etc);
(2) The number of faculty or attorneys at the institution;
(3) The number of students at the institution;
(4) The number of physical locations that will be provided access to HeinOnline.

An annual subscription to HeinOnline entitles the institution to full access to all of the materials currently included in the HeinOnline collection, as well as instant access to all new material added during the annual subscription period. Subscribers may opt for the **Core Subscription Package** or choose from among 24 **A-La-Carte Libraries**.

Individuals may also access HeinOnline on a 24-hour, 48-hour, or weekly basis using a credit card. The costs are $19.95, $29.95, and $49.95 respectively.

Besides winning the AALL award for Best New Product in 2001 and 2009 and the Best Commercial Website Award from the IALL in 2002, Hein was added to EContent's list of 100 most important companies in the digital content industry in 2007. In 2010, **Choice Magazine** selected HeinOnline's World Constitutions Illustrated: Contemporary & Historical Documents & Resources for inclusion on the Outstanding Academic Title list.

HeinOnline is built on the latest version of Dienst Technology, an open architecture for distributed digital libraries. The reputation it has achieved for the quality of its images has led the Library of Congress to use the company's images in the development of its own collections.

Further information regarding the features, content and pricing of HeinOnline may be found at:

http://www.heinonline.org/.

Chapter 20: Legal Newspapers

The first legal newspapers in the United States emerged in the mid-nineteenth century with the appearance of the Philadelphia Legal Intelligencer in 1843 and the Chicago Legal News in 1854. These early legal newspapers served primarily as vehicles for the publication of local legal news, the decisions of state courts, and local legal notices required by law. More legal newspapers appeared in the state of Pennsylvania than in any other state. In fact, the rather unique practice of publishing trial court decisions in Pennsylvania may be traced to their initial appearance in these early county legal newspapers.

The National Law Journal, the first legal newspaper truly national in scope, did not appear until 1978 (its parent company, New York Law Publishing, had published the New York Law Journal since 1888). The National Law Journal was quickly followed by the Legal Times of Washington (now Legal Times), also in 1978, and the American Lawyer in 1979. In 2009, Legal Times was absorbed by the National Law Journal, but infusing the it with the former's Washington, DC-based coverage. The most recent entry into the field is the Lawyers Weekly USA, a product of Lawyers Weekly Publications of Boston. In addition to these four major national legal newspapers, there are several leading daily legal newspapers in major cities which concentrate primarily on legal news of local importance, with minimal coverage of national news. These include the New York Law Journal, the Chicago Daily Law Bulletin, and the Los Angeles Daily Journal. Finally, most states and larger cities have legal newspapers which serve as the leading sources for news of current court decisions, legislative activity, general legal developments, and legal notices in their jurisdictions.

For the active practitioner, a subscription to both a national and a local legal newspapers is a virtually necessity. In most instances, the local legal newspaper provides the attorney with his or her first knowledge of state appellate and important trial court decisions and docket information. Short of a Westlaw or Lexis search, a regular reading of the local legal newspaper, whether in print or online, is probably the most important means by which the attorney can update caselaw research for his or her jurisdiction--research already conducted by using secondary sources, case digests, case reporters, advance sheets, and citator services. While the decisions of state appellate courts are generally not reproduced in full, they may now be obtained routinely from state court Web sites. The national legal newspaper provides greater attention to decisions and developments of broader national significance, including those of the U.S. Supreme Court, and U.S. Courts of Appeals, decisions that may be obtained in full text from federal court Web sites, or one of various online legal services.

In 2007, Incisive Media, a corporation based in the United Kingdom, purchased ALM (formerly American Lawyer Media) for $630 million. ALM had been owned by Bruce Wasserstein's investment and PE firm, Wasserstein & Co. In addition to the American Lawyer, Legal Times, and National Law Journal, Incisive Media acquired ALM's stable of 33 state and local legal newspapers, and a large collection of book titles. Its legal newspapers have a combined readership of 330,00 lawyers and other legal professionals. In 2009, Incisive Media reintroduced the ALM brand for its American-based holdings, while retaining the Incisive Media brand for its UK holdings.

The entries which follow provide the attorney with full descriptions of all the national legal newspapers and several of the leading local newspapers. A listing of many state and local legal newspapers is included in Appendix G. The national and major local legal newspapers are indexed in LegalTrac, the Gale Group's legal periodical index available on CD-ROM, Westlaw, LexisNexis, and the Internet.

National Legal Newspapers

American Lawyer. Published monthly by Incisive Media. Main Office: 120 Broadway, New York, NY 10271. (800) 755-2773. customersvc@incisivemedia.com
Subscription rates: Digital and Print Editions: $34.99 per month/$419.88 per
year; Digital: $29.99 per month/$359.88 per year. Includes unlimited access to the new mobile app & mobile optimized site; monthly magazine delivery, including **The Asian Lawyer** and Focus Europe supplements; Survey access from Global 100 to The Am Law 200; Digital subscription to the Amlaw Daily digital newsletter. Selected contents on the Internet at:
www.americanlawyer.com/contents1205.shtml

First published in 1979, the **American Lawyer** is most commonly described as the **People** magazine of legal publishing because of its focus on personalities and ostentatious lifestyles. Articles typically highlight leading individuals in both the private sector and government, as well as law firms. Each issue includes 4-5 feature stories, several management stories, and departments entitled: Bar Talk, In the News, Heavy Hitter, Taking Issues, Opinion, Books, Inside Moves, Courtly Manners, Big Suits, and Big Deals. Each issue includes an index to all law firms, solo practitioners, companies, and public interest organizations mentioned. There are Directories of Trial Consultants and Support Services. Digital editions include **AmLaw Daily, Litigation Daily, The Asian Lawyer**, and **Surveys and Rankings**, Special issues include the annual **Technology Directory**, the annual rating of law firms by summer law clerks, and such special reports as **The A List, The Am Law 100, The Am Law 200, The Corporate Scorecard**, and the **25th Anniversary Issue**. Includes monthly subscription to **American Law Technology**. Limited content is also available on the **American Lawyer's** web site http://www.americanlawyer.com/index.shtml.

While the **American Lawyer** makes interesting and entertaining reading, it is no substitute for one of the more substantive legal newspapers and should be viewed only as a supplement to one of the following:

Lawyers USA. Published every other Monday by Lawyers Weekly Publications, 41 West St., Boston, MA 02111. Telephone: (800) 451-9998 (circulation).
Subscription rate (print & web): Ceased publication 2013 (2014).

An excellent source for summaries of noteworthy court decisions on the state and federal levels. The editors purport to read every slip opinion from the U.S. Supreme Court, the U.S. Courts of

Appeals, the U.S. Tax Court, every state supreme court, and those of many other courts and agencies. Also includes feature articles, and a Washington Report which provides the status of important bills in Congress. The second "In Practice" section provides attorneys with timely articles on law office management, office technology, legal research, verdicts and settlements, as well as the following classified departments: Legal Product Marketplace, Lawyer-to-Lawyer, Legal Support, Expert Witnesses, Great Escape (real estate) and Career Services.

A subscription to **Lawyers USA** includes access to subscriber-only areas features of the **Lawyers USA** Website which requires a username and password. These subscriber-only benefits include Daily Email Alerts, Weekly Practice Alerts, Preview Alerts, and Rules Service Alert. The **Lawyers USA** web site also provides links to state and federal government web sites for court opinions and statutes.

State Legal Newspapers. Lawyers Weekly, Inc. also publishers legal newspapers for the following states: Maryland, Massachusetts, Michigan, Minnesota, Missouri, New York, North Carolina, Rhode Island, South Carolina, Virginia, and Wisconsin. See Appendix D for addresses and telephone numbers.

Legal Times [see **National Law Journal**]

The National Law Journal. Published weekly by Incisive Media, 345 Park Avenue South, New York, NY 10010. Telephone: (212) 545-6029. Subscription Department: P.O. Box 5012, Brentwood, TN 37024. Subscription inquiries: (800) 274-2893. Published weekly, except two issues combined at year-end. Selected articles and archive also available on the Web at: http://www.nlj.com
Subscription rates: print and digital combination: $29.99 per month/$359.88 per year; digital only: $24.99 per month/$299,88 per year.
Since 1978, this weekly, tabloid-sized legal newspaper has provided members of the profession with timely coverage of current developments in law, government, and business. In March, 2009, it merged with its sister publication, **Legal Times**. The combined publication provides coverage on national issues with a special emphasis on the Washington legal scene. The merger brought together two rival publications which had remained separate even after their parent companies—American Lawyer Media and National Law Publishing—merged in 1997. Although both newspapers were published in 1978, the **National Law Journal** had the largest circulation of any weekly legal publication. Each issue includes several lead articles, usually detailing significant legislative initiatives, major trials, or important legal trends. Regular features include: Sidebar--News of the Profession and the following Departments: Verdicts and Settlements, Regional Reports, Law Schools, Washington Brief and Agency Watch. A Commentary section is devoted to editorials, opinion pieces, and letters to the editor.

Section B provides coverage of law-related business news, court decisions, and developments in such areas as tax, environmental, and family law. A Law Office Management Section addresses such matters as law firm hiring practices, compensation, law firm billing, computerization, and retirement planning. A Technology Resource Guide includes advertisements for law-related products and publications. A "Worth Reading" column highlights current and noteworthy books and articles. There are also pages devoted to coverage of recent decisions of the U.S. Supreme Court, the U.S. Courts of Appeals, and State Courts. Job openings are listed under both Career Opportunities and Corporate Counsel. A Lawyers' Service Directory includes classified ads for a variety of products and services.

Major Local Legal Newspapers

Chicago Daily Law Bulletin. Published daily by the Law Bulletin Publishing Company, 415 North State Street, Chicago, IL 60610 4674. Telephone: (312) 644-7800; http://www.lawbulletin.com/legal/newspapers-and-magazines
Subscription rates (include online access): 1 year: $299.00; 2 years: $499.00; 3 years: $699; 6 months: $225; include online access; 250 issues per year (2014).

Founded in 1854, and billed as the oldest daily courts newspaper in the United States, the **Chicago Daily Law Bulletin** provides coverage of Illinois appellate and trial courts, legislative activity, and selective national and international legal news. Each issue also includes court calendars, a calendar of law-related seminars and lectures, new law suits, classifieds, and public notices. "The insertion of legal notices in the **Chicago Daily Law Bulletin** is sufficient publication under the decision of the Supreme Court of Illinois."

The Legal Intelligencer. Published daily, except Saturdays, Sundays and holidays, by ALM, [formerly Incisive Media], 1617 JFK Boulevard, Suite 1750. Philadelphia, PA 19103. Telephone: (800) 999-1916 or (215) 557-2310.
Subscription rates: Digital and print: $36.99 per month/$443.88 per year; Digital access alone: $29.99 per month/$359.88 per year (20134).

The oldest legal newspaper in the United States, **The Legal Intelligencer** has served Philadelphia lawyers as the leading source for legal information since 1843. This tabloid-sized newspaper contains articles on leading local law-related happenings, national legal developments, Pennsylvania news, digests of recent Pennsylvania appellate and trial court decisions, sheriff's sale notices, classifieds, and public notices. Special supplements and sections provide in-depth coverage of such topics as real estate, litigation, and business law. Legal Communications, also the publisher of **Pennsylvania Law Weekly**, rules of Pennsylvania county courts, and the **Pennsylvania District and County Reports**, was acquired in 1998 by American Lawyer Media, a property of U.S. Equity Partners, L.P., a private equity fund sponsored by Wasserstein Perella. In 2007, American Lawyers Media was acquired by London-based Incisive Media, adopting the latter's name. In 2009, Incisive's American properties were re-branded with the ALM name.

Los Angeles Daily Journal. Published daily by the Daily Journal Corporation, 915 East First Street, Los Angeles, CA 90012. Telephone: (213) 229-5412. Print subscription includes online access to DJC Law.
Subscription rate: $750.00 per year (260 issues); $445.00 six months; $297.00 for three months. Subscription includes website access (2014).

Published since 1888, the **Los Angeles Daily Journal** provides the Southern California legal community with timely reporting of activity in the California trial and appellate courts. In addition to several lead stories, each issue includes Daily Appellate Report Summaries, California Verdicts and Settlements, legal notices, and classifieds. A separate Daily Appellate Report pamphlet contains the full text of decisions of all published opinions of the U.S. Supreme Court, the Ninth U.S. Circuit Court of Appeals, the California Supreme Court, the California Courts of Appeal, the Ninth U.S. Circuit Bankruptcy Appellate Panel, the U.S. District Courts in California, the Federal U.S. Circuit Court of Appeals, and the State Bar Court. The online service finally became operational in December, 2000.

New Jersey Law Journal. Published weekly, each Monday, by ALM, 238 Mulberry Street, P.O. Box 20081, Newark, NJ 07101-6081. Telephone: (973) 642-0075.
Subscription rates: print and digital combination: $29.99 per month/$359.88 per year; digital only: $24.99 per month/$299,88 per year (2014).
A complete legal newspaper in three sections. Section one provides coverage of national and state legal news, feature articles, commentary, computer technology, a Calendar of functions and seminars, continuing legal education classes, and classifieds. Section two includes case digests from New Jersey state courts and administrative agencies, U.S. District Court decisions, and decisions of the U.S. Court of Appeals for the Third Circuit (with full text posted on line on Lexis Counsel Connect New Jersey), Public Notices, and Experts and Services listings. Section three is a Special Advertising Supplement focusing on legal support services or other law-related fields of interest. These include both articles and advertisements in that area. The **New Jersey Law Journal** gives greater attention to substantive news articles, special features, and case digests than it does to public notices. In 2007, American Lawyers Media was acquired by London-based Incisive Media, adopting the latter's name. In 2009, Incisive's American properties were re-branded with the ALM name.

New York Law Journal. Published daily except Saturdays, Sundays and legal holidays by New York Law Publishing Company, a subsidiary of ALM, 120 Broadway, 5th Floor, New York, NY 10271.
Telephone: (800) 888-8300. In Albany: (518) 371-7404.
Subscription rate: print and digital combination: $36.99 per month/$443.88 per year; digital only: $29.99 per month/$359,88 per year (2014).
With the exception of a few articles with a national focus, the **New York Law Journal** concentrates on reporting news of the New York trial and appellate courts. Published since 1888, it is the official law paper for the First and Second Judicial Departments, the U.S. District Court, and the New York Court of Appeals. There are summaries of opinions from the U.S. Court of Appeals for the Second Circuit as well as decisions of the New York trial and appellate courts. A major portion of each issue is taken up with New York trial court calendars, legal notices, and classifieds, including Classified Employment.

For a complete list of State and Local Legal Newspapers see **Appendix D**.

Chapter 21: Legal Newsletters

One category of legal periodical literature which has seen significant growth over the past 30 years is the commercial newsletter. These newsletters are, in large measure, a response to the growing specialization of the legal profession and the need for timely topical information which might otherwise have to be gleaned from the painstaking review of a number of general legal newspapers, advance sheets, and other publications. These newsletters perform a valuable service for their readerships by providing a timely review of current developments, as well as abstracts of relevant court decisions, legislative activity, and administrative rulings in one convenient format.

One explanation for the proliferation in the number of specialized newsletters is the steady growth in the number of trial attorneys in the United States and the corresponding need for many of them to exploit specialized practice niches. The field of products liability litigation, for example, has provided a rich vein of potential lawsuits, including those involving drugs and medical devices, asbestos, mold, tobacco, lead, welding rods, to name just a few. Publishers of these specialized newsletters also sponsor litigation conferences in such areas as pharmaceutical litigation for which costly registration fees are charged. Such conferences draw thousands of lawyers annually eager to hone their skills in enhancing their potential contingency fees or in developing a potentially lucrative litigation niche. The registration fee for a recent two-day VIOXX litigation conference, for example, was $1,095,00 per attendee. Mealey's Emerging Drugs & Devices newsletter from LexisNexis costs $2,148.00 per year.

Although these newsletters may sometimes be the only sources available in narrow areas of specialization, they can also be quite costly and must be selected with care. Also, their brief format and emphasis on items of current interest also means that they tend to lack permanent reference value. While nearly 300 law-related newsletters may be accessed through a variety of on-line databases, they rarely find their way into the general legal periodical indexing services, which provide access from a general perspective. As a consequence, the full benefit of these publications can only be gained when the subscriber routinely reads them from cover to cover and converts the information into his or her mental or office data bank.

The frequency of legal newsletters varies widely, ranging from daily to semi-annual. Some are provided free with a membership in the sponsoring organization or simply as a public service. The quarterly Center for Law and Education Newsnotes falls in this category, as do many ABA sectional newsletters. At the high end is BNA's Daily Report for Executives which runs over $10,000.00 annually (over $9,000.00 on the Web). As might be imagined, the newsletters which are the most reasonable in price tend to be those published by the sections of the American Bar Association and the state bar associations. However, it is common for commercially published newsletters to cost anywhere from $200-$1,000 per year depending their length and frequency.

Leading Selection Tool

Before deciding to subscribe to a legal newsletter, particularly if its price exceeds $100 annually, the reader is advised to consult Legal Newsletters in Print (Infosources Publishing), an annual directory of available titles compiled and edited by Arlene L. Eis. Eis provides complete bibliographic data on more than 2,300 legal newsletters as well indices organized by publisher, on-line vendor, and subject. She includes a variety of publications, including "standard-type newsletters, bulletins, newsletter reporting services, and all reporting services that are used periodically and stored in looseleaf binders." Electronic and FAX newsletters are also included. A list of deletions from previous editions alerts users to the fact that many legal newsletters are transitory in nature and may not survive for an extended period of time. Legal Newsletters in Print is available both in print and as a part of LawTrio, a database also containing Legal Looseleafs in Print, and the Directory of Law-Related CD-ROMs.

The subject index provides an easy way to determine what titles are available in a particular area of practice before making a commitment. Those interested in newsletters in the field of entertainment law, for example, have a choice of seven newsletters ranging in price from bar association newsletters provided free to members (three-four issues per year) to a much more substantial commercially published newsletter costing more than $800 annually (24 issues per year).
The major publishers of legal newsletters (exclusive of state bar associations) include the following:

Andrews Publications (Thomson Reuters)	American Bar Association
Aspen Publishers (Wolters Kluwer)	Barclays (Thomson Reuters)
Matthew Bender & Co., Inc. (LexisNexis)	Bureau of National Affairs
Business Laws, Inc. (Thomson Reuters)	Business Publishers, Inc.
CCH, Inc. (Wolters Kluwer)	Leader Publications (LexisNexis)
LRP Publications	LexisNexis
Mealey Publications, Inc. (LexisNexis)	M. Lee Smith Publishers & Printers
Quinlan Publishing Group (Thomson Reuters)	Strafford Publications, Inc.
Thomson West	Warren, Gorham & Lamont (Thomson Reuters)

Not surprisingly, the trends that have impacted legal publishing generally have also affected the field of legal newsletter publishing. Under an almost non-existent antitrust regime, smaller legal newsletter publishers have been swept up by the legal publishing oligopoly, the latest being Quinlan Publishing Group, acquired by Thomson in 2006, and Leader Publications, acquired by LexisNexis the same year. This phenomenon has swiftly eroded the theory that this concentration of economic power is benign because there are no barriers to the entry of new companies. The fact that there may be no initial barriers to market entry is meaningless, however, if the resulting start-ups are soon consumed by one of the existing behemoths. Indeed, how much longer will the other legal newsletter publishers in the above list remain independent?

The online newsletter directory **Newsletter Access** provides basic information on 9,622 newsletters, 458 of which are legal in nature. This service may also be used to request information on the listed newsletters or request a sample issue. **Newsletter Access** may be reached at:

http://newsletteraccess.com

Cost Saving Tip

One way to avoid the high annul subscription costs of many of these specialized legal newsletters is to access them online on a per-use basis. The complete line of newsletters published by Mealey Publications, for example, is now available via the Mealey's Online Research Service at the LexisNexis web site at: http://www.mealeysonline.com/mealey/ppv/searchPage.do

Researchers have immediate access to current issues the day they are published as well as an editorial archive of all titles from 1990. **Mealey's Insurance and Insurance Insolvency** reports are available back to 1984 and 1989 respectively. All published and advertised court and other documents are downloadable as PDF files and are available from April 2002 to date. Users may search all Mealey products and review the headline results at no charge. Articles are available at $25.00 each; court documents are $35.00, both payable via credit card.

Perils of Newsletter Solicitations

Caution: A not uncommon tactic employed by some commercial newsletter publishers is to send you a trial subscription for a few months, followed by a solicitation disguised as an invoice. Some of these solicitations suggest that your subscription is expiring, a clever psychological ploy based on the assumption that you are more likely to enter a full subscription if you are under the assumption that you already subscribe. The attorney who fails to maintain control over the acquisition of new materials in his or her office library is apt to assume that the subscription was consciously ordered and mistakenly pay the solicitation/invoice. Or, perhaps, your secretary will likewise assume that you ordered the item and pay the invoice. In either event, you will have been tricked into subscribing to a publication you may not have desired in the first place. You are, of course, never obligated to pay for a subscription which you did not order. Unsolicited shipments fall under the language of U.S. Postal law (39 **U.S.C.** § 3009) which states that you are under no obligation to return the merchandise or notify the seller.

Chapter 22: General Law Related Reference Titles

The American Bar Association Complete Personal Legal Guide: The Essential Guide for Every Household. 4th ed. Chicago: American Bar Association, 2008. 1 vol. (784 pp.). Softcover.

Cost: Out-of-Print; from $26.23 on amazon.com (2014).

Published in cooperation with the American Bar Association's Division for Public Education, this is the most comprehensive single-volume legal reference book written for the layperson. The coverage extends to a multitude of topics of greatest interest and value to the general public, including automobiles, computers, credit and bankruptcy, contracts and consumer law, criminal justice, divorce and child custody/support, elder law, estate planning, health care, home ownership, personal injury, real estate, small business, and workplace law. Presented in an easy-to-use question and answer format. Particularly recommended for public libraries and law libraries which serve the general public.

AALS Directory of Law Teachers. Washington, DC: American Association of Law Schools. Annual.

Cost: 2012-2013: $250.00; or $110.00 to member schools, government, non-profits, press (2014). (202) 296-8851.

Begun in 1922, this annual directory of full-time faculty and professional staff of all member and fee-paid law schools, with biographical sketches of over 10,000 full-time teachers and law librarians and lists of full-time teachers by subject taught. There are also separate listings of minority law teachers and of law school professional staff such as directors of admissions, development, placement, or alumni relations. It also lists the Canadian law schools and their full-time faculty. An excellent tool for locating expert witnesses. Available online via password to faculty and staff members listed in the **AALS Directory.**

Almanac of the Federal Judiciary. Washington, D.C.: Wolters Kluwer Law & Business, 1984-date. 2 vols. Supplemented 2-3 times annually.

Cost: $2,099.00; supplementation: 1995: $588; 1996: $590; 1997: $670; 1998: $554; 1999: $428; 2000: $655; 2001: $712; 2002: $779; 2003: $1007; 2004: $1,046; 2005: $1,074; 2006: $1,146; 2007: $1,242; 2008: $1,300; 2009: $1,390;
2010: $1,151; 2011: $2.007; 2012: $2,541; 2013: $2,720.

A unique biographical directory to the judges of the federal courts, from the U.S. District Courts to the United States Supreme Court. In addition to basic biographical data, each judge's entry includes media coverage, and lawyers' evaluations. These candid evaluations provide insights into the intellectual, professional, and personal qualities of the judges as well as critiques of the way in which the judges handle their courtrooms and treat attorneys appearing before them. The entries are a must-read for any attorney preparing to appear before a judge for the first time. In light of the extraordinarily high annual supplementation cost (over $2,720.00 in 2013), the cost-conscious attorney should consult this volume at the public law library or purchase the set anew every few years. The vast majority of the material in these volumes will never be consulted by the average attorney who practices in one only district and one circuit.

ALWD Citation Manual: A Professional System of Citation. Edited by Darby Dickinson. 4th ed. Gaithersburg, MD: Aspen Publishers, 2010 [Wolters Kluwer Law & Business]. 1 vol. (608 pp.). Spiralbound.

Cost: $40.00; kindle: $38.55; from $13.70 on amazon.com (2014).

This new citation manual was a response by the Association Legal Writing Directors (ALWD) to the chronic deficiencies of the **Blue Book**. It is an attempt to provide a restatement of the rules of citation based on the citation form actually used by experts. Its aims include a simplification of some of the rules, a reduction of inconsistencies, a desire to make the rules responsive to the needs of lawyers as well as scholars, and to provide stability and uniformity of citation rules over the long term. The **ALWD Manual** contains one system of citation for all documents, making no distinction between law review articles and other types of writing. It was adopted by 80 law schools in the first three months following its publication. Edited by Darby Dickerson.

American Association of Law Libraries. Committee on Citation Formats. **Universal Citation Guide**. 3d ed. Buffalo, NY: William S. Hein & Co., Inc., 2014.

Cost: $42.50 (2014). (800) 828-7571. Also available in PDF format on the AALL Web site:
[http://www.aallnet.org/main-menu/Publications/products/pub-universal.html].

A Project of the Citation Formats Committee of the American Association of Law Libraries, the **UCG** sets forth rules for citing court decisions, statutory materials, and administrative regulations whether these materials are found in a print source or in an electronic form, such as an online service or web site. The **Guide** includes explanatory materials describing citation issues presented by each type of authority and how they are resolved by the **UCG**. Each rule is followed by numerous examples illustrating its use. The Appendix includes a state-by-state list of model citations.

The American Bench: Judges of the Nation. Sacramento, CA: Forster-Long, Inc. Published annually every October. Current edition is: 2014. 2 vol. (over 3.300 pp.). (800) 328-5091.

Cost: 2014 ed.: $495 + shipping; online version (single user; one year access): $595.00; 2010 print ed: from $84.66 on amazon.com (2014).

The definitive guide to the judges of the nation. Contains a complete listing of all appellate and trial court judges for the federal courts, the 50 states, and the District of Columbia. Features biographies of over 20,000 judges, with addresses and telephone numbers. All judges of the U.S. Supreme Court, U.S. Courts of Appeals, and special federal courts are gathered together in one section. Federal district court judges are grouped together with the judges of the individual states. There is a complete alphabetical name index to all judges listed. The volume also includes the names, addresses, and telephone numbers of clerks of court. All federal and state sections include narrative descriptions of each court, including their jurisdiction and method of appointment, with maps of judicial district boundaries. Even if you don't purchase every edition, this volume will provide you with ready access to information regarding courts, their organization, and telephone numbers.

Annotated Model Rules of Professional Conduct. 7th ed. Chicago: Center for Professional Responsibility, American Bar Association, 2011. 1 vol. (800 pp.) with companion of complete book.

Cost: $159.95; ABA members: $143.95; CPR members: $119.95

(2014).
Adopted by the American Bar Association's House of Delegates on August 2, 1983, the Model Rules of Professional Conduct have now been incorporated into the professional codes of more than 35 states. Each rule is accompanied by comments and detailed legal background, with citations to relevant case law. The Rules are also compared to the prior Model Code of Professional Responsibility that was adopted in 1969. An essential desktop guide for the attorney who wishes to remain on the ethical high road. Highly recommended.

Armstrong, J.D.S. and Christopher A. Knott. **Where the Law Is: An Introduction to Advanced Legal Research**. 4th ed. St. Paul, MN: West, 2013. Paperbound.
Cost: $77.00; from $68.41 on amazon.com (2014).
This estimable textbook is designed for use in advanced legal research classes or as a supplement to basic legal research texts. Unlike traditional research texts that focus on discrete sources of legal information, this text navigates a wider world of suppliers, formats and combinations. Following an introductory discussion of the legal research plan, citations, format, sources, full text searching, field-limited searching, and the best uses of searching subject indexed/edited data, the authors explore in depth the major sources of law, both general and specific, including statutes, legislative history, law review articles, cases, treatises and other overviews, form books and jury instructions, sources of administrative law, looseleaf services, court rules, legal ethics research, foreign law research, international law, municipal law research. The concluding chapter (Where the Law Is) provides valuable insights on the research process and the evaluation of sources. While intended as a textbook for classes in advanced legal research, this volume would be of significant benefit to any attorney or legal researcher who wishes to enhance his or her skills beyond the basic level. J.D.S. Armstrong is Associate Director of Educational and Research Services, Arthur w. Diamond Law Library, Columbia University School of Law. Christpher A. Knott s Associate Dean for Information Services and Technology, and Professor of Law, Wake Forest University School of Law.

Barkan, Steven M., Roy M. Mersky and Donald J. Dunn. **Fundamentals of Legal Research**. 9th ed. Mineola, NY: Foundation Press, 2009. University Textbook Series. Available from West Academic.
Cost: $106.00; from $53.35 on amazon.com (paper) (2014).
Building on the work of the late Roy Mersky and Donald Dunn, Steven M. Barkan has updated this classic text to reflect the latest developments in legal bibliography and research. While intended as a law student textbook for use in courses in legal research and writing, this is also an inexpensive source of legal research assistance to the practicing attorney. Contains a discussion of both computer-assisted legal research and traditional print sources. Includes useful guides to research procedure in various subject areas as well as a table of legal abbreviations. An assignment book is also available for $33.00 ($4.79 on amazon.com).

Barris, Linda J. **Understanding and Mastering the Bluebook: a Guide for Students and Practitioners**. 2d ed. Durham, NC, Carolina Academic Press, 2010. 1 vol. (136 pp.). Spiral-bound.
Cost: $28.00 (10% Internet discount); student workbook: $25.00 (2014).
This invaluable companion to the **Bluebook** guides users through its complicated citation rules with hundreds of illustrations and explanations organized by source type. The author provides step-by-step instructions for building citations to the most common authorities. Students are cautioned by means of tips, cautions and hints to avid common citation pitfalls. All the important rules and sub-rules are fully described and illustrated. Linda Barris is Assistant Professor of Law at Shepard Broad Law Center of Nova Southeastern University.

Berring, Robert C. and Elizabeth A. Edinger. **Finding the Law**. 12th ed. St. Paul, MN: West Publishing Co., 2005. Casebook Series. 1 vol. (393 pp.). Now available from West Academic.
Cost: $81.00 (2014).
An excellent single-volume guide to legal research written from a bibliographical perspective. The chapters cover the context of legal research, court reports, citators, case finding, statutes, legislative history, constitutional law, administrative and executive publications, court rules and practice, secondary authority, and research strategies. The Appendices include a list of state legal research guides and sources of federal regulatory agency rules, regulations, and adjudications. This is a more current, but abridged, version of the author's **How to Find the Law** (9th ed.), which was last updated in 1989.

Bieber's Dictionary of Legal Abbreviations. 6th ed. compiled by Mary Miles Prince. Buffalo, NY: William S. Hein & Co., 2009. 1 vol. (1,181 pp.).
Cost: $65.00 (2014).
The most complete dictionary devoted to legal abbreviations. Contains 35,000 entries and alternative entries for prominent and obscure legal sources, both current and historical. Although new editions appear every few years, largely in response to the specialized needs of law librarians, the average law office should only have to buy this work once. This edition provides more than 1,500 new or expanded entries.

Bieber's Dictionary of Legal Citations (see Prince's **Bieber Dictionary of Legal Citations**)

Black's Law Dictionary. 9th edited by Bryan A. Garner. St. Paul, MN: West, 2009. 1 vol. (1,810 pp.)
Cost: $130.00 (Deluxe hardcover); $79.95 (regular hardcover); from $48.84 on amazon.com (2014).
Originally compiled by Henry Campbell Black and first published in 1891, this work has become the legal profession's leading and most heavily quoted legal dictionary. Legal definitions are accompanied by citations to cases and statutes as an aid to the researcher. The ninth edition includes more than 45,000 terms, alternate spellings, or equivalent expressions for more than 5,300 terms and West key numbers, including 2,000 more terms than found in the 8th edition. Noted legal scholar and legal style expert Bryan Garner has been the editor-in-chief of **Black's Law Dictionary** since the 7th edition.

Blazek, Ron, and Anna H. Perrault. **United States History: A Selective Guide to Information Sources.** 2d ed. Englewood, CO: Libraries Unlimited, 2003. 1 vol. (411 pp.).
Cost: Out-of-Print (2014).
Useful for both research and collection development, this bibliographical guide contains over 1,250 selected sources,

including both standard references and information sources that address the more recent social science focus on American history. Formats include print, online sources of print works, online databases, CD-ROMs, and microforms. Selections were made on the basis of firsthand knowledge and positive reviews in such publications as **Reference Books Bulletin**, **American Reference Books Annual**, **Choice**, **Library Journal**, and **Reference Services Review**. This work includes a useful overview of research trends in the field of history and reference source publishing, which embraces electronic sources and networked materials. Part 1 covers general sources, including biographical, chronological, statistical, geographical, and demographic. Part 2 follows a broad topical and subtopic arrangement. Annotations, which range from 85 to 250 words in length, often suggest search strategies. The Web sites that are listed are current as of November 7, 2002. The introduction offers users an overview of trends in historical research and reference-source publishing, including electronic sources and networked materials. For example, chapter 6, "Social, Cultural, and Intellectual History," includes sections on Jewish genealogy, women's suffrage, Korean Americans, higher education, capital punishment, radio and television, and baseball, among others. Each chapter and many of the sections begin with an overview noting relevant organizations and their publications and directions in research. Besides bibliographic information, the annotated entries offer descriptions and often suggest search strategies. Annotations are 85 to 250 words in length. An author-title index and a subject index are provided.

The Bluebook: A Uniform System of Citation. 19th ed. Cambridge, MA: Harvard Law Review Association, 2010. 1 vol. Spiral-bound format.
Cost: $34.00; online edition: $32.00 (1 year); renewals: $15.00 per year (2014).
Begun in 1923, this is the oldest and still one of the most authoritative guides to legal citation compiled by the editors of the Columbia Law Review, Harvard Law Review, University of Pennsylvania Law Review, and Yale Law Journal. See also: Good, Edward C., **Citing & Typing the Law**, 4th ed. (1999). Dissatisfaction with this guide among legal writing professionals prompted the drafting of an alternative **ALWD Citation Manual: A Professional System of Citation**, published by Aspen Law & Business [now Wolters Kluwer Law & Business] under the auspices of the Association of Legal Writers. More recently, the 19th edition has come in for some harsh criticism from no less than Richard Posner who contends that it "exemplifies hypertrophy in the anthropological sense. It is a monstrous growth, remote from the functional need for legal citation forms, that serves obscure needs of the legal culture and its student subculture." Posner, who has been a critic of the Bluebook since 1986, has devised his own simplified system of citation that doesn't sacrifice anything essential for readers to be able to check citations.

BNA's Directory of State and Federal Courts, Judges & Clerks. 2014 Edition. Edited by Catherine A. Kitchell and the BNA Library staff. Washington, DC: BNA Books, 2014. Annual. 1 vol. (781 pp.).
Cost: $235.00 (2014).
Provides detailed coverage of 2,133 state courts, 216 federal courts, 16,025 judges, and 5,319 clerks. Includes addresses and telephone numbers, as well as Web sites and E-mail addresses, when available. It also includes federal and state court organizational charts, Internet sites for federal and state courts, geographic jurisdiction indexes, and a personal name index.

Botluk, Diana. **The Legal List: Research on the Internet**. St. Paul, MN: Thomson West, 2013-2014 ed. Annual.
Cost: $419.00; Assured Print Price: $35 per month/$420 per year (2014).
An updated version of Erik Heels' **The Legal List: Internet Desk Reference**, this volume provides more substantive Internet research instruction than does its predecessor. The author covers such topics as Internet history, Internet tools, getting connected, world wide web directories, search engines, e-mail, list servs, search engines, and meta search finders. Chapter three, entitled "Beginning an Internet Research Project" contains annotated listings of leading legal Internet sites and explains how to choose general finding tools and locate specific information. Additional chapters provide listings of resources for legislative, administrative and judicial materials as well as secondary authority, news and media, legal ethics and professional responsibility, and international and foreign law materials. As with hundreds of West publications, the cost has gotten completely out-of-control, however, rising 20% in 2009 and 17% in 2010. The Assured Print Price (APP) just locks you into these excessive costs. As a cost-effective alternative, consult the reasonably priced volumes written by Carol Leavitt and Mark Rosch (see below), or compile your own list of sites important to your practice.

Bouchoux, Deborah E. **Cite-Checker: A Hands-On Guide to Using the Bluebook**. 3d ed. New York: Wolters Kluwer Law & Business, 2010. 1 vol. (192 pp.).
Cost: $48.95; from $11.35 on amazon.com (2014).
Proper citation form is designed to allow readers of legal documents to locate and review the authorities cited. The **Uniform System of Citation**, commonly referred to as the **Blue Book**, is a frequently confusing 300-page book that provides law students and legal practitioners with a nationally recognized standard for citing cases, statutes, regulations, and other legal authorities. This brief guide, on the other hand, is designed to provide practitioners with a concise and lucid explanation of the basic rules of legal citation according to the accepted **Blue Book** standard. Attention is given to typeface conventions, and citation form for cases, statutes, regulations, secondary sources, administrative and executive materials, electronic databases, the Internet, public domain citations, and other legal authorities and documents. The author also addresses such subjects as punctuation, quotations, omissions, alterations, short forms, signals, related authority, and capitalization. A Final Review chapter provides a variety of review exercises designed to inculcate the rules discussed. Attorney Deborah Bouchoux teaches legal research and writing at Georgetown University's paralegal program, and is the author of **Legal Research Explained**, also published by Wolters Kluwer.

Burton, William C. **Legal Thesaurus**. 5th ed. New York: McGraw-Hill, 2013.
1 vol. (1,136 pp.). Paperbound.
Cost: $42.95 (paper); from $27.71 on amazon.com (2014).
Originally published in 1980, this was the first work that addressed the needs of lawyers for a specialized thesaurus. Includes words that are strictly legal, words that are not strictly legal but which are commonly used by members of the legal

profession, and words that are neither legal nor used by lawyers but which are sufficiently sophisticated to warrant their use by attorneys. In addition to a main section containing thousands of words, there is an index to assist the attorney is locating synonyms. The compiler, William C. Burton, is vice president and director of governmental affairs for the Continental Insurance Companies. An essential tool for any attorney regularly engaged in legal writing and drafting. The 5th edition is augmented with more than 1,000 new terms, ranging from “cyberbullying” to “whistleblower.”

Checklist of Statutes. 67th ed. Buffalo, NY: William S. Hein & Co. Semi-annual.
1 vol. (354 pp.).
Cost: $71.00 (October, 2013); or no cost to Hein customers who purchase statutory products (2014).
A useful tool for ascertaining the currency of the individual volumes in your state and territorial codes, this volume now also includes the individual volumes in the **Code of Federal Regulations**.

The Chicago Manual of Style. 16th ed. Chicago, IL: University of Chicago Press, 2010. 1 vol. (1,026 pp.).
Cost: $65.00; online (prepaid): $35.00 annually ($30.00 with 2/yr. subscription); print from $37.70 on amazon.com (2014).
Over the past 100 years, the **Chicago Manual of Style** has grown to become the preeminent literary style manual in the field of professional and scholarly publishing. Begun in the 1890s as a single page of typographic fundamentals prepared by a proofreader at the University of Chicago Press, the first edition of the **Manual of Style** appeared in 1906 and is now the most widely used reference for authors, editors, proofreaders, indexers, copyrighters, designers, scholars, and publishers. It is a veritable bible on matters of editorial style and citation, grammar and usage. Although the **Chicago Manual of Style** is generally revised every 10 years, the 16th edition is the most extensive revision in decades, reflecting current style, technology, and electronic publishing practices. The 16th edition also includes a new chapter on American English grammar and usage by Bryan Garner, revised chapters on documentation and the citation of electronic sources, and updated coverage of design and production processes. The **Manual** also provides advice on how to prepare and edit of manuscripts online and prepare mathematical copy. There is an entire chapter devoted to rights and permissions authored by attorney William S. Strong. The 16th edition is a product of the **Manual**’s first advisory board, composed of a distinguished group of scholars, authors and professionals from a variety of business and publishing environments. A fully searchable online version, with Q & A, was introduced in 2006.

City Crime Rankings 2013: Crime in Metropolitan America. Edited by Kathleen O’Leary Morgan and Scott Morgan. Washington, DC: CQ Press, 2013. 1 vol. (388 pp.). Paperbound.
Cost: $95.00 (2014).
This reference work provides an easily accessible source of comparative crime data for cities and metropolitan areas throughout the United States. Statistics are provided for metropolitan areas and cities greater than 75,000 in population, including rates, and trends for total crime, violent crime, murder, rape, robbery, aggravated assault, property crime, burglary, larceny-theft, and motor vehicle theft. Statistics are presented in both alphabetical and rank order. Numbers and rates of police in cities are also included. A useful statistical tool for public officials, law enforcement, policy makers, scholars, journalists, students, and the general public.

Codes of Professional Responsibility. 4th ed. by Rena A. Gorlin. Washington, DC: BNA Books, 1999. 1 vol. (1,166 pp.).
Cost: OUT-OF-PRINT; from $4.78 on amazon.com (2014).
A compilation of 59 codes of professional ethics in the fields of business, health, and law covering such areas as confidentiality, conflicts of interest, fees, competence, advertising, licensing/accreditation, consultation/referral, peer review, and independence. It also includes brief introductory descriptions of organizations, including contacts, membership information, code authority, online availability, organizational resources, programs and services, informational resources, descriptions of activities and goals, discussion of code history, and enforcement. The volume is indexed by organization, profession and ethics topic.

Cohen, Morris and Kent C. Olson. **Legal Research in a Nutshell**. 11th ed. St. Paul, MN: West Academic, 2013. 1 vol. (528 pp.). Paperbound.
Cost: $41; from $31.95 on amazon.com (2014).
A concise introduction to legal research by two leading authorities in the field. Designed primarily as a law school text, this volume covers the legal research process, courts reports, digests and citators, annotations and encyclopedias, electronic resources, statutes and constitutions, legislative history, administrative law, secondary materials, specialized and practice materials, reference resources, international law: U.S. sources, international law: general sources, English and Commonwealth law, and the civil law system. The late Morris Cohen (1927-2010) was Law Librarian (Retired) and Emeritus Professor of Law, Yale Law School. Kent Olson is Lecturer and Assistant Librarian for Public Services, University of Virginia School of Law.

A Concise Encyclopedia of the United Nations. Edited by Helmut Volger. 2d rev. ed. Boston: Martinus Nijhoff Publishers, 2010. 1 vol. (962 pp.).
Cost: $354; from $292.74 on amazon.com (2014).
This is the English edition of the German language *Lexikon der Vereinten Nationen*, a comprehensive encyclopedic reference guide to the United Nations, its structure, agencies, systems, goals, functions, offices, legal concepts and entities, and related international bodies and protocols, as well as recent developments and reform efforts in the face of global opportunities and challenges. The contributing authors include scores of academic scholars of international law, economics and political sciences; active and former diplomats and UN officials; journalists and members of non-governmental organizations (NGOs). The entries are provided with Internet addresses for further information and are supplemented in the annex with a trilingual list (English-French-German) of the most important institutions and items of the official terminology and a list of information facilities concerning the UN. An important addition to any legal collection with a foreign/international component.

Congress and the Nation: Volume XII: 2005-2008. Politics and Policy in the 109th and 110th Congresses. Washington, DC: CQ Press, 2010. 1 vol. (1,260 pp.). Also available in an online format.
Cost: $305.00 (2014).
Since 1965, Congressional Quarterly and CQ Press have been

producing these seminal reference works on the activity of the United States Congresses. This latest (12th) edition provides detailed coverage for the fours years of the 109th and 110th Congresses (2005-2008), constituting the second term of the Bush Presidency. Chapters covering broad areas of public policy each follow a chronological sequence in which the activities of each legislative year are detailed. These include: Politics and National Issues (2) Economic Policy; (3) Homeland Security; (4) Foreign Policy; (5) Defense Policy; (6) Transportation, Commerce, and Communications; (7) Energy and Environment; (8) Agriculture; (9) Health and Human Services; (10) Education; (11) Housing and Urban Aid; (12) Labor and Pensions; (13) Law and Justice; (14) General Government; (15) Inside Congress; and (16) The Bush Presidency. The Appendices contain a number of invaluable features, including lists, charts, figures, boxes, and tables, including a glossary of Congressional terms, the legislative process in brief, key votes by session (2005-2008), Congress and its members, Senate cloture votes, Presidential vetoes, and the text of selective remarks by the President, and members of Congress, and Presidential nominees. This is the most comprehensive single-volume compendium of information on the work of Congress during the years in question. An indispensable tool for any student, journalist, policymaker, Congressional staffer, lobbyist, researcher, lawyer, or citizen interested in the work of Congress. The series as a whole, which spans the years 1945-2008, is also available in an online format.

Congressional Information Service. **CIS/Annual Legislative Histories**. Washington, DC: Congressional Information Service (LexisNexis). Annual, 1984-date.
Cost: 1984-2009: $570.00 each; also available online as part of LexisNexis Congressional with pricing determined by user population. Inquire.
These annual Legislative Histories volumes provide convenient access to the legislative histories of federal laws with citations to legislative documents. An essential tool for any law firm or law library that supports legislative research.
For further information, see “Federal Legislative History” in Zimmerman’s Research Guide: http://law.lexisnexis.com/infopro/zimmermans/disp.aspx?z=1465

Congressional Quarterly’s Guide to the U.S. Supreme Court. 5th ed. Edited by David Savage. Washington, DC: Congressional Quarterly, Inc., 2010. 2 vols. (1,300 pp.). Periodic new editions.
Cost: $465; $437.28 on amazon.com (2014).
This comprehensive reference work provides detailed examination and explanation of the operations of the U.S. Supreme Court, including its history, leading personalities, and decisions which have helped shape American life. The two volumes are organized into six parts and 20 chapters, addressing the origin and development of the court to 1996, the court and the federal system, the court and the individual, pressures on the court, the court at work, and members of the court. The fourth edition provides discussion and analysis of recent events, and decisions and controversies which have consumed the attention of the Rehnquist Court, including the Bush-Gore election case, the homosexual rights case of Lawrence v. Texas, the University of Michigan affirmative action decision, and decisions involving states rights, among others. The author also provides extensive coverage of the court’s history, including its internal operations, the evolution of its relations with the other branches of government and the states, and its impact on individual rights and liberties. The Appendices include the text of the Judiciary Acts of 1789 and 1925, a list of Acts of Congress ruled unconstitutional by the Court, and subject and case indexes. While aimed at a general audience, this reference work nevertheless serves as a useful source of information on the U.S. Supreme Court for scholars and legal professionals. David Savage is the Supreme Court Reporter for the Los Angeles Times.

Court Reporters Sourcebook. Vienna, VA: National Court Reporters Association. Annual (October). Paperbound.
Cost: 2013 Edition: $12.93 (800) 272-6272 (2014).
A state-by-state directory of over 20,000 court reporters. Particularly useful for those seeking to take out-of-town depositions.

Crawford, Tad and Kay Murray. **The Writer’s Legal Guide: An Authors Guild Desk Reference**. 4th ed. New York: Allworth Press, 2013. 1 vol. (352 pp.).
Cost: $19.95; from $11.79 on amazon.com; kindle: $9.99 (2014).
This practical handbook for professional writers and publishers addresses the many legal issues likely to be encountered in the world of publishing, particularly those involving intellectual property rights under the law. The authors, whose backgrounds embrace the worlds of both the law and publishing, provide the latest information on electronic rights, fair use and permissions. The third edition also addresses the latest changes in the law of copyright, book contracts, collaboration agreements, limits of expression, agency contracts, the Freedom of Information Act, and tax laws. It also includes a number of sample forms, including an electronic rights clause, a model contract for licensing articles to magazines, a checklist for avoiding defamation and invasion of privacy, among others. The work is co-published with the Authors Guild. Lead author Tad Crawford is the attorney, and artists’ rights advocate who founded Allworth Press in 1989.

Crime in the United States, 2014: Uniform Crime Reports. Blue Ridge Summit, PA: Bernan Press, 2014. 1 vol. Paperbound.
Cost: 2014 edition $105.00; 2013 edition: from $49.90 on amazon.com (2014). The final report issued by the FBI in 2011 is available at: http://www.fbi.gov/ucr/ucr.htm#cius
Although no longer published by the FBI, this compilation contains findings that the Federal Bureau of Investigation releases annually from its Uniform Crime Reporting Program. It provides a nationwide view of crime and trends based on statistics contributed by State and local law enforcement agencies. The Uniform Crime Reporting (UCR) Program is a nationwide, cooperative statistical effort of more than 17,000 city, university and college, county, state, tribal, and federal law enforcement agencies voluntarily reporting data on crimes brought to their attention. During 2004, law enforcement agencies active in the UCR Program represented 94.2 percent of the total population. Among the crimes reports are violent crime (including murder, robbery, aggravated assault, and forcible rape); property crime (including burglary, larceny-theft, motor vehicle theft, and arson); and hate, or bias, crimes, that are motivated, in whole or in part, by the offender’s bias against a race, religion, disability, sexual orientation, or ethnicity/national origin. The report consists chiefly of tables and statistics. Current edition released April 2013.

Criminal Justice Information: How to Find It, How to Use It. Edited by Dennis C. Benamati, Phyllis A. Schultze, Adam C. Bouloukos, and Graeme R. Newman. Phoenix, AZ: Oryx Press

(Greenwood Publishing Group), 1998. 1 vol. (248 pp.).
Cost: $87.95; from $1.27 on amazon.com (2014).
This reference guide is a response to the effects of the information explosion and the Internet on the task of locating criminal justice information. Its intended audience includes criminal justice researchers, criminal justice professionals, legal professionals, governmental and nongovernmental organizations, and citizens. Although it contains descriptions of hundreds of books, articles and Web sites, it focuses more on process than on a listing of resources. Accordingly, Chapters 1-2 address the nature of criminal justice research in an evolving information environment, and the process of locating authorities and establishing professional connections. The remaining seven chapters discuss sources of basic information; tools for locating books, periodicals, documents and other information sources; periodicals, news sources, indexes, and abstracts; statistical sources; government agencies as generators of criminal justice information; legal research; and international criminal justice information. It also includes an extensive listing of Web sites related to criminal justice.

DeVries. Mary A. **Legal Secretary's Complete Handbook**. 4th ed. Old Tappan, NJ: Prentice Hall, 1992. 1 vol. (650 pp.) (800) 947-7700
Cost: $18.88; from $.01 (paper) on amazon.com (2014).
An excellent compendium of information for the law office secretary, including general duties in the law office, law office automation, production of documents, contacts with clients, maintenance of files, legal and business correspondence, record keeping, client billing, legal research tools, preparation of legal instruments and documents, handling powers of attorney and wills, preparing court papers, handling records on appeal, legal briefs, and legal citation form. Also contains specific guidelines for assisting the attorney in specialized areas of law, including corporations, real estate and foreclosures, probate and estate administration, and commercial collections. Concludes with forms of addresses for judges, Latin words and phrases, a glossary of legal terms, and a listing of courts of record and judicial circuits.

Directory of Corporate Counsel. New York: Wolters Kluwer Law & Business (Aspen). 2 vols. (2,500 pp.). Annual. Hardbound.
Cost: 2013-2014 ed.: print: $1,185.00; also available on LexisNexis (2014).
This directory provides names, addresses and biographies of over 30,000 in-house counsel to leading corporations, and 8,000 corporate legal departments. Individual entries provide information on company organization, department structure and hierarchy, as well as the specialties and background of the attorneys. Indexes also provide access by corporation or organization, geographical area, attorney name, law school, and nonprofit organization.

Directory of Law-Related CD-ROMs. Compiled and edited by Arlene L. Eis. Teaneck, NJ: Infosources Publishing. Annual. (201) 836-7072.
Cost: No longer available in print format; 2012 forward only available as part of LawTrio on the web, combining the **Directory of Law-Related CD-ROMs**, **Legal Looseleafs in Print**, and **Legal Newsletters in Print** at a cost of $339.00/yr; **Directory of Law-Related CD-ROMs** alone: $244.00; one month pass: $95.00 (2014).
The most complete and accurate guide available to legal CD-ROM titles on the market, including those on the Internet.. The 2013 edition includes detailed information on more than 1,600 CD-ROM products published by over 180 publishers in the United States and abroad in the areas of law, legislation, and regulation. In addition to the product listings, there are indices by publisher/distributor, search software, Macintosh titles, and subject. Includes citations to product reviews published in law-related publications.

Dworsky, Alan L. **User's Guide to the Bluebook.** Rev. for the 19th ed. Buffalo, NY: William S. Hein & Co., 2010. 1 vol. (49 pp.).
Cost: $14.50 (2014).
An easy to understand guide to the intricacies of the **Bluebook** and proper citation form designed for law students and lawyers alike.

Economic Freedom of the World: 2013 Annual Report. Compiled by James Gwartney, Robert Lawson, and Joshua Hall. Vancouver, DC: The Fraser Institute, 2014. 1 vol. (322 pp.).
Cost: available at no cost at: http://www.freetheworld.com/release.html (2014)
The roots of this index have their origins in a series of conferences hosted by Michael Walker of the Fraser Institute and Nobel Laureate Milton Friedman from 1986 to 1994. These conferences, which attracted 60 of the worlds leading scholars, focused on the relationship between a nation's institutions and policies and its level of economic freedom. Its first report, **Economic Freedom of the World: 1975-1995**, was published in 1996. This annual report measures the degree to which the policies and institutions of countries are supportive of economic freedom, the cornerstones of which are (1) personal choice; (2) voluntary exchange; (3) freedom to compete; and (4) the security of privately-owned property. This report provides ratings of 141 nations for the year 2008, the most recent year for which data is available. Forty-two data points are used to construct a summary index and to measure the degree of economic freedom in five areas: (1) size of government; (2) legal structure and security of property rights; (3) access to sound money; (4) freedom to trade internationally; and (5) regulation of credit, labor, and business. In this most recent report, for example, nations in the top quartile of economic freedom have an average per capita GDP of $32,744 (U.S.) compared to $3,858 for those in the bottom quartile. Life expectancy in the most free quartile is 79.3 years; in the least free quartile: 59.9 years. James Gwartney is professor of economics at Florida State University where he directs the Gus A. Stavros Center for the Advancement of Free Enterprise and Economic Education. He was assisted by Robert Lawson of Auburn University and Joshua Hall of Beloit College.

Elections A to Z. 4th ed. Edited by David Tarr and Bob Benenson, Washington, DC, CQ Press, 2012. 1 vol. (768 pp.). Also available in online edition.
Cost: $140.00; online edition: inquire: librarysales@sagepub.com; from $39.66 on amazon.com (2014).
A detailed reference work to American political campaigns and elections, including discussion and analysis of how voters, candidates, political parties, special interest groups, and others participate in the electoral process. The alphabetically organized topical entries, with both an historical and current focus, cover

every aspect of the electoral process, including entries for 527 political organizations. The text includes numerous sidebars and cross-references. The third edition includes a number of new topics, including Internet politics, lobbying and elections, and mid-decade redistricting. The author, who has been covering elections for nearly three decades, including the 24 years with **Congressional Quarterly**, is politics editor for CQPolitics.com.

Elgar Encyclopedia of Comparative Law. 2d ed. Edited by Jan M. Smits. Northampton, MA: Edward Elgar, 2012. 1 vol. (1000 pp.).
Cost: $365.00; $328.50 ordered online; from $243.20 on amazon.com (2014).
The rise of comparative law as a scholarly discipline in recent decades, reflecting increased globalization and interest in particular legal structures and practices, has generated a flood of research on both the methodological and substantive law fronts. This compilation of current comparative law scholarship represents the first attempt to provide a comprehensive descriptive and analytical overview of substantive law and specific legal systems. Edited by Jan M. Smits, Professor of European Private Law at Maastricht University, The Netherlands. it contains 76 scholarly essays contributed by a total of 85 authors, each a respected scholar in his or her field of specialty. Forty-two of these articles address specific areas of the law, from accident compensation and administrative law to product liability and unjust enrichment, each providing an invaluable summary of the current state of scholarship. Ten articles deal with methodological issues in comparative law, including the idea of a European civil code and the aims of a comparative law. Twenty-four articles provide lucid overviews of the legal systems of specific countries, including, Australia, Belgium, Canada, China, The Czech Republic, England and Wales, Finland, France, Germany, Greece, Israel, Italy, Japan, Lithuania, The Netherlands, Poland, Russia, Scotland South Africa, Spain, Sweden, Switzerland, Turkey, and the United States. Of particular interest are essays on Mixed Systems, and Legal History and Comparative Law. Each essay provides the reader with citations to the work of leading scholars in the field, concluding with a list of references.

Encyclopedia of American Civil Rights and Liberties. Edited by Otis H. Stephens, John M. Scheb, and Kara E. Stooksbury, Westport, CT, Greenwood Press (ABC-CLIO), 2006. 3 vols. (1,448 pp.).
Cost: $349.95; from $43.55 on amazon.com (2014).
This three-volume comprehensive encyclopedia contains over six hundred entries detailing various aspects of civil rights and civil liberties in the United States. These entries embrace such categories as historical events and developments, fundamental concepts, significant trials and court decisions, legal doctrines, important legislation, leading civil liberties organizations, relevant governmental agencies, and key personalities, most with references, and a bibliography. Historically, the entries range from the antecedents of the Bill of Rights to contemporary controversies over such issues as abortion, racial and sexual equality, religious freedom, free speech, voting rights, and the civil liberties issues raised by the war on terrorism. The alphabetically arranged entries are balanced in outlook and moderate in tone. Designed as a scholarly resource, this resource is useful to students at all levels, teachers, and the general public. The third volume concludes with over three-dozen significant primary documents, including key statutes, court decisions, and influential essays, from the Alien and Sedition Acts (1798) to the USA Patriot Act (2001). Volume three also contains a table of cases and subject index. The entries are written by a team of attorneys, judges, and legal scholars.

Encyclopedia of the Fourth Amendment. Edited by John R. Vile and David L. Hudson, Jr. Washington, DC: CQ Press, 2013. 2 vol.
Cost: $350.00; from $320.65 on amazon.com (2014).
The Fourth Amendment to the United States Constitution specifies that "the right of the people to be secure in their persons, houses, papers, and effects, against unreasonable searches and seizures, shall not be violated, and no Warrants shall issue, but upon probable cause, supported by Oath or affirmation, and particularly describing the place to be searched, and the persons or things to be seized." This two-volume reference work covers the key concepts, laws and legal doctrines, court decisions, events, and litigators and litigants that have defined the Fourth Amendment since 1791. It contains over 900 A to Z entries that address the key issues surrounding this critical component of the Bill of Rights, and an essential pillar of our right to privacy. This includes the application of the 4th Amendment to advances in technology and the threat of terrorism, which has resulted in increased governmental surveillance into our personal lives. Entries also include cross-references and bibliographic entries. The work also includes both alphabetical and topical tables of contents as well as a comprehensive subject and case indices.

Federal Regulatory Directory. 16th ed. Washington, D.C.: CQ Press, 2013. Published every two years.
Cost: $185.00; from $159.49 on amazon.com (2014).
A detailed guide to federal regulatory departments, agencies, offices, commissions, boards, etc. Contains organizational charts and names and telephone numbers of officials and government functionaries. Also features detailed descriptions of regulatory agencies and sub-agencies, including information sources, sources of rules and regulations, administrative proceedings, dockets, data and statistics, publications, and leading legislation. An essential resource for the attorney practicing before regulatory bodies.

Filson, Lawrence E. and Sandra L. Strokoff. **The Legislative Drafter's Desk Reference**. 2d ed. Washington, DC: CQ Press, 2007. 1 vol. (583 pp.).
Cost: $130.00 (2014).
A conceptual and procedural guide to the drafting of legislative bills and administrative regulations intended for use by legislative staff, lobbyists, legal professionals and students. This step-by-step guide to bill drafting, which updates the 1992 edition, reflects the impact of the Internet and word processing technology on the legislative process. Its parts include: general overview; the first stage: preparing to put pen to paper; writing the bill: preliminary considerations; writing the provisions of a prototypical bills; writing Amendatory provisions; style, form and usage generally; the role of the courts; the uniquely federal forms and styles; and state and regulatory drafting considerations. A useful summary of the rules of statutory construction appears in chapter 8. The volume concludes with a "Quick Guide to **The Legislative Drafter's Desk Reference**," in outline form.

Forensic Services Directory. San Diego, CA: National Forensic Center. Updated continuously.
Cost: Available online at no charge at: http://www.national-experts.com/
The Internet Online Directory is a continuously updated online edition of the **National Directory of Expert Witnesses**. It includes over 2,000 expert listings from across the nation in over 400 categories of technical, scientific and medical expertise. The experts listed in the online directory can be searched by keyword, browsed by detailed subject category, or listed by name or company name. There is no charge for accessing the Internet Online Directory. The experts and organizations included in the directory pay a fee for their listings.

Fox, Elyse H. **How to File Looseleaf Services**. Chapel Hill, NC: Legal Information Services, 2004. 1 vol. (100 pp.). Spiralbound.
Cost: $45.00 (2014).
This comprehensive guide to looseleaf services addresses all aspects of their filing and maintenance. Written by Elyse H. Fox of Legal Information Services (see Appendices A & B for contact information), **How to File Looseleaf Services** is a detailed examination of all types of publications issued in a looseleaf format, including discussion of the nature and organization of looseleaf services generally, filing instructions and procedures, shifting among binders, transfer binders, filing problems, and suggestions from other looseleaf filers. It also includes sample filing instructions from sixteen looseleaf publishers, with annotations by the author, and a filer's quiz with answers.

Fox, Elyse. **Legal Research Q & A: 401 Flashcards with Companion Book.** Charlotte, NC: Legal Information Services, 2011. 1 vol. (looseleaf format) with 401 flashcards.
Cost: $85.00 (2014).
This invaluable pedagogical tool provides law students, law librarians, lawyers, and summer associates with an effective means of mastering the basics of legal research and legal bibliography. The flashcards ask three types of questions: fill-in-the-blank, true/false, and multiple choice. The questions cover the following types of publications or topical areas: legal research generally, authority, court reports, statutes, legislative history, administrative law, court rules, attorney general opinions, digests, citation, citators, and law books. The questions and answers are replicated in the pages of the looseleaf binder. The flashcards are printed on heavy card stock with a storage bag and companion looseleaf book. Elyse Fox received her B.A. in 1972 from the University of Michigan, her J.D. in 1975 from the University of Michigan Law School, and her M.S.L.S. in 1981 from Simmons College Graduate School of Library and Information Science. She is the editor of the **Legal Information Management Index, Law Librarian's Bulletin Board**, and author of **How to File Looseleaf Services, The Legal Research Dictionary**, and the **Jury Instructions Drafting Manual and Resource Guide**.

French, Mary Mel. **United States Protocol: The Guide to Official Diplomatic Etiquette**. Lanham, MD: Rowman & Littlefield, 2010 (June). 1 vol. (472 pp.).
Cost: $49.95; e-book: $43.99; from $30.35 on amazon.com (2014).
An essential reference guide for those whose responsibilities involve interaction and communication with government and business officials, international organizations, and high-level military personnel in the United States and abroad. The volume includes meticulous instructions, in-depth diagrams and tables, a comprehensive table of contents, and a variety of examples drawn from the author's experience in the White House. Ambassador Mary Mel French, a graduate of the University of Arkansas (B.A. International Relations) served as the nation's Chief of Protocol during the Clinton administration.

Furi-Perry, Ursula, ed. **The Legal Assistant's Complete Desk Reference: A Handbook for Paralegals and Assistants**. Chicago: American Bar Association, 2011. 1 vol. (454 pp.). with companion CD-ROM. Paperbound.
Cost: $199.95; from $74.99 on amazon.com (2013).
According to the ABA, "a legal assistant or paralegal is a person qualified by education, training or work experience who is employed or trained by a lawyer, law office, corporation, governmental agency or other entity who performs specifically designated substantive legal work for which a lawyer is responsible." The type of tasks which a paralegal may perform is limited only by statutory or court authority or by a supervising attorney's determination. In addition to generalized support tasks, paralegals have expanded their practice into a variety of highly technical and specialized subject areas. This comprehensive text provides paralegals with an overview of the most common areas of legal practice in which they operate and the career opportunities open to them. Opening with a look at a typical day in the life of a legal assistant, the author examines court systems and procedures; the preparation of legal instruments, documents and court filings; legal research and writing; trial preparation; and summaries of some of the leading areas of practice in which paralegals are likely to be involved, including bankruptcy and collections, corporate and business law, labor and employment, estate planning, family law, real estate, and intellectual property. The volume also includes a CD-ROM of sample forms and letters, a state-by-state listing of online resources, a glossary of legal terms, and subject index. This book is an essential primer for any person contemplating or beginning a career as a paralegal or legal assistant. Attorney Ursula Furi-Perry is author of eight books and over 300 articles on various aspects of legal practice.

Gallacher, Ian. **A Form and Style Manual for Paralegals**. Durham, NC: Carolina Academic Press, 2007. 1 vol. (218 pp.).
Cost: $25.00; from $17.89 on amazon.com (2014).
Designed for paralegals and paralegal students, this brief manual guides users through all stages of the writing process, from preparing to write to completing a finished draft. It uses easy to understand and jargon-free language to provide practical suggestions on grammar, punctuation, usage, document formatting, editing and proofreading. It is designed to provide paralegals with a concise overview of the mechanics of writing lucid, technically accurate, and effective legal documents. Ian Gallacher is a Professor of Law and Director of Legal Research and Writing program at Syracuse University College of Law and formerly a partner at the law firm Goodell, DeVries, Leech and Dann in Baltimore.

Garner, Bryan A. **The Elements of Legal Style**. 2d ed. New York: Oxford University Press, 2002. 1 vol. (288 pp.).
Cost: $30.00; from $10.20 on amazon.com (2014).
An essential guide to legal writing and style by the leading authority in the field. The author addresses matters of punctuation, grammar, word choice, syntax, and the manner in which these are incorporated into the legal brief, opinion, or

memorandum. There is also discussion of writing style, words and expressions used and misused, footnotes, citations, and contractions, among other topics. The list of rules covered in the book is printed on the front and back inside covers for easy reference. The detailed index includes references to rules and to the authors quoted throughout the text. A professor of law at Southern Methodist University School of Law, Bryan Garner is the author of numerous reference books on legal writing and style and served as editor-in-chief of the 7th edition of **Black's Law Dictionary**. The **ABA Appellate Practice Journal** has described him as "the preeminent expert in America on good legal writing.

Garner, Bryan A. **Garner's Dictionary of Legal Usage**. 3d ed. New York: Oxford University Press, 2011. 1 vol. (1,032 pp.).
Cost: $65.00 (hardbound); $49.99 (paper); from $8.79 (paper) on amazon.com (2014).
What Henry Fowler did for the English language generally, Bryan Garner has done for the language of the law. Drawing upon judicial opinions for his examples, Garner addresses many problems that arise in the course of legal writing. This reference work is designed to assist the legal draftsman on matters of grammar, syntax, rhetoric, and style and in using legal terms with clarity and precision. An ideal tool for the attorney who wishes to approach legal writing from a fresh perspective.

Garner, Bryan A. **The Redbook: A Manual on Legal Style**. 3d ed. St. Paul, MN: West, 2013. 1 vol. (510 pp.). Paperbound. Available from West Academic.
Cost: $48.00; online: $34; from $40.41 on amazon.com (2014).
A comprehensive guide to the rules of legal writing by the nation's leading authority on the subject. The book includes discussion of the mechanics of legal writing, grammar and usage, and the preparation of a variety of legal documents, including briefs and other court documents, opinion and demand letters, research memos, and contracts. The author discusses the correct usage of more than one thousand words which are most troublesome to writers, and two hundreds terms that have a new meaning in a legal context, and cautions for avoiding stuffy phrases and awkward legalisms, among other features. Bryan Garner has established himself as the nation's leading authority on legal writing, usage, and drafting. A Professor of Law at the Southern Methodist University School of Law, he is the author or co-author of eighteen books on legal writing.

Garner, Bryan A. **The Winning Brief: 100 Tips for Persuasive Briefing in Trial and Appellate Courts**. 3d ed. New York: Oxford University Press, 2013. 1 vol. (528 pp.).
Cost: $59.95; from $51.76 on amazon.com (2014).
Based on the author's famous CLE seminars, this volume covers every detail of brief writing, from organization and design to sentence structure and the presentation of evidence. His effective, point-by-point presentation makes use of many before-and-after examples and choice quotations. Bryan Garner is Professor at Southern Methodist University School of Law and president of LawProse, a Dallas-based company specializing in legal-writing workshops. His many publications include the **Dictionary of Modern Legal Usage** and the **Elements of Legal Style**. He was also the editor-in-chief of the 7th edition of **Black's Law Dictionary**. An essential addition to every law library and library of any lawyer who writes legal briefs.

Gold, Martin B. **Senate Procedure and Practice**. 3d ed. Lanham, MD: Rowman & Littlefield Publishers, 2013. 1 vol. (318 pp.). Paperbound.
Cost: $45.00; from $39.76 on amazon.com; kindle: $26.49 (2014).
The United States Senate is a 21st century institution operating with a core of 18th century rules. Its rules of procedure rest on four pillars, each of which is an exercise of the Senate's power to govern itself pursuant to Article 1, Section 5 of the U.S. Constitution. These pillars include: (1) the Standing Rules of the Senate adopted pursuant Article 1, Section 5 of the U.S. Constitution; (2) special procedures found in rule-making statutes, also written pursuant to the Senate's rule-making power; (3) precedents that interpret the Standing Rules, interpret provisions in rule-making statutes, and interpret other precedents; and (4) unanimous consent orders. This volume provides a lucid explanation of these rules, accompanied by stories and insights which illustrate the intricacies of Senate operations. Martin Gold, a partner in the Washington, DC firm of Covington & Burling, is chairman of its Legislative Practice Group. One of the country's leading experts on congressional procedure, he is a former floor advisor and counsel to Senate Majority Leader Bill Frist and former member of the faculty of Congressional Quarterly.

Gordon, Stacey L. **Online Legal Research: A Guide to Legal Research Services and Other Internet Tools**. Buffalo, NY: William S. Hein & Co., 2003. 1 vol. (427 pp.).
Cost: $79.95; from $74.81 on amazon.com (2014).
Online legal research is developing at a pace almost too rapid for even the most skilled information professionals. Whether in the form of new online services or enhancements to existing services, these developments demand constant attention to continuing education and new product training. This online legal research manual by Stacey Gordon provides legal information professionals with an invaluable tool for maximizing the research potential of both the major and a variety of alternative online legal research services. Her discussion commences with a consideration of the basics of online legal research and examines the criteria by which researchers choose between print and online tools to optimize their research results. She also discusses the process of selecting and evaluating commercial online legal research tools and evaluating information available at no cost on the Internet. The bulk of the book's substantive content is devoted to detailed discussion of the content, features and search techniques for using LexisNexis and Westlaw. However, she also devotes some attention to Loislaw, VersusLaw, HeinOnline, and, to a lesser degree, Fastcase, the most recent entry into the field. The book's concluding chapters examine legal research on the Internet, including directories and portals, search engines, search engine tips, and a description of the leading search engines. She concludes with a consideration of legal research tools and substantive practice areas on the Internet. Two appendices provide lists of leading federal court and state legal and government websites. An invaluable contribution to the literature on online legal research in its broadest sense. Stacey L. Gordon is Director of the William J. Jameson Law Library at the University of Montana.

The Gregg Reference Manual. By William A. Sabin. Tribute Edition. New York: McGraw-Hill/Irwin, 2010. 1 vol. (784 pp.). Spiralbound.
Cost: $95.67; from $42.90 on amazon.com; kindle: $52.82 (2014).
Arguably the best reference guide to the rules of writing, gram-

mar, usage, style, and format in business and academic environments. An essential tool for anyone who writes, edits or prepares copy for final distribution. Rules are illustrated with numerous examples. Includes information on editing, proofreading, and filing, letters and memos, report and manuscripts, notes and bibliographies, tables, and forms of address. Also includes glossaries of grammatical and computer terms.

Guide to International Legal Research. George Washington University Law School International Law Review. 5th ed. Newark, NJ: LexisNexis Matthew Bender, 2013. 1 vol. Softbound.
Cost: $301.00; ebook: $330.00; kindle edition: $240.00; from $238.88 on amazon.com (2014).
This practical guide provides both novices and experienced researchers with the tools necessary to research issues and problems in international legal research. Chapter one examines the researching of international law in an age of globalization. Chapters 2-4 describe and explain the use of primary and secondary sources, research tools, and online databases in international legal research. Chapter 5 examines international legal research techniques and resources by geographic and geopolitical region, including Africa, Asia, Russia, European Union, the Middle East, and Latin America.

Guide to Congress. 7th ed. Washington, D.C.: CQ Press, 2012. 2 vols. (1,668 pp.).
Cost: $445.00; from $129.99 on amazon.com (2014).
A comprehensive reference work on the history, structure, powers, procedures, and political environment of the United States Congress. Authored by the CQ Press editors, the seventh edition addresses the origins and development of Congress, its powers and procedures, pressures on Congress, housing and support, pay and perquisites, Congress and the electorate, and qualifications and conduct. It also examines such topics as the power of the purse, foreign policy powers, impeachment power, party leadership, the legislative process, committee structure, Congressional staff, constituent pressures, media and internal pressures, Supreme Court, the President, the Library of Congress, the Capitol and congressional office buildings, lobbying activities, pay and perquisites, allowances and other benefits, campaign financing, Congress and the electorate, political parties, and elections. Also considered are reapportionment and redistricting, qualifications and conduct, seating and disciplining of members, ethics and criminal prosecutions, rules of the House and Senate, the process by which a bill becomes law, and much more. The text is enhanced by numerous charts, illustrations, and bibliographies, primary source documents, and a complete list of members of Congress from 1789-2011. An invaluable reference work for any law, academic or public library, student, scholar of the American political process, member of Congress, or group or individual with business before Congress. Periodic new editions. Prior edition published in 2007.

Guide to Foreign Law Firms. Edited by James R. Silkenat and William M. Hannay. 5th ed. Chicago: American Bar Association, 2010. 1 vol. (496 pp.). Paperbound.
Cost: $64.95 ($49.95 to members); from $14.90 on amazon.com (2014).
This directory of foreign law firms in 148 jurisdictions is designed to assist lawyers in both the United States and elsewhere in locating qualified legal counsel in countries with which they are likely to conduct business, principally international commercial business transactions. American firms with foreign offices are included only if they possess a strong indigenous foreign law capacity. The volume concludes with chapters on selecting and dealing with foreign lawyers, and selecting and working with foreign counsel.

Guide to the Presidency. 5th ed. Edited by Michael Nelson, Washington, DC: CQ Press, 2012. 2 vols. (2,141 pp.).
Cost: $470.00; from $398.10 on amazon.com (2014).
This massive and magisterial compendium assembles a wealth of factual, historical, descriptive and analytical information on the American Presidency and Vice Presidency. Under the general editorship of Michael Nelson, professor of political science, Rhodes College, twenty scholars in the fields of history, political science, and communications contributed articles to this monumental undertaking. Its thirty-four chapters are grouped under seven parts, including those devoted to the Origins and Development of the Presidency; Selection and Removal of the President; Powers of the Presidency; The President, the Public and the Parties; The Presidency and the Executive Branch; Chief Executive and Federal Government; and Presidents, Their Families, and Life in the White House and Beyond. Part VIII contains biographies of every President, Vice-President, and First Lady. Volume two concludes with a selection of the most significant American political documents, including the U.S. Constitution, a number of leading Presidential speeches and addresses, and a number of valuable tables and graphs relating to the history of the Presidents and Presidential, elections. Each article is accompanied by extensive footnotes to sources, and a selected bibliography. The articles are models of intellectual precision and clarity, combining an admirable combination of sweeping overview and captivating detail, and reflecting a balanced philosophical tone. An essential reference work for any law, academic or public library, scholar of the American political process, member of Congress, or contender for the Presidency.

Hadden, Sally E. and Alfred L. Brophy, eds. **A Companion to American Legal History**. Malden, MA: Wiley-Blackwell, 2013. 1 vol. (582 pp.).
Cost: $200.95; from $147.80 on amazon.com (2014).
This collection of historiographical essays tracks recent scholarship on American legal history from the 17th century to the present day. The first six essays in Part I are chronological in nature, covering the 17th century, 1700-1775, 1775-1815; the Antebellum era through the Civil War, 1865-1920, and 1920-1970. The seven essays in Part II address various individual and groups, beginning with Native Americans, and continuing through African-Americans, women, families, immigrants, and the legal profession. Part III looks at a number of significant subject areas, from various aspects of law and the economy to law and labor, legal history and poverty, taxes, law and the administrative state, law and religion, legal history and the military, criminal law and justice, and intellectual property. Part IV examines legal thought, including law and literature, legal thought from Blackstone to Kent to Story, American jurisprudence in the 19th and early 20th centuries, critical legal studies, and the international context. Each essay is accompanied by a list of references. This is a significant contribution to the area of legal history and an indispensable resource and springboard to any scholar working in the field. Sally E. Hadden is Associate Professor History at Western Michigan University. Alfred L. Brophy is the Judge John J. Parker Distinguished Professor of

Law at the University of North Carolina.

Hasl-Kelchner, Hanna. **The Business Guide to Legal Literacy: What Every Manager Should Know About the Law**. San Francisco: Jossey-Bass, 2006. 1 vol. (372 pp.).
Cost: from $11.89 on amazon.com (2014).
Navigating the legal landscape in an increasingly complex and competitive regulatory, environmental and ethical environment is a daunting responsibility for any business manager. Awareness of the legal environment in which business operates will not only help reduce potential risks and liabilities, but also position a company for maximum competitive advantage. This volume addresses a number of topics of critical importance to the modern business manager, drawing upon the nexis between business, law, decision-making psychology, quality management, organizational change, and qualities of leadership to reduce a company's risk profile, raise its level of corporate compliance, and position it for growth and profitability. The author, a corporate lawyer and former adjunct professor at the Duke University Fuqua School of Business, provides managers with a invaluable roadmap to creating a culture of compliance in any corporate structure, using dozens of real life examples to illustrate important concepts and guidelines. This book should be required reading for any corporate manager.

Hazelton, Penny A., ed. **Specialized Legal Research**. Seattle, WA: University of Washington Law Library (formerly Aspen Publishers), 1997-date. 1 vol. (various pagings). Supplemented annually.
Cost: $350.00 (new edition); supplementation: 2000: $122; 2001: $130; 2002: $142; 2003: $165; 2004: $183; 2005: $196; 2006: $182; 2007: $194; 2008: $208; 2009: $228; 2010: $244; 2011: $262; 2012: $280; 2013: $195.
An in-depth guide to legal research in thirteen specialized area of the law, including securities regulation, the Uniform Commercial Code, Federal income taxation, copyright law, Federal labor and employment law, environmental law and land use planning, admiralty and maritime law, immigration law, military and veterans law, banking law, Federal patent and trademark law, government contracts, customs law. Originally published by Little, Brown, the editorship has now passed to Penny A. Hazelton, Professor of Law and Law Librarian, University of Washington School of Law and Associate Dean of Library and Computing Service. Withdrawn from the Wolters Kluwer catalog in 2013. Now published by the University of Washington M.G. Gallagher Law Library, with a new edition issued in May, 2014.

Hewette, Amber and Diane Hurley. **Law for the Layperson: An Annotated Bibliography of Self-Help Law Books**. 3d ed. Buffalo, NY: William S. Hein & Co., 2006. 1 vol. (486 pp.).
Cost: $78.00; from $29.00 on amazon.com (2014).
A useful annotated bibliography of legal self-help books organized under 68 topical headings. An update of Frank G. Houdek's **Law for the Layman** (1991),and Jean McKnight's **Law for the Layperson** (1997). It also includes author, title, and jurisdiction indices, and a list of publishers.

Hoffman, Marci and Robert C. Berring. **International Legal Research in a Nutshell**. St. Paul, MN: West Academic, 2008. 1 vol. (313 p.). Paperbound.
Cost: $41; from $13.86 on amazon.com (2014).
This basic introduction to international legal research for the non-specialist examines foreign law sources, the law sources of international and regional legal bodies, and treaties. Attention is given to public, private, foreign, international, and supranational law. Includes discussion of United Nations and European Union document and materials. Both print and Internet sources are discussed.

Index to Course Handbooks. New York: Practising Law Institute. Annual.
Cost: No charge, but only available to subscribers to one or more PLI course handbook series.
A useful means of ascertaining the contents of PLI seminar Handbooks; particularly useful in the case of emerging topics.

Insider's Guide to the Key Committee Staff of the U.S. Congress [formerly The Almanac of the Unelected]. Edited by Lisa Friedman. 22nd edition. Lanham, MD: Bernan Press, 2009. 1 vol. (788 pp.). Annual (September).
Cost: $99.95 (paper); from $73.43 on amazon.com (2014).
This guide provide valuable information regarding the individuals who provide legislative and policy support to members of the United States Congress. It includes profiles of staffers to Senate and House leadership as well as those with policy expertise assigned to specific Senate and House Committees. Each profile, submitted by the staffer in question, includes a description of his or her background and policy expertise. Unlike entries in other biographical directories, these profiles are often written from a partisan perspective, reflecting the views of the staffers' party or member of Congress.

Jones, Rachel W., ed. **Federal Regulatory Research: Selected Agency Knowledge Paths**. Binghamton, NY: Routledge Publishers/Haworth, 2002. 1 vol. (123 pp.).
Cost: $60.00 (hardcover); $31.95 (softcover); from $1.99 on amazon.com; kindle: $24.85 (2014).
A useful guide to performing research in seven federal regulatory venues, including the National Library of Education, Environmental Protection Agency, Federal Reserve System, Federal Trade Commission, U.S. Patent and Trademark Office, Federal Deposit Insurance Corporation, and the Department of Justice. Originally produced by the Law Librarians' Society of Washington, DC and published as a special issue of the **Legal Reference Services Quarterly**, each pathfinder guides the user through the maze of relevant federal statutes, regulations, interpretative releases, memoranda, dockets, etc.

The Judicial Branch of Federal Government: People, Process, and Politics. Edited by Charles L. Zelden. Santa Barbara, CA: ABC-CLIO, Inc., 2007. 1 vol. (441pp.)
Cost: $95.00; from $0.99 on amazon.com (2014).
This useful overview of the federal judicial branch of government combines an examination of the judicial process with the encyclopedic features of a library reference work. The contributors bring an historical perspective to the discussion of the federal courts at all levels, with five substantive chapters devoted to the roles, functions and powers of the courts, their structure and process, the individuals who serve in the judicial capacity, the politics of the courts, and interactions with other branches of government. The volume also includes a glossary of concepts, laws, and people; a list of federal judges and the Presidents who nominated them; a list of judges and their race, gender and ethnicity; significant documents related to the history of

the federal judiciary, including selected laws and articles of the Constitution; and landmark decisions of he U.S. Supreme Court. The volume wisely focuses on the entire federal judiciary. For while the Supreme Court now handles about 8,000 certiorari petitions per year, it disposes of less than 100 cases on their merits. This leaves a tremendous volume of cases disposed at the level of the district courts or courts of appeals. Charles L. Zelden is professor of history at Nova Southeastern University, Fort Lauderdale, FL. The contributing authors are all historians. The volume is a component of the publisher's *About Federal Government* reference set.

Kunz, Christina L., et al. **The Process of Legal Research: Authorities and Options**. 8th ed. New York: Wolters Kluwer Law & Business, 2012. 1 vol. (274 pp.). Paperbound.
Cost: $95.00; from $29.90 on amazon.com (2014).
A lucid and well-illustrated introduction to legal research by a team of experienced law librarians from William Mitchell College of Law. Chapters cover literacy in the law, focusing on our client's situation, framing your legal research, case law research, research in enacted law, research in legislative history materials, research in administrative materials, research in rules of procedure, and international law and tribal law. The text is augmented with useful charts, illustrations, and sample pages to guide the novice through the complexities of the legal research process.

Larson, Joni and Dan Sheaffer. **Federal Tax Research**. 2d ed. Durham, NC: Carolina Academic Press, 2011. 1 vol. (369 pp.). Hardbound.
Cost: $57.00; from $18.38 on amazon.com (2014).
Federal tax research is similar in many ways with other types of legal research. These commonalities include the need to gather the relevant facts, isolate the legal issue(s) involved, ascertain what law applies to the resolution of the issue, determine how the issue is resolved when the law is applied to the relevant facts, and communicate the results of the research. Federal tax law may be found in a variety of sources, including the Internal Revenue Code (Title 26 of the United States Code), tax regulations, federal court decisions, legislative history, and both public and taxpayer specific guidance from the Office of Chief Counsel of the Internal Revenue Service (IRS). Forms of Public Guidance include Revenue Rulings, Revenue Procedures, Notices and Announcements, Actions on Decisions, and IRS Publications. These and other federal tax documents are published in the Internal Revenue Bulletin. Taxpayer specific guidance may take the form of Private Letter Rulings, Determination Letters, Information Letters, and Technical Advice Memoranda. In addition, there is a wealth of documents generated by the Office of Chief Counsel for Internal Use, including Field Service Advice, Technical Assistance, Service Center Advice, General Counsel Memoranda, Legal Memoranda, and more. In addition to a thorough exposition of all the relevant sources for federal tax research, the authors also discuss the research process; international tax research, cite checking, law reviews, journals and other publications; and the process of organizing the research into a finished product. The volume also includes a useful chart indicating sources for judicial opinions, both official and commercial. As a law school textbook, each chapter includes citations to related articles for further reading, and multiple choice problems for student use. The authors are professors of law, Thomas M. Cooley Law School.

Law Books and Serials in Print: A Multimedia Sourcebook. New Providence, NJ: R. R. Bowker. Annual (June). 3 vols. Purchase includes mid-year cumulative supplement.
Cost: 2013 Edition (June): $1,210.00 (includes cumulative supplement); 10% discount in first year to standing order customers; 5% discount in subsequent years.
A comprehensive guide to more than 90,000 legal titles, including books, serials, microfiche, videocassettes, software and online databases. Some entries include brief annotations. Generally recommended for purchase only by larger law libraries. Attorneys are encouraged to consult this resource in their local state, court, county, bar association, or academic library. While the information is generally reliable, independent verification is recommended given the breadth of coverage.

The Lawyer's Almanac 2014: The Leading Reference of Vital Facts and Figures About the Legal Profession. New York: Wolters Kluwer Law & Business, 2013. 1 vol. (various pagings). Annual (Dec.). Paperbound.
Cost: 2014 Edition: $445.00.
A valuable compendium of facts and figures on the courts, government, law schools, and the legal profession. Includes a detailed listing of the nation's 700 largest law firms, with rates of compensation, and billing rates, CLE requirements for the 40 states with have them, federal and state court judges, bar associations, litigation statistics, leading Internet legal research sites, and much more.

Lawyers Desk Reference. 9th ed. Compiled by Harry M. Philo. St. Paul, MN: West Group, 2001-date. 4 vols. Annual supplementation. Also available on twice annual CD-ROM.
Cost: $751.00; ProView eBook: $380; supplementation: 1994: $160.00; 1995: $150.00; 1996: $195.00; 1997: $195.00; 1998: $197.50; 1999: $ 213.00; 2000: $265.00; 2001: new edition; 2003: $95.00; 2003: $108.00; 2004: $108.00; 2005: $119.50; 2006: $119.50; 2007: $148.00; 2008: $175.00; 2009: $198.50; 2010: $232.00; 2011: $255; 2012: $283; 2013: $304. **Assured Print Pricing (APP)**: $37.00 mo./$444.00 yr.
Written primarily for the plaintiff's trial lawyer or law firm, this three-volume set provides exhaustive listings of expert witnesses, safety organizations, safety standards and codes, safety films, government information centers, citations to OSHA standards in the CFR, international safety sources, technical safety publications, medical sources, drug product investigation sources, biotechnology and the law, environmental sources, and a host of other areas. An essential tool for the personal injury law firm.

Legal Information Alert. Chicago: Alert Publications, Inc., 1981-date. Published 10 times a year.
Cost: Discontinued; Published from 1981-2011 (v. 30, No.1)
The leading current awareness product in the world of legal information. Editor and publisher Donna Tuke Heroy and her team of editors and contributors provide readers with a timely collection of feature articles and reviews of current legal information sources, both print and electronic. An essential tool for any legal information professional. Both **Legal Information Alert** and **Business Information Alert** ceased publication in 2011.

Legal Information Management Index. Chapel Hill, NC: Legal Information Services, 1984-date. Bimonthly with annual cumulation. (980) 333-3049.
Cost: Discontinued in 2013. Was $188.00 per year ($178.00 online); combination print and online: $238.00 (includes annual cumulation); Online Historic Access only: $100.00 (2014).
This index was edited and published for thirty years by law librarian and attorney Elyse Fox. It indexed 92 periodicals published in the United States, Canada and abroad. Indexed literature includes substantive English-language articles, bibliographies and surveys, and critical reviews of monographs, serials, software and hardware, online databases, microforms, CD-ROMs, looseleaf services, and audio-visual materials. Articles are indexed by key word, and by author. Book reviews are indexed by title. For law librarians, this is the best vehicle for keeping up with the flood of information in the fields of law librarianship and legal information management. Online access was added in 2006. In 2013, the **LIMI** decided to cease publication and offered access to historical information in the database (Vol. 22 - Vol. 30).

Legal Looseleafs in Print. Compiled and edited by Arlene L. Eis. Teaneck, NJ: Infosources Publishing, 1981-date. Updated continuously.
Cost: Available as online subscription only: $199 per year individually; or as part of **LawTRIO Law Publications Database**, combining the **Directory of Law-Related CD-ROMs**, **Legal Looseleafs in Print**, and **Legal Newsletters in Print** at a cost of $339.00 per year.
An exhaustive compilation of bibliographical data for over 3,600 looseleaf publications from 270 different publishers. Includes true looseleaf services, such as those from CCH, BNA, and RIA, and post-binder publication such as those published by Matthew Bender. Basically, coverage includes legal publications contained in ring or post-bound (compression) binders as opposed to permanently bound books. Each entry includes title, author, publisher, date of publication, number of volumes, cost and supplementation cost, frequency of supplementation, recent supplementation cost, Library of Congress control number/ OCLC control number/LC classification, and indicates whether it is available online or on CD-ROM. Entries are indexed by publisher, subject, and electronic format. A publishers' directory provides addresses and telephone numbers for all publishers represented. A valuable guide to what is generally an expensive form of publication.

Legal Newsletters in Print. Compiled and edited by Arlene L. Eis. Teaneck, NJ: Infosources Publishing, 1981-date. Updated continuously.
Cost: Available as online subscription only: $199 per year individually; or as part of **LawTRIO Law Publications Database**, combining the **Directory of Law-Related CD-ROMs**, **Legal Looseleafs in Print**, and **Legal Newsletters in Print** at a cost of $339.00 per year.
A comprehensive guide to more than 2,200 legal newsletters, including standard-type newsletters, bulletins, newsletter-reporting services, and all reporting services issued periodically and stored in looseleaf binders. Does not include publications that require interfiling (see Legal Looseleafs in Print). Each entry includes full bibliographical detail, including sources of indexing, online availability, and description. In addition to the main Title List, there is a publisher index, list of newsletters online, database list, database index, a list of newsletters registered with the Copyright Clearance Center, newsletters that accept advertising, and a subject index. An excellent resource for the attorney or law firm interested in tracking down newsletters in specific subject areas and evaluating available alternatives. Entries include annual subscription costs.

Legal Researchers Desk Reference. Compiled and edited by Arlene Eis. Teaneck, NJ: Infosources Publishing. 1 vol. (424 pp.). Companion web site available on the Internet via password at: www.infosourcespub.com
Cost: 2013-2014 Edition: $75.00; newsletter: $99 (6x) (2014).
An excellent desktop reference tool containing a variety of basic directory information useful to the legal researcher. Information is organized under thirteen broad subject headings: federal government, legislative information, state information, international information, law library suppliers directory, associations and organizations, law librarianship, law schools in the U.S. and Canada, bar admission, legal periodicals, financial and economic information, and miscellaneous information.

The Legislative Drafter's Desk Reference. 2d ed. Washington, DC: CQ Press, 2007. 1 vol. (583 pp.).
Cost: $130.00 (2014).
A conceptual and procedural guide to the drafting of legislative bills and administrative regulations intended for use by legislative staff, lobbyists, legal professionals and students. This step-by-step guide to the bill drafting, which updates the 1992 edition, reflects the impact of the Internet and word processing technology on the legislative process.

Leiter, Richard A., ed. **National Survey of State Laws**. 6th ed. Detroit: Gale Cengage Learning, 2007. 1 vol. (808 pp.). Hardbound.
Cost: $168.00; also available as e-book; from $1.13 on amazon.com (2014).
A valuable overview of state laws in forty-two of the most important and controversial subject areas. The information is presented in chart format with citations to applicable state statutes. The forty-two topics fall within eight broad legal categories: business and commercial laws, criminal laws, education laws, employment laws, family laws, general civil laws, real estate law, and tax laws. An excellent resource for the law firm which owns few state codes, but requires occasional access to comparative information regarding the laws of other states. Since this work is not supplemented (except in the form of new editions), the user must be careful to verify the currency of the information contained therein by consulting the appropriate current state code.

Levitt, Carole A. and Mark E. Rosch. **The Cybersleuth's Guide to the Internet: Conducting Effective Investigative & Legal Research on the Web.** 12th ed. Rio Rancho, NM: Internet for Lawyers, 2012. 1 vol. (560 pp.).
Cost: $64.95 (2014).
Formerly titled **Internet for Legal & Investigative Research: A Guide for Legal Professionals**, this volume provides legal researchers and investigators with tools and techniques for conducting low-cost research on the Internet, including sources for locating missing persons, personal information, phone numbers, public records, property records, birth and death records, social security numbers, employers, aliases, and negative information to attack a person's credibility, much of it available on free

Internet sources. The author also provides sources for conducting free legal research on the Internet, including sources of caselaw, federal state and local primary law, secondary sources, and legal practice materials. The author is a nationally recognized author and speaker on Internet legal research, with over twenty years of experience in the legal field as a law librarian, professor of law, attorney and Internet trainer. She is President and founder of Internet For Lawyers.

Levitt, Carole A. and Mark E. Rosch. **Finding Info Like a Pro: Mining the Internet's Public Records for Investigative Research**. Chicago: American Bar Association, 2011. 1 vol. (280 pp.). Paperbound.
Cost: $79.95 ($47.95 to members); from $45.94 on amazon.com (2014).
This invaluable resource is designed to assist those interested in conducting investigative and or background research at little or no cost. With clearly written language, helpful graphics, and illustrative screen shots, the authors guide the researcher through the intricacies of Internet research in a host of public and private records databases, social networking sites, genealogical sites, news, expert witness databases, consumer credit reports, telephone and address records, and online communities. They also provide helpful guidance In using search engines, summarization search engines, and meta search sites for investigative research. Highlighted websites are accompanied by helpful graphics indicating whether the site is free, feed-based, or requires registration. A companion CD-ROM contains a hyperlinked index of the web sites listed in the book. This volume represents Levitt and Rosch's updating of Joshua Blackman's **The Internet Fact Finder for Lawyers** (ABA), which they re-titled **The Lawyers Guide to Fact Finding on the Internet**. Volume 2: **Mining the Internet's Public Records for Investigative Research** is also available from the ABA at the same price as volume one.

Levitt, Carole A. and Mark E. Rosch. **Google for Lawyers: Essential Search Tips and Productivity Tools**. Chicago: American Bar Association, 2010. 1 vol. (514 pp.). Paperbound.
Cost: $79.95 ($47.95 to members); from $39 on amazon.com (2014).
Launched in March, 1996 by two Stanford University PhD students, Larry Page and Sergey Brin, Google has grown to become the world's leading Internet search tool and a major corporate entity which was added to the Standard & Poor 500 in 2006. Initially funded by the National Science Foundation and other federal agencies, the Stanford Digital Library Project's (SDLP) goal was "to develop the enabling technologies for a single, integrated and universal digital library." At its peak in 2004, Google was responsible for 84.7% of all search requests on the Internet through its own website and its partnerships with such Internet clients as Yahoo!, AOL, and CNN. Google's success may be attributed to its superior search capability, its clean and uncluttered design, its use of personal data to improve searching based on the user profiles, and to corporate acquisitions that have added to its competitive ability to use information gleaned from blog postings to improve the speed and relevance of articles contained in a companion product to the search engine, Google News. Harnessing the power of Google for legal and law-related research is the subject of this excellent desktop research companion. **Google for Lawyers** is intended as a practical desktop guide for lawyers who want to get the most out of Google for their research and technology needs, and who want to use free and low-cost tools to compete with large firms with superior research and technology budgets. Following an introduction to the Internet, Google, and basic and advanced search strategies, the authors explain the use and manipulation of search results, and a variety of specific Google tools and applications, including Google News, Google Groups, Google Image Search, Google Blog Search, Google Finance, Google Glossary, Google Translate, Google Books, Google maps. Knowledge Management Tools, Google Scholar, Google Apps, Google Voice, Google Search Shortcuts, Google's Uncle Sam Search, and Google Analytics, Google Advertising Services., and more. Instructions are clearly written, easy to follow, and enhanced with numerous sample screens. The text also features practice tips, ethics alerts, and "war stories" gathered from a variety of legal professionals. The Appendices include eight case studies drawn from actual court decisions, a web site credibility check list, Google Scholar Alerts, Google Drawings, and Index. Carole Levitt is a nationally recognized author and speaker on Internet legal research, with over twenty years of experience in the legal field as a law librarian, professor of law, attorney and Internet trainer. She is President and founder of Internet For Lawyers. Mark Rosch is Vice President of Internet for Lawyers and developer and manager of the Internet for Lawyers web site. A frequent speaker on Internet research and technology issues, he is co-author (with Carole Levitt) of numerous titles on Internet research for the legal profession.

Long, Judy A. **Office Procedures for the Legal Professional** (West Legal Studies Series). Clinton Park, NY: Thomson/ Delmar Learning, 2005. 1 vol. (411 pp.).
Cost: $129.95; $43.95 (paper); from $2.84 on amazon.com (2014).
An introductory textbook providing guidance in law office procedures and practices, with attention to trial procedures in civil and criminal contexts, and practices in the specific fields of estate planning, probate, family law, business organizations, bankruptcy, real property, and contracts. Designed as a textbook for paralegal students, this work is also useful as an introductory office procedures manual. The author is an attorney and retired professor and program director of paralegal studies.

Maddex, Robert L. **Encyclopedia of Sexual Behavior and the Law**.
Washington, DC: CQ Press, 2006. 1 vol. (419 pp.).
Cost: $155.00; from $2.09 on amazon.com (2014).
An encyclopedic dictionary of over 150 key concepts, sexual practices, perversions, organizations, legal terms, court decisions, government agencies, personalities, and statutes at the intersection of sexual behavior and the law. The entries, which average 2-3 pages, provide the reader with a useful combination of descriptive, historical, and analytical information as a basis for further exploration of the subject. A number of the entries also include useful tabular information, providing an overview of state laws in such areas as marriage, abortion, genetic privacy, and embryonic and fetal research. Prefatory material includes a chronological list of milestones in sexual behavior and the law. Includes a selective bibliography and detailed subject index. Robert L. Maddex is an attorney specializing in international law who serves as an advisor on constitutional procedures and issues. He is the author of **Congressional Quarterly's Constitutions of**

the World, **Illustrated Dictionary of Constitutional Concepts**, and **State Constitutions of the United States**.

The Manual to Online Public Records: The Researchers Tool to Online Resources of Public Records and Public Information. 3nd ed. Michael L. Sankey and Cynthia Hetherington, eds. Tempe, AZ: BRB Publications, 2013. 1 vol. (572 pp.). Softcover. Available from National Book Network, 4501 Forbes Blvd. Suite 200. Lanham, MD 20706. (301) 459-3366.
Cost: $22.50; from $14.01 on amazon.com (2014).
This essential reference work covers nearly 10,000 online databases, including both government agencies and private sources. The fourth edition contains a 75-page Public Record Primer providing an informative and descriptive explanation of the complexities of public record research, as well as detailed profiles on public record websites for all 50 states, including county, state and federal government agencies. The book also includes a directory of recommended government sites, profiles of over 220 private companies that distribute public records, and a directory of nearly 4,500 no-cost databases. The authors have also published **Find It Online**, **Online Competitive Intelligence**, and **The Sourcebook to Public Record Information** among other titles dedicated to the searching and understanding of public records.

Manz, William H. **Guide to State Legislative and Administrative Materials**. 7th ed. Buffalo, NY: William S. Hein & Co., 2008. 1 vol. (#61 in the AALL Publications Series). Paperbound. 1 vol. (465 pp.).
Cost: $85.00; fro $59.50 on amazon.com (2014).
A guide to the print and electronic sources of administrative and legislative information for the fifty states, the District of Columbia, and the commonwealths and territories. Provides citations to hundreds of free websites. Previously published in 1988 and 2000.

Marke, Julius J. and Richard Sloane. **Legal Research and Law Library Management**. Revised ed. By Linda M. Ryan. New York: Law Journal Press, Inc., 2006-date. 1 vol. (1,000 pp.). Looseleaf format. Updated twice annually.
Cost: $595 (print and online inclusive package); online version only: $560.00; supplementation to prior editions: 1995: $47; 1996: $97; 1997: $110; 1998: $105; 1999: $111; 2000: $111; 2001: $136; 2002: $150; 2003: $163; 2004: $183; 2005: $196; 2006: new edition: $259; 2007: $179; 2008: $295; 2009: $322; 2010: $350; 2011: $434; 2012: $499; from $260.66 on amazon.com (2014).
Intended for both lawyers and law librarians, this work provides detailed practical advice on legal research and law library management, including discussions of legal research technologies, legislative history and intent, business information services, and law library economics. The chapters are based upon articles written by the authors over the years for the **New York Law Journal**. While the book is more a collection of random topics than a systematically organized guide, it contains much material of great value to both lawyers and law librarians. Originally written by the late Julius Marke and the late Richard Sloane, it is now updated by Linda Ryan, Assistant Dean, Library and Information Resources, St. John's University School of Law.

Cost Saving Tip: Unfortunately, under ALM, Law Journal Press has instituted a new pricing model that makes this volume far more costly to purchase and maintain. Formerly, the book was available at $289.00 (discounted to $207.20). Now, the only option is to buy the book as a package with the next year's supplementation and online access for $595.00. Supplementation (including online access) in future years is at $540.00 in 2014, compared to $350.00 (2 x $175.00) in 2010. It is no longer possible to buy the book alone (outside of the package with supplementation). This raises the minimum cost of acquiring this volume from $207.20 to $595.00, (a 187% increase); and supplementation from $350.00 to $434.00 (a 25% increase). In my view, the publisher has clumsily instituted a pricing model best employed with substantive law titles for which supplementation is arguably more critical. The best solution is to purchase this volume at infrequent intervals to counteract the publishers attempt to extract exorbitant and unnecessary annual costs on the purchaser. I recommend buying the package no more than once every five years.

Martindale-Hubbell Law Directory. New Providence, NJ: LexisNexis/Martindale-Hubbell, Inc. 9 vols. 1868-date. Annual. (800) 526-4902.
Cost: 2014 edition: $750.00 (full set); DVD: $1,403.00; individual volumes: $81.00 each; individual state law digests at lexisnexis.com @ $29.00 each; law digest volumes no longer available in print or CD-ROM; Partial data also available on the Web at no charge at: http://www.martindale.com
Published annually since 1868, this is the most comprehensive directory of lawyers in the United States. It includes Basic Practice Profile data on virtually every lawyer in the United States, professional biographies, lawyer and law firm ratings, corporate and government lawyers, and links to law firm web sites. Lawyers who don't wish to purchase the complete directory can acquire individual volumes for $76.00 each, or consult them at their nearest law library. Of particular value are the law digests for individual jurisdictions, including all 50 states, the Canadian provinces, and over 160 foreign countries, now only available as purchasable pdfs on the LexisNexis store: http://www.lexisnexis.com/store. These digests are prepared by leading firms in each jurisdiction and provide an excellent overview of the leading areas of the law, providing helpful citations to state statutory codes and case law.

Matthews, Elizabeth W. **The Law Library Reference Shelf: Annotated Subject Guide**. 5th ed. Buffalo, NY: William S. Hein & Co., Inc., 2003. 1 vol. (156 pp.).
Cost: $55.00; from $29.95 on amazon.com (2014).
An annotated bibliography containing descriptions of hundreds of the most useful reference books for the law library. Included are general almanacs, encyclopedias, biographical works, dictionaries, directories, practice and procedure titles, quotation books, research and bibliographical titles, statistical handbooks, style manuals, and bar association publications. Includes an author/title index. Also available on **Spinelli's Law Library Reference Shelf** on **Hein Online**.

Morehead, Joe. **Introduction to United States Government Information Sources**. 6th ed. Englewood, CO: Libraries Unlimited, 1999. 1 vol. (491 pp.).
Cost: cloth: $65.00; paper: $55.00; from $33.50 on amazon.com (2014).
A lucid and comprehensive guide to United States govern-

ment publications which has deservedly earned a place as one of the standard reference tools in the field and served as a popular student text in courses in government publications. Chapters include: Transformation of Government Information, Government Printing Office Programs and Services, The Federal Depository Library Program, General Finding Aids and Selected Reference Sources, Legislative Branch Information Sources, The Presidency, Administrative Law: Regulations and Decisions, Legal Information Sources, Statistical Sources, Intellectual Property, Selected Departments and Agencies by Function, and Geographic Information Sources. Appendices include: The Impeachment and Trial of the President: A Chronology of Primary Source Materials, a Title/Series Index, and Subject/ Name Index. Joe Morehead is Professor in School of Information Science and Policy at the University at Albany, New York and one of the nation's leading authorities on the subject of United States government publications.

NALP Directory of Law Schools, 2013-2014. Washington, DC: National Association for Law Placement, 2013. Annual (April). Further information available online at: http://www.nalplawschoolsonline.org/index.asp
Cost: online only: no cost to students (2014).
This directory is designed to provide recruitment professionals with information regarding on-campus interviewing schedules and contacts at U.S. and Canadian law schools. It also includes law school enrollment demographics, courses of study, special programs, honors, grading systems and more. It is designed to assist recruiters in learning the recruitment procedures of various law schools and interpreting the resumes of law graduates. All U.S. law schools included in the Directory have received at least provisional ABA accreditation.

NALP Directory of Legal Employers, 2013-2014. Washington, DC: National Association for Law Placement, 2013. Annual (May). Also available online only at: http://www.nalpdirectory.com/
Cost: online only: no cost (2014).
A massive compendium of detailed job-related information for law students and legal professionals. It contains essential information on the hiring needs and employment plans of over 1,700 law firms, government agencies, corporations, and public interest organizations. Information and data are presented in a series of uniform, one-page reports containing an organization's demographics, primary practice areas, employment information, salaries, benefits, minority recruitment efforts, non-discrimination policy, partnership data, other offices, and campus inter-view sites. Each entry also includes a narrative statement summarizing the organization's history, structure, and job climate. Preceding this 1297-page section of firm listings is a series of Fast Find Indexes which list law firms and corporations alphabetically and by state; and public interest organizations and government agencies alphabetically and by state. It also lists all employers by practice area and by office size. Produced under the auspices of the National Association for Law Placement, the **National Directory of Legal Employers** also features useful introductory suggestions for the job applicant and the Principles and Standards for Law Placement and Recruitment Activities.

The National Directory of Expert Witnesses. San Diego, CA: National Directory of Expert Witnesses, 2014. 1 vol. (400 pp.) Annual (in July). Paperbound. (800) 735-6660.
Cost: 2014 ed.: $45.00 + $7.00 s & h (2014).
This volume provides a listing of over 2,000 individuals and organizations offering their services in 400 specific areas of technical, scientific, and medical expertise. An equivalent Internet version is available at no charge at: www.national-experts.com/online.html

National Directory of Process Servers. Portland, OR: National Association of Professional Process Servers, Inc.
Cost: Available online at no cost at: http://napps.org/
(800) 532-6377.
Printed twice annually, this directory is designed to assist in the location of process servers throughout the United States. Entries in Index A are organized alphabetically by state and then by city. Index B is a City-County index providing references to the counties in which cities and towns are located. Index C lists process servers alphabetically by County. The directory contains more than 4,000 listings. Statewide process servers are also identified. The print directory is supplied to all members at no additional cost. The web site allows users to search the organization's database of process servers by zip code. An alternate site, provided by the International Process Servers Association, is located at: http://www.iprocessservers.com/index.asp

Nyberg, Cheryl Rae and Carol Boast Robertson. **State Administrative Law Bibliography: Print and Electronic Sources**. Twin Falls, ID: Carol Boast Robertson and Cheryl Rae Nyberg, 2000. 1 vol. (597 pp.).
Cost: Orders go to: Boast/Nyberg, 1347 Maple Ave, Twin Falls, ID 83301.
A major assault on one of the last redoubts of legal bibliography by a leading law librarian and bibliographer. Cheryl Nyberg and Carol Boast have produced a comprehensive guide to state administrative codes and registers, as well as the more illusive cases, adjudications, findings, interpretations, opinions, orders, rulings issued by state administrative agencies. Subject categories include administrative codes, administrative registers, assorted agencies, attorney ethics, attorney general, campaign finance, civil rights, education, environment, ethics, executive orders, insurance, judicial ethics, legislative ethics, public employees, securities, taxation, unemployment, utilities, and workers' compensation. Coverage includes both print and electronic sources. Orders go to: Boast/Nyberg 1347 Maple Ave. Twin Falls, ID 83301.

Nyberg, Cheryl and Carol Boast Robertson. **Subject Compilations of State Laws**. Twin Falls, ID: C. Boast & C. Nyberg, 1981-date. 23 vols.
Cost: Now available on HeinOnline as well in print.
This bibliographical reference tool contains 50-state surveys on a wide variety of topics as they have appeared in law review articles, judicial opinions, web sites, and the 50-state surveys available on Westlaw and Lexis. The first volume in this series appeared in 1981 and covered the years 1960-1979. Supplementary volumes appeared covering the years 1979-83, 1983-85, 1985-88, and 1988-90. Since 1991, bound volumes have appeared on an annual basis. An electronic version, containing more than 20,000 bibliographical records, was released on Hein Online in 2008, which provides comprehensive coverage of the entire series, from 1960-2012. It won the AALL New Product Award in 2009. Latest volume is the 2011-2012. Orders go to: Boast/Nyberg 1347 Maple Ave.Twin Falls, ID 83301.

Oleszek, Walter J. **Congressional Procedures and the Policy Process**. 9th ed. Washington, DC: CQ Press, 2013. 1 vol. (484 pp.). Paperbound.
Cost: $55.95; from $46.00 on amazon.com; kindle: $48.00 (2014).
Congressional rules and procedures constitute an elaborate apparatus that can be employed to expedite, slow down, or stop legislative action. Part of this complexity lies in the framers' deliberate designs in erecting contrasting deliberative mechanisms for the more responsive House of Representatives and the more deliberative Senate. Since its first appearance in 1978, Walter Oleszek's **Congressional Procedures and Policy Process** has served as an essential and definitive guide to Congressional procedures. This volume provides the reader with a thorough grounding in the intricacies of Congressional procedure, from the budget process and preliminary legislative action to the scheduling of legislation, House floor procedure, scheduling legislation in the Senate, Senate floor procedure, the resolution of House-Senate differences, and legislative oversight of administrative actions. A concluding chapter examines legislative activity as a dynamic process. Numerous real-life examples from the annals of Congress provide valuable insights into the manner in which Congressional procedures are played out in practice. The volume is enhanced with a glossary of Congressional terms, a selected bibliography, a list of Internet sources, and index. Walter Oleszek is a senior specialist in the legislative process at the Congressional Research Service, with extensive experience as a staff aid or consultant to every major Congressional reorganization effort, beginning with the passage of the Legislative Reorganization Act of 1970. The 9th edition brings the discussion down to the first of the Obama administration.

Olson, Kent C. **Legal Information: How to Find It, How to Use It**. Phoenix, AZ: Oryx Press, 1999. 1 vol. (342 pp.).
Cost: $85.00; from $.01 on amazon.com; kindle: $42.35 (2014).
This volume can serve both as an introduction to the major bodies of legal literature and as a supplement to such basic legal research texts as **How to Find the Law**, of which Olson is a co-author. Designed to place the various categories of legal literature in their proper context, it is characterized by excellent organization, clarity of expression, and breadth of coverage. Its twelve chapters cover such topics as an overview of the American legal system, understanding legal information, general reference sources, law books, journals and periodicals, finding lawyers and institutions, the Constitution and the Supreme Court, federal legislation, federal courts, federal administrative law, state legislation and administrative law, and state courts. While the author's primary emphasis is on printed sources, references to electronic sources and the Internet are integrated throughout the text. An essential reference tool for any well-equipped law library or law office. Winner of AALL's Joseph L. Andrews Bibliography Award for 2000. The author is assistant librarian for public services at the University of Virginia School of Law.

Olson, Kent C. **Principles of Legal Research**. St. Paul, MN: West Academic, 2009. 1 vol. (499 pp.). Concise Hornbook Series. Paperbound.
Cost: $48.00; from $8.47 on amazon.com (2014).
This legal research text traces its origins back to the first edition of **How to Find the Law**, first published in 1931. The ninth edition, published in 1989, was long overdue for revision. While this work exhibits some of the characteristics of **How to Find the Law**, it bears the distinctive stamp of its new author. Following a chapter on the context and process of legal research, the author tackles research in constitutional law, the legislature (including statutes and legislative information), the executive branch, the judiciary (including an introduction, case law sources, case law research, and other court information), secondary sources (including encyclopedias, restatements, texts, periodicals, and reference resources), international law, and the law of other countries. The Appendices include a bibliography of legal treatises and looseleaf services by subject, and Resource Index. The author, Director of Reference, Research and Instruction at the University of Virginia Law Library, is the author of **Legal Information: How to Find It, How to Use It** and a co-author, with Morris Cohen, of **Legal Research in a Nutshell.**

The Oxford Companion to American Law. Kermit L. Hall, Editor-in-Chief. New York: Oxford University Press, 2002. 1 vol. (912 pp.).
Cost: $79.95; from $.01 on amazon.com (2014).
A scholarly, encyclopedic dictionary of American law containing both brief and extended articles on a variety of legal concepts, terms, court decisions, statutes, historical figures, events, and controversies, as well as broad interpretative essays summarizing important substantive, historical and procedural areas of American law. The entries were written by more than three hundred legal scholars, historians, and academics. Unlike David M. Walker's **Oxford Companion to Law** (1980), which focused on British law, this work provides a distinctly American orientation with longer and more inclusive articles. This is a core reference title for law libraries of all types and sizes, and for academic libraries serving both undergraduate and graduate populations.

Oxford Companion to the Supreme Court of the United States. 2d ed. Edited by Kermit L. Hall. New York: Oxford University Press, 2005. 1 vol. (1,272 pp.).
Cost: $65.00; from $9.63 on amazon.com (2014).
This comprehensive and authoritative scholarly reference contains over 1,200 entries detailing all aspects of Supreme Court history and jurisprudence, including biographies of justices, discussion of leading cases, and analysis of legal constitutional issues and controversies. The second edition provides 66 new articles, including discussion of the impeachment trial of President Bill Clinton, the role of the Rehnquist Court, and the controversial 2000 election decision, and updated discussion of such hot button issues as abortion, affirmative action, eminent domain, school desegregation, freedom of speech. school desegregation, religion, hate speech, campaign finance, and gay rights. This is an essential acquisition for any law, academic or public library.

The Oxford Dictionary of American Legal Quotations. Edited by Fred R. Shapiro. New York: Oxford University Press, 1993. 1 vol. (582 pp.).
Cost: $75.00; from $7.98 on amazon.com (2014).
A detailed and scholarly compendium of more than 3,500 legal quotations covering the period 1620 to the appointment of Clarence Thomas in 1991. An excellent resource for any attorney, judge or legal scholar who wishes to locate appropriate quotations with which to spice up his or her legal writing, oral arguments or speechmaking. Fred R. Shapiro is the Associate

Librarian and Lecturer in Legal Research at the Yale Law School and the editor of the **Yale Book of Quotations**.

Oxford Dictionary of Political Quotations. 3d ed. Edited by Antony Jay. New York: Oxford University Press, 2006. 1 vol. (560 pp.).
Cost: $46.00 (hardcover); from $0.01 on amazon.com (2014).
A useful collection of over 5,000 political quotations drawn, primarily, from 2,500 years of western political history, and ranging from the experience of the Greek city-states to contemporary American civic life. The editor's selections include quotations both by and about politicians; and involving political issues as current as the war in Iraq. Coverage includes quotations attributed to individuals as well newspaper headlines and political slogans.

The Oxford Handbook of Empirical Legal Research. Edited by Peter Cane and Herbert Kritzer. New York: Oxford University Press, 2010. 1 vol. (xv, 1,094 pp.). Paperbound.
Cost: $55.00; from $43.60 on amazon.com; kindle: $35.74 (20134).
One of the most significant intellectual developments in the history of modern legal research is the emergence of the Empirical Legal Studies (ELS) movement at the end of the 20th century. This monumental research guide, however, acknowledges the contributions of three additional areas of empirical research on law, legal systems, and legal institutions that predate the ELS movement, including (1) socio-legal/law and society; (2) empirically-oriented law and economics; and (3) judicial behavior/politics. Following an essay that delineates the development and institutional context of empirical legal research, this volume assembles 43 surveys, reflecting both qualitative and quantitative approaches to social science research, each of which provides an overview of the current state of scholarship, its predominant methodologies, methodological challenges, and possibilities. Thirty-five of these surveys address substantive areas of the law, while ten examine various approaches to empirical legal research and its use in academic and policymaking settings. Among the substantive research surveys are those addressing policing, crime and criminals, consumer protection, personal injury litigation, families, labor and employment laws, constitutions, environmental regulation, administrative justice, evidence law, trial courts and adjudication, appellate courts, and legal education and the legal academy, among others. This is an invaluable starting place for any researcher about to embark on a research project in any of the subject areas addressed by this volume. Each survey is accompanied by a selective bibliography of references. This volume is an essential component of any legal reference collection.

The Oxford Handbook of Legal Studies. Edited by Peter Crane and Mark Tushnet. Oxford, UK: Oxford University Press, 2009. 1 vol. (1,094 pp.).
Cost: $80.00 (out-of-print); from $225.00 on amazon.com (2014).
This collection of 43 incisive scholarly essays provides a conceptually wide-ranging, yet probing, insight into a variety of contemporary legal fields, topics, and issues. The aim is provide a theoretical framework for a broad understanding the law in both its private and public aspects, particularly for the non-specialist in those fields. The book's essays are grouped into six parts: Property and Obligations; Citizens and Government; Wealth Redistribution and Welfare; Business and Commerce; Technology; and Processes. Thus, Parts 1 and 6 will appeal primarily to the academic legal community; while Parts 2-5 will largely, but not exclusively, appeal to those in the fields of political science and government. The essays in Part 1, for example, examine such traditional common law concepts as contracts, torts, restitution, property and equity. Those in Part 6 cover the transnational concept of law, historical research in law, empirical research in law, legal education, the role of academics in the legal system, a century of legal studies, and law as an autonomous concept. The essays in Parts 2-5 examine topics significant in both their legal and public policy implications. While the book's audience is primarily an academic one, it also consists of those students of the law who desire a richer understanding of the law beyond its practical application.

Parry and Grant Encyclopedic Dictionary of International Law. 3d ed. Edited by John P. Grant and J. Craig Barker. New York, NY: Oxford University Press, 2009. 1 vol. (702 pp.).
Cost: $185.00; from $52.97 on amazon.com (2014).
Now in its second edition, this classic reference work provides concise definitions of over 2,400 terms, concepts, doctrines, people, statutes, cases, and treaties in the field of international law. The cross-referenced entries place each term in the context of international law while explaining its historical origins and contemporary significance. Each entry also provides references for further research, including treaties, journal articles, and web sites. The second edition includes over 500 new entries, twenty years of new material, and references to web sites. John P. Grant is professor of law at the Lewis & Clark School of Law. J. Craig Barker is professor of law at the University of Reading School of Law.

Post, Peggy. **Emily Post's Etiquette**. 18th ed. New York: HarperCollins, 2011. 1 vol. (736 pp.).
Cost: $39.99; from $18.05 on amazon.com (2014).
First published in 1922, and now rewritten for the first time since its initial appearance, this classic guide to social etiquette provides expert advice on entertaining, social protocol, table manners, religious ceremonies, expressing condolences, introductions, wedding planning, toasts, sportsmanship, and many other areas of social interaction. The 17th edition also addresses hundreds of contemporary etiquette concerns, including rudeness, netiquette, noxious neighbors, road rage, family harmony, on-line dating, cell phone courtesy, raising respectful children and teens, and travel etiquette. Peggy Post is Emily Post's great-granddaughter-in-law, and the spokesperson and author for the Emily Post Institute.

Prince's Dictionary of Legal Citations. Edited by Mary Miles **Prince.** 8th ed. Buffalo, NY: William S. Hein & Co., Inc., 2011. 1 vol. (542 pp.).
Cost: $49.50; from $11.00 on amazon.com (2014).
This guide to legal citations is based on the rules set out in the 19th edition of **A Uniform System of Citation** and is intended as a companion to the **Bluebook**. Each entry includes the abbreviation as used in the **Bluebook** together with one or more examples of the citation used in context. A useful tool for lawyers, legal secretaries, paralegals, and law students. This edition includes the full text of the **Bluebook**.

Robert, Henry M. **Robert's Rules of Order**. 11th ed. Cambridge, MA: Da Capo Press, 2011. 1 vol. (816 pp.).
Cost: Available through amazon.com: $39.95 (hardcover); $18.95 (paperbound); from $7.86 on amazon.com (2014).
First published in 1875, Robert's Rules of Order has become the national authority on parliamentary procedure. While not necessarily the best of its genre, **Robert's Rules** has become the most widely used. However, because the name and copyright have passed into the public domain, there are several imitators which use the name **Robert's**. This tenth edition has been updated to reflect current technological practices and usages, including how to conduct meetings over the telephone, on the Internet, and via video conferencing.

Schultz, Jon S. **Statutes Compared: A U.S., Canadian, Multinational Research Guide to Statutes by Subject**. 2d ed. Buffalo, NY: William S. Hein & Co., Inc., 2001-date. 1 vol. Looseleaf format.
Cost: $95.00 (2014).
An annotated subject index to periodically published compilations of U.S. state statutes, Canadian provincial laws, and the laws of foreign countries. Designed as an aid to the legal researcher conducting comparative statutory analysis

Shimpock, Kathy. **Business Research Handbook: Methods and Sources for Lawyers and Business Professionals**. New York: Aspen Publishers, 1996-date. 1 vol. Looseleaf format. Supplemented twice annually.
Cost: $859; supplementation: 1997: $75; 1998: $158; 1999: $183; 2000: $208; 2001: $404; 2002: $145; 2003: $355; 2004: $399; 2005: $428; 2006: $450; 2007: $473; 2008: $497; 2009: $560; 2010: $580; 2011: $620.00; 2012: $684; 2013: $732
A comprehensive, annotated guide to business information sources in all formats. The author/editor covers basic research strategies, basic research tools, retrieving information from a variety of sources, biographical research and expert witness profiles, finding government documents and statistics, business and corporate sources, and insurance sources. The appendices include a research strategy worksheet, and subject and title index.
Cost Saving Tip: The high cost of this volume and its accompanying annual cost of supplementation ($732.00 in 2013) make this book an ideal candidate for periodic re-purchase. Avoid the standing order.

Silbiger, Steven. **The Ten Day MBA: A Step By-Step Guide to Mastering the Skills Taught in America's Top Business Schools**. 4th edition. New York: Collins, 2012. 1 vol. (448 pp.).
Cost: $19.99 (paperback); from $11.24 on amazon.com; kindle: $11.89 (2014).
A succinct summary of the key principles and content taught in the top MBA programs, including marketing, ethics, accounting, organizational behavior, quantitative analysis, finance, operations, economics, strategy, research, public speaking, negotiating, international business. Also includes an MBA abbreviation lexicon, quantitative analysis tables, and bibliography. Of particular value to lawyers and librarians who lack business training.

The Sourcebook to Public Record Information. 10th ed. Tempe, AZ: BRB Publications, Inc., 2009. 1 vol. (2,000 pp.). Also available online as the **Public Record Research System-Web** (PRRS-Web).
Cost: print: $24.00; PRRS Web: $124.00 per year; print from $40.83 on amazon.com (2014).
A massive compendium of public records information sources, including 20,000 government agencies at the local, state, and federal level. Includes public record sources for accident records, assessor, aviation, bankruptcy, civil court cases, corporations, criminal records, birth records, marriage records, death records, driver records, fictitious names, GED certificates, judgments, state and federal laws and regulations, LLCs and LLPs, real estate, tax liens, trademarks, UCCs, unlawful detainers, vehicle title and registration, vessel title and registration, voter registration, and workers compensation records. Contains county court contact information for every county in the United States and directions for conducting name searches and records requests. Contains county locators for every state which provide users with ability to determine the county in which every city is situated. Volume also includes a public records primer that explains the basics of using public records. An essential tool for lawyers, paralegals, genealogists, investigators, and others who make frequent use of public records. The PRRS web site provides links to 28,000 government and private agencies that provide free online access to public record information. It provides a comprehensive resource of access methods, restrictions, fees, and search procedures for information not accessible via Google or search engines (see: www.brbpub.com).

Sources of Compiled Legislative Histories: A Bibliography of Government Documents, Periodical Articles, and Books, 1st Congress-108th Congress. 2d ed. Compiled by Nancy P. Johnson. Littleton, CO, Fred B. Rothman [William S. Hein & Co.], 2012-date. 1 vol. AALL Publication Series #14.
Cost: $75.00 (2014). Also available on HeinOnline.
Now in a revised second edition, this bibliography is an invaluable guide to published compilations of legislative histories, as well as sources which discuss the documents contained therein. **Sources of Compiled Legislative History** is also available on **HeinOnline**, which not only provides links to the listed legislative histories, but also to legislative histories that are included in **HeinOnline** and all the articles on those legislative histories, whether they include the legislative history or just have additional information from the **HeinOnline** law review database.

State Rankings 2014: A Statistical View of America. Edited by Kathleen O'Leary Morgan and Scott Morgan. Washington, DC: CQ Press, 2012. 1 vol. (604 pp.).
Cost: cloth: $150.00; paper: $95.00 (2014).
Compiled from a range of official and private sector sources, this reference book presents rankings of all fifty states and the District of Columbia in the form of 567 tables in fifteen significant livability categories. These categories include agriculture, crime and law enforcement, defense, economy, education, employment and labor, energy and environment, geography, government finances: federal, government finances: state and local, health, households and housing, population, social welfare, and transportation. Each table is presented in both alphabetical order and rank order, together with national averages. An excellent source of statistical and comparative data for researchers, legislators, policy analysts, journalists, students, scholars, and the general public.

Statistical Abstract of the United States, 2012-2013: The National Data Book. 131st ed. Washington, DC: U.S. Dept. of Commerce, 2012. Available from Skyhorse Publishing. 1 vol. (992 pp.)
Cost: $44.00 (hardcover); $16.95 (softcover); from $9.10 on amazon.com (2014).
Published since 1878, this is the standard summary of statistics on the social, political and economic organization of the United States, with statistical data culled from hundreds of governmental and private publications. Contains over 1,400 tables and graphics.

The Supreme Court Compendium: Data, Decisions and Developments. Edited by Lee Epstein, Jeffrey A. Segal, Harold J. Spaeth, and Thomas G. Walker. 5th ed. Washington, DC: CQ Press, 2012. 1 vol. (836 pp.).
Cost: $175.00; from $158.28 on amazon.com (2014).
This compilation of data on the United States Supreme Court serves as an invaluable tool for judges, legal scholars, students, journalists, and citizens generally, who interested in the workings of the third branch of government and its impact upon society. The editors have assembled 177 tables which examine the Supreme Court from every possible perspective, including the court as an institution; its review process, caseload and cases; its decision, opinion and outcome trends; the backgrounds, nominations and confirmations of justices; post-confirmation activities and departures from the court; oral arguments, votes and opinions; its political and legal environments; the Supreme Court and public opinion; and the impact of the Supreme Court. It also includes a bibliography of selected readings. An essential acquisition for any law, academic or public library.

Svengalis, Kendall F. **Legal Information Buyer's Guide and Reference Manual, 2014.** 18th ed. North Stonington, CT, New England LawPress, 2014. 1 vol. (878+ pp.). Paperbound. Published annually since 1996.
Cost: $169.00 + $7.00 postage (2014).
A comprehensive guide to the purchase of United States legal information in all its categories and formats, combined with a number of unique reference features. Provides general guidance to those establishing a law office library as well as guidance in the selection of specific categories of information, including statutes, case reporters, digests, citators, reference titles, CD-ROMs, and online services, to name just a few. Contains the most extensive annotated bibliography of legal treatises on the market (over 2,100 titles), organized under sixty-one subject headings, each of which is also represented in a unique spreadsheet providing basic bibliographic, cost, and 5-year supplementation cost data. Also includes an extensive guide to basic legal publications and information sources for all fifty states and the District of Columbia, with prices. Appendices include a guide to the histories and product lines of dozens of leading legal publishers, a directory of legal publishers with addresses, telephone numbers and Web sites, used and rare law book dealers, representative used law book prices, a selective list of looseleaf services, cost saving tips, spreadsheet of CALR case law coverage for twelve vendors, an extensive bibliography, and index. Winner of the 1998 Joseph L. Andrews Bibliographical Award from the American Association of Law Libraries. An essential reference tool for any legal professional who purchases or uses legal information. Previous editions published in 1996, 1997-98, 1998-99, 2000, and 2001-2013. Earlier editions (1996-2010) are now available on the Spinelli's Law Librarian's Reference Shelf on HeinOnline. In 2011, the company name was changed to that of New England LawPress.

Tanenhaus, David S., ed. **Encyclopedia of the Supreme Court of the United States**. Detroit: Macmillan Reference USA, 2008. 5 vols. (2,631 pp.).
Cost: $682.00; from $229.00 on amazon.com (2014).
This comprehensive reference work on the United States Supreme Court contains 1,100 entries, embracing 523 essays on specific court decisions, 468 thematic essays, and 109 biographies, written by leading legal scholars and historians of the court. It includes historical essays on all 17 Supreme Court Chief Justices, leading Associate Justices, court staff, landmark Supreme Court decisions, legal concepts and procedures, theories of law and interpretation, essays on major legal issues, biographical articles on leading political figures, scholars, and lawyers appearing before the court. Ranging in length from 250 to 6,500 words, each signed entry is accompanied by a bibliography and citations to related articles. The appendices in volume five include a chronology of landmark decisions, U.S. history and legislation; foundational documents; a list of Justices; glossary of terms; and subject index. The contributors include some of the leading experts in their respective fields, such Professor Herbert Hovenkamp who wrote the entry on Antitrust. The audience for this five-volume set ranges from advance placement high school students and undergraduates to graduate students, professors, lawyers, journalists and judges.

Turabian, Kate L. ***A Manual for Writers of Research Papers, Theses, and Dissertations: Chicago Style for Students and Researchers.*** 8th ed. Revised by Wayne C. Booth, Gregory G. Colomb, Joseph M. Williams, and the University of Chicago Press Editorial Staff. Chicago: University of Chicago Press, 2013. 1 vol. (436 pp.). Paperbound.
Cost: $18.00; from $10.75 on amazon.com (2014).
Kate Turabian (1893-1987), who served for decades as the dissertation secretary at the University of Chicago, first published this book in 1937 as an aide to students, professors and scholars. Based on her experience with research projects across all subject fields, this guide has sold more than seven million copies since it was first published. Now updated under the supervision of the University of Chicago Press editorial staff, and in its seventh edition, Turabian's *Manual* has been heavily revised to embrace both standard scholarly sources in print as well as new media.

The United States Government Internet Directory. Edited by Shana Hertz-Hattis. Lanham, MD: Bernan Press, 2013. 10th ed. 1 vol. (608 pp.). Paperbound.
Cost: $72.00; from $61.78 on amazon.com (2014).
An annotated guide to more than 2,000 U.S. government web sites organized under the following topical chapters: agriculture, fishing and forestry; business and economics, culture and recreation; defense and intelligence; demographics and sociology; education; employment; energy; engineering hand technology. The subject-based approach of this book allows the user to browse for relevant sites in the chosen field of interest rather than trying to guess the relevant government agency to consult

The United States Government Manual 2013. Washington, DC: U.S. Government Printing Office, 2013 (March 1). Available from Skyhorse Publishing. 1 vol. (682 pp.). Paperbound.
Cost: $17.95 (softcover); from $.11 on amazon.com (2014).
The standard reference work to the U.S. government provides comprehensive information on the agencies of the legislative, judicial, and, primarily, executive branches, as well as quasi-official agencies, international organizations in which the United States participates, including boards, commissions, and committees. Each agency's description includes a summary statement of the agency's purpose and role in the federal government, a brief history of the agency, its legislative and executive authority, a list of principal officials. It also includes a description of consumer activities, contracts and grants, employment, and publications. The **Manual**, which is published as a special edition of the **Federal Register**, is also available on GPO Access, which provides online access to each edition from 1995-96 to date. The new edition of the **Manual** is available to the Public each year in the late summer.

United States Government Printing Office Style Manual, 2008. 30th ed. Washington, DC: U.S. Government Printing Office, 2012. 1 vol. (460 pp.).
Cost: $34.95 (cloth); $27.99 (paperbound); from $24.19 on amazon.com (2014).
The **GPO Style Manual** is issued by the Public Printer under the authority of Section 1105 of Title 44, **United States Code**. Designed to achieve uniform word and type treatment and economy of word use in the form and style of government printing, it also used as a style manual by numerous state and federal government departments and agencies. The prior edition was published in 2000. Also available online at no cost: http://www.gpoaccess.gov/stylemanual/browse.html

The U.S. Justice System: An Encyclopedia. Edited by Steven Harmon Wilson. Santa Barbara, CA: ABC-CLIO, Inc., 2012. 3 v. (1,276 pp.).
Cost: $294.00; from $124.00 on amazon.com (2014).
This three-volume reference work provides a roadmap to the structure and function of the American legal system. Its content consists of long analytical essays, short entries and original documents which elucidate the history and development of the federal, state, and local courts and the political and legal institutions with which they interact. The long essays (chapters) in volume one provide a useful overview of the law and Constitution in early America, the structure and function of the federal government, the federal and state judiciaries, judicial procedure, administrative law and enforcement, the civil justice system, public law litigation, the criminal justice system, and criminal procedure. Volume two consists of short entries regarding people, groups, cases, and constitutional and legal principles. Volume three contains many of the most significant legal and political documents that define the American legal system, a glossary of legal terms, and an extensive general bibliography. It comprises the contributions of nearly seventy scholars and legal practitioners.

Volokh, Eugene. **Academic Legal Writing: Law Review Articles, Student Notes, and Seminar Papers**.
4th ed. New York, NY: Foundation Press, 2010. 1 vol. (411 pp.). Softbound. Available from West Academic.
Cost: $53; from $36.86 on amazon.com; kindle: $28.80 (2014).
An introductory manual on legal writing designed to assist the law student in drafting term papers, law review articles and student notes. The author addresses both the mechanics of legal writing and the publication process. Attention is given to the research process, writing style, use of evidence, cite-checking, publishing and publicizing, and academic ethics. Appendices include a list of clumsy words and phrases, answers to exercises, and sample cover letters. Unlike some of the more exhaustive and intimidating legal style manuals, this one is designed to be consumed and digested by the law student and would-be scholar early in his or her career. Law professor Eugene Volokh, who is the third most cited professor among those who entered the profession after 1992, publishes the online blog "The Volokh Conspiracy." at: http://volokh.com/. An extract of this title I available at: www2.law.ucla.edu/volokh/writing/aextract.pdf

Washington Information Directory. Washington, D.C.: CQ Press. Annual (July). 1 vol. (1,888 pp.). Cloth.
Cost: 2013-2014 (available July, 2013): $160.00; from $151.48 on amazon.com; 2012-2013 ed.: from $.01 (2014).
An invaluable compendium of information on federal government departments and agencies, as well as 2,500 nonprofit organizations. Includes names, addresses, telephone numbers and descriptive entries for executive branch agencies, Congress, foreign embassies, labor unions, and leading state officials. An essential desk reference for tracking down the appropriate governmental official or office. Also includes organizational charts.

Words and Phrases. St. Paul, MN: West Publishing Co., 1940-date. 132 vols. Includes annual pocket parts and periodic revised volumes.
Cost: $6,965; supplementation: 2005: $1,652.00; 2006: $2,540.50; 2007: $3,179.50; 2008: $4,139 (including pocket parts and 30 revised volumes); 2009: $1,053.50 (pocket parts only); 2010: $1,284 (pocket parts only); 2011: $1,844; 2012: $1,896; 2013: $1,958. **Assured Print Price** (APP): $274/mo./$3,288/yr.).
This multi-volume set contains alphabetically arranged judicial definitions of words and phrases from both state and federal courts, from 1658-date. The definitions, which are essentially headnote abstracts from West reporters, may pertain to statutory language, court rules, administrative regulations, or business documents, among other sources. Each definition contains a citation from the court that provided the definition and is also classified to the West Key Number System by the West editors.

Cost Saving Tip: While useful, this set is far too costly to justify its purchase or continued supplementation, particularly for the practitioner. Moreover, the function of this set has been significantly eclipsed by computer-assisted legal research. A discontinued set can still serve as a useful resource for law libraries, providing thousands of definitions from 1658 to the date of cancellation. The 2008 issuance of 30 revised volumes to subscribers was a huge unanticipated cost for which they were unprepared, and a stark indication of what may befall the unwary legal information consumer, particularly from this publisher. The five-year cost of supplementation was $12,186.00. West's new **Monthly Assured Print Price** adds a new twist to the equation, although it remains to be seen if it will be an advantage over the per item (discounted to subscribers) pricing model. For example, the six-year supplementation cost average was $2,307, versus the $3,396 now charged under the

Monthly Assured Print Price.

World Law School Directory. Edited by Michael Beaird. 3d ed. Buffalo, NY: William S. Hein & Co., 2003. 1 vol. (511 pp.).
Cost: $110.00 (2014).
A comprehensive directory of law schools and law related institutions around the world, including address, phone and fax numbers, degrees offered, primary language, whether or not foreign students are admitted, and key names to contact for additional information on a particular school. The third edition includes 500 new entries as well as e-mail and website information. This book is also included as part of the Indices volume of Hein's **Modern Legal Systems Cyclopedia**. Libraries or individuals with limited budgets and/or only occasional need for this information may wish to take advantage of the free, yet more basic, directory information available on the HierosGamos web site: http://www.hg.org/schools.html#dir

Wren, Christopher G. and Jill Robinson Wren. **The Legal Research Manual: A Game Plan for Legal Research and Analysis**. 2d ed. Madison, WI: Legal Education Publishing (State Bar of Wisconsin), 1999.
Cost; OUT-OF-PRINT; from $.01 on amazon.com (2014).
Unlike Cohen and Berring's *How to Find the Law*, this volume approaches legal research as a process and breaks it down into its component phases. Chapters include sources of the law, citations, gathering and analyzing your facts and identifying and organizing the legal issues, finding the law, reading the law, updating the law, how to take effective notes, and when to stop. The appendices include a discussion of computerized legal research, other research sources, and civil procedure. A useful complement to the bibliographical approach to legal research. An ideal review for the new associate who requires a practical perspective on the legal research process.

Yale Book of Quotations. Edited by Fred R. Shapiro. New Haven, CT: Yale University Press, 2006. 1 vol. (1,104 pp.).
Cost: $55.00; from $4.48 on amazon.com (2014).
A refreshing addition to the library of quotations books, this exhaustive compendium encompasses over 12,000 historic and modern American quotations drawn from both traditional and non-traditional sources, including the worlds of film, folk song, proverb, television, sports, law, science and advertising. While the editor has provided an abundant sampling of historical and literary quotations, he also provides a wealth of contemporary quotations more apt to appeal to the reader, author or scholar. Each entry is annotated to provide source and date of first use, many of which correct quotations previously misattributed to other parties, and which reflect the author's sophisticated use of computerized databases. Shakespeare and Milton, Karl Marx and Groucho Marx, Mae West and Yogi Berra are all represented here in the most delightful new quotations book published in years. Fred R. Shapiro is the Associate Librarian and Lecturer in Legal Research at the Yale Law School and the editor of the **Oxford Dictionary of American Legal Quotations**.

Your Nation's Courts Online. Washington, DC: CQ Press. Updated continuously.
Cost: $195.00 (2013).
This online directory, combining the **Directory of State Court Clerks & County Courthouses** and the **Federal-State Court Directory**, provides access to a wealth of vital information, including sources of court decisions, real estate records, UCC and tax liens, criminal convictions and other records maintained by state appellate and trial courts and county courthouses. It includes names, addresses and phone numbers of State appellate, trial court, and county clerks for all 50 states. It also includes a State-by-State guide to corporate and UCC filings, State offices of vital statistics, the procedures for ordering records, trends in State court litigation, and a listing of State court websites.

Chapter 23: Legal Acquisitions Toolbox

Law librarians have at their disposal a wide variety of tools useful in building and developing legal collections. Bibliographies, checklists, directories, manuals, review media, and Web sites provide legal information professionals with the means of sorting through the dozens of publishers' announcements, circulars, and catalogs which land on their desks each day. While many of the publications listed below will not be appropriate acquisitions for the average law firm library, they can be consulted at a local academic or research law library in your area. Others, like the annual **Legal Information Buyer's Guide and Reference Manual,** were specifically designed to assist law firms and law libraries in choosing from among the vast, and often costly, literature in the field of law.

The thirty-five titles or Web sites listed below represent the most significant resources consulted by legal information professionals in the work of acquisitions and collection development. Included in the list are titles which can be employed in retrospective acquisitions, current acquisitions, locating book reviews (both general and legal), acquiring books (new and used), and in monitoring the practices of legal publishers. The author welcomes suggestions for additions to this list (E-mail: rilawpress@comcast.net).

Retrospective Acquisitions

Association of American Law Schools. **Law Books Recommended for Libraries**. South Hackensack, N.J.: F.B. Rothman, 1967-1976. 6 vols. + 4 supplements. Looseleaf format. Available from W.S. Hein & Co. Also available on HeinOnline.
Cost: $650.00 (2014).
Conceived by the Association for American Law Schools and produced by the AALS Library Studies Project, under the direction of Miles O. Price and Harry Bitner, **Law Books Recommended for Libraries** made recommendations in 46 subject categories which were published by Fred B. Rothman from 1967-1976, with coverage to about 1970. Each entry is assigned a letter to designate its suitability for various types of libraries (A=Basic Collection; B=Intermediate Collection; C=Indepth Research Collection). Although the product itself was discontinued due to a lack of funding, it was later supplemented by annual volumes of recommended titles edited by Oscar J. Miller and Mortimer D. Schwartz (See entry for **Recommended Publications for Legal Research** below). Although out of print for a number of years, this set, which is owned by many academic and research law libraries, can provide much useful information for retrospective collection development. Also available on HeinOnline.

Cohen, Morris L. **Bibliography of Early American Law**. Buffalo, NY: William S. Hein & Co., 1998. 7 vols. (5,868 pp. + 2003 supplement (v. 7).
Cost: print: $1,750.00; print and CD-ROM: $1,850.00; CD-ROM only: $1,650.00; also available on HeinOnline (2014).
This monumental scholarly reference work lists and describes the monographic and trial literature of American law published in the United States from its colonial founding to the end of 1860. It also includes works on foreign, comparative, and international which were published in the United States during that time. The **Bibliography of Early American Law** (BEAL) is divided into four sections: Monographs, Civil Trials, Criminal Trials, and Special Proceedings. Special Proceedings embraces selective legislative and administrative proceedings of an adjudicatory nature, and arbitrations. Access to individual entries is provided by means of indexes of authors, titles, specific subjects, names of parties to litigations, jurisdiction, language (if other than English), place of publication and publisher, and year of publication. The work is the product of thirty-five years research in early American bibliography for which the late Morris Cohen received the Joseph L. Andrews Bibliographical Award from the American Association of Law Libraries in 1999. The definitive bibliography for pre-1860 American legal imprints. Also available on HeinOnline.

Index to Legal Periodicals Retrospective: 1908-1981. Bronx, NY: HW Wilson/EBSCO
Cost: Inquire. Call: 978-356-6500.
Released in July, 2004, this retrospective database covers over 500 legal periodicals published in the United States, Canada, Great Britain, Ireland, Australia, and New Zealand. Contains the indexing from 28 of the publisher's bound cumulations of the **Index to Legal Periodicals**, including 750 periodicals and 540,000 records, including book reviews and case citations. Wilson and EBSCO merged in 2011.

Law Books, 1876-1981: Books and Serials on Law and Related Subjects. New York: R.R. Bowker Co., 1981. 4 vols.
Cost: Originally $495.00, but out-of-print; used prices extremely volatile; sets currently available on amazon.com for $1,998.00.
An invaluable source of retrospective bibliographical information on more than 130,000 law or law-related book titles and 4,000 serial titles. Employing a combination of sources for the period covered, including the **American Book Publishing Record**, the **National Union Catalog**, and MARC tapes, the editors have selected entries from a total of more than 500,000 titles examined. Bibliographical entries in volumes 1-3 are organized by main entry within each subject, employing more than 39,000 Library of Congress subject headings. Vol. 4 includes author and titles indices, subject and titles serials indices, a listing of law and law related publishers and distributors, and a listing of law and law related on-line database producers and vendors. Excluded are juvenile literature, handbooks, manuals, looseleafs, or pamphlets that do not indicate a sense of permanency. Ideally consulted in a publicly accessible a law library.

McDermott, James A., ed. **Recommended Law Books**. 2d ed. Chicago: American Bar Association, Section of Corporation, Banking and Business Law, Committee on Business Law Libraries, 1986. 1 vol.
Cost: OUT-OF-PRINT, but available used on amazon.com from $9.01 (2014).
An early attempt to provide practicing lawyers with an annotated list of the best and most useful books for legal research in fifty-nine branches of the law, as well as the most useful legal reference works. The initial selections were made in consultation with members of the ABA's Section of Corporation, Banking and Business Law through a survey which appeared in the November, 1967 issue of **The Business Lawyer** and published

in the July, 1968 issue. This is the second edition of a work first edited by Richard Sloane and published in 1969. The second edition was edited by James A. McDermott, Chairman of the Business Law Libraries Committee of the ABA, with contributions from hundreds of practicing attorneys, law office librarians, and law professors. While now dated, it nevertheless provides a useful tool for retrospective acquisitions and an insight into law books that have stood the test of time.

Recommended Publications for Legal Research. Compiled by Oscar J. Miller and Mortimer D. Schwartz. Littleton, CO: Fred B. Rothman Publications [now a division of William S. Hein & Co., Inc.], 1970/71-2011. Annual. Paper.
Cost: $83.00 per year (2006-2012 only); $2,150.00 for set (42 vols.) (2014).
This series of annual volumes was designed to supplement the 10-volume **Law Books Recommended for Law Libraries** originally published by the Association of American Law Schools and its Library Studies Project. It consequently fills the void left that by the cessation of that project with its coverage to 1970. Oscar J. Miller and Mortimer D. Schwartz compiled 30 annual volumes before turning the editorship over to Mary Miller, Associate Director and Head of Acquisitions at the University of Buffalo, Charles B. Sears Law Library, State University of New York. Entries are organized into fifty subject areas, arranged alphabetically by main entry. Each entry is assigned a letter to designate its suitability for various types of libraries (A=Basic Collection; B=Intermediate Collection; C=In-depth Research Collection). Over the course of the thirty years, the editors examined over 95,000 items and selected over 26,000 for inclusion and ranking.

Shapiro, Fred R. "The Most-Cited Legal Books: A New Tool for Law Library Collection Development." **Legal Information Alert**. 18 (Sept., 1999): 1-6.
Over the years, Fred Shapiro has produced a number of useful studies of the most heavily cited law review articles. In this study, he draws upon the Institute for Scientific Information's (ISI) **Social Sciences Citation Index** for the years 1981-1997 and runs these results through **SOCSCISRCH**, Westlaw's version of the **Social Sciences Citation Index** (which includes over 100 legal periodicals and over 1,000 social science periodicals) through March, 1999. The results are presented in four tables: the most-cited legal books (other than treatises and texts); the most-cited treatises and texts; British legal books most-cited in Social Science Citation Index; and non-legal books most-cited in legal periodicals. All four lists cover the period 1978-March, 1999. These lists can serve as extremely useful and objective tools for law library acquisitions, particularly in an academic law library environment.

Current Acquisition Tools: Books/Online Services

Chiorazzi, Michael and Gordon Russell, eds. **Law Library Collection Development in the Digital Age**. New York: Haworth Press (Taylor & Francis Group), 2002. 1 vol. (322 pp.).
Cost: OUT-OF-PRINT; from $29.95 on amazon.com (2014).
This collection of articles, published simultaneously as Legal Reference Services Quarterly, Volume 21, Numbers 2/3 and 4 (2002), addresses a number of timely issues related to impact of digital technology on law library collection development. Taking as their springboard a seminal paper by Penny Hazelton entitled "How Much of Your Print Collection Is Really on Westlaw or LEXIS-NEXIS," Chiorazzi and Russell and their contributors examine both the philosophical and practical implications of Hazelton's thesis for collection development, legal research, and the physical law libraries of the future. Articles also address such topics as strategic planning for distance learning, long term access to digital information, legal scholarship and digital publishing, consolidation of the legal publishing industry, access versus ownership, electronic journals in the academic law library, and the changing role of law library vendors. An essential acquisition for every law library.

Directory of Law-Related CD-ROMs. Compiled and edited by Arlene L. Eis. Teaneck, NJ: Infosources Publishing. Annual. (201) 836-7072.
Cost: No longer available in print format; 2012 forward only available as part of LawTrio on the web, combining the **Directory of Law-Related CD-ROMs**, **Legal Looseleafs in Print**, and **Legal Newsletters in Print** at a cost of $339.00/yr; **Directory of Law-Related CD-ROMs** alone: $244.00; one month pass: $95.00 (2014).
The most complete and accurate guide available to legal CD-ROM titles on the market, including those on the Internet.. The 2013 edition includes detailed information on more than 1,600 CD-ROM products published by over 180 publishers in the United States and abroad in the areas of law, legislation, and regulation. In addition to the product listings, there are indices by publisher/distributor, search software, Macintosh titles, and subject. Includes citations to product reviews published in law-related publications.

Garces, Vincente E. **Survey on Collection Development Policies and Selection Practices**. Buffalo, NY: William S. Hein & Co., 2006. 1 vol.
Cost: $50.00 (2014).
This brief survey examines the types of materials collected by law libraries and the processes employed in their acquisition.

Hein Checklist of Statutes (State and Territorial). 67th ed. Buffalo, NY: William S. Hein & Co., Inc., 2013. 1 vol. (338 pp.).
Cost: $75.00 (2014).
Revised as of October 31, 2013, this volume provides libraries with a current state-by-state checklist for verifying the completeness of current statutory holdings, as well as the **Code of Federal Regulations**.

Hewette, Amber and Diane Hurley. **Law for the Layperson: An Annotated Bibliography of Self-Help Law Books**. 3d ed. Buffalo, NY: William S. Hein & Co., 2006. 1 vol. (486 pp.).
Cost: OUT-OF-PRINT; from $29.00 on amazon.com (2014).
A useful annotated bibliography of legal self-help books organized under 68 topical headings. An update of Frank G. Houdek's **Law for the Layman** (1991),and Jean McKnight's **Law for the Layperson** (1997). It also includes author, title, and jurisdiction indices, and a list of publishers.

IndexMaster. 1057 Jaycox Road, Avon, Ohio 44011. [Available at: www.indexmaster.com]
Cost: $45.00-$595.00 per year depending on size of firm, or type of library.

(2014); (800) 829-1836.
A state-of-the-art mega index to the tables and contents and indexes of more than 10,000 legal treatises from dozens of the leading legal publishers across the country. Subscribers can search by keyword, author, title, or publisher and then view the specific index and table of contents pages which contain the desired terms, with search results ranked in order of their relevance. Provides libraries with a means of achieving maximum utilization of the titles already in the collections as well as the means of making informed decisions about which new titles to acquire. For a more complete description of IndexMaster, see the introduction to chapter 27: Legal Treatises and Other Subject Specialty Materials.

Law Books and Serials in Print: A Multimedia Sourcebook. Amenia, NY: Grey House Publishing. Annual (June). 3 vols. Purchase includes mid-year cumulative supplement.
Cost: 2014 Edition (June 2014): $1,335.00 (includes cumulative supplement); 10% discount in first year to standing order customers; 5% discount in subsequent years.
A comprehensive guide to more than 90,000 legal titles, including books, serials, microfiche, videocassettes, software and online databases. Some entries include brief annotations. Generally recommended for purchase only by larger law libraries. Attorneys are encouraged to consult this resource in their local state, court, county, bar association, or academic library. While the information is generally reliable, and thorough, independent verification is recommended given the breadth of coverage. A close examination will reveal numerous omissions, including subsequent editions of earlier published works. For example, the 2002 edition not only omitted the 1999 (5th) edition of Lawrence Taylor's **Drunk Driving Defense** but the 1995 (4th) edition as well. A useful, but not exhaustive, bibliographical research tool. Print edition acquired from R.R. Bowker effective January 1, 2010.

Law Books in Print. Online edition. [www.oceanalaw.com]. Dobbs Ferry, NY: Glanville Publishers/Oceana Group [acquired by Oxford University Press on Sept. 30, 2005], 2002-2006. Title discontinued in 2006.
Cost: OUT-OF-PRINT.
Provides complete bibliographic information for law and law-related monographs, series, reports, closed sets of case reports, looseleaf continuations, audio and video cassettes, microforms, computer diskettes and CD-ROMs currently in print and published in English throughout the world. First published in 1957 under the editorship of Meira G. Pimsleur and J. Myron Jacobstein, and later by Robert Buckwalter, and Nicholas Triffin. The last General Editor of **Law Books in Print Online** was Merle Slyhoff, University of Pennsylvania School of Law. Previous editions were published in 1957, 1965, 1971, 1976, 1982, 1987, 1991, 1994, and 1997. A competitor to the annual **Law Books and Serials in Print** (R.R. Bowker). The 8th print edition is now out-of-print. It was replaced in 2002 by the online only version accessible at the Oceana Group Web site and discontinued in 2006.

Law Library Journal (quarterly). Chicago, IL: American Association of Law Libraries, 53 W. Jackson Blvd., Ste. 940. (312) 939-4764.
Cost: $110.00 per year to non-members; $27.50 per issue (2014).
In addition to a variety of scholarly articles on all aspects of law librarianship, **Law Library Journal** contains subject bibliographies, and an annual Legal Reference Books Review (e.g. see Fall, 2003 issue). The **Law Library Journal** is available on Lexis-Nexis™, WESTLAW, H.W. Wilson and Hein-On-Line. The complete back run is available to AALL members on the aallnet.org web site.

Legal Looseleafs in Print. Compiled and edited by Arlene L. Eis. Teaneck, NJ: Infosources Publishing, 1981-date. Updated continuously.
Cost: Available as online subscription only: $199 per year individually; or as part of LawTRIO Law Publications Database, combining the **Directory of Law-Related CD-ROMs, Legal Looseleafs in Print, and Legal Newsletters in Print** at a cost of $339.00 per year (2014).
An exhaustive compilation of bibliographical data for over 3,600 looseleaf publications from 270 different publishers. Includes true looseleaf services, such as those from CCH, BNA, and RIA, and post-binder publication such as those published by Matthew Bender. Basically, coverage includes legal publications contained in ring or post-bound (compression) binders as opposed to permanently bound books. Each entry includes title, author, publisher, date of publication, number of volumes, cost and supplementation cost, frequency of supplementation, recent supplementation cost, Library of Congress control number/ OCLC control number/LC classification, and indicates whether it is available online or on CD-ROM. Entries are indexed by publisher, subject, and electronic format. A publishers' directory provides addresses and telephone numbers for all publishers represented. A valuable guide to what is generally an expensive form of publication.

Legal Newsletters in Print. Compiled and edited by Arlene L. Eis. Teaneck, NJ: Infosources Publishing, 1981-date. Updated continuously.
Cost: Available as online subscription only: $199 per year individually; or as part of **LawTRIO Law Publications Database**, combining the **Directory of Law-Related CD-ROMs**, **Legal Looseleafs in Print**, and **Legal Newsletters in Print** at a cost of $339.00 per year.
A comprehensive guide to more than 2,200 legal newsletters, including standard-type newsletters, bulletins, newsletter-reporting services, and all reporting services issued periodically and stored in looseleaf binders. Does not include publications that require interfiling (see Legal Looseleafs in Print). Each entry includes full bibliographical detail, including sources of indexing, online availability, and description. In addition to the main Title List, there is a publisher index, list of newsletters online, database list, database index, a list of newsletters registered with the Copyright Clearance Center, newsletters that accept advertising, and a subject index. An excellent resource for the attorney or law firm interested in tracking down newsletters in specific subject areas and evaluating available alternatives. Entries include annual subscription costs.

Lipinski, Tomas A. **The Librarian's Legal Companion for Licensing Information Resources and Services**. Edison, NJ: Neal-Schuman Publishers, Inc., 2012.
1 vol. (220 pp). Available from ALA Store.

Cost: $130.00; ebook: $104; from $2.95 on amazon.com (2014). This legal companion provides essential information regarding the legal basis for the many practices involved in library acquisitions, including basic fair trade and contract law concepts; contract formation; compliance, contract and license negotiation; breech and remedy issues; developments in online and information contracting; the advantages and disadvantages of licensing; the deciphering of the legalese in agreements; and detailed explanations of specific types of licenses (web-link, shrink-wrap, etc.). There is also discussion of jurisdictional issues regarding online and information contracting. The book references real-world cases involving the acquisitions process. An Associate Professor in the School of Information Studies, University of Wisconsin—Milwaukee, Tomas A. Lipinski received Ph.D. from the Graduate School of Library and Information Science, University of Illinois at Urbana-Champaign and JD from Marquette University Law School. He is the author of numerous books on law in the library environment.
This book is an updating of the author's **Librarian's Legal Companion for Buying and Licensing Information Resources**.

Matthews, Elizabeth W. **The Law Library Reference Shelf: Annotated Subject Guide**. 5th ed. Buffalo, NY: William S. Hein & Co., Inc., 2003. 1 vol. (156 pp.).
Cost: OUT-OF-PRINT; from $29.95 on amazon.com (2014).
An annotated bibliography containing descriptions of hundreds of the most useful reference books for the law library. Included are general almanacs, encyclopedias, biographical works, dictionaries, directories, practice and procedure titles, quotation books, research and bibliographical titles, statistical handbooks, style manuals, and bar association publications. Includes an author/title index.

Recommended Publications for Legal Research. Compiled by Oscar J. Miller and Mortimer D. Schwartz. Littleton, CO: Fred B. Rothman Publications [now a division of William S. Hein & Co., Inc.], 1970/71-2011. Annual. Paper.
Cost: $83.00 per year (2006-2012 only); $2,150.00 for set (42 vols.) (2014).
This series of annual volumes was designed to supplement the 10-volume **Law Books Recommended for Law Libraries** originally published by the Association of American Law Schools and its Library Studies Project. It consequently fills the void left that by the cessation of that project with its coverage to 1970. Oscar J. Miller and Mortimer D. Schwartz compiled 30 annual volumes before turning the editorship over to Mary Miller, Associate Director and Head of Acquisitions at the University of Buffalo, Charles B. Sears Law Library, State University of New York. Entries are organized into fifty subject areas, arranged alphabetically by main entry. Each entry is assigned a letter to designate its suitability for various types of libraries (A=Basic Collection; B=Intermediate Collection; C=In-depth Research Collection). Over the course of the thirty years, the editors examined over 95,000 items and selected over 26,000 for inclusion and ranking.

Svengalis, Kendall F. **Legal Information Buyer's Guide and Reference Manual**. 18th ed. North Stonington, CT: New England LawPress (formerly Rhode Island LawPress) 2014. 1 vol. (878+ pp.). Paperbound. Published annually since 1996.
Cost: $169.00 + $7.00 s+h (2014).
A comprehensive guide to the purchase of United States legal information in all its categories and formats, combined with a number of unique reference features. Provides general guidance to those establishing a law office library as well as guidance in the selection of specific categories of information, including statutes, case reporters, digests, citators, reference titles, CD-ROMs, and online services, to name just a few. Contains the most extensive annotated bibliography of legal treatises on the market (over 2,150 titles), organized under sixty-one subject headings, each of which is also represented in a unique spreadsheet providing basic bibliographic, cost, and 5-year supplementation cost data. Also includes an extensive guide to basic legal publications and information sources for all fifty states and the District of Columbia, with prices. Appendices include a guide to the histories and product lines of dozens of leading legal publishers, a directory of legal publishers with addresses, telephone numbers and Web sites, used and rare law book dealers, representative used law book prices, a selective list of looseleaf services, cost saving tips, spreadsheet of CALR case law coverage for eight vendors, an extensive bibliography, and index. Winner of the 1998 Joseph L. Andrews Bibliographical Award from the American Association of Law Libraries. An essential reference tool for any legal professional who purchases or uses legal information. Previous editions published in 1996, 1997-98, 1998-99, and 2000 through 2013. Earlier editions (1996-2010) are now available on the Spinelli's Law Librarian's Reference Shelf on HeinOnline. In 2011, the company name was changed to New England LawPress.

Current Acquisitions: General Review Sources

Against the Grain. 209 Richardson Avenue, MSC 98, The Citadel, Charleston, SC 29409. Published in February, April, June, September, November and December/January. Web site: http://www.against-the-grain.com/
Cost: $50.00 per year (6 issues). If **Publishers Weekly** is the bible of the publishing industry," **Against the Grain** is the bible for the world of library acquisitions, providing news about libraries, publishers, book jobbers and subscription agents, and the issues, literature and people that impact the world of books and journals. Articles are insightful, informative, and well-written. An essential read for the acquisitions librarian who wishes to remain informed about issues important to the profession. Subscription includes online access to an archival collection of articles. Tables of Contents available on the Web at: http://www.against-the-grain.com/

Choice: Current Reviews for Academic Libraries. Middletown, CT: Association of College & Research Libraries, 1964-date. Published 11x/yr. (July/August combined).
Cost: $415.00 per year (magazine); Reviews on Cards: $515.00 per year; Choice Reviews Online: rates:
http://www.ala.org/acrl/choice/subscription-rates#crorates (2014).
Subscriptions:100 Riverview Center, Middletown, CT 06457. (860) 347-6933.
Each issue contains approximately 600 brief reviews of recent books and electronic media written by subject matter experts. Reviews are addressed specifically to librarians and faculty members who select materials for academic libraries, especially for undergraduate research and teaching. Reviews cover more

than 50 sub-disciplines spanning the humanities, science and technology, and the social and behavioral sciences. Choice Reviews Online provides access to more than 145,000 Choice reviews plus all the editorial content from Choice magazine. A publication of the Association of College and Research Libraries, a division of the American Library Association.

Library Journal. New York: Cahners Publishing Co., 1876-date. 245 W. 17th St., New York, NY 10011. (800) 677-6694. Published 20 times per year. Also available on the Web at: http://libraryjournal.reviewsnews.com
Cost: print/online subscription: $157.99 per year ($101.99) (with credit card); **Book Verdict Pro Plus** : $143.99 (2014)
First published in 1876, **Library Journal** is the oldest independent national library publication, with a claimed readership of over 100,000 library directors, administrators, and others in public, academic and business libraries. Each issue includes reviews of 250-350 general adult books, most prior to publication. Reviews are addressed to the educated generalist and usually run from 125-150 words. The **Book Verdict Pro Plus** is available for 143.99. It provides the full text of **LJ** reviews as well as Pro functionality that allows the user to create, manage, and tag lists, save searches and export metadata.

Library Use of eBooks, 2011 Edition. New York, NY: Primary Research Group, Inc., 2013. 1 vol. (110 pp.).
Cost: $89.00 (print or PDF) (2014).
This 103-page study is based on data from 68 public, academic, corporate, legal and government libraries, with data broken out by type of library, size of library and other criteria. The study examines how libraries are using eBooks and addresses such issues as spending, budgets, contracts, licensing, number of licenses maintained, and aggregator and publisher preferences and aggregator vs publisher sales as a percentage of total eBook spending. The report also provides detailed data on library spending on particular retail vendors, including Amazon, Barnes & Noble and all other online book vendors. The report also presents data on e-audio books, use of consortium purchasing arrangements for eBooks, the impact of eBooks on interlibrary loan, range of titles typically available for eBook rental at libraries, the impact of tablets and other eBook reading devices, the impact of eBooks on course reserves for higher education libraries, the evolving state of dedicated endowments for eBooks, use of and spending on eDirectories, trends in eBook pricing as experienced by libraries, trends in eBook collection planning, use of eTextbooks and more.

New York Review of Books. New York: NYREV, Inc. 250 W. 57th St., New York, NY 10107. 20 issues per year. (800) 829-5088.
Cost: print: $74.95 per year (includes electronic access to five-year archive);
Two years: $139.00 (2014).
The New York Review of Books has been described by **Esquire** magazine as "the premier literary intellectual magazine in the English language. First published in 1963, it now has a circulation of over 115,000 readers. It publishes lengthy reviews of both current fiction and non-fiction and features lengthy essays addressing most of the important political, cultural, and intellectual issues of the age written by leading writers, critics, intellectuals. Includes reviews of many law-related titles, including those in politics, history, and economics.

New York Times Book Review. New York: New York Times Co. Weekly. 229 W. 43d St., New York, NY 10036. (800) 631-2580
Cost: Online access to NY Times: $99.00 per year; also free online at: http://www.nytimes.com/pages/books/review/index.html (2014).
One of the leading sources in the United States for critical reviews of the best in current fiction and non-fiction, poetry. Also available in a free online version.

Publishers Weekly. The International News Magazine of Book Publishing and Bookselling. 245 W. 17th St., New York, NY 10011. (212) 463-6758. Weekly. Available online at: www.publishersweekly.com
Cost: $249.99 per year (includes online access); digital only: $209.00 (2014).
The leading publication for the publishing industry, **Publishers Weekly** serves as the publication of record for industry news, trends, and data. It is also the source for more than 7,500 succinct reviews of forthcoming books annually. With a subscriber base of 40,000, it reaches a total audience of nearly 100,000 in bookstores, libraries, and the publishing industry. The web site includes exclusive access to an archive of book reviews and articles.

The Survey of Library Database Licensing Practices. 2011 Edition. New York, NY: Primary Research Group, Inc., 2011. 1 vol. (110 pp.).
Cost: $89.50 (print or PDF) (2014).
This invaluable survey of library database licensing practices draws upon responses from 90 libraries, including corporate, legal, college, public, state, and non-profit libraries. More than half of the participating libraries are based in the United States; the remainder are from Australia, Canada, the United Kingdom, and several other countries. The survey data is broken out by type and size of library, we well as by overall level of database expenditure. More than 400 tables provide detailed evidence of library spending on electronic databases, including spending through consortia, the growth rate in the number of licenses, spending on licenses for directories, electronic journals, e-books, and magazine/newspaper databases; and future spending plans on all of the above. The survey also examines price inflation experienced for electronic resources in business, medical, humanities, financial, market research, social sciences and many other information categories, as well as price inflation for e-books, electronic directories, journals, and newspaper/magazine databases. The survey also examines a number of related issues, including the percentage of licenses that require passwords and simultaneous access restrictions; spending on legal services related to licenses, percentage of libraries that have threatened to sue a database vendor; percentage of libraries that have been threatened with suits by database vendors; and the number of hours spent in reviewing license contracts. Of particular interest to law libraries, the survey also reports the percentage of contracts that require that their terms be kept secret; and level of awareness of the terms of other libraries contracts. With the substantial sums spent by libraries for electronic databases, these findings will prove an invaluable resource to library administrators and acquisitions librarians.

Current Acquisitions: Bibliographies and Reviews of Legal Materials

Advanced Bibliography of Law and Related Fields [Hein Green Slips]. Buffalo, NY: William S. Hein & Co., Inc. [formerly Fred B. Rothman]. Weekly.
Cost: Annual subscription cost varies based on the size and type of the organization (2013). Call: 1-800-828-7571.
Reports of new law and law-related titles in the form of 3" x 5" green slips of paper shipped to subscribers approximately every week. Each Hein green slip contains complete bibliographical information and price, and, in some instances, a brief description of contents. Titles are chosen from a variety of sources, including the **ABA Journal, CHOICE, Forthcoming Books, Legal Information Alert, Library Journal**, Library of Congress slips, etc. Books can be ordered by returning the Green slips to Hein. See also **Current Publications in Legal and Related Fields** (below).

Current Law Index. Farmington Hills, MI: Gale Cengage Learning, 1980-date. Monthly with annual bound cumulation.
Cost: 2013 Edition: $1,269.00 per year (2014). 1-800-877-4253.
Current Law Index is a monthly publication indexing the content of more than 900 leading law journals, legal newspapers and specialty publications from the United States, Canada, the United Kingdom, Ireland, Australia and New Zealand. Indexed titles include academic law reviews, bar association journals, specialty journals and selected journals treating law-related disciplines such as criminology, accounting, business, criminal, international law, taxation, and estate planning. Produced in cooperation with the American Association of Law Libraries, **Current Law Index** provides the most comprehensive indexing of law-related articles available in print. Subscription includes annual cumulative volume. Content also available online on **Legal Trac**.

Current Publications in Legal and Related Fields. Fred B. Rothman, a division of William S. Hein & Co., Inc.] Looseleaf. Published nine times per year (monthly except June, July, and September) with an annual cumulation (April).
Cost: $280.00 per year; subscription without annual cumulation: $199.00; annual cumulation alone: $125.00 (2014).
This current awareness bibliography draws new titles from the following publications: **American Book Publishing Record, Bowker's Legal Publishing Preview, Forthcoming Books**, Fred B. Rothman & Co. green slips, Law publishers' circulars and advance catalogs, **Library Journal**, Library of Congress proof slips (C.I.P.), newspaper articles, **Publishers Weekly**, University press catalogs. Reports on more 3,000 titles annually. This current awareness tool for law library acquisitions departments is an economical alternative to the Hein green slips, though lacking the latter's convenience for ordering purposes.

Index to Legal Periodicals and Books. Hackensack, NJ: H.W. Grey House Publishing (formerly H.W. Wilson) , 1908-date. Monthly (except September) with quarterly and annual cumulations. Print available from Grey House Publishing, online database from H.W. Wilson.
Cost: print: $655.00 per year ($725.00 outside of U.S. and Canada); Inquire for current electronic pricing.
First published in 1908, this index was originally titled the **Index to Legal Periodicals**, and, until 1980, was the only extensive index of legal periodical literature. It now indexes more than 1,025 English language legal periodicals published in the United States, Canada, Great Britain, Ireland, Australia, and New Zealand, and 300 law reviews. In 1994, the title was changed to **Index to Legal Periodicals and Books** and approximately 1,400 monographs were added to the coverage. Also available on **WilsonWeb** in index and full text (see below), and retrospective versions (see Retrospective Acquisitions).

Legal Source: Bronx, NY: H.W. Wilson Company, 1981/94-date.
Cost: Inquire for current pricing.
Formerly **Index to Legal Periodicals & Books on WilsonWeb, Legal Source** represents a merger of the H.W. Wilson and EBSCO databases to provide the full text of more than 880 law journals, and detailed indexing of legal journals, law reviews, yearbooks, institutes, statutes, bar association and government publications. It also includes indexing of more than 1,400 monographs annually. It also links to content available via **Hein OnLine** and the **EBSCO Legal Collection**, comprising 1225 full text journals, and over 2.5 million records.

Law and Politics Book Review. College Park, MD: Law and Courts Section, American Political Science Association, 1991-date. Wayne McIntosh, University of Maryland, Department of Government & Politics. University of Maryland, Editor.
Available at: http://www.gvpt.umd.edu/lpbr/index.htm
The **Law and Politics Book Review** is sponsored by the Law and Courts Section of the American Political Science Association. Its web site functions as a searchable archive for all reviews published in this electronic journal since its founding in 1991. Supported by the Section and by the University of Maryland, it is the principal resource for reviews of English language books published in the "Law and Politics" field, broadly construed. Being published on the Internet, its readers receive the reviews automatically in their e-mail box upon publication. The Section has a membership of almost 900 and presently sends the Review to over 1,300 readers in 39 countries. The electronic medium allows the **LPBR** to review almost every book about the legal process and politics, to do longer reviews than are usually published, and to make the reviews available within six months of receipt. Reviews reflect the full range of scholarly and political opinion and typically run from 2,500 to 5,000 words. The Review presently remains available for an indefinite period on the Review's World Wide Web home page [currently: http://www.bsos.umd.edu/gvpt/lpbr].

Legal Information Management Index. Chapel Hill, NC: Legal Information Services, 1984-date. Bimonthly with annual cumulation. (919) 408-0267; FAX: (919) 408-0267.
Cost: Discontinued in December 2013. Was $188.00 per year ($178.00 online); combination print and online: $238.00 (includes annual cumulation); Online Historic Access only: $100.00 (2014).
Edited by law librarian and attorney Elyse Fox, this publication indexes 92 periodicals published in the United States, Canada and abroad. Indexed literature includes substantive English-

language articles, bibliographies and surveys, and critical reviews of monographs, serials, software and hardware, online databases, microforms, CD-ROMs, looseleaf services, and audio-visual materials. Articles are indexed by key word, and by author. Book reviews are indexed by title. For law librarians, this is the best vehicle for keeping up with the flood of information in the fields of law librarianship and legal information management.

LegalTrac (1980-Present). Farmington Hills, MI: Thomson Gale, 1980-date.
Cost: contact Gale Cengage Learning at 1-800-877-4253.
LegalTrac is a Web-based database offering indexing for all major law reviews, legal newspapers, specialty law publications, bar association journals, and law-related articles from general interest publications. LegalTrac indexes over 1500 major law reviews, legal newspapers, and specialty publications, bar association journals, and international legal journals in the United States, Canada, the United Kingdom, Australia, and other major English speaking countries. It also includes the full text of 250 titles, as well as many full-text book reviews. Coverage dates from 1980 for most periodicals indexed. Updated monthly. Corresponds to the print **Current Law Index**.

LexisNexis Directory of Law Reviews: Online Directory of Law Reviews and Scholarly Legal Periodicals. Compiled by Michael H. Hoffheimer. Available at:
http://www.lexisnexis.com/lawschool/prodev/lawreview/
(with password).
This online directory includes Title Index, General Student-Edited Law Reviews, Special Focus Student-Edited Law Journals, Non-Student Edited Peer Review and Trade Journals, University Presses, and bibliography of sources in the field of legal writing. A print directory was distributed to law faculty in 2005.

Essential Web Sites

ACQWEB Vanderbilt University. School of Law. Available at:
http://www.acqweb.org/
Since 1994, **AcqWeb** has served as a "gathering place for librarians and other professionals interested in acquisitions and collection development." It is designed to serve the staff who select and purchase the books, serials and related information resources for libraries. Among its numerous tools, AcqWeb provides an extensive

Directory of Law Publishers
http://www.acqweb.org/pubr/law.html

and

WWW Resources for Law Librarians in Acquisitions and Collection Development. Vanderbilt University. School of Law. Available at: http://www.acqweb.org/law.html
Those who deal regularly with legal publishers and vendors should bookmark this site. The library profession is much indebted to the efforts of Vanderbilt's Anna Belle Leiserson for its creation.

AddAll.com
This book search and price comparison site allows users to search and compare among more than 40 sites, 20,000 sellers, and millions of books. Users may search by author, title, key word and ISBN.

Alibris.com
The world's leading supplier of new, out-of-print and hard to find books. Its inventory encompasses the holdings of hundreds of independent booksellers around the world and boasts a database of 35 million books, manuscripts, maps, photos, prints, and autographs. Located in the San Francisco Bay area, Alibris operates additional facilities across the United States for bookseller relations, technology development, and distribution. Visitors to the Web site can search its inventory or browse by subject area.

Amazon.com
A revolutionary way of acquiring books, e-books, audio, video, and other forms of media. Amazon.com stocks thousands of legal, law-related, and general titles. Entries include thousands of user-generated reviews. It also includes many subject matter bibliographies and customer-inspired recommendations. Provides a search service for out-of-print titles (10% of its sales). While amazon.com has accepted credit card orders from its inception, it is now prepared to service institutional accounts which require invoicing (see **Against the Grain**, Nov., 2001, pp. 60-67). Amazon.com also provides users with the ability to sell new or used books online.

Book Depot. Available at:
http://www.bookdepot.com
One of North America's largest wholesalers of discount and remainder books, the Book Depot has been wholesaling for more than 10 years, and selling online since 1997. Has an inventory of over 5 million books which can be located and purchased online.

CRIV Vendor Relation Page. American Association of Law Libraries, Committee on Relations with Information Vendors (CRIV). Available at:
www.aallnet.org/main-menu/Advocacy/vendorrelations/
The Committee on Relations with Information Vendors is charged with facilitating communications between information vendors and the members of the American Association of Law Libraries and the Executive Board in matters relating to provision of information in any format. The committee monitors complaints and provides constructive suggestions to vendors. The **CRIV Vendor Relation Page** is an extremely useful site for anyone who acquires legal information, providing valuable insight into the issues, responses, and tools employed by professional law librarians in dealing with information vendors. The **CRIV Vendor Relation Page's** CRIV Tools, includes a number of useful features, including tips for dealing with telemarketers and customer service departments, lists of divested titles, a glossary of publishing terms, a guide to negotiating Internet subscriptions, sample letters, a sample publisher log, and vendor contact information. The site should be bookmarked by anyone who regularly deals with legal information vendors

Jurist: The Law Professors' Network. University of Pittsburg. School of Law. Available at: http://jurist.law.pitt.edu/
According to its information page, Jurist is dedicated to advancing academic, professional, and public legal education by providing an online forum where law professors can find information important to the daily work as teachers and scholars, and where they can share knowledge and exchange ideas with a worldwide community of colleagues, law students, lawyers and interested citizens. Monthly book reviews are available in the Books-on-Law section and in an archive than goes back to April, 1998. Contains scholarly reviews of law and law-related titles by legal scholars from across the country. Reviews are available at: http://jurist.law.pitt.edu/lawbooks/index.htm.

The Lawbook Exchange, Ltd. 33 Terminal Ave., Clark, NJ 07066-1321 Available at: http://www.lawbookexc.com/
This New Jersey-based dealer specializes in new, used and rare law books for law libraries, practitioners and scholars. Its monthly online catalogs provide the most extensive current price lists for new, used, antiquarian, and reprinted law books, as well as detailed descriptions of rare and antiquarian titles.

Law-lib list-serv.
More than 3,000 law librarians associated with academic, governmental, law firm, and corporate law libraries are signed on to this list-serv, as well as representatives of legal publishers who use law-lib to monitor the opinions of their largest identifiable block of consumers. If you don't mind sifting through dozens of irrelevant postings, monitoring law-lib is probably the best way of keeping attuned to the practices of the legal publishing industry. To subscribe, send the following message to: listproc@ucdavis.edu: "Subscribe [insert your first and last name]"

Law Librarian Blog:
http://lawprofessors.typepad.com/law_librarian_blog/
Maintained by law librarian Joseph Hodnicki, Director of the Butler County (OH) Law Library, with contributions by Mark Giangrande, Caren Biberman, Sarah Glassmeyer, Victoria Szymczak, and David C. Walker, this blog tracks developments in law libraries, the law librarian job market, and the world of legal publishing. Its archive is a valuable resource for a variety of topics related to the profession and publishing realms.

Law Library Collection Development Policies: Policy Documents and Resources. American Association of Law Libraries. Project of the Acquisitions Committee, Technical Services Special Interest Section. Available at:
http://www.aallnet.org/sis/tssis/committees/acquisitions/collectiondevelopmentpolicies/
This site represents a collective effort by law librarians in many countries to create a virtual collection of collection development policy documents for law libraries, and a bibliography of models, standards, and guides for creating law library collection development policies. The site will eventually include policies from a broad range of law libraries: private, court, agency, public, prison, academic, other. The site also provides access to collection development policy documents for special types of legal materials, such as government documents. Further, the site provides access to related materials of interest, including relevant collection development policies for other types of libraries and special formats, and to bibliographical information on collection policy documents in print, collection development standards, and guides to creating collection development policies. Law libraries are encouraged to contribute their collection development policy to the list. The site is edited by Alan Keely, Wake Forest University Professional Center Library.

Legal Publishers' List: Corporate Affiliations of Legal Publishers. Committee on Relations with Information Vendors. American Association of Law Libraries.
Available at:
http://www.aallnet.org/committee/criv/resources/tools/list/index.htm
This site, formerly maintained by Rob Richards of the University of Colorado Law Library, provides a sporadically updated organizational outline of legal publishers and their corporate affiliations, together with news reports of developments in the world of legal publishing. News items are contributed by law librarians from across the country. Responsibility for this Web site is assumed by AALL's Committee on Relations with Information Vendors (CRIV); however, it was last updated in April 2006.

Law Library Catalogs. Washburn School of Law. Available at: http://www.washlaw.edu/lawcat/
This site provides direct links to several hundred academic and public law library catalogs. Some feature RSS Feeds. "RSS" stands for Really Simple Syndication or Rich Site Summary, a standard for publishing regular updates to web-based content, in this case, recent acquisitions.

New Acquisitions Lists [various]. Available at:
http://www.acqweb.org/law.html#newbooks
A number of law libraries post recent acquisitions lists on their web sites. While many of these lists include titles acquired in recent months, others may contain an archive of titles acquired over the past several years.

Powells.com. Portland, OR: Powell's Books. 1994-date.
Powell's Books, headquartered in Portland, Oregon, is the largest independent retail bookstore in the U.S. With seven locations in the Portland metropolitan area, it also has one of the book world's most successful online businesses (www.powells.com), serving customers worldwide. Their online site is the largest independent online bookseller for hard-to-find and rare books, as well as for new books. The site employs more than 60 full-time Internet personnel.

Principles for Licensing Electronic Resources.
www.arl.org/sc/marketplace/license/licprinciples.shtml
In 1997, the American Association of Law Libraries joined five other library associations in adopting principles to guide libraries in negotiating access to electronic resources and informing vendors of electronic products about issues important to the library community.

Chapter 24: Legal References on CD

One of the more exciting developments in the recent history of legal publishing was the introduction of legal materials in the CD-ROM format. Legal publishing in the English-speaking world goes back more than 500 years and, during much of that time, traditional forms of publication have dominated the field. In fact, the most significant departures from a field dominated by the hardbound book have consisted of the advance sheet pioneered by the West Publishing Company in 1876, the looseleaf service introduced by the Corporation Trust Company (later CCH) in 1907, and the pocket part which West first employed in its 1916 **McKinney's Consolidated Laws of New York**.

The first major break with this 500-year-old tradition of the law in printed form took place in 1973 when Mead Data Central introduced Lexis, the first commercial application of computer technology to the delivery of legal information. Two years later, in 1975, the West Publishing Company brought forth its own computer-assisted legal research system called Westlaw. Together, these systems opened up a whole new world of sophisticated legal research previously unmatched by print finding tools. Significant as these developments were from the delivery side, however, they were compromised by pricing models which prevented their widespread acceptance among many segments of the practicing bar. Clearly, many members of the bar sat on the sidelines in anticipation of a more user-friendly computer-assisted research medium which could provide the power of full-text searching combined with lower and more predictable costs.

As the popularity of CD-ROM wanes, it is important to remember the impact which its introduction had on the pricing of computer-assisted legal research. The application of CD-ROM technology to computer-assisted legal research set into motion a new dynamic in the delivery of legal information. Its presence in the marketplace also served as a catalyst in promoting more attractive fixed-rate pricing models for LexisNexis and Westlaw. It soon became clear, however, that CD-ROM was destined to serve as an interim technology that would be eclipsed by the more timely and technologically more sophisticated online services now readily accessible on the Internet. While a significant number of law-related CD-ROM titles are still produced, the cutting edge of technology and marketing has shifted dramatically to the commercial Internet.

In recent years, the annual subscriptions charges for most West CD-ROM products have risen so dramatically that the equivalent product on Westlaw is by far the better value. In fact, it would appear that West is consciously driving up the cost of both its print and CD-ROM products in order to drive customers toward WestlawNext, which is replacing Classic Westlaw.. WestlawNext sales representatives are in a position to offer attractive packages combining both primary law and desired secondary and analytical products.

CD-ROM Technology

CD-ROM stands for Compact Disk-Read Only Memory. A CD-ROM disc is a laser-encoded optical storage medium similar in appearance to a disc that holds music, except that it may hold pictures and text as well as sound. One CD-ROM disc can hold 600 megabytes of text (600 million characters), the equivalent of 300,000 typewritten pages. Even this capacity can be doubled by using specialized compression software. Information contained on a disc may be accessed by using a CD-ROM disc drive which is either an external unit attached to a PC or a built-in part of a computer's central processing unit (CPU). The search software (also called search engine or search interface) used to access the information may be contained either on the CD-ROM disc itself or on a floppy disc which is loaded onto your PC's hard drive.

Unlike the information contained on a floppy disc, the information on a CD-ROM cannot be altered; however, selected information can be copied to a hard drive and them manipulated with word processing software. A typical CD-ROM disc can hold the equivalent of 300 printed volumes of 1,000 pages each, or 600 compressed volumes of the same length. The production of high-speed CD-ROM drives has reduced access times to a fraction of a second. Attorneys contemplating a hardware purchase or upgrade should consider a system with at least a 56X (speed) CD-ROM drive. The introduction of the DVD format has markedly increased the storage capacity of the medium. The storage capacity of the most common CD-ROM is 700 MB, as opposed to the 4.7 GB storage capacity of the DVD. A DVD contains approximately six times the storage space of a CD-ROM

Searching

Using CD-ROM technology, a researcher can quickly scan the contents of hundreds of volumes of text for specific keywords or phrases or combinations of words or phrases using Boolean connectors [e.g. and, or, but not] between search terms. Unlike Key Number searches in the West digests which are dependent on the identification of specific legal principles, research on a CD-ROM allows the user to locate every instance in which a particular word or phrase appears, regardless of its context. This search capability transcends the limitations inherent in any system which relies upon editorial judgment to assign the legal issues in cases to specific topics and key numbers. It does not replace the Key Number system, but provides an invaluable means of supplementing its limitations. The beauty of CD-ROM is that one can freely adjust the combination of search terms to achieve optimum results without incurring additional online charges. In recent years, however, fixed-rate online plans have providers legal information consumers with a superior alternative.

Currency

One of the most significant difference between CD-ROM and online services is in the level of currency. Information (cases, statutes, regulations, etc.) on Lexis, WestlawNext, Casemaker, Fastcase, VersusLaw and other online services, is usually available within 24-48 hours of its issuance. The currency of the data on a quarterly CD-ROM product, on the other hand, can range from 4-6 weeks upon receipt from the publisher and 16-17 weeks as it reaches the end of its useful life, at which time it is replaced by the next quarterly release. Most CD-ROM publishers, however, including LexisNexis and West, have compensated for this limitation by providing links to the publisher's online database to cover the gap. Thus, with Internet access, the subscriber can achieve the same level of currency as the online subscriber. The primary advantage of this combination is that the subscriber pays a much lower, flat-rate charge for the vast majority of the information and no charge, other than telecommunication charges, for accessing the most recent online information, as long as he or she does not venture into other fee-based databases. However, it is important to compare the cost of a state CD-ROM product with the comparable cost of the same bodies of primary law on an Internet subscription, such as that offered by a WestlawNext plan.

For example, take **Indiana Cases**, the Premise CD-ROM product produced by Thomson Reuters. This product, which contains only appellate caselaw, now costs $806.75 per month, or $9,681 per year, to maintain. Separate CD-ROM containing the Indiana statutes and the **West's Indiana Digest** that once cost an additional $9,400 annually (but have now been discontinued by West), brought the total cost to more than $19,000 annually. By contrast, an unlimited-use **Indiana Primary Law Resources Plus** subscription for a solo practitioner on WestlawNext, including Indiana caselaw (including federal caselaw for the relevant circuit), the annotated Indiana code, the United States Code Annotated, the KeyCite citation service, the ability to search the West Digest System, and other useful libraries, can be obtained for $3,804 annually.

Search Engines

Initially, legal publishers approached the development of CD-ROM search software with the view that lawyers are too busy to spend much time learning search protocols and exhibit a degree of computer-phobia Thus, the search software tends to be extremely user-friendly, requiring the use of only a few keys to perform its major functions. CD-ROM discs can be searched using Boolean connectors and, in the case of West products, Key Numbers. CD-ROM products also feature hypertext links that permit the user to jump from citations in a case to the case or statute cited, and back again, or from a headnote to that portion of an opinion to which the headnote refers. Another feature that greatly enhances the utility of CD-ROM products is the cut and paste option which allows the user to block desired portions of text for insertion into a PC's notebook or into a word processing document. Many CD-ROM vendors issue their titles in Windows, and Macintosh versions.

One of the disadvantages of CD-ROM is the lack of a consistent search interface among the many legal information vendors. Observers had anticipated that, over time, a consolidation in the number of separate search engines would take place as smaller vendors adopted one of the more popular systems. In recent years, however, the number of unique search engines has increased from 80 to more than 100. The various Folio search engines lead the field, followed by West's Premise. Other search engines with a measurable share of the market include Adobe Acrobat and its variations, ASCII, Books on Screen, Dataware, LawDesk, LivePublish, PITA, SPIRS (Silver Platter), Word, and WordPerfect. These, together with Folio and Premise, currently make up more than 80% of the market. There are also a number of Proprietary search engines on the market. In 1996, Matthew Bender decided to convert its Search Master CD-ROMs to Authority, a Folio search and retrieval engine. For a complete list of legal CD-ROM products organized by search engine, see the Search Software Index of the Directory of Law-Related CD-ROMs.

History and Development

Once the potential of CD-ROM technology became apparent, most observers anticipated that West Publishing would begin issuing its various reporter series on CD-ROM. However, West and other major publishers were initially reluctant to begin issuing legal information in this format for the same reasons which delayed their acceptance of online systems in the early 1970's. Their chief concern was how to advance the new technology without harming their existing print and online business. Thus, West's first entries in the world of CD-ROM were specialized libraries which drew upon, but did not replicate, existing reporter series. Legal publishers have long since realized that advances in technology cannot be resisted in the face of rising consumer expectation and demand and with competitors who are prepared to take advantage of available opportunities.

With a marketplace eager for state-specific primary law products, West chose not to compete against either its print or online business. Its specialized products included Federal Bankruptcy, Civil Practice, Federal Securities, and Government Contracts, among others. In fact, a central feature of West's specialized "libraries" was an online link to WestlawNext which, although sold for a fixed monthly charge along with the CD-ROM library, was no doubt designed to stimulate the use of other WestlawNext databases. Matthew Bender was another company which made an early jump into CD-ROM with its Search Master state practice libraries and topical products, although it has now converted all its titles to the Folio search engine.

The major consequence of West's delay in producing state primary law products on CD-ROM was the appearance of a number of smaller CD-ROM vendors who were anxious to tap this significant market. Law Office Information Systems (now Loislaw), of Van Buren, Arkansas, was one of these smaller vendors which took advantage of West's reticence by introducing the CaseBase line of CD-ROM products in such states as Arkansas, Connecticut, Massachusetts, Rhode Island, and Kansas. Without a print or online product upon which to compete, LOIS took a more aggressive approach to securing state primary materials from state courts, legislatures, and administrative bodies, and it provided greater historical case coverage than that offered on the CD-ROMs that West later introduced. Since that time, however, both West and Lexis have pushed their coverage in all states back to the earliest reported decisions.

A few years after releasing its first CD-ROM products, LOIS sold its CaseBase line to Lawyers Cooperative Publishing Company which has since become a part of West, now a division of Thomson Reuters. These original KAware products were then converted to the Folio search engine under the names CaseBase Platinum, or LawDesk. LOIS returned with a greatly enhanced, 32-bit proprietary search engine called PITA. Now, however, Loislaw has abandoned the CD-ROM format and shifted its emphasis to the Internet. At the same time, Lexis Publishing (formerly the Michie Company) issued an extensive line of state CD-ROM products using the Folio search engine. Thus, lawyers in many states had, for a time, multiple state primary law products competing for their CD-ROM business.

Following the merger of West Publishing and Thomson in 1996, the newly created West Group found itself the owner of competing CD-ROM products in many jurisdictions. West had already blanketed the nation with a line of primary law products employing its proprietary Premise search engine. With the addition of the former Lawyers Cooperative line of LawDesk products on Folio, the new West Group was placed in the position of supporting two separate lines of state CD-ROM products, each with its own search engine. West has been consolidating these separate product lines and utilizing the best features of both, although both Premise and LawDesk (Folio) products continue to exist for many jurisdictions.

Titles on CD-ROM

The 2014 edition of Arlene Eis's **Directory of Law-Related CD-ROMs** lists a total of over 1,600 available titles, down from more than 1,700 in 2006. While the initial growth in CD-ROM titles was for products containing state and federal primary law, secondary materials have become increasingly popular in recent years. Bar association materials, legal forms, and textbooks make up another important segment of materials on disc. Even the **Legal Information Buyer's Guide & Reference Manual** is available on CD-ROM for users who wish to conduct full text searching. Shepard's Citations, which made a brief appearance in the CD-ROM format, disappeared with the introduction of the vastly superior Shepard's Citations on Lexis. Finally, many publishers of legal treatises and practice books have adopted the CD-ROM format as a delivery vehicle for companion forms and other appendices.

Looseleaf publishers like BNA, CCH and RIA all offered some of their print products on both CD-ROM and the Internet and have seen their sales shift dramatically to the Internet. And while primary law titles have proven the most popular of all legal CD-ROMs, a number of secondary sources also appeared for a time, including titles from Wolters Kluwer Law & Business (formerly Aspen Law & Business), Matthew Bender, LexisNexis, and Thomson Reuters (West). These are now rapidly giving way to the ebook. Vendors like Loislaw, who initiated the practice of providing the full range of primary sources on the same disc, have forced other companies to provide a similar range of materials on WestlawNext. Under the circumstances, a WestlawNext subscription now a the far better alternative than the combination of separate CD-ROM products they once produced.

CD-ROM versus Books

The acquisition of legal materials on CD-ROM provided subscribers not only with a greatly enhanced searching capability at a fixed cost, but a valuable archival storage medium for bound volumes which may have formerly occupied row upon row of costly shelf space. CD-ROM technology gave the user the opportunity to replace hundreds, or thousands, of casebound volumes with a few CD-ROM discs.

Now, of course, those materials are now readily available in attractively priced online packages, rendering both hardcopy and CD-ROM obsolete. It has also become clear that rapidly escalating subscription costs for many of West's CD-ROM products are part of a calculated plan to drive customers toward WestlawNext. Based on print and CD-ROM subscription cost trends, it makes far more sense to abandon these formats and simply obtain the current information on WestlawNext. Retaining cancelled print materials on the shelves of your law office can still provide a source for initial research, but not be relied upon for currency.

The decision to purchase legal materials on CD-ROM once depended on a number of interrelated factors, including the organizational structure of the materials themselves, coverage, cost, discounts, utility of existing print indices, your current ownership of the title in print, and available law office space for expanding print collections. Now, however, the pricing trajectory of Thomas Reuters CD-ROM products has now rendered it far more cost effective to access these materials on WestlawNext than on CD-ROM.

Some of the articles describing the application of CD-ROM technology in the law firm environment refer to law firms' substantial "investment" in books. This is inaccurate. However much the firm may have spent over the years to build a book collection, the current value of those casebound volumes is a mere fraction of what they initially cost (See **Chapter 8: Used Law Books**). Used sets of case reporters and other law titles have always sold at prices far below the cumulative cost of acquiring them new. With the advent of CD-ROM and the Internet, their prices have fallen even farther. This phenomenon has been amply demonstrated over the past few years as many law libraries and firms have begun offering most of the major reporter series, and other sets, over Internet list-servs to any taker willing to pay the cost of postage. So the term "investment" no longer has much relevance when one is speaking of used sets of casebound law books. While the sale of your print collection may net you a few dollars, the decision to convert your library to a proprietary online service via the Internet must ultimately be made on its own merits and independently of the residual value of your print collection.

CD-ROM versus Online Research

While CD-ROM technology offered some advantages over online services, it has now being eclipsed by a variety of fixed-cost online options. Once the CD-ROM permeated the market, consumers began to demand similar fixed-rate pricing options from online vendors. In that regard, the CD-ROM not only helped bring online costs under control for such materials, but also provided users with the freedom to make mistakes, start over again, refine searches, and read in a relaxed fashion without worrying about mounting online charges. For those firms with both online capability and CD-ROM, the CD-ROM provided the opportunity to test and refine queries before going online for updating purposes. They helped guarantee that online sessions would be short, successful, and less expensive. CD-ROMs also provided a back-up to books which may be missing from library shelves, a role previously filled by online services. Also, with potential online transmission problems, CD-ROM provided greater law firm self-sufficiency. These considerations have now been rendered moot by high-speed and reliable Internet connections. It is only a question of time before CD-ROMs disappear from the marketplace.

One of the primary disadvantage of CD-ROMs is that, by themselves, they are not as current as online services. The availability of attractive fixed-rate online plans is driving many customers to abandon the use of CD-ROMs entirely. Another distinct disadvantage of CD-ROMs when compared to online access is that the ability to conduct cross-file searching and linking is limited to the CD-ROMs to which you subscribe and have been mounted on your network. For example, a WestlawNext subscription which provides access to decisions of your state appellate courts and federal circuit, as well as to those of the U.S. Supreme Court, gives you the ability to search and link to any case covered by your subscription. Accomplishing the same task on CD-ROM is highly impractical.

Another disadvantage is that almost all legal CD-ROM discs are leased from the publisher and expire when the replacement is received (usually quarterly). In most instances, this precludes the purchaser from buying one disc for its historical coverage and canceling the updates.

CD-ROM Licenses

One major difference between legal information on CD-ROM and that in print is that the CD-ROM is usually leased to the subscriber. CD-ROM vendors retain a greater degree of control over the information than print publishers did. The purchaser of a print product has almost total freedom to do what he or she wishes with the physical item. The buyer may keep the item, sell it on the used market, or give it away. With CD-ROM, ownership is retained by the vendor and products which do not have to be returned will generally self-destruct (time expire) after a set period of time, usually several weeks after the anticipated receipt of its replacement. CD-ROMs may not be resold, nor may the licenses be reassigned.

The license agreements may limit the degree to which the data may be copied or converted to another medium. Vendors usually permit the making of backup copies, but they do not want subscribers converting the entire database or large portions of it to another medium. Without these license provisions, vendors would be unable to control the used trade in their discs for their archival value. CD-ROM licenses also provide restrictions on using the product in a multiple-user environment, unless network charges are paid. Obviously, vendors are not going to sacrifice multi-user online contracts or multiple sales of their own print products to customers who plan to network the data unless they are adequately compensated. License agreements may prohibit LAN (local area network) applications, permit them for an additional charge, or permit them without charge. The solution for those consumers anxious to avoid such networking charges is to locate CD-ROM publishers who do not force such fees on the consumer. For example, Loislaw.com products may be networked without charge. Similar restrictions may apply to the use of CD-ROMs on a wide area network (WAN).

The provisions of a CD-ROM license agreement are, in essence, a offer made by the vendor. The customer is free to accept the terms, reject them, or make a counter offer. A customer who desires to modify the terms of the license agreement should be prepared for additional charges if the nature of the changes is such that the vendor stands to lose income. In these and all other instances, the prospective purchaser should closely examine the fine print to determine the exact nature of the agreement and the restrictions which govern use of the data. In evaluating licensing agreements, the prospective licensee should consider such factors as: the parties to the agreement, ownership rights, lease rights, permitted users, access, use of the database, use of search results, use of the software, product maintenance, control of access, hidden costs and penalties, contract terms and termination, warranties, liability and indemnity clauses, and confidentiality issues.

Buying Law-Related CD-ROM Titles

Legal titles on CD-ROM are not necessarily cheaper than print, but invariably more expensive than WestlawNext. It is true now that vendors have dropped the substantial up-front licensing fees which have been associated with legal CD-ROM titles, but West has substantially increased the annual subscription charges at the same time.

CD ROM Selection Criteria

Before selecting a CD-ROM product, the prospective buyer should take into account the following factors:

1. The annual subscription cost. Compare the costs of the various competing products.
2. What libraries of information are contained on the disc(s)? Does it contain statutes, reports, court rules, and administrative regulations on one disc or must you buy several products to assemble the same information? What is the historical coverage? Must you retain some older case reporters in bound volumes to maintain a complete library of cases?
3. Are the discs sold or leased? If leased, what limitations does the vendor place on your use of the product?
4. Will the product run on your computer system (Windows, Macintosh).
5. Does the publisher offer a discount to customers who maintain the print along with the CD-ROM? If it does not, at present, offer such a deal, negotiate one to maintain both.
6. How many discs comprise the entire product?
7. How frequently are the discs updated?
8. Is there an on-line updating service and what charges, if any, are attached to it?
9. Does the vendor provide toll-free assistance and at what hours or offer an online tutorial?
10. Does the vendor provide on-site training?
11. What are the hard disc and memory (RAM) requirements?
12. Can the product be run on a network and are there additional fees to do so?
13. Can the information on the discs be loaded directly onto a server (some publishers don't allow this)?
14. Can the information be downloaded to a disc using a word processing program such as WordPerfect?

15. Is your network CD-ROM compatible?
16. Is the product accompanied by easy-to-understand documentation?
17. Is the product user-friendly or is considerable training required?
18. Is the search engine compatible with the majority of the CD-ROMs in your office or law library? If not, are you prepared to manage the additional training required?
19. Do the discs "self destruct" (time expire) after a period of time following receipt of the updates?
20. Does the publisher offer special discounts on CD-ROM drives, or towers? Most publishers have gotten out of the equipment business after some initial forays in to this area.
21. Will the purchase of this product place you in a more vulnerable position vis-a-vis the publisher than you were when you owned only the print? For example, will you be forced to purchase all quarterly updates when you would prefer them annually?
22. Is the CD-ROM product more current or less current than the print version? Most CD-ROMs are updated monthly or quarterly while the print versions are updated weekly.
23. And finally, how does the CD-ROM product compare with the equivalent information online? You may discover that the package of information available on a WestlawNext subscription or a LexisNexis Advantage subscription provides distinct advantages over CD-ROM when coverage, ease of use, and cost are compared.

Significant Legal CD-ROM Vendors

AccessLaw. Continuing Education of the Bar.
2100Franklin St., Suite 500
Oakland, CA 94612-3098. 1-800-232-3444
www.accesslaw.com
Publisher of CalDisc, a complete collection of California law, including court decisions, state codes, state constitution, and court rules. Available on DVD, and the AccessLaw Online Service. AccessLaw Online Service is priced at $468.00 per year ($39.00 per month), the CalDisc/CalDVD Integrated Law Library is priced at $264.00 initially, plus $$419.00 annually for four quarterly updates, for a total of $683.80 in the first year. On February 1, 2012, the Continuing Education of the Bar, California (CEB) acquired AccessLaw.

American Bar Association. 750 N. Lake Shore Drive, Chicago, IL 60611. (800) 285-2221
www.abanet.org/abapubs/
The ABA publishes dozens of practitioner titles either on CD-ROM, or with a companion CD-ROM containing the book text and/or appendices, forms, or other supporting material. These titles include **Commercial Real Estate Law Practice Manual with Forms, The Family Lawyer's Guide to Bankruptcy, The NEPA Caselaw Digest**, and many more.

American Maritime Cases, Inc. 28 E. 21st St., Baltimore, MD 21218-5932. (410) 243-2426.
http://www.americanmaritimecases.com/
Publisher of **American Maritime Cases** (1923 to date), utilizing the Folio search engine. The library of cases, which had been converted to the DVD format, is now available solely online.

Wolters Kluwer Law & Business. 1185 Avenue of the Americas, 37th Floor, New York, NY 10036. (800) 447-1717.
http://www.aspenpublishers.com/
Publisher of several dozen law-related titles on CD-ROM or with companion CD-ROMs, including **Corporation Plus; Mergers, Acquisitions and Buyouts; Directory of Corporate Counsel; Ginsburg and Martin on Bankruptcy**, and the **Hospital Law Manual**, among others. Aspen took over the operation of Loislaw.com following the latter's acquisition by Wolters Kluwer in 2000. The Aspen Law & Business titles have now migrated to the Wolters Kluwer Law & Business brand. Many of the Wolters Kluwer Law & Business titles are now also available as practice libraries on the Loislaw.com estore.

Matthew Bender (see LexisNexis Matthew Bender).1275 Broadway, Albany, NY 12204. (800) 223-1940.
http://bookstore.lexis.com/bookstore/catalog/
Originally utilizing the proprietary Search Master search engine, Matthew Bender converted to the industry standard Folio in 1996 with its Authority line. It has released most of its hard copy treatises on CD-ROM, many of which are also combined into specialized subject libraries (e.g. the Bankruptcy Law Library). For a brief period, Bender was supplying the CD-ROMs to print subscribers at no additional charge, but abandoned this program after adopting the Folio standard (with its attendant licensing costs). CD-ROM products are sold on an annual subscription basis with annual renewals. Customers choosing not to renew their subscription will eventually lose access to the information since the discs are programmed to self-destruct a few months after the end of the subscription period. Naturally, it is not necessary to return the discs to the publisher. Whether purchased in print, on CD-ROM, or as Internet products, the costs are roughly equivalent (see Chapter 27 for information regarding specific titles). Subscriptions also include the LexisNexis Online Connection for the most current case law at no extra charge. The plan is to discontinue CD-ROMs eventually.

George T. Bisel Co. 710 S. Washington Sq., Philadelphia, PA 19106. (800) 247-3526.
www.bisel.com
Publisher of BISEL-LINK CD-ROM, a compilation of seven Pennsylvania specific titles (compromising 30 volumes) on Folio.

Bradford Publishing. 1743 Wazee St., Denver, CO 80202 (800) 446-2831.
www.bradfordpublishing.com
Publisher of a variety of Colorado state practice titles. Its titles have now been converted to ebooks.

Bloomberg BNA. 1231 25th St., Washington, DC 20037. (800) 372-1033.
www.bna.com
This major publisher of looseleaf services has now transferred most of its CD-ROM products to the Internet, including those in tax, labor and employment law, human resources, environmental law, and human resources. Sales have shifted heavily from both print and CD-ROM to the online formats.

Clark Boardman Callaghan (see Thomson Reuters West).
The former Clark Boardman Callaghan (CBC) issued a number of its major subject-specific treatise products in the CD-ROM format utilizing the Folio search engine running on Windows, including **Couch on Insurance, Environmental Law Reporter, Fletcher Corporate LawLink, Nichols Electronic Cyclopedia of Legal Forms, Norton Bankruptcy Service Plus, Products Liability PowerLink, and Social Security Plus**. Some of these products contain integrated libraries of related titles, such as **UCCSEARCH** which contains the **UCC Reporting Service, UCC Case Digest, PEB Commentaries**, etc., and optional access to the **Hawkland UCC Series** and **Anderson UCC 3d**. Following the 1996 merger of Thomson and West, and its subsequent merger with Reuters, these titles have now become part of the Thomson Reuters (West) product line. Most have been removed from the current catalog, although the publisher may be maintaining some for existing customers.

CCH Inc. (**Wolters Kluwer**). 2700 Lake Cook Rd., Riverwoods, IL 60015. (800) 835-0105
www.cch.com
Commerce Clearing House (CCH) offers CD-ROM and Internet versions of a number of its looseleaf services, including those in the fields of federal and state taxation, labor and employment, health, medical and entitlements, federal securities, human resources, pensions, federal acquisitions, and consumer credit. These products use a proprietary search engine. Products have moved significantly to the Internet.

The Gale Group. 27500 Drake Road, Farmington Hills, MI 48331-3535. (800) 877-4253.
www.gale.com
The Gale Group is a subsidiary of Cengage Learning (formerly Thomson Learning), a division of the Thomson Reuters. This vendor produces **Legal Trac**, of more than 1,500 legal periodical titles, which has now migrated to the Internet. .

Geronimo Development Corp. 606 25th Ave., South, Suite 206, St. Cloud, MN 56301. (800) 457-6045.
www.casefinder.com
Although based in Minnesota, this company produces a comprehensive CD-ROM of Virginia state and federal primary law using the ISYS search engine from Odyssey Development. It has now added online access to its CD-ROM products.

Gould Publications, Inc. 1333 N. U.S. Highway 17-92, Longwood, FL 32750-3724. (800) 717-7917.
http://www.lexisnexis.com/lawenforcement/
Originally a publisher of federal and some state unannotated codes in print, as well as titles in the field of law enforcement, Gould Publications was acquired by Reed Elsevier in 2004. The former Gould titles in such fields as criminal law, law enforcement, motor vehicles, many of which are on CD-ROM, are now part of the LexisNexis family of products.

Government Institutes, Inc. 4 Research Place, Suite 200, Rockville, MD 20850.
https://rowman.com/GovernmentInstitutes
Now an imprint of the Rowman & Littlefield Group, this specialized publisher of environmental books and CD-ROMs has issued products containing federal regulations in the fields of occupational safety and health (OSHA), environmental health and safety, food and drugs, RCRA hazardous waste, and telecommunications.

William S. Hein & Co., Inc. 1285 Main Street, Buffalo, NY 14209-1987.
http://www.wshein.com/
A company of many talents and services, William S. Hein has served for many years as one of the leading agents for the law library community, as well as a lawbook and micropublisher, used book dealer, etc. It has produced the **Bibliography of Early American Law (Cohen), Hein's United States Treaty Index on CD-ROM, the United Nations Treaty Indexing Service, and Law School Catalogs on CD-ROM**. Many of these have now migrated to Hein's award-winning online library, HeinOnline.

Kleinrock Publishing, Inc. (see CCH)
Formerly an independent publisher of federal tax materials and forms on CD-ROM and the Internet, including **Kleinrock's Tax Expert**, Kleinrock was acquired by Wolters Kluwer in 2006 and is now part of the CCH product line.

Lawyers Cooperative Publishing Company. (see West).

LexisNexis (Reed Elsevier). 1275 Broadway, Albany, NY 12204. (800) 223-1940
http://bookstore.lexis.com/bookstore/catalog
LexisNexis produces primary law products on CD-ROM for more than 40 states utilizing the Folio search engine. It also produces a number of specialty law titles. The state products may include appellate court decisions, court rules, state statutes, and administrative regulations or some combination of these databases. LexisNexis products are sold on an annual or monthly basis. Additional charges apply to network installations. Subscriptions also include the LexisNexis Online Connection for the most current case law at no extra charge.

Loislaw, a Division of Aspen Publishers (a Wolters Kluwer Company). 105 North 28th St., Van Buren, AR 72956. (800) 364-2512.
http://www.loislaw.com
Loislaw was the original developer of the CaseBase line of CD-ROM products for the states of Arkansas, Connecticut, Georgia, Kansas, Louisiana, Massachusetts, Mississippi, North Carolina, and Rhode Island. In 1993, LOIS sold all but the Louisiana product to the Thomson Corporation which assigned them to the Lawyers Cooperative Publishing Company. Following the expiration of covenants not to compete, LOIS began producing new CD-ROM products for many of the same states using the PITA search engine. By February, 2000, LOIS was marketing primary law databases for all thirteen federal circuits and all fifty states, as well as a product containing decisions of the U.S. Supreme Court from 1898 to date. In 1999, however, LOIS shifted its focus to loislaw.com, its Internet site. The cost of its complete National Collection is $1,512.00 per year. Loislaw.com was acquired by Wolters Kluwer in 2000 and is now a part of Wolters Kluwer Law and Business.

LRP Publications. 747 Dresher Road (Dept. 425), Horsham, PA 19044-0980. (800) 341-7874, Ext. 245.
www.shoplrp.com
Originally a publisher of legal and law-related looseleaf services in the fields of arbitration, bankruptcy, disability law, education,

and jury verdicts, LRP converted many of those titles to CD-ROM. While it still produces some products on CD-ROM, its emphasis has now shifted to online delivery. Many of its labor law products were acquired by Thomson Reuters.

National Technical Information Service. 5285 Port Royal Road, Springfield, VA,
http://www.ntis.gov/
A publisher of federal regulatory and environmental products, NTIS has issued the complete CFR on CD-ROM and titles on toxic releases and substances control, and defense.

Pike & Fischer, Inc. 4600 East-West Hwy., Suite 200, Bethesda, MD 20814-1438. (800) 255-8131.
http://www.bna.com/legal-business-t5009/
This subsidiary of the Bloomberg BNA produced several CD-ROM products, including the **BNA Criminal Practice Manual, Broadcast Regulation, Communications Regulation, Equipment Regulation, Private Radio Regulation, and Radio Common Carrier Regulation**. All use the Folio search engine. The former Pike and Fischer titles have now migrated to the Bloomberg BNA Internet product line.

Practising Law Institute. 810 Seventh Avenue, New York, NY 10019. (800) 260-4754.
www.pli.edu
One of the largest producers of continuing legal education seminars for the legal profession, PLI issues its programs and materials on both CD-ROM and DVD. Its Interactive Media Division has issued the titles Be **Prepared for Your Deposition** and **The Interactive Courtroom**, a CD-ROM series illustrating trial procedure and tactics. PLI's delivery of CLE programs are now delivered primarily in the form of On-Demand Web programs over the Internet.

Public Utilities Reports, Inc. 8229 Boone Blvd., Suite 401, Vienna, VA 22182. (800) 368-5001.
www.pur.com
A specialist in public utilities publications, PUR, Inc. has issued **PURbase**, a DVD containing state public utilities decisions in its Public Utilities Reports, Fourth Series (PUR4th) (1974 to date).

Research Institute of America Group (RIA). 395 Hudson Street, New York, NY 10014. (800) 431-9025.
http://ria.thomsonreuters.com/
A subsidiary of the Thomson Reuters, RIA CD-ROM titles have largely been converted to the Internet, including titles in the fields of taxation, estate planning, compensation and benefits, pensions, human resources, and payroll, all using the Folio search engine. Many of its products are also available in print and online.

Fred B. Rothman & Co. (see Hein, William F.)

Solutions Software Corp., a division of RegScan, Inc. 800 West 4th Street, Williamsport, PA 17701. (877) 373-4726.
www.env-sol.com
Solutions Software specializes in state and federal regulatory online and CD-ROM products, including the those containing the **CFR, Federal Register**, and the **U.S. Government Manual**. It has also converted many of its products to an ebook format. Adobe Acrobat is the search engine.

Tax Analysts. 6830 N. Fairfax Drive, Arlington, VA 22213. (800) 955-2444.
www.taxanalysts.com/
A producer of specialty tax products, Tax Analysts has now shifted its tax products to the Internet, including the **Federal Tax News, Federal Research Library, OneDisc Premium DVD, Internal Revenue Manual Disc, State Tax Today, International Tax News, and Exempt Organization Tax Review**.

Tax Management, Inc. (see Bloomberg BNA). Bloomberg BNA Customer Contact Center, 3 Bethesda Metro Center, Suite 250, Bethesda, MD 20814-5377 (800) 372-1033.
www.bna.com/tax-accounting-t5000/
This subsidiary of BNA once published a number of tax resources on CD-ROM. These have now been integrated in to the Bloomberg BNA product line and transitioned to the online format.

Thomson Reuters West. 610 Opperman Drive, Eagan, MN 55123. (800) 888-9907.
http://store.westlaw.com/default.aspx
The West Publishing Company began issuing specialized products on CD-ROM in 1987, including libraries covering bankruptcy, civil practice, federal securities, government contracts, and federal taxation. Initially West resisted issuing its reporters on CD-ROM for fear of competing against its own online service WESTLAWNEXT. When it became obvious that other CD-ROM vendors were about to grab a major share of this market, West began producing its own state-specific primary law products. West now has products for all 50 states which contain cases, statutes, administrative regulations, and attorney general opinions or some of combination of these sources. West is also issuing state Key Number digests on CD-ROM for many states as well as those for the **Supreme Court Reporter, Federal Reporter, Federal Supplement, Federal Rules Decisions**, its regional reporters, and the **United States Code Annotated**, among others. With the addition of the separate CD-ROM product lines of Lawyers Cooperative and Clark Boardman Callaghan following the West Thomson merger in 1996, the West Group (now West) became the largest owner/producer of CD-ROM products in the United States. Its products use both the Folio (LawDesk) and Premise search engines. In recent years, West has discontinued a number if its less popular CD-ROM products, including many state digests. Also, annual subscriptions costs have risen dramatically in recent years, making CD-ROM a far less attractive alternative than the same products on WestlawNext. Many CD-ROM products have been removed from the Thomson Reuters online catalog over the past year.

U.S. Government Printing Office. (Superintendent of Documents). P.O. Box 371954, Pittsburgh, PA 15250-7954. (888)293-6498.
http://bookstore.gpo.gov/
The U.S. Government Printing Office has released a number of its print products on CD-ROM, including the **United States Code**, the **U.S. Government Manual**, the **Monthly Catalog of U.S. Government Publications**, the **EPA Toxic Release Inventory,** and the **National Criminal Justice Document Data Base**. They use a variety of search engines, including I-SEARCH, and Adobe Acrobat.

U.S. Patent & Trademark Office. Information Products Division.. Crystal Park 3, Suite 441, Washington, DC 20231. (800) 786-9199.

http://www.uspto.gov/

A number of products, covering all manner of patent and trademark publications, research tools, and records of patents and trademarks, are produced by the Office of Electronic Information Products. These have now been converted to an online format.

Warren, Gorham & Lamont (see RIA). 395 Hudson Street, New York, NY 10014. (800) 950-1210.

http://ria.thomsonreuters.com/TaxResearch/

Most titles are now available only in print and online formats. Visit the RIA web site for information on specific titles.

A note on computer configurations:

In order to access the Internet and to efficiently use the large number of CD-ROMs and DVDs on the market, the well-equipped law office should maintain an up-to-date computer system. When we first provided these guidelines, most law offices were using stand-alone systems for word processing, billing, and Internet access. Today's multi-user, networked law offices often have their own full-time IT (Information Technology) person, and advanced pc workstations. But for the smaller firms and startup solo practitioners, we offer the following guidelines:

1. **Operating system**: You should be using Windows 7, Vista, or XP Professional. A mix and match approach, with different operating systems on different computers can result in incompatibility problems. In addition, users of Microsoft Office should be aware of this problem as well. Office 2011, 2010, and 2007 create files that are incompatible with Office 2003 files, unless saved in the older format. This can be especially true if the practitioners e-mail Word attachments to their clients. Those clients with older versions of Word may not be able to open .docx (newer version files)

2. **Memory**: Most of the standard programs can do well with 1 GB (gigabyte) of Random Access Memory (RAM). Up to 4 GBs are now offered on newer computers. This can be a factor when multi-tasking—having two or three programs running simultaneously. The more memory, the more efficient the computer can be.

3. **Processor speed**: 2.8 GHz (gigahertz) or higher, is recommended. This is the speed at which the computer loads programs and files into the random access memory, and the speed at which the computer processes calculations, data searches, file saves, etc. The higher the speed, the faster that the calculations, searches and similar tasks can be done.

4. **Optical Drives:** CD-ROM read/write drive, as well as a DVD read/write drive is now standard equipment.

5. **Storage** (hard drive): 500 GB (gigabyte) -1 TB (terabyte). For systems on a network, the network server can be used to store backup files, so the amount of storage on the workstation is not as important.

6. **External storage**: : As mentioned above, the network server, with each practitioner having his or her own folder, can provide backup/external storage. For the standalone workstation, an external USB connected hard drive of 500 GB – 1 TB might be a good choice. Network servers can crash occasionally, leaving the practitioners without access to their files. The external USB backup drive can be good insurance. They are generally less than $100. Removable USB flash drives are also very popular. An 16 GB flash drive can now be purchased for $10 or less. These can allow easy transfer of files from office desktop to home or laptop computer**7. Costs**: A complete desktop system with all of the above features can be found at most retail computer stores for about $400-800. Most good notebook computers are still in the over $1,000 range.

7. A complete desktop system with all of the above features can be found at most retail computer stores for about $400-800. Most good notebook computers can be purchased for under $400.00.

8. **Printer**: Most law offices now have network laser printers. In addition, many copy machines now have network connections as well. This can permit the practitioner to produce multiple copies of multi-page documents at very fast speeds, directly from their workstation, thus saving time not having to stand (or wait in line) at the copy machine.

8. **A notebook (laptop) system** is becoming increasingly popular for work in the field and in courtrooms. Wi-fi Internet capabilities are now built in, allowing roaming Internet access. With a VPN (virtual private network) connection, the practitioner can be connected to the office network from a remote location. This allows work from home, on the road, etc. With security a growing issue, a VPN connection can allow the practitioner password access to his/her files on the office network, with a laptop in the field, or a desktop system in the practitioner's home.

Chapter 25: Computer-Assisted Legal Research

Computer-assisted legal research (CALR) has, over the past 35 years, transformed the way lawyers perform legal research. This chapter will direct its attention to an examination of the commercial CALR systems currently on the market as an aid to your selection of a system best suited to your research requirements and budget.

There are currently ten commercial CALR services on the market which will be examined here: three premium services (LexisNexis, Westlaw and Bloomberg Law), and seven alternative services that offer various levels of substantive content and functionality. These seven alternative services presently include CaseClerk, Casemaker, Fastcase, Loislaw.com, TheLaw.net, RegScanLaw, and VersusLaw. In addition to these ten commercial services, legal researchers can access more limited bodies of primary law on several free Internet sites, including FindLaw, lexisOne, Google Scholar, and those maintained by state and federal governmental entities. However, as the tired cliché goes, "you get what you pay for." These free Internet sites have their uses, but cannot match the technical sophistication, depth and breadth of coverage, speed of access, and cross-jurisdictional searching capabilities of the commercial services. For the serious legal researcher, a commercial CALR service is a virtual necessity.

This chapter will examine, in order: (1) the three premium CALR services (Bloomberg Law, LexisNexis and WestlawNext), (2) the four most noteworthy of the alternative CALR services (Casemaker, Fastcase, Loislaw.com, and VersusLaw), and, (3) will conclude with descriptions of the three remaining alternative services (CaseClerk, TheLaw.net, and RegScanLaw). Consideration will also be given to ways in which some of the premium CALR services can be combined with one of the alternative services as a means of reducing overall online costs.

Arguably the leading system for evaluating online legal information services is that developed by the Southern California Online Users Group (SCOUG) at its Fourth Annual Retreat in 1990. The SCOUG Rating Scale employs ten broad categories for evaluating online information services. Attorney T.R. Halvorson, who has authored numerous reviews of CALR systems for llrx.com, employs the SCOUG Rating Scale in his evaluations. These evaluative categories include: (1) coverage and scope, (2) integration, (3) timeliness, (4) output, (5) accuracy/error rate, (6) documentation, (7) accessibility/ease of use, (8) customer support and training,)9) consistency, and (10) value-to-cost ratio. A complete evaluation of CALR services should include these evaluative categories. For a comparative overview of historical caselaw coverage for all nine CALR services, as well as official state government sites, consult Appendix I.

The Emergence of Computer-Assisted Legal Research

When Mead Data Central unveiled Lexis in 1973, it heralded the dawn of a new era in the field of legal research. Prior to that time, finding "the law" was a process heavily dependent upon the intellectual input of indexers and classifiers who served as jurisprudential "gatekeepers" to the legal profession. Unless the indexers used terms and index headings likely to be chosen by researchers, the cases, statutes or regulations remained hidden from view. The West Key Number System, for example, remains a fairly sophisticated means of classifying the law and assigning points of law in particular cases to specific topics and subtopics for later retrieval. However, unless the West editor assigns a particular issue to the "right" topic and key number, the task of locating a case becomes far more difficult.

The introduction of computer-assisted legal research reduced this reliance on indexers' classifications decisions. With Lexis and Westlaw, there is no gatekeeper standing between the researcher and the material being researched. The researcher becomes his or her own indexer--selecting words which he or she believes are found in the text of the material itself. With the aid of the computer, the researcher can, in a matter of seconds, locate relevant materials which would have taken hours to retrieve manually. Computer-assisted legal research offers several distinct advantages over manual research in books: (1) vast libraries of both published and unpublished legal materials, (2) speed of access, (3) timeliness of coverage, and (4) the ability to retrieve materials across data fields.

In the 35 years since CALR arrived on the scene, the legal profession has embraced both Lexis and Westlaw with great enthusiasm. From the outset, database vendors were aware that the future of computer-driven systems was dependent on their use and acceptance by law students who would continue to demand such services when they went into practice. Those first law students who benefited from virtually unlimited access to Lexis and Westlaw in their law school libraries are now in their late-forties and early fifties and in positions to decide the kind of research services which their firms will acquire.

The one significant drawback to this cost-free access in one's law school years is the tendency among many attorneys to leap to the computer without first conducting manual research, or to use CALR exclusively without consulting other, less costly, sources. During the heady days of law firm expansion in the 1980's, law firms had little concern about online costs, and vendors felt little pressure to provide alternatives to expensive online access, or discounts for heavy users. This failure by vendors was felt most particularly in law firms making repeated online use of the law of their own jurisdictions. In this pre-CD-ROM era, law firms chalked up millions upon millions of dollars in online charges for repeated access to the same limited jurisdictional databases. At the same time, many solo practitioners and small firms resisted the adoption of online legal research services because they feared the high costs.

At the end of the 1980's, hard times forced many law firms to question the cost of online computer access and apply controls to such access. Much of this concern was prompted by clients who began to question many of the supplemental charges which law firms had been tacking on to their bills for legal services. Since then, early concerns about the high cost of online access have declined in the face of steadily falling costs, particularly for the small law office market. Indeed, online access is now dramatically cheaper than the cost of maintaining print resources.

Limitations of CALR

Despite the impressive capabilities of computer-assisted legal research, there are inherent limitations in such systems. These limitations were identified in a seminal paper written in 1985 by Professors David C. Blair of the University of Michigan and M.E. Maron of the University of California at Berkeley, entitled "An Evaluation of Retrieval Effectiveness for a Full-Text Document-Retrieval System," and published in the March, 1985 issue of **Communications of the Association of Computing Machinery**. Blair and Maron's controlled study evaluated the effectiveness of IBM STAIRS, a full-text document retrieval system which was used to organize a database of 350,000 documents relating to litigation surrounding the failure of one the Bay Area Rapid Transit (BART) robot cars which drove through the Fremont, CA station and into the parking lot.

Blair and Maron's study revealed that, although an average of 79 out of every 100 documents a search request retrieved proved to be relevant, the queries retrieved only 20 out of every 100 relevant documents in the 350,000 document database. They concluded that even experienced CALR users can have difficulty estimating the effectiveness of a search. While computer-assisted legal research systems may retrieve a number of relevant documents, there is no way to determine how many other equally relevant documents are not found. This is particular true when one is researching a concept that people may express in a variety of ways. Blair and Maron also underscored the need to guard against a false sense that a search is comprehensive when a high percentage of retrieved documents are relevant.

In light of these findings, the careful legal researcher must employ a variety of tools to ensure that a comprehensive search is conducted, including various print tools, online services or CD-ROM, and **Shepard's Citations** or **KeyCite**. For example, print sources provide the kind of analytical and contextual framework only partially available on full text retrieval systems. Although its use is rapidly waning, CD-ROM can provide a more cost-effective medium for conducting the kind alternative search strategies often necessary to ensure that a higher percentage of the total relevant documents are located. Online services can provide broad-based searching and a level of currency which cannot be matched by print publications or periodic CD-ROM updates. Online services can also perform field or segment searching, a task that is impossible using books.

The Shift from Rule-based to Fact-based Legal Analysis

Despite the obvious advantages of computer-assisted legal research, most legal researchers have failed to fully consider its inherent shortcomings. In a fascinating and thought-provoking article in **Law Library Journal** (Summer, 1996), Barbara Bintliff, pointed out that the shift from book-based to computer-based research is transforming the way in which we think about legal problems. This is being manifested in the transformation of the rule- or concept-based system of legal analysis into a fact-based system of analysis. Book-based research, which provided the structural foundation for a rule-based system of legal analysis is giving way to computer-based research which is providing the foundation for a fact-based approach to legal analysis. Computer-assisted legal research systems are excellent tools for matching factual situations, but they have serious limitations in providing access to the underlying rules or concepts which provide intellectual context to the law. In a computer-dominated world of legal research, that context must be supplied by the researcher based upon his or her analysis of a number of factually similar cases. Computer-based legal research systems, which are organized by words, are not yet sophisticated enough to permit rule-based research. Moreover, the natural language search mechanisms, which attempt to provide the ability to search by legal concept or phrase, have proved only marginally better than traditional Boolean searching in this regard.

Bintliff's analysis has profound implications for those generations of law students and lawyers who are more comfortable with computer-based legal research than with books. Research on computer, according to published studies, creates a false sense of security which did not exist when books were the dominant research tool. Relying solely upon the results of a fact-based computer search, the attorney may not ascertain the underlying rules which provide the conceptual framework to predict the outcome of a case. In light of these observations, such concept-based legal research tools as the traditional key-number digest, legal encyclopedia, law review article, and legal treatise provide a necessary complement to computer-assisted legal research systems.

Deciding When to Use CALR

Despite the inherent limitations of computer-assisted legal research, there are a number of instances in which it is clearly more advantageous or cost-effective, including:

1. When the issue is narrow and well-defined.
2. When the issue can be formulated in clear and unambiguous terms.
3. When your law office library lacks the hardcopy sources.
4. When locating the specific document in print would cost more than online charges.
5. When researching specific factual situations.
6. When acquiring a specific case, statute, regulation, article or other document.
7. When performing cite checks to determine case status and to find related cases.
8. When researching the most current law and other information.

Steps Before Going Online

Except in some clearly defined circumstances, legal researchers should resist the use of CALR until less expensive alternatives have been exhausted. Law firm and court librarians, in particular, have to contend with recent law school graduates whose first instinct is to use Westlaw or Lexis without first using manual, CD-ROM, or less expensive online alternatives. These bad habits were exacerbated when Lexis and Westlaw began allowing law students to access their databases at home, an arrangement which encouraged students to read materials online. Breaking the bad habits formed by three or more years of unlimited law school access is a continuing challenge for law firms and governmental entities concerned about controlling CALR costs. Establishing clear guidelines for CALR and monitoring actual online usage will reap repeated dividends in the form of lower online charges. In addition, the following steps should be taken prior to conducting online research:

1. Formulate your query in advance using print sources or CD-ROM.
2. Identify likely synonyms, connectors, date restrictions, and other delimiters in advance.
3. Do not use premium on-line services until print and less costly online resources are exhausted.
4. Do not confine your search to Westlaw or LexisNexis just because you happen to be more familiar with them.
5. Know the pricing policies of each CALR vendor and use the most appropriate vendor for the type of search you are performing.
6. Call upon the Westlaw or LexisNexis research attorneys for assistance by using the vendors' 800 numbers.
7. Determine which database you wish to use prior to signing on.
8. Determine in advance whether a smaller or subject-specific database will satisfy your need.
9. Purchase the fastest modem you can afford to reduce connect time.
10. Use the databases in your Westlaw PRO or PRO PLUS, or Lexis Advantage flat-rate subscription to gain a firm understanding of the law and nomenclature of a legal issue before venturing into databases for which additional charges will be incurred.
11. Use less expensive alternative online sources such as VersusLaw or Casemaker to gain that initial basic understanding of a legal issue. Consider a policy of requiring attorneys to use a service such as Fastcase, VersusLaw or Casemaker as their default online service, particularly in the initial stages of research. This will help guarantee that, when they later use Westlaw or LexisNexis, their searching is likely to better focused and more cost-efficient.

Cost Saving Techniques Once You Are Online

1. Proofread your query before proceeding.
2. Retrieve documents in one step using the Westlaw "find" command or the Lexis "LEXSEE" or "LEXSTAT" commands.
3. Scan documents quickly using the Westlaw "locate" and Lexis "focus" commands to determine their relevance.
4. Once you know you are on the right track, print a list of case citations to which you can return later, if necessary.
5. Use the Westlaw and Lexis linking features to move rapidly between documents.
6. Use the appropriate stack commands to bypass the menu screens and reduce connect time.
7. Use Westlaw's PDQ or Lexis's Eclipse to run automatic searches at regular intervals.
8. Keep an indexed record of your searches for future use.
9. Use documentation, help screens and other search aids.

Selecting an Online Legal Research Vendor

There was a time when Westlaw and LexisNexis were the only major competitors for your online legal research business. With the rise of Internet technology, however, the market positions formerly exercised by Westlaw and LexisNexis are no longer as dominant. As more vendors get into the online legal research business, and more governmental units and other entities start providing primary law on the Internet, the need for Westlaw and LexisNexis will decline as a percentage of the overall online legal research market.

The legal professional with an eye on the bottom line has some significant opportunities to reduce legal information costs by: (1) determining what public Internet sites exist in his or her area(s) of interest; (2) conducting a comparative analysis of the costs of Westlaw, Bloomberg Law or LexisNexis on the one hand and Casemaker, VersusLaw or other alternative CALR vendors on the other; and (3) determining the exact type of subscription and configuration of databases to be purchased from the preferred online vendor or vendors. Leaving a fuller discussion of the Internet for Chapter 26, this chapter will focus its attention on the three major online vendors, LexisNexis, Westlaw and Bloomberg Law, and on several alternative CALR providers.

Selecting any online vendor will necessarily involve a consideration of the following factors:

1. Does the vendor have the content necessary for you to carry on your legal practice? For example, does the vendor have the primary law content for the jurisdictions in which you practice or the topical coverage in your areas(s) of specialty? What about proprietary news and business intelligence?

2. Is the information current? For example, how quickly does the vendor mount the case law or statutes for your jurisdiction?

3. What kind of training and customer support is provided by the vendor, and during what hours is it available?

4. What kinds of subscriptions, or pricing plans, does the vendor offer for your type of organization (e.g. private, government, academic, corporate)? These pricing plans may include hourly, transactional, flat-rate (both standard and negotiated) and may involve the vendor's entire database or selected slices of it.

5. Assuming you have selected some flat-rate pricing option, what are the monthly, or annual, costs for the databases you require?

6. Does the service provide editorial enhancements and are these important enough to your research to warrant paying the additional costs which will inevitably be associated with those enhancements?

7. Are the vendor charges based on the number of attorneys in your firm, regardless of the number of likely simultaneous users or the number of passwords purchased? What is the cost for each additional password?

8. Does the vendor require that you sign a confidentiality agreement preventing you from revealing the terms of your flat-rate contract to others?

9. Do the practices of the vendor hinder or enhance open market competition? Has the vendor been a driving force in the lowering of costs for computer-assisted legal research?

10. How easy is it to navigate the vendor's web-based browser?

11. Based on your level and pattern of usage, might a more streamlined online service be considered as a means of holding down usage (and costs) for your enhanced service? What protocols might you implement in your firm to help guarantee that your users exhaust the resources of the streamlined service prior to using the enhanced service? For example, you may wish to consider a Westlaw or LexisNexis subscription for your own state and circuit, but complement this with a far less expensive subscription to VersusLaw for coverage of other jurisdictions, or take advantage of a bar association provided benefit like Casemaker. This consideration may not be as significant in a firm of less than 40 attorneys for which flat-rate plans are available, but may be critical in a larger firm where increased usage will directly affect future online contracts.

Bloomberg Law

After 35 years in which the market for premium computer-assisted legal research was dominated by two legal publishing giants who thought they had the market to themselves, a new kid has finally come to town. **Bloomberg Law**, which debuted in December, 2009, builds upon a service that had already established itself as a premier source of proprietary news and financial intelligence. Bloomberg has expended enormous capital in developing a competitive, high-end legal research service. The results are impressive.

Bloomberg Law has managed to integrate its highly valued business and news service with a comprehensive legal research service featuring the full panoply of primary law offerings, including comprehensive caselaw coverage, statutes, regulations, a legislative watch, dockets, practice area law alerts, and a Bloomberg law digest. A Bloomberg Law Database Directory provides a detailed listing of its contents.

Bloomberg Law is also developing a variety of editorial enhancements, including its own case headnotes, and has developed a citator service to rival the capabilities of Shepard's and KeyCite. The Bloomberg Law Citator provides case extracts that provide the researcher with a quick overview of the case portion being cited. It also provides court signals and quotations to indicate how the cited reference was used by subsequent courts, and the ability to make side-by-side evaluative comparisons of cited authorities. While Bloomberg Law currently has less in the way of secondary law material, it is moving ahead on that front as well, primarily with the full PLI treatise collection. With a team over 500 lawyers, Bloomberg Law is also drafting its own editorial headnotes, tagging cases, and developing a Law Digest that links index entries to primary law. While many of the features are mere shells of what they will become, the basic ingredients are all in place. Indeed, what impresses the observer is how far Bloomberg Law has come in a relatively short period of time. After all, LexisNexis and Westlaw had 35 years to make themselves into what they are today. Bloomberg has managed to achieve most of this in a fraction of the time, although with obvious indebtedness to its predecessors who blazed the trail.

The search interface is clean and intuitive and employs either Boolean or natural language protocols. The Boolean operators include the standard search terms and proximity delineators, all explained in easy-to-use explanatory boxes. Queries can be run across a range of content types (e.g. cases, statutes and dockets) or more narrowly circumscribed by jurisdiction, industry, or practice area. Moreover, the merger of legal, business and news sources, allows the researcher to monitor company news, including recent court filings drawn from court dockets and SEC filings.

A sophisticated citator feature allows the researcher to view a case while simultaneously monitoring its status in a graphical summary to the right. When expanded, this graphical summary provides a detailed analysis embracing direct history, citation history, and a list of the cases it has cited.

Bloomberg Law, while still a work in progress, already presents the foundations and much of the content of a legal information retrieval service to rival Westlaw and LexisNexis. What it lacks in secondary content, it makes up in its panoply of sophisticated news and business offerings. For the typical practicing attorney, it has all the jurisdictional content offered by its competitors. Unlike its competitors, however, whose pricing structures present an often confusing array of options tailored to specific databases, Bloomberg Law's pricing is completely straightforward and all-inclusive: $450.00 per user per month, but with delayed billing in the first year that will reduce the initial average monthly cost. A floating license plan at a rate of $1,250 per month allows five attorneys to share one password, only one of whom can use it at a time. This plan effectively reduces the per attorney cost to $250.00 per month.

Compared to the most popular WestlawNext PRO plans or to the Lexis Advantage, Bloomberg Law is very competitively priced. The key distinction is that whereas Westlaw and LexisNexis give subscribers the option of subscribing to databases tailored to individual state or federal jurisdictions, Bloomberg does not. What it offers is unlimited access to its entire national database, as well as its news and business offerings. This makes it particularly attractive to law firms representing business entities, or engaged in practices with a significant business, financial or securities focus. Its pricing model should make it attractive to large and mid-sized firms, as well as those with the appropriate client focus. Whether it can attract the firms of 10 attorneys or less, where roughly 70% of lawyers practice, remains to be seen. For the present, Bloomberg Law appears willing to maintain its flat-rate pricing structure and hope lawyers are willing to make the leap to its threshold of full course offerings.

In short, the technical sophistication and wide-ranging content offerings of Bloomberg Law make it a prime candidate to serve the research needs of the legal professional. In 2011, Bloomberg acquired BNA, formerly Bureau of National Affairs, and its sister company, BNA Books. On March 22, 2012, Bloomberg Law was named the recipient of the 2012 New Product Award by the American Association of Law Libraries (AALL). As a part of the Bloomberg news and information empire, Bloomberg Professional service has more than 310,000 subscribers worldwide, of which Bloomberg Law, Bloomberg Government, Bloomberg New Energy, Finance, Bloomberg News, and Bloomberg BNA are essential components. In July 2011, Bloomberg Law released the latest version of its web platform, making the system even faster and easier to use. Bloomberg hopes to replace Lexis as the second provider of online legal research. This is unlikely to happen because they simply entered the field too late. Old habits die hard, however, and it's unlikely that Bloomberg Law will be able to crack the Westlaw/Lexis duopoly in the legal marketplace. Even with its acquisition of BNA, Bloomberg Law still lacks a body of analytical and secondary material capable competing with its content-rich rivals.

LexisNexis

One of the most dramatic developments to take place in the world of computer-assisted legal research was the unveiling of the **LexisNexis.com** web browser-based interface in August, 1997, a product of extensive customer research and technical development. The **LexisNexis.com** browser-based interface is a comprehensive integrated research system that adds a new level of power and functionality to the traditional LexisNexis service.

Users of the new **LexisNexis.com** research system operate from an updated and enhanced Research page which allows researchers to: (1) perform a traditional Lexis search, but with the benefit of suggested words and concepts, (2) use the **Lexis Search Advisor** to find an appropriate legal topic and choose an appropriate database, (3) get a document, and (4) check a citation. In addition, each case in the Lexis database has been enhanced with an editorial summary and core terms, a list of the essential legal terms extracted from the opinion which provides a quick indication of its subject content. Together, these powerful new and enhanced features provide an effective alternative to the West key number system and the editorial content of the West case synopses and headnotes.

The most significant of these new features is the **Lexis Search Advisor**, a detailed classification system which combines the editorial subject expertise of Matthew Bender with the vast resources of the Lexis database. **Lexis Search Advisor** is based on a list of 40 broad legal subjects which correspond to established areas of the law and the subject matter covered in the law school curriculum. A researcher can either type in a legal topic and be guided to the appropriate location in the **Search Advisor** classification system, or click on an appropriate topic and navigate to a subtopic which best encompasses the subject of his inquiry. Once one has identified an appropriate topic, a hidden search, constructed in advance by attorneys on the **Search Advisor** editorial team, will be run automatically.
These search requests combine basic searching, including simple terms and connectors, with more specialized techniques, including segment searching, precise search terms, and complex search syntax. The **Search Advisor** attorney-editors incorporate synonyms, word variations, and statutory citations into the search requests where appropriate. Their aim is to achieve a balance between comprehensiveness and precision, thereby locating leading cases and eliminating irrelevant ones.

Core Term and Case Summaries

LexisNexis has devoted considerable financial resources to create a full range of research enhancing tools for the legal researcher. Its core terms project was based on extensive research and testing by lawyers, linguists and law librarians. Operating off a computer algorithm, it searches through documents (cases) to select the top 20-30 terms, while excluding those least relevant. It has also embarked on a case summaries project which is now providing case summaries, core concepts, procedural posture, and outcome for all prospective court decisions and a still to be determined body of retrospective decisions.

Up until now, Westlaw has been able to maintain its advantage in the area of caselaw research because of its book-based headnotes, synopses, and key number system, tools familiar to most lawyers. The key number system, however, despite laudatory attempts to keep it vital, is nevertheless rooted in the 19th century legal terminology. Consequently, West's editorial advantages can also be liabilities as it struggles to make its system serve the needs of lawyers in the 21st century. LexisNexis, while it lacks these book-based editorial components, is nevertheless in a strong position to develop new computer-based legal research software which reflects the latest design and editorial features conducive to effective legal research in the modern world. It is a system of tools as flexible as the next load of computer software. Lexis-Nexis is now in possession of panoply of computer-based legal research tools which will allow it to match, if not exceed, anything Westlaw has to offer. Its case summaries, for example, employ language exactly as it is used by the courts. And if imitation is the highest form of flattery, one has only to take a glance at Westlaw's KeySearch tool to realize that LexisNexis was on to something.

Shepard's Citations

Another significant addition to **LexisNexis.com** is the power of an enhanced Shepard's Citations service which combines traditional Shepard's' editorial expertise with a number of new features made possible by computer technology. One of the most important of these features is the merging of all Shepard's information from parallel citations into one search result. It is no longer necessary to check separate online documents if a case is listed in more than one Shepard's citator. The new Shepard's also combines the features previously available in AutoCite, LexCite, and Shepard's. Researchers may now obtain analysis of unpublished decisions and law reviews as well as other sources. They may also obtain references to statutes when a case is listed in the annotations of an annotated code, a feature not previously available in a Shepard's Citations list of citing references.
Shepard's also gives the researcher the power to limit the citation results from a Restrictions screen. Once a case has been Shepardized, the Restrictions screen gives the researcher the

ability to limit the citation list to cases from a given court, specific West or official headnote, or area of literature (law reviews, ALRs, etc.). It also combines the power of the old LEXIS Focus feature with Shepard's. It is now possible to employ the Focus feature with a Shepard's citation list to conduct a new, more focused search using a select body of cases.

Finally, subscribers to Shepard's on LexisNexis.com also have the ability to retrieve the full text of any authority in the Lexis database by citation. One can either type in the citation to a case and view (and print) its full text or click on any case retrieved in the process of Shepardizing another citation and view the full text. This one feature opens the content of the complete Lexis database to researchers who have a citation to guide them. Adding all jurisdictional Shepard's to a LexisNexis Advantage subscription has now become one of the best values in legal publishing.

Like Westlaw, Lexis contains an enormous library of both primary and secondary legal source materials, including cases, administrative opinions, statutes, regulations, attorney general opinions, law reviews, legal periodical indices, legislative histories, and looseleaf services. Lexis also serves as a gateway to Nexis, a current awareness news and information service which contains over 8,600 world-wide full-text news and business sources. The LexisNexis database also contains many unpublished judicial opinions not appearing in the standard reporter series. In 1999, Lexis introduced core terms to all cases in its database.

LexisNexis Total Practice Advantage

LexisNexis Total Practice Advantage™ is a sophisticated integrated package of tools and resources for client development, legal research, practice management, and litigation services. It was designed to give attorneys the power and flexibility to increase productivity and profitability, reduce malpractice risk, enhance client interaction, and make well-informed decisions regarding cases and other legal matters. Employing a task-based interface, it provides the ability to conduct research, provide calendar management, draft and file documents, identify prospective clients, and bill for services, all from one online location and from a single sign-on.

LexisNexis Total Practice Advantage also lets you organize all activity related to a particular client or matter, including research, contracts, case details, and documents, so that it can be searched and retrieved, and accessed by any authorized member of your firm.

On September 27, 2007, LexisNexis introduced an innovative new search functionality on lexis.com® called "Search by Topic or Headnote" that enables legal professionals to perform a single search across multiple sources as part of one unified process. The new search platform enables users to search by topic across such content sources as national and state Matthew Bender® titles, primary source material, law review articles, restatements, legal news, and practice forms.

Those interested in more information on the lexisnexis.com Practice Advantage Content Search capability please visit:
http://law.lexisnexis.com/total-practice-advantage/content.

Lexis Pricing

LexisNexis has an array of pricing plans designed to meet the needs of individual customers, firms or organizations. These include: (1) hourly pricing; (2) transactional pricing; (3) LexisNexis Advantage Flat-Rate Libraries, and (4) negotiated fixed-rate plans. Contact your local sales representative for complete information regarding these pricing options.

Hourly Pricing

For a number of years after its introduction in 1973, hourly pricing was the only option available to subscribers. Hourly charges varied considerably based on the size of the database being accessed. Large files, such as those containing all state or all federal cases, were priced at multiples of the cost of accessing the law of a single state. As competitive pressures mounted, LexisNexis designed other pricing models to attract customers previously deterred by the high cost of online access. While hourly pricing still exists, and may be necessary for occasional access to databases outside of one's fixed-rate plan, or contract, it is not recommended as a standard model for online access. Serious users of computer-assisted legal research should select some form of fixed-rate pricing based on the types of databases necessary to support their practice.

Transactional Pricing

Transactional pricing applies a fixed cost per search based upon the type of file being accessed. For more information regarding transactional pricing, contact your local LexisNexis sales representative.

Lexis Advance

The free case law formerly provided by LexisOne has been replaced by Lexis Advance or lexis.com. LexisNexis continues to provide access to a variety of free legal resources and information through the LexisNexis® Communities pages. Go to:
www.lexisnexis.com/community/portal/content/lexisonelanding-page.aspx

Consumers are able to obtain monthly pricing for individual libraries based on size of firm.

LexisNexis Fixed-Rate Plans

Several years ago, LEXIS unveiled a program for solo practitioners and small firms called **MVP** (Maximum Value Products) designed to bring a level of predictability to the costs of computer-assisted legal research. This program has been transformed into Lexis Advantage.

Contact your LexisNexis sales representative for details and specific pricing options.

Special Practice Areas

LexisNexis has also assembled packages for specialists, providing unlimited access to a collection of state and federal statutes, cases and regulations as well as a variety of secondary publications. These specialties include accounting, admiralty, banking, bankruptcy, business & finance, commercial law, communications, compliance/regulated industries, construction law, criminal, cyberlaw, e-commerce, elder law, energy/utilities, environment, family, Federal immigration, intellectual property, international, law, labor & employment, military, public contracts, real estate, securities, social security disability, tax, and tort & insurance. It will also combine multiple specialties and states into a research library designed to support the needs of the specialist practitioner. This service also provides access to any case, statute, or law review article outside of your flat rate library at no extra cost. Access to Shepard's (now incorporating Auto-Cite) is provided for a relatively modest additional charge. Subscribers selecting a package with at least two states will likely be offered Shepard's at no additional charge. Contact the LexisNexis sales representative for pricing and other details.

The above programs are attractive options, particular for the attorney who practices in one or a few jurisdictions and in one of the available legal specialties. LexisNexis is open to other fixed-cost arrangements for other narrow slices of its database. The cost-conscious attorney should investigate all possible fixed-cost plans as a means of bringing online costs under control, particularly in an era in which passing online charges on to clients is becoming increasingly problematic.

One possible disadvantage of the Lexis fixed-rate program is that LexisNexis, like Westlaw, requires that each member of a firm be counted when pricing is calculated, regardless of the likelihood that they will actually utilize the service. This pricing may be quite advantageous if all members of the firm are heavy users of CALR, but less advantageous if usage is concentrated among a smaller group. In the latter type of research environment, this per-attorney pricing model may end up costing more than total firm usage would warrant. This contrasts sharply with the pricing philosophy at Loislaw.com, which allows all members of a firm to share one password and reap the economies associated with cooperative scheduling of online access.

However, LexisNexis is a vastly superior research service and is willing to negotiate special packages which may include state materials, federal materials, a national primary law package, specialized national databases, and all legal materials on Lexis, to name just a few. For a complete review of Lexis databases, pricing, and special package discounts contact your local sales representative. The following Lexis state primary law pricing plans are intended only as a basic introduction to pricing plans available. Consult your local LexisNexis sales representative for the latest pricing options available for your jurisdiction and practice specialty.

Sample LexisNexis Fixed Rate Plans*

State Primary Law, Primary Law Enhanced, and Primary Law Enhanced with Full Federal

STATE	Primary Law	Primary Law Enhanced	Enhanced w/ Full Federal
California	$1,200.00	$1,800.00	$2,400.00
Connecticut	$1,200.00	$1,440.00	$1,920.00
Louisiana	$1,200.00	$1,800.00	$2,400.00
Massachusetts	$1,200.00	$1,800.00	$2,400.00
Michigan	$1,200.00	$1,800.00	$2,400.00
New York	$1,500.00	$1,800.00	$2,400.00
S. Carolina	$1,200.00	$1,800.00	$2,400.00

State Primary typically includes state constitution, statutes, court cases, bills, bill tracking, state and federal court rules, and the full Shepard's Citation service.

Primary Enhanced typically includes state constitution, statutes, state regulatory and administrative materials, state court cases, federal court cases from the respective circuit, attorney general opinions, bills, bill tracking, state and federal court rules, 300+ law reviews and journals, and the full Shepard's Citation service.

State Enhanced with Full Federal adds to the above materials the full library of federal cases from all federal courts of appeal, U,S. District Courts, and specialized federal courts.

The following telephone number will put you in contact with LexisNexis customer and technical support: 1-800-543-6862

A complete list of customer service contact numbers may be accessed at: http://www.lexisnexis.com/custserv/Contact/

As of **April 5, 2011** LexisNexis will no longer offer the website LexisNexis® by Credit Card http://web.lexis.com/xchange/ccsubs/cc_prods.asp, nor the Research Value Packages or transactional access to enhanced case law available at lexisONE®. Customers who have purchased a Research Value Package subscription prior to April 5, 2011, will have access to the content for the duration of the subscription contract. This decision is part of the company's effort to create and support products that better meet those needs identified through collaboration with customers, including tools that help small law attorneys conduct more efficient legal research. In addition to product innovations such as Lexis® Advance for Solos and Lexis® for Microsoft® Office, LexisNexis continues to offer and enhance its free open-Web service, via Lexis® Web at www.lexisweb.com and more than 28 practice area communities located at LexisNexis Communities which provide free up-to-date content and resources such as blogs, content and news. For continued access to convenient and affordable LexisNexis research content, please contact a representative at **888-285-3947 – Option 2** to learn more about lexis.com® subscription options.

Westlaw

Since its introduction in 1975, Westlaw has grown into a massive database containing millions of law-related documents including appellate court decisions at both the state and federal levels, federal and state statutes, regulations, administrative rulings, legislative histories, legal newspapers, legal periodicals, general news, and an array of secondary materials from other publishers. Databases on DIALOG allow researches to locate information on business, medicine, science and technology, intellectual property and other topics. Westlaw provides a citator service called KeyCite, a case history and verification service called Insta-Cite, Dun & Bradstreet Services Online, and the public records database Information America.

Westlaw on the Web

On March 26, 1998, the West Group introduced **westlaw.com**, its Web-based, full-featured legal research service. Accessible by anyone with a Web browser, westlaw.com offers the same research power and content as the traditional WESTMATE® software with the look and feel of desktop book research. Now the preferred mode of access, **westlaw.com** employs content and context frames, book-style printing (including dual column formatting), natural language or Boolean searching, and customized database query templates. It also provides the same services previously available through WESTMATE®, including KeyCite™, Key Number service, Table of Authorities service, Table of Contents service, Find service, Westlaw printing and downloading.

ResultsPlus

One particularly powerful feature available to users of Westlaw is ResultsPlus, a listing of analytical materials relevant to the topic being researched. Each time you run a search on Westlaw, ResultsPlus will suggest additional sources of information from among its vast library of topical content, state-specific content, and materials related to the individual cases. ResultsPlus may include citations to **American Law Reports**, **American Jurisprudence 2d**, **Am Jur Trials**, **Am Jur Proof of Facts**, relevant legal treatises, law reviews, West key numbers, state specific practice guides and handbooks, and a library of over 800,000 legal briefs.

WestlawNext

WestlawNext represents a new technological breakthrough in legal research. Introduced on February 1, 2010 at LegalTech New York, WestlawNext is the culmination of five years of development, and the contributions of hundreds of West employees, including algorithm experts, web designers, lawyer and editors. Furthermore, Thomson West surveyed thousands of lawyers, law librarians and other legal researchers to design a system to meet their needs.

What they came up with is an entirely redesigned search interface and underlying search engine that is easier to use, more intuitive, better organized and functional, and which provides a greatly enhanced search capability. One could describe it as more Google-like in that it replaces the database directories with a clean search page. With the WestSearch technology, it is no longer necessary to choose a database because WestSearch will search all relevant databases within a given jurisdiction. The search protocol allows the researcher to enter a query based on the way he or she is used to searching, or speaking, or will search by citation. Documents are retrieved by document type and ranked by relevance. Those documents can be viewed in as much detail as desired. Related material can also be accessed.

WestlawNext builds upon the vast library of primary and editorially enhanced content West has assembled over its 138-year existence. This includes not only editorial case headnotes, but content rich analytical products, such as legal encyclopedias, legal treatises in dozens of subject areas, legal forms, annotated reports, practice books, statutory annotations, and much more.

WestlawNext also provides a convenient mechanism for the researcher to “drag an drop” relevant documents, or snippets of documents, into folders, highlight relevant portions of text, and add notes.

WestlawNext Pricing

WestlawNext is more expensive than traditional Westlaw, no doubt reflecting the desire to recoup the more than $1 billion Thomson Reuters spent to engineer the upgrade. Their representatives are less than transparent about revealing their pricing in published articles and public forums. Moreover, in typical West fashion, customers are asked not to disclose the terms of proposed contracts. However, this has not deterred various writers from posting their negotiating experiences on such blogs as Lisa Solomon’s Legal Research and Writing Pro: (http://legalresearchandwritingpro.com).

The key to all this is negotiation. West sales representatives have wide latitude in negotiating contracts and may be prepared to offer WestlawNext and additional databases for a modest premium over your current rates. Your negotiations may have to move up the food chain to achieve their ultimate objective, and you must prepared to walk away or threaten giving your business to a competitor to get the best deal.

Another factor to keep in mind is the savings you can achieve by accessing West’s primary law and analytical content online rather than in print format. Users of both traditional Westlaw and WestlawNext should abandon print resources, with their extraordinarily high supplementation costs, and apply those savings to either content enhancements to their contractual plan, or per use charges for content outside of their plan. In the current pricing and supplementation cost environment, it makes little sense to maintain subscriptions to print materials that are heavily underutilized. The cost effective solution is to pay on a per use basis and avoid the high maintenance costs of print subscriptions.

Another factor to keep in mind is the savings you can achieve by accessing West’s primary law and analytical content online rather than in print format. Users of both traditional Westlaw and WestlawNext should abandon print resources, with their extraordinarily high supplementation costs, and apply those savings to either content enhancements to their contractual plan, or per use charges for content outside of their plan. In the current pricing and supplementation cost environment, it makes little sense to maintain subscriptions to print materials that are heavily underutilized. The cost effective solution is to pay on a per use basis and avoid the high maintenance costs of print subscriptions.

Westlaw Pricing

Like LEXIS-NEXIS, Westlaw offers three basic pricing models: (1) Pay As You Go; (2) Low Fixed-Cost Pricing (WestlawNext PRO), and (3) Customized fixed-rate plans.

Pay As You Go Pricing

Upon accessing Westlaw, a user may elect either hourly or transactional billing in the Options Directory (Go to "More" and then "Options"). Such billing election will be effective for that Westlaw session and all subsequent sessions unless the election is changed. For further information regarding hourly pricing, contact your local Westlaw sales representative or request a copy of the Schedule A to Westlaw Subscriber Agreement, Plan 1: Private Dial-Up Service, or Plan 2: Government Service. While hourly pricing can be justified for occasional Westlaw use, those who require frequent access to Westlaw are better served by one of the fixed-rate options described below.

WestlawNext PRO Program (Predictable Research Online)

Westlaw PRO (short for Predictable Research Online) was designed to meet the needs of law firms of 1-40 attorneys, government entities, corporate legal departments with 1-5 attorneys, and judges in state trial courts whose use of computer-assisted legal research is primarily limited to the law of particular jurisdictions or subject areas. For example, **Westlaw PRO** provides the subscriber with unlimited access to the databases of a specific state or region for a fixed monthly charge. Once the base jurisdictional product is purchased, the firm may select from a number of optional add-ons. For example a California solo practitioner who purchases a subscription for unlimited access to its state materials with KeyCite for $232 per month ($2,784 per year) or their Federal District, Federal Circuit and U.S. Supreme Court decisions, the **U.S. Code Annotated, and KeyCite All** for an additional $73 per month ($876 per year), for a total of $305 per month ($3,660 per year). The following are just a few representative samples of **WestlawNext Pro** pricing aimed at firms of 1-3 attorneys:

WestlawNext PRO Sample Annual Charges

STATE	PRIMARY LAW RESOURCES	PRIMARY LAW RESOURCES PLUS
Alabama	$3,156.00	$3,804.00
Alaska	$2,724.00	$3,228.00
Arizona	$2,724.00	$3,228.00
Arkansas	$2,724.00	$3,228.00
California	$3,636.00	$4,380.00
Colorado	$3,156.00	$3,804.00
Connecticut	$3,156.00	$3,804.00
Delaware	$2,724.00	$3,228.00
District of Columbia	$2,724.00	$3,228.00
Florida	$3,636.00	$4,380.00
Georgia	$3,636.00	$4,380.00
Hawaii	$2,724.00	$3,228.00
Idaho	$2,724.00	$3,228.00
Illinois	$3,156.00	$3,804.00
Indiana	$3,156.00	$3,804.00
Iowa	$2,724.00	$3,228.00
Kansas	$2,724.00	$3,228.00
Kentucky	$3,156.00	$3,804.00
Louisiana	$3,636.00	$4,380.00
Maine	$2,724.00	$3,228.00
Maryland	$3,156.00	$3,804.00
Massachusetts	$3,636.00	$4,380.00
Michigan	$3,156.00	$3,804.00
Minnesota	$3,636.00	$4,380.00
Mississippi	$3,156.00	$3,804.00
Missouri	$3,636.00	$4,380.00
Montana	$2,724.00	$3,228.00
Nebraska	$2,724.00	$3,228.00
Nevada	$2,724.00	$3,228.00
New Hampshire	$2,724.00	$3,228.00
New Jersey	$3,636.00	$4,380.00
New Mexico	$2,724.00	$3,228.00
New York	$3,636.00	$4,380.00
North Carolina	$3,156.00	$3,804.00
North Dakota	$2,724.00	$3,228.00
Ohio	$3,156.00	$3,804.00
Oklahoma	$3,156.00	$3,804.00
Oregon	$2,724.00	$3,228.00
Pennsylvania	$3,636.00	$4,380.00
Rhode Island	$2,724.00	$3,228.00
South Carolina	$3,156.00	$3,804.00
South Dakota	$2,724.00	$3,228.00
Tennessee	$3,156.00	$3,804.00
Texas	$3,636.00	$4,380.00
Utah	$2,724.00	$3,228.00
Vermont	$2,724.00	$3,228.00
Virginia	$2,724.00	$3,228.00
Washington	$3,156.00	$3,804.00
West Virginia	$2,724.00	$3,228.00
Wisconsin	$3,156.00	$3,804.00
Wyoming	$2,724.00	$3,228.00

State Primary Law Resources on WestlawNext PRO provides users access to state cases and decisions from the U.S. Supreme Court, U.S. Courts of Appeals, Second Circuit, and U.S. District Courts for the jurisdiction in question. Most of these cases include Full Text Plus™ editorial enhancements, including full classification under the West Key Number System®. Users also have access to that state's annotated statutes, the *United States Code Annotated®*, topical materials, and more.

State Primary Law Resources Plus on WestlawNext PRO provides case law from all 50 states, the District of Columbia, Puerto Rico, Guam, and the U.S. Virgin Islands plus annotated statutes and state court rules from all 50 states, administrative regulations for the state in question, federal case law from the U.S. Supreme Court, U.S. Courts of Appeals, U.S. District Courts, specialized case law, and *United States Code Annotated®*, the U.S. Constitution, and federal court rules.

Thomson Reuters also offers state Essentials plans with less content than the above plans. A CT Essentials plan, for example, is only $162.90 per month or $1,954.80 per year on a two-year contract

WestlawNext PRO has a full panoply of product offerings that can be customized to the needs of the specific attorney, firm, corporation, government entity, etc. Among the most popular add-ons for smaller firms are the following:

Popular WestlawNext PRO Add-Ons

Title	WestlawNext	WestlawNext
	Monthly	Annual
American Jurisprudence 2d	$147.00	$1,764.00
Am Jur Legal Forms	$106.00	$1,272.00
Am Jur Pl. & Prac Forms	$106.00	$1,272.00
American Law Reports	$174.00	$2,088.00
Am Jur Trials	$106.00	$1,272.00
Am Jur Proof of Facts	$106.00	$1,272.00
Am Jur Trials & POF	$133.00	$1,596.00
All Am Jur Library*	$236.00	$2,832.00

*Includes **American Jurisprudence 2d, American Law Reports Library** (1st-6th and Fed 1st and 2d), **ALR Index, Am Jur Legal Forms, Am Jur Trials,** and **Am Jur Proof of Facts**. These list prices, however, can be sharply discounted when added to a state plan and when dealing with a sales representative. The **All Am Jur Library** is only $1,996.80 per year when added to a state plan on a one-year contract, or $1,747.00 per year on a two-year contract.

Contrast the cost of these offerings with cost of the equivalent print resources, both annual print set maintenance costs (2012) and the costs of individual volumes:

Title	Annual upkeep	Bound volumes (ea.)
American Jurisprudence 2d	$8,938.00	$539.00
Am Jur Legal Forms	$3,789.00	$458.00
Am Jur Pl. & Prac Forms	$5,477.00	$585.00
American Law Reports	$14,572.00	$451.00
Am Jur Trials	$6,702.00	$638.00
Am Jur Proof of Facts	$6,686.00	$629.00
Am Jur Trials & POF	$13,388.00	n/a
All Am Jur Library	$46,164.00	n/a

*Remember that pricing for these packages or add-ons is negotiable. Contact your Westlaw sales representative for details.

Cost Saving Tips: Given the rising cost of print, a WestlawNext PRO package can provide significant cost savings to any law firm. This applies not only to packages of state, and state plus federal materials, but to leading add-on secondary products like **American Jurisprudence 2d** and the **American Law Reports**. Contracts for firms of larger than three are negotiated based on firm size and specific content selected. For details and special promotions, contact your Westlaw representative.

It is imperative that the potential customer discuss various pricing options with his or her sales representative. Westlaw is prepared to offer a variety of special package plans for specialty and secondary law products which are priced significantly below the cost of the same products in print. For example, the **All AmJur Library with ALR** package offers **American Jurisprudence 2d, Am Jur Legal Forms, Am Jur Pleading & Practice Forms, Am Jur Trials**, and **Am Jur Proof of Facts, and the ALRs** at an annual cost far below the cost maintaining these titles in print.

How many of the above publications is your law firm subscribing to in print? If you are currently subscribing to the entire **AmJur Library** in print, you can save your firm tens of thousands of dollars annually by converting these titles to Westlaw. If you still prefer to read these materials in print, you will still have access to your existing print collection for your initial research. Only now, your print subscriptions will essentially be replaced or updated by WestlawNext access.

Another way to avoid the high costs of Westlaw access is to limit your Westlaw databases for the firm to those absolutely necessary and obtain your national coverage from Casemaker (free with bar membership in most states), Google Scholar, Versuslaw, Fastcase, or one of the other low-cost alternative CALR services. Remember, that whatever Westlaw databases you select will be applied to all attorneys in the firm and priced accordingly.

Customized Fixed-Rate Westlaw Plans

Larger firms and organizations, including governmental entities, typically find it easier and more cost-effective to subscribe to a broad selection of Westlaw databases as part of a single customized negotiated plan that provides access for all legal professionals in the organization. These plans may be applied in large firms, state and federal court systems, state and federal agencies, and other large organizations. Your West representative will help you create a customized subscription plan that can include federal and state primary law, secondary law sources, as well as online news, forms, and public records sources. The primary risk with these types of plans is that your organization's users may become so accustomed to their use that your negotiating flexibility is compromised. Successive contracts may involve annual increases of 10-15% over the previous contract. As a negotiating strategy, don't be afraid to drop one premium service for another in order to short-circuit this pricing spiral. Keep your online provider on a short leash.

Strategies for Substantial Cost Savings

One of the most effective strategies for controlling online legal research costs is based on understanding that, even if you prefer one of the major online services for most of your research, it is neither necessary nor cost-efficient to use that vendor for all your research needs. For example, the cost-conscious attorney can pair a more limited **WestlawNext PRO** subscription with the use of Casemaker (in selected states) or Versuslaw to provide access to primary law from all other state and federal jurisdictions.

Significant annual savings can be achieved by this kind of pairing of WestlawNext with a less expensive national database like VersusLaw or Casemaker. This option assumes that you will use Westlaw for research in your state, while using VersusLaw or Casemaker for those instances in which you do research outside your jurisdiction (i.e. for that law which is persuasive). Granted, Westlaw offers the researcher a wealth of features not found on the more streamlined Versuslaw service. However, Versuslaw provides an excellent means of conducting preliminary research in foreign jurisdictions which can later be expanded on Westlaw, if necessary.

KeyCite

In July 1997, the West Group introduced an impressive new citator service called KeyCite. KeyCite is an integrated citation service on Westlaw which gives the legal researcher the ability to trace the history of a case, statute, or other legal authority, retrieve a list of all cases on Westlaw that cite a case, and selectively track legal issues by using West topics and key numbers. KeyCite was created by employing a combination of artificial intelligence, human editorial input, the vast Westlaw database, and upgraded mainframe computers.

Although KeyCite has been under development for nearly three years, its debut at the American Association of Law Libraries (AALL) Annual Meeting in Baltimore on July 21, 1997 appeared to suggest a special urgency to head-off possible competitive challenges from rival LexisNexis which purchased Shepard's in a strategic partnership with Matthew Bender in 1996 (Reed Elsevier, the parent company of LexisNexis, acquired complete ownership of both Shepard's and Matthew Bender in 1998). With the withdrawal of Shepard's from Westlaw on July 1, 1999, KeyCite became the only citator service available on Westlaw.

One the most impressive features of KeyCite is its sophisticated integration with the Westlaw database and West's patented key number system. KeyCite is accessible through a tab on the Westlaw search screen. The KeyCite function may also be accessed by clicking on the case status flag in the upper left-hand corner of a case you are viewing. KeyCite uses three graphic icons to indicate the current status of a case. A red flag indicates that a case (or at least part of a case) is no longer good law. A yellow flag indicates that the case has some negative history, but has not been reversed or overruled. A blue "H" indicates that there is some other direct history that is not of a negative variety. The absence of a flag or a blue "H" indicates that there is no direct history or negative indirect history for the case.

Once a case is KeyCited, the Citations to the Case window displays all the cases on Westlaw and secondary sources which have cited it. All negative cases are displayed first, followed by a list of all those other cases citing your case. A significant feature of KeyCite is that the cases are categorized according to the depth of treatment they give to your case. This depth of treatment is indicated by the use of one to four stars, with four stars indicting the most extended discussion and one star usually indicating its appearance in a string citation.

Another impressive feature of KeyCite is its effective blending of the citation service with the power of West's key number system. Citing references may be limited to those citing particular West topics and headnotes by clicking on the Limit Citations button when viewing the Citations to the Case window. By clicking the Limit Citations button, the Limit Citations window displays all the headnotes which appear in the cited case. The researcher can then check only those headnotes which specifically impact the legal issues being researched and, by clicking "O.K.," retrieve a list of citations restricted to those citing only the desired headnotes. A demonstration of the KeyCite citation service can be found on the West home page at: http://www.westlaw.com/Tours/keycite/keycite_full.wl

The introduction of KeyCite also addresses what had become a confusing array of citator services, including Shepard's, InstaCite, QuickCite, and Shepard's PreView. Because KeyCite is available the same day a case is posted on Westlaw, it eliminates the four to six week time lag which formerly existed between the appearance of case of Westlaw and its appearance in Shepard's PreView. It also provides the equivalent of the QuickCite function by which Westlaw was used as a citator, but by adding improved features, graphic and otherwise.

The major question on the minds of industry observers, however, was the likely competitive impact upon Shepard's, which has been the dominant citator service for 125 years. Nearly six years after its introduction, KeyCite has proved to be a worthy rival to Shepard's in terms of functionality, accuracy, and market penetration. In tests which compared KeyCite with a human edited citator like InstaCite, West developers found that KeyCite performed almost flawlessly at catching negative history. KeyCite All is now added as a matter of course to any of the WestlawNext primary law or specialty plans plans.

Choosing Between Lexis and Westlaw

For some time after the introduction of Lexis and Westlaw, it was common for reviewers to draw comparisons based on the size and scope of their respective databases. Prospective subscribers were often persuaded to adopt one system or the other because the case law for their jurisdiction was more extensive, for example. For several years, Lexis was perceived as having an advantage because it included the text of unpublished opinions. As time passed the subject matter and chronological coverage of both systems grew so extensive that such comparisons were largely futile. If one vendor added a database which gave it a perceived advantage, the other vendor followed suit or jumped ahead in another area. This competitive process of leapfrogging has helped ensure that both Lexis and Westlaw have databases so large that very few subscribers will ever begin to tap their full potential. As the databases reached a rough parity in terms of content (and with both achieving full historical caselaw coverage), Westlaw's synopsis, headnote, and key number searching, in addition to full text, provided it with an advantage over Lexis in the area of case law research. Since LexisNexis has introduced such enhancements as Lexis Search Advisor, core terms, and case summaries, however, the playing field has been considerably leveled.

For those who wish to know which of the two systems is best, I can only say that "it depends." Each system has its strengths and both share the weaknesses of online information retrieval outlined by Blair and Maron. In fact, there are distinct advantages to having both systems if yours is a firm which expects to conduct considerable online research. In addition to rough parity in terms of database coverage, both Lexis and Westlaw provide users with the ability to conduct both Boolean and natural language searching.

The one major advantage Westlaw enjoyed was an outgrowth of its dominance in the area of print court reporters and finding tools, although this advantage has narrowed considerably with the introduction of more case summaries and core terms to the cases to the LexisNexis database. The Lexis core terms are a useful indication of case content once a case has been retrieved, but they do not add terms which are not already in the opinions themselves, as the West headnotes and synopses do. However, this comparative advantage applies primarily to case law and does not necessarily impact research in statutory or regulatory law or in the hundreds of other areas, both legal and non-legal, for which both services provide extensive coverage. The Lexis Search Advisor, as stated above, also helps narrow the research advantage formerly held by Westlaw in the case law arena.

For a time, Lexis held the edge in terms of cost, largely due to its transactional pricing. This advantage undoubtedly increased with Lexis's elimination of telecommunications and connect charges. Earlier studies revealed that LEXIS was the cheaper of the two services most of the time. The advantage was particularly marked in the case of lengthy search sessions (30-60 minutes). Westlaw was the cheaper service for shorter search sessions. Since that time, Westlaw and Lexis have both introduced transactional pricing and fixed-rate plans tailored for the small law office, rendering these earlier cost comparisons obsolete. These developments have sharply narrowed the cost differential between these two major online services.

With, arguably, a rough parity between the editorial content and pricing of the two citator services, Shepard's and KeyCite, offered by Lexis and Westlaw, Lexis comes out ahead because an All Jurisdictional Shepard's subscription allows the user to access and print any case for which he or she has a cite or to which he or she can link from a list of citing references. By contrast, a KeyCite user on Westlaw can only gain "free" access to documents which fall within his or her Westlaw PRO plan. For all others, there is a per document charge.

Fixed-Rate Contracts for CALR

Despite the fact that LexisNexis and Westlaw have been strong competitors for nearly 30 years, little information exists regarding fixed-rate contracts for online services in large law firms and other institutions. Yet, in an era when clients have begun to question charges for online computer services and law firms are forced to treat them as a part of overhead, renewed attention is being devoted to contractual arrangements under which online costs are fixed. While many large firms have entered into such contracts, the such agreements typically contain confidentiality clauses.

Law firms contemplating a subscription to one of the major online legal research systems would do best to secure proposals from both LexisNexis and Westlaw and play one off against the other to secure the best deal. Large firms entering into such contracts should, nevertheless, be warned to control costs since higher usage will be factored into the next fixed-rate proposal and/or contract. Thus, the window of opportunity which may exist for a time as the lawyers in your firm take advantage of the fixed-rate contract to increase usage will be closed when the next contract is negotiated at a higher price level. These considerations are less important in law firms whose smaller size qualifies them for the Westlaw PRO or LexisNexis Advantage plans since their banded pricing does not increase with higher levels of usage.

In this regard, a VersusLaw subscription can serve as an excellent means of controlling usage with one of the two major online vendors. Firms should also resist contractual provisions which prevent disclosure of the terms of the fixed-rate contract. This practice is a reflection of the heretofore limited number of CALR vendors. More recent entrants into the field, such as VersusLaw, Loislaw.com and Fastcase, have completely transparent pricing options, a development which should induce the major CALR providers to discontinue their efforts to keep customers from freely sharing contractual terms.

One strategy which holds the greatest promise of holding down usage and costs for Westlaw and LexisNexis is a subscription to VersusLaw which permits unlimited searching for a flat annual fee. Law firms which can resist the urge to use Westlaw or LexisNexis for many of their common searches, or for such comforting, but unnecessary, features as dual-column printing, will be in the best position to negotiate lower flat-rate contracts when these are up for renewal. Establishing protocols for accessing the various online services can help control the often lazy research habits of recent law school graduates who enjoyed virtually unlimited access to Westlaw and LexisNexis in a rarefied world devoid of real-world financial constraints. In the more than 25 states where it is now available, Casemaker can also serve as the low cost default online service.

It comes down to the value-added by the WestlawNext and Lexis, and if the content and sophistication of their offerings and retrieval is worth the cost. In a large firm with well-heeled clients it may be. In a small firm, where most lawyers practice, not so much. This is why Thomson Reuters and LexisNexis have fashioned WestlawNext PRO and Lexis Advantage plans for small law offices, plans that will not jump in price with the next contractual go-around based on Westlaw and Lexis usage during the prior contractual period. For an interesting take on research training and Westlaw and Lexis pricing, see Jean Grady's thoughtful article: "The Myth and the Madness of Cost Effective Lexis and Westlaw Research Training," at:
http://deweybstrategic.blogspot.com/2011/05/myth-and-madness-of-cost-effective.html

Alternative CALR Services

Casemaker

One of the alternative computer-assisted legal research services which has had a significant impact on computer-assisted legal research in some markets is Casemaker. Developed by Cincinnati lawyer Joseph Shea and the Lawriter Corporation, an electronic legal publisher, Casemaker began as a highly popular CD-ROM product marketed to Ohio attorneys in 1988. Joining forces with the Ohio State Bar Association, Casemaker moved to the Internet in 1998, offering Ohio State Bar members access to a complete library of Ohio legal materials. Since that time, additional state bar associations have approached Casemaker to join the Casemaker consortium. As of April, 2013, more than 23 state bar associations have done so, including all six New England states, as well as Alabama, Alaska, Colorado, Idaho, Indiana, Kansas, Kentucky, Michigan, Mississippi, Nebraska, North Dakota, Ohio, South Carolina, Texas, Utah, Vermont, Washington, and Wyoming.

Casemaker has made substantial upgrades to its database coverage in 2006 and 2007. It now includes decisions of the United States Supreme Court from 1754, Courts of Appeal from 1950 (with some as early as 1921) and appellate decisions of the remaining states not presently members of the Consortium from (on average) 1927. Casemaker has already made a significant impact in Ohio, where bar association surveys have shown it to be the most heavily user CALR service. Casemaker is only available to members of the participating bar associations. We include Casemaker among the leading alterative CALR services because it has become the default CALR service for most bar members in the aforementioned states. In fact, more than 400,000 attorneys now have access to Casemaker as a part of their bar membership, a development which is already having an impact on Westlaw PRO and LexisNexis Advantage subscription costs which have remained relatively flat for the past couple of years.

Content for each of the states currently in the consortium features the full range of primary law, including case law, applicable federal court decisions, state codes and constitutions, session laws, regulations, rules of professional conduct, attorney general opinions, workers' compensation opinions, bar journals, and more. Moreover, Casemaker's coverage is not limited to the highest appellate courts and local federal courts, but extends to the courts of appeals, and some trial courts. Content is selected in consultation with each state bar association and, as such, it reflects the specific needs and desires of the practitioners in those states. The Casemaker search engine employs an intuitive technology which includes both Boolean and natural language protocols, a Thesaurus function, and a case history citator. It is simple to navigate and allows users to conduct in each database.

Casemaker's success is a striking indication of the need for low-cost CALR by attorneys across the country. Ohio State Bar Association surveys have revealed that utilization of Casemaker now exceeds that of any other computer-assisted legal research service. And it is not difficult to understand why. Casemaker is rapidly becoming one of the most popular benefits of state bar association membership. In states with a unified (mandatory) bar, Casemaker is being made available to every bar member. In states with a voluntary bar, Casemaker has become the single greatest factor driving the enrollment of new members. With thousands of bar members using Casemaker, the real per member cost averages a mere $20.00 per year. The strength of numbers has made Casemaker into a major success story for users of computer-assisted legal research in some states.

Casemaker will no doubt have a significant impact upon the legal research habits of lawyers in states whose bar associations are part of the consortium. The growth in the size of its database is a one of the most positive developments for legal information consumers in recent years. The major question, however, is whether Casemaker can further enhance its national database of primary and secondary materials with a cross-file searching capability which will make it a major player at the national level. At present, each state's database must be searched independently. Moreover, there is no one site on the Internet where comprehensive information on Casemaker's database coverage may be found. Users are dependent upon the information supplied by the individual bar association sites regarding coverage of the other state sites. While Casemaker's growth is somewhat unhurried and deliberate, it is reflective of the interest of the state bar associations and Casemaker's own desire to remain debt-free. Casemaker is already having a significant impact on the market for computer-assisted legal research in those states whose bar associations have chosen to participate, while restricting the ability of Westlaw and LexisNexis to expand in those states. That impact will spread gradually to other states as they come on board. This will provide a healthy consumer-oriented effect on the online legal research marketplace. Already 475,000 lawyers have access to Casemaker through their bar membership.

Fastcase

A recent entrant into the growing field of CALR providers is Fastcase, an Arlington, VA-based legal research system with an impressive combination of features, including an intuitive search engine, unique navigational tools, and a substantial body of primary law, providing access top over 6 million documents. Unlike other alternative CALR providers, however, Fastcase includes such unique search tools as **Authority Check**, a citator-like service that not only locates other cases citing your authority, but also provides the text surrounding the citation being checked. A **Briefcase** feature allows the researcher to save documents for future use and store up to 18 recent queries. In addition, search results can be sorted according to various criteria of relevance, including most cited within search results, most cited generally, date, and court hierarchy. Search results can also be viewed by title only, by the first paragraph, or by the most relevant paragraph.

Searching on Fastcase is performed using either standard Boolean operators or natural language and pattern searching (which employs expanded versions and variations of search terms). The format and design are professional and aesthetically pleasing in appearance. West and official pagination are provided when available. Other features include dual column printing, hyperlinked case citations, and multiple citation lookup and extraction. The primary law databases include more than 5.5 million documents, including federal court of appeals decisions form 1924 to date, federal district court decisions from 1912 to date, and state appellate court decision from 1950 to date. Statutes and administrative regulations are provided by linking to official government web sites, but searching is conducted by using the Fastcase search engine. Decisions of the U.S. Supreme Court date back to volume one of the United States Reports (i.e. 1754). Documentation and customer support are provided via tutorials, search tips, frequently asked questions (FAQ), and E-mail. Additional help is provided by means of online chat.

At present, more than 380,000 lawyers have access to Fastcase through 33 bar associations and other organizations that have purchased the service for all of their members.

Fastcase features include the following:

* Boolean and natural language searching
* Multiple citation lookup and extraction
* Sorting by search relevance
* Sorting by document authority (most cited)
* Searching by date range, jurisdiction, and other fields
* Dual-column printing
* Hyperlinked case citations
* Page numbers listed throughout cases
* Fast document navigation and term navigation
* Most relevant sections displayed in search results

Fastcase offers the following subscription plans:

Premium Plan - $995 per year for a solo practitioner.
Annual subscription to the full national law library, including federal and 50-state caselaw, statutes, and regulations, including federal district courts, bankruptcy and tax courts.

National Appellate-Only Plan - $695 per year for a solo practitioner.
Comprehensive federal and 50-state database of appellate caselaw, statutes and regulations.

Pricing for larger firms follows a banded pricing model similar in structure to that employed by LexisNexis and Westlaw. Thus, Premium Plan pricing for 2 attorneys is $1,745.00 per year; 3-5 attorneys $2,495.00 per year; 6-10 attorneys $3,995.00 per year, and so forth. Pricing for larger firms may be negotiated. Special promotions may also be offered at various times. A number of large firms are using Fastcase as a means of reducing costs for Lexis and Westlaw.

In 2006, Fastcase negotiated an agreement to provide 76,000 members of the Florida Bar with access to Florida and Fifth Circuit legal materials as a membership benefit, while providing access to its Premium National subscription at the special rate of $195 per year, a savings of $800 per year over the retail price for Fastcase. This annual price for the complete national database is less than the monthly cost for a single state on most other premium legal research services.

In 2005, Fastcase negotiated a deal to provide its 50-state database as a membership benefit to the nearly 20,000 members of the Louisiana State Bar Association. It has negotiated similar arrangements to make its service available to attorneys in other states and localities.

A review of Fastcase by T.R. Halvorson appearing in the August 1, 2002 issue of llrx.com, is located at: http://www.llrx.com/features/idm_fastcase.htm

Loislaw.com

Loislaw.com (formerly LOIS) is an Arkansas-based electronic publisher of comprehensive libraries of state and federal primary law on the Internet and CD-ROM. Founded by practicing attorney Kyle D. Parker in 1987 as a response to the absence of a low-cost alternative to the major online legal services, LOIS was the first company to develop and market a comprehensive library of primary law on CD-ROM: CaseBase-Arkansas (1989). LOIS went on to develop state CD-ROM products for Connecticut, Georgia, Louisiana, Massachusetts, Missouri, Nebraska, North Carolina, Oklahoma, Rhode Island, South Carolina, Wisconsin and other states, as well as CD-ROM libraries containing decisions of the U.S. Supreme Court and U.S. Courts of Appeals.

In 1996, LOIS unveiled a Web site providing up-to-date coverage of the same state and federal primary law previously available on CD-ROM. Its law libraries of state materials typically include Supreme Court and Appeals Court decisions, statutes, session laws, attorney general opinions, administrative regulations, ethics opinions, and court rules. U.S. Supreme Court decisions are available back to 1790 and Court of Appeals decisions back to 1972. Partnerships with a number of state bar associations have resulted in the inclusion of state bar CLE materials in such states as Arkansas, Indiana, Massachusetts, Missouri and Wisconsin. In 2000, Loislaw.com achieved it goal of making available comprehensive libraries for all fifty states and the federal government.

Since its introduction in 1987, LOIS has done much to stimulate competition in the online legal research market. With its low-cost CD-ROM and Internet products, Loislaw.com has forced both Westlaw and LexisNexis to address the needs of the attorney in the smaller law office who had previously been paying high hourly costs for repeated access to the law of his or her jurisdiction. The appearance of LOIS's state CD-ROM products forced West, which had initially resisted competing against its print products and Westlaw service, to develop and market its own line of state and federal CD-ROM products. LOIS was the first vendor to abandon the upfront licensing fees for CD-ROM products and the first to sell CD-ROMs without a built-in time expiration feature. It was also the first legal CD-ROM vendor to sell individual CD-ROMs without requiring the purchase of a subscription (although subsequently abandoned), and the first to offer a no-cost online uplink from its CD-ROM products.

Moving to the Web

Loislaw.com unveiled its Web-based product in 1996. By the first quarter of 2000, it was providing complete law libraries for all 50 states, decisions of the U.S. Courts of Appeals from 1971 to date, decisions of the U.S. Supreme Court from 1899 to date, the **United States Code**, **Code of Federal Regulations**, and **Federal Register**. In the process it also shifted its product focus from CD-ROM to the Internet. Its **National Collection** provides a comprehensive database of state and federal materials and is an alternative for attorneys who desire lower cost access to the primary law of all state and federal jurisdictions. For the attorney interested in the law of more than one state, the **National Collection** has become an alternative, priced at $1,512 per year. Single state libraries are priced at $1,180 per year, making the National Collection a preferred alternative. Loislaw.com was acquired by Wolters Kluwer in 2000 and is now a part of Aspen Publishers.

From the consumer's perspective, there are several factors which make Loislaw.com attractive as an alternative to the major online services:

1. Loislaw.com will sell only as many passwords (permitting simultaneous access) as a firm desires.

2. Loislaw.com's flat-rate pricing is completely open. While there may be special promotions, there are no special flat-rate deals hidden by non-disclosure provisions.

3. The Loislaw.com service is available to firms and libraries of all sizes and varieties.

Loislaw.com Pricing Options (annual, paid in full)	
Single state plus federal circuits	$1,200 per year
National Collection	$1,512 per year

Passwords for Loislaw's **National Collection** have been reduced to $1,512 each. This places Loislaw in a somewhat better competitive position vis-a-vis rivals VersusLaw and Fastcase which provide similar primary law coverage at lower cost. But while the price differential is still significant for the solo practitioner, it is less so in firms of larger size in which a single password may be shared. Were it not for the fact that Loislaw.com is one of the few online providers which does not tie the sale of passwords to firm size, it would have difficulty competing with VersusLaw in a side-by-side comparison. For example, the same $1,512 it costs to buy one Loislaw.com password will buy individual VersusLaw Premium Plan passwords for 5 lawyers. That single Loislaw.com password must be shared, however, and only one attorney can have access at a time. Each additional password must be purchased at a cost of $1,512, although discounting may be available for multiple passwords or for those who also acquire Aspen subject content libraries. Loislaw is also receiving a stiff challenge from Casemaker which has become the default online service for many bar members whose bar associations have become part of he Casemaker consortium and provide the service as a membership benefit.

As a Wolters Kluwer company, Loislaw also provides subscriptions to treatises and forms in specific subject areas, including Bankruptcy Law, Business Law, Construction Law, DUI Law, Elder Law, Employment Law, Estate Law, Evidence Law, Family Law, General Litigation, Internet and E-Commerce Law, Limited Liability Company Law, Personal Injury Law, Product Liability Law, and Real Estate Law.

An in-depth review of Loislaw.com by T. R. Halvorson appeared in the March 1, 1999 issue of LLRX (See: www.llrx.com/features/lois2.htm). A more recent survey of CALR vendors (including Loislaw.com and VersusLaw) by Fritz Snyder and Stacey Gordon appeared in the November/December, 2000 issue of **Legal Information Alert**. In December, 2000, Loislaw.com was acquired by the Dutch conglomerate Wolters Kluwer and is a part of the Wolters Kluwer Law & Business product line.

Versus Law

Founded in 1985 by Joe Acton, VersusLaw provides lawyers with an excellent online research service at an affordable price. It was formerly known as Timeline Publishing's Lawyers Legal Research Online. In 1992, VersusLaw began working with the U.S. Supreme Court, federal circuit and state appellate courts to assemble an affordable online database of court decisions. Initially a bulletin board service (BBS), Versus Law moved to the Internet in 1995. In 1996, it changed the name of Lawyers Legal Research into V. (pronounced "vee"). Its database includes U.S. Supreme Court opinions back to 1900, most circuit court decisions back to 1930, and state court decisions as far back as 1930. The full-text searchable archive of court decisions is updated daily. Searching may be conducted via Boolean operators or natural language. The search software also supports cross-file searching. The databases also include, for an extra charge, the U.S. Code and Code of Federal Regulations, which are among the most current versions available.

VersusLaw Subscription Plans (Per Attorney)

Standard plan*	$13.95 per month or $167.40 per year
Premium Plan**	$24.95 per month or $299.40 per year
Professional Plan***	$39.95 per month or $479.40 per year

*The **Standard Plan** provides access to decisions of the U.S. Supreme Court from 1900 to date, U.S. Courts of Appeals from 1930 to date, current decision of selected Federal District Courts, decisions of state appellate courts (see Appendix J for specific state coverage), and selected tribal and foreign courts.

The **Premium Plan builds on the databases provided under the Standard Plan and adds an archive of Federal District Court decisions back to 1950 (93 districts), selected states statutes (currently 46) and regulations (currently 32), and additional search capabilities.

***The **Professional Plan** includes the content of the Premium Plan plus the United States Code, Code of Federal Regulations, other federal courts, and selected Special Practice Collections.

Both Premium and Professional Plan subscribers have the ability to conduct searches of all federal court libraries (i.e., Circuit Courts of Appeals, District Courts and the Supreme Court), as well as all state courts.

VersusLaw's flat-rate per attorney pricing structure is based on the realization that even if some attorneys are not users, the actual users are performing research for the non-users. It reflects the fact that larger firms will be using more bandwidth than small firms and should pay accordingly. All three of VersusLaw's pricing plans are arguably among the best bargains in the industry, whether for the solo practitioner or for lawyers in medium-sized and large firms.

VersusLaw's plans to provide additional coverage of state and federal cases, statute statues and regulations. Further information regarding subscriptions and may be obtained by contacting VersusLaw at 425-250-0142, or locating VersusLaw on the Internet at: www.versuslaw.com

For a comprehensive, albeit slightly dated, review of VersusLaw, see the review by T. R. Halvorson appearing in llrx at: www.llrx.com/features/v.htm

See also Appendix I for a comparative overview of VersusLaw's caselaw coverage by jurisdiction.

Other Fee-Based Legal Research Services

While the above discussion has focused on the three premium CALR services and the four leading alternative CALR providers, there are at least three other fee-based services worthy of mention. These include:

CaseClerk.com

CaseClerk.com is a reseller of CLE programs offered by VersusLaw, including eLLR, the electronic version of VersusLaw's ethics newsletter Lawyers' Liability Review. It is also a reseller of caselaw, also obtained from VersusLaw. As such, its historical caselaw coverage is identical to that of VersusLaw. The CaseClerk web site also provides users with access to federal and state statutes and regulations by means of links to official government or free commercial web sites. Data is obtained directly from official sources and the query language is standard Boolean with the ability to conduct cross-file searching. CaseClerk has a number of pricing options, including the annual plan ($49.95 per month with an annual subscription/$599.40), monthly plan ($69.95 per month with a monthly subscription), daily plan ($29.95 per day with a 24-hour subscription. Those with further interest are directed to the CaseClerk web site, located at: http://www.caseclerk.com and to the review by T.R. Halvorson appearing in llrx at:

http://www.llrx.com/features/caseclerk.htm

CaseClerk may be contacted by telephone at: (865) 397-7900, ext. 116.
See also Appendix J for a comparative overview of CaseClerk's caselaw coverage by jurisdiction.

TheLaw.net

TheLaw.net, an independently held software company headquartered in San Diego, is a computer-assisted legal research service which provides access to four million court decisions from state and federal jurisdictions and facilitates access to Web-based legal information. The caselaw content on TheLaw.net is supplied by VersusLaw. As such, it replicates VersusLaw's breadth and depth of coverage. As with VersusLaw, The Law.net provides users with the ability to conduct Boolean, natural language, and Cite Lookup. Cross-file searching in the caselaw database. What makes The Law.net unique, however, is its stand alone Internet browser program which incorporates an extensive collection of more than 60,000 links to law-related Internet sites, largely free government sites which host statutes, regulations, forms, and other law-related content. The Internet browser is a specialized version of Opera, an alternative to Netscape and Internet Explorer which was developed by computer programmers from Norway. Also, TheLaw.net's Reference Desk Menu includes approximately 1000 resources in more than 75 sub-directories.

Caselaw coverage encompasses 1 **U.S. Reports** to date, 1 **Federal Reporter** 2d to date, 1 **Federal Supplement** to date, 1 **Bankruptcy Reporter** to date, and the 50 states from at least 1950 to date, some earlier. The database also includes the **United States Code** and statutes for all 50 states, federal regulations, judicial and administrative rules and forms, legislative and executive agency materials, hundreds of news resources, a built-in reference desk and much more.

For reviews of TheLaw.net, see article by Roger V. Skalbeck in llrx located at: http://www.llrx.com/features/thelawnet.htm and T.R. Halvorson located at: http://www.llrx.com/features/reed.htm

See also Appendix J for a comparative overview of TheLaw.net's caselaw coverage by jurisdiction.

TheLaw.net is priced at $575 per year for a solo practitioner, $495 for one lawyer and one paralegal, $995 for two lawyers and two paralegals, $1,395 for three lawyers and three paralegals, $1,795 for four lawyers and four paralegals, $1,995 for five lawyers and five paralegals. Additional packages are available.

RegScan

RegScan GCS (formerly Eastlaw and RegScanLaw), an electronic legal publisher based in Williamsport, PA, was founded by former Congressman and Attorney, Allen E. Ertel in 1987. Its original goal was to provide users with a current and fully-searchable database of federal regulations. Its offerings now include the current **Code of Federal Regulations**, **Federal Register** as well as state environmental regulations and OSHA Plans. RegScan began offering low-cost access to state and federal appellate caselaw on November 2, 2000 under the name Eastlaw, through a partnership with VersusLaw, and more recently under the name RegScanLaw. In 2003, however, it changed its name to RegScan and dropped its **United States Code** and state and federal caselaw databases and re-focused its attention on its regulatory offerings. Visit RegScan GCS at:

http://www.regscan.com/

For further information on RegScan, readers are directed to a review of Eastlaw by T. R. Halvorson which appeared in the January 2, 2001 issue of llrx at: http://www.llrx.com/features/eastlaw.htm

RegScan's pricing may be obtained by telephone at: (800) 734-7226 x1105

Google Scholar

http://scholar.google.com

Google Scholar describes itself as a simple way to broadly search for scholarly literature. It provides researchers with the ability to search across many disciplines and sources, including articles, theses, books, abstracts and court opinions, from academic publishers, professional societies, online repositories, universities and other web sites. Google Scholar ranks documents the way researchers do, by weighing the full text of each document, where it was published, its authorship, and how recently it has been cited in other scholarly literature. Google Scholar works with scholarly publishers to index works from all research disciplines and make them searchable on its platform.

Google Scholar groups multiple versions of a work to improve its ranking. These may include preprints and conference papers which appear before being published as journal articles. Grouping these various versions allows Google Scholar to collect all citations to all versions of a work, a factor that can significantly improve the position of an article in the search results. When multiple versions of a work are indexed, Google Scholar selects the full and authoritative text from the publisher as the primary version. Publishers maintain control over access to their articles, and only cache articles and papers that are not access-controlled.

Google Scholar users are offered at minimum a complete article abstract. For papers with access restrictions, a full author-written abstract helps users choose among the results for the paper most likely to have the desired information. Google Scholar responds to complaints regarding alleged copyright infringement that comply with the Digital Millennium Copyright Act.

At present, Google Scholar has a substantial number of full text decisions in its database, including all U.S. Supreme Court decisions, and many decisions of state and federal courts. The Advanced Scholar Search permits the researcher to conduct a word search, or locate articles or decisions by author, publication title, date or date range, and subject area. A search may be limited to United States federal court opinions, or one or more state jurisdiction. A citation feature allows the researcher to locate citations to thousands of articles or books citing the publication in question. There are, for example, links to 1,182 books and articles citing Robert Bork's **The Antitrust Paradox**, each of which may be cited by hundreds of articles itself.

Google Scholar Preferences allow the researcher to select the interface language, pages within certain designated languages, selected physical libraries where a title is held, WorldCat holdings. In many cases, full text is available as well as citations to articles and books citing the publication in question. In short, Google Scholar provides free and unfettered access to a wealth of information heretofore unavailable outside of libraries. In other instances, it provides access to an abstract or a cited page, with the ability to purchase the complete book or article.

Public Law Library CALR Access

For many medium-sized and large firms, LexisNexis and/or Westlaw are absolutely essential research tools. However, most solo practitioners and many small law firms do not use CALR with sufficient frequency to warrant having their own subscriptions beyond what they may receive as a bar association benefit, e.g. Casemaker or Fastcase. In these instances, access to a public Westlaw or LexisNexis terminal at your local public, bar, or academic law library may be the most cost-effective option, particularly when that access is accompanied by the expert assistance of a trained law librarian with extensive experience in performing online research. This service is priced on a per use basis and generally reflects either the actual cost of online time or a small premium over the library's cost. Typically, there is no charge for the assistance of a trained library professional in formulating your search. If your trips to the local law library for the purpose of online research become frequent, however, you may wish to secure your own subscription with one of the online vendors discussed above.

Chapter 26: Finding Law On the Internet

No attorney practicing law at the beginning of the 21st century can afford to ignore the potential of the Internet as a tool for accessing legal information and reducing the costs of acquiring legal information. According to the ABA's 2013 Legal Technology Survey Report on Online Research, more than 98% of respondents conduct legal research online. Of these, a majority uses a fee-based online research resource first. Attorneys who fail use the Internet now constitute a distinct minority. Not only are they depriving themselves of many opportunities to control legal research costs, but they are missing out on many of the opportunities to improve communications with clients, potential clients and colleagues.

While the Internet still pales in comparison to the size of the LexisNexis and Westlaw databases, it now contains a significant enough body of legal information to make it a viable alternative to either print or online sources in selected instances. Thus, a consideration of the availability of Internet legal sources should start to play some role in the assembly of a law office library. Nevertheless, there are some significant differences between LEXISNEXIS and WESTLAW on the one hand, and the Internet on the other:

LEXISNEXIS AND WESTLAW	World Wide Web
Comprehensive databases	More limited databases
Reliable data	Reliability of data varies by provider
Sophisticated search engines	Varied and less sophisticated search engines
Generally expensive	Free or relatively inexpensive
Available 24 hours/day	Available 24 hours/day
Superior tech support for searching	Limited or no tech support for searching
Centralized	Decentralized
Standard interface	Varied interfaces
Hypertext links	Hypertext links
Standard search commands	Varied search commands
No E-Mail	E-Mail
Limited list servs or newsgroups	Varied list servs and newsgroups
Reliable access	Reliable access
Single source for same information	Multiple sources for same information
Higher cost for "exploration" outside of plan	Little or no direct cost for "exploration"

A number of these generalizations require some degree of qualification. For example, the LexisNexis database is estimated, as of April, 2013, to contain documents from more than 45,000 legal, news and business sources, to which more than 15 million documents per week are being added. While the various Internet search engines are less sophisticated than those of LexisNexis and Westlaw, they do permit searching across disparate databases and have capabilities only dreamt of a few years ago. LexisNexis and Westlaw are generally more expensive, but have begun offering more economical pricing options to small law firms. Free databases on the Internet, such Google Scholar, offer virtually no direct technical support, save for help screens, but the proprietary services do provide such services

Accuracy of Information on the Internet

Despite the growing popularity of the Internet as a tool for legal research, questions remain regarding the accuracy and reliability of the information found there. This is a natural response for information professionals or members of the legal profession. Of course, one should speak less of the Internet as a whole than of those particular Web sites which may contain information of potential value. Much also depends on the nature of the uses to which the information is to be put. For example, a Web site may be quite valuable as a means of locating the law, but may not be a source which you would feel comfortable quoting. Genie Tyburski, Research Librarian for Ballard Spahr Andrews & Ingersoll in Philadelphia, and editor of **The Virtual Chase Web Site**, has identified six characteristics of a superior Web site: timeliness, expediency, accuracy, objectivity, and authenticity. In light of these observations, the careful researcher should:

1. Determine the ultimate source of the information he or she is using. This may not be the Web site initially accessed, but another site to which the user has been linked.
2. Determine the currency of the information.
3. Use the Internet primarily for informational purposes, rather than as a citable source of information.
4. Use an official source when citing or quoting specific information, rather than an unverified Internet source. Use the official source to help gauge the reliability of the Internet source.
5. Use the Internet as a starting point for research, not the final destination.
6. Verify the source and currency of the information, even when that information is obtained from a government Web site.

E-mail

Electronic mail, or e-mail, is a basic tool of the Internet, and actually pre-dates the development of the World Wide Web. Virtually everyone, it seems, now has an e-mail address, and participates in this medium of communication, with friends, relatives, colleagues, clients, and business associates. Its near instantaneous speed provides an increasingly popular alternative to 'snail-mail' and the frustrating game of 'phone tag.' The down side of e-mail, however, involves the problems of 'spam' or unsolicited advertising sent simultaneously to hundreds or thousands of users, and computer viruses, which are sent through e-mail attachments to unsuspecting users. Computer viruses can infect and virtually destroy the computers of an entire business, if the computers are connected to a network

The listserv

The listserv takes E-mail one step farther. Think of it as an electronic mailing list. If you subscribe to a listserv, you have the ability to send E-mail messages to every other person who subscribes to the listserv. This has proven to be a powerful tool for law librarians and lawyers alike. Have an obscure legal question? Pose it to the hundreds, or thousands, of subscribers to the right listserv and wait for a reply. In fact, you are likely to receive more replies than you would have imagined. This is particularly true with the listservs frequented by law librarians who are part of a remarkably knowledgeable and generous profession.

Unlike regular E-mail which permits you to communicate with one person at a time (or more if you enter additional E-mail addresses), a listserv allows you to communicate with all its subscribers at the same time by typing in a single listserv address. Subscribing to a listserv will guarantee that your question or comment reaches a wide audience of like-minded ation about the listserv by typing the following:
information [listserv name] [your name]

Listservs are a particularly powerful means of communication. For the practicing attorney, they can serve as excellent vehicles for obtaining advice on a difficult legal issue or research question, or reaching potential clients. Law librarians commonly use them to answer perplexing reference questions after the normal channels have been exhausted or as a means of alerting other law librarians regarding the acceptable practices of certain legal publishers while they still have time to take action (e.g. the unsolicited shipment of books or supplements, rising costs, etc.) In the past, such information was communicated much more slowly, if at all. Also, with most legal publishers monitoring the most critical listservs, problems are often addressed far more swiftly than in the days of private mail communications or telephone calls.

The News Group

Newsgroups provide another important means of communication on the Internet. Unlike the originator of a listserv posting, however, who sends an E-Mail message to everyone on the mailing list, the originator of a newsgroup message posts the message to an electronic bulletin board (or special newsgroups news server). In this way, the individual interested in reading or responding to postings on a specialized newsgroup can contact the newsgroup at his or her option without being forced to read a mass of unwanted messages as E-Mail. Specialized newsgroups can be founded through a number of law-related sites, including:

Katsuey's Legal Gateway
http://www.katsuey.com/results.cfm?categoryID=25
A directory of legal lists by subject category.

The Leading Law-Related Internet Sites

The following list includes a number of the most useful law-related sites for conducting legal research. Web sites for individual state may be found in the State Publications chapter of this book. For further information, the reader is directed to the many guides to law on the Internet listed in the bibliography at the end of this chapter.

I. Federal Law

A. Judicial Branch

1. U.S. Supreme Court decisions

a. Legal Information Institute Cornell University School of Law
http://www.law.cornell.edu/supct/
These are bench decisions received under the auspices of Project HERMES, an electronic opinion dissemination service of the U.S. Supreme Court which cover the period from May,1990 to the present. Over 600 historic pre-1991 decisions (1793-1966) provided by Infosynthesis are also available.

b. FindLaw Supreme Court Opinions
http://www.findlaw.com/casecode/supreme.html
This site contains a fully searchable database of all the U.S. Supreme Court decisions published from 1893 (volume 150 of the **U.S. Reports**) to date.

c. Oyez
http://www.oyez.org/
Oyez is the most comprehensive website covering the U.S. Supreme Court, containing information about past and present Justices, cases and issues before the Court, oral arguments, and more.

2. U.S. Courts of Appeal decisions

a. Federal Courts Locator. Villanova University School of Law.
http://libguides.law.villanova.edu/fed_ct_locator
Provides a convenient link to the decisions of all thirteen Federal Courts of Appeal and U.S. District Courts. Coverage varies by circuit, beginning as early as 1992.

b. U.S. Courts – The Federal Judiciary
http://www.uscourts.gov/Home.aspx
The official web site of the Administrative Office of the U.S. Court providing access to the various federal courts, and their administrative offices.

c. Commercial subscription services. A listing is available at:
http://www.findlaw.com/casecode/commercial.html

3. U.S. District Court decisions

a. Administrative Office of the U.S. Courts – The Federal Judiciary
http://www.uscourts.gov/court_locator.aspx
This site provides access to all U.S. district courts web sites.

b. FedLaw General Services Administration
http://www.thecre.com/fedlaw/legal32.htm
Provides links to more than 90 U.S. District Courts (as of April 1, 2014).

4. Federal Judicial Branch Agencies

a. The Federal Judiciary Home Page - Administrative Office of the U.S. Courts
http://www.uscourts.gov/adminoff.html
This site functions as a clearinghouse for information from and about the Judicial Branch of the U.S. Government. It includes press releases, court

vacancies, documents explaining the role of the federal courts, a Directory of Electronic Public Access Services, and notices regarding proposed changes in federal rules of procedure and standard citations form for federal opinions.

b. Federal Judicial Center Judicial Conference of the United States
http://www.fjc.gov
The Federal Judicial Center is the Judicial Conference of the United States' agency for research and continuing education, established by Congress in 1967. Contains information about the Federal Judicial Center, the Center's Annual Report, vacancy announcements, and telephone numbers. It also contains an extensive library of full-text publications regarding the role of the federal judiciary, and links to other WWW servers.

B. Legislative Branch.

1. United States Constitution and United States Code

a. FindLaw - United States Constitution with Annotations
http://www.findlaw.com/casecode/constitution
This annotated, searchable version of the U.S. Constitution was prepared by the Congressional Research Service of the Library of Congress. It contains links to cited Supreme Court cases.

b. United States Government Printing Office
http://www.gpo.gov/fdsys/

One of numerous gateways to GPO Access which contains the full-text searchable database of the **United States Constitution**, **United States Code**, and over 70 additional federal databases.

c. Internet Law Library - U.S. House of Representatives, Office of the Law Revision Counsel
http://uscode.house.gov/
The full, searchable text of the **United States Code** current through February 4, 2013. Based on the 2012 Edition of the **Code**, plus Amendments as shown in the tables provided by the Office of the Law Revision Counsel.

d. Legal Information Institute - Cornell University School of Law
http://www.law.cornell.edu/uscode/text
This fully searchable version of the U.S. Code was generated from the most recent version of the U.S. Government Printing Office CD-ROM as is current as of January 26, 1994. The Legal Information Institute provides three ways in which the Code can be updated using the sources of Thomas, the information retrieval system of the Library of Congress.

2. United States Public Laws

a. GPO Access - United States Government Printing Office
http://www.gpoaccess.gov/multidb.html
One of numerous gateways to GPO Access which contains the full-text searchable database of the Public Laws of the United States for the108th Congress (2003-2004) forward.

b. Thomas - Library of Congress
http://thomas.loc.gov/home/thomas.php
Contains the full text of the United States Public Laws from the 104th Congress (1995-1996) to date, searchable by Public Law No.

3. United States Congressional Bills –

a. GPO Access - United States Government Printing Office
http://www.gpoaccess.gov/multidb.html
A full-text searchable database of the Congressional bills for the 103rd Congress (1993-1994) forward. Includes complete instructions for constructing Boolean searches.

b. Thomas - Library of Congress
http://thomas.loc.gov
A full text database of the Congressional bills for the 101st Congress (1989-90) forward, searchable by word/phrase, subject term, bill/amendment number, stage in the legislative process, date, sponsor/cosponsor, or committee.

C. Executive Branch

1. Executive Orders

a. White House Virtual Library
http://www.whitehouse.gov/

2. Code of Federal Regulations - U.S. Government Printing Office
http://www.gpoaccess.gov/cfr/index.html
The full text of all 50 titles of the **Code of Federal Regulations** is available on the specialized search pages which allow more specific field searches.

3. Federal Register

a. GPO Access - U.S. Government Printing Office http://www.gpoaccess.gov/fr/index.html
The **Federal Register** is one of over 70 databases available at this site. The full text of the years 1994 to date is included.

4. Treaties in Force

a. Department of State – Treaties in Force
http://www.state.gov/s/l/treaty/tif/index.htm
A List of Treaties and Other International Agreements of the United States in Force on January 1, 2011

5. Official Federal Government Web Sites - Library of Congress
http://www.loc.gov/rr/news/fedgov.html
This page contains Executive Branch sites only

II. State Law

A. Appellate Court Decisions

1. State Law Resources - FindLaw
http://statelaws.findlaw.com/
A compilation of links to the official legal resources of all fifty states and the District of Columbia, including those to state appellate court decisions. The site provides a search engine powered by AltaVista which will search across data fields in an individual state. There are also links to commercial sites, particularly useful in those instances when a state has not mounted its court decisions on the Web or when the state's official server nly

limited historical coverage of decisions.

2. **State Court Locator - National Center for State Courts**
http://www.ncsc.org/information-and-resources/browse-by-state/state-court-websites.aspx
Contains links to a variety of state legal information sources, including court decisions, legislative and executive branch sites.

B. **Statutory Law**

1. **State Resources - FindLaw**
http://www.statelaws.findlaw.com
A compilation of links to the official legal resources of all fifty states and the District of Columbia including those to state statutory codes, session laws, and legislative bills. The site provides a search engine powered by AltaVista which will search across data fields in an individual state. There are also links to commercial sites, particularly useful in those instances when a state has not mounted its court decisions on the Web or when the state's official server provides only limited historical coverage of decisions.

2. **WashLaw Web - Washburn University School of Law**
http://www.washlaw.edu/
A compilation of links to official Web sites containing state statutory codes, Constitutions, session laws, and legislative bills, as well as other legal information. Permits full text search of state laws.

C. **Administrative Law**

1. **National Association of Secretaries of State Administrative Codes and Registers**
http://www.administrativerules.org/

This is the best means of accessing the administrative codes and registers for all fifty states, the District of Columbia, and U.S. territories. Forty-eight states now have their administrative codes on the Web.

2. **See the Statutory Law Web sites listed above**
Internet coverage of state regulatory information, including links to state administrative agencies may be accessed through the Findlaw, and Washburn sites listed above.

III. Leading Law-Related Internet Sites

A. **Legal Associations and Organizations - FindLaw**
http://www.hg.org/bar.html
A collection of national and state bar associations, foreign bar associations, and other legal organizations.

B. **Academic Law Journals**

1. **FindLaw**
http://stu.findlaw.com/journals/
Contains lists of academic law journals, arranged alphabetically, topically, and by law school. It provides access to both online journals and abstracts of articles.

2. **Google Scholar**
http://scholar.google.com
Google Scholar is a freely accessible web search engine that indexes the full text of scholarly literature across an array of publishing formats and disciplines. Released in beta in Nove ber 2004, the Google Scholar index includes most peer-reviewed online journals of Europe and America's largest scholarly publishers, plus scholarly books and other non-peer reviewed journals.

C. **Directory of Legal Publishers and Vendors - Vanderbilt University School of Law**
http://www.acqweb.org/pubr/law.html
A detailed listing of legal publishers and vendors, purchasing resources, catalogs, journals, newsletters, and listserv archives, all with hypertext links.

D. **West's Legal Directory – Thomson Reuters (West).**
http://lawyers.findlaw.com/
This free service of the West Publishing Company on the Findlaw site provides biographical information about lawyers, law firms, government officers, and corporate law offices in the United States and Canada. It also provides information regarding expert witnesses.

E. **Continuing Legal Education - ALI-ABA**
http://www.ALI-ABA.org
A complete guide to post-admission legal education, including a listing of the MCLE requirements of each state, publications, video and audio tapes, periodicals, etc.

F. **Discussion Groups – Katsuey's Legal Gateways**
http://www.katsuey.com/index.cfm
A comprehensive database of law lists (discussion groups) arranged from A-Z with instructions on their use. The site also contains a list of law-related usenet groups.

G. **Law Lexicon - The 'Lectric Law Library**
http://www.lectlaw.com/ref.html
Among this site's numerous offerings is a large collection of legal practice and business forms, a Lexicon containing thousands of law-related words, terms, and phrases, and specific topic areas. This is also a site with a unique sense of humor.

H. **Law Professors Blog Network**
http://lawprofessors.typepad.com/
Blogs By Law Professors For Law Professors
Law Professor Blogs is a network of blogs designed to assist law professors in their scholarship and teaching. Each site focuses on a particular area of law and combines both (1) regularly-updated permanent resources and links, and (2) daily news and information of interest to law professors. The editors are leading scholars and teachers who are committed to providing ***the*** web destination for law professors in their fields. This site is also useful to independent scholars and citizens interested in tracking developments in dozens of legal specialties. The Law Librarian Blob, edited by Joe Hodnicki and Mark Giangrande, with contributions from Caren Biberman and Sarah Glassmeyer, is an excellent source for news about the world of law librarianship and legal publishing.

IV. Comprehensive Legal Resources

A. **FindLaw: Internet Legal Resources**
http://www.findlaw.com
This site encompasses a wide range of legal resources, from law schools and statutes to law reviews and subject indexes of substantive legal resources. Features the LawCrawler search engine.

B. **Heiros Gamos - Lex Mundi, A Global Association of 143 Independent Law Firms**
http://www.hg.org
Hieros Gamos bills itself as the largest and only comprehensive legal site with over 20,000 original pages and more than 70,000 links. **HG 1** contains information on over 6,000 legal organizations including every government in the world. **HG 2**

includes over 200 practice areas, over 300 discussion groups, and 50 doing business guides, as well as hundreds of hours of online seminars. **HG 3** contains self-listing modifiable databases for meetings, publications, employment. law firms, experts, court reporters, ADR professionals, private investigators and process servers. HG 3 also includes News, the Law Library, the Students' Page, Journals. A Search feature accesses 15,000 law-related URL's.

C. Legal Information Institute - Cornell Law School
http://www.law.cornell.edu
Contains a varied collection of legal documents and links to other law-related sites. Created in 1992 by the National Center for Automated Information and Cornell Law School, this site contains opinions of the U.S. Supreme Court, New York Court of Appeals, and the U.S. Code. There are also menus of legal topics, sources, organizations, and people.

D. WashLaw Web - Washburn University School of Law
http://www.washlaw.edu/
Easily accessible links to a wide variety of law-related Web sites and a full-text search engine make this site an excellent research tool.

E. Yahoo's Law Guide
http://www.yahoo.com/Government/Law
The government and law section of the Yahoo directory provides an alternative to searching Yahoo for legal topics from a broader perspective.

F. Zimmerman's Research Guide
aw.lexisnexis.com/infopro/zimmermans/
An Online Encyclopedia for Legal Researchers by Andrew Zimmerman. A comprehensive directory of links to sources of legal information by law firm librarian, Andrew Zimmerman.

G. Law Library of Congress: Guide to Online Law
http://www.loc.gov/law/help/guide.php
This Guide to Law Online, prepared by the Law Library of Congress Public Services Division, is an annotated guide to online sources of information on government and law. It includes selected links to useful and reliable sites for legal information.

H. Justia.com
Justia provides access to state and federal statutes, a free daily newsletter of opinion summaries for the United States Supreme Court, practice area opinion summaries, a directory of expert witnesses, links to over 2,000 legal blogs, and much more. Justia also lets consumers ask questions online and get answers from attorneys.

V. General Search Services

A. Google
www.google.com
Perhaps the most popular search engine. Google can find structuring of Boolean operators, including phrases in quotation marks.

C. Yahoo
www.yahoo.com
A popular search engine portal. You can use either the directory feature or its search index which looks for web pages that use your search terms.

Guides to Law on the Internet

The growth and acceptance of the Internet as a legal research and law practice management tool has engendered a surfeit of useful books and newsletters on the subject. While the number of books continues to grow, the number of newsletters has dwindled somewhat as readers have become more sophisticated and independent surfers who are less interested in monthly publications with listings of new law-related web sites. Those newsletters surviving this sifting-out process are more likely to provide timely articles on cutting-edge issues of interest to their readership. The average user of law-related information on the Internet is best served by one or more of the excellent guides to law on the Internet described below.

Books

Ambrogi, Robert J. **The Essential Guide to the Best (and Worst) Legal Sites on the Web**. 2d ed. New York: Incisive Media, LLC, 2004. 1 vol. (400 pp.).
Cost: $49.95; from $1.97 on amazon.com (2014).
This encyclopedia of legal resources is organized into more than 30 specific subject categories, including administrative law, bankruptcy, consumer protection, estate planning, immigration, job listings, public records, real estate, etc. The author is director of American Lawyer Media's news service and the author of The Internet Guide for Massachusetts Lawyers, the syndicated column "legal.online," and the monthly column "Web Watch" in Law Technology News.

Botluk, Diana. **The Legal List: Research on the Internet.** St. Paul, MN: West Group, 2014. 1 vol. Paperbound.
Cost: $419.00 (exclusive of discount); monthly assured print price: $32.00/$384 per year (2014).
An updated version of Erik Heels' **The Legal List: Internet Desk Reference**, this volume provides more substantive Internet research instruction than its predecessor. The author covers such topics as history, tools, getting connected, world wide web directories, search engines, E-Mail, list servs, search engines, and meta search finders. Chapter three, entitled "Beginning an Internet Research Project," contains annotated listings of leading legal sites and explains how to choose general finding tools and locate specific information. Additional chapters provide listings of resources for legislative, administrative and judicial materials as well as secondary authority, news and media, legal ethics and professional responsibility, and international and foreign law materials. While this is a useful tool, the cost is a reflection of what happens to most books under Thomson Reuter's control. Look for a used copy or a less costly alternative.

Garvin, Peggy, ed. **The United States Government Internet Manual**. Lanham, MD: Bernan Press, 2008. 1 vol. (680 pp.). Paperbound.
Cost: 2008 Edition: $62.00; from $.46 on amazon.com (2014).
An annotated guide to more than 2,000 U.S. government web sites organized under the following topical chapters: agriculture, fishing and forestry; business and economics, culture and recreation; defense and intelligence; demographics and sociology; education; employment; energy; engineering hand technology;
Environment and nature; government and politics; health and safety; international relations; law and law enforcement; legislative branch; presidency; science and space; social welfare; and transportation. Each entry includes the URL, sponsor, description, and subjects. Appendices include web sites and e-ails addresses for members of Congress, web sites for Congressional committees, a sponsor name/site name index, an index of online publications, and a master index of subjects, sponsors and titles.

Gordon, Stacey L. **Online Legal Research: A Guide to Legal Research Services and Other Internet Tools**. Buffalo, NY: William S. Hein & Co., Inc., 2003. 1 vol. (427 pp.).
Cost: $79.95; from $74.69 on amazon.com (2014).
This online legal research manual by Stacey Gordon provides legal information professionals with an invaluable tool for maximizing the research potential of both the major and a variety of alternative online legal research services. Her discussion commences with a consideration of the basics of online legal research and examines the criteria by which researchers choose between print and online tools to optimize their research results. She also discusses the process of selecting and evaluating commercial online legal research tools and evaluating information available at no cost on the Internet. The bulk of the book's substantive content is devoted to detailed discussion of the content, features and search techniques for using LexisNexis and Westlaw. However, she also devotes some attention to Loislaw, VersusLaw, HeinOnline, and, to a lesser degree, Fastcase, the most recent entry into the field. The book's concluding chapters examine legal research on the Internet, including directories and portals, search engines, search engine tips, and a description of the leading search engines. She concludes with a consideration of legal research tools and substantive practice areas on the Internet. Two appendices provide lists of leading federal court and state legal and government websites.

Hernon, Peter, John A. Shuler, and Robert E. Dugan. **U.S. Government on the Web: Getting the Information You Need**. 3d ed. Englewood, CO: Libraries Unlimited Inc., 2003. 1 vol. (492 pp.).
Cost: from $.01 on amazon.com (2014).
A well-organized and authoritative directory of more than 1,000 federal government agencies providing information on the Web. The author, a Professor in the Graduate School of Library and Information Science, Simmons College, also provides clearly-written descriptions of the agencies from which the Web sites originate.

Jeanneney, Jean-Noel. **Google and the Myth of Universal Knowledge**. Chicago: University of Chicago Press, 2007. 1 vol. (92 pp.).
Cost: $18; paper: $11; from $.01 on amazon.com (2014).
This book is a response to the recent announcement by Google that it plans to create a library of universal knowledge by digitizing the holdings of several major American research libraries. Written by leading librarian and president of the Bibliothèque Nationale de France, this small volume addresses a number of critical concerns posed by this project, now called the "Google Book Search," among them the potential for copyright infringement, the subordination of scholarly and cultural values to economic ones, the unsystematic nature of the digitization project, the misguided and unbalanced reliance on works written in English, and its potential to "misrepresent—and even damage—the world's cultural heritage." While sympathetic to the potential of a universal library, Jeanneney questions short-term thinking which fails to address the significant long-term potential of a culturally balanced and multicultural digitized library.

Kozlowski, Ken. **The Internet Guide for the Legal Researcher**. 3d ed. Teaneck, NJ: Infosources Publishing, 2001. 1 vol. (approx. 400 pp.). Includes access to companion web site updated every 60-90 days.
Cost: $75; from $47.17 used on amazon.com (2014). (201) 836-7072.
An annotated bibliography of law-related Internet resources with an explanation of basic terms and concepts. Includes discussion of Internet communications, web page construction, search engines and indexes, portals, browsing, bookmarks, utilities, citation of Internet sources, electronic journals, reference resources, and more.

Lane, Carole A. **Naked in Cyberspace: How to Find Personal Information Online**. 2d ed. Chicago: CyberAge Books, 2012. 1 vol. (528 pp.). (800) 800-4741.
Cost: $29.95; from $.47 on amazon.com; Kindle: $16.09 (2014).
A guide to the kinds of personal information which is available online, as well as that available on proprietary CD-ROM products and online services. Lane, who founded her own information brokerage in 1993, explains the intricacies of mailing lists, telephone directories, bank records, news databases, consumer credit information, moor vehicle registrations, death and tax records, genealogical information, and other sources of personal information. The author is also knowledgeable about privacy laws and the growing difficulty of concealing personal data. Not as useful as the Levitt title below.

Levitt, Carole A. and Mark E. Rosch. **The Cybersleuth's Guide to the Internet: Conducting Effective Investigative & Legal Research on the Web.** 12th ed. Rio Rancho, NM: Internet for Lawyers, 2012. 1 vol. (560 pp.).
Cost: $64.95 (2014).
Formerly titled **Internet for Legal & Investigative Research: A Guide for Legal Professionals**, this volume provides legal researchers and investigators with tools and techniques for conducting low-cost research on the Internet, including sources for locating missing persons, personal information, phone numbers, public records, property records, birth and death records, social security numbers, employers, aliases, and negative information to attack a person's credibility, much of it available on free Internet sources. The author also provides sources for conducting free legal research on the Internet, including sources of caselaw, federal state and local primary law, secondary sources, and legal practice materials. The author is a nationally recognized author and speaker on Internet legal research, with over twenty years of experience in the legal field as a law librarian, professor of law, attorney and Internet trainer. She is President and founder of Internet For Lawyers.

Levitt, Carole A. and Mark E. Rosch. **Finding Info Like a Pro: Mining the Internet's Public Records for Investigative Research**. Chicago: American Bar Association, 2011. 1 vol. (280 pp.). Paperbound.
Cost: $79.95 ($47.95 to members); from $45.94 on amazon.com (2014).
This invaluable resource is designed to assist those interested in conducting investigative and or background research at little or no cost. With clearly written language, helpful graphics, and illustrative screen shots, the authors guide the researcher through the intricacies of Internet research in a host of public and private records databases, social networking sites, genealogical sites, news, expert witness databases, consumer credit reports, telephone and address records, and online communities. They also provide helpful guidance In using search engines, summarization search engines, and meta search sites for investigative research. Highlighted websites are accompanied by helpful graphics indicating whether the site is free, feed-based, or requires registration. A companion CD-ROM contains a hyperlinked index of the web sites listed in the book. This volume represents Levitt and Rosch's updating of Joshua Blackman's **The Internet Fact Finder for Lawyers** (ABA), which they re-titled **The Lawyers Guide to Fact Finding on the Internet**. Volume 2: **Mining the Internet's Public Records for Investigative Research** is also available from the ABA at the same price as volume one.

Levitt, Carole A. and Mark E. Rosch. **Finding Info Like a Pro, Volume 2: Mining the Internet's Publicly Available Resources for Investigative Research**. Chicago: American Bar Association, 2012. 1 vol. (280 pp.). Paperbound.
Cost: $79.95 ($47.95 to members); from $38.84 on amazon.com (2014).
This guide directs the user to hundreds of sources for public information on the Internet, both governmental and non-governmental. It includes sites for finding assets, evaluating potential business partners, tracking missing witnesses, clients, or heirs, and other sources for investigative research. A companion CD-ROM provides the user with clickable links to the sites referenced in the book.

Levitt, Carole A. and Mark E. Rosch. **Google for Lawyers: Essential Search Tips and Productivity Tools**. Chicago: American Bar Association, 2010. 1 vol. (514 pp.). Paperbound.
Cost: $79.95 ($49.03 to members); from $39.00 on amazon.com (2014).
Launched in March, 1996 by two Stanford University PhD students, Larry Page and Sergey Brin, Google has grown to become the world's leading Internet search tool and a major corporate entity which was added to the Standard & Poor 500 in 2006. Initially funded by the National Science Foundation and other federal agencies, the Stanford Digital Library Project's (SDLP) goal was "to develop the enabling technologies for a single, integrated and universal digital library." At its peak in 2004, Google was responsible for 84.7% of all search requests on the Internet through its own website and its partnerships with such Intenet clients as Yahoo!, AOL, and CNN. Google's success may be attributed to its superior search capability, its clean and uncluttered design, its use of personal data to improve searching based on the user profiles, and to corporate acquisitions that have added to its competitive ability to use information gleaned from blog postings to improve the speed and relevance of articles contained in a companion product to the search engine,Google News. Harnessing the power of Google for legal and law-related research is the subject of this excellent desktop research companion. **Google for Lawyers** is intended as a practical desktop guide for lawyers who want to get the most out of Google for their research and technology needs, and who want to use free and low-cost tools to compete with large firms with superior research and technology budgets. Following an introduction to the Internet, Google, and basic and advanced search strategies, the authors explain the use and manipulation of search results, and a variety of specific Google tools and applications, including Google News, Google Groups, Google Image Search, Google Blog Search, Google Finance, Google Glossary, Google Translate, Google Books, Google maps. Knowledge Management Tools, Google Scholar, Google Apps, Google Voice, Google Search Shortcuts, Google's Uncle Sam Search, and Google Analytics, Google Advertising Services., and more. Instructions are clearly written, easy to follow, and enhanced with numerous sample screens. The text also features practice tips, ethics alerts, and "war stories" gathered from a variety of legal professionals. The Appendices include eight case studies drawn from actual court decisions, a web site credibility check list, Google Scholar Alerts, Google Drawings, and Index. Carole Levitt is a nationally recognized author and speaker on Internet legal research, with over twenty years of experience in the legal field as a law librarian, professor of law, attorney and Internet trainer. She is President and founder of Internet For Lawyers. Mark Rosch is Vice President of Internet for Lawyers and developer and manager of the Internet for Lawyers web site. A frequent speaker on Internet research and technology issues, he is co-author (with Carole Levitt) of numerous titles on Internet research for the legal profession.

Levitt, Carole A. and Mark E. Rosch. **The Lawyer's Guide to Fact Finding on the Internet**. 3d ed. Chicago: American Bar Association, Law Practice Management Section, 2006. 1 vol. (712 pp.). Paperbound.
Cost: $99.95 ($84.95 to LPM Section members); from $9.87 on amazon.com (2014).
A complete, hands-on guide to the best sites, secrets, and shortcuts for conducting efficient research written for legal professionals. It explains the intricacies of search engines and the strategies for conducting focused and efficient searches on the Internet. The book's chapters cover the use of the Internet for factual research, Internet tools and protocols, search strategies, search tools, general factual research, government resources online, finding and backgrounding people accessing public records, finding and backgrounding expert witnesses, company research, comparative intelligence research, medical research, scientific research, environmental research, foreign and international research, law practice management and professional development, statistical research, transportation research, entertainment industry research, and intellectual property. The book includes a CD-ROM with all the links Included with the book. The authors are both experienced Internet trainers and writers on Internet-related topics.

Oldham, Rosie. **Medical Legal Internet Directory [on CD-ROM]**. 3d ed. Tucson, AZ: Lawyers & Judges Publishing Co., 2003. 1 vol. (688 pp.).
Cost: $59; from $2.34 on amazon.com (2014).
A detailed guide to medical and legal sources on the Internet with explanations of Internet sources and search engines, including those for hundreds of medical specialties. Also includes an Internet primer. Now on CD-ROM.

Siskind, Gregory H., Deborah McMurray, and Richard P. Klau. **The Lawyer's Guide to Marketing on the Internet.** 3d ed. Chicago: American Bar Association, Law Practice Management Section, 2007. 1 vol. (192 pp.).
Cost: $84.95 ($74.95 to members); from $50.25 on amazon.com (2014).
A guide and tutorial to integrating a web presence and a comprehensive marketing strategy by an experienced immigration lawyer who developed the first immigration practice web site. The chapters address such topics as developing an Internet marketing plan, web site design issues, promotional content, informational content, navigational tools, interactive tools, choosing your web consultants, e-mail marketing, weblogs and podcasts, web seminar and social networking sites, advertising and search engine optimization, measuring the results of your Internet efforts, and the ethics of client development through technology. The authors' also maintain a valuable weblog on law firm marketing which provides updates to the book and other useful information on marketing techniques and strategies. See: http://www.bookblogs.com/lawmarketing/

Periodicals and Newsletters

Law Practice (formerly Law Practice Management). Chicago: American Bar Association, Section of Law Practice Management, 1975-date. Published eight times per year.
Cost: included in annual dues of $50 to members of the ABA Law Practice Management Section; $64 per year to non-members (800) 285-2221
The flagship publication of the ABA's Law Practice Management Section, **Law Practice Management** provides a variety of timely articles on all aspects of law firm management. It includes a monthly column on Internet topics by attorney Robert J. Ambrogi.

Law Technology News - Products, Systems & Services for Legal Professionals. New York: American Lawyer Media, Inc., 1999-date. Monthly.
With the largest circulation of any legal technology publication, this monthly magazine provides timely articles on legal technology issues and reviews of new law office technologies. Each monthly issue contains articles and columns written by industry experts and notices of more than 200 new products, systems and services. Technology now constitutes the third-largest expense for legal organizations.
Cost: free digitally to U.S. residents; International subscriptions: $230.00 (one year); $400.00 (two years) (2014).

Chapter 27: Legal Treatises & Other Subject Specialty Materials

Admiralty Law - Zoning Law

Among the most valuable reference works for the practicing attorney are the specialized legal treatises, practice books, and other subject-specific compilations of primary law, or primary law and analysis. Unlike the bland and common law dominated text of legal encyclopedias, legal treatises not only describe and analyze the state of the law in particular subject areas, but may provide historical perspective, reflective commentary, and a wealth of special features of great value to the practicing attorney. These special features may include forms, tables, bibliographies, jury instructions, interrogatories, and practice tips. However, just as the law has become a field characterized by specialization, legal treatises increasingly reflect the more narrow research interests of their authors. Thus, works like **Wigmore on Evidence** have given way to **Engineering Evidence** and **Statistical Evidence in Litigation.**

Treatises vary widely in their quality and scholarly authority. This was as true a hundred years ago as it is today. Some legal treatises represent a lifetime of scholarly investigation and writing, reflecting the unified perspective of an influential legal scholar. Others combine some of the features of scholarly research with a more practical, hands-on approach useful for the active practitioner. Some are largely products of in-house editorial staffs which read like well-organized strings of case annotations. Finally, others are written as law school texts, providing introductory description and analysis from a scholarly perspective. The lengthy annotated bibliography of legal treatises and other legal specialty materials which follows this introduction includes works from the following, sometimes overlapping, categories:

(1) Encyclopedic treatises. Treatises in this category are generally multi-volume analytical and encyclopedic expositions of the law representing either the lifetime efforts of a legal scholar or the combined efforts of leading authorities and in-house editorial staffs. Such works include **Wigmore on Evidence**, **Benedict on Admiralty**, Casner's **Estate Planning**, **Corbin on Contracts**, **Williston on Contracts**, **Scott on Trusts, Weinstein's Evidence, Moore's Federal Practice**, **Collier on Bankruptcy,** Larson's **The Law of Workmen's Compensation**, **Powell on Real Property**, and others. While most of these authors are now deceased, publishers continue to employ their names and reputations to sell works which are now updated by other scholars or by in-house editorial staffs. Courts continue to assign greater authority to such works, but their authoritative weight is not as significant as it was when their authors were still involved in their preparation. It is amusing to observe the attempts by some younger writers to attach their own names to the titles of the books they have written in the manner of a **Scott on Trusts**, despite the fact that their names carry little of the scholarly weight which is generally assigned to a scholar of Scott's reputation by the legal community.

Other encyclopedic treatises are written by teams of in-house editorial staff and often provide a wealth of practical features of great value to the practicing attorney. They lack the unified analytical vision of a single scholar, but partially compensate for this by more frequent supplementation (a mixed blessing) and a level of continuity which transcends the scholarly careers of individual authors. Such works include **Damages in Tort Actions** (LexisNexis Matthew Bender), **Federal Procedure** (Thomson Reuters), and Frumer and Friedman's **Products Liability** (LexisNexis Matthew Bender). Editorial supervision and control can be uneven, however. Great latitude is frequently assigned to outside authors whose work product is sometimes published with little or no editorial review. I am acquainted with an attorney who was hired to write one chapter of an existing multi-volume treatise for a major legal publishing house. Not only was her work printed without substantive editing, but she noted numerous significant omissions in the work of the previous author which should have been corrected before the text went to print. What this simply means is that all secondary sources, regardless of their purported authority, must be used with caution and that the careful attorney will use them as one source for locating the primary law which undergirds the treatise text.

(2) Practitioner Treatises. These include both single-volume and multi-volume works which, while they may reflect many of the scholarly attributes of the encyclopedic treatises, are generally designed for the use of the practicing attorney. The coverage combines both discussion and analysis of the substantive law with practical guidance on procedural matters. Citations to primary and other secondary authorities tend to be more limited than those provided in the more scholarly encyclopedic treatises. Examples of treatises in this category include the **American Law of Products Liability** (Thomson Reuters), Rodgers' **Environmental Law** (Thomson Reuters), and **Lindey on Entertainment, Publishing and the Arts** (Thomson Reuters).

(3) Law School Texts. While written primarily for the law school student market, many of these works are excellent introductory overviews of the subject matter for practitioners, most written by legal scholars who serve as law school faculty. Once in practice, many attorneys continue to rely upon these texts for review, both in and outside their areas of specialty. The Hornbook series published by West Publishing and the texts published by Foundation Press (a Thomson Reuters subsidiary) are the most popular of these works. In recent years, West has begun issuing one and two-volume expansions of these Hornbooks in what it calls its Practitioner Treatise Series. These combine expanded scholarly text, with more extensive footnotes, tables, Westlaw Research Guides, and sometimes, forms. An added advantage of these works is that they tend to be much cheaper than the competition because they are mass-produced for the law school market. On the other hand, the higher prices for the Practitioner Treatises tend to more closely parallel the prices of other practitioner-oriented titles. The West Nutshell Series offers the practitioner a wide range of inexpensive paperback summaries of most areas of the law, but without the more in-depth analysis and extensive primary law citations available in the Hornbooks or Practitioner's treatises. CaseBooks, with their extensive reprinting of representative cases for classroom use, are included here only selectively, largely in subject areas lacking a sufficient number of more analytical works. Law school texts and caseBooks are also published by Wolters Kluwer Law & Business, LexisNexis Matthew Bender, Carolina Academic Press, and Oxford University Press, among others.

(4) Looseleaf services (print, CD-ROM, and Internet). Looseleaf services provide convenient subject-matter access to a variety of primary sources, including statutes, administrative regulations, court decisions, administrative rulings and other regulatory determinations and publications. Although these publications had their origins in a print looseleaf format, they are now available on CD-ROM, and online, with hypertext links from analytical discussion to the applicable primary law.

(5) Subject-specific CD-ROM products. Among the most valuable of the new CD-ROM products are those subject-matter titles which combine the full text of the analytical treatise with applicable primary law. Because these products pull together primary law, particularly court decisions, from a variety of jurisdictions, they can serve as significant time and cost savers to attorneys in legal specialty areas. Leading examples of such products are **Copyright on CD-ROM** (Wolters Kluwer Law & Business), **UCC Search** (Thomson Reuters), and **Antitrust Law Developments** (ABA). Other specialty CD-ROM titles assemble primary law from a variety of jurisdictions, but lack the analytical component more common to the major publishers of secondary legal materials.

(6) Scholarly monographs. A scholarly monograph is generally defined as a book that stands alone and is not part of a series, or subject to supplementation, although it may appear in a new, updated, or expanded edition. A scholarly monograph usually offers an original thesis or set of arguments and attempts to expand the frontiers of knowledge in a particular subject area. Based on thorough research, often including original documents, it is usually aimed at other scholars and students in the field rather than the general public.

(7) Law books for the lay person. Recent years have witnessed the proliferation of law books directed at the lay or popular market. These books deal with subjects of particular interest to the general public, including accidents, bankruptcy, landlord-tenant relations, formation of a business entity, criminal law, divorce and family law, employment, immigration, small claims, patent and trademark, personal finance, wills, trusts & probate, real estate matters, and taxes. While these books lack the scholarly attributes (e.g. citations) most commonly found in books aimed at the lawyer or academic audience, they provide a wealth of practical advice, including examples and case studies, designed to guide the lay person through the intricacies of the legal process. NOLO is the most prominent publisher in this area.

Supplementation. Supplementation to legal treatises and subject-specific compilations varies widely. Some titles are supplemented as often as weekly, and may include on-line updating. At the other extreme, some of the law school oriented treatises published by West, LexisNexis/Matthew Bender and others are monographic in nature, and not supplemented at all, except in the form of periodic new editions. The average title is still supplemented on an annual basis, although there is a gradual trend towards more frequent supplementation from publishers who have moved from casebound volumes with annual pocket parts to looseleaf binders which can be supplemented with greater frequency. Given the fact that legal treatises are more significant as case finders than as citable authorities, annual supplementation is more than sufficient in the vast majority of cases. As long as you realize that supplementation decisions are based upon the publisher's need for revenue, rather than the need for currency, you should feel free to update these secondary sources as frequently as you wish based upon the nature of your practice, the frequency with which you plan to use a particular title, and the steps you plan to take to update your research beyond what you find in the treatise itself. For further discussion of this issue, see **Chapter 6: The Question of Supplements.**

An important note about annual supplementation cost figures

Every effort has been made to obtain actual (or subscriber) costs of supplementation for each of the titles reviewed in this chapter and provided in Appendix H in order to provide subscribers or prospective purchasers with an accurate picture of their annual financial outlay to support these titles. In this quest, I have received substantial direct assistance from the following legal publishers: Wolters Kluwer Law & Business, Bloomberg BNA (and Bloomberg BNA Books), Commerce Clearing House, James Publishing, Juris Publishing, LexisNexis (including Matthew Bender, Michie and Shepard's), Practising Law Institute, and numerous smaller publishers. Supplementation cost figures for Thomson/West titles were obtained with the assistance from many law librarians, some of whose names are listed in my acknowledgements.

West now provides customers with substantial supplementation cost information on its web site (by selecting "chose volumes" on most product listing pages); however, these are retail "fill-up" costs, not subscriber costs, and will almost invariably reflect a higher cost than that charged to standing order subscribers. Moreover, there are substantial risks to using this feature as a barometer of annual supplementation costs because the supplements listed are often incomplete and may include complete content replacements you already own. Consequently, it has been our practice to seek out these annual subscriber supplementation costs as a more accurate representation of the true cost of supplementation for those on standing order. Of course, these figures will not apply if the customer chooses to abandon the standing order for greater long-term cost-savings and pay the higher "fill-up" cost to periodically update a publication. For example, the subscriber cost to update **West's Federal Administrative Practice** in 2006 was $529.00, while the non-subscriber "fill-up" cost (reflected on the West web site) was $625.00, i.e. 15% higher. In general, the subscriber supplementation cost of Thomson/West treatise titles runs about 80% of list.

West's reticence about providing the subscriber supplementation cost figures maintained in their internal system appears to reflect concerns that such figures can be misleading to those who take advantage of Library Maintenance Agreements (LMAs), and various package plans which they offer. Nevertheless, the

Subject Areas

Administrative Law	Constitutional Law	Health and Hospital Law	Patents, Trademarks and Intellectual Property
Admiralty and Maritme Law	Construction Law	Immigration Law	Products Liability
Advertising Law	Contract Law	Indian Law	Public Utilities
Agency Law	Copyright Law	Insurance Law	Real Property
Antitrust Law	Corporations	Judges and Judicial Conduct	Religion and the Law
Appellate Practice	Criminal Law	Juries and Jury Instructions	Restatements of the Law
Arbitration	Disabilities Law	Labor and Employment Law	Securities Law
Arts, Entertainment and Sports Law	Education Law	Legal Forms	Social Security Law
Automobile Law and Practice	Elder Law	Legal Profession	Statutory Construction
Banking and Finance Law	Environmental Law	Medical Jurisprudence	Taxation
Bankruptcy Law	Equity Jurisprudence	Military Law and National Security	Telecommunications
Civil Rights	Evidence Law	Municipal Corporations	Tort Law
Class Actions	Family Law	Natural Resources and Energy Law	Trial Practice
Commercial Law	Federal Practice and Procedure	Nonprofit Corporations	Trust and Estates
Computer Law	Gambling Law	Partnership	Workers' Compensation
	Zoning and Planning Law		

***Prices of listed products were collected in February-April, 2014.**

supplementation cost figures for individual titles reflected in this chapter (and in Appendix H) provide an important benchmark against which the Library Maintenance Agreements may be measured. The author looks forward to the time when West will facilitate the collection of this data both for the purposes of this book and for the **AALL Price Index for Legal Publications**, or provide historical upkeep costs for each title on its web site.

New to this edition is the **Monthly Assured Print Price (APP)** for all the West titles represented in this chapter. This plan, which is offered to new, non-library, customers, provides a fixed monthly/annual cost of the title in question. Thus, unlike the subscriber discounted supplementation cost, the **APP** also amortizes the initial cost of the publication into the monthly/annual cost for the new subscriber. In the case of the legal treatises included here, the **APP** represents the first year cost. Increases in the second and third years are dependent upon whether a two- or three-year contract is chosen, involving 6% or 5% increases, respectively. The aim of this program is to convince new customers to enter a standing order for supplementation, thus providing Thomson West with a steady, although reduced, revenue stream. With traditional subscriber discounted supplementation costs increasing at a rate of 11-12 % annually, West is attempting to arrest the cancellation of standing orders by promising lower fixed supplementation costs. The **APP** represents no bargain, however, as the monthly/annual charges come after a decade or more of steady price inflation.

Users of this volume should be aware that ThomsonWest, LexisNexis, and other publishers now offer online equivalents of the many titles in their catalogs. This volume now provides benchmarks in the form of print and eBook pricing and supplementation costs. However, many of these titles may be included within WestlawNext subject or state-specific packages which offer substantial savings over their print equivalents. For these, consumers should contact their local sales representatives to determine the cost of these alternative online formats.

Also, the past year has seen a decided reduction in the number of Thomson/West titles offered in the CD-ROM format, including both treatise and state specific titles. Also, it should be noted that the West bookstore now provides potential customers with the ability to ascertain the cost of various Westlaw services, including WestlawPRO libraries for the fifty states and the District of Columbia.

Finally, Thomson Reuters (West) offers periodic sales promotions that reduce list prices by 25%-30% from the prices listed below. Promotions in February-March 2013, for example, offered a 25% discount on any orders over $250.00 and a 15% discount on orders over $150.00. The wise consumer is urged to wait for these promotions before making a purchase of any magnitude. Ask your sales representative to alert you when these promotions are effect.

IndexMaster:

A State of the Art Tool for Locating Legal Treatises

In the days when the treatise collections of most law libraries numbered in the hundreds, a good law librarian could probably rely on his or her memory to locate a treatise with the specific content or analysis required to answer a reference question or satisfy a patron's requirements. The proliferation of specialized legal treatises over the past twenty years, however, has made it increasingly unlikely that any law librarian could hope to learn the contents of such a rapidly expanding body of material. Of the more than 60,000 titles in the 2007 edition of R.R. Bowker's **Law Books & Serials in Print**, the most experienced legal reference librarian can hope to develop a working familiarity with just a small percentage. Access to the remainder is typically a hit-or-miss proposition, combining a search of the library's catalog, legal bibliographies, publishers' catalogs, browsing the shelves and examining indexes of likely sources, professional recommendations, and postings on law librarian listservs. Unlike bodies of primary law, however, for which multi-state or multi-jurisdictional searching can be conducted in massive on-line databases, the content of legal treatises has often eluded the attention of researchers.

In 1988, R.R. Bowker attempted to bridge this gap in the legal reference literature with the publication of its **Index to Legal Books**, a massive six-volume set which merged the indexes of more than 1,000 legal treatises in 58 subject areas and contained more than 1 million index entries filling over 10,000 pages. Despite its unique value as a legal reference tool, **Index to Legal Books** suffered from a combination of mounting production problems and a weak subscriber base. In announcing his company's decision in 1990 to cease publication, editor Fred Barstein expressed his appreciation to its supporters, while lamenting the fact that "too few cast their vote in favor of this ambitious publication." **Index to Legal Books** was priced at $600 and annual supplementation at $400. However, the concept of a master index to legal treatises was far too significant to disappear for long.

Released in February of 1998, **IndexMaster** is a state-of-the art mega-index to legal treatises which takes the original concept of the **Index to Legal Books** to the next level. Using sophisticated, yet easy to use, Internet technology as its delivery mechanism, **IndexMaster** allows a researcher to search and view the indices and tables of contents of more than 8,000 legal treatises from more than 90 legal publishers across the country. Subscribers can search by keyword, author, title, or publisher and then view the specific index and table of contents pages which contain the desired terms, with search results ranked in order of their relevance. **IndexMaster** not only assists law libraries in achieving a maximum utilization of the treatises already in their collections, but also provides them with the means of making informed choices about which new titles to acquire. Those desiring to purchase a relevant title can do so after being routed to the appropriate publisher's Web site.

IndexMaster is actively working with additional publishers to join those already participating. While designed primarily as a legal research tool, **IndexMaster** has the potential to become an important tool for acquisitions and interlibrary loan librarians, as well as a significant marketing tool for legal publishers. In fact, both small and large legal publishers stand to benefit greatly as a result of the increased exposure which **IndexMaster** will give to their product line. Their participation will also help ensure that the searching performed by legal researchers and librarians is as complete as possible. **IndexMaster** is available on a 12-month subscription, with fees determined by size of firm or type of law library:

Annual subscription rates include unlimited access for all firm members, including all locations worldwide. A ten-day free trial is available. A complete description of the IndexMaster product may be found on its Web site located at: **http://www.indexmaster.com**

Firm Size or Library Type	Annual Subscription Fee
Pay-As-You-Go (48-hour access)	$25 per year
1-15 Attorneys	$45 per year
16-50 Attorneys	$295 per year
51-100	$395 per year
101-500 Attorneys	$495 per year
501+ Attorneys	$595 per year
Corporate Legal Departments	$395 per year
Public Law Libraries	$395 per year
Law School Libraries	$495 per year

(with free passwords for registered students)

Administrative Law

Aman, Alfred C. and William T. Mayton. **Administrative Law**. 2d ed. St. Paul, MN: West Academic Publishing, 2001. 1 vol. (971 pp.). No supplementation between editions.
Cost: $103 (2014).
An introductory, one-volume treatise in the publishers Hornbook Series intended as a textbook for administrative law students and as an overview for the practitioner. Covers legislative power in agencies, agency adjudication, consistency in agency action, control of agency discretion, and information. Appendices include a guide to conducting administrative law research on WESTLAW, relevant statutes, a table of cases, table of statutes, and index.

American Bar Association. Judicial Division. **Model Code of Judicial Conduct for Federal Administrative Law Judges.** Chicago: American Bar Association, 1989. 1 vol. (25 pp.). Paperbound.
Cost: $5.00; member price: $3.00 (2014)
The federal administrative legal system is based on the principle that an independent, fair and competent administrative judiciary will interpret and apply the laws that govern consistent with American concepts of justice. Accordingly, this brief pamphlet sets out the rules of ethical conduct for federal administrative law judges as adopted by the National Conference of Administrative Law Judges (NCALJ) and published in cooperation with the ABA's Judicial Division in 1989. The rules govern the conduct of judges in both their official capacities before federal administrative law tribunals and their conduct off the bench.

American Bar Association. Judicial Division. **Model Code of Judicial Conduct for State Administrative Law Judges.** Chicago: American Bar Association, 1995. 1 vol. (25 pp.). Paperbound.
Cost: OUT-OF-PRINT; was $5.00; from $50.86 on amazon.com
This pamphlet sets out the rules of ethical conduct for state administrative law judges as adopted by the National Conference of Administrative Law Judges (NCALJ) in 1995. No longer available online.

Anderson, William R. **Mastering Administrative Law**. Durham, NC: Carolina Academic Press, 2010. 1 vol. (261 pp.).
Cost: $30; from $21.00 on amazon.com; eBook: $14.77 (2014).
In a law school curriculum dominated by case law analysis, the subject of administrative law is somewhat of an anomaly to the uninitiated. Yet, the vast administrative bureaucracy, whether at the federal or state level, is what comprises the vast majority of government activity. Its activities often take on a life on their own, generally with minimal and perfunctory Congressional oversight. This well-written and crisply organized handbook provides a lucid overview of leading administrative law concepts and subject matter.

The content surveys the role of administrative law, the rulemaking process, adjudication, Constitutional requirements for fair process, the availability of judicial review, the scope of judicial review of agency actions, and the flow of information to agencies and to the public. Numerous charts and illustrations provide graphic depiction of organizational structures as well as concepts and processes. Each chapter includes a preliminary Roadmap of its coverage, and concludes with Checkpoints which review key concepts. The volume concludes with a Master Check List of administrative law concepts, and the text of the Federal Administrative Procedures Act. Inaugurated in 2008, the volumes in the Carolina Academic Press Mastering Series are intended to provide law students with a basic understanding of substance and content of courses in the law school curriculum. Priced comparable to, or below, the cost of the West Nutshell series, these volumes are superior in most respects to their competitors.

Beermann, Jack M. **Inside Administrative Law: What Matters and Why**. New York: Wolters Kluwer Law & Business, 2011. 1 vol. (372 pp.). Paperbound.
Cost: $41.95; from $30.99 on amazon.com; eBook: $35.49 (2014).
Administrative law is that branch of law that regulates the exercise of authority by government officials and agencies executing the law under authority granted by the legislature. Administrative law is crafted to implement the intent of statute, but drawing upon the substantive subject matter expertise residing in the agency or department named in the statute. Although originating in common law actions directed at officials exercising government power, it is largely constitutional and statutory, with substantial authority derived from the 1946 Administrative Procedures Act. This textbook is designed to be used in law school classes on administrative law, as well as by non-law students in political science and paralegal studies. Each of the fourteen chapters provides an overview of the topic, frequently asked questions, sidebars offering parenthetical insights, definitions of key terms, a chapter summary, and connections to material in other chapters. Following an excellent overview of administrative law, the author covers separation of powers and administrative law, judicial review of administrative decisions, scope of judicial review, advanced issues in agency decision-making, agency choice of decision-making, the APA rulemaking process, agency adjudication and due process, agency and private enforcement, license and ratemaking, agency inspections and information gathering, preemption and primary jurisdiction, liability of agencies and officials, and freedom of information and open meetings. The author provides a sophisticated analysis of the often complex relationship between the legislature, from whose authority the agencies derive their rulemaking authority, the administrative agencies charged with implementation, and the courts charged with navigating between the legislative and administrative functions. The author is Professor Law and Harry Elwood Warren Schoiar, Boston University School of Law.

Breger, Marshall J., ed. **Federal Administrative Dispute Resolution Deskbook**. Chicago: American Bar Association, 2001. 1 vol. (764 pp.). Paperbound.
Cost: OUT-OF-PRINT (2014).
Alternative dispute resolution has taken on a significant role at the federal level. This reference work outlines the variety of alternative dispute resolution mechanisms, which are currently employed by federal departments and agencies. The authors examine the legal authority for alternative dispute resolution before federal agencies, negotiated rulemaking, and the various areas in which ADR is currently employed, including enforcement activities, bid protests, contract disputes, environmental disputes, and workplace disputes. Also considered are ADR techniques, the use of neutrals, and ADR training programs.

Federal Administrative Procedure SourceBook. William Funk, Jeffrey S. Lubbers and Charles Pou, Jr., eds. Chicago: American Bar Association, 2008. 4th ed. 1 vol. (1,172 pp.). Updated by new editions.
Cost: $79.95 ($49.95 to Administrative Law Section members and gov't. personnel); from $24.90 on amazon.com (2014).
This desk book provides a convenient, consolidated source for a variety of laws and regulations applicable to federal agencies and officials. First issued in 1985 as a publication of the Administrative Conference of the United States, this volume was taken over by the American Bar Association's Section of Administrative Law and Regulatory Practice in 1995. The introductory chapters contain the full text of the Administrative Procedure Act and discuss judicial review of agency action, Congressional review of agency rulemaking, and White House Orders and Memoranda on Rulemaking. Additional chapters contain the Administrative Dispute Resolution Act, the Agency Practice Act, Contract Disputes Act, Equal Access to Justice Act, Federal Advisory Committee Act, Federal Register Act, Federal Tort Claims Act, Freedom of Information Act, Government in the Sunshine Act, Government Performance and Results Act, National Environmental Policy Act, Negotiated Rulemaking Act, Paperwork Reduction Act, Privacy Act, Regulatory Flexibility Act, and Unfunded Mandates Reform Act. Each chapter also includes citations to the text of the law, a description of the lead agency involved in its implementation, an overview of the act, a brief legislative history, overview of significant case law, a source note, and a bibliography of primary documents and secondary sources.

Federal Procedure. Lawyers Edition. St. Paul, MN: West Group (Lawyers Cooperative Publishing Co.), 1981-date. 76 vols. Annual cumulative supplements with periodic revised (recompiled) volumes.
Cost: $10,381; supplementation: 1991: $482; 1992: $491; 1993: $451.50; 1994: $830.80; 1995: $830.80; 1996: $1,081.50; 1997:

$858; 1998: $973; 1999: $1,300; 2000: $1,390; 2001: $1,634; 2002: $2,181; 2003: $2,331; 2004: $2,295; 2005: $3,293; 2006: $2,995; 2007: $3,784.50; 2008: $1,396; 2009: $4,190.50; 2010: $4,652; 2011: $4,957.50; 2012: $6,969.50; 2013: $7,414; current volumes: $499 (list). **Monthly Assured Print Price (APP)** (includes new set): $576/$6,912 (2014). Best acquired as a WestlawNext add-on.

An encyclopedic reference which treats all three parts of the federal adjudicatory system: traditional courts, specialized courts, and administrative agencies and their tribunals, in 80 individual chapters contained in 33 volumes. The 80 chapters are divided into two types of coverage; core coverage encompassing general principles of procedure in all three levels of the federal court system; and topical coverage encompassing the application of general and specific procedural rules in specific types of actions or proceedings, e.g., banking and financing, bankruptcy, civil rights, environmental protection, and employment discrimination. The topical chapters cover the specialized courts and administrative agencies to which the specific action applies. This set includes a variety of practice aids, practice pointers, checklists, and law review commentary as well as collateral references to other relevant titles in the Total Client-Service Library, such as **Am. Jur. 2d**, the **ALR** series, **Am. Jur Trials**, **Am. Jur. Proof of Facts**, etc. An excellent choice for the firm heavily involved in practice before federal administrative agencies and courts. However, while the supplementation cost was initially less expensive than that for the competing set from Matthew Bender (Stein, et al.), it now exceeds the cost of that set by about $3,000 per year (2014).

Cost Saving Tip: If you prefer this set in print, but wish to avoid the high update costs, acquire a used set or drop the standing order and add it to your Westlaw subscription. The monthly/annual cost of the **Monthly Assured Print Price** (offered to new purchasers only), is now $6,912, a substantial increase since 2011, and is designed to keep the customer on standing order. Also, the new set cost has increased substantially since 2010.

Federal Regulatory Directory. 16th ed. Washington, D.C.: CQ Press. Published every two years. Current edition: 2013. 1 vol. (1,007 pp.).
Cost: $185; from $159.50 on amazon.com (2014).
A detailed guide to the vast federal regulatory system, including its many departments, agencies, offices, commissions, and boards that have taken on a life of their own in the federal administrative state . An introductory essay provides an excellent overview of federal regulation, including discussion of its justification, history, growth, tools, implementation techniques, dispute resolution, methods of analysis, personnel, accountability and oversight, reform, and future prospects. There are detailed descriptions of the major regulatory agencies, including the EPA, FCC, FTC, Food and Drug Administration and Federal Reserve System, as well many smaller ones, each with a description of its functions and legislative history. The volume also contains organizational charts, and names and telephone numbers of officials and government functionaries, information sources, sources of rules and regulations, administrative proceedings, dockets, data and statistics, publications, and leading legislation. An essential resource for the attorney practicing before regulatory bodies.

Fox, William F., Jr. **Understanding Administrative Law**. 6th ed. New York: Matthew Bender & Co., 2012. 1 vol. (522 pp.). Paperbound.
Cost: $45; eBook: $36; from $35.00 on amazon.com; kindle: $28.44 (2014).
Now in its sixth edition, this title provides a succinct overview of the fundamental concepts of administrative law, with particular emphasis on the administrative decision-making process. While intended as a law school text, this volume also provides practitioners with insight into workings of administrative agencies and the process by which legal issues and disputes are resolved at the administrative level. The author also provides a discussion of trends in administrative law, including alternative dispute resolution, regulatory reform, and deregulation, as well as some insight into administrative law at the state level. The author is Professor of Law and Associate Dean for Academic Affairs at Catholic University School of Law. Consumers may access the first chapters of all titles in the *Understanding* series at: http://www.lexisnexis.com/lawschool/study/understanding/
Downloadable updates and and supplements to this title may be found at:
http://www.lexisnexis.com/lawschool

Funk, William F., Sidney A. Shapiro and Russell L. Weaver. **Funk, Shapiro and Weaver's Selected Federal and State Administrative and Regulatory Laws**. St. Paul, MN: West Academic, 2007-date. 1 vol. Paperbound (494 pp.). Supplemented by periodic new editions.
Cost: $40.00 (2014).
Designed as a companion to the standard administrative law caseBook, this volume contains the full text of a variety of laws useful in an administrative and regulatory law context, including the Administrative Procedure Act, Executive Order 12866, Freedom of Information Act, Privacy Act of 1974, Government in the Sunshine Act, Negotiated Rulemaking Act, Administrative Dispute Resolution Act, Regulatory Flexibility Act, Assessment of Federal Regulations and Policies on Families, Congressional Review of Agency Rulemaking, Lobbying Disclosure Act of 1995, Unfunded Mandates Reform Act/Regulatory Accountability and Reform Act, National Environmental Policy Act, Federal Register Act, Paperwork Reduction Act, Equal Access to Justice Act, Federal Trade Commission Act, Ethics in Government Act, National Labor Relations Act, Model State Administrative Procedure Act (1981), Model State Administrative Procedure Act (1961), California Code of Civil Procedure, and the California Government Code.

Gellhorn, Ernest and Ronald M. Levin. **Administrative Law and Process in a Nutshell**. 5th ed. St. Paul, MN: West Academic, 2006. 1 vol. (480 pp.). No supplementation between editions.
Cost: $41; from $23.00 on amazon.com (2014).
A brief introductory survey of federal administrative law intended for use as a basic law school text, but useful to the practitioner looking for a concise overview of the topic.

Gidiere, Stephen, III. **The Federal Information Manual: How the Government Collects, Manages, and Discloses Information under FOIA and Other Statutes**. 2d ed. Chicago: American Bar Association, 2013. 1 vol. (504 pp.).

Cost: $99.95 ($84.95 to ABA members); from $54.82 on amazon.com (2014).

The Freedom of Information Act (FOIA), enacted on July 4, 1966,and amended in 2002 (5 U.S.C. §552), was designed to address the growth of government secrecy, and provide the public greater access to executive branch records.

Federal information policy is governed by an often confusing melange of statutes, regulations, common law, executive orders and court decisions, of which the Freedom of Information Act (FOIA) is the most significant. This volume provides an invaluable examination of federal information gathering, information policy, and disclosure. Chapters address federal information disputes, agency collection of information, agency records management, classified information, access to federal records, electronic records and federal public websites, the elements of a successful FOIA request, reasons for the withholding of agency records, and homeland security information. A glossaries of abbreviations and federal information statutes are included. A partner with the firm of Balch & Bingham LLP and a member of the firm's Environmental and Natural Resources Section, author Stephen Gidiere's practice encompasses a variety of environmental, resources, energy, and administrative law matters, with a focus on government information law. His writings have addressed the intersection of national security and federal information law and policy. Mr. Gidiere is also Executive Editor of the ABA's quarterly journal Natural Resources & Environment.

Kerwin, Cornelius M. and Scott R. Furlong. **Rulemaking: How Government Agencies Write Law and Make Policy**. 4th ed. Washington, DC: CQ Press, 2010. 1 vol. (327 pp.). Paperbound.

Cost: $58; from $51.28 on amazon.com (2014).

Administrative rulemaking has emerged as a key battleground in the political battle between the Obama White House and the Republican-controlled House of Representatives, with the EPA's regulation of so-called "greenhouse" gases at center stage. Having failed to enact "cap and trade" legislation in 2009, the Obama administration is using the administrative process to achieve via the back door what it could not achieve through the legislative process. Yet, despite the importance of this activity, most Americans are woefully uninformed regarding the field of this so-called "delegated legislation," as well as the power wielded by unelected bureaucrats in the Executive Branch. Indeed, the authors acknowledge that rulemaking is the "single most important function performed by agencies of government." While Congress and the White House provide the general statutory framework for government policy, it is the rulemaking performed by the administrative agencies, utilizing the subject matter expertise of professional staff, that gives it form and substance. This estimable analytical work provides the reader with an understanding of the both the mechanics and the political dimensions of the administrative rulemaking process. The authors explain the nature, history, and rationale for rulemaking, as well as the process of rulemaking under the Administrative Procedures Act of 1946 (5 U.S.C.§ 500 et seq.), which has served as a model for similar statutes adopted by most states. They also examine the issues and contradictions of rulemaking, its management, participation, and oversight, concluding with a discussion of rulemaking theories and reform proposals. The 4th edition is updated to reflect analysis of interest group participation, current data, and the early actions of the Obama administration, including executive orders, appointment of key personnel, and agency responses to political changes in Washington. Cornelius Kerwin is president of American University and a professor of public administration in its School of Public Affairs. New co-author Scott Furlong is dean of the College of Liberal Arts and Sciences and professor of political science and public affairs at the University of Wisconsin-Green Bay. This seminal text is an essential read for anyone seeking to understand the federal regulatory process.

Klosck, Jacqueline. **The Right To Know: Your Guide to Using and Defending Freedom of Information Law in the United States**. Santa Barbara, CA: ABC-CLIO, 2009. 1 vol. (227 pp.).

Cost: $44.95; from $34.65 on amazon.com; kindle: $36.00 (2014).

Freedom of information is an essential characteristic of a democratic society and the public's right to know. Enacted in 1966, the Freedom of Information Act (FOIA) (Public Law 89-554, 5 U.S.C.§ 552) provides for the full or partial disclosure of previously unreleased information and documents controlled by Executive Branch agencies of the United States Government. Among its provisions, the Act defines agency records subject to disclosure, outlines mandatory disclosure procedures and grants nine exemptions to the statute. Following a brief history of freedom of Information law, the first manifestation of which was enacted in Sweden in 1766, the author examines the origins and development of the FOIA in the United States. She then directs her attention to the application of the FOIA to such areas as environmental protection, protection of human health and safety, the fight against corruption and government waste, and the protection of human rights and civil liberties. She also addresses what she characterizes as a trend away from openness and toward secrecy in the wake of national security concerns prompted by the terrorist attacks of 9/11. Ironically, the application of the FOIA to environmental concerns cuts both ways, as the recent "Climategate" scandal, which came to light after the release of this title, has revealed. In that episode, thousands of leaked e-mails and other documents have conclusively implicated top climate alarmists in the United States and the UK, including Phil Jones, Michael Mann (author of the infamous hockey stick graph), James Hansen and Barack Obama's science czar John Holdren, all of whom were involved in an effort to hide climate data upon which their alarmist predictions were based, and impugn the integrity and prevent the publication of climate skeptics in the peer-reviewed journals. The Climate Research Unit at the University of East Anglia, the leading source for global warming data, had repeatedly refused FOIA requests for release of the data upon which their computer models and conclusions about global warming were based (revealing, the data from East Anglia now indicates globally-averaged temperatures have remained steady at 14.5 degrees Celsius since 1997). Obstruction of the release of information under the FOIA is a crime in both the UK and the USA, and the guilty scientists can be punished with fines or jail time. Moreover, NASA and its Goddard Institute for Space Studies (GISS) have refused for nearly three years to provide documents related to global warming research requested under the FOIA. The author of this volume, who may be fairly characterized as being in the global warming alarmist camp, quotes approvingly the U.N. Intergovernmental Panel on Climate Change and Al Gore's **An Inconvenient Truth**, both of which have relied heavily on this now discredited research. This example is another indication of a phenomenon not uncommon in the legal literature, that authors without professional training in a scientific or technical field may simply accept the views of those for which they may have an ideological affinity. Jacqueline Klosck is a senior counsel for business at Goodwin Proctor LLP in New York where she represents clients in intellectual property, data privacy, and technology security cases.

Koch, Charles H., Jr. **Administrative Law & Practice**. 3d ed. St. Paul, MN: West Group, 2010-date. 5 vols. Annual cumulative pocket parts, with annual Appendix, Tables, and Index volume
Cost: $591; ProView eBook: $574; supplementation: 2011: $60; 2012: $114; 2013: $128; 2d ed.: 1998: $30; 1999: $43; 2000: $47.50; 2001: $48; 2002: $57; 2003: $64.50; 2004: $72; 2005: $79.50; 2006: $88.50; 2007: $99; 2008: $109.50; supplementation to 1st ed.: 1990: $31; 1992: $43.50; 1993: $62; 1994: $62; 1995: $62; 1996: $73; **Monthly Assured Print Price (APP)**: $17/$204.
This three-volume treatise is written by a member of the faculty at the Marshall-Wythe School of Law at the College of William and Mary and a former member of the Federal Trade Commission. Coverage includes internal processes of the administrative system, agency rulemaking, elements of adjudication, due process rights, informal adjudication, judicial action, standards of review, and public information. Appendices include the Administrative Procedure Act, Freedom of Information Act, Privacy Act, the Model State Administrative Procedures Act, table of statutes, table of cases and subject index. Annual pocket supplements include a WESTLAW Electronic Research Guide as an aide to further research.

Cost Saving Alert; Given the historic pattern of supplementation to this set, the APP pricing model is a bad deal as it pegs the programmed annual cost far above the actual cost of supplementation. Note: Though it was lowered in 2011, the APP is still substantially higher than the actual cost of supplementation.

Lubbers, Jeffrey S. **A Guide to Federal Agency Rulemaking**. 5th ed. Chicago: American Bar Association, 2012. 1 vol. (723 pp.). Updated by periodic new editions.
Cost: $139.95 ($119.95 to government lawyers, non-profit organizations, and students); from $110 on amazon.com (2014).
An ideal overview of federal rulemaking process for both novices and experienced hands. Originally published by the Administrative Conference of the United States (ACUS), it provides a complete review of the historical development of rulemaking, the statutory structure of rulemaking under the Administrative Procedures Act and other relevant statutes, and a step-by-step description of the informal rulemaking process, from preliminary considerations to the adoption of the final rule. The author also examines the judicial role in reviewing agency rulemaking activity, including decisions which address agency inaction. The appendices include leading federal statutes and other rulemaking documents. A table cases provides page references to relevant discussion in the body of the text. The author is Professor of Law at George Mason University and former Chair of the ABA Section on Administrative Law & Regulatory Practice.

Luneburg, William V. and Tho,as M. Susman. **The Lobbying Manual: A Complete Guide to Federal Law Governing Lawyers and Lobbyists**. 4th ed.
Chicago: American Bar Association, 2009. 1 vol. (865 pp.).
Cost: $199.95 ($179.95 to ABA members); from $74.99 on amazon.com; supplementation: 2011: $59.95 (2014).
The number of paid lobbyists in Washington has more than doubled since 2000, growing to more than 35,000. As a profession, lobbying attracts nearly half of all lawmakers who return to the private sector. Lobbyists represent corporations, industry associations, labor unions, and a broad range of private advocacy groups, all attempting to influence government policy in some way. Lobbying has also grown in tandem with the rise of the modern regulatory state. This volume examines the ways in which the Congress has attempted to regulate lobbying activity, particularly in the form of the Lobbying Disclosure Act of 1995, which established criteria for determining whether an organization or firm should register their employees as lobbyists. Lobbyists register with the Secretary of the Senate Office of Public Records, which makes these registrations available for public inspection. This book provides lobbyists, whether lawyers or private advocates, with the information they need to comply with federal law and ethical guidelines, including federal laws and applicable registration forms. Author William V. Luneburg is professor of law at the University of Pittsburgh School of Law where he specializes in the fields of legislation, administrative law, civil procedure, and environmental law. Thomas M. Susman is a partner in the Washington office of Ropes & Gray, LLP and coordinates the firm's regulatory and legislative practice.

McDermott, Patrice. **Who Needs To Know? The State of Public Access to Federal Government Information**. Lanham, MD: Bernan Essential Reference Publications, 2007. 1 vol. (304 pp.).
Cost: $19.95; from $9.98 on amazon.com (2014).
This important study examines the current state of the public's ability to locate, obtain and use federal government information in a post 9/11 world. A major portion of the author's inquiry relates to the availability of information in an era in which national security or homeland security concerns are of paramount importance. But while the author is critical of recent efforts to limit access on national security grounds, she also addresses limitations on public access to information in non-security related areas, which directly impact the ability of members of the general public to affect public policy and hold policy makers accountable. The author is Director of OpenTheGovernment.org, and an advocate for open access to government information.

Morriss, Andrew P., Bruce Yandle, and Andrew Dorchak. **Regulation By Litigation**. New Haven, CT: Yale University Press, 2009. 1 vol. (282 pp.).
Cost: $50; from $42.65 on amazon.com (2014).
A significant trend has emerged in the field of modern administrative law, namely the increasing use of litigation as a tool for advancing regulatory objectives. The growth of the administrative bureaucracy at both the state and federal levels is increasingly being promoted by means of litigation as an alternative to traditional administrative rulemaking procedures. The authors of this volume examine three significant cases in which litigation has been used to achieve regulatory ends, including the EPA's suit against manufacturers of heavy-duty diesel engines, the asbestos and silica dust litigation by private

attorneys, and state and private lawsuits against cigarette manufacturers. In this sophisticated, the authors contend that litigation is an inappropriate means of implementing substantive regulatory measures and suggest a variety of reforms to help reduce the reliance on the courts and the negative impact of an unbridled regulatory state on an already overburdened private sector. Andrew Morriss is a professor of law and business at the University of Illinois, Urbana-Champaign. Bruce Yandle is professor of economics emeritus at Clemson University. Andrew Dorchak is Head of Reference and Foreign/International Law Specialist, Case Western Reserve University School of Law Library.

O'Reilly, James T. **Administrative Rulemaking: Structuring, Opposing, and Defending Federal Agency Regulations**. 2013 ed. St. Paul, MN: Thomson Reuters West (Lawyers Cooperative Publishing Co.), 2013. Annual replacement volumes. 1 vol. (868 pp.). Paperbound.
Cost: $371; supplementation: 1st ed.: 1991: $40; 1992: $62; 1993: $45; 1994: $45; 1996: $50; 1997: $52; 1998: $55; 1999: $60; 2000: $65; 2001: $74; 2002: $81.50; 2003: $92.50; 2004: $94.50; 2005: $119; 2006: $115.50; 2007: new edition; 2008: $175; 2009 (1st annual replacement ed.): $196; 2010: $215; 2011: $235; 2012: $272; 2013: $297; **Monthly Assured Print Price (APP):** $31/$372.
A one-volume practitioner-oriented treatment of the federal regulatory process with emphasis upon the pre-litigation stages of federal rulemaking. The author provides suggestions for the least expensive solutions to regulatory problems. Includes useful flow charts which diagram specific regulatory processes. Originally published by Shepard's McGraw-Hill. The bound volume second edition was replaced by a paperbound second edition in 2009, presumably portending paperbound replacement volumes in future years.

O'Reilly, James T. **Careers in Administrative Law & Regulatory Practice**. Chicago: American Bar Association, 2010. 1 vol. (161 pp.). Paperbound.
Cost: $49.95 ($39.95 to members); from $29.35 on amazon.com (2014).
This concise volume by a leading authority on administrative law, and other contributors, provides valuable and perceptive insights into the nature of administrative law practice and the varied career avenues open to specialists in the field. Included is a consideration of preparation, comparisons to other legal specialties, cross-training, pre-law preparation, stability as an attractive feature, political awareness, skill sets, risks of diminished success, awards and recognition, career advancement, networking, readings to prepare, and perspectives from the law school career services center. Essays by 17 administrative law veterans provide unique perspectives on the various career paths that can be pursued by those interested in the field of administrative law, ranging from environmental law, immigration, food and drugs, election law, professor of administrative law, municipal administrative law, Congressional research attorney, U.S. administrative law judge, product safety lawyer, workers' compensation specialist, association lawyer, adjudicator, antitrust lawyer, and regulations lawyer. James T. O'Reilly is a professor of law at the University of Cincinnati College of Law and former Chair of the ABA Section of Administrative Law. He is the author of 42 textbooks, five of them with ABA Press.

Pierce, Richard J., Jr., Sidney A. Shapiro, and Paul R. Verkuil. **Administrative Law and Process**. 6th ed. St. Paul, MN: Foundation Press, 2014. 1 vol. (659 pp.). University Textbook Series. Online only. No supplementation. Available from Thomson Reuters West.
Cost: Online book: $62.00 (2014).
This text is intended as a collateral reading source for law school or graduate level courses on administrative law. The authors examine a number of topics with an impact on the regulatory process, including the political and legal natures of the administrative process, legislative control of administrative discretion, and executive control of administrative discretion. Also considered are threshold, procedural, and substantive issues in the judicial control of administrative discretion. Finally, the authors discuss access to private and public information, and the issues of fairness and political accountability. The text includes selective citations to applicable cases, statutes, regulations, and secondary authorities. Richard J. Pierce is the Lyle T. Alverson Professor of Law George Washington University Law School. Sidney A. Shapiro is the John M. Rounds Professor of Law, University of Kansas School of Law. Paul R. Verkuil is Dean and Professor of Law, Cardozo School of Law, Yeshiva University.

Pierce, Richard J., Jr. **Administrative Law Treatise**. 5th ed. New York: Wolters Kluwer Law & Business, 2009-date. 3 vols.
Cost: $959; supplementation: 2010: 0; 2011: $172; 2012: $184; 2013: $210; 4th ed: 2003: $171; 2004: $183; 2005: $192; 2006: $204; 2007: $217; 2008: $238; 3d ed.: 1995: $125; 1996: $140; 1997: $148; 1998: $156; 1999: $170; 2000: $195; 2001: 0; 2002: new edition.
The previous editions of this work have been ranked among the most authoritative and significant of all scholarly treatises and were, arguably, the most heavily cited secondary sources in judicial opinions. Professor Davis is universally considered to be the greatest living authority on the subject of administrative law. This third edition is an up-to-date and complete revision of the second edition written by Richard Pierce, the Paul J. Kellner Professor of Law at Columbia University, at the invitation of Professor Davis. As a life-long student of Professor Davis' work, Professor Pierce views are nearly identical to those of his mentor. In fact, in his preface, Professor Pierce identifies only one substantive issue on which their views differ significantly: the scope of the Due Process Clause which appears in 9.2A. A "Comment" by Professor Davis accordingly sets forth his agreement on the Due Process Protection of a Group. The Appendices to this three-volume set include the U.S. Constitution, the Administrative Procedures Act, the Freedom of Information Act, Privacy Act, Government in the Sunshine Act, Negotiated Rulemaking Act, Alternative Dispute Resolution Act, Federal Advisory Committee Act, Equal Access to Justice Act, Federal Tort Claims Act, National Environmental Policy Act, and the Paperwork Reduction Act. Originally published by Little, Brown, this and the rest of Little, Brown's legal titles were sold to John Wiley & Sons in 1996, which was itself purchased by Wolters Kluwer in 1997 and merged with the Aspen product line (now Wolters Kluwer Law & Business).

Reese, John H. **Administrative Law Desk Reference for Lawyers**. Newark, NJ: LexisNexis (Matthew Bender), 2003. 1 vol. (698 pp.). No supplementation between editions.
Cost: $133; from $115.99 on amazon.com (2014).
This concise reference tool is designed for attorneys who practice before federal administrative agencies. It provides a complete overview of administrative law principles and the federal rulemaking process, as well as coverage of the administrative adjudication process, the procedural rights of persons and parties, and the formal hearing process under the Administrative Procedures Act. The author also provides discussion and analysis of agency decisions, sanctions, and licensing. The volume concludes with four chapters encompassing the subject s of judicial review, issues of justiciability, scope, sovereign immunity, timing, and relief pending review. The volume includes a number of charts and graphics which illustrate the administrative process, comparative coverage of APA's for 17 states, and cross reference to the publisher's six-volume **Administrative Law** treatise (Stein, below). The volume also includes tables of cases, statutes, and regulations. The author is Professor of Law at the University of Denver and author of the widely used caseBook **Administrative Law: Principles and Practice** (West). A worthy and cost-effective alternative to some of the more highly priced works on the market.

Rose-Ackerman, Susan, ed. **Economics of Administrative Law**. Northampton, MA: Edward Elgar Publishing, 2007. 1 vol. (637 pp.).
Cost: $315 ($283.50 online discount); from $206.23 on amazon.com (2014).
In the field of administrative law, all representative democracies need to balance democratic accountability with the competent implementation of complex statutes. There is an inherent tension between the power exercised by an administrative, or managerial, bureaucracy and the people to whom they are, albeit indirectly, answerable.This collection of articles examines the economics of administrative law from theoretical, legal and empirical perspectives, drawing upon insights from economics and political economy. The aim is to provide an understanding of why delegation, accompanied by judicial review, takes place and how the self-interest of political, bureaucratic, and judicial actors interacts with institutional structures to determine the outcomes. Congressional and public input is provided for in the rule-making provisions of the Administrative Procedures Act (1946), which provides for Congressional oversight and input from those outside the government. The articles address such broad topics as the political economy of delegation to agencies, Congressional oversight, agency discretion and government institutions, politics and agency rulemaking, the politics of cost-benefit analysis and the role of the President, judicial review in the regulatory state, and comparative administrative law and democratic legitimacy. Susan Rose-Ackerman is the Henry R. Luce Professor of Jurisprudence (Law and Political Science) at Yale University and a widely respected expert in the field of economics and administrative law.

Stein, Jacob A., Glenn A. Mitchell, and Basil J. Mezines. **Administrative Law**. New York: Matthew Bender & Co., 1977-date. 6 vols. Looseleaf format. Updated three times per year. Also available on CD-ROM and ebook.
Cost: $3,578 (includes annual subscription); renewal: 1995: $762; 1996: $803; 1997: $803; 1998: $840; 1999: $880; 2000: $940; 2001: $1,006; 2002: $1,077; 2003: $1,099; 2004: $1,188; 2005: $1,271; 2006: $1,424; 2007: $1,601; 2008: $1,761; 2009: $1,937; 2010: $2,074; 2011: $2,136; 2012: $2,264; 2013: $2,561; 2014: $2,644; CD-ROM: $3,136; renewal: 2014: $2,381.70; eBook: $3,253; renewal: 2014: $2,644.
An exhaustive examination of administrative law with an emphasis on federal procedural principle rather than substantive law. Topics covered include the history and development of the administrative process, administrative establishments, organization and structure, the acquisition use and disclosure of government information, the Freedom of Information, Privacy, and Sunshine Acts, rules and rulemaking, evidence, hearings and adjudication, administrative decision-making, licensing, administrative sanctions, attorney conduct, judicial review, and federal grant dispute resolution. There is also a discussion of the Electronic Freedom of Information Act Amendments of 1996. Matthew Bender has streamlined its editorial processes to reduce the time lag between the current state of the law and the shipment of print supplements. In addition, the CD-ROM or Internet subscriptions allow subscribers to uplink to the LEXIS-NEXIS online update database for the most current case law at no additional charge.

Cost Saving Tip: If you intend to use this product primarily for its core description and analysis, consider buying a new set and dropping the supplementation after the initial year's subscription expires. Then, simply purchase another used set at some future date when you feeled compelled to update it. If you expect to use this title intensively, the CD-ROM or Internet product will not only provide you with more timely full text search capability, but the ability to uplink to the LexisNexis update database for the most current case law at no additional charge. It appears LexisNexis Matthew Bender is transitioning from the CD-ROM and Internet versions to the eBook format.

West's Federal Administrative Practice. 3d-4th eds. St. Paul, MN: West Group, 1999-date. 9 vols. Annual pocket supplements and periodic revised volumes.
Cost: $1,290; supplementation: 1997: $155.50; 1998: $165; 1999: $466; 2000: $535; 2001: $447; 2002: $373.50; 2003: $359; 2004: $323.75; 2005: $354; 2006: $529; 2007: $588; 2008: $490; 2009: $545.50; 2010: $604; 2011: $659.50; 2012: $720; 2013: $780. **Monthly Assured Print Price (APP)**: $87/$1,044.
Formerly titled **West's Federal Practice Manual**, this multi-volume and topically organized reference tool is intended to provide lawyers who are not necessarily specialists with guidance in handling matters before various federal departments and agencies. In addition to substantive discussion and guidance on matters of federal administrative practice, the set includes checklists, forms, instructions, and citations to relevant primary authorities. Less costly to update than some competing products (e.g. Matthew Bender's **Administrative Law**). The set has undergone substantial revision since 1999 in the process of its conversion to the 4th edition.

Cost Saving Alert: While under the **APP** program the new customer receives the complete set under the terms of a fixed monthly cost, the long-term monthly cost comparable to the traditional subscriber discount (currently $1,044/yr. vs. $780).

The cost of the APP program is also substantially higher than that of the customer who buys annual supplements at irregular intervals, say every 2-3 years. The supplementation is overpriced for a 9-volume set.

Additional titles in the field of Administrative Law are available from the following publishers: American Bar Association, Aspen, Bernan, Carolina Academic Press, Cornell University Press, Delmar Publishers, Edward Elgar, Federal Bar Association, LexisNexis, Manhattan Publishing Co., Sage Publications, Thomson Reuters West, West Academic, Yale University Press. See Appendix B for addresses and telephone numbers.

Admiralty and Maritime Law

American Maritime Cases on DVD. Baltimore, MD: American Maritime Cases, Inc., 1923- Online. Updated regularly.
Cost: print: $1,125 per year; monthly issues only: $945; most recent five-year Digest (2003-2007): $675.00; electronic access (12 mos. unlimited): $350.00 (introductory); 24-hour access: $60.00 (2014).
Contains the full text of state and federal **American Maritime Cases** from 1923 to date from the publishers print reporter series. Cases may be searched by full text or by the publisher's own attorney-drafted headnotes, table of cases or cross-reference tables. This is the leading specialized source for cases on American maritime law. In 2007, the CD-ROM product was converted to a DVD format, and in 2010 to online access.

Benedict on Admiralty. 7th ed. by Steven F. Friedell. New York: Matthew Bender & Co., 1958-date. 31 vols. Looseleaf format.
Cost: $6,273 (includes annual subscription); annual renewal: 1995: $1,698.50; 1996: $1,782; 1997: $1,782; 1998: $1,870; 1999: $1,950; 2000: $2,090; 2001: $2,236; 2002: $2,393; 2003: $2,513. 2004: $2,639; 2005: $2,824; 2006: $2,937; 2007: $3,113; 2008: $3.300; 2009: $3,498; 2010: $3,638; 2011: $3,747; 2012: $3,972; 2013: $4,434; 2014: $4,682; eBook: $5,702; renewal: 2014: $4,778.70; **Cruise Ship Law** may be purchased separately at a cost of $328.
This is the seventh edition of probably the oldest continuously published legal treatise in the United States. Originally authored by Erastus C. Benedict in 1850 and carried on members of the Benedict family until 1910, the seventh edition is authored by Steven F. Friedell, a Professor of Law at Rutgers University. This is the most authoritative multi-volume treatise on all aspects of maritime law with the exception of marine insurance. The set includes three volumes formerly published separately: **Longley on Common Carriage of Cargo**; **Poor on Charter Parties and Ocean Bills of Lading**; and **Norris on the Law of Salvage**. In additional to those areas of the law traditionally falling with the filed of admiralty law, this set also provides discussion of cruise ship law, including discussion of government regulation of cruise ships, and responsibilities to passengers, crew members, concessionaires, invitees, licensees, and stowaways,

Cost Saving Tips: The high annual renewal cost for **Benedict**, frozen between 1992 and 1995 at $1,698.50, had increased to $4,682 by 2014. This annual renewal cost provides a strong justification to buy this set with its one-year service and then drop the automatic supplementation. You can update by purchasing a new set at some future date. This decision will no doubt depend on the nature of your practice and the frequency with which you expect to serve as more than a basic reference. Knowing the limitations of the set in your office, you can then update the statutes and cases you find relevant by using the appropriate statute books, case digests, on-line services, and citator services. The editorial lag-time, formerly 6-8 months with print, has been reduced somewhat with the advent of its availability in electronic formats. Consider purchasing the one-volume **Benedict on Admiralty Desk Reference** (also vol. 8 of Benedict) at $381.00 instead of the full set.

Birnbaum, Steven M., et al., eds. **The Longshore Textbook**. 6th ed. Tucson, AZ: Lawyers & Judges Publishing Co., 2010. 1 vol. (450 pp.).
Cost: $99; from $74.80 on amazon.com; kindle: $71.06 (2014).
Designed for use by attorneys, insurance adjusters, physicians, and vocational counselors, this collection of twenty-eight articles addresses various aspects of worker's compensation under the Longshore Act and Harbor Workers' Act and its Extensions. Articles address administrative claims handling at the District Director's Office, application of the AMA Guidelines, the Benefits Review Board appeal, claims administration for nonappropriated fund employees, concurrent jurisdiction, coverage boundaries, jurisdictional considerations under the Defense Base Act, death benefits, disability, retained wage-earning capacity, employer considerations, fees for service, rehabilitation, vessel and vessel owner considerations, and more. The appendices include the full text of the Longshore and Harbor Workers' Compensation Act and its Extensions, related federal regulations under the Act, Longshore forms, maximum and minimum compensation rates, a directory of OWCP/Longshore offices, and an index. The volume would benefit greatly from an introductory essay explaining the Longshore Act and the claims process generally.

Force, Robert. **Admiralty and Maritime Law**. Washington, DC: Federal Judicial Center, 2004. 1 vol. (242 pages).
Cost: Available free of charge from the Federal Judicial Center via Adobe Acrobat download. Go to: https://public.resource.org/scribd/8763552.pdf
This monograph is designed to introduce federal judges to admiralty and maritime law, including both general maritime and statutory law. The author examines the rules of jurisdiction and procedure and those areas related to commercial law, including charter parties, carriage of goods, and marine insurance. He also discusses the Carriage of Goods by Sea Act, the Pomerene Act, and the Harter Act, as well as the body of law dealing with maritime personal injury and death, including damages and seamen's remedies, the Jones Act, and the Longshore and Harbor Workers' Compensation Act. Other topics addressed are the law of collision, towage, pilotage, salvage, limitation of liability, maritime liens, and general average.

Healy, Nicholas and Joseph C. Sweeney. **The Law of Marine Collision**. Centerville, MD: Cornell Maritime Press [Schiffer

Books], 1998. 1 vol. (672 pp.).
Cost: $150; from $75.00 on amazon.com (2014).
A significant contribution to the admiralty law literature, this is the first comprehensive treatment of the law of maritime collisions since the publication of John Sweeney's **The American Law of Collision** in 1949. In particular, it incorporates the 1972 COLREGS (effective in 1977), the first complete revision of the International Rules since 1889, and the U.S. Inland Rules. The authors also discuss maritime damages generally, both-to-blame collisions, official investigations, pilotage, towage, marine pollution, limitation of liability, marine insurance, salvage, and general average. Nicholas Healy has practiced admiralty law since 1936 and taught at New York University for 39 years, also serving as editor of the Journal of Maritime Law and Commerce from 1980 to 1990. Joseph Sweeney, a former admiralty practitioner himself, has taught admiralty law and other subjects at Fordham University for more than 30 years. He has served as editor of the **Maritime Law Newsletter**, published by Lloyd's of London Press, since its inception in1983. An essential tool for the maritime law practitioner.

Maraist, Frank L. and Thomas C. Galligan. **Admiralty Law in a Nutshell**. 6th ed. St. Paul, MN: West Group, 2010. 1 vol. (365 pp.). Available from West Academic.
Cost: $41; from $31.96 on amazon.com; kindle: $23.77 (2014).
A compact summary of admiralty law intended for the law student or the general practitioner. Chapters cover the development of general maritime law and American admiralty law, jurisdiction, the scope of maritime jurisdiction, substantive maritime law, contracts for carriage of goods, liens on maritime property, employment contracts, marine insurance, towage, salvage, general average, maritime tort law, collision law, worker's compensation claims, wrongful death, sovereign immunity, limitation on liability, and jurisdiction and procedure in maritime claims.

Messer, Tuuli Anna. **Master's Handbook on Ship's Business**. 3d ed.Atglen, PA: Schiffer Publishing, 2001. 1 vol. (404 pp.).
Cost: $50; from $29.88 on amazon.com (2014).
This manual is designed to provide guidance to a shipmaster in the performance of his duties the completion of all necessary paperwork incidental to a ship's operation. It includes an overview of United States laws and international codes and conventions, including those governing the civil and criminal liability of the master, as well as a variety of environmental and safety concerns. Additional chapters address such topics as vessel accidents, communications, shipping articles, logbooks, documents and certificates, customs, immigration, ocean bill of lading, charter parties, foreign ports and canals, and flag etiquette. The appendices include shipping articles, sample forms, conversion factors, agencies and contracts, foreign medical evacuation and travelers' insurance companies, and acronyms. An excellent overview of ship operations for those charged with representing their legal interests.

Nordquist, Myron H., Tommy T.B. Koh and John Norton Moore, eds. **Freedom of the Seas, Passage Rights and the 1982 Law of the Sea Convention**. Leiden/Boston: Martinus Nijhoff Publishers, 2009. 1 vol. (623 pp.).
Cost: $232; from $235.42 on amazon.com (2014).
Until very recently in maritime history, seafarers were largely free to navigate the oceans without restriction as long as they were more than three miles offshore. Naval operations, too, exercised the freedom of the high seas, largely unrestrained by international conventions and protocols. On an ecological front, they were also free to ignore the environmental regulations of coastal states, even to the point of discharging raw sewage directly into harbors. More recently, however, seafarers have been made subject to a variety of international and regional agreements on such matters as environmental pollution, use of shipping lanes, reporting requirements, and the type of passage they are exercising. With the enactment of the United Nations Convention on the Law of the Sea (UNCLOS) in 1982, the nations of the world created a legal order for the seas and oceans to facilitate international communications, promote their peaceful use, the equitable and efficient utilization of their resources, the conservation of their living resources, and the study, protection and preservation of the marine environment. This volume assembles the papers presented at the 32nd Oceans Conference on "Freedom of the Seas, Passage Rights and the 1982 Law of the Sea Convention" held in Singapore in 2008, and sponsored by the University of Virginia School of Law's Center for Ocean Law and Policy and the S. Rajaratnam School of International Studies. It contains the texts of two keynote addresses and seven panel discussions (27 papers in all) on a variety of topics and issues related to the freedom of navigation, scientific surveys and hydrographic surveys in the Exclusive Economic Zone (EEZ), military activities in EEZ, transit passage through straits used for international navigation, archipelagic sea lanes passage, vessel source pollution and protection of the marine environment, non-flag state enforcement and protection of the marine environment. Two supplementary papers address navies and maritime security, and piracy issues. Together, they provide a 25-year perspective on UNCLOS and its impact on the freedom of the seas and related issues. Contributors include government officials, senior naval and coast guard commanders, leading jurists, and academic specialists. A companion CD-ROM contains a variety of visuals, slides and maps contained in the speakers' PowerPoint presentations.

Norris, Martin J. and Robert Force. **The Law of Maritime Personal Injuries**. 5th ed. St. Paul, MN: West Group (Clark Boardman Callaghan), 2009/2011-date. 2 vols. Annual cumulative pocket parts.
Cost: $475; supplementation: 1993: $81; 1994: $92; 1995: $110; 1996: $135; 1997: $145; 1998: $153; 1999: $165; 2000: $179; 2001: $208; 2002: $244; 2003: $278; 2004: $311; 2005: $357.50; 2006: $56; 2007: $52.50; 2008: $104.50; 2009: $126; 2010: $139; 2011: $151.50; 2012: $165.50; 2013: $65; **Monthly Assured Print Price (APP):** $23/$276.
This two-volume treatise provides a comprehensive analysis of the law as it applies to harbor workers, passengers and visitors, the Longshore and Harbor Workers' Compensation Act, and the rights and responsibilities of all those involved in maritime personal injury actions. Coverage includes chapters on bringing an action, wrongful death, limitation of liability, suits against the government, negligence, products liability, practice and procedure, and indemnification. Appendices in volume two include the Longshore and Harbor Workers' Compensation Act,

Federal Rules of Appellate Procedure, federal Rules of Civil Procedure, and forms. Also includes a table of personal injury cases, table of cases, table of statutes, and subject index. Avoid APP pricing, which exceeds recent history of supplementation costs.

Norris, Martin J. **The Law of Seamen**. 5th ed. St. Paul, MN: West Group (Clark Boardman Callaghan), 2003-date. 3 vols. (712, 1032, 887 pp.). Annual cumulative pocket parts.
Cost: $590; supplementation: 2004: $90; supplementation to 4th ed.: 1993: $98; 1994: $110; 1995: $150; 1996: $170; 1997: $195; 1998: $206.70; 1999: $223; 2000: $236; 2001: $279; 2002: $307.50; 2003: $348; 2004: $90; 2005: $114; 2006: $110; 2007: $122.50; 2008: $137; 2009: $223; 2010: $221.50; 2011: $241.50; 2012: $265.50; 2013: $65; **Monthly Assured Print Price (APP):** $34/$408.
This three-volume treatise provides full coverage of the law governing the rights and obligations of those who work upon vessels in navigation (as opposed to those work on the shore), including masters, officers, crew members, stowaways, and aliens. Coverage extends to the duties of American consuls, the relation of consuls to seamen, maritime administrative law, the shipping articles (contracts between master and seamen), log books, desertion, crew salvage, criminal offenses, loss of clothing and personal effects, wages, change of rating, maintenance and cure, seaworthiness, suits against the government, death on the high seas, the Jones Act, products liability, and practice and procedure. Appendices in volume three include a topical compilation of maritime injury cases, applicable laws, and Tables of Cases, Statutes, Rules and Forms. Formerly published by Lawyers Cooperative.

Cost-Saving Tip: Avoid APP pricing which exceeds recent supplement cost history.

Parks, Alex L. and Edward V. Cattell, Jr. **The Law of Tug, Tow, and Pilotage**. 3rd ed. Atglen, PA: Schiffer Publishing, 1994. 1 vol. (1230 pp.).
Available through Maryland Nautical Sales, Inc., Baltimore, MD.
Cost: $175.00; from $100.00 on amazon.com (2014).
This comprehensive and scholarly treatise is designed to meet the needs of towing company executives, insurance professionals and practicing attorneys. Building on the work of the late Alex Parks, a lifelong maritime lawyer and adjunct professor of admiralty law at Willamette University College of Law, Edward Cattell has fashioned a work which summarizes and distills the case law governing the towing industry and such collateral areas as insurance law, cargo law, and collision law. The authors cite the relevant case law, including citations to cases published in the **American Maritime Cases** (**AMC**). The researcher is aided by the addition of the case holdings in parentheses following the case citations. The authors also provide citations to relevant cases and statutes from Great Britain and Commonwealth nations. Chapters are devoted to the historical development, the application of admiralty principles to tug and tow, general principles specifically applicable to towing, duty of the tug generally, duty of tow generally, collision and limitation of liability, governmental regulation, marine insurance, maritime liens, charters, pilotage, and salvage. The appendices include a bareboat charter form. sample towage agreements, a time charter, and standard conditions for several foreign jurisdictions, as well as a detailed subject index. The text is preceded by an extensive table of cases.

Schoenbaum, Thomas J. **Admiralty and Maritime Law**. 5th ed. St. Paul, MN: West Academic, 2011-date. 1 vol. (1,030 pp.). Irregular supplementation.
Cost: $113; supplementation: 2013: $35.00; 4th ed.: 2004: 0; 2005: $13; 2006: $13; 2007: $15; 2008: $18; 2009: $20; supplementation to 3d ed.: 2001: 0; 2002: $12; 2003: new edition.
A one-volume review of the basic issues in admiralty and maritime law. A more succinct, student-oriented version of what appears in the author's three-volume Practitioner's Edition. The Appendix includes a variety of forms and documents, a WESTLAW research guide, Table of Cases, and Index. Cost of volume and supplementation are both reasonable.

Schoenbaum, Thomas J. **Admiralty and Maritime Law**. 5th ed. St. Paul, MN: Thomson Reuters, 2011-date. 3 vols. Annual supplementation.
Cost: $291; supplementation: 2013: $71; 4th ed.: 2004: $390 (includes new edition); 2005: $42; 2006: $50; 2007: $56; 2008: $62; 2009: $73.50; 2010: $80.00; 2011: new ed.: $240; supplementation to 3d ed.: 2001: 0; 2002: $32; 2003: $36; 2004: 0; 2006: $45; 2007: $45; supplementation to 2d ed.: 1995: $14; 1996: $17; 1997: $17; 1998: 0; 1999: $29; **Monthly Assured Print Price (APP):** $15/$180.
This Practitioner's edition is an expansion of the author's one-volume Hornbook, exploring in greater depth the principles and issues in admiralty and maritime law. Individual chapters cover the historical background, international maritime jurisdiction and law of the sea, admiralty jurisdiction, general maritime law, seamen, longshore and harbor workers, wrongful death, maritime liens and ship mortgages, carriage of goods, charter parties, towage, pilotage, collision and marine casualty, limitation of liability, salvage, general average, maritime pollution, maritime insurance, sovereign immunity, and admiralty practice and procedure. The Appendix includes a variety of forms and documents, a WESTLAW research guide, Table of Cases, and Index. Highly recommended; an excellent value with extremely reasonable supplementation costs. Avoid the APP pricing option.

Sohn, Louis B., Kristen Gustafson Juras, and John E. Noyes. **The Law of the Sea in a Nutshell.** 2d ed. St. Paul, MN: West Publishing Co., 2010. 1 vol. (613 pp.). No supplementation between editions. Available from West Academic.
Cost: $41; from $32.00 on amazon.com (2014).
A brief handbook on the major issues in admiralty law, including nationality of vessels, duties and jurisdiction of flag states and restrictions on jurisdiction of states over foreign vessels, baseline for determining zones of national jurisdiction, boundaries of maritime jurisdiction between adjacent and opposite states, internal waters and ports, the territorial sea, exclusive economic zone, continental shelf, exploitation of the mineral resources of the deep seabed, protection and preservation of marine environment. high seas freedom, and settlement of disputes. Also includes a table of relevant treaties, table of cases, and index.

Talley, Wayne K., et al. **Maritime Safety, Security and Piracy.** London: informa, 2008. 1 vol. (344 pp.).
Cost: $269.95; kindle: $215.96 on amazon.com (2014).
The issues of maritime safety, security and piracy are of central importance to a world in which more than 90% of global trade is conveyed by international shipping. Although the first maritime treaties date back to the 19th century, it was the sinking of the Titanic in 1912 that led to the promulgation of the first international convention that addressed safety of life at sea (SOLAS), adopted in 1914. As a specialized agency of the United Nations, the International Maritime Organization (IMO) was created pursuant to a convention adopted in Geneva in 1948. Since its first meeting in 1959, the IMO's primary task has been to develop and maintain a comprehensive regulatory framework for shipping, its safety, environmental concerns, legal matters, technical co-operation, maritime security and shipping efficiency. The conventions adopted by the IMO provide mechanisms whereby member states, in their sovereign capacity, can monitor and enforce international regulations governing activities on the seas, and the safety of ships, cargo and seafarers. This is accomplished through the process by which the more than 50,000 ships involved in international shipping are registered (flagged) by member states, and their activities and safe conduct monitored and controlled. The chapters in this volume provide expert and invaluable discussion of topics of interest to maritime law practitioners, including international ship safety regulations; ship formal safety assessment; US ship accident research; security of ships and shipping operations; piracy in shipping; ship piracy: ship type and flag; port safety and workers; port state control, inspection and vessel detention; port ship accidents and risks; port security: a risk based assessment; and property damage, personal injury, and theft. Many include illustrative charts and graphs detailing such topics as ships accidents, risk assessment, piracy attacks, occupational injuries, parameters of maritime accidents, probability of detention, among others. Perhaps the most timely discussion is that related to the analysis, both narrative and econometric, of piracy activities around the globe. Wayne K. Talley, Executive Director of the International Maritime, Ports and Logistics Management Institute and Professor of Economics at Old Dominion University, heads an impressive list of 22 academic experts who contributed to this estimable peer-reviewed volume, each chapter of which is accompanied by a bibliography of essential references. This work represents a major contribution to the literature of maritime law and the safety and security issues with which it is inextricably linked. It should be essential reading to any practitioner, ship-owner, insurer, or scholar interested in gaining a more complete understanding of this important and multi-faceted field.

Additional titles in the field of Admiralty and Maritime Law are available from the following publishers: American Maritime Cases, Carolina Academic Press, Cornell Maritime Press, Edward Elgar, Informa, Juta & Co., Kluwer Academic Press, Law of the Sea Institute (U. of Maine), Lawyers & Judges Publishing, LexisNexis, Marine Education Textbooks, Marine Law Institute, Martinus Nijhoff, and Thomson Reuters West, West Academic. See Appendix B for addresses and telephone numbers.

Advertising Law

Brody, Steven G., Bruce E. H. Johnson. **Advertising and Commercial Speech: A First Amendment Guide**. 2d ed. New York: Practising Law Institute, 2004-date. 1 vol. (611 pp.). Looseleaf format.
Cost: $335; supplementation: 2005: $95.00; 2006: $73; 2007: $111; 2008: $119; 2009: $133; 2010: $140; 2011: $165; 2012: $168; 2013: $173.00; 1st ed.: 2000: $66; 2001: $73; 2002: $79; 2003: $88; 2004: new edition.
This work addresses the legal issues surrounding the emergence of the doctrine of commercial speech and the limitations on legislation controlling advertising. It examines the rise of limitations on advertising and commercial speech, largely at the state level, and the subsequent application of the First Amendment to the states through the Due Process Clause of the 14th Amendment. In addition to chapters detailing the historical evolution of the commercial speech doctrine, the authors discuss such topics as defamation, disparagement, the right to refuse advertising, regulation of the advertising medium, and regulation of advertising content. The second edition includes a new chapter on compelled commercial speech and its relationship to the compelled speech doctrine, and new material on the validity of billboard regulations, the FTC's telemarketing regulations establishing the "Do Not Call" registry; and federal and state regulation of e-mail advertising. Steven G. Brody is a partner with the New York City form of King & Spalding. Bruce Johnson is a partner with the firm of Davis Wright & Tremaine in Seattle. The volume includes extensive citations to the relevant case law.

Flink, Lawrence J. **Guidelines for Advertiser/Agency Contracts**. 2d ed. New York: Association of National Advertisers, 2003. 1 vol. (62 pp.). Paperbound.
Cost: available online to ANA members only (2014).
The Association of National Advertisers (ANA) is the advertising industry's leading trade association dedicated exclusively to marketing and brand building, representing more than 300 companies with 8,000 brands that collectively spend more than $100 billion marketing its members products. This slim volume provides the ANA's Guidelines for Advertiser/Agency Contracts and provides advice on the three basic phases of contract development: (1) initial negotiation of terms, (2) drafting an Interim Letter of Understanding, and (3) the final written contract. Also discussed are issues of defining agency services and compensation, annual reviews, establishing agreements on ownership of materials, and conflict standards. Also includes a sample contract. The author is an advertising agency veteran and contract consultant.

Moore, Roy L., Ronald T. Farrar, and Erik L. Collins. **Advertising and Public Relations Law.** 2d ed. New York: Routledge, 2010. 1 vol. (512 pp.). Paperbound.
Cost: $94.95; from $23.26 on amazon.com (2014).
Intended primarily as a text for undergraduate and graduate students of advertising and public relations, this volume provides both theoretical and practical discussion and insights into the legal milieu in which advertising and public relations are conducted. The authors provide an excellent introduction to such

topics as the First Amendment, commercial speech doctrine, and the state and federal regulatory framework for advertising. They also discuss commercial speech torts, industry self-regulation, intellectual property, and public access to information, as well as such topics as right of publicity, invasion of privacy, disparagement, false light, SEC jurisdiction, journalistic privilege, and obscenity and indecency. Intellectual property issues, such as copyright, trademarks, patents, and trade secrets are also co0nsidertesd. Appendices include professional codes, the U.S. Constitution, an overview of the U.S. court system, copyright registration forms, trademark registration forms, and model releases. Roy L. Moore is Professor of Journalism and Associate Dean for Graduate Studies in the University of Kentucky College of Communications and Information Studies. A practicing attorney, he holds both a Ph.D. in Mass Communications from the University of Wisconsin-Madison and a J.D. in Law from Georgia State University.

Parkinson, Michael G. and L. Marie Parkinson. **Law for Advertising, Broadcasting, Journalism, and Public Relations: A Comprehensive Text for Students and Practitioners**. New York: Routledge, 2006. 1 vol. (528 pp.). Paperbound.
Cost: $86.95; from $5.70 on amazon.com (2014).
A useful overview of the essentials of communication law for students and practitioners in the fields of advertising, public relations and journalism, both print and electronic. Chapters cover the basics of the legal system, legal procedures, structures, and jurisdictions, the First Amendment, electronic media regulations, intellectual property law; employment and agency law, commercial communication law, and special laws and regulations that impact reporters, public relations practitioners, and advertisers who deal with stock sales. The text is illustrated with sample cases, key words and phrases, legal documents, jury instructions, and a sample brief. The authors are practicing attorneys with extensive experience teaching the communications law.

Rosden, Peter Eric and George Eric Rosden. **The Law of Advertising**. New York: Matthew Bender & Co., 1973-date. 4 vols. Looseleaf format. Updated three times per year.
Cost: $2,672 (includes annual subscription); renewal: 1998: $730; 1999: $767; 2000: $810; 2001: $867; 2002: $928; 2003: $975; 2004: $1,024; 2005: $1,096; 2006: $1,173; 2007: $1,319; 2008: $1,425; 2009: $1,511; 2010: $1,541; 2011: $1,618; 2012; $1,715; 2013: $1,962; 2014: $1,966; eBook: $2,429; renewal: 2014: $1,966.
This comprehensive examination of the law related to advertising explores the rules governing each party to the advertising contract, including the media, consumers, advertisers, and advertising agencies. The authors cover such topics as telemarketing, consumers' federal remedies, Federal Trade Commission developments, corrective advertising, children's advertising, legal and medical advertising, tax treatment of advertising income, lotteries and games of chance, tobacco product advertising, First Amendment considerations, and direct marketing. An intellectual property attorney with a specialty in advertising law, Peter Rosden has spent more than 20 years co-authoring The Law of Advertising for Matthew Bender. A graduate of Dartmouth College and Columbia University School of Law, Mr. Rosden worked as a senior enforcement attorney with the U.S. Treasury Department and as a member of the intellectual property law firm of Sixbey, Friedman and Leedom before staring his own firm in Charlottesville, VA.

Cost Saving Tips: Based on your level of usage, you may wish to cancel after the initial one-year subscription has expired and purchase this set again in a few years. In the interim, updating can be performed by checking the relevant primary law, Shepardizing, etc.

Wilson, Lee. **The Advertising Law Guide: A Friendly Guide for Everyone in Advertising.** New York: Allworth Press, 2000. 1 vol. (256 pp.). Paperbound.
Cost: OUT-OF-PRINT; from $0.01 on amazon.com (2014).
This introduction to advertising law addresses the practical needs of copywriters, art directors, photographers, graphic designers, advertising and marketing professionals, and business executives. Chapters cover legal issues in advertising, avoiding false advertising challenges from competitors, libel, right of privacy, the right of publicity, copyright infringement, choosing protectable trademarks, clearing trademarks for use, using other people's trademarks—safely, trademarks in cyberspace, making and managing contracts. The volume also includes a variety of useful appendices, including forms, federal and trade association resources, and a glossary. The author is a practicing attorney with 20 years experience in intellectual property law.

Wood, Douglas J. **Please Be Ad-vised**. 4th ed. Seattle, WA: Amazon Digital Servives, Inc., 2013. 1 vol. (462 pp.).
Cost: available online to ANA members only (2014).
This comprehensive legal reference guide to advertising and marketing law is designed as a practical tool for the use of industry professionals. Arguably the most heavily consulted work in the field, this handbook is designed to help advertising executives avoid legal pitfalls, and addresses both the creative and business sides of advertising. Among the topics discussed are the ownership of ideas, the handling of unsolicited ideas, the relationship of the agency to the client, the ownership and protection of creative work. Additional chapters discuss such topics as copyright and trademark infringement, rights of privacy and publicity, comparative advertising, sales promotion, marketing on the internet, CD-ROM and interactive multimedia, infomercials, home shopping, telemarketing, dealing with the media, dealing with actors, agents, and talent brokers, and more. The 4th edition also includes a CD-ROM with over 20 contracts discussed in the book. Douglas J. Wood is Partner in the New York City law firm of Hall Dickler Kent Goldstein & Wood LLP.

Additional titles in the field of Advertising Law are available from the following publishers: Allworth Press, American Bankers Association, American Bar Association, Association of National Advertisers, CCH, Inc., Lawrence Erlbaum Associates, Greenwood Press, International Advertising Association, LexisNexis, Practising Law Institute, Routledge, Thompson Publishing Group, Thomson Reuters West, West Academic. See Appendix B for addresses and telephone numbers.

Agency Law

American Law Institute. **Restatement of the Law Third. Agency.** St. Paul, MN: American Law Institute, 2006-date. 2 vols. (994 pp.). Periodic Appendix volumes published. Pocket part appears in the back of the most recent Appendix volume only. Also available on CD-ROM.
Cost: $196 for complete set ($75 paperbound); Appendix 1 (2013): $135; ; 2d: 1995: $16; 1996: $17; 1997: $18; 1998: $19; 1999: $23; 2000: $74; 2001: $21; 2002: $22.75; 2003: $25; 2004: $25; 2005: $25; 2006: $25; 2007: $34; 2008: $36; 2009: $39; 2010: $39; 2011: $39; 2012: $40.00; 2013: $135 (Appendix 1).
The **Restatements** represent the most significant attempt by the American legal community to draft common law principles based upon the vast body of published appellate court decisions which appear in the various reporter series. Drafted and published under the auspices of the American Law Institute, the **Restatements** reflect the combined efforts of a committee of distinguished legal scholars and jurists. Work on the third edition of the **Restatement of the Law of Agency** was begun in 2000 and published in 2006.

Gregory, William A. **Law of Agency and Partnership**. 3rd ed. St. Paul, MN: West Academic, 2001. 1 vol. (683 pp.). No supplementation between editions.
Cost: $103; from $43.61 on amazon.com (2014).
This West Hornbook provides the kind of basic coverage one would expect from a course text, including the elements of the agency relationship, ratification, termination of agent's powers, master and servant, notice and knowledge, duties of agent to principal, principal to third party, third person to principal, agent to third party, and third party to agent. Also discusses common law rules and statutory modifications, and the sole proprietorship. Harold Reuschlein is a Professor of Law at Villanova University School of Law and William Gregory Professor Law at Georgia State University.

Hynes, J. Dennis. **Agency-Partnership and the LCC in a Nutshell**. 5th ed. St. Paul, MN: West Academic, 2012. 1 vol. (704 pp.). No supplementation between editions.
Cost: $41; from $29.60 on amazon.com; kindle edition: $24.05 (2014).
A one-volume paperback summary of the main areas of the law of agency and partnership, but with far fewer citations to legal authority than the West Hornbook. Combined with partnership to parallel academic course content.

Jordan, Michael M. L. **Durable Powers of Attorney and Health Care Directives**. 4th ed. St. Paul, MN: Thomson Reuters West (Clark Boardman Callaghan), 2004-date. 2 vols. Looseleaf format. Includes CD-ROM.
Cost: $362 ($291.00 w/o CD-ROM); supplementation: 2005: $100; 2006: $150; 2007: $78; 2008: $87; 2009: $102; 2010: $132; 2011: $121; 2012: $129; 2013: $153; 3d ed.: 1995: $60; 1996: $100; 1997: $285; 1998: $100; 1999: $354; 2000: $384; 2001: $148.50; 2002: $170; 2003: $100; 2004: $100; **Monthly Assured Print Price (APP):** $27/$324.
This treatise provides coverage of those legal issues involved in the exercise of powers of attorney during the incapacity of the grantor of that power, including issues related to the grantor's property, life, health, etc. This set covers durable powers of attorney for health care, property management, the fiduciary status of the agent, the third party perspective, and the drafting of the durable power. The set also includes forms on CD-ROM, drafting checklists, and comments for each of the fifty states and a number of relevant appendices, including the Uniform Rights of the Terminally Ill Act, and Principles and Guidelines Concerning the Foregoing of Life-Sustaining Treatment for Adult Patients. Also includes Tables of Cases and Statutes, and an Index. Well-written and adequately footnoted text. The only drawback is that the substantive text comprises probably less than 20% of the total pages in both volumes, with the bulk of the coverage devoted to state comments. If your practice is limited to one or two states, or if you have little need to research comparative state law, you may be paying for a great deal of material you will consult infrequently, if at all. Originally published by Shepard's/McGraw-Hill, it is now published by Thomson/West.

Cost-Saving Tip: Avoid subsequent CD-ROM to save costs; also avoid APP pricing option which is more expensive than history of supplementation.

Additional titles in the field of Agency Law are available from the following publishers: American Law Institute, Aspen Publishing, Matthew Bender, Casenotes Publishing Co., Carolina Academic Press, Corwin Press, Foundation Press, Kendall-Hunt, Kluwer Law International, LexisNexis, and Thomson Reuters West, West Academic. See Appendix B for addresses and telephone numbers.

Antitrust Law

ABA Section of Antitrust Law. **Antitrust Class Actions Handbook**. Chicago: American Bar Association, 2010. 1 vol. (267 pp.). Paperbound.
Cost: $159.00 ($129.00 to members) (2014).
The antitrust class action is the primary mechanism by which private sector actors attempt to enforce the antitrust laws, with at least 90% of United States antitrust enforcement generated through private actions. Moreover, the volume of private antitrust actions has increased markedly in recent years, leading to changes in class action procedures, of which the Class Action Fairness Act of 2005 is primary example. This volume provides a comprehensive discussion of the issues that arise before, during and after the filing of a private antitrust action, as well as the legal standards and strategic decisions that guide these complex cases. Following an illuminating overview of the private antitrust action, including its history and future trends, the authors address the filing of the class action, antitrust claims suitable for a class action treatment, the decision of whether to opt out of the class action, class certification procedure, antitrust class certification standards, the role of experts in antitrust class certification, and antitrust class action settlements. Extensively annotated with citations to primary and secondary authorities, the volume also includes a table of cases and index. More than 40 members

of the ABA's Trial Practice Committee of the Section of Antitrust Law contributed to this volume.

ABA Section of Antitrust Law. **Antitrust Counterattack in Intellectual Property Litigation Handbook**. Chicago: American Bar Association, 2010. 1 vol. (249 pp.). Paperbound.
Cost: $159.00 ($129.00 to members) (2014).
The United States patent system was created pursuant to the U.S. Constitution's grant to Congress of the "power... to promote the progress of science and useful arts by securing for limited times to authors and inventors the exclusive right to their respective writings and discoveries." Pursuant to this authority, Congress passed the United States Patent Act in 1790 and replaced it with the Patent Act of 1793. The Act's definition of patentable subject matter has been unchanged since that time, and, up to December 31, 2009, 7,640,592 patents have been issued. Cases involving antitrust liability typically arise in patent cases most commonly, when the alleged infringer claims that the patent was procured by fraud, or the party knowingly asserts baseless claims of patent infringement. Antitrust issues may also arise in the course of other activities, including licensing pools and tying arrangements involving patents or other types of intellectual property such as copyrights, trademarks, and trade secrets. This volume is an introduction and practical resource on the antitrust issues likely to arise in intellectual property litigation. It seeks to provide antitrust practitioners with a basic understanding of the various forms of intellectual property, with particular attention to utility (i.e. useful) patent laws and procedures. It also seeks to explain those matters relevant to antitrust claims, such those bearing on the validity, enforceability, interpretation and scope, infringement, implied license, exhaustion, waiver, and estoppel. Additional chapters explain the legal claims that may be asserted by a party accused of violating another party's patents, with attention to the antitrust laws and the patent misuse doctrine generally; strategic issues for prospective litigants; discovery issues; bifurcation and consolidation issues for patent and antitrust claims; appeals to the federal circuit; and settlement of patent litigation.

ABA Section of Antitrust Law. **Competition as Public Policy**. Chicago: American Bar Association, 2010. 1 vol. (349 pp.). Paperbound.
Cost: $159.00 ($129.00 to members) (2014).
This compilation of papers, speeches, and roundtable discussions delivered at the ABA's Antitrust Symposium on Competition as Public Policy in May, 2009, addresses the central question of "whether competition will continue to serve as the foundation for economic policy and legislation." In the wake of the worst economic downturn since the Great Depression, it addresses some of the most significant competition policy issues in the United States and around the world, with a focus upon the role of antitrust policy and government regulation. The presentation range from an examination of competition as public policy to competition in distressed industries, regulatory change: then and now, financial regulation and the current crisis, competition policy and organizational fragmentation in healthcare, the visible hand: government hand-outs and hand-ups, electricity as a case study, financial issues, the role of competition in the market for health care, and more. The presentations vary in quality. For example, Carl Shapiro's otherwise sound historical analysis of antitrust policy is compromised by his support for Keynesian economic stimulus during the Depression, a policy which, in reality, prolonged the economic downturn, a policy failure acknowledged by Treasury Secretary Henry Morgenthau. The failure to grasp that lesson led President Obama to attempt a similar Keynesian solution with his $787 billion economic stimulus in 2009, a policy that only added to the national debt while shifting funds from private capital markets to favored public sector labor unions, state governments, and selected industries. Extensively annotated with citations to primary and secondary authorities, the volume also includes a table of cases and index. More than 20 members of the ABA's Trial Practice Committee of the Section of Antitrust Law contributed to this volume.

Antitrust and Trade Regulation Resource Center. Washington, DC: Bloomberg BNA, 1961-date. Updated continuously.
Cost: $2,584 (1 user (2014).
This is a comprehensive weekly notification looseleaf service which contains the text of statutes, regulations, court decisions, and reports on current legislative and administrative developments in the field. The service features four major sections: **News and Comment** (including significant decisional, legislative and regulative developments affecting the enforcement of competition and the deceptive trade practice laws); **State Developments** (including significant decisional, legislative and regulatory developments affecting competition and deceptive trade practices on the state level; **Franchising** (encompassing both state and federal decisional, legislative, and regulatory developments affecting franchised distribution systems); and **International Developments** (reports of decisional, legislative and regulatory developments in the European Economic Community, Great Britain, Germany, Japan, and Australia). Includes reports of "Official Actions" and a "Calendar of Events" of particular value to the active practitioner. It also features periodic bibliographies containing recent antitrust books and law review articles. This publication is designed for the antitrust law specialist interested in tracking recent developments. The purchaser is buying a subscription to a current notification service; therefore, used sets have negligible value.

Antitrust Health Care Handbook. 4th ed. Chicago: American Bar Association, 2010. 1 vol. (327 pp.).
Cost: $159.00 ($129.00 to members) (2014).
Although the United States has historically relied upon market forces to allocate health care resources, rising health care costs, driven primarily by the third-party system of payment, have increasingly attracted the attention of federal and state antitrust authorities. In 2008, health care expenditures totaled $2.3 trillion, or 16.2% of the U.S. GDP, and the aggregate cost of a family health care plan was $12,680, of which the average worker's annual contribution was $3,354. Prior to the 1970s, antitrust cases in the health care sector were rare, a situation driven by the view that medicine was a "learned profession," rather than a business, and was mostly local in nature. With the issuance of several important Supreme Court decisions, specifically the case of Goldfarb v. Virginia (1975) that there is no "learned profession" exemption from antitrust coverage, the government has increasingly treated health care providers in a manner similar to other sectors of the economy. This volume, prepared under the auspices of the ABA's Health Care and Pharmaceuticals Committee of the Section of Antitrust

Law, applies antitrust principles and doctrines to health care industries. Following an overview of antitrust law concepts and principles, the authors look at the relevant markets for health care, pricing conduct in health care industries, nonprice conduct in health care industries, and preventing and minimizing antitrust problems. Intended primarily for health care professionals and administrators, as well as their legal counsel, this volume provides a learned and thorough overview of the primary issues related to antitrust in the health care sector. The text includes numerous citations to primary and secondary authorities. The volume was produced with contributions from Jeff Miles and other members of the ABA's Health Care and Pharmaceuticals Committee.

Antitrust Law Developments. Section of Antitrust Law. 7th ed. Chicago: American Bar Association, 2012-date. 2 vols. (2,032 pp.). Annual supplementation. CD-ROM available from Matthew Bender (LexisNexis).
Cost: $475 ($400 to Antitrust Law Section members); supplementation: 2013: $169 (2012 Annual Review); Discounts to Antitrust Section members (2014).
This comprehensive review of the federal antitrust laws was produced through the combined efforts of hundreds of lawyers and legal scholars who are members of the ABA's Antitrust Law Section. Each chapter was prepared by the specific Antitrust Law Section Committee responsible for that subspecialty of the law. The current 2012 edition, current through 2011, replaces the 6th edition published in 2007. This new seventh edition covers a number of recent developments, including the Supreme Court's decisions in Twombly, Leegin, American Needle, linkLine, and Weyerhaeuser as well as their treatment in the lower courts. Developments in the courts of appeals relating to bundled discounts and the antitrust-intellectual property interface all receive comprehensive treatment. A chapter on mergers and acquisitions has been heavily revised to reflect the new DOJ/FTC Horizontal Merger Guidelines and new foreign merger control regimes; and the misuse doctrine in the chapter on intellectual property has been reorganized and revised. The American Bar Association's Antitrust Law Section is a rich source for additional books on the subject.

Axinn, Stephen M, et al. **Acquisitions Under the Hart-Scott-Rodino Antitrust Improvement Act**. 3d ed. New York: Law Journal Press, 2008-date. 3 vols. (3,300+ pp.) Looseleaf format. Supplemented twice annually.
Cost: $995 (annual subscription); supplementation: 2009: 0; 2010: $419; 2011: $309; 2012: $949; 2013: $995; 2d ed.: 1995: $65; 1996: $72; 1997: $65; 1998: $110; 1999: $118; 2000: $95; 2001: $244; 2002: $179; 2003: $210; 2004: $245; 2005: 0; 2006; $369; 2007: $389; 2008: $838 (new edition).
A comprehensive antitrust compliance guide to the Hart-Scott-Rodino Act and rules. Provides step-by-step procedural guidance through the Act's pre-merger notification provisions and regulations, including completion of the notification and report form. The authors cover the jurisdictional requirements of the Act, exemptions from the Act's coverage, notification and waiting period procedures, and realistic compliance methods, including responses to government requests and investigations. The work also includes an analysis of the history of the Act and rules, including preliminary drafts and public comments. The Appendices include numerous illustrations and a checklist to determine if a client's transactions are in compliance with the law. Stephen Axinn is a partner in the New York firm of Axinn, Veltrop & Harkrider LLP.

Cost Saving Tips: Given the decision by Law Journal Press to migrate to annual subscription pricing, this and other LJP titles have become far more expense to maintain. In light of this, the savvy consumer will look for products from publishers with more reasonable supplementation costs, or, as an alternative, purchase a new LJP copy every 2-3 years and employ alternate meams of updating.

Bloom, Charles J., et al. **Antitrust Litigation Best Practices: Leading Lawyers on Developing a Defense Strategy, Evaluating Settlement Opportunities, and Avoiding Common Client Mistakes.** Boston: Thomson Reuters/Aspatore Books, 2008. 1 vol. (189 pp.).
Cost: $110; from $85.00 on amazon.com (2014).
Antitrust litigation can have a devastating financial impact on a company or business. In addition to its length and cost, it can prove damaging to a company's operations, productivity, and reputation. Antitrust violations can lead to both criminal and civil penalties. Under the Antitrust Criminal Penalty Enforcement and Reform Act of 2004, the maximum term for a felony conviction was increased to ten years and maximum corporate fine to $100 million. In private civil actions, the prevailing plaintiff can automatically recover treble damages and attorneys' fees. And for companies that contract with the federal government, violations of the antitrust laws frequently lead to debarment. Yet, since 1980, it has become increasingly difficult to advance claims under the Sherman Antitrust Act. The Supreme Court has made antitrust claims more difficult to prove, required virtually impossible proofs, and excised certain forms of conduct from the per se violations list under the Act. This volume brings together eight leading antitrust practitioners to provide authoritative insiders' perspectives on the best practices for litigating antitrust cases. They provide sophisticated advice on how to develop an effective defense strategy, evaluate opportunities for settlement, minimize repercussions, avoid mistakes, translate complex economic concepts for the court, hire experts, manage documentation, and successfully navigate the antitrust laws to advance business objectives. The Appendices include the Federal Trade Commission and U.S. Department of Justice Antitrust Guidelines, a Protective Order Regarding Confidential Information, a Stipulation Regarding the Production of Documents and Electronically Stored Information, and an Antitrust Primer for Federal Law Enforcement Personnel from the U.S. Dept. of Justice that addresses price fixing, bid rigging, and market allocation. The authors are partners and chairs from some of the nation's leading antitrust firms.

Broder, Douglas. **U.S. Antitrust Law and Enforcement: A Practice Introduction**. 2d ed. New York: Oxford University Press, 2011. 1 vol. (312 pp.). Paperbound.
Cost: $185; from $142.00 on amazon.com (2014).
The federal antitrust laws are the most important component of the United States economic regulatory framework. They are designed, at least in theory, to protect free markets and a healthy competitive environment by controlling the collusive and predatory

conduct and monopolistic practices that may be engaged in by businesses operating in a relatively free market. Since the passage of the Sherman Antitrust Act in 1890, the United States has enacted a series of statutes designed to combat oligopolistic cartels, or trusts, whose collusion has threatened to compromise the competitive marketplace. These have included the Clayton Act (1914), the Federal Trade Commission Act (1914), the Robinson-Patman Act (1936), the Cellar-Kefauver Amendments to the Clayton Act (1950), and the Hart-Scott-Rodino Antitrust Improvements to the Robinson-Patman Act (1976). These statutes outlaw a variety of unacceptable business practices, including monopolies, price fixing, certain tying arrangements, bid rigging, anticompetitive mergers and acquisitions, price discrimination, predatory pricing, and other unfair methods of competition in conflict with an open and competitive market environment. This introductory overview covers both the legal and procedural aspects of antitrust law, including chapters on the history of U.S. antitrust enforcement, the Federal antitrust statutes, agreements in restraint of trade, monopolization and attempted monopolization, mergers, acquisitions and joint ventures, premerger notification under the Hart-Scott-Rodino Act, price discrimination under the Robinson-Patman Act, and antitrust enforcement. It concludes with a summary of the United States Federal judicial systems, a glossary of antitrust and related terms, table of cases and index. The author is co-chair of the global antitrust practice at K&L Gates LLP and has practiced antitrust law and litigation in New York City since 1977. He is the author of two previous books and numerous book chapters and articles on antitrust and written advocacy.

Callmann, Rudolf and Malla Pollack. **The Law of Unfair Competition, Trademarks and Monopolies.** 4th ed. St. Paul, MN: Thomson/West (Clark Boardman Callaghan), 2003-date. 10 vols. Looseleaf format. Periodic supplementation.
Cost: $4,697; supplementation: 1993: $440; 1994: $504; 1995: $335; 1996: $653; 1997: $675.65; 1998: $716; 1999: $754; 2000: $834.25; 2001: $937; 2002: $1,045; 2003: $1,193; 2004: $1,332; 2005: $1,459.50; 2006: $1,638.50; 2007: $1,824; 2008: $2,742; 2009: $2,274.50; 2010: $2,501.50; 2011: $1,669.50; 2012: $2,972; 2013: $3,531; **Monthly Assured Print Price (APP):** $342/$4,104.
This multi-volume treatise is the most complete exposition of the law of unfair competition on the market, combining a broad theoretical foundation of the law with an integration of antitrust law. The author treats the basic concepts of protection against unfair competition, government and business competition, and competition and monopolies. He also examines unfair advertising and pricing, unfair interference with a competitor's business relations, misappropriation of a competitor's values, the unlawful conduct of business, the law of trademarks and product simulation, parties, defenses, remedies and procedure and international protection. There is also discussion and analysis of the jurisdiction of the courts, and the jurisdiction and procedure of the Federal Trade Commission. The exhaustive footnotes often dominate the substantive text. The supplementary references are keyed to the text in the body of the set. The Appendices include federal antitrust statutes, guidelines and regulations, and a variety of relevant federal; statutes governing the areas of trade secrets, privacy, commercial bribery, unfair trade practices, control of advertising, trademark statutes, forms and treaties. The 4th edition was prepared by Louis Altman.

Cost-Saving Tip: Take advantage of the discounted initial price (usually 25%) and purchase a new set every 3-4 years to avoid high supplementation costs.

Federal Statutory Exemptions from Antitrust Law. Chicago, IL, American Bar Association, 2007. 1 vol. (426 pp.). Paperbound.
Cost: $149 ($119 to Section members) (2014).
A comprehensive survey of the more than twenty statutory antitrust exemptions in the U.S. Code which address various aspects of commerce. This monograph provides a comprehensive survey of the statutes currently in force that modify or limit federal antitrust law, the economic theories by which they are usually justified, and an analysis their costs and benefits. Though increasingly fewer, some of these statutes completely exempt whole industries from antitrust, while others provide only limited or non-existent scrutiny. Part II includes case studies in three areas in which exemptions are still in force, including agriculture, insurance and ocean shipping and evaluates the applicability of these economic theories to the applicable statutes. Part III addresses three focused exemptions, including railroads, the broadcasting of professional sports games, and newspaper joint publishing arrangements. Part IV analyses the statutes modifying antitrust law, as they are applied to joint ventures and agreements among competitors on research, production and standards setting, and local government restraints on competition. Part V examines these case studies and makes some observations about the legislative process of exemptions from antitrust law.

Gellhorn, Ernest, William E. Kovacic, and Stephen Calkins. **Antitrust Law and Economics in a Nutshell.** 5th ed. St. Paul, MN: West, 2004. 1 vol. (520 pp.). Paperbound. Available from West Academic.
Cost: $41; from $10.86 on amazon.com (2014).
A brief overview of the basic principles of antitrust in the publishers "Nutshell" series. Intended as a student text, but also useful as a review for practitioners, this volume attempts to provide a „basic understanding of the legal and economic principles that govern modern antitrust law." Ernest Gellhorn is the former T. Munford Boyd Professor of Law at the University of Virginia and present Dean of Case Western Reserve University. His co-author, William E. Kovacic, is Professor of Law at George Mason University School of Law and Of-Counsel to the Washington, DC firm of Bryan Cave. In laying out the landscape of modern antitrust law, the authors describe the wide swings which have characterized both doctrine and policy in the courts and the federal enforcement agencies. Due attention is paid to the role of economic analysis in the development of antitrust standards, as well as the increasing globalization of antitrust concerns.

Ginsburg, Martin D. and Jack S. Levin. **Mergers, Acquisitions and Buyouts: A Transactional Analysis of the Governing Tax, Legal, and Accounting Considerations**. 2d ed. New York: Wolters Kluwer Law & Business, 2000-date. 5 vols. Both the print edition and the CD-ROM are completely revised every six months.
Cost: $1,178 (September, 2013 Edition: $589); CD-ROM: $605; print and CD-ROM: $915 (2014).
A comprehensive transactional and analytical guide to all the steps which must be considered when structuring or

examining a corporate merger or acquisition. Volumes 1-4 provide transactional analysis, including such particulars as tax ramifications, covenants not to compete, the handling of stock options, executive compensation, SEC considerations, accounting rules, fraudulent conveyance pitfalls, and include numerous examples and diagrams. Volume 5 contains sample acquisition agreements with extensive annotations and detailed tax and legal analysis. Martin Ginsburg is a Professor of Law at Georgetown University Law Center. Jack Levin is a senior partner with the Chicago firm of Kirkland & Ellis and a lecturer at the University of Chicago and Harvard Law Schools.

Cost Saving Tip: Given the frequency of supplementation and the practice of completely replacing all five volumes every six months, you may wish to drop the standing order and simply purchase a new edition as frequently as you require. In other words, if annual supplementation will suffice, you can cut your annual outlay in half. If you purchase once every two years, you can cut your cost by 75%.

Ginsburg, Martin D. and Jack S. Levin. **Mergers, Acquisitions and Buyouts** [on CD-ROM]. New York: Wolters Kluwer Law & Business, 2000-date. One disc. Updated twice annually. Available for Windows. Search Engine: Folio. Revised every six months.
Cost: September, 2013 Edition: $605 ($1,210 per year) (2014).
Contains the identical substantive content as the entry above. The CD-ROM version is augmented, however, by hypertext links to the full text of relevant cases, statutes, treasury regulations and revenue rulings.

Holmes, William C. **Antitrust Law Handbook**. St. Paul, Thomson Reuters, 2013. 1 vol. Annual. Paperbound or ProView eBook.
Cost: 2013-2014 Edition: $916; **Monthly Assured Print Price (APP):** $76/$912 (2014).
This volume provides a current overview of the state of antitrust law in the United States, with particular attention to the most significant federal antirust statutes, including the Sherman Act, Robinson Patman Act, Clayton Act, and FTC Act. The author also discusses antitrust exemptions and immunities and litigation procedure. A chapter is also devoted to recent developments in the field.

Hovenkamp, Herbert; Phillip Areeda; and Donald F. Turner. **Antitrust: An Analysis of Antitrust Principles and Their Application**. 5th ed. New York: Wolters Kluwer Law & Business, 1978-date. 21 vols. Annual bound supplement.
Cost: $3,925; supplementation: 1995: $450; 1996: $500; 1997: $620; 1998: $795; 1999: $810; 2000: $380; 2001: $395; 2002: $436; 2003: $507; 2004: $1,105; 2005: $1,134; 2006: $1,195; 2007: $1,273; 2008: $1,364; 2009: $1,470; 2010: $754; 2011: $914; 2012: $1,874; 2013: $229; Internet version: $1,944
This monumental exposition of the law of antitrust is the product of two leading legal scholars who have served for many years on the faculty of the Harvard Law School. According to Ira Millstein (99 **Harvard Law Review** pp. 618-632), Professors Areeda (1930-1995) and Turner stake out a middle ground between those who urge a greater use of the antitrust laws to effectuate a reduction in the power of conglomerate mergers and those, such as John K. Galbraith, who view antitrust law as a charade which provides cover for its enemies who, in reality, seek to „conceal the reality of industrial planning and associated price control by the great corporation." This is not a work for the novice, but for the scholar and experienced practitioner who seek to discover less what the law is than what it should be. Likewise, it is a source for the legislator who may be considering future legislative action, or the regulator contemplating new governmental directives. Professor Areeda was joined in the first five volumes by Professor Donald F. Turner, also of Harvard Law School. Following the death of Professor Areeda in 1995, the task of carrying on this work has fallen to Professor Herbert Hovenkamp, the Ben V. & Dorothy Willie Professor of Law at the University of Iowa who has also contributed to revised editions of several of the current 21 volumes. Additional contributors have included Mark Janis and Mark Lemley, authors of **IP and Antitrust Law**, as well as Professor John L. Solow, Associate Professor of Economics, University of Iowa, and Professor Einer Elhauge, Professor of Law, Harvard Law School. This work has had a profound impact upon the courts and relevant government agencies. Both the U.S. Supreme Court and U.S. Courts of Appeal have cited Areeda more than any other treatise in the field. The work is divided into three broad subject areas: Part I: antitrust goals, coverage, procedure and economics (vols. I, II (rev. ed.), and IIA); Part II: market structure issues (vols. IIA, III, IV, and V); Part III: restraints of trade: horizontal and vertical (vols. VI, VII, VIII, IX, X et seq.). Volume one includes a statutory appendix with the text of the Sherman and Clayton Acts, the Federal Trade Commission Act, and other relevant statutes. The final volume includes an index and table of cases. Supplementation is contained in one large annual bound volume rather than individual pocket parts. Originally published by Little, Brown, this title was taken over by Aspen Law & Business (now Wolters Kluwer Law & Business) in 1996.

Cost Saving Tips: Depending on your need for currency, you may wish to consider buying the cumulative bound supplement in alternate years, thereby saving significantly on supplementation costs. I would recommend, however, that you purchase the revised volumes as issued since these must be purchased eventually to maintain the integrity of the set.

Hovenkamp, Herbert. **Federal Antitrust Policy: The Law of Competition & Its Practice**. 4th ed. St. Paul, MN: West, 2011. 1 vol. (944 pp.) No supplementation between editions.
Cost: $103; online book: $69.00; from $75.00 on amazon.com (2014).
A basic exposition of antitrust law and its policy implications written as an introductory student text , but also useful for the practitioner. The author, now Professor of Law at the University of Iowa, is one of the most respected scholars in the field, having authored numerous books and articles on various aspects of antitrust law and policy. His credits include **Economics & Federal Antitrust Law** (West, 1985), **Enterprise and American Law, 1836-1937** (Harvard, 1991), and, more recently, following the death of Phillip Areeda, editorship of Areeda's ten-volume treatise published by Aspen. This work examines prices, markets, monopolies, facts, values and antitrust, measuring market power, cartels, joint ventures, monopolization, mergers of competitors, price discrimination and the Robinson-Patman Act,

private enforcement, damages, and judicial estimates of antitrust damages, and more. A useful and economical introductory explanation and analysis of the major areas of antitrust law with selective citations to primary law and secondary sources.

Hovenkamp, Herbert and Philip Areeda. **Fundamentals of Antitrust Law**. 4th ed. New York: Wolters Kluwer Law & Business, 2011. 1 vol. Looseleaf format. Annual.
Cost: $399 (2014).
This one-volume abridgement of the authors' 21-volume treatise (see previous entry) provides the antitrust professional with the full sections of the complete work cited most frequently by the courts, and those topics most litigated. Designed as a more convenient and less costly alternative to the complete work, it also features cross references back to the full treatise. The work is the product of Herbert Hovenkamp who builds on the magnum opus of the late Phillip Areeda (1930-1995).

Kintner, Earl W. **Federal Antitrust Law.** Newark, NJ: LexisNexis Matthew Bender (Anderson Publishing), 1980-date. 13 vols. Annual pocket supplements.
Cost: $3,127; e-book edition: $3,127; supplementation: 1994: $275; 1995: $425; 1996: $375; 1997: $375; 1998: $400; 1999: $400; 2000: $400; 2001: $400; 2002: $500; 2003: $585; 2004: $483; 2005: $513; 2006: $543; 2007: $587; 2008: $663; 2009: $718; 2010: $775; 2011: $869; 2012: $930; 2013: $1,033; 2014: $1,063.
This major exposition of the law of antitrust was written by the late Earl W. Kintner and members of the Washington, DC law firm of Arent, Fox, Kintner, Plotkin & Kahn. Mr. Kintner was a former Chairman and General Counsel of the Federal Trade Commission, as well as a member of the Indiana and District of Columbia bars. Additional volumes were written by Joseph P. Bauer, Professor of Law, University of Notre Dame and William Kratzke. This is a comprehensive, yet practical text which seeks to provide analysis of all the major areas of federal antitrust law. More basic in its approach than Areeda, this work eschews innovation in favor a basic description of the antitrust statutes and supporting case law. The text is accompanied by exhaustive annotated footnotes which draw upon both primary law and significant secondary sources. Coverage includes basic economic theory, common law principles, an introduction to the Sherman Act, practices prohibited by the Sherman Act, the Robinson-Patman Act, the Clayton Act, the Federal Trade Commission, antitrust exemptions, practice, procedure and enforcement. Cited less frequently by the U.S. Supreme Court and federal appeals courts than **Areeda**, but more frequently than **Von Kalinowski**. Supplementation cost has risen steadily in recent years as the set as expanded in size, but not to the level of **Areeda** or, more particularly, **Von Kalinowski**.

Cost Saving Tip: Purchase pocket supplements in alternate years to reduce your expenditure by more than $1000 every other year. Update through primary sources, digests, Shepard's, KeyCite, etc.

Lifland, William T. **State Antitrust Law.** New York: Law Journal Press, 1984-date. 1 vol. (530+ pp.) Looseleaf format + eBook. Annual supplementation. Annual subscription pricing.
Cost: $313; supplementation: 1996: $46; 1997: $52; 1998: $52; 1998: $57; 1999: $57; 2000: $64; 2001: $130; 2002: $144; 2003: $74; 2004: $74; 2005: $85; 2006: $109; 2006: $228; 2007: $119; 2008: $256; 2009: $258; 2010: $260; 2011: $175; 2012: $149; 2013: $313.
Although federal law dominates the field of antitrust, there are unique aspects to the antitrust laws of each state, laws which also encompass such closely related areas as price-fixing, cartel-like conduct, business acquisitions, and other business practices which may have the effect of hindering competition. For the purposes of this volume, the laws of the states are organized into eight specific subject areas: application of state antitrust law, monopolization and unfair competition, inter-competitor agreements, covenants not to compete, supplier-customer arrangements, acquisitions and mergers, affirmative defenses, and remedies in state antitrust actions. Appropriate federal laws are also referenced in these sections. The appendices include the Uniform State Antitrust Act, selected state antitrust provisions, antitrust laws of the states, vertical restraints guidelines, and the horizontal merger guidelines of the National Association of Attorneys General, as well as a table of cases and subject index. The case citations are more representative than exhaustive, reflecting more recent federal and state case law. The author is a member of the New York, New Jersey and District of Columbia bars.

Cost Saving Tip: Beware! Purchasing this title will enroll you in the publisher's automatic subscription program. LJP no longer sells supplements by the release, but as part of an automatic supplementation program. If you desire the base text, buy it without the supplementation, and simply re-purchase it every 2-3 years, if al all.

Marshall, Kevin S., ed. The Economics of Antitrust Injury and Firm-Specific Damages. Tucson, AZ: Lawyers & Judges Publishing Co., 2008. 1 vol. (375 pp.).
Cost: $55.00; from $48.51 amazon.com; kindle: $46.08 (2014).
Since the 1970s and the emergence of the so-called "Chicago School" of economic analysis, the field of antitrust law has evolved into a field characterized by its increasing economic sophistication. Under this regime, promotion of consumer welfare has emerged as the only legitimate goal of the antitrust laws. Successful instruction in the field of antitrust law involves achieving a balance in the integration of law and economics and filtering the economic analysis through the prism of certain economic assumptions, chief among them the economic model of perfect competition. This economic model embraces such assumptions as (1) the existence of numerous buyers and sellers, each acting independently; (2) each buyer and seller consuming or producing such a negligible share of total output that none can influence price; (3) no entry or exit barriers with respect to consumer or producer markets; (4) all market participants are fully informed (5) all products being homogenous, and constituting interchangeable substitutes for each other; and (6) the forces of supply and demand are free to determine the quantity of output in the relevant market, and determine a market-clearing, competitive price with respect to that output. An essential aspect of antitrust analysis is determining whether such conditions or prevail and, if not, to identify conduct which constitutes an unreasonable restraint of trade or an unfair method of competition. This collection of scholarly articles addresses a variety of specific

topics from both economic and legal perspectives, including the economics of competitive injury, quality control of economic expert testimony, antitrust damages from lost opportunities, the valuation of lost opportunity, economic authority and the limits of expertise in antitrust cases, and the tension between jurisprudential economics and microeconomics. The editor is an Associate Professor of Law at the University of La Verne College of Law, with doctoral degrees in both law and political economy.

Mergers and Acquisitions: Understanding the Antitrust Issues. 3d ed. Chicago: American Bar Association, 2008. 1 vol. (1,201 pp.). Paperbound.
Cost: $199.00; $169.00 to members of the ABA Section of Antitrust Law (2014).
The aim of the United States antitrust laws is to preserve competition in the U.S. economy for the benefit of the consuming public. In the realm of mergers and acquisitions, the antitrust laws seek to prevent one or more firms from exercising sufficient market power to raise prices above competitive levels for a significant period of time. This monumental resource is designed to be a comprehensive review of the substantive merger law in the United States for use by counsel evaluating or advocating a merger. Produced by members of the Mergers and Acquisitions Committee of the ABA's Section of Antitrust Law, this volume guides the reader through the various aspects of merger analysis, beginning with an overview of the applicable U.S. antitrust laws. The additional chapters consider U.S. enforcement policy and procedure, market definition and measurement, horizontal mergers, rebutting the structural inference, efficiencies, possible defenses, joint ventures, potential competition doctrine, vertical mergers, conglomerate mergers, application of merger laws to multinational transactions, and judicial relief and remedies. Each of the thirteen chapters contains extensive citations to court decisions, statutes, agency decisions, and reports. Eighteen appendices contain a number of relevant federal statutes, DOJ and FTC merger and other guidelines, and a table of cases. Under the general editorship of Robert S. Schlossberg, Chair of the Mergers and Acquisitions Committee, more than thirty committee members contributed to the production of this volume. Previous editions were issued in 2000 and 2004.

Miles, John J. **Health Care & Antitrust Law**. St. Paul, MN: West (Clark Boardman Callaghan), 1992-date. 4 vols. Looseleaf format.
Cost: $2,837; supplementation: 1995: $345; 1996: $395; 1997: $411; 1998: $435; 1999: $471; 2000: $503; 2001: $580.50; 2002: $639; 2003: $727.50; 2004: $543; 2005: $1,190; 2006: $1,025; 2007: $1,107; 2008: $1,231.50; 2009: $1.375.50; 2010: $1,513.50; 2011: $1,650; 2012: $1,800; 2013: $2,083; **Monthly Assured Print Price (APP):** $207/$2,484.
A detailed analysis of those areas of the law where health care and antitrust law converge. Volumes one and two provide a comprehensive analytical treatment of the law, with attention to the most significant cases and other legal authorities. Volumes three and four contain an extensive collection of forms, letters, speeches and other sources useful to those practicing in this area. This work covers such specific issues as hospital staff-privilege antitrust problems, provider diversification, ethical restraints and related antitrust concerns, antitrust enforcement issues.

Cost-Saving Tip: Wait for one of Thomson Reuters' periodic promotions to purchase this title. A recent 25% off sale reduced the prioce to $1,952.25. The discounted initial cost will provide added incentive for the cost-conscious consumer to simply re-purchase the set every few years in lieu of remaining on standing order and paying the high cost of supplementation.

Pitofsky, Robert, ed. **How the Chicago School Overshot the Mark: The Effects of Conservative Economic Analysis on U.S. Antitrust**. New York; Oxford University Press 2008. 1 vol. (309 pp.).
Cost: $45; from $27.33 on amazon.com; kindle: $25.99 (2014).
This collection of essays examines the impact of the so-called "Chicago School" of antitrust analysis which emerged in the 1960s in the economics department of the University of Chicago. The book is prompted by a concern that the antitrust system of regulation, which enjoyed wide public and professional support for over a hundred years, is now characterized by more limited support by the Supreme Court and federal regulatory authorities. The contributors to this volume, representing the full ideological spectrum of legal and scholarly opinion, agree that U.S. antitrust enforcement is better today as a consequence of conservative economic analysis. However, they also question the direction of antitrust interpretation and enforcement on the following grounds: (1) the preference for economic models over facts; (2) the tendency to assume that free market mechanisms will cure all market imperfections; (3) the belief that only efficiency matters; (4) outright mistakes by regulators in matters of doctrine; and (5) lack of support for rigorous enforcement and willingness of enforcers to approve questionable transactions if there is even a whiff of a defense. This is a significant and timely contribution to the literature on antitrust which, while acknowledging the many benefits accruing from Chicago School analysis, nevertheless expresses serious reservations regarding the direction in which that analysis has taken antitrust enforcement. The fourteen essays address the following topics: (1) Conservative economic analysis and its effects; (2) Is efficiency all that counts?; (3) Chicago School and dominant firm behavior; (4) Can vertical arrangements injure; (5) Has the free rider explanation for vertical arrangements been unrealistically expanded; and (6) Reinvigorating merger enforcement that has declined as a result of conservative economic analysis. Editor Robert Pitofsky, currently the Sheehy Professor of Trade Regulation Law at Georgetown University Law Center and Of Counsel at Arnold & Porter, is a former Chairman of the Federal Trade Commission, Director of the Bureau of Consumer Protection of Commissioner at the FTC, law professor, and author of numerous books and articles on the subject of antitrust. He is joined by a number of distinguished legal scholars with experience in both academia and government. This is an essential read for anyone attempting to understand the current state of antitrust analysis and enforcement.

Proof of Conspiracy Under the Federal Antitrust Laws. Chicago: American Bar Association, 2010. 1 vol. (297 pp.). Paperbound.
Cost: $159.00 ($129.00 to members) (2014).
The Sherman Antitrust Act prohibits conspiracies in restraint of trade, and Section 1 of the Act requires proof of such a conspiracy agreement. These agreements may be express

or implied, formal or informal, concrete or flexible, simple or complex, written, spoken, or even communicated with a wink of the eye. This book explains the current state of the law for proving such agreements and discusses the use of direct and indirect evidence to get at the heart of what constitutes an agreement. It explains the dramatic changes the Supreme Court has made to antitrust law in recent years, including case law on pleading standards, on motions to dismiss, a circuit-by-circuit exposition of summary judgment standards, and a review of the uses of economic experts and their testimony. The nine chapters cover the congressional intent of Section 1 of the Act; the fundamental question of what constitutes an agreement; the basic issues proving an agreement; special issues of proof, including how the Federal Rules of Evidence deal with co-conspirator statements, the invocation of the Fifth Amendment right against self-incrimination, participation in the Department of Justice Antitrust Division's leniency program, and the effect of guilty please; proof relating to specific types of agreements, including intra-firm agreements and collaborative ventures; the Supreme Court's recently revised motions to dismiss standard; motions for summary judgment; how economic expert evidence may be used in proving an agreement; and concluding with a practical look at a trial of an antitrust conspiracy case. This volume is produced under the auspices of the ABA's Section of Antitrust Law under the chairmanship of Thomas J. Collin.

Reback, Gary L. **Free the Market: Why Only Government Can Keep the Marketplace Competitive**. New York: Portfolio, 2009. 1 vol. (416 pp.).
Cost: $26.95; from $4.25 on amazon.com; Kindle edition: $5.99 (2014).
Antitrust law in the United States consists of that body of statutes, federal regulations, court decisions, and enforcement guidelines and activities designed to control business activities that pose a threat to free market competition. It is predicated upon a fundamental belief that economic issues are best left to private, independent and competitive decision-making enterprises that seek to attract customers who are motivated to achieve maximum advantage by selecting from among market alternatives. The aim of antitrust law is to preserve the conditions for free and open competition by prohibiting and prosecuting cases of collusion, exclusion, and monopoly that limit competition and pose the threat of higher prices, and reduced output, quality and innovation. Since the enactment of the Sherman Antitrust Act in 1890, and the Clayton Act in 1914, the philosophy and enforcement of the antitrust laws has been uneven and sometimes contradictory, reflecting wide swings in legal philosophy, the political environment, and administrative enforcement. In this well-researched and detailed examination of the world of antitrust, Gary Reback provides an informed analysis of antitrust enforcement since enactment of the Sherman Antitrust Act and the changing judicial philosophies that have guided the Supreme Court over the course of the 20th century. Like other observers, Reback believes the pendulum has swung to far in the direction of an unbridled free market, reflecting the influence of the Chicago School of economists and legal scholars which took hold at the Justice Department's Antitrust Division and the Supreme Court in the 1980s. While salutary in many respects, particularly when compared with the overly strict enforcement that prevailed in the 1950s and 1960s, the current antitrust environment has permitted the creation of overpowering corporations with monopolistic powers that have been able to secure excessive patent and copyright protection over intellectual property, curb price competition, and exclude new challengers from markets. Reback brings his extensive experience as an antitrust attorney to the task, including his high profile cases involving Apple, Microsoft, IBM, Oracle, and AT&T. He also brings his own unique insights to the world of legal publishing, having represented LexisNexis in its effort to oppose the acquisition of West Publishing by the Thomson Corporation in 1996. It was during the travel of that case that the first edition of the **Legal Information Buyer's Guide & Reference Manual** first appeared, and this author consulted with Reback on the subject of Thomson-West's future market power. Needless to say, the predictions made back in 1996 regarding the potential impact of Thomson West's (now Thomson Reuters') acquisitions have been fully realized in the highest prices and profit margins in the industry. And those prices have been the proximite cause of untold financial devastation to law libraries across the country, particularly those serving the public. This book is an essential read for anyone who wishes to understand the current state of antitrust law in the United States. A Graduate of Yale University and Stanford University School of Law, Gary Reback has been named one of the 100 Most Influential Lawyers in America by the **National Law Journal**.

Rockefeller, Edwin S. **The Antitrust Religion**. San Francisco, CA: Cato Institute, 2007. 1 vol. (123 pp.).
Cost: $16.95; from $4.16 on amazon.com; kindle: $4.79 (2014).
In this compelling take on the subject of antitrust, the author contends that lawmakers, bureaucrats, academics, and journalists use arbitrary and irrational laws and enforcement mechanisms to punish capitalists rather than promote competition. He argues that the prevailing view that antitrust laws were enacted to protect competition, and the public, is mistaken, and that, in practice, these laws have been primarily used by some businesses to eliminate their competitors. In a brash and witty style, laced with cynicism, the author denudes the notion that there is any coherent economic or legal theory underlying antitrust law or the concept of antitrust. He suggests that in order to become a member of the "antitrust community" "one must be smart enough to be good at it and dumb enough to take it seriously." He describes the ABA's Antitrust Section (with its 11,000 dues-paying members), the driving force behind the antitrust world, as "a cheerleader for whatever government activity is currently in fashion," and lacking any systematic review of its activism, or self-reflection or evaluation of its efforts. Indeed, the author's cynicism is borne out by the refusal of the commission created under the Antitrust Modernization Commission Act of 2002 to study the effects of antitrust enforcement on the grounds that "a study of any empirical data...would be too difficult because the data are not available, and the commission had better uses for its time." As the book's title suggests, the author views antitrust not as the embodiment of the rule of law, but as a religion; and antitrust enforcement as arbitrary, political regulation of commercial activity, employing "economic theories that bestow a veneer of objectivity and credibility on law enforcement practices that actually rely on hunch and whim." This book should be read by every student of antitrust law and practice willing to question the current state of the field. A past chairman of the Section of Antitrust Law of the American Bar Association and an adjunct professor of law at the Georgetown University Law

Center, Edwin S. Rockefeller has also served on the staff of the Federal Trade Commission, and, since 1961, has been chairman of the Advisory Board of the Bloomberg BNA's **Antitrust & Trade Regulation Report**.

Scher, Irving. **Antitrust Advisor**. 4th ed. St. Paul, MN: West Group (Clark Boardman Callaghan), 1995-date. 2 vols. Looseleaf format.
Cost: $249; supplementation: 1997: $70; 1998: $74; 1999: $78; 2000: 0; 2001: $106; 2002: $106; 2003: $120.50; 2004: $120.50; 2005: $132; 2006: $135; 2007: $150; 2008: 0; 2009: $170; 2010: 0; 2011: $195; 2012: 0; 2013: 0; **Monthly Assured Print Price (APP):** $11/$132.
This mammoth one-volume treatise is actually the product of a team of authors working under the general editorship of Irving Scher, a partner with the New York firm of Weil, Gotshal & Manges and adjunct professor of law at New York University School of Law. Originally authored and edited by Carla A. Hills, the former U.S. trade representative, the work has been supplemented by Scher since 1989. A graduate of Columbia University Law School, Mr. Scher is a past chair of both the ABA and New York Bar Association's Antitrust Law Sections. An additional twelve authors have contributed chapters. The work was written as a practical manual for the practicing attorney representing clients involved in antitrust matters and confronting antitrust investigations and controversies. The work has been expanded in recent years to embrace issues relative to the globalization of antitrust issues. Mr. Scher has written chapters detailing the law of horizontal restraints and monopolization, and product distribution. Contributing authors cover such topics as mergers and acquisitions, price discrimination, intellectual property and the antitrust laws, antitrust law in the international marketplace, antitrust exemptions and immunities, Justice Department enforcement, the Federal Trade Commission and the Federal Trade Commission Act, private enforcement of the antitrust laws, and compliance. The Appendices contain the text of basic antitrust statutes, tables of cases and statutes, and a subject index. The body of the text is also preceded by a Short Reference List of frequently cited laws as well as their sources in both the **Statutes-at-Large** and **U.S. Code**. Originally published by Shepard's/McGraw-Hill, this work was acquired by the Thomson Corporation in December, 1995 and assigned to CBC, now part of the West Group. The initial purchase price of this work is quite reasonable given its substantial size.

State Antitrust Enforcement Handbook. 2d ed. Chicago: American Bar Association, Section of Antitrust Law, 2008. 1 vol. (368 pp.). Paperbound.
Cost: $169 ($139 to Section members); also available with **State Antitrust Practice and Statutes** for $567 (2014).
State enforcement of antitrust law operates under the umbrella of federal antitrust law supplemented by the authority and claims of state law. Following a review of the kinds of authority upon which states attorneys general rely for their enforcement authority, the authors examine challenges to that authority, multistate investigations and litigations, state merger enforcement, state criminal enforcement, health care markets, confidentiality issues, and state settlements. The book's appendices include a number of guidelines adopted by the National Association of Attorneys General, including the vertical restraint guidelines, horizontal merger guidelines, and the pre-merger disclosure guidelines, as well as sample letters, and a table of cases. Authored by the ABA's Section of Antitrust Law, this volume provides a useful overview of the role of state governments in antitrust enforcement.

State Antitrust Practice and Statutes. Keith D. Shugarman, editor in chief. 4th ed. Chicago: American Bar Association, Section of Antitrust Law, 2009. 3 vols. (2,400 pp.).
Cost: $499 ($449 to Antitrust Section members) (2014).
Although federal antitrust statutes and caselaw dominate the field, state antitrust law has taken on increased importance in recent years. This three-volume reference work provides practitioners with concise overviews of the civil and criminal antitrust statutes and caselaw of all fifty states. An introductory chapter is followed by chapters devoted to the antitrust law of the fifty states, each organized around federal antitrust law principles. Authored by a team of antitrust law practitioners, the work examines the similarities and differences between the various state antitrust environments. Among the subjects addressed are the remedies available under state law, statutes of limitations, public investigatory tools, private causes of action, private enforcement trends, enforcement policy, and the areas most likely to attract the activities of state attorneys general, with particular attention to antitrust enforcement in the health care industry. An essential reference tool for attorneys involved in either antitrust enforcement or defense.

Sullivan, Lawrence Anthony and Warren S. Grimes. **The Law of Antitrust: An Integrated Handbook**. 2d ed. St. Paul, MN: West, 2006. 1 vol. (1,274 pp.). Available from West Academic.
Cost: $103; online: $69.00; from $62.62 on amazon.com (2014).
This comprehensive overview of the law of antitrust is an updated and expanded version of Lawrence Sullivan's earlier **Handbook of the Law of Antitrust** (1977). Professor Sullivan and co-author Warren S. Grimes discuss and analyze both basic rules of antitrust law and a wide variety of related topics. Their discussion of antitrust and the market mechanism includes a consideration of market effects and the use of measurement in antitrust enforcement. They also consider such topics as monopoly, price predation, horizontal restraints, intrabrand restraints in distribution, foreclosure restraints, franchise antitrust claims, mergers, joint ventures, antitrust and competition policy in regulated markets, antitrust and intellectual property, government enforcement. private enforcement, and the applicable of antitrust principles in global markets. Appendices include a Westlaw research guide, selected U.S. antitrust statutes, and a variety of antitrust enforcement guidelines. Lawrence A. Sullivan is professor of law at Southwestern University School of Law and an internationally recognized authority on antitrust law whose **Handbook of the Law of Antitrust** has been cited in hundreds of U.S. Supreme Court and other federal court opinions. Warren S. Grimes, also a professor of law at Southwestern University, has wide-ranging experience in the field of antitrust law, in government, the private sector, and academia.

Sullivan, E. Thomas and Jeffrey L. Harrison. **Understanding Antitrust and Its Economic Implications.** 5th ed. New York: Matthew Bender & Co., 2009 1 vol. (376 pp.). Legal Text Series.
Cost: $45 (2014).

A comprehensive one-volume treatment of antitrust law which reflects its evolution in the era following the Supreme Court's decision in Continental T.V., Inc. v. GTE Sylvania, which removed nonprice vertical restraints from the *per se* category. Designed as a law student text, the work examines antitrust policy, antitrust economics, antitrust coverage (jurisdiction, enforcement and exceptions), horizontal restraints and cartel behavior, vertical restraints, monopolization and related offenses, mergers and acquisitions, and price discrimination. The authors, professors of law at the Universities of Arizona and Florida, have attempted to provide a balanced approach to the field which acknowledges both the contributions and positions of the "Chicago School" and contrary views. Includes numerous citations to both primary and secondary authorities.

Trade Regulation Reporter. Riverwoods, IL: Wolters Kluwer Law & Business, Inc. (CCH), 1914-date. 7 vols. Looseleaf format. Also available on the Internet. Weekly updates (print); Monthly updates (Internet).
Cost: $5,280 per year (2014).
An essential tool for the antitrust and trade regulation specialist. This is one of two looseleaf services on the market which track current developments and provide access to a variety of current decisional, statutory, and regulatory developments, the other published by BNA. Includes the text of numerous decisions which do not appear in the regular reporter series. Decisions originally appearing in looseleaf format are replaced periodically by permanent bound volumes. Similar in approach to Bloomberg BNA's **Antitrust and Trade Regulation Developments**, Commerce Clearing House's **Trade Regulation Reports** provides a weekly current awareness service of antitrust and trade regulation developments. It provides the full text of the antitrust laws and recent significant decisions. Subscription includes bound volumes of **Trade Cases** which replace decisional material in the looseleaf binders.

Cost Saving Tips: Subscribing to the Internet version will provide more convenient access to the supporting documents and spare you and your staff considerable filing time. There is little point in purchasing a current awareness tool like this unless you plan to consult it with some frequency. If you do not require a service with weekly updating, consider a comprehensive treatise with annual supplementation. If you acquire the print version, you must also be prepared for the secretarial time required to file this service on a weekly basis.

Vakerics, Thomas V. **Antitrust Basics.** New York: Law Journal Press, 1985-date. 1 vol. (900 pp.). Looseleaf and online formats.
Cost: $535 (print and online) ($510.00 eBook and online); supplementation: 1995: $100 1996: $48; 1997: $100; 1998: $100; 1999: $57; 2000: 0; 2001: $130; 2002: $152; 2003: $85; 2004: $92; 2005: $95; 2006: $228; 2007: $85; 2008: $298; 2009: $327; 2010: $330; 2011: volume converted to annual subscription pricing.
An excellent overview of antitrust law which can be of great benefit to both the novice and experienced practitioner. The author, a member of the Washington, DC firm of Perkins Coie, has extensive experience in both the public and private spheres, having served as an antitrust trial attorney at the FTC prior to his association with a number of leading DC firms. He maintains his neutrality throughout the text while carefully avoiding personal statements regarding the proper state of antitrust law. The text provides due attention to the influence of international trade upon the development of antitrust law. Following a brief review of the fundamental concepts of antitrust law, the author provides a discussion of such topics as government antitrust enforcement, private antitrust enforcement, price fixing, monopolization, horizontal restraints, vertical restraints, price discrimination (Robinson-Patman), mergers and acquisitions, joint ventures, technology transfer, international trade and antitrust, and antitrust exemptions and immunities. The Appendices contain a number of relevant primary law documents, including government policy statements and guidelines. The text is more than adequately supplemented with citations to primary authority for a work of this size.

Cost Saving Tips: Law Journal Press has instituted a decidedly unfriendly annual subscription pricing model that substantially raises both the initial and continuing cost of this publication. If possible, look elsewhere for books on antitrust law. If you do purchase this volume, buy the print volume and drop the standing order after the one-year subscription has expired.

Von Kalinowski, Julian O., et al. **Antitrust Counseling and Litigation Techniques.** New York: Matthew Bender & Co., 1984-date. 5 vols. Looseleaf format. Also available on CD-ROM and Internet. Authority CD-ROM includes no-cost online updating via LEXIS-NEXIS.
Cost: $2,236 (annual subscription included); annual renewal: 1987: $125; 1988: $187; 1989: $195; 1990: 339; 1991: 214; 1992: 483; 1993: $483; 1994: $483; 1995: $483; 1996: $507; 1997: $507; 1998: $530; 1999: $555; 2000: $590; 2001: $631; 2002: $676; 2003: $710; 2004: $789; 2005: $829; 2006: $888; 2007: $959; 2008: $1,093; 2009: $1,175; 2010: $1,275; 2011: $1,339; 2012: $1,419; 2013: $1,612; 2014: $1,657; eBook: $2,033 per year; renewal: 2014: $1,657.
A companion work to Von Kalinowski's **Antitrust Laws and Trade Regulation**, this treatise provides detailed coverage of counseling issues, antitrust compliance, document control, corporate mergers and acquisitions, intellectual property, and international antitrust. It also examines in detail private civil actions, government civil actions, and criminal antitrust litigation.

Cost Saving Tips: The attorney who wishes to control supplementation costs may wish to consider dropping the standing order once the initial one-year subscription has elapsed, and re-purchasing the entire work at some later date when he feels sufficient cost savings have been achieved and he feels the need for an updated text. There is much value in the core treatise even without a standing order to the supplementation, most of which consists of voluminous summaries of current case law probably not relevant to your situation. Given the fact that the conscientious researcher must still update the material in the primary sources, and Shepardize relevant cases and statutes, a lapsed set can still be of great value, particularly if the user also subscribes to a current awareness newsletter or service.

Von Kalinowski, Julian O., Peter Sullivan, and Maureen McGuirl. **Antitrust Laws and Trade Regulation.** 2d ed. New York: Matthew Bender & Co., 1997-date. 10 vols. Looseleaf format.

Supplemented three times per year. Also includes Monthly **Antitrust Report** newsletter. Authority CD-ROM or Internet subscription includes no-cost online updating via LEXIS-NEXIS.
Cost: $4,661 (includes annual subscription); renewal: 1987: $595; 1988: $675; 1989: 825; 1990: $825; 1991: $860; 1992: $1,060; 1993: $1,060; 1994: $1,060; 1995: $1,060; 1996: $1,112; 1997: $1,112; 1998: $1,140; 1999: $1,180; 2000: $1,300; 2001: $1,391; 2002: $1,433; 2003: $1,540; 2004: $1,617; 2005: 1746; 2006: $1869; 2007: $2,019; 2008: $2,261; 2009: $2,442; 2010: $2,564; 2011: $2,854; 2012: $2,854; 2013: $3,054; 2014: $3,333; eBook: $4,237; renewal: 2014: $3,333. Monthly **Antitrust Report** newsletter available separately for $956 per year.
This is easily the most comprehensive examination of antitrust law on the market. More practical and less theoretical than Areeda's classic text, its coverage extends to every significant aspect of antitrust law, including an examination of the Sherman, Clayton, Robinson-Patman and Federal Trade Commission Acts, and the powers of the Justice Department's Antitrust Division. The authors lay out the current state of the law with exhaustive citations to relevant primary law, both at the state and federal levels. This work also provides detailed analysis of those business practices which are likely to conflict with the antitrust laws. Frequently cited by the federal courts, although not to the same degree as **Areeda** or **Kintner**. Also sold as volumes 16-16M of Matthew Bender's Business Organization series. Subscription includes the monthly **Antitrust Report**, a current awareness newsletter.

Matthew Bender introduced a second edition in 1997 with coverage of the following topical coverage: statutory overview and historical background, restraints of trade, monopolization, mergers and acquisitions, joint ventures, and interlocking directorates, price discrimination, immunities and exemptions, regulated industries and markets, health care and the learned professions, intellectual property, Federal Trade Commission enforcement, Department of Justice enforcement, state antitrust and trade regulation laws, and private antitrust actions. Volumes 9 and 10 (to be issued in late 1998 and early 1999) will provide coverage of international antitrust issues and foreign competition laws. A Primary Source Pamphlet is generally issued annually.

Cost Saving Tips: A major expense for any practitioner, this work is definitely designed for the specialist given its high initial and, more significantly, high annual supplementation cost. Even without supplementation, the purchaser will find the core analysis of great value as a springboard for further research in the primary sources. Remember that the time lag between the editorial cut-off date of the supplementary materials and the date they are received by the subscriber still requires updating in the primary sources. The monthly newsletter included with the annual subscription can be of great benefit in bridging this editorial gap. The cost-conscious attorney may wish to consider buying the treatise with its one-year supplementation and then dropping the supplementation once the year has elapsed. She can then re-purchase the entire treatise again at some future date when she feels the need to update the core analysis and when sufficient cost savings have been achieved. Also, consider the two-volume abridged edition either as an alternative to the complete edition or as a current supplementary companion to the lapsed complete set. Matthew Bender went to annual renewal pricing in 1996.

Von Kalinowski, Julian O., et al. **Antitrust Laws and Trade Regulation.** Desk Edition. 2d ed. New York: Matthew Bender & Co., 1997-date. 2 vols. and Primary Source Pamphlet. Looseleaf format. Updated once annually.
Cost: $1,999 (annual subscription included); annual renewal: 1995: $410; 1996: $410; 1997: $410; 1998: $420; 1999: $440; 2000: $470; 2001: $503; 2002: $503; 2003: $529; 2004: $555; 2005: $594; 2006: $636; 2007: $696; 2008: $775; 2009: $876; 2010: $964; 2011: $1,060; 2012: $1,177; 2013: $1,259; 2014: $1,375; eBook: $1,817; renewal: 2014: $1,375; not available on CD-ROM except as a part of the entire **Business Law Library** which is priced at $37,053; renewal: 2014: $32,948; Internet: See sales rep. for details.
This two-volume abridgment of the ten-volume treatise provides detailed discussion of all the major antitrust issues without the exhaustive citation of the latter. It provides analysis and full text of the Sherman Clayton, Robinson-Patman, Hart-Scott-Rodino and Federal Trade Commission Acts, discussion of criminal and civil enforcement of the federal antitrust laws, and those business practices which are likely to invite antitrust examination by state and federal authorities. The text was extensively re-written in 1997 to correspond to the second edition of the main treatise. Also includes a primary source pamphlet containing the Sherman Act, the Clayton Act, and the Robinson-Patman Act.

Cost Saving Tips: For the antitrust lawyer, this set is the ideal alternative to the more expensive 16-volume treatise. Given the fact that the cost of its supplementation is a fraction of the full set, the active antitrust practitioner is not encouraged to allow this work to lapse. The owner of the full set may want to use this condensed set as his or her updating medium for significant developments in the field.

Additional titles in the field of Antitrust Law are available from the following publishers: American Bar Association, American Enterprise Institute, Business Laws, Inc., Foundation Press, Greenwood Publishing Group, Juris Publishing, Kluwer Academic, Kluwer Law International, Law Journal Press, LexisNexis, MIT Press, Practising Law Institute, United States Gov't. Printing Office, University of Chicago Press, and Thomason Reuters West, West Academic. See Appendix B for addresses and telephone numbers.

Appellate Practice

American Bar Association. Judicial Administration Division. Standards Relating to Appellate Courts. 1994 Edition. Chicago: American Bar Association, 1995. 1 vol. (134 pp.).
Cost: $25 (2014).
First approved by the American Bar Association House of Delegates in February, 1977, these standards were amended by the same body in August, 1994. They address the structure of appellate court systems, opportunities for appellate review, assistance of counsel, decision-making procedure, appellate court administration, caseflow management and delay reduction, administrative services and facilities, review of proceedings involving limited amounts and infractions, and appellate court technology.

Baum, Lawrence. **The Supreme Court**. 11th ed. Washington, DC: CQ Press, 2012. 1 vol. (229 pp.). Paperbound.
Cost: $46.00 (paperbound); from $37.94 on amazon.com (2014).
This scholarly overview examines both the legal and political dimensions of the U.S. Supreme Court and the appellate process. Intended as a student text for classes in political science, constitutional law, and judicial politics, this volume provides discussion and analysis of the court, the justices, leading cases, the decision-making process, policy outputs, and the court's impact on society. The text is informed by the latest empirical knowledge regarding the internal workings of the court and the behavior of the justices in a politically charged environment. The author is professor of political science at Ohio State University and a noted scholar of the Supreme Court and the judicial process.

Childress, Steven Alan and Martha S. Davis. **Federal Standards of Review**. 4th ed. Charlottesville, VA: LexisNexis, 2010-date. 3 vols. Annual pocket parts.
Cost: $439; eBook: $439; print supplementation: 2011: $370; 2012: $396; 2013: $426; 3rd ed.: 2000: $50; 2001: $65; 2002: $84; 2003: $91; 2004: $97; 2005: $97; 2006: $103; 2007: $110; 2008: $119; 2009: $318; 2d ed.: 1995: $48; 1996: $50; 1997: $56.
Decisions of the federal courts of appeals are the final word in 98.6% of appealed cases. The discretion exercised by these courts over decisions of the federal district courts is grounded in specific standards of review which determine in what manner the appellate court may review the actions of the district court judge, jury or administrative agency. In this two-volume work, the authors provide both the theoretical underpinnings and the practical application of standards of review in the federal courts. However, their discussion is also extended to review in the state courts, including those which have substantially adopted the federal rules and those which have not. It is intended to assist attorneys, judges and scholars in understanding the scope and mission of judicial review and in focusing their attention on those issues which lie at the heart of the appeal. Following a introductory analysis of standards of review generally, the authors provide detailed examination of the application of these standards in civil, criminal and administrative contexts, while addressing the role of the trial judge, jury and administrative agency in the process. Steven Alan Childress, a practicing attorney and professor of law, has extensive experience as both a law clerk and extern in the federal courts. This work is the culmination of his scholarly examination of standards of review in various federal courts of appeals. Professor Martha Davis, a former clerk in the U.S. District Court, provides a complementary perspective of the review functions of the district courts and the review of its decisions by the courts of appeals. The text is adequately supported by citations to primary and secondary sources and includes both a table of cases and index.

Ciampi, Maria L. and William H. Manz. **The Question Presented: Model Appellate Briefs**. 4th ed. Newark, NJ: LexisNexis (Anderson Publishing Co.), 2000. 1 vol. (278 pp.). Paperbound.
Cost: $51 (2014).
An annotated collection of outstanding appellate briefs, as determined by appellate judges, addressing such issues as the theft of Native-American artifacts, freedom of speech, securities fraud, and conflict of interest. The corresponding court opinions are also included. An introductory chapter discusses what appellate court judges believe to be the ingredients of a well-written brief.

Clary, Bradley G., Sharon Reich Paulsen, and Michael J. Vanselow. **Advocacy on Appeal**. 3d ed. St. Paul, West, 2008. 1 vol. (254 pp.). Paperbound, Available from West Academic.
Cost: $77.00; from $30.35 on amazon.com (2014).
This brief volume provides an overview of the basic principles of good appellate advocacy, both written and oral, designed for both the law student and as a review for the practicing attorney. Laid out in three parts, the volume begins with a conceptual approach to advocacy that discusses the basic three-part recipe to effective advocacy: decide where you are going; give the court a reason to want to go there; and give the court a permissible legal route. The approach also includes the importance of a theme, the importance of balance (i.e. by comprehending the court's weighing of choices in light of the facts and law), the importance of roadmapping, and the two fundamental sources of legal rules: case law and statutory law. The remainder of the volume is divided between a consideration of the brief, and the oral argument, with a variety of specific recommendations for effective presentation of each. The Appendices include a number sample case documents, such as stipulations, affidavits, transcripts of court proceedings, orders, oral arguments, and memorandum opinions. Bradley G. Clary is Clinical Professor and Director of Applied Legal Instruction, University of Minnesota. His co-authors are adjunct professors of law at the University of Minnesota.

Congressional Quarterly's Guide to the U.S. Supreme Court. 5th ed. Edited by David Savage. Washington, DC: Congressional Quarterly, Inc., 2010. 2 vols. (1,449 pp.). Periodic new editions.
Cost: $465; from $339.98 on amazon.com (2014).
A valuable compendium of information on the United States Supreme Court, including its history, organization, political milieu, and a discussion of some of the major issues which with it has grappled over its 220-year history. The two volumes are organized into six parts and 20 chapters, addressing the origin and development of the court to 1996, the court and the federal system, the court and the individual, pressures on the court, the court at work, and members of the court. The appendices include a number of major constitutional and statutory documents, the text of several leading Supreme Court decisions, a listing of Supreme Court nominations, glossary of common legal terms, Acts of Congress held unconstitutional, and a chronology of major decisions of the court from 1790-1996. While aimed at a general audience, this reference work nevertheless serves as a useful source of information on the U.S. Supreme Court for scholars and legal professionals. The fourth edition is updated through 2008-2009 and the appointments of Chief Justice John Roberts and Associate Jusices Samuel Alito and Sonia Sotomayor.

Federal Appellate Practice. 2d ed. Mayer Brown LLP. Editor-in-Chief Philip Allen Lacovara. Arlington, VA: Bloomberg BNA

Books, 2013. 1 vol. (1,000 pp.).
Cost: $385.00 (2014).
Written by two dozen prominent national practitioners in Mayer Brown's Supreme Court and Appellate Practice Group, this manual provides detailed practical guidance through the intricacies of federal appellate practice, primarily civil, as well as cases involving review of federal administrative agency decisions. The authors address such matters as preserving issues for appeal, appellate jurisdiction, motions, discretionary interlocutory appeals and mandamus, the record on appeal and the appendix, effective brief writing, the opening brief, the responsive brief, the reply brief, the amicus curiae briefs, oral argument, rehearing, costs and attorneys' fees, criminal appeals, the federal circuit, and considering Supreme Court review. An essential resource for any attorney or firm involved in federal appellate practice and administrative appeals.

Fine, Ralph Adam. **The "How-To-Win" Appeal Manual**. 3d ed. Huntington, NY: Juris Publishing, 2012. 1 vol. (310 pp.).
Cost: $95 (2014).
This is a refreshingly candid and unvarnished examination of the real world of appellate advocacy that strips away the myths surrounding the judicial decision-making process, which generally portray it as a neutral and dispassionate search for truth. Indeed, author Robert Fine, paraphrasing the late Harold Leventhal of the D.C. Circuit Court of Appeals who wrote that "judges parse precedent like a person entering a crowded cocktail party: he or she looks over the heads of strangers to find friends." Cognizant of the reality that appellate judges often reach conclusions instinctively and then marshal the facts and arguments to support those conclusions, the author guides the appellate advocate through this often perilous landscape towards strategies most likely to garner a successful outcome. He also provides insights into the drafting of briefs, the oral argument, standards of review, getting rid of clutter in briefs, and advocacy in the real world, all of which draw upon the author's rich and wide-ranging knowledge of courtroom literature and personal anecdote. Ralph Adam Fine has taught trial advocacy, evidence, and appellate advocacy at more than 100 continuing legal education programs around the country and conducted in-house trial advocacy programs to many law firm litigation departments. Currently a judge on the Wisconsin Court of Appeals, he presided over more than 350 jury trials during his tenure on the Wisconsin circuit court from 1979 to 1988.

Flango, Carol R. and David B. Rottman. **Appellate Court Procedures**. Williamsburg, VA: National Center of State Courts, 1998. 1 vol. (320 pp.). Updated by periodic new editions. Available at:
http://cdm16501.contentdm.oclc.org/cdm/ref/collection/appellate/id/57
Cost: available at no cost in pdf format on ncsc website (2014).
A comparative guide to appellate procedure in all fifty states and the District of Columbia. Organized in a tabular format, this work provides information appellate court jurisdiction, steps in the appellate procedural process, decision making in appellate courts, expedited appellate procedures, the appellate bench, clerks, and judicial support staff, technology, and representation. Appendices include a list of appellate court clerks, and a bibliography. An essential resource for anyone interested in conducting a comparative analysis of procedures and practices of state appellate courts. One of numerous invaluable court-related studies available from the NCSC.

Fontham, Michael R., David W. Miller, and Michael Vitiello. **Persuasive Written and Oral Advocacy: In Trial and Appellate Courts**. 3d ed. New York: Wolters Kluwer Law & Business, 2013. 1 vol. (496 pp.).
Cost: $95 (2014).
This volume provides detailed practical guidance to the practicing attorney involved in advocacy before both trial and appellate courts. The authors take the reader through the entire process of writing, editing, and presenting arguments before the court. They offer practical suggestions for improving writing skills, making effective arguments, and making and delivering oral arguments. They also discuss appellate rules and procedural requirements and how best to comply with them, including such matters as preserving issues, taking appeals, seeking writs, and meeting technical requirements in brief preparation. Michael R. Fontham is a practicing attorney with the New Orleans firm of Stone, Pigman, Walther & Wittmann. David W. Miller and Michael Vitiello are Professors of Law at McGeorge School of Law, University of the Pacific.

Frederick, David C. **Supreme Court and Appellate Advocacy**. 2d ed. St. Paul, MN: Thomson Reuters West, 2010. 1 vol. (383 pp.). Practitioner Treatise Series.
Cost: $74; from $55.00 on amazon.com (2014).
This most recent addition to the literature of appellate advocacy presents a comprehensive approach to the preparation and delivery of oral arguments before appellate courts, including the U.S. Supreme Court. The author discusses the specifics for mastering the case record from below and the significant court decisions that comprise the existing body of common law. He also explains how to anticipate the type of questioning which will be encountered at oral arguments, how to handle hypothetical questions, and prepare closing arguments. The volume also includes both checklists and model arguments. David C. Frederick is a partner in a Washington, D.C., law firm and former law clerk to Justice Byron R. White.

Garner, Bryan A. **The Winning Oral Argument: Enduring Principles with Supporting Comments from the Literature**. St. Paul, MN: West, 2009. 1 vol. (262 pp.). Paperbound. Available from West Academic.
Cost: $64; from $27.24 on amazon.com (2014).
Although many Supreme Court Justices have stressed the often decisive importance of the oral argument in the ultimate determination of a case, they have also frequently voiced negative assessments regarding the quality of the appellate advocates appearing before the Court. Observer Stephen M. Shapiro likened the oral argument to "an initial conference convened to settle the case, [with counsel] invited into the conference for two purposes: to serve as a resource providing information needed to clarify the thinking of the Justices, and to bring an organizing theme, emphasis, and note of drama needed to marshal the information in a meaningful way." This

is a collection of comments drawn from the extensive literature on subject of the oral argument. It has its origins in another book the author co-authored with Justice Antonin Scalia, entitled **Making Your Case: The Art of Persuading Judges**. In addition to quotations on the importance, purpose and quality of oral argument, the editor assembles quotations on the following topics: preparing yourself generally as a public speaker, preparing for oral argument, the manner of your argument, the matter of your argument, responding to the bench, rebutting, and final thoughts. He concludes with an extensive bibliography of works cited and an index. Arguably the nation's leading authority on legal writing and legal style, Bryan Garner is also editor of the current editions of **Black's Law Dictionary**, as well as **Garner's Modern American Usage**, widely considered the leading authority on general English usage. He is Distinguished Research Professor of Law at Southern Methodist University Dedman School. This is an essential resource for any appellate advocate.

Hornstein, Alan D. **Hornstein's Appellate Advocacy in a Nutshell**. 2d ed. St. Paul, MN: West Group, 1998. 1 vol. (323 pp.). Available from West Academic.
Cost: $41; from $9.94 on amazon.com (2014).
Although written primarily as a law school text, this concise entry in West's Nutshell Series also provide the practicing attorney with a review of the principles and practices of effective written and oral appellate advocacy. The author examines the appellate process, the characteristics of various kinds of appellate arguments, and how those arguments differ based on the level of appellate court being addressed. He also discusses the classification of cases in the process of preparing arguments, including cases dealing with contacts, torts, administrative law, statutory questions, and constitutional issues. The appellate brief and its formal subdivisions are also considered. Finally, he addresses the preparation of oral arguments and protocols to observe in making them, including style, formality, order, rebuttal, authority, hot and cold benches, questions, and concluding arguments. The author is Professor of Law at the University of Maryland School of Law.

Houts, Marshall and Walter Rogosheske. **Art of Advocacy: Appeals.** New York: Matthew Bender & Co., 1987-date. 1 vol. Looseleaf format.
Cost: $430; supplementation: 1997: $103 (annual cost frozen since 1993); 1998: $110; 1999: $117; 2000: $125; 2001: $134; 2002: $144; 2003: $152; 2004: $152; 2005: $164; 2006: $184; 2007: $207; 2008: $230; 2009: $255; 2010: $284; 2011: $295; 2012: $327; 2013: $337; 2014: $361; e-book on amazon.com: $344.
A comprehensive guide to appellate practice in personal injury actions. This volume provides the practicing appellate litigator with an impressive combination of substantive and practical information related to the appeals process, as well as sample briefs, motions, arguments and practice commentary. The book is organized into five major sections: the appeals process, the written argument, oral argument, deciding the case, and, finally, motions, petitions, extraordinary writs and post-decision proceedings. Judge Rogosheske's chapter entitled „How One Appellate Judge „Reads" the Briefs," including a list of „Persuasive DO's" and „Irritating DON'T's," is a must for the appellate advocate. Marshall Houts is the creator of the Trauma series, and author of numerous books on courtroom medicine and Walter Rogosheske is a former Senior Justice of the Minnesota Supreme Court, past Chairman of the ABA Committee on the Prosecution and Defense Functions, and, currently, Distinguished Lawyer in Residence, University of Minnesota Law School where he teaches trial jurisprudence and appellate jurisprudence.

Cost Savings Tips: Trial practice titles like this can be used effectively without subscribing to the updates. Forego the standing order and simply re-purchase it when you feel you would like a more current version.

Klein, David E. **Making Law in the United States Courts of Appeals**. New York: Cambridge University Press, 2002. 1 vol. (190 pp.).
Cost: $79.00 (hardcover); $29.99 (softcover); e-book: $234; from $2.50 on amazon.com (2014).
This book melds legal and behavioral scholarship into an insightful analysis of how federal court judges decide cases in the face of unsettled issues of law, and particularly how their decisions are influenced by the rulings of both higher courts and courts at the same level. Based on statistical analyses of decisions and interviews with federal appeals judges, this work provides a close examination of the decision-making process. The author concludes that federal appeals court judges attach serious weight to the decisions of other judges at the same level, while exercising considerable independence from the judgments of the Supreme Court. The author is an Assistant Professor in the Woodrow Wilson Department of Politics at the University of Virginia.

Knibb, David G. **Federal Court of Appeals Manual**. 6th ed. St. Paul, MN: West Group, 2013-date. 1 vol. (595 pp.). Annual supplementation.
Cost: $197; supplementation: 2008: $33.50; 2009: $37.50; 2010: $42; 2011: $45; 2012: $49; 2013: new ed.; 4th ed.: 2001: $52.25; 2002: $26.50; 2003: $23; 2004: $25.75; 2005: $28.50; 2006: $31; 2007: new edition ($105). Local Rules book (2009 ed.): $69; **Monthly Assured Print Price (APP):** $12/$144.
This practical guide explains the federal rules of appellate procedure used before the U.S. Courts of Appeal. Chapters are devoted to a consideration of the entire appellate process, including such topics as how to file a timely appeal, what to consider before taking an appeal, brief writing, preparation of the oral argument, and why the appeals process works the way it does in special situations. Includes an annual pamphlet that details the current circuit court rules.

Levy, Herbert Monte. **How To Handle an Appeal**. 4th ed. New York: Practising Law Institute, 1999-date. 1 vol. Looseleaf format. Annual supplementation anticipated.
Cost: $335; from $81.50 on amazon.com; supplementation: 2001: $74.25; 2002: 82; 2003: $94; 2004: $104; 2005: $99; 2006: $91; 2007: $105; 2008: $109; 2009: $139; 2010: $150; 2011: $154; 2012: $160; 2013: $185.

A comprehensive guide to the appellate process by an attorney experienced in both trial and appellate work. The author covers the full range of topics related to the appellate process, including the preservation of points for appeal, relations with other counsel, fees, technical problems on appeals. perfecting the appeal, the appellate brief, relations with clients and other attorneys, oral argument, the decision, and practical suggestions for practice in the U.S. Courts of Appeals and U.S. Supreme Court. The appendices include a checklist for appellate practice, forms, sample briefs, the Federal Rules of Appellate Procedure, the Rules of the Supreme Court of the United States, and rules on typeface, type style, and type volume. The author provides a lucid and practical approach to appellate procedure free of excessive citations to cases and statutes.

Meador, Daniel J. and Thomas E. Baker. **Appellate Courts: Structures, Functions, Processes and Personnel**. 2d ed. Newark, NJ: LexisNexis.Matthew Bender, 2006. 1 vol. (1,235 pp.). No supplementation between editions.
Cost: $174; looseleaf: $139; 2001 edition on amazon.com: $5.41 (2014).
Unlike trial courts, appellate courts have traditionally maintained a low level of visibility in the American consciousness, although they are responsible for the considerable body of case law that forms a significant segment of our American jurisprudence. This volume provides insightful and in-depth examination of appellate courts and the appellate process in the United States. The author, a Professor of Law at the University of Virginia School of Law, takes a close look at the internal operations of appellate courts, including their structure, jurisdiction, procedures, and personnel.

Moskovitz, Myron. **Winning an Appeal: a step-by-step explanation of how to prepare and present your case efficiently and effectively, with sample briefs**. 4th ed. New York: Matthew Bender & Co., 2007. 1 vol. (242 pp.).
Cost: $51; eBook: $35.00; from $12.70 on amazon.com (2014).
This succinct overview of the appellate process provides attorneys with a practical approach to the principles of appellate advocacy and the steps necessary to present a winning case, both written and oral. The author is Professor Law at Golden Gate University School of Law.

Re, Edward D. and Joseph R. Re. **Brief Writing and Oral Argument**. 9th ed. Dobbs Ferry, NY: Oceana Publications, Inc., 2005. Available from Oxford University Press. 1 vol. (312 pp.). Paperbound.
Cost: $47; from $20.00 on amazon.com (2014).
This classic work provides authoritative guidance in the arts of oral and written advocacy. Designed to bridge the gap between the law school and law practice, it is also an excellent review for practitioners. The authors discuss the elements of good legal writing, both from a general perspective and as it is applied to the drafting of specific legal documents, including opinion letters, trial memoranda and briefs, and appellate briefs. The authors consider the brief as a preparation for oral argument. Their discussion of oral argument examines such matters as preparation, the importance of oral argument, the respondent's oral argument, the appellant's rebuttal, and considerations after oral argument. The authors also include a useful discussion of legal citation and the relative importance of various types of legal authority in crafting the legal brief.. The appendices include a sample appellant's briefs, a Petition for Writ of Certiorari, an Appellee's brief to the U.S. Court of Appeals, claim or demand letters, a trial memorandum, and an office memorandum of law. Edward D. Re is Chief Justice Emeritus of the U.S. Court of International Trade and a Distinguished Professor of Law at St. John's University.

Rambo, Teresa J. Reid and Leanne J. Pflaum. **Legal Writing by Design: A Guide to Great Briefs and Memos**. 2d ed. Durham, NC: Carolina Academic Press, 2013. 1 vol. (684 pp.). Paperbound.
Cost: $60.00; from 0.31 on amazon.com (2014).
The underlying aim of this book is the transformation of reasoning into written form. Indeed, legal analysis, reasoning, and writing are among the essential skills law firms expect of their new hires, along with legal research skills, oral communication, computer legal research, and sensitivity to legal ethics. Good legal writing is clear, concise, cohesive, flows well from point to point, and is absolutely accurate as to the facts, the law, and how the law applies to the client's case. Intended as a textbook for classes in legal skills, the authors devote considerable attention to the design of legal reasoning, in its deductive, inductive and analogical forms, the organization of thought, reading and interpreting cases, and using them effectively in legal argumentation. They examine both persuasive and predictive legal memoranda, their structure and content. Section III is devoted to a point-by-point discussion of persuasive analysis as reflected in the content of legal briefs and oral arguments at the appellate level. The chapters in Section IV provide in-depth analysis of the beginning, middle and ending of the legal memo or brief, with attention to editing, citations, quotations and style, case briefing, and ethics and professionalism. Section V discusses the basics of clear and effective legal writing, including brevity, artistry, simplicity, impact, cohesion and style. The concluding section provides samples of a court opinion, legal memo, appellant's brief, appellee's brief, and reply brief. The text is augmented with numerous examples, charts, templates, exercises, and chapter reviews. This text is model of organization and clarity, explaining the writing process thoroughly and effectively. While intended primarily for law students, this is also an excellent tool for anyone who wants to improve their ability to analyze issues, and write clearly and persuasively, including attorneys, legal assistants, pro se litigants, undergraduate students, or members of the general public. The authors are legal skills professors at the University of Florida Fredric G. Levin College of Law, with a combined forty-plus years of teaching legal writing and appellate advocacy to law students.

Roberts, Matthew M.C. **Oral Argument and Amicus Curiae**. El Paso, TX: LFB Scholarly Publishing, 2012. 1 vol. (168 pp). Hardcover.
Cost: $65.00; from $49.99 on amazon.com (2014).
An *amicus curiae* (also *amicus curiæ*; plural amici curiae, literally "*friend of the court*") is someone not a party to a case who offers information bearing on the case to the court in question that has

not been solicited by any of the parties. This information, which is admitted at the discretion of the court, may take of the form of legal opinion, oral testimony or learned treatise (the amicus brief). It is a way to introduce concerns ensuring that the possibly broad legal effects of a court decision will not depend solely on the parties directly involved in the case. Another characteristic of the amicus is that it is less likely to represent the author of the brief than the sponsoring organization. In this pioneering study, Matthew Roberts examines the role played by amici in influencing the Supreme court's decision-making process, with particular attention to those cases in which the court allows these extra groups to participate not only by filing briefs, but by making oral argument before the court. In doing so, he draws upon a number of statistical analyses of amici influence on the court's decisions in concluding that the Court is often driven by more than political considerations of ideology and party loyalty. The author is professor of political science at the Grand Valley State University (MI).

Scalia, Antonin and Bryan A. Garner. **Making Your Case: The Art of Persuading Judges**. St. Paul, MN: Thomson/West, 2008. 1 vol. (245 pp.).
Cost: $29.95; eBook: $29.95; Kindle edition: $27.03; from $24.45 on amazon.com (2014).
The art of persuasion and the principles of argumentation are skills useful not only in the courtroom, but in many aspects of daily life. In this succinct guide to written and oral argument, Supreme Court Justice Antonin Scalia and Bryan Garner provide attorneys with pithy and insightful discussion of the major elements of appellate advocacy. Their practical and common sense wisdom, laced with humor, is delivered in the form of 115 short chapters which address the general principles of argumentation, legal reasoning, briefing, and oral argument. The authors urge their readers to think syllogistically and to apply the rules of logic to their arguments. They must know and apply the rules of textual interpretation to the governing legal authorities, whether cases, statutes, regulations, ordinances, contracts, and the like. And, when necessary, they must be prepared to defend an interpretation by resort to legislative history (ironically, a process with which Justice Scalia has previously expressed reservations). While their advice is directed primarily at appellate advocacy, it also draws a useful contrast with the aims of trial advocacy where judges are more disposed to the observance of governing caselaw. They urge advocates to learn as much as possible about the judge who will decide the case, including not only their judicial philosophy, but elements of their personal and professional background which might provide clues about the types of arguments which will find a receptive audience. They observe that many law firms keep 'book' on all the judges before whom they appear, recording their personal idiosyncrasies, prejudices, and foibles. There is excellent advice here regarding the briefing process, writing style, courtroom demeanor, the substance and manner of argumentation, and the handling of questions. It concludes with a useful bibliography of sources. For law students, and students of the legal system generally, this volume provides an excellent tool for comprehending the end result of one of the central aims of legal education, namely, to develop a conceptual and practical understanding of caselaw and other legal authorities. Consequently, it can be read and re-read to great benefit by both first-year law students and experienced appellate advocates. Antonin Scalia has served as Associate Justice of the U.S. Supreme Court since 1986. He is a passionate advocate for the principle of textualism in statutory interpretation and an originalist in matters of constitutional interpretation. A professor at Southern Methodist University School of Law, Bryan Garner is a widely recognized author in the field of legal writing and style. He has edited **Black's Law Dictionary** since the 7th edition and written many books and articles, including **A Dictionary of Modern Legal Usage**, **The Elements of Legal Style**, **The Winning Brief**, and **Legal Writing in Plain English**.

Supreme Court Practice. Gressman, Eugene; Stephen M. Shapiro; Kenneth S. Geller; Timothy S. Bishop; and Edward A. Hartnett, eds. 10th ed. Washington, DC: Bloomberg BNA Books, 2013-date. 1 vol. (1,450 pp.)
Cost: $495; no supplementation to date; 8th edition: 1995: $45; 1996: 0; 1997: $65 (2014).
The „bible" for those practicing before the United States Supreme Court. This edition was prompted by Congressional repeal of most of the statutory provisions allowing direct appeals to the Supreme Court, providing for certiorari as the only route of appeal in all but a few cases. It is also a response to the issuance of a new set of rules by the Supreme Court effective October, 2007. Robert Stern and Eugene Gressman have been co-authors of this work since its initial appearance in 1950 when they served. Robert Stern was also a member of the Court committee that drafted the 1954 rules which prompted the second edition of this work. This volume provides a complete and scholarly description and analysis of the process of appealing a case to the United States Supreme Court. Includes a historical introduction to the Supreme Court, discussion of jurisdiction to review decisions of the federal and state courts, factors motivating the exercise of the Court's certiorari jurisdiction, procedure on appeals, certified questions, original cases, extraordinary writs, briefs on the merits, oral argument, petitions for rehearing and final disposition of cases, motions and applications, bails and stays, justiciability, admissions to the bar and disbarment, and forms. Appendices include Rules of the Supreme Court, Guide for Counsel in Cases To Be Argued Before the Supreme Court of the United States, Statutes, and Depositories for Supreme Court Briefs. There is both a table of cases and a subject and rules index. This 9th edition reflects changes in Supreme Court Rules, particularly the revised formatting requirements for booklet-format briefs and the introduction of new procedures for the submission of amicus briefs at the certiorari stage. As the Court adopts new rules, it integrates them into the existing structure and promulgates the entire set of rules anew. The 9th edition is the product of these most recent revisions. This is an indispensable guide to anyone planning to bring a case before the U.S. Supreme Court.

Tanenhaus, David S., ed. **Encyclopedia of the Supreme Court of the United States**. Detroit: Macmillan Reference USA, 2008. 5 vols. (2,631 pp.).
Cost: $786; from $229 on amazon.com (2014).
This comprehensive reference work on the United States Supreme Court contains 1,100 entries, embracing 523 essays on specific court decisions, 468 thematic essays, and 109 biographies, written by leading legal scholars and historians of

the court. It includes historical essays on all 17 Supreme Court Chief Justices, leading Associate Justices, court staff, landmark Supreme Court decisions, legal concepts and procedures, theories of law and interpretation, essays on major legal issues, biographical articles on leading political figures, scholars, and lawyers appearing before the court. Ranging in length from 250 to 6,500 words, each signed entry is accompanied by a bibliography and citations to related articles. The appendices in volume five include a chronology of landmark decisions, U.S. history and legislation; foundational documents; a list of Justices; glossary of terms; and subject index. The contributors include some of the leading experts in their respective fields, such Professor Herbert Hovenkamp who wrote the entry on Antitrust. The audience for this five-volume set ranges from advance placement high school students and undergraduates to graduate students, professors, lawyers, journalists and judges.

Tigar, Michael E. **Federal Appeals: Jurisdiction and Practice.** 3d ed. St. Paul, MN: Thomson/West (Clark Boardman Callaghan), 1999-date. 1 vol. Annual pocket part.
Cost: $186; supplementation: 2000: $32.50; 2001: $32.50; 2002: $43.50; 2003: $43; 2004: $45; 2005: $49; 2006: $55; 2007: $61; 2008: $68; 2009: $81.50; 2010: $95; 2011: $105; 2012: $116; 2013: $125; 2d edition: 1994: $42; 1995: $45; 1996: $50; 1997: 0; 1998: $56; **Monthly Assured Print Price (APP):** $13/ $156.
This single-volume guide to the federal appellate process, authored by a leading federal trial attorney, provides guidance to those bringing and defending federal appeals. The third edition is updated to reflect changes in the federal rules. Includes advice on how to write effective briefs, make persuasive oral arguments, evaluate cases, and set realistic fees. This volume covers the art, science, and tactics of appellate advocacy; the nature of federal appellate jurisdiction, appellate orders, where to appeal, whether to appeal, fees, preparation, handling the record, motions practice, the brief, rehearing, and rehearing en banc. It provides useful advice on discerning the critical factors of timing and jurisdiction, how to read judicial attitudes, making the most of oral argument, and improving the chances of obtaining rehearing.

U.S. Law Week. Washington, D.C.: Bloomberg BNA, 1933-date. 2 vols. Weekly.
Cost: $2,070 per year (includes online access to cases); Internet (single user):$3,735; print discounted when acquired in combination with Internet. (2014).
This two-volume service provides timely reporting of current United States Supreme Court decisions. Although issues generally appear on a weekly basis, extra issues are released during the term's busy weeks. Releases also include Supreme Court Proceedings containing lists and summaries of newly docketed cases, news developments and reports on oral arguments. The General Law Sections include news and abstracts of decisions from other federal and state courts.

Wisotsky, Steven. **Professional Judgment on Appeal: Bringing and Opposing Appeals**. 2d ed. Durham, NC: Carolina Academic Press, 2009. 1 vol. (436 pp.).
Cost: $75; from $71.25 on amazon.com (2014).
How many times have you heard people say they plan to appeal their case all the way to the U.S. Supreme Court? Yet, most potential appellants have no idea what this entails, nor what their chances of success are likely to be. In reality, the overwhelming majority of appeals, both civil and criminal, and in both state and federal courts, fail. Nationally, only 10-15% of cases are reversed upon appeal. And while books on the appellate process, brief writing and oral argument abound, there is no single source that addresses the predictors of the success or failure of appeals. Moreover, most lawyers and their clients simply fail to understand or acknowledge that once a case is lost at trial, it will or should fail upon appeal. The reasons for this are not difficult to ascertain. Restricted appellate review, the preservation of error barrier, deferential standards of review on matters of fact or discretion, and the harmless error rule all provide a strong momentum in favor of affirming the lower court ruling. To mount a successful appeal, the attorney must comprehend these potential barriers and formulate a plan to overcome them. In this essential reference for the appellate attorney, Steven Wisotsky examines the appellate system, views from the bench, the decision to appeal, predicting outcomes, appellate mediation in the federal courts of appeals, finality and appealability, preservation of error, standards of review, harmless error, post-decision practice: rehearings and Supreme Court review, frivolous appeals, appellate malpractice, extraordinary writs, and the ethical dimensions of appellate practice. He draws not only upon the latest cases, rules, and scholarly writings, but upon the assembled wisdom of leading jurists, living and dead. The author brings 30 years experience to the task, much of involving litigation in high-stakes, multi-party appeals involving multiple law firms. He recognizes that few cases receive plenary review and that the decisions of appellate judges are largely driven by the fundamental standards of appellate review.

Wrightsman, Lawrence S. **Oral Arguments Before the Supreme Court: An Empirical Approach**. New York: Oxford University Press, 2008. 1 vol. (187 pp.).
Cost: $75; from $16.00 on amazon.com; kindle: $67.69 (2014).
Of all the steps in the U.S. Supreme Court's decision-making process, the oral argument is the only one not shrouded in secrecy. And, contrary to the views of some critics who view it as a useless exercise, Lawrence Wrightman contends that oral arguments are an important part of the court's decision-making process. They give the Justices an opportunity to test the limits of the claims made by advocates in their briefs, to gauge the feelings of the other Justices, and, possibly, to persuade their colleagues during the questioning process. This empirical study of Supreme Court oral arguments provides penetrating insights into the nature of oral advocacy and its impact on ultimate court rulings. Among the issues addressed by the author is whether oral arguments are still an essential part of the process. He also evaluates the views of the Justices regard8ing oral arguments, the behavior of advocates before the Supreme Court, Justices' questions and statements, the idiosyncratic nature of Justices' behavior during oral arguments, oral arguments in a landmark case, and predicting votes from oral arguments. He concludes with a consideration of three contentious issues: (1) should oral arguments be televised? (2) are parties before the court treated fairly? and (3) does the procedure of oral argument work? Drawing upon a wealth of empirically-based observations, a

review of Justices' statements, and transcripts of actual oral arguments, the author provides significant insights into this important part of the Supreme Court's decision-making process. This is an essential reference for any advocate faced with making an oral argument before the Supreme Court, or any student of the appellate process generally.

Additional titles in the field of Appellate Practice are available from the following publishers: American Bar Association, Wolters Kluwer Law & Business, Bloomberg BNA Books, Cambridge University Press, Carolina Academic Press (CAP), CQ Press, Diane Publishing Company, Federal Bar Association, Greenwood Publishing Group, Juris Publishing, Law Journal Press, Macmillan Reference, Matthew Bender, LexisNexis, National Institute for Trial Advocacy, National Center for State Courts, W.W. Norton & Co., Oxford University Press, Practising Law Institute, Thomson Reuters West, West Academic. See Appendix B for addresses and telephone numbers.

Arbitration and Alternative Dispute Resolution

American Arbitration Association. **ADR Yearbook on Arbitration and the Law**. 25th ed. Huntington, NY: Juris Publishing, 2013. 1 vol. (400 pp.). Also available as downloadable e-book.
Cost: 25th Edition: $95; 24th Edition: $95 (2014).
The latest in a series of annual volumes which contain summaries of the latest state and federal court decisions about alternative dispute resolution, with an emphasis on commercial matters. It also contains commentaries on ADR practice and procedure in the United States by practitioners and scholars, as well as other current developments. These annual volumes are a joint project of the American Arbitration Association, Fordham University School of Law, and Juris Publishing. An excellent addition to any ADR collection and an excellent tool by which scholars and practitioners can keep abreast of developments in the field. A companion CD-ROM, introduced with the 2003 edition, contains the text of the American Arbitration Association's ADR rules and procedures, the recent AAA/ABA code of Ethics for Arbitration in Commercial Disputes, a directory of AAA offices, and other useful materials.

American Arbitration Association. **Handbook on Arbitration Practice**. Huntington, NY: JurisNet, 2010. 1 vol. (428 pp.). Also available as downloadable e-book.
Cost: $95.00 (print or eBook) (2014).
Since the early 1990s, businesses have been moving away from the resolution of commercial and business disputes via the litigation route in favor of arbitration. For most business-to-business disputes, arbitration is the more economical alternative, both in terms of time and money, including lower discovery costs, fewer pre-trial motions, and a more limited right to appeal. While courtroom litigation is administered by independent administrative staff, arbitration is administered by a neutral administrative body only if the parties agree to it. Arbitral awards may be complied with voluntarily by the losing party, but it is often necessary for them to be recorded with a court of law in order to ensure their enforcement. This collection of articles on various aspects of arbitration is a joint project of the American Arbitration Association (AAA) and Juris Publishing. The 32 articles are grouped under the following topical areas: (1) issues in arbitration practice and procedure; (2) arbitrator selection and conduct; (3) arbitration procedure; (4) discovery and evidence in arbitration; (5) ethics in administrative practice; 6) and damages, review and enforcement of arbitration awards. The articles provide a wealth of practical advice bearing on the various phases of the arbitration process, including the pre-hearing phase, the hearing phase, and the post-hearing phase, and such particulars as the preliminary conference, pre-hearing briefs, declarations, and transcripts. More than 30 experts in the field, primarily lawyers and professional arbitrators, contributed to this joint effort.

American Arbitration Association. **Handbook on Construction Arbitration & ADR**. 2d ed. Huntington, NY: Juris, Net, LLC, 2010. 1 vol. (541 pp.). Also available as downloadable e-book.
Cost: $95.00 (print or eBook) (2014).
The field of construction is no different than many other areas of commercial activity that experience disagreements between parties to transactions, either during the contractual phase or during some stage of its execution. This collection of articles on various aspects of construction arbitration and alternative dispute resolution (ADR) is a joint project of the American Arbitration Association (AAA) and Juris Publishing. The 54 succinct chapters are grouped under topics ranging from managing risk and avoiding disputes, ADR in the construction industry, mediation, partnering, arbitration, small claims management, large and complex case management, and dispute resolution boards. The articles are a response to a pressing need for substantive information about conflict resolution techniques and strategies that will help alleviate the high costs of formal litigation. It represents an attempt by the AAA to improve accessibility of arbitration and mediation and related services and information to a worldwide audience. More than 40 authors contributed articles to this volume, providing a wealth of information to any organization or individual contemplating the use of ADR in the construction field.

American Arbitration Association Handbook on Labor Arbitration. 2d ed. Thomas E. Carbonneau, Philip J. McConnaughay, and Crystal L. Stryker, eds. Huntington, NY: JurisNet, LLC, 2010. 1 vol. (267+ pp.). Also available as downloadable e-book.
Cost: $95 (print or eBook) (2014).
One in a series of Handbooks produced by Pennsylvania State University's Dickinson School of Law and the Institute for Dispute Resolution, this valuable collection assembles eighteen articles by leading arbitration experts on various aspects of labor arbitration and practice and drawn from a number of scholarly and professional publications. The articles discuss a variety of topics related to labor arbitration, labor arbitration procedures, advocates' and arbitrators' issues, and the judicial review of labor arbitration. Specific articles discuss the Eight Essential Steps of Grievance Processing, Job Discrimination Claims under Collective Bargaining, and Arbitration in Public Sector Labor Disputes, among others. Thomas E. Charbonneau is the Orlando Distinguished professor of Law at Penn State University.

Born, Gary B. **International Commercial Arbitration**. Austin, TX: Wolters Kluwer, 2009. 2 vols. (3,440 pp.).
Cost: $482; from $362 on amazon.com (2014).
With the expansion of the volume and complexity of international trade and commerce in recent decades, business entities have demonstrated a decided preference for arbitration as a means of resolving commercial disputes. This massive treatise attempts to provide a comprehensive description and analysis of the contemporary constitutional structure, law, practice and policy of international commercial arbitration, and advance a successful model for providing a fair, neutral, expert and efficient mechanism for resolving difficult and complex transnational issues. It has usually provided a superior method to the litigation procedures offered by national courts. Volumes of this size and scope are generally assembled by one or more editors and authored by a team of authors, each contributing a chapter representing his or her specialty. By contrast, one man, Gary Born, authored this volume. His grasp of the complexities of the field, and ability to articulate it in scholarly and readable prose, is unparalleled. This massive text encompasses everything from the history and legal framework of international commercial arbitration to international arbitration agreements and the separability presumption, choice of law issues, the formation, validity and legality of international arbitration agreements, arbitrator's competence, effects and enforcement, interpretation of international arbitration agreements, parties, the legal framework for international arbitral proceedings, selection, challenge and replacement of arbitrators, rights and duties of arbitrators, selection of the arbitral seat, procedures, disclosure and discovery, choice of substantive law, confidentiality, legal representation and professional conduct, and the various aspects of international arbitral awards, among other topics. The text is supported by exhaustive citations to primary and secondary authorities, including those to applicable arbitration rulings. In addition, the exhaustive appendices include an extensive bibliography of commentaries, treatises, monographs and articles, lists of international conventions, instruments, constitutions, statutes, arbitration rules, U.N. documents, index of arbitral awards, index and cases and subject index. This is a revised and expanded edition of the author's International **Commercial Arbitration: Commentary and Materials**, published in 2001. This is the single most important reference tool in the field of international commercial arbitration that should be acquired by every lawyer specializing in international or domestic commercial arbitration.

Brand, Norman and Melissa H. Biren, eds. **Discipline and Discharge in Arbitration**. 2d ed. Washington, DC: Bloomberg BNA Books, 2008. 1 vol. (765 pp.). Updated by new editions.
Cost: $195 (10% discount for web purchase); no supplementation to date; from $164.90 on amazon.com (2014).
This substantial revision of the original 1998 work, brings the latest thought and analysis to bear on a field which has undergone substantial change over the past ten years. Produced in association with the Committee on ADR in Labor and Employment Law, Section of Labor and Employment Law, American Bar Association, this title is one in a series of volumes which provide legal practitioners with guidance in labor and employment law. This text is an extended discussion of just cause, or the equitable principle by which arbitrators determine whether the discipline or discharge of an employee should be upheld. Following an introductory overview of the subject of arbitration advocacy, the authors address a number of specific contexts in which the theory of just cause may be applied. Specific disciplinary issues discussed include attendance, job performance, refusals to perform work or cooperate, substance abuse, dishonesty and disloyalty, workplace misconduct, off-duty conduct, and union activities. Additional chapters examine evidentiary and procedural considerations, remedies for inappropriate discipline, external law, and finality of awards and court actions. The text is amply supported with citations to labor arbitration and court decisions. The second edition examines a number of new rules being applied to new forms of activity, including those designed to prevent employees from surfing the Internet, those to avoid work place behavior that results in litigation, and those to enforce work place rules. These new rules governing the use of computers for personal business or pleasure impose both content and use restrictions and impact the application of progressive discipline. Norman Brand and Melissa Biren are practicing attorneys, arbitrators and mediators. The contributing authors include more than fifteen leading arbitrators and mediators. A companion volume to Elkouri and Elkouri's **How Arbitration Works** and an expansion of the standards discussed in Chapter 15 of that work.

Carbonneau, Thomas E. and Jeanette A. Jaeggi, eds. **AAA Handbook on Commercial Arbitration**. 2d ed. Huntington, NY: Juris Publishing, 2011. 1 vol. (482 pp.). Also available as downloadable e-book.
Cost: $95 (print or eBook); no supplementation to date (2014).
When the American Arbitration Association was founded in 1926, its organizers were motivated by a desire to avoid the costs, delays and risks associated with a litigation system slow to respond to the needs of an industrial age. The motivations of its founders are even more pertinent today in an age of rapid technological, industrial, and informational change. This collection of articles on the basics of commercial arbitration written by leading practitioners and scholars is The Mediator's Handbookdrawn from the pages of the AAA's **Dispute Resolution Journal** and is intended as an introduction to the field. The 47 articles in this volume, written by a team of respected experts, scholars, and practitioners, examine such topics a s the fairness of arbitration, the benefits of business arbitration, new techniques to manage complex commercial disputes, political correctness—a barrier to arbitration efficiency, arbitration clauses and the Internet, the essential qualities of an arbitrator, expert testimony, discovery, arbitration confidentiality, the use of sanctions in arbitration, writing arbitration awards, and state arbitration law, among others. One of a series of volumes on arbitration and ADR produced by the joint efforts of the American Arbitration Association, Juris Publishing, and Penn State University. Thomas E. Carbonneau is the Samuel P. Orlando Distinguished Professor of Law at Penn State's Dickinson School of Law and one of the world's leading experts on domestic and international arbitration. Jeanette A. Jaeggi is Executive Director of Penn State University's Institute for Arbitration Law and Practice.

Carbonneau, Thomas E., Philip J. McConnaughay, and Crystal L. Stryker. **Handbook on Employment Arbitration and ADR**. 2d ed. New York, NY: American Arbitration Association, Inc.,

2010. 1 vol. (372 pp.). Also available as downloadable e-book.
Cost: $95 (print or eBook) (2014).
Drawn from the pages of the AAA's **Dispute Resolution Journal** and other sources, this volume assembles the writings of dozens of specialists on the application of arbitration and alternative dispute resolution to a variety of fields. Among the topics covered in this volume are workplace conflict resolution options, ADR: the Halliburton experience, Is interest-based bargaining really new?, resolving sexual harassment disputes in the workplace: the central role of mediation in an employment contract, issues in employment arbitration after Circuit City, the debate over mandatory arbitration, among other topics. Thomas E. Carbonneau is the Samuel P. Orlando Distinguished Professor of Law at Penn State s Dickinson School of Law and is generally regarded as one of the world's leading experts on domestic and international arbitration. He is the editor-in-chief of leading professional publications, the **World Arbitration and Mediation Report** and the **Journal of American Arbitration.**

Carbonneau, Thomas E. **The Law and Practice of Arbitration**. 4th ed. Huntington, NY: Juris Publishing, 2012. 1 vol. (729 pp.). Also available as downloadable e-book.
Cost: OUT-OF-PRINT; was $150 (print or eBook) (2014).
Arbitration is a private, informal, and extrajudicial process for the adjudication of disputes which serves as a major alternative to litigation. It has become the chief remedy for the resolution of civil disputes both the United States and internationally, and is applied to an ever expanding universe of disputes. Using the Federal Arbitration Act (FAA) as its basis, the U.S. Supreme Court has ruled that arbitration is a legitimate exercise of the freedom to enter into contracts. This treatise provides an in-depth examination of the law governing both domestic and international arbitration and the procedural aspects of its utilization as a tool of dispute resolution. The author discusses the basic concepts and principles of arbitration, the law of arbitration, the FAA and the Uniform Law, arbitration and federalism, contract freedom and arbitrability, old and new applications, workplace arbitration, the enforcement of arbitral awards, international commercial arbitration, transborder regimes, substantive international law, special issues, and writing arbitration agreements. The author provides extensive citations to supporting authorities, including court decisions, statutes. International conventions, and secondary sources. Thomas E. Charbonneau is the Orlando Distinguished professor of Law at Penn State University.

Colosi, Thomas R. and Arthur Eliot Berkeley. **Collective Bargaining: How It Works and Why**. 3d ed. Huntington, NY: Juris Publishing, 2006. 1 vol. (216 pp.). Also available as downloadable e-book.
Cost: $55 (print or eBook); no supplementation to date; from $44.99 on amazon.com (2014).
This manual on the theory and practice of collective bargaining distills the experiences of countless practitioners in light of the current state of labor-management relations. Less a "how to" manual with numerous examples than a succinct description of how collective bargaining should work in practice, it discusses the nature of negotiations, the parties to negotiation, the conflict, the battlefield, the battle, the table process, multilateral bargaining, the table process analyzed, preparation for bargaining, participation and democracy, the framework for bargaining, the continuum of peacemaking peace processes, table manners, table talk, table dynamics, table tact8ics, and promise checking: grievance arbitration. Thomas R. Colosi is an ADR trainer, mediator, lecturer and author who retired in 1999 after 28 years as the AAA's vice-president of ADR education.
Arthur Berkeley is a former professor of alternative dispute resolution at Memphis State University, arbitrator, and ADR trainer.

Cooley, John W. **The Mediator's Handbook**. 2d ed. Notre Dame, IN: National Institute for Trial Advocacy, 2006. Paperbound. 1 vol. (510 pp.). Available from LexisNexis.
Cost: $75; from $68 on amazon.com (2014).
Written for practicing and experienced mediators, including both lawyers and nonlawyers, as well as those involved in litigation and litigation-related disputes, this volume is designed as a practical handbook to be used during every sequential stage of the mediation process. The author, a nationally recognized mediator, arbitrator, trainer and consultant, provides a general description of the mediation process, the role of the mediator as an effective communicator, the mediator's pre-conference functions and duties, conference functions and duties, and post-conference functions and duties. He also describes the hybrid processes, including co-mediation, medical arbitration (med-arb), binding mediation, arb-med, and co-med-arb, and the process of conducting effective cybermediation. The appendices include a variety of checklists do guide practitioner's through the mediation process.

Coulson, Robert. **Labor Arbitration: What You Need To Know**. Revised 5th ed. Huntington, NY: Juris Publishing, 2003. 1 vol. (136 pp.). Available as downloadable e-book.
Cost: OUT-OF-PRINT; was $35 (2014).
This brief guide to the process of labor arbitration is intended as introductory, practical overview for those involved in a labor arbitration case, whether from the labor or management side. It addresses such basic matters as the labor grievance, the selection of a labor arbitrator, the arbitration hearing, and arbitration in the public sector. Appendices include the AAA's Labor Arbitration Rules, a glossary of arbitration jargon, summaries of court and NLRB decisions that have contributed to the language of labor-management arbitration, the just cause standard in discipline and discharge cases, and other useful tools. Robert Coulson is the former President of the America Arbitration Association and a leading expert and author on arbitration and dispute resolution.

Domke, Martin. **Domke on Commercial Arbitration.** 3d Revised ed. by Gabriel M. Wilner. St. Paul, MN: West Group (Clark Boardman Callaghan), 1994-date. 2 vols. Looseleaf format. Annual supplementation.
Cost: $591; supplementation: 1993: $65; 1994: $84; 1995: $140; 1996: $176; 1997: $184.80; 1998: $196.50; 1999: $212.50; 2000: $230.50; 2001: $272.50; 2002: $329; 2003: $362; 2004: $49; 2005; $148.50; 2006: $170; 2007: $190; 2008: $211; 2009: $149; 2010: $309.50; 2011: $296.50; 2012: $209; 2013: $227;
Monthly Assured Print Price (APP): $39/$468.
This is a thorough exposition of the subject of commercial arbitration which combines attention to scholarly detail with features valuable to the practitioner. Subject coverage includes

a consideration of the nature of commercial arbitration, the development of commercial arbitration law, the arbitration agreement, arbitrability, initiation of arbitration, statutory enforcement, the role of the arbitrator, hearings, relief by courts in pending arbitration, awards, challenges of awards, enforcement (both general and interstate), costs and expenses of arbitration, and enforcement in international transactions. Includes a table of cases and subject index. Volume two provides a variety of valuable appendices, including citations to general arbitration statutes in the United States, the Uniform Arbitration Act, and a variety of relevant national and international rules and conventions. Includes the rules promulgated by the American Arbitration Association in the areas of patent, securities, and accident law and the Maritime Arbitration Rules of the Society of Maritime Arbitrators. A Practice Guide, prepared by Rodolphe J. A. de Seife, guides the practitioner through the arbitration process with a brief history of arbitration, a step-by-step guide to arbitration, practice checklists, and forms. The revised edition of this two-volume treatise was prepared by Gabriel M. Wilner, the Thomas Kirbo Professor of Law at the University of Georgia School of Law and an assistant to Professor Domke who had long been considered this country's foremost authority on the subject of commercial arbitration law. In fact, Professor Wilner, with the assistance of the American Arbitration Association, has been responsible for the revisions to this work since its initial publication by Professor Domke in 1968.

Cost Saving Tip: Buy discounted set and let the supplementation lapse. Re-purchase at periodic intervals. Treat this product as a monograph and update the authorities you find here elsewhere.

Elkouri, Frank and Edna Asper Elkouri. **How Arbitration Works.** 7th ed. Washington, DC: Bloomberg BNA Books, 2012-date. 1 vol. (1,828 pp.). Irregular supplementation.
Cost: $325; no supplementation to date; 2004-2007: 0; 2008: $170; 2009: 0; 2010: $205; 2011: $82.00; supp. To 5th ed.: 1999: $70; 2000: 0; 2001: 0; 2002: $70; 2003: new edition;.
Long considered to be the leading work in the field, **How Arbitration Works** provides the labor practitioner with an analysis of practice and procedure in the field of labor arbitration. There is a valuable introductory chapter on arbitration and its setting which examines the possible uses for arbitration, compulsory arbitration, arbitration costs and the leading organizations in the field. Chapters also examine in depth such topics as the legal status of arbitration, the scope of labor arbitration, the arbitration tribunal, grievances--the prelude to arbitration, determining arbitrability, arbitration procedures and techniques, evidence, standards for interpreting contract language, the use of substantive rules of law, custom and past practice, management rights, seniority, discharge and discipline, safety and health, employee rights and benefits, and standards in arbitration of interest disputes. The text is heavily documented with references to decisions and orders of the NLRB and the courts, as well as statutes, regulations, books and articles.

Golann, Dwight. **Mediating Legal Disputes: Effective Strategies for Neutrals and Advocates**. Chicago: American Bar Association, Section of Dispute Resolution, 2009. 1 vol. (370 pp.).
Cost: $69.95; from $19.48 on amazon.com (2014).
Unlike most guides to mediation that assume a desire between parties to work towards a mutually satisfactory resolution of differences, this book is aimed at the resolution of serious legal disputes by parties who already have a strained relationship that stands in the way of dispute resolution. In an effort to overcome these special barriers to settlement, this book examines both traditional and non-traditional mediation strategies, often involving the services of a professional neutral who can help work through years of animosity and bitterness that have manifested themselves in the form of legal warfare. The author shows how to mediate effectively between parties who want to communicate only through lawyers, deal with hard-money bargaining techniques such as insulting first offers and other adversarial tactics, change parties' assessments of the likelihood that they will win in court, and overcome stubborn impasses with such techniques as the "confidential listener," "range" bargaining, and the "mediator's proposal." The book includes examples of the application of these techniques to many real-life mediated cases. Chapters cover everything from basic strategy and the stages of mediation, to process obstacles, psychological issues, merits barriers, resolving impasse and closure, ethical and legal issues, and advocacy at specific stages. Additional chapters apply these strategies to specific areas of practice, including employment disputes, insured claims and other monetary disputes, the intellectual property case, environmental contamination disputes, and mega-disputes and class actions. A companion DVD provides a demonstration of many of these techniques described in the text. Dwight Golann is professor of law at Suffolk University in Boston where he teaches mediation and negotiation. He is joined by a team of nine contributing authors.

Guasco, Matthew P. and Peter R. Robinson. **Principles of Negotiation**.
Irvine, CA: Entrepreneur Press, 2007. 1 vol. (203 pp.). Includes essential legal forms and documents on CD-ROM.
Cost: $32.95; from $7.99 on amazon.com (2014).
The development of superior negotiating skills can translate into better deals, increased profits, more satisfactory litigation outcomes, and less stressful conflict resolutions. The strategies and tactics revealed in this practical guide are the products of research in effective communication theory, game theory, psychology, and classroom simulations. The authors accomplish this by thoughtful examination of what every negotiator should know before the negotiation begins, competitive negotiation, cooperative negotiation, difficult negotiation situations, strategic negotiation in action, ethics in negotiation, and common problems and recommended solutions. Their discussion of the predictability of competitive negotiations involving the division of a fixed pie is particularly insightful. In these negotiations, the question of who makes the first offer is critical. While it has both advantages and disadvantages, making the first offer gives the negotiator making it the greatest opportunity to manage the recipient's expectations. In this context, the authors also explain the strategies for making an offer, what it should be, how to phrase it, and how to use psychology to anchor the offer in such a way to encourage risk avoidance. Similar analysis is applied to other forms of negotiation. This is an excellent introduction to the both the theory and practice of negotiation. Matthew Guasco is an attorney and professional mediator and an adjunct professor at Pepperdine University

School of Law. Peter Robinson is the managing director of the Straus Institute for Dispute Resolution and associate professor at Pepperdine School of Law.

Hill, Marvin F., Jr., Anthony V. Sinicropi, and Amy L. Evenson. **Winning Arbitration Advocacy**. Washington, DC: Bloomberg BNA Books, 1997. 1 vol. (552 pp.).
Cost: $75; from $22.00 on amazon.com (2014).
A useful introductory overview of labor arbitration procedures with attention to several substantive issues encountered in the course of arbitration, including drug and alcohol cases, employment discrimination disputes, and off-duty misconduct. The authors address the arbitration process generally, prehearing considerations, the presentation of the arbitration case, selected issues in litigating an arbitration case, posthearing considerations, public sector advocacy: fact-finding and interest arbitration considerations, and major mistakes made by arbitration advocates. The Appendix contains the Voluntary Labor Arbitration Rules of the American Arbitration Association. There is also a glossary of significant terms used in the arbitration arena.

Horn, Ben and Roger Hopkins, eds. **Arbitration Law Handbook**. London: informa, 2007. 1 vol. (1016 pp.).
Cost: $475; from $288.74 on amazon.com (2014).
International commercial arbitration has become an increasingly more common form of dispute resolution in cross-border contracts. Yet, practitioners trained in both the substantive law and procedural rules of one country may be obliged to arbitrate disputes in other jurisdictions and involving rules and procedures specific to the seat of the dispute. This volume assembles the arbitration rules employed in a number of leading arbitration centers across the globe, including those in Australia, Austria, Belgium, Brazil, Canada, China, France, Germany, Hong Kong, India, Ireland, Japan, Korea, Mexico, Netherlands, Norway, the Russian Federation, Singapore, Sweden, Switzerland, Ukraine, United Arab Emirates, United Kingdom and the United States. The volume also reproduces each country's separate maritime arbitration rules where these apply. The volume also includes the United Nations Commission on International Trade Law (UNCITRAL) Model Law on International Commercial Arbitration (1994), which parties may designate for the conduct of the procedural aspects of a dispute, the UNCITRAL Arbitration Rules (1976), the World Intellectual Property Organization (WIPO) Arbitration and Expedited Arbitration Rules (2002), the International Centre for Settlement of Investment Disputes (ICSID) Arbitration Rules (1965), and the United Nations Convention on the Recognition and Enforcement of Foreign Arbitral Awards--"New York Convention" (1958), the Federal Arbitration Act, and the Maritime Arbitration Rules. Each set of rules is accompanied by a brief introduction that explains relevant treaty obligations, the primary arbitral bodies, and the principal laws in force. An essential reference book for lawyers and other parties involved in international arbitration, cross-border contracts, or international shipping.

Littler Mendelson. **Employment Arbitration Agreements: A Practical Guide**. New York: Wolters Kluwer Law & Business, 2009-date. 1 vol. Looseleaf format.
Cost: OUT-OF-PRINT; was $349 (2014).
Enacted by Congress in 1925, the Federal Arbitration Act provides for judicial facilitation of private dispute resolution through arbitration, and is applicable in both state and federal courts. In recent years, decisions of the U.S. Supreme Court have affirmed arbitration as an efficient and cost-effective alternative to litigation. For these and other reasons, employers have often included arbitration provisions in their employee agreements. Arbitration programs are usually created in the wake of these contractual agreements. A critical question, then, is to what extent these arbitration agreements should reflect the substantive and procedural requirements applicable in the courts. This volume, written by lawyers at the firm of Littler Mendelson, provides guidance to lawyers, corporate counsel and managers in designing employment arbitration programs in non-union settings that meet the procedural guidelines of the jurisdictions in which they are to be implemented. The authors consider other means of non-jury dispute resolution compared with arbitration, the nature of arbitration, the pros and cons of contractual arbitration, state v. federal law, coverage of the arbitration agreement, specific arbitration clauses, and sample arbitration clauses. A variety of useful appendices provide 50-state surveys of the laws and experiences applicable across the country. The volume includes numerous references to applicable state and federal statutes, and cases.

Menkel-Meadow, Carrie, Lela Porter Love, and Andrea Kupfer Schneider. **Mediation: Practice, Policy, and Ethics**. 3d ed. New York: Wolters Kluwer Law & Business, 2013. 1 vol. (672 pp.). Paperbound.
Cost: $116; from $100.00 on amazon.com (2014).
This law school text is designed for use in classes in alternative dispute resolution. The authors view mediation, or facilitated negotiation, as having reached an important point of development in the modern legal and educational environment. It is an environment no longer left solely to adversarial modes of dispute resolution, involving argument, case analysis, and adjudication, but embracing self-empowerment and "process pluralism" in the form of client counseling, negotiation, mediation, advocacy, "neutraling," facilitation, and dispute system design. As such, this volume is dedicated to the study, teaching and performance of all the roles involved in the mediation process, including the foundations of mediation, the mediation process, and the applications of the mediation process. Among the topics covered are processes for handling conflicts and disputes, animating values for conflict and dispute resolution, negotiation, negotiator style, mediation concepts and models, representation in mediation, mediator skills and practices, legal and policy issues in mediation, confidentiality, ethical issues, applications, counseling and planning, multiparty mediation, consensus building, facilitated processes, mediation, arbitration and other hybrid processes, international mediation, and thinking critically about mediation. The appendices include a number of model acts, standards, and guidelines. The text is richly illustrated with excerpts from the writings of numerous scholars and practitioners in the field. The volume also includes Notes and Questions useful in a classroom setting. Useful as both an academic text and as an excellent practitioner review of important concepts and strategies.

Miller, Henry G. **Art of Advocacy: Settlement**. New York: Matthew Bender & Co., 1983-date. 1 vol. Looseleaf format and eBook.
Cost: $430; supplementation: 1994: $103; 1995: $103; 1996: $103; 1997: $103; 1998: $110; 1999: $117; 2000: $125; 2001: $134; 2002: $144; 2003: $152; 2004: $152; 2005: $164; 2006: $184; 2007: $207: 2008: $230; 2009: $255; 2010: $284; 2011: $295; 2012: $330; 2013: $330; 2014: $330.
This is a comprehensive guide to the settlement of personal injury cases. The author, an experienced trial lawyer with the firm of Clark, Gigliardi & Miller of White Plains, New York is a Past President of the New York Bar Association and Director of the New York State Trial Lawyers Association. His philosophy of settlement is predicated on the notion that it takes a good trial lawyer to be a good settler. Courtroom veterans "will find you out if you only come to settle," he argues. He suggests that are no definitive rules or formulas for settlement. It is more art than science, requiring good judgment. The individual chapters are both general and specific. There are general chapters examining such topics as the wisdom of settlement, impediments, dealing with your client, evaluating the case, bargaining, dealing with insurance companies, and settlement techniques. Specific chapters cover settlement in products liability and medical malpractice cases. The chapter on structured settlement, written by Richard G. Halpern, is laced with specific examples. The volume also examines the law of settlement, including bad faith, the attorney's role in settlement negotiations, Mary Carter agreements, the partial settlement, documents of settlement, and the ethics of settlement, concluding with the author's "Ten Commandments of Settlement." This volume is accompanied by **Present Value and Total Payout Tables,** also by Richard G. Halpern, a valuable pamphlet which explains the calculation of present values and the approximation of the present value of a future income stream, together with present value and total payout tables. These can be of significant benefit to those handling personal injury and wrongful death actions.

Cost Savings Tips: The volumes in this series should simply be treated as monographs and re-purchased at periodic intervals, if necessary, in order to avoid the ongoing cost of supplementation.

Newman, Lawrence W. and Richard D. Hill, eds. **The Leading Arbitrators' Guide to International Arbitration**. 2d ed. Huntington, NY: Juris Publishing, Inc., 2008. 1 vol. (860 pp.).
Cost: $175; from $116.01 on amazon.com; no supplementation to date (2014).
Designed as practical and practice-oriented tool for international arbitrators, this contribution to the literature provides a coherent collection of chapters authored by some of the leading representatives of the international arbitration community. It was the intent of the editors to produce a work combining the characteristics of a comprehensive course book with those of a full-blown apprenticeship. The emphasis is upon "very large, financially important, lawyer-driven processes, mostly institutional in structure, of a kind practiced especially in the larger commercial centers of the Northern Hemisphere." The chapters commence with a history of international commercial arbitration, with an emphasis on the years since 1950, during which the various types of commercial arbitration have radically, and rather abruptly, changed. Other chapters discuss the tribunal's appointment, the party-appointed arbitrator, the role of the chairman, the duties of the arbitrator, objections to jurisdiction, arbitration involving states, organizing an international arbitration: practice pointers, ADR and arbitration, discovery, conduct of the hearings, the tribunal's deliberations, the arbitral awards, and confidentiality, among others. The team of highly qualified and experienced contributors are arbitrators from Australia, Belgium, Canada, Denmark, England, France, Germany, Italy, The Netherlands, Italy, Spain, Sweden, Switzerland and the United States. They, therefore, represent both the common law and civil law traditions. The book's intended purpose is to serve the needs of those who may be called to serve as international arbitrators and those who serve as advocates before such bodies. Bringing together a discussion of the various international arbitration doctrines, agreements, and protocols, this volume is undoubtedly the most significant contribution to the field since the publication of the 1996 UNCITRAL **Notes on Organizing Arbitral Proceedings**. Lawrence W. Newman has been a partner in the New York office of Baker & McKenzie and the author/editor of four books on international litigation/arbitration. Richard Hill is a Partner in the Dispute Resolution Department of Fulbright & Jaworski, London.

Nolan-Haley, Jacqueline M. **Alternative Dispute Resolution in a Nutshell**. 4th ed. St. Paul, MN: West Group, 2013. 1 vol. (552 pp.). No supplementation between editions. Available from West Academic.
Cost: $41; from $38.75 on amazon.com (2014).
This succinct law student-oriented text was written with the goal of encouraging students to view litigation, not as the norm, but as just one means of resolving legal disputes. The author, an Associate Clinical Professor of Law at Fordham University School of Law, discusses the background of the ADR movement, negotiation, mediation, arbitration, dispute resolution in the court system, and hybrid dispute resolution procedures. The appendices contain a variety of federal rules, standards, and acts governing arbitration and other forms of ADR. An inexpensive alternative to the lengthier and more frequently supplemented works.

Oehmke, Thomas. **Commercial Arbitration**. 3d ed. St. Paul, MN: West Group (Clark Boardman Callaghan), 2008-2009-date. 5 vols. Annual cumulative pocket supplements. ProView eBook also available.
Cost: $1,781; supplementation: 1992: $58; 1993: $67; 1994: $74; 1995: $150; 1996: $102; 1997: $107.10; 1998: $161; 1999: $191.50; 2000: $186.50; 2001: $220; 2002: $263.50; 2003: $270; 2004: $475; 2005: $580; 2006: $616; 2007: $492; 2008: $1,004; 2009: $1,079.50; 2010: $1,203; 2011: $791; 2012: $1,345; 2013: $1,339; **Monthly Assured Print Price (APP):** $130/$1,560; ProView eBook: $1,635.00.
Formerly published by Lawyers Cooperative, this five-volume work provides a basic overview of commercial arbitration practice, both domestic and international, with appropriate checklists. Appendix includes both AAA and non-AAA forms, litigation forms, federal arbitration statutes, and reprints of various arbitration rules, including those for the construction industry, employment matters, accident claims, real estate matters, election and patent arbitration.
The set was completed revised and expanded in 2008-2009.

Cost saving tip: High cost of supplementation is unnecessary for a work of this nature. Drop the standing order and re-purchase the discounted volume at infrequent intervals for substantial savings. Naturally, the eBook format locks you into annual updating costs, which should be entered into with great trepidation, particularly if the base print version provides you with most of what you need.

Poon, Gary P. **The Corporate Counsel's Guide to Mediation**. Chicago: American Bar Association, 2010. 1 vol. (131 pp.). Paperbound.
Cost: $79.95 ($63.95 to members); from $30.50 on amazon.com (2014).
Mediation is a form of alternative dispute resolution (ADR) designed to help parties settle disputes. The International Chamber of Commerce defines mediation as a "settlement technique in which the neutral acts as a facilitator to help the parties try to arrive at a negotiated settlement of their dispute." It does not include attempts made by the judge to settle a dispute within the course of a judicial proceeding. And it differs from arbitration in that the decision of the mediator is not binding on the parties, as is the decision of an arbitrator. The mediator at all times maintains his or her neutrality and impartiality. The parties play an active role in mediation, identifying interests, suggesting solutions, making decisions regarding he proposals made by the other party. Conciliation is like mediation in that the proposed solution is not binding. But in conciliation, the conciliator plays a more active role in making an actual proposal for settlement. To some observers, it comes down to a matter of style, but with the conciliator playing a more active role. This brief volume provides an overview of the entire mediation process, including a discussion of mediation as an alternative form of dispute resolution, the drafting of mediation clauses, court-directed mediations, selection of a mediator, pre-mediation preparation, the mediation session, post-mediation follow-up, cross cultural mediations, and conclusions. The Appendices include a sample confidentiality agreement, sample mediation rules, and the Model Standards of Conduct. The author is a lawyer, business advisor and a court-approved mediator for the District of Columbia Superior Court.

Rhoades, Rufus V., Daniel M. Kolkey, and Richard Chernick, eds. **Practitioner's Handbook on International Arbitration and Mediation**. 3d ed. Huntington, NY: Juris Publishing, Inc., 2012. 1 vol. (1,006 pp.). Also available in an eBook version.
Cost: $225 (print or eBook) (2014).
A unified collection of in-depth articles on international arbitration and
written by experienced practitioners and experts in the field. The twenty-one chapters are grouped into three Parts which cover: (1) arbitration; (2) mediation; (3) chapters devoted to the description and analysis of arbitration and mediation in nine countries, including Canada, China, Hong Kong, England, France, Germany, Japan, Sweden, and Switzerland. The general arbitration and mediation chapters cover why arbitrate, drafting an enforceable arbitration clause, how to commence an international arbitration, selecting the site for arbitration, procedural issues to consider, practical considerations for conducting the hearing, the award, enforcement of international arbitral awards, becoming an international arbitrator, international mediation basics, initiating an international mediation, and representing clients in arbitration. Each chapter includes expert commentary and practice hints, as well as numerous citations to cases, statutes, arbitration decisions, rules, and secondary sources. And, unlike many compilations of chapters by numerous authors, these chapters are part of a unified whole, with a consistent format throughout and numerous cross-references. A companion CD-ROM contains numerous original source documents in support of the text, all of which are listed in the book's table of contents. Twenty-one specialists in the field of international arbitration contributed to this volume.

Robbins, David E. **Securities Arbitration Procedure Manual**. 5th ed. Charlottesville, VA: LexisNexis, 2001-date. 2 vols. Looseleaf format. Annual supplementation. Also available as e-Book.
Cost: $241 (print or eBook): supplementation: 2002: $93; 2003: $97; 2004-2007: 0; 2008: $135; 2009: $149; 2010: $157; 2011: $163; 2012: $174; 2013: $180.
A systematic overview of the primary issues that arise in the course of a securities arbitration dispute, as well as a discussion of case evaluation, and the preparation and presentation of cases before arbitration panels. Chapters include: arbitration versus litigation, the arbitration agreement, a review of the law, arbitrability of securities disputes, case evaluation, attorneys, experts and pre-filing issues, commencing arbitration, responsive pleadings and motions, discovery at the SRO and the AAA, arbitrator at the SROs and AAA, hearing rules explained, hearing presentation techniques, deliberation and award, available relief and effect of awards, industry arbitration, and securities arbitration. The appendices contain a number of state and federal arbitration statutes, private rules of procedure, and arbitrator's guides and manuals.

St. Antoine, Theodore J., ed. **The Common Law of the Workplace**. 2d ed. Washington, DC: Bloomberg BNA Books, 2005. 1 vol. (454 pp.).
Cost: $125; no supplementation; from $84.70 on amazon.com (2014).
A bold attempt to summarize some of the leading arbitral principles developed in the field of grievance and arbitration since the founding of the National Academy of Arbitrators in 1947. The work's sixteen authors and editors have not attempted to set forth definitive rules, however, due to the nature of specific contractual relationships which govern the workplace. The body of the work consists of short, black letter statements which are accompanied by comments, many with citations to relevant case law. Other entries also include illustrations, and references. Topics include practice and procedure, contract interpretation, management and union rights, job assignments, seniority, discipline and discharge, wages and hours, safety and health, fringe benefits, and remedies.

Senger, Jeffrey M. **Federal Dispute Resolution: Using ADR with the United States Government**. San Francisco, CA: Jossey-Bass, in cooperation with the American Bar Association, Section of Dispute Resolution, 2004. 1 vol. (401 pp.).

Cost: $50; from $2.97 on amazon.com (2014).
Government officials and citizens are increasingly looking for alternatives to litigation because the costs of litigation are too high, too time-consuming, and often leave the underlying controversies unresolved. The use of alternative dispute resolution (ADR), involving the use of neutral professionals, often results in solutions which are quicker, cheaper and more satisfying to all parties. Moreover, giving opposing parties the opportunity to talk directly with each other helps them identify their underlying interests and craft more satisfactory and creative solutions. This guide to alternative dispute resolution addresses disputes involving the federal government both for those who represent the government and those who have disputes with the government. The author discusses the process of selecting cases and processes for federal ADR and the process of selecting and hiring neutral professionals. Additional chapters discuss preparing for federal ADR, advocacy, federal workplace and contracting cases, confidentiality, Federal ADR program design, management and training, and the evaluation of Federal ADR programs. Appendices include the text of the Administrative Dispute Resolution Acts of 1996 and 1998, and other useful federal documents. Jeffrey Senger is senior counsel in the Office of Dispute Resolution at the U.S. Dept. of Justice. A faculty member of Harvard Law School's Program on Negotiation, and the National Institute of Trial Advocacy, he trains federal lawyers around the country in negotiation and ADR.

Teply, Larry L. **Legal Negotiation in a Nutshell**. 2d ed. St. Paul, MN: West, 2005. 1 vol. (351 pp.). No supplementation between editions. Available from West Academic.
Cost: $41; from $30.38 on amazon.com (2014).
This brief volume discusses negotiation in a variety of legal contexts. The author, Professor of Law at Creighton University, provides an overview of the obligations and rules governing the representation of clients in various legal negotiations, including contractual transactions, civil disputes, labor-management negotiations, criminal cases, divorce and domestic relations cases and international legal disputes. He also addresses such general matters as case evaluation, basic negotiating styles and strategies, the stages of legal negotiation, opening the negotiation, bargaining, information exchange, tactics, and persuasion. An inexpensive alternative to some of the longer and more frequently supplemented works.

Additional titles in the field of Arbitration are available from the following publishers: American Bar Association, Wolters Kluwer Law & Business, Bloomberg BNA, Bloomberg BNA Books, Informa, Jossey-Bass, Juris Publishing, JurisNet, Kluwer Academic, Lexis Publishing, Lloyd's of London, LRP Publications, National Institute for Trial Advocacy (NITA), Oxford University Press, Thomson Reuters West, West Academic, John Wiley & Sons. See Appendix B for addresses and telephone numbers.

Arts, Entertainment and Sports Law

Champion, Walter T. **Fundamentals of Sports Law.** 2d ed. St. Paul, MN: West (Clark Boardman Callaghan), 2004-date. 1 vol. (535 pp.).
Cost: $255; supplementation: 1993: $55.50; 1995: $87.50; 1996: $99.95; 1997: $105; 1998: $111; 1999: $120; 2000: $130; 2001: $153.50; 2002: $190; 2003: $0; 2004: $225 (includes new 2d ed.); 2005: $109.50; 2006: 0; 2007: $69; 2008: $77; 2009: $91; 2010: $100; 2011: $110; 2012: $130; 2013: $139; **Monthly Assured Print Price (APP):** $15/$180.
A useful introductory text covering the law of both amateur and professional sports. Written by an Associate Professor of Law at Texas Southern University School of Law who teaches sports law, Walter Champion's work addresses six main subject areas: torts, constitutional implications, contracts, financial considerations, labor law and antitrust. The Appendices include a few sample forms and a Subject Index. As with a number of the one-volume subject specific textbooks formerly published by Lawyers Cooperative and now taken over by sister company Clark Boardman Callaghan, this volume employs a large type face and generous use of white space. Consequently, the number of words per page is considerably less than that found in other CBC titles (e.g. Uberstein) or books from other legal publishers. Coverage is broad, but lacks the depth of competing works. There are adequate citations to primary and secondary authorities and, more significantly, references to relevant articles or books in the West Group's Total Client-Service Library.

Champion, Walter T. **Sports Law in a Nutshell.** 4th ed. St. Paul, MN: West Group, 2009. 1 vol. (325 pp.). Available from West Academic.
Cost: $41; from $9.99 on amazon.com; Kindle: $21.52 (2014).
This brief analysis of sports law in West's Nutshell Series is intended for use as a course text, a student outline or a primer for future sports professionals. Includes discussion and analysis of the most common aspects of the field, including sports contracts, agents, financial considerations, labor law, antitrust matters, torts, participant injuries, spectator injuries, school liability, coach liability, referee liability, defamation, tort defenses, workers' compensation, criminal liability, amateur sports, eligibility, the handicapped athlete, college scholarships, international sports, discipline and penalties, drug testing, and sex discrimination. The Appendix includes a uniform player's contract.

Conway, Michael M. and Miki Vucic Tesija. **Media Law Litigation: The Effective Use of Depositions**. Huntington, NY: Juris Publishing, 2005. 1 vol. (369 pp.).
Cost: $125; from $11.00 on amazon.com; no supplementation (2014).
A practical guide to taking depositions in defamation, privacy, and media cases, this volume addresses a number of both traditional and cutting-edge actions arising through advances in technology, including broadcasting over the Internet and the use of electronic surveillance equipment or wiretaps in newsgathering. Following a useful introduction to media cases involving defamation and libel, chapters examine the necessity for depositions, special considerations involved in media law

depositions, the essential elements of a defamation claim, defenses to defamation, challenging defenses to defamation, the plaintiff as "fair game," claims against news organizations for publishing wiretapped communications, and privacy issues in media law litigation. Included are numerous sample questions and answers employed in examinations of plaintiffs and defendants, as well as citations to relevant state and federal court decisions, and a subject index.

Creech, Kenneth C. **Electronic Media Law and Regulation**. 6th ed. New York: Routledge, 2014. 1 vol. (372 pp.). Paperbound.
Cost: $79.95; from $62.04 on amazon.com; kindle: $63.96 (2014).
The textbook provides a broad, case-based, overview of media law in the United States, beginning with an examination of the First Amendment and embracing an analysis of broadcast regulation, cable and satellite (DSS) television regulation, regulation of electronic media content, regulation of commercial practices, media ownership, intellectual property issues, privacy and electronic media, right of publicity, defamation libel and the media, the conflicting rights involved in free press versus fair trial, issues in information gathering, and communications regulation of new technologies and the Internet. Following a discussion of the U.S. legal system generally, and the federal administrative structure specifically, the author examines the regulatory environment governing communications, particularly the Federal Communications Commission (FCC) and its seven bureaus: Media Bureau, Wireline Competition Bureau, Consumer and Governmental Affairs Bureau, the International Bureau, the Enforcement Bureau, the Wireless Telecommunications Bureau, and the Public Safety and Homeland Security Bureau. The text is accompanied by numerous case studies, and excerpts of U.S. Supreme Court and lower federal court decisions. The text is intended to provide students in journalism and media studies programs with a basic grounding in the legal environmental governing various forms of electronic media in the United States. Kenneth C. Creech is Fairbanks Professor and Department Head of Media Arts at Butler University in Indianapolis, with experience in both commercial and public broadcasting.

Darraby, Jessica L. **Art, Artifact & Architecture Law.** St. Paul, MN: Thomson/West (Clark Boardman Callaghan). 2013-14 edition. 2 vols. Paperbound (formerly looseleaf). Annual replacement editions.
Cost: 2013-14 ed.: $824; supplementation to previous editions: 1996: $95; 1997: $120; 1998: 0; 1999: $260; 2000: $141; 2001: $163; 2003: $257; 2004: $288; 2005: $315; 2006: $313; 2007: $348; 2008: $462; 2010 ed: $756 ($605 to subscribers); **Monthly Assured Print Price (APP):** $75/$900.
This comprehensive treatment of the law regarding the visual arts encompasses the substantive, procedural and evidentiary elements of the field. The author, a member of the California bar and an adjunct professor of law at Pepperdine University School of Law, brings wide-ranging experience to the subject as a court-appointed expert in the area of art law, former art gallery director, and art law columnist for the **Los Angeles Daily Journal**. This volume provides wide-ranging coverage of art issues in relationship to taxation, bankruptcy, copyright, fraud and forgery, import/export, international trade and cultural property, RICO, trademarks, trusts and estates, and the Uniform Commercial Code, among others. It examines such art topics as artist-dealer agreements, auctions, corporate collectors, historical preservation, museums, provenance, public art, valuation and appraisals. Its coverage also extends to the 1990 Visual Artists Rights Act which amended the copyright law to protect certain categories of visual art from destruction and mutilation and preserve the moral rights of artists. The Appendices contain a variety of federal and state laws and regulations and international conventions impacting the world of art, including the Harmonized Tariff Schedules of the United States, the Convention on Cultural Property Implementation Act, the UNESCO Convention on Means of Prohibiting and Preventing Illicit Import, Expert and Transfer Ownership of Cultural Property, and the Hague Convention for the Protection of Cultural Property in the Event of Armed Conflict.

Cost-Saving Tip: Note that the **Monthly Assured Print Price** is higher than the actual cost of the annual replacement volumes. This is an ideal candidate for the "buy and cancel standing order" program. Simply re-purchase at a later date when you want a more up-to-date set, thereby saving yourself thousands in unnecessary supplementation costs.

Dienes, C. Thomas, Lee Levine and Robert C. Lind. **Newsgathering and the Law**. 3d ed. Newark, NJ: LexisNexis, 2005-date. 1 vol. (1,296 pp.).
Cost: $199 (print or e-book); from $22 on amazon.com; supplementation: 2006: $48; 2007: $52; 2008: $45; 2009: $53; 2010: 0; 2011: 0; 2012: 0; 2013: $58; 2d ed.: 2000: $35; 2001: $50; 2002: $51; 2003: $68; 2004: 0; supplementation to 1st edition: 1998: $40; 1999: $40.
A scholarly examination of the law as it applies to newsgathering and freedom of the press. This is an ideal tool for attorneys representing news organizations, as well as reporters, editors and others employed by media organizations. It is also an excellent source of information for reporters about access to specific governmental activities and the means of newsgathering under state and federal laws. The individual chapters examine: fashioning the newsgathering right, access to judicial proceedings: the constitutional foundations, access to judicial proceedings: the lower courts, cameras in the courtroom, access to judicial records: criminal proceedings, access to judicial records: civil proceedings, access to participants in the judicial process, access to public places and events, access to executive and legislative branches, access to federal government records, access to state government records, newsgathering in nongovernmental places, the means of newsgathering, evolution of the journalists' privilege, state shield laws and federal codifications, and constitutional and common law privileges. The authors are professors at George Washington University Law School and Southwestern University School of Law. A unique contribution to the literature on media law, this volume contains exhaustive citations to primary law and the secondary literature.

DuBoff, Leonard D. **Art Law in a Nutshell.** 4th ed. St. Paul, MN: West, 2006. 1 vol. (350 pp.). Available from West Academic.
Cost: $41; from $37.21 on amazon.com (2014).
Leonard D. DuBoff, a leading expert on art law and author of the massive two-volume **Deskbook of Art Law** (Oceana), has written this concise overview of the subject intended for the

law student and practicing attorney, but also accessible to the lay person. The chapter coverage includes art: the customs definition, art: the international movement, art: the victim of war, art as an investment, auctions, authentications, insurance, tax problems: collectors and dealers, the working artist, aid to the arts, tax problems: artists, copyright, trademark, moral and economic rights, freedom of expression, and museums. In keeping with the role of the Nutshell series, there are only selective citations to court decisions

DuBoff, Leonard D. and Sally H. Caplan. **The Deskbook of Art Law.** 2d ed. New York: Oxford University Press, 1993-date. 2 vols. Looseleaf format. Print-on-demand. Supplemented 1-2 times per year.
Cost: $644; supplementation: 1997: $225; 1998: $150; 1999: $335; 2000: $190; 2001: $185; 2002: 0; 2003: $380 (2); 2004: $570 (3); 2005: $565 (3); 2006: $390 (2); 2007: $390; 2008: $210; 2009: $675 (3); 2010: $460 (2); 2011: $490 (2); 2012: $240 (1); 2013: $247 (1).
Intended as a combination practitioner's text and caseBook, this massive compendium embraces all aspects of art law, including the custom definition, international movement of art, art as victim of war, protest art, censorship, obscenity, pornography, government assistance to the arts, art as an investment, authentication, insurance, auctions, tax problems, collectors, dealers, tax problems for artists, copyright, the working artist, moral and economic rights, museum organization, and internal museum problems. The Appendices include a number of U.S. and foreign art laws and international treaties, contracts and agreements, fire insurance policies, museum policies, etc. There are Tables of Cases, Statutes, Treaties, Conventions and Resolutions. There is an extensive Table of Secondary Authorities, both legal and non-legal, and a Subject Index. Many cases listed in the Table of Cases have been reproduced in whole or in part. There are extensive citations to primary and secondary authority and numerous illustrations of works of art. Leonard DuBoff is a Professor of Law at Lewis & Clark's College's Northwestern School of Law who has dedicated his professional life to the specialty of art law. Both the first edition of this work, issued in 1977, and its 1984 supplement were published by Federal Publications. The second edition was published by Oceana in 1993. With the purchase of Oceana by Oxford University Press this title is now published by Oxford Law, and is now available from Print-On-Demand.

Cost Saving Tip: With the cost of supplementation, you are better off dropping the standing order and placing this volume on a cyclical re-ordering schedule.

Farber, Donald C., ed. **Entertainment Industry Contracts**. New York: Matthew Bender & Co., 1986-date. 10 vols. Looseleaf format. Periodic updates. Also available on CD-ROM (see entry, below).
Cost: $2,341 (print or eBook) (includes annual subscription); renewal: 1996: $637; 1997: $637; 1998: $670; 1999: $695; 2000: $740; 2001: $792; 2002: $848; 2003: $891; 2004: $936; 2005: $1,002; 2006: $1,073; 2007: $1,137; 2008: $1,228; 2009: $1,302; 2010: $1,341; 2011: $1,408; 2012: $1,565; 2013: $1,716; 2014: $1,741; eBook: $2,128; 2014: $1,742.
The most exhaustive and authoritative source on the market for entertainment industry contracts and commentary designed for use by attorneys, agents, producers. Each section has been drafted by an expert in the field and includes contracts, alternative clauses, instructions, and commentary. More than 300 contracts encompass such major industry areas as motion pictures, music, television, book publishing, art, theater, electronic publishing, and sports, including multimedia and the Internet. Includes a table of contract clauses, and table of forms by party.

Cost Saving Tip: Allow the print subscription to lapse after one year and re-purchase it at some future date. The cyclical re-purchase of Matthew Bender print publications can save you significant supplementation costs over the course of your practice. These savings are not available with the CD-ROM and Internet formats.

Ferris, Charles D., Frank W. Lloyd, and Thomas J. Casey. **Telecommunications Regulation: Cable, Broadcasting, Satellite, and the Internet.** New York: Matthew Bender & Co., 1983-date. 4 vols. Looseleaf format. Updated 2-3 times annually. Also availableas eBook.
Cost: $1,747 (includes annual subscription); renewal: 1997: $490; 1998: $490; 1999: $505; 2000: $540; 2001: $578 2002: $619; 2003: $650; 2004: 2005: $731; 2006: $783; 2007: $846; 2008: $914; 2009: $983; 2010: $998; 2011: $1,048; 2012: $1,111; 2013: $1,167; 2014: $1,273; eBook: $1,588; renewal: 2014: $1,273.
This treatise provides detailed coverage of the substantive, procedural, and strategic aspects of the law governing the cable television industry, and video technologies, with a special emphasis on the Telecommunications Act of 1996. The authors explore such topics as franchising of cable television systems, local and federal regulation of cable television, copyright issues, antitrust, defamation, securities and tax issues, international developments, and the regulation of such new technologies as the Internet, high definition television (HDTV), subscription television (STV), multi-point distribution service (MDS), direct broadcast satellite (DBS), satellite master antenna television (SMATV), and electronic publishing. The work includes the text of relevant federal statutes and regulations as well as sample FCC, Copyright Office, and state forms. The authors are associated with the Washington, D.C-based law firm of Mintz, Levin, Cohn, Ferris, Glovsky and Popeo, P.C. Formerly entitled **Cable Television Law: A Video Communications Practice Guide**.

Fischer, Mark A., E. Gabriel Perle, and John Taylor Williams. **Perle & Williams on Publishing Law**. 4th ed. New York: Wolters Kluwer Law & Business, 2013-date. 2 vols. Looseleaf format. Annual supplementation.
Cost: $535; from $325; no supplementation to date; 3d ed.: 2000: 0; 2001: $164; 2002: $180; 2003: $248; 2004: $254; 2005: $250; 2006: $263; 2007: $280; 2008: $300; 2009: $325; 2010: $348; 2011: $372; 2012: $398; 2013: $426 & new ed.
A complete and authoritative guide to the legal issues and practical aspects of all segments of the publishing industry, including books, newspapers, magazines, audio, visual, multimedia, and electronic publishing. Designed as a desktop

reference for publishing industry professionals and those representing publishing interests, this two-volume set provides valuable information on such timely issues as copyright, privacy, defamation, right of publicity, contract negotiation, sales and marketing policies, obscenity, licensing, consumer protection, fraud, advertising, liability due to negligence, and much more. The text not only includes citations to scores of relevant cases, statutes and regulations, but is accompanied by dozens of sample guidelines, checklists, releases, and model agreements. E. Gabriel Perle is Senior Counsel at Ohlandt, Greeley, Ruggiero & Perle in Stamford, CT and former Corporate Vice President-Law and Chief Counsel at Time, Inc. where he supervised the legal affairs of a number of leading publishing ventures, including Fortune, Sports Illustrated, Book-of-the-Month Club, Home Box Office, and Little, Brown and Company. John Taylor Williams is a partner and director of the Publishing and Entertainment Law Group at Palmer & Dodge in Boston. He brings wide experience representing national publishers of books, newspapers, and magazines, as well as producers of television and film. He has written extensively on publishing, libel, and First Amendment issues.

Fisher, Jim. **Ten Percent of Nothing: The Case of the Literary Agent from Hell**. Carbondale: Southern Illinois University Press, 2004. 1 vol. (211 pp.).
Cost: $27.50; from $5.85 on amazon.com (2014).
A fascinating look at the inside world of literary agents through the examination of one agent whose fraudulent operations and vanity press bilked would-be authors of $1.5 million as well as their hopes and dreams of literary glory. Jim Fisher, a professor in the Department of Political Science and Criminal Justice at Edinboro University of Pennsylvania, is a graduate of Vanderbilt University School of Law, a former FBI agent, and author of six non-fiction mystery books. This book examines the case of Dorothy L. Deering, a high school graduate with no publishing or editing experience, who operated a fee-based literary agency out of her garage and racked up more than $1.5 million in reading and marketing fees before Fisher's investigative journalism and an FBI investigation led to her conviction and a 46-month prison sentence. This is a fascinating look into the world of literary agents, vanity publishing, and publishing contracts.

Fremlin, Robert and Michael Landau. **Entertainment Law.** Rev. ed. St. Paul, MN: Thomson/West Clark Boardman Callaghan), 2007-date. 1 vol. (1,050 pp.) Annual pocket part.
Cost: $321; supplementation: 1993: $57; 1994: $65; 1995: $75; 1996: $87; 1997: $92; 1998: $97; 1999: $105; 2000: $114; 2001: $132; 2002: $161; 2003: $175; 2004: $175; 2005: $175.00; 2006: $215; 2007: $75; 2008: $83.50; 2009: $94.50; 2010: $104; 2011: $114.50; 2012: $166; 2013: $136; **Monthly Assured Print Price (APP):** $17/$204.
Written by Robert Fremlin, an attorney with the San Francisco firm of Lillick & Charles, this is a selective discussion and analysis of the law of entertainment, encompassing the performers' credits and billing, defamation, privacy, publicity, copyright, trademarks and unfair competition, performers' agreements, representing performers, and incitement. The author's analysis in accompanied by a lucid summary of applicable court decisions, particularly those from the Courts of Appeals and U.S. Supreme Court. The text is supported by extensive citations to court decisions.

Greenberg, Martin J. **Sports Law Practice.** 3d ed. Charlottesville, VA: LexisNexis, 2009-date. 2 vols. Annual pocket parts.
Cost: $370; supplementation: 2009: $93; 2010: $106; 2011: $112; 2012: $120; 2013: $124; 1st ed.: 1993: $60; 1994: $65; 1995: 0; 1996: $90; 1997: $100; 1998: 2d ed.; 1999: $70; 2000: $70; 2001: $50; 2002: $51; 2003: $61; 2004: $65; 2005: $65; 2006: $69; 2007: $73; 2008: $79; e-book: $370.
An indispensable reference for the sports attorney, player agent or manager. Provides both coverage of the legal issues involved and relevant practice aids. The text examines such issues as regulation of amateur and professional athletics, legal relationships in professional sports, sports contracts, antitrust aspects of sports law, collective bargaining, injury liability, and taxation of sports activities. There is analysis of contractual issues, including advice on how to structure contracts and addendums, sample forms, checklists, a discussion of ethical considerations, tax planning, and the qualifications and regulations of sports agents. Supplementation costs for LexisNexis titles tend to be on the low side for the industry. Thus, a standing order to this title is recommended.

Heinke, Rex S. **Media Law**. Washington, DC: Bloomberg BNA Books, 1994-date. 1 vol. (632 pp.). Periodic supplementation.
Cost: $275 (includes current supplement); supplementation: 2000: $125; 2001-2013: 0.
A detailed treatise on the law as it relates to information gathering and publication in its various forms. A particular useful tool for the attorney suing or representing media organizations. The author discusses such subjects as news gathering, defamation, false light, private facts, intrusion, trespass, wiretapping, appropriation and the right of publicity, media liability for false advertisements, imitation and incitement, application of general laws to the media, prior restraints, commercial speech, time, place and manner restrictions, access to the media, confidential sources and related problems. Contains extensive citations to applicable cases and statutory law, as well, as a case table and index. The author, a partner in the Los Angels-based form of Greines, Martin, Stein & Richland, has represented the Los Angeles Times, the Washington Post, The New York Times, NBC, Paramount Pictures, and King World, among other media clients.

LDRC 50-State Survey: Media Privacy and Related Law. Edited by the Libel Defense Resource Center, Inc. New York: Media Law Resource Center, Inc., 2014. 1 vol. (1,523 pp.). Published annually in July. Paperbound.
Cost: 2014-2015 ed.: $175.00 (members); $225 (non-members) (2014).
A state-by-state survey of the basic law of privacy and related tort claims against the media. Individual surveys describe and analyze the state of the law in each of the fifty states, the District of Columbia, and all eleven federal circuits, drawing upon the expertise of practitioners in each jurisdiction. An additional survey covers the Federal law of electronic eavesdropping. Each survey follows a uniform format laid out in the front of the volume

and references both case and statutory law. Topics covered include false light, private facts, intrusion, eavesdropping hidden cameras, misappropriation, right of publicity, infliction of emotional distress, prima facie tort, injurious falsehood, unfair competition, conspiracy, tortious interference with contract, and negligent media publication. Chiefly useful to attorneys representing media organizations. The LDRC also publishes the **LDRC 50-State Survey: Media Libel Law, 2013-2014** (Nov. 2013).

Lerner, Ralph E. and Judith Bresler. **Art Law: The Guide for Collectors, Investors, Dealers. and Artists**. 4th ed. New York: Practising Law Institute, 2012. 2 vols. (2,074 pp.) Also available on Kindle. Revised as necessary.
Cost: $295; no supplementation to date; from $175.91 on amazon.com; $170.52 on Kindle (2014).
This is a three-volume guide to the legal implications of art transactions which can serve as a valuable resource for artists, collectors, investors, dealers, museum administrators and lawyers representing various arts related interests. Among the legal issues covered are questions of title, auctions, museum loans, financing, copyright and authenticity, moral rights, First Amendment freedom of expression considerations, resale rights, charitable donations, the impact of the Uniform Commercial Code upon art transactions, tax and estate planning considerations, museums, and the impact of such emerging technologies as the Internet upon the art world. Contains representative forms and documents and numerous citations to relevant cases and statutes. An ideal, practical tool for those in any way involved in arts-related legal issues.

Lindey, Alexander. **Lindey on Entertainment, Publishing and the Arts: Agreements and the Law.** 3d ed. St. Paul, MN: West Group (Clark Boardman Callaghan), 2004-date. 9 vols. With CD-ROM. Looseleaf format. Supplemented three times annually. The annual **Entertainment, Publishing and the Arts Handbook** is no longer automatically part of the subscription.
Cost: $2,294; supplementation: 1993: $330; 1994: $384; 1995: $442.50; 1996: $480; 1997: $504; 1998: $534; 1999: $609; 2000: $852; 2001: $755; 2002: $816; 2003: $917; 2004: $1,155; 2005: $1,197.50; 2006: $1,403; 2007: $865; 2008: $871.50; 2009: $970.50; 2010: $1,087.50; 2011: $1,228.50; 2012: $1,375; 2013: $1,639; **Monthly Assured Print Price (APP):** $161/$1,932.
This four-volume work combines both discussion and analysis of the legal issues involved in the entertainment law field, and a wealth of practical forms covering the full range of entertainment and publishing transactions. The first two editions were originally authored by Alexander Lindey, an practicing attorney with more than fifty years experience in the field of intellectual property. Following his death, the general editorship of his work passed to Michael Landau, Associate Professor of Law at Georgia State University College of Law and formerly a practicing attorney with Cravath, Swaine & Moore and Skadden, Arps, Slate, Meagher & Flom who handled matters for media, entertainment and technology clients. Volume one includes a useful Introduction to Contract Drafting in the Entertainment Industry as well as a summary of legal developments in such areas as copyright, the First Amendment, Content Regulation of Publications, Newsgathering, Moral Rights of Authors, and Trademarks and Unfair Competition. The forms component encompasses the following subject areas: books, magazines, newspapers, plays, motion pictures, television and radio, music, sound recordings, music video, art work, photographs, advertising, publicity, commercial exploitation: merchandising, agency agreements, tax considerations, photocopying, computers, and other miscellaneous agreements and clauses. There are also comments annotations which accompany each corresponding section of the text. Although the analytical component of this work is somewhat limited, the multiplicity of forms makes it an essential guide to the attorney involved in the field of entertainment law. For more in-depth coverage of the law of copyright, defamation, libel, privacy and publicity, trademarks and unfair competition, the researcher would be advised to consult the more specialized titles available in these areas.

Cost Saving Tips: This set carries with it a substantial supplementation cost which can be avoided if the standing order is dropped and the set repurchased every few years. There is enough boiler plate language contained in these forms for the set to be of great value even if the subscription is not maintained. Citations should all be updated for currency in the primary sources themselves and Shepardized or KeyCited. If you are more interested in substantive content, the **Entertainment Law** text by Selz, et al. is the more complete and economical alternative. The optional **Entertainment, Publishing and the Arts Handbook** is a separate collection of both original and reprinted articles and is no longer an automatic subscription item. The initial price for this set increased $425 in 2004 to $2,095 in 2013, with higher costs for supplementation as well. The introduction of the discounted initial price in 2011 (available at periodic times of the year), however, makes it more advantageous to buy, drop the standing order, and simply re-purchase the set at a later date.

McCarthy, J. Thomas. **The Rights of Publicity and Privacy.** 2d ed. St. Paul, MN: West Group (Clark Boardman Callaghan), 2010-date. 2 vols. Paperbound. Revised and replaced annually.
Cost: 2013 Edition: $1,166; ProView eBook: $1,166; supplementation: 2000: $132; supplementation to 1st edition: 1995: $160; 1996: $183; 1997: $194; 1998: $206; 1999: $244; 2000: $120; 2001: $279; 2002: $330; 2003: $350; 2004: $392; 2005: $429; 2006: $478; 2007: $532; 2008: $558; 2009: $621; 2010: $677; 2011: $738; 2012: $1,070; 2013: $932.80; **Monthly Assured Print Price (APP):** $97/$1,164.
This two-volume treatise focuses on the right of publicity--the inherent right of each individual to control the commercial use of his or her own identity. The author explores the connection between the right of privacy and the right of publicity. Examines legal labels, exploitation, policy reasons for the right of publicity, the elements of infringement of the right of publicity, those protected by the right of publicity, infringement of the use of personal identity in a commercial setting, and infringing the use of personal identity in the media. Cost has risen substantially as the two volume set is revised and replaced every year.

Cost Saving Tip: Avoid standing order and re-purchase only as necessary for core content.

Media Law Reporter [Print with e-mail updates]. Washington, D.C.: Bloomberg BNA, 1977-date. 1 vol. Available on DVD. Weekly reports. Index Digest issued every eight weeks. Annual bound decisional volumes.
Cost: $2,753 per year; Internet: $3,025 (1 user) (2014).
A weekly service providing full-text, indexed coverage of all U.S. Supreme Court decisions and significant federal and state court and administrative decisions in the field of media law. Decisions in both the current looseleaf binder and annual bound decisional volumes are organized according to Bloomberg BNA's unique Classification Guide, the major subject divisions of which are: regulation of media content, regulation of media distribution, newsgathering, and media ownership. Subject access is provided by means of the Index Digest which features headnotes of decisions arranged according to the Classification Guide, with citations to the full-text in the **Media Law Reporter**.

Mitten, Matthew, et al. **Sports Law: Governance and Regulation**. Frederick, MD: Wolter Kluwer Law & Business, 2013. 1 vol. (486 pp.). Paperbound.
Cost: $106.95; from $87.74 on amazon.com (2014).
There is considerable debate on the issue of whether sport law should be regarded as an independent substantive area of the law or nothing more than an amalgam of various substantive areas of law that are also relevant in the sports context. Regardless of one's position on the issue, it is clear that sports impacts diverse substantive areas of law. Intended primarily for undergraduate and graduate sports management programs, this casebook provides an excellent to the law governing both professional and amateur sports. On the professional side, it acquaints the reader with the issues of contracts, agency, labor and employment law, health and safety, and intellectual property rights for marketing. On the amateur side, it explores sports regulation at the high school, college and Olympic levels, and issues of gender/racial equality. Adapted from the authors' successful law school casebook, the coverage embraces the regulation of interscholastic athletics, NCAA internal governance of intercollegiate athletics, the legal relationships between the university and student athletes, coaches' contracts and related issues, gender and racial equity in athletics, health, safety and risk management issues in sports, professional sports league governance and legal regulation, professional sports labor law and relations, representation of players and teams, Olympic and international sports issues, and intellectual property issues in the sports. As befits a student text, each chapter includes excerpts of representative court decisions, key terms, questions, and notes, and problems for consideration or class discussion. The volume also includes a glossary, table of cases, and subject index. Matthew Mitten is Professor of Law and Director, National Sports Law Institute, Marquette University Law School. His co-authors are faculty members at Wake Forest University School of Law, the University of Pennsylvania, the University of North Carolina, and Thomas Jefferson School of Law.

Nafziger, James A. R. and Stephen F. Ross, eds. **Handbook on International Sports Law**. Northampton, MA: Edward Elgar Publishing, 2013. 1 vol. (567 pp.). Hardcover or softcover.
Cost: On-line price: $234 (hardcover); $48.00 (softcover); from $57.00 on amazon.com (paper) (2014).
The contemporary world of sports law reflects a blending of traditional legal rules and procedures that transcend athletic activity with a distinctive and coherent body of what has come to be called "sports law." The latter embraces not only the rules of the game that define a particular field of play, but also the overarching organizational rules and practices that govern organized sporting activities. This volume assembles nineteen articles that collectively aim to address the full range of sports-related subjects on an international scale. These articles include consideration of the foundation and structure of international sports, the protection of competition and athletes, and commercial issues as they relate to sports activity. In his introductory essay, James Nofziger provides a particularly valuable and cogent overview of the current state of international sports law, with attention to such important matters as the international organization structure, the Olympic movement, leading legal issues (politics, commercialism, eligibility, and doping), dispute resolution, and the principle of fairness. The other contributors address such issues as the Court of Arbitration for Sport, the mediation of sports disputes, European and North American models of sports organization, models of sport governance within the European Union, gambling, athlete eligibility, anti-discrimination law, protection of young athletes, media rights, intellectual property rights, image rights, and players' agents, among others. The contributors include a number of leading world authorities on sports law.

Rosden, Peter Eric and George Eric Rosden. **The Law of Advertising**. New York: Matthew Bender & Co., 1973-date. 4 vols. Looseleaf format. Updated 2-3 times per year.
Cost: $2,672 (includes annual subscription); renewal: 1998: $730; 1999: $767; 2000: $810; 2001: $867; 2002: $928; 2003: $975; 2004: $1,024; 2005: $1,096; 2006: $1,173; 2007: $1,319; 2008: $1,425; 2009: $1,511; 2010: $1,541; 2011: $1,618; 2012: $1,715; 2013: $1,962; 2014: $1,966; eBook: $2,429; renewal: 2014: $1,966.
This comprehensive examination of the law related to advertising explores the rules governing each party to the advertising contract, including the media, consumers, advertisers, and advertising agencies. The authors cover such topics as telemarketing, consumers' federal remedies, Federal Trade Commission developments, corrective advertising, children's advertising, legal and medical advertising, tax treatment of advertising income, lotteries and games of chance, tobacco product advertising, First Amendment considerations, and direct marketing. An intellectual property attorney with a specialty in advertising law, Peter Rosden has spent more than 20 years co-authoring **The Law of Advertising** for Matthew Bender. A graduate of Dartmouth College and Columbia University School of Law, Mr. Rosden worked as a senior enforcement attorney with the U.S. Treasury Department and as a member of the intellectual property law firm of Sixbey, Friedman and Leedom before staring his own firm in Charlottesville, VA.

Cost Saving Tips: Based on your level of usage, you may wish to cancel after the initial one-year subscription has expired and purchase this set again in a few years. In the interim, updating can be performed by checking the relevant primary law, Shepardizing, etc.

Sack, Robert D., and Sandra S. Baron. **Sack on Defamation: Libel, Slander, and Related Problems.** 4th ed. New York: Practising Law Institute, 2010-date.
2 vols. (1,400 pp.) or Kindle. Annual supplementation.
Cost: $395; supplementation: 2011: $175; 2012: $190; 2013: $196; 3d ed.: 2000: 0; 2001: $87.25; 2002: $102; 2003: $110; 2004: $115; 2005: $102; 2006: $104; 2007: $125; 2008: $173; 2009: $225; previous edition: 1997: $67.50; 1998: $72.25.
This volume is one of the few indispensable reference sources in the field of defamation law, designed for use by practitioners, judges, journalists, and business executives. It treats both the common law and constitutional law aspects of defamation law, and includes such important issues as First Amendment protections, republication, fair report and neutral reportage, punitive damages, invasion of privacy, injurious falsehood, prima facie torts, and the intentional infliction of emotional distress. Additional chapters cover such topics as jurisdiction and choice of law, motion practice and appeal, insurance, statutes of limitation, retraction and shield statutes.

Scott, Michael D. and James N. Talbott. **Scott on Multimedia Law**. 3d ed. New York: Wolters Kluwer Law & Business, 2008-date. 1 vol. (1,600 pp.). Looseleaf format. Supplemented annually. Includes two discs of forms.
Cost: $525; supplementation: 2009: $155.00; 2010: $165; 2011: $195; 2012: $374; 2013: $200; 2d ed.: 1997: $86; 1998: $89; 1999: $97; 2000: $115; 2001: $115; 2002: $143; 2003; $235; 2004: $254; 2005: $250; 2006: $255; 2007: $272.
A one-volume guide to the entire multimedia industry by an attorney with wide-ranging experience in the computer and intellectual property fields, including 19 years as a computer law practitioner. Michael Scott is currently counsel to the San Francisco law firm of Steinhart & Falconer and was formerly Vice President of Wildwood Interactive, a firm providing services and financing to the interactive multimedia industry. He is also the author of Scott on Computers and is the founder of both the Computer Law Journal and Software Law Journal. This volume addresses such issues as patent requirements, ownership rights, privacy issues, government regulation, rights to pre-existing works and the process of creating rights to new products. It provides an overview of the entire multimedia industry, including legal, business and technical issues, discussion of the source materials used in multimedia works, expert guidance on the legal aspects of creating and distributing multimedia works, including intellectual property law, torts, licensing, contracts and government regulation. The work also provides advice on how to deal with unions, guilds, licensing societies and other organizations on questions of rights to source materials. There are model agreements and sample contract clauses. Finally, the volume provides access to source materials, citations to relevant statutes, a resources directory, glossary of terms, bibliography, etc. Supplementation cost is reasonably priced given the depth and variety of materials. A standing order is recommended for the attorney specializing in this area.

Selz, Thomas D., Melvin Simensky and Patricia Nassif Acton. **Entertainment Law: Legal Concepts and Business Practices.** 3d ed. St. Paul, MN: West (Clark Boardman Callaghan), 2006-date. 4 vols. (approx. 4,000 pp.) Looseleaf format. Supplemented annually.
Cost: $1,157; supplementation: 1993: $80; 1994: $85; 1995: $90; 1996: $98; 1997: $103; 1998: $109; 1999: $229; 2000: $240; 2001: $284; 2002: $350; 2003: $187.50; 2004: $187.50; 2005; $187.50; 2006: $401; 2007: $231; 2008: $624; 2009: $189; 2010: 0; 2011: $416; 2012: $453; 2013: $245; **Monthly Assured Print Price (APP):** $46/$552.
The authors of this four-volume treatise include Thomas D. Selz and Melvin Simensky, both practicing attorneys and Adjunct Professors of Law at New York University School of Law, and Patricia Acton, Clinical Professor of Law, University of Iowa College of Law. Unlike Lindey, this is a treatise with greater attention to the discussion and analysis of the legal issues involved in entertainment law. Sample forms are concentrated in volume four. The treatise component provides analysis of industry structure, investments, risk, power of distributors, credit, billing, contracts, unfair competition, right of publicity, defamation, remedies in credit disputes, artistic control, grant of rights, representations, warranties and indemnities, and compensation. There is also a glossary of industry and entertainment terms, tables of cases, statutes and authorities, and a subject index. Volume four contains a variety of sample entertainment industry forms. This is an excellent alternative to Lindey, particularly if you have a greater interest in the substantive discussion and analysis of entertainment law issues but still require sample forms. The cost for annual supplements is also considerably less than that of Lindey.

Shanker, Jay; David E. Guinn; and Harold Orenstein. **Entertainment Law and Business**. 3d ed. Huntington, NY: Juris Publishing, 2009. 1 vol. (800 pp.). Includes sample forms on CD-ROM.
Cost: print: $150; eBook: $150.00; supplementation: 2011: $95; 2012: $95; 2013: $90 (2014).
According to the authors, "entertainment law is that developing body of laws concerned with the creation, development, transfer and exploitation of artistic properties for purposes of education, artistic enlightenment, and amusement. Artistic properties may be further defined as encompassing the areas of intellectual property (i.e. copyrights and trademarks) and intangible personal property such as reputation, the rights of publicity and privacy, unfair competition, droit moral, and other such related forms of intangible property relating to the creator of intellectual property." This volume provides a useful survey of the law governing entertainment, the Berne and Universal Copyright Conventions, and the practice of entertainment law in the fields of theatre, motion pictures and television, publishing, and music. The authors also address the role of agents, managers and lawyers in the field of entertainment, and the growing role of the Internet. A companion CD-ROM contains a number of forms and agreements keyed to the content of individual chapters. Jay Shanker, JD, is Of Counsel to McAfee & Taft and a veteran entertainment industry attorney whose practice encompasses a wide array of film, television, theatre, music, new media, fine arts and publishing transactions for individual and corporate clients in the United States and abroad. David E. Guinn, JD, PhD, has over twenty years experience in the entertainment industry, having started his career working in the theatre, as a designer, director, and manager, working in stock, regional theatre, Off-Broadway, and On Broadway. While acquiring his law degree, he spent three years working in the business department of the William Morris Agency, before moving into private practice. The late Mr.

Orenstein was a doyen of the entertainment field, who began his career representing one of the major theatrical composer-writers in the 1950s, and continuing as a lawyer for many of the biggest music performers or the 1960s and 1970s.

Shepard, Jason M. **Privileging the Press: Confidential Sources, Journalism Ethics and the First Amendment**. El Paso, TX: LFB Scholarly Publishing, 2011. 1 vol. (316 pp.). Hardbound and softbound.
Cost: $80.00; paperbound: $35.95 from $28.00 on amazon.com (2014).
The confidentiality of a reporter's sources is an essential ingredient of the First Amendment's guarantee of a free press. Simply put, it means that the authorities, including the courts, cannot compel a journalist to reveal the identity of an anonymous source for a story. Without that right, and the privilege of anonymity, many people will hesitate to share information with journalists and advance the public's right to know. In the modern era of telecommunications, journalists' ability to protect their sources increasingly depends also on the adequacy of the computer and communications security measures they employ. The author of this volume, an assistant professor of communications at California State University, Fullerton, examines how subpoenas for newsgathering information have raised both old and new legal and ethical problems for journalists seeking to protect confidential sources. He explores the ethical and legal evolution of the journalistic privilege, exploring its roots in the colonial era and 19th century. He also traces the mid-20th century assertion of First Amendment claims as a basis for the protection of confidential sources by journalists, and the subsequent shift away from the qualified privilege in light of the Supreme Court's decision in *Branzburg v. Hayes* (1972) and Judge Richard Posner's 7th Circuit opinion in *McKevitt v. Pallasch* (2003). In tracing the development of the journalist's privilege from colonial times to the present, Shepard finds a dynamic interaction among journalism ethics, free-press theory, and legal jurisprudence that supports qualified legal protections for journalists. The author concludes that the historical development of the journalist's privilege in practice supports the use of ethical principles to inform the law in three respects: (1) in support of a qualified, rather than an absolute, privilege; (2) in the inclusion of a "public-interest" balancing prong that is currently included in statutory and common law proposals; and (3) in determining who qualifies as a journalist for privilege protection.

Smolla, Rodney A. **Law of Defamation.** 2d ed. St. Paul, MN: West (Clark Boardman Callaghan), 1999-date. 1 vol. Looseleaf format. Annual supplementation. Also available as ProView eBook.
Cost: $1,116; ProView eBook: $1,024; supplementation: 2000: $206; 2001: $238; 2002: $160; 2003: $320; 2004: $320; 2005: $320; 2006: $390; 2007: $434; 2008: $482.50; 2009: $541; 2010: $595; 2011: $649; 2012: $770; 2013: $819.20; 1st ed.: 1993: $153; 1994: $97.50; 1995: $115; 1996: $130; 1997: $137; 1998: $145; 1999: new edition; **Monthly Assured Print Price (APP):** $81/$972.
Smolla, a nationally recognized expert on the First Amendment, provides analysis of all areas of libel litigation, including the fault requirements for defamation, establishing negligence and malice, separating fact, opinion and fair comment, "truth" as a defense, common law privileges, counseling media clients, damages and alternative remedies, and insurance considerations. Smolla also examines the "public figures" question in depth, including a consideration of the distinctions between public figures and officials" and "private figures." His analysis includes an examination of the major court decisions which have shaped this field of the law. This treatise includes ample citations to primary authorities. Smolla is dean and Roy L. Steinheimer, Jr. Professor of Law at Washington and Lee University School of Law in Lexington, Virginia.

Cost-Saving Tip: Aided by the discounted price of a new set, drop the standing order and re-purchase the set every few years. Avoid the APP model which will only lock you in to unnecessarily high supplementation costs.

Stim, Richard. **The Craft Artist's Legal Guide: Protect Your Work, Save on Taxes, Maximize Profits**. Berkeley, CA: Nolo Press, 2010. 1 vol. (400 pp.). Paperbound.
Cost: $39.99; from $16.25 on amazon.com (2014).
This book is directed at all those who make and profit from crafts, but need guidance in dealing with the various legal aspects of these activities, including the process of obtaining supplies, renting a studio or retail space, insuring the business, protecting your artwork or other intellectual property, doing taxes, and executing contracts. The author also provides advice on such matters as the pricing of products, selling wholesale, selling retail, selling at crafts shows, selling on consignment, the crafts studio, zoning laws, the use of the Internet, hiring workers and sales representatives, business and legal liability, protecting appearances with copyright, design patents, and trade dress, names and trademarks, licensing, tax compliance, lawyers, contract and lawsuits. A number of useful forms are provided on a companion CD-ROM. Clearly accessible to those without formal training, this volume provides a wealth of practical information to crafters and those who sell craft items. Author Richard Stim who represents crafts and visual artists, is the author of **Music Law** and **Running a Side Business**.

Taberner, Aimee L. **Cultural Property Acquisitions: Navigating the Shifting Landscape**. Walnut Creek, CA: Left Coast Press, 2012. 1 vol. (209 pp.). Paperbound.
Cost: $26.95; from $12.44 on amazon.com (2014).
The acquisition of cultural properties, particularly antiquities and archaeological artifacts, presents museum staff with both legal and ethical concerns that can be a challenge to both novice and seasoned personnel. Since the 1970s, the number of laws that restrict the acquisition of cultural properties in the United States has increased markedly, as have their interpretation and application, prompted by an increase in the negative press given to the allegedly illegal and unethical collection of antiquities by some museums. The author's recommendations are based on a thorough understanding of the common law principles governing property acquisitions, as well as the foreign and domestic legal means by which cultural properties are controlled or distributed. Such practices require a greater degree of transparency and cooperation among the various stakeholders than in years past. In consultation with the faculty at Harvard Law School and the results of surveys from museum personnel at over thirty museums worldwide, the author describes the legal landscape

of museum acquisitions, the crafting of an acquisitions policy, implementation of an acquisitions policy, acquisitions review procedures, reviewing the basic criteria for the acquisition of domestic and foreign cultural property, and the future of museum collecting, motivated by preservation and education. The appendices contain a number of sample documents, including acquisitions guidelines and questionnaire, examples of basic criteria for acquisitions of domestic and foreign cultural material, and a bibliography. Aimee Taberner received her Master's degree in Museum Studies with distinction from Harvard University Extension and is a board member of the New England Chapter of the Society of Architectural Historians.

Trager, Robert, Joseph Russomanno and Susan Dente Ross. **The Law of Journalism & Mass Communication**. 3d ed. Washington, DC: CQ Press, 2010. 1 vol. (754 pp.).
Cost: $107; eBook: $67.45; from $54.05 on amazon.com; Kindle: $85.60 (2014).
Designed as an undergraduate textbook for use in courses in journalism and mass communications, this volume provides a comprehensive overview of the legal concepts and issues central to the field. The authors begin with an overview of the American legal system, sources of law, the case process, and legal research, illustrated with the text of two landmark Supreme Court decisions. Subsequent chapters are devoted to a consideration of the First Amendment, disruptive speech, libel from the plaintiff's perspective, libel from the defendant's perspective, privacy, emotional distress and physical harm, newsgathering, reporter's privilege, the media and the courts, electronic media regulation, obscenity, indecency and violence, intellectual property, and advertising. Each chapter includes a variety of illuminating features, including timelines of landmark decisions, cases for study, points of law, judicial biographies, charts, photographs, and Real World Law boxes telling stories of the law in practice. Moreover, a companion web site at http://college.cqpress.com/medialaw contains chapter summaries, learning objectives, practice quizzes, interactive flashcards, and annotated web links designed to reinforce the concepts and lessons in the base text. Instructors resources, including test questions, PowerPoint lecture slides and sample classroom activities, are also available at a password protected web site. Appendices include endnotes, a glossary of legal and media-related terms, a list of recommended readings, and case and subject indices. This well-written text will serve as an excellent introduction to the legal issues impacting the field of journalism and mass communications, as well as a useful tool for those practicing in the field.

Uberstein, Gary A., ed. **Law of Professional and Amateur Sports.** St. Paul, MN: West (Clark Boardman Callaghan), 1988-date. 3 vols. Looseleaf format. Supplemented annually.
Cost: $907; supplementation: 1993: $77.50; 1994: $174.50; 1995: $115; 1996: $130; 1997: $137; 1998: $145; 1999: $157; 2000: $170; 2001: $201; 2002: $221.25; 2003: $250; 2004: $250; 2005: $276; 2006: $400; 2007: $343; 2008: $603.75' 2009: $439; 2010: $483; 2011: $526.50; 2012: $610; 2013: $665; **Monthly Assured Print Price (APP):** $66/$792.
This is a well-organized treatise combining the efforts of twenty-four legal scholars, practicing sports attorneys, and professional sports managers, all under the editorship of Gary Uberstein, an attorney with a Los Angeles-based firm specializing in sports law, licensing and commercial litigation. This volume provides in-depth, well-documented coverage of the full range of sports law issues, including regulation of player agents and lawyers, financial planning for the athlete, collective bargaining, negotiations, enforceability of sports industry employment agreements, eligibility and disciplinary rules, NCAA rule enforcement procedures, sex discrimination in amateur and professional sports, injury liability, workers' compensation, violence in professional sports, sports broadcasting, antitrust issues, facility development, taxation of athletes and sports franchises, and endorsement contracts. There are citations to case law, statutory law, regulations and legislative history documents, and a number of sample agreements and contracts. This work will be of great value to practicing sports lawyers/agents, school athletic departments and administrators and sports media personnel. A particular strength of this volume is that the individual chapters have been written by specialists in that area who can provide greater insight than could one author attempting to cover the entire field. Both the initial cost and the supplementation are rather steep for a single-volume work. The cost conscious purchaser may wish to consider a title like Greenberg's two-volume **Sports Law Practice** which costs $231 and only $65 to update (2005).

Wong, Glenn M. **Essentials of Sports Law**. 4th ed. Westport, CT: Praeger Publishers, 2010. 1 vol. (807 pp.). No supplementation. Also available as eBook.
Cost: 94.95; from $68.53 on amazon.com (2014).
An introductory, yet detailed, narrative analysis of the law of amateur and professional sports intended for use by sports lawyers and professionals, sports managers, educational administrators, and students, including those in law and sports management programs. Following basic introductions to the legal system and sports industry, the author addresses the legal principles involved in tort law, the application of tort law to sports, athletic associations, the athlete and constitutional law, drug testing and policies, gender discrimination in athletics, contract law, antitrust law, labor law, agency law, intellectual property law, television and broadcasting, and business law. The third edition reflects numerous developments which have enveloped the field in recent years, including the impact of the Americans with Disabilities Act, the Civil Rights Restoration Act, copyright and patent law, and the blurring of the distinction between professional and amateur sports. The author, a lawyer and former sports manager, is currently Professor of Sports Management at the University of Massachusetts, Amherst. An instructor's manual, caseBook, and supporting web site are also planned.

Additional titles in the field of Arts, Entertainment and Sports Law are available from the following publishers: Allworth Press, American Bar Association, Matthew Bender, Bloomberg BNA, Bloomberg BNA Books, Carolina Academic Press, CQ Press, Greenwood Publishing Group, Indiana University Press, Juris Publishing, Kendall-Hunt Publishing Co., Kluwer Law International, Law-Arts Publishers, LexisNexis, National Association of Broadcasters, Oxford University Press, Practising Law Institute, Praeger, Thomson Reuters West, West Academic, Wolters Kluer Law & Business. See Appendix B for addresses and telephone numbers.

Automobile Law and Practice

Bartell, Don and Anne ImObersteg. **Attacking and Defending Drunk Driving Tests**. Costa Mesa, CA: James Publishing, 2007-date. 1 vol. Looseleaf format.
Cost: $119.00; supplementation: 2008-2014: $69.99.
Drunk driving, or DUI (drinking under the influence), is a serious offense to which considerable law enforcement resources have been devoted in recent years. DUI cases involve everything from Fourth Amendment search and seizure issues to scientific evidence in the form of breath and blood tests. This practical tool provides defense counsel with trial-tested questions and strategies designed to increase the effectiveness of questioning arresting officers and other prosecution witnesses. The volume also includes pattern examinations and strategy discussions, as well as explanatory text. Useful for both prosecution and defense counsel. Don Bartell, a graduate of Notre Dame School of Law, is an experienced DUI practitioner and contributing editor of *California Drunk Driving Law*. Anne ImObersteg, a former Senior Forensic Chemist and Forensic Alcohol Supervisor, has 22 years experience in the field of forensic toxicology. One of many excellent and low-cost resources available from James Publishing.

Blashfield, De Witt Clinton. **Automobile Law and Practice**. 3d ed. St. Paul, MN:Thomson Reuters, 1965-date. 17 vols. Annual pocket parts.
Cost: $2,986; supplementation: 1994: $158; 1995: $158.75; 1996: $181.25; 1997: $273.75; 1998: $213; 1999: $270; 2000: $294; 2001: $178.50; 2002: $382; 2003: $604; 2004: $676.75; 2005: $741; 2006: $565.50; 2007: $1,043.50; 2008: $1,010; 2009: $1,153; 2010: $1,472.50; 2011: $1,611.50; 2012: $2,200; 2013: $2,414.20; **Monthly Assured Print Price (APP):** $214/$2,568.
A multi-volume guide to the practice of automobile and motor vehicle law with substantive discussion, practice tips, forms and checklists. Coverage includes investigation and trial preparation, liability, trial evidence, medical/legal aspects, damages, insurance (including no-fault), civil procedure, registration and licensing, products liability, crimes, etc.

Cost Saving Tip: While useful, this resource does not justify its high supplementation cost. Consider buying pocket supplements in alternate years, or less often, as your needs dictate. The wise consumer will purchase this set during one of Thomson Reuter's periodic sales, drop the standing order, and re-purchase at periodic intervals. Avoid the APP option which only locks you into high annual supplementation costs..

Brown, David W. **Beat Your Ticket: Go to Court and Win**. 7th ed. Berkeley, CA: Nolo Press, 2013. 1 vol. (336 pp.). Paperbound.
Cost: $24.99; from $13.07 on amazon.com (2014).
Tickets for traffic violations are a means of protecting public safety, but can also be a result of officer error, equipment malfunction, a municipality's desire for revenue, or an officer's ticket quota. And since a traffic ticket may result in a steep fine, adversely affect your driving record, result in the suspension of your driver's license, or an increase in your insurance rates, it may be advisable to contest the traffic ticket rather than simply paying it. This layman's manual provides the citizen with the tools necessary to understand and fight traffic tickets in any state court. This can be accomplished by first understanding the law under which you have been charged and an evaluation of whether or not you should fight the ticket. The author also discusses the role of lawyers, speed violations, speed detection, other moving violations, driving under the influence, use of discovery to build your case, preparation for trial, the officer's testimony and cross-examination, trial before a judge, and jury trials. The text is supplemented with numerous examples, tips, charts, and illustrations. The author practices law in Monterey, CA and is the other of several Nolo books, including Fight Your Ticket and Win in California.

Campbell, James F., et al. **Defense of Speeding, Reckless Driving and Vehicular Homicide**. New York: Matthew Bender, 1984-date. 4 vols. Looseleaf format.
Cost: $1,208 (includes annual subscription); annual renewal: 1995: $293 (cost frozen since 1992); 1996: $307; 1997: $307; 1998: $320; 1999: $335; 2000: $360; 2001: $385; 2002: $412; 2003: $433; 2004: $455; 2005: $487; 2006: $522; 2007: $564; 2008: $609; 2009: $658; 2010: $691; 2011: $726; 2012: $770; 2013: $824; 2014: $899. Also available as e-book: $1,098; renewal: 2014: $882.
A comprehensive treatise and practice guide on the defense of speeding, reckless driving and vehicular homicide cases. Contains detailed, well-documented analysis of legal and technical matters combined with relevant litigation techniques. Chapters discuss legal elements of speeding offenses, speed enforcement and measurement, radar equipment, and the trial of speeding, reckless driving and homicide cases.

Cost Saving Tip: If your usage is likely to be infrequent, simply cancel the supplementation and purchase a new set at a later date as your needs dictate. You will probably gain sufficient value from the core treatise without buying all the supplements as long as you have your own system of keeping up with local cases and statutes. Be aware that one should use a secondary source only as a starting point in the research process and that one must check primary sources in your jurisdiction directly, and Shepardize or KeyCite those relevant cases and statutes to keep abreast of the law. These heavily updated legal treatises are an extremely expensive means of doing this.

Cohen, Harvey M. and Joseph B. Green. **Apprehending and Prosecuting the Drunk Driver: A Manual for Police and Prosecution**. New York: Matthew Bender & Co., 1992-date. 1 vol. Looseleaf format. Includes pocket manual.
Cost: $361; supplementation: 1999: $63; 2000: $67; 2001: $72; 2002: $78; 2003: $82; 2004: $86; 2005: $92; 2006: $99. 2007: $107; 2008: $116; 2009: $125; 2010: $131; 2011: $137; 2012: $146; 2013: $165; 2014: $170. Also available as e-book: $361.
This manual is designed to assist law enforcement officers and prosecutors with drunk driving arrests and prosecutions. It includes discussion of such topics as recognizing drunk drivers in motion, operating roadblocks, evaluating sensory clues of alcohol and drug impairment, the administration of field sobriety tests, the determination of probable cause, labeling and preserving test samples, videotaping suspects, evaluating a case before trial, deciding between plea bargain and trial, selecting a jury, and presenting the state's case at trial. Includes a bonus pocket manual for police officers.

Digest of Motor Laws. Washington, DC: American Automobile Association, Traffic Safety and Engineering. Annual. 1930-date. (202) 942-2071
Cost: Print discontinued with 2010 edition. Only available online at: http://drivinglaws.aaa.com/
An invaluable desktop companion to the motor vehicle laws of the fifty states, U.S. territories and Canadian provinces. Contains the following information for each jurisdiction represented: Registration and Proof of Ownership, Taxes, Driver's License, Traffic Rules, Cellular Telephones, Diesel Fuel Permits, Passenger Car Trailer Information, Motorcycle Information, Mopeds, Liability Laws, Accident Reports, AAA Guaranteed Arrest Bond Certificates, Nonresident Driving Privileges and Registration, Guest Suit Laws, Nonresident Violator Compact, Chemical Test Laws, Child Restraint Laws, State Police or Highway Patrol. The Appendix includes 50-state charts for driver's license laws, alcohol laws, vehicle registration laws, and state safety laws.

Disbrow, Vivian A., et al. **No-Fault and Uninsured Motorist Automobile Coverage**. New York: Matthew Bender, 1984-date. 4 vols. Looseleaf format. Supplemented several times annually. No CD-ROM or Internet.
Cost: $2,439 (includes annual subscription); annual renewal: 1995: $564.50 (price frozen since 1992); 1996: $592; 1997: $592; $1998: $625; 1999: $645; 2000: $690; 2001: $738; 2002: $761; 2003: $800; 2004: $840; 2005: $899; 2006: $962; 2007: $1,039; 2008: $1,133; 2009: $1,235; 2010: $1,309; 2011: $1,401; 2012: $1,485; 2013: $1,692; 2014: $1,734; eBook: $2,217; 2014: $1,734.
The individual chapters in this set are authored by no less than 28 legal practitioners and scholars. Detailed, heavily footnoted text covers the full range of no-fault insurance issues, including statutory basis, scope of coverage, exclusions, arbitration, attorney's fees, tort recovery, impact of no-fault plans, statutory uninsured motorist coverage, hit and run accidents, settlement of uninsured motorist claims, litigation, underinsured motorist coverage, conflict of laws, stacking of benefits, and state funds. Appendices include no-fault statutes, uninsured motorist citations, accident claims arbitration rules, etc., as well as tables of statutes, cases, and an index.

Cost Saving Tip: A thorough, but costly set. If the exhaustive coverage meets your needs, you may consider buying the set with its one-year subscription and then letting it lapse. You can supplement the text of the lapsed set with a less expensive alternative text or simply update your research in the primary sources and Shepardize or KeyCite the relevant cases and statutes. "Updates" are months old by the time you receive them and may omit critical citations to more recent cases or statutes, such as those from your state. There is no substitute to doing your own updating when a client's interests are at stake. Remember a secondary source such as this is only a starting place in the research process. Stopping here could be considered grounds for a malpractice suit.

Eades, Ronald W. **Jury Instructions in Automobile Actions.** 4th ed. Charlottesville, VA: LexisNexis, 2004-date. 1 vol. (809 pp.) Annual pocket part.
Also available as e-book.
Cost: $145 (print or eBook); supplementation: 2005: $20; 2006: $26; 2008: $86; 2009: $100; 2010: $102; 2011: $110; 2012: $116; 2013: $128; 3d ed.: 1997: $32.50; 1998: $35; 1999: $40; 2000: $50; 2001: 0; 2002: $60; 2003: $20; 2004: $70; 2d ed.: 1993: $25; 1994: 0; 1995: $35; 1996: 0;
A collection of sample jury instructions in automobile negligence actions with supportive legal authorities and commentaries. Subjects covered include negligence and proof thereof, particular classes of operator of vehicle, condition of operator, condition of vehicle, condition of roadway, liability from ownership land or custody of animals, railroad crossings, liability for negligence of another, duty and control in operation of vehicle, persons injured and their status, contributory and comparative negligence, other defenses, and no-fault insurance. Although supplementation may be less necessary in a volume of this kind, Michie's supplementation costs are considerably more reasonable than those of most legal publishers.

Erwin, Richard E., et al. **Defense of Drunk Driving Cases: Criminal - Civil**. 3d ed. New York: Matthew Bender, 1971-date. 4 vols. Looseleaf format and eBook. Authority CD-ROM includes no-cost online updating via LEXIS-NEXIS.
Cost: $1,950 (includes annual subscription); annual renewal: 1995: $568 (cost frozen since 1992); 1996: $596; 1997: $596; 1998: $630; 1999: $655; 2000: $655; 2001: $701; 2002: $751; 2003: $789; 2004: $828; 2005: $886; 2006: $949; 2007: $1,011; 2008: $1,072; 2009: $1,136; 2010: $1,171; 2011: $1,206; 2012: $1,254; 2013: $1,383; 2014: $1,420; eBook: $1,773; renewal: 2014: $1.383.
An in-depth analysis of the law governing drunk driving and related offenses. Chapters cover double jeopardy, preliminary hearings, penalties, case evaluation, trial procedures and techniques, jury selection, field sobriety tests, examining physicians, physician-patient privilege, chemical tests, blood analysis, the intoximeter and other testing devices, chain of evidence, affirmative defenses, refusal to submit, constitutional objections, implied consent legislation, expert and character witnesses, jury instructions, etc. Also includes a bibliography, index and table of cases. This work is also heavily laced with citations to primary authority, forms and interrogatories. Statutory appendix includes citations and descriptions of drunk driving offenses for all fifty states.

Cost Saving Tip: While this is an exhaustive work with many features to recommend it, you may balk at the high supplementation cost. If so, drop the standing order after one year and update in the traditional manner using primary sources, Shepards, etc. If you have a continuing need for this set, purchase a new set every 3-4 years. Also consider buying the set used in the first place, particularly if you have no desire to keep it up-to-date and If you monitor relevant cases in your own jurisdiction. Combination discounts may be available.

Fitzgerald, Edward F. **Intoxication Test Evidence**. 2d ed. St. Paul, MN: West (Clark Boardman Callaghan), 1995-date. 3 vols. Looseleaf format.
Cost: $777; ProView eBook: $754; supplementation: 1996: $100; 1997: $110; 1998: $127; 1999: $125; 2000: $136; 2001: $161; 2002: $188.50; 2003: $215; 2004: $240; 2005: $263; 2006: $293; 2007: $326; 2008: $363; 2009: $407; 2010: $531; 2011: $585.60; 2012: $562.40; 2013: $562.40; **Monthly Assured Print Price (APP):** $60/$720.
This two-volume treatise provides a wealth of practical and scientific information regarding the types of evidence used to prove intoxication in both civil and criminal cases. Courts have come to accept a variety of chemical tests as evidence, including blood, breath, urine and other body samples, all of which are addressed in these volumes. Seventy-nine chapters and appendices have been organized in ten parts: alcohol consumption, human physiology, and individual differences; basic alcohol calculations for the law office and courtroom; blood alcohol testing: an overview of some inherent problems; breath alcohol testing and reporting; basic mathematical and scientific concepts, terms and measurements; breath test results in criminal cases: some pre-trial challenges; evaluating alcohol test evidence in civil cases: getting the most from depositions; preparation and testimony of the expert witness in alcohol test cases; checklists; and appendices. The author is a Massachusetts attorney with extensive experience handling drinking-driving litigation.

Cost Saving Tip: Avoid APP option which is more costly than regular subscriber discount. Better yet, drop supplementation and re-purchase set periodically when 20% discount is offered.

Genson, Laura Ruhl and Anita M. Kerezman, eds. **Truck Accident Litigation.** 3d ed. Chicago: American Bar Association, Tort Trial and Insurance Law Section, 2013. 1 vol. (504 pp.). Paperbound.
Cost: $149.95; $135.95 to Tort Trial and Insurance Practice Section members; from $94.47 on amazon.com (2014).
Ever wonder what rules govern those semi-trailers and their drivers as they zip by you on the highway, drive on your tail. or nearly blow you off the road? This invaluable collection of articles addresses a variety of topics related to the trucking industry, and the applicable standards for motor carriers and drivers as they relate to their legal liability and other matters. More than forty authors contributed a total of 34 chapters bearing on such topics as an overview of trucking, commercial driver's license requirements, records retention, Federal Motor Carrier Safety Regulations, the truck accident investigation, data collection, spoliation of evidence, the truck driver, special driving situations—hazardous materials, truck driver fatigue, hours of service regulations, cargo securement, on-board electronics, tires and wheels, brakes inspection, the safety rating process, the trial, and much more. Laura Ruhl Genson is general counsel to Ruhl Forensic, Inc and a specialist in vehicle litigation. Anita Kerezman is a professional truck driver and a truck driving and training specialist.

Cost Saving Tip: An interesting phenomenon has emerged on amazon.com. With this and other out-of-print titles, the market has spawned a number of used book sellers charging exhorbitant prices for books originally costing a fraction ofis now being asked. This 2d edition of this title has sellers asking prices ranging from $1,000 to $2,000. Thankfully, a third edition of this title was issued in 2013.

Goodman, Richard M. and Center for Auto Safety. **Automobile Design Liability**. 3d ed. St. Paul, MN: West (CBC), 1991-date. 6 vols. Looseleaf format. Annual supplementation.
Cost: $1,351; supplementation: 1999: $244; 2000: $258; 2001: $300; 2002: $325; 2003: $365.50; 2004: $415; 2005: $389; 2006: $507; 2007: $733.50; 2008: $593.50; 2009: $660.50; 2010: $735; 2011: $816; 2012: $905; 2013: $995; **Monthly Assured Print Price (APP):** $100/$1,200.
This three-volume reference guide is designed to serve the needs of trial attorneys involved in litigating automobile products liability actions. Volume one contains a summary of automobile products liability law, a guide to cases by product defect, and the text of federal, state, and private safety standards, including applicable references to the U.S. Code and Code of Federal Regulations. Volume two contains summaries of major automobile product recalls organized by manufacturer and component. Volume three provides a comprehensive guide to sources of information on auto defects, listings of government safety investigations, and lists of experts and consultants in the field of automobile safety, cross-referenced by area of expertise and state. It concludes with a detailed technical bibliography. The volumes include extensive citations to primary law and secondary sources, including references to other Thomson Reuters (formerly Lawyers Cooperative) Total Client-Service Library products. Richard M. Goodman is a practicing attorney and member of the California and Michigan bars. Generous assistance was provided the staff of the Center for Auto Safety.

Cost Saving Tip: Avoid APP option which is more costly that regular subscriber discounted supplementation. Better yet, drop supplementation and re-purchase discounted set at periodic intervals.

Kenworthy, William E. **Killer Roads: From Crash to Verdict**. 2d ed. Charlottesville, VA: LexisNexis, 1999-date. 1 vol. (698 pp.). and eBook.
Cost: $198 (print and eBook); supplementation: 2000: $30; 2001: $39; 2002: $43; 2003: $90; 2004: $46; 2005: $49; 2006: $53; 2007: $56; 2008: $61; 2009: $78; 2010: $84.00; 2011: $91; 2012: $97; 2013: $101; 1st edition: 1998: $30.
A one-volume handbook dealing with transportation facility negligence cases intended for both plaintiff and defense attorneys, including a consideration of the doctrine of sovereign

immunity. Covers case evaluation and practical trial skills as well as a well-documented discussion of legal issues involved in such cases.

Kenworthy, William E. **Transportation Safety and Insurance Law**. 3d ed. Newark, NJ: LexisNexis, 2004-date. 2 vols. Looseleaf format and eBook. Annual supplementation.
Cost: $348 (print and eBook); supplementation: 2005: 0; 2006: $55.00; 2007: $80; 2008: $93; 2009: $109; 2010: $117; 2011: $124; 2012: $133; 2013: $136; 2d ed.: 2001: $57.75; 2002: $63; 2003: $66; 2004: $70.
Federal regulations and the common law both play a significant role in the conduct of those who transport goods by railroad or highway. This treatise was developed as a resource for the attorney who advises common carriers on matters of regulatory and legal compliance as a means of reducing potential liability. The author begins with a discussion of the common law liability of common carriers and sources of indemnity and contribution, including agencies, contractors and equipment suppliers. He follows with a consideration of the commerce clause and the role of federal versus state safety regulation, the federal statutory background of motor carriers and railroads, motor carrier safety fitness ratings, motor carrier enforcement penalties and proceedings, railroad enforcement penalties and proceedings, drug and alcohol abuse, transportation of hazardous materials, and transportation equipment. Additional topics include employee qualifications, hours of service, and records, transportation contracts and safety, terminal and shop safety, motor carrier size and weight laws, accident and incident reporting, motor carrier insurance, and duty to give notice. William Kenworthy is a former partner in the Washington, DC firm of Rea, Cross & Auchincloss, where he focused on transportation safety and hazardous materials. He has also served as general counsel to Rocky Mountain Motor Tariff Bureau in Denver, Colorado and counsel to Navajo Freight Lines, Inc. He is the author of numerous books and articles for legal journals, and also serves as contributing editor to a trucking management magazine.

Limpert, Rudolf. **Motor Vehicle Accident Reconstruction and Cause Analysis.** 7th ed. Charlottesville, VA: LexisNexis, 2012-date. 1 vol. (746 pp.). Annual supplementation. Also on eBook.
Cost: $218 (print and eBook); supplementation: 2013: $100; 6th ed.: 2011: $96; 2012: new edition; 5th ed.:2000: 0; 2001: $65; 2002: $65; 2003: $67; 2004: $70; 2005: $74; 2006: $78; 2007: $85; 4th edition: 1998: $30.
The author of this volume is a mechanical engineer with over 25 years experience as a teacher and consultant in the area of accident reconstruction and mechanical engineering who has also served as safety standards engineer for the National Highway Traffic Safety Administration. The book's emphasis is upon accident reconstruction and those design features bearing upon accident causation which can provide valuable technical information as a background to trial practice texts.

Nissenberg, David N. **The Law of Commercial Trucking: Damages to Persons and Property**. 3d ed. Newark, NJ: LexisNexis, 2005-date. 2 vols. Annual supplementation.
Cost: $235 (print or eBook); supplementation: 2001: $55; 2002: $55; 2003: $65; 2004: $61; 2005: $65; 2006: $69; 2007: $74; 2008: $80; 2009: $91; 2010: $96.00; 2011: $101; 2012: $108; 2013: $116.
Truck-related accidents now account for more than 5,000 deaths and tens of thousands of injuries each year, not to mention millions of dollars in property damage. This is the only comprehensive work on the subject of commercial trucking law in the United States. The author examines the laws and federal regulations relating to commercial trucking, discusses insurance coverage issues, and considers the various types of liability, including those resulting from unloading and unloading, freight claims, and hazardous cargo. The text is supported with citations to thousands of cases.

Reiff, Robert S. and H. Scott Fingerhut. **Drunk Driving and Related Vehicular Offenses**. 5th ed. Newark, NJ: LexisNexis Matthew Bender, 2010-date. 1 vol. (813 pp.).
Cost: $195 (print and eBook) (2014).
Designed for both defense counsel and prosecutors, this volume examines her wide range of issues involved in handling cases involving those charged with operating a motor vehicle while under the influence of alcohol or drugs. The author, an experienced DUI advocate, provides expert guidance on such topics as the initial client meeting, the stop and arrest, accident reconstruction, expert witnesses, sobriety exercises, breath, urine and blood tests, refusal to submit to a breath test, administrative driver's license hearings, limitations on prosecutions, jury selection, cross-examination of the arresting officer, DUI and drug recognition, murder, manslaughter and vehicle homicide, DUI and entrapment, closing argument, jury instructions, and sentencing. Attention is also given to cases involving boating under the influence. A graduate of Boston University School of Law, Mr. Reiff is one the country's leading DUI experts, and has lectured widely on the topic.

Schermer, Irvin E. **Automobile Liability Insurance**. 4th ed. (revised). St. Paul, MN: West (Clark Boardman Callaghan), 2008/2009-date. 5 vols. Looseleaf format.
Cost: $751; supplementation: 2009: $270.50; 2010: $370; 2011: $326; 2012: $188.80; 2013: $94.40; 3d ed.: 1992: $275; 1993: $297.50; 1994: $303; 1995: $410; 1996: $240; 1997: $130; 1998: $138; 1999: $300; 2000: $159; 2001: $378; 2002: $417; 2003: $461; 4th ed.: 2004: $257.50; 2005: $170; 2006: $406; 2007: $261; 2008: $950 (new ed.); **Monthly Assured Print Price (APP)**: $47/$564.
Written by a senior partner in a Minneapolis law firm who practices primarily in the field of personal injury law, this three-volume treatise provides coverage of both voluntarily and statutorily required policies. Purportedly the only definitive text which treats the operation of financial responsibility acts upon both voluntarily carried and statutorily required liability policies. Features a digest of legislation in each state and the operation of no-fault laws. Includes a discussion of the constitutionality of no-fault laws, conflict of laws, multiple coverage, subrogation, the Financial Responsibility Act, the motor vehicle liability policy, uninsured motorists, and underinsured motorists.

Cost Saving Tip: Your decision to purchase this particular treatise should be based on your need for information which is more exhaustive and somewhat more timely than that offered by the treatise which is supplemented annually. If you intend to use it less frequently and/or for background reference only, you may wish to consider a less costly alternative. You should be prepared for the fact that the cost of three releases annually approaches the cost of the initial set. Moreover, use of a secondary source like this does not relieve the user of updating the information contained therein, whether by Shepardizing or KeyCiting, monitoring applicable local statutes, case law, etc. Periodic re-purchase of discounted new set is recommended. Avoid the APP option.

Sheldon, Jonathan. and Carolyn Carter. **Automobile Fraud: Odometer Tampering, Lemon Laundering, and Concealment of Salvage or Other Adverse History**. 4th ed. Boston, MA: National Consumer Law Center, 2011. 1 vol. (711 pp.). Paperbound.

Cost: $140 (with 2013 supplement); supplementation: 2013: $52; 3d ed.: 2008: $44; 2009: $52; 2010: $52; 2011: new ed. (2014).

Various forms of automobile fraud cost unwary consumers millions of dollars per year. These involve the failure of dealers to disclose a vehicle's wreck or salvage history, the prior use of a vehicle as a rental, lease, taxi, or police vehicle, a vehicle's prior history as a lemon law buyback, repaired damage to new cars, or other mechanical defects. This manual provides practitioners with the information necessary to obtain rescission of an automobile sale, treble damages, $1500 statutory damages, punitive damages, and attorney's fees. The authors provide detailed information about federal and state requirements regarding motor vehicle titles and odometer readings, methods for detecting fraud involving salvage and prior wreck history and obtaining a vehicle's title history. They also provide valuable advice regarding litigation techniques, common law fraud punitive damage claims, various statutory claims, and how to find hidden dealer assets. An accompanying CD-ROM contains a variety of valuable forms, including sample complaints, discovery requests, class action pleadings, jury instructions, sample title documents, and more. Jonathan A. Sheldon is a staff with the National Consumer Law Center in Boston. Supplementary information on companion website: http://shop.consumerlaw.org/pdf/auto-web.pdf

Taylor, Lawrence. **Drunk Driving Defense**. 7th ed. New York: Wolters Kluwer Law & Business, 2010-date. 1 vol. (960 pp.). Looseleaf format. Includes companion CD-ROM. Annual supplementation.

Cost: $365; supplementation: 2011: $115; 2012: $125; 2013; $135; 6th ed.: 2006: $95; 2007: $105; 2008: $112; 2009: $155; 2010: new edition; 5th ed.: 2000: $85; 2001: $90; 2002: $115; 2003: $132; 2004: $137; 2005: new ed.; 4th edition: 1996: $50; 1997: $55; 1998: $64.

A comprehensive guide to drunk driving defense strategies by one of the nation's leading authorities on DUI litigation. This practice tool provides the defense attorney with hundreds of methods to identify weaknesses in the prosecution's position, including the latest developments in blood, breath, and urine analysis, methods used to discredit field sobriety tests, the use of pretrial discovery and suppression motions to get a case dismissed, etc. The author also outlines the facts and strategies to challenge the evidence gathered from such devices as the Intoxilyzer 5000, Intoximeter 3000, and the Datamaster, and explains how to properly employ voir dire at the start of trial and how to make a powerful summation to the jury.

Vehicular Crimes Library – CD-ROM. Newark, NJ: LexisNexis Matthew Bender, 2001-date. One Authority CD-ROM includes the following titles: Defense of Speeding, Reckless Driving & Vehicular Homicide; Defense of Drunk Driving Cases: Criminal–Civil; Apprehending and Prosecuting the Drunk Driver; and relevant primary source material.

Cost: $1,543 (includes one year subscription); supplementation: 2006: $637.00; 2007: $678; 2008: $753; 2009: $813; 2010: $855; 2011: $906; 2012: $998; 2013: $1,068; 2013: $1,143; 2014: $1,176.

Whited, Flem K., III. **Drinking/Driving Litigation: Criminal and Civil**. 2d ed. St. Paul, MN: West (Clark Boardman Callaghan), 1998-date. 4 vols. Looseleaf format.

Cost: $1,324; supplementation: 1992: $184.50; 1993: $224; 1994: $270; 1995: $449.50; 1996: $509; 1997: $605; 1998: $614; 1999: $275; 2000: $405; 2001: $477; 2002: $525; 2003: $597; 2004: $630; 2005: $795; 2006: $975; 2007: $468; 2008: $825.50; 2009: $540; 2010: $594; 2011: $654; 2012: $654; 2012: $777; 2013: $870; **Monthly Assured Print Price (APP):** $87/$1,044.

Authored by one of the most respected names in the field, this five-volume treatise is a complete practical guide to both the law and practice of drunk driving litigation. It covers such areas as pretrial motions, arrest procedures, chemical tests, effects of alcohol, breathalyzer and other measuring devices, blood and urine testing, postmortem problems, blood alcohol, roadblocks, dram shop cases, trial issues, effects of alcohol and the variables that may affect them. Also includes jury instructions and a consideration of sentencing, appeal, and other issues involved in liquor liability. Supplementation costs vary from year-to-year, depending upon the volume of changes to the text. Generally speaking, the supplements are reasonably priced given the initial purchase price. Supplementation includes both cumulative front matter and interfiled pages, which means that updating a lapsed subscription may entail considerable filing.

Cost Saving Tips: Lapsed subscribers may find it less expensive and time-consuming to purchase a new set (or all new contents) periodically if a sufficient number of years have elapsed. The attorney who has a handle on the law of his or her jurisdiction will not require the frequent and costly supplementation of a work which is national in scope. Investigate the purchase of a fairly current used set at periodic intervals for best savings (provided they are available). A slightly out-of-date used set should sell in the $150-$200 range. If not, purchase the set new and drop the standing order. Avoid the APP option, which far exceeds the average annual cost of suipplementation and will lock you into continuous updating costs.

Additional titles in the field of Automobile Law and Practice are available from the following publishers: American Bar Association, American Automobile Association (AAA), American Law Institute, Wolters Kluwer Law & Business, Matthew Bender, Gould, J.J. Keller, Kluwer Law International, Knowles Publishing, LexisNexis, Looseleaf Law Publications, Pocket Press, Inc., National Consumer Law Center, Practising Law Institute, Simon & Schuster Trade Paperbacks, Stephens-Peck, Inc., Thomson Reuters West. See Appendix B for addresses and telephone numbers.

Banking and Finance Law

Bailey, Henry J. and Richard B. Hagedorn. **Brady on Bank Checks and Fund Transfers.** 8th ed. LexisNexis A.S. Pratt, 1997-date. 1 vol. (various pagings). Supplemented three times annually.
Cost: $623 per year; eBook: $582 per year (2014).
First published in 1915, this book, formerly titled Brady on Bank Checks, this treatise provides the most thorough coverage available of the law of bank checks, including such matters as stopping payments, unauthorized deposits, wrongful dishonor and the return of unpaid checks, embezzlement and fraud resulting from check alteration. The eighth edition also covers Revised **UCC** Articles 3 and 4, and wire transfers under Article 4A. Thoroughly footnoted with references to primary authority, including statutes, cases and Federal regulations. Formerly published by Warren, Gorham & Lamont.

Cost Saving Tips: For the attorney specializing in commercial law, this is one of the most authoritative sources available; however, significant savings can be achieved by dropping the standing order and purchasing the book, with its one year subscription, every 2-3 years. When A.S. Pratt & Sons took control of this title in 1997, it converted it to a subscription service and effectively precluded customers from purchasing one of the three cumulative supplements each year. This, in effect, raised the annual supplementation cost from approximately $70 (for those electing to purchase one supplement per year) to, now, $623 per year. By subscribing for one year and skipping one year, you will be able to reduce your average annual cost to about $310 per year while going about one year between updating.

Baker, Donald I., Roland E. Brandel, and James H. Pannabecker. **The Law of Electronic Fund Transfer Systems.** 3d ed. Chicago: LexisNexis A. S. Pratt, 1995-date. One looseleaf volume.
Cost: $623 per year (2014).
A complete guide to the law of electronic fund transfer, including business trends, technological innovations, consumer privacy and state and federal regulations. Examines the rights, duties and liabilities of financial institutions and their clients. Includes a discussion of the legal issues as they relate to the **Uniform Commercial Code**, antitrust actions, ATM networks, POS systems, etc. Now part of the LexisNexis family.

Cost Saving Tips: When A.S. Pratt & Sons took control of this title in 1997, it converted it to a subscription service at an annual cost of $355 and effectively precluded the customer from purchasing the cumulative supplements at intervals appropriate to his or her needs. Significant savings can be achieved by dropping the standing order and purchasing the book, with its one year subscription, every 2-3 years. This, in effect, raised the annual supplementation cost from approximately $65 (for those electing to purchase one supplement per year) to, now, $623 per year in 2013, an annual increase of $558. By subscribing for one year and skipping one year, you will be able to reduce your average annual cost to about $310 per year while going about one year between updating.

Bank Compliance Guide. Riverwoods, IL: Wolters Kluwer Law & Business, Inc. (CCH). 2 vols. Also available on CD-ROM and Internet.
Cost: Print: $967; CD-ROM: $967; Internet: $1,084 (2014). All updated monthly.
Bank attorneys, auditors, and compliance officers, as well as federal and state regulators, will find this a convenient resource for compliance laws, regulations, and explanations as they relate to deposit taking, lending and general bank operations. The text is supplemented by compliance checklists, sample policy statements and sample procedures. Tom Thomas, a compliance expert with Thomas Compliance Associates, provides the analysis of major banking laws and regulations, together with practical "Compliance Notes." CCH now offers this service in multiple formats at roughly comparable prices.

Banking & Commercial Law Library. New York: Matthew Bender & Co. One disc. Updated quarterly. Available for Windows. Search Engine: Folio. Includes toll-free support. CD-ROM includes no-cost online updating via LexisNexis.
Cost: $21,406; renewal: 1998: $5,710; 1999: $5,940; 2000: $6,300; 2001: $6,741; 2002: $7,213; 2003: $7,574; 2004: $7,953; 2005: $8,589; 2006: $9,191; 2007: $9,926; 2008: $10,770; 2009: $11,632; 2010: $12,214; 2011: $12,825; 2012: $13,595; 2013: $14,546; 2014: $16,194.54.
The complete CD-ROM library includes the following Matthew Bender titles: **Banking Law**, **Goods in Transit**, **Commercial Damages: A Guide to Remedies in Business Litigation**, **Secured Transactions Under the U.C.C.**, **U.C.C. Reporter-Digest,** and **Forms and Procedures under the U.C.C.** Various combinations of titles may be selected by the subscriber.

Banking Law. A. Graham et al. et al. New York: Matthew Bender & Co.,1981-date. 20 vols. Looseleaf format. Four releases per year. Also available on CD-ROM and Internet. Authority CD-ROM includes no-cost online updating via LEXIS-NEXIS.
Cost: $5,195 (includes annual subscription); annual renewal: 1995: $1,260 (price frozen from1992-97); 1996: $1,321; 1997: $1,321; 1998: $1,390; 1999: $1445; 2000: $1,550; 2001: $1,659; 2002: $1,776; 2003: $1,865; 2004: $1,958; 2005: $2,115; 2006: $2,264; 2007: $2,445; 2008: $2,653; 2009: $2,865; 2010: $2,937; 2011: $3,099; 2012: $3,330; 2013: $3,531; 2014: $3,854; CD-ROM: $4,351; renewal: 1998: $1,325; 1999: $1,445; 2000: $1,550; 2001: $1,659; 2002: $1,776; 2003: $1,865; 2004: $1,958; 2005: $2,115; 2006: $2,264; 2007: $2,445; 2008: $2,653; 2009: $2,879; 2010: $3,009; 2011: $3,159; 2012: $3,349; 2013: $3,583; 2014: $3,989. Volumes 7, 8, 9 and 10 are sold separately under

the title **Consumer Credit: Law, Transactions and Firms**; Volumes 5 and 5 are sold under the title **Checks, Drafts and Notes**. A major research tool in the area of commercial banking which examines such matters as bank organization, operation, examination, regulation and liquidation, as well as federal income tax law, consumer credit and protection, and federal securities. Unlike **Michie on Banking**, this set analyzes the statutory and regulatory aspects of the banking field as well as the common law side. Useful as an operational manual for banks officers as well for attorneys. The most comprehensive banking law treatise on the market. In 1998, banking law developments pamphlets, written by expert practitioners and legal scholars, were added to the **Banking Law** release cycle and will be issued on a regular basis, as warranted.

Cost Saving Tips: While this is an excellent core resource, the annual supplementation costs might exceed your budget, in which case you would be better off accessing it a local law library. Take heed that your decision to keep it "current " reflects your actual usage, rather than a failure to re-examine your library needs and priorities. As long as you are aware of the limitations of a lapsed set, you can drop the standing order until your own circumstances warrant the purchase of a new one, and do your own updating in the primary sources, case digests, and Shepard's. At the risk of sounding cynical, it is clear that legal publishers are motivated more by a desire for supplementation revenue than a desire to keep supplementation costs under control and to tailor their updating efforts to significant developments rather routine decisional reporting.

Banking Laws and Regulation Deskbook. New York: Wolters Kluwer Law & Business, 2010-date. 3 vols. Looseleaf format. Annual subscription title. Updated monthly.
Cost: $725.00 per year (2014).
The laws and regulations governing banking and financial institutions are of enormous breadth and complexity. That complexity has been heightened by the passage, most recently, of the Dodd-Frank Wall Street Reform and Consumer Protection Act of 2010 that effected the most significant changes to financial regulation in the United States since the regulatory reforms of the New Deal, and made changes in the regulatory environment that affect all federal financial regulatory agencies and almost every part of the nation's financial services industry. This three volume set assembles all the important laws and regulations that govern the various segments and requirements of the industry and its governing agencies, from national bands and the Federal Reserve System to foreign banking, Federal Home Loan Banks, National Housing, the Federal Deposit Insurance Corporation, bank holding companies, financial recordkeeping, the Community Reinvestment Act of 1977, Bank Protection Act, International Banking Act, the Gramm-Leach-Bliley Act, the Fair Debt Collection Practices Act, the Emergency Economic Stabilization Act of 2006, and much more. This service provides convenient access to a wealth of legal and regulatory provisions and changes governing the industry. This is annual subscription service which is updated monthly by interfiled pages.

Banking Report. Washington, DC: Bloomberg BNA, 1965-date. 2 vols. Looseleaf format. Weekly reports. Index issued quarterly and cumulated annually. Also available via the Web.
Cost: $2,575 per year; Internet: $2,877 per year (single user). Combination discounts available (2014).
A current awareness service providing news and commentary on banking and thrift institutions, including rules, proposals, litigation, and legislation. The text of proposed regulations is accompanied by expert summaries, intent, and comment deadlines. The service includes the following sections: Highlights, In This Issue, Topical Index, Table of Cases, News, Bank Notes, Thrift News, Legal Developments, International News, Journal, Text, Analysis and Perspective, Special Reports, and Electronic Resources. An excellent tool for keeping up with current topics and emerging issues.

Beckford, Joseph G. **Bank Holding Company Compliance Manual**. 2d ed. New York: Matthew Bender & Co., 1986-date. 1 vol. Looseleaf format. Updated twice a year. No CD-ROM or Internet.
Cost: $734 (includes annual subscription); renewal: 1998: $200; 1999: $210; 2000: $225; 2001: $241; 2002: $258; 2003: $271; 2004: $285; 2005: $305; 2006: $342; 2007: $384; 2008: $415; 2009: $446; 2010: $467; 2011: $488; 2012: $515; 2013: $551; 2014: $163.02; eBook: $734; renewal: 2014: $589.
Intended chiefly for bank holding company compliance officers and banking law attorneys, this manual provides coverage of the day-to-day compliance responsibilities faced by bank holding companies. The coverage embraces such subjects as Federal Reserve Board requirements for banks and non-bank acquisitions; permissible non-banking activities for bank holding companies; capital and financial requirements, the institution of internal compliance control systems, and on-going compliance. The text features simple and clearly written explanations accompanied by notes, examples and practical hints.

Cappello, A. Barry. **Lender Liability**. 4th ed. Huntington, NY: Juris Publishing, 2009. 1 vol. (various pagings). Looseleaf format.
Cost: $195; no supplementation to date (2014).
Lending institutions may be subject to liability for a variety of acts committed against borrowers, including, but not limited to, failure to uphold loan commitments, misrepresentations, and improper interference with customer business operations. In recent years, lender liability has emerged as a distinct body of law which has become more uniform across jurisdictional lines, and which has resulted in an expanding body of published literature, lawsuits, and court decisions. In this comprehensive volume, the author explains how and where these problems arise between lenders and borrowers, the various common law theories of liability, including breach of contact, breach of fiduciary duty, fraud, improper control, interference, negligence, duress, and conversion. Similarly, he details the various statutory theories of liability, under both federal and state laws. Attention is also given to bankruptcy concerns which arise as a consequence of, lender conduct, and lawsuits against failing or failed financial institutions. The text features numerous citations to supporting court decisions, statutes, regulations, and secondary authorities. The appendices include sample forms, including a sample complaint, request for production of documents, sample interrogatories, and jury instructions, as well as the full text of the Truth in Lending Act, Equal Credit Opportunity Act, and Fair Debt Collection Practices Act. There are also separate tables of

general cases, federal cases, state cases, statutes, rules and regulations, and secondary authorities. An excellent resource for the experienced practitioner or the neophyte involved in representing an institution or client whose interests involve bank liability. A. Barry Cappello is Managing Partner of Cappello & Noël LLP, based in Santa Barbara, California. A successful trial who has obtained verdicts in excess of $200 million and settlements of nearly $1 billion, he has written over 100 articles on lender liability and trial strategy, and is a frequent speaker on these and other topics. Mr. Cappello is listed in Best Lawyers in America, and speaks nationally on trial techniques in complex litigation.

Clark, Barkley. **The Law of Bank Deposits, Collections and Credit Cards.** 4th ed. Chicago: LexisNexis A. S. Pratt, 1995-date. 1 vol. Looseleaf format and eBook. This title was converted to a service publication in 1997.
Cost: $623 per year (2014).
This work is unquestionably the "bible" in the field regarding the law of collections, credit cards, bank deposits, and letters of credit. It includes a discussion of collection of documentary drafts, electronic funds transfer, adverse claims to a deposit account, bank setoff, funds availability and check collection under Regulation CC, check kiting, truth-in-savings, allocation of fraud loss for forged endorsements, letters of credit, and much more. This work is impressive in both its breadth and in-depth analysis, with substantial citations to relevant UCC Sections, cases, statutes, etc.

Cost Saving Tips: For the attorney specializing in commercial law, this is one of the most authoritative sources available; however, significant savings can be achieved by dropping the standing order and purchasing the book, with its one year subscription, every 2-3 years. When A.S. Pratt & Sons took control of this title in 1997, it converted it to a subscription service and effectively precluded customers from purchasing one of the three cumulative supplements each year. This, in effect, raised the annual supplementation cost from approximately $70 (for those electing to purchase one supplement per year) to $623 per year in 2014. By subscribing for one year and skipping one year, you will be able to reduce your average annual cost to about $310 per year while going about one year between updating.

Clore, Duncan L., ed. **Financial Institution Bonds**. 3d ed. Chicago: American Bar Association, 2008. 1 vol. (1033 pp.).
Cost: $129.95 ($99.95 to members) (2014).
Financial institution bonds, which were first developed at the start of the 20th century, had their origins in surety bonds that have existed since ancient times. Surety bonds are three party agreements by which one party (the surety) agrees to guarantee the obligation owed by a second party (the principal) to a third party (the obligee). As such, they provide the benefit of financial security in the event that an obligation is not performed by the principal. Financial security bonds have been used to ensure the honesty of employees. As the banking industry expanded at the beginning of the 20th century, it felt compelled to mitigate their exposure to various forms of employee dishonesty, as well as robbery, theft and other problems. In 1912, the State of New York allowed insurers to combine various forms of unrelated coverages in the form of a single bond. This volume provides detailed discussion of various issues involved in the coverage offered by financial institution bonds, including employee dishonesty, covered employees, discovery of loss, the loan loss exclusion, potential income exclusion, loss and causation, conditions to recovery, recovery of loss, the insured's guide to effective claims, managing the insurer's response to the claim, and litigation strategies from both the insured's and insurer's perspectives. It concludes with a variety of sample policies and forms. The 18 chapters, written by 32 experts in the field of surety law, draw upon the latest supporting case law. The editor is a partner with the firm of Strasburger & Price, LLP in Dallas and past chair of the ABA's Fidelity and Surety Law Committee of the Tort and Insurance Practice Section. As the most authoritative and comprehensive reference on the subject, this volume was prepared in conjunction with 5th national program on Financial Institution Bonds held in Baltimore in 2008.

Federal Banking Law Reporter. Riverwoods, IL: Wolters Kluwer Law & Business (CCH), 1945-date. Looseleaf service. 8 vols. Available in print, and on the Internet. Updated weekly.
Cost: print: $3,756 per year; Internet: $3,756 per year (2014).
This eight-volume looseleaf service provides detailed current coverage of federal laws and regulations governing banks and thrift institutions. Supplemented on a weekly basis, the binders contain the full text of all federal banking laws as codified in Title 12 of the **U.S. Code** and all federal banking regulations as promulgated by various federal banking agencies. It also contains federal banking agency releases, opinion letters, bulletins, notices, commentaries, and other regulatory issuances. Current materials, including legislative documents, regulatory releases and issuances, agency letters and opinions, and court decisions, appear in the Current volume of the set. These current and decisional materials are later moved to transfer binders for permanent retention. An important tool for the attorney working for banking institutions or on banking matters. Its chief value lies in the fact that it brings a wide variety of otherwise diffuse statutory, regulatory, and decisional materials together in one set.

Federal Banking Laws and Regulations. 2013 Edition with CD-ROM. Charlottesville, VA: LexisNexis (Michie). 1 vol. (2064 pp.). Paperbound.
Cost: $69 Print or eBook): $65 (2014).
This handy paperbound volume contains all the banking and banking-related statutes from various titles of the **United States Code** together with the with banking regulations from the **Code of Federal Regulations**. For the banking law specialist, this is an excellent alternative to buying the entire **U.S. Code** and **CFR**.

Fein, Melanie L. **Securities Activities of Banks**. 4th ed. New York: Wolters Kluwer Law & Business, 2012. 1 vol. (1,302 pp.)
Cost: $389; supplementation: 2013: $199 (2014).
The first edition of this book was published in 1991 after banks secured the right under the Glass-Steagall Act, and other laws, to offer securities and other related services, subject to certain legal restrictions, of course. Subsequent editions were released as banks became major players in the securities business, and after the Gramm-Leach-Bliley Act of 1999 removed some of

the Glass-Steagall restrictions, and authorized financial holding companies to facilitate affiliations between banks and securities firms. This fourth edition is issued in the wake of the passage of the Dodd-Frank Wall Street Reform and Consumer Protection Act, a major piece of legislation that attempts to address some of the regulatory shortcomings that led to the banking and financial crisis of 2008-2009. Despite these Congressional actions, however, the success of the banking industry in gaining access to the securities market was due more to its persistent efforts to overcome legal barriers through innovative legal interpretations that were endorsed by the federal banking agencies and upheld by the courts. This volume examines in depth the evolution of bank securities activities and the environment in which that evolution took place. Accordingly, the author considers the bank regulatory framework, the securities regulatory framework, and the Glass-Steagall Act (1933), that, until 1999, prohibited affiliations and interlocks between member banks of the Federal Reserve System and firms engaged principally or primarily in the underwriting and distribution of securities. She also addresses such subjects as investment advice, brokerage activities, investment and trading activities, merchant banking activities, underwriting and dealing, private placement activities, mutual fund activities, fiduciary activities, the securitization of assets, derivatives, and deposit and loan activities. It was Gramm-Leach-Bliley that paved the way for the modern regulatory environment that could accommodate these and other activities heretofore prohibited to it by Glass-Steagall. This volume provides detailed guidance to banks and their legal advisors charged with building their securities business and ensuring regulatory compliance. The text is extensively supported with citations to applicable statutes, regulations, cases, Federal Reserve Board and other regulatory documents. Melanie Fein brings years of experience at the intersection of banking and securities, including the Legal Division of the Board of Governors of the Federal Reserve System where she was involved in regulatory matters involving bank holding companies and their securities activities. Formerly with Arnold & Porter and an adjunct faulty member at Yale School, she is author of the leading treatises on *Federal Bank Holding Company Law* and *Securities Activities of Banks*, among other books and publications. She also chaired the American Bar Association's Banking Law Committee Task Force on the Causes of the Financial Crisis.

Felsenfeld, Carl and David L. Glass. **Banking Regulation in the United States**. 3d ed. Huntington, NY: Juris Publishing, 2011. 1 vol. (xiii, 467 pp.). Also available as a pdf download.
Cost: $125.00 (print or eBook); no supplementation to date (2014).
The regulatory system that governs the banking and financial industry in the United States is a complex, and often redundant and overlapping, amalgam of federal and state agencies and attendant regulatory provisions. In this introductory overview of the U.S. banking regulatory system, the authors survey the legal and regulatory landscape governing banking and financial practices, including the types of bank charters, the regulatory framework, the dual banking system, bank activities, deposits and accounts, usury rate laws, the Federal Deposit Insurance Corporation (FDIC), bank holding companies, bank subsidiaries, interstate banking, branching (including interstate branching), bank securities operations and the Glass-Steagall Act, insurance activities, real estate development, data processing activities, thrifts, S&Ls, savings banks, and credit unions. This volume was published in the wake of the passage of the Dodd-Frank Wall Street Reform and Consumer Protection Act (Pub.L. 111-203), an act that, despite its length and promulgation of more than 240 new regulations, made little change in the fundamental banking regulatory structure. Only one small regulatory Agency—the Office of Thrift Supervision—was abolished and two new agencies created: the Financial Stability Oversight Council and a Bureau of Consumer Protection that will be part of the Federal Reserve. However, the full impact of the legislation has yet to be fully realized.

Franklin, Talcott J. and Thomas F. Nealon III. **Mortgage and Asset Backed Securities Litigation Handbook**. Eagan, MN: West, 2009-date. 1 vol. (various pagings). Looseleaf format.
Cost: $525; supplementation: 2010: $187; 2011: $221; 2012: $276; 2013: $280 (2014).
Mortgage-backed securities (MBS) are asset-backed securities or debt obligations that represent a claim on the cash flows from mortgage loans, most commonly those on residential properties. Mortgage loans are purchased from banks, mortgage companies, and other originators, then assembled into pools by government agencies, government-sponsored enterprises (such as Fannie Mae and Freddie Mac), and private entities. One of the advantages of these securities is that they, at least theoretically, contain features to mitigate the risks of default associated with these mortgages. Mortgage-backed securities represent claims on the principal and payments on the loans in the pool, through a process known as securitization. These securities are usually sold as bonds, but financial innovation has created a variety of securities that derive their ultimate value from mortgage pools. The securitization of residential loans originated in the 1970s; however, commercial loans also became the subject of securitization programs in the early 1990s. While mortgage-backed securities existed in relative obscurity until recently, the subprime mortgage crisis in the period since 2008 exposed their vulnerabilities to the wider public and brought them into the litigation mainstream. This volume provides a comprehensive overview of this rapidly evolving area of law and litigation. Its chapters provide coverage of the industry generally, an overview of securitization litigation, securitization claims, borrower litigation, rating agency claims, bankruptcy considerations, trends in the industry, taxation, suits against the United States government, suits by municipalities, credit default swaps, covered bonds and accounting issues related to securitization. The Appendix contains a glossary of both commercial- and residential-backed securities (CMBS and RMBS), a table of cases and index. Under the general authorship and editorship of Talcott J. Franklin, formerly of Patton Boggs LLP in Dallas, and Thomas P. Nealon, Group General Counsel and Director of Training, Real Estate Finance and Servicing Group, LNR Partners in Miami Beach, FL, this volume's contributors includes several dozen attorney expert in the fields of real estate, securitization, and securities law. A particularly timely addition to the literature on mortgages and securitization issues.

Cost-Saving Tip: Drop standing order and re-purchase volume every few years. Initial price was increased from $289 to $525.00 between 2013 and 2014.

Geva, Benjamin. **The Law of Electronic Fund Transfers**. New York: Matthew Bender, 1992-date. 1 vol. Looseleaf or eBook format. Updated once a year.
Cost: $338 (print or eBook) (annual subscription); renewal: 1998: $70; 1999: $73; 2000: $78; 2001: $83; 2002: $104; 2003: $110; 2004: $116; 2005: $125; 2006: $140; 2007: $158; 2008: $167; 2009: $176; 2010: $181; 2011: $186; 2012: $202; 2013: $214.
This one-volume work provides analysis of the law governing electronic funds transfers, with emphasis on global and domestic wire transfers, ACH payments, and consumer transactions. It includes a concise analysis of U.C.C. Article 4A, EFTA, Regulation E, and other pertinent law. It also includes a discussion of such topics as acceptance, rejection and execution; sender's payment obligation to accepting bank liability for unauthorized payment orders; errors in payment orders and acceptance; cancellations, amendment, and reversal; damages for improper execution; and beneficiary's rights, including notice, payment, and discharge. Includes relevant primary law, including U.C.C. Article 4A, the EFTA and Regulation E, as well as illustrations, charts, and practical hints.

Goolik, Lisa M., et al. **Dodd-Frank Manual Series. Depository institutions (Title III).** New York: Wolters Kluwer Law & Business (CCH), 2012. 1 vol. (1,080 pp.). Paperbound.
Cost: $99.00 (2014).
One in a series of manuals designed to provide explanation and analysis of the *Dodd-Frank Wall Street Reform and Consumer Protection Act of 2010,* Pub. Law. 111-203, 124 Stat. 1376 (July 21, 2010). This volume covers Art. III of the Act dealing with depository institutions. Also published in 2012, other volumes in the series address Financial Stability (Titles I, II and VIII), Private Fund Advisors (Title IV) Bank and Thrift Regulation—Volker Rule (Title VI), Derivatives (Title VII), and Securities Regulation and Corporate Governance (Title IX). The volume is divided into three main sections: explanations, laws, and regulations. At 2,300 pages, the Act is one of the most far-reaching and complex pieces of financial legislation ever enacted, and the most significant legislative change to financial supervision since the 1930s. The stated aims of the Act are to "To promote the financial stability of the United States by improving accountability and transparency in the financial system, to end "too big to fail", to protect the American taxpayer by ending bailouts, to protect consumers from abusive financial services practices, and for other purposes." Still to be fleshed out, the regulatory edifice that it expands also imposes massive burdens on financial institutions, particularly smaller institutions without the resources to absorb the attendant costs and unintended consequences. Ironically, "too big to fail," one of the evils *Dodd-Frank* was supposedly designed to curtail, has simply been renamed "systemically important" for the purposes of making bailouts a permanent fixture of federal fiscal policy. It has been preliminarily estimated that the Act will require 243 rulemakings, 67 one-time reports or studies, and 22 new periodic reports from a total of 11 administrative agencies. This volume will help financial institutions to comprehend the depth of the burdens imposed on them under the Act. The publisher also provides access to the **Dodd-Frank Widget**, providing access to the latest regulatory reform updates:
http://financialreform.wolterskluwerlb.com/financial-reform-widget.html

Hardy, Peter D. **Criminal Tax, Money Laundering, and Bank Secrecy Act Litigation**. Arlington, VA: Bloomberg BNA Books, 2010. 1 vol. (1,669 pp.).
Cost: $525.00 (includes 2012 supp.); supplementation: 2011: $295; 2012: $300; 2013: 0 (2014).
The Internal Revenue Service is the only investigatory agency with jurisdiction over federal criminal tax offenses. Its role has expanded in recent years with the growth of sophisticated criminal activity involving money laundering operations, offshore bank accounts, tax evasion by individuals and corporations, and violations of the Bank Secrecy Act (BSA). The average criminal IRS case is more likely to involve complex fact patterns, technical law, legal privileges, logistical challenges, and difficult questions regarding what constitutes a criminal mental state. Enforcement of the tax code can increase the litigation exposure of corporations, and involve attorney-client privilege, parallel civil and criminal proceedings, deferred prosecution agreements, evidence and conduct in foreign jurisdictions, and the difficulties involved in drawing a line between civil and criminal violations. Moreover, the IRS is now using the Bank Secrecy Act to pursue not only traditional currency reporting offenses, but to step up enforcement of offshore reporting requirements, and to require and enforce anti-money-laundering requirements for financial institutions. The monumental scope of this volume is a reflection of the complexity of the criminal cases now handled by the IRS and federal prosecutors at the Justice Department. It addresses not only current law and procedure, but offers expert practical guidance in handling a federal criminal case from beginning to end, including the full range of complex legal, factual, logistical, and tactical issues which accompany such litigation. While its primary focus is on criminal cases handled by the IRS, this volume also explores the important legal issues that may exist in a complex white-collar practice, including offshore accounts, tax shelter prosecutions, corporate prosecutions, sentencing in white collar cases, and the Supreme Court's recent interpretation of the money laundering statutes. Following an illuminating overview of the nature of IRS criminal enforcement, chapters are devoted to the consideration of the criminal tax statutes, money laundering, the Bank Secrecy Act, the investigation and review process, special issues, pleas agreements, pretrial practice, trial, and sentencing. The text is heavily supported with citations to relevant primary and secondary authorities, including IRS code sections and regulations, and federal court decisions. Designed for use by both prosecutors and defense counsel, this volume will also serve as an essential reference tool for corporate counsel, financial institutions, business and tax professionals, and federal government agencies. The Appendices include a variety relevant federal documents, including a currency transaction report, depository institution suspicious activity report, and a sample agreements involving deferred prosecution of a financial audit, tax and advisory services firm, among others. Peter D. Hardy is a principal in the Philadelphia firm of Post & Schell's national White Collar Defense, Compliance & Risk Management Practice Group. A former federal prosecutor, his practice focuses on the counseling and defense of corporations, directors, officers, managers, professionals and others who may face allegations of business-related or other misconduct.

Kider, Mitchel H. and Don J. Halpern. **Secondary Mortgage Market Guide**. 2d ed. Huntington, NY: Juris Publishing, 2004.

1 vol. (various pagings).
Cost: $125 (print or eBook); no supplementation to date (2014).
The secondary mortgage market is the market for the sale of securities or bonds which have been collateralized by the value of mortgage loans. Mortgage lenders, whether individual banks or specialized mortgage firms, typically group many mortgage loans together and sell them as securities called collateralized mortgage obligations (CMOs). Thus, the risk of the individual loans is reduced by this aggregation process. This guide to the secondary mortgage market analyzes the dramatic transformation of the industry since the 1930s, when the market was characterized by substantial down payments and short-term loans, to the present day's liberalization of mortgage terms, including low (or no) down payments, extended maturities, and creative loan products. The market has also been transformed by technology which has affected property appraisals, automated underwriting, loan origination, and the real estate business. This volume covers the full range of mortgage market topics, including the evolution of the mortgage market, the types of residential mortgages, the primary mortgage market, secondary mortgage market, government sponsored secondary market institutions, development of the private secondary mortgage market, types of mortgage securities, business considerations, buyer's warranty demands, federal regulation of real estate lending, securities law regulations of mortgage-backed securities, and tax considerations. The authors are partners in the Washington, DC firm of Weiner Brodsky Sidman Kider PC, which specializes in real estate finance and mortgage banking.

Kirsch, Clifford E., ed. **Financial Product Fundamentals: Law, Business, Compliance**. 2d ed. New York: Practising Law Institute, 2012-date. 1 vol. (895 pp.). Looseleaf format.
Cost: $335; supplementation: 2013; $376; 1st ed.: 2003: $90; 2004: 0; 2005: $95; 2006: $95; 2007: $105; 2008: $120; 2009: $132; 2010: $273; 2011: $290; 2012: new edition.
This volume provides a basic introduction to a variety of financial instruments, both new and traditional, with which attorneys must deal in servicing their clients. These instruments include products that are offered in capital markets that help companies in their growth and expansion, as well as specific collective investment vehicles. The authors also consider the legal and regulatory regimens imposed on them, their advantages and drawbacks, and the means by which they are priced, distributed and marketed. The volume is enhanced by the addition of a number of sample forms, charts, tables and graphs. More than fifteen attorneys contributed chapters. The editor is Chief Counsel, Variable Products, for the Prudential Insurance Company of America and a former Assistant Director of the SEC's Division of Investment Management.

Lapine, Kenneth M. **Consumer Credit: Law, Transactions and Forms**. New York: Matthew Bender & Co., 1984-date. 4 vols. Looseleaf format. Updated twice a year. Also volumes 7, 8, 9 and 10 of **Banking Law**. No CD-ROM or Internet.
Cost: $1,740 (includes annual subscription); renewal: 1997: $505; 1998: $505; 1999: $525; 2000: $560; 2001: $599; 2002; $641; 2003: $674; 2004: $708; 2005: $758; 2006: $789; 2007: $836; 2008: $890; 2009: $948; 2010: $981; 2011: $1,015; 2012: $1,081; 2013: $1,157; 2014: $1,238; eBook: $1,581; renewal: 2013: $1,238; 2014: $1,243.
A complete guide to the law governing consumer credit and credit transactions. Provides extensive treatment of the law, with practical, step-by-step, guidance for each stage of a consumer credit transaction. The author provides expert commentary and interpretation of the major consumer credit laws, including: truth-in-lending, fair credit reporting; community reinvestment; and real estate settlement procedures. The transactional analysis covers a number of topics, ranging from consumer credit advertising through the loan application and approval and repayment processes. Each significant aspect of the consumer credit transaction is examined to reveal the rules and regulations which apply. Includes the text of relevant statutes, regulations, interpretations and policies. The model forms, checklists, examples and tables are accompanied by compliance hints.

Lovett, William A. **Banking and Financial Institutions Law in a Nutshell**. 7th ed. St. Paul, MN: West, 2009. 1 vol. (491 pp.). Available from West Academic.
Cost: $41; from $30.00 on amazon.com (2014).
The United States was engulfed by a wave of bank failures and losses in 2008 that was reminiscent of the Great Depression. While predatory lenders no doubt contributed to the crisis, a variety of political actors were chiefly to blame, having urged, even demanded, that financial institutions provide mortgages to those with insufficient cash reserves or credit worthiness. The moral hazard created by these loose lending practices was compounded by the increasing popularity of mortgage-backed securities that were packaged into what would become toxic assets in a declining real estate market. This succinct overview of the law of banking and financial institutions in current through the national financial crisis and efforts by the federal government to address it. While primarily intended as a supplementary law school text, it can serve as an useful aid to lawyers, bankers, and financial professionals who wish a summary of banking law, its history, money and banking, the regulatory environment, thrift institutions, securities market regulation, insurance regulation, pension funds, retirement accounts and social security, and controversies and prospects. It is also a useful and inexpensive primer on banking law for general academic or public libraries. The author is the Joseph Merrick Jones Professor of Law and Economics at Tulane Law School, New Orleans.

Malloy, Michael P. **Banking Law and Regulation.** 2d ed. New York: Wolters Kluwer Law & Business, 2005-date. 3 vols. Looseleaf format. Completely revised in 2004.
Cost: $1,749; supplementation: 1996: $184; 1997: $196; 1998: $410; 1999: $410; 2000: $600; 2001: $600; 2002: $640; 2003: $442; 2004: $1,057 (2004-1 supp. and new ed.); 2005: $924; 2006: $940; 2007: $1,002; 2008: $1,074; 2009: $1,112; 2010: $1,232; 2011: $1,350; 2012: $734; 2013: $809.
This three-volume treatise provides a clearly written and well-organized exposition of the law of banks and banking. The text properly reflects all those developments which have impacted the banking world over the past 15 years, including the passage of the Financial Institutions Reform, Recovery, and Enforcement Act of 1989, and the Federal Deposit Insurance Corporation Act of 1991, as well as increased competition from foreign banks, the collapse of the savings and loan industry, and the new regulatory climate. Chapters cover the regulatory environment, organization of the entity, management of depository institutions, exercise of

control, issuance of securities, trading in bank- and thrift-issued securities, securities activities of depository institutions, holding company formation, mergers and acquisitions, conversions, and supervision of troubled and falling institutions. Volume three includes a useful selected bibliography of materials published since 1951, a Table of Cases, Table of Statutes, and Table of Rules and Regulations, and Index. The text of this work is amply documented with citations to statutory law, regulations and, to a lesser degree, case law. It also includes a number of useful charts, graphs and diagrams, including, for example, a particularly valuable annotated, chronological table of regulatory developments which followed the passage of FIRREA. Michael P. Malloy is Professor of Law and Director of Graduate Studies, Fordham University School of Law

Malloy, Michael P. **Principles of Bank Regulation**. 3d ed. St. Paul, MN: West, 2011. 1 vol. (495 pp.). Concise Hornbook Serties. Available from West Academic.
Cost: $48; from $38.00 on amazon.com (2014).
Banking is governed by a variety of statutory and regulatory provisions, both at the federal and state levels. Federal law imposes disclosure requirements typical of the securities industry generally as well as substantive requirements of transactional and corporate law, including incorporation under federal law. Designed primarily for the law student, this book can also serve as a useful overview for the practitioner. The chapters in this volume examine such topics as the regulated environment of banking, entry rules, control transactions, transactional rules, holding company activities, securities regulation, resolution of institution failures, international banking, and bank regulation and social policy. The Appendices include a guide to researching banking regulation on WESTLAW. The author, a Professor of Law at Fordham University School of Law, is also author of the more exhaustive three-volume **Banking Law and Regulation** treatise published by Wolters Kluwer Law & Business.

McCoy, Patricia A. **Banking Law Manual**. 2d ed. New York: Matthew Bender & Co., 2000-date. 1 vol. Looseleaf format or eBook. Updated twice annually.
Cost: $437 (print or eBook) (includes annual subscription); renewal: 1997: $120; 1998: $120; 1999: $127; 2000: new edition; 2001: $144; 2002: $155; 2003: $242; 2004: $171; 2005: $185; 2006: $193; 2007: $205; 2008: $218; 2009: $232; 2010: $244; 2011: $252; 2012: $281; 2013: $301; 2014: $309.
Designed as a desk reference, procedural guide, and training manual for the banking professional, this volume provides expert interpretations and policy discussions on issues of bank regulation, with special attention to the Gramm-Leach-Bliley Act of 1999, and Dodd-Frank. It addresses such topics as securities powers of bank and bank holding companies, geographic restrictions on bank operations, with emphasis on the implications of the Riegle-Neal Interstate Banking and Branching Efficiency Act, responsibilities of officers, directors and outside professionals, safety and soundness regulation of bank activities, federal deposit insurance and its implications, bank supervision and examinations, Bank Secrecy Act requirements, closure of failed financial institutions and resolution techniques, financial institution mergers and antitrust review; and consumer credit laws. Professor Patricia McCoy is a professor of law at Cleveland-Marshall School of Law, Cleveland State University, where she specializes in financial services regulation and the law of corporate governance. She is a former partner at the Washington, DC office of Mayer, Brown & Platt.

Michie on Banks and Banking. Charlottesville, VA: LexisNexis, 1995-date. 14 vols. Annual supplementation. Print or eBook.
Cost: $848; supplementation: 1994: $240; 1995: $240; 1996: $180; 1997: $185; 1998: $195; 1999: $205; 2000: $215; 2001: $230; 2002: $240; 2003: $249; 2004: $249; 2005: $268; 2006: $288; 2007: $451; 2008: $308; 2009: $541; 2010: $651; 2011: $690; 2012: $837; 2013: $774.
This encyclopedic treatise is based on the analysis of case law regarding the organization, functions, rights, duties, powers and liabilities of banks and other financial institutions. Chapters cover control and regulation in general, incorporation, organization and incidents or existence, officers and agents, capital, stock and dividends, stockholders, insolvency and dissolution, banking franchises and powers and their exercise in general, representation of bank by officers and agents, deposits, collections, loans and discounts, exchange, money, securities and investments, circulating notes, actions, national banks, savings banks, loan, trust and investment companies, clearinghouses, and taxation. Index. Annual paperbound volume contains the Regulations of the Board of Governors of the Federal Reserve System. While this is one of the few multi-volume banking law sets on the market, it is not likely to please the specialist who is apt to be disappointed by its concentration on case law and lack of statutory analysis. The subject arrangement leans heavily on the organization of the Banks and Banking topics in the West key number digests. In fact, many of the case annotations are recycled headnotes which have been borrowed from West publishing under a cooperative arrangement. All but three of the bound volumes have been revised since 1987. This set leaves the user wanting for more probing and integrated analysis of case and statutory law, and federal regulations.

Cost Saving Tips: Because of its exclusion of statutory law, this set will have to be supplemented with a work providing greater attention to statutory matters, such as **Banking Law** from Matthew Bender. If you have access to other means of updating, you may not need these pocket parts on an annual basis.

Norton, Joseph Jude, ed. **Commercial Loan Documentation Guide.** New York: Matthew Bender & Co., 1989-date. 2 vols. Looseleaf format or eBook. Supplemented annually.
Cost: $485 (print or eBook) (annual subscription); annual renewal: 1995: $89 (frozen since 1992). 1996: $93; 1997: $93; 1998: $100; 1999: $107; 2000: $115; 2001: $123; 2002: $133; 2003: $140; 2004: $147; 2005: $156; 2006: $167; 2007: $180; 2008: $191; 2009: $207; 2010: $224; 2011: $237; 2012: $251; 2013: $288; 2014: $297; eBook: $485; renewal: 2014: $297.
An excellent one-volume overview and analysis of the basic loan process and loan documents. Provides both lender's and borrower's perspective on commercial loan transactions with attention to loan pricing, commitment letters, commercial loan agreements, commitments to lend, alternate interest rate terms, representations and warranties, default and remedies, collateral

security, guaranties and third-party credit supports, lawyers and legal opinions, and basic accounting concepts. The introduction also provides an overview of the regulatory environment. Includes sample forms and practical hints.

Pollard, Alfred M. and Joseph P. Daly. **Banking Law in the United States**. 4th ed. Huntington, NY: Juris Publishing, 2011-date. 2 vols. (1,426 pp.). Looseleaf format or downloadable eBook.

Cost: $395.00; supplementation: 2012: $95.00; 2013: $95; print and eBook combination: $592.50

Banking law embraces not only the corporate establishment and operation of banks, but also the various financial services that are subject to government regulation. This treatise focuses specifically on the laws governing the operations of commercial banking in the United States, that is, those roughly 8,000 institutions accepting deposits and making commercial loans. The scope of commercial bank activity mirrors the marketplaces and communities, large or small, in which they operate. This work, which combines the features of both a textbook and casebook, places primary emphasis on the legal framework and regulatory scheme governing commercial banking practices, as well as the monumental changes that have impacted the industry in the last twenty years. It begins by providing a invaluable overview of legislative, regulatory and judicial action that has transformed the industry, particularly since 1988, including Gramm-Leach-Bliley, the Emergency Economic Stabilization Act of 2008, the Housing and Economic Recovery Act of 2008, and the Dodd-Frank Wall Street Reform and Commercial Protection Act of 2010. Additional chapters trace the history of banking regulation, the nature of commercial banks and bank holding companies, the various legislative and regulatory bodies that govern banking activities, the enforcement powers of the regulators, the banking structure in the modern legal framework, the process of chartering banks and forming holding companies, and national bank powers. The authors then turn their attention to such bank operations as national bank lending limits, restricted transactions with bank affiliates and insiders, capital and reserve requirements, crimes and torts, holding company nonbanking businesses, securities activities, retail banking, privacy of financial records, international banking, taxation of banks, mergers and acquisitions, failing and failed banks, and conclude with a look at directions in banking law and regulation. The authors have done an admirable job of distilling a complex body of legal and regulatory information into a succinct and well-organized form, without sacrificing critical content or annotated citations to significant statutes, regulations and caselaw. Alfred M. Pollard, who received his undergraduate and law degrees from the University of North Carolina at Chapel Hill and his doctorate in foreign affairs from the University of Virginia, is General Counsel at the Federal Housing Finance Agency (FHFA) in Washington, D.C. Joseph P. Daly, formerly an attorney with the Office of the Comptroller of the Currency, is a Partner with the banking law firm of Luse Gorman Pomerenk & Schick, PC, Washington, D.C. He received his law degree from George Washington University National Law Center.

Rosenthal, Samuel. **Director and Officer Liability in Financial Institutions: A Deskbook**. Arlington, VA: Bloomberg BNA, 2012. 1 vol. (1,045 pp.). Hardcover.

Cost: $395 (2014).

Directors and officers of financial institutions may find themselves the targets of civil, criminal or regulatory actions when their institutions suffer financial crises, or are implicated in such activities as money laundering, Bank Secrecy Act violations, or violations of consumer privacy or consumer protection statutes. In their zeal to find individual scapegoats, however, prosecutors may fail to recognize the often complex political, economic and regulatory nexus that combines to put financial institutions, and their officers, in jeopardy. Indeed, they may make it difficult for defendants to introduce affirmative defenses that might shift the blame to regulators. This was the conclusion reached by the FDIC itself, which concluded that "the rise in the number of bank failures in the 1980s had no single causes or short list of causes," among them broad national forces, a series of severe regional and sectoral recessions that hit banks in a number of markets and led to a majority of the failures, and regulatory authorities that failed to restrain banks that engaged in excessive risk. In the author's view, defending claims made against directors and officers of financial institutions may lie in a proper understanding of the causes of previous financial crises, such as those experienced in the 1980s and 1990s. This volume is designed to assist legal counsel in protecting bank officers and directors at the forefront of liability, and to provide guidance in defending them against civil, criminal, and administrative proceedings by either governmental or private parties. It does this by addressing three main areas of concern in its 19 chapters: (1) sources of liability, including statutory responsibilities, duties of directors and officers, civil liabilities, criminal liabilities, consumer protection and privacy, and administrative actions; (2) governmental enforcement, including agencies involved in enforcement actions, recent civil actions and policies by federal agencies, recent criminal actions against officers ands directors, and government investigation; and (3) defense techniques and factors, including prelitigation defense investigation, the civil case, criminal proceedings, special problems of parallel proceedings, joint-defense agreements and privileges, and paying for the cost of defense. The author brings to the table an impressive understanding of the complex regulatory environment in which financial institutions operate, an environment made even more treacherous with the passage of Dodd-Frank Wall Street Reform and Consumer Protection Act in 2010. Samuel Rosenthal is chair of the Government Investigations and Litigation practice group at Patton Boggs LLP, where he has represented individuals and entities in a range of white collar criminal matters, including those involving director and officer liability. Previously, he served as the chief of the Appellate Section, Criminal Division, with the Department of Justice in Washington.

Ryder, Nicholas. **Financial Crime in the 21st Century: Law and Policy**. Northampton, MA: Edward Elgar, 2011. 1 vol. (340 pp.).

Cost: hardcover: $135 (online price: $121.50); softcover: $47.00 (online price: $37.60); from $40.90 on amazon.com (2014).

Since the 1970s, the war against crime has taken on a global dimension, the financial incarnation of which embraces efforts to combat the illegal drug trade, human trafficking, organized crime, and terrorism. These activities have been aided by loopholes in the financial structure that permit illicit funds to be transferred through the system electronically. As various forms of financial crime have manifested themselves, governments have responded by enacting laws and instituting policies and procedures to combat money laundering and related offenses. These efforts were accelerated as a result of the attacks of 9/11, the collapse of the Barings Bank, Enron and the WorldCom. The United Nations responded by introducing a number of legal protocols designed to address the problems of global money laundering, and the Financial Action Task Force (FATF) was established to make recommendations for confronting the problem of money laundering. Since 9/11, much of the United States' effort has been directed toward the goal of undermining terrorist financing. The purpose of this book is to provide a detailed commentary and analytical review of the financial crime policies adopted by the international community and how these have been implemented in the United States and the United Kingdom. Chapters address money laundering, terrorist financing, fraud, insider trading, the confiscation and forfeiture of the illicit proceeds of crime, regulators and agencies, and sentencing in financial crime. It includes an extensive bibliography of sources. The author/editor is Reader in Law and Head of the Commercial Law Research Unit at the Bristol Law School, University of the West of England, UK. He is joined by Andrew H. Baker, Liverpool John Moore's University, and Karen Harrison, University of Hull.

Schroeder, Milton R. **The Law and Regulation of Financial Institutions**. Sheshunoff/Pratt/LexisNexis, 2014. 3 vols. Looseleaf format.
Cost: $623.00 (2014).
The financial industry has undergone massive upheaval in recent years, most significantly in the Great Recession of 2008, and its aftermath. Some have attributed this upheaval to the changes in banking laws, specifically the amendments to the Glass–Steagall Act of 1932 and the U.S. Banking Act of 1933 that had created distinct categories of financial institutions, and limited commercial bank securities activities and affiliations within commercial banks and securities firms. Since the 1960s, however, the restrictions between commercial banks and securities firms were gradually relaxed, culminating in the passage of the Gramm–Leach–Bliley Act (GLB) (1999) that permitted the consolidation of commercial banks, investment banks, securities firms, and insurance companies. At the same time, massive federal intrusions into the housing market exacerbated by Federal Reserve and government housing policies, specifically as executed by Freddie Mac and Fannie Mae, created giant government-sponsored enterprises (GSEs) whose misregulation threatened the country's economic health. This in-depth guide provides an explanation and analysis of all the major laws and regulations governing financial institutions, their transactions and compliance. It explains the laws that control and limit the activities of such institutions, and identifies the legal rights and duties that apply to financial institution transactions involving checks, credit cards, electronic transfers, consumer credit, secured financing, letters of credit, and bankruptcy. Beginning with a review of banking history and regulation, and the federal statutes governing its operations, including the Dodd-Frank Wall Street Reform and Consumer Protection Act of 2010, the author addresses a number of issues impacting the operation of financial institutions, including the operation of the Federal Reserve, bank holding companies, bank expansion, interstate banking, supervision of bank safety and soundness, enforcement of the Federal Consumer Protection Law, securities activities of banks and bank holding companies, capital adequacy, Federal Deposit Insurance, insolvency and reorganization of depository institutions and financial companies, money laundering, terrorist financing, and the duty to record and report transactions. He also devotes considerable attention to the application of the Uniform Commercial Code, payment and credit transactions, bank collection and payment, secured transactions, consumer credit and interest rate regulation, and bankruptcy. There are extensive references to primary law sources, law reviews, professional journals, and other secondary sources. This is a thorough, but less exhaustive (and expensive), treatment of the law of financial institutions than that offered by Matthew Bender's **Banking Law**, CCH's **Federal Banking Law Reporter,** or **Banking Law and Regulation** from Wolters Kluwer Law & Business. Milton Schroeder is Emeritus Professor of Law, Arizona State University who has taught and written on banking-related, contracts and commercial transactions issues for more than thirty-five years. In 2013, LexisNexis acquired the publishing brands and businesses of Sheshunoff and A.S. Pratt from the Thompson Media Group.

The State Banking Law Reporter. Riverwoods, IL: Wolters Kluwer Law & Business (CCH). Internet only. Consists of the following components: **Northeastern States**, **Central States**, **Southern States**, and **Western States**. Internet updated monthly.
Cost: All-states: approx. $3,300 per year; inquire (2014).
Northeastern States: approx. $1,200 per year; inquire
Central States: approx. $1,200 per year; inquire
Southern States: approx. $1,200 per year; inquire
Western States: approx. $1,200 per year; inquire
A full-text compilation of state banking laws, regulations, agency issuances and selected state UCC laws in full text organized to facilitate comparison of laws and regulations across state lines. Designed for the use of financial institutions and legal counsel who do business with institutions in multiple jurisdictions.

Tatge, David B., David Flaxman, and Jeremy B. Tatge. **American Factoring Law**. Arlington, VA: Bloomberg BNA Books, 2009-date. 1 vol. (856 pp.). Hardbound.
Cost: $465.00; supplementation: 2011: $200; 2012: $210; 2013: $215.
Factoring is a financial transaction in which a business sells its accounts receivable to a third party (a factor) at a discount. In "advance" factoring, the factor provides financing to the seller of the accounts in the form of a cash "advance," often 70-85% of the purchase price of the accounts, with the balance of the purchase price being paid, net of the factor's discount fee (commission) and other charges, upon collection. Factors are a significant source of financing for American businesses, both as a stand-alone source of financing through advances on purchased accounts and in partnership with commercial banks. The relationship between factors and their clients involves a host of financial transactions and legal issues addresses by this comprehensive treatise. Among these are the history of American factoring law, the various roles of factors, the factoring contract, the treatment of credit risk and "true sale" issues, litigation between the factor and his client, litigation between factors and account debtors, factor and guarantors of client obligations,

the factor and funding sources, factors and third-party lenders/ creditors, bankruptcy issues, the factor and tax authorities, and factoring accounting. Among the other issues explored is the role of factors as commission sales agents and financiers. There is detailed discussion of the acquisitions of many factors by major financial institutions and the development of the factoring markets in the United States. The authors also address the varieties of fees, discounts and yields short of barter, as well as representations and warranties regarding the accounts, as well as the mechanics of chargebacks and collections. The text is exhaustively footnoted with citations to both primary law and secondary sources, and contains a glossary of factoring terms, and bibliography. David B. Tatge is a partner in the law firm of Epstein, Becker & Green, P.C., Washington, D.C. His co-author, David Flaxman, is a principal with the third generation New York City factoring firm of Rosenthal & Rosenthal. His son, Jeremy B. Tage, is with the financial institution of Brown Brothers Harriman, Boston, MA. This is an essential resource for any attorney or financial executive involved in factoring deals.

Thorndike Encyclopedia of Banking and Financial Tables. 4th ed. Arlington, VA: A.S. Pratt & Sons, 2002. 1 vol. Paperbound.
Cost: OUT-OF-PRINT; was $195; from $42.29 on amazon.com (2014).
A complete encyclopedia for the banking or investment professional, trust attorney, or financial consultant. Includes loan payment and amortization schedules, tables for compound interest and annuity, interest, savings and withdrawal, installment loans, investments, taxes, stock growth, retirement payments, international weights and measures. Users can flip from table to table to see how changes in rates or periodicity affect the costs and/or yield on loans, IRA's, bonds, Rule of 78 transactions. An essential desktop reference for any professional involved with financial transactions. Currently out-of-print. All A.S. Pratt acquired by LexisNexis.

Villa, John K. **Banking Crimes: Fraud, Money Laundering & Embezzlement**. St. Paul, MN: Thomson Reuters, 1987-date. 2 vols. Looseleaf format. Annual supplementation.
Cost: $528; supplementation: 1996: $225; 1997: $224; 1998: $220; 1999: $119; 2000: $129; 2001: $152; 2002: $53.50; 2003: $61; 2004: $120; 2005: $115; 2006: $250; 2007: $192.50; 2008: $147.50; 2009: $255; 2010: $44; 2011: $162; 2012: $179; 2013: $193.60; **Monthly Assured Print Price (APP):** $38/$456.
A comprehensive overview of the law governing crimes against banking and financial institutions designed for use by attorneys working to ensure compliance with the laws, or defending or prosecuting those charged with violations against financial institutions. The contents include chapters on the federal criminal justice system, criminal referrals, misapplications of funds, embezzlement, false statements made to a federally issued financial institution, bank bribery, bank secrecy, mail and wire fraud, money laundering and the right to financial privacy, and civil and criminal asset forfeiture. John Villa is a practicing attorney with extensive experience representing financial institutions.

Weisblatt, Harold. **Checks, Drafts and Notes**. New York: Matthew Bender & Co., 1984-date. 3 vols. Looseleaf format or eBook. Periodic revisions.
Cost: $593 (print or eBook) (includes annual subscription); renewal: 1997: $170; 1998: $170; 1999: $177; 2000: $190; 2001: $203; 2002: $218; 2003: $229; 2004: $240; 2005: $257; 2006: $268; 2007: $284; 2008: $304; 2009: $325; 2010: $339; 2011: $351: 2012: $374; 2013: $400; 2014: $436; eBook: $539; renewal: 2014: $445.74.
A summary and analysis of Articles 3 and 4 of the **Uniform Commerce Code**, including interpretation of the most recent case law, and statutory and regulatory amendments. Includes a discussion of such topics as signature requirements; transfer and negotiation; holder in due course rule; contract of the parties; bank liabilities and defenses; overdrafts and Regulation CC. Also Volumes 5 and 6 of **Banking Law**.

Williams, Harding de C. **Federal Banking Law and Regulation: a Handbook for Lawyers**. Chicago: American Bar Association, 2006. 1 vol. (361 pp.).
Cost: OUT-OF-PRINT; from $67.66 on amazon.com (2014)
This primer on banking law and regulation outlines the legal and regulatory framework and the state and federal charters within which banks and other financial institutions operate. The author provides a useful overview of the primary historical, political and economic developments that have shaped the current banking system since the creation of the present federal banking agency, the Office of the Comptroller of the Currency, in 1863. Other topics covered include deposit insurance; bank examinations, enforcement, conservatorships, and receiverships; branches and interstate banking; holding companies; subsidiaries, corporate governance rules; audits, audit committees and financial reporting; securities activities of banks; and capital. The author also discusses the impact of the Sarbanes Oxley Act as it applies to publicly-held holding companies, free-standing stock institutions, mutual institutions, and non-public holding companies. The author's lucid style makes this an ideal resource for the attorney new to the field.

Zisman, Barry Stuart, et al. **Banks and Thrifts: Government Enforcement and Receivership.** New York: Matthew Bender & Co., 1991-date. 1 vol. Looseleaf format or eBook. Updated annually.
Cost: $412 (print or eBook); supplementation: 1995: $47 (frozen since 1992); 1996: $50; 1997: $50; 1998: $60; 1999: $63; 2000: $67; 2001: $72; 2002: $93; 2003: $98; 2004: $103; 2005: $110; 2006: $124; 2007: $140; 2008: $153; 2009: $166; 2010: $184; 2011: $186; 2012: $205; 2013: $230; 2014: $236.
Authored by Barry Zisman and a team of thirty practicing attorneys, this one-volume banking law handbook is designed as a complete guide to enforcement and receivership law, and the role of the Federal Deposit Insurance Corporation. Includes a well-documented treatment of federal regulatory law as its applies to the application and examination processes, directory and officer liability, liability of outside professionals, insurance and bond claims, the formal and informal enforcement processes, parallel civil and criminal proceedings, open institution assistance, regulatory seizure, failed transactions, bank and thrift receiverships, receivers' rights and obligations, claims

procedures against receivers, and more. Includes extensive citations to primary law and practical hints.

Additional titles in the field of Banking Law are available from the following publishers: Adams & Reese, American Bankers Association, CCH, Inc., Dearborn Financial Publishing, Greenwood Publishing Group, Harcourt Legal, HIS Financial Products, Institute of International Banking, International Monetary Fund, Kluwer Academic, Kluwer Law International, LexisNexis, Matthew Bender, McGraw-Hill Professional, Oxford University Press, Panel Publishers, Practising Law Institute, A.S. Pratt, Prentice-Hall, Thomson Reuters West, Warren, Gorham & Lamont, West Academic, World Bank. See Appendix B for addresses and telephone numbers.

Bankruptcy Law

Bankruptcy Code and Rules. 2014 Compact Edition. St. Paul, MN: West Group, 2013. 1 vol. Annual. Paperbound or ProView eBook.
Cost: 2014 Edition: $168; ProView eBook: $168; **Monthly Assured Print Price (APP):** $14/$168 (2014).
This handy edition to the Bankruptcy Code and Rules includes the complete text of Title 11 of the U.S.Code, with cross references, relevant sections of Titles 18 and 28, the Federal Rules of Bankruptcy Procedure, Federal Rules of Civil Procedure, and the Federal Rules of Evidence.

Bankruptcy Court Decisions. St. Paul, MN: Thomson Reuters (West) (formerly LRP), 2011-date. 2 vols. Weekly issues. Looseleaf format.
Cost: $2,400.60 per year; **Monthly Assured Print Price (APP):** $200.05/$2,400.60 (2014).
Provides full-text coverage of the country's leading bankruptcy cases, released 4-6 weeks after their release by the court. Also provides news and comment.

Cost Saving Tip: Recently acquired by Thomson Reuters, the cost of this annual subscription leaped from $1,315 per year in 2010 to $1,914 in 2012, and $2,400.60 in 2013, an 82.55% increase in three years. Comparable in cost to **Collier Bankruptcy Cases**.

Bankruptcy Desk Guide. St. Paul, MN: Thomson Reuters/ West. (Clark Boardman Callaghan), 1990-date. 5 vols. Looseleaf format.
Cost: $2,560; supplementation: 1993: $221; 1994: $250; 1995: $281.95; 1996: $332; 1997: $349; 1998: $426; 1999: $468; 2000: $434; 2001: $551; 2002: $582; 2003: $691; 2004: $741; 2005: $882; 2006: $1,200; 2007: $1,057; 2008: $1,127; 2009: $1,353.50; 2010: $1,366.50; 2011: $1,490; 2012: $1,622; 2013: $1,816. **Bankruptcy Law Letter** may be purchased separately at $1,013.52 per year; **Monthly Assured Print Price (APP):** $187/$2,244.
This five-volume set provides analysis of both substantive and procedural aspects of bankruptcy law. This set may be distinguished from the publisher's larger **Bankruptcy Service** by its topical, rather than code section, arrangement and by its attention to matters of procedure. Includes three volumes of text, one volume containing Index and Tables, and one volume of Forms. Features include Comments, Cautions, Observations, Practice Pointers and Law Review Commentaries. Main body of text includes citations to primary authorities, while Case Annotations and Practice Updates are included in the twice annual cumulative supplements. The five looseleaf binders consist of chapters in pamphlet form. This makes updating quick and convenient and allows for easy removal of appropriate sections for use in court. Although libraries may experience more frequent theft of individual pamphlets, the format makes it easier to replace missing material by contacting the publisher toll-free.

Cost Saving Tip: A less costly, albeit less exhaustive, alternative to the **Bankruptcy Service**. If possible, investigate purchase of a current used set and then enter a standing order for updates with your West sales representative. You may be able to save hundreds of dollars on your initial purchase and then be just as current as the purchaser of a new set. As with many Thomson Reuters titles, you can allow your standing order to lapse once the no-charge supplementation has expired and simply re-purchase the set at a later date when sufficient savings have been achieved.

Bankruptcy Law Library. New York: Wolters Kluwer. Online.
Cost: $540.00 per year (2014).
This package of bankruptcy law treatises and practice sets includes **Ginsberg & Martin on Bankruptcy, Bankruptcy Litigation & Practice: A Practitioner Guide, Bankruptcy Litigation Manual, Strategies for Creditors in Bankruptcy Proceedings, Advanced Chapter 11 Bankruptcy Practice, Ordin on Contesting Confirmation, Tax Planning for Troubled Corporations,**

Bankruptcy Law Reporter. Riverwoods, IL: Wolters Kluwer Law & Business (CCH), 1979-date. 3 vols. Looseleaf format and Internet. Updated biweekly.
Cost: $2,822 per year; Internet: call for pricing (2014).
A comprehensive research service providing timely coverage of current bankruptcy statutes, regulations, and cases as well as detailed information on the case administration. The three looseleaf binders provide coverage of current Supreme Court decisions, the Bankruptcy Code and amendments, forms, Supreme Court Rules of Procedure, Congressional committee reports, and state exemption statutes. A Legislative Record section provides coverage of current Congressional activity. The case administration section treats such topics as creditors, debtors, estates, liquidation, debts of municipalities, and reorganization. The text is accompanied by numerous editorial explanations, annotations and historical comments. The annual subscription includes transfer binders containing decisions issued between 1995 and 1997.

Bankruptcy Library [CD-ROM]. Eagan, MN: Thomson Reuters/ West. Updated quarterly. Five discs. Available for Windows, and

Macintosh. Search Engine: Premise. Toll-free support (800-255-2549).
Cost: $10,092 per year (2013).
This Premise product contains the full text West's **Bankruptcy Reporter** (1979 to date**), Bankruptcy Annotated Code, Rules and Forms**, **West's Bankruptcy Digest**, **Norton Bankruptcy Law & Practice, Bankruptcy Bibliography**, **Russell's Bankruptcy Evidence Manual**, and Bankruptcy Table of Cases. Includes hypertext links from analytical discussion in the legal treatises to the relevant primary law. The product runs best on a CD-ROM tower or loaded on a hard drive; otherwise, a shuffling of the multiple disc is required. Also includes a no-cost uplink to current bankruptcy cases on the WESTLAW database.

Bankruptcy Service. Lawyers Edition. St. Paul, MN: Thomson/West (Clark Boardman Callaghan), 1979-date. 23 vols. Looseleaf format. Quarterly supplementation. Includes monthly current Awareness Alert newsletter. Comes with six months free service. Formerly published by Lawyers Cooperative.
Cost: $9,665; supplementation: $832.50; 1993: $932; 1994: $983; 1995: $1,139.95; 1996: $1,310; 1997: $1,325; 1998: $1,383; 1999: $1,404; 2000: $1,502; 2001: $1,863; 2002: $2,054; 2003: $2,354; 2004: $2,750; 2005: $3,100; 2006: $3,467; 2007: $3,978; 2008: $4,324; 2009: $4,974; 2010: $5,546; 2011: $5,700; 2012: $6,121; 2013: $6,855. **Bankruptcy Law Letter** may be purchased separately at $1013.52 per year. **Monthly Assured Print Price (APP):** $566/$6,792. See sales representative for applicable discounts.
One of the most exhaustive treatments of bankruptcy law on the market this set provides coverage organized by both topic and code section. Chapter coverage includes, among others, such topics as what constitutes property of the estates, redemption of property in chapter 7, abandonment of property, bankruptcy crimes involving property of the estate, operating debtor's business use, sale or lease of property, code commentary and analysis, rules, commentary and analysis, forms and research aids. The bulk of this set (8 vols.) consists of Code Commentary and Analysis, organized according to the sections of the Federal Bankruptcy Code in Title 11 of the U.S. Code. Valuable features include Cross-References to other useful reference books, Illustrations, State Aspects, and Law Review Commentaries. Case Annotations are essentially those appearing in the **United States Code Service**. Each chapter includes collateral references to other Clark Boardman and Lawyers Cooperative publications and features extensive citations to appropriate primary authorities, including cases, statutes, bankruptcy rules, and legislative history, as well as to appropriate forms and ALR annotations and texts. Quarterly cumulative supplements include summaries of current cases and Statutory Updates, as well as Legislative Alerts and Practice Updates. The use of pamphlets in the looseleaf binders makes filing far more convenient than those sets with interfiled pages and makes replacement of missing material easier. Pamphlet format also makes it easier to remove desired portions for use in court.

Cost Saving Tips: The high initial cost (which more than doubled from $3,249 to $8,870 between 2006 and 2013) and updating costs for this set make it a costly ongoing expense which should be resisted. Those purchasers not in need of regular updating service may consider purchasing another new set at periodic intervals in lieu of entering a standing order with the publisher for supplementation. A current awareness newsletter may then be purchased for more timely information. As long as you are aware that the used set has its limitations, you can employ the core content to great advantage, but not depend on it for the most up-to-date coverage. This should be an informed decision based on the nature of your practice, available financial resources, and your comfort level with a used set. Although there are obviously a variety of possible options, you may decide to purchase one of the smaller, multi-volume treatises, such as the **Collier Bankruptcy Manual** and use the **Bankruptcy Service** for your initial or more in-depth research. The **Bankruptcy Service** will cost you more than $8,000 in initial and supplementation costs over the first 12 months. Annual updating costs will have been reduced to approximately $1,300 (newsletter and annual subscription to the **Collier Bankruptcy Manual**).

Bernstein, Stan, Susan H. Seabury and Jack F. Williams. **Business Bankruptcy Essentials**. Chicago: American Bar Association, 2009. 1 vol. (246 pp.).
Cost: $89.95; $69.95 to members; from $44.94 on amazon.com (2014).
This is an introduction to the world of business bankruptcy for the non-bankruptcy practitioner, with an emphasis upon bankruptcies among middle market ($25-$100 million) or small ($2-$25 million) businesses. The latter, generally privately held, range from small family groceries to independent pharmacies, local car repair garages, suburban restaurants, printing establishments, and small retail chains to other businesses defined under the Bankruptcy Abuse Prevention and Consumer Act of 2005. Also discussed are single asset real estate cases (SAREs). The book looks at bankruptcy from the perspective of the client who is dealing with a customer or borrower in bankruptcy. The chapters cover handling the bankruptcy cases from the client's perspective, an introduction to sources of vital information in a business bankruptcy case, the history and structure of the Bankruptcy Code, types of bankruptcies, bankruptcy as a tool, who may be a debtor in bankruptcy, getting paid, the automatic stay, the bankruptcy estate, the Chapter 11 case, cash collateral and debtor transactions, executory contracts and unexpired leases, avoidance powers, claims and distributions, the discharge, substantive consolidation, pos-conformation issues, and alternatives to bankruptcy relief. Stan Bernstein is a former U.S. bankruptcy judge. Susan Seabury specializes in commercial bankruptcy-related issues and provides financial advisory services in bankruptcy and insolvency matters. Jack Williams is a professor of law at Georgia State University where he teaches courses in bankruptcy, business, commercial law, and taxation.

Collier Bankruptcy Case Update. New York: Matthew Bender & Co. Weekly subscription via print or e-mail.
Cost: $899 per year (print); $817 (eBook); e-mail edition: $656 (2014).
This service provides concise summaries of current bankruptcy law cases organized by Bankruptcy Code section and Bankruptcy Rule number. Coverage includes decisions of the U.S. Supreme Court, the Circuit Courts of Appeals, District Courts, Bankruptcy Appellate Panels and Bankruptcy Courts.

The subscription also includes an annual set of Tables which indexes decisions published in the Update for the prior year. A cost-saving alternative to the full text coverage provided by the **Collier Bankruptcy Cases**.

Collier Bankruptcy Cases. Second Series. New York: Matthew Bender & Co., 1979-date. 7 looseleaf vols. with 3 bound vols. per year). Biweekly releases.
Cost: $3,060 (with annual subscription); annual renewal: 1995: $525; 1996: $551; 1997: $551; 1998: $580; 1999: $605; 2000: $650; 2001: $696; 2002: $745; 2003: $857; 2004: $900; 2005: 1,050; 2006: $1,208; 2007: $1,358; 2008: $1,507; 2009: $1,702; 2010: $1,805; 2011: $1,895; 2012: $2,009; 2013: $2,150; 2014: $2,242.
This service includes full text of significant cases decided under the Bankruptcy Act, each of which is preceded by a summary of the case and points of law. Cases are cross-referenced to the 15th edition of **Collier on Bankruptcy**. A Codex provides eight research aids updated on a regular basis. The biweekly releases are each accompanied by a newsletter. Although not a treatise, this service is usually marketed with **Collier on Bankruptcy** or the **Collier Bankruptcy Practice Guide** and will, thus, be of interest to the bankruptcy practitioner.

Collier Bankruptcy Library [CD-ROM]. New York: Matthew Bender & Co. One disc. Updated quarterly. Available for Windows. Search Engine: Folio.
Cost: $14,246 (includes annual subscription); renewal: 1998: $3,225; 1999: $3,355; 2000: $3,500; 2001: $3,745; 2002: $4,008; 2003: $4,209; 2004: $4,419; 2005: $4,773; 2006: $5,489; 2007: $5,928; 2008: $6,402; 2009: $6,914; 2010: $7,053; 2011: $7,794; 2012: $8,262; 2013: $8.840; 2014: $9,840.
This product contains all or any combination of the full text of the following Matthew Bender treatises: **Collier on Bankruptcy** (15th ed. rev.), **Collier Bankruptcy Practice Guide**, **Collier Pamphlet Edition**, **Collier Lending Institutions and the Bankruptcy Code**, **Collier Family Law and the Bankruptcy Code**, **Collier Real Estate Transactions and the Bankruptcy Code**, **Collier Handbook for Trustees and Debtors in Possession**, **Collier Business Workout Guide**, **Collier Handbook for Creditors' Committees**, **Collier Compensation, Employment and Appointment of Trustees and Professionals in Bankruptcy Cases**. **Collier Bankruptcy Cases** is also available.

Cost Saving Tips: This CD-ROM package is designed for the law firm with a serious and active bankruptcy practice and already offers significant savings over the combined cost of buying the individual titles separately. Investigate the purchase of smaller packaged options.

Collier Bankruptcy Manual. 4th ed. Revised. Lawrence P. King, Editor-in-Chief. New York: Matthew Bender & Co., 2011-date. 3 vols. Looseleaf format. Updated two times per year. Also available on eBook
Cost: $1,338 (annual subscription); renewal: 1998: $345; 1999: $360; 2000: $360; 2001: $385; 2002: $441; 2003: $464; 2004: $487; 2005: $510; 2006: $560; 2007: $605; 2008: $653; 2009: $705; 2010: $770; 2011: $770; 2012: $770; 2013: $824; 2014: $899; eBook: $1,217 per year; renewal: 2014: $899.
Released at the end of 1997, this is an abridged version of the first eight volumes of **Collier on Bankruptcy**, 15th Edition Revised. It provides section-by-section analysis of the Bankruptcy Code, including those falling under Chapters 7, 11, 12, and 13, and provides a step-by-step guide to filing bankruptcy under any chapter of the Code. It includes a discussion of liquidation, reorganization, debt adjustment for family farmers and individuals and fully correlates the viewpoints of debtors, creditors, and trustees. An ideal alternative to the complete **Collier on Bankruptcy** for the cost-conscious attorney.

Cost-Saving Tip: Acquire this far less costly alternative to the full **Collier on Bankruptcy**, which will provide all the essentials and the currency without the laborious detail and high cost.

Collier Bankruptcy Practice Guide. Asa S. Herzog and Lawrence P. King, Co-Editors-in-Chief. New York: Matthew Bender & Co., 1981-date. 8 vols. Looseleaf format. Supplemented several times per year. Includes the **Collier Local Bankruptcy Court Rules** pamphlet as a part of the subscription. These volumes, cover all federal circuits (4th and D.C. circuits are combined
Cost: $3,808 (includes annual subscription); annual renewal: 1995: $795 (price frozen since 1992); 1996: $795; 1997: $795; 1998: $810; 1999: $840; 2000: $880: 2001: $942; 2002: $1,008; 2003: $1,059; 2004: $1,112; 2005: $1,168; 2006: $1,577; 2007: $1,680; 2008: $1,814; 2009: $1,995; 2010: $2,148; 2011: $2,309; 2012: $2,344; 2013: $2,508; 2014: $2,737.
Intended as a complement to **Collier on Bankruptcy**, this set has been edited by Asa Herzog, Bankruptcy Judge, Southern District of New York (Ret.) and Lawrence P. King, Charles Seligson Professor of Law, New York University School of Law, and written by 43 contributing authors. It is intended to guide the attorney through the complete bankruptcy process, beginning with the initial client interview. Organizationally, it is divided into twelve parts, reflecting the major areas encountered when handling a case under the Federal Bankruptcy Code. Each of the Chapters is then divided into Practice Discussion, featuring procedural analysis, and Practice Aids, including checklists, forms and a research guide listing applicable code sections, bankruptcy rules, and secondary sources. Footnotes provide citations to applicable case law and statutes.

Cost Saving Tips: Given the high supplementation cost ($2,737 in 2014), you may choose to forego supplementing this set and get your updating in some other form. If you desire the detailed analysis of procedural aspects of bankruptcy, the core treatise may serve you well without supplementation from the publisher. You always have the option of choosing a less costly set which addresses the procedural aspects and supplementing this with a newsletter or other updating vehicle. A standing order to the bankruptcy code and rules pamphlets from LexisNexis Matthew Bender, Thomson/West, or another publisher will provide you with all but the most recent changes in the law and rules. A long as you are aware of the limitations of the lapsed set and take appropriate steps to provide updating in other forms, you can save on both initial and updating costs.

Collier Consumer Bankruptcy Practice Guide with Forms. Sommer, Henry J. Lawrence P. King, Editor-in-Chief. New York: Matthew Bender & Co., 1997-date. 3 vols. Looseleaf format and eBook. Updated annually.
Cost: $1,265 (includes annual subscription); renewal: 2004: $355; 2005: $383; 2006: $412; 2007: $465; 2008: $495; 2009: $528; 2010: $599; 2011: $620; 2012: $733; 2013: $693; 2014: $756; eBook: $1,150; renewal: 2013: $693; 2014: $756.
A tool designed to guide the attorney through all phases of the consumer bankruptcy case, from initial client interview to filing an appeal. Designed primarily for solo practitioners and small consumer bankruptcy firms, it provides discussion of such topics as: methods and strategies for interviewing the debtor; counseling the debtor about bankruptcy options; choosing the type of case offering the greatest advantage to the client; agreements for and disclosure of attorneys fees; preparation and filing of bankruptcy forms, statements and schedules used in the typical bankruptcy case; enforcing the automatic stay and the Chapter 13 co-debtor stay, as well as motions for relief from the stay; claiming and objecting to exemptions; preparing and meeting of creditors, the avoiding powers of the trustee; filing and objections to proofs of claim; obtaining a discharge of the debtor and the dischargeability of particular debts; the essentials of a successful Chapter 13 plan; reaffirmation of debts; and litigation procedures in bankruptcy cases. The text is accompanied by such special features as Practice Notes, Planning Notes. Illustrations, and Warnings, which appear in text boxes highlighting tactical and strategic information. Henry J. Sommer is a noted expert in the area of consumer bankruptcy. Includes a complete set of forms covering every aspect of consumer bankruptcy proceedings, this work is organized topically to follow the sequence of tasks performed by bankruptcy practitioners. The forms are integrated with the discussion in the **Consumer Bankruptcy Practice Guide** through extensive cross-references.

Collier on Bankruptcy. Lawrence P. King, Editor-in-Chief. 15th ed. New York: Matthew Bender & Co., 1985-date. 27 vols. Looseleaf format. Quarterly supplements. **Collier on Bankruptcy Practice Package** on CD-ROM features relevant case law and LexisNexis online connection at no extra charge.
Cost: $9,415 (includes annual subscription); annual renewal: 1995: $1,747 (frozen since 1992); 1996: $1,747; 1997: $1,747.50; 1998: $1,785; 1999: $1,860; 2000: $1,930; 2001: $2,065; 2002: $2,210; 2003: $2,265; 2004: $2.295; 2005: $2,433; 2006: $3,650.00; 2007: $3,887; 2008: $4,198; 2009: $4,534; 2010: $4,647; 2011: $5,088; 2012: $5,088; 2013: $5,444; 2014: $5,942; e-book: $7,999; renewal: 2013: $4,011; 2014: $5,553.
The classic treatise on the law of bankruptcy which has been published continuously by the Matthew Bender Company since the passage of the Bankruptcy Act of 1898. The 15th edition is the first edition published since the Bankruptcy Reform Act of 1978. It provides an in-depth analysis of the Bankruptcy Code, including the 1978 amendments to the Code and the Bankruptcy Reform Act of 1994. Includes a historical analysis of he bankruptcy legislation, discussion of the bankruptcy courts, jurisdiction and venue, the Panel of Private Trustees, United States Trustees, bankruptcy crimes, case administration, creditors, debtors and the estate, liquidation, adjustments of municipal debts, reorganization, and much more. The set also includes forms, a listing of State Exemptions, Bankruptcy Rules, a Finding Aids volume, and four volumes of Appendices, which includes the text of the Bankruptcy Acts and related legislative history. In 1997, Matthew Bender issued a completely new and revised 15th edition of **Collier on Bankruptcy** which replaces the former 15th edition. The editors of the new **Collier on Bankruptcy** have at least four major goals: (1) to place less focus on historical analysis and more on current law (moving historical commentary to the ends of each chapter); (2) to make the textual discussion more reflective of the current state of law; (3) to take more definitive positions where the law is unclear or where the courts are divided; and (4) to make the publication easier to use in both print and electronic formats. In support of this last goal, the editors have divided each chapter in more paragraphs and subparagraphs with greater use of descriptive captions. In addition, the accompanying forms have been updated, improved and reorganized into two volumes of commercial bankruptcy forms and one volume of consumer bankruptcy forms. The Appendix volumes have been reorganized to make it easier to locate primary source materials, including the text of legislation and recent legislative history. The whole revision process has been guided by Collier Editor-in-Chief, Professor Lawrence P. King of the New York University School of Law, a newly appointed Board of Editors, and a number of contributing authors.

Cost Saving Tips: **Collier on Bankruptcy** is, without question, a major purchase for any law firm or law library. If yours is a specialized bankruptcy practice, perhaps you require the in-depth treatment which Collier provides. You should be prepared, however, for the significant cost of maintaining this set on a current basis ($5,942 in 2014). Both the purchase and supplementation costs of this set should cause you to evaluate all options carefully. As with most Bender treatises, you always have the option of subscribing for one year and then letting the subscription lapse. This will leave you with a core treatise capable of answering the vast majority of your bankruptcy questions. You can fall back on a less expensive alternative treatise with annual pocket parts, supplemented with a newsletter, and the current year's **Bankruptcy Code** and **Bankruptcy Rules**. You must be prepared to update your research in these and applicable **U.S. Code** sections and U.S. bankruptcy cases, employing **Shepard's Citations** when necessary. Your local public law library can be of great benefit in this regard. Don't forget that, if you are a subscriber to the **U.S. Code Service** or **U.S. Code Annotated**, you will be duplicating much of the coverage, including the statutory amendments and case annotations you already have in one of those sources. It is the textual analysis which is the most unique and valuable part of **Collier's. Collier on Bankruptcy** may also available on the used lawbook market for anywhere from $295 to $595 depending on the currency of the set. A set at the high end of that range was probably purchased by the used book dealer within the last month or two. Be aware, however, that if it is your intention to bring it up-to-date, there is no point in buying a used set since Bender titles are now all subscription publications with one year's service. This option is only for that person who wishes to maintain a slightly dated set and, then, perhaps, update it periodically by buying another used set. Going this route may initially save you more than $5,000, and more than $4,000 per year thereafter. See Chapter on Used Law Book Dealers for further information. Your decision to acquire an electronic version will depend, therefore, upon your objective evaluation of those products on their own merits. Remember

that, should you choose either of these two options, you must maintain the annual subscription or lose the information.
Another alternative is **the Collier on Bankruptcy Practice Package** on CD-ROM, priced roughly the same as Collier on Bankruptcy, but also including the **Collier on Bankruptcy Practice Guide**, priced at $3,808 by itself.

Collier Bankruptcy Act Pamphlet Edition. New York: Matthew Bender, 1938-date. Annual. 3 vols. Paperbound.
Cost: 2013 Edition: $289.
These desktop reference tools provide access to the full text of the **Bankruptcy Code** and the **Federal Rules of Bankruptcy Procedure**, together with expert commentary and analysis, comments on Amendments, discussion of related **Code** sections and **Rules**, case annotations, legislative history and Advisory Committee Notes, and research references to other Collier publications. Volume one contains the annotated **Bankruptcy Code** and volume two the annotated **Federal Rules of Bankruptcy Procedure**. Volume three, the **Collier Portable Pamphlet**, contains the full text of the **Code**, relevant statutory provisions and the **Federal Rules of Bankruptcy Procedure**. The commentaries are written by Professor David G. Epstein, the Charles E. Tweedy Jr. Professor of Law at the University of Alabama and of counsel at King & Spalding in Atlanta, Hon. Mary Davies Scott, U.S. Bankruptcy Judge for the Eastern and Western Districts of Arkansas and member of the Bankruptcy Appellate Panel for the Eighth Circuit Court of Appeals, and Collier Editor-in-Chief Lawrence P. King, the Charles Seligson Professor of Law at New York University and of counsel at Wachtell, Lipton, Rosen & Katz, New York.

Drake, W. Homer, Jr. **Bankruptcy Practice for the General Practitioner**. 3d ed. St. Paul, MN: West (Clark Boardman Callaghan), 1995-date. 1 vol. Annual replacement volume.
Cost: 2013 Edition: $223; supplementation: 1996: $105; 1997: $120; 1998: $116.85; 1999: $128; 2000: $137; 2001: $162; 2002: $177; 2003: $31; 2004: $42; 2005: $46; 2006: $82; 2007: $101.50; 2008: $196.50; 2009: $50.50; 2010: annual editions instituted; **Monthly Assured Print Price (APP):** $20/$240.
Written by Judge Homer Drake, United States Bankruptcy Judge for the Northern District of Georgia, this is a practitioner-oriented guide to the Bankruptcy Reform Act of 1978 and its subsequent amendments. Volume one contains chapters on the background of the Code, the United States Trustee, obtaining relief from a bankruptcy court, jurisdiction, venue and appeals, the debtor's estate, duties and benefits of debtors, creditors and claims, estate administrative provisions, estate administrative powers, officers of the estate, straight bankruptcy (liquidation), reorganization, debt repayment for individual with regular income, and debt repayment for the family farmer with regular annual income. Appendices include the Bankruptcy Reform Act of 1978, as amended, Judicial Code Provisions Applicable to Bankruptcy Practice, and the Bankruptcy Tax Act of 1980. Volume two contains the Bankruptcy Rules, Proposed Bankruptcy Rules, Forms (including Official Forms issued by the Judicial Conference of the United States, the Director's Procedural Forms, the author's suggested forms, tables and subject index. An excellent set combining features of the legal treatise and the practitioner's handbook. Annual supplementation cost is reasonable considering he fact that this is a two-volume set with semi-annual updates. A good choice for the practitioner desiring more frequent supplementation than that offered by Cowans and Epstein, but less than that of the larger multi-volume works such as **Collier on Bankruptcy**.

Epstein, David G., and Steve H. Nichols. **Principles of Bankruptcy Law**. St. Paul, MN: West, 2007. 1 vol. (310 pp.). Available from West Academic. Concise Hornbook Series.
Cost: $48 (2014).
This West Hornbook contains the material embraced by the typical law school course in bankruptcy. It tracks the progress of a bankruptcy case and examines Chapter 7, Chapter 11, Chapter 13 bankruptcies. West Academic is a new entity that acquirecd the Hornbooks and Nutshells formerly owned by Thomson Reuters.

Ginsburg, Robert E., Robert D. Martin and Susan V. Kelley. **Ginsburg & Martin on Bankruptcy**. 5th ed. New York: Wolters Kluwer Law & Business, 2010-date. 4 vols. With 2 forms discs. Looseleaf format. Annual supplementation.
Cost: $879; supplementation: 2009: $490; 2010: new edition; 2011: $825; 2012: $885; 2013: $1,077; prior eds.: 1997: $175; 1998: $149; 2000: $194; 2001: $215; 2002: $220; 2003: $270; 2004: $330; 2005: $330; 2006: $395; 2007: $395; 2008: new edition.
This practitioner's guide to the key areas of bankruptcy law combines discussion and analysis of the relevant law with the most recent case strategies from both the debtor's and creditor's perspective. Chapters examine such topics as voluntary and involuntary petitions, the automatic stay, selection and compensation of trustees, professionals and committees, the property of the estate, exemptions, executory contracts, the trustee's avoiding powers, the strongarm clause, fraudulent transfer actions, proof, allowance and priority of claims, discharge and dischargeability, cases under Chapters 7, 11, 12 and 13, and tax issues. Each of the more than 400 model bankruptcy forms, available in both print and disc, is acccompanied by detailed practice notes and commentary. The authors are both federal bankruptcy judges and former law professors. They are joined by a team of more than two dozen contributing editors.

Jacob, Marvin E. and Sharon Youdelman, eds. **Reorganizing Failing Businesses: A Comprehensive Review and Analysis of Financial Restructuring and Business Reorganization**. Revised Edition. Weil, Gotshal & Manges LLP. Chicago: American Bar Association, 2006. 2 vols. (1,100 pp.). Looseleaf format.
Cost: $315.95 ($250.95 to Bankruptcy Section members); from $174.96 on amazon.com (2014).
The results of corporate failure are complicated and far-reaching. This work was written to benefit the various professionals involved in restructurings, including corporate lawyers and litigators, executives, bankers and accountants. It is organized in four parts: out-of-court restructurings, Chapter 11 proceedings, specialized restructurings, and general considerations, and is the result of a two-year collaboration by attorneys with the New York firm of Weil, Gotshal & Manges LLP, the leading U.S. firm with experience in the areas of corporate restructurings, turnabouts, and workouts. Both practical and scholarly, this work

is highly recommended for any attorney involved in the issues of corporate failures or restructuring.

Norton, William L., Jr. **Norton Bankruptcy Law and Practice**. 3d ed. St. Paul, MN: Thomson/West (Clark Boardman Callaghan), 1994-date. 12 vols. Looseleaf format. Updated quarterly. Subscription also includes **Norton Bankruptcy Law Advisor**, a monthly newsletter.
Cost: $4,608; annual supplementation: 1993: $545; 1994: $595; 1995: $595; 1996: $575; 1997: $380; 1998: $782; 1999: $845; 2000: $895; 2001: $1,037; 2002: $1,140; 2003: $1,056; 2004: $1,452.50; 2005: $1,659; 2006: $1,782; 2007: $1,782; 2008: $2,566.04; 2009: $2,392; 2010: $2,608.50; 2011: $2,843.52; 2012: $3,099; 2013: $3,682. **Monthly Assured Print Price (APP):** $352.29/$4,227.48; **Norton Bankruptcy Law Adviser** newsletter also available separately at $1,636.56 per year. Also includes forms.
This comprehensive survey of all areas of bankruptcy law is arranged topically to track the course of a typical bankruptcy case. It covers both the legal and procedural aspects from the practitioner's perspective. Contents include court organization and powers, the estate, tax consequences, stockbroker liquidations, debtor in possession, adjustment of debts of an individual with regular income, Bankruptcy Code and Rules, index and forms. Includes statutory tables. A separate monographic volume provides discussion of significant bankruptcy topics such as bankruptcy ethics and the exclusion of the debtor's interest in ERISA.

Cost Saving Tip: If you are unable to locate a used set, your best savings can be achieved by buying the set with its annual subscription and then allowing it to lapse after one year. You will have to determine how valuable the quarterly updates are to your practice to warrant spending over $2,500 annually to maintain it. Much will depend upon the other resources in your library.

Norton Bankruptcy Law (WestLawNext PRO]. Eagan, MN: Thomson Reuters West. Updated continually. Minimum 12-month subscription required.
Toll-free support: 1-800-290-9378.
Cost: $1,596 per year (2014).
Contains a full library of Nrton Bankruptcy titles, including the full text of the **Norton Bankruptcy Law and Practice 3d, Norton Creditors' Rights Handbook**, **Norton Journal of Bankruptcy Law & Practice**, **Norton Bankruptcy Law Adviser**, **Norton Bankruptcy Dictionary**, **Norton Bankruptcy Law Adviser**, 12 additional titles, over 55,000 bankruptcy cases, and the bankruptcy code and rules, all with hypertext links. For a fuller description of the print **Norton Bankruptcy Law**, visit the West online product description.

Steinfeld, Shayna M. and Bruce R. Steinfeld. **The Family Lawyer's Guide to Bankruptcy: Forms, Tips and Strategies**. 2d ed. Chicago: American Bar Association, 2008. 1 vol. (376 pp.).
Cost: $129.95 ($109.95 to members); from $123.45 on amazon.com (2014).
Bankruptcy is a system of laws and procedures designed to deal with the management and settlement of the debts of either an individual or corporation that is in serious financial difficulty, and to allow them to a fresh start with their financial lives. The volume addresses the impact of bankruptcy on divorce and the inherent conflict between bankruptcy and divorce law. While it did not change the basics of bankruptcy under the Bankruptcy Code, the passage of the Bankruptcy Abuse Prevention and Consumer protection Act of 2005 (BAPCPA) made it substantially more difficult for a debtor to escape a divorce-related obligation. The two substantive chapters in this book cover bankruptcy law for the divorce practitioner, and bankruptcy 101 with an emphasis on divorce ramifications. The remainder consists of a number of useful appendices, including pre-bankruptcy planning for the divorce practitioner, pre-BAPCPA: a discussion of prior law under §523(a)(15)'s balancing test, a dictionary of bankruptcy terms, official forms, tax forms, a bankruptcy court directory, exemption statutes, and index. The text is rather exhaustively footnoted for a book of this length. The Appendices, including forms, are reproduced on a companion CD-ROM. Bruce Steinfeld is a fellow of the American Academy of Matrimonial Lawyers and a family law practitioner in Georgia. Shayna Steinfeld practices in the fields of bankruptcy and corporate reorganization and has held numerous positions in Georgia Association for Women Lawyers and the Atlanta Bar Association, and has been a frequent lecturer in continuing legal education programs and bar programs.

Additional titles in the field of Bankruptcy Law are available from the following publishers: American Law Institute, CCH, Inc., Federal Bar Association, Gaunt, Gould, Juris Publishing, LRP Publications, LexisNexis, Matthew Bender, National Association of Credit Management, New Generation Research, Nolo, Panel Publishers, Practising Law Institute, Robert Morris Associates. Thomson Reuters West, Warren, Gorham & Lamont, West Academic. See Appendix B for addresses and telephone numbers.

Civil Rights
(see also Constitutional Law and Criminal Law)

Barron, Jerome A. and C. Thomas Dienes. **First Amendment Law in a Nutshell**. 4th ed. St. Paul, MN: West, 2009. 1 vol. (576 pp.). Paperbound. Available from West Academic.
Cost: $41; from $18 on amazon.com (2014).
A concise overview of the philosophical underpinnings and case law which define the current state of First Amendment law, including the constitutional guarantees of freedom of speech, press, and religion. While intended chiefly as introductory students texts, the volumes in the Nutshell Series provide ideal overviews for practicing attorneys who wish a quick explication of new or unfamiliar topics without all the burdensome footnotes. Jerome Barron is the Lyle T. Alverson Professor of Law, George Washington University Law School. C. Thomas Dienes is the Patricia Roberts Harris Research Professor of Law at the same institution.

Bodensteiner, Ivan E. and Rosalie Berger Levinson. **State & Local Government Civil Rights Liability**. 2d ed. St. Paul, MN: West (Clark Boardman Callaghan), 2011-date. 4 vols. Looseleaf format. Annual supplementation.
Cost: $1,144; ProView eBook: $1,049; supplementation: 1993: $60; 1994: $67; 1995: $45; 1996: $87; 1997: $87; 1998: $96; 1999: $173.75; 2000: $194; 2001: $225.25; 2002: $247.75; 2003: $325; 2004: $320; 2005: $350.50; 2006: $391; 2007: $435; 2008: $484.50; 2009: $553.50; 2010: $617; 2011: $808; 2012: $889; 2013; $840; **Monthly Assured Print Price (APP):** $83/$996.
This two-volume treatise examines the grounds upon which state and local governments are subject to suit under federal civil rights acts. It provides attorneys and local governments with guidance on how to defend against civil rights actions and how to prevent liability in the first place. Outlines strategies and tactics used by plaintiffs in such cases. Provides advice on such matters as jurisdiction, procedure, defenses, immunities, enforcement, remedies, types of conduct regulated, proof of claims and attorneys fees. Also discusses the protection of Federal rights under §1983, employment discrimination, the Age Discrimination in Employment Act, and litigating federal claims in state courts.

Cook, Joseph G. and John L. Sobieski. **Civil Rights Actions**. New York: Matthew Bender and Co., 1983-date. 7 vols. Looseleaf format. Supplemented twice annually. eBook version also available with hypertext links to cases.
Cost: $2.492 (includes annual subscription); annual renewal: 1995: $630 (price frozen since 1992); 1996: $661; 1997: $661; 1998: $695; 1999: $730; 2000: $835; 2002: $894; 2003: $939; 2004: $986; 2005: $1,055; 2006: $1,129; 2007: $1,219; 2008: $1,317; 2009: $1,396; 2010: $1.439; 2011: $1,511; 2012: $1,602; 2013: $1,714; 2014: $1,870; eBook: $2.265; renewal: 2014: $1,870.
The most in-depth treatment of civil rights law available. This set provides extensive treatment of the history of civil rights law and legislation, from the Constitutional Convention through the modern era. Other topics considered include institutional and individual immunity, the relationship between state and federal courts, the procedural and remedial framework of civil rights actions, equal rights under the law, property rights, deprivation of rights under state law (as applied to elections, education, law enforcement, prisons, public employment, business licenses and professional privileges, family relations, mental institutions, public administration and facilities, and due process), conspiracies to interfere with civil rights, implied causes of action, discrimination in public accommodations, discrimination in public education, discrimination in federally assisted programs, voting rights, fair housing, equal pay for equal work, discrimination based on race, color, religion, sex or national origin, age discrimination, discrimination in credit, wiretapping and eavesdropping and privacy protection. Includes two volumes of forms, both general and specialized.

Cost Saving Tip: If you require the detailed coverage provided by this set, but are unwilling to absorb the high supplementation costs, allow it to lapse after the initial one-year subscription period has expired. There is no longer any point in purchasing a used set and updating it through the publisher since all Bender publications are now on an annual subscription basis. Your lapsed set can be updated by consulting primary sources (cases, statutes) directly, using digests, **Shepard's Citations**, etc. Or you may wish to consider maintaining a current subscription to a less expensive work like Smolla's **Federal Civil Rights Acts** for the sake of currency, using Cook as a starting point.

Edwards, Marcy, et al. **Freedom of Speech in the Public Workplace**. Chicago: American Bar Association, Section of State and Local Government Law, 1998. 1 vol. (158 pp.). Paperbound.
Cost: $8.13 (50% off); from $15.00 on amazon.com (2014).
A basic guide to the legal aspects of free speech in the public employment environment written for lawyers who represent employees and employers, as well as elected officials, personnel directors, and union representatives. It includes a consideration of employees First Amendment speech rights, guidelines on employers' restrictions on employees' political activities, whistle blowing, criticism of supervisors, and the role of the First Amendment in issues of race, sex, sexual orientation, and religion. The authors also address speech in schools, public safety and fire protection agencies, as well as privatization and the First Amendment protection afforded independent contractors. Marcy Edwards is a labor and employment law associate with the firm of Seyfarth, Fairweather & Geraldson with experience representing both public and private sector clients.

Employment Discrimination Coordinator. Eagan, MN: Thomson West (Clark Boarman Callaghan). 8 volumes. Updated periodically.
Cost: $2,160 per year (2014).
This practice set provides expert analysis and guidance on issues of employment discrimination in both public and private employment, including consideration of state and federal laws and regulations, particular employment practices, remedies, attorneys' fees, practice and procedure, wrongful termination, State tort claims in racial or sexual harassment suits, forms, pleadings and other practoice aids, and finding aids. The authors provide cautions, observations, illustrations and recommendations, and include state-by-state coverage highlighting key differences between state and federal law.

Employment Discrimination Coordinator (WestlawNext PRO). Eagan, MN: Thomson West. Updated continuously.
Cost: $2,160 per year (2014).
This library provides expert analysis and guidance on issues of employment discrimination, including consideration of state and federal laws and regulations with full-text search capability. The library contains the text of all significant state and federal employment discrimination statutes, regulations, executive orders, and the full text of all the cases cited in the substantive discussion. The authors provide cautions, observations, illustrations and recommendations, and include state-by-state coverage highlighting key differences between state and federal law.

Encyclopedia of American Civil Rights and Liberties. Edited by Otis H. Stephens, John M. Scheb, and Kara E. Stooksbury, Westport, CT, Greenwood Press, 2006. 3 vols. (1,448 pp.).
Cost: $349.95; from $43.65 on amazon.com (2014).
This three-volume comprehensive encyclopedia contains over six hundred entries detailing various aspects of civil rights and civil liberties in the United States. These entries embrace such categories as historical events and developments, fundamental concepts, significant trials and court decisions, legal doctrines, important legislation, leading civil liberties organizations, relevant governmental agencies, and key personalities, most with references, and a bibliography. Historically, the entries range from the antecedents of the Bill of Rights to contemporary controversies over such issues as abortion, racial and sexual equality, religious freedom, free speech, voting rights, and the civil liberties issues raised by the war on terrorism. The alphabetically arranged entries are balanced in outlook and moderate in tone. Designed as a scholarly resource, this reference book is useful to students at all levels, teachers, and the general public. The third volume concludes with over three-dozen significant primary documents, including key statutes, court decisions, and influential essays, from the Alien and Sedition Acts (1798) to the USA Patriot Act (2001). Volume three also contains a table of cases and subject index. The entries are written by a team of attorneys, judges, and legal scholars.

Freeman, D. Reed, Jr. and J. Trevor Hughes. **Privacy Law in Marketing**. Chicago, IL: CCH, Wolters Kluwer Law & Business, 2007-date. 2 vols. Looseleaf format. Updated monthly.
Cost: print: approx. $1,025 per year (2014).
This two-volume work combines the full text of relevant privacy statutes, regulations and enforcement actions from forty-six states, privacy laws from thirty-five foreign jurisdictions and the European Union, together with the authors' expert commentary. The full text of key court decisions, regulatory enforcement actions and policy documents are all headnoted. A monthly Report Letter provides news of current developments. An invaluable resource for lawyers and other professionals in marketing operations who are charged with monitoring and staying in compliance with U.S. and international privacy laws, including those dealing with telemarketing, e-mail marketing, cookies and Web beacons, phishing, children's privacy, information security/data breach, identity theft, use of social security numbers, fax marketing.

Griffith, Benjamin E., ed. **America Votes!: A Guide to Modern Election Law and Voting Rights**. 2d ed. Chicago: American Bar Association, Section of State and Local Government Law, 2012. 1 vol. (447 pp.). Paperbound.
Cost: $55.95 ($44.95 to ABA and Section members) from $2.86 on amazon.com (2014).
Election law and procedure, and voting rights, have become increasingly contentious subjects of debate in recent years, fueled by a number of extremely close and disputed election results, of which the 2000 presidential election is the most obvious example. This collection of articles tackles a variety of important and contentious issues, from the lessons of the 2000 and 2004 presidential elections, to language assistance provisions of the Voting Rights Act, voter protection on election day, election day registration, felon disenfranchisement, Section 5 and the Voting Rights Act, the role of demographic and statistical experts in election law disputes, government-issued photo identification and proof of citizenship requirements, voting technology and the law, the growth of early and non-precinct place balloting, election challenges involving candidates for federal office, bailout (exemption) under the Voting Rights Act, and the origins and impact of the Help America Vote Act of 2000. Twenty-six scholars and litigators, all with significant experience in the field of voting rights and election law, contributed to the seventeen chapters in this volume. While at least half of the authors bring a nonpartisan or neutral scholarly perspective to the task, those with a left-of-center partisan background outnumber those on the right by a factor of about five to one. Each of the articles is supported with citations to relevant authorities, including cases, statutes, and scholarly articles. The editor, who is chair of the ABA Section of State and Local Government Law, brings extensive experience as a litigator on behalf of state and local government entities and officials in actions involving the Voting Rights Act, election law, civil rights actions 42 U.S.C. Section §1983, public sector insurance coverage, and environmental law. In addition to wide-ranging professional activities, he has written and edited numerous publications in his areas of expertise.

Lane, Frederick S. **American Privacy: The 400-Year History of Our Most Contested Right**. Boston: Beacon Press, 2009. 1 vol. (282 pp.).
Cost: $29.95; $21.00 in paper; from $1.42 on amazon.com (2014).
The right to privacy in the United States has experienced a checkered history over the course of the past 400 years, from colonization to the modern digitized age. While enshrined in the Fourth Amendment's "right of the people to be secure in their persons, houses, papers, and effects, against unreasonable searches and seizures," the right of privacy has been violated in various ways by government and private entities. Americans have also been complicit in these violations, not only during times of war, when surveillance has been excused and defended on national security grounds, but by their behavior as electronic consumers, allowing retailers to compile extensive dossiers on their consumer habits and preferences. In the computer age, thousands of programs have been written to store a wealth of personal information, and, unbeknownst to all but a few technologically-savvy individuals, that information has taken on a life of its own. In our zest to embrace new technologies, we have lost sight of their negative consequences, namely, the loss of personal privacy. In this fascinating study, Frederick Lane explores the history of privacy in the United States, from the colonial era, in which Governor Bradford opened colonists' mail bound for England, to the modern era of Google, twitter, webcrawlers, and social networks which capture and store trillions of bits of personal information. He concludes by calling on Congress to comprehend that innovation and the infringement of the right of privacy go hand-in-hand, and to take steps to protect privacy before it is lost completely. This is an essential read for anyone attempting to understand the threat to personal privacy posed by modern technology.

Lee, David W. **Handbook of Section 1983 Litigation**. 2013 Edition. New York: Wolters Kluwer Law & Business, 2013. 1 vol.

(720 pp.). Annual editions.
Cost: 2013 Edition: $384 (2014).
Section 1983 of the Civil Rights Act of 1871 was enacted to provide redress for violations of federally protected rights committed by persons acting under color of law. Now a part of Title 42 of the United States Code, Section 1983 gives an individual the right to sue state government employees and others acting "under color of state law" for civil rights violations and is the source of a significant body of the civil rights litigation brought in the United States. This deskbook is designed to provide convenient answers to issues that frequently arise in Section 1983 cases, including such matters as police misconduct, affirmative actions, and gender and race discrimination. Organized to provide assistance to both plaintiff's and defendant's counsel, it provides concise statements of the law governing every aspect of a Section 1983 claim, as well as extensive citations to supporting caselaw, including every major Supreme Court and many U.S. Circuit Court opinions. Among the topics discussed are supervisory, municipal, county, and school district liability, incarcerated and confined persons, due process, the First Amendment, immunity, pleadings, motions, affirmative defenses, injunctions and declaratory relief, damages, discovery, and attorney's fees. David W. Lee is Managing Partner of the Oklahoma City form of Lee & Gooch and an adjunct professor of law at the Oklahoma City University School of Law and the University of Oklahoma College of Law.

Nahmod, Sheldon H. **Civil Rights and Civil Liberties Litigation: The Law of Section 1983**. 4th ed. St. Paul, MN: West Group (Clark Boardman Callaghan), 2008-date. 2 vols. Supplemented annually.
Cost: $467; ProView eBook: $429; supplementation: 2009: $229.50; 2010: $252; 2011: $274.50; 2012: $324; 2013: $343.20; 2d ed. 1992: $65; 1993: $70; 1994: $70; 1995: $80; 1996: $88; 1997: 3d ed.: $235; 1998: $64; 1999: $69; 2000: $74; 2001: $91; 2002: $106.50; 2003: $121; 2004: $125; 2005: $137; 2006: $201; 2007: $255; 2008: new edition; **Monthly Assured Print Price (APP):** $34/$408; 3d ed. from $200 on amazon.com (2014).
A comprehensive guide to §1983 litigation intended for lawyers and federal and state judges. The author reviews and analyzes relevant decisions of the United States Supreme Court, U.S. Courts of Appeal, and state courts. The discussion and analysis is based on the author's personal reading of every §1983 case decided by the Supreme Court and all federal appeals courts. Contents include a complete discussion of the Section 1983 cause of action, history, jurisdiction and procedural matters, deprivation of rights, damages, prospective relief and related defenses, governmental liability, individual immunity of legislators, judges, prosecutors, etc., qualified immunity, procedural defenses, and attorney's fees. Includes Section 1983 checklists, leading cases, forms, table of cases, and subject index. Includes extensive footnotes and explanatory notes. Supplementation cost is reasonable for a two-volume set in the current legal publishing environment. Formerly published by Shepard's/McGraw-Hill, this set was acquired by the Thomson Corporation in December, 1995 and transferred to Clark Boardman Callaghan (now part of West).

Perritt, Henry H. **Civil Rights in the Workplace.** 3d ed. Somerset, NJ: Wolters Kluwer Law & Business, 2000-date. 2 vols. Annual supplementation. (Employment Law Library)
Cost: $395; supplementation: 2001: 0; 2002: $115; 2003: $129; 2004: $149; 2005: $159; 2006: $175; 2007: $189; 2008: $205; 2009: $225; 2010: $225; 2011: $265; 2012: $285; 2013: $315; 2d edition: 1996: $70; 1997: $76; 1998: $86; 1999: $89.
A discussion and analysis of the Civil Rights Act of 1991 and its impact on employment law written by Henry H. Perritt, Jr., Professor of Law at Villanova University School of Law, former head labor lawyer for the Consolidated Rail Corp. and deputy Undersecretary of labor in the Ford administration. Professor Perritt is the author of six books and more than 30 articles in the field of labor, employment and disability law. This treatise includes a useful overview of the Civil Rights Act of 1991 including a discussion of the events leading to its adoption, both judicial and legislative. The author treats discrimination under civil rights statutes as well as that falling under the Age Discrimination in Employment Act and the Americans with Disabilities Act. There are chapters devoted to Section 1981 of Title 42 (which authorizes damages for intentional race discrimination), jury trials, compensatory and punitive damages, proof of disparate impact. proof of disparate treatment, statutes of limitations, attorneys' fees and costs, intervention and preclusive effect, and age discrimination. Appendices include the full text of the Civil Rights Act of 1991 and changes to existing law. There are also tables of cases and federal statutes contained in the **United States Code** and an Index. The author provides a clear and concise explanation of the law which is adequately supported by references to both primary and secondary sources, including cases, statutes, and legislative history documents. I would question the necessity of reproducing the full text of at least 13 leading U.S. Supreme Court decisions in volumes which are not particularly lengthy to begin with. For example, nearly 100 pages of the 330 pages in volume one consist of these full text decisions. By eliminating these decisions, the publisher could have easily consolidated these two volumes and reduced both the purchase price and supplementation cost accordingly.

Renstrom, Peter G. **Constitutional Rights SourceBook.** Santa Barbara, CA: ABC-CLIO, 1999. 1 vol. (770 pp.).
Cost: $75; from $4.07 on amazon.com (2014).
A reference guide to fundamental concepts of constitutional law, particularly as embodied in the First, Fourth, Fifth, Sixth, Eighth and Fourteenth Amendments to the U.S. Constitution. Written in a narrative style, each chapter provides a general overview of the Amendment and addresses the most significant issues falling within the scope of that Amendment. In the case of the First Amendment, for example, the author addresses Establishment of Religion, Free Exercise of Religion, Freedom of Speech, and Freedom of the Press. Each of these First Amendment rights is further subdivided into a number of individual concepts. For example, Establishment of Religion section address such concepts as the child benefit doctrine, establishment standards, public displays, school prayer, aid to nonpublic education, and public access. Each subtopic is built around the most significant U.S. Supreme Court decision while addressing other relevant decisions of significance, all with citations to the official **U.S. Reports**. The volume also includes a glossary of over 140 legal words and phrases, the text of the Constitution, and an index. The author is Professor of Political Science, Western Michigan

University. A worthy addition to most academic and law libraries.

Rosenstock, Richard and William S. Palmieri. **Rosenstock's Section 1983 Civil Rights Digest**. Costa Mesa, CA: James Publishing, 1997-date. 1 vol. (648 pp.). Annual. Free at: http://www.jameseducationcenter.com/shop/rosenstocks-section-1983-civil-rights-digest/
Cost: free via James' Attorney Education Center; supplementation: 2001: $59.99; 2002: $59.99; 2003: $69.99; 2004: $69.99; 2005: $69.99; 2006-2013: $79.99.
This unique digest of Section 1983 cases contains summaries of over 2,000 cases dating back to 1983 grouped into more than 250 specific sub-headings. Cases are classified under 14 broad subject areas, including action under color of state law, First Amendment, Fourth Amendment, self-incrimination, procedural due process, substantive due process, equal protection, Eighth Amendment, attorneys, supervisory liability, defenses, discovery, summary judgment, and remedies. The author has over 23 years experience representing plaintiffs in civil rights claims against various governmental entities and is listed in **Best Lawyers in America**.

Ross, Mary Massaron and Edwin P. Voss, Jr. eds. **Sword & Shield: A Practical Approach to Section 1983 Litigation**. 3d ed. Chicago: American Bar Association, State and Local Government Law Section, 2006. 1 vol. (556 pp.).
Cost: $124.95 ($114.95 to State and Local Government Law Section members); from $74.68 on amazon.com (2014).
Section 1983 claims under Title 42 of the **United States Code** constitute an ever expanding and complex field of civil rights law. This anthology of scholarly articles addresses the application of Section 1983 in various contexts, and reflects the fact that every official policy or governmental action is potentially subject to a lawsuit on some constitutional or statutory theory of liability. The contributing authors address such topics as the fundamentals of Section 1983 litigation, pre-litigation considerations for plaintiff's counsel, state court Section 1983 litigation, municipal liability under Section 1983, Fourth Amendment federalism, the court's vacillating mistrust and trust of state search and seizure laws, constitutional rights of public employees, the Section 1983 land use case, students' constitutional rights in public schools, and individual immunity defenses under Section 1983. Contributing authors include Steven H. Steinglass, Martin A. Schwartz, Michael S. Bogren, and Kathryn R. Urbonya.

Schwartz, Martin A. and John E. Kirklin. **Section 1983 Litigation: Claims, Defenses, and Fees**. 3d ed. New York: Wolters Kluwer Law & Business, 1997-date. 6 vols. Supplemented semi-annually.
Cost: $1,469; supplementation: 1998: $271.98; 1999: $350; 2000: $473; 2001: $795; 2002: $940; 2003: $990; 2004: $753; 2005: $935; 2006: $1,291; 2007: $1,237; 2008: $1,271; 2009: $1,324; 2010: $1,195; 2011: $1,569; 2012: $1,679; 2013: $1,796.
An detailed analysis of §1983 of the U.S. Code which authorizes relief when state or local officials violate rights protected under federal law. Covers origins, function, jurisdiction and choice of forum, persons protected, protected rights, culpable conduct, color of law and state action, the Eleventh Amendment, government liability and immunity, common law immunities, individual liability, exhaustion of state remedies, law applied in §1983 actions, abstention doctrines, damages and other relief, and extensive coverage of attorneys fees and awards under §1988.

Cost saving tip: Purchase cumulative supplements every 2-3 years to sharply reduce annual update cost, or simply re-purchase the set at periodic intervals.

Section 1983 Litigation Library on LoisLawConnect. New York: Wolters Kluwer Law & Business.
Cost: $540.00 per year (solo practitioner) (2014).
This library provides in-depth analysis of civil rights cases under Section 1983 of Tittle 42 of the U.S. Code, including case law, jury instructions, attorney's fees, evidenciary issues, etc. The titles in this library include Claims and Defenses, Statutory Attorney Fees, Federal Evidence, Jury Instructions, Handbook of Section 1983 Litigation, as well as access to cases, statutes, jus instructions, and recent developments. A cost-effective alternative to buying each of the volumes in hardcopy.

Smolla, Rodney. **Federal Civil Rights Acts**. 3d ed. St. Paul: West Group (Clark Boardman Callaghan), 1994-date. 2 vols. (3,540 pp.). Two annual paperbound volumes revised twice annually (replacing loose-leaf volumes in 2011).
Cost: 2014-1 Ed.: $1,190; supplementation: 1995: $189; 1996: $215; 1997: $220; 1998: $234; 1999: $252; 2000: $268; 2001: $310; 2002: $341; 2003: $388; 2004: $388; 2005: $463; 2006: $474; 2007: $598; 2008: $694; 2009: $275; 2010: $451.50; 2011: $994; 2012: $825; 2013: $2,380; **Monthly Assured Print Price (APP):** $161/$1,932.
The third edition of this treatise is written by Rodney Smolla, Dean of the University of Richmond School of Law, replacing Chester Antieau who authored the first two editions. Chapters include: the interplay of constitutional and statutory law in civil rights enforcement, voting rights, housing discrimination, involuntary servitude, the Religious Freedom Restoration Act, the Indian Civil Rights Act, discrimination in places of public accommodation, discrimination in Federally assisted programs, employment discrimination because of race, color, religion, sex, or national origin, the Equal Pay Act, the Age Discrimination in Employment Act, rights of the disabled, discrimination in property, contract, and economic rights (§§ 1981 and 1982), deprivation of rights under color of law: §1983, *Bivens* actions and related issues, conspiracies to violate civil rights, and attorneys fees. Appendix includes all relevant Federal acts and U.S. Code sections as well as Table of Cases and Index. This is a well-organized and lucidly written treatise which addresses all the major civil rights laws and their practical application. Coverage includes an analysis of the Americans with Disabilities Act and the Religious Freedom Restoration Act of 1993. Work is heavily footnoted to both primary and secondary sources, including relevant law review articles. A useful choice for the civil rights specialist, but best utilized in a law library to avoid the high cost.

Cost Saving Tip: Both the initial and annual supplementation cost of this two-volume set have risen steeply in recent years. In 2011, the two volume looseleaf edition was replaced by twice annual replacement volumes, now costing $1,190 (discounted periodically), or $2,380 per year. Acquiring the sem-annual set every 2-3 years will allow you to reduce your annual supplementation costs by more than 80%. Even purchasing them annually will cut your cost by 50%.

Steinglass, Steven H. **Section 1983 Litigation in State Courts**. St. Paul: West Group (Clark Boardman Callaghan), 1987-date. 2 vols. (2,500 pp.). Looseleaf format. Generally supplemented twice annually.
Cost: $675; ProView eBook: $655; supplementation: 1993: $156.50; 1994: $200; 1995: $225; 1996: $260; 1997: $320; 1998: $185; 1999: $300; 2000: $162; 2001: $190; 2002: $112; 2003: $119; 2004: $131; 2005: $149; 2006: $168; 2007: $435; 2008: $363; 2009: $74.50; 2010: $270; 2011: $294.50; 2012: $400; 2013: $448; **Monthly Assured Print Price (APP):** $44/$528.
A guide to litigating §1983 cases in state courts. Includes discussion of choosing state or federal courts, tactical choice of forum considerations, state court duty to hear §1983 actions, framing the state court §1983 action, the federally defined §1983 action, damages, exhaustion of administrative remedies, use of state policies, statutes of limitations, attorneys fees, and removal of §1983 actions to federal court. Provides detailed treatment of federal and state immunity doctrines. Appendices includes applicable federal civil rights, other relevant federal statutes, leading state court §1983 cases, state court §1988 attorney fees cases, §1983 choice of forum checklist, and §1983 cases on remedial and procedural issues organized by state.

Vieira, Norman. **Constitutional Civil Rights in a Nutshell**. 3d ed. St. Paul, MN: West, 1998. 1 vol. (330 pp.). Available from West Academic.
Cost: $41; from $0.10 on amazon.com (2014).
A succinct, student-oriented exposition of constitutional law directed chiefly at a consideration of the case law applicable to the 14th Amendment. The author, a Professor of Law at Southern Illinois University, examines substantive due process, procedural due process, equal protection, state action, and state actions under Section 1983 of Title 42 of the U.S. Code. For purposes of brevity, the author omits a discussion of criminal procedural problems, and the First Amendment. The Appendix contains selected constitutional and statutory law provisions. The volumes includes a table of cases and index.

Wang, Lu-in. **Hate Crimes Law**. St. Paul, MN: West, 1993-date. 1 vol. Revised and replaced annually. Softbound.
Cost: 2013 Edition: $284; **Monthly Assured Print Price (APP):** $24/$288 (2014).
The rise of hate crime across the United States has prompted the introduction of hate crime legislation at both the state and federal levels. These include criminal statutes directed at predicate offenses that are animated by animus of a racial or religious nature or having their origin in bias based upon sexual-orientation ethnicity/national origin bias or disability. Other, more controversial, statutes are directed to the utterance of racist or bigoted speech, or the commission of bigoted acts that are substantially equivalent to speech. This treatise provides a comprehensive look at state and federal statutes that address the problem of hate crime. Federal statutes discussed include the Hate Crime Statistics Act of 1990, conspiracy against rights under 18 U.S.C. § 241, deprivation of rights under color of law under 18 U.S.C. § 242, federally protected activities under 18 U.S.C. § 245, damage to religious property and obstruction of persons inn the free exercise of religious beliefs under 18 U.S.C. §§ 247 and 248, and prevention if intimidation provision of Fair Housing Act under 42 U.S.C., § 3631. The author also discusses federal sentencing issues, state hate crime statutes, bias-motivated violence and intimidation, malicious harassment, an related state statutes, state antimask statutes, state cross burning statutes, and more. There is also a discussion of state civil actions, including private causes of action and attorney general/district attorney civil actions. The appendices include provisions of federal law relevant to hare crimes, jurisdiction review—state statutory provisions relevant to hate crimes, and a selected bibliography. The volume includes numerous citation to applicable cases and statutes and research references to other West Group research tools, including West Digests, ALR annotations. The author is Associate Professor of law at the University of Pittsburgh School of Law.

Additional titles in the field of Civil Rights are available from the following publishers: American Bar Association, Amnesty International, Wolters Kluwer Law & Business, Matthew Bender, Carolina Academic Press, Cato Institute, Congressional Quarterly, Federal Bar Association, Garland Publishing Co., Gaunt, Greenwood Publishing Group, William S. Hein & Co., James Publishing, Kluwer Academic, LexisNexis, Oxford University Press, Practising Law Institute, Thomson Reuters West, West Academic, Yale University Press. See Appendix B for addresses and telephone numbers.

Class Actions

Anderson, Brian and Andrew Trask. **The Class Action Playbook**. 3d ed. New York: Oxford University Press, 2014. 1 vol. (352 pp.). Paperbound or eBook. Availlable from LexisNexis.
Cost: $159 (2014)
Primarily a United States phenomenon, class actions are lawsuits filed on behalf of a class of people with similar claims against a defendant. Once the action is filed by one, or a few, class representatives, or named plaintiffs, it is up the court to determine whether it is appropriate to proceed as a class action based upon four factors: (1) numerosity: whether there are enough claims to use the class action form; (2) commonality: whether the claims are sufficiently alike to use the class action form; (3) typicity: whether the class representatives' claims are typical of all claims; and (4) adequacy: whether the representatives are up to the task of representing the class fairly and well. Unlike treatises which address the law of class actions, or analytical works which argue for or against class actions from a theoretical perspective, this is a practical guide to how class actions work and the strategic decisions that attorneys must make when prosecuting or defending class actions. In this work, the authors refrain from passing judgment on class actions and attempt to bridge the ideological divide between plaintiffs' and defendants' lawyers who may see such actions as either honorable attempts to represent large numbers of "victimized" plaintiffs who would otherwise be unable to bring such actions on their own, or as a means by

which profit-motivated attorneys can extract windfall settlements from unpopular (or soon to be) companies or industries. In the view of the authors, from a strategic perspective, it matters less which side is right than which side is making the right moves. It is from this philosophical angle that they address the types of decisions that must be made in the course of bringing a class action, and the considerations that drive certain strategies at each stage of the litigation process. Toward that end, they lay out the nature the class actions and why they exist, class certification requirements, the construction of a class action lawsuit, pre-certification steps, the class certification motion, post-certification steps, trial preparation, settlement, class action judgments, and international class action practice. The authors accomplish these aims with both scholarly erudition and clarity of expression. This second edition, published just two years after the first, addresses six U.S. Supreme Court cases that affected class action law, as well as other developments in the field. Brian Anderson, a partner with the Washington, DC office of O'Melveny & Myers LLP, has defended over 400 aggregated actions and class actions in state and federal courts. Andrew Trask, counsel in the London office of McGuire Woods LLP, has defended more than 100 class actions, and maintains the Class Action Countermeasures blog at: classactioncountermeasures.com.

Bogus, Cart T. **Why Lawsuits are Good for America: Disciplined Democracy, Big Business, and the Common Law**. New York: New York University Press, 2001. 1 vol. (272 pp.).
Cost: $75 (hardcover); $24 (paperbound); from $0.99 on amazon.com; kindle edition: $12.24 (2014).
Unlike critics of the current tort system, Carl Bogus argues that lawsuits and the common law are an essential element of American democracy, providing ordinary citizens without money or political influence with a mechanism to challenge far more powerful interests on an almost level playing field. The contingent fee system, he argues, allows ordinary individuals to engage first-rate legal talent and seek redress from large corporations. Bogus focuses his attention primarily upon the law of products liability, a subfield of tort law under which individuals injured by unreasonably dangerous products can seek damages in a court of law. In fact, Bogus contends that the judicial system performs an important regulatory function through its decision-making in products liability cases because it creates incentives for businesses to improve their products. Sadly, he gives insufficient attention to the rising level of frivolous claims brought against corporations with deep pockets that simply adds to the cost of doing business, although his message will certainly find support among the trial attorneys bringing such claims. The chapters of this book address the war on the common law, the third branch of government, disciplined democracy and the American jury system, the American common law tradition, the three revolutions in products liability, and the future of common law. This book is an important contribution to the debate on tort reform. The author is Associate Professor of Law at Roger Williams University School of Law in Rhode Island. For an opposing view on tort reform, see Walter Olson, **The Rule of Lawyers** (below).

Dickerson, Thomas A. **Class Actions: The Law of 50 States**. New York: Law Journal Press, 1988-date. 1 vol. Looseleaf format and online. Supplemented 1-2 times per year. Annual subscription pricing.
Cost: $555; eBook and online: $530; supplementation: 1995: $45; 1996: $48; 1997: $100; 1998: $54; 1999: $54; 2000: $59; 2001: $130; 2002: $130; 2003: $69; 2004: $79; 2005: $174; 2006: $190; 2007: $126; 2008: $149; 2009: $157.02; 2010: $165; 2011: $517; 2012: $517; 2013: $555.
A practice-oriented guideBook to the conduct of a class action lawsuit. The author explains how to identify a potential class action, select a proper class representative, prepare pleadings and pre-certification motion papers, respond to motions and counterclaims of opposing counsel, satisfy requirements for class certification, notify class members, conduct discovery and settlement negotiations, handle pre-settlement certification, obtain court approval, and satisfy guidelines governing fee awards. The book also contains a state-by-state listing of class action decisions organized by subject matter.

Cost Saving Alert: Under ALM ownership, Law Journal Press has instituted a new pricing model that substantially drives up the cost of owning these volumes. The initial cost of this title was increased 79% between 2010 and 2012, from $289 to $555 for a print/online package and one year's supplementation. To avoid this high cost, purchase the volume and drop the standing order beyond the first year. Re-purchase several years down the road, or as necessary.

Greer, Marcy Hogan. **A Practitioner's Guide to Class Actions**. Chicago, IL: American Bar Association, 2010. 1 vol. (1,354 pp.).
Cost: $299.95 ($275.95 to members); supplementation: 2012: $49.95 ($39.95 to members) (2014).
This comprehensive treatment of the subject of class actions examines the precertification process, the ethical and practical issues involved in communicating with members of class, interlocutory appeals, settlements, claims administration, the Class Action Fairness Act, bankruptcy and class actions, and arbitration. In addition to a detailed analysis of the intricacies of a class action lawsuit, the volume provides a state-by-state analysis of the ways in which class actions differ from the Federal Rule of Civil Procedure 23 governing class actions. The book is divided into three parts: (1) Anatomy of a Class Action; (2) Special Issues in Class Actions; and (3) Jurisdictional Survey of Local Requirements Governing Class Actions. The multiple authors include 12 leading litigators at the firm of Fulbright and Jaworski.

Hensler, Deborah R., et al. **Class Action Dilemmas**. Santa Monica, CA: Rand Corporation, 2000. 1 vol. (625 pp).
Cost: hardcover: $34.50 ($31.05 web discount); paperbound: from $29.22 on amazon.com; kindle ed.: $8.49 (2014).
The current controversy regarding the use of class action litigation was ignited in 1966 when the federal courts amended Rule 23, the procedural rule that permits class actions in federal courts. Prior to the amendment, individuals seeking money damages had to affirmatively sign on to such suits. Following the amendment, those whom the plaintiff claimed to represent would be considered part of the lawsuit unless they explicitly withdrew.

This rule precipitated a dramatic rise in number of money damage lawsuits and significantly increased the exposure of corporations. This study takes an objective and analytical look at the issue of mass (class action) torts litigation in the United States and its implications for the American legal system. Unlike the more polemical books on the subject, which have appeared in recent years, it provides an objective look at the issue of mass tort litigation and uncovers the deep fissure that exists within the legal community regarding their use. This study is based on interviews with hundreds of lawyers, judges, public officials, and representatives of business, consumer, and public interest groups. While the battleground of such litigation will largely remain in the courts, the issue has also shifted to Congress, where proposals to limit the size of damage awards are being hotly debated. Judith Hensler, the lead author, is a Senior Fellow at the Rand Institute for Civil Justice, a Santa Monica, CA-based think tank. An executive summary of this study may be found at: www.rand.org/

Klonoff, Robert H. **Class Actions and Other Multi-Party Litigations in a Nutshell**. 4th ed. St. Paul, MN: Thomson Reuters West, 2012. 1 vol. (400 pp.). Paperbound. Available from West Academic.
Cost: $41; online (from West): $29; from $38.95 on amazon.com (2014).
A brief overview of class action law and practice. Includes discussion of commencement of a class action, requirements for class certification, discovery, notice to class members, "opt-out" rights, 7th Amendment and due process issues, class settlements, remedies, appellate review, issue and claim preclusion, constitutional and procedural issues, securities, mass torts, attorneys fees, defendant class actions, shareholder derivative suits, and ethical and policy issues. The author is a Partner in the Washington, DC firm of Jones, Day, Reavis & Pogue, and an Adjunct Professor of Law at Georgetown University Law Center.
Unlike most Nutshells, this one is still with West, rather than West Academic.

Koenig, Thomas H. and Michael L. Rustad. **In Defense of Tort Law**. New York: New York University Press, 2002. 1 vol. (320 pp.).
Cost: $75 (cloth); $25 (paper); from $3.83 on amazon.com; kindle ed.: $11.49 (2014).
A well-argued and meticulously researched examination of the tort reform debate that considers its social, legal, and policy dimensions. The authors challenge the common misperceptions about some of the most widely publicized "frivolous" lawsuits with empirical data, and argue that tort law plays an important role in protecting consumers from dangerous products and hazards. They address such important policy questions as the wisdom of capping damage awards. They also argue that the legal system contains a number of serious gender inequities since women are, for example, disproportionately injured by defective medical products. Thomas H. Koenig is Professor of Sociology and a founding member of the Law, Policy, and Society doctoral program at Northeastern University in Boston. Michael L. Rustad is Professor of Law and Director of the High Technology Law Program at Suffolk University Law School in Boston.

Newberg, Herbert B. and Alba Conte. **Newberg on Class Actions**. 4th-5th ed. St. Paul, MN: Thomson Reuters West (Shepard's/McGraw-Hill/Lawyers Cooperative), 2002-date. 11 vols. Looseleaf (pamphlet) format. Annual supplementation.
Cost: $1,823; supplementation: 1996: $200; 1997: $130; 1998: $272; 1999: $294; 2000: $317.50; 2001: $376; 2002: 376; 2003: $274.50; 2004: $307.75; 2005: $181; 2006: $206; 2007: $417; 2008: $465; 2009: $525; 2010: $577.50; 2011: $741.50; 2012: $861.50; 2013: $657; **Monthly Assured Print Price (APP):** $104/$1,248.
Class actions are a means whereby individuals with similar claims against a defendant can be joined together to prosecute their claims in a more efficient manner. In order to initiate a class action, one of these parties, whose claims are typical of the of the other members of the class, must agree to serve as the class representative and be approved by the court. Newberg is the premier work on the law and conduct of class actions. Designed as both a theoretical and practical reference, the book's chapters are organized into three broad sections: theory and basic requirements of class actions, general application of Rule 23, and application in specific areas. The chapters examine such topics as mass tort litigation, Chapter 11 proceedings, antitrust, employment discrimination, and other types of class actions issues. Originally published by Shepard's/McGraw-Hill, this work was purchased by the Thomson Corporation in December 1995. It was added to the West Group product line following Thomson's acquisition of West Publishing in 1996.

Cost Saving Tip: This title stands as a good example of why the **Monthly Assured Print Price** is a bad deal for consumers. Although Thomson Reuters West provides the new set as a part of the APP contract, this savings does not offset the cumulative costs of substantially higher supplementation charges in future years. For example, during the years 2006-2011, annual supplementation costs averaged about $400 per year. Under the APP model, however, annual supplementation starts at $1,200.00 and rises 5-6% annually depending upon whether a 2- or 3-year contract is chosen. The ultimate aim of APP is, of course, to lock the custumer into the standing order for future supplementation and preserve the publisher's revenue stream, amortizing the initial cost of the set into the monthly payments. Rather than providing the standing order customer with a discount, however, West has taken the opportunity to substantially adjust supplementation costs upward, thereby guaranteeing a more substantial revenue stream in future years. And what might appear on the surface to reflect a lower annual supplementation cost increase (5-6% vs. the typical 11-12% increase) is more than offset by the substantial cost adjustment at the outset. Moreover, even the limited history of APP's demonstrates that Thomson Reuters has substantially raised their costs from those originally established. Bottom line: West does everything with the goal of substantially maximizing revenue. The APP is no exception.

Olson, Walter. **The Rule of Lawyers**. New York: St. Martin's Press, 2003. 1 vol. (358 pp.).
Cost: $22.99 (paperbound); from $2.64 on amazon.com; Kindle: $7.59 (2014).
A well-documented and impassioned polemic regarding the abuse of the American legal system by trial lawyers who use

class actions to extract massive verdicts and settlements from big business. Olson focuses his attentions upon class action lawsuits against producers of such products as automobiles, pharmaceuticals, tobacco, asbestos and guns, arguing that such class action suits attempt to achieve in the courtroom what various political interests are unable to achieve through the legislative process. His is one of numerous attacks on trial lawyers that have appeared in recent years from such figures as Peter Huber, Michael Fumento, and commentators John Stossel and Catherine Crier, which provide the intellectual and political basis for tort and products liability reform. His Web site Overlawyered.com chronicles some of the more egregious examples of tort excess. Walter Olson is a Senior Fellow at the Manhattan Institute, a New York-based think tank that advocates market-oriented solutions to public policy questions. For opposing views on tort reform and class actions see: Bogus, Carl T., **Why Lawsuits are Good for America**; and Koenig, Thomas H., **In Defense of Tort Law** (above).

Pace, Nicholas M., et al. **Insurance Class Actions in the United States**. Santa Monica, CA, Rand Corp., 2007. 1 vol. (170 pp.).
Cost: $32; web price: $28.80; from $2.49 on amazon.com (2014).
Class actions are civil cases in which parties initiate a lawsuit on behalf of other plaintiffs who are not specifically named in the complaint. The role of class action lawsuits as a procedural device has garnered increasing attention in recent years, particularly in the context of debate over the Class Action Fairness Act of 2005 (CAFA) (Public Law 109-2). Class action settlements may affect millions of class members and millions of dollars in restitution. The paucity of information on class actions generally, however, prompted this RAND study that used a defendant-based survey to collect original data on both state and federal insurance class actions. It also surveyed state departments of insurance to better understand the interests of regulators in the issues litigated by the parties in these cases. This book presents the results of a survey of the experiences of U.S. insurance companies over a 10–year period. The data collected allowed the authors to describe the significant characteristics of the litigation, including the types of classes, where the cases are being filed, what allegations are being made, how these cases are resolved, the length of time required for resolution, and impact of the Class Action Fairness Act of 2005. The authors are members of the research staff at the RAND Institute for Civil Justice, "a nonprofit research organization providing objective analysis and effective solutions that address challenges in the private and public sectors around the world."

Rossman, Stuart T., Charles Delbaum, and Arielle Cohen. **Consumer Class Actions**. 8th ed. Boston, MA: National Consumer Law Center, 2013. 1 vol. Paperbound.
Cost: $210.00 (2014).
A class action is a civil court procedure under which one party, or a group of parties, sue as representatives of a larger class. Class actions are an exception to the general rule that litigation is conducted by and on behalf of individual named parties only. There are many advantages to the unitary resolution of multiple claims, the chief being efficiency. A class action saves the resources of the court and the parties by allowing an issue potentially affecting every class member to be litigated in an economical fashion. Consumer class actions are the only economically viable way to provide legal representation for clients with relatively small claims. In many instances, in the absence of class action, there will never be a recovery for anyone at any time. As Judge Richard Posner put it: "The realistic alternative to a class action is not 17 million individual suits, but zero individual suits, as only a lunatic or a fanatic sues for $30." But beyond the relatively small monetary awards to individual members of the class, class actions create a disincentive for the defendant to engage in wrongful conduct in the future. Such actions are generally brought when consumers complain of injury as a result of a company's systematic and illegal practices, including such things as illegal charges on bills, illegal penalties for late-payments, defective products, and failure to comply with consumer protection laws. Only the class members who opt out are not bound by the judgment in the case. This treatise is a practice guide for plaintiffs' attorneys who litigate consumer class actions. The detailed chapters provide a roadmap through the litigation process, from forum selection and choice of venue to drafting the complaint, discovery, class certification, the class motion and briefs, class notice, negotiations and settlement, the court settlement approval process, claims administration and distribution of benefits, the class action trial, res judicata and collateral estoppel, and attorney fees, and more. The text is amply supported by citations to primary and secondary authorities as an aid to further research. Appendices include the Federal Rule of Civil Procedure 23 (class actions) and Advisory Committee Notes, federal class action legislation (represented by the Class Action Fairness Act of 2005, Pub. L. No. 109-2, 119 Stat. 4), a survey of state class action law (2012), NACA class action guidelines, sample agreements with named plaintiffs, consumer class action web addresses, a guide to finding pleadings and primary sources on the companion web site, and index. The companion web site provides keyword access to the book's entire text. Stuart Rossman is NCLC's director of litigation, formerly chief of the Trial Division and of the Business and Labor Protection Bureau at the Massachusetts attorney general's office. He is joined by twelve contributing authors, representing the NCLC, academia, and private firms.

Additional titles in the field of Class Actions are available from the following publishers: National Consumer Law Center, New York University Press, Rand Corp., St. Martin's Press, Thomson Reuters West, West Academic. See Appendix B for addresses and telephone numbers.

Commercial Law

Alces, Peter A. et al. **Uniform Commercial Code Transaction Guide: Analysis and Forms.** St. Paul, MN: Thomson Reuters West (Clark Boardman Callaghan), 1988-date. 4 vols. (4,525 pp.). Looseleaf format.
Cost: $1,475; supplementation: 1993: $105; 1994: $155; 1995: $194; 1996: $213; 1997: $223.65; 1998: $237.50; 1999: $256.50; 2000: $277; 2001: $335; 2002: $392.50; 2003: $446.50; 2004: $446.50; 2005: $493.50; 2006: $502; 2007: $606.50; 2008: $676; 2009: $756.50; 2010: $832; 2011: $907; 2012: 1,100; 2013:

$1,232. **Monthly Assured Print Price (APP):** $114/$1,368. This is practitioner's drafting manual and forms set covering the most common types of commercial transactions, including sales contracts, leases, bank collections, commercial paper, letters of credit, bulk transfers, documents of title, secured transactions, investment securities, inventory financing. It includes financing forms for all fifty states. The forms are tied to applicable UCC requirements and are accompanied by strategic advice applicable to drafting and negotiation of agreements. Includes both complete forms and a variety of specific clauses in each subject area with practice aids and bibliographies. Also includes a profusion of citations to relevant statutory and case law.

American Law Institute. **Restatement of the Law Third. Suretyship and Guaranty.** St. Paul, MN: American Law Institute, 1996-date. 1 vol. (361 pp.).
Cost: $72; supplementation: 1997: $18; 1998: $19; 1999: $20; 2000: $21; 2001: $21; 2002: $22.75; 2003: $25; 2004: $25; 2005: $25; 2006: $25; 2007: $28; 2008: $29.50; 2009: $32; 2010: $32; 2011: $32; 2012: $33; 2013: $39.
Suretyship law governs the relationships created when a "secondary obligor" assumes liability for performing a duty of the primary obligor. Although the law is largely uncodified and often escapes attention, it has become more critical in modern business practices. This volume is the first comprehensive reformulation of suretyship law in more than 50 years, completely replacing Division II of the Restatement of Security (1941), the American Law Institute's previous coverage of the subject. It expands upon modern contract theory and those principles embodied in the Uniform Commercial Code.

American Law Institute. **Restatement of the Law Second. Unfair Competition 3d.** St. Paul, MN: American Law Institute, 1995-date. 1 vol. (683 pp.). Also available on CD-ROM.
Cost: $85; supplementation: 1997: $18; 1998: $19; 1999: $20; 2000: $21; 2001: $21; 2002: $22.75; 2003: $25; 2004: $25; 2005: $25; 2006: $25; 2007: $28; 2008: $29.50; 2009: $32; 2010: $32; 2011: $32; 2012: $33; 2013: $39.
The common law action for unfair competition evolved originally to afford relief against a competitor's misrepresentation of the source of goods or services. The term "unfair competition" now describes an array of legal actions addressing methods of competition that improperly interfere with the legitimate commercial interests of other sellers in the marketplace. The **Restatement of Unfair Competition** represents the first time that the American Law Institute has addressed the subject since publication of the original **Restatement of Torts** more than 50 years ago. Since that time, the field has been transformed by a variety of legislative enactments, including the Unfair Trade Practice and Consumer Protection Act, the Lanham Act, state antidilution acts, as well as analogous common law developments.

American Law Institute and National Conference of Commissioners on Uniform State Laws. **Uniform Commercial Code**, 2013-2014 ed. St. Paul, MN: West Group, 2013. 1 vol. (2,016 pp.). Paperbound.
Cost: $146 (2014).
Prepared under the joint sponsorship of the American Law Institute and the National Conference of Commissioners on Uniform State Laws, this volume provides a complete modernization of various statutes related to commercial transactions, including sales, leases, bank deposits and collections, negotiable instruments, fund transfers, letters of credit, bulk sales, documents of title, investment securities, and secured transactions. This edition also contains the Revised Article 9 on Secured Transactions which was promulgated in 1999. The text of the **Uniform Commercial Code** is accompanied by Official Comments drafted by the ALI and NCCUSL. An inexpensive source for the text of the **UCC**.

Bailey, Henry J. and Richard B. Hagedorn. **Brady on Bank Checks and Fund Transfers.** 8th ed. LexisNexis A.S. Pratt, 1997-date. 1 vol. (various pagings). Supplemented three times annually.
Cost: $623 per year; eBook: $582 per year (2014).
First published in 1915, this book, formerly titled Brady on Bank Checks, this treatise provides the most thorough coverage available of the law of bank checks, including such matters as stopping payments, unauthorized deposits, wrongful dishonor and the return of unpaid checks, embezzlement and fraud resulting from check alteration. The eighth edition also covers Revised **UCC** Articles 3 and 4, and wire transfers under Article 4A. Thoroughly footnoted with references to primary authority, including statutes, cases and Federal regulations. Formerly published by Warren, Gorham & Lamont.

Cost Saving Tips: For the attorney specializing in commercial law, this is one of the most authoritative sources available; however, significant savings can be achieved by dropping the standing order and purchasing the book, with its one year subscription, every 2-3 years. When Sheshunoff Pratt took control of this title in 1997, it converted it to a subscription service and effectively precluded customers from purchasing one of the three cumulative supplements each year. This, in effect, raised the annual supplementation cost from approximately $70 (for those electing to purchase one supplement per year) to $499 per year. Under the LexisNexis umbrella the annual cost has increased to $623.00 per year. By subscribing in alternate years, you will be able to reduce your average annual cost to $311 per year while going about one year between updating. The eBook version includes access to supporting primary law documents.

Banking & Commercial Law Library [CD-ROM and Internet]. New York: Matthew Bender & Co. One disc. Updated quarterly. Available for Windows. Search Engine: Folio. Includes toll-free support.
Cost: $21,406; renewal: 1998: $5,710; 1999: $5,940; 2000: $6,300; 2001: $6,741; 2002: $7,213; 2003: $7,574; 2004: $7,953; 2005: $8,589; 2006: $9,191; 2007: $9,926; 2008: $10,770; 2009: $11,631; 2010: $12,214; 2011: $12,825; 2012: $13,595; 2013: $14,546; 2014: $16,194.54.
The complete library includes the following Matthew Bender titles: **Banking Law**, **Goods in Transit**, **Commercial Damages: A Guide to Remedies in Business Litigation**, **Secured Transactions Under the U.C.C.**, **U.C.C. Reporter-Digest**, **Collier Lending Institutions under the Bankruptcy Code**, and **Forms and Procedures under the U.C.C.** Various combinations of titles may be selected by the subscriber.

Batman, Jean L. **Advising the Small Business: Forms and Advice for the Legal Practitioner**. 2d ed. Chicago: American Bar Association, 2011. 1 vol. (843 pp.).
Cost: $159.95 ($145.95 to members) (2014).
Designed for general practitioners, small firm attorneys, and lawyers engaged in providing legal advice to small businesses, this volume provides advice and forms in a number of areas central to small business activity. The chapters cover representation of small businesses, the protection of intellectual property, business plans, contracts for small businesses, legal structures fort small businesses, organizing and cleaning up a corporation, organizing and cleaning up an LLC, organizing and cleaning up a partnership, founders and advisors, raising money through private placements, seed financing and angel investors, venture capital, hiring employees, providing equity incentives to employees, and liquidity events. The boilerplate forms, on a companion CD-ROM, can be easily adapted to individual circumstances. An ideal desktop companion for any attorney representing small business entities. Formerly a partner in the San Francisco firm of Duane Morris LLP, the author founded Legal Venture Counsel, Inc. in 2004 for the purpose of providing outside general counsel services to investors, entrepreneurs, and small businesses.

Betsos, Peter J. and Frances P. Hays. **Modern UCC Litigation Forms.** New York: Matthew Bender Co., 1969-date. 3 vols. Looseleaf format. Supplemented several times annually.
Cost: $1,257 (print or eBook) (includes annual subscription); annual renewal: 1995: $298 (frozen since 1992); 1996: $313; 1997: $313; 1998: $325; 1999: $340; 2000: $365; 2001: $391; 2002: $438; 2003: $460; 2004: $483; 2005: $512; 2006: $548; 2007: $592; 2008: $639; 2009: $690; 2010: $726; 2011: $759; 2012: $805; 2013: $861; 2014: $941.
A collection of UCC forms adapted from actual cases for use in the preparation and trial of law suits. Includes explanatory material, alternative procedures and commentary.

Cost Saving Tips: This subscription may be canceled at any time following the initial year's service should you decide that the coverage or cost is not what you desire. Is your use sufficient to justify the annual supplementation cost? If not, don't fall into the trap of supplementing what you do not use with sufficient regularity Library costs can escalate rapidly if attention is not paid to usage. If you do cancel, you will still have a useful resource for boiler plate form language which can be adapted to your purposes.

Business Law Library [CD-ROM and Internet]. New York: Matthew Bender & Co. One disc. Updated quarterly. Available for Windows. Search Engine: Folio. Includes toll-free support. Also available on the Internet.
Cost: $37,053 (includes annual subscription); renewal: 1998: $12,035; 1999: $12,525; 2000: $13,000; 2001: $13,910; 2002: $14,884; 2003: $15,629; 2004: $16,410; 2005: $17,559; 2006: $18,789; 2007: $20,292; 2008: $21,915; 2009: $23,668; 2010: $24,852; 2011: $26,095; 2012: $27,661; 2013: $29,597; 2014: $32,948. Lesser combinations also available.
The complete library includes the following Matthew Bender titles: **Current Legal Forms with Tax Analysis, Warren's Forms of Agreement, Antitrust Counseling & Litigation Techniques, Commercial Damages, Blue Sky Regulation, Business Torts, Cable Television Law, Business Organizations with Tax Planning, Debtor-Creditor Law, Administrative Law, Corporate Acquisitions and Mergers, Franchising, Professional Corporations & Associations, Federal Securities Exchange Act of 1934, Federal Securities Act of 1933, Securities Law Techniques, Primary Law SourceBook, Antitrust Laws and Trade Regulation**, and six Tax Analysts titles."

Business Practice Law Library on LoislawConnect. New York: Wolters Kluwer Law & Business. Online.
Cost: $525.00 per year (2014).
This library of business law treatises and practice titles addresses everything from business formation to operations. The titles in the library include **Choosing the Right Business Entity, Limited Liability Company & Partnership Answer Book, Drafting Limited Liability Company Operating Agreements, S Corporation Taxation Guide,** and **Financing Start-Ups.** Provides significant savings over the total cost of these titles priced individually.

Business Torts Library on LoislawConnect. New York: Wolters Kluwer Law & Business. Online.
Cost: $525.00 per year (2014).
The Business Torts Library provides users with recent developments, analysis, statutes and court decisions for commercial tort actions. The titles include **Business Torts Reporter**, **Business Torts: A Fifty-State Guide**, **Civil False Claims and Qui Tam Actions**, **Civil RICO Practice Manual**, and **Smart Charts**, which provide a way to quickly conduct multi-jurisdictional research by topic
Provides significant savings over the total cost of these titles priced individually.

Clark, Barkley. **The Law of Bank Deposits, Collections and Credit Cards.** 4th ed. Chicago: LexisNexis A. S. Pratt, 1995-date. 1 vol. Looseleaf format and eBook. This title was converted to a service publication in 1997.
Cost: $623 per year (2014).
This work is unquestionably the «bible» in the field regarding the law of collections, credit cards, bank deposits, and letters of credit. It includes a discussion of collection of documentary drafts, electronic funds transfer, adverse claims to a deposit account, bank setoff, funds availability and check collection under Regulation CC, check kiting, truth-in-savings, allocation of fraud loss for forged endorsements, letters of credit, and much more. This work is impressive in both its breadth and in-depth analysis, with substantial citations to relevant UCC Sections, cases, statutes, etc.

Cost Saving Tips: For the attorney specializing in commercial law, this is one of the most authoritative sources available; however, significant savings can be achieved by dropping the standing order and purchasing the book, with its one year subscription, every 2-3 years. When A.S. Pratt & Sons took control of this title in 1997, it converted it to a subscription service and effectively precluded customers from purchasing one of the three cumulative supplements each year. This, in effect, raised the annual supplementation cost from approximately $70 (for those electing to purchase one supplement per year) to $623 per year in 2014. By subscribing for one year and skipping one year, you will be able to reduce your average annual cost to about $310 per year while going about one year between updating.

Commercial Finance Guide. Revised ed. Jeffrey J. Wong and Michael A. Leichtling, Editors-in-Chief. New York: Matthew Bender & Co., 1997-date. 2 vols. Looseleaf format. Updated annually.
Cost: $523 (print or eBook); supplementation: 1998: $90; 1999: $96; 2000: $105; 2001: $112; 2002: $139; 2003: $146; 2004: $153; 2005: $164' 2006: $176; 2007: $190; 2008: $205; 2009: $221; 2010: $251; 2011: $252; 2012: $264; 2013: $282; 2014: $307; eBook: 2014: $523.
Completely revised in 1997, this publication provides a practical examination of the specific types of secured lending transactions and specific legal issues that may arise in such transactions. It provides extensive coverage of commercial financial products other than basic loan agreements. See companion **Commercial Loan Documentation Guide** (below).

Commercial Loan Documentation Guide. Revised ed. Jeffrey J. Wong and Michael A. Leichtling, Editors-in-Chief. New York: Matthew Bender & Co., 1988-date. 2 vols. Looseleaf format. Updated annually.
Cost: $485; renewal: 1998: $100; 1999: $107; 2000: $115; 2001: $123; 2002: $133; 2003: $140; 2004: $147; 2005: $156; 2006: $167; 2007: $180; 2008: $191; 2009: $206; 2010: $207; 2011: $237; 2012: $269; 2013: $288; 2014: $297;
e-book: $485; renewal: 2014: $297.
This companion volume to the **Commercial Finance Guide** documents the complete spectrum of commercial loan and finance transactions, and provides an extensive collection of relevant practice forms.

Consumer Credit Guide. Riverwoods, IL: Wolters Kluwer Law & Business (CCH), 2004-date. 8 vols. Looseleaf format. Updated biweekly. Internet also available (see next entry).
Cost: $3,204 per year; Internet: call for pricing (2014).
This looseleaf service provides access to a variety of federal and state laws and regulations impacting the operation of the consumer credit industry. The coverage extends to such topics as truth-in-lending, equal credit opportunity, fair debt collection practices, retail installment sales, small loans, interest and usury. An invaluable resource for those employed in bank legal departments, representing banking interests, or otherwise impacted by the federal banking and credit regulatory apparatus.

Consumer Credit Guide [Internet]. Riverwoods, IL: Wolters Kluwer Law & Business (CCH). Available for Windows. Search Engine: Proprietary. Updated monthly. Internet updated biweekly.
Cost: Internet: approx. $3,204 per year (contact sales rep. for exact pricing) (2014).
This Internet version contains the equivalent of the eight-volume looseleaf service described above, with all the benefits of online continuous updating.

Consumer Finance Law Library on LoislawConnect.. New York: Wolters Kluwer Law & Business. Online.
Cost: $540.00 per year (solo practitioner) (2014).
This library includes a variety of consumer finance related treatise titles which examine such topics as derivatives regulation, bankruptcy abuse, credit collection, and commecial real estate workouts. Titles include **Dodd-Frank Wall Street Reform and Consumer Protection Act: Law, Explanations & Analysis; Bankruptcy Abuse Prevention and Consumer Protection Act of 2005: Law and Practice**; **Complete Guide to Credit and Collection Law**; **Derivatives Regulation**; **Securities and Derivatives Reform in 2010: A Guide to the Legislation**; **Structuring Commercial Real Estate Workouts: Alternatives to Bankruptcy and Foreclosure.** A cost-effective alternative to buying all the titles separately.

Duesenberg, Richard W. and Lawrence P. King. **Sales and Bulk Transfers Under the UCC.** New York: Matthew Bender & Co., 1966-date. 2 vols. Looseleaf format and eBook. Supplemented several times annually.
Cost: $1,224 (print) $1,113 (eBook) (includes annual subscription); annual renewal: 1995: $295 (frozen since 1992); 1996: $309; 1997: $309; 1998: $325; 1999: $340; 2000: $365; 2001: $391; 2002: $419; 2003: $440; 2004: $462; 2005: $494; 2006: $529; 2007: $571; 2008: $617; 2009: $666; 2010: $700; 2011: $732; 2012: $776; 2013: $830; 2014: $906.
This substantial treatise examines sales and bulk transfer issues arising under Articles 2 and 6 of the **UCC**. Includes alternative drafting and litigation strategies for both the buyer and the seller. Provides analysis of relevant pre-Code and non-Code law. Multitudinous citations to relevant primary authority.

Cost Saving Tips: This subscription may be canceled at any time following the initial year's service should you decide that the coverage or cost is not what you desire, or your use insufficient to justify the annual supplementation cost. Don't fall into the trap of supplementing what you do not use with sufficient regularity. Library costs can escalate rapidly if attention is not paid to usage. If you do cancel, you will still have a useful resource which can be updated in the primary sources, etc.

Eisenberg, Theodore, ed. **Debtor-Creditor Law.** New York: Matthew Bender & Co./LexisNexis Electronic, 1982-date. 10 vols. Looseleaf format or eBook. Supplemented about 3 times per year.
Cost: $4,290 (print); $3,645 (eBook) (includes annual subscription); annual renewal: 1995: $1,086 (price frozen since 1992); 1996: $1,139; 1997: $1,139; 1998: $1,200; 1999: $1,255; 2000: $1,260; 2001: $1,348; 2002: $1,443; 2003: $1,660; 2004: $1,743; 2005: $1,865; 2006: $1,996; 2007: $2,155; 2008: $2,317; 2009: $2,502; 2010: $2,566; 2011: $2,643; 2012: $2,749; 2013: $2,941; 2014: $3,210.
Authored by a team of twenty legal scholars and practitioners, this treatise is an exhaustive examination of the debtor-creditor relationship from creation to enforcement. Contents includes a review of such consumer legislation as the Truth in Lending Act, Fair Debt Collection Practices Act, Unfair and Deceptive Acts or Practices, Consumer Leasing Act, Fair Credit Reporting, Federal Restrictions on Wage Garnishment, Uniform Commercial Code, usurious transactions, third parties, non-

judicial remedies, possessory proceedings, judicial remedies and insolvency, enforcement of judgments and federal tax liens. Last volume includes Table of Cases, Table of Statutes and Index. Relevant forms are placed strategically throughout the text. This is an impressive work with detailed coverage of all relevant subject areas and a multitude of citations to supporting primary authorities. The eBook version provides links to caselaw in Lexis.

Cost Saving Tips: By its scope and frequency of supplementation, this set is obviously designed for the specialist. As with any Bender treatise, however, the subscriber always has the option of canceling the standing order after one year and then updating by buying a new set at some future date. This is a decision you must make based on your need for current analysis and citations. As with any secondary source, there is a certain lag time between the editorial cut-off and your receipt of the supplement. Under these circumstances, updating directly in primary sources and Shepardizing relevant citations is essential. Used correctly, the core material may provide you with sufficient utility that you can forego the more costly standing order. Although subject specific treatises like this are not readily available used, you may be able to locate a fairly current used set at considerable savings.

Fonseca, John R., and Patricia Fonseca. **The Law of Modern Commercial Practices.** 2d revised ed. St. Paul, MN: West Group, 1998-date. 3 vols. Annual replacement volumes.
Cost: 2013 Edition: $462; 2012: $453; supp.: 1993: $90; 1994: $103.50; 1995: $174; 1996: $192; 1997: $201.60; 1998: $325; 1999: $231; 2000: $250; 2001: $449; 2002: $116; 2003: $132; 2004: $148; 2005: $163.50; $182.50; 2007: $203; 2008: $360.50; 2009: $253.50; 2010: $279; 2010: $303; 2011: $312; **Monthly Assured Print Price (APP):** $39/$468.
This two-volume practitioner's treatise is basically a condensed guide to Articles 1-9 of the **Uniform Commercial Code** combined with analysis of the Magnuson-Moss Warranty Act. A clearly written and well documented work which provides useful Notes and Practical Hints. The authors document numerous instances in which their work was cited by the courts as authority for various propositions. The impact of this set on the courts make it a worthy competitor to White and Summers. An excellent choice for the attorney looking for a less detailed and expensive alternative to multi-volume treatises by Anderson and Hawkland or Bender's.

Fonseca, John R. **Williston on Sales.** 5th ed. St. Paul, MN: West Group (Clark Boardman Callaghan), 1994-date. 4 vols. Annual pocket supplements.
Cost: $647; supp.: 1993: $225; 1994: $229; 1995: $267; 1996: $305; 1997: $162.75; 1998: $173; 1999: $187; 2000: $202; 2001: $238.50; 2002: $279; 2003: $318; 2004: $380; 2005: $300; 2006: $397.50; 2007: $67.50; 2008: $75; 2009: $88.50; 2010: $97.50; 2011: $106.50; 2012: $120; 2013: $132; **Monthly Assured Print Price (APP):** $22/$264.
A detailed analysis of the law of sales under Article 2 of the Uniform Commercial Code which encompasses the history and general principles of sales law under the UCC, sales transactions, contracts of sale, statute of frauds, warranties, title, creditor and good faith purchases, remedies after the buyer's breach, and buyer's remedies. Originally published by Lawyers Cooperative, this title was taken over by CBC following the reorganization of product lines under the Thomson Corporation. In 1997, it was placed under the West Group, now a part of Thomson Reuters.

Haig, Robert L., ed. **Business and Commercial Litigation in Federal Courts**. 3d ed. St. Paul, MN: West Group, jointly with the American Bar Association, Section of Litigation, 2011-12-date. 12 vols. Annual supplementation. Includes a CD-ROM containing 319 jury charges and 349 essential litigation forms.
Cost: $1,434; supplementation: 2012: $264; 2013: $296; 2d ed.:1999: $100; 2000: $106; 2001: $121; 2002: $142; 2003: $156.50; 2004: $166; 2005: $600; 2006: $750; 2007: $167; 2008: $186; 2009: $220; 2010: $242; 2011: new edition; **Monthly Assured Print Price (APP):** $60/$720.
A comprehensive collection of materials on both the substantive and procedural aspects of commercial litigation in the federal courts. Eighty individual chapters are authored by 152 experienced federal litigators each of which is a leading expert in the field. These chapters address topics ranging from personal jurisdiction and service, motion practice and expert witnesses to such substantive matters as antitrust, securities, admiralty, banking, insurance and contracts, to name just a few. Coverage embraces pretrial phases of litigation, the trial itself, expert witnesses and testimony, damages and remedies, and appeals. Each of the substantive topics covered in this set examines those specific procedural and strategic issues which characterize that field of law. Editor-in-Chief Robert L. Haig is a partner in the New York City firm of Kelley Drye & Warren LLP and is co-chair of the Commercial Courts Task Force which created the Commercial Division of the New York State Supreme Court.

Hart, Frederick M. **Forms and Procedures Under the UCC.** New York: Matthew Bender & Co./LexisNexis Electronic, 1963-date. 8 vols. Looseleaf format or eBook. Supplemented several times annually. Also in CD-ROM format as of the publisher's Authority Banking and Commercial Law Library.
Cost: $3,087 (includes annual subscription); annual renewal: 1995: $750 (price frozen since 1992); 1996: $787; 1997: $787; 1998: $825; 1999: $860; 2000: $920; 2001: $966; 2002: $1,034; 2003: $1,086; 2004: $1,140; 2005: $1,231; 2006: $1,318; 2007: $1,423; 2008: $1,537; 2009: $1,660; 2010: $1,743; 2011: $1,830; 2012: $1,940; 2013: $2,076; 2014: $2,265; e-book: $2,807; 2013: $2,076; 2014: $2,265.
A procedural guide to the **UCC** with forms, checklists, and examples which apply the **UCC** to specific situations. This set provides detailed procedural analysis of the **UCC** and related Federal statutes.

Cost Saving Tips: Subscription may be canceled at any time following the initial year's service should you decide that the coverage or cost is not what you desire. If you do cancel, you will still have a useful secondary resource which can be updated in the primary sources and Shepard's.

Hawkland, William D. **Uniform Commercial Code Series.** St. Paul, MN: West (Clark Boardman Callaghan), 1982-date. 20 vols. Looseleaf format. Annual supplementation.
Cost: $3,171; supplementation: 1993: $423; 1994: $417; 1995:

$471; 1996: $486; 1997: $570.70; 1998: $575; 1999: $565.50; 2000: $695.50; 2001: $922; 2002: $598.50; 2003: $578; 2004: $705; 2005: $750; 2006: $1,087; 2007: $1,153; 2008: $1,417; 2009: $1,554; 2010: $1,714.50; 2011: $1,466.50; 2012: $2,187; 2013: $1,706; **Monthly Assured Print Price (APP):** $223/$2,676; Hawkland is also available as a part of West's **Commercial/UCC Practitioner Counselor** on WestlawNext™ PRO), a comprehensive library priced at $2,700.00 per year.
Written by the Chancellor Emeritus of the Louisiana State University Law Center and other leading authorities in the field, this nine-volume treatise provides exhaustive coverage of each of the articles of the Uniform Commercial Code. In addition to analysis of each code section, the authors provide analysis of the major differences in the UCC provisions of the individual states. It provides verbatim text of the complete UCC with recent changes underlined. Includes official commentaries and history of each section. Supplements provide both changes to text and annotated references to recent case law. There is a Master Index to the entire set as well as indexes to each article. A detailed concordance to both Words and Phrases in volume one provides an additional method of access to relevant material. This is a well-written, scholarly work in an easy to read format. A recommended publication for the busy **UCC** practitioner who may wish more detailed coverage than that provided by White and Summers and is willing to pay the additional cost, both for the base volumes and for annual supplementation.

Cost Saving Tips: Best acquired as a part of West's **Commercial/UCC Practitioner Counselor** on WestlawNext™ PRO), a comprehensive library priced at $2,700. per year.

Knapp, Charles L. et al. **Commercial Damages: A Guide to Remedies in Business Litigation**. New York: Matthew Bender & Co., 1986-date. 3 vols. Looseleaf format. Supplemented several times annually.
Cost: $1,688 (includes annual subscription); annual renewal: 1995: $465 (price frozen since 1992); 1996: $488; 1997: $488; 1998: $515; 1999: $535; 2000: $540; 2001: $540; 2002: $578; 2003: $607; 2004: $683; 2005: $688; 2006: $737; 2007: $796; 2008: $860; 2009: $929; 2010: $975; 2011: $1,014; 2012: $1,075; 2013: $1,150; 2014: $1,255; eBook: $1,534; renewal: 2014: $1,255.
Written by over forty legal scholars and practitioners, this three-volume treatise provides discussion and analysis of remedies available in the context of commercial affairs. Specific coverage includes general remedial principles, the law of damages, specific relief and other remedies, practical considerations in evaluating the case, the business enterprise as buyer or seller of property or services, remedies for wrongful interference, and the business enterprise as investment. Contains a Table of Cases, Table of Statutes and Index.

Cost Saving Tips: Subscription may be canceled at any time following the initial year's service should you decide that the coverage or cost is not what you desire. If you do cancel, you will still have a useful secondary resource which can be updated in the primary sources and Shepard's. This option is only available with the print version, however; cancellation of the Internet versions leaves you without a basic, albeit, out-of-date, reference.

Lapine, Kenneth M. **Consumer Credit: Law, Transactions and Forms**. New York: Matthew Bender & Co., 1984-date. 6 vols. Looseleaf format and eBook. Updated twice a year. Also volumes 7, 8, 9 and 10 of **Banking Law**.
Cost: $1,740 (print); $1,581 (eBook) (includes annual subscription); renewal: 1998: $505; 1999: $525; 2000: $560; 2001: $599; 2002: $641; 2003: $674; 2004: $708; 2005: $758; 2006: $789; 2007: $836; 2008: $890; 2009: $961; 2010: $981; 2011: $1,015; 2012: $1,081; 2013: $1,157; 2014: $1,263; Available on Internet as part of **Banking Law** set.
A complete guide to the law governing consumer credit and credit transactions. Provides extensive treatment of the law, with practical, step-by-step, guidance for each stage of a consumer credit transaction. The author provides expert commentary and interpretation of the major consumer credit laws, including: truth-in-lending, fair credit reporting; community reinvestment; and real estate settlement procedures. The transactional analysis covers a number of topics, ranging from consumer credit advertising through the loan application and approval and repayment processes. Each significant aspect of the consumer credit transaction is examined to reveal the rules and regulations which apply. Includes the text of relevant statutes, regulations, interpretations and policies. The model forms, checklists, examples and tables are accompanied by compliance hints.

Lawrence, Lary. **Lawrence's Anderson on the Uniform Commercial Code.** 3d ed. St. Paul, MN: West (Clark Boardman Callaghan), 1983-date. 11 vols. Annual pocket supplements. Also available on West's **Commercial/UCC Practitioner Counselor on WestlawNext PRO.**
Cost: $4,667; supplementation: 1993: $290; 1994: $500; 1995: $590; 1996: $633; 1997: $672.65; 1998: $589.50; 1999: $638.50; 2000: $622; 2001: $804; 2002: $725; 2003: $811.50; 2004: $1,122.48; 2005: $1,105; 2006: $1,285; 2007: $1,503; 2008: $1,381; 2009: $2,236; 2010: $2,460; 2011: $961; 2012: $2,600; 2013: $2,847; **Monthly Assured Print Price (APP):** $294/$3,528; Also available as part of **West's Commercial/UCC Practitioner Counselor** on WestlawNext PRO at $2,700.00 per year.
This multi-volume treatise, which reflects the tremendous expansion of commercial law over the past thirty years, is organized by **UCC** section and includes the text of both the Code and official Code commentary, followed by the author's analysis which relates both Code and non-Code law. Subject coverage includes the law of sales, commercial paper, bank deposits and collections, letters of credit, bulk transfers, documents of title, bills of lading, warehouse receipts, investment securities, secure transactions, sales of accounts, contracts, and chattel paper. Pocket supplements provide both amendments to code provisions and annotations to recent court decisions. Both bound volumes and pocket parts provide citations to local statutory citations and variations. Lary Lawrence is the Harriet L. Bradley Chair in Contract Law at Loyola Law School in Los Angeles where he teaches commercial and contract law. Professor Lawrence is a member of the California State Bar Association, UCC Committee of Business Law Section, and a former member of the American Bar Association Task Force on Article 1 of Uniform Commercial Code. He has assumed editorial responsibility for a work originally written by Ronald A. Anderson, who also authored the second edition of **Couch on Insurance**.

Cost Saving Tips: This set has been thoroughly updated in recent years; however, both the initial and annual cost of supplementation have bene increased substantially. Between 2012 and 2013, for example, the purchase price was increased 38.5%. This makes the purchase of a WestlawNext PRO **Commercial/UCC Practitioner Counselor** package the best option.

Lawrence, William H. **Understanding Negotiable Instruments and Payment Systems**. Newark, NJ: Matthew Bender, 2002. 1 vol. (423 pp.).
Cost: $45; eBook: $36 (2014).
This introductory textbook examines the subjects covered by Articles 3, 4 and 4A of the Uniform Commercial Code, the Truth in Lending Act, the Fair Credit Billing Act, the Electronic Funds Transfer Act, and Regulations E, J, Z, and CC. The author also discusses the legal structure that undergirds existing payment systems, embracing payment by cash, checks and other drafts, debit cards, credit cards, automated clearinghouses, automated teller machines, and wholesale fund transfers. There is a lucid description of these different systems for the benefit of the uninitiated. William H. Lawrence is a Professor at the University of San Diego School of Law. Nationally recognized for his work in commercial law and solar energy law, he is the author of numerous articles and books, including the two-volume Commercial Paper and Payment Systems (Matthew Bender) and co-author of The Law of Personal Property Leasing (Thomson Reuters).

Lawrence, William H., William H. Henning, and R. Wilson Freyermuth. **Understanding Secured Transactions**. 5th ed. New York: Matthew Bender & Co., 2012. 1 vol. (418 pp.). Legal Text Series.
9Cost: $45; eBook: $36 (2014).
This is an introductory student text designed to illuminate Article 9 of the Uniform Commercial Code and selected provisions of the federal Bankruptcy Reform Act. The organization of the work is based upon the traditional five-part approach to the law of secured transactions: scope, creation, perfection, priorities, and default. There are numerous, but not exhaustive, citations to relevant statutes and cases. The authors are professors at the University of San Diego and the University of Missouri-Columbia law schools. An inexpensive alternative to some of the practitioner-oriented treatises.

Limited Liability Company Law Treatise Library on LoisLawConnect. New York: Wolters Kluwer Law & Business. Online.
Cost: $540.00 per year (solo practitioner) (2014).
The collection provides expert guidance on the drafting of limited liability operating agreements, state and federal law and taxation. Titles include: **Drafting Limited Liability Company Operating Agreements, Federal and State Taxation of Limited Liability Companies, State Limited Liability Company & Partnership Laws**.

Loonin, Deanne and Geoff Walsh. **Student Loan Law**. 4th ed. Boston, MA: National Consumer Law Center, 2010. 1 vol. ()690 pp.). Paperbound. Includes current supplement (2013).
Cost: $130.00; supplementation: 2013: $72.00 (2014).
Student loan debt in the United States recently surpassed $1 trillion, an amount higher than all the debt owed to credit card companies. Defaults on student loan debt have already reached crisis proportions, with a FY 2011 2-year national cohort default rate of 10.0 percent. Two-thirds of college students now graduate with student loan debt. The average debt of graduating seniors has risen from $23,200 in 2008 to $29,400 in 2013, an increase of 26%. In 2010, nearly 100% of graduates from private for-profit universities had student loans versus 85% in 2004. Defaulting on a student loan has serious consequences. The school, the financial institution that made or owns your loan, the loan guarantor, and the federal government can all take steps to recover the money owed, including interception of income tax refunds, wage garnishment, reduction in federal benefits, or a lawsuit to recover money owed. The federal government has collection powers far beyond those of most unsecured creditors. For many young people, student loan debt has become the new mortgage, making it difficult to buy a home, start a business, or save for the future. Even adults age 60 and older are seeing their Social Security checks garnished because they have fallen behind on student-loan payments. The total amount of outstanding student-loan debt among people over age 50 reached $155-billion in 2012. This manual is designed to help advocates navigate the world of student financial assistance, specifically federal student loan programs, but also private student lending. The first chapter provides a useful introduction to the world of federal student assistant, including grants and loans, assistance to military service members, the application process, eligibility requirements, academic requirements, consumer information requirements, and a checklist for handing student loan issues. Other chapters cover such topics as taking out a Federal student loan, pre-default repayment options, postponing repayment, implications of student loan defaults, repayment strategies for getting out of default, federal student loan collection, property and asset seizures, statutory discharge, discharge of loans in bankruptcy, private student loans, and proprietary school and other student loan litigation. The appendices, which comprise more than half of the volume, include federal student loan statutes, regulations, Department of Education policy guidance letters, student assistance forms, ample pleadings and letters, sample discovery and FOIA requests, a directory of guaranty agencies, student loan collection agencies, frequently asked questions, and more. Deanne Loonin is an NCLC staff attorney focusing on student loan law. Geoff Wolf is also an NCLC staff attorney, after having served as a Legal Services attorney for over 25 years. Founded in 1969, the National Consumer Law Center is a non-profit corporation that serves consumers, advocates, and public policy makers. As with most NCLC publications, this volume provides an exhaustive treatment of the subject matter together with primary documents and other useful aids.

Marsh, Gene A. **Consumer Protection Law in a Nutshell**. 3d ed. St. Paul, MN: West, 1999. 1 vol. (445 pp.). Available from West Academic.
Cost: $41; from $16.48 on amazon.com (2014).
Like most titles in West's Nutshell series, this volume provides

an introductory overview of consumer protection law for students and a succinct review of basic principles and laws for the practitioner. The author's discussion reflects the many changes which have taken place in the world of consumer law as paper transactions have been increasingly replaced by electronic ones and credit has become far more widespread as a method of payment. Chapters include: an introduction to consumer transaction law, public and private actions to regulate commerce markets, methods of inducing consumer transaction, the consumer credit market, credit reports, identity theft, credit repair and equal access to credit, disclosure of terms in consumer credit transactions, regulating the cost of credit, regulation of other terms in consumer transactions, and post-transaction problems. The text includes selective citations to cases, statutes and regulations. Gene Marsh is a Professor of Law at the University of Alabama School of Law.

McDonnell, Julian B. et al. **Secured Transactions Under the UCC.** New York: Matthew Bender & Co., 1963-date. 5 vols. Looseleaf format. Supplemented several times annually. Also in eBook format.
Cost: $2,812 (includes annual subscription); annual renewal: 1995: $688 (price frozen since 1992); 1996: $722; 1997: $722; 1998: $760; 1999: $790; 2000: $850; 2001: $884; 2002: $946; 2003: $994; 2004: $1,044; 2005: $1,160; 2006: $1,196; 2007: $1,292; 2008: $1,395; 2009: $1,506; 2010: $1,605; 2011: $1,685; 2012: $1,786; 2013: $1,911; 2014: $2,085; eBook: $2,556; renewal: 2014: $2,085.
CD-ROM also available as a part of Matthew Bender's **Authority Banking & Commercial Law Library** which includes no-cost online updating via LEXIS-NEXIS. A thorough examination of **UCC** Article 9 covering secured lending with attention to related non-Code areas as well as federal tax liens and bankruptcy matters.

Cost Saving Tips: With annual supplementation costs approaching the cost of a new set, it is far more cost-effective to simply re-purchase this set every three years, or more, depending on your need for currency. Remember that a new purchase includes one year's supplementation.

Miller, Frederick H. **Sales and Leases of Goods in a Nutshell.** 4th ed. St. Paul, MN: West Academic, 2003. 1 vol. (425 pp.). No supplementation between editions.
Cost: $41; from $9.62 on amazon.com (2014).
A brief overview of the law of sales and leases under articles 2 and 2A of the Uniform Commercial Code, with some attention to related subject governed by Articles 5 and 7. Includes full text of Code provisions with analysis, although citations to case authority are provided only in the Table of Cases. Also contains a Table of Statutes and Index. A succinct, briefcase-sized handbook. For fuller treatment see White and Summers.

Nickles, Steve H. and Mary Beth Mathews. **Payments Law in a Nutshell.** St. Paul, MN: West, 2005. 1 vol. (485 pp.). Available from West Academic.
Cost: $41; from $20.98 on amazon.com (2014).
This introductory law student text explains the fundamentals of negotiable instruments, including promissory notes, drafts, checks, and certificates of deposit as they appear in Articles 3 and 4 of the **Uniform Commercial Code**. It also provides an overview of the requisites of negotiability contract liability, secondary liability conditions, and discharge liability. Instruments of property are also discussed, including enforcement, transfer, and negotiation. The authors also address such topics as warranty, restitution, claims, defenses to instruments, holder in due course, and the check collection process and examine the customer/payor bank relationship and risk allocation. Includes a Table of Statutes, index to the **UCC** Sections discussed and representative citations to case authority.

Nottonson, Ira and Theresa A. Pickner. **The Small Business Legal Tool Kit**.
Irvine, CA: Entrepreneur Press, 2007. 1 vol. (350 pp.). Includes essential legal forms and documents on CD-ROM.
Cost: $29.95; from $0.01 on amazon.com (2014).
Designed as an introductory tool for the person unfamiliar with the basics of starting and running a business, this book provides an ideal starting point for the prospective entrepreneur. The authors offer detailed and specific guidance on all aspects of business creation and operation, including the self-assessment process necessary before deciding to go into business. There is discussion of limited liability protection and the various forms of business organization, including sole proprietorships, general partnerships, and limited partnerships, limited liability companies, S corporations, and C corporations, as well as the considerations involved in choosing each business entity. Obtaining a federal employee identification number and identity theft are also discussed, as are sales, franchise, personal property and income taxes. Other important aspects of business operations are also addressed including various employment matters, legal contracts (both general and specific), financing, and business ethics, and the decision to start a new business or purchase an existing one. Finally, the authors offer advice on dealing with the decision to turn over a family business, or sell it to an outside party, including business valuation and important considerations involved in making a sale. The appendices include tables of 50-state sales, use, franchise, and state income taxes, and a glossary of key business terms. A companion CD-ROM contains a number basic legal forms for small business. Ira Nottonson is a legal consultant to businesses and a graduate of Boston College Law School. Theresa Pickner, specializes in business, taxation, and estate planning law.

Pratt, Shannon and Alina V. Niculita. **The Lawyer's Business Valuation Handbook: Understanding Financial Statements, Appraisal Reports, and Expert Testimony**. 2d ed. Chicago: American Bar Association, 2010. 1 vol. (625 pp.). Paperbound.
Cost: $149.95 ($124.95 to members); from $91.94 on amazon.com (2014).
The valuation of a business entity is of critical importance from a variety of specific perspectives, including tax, family law, and corporate law, among others. Determining value is a relative matter, depending on the purposes for which the valuation is being conducted. Value may be a reflection of fair market value, fair value under state statutes, fair value for financial reporting, investment value, and intrinsic or fundamental value, or be calculated by such other determinants as acquisition value, book value, going concern value, enterprise value, liquidation

value, strategic value, or transaction value. Various sources of authority may be employed to determine value, among them: federal and state statutory law, legally binding rules and regulations, contractual definitions of value, non-legally binding administrative rulings, precedential court decisions, direction from the court, direction from the lawyer, the use of IRS authority in non-tax situations, and opinions of other lawyers and appraisers. Sorting through these various determinants of value and their use in specific factual and legal contexts is the subject of this authoritative treatise and practice guide. The authors examine the levels and premises of value and provide an overview of business valuation approaches, methods and procedures. They consider financial disclosure terminology, and the major approaches to business valuation: the income approach, the market approach, the asset-based approach, and the excess earnings method. They also examine rules of thumb which may be used, not as primary appraisal methods, but to provide "ballpark" estimates of value. They also consider such topics as personal versus enterprise goodwill, reasonable compensation, financial statement adjustments, comparative financial statement analysis, economic and industry analysis, discounts and premiums, and valuations for federal tax matters. Attention is also devoted to valuations in the context of shareholder and partner disputes, and marital dissolution; as well as to employee stock ownership plans, and the valuation of professional practices and small service businesses. They also discuss valuation reports from both a methodological and procedural perspective. Finally, they examine valuation from a litigation perspective, including the admissibility and impact of expert business valuation evidence, discovery and the business valuation expert, alternative dispute resolution, business valuation standards and credentials, and the cross-examination of a business valuation expert. The text is accompanied by more than 70 exhibits that explain and illustrate determinations of value and other financial calculations. The volume also includes an extensive bibliography of sources, table of cases and index. Shannon Pratt, Chairman and CEO of Shannon Pratt Valuations, is widely considered to be a leading business valuation guru, with more than 40 years experience in the field. Alina Niculita is President and COO of Shannon Pratt Valuations, and a widely published author in the field of business valuation.

Renuart, Elizabeth and Kathleen E. Keest. **Truth in Lending with CD-ROM**. 8th ed. Boston: National Consumer Law Center, 2012-date. 2 vols. (1,300+ pp.) with companion website. Includes current supplement.
Cost: $240; supplementation: 2013: $50.00; 7th ed.: 2008: $50; 2009: $52; 5th ed.: 2004: $52; 2005: $53; 2006: $56; 2007: $50.
A comprehensive and convenient source of primary law, analysis and practice aids for the consumer law practitioner designed for use in all states. This volume covers the full range of consumer credit issues, including truth in lending, finance charges, closed-end credit disclosures, open-end credit disclosures, billing rights, credit cards, rescission rights, creditor defenses and counterclaims, consumer remedies, high-rate home equity loan protections, and consumer leasing statutes. The CD-ROM contains the full text of all the relevant federal consumer law statutes and regulations, pleadings, interrogatories, jury instructions, and worksheets. One of sixteen such manuals published by the National Consumer Law Center, the nation's leading advocacy organization devoted to the interests of consumers in the marketplace. These manuals are among the best values in legal publishing, providing an uncommonly rich body of both theoretical and practical information at low cost. Each manual in the series is highly recommended to attorneys practicing in these consumer law fields.

Ribstein, Larry E. and Peter V. Letsou. **Business Associations**. 4th ed. New York: Matthew Bender & Co., 2003. 1 vol. Paperbound. Legal Text Series.
Cost: $169; from $34.30 on amazon.com (2014).
This comprehensive overview of the law of business associations encompasses such topics as agency, partnership, corporate structure and operation, and federal securities law and regulation. Includes numerous problems for student analysis. Contains numerous citations to primary authority.

Rossman, Stuart T., Charles Delbaum, and Arielle Cohen. **Consumer Class Actions**. 8th ed. Boston, MA: Consumer Law Center, 2013. 1 vol. Paperbound.
Cost: $210.00 (2014).
A class action is a civil court procedure under which one party, or a group of parties, sue as representatives of a larger class. Class actions are an exception to the general rule that litigation is conducted by and on behalf of individual named parties only. There are many advantages to the unitary resolution of multiple claims, the chief being efficiency. A class action saves the resources of the court and the parties by allowing an issue potentially affecting every class member to be litigated in an economical fashion. Consumer class actions are the only economically viable way to provide legal representation for clients with relatively small claims. In many instances, in the absence of class action, there will never be a recovery for anyone at any time. As Judge Richard Posner put it: "The realistic alternative to a class action is not 17 million individual suits, but zero individual suits, as only a lunatic or a fanatic sues for $30." But beyond the relatively small monetary awards to individual members of the class, class actions create a disincentive for the defendant to engage in wrongful conduct in the future. Such actions are generally brought when consumers complain of injury as a result of a company's systematic and illegal practices, including such things as illegal charges on bills, illegal penalties for late-payments, defective products, and failure to comply with consumer protection laws. Only the class members who opt out are not bound by the judgment in the case. This treatise is a practice guide for plaintiffs' attorneys who litigate consumer class actions. The detailed chapters provide a roadmap through the litigation process, from forum selection and choice of venue to drafting the complaint, discovery, class certification, the class motion and briefs, class notice, negotiations and settlement, the court settlement approval process, claims administration and distribution of benefits, the class action trial, res judicata and collateral estoppel, and attorney fees, and more. The text is amply supported by citations to primary and secondary authorities as an aid to further research. Appendices include the Federal Rule of Civil Procedure 23 (class actions) and Advisory Committee Notes, federal class action legislation (represented by the Class Action Fairness Act of 2005, Pub. L. No. 109-2, 119 Stat. 4), a survey of state class action law (2012), NACA class action guidelines, sample agreements with named plaintiffs, consumer class action web addresses, a guide to finding

pleadings and primary sources on the companion web site, and index. The companion web site provides keyword access to the book's entire text. Stuart Rossman is NCLC's director of litigation, formerly chief of the Trial Division and of the Business and Labor Protection Bureau at the Massachusetts attorney general's office. He is joined by twelve contributing authors, representing the NCLC, academia, and private firms.

Secured Transactions Guide. Riverwoods, IL: Wolters Kluwer Law & Business, 1969-date. 5 vols. Looseleaf format. Updated biweekly. Also available on the Internet.
Cost: $3,113 per year; Internet: comparable, but contact sales representative for specifics (2014).
A comprehensive guide to the state laws and regulations which govern the security interests of secured lenders, including the process by which a security interest is established and maintained against third-party claims. The service follows a uniform topical and paragraph arrangement and includes court decisions, Attorney General opinions, UCC coverage, and various compliance aids.

Spires, Jeremiah J. et al. **Doing Business in the United States.** New York: Matthew Bender, 1978-date. 6 vols. Looseleaf format or eBook. Supplements are issued twice annually.
Cost: $2,920 (print); $2,578 (eBook) (includes annual subscription); annual renewal: 1995: $796 (frozen since 1992); 1996: $835; 1997: $835; 1998: $880; 1999: $920; 2000: $980; 2001: $1,049; 2002: $1,123; 2003: $1,180; 2004: $1,179; 2005: $1,262; 2006: $1,313; 2007: $1,392; 2008: $1,489; 2009: $1,593; 2010: $1,658; 2011: $1,708; 2012: $1,845; 2013: $1,974; 2014: $2.155; eBook: $2,578; renewal: $2,112.
This multi-volume treatise provides an excellent, detailed overview of the American legal system with summary and analysis of the leading areas of United States business law. Intended for lawyers, accountants, business owners, and business planners, the chapter coverage encompasses a well written explanation of government and the legal order in the U.S., Federal administrative law, resolution of disputes, contracts, sales contracts, entry of foreign business personnel in the U.S., forms of business organization, accounting, real property, industrial and intellectual property, taxation, **Uniform Commercial Code**, import-export transactions, business regulation, labor relations, business organization, corporate law, and regulated businesses. Includes a glossary of business and legal terms and a detailed Index. Text is supported by extensive citations to primary authority. Supplements provide amendments to text as well as case summaries and citations to other primary authority.

Cost Saving Tips: While this a highly recommended resource, the primary value lies in its general overview of the American legal system and summary of major areas of business law. If you do not require it to provide a relatively up-to-date source of recent analysis, or citations to primary authority, you may wish to consider dropping the standing order after the initial year to save on updating costs. A new set can be purchased at some future date as you feel it necessary.

Steingold, Fred S. **The Complete Guide to Selling a Business**. 4th ed. Berkeley, CA: Nolo Press, 2012. 1 vol. (496 pp.). Paperbound.
Cost: $34.99; from $19.35 on amazon.com; kindle ed.: $19.49 (2014).
Selling a business may appear intimidating for someone who has never been through the process before. Of the more than 750,000 businesses that change hands each year, many require some form of legal, accounting, real estate, or other professional assistance to complete the deal. Finding a qualified buyer and selling the business on favorable terms will often require planning and hard work.
This book, which focuses on small and medium-sized businesses, provides a roadmap to simplify the process and eliminate unnecessary complications. In 22 illuminating chapters, the author provides an overview of the selling process, the process of getting ready for sale, preparing the sales agreement, the preparation of the promissory note and other sales documents, and the closing of the deal. While the advice rendered here is designed to help the seller avoid having to hire professional assistance, it also provides guidance to those working with lawyers, accountants, and brokers. Here you will also learn how to valuate a business, deciding whether and when to sell, the key legal and tax issues to be addressed, terms of payment. structuring the sale, and much more. The Appendices include an explanation of how to use the CD-ROM, several sample sales agreements, and index. A companion CD-ROM includes more than two dozen legal documents. Fred Steingold is author of three Nolo titles, including **Nolo's Guide for Starting and Running a Small Business**, the **Complete Guide to Buying a Business**, and **The Employer's Legal Handbook**, and writes a monthly column, **The Legal Adviser**, for trade publications around the country.

Stone, Bradford. **Uniform Commercial Code in a Nutshell.** 8th ed. St. Paul, MN: West, 2012. 1 vol. (579 pp.). Available from West Academic.
Cost: $41; from $21.00 on amazon.com; kindle ed.: $18.07 (2014).
This brief summary of the law and principles of the **Uniform Commercial Code** is based on the 1987 Code which added Article 2 on Leases as well as recent amendments to the Bankruptcy Code, the Federal Expedited Funds Availability Act, the Federal Food Security Act, the FTC Credit Practices Rules, and the Uniform Fraudulent Transfer Act. Those UCC sections discussed are accompanied by the full text . Although this volume is intended as a law school text, it can be of great value as a review of basic UCC principles for the practitioner.

Uniform Commercial Code Case Digest. St. Paul, MN: West Group (Clark Boardman Callaghan), 1976-date. 52 casebound volumes, including Finding Aids volume (as of March, 2014). Pocket supplements issued three times per year, as well as periodic revised volumes.
Cost: $9,686; supplementation: 1993: $817; 1994: $863; 1995: $590; 1996: $633; 1997: $670.65; 1998: $1,236.50; 1999: $1,423.75; 2000: $1,417; 2001: $1,765; 2002: $2,049; 2003: $2,167.50; 2004: $2,413; 2005: $2,619; 2006: $2,921; 2007: $3,180; 2008: $2,893.50; 2009: $4,171; 2010: $4,388; 2011: $4,914; 2012: $6,400; 2013: $4,057; **Monthly Assured Print Price (APP):** $654/$7,848.
A multi-jurisdictional digest to **UCC** decisions organized by Code

section. The body of this finding tool consists of clearly-written headnotes summarizing individual decisions. Within each section of the Code, headnotes, whether of state or federal decisions, are arranged alphabetically within each state. A Finding Aids volume contains a **UCC** Digest Finder, Cumulative Table of Cases, and a Digest Index. This is a well-organized and easy to use finding tool to relevant **UCC** cases. Originally published by Callaghan & Company, this title moved to Clark Boardman Callaghan in 1992, and, finally, to the West Group in 1997.

Cost Saving Tips: Given the high cost of supplementation, this is a resource that should be consulted in a law library rather than purchased. If you do purchase it, acquire the pocket supplements on an irregular basis. The thrice-yearly pocket parts are clearly excessive in a field like commercial law and are really just a cash cow for the publisher. For example one set of pocket parts every two years will cost you about $1,800, as opposed to the more than $10,000 - $12,000 two-year cost for subscribers. The advantage of the casebound format is that you can purchase the latest pocket parts and any revised volumes and be current again. Even the out-of-date set can provide you with access to a substantial amount of case law which can be updated in your own state's annotated code and, then, Shepardized or KeyCited.

Uniform Commercial Code Reporter-Digest. New York: Matthew Bender & Co., 1965-date. 24+ vols. Looseleaf format. Updated quarterly. Also available in CD-ROM format.
Cost: $4,692 (print); $4,265 (eBook) (includes annual subscription); annual renewal: 1995: $1,358.50 (frozen since 1992); 1996: $1,425; 1997: $1,425; 1998: $1,500; 1999: $1,565; 2000: $1,610; 2001: $1,691; 2002: $1,810; 2003: $1,864; 2004: $1,957; 2005: $2,074; 2006: $2,220; 2007: $2,398; 2008: $ 2,542; 2009: $2,745; 2010: $2,776; 2011: $2,859; 2012: $2,973; 2013: $3.181; 2014: $3,472; eBook: $4,265; renewal: 2014: $3,472. Also available on CD-ROM as part of the **Authority Banking & Commercial Law Library**.
This service provides the full text of the **UCC** with all state variations, case digests arranged by Code Section, text of decisions from all states, and drafting history and Permanent Editorial Board reports.

Uniform Commercial Code Reporting Service 2d. St. Paul, MN: West (Clark Boardman Callaghan), 1965-date. 67 vols. Monthly case releases, replaced with bound volumes.
Cost: $15,387.60; supplementation: 1993: $1,250; 1994: $1,270; 1995: $1,270; 1996: $1,537; 1997: $1,537; 1998: $1,614; 1999: $1,743; 2000: $1,848; 2001: $2,096; 2002: $2,305; 2003: $2,580; 2004: $2,915.50; 2005: $3,222; 2006: $3,598; 2007: $3,993.96; 2008: $4,445.52; 2009: $4,948; 2010: $5,937.48; 2011: $7,125; 2012: $10,500; 2013: $12,312. **Monthly Assured Print Price (APP):** $1,068.58/$12,822.95.
This service provides full text of practically all state appellate and federal decisions construing provisions of the **UCC**, including bankruptcy decisions and attorney general opinions. Additional volumes include full text of the Code with official comments, a one-volume Findex providing easy access to specific opinions by Code section, a volume highlighting the differences between the official Code and the state variations, and a monthly newsletter entitled **UCC Bulletin**. The current library includes 67 volumes in the second series. Decisions appear initially in looseleaf format and are subsequently replaced by casebound reporter volumes. Originally published by Callaghan & Company, this title moved to Clark Boardman Callaghan in 1992, and, finally, to the West Group in 1997.

Cost Saving Tips: This set is obviously intended for the firm with a substantial commercial practice which requires regular and up-to-date access to both past and current **UCC** decisions in full text. Given the high cost of supplementation, obtain decisions on WestlawNext PRO.

White, James J. and Robert S. Summers. **Uniform Commercial Code.** 6th ed. St. Paul, MN: Thomson Reuters, 2005-date. 5 vols. Annual pocket supplements. Practitioner's Edition.
Cost: $827; supplementation: 1996: $30.50; 1997: $35; 1998: $37; 1999: $41; 2000: $45; 2001: $60; 2002: $175; 2003: $75; 2004: $80; 2005: $85; 2006: $164; 2007: $179; 2008: $220; 2009: $75; 2010: $155; 2011: $169; 2012: $184; 2013: $310; **Monthly Assured Print Price (APP):** $34/$408.
Authored by Professors from the University of Michigan and Cornell University Schools of Law, this four-volume treatise is an expansion of the authors' one-volume Hornbook. Topical organization parallels the order of the articles in the **Uniform Commercial Code**. The authors have attempted to meet the needs of both law students and practitioners by presenting a clear exposition of the law, but one adequately laden with footnote citations to relevant case and statutory law. The four-volume edition includes chapters on warehouse receipts and bills of lading which do not appear in the one volume Hornbook. Both editions includes discussion of recent case developments, new federal and state statutes, and a new chapter covering NSF checks, documentary drafts, and forged checks, liability of payers and collecting banks, final payment, and delay. While the statutory law has grown considerably in recent years, the authors have tried to present a multi-jurisdictional treatise on the Code. The original volumes one and two were published in 1988. Volume 1A, published in 1991, covers the new Article 2A on leases of goods. Volume 1B, published in 1993, covers revised articles 3, 4 and 4A, while its appendix includes revisions of the CHIP rules and NACHA regulations. A revised volume 4 provides updated coverage of the amended Article 9. Appendices in volume two include The Uniform Customs and Practices for Documentary Credits, Sample Forms for Standby Letters of Credit, WESTLAW references, a table of cases, table of statutes, and subject index. Like most West Practitioner's Editions, this is a thorough, scholarly work with excellent editorial features. An excellent value with a history of reasonably priced annual supplementation.

White, James J. and Robert S. Summers. **Uniform Commercial Code**. 6th ed. St. Paul, MN: West, 2010. 1 vol. (1,586 pp.). Available from West Academic.
Cost: $103; from $55.24 on amazon.com (2014).
This law school Hornbook provides an in-depth introduction to the UCC without the detail and case citations found in the author's more extensive Practitioner's Edition. All articles of the UCC are covered; however, the chapters on Articles 5 and 9

have been completely rewritten to reflect recent amendments to the Code. One of the book's two appendices contains a guide to Researching Uniform Commercial Code Law on Westlaw

Wright, Benjamin and Jane K. Winn. **The Law of Electronic Commerce**. 4th ed. New York: Wolters Kluwer Law & Business, 2000-date. 1 vol. Looseleaf format
Cost: $535; supplementation: 2002: $115; 2003: $115; 2004: $254; 2005: $268; 2006: $284; 2007: $304; 2008: $326; 2009: $337; 2010: $372; 2011: $390; 2012: $416; 2013: $462; 3d edition: 1999: $144.
The rapid acceptance of commerce over the Internet has raised a number of legal and technological questions. Chief among these is the issue of security for electronic transactions involving the use of credit cards. Although millions of dollars have been invested in the development of the Secure Electronic Transaction (SET) protocol to protect credit card numbers, this protocol is having no impact upon the growth of electronic merchandising. In practice, credit card numbers are being protected by the automatic Secure Socket Layer (SSL), security built into Web browsers. This volume addresses security and other issues driven by commerce in an increasingly electronic environment. Its 21 chapters are grouped into five Parts: the Context of Electronic Commerce, Legal Proof Issues, Recordkeeping and Internal Control, Electronic Issues, and Network Service Providers and Customers. The appendices contain a number of model agreements and other documents useful in an electronic commerce context. Also included are a glossary, table of cases, table of statutes and related sources, and index.

Additional titles in the field of Commercial Law are available from the following publishers: American Bar Association, Matthew Bender, Foundation Press, Greenwood Publishing Group, William S. Hein & Co., Inc., Institute of International Banking Law & Practice, Irwin McGraw-Hill, Kluwer Academic, Kluwer Law International, LexisNexis, National Consumer Law Center, Oxford Law, Panel Publishers, Practising Law Institute, Thomson Reuters West, Warren, Gorham & Lamont. West Academic. See Appendix B for addresses and telephone numbers.

Computer Law

Battersby, Gregory J. and Charles W. Grimes. **Drafting Internet Agreements**. 2d ed. New York: Wolters Kluwer Law & Business, 2010-date. 1 vol. Looseleaf format.
Cost: $359; supplementation: 2011: $150; 2012: $160; 2013: $199; 1st ed.: 2001: 0; 2002: $110; 2003: $135; 2004: $137; 2005: $144; 2006: $153; 2007: $163; 2008: $175; 2009: $192; 2010: new edition.
An exhaustive collection of sample Internet agreements including those on Internet advertising, Internet consulting, electronic commerce, joint ventures, licensing, technology development, and Website agreements. Each of the more than 40 agreements includes a general description, checklists to aid in the drafting of agreements, and practice tips which identify the sections most likely to require the most negotiation and which provide guidance in how to handle those issues. Includes citations to relevant cases. The author/editors are members of the Stamford, CT form of Grimes and Battersby which specializes in all areas of intellectual property law, and authors of numerous books in the field of intellectual property.

Bender, David. **Computer Law**. New York: Matthew Bender & Co., 1978-date. 4 vols. Looseleaf format. Supplemented twice annually. On print and eBook. Also on **Authority Intellectual Property Law Library on CD-ROM**.
Cost: $1,510 (annual subscription); renewal: 1998: $405; 1999: $420; 2000: $450; 2001: $482; 2002: $516; 2003: $542; 2004: $569; 2005: $609; 2006: $652; 2007: $733; 2008: $792; 2009: $855; 2010: $865; 2011: $908; 2012: $962; 2013: $1,010; 2014: $1,102; eBook: $1,373; renewal: 2014: $1,102.
This comprehensive research tool is designed to provide the practicing attorney with both the conceptual underpinnings and the practice techniques of both evidence and discovery procedures as they relate to computer-based information and the protection of computer software under the laws governing intellectual property. The author addresses the three primary problems presented by computer-related problems: (1) understanding the technology sufficiently to understand where the problems lie; (2) communicating with computer experts, and (3) applying the law in this technological environment. The set's 20 chapters examine such topics as the computer industry, computer technology, software protection, multimedia issues, Internet issues, copyright protection of software, trade secret, contractual, and extralegal protection of software, computer applications and illustrative legal problems, general evidentiary principles, the rule against hearsay evidence, privileges, probative value, computer litigation support systems, discovery examples, applied computer evidence and procedure, and computer-related torts.

Cost Saving Tips: Although customers have the option of dropping the subscription to this publication after the first year, a standing order is recommended in this highly volatile field. If the renewal cost is more than you wish to pay, however, consider one of the annually supplemented single-volume alternatives.

Blakeslee, Melise R. **Internet Crimes, Torts and Scams: Investigation and Remedies**. New York: Oxford University Press, 2013. 1 vol. (480 pp.). Paperbound.
Cost: $185; from $147.87 on amazon.com (2014).
Internet scams, usually originating in some foreign jurisdiction, that seek to separate us from our bank accounts have become ubiquitous on the Internet. Indeed, the Internet has given life to older scams and cons, but now shrouded in the impersonal and anonymous garb of instantaneous electronic communication and financial transmission. In this comprehensive and practical guide to cybercrime, author Melise Blakeslee details the range of illegal and malicious internet activity that preys upon the unwary, and explains the expanding range of response or enforcement options available to victims and law enforcement agencies. Her practical and problem-oriented approach addresses a variety of practical topics, including intellectual property enforcement, libel, third-party liability, forensics, global jurisdictional issues, interpretation of email headers, investigation of counterfeiters, the problems of anonymity on the Internet, and the preparation

of complaints. It provides the practitioner the tools not only identify the types of Internet-related risks faced by clients, but how to investigate and best respond to those risks. The extensive appendices include ICANN complaints, motions, a list of online resources, and guidelines for the seizure of electronic evidence. The founder and president of Ecrimetools.com, a firm devoted to assisting legal professionals fight cybercrime, Melise Blakeslee is also managing partner at Sequel Technology & IP Law, LLP. She draws upon extensive experience investigating and litigating internet-based legal problems, Internet crimes, complex software, and copyright disputes.

Campbell, Dennis, ed. **The Internet: Laws and Regulatory Regimes**. 2d ed. Huntington, NY: Juris Publishing, 2010. 1 vol. Looseleaf format. Annual supplements.
Cost: $175 (print or eBook); supplementation: 2012: $65; 2013: $70.00; from $116 on amazon.com (2014).
This volume provides surveys of the Internet laws and regulatory regimes of 23 jurisdictions around the world, including Anguilla, Argentina, Australia, Austria, Brazil, Canada, Chile, Cyprus, the Czech Republic, Estonia, France, Israel, Japan, Luxembourg, Malta, Norway, Singapore, Spain, Switzerland, Taiwan, Thailand, United Kingdom, and the United States. Most of the surveys address the following areas: intellectual property, privacy and data, communications and defamation, fraud and Internet crime, contractual matters, jurisdiction and dispute resolution, and Internet standards. Each survey is introduced by a useful overview of the jurisdiction's legal environment, applicable law, and E-Commerce environment. The authors are practicing attorneys in the respective jurisdictions. A useful resource for attorneys engaged in transnational E-Commerce and related Internet law issues.

Clifford, Ralph D., ed. **Cybercrime: The Investigation, Prosecution and Defense of a Computer-Related Crime**. 3d ed. Durham, NC: Carolina Academic Press, 2011. 1 vol. (312 pp.). Paperbound.
Cost: $38; from $27.49 on amazon.com (2014).
Cybercrime embraces those various criminal acts involving the use of computer technology. The earlier term, computer crime, was generally used to describe acts in which computer technology was used to commit a traditionally recognized crime. But technological advances and increased sophistication on the part of criminals have generated new forms of criminal behavior that would not have been possible without the use of computer technology. And while computer crimes were committed primarily by insiders prior to 1989, the privatization and commercialization of the Internet unleashed a new wave of computer-related crime in which perpetrators are just as likely to reside outside an organization as within it. Following an introduction by the editor, this volume brings together several cybercrime experts to address such topics as: defining cybercrime: a review of state and federal law; the investigation and prosecution of a cybercrime; defending cybercrime cases: selected statutes and defenses; and international cybercrime: recent developments in the law. Each chapter includes citations to relevant authorities. Ralph Clifford is a professor of law at Southern New England School, of Law. The contributing authors are all recognized experts in cybercrime from the fields of academia, private practice, and the U.S. government.

Curtis, George. **The Law of Cybercrimes and Their Investigations**. New York: CRC Press, 2012. Vol. (398 pp.). Hardbound.
Cost: $98.95; from $72.09 on amazon.com; kindle: $71.96 (2014).
Cybercrime may be defined as unlawful conduct involving the use of a computer or other digital device in the commission of a crime. This volume examines crimes committed: (1) by use of a computer, digital or electronic device as the instrumentality of the crime; (2) upon a computer, digital, or electronic device, in which the device is the victim of the crime; and (3) by the use of a computer, digital, or electronic device for the storage of evidence of a crime. Prior to 1984, crimes involving computers were prosecuted under existing federal criminal statutes (e.g. wire fraud). In 1984, however, the first statute was enacted that specifically addressed computer crime, namely, the Counterfeit Access and Computer Fraud Act of 1984 (Pub, L. 98-473). The current federal computer law appears at 18 U.S.C § 1030 (a), commonly known as the Computer Fraud and Abuse Law, which includes seven categories of criminal conduct. This textbook covers crimes involving the use of computers, information warfare and cyberterrorism, crimes against morality, crimes threatening or resulting in physical or mental harm, Internet frauds, data privacy crimes, and intellectual property fraud. The remainder of the volume covers the investigation and enforcement of cybercrimes, including search and seizure, wiretapping and eavesdropping, access to stored communications, pen register, trap and trace, and GPS devices, digital evidence and forensic analysis, and international issues involving the investigation and prosecution of cybercrimes. Each chapter includes excerpts from sample cases, key words and phrases, review problems and web links. George E. Curtis is professor of criminal justice at Utica College, where he teaches undergraduate classes in economic crime and cybercrime. A graduate of Brooklyn Law School, he served as a confidential clerk to the New York Court System for 26 years, and currently has an appellate practice.

Delta, George B. and Jeffrey H. Matsuura. **Law of the Internet**. 3d ed. New York: Wolters Kluwer Law & Business, 2008-date. 1 vol. Looseleaf format. Annual supplementation.
Cost: $545; supplementation: 2009: $155; 2010: $330; 2011: $350; 2012: $374; 2013: $415; 2d ed.: 1998: $76; 1999: $82; 1999: $167; 2001: $210; 2002: $130; 2003: $130; 2004: $162; 2005: $300; 2006: $318; 2007: $340; 2008: $395 (new edition).
In the relatively short time that it has been embraced by the general population, the Internet has already had a profound effect on a wide range of human activities, from communication, business transactions, and research to entertainment, information storage, and personal relationships. This volume operates on the assumption that there is no Internet law as such, but only a new context in which traditional legal principles are applied. Following an introductory overview of the Internet and its relationship to the law, the authors address such topics as the regulation of access, interoperability and services, jurisdictional issues in cyberspace, antitrust, intellectual property, privacy issues, defamation, obscene and indecent materials, commerce, tax issues and electronic commerce, and export controls. The volume also concludes thirteen valuable appendices, including security and management check-lists, sample agreements, and guidelines. George B. Delta is Of Counsel to the Washington, DC firm of Gray & Goodman Ltd. where he specializes

in commercial, tax and financial matters, and electronic commerce. Jeffrey H. Matsuura is a principal in Roundtable Research Commercialization, Inc., a Virginia-based consulting firm that assists high technology bring scientific research and technological innovation to market.

Guide to Computer Law. Riverwoods, IL: Wolters Kluwer Law & Business (CCH), 1989-date. 2 vols. Looseleaf format. Monthly updates. Also available in CD-ROM and Internet formats. All formats updated monthly.
Cost: $1,461 per year; Internet: comparable, but call 888-224-7377 for specifics (2014).
An authoritative and convenient guide to the major issues involving computers, including intellectual property, communications, computer software, Internet, and electronic commerce issues. The coverage embraces material that falls under the key areas of intellectual property law, including patent law, copyright law, trade secrets, and trademark law. Includes the text of relevant statutes and cases, together with explanatory text. It also provides information regarding the historical sources of computer law based in the law of copyright, patent, trade secrets, and trademark. Also covered are such matters as antitrust, privacy, security, torts, evidence, and unfair trade issues as they apply to the computer industry. The user will also find information on the topics of computer sales, digital signatures, leases, licenses, semiconductor chip protection, and computer crime. New developments in the field are highlighted in each monthly release. Intended for the specialist who requires timely and authoritative information on computer-related issues.

Hamadi, Rob. **Identity Theft: What it is, how to prevent it, and what to do if it happens to you**. London, Vision, 2004. 1 vol. (241 pp.).
Cost: $17.95; from $0.08 on amazon.com (2014).
In this examination of identity theft from an international perspective, the author explains the methods by which identities are stolen, including the theft of ATM pin and social security numbers, the cracking of online accounts, the copying of credit cards, and the searching of trash. He also outlines the steps which can be taken to prevent identity theft and recover it after has been stolen. The book pays particular attention to the identity theft environment in the United States and United Kingdom. The author is head of communications at the Publishers Association, United Kingdom, and is the founding chair of the Digital Content Forum's Cybercrime Industry Action Group.

Hannon, Michael. **Digital Evidence: Computer Forensics and Legal Issues Arising From Computer Investigations**. Buffalo, NY: William S. Hein & Co. Inc., 2012. 1 vol. (368 pp.).
Cost: $74.95; from $59.99 on amazon.com (2014).
Digital evidence consists of information or data stored or transmitted in binary form that may be relied on in court proceedings. Such information may be stored in a variety of locations, including on a computer hard drive, a mobile phone, a personal digital assistant (PDA), a CD, and a flash card in a digital camera. Although digital evidence is commonly associated with electronic crime, or e-crime, it is also used to prosecute all types of crimes. In their effort to fight e-crime and to collect relevant digital evidence for all crimes, law enforcement agencies are increasingly engaged in the collection and analysis of digital evidence, also known as computer forensics, and incorporating it into their infrastructure. In pursuance of this effort, law enforcement agencies must train officers to collect digital evidence and keep up with evolving technologies, including computer operating systems. This intent of this volume is to provide judges, attorneys and law enforcement officers with a thorough grounding in digital evidence and computer-related Fourth Amendment issues and to explain the technical and legal issues that arise in the course of investigations involving computers, digital devices and network communications, whether of a civil or criminal nature. Chapters are devoted to hard drive technology, file systems, and computer forensics; computer forensic techniques and sources of digital evidence; child pornography investigations; the Fourth Amendment and computers; and federal privacy statutes. The appendix includes a list of important web resources in the field. Michael Hannon is Associate Director for Library and Educational Technology at the University of Minnesota.

Hart, Jonathan D. **Internet Law: A Field Guide**. 6th ed. Washington D.C.: Bloomberg BNA Books, 2009. 1 vol. (831 pp.).
Cost: $195; from $10.27 on amazon.com (2014).
This comprehensive treatise and practice guide both explains and analyzes the law as it relates to Internet publishing. These legal issues range from First Amendment concerns, including libel and defamation, privacy and data collection (including COPPA, HIPPA, ECPA, and the USA PATRIOT Act), electronic signatures and contracts, domain name disputes, advertising regulations, trademark rights, protection of web site content, the risks of producing web site content, Internet taxation, copyright infringement, and the legal implications of the CAN-SPAM Act of 2003 (Public Law No. 108-187), FTC privacy regulations, and publication of materials that are available internationally. The volume includes a comprehensive index and detailed table of contents. The volume also includes a fully searchable CD-ROM with the complete contents of the book and the text of the statutes, regulations, and judicial opinions referenced therein. The author discusses each topic in the context of general area of law in which it arises. A nationally recognized expert on Internet law, Jonathan Hart is a member Washington, DC firm of Dow, Lohnes & Albertson where he specializes in the representation of media and technology companies on a broad range of commercial, transactional, operational, and content matters. His clients include dozens of web publishers, software and technology companies, newspapers, magazines, and broadcasters. This is an essential resource for any attorney who practices Internet law or in areas impacted by the Internet.

Hollaar, Lee A. **Legal Protection of Digital Information**. Washington, DC: Bloomberg BNA Books, 2002. 1 vol. (498 pp.). Softbound.
Cost: $155; from $90.00 on amazon.com (2014).
A useful introductory exposition of copyright and patent law as it applies to digital information. The author, a professor of computer science at the University of Utah, registered patent agent, and hardware and software developer, shares his insights regarding copyright law generally, the copyright of

computer programs, copyright of digital information, patent law, and software-based inventions. His coverage extends to the history of copyright legislation, court decisions, and current legal doctrines applicable to computer software, including the CONTU recommendations, the Digital Millennium Copyright Act (DMCA) and the scope of software copyright. He argues that copyright laws are ill-suited for protecting digital information, analyzes the problem of file sharing within the parameters of the Copyright Act's six exclusive rights as specified in Section 106, and offers possible solutions to this dilemma. The author also discusses patent law and the protection of business methods. The volume's appendices include the text of a number of applicable statutes, as well as tables of cases, statutes and rules. The complete text is contained on a companion CD-ROM.

Internet and e-Commerce Law Treatise Library on LoisLawConnect. New York: Wolters Kluwer Law & Business.
Cost: $540.00 per year (solo practitioner) (2014).
This package of titles provides expert guidance on drafting internet contracts, licensing agreements, and litigating e-commerce cases. The titles include: **Law of the Internet, Drafting Internet Agreements, Scott on Multimedia Law, Computer & Internet Lawyer, Law of Electronic Commerce,**
and **Internet and Technology Law Desk Reference.** A cost-effective alternative to acquiring the individual titles in print format.

Internet LawResource Center. Arlington, VA: Bloomberg BNA, 1999-date. Now available only on the Internet; updated every business day.
Cost: $2,720 (2014).
A comprehensive resource on Internet law which brings together primary law and analytical commentary by leading practitioners in the field. Substantive areas covered by this resource include Internet commerce, intellectual property, privacy, freedom of speech, jurisdiction, criminal liability, securities, taxation, encryption/cryptography, and the FCC and the Internet. Primary law documents include laws and policy, cases, pleadings, motions, briefs. The Topical Digests section of Internet Law & Regulation provides subscribes with a uniquely powerful way to compare how similar Internet law issues are treated in different jurisdictions and by different parties. All decisions, complaints, briefs, and motions included in **Internet Law & Regulation** are extensively headnoted by a staff of lawyer/editors and made available through a topical digesting system. Cases and Digests sections are thoroughly cross-linked, so that it is easy to move from case to digest and from digest to full text of an opinion or pleading. Formerly **Internet Law & Regulation** the now retitled **Internet Law Resource Center** also includes recent articles on Internet-related topics. Bloomberg BNA took this title over from its Pike & Fisher subsidiary in 2010.

Lundberg, Steven W., Stephen C. Durant and Ann M. McCrackin, eds. **Electronic and Software Patents: Law and Practice**. 3d ed. Arlington, VA: BNA Books, 2011. with 2012 Supplement. Hardcover.
Cost: $495; supplementation: 2012: $210; 2013: $220.
This volume assembles a blend of academic and practically oriented chapters on how to draft and prosecute successful electronic and software parents. Its aim is to guide applicants through the patent application process with an understanding of the latest technological developments in the field of software design, current USPTO policies, and significant court rulings, including analysis of the U.S. Supreme Court's decision in *Bilski v. Kappos,* which rejected the "machine-or-transformation test" as the sole test for patent eligibility of claims reciting a process. An outgrowth of BNA's collaboration with the American Intellectual Property Law Association (AIPLA), the sixteen chapters in this volume address the following broad topics: (1) deciding whether or not to seek patent protection; (2) drafting and prosecuting an application in the United States; (3) drafting and prosecuting international applications, (4) business method patents and design patents; and (5) managing patents in business and litigation. Individual chapters address such subjects as whether to seek patent protection at all, how to search for and evaluate prior art, how to use trade secret and copyright law in conjunction with patent strategy, and how to draft claims for broad yet distinct interpretation. Appendices include a Patent Application Checklist, a sample software patent, a sample electronics patent, a sample business method patent, and a sample design patent. Twenty-three authors, each an expert in his or her field, have written, or co-authored, the sixteen chapters. The text includes numerous citations to the U.S. Code, federal regulations, federal court decisions, USPTO guidelines, and other patent related documents. The third edition is unique in offering an international survey of the statutes, regulations, and case law of more than 40countries, in addition to basic global principles of patentability. It also includes guidance for writing specifications in view of the Federal Circuit's decision in *Ariad Pharmaceuticals, Inc. v. Eli Lilly & Co.* (2008).

Nimmer, Raymond T. **The Law of Computer Technology: Rights, Licenses, Liabilities**. 4th ed. St. Paul, MN: Thomson Reuters/West, 2007-date. 4 vols. (2,030 pp.). Looseleaf format. Supplemented twice annually.
Cost: $945; ProView eBook: $917; supplementation: 2003: $276; 2004: $320; 2005: $304; 2006: $346.50; 2007: $386; 2008: $551; 2009: $631; 2010: $275; 2011: $321; 2012: $350; 2013: $382; **Monthly Assured Print Price (APP):** $47/$564.
The computer revolution has had a profound impact on modern society, including business, industry, government and education. The speed of technological innovation, however, has generated a myriad of legal issues which must be addressed on a variety of levels. This comprehensive work examines a wide range of legal issues which have been impacted by this rapid pace of change. The author, a leading expert on computer law, examines such topics as copyright and computer technology, patent law, software systems and protection, trade secrets and confidentiality, research, development and ownership, international intellectual property issues, computer system sales contracts, technology licensing, computer and software leasing, information services contracts, fraud and computer-related torts, international technology export and import, computer crime, computer error and use liability, electronic transaction environments, information products, electronic publishing, and privacy, data protection, and access to information. The author is the Leonard Childs Professor of Law, University of Houston Law Center.

Payton, Theresa M. and Ted Claypoole. **Privacy in the Age of Big Data**. Lanham, MD: Rowman & Littlefield, 2013. 1 vol. (239 pp.).
Cost: $35.00; from $27.20 on amazon.com; kindle: $19.24 (2014).
Digital data collection and surveillance are becoming more pervasive by the day. IBM has estimated that 90% of the data in existence in the world was created in 2011-2012, and the Computer Science Corporation projects that the creation of data will be forty-four times greater in 2020 than it was in 2009. This massive data collection presents both promise and peril. We know that Google monitors our online searching to enable advertisers to better target us; and that our personal information is widely disseminated on social media sites. Most computer users take advantage of benefits offered by online access, but have little comprehension of the full extent to which data is collected, stored, aggregated, and used to compromise their personal privacy. As the authors explain, we are at risk not only from sharing personal data on the Internet, but from government data collection, smartphone usage, surveillance cameras, smart cars, medical records, computerized smart grids, cable service providers, sexual predators, and home digital networks. This volume introduces readers to the ways in which our privacy is compromised electronically at home, in one's car, on the street, or in our interactions with government, medical providers, or business relationships and suggests ways in which we can adjust our behavior and activities to recapture it. The concluding chapters examine the future of technology and privacy, and laws and regulations that could help preserve privacy. Theresa Payton, an authority of Internet security, net crime and technology implementation, was the first female White House Chief Information Officer from 2006 to 2008. Ted Claypoole is leader of the Privacy and Data Management team at the law firm of Womble Carlyle and co-chair of the Cyberspace Privacy and Data Security Subcommittee for the ABA's Business Law Section.

Perritt, Henry H., Jr. **Digital Communications Law**. Gaithersburg, MD: Wolters Kluwer Law & Business, 2010-date. 1 vol. (488 pp.). Looseleaf format. Annual supplementation.
Cost: $429; supplementation: 2011: $130; 2012: $139; 2013: $199; supplementation to predecessor title: 2001: $105; 2002: $130; 2003: $182; 2004: $193; 2005: $203; 2006: $216; 2007: $230; 2008: $247; 2009: $269; 2010: 0; 1st edition: 1997: $57; 1998: $64; 1999: $76.
Rapid changes in information technology have raised a host of legal issues which must be addressed by either the government, the market, or the legal system, including property rights, contract and commercial issues, adjudication of competing claims for access to distribution channels for information, and the rights to obtain and sell government information. Moreover, the worldwide production and distribution of information raises jurisdictional and other questions which transcend the boundaries of sovereign nations and their individual legal traditions. Inevitably, responses by the legal system lag behind these developments in the technological sphere, increasing the likelihood of conflict. Henry Perritt has been at the forefront of these issues for a number of years, both as a widely published professor of law at Chicago-Kent School of Law and as an advisor to numerous national and international commissions. Chairman of the ABA Section on Administrative Law and Regulatory Practice, Perritt brings a unique combination of computer expertise and legal knowledge to bear on many of these highly technical issues. The chapters in this volume examine the National Information Infrastructure as a source of legal issues, access to networks and facilities, privacy, liability for harmful communications, liability for service failures, constitutional considerations, regulation, interoperability and compatibility, electronic commerce, contracting, intellectual property, public information, civil dispute resolution and procedure, criminal law, and international law and trade. The 1998 supplement examines the efforts to reform the Internet's domain name system and the potential for private international self-regulation, among other issues. This book is an essential reference for the attorney actively involved in computer and information technology issues. When Wiley Law Publications was acquired by Wolters Kluwer in 1997, this title was assigned to Wolters Kluwer Law & Business. This title replaces the author's **Law of the Information Superhighway**.

Rustad, Michael. **Global Internet Law in a Nutshell**. 2d ed. St. Paul, MN: West Academic, 2013. 1 vol. (587 pp.). Paperbound.
Cost: $41.00; from $27.47 on amazon.com (2014).
First predicted in 1967 by Harvard law professor Benjamin Kaplan in his book **An Unhurried View of Copyright**, the Internet has blossomed into a transformative technology with a profound impact on the world of information creation, transfer, searching, and storage, as well as substantive contributions to every field of human endeavor. Beginning with an overview of the history and technical infrastructure that comprises the Internet, this concise volume provides readers with an outline of the central features, developments, legal issues, and theories of the Internet, as well as the relevant case law and statutory developments which have addressed it. The author examines the competing theories of Internet governance, the development and implications of Web 3, cyber jurisdiction and enforcement of judgments, choice and conflicts of law, cyber-torts, online contracting and licensing, the protection of online intellectual property assets, the protection of online privacy, criminal liability for Internet activity, and European Community Directives such as the E-Commerce Directive, Brussels Regulation, and the Rome I Regulation. He also addresses such topics as electronic commerce, consumer regulation, content regulation, copyrights, trademarks, trade secrets, and Internet-related patents. While intended as a concise review for law students, it is an excellent resource for anyone who works online, or has a personal or business Web presence, including high-tech and e-commerce companies, traditional businesses with websites, graphic artists, Internet developers, and software programmers. The second edition presents a comprehensive review of cybertort and cybercrime developments including foreign cases. Each chapter of this revised edition reviews statutory and caselaw developments from the European Union as well as other foreign countries. An excellent introductory exposition of most Internet-related issues.

Rustad, Michael L. **Software Licensing: Principles and Practical Strategies**. New York: Oxford University Press, 2010. 1 vol. (785 pp.). Paperbound.
Cost: $200; amazon.com kindle ed.: $113.49 (2014).
The computer software industry has grown into the third largest industry in the United States, yet the field of software licensing

law is still relatively undeveloped and fraught with potential hazards. Software licenses have become a subject of concern to lawyers that represent licensors or licensees, those who draft specialized software agreements, or grapple with related legal, business and policy issues. In addition, business and intellectual property lawyers should become familiar with the basic structure of a software license since licensing has become a leading mechanism for transferring value in an information-based economy. This comprehensive survey of the law of software licensing draws upon best practices, as well as legal doctrine imported from the American Law Institute's *Principles of the Law of Software Contracts*, the Uniform Computer Information Transactions Act (UCITA), UCC Article 2, and international commercial law, supplemented by interviews with leading software attorneys. The author provides a detailed discussion and analysis of the concepts and methods of software licensing with special attention to the contract and intellectual property interface of this process. The book's 13 chapters provide an overview of the field of software licensing; the nuts and bolts of software licenses; indemnification and warranties; breach, termination and remedies; standard-form licenses; managing open source; software from scratch; development agreements; source code escrow in development contracts; a practitioner's guide to the UCITA minefield; the principles of law of software contracts; understanding secured credit and bankruptcy issues; global software licensing; and avoiding licensing lost in translation. Michael Rustad is the Thomas F. Lambert Jr. Professor Law and Co-Director of the Intellectual Property Law Concentration at Suffolk University Law School in Boston, where he has taught courses in software licensing for almost 20 years.

Scott, A. Hugh. **Computer and Intellectual Property Crime: Federal and State Law**. Washington, DC: Bloomberg BNA Books, 2001. 1 vol. (1,574 pp.).
Cost: $340; supplementation: 2003: $155; 2004: $165; 2005: $175; 2006: $175; 2007-2013: 0.
A comprehensive examination of federal and state criminal law as it applies to computers and intellectual property. The work opens with an overview and history of computer and intellectual property crime and the Internet. The author's discussion of federal laws includes those, which specifically address computer and intellectual property crime as well as general criminal statutes, which can be applied to crimes in these areas. Coverage includes a summary of the area, the text of the law, discussion of applicable caselaw, legislative history, the elements of the offense, instructions to juries, and available civil remedies. There is also discussion of the federal prosecution process, jurisdiction and venue, federal investigations, search and seizures of computers, and the use of federal sentencing guidelines. The federal statutes discussed include the Computer Fraud and Abuse Act, Electronic Privacy Act, Child Sexual Exploitation and Pornography Act, Racketeer Influenced Corrupt Organizations Act, and thirteen others. A state-by-state treatment of state statutes follows, with a list of enforcement agencies and remedies for victims. The unique and comprehensive coverage of this book makes it an essential acquisition for research law libraries, prosecutors and defense counsel, IP firms, and scholars and students of computer and IP crime.

Shane, Peter M. and Jeffrey Hunker, eds. **Cybersecurity: Shared Risks, Shared Responsibilities**. Durham, NC: Carolina Academic Press, 2013. 1 vol. (330 pp.). Paperbound.
Cost: $43.00; from $27.87 on amazon.com (2014).
Recent revelations implicating China in a major cyber-espionage campaign to steal sensitive data from organizations in the United States and other countries raise serious concerns implicating national, financial, and economic security. First coined in 1994, the term cybersecurity refers to the body of technologies, processes and practices designed to protect networks, computers, programs and data from attack, damage or unauthorized access. Major elements of cybersecurity include application security, information security, network security, disaster recovery, business continuity planning, and end-user education. This introduction to cybersecurity describes and evaluates the role of cybersecurity and the institutional struggles involved in a world transformed by technology, including the inherent limitations of government policy in addressing the threat. The contributing authors provide an insightful examination of U.S. global leadership in cybersecurity, the roles of government and private sector in addressing the information security to the U.S. financial services industry, the shared domain: the Cybersecurity governance imperative, Cybersecurity and conflict response, Cyber relationships in the United States government, threat assessment in Cyberspace, the application of international environmental legal norms to Cyber statecraft, making good Cybersecurity law and policy, Cybersecurity ideas whose time has not come—and shouldn't, and Cybersecurity policy as if ordinary citizens mattered. The authors tap the full range of government and private sector documents on cybersecurity policies and issues. Peter Shane teaches law at Ohio State University's Moritz College of Law. Jeffrey Hunker is Visiting Scholar at the University of California at Davis Computer Science Department.

Stobbs, Gregory A. **Software Patents**. 3d ed. New York: Wolters Kluwer Law & Business, 2012-date. 1 vol. (650 pp.) Annual supplementation.
Cost: $409; no supplementation to date; 2d ed. 2001: $115; 2002: $150; 2003: $175; 2004: $198; 2005: $198; 2006: $205; 2007: $218; 2008: $234; 2009: $255; 2010: $272; 2011: $290; 2013: $311; 1st ed.: 1997: $59; 1998: $67; 1999: $85.
As a burgeoning form of intellectual property, computer software has opened up a promising new practice area for the legal profession. With copyright law inadequate to protect the interests of software developers, the importance of drafting complete and accurate patent applications has taken on increased importance for those who wish to protect their commercial interests. This volume provides an complete breakdown of the patent application process and discusses the requirements of U.S. Code Section 112. It also provides examples of public testimony that has been presented in public hearings before the U.S. Patent Office by a number of major corporations, analyzes significant Supreme Court decisions affecting software patents, and examines applicable foreign case law. When Wiley Law Publications was acquired by Wolters Kluwer in 1997, this title was assigned to Aspen Publishers (now Wolters Kluwer Law & Business).

Street, F. Lawrence. **Law of the Internet.** 3d ed. Charlottesville, VA: LexisNexis, 2001. 1 vol.
Cost: $290 (print or eBook); supplementation: 2002: $179.50;

2003: $132; 2004: $140; 2005: $140; 2006: $148; 2007: $156; 2008: $164; 2009: $199; 2011: $211; 2012: $240; 2013: $248.
The rise of the Internet as a significant medium of mass communication has generated a host of legal issues in such areas as contracts, privacy, trademarks, copyright, defamation, censorship, taxation, securities regulation, and Internet legal research and practice. The author, a partner in the Technology Group of Morris, Manning & Martinof Atlanta, GA, analyzes the body of law which has emerged from Internet litigation, provides summaries of major cases and statutes, and includes form documents which can be employed in an Internet legal practice.

Stuckey, Kent D. **Internet and Online Law**. New York: Law Journal Press, 1996-date. 1 vol. (600+ pp.). Supplemented twice annually. Converted to annual subscription service in 2010.
Cost: $540 (print + online + ebook combination); online + ebook: $515; supplementation: 1997: $45; 1998: $96; 1999: 0; 2000: 0; 2001: $214; 2002: $166; 2003: $89; 2004: $94; 2005: $105; 2006: $231; 2007: $264; 2008: $328; 2009: $357.02; 2010: converted to annual subscription pricing (see note below); 2012: $477.
A detailed introduction to the law of the Internet and online services designed to meet the needs of the practicing attorney and the business executive. The author, former General Counsel and Secretary of CompuServe before becoming its Director of Business Development and Vice President of CompuServe Ventures, Inc., is joined by a number of contributing authors with expertise in specific areas of the law. Topics covered include contracting in the electronic environment, defamation, factual misstatements, obscenity and indecency, privacy and related issues, copyright, trademark and unfair competition issues, patents, regulatory issues, procedural issues, and securities law and the Internet.

Cost Saving Alert: Law Journal Press, has taken the road of converting many of its titles to annual subscription pricing, thereby substantially increasing he cost of both their initial cost and maintenance. It remains to be seen how supplementation costs in future years will compare with the initial cost. If you desire the core content, but wish to avoid the high maintenance cost, simply cancel your subscription after the initial year and re-purchase the volume periodically.

Wright, Benjamin and Jane K. Winn. **The Law of Electronic Commerce**. 4th ed. New York: Wolters Kluwer Law & Business, 2001-date. 1 vol. Looseleaf format
Cost: $535; supplementation: 2001: 0; 2002: $115; 2003: $115; 2004: $254; 2005: $268; 2006: $284; 2007: $304; 2008: $326; 2009: $337; 2010: $372; 2011: $390; 2012: $416; 2013: $462; 3d ed.: 1999: $144.
The rapid acceptance of commerce over the Internet has raised a number of legal and technological questions. Chief among these is the issue of security for electronic transactions involving the use of credit cards. Although millions of dollars have been invested in the development of the Secure Electronic Transaction (SET) protocol to protect credit card numbers, this protocol is having no impact upon the growth of electronic merchandising. In practice, credit card numbers are being protected by the automatic Secure Socket Layer (SSL), security built into Web browsers. This volume addresses security and other issues driven by commerce in an increasingly electronic environment. Its 21 chapters are grouped into five Parts: the Context of Electronic Commerce, Legal Proof Issues, Recordkeeping and Internal Control, Electronic Issues, and Network Service Providers and Customers. The appendices contain a number of model agreements and other documents useful in an electronic commerce context. Also included are a glossary, table of cases, table of statutes and related sources, and index.

Cost-Saving Tip: With the cost of supplementation fast approaching the cost of a new volume, the smart consumer would be wise to simply re-purchase the volume every 2-3 years.

Additional titles in the field of Computer Law are available from the following publishers: American Bar Association, Wolters Kluwer Law & Business, Bloomberg BNA Books, Computer Law Association, Gaunt, Greenwood Publishing Group, Harcourt Legal, Juris Publishing, Kluwer Law International, Law Journal Press, LexisNexis, McFarland & Co., McGraw-Hill, Panel Publishers, Routledge, STP, Thomson Reuters West, Trans-Atlantic Publications, Warren, Gorham & Lamont, West Academic. See Appendix B for addresses and telephone numbers.

Constitutional Law
(see also Civil Rights and Criminal Law)

Antieau, Chester J. and William J. Rich. **Modern Constitutional Law**. 3d ed. St. Paul, MN: West Group (Lawyers Cooperative Publishing Co.), 2010-date. 3 vols. Annual pocket parts.
Cost: $392; supplementation: 2011: $345; 2012: $379; 2013: $96; 2d ed.: 1998: $39; 1999: $42.50; 2000: $46; 2001: $54; 2002: $64.50; 2003: $73.50; 2004: $82.50; 2005: $90; 2006: $100; 2007: $100.50; 2008: $126; 2009: $148.50; 2010:$270.
Monthly Assured Print Price (APP): $15/$180.
Authored by a Chester Antieau, Professor Emeritus of Constitutional Law and Local Government Law, Georgetown University Law Center, this two-volume treatise discusses both the scope of individual rights and society's interests in privacy, private property and individual freedoms and examines judicial review, the powers of the President and Congress, and the obligations of the federal government to the states. William J. Rich is Professor of Law, Washburn University School of Law.

Attanasio, John and Joel K. Goldstein. **Understanding Constitutional Law.** 4th ed. New York: Matthew Bender & Co., 2012. 1 vol. Legal Text Series. No supplementation.
Cost: $45; eBook: $36; from $27.00 on amazon.com; kindle: $28.44 (2014).
A basic introduction to constitutional law designed for student use, but also useful as an overview for the practicing attorney. Covers the structure of government, federalism, separation of powers, Congressional power, the Commerce Clause, Executive power, individual rights and liberties, due process, equal protection, and first amendment, racial equality, affirmative action, equal rights for the sexes, political speech and association, government and the media, speech in public places, government and religious

freedom, and more. intended as a conceptual supplement to the class caseBook. Norman Redlich is Dean Emeritus and Judge Edward Weinfeld Professor of Law Emeritus at New York University. Bernard Schwartz is the Chapman Distinguished Professor of Law, University of Tulsa; and John Attanasio is Dean and Professor of Law, St. Louis University.

Baker, Thomas E. and Jerre S. Williams. **Constitutional Analysis in a Nutshell**. 2d ed. St. Paul, MN: West, 2003. 1 vol. (514 pp.). Paperbound. Available from West Academic.
Cost: $41; from $7.99 on amazon.com (2014).
An introductory overview and analysis of the basic principals of constitutional law intended for the law school student. Chapters examine the topics of American constitutionalism, judicial review, constitutional analysis, constitutional liberty, government powers, structure of the Constitution, and constitutional theory. The volume also includes a Leading Case Outline of Constitutional Liberty, the text of the U.S. Constitution, and diagrams designed to aid in the understanding of the American system of government. Thomas E. Baker is Professor of Law, University of Florida College of Law, a noted Constitutional law scholar, and the author of six books and more than 90 articles. The late Jerre S. Williams was a judge on the U.S. Court of Appeals for the 5th Circuit and a Professor of Law at the University of Texas.

Barnett, Randy E. **Restoring the Lost Constitution: The Presumption of Liberty**. Revised ed. Princeton, NJ: Princeton University Press, 2014. 1 vol. (430 pp.). Paperbound.
Cost: $22.95; from $17.41 on amazon.com; kindle: $13.77 (2014)
In this path breaking work of originalist interpretation, Professor Randy Barnett argues that the U.S. Constitution enforced by the Supreme Court today bears little resemblance to the document drafted by the Founding Fathers, particularly since the 1930s. Barnett views constitutional legitimacy as flowing from natural (or liberty) rights, rather than the principle of popular sovereignty or consent of the governed. He contends that the conditions required to make the 'consent of the governed' argument did not exist at the time the Constitution was adopted, and was, therefore, a fiction. Furthermore, while people can be bound by their consent, that consent must be unanimous, not majoritarian. Anything less cannot bind nonconsenting parties. Barnett contends that a constitution to which everyone does not consent could still be legitimate if it establishes a procedure that makes it more likely than not that the laws being imposed on nonconsenting persons (a) do not improperly violate the rights of these persons and (b) are necessary to protect the rights of others. A fundamental premise of the U.S. Constitution, beyond the governmental structure it fashioned, is that it is a constraint on the power of government. Yet, the history of constitutional interpretation by the Supreme Court is one in which the Constitution has been drained of its power-constraining language. Over the years, but particularly since the 1930s, the Court has affirmed the proposition that the Constitution does not mean what it plainly says. Barnett argues that, according to the Supreme Court, a majority in Congress can restrict the liberties of the people any way they wish unless prohibited by a specific provision of the Constitution. As a consequence, it has gradually eroded the original Constitution and its amendments to eliminate those parts that protect liberty from the power of government. Thus, the Commerce Clause, the Necessary and Proper Clause, the Ninth and Tenth Amendments, the Privileges and Immunities Clause of the 14th Amendment have all been stripped of their authority. In thirteen chapters, Barnett grapples with issues of Constitutional Legitimacy, Constitutional Method, Constitutional Limits, and Constitutional Powers. In an Afterward entitled "What I Have Learned Since the First Edition", Barnett relates what has happened in the realms of both constitutional interpretation and constitutional law since 2004, when **Restoring the Lost Constitution** first appeared. This is a brilliant and thought-provoking book that probes one of the fundamental enduring political and constitutional issues of our time. Randy Barnett is the Carmack Waterhouse Professor of Political Theory at the Georgetown University Law Center, and author of **The Structure of Liberty: Justice and the Rule of Law** (2014).

Barron, Jerome A. and C. Thomas Dienes. **Constitutional Law in a Nutshell**. 8th ed. St. Paul, MN: West Academic, 2013. 1 vol. (811 pp.). Paperbound.
Cost: $41; from $26.50 on amazon.com (2014).
This student-oriented overview of the principles of constitutional law includes a consideration of such topics as judicial review and its limits, national legislative powers, state power in American federalism, Congress and the executive power, due process of law; equal protection, freedom of expression and religion, state action, and congressional legislation in civil rights and liberties. The 8th edition includes the opinions of the Justices of the Supreme Court opinions in the Affordable Care Act decision, *National Federation of Independent Business v. Sebelius* (2012) and examines the impact of the decision on the law concerning the Taxing Power, the Spending Clause and the Commerce Clause, among other recent decisions.

Barron, Jerome A. and C. Thomas Dienes. **First Amendment Law in a Nutshell**. 4th ed. St. Paul, MN: West, 2009. 1 vol. (632 pp.). Paperbound. Available from West Academic.
Cost: $41; from $18.00 on amazon.com (2014).
A concise overview of the philosophical underpinnings and case law which define the current state of First Amendment law, including the constitutional guarantees of freedom of speech, press, and religion. While intended chiefly as introductory students texts, the volumes in the Nutshell Series provide ideal overviews for practicing attorneys who wish a quick explication of new or unfamiliar topics without all the burdensome footnotes. Jerome Barron is the Lyle T. Alverson Professor of Law, George Washington University Law School. C. Thomas Dienes is the Patricia Roberts Harris Research Professor of Law at the same institution.

Bloch, Susan Low and Vicki C. Jackson. **Federalism: A Reference Guide to the United States Constitution**. Santa Barbara, CA: Praeger, 2013. 1 vol. (315 pp.).
Cost: $95.00; from $81.25 on amazon.com; kindle: $76.00 (2014).
The concept of federalism, enshrined in the U.S. Constitution, provides for a sharing of power between the national, state and local governments, each of which are granted certain exclusive

powers and share other powers. It is born of the Founders fear of a centralized government and a desire to hold it in check, a fear more recently manifest in the abuse of executive branch authority. This historical overview examines the development of the concept of federalism as enunciated in U.S. Supreme court decisions since the nation's founding. By "federalism" the authors refer to the constitutional allocations of authority (legislative, executive, judicial) to the national and state governments and to the relationship between and among those levels and branches of government. Depending on the particular era, the Supreme Court's jurisprudence has vacillated between periods of expansion of national power and periods, specifically the post-Warren era, when federalism-based limits on national power were dominant. Over the country's history, there has been a significant evolution of major points of doctrine, including Congress's power under the Commerce Clause, the reach of Congress's powers under the Fourteenth and other post-Civil War Amendments, the state's authority to regulate commercial and economic matters when Congress is silent on the issue, the principle of the supremacy of federal (national) law and the law of preemption that follows it, intergovernmental and sovereign immunities, the obligation of state courts to enforce federal laws, and the scope of federal (national) power to regulate or impose obligations on the states. And while the authors' analytical focus is largely devoted to a consideration of U.S. Supreme Court decisions, they acknowledge that the influence of those decisions on the country's historical development is also formed by simultaneous political events and broader social developments. This historical analysis of the points of federalism-related doctrine impacted by the Supreme Court's decision-making is organized into five chapters: The Founding to the Civil War; The Civil War and Its Aftermath; The Early Twentieth Century; The New Deal Court Through the Warren Court; and The "New" Federalism and Its Future, each of which is supported by extensive endnotes. The volume concludes with a Note on Theories of Federalism and Bibliography, a Table of Cases, and Index. This volume is a major contribution to an understanding of the Supreme Court's impact on the evolution of both the theory and practice of federalism in the United States. Susan Low Bloch is a professor of constitutional law at Georgetown University Law Center. Vicki Jackson is the Thurmond Marshall Professor of constitutional law at Harvard Law School.

Chandler, Ralph C., Richard A. Enslen, and Peter G. Renstrom. **Constitutional Law Deskbook: Individual Rights**. 2d ed. St. Paul, MN: West (Lawyers Cooperative Publishing Co.), 2008-date. 1 vol. (765 pp.). Supplemented with cumulative annual pamphlet.
Cost: $297; supplementation: 2009: $155; 2010: $171; 2011: $188; 2012: $232; 2013: $238; 1st ed.: 1994: $27; 1995: $27; 1996: $30; 1997: $30; 1998: $48.25; 1999: $52; 2000: $56.50; 2001: $65; 2002: $71.50; 2003: $81.50; 2004: $91.25; 2005: $100; 2006: $111.50; 2007: $124; 2008: new edition; **Monthly Assured Print Price (APP):** $25/$300.
This one volume treatise presents a succinct explanation of American constitutional law as it pertains to individual rights. Its potential audience is the general practitioner who requires a basic and current overview of constitutional law defenses. Includes a useful summary of the concept of constitutionalism and its historical development, chapters on the first, fourth, fifth, sixth and eighth amendments, and equal protection and privacy. Chapter 8 includes a particularly useful glossary of significant legal words and phrases with citations to leading Supreme Court decisions. Appendices include the U.S. Constitution, a listing of Justices of the Supreme Court, court composition since 1900, Table of Cases, and Index. Chapters also include topical tables of Case References to significant U.S. Supreme Court decisions, Research References, and Annotation References. This volume should be viewed as a useful companion to one or more of the more substantial treatises on constitutional law and as a quick reference for the general practitioner. While useful, it lacks the depth and breadth of the works by Rotunda or Tribe. Supplementation cost is substantial for a single-volume work.

Congressional Quarterly's Guide to the U.S. Supreme Court. 5th ed. Edited by David Savage. Washington, DC: Congressional Quarterly, Inc., 2010. 2 vols. (1,449 pp.). Periodic new editions.
Cost: $465; from $349.07 on amazon.com (2014).
A valuable compendium of information on the United States Supreme Court, including its history, organization, political milieu, and a discussion of some of the major issues which with it has grappled over its 220-year history. The two volumes are organized into six parts and 20 chapters, addressing the origin and development of the court to 1996, the court and the federal system, the court and the individual, pressures on the court, the court at work, and members of the court. The appendices include a number of major constitutional and statutory documents, the text of several leading Supreme Court decisions, a listing of Supreme Court nominations, glossary of common legal terms, Acts of Congress held unconstitutional, and a chronology of major decisions of the court from 1790-1996. While aimed at a general audience, this reference work nevertheless serves as a useful source of information on the U.S. Supreme Court for scholars and legal professionals. The fourth edition is updated through 2008-2009 and the appointments of Chief Justice John Roberts and Associate Jusices Samuel Alito and Sonia Sotomayor.

Constitution of the United States of America – Analysis and Interpretation. Prepared by the Library of Congress, Congressional Research Service. Washington, DC: U.S. Government Printing Office, 2004. 2 vols. (2,608 pp.).
Available at no cost at: http://www.gpo.gov/fdsys/pkg/GPO-CONAN-2013/content-detail.html
Cost: $290; supplementation: 2004: $6.50; 2008: $21.00; 2010: $15.00 (2014).
Prepared by the staff of the Congressional Research Service, this two-volume Centennial Edition provides analysis and interpretation of each article and amendment of the U.S. Constitution over the past fifty years, with particular emphasis on the ten year period since publication of the previous edition in 1994. Includes annotations to June 28, 2002. A supplement by constitutional scholars Johnny H. Killian, George A. Costello and Kenneth R. Thomas provides coverage to June 29, 2004. An essential acquisition for any constitutional law collection.

Dinan, John J. **The American State Constitutional Tradition**. Lawrence, KS: University Press of Kansas, 2006. 1 vol. (430 pp.).
Cost: $39.95; $22.50 (paper); from $14.28 on amazon.com (2014).

The tradition of constitutional analysis in the United States has focused predominantly on the national constitution. This pioneering comparative study examines the degree to which state constitutional conventions have deliberated the basic governing principles which were argued and adopted by the Constitutional Convention in 1787. But unlike the founding fathers, who erected significant barriers to constitutional revision and amendment such that no additional conventions have been held, delegates to constitutional conventions in the fifty states have held 233 constitutional conventions, adopted 146 constitutions, and ratified more than 6,000 amendments to their constitutions. This study, which examines the extant records of debates of 114 state constitutions conventions, concludes that a number of governing principles and institutions preserved in the national constitution have been revised or rejected in state constitutional conventions. Following an historical overview of state constitutional conventions, the author focuses his scholarly attention on the issues of amendment and revision, representation, separation of powers, bicameralism, rights, and the formation citizen character. The author, an associate professor of political science at Wake Forest University, has based his findings on exhaustive research into state constitutional documents as well as contemporary commentary and scholarly literature. This is an essential acquisition for any constitutional law collection.

Dorf, Michael C. and Trevor W. Morrison. **The Oxford Introductions to U.S. Law: Constitutional Law**. New York: Oxford University Press, 2010. 1 vol. (254 pp.). Paperbound.
Cost: $19.95, from $1.01 on amazon.com; kindle ed.: $9.99 (2014).
An erudite, yet accessible introduction to some of the leading topics in the field of U.S. constitutional law, including judicial review, constitutional interpretation, federalism, separation of powers, equal protection, enumerated rights under the First Amendment, unenumerated rights, and Congressional enforcement of constitutional rights. The authors acknowledge that one of the most important functions performed by the Constitution and the thousands of federal cases interpreting it is the allocation of decision-making, such as when courts rule that the Constitution takes some issue outside of the political domain? Of particular note are the authors' analyses of the various interpretative theories that guide constitutional decision-making, ranging from judicial restraint to natural law and moral reading, representation reinforcement ("process theory"), originalism, and eclecticism. And while they acknowledge that complete cynicism toward judicial decision making is unwarranted, even while recognizing that ideology may explain a great deal, they, nevertheless, argue that most judges try to control for ideological bias and may vote "against type" because they are persuaded by the force of legal arguments that the Constitution requires something different than that which they would favor as a matter of policy. This is particularly true in the case of trial and intermediate appellate courts in which precedent and fear of reversal on appeal constrains judges. All in all, this is a well-reasoned and balanced introduction to the field of constitutional law which can be of great value to the law student and the general reader, as well as the more seasoned legal practitioner. Michael C. Dorf is the Robert S. Stevens Professor of Law at Cornell University Law School and former law clerk to Justice Anthony M. Kennedy. Trevor W. Morrison is Professor of Law at Columbia Law School and former law clerk to Justice Ruth Bader Ginsburg.

Encyclopedia of the American Constitution. 2d ed. Edited by Leonard W. Levy and Kenneth L. Karst. New York: Macmillan Reference USA, 2000. 6 vols. (3,164 pp.). Also available in an e-book version.
Cost: print: $1,028; e-book: contact publisher; from $200.00 on amazon.com (2014)
This was the first major reference work to treat the United States Constitution in a comprehensive and multidisciplinary manner. Published initially in 1986 to commemorate the bicentennial of the Constitution, this Encyclopedia provides detailed scholarly entries on a broad range of topics falling into five general categories: doctrinal concepts of constitutional law (55% of the total words), people (15%), judicial decisions (15%), public acts (5%), and historical periods (10%). Its more than 2,460 signed articles were written by 237 authors, including historians, lawyers (including law professors, practitioners, and judges), and political scientists. The 2000 edition consolidates and updates the topics covered in the original four-volume set, a supplementary volume published in 1992, and includes new articles which detail developments in the 1990s. The well-written narrative articles provide both scholars and students with valuable overviews of the issues, decisions, laws, legal theories, and individuals important to an understanding of the Constitution and its role in American political and social life. The authors were encouraged to not only describe and analyze their subjects, but to offer their own views. In the case of controversial topics (e.g. abortion), the contributions of those with divergent views were included. Most entries include selective bibliographical references. Full citations to the, mostly, U.S. Supreme Court decisions are omitted in favor of a case index (vol.6) which provides citations to the appropriate case reporters. Appendices include The Call for the Federal Constitutional Convention, the Articles of Confederation, the United States Constitution, the Resolution Transmitting the Constitution to Congress, Washington's Letter of Transmittal, chronologies of Constitutional history, a glossary of legal terms, case index, name index, and subject index.

Epstein, Lee and Thomas G. Walker. **Constitutional Law for a Changing America: Institutional Powers and Constraints**. 8th ed. Washington, DC: CQ Press, 2013. 1 vol. (764 pp.). Paperbound with online case archive.
Cost: $109; from $70.71 on amazon.com (2014).
This constitutional law caseBook examines the three branches of American government, key constitutional law concepts, and the powers of the national government under the Constitution. Each of the volume's eleven chapters includes an introductory essay followed by discussion of key U.S. Supreme Court rulings which impact the topic under consideration, summaries of the oral arguments, and excerpts of majority and dissenting opinions. The chapters are organized into four major sections: (1) the U.S. Constitution; (2) institutional authority; (3) nation-state relations, and (4) economic liberties. Individual chapters examine the U.S. Supreme Court, the federal judiciary generally, the legislature, the Executive, the doctrine of separation of powers, the doctrine of federalism, the commerce power, the power to tax and spend, the contract clause, economic substantive due process, and the takings clause. The analytical commentary, accompanied by

illuminating tables, figures, boxes, and photos, places key U.S. Supreme Court decisions in an historical context which combines the traditional pedagogical approach to constitutional law with the political dynamics of the litigation. "Aftermath" boxes also provide readers with an understanding of the impact the decisions have had on lives of the American people. A chronological table of cases lists 106 leading Supreme Court cases discussed in the book precedes the chapters. A companion web site includes an online archive of more than 300 supplemental excerpted cases, as well as landmark cases after the conclusion of every Supreme Court term. Lee Epstein is a professor law at Northwestern University School of Law. Thomas G. Walker is a professor of political science at Emory University. It is intended as a textbook for undergraduate and graduate classes in political science, public law, and constitutional law.

Fallon, Richard J., Jr. **The Dynamic Constitution: An Introduction to American Constitutional Law and Practice**. 2d ed. New York: Cambridge University Press, 2013. 1 vol. (401 pp.). Paperbound.
Cost: $29.99; from $20.00 on amazon.com (2014).
In view of Richard Fallon, American constitutional law is a complex web of social, cultural and political factors within which the written Constitution and its interpretative Supreme Court decisions are couched. Interpretation of the Constitution is dependent on a variety of factors external to the text, including the historical practices of Congress and the President, previous precedents, public expectations, practical considerations, and moral and political values. Directed at a nonlawyer readership, this introductory overview of American constitutional law departs from the prior chronological treatment of Robert McCloskey's **The American Supreme Court** (1960) by looking at the subject matter through a more contemporary prism, yet grounded in an appreciation of the historical context from which its rulings emerge. He attempts to deal openly with the concerns that Supreme Court jurisprudence is a veiled form of judicial politics, determined by the political balance of the justices. Though a consideration of the Affordable Care Act decision and other vignettes, he attempts to paint a portrait of Supreme Court jurisprudence that defies easy classification, but one that is complex, multifaceted, tension ridden, and occasionally inspiring. He does by first addressing the dynamism of the Constitution, followed by consideration of the Supreme Court's jurisprudence in the areas of freedom of speech, freedom of religion, protection of economic liberties, fundamental rights enumerated in the Bill of Rights, equal protection of the laws, unenumerated fundamental rights, the powers of Congress, executive power, judicial power, structural limits on state power, the Constitution in war and emergency, and the reach of the Constitution and Congress's enforcement power. This is a deftly constructed, clearly written, and nuanced treatment of constitutional law that embraces the various judicial and political forces that form its intricate fabric. Richard H. Fallon is the Ralph S. Tyler, Jr. Professor of Constitutional Law at Harvard University Law School.

Finkleman, Paul and Melvin I. Urofsky. **Landmark Decisions of the United States Supreme Court**. 2d ed. Washington, DC: CQ Press, 2008. 1 vol. (791 pp.). Hardbound.
Cost: $295; from $219 on amazon.com (2014).
Contains succinct, carefully written summaries of more than 1,200 of the Supreme Court's most important decisions. Organized chronologically, by decade, each decision includes its citation to the official U.S. Reports and/or Supreme Court Reporter, date, vote, and author of the majority opinion. The entries also indicate whether the case was affected by later decisions or statutory enactments. The summaries span the years 1791-2007, and include 67 decisions handed down in the last six years. The Introduction provides a useful and highly readable overview of the Supreme Court's history. The appendices include the Constitution of the United States, a table of confirmed Supreme Court nominations by nominating President, 1789-2007; and membership changes in the U.S. Supreme Court by Chief Justice, 1789-2007. There are also portraits and photographs of Supreme Court Justices and Courts, from John Jay to the 2006 Roberts Court. While chiefly useful to academic and public libraries, and scholars lacking a collection of U.S. Supreme Court reporters, this volume will also serve as an excellent resource in law libraries of all types and sizes.

Fisher, Louis and Katy J. Harringer. **American Constitutional Law**. 10th ed. Durham, NC: Carolina Academic Press, 2013. 1 vol. (1,180 pp.).
Cost: $100.00 (with 10% Internet discount); from $82.79 on amazon.com (2014).
A comprehensive analysis of constitutional law that examines not only Supreme Court decisions, but the role played by legislatures, executives, the states, and the general public in the ongoing political process. The authors draw upon new developments in case law, congressional statutes, presidential policies, and initiatives undertaken by states under their own constitutions. A substantially revised chapter on equal protection addresses immigration law and the rights of aliens, with readings from cases, congressional floor debates, committee reports, committee hearings, presidential vetoes and other statements, state actions, Federalist papers, and professional journals. Unlike other textbooks, American Constitutional Law explores the interaction of judicial and non-judicial forces in shaping legal doctrines and practices. The authors also cover state involvement in constitutional law and how they often depart from U.S. Supreme Court doctrines in the interpretation of their own constitutions. This is a skillful blend of the caseBook and textbook. The authors cover such topics as constitutional politics, the doctrine of judicial review, threshold requirements, judicial organization, decision making, separation of powers, federal-state relations, economic liberties, free speech, freedom of the press, religious freedom, due process of law, search and seizure, racial discrimination, the expansion of equal protection, rights of privacy, political participation, and efforts to curb the court. Contains a well-chosen selection of court decisions and political documents. Each chapter includes conclusions and a list of selected readings. Appendices include the text of the U.S. Constitution, a glossary of legal terms, a guide to researching the law, table of cases, and index. Louis Fisher is the Senior Specialist in Separation of Powers for the Congressional Research Service of the Library of Congress, and the author of many books and articles on Constitutional law and American political process. Katy Harriger is a professor of political science at Wake Forest University.

Fisher, Louis. **On the Supreme Court: Without Illusion or Idolatry**. Boulder, CO: Paradigm Publishers,2014. 1 vol. (242 pp.). Paperbound.

Cost: $28.95; from $23.73 on amazon.com (2014).

This estimable volume is a reflection of the author's philosophy that the Supreme Court's role is a "joint exercise," sharing statutory and constitutional interpretation with the elected branches of government, the fifty states, and the American people. In Fisher's considered view, it was never the framer's intention to vest the Court with final authority on matters of constitutional significance, a view echoed by Chief Justice Roberts and Justice Samuel Alito, who have argued that the Supreme Court does not possess a judicial monopoly, but that all public servants have a role in shaping the law. The author contends that the Court is neither final nor infallible, and that the Justices themselves would doubtless acknowledge, as did Justice Robert H. Jackson in 1953, that "long-sustained public opinion does influence the process of constitutional interpretation." With this realist understanding of the Court's role, the author examines many of the seminal decisions of the Supreme Court over its more than 220-year history, beginning with the principle of judicial review and weaving his way through the decision-making process, the Court's self-inflicted wounds, judicial failings after World War II, and individual and minority rights. In doing so, he succinctly illustrates in lucid prose and incisive commentary, laced with selective citations to both judicial and non-judicial authorities, the politically infused environment in which the Court operates. And contrary to the Court's assertions, Fisher argues that there is nothing in our national experience that justifies the claim that "when the Supreme Court decides a constitutional issue, its ruling is final and binding on the elected branches." He makes his case by tackling such politically sensitive issues as abortion rights, state secrecy, campaign finance, religious liberties, minority rights, and the Presidential election of 2000, among others. Louis Fisher received his doctorate in political science from The New School for Social Research and served four decades as Senior Specialist in Separation of Powers at the Congressional Research Service at the Library of Congress. He is the author of more than twenty books, including the widely used textbook, **American Constitutional Law** (see above).

Friedman, Lawrence M. **Guarding Life's Dark Secrets: Legal and Social Controls Over Reputation, Propriety and Privacy.** Palo Alto, CA: Stanford University Press, 2007. 1 vol. (352 pp).

Cost: $29.95; kindle: $16.47; from $0.83 on amazon.com (2014).

In this engaging and illuminating study, Lawrence Friedman probes the legal and social culture of the United States to expose the network of doctrines which were designed to protect reputation. His story traces these doctrines from their Victorian-era roots, when decency and propriety were subject to strict and unbending rules which, nevertheless, provided ways to protect the reputations of respectable men and women who violated them. This "Victorian compromise," which erected a zone of privacy, particularly in areas of sexual behavior, was demolished, first by 19th century moralists for its tolerance of sin, and, then, by the permissive drift of the 20th century. Friedman contends that, as this zone of privacy has been eroded, elites and public figures have lost some of their privacy rights, while ordinary people have gained more privacy. His analysis embraces such legal issues as defamation, blackmail, breach of promise, censorship, privacy, reputation, and the threat of technology in a world of surveillance. A professor of law at Stanford University Law School, Lawrence Friedman is a renowned legal historian, and author of the award-winning **History of American Law** (1973).

Gibson, Alan Ray. **Understanding the Founding: the Crucial Questions**. 2d ed. Lawrence, KS: University Press of Kansas, 2010. 1 vol. (418 pp.).

Cost: $24.95; from $7.91 on amazon.com (2014).

The Founding Fathers and their role in drafting the U.S. Constitution occupy a central place in the history of American political thought. Scholars have long debated the precise nature of that role on a number of contentious questions. In this synoptic study of scholarship on the Founders over the last century, Alan Gibson examines four central questions which comprise that debate: (1) Were the Framers motivated by their economic interests? (2) How democratic was the Framer's Constitution? (3) Should we interpret the Founding using philosophical or strictly historical approaches? and (4) What traditions of political thought were most important to the Framers? His analysis of the competing interpretive schools of thought on these and other questions draws upon a wide-ranging pool of historians and political theorists. This balanced and erudite historiographical study of the Founders and their thought will serve as an invaluable overview for legal scholars and judges who must grapple with modern constitutional questions. Alan Ray Gibson is associate professor of political science at California State University—Chico, and the author of **Interpreting the Founding: Guide to the Enduring Debates over the Origins and Foundations of the American Republic**.

Greenburg, Jan Crawford. **Supreme Conflict: the Inside Story of the Struggle for Control of the United States Supreme Court**. East Rutherford, NJ: Penguin-Putnam Inc., 2007. 1 vol. (340 pp.).

Cost: $28.95 (hardbound); $17.00 (softbound); from $.01 on amazon.com; kindle ed.: $11.84 (2014).

The death of Chief Justice William Rehnquist in 2005 and the retirement of Associate Justice Sandra Day O'Connor in January 2006 brought to an end the longest period (1993-2005) that nine Supreme Court justices had served together without a change in the court's membership. It was an era marked by conflicting political and ideological forces grappling with some of the thorniest legal issues. During that time, the court was precariously balanced between its conservative and liberal wings, with many cases decided by 5-4 votes. Justice O'Connor's was often the deciding vote, a fact not lost on lawyers who framed their arguments with her views in mind. The fact that seven of the nine Justices had been appointed by Republican Presidents was no guarantee that their votes would follow a conservative line. And despite the goals of conservatives, who had hoped to overturn controversial rulings on abortion, affirmative action, and religion, the court's decisions often failed to provide the clear resolutions they desired. In this intimate portrait, journalist Jan Crawford Greenburg provides a fair-minded and illuminating examination of the inner workings of the Supreme Court, its personalities, operations, its conflicts, and shifting majorities. She also describes the behind-the-scenes political maneuvering which accompanied the abortive nomination of Harriet Miers and the successful, but contentious, confirmation hearings which followed the nominations of Chief Justice Roberts and Associate

Justice Alito. A graduate of the University of Chicago Law School, Jan Crawford Greenburg is a correspondent for ABC News who covers law and politics for World News Tonight, Nightline and Good Morning America. This book is based on extensive interviews with nine Supreme Court Justices, high-level sources in the White House, members of Congress, and officials in the Justice Department. It is arguably the richest and most valuable journalistic examination of the Supreme Court since Woodward and Bernstein's ***The Brethren*** (1979).

Kuhn, Martin. **Federal Dataveillance: Implications for Constitutional Privacy Protections**. New York: LFB Publishing, 2007. 1 vol. (223 pp.).
Cost: $65; from $61.75 on amazon.com; kindle ed.: $58.66 (2014).
The constitutional right to information privacy has taken on a new urgency in the information age as a result of (1) the development of new and cost-efficient information technologies which have permitted the collection and processing of vast quantities of personal information; and (2) the use of these new information technologies by federal law enforcement entities to access privately held data for the purposes of combating terrorism. Data mining, or knowledge discovery in databases (KDD), is the tool used by law enforcement to detect patterns of activity which replicate those from previous terrorist attacks. Reconceptualizing constitutional privacy rights in this new age of information technology is the subject of this study, both within the context of the First and Fourth Amendments, and within the broader context of information privacy jurisprudence, including privacy as space, privacy as secrecy, and privacy as information control. Because these historic protections are inadequate against federal dataveillance programs, the author suggests using a theoretical perspective from which privacy law can function to balance personal privacy and national security by limiting the government's ability to access, manipulate, and control personal information. The author's new conceptualizations of constitutional privacy, include (1) privacy-as-confidentiality (now emerging in federal circuit court information privacy cases), and (2) the privacy-as-knowledge-control needed to provide protection for federally created knowledge about specific individuals. He also posits an information privacy theory that will assist future courts in balancing individual privacy interests against the government's interests in disclosure. Martin Kuhn received his Ph.D. from the University of North Carolina at Chapel Hill and currently holds a Presidential Management Fellowship within the U.S. Department of Justice. Previously, he was the marketing director for a commercial printing company that provided direct mail marketing services.

Lieberman, Jethro K. **A Practical Companion to the Constitution: How the Supreme Court Has Rules on Issues from Abortion to Zoning**. Berkeley, CA: University of California Press, 1999. 1 vol. (796 pp.). Paperbound.
Cost: $47.95; from $3.95 on amazon.com (2014).
Since 1803, the United States Supreme Court has decided more than 7,500 cases that deal with the Constitution in some form or manner. This reference guide treats these decisions in the form of more than 1,000 topically arranged entries, each providing a brief history of the subject or legal doctrine and a summary of the manner in which the U.S. Supreme Court has dealt with it over the years. The volume also includes a guided tour of the Constitution, the text of the Constitution, a Concordance, a time chart of Supreme Court Justices, biographical notes on the Justices, a table of all the cases discussed in the topical entries, and endnotes to the text. Written for both the legal scholar and the layperson. The author/editor is professor of law and director of the writing program at New York Law School and the author of more than twenty books on American law and legal history. This is an updated and expanded edition of the author's **The Evolving Constitution,** though it is now somewhat outdated itself.

Linton, Paul Benjamin. **Abortion Under State Constitutions: a State-by-State Analysis**. 2nd ed. Carolina Academic Press, 2012. 1 vol. (703 pp.).
Cost: $87.00 (10% discount on Internet); from $8.69 on amazon.com (2014).
While the U.S, Supreme Court has spoken decisively on the issue of abortion, State constitutions may also protect the right to an abortion, and determine whether the State has the power to enact and enforce laws regulating the practice. This is the first full-length effort to examine the act of abortion under State constitutions and the legal theories under which it is protected, including privacy, due process of law, equality of rights, equal protection, and privileges and immunities. The author considers what the situation would be in the event that Roe v. Wade were overturned, in which case abortion rights would be protected in thirteen states independent of the right to abortion enunciated in Roe v. Wade, and thirty-seven states in which it would not be protected. Accordingly, the author examines the constitutional provisions of each of the fifty states that address abortion rights and the appellate court decisions that have interpreted them. He also examines relevant constitutional history of each state, pre-Roe prohibitions of abortion and their interpretation by state courts, post-Roe regulations of abortion, and what rights state law has granted to unborn children outside of the context of abortion. An essential reference tool for any attorney, judge, legal scholar, or individual who wants to have a better understanding of how the issue of abortion has been treated at the state level. The author is Special Counsel for the Thomas More Society, a public interest law firm based in Chicago and former General Counsel for Americans United for Life. He has represented amici curiae in numerous landmark decisions of the U.S. Supreme Court on the issue of abortion rights.

Maddox, Robert L. **State Constitutions of the United States**. 2d ed. Washington, DC: CQ Press, 2005. 1 vol. (592 pp.).
Cost: $175 (2014).
This reference volume contains the Constitutions of all U.S. states and territories. Each Constitution is preceded by a brief introduction consisting of general information and Constitutional history. The basic structure of each state's government is also represented in tabular form. The appendices include the U.S. Constitution, a table of cases, glossary of terms, a bibliography of sources, and index. An excellent resource for the student, attorney or legal scholar who requires convenient access to all state Constitutions.

Meese, Edwin, ed. **The Heritage Guide to the Constitution**. Washington, DC: Regnery Publishing: Heritage Foundation, 2005. 1 vol. (475 pp.).
Cost: $35; from $6.82 on amazon.com (2014).
A line-by-line analysis of the U.S. Constitution by 108 of the country's leading constitutional scholars. Produced under the editorship of former attorney general Edwin Meese and through the auspices of the Heritage Foundation, this volume provides a close examination of the original intent of the Constitution as the authoritative standard of constitutional interpretation. In addition to the text of the document itself, the contributors draw upon James Madison's notes taken at the Constitutional Convention, the **Federalist Papers**, and Justice Joseph Story's classic **Commentaries on the Constitution of the United States**. The book includes preliminary essays by Edwin Meese on the Meaning of the Constitution, Matthew Spalding on the Formation of the Constitution, and David Forte on the Originalist Perspective. Among the many scholars represented are Richard A. Epstein, John McGinnis, Gary Lawson, Charles Kessler, Eugene Volokh, Douglass Kmiec, Charles Fried, Douglas Ginsburg, Ronald Rotunda, Jonathan Turley, and Forrest McDonald. Each of the book's essays is accompanied by a list of significant cases and selective bibliography, features which are cumulated in the appendices. A valuable resource for understanding the Originalist view of the Constitution.

Melone, Albert P. **Researching Constitutional Law**. 3d ed. Dubuque, IA: Kendall Hunt Publishing, 2013. 1 vol. (390 pp.). Paperbound. Instructor's manual also available.
Cost: $42.00; from $35.91 on amazon.com (2014).
This guide to the process of conducting research on constitutional law is directed primarily at the needs of undergraduate, pre-law and political science students. The author provides a clearly written exposition of research sources and methodology, including case briefing, quantitative applications, and writing and documentation. In addition to a discussion of primary and secondary law sources, this volume also includes summaries of leading Supreme Court decisions, sample citations, a glossary of terms, and an extensive bibliography of sources. The author is Professor of Political Science at Southern Illinois University.

Nowak, John E. and Ronald D. Rotunda. **Constitutional Law**. 8th ed. St. Paul, MN: West, 2010. 1 vol. (1,802 pp.). Hornbook Series. Student Edition.
Available from West Academic.
Cost: $113; e-book: $76 (Thomson Reuters West); from $78.88 on amazon.com (2014).
Over 32 years have elapsed since the first edition of this estimable Hornbook on constitutional law was released in 1978. Intended as law school text, it provides detailed description and analysis of the structure of the national government and the provisions and doctrines of the U.S. Constitution. Chapters cover the origins of judicial review, federal jurisdiction, sources of national authority, the federal commerce power, federal fiscal powers, international affairs, the President and Congress, the commerce clause and restrictions on state regulatory powers, federal regulation and state authority, individual liberties, substantive due process, state action, procedural due process, equal protection, congressional enforcement of civil rights, freedom of speech, and freedom of religion. The text features extensive citations to U.S. Supreme Court decisions, and relevant scholarly authorities. Appendices includes the Constitution of United States, a WESTLAW research guide, table of cases, and subject index. John E. Nowak is Raymond and Mary Simon Chair in Conbstitutional Law at Loyola University Chicago School of Law. Ronald D. Rotunda is the Day and Dee Henley Chair and Distinguished Professor of Jurisprudence, Chapman University School of Law.

The Oxford Companion to the Supreme Court of the United States. 2d ed. Kermit L. Hall, Editor-in-Chief. New York: Oxford University Press, 2005. 1 vol. (1,080 pp.).
Cost: $65; from $12.64 on amazon.com (2014).
The United States Supreme Court has, for more than 200 years, played a pivotal role in the development of the American nation. Many of the most controversial political, social and economic issues have come before the court for resolution. This reference work presents the broad sweep of the Court's history in more than a thousand alphabetically arranged entries. These entries include summaries of more than four hundred of the court's leading decisions, biographies of justices and other important jurists and attorneys, extended essays on the major issues that have confronted the court, biographies of Presidents who have had a significant impact on the court, and essays on judicial matters and legal terms. More than 300 leading legal scholars contributed the more than 1200 entries. The second edition includes 60 new entries on key decisions and critical areas of constitutional law, including abortion, freedom of religion, school desegregation, freedom of speech, voting rights, military tribunals, the rights of the accused, campaign finance, hate speech, Native Americans, sexual harassment, and Internet and computer access. The appendices include the Constitution of the United States, Supreme Court nominations, and court trivia. it also includes case and topical indexes. An essential reference book for any practicing attorney, legal scholar, or law library. Kermit L. Hall is the president of Utah State University and the editor of The Oxford Companion to American Law. James W. Ely, Jr. is Milton R. Underwood Professor of Law and History, Vanderbilt University. Joel B. Grossman is Professor of Political Science, Johns Hopkins University.

Patrick, John J. and Gerald P. Long, eds. **Constitutional Debates on Freedom of Religion: A Documentary History**. Westport, CT: Greenwood Press, 1999. 1 vol. (360 pp.).
Cost: $65; kindle edition: $52.00; from $7.94 on amazon.com (2014).
A collection of over 70 primary documents detailing the history of religious liberty and freedom of religion in the United States. Following a chronology of key events, the editors present a variety of relevant documents in five chapters: Colonial Roots of Religious Liberty, 1606-1776; Religious Liberty in the Founding of the United States, 1776-1791; The Constitutional Right to Free Exercise of Religion, 1791-1991; The Constitutional Prohibition of an Establishment of Religion, 1791-1991; and Constitutional Issues on Freedom of Religion, 1991-1998. The assembled documents include colonial Acts and Charters, statements of leading figures and religious leaders, statements of delegates to the Constitutional Convention, and the text of leading U.S. Supreme Court decisions. A valuable addition to any collection of materials on constitutional law and issues.

Persily, Nathaniel; Jack C. Citrin; and Patrick J. Egan, eds. **Public Opinion and Constitutional Controversy**. New York: Oxford University Press, 2008. 1 vol. (264 pp.). Paperbound.
Cost: $29.95; kindle: $16.17; from $19.50 on amazon.com (2014).
An illuminating empirical examination of public opinion on fourteen contentious American political issues, including desegregation, the rights of the accused, school prayer, abortion, the death penalty, gender equality, affirmative action, flag burning, federalism, gay rights, the right to die, government takings of private property, the war on terror an civil liberties, and the 2000 Presidential election controversy. Twenty-five scholars contributed to the fourteen substantive chapters, each of which provides an historical overview of public opinion polling trends over the previous half century. This is the first time that public opinion data on the most controversial constitutional issues has been assembled in one book. Interestingly, the editors note that the decisions of the U.S. Supreme Court and other courts have had almost no effect on the weight of public opinion. Thus, a popular constitutionalism stands as a counterweight to the monopoly that the Supreme Court has attempted to assert in the political process. For others, however, the Court's "countermajoritarian" position provides essential protections to "discrete and insular minorities" or unpopular individuals exercising rights protected by the Constitution. This important contribution to the empirical literature on public opinion provides valuable context to many of the hotly contested issues in which the Supreme Court has been embroiled over the past half century. The three editors are professors of law or political science at Columbia, UC Berkeley, and New York University.

Pyle, Christopher H. and Richard M. Pious. **The Constitution Under Siege: Presidential Power Versus the Rule of Law**. Durham, NC: Carolina Academic Press, 2010. 1 vol. (374 pp.).
Cost: $49.00; from $40.50 on amazon.com (2014).
This is a book about the powers exercised by the President the armed forces, and intelligence agencies in a Constitutional Republic of limited and circumscribed powers. It is also a book about the legitimacy of claims to power that would alter the historical balance of policy-making authority. Beginning with a consideration of such constitutional first principles as limited government, guaranteed liberties, separation of powers, checks and balances, popular sovereignty, representative government, and the rule of law, the authors draw upon historical examples and primary source materials to illuminate many of the dubious assertions of power that have been made by the President and Congress over our history. These assertions of power have been the means by which the President and other governmental authorities have waged clandestine wars, detained people without trial, suspended the writ of habeas corpus, operated secret prisons, tortured prisoners, and assassinated both citizens and foreigners without accountability. Unlike typical law school caseBooks which rely primarily on selected cases to illustrate legal points, the documents in this volume draw not only upon the opinions of judges, but those of historians, philosophers, political scientists, and law professors. Additional chapters consider the subject of emergency powers; foreign affairs powers; military force, paramilitary force and covert action; and secret government versus the rule of law. Christopher H. Pyle is the Class of 1926 Professor of Politics at Mount Holyoke College and the author of works on military surveillance, human rights, torture and war crimes. Richard M. Pious is the Adolph and Effie Ochs Professor at both Barnard College and the Graduate School of Arts and Sciences at Columbia University where he teaches and writes on the subjects of the American presidency and executive power, military tribunals, war powers, and the war on terrorism.

Renstrom, Peter G. **Constitutional Rights SourceBook**. Santa Barbara, CA: ABC-CLIO, 1999. 1 vol. (770 pp.).
Cost: $75.00; from $4.06 on amazon.com (2014).
A reference guide to fundamental concepts of constitutional law, particularly as embodied in the First, Fourth, Fifth, Sixth, Eighth and Fourteenth Amendments to the U.S. Constitution. Written in a narrative style, each chapter provides a general overview of the Amendment and addresses the most significant issues falling within the scope of that Amendment. In the case of the First Amendment, for example, the author addresses Establishment of Religion, Free Exercise of Religion, Freedom of Speech, and Freedom of the Press. Each of these First Amendment rights is further subdivided into a number of individual concepts. For example, Establishment of Religion section address such concepts as the child benefit doctrine, establishment standards, public displays, school prayer, aid to nonpublic education, and public access. Each subtopic is built around the most significant U.S. Supreme Court decision while addressing other relevant decisions of significance, all with citations to the official **U.S. Reports**. The volume also includes a glossary of over 140 legal words and phrases, the text of the Constitution, and an index. The author is Professor of Political Science, Western Michigan University. A worthy addition to most academic and law libraries.

Rotunda, Ronald D. and John E. Nowak. **Treatise on Constitutional Law: Substance and Procedure**. 5th ed. St. Paul, MN: West, 2012-date. 6 vols. Annual pocket parts and periodic revised volumes.
Cost: $927; supplementation to 3rd ed.: 2000: $70; 2001: $79; 2002: $115; 2003: $99.50; 2004: $111.50; 2005: $122; 2006: $136; 2007: $349; 2008: $570; 2009: $55.50; 2010; $60.50; 2011: $66; 2012: $74; 2013: $74; 2d edition: 1995: $47.50; 1996: $49; 1997: $54; 1998: $57; **Monthly Assured Print Price (APP):** $47/$564.
The most exhaustive general treatise on the subject of constitutional law on the market. The four volumes cover the range of constitutional law topics from judicial review and Presidential powers to equal protection, due process and freedom of speech and religion. Volume five appendices include a variety of significant legal documents from the Declaration of Independence to the modern civil rights statutes. It also includes a guide to conducting constitutional law research on WESTLAW, a Table of Cases, Table of Authorities, and Index. While the $562 initial cost is not inconsequential, the annual supplementation cost is a real bargain in today's legal publishing market.

Savage, David. **The Supreme Court and Individual Rights**. 5th ed. Washington, D.C.: CQ Press, 2009. 1 vol. (360 pp.). Paperbound.
Cost: $60; from $3.42 on amazon.com (2014).
This reference book examines the revolution in constitutional law that has taken place over the last century, particularly as it

has impacted freedom for ideas, rights of political participation, due process and criminal rights, and equal rights and personal liberties. The book also addresses the freedoms provided in the Bill of Rights the book provides full coverage of the freedoms outlined in the Bill of Rights, the right to vote and to engage in political participation, the individual's right to due process under the law, and modern equality issues, including such controversial issues as affirmative action and rights allowed illegal immigrants to the United States. The Appendixes include a glossary of legal terms, an explanation of how to read a legal citation, and biographies of the Justices of the United States Supreme Court. The author is the Supreme Court Reporter for the Los Angeles Times.

Sollenberger, Mitchell A. **The President Shall Nominate: How Congress Trumps Executive Power**. Lawrence: University Press of Kansas, 2008. 1 vol. (312 pp.).
Cost: $39.95; from $31.01 on amazon.com (2014).
Although the Constitution gives the President power to nominate individuals to positions in the executive and judicial branches of government, with the advice and consent of the Senate, the process is more complicated than the language of the Constitution might imply. Unlike books that focus on the confirmation process, this book examines the pre-nomination process and describes in depth how the political process has shaped the power that the Constitution has declared must be shared by the executive and legislative branches. It examines how this political process has played out from the administrations of President Washington to that of George W. Bush, and how particular appointments have affected the fundamental principle of shared power. In doing so, the author also considers such issues as the express and implied powers, the validity of the executive model, the tension between politics and professionalism, and the limits of originalism and textualism in evaluating the appointment process. Following an introductory chapter that examines the constitutional principles of the appointment process, the author traces the evolution of the process through seven eras of presidential leadership: 1789-1829, 1829-1845, 1845-1869, 1869-1881, 1881-1897, 1897-1977, and 1977-2007. A concluding chapter provides the author's analysis and conclusions and suggests how the appointment clause should ideally operate in a republican form of government. Michael A. Sollenberger is a visiting associate professor in the Public and International Affairs Department at George Mason University.

Supreme Court Practice. Gressman, Eugene; Stephen M. Shapiro; Kenneth S. Geller; Timothy S. Bishop; and Edward A. Hartnett, eds. 10th ed. Washington, DC: Bloomberg BNA Books, 2013-date. 1 vol. (1,450 pp.)
Cost: $495; no supplementation to date; 8th edition: 1995: $45; 1996: 0; 1997: $65 (2014).
The „bible" for those practicing before the United States Supreme Court. This edition was prompted by Congressional repeal of most of the statutory provisions allowing direct appeals to the Supreme Court, and providing for certiorari as the only route of appeal in all but a few cases. It is also a response to the issuance of a new set of rules by the Supreme Court effective October, 2007. Robert Stern, who died in 2000, and Eugene Gressman were the co-authors of this work since its initial appearance in 1950, and served on the committee that drafted the 1954 Rules, which prompted the second edition of this work. This volume provides a complete and scholarly description and analysis of the process of appealing a case to the United States Supreme Court. Includes a historical introduction to the Supreme Court, discussion of jurisdiction to review decisions of the federal and state courts, factors motivating the exercise of the Court's certiorari jurisdiction, procedure on appeals, certified questions, original cases, extraordinary writs, briefs on the merits, oral argument, petitions for rehearing and final disposition of cases, motions and applications, bails and stays, justiciability, admissions to the bar and disbarment, and forms. Appendices include Rules of the Supreme Court, Guide for Counsel in Cases To Be Argued Before the Supreme Court of the United States, Statutes, and Depositories for Supreme Court Briefs. There is both a table of cases and a subject and rules index. This 9th edition reflects changes in Supreme Court Rules, particularly the revised formatting requirements for booklet-format briefs and the introduction of new procedures for the submission of amicus briefs at the certiorari stage. As the Court adopts new rules, it integrates them into the existing structure and promulgates the entire set of rules anew. The 9th edition is the product of these most recent revisions. This is an indispensable guide to anyone planning to bring a case before the U.S. Supreme Court.

The Supreme Court Yearbook. Washington, D.C.: CQ Press, 1989-date. Annual. Online edition.
Cost: 1989-2012 online edition: $500 per year (2014).
This series of **Yearbooks**, commencing with the 1989-1990 term, provides summaries of every case decided by the United States Supreme Court between 1989 and 2012. Each volume includes a topically arranged summary of the court's decisions during the term, including background, analysis and future impact, excerpts of the more significant decisions, biographies of the Justices, and a glossary of legal terms.

Tribe, Lawrence H. **Constitutional Law**. 3d ed. Mineola, NY: Foundation Press, 1999. 1 vol. No supplementation. University Textbook Series. Available from West Academic.
Cost: $106; from $37.00 on amazon.com (2014).
Written by one of America's leading constitutional scholars, this exhaustive and well-documented treatise is intended as a student textbook, but is complete enough to be effectively utilized by the practitioner. Tribe's chapter coverage encompasses approaches to constitutional analysis, the model of separated and divided powers, federal judicial power, federal executive power, federal legislative power, federally based limits on state and local power, direct protection of individuals and groups, the model of implied limitations on government, the model of settled expectations, uncompensated takings and contract impairments, the model of governmental regularity, ex post facto laws, bills of attainder, and procedural due process, liberty beyond contract, rights of communication and expression, rights of political participation, rights of privacy and personhood, the model of equal protection, toward a model of structural justice, and the problem of state action. Appendices include a listing of Justices of the U.S. Supreme Court, table of authorities, and subject index. As is typical of most student texts, the only limitation is the lack of supplementation. Student texts tend to be updated only

by new editions rather than periodic pocket parts. Volume one, corresponding to the first ten chapters of the second edition, appeared in August, 1999. Volume two, when it finally appears, will address in greater detail the substantive rights and liberties outlined in volume one. As is typical of most student texts, the only limitation is the lack of supplementation. Student texts tend to be updated only by new editions, not periodic pocket parts. In 2005, Professor Tribe announced that he was foregoing further editions of his constitutional law textbook because, in his view, the court's jurisprudence was so contradictory and lacking in grand theory or cohering principle as to render the writing of a lucid, intelligible text impossible.

Tushnet, Mark. **The Constitution of the United States: A Contextual Analysis**. Portland, OR: Hart Publishing, 2009. 1 vol. (296 pp.). Paperbound.
Cost: $31.00; from $22.37 on amazon.com; kindle ed.: $19.89 (2014).
Since its adoption in 1789, the U.S. Constitution has been amended only twenty-seven times. In the view of Mark Tushnet, its age, brevity (less than 6,000 words), and near-unamendability contribute to a critical distinction between the canonical text of the document and what 19th century the English economist and journalist Walter Bagehot described as the "efficient" Constitution. In this sense, the U.S. Constitution is just one of various written forms which define the operation and parameters of governmental activity and allow it to adapt to the significant changes in technology, values and attitudes which have arisen since 1789. In the absence of constitutional amendments, the decisions of the Supreme Court and the actions of various political actors provide the means whereby various policy objectives are pursued. For example, the efficient constitution has provided a vehicle for accommodating the demand for regulation even though the canonical text has remained virtually unchanged. In this examination of the current state constitutional law, Professor Tushnet examines the way politics has given meaning to the Constitution and provided the means for adapting to current exigencies and policy demands. Tushnet sets the stage for his analysis with a useful overview of the history of the U.S. Constitution. He follows this with a consideration of the constitutional politics of the legislative, executive and judicial branches of government; and addresses the issues of federalism, individual rights under the Constitution, and the processes of constitutional change. Mark Tushnet is the William Nelson Cromwell Professor of Law at Harvard Law School.

U.S. Law Week. Washington, D.C.: Bloomberg BNA, 1933-date. 2 vols. Weekly.
Cost: $1,990 per year (includes online access to cases); Internet (single user): $3,735; print discounted when acquired in combination with Internet. (2014).
This two-volume service provides timely reporting of current United States Supreme Court decisions. Although issues generally appear on a weekly basis, extra issues are released during the term's busy weeks. Releases also include Supreme Court Proceedings containing lists and summaries of newly docketed cases, news developments and reports on oral arguments. The General Law Sections include news and abstracts of decisions from other federal and state courts.

Viera, Norman. **Constitutional Civil Rights in a Nutshell**. 3d ed. St. Paul, MN: West, 1998. 1 vol. Available from West Academic.
Cost: $41; from $0.10 on amazon.com (2014).
A succinct, student-oriented exposition of constitutional law directed chiefly at a consideration of the case law applicable to the 14th Amendment. The author, a Professor of Law at Southern Illinois University, examines substantive due process, procedural due process, equal protection, state action, and state actions under Section 1983 of Title 42 of the **U.S. Code**. For purposes of brevity, the author omits a discussion of criminal procedural problems, and the First Amendment. The Appendix contains selected constitutional and statutory law provisions.

Vile, John R. **Encyclopedia of Constitutional Amendments, Proposed Amendments, and Amending Issues, 1789-2002**. 2d ed. Santa Barbara, CA: ABC-CLIO, 2003. 1 vol. (427 pp.).
Cost: $85.00; from $8.45 on amazon.com (2014).
In the 200 years between 1791 and 1992, 27 Amendments to the United States Constitution have been ratified, the last a long dormant proposal regarding congressional pay raises that had been introduced in 1789 as a part of the original Bill of Rights. Drawing on the earlier work of Herman Ames (1896) and M. A. Musmanno (1929), the author has compiled a guide to the U.S. Constitution, the existing 27 Amendments, and the more than 10,900 others that have been proposed. These 10,900 proposed Amendments, however, are compressed into only slightly more than 400 topical entries because of their duplicative and overlapping subject matter. For example, over 1,000 proposals for an equal rights amendment have been introduced, but are treated here in a single essay. Additional entries deal with major Constitutional reforms introduced outside of Congress, influential individuals and organizations, Supreme Court decisions, unresolved issues, and miscellaneous topics such as the Articles of Confederation. Appendices includes the text of the Constitution and its Amendments, a listing of the dates Amendments were proposed and ratified, a listing of the Amendments by decade, a listing of the most popular amending proposals by year, an extended bibliography, and index. The author is Professor of Law, Chair of the Department of political science at Middle Tennessee State University, and the author of six books on the constitutional amendment process.

Vile, John R. **Essential Supreme Court Decisions: Summaries of Leading Cases in U.S. Constitutional Law**. 15th ed. Lanham, MD: Rowman & Littlefield, Publishers, 2010. 1 vol. 533 pp.). Paperbound.
Cost: $24.95; from $15.00 on amazon.com; kindle: $16.49 (2014).
For more than 50 years, the authors of this volume has been distilling the rulings of leading U.S. Supreme Court decisions for a general academic audience, including undergraduate and graduate students in the fields of history, political science, and law, as well as lawyers and general readers. Now in its 15th edition, and with more than 450 seminal cases briefed, each entry follows a standard format that includes: (1) the Facts; (2)

the Question; (3) the Decision; and (4) the Reasons (including the vote). The Reasons embrace not only the majority opinion, but significant concurring and dissenting opinions as well. The entries are grouped under fifteen topics (each prefaced by a brief essay), and chronologically within each topic. The topics include: (1) Article I: the Legislative Branch; (2) Article II: The Executive Branch; (3) Articles I and II: Distinct Yet Overlapping Powers; (4) Article III: The Judicial Branch; (5) Articles IV and VI: Federalism; (6) Articles V and VI: Constitutional Amending Process and Ratification of the Constitution; (7) Property Rights; (8) The Bill of Rights and Its Application to the States; (9) First Amendment: Religious Rights; (10) First Amendment: Political Rights; (11) Second, Third and Fourth Amendments; (12) Fifth, Sixth, Seventh and Eighth Amendments; (13) Ninth Amendment, Right to Privacy, and Other Unenumerated Rights; (14) Thirteenth and Fourteenth Amendments; and (15) Voting Rights. The individual entries are models of clarity that employ, selectively, the language of Justices themselves. The Appendices include a list of the Supreme Court Justices, the Text of the Constitution, a glossary of legal terms, an alphabetical list of cases briefed, a chronological list of cases by Chief Justice, and an index. John R. Vile, professor of political science at Middle Tennessee State University, is the author of numerous reference books on the Constitution, and its amendments. He assumed authorship of this volume more than 30 years ago.

Wilkinson, J. Harvie, III. **Cosmic Constitutional Theory: Why Americans are Losing Their Inalienable Right to Self-Governance**. New York: Oxford University Press, 2012. 1 vol. (161 pp.).
Cost: $21.95; from $14.97 on amazon.com; kindle: $9.99 (2014).
Judge Harvie Wilkinson makes a compelling case that American constitutional law has undergone a dramatic transformation in the last fifty years. Issues that were once decided by the democratic process through popularly elected legislatures have increasingly become the province of the courts. Subjects as wide-ranging as abortion rights, firearms regulations, health care reform and counterterrorism efforts, not to mention the 2000 presidential election, have been left to the prerogative of judges. He argues that judges with views as diverse as William Brennan and Antonin Scalia, and professors John Hart Ely, Robert Bork and Richard Posner have formulated what he terms "cosmic" constitutional theories that, for all their brilliance, circumvent the goal of judicial restraint, erode the role of representative institutions in America, and leave our children bereft of democratic liberty. He contends that the judicial modesty once practiced by such seminal legal thinkers as Learned Hand, John Harlan, and Oliver Wendell Holmes has given way to competing schools of liberal and conservative activism seeking sanctuary in one legal theory or another, be it Living Constitutionalism, Originalism, Process Theory, or the supposedly anti-theoretical creed of Pragmatism. In each case, the favored theory offers its proponents an intellectually respectable route to a desired political outcome from the bench, rather than from elected representatives beholden to the voters. The losers in all the theorizing from the bench are the venerable and honorable traditions of judicial restraint. and democratic governance that may be impossible to reconstruct as long as the cosmic constitutionalists continue to dominate contemporary legal thought. J. Harvie Wilkinson III was appointed to the United States Court of Appeals for the Fourth Circuit by Ronald Reagan. He has served on that court since 1984 and as its Chief Judge from 1996 to 2003. He has been frequently on the short list of prospects for the Supreme Court and is regarded as one of the country's leading appellate jurists.

Additional titles in the field of Constitutional Law are available from the following publishers: ABC-CLIO, American Bar Association, Anderson Publishing, Belknap Press, Brookings Foundation, Carolina Academic Press, Duke University Press, Foundation Press, Garland Publishing, Greenwood Publishing Group, Harvard University Press, William S. Hein & Co., Inc., Johns Hopkins University Press, LexisNexis, Liberty Fund, Madison House, RJS Publications, Rowman & Littlefield Publications, Inc., Temple University Press, Thomson Reuters West, University of Chicago Press, University of Oklahoma Press, University Press of America, University Press of Kansas, West Academic, Wolters Kluwer Law & Business. See Appendix B for addresses and telephone numbers.

Construction Law

Acret, James. **Construction Arbitration Handbook**. 2d ed. St. Paul, MN: West (Clark Boardman Callaghan), 2006-date. 1 vol. (375 pp.). Annual replacement volume.
Cost: 2013 Edition: $112; supplementation: 2007: $25; 2008: $30; 2009: $30; 2010: $68; 2011: 1st annual replacement vol.; 2012: $110; 1st ed.: 1995: 0; 1996: $62; 1997: $65.10; 1998: $69; 1999: $75; 2000: $82; 2001: $95; 2002: $117; 2003: $128; 2004: $143.50; 2005: $158; 2006: $176.50 (new ed.); **Monthly Assured Print Price (APP):** $10/$120.
Negotiation, arbitration, or litigation may achieve the settlement of disputes in the construction industry. While most disputes are settled through negotiation, parties may voluntarily agree to arbitration as a less costly alternative to litigation. This volume provides a basic overview of the practical problems faced by attorneys who represent clients in the private arbitration forum. Individual chapters cover the arbitration system, conflicts of law, enforceability of arbitration agreements, provisional remedies, consolidation and joinder, selection of the arbitrator, the arbitrator, preparing for the hearing, conduct of the hearings, the award, appealable and nonappealable orders, limitations, and opting for arbitration. Discussion of, and citations to, the relevant case law amply support the text. The author, a practicing attorney for over 30 years, is a national authority on construction and real estate law with a specialization in the arbitration of construction law disputes.

Allen, Richard K. and Stanley A. Martin. **Construction Law Handbook**. 2d ed. New York: Wolters Kluwer Law & Business, 2008-date. 2 vols. (2,136 pp.). Updated annually.
Cost: $485 (new edition); supplementation: 2002: $125; 2003: $173; 2004: $181; 2005: $190; 2006: $190; 2007: $197; 2008: $213; 2009: $99; 2010: $105; 2011: $120; 2012: $128; 2013: $159.
This is a comprehensive reference on the current state of construction and construction law written by a panel of over 70 construction industry professionals. Each chapter examines

a major legal or business issue from the perspective of the participants. It includes discussion of all the major issues likely to be encountered during the construction process, including drafting and negotiating construction contracts, understanding the duties and liabilities of each of the parties to a project, financing, management, identification and allocation of risk, calculation of construction claims, understanding the surety's rights and obligations, bankruptcy procedures and other solutions for financially distressed enterprises. A useful resource for attorneys, architects, engineers, public and private owners, bankers, accountants and other industry participants.

Branca, Michael A., Aaron P. Silberman, and John S. Vento. **Federal Government Construction Contracts**. 2d ed. Chicago: American Bar Association, 2010. 1 vol. (863 pp.). Paperbound.

Cost: $189.95 ($159.95 to members); from $158.85 on amazon.com (2014).

With the passage of the American Reinvestment and Recovery Act of 2009 (Pub.L. 111-5) (the so-called economic stimulus), the federal government will continue to be the world's largest purchaser of construction services. Most construction lawyers will inevitably handle some government contract cases at some point in their careers, and face the daunting prospect of grappling with the voluminous and complex regulations, clauses and case law that govern federal construction contracts. These regulations permeate every aspect of construction contracting, from procurement of construction services, to compliance, risk allocation between the government and the contractor, prevention of waste, fraud and abuse, and the final payment. This exhaustive and authoritative volume examines the full range of contract formation issues, from FARs, sealed bidding, competitive negotiations, architect/engineer contracting, design-build, construction management, IDIQ task order contracts, bid protests, and other provisions and issues unique to federal government construction contracts. It also considers the various aspects of performance, from contractual changes, differing site conditions, inspection, acceptance, warranties, payment and contract funding, termination for convenience and default, equitable adjustments and claims, surety bonds, overhead costs, as well as funding and other issues related to projects outside of the U.S. Finally, it addresses the various aspects of dispute resolution, including ADR, litigation, claim procedures, defective specifications, the False Claims Act and other fraud statutes. Additional chapters examine such topics as subcontracting, pricing of claims, and federal grants. The text is supported with numerous citations to federal statutes, regulations, and case law. Thirty-nine experts in the field of federal construction contracts contributed to the book's 26 chapters, each with extensive legal or construction contract experience. Already well respected in the field, this new second edition will continue to serve as a "bible" for lawyers immersed in the intricacies of federal government construction contracts.

Bruner, Philip L and Patrick J. O'Connor. **Bruner & O'Connor on Construction Law**. St. Paul, MN: Thomson Reuters West, 2002-date. 7 vols.

Cost: $1,187; supplementation: 2003: $80.50; 2004: $78.50; 2005: $86; 2006: $96; 2007: $197; 2008: $267; 2009: $367; 2010: $391.50; 2011: $380; 2012: $415; 2013: $454; **Monthly Assured Print Price (APP):** $58/$696.

Construction law is an enormously complex field involving the contributions of a variety of professionals and non-professionals, including owners, architects, contractors, regulators, representatives of financial institutions, and environmental organizations, as well as land, materials, machinery, and workers. Although previously not recognized as a distinct field of law, construction law has, in recent years, spawned a greater number and variety of research tools. This comprehensive treatise provides information on the types of legal issues involved in most construction projects from the basic to the complex. Unlike the existing offerings in the field of construction law, the coverage of this set extends to a wider variety of topics and issues, including contract formation and interpretation, project delivery methods and contract pricing arrangements, risk management, the payment process and financing, warranties, indemnity and contribution, insurance, suretyship, inspection and acceptance of work, differing site conditions, risks of construction time, government regulation (including licensing and permitting), roles and responsibilities of design professionals, contract breach and termination, remedies and damage measures, arbitration, and international construction. The authors' collaboration began more than 20 years ago in the pages of the annual Construction Review and the present work is the result of more than 11 years research and writing. Philip Bruner has practiced law for more than 37 years, has litigated complex construction law cases in more than 25 states, and is a Founding Fellow of the American College of Construction Lawyers. Patrick J. O'Connor, Jr. has practiced law for more than 20 years, is Chair of the Bond and Insurance Division of the ABA's Forum on the Construction Industry, and is an advisor to the American Law Institute's Restatement of the Law Third, Suretyship and Guaranty. A worthy alternative to Stein, Construction, published by Matthew Bender. While the authors' credentials are impeccable, it is unfortunate that they and/or their publishers have resorted to that increasingly archaic practice of including the authors' names in the title when they should know full well that the task of keeping the set current will eventually fall to others and/or the publishers' editorial staff.

Bruner, Philip L. and Tracey L. Haley, eds. **Managing and Litigating the Complex Surety Case**. 2nd ed. Chicago: American Bar Association, 2007.
1 vol. (843 pp.).

Cost: $99.95 ($84.95 to members) (2014).

The law of suretyship and guaranty involves a person or party who agrees to be responsible for the debt or obligation of another in situations in which the ability of the principal to perform its obligations under a contract is in question, or when there is some public or private interest which requires protection from the principal's default or delinquency. In most common law jurisdictions, a contract of suretyship is subject to the statute of frauds (or its equivalent local laws) and is only enforceable if memorialized by a writing signed by the surety. One of the most complex areas of legal practice is the litigation of surety cases involving multiple parties involved in major construction projects. These cases often involve multiple parties, multiple project locations, multiple claimants, multiple sources for "salvage", multiple forums for dispute resolution, and a variety of technical engineering, accounting, and construction issues. This guide provides instruction on topics ranging from the evaluation of evaluating a surety's performance bond exposure, trial proceedings, post hearing motions, and appeals. Philip L. Bruner is one of the most highly regarded attorneys in the field of construction law. He has 43 years experience in the field of construction law, 17 of these as a partner with the Minneapolis form of Faegre & Benson. He is now a member of JAMS, The Resolution Experts, the nation's largest private provider of ADR services, having become Director of JAMS' Global Engineering and Construction (GEC) Group.

Callahan, Michael T, Barry B. Bramble, and Frank M. Rapoport. **Discovery in Construction Litigation**. 4th ed. Charlottesville, VA: LexisNexis, 2003-date. 1 vol. (630 pp.). Hardbound or eBook.
Cost: $248; e-book: $296; supplementation: 2004: $68; 2005: $80; 2006: $85; 2007: $90; 2008: $95; 2009: $129; 2010: $135; 2011: $144; 2012: $154; 2013: $149; 3d ed.: 1996: $30; 1997: $35; 1998: $35; 1999: $50; 2000: $55; 2001: $60; 2002: $65; eBook: $248.
A useful guide to maximizing discovery efforts in a highly complex area of law which often involves complicated claims, counterclaims, large numbers of participants, and highly technical variables. Discusses discovery in a variety of forums, including arbitration, litigation, administrative courts and special courts.

Circo, Carl J. And Christopher H. Little, eds. **A State-By-State Guide to Construction Law: Current Statutes and Practices**. 2d ed. Chicago: American Bar Association, Section on Real Property, Trusts & Estate Law, 2011. 1 vol. (1,169 pp.).
Cost: $179.95 ($159.95 to members); from $84.99 on amazon.com (2014).
This practical, easy to navigate compendium provides essential information about design and construction law and contracting practices in all 50 states plus the District of Columbia and Puerto Rico. Chiefly useful for lawyers negotiating or reviewing construction or design contracts for projects outside their own jurisdictions. Information for each state follows a standard organizational outline, allowing the reader to easily compare how different jurisdictions treat the same issue. The topics addressed in each state chapter include: (1) Considerations Relating to Project Delivery Systems; (2) Design and Construction Professionals; (3) Considerations Applicable to Payments to Contractors and to Subcontractors; (4) Warranties: (5) Principles Applicable to Indemnification Agreement; (6) Insurance; (7) Suretyship and Bond; (8) Damages; (9) Construction Liens; (10) Arbitration, Mediation, and Other ADR; (11) Other Special Considerations Applicable to Construction Contract Practices Generally; (12) Consumer Protection Laws Applicable to Design and Construction Contracts; and (13) Environmental Considerations. The text is supported by references to both case law and statutes. The chapters were written by experienced real estate practitioners in each jurisdiction, involving a total of 75 lawyer contributors with a specialization in construction and design law. This is an essential reference for any attorney or construction professional, particularly those with a multi-state practice or construction business.

Construction Checklists: A Guide to Frequently Encountered Construction Issues. Edited by Fred D. Wilshusen, Eric E. Berg, Terrence L. Brookie, and Carrie Lynn H. Okizaki. Chicago: American Bar Association, Forum on the Construction Industry, 2008. 1 vol. (556 pp.). Paperbound, with companion CD-ROM.
Cost: $189.95 ($159.95 to members) (2014).
In addition to contract and general business law, construction attorneys must be conversant with a number of other areas of the law, among them the concepts of principal and surety, real estate law, trial and arbitration law and procedure, labor and employment law, and other areas specific to the construction industry. This practical, hands-on, guide provides detailed checklists designed to assist a variety of professionals involved in various aspects and stages of the construction process, from contract formation and contract administration to claims and disputes. Additional checklists address a variety of specific topics, including labor and employment issues, government contracting, international contracting, bankruptcy considerations, catastrophic construction events, time and schedule issues, contractor's delay and acceleration clauses, and owner's defense of delay and acceleration clauses. More than sixty-five construction attorneys contributed the seventy-four checklists contained in this volume. The checklists are reproduced on a companion CD-ROM.

Construction Financial Management Association (CFMA). **Financial Management and Accounting for the Construction Industry**. New York: Matthew Bender & Co., 1988-date. 2 vols. Looseleaf format or eBook.
Cost: $395; supp.: 1999: $147; 2000: $145; 2001: $155; 2002: $166; 2003: $175; 2004: $184; 2005: $184; 2006: $212; 2007: $218; 2008: $227; 2009: $245; 2010: $253; 2011: $261; 2012: $278; 2013: $153; 2014: $313; eBook: $395; renewal: 2014: $313.
While this resource was written primarily for accountants working with the construction business, it also provides information of critical value to corporation legal counsel, including income recognition, planning for income taxes, preparing bids and estimates, and other matters for which legal review is critical, if not essential. It includes an analysis of all aspects of project management, from bidding through completion. Additional subjects covered include risk management and insurance, surety, government contracts, cash management, budgeting and planning, privatization, employee benefits, activity-based costing, and more. Sponsored by the Construction Financial Management Association, this work is the product of a team of experienced practitioners from leading construction and accounting firms.

Construction Law Library on LoislawConnect.. New York: Wolters Kluwer Law & Business. Online service.
Cost: $660 per year (2014).
Contains the text of the following Wolters Kluwer Law & Business construction law titles, including **Proving and Pricing Construction Claims**, **Construction Delay Claims**, **Legal Guide to AIA Documents**, **Construction Change Order Claims**, **Calculating Construction Damages**, **Fifty State Construction Lien and Bond Law**, **Alternative Clauses to Standard Construction Contracts**, **Construction Law Handbook**, **Design-Build Contracting Formbook**, **Design-**

Build Contracting Handbook, **State-by-State Guide to Architect, Engineer and Contractor Licensing, and Sweet on Construction Industry Contracts**. Includes links to cases, statutes, etc. from the Loislaw database. Other online libraries available.

Cushman, Robert F. **Construction Litigation: Representing the Owner**. 2d ed. New York: Wolters Kluwer Law & Business, 1994-date. 2 vols. Annual supplementation.
Cost: $315; supplementation: 1996: $86; 1997: $96; 1998: 0; 1999: $114; 2000: 0; 2001: $125; 2002: $142; 2003: $140; 2004: $155; 2005: $163; 2006: $174; 2007: $229; 2008: $200; 2009: $200; 2010: $200; 2011: $214; 2012: $257; 2013: $279.
A practical guide to representing the legal interests of owners of construction projects. Useful not only to attorneys, but to construction professionals involved in various phases of the construction process.

Cushman, Robert F. **Fifty State Construction Lien and Bond Law**. 3d ed. Frederick, MD: Wolters Kluwer Law & Business, 2013-date. 3 vols. Annual supplementation.
Cost: $599; no supplementation to date. 2d ed.: 1996: $86; 1997: $96; 1998: 0; 1999: $98; 2000: $86; 2001: $86; 2002: $137; 2003: $166; 2004: $185; 2005: $384; 2006: $215; 2007: $170; 2008: $246; 2009: $279; 2010: $288; 2011: $305; 2012: $349; 2013; $373 & new ed.
Designed for use by attorneys who must deal with construction lien and bond laws in multiple jurisdictions, this set provides attorney-written summaries of the construction lien and bond laws for all fifty states. It also provides discussion of the requirements of both public and private construction projects, Miller Act Remedies, construction remedies in bankruptcy, and forms for preserving lien and bond rights in each of the fifty states.

Dib, Albert. **Forms and Agreements for Architects, Engineers and Contractors**. Revised ed. St. Paul, MN: Thomson Reuters West (Clark Boardman Callaghan), 2008/2009-date. 5 vols. Looseleaf format. Supplemented three times per year.
Cost: $4,299; supplementation: 2009: $1,299; 2010: $1,558.50; 2011: $1,870.50; 2012: $3,242; 2013: $3,232; prior edition: 1995: $450; 1996: $340; 1997: $542; 1998: $542; 1999: $921; 2000: $669; 2001: $880; 2002: $870.50; 2003: $840; 2004: $940.50; 2005: $975; 2006: $1,048.50; 2007: $1,048.50; 2008: new edition; **Monthly Assured Print Price (APP):** $327/$3,924.
This work provides lawyers and construction industry contract representatives with the tools for evaluating and drafting construction documents, including sample forms, alternative clauses, annotations, and citations to applicable case law. Also included are the more common procurement clauses used in industrial purchasing for capital construction and plant renewal and modification, such as the acquisition of raw materials, engineered components and assemblies. Includes documents for project planning and contracting, the architectural engineering contract, construction contracts, procurement, third party liability, purchasing, warranties and other remedies, nondisclosure and restrictive agreements, joint ventures, consulting, financing expansion, contract administration, pattern project cases, alternate dispute resolution, and pleadings. Albert Dib, a practicing attorney associated with the firm of Buhler King and Buhler and special counsel to an engineering construction firm, is the Charter Chairman of AIChE's Engineering and Construction Contracting Committee.

Cost Saving Tip: With high supplementation costs, you are better off dropping the standing order for supplementation. You will find more than enough value in the base set without incurring the additional expense of frequent updates which provide summaries of new cases you can find elsewhere. The Monthly Assured Print Price, which increased 20.7% in 2011, rose another 20% from 2011 to 2012. At this rate, the only thing assured about it will be the draining of your wallet.

Driscoll, Thomas J., et al. **Construction Scheduling: Preparation, Liability, and Claims**. 3d ed. New York: Wolters Kluwer Law & Business, 2009-date. 1 vol. (560 pp.). Annual supplementation.
Cost: $315; supplementation: 2010: $245; 2011: $107; 2012: $125; 2013: $135; 2d ed.: 1997: $80; 1998: $86; 1999: $90; 2000: $120; 2001: $130; 2002: 0; 2003: $154; 2004: $154; 2005: $306; 2006: $162; 2007: $170; 2008: $182; 2009: new edition.
The volume addresses both the mechanics and legal implications of scheduling construction projects, including a consideration of responsibility for scheduling, the use of scheduling to calculate delay, acceleration, and lost productivity claims.

Enhada, Carina Y., Cheri Turnage Gatlin, and Fred D. Wilshusen, eds. **Fundamentals of Construction Law**. Chicago: American Bar Association, 2001. 1 vol. (381 pp.). Paperbound.
Cost: $129.95 ($109.95 to members); from $85.00 on amazon.com (2014).
A product of the ABA's Forum on the Construction Industry, this volume addresses a variety of issues basic to an understanding of the legal and practical aspects of the construction industry. Its premise is that the lawyer must have an adequate understanding of the construction industry in order to provide proper advice to his or her clients. Topics covered include: the owner's perspective, the rights and responsibilities of the design professional, role of the prime contractor, role of the subcontractor, a primer in contract surety law, delivery systems, payment provisions, scheduling for a construction project, changes in the work, default termination, construction damages, construction insurance, and alternative dispute resolution. Appendices include a summary of significant construction law cases, a glossary of terms, and a guide to useful Websites for the construction lawyer. The volume includes minimal citations to primary law.

Hutchings, Jonathan F. **National Building Codes Handbook**. New York: McGraw-Hill Professional, 1998. 1 vol. (545 pp.).
Cost: from $1.15 on amazon.com (2014).
Designed for building professionals and their legal advisers, the **National Building Codes Handbook** explains and clarifies the most commonly encountered provisions of the SBCCI, ICBO and BOCA codes, as well as HUD, HVAC and other federal regulations. The volume also includes many tables and diagrams that explain practical building techniques and applications, designed to assist the user in passing building inspections. Chapter contents include administration, terms and

definitions, occupancy, general building limitations, types of code construction, fire-resistant materials and construction, interior finishes, fire protection systems, means of egress, exterior walls, roof structures, structural loads, foundations and retaining walls, concrete, electrical, wood and framing, board and plaster, code specification tables, and index.

Joy, S. Gregory and Eugene J. Heady. **Alternative Clauses to Standard Construction Contracts**. 4th ed. New York: Wolters Kluwer Law & Business, 2013-date. 1 vol. (1,000 pp.) Annual supplementation.
Cost: $349; no supplementation to date; 3d ed.: 2010: $135; 2011: $144; 2012: $154; 2d ed.: 1997: $69; 1998: $75; 1999: $75; 2000: $94; 2001: $100; 2002: $120; 2003: $141; 2004: $147; 2005: $154; 2006: $162; 2007: $168; 2008: $180; 2009: $259 (new edition).
A comprehensive collection of alternate clauses to standard AIA contracts designed to address the needs of owners, developers, contractors and subcontractors. The commentary provides analysis of the benefits and limitations of each clause from the vantage point of the various parties involved.

Kelleher, Thomas J., Brian G. Corgan, and William E. Dorris. **Construction Disputes: Practice Guide with Forms**. 2d ed. New York: Wolters Kluwer Law & Business, 1994-date. 2 vols. Annual supplementation.
Cost: $575; supplementation: 2001: $125; 2002: $136; 2003: $149; 2004: $145; 2005: $120; 2006: $128; 2007: $136; 2008: $146; 2009: $161; 2010: $172; 2011: $164; 2012: $197; 2013: $209.
A comprehensive guide to all aspects of construction litigation, from case analysis and pre-trial activities to substantive damage claims resulting from delay and acceleration, lost productivity, etc. The authors also examine such trial issues as defense and cross examination, appeals, settlement, and releases. The set also includes checklists for the drafting of many of the documents used in construction litigation.

Kelley, Gail S. **Construction Law: An Introduction for Engineers, Architects, and Contractors**. Hoboken, NJ: John Wiley & Sons, 2013. 1 vol. (287 pp.).
Cost: $115.00; from $61.36 on amazon.com; kindle: $78.11 (2014).
This volume provides a succinct, yet comprehensive, overview of the legal environment governing the activities of the design and construction industries. It provides a basic introduction to the American legal system, its sources and hierarchy of law, legal principles, doctrines, and causes of action. It also examines the basic legal principles involved in the construction field, including contract, agency and tort law. It looks at the various project participants, project delivery systems, construction contracts, the design process, procurement, the pricing of construction projects, subcontractors and suppliers, time for performance, construction scheduling, contract administration, the payment process, changes to the work, differing site conditions, termination of the construction con tract, mechanics liens, insurance, surety bonds, liability for defective construction, calculations of damages, the economic loss doctrine, and alternative dispute resolution. The appendices include a list of abbreviations common to the field, a table of cases, glossary and index. While multi-volume legal treatises on construction abound, this is arguably the best single-volume overview of construction law on the market written for those in the design and construction industries, and laypersons with an interest in the field. Gail S. Kelley is a professional engineer and LEED Accredited Professional as well as a practicing attorney, with extensive experience in construction management, structural design, and structural evaluation.

Moelmann, Lawrence R., Matthew M. Horowitz, and Kevin L. Lybeck, eds. **The Law of Performance Bonds**. 2d ed. Chicago: American Bar Association, Tort, Trial and Insurance Practice Section, 2009. 1 vol. (898 pp.).
Cost: $129.95; $99.95 to members (2014).
Performance bonds are surety bonds issued by a bank or insurance company to guarantee the completion of a construction project in accordance with the specifications laid out in the contract. As contracts, they are ultimately nothing more than that to which the parties to them agree. The concept of suretyship goes back to at least the third century B.C. Almost all states, excepting Louisiana, require that the contract be in writing and signed by the party to be charged as a condition precedent to enforcement of a promise of suretyship. Government regulation of the surety industry has generally paralleled that of the insurance industry, although suretyship reflects certain fundamental differences with the traditional insurance. A surety bond, for example, is a guarantee, in which the surety guarantees that the contractor, called the "principal" in the bond, will perform the "obligation" stated in the bond. The 14 chapters in this volume address the creation of he relationship, conditions precedent to asserting a performance bond claim, performance options available to the surety, the performance bond surety's rights to the contract funds, rights of recovery against principals and indemnitors, surety's rights under the general indemnity agreement to minimize loss, right of the surety to pursue claims against third parties, liability of he performance bond surety for damages, extra-contractual liability of performance bond sureties, claims and defenses, defenses available to the surety, litigation issues, effect of an arbitration provision, and bankruptcy. The text includes numerous references to the relevant primary and secondary literature. Thirty-five authors contributed to the 14 chapters in this volume.

Sabo, Werner. **Legal Guide to AIA Documents**. 5th ed. New York: Wolters Kluwer Law & Business, 2008-date. 1 vol. (901 pp.). Annual supplementation.
Cost: $325; supplementation: 2009: $119; 2010: $127; 2011: $135; 2012: $144; 2013: $154; 4th ed.: 1999: $60; 2000: $78; 2001: $90; 2002: $110; 2003: $149; 2004: $135; 2005: $145; 2006: $155; 2007: $165; 2008: new edition; from $34.12 on amazon.com (2014).
A detailed examination from the architect's perspective of four of the most significant 1987 standard AIA documents: B141, A201, C141, and A101. Werner Sabo, an attorney and licensed architect, provides detailed explanation of the AIA clauses for each document, along with expert commentary and case citations. Alternate language for each of the documents is also considered.

Schwartzkopf, William, John J. McNamara, and Julian F. Hoffar. **Calculating Construction Damages**. 2d ed. New York: Wolters Kluwer Law & Business, 2000-date. 1 vol. (253 pp.). Annual supplementation.
Cost: $315; supplementation: 1997: $67; 1998: $86; 1999: $92; 2000: $95; 2001: $90; 2002: $110; 2003: $126; 2004: $98; 2005: $121; 2006: $129; 2007: $137; 2008: $147; 2009: $159; 2010: $180; 2011: $182; 2012: $194; 2013: $219; from $199.65 on amazon.com
A practical tool for calculating the value of a construction damage claim and the legal basis by which such damages are determined, including cost overruns for labor, equipment, tools, home office overhead.

Stein, Steven G. M. **The American Institute of Architects Legal Citator**. New York: Matthew Bender & Co., 1996-date. 1 vol. Softcover. Annual.
Cost: 2014 Edition: $319.
For attorneys practicing in the area of construction law, this tool provides an efficient mechanism for locating federal and state court decisions which have interpreted specific provisions of AIA construction contracts and related documents. Each AIA document is broken down into specific provisions and each provision is followed by a list of relevant cases. The Document-to-Document Charts list three types of cases: those involving an AIA document provision or identical language, cases probably involving an AIA document provision or similar language, and cases that are analogous and helpful. The author/editor is a senior partner in the Chicago law firm of Stein, Ray and Conway, Adjunct Professor at ITT-Kent College of Law, and a nationally known speaker on design and construction law.

Stein, Steven G. M., ed. **Construction Law**. New York: Matthew Bender, 1986-date. 6 vols. Looseleaf format. Supplemented 2-3 times per year. Also available on Authority CD-ROM which includes no-cost online updating via LEXISNEXIS.
Cost: $1,844 (includes annual subscription); renewal: 1996: $559; 1997: $559; 1998: $585; 1999: $605; 2000: $605; 2001: $647; 2002: $675; 2003: $725; 2004: $761; 2005: $761; 2006: $855; 2007: $911; 2008: $979; 2009: $1,057; 2010: $1,069; 2011: $1,080; 2012: $1,112; 2013: $1,213; 2014: $1,299; eBook: $1,677; renewal: 2014: $1,299.
This comprehensive resource mirrors the full complexity of the construction law practice, from bidding and contract negotiation to subsequent litigation. Editor-in-Chief Steven Stein, a leading construction law attorney and Adjunct Professor of Law at ITT/Chicago-Kent College of Law, brings together forty experts with specific expertise in the various phases of construction law. Volumes 1-4 contain the substantive text, accompanied by relevant forms, documents, statutes, and rules. Individual chapters are dedicated to bidding and construction contracts, timeliness of performance, payment, documenting and presenting construction claims, construction lien law, workers' injuries, remedies and damages, arbitration, risk management and indemnity, construction financing, government contracting and regulation, bankruptcy, construction bonds, warranties, labor relations, and intellectual property--protection of the design. The Appendices include selected AIA documents, selected Associated General Contractors (AGC) documents, a table of cases, and index. Volumes 5-6 comprise a two-volume AIA Building Construction Legal Citator which provides lists and digests of significant cases that have interpreted the commonly used AIA construction documents. Among the work's special features is a state-by-state lien and bond claim summary laying out in chart form the notice and filing requirements for preserving rights involving mechanics' liens and bond claims. This is the most exhaustive work available on the subject of construction law.

Sweet, Justin and Jonathan J. Sweet. **Sweet on Construction Industry Contracts: Major AIA Documents**. 5th ed. New York: Wolters Kluwer Law & Business, 2008-date. 2 vols. (1,300 pp.) Annual supplementation.
Cost: $499; supplementation: 2009: $110; 2010: $118; 2011: $126; 2012: $135; 2013: $145; 4th ed.: 2001: $109; 2002: $115; 2003: $154; 2004: $161; 2005: $169; 2006: $179; 2007: $191; 2008: new edition; 3d edition: 1997: $75.00; 1998: $86.00; 1999: 0.
A practical and analytical guide to the most important construction industry contracts prepared by the American Institute of Architects, including AIA small project documents A105, B155 and A205; new AGC, FIDIC, and EJCDC contracts; an, negotiation, and litigation. Formerly published by Wiley Law Publications, this title became part of the Aspen Law & Business product line following the acquisition of the Wiley Law Publications by Wolters Kluwer in 1997.

Sweet, Justin. **Sweet on Construction Law**. Chicago: American Bar Association, Forum on the Construction Industry, 1997. 1 vol.
Cost: $109.95 ($99.95 to Forum Committee on the Construction Industry members); from $89.70 on amazon.com (2014).
Based on a series of lectures delivered by Professor Sweet at the University of Tel-Aviv, this volume presents an overview of the construction process delivered in a conversational style which relies on anecdotes and the author's personal experiences. Professor Sweet considers the various types of contracts, cost methods, construction planning, and litigation.

Walker, Stephen G., Richard A. Holderness, and Stephen D. Butler. **State-By-State Guide to Architect, Engineer, and Contractor Licensing**. 2d ed. New York: Wolters Kluwer Law & Business, 2012-date. 2 vols. (2,800 pp.). Annual supplementation.
Cost: $559; supplementation: 2013: $179; 1st edition: 2000: $94; 2001: $115; 2002: $150; 2003: $172; 2004: $224; 2005: $175; 2006: $200; 2007: $213; 2008: $228; 2009: $249; 2010: $266; 2011: $285; 2012: new edition.
For construction companies, and engineering and architectural firms doing business in more than one state, this volume provides a convenient resource for determining the licensing requirements likely to be required for various types of construction projects. Each state section is authored by local counsel with expertise on licensing issues. A typical state chapter treats the detailed requirements of architecture, engineering, and contractor license law, addressing such concerns as entitlement to practice, entities allowed, when is licensing required, the qualification process, exemptions, reciprocity, sealing and signing requirements, liability for engineers, violations, and disciplinary procedures.

Stephen G. Walker and Stephen Butler are Senior Counsel and Manager of the Litigation Group, respectively, of the Bechtel Corporation in San Francisco. Richard Holderness is a partner in the Construction Practice Group of the San Francisco firm of McKenna & Cuneo.

Additional titles in the field of Construction Law are available from the following publishers: American Bar Association, American Law Institute, American Society of Civil Engineers, Wolters Kluwer Law & Business, Associated General Contractors of America, Builders Publishing Co., Construction Publications, Home Builder Press, J.J. Keller & Associates, LexisNexis, Matthew Bender, McGraw-Hill Professional, Practising Law Institute, Thomson Reuters West, West Academic. See Appendix B for addresses and telephone numbers.

Contract Law

Adams, Kenneth A. **A Manual of Style for Contract Drafting**. 2d ed. Chicago: American Bar Association, Section of Business Law, 2008. 1 vol. (253 pp.). Paperbound.
Cost: $74.95 ($59.95 to Section members); from $56 on amazon.com; kindle: $39.99 (2014).
Written for both contract drafters and litigators, this book explains how to draft contracts in language most likely to pass legal scrutiny whether in or outside of the courtroom. The author, an experienced corporate attorney and authority on legal drafting, addresses common sources of inefficiency, dispute, and misunderstanding and suggests ways to avoid them. Among the subjects covered are the introductory and concluding parts of a contract; the different categories of contract language, organizing sections, subsections, enumerated clauses, vagueness, ambiguity, the use of defined terms, and the drafting corporate resolutions, among other topics. Its level of practical detail distinguishes it from other books on drafting. Highly recommended for any attorney who drafts contracts.

American Law Institute. **Restatement of the Law Second. Contracts.** St. Paul, MN: American Law Institute, 1981-date. 12 vols. Annual pocket parts. Periodic Appendix volumes published. Pocket part appears in the back of the most recent Appendix volume only.
Cost: $823.50; vols. 1-3 (base vols.) only: $190.50 ($46.00 in softcover); vols. 4-11 (Appendices) only: $633; supplementation: 1995: $19.00; 1996: $19; 1997: $72; 1998: $19; 1999: $20; 2000: $21; 2001: $21; 2002: $22.75; 2003: $25; 2004: $25; 2005: $25; 2006: $29; 2007: $30.00; 2008: $114.50; 2009: $32.00; 2010: $32.00; 2011: $32; 2012: $40.00; 2013: $59.
The **Restatements** represent the most significant attempt by the American legal community to draft common law principles based upon the vast body of published appellate court decisions which appear in the various reporter series. Drafted and published under the auspices of the American Law Institute, the **Restatements** reflect the combined efforts of a committee of distinguished legal scholars and jurists. Work on the **Restatement (Second) of the Law of Contracts** was begun in 1962 and first volume was published in 1981. The main body of the work is contained in volumes one through three, while the Appendices, containing Reporter's Notes and Annotations of court decisions, appear in volumes four through nine. Supplementation is published only for certain Appendix volumes.

The Annotated Construction Law Glossary. Edited by A, Elizabeth Patrick, et al. Chicago: American Bar Association, 2010. 1 vol. (191 pp.). Paperbound.
Cost: $79.95 ($69.95 to members); from $56.58 on amazon.com (2014).
This useful glossary provides annotated definitions of more than 300 construction and construction-related terms. Each entry not only defines the term, but also provides additional substantive commentary, and identifies the source of the definition so that it can be used with authority in legal opinions, court decisions, pleadings, and legal research and literature. Written by over 60 experienced construction lawyers, the authors have incorporated research from the widest range of information sources in their definitions, including legal treatises, law review articles, judicial decisions, engineering texts, industry literature, and many other secondary sources. A chart of acronyms and abbreviations is provided for ease of reference when using the book. A useful for tool for law students, young lawyers, construction project managers, and experienced construction attorneys. Lead editor A. Elizabeth Patrick, founder of the Patrick Law Group, has negotiated hundreds of commercial, construction, and procurement contracts. The book is a product of the ABA's Forum on the Construction Industry.

Branca, Michael A., Aaron P. Silberman, and John S. Vento. **Federal Government Construction Contracts**. 2d ed. Chicago: American Bar Association, 2010. 1 vol. (863 pp.). Paperbound.
Cost: $189.95 ($159.95 to members); from $158.85 on amazon.com (2014).
With the passage of the American Reinvestment and Recovery Act of 2009 (Pub.L. 111-5) (the so-called economic stimulus), the federal government will continue to be the world's largest purchaser of construction services. Most construction lawyers will inevitably handle some government contract cases at some point in their careers, and face the daunting prospect of grappling with the voluminous and complex regulations, clauses and case law that govern federal construction contracts. These regulations permeate every aspect of construction contracting, from procurement of construction services, to compliance, risk allocation between the government and the contractor, prevention of waste, fraud and abuse, and the final payment. This exhaustive and authoritative volume examines the full range of contract formation issues, from FARs, sealed bidding, competitive negotiations, architect/engineer contracting, design-build, construction management, IDIQ task order contracts, bid protests, and other provisions and issues unique to federal government construction contracts. It also considers the various aspects of performance, from contractual changes, differing site conditions, inspection, acceptance, warranties, payment and contract funding, termination for convenience and default, equitable adjustments and claims, surety bonds, overhead costs, as well as funding and other issues related to projects outside of the U.S. Finally, it addresses the various aspects of dispute

resolution, including ADR, litigation, claim procedures, defective specifications, the False Claims Act and other fraud statutes. Additional chapters examine such topics as subcontracting, pricing of claims, and federal grants. The text is supported with numerous citations to federal statutes, regulations, and case law. Thirty-nine experts in the field of federal construction contracts contributed to the book's 26 chapters, each with extensive legal or construction contract experience. Already well respected in the field, this new second edition will continue to serve as a "bible" for lawyers immersed in the intricacies of federal government construction contracts.

Burnham, Scott J. **Drafting and Analyzing Contracts: A Guide to the Practical Application of the Principles of Contract Law.** 3d ed. Charlottesville, VA: LexisNexis, 2003. 1 vol. (382 pp.). No supplementation between editions.
Cost: $39; from $28.69 on amazon.com (2014).
This student textbook is organized around the topics presented in the first year course in contract law, including offer and acceptance, consideration, indefiniteness, enforceability, capacity, parol evidence, interpretation, mistake, force majeure, promise and condition, modification and discharge, warranties, damages, and third parties. The author also addresses the principles of drafting as exemplified in contracts, including the framework of a contract, operative language and boilerplate terms, the language of drafting, plain language, and drafting with a computer. Finally, he discusses the various passes through which contract language is to be scrutinized, including the issues of orientation, explication, implication, remediation, and evaluation conclusion. The book is also useful as a review of contract drafting principles and analysis for the practitioner. Scott J. Burnham is Professor of Law at the University of Montana School of Law.

Calamari, John D. and Joseph M. Perillo. **The Law of Contracts.** 7th ed. St. Paul, MN: West Academic, 2013. 1 vol. (915 pp.) No supplementation.
Cost: $103; e-book; $69 (Thomson Reuters); 6th ed. from $26.76 on amazon.com (2014).
This is a one-volume Hornbook intended as a student text, but also useful to the practicing attorney who requires a good overview of the subject matter. The authors explain and analyze such topics as the offer and acceptance, parole evidence and interpretation, the consideration, promissory estoppel, contracts under seal, capacity, avoidance or reformation for misconduct or mistake, conditions, performance and breach, damages, restitution for breach, specific performance, assignment and delegation, the statute of frauds, discharge, and illegal bargains, In addition to the standard coverage of the field of contractual law, the volume features WESTLAW References scattered throughout the text. The authors also provide liberal citations to both primary and secondary sources. Appendices include a guide to WESTLAW research guide, with examples illustrating contract law queries. There are also Tables of Cases, **UCC** Citations, and an Index. As with most West Hornbooks, there is no supplementation between editions. Thus, more current material must be located in supplemented treatises or primary sources after using this volume as a first step in the research process. The work was first published in 1970 by Joseph M. Perillo, now Distinguished Professor of Law, Fordham University, and the late John D. Calamari.

Cibinic, John, and Ralph C. Nash. **Administration of Government Contracts**. 4th ed. Washington, DC: George Washington Univ. Law School, Government Contracts Program, 2010. 1 vol. Softbound. Available from CCH, Inc.
Cost: hardcover: $150; softcover: $105; from $89.25 on amazon.com; kindle: $85.99 (2014).
A companion to the authors' **Formation of Government Contracts** (see next entry), this volume provides expert guidance in the administration and management of government contracts, including such matters as contract interpretation, renegotiation, management of delays and damages, price adjustments, dispute resolution without litigation, payment policies, and contract termination. Chapters include: contract administration and personnel, contract interpretation, risk allocation, changes, differing site conditions, delays, government property, pricing of adjustments, inspection, acceptance and warranties, default termination, damages and liquidated damages, termination for convenience, payment and discharge, and disputes. The Appendices include Standard FAR clauses, statutes, regulations, citations to more than 3,400 of court, board, and Comptroller General decisions, B-Numbers, and a detailed subject index. John Cibinic, a Professor Emeritus of Law at George Washington University Law School and director of the Law School's Government Contracts Program from 1965 to 1974, is a frequent government contracting seminar speaker and consultant. Ralph Nash is the founder of the Government Contracts Program at George Washington University Law School and Professor Emeritus.

Cibinic, John, and Ralph C. Nash. **Formation of Government Contracts**. 4th ed. Washington, DC: George Washington University Law School, Government Contracts Program, 1998. 1 vol. Softbound. Available from CCH, Inc.
Cost: $150; from $76.97 on amazon.com (2014).
A complete guide to process of government contracting and procurement, including the solicitation, bidding, and award processes under the Executive Branch. It incorporates the changes brought about by the rewrite of FAR Part 15, the Federal Acquisition Streamlining Act of 1994 (FASA), the Clinger-Cohen Act of 1996, and the Administrative Disputes Resolution Act of 1996. Individual chapters examine: basic principles of federal procurement, contract formation principles, acquisition planning, contractor qualification, sealed bidding, basic negotiation procedures, special negotiation procedures, types of contracts, contract pricing, collateral policies, and contract award controversies. The third edition provides an updating of the last ten years of Comptroller General, court, and board decisions. It also includes a table of authorities and detailed subject index. John Cibinic, a Professor Emeritus of Law at George Washington University Law School and director of the Law School's Government Contracts Program from 1965 to 1974, is a frequent government contracting seminar speaker and consultant. Ralph Nash is the founder of the Government Contracts Program at George Washington University Law School and Professor Emeritus.

Contract Appeals Decisions. Riverwoods, IL: Wolters Kluwer Law & Business (CCH Inc.), 1965-date. 1vol. Also available on the Internet.
Cost: Print: $2,825 per year; Internet: similar in cost, but inquire (2014).
Tracking down decisions of the various federal Boards of Contract Appeals can be a bewildering task for the busy practitioner. This product assembles full-text decisions of the Board of Contract Appeals for the ASBCA, GSBCA, ENG, BCA, AGBCA, HUD BCA, IBCA, LBCA, DOT BCA, EBCA, NASA BCA, PSBCA and VABCA. going back to 1956. The product also includes a citator which allows the researcher to determine if a case has been subsequently cited or discussed.

Corbin, Arthur Linton. **Corbin on Contracts: A Comprehensive Treatise on the Working Rules of Contract Law**. Revised edition. Charlottesville, VA: LexisNexis, 1993-date. 15 vols. Hardbound or eBook. Supplemented annually.
Cost: $1,720; supplementation: 1994: $91; 1995: $102; 1996: $113.50; 1997: $114; 1998: $130; 1999: $135; 2000: $255; 2001: $245; 2002: $169; 2003: $315; 2004: $367; 2005: $378; 2006: $390; 2007: $408; 2008: $458; 2009: $696; 2010: $725; 2011: $826; 2012: $884; 2013: $689; eBook: $1,720; renewal: 2013: $809.
A long-awaited revision of Corbin's classic treatise by Professor Joseph M. Perillo. A monumental achievement in the history of legal scholarship, Professor Corbin's magnum opus is a reflection of the author's view that the law is rooted in reality, not dogma and that the generalizations made in legal treatises must be based upon the reading and close analysis and reevaluation of the great mass of court decisions. The more than 90 chapters are organized into the following parts: formation of the contract; statute of frauds; interpretation--parol evidence--mistake; construction and legal operation of contract--conditions of legal duty; rights of third parties--assignment--joint and several contracts; breach of contracts--judicial remedies; discharge and impossibility; and illegal bargains. There is a separate volume containing Tables and Index. Original and revised volumes of the first edition were published between 1950 and 1962. The first volume of the Revised Edition, authored by Joseph M. Perillo, the Alpin J. Cameron Professor of Law, Fordham University School of Law, was published in 1993. The text is amply supported by the inclusion of numerous citations to, and digests of, relevant state and federal court decisions. Includes Library References to both **Corpus Juris Secundum** and the West Key Number Digests. Reasonable annual supplementation costs make the standing order a safe bet for the attorney concerned about costs. As a part of the merger between Thomson Professional Publishing and West Publishing Company in 1996, the Justice Department required West to divest itself of this and 50 other titles. Reed Elsevier acquired the entire package in January 1997 and assigned it to LexisNexis.

Cost Saving Tip: Acquire the Desk edition (see Murray, below) as a cost-effective alternative and avoid the high initial and supplementation costs.

Farnsworth, E. Allen. **Contracts**. 4th ed. New York: Wolters Kluwer Law & Business, 2004. 1 vol. (940 pp.). No supplementation between editions.
Cost: Hardcover: $98; paperbound: $79 (2014).
This student textbook provides comprehensive coverage of all the topics and issues which are addressed in the typical first-year course in contract law. The volume represents a distillation of the author's more expansive three-volume practitioner-oriented treatise **Farnsworth on Contracts**.

Farnsworth, E. Allan. **Farnsworth on Contracts**. 3d ed. New York: Wolters Kluwer Law & Business, 2004-date. 3 vols. Periodic supplementation.
Cost: $845; supplementation: 2005-2007: 0; 2008: $224; 2009: $249; 2010: $266; 2011: $295; 2012: $710; 2013: $698; 2d ed.: 1993: $69.50; 1994: $125; 1995: $137.50; 1996: $145; 1998: $151; 1999: $165; 2000: $140; 2001: 0; 2002: $150; 2003: $185; 2004: new edition.
This three-volume treatise is an expansion of the author's one-volume textbook and is an outgrowth of his work as a Reporter for the **Restatement 2d of Contracts.** As a professor of contract law at Columbia University School of Law, Allan Farnsworth has expanded upon his textbook by adding sections of interest to the practitioner, expanding other sections, and by providing additional footnotes to cases, statutes and secondary sources. Chapter coverage includes a useful introduction which summarizes the general scope of contract law, and chapters on enforceability of promises, scope and effect of promises, rights of third parties and enforcement of promises. The author also relates contractual law to the **Uniform Commercial Code**. The author's clear prose style is matched by a well-organized presentation which can satisfy both the student and the experienced practitioner. Volume three also includes a biographical appendix, Table of Cases, Table of Uniform Commercial Code Sections, a Table of Restatements of the Law, Table of Authorities, and Index. An ideal mid-sized treatise for the practitioner who wants more than a Hornbook, but less than a multi-volume treatise like **Corbin** or **Williston**.

Feldman, Robert A. and Raymond T. Nimmer. **Drafting Effective Contracts: A Practitioner's Guide**. 2d ed. New York: Wolters Kluwer Law & Business, 1999-date. 1 vol. (900 pp.). Looseleaf format.
Cost: $409; supplementation: 2000: 0; 2001: $115; 2002: $120; 2003: $178; 2004: $178; 2005: $187; 2006: $199; 2007: $212; 2008: $227; 2009: $249; 2010: $272; 2011: $291; 2012: $305; 2013: $349.
This is less a book of sample forms than an entire form drafting reference guide with principles which can be used to draft a variety of contracts. The authors begin with a comprehensive and practical review of the contract process, from initial client interview to closing the deal. This is followed by a discussion of the 11 drafting elements essential to every contract: parties, recitals, subject, consideration, warranties and representations, risk allocation, conditions, performance, dates and term, boilerplate, and signatures, each of which is covered in detail in the Structural Analysis chapters that follow. This edition incorporates the significant legal developments over the last decade which have impacted contract drafting, including the new Article Nine of the **Uniform Commercial Code** and judicial interpretations of various contract provisions. Robert Feldman is Deputy General Counsel for Computer Sciences Corporation and a practitioner with over 30 years experience handling transactions both large

and small. Raymond Nimmer is the Leonard Childs Professor of Law at the University of Houston Law Center and counsel to the firm of Weil, Gotshal & Manges. He is currently the Reporter to the Drafting Committee on **Uniform Commercial Code** Article 2B-Licenses and the author of over ten books, including **The Law of Computer Technology and Information Law**.

Feldman, Steven W. **Government Contract Awards: Negotiation & Sealed Bidding.** St. Paul, MN: West (Clark Boardman Callaghan), 1994-date. 3 vols. Recently converted to annual replacement volumes.
Cost: 2013-2014 ed.: $855; supplementation: 1996: $125; 1997: $131.25; 1998: $189.50; 1999: $150.50; 2000: $162.50; 2001: $188.50; 2002: $235; 2003: $252; 2004: $282; 2005: $282; 2006: $314.50; 2007: $350; 2008: $390.50; 2009: $448; 2010: $496.50; 2011 (1st annual replacement): $660; **Monthly Assured Print Pricing (APP):** $71/$852.
A well-organized and readable exposition of the law governing government contract awards. Topics covered include presolicitation rules and activities, solicitation processes, evaluation processes, award processes, special categories of negotiated acquisition, and sealed bidding essentials. Primary attention is devoted to the procurement processes contained in the Federal Acquisition Regulation (FAR) and to the protests, particularly of negotiated contracts, brought before the General Accounting Office (GAO), the General Services Administration Board of Contract Appeals (GSBCA), the federal district courts, and the United States Court of Claims. While this set provides more than adequate citations to primary authority, it lacks the extensive primary source material and extensive cross-references contained in the West's **Government Contracts**.

Filipp, Mark R. **Covenants Not To Compete**. 3d ed. New York: Wolters Kluwer Law & Business, 2005-date. 2 vols. (880 pp.). Annual supplementation.
Cost: $489; supplementation: 2006: $169; 2007: $179; 2008: $189; 2009: $199; 2010: $215; 2011: $239; 2012: $255; 2013: $285; 2d ed.: 1998: $103; 1999: $96; 2000: $96; 2001: $105; 2002: $145; 2004: $151; 2005: new ed.
Protecting trade secrets and other sensitive information from competitors is a growing concern to employers. Drafting well-tailored non-competition agreements is essential in order to avoid potential litigation or to ensure success in the event litigation results. This two-volume work combines a discussion of the basic theories governing employment law and non-competition agreements with practical guidance on the drafting of such agreements. The author also discusses various pre-litigation and litigation concerns and includes sample employment agreements and litigation forms. Volume two includes a state case digest and various American Arbitration Association rules and procedures.

Cost Saving Tip: Since the most valuable portions of this work are contained in volume one, the cost-conscious attorney may wish to forego purchasing volume two, particular if he or she owns the arbitration rules in other forms and has access to state case law. Dropping the standing order for supplementation will provide an additional $250+ savings per year.

Government Contract Law: The Deskbook for Procurement Professionals. 3d ed. Chicago: American Bar Association, Section of Public Contract Law, 1999. 1 vol. (473 pp.). Paperbound.
Cost: $99.95 ($94.95 to Section members); from $99.95 on amazon.com (2014).
The basis for this volume is the government contracts text developed by the Contract Law Department at the Judge Advocate General's School of the U.S. Army in Charlottesville, VA which is recognized as a standard reference in government, industry and academia. The individual chapters are in outline form and have been developed and updated by the government contracts law instructors who incorporate the content of new statutes, regulations and court decisions. The chapters include an overview of the contract attorneys' course (CAC), contract law research materials, authority to contract, types of contracts, competition, sealed bidding, socioeconomic policies, negotiations, simplified and commercial item acquisitions, government information practices, bid protests, ethics in government contracting, construction contracting, funding and fund limitations, contract changes, selected labor standards, pricing of contract adjustments, procurement fraud, contracting for services, and more. This second edition incorporates the Federal Acquisition Regulations implementation of the Federal Acquisition Streamlining Act of 1994, changes enacted in the Federal Acquisition Reform Act, the Administrative Dispute Resolution Act of 1996, and the re-write of FAR Part 15. The volume contains extensive citations to cases, statutes and federal regulations.

Government Contracts Reporter [Internet]. Riverwoods, IL: Wolters Kluwer Law & Business (CCH Inc.), 2003-date. onthly; Internet updated weekly. Includes toll-free support.
Cost: No print; Internet: approx. $5,123 per yr., but inquire (2014).
This exhaustive compilation of full text federal procurement laws and regulations, including current Federal Acquisition Regulation (FAR) and its supplements. also contains detailed analyses of 35,000 court and agency decisions. The print version was eliminated from the CCH product line in1998.

Hunter, Howard O. **Modern Law of Contracts.** St. Paul, MN: West, 1993-date. 2 vols. Paperbound. Replaced annually.
Cost: 2014 Edition: $550; ProView eBook: $504; supplementation: 1994: $128; 1995: $132; 1996: $146; 1997: $154; 1998: $160.50; 1999: $188.50; 2000: $108; 2001: $128; 2002: $150; 2003: $171; 2004: $192; 2005: $220; 2006: $338.50; 2007: $300; 2008: $238; 2009: $265; 2010: $289; 2011: $319. **Monthly Assured Print Price (APP):** $42/$504.
A one-volume comprehensive practitioner's treatise on contractual law. In addition to the standard topical coverage, Part V analyzes the specific application to employment relationships and the Convention on the International Sale of Goods. Includes a Cumulative Table of Cases and Index. The author writes in a clear and easily understandable style. Includes numerous citations to relevant primary authority. The title was transferred from Warren, Gorham & Lamont to West in August, 1997.

Cost Saving Tips: Consider dropping the standing order and being placed on a prior notification basis for supplementation. Since the volumes are cumulative, you can simply order one whenever you believe your set should be updated. In the meantime, the base text will satisfy most of your needs and you can update relevant authorities in the primary sources and Shepardize. Don't make the mistake of maintaining the standing order if the volume is not used. For example, the five-year cost of updating this two-volume work will probably exceed $2,500 given the likely increases in the cost of the annual replacement volumes; and a comparable amount if the **APP** is selected.

Keyes, W. Noel. **Government Contracts in a Nutshell.** 5th ed. St. Paul, MN: West, 2011. 1 vol. (557 pp.)Available from West Academic.

Cost: $41; from $20.49 on amazon.com; kindle: $21.62 (2014)

A volume in the West "Nutshell" series, this work is intended as an aid to lawyers and contract administrators in the business world who deal with government and those in government who deal with private industry. While brief, it does offer critical commentary on those courts and boards which do not follow the law. It treats the Federal Acquisition Regulation (FAR) System, acquisition planning, contracting methods and contract types, general contracting requirements, special categories of contracting, contract management, and clauses and forms. Includes a table of cases and subject index.

Malsberger, Brian M. **Covenants Not To Compete: A State-By-State Survey**. 9th ed. Washington, DC: Bloomberg BNA Books, 2013-date. 3 vols. (6,000 pp.). Periodic supplementation.

Cost: $705; no supplementation to date; 7th ed.: 2011: $225; 6th ed.: 2009: $215; 5th ed.: 2007: $185; 4th ed.: 2005: $175; 3d ed.: 2003: $215; 2d ed.: 1997: $135; 1998: $215; 1999: $215; 2000: $245; 2001: $255.

Protecting company interests and information from use by competitors or potential competitors is a serious concern for many businesses. This resource is designed to assist attorneys representing employers with drafting, counseling, and litigating restrictive covenants, otherwise known as covenants not to compete. Organized alphabetically by state, it addresses 150 important legal issues, including state statutes governing enforceability of such covenants, employer's protectable interests, proof of existence of a covenant, courts' power to modify a covenant, obtaining a preliminary injunction, establishing irreparable harm, the standard of review on appeal, enforceability after firing, damages recoverable by an employer, liquidated damages clauses, applicable choice of law rules, and many more. Each state entry also provides a list of relevant law review articles and appellate decisions. A particularly valuable resource for the attorney with clients having multi-state operations.

McKenna Long Aldridge LLP and Ronald A. Kienlen. **Government Contract Disputes**. Eagan, MN: Thomson Reuters West, 2010. 1 vol. (517+ pp.).

Cost: $225; supplementation: 2011: $45; 2012: $37; 2013: $32.

From formation through administration, contracting with the federal government is a highly regulated process. Unlike commercial contracting, which is governed generally by the Uniform Commercial Code and the common law, federal government contracting is governed by a maze of statutes and regulations. Claims and disputes that arise under federal government contracts may take many forms, including claims asserted under the Contract Disputes Act of 1978 (CDA), as amended, implemented through the Federal Acquisition Regulations (FAR), and resolved by the boards of contract appeals, U.S. Federal Court of Federal Claims (COFC), or the U.S. Court of Appeals for the Federal Circuit. This volume examines the various venues and procedures through which federal contract claims and disputes are resolved, with special attention to those under the Contract Disputes Act of 1978. Following a brief summary of federal claims and disputes in Part I, Part II reviews the coverage of the Contract Disputes Act, claims process and procedures, and the contracting officer's final decisions and appeal prerequisites. Part III examines the various dispute resolution forums, including the Board of Contract Appeals, the U.S. Court of Federal Claims, the U.S. Court of Appeals for the Federal Circuit, the Federal Aviation Administration Office of Dispute Resolution for Acquisitions, and payment and interest. Additional parts examine actions affecting jurisdiction, other avenues of relief and forums in contract cases, alternative dispute resolution, subcontractor disputes, and other remedies. There is also discussion of the Freedom of Information Act (FOIA), equal access to justice, government and contractor tort liability, criminal liabilities, and suspension and disbarment. The Appendices include a table of abbreviations, table of laws and rules, table of cases and index. The text is heavily annotated with citations to statutes, rules, and administrative and federal court decisions. Each chapter is prefaced by research references, including appropriate Westlaw databases, ALR citations, treatises and practice aids, trial strategy citations, and law reviews and other periodicals. The book was written by members of the law firm of McKenna Long Aldridge LLP and Ronald A. Kienlen, a retired member of the Armed Services Board of Contract Appeals.

Murray, John E., Jr. **Corbin on Contracts**. Desk Edition. Newark, NJ: LexisNexis, 2013. 1 vol. (various pagings). Paperbound or eBook.

Cost: 2013 Edition: $371; 2012 Edition: $349.00; eBook: $379 (2014).

A chapter-by-chapter summary of the key legal concepts and principles laid out in the 89 chapters of the multi-volume treatise **Corbin on Contracts**. The author of this volume has made no effort to emulate the style or language of the original, except for those phrases or statements that have become standard language in contract law. Rather, he presents a largely original text that tracks the topics in the original. The text includes numerous "Practice Resource" references to the applicable sections of the multi-volume Corbin treatise where the reader can find more in-depth treatment of the subject matter. Citations to applicable cases and statutes are selective, rather than exhaustive. The author is University Chancellor and Professor of Law at Duquesne University School of Law. This is an ideal alternative for the cost-conscious attorney who wishes to have immediate access to the key legal concepts of contract law without the expense associated with the multi-volume treatise, which can be consulted in the nearest academic of public law library as necessary. See entry for **Corbin on Contracts** (above).

Nagle, James F. **How to Review a Federal Contract: Understanding and Researching Government Solicitations and Contracts**. 2d ed. Chicago: American Bar Association, 2000. 1 vol. (328 pp.). Paperbound.
Cost: OUT-OF-PRINT; from $89.00 on amazon.com (2014).
Intended as a primer for those new to Federal contracting, this volume can also serve as a useful review reference for the experienced practitioner. The author takes a step-by-step look at the federal contracting process and the statutes and decisions which govern it. He also explains how the Federal Acquisition Regulation system (FAR) operates, and where to go for interpretations and guidance. The bulk of the book examines the three most common types of contracting: supply and service contracting (where most federal dollars are spent), commercial contracting, and construction contracting. The appendices include with a variety of resources for understanding and preparing federal contracts, including standard sample forms used by the government in its contracts, and sample sections of contracts to illustrate how the federal government prepares and arranges its contracts. It also includes a glossary of government acronyms, listings of the GSA's Small Business Centers, the SBA's Procurement Center Representatives, and matrices for solicitations and contracts. The second edition also includes a listing of current Internet sites for further research. James Nagle is a partner in the Seattle firm of Oles Morrison Rinker & Baker. He has written four books on federal contracting and has received the Federal Bar Foundation Award for Distinguished Accomplishment in the Study of Procurement Law.

Nash & Cibinic eSeries. Riverwoods, IL: CCH, Inc., 2003-date. Online.
Cost: approx. $1,100 per year (2014).
This online service includes five of the most popular books from the George Washington University Law School's Government Contracts Program, including **Administration of Government Contracts**, Formation of Government Contracts, **Competitive Negotiation: The Source Selection Process, Acronyms and Abbreviations in Government Contracting,** and the **Government Contracts Reference Book: A Comprehensive Guide to the Language of Procurement, as well as** citations for more than 3,400 court, BCA and Comptroller General decisions.

Nash, Ralph C., Steven L. Schooner, and Karen R. O'Brien. **The Government Contracts Reference Book: A Comprehensive Guide to the Language of Procurement**. 4th ed. Washington, DC: George Washington University Law School, Government Contracts Program, 2013. 1 vol. (587 pp.). Available from CCH, Inc. Perfect bound.
Cost: 2013 Edition: $80 (hardcover); $65.00 (softcover) (2014).
An indispensable reference tool for those involved in government contracting, this volume provides an alphabetical listing of definitions of more than 1,400 terms, phrases, and acronyms used in all stages of the contracting process. It includes both general and agency-specific terms used in such agencies as the Department of Defense, General Services Administration, and the Department of Energy. It also includes valuable cross-references to **Formation of Government Contracts** and **Administration of Government Contracts** by John Cibinic and Ralph C. Nash. These three volumes form the basis of any complete government contracting library.

Rohwer, Claude D. and Anthony M. Skrocki. **Contracts in a Nutshell.** 7th ed. St. Paul, MN: West, 2010. 1 vol. (577 pp.). Available from West Academic.
Cost: $41; from $16.99 on amazon.com (2014).
A succinct overview of contract law intended for the law student, but also useful for the practitioner. Covers such topics as forming contracts, restitution, statute of frauds, contract interpretation, modification, remedies, performance, and third-party beneficiaries.

Stim, Richard. **Contracts: The Essential Business Desk Reference**. Berkeley, CA: Nolo. 2010. 1 vol. (475 pp.). Paperbound.
Cost: $39.99; from $23.43 on amazon.com (2014).
Legal and binding contracts are a pervasive feature of life in a modern society, involving everything from purchase of a home or business to the simple act of using a toll bridge. A contract is an agreement entered into voluntarily by two parties or more with the intention of creating a legal obligation. Although most contracts are in writing, they may also be made orally. The primary aims of this book are to explain how to write a contract or contract provision, how to comprehend particular contract provisions, and how to ensure that you can enforce business contracts at a later date. The core content of this volume is a dictionary of more than 300 contractual terms. The definitions are enhanced by the inclusion of common negotiation strategies, sample contract provisions, sample contracts with explanations, explanations of electronic contracts, tips for amending and modifying contracts, and a discussion of what to expect when contracts are broken. Like all Nolo titles, this volume is noteworthy for its clarity and avoidance of legalese. While directed primarily at small business owners, it is also an invaluable reference for anyone whose business or life requires an understanding of legally enforceable agreements. Richard Stim is a San Francisco-based practitioner who specializes in small business and intellectual property issues. He has written numerous books for Nolo, particularly in areas of intellectual property.

Williston, Samuel. **A Treatise on the Law of Contracts.** 4th ed. by Richard A. Lord. St. Paul, MN: West (Lawyers Cooperative Publishing Co.), 1990-date. 41 vols. (including five forms vols.)
Cost: $4,606; supplementation: 1994: $40.00; 1995: $50 (excluding new volumes); 1994: $315; 1995: $315; 1996: $147.50; 1997: $370; 1998: $164.50; 1999: $494.50; 2000: $771.50; 2001: $1,108; 2002: $345; 2003: $1,075; 2004: $1,480.50; 2005: $545; 2006: $607.50; 2007: $1,438; 2008: $1,603; 2009: $1,833; 2010: $2,017.50; 2011: $2,203; 2012: $2,600; 2013: $3,082; **Monthly Assured Print Price (APP):** $326/$3,912.
A classic treatment of contract law originally authored by Samuel Williston, the Dane Professor of Law, Harvard Law School and updated by Walter Jaeger, currently Professor Law at ITT Chicago-Kent College of Law. The 4th edition was prepared by Professor Richard A. Lord, Professor of Law, Campbell University School of Law. It provides complete coverage of the full range of contract related issues, including informal contracts, offers, acceptance, consideration, capacity of parties, married women, corporations and others, contracts of agents and fiduciaries, contracts for the benefit of third parties, contracts for the sale of goods, the parole evidence rule, usage and custom, express

conditions, nonperformance, negotiable instruments, breach, specific performance and other equitable remedies, fraud and misrepresentation, mistake, duress, release, and much more. Set includes tables and index volumes and five volumes of forms. Professor Lord's stated intent in preparing this 4th edition is to report, analyze and synthesize the approaches to contract law as reflected in judicial decisions, while integrating provisions of the **Uniform Commercial Code** and **Restatement (Second) of Contracts** which have had a significant impact upon contract law. While there has been a proliferation of treatises in specialized areas of contract law, the author's intention is to produce a work which remains comprehensive in its scope.

Cost-saving Tip: High supplementation costs makes this a poor choice unless acquired as part of a WestlawNext package. **Couch on Insurance** on WestlawNext is priced at only $1,728 per year, or about half the cost of Williston.

Yorio, Edward and Steve Thel. **Contract Enforcement: Specific Performance and Injunctions.** 2d ed. New York: Wolters Kluwer Law & Business (Aspen), 2011-date. 1 vol. (602 pp.). Annual supplemention.
Cost: $339; supplementation: 2012: $160; 2013: $171; 1st ed.: 1993: $55; 1994: $75; 1995: $80; 1996: $85; 1997: $88; 1998: $97; 1999: $104; 2000: $112; 2001: $118; 2002: $125; 2003: $143; 2004: $175; 2005: $180; 2006: $189; 2007: $201; 2008: $216; 2009: $236; 2010: $253; 2011: new ed.
This is the first book on the law of specific performance since the publication of the third edition of Pomeroy's **A Treatise on the Specific Performance of Contracts** in 1926. The text covers general principles of equitable relief, including various types of contract remedies, the relationship between legal and equitable relief, a survey of particular contracts, agreed remedies, procedure, and theory and comparative law. The particular contracts analyzed include those covering real estate, sale of goods, intangible personalty, construction contracts, employment contracts, service contracts, covenants not to compete, exclusive dealing contracts, contracts to pay money, and wills and other property settlements. Appendices includes a table of cases, **Restatement (Second) of Contracts** provisions, **UCC** provisions, and a subject index. Text is adequately buttressed with footnotes to primary sources.

Additional titles in the field of Contract Law are available from the following publishers: AMACOM, Wolters Kluwer Law & Business, Matthew Bender & Co., Casenotes Publishing Co., CCH, Inc., Gaunt, Kluwer Academic, LexisNexis, Lloyd's of London Press, National Contract Management, NYU Press, Oxford University Press, Panel Publishers, Practising Law Institute, Prentice-Hall, Thomson Reuters West, Warren, Gorham & Lamont, West Academic. See Appendix B for addresses and telephone numbers.

Copyright Law

Clarida, Robert W. **Copyright Law Deskbook**. Arlington, VA: BNA Books, 2009. 1 vol. with Case Digest CD-ROM and 2012 Cumulative Supplement.
Cost: $505; supplementation: 2012: $210; 2013: $215.
This impressive reference work aims to describe the law of copyright as it has been applied by the courts in a variety of specific factual circumstances. Accordingly, each chapter or sub-chapter begins with a description of applicable sections(s) of the copyright law and follows this with a discussion of the cases in order of greatest interest to the practitioner. It aims to summarize the applicable standard and then consider whether that standard has or has not been satisfied. Chapter one on Jurisdiction and Procedure, for example, examines subject matter jurisdiction, personal jurisdiction, standing, pleadings, jury trial, and declaratory judgment, and the manner in which the courts have ruled in each area. Subsequent chapters cover the issues of copyrightability, ownership, formalities, infringement, fair use, other disputes, remedies, preemption, the Digital Millennium Copyright Act, international issues, and tax, insurance, antitrust and bankruptcy. As the author himself describes it, the result is not so much a treatise or hornbook, but a professional reference that seeks to be useful to the practitioner rather than monumental. In other words, his aim is to describe the law as it is instead of what it ought to be. Indeed, it is the clarity of expression in discussing the applicable cases that the practitioner will find most valuable. The companion CD-ROM provides a 2009 cumulative Case Digest of decisions form 1993-2008. A graduate of Columbia University Law School, the author is member of the New York firm of Reitler, Kailas & Rosenblatt LLC. He is widely recognized for his wide-ranging expertise in the field of intellectual property law.

Decherney, Peter. **Hollywood's Copyright Wars: From Edison to the Internet**. New York; Columbia University Press 2013. 1 vol. (287 pp.). Paperbound.
Cost: $26.00; from $15.00 on amazon.com; kindle: $18.35 (2014).
To fully understand the Hollywood film industry, one must grasp the legal context in which films are created, disseminated, and protected from piracy and violation of copyright, particularly in a universe of expanding media producers, amateur video makers, file sharers, and Internet entrepreneurs. And while legal historians often limit themselves to analyses of landmark court decisions and major policy developments, Hollywood's studio heads and filmmakers have turned to various forms of self-regulation to resolve issues of intellectual property, including the involvement of Hollywood's talent guilds to arbitrate disputes over authorship. In this lively and entertaining book, Peter Decherney examines regulation as one of the most important drivers of the film and television industries. That regulation may include court decisions, legislative enactments, or internal, self-regulating, company policies that constitute a means of sidestepping legal regulation. Indeed, much of Hollywood's engagement with the copyright laws has taken place outside of the courtroom or the legislative hall. Decherney traces the history of Hollywood's engagement with copyright and intellectual property issues from the silent era to the advent of the digital revolution, drawing upon many high profile legal disputes. The copyright wars that have ensued have consistently pitted incumbent owners of copyrighted material against pirates pushing the bounds of art and technology. Yet, ironically, recorded music, radio and cable television exist today because the copyright laws have changed or evolved to permit

practices once considered piracy. This phenomenon reflects the manner in which the copyright laws attempt to balance the interests of copyright holders and users. This book will be of interest to anyone with an interest in copyright issues involving the film and television industries and the types of legal disputes that have arisen therein. The author is a professor of cinema studies and English at the University of Pennsylvania and the author of **Hollywood and the Culture Elite: How the Movies Became American**.

Gassaway, Laura N. **Copyright Questions and Answers for Information Professionals: From the Columns of *Against the Grain***. West Lafayette, IN: Purdue University Press, 2013. 1 vol. (284 pp.). Paperbound.

Cost: $24.95; from $11.39 on amazon.com; kindle: $8.69 (2014).

This engaging and highly readable volume reproduces, and updates, the author's "Copyright Questions and Answers" column appearing over a 15-year period in *Against the Grain*, the leading periodical for acquisitions librarians. These responses to librarians' questions on copyright issues have been grouped under logical chapters, each of which is prefaced by a short introductory essay on the subject. These 336 questions are those that have been posed by librarians, publishers, college faculty, K-12 teachers, and authors, whether at the author's copyright seminars, or via telephone or e-mail, and address those issues most commonly asked by such professionals. These chapters include Copyright Basics; Copies for Users; Library Reserves; Permissions and Licensing; Performance and Display: Libraries and Other Organizations; Performance and Display: Nonprofit Educational Institutions; Audiovisual Works; Sound Recordings and Software; Photographs and Graphics; the Internet and the Web; Interlibrary Loan and Document Delivery; Preservation and Archiving; Digitization; and Miscellaneous Issues. An epilogue explores Emerging Challenges in Copyright. The Appendix includes a useful chart for determining When U.S. Works Pass into the Public Domain. This book should be kept within easy reach on the desk of every librarian or information professional and available in every library or educational institution. Laura Gassaway is the Paul B. Eaton Distinguished Professor of Law at the University of North Carolina, a nationally known authority on copyright law, frequent speaker at copyright seminars and professional conferences, consultant to libraries and educational institutions, and the only librarian serving on the Board of Directors of the Copyright Clearance Center.

Goldstein, Paul. **Goldstein on Copyright.** 3d ed. New York: Wolters Kluwer Law & Business, 2005-date. 4 vols. (3,425 pp.). Looseleaf format. Annual updates.

Cost: $985; supplementation: 2006: $395; 2007: $421; 2008: $451; 2009: $483; 2010: $516; 2011: $550; 2012: $1,180; 2013: $631; 2d ed,: 1997: $225; 1998: $238; 1999: $265; 2000: $325; 2001: $310; 2002: $326; 2003: $395; 2004: $395; 2005: new edition.

Paul Goldstein, the Stella W. and Ira S. Lillick Professor of Law at Stanford University School of Law, has written a detailed and scholarly treatise for lawyers, judges, legal researchers and public policymakers. Its discussion and analysis of copyright doctrine under the 1976 Copyright Act is accompanied by a consideration of such related issues as contract protection for ideas, unfair competition, trade secrets and the right of publicity. It also treats the courts' role in shaping copyright law, particularly as it involves such unresolved questions as what constitutes original authorship qualifying for protection, where should the line be drawn between a work's unprotectible ideas and its protectible expression, and what constitutes infringement? He also examines the role of the Copyright Office which shapes the law by providing advice to Congress and to the many artists, writers and composers who seek protection for their works.

The set's 13 chapters address the topography of copyright; subject matter; publication and formalities, title, term and termination of transfers; exclusive rights in copyrighted works; contributory infringement and vicarious liability, the elements of infringement; infringement of rights in literary, visual, musical, factual and functional works; legal and equitable defenses; fair use; injunctions, ancillary and declaratory relief, criminal proceedings; monetary awards; jurisdiction, venue, etc. The Appendices include relevant statutes, legislative reports and regulations, copyright conventions, and form. There are also a tables of cases and statutes and an index. There are extensive citations to primary and secondary authorities, including cases, statutes, regulations, legislative history documents, and books and articles. An excellent and well-written work which can be used with equal utility by the novice as well as the specialist. Originally published by Little, Brown, this title was purchased in 1996 by Wolters Kluwer and merged with the Aspen product line (now Wolters Kluwer Law & Business). The Internet verson, which contains every case, statute, and point of legal analysis cited in the body of the text, has now been transferred to sister company, CCH.

Hawes, James E. **Copyright Registration Practice**. 2d ed. St. Paul, MN: Thomson Reuters West, 1999-date. 1 vol. Looseleaf format. Annual supplementation.

Cost: $1,233; supplementation: 2002: $296; 2003: $313; 2004: $351; 2005: $384; 2006: $430; 2007: $479; 2008: $533; 2009: $597; 2010: $657; 2011: $761; 2012: $415; 2013: $904; **Monthly Assured Print Price (APP):** $90/$1,080.

A comprehensive guide to the copyright registration process as it applies to various forms of intellectual property. The author discusses what is copyrightable matter and provides an introduction to the copyright office and the copyright application in general. Other topics addressed include title and author considerations, creation and publication considerations, copyright claimant considerations, previous registration considerations, derivative works and compilation considerations, manufacturing considerations, nondramatic literary work applications, visual arts applications, computer related applications, the copyright registration, renewal of copyright registrations, copyright notice requirements, deposit requirements, rights secured by copyright, assignment and licensing of copyrights, and accessing copyright office records. The author, a practicing attorney and former Examiner in the U.S. Patent and Trademark Office, has wide ranging experience in the field of intellectual property and is the author of four treatises in the field of intellectual property.

Heller, James S., Paul Hellyer, and Benjamin J. Keele. **The Librarian's Copyright Companion**. 2d ed. Buffalo, N.Y.:

William S. Hein & Co., 2012. 1 vol. (324 pp.).
Cost: $49 (2014).
Now in a second, expanded edition, this manual provides a practical overview of the general principles governing copyright law and their application to the library environment. Following an introduction to U.S. Copyright law and applicable international treaties, the authors provide an in-depth discussion and analysis of the law's provisions most applicable to the library environment, including restrictions on the use of copyrighted materials (Sec. 106); liability for infringement (Sec. 504 and 507); fair use (Sec. 107); the library exemption (Sec. 108); the public performance exemption (Sec. 110), and digital information and software (Sec. 117), as well as a discussion of the use of print, digital, and audiovisual works. The analysis extends to the court decisions which have interpreted the 1976 Copyright Act and its amendments. The author is Professor of Law and Director of the Law Library at the Marshall-Wythe School of Law at the College of William & Mary and a past-president of the American Association of Law Libraries. His co-authors are reference librarians, also at Willliam & Mary.

Keller, Bruce, and Jefrey P. Cunard. **Copyright Law: A Practitioner's Guide**. 5th ed. New York: Practising Law Institute, 2004-date. 1 vol. (697 pp.). Looseleaf format. Updated annually.
Cost: $295; supplementation: 2005: $198; 2006: $101; 2007: $111; 2008: 0; 2009: $155; 2010: $158; 2011: $175; 2012-2013: 0; 4th ed.: 2003: $90; 2004: $180.
This volume provides coverage of the fundamental tenets of copyright law in both the real and virtual realms. The authors address the constitutional and statutory bases of copyright law, what qualifies for protection, the ownership and transfer of copyright, exclusive rights, deposit, registration and recordation, publication and notice, duration and renewal, the fair use doctrine, specific limits on a copyright owner's exclusive rights, clearing rights, infringement, remedies, the Copyright Office, and copyright in the digital age. They also provide firsthand analysis of several leading copyright cases. The volume also includes checklists, practice tips, and pointers for both plaintiff and defendant. The authors are members of the Washington, DC firm of Debevoise & Plimpton. This volume replaces PLI's earlier offering in the field, **Henn on Copyright Law** (1991).

Leaffer, Marshall. **Understanding Copyright Law**. 5th ed. New York: Matthew Bender & Co., 2010. 1 vol. (500 pp.); no supplementation between new editions.
Cost: $45; eBook: $36 (2014).
This comprehensive student treatise on copyright law is approached from institutional, economic, and historical perspectives. The Copyright Act of 1976 is the point of departure for an analysis of the relevant case law and statutory developments, including factual works, works made for hire, renewal rights, parody as fair use, and the protection of computer software.

Lipinski, Tomas A. **The Complete Copyright Liability Handbook for Librarians and Educators**. New York: Neal-Schumann Publishers, 2006. 1 vol. (413 pp.). Paperbound.
Cost: $130; from $1.00 on amazon.com (2014).
This detailed overview of copyright issues is designed to provide librarians and educators with the background necessary to understand their responsibilities under the law and the potential liabilities for non-compliance, liabilities that have increased dramatically with the digital revolution. While both individuals and institutions can benefit from the copyright law's specific use provisions, they are correspondingly obliged to comply with the full scope of the law. By erecting a proper environment of copyright compliance, librarians and other institutions are more likely to avoid violating the rights of copyright holders and running the risks of legal action. The author addresses the three types of copyright liability: direct copyright infringement, contributory infringement, and vicarious infringement. He also explains the penalties and immunities in copyright law for schools and libraries, including potential damages and their limitation, how to obtain immunity, and the Section 512 Safe Harbor. In Parts 3 and 4, he considers the Digital Millennium Copyright Act and its impact on library and educational environments; and ways in which schools and libraries can limit their legal exposure. The volume also contains a number is useful appendices, including a copyright compliance audit, an implementation checklist for Section 512 registered agents, and 16 sample copyright policy provisions. Prefatory materials include a glossary of essential terms used in the book. The text includes extensive citations to primary and secondary sources, including relevant cases, statutes, and Congressional documents. Tomas Lipinski received his law degree from Marquette University Law School and is currently co-director of the Center for Information Policy Research at the University of Wisconsin-Milwaukee. He is a frequent speaker on various topics related to copyright, information policy, free speech, and privacy rights.

Miller, Arthur and Michael H. Davis. **Intellectual Property: Patents,Trademarks, and Copyright in a Nutshell.** 5th ed. St. Paul, MN: West, 2012. 1 vol. Available from West Academic.
Cost: $41; from $24.10 on amazon.com; kindle: $20.84 (2014).
This brief, student-oriented text was authored by the famous Arthur Miller of Harvard Law School and Michael Davis, Associate Professor of Law at Cleveland State University's Cleveland-Marshall College of Law. Provides a succinct overview of all three fields with limited citations to relevant case law.

Nimmer, Melville and David Nimmer. **Nimmer on Copyright: A Treatise on the Law of Literary, Musical and Artistic Property, and the Protection of Ideas.** New York: Matthew Bender & Co., 1963-date. 10 vols. Looseleaf format, CD-ROM and eBook. Supplemented approximately twice a year. Authority CD-ROM version includes no-cost online updating via LexisNexis.
Cost: $3,087 (includes annual subscription); renewal: 1995: $600 (price frozen since 1992); 1996: $800; 1997: $800; 1998: $840; 1999: $880; 2000: 940; 2001: $1,006; 2002: $1,077; 2003: $1,131; 2004: $1,188; 2005: $1,188; 2006: $1,373; 2007: $1,483; 2008: $1,602; 2009: $1,730; 2010: $1,818; 2011: $1,909; 2012: $2,024; 2013: $2,166; 2014: $2,364; CD-ROM: $3,121; renewal: $840; 1999: $880; 2000: $940; 2001: $1,006; 2002: $1,077; 2003: $1,131; 2004: $1,188; 2005: $1,283; 2006: $1,373; 2007: $1,483; 2008: $1,616; 2009: $1,745; 2010: $1,833; 2011: $1,925; 2012: $2,041; 2013: $2,184; 2014: $2,431.68; eBook: $2,807; renewal: 2014: $2,364.

Originally authored by Melville Nimmer (1923-1985), late Professor of Law at UCLA, and carried on by his son David Nimmer, currently associated with the Los Angeles firm of Irell & Manella, this is considered to be the most authoritative work in the area of copyright law and the most heavily cited by the courts. The text is lucidly written and well documented throughout and employs a type face which is easy on the eye. The analysis encompasses the constitutional, statutory and common law aspects of copyright and applies these to transactions in various creative fields. The work embraces both the substantive and the procedural aspects of copyright including the application process, infringement actions, criminal actions, the enforcement and litigating of copyright claims, trial procedure and appeals. The set includes the full text of relevant laws, regulations, international conventions, and legislative reports, as well as applicable forms and jury instructions. The text is exhaustively documented with citations to primary and secondary authorities, including cases, statutes, and legislative history documents. Although originally written in 1963, the set was completely revised in 1978. This is a first-rate work of scholarship designed for the copyright and intellectual property specialist.

Cost Saving Tips: Allow the subscription to lapse after one year and repurchase it 2-3 years later. Find another medium for current developments. New set cost rose 21% in 2013.

Rosen, Ronald S. **Music and Copyright**. LexisNexis, 2013. 1 vol. (596 pp). Paperbound and kindle.
Cost: $219.00; amazon kindle: $175.20 (2014).
This is a scholarly and practical exposition of music infringement issues within the context of copyright law and litigation. Designed as a practical guide to the music infringement litigation process, it combines a through understanding of the various forms of musical expression with the advice from a seasoned litigator. Following a general discussion of copyright law and remedies for infringement, the author addresses the basic elements of musical language and ideas from a copyright perspective, infringement and the commencement of litigation, the importance of the expert, fair use, discovery, music and summary judgment, copyright and music in the courtroom, and music, copyright ad the impact of new technology. The author's analysis reflects a deep understanding of both the legal issues and musical content, as well as the judicial response to infringement cases in a variety of contexts, from forms of popular musical expression, including parody, to more serious forms of musical composition. This is an essential acquisition for any litigator involved in music infringement cases. Ronald Rosen is a partner with the Los Angeles firm of TroyGould where he specializes in entertainment, intellectual property, and commercial litigation. He is a leading expert in copyright litigation and other disputes involving such creative works as musical compositions, motion pictures, and television productions.

Stim, Richard. **Getting Permission: How to License & Clear Copyrighted Materials Online and Off**. 5th ed. Berkeley, CA: Nolo, 2013. 1 vol. (528 pp.). Paperbound.
Cost: $34.99; from $17.54 on amazon.com; kindle: $19.24 (2014).
The use of copyrighted creative material may require getting permission from the copyright holder to avoid legal repercussions. Those who wish to use some or all of a play, poem, song, novel, work of nonfiction or other work covered by the copyright laws need to obtain legal permission prior to using that material in another work. This guide explains the processing of obtaining permission from the copyright holder, determining when material is in the public domain, how to determine who owns the copyright, the "fair use" rule, website permissions, and license and merchandise agreements. A companion CD-ROM containing licensing forms is included. Following an introduction to the permissions process, the author explains the process of getting permission to use text, photographs, artwork, music, and website materials. He also addresses academic and educational permissions, the public domain, fair use, permission to use trademarks, art and merchandise licenses, releases, and copyright research. Additional chapters cover what happens after permission is granted, assignments and works made for hire, and resources for additional assistance beyond this book. The text includes numerous examples, sample forms, and cautions, all of which combine to provide a lucid explanation of the permission process. The author is an intellectual property attorney, a legal editor at Nolo, and author of the permissions blog: Dear Rich: Nolo's Patent, Copyright & Trademark Blog

Additional titles in the field of Copyright Law are available from the following publishers: American Bar Association, Bloomberg BNA Books, Matthew Bender, CCH, Inc., Federal Bar Association, Foundation Press, Gordon Press, Greenwood Publishing Group, William S. Hein & Co., Inc., Law Arts, LexisNexis, Nolo Press, Panel Publishers, Practising Law Institute, Thomson Reuters West, Warren, Gorham & Lamont, West Academic. See Appendix B for addresses and telephone numbers.

Corporations

Adams, Edward S. **Corporate Counselor's Business Handbook**. New York: Wolters Kluwer Law & Business, 2011-date. 1 vol. (various pagings). Looseleaf format.
Cost: $299.00; supplementation: 2011: $199; 2012: $229; 2013: $265.
A basic understanding of accounting principles and practices is essential for any corporate counsel to understand the financial condition of the company he represents. Whether dealing with transactional or litigation matters, corporate counsel must have a familiarity with accounting and finance to perform his job effectively. This volume provides a basic grounding in accounting principles, annual reports and financial statements, cash flow analysis, core financial formulas and their application and relevance, capital structure policy, and a company's mixture of debt and equity. Among the issues addressed are the generally accepted accounting standards (GAAP) promulgated in large part by the private independent Financial Accounting Standards Board (FASB). Indeed, failure to observe these standards may expose a company to liability or loss of credit. Individual chapters are devoted to an overview of accounting and scope, three types of financial statements, fundamental principles, the balance sheet, the income statement, the statement of cash flows,

valuation, three example approaches to valuation, the corporate finance framework, corporate finance and the financial markets, valuing the corporation, Bank of America: a case study, and Dreamworks Animation: a case study. For illustrative purposes, the text also examines some of the leading cases in the news involving financial fraud and financial statement review, including Enron, MCI-Worldcom, Tyco, and Fannie Mae and Freddie Mac. The author, a graduate of the University of Chicago School of Law, holds the Howard E. Buhse endowed chair in finance and law at the University of Minnesota School of Law, and is an internationally recognized expert in accounting and corporate finance, corporate law, securities, commercial paper, bankruptcy and entrepreneurship.

American Bar Association. Committee on Corporate Laws, Section, of Business Law. **Corporate Director's GuideBook**. 6th ed. Chicago: American Bar Association, 2012. 1 vol. (118 pp.). Paperbound.
Cost: $64.95 ($49.95 to members); from $29.00 on amazon.com (2014).
Recent scandals involving such companies as Enron and WorldCom have caused considerable soul-searching among the nation's corporate directors who believe that CEO's, senior management, boards of directors, and audit committees should play a much greater role in ensuring good corporate governance and a higher ethical business culture. This succinct guide to the role of corporate directors and boards addresses these responsibilities in the new corporate environment in which higher ethical standards and government oversight have assumed greater importance. First published in 1978, the 5th edition in this post-Sarbanes-Oxley Act era focuses attention on greater and more effective board involvement in corporate decision-making, responsiveness to shareholder and the public, the importance of thorough understanding of the business, finances and major transactions presented to the board, legal and regulatory corporate compliance driving change in Boardroom dynamics, and compensation issues. An appendix lists corporate governance websites and includes concise quotes to assist in applying the GuideBook on a daily basis. The volume is a product of the ABA's Committee on Corporate Laws.

American Bar Association. **Legal Guide for Small Business**. 2d ed. New York: Random House Reference, 2010. 1 vol. (472 pp.). Paperbound.
Cost: $16.99; from $5.51 on amazon.com (2014).
This practical desktop guide to business formation and operations is designed to assist business owners and operators with a basic understanding of their legal rights and responsibilities and the pros and cons of various courses of action. The author addresses the basics of business formation, legal assistance, and operations, beginning with the choice of business organization and extending from employee and customer relations, contracts, intellectual property rights, taxes, and financial difficulties to the sale of the business, and retirement planning. Author Robert Sprague is an assistant professor at the University of Wyoming College of Business Department of Management & Marketing, where he teaches Law for Managers, Business Law for Entrepreneurs and Commercial Law courses. This is one in a series of ABA Guides published by Random House Reference.

American Law Institute. **Principles of Corporate Governance: Analysis and Recommendations**. Philadelphia: American Law Institute, 1994. 2 vols. (909 pp.).
Cost: $153 (hardbound); $39 (softbound); supplementation: 2008: $64.50; 2009: $68; 2010: $68; 2011: $68; 2012: $68; 2013: $78.
The American Law Institute's first comprehensive treatment of corporate law, this work describes and examines the duties and responsibilities of directors and officers of business corporations to both their corporations and shareholders. In preparation for more than 15 years by Reporters who are leading authorities in the field, it combines analysis of current legal requirements with recommendations for clarifications or changes in the law. Topics include the objective and conduct of the business corporation, the structure of the corporation, duty of care and the business judgment rule, the duty of fair dealing, the role of directors and shareholders in transactions in control and tender offers, and corporate remedies.

Baran, Jan Witold. **The Election Law Primer for Corporations**. 5th ed. Chicago: American Bar Association, Section of Business Law, 2008. 1 vol. (431 pp.).
Cost: $69.95 ($49.95 to members); from $43.00 on amazon.com (2014).
This volume lays out the basic principles of the federal campaign finance laws that regulate political activity by corporations executives, employees, and stockholders, as well as the related areas of lobbying, ethics, and taxation. Naturally, this edition was published prior to the Supreme Court's decision in *Citizens United v. Federal Election Commission*, that overruled two precedents: Austin v. Michigan Chamber of Commerce, a 1990 decision that upheld restrictions on corporate spending to support or oppose political candidates, and McConnell v. Federal Election Commission, a 2003 decision that upheld the part of the Bipartisan Campaign Reform Act of 2002 (McCain-Feingold) that restricted campaign spending by corporations and unions. The 2002 law banned the broadcast, cable or satellite transmission of "electioneering communications" paid for by corporations or labor unions from their general funds in the 30 days before a presidential primary and in the 60 days before the general elections. The Court argued that the First Amendment "prohibits Congress from fining or jailing citizens, or associations of citizens, for simply engaging in political speech." Among the subjects addressed by this volume are political action committees, corporate facilities for political purposes, political communications by a corporation, corporate relations with government officials, contributions by foreign corporations and their U.S. subsidiaries, state and local elections and soft money, tax considerations, and the Federal Election Commission and enforcement. Appendices include FEC Forms and Instructions, sample PAC articles of organization, federal contribution limits, lobbying forms and guidance, summary of state contribution limits for corporations, state campaign finance and ethics/lobbying web sites, IRS forms and information, and FEC Notices and Guidance Regarding PAC Administration. Author Jan Witold Baran is a partner with Wiley Rein, LLP in Washington, D.C.

Basri, Carole and Irving Kagan. **Corporate Legal Departments**. 4th ed. New York: Practising Law Institute, 2011-date. 1 vol.

(approx. 430 pp.). Looseleaf format. Annual supplementation.
Cost: $365; supplementation: 2012: $326; 2013: $340; 3d ed.: 1998: $60; 1999-2002: 0; 2003: $90; 2004: 0; 2005: $174; 2006: $101; 2007: $236; 2008: $248; 2009: $136; 2010: $152; 2011: new edition.
The practice of law in corporate America has become increasingly complex and demanding. The role of in-house counsel demands an intimate knowledge of corporate affairs and a variety of new skills. This volume takes an in-depth look at such issues as ethics in the corporate environment, possible conflicts of interest between officers and the corporation, the attorney-client privilege, malpractice, confidentiality, whistleblowing, internal investigations, corporate governance, recruitment of legal staff, the use of outsourcing and non-legal staff to boost productivity, time and cost accountability, use of outside counsel, and the use of such cutting-edge techniques as re-engineering and benchmarking. The volume includes hundreds of case studies and techniques for improving productivity. Carole Basri, formerly assistant general counsel at Maidenform, Inc. and now consultant to Deloitte & Touche and Executive Director of the Greater New York Chapter of the American Corporate Counsel Association, is an adjunct professor of law at NYU School of Law. Irving Kagan is a partner and counsel to Madison Partners, L.L.C., an investment and management consulting group based in New York City.

Block, Dennis J., Nancy E. Barton and Stephen A. Radin. **The Business Judgment Rule: Fiduciary Duties of Corporate Directors**. 6th ed. New York: Wolters Kluwer Law & Business, 2009-date. 4 vols. (6,112 pp.). Annual supplementation.
Cost: $785; supplementation: 2012: $450; 2013: 0; 3rd ed.: 2001: $170; 2002: $195; 2003-2009: 0.
Officers and directors of corporations have certain presumed duties and responsibilities to both their corporations and shareholders. This work addresses in detail the variety and extent of these responsibilities in the corporate environment. The authors explore such topics as the duties of care and loyalty, director protection statutes, interested director transactions, the corporate opportunity doctrine, director and officer compensation, controlling shareholder transactions, disclosure rules, wrongful coercion and preclusive conduct, duties of directors of financially troubled corporations, transactions including corporate control, merger of equals, defensive measures, poison pill shareholder rights plans, and the pre-litigation demand requirement in derivative litigation. This is a substantial scholarly contribution to the field with over 12,000 footnotes to relevant cases and statutes. Dennis Block is a senior partner in the New York firm of Cadwalader, Wickersham & Taft. Nancy E. Barton is a Senior Vice President and General Counsel at General Electric Capital Corporation in Stamford, CT. Stephen Radin is a member of the firm of Weil, Gotshal & Manges. All three have extensive experience as authors and speakers on the subjects of corporate governance, the business judgment rule, class and derivative litigation and related topics.

Block, Dennis J. and Michael A. Epstein, eds. **The Corporate Counsellor's Deskbook**. 5th ed. New York: Wolters Kluwer Law & Business, 1999-date. 1 vol. (1,600 pp.). Looseleaf format.
Cost: $489; supplementation: 2005: $145; 2006: $199; 2007: $226; 2008: $242; 2009: $269; 2010: $284; 2011: $498; 2012: $558; 2013: $577.
Designed as a desktop reference for the corporate practitioner, this valuable collection of materials addresses many key areas of corporate practice. Assembled under the editorship of two experienced corporate attorneys with major New York law firms, the chapters in this volume were prepared by more than 25 leading corporate attorneys. The subjects include: internal corporate investigations, indemnification and insurance of corporate officials, the corporation's obligation to protect against insider trading, counselling on intellectual property, noncompetition agreements, managing complex litigation, alternative dispute resolution, corporate law, employment law, executive compensation, bankruptcy law, the corporate counsellor and antitrust, import regulation, environmental law concerns, advances in law department technology, and more. The substantive discussion is illustrated with a variety of practical tools, including litigation projections, negotiation checklists, sample work plans, real estate checklists, company policies, and non-disclosure agreements.

Blumberg, Phillip I. et al. **Blumberg on Corporate Groups.** 2d ed. New York: Wolters Kluwer Law & Business, 2005-date. 5 vols. Annual supplementation.
Cost: $739; supplementation: 2006: $165; 2007: $175; 2008: $188; 2009: $208; 2010: $216; 2011: $230; 2012: $502; 2013: $560; supplementation to 7-vol. 1st edition: 2000: $878; 2001: $738; 2002: $835; 2003-2005: 0.
Traditional corporation law and piercing the veil doctrines no longer provide adequate guides to the law of parent and subsidiary corporations. In numerous areas of corporate law, courts and legislatures are allocating legal rights and liabilities according to modern enterprise principles. This is the second edition of Professor Blumberg's monumental treatise on the law of corporate groups and the relationship between parent, subsidiary, and affiliated companies. Now consolidated into a unified five-volume set, it replaces the seven volumes of the first edition with their confusing individual subtitles. Professor Blumberg provides detailed analysis of the federal and state statutory and common law that impacts parent and subsidiary corporations, franchisors and franchisees, licensors and licensees, health care institutions and medical staff, and other corporate entities. He also provides comprehensive coverage of the law as it is applied to either the whole multi-corporation enterprise or the individual corporate entity. Professor Blumberg's analysis draws upon thousands of cases and regulatory provisions to elucidate the new legal principles supporting these new enterprise principles.

Volume one provides an introduction to the law of corporate groups, piercing the veil theory, and jurisdiction, practice and procedure. Volume two addresses the application of the substantive common law to the areas of contracts, torts, property, conflicts of law, and bankruptcy. Volume three discusses the application of the general statutory law with specific attention to enterprise principles. Volume four addresses the topics or world trade and enterprise regulation. Volume five examines franchising and other relational law, including that involving successors, licensors, and subcontractors. It also includes a table of cases, table of statutes, and index. Phillip Blumberg is Dean and Professor of Law Emeritus at the University of Connecticut School of Law. Originally published by Little, Brown, this work was purchased in 1996 by Wolters Kluwer and merged into the with Aspen Publishing product line.

Brodsky, Edward and M. Patricia Adamski. **Law of Corporate Officers and Directors: Rights, Duties. and Liabilities**. St. Paul: Thomson Reuters West (Clark Boardman Callaghan), 1984-date. 1 vol. Annual replacement volumes.
Cost: 2012-2013 Edition: $760; supplementation: 1995: $106; 1996: $70; 1997: $117.60; 1998: $78; 1999: $131.50; 2000: $91; 2001: $161; 2002: $124.50; 2003: $214; 2004: $159; 2005: $205; 2006: $199; 2007 $319.50; 2008: $252.50; 2009: $123; 2010: $324; 2011: annual replacement volume:$602. **Monthly Assured Print Price (APP):** $63/$756.
Written for legal counsel to corporate officers and directors, this work provides a thorough discussion of the types of legal issues which should form the basis of thorough and effective counseling, including accountability to shareholders, duty of care, conflict of interest. sale of control, management opposition to tender offers and other shifts in control, corporate attorney-client privilege, shareholder derivative suits, and duties of directors of non-profit corporations. An effective tool for helping officers and directors avoid liability for their actions.

Brown, J. Robert, Jr. **The Regulation of Corporate Disclosure**. 3d ed. New York: Wolters Kluwer Law & Business, 1999-date. 1 vol. (750 pp.). Looseleaf format.
Cost: $699; supplementation: 2000: 0; 2001: $126; 2002: 0; 2003: $189; 2004: $343; 2005: $350; 2006: $358; 2007: $382; 2008: $410; 2009: $453; 2010: $490; 2011: $525; 2012: $558; 2013: $620.
Corporations are potentially liable for violations of both federal and state securities laws regarding corporate disclosures, which make take the form of speeches, press releases, letters to shareholders, or communications on the Web. This volume is designed to assist corporations, their directors, and legal counsel develop communications policies which will reduce legal exposure and further business objectives. The author begins with a discussion of the problem of excessive litigation and an overview of the regulatory environment. He follows this with a consideration of the duty to disclose, dissemination of corporate information, material facts, particular disclosure issues, sensitive disclosure periods, dealing with analysts, electronic communications, liability of officers and directors, state disclosure obligations, corporate communication policies, shareholder communications, the summary annual report, and communicating with beneficial owners. J. Robert Brown, Jr., Professor of Law at the University of Denver College of Law and a former legal counsel at the Securities and Exchange Commission, has written extensively on corporate security and disclosure issues.

Business Law Monographs. New York: Matthew Bender & Co., 1984-date. 36 vols. Looseleaf format. Updated quarterly. New monographs issued periodically.
Cost: $3,645 (full set); $103 per volume; annual supplementation: 1998: $855; 1999: $890; 2000: $950; 2001: $950; 2002: $1,017; 2003: $1,068; 2004: $1,121; 2005: $1,200; 2006: $1,284; 2007: $1,387; 2008: $1,498; 2009: $1,618; 2010: $1,699; 2011: $1,784; 2012: $1,927; 2013: $2,062; 2014: $2,250.
This collection of practice guides is designed specifically for corporate counsel and the general corporate attorney. The volumes in the set are grouped into nine Series, encompassing the practice areas of Antitrust, Corporate, Employment, General Business, Insurance, Intellectual Property, International, Litigation, and Securities. Each color-coded volume addresses a discretely focused subject area and is written by an experienced attorney in the field. A review of the law is accompanied by practice notes, checklists, forms, and primary sources.

Cavitch, Zolman. **Business Organizations with Tax Planning.** New York: Matthew Bender and Co., 1963-date. 16 vols. Looseleaf format and eBook.
Cost: $6,433 (includes annual subscription); annual renewal: 1995: $1,644 (price frozen since 1992); 1996: $1,725; 1997: $1,725; 1998: $ 1,810; 1999: $1,880; 2000: $2,010; 2001: $2,151; 2002: $2,151; 2003: $2,259; 2004: $2,372; 2005: $2,538; 2006: $2,640; 2007: $2,851; 2008: $3,065; 2009: $3,310; 2010: $3,399; 2011: $3,569; 2012: $3,747; 2013: $4,009; 2014: $4,375; eBook: $5,849; 2014: $4,275.
A complete and exhaustive treatise and practice guide to the law of business organizations. Contains full discussion and analysis of every aspect of corporate law with attention to relevant areas of federal taxation. Includes a discussion of federal corporate taxation, limited partnerships, antitrust law, securities law, employment discrimination, environmental law, bankruptcy, products liability, copyright, franchising, state taxation and federal contracting. Features citations to statutes and case law from all jurisdictions, as well as relevant law review articles and legal treatises. Written by Zolman Cavitch and the Matthew Bender editorial staff. Without question, this is a fist-rate work of scholarship loaded with numerous practice aids. Highly recommended.

Cost Saving Tips: Due to the high supplementation cost, drop the standing order after the year's subscription has expired. Buy another new set at some future date as your needs dictate. One strategy is to buy a new set every three years, i.e. have a current subscription for one year and allow it to lapse for two years. This will save you more than $8,700 in every three-year cycle.

Cohen, Adam I. **Social Media: Legal Risk and Corporate Policy**. New York: Wolters Kluwer Law & Business, 2013. 1 vol. (521 pp.). Paperbound.
Cost: $85.00; from $49.95 on amazon.com; kindle: $68 (2014).
The proliferation of social media channels and content have vastly expanded opportunities for corporate outreach and marketing. Yet, corporate policymakers, lawyers, judges and government regulatory agencies have only just begun to grapple with the practical business impacts and other legal risks posed by employee use of these forms of communication. Indeed, global social media postings raise the stakes and the potential for negative impacts on corporate activity. Social media has become fair game in litigation, raising evidentiary issues, false expectations of privacy, and raising issues of obtaining social media discovery from service providers. Information gleaned from social media sources may be used in cases involving employment, breach of contract, defamation, personal injury, intellectual property, false advertising, civil rights, taxation, and

other issues. This volume, which predicts a coming avalanche of social media-related litigation, seeks to reduce or mitigate the potential liabilities stemming from such activity by corporate employees. Based on an analysis of the social media cases that have already been litigated, it provides a rationale for a corporate social media compliance policy and the fundamental areas to be covered by such a policy if it wants to maximize what little control the corporation has over information shared by its employees. It includes a policy creation "toolkit" that organizes and provides sample provisions that can be used to build a social media policy. These sample provisions are classified by topic and represent the various ways corporations can communicate and document their policy on social media. It also examines class action litigation that has been filed against social media services regarding their use of personally identifiable information, and identifies the privacy policies provisions of five major social media service providers. It also provides a privacy policy comparison of Facebook, MySpace, Twitter, LinkedIn, and Google, and a taxonomy of social media service privacy policies. The appendices include a variety of state and federal legislative proposals addressing various social networking privacy and ethical concerns. Adam Cohen is an attorney, consultant, and professor whose principal focus is electronic discovery and information management. He is an adjunct professor at Fordham and Pace law schools.

Contemporary Corporation Forms. 2d ed. New York: Wolters Kluwer Law & Business, 1998-date. 5 vols. plus CD-ROM. Looseleaf format. Supplemented three times annually.
Cost: $1,749; supplementation: 1993: $145; 1994: $275; 1995: $234; 1996: $482; 1997: $320; 1998: $375; 1999: $368; 2000: $591; 2001: $625; 2002: $690; 2003: $285; 2004: $882; 2005: $900; 2006: $920; 2007: $990; 2008: $1,062; 2009: $1,137; 2010: $1,218; 2011: $1,302; 2012: $1,405; 2013: $1,524.
A collection of more than 500 corporate forms drawn from some of the country's leading law firms and keyed to the substantive text in the publisher's 8-volume **Corporation: A Service**. The forms are accompanied by text and commentary with valuable citations to applicable state statutes.

Corporate Director's GuideBook. 6th ed. Chicago: American Bar Association, Corporate Laws Committee, 2011. 1 vol. (147 pp.). Paperbound.
Cost: $64.95; $49.95 to members; from $34.99 on amazon.com (2014).
This brief volume covers the relationship between boards of directors and their CEOs, other senior management personnel, and shareholders. Directors, who are elected by the shareholders, have a duty to advance the interests of the corporation to the exclusion of their own personal interests. This book is directed to individual directors of public companies or those with public shareholders and a trading market for their shares, and the responsibilities which such positions entail. It provides an overview of boards of directors; the act of joining a board of directors; the responsibilities, rights and duties of a corporate director; risk management, compliance and oversight; board structure, process and operations; committees of the board; the audit committee; the compensation committee; nominating and governance committee; the relationship between the board of directors and shareholders; duties under the federal securities laws; and liabilities, indemnification, and insurance. The sixth edition is published in the wake of passage of the Dodd-Frank Wall Street Reform and Consumer Protection Act, and consequently emphasizes certain issues that arose out of the crisis that led to its passage and that are important to all directors. The Appendix includes an invaluable list of online resources for corporate governance.

Corporation Service. Gaithersburg, MD: Wolters Kluwer Law & Business, 1964-date. 8 vols. Looseleaf format. Quarterly updates with semi-monthly report bulletins.
Cost: $2,875 per year; **Corporation Plus on CD-ROM**: $1,866; **Corporation Law Integrated Library** (online) (contact CCH): approx. $2,625 per year (2014).
This looseleaf service provides full-text coverage of the business corporation laws and Limited Liability Company acts of all 50 states and the District of Columbia with annotations of important cases. It also includes a practice guide providing expert analysis of corporate law issues. Also available on CD-ROM. The online version is available from Aspen's sister company, CCH.

Corporation Governance Integrated Library. Riverwoods, IL: Wolters Kluwer Law & Business (CCH). Updated monthly.
Cost: approx. $2,600 per year (single user) (2014).
Contains a practice guide and the text of the business laws of all fifty states and the District of Columbia, case law annotations of both reported and unreported decisions, yearly analysis of Delaware law , practical advice, limited liability statutes, corporate checklists, state corporation taxes, and a table of cases. Contains information on corporate practice and procedure, corporate organization, close corporations, directors and officers, stockholders, corporate financing, dividends, combination, reorganization and dissolution. Also includes hundreds of hypertext links to facilitate cross-referencing across state lines, and the contents of the publisher's five-volume **Contemporary Corporation Forms** for every type of corporate transaction. The service has a time-saving "What's New" feature that summarizes and updates highlights of legislative and case law developments every two weeks.

Delikat, Michael and Renee Phillips. **Corporate Whistleblowing in the Sarbanes-Oxley/Dodd-Frank Era**. 2d ed. New York: Practising Law Institute, 2011-date. Supplemented annually.
Cost: $335.00; from $157.45 on amazon.com; kindle: $286.42 (2014).
A reaction to a number of major corporate and accounting scandals, the Sarbanes–Oxley Act of 2002 (Pub.L. 107–204, 116 Stat. 745, July 30, 2002), also known as the Public Company Accounting Reform and Investor Protection, or more commonly Sarbanes–Oxley, or SOX, is a federal law that set new or enhanced standards for all U.S. public company boards, management and public accounting firms. The Dodd–Frank Wall Street Reform and Consumer Protection Act (Pub.L. 111–203, H.R. 4173, July 21, 2010), commonly referred to as **Dodd-Frank**), enacted in response to the financial crisis of 2008 and recession that followed, was the most comprehensive financial reform measure since the Glass-Steagall Act of 1933, which sought to regulate the financial markets, and the Gramm-Leach-Bliley Act (Pub.L. 106-102, 113 Stat. 1338, November 12, 1999),

which repealed Glass-Steagall. It made significant changes in the American financial regulatory environment that affected all federal financial regulatory agencies and almost every part of the nation's financial services industry. This volume is designed to provide practitioners, corporations, and individuals who believe they have claims under the Sarbanes-Oxley Act or Dodd-Frank Act with a detailed understanding of the whistleblower provisions of those Acts, the regulation promulgated pursuant to the Acts, and the burgeoning case law that has appeared from both administrative agencies and the federal courts. It also explains how to appeal OSHA determinations and administrative law judge decisions, how to successfully litigate whistleblower claims before federal administrative agencies, in federal court, and how to minimize potential exposure under the Sarbanes-Oxley and Dodd-Frank Acts. It explains the administrative process, federal district court and alternative forums, the elements of a prima facie case and employer defenses, remedies, codes of ethics, internal investigations, and much more. This is an essential resource for corporate attorneys, managers, human resources professionals, litigators representing both employers and employees, as well as compliance officers and federal regulators. Half the volume provides convenient access to the text and legislative history of the two Acts, Rules of Practice and Procedure before the Office of Administrative Law Judges, federal and state whistleblower statutes, the OSHA Whistleblower Investigations Manual, and federal regulations governing Federal Securities Whistleblower Incentives and Protections, among other primary documents. This volume should on the shelf of every lawyer involved in litigating whistleblower claims. Michael Delikat is a partner and Chair of Orrick, Harrington & Sutcliffe LLP with significant experience in litigating whistleblower claims and representing corporations in matters under the provisions of Sarbanes-Oxley and Dodd-Frank. Rene Phillips Sarbanes-Oxley and Dodd-Frank whistleblower issues.

Fletcher Corporation Forms Annotated. 4th ed. By Lenore M. Zajdel. St. Paul, MN: West (Clark Boardman Callaghan), 1980-date. 21 vols. Annual pocket parts and periodic revised volumes.

Cost: $5,220; supplementation: 1993: $429; 1994: $528; 1995: $511; 1996: $519; 1997: $599.70; 1998: $750; 1999: $918.40; 2000: $1,097; 2001: $1,302; 2002: $1,052; 2003: $1,152; 2004: $1,291; 2005: $1,788.50; 2006: $2,027.50; 2007: $1,575; 2008: $2,909; 2009: $2,366; 2010: $2,638.50; 2011: $2,793; 2012: $3,503; 2013: $2,728; **Monthly Assured Print Price (APP):** $292/$3,504.

This exhaustive collection of corporate forms, which is cross-referenced to **Fletcher Cyclopedia of Corporations**, includes actual forms used by attorneys, official state and federal forms, and unofficial model forms. Each chapter of forms is preceded by explanatory text which lays out the scope of the chapter and explains where to find the law. There are forms for preincorporation contracts and articles of incorporation, bylaws of incorporation, corporate organization, stock and capital, contracts and arrangements, corporate bonds, acknowledgments, affidavits and certificates, consolidations and mergers, foreign corporations, nonprofit corporations, and more.

Cost Saving Tips: Savings can be achieved by going two or more years between pocket parts. The incremental value of each year's pocket parts and revised volumes is hardly worth the recent cost of supplementing this set. Given the current cost of annual supplementation, buy a new set every 3-4 years instead of remaining on standing order. In the last analysis, there is plenty of boiler-plate language in this set to provide a sound basis for drafting your own forms regardless of its currency, provided you are attuned to statutory changes which may impact their use.

Fletcher, William Meade. **Fletcher Cyclopedia of the Law of Private Corporations.** St. Paul, MN: West (Clark Boardman Callaghan), 1971-date. 36 vols. Annual pocket parts and periodic revised volumes.

Cost: $7,534; supplementation: 1993: $754; 1994: $824; 1995: $924; 1996: $1,037; 1997: $1,083.65; 1998: $1,150; 1999: $1,328; 2000: $1,334; 2001: $1,561; 2002: $1,984; 2003: $1,924; 2004: $2,196; 2005: $2,531.50; 2006: $2,820.50; 2007: $2,923; 2008: $3,257; 2009: $3,657; 2010: $4,007; 2011: $4,367; 2012: $5,198; 2013: $5,529; **Monthly Assured Print Price (APP):** $441/$5,292.

The classic treatise on corporate law. Originally authored by William Meade Fletcher and updated since his death by the publisher's editorial staff, this is the easily the most complete and authoritative work ever produced on the law governing all types of corporate entities, public and private. Recent bound volume revisions have incorporated developments which have taken place since the introduction or revision of four revised model acts: the Revised Model Business Corporation Act, the Revised Model Nonprofit Corporation Act, and the supplements to the Model Statutory Close Corporation Act, and Model Professional Corporation Act. Heavily cited by the courts, Fletcher examines all aspects of corporate law from incorporation and management to powers, charters, organization, liability, stock and stockholders, government control, taxation, combination and merger, reorganization, insolvency and bankruptcy, receivers, trusts and associations, and foreign corporations. Volume 19 is a deskbook, encapsulating the most significant portions of the complete set and designed to be used by itself. Use is facilitated by a thorough indexing, an eye-pleasing type face, and exhaustive citations to cases, statutes and secondary sources. A must purchase for any lawyer or firm with a specialty in corporate law.

Freund, James C. **Anatomy of a Merger: Strategies and Techniques for Negotiating Corporate Acquisitions**. New York: Law Journal Press, 1975. 1 vol. (559 pp.). and online. No supplementation.

Cost: Print, online & eBook combo: $310 (2014).

This classic analysis of the corporate merger process examines strategies and techniques for negotiating corporate acquisitions. Freund considers strategies designed to achieve a workable compromise between parties, as well as those designed to gain advantage over adversaries, and how these conflicting goals can be achieved. He devotes much discussion to the jockeying for position which characterizes the early stages of negotiation. Other chapters are devoted to a consideration of the basic acquisition agreement, bargaining techniques applicable to such substantive issues as purchase price, representations and warranties, indemnification, employment contracts, and the period between signing and closing when deals can go sour. James Freund is Of Counsel to the New York firm of Skadden, Arps, Slate, Meagher & Flom LLP and the author of **Lawyering:**

A Realistic Approach to Legal Practice.

Gevurtz, Franklin A. **Corporation Law**. 2d ed. St. Paul, MN: West, 2010. 1 vol. (792 pp.). Hornbook Series. Available from West Academic.
Cost: $103; eBook: $69 (West) (2014).
While intended primarily as a law school textbook, this West Hornbook provides an excellent introduction and overview for practicing attorneys, judges, and other professionals. Adopting an easy, conversational style, the author discusses the formation of corporations, their financial structure, governance, the duties of officers and directors, special problems related to closely held corporations, securities fraud and regulation, and mergers and acquisitions. As an aid to further research, he has included citations to relevant cases and statutes, and Research References to other West publications. The Appendix includes a guide to Researching Corporation Law on Westlaw. The author is professor of Law, University of the Pacific, McGeorge School of Law.

Glazer, Donald W., Scott Fitzgibbon, and Steven O. Weise. **Glazer and Fitzgibbon on Legal Opinions**. 3d ed. New York: Wolters Kluwer Law & Business, 2008-date. 1 vol. (536 pp. + appendices).
Cost: $395; supplementation: 2009: $285; 2010: $193; 2011: $225; 2012: $247; 2013: $269; 2d ed.: 2003: $145; 2004: $171; 2005: 0; 2006: $190; 2007: 0; 2008: new edition.
Third-party closing opinions are opinions drafted by legal counsel to one party to a financial transaction to the party on the other side. Such opinions are routinely prepared by either inside or outside counsel as a means of determining if a corporate transaction works from a legal standpoint. The intent of this volume is " to provide practicing lawyers with guidance on the form and meaning of legal opinions and the work required to support them." Following an explanation of the opinion framework, the authors examine unqualified, qualified, and reasoned opinions, the establishment of a factual basis for the opinion, and the responsibility of principal for opinions of other counsel. They then address the standard opinion clauses, including company's status as a corporation, its qualifications to do business and its good standing in jurisdictions other than the state of incorporation. Also considered are matters of corporate power, the enforceability opinion, validity of stock issues, secondary sales of stock, security interests in personal property, no violation of law opinions, and compliance with court and administrative orders, and more. Twenty-six appendices reproduce a number of bar association reports which attempt to reflect a consensus about standard opinion language and the work required to support commonly-rendered opinions. These reports reflect a growing consensus toward uniformity, propelled, in large part, by the **ABA's 1998 Legal Opinion Principles** and the **TriBar Opinion Committee's 1998 Report**. The volume also includes a table of cases, select bibliography, and index. Additional bar association are included on an accompanying CD-ROM. Donald Glazer is an attorney with the Boston firm of Goodwin Proctor; Scott Fitzgibbon is professor law at Boston College Law School; Steven Weise is an attorney with the Los Angeles firm of Heller, Ehrman, White & McAuliffe. This is an essential resource for a firm which prepares closing opinions.

Goodman, Amy L. and Bart Schwartz. **Corporate Governance: Law and Practice**. Newark, NJ: LexisNexis Matthew Bender, 2004-date. 2 vols. Looseleaf format and eBook.
Cost: $601; supplementation: 2006: $226; 2007: $246; 2008: $266; 2009: $319; 2010: $317; 2011: $326; 2012: $336; 2013: $360; 2014: $393; e-book: $547; renewal; 2014: $393.
A lucid overview of the governing principles and practices of corporations, including the various statutory, regulatory and common law regimes by which they are impacted. Discussion also embraces stock market listing requirements, best practices guidelines, rights of shareholders, obligations of corporate director and managers, the business judgment rule, board structure and specific board processes, limitations on director and officer liability, indemnification, insurance, exculpation under the Delaware General Corporation Law, codes of best practices, nominating process, audit and compensation committees, scrutiny exercised by courts, actions and responses preparatory to takeover proposals, going private and hostile tender offers, corporate codes of conduct, and the roles and responsibilities of the major non-board participants in corporate governance, including the CEO; the CFO, the head of the internal audit; the corporate secretary; the chief governance officer; the chief compliance officer; the general counsel and independent public accountants. The authors also review the impact of Sarbanes-Oxley Act, as ell as SEC and SRO code of conduct requirements. Amy L. Goodman is a Partner at Gibson, Dunn & Crutcher LLP in Washington, D.C. She is a member of the firm's Securities Regulation and Corporate Transactions groups. Bart Schwartz is Deputy General Counsel and Corporate Secretary of Marsh & McLennan Companies, Inc., a holding company for financial services businesses. This title replaces **Corporate Governance** by Douglas Branson, which is now out-of-print.

Gross, Kenneth A. et al. **Corporate Political Activities Deskbook**. New York: Practising Law Institute, 2012. 1 vol. (various pagings). Looseleaf format.
Cost: $335; supplementation: 2013: $95.00; from $164.55 on amazon.com; kindle: $261.25 (2014).
This book is an outgrowth of issues that have arisen regarding corporate political activity and the associated legal requirements regarding the disclosure of corporate political contributions, lobbying and related activities. These disclosure-related issues often arise in the form of demands and pressure by shareholders that corporations more fully account for their political activities. And while transparency and corporate oversight of political spending have increased, a recent study of S&P 500 companies revealed that thorough disclosure to shareholders still remains low. This volume is primarily a practice manual for in-house attorneys advising corporations about their involvement in the political process. It does this by describing the current state of federal and state campaign finance law, pay-to-play, lobbying, and gift compliance. Less an analytical legal treatise, the emphasis is on the rules of campaign finance together with best practices and "do's and dont's." It includes numerous charts of state and federal campaign finance, gift and lobbying laws, summaries of significant federal court decisions (including the full text of Citizens United v. FEC), advisory opinions, statutes, regulations, forms, and practice tips. Kenneth A. Gross is a partner in the firm of Skadden, Arps, Slate, Meagher & Flom in Washington, DC, where he advises clients on matters regarding the regulation of political activity. This is an essential resource

for an in-house or consulting attorney advising corporations on matters of political activity and compliance.

Haas, Jeffrey J. **Corporate Finance in a Nutshell**. 2d ed. St. Paul, MN:West, 2011. 1 vol. (799 pp.). Paperbound. Available from West Academic.
Cost: $41; from $32.00 on amazon.com; kindle: $21.66 (2014).
A comprehensive overview of the field of corporate finance which is current enough to include a discussion of the Dodd-Frank Wall Street Reform and Consumer Protection Act (Pub.L. 111-203), enacted on July 21, 2010. Its coverage, which embraces the fields of mathematics, accounting, economics and macroeconomics, ranges from a consideration of the valuation of the going-concern (including both publicly-traded and privately-held companies), working with financial statements, the time value of money, future value and present value, bond valuation, valuing companies, efficient capital market hypothesis, and valuation in the courtroom. Additional chapters cover measures of risk, derivative instruments, debt holders, preferred stockholders, convertible security holders, common shareholders, fundamental concepts of mergers and acquisitions, federal law aspects, and state law aspects. Intended primarily as a student text, it also provides sample valuation problems, answers, and explanations. The text explains financial concepts in clear language and is supported selectively with citations to primary and secondary authorities. The author is a professor of law at New York Law School.

Hamilton, Robert W. and Richard D. Freer **The Law of Corporations in a Nutshell**. 6th ed. St. Paul, MN: West, 2010. 1 vol. (713 pp.). Available from West Academic.
Cost: $41; from $16.11 on amazon.com; kindle: $18.12 (2014).
This brief student overview of the law of corporations was written by the Minerva House Drysdale Regents Chair in Law at the University of Texas at Austin. The covered topics include the corporation in perspective, selection of the most appropriate business form for a venture, the formation of corporations, the limited role of ultra vires, preincorporation transactions, piercing the corporate veil, financing, distribution of powers, shares and share-holders, directors, officers, closely held corporations, publicly held corporation, duties of directors, inspection of books and records, dividends, shareholder suits, organic changes, amendments, mergers and dissolution. Includes only selective citations to case law.

Handbook for the Conduct of Shareholders' Meetings. 2d ed. Chicago: American Bar Association, Section of Business Law, 2011. 1 vol. (233 pp.) Spiralbound.
Cost: $69.95; ($49.95 to section members); from $40.91 on amazon.com (2014).
A practical manual for corporate attorneys and executives charged with the responsibility of ensuring productive and successful shareholder's meetings. Covers such topics as the overriding principles of interpretation, opening the meeting, powers of the chair, shareholder participation, voting, and concluding the meeting. The appendices include forms of board resolutions, bylaw provisions, agendas, supplemental rules, script, shareholder verification procedures, Secretary's Certificate as to Mailing Notice, and Certificate of Inspectors. Includes annotations to relevant court decisions from across the country.

Internal Corporate Investigations. 3rd ed. Edited by Barry F. McNeil and Brad D. Brian. Chicago: American Bar Association, 2007. 1 vol. (526 pp.).
Cost: $115 ($95 to members); from $59.22 on amazon.com (2014).
In the aftermath of a number of highly publicized scandals and the enactment of the Sarbanes-Oxley Act, the internal operations of corporations have been exposed to heightened scrutiny and investigation. This book is designed to be used by both in-house and outside counsel who are charged with conducting internal investigations of corporate operations. The chapters provide step-by-step guidance to those conducting the internal investigation, addressing such topics as the different types of internal investigations, the initial meeting, the implications of the attorney-client privilege and work-product doctrine, the witness interview process, perjury and obstruction of justice, gathering and organizing relevant documents, parallel proceedings, disclosure of results of international investigations to government or third parties, the special litigation committee investigation, unique problems associated with internal investigations in environmental cases, report of the investigation, internal investigations for government contractors, internal investigations into violations of securities laws, internal investigations into health care, internal investigations from the in-house perspective, internal investigations in antitrust matters, and internal investigations in a *Sarbanes-Oxley* world. This volume is an essential tool to anyone involved in conducting internal investigations, each chapter of which describes the methods and skills involved and the advises how to avoid the pitfalls of such investigations. Brad D. Brian is partner in the Los Angeles firm of Munger, Tolles & Olson LLP, a fellow in the American College of Trial Lawyers, and is listed in the ***Best Lawyers in America***. His co-editor, Barry F. McNeil, is partner with the Dallas firm of Haynes & Boone, also a fellow in the American College of Trial Lawyers, and an experienced corporate litigator with over 35 years experience.

Jelsma, Phillip L and Pamela Everett Nollkamper. **The Limited Liability Company.** Costa Mesa, CA: James Publishing Co., 2012-date. 1 vol. with CD-ROM. Annual supplementation.
Cost: $99; supplementation to date: 2013: $69.
The limited liability company is a statutory business entity that falls between the corporation and the partnership. For a number of reasons, the limited liability corporation is replacing the general partnership, the limited partnership, the S corporation and the closely held corporation as a superior alternative form of corporate organization. Among these reasons are the limited liability, the flow- through tax treatment, and the flexibility. This is a detailed, practical guide to the organization and operation of the limited liability company which is now permitted by the laws of forty-six states. Includes discussion and analysis, forms, and sample articles of incorporation. This edition provides model formation and operation documents, drafting tips, sample client letters, comparison charts, IRS revenue rulings andother documents. The authors discuss each state act separately in a detailed state-by-state analysis that includes checklists and forms. The work replaces the two volume set by Bagley and Whynott, published in 2000.

Knepper, William E. and Dan A. Bailey. **Liability of Corporate Officers and Directors.** 8th ed. Charlottesville, VA: LexisNexis, 2009-date. 2 vols. Looseleaf format. Irregular supplementation.
Cost: $514; supplementation: 2010: $218; 2011: $231; 2012: $247; 2013: $315; 7th ed.: 2003: $160; 2004: $185; 2005: $95; 2006: $105; 2007: $119; 2008: $173; 2009: new edition; 6th ed.: 1999: $60; 2000: $70; 2001: $89; 2002: new edition; 5th edition:1994: $40; 1995: $50; 1996: $55; 1997: $60; 1998: new edition; eBook: $514; supplement: 2013: $271; 2014: $315.
The 8th edition of this treatise is a response to the increasingly unsettled corporate and regulatory environment which has placed officers and directors in greater risk of personal liabilities, both civil and criminal. The authors, partners in the firm of Arter and Hadden, have written a guide which addresses the basic duties of corporate officers and directors, the specific liabilities to which they may be liable, and types of liability which may impact them in various business situations. They also discuss the state statutes limiting liability, defenses, protective measures and compliance programs, actions, legal representation, good faith and fair dealing, allocation, indemnification, insurance for directors. There is also a valuable liability and market survey conducted by the Wyatt Company. An excellent resource for the attorney or firm representing and advising corporate clients on liability issues.

Levy, Steven Mark. **Corporate Financial Disclosure Answer Book**. Austin, TX: Wolters Kluwer Law & Business, 2009-date. 1 vol. Looseleaf format.
Cost: $359; supplementation: 2010: $330; 2011: $177; 2012; $189; 2013: $210; from $70.00 on amazon.com (2014).
Companies that issue securities are required by federal law to disclose significant corporate information and financial results to the public. This information may be disclosed in the company's prospectus (assuming it is making a public offering) or in its annual or quarterly reports, prepared in accordance with general accepted accounting principles (GAAP). This information should include a description of the company's business and financial condition, sufficient financial data to provide trend analysis, and other financial statements to aid the prospective purchaser in making an informed decision whether or not to acquire the company's shares. Those central to the financial reporting process include company management, an independent auditor, an audit committee, and regulatory and law enforcement agencies. This volume provides an exhaustive guide to the financial reporting process, organized in a logical and clearly-written question-answer format. The introduction provides a complete listing of all the questions answered in the course of the book's 29 chapters. These questions address everything from the details of the regulatory framework and agencies to the nature of financial reporting, financial statement audits, international standards, electronic filing, SEC requirements, stock exchange requirements, and Public Company Accounting Oversight Board (PCAOB) standards under the Sarbanes-Oxley Act of 2002. The answers reference the appropriate federal statutes, regulations, SEC Rules of Practice, and other relevant sources. An ideal desktop reference book for any attorney or financial officer charged with the financial reporting process. Steven Mark Levy is a former senior partner in the Los Angeles firm of Lewis Brisbois Bisgaard & Smith whose practice consists of counseling public companies, financial institutions, securities professionals, and others, on regulatory and compliance issues. He has written two books and numerous articles in the field of securities regulation and money laundering.

Cost-Saving Tip: Supplementation frequency varies between one and two per year. In 2010, for example, the two supplements cost more than the initial purchase price. You can save substantially by purchasing a new set every two years (or less frequently, if possible, depending on your use).

Macey, Jonathan R. **Macey on Corporation Laws**. 2d ed. New York: Wolters Kluwer Law & Business, 2010-date. 2 vols. Looseleaf format. Annual supplementation. Includes CD-ROM.
Cost: $762; supplementation: 2011: $550; 2012: $894; 2013: $956; 1st ed.: 1999: $125; 2000: $393; 2001: $270; 2002: $280; 2003: $155; 2004: $384; 2005: $199; 2006: $625; 2007: $454; 2008: $486; 2009: $530; 2010: new edition.
This treatise provides a detailed examination of three of the most important bodies of corporation law: the Model Business Corporation Act, the Delaware General Corporation Law, and the American Law Institute's Principles of Corporate Governance. Following the organization of the MBCA, the work examines the corporation statutory form, matters of incorporation and corporate structure, duties, responsibilities and powers of the corporate entity, shares and shareholders, and directors and officers of the corporation. The relevant provisions of the Delaware General Corporation Law, ALI Principles of Corporate Governance, and significant state statutes are reprinted and analyzed under their appropriate subject topical headings. Jonathan Macey is the J. DuPratt White Professor of Law at Cornell University, a former reporter for the ABA's Committee on Corporate Laws' Model Business Corporation Act Revision Project, and a widely published authority in the field of corporate law. An accompanying CD-ROM contains the full text of the three model laws, with annotations.

Mancuso, Anthony. **The Corporate Records Handbook: Meetings, Minutes & Resolutions**. 5th ed. Berkeley, CA: NOLO, 2010. 1 vol. (606 pp.). Paperbound.
Cost: $69.99; from $42.24 on amazon.com; kindle: $37.99 (2014).
The legal formation of a corporate entity is just the first step in its proper operation. This practical handbook provides detailed guidance in dealing with all the paperwork and legal formalities of running a corporation, including the holding and documenting of corporate meetings of shareholders and directors, the documenting of corporate actions without a meeting, and the approval of common ongoing corporate legal, tax, and other business decisions. Sample forms, charts, reminders, cautions, special instructions, tips, and resources accompany the step-by-step instructions. The forms are provided both as tear-outs and on a companion CD-ROM. Anthony Mancuso is a corporations expert and author of several other NOLO business titles, including **How to Form a Nonprofit Corporation** and **Form Your Own Limited Liability Company**. NOLO books are among the most useful and economical self-help publications on the market, priced at just a fraction of what the major legal publishers charge.

Model Business Corporation Act: Official Text with Official Comments and Statutory Cross-References Revised Through December 2010.. Chicago, American Bar Association, Corporate Laws Committee, 2011. 1 vol. (various pagings). Paperbound.
Cost: $329.95; from $194.27 on amazon.com (2014).
First promulgated by the ABA's Committee on Corporate Laws of the Section of Corporation, Banking and Business Law (now the Section of Business Law) in 1950, the **Model Business Corporation Act** was completely revised and published in 1984. Today, it stands as the model for the general corporation statutes of 30 states and the source of many provisions of the general corporation statutes of states that have not adopted the **Model Act** its entirety. This official text includes official comments, cross-references, cross reference tables, table of cases, and subject index. The text of the Model Act addresses such matters as general provisions, incorporation, purposes and powers, name, office and agent, shares and distributions, shareholders, directors and officers, domestication and conversion, amendment of articles of incorporation, mergers and share exchanges, disposition of assets, appraisal rights, dissolution, foreign corporations, records and reports, and transition provisions.

Model Business Corporation Act Annotated. 4th ed. Chicago: American Bar Association, 2008-date. 4 vols. Looseleaf format. Infrequent supplementation.
Cost: $685.95 ($525.95 to Business Law Section and ABA members); supplementation: 2009: $99.95 ($79.95 to Section members); 2010: 0; 2011: $249.95; 2012: 0; 2013: $249.95 (member: $199.95); previous ed. supps.: 1991: $150; 1992: $150; 1993: $150; 1994: $145; 1995: $165; 1996: $165; 2002: $145.95; 2003: $170; 2004-2007: 0; 2008: new edition.
First promulgated in 1950, the **Model Business Corporation Act Annotated** is designed as a free-standing general corporation statute that can be adopted either in its entirety, or selectively, by state legislatures. As of 2007, thirty states had adopted all, or substantially all, of the **MBCA**, while others had adopted selective portions of the Act. The Contents of the Act (contained in four looseleaf volumes), include: General Provisions, Incorporation, Purposes and Powers, Name, Office and Agent, Shares and Distribution, Shareholders, Directors and Officers, Domestication and Conversion, Amendment of Articles of Incorporation and Bylaws, Mergers and Share Exchanges, Disposition of Assets, Appraisal Rights, Dissolution, Foreign Corporations, Records and Reports, and Transition Provisions. The set also includes cross-reference tables, a table of cases, and index. The fourth edition contains all amendments to the text and Official Comments through December 2007, as well as summaries of relevant court decisions, ALR and law review citations, selected references to leading secondary sources, and amendments to the corporation statutes of all fifty states. DC, and Puerto Rico. Provides comparisons of the **MBCA** and state statutes. An excellent resource for the corporate attorney. Formerly published by Wolters Kluwer Law & Business, the third (1997) and, now, fourth editions were taken over by the American Bar Association's Section of Business Law.

Olson, Brent A. **Publicly Traded Corporations: Governance and Regulation**. 3d ed. St. Paul, MN: Thomson Reuters West (CBC), 2010-date. 2 vols. Twice annual replacement volumes beginning in 2010.
Cost: 2013-2 Edition: $348; supplementation: 2d ed.: 2002: $130; 2003: $125; 2004: $143; 2005: $180; 2006: $218; 2007: $194; 2008: $216; 2009: $244; 2010: $400; 2011: $292; **Monthly Assured Print Price (APP):** $51/$612.
A practical guide to the essential aspects of corporate and securities law for the attorney who represents directors, shareholders, and stockholders of publicly traded corporations. Following an introduction to the publicly traded corporation, there are chapters devoted to management and control of the publicly traded corporation, communications in connection with shareholder meetings, shareholder communications not in connection with shareholder meetings, corporate misrepresentation, duty to disclose, the Private Securities Litigation Control Act of 1995, regulation of securities transactions of corporate insiders, tender offers, takeover tactics and defenses, and conflict of interest in going private transactions.

Cost-Saving Tip: Beware the twice annual replacement editions which raise the annual updating cost to nearly $700.00. Avoid the standing order and re-purchase as necessary.

O'Neal, F. Hodge and Robert B. Thompson. **O'Neal and Thompson's Close Corporations and LLCs: Law and Practice.** Rev. 3d ed. St. Paul, MN: West (Clark Boardman Callaghan), 2004-date. 2 vols. Looseleaf format and ProView eBook.=. Annual supplements.
Cost: $876; ProView eBook: $850; supplementation: 2004: $313.00 (new edition); 2005: $266; 2006: $369; 2007: $295; 2008: $664; 2009: $459; 2010: $532.50; 2011: $441; 2012: $400; 2013: $448; 2d ed.: 1993: $68; 1994: $121; 1995: $93; 1996: $158; 1997: $107; 1998: $168.50; 1999: $122.50; 2000: $192; 2001: $155; 2002: $274.50; 2003: $194.50; **Monthly Assured Print Price (APP):** $62/$744.
A practical guide to the law, planning, and operation of the close corporation, including the drafting of forms suitable to the specific needs of the corporate entity. Originally written by F. Hodge O'Neal (1917-1991) former Dean and George Alexander Madill Professor of Law, Washington University, the work has been revised and updated by Robert Thompson Professor of Law, Washington University and Faye L. Katt of the Chicago firm of Bell, Boyd & Lloyd. It describes the distinctive needs of close corporations, the steps preceding the organization of a close corporation, molding the corporate form by charter and bylaw provision, control distribution devices, protecting the tenure and status of shareholder-employees and key personnel, stock transfer restrictions, and problems of operation. There are extensive specimen provisions for charters, bylaws, shareholder agreements and other documents. The appendices include a table of United States statutes, regulations and rulings, table of state statutes, model and uniform acts, table of cases and index. There are extensive citations to relevant cases and statutes.

Overton, Bruce and Susan E. Stoffer. **Executive Compensation Answer Book**. 8th ed. New York: Wolters Kluwer Law & Business, 2012. 1 vol. (1077 pp.).
Cost: $385.00; supplementation: 2013: $285.
Executive compensation programs are an essential ingredient

to attracting and retaining top-flight executives and managers. A typical executive package includes base salary, annual incentives, long-term incentives, benefits, and perquisites. The specific design of the package is driven by competitive practices, tax and accounting rules and regulations, and company values and strategies. The question-answer format of this volume provides exhaustive and clearly-explained coverage of the full range of issues involved in building and implementing an effective executive compensation program, including the fundamental concepts of executive compensation, the structuring of a total compensation strategy, identifying and evaluating executive candidates, base salary considerations, deferred compensation, employment agreements, incentive plans, retirement plans, life and disability coverage, early retirement programs, and ERISA aspects of deferred compensation. Also addressed are small versus large company practices, publicly traded company issues, compensation in the non-profit environment, public sector compensation, compensation in high technology and start-up companies, compensation for division executives, U.S, executives working overseas, compensation for boards of directors, administration and communication of executive compensation, and trends in executive compensation, among other topics. The appendices include a number of illustrative agreements and plans. The text is augmented by numerous financial and benefit examples. This is an essential acquisition for any business or corporation involved in structuring or implementing an executive compensation program. Bruce Overton is President of the Overton Consulting, Inc., an executive compensation consulting firm in Atlanta. Susan E. Stoffer is a partner in the Executive Compensation and Employee Benefits practice group at the national law firm Nelson, Mullins, Riley & Scarborough LLP.

Poon, Gary P. **The Corporate Counsel's Guide to Mediation**. Chicago: American Bar Association, 2010. 1 vol. (131 pp.). Paperbound.
Cost: $79.95 ($63.95 to members); from $60.73 on amazon.com (2014).
Mediation is a form of alternative dispute resolution (ADR) designed to help parties settle disputes. The International Chamber of Commerce defines mediation as a "settlement technique in which the neutral acts as a facilitator to help the parties try to arrive at a negotiated settlement of their dispute." It does not include attempts made by the judge to settle a dispute within the course of a judicial proceeding. And it differs from arbitration in that the decision of the mediator is not binding on the parties, as is the decision of an arbitrator. The mediator at all times maintains his or her neutrality and impartiality. The parties play an active role in mediation, identifying interests, suggesting solutions, making decisions regarding he proposals made by the other party. Conciliation is like mediation in that the proposed solution is not binding. But in conciliation, the conciliator plays a more active role in making an actual proposal for settlement. To some observers, it comes down to a matter of style, but with the conciliator playing a more active role. This brief volume provides an overview of the entire mediation process, including a discussion of mediation as an alternative form of dispute resolution, the drafting of mediation clauses, court-directed mediations, selection of a mediator, pre-mediation preparation, the mediation session, post-mediation follow-up, cross cultural mediations, and conclusions. The Appendices include a sample confidentiality agreement, sample mediation rules, and the Model Standards of Conduct. The author is a lawyer, business advisor and a court-approved mediator for the District of Columbia Superior Court.

Presser, Stephen B. **Piercing the Corporate Veil.** St. Paul, MN: Thomson Reuters West (Clark Boardman Callaghan), 1991-date. 1 vol. Looseleaf format. Annual replacement volumes beginning in 2011.
Cost: 2013 Edition: $548; supplementation: 1994: $59; 1995: $74; 1996: $81; 1997: $85; 1998: $90; 1999: $97.25; 2000: $103; 2001: $120; 2002: $132; 2003: $150.50; 2004: $168.50; 2005: $237; 2006: $472.50; 2007: $228.50; 2008: $254.50; 2009: $283.50; 2010: $312; 2011: $347; 2012: $505; **Monthly Assured Print Price (APP):** $46/$552.
The primary aim of this treatise is to address the question of when the corporate entity is ignored in order to place civil liability on individual or corporate shareholders. The author, Professor of Law at Northwestern University, confronts this question in three ways: (1) by providing an analytical review of the principles of veil-piercing with attention to its historical development and arguments pro and con; (2) state-by-state summaries of the law with in-depth analysis of at least one significant case from that state; and (3) summaries of federal law for both the Supreme Court , each of the Federal Circuits, and the application of veil-piercing doctrines to various areas of federal law. Includes a Table of Cases and Index. This volume is most useful for its excellent analytical summaries of veil-piercing law in the fifty states and federal circuits.

Smiddy, Linda O. and Lawrence A. Cunningham. **Soderquist on Corporate Law & Practice**. 4th ed. New York: Practising Law Institute, 2012-date. 1 vol. (395 pp.). Periodic supplementation.
Cost: $295; supplementation: 2013: $186; 3d ed.: 2008: $118; 2009: $160; 2010: $304; 2011: $159; 2012: new edition.
An excellent introduction to the law of corporate practice which reflects changes brought about by the adoption of the revised Model Business Corporation Act in many states. The chapters address every aspect of corporate practice, corporate organization and operation, including an historical and contemporary overview of the corporation in America, the basics of corporation law, choosing the corporate form, preincorporation transactions, incorporation, capitalization, organizing the corporation, disregard of the corporate entity, corporate authority, directors' duty of care, directors' and shareholders' duties of fairness, dividends and distributions, control distribution devices, merger and acquisitions, and an introduction to securities law. The appendices include selected provisions of the Model Business Corporation Act and a guide to reading financial statements. The work includes citations to relevant cases and statutes. Larry Soderquist is a Professor of Law and Director of the Corporate and Securities Law Institute at Vanderbilt University. He is joined by co-authors from both the academic world and private practice.\\\

Spadaccini, Michael. **Business Structures**. Irvine, CA: Entrepreneur Press, 2007. 1 vol. (442 pp.). Includes sample forms and documents on CD-ROM.
Cost: $32.95; from $3.49 on amazon.com (2014).

This popular introduction to business structures explains in clear language how to form a corporation, an LLC, a partnership and a sole proprietorship. The features of each business form are explained in detail, as are the organizational and operational characteristics, and advantages and disadvantages of each form. The author also discusses liability protection, including the process of suing or being sued as an LLC or corporation, individual suits, derivative suits, liability protection rules, and liability and veil piercing. The appendices contain forms applicable to partnerships and LLCs, and reference tables to the laws and procedures applicable in all fifty states and the District of Columbia. The intended audience includes not only businesspersons, but lawyers, accountants, and managers. The author is a graduate of Quinnipiac University School of Law and a practicing attorney specializing in business, trademark, securities and Internet law. He has written several self-help books in the Entrepreneur Press Legal Guide Series, including **Incorporate Your Business** and the **Small Claims Court GuideBook**.

Spadaccini, Michael. **Incorporate Your Business in Any State**. Irvine, CA: Entrepreneur Press, 2007. 1 vol. (262 pp.). Includes sample forms and documents on CD-ROM.
Cost: $32.95; from $3.25 on amazon.com (2014).
Incorporation of a business offers multiple advantages, but also a host of potential problems if is not executed or maintained properly. Corporations allow their owners to protect their assets, reduce their tax burden, and minimize their potential liabilities. The author addresses the various alternative business forms, from sole proprietorships to limited liability companies and discusses the types of considerations applicable to all businesses, regardless of form. This volume sets out the thirteen steps involved in self-incorporation, including: (1) where to incorporate; (2) selection of corporate name; (3) selection of type of corporation; (4) selection of registered agent; (5) whether it should be done yourself or by your attorney; (6) determining the stock structure; (7) drafting and filing articles of incorporation; (8) ordering your corporate kit and sea; (9) selection and appointment of corporate directors; (10) preparing and approving corporate bylaws; (11) the director's organizational meeting; (12) obtaining your F.E.I.N.; and (13) observing formalities and maintaining good standing. Various aspects of business operations are also addressed, including protection from liability, reporting requirements, the amendment of articles of incorporation, suing and being sued, managing liability protection, government claims, and more. More than half the volume is devoted to sample corporation forms and documents, all of which are included on a companion CD-ROM. Michael Spadaccini is a graduate of Quinnipiac University School of Law who specializes in business, trademark, securities and Internet law. He has written several self-help books in the Entrepreneur Press Legal Guide Series.

Spadaccini, Michael. **The Operations Manual for Corporations**. Irvine, CA: Entrepreneur Press, 2008. 1 viol. (348 pp.). Includes sample forms and documents on CD-ROM.
Cost: $32.95; from $5.63 on amazon.com (2014).
This book provides business owners with a clearly written overview of the basic principles and practices of corporate operations, including their formalities and mechanics. Accordingly, the author explains and defines the various business corporations acts, articles or incorporation and bylaws which govern corporate operations, the participants in the corporate enterprise, the types of paperwork which must be completed to maintain corporate statues. He also discusses the meetings of directors and shareholders, corporate lawsuits and liability protection, and such related concepts as professional corporations, not-for-profit corporations, close corporations, and limited liability companies. Essential legal forms are contained on a companion CD-ROM. The author, a graduate of Quinnipiac University School of Law, is a practicing attorney specializing in business, trademark, securities and Internet law. He has written several self-help books in the Entrepreneur Press Legal Guide Series, including Incorporate Your Business and Small Claims Court GuideBook.

Villa, John K. **Corporate Counsel Guidelines**. St. Paul, MN: Thomson Reuters West, 1999-date. 2 vols. Looseleaf format.
Cost: $313; supplementation: 2000: $48; 2001: $55.50; 2002: $61.50; 2003: $70; 2004: $70; 2005: $85; 2006: $87.50; 2007: $97.50; 2008: $109; 2009: $129; 2010: $142; 2011: $165; 2012: $181; 2013: $196.80; **Monthly Assured Print Price (APP):** $21/$252.
A joint project of the American Corporate Counsel and the West, this volume addresses the types of legal problems most likely to be encountered by corporate counsel. Each of the book's six sections examines a broad subject area, provides an overview and analysis of controlling legal principles, and applies these principles to real-life situations. Each of these real-life situations is accompanied by specific forms and steps to be undertaken. This work is destined to become an essential desktop reference for corporate counsel. Chapters examine the attorney-client privilege and in-house corporate counsel, the work product doctrine and in-house corporate counsel, ethical issues for inside counsel, overseeing civil litigation, overseeing corporate criminal investigations and litigation, and individual rights and liabilities or corporate counsel. Tables of statutes, rules, cases and index.

Weise, Richard H. **Representing the Corporation: Strategies for Legal Counsel.** 2d ed. New York: Wolters Kluwer Law & Business, 2001-date. 2 vols. Looseleaf format.
Cost: $695; supplementation: 1998: $88; 1999: $190; 2000: $211; 2001: $294; 2002: $316; 2003: $218; 2004: $218; 2005: $290; 2006: $275; 2007: $308; 2008: $330; 2009: $364; 2010: $390; 2011: $420; 2012: $450; 2013: $500.
This two-volume guide to corporate law department management began as an outgrowth of the author's experience as Senior Vice President, General Counsel & Secretary of Motorola, Inc. and a participant in that company's quality improvement program in the late 1970's. Weise lays a detailed strategy for streamlining and improving the quality of law department management. He addresses quality criteria, designing management systems for corporate counsel, full client utilization, annual client operations reviews, knowledge reuse through automation, automated management systems, outside counsel relationships, transactions in a corporate law department, securities practice in a law department, government contract practice, corporate compliance, lawyers and integrity, and more. Each chapter is accompanied by a chapter of valuable exhibits drawn from

leading corporate law departments. The author provides some particularly candid advice regarding attorney recruitment, development, and dismissal. This is a revised edition of the author's **Representing the Corporate Client: Designs for Quality**, first published in 1991.

Additional titles in the field of Corporate Law are available from the following publishers: Altman Weil, ALI-ABA, American Bar Association, American Enterprise Institute, Wolters Kluwer Law & Business, BNA, Business Laws, Inc., CCH, Inc., Gaunt, Greenwood Publishing Group, Harcourt Legal, Harvard University Press, William S. Hein & Co., Inc., Kluwer Academic, Law Journal Press, LexisNexis, Looseleaf Law, Matthew Bender, Nolo Press, Oxford University Press, Practising Law Institute, Routledge, Thomson Reuters West, Warren, Gorham & Lamont, West Academic. See Appendix B for addresses and telephone numbers.

Criminal Law

(see also Civil Rights and Constitutional Law)

Abbell, Michael. **Extradition to and from the United States**. 2010. Boston: Martinus Nijhoff, 2010. 1 vol. (588 pp.).
Cost: $238.00 (2014).
Extradition is the process by which one nation or state surrenders a suspected or convicted criminal to another nation or state. Although the term "extradition" has only been used since the late 18th century, the process of returning a fugitive to another jurisdiction has been employed since antiquity. In recent years, the explosion in the level of transnational criminal activity and the greater mobility of criminals has prompted a corresponding increase in requests for extradition. In 2008 alone, 589 individuals were extradited to the United States and many others by it to other countries. By contrast, as recently as the early 1970s, the United States typically made and received only 40 requests annually for international extradition. While interstate extradition is governed by Article IV, sec. 2 of the U.S. Constitution, international extradition is governed by the many bilateral treaties between United States and other nations. In this thorough and well-sourced volume, the author provides a lively exposition of the development of international extradition in the United States and the basis, in federal statute and treaty, for extradition from the United States, with attention to substantive treaty provisions. He also addresses the practical aspects of extradition, including the process prior to the extradition hearing, the hearing itself, the proofs required on behalf of the requesting country, defenses of requested persons, the decision of the extradition magistrate, judicial review, processing by the Department of State, and deportation from the United States as an alternative to extradition. The author also examines the statutes and treaties governing extradition to the United States, with attention to substantive treaty provisions, as well as the process of extradition. Additional chapters are devoted to the effect of extradition on subsequent prosecution in the United States, and international transfer of proceedings in criminal matters from a U.S. perspective. Appendices include the applicable U.S. Code provisions, a list of extradition treaties, substantive treaty provisions, the United States Attorneys Manual for Extradition, other primary documents. The author, a graduate of Harvard Law School, is a consultant on international criminal legal matters and the author of **International Prisoner Transfer** and **Obtaining Evidence from Abroad in Criminal Cases**. Available on amazon.com, but at prices higher than that from the publisher.

Adams, James A. and Daniel D. Blinka. **Prosecutor's Manual for Arrest, Search and Seizure.** 2d ed. Charlottesville, VA: LexisNexis, 2004-date. 1 vol. Annual supplementation. Print or eBook.
Cost: $186; supplementation: 2005: $48; 2006: $53; 2007: $58; 2008: $60; 2009: $70; 2010: $74; 2011: $81; 2012: $87; 2013: $90; 1st ed.: 1999: $35; 2000: 0; 2001: $47; 2002: $50; 2003: $45.
Most criminal prosecutions hinge on critical Fourth Amendment issues involving the legality of an arrest or evidence seized by police. This volume examines the most significant of these issues from the prosecutor's perspective, including Fourth Amendment standing and suppression motions, the exclusionary rule and its exceptions, search warrants, extraordinary searches, arrests on warrants, warrantless police-citizen interactions, automobile intrusions, consent searches, inventories, border stops and searches, stops and searches at sea, exigent circumstances, special needs searches, administrative searches, warrantless administrative searches of "closely regulated" businesses, devices used to augment an officer's sensory perception, police investigatory activity and seizures not considered searches or seizures under the Fourth Amendment. James Adams is the Richard M. and Anita Calkins Distinguished Professor of Law at Drake University and a former Assistant U.S. Attorney for the District of Columbia. Daniel Blinka is Professor of Law at Marquette University Law School, where he teaches evidence, criminal law, criminal procedure, trial practice, and legal history. He was a former Assistant District Attorney in Milwaukee County, Wisconsin.

Androphy, Joel M. **White Collar Crime.** 2d ed. St. Paul, MN: Thomson Reuters West (Clark Boardman Callaghan), 2001-date. 4 vols. Supplemented 2 times per year. Also comes with a Word Perfect forms disc.
Cost: $671; supplementation: 2002: $64; 2003: $73; 2004: $167; 2005: $118.50; 2006: $232; 2007: $258; 2008: $479; 2009: $322; 2010: $354; 2011: $389.50; 2012: $428.50; 2013: $480; 1st ed.: 1993: $92; 1994: $130; 1995: $130; 1996: $130; 1997: $150; 1998: $150; 1999: $162; 2000: $88; 2001: $192 (new edition); **Monthly Assured Print Price (APP):** $49/$588.
Authored by a partner in the Houston law firm of Berg & Androphy, this substantial four-volume work is intended to aid the criminal lawyer in handling white collar criminal cases from indictment through sentencing. Each chapter of this well-organized and lucidly written text is accompanied by relevant forms, motions, letters, and orders. Chapters cover not only general legal and procedural aspects of the field, but substantive crimes such as those involving banks, securities, RICO, taxation, perjury, money laundering, etc.

Bailey, F. Lee and Henry B. Rothblatt. **Crimes of Violence: Homicide and Assault.** St. Paul, MN: Thomson Reuters West

(Clark Boardman Callaghan), 1973-date. 1 vol. Looseleaf format. Annual supplementation.

Cost: $835; from $198.31 on amazon.com; supplementation: 1994: $65; 1995: $85; 1996: $96; 1997: $105; 1998: $113; 1999: $121.50; 2000: $132; 2001: $153.50; 2002: $180; 2003: $205; 2004: $229.50; 2005: $239.50; 2006: $282.50; 2007: $314.50; 2008: $351; 2009: $404.50; 2010: $445; 2011: $485; 2012: $528; 2013: $613; **Monthly Assured Print Price (APP):** $61/$732.

A practical guide which can be of use to both defense attorneys and prosecutors. Covers the range of procedural matters in handling a criminal case with specific attention to various crimes of violence, including assault, homicide, and kidnapping. Includes a discussion of the elements of culpable homicide, participants in the crime, self defense, capacity to commit crime, and miscellaneous excuses or defenses. Includes forms and a subject index.

Cost Saving Tip: The Bailey and Rothblatt titles are long overdue for revision. Ironically, West continues to increase the price of the base volumes (now $766 each), as well as the cost of supplementation. Used purchase is therefore highly recommended ($62.55 on amazon) if you buy them at all.

Bailey, F. Lee and Henry B. Rothblatt. **Crimes of Violence: Rape and Other Sex Crimes.** St. Paul, MN: West (Clark Boardman Callaghan), 1973-date. 1 vol. Looseleaf format. Annual supplementation.

Cost: $835; from 0.73 on amazon.com; supplementation: 1994: $65; 1995: $85; 1996: $96; 1997: $105; 1998: $112.50; 1999: $121.50; 2000: $132; 2001: $153; 2002: $179; 2003: $204; 2004: $229.50; 2005: $239.50; 2006: $282.50; 2007: $314.50; 2008: $351; 2009: $404.50; 2010: $445; 2011: $485; 2012: $528; 2013: $613; **Monthly Assured Print Price (APP):** $61/$732.

Intended for the criminal defense attorney, this practical handbook provides step-by-step guidance in the defense of the sex crime case, from arrest to trial. Chapters cover general principles, the fee, fact sheet, surrendering your client, initial judicial proceedings, bail, investigation aids and procedures, locating witnesses, interviewing witnesses, preliminary hearing, grand jury, indictment, change of venue, severance, discovery, suppression of evidence, plea bargaining, the jury, opening statement, cross-examination, direct examination, expert opinion and testimony, insanity defense, summation, rape, prostitution and related offenses, incest, obscenity, sodomy, homosexuality, and the sexual psychopath. Includes relevant forms, suggested questions and index.

Cost-Saving Tip: Available used on amazon.com for $0.73.

Bailey, F. Lee and Kenneth J. Fishman. **Handling Misdemeanor Cases.** 2d ed. St. Paul, MN: Thomson Reuters West (Clark Boardman Callaghan), 1993-date. 1 vol. Looseleaf format.

Cost: $686; supplementation: 1993: $59; 1994: $64; 1995: $75; 1996: $80.00; 1997: $90; 1998: $94.50; 1999: $102; 2000: $110; 2001: $130; 2002: $152; 2003: $173.50; 2004: $194.50; 2005: $247; 2006: $239.50; 2007: $266.50; 2008: $296.50; 2009: $322; 2010: $365; 2011: $398; 2012: $434; 2013: $473; **Monthly Assured Print Print Price (APP):** $50/$600.

This one-volume work is organized into 29 chapters covering topics ranging from arrests and arraignment, plea bargaining and jury trials to defending the juvenile client and specific misdemeanors, such as drunk driving, gambling, offenses against property, lewdness, obscenity, prostitution, reckless driving, unauthorized practice of medicine, and federal misdemeanors. In the looseleaf format, each individual chapter is placed under a corresponding subject tab and is in a pamphlet format for ease of updating. This is a succinct, clearly written overview of a variety of misdemeanors with useful Research References to both Lawyers Cooperative and CBC publications, including Annotation References to the **American Law Reports**. Case citations are limited, but adequate, given the nature of the work. Written for the practicing attorney who needs a brief, but practical, guide to aid his defense of individuals charged with various misdemeanor offenses.

Batista, Paul A. **Civil RICO Practice Manual**. 3d ed. New York: Wolters Kluwer Law & Business, 2008-date. 1 vol. Looseleaf format. Periodic supplementation.

Cost: $365.00; supplementation: 2009: $135; 2010: $146; 2011: $160; 2012: $182; 2013: $209.

The Racketeer Influenced Corrupt Organizations Act, otherwise known as RICO,

was originally enacted as Title X of the Organized Crime Control Act of 1970 (OCCA). Initially employed by federal criminal prosecutors as tool to prosecute various forms or organized criminal activity, it emerged in the early 1980s as a stealth litigation weapon used by both plaintiffs and defendants asserting a variety of novel claims, many of which were propelled by its statutory provisions for treble damages. The broad language of the statute provided civil litigants, who normally figure as defendants, with the tools to assert novel claims as plaintiffs. This exhaustive resource provides a neutral perspective on the various uses to which the RICO statute may be employed as a litigation weapon. Accordingly, the author discusses both the offensive use of RICO and the defenses to civil RICO, including the procedural dimensions of civil RICO litigation from discovery through appeal, special problems of civil RICO cases and the criminal uses of RICO and their relation to civil racketeering litigation. Indeed, the use of RICO to prosecute federal criminal activity has proven an effective tool for gaining convictions. The appendices include the text of the RICO Act, and a variety of forms, including a model civil RICO complaint. The author is a nationally known trial lawyer with more than 30 years experience, a frequent commentator on Court TV and other news programs, and author of the best selling novel ***Death's Witness*** (2007).

Beale, Sara Sun and William C. Bryson. **Grand Jury Law and Practice.** 2d ed. St. Paul, MN: Thomson Reuters West (Clark Boardman Callaghan), 1997-date. 2 vols. Looseleaf format. Annual supplements.

Cost: $340; supplementation: 1998: $65; 1999: $70; 2000: $76; 2001: $90; 2002: $100; 2003: $100; 2004: $100; 2005: $64; 2006: $71; 2007: $79; 2008: $128; 2009: $105.50; 2010: $116; 2011: $126.50; 2012: $138; 2013: $63; 1st ed.: 1993: $71.50; 1994: $102.50; 1995: $115; 1996: $131; 1997: new edition; **Monthly Assured Print Price (APP):** $19/$228.

This treatise was written in response to the heightened litigation over a variety of grand jury matters, including their composition, prosecutorial conduct, secrecy, and investigative procedures. Chapter coverage includes an introduction (with history), the role of the grand jury in state and federal practice, grand jury reports, selecting and summoning grand jurors, organization and administration, conduct of proceedings and issuance of the indictment, secrecy of grand jury proceedings, parallel civil and criminal proceedings, grants of immunity to witnesses, prosecutorial misconduct, abuse of grand jury, judicial review, and grand jury offenses. Clearly written and organized, this text provides extensive citations to relevant cases and statutes, both state and federal.

Brenner, Susan W. and Lori E. Shaw. **Federal Grand Jury: A Guide to Law and Practice**. 2d ed. St. Paul: West, 2006-date. 2 vols. Annual pocket parts.
Cost: $262; supplemetation: 2007: $44; 2008: $60; 2009: $70.50; 2010: $96; 2011: $85; 2012: $92.50; 2013: $100.50; supplementation to 1st ed.: 1998: $62; 1999: $35; 2000: $38; 2001: $45; 2002: $53.50; 2003: $0; 2004: $108; 2005: $70; 2006: new edition ($170); **Monthly Assured Print Price (APP):** $12/$144.
A thorough and practical guide to practice before federal grand juries written by a professor of law at the University of Dayton and an Assistant United States Attorney for the Southern District of Ohio. The authors place the federal grand jury in its historical context and examine such topics as concurrent federal and state proceedings, selection of grand jurors, convening of the grand jury, the role of the prosecutor, grand jury secrecy, disclosure of proceedings and evidence, securing evidence, securing testimony, parallel proceedings, indictments, grand jury abuse and ethical issues in grand jury proceedings. Appendices include forms, and tables of statutes, court rules, and cases. The text is proceeded by both guidelines for grand jury practice and checklists for the major procedural stages in grand jury proceedings. It is also adequately supported with citations to primary law and relevant secondary sources. The volume also includes a WESTLAW Electronic Research Guide with examples drawn specifically from relevant criminal cases and statutes. Although contained in only one volume, this treatise is comparable in length to the competing two-volume **Grand Jury Law and Practice** (West), and a better value. Supplementation is also likely to be less costly.

Business Crime: Criminal Liability of the Business Community. Stanley S. Arkin et al. New York: Matthew Bender & Co., 1981-date. 8 vols. Looseleaf format. Supplemented usually twice annually. No CD-ROM or Internet.
Cost: $3,347 (includes annual subscription); annual renewal: 1995: $884.50 (frozen since 1992); 1996: $928; 1997: $928; 1998: $975; 1999: $1,010; 2000: $1,080; 2001: $1,156; 2002: $1,237; 2003: $1,299; 2004: $1,364; 2005: $1,395; 2006: $1,493; 2007: $1,612; 2008: $1,741; 2009: $1,880; 2010: $1,975; 2011: $2,034; 2012: $2,115; 2012: $2,221; 2013: $2,424; 2014: $2,424; Ebook: $3,043; 2014: $2,424.
A detailed examination of the wide variety of criminal activity which may arise in the course of business practices. This work provides guidance on how to set up compliance programs to prevent criminal activity or liability in a business setting, offers expert advice to business clients on how to conduct internal investigations, and explains how to handle administrative, civil and criminal cases on behalf of your clients. Includes a discussion of federal and state laws as they apply to areas in which government investigation and prosecution is likely. Provides tactical advice and numerous forms for every stage of a business crime practice. Also includes model direct and cross-examinations, opening and closing arguments, checklists, bibliographies and an index.

Cost Saving Tips: The initial and, more particularly, supplementation cost, may cause you to consider ways to gain the benefits of this set on a more cost-effective basis. As with all Matthew Bender sets, this one is sold with a one year subscription. Consider dropping the subscription after one year and updating by buying a new set when you feel it is necessary. In the meantime, you can check primary sources, Shepardize the relevant cases and statutes, and do all those things which must be done after consulting a secondary source. Remember, there is always a lag time between the editorial cut-off date of most supplements and your receipt of them--so beware.

Carr, James G. **The Law of Electronic Surveillance.** 2d ed. St. Paul, MN: Thomson Reuters West (Clark Boardman Callaghan), 1986-date. 2 vols. Twice annual replacement editions or eBook, 2011-date.
Cost: 2014-1 Edition (print or eBook): $360 ($720.00 per year); supplementation: 1993: $127; 1994: $134.50; 1995: $150; 1996: $190; 1997: $210; 1998: $220; 1999: $238; 2000: $252; 2001: $292; 2002: $321; 2003: $366; 2004: $410; 2005: $440; 2006: $461; 2007: $558; 2008: $621; 2009: $691; 2010: $753; 2011: $836; 2012: $928; **Monthly Assured Print Price (APP):** $97/$1,164.
This treatise examines the law of electronic surveillance, particularly as it has evolved under Title III of the Omnibus Crime Control and Safe Streets Act of 1968 and is intended for the use of lawyers, judges and law enforcement personnel. Chapters cover a history of electronic surveillance prior to the adoption of Title III, the enactment and constitutionality of Title III, surveillance without a court order, contents of applications and orders for court-ordered electronic surveillance, executing an electronic search, proceedings to determine compliance with Title III, Retrieval, Discovery, and Use of Information and Evidence from Electronic Surveillance, Criminal Penalties and Civil Remedies for Illegal Electronic Surveillance, Foreign Intelligence Surveillance. Appendix includes selected statutory material relating to electronic surveillance. A detailed and clearly written text with several thousand citations to relevant cases and statutes. Discussion of state law and procedure often includes references and citations to applicable law. Includes a table of cases and index.

Carter, Linda E., Ellen S. Kreitzberg, and Scott W. Howe. **Understanding Capital Punishment Law**. 3d ed. New York: LexisNexis, 2012. 1 vol. (369 pp.). Paperbound.
Cost: $45; eBook: $36 (2014).
The use of capital punishment is a subject of widespread and heated debate throughout the world. Sixty-nine countries, including the United States, and countries in Asia and the Middle East, continue to impose the death penalty for a number of

serious crimes, including murder, rape, robbery, adultery, and corruption. On the other hand, 128 countries, including those in Europe, have abolished the death penalty. Even in the United States, there is a division between the majority of states that impose the death penalty and the remainder that do not. And among those that authorize it, there is a split over the manner in which it is applied. This volume in the Understanding Series provides a useful introduction to the law of capital punishment, the primary arguments pro and con of the debate, and the legal basis for its application. The authors also provide insightful discussion and analysis of a number of relevant issues, including challenges to the constitutionality of the death penalty, methods of execution, modern death penalty statutes, the death penalty trial, categorical bars to the death penalty, aggravating circumstances and evidence, the selection process and mitigation, the life or death decision, direct appeals, post-conviction proceedings, innocence, clemency, death row issues, gender bias, and the federal death penalty, among others. The text is accompanied by selective citations to legal authorities. Linda Carter is Professor of Law at McGeorge School of Law; Ellen Kreitzberg is Professor of Law and Director, Death Penalty College, Santa Clara University School of Law; Scott Howe is Professor of Criminal Law at Chapman University School of Law.

Cassella, Stefan D. **Asset Forfeiture Law in the United States**. 2d ed. Huntington, NY: JurisNet, LLC, 2013-date. 1 vol. (1,252 pp.).
Cost: $175; supplementation to prior ed.: 2008: 0; 2009: 0; 2010: $75; 2011: 0; 2013: new ed.
As an essential and commonly used tool of federal law enforcement, thousands of civil and criminal asset forfeiture cases are filed in the federal courts every year and tens of thousands of seizures take place. The U.S. Supreme Court has decided numerous forfeiture cases in recent years, addressing such fundamental issues of constitutional law as due process, search and seizure, right to counsel, double jeopardy, and the proportionality of the property seized to the crime involved. In 2000, Congress enacted the Civil Asset Forfeiture Reform Act (CAFRA), which added a number of due process protections to the existing body of forfeiture statutes. And since that time, the Supreme Court has amended the Federal Rules of Criminal Procedure and Rules of Civil Procedure to deal more systematically with forfeiture matters. This comprehensive volume explains the law of forfeitures and how it is supposed to work. Its preparation was predicated on the fact that most of the fundamental issues regarding forfeiture have now been settled, allowing the author to accurately describe the current state of the law and provide practitioners with a practical guide to litigation in the federal courts. The book's 28 chapters are grouped under the following Parts: (1) Overview and History; (2) Administrative and Civil Forfeiture; (3) Criminal Forfeiture Procedure; (4) What if Forfeitable; and (5) Excessive Fines Clause of the 8th Amendment. This detailed and heavily annotated text features numerous citations to supporting court decisions, statutes, and federal rules, as well as a subject index. A companion CD-ROM provides a chart of each federal criminal offense with the corresponding forfeiture statute. It is authored by Stefan D. Cassella, one of the federal government's leading experts on asset forfeiture law. As a federal prosecutor, he has been litigating asset forfeiture cases since the late 1980's and is now the Deputy Chief of the Justice Department's Asset Forfeiture and Money Laundering Section. He teaches asset forfeiture procedure at the Federal National Advocacy Center at the University of South Carolina. A graduate of Georgetown University Law School, Mr. Cassella was also Senior Counsel to the U.S. Senate Judiciary Committee.

Clifford, Ralph D. **Cybercrime: The Investigation, Prosecution and Defense of a Computer-Related Crime**. 3d ed. Durham, NC: Carolina Academic Press, 2011. 1 vol. (301 pp.). Paperbound.
Cost: $38.00; from $31.45 on amazon.com (2014).
Computer users are increasingly the victims of, or vulnerable to, various forms of computer-related crime. The term cybercrime is the most commonly used term to describe the use of computer technology to engage in illegal activity. Cybercrime, as distinct from cyberwarfare or cyber terrorism, may involve either crimes of the traditional variety (e.g. theft, arson, extortion), or of a nature unique to modern technology, such as the distributed denial of service (DDoS) attack in which a multitude of compromised systems attack a single target and thereby causing a denial of service for users of the targeted system. Recent years have also witnessed a significant evolution in the nature of cybercrime, from one in which banking and financial cyber threats were the primary concerns to one in which child pornography, cyberharassment, and identity theft have become more predominant. There are now more than 40 federal statutes that can be engaged to prosecute cybercrime. Some of these statutes, including those addressing wire fraud, predate the rise of cybercrime. Others deal specifically with such cybercrimes as hacking, cracking, virus dissemination, and child pornography. This volume covers not only the various types of cybercrime under federal law, the investigatory process, the defense of cybercrime cases, and international cybercrime. The author, who has computer science education, is professor of law at the University of Massachusetts School of Law-Dartmouth where he has taught computer and cyber law for 25 years. As a former computer systems analyst and programmer, he has also written and spoken widely on the topic.

Cohen, Harvey M. and Joseph B. Green. **Apprehending and Prosecuting the Drunk Driver: A Manual for Police and Prosecution**. New York: Matthew Bender & Co., 1992-date. 1 vol. Looseleaf format. Includes pocket manual.
Cost: $361; supplementation: 1999: $63; 2000: $67; 2001: $72; 2002: $78; 2003: $82; 2004: $86; 2005: $92; 2006: $99; 2007: $107; 2008: $116; 2009: $125; 2010: $131; 2011: $137; 2012: $156; 2013: $170; 2014: $170; eBook: $361; renewal: 2014: $170.
This manual is designed to assist law enforcement officers and prosecutors with drunk driving arrests and prosecutions. It includes discussion of such topics as recognizing drunk drivers in motion, operating roadblocks, evaluating sensory clues of alcohol and drug impairment, the administration of field sobriety tests, the determination of probable cause, labeling and preserving test samples, videotaping suspects, evaluating a case before trial, deciding between plea bargain and trial, selecting a jury, and presenting the state's case at trial. Includes a bonus pocket manual for police officers.

Cook, Joseph G. **Constitutional Rights of the Accused.** 3d ed. St. Paul, MN: Thomson Reuters West (Clark Boardman Callaghan), 1996-date. 3 vols. Annual supplementation. Formerly published by Lawyers Cooperative.
Cost: $992; ProView eBook: $963; supplementation: 1997: $137.50; 1998: $145; 1999: $157; 2000: $169; 2001: $198; 2002: $233; 2003: $265; 2004: $297; 2005: $325; 2006: $365.50; 2007: $407; 2008: $779; 2009: $507.50; 2010: $558.50; 2011: $609; 2012: $883; 2013: $989; 2d edition: 1993: $80; 1994: $105; 1995: $125; **Monthly Assured Print Price (APP):** $77/$924.
An analysis of the constitutional rights of individuals accused of crimes by a leading authority in the area of civil rights and constitutional law. This three-volume set provides commentary on the development of the United States Supreme Court's position on such matters as standards of reasonableness under the 4th Amendment, the exclusion of evidence, admissibility of confessions, self-representation, and punishment. Chapters cover detention and arrest, search and seizure, entrapment, confessions, identification, right to counsel, self-representation, psychiatric examinations, lie detector tests, bail, indictment by grand jury, nature and causes of accusation, guilty pleas, speedy trial, public trial, trial by jury, the trial, appeals, punishment, probation and parole, pardons and communications, double jeopardy, habeas corpus. The text is not as dense or deeply analytical as other works in this area, but does include exhaustive citations to case law and Total Client-Service Library References to former Lawyers Cooperative publications, including the **American Law Reports**.

Criminal Defense Techniques. Edited by Michael Michelle A. Zeppetello and Ann W. Latner. New York: Matthew Bender & Co., 1969-date. 10 vols. Looseleaf format. Supplemented periodically. Also available on eBook.
Cost: $4,559 (includes annual subscription); e-book: $4,144; annual renewal: 1995: $1,237.50 (price frozen since 1992); 1996: $1,298; 1997: $1,298; 1998: $1,360; 1999: $1,415; 2000: $1,490; 2001: $1,594; 2002: $1,706; 2003: $1,792.00; 2004: $1,882; 2005: $1,976; 2006: $2,115; 2007: $2,284; 2008: $2,467; 2009: $2,664; 2010: $2,798; 2011: $2,882; 2012: $2,997; 2013: $3,087; 2014: $3,369; eBook: $4,144; renewal: 2014: $3,369.
This set provides detailed guidance to the criminal lawyer on all aspects of criminal defense. Individual chapters are authored by a team of more than 130 experts. **Criminal Defense Techniques** covers all phases of the criminal process from pre-trial motion tactics and techniques to criminal appeals. Included are such topics as bail and pre-trial release, search and seizure, wiretapping, discovery, evidence, direct and cross-examination, opening and closing statements, probation and parole, homicide, obscenity, military proceedings, use of forensic pathology, psychological evidence, behavior modification, the ABA criminal justice standards, and many more. One of the most exhaustive works of its kind in print.

Cost Saving Tips: As with most legal treatises, the primary cost is that for ongoing supplementation. This one is no exception. As with all Matthew Bender sets, this one is sold with a one year subscription. Consider dropping the subscription after one year and updating by buying a new set when you feel it is necessary. Don't be influenced by the publisher's desire to sell you costly supplements, particular for a secondary source that is only the starting point for your research. Don't hesitate to drop the subscription and buy another set at some future date, updating in the primary sources and with citator services. You will save yourself thousands in supplementation costs.

Criminal Law Advocacy. Written by Mark J. Kadish et al. with revisions by Matthew Bender editorial staff. New York: Matthew Bender & Co., 1982-date. 7 vols. Looseleaf format. Periodic supplementation.
Cost: $2,924 (includes annual subscription); annual renewal: 1995: $792 (price frozen since 1992); 1996: $831; 1997: $831: 1998: $870; 1999: $910; 2000: $910; 2001: $974; 2002: $1,043; 2003: $1,096; 2004: $1,151; 2005: $1,232. 2006: $1,319. 2007: $1,425; 2008: $1,539; 2009: $1,662; 2010: $1,746; 2011: $1,798. 2012: $1,870; 2013: $2,001; 2014: $2,184; eBook: $2,581; 2014: $2,184.
This seven-volume work is a detailed practitioner's guide to criminal law and practice. Individual volumes deal with: Trial Investigation and Preparation, Guilty Pleas, Trial Proof, Witness Examination (vols. 4 & 5), Argument to the Jury and Jury Selection. It addresses both substantive and procedural aspects of criminal law with examples of testimony, forms, and checklists. Volume one has particularly valuable and detailed discussion of the steps in the criminal process, including a chapter on case management. Other chapters examine discovery techniques, suppression of evidence, motion practice, plea bargaining, constitutional standards for accepting pleas, real evidence, elements of guilt, privileges, objections, operation of the rules of evidence, direct and cross-examination, perjury, successful opening and closing statements, eyewitness identification. Includes examples of arguments for real trials.

Cost Saving Tips: Drop the standing order after the initial year's service has expired, and buy another set at some future date, as necessary.

Decker, John F. and Bruce L. **Arson Law and Prosecution**. Durham, NC: Carolina Academic, 2009. 1 vol. (596 pp.).
Cost: $76; from $36.50 on amazon.com (2014).
The FBI's Uniform Crime Reporting Program defines arson as "any willful or malicious burning or attempt to burn, with or without intent to defraud, a dwelling house, public building, motor vehicle or aircraft, personal property of another, etc." Arson crimes, totaling 69,055 in 2006, are the cause of significant death, injury, and property damage, as well as significant financial loss from insurance fraud. This volume provides an in-depth of examination of what fire investigators, prosecutors, and defense attorneys should know about arson crime scene investigation and fire science, the procedures they must follow in conducting an investigation, and their role as expert witnesses in arson prosecutions. It also considers the relevant law of search and seizure and the police interrogation of witnesses and suspects. Additional chapters address the use of grand juries in arson cases, and the privilege against self-incrimination, state sharing statutes in the fifty states and the District of Columbia governing arson, the important relevant federal statutes, the law governing accessories and inchoate liability, and the defenses commonly raised in arson prosecutions. The concluding chapter is an edited transcript of the prosecution's evidence in an arson

trial that demonstrates the real-life juxtaposition of crime scene investigation and law. Intended as law school caseBook, this volume nevertheless provides a solid analytical discussion of the subject matter combined with excerpts of leading arson cases from across the country. John F. Decker is professor of Law Emeritus at DePaul University. Bruce L. Ottley Professor of Law at DePaul University.

The Department of Justice Manual. 3d ed. Gaithersburg, NY: Wolters Kluwer Law & Business, 2012-date. 8 vols. Looseleaf format. Supplemented 3-4 times annually.
Cost: $2,569; supplementation: 2000: $708; 2001: $720; 2002: $793; 2003: $813; 2004: $822; 2005: $1,152; 2006: $1,208; 2007: $1,288; 2008: $1,749; 2009: $1,476; 2010: $1,607; 2011: $1,808; 2012: $3,684 (including new ed.); 2013: $2,076.
This expanded eight-volume resource assembles the basic manuals, guidelines, policy statements, and procedures distributed by the Department of Justice which govern the actions of U.S. Attorneys working in the Justice Department's Civil, Environment and Natural Resources, Tax, Antitrust, Civil Rights, and Criminal Divisions, and U.S. Attorneys' Offices nationwide. Among these is the **United States Attorneys' Manual**, first published in 1980 and now available online at http://www.usdoj.gov/usao/eousa/foia_reading_room/usam. It is designed as a ready reference for U.S. Attorneys responsible for the prosecution of violations of federal law. It is intended a source of internal Department of Justice guidance and is not intended to create any rights, enforceable by law by any party in any civil or criminal matter. The Manual is divided into nine titles: General, Appeals, Executive Office for United States Attorneys, Civil, Environment and Natural Resources, Tax, Antitrust, Civil Rights, and Criminal. An essential resource for federal attorneys and those representing litigants or defendants in matters involving the application of federal law in the above named subject areas.

DerOhannesian, Paul. **Sexual Assault Trials**. 3d ed. Charlottesville, VA: LexisNexis, 2006-date. 2 vols. (1,099 pp.). Annual supplementation.
Cost: $220 (print or eBook); supplementation: 2007: $65; 2008: $69; 2009: $71; 2010: $74; 2011: $77; 2012: $81; 2013: $81; 2d ed.: 1999: $55; 2000: $65; 2001: $60; 2002: $68.00; 2003: $71; 2004: 0; 2005: 0; 2006: new edition.
This procedural guide to the conduct of a sexual assault trial is arranged chronologically from pretrial issues through summation. The author considers a panoply of issues which may arise in the course of trial, including child witness suggestibility, accommodating the sexual assault victim in the courtroom, the rape shield statute, cross-examination of a sexual assault complainant, and DNA and other scientific evidence. The author is a trial attorney who has served as Assistant District Attorney for Albany County, New York since 1979, and has prosecuted a significant number of sexual assault cases.

Dressler, Joshua. **Understanding Criminal Law**. 6th ed. New York: Matthew Bender & Co., 2012. 1 vol. (639 pp.). Legal Text Series.
Cost: $45; eBook: $36; from $27.94 on amazon.com; kindle: $30.49 (2014).
A basic, but comprehensive, guide to substantive criminal law which examines the elements of individual criminal responsibility. The author, a professor of law at McGeorge School of Law, University of the Pacific, describes and analyzes the basic elements of, and defenses to, all manner of criminal acts, including homicide, rape, theft, and assault. Comparisons are drawn between the common law rules and the Model Penal Code. The author also gives due consideration to the operation of the criminal justice system and to the utilitarian and retributivist philosophies which provide its theoretical foundation. For both the student and practitioner, there are numerous citations to primary law and secondary sources. This is a well-written, yet inexpensive, alternative to most of the practitioner-oriented treatises on the market.

Dressler, Joshua. **Understanding Criminal Procedure.** 6th ed. New York: Matthew Bender & Co., 2010. 2 vols. Legal Text Series.
Cost: $90 ($45 ea.); eBook: $72; vol. 1: from $35.83; vol. 2: $27.00 on amazon.com; kindle: vol. 1: $28.44; vol. 2: $28.44 (2014).
Designed to be used by law school criminal procedure classes, this set has been expanded to two volumes. Volume covers investigation; volume two, the adjudicative process. The authors provide a thorough treatment of the subject matter with some consideration of the values that have shaped the criminal justice system. The author, a professor of law at McGeorge School of Law, University of the Pacific, covers the overarching policy issues in criminal procedure, the incorporation of the Bill of Rights, general constitutional law doctrines, the fourth amendment (with an in depth examination of the subject of search and seizure and probable cause), arrests, search warrants, searches incident to lawful arrests, searches of cars and containers therein, "plain view" and related doctrines, inventory searches, consent searches, the "reasonableness" balancing standard in criminal investigations, standing, the exclusionary rule, interrogation law, coerced confessions, Miranda v. Arizona, right to counsel, privilege against self-incrimination, eyewitness identification, entrapment, right to counsel, pretrial release, plea bargaining and guilt pleas, and double jeopardy. The author provides sufficient citations to relevant Supreme Court decisions, the Federal Rules of Criminal Procedure, other leading cases and statutes, as well as the scholarly literature, to make this a useful and low cost basic handbook for the criminal law practitioner.

Erwin, Richard E., et al. **Defense of Drunk Driving Cases: Criminal - Civil**. 3d ed. New York: Matthew Bender, 1971-date. 4 vols. Looseleaf format and eBook. Authority CD-ROM includes no-cost online updating via LEXIS-NEXIS.
Cost: $1,950 (includes annual subscription); annual renewal: 1995: $568 (cost frozen since 1992); 1996: $596; 1997: $596; 1998: $630; 1999: $655; 2000: $655; 2001: $701; 2002: $751; 2003: $789; 2004: $828; 2005: $886; 2006: $949; 2007: $1,011; 2008: $1,072; 2009: $1,136; 2010: $1,171; 2011: $1,206; 2012: $1,254; 2013: $1,383; 2014: $1,437; CD-ROM: $2,406; renewal: 1998: $595; 1999: $655; 2000: $700; 2001: $749; 2002: $802; 2003: $843; 2004: $885. 2005: $947; 2006: $1,014; 2007: $1,080; 2008: $1,177; 2009: $1,248; 2010: $1,336; 2011: $1,416; 2012; $1,515; 2013: $1,621; 2014: $1,804.38; eBook:

$1,773; renewal: 2014: $1,437.
An in-depth analysis of the law governing drunk driving and related offenses. Chapters cover double jeopardy, preliminary hearings, penalties, case evaluation, trial procedures and techniques, jury selection, field sobriety tests, examining physicians, physician-patient privilege, chemical tests, blood analysis, the intoximeter and other testing devices, chain of evidence, affirmative defenses, refusal to submit, constitutional objections, implied consent legislation, expert and character witnesses, jury instructions, etc. Also includes a bibliography, index and table of cases. This work is also heavily laced with citations to primary authority, forms and interrogatories. Statutory appendix includes citations and descriptions of drunk driving offenses for all fifty states.

Cost Saving Tip: While this is an exhaustive work with many features to recommend it, you may balk at the high supplementation cost. If so, simply treat it as a non-supplemented monograph and update in the traditional manner using primary sources, Shepards, etc. If you have a continuing need for this set, you may decide to purchase a new set, say, every 3-4 years. Also consider buying the set used in the first place, particularly if you have no desire to keep it up-to-date.

Ewing, Charles Patrick. **Insanity: Murder, Madness, and the Law**. New York: Oxford University Press 2008. 1 vol. (188 pp.).
Cost: $39.95; from $25.99 on amazon.com; kindle: $31.16 (2014).
The use of the insanity defense in murder cases has a venerable history in the American legal system. Employed as a defense to many crimes, its use is generally controversial only in murder cases where the public is highly suspicious of its use and tends to view it as a device to escape punishment, and as a product of the influence of lawyers and psychologists rather than the defendant's true mental state. This volume includes ten in-depth analyses of the most influential, or infamous, cases in which the insanity defense was invoked, each of which involved extensive testimony by psychologists and psychiatrists. Following a brief introduction and historical overview of the insanity defense, the author examines the real-life cases of Jacob Rubenstein (Jack Ruby), Robert Torsney, David Berkowitz ("Son of Sam"), John Wayne Gacy, Arthur Shawcross, Scott Panetti, Eric Smith, Andrew Goldstein, Eric Michael Clark, and Andrea Yates. Charles Patrick Ewing is a forensic psychologist, attorney, and Distinguished Service Professor at the State University of New York. He is the author of **Minds on Trial: Great Cases in Law and Psychology** (2006). This volume provides illuminating insight into the manner in which the insanity defense was employed in the courtroom.

Farrell, Thomas J. **Criminal Defense Tools and Techniques**. Santa Ana, CA: James Publishing, 2008-date. 2 vols. (various pagings). Looseleaf format.
Cost: $149; supplementation: 2009-2014: $69.99 per year.
A complete step-by-step guide to the process of criminal defense, from initial representation to appeal. The author provides detailed guidance on matters of both law and procedure, with selective citations to the applicable case, statutes and court rules. Individual chapters cover the representation agreement, arrest and initial appearance, bail and pre-trial release, extradition, experts and investigators, search and seizure, interrogations, confessions and other statements, identification procedures, preliminary hearings, forfeiture, grand jury practice, mental health issues, discovery, motion practice, plea bargaining, representing victims and witnesses, related civil litigation, trial, post-trial motions, sentencing, probation, parole and other post-release supervision, and appeals. Organized in a convenient outline form, the text is supplemented with applicable forms and practice tips. The complete text and forms are replicated on a fully searchable CD-ROM. Thomas J. Farrell is a partner with the Pittsburgh firm of Dreier L.L.P. where he maintains a wide-ranging criminal defense practice. He was selected as one of the Best Lawyers in America in 2006 and 2007 for white collar and non-white collar criminal defense.

Fishman, Clifford S. and Anne T. McKenna. **Wiretapping and Eavesdropping: Surveillance in the Internet Age.** 3d ed. St. Paul, MN: Thomson Reuters West (Clark Boardman Callaghan), 2008-date. 4 vols. or ProView eBook. Annual supplementation.
Cost: $845; ProView eBook: $820; supplementation: 2009: $112; 2010: $244; 2011: $268; 2012: $295; 2013: $337; 2d ed.: 1996: $110; 1997: $70; 1998: $74; 1999: $80; 2000: $87; 2001: $101; 2002: $153; 2003: $153; 2004: $134.50; 2005: $165; 2006: $184; 2007: $499; 2008: $599; **Monthly Assured Print Price (APP):** $35/$420.
A general overview of the law of electronic surveillance. Chapter coverage includes general matters, consensual interceptions, non-consensual exceptions to warrant requirement, decision to seek warrant, the application, the warrant, establishing the listening post, executing warrants, extensions and second generation warrants, post-execution procedures, eavesdropping evidence and the grand jury, preliminary defense strategy and motions, grounds for suppression, litigating the suppression motion, trial issues relating to tapes and transcripts, the trial, and equipment and tape control procedures. Larger print and greater use of white space render this volume less detailed than Carr's **The Law of Electronic Surveillance**, also a one volume work from the CBC.

Floyd, John E. **RICO State by State: A Guide to Litigation Under the State Racketeering Statutes**. 2d ed. Chicago: Section of Antitrust Law, American Bar Association, 2011. 1 vol. (1,372 pp.).
Cost: $249; $199 to members (2014).
A collection of laws and decisions from the thirty-three states which have adopted a statute patterned after the federal Racketeer Influenced and Corrupt Organizations (RICO) statute. The state laws are preceded by a succinct 60-page overview of RICO law.

Gershman, Bennett L. **Prosecutorial Misconduct**. St. Paul, MN: Thomson Reuters West, 2002-date. 1 vol. Paperbound. Annual replacement editions or ProView eBook.
Cost: 2013-2014 Edition: $481; 2010-2011: $371; 2011-2012: $404; 2012-2013 Edition: $441 (2014).
This volume provides critical and systematic examination of the guidelines for prosecutorial behavior and when that behavior

crosses the line into misconduct. The chapters focus on specific manifestations of prosecutorial misconduct, including investigative misconduct, prosecutorial misconduct in the grand jury, abuse of process, abuse of the charging function, suppression of evidence, misconduct in the plea bargaining process, delay, misconduct in the presentation of evidence, forensic misconduct, prosecutorial-provoked mistrials and double jeopardy, and misconduct on sentencing. The author also examines the relationship between the prosecutor and the media. The text is buttressed with citations to thousands of court decisions, including extensive discussion of the case of DeShaney v. Winnebago County Dept. of Social Services, 489 U.S. 189 (1989). Originally published in 1985 by the Clark Boardman Company (now part of the West).

Gershman, Bennett L. **Trial Error and Misconduct**. 2d ed. Charlottesville, VA: LexisNexis, 2007-date. 1 vol. (577 pp.) or eBook. Annual supplementation.
Cost: $161; supplementation: 2008: $60; 2009: $70; 2010: $74; 2011: $81; 2012: $87; 2013: $90; 1st ed.: 1999: $45; 2001: $55; 2002: $68; 2003: $71; 2004: $75; 2005: $79; 2006: $83; 2007: new edition.
This volumes addresses what the author terms the "pathologies" of the criminal trial and examines the roles of four key participants in the process: judges, prosecutors, defense lawyers, and juries. Each of these key participants is capable of infecting the trial process by violating the rules of proper trial conduct. These rules of trial conduct are rooted in the Sixth Amendment and the due process clause, supported by the procedural and evidentiary codes, and buttressed by the common law, ethical rules, and individual conscience. The first four chapters provide an in-depth examination of specific actions taken by judge, prosecutor, defense counsel, and jury that may constitute either error or rise to the level of misconduct. Chapter five examines a variety of special issues arising in the context of trial error and misconduct, including permissible and impermissible bolstering of witness credibility, polygraph tests, alibi witnesses, children's testimony, eyewitnesses, spies and stool pigeons, multiple defendants, and experts. Chapter six provides a review of the various means by which error and misconduct are reviewed and remedied, and the standards to be applied by appellate courts in conducting that review. The author, a former prosecutor in the New York State Anti-Corruption Unit and special assistant to the Attorney General, is a Professor of Law, Pace University School of Law.

Hankin, Ron. **Navigating the Legal Minefields of Private Investigations: A Career-Saving Guide for Private Investigators, Detectives, and Security Police**. Flushing, NY: Looseleaf Law Publications, 2009. 1 vol. (210 pp.). Paperbound.
Cost: $24.95; from $12.73 on amazon.com (2014).
Private investigators, whether designated as private detectives or private security officers, derive their authority from the state in which they are licensed. The typical state licensing act limits their issuance to applicants of good moral character with prior government-police or police-like civilian experience. The rationale for strict licensing requirements for private investigators lies in the fact that such operatives lack a hierarchy of authority which attends those employed by governmental entities. Not surprisingly, private investigators operate in a legal environment that exposes them to great personal and professional liability. The aim of this manual is to alert private investigators and special police to those areas of practice which may expose them to liability under state or federal law, or to civil liability. Among the topics addressed are the lawful authority of private investigators or private security operatives, the liability of private operatives, ruse, impersonation, obstruction; surveillance, stalking, trespass or invasion of privacy, defamation, false accusations, power of the subpoena of operative's file during litigation; eavesdropping, picture taking, tracking devices, polygraph, interrogation of subjects, arrest authority of private special police, search and seizure, warrants, stop and frisk, and more. The author has experience as both a police investigator and a licensed private investigator. This is an essential read for any private investigator or the attorney who provides them with legal counsel.

Hardy, Peter D. **Criminal Tax, Money Laundering, and Bank Secrecy Act Litigation**. Arlington, VA: Bloomberg BNA Books, 2010. 1 vol. (1,669 pp.).
Cost: $525.00; supplementation: 2011: $295; 2012: $300; 2013: 0 (2014).
The Internal Revenue Service is the only investigatory agency with jurisdiction over federal criminal tax offenses. Its role has expanded in recent years with the growth of sophisticated criminal activity involving money laundering operations, offshore bank accounts, tax evasion by individuals and corporations, and violations of the Bank Secrecy Act (BSA). The average criminal IRS case is more likely to involve complex fact patterns, technical law, legal privileges, logistical challenges, and difficult questions regarding what constitutes a criminal mental state. Enforcement of the tax code can increase the litigation exposure of corporations, and involve attorney-client privilege, parallel civil and criminal proceedings, deferred prosecution agreements, evidence and conduct in foreign jurisdictions, and the difficulties involved in drawing a line between civil and criminal violations. Moreover, the IRS is now using the Bank Secrecy Act to pursue not only traditional currency reporting offenses, but to step up enforcement of offshore reporting requirements, and to require and enforce anti-money-laundering requirements for financial institutions. The monumental scope of this volume is a reflection of the complexity of the criminal cases now handled by the IRS and federal prosecutors at the Justice Department. It addresses not only current law and procedure, but offers expert practical guidance in handling a federal criminal case from beginning to end, including the full range of complex legal, factual, logistical, and tactical issues which accompany such litigation. While its primary focus is on criminal cases handled by the IRS, this volume also explores the important legal issues that may exist in a complex white-collar practice, including offshore accounts, tax shelter prosecutions, corporate prosecutions, sentencing in white collar cases, and the Supreme Court's recent interpretation of the money laundering statutes. Following an illuminating overview of the nature of IRS criminal enforcement, chapters are devoted to the consideration of the criminal tax statutes, money laundering, the Bank Secrecy Act, the investigation and review process, special issues, pleas agreements, pretrial practice, trial, and sentencing. The text is heavily supported with citations to relevant primary and secondary authorities, including IRS code sections and regulations, and federal court decisions. Designed for use by both prosecutors and defense counsel, this volume will also serve as an essential reference tool for corporate counsel, financial institutions, business and tax professionals, and federal

government agencies. The Appendices include a variety relevant federal documents, including a currency transaction report, depository institution suspicious activity report, and a sample agreements involving deferred prosecution of a financial audit, tax and advisory services firm, among others. Peter D. Hardy is a principal in the Philadelphia firm of Post & Schell's national White Collar Defense, Compliance & Risk Management Practice Group. A former federal prosecutor, his practice focuses on the counseling and defense of corporations, directors, officers, managers, professionals and others who may face allegations of business-related or other misconduct.

Hertz, Randy and James S. Liebman. **Federal Habeas Corpus Practice and Procedure**. 7th ed. Newark, NJ: LexisNexis/Matthew Bender, 2011-date. 2 vols. (2,465 pp.), CD, or eBook. Annual supplementation.

Cost: $481 (print or eBook); supplementation: 2012: 0; 2013: 0 6th ed.: 2006: $46; 2007: $53; 2008: $80; 2009: $88; CD-ROM with book: $753.

This comprehensive scholarly examination of habeas corpus relief in capital and non-capital cases, was substantially revised following passage of the Antiterrorism and Effective Death Penalty Act of 1996 (AEDPA), which itself revised and superseded certain provisions of prior habeas corpus law while leaving other provisions substantially unchanged. First published in 1988, this 5th edition brings clarity to a field of law rendered more confusing by successive congressional enactments and conflicting constitutional and interpretive issues. Described as an introduction to the procedures available for securing federal habeas corpus review this book's 42 chapters include an introductory examination of habeas corpus, an overview of federal habeas corpus process under AEDPA, and the client. The remaining chapters address the timing of a federal habeas corpus petition and state remedies, habeas corpus jurisdiction, ancillary and summary proceedings upon filing, magistrate judge practice and fact development procedures, procedural defenses, adjudication of the merits, post judgment proceedings and appeals, and federal prisoners and detainees. The authors' analysis embraces not only the substantial body of federal case law, but the federal statues (particularly AEDPA), and the vast secondary scholarly literature. The text is enhanced with exhaustive footnotes and case summaries, and its appendices include the text of relevant statutes, federal court rules, and legislative history materials. There are also tables of cases, constitutional provisions, federal statutes, state statutes and rules, foreign statutes, legislative sources and, federal rules and regulations, and secondary authorities.

Hutchison, Thomas W., et al. **Federal Sentencing Law and Practice**. St. Paul, MN: Thomson Reuters West, 1997-date. 1 vol. (1,616 pp.). Courtroom Practice Series. Annual editions. Softbound or ProView eBook.

Cost: 2014 Edition: $303; **Monthly Assured Print Price (APP):** $22/$264 (2014).

Federal sentencing law was significantly altered by the Sentencing Reform Act of 1984 which curtailed the discretion of the sentencing judge, abolished parole, reduced good time credit, and authorized the appeal of sentences by the prosecution and the defense. The Federal Sentencing Commission created under this act was charged with the preparation of a detailed manual to the federal sentencing guidelines designed for use by judges, prosecutors, defense attorneys, probation officers, and others. The first eight chapters of this volume annotate the eight chapters of the United States Sentencing Commission's **Guidelines Manual**, the official version of the guidelines and include Author's Comments written by the authors of this book. Chapters 9-10 provide the authors' explanation and analysis of departures from the guidelines and appellate review of sentences.

Imwinkelried, Edward J., Paul C. Giannelli, Francis A. Gilligan, Frederic I. Lederer. **Courtroom Criminal Evidence**. 5th ed. Charlottesville, VA: LexisNexis, 2005-date. 2 vols. or eBook. Annual supplementation.

Cost: $230; supplementation: 2006: $72; 2007: $42; 2008: $42; 2009: $49; 2010: $55; 2011: $45; 2012: $48; 2013: $51; 2d ed.: 1994: $30; 1995: $40; 1996: $47.50; 1997: $52.50; 1998: 3d edition; 1999: $40; 2000: $62; 2001: $73; 2002: $74; 2003: $77; 2004: $81; 2005: $86.

Operating from the basic premise that an understanding of the rules of evidence is second in importance only to a knowledge of procedure, the authors of this textbook have attempted to write a work designed for courtroom use by the trial attorney. The authors contrast this text to such scholarly texts as those written by Wigmore, Weinstein, Wright and Graham, LaFave, and Whitebread intended for use in preparation of formal legal documents such as briefs and memoranda. Consequently, the authors have attempted to limit the number of citations in favor of substantive text which can provide guidance to the attorney in an courtroom environment. This volume provides an up-to-date overview of the current status of the law of evidence in criminal trials, encompassing the common law, the Federal Rules of Evidence, federal statutes, and exclusionary rules enunciated by the U.S. Supreme Court. Topics covered include scientific evidence (including DNA), character and habit evidence, hearsay exceptions, as well as the exclusionary rule. Chapters cover an introductory overview of the origins of the law of evidence, trial procedures, competency of witnesses, relevance, authentication, real evidence, credibility, uncharged misconduct, expert and lay opinion testimony, best evidence rule, privileges for confidential relations, search or seizure, probable cause and warrants, warrantless searches, voluntariness, the Miranda doctrine, right to counsel, suppression of confessions, eyewitness identification, burdens of production and proof, judicial notice, and stipulations. Both in substance and style, this in an excellent companion to the scholarly works on evidence and is highly recommended for the criminal trial attorney.

Imwinkelried, Edward J. and Daniel D. Blinka. **Criminal Evidentiary Foundations**. 2d ed. Newark, NJ: Lexis Law Publishing, 2007-date. 1 vol. (562 pp.) Print or eBook. Annual supplementation.

Cost: $137 (print or eBook); supplementation: 1997: $20; 1999: $30; 2000: $35; 2001: $44; 2002: $44; 2003: 0; 2004: $48; 2005: $51; 2006: $54; 2007: new edition; 2008: $108; 2010: $52; 2011: $55; 2012: $58; 2013: $61.

Laying the groundwork for the introduction of evidence in criminal trials requires skill and preparation. This practitioner's handbook provides specific guidance to criminal litigators who wish to introduce and control the introduction of evidence. The authors provide explanations for the phrasing of questions on direct and cross-examination and numerous sample questions adapted for criminal trials. The book chapters examine such topics as the competency of witnesses, authentication, Rule 403 and legal relevance limitations on credible evidence, legal relevance limitations on evidence that is relevant to the historical merits of the case, privileges and similar doctrines, the best evidence rule, opinion evidence, the hearsay rule, its exemptions, and its exceptions, substitutes for evidence, and motion to suppress evidence. Edward Imwinkelried, Professor of Law at the University of California at Davis, is one of the nation's leading authorities on the subjects of evidence and criminal law. Daniel Blinka, Associate Professor of Law at Marquette University School of Law, former District Attorney, and co-author of Pretrial Motions in Criminal Prosecutions.

Imwinkelried, Edward J. and Norman M. Garland. **Exculpatory Evidence: The Accused's Constitutional Right to Introduce Favorable Evidence**. 3d ed. Charlottesville, VA: LexisNexis, 2012-date. 1 vol. (572 pp.). Print or eBook. Annual pocket supplement.
Cost: $194; supplementation: 2005: $84; 2006: $88; 2007: $105; 2008: $113; 2009: $130; 2010: $134; 2011: $138; 2012: $148; 2013: $153; 2d ed.: 1997: $35; 1998: $40; 1999: $45; 2000: $60; 2001: $71; 2002: $75; 2003: $79.
The American criminal justice system provides individual defendants the right to present evidence supporting their theory of a case, a right raised to constitutional status by the U.S. Supreme Court in the case of Washington v. Texas, 388 U.S. 14 (1967). Although several law review articles have examined this development in the case law, this is the first comprehensive, book-length study of the constitutional right to present exculpatory evidence in criminal proceedings. Edward J. Imwinkelried, Professor of Law at the University of California at Davis, is one of the most prolific scholars in the field, having authored at least a dozen books and numerous law review articles on various aspects of evidence. His co-author is Professor of Law at Southwestern University Law School. This volumes includes numerous citations to case and statutory law, as well as a bibliography of related books and articles on the subject.

Kreit, Alex. **Controlled Substances: Crime, Regulation, and Policy**. Durham, NC: Carolina Academic Press, 2013. 1 vol. (983 pp.).
Cost: $100.00; from $95.00 on amazon.com (2014).
Drug offenses and convictions constitute the single largest category of crime in the United States, with more than 1.5 million arrests in 2011. Drug convictions have also fueled an explosion in the U.S. prison population, constituting nearly one-quarter of those incarcerated. This has taken place despite the war on drugs, which has consumed an enormous amount of human and financial resources since 1970. This casebook provides a comprehensive overview of drug-related crime, its regulation, and its public policy implications. The book begins with materials bearing on the debate between advocates of prohibition and alternative responses to the drug problem, with particular attention on the modern "war on drugs" model of prohibition. With this foundation, the book turns its attention to an examination of the drug laws themselves, and in-depth look at controlled substances offenses, drug sentencing, and the investigation of drug crimes. It also examines the body of administrative law that governs the classification of controlled substances and the use and distribution of controlled substance for medical purposes. It concludes with an overview of international and comparative issues in drug law. The volume contains an illuminating selection of court decisions, law review articles, and other readings. Alex Kreit is Associate Professor of Law, Thomas Jefferson School of Law.

LaFave, Wayne R., Jerold H. Israel, Nancy J. King, and Orin S. Kerr. **Criminal Procedure**. 5th ed. St. Paul, MN: West, 2009-date. 1 vol. (1,452 pp.). Annual supplementation. Hornbook Series. Available from West Academic. Online ed. available from Thomson Reuters West.
Cost: $92; online edition; $62; supplementation: $20.00; 2009: new ed.; 3d ed: 2000: $8.95; 2001: 0; 2002: $10; 2003: $10; 2004: 4th ed.; 2005: $12.00; 2006: $12; 2007: $12; 2008: $20; 2009: new edition.
This inexpensive student Hornbook covers all the major stages in the criminal justice process. Beginning with an introduction to the criminal justice process and the constitutionalization of criminal procedure, its chapters cover the entire criminal process from the detection and investigation of crime to the commencement of formal proceedings, the adversary system and the determination of guilt or innocence. Provides sufficient detail to be significant value to the attorney in criminal practice. Contains selective citations to primary and secondary authorities. Appendices include a Westlaw research guide with a focus on criminal procedure issues, table of cases, and index.

LaFave, Wayne R., Jerold H. Israel and Nancy J. King. **Criminal Procedure.** 3d ed. St. Paul, MN: Thomson Reuters West, 2007-date. 7 vols. Irregular supplementation. Criminal Practice Series.
Cost: $874; supplementation: 2007: $521.50 (new vols.); 2008: $105; 2009: $122.50; 2010: $180; 2011: $158; 2012: $175; 2013: $192.50; 2d ed.: 2000: $173; 2001: $194; 2002; $228; 2003: $262.50; 2004: $298; 2005: $219; 2006: $248.50; **Monthly Assured Print Price (APP):** $31/$372.
An in-depth analysis of the complete criminal justice process from investigation to post-appeal collateral attacks. The authors have attempted to devote greater coverage to the more significant procedural aspects of the law, particularly those not addressed by other specialized treatises. Discussion also treats historical origins and policy considerations in addition to bare description. Chapters are devoted to an overview of the criminal justice process, due process, arrest, search and seizure, wiretapping and electronic surveillance, police "encouragement" and the entrapment defense, interrogation and confessions, identification procedures, grand jury investigation, scope and administration of exclusionary rules, right to counsel, pretrial release, decision whether to prosecute, preliminary hearing, grand jury review, location of the prosecution, joinder and severance, speedy trial,, guilty pleas, jury trials, fair trial and free press, criminal trial, double jeopardy, sentencing procedures, appeals, collateral review. Appendices include selected provisions of the U.S. Constitution, selected federal statutes, federal rules of criminal

procedure, Federal Rules of Criminal Procedure for the U.S. District Court, selected state statutes, etc. With the release of the long-awaited 2d edition, this remains an excellent resource for the law of criminal procedure with reasonably priced annual pocket parts.

LaFave, Wayne R. **Search and Seizure: A Treatise on the Fourth Amendment.** 5th ed. St. Paul, MN: Thomson Reuters West, 2012-date. 6 vols. Annual pocket parts. Criminal Practice Series.
Cost: $1,028; supplementation: 2013: $160; to 4th ed: 2005: $129; 2006: $135; 2007: $150.50; 2008: $168; 2009: $193.50; 2010: $213; 2011: $250; 2012: new ed.; 3d ed.: 1996: $40; 1997: $49; 1998: $55; 1999: $64; 2000: $75; 2001: $89; 2002: $96; 2003: $109.50; 2004: $471 (new edition); **Monthly Assured Print Price (APP):** $47/$564.
An exhaustive analysis of the law of search and seizure under the Fourth Amendment. The author's intent is to provide a systematic examination of the current state of Fourth Amendment law as well as a critical assessment of the manner in which the Supreme Court and lower courts have dealt with search and seizure issues. While heavily documented, this work does not attempt to provide an exhaustive list of cases for each jurisdiction, but does provide extensive discussion of the many subtle differences in a field of jurisprudence which is highly fact-oriented. The chapters in this four-volume set cover the exclusionary rule and other remedies, protected areas and interests, probable cause, search warrants, seizure and search of persons and personal effects, entry and search of premises, search and seizure of vehicles, consent searches, stop-and-frisk and similar lesser intrusions, inspections and regulatory searches, and administration of the exclusionary rule. Volume four contains a Tables of Cases, Statutes, and Rules and Regulations, and a subject index. An excellent resource and value. The author does a fine job of interweaving a discussion of examples and distinctive aspects of the law into his well written comprehensive analysis. Supplementation cost has historically been quite reasonable for a four-volume set.

LaFave, Wayne R. and Austin W. Scott, Jr. **Substantive Criminal Law**. 2d ed. St. Paul, MN: Thomson Reuters West, 1986-date. 3 vols. Annual pocket parts. Criminal Practice Series.
Cost: $492; supplementation: 1995: $35; 1996: $35; 1997: $39; 1998: $42; 1999:; 2000: $53; 2001: $62; 2002: $73; 2003: $289.50; 2004: $54; 2005: $59.25; 2006: $67.50; 2007: $75; 2008: $84; 2009: $109.50; 2010: $120; 2011: $132; 2012: $154; 2013: $180; **Monthly Assured Print Price (APP)**: $22/$264.
This two-volume general overview of criminal law is an updating of the authors' earlier Criminal Law Hornbook. Wayne LaFave is the David C. Baum Professor of Law and Professor in the Center for Advanced Study, University of Illinois. The late Austin W. Scott, Jr. was Professor of Law at the University of Colorado. It is intended for use by prosecutors, defense attorneys, and trial and appellate judges and others with interest in the practical application of the law. It is not an procedural handbook, however, but a exposition of the more theoretical aspects of criminal law based on a close examination of appellate case law. Chapters cover introduction and general overview of criminal law, sources and general limitations, basic premises of the criminal law, responsibility, justification and excuse, anticipatory offenses, parties, crimes against the person, and crimes relating to property. Appendices include the Model Penal Code, WESTLAW references, table of cases, table of statutes and Model Penal Code references, table of authorities, and subject index. WESTLAW references are liberally sprinkled throughout the text as aid to on-line research. An excellent scholarly resource with extensive citations to primary authority. Supplementation costs are reasonable for a three-volume set. A better value than the four-volume **Wharton's Criminal Law** (CBC).

Lane, Fred and Irving Goldstein. **Lane's Goldstein Trial Technique.** 3d ed. St. Paul, MN: Thomson Reuters West (Clark Boardman Callaghan), 1984-date. 3 vols. Looseleaf format or ProView eBook. Annual supplementation.
Cost: $1,923; supplementation: 1993: $102; 1994: $125; 1995: $211; 1996: $220; 1997: $250; 1998: $250; 1999: $270; 2000: $293; 2001: $346; 2002: $405; 2003: $462; 2004: $517; 2005: $530; 2006: $729; 2007: $729; 2008: $812.50; 2009: $931; 2010: $1,024; 2011: $1,116; 2012: $1,227; 2013: $516; **Monthly Assured Print Price (APP):** $140/$1,680.
This work had its origins in Judge Irving Goldstein's long association with the Trial Technique Institute in Chicago where he taught for many years. The first edition was Judge Goldstein's attempt to provide attorneys with a practical compendium of the procedures and techniques necessary for successful litigation. Fred Lane, a practicing attorney with the firm of Lane & Munday, is Dean of the Trial Technique Institute and past-President of the Illinois Bar Association, began teaching at the Institute with Judge Goldstein in the early 1960's. Consequently, this work reflects the experience of attorneys from every jurisdiction in the country who have studied at the Institute over the years. This is a well-organized and highly readable work of a length which properly balances the need for completeness with the requirements of economy. It covers each stage of the litigation process, from trial preparation to appellate practice. The text, which addresses both substantive and procedural matters, is supplemented with pleading forms, sample trial questions, questionnaires, memoranda of law, opening and closing statements. There are adequate, but not overpowering, citations to primary law and secondary sources. Where appropriate, the author cites to case law from both the U.S. courts and individual states. An excellent and highly recommended resource for the trial attorney. Purportedly, one of the best selling practice books on the market .

Cost Saving Tips: If you acquire this set as a general reference on trial technique, drop the standing order to the costly supplementation. This is little more than a cash cow for the publisher. There are much less costly ways of keeping up-to-date on the substantive criminal law.

Lanier, Charles S., William J. Bowers, and James R. Acker, eds. **The Future of America's Death Penalty: An Agenda for the Next Generation of Capital Punishment Research**. Durham, NC: Carolina Academic Press, 2009. 1 vol. (552 pp.). Paperbound.
Cost: $56; from $28.04 on amazon.com (2014).
Capital punishment is the killing of a person by judicial process

as punishment for an offense. Those crimes that can result in a death penalty are known as *capital crimes* or *capital offences*. Although over the course of human history capital punishment has been practiced in virtually every society, only 58 nations currently practice it, while 95 countries have abolished it. Scholarly research on the subject of capital punishment is often considered by legislatures and courts in the implementation of legislative or judicial remedies. These may involve a variety of public policy efforts, including attempts at reform, the declaration of a moratorium while the issue is studied comprehensively, or its outright abolishment. This collection of scholarly studies attempts to survey not what we know, but what we need to know about the death penalty. The authors were asked to identify questions in their areas of expertise that are most urgently in need of answers and to sketch out how best to obtain those answers. This book has its origins in a symposium held by the Capital Punishment Research Initiative of the University of Albany School of Criminal Justice in October 2006. The 23 essays fall under five broad categories of investigation: general research directions and challenges, the process leading to a capital sentence, the process beyond the sentencing decision, the utility and efficacy of the capital sanction, and examining the punishment of death. Each examines the current state of research, outlines key findings, points to future areas on inquiry, and draws certain tentative conclusions. Each is also accompanied by a list of references. The concluding chapter lays out an agenda for the next generation of capital punishment research. The editors are all professors at the University of Albany School of Criminal Justice. An excellent source of cutting edge research for lawyers and scholars involved in the field of criminal law generally, and capital cases specifically.

Lawless, Joseph F. **Prosecutorial Misconduct: Law, Procedure, and Forms**. 4th ed. Charlottesville, VA: LexisNexis Matthew Bender, 2008. 1 vol. Print or eBook. Annual supplementation.

Cost: $215; supplementation: 2009: $44; 2010: $46; 2011: $48; 2012: $51; 2013: $54; 3d ed.: 2004: $50; 2005: $53; 2006: $56; 2007: $59; 2008: new edition.

The expansion of government power to investigate and prosecute criminal activity can lead to abuse on the part of both state and federal prosecutors. Now in its third edition, this volume provides comprehensive and analytical coverage of every stage in the trial process, from criminal investigation to appeal and post-conviction remedies. The author provides an overview of the prosecution function, grand jury abuses and how to combat them, and prosecutorial abuse of the decision to charge. Additional chapters address the press and prosecutor, abuses of the discovery process, plea negotiations, agreements, and strategy, unnecessary delay, prosecutorial abuses in jury selection, abuses in opening and closing arguments, misconduct in evidentiary proceedings, mistrials, double jeopardy, retrial problems, prosecutorial misconduct at sentencing, actions, sanctions for misconduct, stings, scams, entrapment, and collateral attacks. Appendices include tables of cases, statutes and other authorities, and an index. The third edition includes a complete collection of motions, briefs, and arguments from actual cases handled by noted criminal defense attorneys, including Gary Spence, David Kendall, and Michael Tigar, and including the Jason Williams murder case, the Clinton/Lewinsky grand jury probe, and the Buddhist Temple fundraising case, among others. Joseph F. Lawless is a highly regarded criminal defense attorney who maintains a national practice in white-collar criminal defense and complex civil litigation from Philadelphia. He has successfully represented corporate and individual defendants in grand jury investigations, at trial and on appeal in federal and state courts, before Congress and other government agencies on charges ranging from bank fraud, bribery, government contracting fraud, racketeering, public corruption, and other matters. He is past Chair of the Criminal Law Section of the Association of Trial Lawyers of America.

Leitzel, Jim. **Regulating Vice: Misguided Prohibitions and Realistic Controls**. Port Chester, NY, Cambridge University Press, 2008. 1 vol. (318 pp.).

Cost: $108 (hardcover); $36.99 (paper); eBook: $30.00; from $0.01 in paper on amazon.com (2014).

The traditional regulation of gambling, drugs, alcohol, prostitution, and other vices, while generally misguided, is a not irrational response to the negative consequences of unlimited access to such behaviors and substances. This interdisciplinary and scholarly study of the various vices examines the issue of whether or not vices can be controlled, and the best policies for controlling or minimizing their impact. Sin taxes, advertising restrictions, licensing, and governmental subsidies for treatment are all potentially desirable components of balanced vice policies. The author argues that public policies toward various addictive practices should work well in many circumstances, including those in which the participants are rational and fully informed, as well as situations in which vice-related choices are characterized by lapses of self-control or irrationality. His analysis rules out the prohibition of most private adult vices while supporting the application of controls on access to such substances as alcohol, tobacco, and cocaine. Chapters include: (1) The harm principle; (2) Addiction: rational and otherwise; (3) The robustness principle; (4) Prohibition; (5) Taxation, licensing, and advertising controls; (6) Commercial sex; (7) The Internet and vice; (8) Free trade and federalism; Conclusions. The appendices include various vice statistics and references. Jim Leitzel, who received his PhD in economics from Duke University, teaches public policy and economics at the University of Chicago. He is the founding member of Vice Squad (vicesquad.blogspot.com), a blog devoted to vice policy.

Levy, Steven Mark. **Federal Money Laundering Regulation: Banking, Corporate, and Securities Compliance**. 2d ed. New York: Wolters Kluwer Law & Business, 2008-date. 1 vol. Looseleaf format. Annual supplementation (June).

Cost: $359; supplementation: 2009: $189; 2010: $199; 2011: $210; 2012: $225; 2013: $241; 1st ed.: 2004: $48; 2005: $147; 2006: $55; 2007: $165; 2008: new edition (2014).

The role of money laundering in various types of criminal activity--particularly drug trafficking, organized crime and international terrorism--has brought with it increased attention from law enforcement authorities. Financial institutions, corporations and securities dealers are particularly at risk from money laundering. In addition, financial institutions are at risk of inadvertent non-compliance with the laws and regulations promulgated to combat these criminal activities. Both authoritative and practical, this publication provides timely analysis and discussion of money laundering and asset forfeiture for attorneys, executives, business owners, financial personnel, government regulators, investors and those accused of money laundering. Twenty-seven chapters address such topics as how money is laundered, U.S. money laundering laws, law enforcement and regulatory requirements, recordkeeping and reporting, reporting requirements, Suspicious Activity Report (SAR), Currency Transaction Report (CTR), anti-money laundering programs for institutions, money laundering crimes, asset forfeiture, state money laundering laws, and worldwide efforts against money laundering. Appendices include the Bank Secrecy Act (BSA), Internal Revenue Code 6050I, and significant federal statutes relating to money laundering crimes and forfeitures.

Loftus, Elizabeth F., James M. Doyle, and Jennifer E. Dysart. **Eyewitness Testimony: Civil and Criminal**. 5th ed. Charlottesville, VA: LexisNexis, 2013-date. 1 vol. (415 pp.) Print or eBook.
Cost: $190 (print or e-book); no supplementation to date; 4th edition: 2009: $74; 2010: $77; 2011: $84; 2012: $85; 2013: new edition; 3d ed.: 2002: $51; 2003: $46; 2004: $50; 2005: $54; 2006: $58; 2007: 0; 2008: $63.
An in-depth discussion and analysis of eyewitness testimony from both legal and psychological perspectives. The authors address the latest psychological research on such matters as jurors' beliefs about eyewitness testimony, perception, the three components of memory, and factors that interfere with memory. Additional chapters discuss factors determining retention and retrieval of events, recognizing people, pretrial proceedings in civil cases, pretrial proceedings in criminal cases, jury education and selection, opening statements, direct and redirect examinations, cross-examination: strategies and tactics, presenting expert testimony, jury instructions, and closing argument. Elizabeth Loftus is a Professor of Psychology at the University of Washington and a leading psychological authority in the field of eyewitness testimony, who has published more than a dozen books and hundreds of scholarly articles in the field. James M. Doyle is of counsel to the Boston firm of Carney & Bassil where he specializes in trial and appellate litigation. He has written and spoken widely on the subjects of trial advocacy and eyewitness trials.

Love, Margaret Colgate. **Relief from the Collateral Consequences of a Criminal Conviction: A State-by-State Resource Guide**. Buffalo, NY: William S. Hein & Co., Inc., 2006. 1 vol. Paperbound.
Cost: $68 (2014).
Individuals convicted of crimes in United States jurisdictions are subject to a variety of collateral penalties and disabilities over and above the sentences imposed by the courts. This volume details the legal process by which such individuals avoid or mitigate these penalties. The legal mechanisms range from executive pardon and judicial expungement to the restoration of the right to vote and the opportunity to obtain employment in such fields as education, transportation and health care. The introductory materials include summaries of pardoning policies and practice in the United States, judicial expungement of adult felony convictions, regaining of the right to vote and corresponding jurisdictional tables. The remainder of the volume consists of state-by-state jurisdictional profiles which summarize the laws regarding the manner in which these collateral penalties are treated. Margaret Love is an attorney specializing in executive clemency and restoration of rights, sentencing and corrections policy, and legal and government ethics. She has written and lectured widely on pardon policy and practice, and on the collateral consequences of a criminal conviction. She served as U.S. Pardon Attorney between 1990 and 1997, and currently directs the ABA Commission on Effective Criminal Sanctions.

Mahoney, Kevin J. **Relentless Criminal Cross-Examination**. Santa Ana, CA: James Publishing, 2008-date. 1 vol. (various pagings). Looseleaf format.
Cost: $99; supplementation: 2009-2014: $59.99 per year.
The Sixth Amendment to the U.S. Constitution grants the accused the right to confront, but not necessarily to cross-examine, witnesses. In the view of the Framers, however, the right to confront and challenge government witnesses was critical to protecting the innocent from unwarranted convictions and providing a check on excessive governmental power. Since the late 18th century, the right to cross-examine witnesses has become more securely enshrined in our legal system through a succession of U.S. Supreme Court decisions. In this detailed and well-crafted guide to successful cross-examination techniques, defense attorney Kevin Mahoney draws upon a wealth a successful trial court experience to aid defense counsel in protecting the rights of their clients and achieve acquittals. He opens with a general discussion of the governing principles and strategies for cross-examination, a consideration of the theory of the case, the opening statement, and the closing argument. Specific attention is then devoted to the cross-examination of specific witnesses, including the arresting officer, the detective who obtained the confession, informants and accomplices, eyewitnesses, and expert witnesses, together with the tactics appropriate to each type of witness or situation. Attention is given to cross-examining bystanders, the consummate liar, the miscreant co-defendant, the innocent bystander, the wealthy defendant, the prison informant, the recanting informant, and much more. Finally, the author discusses the application of cross-examination techniques to sexual assault and DWI cases. Each chapter is replete with case and rule citations, practice points, technique tips, sample cross-examinations, and forms. The entire text of the book, with forms, table of cases and index, is contained on a fully searchable companion CD-ROM. Kevin J. Mahoney is a criminal defense attorney in Cambridge, Massachusetts. A legal analyst for Fox News Live, Fox & Friends, CNN, and Court TV, he has won 36 of his last 38 trials. This is another outstanding and economical trial practice title from James Publishing.

Marcus, Paul. **The Entrapment Defense**. 4th ed. Newark, NJ: LexisNexis (Michie), 2009-date. 1 vol. (793 pp.) Print or eBook.
Cost: $192 (print or eBook); supplementation: 2010: $42; 2011: $45; 2012: $45; 2013: $50; 3d ed.: 2003: $40; 2004: $42; 2005: $45; 2006: $48; 2007: $51; 2008: $64.
Entrapment is the active involvement of governmental entities or agents in the inducing of crime by those not predisposed to commit the induced crime. The entrapment defense first appeared in American legal practice in the late 19th century and

has been gaining ground throughout the 20th century, although it has generally not found acceptance in English courts. This volume provides both a theoretical and practical approach to the law of entrapment, addressing such topics as the subjective test, the objective test, proving entrapment, trial procedure, practical considerations for the entrapment defense, jury instructions, and the future of the entrapment defense. The volume also includes the text of twenty of the leading entrapment cases, and the entrapment statutes for twenty-five states. The author is the Haynes Professor of Law at the College of William and Mary, Marshall-Wythe School of Law and a leading authority on evidentiary and constitutional issues involved in criminal prosecutions. He has written numerous books and articles on criminal law and evidence, including **Criminal Law**, and the **Prosecution and Defense of Criminal Conspiracy Cases**, and served as the reporter to the Federal Judicial Conference Committee on Federal Criminal Jury Instructions.

Mauriello, Thomas P. **Criminal Investigation Handbook: Strategy, Law and Science**. New York: Matthew Bender & Co., 1990-date. 1 vol. Looseleaf format. or eBook. Annual supplementation.
Cost: $327 (print); supplementation: 1999: $78; 2000: $83; 2001: $89; 2002: $96; 2003: $101; 2004: $106; 2005: $113; 2006: $127; 2007: $139; 2008: $158; 2009: $181. 2010: $186; 2011: $195; 2012: $205; 2013: $215; 2014: $208; eBook: $327; 2014: $208.
This comprehensive handbook and treatise was designed for use by all individuals responsible for conducting criminal investigations and those who require an in-depth understanding of the criminal investigative process. It provides a road map on how to conduct a criminal investigation and a detailed discussion of the process of determining what evidence has the most probative value in the courtroom. Formerly titled **Police Investigative Handbook**, the work provides information of the investigative protocol, the collection, preparation and preservation of physical evidence, interviewing witnesses, the investigation case file, scientific laboratory examination requirements, legal considerations, forensic interviewing of suspects, presenting the case to court, expert testimony, identifying weaknesses in the investigatory process, and developing a strategic view of the entire investigative process. The volume also includes detailed checklists, sample investigative forms, scientific evidence processing requirements, illustrations and photographs, and a list of state, local and federal agency support services. The author is an experienced professional investigator with extensive experience in a number of federal agencies. He is currently Director of Interagency Operations Security Support Staff at the U.S. Department of Defense.

Morosco, B. Anthony. **The Prosecution and Defense of Sex Crimes.** New York: Matthew Bender & Co., 1976-date. 1 vol. Looseleaf format or eBook. Twice annual supplements.
Cost: $665; (includes one-year subscription); annual renewal: 1995: $164.50 (price frozen since 1992); 1996: $173; 1997: $173; 1998: $185; 1999: $192; 2000: $205; 2001: $219; 2002: $235; 2003: $247; 2004: $259; 2005: $277; 2006: $297; 2007: $321; 2008: $347; 2009: $375; 2010: $394; 2011: $414; 2012: $439; 2013: $470; 2014: $512; eBook: $605; renewal: 2014: $503.
Written by a member of the New York and Virginia Bars and Adjunct Associate Professor of Law at the Lubin School of Business, Pace University, this substantial one-volume treatise provides in-depth coverage of both the substantive and procedural aspects of a variety of sexual offenses. As the author states, however, "it is intended to be a useful desk reference, and a **starting point for research**." Chapters cover sex offenses, motion practice in sex cases, corroboration of sex cases, forcible sex crimes, jury instructions, Aids legal issues, non-forcible heterosexual sex offenses, defense of consensual sodomy and public lewdness, obscenity and pornography, child sexual assault, prostitution, child abuse, spouse abuse and marital rape, sentencing, expert witnesses, DNA evidence, jury selection, and appeals. Includes forms and voir dire questions. Cumulative supplements include case summaries keyed to footnotes as well as interfiled revisions to base text.

Parry, John. **Criminal Mental Health and Disability Law, Evidence and Testimony: A Comprehensive Reference Manual for Lawyers, Judges and Criminal Justice Professionals.** Chicago: American Bar Association, Commission on Mental and Physical Disability Law, Criminal Justice Section, 2009. 1 vol. (462 pp.). Paperbound.
Cost: $110 ($99 for members; $94 for entity memnbers) (2014).
This volume provides lawyers, judges and other criminal justice professionals with an in-depth examination of two interrelated aspects of criminal law—mental health and disability discrimination. Now well-established, criminal mental health law has its origins in the 19th century, if not earlier. Criminal disability discrimination did not take root until the 1980s, particularly following passage of the Americans with Disabilities Act in 1990. This volume builds upon a number of other ABA publications, including the **Mental & Physical Disability Law Reporter**, first published in 1976, **Mental Disability Law, Evidence and Testimony** (2007) and **Disability Discrimination Law, Evidence and Testimony** (2008). The book's 13 chapters cover the legal history of mental health and disability discrimination in the criminal justice system, a mental health and disability law overview, criminal competency, insanity and diminished capacity, dangerousness in the criminal law, jails, prisons and secure "treatment" facilities, admissibility of expert evidence and testimony, mental health diagnosis and assessments, criminal incompetency, evidence of insanity and diminished culpability, dangerousness to self and others, care and treatment of inmates, and disability discrimination involving inmates in corrections facilities. The volume also includes a glossary of key terms, definitions and Supreme Court decisions, index and table of cases. Attorney John Parry is Director of the ABA Commission on Mental and Physical Disability.

Phelps, Kathy Bazoian, and Hon. Steven Rhodes. **The Ponzi Book: a Legal Resource for Unraveling Ponzi Schemes.** New Providence, NJ: LexisNexis, 2012. 1 vol. (various pagings). Also in eBook format.
Cost: $225 (2014).
A Ponzi scheme is a fraudulent investment scam that promises high rates of return by paying investors from their own money or the money paid by subsequent investors, rather than from profits earned by the underlying business venture. The Ponzi scheme usually entices new investors by offering higher returns

than other investments, but which are, in reality, illusory because the profits are non-existent. Perpetuation of the high returns requires an ever-increasing flow of money from new investors to keep the scheme going. Eventually, these schemes collapse on themselves when the supply of new investors dries up, resulting in bankruptcy or receivership. Named for Charles Ponzi, a Boston clerk who operated such a scheme in 1919, it was more recently perpetrated by Bernie Madoff in what many consider the largest financial fraud in American history. This volume examines the intricacies of Ponzi schemes with the intent of unraveling the complex financial machinations by which investors have been deprived of their assets and making them whole. It does this by examining the competing claims and defenses of affected parties, actual fraudulent transfer claims, constructive fraudulent transfer claims, as well as the defenses that investors, brokers and others can assert to those claims. The book also provides a detailed discussion of a wide range of litigation claims that can be pursued against defendants with culpability or liability due to its involvement in such schemes. It also address related criminal proceedings, including related Fifth Amendment and other privilege issues as well as a detailed analysis of what happens to competing claims for assets in parallel insolvency and criminal proceedings. It also highlights recent changes in the tax laws to provide tax relief for Ponzi victims and raise awareness of these issues for victims and their tax advisors. This volume is aimed at lawyers, financial advisors and investors involved in the complex unraveling process. The Appendix includes a guide to "Applying the Rising Tide Method of Claims Distribution." Previously described in popular accounts, this is first volume to provide a professional and scholarly analysis of Ponzi schemes and the legal and financial hurdles involved in unraveling them. Kathy Bazoian Phelps is a partner in the law firm of Diamond McCarthy LLP in Los Angeles, who has been representing trustees, federal equity receivers, debtors and creditors in bankruptcy cases for over 20 years. She has published extensively in the field of bankruptcy and financial fraud. The Hon. Steven Rhodes is United States Bankruptcy Judge, Eastern District of Michigan-Detroit, with extensive experience in bankruptcy and commercial matters.

Pieth, Mark, ed. **Recovering Stolen Assets**. Bern, Switzerland: Peter Lang, 2008. 1 vol. (391 pp.). Paperbound.
Cost: $122.95; from $79.95 on amazon.com (2014).
Embezzlement, money laundering, and the illegal transfer of funds to safe havens in foreign jurisdictions have generated increased attention from the international law enforcement community. In a number of infamous cases, the funds embezzled from government coffers by corrupt African rulers have been illegally transferred to major European banks. The significance of this criminal activity is heightened by its impact on the development agenda of the poor countries from which the wealth has been plundered. Since the enactment of the OECD Convention on Bribery in 1997, the international community has enacted a number of protocols to address this growing problem, of which the nonbinding United Nations Convention against Corruption (2003) (UNCAC) is the most significant. While initially directed at combating illegal drug traffic and terrorism, these law enforcement tools are also available to those involved in combating cases of financial corruption. Chief among these tools are search, seizure and freezing of assets, mutual legal assistance requests, forfeiture, and extradition of funds. Despite the enactment of these various legal protocols, however, the recovery of financial assets ultimately depends on the goodwill of the state in which the assets have been found. This collection of insightful articles on international financial corruption and asset recovery is a product of the Basel Institute on Governance, an independent non-profit institution devoted to interdisciplinary research and policy advice in the areas of public, corporate and global governance, with a particular focus on fighting corruption and money laundering. The book's twenty-four chapters are grouped under six topical areas: The Challenges [of asset recovery]; Success Stories; Asset Recovery Systems; Concrete Challenges: Seizure and Confiscation; UNCAC, Technical Assistance and Development Efforts; and What is UNCAC Going to Change? The authors include many of the world's leading experts in the fields of international banking and asset recovery under the editorship of Mark Pieth, Professor of Law at the University of Basel and President of the Basel Institute on Governance.

Ramirez, Linda Friedman, et al. **Cultural Issues in Criminal Defense**. 3d ed. Huntington, NY: Juris Publishing, 2010. 1 vol. (730 pp.). Also available as eBook.
Cost: $175 (print or eBook); from $135.00 on amazon.com (2014).
This insightful volume brings a unique cross-cultural perspective to the subject of criminal defense. Its 24 chapters, presented by a number of contributing authors, grapple with a number of cultural issues in the context of the various stages of criminal defense, from client interview and case evaluation, to pretrial practice, trial practice, and post-trial practice. The chapters deal with such issues as consular resources and litigation strategies, the use of foreign language interpreters, language proficiency and its relationship to language evidence, legal challenges to extradition cases, cultural issues on motions to suppress, selective prosecution, racial profiling, raising cultural defenses, using cultural experts, cultural issues in jury selections, cultural issues in sentencing, and more. Clearly, an essential resource for any defense counsel involved in the defense of clients from different cultures. Linda Ramirez, who practices federal and international criminal law in St. Petersburg, FL, brings extensive international defense and publishing experience to this project. The contributing authors, who bring extensive experience in the cultural aspects of criminal defense, are drawn from both private practice and academia.

Ringel, William E. **Searches & Seizures, Arrests and Confessions.** 2d ed. prepared by Justin D. Franklin and Steven C. Bell. St. Paul, MN: Thomson Reuters West (Clark Boardman Callaghan), 2003/2009-date. 3 vols. Looseleaf format or ProView eBook. Supplemented several times per year.
Cost: $2,572; ProView eBook: $2,360; supplementation: 1993: $365.50; 1994: $307.50; 1995: $345; 1996: $395; 1997: $435; 1998: $435; 1999: $471; 2000: $501; 2001: $579; 2002: $466; 2003: $724.50; 2004: $760.50; 2005: $810; 2006: $903; 2007: $1,005; 2008: $1,119; 2009: $1,245; 2010: $1,369.50; 2011: $1,492.50; 2012: $787; 2013: $1,889; **Monthly Assured Print Price (APP):** $188/$2,256
Intended for use by lawyers, judges and law enforcement officers, this three-volume set explains and analyzes Fourth, Fifth, and Sixth Amendment law, principles and court rulings. Considers such topics as the exclusionary rule, probable cause, formal

requirements for issuance of warrants, searches of vehicles, stop and frisk, motions to suppress, habeas corpus, civil liability for illegal searches, arrest, confessions and admissions, Miranda requirements, suppression of evidence, and much more. While the original edition was written by Judge William E. Ringel, second edition was prepared by the publishers' editorial staff.

Cost Saving Tip: While this a well-written and exhaustive analytical work, LaFave's four-volume **Search and Seizure: A Treatise on the Fourth Amendment** is the better choice, with significantly lower supplementation costs ($160 in 2013 versus $1,889 for Ringel).

Robinson, Paul H. **Criminal Law Defenses.** St. Paul, MN: Thomson Reuters West, 1984-date. 2 vols. Annual pocket parts. Also available as ProView eBook. Criminal Practice Series.
Cost: $357; ProView eBook: $347; supplementation: 1993: $36.50; 1996: $42.50; 1997: $46.00; 1998: $49; 1999: $54; 2000: $60; 2001: $69; 2002: $82.00; 2003: $93.50; 2004: $104.50; 2005: $115; 2006: $129; 2007: $144; 2008: $160; 2009: $181; 2010: $199; 2011: $219; 2012: $241; 2013: $259; **Monthly Assured Print Price (APP):** $28/$336.
The author, Professor of Law, Rutgers University School of Law, cites as his chief aim that of improving "the understanding of criminal law defenses by the bench, bar and legislatures and thereby to improve the quality of American law on the subject." The focus is primarily on statutory law because American criminal law is largely statutory. Chapter coverage includes a guide in how to use the treatise, proving and disproving criminal law defenses, the burden of production, the burden of persuasion, alternative consequences of a successful defense, a systematic analysis of criminal law defenses, defenses relating to offense definitions, justification defenses, excuse defenses, and nonexculpatory defenses. Appendices include Model Criminal Defense Codifications, Selected Provisions of the Model Penal Code, and tables of references to the Model Penal Code, statutes, court rules and authors, as well as a subject index. This is a well-written and heavily documented exposition on criminal procedure with many penetrating insights for the criminal lawyer. Base volumes reflect West's sluggish approach to the revision of bound volumes (an attitude more publishers should adopt), but with reasonably priced pocket part supplementation.

Rudenstein, David S., C. Peter Erlinder and David C. Thomas. **Criminal Constitutional Law.** New York: Matthew Bender & Co., 1990-date. 3 vols. Looseleaf format or eBook. Annual supplements. No CD-ROM or Internet.
Cost: $926 (print or eBook) (includes annual subscription); annual renewal: 1995: $74.50 (price frozen since 1992); 1996: $79; 1997: $79.; 1998: $80; 1999: $83.00; 2000: $89; 2001: $95; 2002: $164; 2003: $173.87; 2004: $182; 2005: $195; 2006: $209; 2007: $222; 2008: $240; 2009: $259; 2010: $281; 2011: $282; 2012: $293; 2013: $308; 2014: $317.
This treatise closely examines those areas in which the United States Constitution places limitations upon the criminal justice process, both at the state and federal levels. Providing a good balance between text and footnotes, the chapters cover search and seizure, exceptions to the warrant requirement, confessions and other incriminating statements, eyewitnesses identification procedures, grand jury procedures, pretrial release, the preliminary hearing, prosecutorial decision-making, disclosure and discovery, pretrial motions, pleas and plea bargaining, right to counsel, trial by jury, conduct of the trial, civil forfeiture, and appeals. Appendix includes a table of cases and subject index. An excellent and reasonably-priced resource for the criminal defense attorney or prosecutor.

Ryder, Nicholas. **Financial Crime in the 21st Century: Law and Policy**. Northampton, MA: Edward Elgar, 2011. 1 vol. (340 pp.). Paperbound.
Cost: $45.00; from $40.25 on amazon.com (2014).
Since the 1970s, the war against crime has taken on a global dimension, the financial incarnation of which embraces efforts to combat the illegal drug trade, human trafficking, organized crime, and terrorism. These activities have been aided by loopholes in the financial structure that permit illicit funds to be transferred through the system electronically. As various forms of financial crime have manifested themselves, governments have responded by enacting laws and instituting policies and procedures to combat money laundering and related offenses. These efforts were accelerated as a result of the attacks of 9/11, the collapse of the Barings Bank, Enron and the WorldCom. The United Nations responded by introducing a number of legal protocols designed to address the problems of global money laundering, and the Financial Action Task Force (FATF) was established to make recommendations for confronting the problem of money laundering. Since 9/11, much of the United States' effort has been directed toward the goal of undermining terrorist financing. The purpose of this book is to provide a detailed commentary and analytical review of the financial crime policies adopted by the international community and how these have been implemented in the United States and the United Kingdom. Chapters address money laundering, terrorist financing, fraud, insider trading, the confiscation and forfeiture of the illicit proceeds of crime, regulators and agencies, and sentencing in financial crime. It includes an extensive bibliography of sources. The author/editor is Reader in Law and Head of the Commercial Law Research Unit at the Bristol Law School, University of the West of England, UK. He is joined by Andrew H. Baker, Liverpool John Moore's University, and Karen Harrison, University of Hull.

Scott, A. Hugh. **Computer and Intellectual Property Crime: Federal and State Law**. Washington, DC: Bloomberg BNA Books, 2001-date. 1 vol. (1,574 pp.).
Cost: $340; supplementation: 2003: $155; 2004: $165; 2005: $175; 2006: $175; 2007-2013: 0.
A comprehensive examination of federal and state criminal law as it applies to computers and intellectual property. The work opens with an overview and history of computer and intellectual property crime and the Internet. The author's discussion of federal laws includes those, which specifically address computer and intellectual property crime as well as general criminal statutes, which can be applied to crimes in these areas. Coverage includes a summary of the area, the text of the law, discussion of applicable caselaw, legislative history, the elements of the offense, instructions to juries, and available civil remedies. There is also discussion of the federal prosecution process, jurisdiction and venue, federal investigations, search and seizures of computers, and the use of federal sentencing guidelines. The federal statutes discussed

include the Computer Fraud and Abuse Act, Electronic Privacy Act, Child Sexual Exploitation and Pornography Act, Racketeer Influenced Corrupt Organizations Act, and thirteen others. A state-by-state treatment of state statutes follows, with a list of enforcement agencies and remedies for victims. The unique and comprehensive coverage of this book makes it an essential acquisition for research law libraries, prosecutors and defense counsel, IP firms, and scholars and students of computer and IP crime.

Silver, Isadore. **Police Civil Liability**. New York: Matthew Bender & Co., 1986-date. 2 vols. Looseleaf format. Updated twice annually. Also available on **Federal Practice Library** CD-ROM (see **Fed. Prac. & Procedure**)
Cost: $963 (print or eBook) (includes annual subscription); supplementation: 1998: $185; 1999: $192; 2000: $205; 2001: $219; 2002: $235; 2003: $247; 2004: 259; 2005: $277; 2006: $297; 2007: $321; 2008: $347; 2009: $714; 2010: $422; 2011: $782; 2012: $842; 2013: $874; 2014: $891.
With charges of police misconduct becoming more common in recent years, this work provides both the practical and analytical tools necessary for evaluating and litigating such cases. Designed for use by personal injury lawyers, civil rights attorneys, government counsel, and law enforcement officers, this two-volume work provides coverage of complaints ranging from personal injury claims to civil rights actions in both federal and state courts. Chapter coverage includes principles of tort liability, general police duties and authority, negligence during police emergencies, false arrest or imprisonment, liability for misuse of weapons, assault and battery, malicious prosecution actions, Section 1983 and other federal civil rights actions, specific constitutional rights and Section 1983, duty to protect, and immunity. Appendices include state emergency vehicle statutes, state immunity statutes, federal civil right statutes, immunity in federal civil rights actions, factual synopses of entrapment cases by court, a bibliography, and subject index. Includes extensive citations to relevant cases and statutes. The author is a Professor of Constitutional Law and History at John Jay College of Criminal Justice, City University of New York University Law School and an authority on criminology and public employment law.

Strader, J. Kelly. **Understanding White Collar Crime**. 3d ed. Newark, NJ: LexisNexis, 2011. 1 vol. (345 pp.). No supplementation between editions.
Cost: $45; eBook: $36; from $26.99 on amazon.com (2014).
White collar crime is based primarily upon a complex set of federal statutes. This volume provides an overview of the principal areas of federal white collar crime with coverage of the related areas of criminal law and procedure. Written primarily to serve the needs of law students in classes in white collar crime, federal criminal law, and corporate crime, it is also a valuable overview for practitioners and judges. unfamiliar with the field. The primary focus is on the applicable federal statutes and their interpretation by the courts. The author also addresses the enforcement policy issues that arise in white collar crime cases. Chapters include: introduction to white collar crime, corporate and individual responsibility, conspiracy, mail fraud, wire fraud and elated offenses, securities fraud, computer crime, environmental crimes, bribery and gratuities, extortion, false statements, perjury, obstruction of justice, tax crimes, currency transaction reporting crimes, money laundering, RICO, grand jury issues, the right against compelled self-incrimination, federal sentences and other sanctions, and forfeitures. The author is Professor of Law at Southwestern University School of Law. A low-cost alternative to Androphy's White Collar Crime (West) and Business Crime (LexisNexis/Matthew Bender).

Tobolowsky, Peggy M., et al. **Crime Victim Rights and Remedies**. 2d ed. Durham, NC: Carolina Academic Press, 2009. 1 vol. (364 pp.).
Cost: $40; from $32 on amazon.com (2014).
Crime victimization impacts millions of Americans annually. In 2008, the National Crime Victimization Survey estimated that Americans aged 12 or over experienced 21,312,4000 violent and property crimes, of which 4,856,510 were for violent offenses of sexual and non-sexual assault and robbery, and 16,435,890 were for property and non-violent offense categories of household burglary, and personal, household and motor vehicle theft. It has also been estimated that the aggregate cost of crime is over $1.7 trillion dollars annually. Until relatively recently, victims of crime had relatively few rights and remedies in the criminal justice system. This began to change when President Reagan convened the Task Force on Victims of Crime in 1982, and when its recommendation were implemented at both the state and federal levels. At present, there are tens of thousands of statutes that directly or indirectly affect crime victim rights and interests, as well as constitutional provisions in a majority of states to protect victim rights. This volume assembles a variety of materials which describe the evolution of victim rights in the United States, the current state of the law, the status of implementation of these rights and remedies, relevant empirical studies, and representative policy analysis. The authors consider the return of crime victim rights and remedies, the rights of participation in the criminal justice process, the right to notice of proceedings and outcomes, the right to be present at criminal justice proceedings, the right to heard at various stages of the criminal justice process (charging, pleas, sentencing, parole), the Constitutional and legislative response, remedies for victim rights violations, restitution, compensation, civil litigation, and the future of crime victim rights and remedies. Appendices include the recommendations of the President's Task Force on Victims of Crime, the proposed Federal Victim Rights Constitutional Amendment, and State Victim Rights Constitutional provisions. The volume includes extensive citations to relevant cases, statutes constitutional provisions, and law review articles. The lead author is professor and chair of Criminal Justice at the University of North Texas. She is joined by colleagues at her institution and at the University New Haven (CT).

Torcia, Charles E. **Wharton's Criminal Law.** 15th ed. St. Paul, MN: West (Clark Boardman Callaghan), 1993-date. 4 vols. Annual pocket parts. Originally published by Lawyers Cooperative.
Cost: $1,480; supplementation: 1994: $215; 1995: $280; 1996: $320; 1997: $199; 1998: $199.00; 1999: $215; 2000: $233; 2001: $276; 2002: $324; 2003: $369; 2004: $413.50; 2005: $450; 2006: $505; 2007: $562; 2008: $627; 2009: $716.50;

2010: $788; 2011: $859; 2012: $1,021; 2013: $1,086; **Monthly Assured Print Price (APP):** $108/$1,296.
A four-volume overview of substantive criminal law, both state and federal, since adoption of the Model Penal Code. Covers classification of crime, parties, defenses, offenses against the person, homicide, murder, man-slaughter, incest, abortion, prostitution, rape, obscenity, offenses against property, receiving stolen property, forgery, libel, obstruction of justice, treason, etc. The bound volumes of this work are due for revision, having been published in 1993. Pocket parts contain extensive annotated case references, but little or no changes to the original text. The emphasis in these volumes is heavily weighted towards case citations rather than densely analytical text and many pages have little or no text. By comparison, LaFave and Scott's **Substantive Criminal Law** has more substantive analytical text in two volumes than this set does in four, and at a fraction of the cost (particularly for supplementation). This is one of the former Lawyers Cooperative texts which probably should have been abandoned after the consolidation, but which is maintained because it has a customer base which pays the substantial cost of the annual pocket parts.

Welling, Sarah N., Pamela H. Bucy, and Sara Sun Beale. **Federal Sentencing Guidelines Manual.** St. Paul, MN: West, 1998-date. 3 vols. (paperback). Criminal Practice Series. Annual replacement volumes.
Cost: 2013 Edition: $123; **Monthly Assured Print Price (APP):** $10/$120 (2014).
This one-volume paperback contains the current text of the Sentencing Guidelines, Commentary and Policy Statements of the United States Sentencing Commission as recently amended effective November 1, 1994. It also includes the highlights of the 1994 Amendments, Supreme Court consideration of the guidelines, highlights of the 1994 crime legislation, selected provisions of the 1994 Crime Act relating to the Guidelines, the most frequently asked questions about the Guidelines, sentencing worksheets. model sentencing forms, related criminal statutes and rules. Also included are a Table of Cases applying the Guidelines and a history of the 1988-1994 Amendments to the Sentencing Reform Act of 1984.

Wharton's Criminal Evidence. 15th ed. by Barbara E. Bergman, Teri Duncan, and Nancy Hollander. St. Paul, MN: West (Clark Boardman Callaghan), 1997-date. 8 vols. Annual pocket parts. Originally published by Lawyers Cooperative.
Cost: $1,014; supplementation: 1993: 79; 1994: $100; 1995: $165; 1996: $170; 1997: $215; 1998: $170; 1999: $270; 2000: $325; 2001: $427; 2002: $205; 2003: $234; 2004: $233.50; 2005: $282; 2006: $319.50; 2007: $355.50; 2008: $396; 2009: $459; 2010: $505.50; 2011: $551; 2012: $799; 2013: $697; **Monthly Assured Print Price (APP):** $71/$660.
Both the 13th and 14th editions of this work were authored by Charles E. Torcia, a law professor who has taught at Dickinson School of Law, the Marshall-Wythe School of Law at the College of William and Mary, and New York University School of Law. This task has now been assumed by Barbara E. Bergman, professor of law at the University of New Mexico, Nancy Hollander, a practicing criminal defense attorney, and Teri Duncan. This edition reflects the promulgation of the Federal Rules of Evidence and the adoption of evidentiary rules in many states. While the author relies primarily upon federal case law in his text and footnotes, some attention is given to state appellate court decisions. Chapters cover the burden and degree of proof, presumption and inferences, relevance and materiality, judicial notice, hearsay evidence, competency of witnesses, examination of witnesses, impeachment of witnesses, attendance of witnesses, documentary evidence, best and secondary evidence, privileged communications, expert and opinion evidence, examinations, tests, and real evidence, co-conspirators and accomplices, confessions and admissions, evidence at preliminary hearing or former trial, judgments and jeopardy, right to counsel, and search and seizure. As in the case of **Wharton's Criminal Procedure**, this set in clearly weighted more toward exhaustive case citation than analytical text. In this regard, the one-volume **Courtroom Criminal Evidence** by Imwinkelried is clearly the better value at $177, with much lower supplementation costs.

Wharton's Criminal Procedure. 14th ed. by Barbara E. Bergman, Teri Duncan, Nancy Hollander, and Melissa Stephenson. St. Paul, MN: West (Clark Boardman Callaghan), 1989/2002-date. 8 vols. Annual pocket parts. Originally published by Lawyers Cooperative Publishing Company.
Cost: $949; supplementation: 1993: $104; 1994: $125; 1995: $165; 1996: $190; 1997: $199; 1998: $199; 1999: $215; 2000: $233; 2001: $274; 2002: $367; 2003: $242; 2004: $345; 2005: $300; 2006: $427; 2007: $477; 2008: $370.50; 2009: $476; 2010: $512; 2011: $334; 2012: $444; 2013: $160; **Monthly Assured Print Price (APP):** $39/$468.
The 14th edition of this eight-volume treatise is written by Barbara E. Bergman, Teri Duncan, Nancy Hollander, and Melissa Stephenson, who replace Charles E. Torcia in that role. Written since the promulgation of the Federal Rules of Evidence in 1975 and the federal Sentencing Reform Act, this treatise tracks the development of a systematic body of procedural principles which guide the criminal law. While the primary emphasis is upon caselaw, particularly at the U.S. Supreme Court and federal court levels, the author makes selective reference to state appellate court decisions as well. Court rules and statutes are considered only to the extent that they play a role in judicial decision-making.

Chapter coverage includes the criminal court, juvenile court, jurisdiction, venue and removal of prosecution, arrest, extradition, preliminary hearing, search and seizure, grand jury, indictment and information, joinder and severance, bail, arraignment and pleas, pretrial motions or objections, discovery, privilege against self-incrimination, immunity, right to counsel, selection of trial jury, accused's capacity to stand trial, presence of accused, control of trial proceedings, opening statements, evidence and objections, withdrawal from jury, charge to jury, separation of jury, deliberations of jury, verdict, post-trial motions, sentence, punishment, appeal, and post-conviction remedies. In contrast to LaFave and Israel's Criminal Procedure, this work's textual content is more heavily weighted toward case citations (many with annotations) than text. Many pages include minimal or no text replaced with extensive case citations under specific footnotes. The distinctions and subtleties are often drawn in the these citations rather than in the textual analysis. The work does provide Total Client-Service Library References to other West products, however, including Annotation References to the American Law Reports series. Annual pocket parts provide summaries of more recent cases and only minimal additions or corrections to text.

Whited, Flem K. III. **Drinking/Driving Litigation: Criminal and Civil**. 2d ed. St. Paul, MN: West (Clark Boardman Callaghan), 1985-date. 5 vols. Looseleaf format.
Cost: $1,324; supplementation: 1992: $184.50; 1993: $224; 1994: $145; 1995: $174.50; 1996: $337; 1997: $605; 1998: $614; 1999: $275; 2000: $405; 2001: $477; 2002: $525; 2003: $597; 2004: $630; 2005: $800; 2006: $856; 2007: $468; 2008: $825.50; 2009: $145; 2010: $594; 2011: $654; 2012: $777; 2013: $866; **Monthly Assured Print Price (APP):** $87/$1,044.
Now authored by Flem K. Whited, this five-volume treatise is a complete practical guide to both the law and practice of drunk driving litigation. It covers such areas as pretrial motions, arrest procedures, chemical tests, effects of alcohol, breathalyzer and other measuring devices, blood and urine testing, postmortem problems, blood alcohol, roadblocks, dram shop cases, trial issues, effects of alcohol and the variables that may affect them. It also includes jury instructions and a consideration of sentencing, appeal, and other issues involved in liquor liability. Supplementation costs are not insignificant, a factor which should influence your decision to remain on a standing order. Supplementation includes both cumulative front matter and interfiled pages, which means that updating a lapsed subscription may entail considerable filing. The author is a noted DWI specialist in Florida with thirty years experience in the field.

Cost Saving Tips: Lapsed subscribers will find it less expensive and time-consuming to purchase a new set periodically provided a sufficient number of years have elapsed.

Wolf, Ross, Charles Mesloh and Robert H. Wood. **Constitutional Limitations of Interviewing and Interrogations in American Policing**. Durham, NC: Carolina Academic Press, 2013. 1 vol. (141 pp.).
Cost: $22.00; from $11.00 on amazon.com (2014).
This volume was written to provide legal and criminal justice practitioners with the knowledge of the Constitution and Supreme Court decisions that impact the conduct of police interviews and interrogations. Applying this evolving federal case law to police encounters, interviews, interrogations, and polygraph testing is a persistent challenge to those in law enforcement if they are to avoid missteps that violate the rights of the accused and jeopardy the efforts of prosecutors. The purpose of this book is to "understand the intricate nature of working within the boundaries of case law when collecting testimonial evidence." The chapters including an introduction to the criminal justice system, summaries of landmark Supreme Court cases, clarifications on Miranda, interviewing juveniles, contact, seizure and arrest, and polygraph testing and privileged communications, Appendices include the text of the 4th, 5th, 6th and 14th Amendments, the Garrity Rule, a selective list of references, glossary, and index.

Wolfe, Zachary. **Hate Crimes Law**. St. Paul, MN: West, 1993-date. 1 vol. Softbound. Annual replacement volume (starting with 2005 edition).
Cost: 2013 Edition: $284; 2012 Edition: $261; supplementation: 2003: $57; 2004: $70; 2005: $95; 2006: $106; 2007: $132.50; 2008: $164; 2009: $175; 2010: $217; 2011: $239; **Monthly Assured Print Price (APP):** $24/$288.
The alleged rise of hate crime across the United States has prompted the introduction of hate crime legislation at both the state and federal levels. These include criminal statutes directed at predicate offenses that are animated by animus of a racial or religious nature or having their origin in bias based upon sexual-orientation ethnicity/national origin bias or disability. Other, more controversial, statutes are directed to the utterance of racist or bigoted speech or the commission of bigoted acts that are substantially equivalent to speech. This treatise provides a comprehensive look at state and federal statutes that address the problem of hate crime. Federal statutes discussed include the Hate Crime Statistics Act of 1990, conspiracy against rights under 18 U.S.C. § 241, deprivation of rights under color of law under 18 U.S.C. § 242, federally protected activities under 18 U.S.C. § 245, damage to religious property and obstruction of persons in the free exercise of religious beliefs under 18 U.S.C. §§ 247 and 248, and prevention of intimidation provisions of the Fair Housing Act under 42 U.S.C. § 3631. The author also discusses federal sentencing issues, state hate crime statutes, bias-motivated violence and intimidation, malicious harassment, and related state statutes, state antimask statutes, state cross burning statutes, and more. There is also a discussion of state civil actions, including private causes of action and attorney general/district attorney civil actions. The appendices include provisions of federal law relevant to hate crimes, jurisdiction review—state statutory provisions relevant to hate crimes, and a selected bibliography. The volume includes numerous citation to applicable cases and statutes and research references to other West research tools, including West Digests, ALR annotations. The author is Associate Professor of Law at the University of Pittsburgh School of Law.

Worrall, John L. and M. Elaine Nugent-Borakove. **The Changing Role of the American Prosecutor**. Albany, NY: State University of New York, 2008. 1 vol. (284 pp.). Paperbound.
Cost: $29.95; from $25.00 on amazon.com (2014).
A useful scholarly analysis of the role of the American prosecutor in the United States from an historical and comparative perspective. The articles trace the development of the prosecution function from its colonial origins in Connecticut, which was the first colony to adopt a system of public prosecution, to its modern manifestations. Twelve chapters address such topics as the state's role in prosecutorial politics, the prosecution policy and errors of justice, performance measures and accountability, prosecutors and treatment diversion, project safe neighborhoods and the changing role of the U.S. Attorney's Office, anticipatory prosecution on terrorism-related cases, community prosecution, prosecutors in problem-solving courts, and the future of local prosecution in America. The editor and lead author is Associate Professor of Criminology at the University of Texas at Dallas. M. Elaine Nugent-Borakove is Director of the Office of Research and Evaluation at the American Prosecutors Research Institute.

Additional titles in the field of Criminal Law are available from the following publishers: American Correctional Association, AMS Press, Ashgate Publishing Co., Wolters Kluwer Law & Business, Carolina Academic Press, Casenotes Publishing, CRC Press, Foundation Press, Garland, Gaunt, Harcourt Legal, William S. Hein & Co., Inc., International Specialized Book Services, Kluwer Law International, L & E Publishers, Lega Books, LexisNexis, McGraw-Hill, National Judicial College, Oxford University Press, Prentice-Hall, Routledge, Thomson Reuters West, University of Chicago Press, West Academic. See Appendix B for addresses and telephone numbers.

Disabilities Law

Americans with Disabilities Act: Employee Rights and Employer Obligations. New York: Matthew Bender & Co., 1992-date. 2 vols. Looseleaf format and eBook. Supplemented annually.
Cost: $359 (print and eBook); supplementation: 1995: $72 (price frozen since 1993); 1996: $42; 1997: $42; 1998: $45; 1999: $47; 2000: $50; 2001: $54; 2002: $58; 2003: $61; 2004: $64; 2005: $179; 2006: $189; 2007: $204; 2008: $220; 2009: $276; 2010: $265; 2011: $296; 2012: $316; 2013: $326; 2014: $349. Also available as a part of the **Employment Law Library** on CD-ROM (see sales representative for details).
This one-volume guide to the ADA was written and edited by attorneys with the Washington, D.C.-based law firm of Ogletree, Deakins, Nash , Smoak & Stewart. Its coverage of the Americans with Disabilities Act of 1990 is primarily directed to an examination of its employment provisions and is designed to assist both employers and employees in the private sector understand their rights and obligations under the Act. It provides background information and the legislative history of the ADA, an overview of the Act, a discussion of the definition of disability under the Act, analysis of a «qualified individual with a disability,» prohibitions against discrimination, reasonable accommodations, «undue hardship,» enforcement of the Act, and Title III: Public Accommodations and Facilities operated by Private Entities. Appendix A contains an extensive summary of state statutes which prohibit discrimination under the Act, and a Practice Guide containing forms, directories and checklists. Appendices B and C contain the full text of the ADA and the EEOC Final Regulations Implementing Title I of the Act (29 **CFR** 1630). This volume contains a wealth of substantive and procedural material for the attorney concerned with disabilities issues. There are Practice Pointers scattered throughout the text as an aid to the practitioner. There are also extensive citations to various forms of primary and secondary authority, a table of cases and subject index.

Cost Saving Tips: An excellent value for the attorney interested in a more concise, yet scholarly, alternative to the West's four-volume **Americans with Disabilities: Practice and Compliance Manual**

Americans with Disabilities Act Manual [complete service]. Washington, DC: Bloomberg BNA, 1992-date. 2 vols. Looseleaf format. Updated monthly. Newsletter issued twice a month.
Cost: $1,931 per year (2014).
Designed for the use of both the litigator and the compliance officer, this comprehensive guide to the Americans with Disabilities Act addresses the application of the Act in a variety of circumstances, including employment, state and local governments, transportation, public accommodations, and telecommunications. Additional chapters are devoted to coverage of definitions and terms, policy and practice, legal developments, statutes and regulations, state disability laws, and technical assistance and resources. An excellent vehicle for monitoring current legal developments, including court decisions, federal and state legislation and regulations. Also available as a part of the Bloomberg BNA's **Labor and Employment Law Library: Disabilities Law on CD**.

Americans with Disabilities: Practice and Compliance Manual. St. Paul, MN: Thomson Reuters West (Lawyers Cooperative Publishing Co.), 1992-date. 6 vols. Looseleaf pamphlet format. Supplemented quarterly. Bound decisions also available.
Cost: $3,195; supplementation: 1993: $195; 1994: $290; 1995: $370; 1996: $329.50; 1997: $235; 1998: $313.50; 1999: $504; 2000: $537; 2001: $855; 2002: $688; 2003: $901; 2004: $1,088; 2005: $1,121.50; 2006: $1,176.50; 2007: $1,635.96; 2008: $1,726.22; 2009: $1,507.50; 2010: $1,678; 2011: $1,709; 2012: $2,144.50; 2013: $701; **Monthly Assured Print Price (APP):** $179/$2,148.
This is a combination treatise and practice manual which covers the federal law governing the civil of rights of individuals with disabilities. Federal legislation addressed includes the Americans with Disabilities Act, of 1990, the Rehabilitation Act of 1973, the Architectural Barriers Act of 1968, the Individuals with Disabilities Education Act and the Fair Housing Amendments Act of 1988. The four binders encompass material on: Programs, Services and Accommodations; Employment; Education; and Housing. The first two binders cover the ADA and other relevant disabilities legislation. Binders 3 and 4 treat those laws enacted prior to the adoption of the ADA. The impressive thing about this set is that it not only provides a well-written textual analysis of the relevant disabilities laws, but provides a wide range of supporting materials, including the full text of applicable laws and regulations (including the ADA Title 1 Manual), relevant **ALR** annotations, forms, and trial strategies from **Am. Jur. Trials.** Each text chapter includes valuable features explaining the Scope of Topic, State Aspects, and a listing of relevant material treated elsewhere in the set. Detailed chapter outlines are followed by General References to applicable statutes, regulations and trial practice materials.

Chapters cover Section 504: Nondiscrimination Under Federal Programs or Activities, State and Local Government Services, Transportation, Public Accommodations, Telecommunications, Programs, Services and Accommodation Forms, American with Disabilities Act, Employment by Federal Government and Federal Contractors, Veterans, Employment Forms, Individuals with Disabilities Education Act (IDEA), Suits Under Section 1983, Education Forms, Fair Housing, and Housing Forms. Special features designated by 4-bar symbols includes Comments, Cautions, Observations, Law Review Commentaries, Practice

Pointers, Illustrations, Notes, Law Under the Rehabilitation Act, State Aspects, and Legislative Intent notes. The text is liberally footnoted with references to primary authorities. As may be expected, the editors provide extensive references to other Total Client-Service Library publications, including the publisher's **Federal Procedure, L. Ed**, **Federal Procedural Forms**, the **ALR** series, and **Am. Jur. Trials**. The subscription also includes a monthly current awareness newsletter. This set is a clearly written and well organized research tool, with excellent indexing. Highly recommended for the attorney practicing in the area of disabilities law, despite relatively high supplementation costs.

Cost Saving Tip: With supplementation costs nearly equal to the cost of a new set, consider purchasing a new set every 2-3 years instead of maintaining a standing order, particularly if you have access to the primary law from other sources. If you purchase anew every two years, you will still only go one year between updates, while netting $1,000 in savings over that period.

Blanck, Peter, Bruce A. Goldstein and William N. Myhill. **Legal Rights of Persons with Disabilities: An Analysis of Federal Law.** 2d ed. Horsham, PA: LRP Publications, 2013-date. 1 vol. (331 pp.). Paper. Annual replacement volumes.
Cost: $365 + $35 s&h; no supplementation to date; 1st ed.: 1994: $107; 1995: $160; 1996: $67.50; 1997: $108; 1998: $58; 1999: $133.50; 2000: $145.45; 2001: $91.70; 2002: $96.40; 2003: $229; 2004: $225.75; 2005: $142; 2006: $289.75; 2007: 0; 2008: $169.50; 2009: $154; 2010: $152.75; 2011: 0.
This two-volume guide to federal disability law is written by Bonnie Tucker, an attorney and Associate Professor of law at Arizona State University College of Law with extensive experience in disability law related issues and organizations. She is a member of the governing board of the Alexander Graham Bell Association for the Deaf and was appointed to the National Advisory Group to the National Technical Institute for the Deaf by the United States Secretary of Education in 1981. Bruce Goldstein, an attorney in private practice and adjunct professor at the State University of New York at Buffalo teaches both disabilities law and education law and has spoken and written widely on these topics.

The authors provide a valuable overview of the practical difficulties facing persons with disabilities. The individual chapters address the constitutional rights of the disabled, Sections 501, 503 and 504 of the Rehabilitation Act of 1973, transportation issues, architectural barriers and housing, the Americans with Disabilities Act of 1990, and extensive coverage of the Education for All Handicapped Children Act enacted in 1975. There is also a chapter on the law governing disabled newborns. The Appendices include the full text of all relevant federal statutes, a sample IEP (Individualized Education Program) form, a suggested checklist for IEP's, a Checklist of Concerns, a Curriculum Checklist, a Checklist of Work Behaviors for Vocational Education, and a list of acronyms. Also included are a table of cases, and subject index. This is a clearly written analysis of the field, particularly as it relates to educational issues. While the set lacks the exhaustive cross references and citations of the Lawyers Cooperative set, it does provide more than adequate citations to relevant primary sources, including cases, statutes, regulations, and legislative history documents. Semi-annual updating ensures that the user is kept reasonably current regarding recent developments and trends. The second has moved to a perfectbound format, presumably presaging annual replacement volumes.

Coleman, John J. **Disability Discrimination in Employment: Law and Litigation.** St. Paul, MN: West (Clark Boardman Callaghan), 1991-date. 1 vol. Looseleaf format. Supplemented annually.
Cost: $631; supplementation: 1993: $57.50; 1994: $66; 1995: $83; 1996: $95; 1997: $99.75; 1998: $106; 1999: $114.50; 2000: $124; 2001: $144; 2002: $168; 2003: $191; 2004: $191; 2005: $203; 2006: $233; 2007: $259.50; 2008: $329.50; 2009: $323.50; 2010: $356; 2011: $388; 2012: $450; 2013: $459; **Monthly Assured Print Price (APP):** $49/$588.
Written by a partner in a Birmingham, Alabama law firm and adjunct professor at Cumberland School of Law, this volume is a practical guide to the law as it applies to discrimination against the disabled in employment. This volume addresses all applicable state and federal laws governing discrimination against the disabled, including the ADA, the Civil Rights Act of 1991, Rehabilitation Act, the Veterans Reemployment Act, etc. Includes a discussion of the obligations of employers, the permissibility of medical tests and inquiries, and «reasonable accommodations.» Includes such practical features as a sample job analysis form and accommodation charts. This volume provides the attorney with guidance in the litigation process, including a discussion of the commencement of an action, statutory schemes, limitation periods, parallel proceedings, remedies, appellate review, proof burdens, and litigation strategy. Includes a summary of the disability laws of all fifty states and the District of Columbia in five areas: parties, protected conditions, commencing the action, proof burdens, and remedies. Appendices include the complete text of the Americans with Disabilities Act of 1990 and the Equal Employment Opportunity for Individuals with Disabilities (29 **CFR** 1630). An excellent resource for the attorney, corporate counsel or human resources administrator.

Goren, William D. **Understanding the Americans with Disabilities Act**. 4th ed. Chicago: American Bar Association, 2013. 1 vol. (328 pp.).
Cost: $99.95 ($85.95 to section members) (2014).
The passage of the Americans with Disabilities Act (ADA) in 1990 marked the first comprehensive attempt at the national level to deal with discrimination against those with disabilities. This book, written by a lawyer with a hearing impairment, describes the wide-ranging changes in the way persons with disabilities are treated in the United States. In addition to the concepts underlying the ADA, the author addresses the issue of the essential functions of a job in the employment context, the concept of undue hardship and reasonable accommodation, the treatment of alcoholics and drug addicts, the issue of pre-employment medical exams and disability-related inquiries, the ADA and health insurance, the ADA in the public sector, places of public accommodation and commercial facilities, the ADA and the health care provider, the relationship between the ADA and other laws, remedies and procedural issues, the ADA and sports, and other areas. The volume also incorporates the more than one dozen ADA-related cases decided by the U.S. Supreme

Court, as well as many appellate decisions as well. The book also includes sample complaints and answers and a table of statues and regulations.

Individuals with Disabilities Education Law Report (IDELR). Horsham, PA: LRP Publications, 1978-date. 2 vols. Updated 24 times per year.
Cost: $1,350 per year + $65 s&h (2014).
A comprehensive reference tool covering a wide range of legal issues in the field of special education, including classroom discipline, mediation of disputes, development of individual education profiles, compliance with state standards and much more. Includes the full text of major federal laws and regulations, IDEA policy rulings, Section 504 policy rulings, federal and state court decisions, and SEA appeals decisions. The subscription also includes the biweekly **IDELR Highlights** and periodic **Special Reports**.

Labor and Employment Law Library: Disabilities Law [Internet]. Washington, DC: Bloomberg BNA. Internet. Available for Windows. Search Engine: Folio. Updated monthly.
Cost: Internet: $1,825; also available with cases (2013).
This product combines the full text of Bloomberg BNA's **Americans with Disabilities Act Manual** (see entry above) with **Americans with Disabilities Act Cases** (which are reported in print as part of the **Labor Relations Reporter**. Monthly updates provide current case law and newsletters, as well as a complete archive of newsletter back issues. The service may updated biweekly by means of an uplink to the BNA Web site. This product features full text searching, hypertext links, a customizing option, a user's handbook, and useful help features.

Levy, Robert M. and Leonard S. Rubenstein. **The Rights of People with Mental Disabilities: The Authoritative ACLU Guide to the Rights of People with Mental Illness and Mental Retardation**. Carbondale, IL: Southern Illinois University Press, 1996. 1 vol. (370 pp.). Paperbound.
Cost: $19.95; from $1.06 on amazon.com (2014).
One in a series of more than twenty ACLU Guides, this volume is designed to explain the law as it applies to the mentally disabled in a language accessible to the layperson. This Guide opens with an historical overview of the evolution of rights for the mentally disabled and a discussion of mental disability itself. Following a question-answer format, additional chapters examine standards for involuntary commitment; procedures for admission and release; personal autonomy, informed consent, and the right to refuse treatment; the right to be free from discrimination; the right to treatment and services; rights in everyday life in institutions and the community; and the legal system. The appendices contain excerpts of the standards recognized in the case of Wyatt v. Stickney (see 344 F. Supp. 373), and bibliographical and organizational resources. Robert M. Levy is a federal magistrate judge in the Eastern District of New York. Leonard S. Rubenstein is executive director of Physicians for Human Rights and an adjunct professor of law at Georgetown University Law Center.

Marx, Gary S. **Disability Law Compliance Manual**. St. Paul, MN: West, 2007/2009-date. 2 vols. Looseleaf format. Subscription servivce billed annually (2014-date).
Cost: $1,071 per year; supplementation: 2002: $278; 2003: $292; 2004: $330; 2005: $365; 2006: $407; 2007: $407; 2008: $477.48; 2009: $531.48; 2010: $706; 2011: $308; 2012: $342; 2013: $379; **Monthly Assured Print Price (APP):** $84/$1,008.
A practical manual designed to provide guidance to lawyers in advising businesses, corporations and other clients in their compliance with the Americans with Disabilities Act (ADA). This set is primarily concerned with the employment and public accommodations provisions of the ADA and includes discussion of statutory language, administrative regulations, common liabilities, and means of accommodation. Chapters include: major life activities/substantial limitations/qualified individuals, reasonable accommodation, employment inquiries/medical examinations, nondiscriminatory employment practices, selection criteria and testing, substance abuse, psychiatric disabilities, overlap of ADA and workers' compensation law and the Family and Medical Leave Act, public accommodations and commercial facilities, and specific oblations of public accommodations.

Cost Saving Tip: This publication provides a window into the publishing philosophy of Thomson Reuters West: maximize revenue from each title in its stable. This title, for example, was converted into an annual subscription mode between 2013 and 2014, thereby increasing the annual maintenance cost from $379 in 2013 to $1,071 in 2014, or 182%. If you like the basic coverage, simply cancel the standing order and don't allow West to automatically bill you annually. Find a less expensive way of keeping up with current developments.

National Disability Law Reporter. Horsham, PA: LRP Publications, 1990-date. 4 vols. Looseleaf service. Updated 22 times per year. Also available on CD-ROM, see **Disability Law on CD-ROM** above.
Cost: $925 + $63.00 s&h (2014).
This comprehensive reference tool combines analytical discussion and practical guidance on the Americans with Disabilities Act, the Individuals with Disabilities Education Act, Social Security Act, Rehabilitation Act of 1973, Civil Rights Act of 1964, etc. Includes the full-text of ADA and other federal and state disability decisions, statutes, and regulations. Finding tools include a topical index, judicial table, judicial citator, and statutory regulatory tracker.

Parry, John. **Disability Discrimination Law, Evidence and Testimony: A Comprehensive Reference Manual for Lawyers, Judges and Disability Professionals**. Chicago: American Bar Association, Commission on Mental and Physical Disability Law, 2008. 1 vol. (703 pp.). Paperbound.
Cost: $105 ($95 to members); from $40.47 on amazon.com (2014).
The history of disability discrimination law dates from only the 1960s, although the first national legislation was enacted in 1948 when a post-World War II Congress outlawed discrimination against "physical handicap" in the U.S. Civil Service. Since that time, Congress has enacted a number of significant pieces of legislation addressing the needs of the physically and mentally handicapped, including the Rehabilitation Act of 1973

and the American with Disabilities Act of 1990. Despite these legislative achievements, the condition of those with disabilities has not improved markedly in many respects. This reference manual provides a comprehensive review of existing disability discrimination laws and the procedures for addressing the chronic condition of the disabled in American society. Fourteen chapters provide discussion and analysis of the history of disability discrimination law; a legal overview of key statutes and sovereign immunity limitations; disability definitions in federal and state discrimination laws; enforcement under federal and state disability discrimination laws; attorneys' fees in federal and state cases; effective representation of clients with disabilities and the client-lawyer relationship; employment discrimination; state and local government and other public services; public accommodations and the private sector; telecommunications and the Internet; housing and zoning; education, exams and licensing; mental disability discrimination law; and expert evidence and testimony. Appendices provide tables of state discrimination laws in employment, public services/state government, public accommodations, and housing, as well as an alphabetical listing of Supreme Court cases, a summary of Supreme Court cases, index and table of cases. This is an invaluable guide to both the substance and procedure of disability discrimination law, with citations to relevant legal authorities. The author is director of the ABA Commission on Mental and Physical Disability Law and author of the **Handbook on Disability Discrimination Law** (2003) and **Mental Disability Law, Evidence, and Testimony** (2007).

Perritt, Henry H., Jr. **Americans with Disabilities Act Handbook.** 4th ed. New York: Wolters Kluwer Law & Business, 2002-date. 4 vols. Published twice annually.
Cost: $839; supplementation: 2003: $165; 2004: $366; 2005: $378; 2006: $394; 2007: $418; 2008: $695; 2009: $520; 2010: $550; 2011: $604; 2012: $670; 2013: $741; 2d ed.: 1994: $60; 1995: $67; 1996: $158; 1997: new edition; 3d ed.: 1998: $192; 1999: $192; 2000: $192; 2001: $210; 2002: $265.
An analytical treatise which examines the implications and intent of the Americans with Disabilities Act and its impact upon businesses and public facilities. Provides detailed guidance for the ADA plaintiff by outlining the procedures for bringing actions and explaining how the provisions of the Act apply. The volume includes the full text of the act, applicable regulations, and an overview of the public accommodations requirements. It also looks at the costs of compliance. Volume two provides the litigator with practical guidance on the steps necessary to avoid litigation as well as techniques to employ when litigation is necessary. Includes a variety of litigation documents, including complaints under Titles I, II and III. Also includes sample memoranda, checklists, forms, guidelines and job descriptions.

Rothstein, Laura F. **Disabilities and the Law**. 4th ed. St. Paul, MN: West, 2009-date. 1 vol. (870 pp.). Revised twice annually.
Cost: 2014-1 Edition: $95; supplementation: 2010: $31.50; 2011: $40; 2012: $160; 2013: $139; 3d ed.: 2007: $34; 2008: $75; 2d ed.: 2002: $75; 2003: $86; 2004: $100; 2005: $100; 2006: new edition; **Monthly Assured Print Price (APP):** $13/$156.
A comprehensive guide to the impact of the Americans with Disabilities Act in the fields of education, employment, public accommodations and services, transportation, and health care. Includes a discussion of the Rehabilitation Act and other disabilities rights laws. Laura Rothstein is Law Foundation Professor of Law at the University of Houston. A former attorney with the Developmental Disabilities Law Project at the University of Pittsburgh, she has written and spoken widely on disability law matters.

Additional titles in the field of Disabilities Law are available from the following publishers: American Bar Association, Wolters Kluwer Law & Business, Matthew Bender, BNA Plus, Business Laws, Inc., CCH, Inc., Cornell University Press, Foundation Press, Gaunt, Greenwood Publishing Group, William S. Hein & Co., Inc., JIST Works, Inc., Kluwer Academic, LexisNexis, LRP Publications, McGraw-Hill Professional Book Group, National Conference of State Legislatures, Prentice-Hall, Society for Human Resources, Thompson Publishing Group, Thomson Reuters West, Warren, Gorham & Lamont, West Academic, and Workers Compensation Research Institute. See Appendix B for addresses and telephone numbers.

Education Law

Alexander, Kern and M. David Alexander. 4th ed. **The Law of Schools, Students, and Teachers in a Nutshell.** St. Paul: West, 2009. 1 vol. (653 pp.).
Available from West Academic.
Cost: $41; from $25.38 on amazon.com; kindle: $20.84 (2014).
This West Nutshell is a useful and economical overview of the major education law issues in the United States. The authors, Professors of Law at the University of Florida and Virginia Tech University, have written a succinct text which can be of use to the law student, the general practitioner and the lay person. They address a range of specifics, including public school attendance, due process, freedom of speech and expression, religious activities in public schools, discipline, search and seizure, student publications, racial segregation, education of the handicapped, sex discrimination, civil liability. student records, testing, teacher employment and dismissal, employment discrimination, etc. Includes selective citations to case law.

Deskbook Encyclopedia of American School Law. Birmingham, AL: Center for Education and Employment Law, 1981-date. 1 vol. (526 pp.). Annual (August). Paperbound. Optional monthly newsletter **Legal Notes for Education**.
Cost: 2013 Edition: $279.00; newsletter only: $159.00; 2012 Edition: from $10.57 on amazon.com (2014).
This is a topically organized digest of state and federal decisions in the field of education law designed for quick access to relevant court decisions. Summaries of hundreds of decisions are organized under fourteen chapter headings: accidents, injuries and deaths; freedom of religion; freedom of speech and association; student rights; employment discrimination; termination, resignation and retirement; tenure and due process; employee reassignments, suspensions and demotions; labor relations; school operations; disabled students' rights; private schools; and interscholastic athletics. The appendices include selected portions of the **U.S. Constitution**, a bibliography of

recent law review articles, glossary, and index.

Dunklee, Dennis R. and Robert J. Shoop. **The Principal's Quick-Reference Guide to School Law: Reducing Liability, Litigation, and Other Legal Tangles**. 2d ed. Thousand Oaks, CA: Corwin Press, 2006. 1 vol. (324 pp.).
Cost: $44.95 (paper); from $25.89 on amazon.com (2014).
This practical handbook is designed to assist school principals in dealing with the legal issues most commonly encountered in the school environment, including staff selection, contracting and evaluation, teachers' constitutional rights and conditions of employment, students' rights, student discipline, the principal's responsibilities in providing special education services, academic issues and student records, copyright law, search and seizure, program management, sexual harassment, and tort liability. Introductory chapters discuss preventive law and the school and the legal environment. Appendices include the text of the constitutional provisions of interest to education, and leading U.S. Supreme Court decisions on education. Dennis Dunklee is on the faculty in the Graduate School of Education at George Mason University, the author of numerous books on education-related topics, and a nationally recognized expert in the area of school law and risk management. Robert J. Shoop is a professor in the Department of Educational Administration and Leadership at Kansas State University, and the author of numerous books on educational leadership.

Dunn, Joshua M. and Martin R. West, eds. **From Schoolhouse to Courthouse: The Judiciary's Role in American Education**. Washington, DC: Brookings Institution Press, 2009. 1 vol. (275 pp.).
Cost: $28.95; from $0.01 on amazon.com; kindle: $15.63 (2014).
In 1948, Supreme Court Justice Robert Jackson warned his colleagues against "establishing themselves as a super board of education for every school district in the nation." Since that time, however, state and federal courts have so intruded into every aspect of school operation that substantial numbers of teachers and administrators practice defensive teaching in order to avoid legal challenges. The number of education cases has expanded dramatically over the past 60 years, from 1,552 in the 1940s to 6,788 in the 1970s, and has fluctuated at that level ever since. But while the majority of pre-1950 cases concerned such subjects as tax policies, bond offerings and district boundaries, those in the post-1950 era encompassed the more highly charged areas of school desegregation, separation of church and state, school discipline, and due process rights of teachers. This volume examines the corpus of decisions in those areas of educational policy in which the judiciary has been and remains most active, as well as their implications for educational policymaking. Yet, despite this activism, the courts have shown themselves to be less than perfect instruments of reform. For as Fordham Institute President Chester Finn contends, "we ought not to be so dazzled by some of the great, transformative court rulings of yesteryear--*Brown* above all--as to suppose that any large fraction of the 7,000 or so education-related decisions now being rendered annually by federal and state judges are having a salutary effect on American schools or children's learning." This volume is a product of collaboration between the Thomas B. Fordham Institute, whose primary concern is primary-secondary education and the expansion of educational achievement and academic performance by needy families and children, and the Brookings Institution. Under the editorship of Joshua Dunn, associate professor of political science at the University of Colorado, and Martin K. West, assistant professor of education at the Harvard Graduate School of Education, the chapters in this volume grapple with such issues as the Supreme Court as school board revisited, court-ordered remedies, school superintendents and the law, school desegregation, school finance litigation, the judiciary's now limited role in special education, high-stakes testing, school choice litigation after *Zelman*, separation of church and state, freedom of speech and students' rights, No Child Left Behind, and school discipline. This sophisticated, balanced and timely analysis of the current state of educational litigation in the United States should be required reading for any litigator or policy maker concerned with education-related issues.

Essex, Nathan L. **School Law and the Public Schools: a Practical Guide for Educational Leaders**. 5th ed. Boston, MA: Allyn and Bacon, 2011. 1 vol. (400 pp.).
Cost: $145.33; from $86.00 on amazon.com; kindle: $83.11 (2014).
Intended for an audience of educational administrators, policy makers, teachers, and graduate students in educational administration, this text addresses a variety of legal issues likely to be faced in the course of school administration. Among the issues considered are school safety, alcohol and breathalyzers, application of the Patriot Act, the theory of evolution, Intelligent Design, the use of personal data assistants, confidentiality in school counseling, the Family Medical Leave Act, intellectual property and fair use, charter schools, child abuse, Title IX retaliation, the reauthorized Individuals with Disabilities Improvement Act, the posting of the Ten Commandments, and more. The text is supplemented with summaries of relevant court decisions, charts and tables. Essential reading for any school administrator who wishes to comply with the law, whether in the form of the U.S. Constitution, state and federal statues, and case law. The frequent editions reflect the book's use as an educational textbook and, at least partially, to undercut the market in used copies.

Fischer, Louis, David Schimmel, and Leslie Stellman. **School Law: What Every Educator Should Know, A User-Friendly Guide**. Boston, MA: Allyn & Bacon, 2007. 1 vol. (192 pp.).
Cost: $30.00; from $13.98 on amazon.com (2014).
Intended as a textbook in teacher education programs, this book provides, in a question and answer format, discussion of the legal issues most likely to be encountered by teachers and students in the school environment. Written in non-technical language, this volume covers the legal aspects of teaching, contracts, collective bargaining, liability, libel and slander, child abuse, copyright, freedom of expression, religious freedom, due process rights, racial discrimination, sex discrimination, students with disabilities, student records, attendance laws, and restrictions on personal appearance. The authors also discuss the issues most likely to face the courts in the next decade. Appendices include selected provisions of the U.S. Constitution, major civil rights laws affecting schools, and legal resources for teachers. Louis

Fischer is Professor Emeritus in the Department of Education, University of Massachusetts. David, also a professor in the Department of Education, received his law degree from Yale Law School. Leslie Stellman is a practicing attorney with the Baltimore firm of Blum, Yumkas, Mailman, Gutman & Denick.

Gajda, Amy. **The Trials of Academe: The New Era of Campus Litigation**. Cambridge, MA: Harvard University Press, 2009. 1 vol. (334 pp.).
Cost: $40.00; $18.72 on amazon.com; kindle ed.: $29.60 (2014).
It should come as no surprise that the litigiousness which has come to infect American society as a whole has also taken root on the college campus. While litigation has been apart of academic life for more than 200 years, the quantity and character of that litigation has changed markedly. Disputes which, in an earlier era, would never have left the halls of academe, or been brought at all, have received increased scrutiny from both courts and legislators. This transformation has been a product of both internal and external forces, including not only the increasing range of federal and state regulation and civil rights laws, but also the fragmentation of the modern «multiversity» and its former sense of community, and an oppressive wave of political correctness, with its preoccupation with race and gender issues. In this engaging book by law professor and legal journalist Amy Gajda, these trends are subjected to close and thoughtful examination. These lawsuits may involve tenure decisions, student grading, alleged race discrimination, hiring or promotion, tuition increases, administrative oversight of course content, defamation actions by rival scholars, and even redress from mentors for faulty advice. By the late 1970s, the courts had overcome their previous reluctance to hearing cases involving academic institutions, and begun to define the rights and responsibilities of the university and its constituent parts. The book's chapters address academic deference, anti-discrimination law on campus, free speech and the First Amendment, battles over intellectual property, privacy and the peer review process, academic defamation, tort law on campus, and contractual issues. The author draws upon the scholarly literature, court decisions, and applicable statutes in framing her thought-provoking and critical analysis of legal trends on the modern university campus.

Gerstein, Ralph and Lois Gerstein. **Education Law: An Essential for Attorneys, Teachers, Administrators, Parents and Students**. 2d ed. Tucson, AZ: Lawyers & Judges Publishing Co., 2007. 1 vol. (515 pp.).
Cost: $99; 1st edition: from $4.87 on amazon.com; kindle ed.: $99 (2014).
An in-depth handbook on a wide variety of legal issues impacting the field of education, including admissions, academic issues, impact of the Americans with Disabilities Act, special education services, administrative proceedings and litigation, regulation of student conduct, disciplinary sanctions against students, disciplinary procedures, weapons and rugs, search and seizure, school violence, First Amendment speech issues, religion and the schools, civil rights and discrimination, student records, civil wrongs, attendance and home schooling, school athletics and cheerleading, and personnel issues. The authors' even-handed approach to a number of contentious issues makes this an excellent tool for both administrators and students. The text is complemented by numerous case studies which illustrate the various legal issues being discussed. Ralph Gerstein is an attorney in private practice with extensive experience handling education-related cases.

Harding, Bertrand M., Jr. **Tax Law of Colleges and Universities**. 3d ed. Washington, DC: Wiley Publishers, 2007-date. 1 vol. Also available as E-Book.
Cost: $230; from $213.88 on amazon.com; kindle: $144.99; no supplementation to date; 2d ed.: 2002: 0; 2003: $75; 2004: $80; 2005: $85; 2006: $90.
IRS audits of colleges and universities result, on average, in assessments of more than $1 million per institution. This resource is designed to provide college financial and legal officers with the tools necessary to improve IRS compliance and reduce these potential tax liabilities. It discusses and analyzes a wide-range of tax issues including unrelated business income tax, FICA and other employment taxes, and withholding and reporting on payments to nonresident aliens. In addition, the book examines the IRS audit process and provides helpful hints and techniques on how to prepare for an IRS audit and how to interact with IRS agents during the course of the audit.

Imber, Michael, Tyll Van Geel, J.C. Blokhuis and Jonathan Feldman. **Education Law**. 5th ed. New York, NY: Routledge, 2013. 1 vol. (552 pp.).
Cost: $265 (hardbound); $109.95 (paper); from $87.19 on amazon.com; kindle ed.: $89.95 (2014).
Designed primarily as a text for educational administrators and policy makers, this comprehensive survey of education law covers a variety of topics which may embroil schools in litigation. While primarily a work of commentary, this edition does include the selective reprinting of illustrative court decisions. Following an overview of education law, the authors tackle such subjects as compulsory education, curriculum, student free speech rights, student discipline, equal educational opportunity: race and gender, students with special needs, school finance, federal constitutional and statutory rights of school employees, teacher employment, collective bargaining, unions, and teacher contracts, and torts. Footnotes provide citations to other relevant court decisions. The volume also includes the text of the U.S. Constitution, a table of cases, and index. Michael Imber id Professor of Educational Policy and Administration in the School of Education at the University of Kansas. Tyll Van Geel is Taylor Professor of Education in the Graduate School of Education, University of Rochester.

Individuals with Disabilities Education Law Report (IDELR). Horsham, PA: LRP Publications, 1978-date. 2 vols. Updated 24 times per year.
Cost: $1,350 per year + $65 s&h (2014).
A comprehensive reference tool covering a wide range of legal issues in the field of special education, including classroom discipline, mediation of disputes, development of individual education profiles, compliance with state standards and much more. Includes the full text of major federal laws and regulations,

IDEA policy rulings, Section 504 policy rulings, federal and state court decisions, and SEA appeals decisions. The subscription also includes the biweekly **IDELR Highlights** and periodic **Special Reports**.

Kaplin, William A. and Barbara A. Lee. **The Law of Higher Education**. 5th ed. San Francisco, CA: Jossey-Bass, 2013. 2 vols. Also available as E-Book.
Cost: $250 (print); kindle: $242.34; no supplementation to date; 2009: $60; 2010-2012: 0; Student version (e-book): $79.99; from $56.89 on amazon.com (2014).
In the past thirty years, higher education has become the locus for a variety of legal conflicts and issues far beyond those of traditional educational administration. This comprehensive and practical guide to the law as it impacts the conduct of higher education examines these issues within the scope of nine chapters, including an overview of postsecondary education law; the college and trustees, administrators and staff; the college and the faculty; the college and the students; the college and the community; the college and the state government, the college and the federal government, the college and educational associations, and the college and the business/industrial community. Among the current issues discussed are sex discrimination, hate speech, academic freedom in religious institutions, athletic scholarships, animal research, and environmental laws. William A. Kaplin is a professor of law at Catholic University Of America where he specializes in education law and policy, constitutional law, and civil rights law. He has also been special counsel to the university since 1981. Barbara A. Lee is Dean of the School of Management and Labor Relations at Rutgers. The first edition of **The Law of Higher Education** was recognized by the American Council on Education as the most outstanding book on higher education for the year 1978.

Kors, Alan Charles and Harvey A. Silverglate. **The Shadow University: The Betrayal of Liberty on America's Campuses**. New York: The Free Press, 1998. 1 vol. (415 pp.).
Cost: $15; from $.01 on amazon.com; kindle ed.: $13.67 (2014)
No understanding of the law of higher education would be complete without an appreciation of the climate of political correctness which grips most modern college campuses and is a root cause of much of the litigation, both open and secret, with which they are increasingly embroiled. Grounded in the theories of the late Marxist theoretician, and member of the Frankfurt School of critical theory, Herbert Marcuse, this new orthodoxy of intolerance is enforced by academic bureaucracies and faculties which promote rights of certain favored groups over individual rights through the mechanisms of speech and conduct codes, student indoctrination, and disciplinary proceedings which make a mockery of due process and constitutional rights. Indeed, the very notion of free speech is rejected by these Marcusians who hold that the supposedly neutral tolerance for ideas in the United States is, in reality, a selective tolerance that reinforces the hegemony of the dominant power structure. For all the talk about diversity on college campuses, there is increasinly less intellectual or political diversity. By advancing racial, cultural or sexual diversity above other considerations, we get more of the same intellectual conformity and an enforced political orthodoxy that has no place in the academy. It is within the context of Marcuse's theories that the far-left, which supported "free speech" for its own ends in the 1960s, now hypocritically seeks to repress the free speech of those who do not accept their totalitarian worldview. This book has its origins in the infamous "Water Buffalo Case" at the University of Pennsylvania in 1993 in which a freshman student by the name of Eden Jacobowitz was wrongfully accused of racial harassment and subjected to the university's ideologically-charged disciplinary process. Alan Charles Kors, a professor of history who came to the student's defense in that case, is joined by Massachusetts criminal and civil rights attorney Harvey Silverglate in writing this incisive and well-documented indictment of higher education's assault on liberty and procedural due process. Their discussion is accompanied by a thorough-going analysis of First Amendment free speech guarantees as enunciated in 20th century American jurisprudence. The authors are also active in the Foundation for Individual Rights in Education (FIRE), a nonprofit educational foundation devoted to free speech, individual liberty, religious freedom, the rights of conscience, legal equality, due process, and academic freedom on the nation's campuses (www.thefire.org).

Latham, Peter S., Patricia Horan Latham, and Myrna R. Mandlawitz. **Special Education Law**. Boston, MA: Allyn and Bacon, 2007. 1 vol. (192pp.)
Cost: $65.00; from $8.88 on amazon.com (2014).
The Individuals with Disabilities Education Act (IDEA), originally adopted in 1975 as the Education for all Handicapped Children Act, mandated that students with disabilities have access to the public education system and be provided appropriate special education and related services. Compliance with this and other applicable federal and state laws and regulations regarding special education is an area which consumes educators at all levels. This volume presents in clear and organized fashion the most significant law regarding special education, including the Individuals with Disabilities in Education Act, the Americans with Disabilities Act, and the special education implications of the No Child Left Behind Act, among others. Peter S. Latham and Patricia Horan Latham are partners in the Washington, DC law firm of Latham & Latham and the publishing company JKL Communications, authors of Terrorism and the Law and eight books on legal issues in employment and education, including Learning Disabilities and the Law and Attention Deficit Disorder and the Law, as well as contributors to nine additional books. They are founders of the National Center for Law and Learning Disabilities.

Lentz, Mary A. **Lentz School Security**. St. Paul, MN: West, 1993-date. 1 vol. Annual editions. Paperbound.
Cost: 2013-2014 Edition: $268; **Monthly Assured Print Price (APP):** $22/$264 (2014).
A comprehensive discussion and analysis of school security issues designed for use by school administrators, attorneys and scholars. The author discusses a wide variety of problems which plague modern schools, including child neglect and abuse, date rape, pornography, bullying, physical aggression, harassment, and weapons. She addresses a number of significant school-related security issues, including school and law enforcement partnerships, criminal behavior in the school environment,

responses to threats, student conflict, intervention and conflict resolution, missing, abused and neglected children, safe and secure schools, safety preparedness, search and seizure, interviewing of children, and special needs children. The appendices include the text of relevant federal education statutes and regulations, including the Teacher Liability Protection Act and the Gun Free School Zones Act. The volume also includes a number of useful forms and checklists, including checklists for maintaining safer schools and a sample sexual harassment policy. Mary A. Lentz is a former public school teacher who practices public and private school law in Chagrin Falls, Ohio and a former legal counsel to the Ohio State Board/Department of Education. An invaluable desktop reference for school administrators and attorneys.

McCarthy, Martha M. Nelda H. Cambron-McCabe, and Stephen B. Thomas. **Legal Rights of Teachers and Students**. 3d ed. Boston: Pearson/Allyn & Bacon, 2013. 1 vol. (336 pp.).
Cost: $106.00; from $71.82 on amazon.com (2014).
An introductory overview of the law governing teachers and students written primarily. for an undergraduate and returning professional audience of teachers. The authors address the issues most commonly encountered in a real-life school setting, including the legal framework of public education, church/state relations, instructional issues, student expression, association and appearance, student classification, rights of students with disabilities, student discipline, terms and conditions of employment, substantive constitutional rights, discrimination in employment, termination of employment, tort liability. The book includes a glossary of legal terms, text of selected Supreme Court decisions, and index. Martha McCarthy is professor of education in the School of Education, Indiana University. Nelda Cambron-McCabe is Professor, Department of Educational Leadership. Miami University (OH). Stephen B. Thomas is a professor in the College and Graduate School of Education, Kent State University. A revised and condensed version of the authors' Public School Law, 5th ed (2004).

McCarthy, Martha M., Nelda H. Cambron-McCabe, and Stephen B. Thomas. **Public School Law: Teachers' and Students' Rights**. 7th ed. Needham Heights, MA: Allyn & Bacon, 2013. 1 vol. (560 pp.).
Cost: $171.80; from $115.46 on amazon.com; kindle: $79.80 (2014).
Designed for courses in School Law, and Law and Education. Also designed as a reference source for school administrators and school attorneys. **Public School Law: Teachers' and Students' Rights**, provides a comprehensive treatment of the evolution and current status of the law governing public schools. The text addresses legal principles applicable to practitioners in a succinct but comprehensive manner. Information in this text should help alleviate concerns voiced by educators who feel that the scales of justice have been tipped against them. In the fourth edition, the content of all chapters has been updated and new sections have been added to reflect emerging issues of legal concern. The 7th edition includes 400 new cases and content updated to July 2012.

Osborne, Allan G. and Russo, Charles J. **Special Education and the Law: A Guide for Practitioners**. 2d ed. Thousand Oaks, CA: Corwin Press, 2006. 1 vol. (304 pp.).
Cost: $90.95 (hardcover); $41.95 (paperbound); from $8.84 on amazon.com (2014).
Special education occupies a central place in American public education and consumes a growing share of its spending. With passage of the Disabilities Education Act (IDEA), Americans with Disabilities Act (ADA) and Section 504 of the Rehabilitation Act, public education has become increasingly vulnerable to lawsuits on special education related matters. This brief guide is designed to provide school teachers and administrators with basic information on federal special education laws and regulations and their implementation. Beginning with a useful introduction to the history and mandates of special education law, the authors proceed to discuss rights to a free appropriate public education, educational services, due process procedures for evaluation, the development of individual education plans (IEPs), student discipline, dispute resolution, and remedies for failure to provide an appropriate public education. Allan G. Osborne is the Principal of Snug Harbor Community School in Quincy, Massachusetts, and a visiting associate professor at Bridgewater State College. Charles J. Russo is the Joseph Panzer Chair of Education in the School of Education and Allied Professions and Adjunct Professor in the School of Law at the University of Dayton.

Poskanzer, Steven G. **Higher Education Law: The Faculty**. Baltimore, MD: Johns Hopkins University Press, 2001. Paperbound. 1 vol. (352 pp.).
Cost: $23.00; from $3.00 on amazon.com; kindle: $15.33 (2014).
A well-written overview of the multitude of legal issues impacting the faculty of colleges and universities. While written primarily to assist faculty and administrators in negotiating the legal minefield that constitutes higher education today, this text is also accessible to employees, students, and the general public. The author provides the reader with an excellent summary of the legal landscape, including its constitutional, statutory, regulatory, and judicial dimensions. The discussion then covers such topics as first amendment principles, contractual obligations, immunity from suit, scholarship, conflicts of interest, academic freedom, copyright and teaching materials, faculty involvement in institutional governance, conferences and symposia, faculty as public citizens, faculty as employees, hiring, promotion and job security, nondiscrimination law, terms of employment, and faculty discipline. A unique and invaluable contribution to the field. Steven G. Poskanzer is President of the State University of New York, New Paltz and a graduate of Harvard Law School.

Rapp, James A. **Education Law.** New York: Matthew Bender & Co., 1984-date. 7 vols. Looseleaf format. Supplemented about twice a year. No CD-ROM or Internet access.
Cost: $1,883 (includes annual subscription); renewal: 1995: $507.00 (frozen since1992); 1996: $532; 1997: $532; 1998: $560; 1999: $585; 2000: $585; 2001: $626; 2002: $670; 2003: $704; 2004: $739; 2005: $791; 2006: $823; 2007: $888; 2008: $959; 2009: $1,036; 2010: $1,088; 2011: $1,142; 2012: $1,199; 2013: $1,283; 2014: $1,408; eBook: $1,712; renewal: 2014: $1,408.

This massive four-volume treatise, providing the most detailed coverage of educational law issues on the market, is edited by James Rapp of the Quincy, Illinois law firm of Hutmacher, Rapp & Ortbal and authored by thirty legal scholars and practitioners with experience in specific aspects of education law. The coverage is designed to satisfy the needs of school administrators and practitioners representing clients with grievances against educational institutions as well as those representing schools, school boards, and educational administrators. While the substantive emphasis is upon those areas with a basis in United States constitutional or statutory law, state specific matters are also addressed. The law governing both public and private institutions is discussed and analyzed. Individual chapters are devoted to discussion and analysis of: education law and the attorney; church, state and education; governing agencies, boards, officers and authorities; operating procedures of educational institutions; funding support, and finances of education; faculty and staff employment and dismissal; labor relation in education; the student-educational institution relationship; student control and discipline; educational opportunities and equality; curriculum and teaching methods, general liabilities and litigation; education records, and intellectual property. Part II contains a variety of appropriate forms, including contracts, model school policies, litigation forms and checklists, in support of the content in Part I. Part III features state statutory tables in a number of specific areas, including student discipline, compulsory education requirements, etc. Volume four also contains a detailed subject index and tables of statutes and cases. The text is heavily supported with citations to case and statutory law and secondary sources.

Cost Saving Tips: By its scope and frequency of supplementation, this set is obviously designed for the specialist. As with any Bender treatise, however, the subscriber always the option of canceling the standing order after one year and then updating by buying a new set at some future date. This is a decision you must make based on your need for current analysis and citations. As with any secondary source, there is an editorial time lag which must be addressed by consulting primary sources and Shepardizing or KeyCiting relevant citations. Used correctly, the core material may provide you with sufficient utility that you can forego the more costly standing order. Although subject specific treatises like this are not readily available, you may be able to locate a fairly current used set at considerable savings.

Redfield, Sarah E. **Thinking Like a Lawyer: An Educator's Guide to Legal Analysis and Research**. 2d ed. Durham, NC: Carolina Academic Press, 2011.
1 vol. (192 pp.). Paperbound.
Cost: $25.00; from $11.00 on amazon.com (2014).
This book, which had its origins in the Education Law Institute at Franklin Pierce Law Center, was written to provide professional educators with an understanding and comprehensive of the increasingly complex legal landscape in which they operate. In addressing both the concepts and sources of law, the author's aim is to train educators to evaluate and analyze legal issues as lawyers would. This is accomplished by examining the sources of law, the process of reading case law, and the process of conducting research in the law. Appendices include an annotated glossary of legal terms and the complete text of the U.S. Supreme Curt decision of Vernonia v. Acton, a school-related search and seizure case involving drug use by student athletes. Sarah Redfield, a professor of education law at Franklin Pierce Law Center, has extensive experience in presenting education law programs to educators in the form of courses and annual conferences sponsored by the Education Law Institute.

Russo, Charles, ed. **Encyclopedia of Law and Higher Education**. Thousand Oaks, CA: Sage Publications, 2010. 1 vol. (557 pp.).
Cost: $110.00; from $87.30 on amazon.com (2014).
Since at least 1817, when the U.S. Supreme Court decided the case of *Trustees of Dartmouth College v. Woodward*, the legal system has exerted an influence over higher education in the United States. This encyclopedic reference provides undergraduate and graduate students, faculty, legal practitioners, and general readers with insightful essays regarding the impact of the law on higher education. Nearly 150 alphabetically arranged entries provide essential information in eleven categories, including cases in higher education law; concepts, theories and legal principles; concepts, rights and issues; faculty rights, governance and finance; organization and institutions; primary sources: excerpts from land mark U.S. Supreme Court cases; religion and freedom of speech; statutes; students rights and welfare; and technology. Each entry is accompanied by "see also" references, a list of further readings, and a list of citations to relevant state and federal appellate court decisions. Preliminary materials include a general introduction explaining the scope of the work and a overview of its content, and a brief explanation of how to work with legal materials. A useful introductory tool for any student or scholar engaged in educational research. The articles were written by 49 academic scholars and school administrators under the general editorship of Charles J. Russo, the Joseph Panzer Chair in Education in the School, of Education and Allied Professions and adjunct professor in the school of law at the University of Dayton, OH.

Russo, Charles J. and Allan G. Osborne, Jr. **Essential Concepts & School-Based Cases in Special Education Law**. Thousand Oaks, CA: Corwin Press (Sage Publications), 2008. 1 vol. (350 pp.).
Cost: $95.95 (hardcover); $44.95 (softbound); from $24.43 on amazon.com (2014).
Originally enacted in 1975, the Education for All Handicapped Children Act (P.L. 94-142), was amended in 1990 and given its current title, the Individuals with Disabilities Education Act (IDEA). This act and its subsequent amendments provide a permanent federal source of funding to states to educate children with disabilities. This volume provides lawyers, educators, education students, and parents with an overview of the law regarding special education and its practical application in school-based settings. After laying the legal framework regarding sources of law generally, and special education specifically, the authors turn their attention to such topics as the entitlement to special education an related services; procedural due process; free appropriate special education; required related services, assistive technology, and transition services; student discipline; dispute resolution; remedies for failure to provide a free appropriate public education; emerging issues, and antidiscrimination

statutes. Appendices include a glossary of terms and relevant web sites. Each chapter includes excerpts drawn from court decisions and statutes. Charles J. Russo, Chair of the School of Education and Allied Professions and Adjunct Professor in the School of Law at the University of Dayton, is the author or editor of 26 books and more than 170 articles in peer-reviewed journals. Allan Osborne, who holds a doctorate in educational leadership from Boston College, is principal of the Snug Harbor Community School in Quincy, MA and the author of numerous educational texts.

Russo, Charles J., ed. **Key Legal Issues for Schools: The Ultimate Resource for School Business Officials**. 2d ed. Rowman & Littlefield, 2013. 1 vol. (193 pp.). Paperbound.
Cost: $33.95; from $23.96 on amazon.com; kindle: $18.14 (2014).
The responsibilities of school business officials (SBOs) extend far beyond matters relating to budgeting and accounting. Their responsibilities often extend to such legal-related issues as contracts, setting policy on state bidding laws, and student and teacher rights, among others, depending on the size and administrative structure of their school districts. The fourteen chapters in this volume address such varied topics as state credentialing laws, effective policy formation, accounting and budget functions, privatization of elementary and secondary education, school finance, transportation, school technology, negligence, building and physical plants, supervision and evaluation of school employees, employment issues, students rights, special education and students with disabilities, and the role of religion in public schools, each of which includes numerous citations to legal and other authorities. The volume brings together more than dozen experts with expertise in various aspects of school administration and governance. Charles J. Russo is the Panzer Chair in Education and adjunct professor of law at the University of Dayton, OH. A past president of the Education Law Association, he is the author of more than 850 publications in the field of education. This volume is an excellent overview of some of the dominant legal issues in the field of education that can be of great value to school business officials and school district legal counsel.

Shoop, Robert J. and Dennis R. Dunklee. **Anatomy of a Lawsuit: What Every Education Leader Should Know About Legal Actions**. Thousand Oaks, CA: Corwin Press, 2005. 1 vol. (142 pp.). Paperbound.
Cost: $72.95 (hardcover); $31.95 (softbound); from $4.74 on amazon.com; kindle ed.: $17.25 (2014).
In our increasingly litigious society, teachers and educational administrators are frequently involved in litigation over a wide variety of legal issues, both civil and criminal. These educators who become involved in the litigation process may do so in a variety of capacities, including that of criminal defendant, civil defendant, criminal plaintiff, civil plaintiff, character witness, factual witness, respondent to interrogatories, consulting expert witness, or a testifying expert witness. Moreover the professional conduct of educators is heavily influenced by the law and the threat of litigation. This useful overview of the litigation process for professional educators includes a review of the legal environment and the function of the law, the organization of the courts, the process of litigation, working with an attorney, the courtroom environment, the trial, management of litigation stress, verdict and analysis, the role of the expert witness, and managing the risk of litigation. .Robert Shoop is professor of education law at Kansas State University. Dennis Dunklee is associate professor in the Education Leadership Department in the Graduate School of Education at George Mason University.

United States School Laws and Rules. 2013 Edition. St. Paul, MN: West, 2003-date. 2 vols. (1406 pp.) Annual. Paperbound.
Cost: 2013 Edition: $266; **Monthly Assured Print Price (APP):** $22/$264 (2014).
Designed for attorneys specializing in education law, school administrators, school board members, labor officials, state policy-makers, students, and faculty, this volume contains the full text of the most significant education-related statutes in the **United States Code**, and regulations from the **Code of Federal Regulations**. Includes portions of Titles 8, 15, 18, 20, 28, 29, 41 and 42. An excellent, cost-effective alternative to the purchasing the entire **United States Code**.

Valente, William D. and Christina M. Valente. **Law in the Schools**. 6th ed. Prentice Hall, 2005. 1 vol. (432 pp.).
Cost: $158.80; from $79.37 on amazon.com (2014).
A guide to the full range of legal issues which now impact schools across the United States. The sixth edition reflects the many changes which have impacted education in recent years, as schools grapple with such issues as violence, drug use, sexual misconduct, increased use of computers and the Internet, student and community group use of public school buildings for prayer and religious expression, rights of students with disabilities, tuition vouchers, and responsibility for medical decisions. Chapters include an overview of education under the American legal system, public schools: programs and services, public schools: religion-related problems, tort liability under state law, professional employees: rights and obligations, personal civil rights—teachers, student rights and discipline, the pyramid of discrimination remedies, ad private education: alternatives to the public schools. Excerpts of selected court decisions appear at the end of each chapter. Intended as a graduate school text, this volume is also a useful reference for school administrators, legal counsel, and teachers. William D. Valente is Professor of Law Emeritus, Villanova University School of Law. Christina M. Valente is an Adjunct Professor of Political Science at Villanova.

Weber, Mark C. **Special Education Law and Litigation Treatise**. 3d ed. Horsham, PA: LRP Publications, 2008. 1 vol. Looseleaf format. Periodic supplementation.
Cost: $295 + $13 s&h; supplementation: 2010: $98.25 + $7.50 s&h; 2011: 0 (2014).
Special education is defined by the Individuals with Disabilities Education Act (IDEA) as "specially designed instruction, at no cost to parents, to meet the unique needs of a child with a disability." Since the enactment of the Education for All Handicapped Children Act in 1975, the field of special education has been subject to a host of legislative and regulatory enactments designed to improve the delivery of educational services to students with disabilities. This comprehensive treatise provides

detailed coverage of the legal environment of special education and the issues unique to the field. Its 23 chapters address a host of topics, from the statutory background of special education, eligibility for special education services, appropriate education, evaluation of students, individualized education programs, placement, accessibility and technology, related services, early childhood and preschool, monitoring and compliance, student discipline, parental status and related issues, records, residency, plans and funding, and personnel development. Additional chapters provide guidance in the litigation side of special education, including due process procedure, procedure and claims, hearings, remedies and appeals, and attorney's fees. The appendices include the full text of the IDEA and appropriate federal regulations. Each chapter is accompanied by substantial citations to statutory authority and case law, including citations to the publisher's **Individual's With Disabilities Education Law Reporter** (**IDELR**). The author is the Vincent de Paul Professor of Law at DePaul University and the author of numerous books and articles, including **Disability Harassment** (NYU Press) and **Understanding Disability Law** (LexisNexis).

Weeks, Kent M. and Derek Davis, eds. **Legal Deskbook for Administrators of Independent Colleges and Universities**. Rev. 2d ed. Waco, TX: J. M. Dawson Institute for Constitutional Studies, Baylor University and National Association of Colleges and University Attorneys, 1993-date. 1 vol. (looseleaf). Annual cumulative supplements.

Cost: DISCONTINUED. Was $59.50; supplementation: 1994-1999: $15.00 each year; 2000-2007: $16.00; from $80 on amazon.com.

Designed as a guide for administrators and legal counsel serving independent colleges and universities, this **Deskbook** places its emphasis upon the preventative application of the law and problem solving. Each of its twelve substantive chapters provides basic discussion of a specific legal problem, identifies critical issues faced by independent institutions of higher education, and outlines planning steps which such institutions can take in these areas. Each chapter includes a list of bibliographical resources, including relevant cases, statutes, articles, and policy statements. References to cases in the public sector are cited in selective instances if they offer policy options which might prove useful to independent institutions. Chapters include introduction, preventive planning, governance, employment, students, physical facilities, tort liability, taxation, religiously affiliated colleges and universities, environment, charitable giving, research and technology transfer issues. Kent Weeks is an attorney with the Nashville firm of Weeks, Turner, Anderson & Russell and Professor of Practice at Vanderbilt University. Derek Davis, Director of the Center for Constitutional Studies, Baylor University, is editor of the Journal of Church and State and author of numerous books and articles in the area of church-state relations. Numerous attorneys contributed chapters or sections in their areas of expertise. Both the main volume and annual cumulative supplements are reasonably priced. The publication was discontinued in 2007 when Derek Davis left Baylor University.

Weinberg, Lawrence D. **Religious Charter Schools: Legalities and Practicalities**. Greenwich, CT: Information Age Publications, Inc., 2007. 1 vol. (158 pp.).

Cost: $85.99 (web price: $73.09) (hardcover); $45.99 (web price: $39.09) (paperbound); from $43.69 on amazon.com (2014).

The failure of the public school monopoly to meet both the educational and religious/moral needs of parents and students has prompted the passage of state laws permitting the creation of autonomous charter schools. This volume addresses the legality of charter schools created for religious purposes. While charter schools cannot endorse or promote a particular form of religious belief, they can accommodate the religious views of their students. Following a consideration of the constitutionality of religious charter schools and their position vis-à-vis the establishment clause of the U.S. Constitution, the author examines the history of privately-funded religious schools in the United States and the more recent introduction of publicly-funded charter schools, including those created to meet religious as well as educational needs. He also looks at charter schools from a policy perspective, and at the legality of a number of specific religiously-based educational practices. The text is supported by citations to the most significant cases, statutes, and secondary sources.

Additional titles in the field of Education Law are available from the following publishers: ABC-CLIO, Allyn & Bacon, Matthew Bender, Casenotes Publishing, Inc., Center for Law & Education, College Administration Publications, College Legal Information, Inc., Corwin Press, Education Law Association, Education Publications, Greenwood Publishing Group, Institute for Educational Leadership, LexisNexis, National Conference of State Legislatures, National School Boards Association, Neal-Schuman, Thomson Reuters West, United States Government Printing Office, West Academic, Wiley Publishers. See Appendix B for addresses and telephone numbers.

Elder Law

(see also Social Security Law and Trusts and Estates)

American Bar Association Commission on Law and Aging/ American Psychological Association. **Assessment of Older Adults with Diminished Capacity: A Handbook for Lawyers**. Washington, DC: ABA Commission on Law and Aging: American Psychological Association, 2005. 1 vol. (72 pp.). Paperbound or PDF download.

Cost: $25 (2014).

This collaborative project of the American Bar Association Commission on Aging and the American Psychological Association is a response to the growing numbers of older Americans with problems in decision-making capacity brought on by various forms of dementia. Lawyers are increasingly called upon to make assessments of mental capacity in a variety of legal transactions, including guardianship determinations. Rather than outlining compulsory actions, this volume aims to offers ideas and effective practices for balancing the competing goals of autonomy and protection. Following an executive summary, the volume addresses the importance of lawyer assessment of client capacity, legal standards of diminished capacity, clinical models of capacity, lawyer assessment of capacity, techniques lawyers can use to enhance client capacity, referrals for consultation or formal assessment, and understanding and using the capacity assessment report. The volume appendices include a capacity worksheet for lawyers, case examples involving legal transactions and guardianship, a brief guide to psychological and neuropsychological instruments, and a dementia overview. This is an essential resource for attorneys who represent the elderly.

American Bar Association Commission on Law and Aging/ American Psychological Association/National College of Probate Judges. **Judicial Determination of Capacity of Older Adults in Guardianship Proceedings**. Washington, DC: ABA Commission on Law and Aging: American Psychological Association, 2006. 1 vol. (42 pp.). Paperbound.
Cost: $25 (2014); also available free of charge at: http://www.abanet.org/aging/publications/onlinepublicationsprofessionals.shtml
A joint product of the American Bar Association Commission on Aging and the American Psychological Association, this volume provides a framework by which judges can make capacity determinations. It provides a discussion of the role of judges in capacity determinations and an overview of capacity assessments. It goes on to explain the six pillars of capacity: (1) medical condition; (2) cognition; (3) everyday functioning; (4) values and preferences patterns; (5) risk of harm and level of supervision needed; and (6) means to enhance capacity. It also explains the steps in the determination process: (1) screening the case; (2) gathering information; (3) conducting the hearing; (4) making determination; and (5) ensuring court oversight. The appendices include a number of essential documents, including a model form for confidential judicial notice, model court investigator report, model order for clinical evaluation, model clinical evaluation report, model order for guardianship of person and estate, model plan for guardian of person and estate, and a model annual report for guardian of person and estate. Also includes a glossary and endnotes.

The American Bar Association Complete Personal Legal Guide. 4th ed. Chicago: American Bar Association, 2009. 1 vol. (784 pp.).
Cost: Currently out-of-print; was $22.95 ($19.50 to members) (softcover) (2014).
Published in cooperation with the American Bar Association's Division for Public Education, this is the most comprehensive single-volume legal reference book written for the layperson. The coverage extends to a multitude of topics of greatest interest and value to the general public, including automobiles, computers, credit and bankruptcy, contracts and consumer law, criminal justice, divorce and child custody/support, elder law, estate planning, health care, home ownership, personal injury, real estate, small business, and workplace law. Presented in an easy-to-use question and answer format. Particularly recommended for public libraries and law libraries which serve the general public.

Begley, Thomas D., Jr. and Jo-Anne Hirina Jeffreys. **Representing the Elderly Client: Law and Practice**. New York: Wolters Kluwer Law & Business, 1999-date. 2 vols. Looseleaf format. With CD-ROM. Annual supplementation.
Cost: $545; supplementation: 2000: 0; 2001: $95; 2002: $115; 2003: $135; 2004: $141; 2005: $148; 2006: $155; 2007: $165; 2008: $177; 2009: $194; 2010: $205; 2011: $215; 2012: $476; 2013: $492.
This desktop reference tool provides convenient access to information on many of the most critical legal issues facing the elderly population, including benefits programs, healthcare issues, probate matters, and domestic issues. The authors, both experienced elder law practitioners, discuss advocacy on behalf of the elderly and the practical dilemmas of representing elderly clients. There is also discussion of the full range of treatment and living facilities available to the elderly, nursing home law and litigation, managed care practice and litigation, non-Medicaid financing or long-term care, Medicaid financing or nursing home care, Medicaid planning strategies, Medicaid liens and estate recovery, Medicaid fair hearings and litigation considerations, public benefit programs, special needs trusts and financial planning for the disabled child, enforcement of the right to die, elder abuse, and operating the elder law practice. This volume also contains numerous practice tools, including checklists, sample letters, flow charts, client intake forms, and reference tables. A separate disc contains a variety of word processing documents, including forms useful in Medicaid planning, Medicaid fair hearings, and the drafting and establishment of special needs trusts.

Brashier, Ralph C. **Mastering Elder Law**. Durham, NC: Carolina Academic Press, 2010. 1 vol. (490 pp.). Paperbound.
Cost: $40.00; from $24.99 on amazon.com; kindle: $18.69 (2014).
This entry in the Carolina Academic Press Mastering Series is devoted to the subject of elder law, a term that embraces those areas of legal practice that chiefly affect the aging population. The elderly are subject to a variety of legal issues, challenges, and perils, ranging from support and maintenance, health care expenses, estate matters, and mental capacity issues that make them vulnerable to undue influence from family members or fiduciaries. Generally speaking, there are three main categories that make up the field of elder law: (1) estate planning and administration, including tax planning; (2) Medicaid, disability and long-term care issues; and (3) guardianship, conservatorship and commitment matters, including fiduciary administration. This volume addresses elder abuse, guardianships and conservatorships, wealth management and property transfers, health-care decision making, age discrimination in employment, Social Security, retirement and pension programs, Medicare, Medicaid, long-term care, the home, and the professional responsibilities of the lawyer. Each chapter is prefaced by a "Roadmap" that outlines the topics to be discussed and concludes with a series of "Checkpoints" for review. These Checkpoints are reproduced in a Master Checklist at he end of the volume. The author is the Cecil C. Humphries Professor of Law at the University of Memphis.

Brown, Baird, Arthur C. Walsh, Kathryn Kaye, and James Grigsby. **Mental Capacity: Legal and Medical Aspects of Assessment and Treatment.** 2d ed. St. Paul, MN: Thomson Reuters West (Clark Boardman Callaghan), 1994-date. 1 vol. Looseleaf format. Annual supplementation.
Cost: $394; supplementation: 1997: $60; 1998: $63; 1999:

$69; 2000: $74; 2001: $86; 2002: $90.50; 2003: $96.50; 2004: $111.50; 2005: $123; 2006: $136; 2007: $151.50; 2008: $168.50; 2009: $189.50; 2010: $202.00; 2011: $215; 2012: $238; 2013: $265; **Monthly Assured Print Price (APP):** $29/$348.
Written by an attorney with extensive experience in elder law, a physician specializing in care of the elderly, and two geriatric psychologists, this work provides an extensive discussion of the legal and medical issues involved in determining mental capacity and representing the elderly on such matters as executing documents, consenting to medical treatment, stipulating medical care contingencies, donative capacity, and contractual capacity. It also addresses the duties of the attorney in such attorney-client relationship and the record of the courts in deciding cases of mental capacity. The volume is accompanied by a 3.5» diskette containing a 30-point questionnaire to help the attorney make an initial determination of mental capacity.

Brown, Robert N. **The Rights of Older Persons: A Basic Guide to the Legal Rights of Older Persons under Current Law.** 2d ed. Carbondale, MN: Southern Illinois University Press, 1989. 1 vol. (413 pp.). An American Civil Liberties Union Handbook.
Cost: $19.95; from $.01 on amazon.com (2014).
Using a question and answer format, this ACLU Handbook is written primarily for the elderly and those individuals responsible for their care and advocacy. Its primary focus is providing information on the rights of older Americans to receive the benefits provided them under law, including social security, Medicare, Medicaid, and pension rights. Additional chapters are devoted to issues of age discrimination in employment, nursing homes, guardianship and civil commitment, and the right to refuse medical treatment. Appendices provide listings of national legal organizations for the elderly, congressional committees, and relevant state offices handling elderly affairs. The text is written by Robert N. Brown, Professor of Law at the University of Detroit School of Law and Director of its Health Law Center, and more than a dozen experts in specific areas of law applicable to the elderly.

Carlson, Eric M. **Long-Term Care Advocacy**. New York: Matthew Bender & Co., 1999-date. 1 vol. Looseleaf format.
Cost: $220 per year; supplementation: 2002: $98; 2003: $103; 2004: $108; 2005: $116; 2006: $121; 2007: $128; 2008: $133; 2009: $144; 2010: $155; 2011: $167; 2012: $132; 2013: $137; 2014: $145.
This is the first book to focus exclusively on issues of law as they relate to long-term care. It is primarily aimed at those who advocate on behalf of residents of health care facilities, but can also serve as an excellent resource for attorneys representing health care providers and relevant government agencies. The author provides the general background of long-term health care law, and discusses such topics as services provided by a nursing facility, admission to a nursing facility, transfers, discharges and readmissions in nursing facilities, residential care facilities, continuing care retirement communities, Medicaid payment for nursing care facility, private of Medicare payment for nursing facility care, insurance payments for long-term care, and litigating against long-term care facilities. The volume also includes discussion of applicable federal and state laws and regulations, checklists, forms, and the text of relevant statutes and model acts. The author provides extensive citations to relevant cases, statutes, regulations, secondary sources, and source documents. CD-ROM version contains Transfer/Discharge Appeal Administrative Decisions

Elder Law Library on LoisLawConnect. New York: Wolters Kluwer Law & Business, 2006-date.
Cost: $539.00 per year (solo practitioner) (2014).
An all-inclusive library of information on all aspects of elder law, covering such issue as long-term care, estate planning, retiremnt planning, health care decision making, rights of the elderly, Social Security, Medicare and Medicaid, special needs trusts. Draws upon the content of Margolis' **Elder Law Portfolio Series** and **Elder Law Forms Manual**. Provides links to applicable cases, statutes and regulations cited in the text.

Encyclopedia of Aging. David J. Ekerdt, Editor in Chief. New York: Macmillan Reference USA, 2002. 4 vols. (2,000 pp.).
Cost: $669; from $23.85 on amazon.com (2014).
The aging of the baby boomer generation places in stark relief the demographic trends enveloping the American population and the associated medical, legal, social, and life-style issues with which society will become increasingly concerned. This four-volume reference work contains over 400 alphabetically arranged articles embracing the fields of biology, medicine, economics, law, psychology, sociology, and history, and addressing such topics as Alzheimer's, criminal victimization, age discrimination, assisted living, centenarians, driving ability, euthanasia and suicide, health insurance, intelligence, leisure, Medicare, retirement planning programs, Social Security Administration, subjective well being, widowhood, and much more. Produced under the editorship of David J. Ekerdt, Gerontology Center, University of Kansas. An excellent reference tool for research law libraries and attorneys practicing in the field of elder law.

The Encyclopedia of Aging: A Comprehensive Resource in Gerontology and Geriatrics. Richard Schultz, Editor-in-Chief. 4th ed. New York: Springer Publications, 2006. 1 vol. (1,440 pp.).
Cost: $460.00; from $159.12 on amazon.com (2014).
A comprehensive and authoritative two-volume reference work embracing the interdisciplinary field of gerontology and geriatrics. Its nearly 600 articles are written by more than 200 scholars in the fields of biology, nursing/medicine, psychology, psychiatry, sociology, and social services, including a number of scholars providing a global perspective. Provides detailed explanation of more than 500 terms and concepts relevant to the aging process. The work also includes a detailed index, and exhaustive bibliography. Written for the educated reader and non-specialist, it provides a wealth of information to those specializing in elder law, including the medical, psychological, sociological, and social welfare issues which impact it. A less exhaustive and costly alternative to the Macmillan Reference work cited above, particularly when a used copy of the previous edition is acquired.

English, David M., Rebecca C. Morgan and John J. Regan. **Tax, Estate & Financial Planning for the Elderly**. New York: Matthew Bender & Co., 1985-date. 1 vol. Looseleaf format. Also

available on Internet and CD-ROM on **Tax Library and Estate Planning Library**.
Cost: $453 (includes annual subscription); renewal: 1996: $166; 1997: $166; 1998: $175. 1999: $182; 2000: $180; 2001: $193; 2002: $207; 2003: $218; 2004: $226; 2005: $238; 2006: $248; 2007: $262; 2008: $271; 2009: $293; 2010: $302; 2011: $288; 2012: $300; 2013: $315; 2014: $337; eBook: $412; renewal: 2014: $337.
This comprehensive practice tool is designed to guide the attorney through all aspects of the elder law practice, from initial client interview through the major areas of law of special concern to elderly clients, including income and pensions, government benefits, health care decision-making, insurance, nursing care, and income, estate and gift taxes. Each chapter is introduced by a series of «Common Client Questions» with references to applicable discussion in the text. These questions address such subjects as financing health care, financial planning, income tax planning, estate planning and lifetime giving, wills and trusts. Other issues, such as elder abuse, are treated as well. David English, a Professor of Law at Santa Clara University, has wide-ranging experience as professor of law, author, and Reporter for a number of elder-related Acts and Codes, including the Uniform Health-Care Decisions Act, and the Uniform Probate Code. Rebecca C. Morgan, a Professor of Law at Stetson University School of Law, has authored a number of books and articles on various aspects of elder law and has served as Secretary of the National Academy of Elder Law Attorneys, among her numerous professional activities.

English, David M., Michael Gilfix, and Rebecca C. Morgan. **Tax, Estate & Financial Planning for the Elderly: Forms & Practice**. New York: Matthew Bender & Co., 1991-date. 2 vols. Looseleaf format.
Cost: $608; supplementation: 1996: $61; 1997: $61; 1998: $85; 1999: $89; 2000: $95; 2001: $102; 2002: $110; 2003: $116; 2004: $116; 2005: $127; 2006: $133; 2007: $141; 2008: $146; 2009: $158; 2010: $204; 2011; $186; 2012: $192; 2013: $205; 2014: $219; eBook: $510; renewal: 2014: $219 per year.
A companion volume to the author's Tax, Estate & Financial Planning for the Elderly, this volume provides forms, checklists, and practice tips in the areas of health care, retirement, tax planning financial considerations. It includes client interview forms, sample letters, annotated forms, and blank forms which can be removed and copied.

Esperti, Robert A. and Renno L. Peterson. **Love, Money, Control: Reinventing Estate Planning**. Denver, CO: Quantum Press LLC, 2004. 1 vol. (543 pp.).
Cost: $29; from $.01 on amazon.com (2014).
Simply put, estate planning is the process of planning for the management and disposition of your assets and resources when you are deceased or no longer able to manage your own affairs. For most individuals or families who fail to plan, state intestacy laws provide a default estate plan. The primary message of this guide to estate planning is that individuals should be motivated to plan out of love for family friends, and personal causes. Indeed, estate planning is more than just tax planning, but a range of inter-related considerations, including family legacy, financial, retirement, disability, charitable, business succession, and gift planning. This manual is the end result of an editorial process involving sixty-nine estate planning attorneys and financial advisors from across the country. Utilizing an easy to comprehend question-answer format, it provides a lucid explanation of critical estate planning issues organized under the broad headings of love, money, and control. The three chapters in Part One (Love) provide an introduction to estate planning, examine the process of planning for loved ones, and planning for loved ones and charity. Part Two (Money) examines tax basics, wealth transfer techniques, and retirement planning. Part Three (Control) considers the administration of the estate, planning for disability, living trust-centered estate planning, business succession planning, asset protection planning, planning for seniors, and finding and working with professional advisors. The appendices include a variety of estate planning and professional resources, and a glossary of terms. The text is illuminated by numerous charts and financial calculations. The authors of more than 24 books in the field, Robert A. Esperti and Renno L. Peterson are nationally recognized estate planning attorneys, and co-founders of the National Network of Estate Planning Attorneys, the Esperti Peterson Institute, The Academy of Multidisciplinary Practice, and The Estate and Wealth Strategies Institute at Michigan State University. An invaluable tool for both estate planning professionals and the general public.

Estate Planning Library [Internet]. Rochester, NY: Thomson Reuters Tax & Accounting, 1995-date. Call (800-950-1216).
Cost: $6,335 per year (solo practitioner); Estate Planning Library w/o treatises: $3,220 per year; treatises also available individually (2014).
Contains the full text of more than 20 RIA and WG&L practice titles, including **Estate** Planning Law and Taxation, Tax Planning for Family Wealth Transfers, Structuring Estate Freezes Under Chapter 14, Structuring Buy-Sell Agreements, Tax Planning with Life Insurance, Federal Income Tax of Estates and Trusts, and 17 more. Prices usually adjust annually in July, so check with the RIA sales representaive for up-to-date pricing.

Fleming, Robert B. **Elder Law Answer Book**. 3d ed. Frederick, MD: Wolters Kluwer Law & Business (Panel), 2012. 1 vol. Periodic new editions.
Cost: $315 (2014).
This volume is a compilation of more than 900 questions and answers in the field of elder law, encompassing the topics of elder care, estate planning, retirement planning, healthcare decision making, and the rights of the elderly. It includes explanations of the current rule or regulation governing the area, as well as citations to applicable cases and statutes. The author's expert analysis includes planning advice, cautionary tips, real life examples, and practical approaches to common problems confronting the elderly. One in series of books in the question/answer format from Panel Publishers. Robert Fleming is a partner in the Tucson, AZ firm of Fleming & Curti, P.L.C., specializing in matters of guardianship, conservatorship, estate planning, and probate. He is an adjunct lecturer for the University of Arizona Department of Gerontology, and active member and past officer of numerous bar associations and elder-related panels, including the White House Conference on Aging.

Frolik, Lawrence A. and Melissa C. Brown. **Advising the Elderly or Disabled Client**. 2d ed. Boston: Warren, Gorham & Lamont, 1992-date. 1 vol. (various pagings). Annual subscription publication with semi-annual supplements.
Also available in online format.
Cost: $360 per year; Internet: $575 per year (2014).
The rise of the elderly population in the United States in recent years together with an increased awareness of the disabled have been accompanied by a growing interest in legal issues of particular concern to these segments of the population. This desktop reference is designed primarily as a planning guide which will help the attorney achieve the best results for his or her client. The individual chapters examine the role of the planner, the initial client interview, and provide an overview of common physical and mental impairments. They also address such particular issues as social security benefits, supplemental security income, other federal and state benefits, private pension plans, health care maintenance, Medicare, Medicaid, alternate housing, special planning concerns of the disabled, the AIDS client, medical treatment decision making for disabled minors and adults, situational incompetency, nonjudicial forms of substitute decision making, adult guardianship and conservatorship, right to die issues, federal income taxation, federal estate and gift taxation, estate planning, and use of trusts. The appendices include a glossary of relevant acronyms and terms, as well as tables of cases, statutes, regulations, and tax rulings. Lawrence Frolik is Professor of Law at the University of Pittsburgh School of Law. Melissa Brown is a member of the California Bar.

Cost Saving Tips: Since this was converted to a service publication, the cost of supplementation has risen significantly. The cost-conscious consumer will subscribe for one year and drop the standing order, then reinstate the subscription every 2-3 years. Even buying every two years, will cut your supplementation costs in half while providing annual updating.

Frolik, Lawrence A. and Richard L. Kaplan. **Elder Law in a Nutshell**. 5th ed. St. Paul, MN: West, 2010. 1 vol. (435 pp.). Softbound. Available from West Academic.
Cost: $41; from $31.71 on amazon.com; kindle ed.: $23.69 (2014).
A succinct, student-oriented overview of the laws affecting older Americans, whose scope ranges from ethical considerations in dealing with older clients to health care ddecision making, Medicare and Medigap, Medicaid, long-term care insurance, nursing homes and assisted living facilities, housing alternatives and options, guardianship, Social Security benefits, veterans' benefits, pension plans, age discrimination in employment, and elder abuse and neglect. In keeping with the editorial philosophy of the Nutshell Series, it contains selective citations to cases, statutes and secondary sources.

Frolik, Lawrence A. and Linda S. Whitton. **Everyday Law for Seniors**. 2nd ed. Boulder, CO: Paradigm Publishers, 2012. 1 vol. (187 pp.) Paperbound.
Cost: $28.95 ($24.61 when ordered online); from $17.50 on amazon.com (2014).
As the American population continues to age, increased attention will be devoted to the specific legal issues and problems affecting senior citizens. This guide provides a clearly written exposition of those laws and legal issues of paramount concern to senior citizens. Written by two of the nation's foremost authorities on elder law, it volume provides an illuminating overview of law as it affects seniors, and addresses such topics as age discrimination in employment, Social Security and Supplemental Security income, employer-provided retirement benefits and IRAs, Medicare, Medicaid and long-term care insurance; housing; mental incapacity, guardianship, and conservatorship; substitute decision-making for health care and property; and elder abuse, neglect, and exploitation. The text is supported with citations to federal laws and regulations. Each chapter concludes with a list of relevant web sites for further information. Lawrence Frolik is Distinguished Faculty Scholar and Professor of Law at the University of Pittsburgh School of Law. Linda S. Whitten is a Professor of Law at Valparaiso University School of Law.

Frolik, Lawrence A. **The Law of Later-Life Health Care and Decision Making**. Chicago: American Bar Association, 2006. 1 vol. (298 pp.).
Cost: $89.95; now half-off at $44.98; (2014).
Dealing with end-of-life health care decisions is one of the most difficult issues faced by the elderly, their children or guardians, doctors, and attorneys. This volume provides a comprehensive overview of the laws which regulate both health care and personal decision-making for the elderly. Among the issues considered are the payment of health care costs, long-term care options and costs, mental incapacity, guardianship, conservatorship, powers of attorney, and critical end-of life decisions. Lawrence Frolik is a professor of Law at the University of Pittsburgh and a nationally recognized expert on elder law and guardianship.

Frolik, Lawrence A. **Residence Options for Older and Disabled Clients**. Chicago: American Bar Association, 2008. 1 vol. (424 pp.). Paperbound.
Cost: $89.95 ($79.95 to members); from $15.16 on amazon.com (2014).
Increased life expectancy, propelled by medical and scientific breakthroughs, have dramatically increased the numbers of older and disabled Americans searching for housing appropriate to their age and physical condition. In former times, the elderly were often cared for in their own homes or by family members. In recent years, the availability of Social Security, Medicaid, and Supplemental Security Income have combined to increase the options available to older Americans, among them nursing homes, continuous care retirement communities, assisted living facilities, and age restricted housing communities. Attorneys serving this population need to be aware of these housing options and the legal issues involved as the elderly transition to them. This volume guides the reader through these various residence options and their legal ramifications. The author begins with an excellent review of the nature of aging, the effects of aging on housing choices, and the factors which influence decisions about housing choices. Additional chapters are devoted to the topics of age restricted housing, aging in place, condominiums and cooperatives, planned communities and homeowner associations, manufactured housing and mobile homes, continuing care retirement communities, congregate housing and assisted living, group homes and other housing for the disabled, personal care and health care in the home, nursing homes, and hospices and hospice care. The volume

includes selective citations to legal authorities, including cases, statutes, and regulations. The forms, agreements and checklists contained in the appendices are reproduced on a companion CD-ROM. Lawrence Frolik is a professor law at the University of Pittsburgh School of Law and author of numerous books on the subject of elder law.

Jordan, Michael M. L. **Durable Powers of Attorney and Health Care Directives**. 4th ed. St. Paul, MN: Thomson Reuters West (Clark Boardman Callaghan), 2004-date. 2 vols. Looseleaf format. Includes CD-ROM.
Cost: $362; supplementation: 2005: $100; 2006: $150; 2007: $78; 2008: $87; 2009: $102; 2010: $132; 2011: $121; 2012: $129; 2013: $138; 3d ed.: 1995: $60; 1996: $100; 1997: $285; 1998: $100; 1999: $354; 2000: $384; 2001: $148.50; 2002: $170; 2003: $100; 2004: $100; **Monthly Assured Print Price (APP):** $27/$324.
This treatise provides coverage of those legal issues involved in the exercise of powers of attorney during the incapacity of the grantor of that power, including issues related to the grantor's property, life, health, etc. This set covers durable powers of attorney for health care, property management, the fiduciary status of the agent, the third party perspective, and the drafting of the durable power. The set also includes forms, drafting checklists, and comments for each of the fifty states and a number of relevant appendices, including the Uniform Rights of the Terminally Ill Act, and Principles and Guidelines Concerning the Foregoing of Life-Sustaining Treatment for Adult Patients. Also includes Tables of Cases and Statutes, and an Index. Well-written and adequately footnoted text. The only drawback would appear to be the fact that the substantive text comprises probably less than 20% of the total pages in both volumes, with the bulk of the coverage devoted to state comments. If your practice is limited to one or two states, or if you have little need to research comparative state law, you may be paying for a great deal of material you will consult infrequently, if at all. Originally published by Shepard's/McGraw-Hill, it is now published by Thomson/West.

Krauskopf, Joan M., et al. **Elderlaw: Advocacy for the Aging**. 2d ed. St. Paul, MN: West, 1993-date. 2 vols. (1,140 pp.).
Cost: $436; supplementation: 1996: $39; 1997: $48; 1998: $50; 1999: $54; 2000: $66; 2001: $77; 2002: $91; 2003: $104; 2004: $116.50; 2005: $126; 2006: $152; 2007: $158.50; 2008: $178; 2009: $209; 2010: $230; 2011: $253; 2012: $278; 2013: $320; **Monthly Assured Print Price (APP):** $32/$384.
Provides guidance in a number of key areas relative to the legal needs of elderly clients, including health care, public benefit programs, long-term care, incapacity, medical decision-making, age discrimination, consumer fraud, veterans' benefits, housing programs, handicap laws, credit protection, and community resources.

Levine, Jeffrey M., ed. **Medical-Legal Aspects of Long-Term Care**. Tucson, AZ: Lawyers & Judges Publishing Co., 2003. 1 vol. (361 pp.).
Cost: $95; from $4.32 on amazon.com; kindle: $70.64 (2014).
The aging of the American population has generated increased awareness of and concern about the issues of long-term medical care. Nursing homes now serve a multitude of functions, from residential communities and social service agencies to family support centers and medical treatment facilities. Moreover, the development of more extensive home and community-based long-term care alternatives have allowed the elderly to remain in their homes far longer than in previous years, raising a different set of medical and legal issues. The chapters in this book address a number of long-term care issues, primarily in the nursing home environment, including the nursing home industry generally, resident assessment and planning, understaffing in nursing homes, dementia care, pain management, nutrition and hydration, would care, adverse drug events, psychopharmacologic medications, falls and related injuries, physical restraints, bed safety, physical abuse and neglect, and effective risk management, and the role of private accreditation. The 17 individual chapters are authored by a number of medical experts with extensive experience in the medical and treatment aspects of long-term care management issues.

Lindemann, Barbara T. and David D. Kadue. **Age Discrimination in Employment Law**. Arlington, VA: BNA Books, 2003. 1 vol. (1,578 pp.).
Cost: $410.00; supplementation: 2013: $210; from $86.87 on amazon.com (2014).
In 1967, Congress enacted the Age Discrimination in Employment Act (ADEA) (Pub. L. No. 90-202, 81 Stat. 602 (Dec. 15, 1967), codified at 29 U.S.C. §§ 621-634) to outlaw discrimination in the United States against anyone at least 40 years of age. Not surprisingly, the law has created problems for employers trying to comply and for judges charged with trying to decide if the law has been violated. Following the enactment of a series of laws prohibiting employment discrimination on the basis of various factors, particularly Title VII of the Civil Rights Act of 1964, courts have grappled with the issue of proving motive. In 1967, the factor of age was added to the list, first of those from age 40 to age 65, then, after 1986, of any age above 40. Outside the context of employment law cases, the issue of motive is rarely raised. This volume probes the complexities of age discrimination litigation, whether in matters of hiring, promotion, monetary compensation, employee benefit programs, exit incentives and early retirement programs, mandatory retirement, reductions if force, harassment, constructive discharge, discharge, and special issues for unions and apprenticeship programs. It also considers age discrimination in the form of disparate treatment through the introduction of circumstantial evidence, as well as the adverse impact model of proof when it is alleged that a practice has a foreseeably and statistically significant adverse impact on a members of a protected class, absent some employer justification based on business necessity to ensure normal operations and for which there is no alternative with a less discriminatory impact. The authors also outline the jurisdiction and procedures governing age discrimination actions and the various aspects of ADEA litigation from discovery, evidence and statistical evidence to summary judgment, jury trials, expert witnesses, defenses, EEOC litigation, public employee litigation and collective actions by certain classes of employees. They also examine alternative forms of conflict resolution, alternative avenues of relief, and resolution, including remedies, attorneys' fees and costs, and tax treatment of awards and settlements.

The Appendices include the text of the ADEA, the text of 21 U.S. Supreme Court decisions on age discrimination, EEOC regulations and guidelines, the Government Employee Rights Act of 1991, sample release forms, and revenue rulings, a table of cases, and a useful table of ADEA (and Amendments) provisions which directs users to their discussion in the text. **Barbara T. Lindemann** is formerly Of Counsel at Seyfarth Shaw and co-author of Bloomberg BNA's **Employment Discrimination Law** and **Workplace Harassment Law**. David D. Kadue is a partner in Seyfarth Shaw, Los Angeles, author of **Preventing Sexual Harassment and Other Workplace Harassment: A Fact Sheet for Employees** and co-author of **Workplace Harassment Law**. They are joined by fifty contributing authors, with extensive experience in varied aspects of age and employment discrimination matters, who contributed chapters or parts of chapters. This book represents a monumental achievement in the field of age discrimination in employment and an indispensable resource to any attorney practicing in the field.

Margolis, Harry S. **Elder Law Forms Manual: Essential Documents for Representing the Older Client**. New York: Wolters Kluwer Law & Business, 1999-date. 2 vols. Looseleaf format. Annual supplementation.
Cost: $435; supplementation: 1997: $78; 1998: 0; 1999: $190; 2000: $95; 2001: $190; 2002: $245; 2003: $139; 2004: $310; 2005: $310; 2006: $330; 2007: $345; 2008: $360; 2009: $386; 2010: $412; 2011: $430; 2012: $460; 2013: $505.
A companion set to the editor's Elder Law Portfolio Series, this two-volume forms set with commentary provides the practitioner with the tools necessary to manage a practice geared to the needs of the older client. Moreover, it provides convenient access to forms which cut across a number of legal specialties. The chapter coverage includes: marketing; law office management; personnel policies; the client meeting; Medicaid planning letter provisions; estate planning letter provisions; guardianship and conservatorship; durable powers of attorney; health care powers of attorney, proxies, and living wills; wills; revocable trusts; irrevocable trusts; the supplemental needs trust; estate administration; the Medicaid application; real estate; and miscellaneous forms. The work is edited by Harry Margolis, founder of ElderLaw Services, a Boston law firm specializing on the legal needs of older clients, and an attorney with extensive community experience working with organizations providing services to the elderly. This resource is an excellent value from a publisher whose supplementation costs are relatively reasonable for the industry.

Margolis, Harry S., ed. **The ElderLaw Portfolio Series**. New York: Wolters Kluwer Law & Business, 1993-date. 2 vols. (1468 pp.) Looseleaf format. Supplemented twice annually.
Cost: $389; supplementation: 1996: $75; 1997: $78; 1998: 0; 1999: 0; 2000: $95; 2001: $190; 2002: $225; 2003: $145; 2004: $310. 2005: $310; 2006: $330; 2007: $340; 2008: $364; 2009: $398; 2010: $416; 2011: $440; 2012: $721; 2013: $753.
Each of the eighteen portfolios in this two-volume looseleaf resource was written by an expert with specialized knowledge in the field. At present, the portfolios cover the practical aspects of managing an elder law practice, Medicaid eligibility, Medicaid trusts, tax implications of transfers of assets, housing options, Medicare, guardianship, long-term care insurance, Medicaid, planning for retirement benefit distributions, Medicaid trusts: estate planning using non-Medicaid disqualifying self-settled trusts, rights of long-term care facility residents, nursing home litigation, veterans' benefits for the elderly, durable powers of attorney, and health care decision making in an elder law practice. It also includes a table of abbreviations and acronyms. The work is edited by Harry Margolis, founder of ElderLaw Services, a Boston law firm specializing on the legal needs of older clients, and an attorney with extensive community experience working with organizations providing services to the elderly. This resource is an excellent value with very reasonable supplementation costs for which a standing order is recommended.

Mezzullo, Louis A. and Mark Woolpert. **Advising the Elderly Client**. St. Paul, MN: Thomson Reuters West (Clark Boardman Callaghan), 1992-date. 3 vols. Semi-annual supplementation. Includes CD-ROM with forms.
Cost: $1,271; supplementation: 1996: $339; 1997: $180; 1998: $190; 1999: $206; 2000: $715; 2001: $555; 2002: $922; 2003: $602; 2004: $338; 2005: $361; 2006: $412; 2007: $459; 2008: $639; 2009: $614.50; 2010: $594; 2011: $647.50; 2012: $706; 2013: $819; **Monthly Assured Print Price (APP):** $93/$1,116.
A comprehensive guide to the variety of sub-specialties which comprise the growing area of elderly law, including estate planning, financial planning, Social Security, Medicare, Medicaid, health care facilities, incapacity, living wills, durable powers of attorney, right-to-die issues, discrimination against the elderly, and more. It provides both analysis and guidance for attorneys who advise elderly clients, and includes comprehensive coverage of the relevant statutes in all fifty states, forms, checklists, and charts. Pleading and practice forms are contained on a separate disc.

Cost Saving Tip: This is a good example of the manner in which supplementation can catch you unawares. Annual costs hovered in the $200 range until 2000, when the publisher issued substantial revisions to the text, with a corresponding jump in the supplementation costs, rising to $922 in 2002 (they have now fallen to $819 in 2013). Placing this title on an "advise before shipment" (or notification) status would have allowed the savvy attorney to avoid these costs and purchase another new set at a later date. The **Monthly Assured Print Price** simply locks you in the higher annual supplementation costs ($1,116 in 2014), thereby reducing your flexibility to cancel when costs become onerous. What the publisher wants, most of all, is a permanent revenue stream via your credit card.

Nursing Home Litigation: Investigation and Case Preparation. Edited by Patricia W. Iyer. 2d ed. Tucson, AZ: Lawyers & Judges Publishing Co., 2005. 1 vol. (702 pp.).
Cost: $149; from $141.55 on amazon.com (2014).
Nursing home cases are among the more complex types of litigation, involving a maze of state and federal regulations, evidentiary standards, expert testimony, and medical terminology, as well as basic understanding of variety of medical subjects from geriatrics to nutrition. The growth of for-profit nursing homes (more than 66% of the total in 2003), the aging of the American population, the growth of federal services to

the elderly, and a growing appreciation for the quality of life for nursing home residents, have led to an increase in the volume of litigation and the size of verdicts. This volume provides a comprehensive look at the topics and issues which comprise the field of nursing home litigation, from initial screening of nursing home cases, investigation and pretrial considerations, assisted living cases, the legal nurse consultant, inside the nursing home from a medico-legal perspective, the foundations of nursing practice, nursing home liability, physician's liability, and administrator and nursing home liability issues. Additional chapters examine a number of specific liability allegations, including falls and restraints, skin trauma, infections, wandering and elopement, pharmacology, pain management issues, billing fraud, and medical record tampering. The volume concludes with three chapters providing defense perspectives. Each chapter is accompanied by numerous references to supporting books and articles from the legal and medical literature. The chapters were authored by a total of thirty specialists in the fields of law, nursing, and nursing home management. This is an essential acquisition for all nursing home administrators and attorneys specializing in nursing home litigation.

O'Reilly, James T. **The Lawyer's Guide to Elder Injury and Accident Compensation.** 2d ed. Chicago: American Bar Association, 2004. 1 vol. (276 pp.).
Cost: OUT-OF-PRINT: was $84.95 ($74.95 to Senior Lawyers Division members) from $29.85 on amazon.com (2014).
This volume is the first comprehensive examination of safety issues as they relate to the elderly. The author is an adjunct professor at the University of Cincinnati and an author of 25 textbooks and articles in the areas of product safety, government regulation, and health law. He brings more than 20 years of practice in the product safety and health fields to this book, as well as his work with an international consumer safety group that studied safety issues and the elderly. The book's 19 chapters are grouped into two main divisions: those which discuss elder injuries generally and the lawyer 's role in preventing injuries and representing victims; and (2) those which examine specific types of injuries which befall elders, including motor vehicle and pedestrian accidents, medicine-related harm; falls, medical devices, abuse, neglect and fraud, nutritional supplements, consumer products, home institution and building safety, nursing home accidents, and medical malpractice. The appendices include a directory of regulations and laws, a directory of federal health and regulatory agencies, a table of major cases, and index.

Cost-Saving Tip: Amazon.com is not always a good deal. For example, when ABA titles go out-of-print, look for indepemdent used booksellers to take advantage of that void to jack up prices above their original. Several sellers on amazon.com have this title listed for prices of as much as $1,955. This title is just one example. This should encourage you to urge the ABA to reprint or come out with a new edition.

Pennell, Jeffrey N. **Estate Planning.** 8th ed. Riverwoods, IL: Wolters Kluwer Law & Business, 2012-date. 2 vols. (1943 pp.). Paperbound and eBook.. Annual revised editions.
Cost: $465 (print or eBook); print 75% off with purchase of eBook; supplementation: 2000: $250; 2001: $165; 2002: $225; 2003: $255; 2004: $269; 2005: $279; 2006: $299; 2007: $625; 2008: $625; 2009: $365; 2010: 0; 2011: 0; 2012: new ed.; 5th ed.: 1992: $175; 1993: $195; 1994: $295; 1995: $295; 1996: $310; 1997: $322; 1998-99: not available.
This two-volume treatise, replacing the three-volume 6th edition, provides complete coverage of the various arrangements which can be made to effectuate the devolution of an individual's wealth. While many estate plans involve the drawing up of a will, many others are based on a variety of inter vivos arrangements, including outright gifts, joint ownership, irrevocable inter vivos trusts, revocable inter vivos trusts, legal present and future interests created inter vivos, and settlements involving the distribution of life insurance proceeds. The authors' discussion is devoted largely to matters involving large estates, but also encompasses small estates. Naturally, a great preponderance of material is concerned with tax issues as they relate to various estate planning mechanisms. Professor Casner, the late Austin Wakeman Scott Professor of Law, Emeritus, Harvard Law School published his first edition of this work in 1953. Jeffrey N. Pennell, the Richard Clark Professor of Law at Emory University School of Law, has assumed the task of preparing the sixth and seventh editions following the death of Professor Casner in 1990. The chapters cover the estate plan created by the operation of law (intestate succession), wills, income taxation of estates, revocable inter vivos trusts, family annuities, non-trust gifts, life insurance, employee benefits, social security, concurrent interests in community property, future interests in an estate plan, generation-skipping transfer tax, powers of appointment, the marital deduction, the charitable deduction, planning for the payment of death costs, estate plans that cross state or national borders. Volume five contains a hypothetical proposed estate plan for Mr. and Mrs. Richard Harry Black III. Volume six contains tables of cases, IRS Code sections, Treasury regulations, Internal Revenue rulings, Internal Revenue Bulletin rulings, Letter rulings, Revenue Procedures, Technical Advice Memoranda, state statutes, Uniform and Model Acts, **Restatements**, and secondary authorities. In 2004, responsibility for the publication and distribution of **Estate Planning** was assumed by Wolters Kluwer's sister company, CCH.

Pension and Benefits Advisor on Checkpoint [Internet]. New York: Research Institute of America Group. Toll-free support (800-431-9025).
Cost: Internet: $3,545 per year (2014).
A complete library of source material, including Internal Revenue Code and Treasury Regulations, ERISA statute and regulations, pension-related forms and instructions. Also includes detailed annotations of significant cases organized by IRS Code or ERISA section numbers and issue. Provides analysis of a wide variety of pension, employee benefit and executive compensation issues with hypertext links to cited materials. Also includes a subscription to the weekly **Pension & Benefits Week** newsletter.

Pension and Benefits Expert on Checkpoint [Internet]. New York: Research Institute of America Group. Toll-free support (800-431-9025).
Cost: Internet: $5.010 (2014).
In addition to the above analysis and commentary on the rules

dealing with qualified and non-qualified retirement plans, non-pension employee benefits, and executive compensation, this product includes a complete library of full text of case law, court materials, revenue rulings, etc. from 1924 to the present.

Pension Plan Guide. Riverwoods, IL: Wolters Kluwer Law & Business (CCH), 1979-date. 10 vols. Looseleaf format. Updated weekly.
Cost: $2,615 per year (2014).
A comprehensive reference tool which provides guidance in establishing, maintaining and revising pension and profit sharing plans, profit sharing, employee benefits and executive compensation programs. Includes full-text reporting of the ERISA and IRC regulations, rulings, releases and other documents. Explanations cover rules and compliance requirements for planning , administration, plan qualification, vesting, funding and plan termination. Also includes coverage of employee benefits litigation, including case digests and full text of Supreme Court decisions. Additional features include interest rates, reporting calendars, and tax tables.

Pension Plan Guide [Internet]. Riverwoods, IL: Wolters Kluwer Law & Business (CCH Inc.). Internet updated monthly. Toll-free support (800-835-0105).
Cost: $2,615 per year (2014).
This CD-ROM product contains the fully searchable text of CCH's **Pension Plan Guide**, including the full-text of the Employment Retirement Income Security Act (ERISA), Internal Revenue Service Code, regulations, letter rulings, opinion letters, IRS, DOL, PBGC and other federal forms, sample plans, as well as CCH explanations, and weekly newsletters. Includes an optional link to the CCH database.

Price, John R. **Price on Contemporary Estate Planning.** 4th ed. Riverwoods, IL: CCH, a Wolters Kluwer business, 2008-date. 1 vol. (1,500 pp.). Periodic revisions.
Cost: 2014 edition: $495.95; supplementation: 2001: $165; 2002: $180; 2004: $199; 2005: n/a; 2006: new edition; 2007: 0; 2008: $215; 2009: $265; 2010: $389; 2011: $410.
A massive one-volume treatment of all aspects of estate planning from the client interview to post-mortem planning. The author, a leading expert in the field of estate planning, examines both tax and non-tax areas, including the durable power of attorney and the living will. His discussion of tax issues includes private annuities and charitable remainder trusts. It also features a variety of practice aids such as forms, worksheets, and checklists. The author provides the practitioner with invaluable practical advice. This title was sold by Wolters Kluwer Law & Business to CCH, Inc. in 2003.

Takacs, Timothy L. **A Guide to Elder Law Practice**. New York: Matthew Bender, 2007. 1 vol. Paperbound.
Cost: $57 (2014).
The elderly are subject to special risks and vulnerabilities as a result of advanced age, medical problems, and real and potential mental incapacity. This excellent introductory guide to the scope and specifics of elder law practice is designed to assist the attorney in serving the needs of this client population. Written for both the novice and the seasoned practitioner venturing into a new area of law, it provides an overview of the areas most likely to be encountered by the attorney venturing into this specialty. The author begins with a survey of the future of elder law practice from a demographic perspective, with special attention to long-term care issues. Additional chapters address the representation of elders, the process of becoming an elder law attorney, the primary responsibilities of the elder law attorney, setting up and managing an elder law practice, and getting and keeping clients. Among the specific topics examined are health care concerns, housing and community services, wealth transfer at death, Medicaid asset protection planning, elder abuse, and nursing home litigation, among others. The appendices include a list of recommended reading, and elder law resources. Timothy L. Takacs is certified as an Elder Law Attorney by the National Elder Law Foundation and as a Certified Elder Law Specialist by the Tennessee Commission on CLE and Specialization, and has been in private law practice in Hendersonville, Tennessee, since 1980. He writes and gives frequent seminars to attorney and other professionals about elder law.

Additional titles in the field of Elder Law are available from the following publishers: American Bar Association, American Law Institute, Matthew Bender, Carolina Academic Press, CCH, Inc., Legal Counsel for the Elderly, LexisNexis, National Clearinghouse for Legal Services, National Conference of State Legislatures, Panel Publishers, Quantum Press, RIA Group, Springer Publications, Thomson Reuters West. West Academic. See Appendix B for addresses and telephone numbers.

Environmental Law

Baur, Donald C., Tim Eichenberg, and Michael Sutton. **Ocean and Coastal Law and Policy**. Chicago: American Bar Association, Section of Environment, Energy, and Resources, 2008. 1 vol. (708 pp.). Paperbound.
Cost: $119.95; from $93.65 on amazon.com (2014).
A useful overview of a variety of environmental issues in the areas of ocean and coastal law and policy. Thirty authors contributed the individual chapters, each of them possessing some expertise in environmental law and/or policy, science, or some combination of both. The book is premised on the contention that the earth's oceans and coasts are severely threatened, and that these threats are the consequence of failure of government, its fragmented laws, confusing and overlapping jurisdictions, and the lack of a clear national ocean policy. Accordingly this volume attempts to identify these problems and the policies necessary to ameliorate them. The authors provide expert description and analysis of such subjects as national and international jurisdictions and boundaries, the Public Trust Doctrine, the role of the states, regulation of costal wetlands, management of coastal development, the National Environmental Policy Act, coastal water quality protection, ocean dumping and marine pollution, domestic fishery management, offshore energy development, the Endangered Species Act and marine species, and more.

A chapter on climate change, however, makes some clearly questionable assertions reflecting more ideological supposition than scientifically verifiable proof. For example, the authors assert that "the world's climate is warming, it is going to get much warmer; and humans are significantly responsible." Anyone familiar with the political and bureaucratic machinations by which the Intergovernmental Panel on Climate Change (IPCC) made a similar assertion (which, incidentally, was never approved by the scientists involved in the process), will not be surprised. Indeed, in a 1997 survey conducted of U.S. State Climatologists, 90% agreed with the statement that the "scientific evidence indicates variations in global temperatures are likely to be naturally occurring and cyclical over very long periods of time." Their scientific opinions are echoed by the more than 31,000 credentialed scientists who signed the Oregon Petition, 2,600 of them climate scientists. Moreover, the so-called global warming consensus was shattered in 2009 when leaked e-mails from the University of Anglia exposed an orchestrated effort to conceal climate data and impugn the integrity of global warming skeptics. Since then, hundreds of leading climate scientists around the world have stepped forward to question the basis upon which this "consensus" was based. Moreover, the global warming hysteria has been untirely undercut by the fact that globally-averaged temperatures, as recorded at East Anglia, have not risen since 1997, and, even when they were rising, amounted to no more than one-third of a degree Celsius from 1978-1997. Not surprisingly, none of the four authors of this chapter has any scientific credentials in the fields of meteorology, climate science, or related disciplines. This is just one of many examples in which individuals with credentials in one area venture outside their area(s) of expertise to make assertions for which they lack authority, either by training or experience.

Beck, Robert E. **Water and Water Rights.** 3d ed. Charlottesville, VA: LexisNexis, 1991-date. 8 vols. Annual pocket parts. Print and eBook.
Cost: $1,298; supplementation: 1993: $180; 1994: $315 (incl. one rev. vol.); 1995: $210; 1996: $356;1997: $245; 1998: $255; 1999: $270; 2000; $280; 2001: $728; 2002; $461; 2003: $163; 2004: $170; 2005: $536; 2006: $557; 2007: $618; 2008: $667; 2009: $998; 2010: $1,028; 2011: $1,058; 2012: $1,100; 2013: $1,177.
This multi-volume treatise is a complete revision of the first edition originally edited by Robert Emmett Clark between 1967 and 1976 which has been recognized as the leading work in the field. Edited by Robert Beck, Professor at the Southern Illinois University School of Law, this edition is written by a team of thirteen legal scholars and practicing attorneys. It provides the environmental attorney with a thorough and rigorous analysis of the law governing water, water rights, riparianism, prior appropriation, quantitative groundwater law, the public right to use water in place, federal and Indian rights, powers and activities, interstate water allocation, international waters, environmental controls, water pollution and water quality control, drainage, flooding and wetlands preservation, and planning. Volume six includes surveys of the laws of the fifty states and major river basins written by local experts, as well as a glossary of relevant terms. Volume eight includes cumulative tables of cases, statutes and index. This work not only addresses the statutory and common law bases of water law, but provides an integrated and thoroughly documented background discussion of substantive topics and issues of interest to the environmental attorney. The authors provide the user with exhaustive citations to applicable state and federal cases and statutes, as well as significant secondary sources such as law review articles and leading governmental and professional studies. There is no other work in the field which matches this one in terms of coverage and scholarly analysis. For the attorney specializing in water and environmental issues, this work should be an essential purchase. Supplementation costs are not unreasonable given the size and scope of the set.

Bergeson, Lynn and Tracy Hester. **Nanotechnology Deskbook.** Washington, DC: Environmental Law Institute, 2008. 1 vol. (393 pp.). Paperbound.
Cost: $109.95; from $19.23 on amazon.com (2014).
Nanotechnology may be defined as research and technology developments at the atomic, molecular, or macromolecular level using a scale of approximately one to one hundred nanometers in any dimension; the creation and use of structures, devices and systems that have novel properties and functions because of their small size; and the ability to control or manipulate matter on an atomic scale (a nanometer being one billionth of a meter). Nanotechnology has potential applications in many areas of the American economy, including health care, transportation, energy, agriculture and a host of consumer products. And while nanotechnology offers the potential to improve our ability to measure, monitor, manage and minimize contaminants in the environment, it may also impose certain environmental risks or hazards. This volume assembles a number of important E.P.A. papers and other documents regarding nanoscale materials and the potential risks thereof which are being addressed at the regulatory level. Lynn Bergeson, Managing Director of Bergeson & Campbell, a Washington, DC Law firm, focuses on conventional and engineered nanoscale chemical, pesticide and other specialty chemical regulation and approval matters. Mr. Tracy Hester heads the environmental law section of the Houston firm of Bracewell & Giuliani where he assists clients in regulatory counseling and enforcement defense.

Brickey, Kathleen F. **Environmental Crime: Law, Policy, Prosecution**. Austin, TX: Wolters Kluwer Law & Business, 2008. 1 vol. (386 pp.). Paperbound.
Cost: $56; from $33.25 on amazon.com (2014).
The enactment of a number of high profile pieces of environmental legislation in the 1970s and 1980s ushered in a new era of enforcement designed to prosecute polluters. This emphasis on criminal enforcement was reinforced by the creation of an Environmental Crimes Section in the Justice Department and an Office of Criminal Enforcement at the Environmental Protection Agency. Intended as a law school text, this volume distinguishes between the criminal enforcement of the federal environmental statutes and their civil counterparts. A central issue is whether the bar for the enforcement of criminal penalties has been set so low that innocent parties are placed at risk of criminal prosecution. The author provides a broad overview of environmenal crimes by examining the intersection of environmental crime and criminal law theory. She also addresses the doctrine of mens rea (guilty mind) to elucidate the various mental states that might satisfy

the standard for criminal prosecution. Other subjects addressed in this volume are individual and organizational liability, water pollution, air pollution, hazardous waste, hazardous and toxic substances, conventional criminal statutes, and enforcement. The volume includes excerpts of court decisions, and discussion questions. The author is the James Carr Professor of Criminal Jurisprudence, Washington University School of Law.

Christie, Donna R. and Richard G. Hildreth. **Coastal and Ocean Management Law in a Nutshell.** 3d ed. St. Paul, MN: West, 2006. 1 vol. (482 pp.). Nutshell Series. Available from West Academic.
Cost: $41; from $21.93 on amazon.com (2014).
Focusing as it does on place, rather than on a generally recognized field of law, coastal management law involves aspects of property law, land use regulation, water law, natural resources law, constitutional law, federal and state statutory law, and international law in the special context of the coastal environment. This Nutshell examines the special interrelationships of land, water and natural resources and the conflicts over public and private rights, boundaries, jurisdictions, and management priorities. Donna Christie is Professor of law at Florida State University College of Law. Richard G. Hildreth is Professor of Law and Co-Director of the Coastal Law Center, University of Oregon School of Law.

Conrad, James W., ed. **Environmental Science Deskbook**. St. Paul, MN: West, 1998-date. 1 vol. (519 pp.) Looseleaf format. Annual supplementation.
Cost: $482; supplementation: 1999: $85; 2000: $92; 2001: $107; 2002: $118; 2003: $134.50; 2004: $150.50; 2005: $163; 2006: $185.50; 2007: $185.50; 2008: $206.50; 2009: $231.50; 2010: $270; 2011: $297; 2012: $326; 2013: $353; **Monthly Assured Print Price (APP):** $35/$420.
This volume attempts to provide a layman's introduction to the scientific and technological background of environmental law. Edited by a Senior Counsel with the Chemical Manufacturers Association and written by seventeen subject specialists, it covers a range of topics likely to be useful to those practicing in the field, including numerical notations and basic statistics, physical analysis, health risk assessment, groundwater, surface water quality and wastewater treatment, solid waste and contaminated soil, air, and wetlands. A chapter-by-chapter listing of additional specialized references is included. Ideally suited to the environmental attorney with a limited understanding of the science, as well as those who require a convenient review of basic scientific principles.

Cooke, Susan M., ed. **The Law of Hazardous Waste: Management, Cleanup, Liability and Litigation.** New York: Matthew Bender & Co., 1987-date. 4 vols. Looseleaf format. Supplemented several times annually.
Cost: $1,994 (includes annual subscription); renewal: 1995: $483.00 (frozen since 1992); 1996: $507; 1997: $507; 1998: $530; 1999: $555; 2000: $590; 2001; $631; 2002: $676; 2003: $710; 2004: $759; 2005: $812; 2006: $869; 2007: $938; 2008: $1013; 2009: $1,094; 2010: $1,139; 2011: $1,196; 2012: $1,236; 2013: $1,357; 2014: $1,481; eBook: $1,813; renewal: 2014: $1,481.
This is a thorough and exhaustive treatise dedicated to discussion and analysis of the legal issues involved in hazardous waste. Written by Susan Cooke and a team of twenty-seven environmental law experts, this four-volume work provides extensive coverage of hazardous waste management issues, including chapters on indemnification of hazardous wastes, requirements for generators, transporters, treatment, storage and disposal facilities, recycling requirements, requirements for underground storage tanks, spill reporting requirements, emergency planning and right-to-know, emerging comprehensive regulation of medical waste, hazardous waste regulation and liability requirements, hazardous substance cleanup and liability, federal and state Superfund and settlement provisions, liability under CERCLA for hazardous waste cleanup, non-CERCLA liability for government cleanup of hazardous waste, statutory liability for private cleanup of hazardous waste, environmental tort liability, criminal enforcement of federal hazardous waste laws, and hazardous waste considerations in conveyance of real property interests. Volume three contains a Glossary of Terms and Index. Detailed appendices following most chapters provide full text of applicable standards for hazardous waste disposal and facilities, EPA forms, tests, model forms and letters. Primary law citations include references to legislative history of applicable statutes.

Cost Saving Tips: In making a decision to enter a standing order to the hard copy, you must weigh your need for currency against the cost. If you intend to use this treatise merely as a starting place for your research, you may wish to forego the supplementation after the initial year's subscription has expired and update your research directly in the primary sources, digests, etc. and purchase another set at some future date. Remember that if you opt for the CD-ROM version, you cannot allow the subscription to lapse without losing the text, which is on time expiration. LexisNexis raised the initial cost of this set 21% in 2013-2014 alone.

Cross, Frank B. **Federal Environmental Regulation of Real Estate**. St. Paul, MN: Thomson Reuters West, 1993-date. 1 vol. Looseleaf format. Supplemented by twice annual replacement volumes.
Cost: 2013-2 Ed.: $387 ($774 annually); supplementation: 2003: $237.20; 2004: $204; 2005: $145; 2006: $279; 2007: $393; 2008: $283.50; 2009: $346; 2010: $385; 2011: $421; **Monthly Assured Print Price (APP):** $57/$684.
This volume provides an examination of every major federal environmental law and regulation which affects real estate ownership, development and acquisition, including environmental cleanup standards under the Comprehensive Environmental Response, Compensation, and Liability Act (CERCLA or "Superfund"), development restrictions involving wetlands and endangered species habitats, compliance with hazardous waste regulations, and implementation of storm water run-off rules governing industrial and construction activities. Also addressed are such topics as underground storage tanks, the Resource Conservation and Recovery Act (RCRA), state-related legislation, and state voluntary cleanup programs. Frank B. Cross is the Herbert D. Kelleher Professor of Business Law at the University of Texas at Austin and the author of eight books and

over 40 articles on environmental law and law and economics. His seminal work on the perils of the precautionary principle have addressed the perverse side effects that undermine the intended benefits of environmental regulation as well as the health risks of political resource misallocation.

Dietrich, David J. and Christian Dietrich. **Conservation Easements: Tax and Real Estate Planning for Landowners and Advisors**. Chicago: American Bar Association, 2011. 1 vol. (402 pp.). Paperbound with companion CD-ROM.
Cost: $139.95; ($119.95); from $85.70 on amazon.com (2014).
A conservation easement is a tool used by landowners to protect natural resources and preserve scenic open space. While ownership in the land still resides in the landowner, he or she relinquishes the right to do certain things on the land so designated in perpetuity. The landowner who gives an easement limits the right to develop and subdivide the land, or some other rights, now and into the future, but still retains ownership. The organization accepting the easement agrees to monitor it forever to ensure compliance with its terms. No public access is required by a conservation easement. The conservation easement creates a legally enforceable land preservation agreement between a landowner and a government agency (municipality, county, state, or federal) or a qualified land protection organization (often called a «land trust»), for the purposes of conservation. On the other hand, a landowner may also qualify for certain tax advantages as a consequence of the donation. While the decision to place a conservation easement on property is, at least nominally, a voluntary act, the decision may be prompted by municipal ordinances or zoning regulations that dictate such donations in certain circumstances, such as the creation of a subdivision from previously undeveloped land. In some jurisdictions, subdivision approval may be conditioned upon donation of a portion of land to a qualified land trust, or, in the absence of a trust willing to accept the land, a requirement that an equivalent amount of cash in lieu of land be donated to the jurisdiction. Under these potential circumstances, a conservation easement may be viewed as a less restrictive alternative. Such requirements, however, call into the question the right to private property and create a conflict of interest for the municipality which stands to benefit from its violation of private property rights. On a broader scale, the introduction of the U.N.'s stealth Agenda 21 into some local communities on the grounds of "sustainable development," reflects a comprehensive global plan of extreme environmentalism, social engineering, and political control that threatens private property rights, freedom, and American sovereignty. This volume provides a solid grounding in the laws governing conservation easements and the tax ramifications of such donations. Chapters address the nature of conservation purposes, easements not exclusively for conservation purposes, tax consequences, valuation and appraisal, tax traps, grantor and grantee, events down the road, hidden dangers, and the encouragement of conservation. The appendices include three sample conservation easements, relevant IRS notices, code sections, and forms related to the tax consequences of qualified easements. The authors are both graduates of the University of Montana Law School. David J. Dietrich maintains an active tax, real estate and agricultural practice. Christian Dietrich practices in the areas of business, real estate, tax and nonprofit law, and has significant experience with conservation easement issues.

Domike, Julie R. and Alec C. Zacaroli. **The Clean Air Act Handbook**. 3d ed. Chicago: American Bar Association, 2011. 1 vol. (739 pp.). Paperbound.
Cost: $179.95; from $95.68 on amazon.com (2014).
The Clean Air Act (42 U.S.C. §7401 et seq.) (1970) is the comprehensive federal law that regulates air emissions from stationary and mobile sources. Among other things, this law authorizes the EPA to establish National Ambient Air Quality Standards (NAAQS) to protect public health and public welfare and to regulate emissions of hazardous air pollutants. In recent years, the Clean Air Act has been used as the tool for circumventing the will of Congress is regulating greenhouse gases, specifically carbon dioxide and five others, that some believe are responsible for "climate change." The controversial U.S. Supreme Court decision in Massachusetts v. EPA (549 U.S. 497) (2007) ruled that greenhouse gas emissions (GHGs) are subject to regulation under the Clean Air Act, a decision that resulted in the largest single expansion of the statute in history. Following the failure of Congress to enact a massive "cap and trade" program, there has been considerable pushback from the Republican-led House and various state governments against the unilateral actions of the EPA under the Obama administration which directly threatens separation of powers. This volume assembles twenty-eight environmental law practitioners with expertise in various aspects of environmental law, including implementation, litigation, enforcement, and corporate counseling. The twenty essays in this volume address number of the most significant issues relative to the Clean Air Act and its implementation. Following an illuminating Introduction to the Clean Air Act: History, Perspectives, and Direction, the authors grapple with such topics as setting national ambient air quality standards, transportation and conformity requirements in state implementation plans, interstate transport and regional implementation plans, the new source review program, the visibility protection program, hazardous air pollutants, regulation of mobile sources, regulation of fuels and fuel additives, the acid rain program, stratospheric ozone protection, the Clean Air Act and global climate change, the title VI operating permit program, civil enforcement, criminal enforcement, and rulemaking and judicial review under the Clean Air Act, among others. Editor Julie R. Domike is a partner in the firm of Kilpatrick, Townsend & Stockton LLP in Washington, DC. Her co-editor is an environmental law practitioner with the same firm. Both have extensive experience in environmental law issues.

Dore, Michael. **The Law of Toxic Torts**. St. Paul, MN: Thomson Reuters West (Clark Boardman Callaghan), 1987-date. 4 vols. Looseleaf format. Supplemented three times annually.
Cost: $3,362; supplementation: 1996: $302; 1997: $503.10; 1998: $534; 1999: $576; 2000: $624; 2001: $723; 2002: $795; 2003: $906; 2004: $650; 2005: $1,068; 2006: $1,191; 2007: $1,326; 2008: $1,476; 2009: $1,642.50; 2010: $1,791; 2011: $1,951.50; 2012: $2,319; 2013: $2,467; **Monthly Assured Print Price (APP):** $245/$2,940.
This four-volume practice tool is designed to aid attorneys representing clients with actual or potential liability in toxic torts cases. It examines the various toxic tort liability theories, defense issues, coordination issues, discovery, the proof of toxic tort claims, insurance coverage, and criminal liability. It

considers such potential sources of liability as product sales, waste disposal, property ownership, and construction; and

evaluates the leading damage theories which may be brought by plaintiffs, including emotional distress, cancerphobia, post-traumatic stress disorder, and various statutory claims. Included are a number of research references which can be used as checklists of matters to be addressed or as models for form drafting, including federal and state statutes and regulations, pleading forms, agreements, discovery stipulations, etc. The author is a partner at the Roseland., NJ firm of Lowenstein, Sandler, Kohl, Fisher & Boylan and has published and lectured widely in the field of toxic torts and litigation.

Driesen, David M. and Robert W. Adler. **Environmental Law: A Conceptual and Pragmatic Approach**. 2d ed. New York: Wolters Kluwer Law & Business, 2007. 1 vol. (700 pp.).
Cost: $178; from 0.58 on amazon.com (2014).
This introductory law school textbook is intended to illustrate the leading concepts of environmental law through a combination of analytical discussion and excerpts from relevant court decisions. Following an overview of the nature and evolution of environmental law, the authors examine the goals for particular regulations, the means of environmental protection, allocation of responsibility, and enforcement. They trace the evolution of environmental law from its common law roots to its administrative and statutory goals and objectives. Individual chapters address such topics as effects-based standards, technology-based standard setting, cost-benefit approaches, traditional regulation, economic incentives, information-based approaches, pollution prevention and recycling, private cleanup responsibility, allocation of government responsibility, detection of violations, government enforcement and citizen enforcement. While the book's legal analysis is generally sound, some of its scientific assertions lack empirical proof, including claims of dramatic sea level rise as a result of "climate change," and increased severity of storms and floods, both of which have been soundly contradicted by the leading scientists operating in these areas, such as Nils-Axel Mörner, the noted Swedish physicist and world-renowned sea level expert whose research indicates that sea levels have been rising at roughly the same rate since the end of the last Ice Age 12,500 years ago. His findings are buttressed by the U.N.'s IPCC which has estimated sea level rise at 8"-18" by the end of the century, a figure entirely in keeping with geologic experience. David Driesen is the Angela Cooney Professor at the Syracuse University College of Law. Robert Adler is Associate Dean and Professor of Law at University of Utah, S.J. Quinney College of Law.

Dwyer, John P. and Marika F. Bergsund. **Dwyer & Bergsund Federal Environmental Laws Annotated**. St. Paul, MN: Thomson Reuters West, 1994-date. 1 vol. (2,300 pp.). Annual.
Cost: 2013 Edition: $371; **Monthly Assured Print Price (APP):** $31/$372 (2014).
This volume provides access to the text of most federal environmental laws, with annotations and cross-references to federal regulations, cases, other federal laws, and leading law review articles. The laws themselves are also summarized for easier access. For the environmental practitioner, this is a low-cost alternative to purchasing the entire U.S. Code.

Environment & Safety Resource Center [Internet]. Washington, D.C.: Bloomberg BNA. Updated daily.
Cost: $23,583 (2014).
The Environment & Safety Resource Center is a comprehensive source for environment, health & safety (EHS) news, analysis, legal and regulatory developments, and significant case law. The Environment & Safety Resource Center integrates the content of Bloomberg BNA's popular Environment & Safety Library with a more intuitive and easy-to-navigate interface, and enhanced functionality and features. Searches can be conducted across a wide array of reference and information products, and cross-product hypertext links to full-text references are also incorporated and fully searchable. The Resource Center provides a powerful, easy-to-use, continuously updated compliance tools with a research collection of federal and state laws, regulations, and documents. Covers air pollution, biotechnology, coastal zone management, community right-to-know, drinking water, food safety, general environment and safety, hazardous materials transportation, hazardous waste, hazardous waste cleanup (Superfund), mining, occupational safety and health, the oil and gas industry, pesticides, radiation, toxis substances, water quality and supply.

Environment Reporter. Washington, D.C.: Bloomberg BNA, 1970-date. 14 vols. Looseleaf service. Print reference material is updated biweekly and indexed semiannually. Print notification is issued weekly and indexed quarterly, cumulating annually. Decisions are published weekly and indexed regularly, with Bound Volumes issued semiannually.
Cost: print: $4,995 per year for full service; Internet: Call for specific pricing (2014).
Although not a treatise, this looseleaf service warrants inclusion in any bibliography devoted to significant sources of environmental law. This is a combination current awareness and reference service which provides coverage of legislative, administrative, and judicial developments in the areas of pollution control and environmental protection. Its 13 volumes include those devoted to Current Developments, Court Decisions, federal laws, federal regulations, and mining laws. Court decisions in looseleaf form are eventually replaced by permanent bound volumes. An important tool for the attorney charged with tracking developments in environmental law. Individual components are also available.

Environmental Law Handbook. Edited by Thomas F. P. Sullivan. Rockville, MD: Government Institutes, 1982-date. 1 vol. (897 pp.). Annual. Paperbound.
Cost: 2011 (21st) edition: $105 (hardbound); $99.99 (eBook) (2014).
This comprehensive, yet succinct, guide to environmental law provides essential information regarding the legal, scientific, and practical aspects of fifteen sub-specialties of the field. Each of the book's sixteen chapters is re-written annually by leading attorneys and law firms specializing in environmental law and is designed to provide environmental managers, engineers, attorneys, consultants and students with informed guidance in statutory and regulatory compliance. Following an introductory chapter entitled "Fundamentals of Environmental Law," the book's

remaining fifteen chapters provide substantive detail on such topics as enforcement and liability, The Resource Conservation and Recovery Act, underground storage tanks, the Clean Air Act, Clean Water Act, Oil Pollution Act, Safe Drinking Water Act, National Environmental Policy Act, Toxic Substances Control Act, pesticides, and the Occupational Safety and Health Act, among others. Each chapter provides citations to the relevant statutes, regulations, and caselaw in the field, as well as a list of research resources for further study, including leading web sites and hotlines. While there are clearly more comprehensive works on the market, there is no other work of this size which provides this combination of comprehensiveness and currency at such a reasonable cost.

Environmental Law Library [CD-ROM]. New York: Matthew Bender & Co. One disc. Updated quarterly. Available for Windows. Search Engine: Folio.
Cost: $10,096 (includes annual subscription); renewal: 1998: $2,070; 1999: $2,150; 2000: $2,300; 2001: $2,461; 2002: $2,634; 2003: $2,766; 2004: $2,904; 2005: $3,107; 2006: $3,325; 2007: $3,591; 2008: $3,914; 2009: $4,227; 2010: $4,439; 2011: $4,661; 2012: $4,941; 2013: $5,287; 2014: $5,657.
The complete library includes the following Matthew Bender titles: **Treatise on Environmental Law, A Guide to Toxic Torts, Law of Hazardous Waste: Management, Cleanup, Liability and Litigation, Environmental Law in Real Estate and Business Transactions, Environmental Law Practice Guide: State and Federal Law, Insurance Coverage for Environmental Claims, Practical Guide to Winning Land Use Approvals and Permits, and Zoning and Land Use Controls.** Various combinations of titles may be selected by the subscriber.

The Environmental Law Reporter. Washington, D.C.: Environmental Law Institute, 1971-date. Online service.
Cost: eAccess subscription (UPDATE, News & Analysis, RLR Online): $1,995 per year (full subscription is online with the exception of the monthly News & Analysis which is also in print); individual components also available; UPDATE: $725; News and Analysis: $725 (2014).
A comprehensive current awareness and analytical tool designed for the environmental law specialist. The service includes five volumes: Current Volume Year, Pending Litigation, Statutes, Regulations, and Indexes. The Current Volume Year contains a news and analysis section that provides an ongoing review of developments in environmental and natural resources law, summaries of recent cases, issues in pending cases, reports on Supreme Court cases accepted or rejected for review, and appeals and petitions filed. It also contains reports on current Congressional activity, including committee and conference committee action, and **Federal Register** notices. The Analysis section provides discussion of a variety of environmental issues written by practitioners, law professors, contributing authors, and the Reporter's editors. This volume also contains a bibliography of books, articles, comments, notes, symposia, and surveys appearing in a variety of legal publications. An annual cumulative bibliography is published in the Index volume. A litigation section reports on important environmental law cases on both the federal and state levels. The Pending Litigation volume tracks current developments in the field through new cases filed. Each entry provides a summary of the facts, describes the claims and arguments, and summarizes the pleadings. The ELI also provides copies of the pleadings to its subscribers at cost. The Statutes volume contains the current, full text of all relevant environmental laws, environmental treaties, conventions, and other international agreements. The Regulations volume contains the full text of selected environmental regulations and executive orders with citations to the **Code of Federal Regulations**. The Indexes volume contains cumulative indexes to all the volume in the service as well as the cumulative annual bibliography. The service is updated by means of «News and Analysis,» a monthly analytical journal which provides both notice of current developments and in-depth articles; and the «Update,» E-mail bulletins published online 36 times a year (3 times a month), which provide concise reports of recent court decisions, legislative developments and agency actions. This is a first-rate, and reasonably priced, current awareness and analytical tool for the environmental law specialist, albeit with a pro-environmentalist activist bias.

Cost Saving Tip: Superior value in comparison to Bloomberg BNA's **Environment Reporter**, which is now priced at nearly $4,000 per annum. Moreover, unlike BNA, the Environmental Law Institute's prices are openly posted on their web site and exhibit minimal price increases.

Environmental Statutes Outline: A Guide to Federal Environmental Laws. 4th ed. Washington, DC: Environmental Law Institute, 2007. 1 vol. (102 pp.). Paperbound.
Cost: $29.95; from $28.00 on amazon.com (2014).
This handy volume contains summaries of fifty-eight most significant federal environmental laws, with summaries of the major provisions of each statute. An ideal tool for the study and review of the major environmental laws. The full text of these statutes appears in the ELI's companion **Environmental Law Deskbook**.

Federal Environmental Laws. St. Paul, MN: Thomson Reuters West. Annual. 1 vol. (approx. 2,000 pp.). Paperbound.
Cost: 2013 Edition: $238; ProView eBook: $238; **Monthly Assured Print Price (APP):** $20/$240 (2014).
A handy compendium of the leading federal environmental statutes covering such areas as air, water and land pollution, coastal zone management, environmental response, compensation, liability, environmental taxes, national climate program, nuclear waste policy, ocean pollution monitoring, and environmental planning.

Findley, Roger W. and Daniel A. Farber. **Environmental Law in a Nutshell.** 8th ed. St. Paul: West, 2010. 1 vol. (328 pp.). Available from West Academic.
Cost: $41; from $25.00 on amazon.com; kindle ed.: $20.84 (2014).
This student handbook provides an overview of the basic issues involved in environmental law, regulations, planning and disputes. It considers the implementation of environmental policies in a legal environment which emphasizes administrative discretion, judicial restraint and deference for the various levels

of governmental authority. Chapters cover judicial review of government decisions, federalism and the environment, pollution control, risk management and scientific uncertainty, control of toxic substances, and preservation of natural areas. It includes a table of acronyms, table of cases and subject index. In keeping with the editorial philosophy of the Nutshell Series, it provides only limited citations to primary authority.

Gaba, Jeffrey M. **Law of Solid Waste, Pollution Prevention and Recycling.** St. Paul, MN: Thomson Reuters West (Clark Boardman Callaghan), 1992-date. 2 vols. Looseleaf format. Supplemented twice annually.
Cost: $822; supp.: 1993: $65; 1994: $155; 1995: $155; 1996: $176; 1997: $184.50; 1998: $195; 1999: $125; 2000: $135; 2001: $158; 2002: $188.50; 2003: $211.50; 2004: $237; 2005: $254; 2006: $295; 2007: $328.50; 2008: $328.50; 2009: $421.50; 2010: $463.50; 2011: $505; 2012: $555; 2013: $585; **Monthly Assured Print Price (APP):** $63/$756.
A part on the publisher's Environmental Law Series, this volume covers the rapidly evolving law of hazardous waste, disposal, recycling and prevention. Examines both state and federal responses to the challenges imposed by solid and hazardous waste under the Resource Conservation Recovery Act. (RCRA) and state law. Chapters cover distinguishing solid waste from hazardous waste, regulation of disposal of nonhazardous solid waste under RCRA, regulation of municipal solid waste, regulation of the disposal and use of sewage sludge, regulation of special wastes under RCRA, regulation of solid wastes under CERCLA, regulation of the recycling of hazardous waste under RCRA, federal pollution, prevention, waste minimization and recycling programs, state regulation of nonhazardous industrial solid waste, state and municipal solid waste recycling programs, solid wastes of special concern and interstate issues in the management of solid waste. Contains a Table of Cases and Index. A good one-volume work for the attorney primarily concerned with solid waste disposal issues. Contains adequate citations to statutes, regulations and case law.

Global Climate Change and U.S. Law. Edited by Michael Gerrard, Chicago: American Bar Association, Section of Environment, Energy, and Resources, 2007. 1 vol. (754 pp.).
Cost: $59.95 ($49.95 to Section members); from $25 on amazon.com (2014).
It's astounding what a negligible increase of 0.8 degrees Celsius in the world's temperature over the past 150 years, coming at the end of the Little Ice Age, will do to fuel the collective, and collectivist, mindset among the nations and citizens of the world. The temperature of the world has variously risen and fallen for eons due to the complex interaction of natural factors. Indeed, some of the most highly qualified climate scientists have painstakingly documented the existence of a 1,500-year climate cycle over the entire globe. A monumental 1983 study of mile deep Greenland ice core samples by Denmark's Willi Dansgaard and Switzerland's Hans Oeschger (results confirmed a few years later on Antarctica, and by scores of proxy studies) revealed a 250,000-year world climate history which reflected the moderate climate cycles of the sun. What characterizes the present era, however, is a lot of bad science anxious to tap virtually unlimited sources of government funding for climate research, a gullible media, quasi-religious environmental organizations, and the nefarious influence of politics upon the scientific enterprise. The fruits of that "research" include Michael Mann's now thoroughly debunked "hockey stick" representation of the most recent 1,000 years of climate history, which, nevertheless, became a prominent feature of Al Gore's global warming sideshow, and which finds naïve acceptance by the editor of this volume (see Figure 1-1). The "presentist" mindset, which interprets the current climate experience as a unique and threatening phenomenon, reveals a sorry lack of historical perspective. Most significantly, the carefully documented climate record reveals that temperatures were 2-4 degrees higher in the medieval warm period (900-1300 A.D.) than they are today, when CO2 levels are higher, and that CO2 levels are actually an 800-year lagging indicator of global warming, not a causal factor. Many of the scientists who contributed to the 1996 Intergovernmental Panel on Climate Change (IPCC) documented these findings, concluding that no such "human fingerprint" had been found in the recent global warming, but their statements were shockingly removed from Chapter 8 of the IPCC's 1996 report by U.N. bureaucrats and U.S. politicians in the Clinton administration anxious to manufacture "consensus" regarding anthropogenic global warming. This is the context in which books like the **Global Climate Change and U.S. Law** are produced. Regardless of the flawed scientific presentation in this volume, however, lawyers stand to make a good living off the complex legal and regulatory schemes detailed in this book, including the implementation of an elaborate system of emission caps and trading programs, as well as the more benign efforts to conserve energy, and develop renewable energy sources. Building upon this flawed scientific analysis, Part I of this volume describes the national and international framework of climate change regulation, the impact of the Kyoto Protocol on U.S. business, clean air regulation, civil remedies, climate change in facility permitting, and international trade and development. Part II describes the emerging regional, state and local actions, together with a 50-state survey of state responses to climate change. Part III examines a variety of corporate actions, including disclosure issues, fiduciary duties, insurance and climate change, and subsidies, tax policy and technological innovations. Part IV examines the legal aspects of efforts to reduce greenhouse gases, such as voluntary efforts, emissions trading, and carbon sequestration. It also includes a list of important resources, a glossary of climate related terms, a list of acronyms; endnotes, and index. Twenty-four authors contributed to this volume under the editorship of Michael Garrard, a partner in the New York office of Arnold & Porter LLP, where he heads its environmental practice group. The views of the individual authors stand alone, irrespective of the views of the other contributors. For more authoritative and balanced views of the science of global climate, see Fred Singer and Dennis Avery's **Unstoppable Global Warming: Every 1,500 Years** (Rowman & Littlefield, 2007); and Henrik Svensmark and Nigel Calder's **The Chilling Stars: A New Theory of Climate Change** (Icon Books, 2007), which argues that the interplay of clouds, the sun, and cosmic rays has a far more profound effect of climate than carbon dioxide. Readers are also directed to Willie Soon and Sallie Baliunas' metanalysis of studies related to the existence of the climate cycle, the Medieval Warming Period, and Little Ice Age (see «Reconstructing Climatic and Environmental Changes of the Past 1000 Years: A Reappraisal,» *Energy and Environment* 14, no. 2/3 (March 2003), 233-296. They discovered 112 studies about the Medieval Warming Period, 92% of which showed evidence of warming, 124 studies

from around the world addressing the existence of the Little Ice Age, 98% of these confirming the era's cooling. Finally, they examined 102 studies containing information on the question of whether the 20th century was the warmest on record, 78% of which found earlier periods lasting at least 50 years that were warmer than any period in the 20th century. Ironically, despite all the hoopla about "global warming" or, increasingly, "climate change," global mean temperatures are now below their 3,000-year average.

Since this review was written, the so-called "Climategate" scandal has implicated the Hadley Centre's Climatic Research Unit at the University of East Anglia in the UK, a leading source for the U.N.'s climate data, in an orchestrated effort to fudge climate data and impugn the integrity of global warming skeptics. Among those involved were the Center's director Phil Jones, and Michael Mann, author of the infamous hockey stick graph referenced above. As a result of the fallout, many scientists are now acknowledging a much higher degree of uncertainty in the climate record. What the "global warming" hysteria amounted to was a hyperbolic reaction to a miniscule one-third of a degree rise in globally averaged temperatures from between 1978 and 1997. And, for the record, the Hadley Centre's data collection since 1997 shows no increase in globally-averaged temperatures, which have held steady at 14.5 degrees Celsius, which is why the activists have lowered the bar to something they now term "climate change," as if perfectly normal climate cycles should be cause for worldwide hysteria.

Grad, Frank P. **Treatise on Environmental Law.** New York: Matthew Bender & Co., 1973-date. 8 vols. Looseleaf format.
Cost: $2,756 (includes annual subscription) renewal: 1995: $650 (frozen since 1992); 1996: $682; 1997: $682; 1998: $725; 1999: $750; 2000: $800; 2001: $856; 2002: $916; 2003: $962; 2004: $999; 2005: $1,069; 2006: $1,144; 2007: $1,235; 2008: $1,359; 2009: $1,468; 2010: $1,570; 2011: $1,617; 2012: $1,714; 2013: $1,382.10; 2014: $2,021; CD-ROM: $2,696; renewal: 1998: $685; 1999: $750; 2000: $800; 2001: $856; 2002: $916; 2003: $962; 2004: $1,010; 2005: $1,081; 2006: $1,157; 2007: $1,249; 2008: $1,249; 2009: $1,349; 2010: $1,639; 2011: $1,688; 2012: $1,688; 2013: $1,834; 2014: $1,989; eBook: $1,990; renewal: 2013: $1,154; 2014: $1,479. Also available as a part of the publisher's Environmental Law Library on CD-ROM (see sales representative for special promotions).
This major environmental treatise is authored by Frank P. Grad, the Chamberlain Professor of Legislation, Columbia Law School and Director of the Legislative Drafting Research Fund at Columbia University. This is a sophisticated, integrated analysis of all major areas of environmental law, including solid waste, hazardous waste, toxic substances, radiation, air, water and noise pollution. The discussion encompasses the National Environmental Policy Act and State "Little NEPA's", the Emergency Planning and Community Right-to-Know Act of 1986, the Resource Conservation and Recovery Act, land use planning issues, public lands and conservation, international issues, attorney's fees and alternative dispute resolution, and more. The author addresses all major environmental laws, regulations, and court decisions and provides thoughtful discussion and analysis of such significant environmental problems as growth, depletion of natural resources, pollution-related health issues, power shortages and aesthetic considerations. The text is updated through both interfiled pages and yellow, front-end supplementary pages. This a particularly valuable general resource for the environmental attorney, government policy specialist, or corporate counsel specializing in environmental issues.

Cost Saving Tips: Given the high supplementation costs, the cost-conscious purchaser of this treatise may wish to consider dropping the standing order after the one year's initial subscription has expired. Be aware that even the most recently issued supplement must be updated in the primary sources, and relevant cases and statutes must be Shepardized to ensure currency. This an excellent introductory avenue for your environmental legal research, but, as with all secondary sources, it is not the last word. Once you feel the text is becoming too dated for it to be useful, simply purchase a new set at some future date depending upon the nature of your practice and your need for more current analysis. If you are an environmental law specialist, however, the standing order may be preferable.

Greenberg, Michael R. **The Environmental Impact Statement After Two Generations: Managing Environmental Power**. New York: Routledge, 2012. 1 vol. (229 pp.). Paperbound.
Cost: $53.95; from $45.60 on amazon.com (2014).
One of the consequences of the National Environmental Policy Act of 1969 (NEPA) (42 U.S.C. 4321-4347) was to require the submission of an environmental impact statement (EIS) for certain actions «significantly affecting the quality of the human environment.» An EIS is part of the preliminary fact-gathering process prior to decision-making by the appropriate regulatory bodies. The author's stated intent to examine the nuances of reading environmental and risk evaluations as a prelude to discussion and negotiation, since most cases are resolved by such negotiation instead of the winner-take-all outcome of litigation. Following a brief history of the NEPA and the role of environmental impact statements generally, the author embarks on an examination of six specific real world environmental case studies and the role played by EISs in the decision-making process. He concludes with an evaluation of NEPA and the environmental challenges of the twenty-first century. The volume also contains an extensive bibliography of sources and subject index. The author is a Professor and Dean at Rutgers University and the author of more than 20 books and 300 articles on environmental policy.

Johnson, John W. **United States Water Law: An Introduction**. Boca Raton, FL: CRC Press, Taylor & Francis Group, 2009. 1 vol. (471 pp.). Hardcover.
Cost: $154.95; from $106.54 on amazon.com; kindle ed.: $101.21 (2014).
Water is a critical natural resource, but is continually being renewed by precipitation, and the pooling and runoff that follow. Nevertheless, suitable water is limited in quantity and the demand for it often exceeds its supply in many locations in the United States and around the globe. This introductory text provides a solid foundation for an understanding of water law in the United States and the rights upon which it is based. These rights are determined by two major legal systems: (1) riparian

rights, based on ownership of the riparian lands which border the body of water, which predominate in the eastern United States; and (2) prior appropriation rights, common in the Western states, which arose as a result of federal ownership of lands and which furthered a system in which water rights were assigned on the basis of beneficial use under statutory requirements. This volume examines the division of authority between federal and state governments, the allocation of interstate water rights, public rights to use surface waters, water ownership, water supply and uses, riparian rights, prior appropriation rights, groundwater, Native American rights, environmental regulation, nuisance and tort law, social theory, Louisiana and Hawaii water law, the future of water resources in the U.S., water corporations, reclamation, Western state water systems and fees, classification of water bodies and types of precipitation, and prominent federal agencies dealing with U.S. waters. The volume is enhanced by a number of valuable appendices containing selected federal statutes, charts and lists, forms and illustrations. John W. Johnson is a graduate of the Seattle University School of Law and a member of the Washington State Bar Association.

King, Raymond C. **Toxic Mold Litigation**. 2d ed. Chicago: American Bar Association, Tort Trial and Insurance Practice Section, 2008. 1 vol. (324 pp.). Paperbound.
Cost: $125; member price: $105.00 (2014).
Molds are microscopic fungi that depend on plant or animal matter for their survival. Once mold spores land and begin digesting their host, they are also dependent on moisture, a nutrient source, and a temperature of between 40 and 100 degrees. The rise of mold-related litigation in recent years is a consequence of a number of factors, among them changes in construction practices, greater media attention, and the awareness of trial lawyers in the income-producing potential of such cases. This book is intended to serve as a practical reference for both lawyers and non-lawyers on the science and law governing toxic mold cases. The book will prove useful to those concerned with the impact of mold on commercial and residential real estate, and schools or hospitals, whether as owners, builders or insurers. Following an historical overview of toxic mold awareness, the author provides a useful summary of recent mold cases in the United States, assessment of the mold claim, preparation for trial, the science behind mold litigation, mold and insurance coverage: the first party claim, mold and insurance coverage: the third-party claim, an update on mold and government regulation, expert witnesses, floods and hurricanes, and the future of toxic mold litigation. The appendices include numerous forms, checklists, interrogatories, and government standards and tests. The author, who practices law in Plano, TX, practiced medicine before receiving his law degree. He has contributed to numerous publications in the fields of law and medicine and advised plaintiffs and defendants in over 250 toxic mold cases.

Lathrop, Mitchell L. **Insurance Coverage for Environmental Claims.** New York: Matthew Bender & Co., 1992-date. 2 vols. Looseleaf format and Internet Supplemented annually.
Cost: $299 (print or eBook); supplementation: 1997: $65; 1998: 0; 1999: $82; 2000: $73; 2001: $76; 2002: $82; 2003: $87; 2004: $99; 2005: $106; 2006: $119; 2007: $134; 2008: $147; 2009: $159; 2010: $181; 2011: $179; 2012: $197; 2013: $211; 2014: $227.
A detailed, state-by-state survey designed to assist practitioners in determining how the courts have treated a number of significant insurance-related environmental insurance questions, including the duty to defend, the meaning of occurrence/accident language in liability insurance policies, and policy exclusions. The author is a partner in the San Diego, CA firm of Luce, Forward, Hamilton & Scripps.

Lee, C. C., ed. **Dictionary of Environmental Legal Terms**. New York: McGraw-Hill Professional, 1997. 1 vol. (818 pp.).
Cost: OUT-OF-PRINT; was $84; from $23.90 on amazon.com (2014).
This dictionary is a systematic compilation of environmental legal terms which appear in U.S. environmental laws and regulations and other sources. Statutory definitions are drawn from all the major environmental laws, including the Clean Air Act, the Clean Water Act, thee Safe Drinking Water Act, the Resource Conservation and Recovery Act, the Toxic Substances Control Act, and the Superfund Act. Regulatory definitions are taken from 40 CFR, Parts 1 to 1517. Health-related environmental definitions are taken from 29 CFR and radioactive waste-related definitions are taken from 10 CFR. Environmental engineering definitions are drawn from EPA publications. Representative chemical listings from each major environmental law and regulation are included. The editor is Research Program Manager, National Risk Management Research Laboratory, U.S. Environmental Protection Agency.

Lomborg, Bjørn, ed. **Global Crises, Global Solutions**. 2d ed. New York: Cambridge University Press, 2009. 1 vol. (648 pp.).
Cost: paperbound: $39.99; e-book: $32.00; from $0.01 on amazon.com (2014).
Now in its second edition, this unique and invaluable examination of global health and environmental problems is an outgrowth of the "Copenhagen Consensus," an ambitious international project designed to prioritize solutions to the world's leading challenges, including climate change, communicable diseases, conflicts, education, financial instability, corruption, migration, malnutrition and hunger, trade barriers, and water access. Its authors include a number of eminent economists who provide arguments and data for prioritizing responses to these problems. In a world of finite financial resources, they apply the latest in scientific knowledge and cost-benefit analysis to various programs in order to gauge how best to achieve the greatest good for the money. Each problem is introduced by a world-renowned expert who analyzes the scale of the problem and evaluates the costs and benefits of a range of policy options to improve the situation. Alternative solutions are also offered by other experts in shorter pieces. All ten challenges are evaluated by a panel of economists from North America, Europe, and China who rank the most promising policy options. For example, the consensus is that it would be far wiser to spend resources on the immediate problem of AIDS in Africa than the more distant one of global warming. At the top of the group's list of 17 projects are control of HIV/AIDS, providing micro nutrients to combat malnutrition, trade liberalization, and control of malaria. At the bottom of the list were guest worker programs for the unskilled and the various projects to address alleged global warming. Bjørn Lomborg is Associate Professor of Statistics at the University of Aarhus and the director of the Danish Environmental Assessment Institute.

He is also the author of the bestselling book **The Skeptical Environmentalist** (2001). This is a fascinating and valuable effort to merge scientific knowledge with an understanding of economic realities in addressing pressing global problems.

Malone, Linda A. **Environmental Regulation of Land Use.** St. Paul, MN: Thomson Reuters West (Clark Boardman), 1990-date. 1 vol. Looseleaf format or ProView eBook.
Cost: $1,049; ProView eBook: $963; supplementation: 2003: $259; 2004: $290; 2005: $313; 2006: $357; 2007: $398.50; 2008: $444; 2009: $507.50; 2010: $594.50; 2011: $648; 2012: $706; 2013: $770; **Monthly Assured Print Price (APP):** $77/$924.
In the context of our modern environmentally sensitive legal and regulatory climate, land use and management decisions are fraught with peril for developers and their legal representatives. In this volume, the author addresses environmental regulation in a variety of areas, with individual chapters devoted to coastal zones, wetlands, soil conservation, farmland preservation, floodplain regulation, preservation of environmental quality, water quality, groundwater, air quality, noise control, special management techniques, growth controls for environmental preservation, critical area regulations, development rights and the taking clause, and habitat conservation requirements. The author discusses the impact of federal, state, and local laws and regulations in the field, the sources of pollution, and the health and economic impacts of land use activities and decisions, and their remedies. The text includes citations to the latest statutes, regulations and court decisions. Linda A. Malone is the Marshall-Wythe Foundation Professor of Law at The College of William and Mary School of Law and author of numerous articles and the author or co-author of ten books on international law, human rights, and environmental law.

Michaels, Patrick J. and Robert C. Balling, Jr. **The Satanic Gases: Clearing the Air about Global Warming**. Washington, DC: Cato Institute, 2000. 1 vol. (234 pp.). Paperbound.
Cost: $10.95; from $.01 on amazon.com (2014).
Alleged global warming, or climate change, has become one of the most significant environmental controversies of our time. Indeed, the level of hysteria generated by the issue has prompted Richard Lindzen, Alfred P. Sloan Professor of Meteorology at MIT, to reflect that «future generations will wonder in bemused amazement that the early 21st century's developed world went into hysterical panic over a globally averaged temperature increase of a few tenths of a degree and, on the basis of gross exaggerations of highly uncertain computer projections combined into implausible chains of inference, proceeded to contemplate a roll-back of the industrial age.» This volume, by two of the nation's leading climatologists, is an invaluable scholarly review of both the science and politics of the global warming debate. The authors, drawing upon a wealth of peer-reviewed scientific literature, examine the scientific evidence for global warming, efforts to model the earth's climate, global warming and mortality, the greening planet, and predictions of rising sea levels. They also address the various policy initiatives which have been offered to address the perceived threat of global warming, including treaties, programs, and protocols, including the Kyoto Protocol. They conclude that climate change will be relatively modest and benign and that such drastic measures as the Kyoto Protocol, which would mandate a reduction in U.S. emissions of 30-43% below expected 2008-2012 levels, would have devastating consequences for the United States and world economies, while achieving negligible results. Patrick Michael is a research professor of environmental sciences at the University of Virginia, a visiting scientist with the Marshall Institute in Washington, DC, and the author of over 200 scientific, technical and popular articles on climate Robert C. Balling is Professor of Geography and Director of the Office of Climatology at Arizona State University, author of over 100 papers in the leading scientific journals of climate and atmospheric sciences, and a world authority on drought and climate change. In 2004, Michaels published **Meltdown: The Predictable Distortion of Global Warming by Scientists, Politicians, and the Media**, which documents hundreds of exaggerations regarding supposed global warming.

Nolan, John R. and Daniel B. Rodriguez, eds. **Losing Ground: A Nation on Edge**. Washington, DC: Environmental Law Institute, 2007. 1 vol. (491 pp.). Paperbound.
Cost: $69.95; from $18.57 on amazon.com (2014).
Many of the environmental disasters that befall the natural environment and impact its citizens are a natural consequence of our penchant for building on the edge of disaster prone areas, including seashores and rivers, in close proximity to highly flammable forests, and in valuable wetlands. In many of these situations, property rights and the expectations of land owners and developers are obstacles to attempts by government to mitigate such potential disasters through regulation. The modern planning philosophy attempts to integrate the natural and built environments, but the end result is a high level of tension when governments try to reduce the economic, social, and human toll of natural disasters. The challenge of public policy is to channel this tension in the service of sensible environmental regulation. This collection of articles addresses a variety of environmental disasters and their mitigation through government regulation and civic involvement. The essays include endnotes to primary and secondary sources, as well as links to online sources. John Nolan is Professor of Law and Counsel to the Land Use Law Center, Pace University School of Law. Daniel B. Rodriguez is the Warren Distinguished Professor of Law, University of San Diego School of Law.

Novick, Sheldon M. et al., eds. **Law of Environmental Protection.** St. Paul, MN: West (Clark Boardman Callaghan), 1987-date. 3 vols. or ProView eBook. Annual replacement volumes. Supplemented twice annually.
Cost: 2013-2 Edition: $825 ($1,650 annually); ProView eBook: $825; supplementation: 1993: $177; 1994: $200; 1995: $245; 1996: $278; $1997: $255; 1998: $271; 1999: $293; 2000: $313; 2001: $363; 2002: $396; 2003: $451; 2004: $505; 2005: $318; 2006: $617; 2007: $1,006.50; 2008: $765; 2009: $861; 2010: $936; 2011: $1,032 (1st annual replacement vols.); **Monthly Assured Print Price (APP):** $121/$1,452.
This work is edited by Sheldon Novick, formerly the Regional Counsel for the Environmental Protection Agency. Written by a team of more than forty attorneys and environmental law experts under the auspices of the Environmental Law Institute, many of them senior litigators and program administrators, this three-volume treatise provides guidance on those areas of environmental law dealing with pollution controls, regulation of

hazardous waste and toxic substances. It analyzes existing law and summarizes those general principles arising from the mass of environmental laws, regulations and case law. Its emphasis is upon the means whereby goals of environmental protection can be achieved, with a call for codification of existing law. Chapters cover Goals of Environmental Protection, Methods of Environmental Protection, Administrative Agencies and Procedures, Ethical and Economic Problems, State Environmental Law and Programs, Environmental Self-Assessment, Enforcement, The National Environmental Policy Act, Media-Specific Programs for Air, Water, Soil and Groundwater, Introduction to Products and Manufacturing Regulation, Toxic Chemicals, Drinking Water, Pesticides, and Biotechnology. Volume three contains a Table of Cases, Table of Statutes, and Index. While the individual chapters were written by different authors, the editors have produced a set which reflects a coherent organizational structure. The authors also address policy considerations in a balanced fashion, giving deference to both economic and environmental concerns. The authors treatment of matters of policy and implementation is particularly valuable because it recognizes and analyzes the various interests which must be balanced in any effective program of implementation. The well-written text is accompanied by exhaustive citations to primary law, secondary treatises and professional studies.

Cost-Saving Tip: The annual cost, which, initially, decreased substantially with introduction of the annual replacement volumes (from $995 to $696), has now skyrocketed to $1,650 annually. The APP option provides minimal savings.
A better option is to purchase in alternate years, or less often.

Pearson, Eric. **Environmental and Natural Resources Law.** 4th ed. Newark, NJ: LexisNexis, 2012. 1 vol. (553 pp.) or eBook.
Cost: $174 (print); $104 (eBook); from $16.40 on amazon.co (2014).
This law school caseBook combines well-written discussion and analysis with a number of carefully chosen case and article excerpts. The author examines such topics as common law considerations, constitutional considerations, the National Environmental Policy Act, Federal lands, the Public Trust Doctrine, the Endangered Species Act, water rights, the Clean Air Act, the Clean Water Act, the Resource Conservation and Recovery Act, and Comprehensive Environmental Response Compensation and Liability Act (CERCLA). The volume also includes an appendix of acronyms, and a valuable list of the canons of statutory interpretation. Unlike some environmental texts, this one is characterized by a balanced perspective on the often controversial and highly-charged issues which dominate the field. Eric Pearson is Professor of Law, Creighton University School of Law.

Rodgers, William H., Jr. **Environmental Law.** St. Paul: Thomson Reuters West, 1986-date. 4 vols. (approx. 2,770 pp.) or ProView eBook. Supplemented twice annually.
Cost: $972; ProView eBook: $892; supplementation: 1994: $52.50; 1995: $61; 1996: $82; 1997: $99.50; 1998: $182; 1999: $196; 2000: $212; 2001: $206; 2002: $207; 2003: $236; 2004: $264.50; 2005: $143; 2006: $326; 2007: $374.50; 2008: $416; 2009: $467; 2010: $514; 2011: $565; 2012: $621.50; 2013: $713; **Monthly Assured Print Price** (APP): $71/$852.
This four-volume treatise is written by William H. Rodgers, Professor of Law at the University of Washington School of Law. It addresses a variety of environmental issues, including air and water pollution (vols. 1-2), pesticides and toxic substances (vol. 3), and hazardous wastes and substances (vol. 4) by analyzing relevant federal statutes, regulations and court decisions. The author's treatment, aimed at both law students and practitioners, recognizes the enormity of the task of adequately covering the field. It is a field he describes as one in which «each statement of facts is a multidisciplinary saga, with loose ends trailing off to the limits of the knowledge of a variety of scientific disciplines.» The author also has a clear appreciation of the transient and dynamic nature of environmental law where «a regulation is inseparable from a revision, a statute not far from an amendment.» In addition to addressing the more common sources of environmental law in statutes, regulations and court decisions, the author has sought out various authoritative studies, such as those commissioned by the Environmental Protection Agency and National Academy of Sciences, and reviewed documents and reports which serve as sources of the deliberative process at the agency level. These studies are well represented among the work's extensive footnotes to primary authority. Chapter coverage includes theoretical considerations, common law and the variations, air pollution, water pollution, pesticides, toxic substances, hazardous wastes, hazardous substances (including the Superfund Law). Volume four includes tables of statutes, regulations, and cases, and a subject index. The front matter to volume four also includes a useful table of acronyms. This well organized and thoroughly documented work provides both analysis of the law and guidance on administrative and procedural matters. The annual supplementation is reasonably priced for a four-volume set.

Rodgers, William H. **Environmental Law**. 2d ed. St. Paul: West, 1994. 1 vol. (1158 pp.). No supplementation between editions.
Cost: $92 (2014).
A student textbook in the publisher's Hornbook Series, this is a well-written consolidation of the material appearing in the author's four volume treatise of the same title. Following a brief and slightly hyperbolic introduction which paints a gloomy picture of our environmental future, the author relates the tremendous growth in environmental legislation to the «decline and collapse of ecological systems.» He provides two useful tables illustrating the growth in the number of U.S. Environmental Laws and the Growth in Number of International Environmental Treaties, as well, as a list of the major pieces of environmental legislation passed since 1899. The book's chapters include: an Introduction to Environmental Law, Common Law and the Variations, Air Pollution, Water Pollution, the Federal Insecticide, Fungicide & Rodenticide Act (FIFRA), Toxic Substances, Hazardous Wastes, Hazardous Substances, the Superfund Law, and the National Environmental Policy Act. The Appendices include a guide to Researching Environmental Law on WESTLAW, a table of cases, table of statutes and regulations, and a subject index. The text is well supported by primary authority and case notes. The author's acceptance of the highly controversial global warming theory, however, is unsupported by the latest temperature data. With this one exception, this is one of the best single-volume environmental treatises on the market and a bargain at that. The trick here is finding a treatise that is also a popular student textbook with high volume sales.

Rohan, Patrick J. **Zoning and Land Use Controls.** New York: Matthew Bender & Co., 1978-date. 10 vols. Looseleaf format. Supplemented about three times yearly.
Cost: $3,542 (includes annual subscription); annual renewal: 1995: $955.50 (price frozen since 1992); 1996: $1,002; 1997: $1,002; 1998: $1,005; 1999: $1,050; 2000: $1,050; 2001: $1,124; 2002: $1,203; 2003: $1,347.00; 2004: $1,327; 2005: $1,420; 2006: $1,520; 2007: $1,619; 2008: $1,749; 2009: $1,889; 2010: $1,946; 2011: $2,004; 2012: $2,124; 2013: $2,273; 2014: $2,480; eBook: $3,220; renewal: 2014; $2,480.
A comprehensive guide to both the law and procedure of zoning and land use planning by Patrick J. Rohan, the Dean and Professor of Law, St. John's University School of Law and author of Powell on Real Property (revised edition), as well as a number of legal scholars. This treatise is typical of many Matthew Bender titles in its exhaustive coverage of the subject matter and frequent supplementation. In 57 chapters, the authors discuss zoning in all its manifestations, from exclusionary and inclusionary zoning to landmark, historic zoning and industrial zoning. Additional chapters are devoted to space zoning, builder exactions, adult entertainment zoning, cluster zoning, aesthetic zoning, sign regulation, floodplains, environmental regulation, environmental impact requirements, municipal comprehensive planning, objectives of zoning, subdivision controls, building permits, zoning procedure, land use arbitration, and judicial review. There are extensive forms and documents, both governmental and litigation forms. There are citations to cases and statutes from all jurisdictions. This set combines first-rate scholarship with all the relevant practical aids necessary for the attorney specializing in zoning and planning matters.

Cost Saving Tips: You can bring the high supplementation costs under control by cyclically repurchasing this set every few years rather than maintaining a standing order for the supplements. Update the text by consulting the relevant primary sources and Shepardizing cases and statutes. LexisNexis Matthew Bender raised the initial price of this set by 21% from 2013 to 2014.

Safety Resource Center. Washington, DC: Bloomberg BNA, 2002-date. Internet Search Engine: Folio. Updated monthly.
Cost: base product: $952.00 per year (2014).
A comprehensive Internet guide to environmental and safety issues. Includes information on carcinogens, combustible materials, electrical hazards, environmental conditions, explosive materials, fire protection, hazardous materials, mechanical hazards, materials handling and storage, occupational health, pathogens, protective equipment, toxic substances, workplace management, selected industries and processes, and work areas and surfaces. Includes relevant federal and state laws and regulations, policies, OSHA documents, cases, Review Commission decisions, and interactive forms, and sample policies. Also includes special Enhanced Topics featuring BNA analysis with links to best outside Web resources, and much more. Safety news alerts are updated daily. Beyond raw data, this Internet library collects, integrates, and organizes federal and state OSH laws, regulations, policy documents, and provides comprehensible guidance and analysis.

Shea, Edward E. **Lead Regulation Handbook**. 2nd ed. Rockville, MD, Government Institutes, Inc., 2007. 1 vol. (298 pp.).
Cost: $100; from $56.99 on amazon.com (2014).
The Environmental Protection Agency (EPA) regulates environmental lead through seven principal statutes: the Toxic Substances Control Act (TSCA), the Resource Conservation and Recovery Act (RCRA), the Comprehensive Environmental Response, Compensation and Liability Act (CERCLA), the Clean Air Act (CAA), the Clean Water Act (CWA), the Safe Drinking Water Act (SDWA) and the Emergency Planning and Community Right to Know Act (EPCRA). This comprehensive handbook discusses all aspects of lead regulation and enforcement, including product regulation, liability, workplace regulations, and litigation resulting from related EPA and OSHA statutes, including the Solid Waste Disposal Act, Consumer Product Safety Act, and Hazardous Materials Transportation Act. The author also discusses Department of Housing and Urban Development regulations, new national emission standards for primary and secondary smelting, new water quality management and planning regulations and regulations at the state level. Edward E. Shea is head of environmental practice of Windels Marx Lane & Mittendorf, LLP, a law firm with offices in the City of New York and in New Brunswick, New Jersey.

Stever, Donald W. **Law of Chemical Regulation and Hazardous Waste**. St. Paul, MN: Thomson Reuters West, 1986-date. 4 vols. Annual supplementation.
Cost: $2,957; ProView eBook: $2,869; supplementation: 1996: $412; 1997: $435; 1998: $461; 1999: $498; 2000: $528; 2001: $627; 2002: $666; 2003: $766.50; 2004: $858; 2005: $918; 2006: $1,047; 2007: $777.50; 2008: $1,297,50; 2009: $1,926; 2010: $1,575; 2011: $1,716; 2012: $1,990; 2013: $2,169; **Monthly Assured Print Price (APP):** $219/$2,628.
This is a comprehensive examination of the law governing the chemical industry and the disposal of hazardous waste. It also examines the regulatory programs that govern the chemical industry and those exposed to its products. While the author's primary aim is to provide the kind of regulatory guidance which will help industry, and its legal counsel, avoid costly litigation, reduce liability risks, and plan defense strategies, this set can also be used by plaintiff's and environmental organizations to understand industry's responsibilities under the law. Coverage also extends to pesticides, chemicals in consumer products, emergency and remedial response to chemical hazard situations, toxic air emissions, wastewater effluents, chemicals in food, and worker exposure to chemicals. Donald W. Stever is a partner in the New York firm of Dewey and Ballantine and has practiced environmental health and safety law for twenty years. Between 1979 and 1982, he headed the Pollution Control and the Environmental Defense Sections in the U.S. Dept. of Justice.

Susskind, Lawrence, Paul F. Levy, and Jennifer Thomas-Larmer. **Negotiating Environmental Agreements: How to Avoid Escalating Confrontation, Needless Costs, and Unnecessary Litigation**. Washington, DC: Island Press, 2000. 1 vol. (337 pp.). No supplementation.
Cost: $45; from $0.17 on amazon.com; kindle: $35.99 (2014).

Produced in conjunction with the MIT-Harvard Public Disputes Program, this volume outlines a variety of strategies and techniques to aid the various parties involved in environmental disputes in arriving at satisfactory and cost-effective agreements through negotiation. While more than 90 percent of all environmental disputes are settled before going to court, many of these agreements are achieved only after costly and bitter struggles between the various interests involved. The authors' proposals are based on a theory of mutual gains negotiation in which the parties clarify their interests and those of other stakeholders. In addition to a complete explanation of mutual gains negotiation, the authors present five simulations designed to test the understanding of the theory and four real-life examples of settlements achieved through the use of negotiation. The volume also includes a bibliography and a listing of mediation and facilitation organizations.

Tarlock, A. Daniel. **Law of Water Rights and Resources**. St. Paul, MN: Thomson Reuters West (Clark Boardman Callaghan), 1988-date. 1 vol. Looseleaf format or ProView eBook. Annual replacement volume.
Cost: 2013 ed.: $798; ProView eBook: $798; supplementation: 2002: $208; 2003: $216; 2004: $242; 2005: $257; 2006: $298; 2007: $332; 2008: $370; 2009: $413.50; 2010: $484; 2011: $672; 2012: $600; **Monthly Assured Print Price (APP):** $87/$1044.
The administration and regulation of water rights as well as the allocation and distribution of water is a major source of concern throughout the United States, but particularly in the Western states where the pressures of development and requirements of irrigation (90% of current usage) press upon limited supplies. This volume in the publisher's Environmental Law Series addresses a variety of environmental and regulatory issues to ensure compliance with federal, state, and local laws and regulations. The volume's coverage includes an overview of water law, the hydrologic cycle, the common law of riparian rights, the law of groundwater allocation, the prior appropriation doctrine, appropriation of groundwater, adjudication of water rights, public water use rights, federal allocation and regulation of water, interstate allocation, and international water allocation. A. Daniel Tarlock is Distinguished Professor of Law and Director of the Program in Environmental and Energy Law at the Chicago-Kent School of Law and an internationally recognized expert in environmental law and the law of land and water use.

Weinberg, Philip. And Kevin A. Reilly. **Understanding Environmental Law**. 3d ed. Newark, NJ: LexisNexis Matthew Bender, 2013. 1 vol. (520 pp.). Paperbound.
Cost: $45; eBook: $36; from $34.82 on amazon.com; kindle ed.: $20.99 (2014).
The field of environmental law is, in reality, an outgrowth of the old English common law, primarily tort and property law and its offshoots. The field has expanded considerably in recent years with the passage of significant pieces of national legislation, and their accompanying regulations pursuant thereto. The authors begin their discussion with a consideration of the administrative, judicial and constitutional aspects of environmental law, the various policy issues involved in the determination and resolution of environmental issues, and the traditional common law remedies which can be brought to bear on them. Substantial attention is given to various federal laws that govern environmental quality, including the National Environmental Policy Act (NEPA), the Clean Air Act, the various federal water pollution statutes, including the Clean Water Act, solid and hazardous wastes, toxic substances, noise, fish and wildlife, land use, energy production and mineral extraction, and international aspects of environmental protection. They conclude with a review of numerous innovations and trends in the field, including the "XL" program designed to encourage industry strategies that exceed the results of government command and control regulatory programs. They also look at community-based projects, self-policing, and resource conservation challenges. Intended as an introductory law school text, this book can also serve as a useful review for practitioners and others interested in the fundamental aspects of environmental law. The authors have endeavored to keep the scientific content at a basic level, in keeping with the authors' admittedly limited scientific expertise. Philip Weinberg, currently an adjunct professor of law at Columbia and Pace Schools of Law, has taught environmental law for more than four decades. Kevin Reilly is an adjunct professor of law at St. John's University School of Law and served as a senior staff attorney for the New York Supreme Court's Appellate Division, First Department for several decades where he was responsible for most environmental and land use appeals.

Williams, Norman, Jr. and John Taylor. **American Land Planning Law: Land Use and the Police Power.** St. Paul, MN: Thomson Reuters West (Clark Boardman Callaghan), 1985-date. 8 vols. Annual pocket supplements.
Cost: $1,058; supplementation: 1993: $175; 1994: $210; 1995: $250; 1996: $284; 1997: $298; 1998: $316; 1999: $341; 2000: $369; 2001: $429; 2002: $502; 2003: $627; 2004: $280; 2005: $303; 2006: $345; 2007: $384; 2008: $427.50; 2009: $480; 2010: $528; 2011: $576.50; 2012: $628; 2013: $681; **Monthly Assured Print Price (APP):** $75/$900.
A comprehensive examination of land use planning and the fundamental changes which have enveloped the field over the past thirty years. The authors closely analyze the relationship between governmental authority and private development as it has manifest itself in the resolution of environmental concerns, exclusionary zoning practices. The authors discuss and analyze over 15,000 cases in all fifty states. The contents encompass such topics as land use planning and controls, comprehensive plans, residential zoning, conflicts between residential and nonresidential land use, nonconforming uses, administrative aspects of zoning, variances, special permits, techniques to implement community design, preservation of open space, state and regional land use controls, and future trends. Volume six contains appendices, illustrations, Tables of Cases and Index. One of the upshots of Thomson Legal Publishing's recent acquisitions is that the West is now the publisher of three multi-volume treatises in the field of zoning and planning law--treatises formerly published independently by Lawyers Cooperative, Clark Boardman, and Callaghan and Company. All three have their strengths. Williams leans more heavily toward the planning side of the field, while Rathkopf and Anderson cover zoning law with greater specificity. Like the other two, Williams features extensive citations to both case and statutory law, and zoning ordinances.

Witkin, James B., ed. **Environmental Aspects of Real Estate and Commercial Transactions: From Brownfields to Green Buildings**. 4th ed. Chicago: American Bar Association, 2011. 1 vol. (793 pp.). Paperbound.
Cost: $199.85; from $185.07 on amazon.com (2014).
This volume explores the intersection of real property and environmental law and the effect of environmental law on real estate and commercial transactions. It aims to bridge the gap between real estate law practitioners and those who practice in the field of environmental law. The subject matter of this fourth edition reflects the growth of environmentally impacted properties, the changes that have taken place on such related issues as environmental insurance, institutional controls, brownfields, and concerns over specific substances like asbestos, lead paint and mold. The book's five parts address: (1) basic issues of liability, both statutory and common law; (2) environmental due diligence, including the environmental audit process, the role of environmental consultants, and the science behind consultants' reports; (3) environmental matters in the transactional and business context, including such matters as how deals are structured and documented to allocate environmental risk, landlord-tenant environmental issues, tax issues related to cleanups, environmental disclosures under the securities laws, and environmentally-related bankruptcy issues; (4) some of the most common environmental problems affecting developed properties, including underground storage tanks, asbestos, lead-based paints, indoor air pollution, and mold; and (5) environmental problems that arise in the context of the land development process, including wetlands, endangered species, stormwater issues, and the constitutional "takings" issues associated with environmental laws. The concluding chapters examine the subjects of environmental justice, conservation easements, issues relative to the remediation and development of former military bases, and the expanding area of "smart growth." Thirty-seven experts in environmental and real estate law were involved in the preparation of the individual chapters in this book. Each chapter is thoroughly sourced to provide the user with other relevant sources of information. The volume also includes a table of cases and subject index. This book should be on the desk of every environmental practitioner involved with real estate or commercial transactions and every real estate practitioner whose work is impacted by environmental issues. James B. Witkin is chair of the Environmental Practice Group of Linowes and Blocher LLP in Bethesda, MD and a graduate of Harvard Law School.

Additional titles in the field of Environmental Law are available from the following publishers: American Enterprise Institute, Matthew Bender, Brookings Institution, Business Legal Reports, Center for Policy Alternatives, Environmental Design Research Center, Federal Bar Association, Garland Publishing Co., Government Institutes, Greenwood Publishing Group, Lewis Publications, LexisNexis, National Conference of State Legislatures, National School Boards Association, Neal-Schuman, Oceana Publications, Practising Law Institute, Rand Corporation, Rocky Mountain Mineral Law Foundation, Thomson Reuters West, West Academic. See Appendix B for addresses and telephone numbers.

Equity Jurisprudence

Pomeroy, John Norton. **Pomeroy on Equity Jurisprudence.** 5th ed. edited by Spencer W. Symons. Rochester, NY: Lawyers Cooperative Publishing Co., 1941. 5 vols. ISBN: 1-886363-05-6. Reprinted, 1995 by Law Book Exchange, Ltd.
Cost: $650 (2014)
Although this work is more than fifty-five years old, it remains the definitive treatise on the subject of equity jurisprudence. Spencer W. Symons, editor of this fifth edition, has preserved the exact text of this classic work, while providing updated commentary in brackets. According to a review in the Virginia Law Review: «Until the time that someone writes a treatise on equity that is all embracing--and no one has done that yet--there will be a real need for the Pomeroy treatise . . . As a book of reference, indeed, it will outrank the Restatements for their style is such that often has to read several times before he knows what is really said and what is avoided. The present book, on the contrary, is couched in the English of our fathers.»

The substantive portion of Pomeroy's work is contained in four volumes and organized into four parts: (1) the Nature and Extent of Equity Jurisprudence, (2) the Maxims and General Principles of Equity Jurisprudence, and the Events Which Are Occasions of Equitable Primary or Remedial Rights, (3) the Equitable Estates, Interests, and Primary Rights Recognized and Protected by the Equity Jurisprudence, and (4) the Remedies and Remedial Rights Which Are Conferred by the Equity Jurisprudence. Volume five contains a Table of Cases, Table of Statutes Cited, Table of Texts, Legal Treatises, Etc., Quoted and Cited, a Table of Annotations Cited, and an Index. This reprinted edition, printed on acid-free paper, again makes available this classic work which, heretofore, was only available on the used book market.

Story, Joseph. **Commentaries on Equity Jurisprudence**. 13th ed. Boston: Little, Brown & Co., 1886. 2 vols. Reprint by William S. Hein & Co., 2006.
Cost: $195 (2014).
A classic exposition of equity jurisprudence by one America's leading 19th century legal scholars. Joseph Story served in Congress, as Speaker of the Massachusetts House of Representatives, and Justice of the Massachusetts Supreme Judicial Court. A founder of Harvard Law School, he wrote and published twelve volumes of commentaries on American law between 1835 and 1845. The thirteenth edition preserves the text and footnotes of the last edition completed by Story himself (4th, 1846). In it, he expounds on the sources and limits of equity jurisprudence and the leading doctrines which guide courts of equity in the exercise of their jurisdiction. Among the legal doctrines addressed are mistake, actual or positive fraud, legacies, confusion of boundaries, dower, marshalling of securities, partition, partnership, matters of rent, peculiar remedies in equity, specific performance, compensation and damages, wills and testaments, implied trusts, and peculiar defenses and proofs in equity.

Additional titles in the field of Equity Jurisprudence are available from the following publishers: Ayer Co. Publications, Foundation Press, Gaunt, William S. Hein & Co., Lawbook Exchange, LexisNexis, Thomson Reuters West. See Appendix B for addresses and telephone numbers.

Evidence

Cohen, Adam E. and David J. Lender. **Electronic Discovery: Law and Practice**. 2d ed. New York: Wolters Kluwer Law & Business, 2011-date. 1 vol. (various pagings). Looseleaf format. Annual supplementation.
Cost: $475; supplementation: 2012: $272; 2013: $289; 1st ed.: 2004: $125; 2005: $128; 2006: $170; 2007: $181; 2008: $194; 2009: $208; 2010: $222; 2011: new edition.
The discovery process has undergone a dramatic transformation in the age of electronic information storage and retrieval, and of the Internet. Most cases now involve some aspect of the discovery of electronic information. Indeed, as early as 1970, the Federal Rules of Civil Procedure, specifically Rule 34(a), contemplated their application to electronic data. Traditional discovery requests, whether in the form of documents, interrogatories or depositions, have all been adapted to this new electronic environment. And those involved in the litigation process must necessarily have a working knowledge of the technical side of information storage and retrieval, particularly since information thought deleted may actually be preserved on one's hard drive. This volume addresses both the legal and technical aspects of electronic discovery and the issues related to the creation, storage and retrieval of electronic information by potential litigants. The authors address such topics as the mechanisms for electronic discovery, spoliation, document retention policies and their application to electronic information, shifting the costs of electronic discovery, evidentiary issues, the attorney-client privilege and email, computerized litigation support systems and the work product doctrine, electronic discovery technology, the inspection of hard discs in civil litigation, privacy concerns, and government documents. The authors, both partners in the litigation department of the New York office of Weil, Gotshal and Manges LLP, bring to this subject a far-reaching understanding of the issues involved in electronic discovery. Adam Cohen specializes in intellectual property and commercial matters for clients in the technology, media, and entertainment industries. David J. Lender is a highly successful litigator, specializing in complex commercial litigation, with a special emphasis on patent and intellectual property law. This volume includes a number of valuable appendices, including white papers on electronic discovery best practices, and federal and state court rules regarding electronic discovery. It also includes extensive references to relevant court decisions. statutes, and regulations.

Costanzo, Mark; Daniel Krauss, and Kathy Pezdek, eds. **Expert Psychological Testimony for the Courts**. Mahwah, NJ: Lawrence Erlbaum Associates, Publishers, 2007. 1 vol. (321 pp.). Paperbound.
Cost: $51.95; from $20.78 on amazon.com (2014).
Recent decades have witnessed a dramatic rise in the use of psychological testimony in the courtroom, expanding from the use of clinical psychological testimony to evaluate the defendants' sanity and competency to stand to the use of testimony from cognitive, developmental, and social psychologists. This which, which draws on the latest scholarly findings in the field, examines use of expert testimony generally, the psychological aspects of forensic identification evidence, and expert testimony on such matters as interrogations and confessions, eyewitness memory, sexual harassment cases, battered women, risk and future dangerousness, risk factors, and child custody evaluations. The editors and chapter authors have wide-ranging experience as scholars and expert witnesses in court proceedings. A useful guide for attorneys who regularly make use of expert psychological testimony.

Cotchett, Joseph W. **Federal Courtroom Evidence**. 5th ed. Charlottesville, VA: LexisNexis, 2003-date. 1 vol. w/CD-ROM. Also on eBook.
Cost: $261 (print or eBook); supplementation: 2004: $81; 2005: $84; 2006: $90; 2007: $95; 2008: $106; 2009: $122; 2010: $128; 2011: $143; 2012: $153; 2013: $157; 4th ed.: 2000: $55; 2001: $65; 2002: $72; 2003: $75;
This book is designed to serve as a ready reference in the courtroom. A one-page index takes the user directly to the major topics, relevant rules, objections, and supporting case law. The book's 33 chapters are grouped into the following parts: general provisions, judicial notes, presumptions in civil actions and proceedings, relevancy and its limits, privileges, witnesses, opinions and expert testimony, hearsay, authentication and identification, content of writings, recordings and photographs, miscellaneous rules, and procedure. The author is a trial lawyer with the California firm of Cotchett, Pitre & Simon and an author of numerous articles on the trial of cases.

Easton, Stephen D. **Attacking Adverse Experts**. Chicago: American Bar Association, 2008. 1 vol. (770 pp.). Paperbound.
Cost: $165 ($135 to members) (2014).
This is a systematic guide to attacking the credibility of adverse witnesses in civil cases. In the author's view, such witnesses are often not only wrong, and unworthy of respect, but "potentially very dangerous in a system designed to be a search for the truth." His strong views are the product of 15 years of full time practice as a trial attorney and a decade of teaching, researching and writing about the law, with a scholarly focus on expert witnesses. At heart is the tendency of expert witnesses to shape their testimony to please the attorneys who retain them. The 22 chapters in this volume provide a methodology for gathering relevant information, deposing the adverse expert, moving to disqualify the adverse expert, launching he attack, crossing the adverse expert, and finishing the job. In addition to citations to relevant primary and secondary authorities, the text also features checklists, cautions, sample cross-examination questions and answers. Appendices, contained on a companion CD-ROM, include checklists and outlines, charts (of the law of multiple jurisdictions), and outlines (of the law for attorneys in specified jurisdictions). The author is a trial attorney with wide-ranging experience in expert-dominated cases, a law professor, and former U.S. Attorney for the District of North Dakota. In 2006, he received the Richard S. Jacobson Award for excellence

in teaching trial advocacy from the Pound Civil Justice Institute.

Evidence Law Treatise Library on LoisLawConnect. New York: Wolters Kluwer Law & Busness.
Cost: $540.00 per year (solo practitioner) (2014).
This treatise library provides coverage of all federal and state evidence rules, with expert analysis and links to related cases on such issues as admissibility, relevancy, privileges, witnesses, hearsay, scientific evidence and expert testimony, and more. Titles include **Wigmore on Evidence, Scientific Evidence and Experts Handbook, Destruction of Evidence Handbook, Evidence: Practice Under the Rules,** and relevant forms and checklists. A cost-effective alternative to buying the titles in print format.

Faigman, David L., David H. Kaye, Michael J. Saks, and Joseph Sanders. **Modern Scientific Evidence: The Law and Science of Expert Testimony**. Continues 2d ed. St. Paul, MN: Thomson Reuters West, 2005-date. 5 vols. Paperbound. Annual replacement editions (2005-date) or ProView eBook.
Cost: 2013-2014 Edition: $390; 2008-2009 ed.: $300; 2010-2011: $300; 2011-2012 Edition: $330; 2012-2013 Edition: $360; supplementation to 2d ed.: 2002: $32.50; 2003: $32.50; 2004: $32.50; 1st edition: 1998: $18.00; 1999: $65.00; 2000; $65.00; 2001: new edition; **Monthly Assured Print Price** (APP): $33/$396.
Evaluating the admissibility of scientific expert testimony evidence in the courtroom is a task which has increasingly arrested the attention of judges in U.S. courts. Ruling in *Daubert v. Merrell Dow Pharmaceuticals*, the Supreme Court held that, under the Federal Rules of Evidence, trial court judges must act as gatekeepers and evaluate the validity of the basis for proffered scientific expertise before permitting experts to testify. While *Daubert* does not expect judges to become trained scientists in order to make admissibility decisions, it does expect them to become sophisticated consumers of science. The authors of this treatise address a number of scientific issues likely to be encountered in the modern courtroom, including insanity and diminished capacity, the battered woman and battered child syndromes, eyewitness identification, hypnosis, repressed memories, polygraph tests, admissibility of DNA evidence and profiling, parentage testing, forensic identification, toxicology, epidemiology, electromagnetic fields, tobacco, and drug testing. The book opens with several valuable chapters which examine the legal standards for the admissibility of scientific evidence, the scientific method, statistical proof, and multiple regression. The entire discussion is accompanied by extensive references to both the scientific and legal literature, as well as to illustrative appellate cases. Each chapter is divided into two sections: a discussion by the core authors of the legal issues related to that scientific topic, and a discussion of the current state of the science in that area by a nationally known expert. The appendices include an extensive glossary, table of cases, and index. A highly recommended resource for the judge or attorney grappling with scientific issues in the courtroom. Once supplemented with annual pocket parts, the volumes are now revised annually at considerably higher cost..

Federal Judicial Center. **Reference Manual on Scientific Evidence**. 3d ed. St. Paul: West, 2012. 1 vol. (1,034 pp.) Annual. Paperbound.
Cost: $79.95 (2014).
A rise in the introduction of scientific evidence in the nation's courts has raised a number of evidentiary issues which must be resolved by judges who often lack the technical expertise to make proper determinations regarding the introduction of such evidence. This volume is designed to assist members of the bench in «implementing effective management of expert evidence involving scientific issues.» Such experts most commonly include physicians, economists, engineers, but also include a variety of scientific and technical experts. This volume contains twelve chapters discussing such topics as the management of expert evidence, the admissibility of expert testimony, and including reference guides on epidemiology, toxicology, survey research, medical testimony, forensic DNA evidence, statistics, multiple regression, and the estimation of economic losses in damages awards. A fascinating essay entitled "How Science Works," by physicist David Goodstein, provides an insightful overview of the role of science and the scientific method. An indispensable guide to the jurist hearing technical cases.

Forensic Sciences. Edited by Cyril H. Wecht. New York: Matthew Bender & Co., 1981-date. 5 vols. Looseleaf format and eBook.
Cost: $1,856; supplementation: 2003: $686; 2004: $720; 2005: $770; 2006: $824; 2007: $890; 2008: $961; 2009: $1,038; 2010: $1,090; 2011: $1,123; 2012: $1,168; 2013: $1,250; 2014: $1,364; eBook: $1,687; renewal: 2014: $1,364.
This five-volume resource provides scholarly and expert discussion of a variety of scientific and medical issues relevant to both criminal and civil litigation and the use of expert testimony in the courtroom. Among the topics included are expert testimony and scientific evidence—admissibility, scope, impeachment, hypothetical questions, privilege; forensic pathology; forensic anthropology and odontology, forensic engineering, forensic toxicology and pharmacology, antemortem and postmortem alcohol determinations, firearm identification, investigation of explosions, AIDS: legal and medical considerations, DNA typing—criminal and civil applications, illustrative testimony, forensic psychiatry and psychology, computer imaging, and automobile accident investigation. The set also includes an index of experts. The editor and co-author is Coroner of Allegheny County, PA and a leading medical-legal author, consultant, and lecturer. Includes contributions by dozens of scientific and medical experts.

Giannelli, Paul C. and Edward J. Imwinkelried. **Scientific Evidence**. 5th ed. New Providence, NJ: LexisNexis, 2012-date. 2 vols. Annual supplementation.
Also available on eBook.
Cost: $350; supplementation: 2013: $105; 4th ed.: 2008: $76; 2009: $88; 2010: $91; 2011: $95; 2012: $100; 3d ed.: 2000: 0; 2001: $60; 2002: $67; 2003: $63; 2004: $66; 2005: $70; 2006: $74; 2007: new edition.
A scholarly and highly regarded exposition of the use of scientific evidence in the courtroom. This revised edition reflects dramatic advances in technology which have impacted the procedures for

obtaining, measuring and interpreting physical evidence. It also reflects new standards for the admission of scientific evidence as articulated by the Supreme Court in *Daubert v. Merrell Dow Pharmaceuticals*. The authors are leading authorities on matters of evidence generally, and scientific evidence in particular. The chapters address such topics as constitutional limitations on obtaining evidence for scientific analysis, securing expert assistance, laboratory reports, chain of custody, polygraph and deception tests, voice identification, neutron activation analysis, hypnosis, statistical evidence, fingerprints, DNA genetic markers, pathology, drug identification, trace evidence, arson, measurement of speed, and more. The text is accompanied by extensive citations to statutes and case law. Paul Giannelli is Weatherhead Professor of Law at Case Western Reserve University. Edward J. Imwinkelried is Professor of Law and Director of Trial Advocacy at the University of California at Davis.

Gidiere, P. Stephan, III. **The Federal Information Manual: How the Government Collects, Manages, and Discloses Information under FOIA and Other Statutes**. 2d ed. Chicago: American Bar Association, 2013. 1 vol. (446 pp.).
Cost: $99.95 ($84.95 to ABA members); $54.82 on amazon.com. (2014)
The Freedom of Information Act (FOIA), enacted on July 4, 1966,and amended in 2002 (5 U.S.C. §552), was designed to address the growth of government secrecy, and provide the public greater access to executive branch records.
Federal information policy is governed by an often confusing melange of statutes, regulations, common law, executive orders and court decisions, of which the Freedom of Information Act (FOIA) is the most significant. This volume provides an invaluable examination of federal information gathering, information policy, and disclosure. Chapters address federal information disputes, agency collection of information, agency records management, classified information, access to federal records, electronic records and federal public websites, the elements of a successful FOIA request, reasons for the withholding of agency records, and homeland security information. A glossaries of abbreviations and federal information statutes are included. A partner with the firm of Balch & Bingham LLP and a member of the firm's Environmental and Natural Resources Section, author Stephen Gidiere's practice encompasses a variety of environmental, resources, energy, and administrative law matters, with a focus on government information law. His writings have addressed the intersection of national security and federal information law and policy. Mr. Gidiere is also Executive Editor of the ABA's quarterly journal Natural Resources & Environment.

Golan, Taj. **Laws of Men and Laws of Nature**: **The History of Scientific Expert Testimony in England and America**. Cambridge, MA: Harvard University Press, 2004. 1 vol. (336 pp.). Softbound.
Cost: $29.50; from $22.61 on amazon.com (2014).
Expert witnesses have been a feature of courtroom trials since the late 18th century. The use of expert testimony increased steadily throughout the 19th and 20th centuries and has become a lucrative profession in its own right. In 1993, the U.S. Supreme Court raised the issue of expert testimony in the case of Daubert v. Merrell Dow Pharmaceuticals, 509 U.S. 579 (1993), in which the court held that federal trial judges are the "gatekeepers" of scientific evidence and, therefore, must evaluate proffered expert witnesses to determine whether their testimony is both "relevant" and "reliable," a two-pronged test of admissibility. This volume views expert witnesses from an historical perspective, asking the question of whether they are spokesmen for objective science or merely partisans in courtroom battles. Using stories taken from real-life trials, the author views the topic from a scholarly perspective which will help provide judges, lawyers, and other participants the ability to distinguish between good science and bad science in the courtroom. Tal Golan is Associate Professor of History of Science at the University of California, San Diego

Graham, Michael H. **Federal Rules of Evidence in a Nutshell.** 8th ed. St. Paul: West, 2011. 1 vol. (800 pp.). Available from West Academic.
Cost: $41; from $23 on amazon.com; kindle ed.: $20.84 (2014).
Professor Graham, Professor of Law at the University of Miami School of Law, authored this volume in the West Nutshell Series with the needs of the law student in mind. Contains the rules and brief analysis, but few case citations. An excellent source for a succinct review of the Federal Rules. Organized according to the XI Articles of the Federal Rules of Evidence.

Graham, Michael H. **Handbook of Federal Evidence.** 7th ed. St. Paul: Thomson Reuters West, 2011-date. 8 vols. Annual supplementation. West's Handbook Series.
Cost: $803; supplementation: 2012: 0; 2013: $184; 6th ed.: 2006: $67; 2007: $69; 2008: $110; 2009: $135; 2010: $154.50; 5th ed.: 2001: $58.50; 2002: $70; 2003: $79.75; 2004: $62; 2005: 0; 2006: new edition; 4th edition: 1997: $40; 1998: $42.50; 1999: $46; **Monthly Assured Print Price (APP):** $38/$456.
This is the fourth edition of a work first authored by Professor Graham of the University of Miami School of Law in 1981. Its stated aim is to provide the «trial attorney and presiding judge «a clear statement of what the law of evidence is in a convenient to use one-volume format.» It is based upon an analysis of every case in reported federal decisions to the Federal Rules of Evidence. The Commentary following each rule is based upon the interpretive authority emerging from this analysis. The author also provides special attention in the text, footnotes and citations to those areas which remain controversial. The substantive part of the text is divided into the eleven articles under which the Rules have been organized, including general provisions, judicial notice, burdens of proof and presumptions in civil and criminal actions and proceedings, relevancy and its limits, privileges, witnesses, opinions and expert testimony, hearsay, authentication and identification, contents of writings and photographs, and miscellaneous rules. Appendices include the Federal Rules of Evidence, table of statutes, table of rules and standards, table of cases, and a subject index.

Imwinkelried, Edward J., Paul C. Giannelli, Francis A. Gilligan, Frederic I. Lederer. **Courtroom Criminal Evidence**. 5th ed. Charlottesville, VA: LexisNexis, 2011-date. 2 vols. Annual supplementation. Also on eBook.
Cost: $230 (print or eBook); supplementation: 2011: $45; 2012: $48; 2013: $51; 4th ed,: 2006: $72; 2007: $78; 2008: $42; 2009:

$49; 2010: $57; 2d ed.: 1994: $30; 1995: $40; 1996: $47.50; 1997: $52.50; 1998: 3d edition; 1999: $40; 2000: $62; 2001: $73; 2002: $74; 2003: $77; 2004: $81; 2005: $86.

Operating from the basic premise that an understanding of the rules of evidence is second in importance only to a knowledge of procedure for the trial attorney, the authors of this textbook have attempted to write a work designed for courtroom use by the trial attorney. The authors contrast this text to such scholarly texts as those written by Wigmore, Weinstein, Wright and Graham, LaFave, and Whitebread intended for use in preparation of formal legal documents such as briefs and memoranda. Consequently, the authors have attempted to limit the number of citations in favor of substantive text which can provide guidance to the attorney in an courtroom environment. This volume provides an up-to-date overview of the current status of the law of evidence in criminal trials, encompassing the common law, the Federal Rules of Evidence, federal statutes, and exclusionary rules enunciated by the U.S. Supreme Court. Topics covered include scientific evidence (including DNA), character and habit evidence, hearsay exceptions, as well as the exclusionary rule. Chapters cover an introductory overview of the origins of the law of evidence, trial procedures, competency of witnesses, relevance, authentication, real evidence, credibility, uncharged misconduct, expert and lay opinion testimony, best evidence rule, privileges for confidential relations, search or seizure, probable cause and warrants, warrantless searches, voluntariness, the Miranda doctrine, right to counsel, suppression of confessions, eyewitness identification, burdens of production and proof, judicial notice, and stipulations. Both in substance and style, this in an excellent companion to the scholarly works on evidence and is highly recommended to the criminal trial attorney.

Imwinkelried, Edward J. and Daniel D. Blinka. **Criminal Evidentiary Foundations**. Charlottesville, VA: LexisNexis, 2007-date. 1 vol. (717 pp.). Annual supplementation. Print or eBook.

Cost: $137 (print or eBook); supplementation: 2008-2010: 0; 2011: $52; 2012: $55; 2013: $59; 2014: $64; 1st ed.: 1997: $20; 1999: $30; 2000: $35; 2001: $44; 2002: $44; 2003: 0; 2004: $48; 2005: $51; 2006: $54; 2007: new edition.

Laying the groundwork for the introduction of evidence in criminal trials requires skill and preparation. This practitioner's handbook provides specific guidance to criminal litigators who wish to introduce and control the introduction of evidence. The authors provide explanations for the phrasing of questions on direct and cross-examination and numerous sample questions adapted for criminal trials. The book chapters examine such topics as the competency of witnesses, authentication, Rule 403 and legal relevance limitations on credible evidence, legal relevance limitations on evidence that is relevant to the historical merits of the case, privileges and similar doctrines, the best evidence rule, opinion evidence, the hearsay rule, its exemptions, and its exceptions, substitutes for evidence, and motion to suppress evidence. Edward Imwinkelried, Professor of Law at the University of California at Davis, is one of the nation's leading authorities on the subjects of evidence and criminal law. Daniel Blinka, Associate Professor of Law at Marquette University School of Law, former District Attorney, and co-author of Pretrial Motions in Criminal Prosecutions.

Imwinkelried, Edward J. **Evidentiary Foundations**. 8th ed. Charlottesville, VA: LexisNexis, 2011. 1 vol. Softbound. No supplementation between editions.

Cost: $131 (2014).

A practical, annotated guide to the process of laying foundations for the introduction of evidence. The text provides a brief description of the pertinent Federal Rules of Evidence and the most recent leading cases construing the Rules. The author covers all the major evidentiary doctrines and explains how to transform abstract doctrines into specific lines of questioning. He also explains how questions should be phrased during direct and cross-examination and supplies several hundred sample foundational questions. An excellent introduction to the theory and practice of laying foundations for the introduction of evidence as part of a broader introduction to trial technique. The author is the Edward L. Barrett, Jr. Professor of Law at the University of California, Davis, and a national authority on evidence matters. He has authored numerous texts on various aspects of evidence.

Imwinkelried, Edward J. and Norman M. Garland. **Exculpatory Evidence: The Accused's Constitutional Right to Introduce Favorable Evidence**. 3d ed. Charlottesville, VA: LexisNexis, 2004-date. 1 vol. (572 pp.). Annual pocket supplement. Print or eBook.

Cost: $194; supplementation: 2005: $84.00; 2006: $88; 2007: $92; 2008: $113; 2009: $130; 2010: $134; 2011: $138; 2012: $148; 2013: $153; 2d ed.: 1997: $35.00; 1998: $40.00; 1999: $45.00; 2000: $60.00; 2001: $71.00; 2002: $75.00; 2003: $79.00.

The American criminal justice system provides individual defendants the right to present evidence supporting their theory of a case, a right raised to constitutional status by the U.S., Supreme Court in the case of Washington v. Texas, 388 U.S. 14 (1967). Although several law review articles have examined this development in the case law, this is the first comprehensive, book-length study of the constitutional right to present exculpatory evidence in criminal proceedings. Edward J. Imwinkelried, Professor of Law at the University of California at Davis, is one of the most prolific scholars in the field, having authored at least a dozen books and numerous law review articles on various aspects of evidence. His co-author is Professor of Law at Southwestern University Law School. This volume includes numerous citations to case and statutory law, as well as a bibliography of related books and articles on the subject.

Imwinkelried, Edward J. and David A. Schlueter. **Federal Evidence Tactics**. New York: Matthew Bender & Co., 1997-date. 1 vol. Annual supplementation anticipated. Also an eBook.

Cost: $541 (print or eBook); supplementation: 1997: new edition; 1998: 0; 1999: $101; 2000: $110; 2001: $118; 2002: $127; 2003: $134; 2004: $137; 2005: $147; 2006: $158; 2007: $171; 2008: $186; 2009: $201; 2010: $228; 2011: $232; 2012: $290; 2013: $298; CD-ROM: $596; renewal: 1999: $99; 2000: $105; 2001: $112; 2002: $120; 2003: $126; 2004: $137; 2005: $147; 2006: $158; 2007: $171; 2008: $186; 2009: $201; 2010: $211; 2011: $228; 2012: $244; 2013: $262; 2014: $296; eBook: $541; 2014: $298.

This is less an examination of the rules of evidence than a guide to the tactical strategies which can be employed by the litigator in evidentiary matters. The authors' introductory chapters discuss the importance of tactics in trial advocacy, the proponent's threshold tactical decision to choose a particular item of evidence to proffer at trial, and the opponent's threshold tactical decision whether to object to an item of evidence proffered by the proponent. Additional chapters examine the eleven articles of the Federal Rules of Evidence, including General Provisions, Judicial Notice, Presumptions in Civil Actions and Proceedings, Relevancy and Its Limits, Privileges, Witnesses, Opinions and Expert Testimony, Hearsay, Authentication and Identification, Contents of Writings, Recordings, and Photographs, and Miscellaneous Rules. Edward Imwinkelried, Director of Trial Advocacy of the University of California, Davis Law School, is one of the nation's foremost authorities on the law of evidence and the author of more than 20 books. David Schlueter, Professor of Law at St. Mary's University, is the author of eight books and numerous law review articles on evidence and criminal procedure.

Jones, Burr W. **Jones on Evidence, Criminal and Civil.** 7th ed. by Clifford S. Fishman. St. Paul, MN: West (Lawyers Cooperative Publishing Co.), 1992-date. 6 vols. Annual pocket parts.
Cost: $1,467; supplementation to vols. 1-3: 1994: $20; 1995: $25; 1996: $34; 1997: $45; 1998: $125; 1999: $100; 2000: $218; 2001: $160; 2002: $187.50; 2003: $552.75; 2004: $430.50; 2005: $385; 2006: $439.50; 2007; $534; 2008: $611; 2009: $716.50; 2010: $1,497; 2011: $853; 2012: $997; 2013: $979; **Monthly Assured Print Price (APP):** $99/$1,188.
Written as a practitioner's tool, this five-volume treatise does not attempt to include the exhaustive citations to authority one finds in works like **Wigmore** or **Weinstein**. Now in its seventh edition, this treatise was originally published in 1896 by Burr W. Jones, Professor of Law at the University of Wisconsin College of Law. This edition, by Professor Clifford S. Fishman, reflects a number of significant developments in the law of evidence including the simplification, and codification of the exclusionary rules, the adoption of the Uniform Rules of Evidence, and the adoption of the Federal Rules of Evidence. One of the aims of this edition is to incorporate into the body of the text references to these codifications for comparative purposes and in order to highlight the differences between state and federal evidence procedures. The chapters encompass the nature and definition of evidence, judicial notice, presumptions and inferences, relevancy, burden of proof, unconstitutionally obtained evidence, best and secondary evidence, hearsay and its exceptions, admissions and confessions, expert and opinion testimony, demonstrative evidence, extrinsic evidence, documentary evidence, depositions, discovery, competency of witnesses, and much more. The author acknowledges that no attempt has been made to assemble all the relevant decisions. Rather he has attempted to provide citations to leading cases which can be employed as a launching pad for further research. The text is a bit thin in comparison with other comparable treatises such as Mueller and Kirkpatrick's **Federal Evidence**, with a generous use of white space. However, it does incorporate references to the publications in former Lawyers Cooperative Total Client-Service Library, including the **American Law Reports**, **American Jurisprudence 2d**, **Proof of Facts**, **Am. Jur. Trials**, etc.

Kuhne, Cecil C. **A Litigator's Guide to Expert Witnesses**. Chicago: American Bar Association, 2006. 1 vol. (225pp.).
Cost: $84.95 ($68.95 to members); from $39 on amazon.com (2014).
According to the author, "the admission of expert witness testimony remains one of the most contentious, critical, and interesting aspects of modern-day litigation practice. And there is little sign that this tendency will abate anytime soon. The courts have struggled—and will continue to struggle—in their efforts to ensure reliable expert witness testimony without unduly invading the jury's province to independently assess the credibility of a particular witness." This volume provides an detailed overview of the role of the expert witness in the litigation process, including a discussion of such topics as an overview of expert testimony, the legal framework, relevant Supreme Court decisions (including Daubert, Kumho and Joiner opinions), the rules of discovery, the rules of evidence, selecting experts, presenting experts, objecting to experts, depositions, direct examination, and cross-examination. The volume also includes the text of the three Supreme Court cases cited above. The author is a member of the litigation section of the Dallas office of the firm of Fulbright & Jaworski where he has represented clients in federal and state court proceedings involving complex commercial disputes, business torts, and product liability.

Leonard, David P., et al. **The New Wigmore: A Treatise on Evidence**. Gaithersburg, MD: Wolters Kluwer Law & Business, 2002-date. 5 vols. Annual supplementation.
Cost: $1,469; supplementation: 1998: $84; 1999: $87; 2000: $114; 2001: $120; 2002: $340; 2003: $252; 2004: $188; 2005: $202; 2006: $218; 2007: $232; 2008: $457; 2009: $489; 2010: $520; 2011: $795; 2012: $900; 2013: $940.
With the death of Professor Wigmore in 1943, numerous scholars have carried on the task of updating his classic and highly regarded treatise. The process of supplementing the fourth edition **of Wigmore on Evidence** continues up to the present day. **The New Wigmore** was undertaken, however, with the understanding that an entirely new approach to the subject matter was warranted and that the classic integrity of the older Wigmore should be preserved intact. As such, this represents an entirely new work, not a 5th edition of **Wigmore on Evidence**. In **The New Wigmore** Professor David Leonard, Professor of Law at Loyola Law School in Los Angeles, who initiated this ambitious scholarly enterprise in 2002, followed by Professors Edward J. Imwinkelried, David H. Kaye, David E. Bernstein, and Jennifer L. Mnookin. At present, the set includes five volumes encompassing the following components: **Evidentiary Privileges** (2 vols.) (2002); **Selected Rules of Limited Admissibility: Regulation of Evidence to Promote Extrinsic Policies and Values** (2002); **Expert Evidence** (2004); and **Evidence and Other Misconduct and Similar Events** (2009). Each volume approaches the topic with scholarly erudition and thoroughness, providing the reader with substantial body of citations to primary and secondary sources. The set is under the general editorship of Richard D. Friedman, Professor of Law at the University of Michigan.

Lipson, Ashley S. **Is It Admissible?** Santa Ana, CA: James Publishing, 1998-date. 1 vol. Updated annually.
Cost: $89.98; supplementation: 2000: $59.99; 2001: $59.99; 2002: $59.99; 2003: $59.99; 2004-2014: $69.99 per year.
A briefcase-sized courtroom reference tool designed to answer the most common questions regarding the introduction of evidence. It divides evidence into four basic categories: testimonial, documentary, real, and demonstrative. The author is an experienced litigator, mathematician and computer scientist with wide-ranging experience in the area of cross-examination. Unlike most of the legal publishing world, James Publishing has not raised either the initial or the supplementation costs of its publications in years. These high quality and practical reference tools are without a doubt the best values in the world of legal publishing.

Loftus, Elizabeth F. and James M. Doyle. **Eyewitness Testimony: Civil and Criminal**. 5th ed. Charlottesville, VA: LexisNexis, 2008-date. 1 vol. (415 pp.). Print or eBook.
Cost: $190 (print or eBook); supplementation: 2009: $74; 2010: $77; 2011: $84; 2012: $85; 2013: $85; 3d ed.: 2002: $51; 2003: $48; 2004: $50; 2005: $53; 2006: $57; 2007: $62; 2008: new edition; kindle: $173.
An in-depth discussion and analysis of eyewitness testimony from both legal and psychological perspectives. The authors address the latest psychological research on such matters as jurors' beliefs about eyewitness testimony, perception, the three components of memory, and factors that interfere with memory. Additional chapters discuss factors determining retention and retrieval of events, recognizing people, pretrial proceedings in civil cases, pretrial proceedings in criminal cases, jury education and selection, opening statements, direct and redirect examinations, cross-examination: strategies and tactics, presenting expert testimony, jury instructions, and closing argument. Elizabeth Loftus is a Professor of Psychology at the University of Washington and a leading psychological authority in the field of eyewitness testimony, who has published more than a dozen books and hundreds of scholarly articles in the field. James M. Doyle is of counsel to the Boston firm of Carney & Bassil where he specializes in trial and appellate litigation. He has written and spoken widely on the subjects of trial advocacy and eyewitness trials.

Longo, Amy Jane; Allen W. Burton; and Allan D. Johnson. **Electronic Discovery Practice Under the Federal Rules**. Washington D.C.: Bloomberg BNA Books, 2013. 1 vol. (180 pp.). Annual.
Cost: 2014 Edition: $160 (2014).
The first in a new Portfolio series examining the history of the changes to the Federal Rules of Civil Procedure (effective December 1, 2007), this work addresses the discovery of electronically stored information (ESI), analyzes the rules revisions in relation to existing discovery practice, and provides practical suggestions and guidelines for their application to civil cases. The Portfolio begins with an analysis of the evolution of each rule change, with discussion of significant changes and points of debate throughout the rulemaking process, and the analysis of such topics as the duty to preserve, reasonable accessibility, cost-shifting and sanctions for spoliation. The Portfolio also discusses each of the subject areas in which the rules were amended, including, among others, initial disclosures under Rule 26, early meeting of counsel and initial pretrial conference before the court, privilege and work product issues, and limitations on sanctions provided by Rule 37(f), which purports to protect certain losses of information which occur in good faith and due to the routine operation of an electronic information system. The volume also provides the authors' own worksheets, which include documents related to activities involving initial disclosures/early meeting, scope of production, form of production, privilege, sanctions, and more. This Portfolio is the first of a planned series on E-Discovery designed to provide practitioners and corporate counsel with in-depth analysis and commentary on timely issues in the field. Amy J. Longo is co-founder and co-chair, O'Melveny & Meyers' Electronic Discovery and Document Retention Practice. Mr. Burton is a member of O'Melveny & Meyers' Securities Litigation Practice and Electronic Discovery and Document Retention Practice. Mr. Johnson is a member of O'Melveny & Meyers' Global Enforcement and Criminal Defense Practice and Electronic Discovery and Document Retention Practice.

McCormick, Charles T. **McCormick on Evidence.** 6th ed. by John William Strong. St. Paul, MN: West, 2006. 1 vol. (633 pp.) Available from West Academic.
Cost: $92 (2014).
This one-volume student Hornbook, originally authored by Professor Charles McCormick in 1954, follows the same organization as the two-volume Practitioner's Edition but is about one-third its length (see title coverage for Practitioner's edition). This edition reflects the substantial growth in the law since that time, particularly with the appearance of the Federal Rules of Evidence and their state counterparts. The text of this edition is substantially the same as the Practitioner's edition; however, the authors have stripped it of the more exhaustive case citations of the latter to reduce «unwanted bulk and expense.» West's student Hornbooks are basically monographs, with updating contained in subsequent editions. Supplementation costs are, therefore, likely to be minimal or nonexistent.
Now published by West Academic Publishers, a subsidiary of Eureka Growth Capital which operates as a stand-alone business with three imprints: West Academic Publishing, Foundation Press, and Gilbert.

McCormick, Charles T. **McCormick on Evidence.** 7th ed. by John William Strong. St. Paul, MN: West, 2013-date. 2 vols. Practitioner Treatise Series. Supplementation is irregular
Cost: $358; no supplementation to date: 2007: 0; 2008: 0; 2009: $59; 2010: 0; 2011: 0; 2012: 0; 2013: new ed.; 5th ed.: 2001: $29.00; 2002: 0; 2003: $37.00; 2004: 0; 2005: 0; 2006: new 6th edition.
First published by Professor Charles Tilford McCormick in 1954, this Hornbook has served countless numbers of law students as their introduction to the law of evidence. This Practitioner's edition is an expansion of the one-volume student edition by the same authors who have, in this fourth edition, attempted to follow Professor McCormick's basic topical organization and analytical division of the subject. The set's thirty-seven chapters are organized into thirteen Titles: Introduction, Examination of Witnesses, Admission and Exclusion, Competency, Privilege: Common Law and Statutory, Privilege: Constitutional, Relevancy

and Its Counterweights, Demonstrative Evidence, Writings, the Hearsay Rule and Its Exceptions, Judicial Notice, Burden of Proof and Presumptions, Administrative Evidence. The Appendices include the Federal Rules of Evidence, a guide to Evidence Law Research on WESTLAW. There are Tables of Cases, Statutes, Rules and a separate Table of Citations in which the Courts have cited the third edition of McCormick. Volume two concludes with a detailed subject index. This is a basic tool for any law office which does not require the more extensive coverage of a Wigmore or Weinstein. It attempts to achieve a balance between the mere recitation of black letter law and the more exhaustive detail of the larger works. The work extensive citations to the primary law.

Michie's Federal Rules of Evidence Manual on CD-ROM: Saltzburg, Martin, and Capra Edition. Charlottesville, VA: LexisNexis, 1995-date. 1 disc. Updated semiannually. Available for Windows. Search Engine: Folio

Cost: $789 per year (2014).

This product contains the full text of the three-volume analytical guide to the Federal Rules of Evidence combined with the full text of several thousand hypertext linked cases cited in the treatise. For a full description of the substantive treatise, see Saltzburg (below).

Mueller, Christopher M. and Laird C. Kirkpatrick. **Federal Evidence.** 4th ed. St. Paul, MN: Thomson Reuters West (Lawyers Cooperative Publishing Co.), 2013-date. 6 vols. Annual pocket parts.

Cost: $944; no supplementation to date; 3d ed: 2008: $146.50; 2009: $167; 2010: $183.50; 2011: $202; 2012: $224; 2d ed.: 1995: $189.50; 1996: $197.50; 1997: $185; 1998: $196; 1999: $212; 2000: $229; 2001: $252; 2002: $295; 2003: $335; 2004: $377; 2005: $404; 2006: $464.50; 2007: new edition; **Monthly Assured Print Price (APP):** $62/$744.

This is the second edition of a work originally written by the late David Louisell and Christopher Mueller. In this edition, Mueller, the Henry S. Lindsley Professor of Law at the University of Colorado School of Law is joined by Laird Kirkpatrick, the Hershner Professor of Jurisprudence, University of Oregon School of Law. The authors have attempted to provide a «practical and usable» text of value to lawyers and judges, but also a work sufficiently theoretical to provide guidance in addressing future issues and questions. Their discussion is directed primarily to an analysis of the sixty-three Federal Rules of Evidence, but also to those areas, including criminal presumptions, privileges and impeachment by contradiction, in which the Federal Rules are silent and to which common law speaks. The citations to primary authority are selective, but thorough and annotated, while older citations have been eliminated for the ease of the user.

Mueller, Christopher B. and Laird C. Kirkpatrick. **Evidence: Practice Under the Rules**. 4th ed. New York: Wolters Kluwer Law & Business, 2012-date. 1 vol. (1,700 pp.) Annual supplementation.

Cost: $359; supplementation: 2013: $155; 3d ed.: 2010: $135; 2011: $144; 2d ed.: 2000: 0; 2001: $126; 2002: 0; 2003: $163; 2004: $178; 2005: $187; 2006: $199; 2007: $212; 2008: $227; 2009: new ed.; 1st ed.: 1996: $80; 1997: $83; 1998: 0.

Written by two leading legal scholars and teachers with more than fifty years combined experience, this massive, one-volume treatise provides the practicing attorney with clear and comprehensive analysis of the law of evidence. Provides comprehensive discussion and analysis of all major issues with summaries of the most significant cases. Chapters include: Preliminary matters, judicial notice, burdens and presumptions, privileges, witnesses, opinions and expert testimony, scientific evidence, hearsay, foundational evidence, authentication, and the best evidence doctrine. Includes a Table of Cases, a Table of Books and Treatises, Table of Law Review Articles, Table of Restatements, and Index. An excellent one-volume choice for the busy practitioner who desires a thorough, yet compact exposition of the law of evidence. This second edition is the successor to the authors' **Modern Evidence**.

Nelson, Sharon D., Bruce A. Olson and John W. Simek. **The Electronic Evidence and Discovery Handbook: Forms, Checklists, and Guidelines**. Chicago: American Bar Association, Law Practice Management Section, 2006.
1 vol. (755 pp.). Paperbound.

Cost: $129.95 ($99.95 to Law Practice Management Section members); from $16.59 on amazon.com (2014).

The past several years have witnessed a dramatic shift in the field of litigation management toward the use of electronic evidence in both law offices and courtrooms. This shift is an inevitable result of the fact that between 93 and 97 percent of all information is now created electronically. Much of this is fueled by the amount of litigation in which corporations, both large and small, find themselves embroiled. The 2005 **Litigation Trends Survey** of 354 corporate counsel conducted by the law firm of Fulbright Jaworski revealed that the median company (with annual gross revenues of $448 million) was involved in 37 lawsuits; and that $1 billion plus companies were involved in 137 lawsuits. For companies of more than $100 million in revenues, the greatest concern was electronic discovery. The result of all this litigation, both real and potential, has been a preoccupation with electronic discovery, document retention and litigation-hold policies. Even small cases are increasingly affected by this phenomenon. And the costs are staggering. U.S. companies spend $4.6 billion annually to analyze e-mails, which comprise 50% of all evidence. Ten percent of corporate lawyers have indicated that they have settled cases rather than endure the costs of e-discovery.

This volume provides lawyers with a comprehensive road map to developing strategies for dealing with electronic evidence and discovery, including those for gathering evidence, the use of third-party experts, preservation and spoliation issues, proposed amendments to the Federal Rules of Civil Procedure, and electronic discovery. Each chapter is accompanied by numerous forms, checklists, guidelines, preservation of evidence letters, interrogatories, requests for production of documents, depositions, motions to compel, motions for protective orders, motions for sanctions, and sample orders. The volume also includes a glossary of terms produced by the Sedona Conference, an Electronic Evidence Digest of 249 cases, table of cases, and index. The forms, case digest, and table of cases are all duplicated on an accompanying CD-ROM.

Sharon Nelson is president of Sensei Enterprises, a computer forensic and legal technology firm headquartered in Fairfax, VA, and a graduate of Georgetown University Law Center. Bruce Olson is a partner in the Milwaukee firm of David & Kuelthau, S.C. and an expert and frequent speaker on legal technology issues.

Obtaining Discovery Abroad. 2d ed. Chicago: American Bar Association, 2005. 1 vol. (361 pp.).
Cost: $124 ($109 to ABA members); from $33.99 on amazon.com (2014).
Securing evidence from parties located in foreign jurisdictions has become an increasingly significant issue as litigation involving foreign parties or involving overseas conduct has increased. Antitrust litigation, in particular, has fueled this global trend. The task of collecting evidence from foreign jurisdictions has been complicated, however, by incompatibilities between U.S. style discovery and those procedures, which apply, in foreign jurisdictions governed by inquisitorial systems of justice. In such systems, the questioning of witnesses and the gathering of evidence are viewed as sovereign functions, which fall under the discretion of judges, not litigators. Consequently, there is a general hostility toward U.S.-style discovery practices. This volume's first two chapters addresses the specific requirements and limitations imposed on the discovery process by the U.S. legal system when evidence is located in a foreign jurisdiction. The third chapter discusses the discovery process under the terms of international discovery treaties and conventions to which the United States is a signatory. The remaining nine chapters discuss the discovery procedures, which apply in Belgium, Canada, France, Germany, Italy, Japan, the Netherlands, Switzerland, and the United Kingdom. Among the topics discussed are party depositions, interrogatories, requests for production of documents, third-party depositions and the manner in which such forms of discovery are treated abroad. For the attorney or law firm engaged in litigation involving parties in foreign jurisdictions, this is an essential reference tool providing guidance in dealing with often complicated foreign legal systems and procedures.

Paul, George L. **Foundations of Digital Evidence**. Chicago: American Bar Association, 2008. 1 vol. (450 pp.). Paperbound.
Cost: $119.95; from $66.67 on amazon.com (2014).
In a span of less than twenty years, the system of written communication that evolved over 5,000 years has been transformed by the digital revolution. The law has responded to this digital revolution just as have the worlds of commerce, government, and public discourse. The rules of evidence have long recognized the superiority of permanent, written evidence under the standards of admissibility. In the new digital world, written communications or records are produced by methods other than people, and may be preserved, modified of destroyed at will by the person handling such records. This volume provides a learned consideration of this new digital realm and its impact on the traditional rules governing the integrity and use of evidence. The author lays a foundation for the examination of this new world of evidence in light of such tested scientific principles as empiricism, the scientific method, and testability. He extends his discussion to a consideration of the digital realm, the existing scheme regarding authenticity, the integrity of information, time [of recording], identity, the application of the doctrine of hearsay to digital evidence, and the new foundation of system reliability. The appendices are devoted to a variety of case studies, a consideration of e-mortgages, evidentiary requirements for electronic notarization and the legalization of certified electronic documents, digital evidence in five nations (Argentina, France, Germany, Japan, and the Russian Federation), and the role of the vendor and specialized software in the handling of digital evidence. Appendix G provides an illuminating case study in the authenticity of a printed electronic document drawn from recent federal court litigation. George L. Paul is a partner in the Business Litigation Section of Lewis & Roca LLP in Phoenix, AZ, with over 25 years experience in business litigation and trial work on behalf of both plaintiffs and defendants. He is the author of numerous books and articles on the subject of document authenticity, discovery, and legal information.

Rice, Paul R. et al. **Electronic Evidence: Law and Practice**. 2d ed. Chicago: American Bar Association, 2008. 1 vol. (406 pp.).
Cost: $120 ($95 to ABA members); from $72.21 on amazon.com (2014).
Lawyers engaging in the discovery process are now faced with a far more complex task reflecting the exponential growth in the amount of electronic evidence produced in recent decades. The task of obtaining evidence in electronic form requires a far more sophisticated understanding of information technology and may involve the assistance of IT professionals to assist in the process of obtaining e-mail or data files and even information supposedly deleted from computer systems. Electronic data is recoverable under the Federal Rules of Civil Procedure 34 because it falls under the definition of "documents." This includes not only current data being utilized by a party, but backup data and deleted data that can be recovered. The author discusses the full range of discovery issues as applied to an electronic environment, including authentication, spoliation, confidentiality and attorney-client privilege, best evidence and the original writing rule, presumption, hearsay, judicial notice, science and technology, and the future's challenge. This is an essential resource for any attorney or firm engaged in complex litigation requiring the discover6y of electronic information. The author is Professor of Law, American University Washington College of Law, and author of Attorney-Client Privilege in the United States (1993) and Attorney-Client Privilege: State Law (1997). He has ruled upon thousands of privilege claims as a special master in the government's divestiture action against American Telephone and Telegraph, as well as private antitrust and patent infringement actions.

Robillard, Walter G., Donald A. Wilson, and Curtis M. Brown. **Evidence and Procedures for Boundary Location**. 5th ed. Hoboken, NJ: John Wiley & Sons, 2011. 1 vol. (640 pp.).
Cost: $145; from $33.97 on amazon.com (2014).
An essential reference for real estate and title attorneys, surveyors, and civil engineers, this, now, classic work provides detailed information on the various types of evidence required to establish legal and accurate boundaries which will survive

legal scrutiny in courts of law. Includes discussion of the nature, scope and definition of evidence, verbal evidence, plats as evidence, water boundaries, historical knowledge, preservation, of evidence, procedures for locating boundaries described in writings and on maps, original surveys and platting laws, unwritten transfers of land ownership, guarantees of title and location, professional liability, professional stature, the surveyor in court, and the professional relationship between the surveyor, the law and evidence. Contains several useful appendices, including the surveyor's report, wooden evidence, the quasi-judicial function of surveyors, geodaesia, and land acts that created the pubic lands. Walter G. Robillard is an attorney at Land Consultants, Inc. of Atlanta, GA. Donald A. Wilson is with Land Boundary, Inc. in New Fields, NH.

Rothstein, Paul F., Myrna S. Raeder and David Crump. **Evidence in a Nutshell**. 5th ed. St. Paul, MN: West, 2007. 1 vol. (816 pp.). Paperbound. Available from West Academic.
Cost: $41; from $19.41 on amazon.com; kindle ed.: $20.84 (2014).
An introductory overview of the basic concepts and rules of evidence, with particular focus on the Federal Rules of Evidence. The rules of evidence are considered in their application to trial, pre-trial and post-trial proceedings. The authors also discuss the theoretical bases for the rules of evidence by examining various schools of evidentiary thought. The text is supported by representative citations to courts decisions. The volume also includes tables of cases and rules to guide the reader to discussion in the text. Paul F.Rothstein is Professor of Law, Georgetown School of Law. Myrna Raeder is Professor of Law at Southwestern University School of Law. David Crump is the John B. Neibel Professor of Law & Director of CLE at the University of Houston Law Center.

Rychlak, Ronald J. **Real and Demonstrative Evidence: A Real World Practice Manual for Winning at Trial**. 3rd ed. Huntington, NY: Juris Publishing, 2013. 1 vol. (779 pp.). Print or eBook.
Cost: $125.00 (print or eBook); from $115.00 on amazon.com (2014).
This is more than a book about demonstrative evidence, but a book about effective trial technique that illustrates the effective use of demonstrative evidence and the kind of modern technologies that bring that evidence to the attention of triers of fact. The modern era of demonstrative evidence is said to have emerged with the publication of the first edition of **McCormick on Evidence** in 1940. With the passage of time, it has becaome essential for counsel to employ physical evidence and visual aids to make an effective and credible case to a judge or jury. The author effectively explains basic trial procedure and strategy, including such matters as common objections, chain of custody examples, laying the foundation, and a checklist for expert deposition. The third edition of this treatise reflects the expanding role technology has had on the presentation of demonstrative evidence in the courtroom. He also deals with real and demonstrative evidence away from trial, laying the foundation for the introduction of evidence, objections, handling exhibits in the courtroom, real evidence at trial, photographic evidence, audio recordings, diagrams, drawings, maps, charts and graphs, models, reenactments, demonstrations and experiments, animations or other computer-generated evidence, documents, new scientific evidence, working with expert witnesses, and remote sensing and satellite imaging. The text is augmented with sample testimony, checklists, and citations to relevant primary and secondary authorities. The appendices include a selected bibliography, Federal Rules of Evidence (amended to Dec. 1, 2011), examples of real and demonstrative evidence, table of cases, and index. Ronald J. Rychlak is Mississippi Defense Lawyers Association Professor of Law at the University of Mississippi where he has taught since 1987. Page for page, this is arguably the best single-volume work on demonstrative evidence on the market. It is a far better value than Lipson's **Art of Advocacy: Demonstrative Evidence**, which not only costs far more ($430.00), but is paired with costly annual supplementation ($350.00 in 2014). In a legal publishing environment dominated by mega-publishers out to extract every last dollar from customers, Juris Publishing is proof that quality legal publications can be produced at reasonable prices.

Saltzburg, Stephen A., Michael M. Martin and Daniel J. Capra. **Federal Rules of Evidence Manual**. 10th ed. Charlottesville, VA: LexisNexis, 2011-date. 5 vols. Annual pocket parts. Print or eBook.
Cost: $830 (print or eBook); supplementation: 2006: $121; 2007: $268; 2008: $152; 2009: $167; 2010: $179; 2011: $192; 2012: $205; 2013: $212; 8th ed.; 2002: $90; 2003: $96; 2004: $101; 2005: $218; 7th ed.: 1995: $90; 1996: $62.50; 1997: $59; 7th edition: 1998: $44.50; 1999: $70; 2000: $85; 2001: $68.
This three-volume analytical guide to the Federal Rules of Evidence is divided into three main Parts: (1) the Background of Codification Generally and the Federal Rules Specifically, (2) Analysis of each Rule, and (3) those Rules proposed by the Advisory Committee on the Federal Rules of Evidence, but rejected by Congress. The bulk of this treatise is devoted to an analysis of each of the Federal Rules of Evidence, including the Official Text of the Rule, an Editorial Explanatory Comment, selective Annotated Cases arranged topically, Legislative History, Advisory Committee Notes, House Subcommittee on Criminal Justice Notes, Report of the House Committee on the Judiciary, Report of the Senate Committee on the Judiciary, Report of the House and Senate Conferees, and Citations to Hearings and Debates. This logical arrangement provides for easy access by the busy practitioner or the legal scholar. Supplementation costs are reasonable in comparison with sets of similar size.

Tarantino, John A. and Gordon P. Cleary. **Trial Evidence Foundations**. Santa Ana, CA: James Publishing, Inc., 1986-date. 1 vol. (250+ pp.). Annual supplementation.
Cost: $99; supplementation: 1998: $59.99; 1999: $62.99; 2000: $64.99; 2001: $64.99; 2002: $64.99; 2003: $64.99; 2004: $64.99; 2005: $64.99; 2006-2014: $59.99 per year.
Laying the proper foundation for the introduction of various types of evidence is critical to a litigator's success at trial. Marshaling his experience as a litigator, the author provides the rule, elements, tactics and key cases for the most commonly employed foundations. The Elements section for each type of evidence foundation provides an invaluable checklist of foundational requirements. This practice book is also useful as a tool for

recognizing the defects in the foundations laid by opponents. Chapters include: introduction--tactics, trial proceedings and motions, witnesses, opinion evidence, authentication, hearsay, privileges, and other evidence rules. John Tarantino is a partner and Chairman of the Litigation Department at the Providence, Rhode Island firm of Adler Pollock & Sheehan.

Torcia, Charles E. **Wharton's Criminal Evidence.** 15th ed. St. Paul, MN: Thomson Reuters West (Clark Boardman Callaghan), 1997-date. 4 vols. Annual pocket parts. Originally published by Lawyers Cooperative.
Cost: $1,014; supplementation: 1993: $79; 1994: $100; 1995: $165; 1996: $170; 1997: $215; 1998: $170; 1999: $270; 2000: $325; 2001: $427; 2002: $205; 2003: $234; 2004: $233.50; 2005: $282; 2006: $319.50; 2007: $355.50; 2008: $396; 2009: $459; 2010: $537; 2011: $586; 2012: $799; 2013: $697; **Monthly Assured Print Price (APP):** $71/$852.
Both the 13th and 14th editions of this work were authored by Charles E. Torcia, a law professor who has taught at Dickinson School of Law, the Marshall-Wythe School of Law at the College of William and Mary, and New York University School of Law. This edition reflects the promulgation of the Federal Rules of Evidence and the adoption of evidentiary rules in many states. While the author relies primarily upon federal case law in his text and footnotes, some attention is given to state appellate court decisions. Chapters cover the burden and degree of proof, presumption and inferences, relevance and materiality, judicial notice, hearsay evidence, competency of witnesses, examination of witnesses, impeachment of witnesses, attendance of witnesses, documentary evidence, best and secondary evidence, privileged communications, expert and opinion evidence, examinations, tests, and real evidence, co-conspirators and accomplices, confessions and admissions, evidence at preliminary hearing or former trial, judgments and jeopardy, right to counsel, and search and seizure. The 15th edition must be purchased with the 14th edition until it is completed. As in the case of Torcia's **Criminal Procedure**, this set in clearly weighted more toward exhaustive case citation than analytical text. In this regard, the one-volume **Courtroom Criminal Evidence** by Imwinkelried is probably the better value at $177.00. However, there are valuable Total Client-Service Library References to the former Lawyers Cooperative (now West) publications, including the **American Law Reports**.

Weinstein, Jack B. and Margaret A. Berger. **Weinstein's Evidence Manual.** 2d ed. New York: Matthew Bender & Co., 1995-date. 1 vol. Looseleaf format. Also on eBook. No CD-ROM or Internet.
Cost: $487 (print or eBook); supplementation: 1996: $139.50; 1997: $139.50; 1998: $145; 1999: $152; 2000: $165; 2001: $170; 2002: $182; 2003: $192; 2004: $199; 2005: $213; 2006: $228; 2007: $246; 2008: $266; 2009: $287; 2010: $317; 2011: $306; 2012: $375; 2013: $401; 2014: $413.
A one-volume condensation of the author's multi-volume treatise on the law of evidence containing both the rules and analytical commentary. It also contains numerous citations to relevant case with cross-references to the complete multi-volume work.

Cost Saving Tip: An excellent alternative for the attorney who wants the expert commentary of Weinstein without the higher cost of the multi-volume set.

Weinstein, Jack B. and Margaret A. Berger. **Weinstein's Federal Evidence.** Revised 2d ed. New York: Matthew Bender & Co., 1997-date. 6 vols. Looseleaf format. Supplemented several times annually. Also available on eBook and Authority CD-ROM with no-cost online updating via LexisNexis.
Cost: $4,735 (includes annual subscription); annual renewal: 1995: $1,231; 1996: $1,231; 1997: $1,231; 1998: $1,260; 1999: $1,305; 2000: $1,370; 2001: $1,411; 2002: $1,453; 2003: $1,526; 2004: $1,648; 2005: $1,699; 2006: $1,888; 2007: $1,963; 2008: $2,120; 2009: $2,290; 2010: $2,313; 2011: $2,429; 2012: $2,990; 2013: $3,199; 2014: $3,491; CD-ROM: $5,138; renewal: 1998: $1,255; 1999: $1,305; 2000: $1,370; 2001: $1,466; 2002: $1,569; 2003: $1,648; 2004: $1,648; 2005: $1,699; 2006: $1,887; 2007: $2,038; 2008: $2,445; 2009: $2,641; 2010: $2,773; 2011: $2,995; 2012: $3,265; 2013: $3,493; 2014: $3,888.24; eBook: $4,305; renewal: 2014: $3,491.
Written by Judge Jack B. Weinstein, U.S. District Court Judge for the Eastern District of New York and Professor of Law at Columbia University School of Law, and Margaret Burger, Professor of Law at Brooklyn Law School, this is a massive analytical work on the Federal Rules of Evidence. Among the themes which run through this treatise is the conviction that the Federal Rules are better interpreted and applied to admit rather than to exclude evidence, that the court's conduct in particular cases requires both flexibility and discretion, and that the Federal Rules of Evidence pave the way for innovations which are responsive to new forces and events. Consequently, the authors attempt to explain the reason behind the rule by devoting attention to legal theory in their commentary. This treatise is considerably enhanced by an organizational structure which lays out the rule and explains its intent, the reason behind the rule, and the philosophy and practice under the Rule. Included are the legislative history, commentary, state adaptation, and Advisory Committee Notes and References to secondary authorities. The set includes exhaustive citations to all relevant federal and state cases which have been decided under the Rule. The content is grouped into individual Articles, including General Provisions, Judicial Notice, Presumptions, Relevancy and Its Limits, Privileges, Witnesses, Opinions and Expert Testimony, Hearsay, Authentication and Identification, Contents of Writings, Recordings and Photographs, and Miscellaneous Rules. Volumes 6 and 7 contain an index, table of statutes and rules, table of cases, and a table of authors and titles (secondary authorities). The revised second edition includes a number of enhancements designed to make the product more «user friendly.» Besides bringing the text up-to-date, the authors have completely reorganized the chapters to provide more subtopics, thus allowing the user to more quickly locate relevant text by scanning the chapter synopsis. Historical developments have been moved to separate historical appendices to allow the user to find the current law more readily. Also, significant analytical points have been moved from the footnotes to the main text to allow their retrieval by using the index and chapter synopsis. In addition, case citations have been grouped by circuit making it easier for the researcher to locate cases from his or her own circuit more quickly. Finally, the old post-binders have been replaced by more convenient ring binders. The contents of the revised

edition were shipped to all existing Weinstein subscribers at no extra cost as a apart of their regular annual service. Subscribers will receive three updates per year, at least one of which will contain direct text revisions. All three releases include Current Developments pamphlets; and all significant developments are incorporated directly into the text at least once per year.

Cost Saving Tip: If the exhaustive coverage meets your needs, you may consider buying this set with its one-year service and then letting it lapse, re-purchasing it on some cyclical schedule more appropriate to your needs and financial resources. You can supplement the text of the lapsed set with a less expensive alternative text or simply update your research in the primary sources and Shepardize relevant cases and statutes. Also, consider the one-volume condensed version as an alternative which will be kept updated (see next entry).

Weissenberger, Glen. and James J. Duane. **Federal Evidence.** 7th ed. Newark, NJ: LexisNexis Matthew Bender, 2011-date. 1 vol. (911 pp.). Annual pocket part.
Print or eBook.
Cost: $226 (print or eBook); supplementation: 2012: $58; 2013: $65; d ed.: 1999: $30.00; 2000: $35.00; 2001: $35.00 and 4th ed; 2002: $39.50.
Glen Weissenberger, Professor of Law at the University of Cincinnati, authored this succinct, one-volume scholarly analysis of the Federal Rules of Evidence. It provides both practical direction for the lawyer or judge and theoretical analysis and discussion for the law student. The text of each Rule is accompanied by a logically arranged analysis with extensive citations to both primary and secondary authorities. Both the initial and supplementation costs are quite reasonable.

Wigmore, John Henry and Arthur Best. **Evidence in Trials at Common Law**. 4th ed. New York: Wolters Kluwer Law & Business, 1961-date. 13 vols. Free-standing supplement issued three times per year.
Cost: $2,950 supplementation: 1993: $110; 1994: $160; 1995: $176; 1996: $185; 1997: $192; 1998: $205; 1999: $448; 2000: $482; 2001: $535; 2002: $660; 2003: $375; 2004: $822; 2005: $852; 2006: $914; 2007: $974; 2008: $1,044; 2009: $1,118; 2010: $1,196; 2011: $1,280; 2012: $2,102; 2013: $2,232.
Originally published in 1904 by Professor John Henry Wigmore of Northwestern University Law School, this monumental work of legal scholarship has had an impact far-reaching in its scope. Wigmore was one this country's most brilliant and productive legal scholars, amassing a prodigious body of scholarship over his 50-year academic career. His intellectual output totaled more than 100 books and 800 law review articles, of which his Evidence in Trials at Common Law is the magnum opus. This work remains the most significant treatise ever published on the law of evidence and one of the most important of all legal treatises on any topic. It continues to be an essential reference source for the attorney, judge or legal scholar researching evidentiary issues. Since the death of Professor Wigmore in 1943, this now thirteen-volume work has been revised and updated by a number of legal scholars, including James Chadbourn of Harvard Law School (vols. II, III, IIIA, IV, V, VI, VII, IX), Peter Tillers of the New England School of Law (vols. I, IA), and James T. McNaughton of Harvard Law School (vol. VIII). More recently, Walter A. Reiser of the University of South Carolina and Arthur Best of the University of Denver College of Law have prepared supplements. Reviews of the subsequent revisions, while generally quite favorable, have noted a falling away from the high standard set by Professor Wigmore (see Frederick Bernays Weiner, 75 Harvard Law Review 441, 453 (1961)), although one must distinguish between the work of the various revisers. The Revised 4th ed.] edition generally follows the organization of the Wigmore's work as well as much of its text, while expanding those areas which have been subject to growth and revision since Wigmore first put pen to paper. For example, a new chapter entitled «Modern Theories of Relevancy» addresses those developments in relevancy theory which have emerged in the middle third of the 20th century. Similarly, there is an expansion of those sections dealing with evidence of habit or custom and with character evidence. As might be expected in a work of this magnitude, there are exhaustive footnotes to both primary and secondary authorities, particularly case law, which often occupy more space on the page than the text itself. Citations to case law are arranged alphabetically by jurisdiction as an aid to the researcher. The substantive text is contained in volumes 1-9. Volume X contains Tables of Statutes and Cases while Volume XI contains the Index and a Table of Authors Cited. The set is updated with in one annual, free-standing cumulative supplement which updates all volumes. The supplementation costs are reasonable for a thirteen volume set, although the introduction of twice-yearly supplements in 1999 doubled the annual supplementation cost. A law library of any size cannot afford to be without this work. Current editor Arthur Best is a professor of law at the University of Denver College of law and a widely published author in the fields of evidence and comparative negligence. Under his editorship, the coverage is, by necessity, less exhaustive than that presented Professor Wigmore. **The New Wigmore: A Treatise on Evidence**, written by Professor David B. Leonard (see Leonard, supra, under this heading), is an entirely new effort not intended to directly update the older Wigmore.

Cost Saving Tips: The cost-conscious owner may wish to drop the standing order and buy the cumulative supplement every 2-3 years. Buying it once every three years, for example, will result in over $2,200 savings over that period.

Additional titles in the field of Evidence Law are available from the following publishers: American Bar Association, Wolters Kluwer Law & Business, Matthew Bender, Foundation Press, James Publishing, LexisNexis, National Institute for Trial Advocacy, Panel Publishers, Practising Law Institute, Thomson Reuters West, West Academic, John Wiley. See Appendix B for addresses and telephone numbers.

Family Law

Altschuler, Mark K. **Value of Pensions in Divorce**. 5th ed. New York: Wolters Kluwer Law & Business, 2013. 1 vol. Looseleaf format.

Cost: $399; no supplementation to date; 4th ed.: 2010: $219; 2011: $249; 2012: $275.

Calculating the value of pensions in a divorce is one of the major determinations which must be made by the parties, attorneys and judges. This volume discusses the preliminary evaluation of a pension plan and an assessment of its relative importance in the distribution of marital assets, and examines the two key options for dealing with pension assets: immediate valuation of the pension, or deferred distribution through a Qualified Domestic Relations Order (QDRO). All the variables which can affect the evaluation of a pension, including plan type, mortality, retirement date, inflation, interest rates, taxes, and federal laws are considered. Mark K. Altschuler, M.S. is Actuary for Pension Analysis Consultants, Inc. As a professional qualified actuary with more than 22 year's experience, with 15 years prior experience as an applied mathematician and analytical enginee, he has performed actuarial work in both the pension and commercial casualty areas.

Formerly authored by Marvin Snyder.

American Law Institute. **Principles of the Law of Family Dissolution: Analysis and Recommendations**. Newark, NJ: Matthew Bender, 2002. 1 vol. (1,187 pp.).

Cost: $196; hardbound available from ALI: $150; supplementation: 2010: $32.00; 2011: $32; 2012: $33; 2013: $39.

These **Principles** are the product of more than ten years effort on the part of the American Law Institute and this project's Reporters, Advisors, and Members Consultative Group. These **Principles** provide a detailed statement of the legal consequences of marital dissolution in the areas of child custody, child support, distribution of marital property, and compensatory payments to former spouses. Unlike the ALI's **Restatements,** which are statements of the common law, the **Principles** are statements of statutory law, the chief source of family law. These **Principles** are accompanied by Commentary, Reporter's Notes and Illustrations. The Reporter's Notes, in particular, provide extensive citations to primary law sources. Designed primarily for use by judges and rulemakers, these principles also constitute an important research and reference tool for family law practitioners. An essential acquisition for research law libraries, equal in importance to ALI's **Restatements of the Law**.

American Law Institute. **Uniform Laws Annotated, Master Edition.** St. Paul: Thomson Reuters West, 1968-date. 10 vols. Annual pocket parts. Matrimonial, family and health laws are contained in volume 9 Pt. 1A, 9 Pt. 1B, 9 Pts. 2-5, 9A Pts. 1-2, 9B, 9C - 10 vols. total).

Cost: $3,578 (full set); supplementation (full set): 1994: $221.00; 1997: $569.50; 1998: $414; 1999: $447.50; 2000: $506; 2001: $694; 2002: $1,499; 2003: n/a/; 2004: $608; 2005: $577; 2006: $833 (list); 2007: $852; 2008: $880; 2009: $981; 2010: $1,094; 2011: $2,280; 2012: $2,531; 2013: $2,389; **Monthly Assured Print Price (APP):** $258/$3,096; volume 9 Pts. 1-6, 9A Pts. 1-2, 9B, and 9C only: $1,433 (10 vols.); supplementation: 1997: $134; 1998: $145; 1999: $175; 2000: n/a; 2001: n/a; 2002: $126; 2003: n/a; 2004: $207; 2005: $176; 2006: $184; 2007: $194; 2008: $236; 2009: $264; 2010: $294; 2011: $296; 2012: $325; 2013: $360; **Assured Print Price (APP):** $152/$1,824.

Prepared under the auspices of the American Law Institute and the National Conference of Commissioners on Uniform State Laws, this multi-volume set provides the complete annotated text of those uniform laws adopted by at least one state. The National Conference of Commissioners on Uniform State Laws was formed in 1892 for the purpose of drafting and promoting the adoption of uniform laws by the states in those fields in which uniformity would be of practical benefit. Over two hundred uniform laws have been approved since 1892 and over one hundred of these have been adopted by at least one state, the most significant of which is the **Uniform Commercial Code** adopted by all fifty states. In addition to the text of the uniform laws, these volumes include Commissioners' notes, explanations of state variations, and references to state court decisions and law review articles. Tables in both the bound volumes and pocket parts list all the states that have adopted each of the laws. An annual pamphlet includes a directory of all the uniform acts, a listing of all the acts adopted by individual states, and a subject index.

Cost Saving Tip: Family law practitioners can benefit by purchasing only the volumes which contain all those uniform laws related to matrimonial, family and health law, including the Child Custody Jurisdiction Act, Interstate Family Support Act, Reciprocal Enforcement of Support Act, and the Uniform Controlled Substances Act, among others. This will reduce annual supplementation costs from over $800 per year to about $360. Note, however, that the cost of individual volumes has now risen to $360 each (list), requiring selectivity in selection. Better yet, consult your local law library.

Atkinson, Jeff. **Modern Child Custody Practice.** 2d ed. Charlottesville, VA: LexisNexis, 2000-date. 2 vols. Looseleaf format. Annual supplementation.

Cost: $353 (print or eBook); supplementation: 2001: $134; 2002: $134; 2003: $141; 2004: $148; 2005: $157; 2006: $168; 2007: $179; 2008: $194; 2009: $222; 2010: $233; 2011: $247; 2012: $264; 2013: $272; 1st edition: 1994: $80; 1995: $85; 1996: $95; 1997: $105; 1998: $112; 1999: $120.

A two-volume practical guide to handling child custody and support matters which examines both the legal and human sides of the field. The user is guided through each step in the custody proceeding from initial interview through appeal. Topics examined include visitation rights of the noncustodial parent and grandparents, joint and split custody, mediation, jurisdictional issues, and the ramifications of the custodial parent moving out-of-state. The volume also includes a variety of forms, checklists, and case histories. The work includes extensive citations to primary authorities.

Chinn, Mark A. **How to Build and Manage a Family Law Practice**. Chicago: American Bar Association, Law Practice Management Section, 2006. 1 vol. (238 pp.) with CD-ROM.

Paperbound.
Cost: $64.95 ($54.95 to Family Law Section members); from $24.79 on amazon.com (2014).
Part of the ABA Law Practice Management Section's Practice-Building Series this lucid overview addresses both the organizational and practical sides of establishing and operating a family law practice. While written primarily for those new to the practice of family law, it also provides useful advice to more seasoned practitioners. Among the topical areas covered are mission and goals, start-up, systems, marketing, intake of a new client, fees and billing, civility, dealing with clients, staff, service, trial preparation and presentation, getting to court, case management, time management, financial management, getting better, taking care of yourself, and parting thoughts. Mark Chinn, a practitioner with more than 25 years in the field of family law, is the author or contributor to several other ABA publications, including **How to Capture and Keep Good Clients** and **Building a Successful Family Law Practice**. Appendices (contained on the accompanying CD-ROM), include a variety of sample forms, mission statements, worksheets, checklists, contracts, questionnaires, letters, and other documents useful to a family law practice.

Clark, Homer H., Jr. **The Law of Domestic Relations in the United States.** 2d ed. St. Paul, MN: West, 1987. 2 vols. (1,688 pp.) No supplementation. Practitioner Treatise Series.
Cost: OUT-OF-PRINT; no supplementation (2014).
This two-volume work provides more in-depth coverage for the practicing attorney than Clark's single volume Hornbook. Chapter coverage includes breach of promise; marriage; domicile in domestic relations; illegitimate children; contraception, sterilization and abortion; legal position of married women; legal disabilities of minors; tort liability within the family; protection for rights of consortium; jurisdiction for divorce, alimony and custody; divorce--grounds and defenses; division of property; alimony; child support orders; separation agreements; termination of parental rights and adoption, etc. A scholarly and highly readable reference tool. The lack of supplementation since its initial publication in 1987 is inexcusable, however. This is a not uncommon occurrence with outside-authored books over which the publisher has less control than pocket parts produced by in-house editorial staff.

Clark, Homer H., Jr. **The Law of Domestic Relations in the United States.** 2d ed. St. Paul, MN: West, 1988-date. 1 vol. (1050 pp.). Available from West Academic..
Cost: $73; from $19.40 on amazon.com (2014).
An excellent, scholarly overview of the law of domestic relations by Homer Clark, the Moses Lasky Professor of Law Emeritus at the University of Colorado. It highlights the many significant changes in the law over the twenty-year period since the publication of the first edition, including increased personal control over contracts, the virtual removal of discrimination against illegitimate children, the replacement of fault-based grounds for divorce with no-fault, and a greater emphasis upon property division over alimony. Chapter coverage includes antenuptial agreements; marriage; the suit to annul; the illegitimate child; contraception, sterilization and abortion; support obligations in the family; the legal position of women; legal disabilities of minors; the care, education and supervision of children; tort liability within the family; protection for rights of consortium; jurisdiction for divorce, alimony and custody; divorce--grounds and defenses; divorce procedure; division of property on divorce; alimony, temporary and permanent; child support orders in divorce decrees, separation agreement, custody of children; and termination of parental rights and obligations. The text is well supported with extensive citations to primary and secondary authorities, many of them annotated. WESTLAW references provide the user with sample on-line queries. The lone deficiency is the lack of regular supplementation. In fact, the publisher has not supplemented this work since its release in 1988.

Doskow, Emily. **Nolo's Essential Guide to Divorce**. 4th ed. Berkeley, CA: Nolo Press, 2012. 1 vol. (496 pp.). Paperbound.
Cost: $24.99; from $12.51 on amazon.com; kindle: $14.74 (2014).
This self-help book is designed to guide parties through the divorce process whether that process is amicable, grudgingly co-operative, or combative. The author considers not only the legal side of divorce, but the social, emotional and financial issues that usually envelope the divorcing parties. The author's intent is to steer the parties toward mediation before litigation as a means of saving time, money and emotional toil. She considers the alternatives to divorce, including separation and annulment. She also addresses the many issues confronting divorces couples, from living arrangements, financial issues, and professional help, to property, custody and support. Chapters are devoted to the uncontested divorce, divorce mediation, contested divorce and trial, custody decisions and parenting, custody disputes, child support, marital property, property division, spousal support and health insurance, military divorce, and preparation of the marital settlement agreement. The author also considers what happens when things really go wrong, from domestic violence and child abuse to kidnapping and bankruptcy. Finally, she considers what happens after the divorce, including relationships with children, modifications of spousal support, the right to Social Security, and more. A final chapter provides advice for getting help, information, legal advice, and doing research. The Appendix includes grounds for divorce, financial inventory worksheets, net worth summary, monthly income calculations, daily expenses, and monthly budget. The author is an attorney-mediator in private practice, the editor of Nolo's family law books, and author of the **Sharing Solution**, **Neighbor Law**, and other Nolo titles.

Dundee, Mark W. **Qualified Domestic Relations Order Answer Book**. 5th ed. Frederick, MD: Wolters Kluwer Law & Business, 2011-date. 1 vol. (832 pp.). Annual.
Cost: 2013 Edition: $385; 4th ed,: $355; 3d edition: 2004: $169.; 2005: $179; 2007: $239; 2008: $189; 2009: $209; 2010: $309; 2d ed.: 2000: $96; 2001; $96; 2002: 0; 2003: new edition.
A qualified domestic relations order (QDRO) is a domestic relations order that assigns to an alternate payee the right to receive all or a portion of the benefits payable to a participant under a qualified retirement plan that meets certain other requirements. A domestic relations order (DRO) is any judgment, decree or order which relates to the provision of child support, alimony payments, or marital property rights to a spouse, former spouse, child or other dependent of a participant and is made pursuant to a State domestic relations law. This volume presents

answers to nearly 600 questions likely to be encountered by plan administrators, ERISA lawyers, family lawyers and other employee benefit professionals in the course of handling the qualified domestic relations order. While presented in a question-answer format, the discussion includes citations to many relevant statutes and cases. The appendices contain applicable Internal Revenue Code sections, ERISA provisions, Treasury regulations, sample amicus briefs regarding attorneys fees and early retirement subsidies, IRS notice and private rulings, Department of Labor Guidance, and tables, glossary and index.

Family Law Reporter. Washington, DC: Bloomberg BNA, 1974-date. 2 vols. Looseleaf service. E-mail updates.
Cost: $1,423 per year; Internet: $1,545 per year (single user); print discounts to electronic subscribers (2014).
This is a combination current awareness and reference service. The **Current Developments** binder includes weekly "Highlights" of current court opinions, legislative activities, reports and proposals, and United States Supreme Court proceedings, full text of significant cases, monographs, and an Index/Table of Cases. **The Reference File and Tax Guide** reproduces the text of relevant federal laws, Uniform and Model Acts, and tax statutes, regulations, legislative history, analysis, and forms in the family law area. It also includes analyses of such topics as gift planning, nonmarital cohabitations, and other income tax matters. The full text of state divorce laws are reprinted along with a tabular summary. The final section provides a number of Practice Aids including sample forms and letters. A useful current awareness tool of national family law developments for the family law specialist. Transfer binders are shipped annually to provide permanent storage of past "Highlights" issues.

Family Law Treatise Library on LoisLawConnect. New York: Wolters Kluwer Law & Business.
Cost: $540.00 per year (solo practitioner) (2014).
This library includes treatises addressing such topics as prenuptial agreements, asset valuation, child support and custody, and divorce settlements. The titles include **Drafting Prenuptial Agreements, Property Division in Divorce Proceedings: A Fifty State Guide, Valuation Strategies in Divorce, Valuing Specific Assets in Divorce, Value of Pensions in Divorce, QualifiedDomestic Relations Order Handbook**, **Child Support Guidelines: Interpretation and Application**, **Psychological Experts in Divorce Actions**, *the* **AmericanJournal of Family Law, Family Law Update**, and relevant forms and checklists from a variety of sources. A cost-effective alternative to acquiring these titles in print format.

Feder, Robert D., Charles T. Rosoff, and Aleza Tadri Friedman, eds. **Valuation Strategies in Divorce**. 4th ed. New York: Wolters Kluwer Law & Business, 2012-date. 1 vol. (various pagings/1,765 pp.). Annual supplementation.
Cost: $289; supplementation: 2013: $269; 3d ed.: 1998: $70; 1999: $77; 2000: $87; 2001: $97; 2002: $115; 2003: $149; 2004: $155; 2005: $163; 2006: 0; 2007: $163; 2008: $174; 2009: $199; 2010: $278; 2011: $210; 2012: $289 (revised ed.).
Most states provide some form of equitable distribution of marital assets upon divorce. That distribution is a three-step process: (1) identification of assets; (2) valuation; and (3) distribution. This comprehensive guide is the definitive resource for locating and valuing assets in divorce cases that can be utilized in both simple and complicated cases. Now combined into one volume, the chapters cover analyzing and adjusting financial statements, analysis of corporate and personal tax returns, valuation of closely held businesses, valuation of professional practices, valuation of pensions, real estate, personal property, collections, fine arts, and specialty or novelty assets, Additional materials include checklists of valuation strategies, discovery in valuation cases, sample valuation reports, critiques and examination questions, direct examination of business appraisers, cross examination of business appraisers, mock transcript of a valuation trial, and legal issues in valuation strategies. The past editor, Robert D. Feder, was formerly partner in the family law department of the Philadelphia firm of Schnader, Harrison, Segal & Lewis, and now Of Counsel to the Family Law Practice Group at Cozen O'Connor, where he specializes in the financial aspects of divorce. Charles T. Rosoff is the presdident of Appraisal Services Associates, an appraisal form specializing in forensic evaluations of fine arts, antiques, decorative arts, residential and office contents. In 2012, Aleza Tadri Friedman has been at appraiser at Appraisal Services Associates since 2002. Fifteen other experts in marital law, business or other asset valuation contributed chapters. The 2012 edition was transformed into a one-volume work, but still retains the 4th edition designation. The cost was also reduced.

Feld, Barry C. **Juvenile Justice Administration in a Nutshell**. 3d ed. St. Paul, MN: West, 2014. 1 vol. (478 pp.). Paperbound. Available from West Academic.
Cost: $41; from $17.01 on amazon.com; kindle ed,: $15.40 (2014)
A basic introduction to the criminal and non-criminal misconduct of juveniles which brings them in contact with the juvenile justice system. The author looks at the manner in which law enforcement, the courts, and the juvenile justice system respond to those who violate the law. Following an introduction to the juvenile justice system, the author discusses juvenile court jurisdiction over delinquent and status offenders, police and juveniles: pre-trial criminal procedure, preliminary procedures: intake and diversion, pretrial detention, waiver of juvenile court jurisdiction, adjudication of delinquency: procedural rights at trial, and the dispositional decision. He also addresses the issue of children's rights as they are impacted by the process of investigating and prosecuting juvenile offenders. Barry C. Feld is the Centennial Professor of Law, University of Minnesota

Felder, Raoul Lionel. **Encyclopedia of Matrimonial Clauses.** New York: Law Journal Press, 1990-date. 1 vol. Looseleaf format. Supplemented twice annually.
Cost: print/online/ebook combo: $570 (ebook and online only: $545); supplementation: 1994: $94 (2); 1995: $48; 1996: $114; 1997: $100; 1998: $59.99;1999: $59; 2000: $59; 2001: $140; 2002: $168; 2003: $180; 2004: $96; 2005: $212; 2006: $226; 2007: $241; 2008: $278; 2009: $313.49; 2010: 0; 2011 (March): converted to online/print combo pricing.
This volume consists entirely of matrimonial clauses with brief

accompanying comments, arranged alphabetically by subject. Sample clauses include subjects ranging from actuarial valuation of pensions and adoption of children to child support, medical expenses, tax refunds, and visitation.

Cost Saving Tips: Under its new ownership, Law Journal Press has, or is in the process of converting all its titles to an annual subscription pricing model, combining online and print. While providing the dual formats, this plan nevertheless nearly doubles the annual supplementation cost of this title, from $289 (with a roughly $300 annual supplement charge) to $570 annually for the print/online combination, or $545 for online only. This represents a better than 75% increase in the initial cost and a roughly 70% increase in the supplementation cost. In its own small way, this particularly egregious plan to substantially increase both initial and supplementation costs of its titles is accomplished by forcing customers into this blatantly manipulative dual format pricing model. Savvy consumers will avoid LJP whenever possible and look for alternate publishers with similar subject coverage.

Gardner, Martin R. **Understanding Juvenile Law**. 3d ed. New York: Matthew Bender & Co., 2009. 1 vol. (377 pp.). Legal Text Series.
Cost: $45; eBook: $36; $31.96 on amazon.com (2014); no supplementation except in the form of future editions.
Young people have traditionally been treated as a distinct class deserving of protection under the law. In certain contexts, this view has been challenged by one which recognizes the autonomy rights of adolescents. It is in light of these conflicting philosophies that the author, the Steinhart Foundation Professor of Law at the University of Nebraska, approaches this scholarly overview of juvenile law. Intended primarily as a law school text, this volume examines the concept of minority as a legal status, the rights of juveniles, the child and the family, child abuse, private law issues outside the family, constitutional rights, the juvenile court movement, jurisdiction, the pre-adjudication process, adjudication, dispositions, and the future of the juvenile justice system. Includes numerous citations to both primary law and various secondary sources.

Goldberg, Barth H. **Valuation of Divorce Assets.** Revised edition. St. Paul, MN: Thomson Reuters West, 2005-date. 2 vols. Annual supplementation.
Cost: $408; supplementation: 2006: $139; 2007: $146; 2008: $163; 2009: $196; 2010: $230; 2011: $252; 2012: $276; 2013: $300; 1st ed.: 1994: $48; 1995: 0; 1996: $48; 1997: 0; 1998: 0; 1999: $55; 2000: $60; 2001: $71; 2002: $83; 2003: $95; 2004: $79.50; 2005: new edition. **Monthly Assured Print Price (APP):** $30/360.
This combination treatise and handbook reflects the major changes which have taken place in the rules regarding the distribution of marital assets. These changes are a product of more exacting standards by courts and more specific standards imposed under state law, including the adoption of equitable distribution statutes in most jurisdictions. This work is designed to aid the practicing attorney in more competently representing clients whose assets are subject to distribution under these new rules. The individual chapters examine the valuation process; experts and how to use them; understanding accounting protocol; use of financial statements; financial statements analysis; valuation of closely held corporations; dealing with corporate stock issues; valuation of professional entities, goodwill and license interests; valuing retirement plans; valuation of wife's services; effect of bankruptcy on dissolution proceedings; particular valuations; tax issues concerning valuations; valuation of collectibles; and a compendium of valuation cases covering specific assets. The volume also includes a Digest of State Valuation Cases derived from West Key Number 253 from the 9th **Decennial Digest** (Part 1, 1976-1981) to date, Tables of Statutes, and Court Rules. An excellent and reasonably priced resource with regular annual updating.

Gold-Bikin, Lynne Z. et al. **Divorce Practice Handbook.** Charlottesville, VA: LexisNexis, 1994. 1 vol. (325 pp.). No supplementation.
Cost: $109 (2014).
This basic guide to divorce practice is written by four specialists in the field of domestic relations law. It addresses such issues as jurisdiction, the client interview, discovery and trial preparation, negotiation tactics, visitation, child support, property division, tax issues and ethical matters. There are a variety of practical aids including forms, checklists and a model client information manual. A reasonably-priced introductory guide for both new lawyers and general practitioners.

Gold-Bikin, Lynne Z. and Stephen A. Kolodny. **Divorce Trial Manual**. Chicago, IL: American Bar Association, Section of Family Law, 2004. 1 vol. (264 pp.). Paperbound.
Cost: $119 ($109.95 to Section members); from $70.85 on amazon.com (2014).
Divorce lawyers spend more time in court than most litigators. This practice-oriented volume provides a step-by-step guide to the process of litigating a divorce action, from the initial interview to the trail and closing argument. Chapters include coverage of the initial client interview, organization for trial, discovery, theory of the case, motions, the closing argument, the opening statement, direct examination, cross-examination, choice and preparation of law witnesses, experts and their reports, evidence, and the development and introduction of exhibits. Based on the collective wisdom gathered from over 17 years experience with the Trial Advocacy Institute for matrimonial lawyers. The authors are both experienced trial lawyers.

Green, Janice. **Divorce After 50: Your Guide to the Unique Legal & Financial Challenges**. 2d ed. Berkeley, CA: Nolo, 2013. 1 vol. (370 pp.). Paperbound.
Cost: $29.99; from $17.17 on amazon.com; kindle: $16.99 (2014).
Unlike divorce among younger spouses, divorce after 50 has its own unique legal, financial and emotional issues and challenges that need to be addressed.
Those divorcing at an older age are more likely to be concerned about issues of health, retirement security, and their adult children's response to events, as well as the heightened level of emotional anxiety that inevitably accompanies such events. The author gives attention not only to the practical, nut-and-bolts, aspects of divorce, but to the personal side of separation

and divorce. The author begins with personal testimonies of those involved in late-life, and proceeds through such matters as getting advice (both professional and personal), divorce options (litigation, arbitration, mediation and collaborative divorce), marital steps, to a fair division, dealing with big ticket items ((home, retirement, business), other assets, debts and taxes, health care, financial survival, estate planning and divorce, and finishing up and moving on. She concludes with a number of survival stories. Appendices include an inventory of assets and liabilities form, state risk pool contact information, assessment of living expenses, and index. Aimed at a general audience, this volume provides a lucid path through the divorce quagmire. The author, a partner in Farris & Green in Austin, TX, has practiced family law for more than 30 years. A fellow in the American Academy of Trial Lawyers and was named to Best Lawyers in America.

Gregory, John DeWitt, Peter N. Swisher and Sheryl L. Scheible-Wolf. **Understanding Family Law**. 4th ed. New York: Matthew Bender & Co., 2013.
1 vol. (612 pp.). Law Text Series. No supplementation between new editions.
Cost: $45; eBook: $36; from $30.96 on amazon.com; kindle ed.: $18.70 (2014).
A lucidly written overview of the legal aspects of family relationships--both traditional and non-traditional. Although aimed primarily at a law student audience, it contains sufficient citations to primary authority to be employed successfully by the practicing attorney. Following an introductory chapter which aims to delineate the history and structure of various family relationships, the chapters explore such topics as marriage, property and support rights during marriage, altering the essentials of marriage by agreement, having children: the alternative choices, unique family issues (interfamily torts, etc.), divorce grounds and defenses, spousal and child support on divorce, equitable distribution of property, and child custody and visitation. Also includes the text of the Uniform Marriage and Support Act, table of cases and index. John De Witt Gregory is the Sidney & Walter Siben Distinguished Professor of Family Law at Hofstra University. Peter Swisher and Sheryl L. Scheible are Professors of Law at the Universities of Richmond and New Mexico.

Haralambie, Ann M. **Handling Child Custody, Abuse and Adoption Cases.** 3d ed. St. Paul, MN: Thomson Reuters West (Clark Boardman Callaghan), 2009-date. 3 vols. Annual pocket parts.
Cost: $675; supplementation: 2010: $135; 2011: $148.50; 2012: $175; 2013: $187; 2d ed.: 1994: $50; 1995: $50; 1996: $56.50; 1997: $60; 1998: $62; 1999: $67; 2000: $72; 2001: $86; 2002: $101; 2003: $120; 2004: $134; 2005: $144.50; 2006: $165; 2007: $184; 2008: $205; 2009: $135; **Monthly Assured Print Price (APP):** $22/$324.
An outstanding resource for the domestic relations attorney concentrating in child custody, adoption and abuse matters. The author, a Certified Domestic Relations Specialist practicing in Tucson, Arizona, has a wide ranging practice representing parents, children, child welfare and adoption agencies. She is a past-president of the National Association of Counsel for Children and a life charter member of the American Professional Society on the Abuse of Children, among other professional associations. The first edition of this treatise received the Harrison Tweed Award for Special Merit from the American Law Institute-American Bar Association. This is a work impressive in both its scholarship and coverage. The author treats the full range of issues relating to child custody, abuse and adoption. Beginning with the historical background of child custody, she examines jurisdictional issues, rights of unmarried parents, custody incident to dissolution of marriage, legal separation or annulment, visitation rights, post decree modification of custody, assisted conception and surrogacy, third-party custody and visitation, dependency and neglect actions and guardianship. Volume two covers termination of parental rights, adoption, the Indian Child Welfare Act, proving physical and sexual abuse, proving neglect, abandonment, and emotional abuse, interference with custody and visitation, child abuse and neglect, torts, trial techniques: basic strategies, use of experts and treatises, using technology, and children's development, memory and testimony. Appendices include Tables of Cases and Secondary Authorities and an Index. A highly recommended resource for the active practitioner in the field. Supplementation cost is quite reasonable for a two-volume set given the depth of coverage.

Herman, Gregg, ed. **101+ Practical Solutions for the Family Lawyer: Sensible to Common Problems.** 3d ed. Chicago: American Bar Association, Section of Family Law, 2009. 1 vol. (695 pp.). Paperbound.
Cost: $139.95 ($119.95 to Family Law Section members); from $75 on amazon.com (2014).
This volume is a selective compendium of the best «Hot Tips From the Experts» programs presented by the Family Law Section at the American Bar Association annual meetings over a five year period. The presenters, chosen from among the best family law practitioners in the country, have no more than five minutes each to state their case to the audience. This volume collects 115 of these «hot tips» in a series of brief chapters. The topics are arranged into 15 headings: client relations, fees, custody, malpractice avoidance, office practices, discovery, premarital relations, taxes, retirement plans, valuation, settlement, torts, trial tactics, evidence, and after the divorce. This is an invaluable resource for the family law practitioner.

Herman, Gregg. **Settlement Negotiation Techniques in Family Law: A Guide to Improved Tactics and Resolution**. Chicago: American Bar Association, 2013. 1 vol. (173 pp.). Paperbound.
Cost: $69.95 ($54.95 to members); from $52.46 on amazon.com (2014).
The fundamental premise of this volume is that most lawyers would prefer to settle, rather than litigate, cases. The problem, as the author sees it, however, is that most legal education is aimed at litigation, rather than negotiation. The fault lies with lawyers who think they need training for the former, but not the latter. This volume is aimed, not at the novice, but at lawyers who have some experience with negotiation, but see need for improvement. And at those who would rather achieve compromise than "zealously advocate for their clients," and thereby abdicate their

responsibilities as attorneys. As such, it collates many of the concepts of divorce settlement negotiations that are discussed in the author's earlier **Joy of Settlement**. The individual chapters cover the goal of getting to "Yes" employing traditional theory, negotiation basics, timing, controlling emotions, preparing the client for settlement, disclosure, position negotiation, negotiating with opposing counsel, negotiating with the pro se party, the four-way meeting, the role of the judge, planned early negotiation, family law-specific settlement issues, mediation, collaborative divorce, cooperative divorce, creative settlement techniques, divorce settlements and game theory, ethical considerations, ten commandments of negotiations, the endgame, and becoming a better negotiator. The author has assembled an illuminating collection of insights, coupled with sage advice, many of which were contributed by a number of family law contributors to the **Joy of Settlement.** The author, who is a shareholder with the firm of Loeb & Herman, S.C,, received his law degree from the University of Wisconsin law school.

Hertz, Frederick. **Counseling Unmarried Couples: Guide to Effective Legal Representation**. Chicago: American Bar Association, 2011. 1 vol. (390 pp.). Paperbound wit companion CD-ROM.
Cost: $99.95 ($79.95 to members); from $61.85 on amazon.com (2014).
Cohabitation is a living arrangement in which an unmarried couple lives together in a long-term relationship that resembles a marriage. Couples cohabit, rather than marry, for a variety of reasons. Some may want to test their compatibility before they commit to a legal union, others may want to maintain their single status for financial reasons. while still others may feel that marriage is unnecessary. Between 1970 and 1990, the number of couples living together outside of marriage quadrupled, from 523,000 to nearly 3 million. Many of the legal issues faced by unmarried couples are similar to those faced by married couples, while others are unique to that status. This volume examines a multitude of issues facing unmarried couples and the strategies for providing them with effective representation. Following a discussion of the broader legal history and social context of family relationships, the author examines the fundamentals of representing unmarried partners; living arrangements, counseling low-asset cohabiting renters; debts, assets, and liabilities; tax consequences, liabilities and benefits; real estate ownership and management; cohabitation and financial agreements; public and private benefits; the rules and practice of parentage; illness and disability planning; estate planning concerns and practices; substantive legal doctrines; and the process of non-marital dissolution. The companion CD-ROM provides the forms needed for representation of unmarried couples. The author is a graduate of Boalt Hall School of Law at UC Berkeley and a real estate and land use law practitioner in Oakland, California, with prior experience in litigation involving unmarried couples.

Hollinger, Joan H. ed. **Adoption Law and Practice.** New York: Matthew Bender & Co., 1988-date. 2 vols. Looseleaf format or eBook. Supplemented annually.
Cost: $536 (print or eBook); supplementation: 1995: $124 (cost frozen since 1992); 1996: $130; 1997: $130; 1998: $140; 1999: $177; 2000: $190; 2001: $203; 2002: $218; 2003: $225; 2004: $236; 2005: $253; 2006: $271; 2007: $292; 2008: $292; 2009: $315; 2010: $348; 2011: $349; 2012: $373; 2013: $399; 2014: $427.
This two-volume guide to adoption law and practice is edited by Joan Heifetz Hollinger, a Professor of Law at the University of Detroit School of Law, and a team of fifteen experts in the field of family law and adoption. This is a comprehensive treatise which provides thorough guidance in handling consent, placement, representation, financial and other issues related to the adoption process. Its intended audience consists of attorneys with a general practice, family law specialists, court officials and support officials in the area of child placement. The substantive discussion and analysis is complemented by annotated coverage of the case and statutory law of all fifty states. Special features include bibliographies accompanying each chapter, forms, and statutory tables. Chapters include an introduction to adoption law and practice, consent to adoption, placing children for adoption, adoption procedure, Uniform Adoption Act, the Attorney's role in independent adoption: dual representation, the attorney's role in independent adoptions: separate representation of each party, attorney's role in agency adoptions, contested adoptions: strategy, adoption assistance for children with special needs, international adoption, the aftermath of adoption: economic consequences--support, inheritance and taxes, legal and social consequences, alternative reproduction and the law of adoption, and adoption of Native American children. There are Tables and Cases and a detailed subject index. An excellent and in-depth resource, thoroughly annotated with references to cases, statutes, and secondary materials. As useful to the general practitioner as to the most experienced family law specialist.

Karp, Leonard and Cheryl L. Karp. **Domestic Torts: Family Violence, Conflict and Sexual Abuse.** Revised edition. St. Paul, MN: Thomson Reuters West (Clark Boardman Callaghan) 2005-date. 1 vol. (759 pp.) Annual pocket parts.
Cost: $258; supplementation: 2006: $80; 2007: $89.50; 2008: $99; 2009: $123; 2010: $124; 2011: $136; 2012: $158; 2013: $171; 1st ed.:1992: $74; 1993: $82; 1994: $96; 1996: $59; 1997: $65; 1998: $68; 1999: $73; 2000: $79; 2001: $92; 2002: $101; 2003: $115; 2004: $129; 2005: new edition; **Monthly Assured Print Price (APP):** $18/$216.
An examination of domestic torts from both the legal and psychological perspectives co-authored by a practicing attorney and psychologist. Subject coverage includes spousal and child abuse, marital rape, sexual exploitation of children, child snatching, sexually transmitted diseases, infliction of emotional distress, third party liability, insurance matters, civil rights issues. Excellent analytical coverage of a variety of sensitive legal issues. Originally published by Shepard's/McGraw-Hill. Sold to the Thomson Corporation in December, 1995.

Kramer, Donald T. **Legal Rights of Children.** Revised 2d ed. St. Paul, MN: Thomson Reuters West (Clark Boardman Callaghan), 2005-date. 3 vols. Annual pocket parts.
Cost: $538; supplementation: 2006: $165; 2007: $183; 2008: $204; 2009: $267; 2010: $268.50; 2011: $295.50; 2012: $345; 2013: $364; 1st ed.: 1995: $46; 1996: $51; 1997: $60; 1998: $65.00; 1999: $70; 2000: $75; 2001: $58.50; 2002: $103.50;

2003: $120; 2004: $135; 2005: new edition; **Monthly Assured Print Price (APP):** $38/$456.
Building on the earlier work of Robert Horowitz and Howard Davidson of the National Legal Resource Center for Child Advocacy and Protection, Young Lawyers Division of the ABA, Donald Kramer, Senior Executive Editor at Shepard's/McGraw-Hill has written a thorough exposition of the issues impacting the rights and welfare of children. This work reflects the many developments in the status and treatment of children which have received increased media focus since the publication of the first edition in 1984, including such issues as child abuse, lack of support, youth incarceration, artificial insemination, surrogate mothers, grandparent visitation rights, the tort of wrongful life, and childhood violence. The three volumes contain 33 chapters organized into ten parts, including children's rights: a look backward and a glance ahead; children and the family relationship; substantive laws and illegitimate children; children in the courtroom; adolescents and their legal rights; child abuse, sexual abuse, and exploitation of children; children in trouble: the juvenile justice system; the state's role in educating children; the state's role in caring for and rearing children; and the state's role in providing assistance for children. There are tables of cases, statutes, rules and regulations, authorities, as well as a detailed subject index. The introduction to each chapter consists of a summaries of recent news items providing scope and context for the detailed analytical discussion which follows. The well organized text is written in a lucid style which is readily comprehensible to the layperson. There are plentiful citations to applicable primary and secondary authority as an aid to the researcher. An excellent resource for the attorney specializing in the field of domestic relations. Originally published by Shepard's/ McGraw-Hill, this book was taken over by Clark Boardman Callaghan in December, 1995 and West Publishing in 1996.

Krause, Harry D. and David D. Meyer. **Family Law in a Nutshell**. 5th ed. St. Paul: West, 2007. 1 vol. (511 pp.). Available from West Academic.
Cost: $41; from $21 on amazon.com (2014).
While primarily intended as an overview for the law students, this volume from West's «Nutshell Series» can also be useful to practicing attorneys, social workers, marriage counselors, mediators and mental health professionals. The author, the Alumni Distinguished Professor of Law at the University of Illinois, covers such topics as the Sources and Application of Family Law, the New Constitutional Family Law, Creation of the Marriage Relationship, Spousal Rights and Obligations in the Ongoing Marriage, the Parent and Child Relationship, Termination of Marital Status, and Economic Consequences of Divorce. Case citations, necessarily limited in a work of this kind, are collected in an introductory table. An inexpensive handbook to the basics of family law.

Lind, Göran. **Common Law Marriage: A Legal Institution for Cohabitation**. New York: Oxford University Press, 2008. 1 vol. (1,221 pp.).
Cost: $139.95; from $84.40 on amazon.com; kindle: $90.34 (2014).
Common law marriage may be loosely defined as an institution that gives the legal effects of formal marriage to qualified couples that, without a formal marriage contract, are in agreement and live together under marriage-like conditions. During the past thirty years, family law in the Western world has experienced decreasing rates of marriage, a dramatic rise in the numbers of unmarried cohabiting couples, and an increase in the numbers of children born to such relationships. These developments have prompted significant activity by both legislative and judicial bodies in a number of countries. Courts, for their part, have attempted to address these family law issues of cohabiting couples by applying property law principles, while legislatures have enacted cohabitation legislation, the effects of which have come to resemble formal marriage. In this exhaustive study of common law marriage, the author examines the historical origins of the institution, the current state of the law, and the future prospects for both common law marriage and modern cohabitation law. The book commences with a useful explanation of the conceptual framework for the study together with a discussion of the sources consulted. The origins of common law marriage may be traced to the Roman and medieval canon law which, in England, was administered through the ecclesiastical, rather than the common law, courts. The reception of common law marriage in the United States in the 19th century may be attributed largely to the influence of Chancellor James Kent, who introduced the concept through decisions of the New York Supreme and his widely influential **Commentaries of American Law**. In his discussion of the current state of the law, the author considers the subjects of legal capacity, the common law marriage contract, implied marriage agreements, cohabitation, holding out and reputation as spouses, burdens of proof and presumptions, conflicts of law, and choice of law. Much of the discussion is focused on the eleven jurisdictions that currently recognize common law marriage and give it full legal effect, namely Alabama, Colorado, District of Columbia, Iowa, Kansas, Montana, Oklahoma, Rhode Island, South Carolina, Texas, and Utah. In his discussion of the future of common law marriage and cohabitation, the author addresses the issue from a demographic and sociological as well as a legal perspective, and draws upon the experiences of countries in Western and Northern Europe, Canada, Australia, and the United States. In his examination of various legislative proposals in the area, he considers the question of whether a reformed formal marriage can constitute an alternative to legalization of informal relationships through common law marriage and existing cohabitation legislation. Based on the author's doctoral dissertation at Uppsala University in Sweden, this exhaustive and well-documented study makes a major contribution to our understanding of common law marriage from an historical and comparative perspective, and analyzes over 2,000 American cases on the subject. Göran Lind is an Associate Professor of Law at Uppsala University and general manager of the JURA Institute.

Lindey, Alexander and Louis Parley. **Lindey and Parley on Separation Agreements and Antenuptial Contracts**. 2d ed. New York: Matthew Bender, 2000-date. 2 vols. Looseleaf format. Print and eBook.
Cost: $860 (includes annual subscription); annual renewal: 2001: $275; 2002: $295; 2003: $289; 2004: $303; 2005: $324; 2006: $347; 2007: $369; 2008: $399; 2009: $431; 2010: $453; 2011: $476; 2012: $505; 2013: $540; 2014: $590; previous edition: 1995: $473 (cost frozen since 1992); 1996: $496; 1997: $496; 1998: $520; 1999: $545; 2000: $545; eBook: $782; renewal: 2014: $590.

This two-volume treatise and practice guide is intended for the domestic relations specialist. It provides detailed examination of separation agreements and antenuptial contracts with attention to statutes regarding equitable distribution and community property. The substantive text is accompanied by hundreds of illustrative forms, practical suggestions, and extensive citations to case law, state statutes, and secondary sources. The authors examine bankruptcy, security arrangements, life insurance issues, and tax matters, among other issues. The second edition also covers subjects as alimony, child custody and support, division of both tangible and intangible assets (including pensions(, income tax aspects of support, and the property rights of cohabiting couples. The text is broken down into five parts, including typical separation agreements, individual clauses to be embodied in separation agreements, related forms, antenuptial and postnuptial agreements, and cohabitation agreements. The Appendices include the full text of a number of Uniform Acts and Guides, including the Uniform Marital Property Act and Uniform Premarital Agreement Act, the Uniform Child Custody Jurisdiction Act, the Uniform Marriage and Divorce Act and the Uniform Reciprocal Enforcement of Support Acts, among others. Includes a Selected Bibliography of Books and Law Review Articles, the latter arranged by subtopic. There is an extensive table of cases and a detailed subject index. Includes over 600 easy to use forms. An excellent reference tool for the specialist, with both substantive and practical coverage. Louis Paley, a prominent member of the Connecticut Bar Association who has written and spoken widely on family law issues, has been the sole author of this work since Alexander Lindey's death in 1987. Highly recommended.

McCahey, John P. et al. **Child Custody & Visitation Law and Practice.** New York: Matthew Bender & Co., 1983-date. 4 vols. Looseleaf format and eBook. Supplemented twice a year.
Cost: $2,167 (print) (includes annual subscription); annual renewal: 1995: $575 (cost frozen since 1992); 1996: $604; 1997: $604; 1998: $635; 1999: $655; 2000: $700; 2001: $749; 2002: $802; 2003: $825; 2004: $850; 2005: $893; 2006: $956; 2007: $1,032; 2008: $1,115; 2009: $1,204; 2010: $1,265; 2011: $1,328; 2012: $1,394; 2013: $1,492; 2014: $1,627; eBook: $1,970; renewal: 2014: $1,627
Written by the Matthew Bender editorial staff in conjunction with nearly forty outside experts, this four-volume set is the most complete resource available on the subject of child custody. The authors treat all phases of the disputed custody or visitation proceeding, as well as the effective use of experts, the substantive law of custody and visitation, case management, an analysis of relevant Uniform Acts and Conventions, child abuse and neglect, the rights of putative fathers, international enforcement of custodial rights, disputes between parents, and between parents and non-parents, and much more. The exhaustive footnotes cite to the law of all fifty states. There are more than 150 litigation forms and a state-by-state analysis of the Uniform Child Custody Jurisdiction Act. There are also bibliographies of significant treatises, law review articles, legal encyclopedias, and **ALR** annotations. Appendices include cases, table of statutes, and subject index. This is a well-written, thoroughly researched, and highly practical guide to custody and visitation issues.

Cost Saving Tips: The depth of coverage and frequency of supplementation make this an expensive set to maintain on an annual basis. If you feel that the basic analysis of the core set is sufficient for your needs, you may wish to drop the standing order and up-date on an as-needed basis. This will save you thousands of dollars over the life of your practice. Much of what you pay for on a standing order will be material you rarely, if ever, consult. The trick, once you have isolated the specific legal issue of concern is to use the primary sources directly to update the cases and analysis you find in this, or any, secondary source. To do this, you must consult the appropriate Shepard's citators, computer-assisted legal research systems, jurisdictional digests, legal newspapers, slip opinions, etc.

Moe, Barbara A. **Adoption: a Reference Handbook**. 2nd ed. Santa Barbara, CA: ABC-CLIO, Inc., 2007. 1 vol. (342pp.).
Cost: $55; no supplementation (2014).
Adoption is a time-honored tradition which was practiced in Roman times and acquired a statutory basis in the United States in the mid-19th century. While most of the more than 125,000 adoptions taking place in the United States today (generally by judicial proceeding), are by other family members, adoptions also take place across racial and cultural lines. Indeed, Americans have adopted more than a quarter million children internationally. This volume, which is directed at a general academic and professional audience, provides a lucid overview of the practice of adoption and summarizes the latest scholarship on the specific and sometimes controversial issues with which adoption has been involved, including transracial and same-sex adoptions, and adoptions by single parents. The author also provides an international perspective with a chapter on how adoption is practiced in countries outside the United States. The author is a consultant to and past director of the Special Needs Program at Adoption Alliance in Denver, CO.

Mosten, Forrest S. **The Complete Guide to Mediation: The Cutting-Edge Approach to Family Law Practice**. Chicago: American Bar Association, Section of Family Law, 1997. 1 vol. (441 pp.).
Cost: $89.95 ($79.95 to Family Law Section members) (2014).
A detailed, practical guide to the often complex process of mediation in the domestic relations context. The author, an international authority in mediation circles, provides readers with an excellent overview of the mediation process, its techniques and benefits. He attempts to disabuse lawyers of the notion that «winning» in a divorce proceeding means vanquishing the other party. He discusses such topics as the use of therapists as mediators, mediation in the courts, mediation training, the lawyer's role during agreement making, prevention of future conflict, marketing mediation-related service products, and index.

Myers, John E. B. **Myers on Evidence of Interpersonal Violence: Child Maltreatment, Intimate Partner Violence, Rape, Stalking, and Elder Abuse**. Successor to the author's **Evidence in Child Abuse and Neglect Cases**. New York: Wolters Kluwer Law & Business, 2011-date. 1 vol. (approx. 1,298 pp.). Annual supplementation.

Cost: $453; supplementation: 2012: $145; 2013: $155.
Written by a leading expert and commentator on child abuse and neglect investigation and litigation, this expanded treatise provides detailed coverage of child abuse and neglect cases, intimate partner abuse, and the crimes of rape, stalking and elder abuse. The author examines the current medical and scientific research regarding evidence in such cases as well as the latest techniques for questioning children, the signs of sexual abuse, the use of videotaped depositions, analysis of character evidence, and the use of expert testimony. Chapters examine child development relevant to interviewing children and litigating allegations of maltreatment, testimonial competence, children in court, physical child abuse, neglect, child sexual abuse, hearsay, and evidence of character and uncharged misconduct, and impeachment, intimate partnet violence, stalking, rape, elder abuse, neglect and exploitation. The volume includes citations to over 2,500 cases and psychological studies, a table of cases, and subject index. John E. B. Myers is a professor of law at the University of the Pacific, McGeorge School of Law.

Nichols, John F., Sr. and Joe Phillips. **Family Law Depositions**. Huntington, NY: Juris Publishing, 2010. 1 vol. Looseleaf format or eBook.
Cost: $225.00; supplementation: 2011: $70; 2012: $80; 2013: $95 (2014).
Depositions In family law matters are generally conducted for the purposes of ascertaining matters of material fact, determining case strategy, and probing the conscience of the deponent and opposing counsel. They are far more likely in cases involving long marriages in which property issues are more important, the difference in earning power of the spouses is significant, or where children or custody issues are involved. This volume provides expert practical guidance and sample depositions in the areas of pre-deposition strategy, the conduct of the deposition, divorce proceedings, custody proceedings and visitation, property proceedings, marriages, family torts, other torts, and damages. Each deposition form consists of a statement of legal background, strategy and facts, and an examination section consisting of the various topics to be addressed by the deposition, many accompanied by helpful explanatory notes. The substantive text is augmented by selective citations to relevant case law and other primary and secondary authorities. For the family law practitioner, this volume provides a an excellent roadmap for conducting depositions and a wealth of invaluable and well-organized sample questions that can be utilized in a variety of specific cases. John Nichols, a graduate of the University of Houston School of Law, is a trial attorney with extensive experience in the fields of family law, personal injury law, and general civil trial litigation. Joe Phillips, a graduate of the University of California Boalt Hall School of Law, has practiced in the areas of family law litigation, complex products liability litigation, class actions, and consumer protection law, among others.

Ramsey, Sarah H. and Douglas E. Abrams. **Children and the Law in a Nutshell**. 4th ed. St. Paul, MN: West, 2011. 1 vol. (623 pp.). Paperbound. Available from West Academic.
Cost: $41; from $29.94 on amazon.com; kindle ed.: $17.05 (2014).
A succinct overview of the primary legal issues involving children, including status, rights and obligations of children, the parent-child relationship, child abuse and neglect, foster care, criminal abuse and neglect, adoption, medical decision-making, financial responsibility and control, regulation of children's conduct, and delinquency. The author also discusses the representation of children, and international law issues as reflected by the UN Convention on the Rights of the Child, and child labor. Sarah Ramsay is Professor of Law, Syracuse University School of Law. Douglas Abrams is Associate Professor of Law, University of Missouri-Columbia School of Law.

Rice, Larry. **The Complete Guide to Divorce Practice: Forms and Procedures for the Lawyer**. 4th ed. Chicago: American Bar Association, General Practice, Solo & Small Firm Section, 2013. 1 vol. (732 pp.)
Cost: $149.95 ($135.95 to Section members); from $90.74 on amazon.com (2014).
This volume represents the author's systematic approach to the practice of divorce law. The order of the documents, forms, checklists and commentary reflect the natural order of the divorce experience, from initial consultation through trial and prenuptial agreements. The book's sections include: law office management, clients, interview, complaint, discovery, marital dissolution agreement, alternative dispute resolution, trial, final decree, petition, motions, orders, consent orders, miscellaneous pleadings, letters, prenuptial and postnuptial agreements, and miscellaneous. The forms are reproduced on a computer disc in WordPerfect format. A specialist in divorce and personal injury litigation, the author is a popular speaker and past Chairperson of the Family Law Section of the Tennessee Bar Association.

Rose, Melody. **Abortion: a Documentary and Reference Guide**. Westport, CT, Greenwood Press, 2008. 1 vol. (272 pp.).
Cost: $85; from $12.90 an amazon.com (2014).
A collection of over 40 primary documents representing the full range of views in the contentious abortion debate. Spanning the 19th century to the present day, the documents represent the views of religious leaders, judges, doctors, feminists, politicians, and political extremists. Each document is accompanied by the author's introduction and subsequent analysis. The documents, arranged in chronological order, trace the evolution of the abortion debate from the 19th century, when it was virtually a non-issue, to the present day, when it has become one of the most hotly contested issues on the political landscape. The documents include the Supreme Court decision of Roe v. Wade, the Partial Birth Abortion Ban, Pope Paul VI's encyclical Humanae Vitae, memoirs of early abortion providers, the personal writings of key conservative and liberal voices, and many more. Each chapter is accompanied by suggestions for further reading or research. The volume also includes a timeline of major events in abortion history, a bibliography of 50 titles on abortion, and over 30 Web links. The author is chair of political science at the Hatfield School of Government at Portland State University and the author of a number of articles and books on social and election policy, most recently including **Safe, Legal, and Unavailable**? (CQ Press, 2007).

Rutkin, Arnold H., ed. **Family Law and Practice.** New York: Matthew Bender & Co., 1985-date. 4 vols. Looseleaf format or

eBook. Supplemented approximately twice annually. No CD-ROM or Internet.
Cost: $2,004 (print); supplementation: 1995: $550 (cost frozen since 1992); 1996: $577; 1997: $577; 1998: $ 605; 1999: $625; 2000: $625; 2001: $669; 2002: $716; 2003: $750; 2004: $775; 2005: $829; 2006: $888; 2007: $959; 2008: $1,036; 2009: $1,119; 2010: $1,175; 2011: $1,234; 2012: $1,308; 2013: $1,400; 2014: $1,528; eBook: $1,822; renewal: 2014: $1,528.
This exhaustive treatise and practice guide is edited by Arnold Rutkin, a well-known family law practitioner who is chairman of the Family Law Section of the Association of Trial Lawyers of America. Mr. Rutkin has assembled a team of seventy-five experts in specific aspects of family law to draft the 67 individual chapters. The coverage includes both substantive legal analysis and practice materials guiding the practitioner through every stage of family law matters. Practice features include family law strategies, state statutes, the Uniform Marriage and Divorce Act, sample forms, and much more. Chapters cover the full range of marriage, divorce, and child matters as well as such issues as domestic torts, cohabitation and paternity. The text is heavily footnoted and includes the full text of many relevant statutes. There are also Tables of Cases and Statutes, and a detailed Subject Index. This is one of the most thorough works of its kind available on the market. The only drawback would the supplementation cost if, in fact, you choose to maintain a standing order.

Cost Saving Tips: This set comes with one year's updates as a part of the initial purchase price. After that, you are free to drop the standing order and supplement by purchasing a new set at some future date. You may find that the basic set provides most of what you require in the way of legal analysis and practical guidance and that you do not really need to maintain a standing order. Remember that there is an editorial time lag even if you maintain a standing order which requires updating in the appropriate digests, statutory codes, and Shepard's citators to completely update your research. In light of this, why subject your self to these high supplementation costs?

Rutkin, Arnold H. et al. **Valuation and Distribution of Marital Property.** New York: Matthew Bender & Co., 1984-date. 3 vols. Looseleaf format and eBook.
Cost: $1,569 (print) (includes annual subscription); renewal: 1995: $426; 1996: $447; 1997: $447; 1998: $470; 1999: $490; 2000: $490; 2001: $524; 2002: $561; 2003: $590; 2004: $620; 2005: $663; 2006: $710; 2007: $755; 2008: $816; 2009: $881; 2010: $926; 2011: $972; 2012: $1,011; 2013: $1,062; 2014: $1,159; eBook: $1,426; renewal: 2014: $1,159.
This exhaustive, three-volume guide to property distribution is written by Arnold Rutkin, a well-known family law practitioner who has served as chairman of the Family Law Section of the Association of Trial Lawyers of America, and a number of experts in matrimonial law. The authors discuss and analyze property distribution in both community property and equitable distribution jurisdictions. Attention is given to the use of accountants, appraisers and pension evaluators, valuation of real property, small businesses, professional practices, intangible assets, ERISA and non-ERISA pension plans. The authors also treat the characterization and division of community property, antenuptial, postnuptial and property settlement agreements, and the possession, sale and distribution of the marital home. This set is typical of most Matthew Bender treatises in the thoroughness of its coverage, wealth of citations, and practice aids. Again, the only drawback is the high cost of supplementation.

Cost Saving Tips: Drop the standing order after the initial one year's supplementation has expired. Purchase again when you feel you require more up-to-date coverage, remembering that even a «current» subscription reflects an editorial lag-time which must be covered by consulting primary sources, digests, Shepard's citations, legal newspapers, slip opinions, etc. If you use this work as a launching pad for further research and do not expect it to provide you with the last word on a given issue, you can save hundreds, if not thousands, of dollars over the life of your practice by following this strategy.

Shaner, Leslie Ann. **Divorce in the Golden Years: Estate Planning, Spousal Support, and Retirement Issues for Clients at Midlife and Beyond**. Chicago: American Bar Association, 2010. 1 vol. (369 pp.). Paperbound.
Cost: $139.95 ($119.95 to members); from $83.26 on amazon.com (2014).
For those who have reached the "Golden Years," or are approaching them, divorce presents a number of challenges that do not obtain with younger Americans. Chief among these is the division of retirement benefits and other estate planning issues. The largest cohort of these older Americans consists of the so-called Baby Boomers, that is, those born between 1946 and 1964, a group that totals 80 million. For a variety of reasons, ranging from verbal, physical or emotional abuse, cheating, alcohol or drug abuse, money problems, falling out of love, etc., couples in their Golden Years divorce, often sacrificing financial and emotional security in the process. Beginning with a useful introduction to the nature of divorce among older Americans, the author provides an in-depth analysis of such topics as nonprobate assets (e.g. life insurance), intestacy, wills and trusts, powers of attorney/medical directives, spousal support and equitable distribution factors, spousal support: methods of payment, amount and specification; and retirement plans. Each of the book's seven chapters is accompanied by citations to relevant cases, statutes, government reports, and other secondary authorities. The Appendices provide invaluable charts detailing the statutes of each state in a variety of areas relevant to divorce matters, including nonprobate assets, dower and curtesy, power of attorney and medical directives, spousal support factors, equitable distribution factors, division of retirement benefits; and sample provisions for property settlements and distribution of assets. A graduate of Washington & Lee University School of Law, the author practices family law in Richmond, VA, with a particular emphasis on the division of retirements in divorce, elder law, and estate planning. The complete book, with Appendices, is replicated on a companion CD-ROM.

Shulman, Gary A. **Qualified Domestic Relations Order Handbook**. 3d ed. New York: Wolters Kluwer Law & Business, 2007-date. 1 vol. (1,304 pp.). Looseleaf format.
Cost: $385; supplementation: 2008: $189; 2009: $205; 2010: $219; 2011: $448; 2012: $259; 2013: $295.
This comprehensive guide to qualified domestic relations orders is the definitive
work on the topic. The author provides clear explanation and

guidance into the intricacies of QDRO issues, with step-by-step instructions. The text is augmented with expert tips, drafting checklists, and a special chapter outlining 29 areas of high liability risk. It includes comprehensive model separation agreement language that can be incorporated directly into decrees to ensure that all of the QDRO issues are properly addressed, guidance on how to draft and administer child support QDROs, instructions and models for dividing federal and state government plans, model discovery letters, step-by-step drafting guidelines, 21 QDRO models for all types of plans and conditions, drafting and compliance checklists, and company policies and procedures manual. The Appendices include related statutory provisions.

Soler, Mark I. et al. **Representing the Child Client.** New York: Matthew Bender & Co., 1987-date. 1 vol. Looseleaf format or eBook. Supplemented 1-2 times per year. No CD-ROM.
Cost: $623 (print) (includes annual subscription); renewal: 1995: $138 (cost frozen since 1992); 1996: $145; 1997: $145; 1998: $155; 1999: $162; 2000: $175; 2001: $187; 2002: $236; 2003: $248; 2004: $260; 2005: $276; 2006: $298; 2007: $322; 2008: $348; 2009: $376; 2010: $395; 2011: $407; 2012: $423; 2013: $453; 2014: $494; eBook: $566; renewal: 2014: $494.
This one-volume guide to the legal representation of children was written by the attorneys and staff of the Youth Law Center headquartered in San Francisco with the assistance of the Matthew Bender editorial staff. The intended audience for this combination treatise and practice guide consists of attorneys who represent children who may find themselves in the position of witnesses, victims or clients. Accordingly, it provides attention to the legal rights of children in a variety of situations. Chapter coverage treats litigation on behalf of children in institutions, legal rights of children in institutions, the legal status of minors, representing children in dependency and juvenile justice and school disciplinary proceedings, the child witness, health care for low income children, and practical considerations in representing children. Each chapter is thoroughly annotated with references to case and statutory law and secondary source literature. There are tables of cases and statutes, and a detailed subject index, reflecting Matthew Bender's new commitment to quality in that regard. This is a thoroughly researched and well-written resource useful for both its analysis of substantive law and its practical advice on child representation matters.

Steinfeld, Shayna M. and Bruce R. Steinfeld. **The Family Lawyer's Guide to Bankruptcy: Forms, Tips and Strategies.** 2d ed. Chicago: American Bar Association, 2008. 1 vol. (376 pp.).
Cost: $129.95; $109.95 to members; from $54.90 on amazon.com (2014).
Bankruptcy is a system of laws and procedures designed to deal with the management and settlement of the debts of either an individual or corporation that is in serious financial difficulty, and to allow them to a fresh start with their financial lives. The volume addresses the impact of bankruptcy on divorce and the inherent conflict between bankruptcy and divorce law. While it did not change the basics of bankruptcy under the Bankruptcy Code, the passage of the Bankruptcy Abuse Prevention and Consumer protection Act of 2005 (BAPCPA) made it substantially more difficult for a debtor to escape a divorce-related obligation. The two substantive chapters in this book cover bankruptcy law for the divorce practitioner, and bankruptcy 101 with an emphasis on divorce ramifications. The remainder consists of a number of useful appendices, including pre-bankruptcy planning for the divorce practitioner, pre-BAPCPA: a discussion of prior law under §523(a)(15)'s balancing test, a dictionary of bankruptcy terms, official forms, tax forms, a bankruptcy court directory, exemption statutes, and index. The text is rather exhaustively footnoted for a book of this length. The Appendices, including forms, are reproduced on a companion CD-ROM. Bruce Steinfeld is a fellow of the American Academy of Matrimonial Lawyers and a family law practitioner in Georgia. Shayna Steinfeld practices in the fields of bankruptcy and corporate reorganization and has held numerous positions in Georgia Association for Women Lawyers and the Atlanta Bar Association, and has been a frequent lecturer in continuing legal education programs and bar programs.

Turner, Brett R. **Equitable Distribution of Property**. 3d ed. St. Paul, MN: Thomson Reuters West, 2005-date. 3 vols. Annual supplementation.
Cost: $380; supplementation: 2006: $75; 2007: $84; 2008: 0; 2009: $130.50; 2010: $141: 2011: $156; 2012: $171; 2013: $185; 2d ed.: 1995: $36; 1996: $50; 1997: $50; 1998: $53; 1999: $57; 2000: $61; 2001: $72.50; 2002: $85; 2003: $97; 2004: $108.50; 2005: new edition; **Monthly Assured Print Price (APP):** $21/$252.
This volume provides detailed coverage of the complex process by which marital assets are classified, valued and divided in a divorce. The author provides practical guidance on such matters as property division systems, procedure, discovery, classification, specific types of property, the mechanics of division, witness selection, retirement benefits, the classification and valuation of professional practices, and constitutionality issues. He also includes forms for discovery and valuation purposes and citations to cases from all equitable distribution states.

Zemmelman, Mimi Lyster. **Building a Parenting Agreement That Works: Child Custody Agreements Step-By-Step**. 7th ed. Berkeley, CA: Nolo, 2010. 1 vol. (335 pp.). Paperbound.
Cost: $29.99; from $7.97 on amazon.com; kindle ed.: $16.99 (2014).
Protecting the best interest of the child should be the primary objective of the custody agreement, but arriving at a fair, equitable and realistic solution can sometimes be a challenge for the parties involved. This guide cuts through the legalese to help the parties fashion a parenting agreement that deals with all the major, and most of the minor, issues that can complicate the drafting of such an agreement. The author discusses such matters as the child's domicile, medical care, holidays, education, insurance, making decisions, resolving disputes, making negative comments, consistency in raising children, labeling the custody arrangement, exchanging information, child care, special occasions and family events, vacations, transportation between parents' homes, improving transition times, maintaining contact, grandparents, relatives and important friends, religious training, psychiatric and other mental health care, and much more. Other chapters deal with such topics as special challenges, child support, alimony and jointly owned property, mediation and arbitration, making changes, understanding the child's needs, multiracial, multicultural and international families, nontraditional

families, state and federal laws affecting child custody, and help beyond the book, including organizational resources and a bibliography. The Appendix includes detailed worksheets and a sample parenting agreement. Mimi Zemmelman has over 20 years experience in family mediation and child custody matters.

Additional titles in the field of Family Law are available from the following publishers: American Bar Association, Wolters Kluwer Law & Business, Matthew Bender, CCH, Inc., Foundation Press, Independent Institute, LexisNexis, National Council of Juvenile Court Judges, Random House, Thomson Reuters West, West Academic. See Appendix B for addresses and telephone numbers.

Federal Practice and Procedure

Bender's Federal Practice Forms. Compiled by Louis R. Frumer and Marvin Waxner. New York: Matthew Bender & Co., 1951-date. 20 vols. Looseleaf format. Also available in CD-ROM format.
Cost: $7,273 (includes annual subscription); annual renewal: 1995: $1,588 (price frozen since 1992); 1996: $1587.50; 1997: $1,587.50; 1998: $1,670; 1999: $1,750; 2000: $1,850; 2001: $1,980; 2002: $2,119; 2003: $2,225; 2004: $2,336; 2005: $2,453; 2006: $2,625; 2007: $2,835; 2008: $3,402; 2009: $3,674; 2010: $4,006; 2011: $4,246; 2012: $4,543; 2013: $4,861; 2014: $5,305; CD-ROM: $7,448; renewal: 1998: $1,675; 1999: $1,750; 2000: $1,850; 2001: $1,980; 2002: $2,142; 2003: $2,225; 2004: $2,336; 2005: $2,453; 2006: $2,625; 2007: $2,835; 2008: $3,434; 2009: $3,709; 2010: $3,878; 2011: $4,110; 2012: $4,585; 2013: $4,906; 2014: $5.461.08; eBook: $6,612; renewal: 2012: $4,543; 2013: $4,861; 2014: $5.305.
A companion to **Moore's Federal Practice**, this set provides the full text of all federal rules, notes to amendments, Advisory Committee Notes, as well as hundreds of relevant forms. Included are the Rules of Civil Procedure, Rules of Criminal Procedure, Federal Rules of Evidence, United States Magistrates, Federal Rules of Appellate Procedure, U.S. Supreme Court Rules, U.S. Tax Court Rules, Bankruptcy Rules, etc. followed by the forms applicable to each rule. Footnotes provide citations to relevant federal decisions. Includes cross-references to **Moore's Federal Practice** as an aid to more in-depth research.

Cost Saving Tips: For those who desire the set in hard copy, used sets have sold for prices in the range of $400-$500. The purchaser may then choose to purchase another used set at some later date, employing a current edition of the Federal Rules to keep up with any actual changes. Annual paperback editions of the rules are available from numerous sources, including West and Matthew Bender. The initial cost of this set rose 21% since last year.

Bender's Federal Practice Forms [CD-ROM]. New York: Matthew Bender & Co. One disc. Updated quarterly. Available for Windows. Search Engine: Authority.
Cost: $7,448 (includes annual subscription); annual renewal: 1997: $1,590; 1998: $1,670; 1999: $1,670; 2000: $1,850; 2001: $1,980; 2002: $2,142; 2003: $2,225; 2004: $2,336; 2005: $2,453; 2006: $2,625; 2007: $2,835; 2008: $3,434; 2009: $3,709; 2010: $3,878; 2011: $4,110; 2012: $4,585; 2013: $4,906; eBook: $6,612; renewal: 2012: $4,543; 2013: $4,861; 2014: $5,461.08.
This CD-ROM version of the 16-volume print set (see description above) is also available as a part of Matthew Bender's Authority Federal Practice Library.

Cost Saving Tips: For the customer interested in reducing annual supplementation costs, the print version is the preferred option since, unlike the Internet or CD-ROM versions, it can be utilized into the future without the time expiration typical of electronic products.

Brunet, Edward J., Martin H. Redish, and Michael A. Reiter. **Summary Judgment: Federal Law and Practice**. 2014 ed. St. Paul, MN: Thomson Reuters West, 2006-date. 1 vol. (620 pp.). Annual supplementation.
Cost: 2014 Edition: $145; supplementation: 2006: $110; 2007: $30; 2008: $33.50; 2009: $45; 2010: $49; 2011: $53; 2012: $58; 2d ed.: 2001: $23.50; 2002: $26; 2003: $29.50; 2004: $32; 2005: $35; supplementation to 1st ed.: 1995: $40; 1996: $40; 1997: $48.00; 1998: $40; 1999: $52; 2000: new edition; **Monthly Assured Print Price** (**APP**): $10/$120.
A comprehensive treatise on the law of summary judgments in the federal courts. Combines a description and substantive evaluation of the state of the law and the complete summary judgment process. It also provides detailed explanation of the procedures involved in summary judgment and practical advice in a number a substantive areas, including personal injury, civil rights, libel, antitrust, real estate ownership, and contract disputes. Additional discussion is devoted to the role of summary judgment generally, burden shifting, timing of motions, and the standard for awarding summary judgment. Includes model forms, citations to cases and statutes, and a complete problem solving guide. Edward Brunet is the Henry J. Casey Professor of Law for Lewis and Clark Law School. Martin Redish is the Louis and Harriet Ancel Professor of Law and Public Policy at Northwestern University School of Law at Northwestern University School of Law and a national expert on civil procedure, constitutional law, and federal jurisdiction. Michael Reiter is a noted trial and appellate attorney, an adjunct professor of law at Northwestern University School of Law, and a faculty member of the National Institute for Trial Advocacy.

Childress, Steven Alan and Martha S. Davis. **Federal Standards of Review**. 4th ed. Charlottesville, VA: LexisNexis, 2010-date. 2 vols. Annual pocket parts.
Cost: $439 (print or eBook); no supplementation to date; 3d ed.: 2000: $65; 2001: $84; 2002: $87; 2003: $91; 2004: $97; 2005: $97; 2006: $103; 2007: $111; 2008: $119; 2009: $318; 2011: $398; 2012: $426; 2013: $151; 2d edition: 1995: $48; 1996: $50; 1997: $56; 1998: $60.
Decisions of the federal courts of appeals are the final word in 98.6% of appealed cases. The discretion exercised by these courts over decisions of the federal district courts is grounded in specific standards of review which determine in what manner

the appellate court may review the actions of the district court judge, jury or administrative agency. In this two-volume work, the authors provide both the theoretical underpinnings and the practical application of standards of review in the federal courts. However, their discussion is also extended to review in the state courts, including those which have substantially adopted the federal rules and those which have not. It is intended to assist attorneys, judges and scholars in understanding the scope and mission of judicial review and in focusing their attention on those issues which lie at the heart of the appeal. Following a introductory analysis of standards of review generally, the authors provide detailed examination of the application of these standards in civil, criminal and administrative contexts, while addressing the role of the trial judge, jury and administrative agency in the process. Steven Alan Childress, a practicing attorney and professor of law, has extensive experience as both a law clerk and extern in the federal courts. This work is the culmination of his scholarly examination of standards of review in various federal courts of appeals. Professor Martha Davis, a former clerk in the U.S. District Court, provides a complementary perspective of the review functions of the district courts and the review of its decisions by the courts of appeals. The text is adequately supported by citations to primary and secondary sources and includes both a table of cases and index.

The Department of Justice Manual. 3d ed. Gaithersburg, NY: Wolters Kluwer Law & Business, 2012-date. 8 vols. Looseleaf format. Supplemented 3-4 times annually.
Cost: $2,569; supplementation: 2000: $708; 2001: $720; 2002: $793; 2003: $813; 2004: $822; 2005: $1,152; 2006: $1,208; 2007: $1,288; 2008: $1,749; 2009: $1,476; 2010: $1,607; 2011: $1,808; 2012: $3,684 (including new ed.); 2013: $2,076.
This five-volume resource assembles the basic manuals, guidelines, policy statements, and procedures distributed by the Department of Justice which govern the actions of U.S. Attorneys working in the Justice Department's Civil, Environment and Natural Resources, Tax, Antitrust, Civil Rights, and Criminal Divisions, and U.S. Attorneys' Offices nationwide. It is designed as a ready reference for U.S. Attorneys responsible for the prosecution of violations of federal law. It is intended a source of internal Department of Justice guidance and is not intended to create any rights, enforceable by law by any party in any civil or criminal matter. The Manual is divided into nine titles: General, Appeals, Executive Office for United States Attorneys, Civil, Environment and Natural Resources, Tax, Antitrust, Civil Rights, and Criminal. An essential resource for federal attorneys and those representing litigants or defendants in matters involving the application of federal law in the above named subject areas.

Deskbook for Chief Judges of the U.S. District Courts. 3d ed. Washington, DC: Federal Judicial Center, 2003. 1 vol. (138 pp.).
Cost: available at no cost at:
www.fjc.gov/public/pdf.nsf/lookup/Deskbook.pdf/$file/Deskbook.pdf
This volume was designed to assist Chief Judges of the U.S. District Courts in meeting the "complex challenges of leading their district courts." It describes those challenges and the statutes and administrative policies that impact the District Courts. The Deskbook includes two kinds of materials: (1) summaries of statutes and Judicial Conference policies and descriptions of relevant sources and assistance available from the Federal Judicial Center and Administrative Office of the U.S. Courts; and (2) suggestions for chief judges to consider when confronting particular matters, those suggestions based upon comments from experienced chief judges and professional literature regarding the management of public and private organizations. The first edition of this volume was published in 1984.

Federal Judicial Center. **Reference Manual on Scientific Evidence**. 3d ed. St. Paul: Thomson/West, 2000. 1 vol. (639 pp.) Annual. Paperbound.
Cost: $79.95 (2014)
A rise in the introduction of scientific evidence in the nation's courts has raised a number of evidentiary issues which must be resolved by judges who often lack the technical expertise to make proper determinations regarding the introduction of such evidence. This volume is designed to assist members of the bench in «implementing effective management of expert evidence involving scientific issues.» Such experts most commonly include physicians, economists, engineers, but also include a variety of scientific and technical experts. This volume contains twelve chapters discussing such topics as the management of expert evidence, the admissibility of expert testimony, and including reference guides on epidemiology, toxicology, survey research, medical testimony, forensic DNA evidence, statistics, multiple regression, and the estimation of economic losses in damages awards. A fascinating essay entitled "How Science Works," by physicist David Goodstein, provides an insightful overview of the role of science and the scientific method. An indispensable guide to the jurist hearing technical cases.

Federal Practice Library [CD-ROM]. New York: Matthew Bender & Co. One disc. Updated quarterly. Available for Windows. Search Engine: Authority.
Cost: $51,212 (includes annual subscription); renewal: 1998: $14,160; 1999: $14,725; 2000: $15,500; 2001: $16,585; 2002: $17,746; 2003: $18,634; 2004: $19,566; 2005: $20,936; 2006: $22,402; 2007: $24,194; 2008: $26,371; 2009: $28,480; 2010: $31,040; 2011: $33,523; 2012: $36,540; 2013: $39,098; 2014: $46,592.58.
The complete library includes the following Matthew Bender titles: Moore's Federal Practice (3rd ed.), Bender's Federal Practice Forms, Federal Litigation Guide, Weinstein's Federal Evidence (2d ed.), Bender's Forms of Discovery, Benedict on Admiralty, Court Awarded Attorney Fees, Federal Evidence Practice Guide, Modern Federal Jury Instructions, Benefits Review Board Service--Longshore Reporter, Civil Rights Actions, Moore's Manual-Federal Practice and Procedure, Moore's Manual-Federal Practice Forms, Moore's Federal Rules Pamphlet, Police Civil Liability, Federal Practice Before Federal Magistrates, Federal Evidence Tactics, and Federal Local Court Rules. Various combinations also available.
This product expewrienced a 21% price increase since 2013.

Federal Procedural Forms. Lawyers Edition. St. Paul, MN: West (Lawyers Cooperative Publishing Co.), 1975-date. 43 vols. Annual pocket parts. CD-ROM product discontinued (see Westlaw).

Cost: $6,335; supplementation: 1991: $433.00; 1992; $335.00; 1993: $491.50; 1994: $479.50; 1995: $604.10; 1996: $726.50; 1997: $574.00; 1998: $680.00; 1999: $872.00; 2000: $942.00; 2001: $1,109.50; 2002: $1,255.00; 2003: $1,222.00; 2004: $1,418.00; 2005: $1,489.50; 2006: $1,826; 2007: $2,033; 2008: $2,053; 2009: $2,585; 2010: $3,125; 2011: $3,512; 2012: $4,142; 2013: $4,815; **Monthly Assured Print Price (APP):** $348/$4,176.

This comprehensive set provides the practitioner with civil, criminal, and administrative forms organized into more than 60 chapters. Each chapter includes a scope note, a listing of matters treated elsewhere within the set, and collateral references to other Lawyers Cooperative publications, including **Am. Jur. 2d.**, **Federal Procedure**, **ALR**, **Am. Jur. P.O.F.**, **Am. Jur. Trials**, **Lawyers Edition Digest**, **Federal Rules Digest: Findex**, and **Federal Rules of Evidence Digest: Findex**. The forms themselves are accompanied by General References to the relevant federal rules and valuable reminders to ensure that your research is complete and up-to-date. Research References refer the use to pertinent sections of other LCP sources to consult when drafting and using the specific forms. Annotation References refer to both **ALR** and **L.Ed**. annotations which discuss the legal issues addressed by the forms. Finally, Procedural Guides provide the attorney with specific advice regarding the drafting and use of the forms and textual analysis of applicable statutes, rules, regulations and case law as they apply to the forms' language. Categories of forms include: notices, jury instructions, complaints, motions, affidavits, judgments, summonses, stipulations, answers, counterclaims, subpoenas, cross claims, orders, interrogatories, and writs. An excellent and exhaustive set of forms. The editorial notes and references provide clear and thorough guidance to the practitioner involved in drafting the forms.

Cost Saving Tips: If you desire to keep this publication current, add it to your WestlawNext subscription. The rising cost of West's print products makes this a dinosaur. If you must have a print set, buy it used or on sale and let the subscription lapse. Even a non-current set will provide useful boiler plate language to the attorney who must draft his own forms. Avoid the **Monthly Assured Print Price** which will just lock you into supplementation you don't need.

Federal Procedure. Lawyers Edition. St. Paul, MN: West Group (Lawyers Cooperative Publishing Co.), 1981-date. 76 vols. Annual cumulative supplements with periodic revised (recompiled) volumes. Also available on CD-ROM.

Cost: $10,381; supplementation: 1991: $482; 1992: $491; 1993: $451.50; 1994: $830.80; 1995: $830.80; 1996: $1,081.50; 1997: $858; 1998: $973; 1999: $1,300; 2000: $1,390; 2001: $1,634; 2002: $2,181; 2003: $2,331; 2004: $2,295; 2005: $3,293.00; 2006: $2,895; 2007: $3,582; 2008: $3,582; 2009: $4,190.50; 2010: $4,652; 2011: $4,957.50; 2012: $6,969.50; 2013: $7,130; **Monthly Assured Print Price (APP):** $576/$6,912. Used sets sell for approx. $800. CD-ROM version discontinued (see WestlawNext).

An encyclopedic reference which treats all three parts of the federal adjudicatory system: traditional courts, specialized courts, and administrative agencies and their tribunals, in 80 individual chapters contained in 33 volumes. The 80 chapters are divided into two types of coverage; core coverage encompassing general principles of procedure in all three levels of the federal court system; and topical coverage encompassing the application of general and specific procedural rules in specific types of actions or proceedings, e.g., banking and financing, bankruptcy, civil rights, environmental protection, and employment discrimination. The topical chapters cover the specialized courts and administrative agencies to which the specific action applies. This set includes a variety of practice aids, practice pointers, checklists, and law review commentary as well as collateral references to other relevant titles in the Total Client-Service Library, such as **Am. Jur. 2d**, the **ALR** series, **Am. Jur Trials**, **Am. Jur. Proof of Facts**, etc. An excellent choice for the firm heavily involved in practice before federal administrative agencies and courts. However, while the supplementation cost was initially less expensive than that for the competing set from Matthew Bender (**Mezines**), it now exceeds the cost of the Bender set by nearly $1,100.00 per year.

Cost Saving Tip: Substantial increases in the both the initial and supplementation for this set make it an ideal candidate for used purchase with maintenance on WestlawNext. The print set will cost more than $10.000 in the first year, and over $7,000 per year for supplementation--a cash cow for West, a gigantic hole in your wallet. You can have the same publication for about $1,000 annually added to your WestlawNext contract. Avoid the Monthly Assured Print Price, which will just lock you into high supplementartion costs.

Gensler, Steven S. **Federal Rules of Civil Procedure: Rules with Commentary**. 13th ed. St. Paul, MN: Thomason Reuters West, 2010-date 2 vols. Annual. Paperbound.

Cost: 2014 Edition: $344; ProView eBook: $344.

First promulgated in 1938, the Federal Rules of Civil Procedure (FRCP) govern civil procedure in the United States (federal) district courts (i.e. the trial courts of the federal judiciary). Officially, the rules are promulgated by the U.S. Supreme Court under the Rules Enabling Act, and then approved by the U.S. Congress. Changes in the rules originate with the Judicial Conference of the United States, which serves as the federal judiciary's internal policy-making body. Major revisions to the FRCP have been made in 1948, 1963, 1966, 1970, 1980, 1983, 1987, 1993, 2000, and 2006. Rules of civil procedure in most states are patterned after the FRCP. First published in 2006, this, now, two-volume resource reproduces each rule, the text of which is accompanied by expert analysis and annotated practice commentary by Steven S. Gensler, Professor of Law at the University of Oklahoma. Volume two contains the appendix material, consisting primarily of the Advisory Committee Notes and Explanatory Statements, forms, supplemental rules, and subject index. The practice commentaries and case annotations provide a lucid and scholarly guide to the manner in which the federal courts have construed the individual rules, and explain how they relate to other rules or procedural matters. The 2009 edition reflects the enactment of Federal Rule of Evidence 502, continuing developments in e-discovery, and the reaction of the federal circuit courts to pleading standards under *Bell Atlantic v. Twombly*. Professor Gensler has been a member of the Civil Rules Advisory Committee since 2005.

Graham, Michael H. **Handbook of Federal Evidence.** 7th ed. St. Paul: Thomson Reuters West, 2011-date. 8 vols. Annual supplementation. West's Handbook Series.
Cost: $803; supplementation: 2013: $184; 6th ed.: 2006: $58; 2007: $69; 2008: $110; 2009: $132; 2010: $154; 5th ed.: 2001: $58.50; 2002: $70; 2003: $79.75; 2004: $62; 2005: 0; 2006: new edition; 4th edition: 1997: $40; 1998: $42.50; 1999: $46; **Monthly Assured Print Price (APP):** $38/$456.
This is the fourth edition of a work first authored by Professor Graham of the University of Miami School of Law in 1981. Its stated aim is to provide the «trial attorney and presiding judge «a clear statement of what the law of evidence is in a convenient to use one-volume format.» It is based upon an analysis of every case in reported federal decisions to the Federal Rules of Evidence. The Commentary following each rule is based upon the interpretive authority emerging from this analysis. The author also provides special attention in the text, footnotes and citations to those areas which remain controversial. The substantive part of the text is divided into the eleven articles under which the Rules have been organized, including general provisions, judicial notice, burdens of proof and presumptions in civil and criminal actions and proceedings, relevancy and its limits, privileges, witnesses, opinions and expert testimony, hearsay, authentication and identification, contents of writings and photographs, and miscellaneous rules. Appendices include the Federal Rules of Evidence, table of statutes, table of rules and standards, table of cases, and a subject index.

Grenig, Jay E. and Jeffrey S. Kinsler. **Handbook of Federal Civil Discovery and Disclosure**. 3d ed. St. Paul, MN: Thomson Reuters West, 2010-date. 1 vol. (871 pp.). Hardbound or ProView eBook. Includes forms on CD-ROM.
Cost: $276; ProView eBook: $268; supplementation: 2011: $97; 2012: $106; 2d ed.: 2003: $22; 2004: $24.75; 2005: $27; 2006: $30; 2007: $33.50; 2008: $37.50; 2009: $41.50; $1st ed.: 1999: $27.50; 2000: 0; 2001: $32.50; 2002: $102.50 (new edition); **Monthly Assured Print Price (APP):** $14/$168.
A thorough analysis of the federal rules governing discovery and disclosure in civil actions. Each rule is also accompanied by discussion of its practical application in real-life situations, and includes citations to supporting case authority, practice tips and checklists. Chapters encompass such topics as the duty of disclosure, depositions before actions or pending appeal, persons before whom depositions may be taken, stipulations regarding discovery procedure, depositions upon oral examination, depositions upon written questions, use of depositions in court proceedings, interrogatories to parties, production of documents and things, physical and mental examination, requests for admission, failure to make discovery or cooperate in discovery: sanctions, electronic discovery, ethics, professionalism and discovery, and obtaining evidence in foreign countries. The appendices includes discovery forms, and the discovery timetable under federal rules. A disc of related federal forms is also included. Jay Grenig is a professor of law at Marquette University Law School. Jeffrey Kinsler is an associate professor at Marquette University Law School and of counsel at Mayer, Brown & Platt. They have authored books on federal civil procedure, discovery and evidence.

Herr, David F. **Annotated Manual for Complex Litigation**. 4th ed. St. Paul, MN: Thomson Reuters West, 2001-date. 1 vol. Annual. Softbound or ProView eBook.
Cost: 2013 Edition: $178 (2014); **Monthly Assured Print Price (APP):** $15/$180.
An essential companion to the Federal Judicial Center's **Manual for Complex Litigation**, this volume provides current and up-to-date information regarding case management that has developed since the last revision of that work in 1994. It includes the complete text of the **Manual for Complex Litigation** together with the author's insightful analysis of recent developments, including the use of "bidding" for selecting lead counsel, the impact on class certification of the Supreme Court's 1999 decision in Ortiz v. Fibreboard Corp., the use of bellweather trials, the operation of Internet-based document depositories, the role of survey evidence, particularly in intellectual property cases, and the evolving standards for the award of attorneys' fees. David Herr is a partner in the Minneapolis firm of Maslon Edelman Borman & Brand LLP, and a member of the faculty of William Mitchell College of Law since 1978. Among his extensive professional activities, he has authored or co-authored more than 20 litigation treatises and guides.

Hunter, Robert S. **Federal Trial Handbook: Civil and Criminal.** 4th ed. St. Paul, MN: Thomson Reuters West (Lawyers Cooperative Publishing Co.), 2003-date. 2 vols. (2,156 pp.). Softbound. Annual editions.
Cost: 2013 Edition: $742; criminal and civil volumes also available individually. Supplementation to prior edition: 1994: $40.00; 1995: $44.75; 1996: $70; 1997: $79; 1998: $64; 1999: $69; 2000: $73; 2001: $84; 2002: $99; 2003: 2005: $175; 2006: $175; 2008: $215; 2009: $356; 2010: $391.50; 2011: new edition. **Monthly Assured Print Price (APP):** $60/$720.
Unlike the exhaustive scholarly treatments of Federal law and practice, this two-volume trial practice guide is intended as a quick, yet comprehensive reference to the law on the myriad of questions that arise in the course of a trials in the Federal courts. This third edition has been divided into two volumes covering Civil and Criminal practice. The author covers topics ranging from evidence and procedure, attorney conduct, motions to jury trials, burden of proof, witnesses, evidence, judicial notice and damages. The text is supported by references to supporting case and statutory law, and includes such Lawyers Cooperative features as references to relevant Annotations in **ALR**, trial practice aids such as **Am. Jur. Trials** and **Proof of Facts**, and practice checklists. There are separate Indexes for each of the two volumes--Civil and Criminal. A well-written and nicely organized practice tool, particularly when one desires a quick answer to a question involving federal practice. Supplementation cost is reasonable for a two-volume work.

Hutchinson, Thomas W., et al. **Federal Sentencing Law and Practice**. St. Paul, MN: West, 1999-date. 1 vol. (2,268 pp.). Courtroom Practice Series. Annual editions. Print or ProView eBook.
Cost: 2014 Edition: $303 (2014).
Federal sentencing law was significantly altered by the Sentencing Reform Act of 1984 which curtailed the discretion of the sentencing judge, abolished parole, reduced good time credit, and authorized the appeal of sentences by the prosecution

and the defense. The Federal Sentencing Commission created under this act was charged with the preparation of a detailed manual to the federal sentencing guidelines designed for use by judges, prosecutors, defense attorneys, probation officers, and others. The first eight chapters of this volume annotate the eight chapters of the United States Sentencing Commission's **Guidelines Manual**, the official version of the guidelines and include Author's Comments written by the authors of this book. Chapters 9-10 provide the authors' explanation and analysis of departures from the guidelines and appellate review of sentences.

Joseph, Gregory P. **Sanctions: The Federal Law of Litigation Abuse**. 5th ed. Charlottesville, VA: LexisNexis (Michie), 2013-date. 1 vol. Or eBook.

Cost: $242; no supplementationto date; 4th ed.: 2010: $65; 2011: $72; 2012: $77; 3rd ed.: 2001: $47; 2002: $49; 2003: $51; 2004: $53; 2005: $53; 2006: $57.

Judges in federal courts have been increasingly willing to impose sanctions, combined with hefty financial fines, upon parties and lawyers who abuse the litigation process, the most significant of which was the $114 million in attorneys' fees and fines imposed for discovery abuse in Bush Ranch, Inc. v. E. I. duPont de Nemours & Co. (11th Cir., 1996). This volume provides a thorough review of the current state of the law regarding sanctions in the federal courts, as well as discussion of such topics as litigation abuse, Rule 11 on pleadings and written motions, Section 1927: multiplying litigation, inherent power of the court in dealing with bad faith litigation abuse, frivolous appeals, pretrial orders and conferences, discovery abuse, and the application of local Federal court rules. The author makes frequent comparisons between the subjective focus of a sanction and its objective standard and includes citations to thousands of relevant cases. Includes useful appendices and a subject index.

Knibb, David G. **Federal Court of Appeals Manual**. 6th ed. St. Paul, MN: Thomson Reuters, 2013. 1 vol. (595 pp.). Annual supplementation.

Cost: $197; supplementation: 2008: $33.50; 2009: $33.50; 2010: $39; 2011: $42; prior editions: 2001: $52.25; 2002: $26.50; 2003: $23; 2004: $25.75; 2005: $28.50; 2006: $31; 2007: new edition: $105; **Monthly Assured Print Price (APP):** $12/$144.

This practical guide explains the federal rules of appellate procedure used before the U.S. Courts of Appeal. Chapters are devoted to a consideration of the entire appellate process, including such topics as how to file a timely appeal, what to consider before taking an appeal, brief writing, preparation of the oral argument, and why the appeals process works the way it does in special situations. Includes an annual pamphlet that details the current circuit court rules.

Moore, James W. et al. **Moore's Federal Practice.** 3d ed. New York: Matthew Bender & Co., 1997-date. 31 vols. Looseleaf format. Supplemented 3-4 times per year. Also available on CD-ROM and eBook.

Cost: $7,421 (includes annual subscription); renewal: 1997: $2,693 (cost frozen since 1992); 1998: $2,750; 1999: $2,860; 2000: $2,860; 2001: $2,917.00; 2002: $2,950; 2003: $2,975; 2004: $2,999; 2005: $3,049; 2006: $3,080; 2007: $3,142; 2008: $3,936; 2009: $4,192; 2010: $4,234; 2011: $4,376; 2012: $4,362; 2013: $4,667; 2014: $5,094; CD-ROM: $9,518; renewal: 1998: $2,695; 1999: $2,860; 2000: $2,860; 2001: $3,060; 2002: $2,950; 2003: $2,975; 2004: $2,999; 2005: $3,209.00; 2006: $3,243; 2007: $3,501; 2008: $4,143; 2009: $4,474; 2010: $4,699; 2011: $5,075; 2012: $5,532; 2013: $5,919; 2014: $6,590.22; eBook: $6,746; renewal: 2012: $4,362; 2013: $4,667; 2014: $5,094. Criminal and Civil volumes available separately.

Originally published in 1938, the second edition of this massive treatise on procedure in the federal courts was issued in 1948, and a completely new and revised third edition appeared in March, 1997. It was originally authored by the late Professor James William Moore of Yale School and a team of co-authors, including Jo Desha Lucas, Professor of Law at the University of Chicago, Professor Howard P. Fink of Ohio State University College of Law, Richard D. Freer, the Robert Howell Hall Professor of Civil Procedure, Emory University, Dean Donald T. Weckstein of the University of San Diego School of Law, and Jeremy C. Wicker, a member of the Federal and Texas Bars. Considered authoritative by the Federal Courts, this is one of the most heavily cited works in the legal literature. This is a complete and authoritative guide to practice before the federal courts which treats such matters as court organization and jurisdiction, complex litigation, venue, the Federal Rules of Civil Procedure, Admiralty, the Judicial Code, the Rules of Criminal Procedure, Magistrates' Rules, Appellate process, the Federal Rules of Evidence and Supreme Court practice and jurisdiction. This treatise is valuable not only for its exhaustive coverage of federal practice matters, but for its historical analysis which examines the origins and development of each federal rule, a feature which distinguishes it from its competitors. The text is thoroughly footnoted with citations and notes to relevant cases and statutes. The Rules volumes provide, in addition to the full text, the history of each rule, including Congressional Committee notes, summary of amendments, etc. Volumes covering the Rules of Criminal Procedure (8-8C) and the Manual for Complex Litigation (vol. 1, Pt. 2) are also available separately. The volumes are supplemented with both interfiled pages and front-matter supplements. This new and modernized third edition of **Moore's Federal Practice** reflects the scholarly standards of its original author, the late Professor James William Moore, but the editorial insights and content revisions of a new editorial board and team of over 50 authors and reviewers. Substantively, the third edition of **Moore's Federal Practice** reflects the following changes: (1) a complete updating of the substantive text; (2) a reorganization of the chapters to provide more subtopic headings; (3) transfer of historical discussion to separate historical appendices that follow each chapter so as not to impede editorial discussion of the current state of the law; (4) greater analysis in the text, rather the footnotes; (5) case citations grouped by circuit; (6) new looseleaf ring binders; and (7) new updating practices to ensure that Moore's content is more up-to-date. Subscribers will receive four updates per year, two of which will include text revisions and all four of which will include Current Developments pamphlets for each volume.

Cost Saving Tips: Both the initial and supplementation cost of this set define it as a resource for the specialist in federal matters. If the hefty purchase price is more than you care to spend, the set should be available on the used law book market for $600-800, a savings of more than $6,700 off the $7,421 new price. Since cost of supplementation is also very high, you may choose to forego purchasing current supplements and buy new sets at periodic intervals. This will save you thousands of dollars in just a few years--dollars you can spend on other publications useful to your practice. Please note that the «current» print supplements («releases») to this set are several months old the day you receive them, although the availability of online formats are helping to reduce this gap. If you appreciate the historical coverage of **Moore's**, you can obtain your current information from a competitive product, such as **Federal Practice and Procedure**, which is far less costly to maintain. Or consider **Moore's Manual** as a lower-cost alternative

Moore, James William. **Moore's Manual--Federal Practice and Procedure.** New York: Matthew Bender & Co., 1962-date. 3 vols. Looseleaf format. Also available on LexisNexis.
Cost: $1,584 (includes annual subscription); renewal: 1995: $501 (price frozen since 1992); 1996: $526; 1997: $526; 1998: $550; 1999: $575; 2000: $870; 2001: $931; 2002: $997; 2003: $625; 2004: $629; 2005: $635; 2006: $642; 2007: $655; 2008: $820; 2009: $869; 2010: $982; 2011: $1,033; 2012: $997; 2013: $1,067; 2014: $1,220; CD-ROM available only as a part of **Authority Federal Practice Library**.
A three-volume condensation of the massive 34-volume **Moore's Federal Practice**. Provides cross-references to both **Moore's Federal Practice** and **Bender's Federal Practlce Forms**. Tracks a case, in abridged form, through the federal courts, addressing such issues as jurisdiction, venue, removal, appeals, etc.

Cost Saving Tips: This is an excellent alternative to the more costly Moore's Federal Practice. However, if the supplementation cost is excessive, simply drop the standing order subscription and re-purchase the set every 2-3 years.

Motions in Federal Court. 3d ed. St. Paul, MN: Thomson Reuters West (Clark Boardman Callaghan), 1996-date. 3 vols. (1,800 pp.). Supplemented annually with pocket parts. Print or ProView eBook.
Cost: $517; ProView eBook: $427; supplementation: 1997: $50; 1998: $56; 1999: $60; 2000: $64; 2001: $37.50; 2002: $82.50; 2003: $93; 2004: $103.50; 2005: $114; 2006: $126; 2007: $141; 2008: $86.50; 2009: $122; 2010: $264; 2011: $132; 2012: $145; 2013: $157; 2014: $170. **Monthly Assured Print Price (APP):** $33/$396.
This three-volume reference tool provides discussion and analysis of 129 of the most commonly used motions under the Federal Rules of Civil Procedure. It also includes checklists to guide the practitioner through the process of drafting, serving and filing motions in the federal courts. There are also explanations of the reasons for using each motion, the best time to file the motions, the factors employed by the courts in ruling upon the motions. Also explained are the grounds upon which the court is likely to grant or deny the motions as well as their appealability. The set is enhanced by a number of practice aids, including answers to motion questions, summaries of relevant Supreme Court decisions, and Research Guides to sources for further research. Originally prepared by the editorial staff of Shepard's/ McGraw-Hill, this book was taken over by Clark Boardman Callaghan in December, 1995.

Mullenix, Linda S., Martin Redish and Georgene Vairo. **Understanding Federal Courts and Jurisdiction**. New York: Matthew Bender & Co., 1998. 1 vol. (596 pp.).
Cost: $45; eBook: $36; from $0.01 on amazon.com; kindle ed.: $28.44 (2014).
Another in the publisher's Understanding series, this law school text provides a comprehensive overview of the constitutional principles and doctrines governing the federal judicial system, including discussion of Article III, the role of Congress in regulating the jurisdiction of the federal courts, the constitutional and statutory bases for federal jurisdiction, litigation before the federal courts, and the relationship between state and federal courts. The authors also examine such matters as justiciability, political questions, federal questions, diversity, removal, personal jurisdiction, multidistrict litigation, abstention doctrine, 11th Amendment, the Erie doctrine, and interstate preclusion. While intended for students in introductory and advanced federal procedure cases, it is also an inexpensive overview of the subject for practitioners. Linda S. Mullenix is the Rita and Morris Atlas Chair in Advocacy at the University of Texas School of Law. Martin H. Redish, the Louis and Harriet Ancel Professor of Law and Public Policy at Northwestern University School of Law, is a nationally renowned authority on the subjects of federal jurisdiction, civil procedure, freedom of expression and constitutional law. Georgene M. Vairo is Professor of Law & William M. Rains Fellow, Loyola of Los Angeles School of Law.

O'Malley, Kevin E., et al. **Federal Jury Practice and Instructions--Civil and Criminal.** 5th/6th ed. St. Paul, MN: Thomson Reuters West, 1999-date. 9 vols. A full set consists of volumes 1, 1A of the 6th ed. and volumes 2, 2A, 2B, 3, 3A, 3B, 3C of the 5th edition. Annual pocket parts. Package includes 12 circuit-specific pattern jury instruction pamphlets. [formerly Devitt and Blackmar]
Cost: $1,259; supplementation: 1994: $47; 1995: $52.50; 1996: $59; 1997: $119; 1998: $75; 1999: $90.50; 2000: $81; 2001: $366; 2002: $139.50; 2003: $159; 2004: $178; 2005: $196.50; 2006: $305; 2007: $243.50; 2008: $538.50; 2009: $481; 2010: $529; 2011: $578; 2012: $1,222; 2013: $909; **Monthly Assured Print Price (APP):** $79/$948.
Judges of the federal district courts have an obligation to instruct the jury as to the law of the case and provide reasonable guidance on the accompanying facts. This of one of the most important functions performed by the trial justice. While the judge has wide discretion in instructing the jury, he or she must observe Civil Rule 51 and Criminal 30 governing jury instruction procedure. Counsel in federal cases may, under the rules, submit requests for instructions at the close of evidence or when the court directs. The court must also advise counsel of proposed action upon these requests prior to closing arguments to the jury in order to allow them to tailor their remarks to the judge's instructions. This four-volume set provides both a discussion of the federal jury practice and instructions, and specific pattern or model instructions in a wide variety of civil and criminal matters. Each pattern instruction is accompanied by a discussion of relevant case law supporting the use of the instruction with numerous specific examples from the various federal circuits. The authors includes Judge William Lee (vol. 1), Kevin E. O'Malley (vols. 1A, 2, 2A), and Jay Grenig (vols. 3, 3A). Critical terms are

clearly defined, again with examples of definitions applied in the federal courts. The free-standing supplement contains tables of cases and statutes, subject index, and a WESTLAW Electronic Research Guide to jury instructions. An indispensable resource for the federal litigator.

Saltzburg, Stephen A., Michael M. Martin and Daniel J. Capra. **Federal Rules of Evidence Manual.** 10th ed. Charlottesville, VA: LexisNexis, 2011-date. 5 vols. Annual pocket parts.
Cost: $830; supplementation: 2007: $268; 2008: $152; 2009: $167; 2010: $179; 2011: $192; 2012: $205; 2013: $212; 8th ed.: 2002: $90.00; 2003: $96.00; 2004: $101.00; 2005: $218.00; 7th ed.: 1995: $90.00; 1996: $62.50; 1997: $59.00; 7th edition: 1998: $44.50; 1999: $70.00; 2000: $85.00; 2001: $68.00.
This three-volume analytical guide to the Federal Rules of Evidence is divided into three main Parts: (1) the Background of Codification Generally and the Federal Rules Specifically, (2) Analysis of each Rule, and (3) those Rules proposed by the Advisory Committee on the Federal Rules of Evidence, but rejected by Congress. The bulk of this treatise is devoted to an analysis of each of the Federal Rules of Evidence, including the Official Text of the Rule, an Editorial Explanatory Comment, selective Annotated Cases arranged topically, Legislative History, Advisory Committee Notes, House Subcommittee on Criminal Justice Notes, Report of the House Committee on the Judiciary, Report of the Senate Committee on the Judiciary, Report of the House and Senate Conferees, and Citations to Hearings and Debates. This logical arrangement provides for easy access by the busy practitioner or the legal scholar. Supplementation costs are reasonable in comparison with sets of similar size.

Sand, Leonard B. et al. **Modern Federal Jury Instructions.** New York: Matthew Bender & Co., 1984-date. 5 vols. Looseleaf format. Supplemented several times annually (24 times between 1984 and 1995). Also on CD-ROM and eBook.
Cost: $2,321 (with annual subscription); renewal: 1995: $633.50 (price frozen since 1992); 1996: $664; 1997: $664; 1998: $700; 1999: $730; 2000: $750; 2001: $803. 2002: $860; 2003: $903; 2004: $975; 2005: $1,034; 2006: $1,076; 2007: $1,141; 2008: 2008: $1,209; 2009: $1,306; 2010: $1,371; 2011: $1,440; 2012: $1,526; 2013: $1,633; 2014: $1,782; CD-ROM: $2,656; renewal: 1998: $665; 1999: $730; 2000: $780; 2001: $835; 2002: $860; 2003: $903; 2004: $975; 2005: $1,043.00; 2006: $1,085.00; 2007: $1,171; 2008: $1,271; 2009: $1,373; 2010: $1,469; 2011: $1,578; 2012: $1,730; 2013: $1,851; 2014: $2,060.40; eBook: $2,110; renewal: 2013: $1,633; 2014: $1,782.
Intended primarily for the use of attorneys who must prepare requests to charge a jury, and judges who must read and consider these requests, this set provides a wide variety of both criminal and civil pattern jury instructions. Borrowing heavily from other published sources, the text of each of the instructions is accompanied by relevant case authorities and a succinct commentary which is designed to inform and instruct the user in the legal issues involved. According to the authors, each recommended charge satisfies the following criteria: (1) it is an accurate statement of the law, (2) it is expressed in language which is comprehensible to the lay juror; and (3) it is as brief as the two criteria will permit. More than just a collection of pattern jury instructions, this reference work provides practitioners with a consider statement of each element in a civil or criminal proceeding which must be proven or disproven at trial. It is also useful to attorneys who must evaluate the probable success of a given case and those who need to determine the elements of a particular cause of action which should be alleged in a particular case. The cases cited under the authority headings provide notice to those interested in tracking trends in the various federal circuits. Includes five numbered volumes (1, 1A, 2, 3, 4) and two paperbound volumes, published periodically, containing pattern jury instructions in civil and criminal matters from the 5th, 6th, 7th, 8th, 9th and 11th circuits and the Federal Judicial Center. A well-organized and lucid reference tool. The instructions are comprehensive and the commentaries clear and concise. The most thorough work of its kind on the market.

Cost Saving Tips: If you don't require the entire set, consider purchasing only the civil or criminal volumes your practice requires. If you do purchase the hard copy, you can always drop the standing order and purchase a new set at some future date. Remember, however, that the CD-ROM product will time expire if you do not maintain the subscription, leaving you with nothing to show for your expense.

Sinclair, Kent B. **Practice Before Federal Magistrates.** New York: Matthew Bender & Co., 1985-date. 1 vol. Looseleaf format. Supplemented annually..
Cost: $557 (includes annual subscription); renewal: 1995: $75; 1996: $79; 1997: $79; 1998: $85; 1999: $89; 2000: $95; 2001: $102; 2002: $110; 2003: $116; 2004: $122; 2005: $131; 2006: $147; 2007: $165; 2008: $178; 2009: $192; 2010: $214; 2011: $213; 2012: $252; 2013: $272; 2014: $281.
This one-volume treatise is authored by Kent Sinclair, Professor Law at the University of Virginia, former Magistrate for the Southern District of New York, and a leading expert on practice before federal magistrates. Following an introductory overview of the magistrates system and the structure of the Magistrates Act and Rules, Sinclair describes and analyzes the role of the federal magistrate within the federal court system in both criminal and civil proceedings. Included are discussions of the criminal defendant's initial appearance, preliminary hearings, criminal «removal» hearings, arraignment, criminal calendar control. The section on civil proceedings addresses civil case referral practice, pretrial conferences and calendar control, subpoenas, writs and warrants, civil discovery, dispositive and non-dispositive civil motions, civil evidentiary hearings, settlement conferences, habeas corpus petitions, special master proceedings, civil trials upon consent, and administrative record reviews in Social Security cases. The Appendices includes the relevant federal statutes and rules governing federal magistrates, as well as tables of cases, statutes, and a subject index.

Supreme Court Practice. 10th ed. Gressman, Eugene; Stephen M. Shapiro; Kenneth S. Geller; Timothy S. Bishop; and Edward A. Hartnett, eds. Washington, DC: Bloomberg BNA Books, 2013-date. 1 vol. (1,450 pp.)
Cost: $495; no supplementation to date; supplementation to 8th edition: 1995: $45; 1996: 0; 1997: $65.
Since 1950, this book has served as the „bible“ for anyone practicing before the United States Supreme Court, that

appellation bestowed by none other than Supreme Court Associate Justice Lewis F. Powell on the occasion of Eugene Gressman's retirement in 1987. The first edition, which appeared in 1950, was co-authored by Robert Stern (1908-2000) and Eugene Gressman (1917-2010), whose collaboration would continue through numerous editions, and Eugene Gressman's through all but the present edition. Their collaboration began in 1949 when Gressman, a five-year law clerk to Justice Murphy joined with Stern, a former lawyer in the Office of Solicitor General who had argued more than sixty cases before the Supreme Court. Their first edition drew upon not only their own wide-ranging knowledge and expertise, but upon advice and counsel from the Office of the Clerk of the Supreme Court, who reviewed their draft document and made corrections and suggestions. Since that time, the book has earned a well-deserved reputation as the definitive resource for practice before the Court.

The 10th edition, which builds upon the impressive work of the previous authors, provides detailed guidance through every aspect of practice before the U.S. Supreme Court. The opening chapter provides an authoritative introduction to the Court, its history, structure and operations. This is followed by chapters detailed the Court's jurisdiction to review decisions of the federal and state courts, the factors motivating the Court's decision to exercise its Certiorari appellate jurisdiction, and he manner and procedures whereby the Court takes such jurisdiction. Additional chapters cover In forma pauperis proceedings, certified questions, original cases, extraordinary writs, the briefs on the merits, oral argument, petitions for rehearing and final disposition of cases, motions and applications, stays, injunctions and bail, capital cases, jurisdiction, standing, mootness and abatement, and admission to the bar and disbarment. The six Appendices contain the Rules of the Supreme Court of the United States, Clerk Guidelines Regarding Filing Cases, Clerk's Guidelines Regarding Cases Selected for Review, Forms, Statutes and Regulations, and Applications and Instructions for Admission to the Bar. The text is accompanied by appropriate citations to relevant Supreme Court and federal appellate court decisions, and applicable federal statutes.

The five current co-authors bring a wealth of experience and scholarly erudition to the 10th edition. Stephen M. Shapiro and Kenneth S. Geller have been co-authors since the sixth and seventh editions, respectively, both now partners with the firm of Mayer Brown, LLP. Each has extensive experience with the Supreme Court, from petitioning and briefing to oral argument. Timothy S. Bishop, also a partner in the firm of Mayer Brown, has experience as clerk to Supreme Court Justice William J. Brennan, Jr. and in briefing and arguing cases before the Court. Edward A. Harnett is the Richard Hughes Professor for Constitutional Law and Public Law and Service at Seton Hall University School of Law who brings federal clerkship experience and an impressive record of scholarly publication to this project. Dan Himmelfarb, also a partner in the appellate litigation for Mayer Brown LPP, served as law clerk to Associate Justice Clarence Thomas and assistant to the Solicitor General of the United States, with extensive experience briefing and arguing cases before the Supreme Court in both public and private capacities.

As with previous editions, the 10th edition incorporates into its discussion recent rules revisions, in this case as amended and effective July 1, 2013, which are otherwise all integrated into the existing 48 rules without being highlighted or designated as new procedures. It also contains updated guidelines and checklists for docketing and processing petitions for certiorari and appeals, and for pursuing a case after review has been granted. And the text and footnotes have been revised and augmented to incorporate recent rulings of the Supreme Court and other legal developments. Nothing in the literature remotely compares to **Supreme Court Practice** as a guide to anyone planning to bring a case before the U.S. Supreme Court.

Tigar, Michael E. **Federal Appeals: Jurisdiction and Practice.** 3d ed. St. Paul, MN: Thomson Reuters West (Clark Boardman Callaghan), 1999-date. 1 vol. Annual pocket part.
Cost: $186; supplementation: 2000: $32.50; 2001: $32.50; 2002: $43.50; 2003: $43; 2004: $45; 2005: $49; 2006: $55; 2007: $61; 2008: $68; 2009: $81.50; 2010: $95; 2011: $105; 2012: $115; 2013: $125; 2d edition:1994: $42; 1995: $45; 1996: $50; 1997: 0; 1998: $56; **Monthly Assured Print Price (APP):** $13/$156.
This single-volume guide to the federal appellate process, authored by a leading federal trial attorney, provides guidance to those bringing and defending federal appeals. The second edition is updated to reflect the 1993 changes in the federal rules. Includes advice on how to write effective briefs, make persuasive oral arguments, evaluate cases, and set realistic fees.

Weinstein, Jack B. and Margaret A. Berger. **Weinstein's Federal Evidence--United States Rules.** 2d ed. New York: Matthew Bender & Co., 1991-date. 6 vols. Looseleaf format. Supplemented several times annually. Also available on CD-ROM.
Cost: $4,735 (includes annual subscription); annual renewal: 1997: $1,231 (frozen since 1992); 1998: $1,250; 1999: $1,305; 2000: $1,370; 2001: $1,411; 2002: $1,569; 2003: $1,526; 2004: $1,648; 2005: $1,763; 2006: $1,818; 2007: $1,963; 2008: $2,120; 2009: $2,216; 2010: $2,313; 2011: $2,429; 2012: $2,990; 2013: $3,199; 2014: $3,491; CD-ROM: $5,138; renewal: 1998: $1,230; 1999: $1,305; 2000: $1,370; 2001: $1,466; 2002: $1,569; 2003: $1,648; 2004: $1,648; 2005: $1,763; 2006: $1,887; 2007: $2,038; 2008: $2,445; 2009: $2,641; 2010: $2,773; 2011: $2,995; 2012: $3,265; 2013: $3,494; 2014: $3,888.24; eBook: $4,305: 2013: $3,199; 2014: $3,491 per year. Also available as a part of the **Federal Practice Library**.
Written by Judge Jack B. Weinstein, U.S. District Court Judge for the Eastern District of New York and Professor of Law at Columbia University School of Law, and Margaret Burger, Professor of Law at Brooklyn Law School, this is a massive analytical work on the Federal Rules of Evidence. Among the themes which run through this treatise is the conviction that the Federal Rules are better interpreted and applied to admit rather than to exclude evidence, that the court's conduct in particular cases requires both flexibility and discretion, and that the Federal Rules of Evidence pave the way for innovations which are responsive to new forces and events. Consequently, the authors attempt to explain the reason behind the rule by devoting attention to legal theory in their commentary. This treatise is considerably enhanced by an organizational structure which lays out the Rule and explains its intent, the reason behind the rule, and the philosophy and practice under the Rule. Included are the legislative history, commentary, state adaptation, and Advisory Committee Notes and References to secondary authorities. The set includes exhaustive citations to all relevant federal

and state cases which have been decided under the Rule. The content is grouped into individual Articles, including General Provisions, Judicial Notice, Presumptions, Relevancy and Its Limits, Privileges, Witnesses, Opinions and Expert Testimony, Hearsay, Authentication and Identification, Contents of Writings, Recordings and Photographs, and Miscellaneous Rules. Volumes 6 and 7 contain an Index, Table of Statutes and Rules, Table of Cases, and a Table of Authors and Titles (secondary authorities).

Cost Saving Tip: A thorough, but costly, set. First, investigate availability of the set on the used law book market. If you buy it new, let it lapse after the one-year subscription expires. You can also supplement the text of the lapsed set with a less expensive alternative text or simply update your research in the primary sources and Shepardize your relevant cases and statutes. So-called «updates» are several months old by the time you receive them and may omit critical citations to more recent cases or statutes, such as those from your state. There is no substitute to doing your own updating when a client's interests are at stake. Remember that a secondary source such as this is only a starting place in the legal research process.

West's Federal Administrative Practice. 3d-4th eds. St. Paul, MN: West Group, 1996-date. 9 vols. Biennial pocket supplements.
Cost: $1,290; supplementation: 1997: $155.50; 1998: $165; 1999: $466; 2000: $535; 2001: $447; 2002: $373.50; 2003: $359; 2004: $323.75; 2005: $337; 2006: $529; 2007: $519; 2008: $490; 2009: $549.50; 2010: $604; 2011: $659.50; 2012: $720; 2013: $780. **Monthly Assured Print Price (APP):** $87/$1,044.
Formerly titled **West's Federal Practice Manual**, this multi-volume and topically organized reference tool is intended to provide lawyers who are not necessarily specialists with guidance in handling matters before various federal departments and agencies. Less costly to update than some competing products (e.g. Matthew Bender's **Administrative Law**) since West takes a more conservative approach to supplementation and recompilation. While some of the bound volumes to this set are due for revision, West has begun to take a stronger interest in its updating, the most recent evidence of which is the title change. For those older bound volumes, the use of pocket supplements is all the more imperative. The West Group's **Federal Procedure** is, at least in terms of its bound volumes, a more up-to-date set, even though both have supplementation. However, the publisher has been significantly updating this set in recent years.

West's Federal Forms. St. Paul, MN: West, 1951-date. 23 vols. Annual pocket parts and periodic revised volumes.
Cost: $2,422; supplementation: 1994: $304.25; 1995: $122; 1996: $149; 1997: $273; 1998: $346; 1999: $195; 2000: $391.50; 2001: $372; 2002: $645.20; 2003: $540; 2004: $604.75; 2005: $315; 2006: $747.50; 2007: $831.50; 2008: $494.50; 2009: $1,133.50; 2010: $626; 2011: $707.50; 2012: $1,472.50; 2013: $1,766; **Monthly Assured Print Price (APP):** $168/$2,016;
A companion to West's **Federal Practice and Procedure,** this set arranges the forms in order by federal rule number for practice before the U.S. District Courts, Courts of Appeals, and United States Supreme Court. There are also separate volumes containing forms for use in both admiralty and bankruptcy actions. The forms are accompanied by explanatory notes and supporting references to primary authority.

Wright, Charles Alan, et al. **Federal Practice and Procedure.** Revised ed. St. Paul, MN: Thomson Reuters West, 1971-date. 55 vols. Annual pocket parts and revised volumes.
Cost: $4,118; supplementation: 1994: $406.25; 1995: $528.50; 1996: $551.50; 1997: $518; 1998: $807.50; 1999: $681; 2000: $728; 2001: $822; 2002: $872; 2003: $935; 2004: $1,171; 2005: $1,524.50; 2006: $1,716; 2007: $2,131; 2008: $2,414; 2009: $2,210; 2010: $2,455; 2011: $2,537.50; 2012: $3,031.50; 2013: $3,389; **Monthly Assured Print Price (APP):** $256/$3,072 (2014).
This is one of the most respected treatises on the subject of federal procedure and probably the most widely used. This multi-volume guide to the Federal Rules of Civil and Criminal Procedure and Federal Rules of Evidence, originally authored by William W. Barron and Judge Alexander Holtzoff, was first published in 1951. It was called the «Rules Edition.» With the death of William Barron, Professor Charles Alan Wright of the University of Texas School of Law assumed editorial responsibility for the work with the assistance of Judge Holtzoff. Their so-called «First Edition» was published in 1969 under the editorial supervision of Professor Wright. In the current Second Edition, Professor Wright has been assisted by a number of noted legal scholars, including Professor Arthur R. Miller of Harvard Law School, Kenneth W. Graham, Professor of Law at the University of Miami, Edward H. Cooper, and Victor Gold. This set is organized into four primary segments: Federal Rules of Criminal Procedure (vols. 1-3A); Federal Rules of Civil Procedure (vols. 4-12); Jurisdiction and Related Matters (vols. 13-19); and the Federal Rules of Evidence (vols. 21-28). The text of each rule is accompanied by Advisory Committee's Notes, excerpts from House and Senate Committee Reports, and the author's expert analysis. The authors' analytical text is exhaustively footnoted with relevant case notes, providing the researcher with near encyclopedic coverage of case law. The inclusion of a number of A and B volumes, brings the size of the complete set to 55 volumes. This set is highly recommended not only for its rare scholarly attributes, but for the reasonable cost of supplementation. The prospective purchaser of such a large set is obviously someone with an extensive federal practice who will make adequate use of such a comprehensive treatment. Those with a less significant federal practice are urged to consider one of the smaller and less exhaustive treatments.

Cost Saving Tips: Given the substantial cost of print supplementation, the wise purchaser will consider obtaining the set as a Westlaw add-on. While it is certainly possible to drop the standing order and buy pocket parts in alternate years, the annual updating cost is more reasonable than that of **Moore's Federal Practice.** If you do prefer print, consider dropping the standing odder for supplementation and simply buy another set (at 20-30% discount) every three or four years.

Wright, Charles Alan and Mary Kay Kane. **Law of Federal Courts.** 7th ed. St. Paul, MN: West, 2011. 1 vol. (929 pp.).

Hornbook series. Available from West Academic.
Cost: $103 (2014).
Authored by the late William B. Bates Chair for the Administration of Justice at the University of Texas and one of this country's leading authorities on the subject of Federal practice and procedure, this student Hornbook serves as a valuable review for the practitioner as well as an excellent introduction for the law student . Professor Wright was involved as an author or co-author of this work since the publication of the first edition in 1963. In this edition, he treats a number of developments which have taken place over the past twelve years, including the reaffirmation of principles of original jurisdiction, the law of standing, the application of the 11th Amendment, as well as statutory changes to the law of diversity, jurisdictional amount, removal and venue. He also discusses changes to the Federal Rules of Civil Procedure, particularly Rule 4 on the service of process. The chapters in this volume cover the federal judicial system, the judicial power of the United States, the Federal Question, Diversity of Citizenship, Jurisdictional Amount, Removal Jurisdiction and Procedure, Venue, Relations of State and Federal Courts, the Law Applied by the Federal Courts, Procedure in the District Courts, Appellate Jurisdiction of the Courts of Appeals, Appellate Jurisdiction of the Supreme Court, and Original Jurisdiction of the Supreme Court. The entire text is thoroughly footnoted with references to cases, statutes, and various secondary sources. For the on-line researcher, there is a valuable Appendix on Researching Federal Court Jurisdiction and Practice on WESTLAW which describes the federal resources available on WESTLAW and explains query formulation using examples from federal law. An excellent and economical resource. An up-to-date West Hornbook is likely to be best value on the market, written and priced as it is for the student market. The only deficiency is that Hornbooks are rarely supplemented and the user must usually await a new edition. The Federal practitioner will obviously require a treatise with regular supplementation to keep up with current developments.

Yackle, Larry W. **Federal Courts**. 3d ed. Durham, NC: Carolina Academic Press, 2009. 1 vol. (714 pp.).
Cost: $68; from $33.84 on amazon.com (2014).
This basic guide to the powers and functions of the federal judiciary is designed for lawyers, judges, magistrates, and law students, and law clerks. The book's organizational structure tracks that of typical law school courses on the federal courts, or federal jurisdiction. Based on a current analysis of constitutional principles, statutes, and court decisions, the author constructs a methodology for resolving cases that involves the allocation of power among the three branches of government and, under the principle of federalism, between the national government and the states. His primary aim is to illuminate the federal courts' role in adjudicating questions of federal law, particularly those involving individual constitutional rights. He does this by examining the history and modern structure of the federal courts, the concept and operation of judicial independence, Article III courts, non-Article III adjudicative bodies, federal questions in state court, the Supreme Court, and federal questions in the district courts. He also analyzes issues of justiciability, including such doctrines as standing, government suits, standing and the merits, ripeness, and mootness; suits against government and government officers, abstention, and habeas corpus. The third edition embraces of variety of new developments, including Supreme Court decisions on jurisdiction in federal-question cases, standing, sovereign immunity, and habeas corpus, and reacts to such recent statutes as the Antiterrorism and Effective Death Penalty Act, the Detainee Treatment Act, the Military Commissions Act, as well as the power of the federal courts to entertain petitions from Guantanamo Bay detainees. The text features extensive citations to primary and secondary authorities, many with the author's illuminating commentary. Larry W. Yackle is a professor of law at Boston University School of Law who has written numerous books and articles on questions of federal judicial powers and is the author of numerous U.S. Supreme Court briefs concerning the federal judicial system.

Additional titles in the field of Federal Law and Procedure are available from the following publishers: Matthew Bender, Bloomberg BNA, Greenwood Publishing Group, Kluwer Academic Publications, LexisNexis, Liberty Fund, National Conference of State Legislatures, Thomson Reuters West, Transaction Publications, West Academic. See Appendix B for addresses and telephone numbers.

Gambling Law

Benedict, Jeff. **Without Reservation: The Making of America's Most Powerful Indian Tribe and Foxwoods, the World's Largest Casino**. New York: HarperCollins, 2000. 1 vol. (376 pp.).
Cost: $14.95 (paperbound); from $.01 on amazon.com (2014).
The rapid expansion of casino gambling across the United States over the past forty years has profoundly impacted American society on a number of levels—economic, governmental and moral--and brought with it a host of social pathologies. Capitalizing on the concept of tribal land sovereignty, Indian tribes, with the complicity of international gambling conglomerates, cash-hungry state governments and inept federal officials, have been able to carve out a significant niche in the world of casino gambling in the United States. In this compelling narrative, Jeff Benedict explains how one Connecticut tribe, the Mashantucket Pequots, was able to rise from near extinction, and a non-existent tribal genealogy, to become the richest tribe in American history through a process of fraud and manipulation. This is a fascinating case study of gambling and the complex legal and political machinations by which the Mashantucket Pequots were able to manipulate state and federal officials and politicians into granting it the recognition it required to achieve its goals. Jeff Benedict is former research director, Center for the Study of Sport in Society, an investigative journalist, lawyer and author of several books, including **Pros and Cons: The Criminals Who Play in the NFL** and **Public Heroes Private Felons: Athletes And Crimes Against Women**. The book includes an extensive bibliography, with source notes.

Balestra, Mark, ed. **Indian Gambling Industry Report.** 12th ed. Newton, MA: Casino City Press, 2012. 1 vol. (202 pp.).
Cost: 2013 Edition: $399.95; Book and Online subscription package: $499.95; CD-ROM subscription alone: $474.95 (2014). Available from River City Group: 1-800-490-1715; or via

IGR Online at: http://www.casinocitypress.com/gamingalmanac/indiangamingreport/
The annual Indian Gaming Industry Report provides current, unique, cutting-edge research on the Indian gaming industry appropriate for executives in the industry, gaming analysts, regulators, consultants, lawyers, lobbyists, academics, and those interested in the state of Indian gaming. The report examines the size and growth of the market and its economic and fiscal impact on the U.S. and various state economies. The 2012 edition provides calendar year 2010 nationwide statistics and state-by-state statistics, including: gaming and non-gaming revenue; Class II vs. Class III gaming; number of facilities, tribes, gaming machines, and table games; trends; and the fiscal impact of Indian gaming, including revenue sharing with state and local governments. The Report also includes comparisons across states, historical perspective on Indian gaming, an examination of the reasons for Indian gaming's current recovery after a slight decline in 2009, comparisons to commercial casinos and racinos, an economic impact analysis examining Indian gaming's contribution to the U.S. economy, and a qualitative future outlook for Indian gaming.

Eadington, William R. and Judy A. Cornelius, eds. **Gambling: Public Policies and the Social Sciences**. Reno, NV: Institute for the Study of Gambling and Commercial Gaming, College of Business Administration, University of Nevada, 1997. 1 vol. (694 pp.).
Cost: $34.95; from $7.24 on amazon.com (2014).
A collection of 39 scholarly articles providing analyses of modern gambling and its impact on society, both in the United States and in selected foreign countries. The articles are organized into eight sections covering the following topics: the spread of gambling, gaming and new jurisdictions, Indian gaming, economic and social impacts of commercial gaming, planning processes and bidding for casino licenses, studies in history and culture of gambling, lotteries, legal and regulatory issues. Useful chiefly as a background reference for policymakers, these articles provide critical analysis of various gambling practices and the experiences of various jurisdictions which have allowed the expansion of gambling, ostensibly to enhance state revenues. William Eadington is professor of economics and director of the Institute for the Study of Gambling and Commercial Gaming at the University of Nevada, Reno. Judy Cornelius is associate director of the Institute.

Eadington, William R., ed. **Indian Gaming and the Law**. Revised 3d ed. Reno, NV: Institute for the Study of Gambling and Commercial Gaming, College of Business Administration, University of Nevada, 2004. 1 vol. (298 pp.). Paper.
Cost: $14.95; from $.97 on amazon.com (2014).
A collection articles addressing the legal ramifications of Indian gaming in the wake of the passage of the Indian Gaming Act of 1988. Originally published in 1990, it assembles papers and comments presented at the North American Conference on the Status of Indian Gaming held in Reno, Nevada in March, 1989. The authors include scholars, government officials, tribal attorneys and leaders. Topics include the Indian Gaming Act and the political process, the views of supporters of the Act, the Fort Mojave Project, observations of tribal leaders, alternative perspectives and implications, and the Canadian experience. Appendices include the full text of the Cabazon decision (480 U.S. 202), and the Indian Gaming Regulatory Act. William Eadington is professor of economics and director of the Institute for the Study of Gambling and Commercial Gaming at the University of Nevada, Reno.

Goodman, Robert. **The Luck Business: The Devastating Consequences of America's Gambling Explosion.** New York: Touchtone Books, 1995. 1 vol. (288 pp.).
Cost: $19.95; from $.01 on amazon.com (2014).
A scholarly examination of the impact of gambling on the United States and its citizens by a Professor at Hampshire College in Massachusetts. Goodman asserts that the gambling industry produces no product and siphons off money not only from retail businesses but also from manufacturing. He claims that gambling interests have enlisted the support of governments by holding out false hopes to naïve legislators and other officials who are eager to find new sources of income without raising taxes. Goodman, who headed the United States Gambling Study of 1992-94, points out that Americans legally gambled almost $400 billion in 1993, producing more than $40 billion in gambling revenues, while causing myriad economic and social problems for the very communities where they are located.

International Gaming Institute. **The Gaming Industry: Introduction and Perspectives.** New York: John Wiley & Sons, Inc., 1996. 1 vol. (270 pp.).
Cost: $97.00; from $23.44 on amazon.com (2014).
Intended primarily as an introductory text for those interested in pursuing careers in the gambling, or «gaming,» industry, this volume discusses the historical development of games of chance and the gambling industry, presents the complexities of gambling operations in relation to various casino functional areas, explains gaming mathematics and utility analysis, and discusses preparation for gambling careers. It also places gaming in the context of the broader hospitality and entertainment industry. The contributing authors are faculty members of the William F. Harrah College of Hotel Administration International Gaming Institute at the University of Nevada Las Vegas, an organization committed to leadership in gaming information and resources, and financed by the founder of Harrah's Entertainment.

Jarvis, Robert M., et al. **Gaming Law: Cases and Materials**, 2003. Newark, NJ: LexisNexis (Matthew Bender), 2003. 1 vol. (604 pp.).
Cost: $157 (2014).
Until recently, gambling has not been the subject of serious scholarly inquiry at the nation's law schools. This accounts for the relative paucity of literature on the law of gambling, or "gaming" as it is now euphemistically called. This justifies the inclusion of this first caseBook in a chapter generally devoted to reviews of analytical treatises. Among the topics covered by the authors/editors are state-sponsored gambling, charitable gaming, pari-mutual gaming, sports gaming, casino gaming, shipboard gaming, Indian gaming and Internet gaming. The 100 selected cases are accompanied by 180 notes providing commentary, and 40 problems. At the very least, this volume can

serve as a useful compendium of primary law for those lawyers practicing in the field. Robert Jarvis is Professor of Law at the Nova Southeastern University Shepard Broad Law Center.

Light, Steven Andrew and Kathryn R.L. Rand. **Indian Gaming and Tribal Sovereignty: The Casino Compromise**. Lawrence, KS: University Press of Kansas, 2005. 1 vol. (240 pp.).
Cost: $29.95 (hardcover); $17.95 (paper); from $10.99 on amazon.com (2014).
The rise of Indian gaming across the United States is a direct result of the assertion of tribal sovereignty as it has emerged under the aegis of congressional authority and the provisions of the Indian Gaming Regulatory Act of 1988. For many tribes, and their financial backers, sovereignty was the legal avenue to establish high-stakes gambling operations on tribal lands or a means to negotiate the creation of casinos on non-tribal properties. Some, like the Masantucket Pequots of Connecticut, were enormously successful; others were less so, or refrained from gambling entirely. This scholarly study of the confluence of tribal sovereignty and Indian gambling provides a detailed examination of the laws and politics which govern this area of American life. The authors also examine the competing legal rights and political interests which are implicated in the issue of Indian gambling, from the strengthening of tribal governments and fortunes to the economic and social costs to society at large. Steven Andrew Light is a professor of political science and public administration at the University of North Dakota. Kathryn R.L. Rand is associate professor of law at the University of North Dakota School of Law. Both are founders and co-directors of the University's Institute for the Study of Tribal Gaming Law and Policy.

Mason, W. Dale. **Indian Gaming: Tribal Sovereignty and American Politics**. Norman, OK: University of Oklahoma Press, 2000. 1 vol. (330 pp.).
Cost: $24.95; from $2.49 on amazon.com (2014).
A valuable examination of the issue of Indian tribal sovereignty within the context of the American political system and the role of gaming as an assertion of that sovereignty. In the wake of the Supreme Court's 1987 Cabazon decision and passage of the Indian Gambling Regulatory Act in 1988, gambling has emerged as the primary focus of efforts by American Indian tribes to assert the right to determine for themselves what they can control on tribal lands. With particular attention to the experiences of tribes in Oklahoma, New Mexico, California, and Minnesota, the author explains how the tribes, through their gambling activities, act as both political entities and interest groups, lobbying state and federal legislative bodies and using the wealth generated by gambling to influence public policy and the electoral process. He also examines the role of tribal governments in the area of intergovernmental relations in the context of the federal Indian policy of self-determination and against the national political movement to devolve power to state governments which are more anxious to extend state sovereignty into Indian territory. The author is an assistant professor of political science at the University of New Mexico. This work is an outgrowth of his doctoral dissertation at the University of Oklahoma. A useful study for anyone seeking to understand the complex nature of emerging Indian sovereign authority within the context of the federal system and the role of gambling in that process.

Rand, Kathryn R.L. and Steven Andrew Light. **Indian Gaming Law and Policy**. Durham, NC: Carolina Academic Press, 2006. 1 vol. (320 pp.). Paperbound.
Cost: $42; from $19.95 on amazon.com (2014).
Over the past twenty years, the rapid expansion of gambling at over 400 Indian casinos in 30 states has generated billions of dollars in revenue. As this side of the gambling industry continues to expand, a host of legal issues has arisen which pits Indian tribal sovereignty against the regulatory authority of state and federal authorities, and local authorities. This has created monumental problems for policy makers who, having sanctioned the existence of sovereigns within sovereigns, are only beginning to grapple with the legal, political, and public policy fall-out. This volume provides readers with a comprehensive overview of the subject of Indian gambling (euphemistically called "gaming"), including discussion of the origins of tribal gambling under the Indian Gaming Regulatory Act Gaming Law and the Supreme Court's decision in the case of *California v. Cabazon Band of Mission Indians*, 480 U.S. 202 (1987) which ruled that neither the State of California nor the county had any authority to enforce its gambling laws within the reservations. The author's discuss in detail the provisions of the Indian Gaming Regulatory Act and the legal and political developments which followed its enactment. They also consider the various classes of gambling and the manner in which gambling has been politicized following the Supreme Court's scrutiny of the Act in *Seminole Tribe v. Florida*, 517 U.S. 44 (1996) in which the court held that Congress did intend to abrogate states' sovereign immunity under the IGRA but that the Indian Commerce Clause (and by implication the Commerce Clause) did not give Congress that power. Under the Eleventh Amendment, all states are regarded as sovereign entities. The widespread legal and policy implications of this subject make it an ideal resource for policymakers and political leaders as well as lawyers and law students. Kathryn R.L. Rand is a professor of law at the University of North Dakota School of Law. Steven Andrew Light is a professor of political science and public administration at the University of North Dakota.

Rand, Kathryn R.L. and Steven Andrew Light. **Indian Gaming Law: Cases and Materials**. Durham, NC: Carolina Academic Press, 2008. 1 vol. (570 pp.).
Cost: $71; from $50.39 on amazon.com (2014).
This law school caseBook combines analytical text with a variety of materials designed to impart understanding of the legal and regulatory issues involved in Indian gambling, including a theoretical framework for comprehending tribal sovereignty. Materials include excerpts from relevant case law, statutes, regulations, book excerpts, journal articles, and testimony by key authorities in the field. The editors also provide specific examples of tribal and state experiences with tribal gambling. Each chapter also includes teaching problems and notes. An ideal companion to the editors' **Indian Gaming Law and Policy.** Kathryn R.L. Rand is a professor of law at the University of North Dakota School of Law. Steven Andrew Light is a professor of political science and public administration at the University of North Dakota. The editors are founders and co-directors of the University's Institute for the Study of Tribal Gaming Law and Policy.

Rose, I. Nelson and Robert A. Loeb. **Blackjack and the Law**. Oakland, CA: RGE Publishing, 1998. 1 vol. (245 pp.).
Cost: $24.95; from $.01 on amazon.com (2014).
In the highly profitable world of casino gambling, blackjack is the only game which does not have a mathematically calculable advantage to the house and which can be legally beaten by a small percentage of skillful players who practice card counting. The subject of blackjack, and the legal implications of casinos' attempts to identify and thwart skilled players through the use of computers, is one of many topics addressed in this 14-year collection of the author's syndicated newspaper column «Gambling and the Law.» The book includes commentary by Attorney Robert A. Loeb. Additional chapters examine such topics as Indian Gaming, the Casino Boom, and the Federal Gaming Commission. A Professor of Law at Whittier Law School, Nelson I. Rose is recognized as one the world's leading authorities on the subject of gambling. Robert Loeb is a criminal defense attorney, an adjunct professor at DePaul University College of Law, and a blackjack players who has represented a number of clients involved in disputes with casinos.

Rose, I. Nelson and Martin D. Owens. **Internet Gaming Law**. 2d ed. New York: Mary Ann Liebert, 2009. 1 vol. (460 pp.).
Cost: $393.00; ebook: $1,180 (institutional site license); from $110.00 on amazon.com (2014).
Prior to the 1990s, individuals who wished to place a casino-type or sports bet had two alternatives: place a bet at a legitimate gambling establishment located in a jurisdiction that permitted gambling or place an illegal wager through a bookmaker. In the mid 1990s, however, the emergence of the Internet spawned an entirely new kind of wagering—online gambling and sport wagering. By 2003, online gambling had grown into a $5 billion business. The global legal framework for Internet gambling is a complicated mix of laws and regulations. In the United States, gambling is governed by a combination of federal and state statutes. Gambling is generally regulated at the state level, with federal law supporting state laws and regulations to ensure that interstate and foreign commerce do not circumvent them. The Federal Wire Act prohibits gambling businesses from using interstate or international telecommunications to knowingly transmit or receive bets. Foreign countries and jurisdictions have taken a variety of approaches to regulating on-line gaming, including legalizing some forms, seeking effective regulatory approaches, and prohibiting it entirely. The major participants in the credit card industry have tried to restrict the use of their cards for Internet gambling by prohibiting cardholders from using the cards to gamble on line. This is a revised edition of the authors' 2005 examination of Internet gambling law—now euphemistically called "gaming,"--authors I. Nelson Rose and Martin Owens consider the impact of state, federal and international law on gambling conducted online. Among the topics discussed are federal legislation related to Internet gambling, the application of U.S. law to advertising for Internet gambling services, the use and abuse of certain of certain bank instruments for gambling purposes, laws regarding the use of telephone lines for wagering, gambling tax issues, intellectual property issues, and more. Professor I. Nelson Rose is one of the nation's leading authorities on gambling law. Martin Owens is an attorney who specializes in online gambling. The book's price has also increased significantly since the appearance of the first edition, from $195 to $393.

Schwartz, David G. **Roll Them Bones: The History of Gambling (Casino Edition)**. 2d ed. Las Vegas, NV: Winchester Books, 2013. 1 vol. (454 pp.). Paperback.
Cost: $21.99; from $16.82 on amazom.com; kindle ed.: $9.99 (2014).
An exhaustive and scholarly history of gambling throughout the ages, from its origins in ancient divination rituals to the global world of high-tech and Internet gambling. The author examines gambling in the Greek and Roman worlds, the Middle Ages, the first casino in Venice, the inception of playing cards in China, the spread of gambling through the British Empire, the United States, Las Vegas, Indian casinos, the impact of state-sponsored gambling, and gambling addiction. An essential resource for anyone attempting to understand the universal compulsion to gamble. David G. Schwartz is an historian at the University of Nevada's Center for Gaming Research. The book was named the National Council on Problem Gambling's Book of the Year for 2006 and won a prestigious Editor's Choice 2006 Trippie Award. The second edition, which adds a chapter 17, addresses the events of the last decade in the gambling world, beginning with a discussion of how Las Vegas casinos changed their approach after the 9/11 recession, becoming less dependent on gambling. It also covers the mid-decade boom that was followed by a crash from which the Las Vegas industry has still not recovered. The second half of chapter 17 provides a short history of online gambling, beginning with the first sites in the mid-1990s and covering the leading regulatory and legal challenges it has faced. The author concludes the book with some thoughts on the present and future of gambling.

Thompson, William. **Gambling in America: An Encyclopedia of History, Issues, and Society**. Santa Barbara, CA: ABC-CLIO, 2001. 1 vol. (350 pp.).
Cost: $85; from $2.03 on amazon.com (2014).
This reference work contains nearly 200 alphabetical entries on multiple aspects of gambling in the United States and the Western Hemisphere, including those devoted to particular personalities, various games of chance, the gambling culture, economics, legality, policies, events, gambling equipment, as well as entires for each state, Canadian province, most Latin American countries, Las Vegas, and Reno. The entries, which range in length from a paragraph to several pages, were written primarily by William Thompson, but also by contributors with financial, legal, and academic backgrounds. It also includes a chronology, a glossary of gambling terms, an annotated list of relevant court cases, a bibliography for further reading, and retailed index. William Thompson is a professor at the University of Nevada, Las Vegas and gambling scholar. Gambling in America examines the «people, places, events, laws and policies, and concepts concerning gambling as well as gambling equipment.» The focus is on gambling in the Western Hemisphere.

Understanding Gaming Law Issues: Leading Lawyers on Understanding Recent Changes in State and Tribal Gambling, Handling Economic and Regulatory Pressures,

and Anticipating Future Legal Trends. Boston, MA: Thomson Reuters/Aspatore, 2010. 1 vol. (307 pp.). Paperbound.
Cost: $95.00; from $92.00 on amazon.com (2014).
Indian gaming law is governed generally by the Federal Indian Gaming Regulatory Act (IGRA), 25 U.S.C. § 2701, et seq. (1988), and regulated at the federal, state and tribal levels. This timely collection of articles on various aspects of Indian gaming law addresses the current regulatory climate and trends; gaming activities in the State of Washington; Indian gaming in the 21st century: regulatory issues for a mature industry; how economic and regulatory pressures threaten to undermine tribal gaming, Indian gaming in Oklahoma, and revisions to Indian gaming law, principally the effort by states to limit the scope of Indian gaming and prevent the acquisition of news lands to be removed from local tax rolls. Six leading attorneys with extensive experience in Indian gaming, and gaming law generally, contributed to this volume. The appendices include a representative Intergovernmental Agreement By and Between the Mashpee Wampanoag Tribe and the Town of Middleborough, Massachusetts, California v. Cabazon Band of Mission Indians, the Gaming on trust Lands Rule, Gaming on Trust Lands Final Rule, and the Supreme Court's decision in *Carcieri v. Salazar* (RI) that limited the Bureau of Indian Affairs to only take Indian Land into trust if the tribe was federally recognized in 1934 at the time of the laws enactment. This holding excluded the Narragansett tribe from turning land over to the BIA as they were not federally recognized until 1983.

U.S. Government Acountability Office. **Internet Gambling: An Overview of the Issues**. New York: Cosimo Books, 2011. 1 vol. (68 pp.).
Cost: $12.99; from $12.99 on amazon.com (2014).
In 2005, roughly 15-20 million gamblers in the United States placed bets online, comprising an online gambling market estimated at $6 billion, or half of the world's online gambling revenues. Ironically, the U.S. government has simultaneously been the world's strongest opponent of online gambling. Under both the Clinton and Bush administrations, the Justice Department has fought efforts to legalize Internet gambling, and legislators have expended considerable effort attempting to enact anti-Internet gambling laws. As of 2011, however, gambling interests in the United States and abroad were renewing efforts to legalize Internet gambling in the United States, having already succeeded in persuading the Obama administration to delay enforcement of the *Unlawful Internet Gambling Enforcement Act of 2006*. Providing critical background to this contentious issue is this 2002 study of the U.S. Government Accountability Office which examined such topics as the legal franework for Internet gambling both in the U.S. and abroad, the use of credit cards to pay for Internet gambling, the views of law enforcement and banking regulators, and the vulnerability of Internet gamblijg to criminal money laundering. Created in 1921, the Government Acountability Office is an investigative arm of the United States Congress.

Volberg, Rachel A. **When the Chips Are Down: Problem Gambling in America**. New York: Century Foundation, 2001. 1 vol. (139 pp.).
Cost: $13.95; from $.01 on amazon.com (2014).
This book addresses one of the most significant social and economic problems to arise in the wake of the widespread legalization of gambling in the United States and the proliferation of casinos. Americans now spend more money on gambling-related activities than on theme parks, movie tickets, sporting events, and video games combined. This book is an analysis of the economic and social costs of gambling, particular pathological gambling which directly afflicts over 5.5 million Americans and places another 15 million at risk for problem gambling. Dr. Rachel Volberg, a member of he Graduate Faculty in the School of Public Health, University of Massachusetts, has conducted numerous studies of problem gambling since 1986.

Von Herrmann, Denise. **The Big Gamble: The Politics of Lottery and Casino Expansion**. Westport, CT: Praeger, 2002. 1 vol. (148 pp.).
Cost: $88.95; from $8.99 on amazon.com; kindle ed.: $64.99 (2014)
An examination of the politics of state and local gambling, particularly as it involves casinos and state lotteries. The author argues that American image of gambling has been largely transformed in recent years, from one focusing on its sordid, sinful and corrupt aspects to one focusing on its benign aspects as a pleasurable entertainment experience. Chapters include: Introduction: Policy Making and Morals, the History and Regulation of Gambling in the United States, the Politics of Gambling Adoptions, State Regulation of Gambling, the Economic and Social Impacts of Gambling and Their Effects on Policy, Rolling the Dice: Assessments and Directions for the Future of Legal Gambling. The author is Chair of the Arts and Sciences Division, University of Southern Mississippi, Gulf Coast.

Additional titles in the field of Gambling Law are available from the following publishers: Alberta Gaming Research Institute, ALI-ABA, Century Foundation, Greenwood Publishing Group, Matthew Bender, Practising Law Institute, Praeger Publishers, RGE Publishing, Thomson Reuters Aspatore, Trace Publications, University of Colorado Press, University of Nevada Bureau of Business and Economic Research, University of Nevada Las Vegas Gaming Studies Research Center John Wiley. See Appendix B for addresses and telephone numbers.

Health and Hospital Law

Alexander, Barry D., et al. **Fundamentals of Health Law**. 5th ed. Washington, DC: American Health Lawyers Association, 2011. 1 vol. (473 pp.). Paperbound with CD-ROM or eBook. Availlable from LexisNexis.
Cost: $129 to AHLA members (2014).
Health law is one of those areas of law that has evolved into a full-blown specialty in keeping with the growth of the health care industry. Health lawyers represent hospitals, doctors, healthcare providers, pharmaceutical companies, and insurance companies. Sixteen health law specialists contributed to this collection of substantive chapters on various aspects of health

care, including patient care, Medicare, fraud and abuse, tax-exempt issues, antitrust law, regulation of insurance, regulation of hospitals, representing physicians, home care providers and long term care, healthcare transactions and contracting, and bioethics. Chapter one includes a glossary of health care terms, and a table of acronyms and abbreviations. Each chapter provides a well-written summary of the topic, accompanied by selected citations to primary and secondary authorities, and a list of references. The American Health Lawyers Association publishes a wide variety of excellent titles in health law specialties, now available from LexisNexis.

The American Bar Association Complete and Easy Guide to Health Care Law: Your Guide to Protecting Your Rights as a Patient, Dealing with Hospitals, Health Insurance, Medicare, and More. New York: Random House Reference, 2001. 1 vol. (427 pp.). Paperbound.
Cost: $15; $12.75 (member price); from $.01 on amazon.com; kindle ed,: $11.84 (2014).
A patient-oriented guide to health care law written in conjunction with the ABA's Division for Health Law and Division for Public Education. The coverage includes the topics most useful to those involved with the health care system, including confidentiality, privacy, the Patient's Bill of Rights, emergency care, informed consent, paying for health services, insurance and managed care, COBRA, reproduction, abortion, sterilization, wrongful birth and pregnancy, people with disabilities, pregnancy, vaccination, tort liability, nursing homes, paying for long-term care, Medicaid planning, regulation of medical professionals. licensing of doctors, nurses and hospitals, organ donation, death and dying, right to refuse life-sustaining treatment, hospices, and assisted suicide. Presented in an easy to understand question-answer format. A valuable acquisition for any public library or law library serving the general public.

Baumann, Linda A., ed. **Health Care Fraud and Abuse: Practical Perspectives**. 3d ed. Chicago: American Bar Association in cooperation with Bloomberg BNA Books, 2013-date. 1 vol. (1,500 pp.). With Companion CD-ROM. Available from Bloomberg BNA Books.
Cost: $415; $352.50 to ABA Health Care Section members; no supplementation to date; 2d ed.: $185; 2009: $195; 2010: $205; 2011: $210; 2012: $220.
The significant rise in the number of health care fraud and abuse cases is a direct result of the complexity of federal laws and regulations and the growing attention by state and federal government agencies to their prosecution. The potential liabilities of health care providers, be they hospitals, nursing homes, physicians, pharmaceutical companies, pharmacies, or pharmacy benefit managers, are often exacerbated because of the often ambiguous rules regarding medical and pharmaceutical reimbursement. Attorneys representing health care providers must be intimately vigilant regarding these rules if they are to protect their clients from potential exposure to investigation or prosecution. Those found to have committed health care or abuse can be subject not only to criminal prosecution but to statutory penalties of several thousand dollars per improper claim as well as treble damages. In addition, fraud and abuse cases may be subject to the Qui Tam provisions of the Federal civil False Claims Act under which private citizens can act as whistleblowers and collect all or part of the penalties imposed. The ten chapters in this substantial volume provide in-depth discussion and analysis of fraud and abuse within the health care industry, with particular attention to federal physician self-referral restrictions, Stark [i.e. Congressman Peter Stark] Phase III regulation, the False Claims Act in health care prosecutions, practical considerations in defending fraud and abuse cases, legal issues surrounding hospital and physician relationships, managed care fraud and abuse, corporate compliance programs, potential liabilities for directors and officers of health care organizations, obligations of legal counsel to inform stockholders and stakeholders about Qui Tam suits or investigations, and the control of fraud, waste and abuse in the Medicare Part D program. Sixteen health care law specialists collaborated in the production of the ten chapters comprising this volume and its appendices. The text is annotated with citations to cases, statutes, regulations, OIG advisory opinions, IRS letter rulings, and other relevant documents. The volume also includes an appendix table of contents and index. All 60 appendix documents are contained on a companion CD-ROM. Published in cooperation with the ABA's Health Law Section. The Editor-in-Chief is a partner in the Washington, DC firm of Arent Fox LLP with extensive experience in a wide variety of health care law transactions and regulatory issues.

Becker, Scott. **Health Care Law: A Practical Guide**. 2d ed. New York: Matthew Bender & Co., 1998-date. 1 vol. Looseleaf format and eBook. Annual supplementation.
Cost: $492; supplementation: 2000: $175; 2001: $187; 2002: $201; 2003: $212; 2004: $223; 2005: $237; 2006: $256; 2007: $276; 2008: $298; 2009: $322; 2010: $343; 2011: $362; 2012: $381; 2013: $418; 2014: $431; eBook: $492; renewal: 2014: $431.
This reference provides comprehensive analysis and practical guidance on legal issues facing health care providers. Now in a second edition, it addresses a wide variety of topics, including medical malpractice, risk management and quality assurance, consent to medical treatment, medical information and confidentiality, reimbursement, antitrust and health care, medical staff matters, patient care issues--admission and discharge, abortion and sterilization, death, autopsies, organ donations, and AIDS issues, tax issues, contractual relations facility licensing and accreditation, licensure of professionals, joint ventures and practice acquisitions, fraud and abuse and self-referral issues. Each chapter includes a concise, comprehensive discussion of the law, an analysis of problems likely to be faced by health care providers, and practical guidelines for addressing them. The author is a partner is partner in the Chicago law firm of Ross & Hardies, an adjunct professor of corporate health care at the Chicago-Kent School of Law, author, and a frequent speaker on health care law issues.

Beers, Donald and Kurt R. Karst. **Generic and Innovator Drugs**. 8th ed. New York: Wolters Kluwer Law & Business, 2013. 1 vol. (various pagings). Looseleaf format.
Cost: $535.00 (2014).
The manufacture and distribution of drugs in the United States is governed by the Food and Drug Administration (FDA), a division of the Department of Health and Human Services. Approval of new human drugs is governed by the FDA's Center for Drug Evaluation and Research (CDER), and, in some instances, a

sister center, the Center for Biologics Evaluation and Research. The statutory authority for the FDA's jurisdiction over drug approvals derives from the Federal Food, Drug and Cosmetic Act (FDCA) (21 U.S.C. § 301 et seq.) and, for human biologic drugs, from both the FDCA and the Public Health Service Act (PHSA) (42 U.S.C. § 262 et seq.). The FDCA was amended by the Drug Price Competition and Patent Term Restoration Act of 1984 (P.L. No. 98-417, 98 Stat. 1585 (1984)), otherwise known as Hatch-Waxman Amendments, which amended the FDCA's premarketing approval process to allow for more expeditious approval of "generic copies" of FDA-approved "pioneer" drug products. Long considered the definitive work on the subject of generic and innovator drug approvals, this estimable legal treatise provides step-by-step guidance through the approval process, particularly as governed by the Hatch-Waxman Amendments, and, more generally, by the FDCA. The book's chapters takes the user through the entire approval process, including (1) FDA Approval Requirement; (2) Full New Drug Applications; (3) Abbreviated New Drug Applications and "505(b)(2) Applications"; (4) Delaying Approval of Competitive Drug Products; (5) Public Availability of Drug and Biologic Data; (6) Potential for Governmental Compensation; (7) the Orphan Drug Amendments; (8) Debarment and Civil Penalties; (9) FDA Fraud Policy; (10) Expanded Access to Investigational Drugs and Accelerated Approvals; (11) Export and Import Requirements; (12) Prescription Drug and Biologic User Fees; and (13) FDA Regulation of Biologic Products. The Appendices contain the full text of the primary documents used by practitioners to understand how FDA currently interprets the law, including the relevant statutory and regulatory provisions. The aim has been to provide attorneys and others with a single resource to be consulted on specific drug approval matters. The eighth edition was prepared by Kurt R. Karst, a Director at Hyman, Phelps & McNamara, P.C. who specializes in providing regulatory counseling to pharmaceutical manufacturers concerning Hatch-Waxman patent and exclusivity issues, and myriad drug development issues. He takes over from Don Beers who left private practice to return to the FDA.

Buckley, John F., IV. **ERISA Law Answer Book**. 8th ed. Austin, TX: Wolters Kluwer Law & Business, 2013-date. 1 vol. (various pagings).
Cost: $399; no supplementation to date: 7th ed.: 2012: $249; 6th ed.: 2009: 0; 2010: $230; 2011: new ed.
This practical desk reference provides authoritative answers to more than 1,300 key ERISA-related questions with clarity and precision. The questions cover everything from benefit arrangements subject to the ERISA provisions, interpretation of ERISA plans, claims procedures, exhaustion of administrative remedies, notice, reporting and disclosure, plan amendment, assignment, waiver and forfeiture, fiduciaries, plan coverage and participation requirements, benefit accrual and vesting, contributions and benefits, plan funding, distributions, plan disqualification and remediation, COBRA, insurance, actions and remedies, preemption, standard of review, and attorneys' fees, among others. The answers provide detailed analyses of ERISA provisions. There is also extensive coverage of such recent developments as the Pension Protection Act of 2006. Each answer includes citations to relevant cases, statutory or regulatory provisions, IRS Code sections and regulations. An essential tool for those in involved in representation of clients on ERISA-related matters or litigation. The author is a senior attorney on the Public Law team of the National Legal Research Group, where he specializes in civil rights, employment discrimination, and local and state government law. He is author or editor of numerous Aspen titles.

Busch, Rebecca Saltiel. **Healthcare Fraud: Auditing and Detection Guide**. 2nd ed. Hoboken, NJ: John Wiley & Sons, Inc., 2012. 1 vol. (340pp.).
Cost: $75.00; from $33.70 on amazon.com; kindle ed.: $42.24 (2014).
Health care fraud is a multi-billion dollar epidemic whose costs affect health care providers, recipients, and payers, as well as U.S. taxpayers. It is defined as "intentional deception or misrepresentation that an individual knows or should know to be false, or does not believe to be true, and makes, knowing the deception could result in some unauthorized benefit to himself or some other person(s)." Such acts are punishable as a federal criminal offense under the Health Insurance Portability and Accountability Act (HIPAA) of 1996, and increasingly involve high-tech, highly skilled, educated, and professional perpetrators. Fraud may be committed by providers, insurance patients, individuals, approvers (employees), rings, nonproviders, agents or vendors. Now in its second edition, this impressive volume is an invaluable reference tool for auditors, healthcare managers, and investigators seeking to identify fraudulent activity in the healthcare sector. The author does this by providing detailed analysis of the healthcare continuum in a variety of contexts which will permit the investigator to identify entities that will most likely impact an episode of care. She also examines various health related pipelines that can aid the investigator in identifying fraud, including the health information pipeline, the accounts receivable pipeline, operational flow activity, product, service and consumer market activity, data management, normal infrastructure, data mapping, data mining, data analysis models, clinical content data analysis, profilers, and market implications. Rebecca S. Busch is the President and CEO of Medical Business Associates Inc. (founded in 1991), a healthcare consulting, auditing, and forensic services firm specializing in how money moves through the healthcare system. She has twenty years of progressive achievement in the healthcare management industry. She is a registered nurse and holds an MBA. She is also a Certified Fraud Examiner (CFE), Healthcare Fellow in Financial Management (FHFMA), a Certified Professional Coder (CPC), Life Care Planning Fellow (FIALCP), a Certified Business Manager (CBM), has a Masters Certificate in Case Management (CCM), and holds a certification in Homeland Security (CHS-III). She is also Strategic Partner, Financial Investigations and Assurance Services with McGovern & Greene, CPAs and Strategic Accountants.

Cacioppo, Paul P. **Health Care Fraud & Abuse: A Guide to Federal Sanctions.** St. Paul, MN: Thomson Reuters West (Clark Boardman Callaghan), 1991-date. 5 vols. Looseleaf format. Regular supplementation.
Cost: $1,338; supplementation: 1995: $158; 1996: $180; 1997: $189; 1998: $200; 1999: $216; 2000: $234; 2001: $272; 2002: $300; 2003: $342; 2004: $383; 2005: $423; 2006: $490; 2007: $525; 2008: $584; 2009: $653; 2010: $800.50; 2011: $775;

2012: $515; 2013: $982; **Monthly Assured Print Price (APP):** $97/$1,164.
An excellent overview of the federal and state laws and regulations governing health care organizations and their treatment of fraud and abuse issues. Includes extensive citations to primary law.

Charrow, Robert P. **Law in the Laboratory: A Guide to the Ethics of Federally Funded Science Research**. Chicago: University of Chicago Press, 2010. 1 vol. (330 pp.). Paperbound.
Cost: $31.00; from $12.95 on amazon.com; kindle ed.: $17.72 (2014).
The National Institutes of Health and the National Science Foundation together fund more than $40 billion annually in scientific research both in the United States around the world. But this federal money comes with significant strings attached that compel the recipient to adhere to strict ethical guidelines, federal statutes, regulations, and generally accepted procedures that dictate how the funds are to be used. This volume focuses its attention of this intersection of law and science as it probes the legal and ethical considerations involved in biomedical research. As the author explains, scientists and lawyers share many characteristics, from the need to state a problem precisely, to the process of gathering facts, and applying the appropriate scientific and legal principles to those facts to produce a solution. Both attempt to produce a rule from this process. For the scientist, this is a testable hypothesis. For the lawyer, it a legal principle that emerges from the mass of case law. This book is a primer for any research scientist or administrator who wishes to ensure that he or she is compliant with all applicable legal and ethical guidelines. Following an illuminating essay on the law, the legal mind, and the legal system, the author proceeds to examine government funding of research in the United States, how the integrity of research is regulated, misconduct, guidelines affecting research on human subjects, financial conflicts of interest, protection of data, intellectual property considerations (including the issue of who owns the products of research), and regulations governing the welfare of laboratory animals. The volume is enhanced by the inclusion of numerous hypothetical case studies that illustrate the issues being discussed.
The text is supported by numerous citations to relevant cases, statutes, regulations, scholarly articles in both law and science, and newspaper articles. This is an essential reference for any academic researcher, graduate or post-doctoral student whose position is funded by federal grants or who is involved in securing grants for scientific research. The author has served as principal deputy general counsel of the U.S. Department of Health and Human Services, a law professor, and chair of the Clinical Research Interest Group of the Health Law Section of the ABA.

Coogan, John F., R. Glenn Hubbard, and Daniel P. Kessler. **Healthy, Wealthy and Wise: Five Steps To a Better Health Care System**. 2d ed. Washington, DC: American Enterprise Institute Press, 2011. 1 vol. (130 pp.).
Cost: $19.95; from $.01 on amazon.com; kindle ed.: $9.99 (2014).
Despite its remarkable achievements in the areas of medical procedures, technology and pharmaceuticals, as well as its success in diagnosis, treatment and cure in recent years, the American health care system is plagued by rising costs and a growing number of uninsured. In this volume, three health care policy experts assess the current state of health care in the United States and offer a series of proposals to address the problems of cost, quality and coverage. These proposals take the form of (1) health care tax reform, including total deductibility of health care expenses, expanded health savings accounts, and tax credits for low income individual and families; (2) insurance reform, including nationwide portable health insurance, and subsidized health insurance for the chronically ill; (3) improved health information, including expansion on the number and scope of report cards on doctors and hospitals, and the promotion of "best practices" through guidelines; (4) control of anticompetitive behavior by providers and insurers; and (5) reform of the malpractice system. John Coogan is a senior fellow at the Hoover Institution; R. Glenn Hubbard is dean of the Graduate School of Business at Columbia University; Daniel Kessler is professor of economics, law and policy at Stanford University's Graduate School of Business.

Fox, Thomas C., Carol Colborn, Carl Krasik, and Joseph W. Metro. **Health Care Financial Transactions Manual**. St. Paul, MN: Thomson Reuters West, 1993-date. Twice annual replacement volumes.
Cost: 2013-2 Edition: $670; supplementation: 1996: $98; 1997: $103; 1998: $109; 1999: $118; 2000: $125; 2001: $151; 2002: $151; 2003: $378.50; 2004: $225.50; 2005: $243; 2006: $515; 2007: $554; 2008: $617; 2009: $694; 2010: $763; 2011: $885; 2012: $1,228; 2013: $1,340; **Monthly Assured Print Price (APP):** $93/$1,116.
Government regulation of health care transactions represents one of the most highly regulated sectors of the American economy. The industry is in the process of transforming itself through the creation of new ownership structures and contractual relationships. This work features an overview of the health care industry, a description and analysis of the various types of providers and suppliers, the role of Medicare and Medicaid, and applicable state and federal statutes and regulations. It also provides a seven-step process for analyzing the issues that may arise in a health care transaction and examines such issues as restrictions on physician financial arrangements, fraud and abuse, and ownership disclosure. Among the transactions examined are changes of ownership, reimbursement implications, risk factors, the corporate practice of medicine, distressed facilities, etc.

Furrow, Barry R., et al. **Health Law**. 2d ed. St. Paul, MN: Thomson Reuters West, 2000. 2 vols. (1,134 pp.). Practitioner Treatise Series. Not supplemented except in the form of future editions. Hornbook available from West Academic.
Cost: $195; Hornbook (1 vol.): $103 (2014).
This two-volume Practitioner's Edition is designed as a reference for those who do business with the health care delivery system, including health care institutions, and individuals within the system. Its coverage extends to tax, corporate, and organizational issues that arise in the health care field. It also examines governmental efforts to control costs and expand access through the Medicare and Medicaid programs, and through private insurance regulation, including government efforts to monitor fraud, abuse, and anti-competitive activities. Finally, it examines such legal and ethical issues as those involving death, reproduction and medical research. Includes

extensive citations to applicable case, statutes and regulations.

Gantt, W. Andrew H., III. **E-Health, Privacy, and Security Law**. 2d ed. Arlington, VA: Bloomberg BNA Books, 2011. 1 vol. (865 pp.). Hardbound, with companion CD-ROM.
Cost: $480; supplementation: 2012: $220; 2013: $225 (2014).
The Integration of the Internet and modern technology with the health care system has ushered in a host of legal issues for patients, health care providers and their legal representatives. Encouraged by government financial support and private industry innovation, the future of e-health promises to deliver efficiencies and cost savings to patients, doctors, and insurers, but not without some significant negative consequences. Among these are ethical, legal and financial risks, as well as privacy and security concerns, of which the Patient Protection Affordable Care Act (2010) and its massive regulatory apparatus is a prime contributor. A product of the ABA's Health Law Section, this volume assembles a team of leading legal experts to address the full range of significant and, often, unfamiliar business and transactional law issues which have arisen in the wake of this e-health explosion. It provides critical insights into the liabilities and ethical issues associated with the increased use of health information technology, social media, and digitized patient records, including FDA regulation of e-health technology, the latest regulations on privacy and security issues under the HITECH Act, and new enforcement techniques and practices. This new second edition provides a comprehensive discussion of new HIPAA enforcement actions, including the first impositions of civil money penalties and jail time for criminal actions under the Act. Much of this activity is tied to the so-called "meaningful use" doctrine, a set of criteria by which the federal government will determine if healthcare providers are using the deployed health IT tools effectively. Compliance with these criteria will be tied to incentives initially and to penalties ultimately. The eighteen chapters in this volume explore in a comprehensive fashion the issues tied to e-health and its implementation, including the e-health explosion, the e-health industry, health information technology, privacy and social media issues, privacy concerns, information security and its breach, e-health liability, FDA regulation of e-health technology and services, due diligence in e-health transactions, antitrust concerns, the intersection of e-health and intellectual property, discovery and admission of electronic information into evidence, and lethal ethics and e-health. The Appendices include an invaluable list of Internet health sites, government agencies, comprehensive e-health glossary, a HIPPA glossary, table of cases and index. The text is amply supported with citations to applicable statutes, regulation, case law, and secondary sources. Twenty-four health law practitioners and law professors contributed to this volume under the editorship of Andrew Gantt, a partner at Cooley LPP in Washington, DC.

Guide to HIPAA Security and the Law. Edited by Stephen S. Wu, Chicago: American Bar Association, 2007.
Cost: OUT-OF-PRINT; $79.95 ($69.95 to members); from $55.96 on amazon.com kindle (2014).
The Health Insurance Portability and Accountability Act (HIPAA), Public Law 104-191, requires the continuity of healthcare coverage for individuals who change jobs, the management of health information, simplification of the administration of health insurance, and the combat of waste, fraud, and abuse in health insurance and health care. Title II includes requirements to ensure the security and privacy of individuals' medical information in order to maintain the right of individuals to keep private information about themselves, and bridges the gap between the law and information security practices. The contributing authors discuss the background and history of HIPAA, HIPAA privacy and security, the scope and applicability of the security rule, the security rule itself, implementation, enforcement, and liability and litigation. They provide a section-by-section analysis of the Security Rule, as well as the applicable enforcement mechanisms. Appendices include the HIPAA administrative simplification provisions, security and privacy regulations, and HIPAA security resources on the Internet. Stephen S. Wu is a partner in the Silicon Valley offices of Cooke Kobrick & Wu LLP, advising clients on data security requirements under the law.

Hall, Mark A., Ira M. Ellman, and David Orenlicher . **Health Care Law and Ethics in a Nutshell**. 3d ed. St. Paul, MN: West, 2011. 1 vol. (464 pp.). Available from West Academic.
Cost: $41; from $14.19 an amazon.com; kindle ed.: $23.08 (2014).
A succinct, student-oriented guide to the legal and financial structure of health care, and bioethics. The authors address the impact of advances in medical technology upon treatment options and costs which have raised more complex ethical issues. Also useful as an overview for the practitioner.

HCFA's Laws, Regulations, Manuals [CD-ROM]. Pittsburgh, PA: U.S. Government Printing Office. One disc. Annual subscription. Updated monthly. Available for Windows. Search Engine: Text ReferenceBook (Dataware).
Cost: $250 per year (2014).
Contains the full text of 20 Health Care Financing Administration Manuals published by the Department of Health and Human Services with related publications and memoranda on Medicare and Medicaid. Also includes the text of Titles 11, 18 and 19 of the Social Security Act and Titles 45 and 52 of the **CFR**.

Health Care Compliance Portfolio Deluxe [Internet]. Riverwoods, IL: CCH, a Wolters Kluwer busiess. Updated as necessary. Search Engine: Proprietary. Includes toll-free product support.
Cost: approx. $2,000 per year; contact sales representative for specifics (2014).
An all-inclusive library designed for attorneys, in-house counsel of managed-care organizations, and risk managers, this product provides coverage of federal and state health care legislative and case law developments, the text of trial and appellate court decisions, and settlement information. The four individual products include the **Health Care Compliance Professional's Manual**, **CCH Healthcare Compliance Reporter**, the **Journal of Health Care Compliance**, and the **CCH Healthcare Compliance Letter**.

Health Care Compliance Professional's Manual. Chicago: Wolters Kluwer Law & Business, 1999-date. 1 vol. (1,238 pp.). Annual updates.
Cost: Print: $399 per year; Internet: contact sales representative (2014).
Designed for use by health plan administrators and legal counsel, this reference service provides the information necessary to ensure that health plans comply with applicable laws and regulations. It guides the reader through the complexities of health plan compliance while providing citations to the underlying laws and regulations. Written by experienced compliance practitioners and HCCA board members, the text addresses the health care legislative environment, and such topics as designing health plans, communicating health plans, enrolling in health plans, administering health plans, processing employee terminations, amending health plans, terminating health plans, avoiding penalties, sanctions and lawsuits, working with specific types of plans, and cafeteria plans. The appendices contain a variety of special features, including forms, model health compliance plan language, checklists, a glossary of terms, topical index, and table of cases. It also includes the full text of applicable laws, regulations, rulings, and notices. The **Manual** is endorsed by the Health Care Compliance Association. This title replaces the former two-volume **CCH Health Care Compliance Guide.**

Health Law & Business Library [print and Internet]. Washington, DC: Bloomberg BNA, 1997-date.
Cost: print: $3,001; $3,287 per year (2014).
This product provides electronic access to the portfolios available in Bloomberg BNA's **Health Law & Business Series** and serves as a reference source to back issues of Bloomberg BNA's **Health Law Reporter**. Written by experienced practitioners, it provides analytical coverage of those areas in which health care law and business concerns intersect. The portfolios analyze such specific topics as antitrust, contracting issues, fraud an abuse, operational issues, structural and legal issues, tax-exempt health care entities, transactional issues. The individual portfolios contain detailed analysis, working papers, checklists, full text of cases, statutes and regulations, model documents, and bibliography. There is a series-wide index and tables. Print portfolios are updated monthly and indexed periodically. The Web portfolios library is updated regulary, includes Web notification coverage.

Health Law Practice Guide. 2d ed. St. Paul, MN: Thomson Reuters West (Clark Boardman Callaghan), 1993-date. 5 vols. Looseleaf format or ProView eBook. Supplemented three times annually.
Cost: $2,875; ProView eBook: $2,637; supplementation: 1996: $272; 1997: $287; 1998: $304; 1999: $329; 2000: $355; 2001: $415; 2002: $477.50; 2003: $551; 2004: $657; 2005: $703; 2006: $825; 2007: $1,263; 2008: $1,405.50; 2009: $937; 2010: $1,781.50; 2011: $1,669.50; 2012: $1,836; 2013: $2,109; **Monthly Assured Print Price (APP):** $168/$2,016.
This comprehensive guide to health law issues is written and produced under the auspices of the National Health Lawyers Association. Its thirty-nine chapters provide analysis and practical advice on a host of law-related health care issues, ranging from operational issues for health care facilities, patient case delivery, payment issues, transactions, and the business environment. Individual chapters explore such topics as professional rights and responsibilities, medical records, environmental issues, health care decision-making, the HIV-infected healthcare worker, insurance payments for healthcare, Medicare payments, fraud and abuse in payment systems, antitrust in transactions, capital finance, the business environment of hospitals, long-term care, HMOs and PPOs, children's hospitals, outpatient/ambulatory services, and cost-containment, and more. The text is supported with sufficient citations to primary law and secondary sources to enhance further research. The authors include more than forty professionals in both the legal and health care fields.

Caution: The cost of this 5-volume set has risen sharply in recent years, from $980.00 In 2006 to $2,637 in 2013 (169%). Similarly, subscriber supplementation costs (which are about 80% of list) have risen 155%, from $825.00 to $2,109.

Hospital Law Manual [Print and Internet]. Gaithersburg, MD: Wolters Kluwer Law & Business, Inc. (Aspen), 1983-date. 5 vols. (4,908 pp.). With CD-ROM. Looseleaf format. Quarterly updates, monthly bulletins, and periodic special reports. Also available on the Internet.
Cost: $2,310 per year; Internet (available from CCH): inquire (but about $2,100 per year) (2014).
Contains the full text of the publishers **Hospital Law Manual** in both the print and on the Web, providing guidance on a variety of issues related to the management of health care facilities. Contents include: Admitting and Discharge, AIDS in health Care, Antitrust, Bankruptcy, Consent to Medical and Surgical Procedures, Dying, Death, and Dead Bodies, Environmental Issues, Reimbursement Issues, Governing Board, Immunity from Liability, Labor, Laboratory, Hospital Licensure, managed Care, Medical Records, Medical Staff, Pharmacy, Principles of Hospital Liability, Reproductive Issues, and Taxation Issues for Health Care Facilities. Volume 5 contains a collection of statutes, regulations, and applicable court decisions. The Internet version is available from Aspen Publisher's sister company, CCH, Inc.

Jordan, Michael M. L. **Durable Powers of Attorney and Health Care Directives**. 4th ed. St. Paul, MN: Thomson Reuters West (Clark Boardman Callaghan), 2004-date. 2 vols. Looseleaf format. Includes CD-ROM.
Cost: $362 ($291 w/o CD-ROM); supplementation: 2005: $100; 2006: $150; 2007: $78; 2008: $87; 2009: $102; 2010: $132; 2011: $121; 2012: $129; 2013: $153; 3d ed.: 1995: $60; 1996: $100; 1997: $285; 1998: $100; 1999: $354; 2000: $384; 2001: $148.50; 2002: $170; 2003: $100; 2004: $100; **Monthly Assured Print Price (APP):** $27/$324.
This treatise provides coverage of those legal issues involved in the exercise of powers of attorney during the incapacity of the grantor of that power, including issues related to the grantor's property, life, health, etc. This set covers durable powers of attorney for health care, property management, the fiduciary status of the agent, the third party perspective, and the drafting of the durable power. The set also includes forms on CD-ROM, drafting checklists, and comments for each of the fifty states and a number of relevant appendices, including the Uniform Rights of the Terminally Ill Act, and Principles and Guidelines Concerning

the Foregoing of Life-Sustaining Treatment for Adult Patients. Also includes Tables of Cases and Statutes, and an Index. Well-written and adequately footnoted text. The only drawback would appear to be the fact that the substantive text comprises probably less than 20% of the total pages in both volumes, with the bulk of the coverage devoted to state comments. If your practice is limited to one or two states, or if you have little need to research comparative state law, you may be paying for a great deal of material you will consult infrequently, if at all. Originally published by Shepard's/McGraw-Hill, it is now published by Thomson/West.

Krohm, Carol and Scott Summers. **Advance Health Care Directives: A Handbook for Professionals**. Chicago: American Bar Association, Senior Law Division, 2002. 1 vol. (352 pp.). Softcover.
Cost: OUT-OF-PRINT; was $99.95 ($89.95 for members); from $20.61 on amazon.com (2014).
Advance health care directives, including living wills and health care powers of attorney, are personal planning documents designed to provide health care personnel with prior instructions regarding the specific treatment to be given to specified patients when decision-makers are not available to give those instructions directly. This book is multidisciplinary in approach, combining legal, medical, spiritual and patient perspectives. Authored by an attorney and a board-certified family practitioner with a specialty in geriatrics, this volume addresses such topics as the difficulties in attempting to control the future, the various kinds of health care directives, ethical issues, client concerns and misconceptions,. the issue of competence and incompetence, special circumstances such as divorce, military status, and organ donations, the role of family and friends as advisors and surrogate decision-makers, alternatives in the absence of directives, the involvement of clergy and other spiritual advisors, and the future of advance health care directives. The Appendices include a number of invaluable documents, including relevant federal statutes, the Uniform Health-Care Decisions Act, Uniform Anatomical Gift Act, representative state statutes, selected religious directives, sample letters and wallet cards, glossary, and bibliography.

Legal Medicine. American College of Legal Medicine Textbook Committee, S. Sandy Sanbar et al. 7th ed. St. Louis, MO: Mosby, 2007. 1 vol. (768 pp.).
Cost: ebook: $229.00**;** from $139.97 on amazon.com; kindle ed.: $229 (2014).
This volume is a product of the American College of Legal Medicine, an organization devoted to furthering knowledge and education in the fields of medical jurisprudence and forensic medicine, and addressing problems that exist at the interface of law and medicine. This text addresses those areas of professional activity which present potential risk of legal liability. The book's fifty chapters discuss a wide range of medico-legal topics, combining discussion of substantive medical conditions and issues with a consideration of the legal ramifications of such activities. Topics include legal medicine and health law education, contracts, agency and partnership, competency and capacity, education and licensure, medical staff peer review, physician as defendant in medical malpractice, medical testimony and the expert witness, medical product liability, health insurance and professional liability insurance, risk management, fetal interests, medical records and disclosure about patients, forensic pathology, human experimentation and research, and many more. Endnotes to each chapter include references to relevant cases, statutes, and medical literature. The authors include more than fifty scholars in the fields of law and medicine, many of these with degrees in both disciplines. An excellent one-volume resource for law, medical, and academic libraries, and practitioners in both fields.

Loucks, Michael K. and Carol C. Lam. **Prosecuting and Defending Health Care Fraud Cases**. 2d ed. Arlington, VA: BNA Books, 2010. 1 vol. (1185 pp.).
Cost: $500.00; supplementation: 2013: $225; from $177.19 on amazon.com (2014).
Our enormously complex health care system in the United States is driven by a third-party payer system that leads inevitably to lack of accountability for medical decisionmaking, an environment in which fraudsters operate. Costs spiral out-of-control due largely to increased demands for the latest medical treatments, and from the fact that a combination of government- and employer-financed health insurance weakens the normal market-based dynamics that would exist between providers and recipients of medical care. Fraud in Medicare alone is estimated to range from $10 billion to $30 billion annually, a problem that was rarely addressed 30 years ago, but has not taken on far greater urgency today. The authors' objective in writing this volume is to guide the health care attorney through the statutes and regulations prohibiting certain conduct by health care providers and to provide practical advice regarding investigations, criminal and/or civil proceedings, and sentencing or settlement, as the case may be. They guide the user through the basics of litigation and counseling, the theories of fraud liability in health care cases (primarily false billing, the Civil False Claims Act, and the Federal Food, Drug and Cosmetic Act), the anti-kickback statute, the Stark prohibitions and related safe harbors, the anti-kickback advisory opinions, the investigation, the charging decision, global resolutions, criminal trial, and sentencing. The relevant Acts and regulations are reproduced in the volume's Appendices. The text is exhaustively accompanied by citations to relevant statutes, regulations, case law, and advisory opinions as an aid to further research. The substantive scope and scholarly treatment of the subject matter make this an essential resource for any attorney charged with prosecuting or defending cases of health care fraud. The 2013 supplement, issued in December, indicates that in 1992 the total health care fraud recovery was $111 million, but that, by 2012, exceeded $7 billion. In addition to updates to the text of the base volume, its Appendix G of Health Care Fraud Settlements of at least $1 million (from Jan. 1, 1991 to July 1, 2013), replaces the Appendix G of the main volume. Michael K. Loucks, former Acting U.S. Attorney and First Assistant U.S. Attorney for the District of Massachusetts, is now a litigation partner with Skadden Arps, LLP in Boston. Carol C. Lam is the former U.S. Attorney for the Southern District of California.

McLaughlin, Daniel B. **Responding to Healthcare Reform: A Strategy Guide for Healthcare Leaders**. Chicago, IL: Health Administration Press, 2011. 1 vol. (169 pp.). Paperbound.

Cost: $76.00; from $41.81 on amazon.com; kindle ed.: $67.16 (2014).
This volume attempts to provide practical guidance through the intricacies of the historic, comprehensive, and highly controversial, Patient Protection and Affordable Care Act (PPACA) of 2010 (now shortened to the Affordable Care Act (ACA)). The task of comprehending the ACA was exacerbated by the fact that it contains over 400 complex sections, a fact that makes a straightforward reading of the Act's language a difficult process. While the author acknowledges that the enactment of the ACA was highly partisan, he suggests that the historical lead up to passage owed much to bipartisan efforts over many years to reform the American healthcare system. Aimed at healthcare leaders, this volume attempts to address these complexities by focusing on three fundamental theories underlying the Act, namely (1) systems: how does each element in the system interact with and affect the other elements to achieve the desired outcomes (patient health)?; (2) funds flow and incentives: how can revenue and payment systems be designed to create change in behaviors to achieve desired outcomes; and (3) markets: how can markets be made to operate effectively to allow "the invisible hand" of capitalism to achieve the desired outcomes (provider market share and profits)? The author acknowledges that the bill's complexity was exacerbated by the fact that it never made it to conference committee where much of the logic of the bill is set, a situation dictated by the peculiar method of its passage. The text is primarily directed at attempting to explain the Act through the implementation of these three basic theories. Ironically, the author contends that the final theory of the ACA is based in liberty and the force of the free market to optimize healthcare costs and value, without rationalizing the place of the health care mandate and the punitive effects of IRS enforcement mechanism in the pursuit of those ideals. Chapter coverage includes a discussion of chronic disease management and primary care, productivity and quality, prevention and wellness, systems view scenarios, payment incentives, the safety net, funds flow scenarios, the perfect market: health insurance reform, market scenarios, and the future. Appendices include discussion questions, the Congressional Research Service Summary of the ACA, and subject index. This is an invaluable explanatory complement to the often confusing original text of the Act. The author is director of the Center for Health and Medical Affairs in the Opus College of Business at the University of St. Thomas in St. Paul.

Medicare and Medicaid Guide. Riverwoods, IL: Wolters Kluwer Law & Business (CCH), 1969-date. 6 vols. Looseleaf service. (approx. 8,000 pp.). Weekly. Also available on Internet (see below).
Cost: $2,859 per year; Internet: Inquire (2014)
This five-volume looseleaf service provides detailed coverage of the programs created by Titles XVIII (Medicare) and XIX (Medicaid) of the Social Security Act. The coverage is primarily devoted to federal laws, although State Medicaid laws are covered in more superficial fashion. Material includes federal laws, regulations, federal agency publications, federal court decisions, administrative agency rulings, and reports to Congress issued by the General Accounting Office (GAO) and the Health and Human Services Office of the Inspector General.

Medicare and Medicaid Guide [Internet]. Riverwoods, IL: Wolters Kluwer Law & Business (CCH), 1989-date. Search Engine: Proprietary. Includes toll-free product support.
Cost: Inquire (2014).
Contains the full text of the print service with full text searching and hypertext linking. This version also includes the optional HCFA Manuals. An optional archive CD-ROM disc contains opinions, decisions, administrative rulings and other documents issued since the beginning of Medicare in 1966.

Melton, Gary B., et al. **Psychological Evaluations for the Courts: A Handbook for Mental Health Professionals and Lawyers**. 3d ed. New York: The Guilford Press, 2007. 1 vol. (930 pp.).
Cost: $120 (online order: $102); from $71.94 on amazon.com; kindle ed.: $86.74 (2014).
The use of expert testimony from mental health professionals is a subject of great controversy, eliciting criticism from both the general public and the legal profession, as well as considerable debate among behavioral science researchers and mental health professionals. The authors of this monumental resource take a moderate position between those advocating outright exclusion of such testimony and those who defend its use. This volume is directed at two audiences: mental health professionals who perform psychological evaluations for the courts; and lawyers and judges who request such evaluations. The eighteen substantive chapters are divided into five parts: (1) General Considerations: embracing chapters on the uneasy alliance between the law and the mental health professions; an overview of the legal system; the nature and method of forensic assessment; the constitutional, common law, and ethical contours of the evaluation process; and managing public and private forensic services; (2) The Criminal Process: encompassing such topics as competency to stand trial; other competencies in the criminal process; mental state at the time of the offense; and sentencing; (3) Noncriminal Adjudications, including chapters on civil commitment; civil competencies; compensating mental injury; and federal antidiscrimination and entitlement laws; (4) Children and Families: including the subjects of juvenile delinquency; child abuse and neglect; child custody in divorce; and education and habilitation; and (5) Communicating with the Courts: including the subjects of consultations, report writing, and expert testimony. Chapter 19 includes a number of sample reports illustrating the subject matter of the prior substantive chapters. The volume concludes with glossaries of legal terms, clinical and research terms. Gary B. Melton, Professor of Psychology and Director of the Institute on Family and Neighborhood Life at Clemson University, is the author of over 300 publications, has lectured in more than 40 countries, and has been cited by the U.S. Supreme Court and lower courts. Previous editions of this book were published in 1987 and 1997.

Miles, John J. **Health Care & Antitrust Law**. St. Paul, MN: Thomson Reuters West (Clark Boardman Callaghan), 1992-date. 4 vols. Looseleaf format.
Cost: $2,837; supplementation: 1995: $345; 1996: $395; 1997: $411; 1998: $435; 1999: $471; 2000: $503; 2001: $580.50; 2002: $639; 2003: $727.50; 2004: $543; 2005: $1,190; 2006: $1,025; 2007: $1,107; 2008: $1,231.50; 2009: $1.375.50; 2010: $1,513.50; 2011: $1,650; 2012: $1,830; 2013: $2,083; **Monthly**

Assured Print Price (APP): $207/$2,484.
A detailed analysis of those areas of the law where health care and antitrust law converge. Volumes one and two provide a comprehensive analytical treatment of the law, with attention to the most significant cases and other legal authorities. Volumes three and four contain an extensive collection of forms, letters, speeches and other sources useful to those practicing in this area. This work covers such specific issues as hospital staff-privilege antitrust problems, provider diversification, ethical restraints and related antitrust concerns, antitrust enforcement issues.

Nelson, James M. **Health and Welfare Benefit Plans**. 3d ed. Huntington, NY: Juris Publishing, Inc., 2009-date. 1 vol. (632 pp.). Also available as downloadable electronic product.
Cost: $175; supplementation: 2010: $20; 2011: $25; 2012: $25; 2013: $25.
This is a guide to the various types of benefits (exclusive of discount pension benefits) that employers choose to provide to their employees, and the mechanisms that they use to administer those benefits. It also explains employee benefit regulation and some of the tax issues that arise in conjunction with the administration of these benefits. And while the Employee Retirement Income Security Act (ERISA) of 1974 does not provide minimum participation, vesting or funding standards for welfare benefit plans, it does control employers who choose to provide benefits by regulating the manner in which those benefits are provided, including reporting and disclosure requirements, fiduciary duty regulations, and enforcement provisions that apply equally to welfare benefit plans and pension plans. This volume provides coverage of the federal income tax laws and regulations applicable to welfare benefits, the various forms of employee welfare benefits, coverage requirements, exclusions and limitations, disclosure of medical information, disability, retiree health issues, ERISA coverage, ERISA preemption, ERISA disclosure and reporting obligations, COBRA continuation health coverage, ERISA fiduciary responsibility, employee benefit discrimination, and EREISA enforcement and litigation. The text is supported with numerous references to federal statutes, regulations, and court decisions. The work is intended as a planning and management guide for attorneys who are not employee benefit specialists, and for human resource professionals who administer employee benefits. Author James M. Nelson is a shareholder in Greenberg Traurig LLP's Labor and Employment and Global Benefits and Compensation practice groups in Sacramento, California, where he represents employers and ERISA plan fiduciaries in matters concerning ERISA compliance, fiduciary responsibility, collective bargaining, wage and hour matters, employee benefits, safety, discrimination, wrongful termination, and other labor and employment issues. He is also editor of the ABA Labor Section Employee Benefit Committee Newsletter.

Obade, Claire C. **Patient Care Decision Making: A Legal Guide for Providers**. St. Paul, MN: Thomson Reuters West (Clark Boardman Callaghan), 2011-date. 1 vol. Annual replacement volume. Paperbound.
Cost: 2013-2014 edition: $758; supplementation to prior edition: 1996: $114; 1997: $120; 1998: $127; 1999: $137; 2000: 0; 2001: $170; 2002: $199; 2003: $226.50; 2004: $226; 2005: $245; 2006: $315; 2007: $312.50; 2008: $348; 2009: $417; 2010: $459.50; 2011: $599; 2012-2013 ed.: $696. **Monthly Assured Print Price (APP):** $63/$756.
Decision-making in the health care field often involves the careful balancing of the rights of patients and the responsibilities of health care providers. This volume provides an analytical framework, including general guidelines and principles, for confronting such issues as consensual treatment (including waivers and special consent requirements), the right to refuse treatment, limitations on surrogate decisions, unnecessary, inappropriate or futile care, forced treatment of the mentally ill, privacy and confidentiality, access to medical information and records by patients and surrogates, and exceptions to and limitations on the right of confidentiality.

Pinheiro, Brian M. et al. **Employer's Guide to Health Care Reform**. New York: Wolters Kluwer Law & Business, 2014. 1 vol. (various pagings). Paperbound. Annual.
Cost: $309.00; from $252.47 on amazon.com (2014).
The Patient Protection and Affordable Care Act of 2010, otherwise known as the Affordable Care Act (ACA) or "Obamacare" (P.L. 111-148, 124 Stat. 119-1025) is the most significant regulatory overhaul of the U.S. healthcare system since the passage of Medicare and Medicaid in 1965. Despite the President's oft repeated statements that "if you like your current insurance, you can keep your current insurance" and "if you like your doctor, you will be able to keep your doctor," the reality is far different. The authors posit that "although the Affordable Care Act does not force individuals to drop or change their coverage, it remains to seen whether employers, through which many individuals currently have health insurance coverage, decide to continue to provide the same type of coverage in light of the health care reform changes." In the meantime, the response by employers will depend on a variety of factors, including the size of the workforce, the average income level of employees, the level of unionization, whether the employer provides coverage to pre- and/or post-Medicare retirees (in addition to active employees) the types of group health plans provided to employees, whether the costs incurred under those plans are self-funded by the employer out of its operating assets or are funded through insurance (or a combination of both), the design of the employer's group health plan and the terms and conditions of coverage, whether the employer is profit or non-profit, and the degree to which health benefits continue to be viewed as an important benefit for the recruitment and retention of employees in the employer's industry. This volume provides a comprehensive overview of the Affordable Care Act and the issues it raises for employers attempting to adapt to its complex network of laws, regulations, administrative directives, and exemptions. Following a review of the evolution of health care reform and the legal challenges to health care reform, they examine health care reform exemptions, the issues of quality, affordability and accessibility, the preservation and expansion of immediate access to coverage, coverage improvements during the transition period, the improvements effective January 1, 2014, issues of transparency and accountability, mandates of exchanges, operational changes for health plans, new taxes and other revenue raisers. Finally, they analyze the impact of health care reform going forward

on both small and large employers. Half the volume consists of applicable regulations from the Federal Register and other official government sources. This is an essential resource for any small or large business or corporation grappling with the intricacies of the new health care law and its implementation. Three of the authors are members of the Employee Benefits and Executive Compensation Group at the law firm of Ballard Spahr LPP. Jean Hemphill is a partner in the Business and Finance Department of Ballard Spahr.

Pozgar, George D. **Legal Aspects of Health Care Administration**. 11th ed. Sudbury, MA: Jones & Bartlett Learning, 2012. 1 vol. (602 pp.).
Cost: $123.95; from $59.72 on amazon.com (2014).
This volume provides a comprehensive treatment of legal and ethical issues in the field of health law as they operate within the complex web that constitutes the American legal system, a web complicated by the passage of **Patient Protection and Affordable Care Act (PPACA),** signed into law by President Barack Obama on March 23, 2010. Intended as a textbook in the field of healthcare administration, its 27 chapters address a wide variety of topics, beginning with a history of hospitals, an overview of the American legal system, and the application of traditional fields of law to the health environment, including tort law, criminal law, contracts and antitrust, civil procedure and trial practice, and corporate structure and legal issues. The author also examines the legal implications as they relate to medical staff, nursing, allied professionals, information management, patient consent, legal reporting requirements, patient rights and responsibilities, AIDS, healthcare ethics, procreation and ethical dilemmas, end-of-life issues, professional liability issues, labor relations, employee discipline and discharge, employee rights and responsibilities, managed care, tort reform and risk reduction, patient safety and zero tolerance. Concluding chapters address the world wide search for healthcare resources on the Internet, and establishing the healthcare war room for improving the quality of patient care. Each chapter contains numerous case studies, references to the applicable law, including summaries of relevant court decisions and statutes; as well as chapter reviews, review questions, and notes. The author is a veteran hospital administrator, author, consultant, and surveyor across 650 hospitals.

O'Reilly, James T. **Food and Drug Administration**. 3d ed. Eagan, MN: Thomson Reuters West, 2007-date. 2 vols. Looseleaf format and eBook.
Cost: $1,250; ProView eBook: $1,146; supplementation: 2010: $666; 2011: $742; 2012: $828; 2013: $919; **Monthly Assured Print Price (APP):** $91/$1,092.
The legislative basis for the Food and Drug Administration (FDA) has its origins in the Food and Drugs Act (1906), out of which arose the Bureau of Chemistry under the USDA. In 1927, the Bureau of Chemistry's regulatory powers were reorganized under a new USDA body, the Food, Drug, and Insecticide organization. This name was shortened to the Food and Drug Administration (FDA) three years later. In 1938, President Franklin Delano Roosevelt signed the new Food, Drug, and Cosmetic Act, a law which significantly increased federal regulatory authority over drugs, set new regulatory standards for foods, and brought cosmetics and therapeutic devices under federal regulatory authority. This law, though extensively amended in subsequent years, remains the central foundation of FDA regulatory authority to the present day. This two-volume treatise provides the practicing attorney with a guide to the practice and procedures of the Food and Drug Administration and the complex regulatory apparatus over which it has responsibility. Organizationally, the 29 chapters in this two-volume work track the FDA's general rulemaking authority, its administrative enforcement apparatus, and its court proceedings. The remainder of volume one and a portion of volume two provide in-depth analysis of the substantive provisions of the Food, Food, and Cosmetic Act. In addition to a review of the structure and history of the FDA, the chapters cover such topics as FDA policy making; hearings; enforcement; civil actions in court; criminal actions in court; food safety and quality issues; food regulation: marketing, nutrition and dietary supplements; food additives; color additives; drug regulation: definitions and approvals; drug conflicts: rejections, enforcement and litigation issues; drug reporting, marketing and international issues; animal drugs and feds; cosmetics; medical devices; radiological products; inspections; product recalls; openness and publicity; good practices regulations; FDA and other Federal agencies; FDA and state governments; products liability; science issues; import and export issues; and the FDA and tobacco products. The Appendices contain the text of he Food, Drug and Cosmetics Act, as amended (1938 et seq.), the Public Health Services Act, as amended (1944 et seq.), selected litigation forms, table of cases, and index. The substantive text is replete with citations to primary and secondary authorities as an aid to further research. This exemplary work is notable for its combination of scholarship and practical utility. James T. O'Reilly currently teaches at the University of Cincinnati College of Law, is a city council member, and serves as a trustee of the regional council of governments in the Cincinnati area. A former journalist and business lawyer, he has lectured widely on recycling and liability throughout the United States, Mexico, and Europe, and has served as a consultant to the Environmental Protection Agency on waste issues.

Showalter, J. Stuart. **The Law of Healthcare Administration**. 6th ed. Chicago: Health Administration Press, 2011. 1 vol. (511 pp.).
Cost: $129; from $89.97 on amazon.com (2014).
Written primarily for students of healthcare administration, this book has had an enormous impact in the field since the appearance of the first edition in 1978. Originally authored by Arthur F. Southwick, it was designed to impart the intricacies of the field of health law from the perspective of the administrator. Following Professor Southwick's death in 1997, J. Stuart Showalter, Director of Compliance at the Orlando Regional Health System, has brought the book up-to-date by incorporating the latest legal developments in the field, including issues arising under the Taxpayer Bill of Rights, developments in antitrust law, and the effects of the Emergency Medical Treatment and Active Labor Act, among others. Following a succinct description of the American legal system, the author discusses such issues as breach of contract and intentional tort, negligence, the organization and management of a corporate healthcare institution, liability of the healthcare institution, taxation of healthcare institutions, antitrust law, healthcare fraud and abuse, admission and discharge, emergency care, consent for treatment and withholding of consent, family planning, medical

records, and medical staff appointments and privileges. Although primarily aimed at students of healthcare administration, this work provides attorneys representing healthcare institutions with an excellent review of the most significant legal issues. The best work of its kind on the market.

Treatise on Health Care Law. New York: Matthew Bender & Co., 1991-date. 4 vols. Looseleaf format. Supplemented twice annually. Also available on eBook. **Cost**: $1,717 (includes annual subscription); renewal: 1996: $238; 1997: $238; 1998: $250; 1999: $265; 2000: $285; 2001: $305; 2002: $327; 2003: $344; 2004: $361; 2005: $386; 2006: $414; 2007: $447; 2008: $483; 2009: $531; 2010: $569; 2011: 2012: $609; 2013: $652; 2014: $712; eBook: $1,561; renewal: 2013: $652; 2014: $712.
The rise of health care to a central position in the public policy agenda in the United States is a reflection of the confluence of a number of factors, including the impact of major biomedical and technical advances, the increasing demand for health care services, the dominant role of third party payors, the growth of a complex regulatory framework, and difficult patient care and treatment issues. This comprehensive work provides analysis and practical guidance in a variety of legal areas central to health care, including corporate organizations, health care contracts, tax implications for health care institutions, facility licensure and accreditation, employment and labor issues, medical staff, economic aspects of the health care delivery system, health care payment systems, Medicare, Medicaid, peer review, alternative delivery systems, fraud and abuse, environmental concerns, access to health care, medical malpractice, tort reform, patient information and confidentiality, consent to medical treatment, and refusal of medical treatment. Each chapter of the text is accompanied by detailed synopses, case citations, statutes, regulations, state-by-state charts, and a table of cases. Written by a team of more than forty legal and health care professionals.

Wigder, Herbert N. and Jeffrey C. Moffat. **Standards of Care in Emergency Medicine: A Practical Guide to Emergency Procedures and Legal Liability**. Gaithersburg, MD: Wolters Kluwer Law & Business, Inc., 1998-date. 1 vol. Looseleaf format.
Cost: $449; supplementation: 1999: $55; 2000: $60; 2001: $119; 2002: $149; 2003: $175; 2004: $183; 2005: $189; 2006: $299; 2007: $209; 2008: $225; 2009: $249; 2010: $255; 2011: $279; 2012: $305; 2013: $359.
This manual is designed to provide guidance to physicians and attorneys concerned about standards of care in the field of emergency medicine. While malpractice concerns have diminished in recent years, there remains a continuing interest in ensuring that proper standards of care are delivered to patients. Part I of this manual is designed to familiarize the attorney with special laws which apply to malpractice actions in various jurisdictions, including duties and standards of care, negligence, duty to warn, res ipsa loquitur, battery and informed consent, negligent infliction of emotional distress, loss of consortium, fraud, falsification of medical records, vicarious liability, causation, affirmative defenses, and limitations on medical malpractice actions and damages. Part II provides information on standards of care in specific emergencies, from appendicitis and drug reaction to myocardial infarction and ruptured spleen. Each of these specialized chapters examines a uniform series of subtopics, including definitions and terminology, diagnostic criteria, medical management, controversies and problem areas, legal considerations, typical medical case, medical analysis, and legal analysis. Each chapter includes citations to relevant legal and medical authorities. The appendices include a glossary of terms, and tables of cases, statutes, and other legal authorities. Herbert Wigder is Associate Director of Emergency Medicine, Lutheran General Hospital, Park Ridge, Illinois and an Clinical Associate Professor, Department of Medicine, Section of Emergency Medicine, University of Chicago. Jeffrey Moffat is an attorney with the Los Angeles firm of Boone, Bridges, Mueller, O'Keefe & Nichols. They were assisted by seven contributing authors.

Zanglein, Jayne E. and Susan J. Stabile. **ERISA Litigation.** 4th ed. Arlington, VA: Bloomberg BNA Books, 2011-date. 1 vol. (1,664 pp.). Annual supplementation.
Cost: $480; supplementation: 2012: $195; 2013: $195; 3d ed.: 2009: $185; 2010: $190.
The Employee Retirement Income Security Act of 1974 (ERISA) is a federal law that establishes minimum standards for most voluntarily created pension and health plans in private industry in order to provide protection for individuals in these plans. Among the ERISA guidelines are those that provide participants with important information about plan features and funding, and establish fiduciary responsibilities for those who manage and control the assets of such plans. The law also requires plans to establish a grievance and appeals process to ensure that participants get benefits from their plans; and gives participants the right to sue for benefits and breaches of fiduciary duty. ERISA has been subject to several significant amendments expanding the protections available to health benefit plan participants and beneficiaries. One of these, the Consolidated Omnibus Budget Reconciliation Act of 1985 (COBRA), provides some workers and their families with the right to continue their health coverage for a limited time after certain events, such as the loss of a job. Another amendment, the Health Insurance Portability and Accountability Act of 1996 (HIPAA), provides protections for working Americans and their families who have preexisting medical conditions or might otherwise suffer discrimination in health coverage. Other amendments include the Newborns' and Mothers' Health Protection Act, the Mental Health Parity Act, and the Women's Health and Cancer Rights Act. More than 10,000 ERISA cases are files annually in the federal courts. This comprehensive guide to ERISA litigation is designed for both the novice and experienced attorneys, with information detailed enough to lead them through the intricacies of the most complex case. The book's 39 chapters encompass every aspect of ERISA litigation procedure, from the initial determination of whether an ERISA welfare or pension plan is involved, to what causes of action are available, who can sue and be sued, available remedies, statute of limitations, what courts have subject matter jurisdiction, service of process, appropriate venue, the court's personal jurisdiction over the defendant, availability of a jury trial, availability of attorneys' fees, appropriate standards of review, pretrial discovery, attorney-client privilege and work product doctrine, and the appropriateness of the class action. Part II encompasses potential causes of action, including wrongful denial of benefits, fiduciary duties, pension plan investments, age discrimination, retiree welfare benefits, spousal rights, termination of pension plans, civil RICO, delinquency actions,

medical privacy, COBRA litigation, contingent workers and employee benefits, and special rules for multiemployer plans. The volume includes exhaustive citations to relevant cases, statutes and regulations. Moreover, each chapter features a Table of Significant Cases, organized by U.S. Supreme Court and federal circuits. The Appendices include an ERISA—U.S. Code Correspondence Table, an exhaustive table of cases, and index. Lead authors Jayne Zanglein and Susan Stabile are joined by a team of 24 contributing authors. This comprehensive and well-organized volume is an essential acquisition to any attorney or law firm engaged in ERISA litigation.

Additional titles in the field of Health and Hospital Law are available from the following publishers: American Bar Association, American Hospital Publishing, Inc., Wolters Kluwer Law & Business, Matthew Bender, Bloomberg BNA, Bloomberg BNA Books, CCH, Inc., Health Administration Press, Government Institutes, Inc., Juris Publishing, Mosby, Practising Law Institute, Thomson Reuters West, Warren, Gorham & Lamont, West Academic. See Appendix B for addresses and telephone numbers.

Immigration Law

AILALink [CD-ROM]. Washington, DC: American Immigration Lawyers Association. Online resaerch database.
Cost: members: $695 per year; non-members: $1,025; academic institutions: $725; government agencies: $749; $125 each for up to five concurrent users (2014).
A comprehensive electronic resource for the immigration law specialist, containing the text of federal statutes, regulations, Board of Immigration Appeals decisions (1983-date), INS Operating Instructions, AILA handbooks and manuals, case summaries, practice advisories, advocacy materials, etc. An online link allows users to download files from the AILA InfoNet Web site and conduct simultaneous searches of both the CD-ROM and downloaded files. Includes online tutorial and technical support.

Akers, Grace E., ed. **Navigating the Fundamentals of Immigration Law: Guidance and Tips for Successful Practice** [eBook]. 2013-2014 Edition. Washington, DC: American Immigration Lawyers Association, 2013. 1 vol. (439 pp.). Online only.
Cost: $199; $109 to AILA members (2014).
This collection of articles by thirty contributing authors addresses general practice strategies as well as a variety of specific aspects of immigration law practice. The editor describes it as a "core curriculum" handbook designed as both a primer for students, paralegals and practitioners new to the immigration law field, and a tool for all practitioners who need a handy reference to the fundamentals of immigration law and procedure. Leading off with a glossary of key definitions and concepts, the practice strategies section also discusses the best practices for immigration law office management, ethical issues for immigration lawyers, initial interviews, and foiling procedures. The remaining article as are grouped under the headings: work authorization, employment-based permanent residence, employment-based nonimmigrant visas, other nonimmigrant visas, adjustment of status/consular proceedings, family-based permanent residency/naturalization and citizenship, and admission, removal, and relief. While the text is augmented by selective citations to applicable cases, statutes, regulations and secondary authorities, its primary value lies in its lucid discussion and explication of the often complex details of immigration law and procedure. The authors are all experienced practitioners in the immigration law field.

Federal Immigration Laws and Regulations. St. Paul, MN: Thomson Reuters West. 1 vol. Published annually. Softbound.
Cost: 2013 Edition: $337; ProView eBook: $337 (2014).
An desktop source for all significant federal immigration and laws and regulations.

Cost-Saving Tip: This is high priced example of what happens when West gets its hands on public domain material and repackages it for public consumption. As an alternative, The **Complete Code of Federal Regulations, Title 8, Aliens And Nationality**, 2012 is available from amazon for $9.95. Both the **U.S. Code** and **Code of Federal Regulations** are available at no cost on the GPO web site.

Anker, Deborah E. **Law of Asylum in the United States**. 4th ed. St. Paul, MN: Thomson Reuters West, 2012. 1 vol. (611+ pp.). Paperbound.
Cost: 2013 Edition: $207.00 (2014).
Asylum, which may be defined as the protection of persons facing persecution, has been a formal part of United States law for more than 30 years. The United Nations Convention relating to the Status of Refugees was ratified by the United States in 1968, but it was not until 1980 that Congress enacted specific statutory provisions to comport with that treaty. Since that time, the United States has enacted a substantial body of law and produced thousands of court decisions, defining the core concert of "refugee" as one who has experienced or fears persecution for reasons of race, religion, nationality, membership in a particular social group, or political opinion. The Refugee Act, enacted in 1980 (P.L. No. 96-212, 94 Stat. 102) was designed to reflect U.S. legal obligations under the U.N. Refugee Convention. Asylum law, which is domestic law based on international law, takes the form of the statute, federal court decisions, precedential and non-precedential administrative decisions of the Board of Immigration Appeals (BIA), regulations, and sub-regulatory instructions and related texts. Following a thorough introduction to asylum law, which includes a review of its sources, the nature of asylum generally, and other immigration statuses, the author examines standards of proof, evidence, persecution, the nexus and grounds of persecution, exclusions from asylum and withholding of removal, and protection under Article 3 of the Convention Against Torture. The text is accompanied by extensive citations to relevant primary and secondary sources, including case annotations, and includes tables of laws, rules and cases. Deborah Anker, is Clinical Professor of Law and Director of the Harvard Law School Immigration and Refugee Clinical Program, where she has taught for more than 25 years.

Boswell, Richard A. **Essentials of Immigration Law**. 3d ed.

Washington, DC: American Immigration Lawyers Association, 2012. 1 vol. (284 pp.). Paperbound.
Cost: $109; $79 to members (2014).
This is arguably the best single-volume overview of the basics of immigration and refugee law, including its history, current state, and practical application, Designed for use by law students, paralegals, law clerks, laypersons, as well as attorneys new to the field, the author provides a clearly written discussion of such topics as the administration and development of immigration law and immigrants' rights under the Constitution; inadmissibility, deportability, waivers, and relief from removal; protection from harm; nonimmigrant visas providing temporary admission to the United States; immigrant visas providing lawful permanent residence; administrative and judicial review, and U.S. citizenship. Useful appendices include key definitions and concepts, abbreviations and acronyms, immigrant classifications and visas, nonimmigrant visa classifications, conversion tables, and a selected bibliography and electronic resources. Includes numerous citations to relevant primary and secondary sources. The author is professor of law at the University of California, Hastings College of the Law, and director of its Immigrants Rights Clinic and Center on Institutional Justice and Human Rights. One of many excellent resources published by the American Immigration Lawyers Association, of which the author is a member and former member of its board of governors.

Divine, Robert C. and R. Blake Chisam. **Immigration Practice**. 2011-2012 Edition. 14th ed. Huntington, NY: Juris Publishing, 2012. 1 vol. (1,710).
Cost: $295; downloadable electronic product: $295 (2014).
A detailed and practical guide to the complexities of immigration law and procedure. Its nineteen chapters provide in-depth coverage of such matters as client contacts, preparation of filings, dealing with agencies, representation by attorneys and non-profit agencies, requests for government files, the sources of law, an introduction to immigration procedures, nonimmigrant visas and status, processing toward permanent status, maintaining permanent residence status, inadmissibility and deportability grounds and their waiver, removal proceedings and relief from them, citizenship, "lotteries" for permanent residence, and family- and employment-based avenues to permanent residence, immigration to avoid persecution and chaos, temporary employment-based classifications, visitors, students and trainees, and employment of aliens. Appendices include a list of abbreviation s used in the immigration practice and an INS/USC conversion table, as well tables of cases, statutes, and index. The text is accompanied by exhaustive citations to relevant cases, statutes, and regulations. A companion CD-ROM contains Appendices C, D & E, with government offices, law and policy, frequently used government forms and suggestions for completing them, and miscellaneous forms, checklists and documents. Robert C. Divine is currently Principal Legal Advisor to the U.S. Citizenship and Immigration Service, a bureau of the Department of Homeland Security. Prior to his appointment, he was leader of the immigration team at the firm of Donelson Bearman Caldwell & Berkowitz. Co-author, and editor of the 2006-2007 edition, R. Blake Chisam is a partner in the firm of Chisam and Majid where his practice is devoted exclusively to immigration law. First published in 1994, followed by annual pocket part supplements, it was converted to an annual publication in 1997.

Fragomen, Austin T. and Steven C. Bell. **Immigration Employment Compliance Handbook**. St. Paul, MN: Thomson Reuters West (Clark Boardman), 1987-date. 1 vol. Paperbound. Annual.
Cost: 2013-2014 Edition: $853; ProView eBook: $853; **Monthly Assured Print Price (APP):** $71/$852 (2014).
This guide is intended to assist employers and their legal counsel in compliance with the provisions of U.S. immigration laws, particularly those contained in the Illegal Immigration Reform and Immigrant Responsibility Act of 1996 (IIRIRA) and the Immigration Reform and Control Act of 1986 (IRCA). The authors provide practical guidance to assist legal counsel in representing clients on a wide variety of immigration-related matters, including litigation involving employer sanctions and discrimination. There is also detailed discussion of the I-9 system whereby the federal government requires employers to help the government police illegal aliens. This annually revised volume also includes the text of applicable federal statutes, regulations, opinion letters, and critical federal immigration policy documents, such as the INS Handbook for Employers, and I-9 forms.

Fragomen, Austin T., Jr., Alfred Del Ray, Jr. and Sam Bernsen. **Immigration Law and Business.** 2d ed. St. Paul, MN: Thomson Reuters West (Clark Boardman Callaghan), 2011-date. 2 vols. Looseleaf format. Supplemented periodically.
Cost: $759; ProView eBook: $737; supplementation: 2012: $213; 2013: $232; 1st ed.: 1993: $200; 1994: $305; 1995: $345; 1996: $445; 1997: $420; 1998: $375; 1999: $405; 2000: $360; 2001: $496; 2002: $345; 2003: $435; 2004: $345; 2005: $360; 2006: $450; 2007: $459; 2008: $511.50; 2009: $570; 2010: $621; 2011: new ed.: $727.50; **Monthly Assured Print Price (APP):** $43/$516
The treatise, prepared by attorneys with the firm of Baker and McKenzie, is designed to provide detailed guidance to business enterprises in their dealings with immigrants and aliens. There is an excellent introductory chapter reviewing the history of immigration legislation since 1882, a complete discussion of the various categories of non-immigrants and procedures, permanent resident status, labor certification, naturalization and citizenship, exclusion and deportation, refugees and asylum, rights of aliens, tax aspects of immigration, administrative and judicial review, and employment of aliens. The Appendices include more than 50 INS forms, Table of Cases, Table of Statutes, and Index. The text is supported with citations to relevant court decisions, Board of Immigration Appeals decisions, statutes, regulations, and other authorities.

Fragomen, Austin T., Alfred J. Del Rey and Steven C. Bell. **Immigration Procedures Handbook**. St. Paul, MN: Thomson Reuters West (Clark Boardman Callaghan), 1985-date. 3 vols. Annual editions. Paperbound.
Cost: 2013-2014 Edition: $984; ProView eBook: $984 (2014).
A comprehensive guide to current federal immigration procedures in the aftermath of the 1996 Immigration Reform Act written for the practitioner. Materials are organized under three chapter headings: (1) Chapter 1: The B Visa Category, including basic

information about the B Category, requirements for classification in the B category, application for the B Visa at a U.S. Consulate, procedure at the border, extension of stay, change of status, the Visa waiver pilot program for B visitors, and proposed regulations for the B category; Chapter 2: The F Visa category, including basic information about the F category, basic requirements for obtaining F-1 status, preparation and presentation of papers to obtain F-1 status, procedures at the border, changing major, schools or educational programs: the notification procedure, failure to complete academic program within anticipated time, employment by students, practical; training for F-1 students, and change of status to the F-1 category; Chapter 3: The E Visa category, including purposes and uses of the E category, rules applicable to the E category, alternatives to the E category, preparation of the papers to obtain E status, and submission of papers and government processing. Despite the high cost for a one volume work, this volume provides convenient access to current immigration procedures for the active practitioner.

Generazio, Marc R. **Immigration Law: A Guide to Laws and Regulations**. Chicago: American Bar Association, 2011. 1 vol. (209 pp.) with CD-ROM. Paperbound.
Cost: $74.95; member price: $59.95; from $25.15 on amazon.com (2014).
While the process of immigration involves all those persons applying to enter the United States with the intention of staying permanently, the particular circumstances of their application and compliance are often complex and detailed. This compact guide provides a convenient summary and overview of immigration laws and regulations and their sources. The coverage embraces immigrants and immigrant visas, immigration classifications, admission into the United States and nonimmigrant visas, inadmissibility and removal, citizenship and naturalization. The text is accompanied by numerous tables that conveniently detail immigrant classifications, deferred inspection sites, nonimmigrant visa classifications, the legal grounds of inadmissibility, waivers and exceptions, and immigration consequences for criminal activity. The volume also contains lists of consulates in the United States, detention facilities, a table that converts provisions of the Immigration and National Act (INA) to their respective U.S. Code sections, and numerous immigration forms. The entire text is replicated on a companion CD-ROM. The author is a former adjudication officer with the Department of Homeland Security, United States Citizenship and Immigration Services in Boston. He confines his practice exclusively to immigration law and teaches immigration law at the University of Massachusetts in Lowell.

Germain, Regina. **AILA's Asylum Primer: A Practical Guide to U.S. Asylum Law and Procedure**. 6th ed. Washington, DC: American Immigration Lawyers Association, 2009. 1 vol. (468 pp.). Periodic new editions.
Cost: $109; $79 to AILA members (2014).
This volume provides a complete review of the legal and procedural rules governing the granting of asylum. The author, Senior Legal Counselor in the Washington Office of the United Nations High Commissioner for Refugees (UNHCR), discusses the current state of U.S. and international law on asylum. She also reviews the substantive criteria and procedures for asylum and withholding of removal, expedited removal, and other forms of relief. The appendices include interviewing techniques, a sample intake form, discussion of the process of completing the application and applying affirmatively, supporting documentation, preparing for the hearing, contacts and resources, charts, and recommended texts and tools.

Gordon, Charles, Stanley Mailman, and Stephen Yale-Loehr. **Immigration Law and Procedure.** Revised edition. New York: Matthew Bender & Co., 1960-date. 20 vols. Looseleaf format. Supplemented quarterly. CD-ROM features relevant case law and LEXIS-NEXIS online connection at no extra charge.
Cost: $3,446 (includes annual subscription); renewal: 1995: $1,100; 1996: $1,100; 1997: $1,100; 1998: $1,160; 1999: $1,200; 2000: $1,200; 2001: $1,284; 2002: $1,374; 2003: $1,443; 2004: $1,515; 2005: $1,576; 2006: $1,640; 2007: $1,738; 2007: $1,738; 2008: $1,738; 2009: $1,877; 2010: $1,972; 2011: $2,071; 2012; $2,133; 2013: $2,282; 2014: $2,491; CD-ROM Library (see entry below): $3,218; renewal: 2000: $820; 2001: $877; 2002: $939; 2003: $986; 2004: $1,035; 2005: $1,108; 2006: $1,186; 2007: $1,280; 2008: $1,357; 2009: $1,466; 2010: $1,496; 2011: $1,616; 2012: $1,881; 2013: $2,013; 2014: $1,964.52; eBook: $3,133; renewal: 2014: $2,265.
Authored by Charles Gordon, a practicing attorney in Washington, DC and former General Counsel to the Immigration and Naturalization Service and Stanley Mailman, a member of the New York law firm of Satterlee Stephens Burke and Burke and Immigration Columnist for the **New York Law Journal**, this 20-volume work provides detailed analysis of all phases of immigration law and practice. Chapters in volumes 1-6 provide an overview of immigration law and discuss relevant governmental institutions and agencies, the process of controlling entry into the United States, non-immigrants, immigrants, entry, exclusion, waivers and parole, deportation, judicial review, civil liabilities and criminal offenses, nationality and citizenship, and practice and strategy in immigration practice. Appendices in volumes 7-10 contain a variety of relevant primary materials, including the Immigration and Nationality Act, regulations, selected statutes, U.N. documents, and Executive Orders, Operations Instructions, the INS Examinations Handbook, Technical Assistance Guide, BALCA Deskbook, Foreign Affairs Manual, Volume 9--Visas and Availability of Documents. The * Volume contains an Index and Tables of Cases and Statutes. The is the most complete analytical treatise available for the immigration attorney and generally considered to be the definitive work in the field. The text is exhaustively footnoted with references to relevant cases, statutes, regulations, and other primary documents. The CD-ROM version includes a wide variety of immigration law statutes, regulations, documents, and handbooks at no extra charge. Recent revisions include analysis of the changes brought about by the Illegal Immigration reform and Immigrant Responsibility Act of 1996. Housed in the new looseleaf format, the set now includes 20 volumes, including both official practice forms and litigation forms, along with such significant primary law material as the **Foreign Affairs Manual**, the INS Operations Instructions, and Immigration and Nationality Act. Subscribers to both the print and CD-ROM products also receive **Bender's Immigration Bulletin**, published twice-monthly, and **Bender's Immigration Regulations Service**, updated monthly, at no extra charge.
Cost Saving Tips: The cost-conscious attorney may wish to

consider the periodic re-purchase of a new set in order to avoid ongoing supplementation costs. The one-volume **Immigration Law and Procedure** Desk Edition (see below) provides the best cost-saving alternative.

Ignatius, Sarah B. and Elisabeth S. Stickney. **Immigration Law and the Family.** St. Paul, MN: Thomson Reuters West (Clark Boardman Callaghan), 1995-date. 1 vol. Annual replacement volume or ProView eBook.
Cost: 2013 Edition: $471 (print or ProView eBook); supplementation to prior editions: 1995: $45; 1996: $67.50; 1997: $75; 1998: $79; 1999: $85; 2000: $92; 2001: $106; 2002: $135; 2003: $153; 2004: $140; 2005: $150; 2006: $190; 2007: $192; 2008: $213.50; 2009: $241; 2010: $268.50; 2011: $298; 2012: $432; **Monthly Assured Print Price (APP):** $39/$468.
A treatise and practice guide designed for the family immigration specialist. Provides guidance for the practitioner involved in cases involving opportunities for U.S. citizens and immigrants who desire to have foreign family members qualify for immigration, asylum, citizenship or naturalization. Covers the preference system, marriage, conditional residents, children and other relatives, documenting and filing the VISA petition, adjustment statutes, consular processing, revocation and recision, waivers, adoption and orphan cases, citizenship and naturalization, and more. Appendices include sample forms, cover letters, IRS and INS forms, etc.

Immigration & Nationality Law Handbook. Washington, DC : American Immigration Lawyers Association, 1991-date. Annual. 1 vol. Paperbound.
Cost: 2011 Edition: $99; $59 to members; prior editions available at reduced prices, and on Amazon.com (2014).
An annual collection of more than sixty cutting-edge articles on a variety of immigration-related issues written by a team of more than 125 experts in the field. Included are articles which address practice management and ethics, removal and relief, strategies before the courts, asylum and other forms of protection, family immigration and adoption, strategies for obtaining LPR status, employment-based immigration visas, employment and security compliance, employment-based nonimmigrant visas, nonimmigrant visas for students, trainees and victims of crime, entry and exit visas, and naturalization. The articles are aimed at the experienced practitioner rather than the novice, who is directed to use Boswell's **Essentials of Immigration Law** (see above). The articles include timely and appropriate documents, citations to primary and secondary authorities, and lists of online resources. An essential resource for any immigration law specialist.

Immigration Case Reporter. New York: Matthew Bender & Co., 1985-date. 3 vols. Looseleaf format. Updated with monthly issues and bulletins, supplements and revised pages.
Cost: $1,627 (includes annual subscription); renewal: 1996: $475; 1997: $475; 1998: $500; 1999: $600; 2000: $640; 2001: $685; 2002: $641; 2003: $770; 2004: $809; 2005: $866; 2006: $812; 2007: $868; 2008: $956; 2009: $1,032; 2010: $1,106; 2011: $1,172; 2012: $1,242; 2013: $1,342; 2014: $1,479; eBook: $1,479; renewal: 2014: $1,479.
Provides current and prospective coverage of all immigration law developments, including full text of federal court decisions, precedential administrative decisions, and selected non-precedential and labor certification (BALCA) cases. Also includes the full and up-to-date text of statutes, regulations, and proposed regulations as well as articles by immigration law experts on timely topics of interest. There are practice pointers covering more than 20 areas of specialty. Includes a monthly bulletin reporting significant developments. CD-ROM includes a full library of immigration laws, regulations, documents, and manuals. See Gordon and Mailman entry (above) for relevant cost-saving tips.

Immigration Law and Defense. National Lawyers Guild. 3d ed. St. Paul, MN: Thomson Reuters West (Clark Boardman Callaghan), 1988-date. 2 vols. Looseleaf format. Supplemented twice annually
Cost: 2014-1 Edition: $536; ProView eBook: $492; supp.: 1993: $168; 1994: $197.50; 1995: $225; 1996: $260; 1997: $270; 1998: $200; 1999: $216; 2000: $216; 2001: $250; 2002: $288; 2003: $295; 2004: $319; 2005 $326; 2006: $405; 2007: $439.50; 2008: $463; 2009: $525; 2010: $561; 2011: $611; 2012: $787; **Monthly Assured Print Price (APP):** $68/$816.
This two-volume practice manual provides the attorney representing immigrants and aliens with a fairly comprehensive look at the history of immigration legislation, non-immigrant visa categories, procedures for obtaining law residence in the United States, exclusion and deportation, administrative and federal appeals and procedures, and requirements for citizenship and naturalization. The work includes more than 70 relevant INS forms as well as suggested defense strategies and tactics. The text incorporates the changes brought by the Immigration Reform and Control Act (IRCA), the Immigration Act of 1990, the Immigration Marriage Fraud Amendments of 1986, Immigration and Nationality Amendments of 1991. Adequately supported with citations to cases, statutes, and legislative history documents.

Immigration Law and Procedure. Desk Edition. New York: Matthew Bender & Co., 1980-date. 1 vol. Looseleaf format.
Cost: $559 (print or eBook) (includes annual subscription); renewal: 1995: $141; 1996: $141; 1997: $141; 1998: $150; 1999: $157; 2000: $170; 2001: $182; 2002: $195; 2003: $205; 2004: $215; 2005: $230; 2006: $247; 2007: $267; 2008: $288; 2009: $311; 2010: $328; 2011: $338; 2012: $352; 2013: $377; 2014: $411.
A distilled edition of the Gordon and Mailman work (see above for description of complete work).

Cost Saving Tip: An excellent cost-effective alternative to the full Gordon and Mailman, **Immigration Law and Procedure** treatise, either by itself or as a current updating vehicle for a lapsed full set.

Immigration Law Library [CD-ROM]. New York: Matthew Bender & Co. One disc. Updated quarterly. Available for Windows. Search Engine: Folio.
Cost: $3,218; renewal: 2000: $820; 2001: $877; 2002: $939; 2003: $986; 2004: $1,035; 2005: $1,108; 2006: $1,186; 2007:

$1,280; 2008: $1,357; 2009: $1,466; 2010: $1,496; 2011: $1,616; 2012: $1,881; 2013: $2,013; 2014: $1,964.52.
This CD-ROM product contains the full text of several of Matthew Bender's analytical works in the field of immigration law together with a collection of relevant primary law. The complete library includes the following Matthew Bender titles: **Immigration Law and Procedure,** and **Bender's INS Regulations Service,** and over twenty additional immigration law titles and government documents. Immigration cases are also available as a subscriber option. Also included on the CD is the **Immigration Practice Expeditor** which currently contains 18 separate tasks that lawyers frequently encounter in immigration law.

Immigration Law Service 2d. Bob Bouchard, Editor-in-Chief. St. Paul, MN: Thomson Reuters West (Clark Boardman Callaghan), 1985-date. 11 vols. Looseleaf pamphlet format.
Cost: $2,474 (annual subscription service) prior year's subscription costs: 1995: $795; 1996: $900; 1997: $940; 1998: $996; 1999: $1,076; 2000: $1,140; 2001: $1,260; 2002: $1,277; 2003: $1,325; 2004: $1,154; 2005: $760; 2006: $848; 2007: $944; 2008: $1,250; 2009: $1,172; 2010: $1,276; 2011: $1,440; 2012: $1,708; 2013: $1,912; **Monthly Assured Print Price (APP):** $181/$2,172.
This combination treatise/practice guide offers the immigration practitioner complete coverage of immigration law and procedures. The core component of this work consists of 54 chapters in five volumes covering everything form the history of United States immigration law through Owners and Masters of International Vessels or Aircraft. Broad topical areas considered include: seeking admission, gaining entry, exclusion and deportation, seeking extension, adjustment or change of status, living in the United States, proving, obtaining, or losing citizenship, and citizenship documents. The Appendices located in volumes 4-7 include the relevant immigration laws, regulations, manuals, guides, and Presidential Documents. An Index and Tables Binder includes a monthly newsletter entitled **Immigration Law Advisory,** and tables of statutes, rules, regulations, cases, and official forms. The substantive portion of the text is accompanied throughout by editorial Comments, Observations, Notes, Illustrations, Practice Pointers, General References to relevant primary and secondary sources. Each chapter includes a description of its scope, citations to similar treatment elsewhere in the set, Collateral References to **ALR** and other secondary sources and Auto-Cite. Forms are located at appropriate places throughout the set. While not on the same scholarly plane as Gordon and Mailman, this is a highly readable and practical resource for the immigration attorney. Location of relevant primary and secondary sources is facilitated by more than adequate footnotes. The pamphlet format sharply reduces filing time and the chance of misfiled pages.

The Immigration Law SourceBook: A Compendium of Immigration-Related Laws and Policy Documents. Chicago: American Bar Association, 2013. 1 vol. (1,602 pp.). Annual. Paperbound.
Cost: 2013 Edition: $249.95; member price: $199,95; from $145.74 on amazon.com (2014).
This massive resource provides a convenient source for the major sources of U.S. immigration law, including the Immigration and Nationality Act of 1952 ("McCarran-Walter Act), as amended (U.S.C. §1101 et seq.); the Immigration Reform and Control Act of 1986 ("Simpson-Mazzoli") (Pub.L. 99-603, 100 Stat. 3359); Title 8 of the Code of Federal Regulations—Aliens and Nationality; and Title 22 of the Code of Federal Regulations—Foreign Relations. A part of the ABA SourceBook Series.

Interpreter Releases. St. Paul, MN: Thomson Reuters West [formerly Federal Publications, Inc.], 1923-date. Published weekly (except the 3rd week in February and June and the last weeks in November and December). Subscription service.
Cost: $1,939 per year (2014).
This weekly pamphlet service provides timely reporting of Immigration & Naturalization Service rulings and regulations, proposed actions and rulings by the Labor, Justice, State and other federal departments, judicial and administrative decisions, and U.S. Supreme Court decisions. Also includes policy letters, field memoranda and attorney/agency correspondence. Significant documents, including selected rulings, proposed regulations and pending legislation, are reproduced in full. Totals over 1700 pages per year. Service includes cumulative General and Decision Indices, and Tables of Cases. Initially published by Federal Publications, which was purchased by Thomson in 1998.

Johnson, Kevin R., et al. **Understanding Immigration Law**. Newark, NJ: LexisNexis, 2009. 1 vol. (522+ pp.). Paperbound.
Cost: $45; eBook: $36; from $31.48 on amazon.com (2014).
Designed to provide a comprehensive overview of immigration law for law students, this volume examines not only the intellectual, historical, and constitutional foundations of U.S. immigration law, but the factors that draw immigrants to the United States and push them out of their native countries. The authors also consider the evolution of U.S. immigration law and policy, the federal immigration powers, state and local involvement in immigration and policy, federal agencies and courts, judicial review, immigrant visas, nonimmigrant visas, inadmissibility grounds and waivers, admission procedures, removal, immigration enforcement, the rights of immigrants, citizenship, and the future of U.S. immigration law. The clearly written text is accompanied by numerous citations to applicable primary law sources and the scholarly literature. The co-authors also provide up-to-date immigration law news and analysis on the ImmigrationProf blog.

Kesselbrenner, Dan and Lory D. Rosenberg. **Immigration Law and Crimes**. National Immigration Project of the National Lawyers Guild. St. Paul, MN: Thomson Reuters West (Clark Boardman Callaghan), 1984-date. 1 vol. Looseleaf format. Updated twice annually.
Cost: 2013-2 Edition: $426; ProView eBook: $426; supplementation: 1993: $122; 1994: $150; 1995: $154.50; 1996: $175; 1997: $190; 1998: $180; 1999: $196; 2000: $144; 2001: $192; 2002: $124; 2003: $240; 2004: $269; 2005: $274; 2006: $345; 2007: $352; 2008: $196; 2009: $442; 2010: $486; 2011: $563; 2012: $705; 2013: $852; **Monthly Assured Print Price (APP):** $59/$708.
Prepared by attorneys with the National Immigration Project of

the National Lawyers Guild, this one-volume looseleaf treatise was written for the benefit of both immigration law and criminal attorneys representing foreign-born defendants. Includes a discussion of all those elements necessary to providing competent defense, including statutory, judicial and regulatory developments, immigration and criminal procedures, trial strategies, and issues involving immigrants and aliens, including conviction for criminal activity, foreign convictions, commission and admission of criminal activity and immigration offenses related to crime. Well-written text is accompanied by detailed subject indexing.

Kramer, Mary E. **Immigration Consequences of Criminal Activity: A Guide to Representing Foreign-Born Defendants**. 5th ed. Washington, DC: American Immigration Lawyers Association, 2013. 1 vol. (494 pp.). Paperbound.
Cost: $199; $119 to AILA members (2014).
Criminal offenses carry with them certain immigration-related consequences for defendants born in foreign countries. Upon a final conviction, the Immigration and Nationality Act (INA) prescribes the process for determining the proper classification of the crime under immigration law. Immigration law provides for two major categories of crime: (1) crimes involving moral turpitude; and (2) aggravated felonies. In addition to crimes falling into these two categories, the INA has provisions which address controlled substances offenses, money laundering, firearms offenses, crimes of domestic violence, alien smuggling, registration and visa/passport violations, and export law violations. This volume is intended for the use of both immigration and criminal attorneys representing foreign-born defendants. Indeed, proper representation of such clients requires an early determination of their immigration status since this will affect the immigration-related consequences of their criminal activity, particularly inadmissibility and deportation. Toward that end, the author provides a useful overview of basic immigration law system and the terms which are applicable to it. She also provides a detailed definition of 'conviction' under the immigration laws, and discusses at length the consequences of criminal activity, specifically removal from the United States and detention inside the United States. She also addresses the critical issue of how specific crimes are classified under immigration law, and the consequences of specific criminal activity. Finally, she considers the defense of immigrants charged or convicted of crimes under the immigration laws and the waivers and other forms of relief which may be employed on their behalf. These include pleas designed to avoid adverse consequences, and negotiations which bring a charge down to a lesser offense or keep the sentence below the threshold for inadmissibility or deportability. Includes an index and table of cases. The author is a sole practitioner in Miami specializing in immigration cases involving persons with criminal records. A past president of the AILA South Florida Chapter, she has written extensively and lectured widely on the immigration consequences of criminal activity.

Kurzban, Ira. **Kurzban's Immigration Law SourceBook: A Comprehensive Outline and Reference Tool**. 14th ed. Washington, D.C.: American Immigration Lawyers Association, 2014.
Cost: $599; $399 to AILA members (2014).
The author of this book is a past president and former General Counsel of the American Immigration Lawyer's Association who has long been in the forefront of public interest class action lawsuits concerning the rights of aliens. This is not a treatise, but an outline of immigration law based upon the author's notes compiled over the years for litigation and teaching purposes. The 13 chapters cover the following topics: history of immigration laws, Federal authority to regulate immigration, exclusion and deportation, refugees and asylees, non-immigrants, permanent resident status, employment based immigration and labor certification, relief from deportation, administrative review, federal judicial review, actions against government officials, employer sanctions, and naturalization and citizenship. The extensive appendices include naturalization charts, tax treatise, a subject matter index, table of cases, an index to citations, and other useful documents. Published about every two years.

LeMay, Michael C. **U.S. Immigration: A Reference Handbook**. Santa Barbara, CA: ABC-CLIO, 2003. 1 vol. (283 pp.)2
Cost: $50; from $1.99 on amazon.com (2014).
This reference guide focuses on immigration policy since 1965 and addresses both domestic policy implications and relevant global issues. It also provides a chronology of significant events in the history of immigration policy, biographical sketches of leading personalities in the field, discussion of key laws and court cases, a directory of significant governmental agencies and non-governmental organizations, a bibliography of leading print and non-print resources, glossary of important terms, and index. Michael C. LeMay is professor of political science and assistant dean of the College of Social and Behavioral Sciences at California State University San Bernardino.

McWhirter, Robert J. **The Criminal Lawyer's Guide to Immigration Law: Questions and Answers**. 2d ed. Chicago: American Bar Association, 2005. 1 vol. (500 pp.).
Cost: $114.95 ($99.95 to ABA members); from $95 on amazon.com (2014)
According to the Center for Immigration Studies, more tha 1.3 million legal and illegal immigrants, on average, have settled in the United States annually.
Current estimates put the number of illegal immigrants currently residing in the country at 8.9 million. The U.S. Bureau projects that U.S. population will rise from its present 288 million to 400 million by the year 2050. Moreover, this phenomenon raises a host of political, economic, social and demographic, and security issues, particularly in border states confronting this tide of illegal immigration. This volume, in question-answer format, provides guidance to criminal defense attorneys representing aliens who have entered the country illegally. Following an introduction to immigration law for criminal lawyers, the the questions and answers tackle such issues as border stops, the immigration consequences of criminal convictions, aggravated felonies, alien employment crimes, marriage fraud, alien smuggling and hostage taking, immigration document fraud and false statements, illegal ,entry and reentry, getting witnesses and evidence from abroad, international extradition, and treaty transfers. The author is an Assistant Federal Public Defender based in Arizona.

Notkin, Deborah J and Becki L. Young, eds. **Immigration Options for Essential Workers**. Washington, DC: American

Immigration Lawyers Association, 2008. 1 vol. (186 pp.).
Cost: OUT-OF-PRINT; was $129.00; $79.00 to AILA members (2014).
Essential workers are concentrated in the hospitality, agriculture, health, child-care, construction, and landscaping sectors of the economy. With each of these sectors facing critical labor shortages in the coming years, there is a need to implement effective immigrant solutions to provide an adequate American labor force. This volume provides practical guidance in the options available to fill critical un-skilled and low-skilled jobs in these industries. These chapters discuss nonimmigrant options for hospitality workers, (including the Q-1 petition, P-3, F-1, M-1, H-2B, E, H-1B, B-1, J-1 and H-3 status); permanent residence options for child-care workers, immigration workers for landscaping and construction industries, H-2B nonimmigrant visa petition for workers to supplement the needs of the construction industry, exchange visitors in the workplace, adjustment status under Section 245(i), worksite enforcement, and more. There is also a discussion of temporary worker proposals unlikely to meet U.S. labor needs. Relevant forms and regulations are included with each chapter. Deborah Notkin is a past president of the American Immigration Lawyers Association and nationally-recognized expert in business immigration. Becki Young has a small immigration practice in Washington, DC. This is one of more than 70 practical guides published by the American Immigration Lawyers Association, a national bar association of more than 11,000 attorneys who practice immigration law and/or work as teaching professionals.

Steel, Richard D. **Steel on Immigration.** 2d ed. St. Paul, MN: Thomson Reuters West (Clark Boardman Callaghan), 2004-date. 1 vol. Annual replacement volumes. Paperbound.
Cost: 2013 Edition: $287; supplementation to prior editions: 2004: $89; 2005: $96; 2006: $125; 2007: $116.50; 2008: $129.50; 2009: $148; 2010: $163; 2011: $241; 2012: $263; 1st ed.: 1993: $59.50; 1994: $137.50; 1995: $147.50; 1996: $167; 1997: $85; 1998: $85; 1999: $184; 2000: $51; 2001: $63.50; 2002: $160; 2003: $175; **Monthly Assured Print Price (APP):** $24/$288.
A concise one-volume treatise providing an up-to-date summary and analysis of the United States Immigration and Nationality Act of 1952 as amended. Covers law and procedures in almost every kind of immigration case. Includes historical overview, basic structure of the immigration law, non-immigrants, permanent status, summary of eligibility and limitations. Includes citations to both the **United States Code** and the **Code of Federal Regulations.**

Additional titles in the field of Immigration Law are available from the following publishers: ABC-CLIO, Allworth Press, American Immigration Center, Matthew Bender, Carolina Academic Press, Federal Bar Association, Greenwood Publishing Group, William S. Hein & Co., Kluwer Academic Press, Kluwer Law International, LexisNexis, Practising Law Institute, S. Illinois University Press, Thomson Reuters West, University Press of America, West Academic. See Appendix B for addresses and telephone numbers.

Indian Law

Benedict, Jeff. **Without Reservation: The Making of America's Most Powerful Indian Tribe and Foxwoods, the World's Largest Casino**. New York: HarperCollins, 2000. 1 vol. (376 pp.).
Cost: $14.95 (paperbound); from $.01 on amazon.com (2014).
The rapid expansion of casino gambling across the United States over the past thirty years has profoundly impacted American society on a number of levels—economic, governmental and moral--and brought with it a host of social pathologies. Capitalizing on the concept of tribal land sovereignty, Indian tribes, with the complicity of international gambling conglomerates, cash-hungry state governments and inept federal officials, have been able to carve out a significant niche in the world of casino gambling in the United States. In this compelling narrative, Jeff Benedict explains how one Connecticut tribe, the Mashantucket Pequots, was able to rise from near extinction, and a non-existent tribal genealogy, to become the richest tribe in American history. This is a fascinating case study of gambling and the complex legal and political machinations by which the Mashantucket Pequots were able to manipulate state and federal officials and politicians into granting it the recognition it required to achieve its goals. Jeff Benedict is former research director, Center for the Study of Sport in Society, an investigative journalist, lawyer and author of several books, including **Pros and Cons: The Criminals Who Play in the NFL** and **Public Heroes Private Felons: Athletes And Crimes Against Women**. The book includes an extensive bibliography, with source notes.

Canby, William C. **American Indian Law in a Nutshell**. 5th ed. St. Paul, MN: West, 2009. 1 vol. (610 pp.). Availlable from West Academic.
Cost: $41; from $28.84 on amazon.com; kindle ed.: $20.84 (2014).
This volume in the West Nutshell series provides an introductory overview of the law as it pertains to the status of Indian tribes and their relationship with the federal government. It addresses four primary themes: Indian tribes as independent entities with inherent powers of self-government, the role of Congress in regulating and modifying the status of the tribes, the exclusively federal power to deal with and regulate the tribes, and the federal responsibility to protect the tribes and their property. The chapters cover such topics as the history of federal Indian law and policy, tribal governments, tribal sovereignty, treaties, civil and criminal jurisdiction in Indian country, federal grant of jurisdiction to the states under Public Law 280, taxation and regulation in Indian country, individual rights and Indian law, Indian lands, water

rights, and Indian hunting and fishing rights.

Cohen, Felix S. **On the Drafting of Tribal Constitutions** (American Indian Law and Policy Series). Edited by David E. Wilkins. Norman, University of Oklahoma Press, 2007. 1 vol. (200 pp.).
Cost: $34.95; from $24.50 on amazon.com (2014).
Originally penned in 1934 following the author's appointment to the Department of the Interior, this essay was the product of a committee charged with assisting Native American tribes in drafting tribal constitutions. Cohen urges the tribes to consider incorporating and preserving their ancient traditions through their tribal constitutions, rather than adopting documents provided by authorities in Washington. The original 1934 essay, entitled "Basic Memorandum on Drafting of Tribal Constitutions," is edited and introduced by David E. Wilkins, Professor of American Indian Studies and Adjunct Professor of Political Science, Law, and American Studies at the University of Minnesota, Twin Cities, and coauthor of **Uneven Ground: American Indian Sovereignty and Federal Law**.

Cohen's Handbook of Federal Indian Law. 2012 ed. Mell Jessup Newton, editor-in-chief. Newark, NJ: LexisNexis (Matthew Bender), 2012. 1 vol. Updated every other year.
Cost: $231; no supplementation to date.
A long-awaited revision of the classic, but seriously outdated, text on American Indian law, this edition assembles a team of thirty authors and editors who have contributed chapters on a wide range of issues affecting American Indian tribes. Chapters address the historical development and background of Indian policy, principles of interpretation, Indian tribal government, the tribal-federal relationship, tribal-state relationship, civil jurisdiction, taxation, criminal jurisdiction, environment regulation in Indian country, the Indiana Child Welfare Act, Indian gambling liquor regulation, civil rights, tribal property, individual Indian property, natural resources, hunting, fishing and gathering rights, water rights, tribal cultural resources, economic development, and government services to Indians. Easily the single most important work in the field. An essential acquisition for any attorney representing Indian tribes or engaged in Indian-related issues.

Originally authored by Felix Cohen and published by the U.S. Government Printing Office in 1942, this work has undergone numerous reprintings and one major revision. Felix Cohen was much respected legal scholar with significant achievements in legal scholarship and government service who held the positions of Special Assistant to the Attorney General and Associate Solicitor of the Department of the Interior. Upon leaving government service in 1948, he was awarded the Interior Department's highest honor, the Distinguished Service Award. He continued to practice Indian law while devoting much of his energy to legal writing and teaching. He died in 1953 at the age of 46.

Conference of Western Attorneys General. **American Indian Law Deskbook**. 4th ed. Boulder, CO: University Press of Colorado, 2008-date. 1 vol. (789 pp.). Annual supplementation. Also available in eBook format.
Cost: $90.00; eBook: $85; from $81.28 amazon.com; supplementation: 2009: $19.95; 2010: $21.95; 2011: $21.95; 2012-2013: 0; 3d ed.: 2004: $16.95; 2005: $19.95; 2006: $29.95; 2007: $29.95; 2d ed.: 1999: $19.95; 2000: $16.95; 2001: $19.95; 2002: $22.95; 2003: 0.
Although Indian law is primarily the province of the federal courts, state courts have also begun to exercise greater authority in this field in recent years. In scope, organization, and depth of scholarship, this has become the premiere work in the field. First published in 1993, it now fills a significant void left by the datedness of Felix Cohen's classic, but less comprehensive, 1942 exposition on American Indian law. Written under the auspices of the Conference of Western Attorneys General and the chairmanship of South Dakota Attorney General Larry Long, this volume assembles the contributions of Indian law practitioners in most of the states represented in the Conference. Chapters address such topics as: Federal Indian Law Policy: Origins and Legal Development; Indian, Indian Tribe, and Indian Country; Indian and Reservation Lands; Criminal Law; General Civil-Regulatory Jurisdiction; Civil-Adjudicatory Jurisdiction; Tribal Sovereign Immunity and the Indian Civil Rights Act; Indian Reserved Water Rights; Hunting and Fishing Regulation; Environmental Regulation; Taxation in Indian Country; Indian Lands Gaming; Indian Child Welfare Act; and State-Tribal Cooperative Agreements. The volume includes extensive citations to primary and secondary authorities, as well as tables of cases, statutes and codes, and a detailed bibliography. This is unquestionably the most important acquisition for any Indian law practitioner. The volume is kept current through annual, and reasonably priced, cumulative supplements.

Eaglewoman, Angelique Townsend and Stacy L. Leeds. **Mastering American Indian Law**. Durham, NC: Carolina Academic Press, 2013. Vol. (172 pp.).
Cost: $25.00 (10% Internet disc.); from $23.75 on amazon.com; kindle: $19.99 (2014).
The law governing Indian tribes predates European colonization from time immemorial. In recent centuries, however, American Indian law refers to two separate bodies of law governing the 560 tribes operating within the boundaries of the U.S. land mass: law created by Tribal nations, and that enacted by the U.S. government. Other sources of Indian law include state laws, agreements, federal and state regulations, judicial decisions, and administrative rulings. And, finally, there is an international overlay to relations between Indian tribes and the U.S. government in the form of international indigenous legal principles. This volume provides readers with a well-organized and succinct overview of American Indian law that address the most critical aspects of the topic. Each of its ten chapters begins with a roadmap setting out the issues to be covered. Chapter One, for example, provides an instructive overview of U.S. Indian Policy Eras, from 1778 to the present, and addresses such subjects as how tribal membership is determined and the sources of tribal law. Additional chapters cover such subjects as American Indian Property Law, Criminal Jurisdiction in Indian Country, Tribal Government, Tribal Business, Industries and Commercial Practices, Family Law in Tribal Communities, Natural Resources, Tribal-State Relations, Sacred Sites and Cultural Property Protection, and International Indigenous Issues and Tribal Nations. The book concludes with

a "Mastering Indian Law Master Checklist" of concepts that the reader should be able to understand. In keeping with the aims of the publisher's Mastering Series, the volume includes selective citations to legal authorities so as not to interrupt the flow of the narrative. Angelique Townsend Eaglewoman is professor of law at the University of Idaho College of Law. Her co-author, Stacy L. Leeds, is Dean, and professor of law at University of Arkansas School of Law.

Finkelman, Paul and Tim Alan Garrison. **Encyclopedia of United States Indian Policy and Law**. Washington, DC: CQ Press, 2008. 2 vols. (1,249 pp.).
Cost: $385; from $334.42 on amazon.com (2014).
This major reference work, produced by a team of scholars, contains hundreds of A-Z entries detailing every aspect of relations between the United States and American Indian tribes from the Continental Congress to the present day, including articles addressing history, politics, sociology, civil rights and culture. Included are biographies of prominent Native Americans in history, articles on military policy, colonial, state and federal Indian policy, anthropology, ethnology, art, film and cultural property, political and philosophical beliefs and doctrines, and legal issues challenging federal and state Indian policy. It includes illustrations by Native artists, maps, tables and charts. The appendices of primary source documents provide a sampling of federal policies and proclamations reflecting Indian policy from 1790 to 2000. Paul Finkelman is the President William McKinley Professor of Law and Public Policy at the University of Albany Law School and author of more than 20 books, including the **Encyclopedia of American Political History**. Tim Alan Garrison is an associate professor of Native American Studies at Portland State University.

Getches, David H., Charles F. Wilkinson, Robert A. Williams, and Harold L. Williams. **Cases and Materials on Federal Indian Law**. 6th ed. St. Paul, MN: Thomson Reuters West, 2011. 1 vol. (1,055 pp.).
Cost: $200; e-book: $143; from $98.11 on amazon.com (2014).
This law school caseBook provides an historical overview of Indian law and policy in the United States. The authors trace the development of legal doctrines affecting the Native Americans from the period of discovery, and the formative era, through what they term the "century of shifting policy" (1871–present). Part II of the book covers federal Indian law from a contemporary perspective, including discussion of the federal tribal relationship, tribal sovereignty, federal supremacy, states' rights, the jurisdictional framework, criminal and civil court jurisdiction, taxation and regulation of reservation economic development, Indian religion and culture, water rights; fishing and hunting rights, rights of Alaska natives and native Hawaiians, and comparative and international legal perspectives. The selected cases are accompanied by the authors' commentary.

Grossman, Mark. **The ABC-CLIO Companion to the Native American Rights Movement**. Santa Barbara, CA: ABC-CLIO, Inc., 1996. 1 vol. (498 pp.).
Cost: $65.00; from $6.94 on amazon.com (2014).
A valuable compendium of information on Native Americans and their struggle for legal and political rights. Its hundreds of entries include those on leading court decisions involving Native American tribes, legislation, treaties, historical events, and biographies of activists, scholars, tribal leaders, and organizations. The coverage overlaps, to a degree, that found in **The Encyclopedia of Native American Legal Tradition** (see Johansen, ed., below), while it provides greater attention to aspects of the struggle for human, civil and political rights.

Johansen, Bruce Elliott, ed. **The Encyclopedia of Native American Legal Tradition**. Westport, CT: Greenwood Press, 1998. 1 vol. (410 pp.).
Cost: $138.95; from $1.85 on amazon.com (2014).
According to its introduction, **The Encyclopedia of Native American Legal Tradition** is the "first attempt in book form to inject Native American political and legal systems into the study of the law in the United States." Unlike texts on Indian law which examine the impact of the Anglo-American legal tradition upon the tribes, this work provides extensive coverage of the indigenous legal traditions and arrangements of the Native American population. The entries include those for nearly two dozen Native American legal and political systems, many of the leading Indian law cases, Congressional acts, treaties, documents, concepts, theories, traditions, and biographies of individuals who have played an important role in the legal and political history of Native Americans. Robert T. Reilly is Professor of Journalism and Native American Studies at the University of Nebraska, Omaha. The contributors include scholars and professors from a variety of disciplines. This is an essential reference tool for any attorney whose practice involves Native American tribes and legal issues.

Landmark Indian Law Cases. By the National Indian Law Library. Buffalo, NY: William S. Hein & Co., 2002. 1 vol. (942 pp.). Also available on HeinOnline.
Cost: $95 (2014).
This book presents fifty-three groundbreaking decisions made by the United States Supreme Court in the area of federal Indian law. Since the last revision (entitled: Top Fifty and first published in 1988), the Court has made new pronouncements on tribal hunting and fishing rights, Alaska Native sovereignty, and tribal sovereign immunity from suit and tribal court jurisdiction. These have helped define the powers of more than American Indian and Alaska Native tribes that represent the third sovereign in the United States (along with the federal government and the states) and provide a glimpse into the future decisions of the Court. The cases examined represent not only the decisions that resolve important questions and set forth broad principles of federal Indian law, but also ones which have practical implications for real-life situations currently affecting American Indian and Alaska Native tribes. The book's subject index of cases provides a quick reference aid, and all cases are listed under one or more relevant subject headings.

Mashantucket Pequot Tribal Laws 2006/2007. Huntington, NY: Juris Publishing, 2004. 1 vol. (443, 117 pp.). Paperbound. Also available as e-book.

Cost: $95; e-book: $40; from $72 on amazon.com. 2012 supplement available at:
http://www.mptnlaw.com/laws/2012%20Supplement%20to%20Mashantucket%20Pequot%20Tribal%20Laws.pdf
This volume contains the complete text of the Mashantucket Pequot Tribal Laws combined with the Mashantucket Pequot Rules of Court. The laws cover the following topics: judiciary, criminal law, gaming, tort claims, child welfare, family relations, traffic safety code, employment, commercial, arbitration, civil actions, workers' compensation code, land use law, administration and claims review of tribally sponsored employee benefit plans under ERISA (TERISA), general revenue and taxation code, liquor control, mandatory school attendance, & truancy, escheat and abandoned property, civil rights code, public safety code, probate law, residential foreclosure and eviction law, tribal food law, land assignment law, right to work law, the non-trial member surviving spouse law, and captive domicile law. While the Mashantucket Pequot's have a questionable history, as explained in detail by Jeff Benedict's **Without Reservation** (see above), their casino in Eastern, Connecticut has grown into the largest in the world and a source of great wealth for the tribe. This detailed legal code, however, reflects the wealth, time and energy devoted to giving the tribe the trappings of legitimacy. A companion to the quarterly **Mashantucket Pequot Reporter**, which contains the opinions of the Mashantucket Pequot Court of Appeals and Tribal Court.

Mason, W. Dale. **Indian Gaming: Tribal Sovereignty and American Politics**. Norman, OK: University of Oklahoma Press, 2000. 1 vol. (330 pp.).
Cost: $24.95; from $2.49 on amazon.com (2014).
A valuable examination of the issue of Indian tribal sovereignty within the context of the American political system and the role of gaming as an assertion of that sovereignty. In the wake of the Supreme Court's 1987 Cabazon decision and passage of the Indian Gambling Regulatory Act in 1988, gambling has emerged as the primary focus of efforts by American Indian tribes to assert the right to determine for themselves what they can control on tribal lands. With particular attention to the experiences of tribes in Oklahoma, New Mexico, California, and Minnesota, the author explains how the tribes, through their gambling activities, act as both political entities and interest groups, lobbying state and federal legislative bodies and using the wealth generated by gambling to influence public policy and the electoral process. He also examines the role of tribal governments in the area of intergovernmental relations in the context of the federal Indian policy of self-determination and against the national political movement to devolve power to state governments which are more anxious to extend state sovereignty into Indian territory. The author is an assistant professor of political science at the University of New Mexico. This work is an outgrowth of his doctoral dissertation at the University of Oklahoma. A useful study for anyone seeking to understand the complex nature of emerging Indian sovereign authority within the context of the federal system and the role of gambling in that process.

McCool, Daniel, Susan M. Olson, and Jennifer L. Robinson. **Native Vote: American Indians, the Voting Rights Act, and the Right to Vote**. Port Chester, NY, Cambridge University Press, 2007. 1 vol. (232 pp.).
Cost: $29.00 (paperbound); from $8.55 on amazon.com (2014).
In a history characterized by the expansion of the franchise, American Indians have encountered an extended struggle to gain the right to vote. That right to the franchise is rooted in the Voting Rights Act and the Equal Protection Clause of the U.S. Constitution. Drawing upon seventy cases brought under the Voting Rights Act, the author assesses the political impact of these cases and the role of American Indians in contemporary politics. Extended analysis is applied to three case studies. Chapters include: (1) From vanishing American to Voter: The Enfranchisement of American Indians; (2) On Account of Race or Color: The Development of the Voting Rights Act; (3) A Milestone on the Reservation: the Voting Rights Act comes to Indian Country; (4) Niha Whol Zhiizh (It's Our Turn): Indian Voting; (5) Going to Court for a Seat at the Table: Fort Belknap versus Blaine County; (6) Lakotas in the Legislature: The Bone Shirt Case; (7) A Fair Opportunity: The Impact of the Voting Rights Act; (8) From Extermination to Electorate: Indians in American Politics. Daniel McCool is a professor of Political Science at the University of Utah and the director of the American West Center and the Environmental Studies program at the University of Utah. He is the author, co-author, or editor of six other books. Jennifer L. Robinson currently works for the Center for Public Policy and Administration at the University of Utah as a research associate.

Pevar, Stephen L. **The Rights of Indians and Tribes: The Basic ACLU Guide to Indian and Tribal Rights**. 3d ed. Carbondale, MN: Southern Illinois University Press, 2002. 1 vol. (338 pp.).
Cost: $25; from $16.00 on amazon.com; kindle ed.: $9.99 (2014).
This basic overview of the rights of Indians and Indian tribes in the United States in one of a series of inexpensive American Civil Liberties Union Handbooks. While the intent of the books in this series is to inform individuals of their legal rights, there is much general information in this volume relating to federal Indian policy. The subjects covered include treaties, trust responsibility, tribal self-government, state power over Indian affairs, civil and criminal jurisdiction in Indian country, taxation, hunting, fishing and gathering rights, water rights, civil rights, the Indian Civil Rights Act, the Indian Child Welfare Act, government services to Indians, and judicial review. While not exhaustively documented, each chapter does include endnotes to relevant cases, statutes, government reports, and secondary sources. The author, an adjunct professor at the University of Denver School of Law, has been. Regional Counsel for the Mountain States Office of the American Civil Liberties Union since 1976. An exceptional value for a legal text.

United States Tribal Courts Directory. 3d ed. Edited by April Schwartz and Mary Jo B. Hunter. Buffalo, NY: William S. Hein & Co., Inc., 2008. 1 vol. (179 pp.). AALL Publication Series No. 70.
Cost: $60 (2014).
As sovereign entities, American Indian tribes have established their own tribal courts for the purposes of adjudicating cases in criminal, civil, domestic, traffic, juvenile, and other matters. This directory, organized alphabetically by state and by tribe, includes

descriptions of the various tribal courts across the United States.

Walters, Lawrence. **Indigenous Peoples, the Environment and Law.**
Durham, NC: Carolina Academic Press, 2004. 1 vol. (460 pp.).
Cost: $48.00; from $18.15 on amazon.com (2014).
Indigenous peoples around the world have a time-honored symbiotic relationship with the land and natural environment. Their history, identity, and tribal sovereignty are directly linked to the land and its resources. This timely anthology of twenty-three scholarly articles focuses on the relationship between various indigenous peoples, the environment, and the law. Embracing a broadly international perspective, the articles address such topics as biodiversity, community and conservation, development, the protection of traditional knowledge, conflict in a comparative context, multinational corporations, globalization, and the emergence of a framework for understanding indigenous peoples and their relationship to various national and international legal frameworks. Thirteen of the articles examine indigenous peoples in specific regional or national contexts, including the Arctic, Scandinavian Japan, Guatemala, Russia, Australia, Bolivia, Canada, Philippines, New Zealand, and the United States. The articles with a United States focus consider Native Hawaiians, sacred sites, water, and whaling. This volume provides an invaluable international perspective to the subject as it relates to Native Americans. The editor is Visiting Professor, Faculty of Law, University of Wuhan, China, and Visiting Professor, Faculty of Law, University of Auckland, New Zealand.

Additional titles in the field of Indian Law are available from the following publishers: ABC-CLIO, American Bar Association, American Indian Resources Institute, Federal Bar Association, Garland Publishing Co., Greenhaven Press, William S. Hein & Co., Institute for the Development of Indian Law (Oklahoma City Univ. School of Law), LexisNexis, National Conference of State Legislatures, Rocky Mountain Mineral Law Foundation, Scholarly Resources, Inc., Thomson Reuters West, University of Oklahoma Press, University of Texas Press, West Academic. See Appendix B for addresses and telephone numbers.

Insurance Law

Anderson, Eugene R., William G. Passannante, and Robert M. Horkovich, eds. **The Policyholder Advisor**. Huntington, NY: Juris Publishing, 2002. 1 vol. (348 pp.).
Cost: $125; from $6.00 on amazon.com (2014).
Both individuals and corporations are exposed to a variety of real and potential losses resulting from accidents, criminal acts, natural disasters, and other calamities for which they obtain insurance policies as a means of transferring risk. This collection of articles, reprinted from the Policyholder Advisor, a series of weekly newsletters published by the law firm of Anderson, Kill & Olick, a leading firm representing individuals and corporations against insurance companies, provide practical guidance on a number of insurance coverage issues. With a bias in favor of policyholders, the articles provide guidance on matters likely to increase the chances of their being able to access the benefits to which they are entitled. The articles are grouped under the following headings: Insurance Coverage Fundamentals; Claims Handling and Defense Issues; Insurance Company Bad Faith; Special Insurance Concerns for Corporate Policyholders; Directors and Officers Liability Insurance; Intellectual Property Insurance; E-Commerce Insurance; First-Party Coverage; Fidelity Bonds, Commercial Crime Coverage, and Financial Institutions Bonds; Healthcare-related Insurance Disputes; Emerging Areas of Insurance Disputes; London Market Issues; Polluter's Exclusions; and Environmental and Long-Tail Liability Insurance Coverage. The articles provide citations to relevant published court decisions. This volume provides a wealth of collected wisdom contributed by more than thirty Anderson, Kill & Olick attorneys. It is edited by founding partner Eugene R. Anderson, who has been described as one of the 20 people who have had the greatest impact on property and casualty insurance over the past 20 years; Robert V. Horkovich, Chair of the firm's Insurance Coverage Practice; and its Co-Chair William G. Passannante.

Appleman, John A. and Jean Appleman. **New Appleman on Insurance Law Library Edition.** 2d ed. Charlottesville, VA: LexisNexis, 1996-date. 69 vols. [44 vols. of 1st ed. & 25 vols. of 2d ed.] Annual pocket parts. Originally published by West Publishing Co. Now available as the Appleman print bundle containing: **New Appleman on Insurance Law Library Edition**, **Appleman on Insurance 2d**, John Appleman, **Insurance Law and Practice**, the 2010 Edition of the **New Appleman Insurance Law Practice Guide** (the practice guide accompaniment to the Library Edition), and **New Appleman on Insurance Law: Current Critical Issues in Insurance Law** (the quarterly on current topics in insurance law).
Cost: $3,529; supplementation: 1994: $134; 1995: $139.75; 1996: $162.50; 1997: $170; 2000: $330; 2001: $505; 2002: $510; 2003: $497.50; 2004: $622; 2005: $372; 2006: $412; 2007: 424; 2008: $305; 2009: $518; 2010: $544; 2011: $550; 2012: $731; 2013: $2,593; eBook: $3,208; renewal: 2,593.
This is one of two major treatises in the field of insurance law. John Appleman, a former head of the legal department at State Farm Insurance and a nationally known expert in insurance law, wrote the initial 25-volume set between 1939 and 1947. Since that time, it has undergone total revision. The task of preparing the pocket parts and revised volumes then passed to the author's daughter, Jean Appleman, an author and law professor. Most recently, the pocket parts have been prepared by Stephen Liebo of the Minnesota and Wisconsin bars and adjunct professor at the William Mitchell College of Law. The 478 chapters in this massive work may be divided into 12 major divisions: personal insurance; property insurance; casualty insurance; uninsured motorists; state funds; no fault; commercial insurance and bonds; the insurance contract; reinsurance and premiums; agents brokers and adjusters, waiver and estoppel; organization, taxation, and liquidation; and procedure and forms. The level of detail is reflected in chapter one which discusses 33 broad categories of contracts of personal insurance representing over 200 different types of policies. The authors have attempted to present their text in a clear and readable form understandable to the lay person. The facts of specific cases are set out in the footnotes, many of which are quoted liberally. The pocket parts contain both summaries of more recent decisions in support of the text and revisions of the text itself. The editors have also

indicated where each section of Appleman has been cited by the courts. One report indicates that Appleman and Couch have been cited with rough equivalency by the courts in recent years. As of 1996, the average copyright date of the 60 bound volumes was 1977, although all have been updated with pocket parts. The first volume of the long-awaited second edition, written by Eric Mills Holmes and Mark S. Rhodes, appeared in December, 1996. As volumes of the projected 57 volume second edition are released, the old volumes are retired This was one of a handful of titles sold by the Thomson Corporation to Reed Elsevier pursuant to the consent decree by which the Department of Justice approved the merger of the Thomson Corporation and West Publishing in 1996.

Cost Saving Tips: Those interested in reducing their annual expenditure should acquire the cumulative pocket parts in alternate years or less often, using Shepard's or KeyCite to update citations.

Ashley, Stephen S. **Bad Faith Actions: Liability and Damages.** 2d ed. St. Paul, MN: Thomson Reuters West (Clark Boardman Callaghan), 1998-date. 1 vol. Looseleaf format and ProView eBook. Updated twice annually.
Cost: $390; ProView eBook: $358; supplementation: 1993: $107; 1994: $54; 1995: $132; 1996: $160; 1997: $85; 1998: $50; 1999: $54; 2000: $58; 2001: $68.50; 2002: $90; 2003: 91.50; 2004: $102.50; 2005: $113.25; 2006: $126; 2007: $141; 2008: $157.50; 2009: $189; 2010: $210; 2011: $233; 2012: $258; 2013: $287; **Monthly Assured Print Price (APP):** $28/$336.
A thorough discussion of bad faith law with appropriate strategies for representing either the plaintiff or defendant in such actions. Provides analysis of the law as it is has been applied by courts in all fifty states. Chapters examine the historical development bad faith as a cause of action, elements of the cause of action, third party cases, first party cases, defenses to actions for bad faith, statutes relevant to insurance cases, bad faith in noninsurance cases, bad faith in employment cases. Includes strategies, tactics and procedures, practice aids, and forms.

Couch on Insurance. Russ, Lee R. and Thomas F. Segalla. 3d ed. St. Paul, MN: Thomson Reuters West (Clark Boardman Callaghan), 1995-date. 19 vols. Looseleaf format. Twice annual pocket parts.
Cost: $6,038; supplementation: 1993: $324; 1994: $410; 1995: $695; 1996: $790; 1997: $830; 1998: $949; 1999: $954; 2000: $1,032; 2001: $1,208; 2002: $1,025; 2003: $1,559; 2004: $1,431.50; 2005: $1,680; 2006: $2,200; 2007: $2,200; 2008: $2,498; 2009: $3,925; 2010: $1,647; 2011: $3,372.50; 2012: $4,165; 2013: $4,623; WestlawNext PRO: $1,728 per year (single user); combination discounts available; **Monthly Assured Print Price (APP):** $391/$4,692.
Couch on Insurance is a complete and detailed treatise originally authored by George J. Couch. The second edition was prepared by Ronald A. Anderson and revised by Mark S. Rhodes. This completely updated and revised third edition is written by Lee R. Russ, an experienced legal writer, with practical insights provided by Thomas F. Segalla, a veteran litigator. It includes description and analysis of all types of insurance, including life, property, marine, health and accident, liability and indemnity, automobile, fidelity guarantee, contract guarantee, reinsurance, group, annuities, governmental life and disability, and servicemen's indemnity. Procedural and as well as substantive issues are addressed on both the state and federal levels with analysis of appellate court decisions at both levels. Provides clear statement of applicable rule followed by exceptions.

Cost Saving Tips: The cost-conscious attorney may want to drop the standing order and purchase the cumulative supplements in alternate years, or less often, depending upon need. Note that in 2013 the annual cost of updating **Appleman** was only $2,593 for 69 volumes versus the $4,623 annual cost to update **Couch**.

Disbrow, Vivian A., et al. **No-Fault and Uninsured Motorist Automobile Coverage**. New York: Matthew Bender, 1984-date. 4 vols. Looseleaf format. No CD-ROM or Internet.
Cost: $2,439 (includes annual subscription); annual renewal: 1995: $564.50 (supplementation cost frozen since 1992); 1996: $592; 1997: $592; 1998: $625; 1999: $645; 2000: $690; 2001: $738; 2002: $761; 2003: $800; 2004: $840; 2005: $899; 2006: $962; 2007: $1,039; 2008: $1.133; 2009: $1,235; 2010: $1,309; 2011: $1,401; 2012: $1,485; 2013: $1,589; 2014: $1,734; eBook: $2,217; renewal: 2014: $1,734.
The individual chapters in this set are authored by no less than 28 legal practitioners and scholars. Detailed, heavily footnoted text covers the full range of no-fault insurance issues, including statutory basis, scope of coverage, exclusions, arbitration, attorney's fees, tort recovery, impact of no-fault plans, statutory uninsured motorist coverage, hit and run accidents, settlement of uninsured motorist claims, litigation, underinsured motorist coverage, conflict of laws, stacking of benefits, and state funds. Appendices include no-fault statutes, uninsured motorist citations, accident claims arbitration rules, etc., as well as tables of statutes, cases, and an index.

Cost Saving Tip: A thorough, but costly set. If the exhaustive coverage meets your needs, you may consider buying the set with its one-year service and then letting it lapse. You can supplement the text of the lapsed set with a less expensive alternative text or simply update your research in the primary sources and Shepardize relevant cases and statutes. There is no substitute for doing your own updating when a client's interests are at stake. Remember, a secondary source such as this is only a starting place.

Dobbyn, John F. **Insurance Law in a Nutshell.** 4th ed. St. Paul, MN: West, 2003. 1 vol. Available from West Academic.
Cost: $41; from $25.15 on amazon.com (2014).
A brief overview of insurance law in the publisher's student Nutshell Series by a Professor of Law at Villanova University. Contains only limited citations to cases and statutes.

Feinman, Jay M. **Professional Liability to Third Parties**. 3nd ed. Chicago: American Bar Association, 2013. 1 vol. (390 pp.).
Cost: $159.95; $145.95 to Section members (2014).
The law of liability to third parties embraces circumstances which involve parties other than the insurer and insured. In

the professional arena, this embraces those parties harmed or injured through actions of the insured acting his or her professional capacity. This newly updated edition outlines explains the doctrines that are applied in third-party liability cases and examines the circumstances that give rise to them. In addition to describing the state of the law, it discusses the strategies for expanding or limiting liability to third-parties liability and assists the user in distinguishing between different types of cases, including those for which there is little or no direct authority. The author also considers the different approaches applied in third-party cases. including the contractual argument to limit liability and the relational argument to expand liability. Further, he explains the various doctrines applied in third-party cases, including privity and near-privity, third-party beneficiary, negligence, and negligent misrepresentation. He also applies third-party liability to a variety of specific professions, including lawyers, accountants, title abstractors, appraisers, surveyors, pest inspectors, and others performing evaluative services, real estate brokers, architects, and engineers. Includes an index and table of authorities. Jay M. Feinman is the Distinguished Professor of Law at Rutgers School of Law – Camden and a member of The American Law Institute, an Advisor for the Restatement Third of Torts: Liability for Economic Loss, and a member of the Board of Legal Scholars of the Academy of Trial Advocacy. At Rutgers, he has served as Associate Dean and Acting Dean of the law school and has authored five books and dozens of law review articles.

Frangiamore, David. **How Insurance Companies Settle Cases.** Costa Mesa, CA: James Publishing Co., 1989-date. 1 vol. Looseleaf format. Annual supplements.
Cost: $99; supplementation: 1993: $53.91; 1994: $54.85; 1995: $49.99; 1996: $54.99; 1997: $58.99; 1998-2014: $59.99 per year.
This volume provides a detailed insider's description and analysis of the process and tactics employed by insurance companies in handling claims. The author, an consult and expert witness with over 27 years experience as a claims adjuster and claims manager, provides insights gained from both sides of the negotiation process. Included are such topics as how to play the claims game, insurance policy defenses and coverage issues, avoiding bad faith traps, unfair settlement techniques, effective coverage techniques, and negotiation tactics. The volume includes sample insurance forms, checklists and letters.

Grace, Martin F. and Robert W. Klein, eds. **The Future of Insurance Regulation in the United States**. Washington, DC: Brookings Institution Press, 2009. 1 vol. (232 pp.).
Cost: $34.95; from $5.89 on amazon.com; kindle ed.: $19.22 (2014).
Insurance companies in the United States have traditionally been regulated by the states. in U.S. v. South-Eastern Underwriters (1944), however, the U.S. Supreme extended the commerce clause to insurance and, in doing so, extended the reach of the federal antitrust laws to insurance companies and their agents. In 1945, the Congress responded by passing the McCarren-Ferguson Act (MFA), which delegated the regulation of insurance companies to the states. With most insurance policies now written by national companies across state lines, many insurance companies view state regulation as an impediment to their efficiency and competitiveness and are calling for a federal regulatory system in the form of an optional federal charter (OFC). The OFC would allow insurance companies and agents to chose to be federally regulated and exempt from state regulation. These proposals are opposed by state governments and by state-oriented segments of the industry. The crisis that has affected financial markets has brought renewed calls for federal regulation of the insurance industry as part of a broader restructuring of the regulatory framework for increasingly interconnected financial institutions. This volume is the product of a conference on the future of insurance regulation sponsored by Georgia State University, the Brookings Institution, and the American Enterprise Institute held in Washington, DC in 2008. Following an introductory chapter on the future of insurance regulation, various industry experts grapple with such topics as the insurance industry and its regulation, an optional Federal Charter for Insurance, dual insurance chartering and its potential consequences, insurance regulation: the need for policy reform, consumer benefits of an Optional Federal Charter, convergence in financial service markets, and U.S. insurance regulation in a competitive world insurance market. Martin Grace is professor of risk management and insurance at Georgia State University. Robert W. Klein is director of the Center for Risk Management and Insurance Research and associate professor of risk management and insurance at George State University.

Harnett, Bertram and Irving I. Lesnick. **The Law of Life and Health Insurance.** New York: Matthew Bender & Co., 1988-date. 6 vols. Looseleaf format. Supplemented annually.
Cost: $1,617 (includes annual subscription); annual renewal: 1995: $269 (price frozen since 1992); 1996: $282; 1997: $282; 1998: $295; 1999: $310; 2000: $330; 2001: $353; 2002: $392; 2003: $412; 2004: $433; 2005: $463; 2006: $519; 2007: $583; 2008: $641; 2009: $705; 2010: $755; 2011: $778; 2012: $809; 2013: $866; 2014: $945; eBook: $1,060; renewal: 2014: $788.
An exhaustive description and analysis of all types of life and health insurance policies with case and statutory analysis, and practice aids. The authors, a retired Justice of the New York State Supreme Court and a practitioner who has taught insurance law at Hofstra University Law School, have written a treatise impressive in both its breadth and detail. They treat the life and health insurance industry, ERISA and employment benefit plans, fraud and misrepresentation, disability policies, annuities, unfair trade and advertising practices, civil rights, etc. There are annotated policies for life, health, group health, Medicare and Medigap insurance. The Appendices include a variety of forms, including policy forms and reinsurance contracts, life insurance underwriting manuals, actuarial tables, etc. Also includes tables of federal and state cases and statutes and a detailed subject index.

Cost Saving Tips: For the attorney specializing in insurance-related cases, the cost of maintaining this work is not particularly onerous, particularly for a five-volume set. Nevertheless, you always have the option of dropping the standing order and updating the cases through your own state digest, Shepard's Citations, KeyCite, etc.

Harnett, Bertram. **Responsibilities of Insurance Agents and Brokers**. New York: Matthew Bender & Co., 1974-date. 4 vols.

Looseleaf format and eBook. Updated periodically.
Cost: $2,220 (includes annual subscription); renewal: 1998: $520; 1999: $545; 2000: $580; 2001: $621; 2002: $665; 2003: $699; 2004: $734; 2005: $793; 2006: $889; 2007: $1,000; 2008: $1,100; 2009: $1,210; 2010: $1,270; 2011: $1,308; 2012: $1,386; 2013: $1,483; 2014: $1,619; eBook: $2,018; renewal: 2014: $1,619.
A comprehensive guide to the legal rights and responsibilities of insurance agents and brokers. The text covers liability issues, licensing, tax issues, professional ethics, advertising, unfair trade practices, ERISA plans, buying and selling agencies and brokerages, debtor/creditor issues, and errors and omissions coverage. The set also includes extensive primary source materials, including insurance statutes for almost all fifty states, model codes of ethics, NAIC model acts, and statutory forms.

Cost Saving Tips: Treat this publication as a monograph rather than a subscription publication. Drop the subscription once the initial one-year period has expired and re-purchase it again in a few years, if necessary.

Insurance Law Treatise Library on LoisLawConnect. New York: Wolters Kluwer Law & Business.
Cost: $540.00 per year (solo practitioner) (2014).
This collection of insurance law titles includes the following titles: **CGL Policy Handbook, Insurance Coverage Litigation, Policyholder's Guide to the Law of Insurance Coverage, Practitioner's Guide to Litigating Insurance Coverage,** and forms and checklists from drawn from the above. A cost-effective alternative to buying these titles in print format.

Jerry, Robert H. **Understanding Insurance Law**. 5th ed. New York: Matthew Bender & Co., 2012. 1 vol. (1,022 pp.). Legal Text Series.
Cost: $47; eBook: $38; from $20.00 on amazon.com; kindle ed.: $30.40 (2014).
This volume provides a comprehensive overview of the field of insurance law, including health insurance, ERISA, and relevant provisions of the Commercial Liability Policy. Intended as a law school text, this resource can also serve as an excellent basic deskbook for the practicing attorney. The second edition has been expanded to encompass a discussion insurance as it applies to AIDS and genetic screening. Also includes new information on the insurer's duty to defend and conflicts of interest. Contains ample citations to relevant cases, statutes, and secondary sources.

Kalis, Peter, Thomas M. Reiter and James R. Segerdahl. **Policyholder's Guide to the Law of Insurance Coverage**. New York: Wolters Kluwer Law & Business, 1997-date. 2 vols. (1,538 pp.). Looseleaf format. Annual supplementation.
Cost: $435; supplementation: 1999: $84; 2000: $92; 2001: $135; 2002: $160; 2003: $160; 2004: $175; 2005: $175; 2006: $186; 2007: $198; 2008: $212; 2009: $239; 2010: $255; 2011: $270; 2012: $309; 2013: $339.
Designed for use by insurance policyholders and their legal counsel, this one volume practitioner's tool provides substantive and strategic guidance to aid in the interpretation of insurance policy language and the litigation of policy coverage disputes. It addresses a variety of general coverage issues as well as those unique to specialized industries or situations. The text is supported with citations to thousands of cases, cross-references, checklists, and other practice aids.

Keeton, Robert E. and Alan I. Widiss. **Insurance Law: A Guide to Fundamental Principles, Legal Doctrines, and Commercial Practices.** Practitioner's Edition. St. Paul, MN: Thomson Reuters West, 1988-date. 1 vol. (1,456 pp.). Available from West Academic.
Cost: $90; from $37.00 on amazon.com (2014).
This one-volume Practitioner's Edition is authored by Robert Keeton, the Langdell Professor Emeritus, Harvard University School of Law, and Alan Widiss, the Josephine R. Witte Professor of Law, University of Iowa. Like the Hornbook, it attempts to facilitate an understanding of the general principles and doctrines governing insurance law, but also to apply those principles to specific types of insurance, but with greater detail and more footnotes. The Appendices include sample policies, WESTLAW References, a Table of Cases, and Subject Index. Contains numerous citations to relevant primary and secondary authorities. Overdue for an updated edition.

Keeton, Robert E. and Alan I. Widiss. **Insurance Law: A Guide to Fundamental Principles. Legal Doctrines, and Commercial Practices.** Student Edition. St. Paul, MN: West, 1988. 1 vol. (1,357 pp.) Available from West Academic.
Cost: $90 (2014).
This one-volume student Hornbook is authored by Robert Keeton, the Langdell Professor Emeritus, Harvard University School of Law, and Alan Widiss, the Josephine R. Witte Professor of Law, University of Iowa. It attempts to facilitate an understanding of the general principles and doctrines governing insurance law, but also to apply those principles to specific types of insurance. The chapters addresses the following topics: insurance: conceptualization and classification; the marketing of insurance; indemnity and insurability; persons and interests protected; the risks transferred; rights at variance with insurance policy provisions; claims: processes and settlements; insurance regulation and government sponsorship of insurance; and resolving disputed claims involving insurance, a table of cases, and subject index. Contains numerous citations to relevant primary and secondary authorities. The only downside is that Hornbooks are rarely supplemented between new editions; and the practitioner will probably require a supplementary title to supply more current material.

Leitner, David L., Reagan W. Simpson, and M. John , eds. **Law and Practice of Insurance Coverage Litigation**. St. Paul, MN: Thomson Reuters West, 2000-date. 5 vols. Looseleaf format. Includes forms on 3.5" discs.
Cost: $671; supplementation: 2001: $86; 2002: $106; 2003: $108; 2004: $121; 2005: $136; 2006: $159; 2007: $89; 2008: $99.50; 2009: $112; 2010: $124; 2011: $136; 2012: $150; 2013: $166; **Monthly Assured Print Price (APP):** $26/$312.
A significant new contribution to the literature of insurance law by the West and the American Bar Association's Tort and Insurance

Practice Section. This is a practical resource which supplements those texts focusing on the substantive law of insurance and is designed for those involved in insurance litigation. The chapters, authored by more than 75 Tort and Insurance Practice Section members, address all aspects of the insurance litigation process generally, and litigation involving specific kinds of insurance policies. General chapters discuss such topics as duty to defend, choice of law, arbitration, and pleadings. Additional chapters discuss specific types of policies, including automobile, homeowners, marine, construction, products liability, and environmental insurance. The text is supported by thousands of references to cases and statutes, and includes valuable checklists, forms, and jury instructions. Includes forms on 3.5" discs.

Lichtor, Joseph M. **Personal Injury Insurance Fraud: The Process of Detection, A Primer for Insurance and Legal Professionals**. Tucson, AZ: Lawyers & Judges Publishing Co., 2002. 1 vol. (190 pp.).
Cost: e-book only: $25 (2014).
Personal injury insurance fraud in the United States and Europe is a problem of significant proportions, the costs of which are passed on to the public in the form of higher insurance premiums. This introductory examination of the subject begins with a history of personal injury scams since the 19th century's "railway spine" epidemic. The author, an orthopedic surgeon, explains the nature of the problem by explaining the mechanics of specific injuries, patient evaluation (including investigation of the patient's accident history), and prevention of claimant and physician deception relating to such alleged injuries as whiplash, back injury, traumatic fibromyalgia, repetitive motion injury, aggravation of pre-existing conditions, and discusses malingering, worker's compensation fraud, and federal fraud. He also analyzes a number of specific accidental injuries, including auto accidents, slip and fall accidents, and various home hazards. Finally, he suggests ways to investigate claims and ascertain the legitimacy of a claimant's injury. He argues that patients, physicians, and medical providers and attorneys all may engage in personal injury insurance fraud and that attempts at eradication must include prevention, investigation, and prosecution.

Magarick, Pat. **Excess Liability: The Rights and Duties of Commercial Risk Insureds and Insurers**. 4th ed. St. Paul, MN: Thomson Reuters West (Clark Boardman Callaghan), 1999-date. 2 vols. Annual replacement volumes.
Cost: 2013 Edition: $350; supplementation: 1993: $105; 1994: $75; 1995: $82.50; 1996: $97.50; 1997: $99.50; 1998: $106; 1999: $114; 2000: $56; 2001: $70.50; 2002: $210; 2003: $94.50; 2004: $106; 2005: $119; 2006: $150; 2007: $144; 2008: $161; 2009: $180.50; 2010: $198.50; 2011: $221; 2012: $320; **Monthly Assured Print Price (APP):** $29/$348.
This one-volume guide provides a detailed examination of the potential and actual excess liability verdicts which may be rendered against insurers. The author considers first and third party insurance relationships and the role of agents and brokers, the measure of good faith duties and the role of the state, the relationship of commercial insured and insurer where the policy has a large deductible or fronted self-retention factor, the potential problems involving fronted self-retained limits on deductible policies, the measurement of risk, adequate insurance limits, insolvencies, and the insured's ability to pay uninsured losses, duties of insurer to excess insurers, reinsurers, the relationship of insurer, claims adjuster and defense counsel, the commercial insurance contract, reservation of rights, nonwaiver agreements, workers' compensation and employment practices coverage issues and financial coverages and other insurance.

Matthiesen, Bradley W., Gary L. Wickert and Douglas W. Lehrer. **Fundamentals of Insurance Coverage in all Fifty States**. 4th ed. Huntington, NY: Juris Publishing, 2013. 1 vol. (1,238 pp.). Also available as eBook.
Cost: $225 (print or eBook); from $213.75 on amazon.com (2014).
This book is a comprehensive overview of the statutes, regulations and case law governing insurance coverage in all fifty states. The narrative treatment of each state follows a similar template, including: the contract of insurance, procedural considerations, construction and interpretation, extent of risks and coverage, rights and obligations of the parties, insurer's duty of good faith and fair dealing, policy defenses, and environmental issues and insurance law. State statutes, regulations, and case law (with citations) are artfully woven into the narrative of each topic. This is an invaluable resource for insurance claims handlers and supervisors who have responsibility for, or occasion to deal with, coverage issues relating to third-party defense litigation, first-party claims litigation, and /or reservation of rights circumstances, as well as attorneys who bring or defend insurance claims, insurance companies, and businesses and individuals concerned about limits of coverage. Of particular note are the rising numbers of disputes between insurers and insured regarding environmental pollution and exclusions, in which exclusions must be meticulously enforced to ensure insurance company profitability. Bradley W. Matthiesen has been employed as an insurance defense trial attorney for thirty-five years. Gary Wickert has over 30 years experience in insurance litigation and is a widely regarded expert in insurance subrogation. Douglas W. Lehrer is an insurance defense practitioner with experience in a wide variety of insurance disputes. All three are partners in the firm of Matthiesen, Wickert & Lehrer, S.C.

Mezzullo, Louis A. **An Estate Planner's Guide to Life Insurance**. 2d ed. Chicago: American Bar Association, Section of Real Property, Trust and Estate Law, 2009. 1 vol. (98 pp.). Includes the text on a companion CD-ROM.
Cost: $139.95; $119.95 to members (2014).
Life insurance plans a significant role in the estate planning of most adults, particularly those married and with children. Estate planning advisors should be fully informed regarding the various life insurance products and the role they play in the financial planning for their clients. This volume provides a good overview of the role of life insurance in the estate planning process, the terminology, the types of policies, employer-provided insurance, information needed for planning, income tax ramifications, transfer taxation, and the irrevocable life insurance trust, as well as sample forms. The second edition brings the book current to December, 2008. Louis A. Mezzullo is a partner in the Rancho Santa FE, CA office of Luce, Forward, Hamilton & Scripps LLP,

where his practice is devoted to taxation, estate and business planning, and employee benefits. He is the author of numerous books and articles in the field of estate planning, taxation, and employee benefit issues.

Miller, Susan J. and Philip Lefebvre. **Miller's Standard Insurance Policies Annotated**. 5th ed. St. Paul, MN: Thomson Reuters West [formerly Legal Research Systems, Inc.] 2009-date. 7 vols. Looseleaf format. Semi-annual supplementation as a rule.
Cost: $1,831; supplementation: 1997: $250; 1998: $250; 1999: $250; 2000: $271; 2001: $304; 2002: $280; 2003: $300; 2004: $150; 2005: $320 (2); 2006: $316; 2007: $338; 2008: $349; 2009: 0; 2010: $948; 2011: $948; 2012: $1,221; 2013: $1,488; also available on WestlawNext PRO: $1,800.00 per year; **Monthly Assured Print Price (APP):** $107/$1,284.
Contains more than 140,000 annotations on property and casualty cases reported since 1978 that have interpreted 93 property and casualty insurance policies and over 700 endorsements linked by policy provision of more than 3,000 topics, words and phrases in Miller's index referencing over 13,000 coverage provisions. The system also allows full-text searching of the subscriber's own personal case notes. Also available on LexisNexis.

Special Alert: Following the acquisition of this title by Thomson Reuters, the initial price has skyrocketed to $1,468 in 2013, a 76% increase in three years, and to $1,831 in 2014, a 24% year over year increase. Supplementation cost has also risen. The periodic user would be well advised to consult this set in a law library and avoid the high maintenance cost. This is a graphic example of what happens in an antitrust vacuum when the Thomson Reuters juggernaut swallows up smaller companies like this one.

New Appleman Insurance Bad Faith Litigation [formerly Shernoff, Gage and Lewis]. 2d ed. New York: Matthew Bender and Co., 1984-date. 1 vol. Looseleaf format or eBook.
Cost: $565 (includes annual subscription); annual renewal: 1995: $157.50 (price frozen since 1992); 1996: $165; 1997: $165; 1998: $175; 1999: $182; 2000: $195; 2001: $209; 2002: $224; 2003: $236; 2004: $248; 2005: $265; 2006: $284; 2007: $306; 2008: $337; 2009: $371; 2010: $401; 2011: $411; 2012: $427; 2013: $457; 2014: $499; eBook: $605; renewal: 2014: $499.
This work provides complete coverage of tort liability of insurers for bad faith or wrongful conduct. Included is a discussion of insurer's duty of good faith and fair dealing in connection with defense and settlement of third-party actions against the insured, insurer's duty of good faith handling claims by insureds under first-party policies, insurer's liability for violation of statutory claims duties, and punitive and compensatory damages. Includes practical guidance regarding pre-trial tactics, a discussion of substantive law, sample forms, and annotated jury instructions.

New Appleman Law of Liability Insurance. New York: Matthew Bender & Co., 1966-date. 5 vols. Looseleaf format or eBook. Supplemented several times annually.
Cost: $3,529 (includes annual subscription); annual renewal: 1995: $788 (price frozen since 1992); 1996: $827; 1997: $827; 1998: $865; 1999: $900; 2000: $960; 2001: $1,027; 2002: $1,099; 2003: $1,106; 2004: $1,212; 2005: $1,297; 2006: $1,453; 2007: $1,634; 2008: $1,797; 2009: $1,977; 2010: $2,145; 2011: $2,145; 2012: $2,220; 2013: $2,375; 2014: $2,593; eBook: $3,208; renewal: 2014: $2,593. No longer available on CD-ROM.
This treatise provides detailed coverage of liability insurance and injuries to both persons and property. Covers the insurer's duty to defend and settle cases in good faith, environmental liability, products liability and professional malpractice. Also treats such topics as contribution, subrogation, uninsured motorist coverage, and no-fault insurance. Appendices include forms for declaratory relief, new policy provisions, and analysis of the effects of revisions to standard commercial general liability insurance policies. The text is exhaustively supported by relevant case authorities.

New Appleman Insurance Law Practice Guide. Edited by Jeffrey E. Thomas, Leo Martinez, Marc S. Mayerson, and Douglas R. Richmond. 2014 Edition. Newark, NJ: LexisNexis, 2013. 3 vols. (various pagings). Paperbound or eBook.
Cost: 2014 Edition: $665 (2014).
Seventy-five experts in the field of insurance law contributed to this refreshing and succinct updating of the publisher's classic 69-volume **Appleman on Insurance**. The wide-ranging subject coverage embraces the full range of insurance concepts, types of insurance and litigation issues. Unlike the standard treatise discussion of traditional works, this three-volume text deftly combines the discussion and analysis of key legal concepts with a variety of practice considerations, including pointers, checklists, examples, cross-references, forms and a, contrasts, counter-attacks, warnings, and forms designed to dramatically heighten its practical utility. The chapters are written from policyholder, insurer, and judicial perspectives, providing step-by-step procedural guidance on each phase of coverage disputes combined with strategies for achieving successful legal outcomes. The text is also laced with citations to supporting legal authorities, and includes numerous LexisNexis search strategies. Those used to the traditional treatise format will find the task-based format conducive to an efficient work flow, the informed determination of the merits of a coverage dispute, and the successful course of action, be it arbitration, mediation, settlement, lawsuit or defense. The **New Appleman** will also help the user understand the pertinent procedural rules and strategies as well as the substantive law applicable to all major insurance lines. It also provides numerous sample searches and cross references to pertinent ISO forms, **Miller's Standard Insurance Forms Annotated**®, and LexisNexis insurance and civil procedure publications. The text is also available on LexisNexis.

Pace, Nicholas M., et al. **Insurance Class Actions in the United States**. Santa Monica, CA, Rand Corp., 2007. 1 vol. (170 pp.).
Cost: $32; from $2.50 on amazon.com (2014).
Class actions are civil cases in which parties initiate a lawsuit on behalf of other plaintiffs who are not specifically named in the complaint. The role of class action lawsuits as a procedural device has garnered increasing attention in recent years, particularly

in the context of debate over the Class Action Fairness Act of 2005 (CAFA) (Public Law 109-2). Class action settlements may affect millions of class members and millions of dollars in restitution. The paucity of information on class actions generally, however, prompted this RAND study that used a defendant-based survey to collect original data on both state and federal insurance class actions. It also surveyed state departments of insurance to better understand the interests of regulators in the issues litigated by the parties in these cases. This book presents the results of a survey of the experiences of U.S. insurance companies over a 10-year period. The data collected allowed the authors to describe the significant characteristics of the litigation, including the types of classes, where the cases are being filed, what allegations are being made, how these cases are resolved, the length of time required for resolution, and impact of the Class Action Fairness Act of 2005. The authors are members of the research staff at the RAND Institute for Civil Justice, "a nonprofit research organization providing objective analysis and effective solutions that address challenges in the private and public sectors around the world."

Pierce, John S., Harold Weston, Robert G. Levy, and Dawn Valentine. **Insurance Practices and Coverage in Liability Defense**. New York: Wolters Kluwer Law & Business, 2005. 1 vol. (various pagings). Looseleaf format. Annual supplementation.
Cost: $299; supplementation: 2006: $115; 2007: $125; 2008: $134; 2009: $149; 2010: $159; 2011: $170; 2012: $182; 2013: $299; from $188.10 on amazon.com (2014).
The duty of an insurer to defend the insured is generally triggered by a lawsuit seeking damages for personal injury or property damage when such injuries are covered by the language of the insurance contract. This volume provides detailed discussion and analysis of the insurer's duty to defend the insured in any suit alleging damages that are covered under the terms of the policy. The authors provide an overview of the duty to defend, examine the nature of the tripartite relationship in insurance defense, the use of staff counsel, billing guidelines, legal audits, conflicts of interest and use of independent counsel, and allocation issues between insurer and insured. Chapter 7 provides a state-by-state jurisdictional survey on the issue of who controls the defense: the insurer, or the insured who has a right to select independent counsel. John Pierce is a senior partner and former managing partner of the San Francisco firm of Barger & Wolen, LLP. Robert Levy and Dawn Valentine are partner and senior associate, respectively, at Barger & Wolen. Harold Weston is an attorney and consultant with Creative Risk Consultants International in Oakland. This volume was formerly entitled **Defending the Insured**.

Quinley, Kevin M., Kenneth A. Satin, et al. **Insurance Settlements**. Costa Mesa, CA: James Publishing, Inc., 1990-date. 2 vols. Looseleaf format. Annual supplementation.
Cost: $129; supplementation: 1998: $64.99; 1999: $64.99; 2000-2014: $69.99 per year.
More than fifty experienced lawyers, claims adjusters, paralegals and other insurance professionals contributed chapters to this comprehensive practitioner's guide to the settlement of insurance cases. Thirty-seven chapters are organized into seven broad categories: claims handling, valuing claims, evaluating coverage, documenting claims, effective negotiation, efficient settlement, specific types of cases. The substantive and practical discussion of the individual topics is accompanied by a wealth of sample forms and insurance documents which would take the average practitioner years to assemble. This is a basic resource for any practitioner involved in the settlement of insurance cases. Previously known as **Insurance Settlement Handbook**.

Rynard, Thomas W. **Insurance and Risk Management for State and Local Governments**. New York: Matthew Bender & Co., 1991-date. 1 vol. Looseleaf format.
Cost: $323; supplementation: 1999: $107; 2000: $115; 2001: $123; 2002: $132; 2003: $139; 2004: $146; 2005: $155; 2006: $166; 2007: $179; 2008: $195; 2009: $211; 2010: $236; 2011: $233; 2012: $294; 2013: $316; 2014: $285; eBook: $323.
Designed for the attorney who advises public entities on legal issues pertaining to risk management. Part I introduces the concepts of risk and risk management; Part II discusses the hazards and perils involving public entities, particularly governmental tort liability; and Part III examines insurance policies and risk management alternatives other than commercial insurance. There are specific chapters devoted to such topics as liability for civil rights violations, liability for law enforcement activities, fire protection activities, and liability for schools. The author also discusses the public official bond, risk sharing, and claims administration. Thomas Rynard is an attorney with the Jefferson City, Missouri office of Craft, Fridkin & Rhyne, practicing in the areas of administrative law, governmental legal issues (including tort defense), environmental law, and insurance regulatory practice. He is the author of numerous articles and other publications in the area of risk management for local government.

Schermer, Irvin E. **Automobile Liability Insurance.** 4th ed. St. Paul, MN: Thomson Reuters West (Clark Boardman Callaghan), 2004-date. 5 vols. Looseleaf format. Updated twice annually.
Cost: $751; supp.: 1996: $240; 1997: $130; 1998: $138; 1999: $300; 2000: $318; 2001: $378; 2002: $238; 2003: $461; 2004: $257.50; 2005: $170; 2006: $190; 2007: $261; 2008: $291; 2009: $270.50; 2010: $370; 2011: $326; 2012: $359; 2013: $394; **Monthly Assured Print Price (APP):** $47/$564.
A practitioner's guide to the law of automobile liability insurance and the handling of actions against or in defense of insurers. It includes a detailed treatment of coverage, exclusion and condition provisions in automobile liability policies and a review of state case law in the field. It also provides an examination of no-fault insurance provisions, with an annotated analysis of state acts, and discussion of conflict of laws as applied to multiple coverage problems. Additional chapter coverage includes the Financial Responsibility Act, the motor vehicle liability policy, cancellation, uninsured motorists, damages recoverable, stacking of coverage, and more.

Sevier, Francis, A. C. **Insurance Depositions: Law, Strategy and Sample Depositions**. Huntington, NY: Juris Publishing, 2000-date. 1 vol. Looseleaf format.
Cost: eBook: $125.00; no supplementation (2014).

A deposition is an out-of-court form of witness oral testimony that is reduced to writing for later use in court and is a part of the discovery process in which litigants gather information in preparation for trial. In the United States and Canada, depositions are usually taken outside of the courtroom. This volume is a collection of depositions relevant to insurance cases, which usually involve one of two categories: (1) coverage (including its denial or existence) and (2) bad faith, both with an emphasis on cases that are litigated in court. The depositions presented in this volume address the areas of personal insurance, liability insurance, casualty insurance, and damages in insurance litigation. Regardless of the type of coverage being litigated (automobile, life and health, homeowners, professional liability or product liability), the approach to the litigation in all of these areas is identical, with a consideration of the following elements: (1) the insurance contract, if any; (2) the particular insurance code of the jurisdiction involved; (3) the case law of the jurisdiction involved; and (4) the available records and documents ensconced in the repository of the insurance company involved, including manuals, correspondence, promotional material, advertising records, etc. According to the author, this volume provides, "in broad outline, the tactical and strategic approach of effectively and efficiently gathering, eliciting, preserving and presenting testimony from potential witnesses." The author's goal is to present a glimpse of some of the problems that arise in the course of insurance litigation and suggest possible methods of addressing them. A retired trial attorney who has litigated more than 300 jury trials, Francis Sevier, a graduate of Temple University School of Law, is currently involved in mediating medical malpractice cases, appearing as an expert witness in insurance matters, and consulting.

Wickert, Gary L. **ERISA and Health Insurance Subrogation: In All 50 States**. 5th ed. Huntington, NY: Juris Publishing, Inc., 2013. 1 vol. (1,300 pp.). Purchase includes online access.
Cost: $225 (print or eBook) (2014).
Legally defined, subrogation is "the substitution of one person in the place of another with reference to a lawful claim or right." As applied to health insurance and ERISA (Employee Retirement Income Security Act), subrogation involves any attempt by an insurance carrier or self-insured entity to recover money which it paid out in a claim or which it is otherwise legally entitled to recover. This volume provides an overview of the law of subrogation, including contractual subrogation, equitable subrogation, and statutory subrogation. More specifically, this volume treats its application in heath and medical contexts, where insureds are paid by the insurer who then acquires the insured's rights for reimbursement (or subrogation) against the party ultimately responsible. Much of this volume consists of summaries of the statutory and case law of the fifty states as it regards health insurance subrogation. The other chapters cover such topics as self-funded ERISA-covered employee medical benefit plan subrogation, preemption, the equitable made whole doctrine, the equitable common fund doctrine, and the law regarding a plan's rights of recovery under its subrogation and/or reimbursement language. An important tool for attorneys representing insurance carriers, self-insured parties, or involved in insurance subrogation matters, this work, replete with citations to case law and statutes, brings order to the otherwise complicated law regarding subrogation issues. Gary Wickert is an insurance trial attorney and leading expert in the field of insurance subrogation who supervises a National recovery Program which includes a network of 300 contracted subrogation firms in all 50 states, Mexico, Canada, and the United Kingdom.

Windt, Allan D. **Insurance Claims and Disputes: Representation of Insurance Companies and Insureds.** 6th ed. St. Paul, MN: Thomson Reuters West (Clark Boardman Callaghan), 2013-date. 3 vols. Print or ProView eBook. Annual pocket parts.
Cost: $510; ProView eBook: $499; supplementation: 2008: $246; 2009: $53.50; 2010: $88; 2011: $98; 2012: $109; 2d ed.: 1993: $42; 1994: $45; 1995: 3d ed.; 1996: $60; 1997: $90; 1998: $95; 1999: $103; 2000: $111; 2001: $198; 4th ed.: 2002: $249; 2003: $68.50; 2004: $54.50; 2005: $72; 2006: $105; 2007: new edition ($198 to subscribers); **Monthly Assured Print Price (APP):** $28/$336.
A practical guide to litigation strategies employed by attorneys representing both insurance companies and insureds, including the determination of the rights and the obligations and potential liabilities of the parties following the filing of a claim under an insurance policy. Covers notice of claim, obligations of insurer, obligations of insured, duty to defend, duty to settle, duty to indemnify, rights and duties as between insurers, declaratory judgment actions, coverage actions, and contribution, subrogation, and indemnity. Includes a table of cases and subject index. Formerly published by Shepard's/McGraw-Hill, this title sold to the Thomson Corporation in 1995, after which it became part of the West product line.

Zulkey, Edward J. **Litigating Insurance Disputes**. Huntington, NY: Juris Publishing, Inc., 2011-date. 1 vol. (608 pp.). Looseleaf format (various pagings). Purchase includes online access and CD-ROM.
Cost: $175; ebook: $175; combo price: $262.50; supplementation: 2013: $75.
Insurance policies are basically contracts between insureds and insurers that provide protection of insureds against liability for claims or suits brought by third parties. This comprehensive resource provides a well-organized and annotated discussion of all types of insurance coverage, including automobile, commercial general liability, professional liability, directors' and officers' liability, and workers compensation, as well as the various layers of coverage, including primary, excess, umbrella and reinsurance. There is also discussion of how to read an insurance policy, the rules of insurance policy construction, the insured's duty of cnotice and cooperation, the insured's duty to defend, reservation rights and conflict of interest, the number of occurrences or claims, deductibles and limits, relationship of multiple insurers, the failure to settle, and the role of the broker. Part II addresses choice-of-law resolution in insurance cases, declaratory judgment litigation issues and strategies, discovery and case management in declaratory judgment actions, and arbitration in insurance disputes. Part III covers litigating directors' and officers' coverage claims, advertising liability coverage, litigating environmental and toxic tort coverage claims, employment liability coverage, and fiduciary responsibility insurance. The text is supported by numerous citations to case law and statutes. A companion CD-ROM provides a variety of forms, agreements, and other supporting documents. This is an invaluable tool for any lawyer who represents policyholders

or insurers. Edward J. Zulkey is a Partner and General Counsel in the Chicago office of Baker & McKenzie where he practices primarily in the fields of liability insurance-related issues and professional liability. He is former Vice-Chair of the ABA/TIPS' Committee on Excess and Reinsurance, Co-Chair of the Legal Malpractice Subcommittee of the ABA/TIPS' Committee on Insurance Coverage Litigation and Chairman, Casualty & Excess Insurance Committee, International Association of Defense Counsel. He has written numerous articles and lectured widely in the field of insurance coverage.

Additional titles in the field of Insurance Law are available from the following publishers: American Insurance Association, Matthew Bender, Chartered Property Casualty Underwriters Society, Foundation Press, Gould, Greenwood Publishing Group, William S. Hein & Co., International Risk Management Institute, James Publishing, Lawyers & Judges Publishing Co., Legal Research Systems, LexisNexis, Lloyd's of London Press, National Association of Insurance Commissioners, Oakstone Legal & Business Publishing, Panel Publishers, Practising Law Institute, S. Illinois University Press, Thomson Reuters West, University Press of America, Warren, Gorham & Lamont, West Academic. See Appendix B for addresses and telephone numbers.

Judges, Courts, and Judicial Conduct

Aldisert, Ruggero J. **The Judicial Process: Text, Materials and Cases**. 2d ed. St. Paul, MN: West, 1996. 1 vol. (790 pp.). No supplementation.
Cost: $158; from $15.85 on amazon.com (2014).
This caseBook provides valuable insights and analyses of the judicial process, including the nuances of precedent, retroactivity, statutory construction, inductive and deductive reasoning, the exercise of discretion, and standards of review in appellate courts. There are also excerpts of teachings from American masters in the law, and discussion of the fundamental theories of philosophy and jurisprudence, with illustrative cases.

Aldisert, Ruggero J. **Opinion Writing**. 3d ed. Durham, NC: Carolina Academic Press, 2012. 1 vol. (362 pp.). Paperbound.
Cost: $40.00; from $30.00 on amazon.com (2014).
According to Judge Ruggero Aldisert, "a judicial opinion may be defined as a reasoned elaboration, publicly stated, that justifies a conclusion or decision. Its purpose is to set forth an explanation for a decision that adjudicates a live case or a controversy that has been presented before a court. This explanatory function of the opinion is paramount. In the common law tradition the court's ability to develop case law finds legitimacy only because the decision is accompanied by a publicly recorded statement of reasons." This guide to opinion writing is the product of the author's more than forty years experience as a judge at both the state and federal levels and an abiding interest in the theory and craft of judicial drafting. The book is divided into four parts: (1) Theoretical Concepts Underlying an Opinion; (2) the Anatomy of an Opinion; (3) Writing Style; and (4) Opinion Writing Checklists. Its audience includes judges at every level: local, state, and federal, including appellate and trial court judges, administrative court judges, hearing officers, and members of the agency, private judges (arbitrators), and law clerks. The author brings to the task eight years as a judge on the Pennsylvania Common Pleas Court and, since 1968, the U.S. Court of Appeals for the Third Circuit, where he served as Chief Judge from 1984 to 1986. He also draws upon his experience as a member of the law faculty at the University of Pittsburgh School of Law from 1963 to 1986 and as a visiting professor at other law schools. This book is an outgrowth of his role as a discussion leader at Senior Judge Seminars sponsored by the Institute of Judicial Administration at New York University and draws upon the interaction with over 300 senior appellate judges, including four U.S. Supreme Court justices, over a span of 20 years.

Annotated Model Code of Judicial Conduct. 2d ed. Chicago: American Bar Association, Judicial Division, 2011. 1 vol.
Cost: $95 ($71.25 to Judicial Division members) (2014).
The **Model Code of Judicial Conduct** is designed to establish standards for ethical conduct of judges and provide guidance to judges and candidates for judicial office and structure for regulating conduct through disciplinary agencies. This authoritative analysis of the judicial ethics rules and the cases, ethics opinions, and other legal authorities essential to understanding them, prepared by the ABA Center for Professional Responsibility and Judicial Division. The book's organization follows the style of the **Annotated Model Rules of Professional Conduct** and builds upon the historical work presented in the 1973 **Reporter's Notes to Code of Judicial Conduct** by E. Wayne Thode and The **Development of the ABA Judicial Code** written by Lisa L. Milord in 1992. **The Model Code of Judicial Conduct** consists of broad statements called Canons, specific rules set forth in Sections under each Canon, a Terminology Section, and an Application Section with Commentary. The text of the Canons and the Sections, including the Terminology and Application Sections, are considered to be authoritative. The book includes citations to nearly 1000 cases, hundreds of ethics opinions and numerous law review articles. It is based upon the 2011 edition of the **Model Code of Judicial Conduct**, including changes to the Application Section made in 2010.

Barton, Benjamin H. **The Lawyer-Judge Bias in the American Legal System**. New York: Cambridge University Press, 2011. 1 vol. (303 pp.). Hardcover.
Cost: $101.00; from $22.09 on amazon.com; kindle ed.: $18.87 (2014).
It is Benjamin Barton's contention that lawyer-judges instinctively favor the legal profession in their decision-making, and that this bias has far-reaching and harmful consequences for the American legal system. Judge Dennis Jacobs, Chief Judge of the U.S. Court of Appeals for the 2d Circuit, concurs, called it an "ambient bias," a frame of mind that closely surrounds and nurtures the legal community. In likening it to the existence of a close-knit professional fraternity, Judge Jacobs gives voice to sentiments that are frank and unusual for a sitting judge. The author contends that this bias occurs regardless of political affiliation, judicial philosophy, race, gender, or religion. The most significant personality characteristic of judges is that they were former lawyers and, as such, have, above all, sympathy and

empathy for fellow lawyers. Despite the historical trappings and aura of judicial majesty and infallibility that surrounds the bench, it is far more common for the public to view judges as human and fallible. His analysis proceeds from a theoretical basis to a close examination of individual cases in a legal system that he describes as "uniquely complex and unwieldy." Following his theoretical observations, the author examines their application in realms of constitutional criminal procedure, civil constitutional law, lawyer regulation, torts, evidence and civil procedure, the business of law, and concludes with a consideration of the ramifications of these findings and possible solutions. The author is the Director of Clinical Programs and Professor of Law at the University of Tennessee college of Law, and winner of the 2010 LSAC Philip D. Shelton Award for outstanding research in legal education. This is one of a number of recent books exposing the underside of the legal profession, including Lester Brickman's. **Lawyers Barons**, Walter Olson's **The Rule or Lawyers**, and Philip K. Howard's **Life Without Lawyers**.

Baum, Lawrence. **Specializing the Courts**. Chicago: University of Chicago Press, 2011. 1 vol. (281 pp.).
Cost: $30.00; from $8.72 on amazon.com; kindle ed.: $16.81 (2014).
Although most judges are generalists who hear cases on a broad range of subject areas, from antitrust to zoning, an increasing number in both federal and state courts hear cases in specialized subject areas. On the federal level, these include courts that hear cases in the areas of tax, bankruptcy and international trade. On the state level, judges sit on specialized courts that hear criminal, environmental, family, housing, juvenile, traffic, probate, small claims, tax, and workers' compensation matters. While such specialization is often reflected in a court system's organizational chart, it is also manifest within the courts themselves. This book provides an in-depth examination of the phenomenon of judicial specialization in the United States that has shown a marked growth since the late 19th century. It also explores the issue of how and why the courts have become more specialized, concluding that they have their origins in a long series of specific decisions based on the belief that specialization would produce desired results in a particular context. The author also addresses the effects of specialization, which are contingent on the conditions under which a particular court operates. Drawing upon these general observations, the author also analyzes specialize courts that deal with foreign affairs and internal security; criminal law; economic issues involving governmental litigation (including claims against the federal government); and economic issues involving private litigation (including patents, bankruptcy, corporate governance, and business courts). A concluding chapter considers the causes and consequences of specialization, the evaluation of judicial specialization, and the future of judicial specialization. This is the first book to examine the subject of specialized courts in a comprehensive and scholarly way. Lawrence Baum is professor of political science at Ohio State University and the author of **Judges and the Audiences**, among other books on the courts.

Binder, Sarah A. and Forrest Maltzman. **Advice & Dissent: The Struggle to Shape the Federal Judiciary**. Washington, DC: Brookings Institution Press, 2009. 1 vol.
Cost: $22.95; from $15.35 on amazon.com; kindle ed.: $13.77 (2014).
The process of judicial selection and confirmation has become increasingly contentious and acrimonious in recent years as the battleground for many policy disputes has shifted to this least democratic branch of government. The founding father's original notion of judges as neutral arbiters of legal disputes has been seriously compromised as partisan and ideological disputes have intruded into the judicial process. In this environment, it is no wonder that the selection and confirmation of federal judges has become just another manifestation of this partisan political divide. In this insightful empirical analysis of the federal judicial confirmation process, the authors seek to reconstruct the history and contemporary practice of advise and consent, to identify the causes of conflict over the makeup of the federal bench in the post-WWII era, and to examine the consequences of battles over appointments to the federal courts. Their focus is directed to the experience with confirmation to the district and courts of appeals which serve as the courts of last resort for the vast majority of federal disputes. Indeed, since 1947, the percentage of nominees to the district courts and courts of appeals has fallen dramatically. Since 1992, for example, the confirmation rate for the courts of appeals has fallen to less than 60%, and less than 50% during some recent Congresses. The consequence of this highly partisan and ideological selection and confirmation logjam is a diminution in the integrity of the judicial process, both substantively and procedurally. Judicial integrity is compromised as society increasingly views judges as simply a new breed of political agents whose decisions are made on the basis of ideology, and justice is delayed and denied as dockets increase in the face-off confirmation disputes. This is an essential resource for anyone interested in understanding the contemporary judicial confirmation process. Sarah Binder is a senior fellow in Governance Studies at the Brookings Institution and a professor of political science at George Washington University. Forrest Maltzman is a professor of political science at George Washington University and co-author of **Crafting Law on the Supreme Court: The Collegial Game**.

Bybee, Keith J. **All Judges Are Political—Except When They Are Not**. Stanford, CA: Stanford University Press, 2010. 1 vol. (177 pp.).
Cost: $19.95; from $13.20 an amazon.com; kindle ed.: $10.99 (2014).
Keith Bybee addresses one of the most fundamental questions in law today: whether judges are neutral and apolitical arbiters providing answers to controversial questions or political actors imposing their own ideological preferences on those issues. Many Americans regard judges as impartial arbiters of the law at the same time that they view many judicial rulings to be politically motivated, leading many to suspect that all the talk about the meaning and requirements of the law is simply empty rhetoric masking a world of legal realism.
The more controversial the decision, the more the public views the courts as political in nature, despite their alleged obeisance to the law and, for example, the application of neutral rules of statutory construction. This thoughtful book explores the fundamental tension that exists between these alternative ways of looking at the judicial function which, despite the apparent hypocrisy, strengthens the law and sustains its legitimacy. The author is professor law at the Syracuse University College of Law.

Coffin, Frank M. **On Appeal: Courts, Lawyering and Judging**. New York: W. W. Norton & Co., 1994. 1 vol. (373 pp.).
Cost: Out-of-print; from $6.03 on amazon.com (2014).
A scholarly examination of the appellate process by the Senior Judge for the United States Court of Appeals for the First Circuit. Based on more than 25 years experience as an appellate judge, this illuminating volume combines the elements of personal reflection and appellate advocate's handbook in outlining the procedures for appeals in various court systems and the relationship between state and federal courts. Coffin reflects on his own work as an appellate judge by describing how he reads lawyers' briefs and prepares for oral argument.

Conn, Kenneth E. **Settlement Conference: A Handbook for Judges and Lawyers**. San Joaquin, CA: San Joaquin Eagle Publishing, 1988. 1 vol.
Cost: $20; from $4.00 on amazon.com (2014).
An experienced trial judge explains the intricacies of the settlement conference as an effective tool to speed civil cases through the judicial system.

Deskbook for Chief Judges of the U.S. District Courts. 3d ed. Washington, DC: Federal Judicial Center, 2003. 1 vol. (138 pp.).
Cost: available at no cost at: FJC web site (do Google search for title).
This volume was designed to assist Chief Judges of the U.S. District Courts in meeting the "complex challenges of leading their district courts." It describes those challenges and the statutes and administrative policies that impact the District Courts. The Deskbook includes two kinds of materials: (1) summaries of statutes and Judicial Conference policies and descriptions of relevant sources and assistance available from the Federal Judicial Center and Administrative Office of the U.S. Courts; and (2) suggestions for chief judges to consider when confronting particular matters, those suggestions based upon comments from experienced chief judges and professional literature regarding the management of public and private organizations. The first edition of this volume was published in 1984.

Flamm, Richard. **Judicial Disqualification: Recusal and Disqualification of Judges**. 2d ed. Berkeley, CA: Banks and Jordan Law Publishing Co., 2007. 1 vol. (1,208 pp.). Irregular supplementation.
Cost: $299; supplementation: $2007: $69; 2009: $99; 2010-2013: 0; 1st ed.: 2005: $89.50 (2014).
A comprehensive guide to the law in every American jurisdiction governing motions to disqualify judges. The author analyzes every legal basis for judicial disqualification, including constitutional provisions, state and federal statutes, court rules, and court decisions. The book's twenty-seven chapters examine every possible aspect of judicial disqualification, including disqualification for cause, preemptory disqualification, bias, appearance of bias, gifts, favors and political support, interest, familial and social relationships, business and professional relationships, background and experience, prior activity as an attorney, judicial knowledge, knowledge obtained in criminal proceedings, ex parte communications, judicial conduct, adverse rulings or comments, procedure, timeliness, legal sufficiency, factors mitigating against disqualification, tactical motivations of moving party, procedure following disqualification, federal disqualification provisions, disqualification under 28 U.S.C.§455, disqualification under 28 U.S.C.§144, the relationship between §§144 and 455, and disqualification in state court. This is the most comprehensive work of its kind on the market and an essential tool for any judge or lawyer involved in judicial disqualification proceedings. The author, a graduate of Rutgers Law School, and adjunct professor at Boalt Hall School of Law, is a nationally recognized expert in the field of legal ethics who specializes in providing representation, advice and expert witness testimony on matters of legal and judicial ethics, legal malpractice, and breach of fiduciary duties. Originally published by Little Brown in 1996, the revised [second] edition was published in 2004.

Garner, Bryan A. **Guidelines for Drafting and Editing Court Rules**. Washington, DC: Administrative Office of the United States Courts, 1996. 1 vol. (36 pp.).
Cost: available online at no cost at: http://www.uscourts.gov/uscourts/RulesAndPolicies/rules/guide.pdf
Originally published and distributed by the Administrative Office of the United States Courts in 1996, these Guidelines were drafted to help explain the drafting and editing choices reflected in the Federal Rules of Appellate Procedure and to open the rulemaking process to public scrutiny and participation. Bryan Garner, as Consultant to the Rules Committees, was also assigned the task of drafting Guidelines to assist the committee members in their work. This volume has undergone several reprintings, the most recent in 2002. Bryan Garner has established himself as the nation's leading authority on legal writing, usage, and drafting. A Professor of Law at the Southern Methodist University School of Law, he is the author or co-author of eighteen books on legal writing.

George, Joyce J. **Judicial Opinion Writing Handbook**. 5th ed. Buffalo, NY: William S. Hein & Co., 2007. 1 vol. (854 pp.).
Cost: $68; from $64.60 on amazon.com (2014).
This reference tool provides guidance to judges in the drafting of judicial opinions. The author reviews existing methods, styles, rules, and techniques of opinion writing and provides guidance in writing opinions which clearly illuminate the legal issues and facts involved. A section discussing Finding of Fact and Conclusion of Law is included for the benefit of the trial judge. The work includes forms and structure outlines. The fourth edition includes two new sections. Judges Views contains comments of judges about how to write effectively. Criticism of Judges Opinions discusses the climate of criticism, both legitimate and illegitimate, and how to respond to it.

Geyh, Charles and W. William Hodes. **Reporters' Notes To the Model Code of Judicial Conduct**. Chicago: American Bar Association, 2009. 1 vol. (151 pp.).
Cost: $29.95 ($19.95 to members) (2014).
The **Model Code of Judicial Conduct** is intended to establish standards for ethical conduct of judges, provide guidance to judges and candidates for judicial office and provide structure for regulating conduct through disciplinary agencies. It consists

of broad statements called Canons with specific rules set forth in Sections under each Canon, a Terminology Section, an Application Section and Commentary. The text of the Canons and the Sections, including the Terminology and Application Sections, is authoritative. Adopted in 1924, the **Canons of Judicial Ethics** consisted of 36 provisions that included both generalized, hortatory admonitions and specific rules of proscribed conduct. In 1972, these were replaced by a new **Code of Judicial Conduct**, a document revised and adopted most recently in 2007, as the **Model Code of Judicial Conduct**. As Reporters, Professors Charles Geyh and W. William Hodes listened to, observed, and helped evaluate the voluminous testimony and comments presented to the ABA Commission to Evaluate the Model Code of Judicial Conduct. This volume is a Rule-by-Rule record of their notes and the comments contributed by participants in that process.

Gray, Cynthia. **An Ethics Guide for Judges and Their Families**. Chicago: American Judicature Society, 2001. 1 vol. (130 pp.).
Cost: $25 (2014)
This guide explores the code of judicial conduct restrictions that affect a judge as a member of a family and the guidance the rules give to family members. It lists examples of permitted and prohibited conduct in areas such as misuse of office, disqualification, hiring family members, and political activity, and provides practical suggestions on issues such as stress and security. A related discussion guide contains materials for use in programs on ethics and related topics for judges and their families.

Gray, Cynthia and Nancy Biro. **An Ethics Guide for Part-time Lawyer Judges**. Chicago: American Judicature Society, 1999. 1 vol. (121 pp.).
Cost: $25 (2014).
This volume address the conduct of part-time judges who are also involved in the practice of law. The discussion reflects the rules of the code of judicial conduct, judicial ethics advisory opinions. It also includes a self-test and discussion questions designed to guide part-time judges in adjusting their conduct accordingly.

Gray, Cynthia. **A Study of State Judicial Discipline Sanctions**. Chicago: American Judicature Society, 2002. 1 vol. (180 pp.).
Cost: $25 (2014).
This examination of state judicial discipline sanctions begins with a brief overview of the state judicial discipline systems, supplemented by tables that identify the sanctions available in each state. The author then examines all the cases decided between 1990 and 2001 in which judges have been removed from office as a result of judicial discipline. proceedings and categorizes each by the type of misconduct. The author also analyzes the cases in which there has been disagreement about the appropriate sanction, either between the commission and the state supreme court or among the members of the supreme court as reflected in dissents. The discussion of appropriate sanctions considers the role of the judge's reputation and the role which remorse plays in applying sanctions. and catalogs the factors supreme courts and conduct commissions have listed as relevant in determining the appropriate sanction and analyzes the cases to discuss issues such as the importance of the judge's reputation in the sanction decision and the role remorse plays. The Study concludes with recommendations for states to consider in their pursuit of a fair and effective system of judicial discipline.

Gray, Cynthia. **When Judges Speak Up**. Chicago: American Judicature Society, 1998. 1 vol. (65 pp.). CD-ROM and video also available.
Cost: $25 (2014).
A multimedia curriculum designed to help judges resolve the conflict between increasing demands for their observations on cases and controversial legal issues and their commitment to maintaining public confidence in the judiciary. The curriculum consists of a videotape and a self-study guide. The video and self-study guide are also available on CD-ROM. An instructor's manual is also available.

Judicial Conduct Reporter. Chicago: American Judicature Society, Center for Judicial Conduct Organizations, 1979-date. Published quarterly. Availlable in online pdfs.
Cost: $40 per year; $10 per issue (2014).
This quarterly newsletter tracks recent developments in the areas of judicial discipline and disability, provides summaries of current court and commission decisions, reviews books and journal articles, and includes an annual survey of commission complaint disposition, staff, and budget. Serves as a current awareness tool for the **Judicial Discipline and Disability Digest** (see next entry).

Judicial Discipline and Disability Digest. Edited by Judith Rosenbaum; assisted by Scott Beller. Chicago: American Judicature Society, 1981-date. 5 vols.
Cost: Bound volumes are out-of-print: 1961-1978 base and some supplementary volumes out-of-print; supplementary volumes: 1979: $50; 1980: $50; 1981-86: $100; 1986-88: $125; 1989-91: $140. See **Judicial Conduct Reporter** (above) for current developments.
The most exhaustive research tool available covering the field of judicial discipline and disability, this publication digests more than 2,000 published and unpublished decisions issued by judicial conduct commissions and courts in disciplinary and related matters. The main volume, encompassing decisions issued during the years 1961-1978, is supplemented by digest volumes covering the years 1979, 1980, 1981-1986, 1986-1988, and 1989-1991. Decisions are arranged under 500 subheadings. Out-of-print. Must be consulted in law libraries.

Keeton, Robert E. **Keeton on Judging in the American Legal System**. Charlottesville, VA: LexisNexis, 1999. 1 vol. No supplementation.
Cost: Out-of-print; from $49.95 on amazon.com (2014).
A valuable manual and sourceBook on the theory and practice of judging by an experienced judge, former law school professor and trial attorney. His audience includes not only new and

experienced members of judiciary, but trial attorneys who wish to understand the mindset of the trial judge. Judge Keeton addresses such topics as the distinction between the law and facts, values in reasoned decision making, limits on state and national governmental powers, making merits and managerial decisions, judge and jury, a judge's writing and speaking, judging statutes, professional roles, overseeing trials and other evidentiary proceedings, judgments, and more. A Professor of Law at Harvard Law School from 1953 to 1979, Judge Keeton has served as a U.S. District Judge for the District of Massachusetts since 1979. He has also served on a number of judicial committees, including the U.S. Judicial Conference Committee on Admission of Attorneys to Federal Practice, the Committee on Court Administration, and the Committee on Rules of Practice and Procedure. Judge Keeton has made a welcome contribution to the literature on the art of judging.

Kuhne, Cecil C., III. **Convincing the Judge: Practical Advice for Litigators**. Chicago: American Bar Association, General Practice, Solo and Small Firm Division, 2008. 1 vol. (197 pp.).
Cost: $84.95 ($68.95 to Section members); from $29.98 on amazon.com (2014).
According to the author of this volume, it took years of practice before he came to the simple, yet poignant, realization that judges are human beings too. Indeed, learning how to deal effectively with both trial court and appellate judges is a skill that often takes years to master because it encompasses a mature understanding of human nature. This practical guide attempts, in the interests of justice, and smooth and efficient case management, to impart the time-tested wisdom and advice of judges for the benefit of courtroom litigators. In 18 succinct chapters, he distills the most important elements of the lawyer's demeanor in the courtroom or chambers likely to win over the judge and advance the interests of his or her client. These include discussion of the judicial role, what judges like, what judges don't like, the difficult judge, case management, discovery disputes, pretrial motions, settlement negotiations, general trial considerations, the void dire, opening statements, evidence, witnesses, closing statements, jury instructions, appeals, appellate briefs, and oral arguments.

Miller, Mark C. **Exploring Judicial Politics**. New York: Oxford University Press, 2009. 1 vol. (368 pp.).
Cost: $53.95; from $.77 on amazon.com (2014).
Unlike the executive and legislative branches of government which are overtly political in their orientation, the courts are both legal and political institutions. Judges stand for election or are appointed by elected officials, yet they, at least theoretically, make decisions based on the rule of law, impartiality, and precedent. This collection of articles, scrutinizes the intersection of law and politics and the role of the judiciary in the political process. While directed primarily at an undergraduate audience, it provides invaluable insights for anyone interested in exploring the political context of the judicial branch and the decision-making process. Mark Miller contributes an illuminating introductory essay on the study of judicial politics and the role of political scientists in that enterprise, with attention to the empirical and behavioralist approaches to scholarship. The contributing authors examine the differences in state judicial election, the role of pressure groups and federal judicial election process, the role of lawyers in the courts and society, the politics of jury reform, the role of state trial courts in achieving justice in civil litigation, the role of the U.S. District courts, state supreme courts as policymakers, the U.S. Courts of Appeals, the role of the Solicitor General, U.S. Supreme Court law clerks, the boundaries of judicial power, women and the law, the federal courts and terrorism, interaction between the federal courts and the other branches, comparative judicial studies, and the role of the U.S. Supreme Court as Super Legislature. Mark C. Miller is associate professor and former chair of the Dept. of Government and International relations at Clark University. The chapter authors are primarily professors of law and political science.

O'Brien, David M., ed. **Judges on Judging: Views From the Bench**. 4th ed. Washington, DC: CQ Press, 2012. 1 vol. (372 pp.). Paperbound.
Cost: $44; from $28.99 on amazon.com (2014).
Many Americans express opinions on the judicial process or specific judges without an adequate understanding of the judge's role or the often conflicting philosophies that guide their determinations. This invaluable collection of extra-judicial essays on the role of the judge assembles the views many of the leading judicial minds in modern history, both living and dead. Among the contributors are Chief Justices Warren Burger, William H. Rehnquist, and John G. Roberts, Associate Justices Felix Frankfurter, Robert H. Jackson, William J. Brennan, Hugo Black, Ruth Bader Ginsburg, Lewis F. Powell, John Paul Stevens, Steven G. Breyer, and Thurgood Marshall; Judges Jerome Frank, Robert Bork, Frank Easterbrook, and Richard A. Posner, among others. The essays address such topics as judicial review and American politics, the dynamics of the judicial process, the judiciary and the Constitution, the judiciary and federal regulation, statutory interpretation, and our dual Constitutional system: the Bill of Rights and the states. The appendices include a selective bibliography of off-the-bench commentaries, Federalist No. 78 on the judicial department, and a time chart of the U.S. Supreme Court justices.

Ostrom, Brian J.. et al. **Trial Courts as Organizations**. Philadelphia: Temple University Press, 2007. 1 vol. (194 pp.).
Cost: $64.50; from $50.00 on amazon.com (2014).
Each of the more than 16,000 trial courts in the United States has its own unique culture which guides its operations and the success it achieves in serving both the ends of justice and the interests of its participants. In this study of trial courts, the authors have applied the ideas, framework and tools used by business school scholars to assess how trial court organizations operate and hope to operate in the future. They identify four different types of trial court cultures--communal, networked, autonomous and hierarchical—based on clusters of particular values, and then apply this analytical structure to 12 courts in three states--California, Florida, and Minnesota. Chapters include: (1) organizational culture in American trial courts; (2) a framework for court culture; (3) measuring court culture; (4) elaborating he four cultures; (5) consequences of court culture; (6) preferences for court culture; and (7) conclusions and implications. A number of appendices organize their findings in the form of charts and tables. The authors explain how courts function as a unit to preserve judicial independence, strengthen

organizational leadership, and influence court performance. Brian J. Ostrom is Principal Research Consultant at the National Center for State Courts. Charles W. Ostrom, Jr. is Professor of Political Science at Michigan State University. Roger A. Hanson is an Adjunct Professor of Law and Political Science at the University of Colorado. Matthew Kleiman is a Senior Court Research Associate at the National Center for State Courts.

Sampson, Kathleen, ed. **Handbook for Judges: An Anthology of Inspirational and Educational Readings**. 4th ed. Chicago: American Judicature Society, 2004. 1 vol. (263 pp.).
Cost: $20 (2014).
An invaluable collection of articles which address a variety of issues of special interest to judges and those interested in understanding the nature of the judicial role. The articles focus on such topics as the personal and professional qualities of a judge, the work of judging, communicating with juries, sentencing criminals, writing opinions, managing cases, the relationship between courts and communities, the judicial role, the judicial reform movement, and more.

Shaman, Jeffrey M., Steven Lubet, and James J. Alfini. **Judicial Conduct and Ethics**. 5th ed. Charlottesville, VA: LexisNexis, 2013-date. 1 vol.
Cost: $184; no supplementation to date; 3d ed.: 2001: $28; 2002: 0; 2003: $28; 2004: $35; 2005-2006: 0; 2007: new edition.
A comprehensive guide to judicial conduct and ethics in federal, state and local courts. The authors' discussion and analysis draws upon and cites to Supreme Court decisions, ethics advisory opinions, and the ABA's 1990 **Model Code of Judicial Conduct.** The chapter coverage examines such topics as the use of power, demeanor, impartiality and competence, disqualification and conflict of interest, ex parte communications, case management and administrative imperatives, personal finances, financial disclosures, civil and charitable activities, personal conduct, speech and association, election and political activities, appointment and confirmation, regulatory organization and procedure, civil and criminal liability, and judicial disability and retirement. An Appendix contains Guidelines for Cases Involving Judicial Disability. The volume also includes a table of cases and index. Jeffrey Shaman is a Professor of Law at DePaul University. Steven Lubet is Professor of Law and Director of the Program on Advocacy and Professionalism at the Northwestern University School of Law. James Alfini is Dean of the Northern Illinois University College of Law.

Sheppard, Jennifer. **In Chambers: a Guide for Judicial Clerks and Externs**. New York: Wolters Kluwer Law & Business, 2012. 1 vol. (228 pp.).
Cost: $43; from $20.00 on amazon.com; kindle: $35.13 (2014).
Landing a judicial clerkship after law school is one of the most valuable initial experiences a newly-minted lawyer can garner. A judicial clerkship provides unique insights into the inner workings of the judicial process, whether at the trial or appellate court level, that can last a lifetime. This book provides essential background into the types of knowledge clerks should possess on their first day on the job, including such basic tasks as reading a docket sheet, working with a case file, drafting jury instructions, understanding standards of review, sources of authority commonly relied upon by the courts, and the ethical considerations which must be observed both during and after court employment. Chapters also address the civil and criminal litigation process, the research process, writing technique when drafting documents to the court, drafting a judicial opinion, drafting a bench memorandum, legal citation, and applying for a clerkship. The author also provides useful checklists for drafting documents, a useful system for note taking, and exercises at the end of chapters to evaluate the reader's comprehension and application of the materials. The text is a product of the author's own experience as a judicial clerk as well as her involvement with the externship programs at Appalachian School of Law and Mercer University School of Law.

Sirico, Louis J., Jr. **Judging: A Book for Student Clerks**. Newark, NJ: LexisNexis Matthew Bender, 2002. 1 vol. (228 pp.). Paperbound.
Cost: Out-of-print; from $3.82 on amazon.com (2014).
This fascinating and sometimes provocative anthology of articles by and about judges provides valuable insights into the types of issues faced by judges at both the state and federal levels. Designed as a textbook for the classroom compoent of a judicial externship, the articles provide an invaluable introduction to the role of the judge for law students contemplating a judicial clerkship, or a judicial career. The readings in each chapter are preceded by an introductory essay and followed by a series of questions designed for classroom discussion. The articles address such topics as sentencing, the judge's role in settlement, the mysteries of judicial decision making, criticism of judges, dissents, the clerks role in drafting appellate court decisions, the juvenile justice system, cameras in the courtroom, the notion of the impartial judge, judicial ethics and private lives, civility among judges, protecting the appearance of judicial impartiality in the face of law clerk employment negotiations, public comments which lead to recusal, charting the bounds of proper criticism by judges of other judges, opinion writing assistance involving law clerks, lending impaired judges a hand, 10 trial mistakes, and responding to judicial alcohol abuse, among others. The author is Professor of Law and Director of the Legal Writing Program, Villanova University School of Law.

Sollenberger, Mitchell A. **Judicial Appointments and Democratic Controls**. Durham, NC: Carolina Academic Press, 2010. 1 vol. (273 pp.). Paperbound.
Cost: $42.00; from $10.95 on amazon.com (2014).
This volume navigates the nuances of the appointment process under the U.S. Constitution in which the President, with the advice and consent of the Senate, appoints judges to the federal courts. The author argues that "republican and structural safeguards matter when assessing governing relationships" and that the democratic controls that guide judicial appointments are rooted in the Constitution. And while the specific mechanisms that guide the appointment process are not found in the Constitution, the process is ultimately rooted in the notion that a fully functioning government must be based on the idea of representation, as James Madison affirmed it in **The Federalist** No. 49. This book takes a close look at the various procedures that comprise the judicial appointment process, from the overarching role of Congress and the courts, to textual

direction, statutory qualification, the pre-nomination process, the role of the Senate Judiciary Committee, Senate floor action, and reform proposals. The concluding chapter examines the issues of democratic controls versus executive governance, and majority rule versus minority rights. The Appendices contain the White House Personal Data Statement Questionnaire, the Executive Branch Personnel Public Financial Disclosure Report, the Senate Judiciary Committee Questionnaire for Judicial Nominees, the Senate Judiciary Committee Financial Disclosure Report, and the "Blue Slip" soliciting the approval or non-approval of nominees by members of the Senate. The volume also includes an extensive bibliography of sources regarding the appointment process, table of cases, and index. The author is an assistant professor of political science at the University of Michigan-Dearborn.

Spohn, Cassia. **How Do Judges Decide? The Search for Fairness and Justice in Punishment**. 2d ed. Los Angeles: Sage Publications, 2009. 1 vol. (357 pp.). Paperbound.
Cost: $64.00; from $18.85 on amazon.com; kindle: $51.20 (2014).
Intended as a text for upper-division and graduate level courses in criminal justice, the judicial system, criminal law, and law and society, this book looks beyond the idealized conception of sentencing as a process by which the judge weighs the facts and circumstances of the case, the background and blameworthiness of the offender, and his own philosophy of punishment. In the author's view, the sentences meted out by judges in state and federal courts are generally the result of a collaborative process Involving legislators, and criminal justice officials in supporting roles, and are often heavily influenced by guidelines that specify minimum sentences to be imposed. Such sentences may not reflect a coherent philosophy of punishment, a rational assessment of the seriousness of the crime, or the culpability of the offender, but rather inconsistencies based on a variety of variables, including the offender's race, social class, ethnicity, or gender. This volume examines the goals of sentencing (including its theoretical models), the sentencing process, the decisional process of the judge, sentencing disparity and discrimination by gender, race and ethnicity, the sentencing reform movement, and the impact of sentencing reform. The author draws upon the latest scholarly research to frame her analysis. The volume also features an extensive bibliography of scholarly sources and chapter discussion questions. The author is professor in the School of Criminology and Criminal Justice at Arizona State University and author of three books in the field of criminal justice.

Standards Relating to Appellate Courts. Chicago: American Bar Association, Judicial Administration Division, 1994. 1 vol. (134 pp.). Paperbound.
Cost: $25 (2014).
This volume contains ABA policy recommendation for appellate courts and addresss such topics as appellate court structure, opportunity for appellate review, assistance of counsel, decision making, appellate court administration, caseflow management and delay reduction, appellate court administration and facilities and technology.

Strauss, Debra. **Behind the Bench: The Guide to Judicial Clerkships**. Chicago: West Academic (Gilbert Law Publishing), 2002. 1 vol. (325 pp.). Paperbound.
Cost: $21.95; from $.02 on amazon.com (2014).
For the recent law school graduate, the judicial clerkship can provide an excellent learning and career-enhancing experience. Most law school graduates never apply for judicial clerkships because they lack knowledge of the process and the potential career benefits. This guide provides prospective applicants with a complete overview of the application and interview process, the nature of the work involved in serving as a clerk, and the life-long career benefits provided. The author is a graduate of Yale Law School and former Director of its udicial Clerkship Counseling and Programs. She has also served as Project Director of the National Judicial Clerkship Study sponsored by the National Association for Law Placement (NALP) and the American Bar Association (ABA), and authored the report on the 2000 National Judicial Clerkship Study.

Wheeler, Russell. **A New Judge's Introduction to Federal Judicial Administration**. Washington, DC: Federal Judicial Center, 2003. 1 vol. (20 pp.).
Cost: Free of charge; a limited number of print copies are available from the FJC upon request (see address in Appendix A); or as a free download at: http://www.fjc.gov
A invaluable overview of the administrative structure of the federal judicial system and of the organizations and agencies that are responsible for the nonjudicial business of the courts, including the Judicial Conference of the United States, the Administrative Office of the U.S. Courts, the Federal Judicial Center, and the Circuit Judicial Council, among others. An essential read for any federal judge or administrative staff member who wishes to understand the organizational structure and operations of federal judicial administration. The Federal Judicial Center was created by act of Congress in 1967 for the purpose of conducting research on federal court operations and procedures and for providing orientation and continuing education for judges and court personnel.

Whinery, Leo H., Theodore P. Roberts and Robert B. Smith. **The Judge's Evidence Bench Book**. St. Paul, MN: Thomson Reuters West, 2004. 1 vol. (1,275 pp.). Looseleaf format.
Cost: Out-of-print; (2014).
Based on the **Federal Rules of Evidence**, this volume is designed to assist judges in making proper evidentiary rulings in trials and preliminary hearings. In addition to the text of the **Federal Rules of Evidence**, it includes official comments, analysis, illustrative examples, summaries of relevant cases, checklists, and cross references. Also useful for trial lawyers dealing with evidentiary issues.

Additional titles on Judges and Judicial Conduct are available from the following publishers: American Judicature Society, American Law Institute, Bloomberg BNA Books, Gordon Press, Greenwood Publishing Group, William S. Hein & Co., National Judicial College, Oxford University Press, Thomson Reuters West, University Press of Florida, West Academic. See Appendix B for addresses and telephone numbers

Juries and Jury Instructions

Beale, Sara Sun, William C. Bryson, James E. Felman, and Michael J. Elston. **Grand Jury Law and Practice.** 2d ed. St. Paul, MN: West (Clark Boardman Callaghan), 1997-date. 2 vols. Looseleaf format. Annual supplementation.
Cost: $340; supplementation: 1995: $115; 1996: $131; 1997: $195; 1998: $65; 1999: $70; 2000: $76; 2001: $90; 2002: $100; 2003: $100; 2004: $108; 2005: $114; 2006: $71; 2007: $79; 2008: $89; 2009: $105.50; 2010: $116; 2011: $126.50; 2012: $138; 2013: $63; **Monthly Assured Print Price (APP):** $19/$228.
This work is a response to the rapid growth in the volume of litigation over grand jury proceedings, particularly the conduct of prosecutors before grand juries. The authors include Sara Sun Beale, Professor of Law at Duke University School of Law and William C. Bryson, Deputy Solicitor General, U.S. Department of Justice. Following an historical overview of grand jury proceedings, the authors examine the role of the grand jury in state and federal practice, grand jury reports, selection of the grand jury, organization and administration, conduct of proceedings, the issuance of the indictment, secrecy of proceedings, parallel civil and criminal proceedings, grants of immunity to witnesses, prosecutorial misconduct, abuse of the grand jury, judicial review, and grand jury offenses. The authors provide extensive citations to applicable cases, statutes, treatises and law review articles to aid in further research. Although this work consists of two looseleaf volumes, the base text is comparable in length to the single volume **Federal Grand Jury**, also published by West.

Brenner, Susan W. and Lori E. Shaw. **Federal Grand Jury: A Guide to Law and Practice**. 2d ed. St. Paul: Thomson Reuters West, 2006-date. 2 vols. Annual pocket parts.
Cost: $262; supplemetation: 2007: $44; 2008: $60; 2009: $70.50; 2010: $96; 2011: $85; 2012: $94; 2013: $101; supplementation to 1st ed.: 1998: $62; 1999: $35; 2000: $38; 2001: $45; 2002: $53.50; 2003: $0; 2004: $108; 2005: $70; 2006: new edition ($170); **Monthly Assured Print Price (APP):** $12/144.
A thorough and practical guide to practice before federal grand juries written by a professor of law at the University of Dayton and an Assistant United States Attorney for the Southern District of Ohio. The authors place the federal grand jury in its historical context and examine such topics as concurrent federal and state proceedings, selection of grand jurors, convening of the grand jury, the role of the prosecutor, grand jury secrecy, disclosure of proceedings and evidence, securing evidence, securing testimony, parallel proceedings, indictments, grand jury abuse and ethical issues in grand jury proceedings. Appendices include forms, and tables of statutes, court rules, and cases. The text is proceeded by both guidelines for grand jury practice and checklists for the major procedural stages in grand jury proceedings. It is also adequately supported with citations to primary law and relevant secondary sources. The volume also includes a WESTLAW Electronic Research Guide with examples drawn specifically from relevant criminal cases and statutes. Although contained in only one volume, this treatise is comparable in length to the competing two-volume **Grand Jury Law and Practice** (West), and a better value. Supplementation is also likely to be less costly.

Eades, Ronald W. **Jury Instructions in Automobile Actions.** 4th ed. Charlottesville, VA: LexisNexis, 2004-date. 1 vol. (809 pp.) Annual pocket part.
Also available as eBook.
Cost: $145 (print or ebook); supplementation: 2005: $20; 2006: $26; 2008: $86; 2009: $100; 2010: $102; 2011: $110; 2012: $116; 2013: $128; 3d ed.: 1997: $32.50; 1998: $35; 1999: $40; 2000: $50; 2001: 0; 2002: $60; 2003: $20; 2004: $70; 2d ed.: 1993: $25; 1994: 0; 1995: $35; 1996: 0;
Provides the litigator and judge with over 200 instructions on the kinds of issues which are likely to arise in the course of automobile negligence cases. Written in language comprehensible to the layperson. Also available as a part of Michie's **Jury Instructions for Personal Injury and Tort Cases** library (4 vols.) which sells for $461, a savings over the single volume prices.

Eades, Ronald W. **Jury Instructions in Commercial Litigation**. Charlottesville, VA: LexisNexis, 1996-date. 1 vol. (411 pp.) Annual pocket part.
Cost: $178 (print or eBook); supplementation: 2010: $95; 2011: $103; 2012: $110; 2013: $113.
A comprehensive collection of jury instructions covering various areas of commercial litigation successfully given by judges and followed by juries in actual commercial trials. Each instruction is accompanied by an explanation to the layman which translates complex legal concepts into common language.

Eades, Ronald W. **Jury Instructions in Real Estate Litigation.** 2d ed. Charlottesville, VA: LexisNexis, 2006-date. 1 vol. Looseleaf format. Periodic supplemetation.
Cost: $174 (print or eBook); supplementation: 2009: $85; 2010: $88; 2011: $93; 2012: $96; 2013: $102; 1st ed.: 1993: $25; 1995: $35; 2000: $35; 2001-2005; 2006: new edition.
Provides the litigator and judge with over 250 instructions from all fifty states on those issues which are likely to arise in the course of real estate litigation, including easements, covenants, deeds, adjoining Landowners, boundaries, adverse possession, dedication, vendor and purchaser, landlord and tenant, eminent domain, waters, nuisance, trespass, waste, real estate brokers, premises liability, ejectment, ouster, slander, and more.

Eades, Ronald W. **Jury Instructions on Damages in Tort Actions.** 5th ed. Newark, NJ: LexisNexis, 2003-date. 1 vol. Looseleaf format. Annual pocket part.
Cost: $163 (print or eBook); supplementation: 2004: $99; 2005: 0; 2006: $55; 2007: $58; 2008: $63; 2009: $72; 2010: $75; 2011: $84; 2012: $90; 2013: $92; 4th ed.: 1999: $30; 2000: $35; 2001: $39; 2002: $49; 3d edition: 1994: $15; 1995: $25; 1996: $29.75; 1997: $35;
Provides the litigator and judge with over 200 instructions on the kinds of issues which are likely to arise in the course of tort actions. Each instruction is supported by case law, **ALR** annotations, and law review articles. Written in language comprehensible to the layperson. Also available as a part of Michie's four-volume **Jury Instructions for Personal Injury and Tort Cases** library which sells for $414, a savings of $95 over the single volume prices.

Eades, Ronald W. and Graham Douthwaite. **Jury Instructions on Medical Issues.** 6th ed. Charlottesville, VA: LexisNexis, 2004-date. 1 vol. (850 pp.) Annual pocket part.
Cost: $144 (print or eBook); supplementation: 2005: $50; 2006: $55; 2007: $57; 2008: $62; 2009: $72; 2010: $74; 2011: $86; 2012: $92; 2013: $95; 5th ed.: 1993: $20; 1994: $35; 1995: $40; 1996: $40; 1997: 0; 1998: $45; 1999: $50; 2000: $55; 2001: $60; 2002: $65; 2003: $48.
Provides the litigator and judge with over 200 instructions on the kinds of issues which are likely to arise in the course of medical litigation, including patient experimentation, childbirth, anesthesiology, pre-existing conditions, and allergies . Written in language comprehensible to the layperson. Also available as a part of Michie's **Jury Instructions for Personal Injury and Tort Cases** library (4 vols.) which sells for $507.00, a savings of over $150.00 over the single volume prices.

Eades, Ronald W. **Jury Instructions on Products Liability.** 4th ed. Charlottesville, VA: LexisNexis, 2006-date. 1 vol. (500 pp.) Annual pocket part.
Cost: $162 (print or eBook); supplementation: 2000: $35; 2001: $44; 2002: $44; 2003: $46; 2004: $48; 2005: $51; 2006: 0; 2007: $50; 2008: $54; 2009: $63; 2010: $69; 2011: $75; 2012: $80; 2013: $83; 2d edition: 1994: $15; 1995: $20; 1996: $33.50; 1997: $37.50; 1998: $44.
Provides the litigator and judge with complete coverage of the types of issues which are likely to arise in the course of a products liability trial. Each instruction is supported by case law, **ALR** annotations, and law review articles. The instructions themselves are written in a style which can be comprehended by the layperson. Also available as a part of Michie's **Jury Instructions for Personal Injury and Tort Cases** library (4 vols.) which sells for $461.00, a savings of $144 over the single volume prices.

Fox, Elyse. **Jury Instructions Drafting Manual and Resource Guide**. Charlotte, NC: Legal Information Services, 2010. 1 vol. (175 pp.). Looseleaf format. Annual updates.
Cost: $85 (includes priority shipping) (2014).
Jury instructions are a form of guidance by which a judge explains to a jury the rules of law they are to apply to the facts of the case in which they are charged with rendering a verdict. These instructions may be general, preliminary, trial, final and supplementary, and may be delivered at verious stages during the course of the trial. Instructions may be written by the judge, with or without the assistance or suggestion of counsel for each side. Failure to correctly instruct the jury on the law may result in an appeal, followed by a remand for new trial. Most federal and state jurisdictions have pattern instructions, also referred to as standard, uniform, suggested or approved jury instructions, whose use is designed to provide uniformity from trial to trial. Jury instructions, which evolve with changes in the law, have shown a marked tendency in recent years to replace legalese with plain English. This valuable reference guide provides users with an explanation of the various kinds of jury instructions, both pattern and non-pattern, guidelines for drafting jury instructions, a bibliography of jury instructions for the federal circuits and states, and federal and state topical jury instructions. It also includes a list of selected jury instruction organizations and conferences, and concludes with a selective bibliography, webliography and resource guide to articles on the subject of jury instructions. The author/compiler received her J.D. from the University of Michigan and M.L.S. from Simmons College. As law librarian, she has published extensively on legal research and bibliography, and is the author or editor of six publications, including **How to File Looseleaf Services**, and the **Legal Information Manegement Index**. This is an essential addition to any legal research collection.

Lieberman, Joel D. and Bruce D. Sales. **Scientific Jury Selection**. Washington, DC: American Psychological Association, 2007. 1 vol. (261 pp.).
Cost: $39.95 ($39.95 to members); from $28.47 on amazon.com (2014)
This volume reviews the most common techniques used to select jurors and subjects these methods to the latest social scientific-based evaluation.
For example, while research findings suggest that trial lawyers are able to influence trial outcomes through the use of voir dire and the use of consultants, the evidence is unclear as to whether these results are actually better than mere chance. Indeed some social scientists have concluded that techniques used by attorneys during jury selection are not very effective and often have minimal effect on the jury's verdict. The authors also examine the use of community surveys, the influence of demographic factors, personality and attitudes, in court questioning of prospective jurors, in court observations of nonverbal behavior, the overall effectiveness of scientific jury selection, additional trial consulting techniques that aid jury selection, ethical and professional issues in scientific jury selection, and the future directions for scientific jury selection, including such proposed reforms as the licensure of consultants and restrictions on voir dire questions and preemptory challenges. The volume includes an extensive list of scholarly references to cited research, a table of authorities, author and subject indexes. This is essential reading for any trial lawyer regularly involved in selecting jurors.

Lundquist, Weyman I. and Alyson Pytte, eds. **The Litigation Manual: Jury Trials**. 3d ed. Chicago: American Bar Association, Section of Litigation, 2008. 1 vol. (403 pp.).
Cost: $89.95; $74.95 to members; from $22.40 on amazon.com (2014).
In the view of Thomas Jefferson, the right to trial by jury is more important than the right to vote and is an indispensable instrument of public justice. Part of the criticism directed at the jury system is a product of the notion that jury trials contribute to the backlog of cases and increase the burden on the courts. Also, various forms of alternative dispute resolution have emerged as alternatives to civil jury trials. Nevertheless, the legal community and general public are overwhelmingly in favor of the system of trial by jury as the fairest method of determining guilt or innocence in criminal trials, or arriving at a just and correct result in civil cases. This volume is, in part, a response to criticisms of the jury system from academicians, politicians, and the general public. The thirty-seven articles in this anthology, reprinted from the ABA's *Litigation Journal*, provide a defense of jury trials in civil cases. The articles are grouped under the following general topics: Should You Have a Jury Trial?; Understanding Today's Jurors; Finding the Juror You Want; Instructing the Jury; Winning Over the Jury; Telling the Jury a Story; Trying the Jury

Case: Courtroom Techniques; Opening Statements; Witnesses; Complex Cases; Closing Argument; and After the Trial. Among the most interesting articles are those that consider: How Jurors Respond to Complex Cases, What You May Not Say to the Jury, and Impeaching Jury Verdicts. The articles, which are characterized by their clarity and general readability, provide an excellent resource for both trial attorneys and those who want a better understanding of the jury system.

Michie's Jury Instructions on CD-ROM. Charlottesville, VA: LexisNexis. 1 CD-ROM. Folio. Updated periodically.
Cost: $758 per year (2014).
A collection of more than 5,000 jury instructions covering virtually every conceivable type of action in both federal and state courts. Employs the Folio search engine.

O'Malley, Kevin E., et al. **Federal Jury Practice and Instructions--Civil and Criminal.** 5th/6th ed. St. Paul, MN: Thomson Reuters West, 1999-date. 26 vols. A full set consists of volumes 1, 1A of the 6th ed. and volumes 2, 2A, 2B, 3, 3A, 3B, 3C of the 5th edition. Annual pocket parts. Package includes 12 circuit-specific pattern jury instruction pamphlets. [formerly Devitt and Blackmar]
Cost: $1,259; supplementation: 1994: $47; 1995: $52.50; 1996: $59; 1997: $119; 1998: $75; 1999: $90.50; 2000: $81; 2001: $366; 2002: $139.50; 2003: $159; 2004: $178; 2005: $196.50; 2006: $305; 2007: $243.50; 2008: $538.50; 2009: $481; 2010: $529; 2011: $578; 2012: $1,222; 2013: $909; **Monthly Assured Print Price (APP):** $79/$948.
Judges of the federal district courts have an obligation to instruct the jury as to the law of the case and provide reasonable guidance on the accompanying facts. This of one of the most important functions performed by the trial justice. While the judge has wide discretion in instructing the jury, he or she must observe Civil Rule 51 and Criminal 30 governing jury instruction procedure. Counsel in federal cases may, under the rules, submit requests for instructions at the close of evidence or when the court directs. The court must also advise counsel of proposed action upon these requests prior to closing arguments to the jury in order to allow them to tailor their remarks to the judge's instructions. This four-volume set provides both a discussion of the federal jury practice and instructions, and specific pattern or model instructions in a wide variety of civil and criminal matters. Each pattern instruction is accompanied by a discussion of relevant case law supporting the use of the instruction with numerous specific examples from the various federal circuits. The authors includes Judge William Lee (vol. 1), Kevin E. O'Malley (vols. 1A, 2, 2A), and Jay Grenig (vols. 3, 3A). Critical terms are clearly defined, again with examples of definitions applied in the federal courts. The free-standing supplement contains tables of cases and statutes, subject index, and a WESTLAW Electronic Research Guide to jury instructions. An indispensable resource for the federal litigator.

Personal Injury Valuation Handbooks. St Paul, Thomson Reuters West (LRP), 1964-date. 9 vols. Looseleaf format. Individual pamphlets replaced as necessary.
Cost: $1,175.04 per year; **Monthly Assured Print Price (APP):** $97.92/$1,175.04 (2014).
This service provides up-to-date coverage of personal injury verdicts organized by part of the anatomy. Individual entries summarize the case and provide the following data: court, attorneys, final demand, final offer, total verdict, compensatory damages, past medical expense claimed, filing date, and trial date. There are also pamphlets covering current award trends, and pamphlets for individual states which can be purchased as an add-ons. The most complete service of its kind for tracking jury verdicts by injury. Acquired by Thomson Reuters in 2011.

Representation of Witnesses Before Federal Grand Juries. National Lawyers Guild Staff and Rikki J. Klieman. 4th ed. St. Paul, MN: West (Clark Boardman Callaghan), 1999-date. 2 vols. Looseleaf format. Supplemented twice annually.
Cost: $1,599; supplementation: 2000: $252; 2001: $292; 2002: $354; 2003: $378; 2004: $410; 2005: $428; 2006: $461; 2007: $621; 2008: $621; 2009: $1,067.50; 2010: $753; 2011: $821; 2012: $895; 2013: $1,038; 3d ed.: 1995: $165; 1996: $210; 1997: $210; 1998: $220; **Monthly Assured Print Price (APP):** $108/$1,296.
Unlike other works dealing with grand jury practice, this two-volume treatise is designed to assist attorneys called upon to represent witnesses before federal grand juries. As a project of the National Lawyers Guild, the authors address both real and potential abuses of the grand jury which, they claim, are not uncommon and are not limited to political dissenters. The chapters provide discussion of grand jury procedure, the subpoena power, injunction and intervention, selection and composition, the statutory and caselaw framework of federal grand juries, constitutional protections, testimonial privileges, grand jury secrecy, abuse of the grand jury process, prosecutorial misconduct, contempt, perjury, false statements, obstruction of justice, post-contempt remedies, and contempt prisoners. Appendices include sample pleadings, the **ABA Prosecution Function Standards**, sample correspondence between the government and a cooperating witness, Justice Department Guidelines for Government Attorneys, Rule 6 of the **Federal Rules of Criminal Procedure**, a glossary, table of cases, and subject index.

Cost Saving Tips: Twice-annual supplementation brings the annual cost of updating this set to more than $1,000. The non-cumulative form of supplementation makes it more advantageous to drop the standing order and buy another set at periodic intervals. In the interim, the user can employ primary sources, digests and citators to update the text. Avoid the **Monthly Assured Print Price** which just assures you high annual supplementation costs.

Sand, Leonard B. et al. **Modern Federal Jury Instructions.** New York: Matthew Bender & Co., 1984-date. 5+ vols. Looseleaf format. Supplemented several times annually (24 times between 1984 and 1995). Also on CD-ROM and eBook.
Cost: $2,321 (with annual subscription); renewal: 1995: $633.50 (price frozen since 1992); 1996: $664; 1997: $664; 1998: $700; 1999: $730; 2000: $750; 2001: $803. 2002: $860; 2003: $903; 2004: $975; 2005: $1,034; 2006: $1,076; 2007: $1,141; 2008: 2008: $1,209; 2009: $1,306; 2010: $1,371; 2011: $1,440; 2012:

$1,526; 2013: $1,633; 2014: $1,782; CD-ROM: $2,656; renewal: 1998: $665; 1999: $730; 2000: $780; 2001: $835; 2002: $860; 2003: $903; 2004: $975; 2005: $1,043.00; 2006: $1,085.00; 2007: $1,171; 2008: $1,271; 2009: $1,373; 2010: $1,469; 2011: $1,578; 2012: $1,730; 2013: $1,851; 2014: $2,060.40; eBook: $2,110; renewal: 2014: $1,782.

Intended primarily for the use of attorneys who must prepare requests to charge a jury, and judges who must read and consider these requests, this set provides a wide variety of both criminal and civil pattern jury instructions. Borrowing heavily from other published sources, the text of each of the instructions is accompanied by relevant case authorities and a succinct commentary which is designed to inform and instruct the user in the legal issues involved. According to the authors, each recommended charge satisfies the following criteria: (1) it is an accurate statement of the law, (2) it is expressed in language which is comprehensible to the lay juror; and (3) it is as brief as the two criteria will permit. More than just a collection of pattern jury instructions, this reference work provides practitioners with a consider statement of each element in a civil or criminal proceeding which must be proven or disproven at trial. It is also useful to attorneys who must evaluate the probable success of a given case and those who need to determine the elements of a particular cause of action which should be alleged in a particular case. The cases cited under the authority headings provide notice to those interested in tracking trends in the various federal circuits. Includes five numbered volumes (1, 1A, 2, 3, 4) and two paperbound volumes, published periodically, containing pattern jury instructions in civil and criminal matters from the 5th, 6th, 7th, 8th, 9th and 11th circuits and the Federal Judicial Center. A well-organized and lucid reference tool. The instructions are comprehensive and the commentaries clear and concise. The most thorough work of its kind on the market.

Cost Saving Tips: If you don't require the entire set, consider purchasing only the civil or criminal volumes as your practice requires. If you do purchase the hard copy, you can always drop the standing order and purchase a new set at some future date. Remember that, unlike the print, the CD-ROM version will time expire if you do not maintain the subscription, leaving you with nothing to show for your expense.

Singer, Amy and Pat Maloney Sr. **Trials and Deliberations Inside the Jury Room**. Revised Edition. St. Paul, MN: Thomson Reuters West, 1999-date. 5 vols. Looseleaf format. Annual supplementation.

Cost: $975; supplementation: 2000: $211; 2001: 0; 2002: $255; 2003: $303; 2004: $339; 2005: $375; 2006: $499; 2007: $519; 2008: $1,147; 2009: $559.50; 2010: 0; 2011: $670.50; 2012: $737.50; 2013: $818.

Based on the results of thousands of mock trials, this five-volume work provides unique insights into the deliberations of jurors in a wide variety of civil and criminal matters. Amy Singer, president and founder of Trial Consultants, Inc., a firm providing jury research and trial consultation to litigators, has drawn upon the results of thousands of mock trials and simulations in providing the tools for predicting how a jury is likely to think and feel on every important issue. She is joined by veteran plaintiff's attorney Pat Maloney who provides practical recommendations at the end of each chapter. Volumes 1-3 cover a variety of personal injury actions, including cardiology, improper diagnosis, infection, air crashes, drunk drivers, security failure, slip and fall, toxic torts, motorcycles, and much more. Volume four covers various types of business litigation, including contracts, banking, insurer's bad faith, securities, and antitrust. Volume five contains criminal and miscellaneous litigation, including eminent domain, drugs, assault by a police officer, defamation, premises liability, discrimination, civil rights, and disparagement. The content includes the actual conversations of jurors, jurors' perceptions of what issues are important, specific voir dire questions, discussion of desirable and undesirable juror personality types, convincing opening statements and closing arguments, recommended direct and cross-examination, and a variety of visual aids.

Cost Saving Tip: In the current legal publishing environment, even titles related to litigation techniques are vulnerable to supplementation exploitation. This work clearly falls into that camp. The wise consumer will treat this work as a monograph and drop the supplementation. To update, simply buy another set at some future date if you feel it necessary, thus cutting your maintenance costs substantially.

Starr, V. Hale and Mark McCormick. **Jury Selection.** Rev. 4th ed. New York: Wolters Kluwer Law & Business, 2010-date. 1 vol. (430 pp.) Looseleaf format.

Cost: $335; supplementation: 2010: $135; 2011: $144; 2012: $154; 2013: $179; 2d ed.: 1993: $30; 1994: $50; 1995: $53; 1996: $55; 1997: $55; 1998: $57; 2000: $94; 3d ed.: 2001: $126; 2002: $138; 2003: $157; 2004: $167; 2005: $175; 2006: $184; 2007: $196; 2008: $210; 2009: 0.

This volume combines a summary of the substantive and procedural law regarding jury selection with a complete analysis of the latest scientific methodology regarding the actual selection process. V. Starr Hale, who holds a doctorate in communications, is a leading expert in the field of jury selection and a founding member of the American Society of Trial Consultants. She has more than 15 years experience as a forensic consultant to trial lawyers. Her co-author is a practicing attorney in the state of Iowa and former member of the Iowa Supreme Court. The authors' coverage includes a history of the law of juries, including the history of the right to trial by jury, the role of statutes, rules and case law in jury selection, and current issues and developments in jury law. The heart of the volume, however, is dedicated to an exhaustive examination of the process and factors involved in selecting jurors, including chapters on pre-trial investigation, the issues study and community attitude assessment, change of venue, trial simulation, demographic analysis of the jury panel, voir dire mechanics and techniques, nonverbal communications (including appearance, voice, and movement), and jury selection in the courtroom. The Afterward includes a discussion of the evaluation and use of trial consultants. The Appendices include a variety of sample documents to be used in the jury selection process including juror questionnaires, community attitude study and change-of-venue training manuals, sample affidavits, basic outlines and voir dire questions for civil and criminal matters, and basic voir dire questions for all types of cases.

Cost Saving Tips: Drop the standing order to the supplementation and re-purcase every 3-4 years, if necessary. As a general rule, the general guidance provided by this volume will suffice, without the need for supplementation.

Wagner, Ward, Jr. **Art of Advocacy: Jury Selection**. New York: Matthew Bender & Co., 1980-date. 1 vol. Looseleaf format or eBook.
Cost: $430; supplementation: 1994: $103; 1995: $103; 1996: $103; 1997: $103; 1998: $110; 1999: $117; 2000: $125; 2001: $134; 2002: $144; 2003: $152; 2004: $152; 2005: $164; 2006: $184; 2007: $207; 2008: $230; 2009: $255; 2010: $284; 2011: $295; 2012: $328; 2013: $351; 2014: $382.
This one-volume practice guide presents both general principles of jury selection and specific strategies to be applied in particular types of cases. Of the book's 26 chapters, two are devoted to general voir dire techniques and the law of jury selection. The remaining 24 address jury selection in a variety of personal injury actions, from medical malpractice and rape to diving injuries and construction site accidents. The lead author, President of the West Palm Beach firm of Wagner, Nugent, Johnson, Roth, Kupfer & Rossin is joined by twenty contributing authors. Each of the specific chapters contains a sample opening of the voir dire, and sample questions covering each stage of the trial proceeding, with commentaries. The volume also includes model questions, bibliography, and index.

Cost Savings Tips: Drop the supplementation and simply re-purchase at periodic intervals when you want a more up-to-date text.

Additional titles on Juries and Jury Instructions are available from the following publishers: American Bar Association, American Judicature Society, Wolters Kluwer Law & Business, Matthew Bender, Greenwood Publishing Group, Lawpress, LexisNexis, Rand Corporation, Thomson Reuters West, Westwood Publishing Co. See Appendix B for addresses and telephone numbers.

Labor and Employment Law

Amar, Dipanwita Deb. **The Labor and Employment Lawyer's Job: a Survival Guide**. Chicago: American Bar Association, 2007. 1 vol. (152 pp.).
Cost: $59.95 ($44.95 to Section members) (2014).
This introductory guide to the new employment or labor lawyer provides basic orientation regarding common job assignments and best methods of proceeding, including the precise questions to be asked. Divided into three parts, the volumes addresses (1) Preliminary Matters -- issues that might arise before an employment matter becomes a court action; (2) Employment Litigation -- major issues that frequently recur, but are not always recognized or property treated; and (3) Substantive Law -- areas that you are likely to encounter in the practice of labor and employment law. An invaluable guide to the novice, and experienced, labor and employment lawyer. Dipanwita Deb Amar is a director with the firm of Howard Rice Nemerovski Canady Falk & Rabkin in San Francisco and a member of its Labor & Employment Group. Her practice involves defending employers in federal and state court in cases involving discrimination, harassment, wrongful termination (including whistleblower claims) and other state law torts.

Basic Patterns in Union Contracts. 14th ed. Washington, DC: Bloomberg BNA Books, 1995. 1 vol. (135 pp.). Paperbound.
Cost: $35 (2014).
An invaluable survey of the major types of union contract provisions and the frequency with which they appear in collective bargaining agreements. Based on a sampling from the Bloomberg BNA files of more than 4,000 collective bargaining agreements, this volume presents a cross-section of industries, unions, number of employees covered, and geography. Provisions are grouped under the following categories: amendment and duration, discharge, discipline and resignation, insurance, pensions, grievances and arbitration, income maintenance, hours and overtime, holidays, layoff, rehiring and work sharing, leave of absence, management and union rights, seniority, strikes and lockouts, union security, vacations, wages, working conditions: safety and health, discrimination. Reprinted from **BNA's Collective Bargaining Negotiations and Contracts.**

Better, Maurice B. **Contract Bargaining Handbook for Local Union Leaders**. Washington, DC: Bloomberg BNA Books, 1993. 1 vol. (336 pp.). Softcover. No supplementation.
Cost: $35; from $32.91 on amazon.com (2014).
Designed as a tool for local labor union leaders and negotiators, this volume can also provide insights for employer representatives as well. It is designed to assist negotiators in recognizing their bargaining strengths and weak-nesses, finding the best strike and non-strike alternatives, making effective use of third party mediators, and avoiding impasses. The author discusses both traditional and win-win negotiations in situations ranging from manufacturing, retail, and service industries to the governmental sector.

Bornstein, Tim and Ann Gosline, general editors. **Labor and Employment Arbitration.** New York: Matthew Bender & Co., 1988-date. 2 vols. Looseleaf format. Supplemented approximately twice a year.
Cost: $1,252 (includes annual subscription); renewal: 1995: $229.50 (price frozen since 1992); 1996: $241; 1997: $241; 1998: $255; 1999: $270; 2000: $290; 2001: $310; 2002: $332; 2003: $349; 2004: $366; 2005: $395; 2006: $423; 2007: $456; 2008: $492; 2009: $531; 2010: $559; 2011: $587; 2012: $628; 2013: $672; 2014: $733; eBook: $1,133; renewal: 2014: $733; CD-ROM available as a part of Matthew Bender's **Employment Law Library**: 2014: $6,158 per year.
Written by a team of more than 70 practicing lawyers, law professors and professional arbitrators, this three-volume treatise thoroughly examines the practice and procedure of labor and employment arbitration. There is detailed attention to each stage in the arbitration process, including discovery and the duty to disclose, arbitration advocacy, witnesses, evidence, medical evidence, the use of arbitral subpoenas, tripartite arbitration, and union rights. Chapters also examine the issue of arbitrability and the general principles of contract interpretation, discipline, discharge and resignation, seniority rights, compensation, benefits, Section 301 actions, external law and judicial review, public sector arbitration, and alternative means of dispute resolution There are also individual chapters devoted to the arbitration of disputes in selected industries, including teachers, police and firefighters, postal service employees, as well as railroad, health care, coal and paper

industry workers. The Appendices include, among other items, the Code of Professional Responsibility for Arbitrators of Labor-Management Disputes, the Labor Arbitration Rules of the American Arbitration Association, and the AAA's Expedited Labor Arbitration Procedures. There is also a table of cases and subject index. This is an ideal resource for those involved in labor or employment arbitration. It provides thorough and scholarly description and analysis of labor arbitration and other forms of employment mediation.

Cost Saving Tips: While the cost of purchasing and updating this set is not unreasonable given the depth of coverage, the cost-conscious attorney may wish to drop the standing order and re-purchase this set at periodic intervals. Updating can be performed using primary sources, Shepard's Citations, West digests, etc. The **Employment Law Library** on CD-ROM includes 13 different employment-related titles at a cost of $6,158 and renewal of $4,681.

Brand, Norman, ed. **Discipline and Discharge in Arbitration**. 2d ed. Washington, DC: Bloomberg BNA Books, 2008. 1 vol. (527pp.).
Cost: $195; from $175.49 on amazon.com; no supplementation to date; 1st ed.: 2001: $65; 2002-2007: 0.
Produced in association with the Committee on ADR in Labor and Employment Law, Section of Labor and Employment Law, American Bar Association, this title is one in a series of volumes which provide legal practitioners with guidance in labor and employment law. This text is an extended discussion of just cause, or the equitable principle by which arbitrators determine whether the discipline or discharge of an employee should be upheld. Following an introductory overview of the subject of arbitration advocacy, the authors address a number of specific contexts in which the theory of just cause may be applied. Specific disciplinary issues discussed include attendance, job performance, refusals to perform work or cooperate, substance abuse, dishonesty and disloyalty, workplace misconduct, off-duty conduct, and union activities. Additional chapters examine evidentiary and procedural considerations, remedies for inappropriate discipline, external law, and finality of awards and court actions. The text is amply supported with citations to labor arbitration and court decisions. The authors include a number of leading arbitrators and mediators. A companion volume to Elkouri and Elkouri's **How Arbitration Works** and an expansion of the standards discussed in Chapter 15 of that work.

Buckley, John F., IV. **ERISA Law Answer Book**. 8th ed. Austin, TX: Wolters Kluwer Law & Business, 2013-date. 1 vol. (various pagings).
Cost: 8th edition: $399; supplementation: 2012: $249; 6th ed.: 2009: 0; 2010: $230; 2011: new ed.
This practical desk reference provides authoritative answers to more than 1,300 key ERISA-related questions with clarity and precision. The questions cover everything from benefit arrangements subject to the ERISA provisions, interpretation of ERISA plans, claims procedures, exhaustion of administrative remedies, notice, reporting and disclosure, plan amendment, assignment, waiver and forfeiture, fiduciaries, plan coverage and participation requirements, benefit accrual and vesting, contributions and benefits, plan funding, distributions, plan disqualification and remediation, COBRA, insurance, actions and remedies, preemption, standard of review, and attorneys' fees, among others. The answers provide detailed analyses of ERISA provisions. There is also extensive coverage of such recent developments as the Pension Protection Act of 2006. Each answer includes citations to relevant cases, statutory or regulatory provisions, IRS Code sections and regulations. An essential tool for those in involved in representation of clients on ERISA-related matters or litigation. The author is a senior attorney on the Public Law team of the National Legal Research Group, where he specializes in civil rights, employment discrimination, and local and state government law. He is author or editor of numerous Aspen titles.

Compensation & Benefits Library [Internet]. Washington, DC: Bloomberg BNA. Internet. Updated continuously.
Cost: $1,817 per year (single user) (2014).
Contains the complete text of BNA's **Compensation & Benefits Guide** together with relevant court decisions, statutes and regulations, including the IRC, ERISA, ADA, FMLA. IRS Revenue Rulings, Revenue Procedures, DOL Advisory Opinions, and IRS publications. The **Guide** portion provides coverage of such issues as compensation, staffing, employment taxes, pensions, health care benefits, and more. Features full text searching, hypertext linking, and interactive forms. An ideal tool for the human resource administrator managing complex benefit programs. Includes a biweekly newsletter in print.

Covington, Robert N. and Kurt H. Decker. **Individual Employee Rights in a Nutshell.** 3d ed. St. Paul, MN: West, 2009. Available from West Academic.
Cost: $41 (2014).
A brief student guide to individual employee rights in the publisher's Nutshell Series by Robert Covington, Professor of Law, Vanderbilt University and Kurt Decker. Adjunct Professor, Widener University School of Law. Chapters cover the developing law of individual employee rights, physical safety, privacy and reputation, discrimination, collective rights, termination of employment, wage and hour regulation, pensions and other employee benefit programs, and general concepts and current issues. Contains selective citations to cases and statutes.

cyberFEDS Complete Library on the Web. Horsham, PA: LRP Publications, 2002-date.
Cost: approx. $2,100 per year (solo practitioner); many other pricing options available depending on customer or agency--call 800-341-7874 for details (2014).
A complete library of federal labor law resources, including the publisher's **Federal Labor Relations Reporter**, **Federal Merit Systems Reporter**, **Federal Pay and Benefits Reporter**, **Federal Equal Opportunity Reporter**, **Quick Star Guides**, daily news updates, **Mentor**, a labor management tool, and a library of case law, statutes, regulations, handbooks, manuals, and more. An economical alternative to subscribing to the individual services.

DelPo, Amy and Lisa Guerin. **The Manager's Legal Handbook**.

7th ed. Berkeley, CA: Nolo, 2014. 1 vol. (528 pp.).
Cost: $49.99; from $31.66 on mazon.com; kindle ed.: $35.85 (2014).
Since its founding in 1971, Nolo has ushered in a revolution in providing self-help legal books to the public, and attorneys as well. Now in its 6th edition, **The Manager's Legal Handbook** provides a comprehensive and easy to understand guide through the maze of employment law and the myriad issues faced by managers in the workplace. Beginning with attention to the hiring process, the authors work their way through issues of compensation and hours, discrimination, personnel basics, time off, privacy, health and safety, unions, independent contractors, trade secrets, handling workplace problems, firing employees, layoffs, and departing workers. Each topic is handled with a keen understanding of the legal issues involved and illustrated with charts of relevant state laws, lessons from the real worlds, frequently asked questions, checklists, legal dos and don'ts, and tests of knowledge (with answers). The appendices include a directory of federal and state employment-related departments and agencies. This is an excellent desktop reference for any business manager. And, unlike the mainstream legal publishers who charge you an arm and leg for supplementation, Nolo posts changes on its web site at no cost: www.nolo.com/back-of-book/ELBA6.html A graduate of the University of North Carolina Law School, author Amy Delpo is an attorney with experience practicing before both federal and state appellate courts and currently a Nolo consulting editor. Lisa Guerin was a staff attorney for the 9th Circuit Court of Appeals before joining Nolo Press as an editor.

Edwards, Marcy, et al. **Freedom of Speech in the Public Workplace**. Chicago: American Bar Association, Section of State and Local Government Law, 1997. 1 vol. (200 pp.). Paperbound.
Cost: Was $16.36, now discounted 50% to $8.13 (2014).
A basic guide to the legal aspects of free speech in the public employment environment written for lawyers who represent employees and employers, as well as elected officials, personnel directors, and union representatives. It includes a consideration of employees First Amendment speech rights, guidelines on employers' restrictions on employees' political activities, whistle blowing, criticism of supervisors, and the role of the First Amendment in issues of race, sex, sexual orientation, and religion. The authors also address speech in schools, public safety and fire protection agencies, as well as privatization and the First Amendment protection afforded independent contractors. Marcy Edwards is a labor and employment law associate with the firm of Seyfarth, Fairweather & Geraldson with experience representing both public and private sector clients.

Eglit, Howard C. **Age Discrimination.** 2d ed. St. Paul, MN: Thomson Reuters West (Clark Boardman Callaghan), 1993-date. 3 vols. Looseleaf format. Annual supplementation.
Cost: $775; supplementation: 1994: $229.50; 1996: $70; 1997: $42; 1998: $105.50; 1999: $132; 2000: $142; 2001: $164; 2002: $103; 2003: $180; 2004: $216; 2005: $237; 2006: $294; 2007: $327; 2008: $364.50; 2009: $372; 2010: $414; 2011: $446; 2012: $486; 2013: $389; **Monthly Assured Print Price (APP):** $57/$684.
The most extensive treatise and practice guide on the market devoted to age discrimination issues. Provides complete discussion and analysis of the Age Discrimination in Employment Act, the Americans with Disabilities Act and the Older Workers Benefit Protection Act. Chapters also analyze the subject of age in American society and workplace, constitutional and other nonstatutory bases for action at the state and federal levels, bars to age discrimination in employment, including federal and state statutes, executive orders and regulations. Covers such procedural matters as the judicial and arbitral forums available, the grievant's, respondent's and decision-maker's roles, remedies, fees and costs. There are extensive citations to relevant primary and secondary sources, including statutes, regulations and excerpts from legislative history documents. The Appendices include the full text of all major statutes and regulations.

Elkouri, Frank and Edna Asper Elkouri. **How Arbitration Works.** 7th ed. Washington, DC: Bloomberg BNA Books, 2012-date. 1 vol. (1,896 pp.). Irregular supplementation.
Cost: $325; ebook: $329.99; no supplementation to date; prior editions supplemented in 1999: $70.00; 2008: $170; 2010: $205.
Long considered to be the leading work in the field, **How Arbitration Works** provides the labor practitioner with an analysis of practice and procedure in the field of labor arbitration. There is a valuable introductory chapter on arbitration and its setting which examines the possible uses for arbitration, compulsory arbitration, arbitration costs and the leading organizations in the field. Chapters also examine in depth such topics as the legal status of arbitration, the scope of labor arbitration, the arbitration tribunal, grievances--the prelude to arbitration, determining arbitrability, arbitration procedures and techniques, evidence, standards for interpreting contract language, the use of substantive rules of law, custom and past practice, management rights, seniority, discharge and discipline, safety and health, employee rights and benefits, and standards in arbitration of interest disputes. The text is heavily documented with references to decisions and orders of the NLRB and the courts, statutes, regulations, books and articles.

Employment Coordinator. St. Paul, MN: Thomson Reuters West (Clark Boardman Callaghan), 1984-date. 17 vols. Supplemented monthly; includes biweekly newsletter.
Cost: $5,912.52; supplementation (renewal): 1997: $1,231.65; 1998: $1,232; 1999: $1,337; 2000: $1,417; 2001: $1,630; 2002: $1,792.50; 2003: $1,820; 2004: $1,848; 2005: $1,940; 2006: $2,115; 2007: $2,283.96; 2008: $2,465; 2009: $2,628.96; 2010: $3,006; 2011: $3.297.96; 2012: $4,713; 2013: $4.632.60; also available as a component of **WestlawNext for Corporate Counsel Plan 3 - Employment and Corporate Counsel Guidance** as Westlaw add-on at $4,740 per year (1 user); A Westlaw subscription is the obviously less expensive choice, particularly when added to a basic subscription. Contact sales representative for details.
This topically arranged looseleaf service provides the user with a clear and concise description and analysis of employment law, updated on a monthly basis. A detailed one-volume index leads the researcher to one of six major subject areas: Benefits, Compensation, Employment Practices, Labor Relations, Personnel Manual, and Workplace Safety. Each subject area

features a Detailed Reference Table of Subjects Discussed which lists each paragraph number and its subtopic. The substantive text includes a number of editorial aids to assist the researcher, including Illustrations, Cautions, Recommendations, and Observations. The text also cites to relevant statutes, regulations, and case law. Federal law is discussed and compared to related state laws and to earlier enactments. All current material is located in the appropriate section of the text. There is no need to consult a separate section. Highly recommended for both the novice and the experienced attorney.

Cost-Saving Tip: The WestlawNext add-on is the obvious better choice as it is priced less than the print subscription alone and includes various employment related tools.

Employment Discrimination Coordinator. St. Paul, MN: West (Clark Boardman Callaghan), 1993-date. 8 vols. Looseleaf format. Updated monthly with biweekly newsletter.
Cost: $4,613.04; renewal: 1998: $1,054; 1999: $1,140; 2000: $1,208; 2001: $1,395; 2002: $1,534; 2003: $1,580; 2004: $1,625; 2005: $1,779; 2006: $1,983.50; 2007: $2,142; 2008: $2,142; 2009: $2,397.96; 2010: $2,614; 2011: $2,849.52; 2012: $3,852.48; 2013: $3,690; also available as a component of **WestlawNext for Corporate Counsel Plan 3 - Employment and Corporate Counsel Guidance** as Westlaw add-on at $4,740 per year (1 user); A Westlaw subscription is the obviously less expensive choice, particularly when added to a basic subscription. Contact sales representative for details.
Reflecting an increase in legal challenges to employment hiring dismissal actions, the eight-volume looseleaf service provides a comprehensive examination of the issues and law of employment discrimination. It includes coverage of both federal and state laws prohibiting employment discrimination in both public and private employment settings, including discussion of such matters as unjust dismissal, wrongful discharge, affirmative action, disciplinary issues, union activities, employment agency involvement, whistle blowing, free speech, administrative and court proceedings. It also provides citations to controlling primary authorities.

Cost-Saving Tip: The WestlawNext add-on is the obvious better choice as it is priced less than the print subscription alone and includes various employment related tools.

Employment Guide [Print and Internet]. Washington, DC: Bloomberg BNA. 1 vol. Updated monthly. Internet updated continuously.
Cost: Print: $1,205; Internet: $1,178 (2014).
A practical guide to the resolution of a variety of employment management issues including those involving hiring to retirement, pay: wages and salaries, employee benefits, rules and discipline, safety and health, and dealing with a union. Includes a brief review of applicable laws and regulations. Each chapter includes four uniform features: overview, policy considerations, model forms and checklists, and sample policies.

Employment Law Deskbook. New York: Matthew Bender & Co., 1989-date. 1 vol. Looseleaf format or eBook. Also available on CD-ROM Employment Law Library.
Cost: $474; supplementation: 1996: $76; 1997: $76; 1998: $80; 1999: $83; 2000: $89; 2001: $95; 2002: $102; 2003: $108; 2004: $113; 2005: $121; 2006: $130; 2007: $140; 2008: $151; 2009: $163; 2010: $183; 2011: $181; 2012: $206; 2013: $220; 2014: $227; eBook: $474; renewal: 2014: $227.
A convenient desktop companion for the employment or labor law specialist or personnel department which provides coverage of such topics as hiring, training, performance evaluations, promotions, wages, hours and competition, terms, conditions and privileges of employment, discipline and discharge, layoffs and reductions in workforce, safety and health, unemployment compensation, workers' compensation, employee benefits law, written employment agreements, common law claims, labor relations, equal employment, affirmative action, drugs and alcohol, record retention, and state labor and employment law. While the emphasis is upon federal law, there is also a summary of significant state employment laws. The text is accompanied by detailed examples, chart summaries, checklists, scope notes and commentary, illustrations, and sample documents and forms. Written by employment law experts at the Baltimore, MD firm of Shawe & Rosenthal. Also available on Authority CD-ROM.

Employment Law Library [CD-ROM]. New York: Matthew Bender & Co. One disc. Updated quarterly. Available for Windows. Search Engine: Folio.
Cost: $6,158 (includes annual subscription); renewal: 1998: $1,780; 1999: $1,850; 2000: $1,980; 2001: $2,119; 2002: $2,268; 2003: $2,382; 2004: $2,501; 2005: $2,676; 2006: $2,864; 2007: $3,083; 2008: $3,371; 2009: $3,641; 2010: $3,823; 2011: $4,014; 2012: $4,255; 2013: $4,553; 2014: $5,068.38.
The complete library includes the following Matthew Bender titles: Employment Discrimination, Wages and Hours: Law and Practice, Americans with Disabilities Act: Employee Rights and Employer Obligations, Unjust Dismissal, Employment Law Deskbook, Employee Rights Litigation: Pleading and Practice, Drafting Employment Contracts & Termination Agreements, Americans with Disabilities Act: Public Accommodations & Commercial Facilities, Labor and Employment Arbitration, Employment Screening, Occupational Safety and Health Act, Employee Benefits Guide, and National Labor Relations Act: Law & Practice. Various combinations of titles may be selected by the subscriber.

The Employment Law SourceBook: Volume 1: A Compendium of Employment-Related Laws and Policy Documents. Chicago: American Bar Association, 2013. 1 vol. (489 pp.) Paperbound.
Cost: 2013 Edition: $249.95; $199.95 to members; from $79.23 on amazon.com (2014).
A collection of employment-related federal statutes and regulations, including the Age Discrimination in Employment At of 1967 (29 U.S.C. § 621 et seq.), the Americans with Disabilities Act of 1990 (42 U.S.C. § 12101 et seq.); the Equal Opportunity Commission Procedural Regulations (29 CFR § 1601 et seq.), the Equal Pay Act of 1963 (29 U.S.C. § 206 et seq.), Executive Order No. 11246 regarding discrimination by contractors and subcontractors, the Fair Labor Standards Act of 1938 (29 U.S.C. § 201 et seq.), the Family and Medical Leave Act of 1993 (29

U.S.C. § 2601 et seq.), the Immigration Reform and Control Act of 1986 (Pub.L. 99-603, 100 Stat. 3359), the Lilly Ledbetter Fair Pay Act of 2009 (P.L. 111-2, 123 Stat. 5), the Occupation Safety and Health Act of 1970 (29 U.S.C. § 651 et seq.), the Portal to Portal Act of 1947 (29 U.S.C. § 251 et. Seq.), the Rehabilitation Act of 1973 (29 U.S.C. § 701 et seq.), Title VII of the Civil Rights Act of 1964 ((Pub.L. 88-352, 78 Stat. 241; 42 U.S.C. §2000e et seq.), and the Worker Adjustment and Retraining Act of 1988 (29 U.S.C. 210l et seq.).

Employment Law Treatise Library on LoisLawConnect. New York: Wolters Kluwer Law & Business.
Cost: $540.00 per year (solo practitioner) (2014).
This treatise package covers such subjects as employment contracts, covenants not to compete, employee benefits, employee dismissal, employment policiesand immigration law. Titles include **Employment Law Answer Book, Employee Dismissal: Law and Practice, Immigration Law in the Workplace, Drafting and Revising Employment Policies, Employment Relationships: Law & Practice, Covenants Not to Complete,** and forms and checklists from a variety of employment law titles. A cost-effective alternative to buying all these titles individually in print format.

The Family and Medical Leave Act. Ossip, Michael J. and Robert M. Hale, Editors-in-Chief. Arlington, VA: Bloomberg BNA Books, 2006. 1 vol. (929 pp.). Hardbound.
Cost: $515.00; supplementation: 2011: $225; 2012: 0; 2013: $245.
The Family Medical Leave Act (FMLA) (Pub.L. 103-3; 29 U.S.C. sec. 2601; 29 CFR 825) was signed into law by President Bill Clinton on February 5, 1993. It was enacted "to balance the demands of the workplace with the needs of families, to promote the stability and economic security of families, and to promote the national interests in preserving family integrity." The law requires businesses of 50 or more employees to provide job-protected unpaid leave for qualified medical and family reasons. These reasons include personal or family illness, military service, family military leave, pregnancy, adoption, or the foster care placement of a child. The FMLA is administered by the Wage and Hour Division of the United States Department of Labor. This volume provides detailed guidance to employers and employees in complying with the provisions of the Act, applicable Department of Labor regulations, federal case law, and DOL opinion letters that have interpreted FMLA provisions. This volume covers the history structure and administration of the FMLA, the coverage of employers, eligibility of employees for leave, entitlement of employees to leave, the length and scheduling of leave, notice and information requirements, pay and benefits during leave, restoration rights, the interrelationship with other laws, employer practices and collective bargaining agreements, interference, discrimination and retaliation claims; and enforcement, remedies and other litigation issues. The appendices include the text of the Act, applicable Department of Labor regulations, FMLA forms, 120 FMLA opinion letters (with conclusions), a summary of state family and medical leave laws, a table of cases, and subject index. An essential tool for corporate counsel and human resources departments, employees, and others impacted by the Act. The text contains exhaustive citations to federal case law, statutes, and regulations. More than forty attorney authors and editors contributed to the final product, each an expert in his or her field.

Federal Equal Opportunity Reporter (FEOR). Horsham. PA: LRP Publications, 1979-date. 3 vols. Looseleaf format. Twenty-two biweekly issues per year; back volumes from 1979 to present also available for additional cost. Also available on Internet as a part of **cyberFEDS Complete Library on the** Web (see above listing).
Cost: print: $1,575 per year; or as part of **cyber Feds Complete Library on Web**: approx. $2,100 per year (call for pricing for your situation) (2014).
This three-volume guide to the creation and operations of a successful EEO program, including the leading decisions rendered by the Equal Opportunity Commission and federal courts.

Federal Labor Laws Pamphlet. St. Paul, MN: Thomson Reuters West, 1974-date. 1 vol. Paperbound.
Cost: 2013 Edition: $192; ProView eBook: $192 (2014).
Contains the complete text of Federal labor law as found in Title 29 of the **United States Code**. The appendix contains the text of more than twenty-five related labor laws. For the specialist in labor law, this volume is a convenient and low-cost alternative to purchasing the entire **U.S. Code**.

Federal Labor Relations Reporter (FLLR). Horsham. PA: LRP Publications, 1970-date. 3 vols. Looseleaf format. Forty-eight weekly issues per year; back volumes from 1970 to present also available for additional cost. Also available on Internet as part of **cyberFEDS Complete Library on the Web** (see above listing).
Cost: No longer available in print, but as part of **cyber Feds Complete Library on Web**: approx. $2,100 per year (call for pricing for your situation) (2014).
This three-volume looseleaf service is a complete source for decisions of the Federal Labor Relations Authority, the Federal Service Impasses Panel, administrative law judges, labor arbitrators, and the federal courts. The Web service contains a complete federal labor law library.

Federal Merit Systems Reporter (FMSR). Horsham. PA: LRP Publications, 1979-date. 3 vols. Looseleaf format. Forty-eight weekly issues per year; back volumes from 1979 to present also available for additional cost. Also available on Internet as a part of **cyberFEDS Complete Library on the** Web (see above listing).
Cost: print: $1,475 per year; or as part of **cyber Feds Complete Library on Web**: approx. $2,100 per year (call for pricing for your situation) (2014).
This three-volume looseleaf service reports decisions of the Merit Systems Protection Board and federal courts. The weekly case updates provide in-depth analyses of such employment issues as absence, accommodation, discrimination, leave, management rights, performance, settlement agreements, etc.

Federal Pay and Benefits Reporter (FPBR). Horsham. PA: LRP Publications, 1974-date. 2 vols. Looseleaf format. Twelve monthly issues per year; back volumes from 1974 to present also available for additional cost. Also available on Internet as a part of **cyberFEDS Complete Library on the** Web (see above listing).
Cost: No longer available in print, but as part of **cyber Feds Complete Library on Web**: approx. $2,100 per year (call for pricing for your situation) (2014).
This two-volume looseleaf service provides the text of Comptroller General decisions pertaining to employee entitlement issues, decisions rendered under the General Accounting Office's authority to review federal employees' legal entitlements related to travel, leave, relocation, and compensation.

Finkel, Noah H., Brett C. Bartlett and Andrew M. Paley. **Wage and Hour Collective and Class Litigation**. New York: Law Journal Press, 2012. 1 vol. (912 pp.). Looseleaf format.
Cost: print and online: $415; print, online & ebook only: $445 (2014).
The Fair Labor Standards Act of 1938 (FLSA) (29U.S.C.A. § 201 et seq.), also called the Wages and Hours Act, was the first action by Congress to regulate wages and hours under interstate commerce. It established a minimum wage of 25 cents per hour, to be increased to 40 cents within seven years. It requires employers to pay covered employees who are not otherwise exempt at least the federal minimum wage and overtime pay of one-and-one-half-times the regular rate of pay. For nonagricultural operations, it restricts the hours that children under age 16 can work and forbids the employment of children under age 18 in certain jobs deemed too dangerous. For agricultural operations, it prohibits the employment of children under age 16 during school hours and in certain jobs deemed too dangerous. The Act is administered by the Employment Standards Administration's Wage and Hour Division within the U.S. Department of Labor. Since the late 1990s, the federal courts have witnessed a significant increase in the number of collective actions filed under FLSA, from 1,890 in 2000 to 7,028 in 2010, not including actions filed at the state level. Wages and hours lawsuits are those in which one or more workers assert that they have not been fully compensated for their labor in accordance with legal requirements. Broadly speaking, this proliferation in the number of lawsuits is a result of a heightened realization, among the plaintiff's bar, of the potentially lucrative fees resulting from wages and hours collective and class litigation, particularly among the fertile grounds of clients previously subject to the white-collar exemption. This volume is arguable the best single-volume treatment of wages and hours collective litigation written from a defense perspective. It provides detailed practical guidance on the law, tactics and strategies that can be effectively employed by defense counsel, while serving as an invaluable countervailing resource to plaintiffs' counsel. More than seventy attorneys and other professionals with the Wage & Hour Litigation Practice Group the firm of Seyfarth Shaw contributed to its production, addressing everything from the genesis of a wage and hour lawsuit, to defense of a FLSA collective action, decertification, discovery issues, arbitration agreements, collective action trials, settlement/mediation, the white collar exemption, independent contractors and joint employers, minimum wage, and deductions from wages, and much more. Each chapter is exhaustively footnoted with citations to supporting authorities in the statutes and federal and state case law. This is an essential resource for any attorney defending wage and hour lawsuits or attorney bringing such actions. The editors are Co-Chairs of Seyfarth Shaw's Wage & Hour Litigation Practice Group.

Cost-Saving Tip: Buy and let lapse for 1-2 years, or more, to avoid high supplementation costs. Annual supplementation is sufficient for any secondary source. Use as a starting place for research only. If you purchase every two years, you will cut your annual cost in half, while going only one year between updates.

Finkin, Matthew W. **Privacy in Employment Law**. 4th ed. Washington, D.C.: Bloomberg BNA Books, 2013-date. 1 vol. (1,300 pp.). Annual supplementation.
Cost: $445; no supplementation to date; 2009: 3d edition; supp.: 2010: $165; 2011: $175; 2012: $185; 2d ed.: 2003: $85; 2004: $105; 2005: $125; 2006: $130; 2007: $145; 2008: $155; 1st ed.: 1998: $105; 1999: $135; 2000; $145; 2001: $155; 2002: 0.
The law of privacy in the workplace is governed by an often confusing array of statutory provisions and court decisions. This work provides a coherent overview of these disparate sources of law governing such areas as medical screening and testing, drug, alcohol and tobacco screening and testing, psychological screening and testing, interview questions, questionnaires, credit checks, references, monitoring employee performance and conduct, control of employees, polygraphy and lie detection, drug testing, use of tobacco, alcohol and unlawful products, and access to personnel records. Part III includes a number of sample business forms. The volume also includes the full text of key federal and state laws. Matthew Finkin, the Albert J. Harno Professor of Law at the University of Illinois, is an international authority on individual employment rights and the author of numerous texts in the field of employment law.

Franckiewicz, Matthew M. **Winning at the NLRB**. 2d ed. Washington, DC: Bloomberg BNA Books, 2009-date. 1 vol. (1,039 pp.). Hardcover. Generally not supplemented between editions.
Cost: $315; no supplementation to date; 1st ed.: 1997: $50; 1998: $50; 1999: $75; 2000: 0; 2001: $95; 2002: $155; 2003: $135; 2004: 0; 2005: $155; 2006-2007: 0.
This is a practical guide for the labor law practitioner who has substantial interaction with the National Labor Relations Board. Intended neither as a treatise on substantive law nor a procedural manual, this is a book of practical advice and opinion which is designed to assist the attorney in achieving favorable outcomes before the NLRB or, more commonly, before its Regional Offices. The author's intent is to be neither pro-union nor pro-management, but «pro-practitioner.» It is intended as companion to **The Developing Labor Law**, BNA's two-volume substantive law treatise. Individual chapters examine the people of the NLRB, information sources, Regional Office investigation and adjudication of unfair labor practice cases, investigation, filing charges, winning investigations, settling, deferral to arbitration, winning trial tactics, procedural aspects of back pay and compliance, substantive back pay law and implications, winning representation cases, elections, post-election proceedings, and other proceedings involving the

NLRB. Despite the practical thrust of this volume, it is more than adequately accompanied by citations to relevant cases, statutes, regulations, and secondary sources. The Appendices include an index of General Counsel's Memoranda, a list of areas to explore in preparing for an unfair labor practice investigation, a list of areas to explore at representation case hearings, charge language, an NLRB Directory, and form cross-references. Also includes tables of cases and a subject index. The author, a graduate of the Massachusetts of Technology and the University Law School, served as attorney and trial specialist with the NLRB, investigating hundreds of unfair labor practice charges and serving as a hearing officer and decision writer in more than 100 representation cases. Since 1987, he has worked as an arbitrator, both on a permanent and an ad hoc basis, and has written extensively in the field.

Friend, Mark A. and James P. Kohn. **Fundamentals of Occupational Safety and Health**. 5th ed. Rockville, MD: Government Institutes, Inc., 2010. 1 vol. (477 pp.).
Cost: $79; from $60.02 on amazon.com; kindle ed.: $42.74 (2014).
In 1970, Congress enacted the Occupational Safety and Health Act which created both the National Institute for Occupational Safety and Health (NIOSH) and the Occupational Safety and Health Administration (OSHA), a branch of the U.S. Department of Labor. This handbook provides a complete and up-to-date overview of the laws and regulations governing occupational safety and health, and discusses the issues faced by professionals in the field. Designed as a reference for both students and professionals, this volume provides practical information regarding technology, management, and regulatory compliance issues, including information regarding organizing, staffing, directing, and evaluating the system. This book also addresses OSHA's required written programs for general industry, information on hazardous materials, workplace violence, and the threat of terrorism. Includes a directory of resources, including safety and health associations, First Responder organizations, and state and federal agencies. Mark A. Friend is professor of Safety and Chair of the Department of Applied Aviation Sciences at Embry-Riddle Aeronautical University, Daytona Beach, Florida. The late James Kohn was associate professor of Industrial Technology at ECU and president of OccuSafe Service Corporation, a Certified Safety Professional, Certified Industrial Hygienist, and Certified Professional Ergonomist.

Frolik, Lawrence A. and Kathryn L. Moore. **Law of Employee Pension and Welfare Benefits**. 3rd ed. New Providence, NJ: LexisNexis, 2012. 1 vol. (639 pp.). Available in hardbound, looseleaf, or eBook formats.
Cost: book: $174; looseleaf: $138; eBook: $104; kindle ed.: $83.20 (2014).
This law school casebook is designed to introduce students and other readers to the breadth and depth of employee benefits law. Employee benefits represent a high percentage of payroll costs ($1.5 trillion paid in 2009), as well s significant tax expenditures because such benefits generally receive favorable income tax treatment, either as a result of the failure to tax, or to defer taxation on what would otherwise be currently taxable income. The book opens with a brief history of employee benefits plans and their role in society. Succeeding chapters examine the full range of employee pension plans, welfare benefits, the regulation of employee benefit plans, preemption, plan administration, enforcement issues, nondiscrimination rules, and plan amendment and termination. Each chapter is accompanied by illustrative excerpts of court decisions, statutes, and law review articles, as well as questions and problems for classroom use. Lawrence A. Frolik is Professor of Law, University of Pittsburgh School of Law, an expert on elder law, and author of numerous books in the field, including the ERISA Litigation (BNA) *The Law of Later-Life Health Care and Decision Making* (ABA). Kathryn L. Moore is the Everett H. Metcalf, Jr. Professor of Law, University of Kentucky College of Law, where she teaches property law, land use planning, employee benefits, and state and local taxation. Her research focuses on employee benefits and Social Security reform.

Garren, Brent, ed. **How to Take a Case Before the NLRB.** 8th ed. Washington, DC: Bloomberg BNA Books, 2008-date. 1 vol. (943 pp.) Periodic new editions.
Cost: $565 (new edition); supplementation: 2009: 0; 2010: 0; 2011: $245; 2012-13: 0; 7th ed.: 2002: $145; 2003: $175; 2004: 0; 2005: $215; 2006-2007: 0; 6th edition: 1997: $125; 1998: $125.
The definitive handbook to procedures before the National Labor Relations Board, this volume is a step-by-step guide through the NLRB's regulations and Casehandling Manual, including representattion proceedings, unfair labor pracxtice proceedings, supplemental proceedings, and records and filing requirements. The authors provide advice and guidance on a number of current issues and developments, including how to determine the appropriate bargaining units in the health care industry, the new right to file reply briefs, alterations in summary judgment proceedings, the filing of appeals, filing by FAX, requesting extensions, and much more. There are numerous cross references to NLRB regulations, sample forms, and flow charts outlining procedures before the Board, and citations to decisions before the NLRB and federal courts. Published since 1949, the book is now revised and updated by specialists from the ABA's Section of Labor and Employment Law.

Cost Saving Tips: The cost of a number of casebound volumes published by Bloomberg BNA Books has risen significantly in recent years, reflecting the niche position assumed by these titles. The budget-conscious purchaser is advised to evaluate all available options before purchasing some of these high-priced single-volume works. On the hand, they are of high quality, and not overly supplemented, as with other publishers.

Gould, William B. IV. **A Primer on American Labor Law**. 5th ed. New York; Cambridge University Press, 2013. 1 vol. (448 pp.). Paperbound.
Cost: $42.99; from $29.95 on amazon.com; kindle: $23.52 (2014).
This descriptive overview of labor law in the United States is intended as an introduction for non-specialists in the field, including representatives of labor and management, foreigners, neutral parties involved in labor dispute resolution, and attorneys in general practice who occasionally represent a union or

company.

The author provides a useful overview of the state of labor law before the advent of modern (i.e. New Deal) legislation, the National Labor Relations Act (1935), and related labor law, unfair labor practices, the establishment of the collective bargaining relationship, including and recognition of bargaining units, the economic pressures and bargaining tactics that exist in established relationships, remedies that exist for those engaged in union activities, the Labor Reform Bill of 1978, and the so-called "Employee Free Choice Bill of 2009, dispute resolution in the established relationship, the duty of fair representation, collective bargaining in the public sector (which is not, by the way, governed by the National Labor Relations Act), and public interest labor law. The author is the Charles A. Beardsley Professor Law, Emeritus at Stanford Law School. A prolific scholar, he brings more than forty years experience in labor-management relations to the task, including service as Chairman of the National Labor Relations Board from 1994-1998. He is the author of ten books and over 60 law review articles.

Granof, Michael H., Jay E. Grenig, and Moira J. Kelly. **How to Cost Your Labor Contract**. 2d ed. Arlington, VA: Bloomberg BNA Books, 2011. 1 vol. (229 pp.). Paperbound.
Cost: $145 (2014).
Over the past 40 years, the costing of labor contracts has been impacted by a number of developments including: (1) a sharp reduction in the number private sector unionized employees and a substantial increase in the number of unionized public employees; (2) the greater ease of conducting complex calculations with the aid of technology; (3) the increased significance of labor costs; (4) legacy costs, including pensions and benefits, have become extraordinarily important in the private sector; and (5) concessions and attempts to keep businesses from moving overseas or closing have become the subtext of many negotiations.. Conducting an honest and accurate assessment of the costs of a labor contract is an essential prerequisite to labor negotiations in the current labor environment. For most organizations, labor costs, both hourly and salaried, are the single most important cost of doing business. This volume represents the only comprehensive approach to costing available in one place. ts primary aim is to assist executives charged with the responsibility of determining the financial consequences of changes in compensation schemes. The chapters include: laying the groundwork for financial analysis; preparing a costing worksheet; evaluating wages and other paid time; evaluating other contract provisions; using the deferred cash flow model; costing proposals during negotiations; using an interest-based negotiation style in economic components of bargaining; alternative dispute resolution: negotiation, mediation, fact finding, and arbitration; and using costing information in negotiating, mediating, fact finding, and arbitration. Lead author, Michael Granof, who authored the first edition of this book in 1973, is Professor of Accounting, University of Texas at Austin.

Grievance Guide. 13th ed. Washington, DC: Bloomberg BNA Books, 2012. 1 vol. (676 pp.). Softcover.
Cost: $100 (2014).
Arbitrators typically apply the standard of "just cause" when ruling on the appropriateness of disciplinary actions taken against employees. This revised handbook addresses the application of this standard to various forms of workplace conduct and is designed to provide guidance to all parties involved in the resolution of labor grievances. Organized into more than 50 common areas of grievance, it provides summaries of arbitrators' rulings as an aid to anticipating likely outcomes. Topical coverage embraces such current issues as off-duty misconduct, sexual harassment, drug testing, AIDS, horseplay, as well as those dealing with such basic areas as discharge and discipline, leave of absence, promotions, vacations, union rights, checkoff, and health and welfare benefits. Each topical area includes Policy Guide summaries which highlight important issues and distinctions, and provide detailed examples and guidelines to aid in evaluating one's position. Each case summary is accompanied by a citation to the full decision appearing in Bloomberg BNA's **Labor Arbitration Reports**, a component of the publisher's **Labor Relations Reporter** service.

Haggard, Thomas R. **Understanding Employment Discrimination**. 2d ed. New York: LexisNexis, 2008. 1 vol. (332 pp.). Paperbound.
Cost: $45; eBook: $36; from $39 on amazon.com; kindle ed.: $28.44 (2014).
This succinct summary of the law government employment discrimination provides an overview and outline of the constitutional, statutory, regulatory, and decisional authorities that prohibit such conduct by employers. The leading constitutional constraint upon such conduct is found in the equal protection clause of the U.S. Constitution. This is reinforced by a number of federal statutes including the Civil Rights Act of 1964, the Civil Rights Acts of 1866 and 1871,the Equal Pay Act of 1963, the Americans with Disabilities Act, and Executive Order No. 11246. The author also addresses such subjects as the role of the 11th Amendment; individual disparate treatment; systemic disparate treatment; disparate impact; special problems relating to race, sex, national origin, and religious discrimination; retaliation; discrimination by labor unions and employment agencies; Title VII procedure; filing and processing charges; litigation; and remedies, among others. A part of the LexisNexis Understanding Series, this volume is intended chiefly as a supplementary text for law school courses in labor and employment law. The text is supported by selective citations to legal authorities. The author is a Distinguished Professor of Law Emeritus at the University of South Carolina School of Law.

Hardin, Patrick, Editor-in-Chief. **The Developing Labor Law: The Boards, The Courts, and the National Labor Relations Act**. 6th ed. Washington, DC: Bloomberg BNA Books, 2012-date. 2 vols. (3,582 pp.) Annual supplementation.
Cost: $710; supplementation: 2013: $210; prior eds.: 2007: $175; 2008: $185; 2009: $190; 2010: $200; 2911: $205; 4th ed.: 2002: $165; 2003: $175; 2004: $195; 2005: $210; 3d ed.: 1994: $75; 1995: $95; 1996: $115; 1997: $135; 1998: $175; 1999: $205; 2000: $125; 2001: new edition.
This essential guide to the National Labor Relations Act and the labor decisions of the NLRB and U.S. Supreme Court was written by more than 400 labor attorneys representing both management and labor. Comprehensive and scholarly, the coverage includes the legal rights and duties of employers, employees and unions, as well as procedures and remedies under the NLRA.

Hogan, Roscoe B., B. Ben Hogan and Robert D. Moran. **Occupational Safety and Health Act.** New York: Matthew Bender & Co., 1977-date. 3 vols. Looseleaf format. Supplemented approximately twice annually.
Cost: $1,299 (includes annual subscription); annual renewal: 1995: $310.50 (price frozen since 1992); 1996: $326; 1997: $326; 1998: $340; 1999: $355; 2000: $380; 2001: $407; 2002: $436; 2003: $458; 2004: $481; 2005: $515; 2006: $552; 2007: $596; 2008: $644; 2009: $696; 2010: $731; 2011: $768; 2012: $814; 2013: $871; 2014: $950; eBook $836; renewal: 2014: $621; also available as a part of Matthew Bender's **Employment Law Library** CD-ROM (see above): 2014: $6,158 per year.
Originally authored by the late Roscoe B. Hogan and Robert D. Moran, this two-volume treatise is now updated by the author's son B. Ben Hogan. With the thoroughness typical of most Matthew Bender treatises, this work addresses both the substantive and procedural issues involving workplace safety and health. Volume one gives attention to the Act's legislative history and jurisdiction over employees, employer defenses to OSHA enforcement, nature of OSHA inspections, and general regulations. Volume two addresses health and safety standards in the mining and construction industries, among others, OSHA enforcement, and private litigation employing OSHA standards. Volume three treats employment discrimination, recordkeeping and reporting requirements, regulation of chemicals, the bloodborne pathogens standard, ergonomics, and state OSHA programs and OSHA-type laws. The text is thoroughly documented with citations to cases, statutes and regulations. An excellent resource for the labor attorney or those involved in workplace safety litigation.

Human Resources Library [Internet]. Washington, DC: Bloomberg BNA. Updated continuously. Subscription includes the weekly **Bulletin to Management** newsletter.
Cost: $2,353 (2014).
An impressive human resources management tool for ensuring compliance with federal and state laws and regulations, this CD-ROM contains the full text of BNA's multi-volume **Policy and Practice Series**. The subscription also includes print subscriptions to the weekly **Bulletin to Management**, the biweekly **Fair Employment Practices Summary of latest Developments**, a variety of periodic special reports and surveys, and interactive government forms.

Kahn, Steven C. et al. **Legal Guide to Human Resources.** St. Paul, MN: Thomson Reuters West, 1995-date. 1 vol. Looseleaf format and ProView eBook. Originally published by Warren, Gorham & Lamont.
Cost: $1,170; ProView eBook: $1,073; supp.: 1995: $120; 1996: $129; 1997: $140; 1998: $164; 1999: $191; 2000: $198; 2001: $224; 2002: $132; 2003: $345; 2004: $336; 2005: $362; 2006: $410; 2007: $508; 2008: $509; 2009: $572; 2010: $688; 2011: $679; 2012: $747; 2013: $859; **Monthly Assured Print Price (APP):** $85/$1,020.
A well organized guide to the laws and regulations affecting human resources management and practices. An ideal desk-top companion for the legal human resources director or corporate legal counsel involved in employment issues. This one-volume looseleaf reference covers a wide range of legal issues, each of which is supported with citations to cases, statutes, regulations, and administrative manuals. Chapters cover employee selection and EEO; affirmative action programs; discrimination in the workplace; performance appraisals; training, promotion and transfer; employment at will; discipline, termination and layoffs; employee privacy and recordkeeping; occupational safety and health; union representation of employees, employer unfair labor practices; union unfair labor practices, strikes, and boycotts, collective bargaining, compensation, and retirement and other benefit plans. Sample forms and letters accompany each chapter. The Appendix contains brief summaries of selected state employment laws. Also contains a table of cases and subject index.

Cost-Saving Tip: This title is typical of the manner in which Thomson Reuters West prices its products. Supplementation costs, already high to begin with, are increased at double-digit rates annually, in this case 15% between 2012 and 2013. The savvy consumer will drop the standing order to supplemented legal treatises and treat them like monographs. You still need to Shepardize or KeyCite all authorities. The supplemented legal treatise is nothing more than a cash cow for the publisher, but you don't have to get milked.

Kearns, Ellen C., ed. **The Fair Labor Standards Act**. 2d ed. Arlington, VA: BNA Books, 2010. 2 vols. with 2012 supplement. Hardcover.
Cost: $755; supplementation: 2012: $265; 2013: $270.
Enacted in 1938, the Fair Labor Standards Act (FLSA) (29U.S.C.A. § 201 et seq.) was the culmination of decades of government efforts to regulate working conditions under interstate commerce. It established minimum wage rates, overtime pay eligibility, recordkeeping, and child labor standards that affected full-time and part-time workers both in the private sector and in federal, state, and local governments. Prior to its enactment, the Supreme Court wrestled over whether it could regulate hours and wages without violating the constitutional doctrine of liberty of contract. Similarly, state legislatures engaged in a balancing act between the preservation of individual liberties and the enactment of minimum standards to protect workers. Since the date of original enactment, the Act has been amended numerous times and subject to court interpretation. This exhaustive two-volume treatise explores every facet of the Fair Labor Standards Act. Volume one explores the history of the Act and its precedents, the operations and functions of the Department of Labor, coverage of the Act, white collar exemptions affecting executive, administrative and professional employees, agricultural exemptions, special certificates, determination of compensable hours worked, determinations of overtime compensation, government employment, child labor, homework, hot goods provisions, retaliation, and recordkeeping. Volume two examines Department of Labor enforcement and remedies, litigation issues, collective actions, and hybrid FLSA/state law class actions. Appendices include the text of the Act, the Department of Labor Coefficient Table for computing extra half-time for overtime, exemptions under the Act, tables of cases and Code of Federal Regulations provisions, and subject index. This massive reference work addresses a wide range of specific issues that arise under the purview of the Act, including such things as travel time from one job site to another within the course of the working day. In each instance, the text is supported with voluminous citations to case law, statutory provisions,

regulations, Department of Labor policy documents, and administrative opinions. An essential tool for any labor lawyer or attorney representing employers, labor unions, government entities, or private parties who wishes to understand the precise applications of specific provisions of the Act. Editor-in-Chief Ellen C. Kearns a managing partner at Constangy, Brooks & Smith, LLP, Boston, MA, where she represents management in labor and employment issues.

Kozak, Barry. **Employee Benefit Plans**. Durham, NC: Carolina Academic Press, 2010. 1 vol. (592 pp.). Paperbound.
Cost: $60.00; from $57 on amazon.com (2014).
There are three primary categories of employee benefits that benefits professionals generally should understand: (1) retirement benefit plans; (2) health and welfare benefit plans; and (3) executive compensation and equity programs. The primary emphasis of this volume is directed to retirement benefit plans, with only one chapter each devoted to health and welfare benefit plans, and executive compensation. The coverage of retirement benefit plans includes an overview of the benefits that employers can offer to their employees, basic tax concepts, the Employee Retirement Income Security Act of 1974 (ERISA), qualified retirement plans, defined contribution plans and defined benefit plans, funding plans, vesting and accruals, annual testing, distributions, the role of the IRS, labor rights and protections in ERISA plans, written plan documents, EROSA causes of action, reporting and disclosure, plan terminations, and the role of the Department of Labor. Additional chapters are devoted to a consideration of the basics of executive compensation; and health and welfare benefit plans, Social Security benefits and individual retirement accounts, ethics issues, career advice essays, and public policy of an aging population. The Appendices contain a primer of Law 101 concepts for non-law students, ERISA and Code organizational charts, ERPA Learning objectives and mapping, a table of statutes and regulations, table of cases and index. The substantive chapters include excerpts of relevant Treasury, Labor and other regulations. Barry Kozak is an attorney, Enrolled Actuary, employee benefits professional, a Chartered Financial Consultant, and professor at the John Marshall and DePaul University law schools, where he teaches classes in employee benefits, income tax, elder law and compensation law. Designed as a law or business school textbook, this volume can also be of value to those pursuing programs in actuarial or human resources management.

Labor Relations Reporter. Washington, DC: Bloomberg BNA, 1937-date. 19 vols. Updated weekly. Looseleaf service. Also available on Internet.
Cost: $9,122 (complete print service); also available in subsets and various combinations. See your sales representative for further details.
A complete weekly looseleaf service providing current coverage of all aspects of labor and employment law with permanent bound case reports. The set includes a **Master Index** (2 v.), **Labor Relations Expeditor** (2 v.), **Analysis/ News Background Information** (1 v.), **Decisions of the Boards and Courts** (1 v.), **Labor Arbitration and Dispute Settlements** (1 v.), **State Labor Laws** (2 v.), **Wages and Hours Cases** (1 v.), **Wages and Hours Manual** (2 v.), **Fair Employment Practices Cases** (1 v.), **Fair Employment Pacifies Manual** (3 v.), **Individual Employment Rights Cases** (1 v.), **Individual Employment Rights Manual** (1 v.), and **Americans with Disabilities Cases** (1 v.). The subscription also includes bound volumes, and digest/indexes for **Labor Arbitration Decisions**, **Labor Relations Reference Manuals** (**Practices**), **Fair Employment Practices Cases**, **Wages and Hours Decisions**, **Individual Employment Rights Cases**, and **American with Disabilities Cases**. A thorough reference service covering both for the lawyer or firm specializing in labor and employment law. Provides complete coverage of both state and federal law in labor-management relations, labor arbitration, wages and hours, fair employment practices, individual employment rights and disabilities law. Employs a classification which allow the researcher to locate similar cases through a series of cumulative digests. Decisions appearing initially in looseleaf form are preserved in permanent bound volumes.

Cost Saving Tip: Given its hefty price tag, this service is designed for the attorney or law firm with a labor and employment law specialization. Information is both thorough and timely; however, you must decide if your potential usage justifies a service with weekly updating. If not, a labor law treatise with less frequent supplementation may be a more appropriate purchase. You need to think twice about purchasing this service if your usage is likely to be infrequent, particularly if it is already available at your local public law library.

Labor and Employment Law Resource Center [Internet] Washington, DC: Bloomberg BNA.
Cost: Core: $4,585; includes the following modules (one user): Labor: $4,367; Employment: $5.570; Employment & Safety: $6,580; Labor & Employment: $8,599; Labor, Employment & Safety: $9,608; also available in subsets and various combinations. See your sales representative for further details (2013).
This comprehensive CD-ROM product contains the full text of the 19-volume **Labor Relations Reporter** and more than 70,000 full-text court decisions from its six component services: **Labor Relations Reference Manuals**, **Wages and Hours Cases**, **Fair Employment Cases**, **Labor Arbitration Cases**, **Individual Employment Rights Cases**, and **Americans with Disabilities Cases.** It also includes digest decisions of the NLRB, tribunal and union listings, biographies of arbitrators, finding aids, reference manuals, the Analysis/News & Background of the **LRR**, the **Fair Employment Practices Summary of Latest Developments** newsletter, and the **Individual Employment Rights** newsletter. Features full-text searching and hypertext linking. For fuller description of the content of this product, see the entry for the **Labor Relations Reporter** below.

Labor Law Library. Riverwoods, IL: Wolters Kluwer Law & Business (CCH), 1934-date. 19 vols. Looseleaf service. Updated weekly.
Cost: **Labor Relations:** print (7 v.): $4,229; online: inquire; **Wages-Hours Reporter:** print (2 v.): $1,667; Internet: inquire; **Labor Arbitration Awards:** print (1 v.): $2,548; Internet: inquire; **Employment Practices Guide:** print (5 v.): $2,283; Internet: inquire; **Accommodating Disabilities Business Management**

Guide: print (3 v.): $873; and Internet: inquire; **Accommodating Disabilities Decisions**: print (only): $873. Contact your sales representative for further details regarding online pricing and special discounts.
This weekly looseleaf service covers all major areas of labor and employment law, including both court and administrative decisions, wages and hours laws and cases, NLRB decisions, employment practices decisions, and arbitration awards. **The Labor Law Library** includes the following components: **Labor Relations**, **Wages-Hours Reports**, **Labor Arbitration Awards**, **Employment Practices Guide**, **Accommodating Disabilities Business Management Guide**, and **Accommodating Disabilities Decisions**. The individual components may be purchased separately if you wish to cut costs and don't require the full service. The CD-ROM and Internet versions also include archives of decisions not available with the current print service.

Lareau, N. Peter, et al. **Labor and Employment Law.** Conklin, New York: Matthew Bender, 2003-date. 11 vols. Looseleaf format. Supplemented approximately four times annually. Also available as vols. 18-18I of the publisher's **Business Organizations** set. Also available on the Internet.
Cost: $3,054 (includes annual subscription); annual renewal: 1995: $865 (price frozen since 1992); 1996: $907; 1997: $907; 1998: $955; 1999: $990; 2000: $1,060; 2001: $1,134; 2002: $1,214; 2003: $1,275; 2004: $998; 2005: $1,078; 2006: $1,154; 2007: $1,246; 2008: $1,346; 2009: $1,454; 2010: $1,527; 2011: $1,603; 2012: $1,715; 2013: $1,835; 2014: $2,003; eBook: $2,777; renewal: 2014: $2,003.
This is unquestionably the most exhaustive and detailed labor law treatise on the market. The team of authors, headed by N. Peter Lareau provides a thorough description and analysis of labor law from both an historical and a practical perspective. There is a discussion of each of the major labor laws and their role in the administration and regulation of industrial relations. The well-written text is fully supported by citations to relevant primary authority, including cases, statutes, legislative history documents, and a variety of secondary sources, including histories, treatises and scholarly articles. Chapter coverage encompasses labor law, employment discrimination, the Americans with Disabilities Act, pensions and benefits, family and medical leave, wages and hours, occupational safety and health, labor and employment arbitration, employment at-will, privacy, and employment contracts, and other issues. The Appendices include the full text of all major labor laws, including the Americans with Disabilities Act. This is an indispensable resource for the labor law specialist. The text is thorough and supported by exhaustive citations and notes. Formerly Kheel, **Labor Law**.

Cost Saving Tips: The periodic re-purchase of this work can provide considerable savings for the attorney who uses it as a springboard for further research and not as the last word on matters of labor law. Buying a new set every three years will result in significant savings over maintaining a standing order.

Larson, Arthur and Lex K. Larson. **The Law of Workmen's Compensation.** New York: Matthew Bender & Co., 1952-date. 12 vols. Looseleaf format. Supplemented approximately three times annually. Authority CD-ROM includes no-cost online updating via LEXIS-NEXIS.
Cost: $5,399 (includes annual subscription); annual renewal: 1995: $1,558.50 (price frozen since 1992); 1996: $1,635; 1997: $1635; 1998: $1,720; 1999: $1,790; 2000: $1,920; 2001: $2,054; 2002: $2,116; 2003: $2,222; 2004: $2,333; 2005: $2,520; 2006: $2,621; 2007: 2,778; 2008: $3,000; 2009: $3,180; 2010: $3,180; 2011: $3,212; 2012: $3,324; 2013: $3,557; 2014: $3,882; CD-ROM: $6,322; annual renewal: 1998: $1,640; 1999: $1,790; 2000: $1,920; 2001: $2,054; 2002: $2,198; 2003: $2,308; 2004: $2,423; 2005: $2,593; 3006: $2,697; 2007: $2,912; 2008: $3,174; 2009: $3,428; 2010: $3,599; 2011: $3,779; 2012: $4,006; 2013: $4,286; 2014: $4,771; eBook: $4,587; renewal: 2014: $3,628.
Although a few competitors have appeared upon the scene, this work remains the classic and definitive work on the subject of workers' compensation. Its author, the late Arthur Larson, was the James B. Duke Professor of Law at Duke University and former Under Secretary of Labor from 1911-1933. Originally published in 1952, the work is now updated by his son Lex K. Larson. President of Employment Law Research, Inc. and a Senior Lecturer at Law at Duke University Law School. This is an exhaustive treatise on the law and practice governing workplace injuries and the rules governing the awarding of cash and medical benefits to the injured workers. The set examines the nature and historical origins of workers compensation, the nature and definition of workplace injuries, specific inclusions or exemptions, disability and personal injury benefits, dependency and death benefits, the exclusiveness of the compensation remedy, employer misconduct, third party actions, adjective law, conflict of laws, insurance, and the relation to other kinds of wage-loss protections. The text is thoroughly supported with citations to relevant cases, with indications of those decisions in which **Larson** is cited by the court. Includes 9 volume of substantive text and two volumes containing the Index and Table of Cases. A virtual necessity for the attorney specializing in workers compensation.

Cost Saving Tips: The periodic re-purchase of this work can provide considerable savings for the attorney who uses it as a springboard for further research and not as the last word on matters of workers compensation law. Buying a new set every three years will result in a considerable savings over the three-year period. If you do not require the exhaustive coverage of the 11-volume work, consider purchasing the 3-volume desk edition, either by itself or as an updating medium for the larger edition.

Larson, Arthur and Lex K. Larson. **The Law of Workmen's Compensation--Desk Edition.** New York: Matthew Bender & Co., 1972-date. 3 vols. Looseleaf format. Also available on CD-ROM and Internet.
Cost: $1,443 (includes annual subscription); annual renewal: 1995: $419.00 (price frozen since 1992); 1996: $440; 1997: $440; 1998: $465; 1999: $485; 2000: $520; 2001: $556; 2002: $573; 2003: $602; 2004: $632; 2005: $683; 2006: $711; 2007: $754; 2008: $814; 2009: $863; 2010: $968; 2011: $1,045; 2012: $903; 2013: $903; 2014: $1,055; CD-ROM: $1,769; annual renewal: 2014: $1,356.60: ebook: $1,312; renewal: 2014; $1,055.
This is an abridgment of the 12-volume treatise with fewer citations to case law. However, even this abridgment has greater coverage than any competitive product.

Cost Saving Tips: Beware: both the print and CD-ROM of this product experienced a 29% price increase between 2013 and 2014 (the eBook is slightly cheaper). It is still, however, a cost-effective alternative to the complete **Larson** at a little more than one-third the initial cost. You can buy the CD-ROM version of the Desk Edition to update a lapsed full set. Remember that the CD-ROM subscription must be maintained or you will eventually lose your ability to access the text due to the built-in time expiration feature.

Larson, Lex K. **Employment Discrimination.** 2d ed. New York: Matthew Bender & Co., 1994-date. 10 vols. Looseleaf format. Supplemented three times annually. Authority CD-ROM subscription includes no-cost online updating via LEXIS-NEXIS.
Cost: $3,328 (includes annual subscription); renewal: 1995: $809 (price frozen since 1992); 1996: $849; 1997: $849; 1998: $895; 1999: $930; 2000: $1,000; 2001: $1,070; 2002: $1,145; 2003: $1,144; 2004: $1,263; 2005: $1,364; 2006: $1,460; 2007: $1,577; 2008: $1,703; 2009: $1,839; 2010: $1,986; 2011: $2,029; 2012: $2,151; 2013: $2,302; 2014: $2,538.78; CD-ROM: $3,390; renewal: 1998: $895; 1999: $930; 2000: $1,000; 2001: $1,070; 2002: $1,089; 2003: $1,144; 2004: $1,201; 2005: $1,297; 2006: $1,388; 2007: $1,499; 2008: $1,634; 2009: $1,765; 2010: $1,853; 2011: $1,946; 2012: $2,063; 2013: $2,207; 2014: $2,458.20; e-book: $3,025; renewal: 2013: $2,538.78.
Originally written by Arthur Larson, the late James B. Duke Professor of Law at Duke University, the task of carrying on this work has fallen to his son Lex Larson, the President of Employment Law Research, Inc. and a Senior Lecturer at Law, Duke University. This is without question the most detailed and scholarly work on the subject of employment discrimination in print. The authors have gone to great lengths to provide complete and balanced coverage of all aspects of employment discrimination in both their substantive and procedural aspects. Beginning with a factual and historical introduction, the authors address Title VII of the Civil Rights Act of 1964, including extensive coverage of both disparate treatment and disparate impact. They also address retaliation, procedural matters, remedies, race differentiation, age, handicap, the Americans with Disabilities Act, homosexuality and transsexuality, veterans' preference, political discrimination, and employment-at-will exceptions. The Appendices include EEOC forms, practice forms, a Table of Cases, and Index. This set is marked by its well-written text and extensive citations and case notes.

Cost Saving Tips: Buying the set on the used law book market could save you 50% or more. If you cannot locate a used set, you can still reduce your long-term expense by buying the set new with its one-year subscription and then letting it lapse, saving over $2,500 per year in supplementation costs. Simply update in the primary sources, digests, Shepard's until such time as you feel it necessary to buy another new set. Remember that the CD-ROM or Internet subscriptions must be maintained or you will eventually lose your ability to access the text.

Lazar, Wendi S. and Gary R. Siniscalco, eds. **Restrictive Covenants and Trade Secrets in Employment Law: An International Survey**. Arlington, VA: Bloomberg BNA Books, 2010-date. 2 vols. (various pagings).
Cost: $800.00; supplementation: 2011: $175; 2012: $259; 2013: $390 (2014).
As the global economy continues to expand, transnational, or international, corporations extend their reach, and employees change jobs, the task of protecting confidential information and trade secrets becomes a greater legal challenge. While corporations have a vested interest in protecting their proprietary information, as well as protecting their investments in customers and employees, their former employees need the flexibility to change jobs, earn a living, utilize the knowledge they have acquired with their former employers, and preserve customer contacts. Drafting and negotiating restrictive covenants or litigating covenants and trade secrets issues at the international level in light of these conflicting interests is a significant challenge for attorneys in the U.S. and in other jurisdictions. Attorneys who represent employers want to ensure that such provisions are enforceable worldwide. And attorneys representing employees want to ensure that their clients are able to retain their employment viability and mobility in the event of a change in employment circumstances. Enforcement on the employer side is particularly difficult in foreign jurisdictions where courts disfavor post-employment restrictions in general, where such restrictions may supersede a U.S. court's decision on the merits, or where statutory or regulatory limits exist on allowable mechanisms. More commonly, a foreign court may set aside U.S. choice of law and jurisdictional provisions contained in an agreement because those provisions violate or run counter to its own legal requirements. In the end, thinking globally about these provisions while being attentive to local rules and customs is essential to attorneys involved in this work. And while each country's law is unique, similarities exist among countries that share the same jurisprudential toots, such as those who share the English common law heritage, those that base their law on the civil law of France or Spain, or those who draw upon the German Civil Code.

This two-volume treatise provides comprehensive and detailed assistance in drafting, negotiating, and litigating restrictive covenants and trade secrets in conformity with the law in key jurisdictions around the world. Volume one includes three introductory chapters that address: (1) confidentiality, trade secrets, and other duties and restrictive covenants in a global economy; (2) restrictive covenants and trade secret issues is Europe; and (3) the challenge of cross-border litigation from a EU perspective. The remainder of the volume is devoted to surveys of the applicable law in European Union, and other European countries. Volume two contains introductory essays that address restrictive covenants and trade secret issues in the U.S. and Canada; Asia; the Middle East and Africa; and Oceania and selected countries in Asia. The remainder of the volume is devoted to country surveys for the Americas (including the United States and Canada), Asia, the Middle East and Africa, and Oceania. The Preface of each volume contains a useful outline of the topics covered in each country survey; and the Appendix of each volume contains the text of the Hague Convention on the Taking of Evidence Abroad in Civil or Commercial Matters; and the U.N. Convention on the Recognition and Enforcement of Foreign Arbitral Awards ("New York Convention"). Produced through the efforts of the ABA's International Labor and Employment Law Committee, Section of Labor and Employment Law, this monumental treatise is an essential tool for any attorney engaged in the representation of employers or employees involved in international restrictive covenant or trade secret issues.

Lewis, Harold S., Jr. and Elizabeth J. Norman. **Employment Discrimination Law and Practice**. 2d ed. St. Paul, MN: Thomson Reuters West, 2004. 1 vol. (917 pp.). Hornbook Series. Available from West Academic.
Cost: $90; from $24.95 on amazon.com (2014).
This student Hornbook provides wide-ranging coverage of the federal laws governing employment discrimination, including the statutory gounds, modes of proof for Title VII claims, Title VII administrative prerequisites, procedures and remedies, affirmative action,Title VII claims against state and local government, the Equal Pay ASct of 1963, prohibitions on race discrimination in federally funded, and sex discrimination in federally funded education programs, court costs and feesm Civil Rights Attorney's Fees Awards Act, programs, the Age Discrimination in Employment Act of 1967, as well as the procedural aspects of such actions. and much more. The author is the Walter F. George Professor of Law at Mercer University.

Lewis, Jackson. **Winning NLRB Elections: Avoiding Unionization Through Preventative Employee Relations Programs**. 4th ed. Chicago: Commerce Clearing House, Inc., 1997. 1 vol. (253 pp.).
Cost: OUT-OF-PRINT; from $24.87 on amazon.com (2014).
According to a 1977 Report of the House Education and Labor Committee, «the National Labor Relations Act proceeds on the understanding that the employer has a right commencing on the date of hire to convince its employees that union representation is not in their interest.» This volume provides management with a comprehensive program for thwarting union organization activities within the limits of the law. The author addresses preventive measures to discourage union organization, conduct during the early stages of organizing, and strategies for winning elections. It includes a number of useful illustrations and forms which can be adapted to particular management efforts.

Lindemann, Barbara T. and David D. Kadue. **Age Discrimination in Employment Law**. Arlington, VA: BNA Books, 2003. 1 vol. (1,578 pp.).
Cost: $410.00; supplementation: 2013: $210; from $86.87 on amazon.com (2014).
In 1967, Congress enacted the Age Discrimination in Employment Act (ADEA) (Pub. L. No. 90-202, 81 Stat. 602 (Dec. 15, 1967), codified at 29 U.S.C. §§ 621-634) to outlaw discrimination in the United States against anyone at least 40 years of age. Not surprisingly, the law has created problems for employers trying to comply and for judges charged with trying to decide if the law has been violated. Following the enactment of a series of laws prohibiting employment discrimination on the basis of various factors, particularly Title VII of the Civil Rights Act of 1964, courts have grappled with the issue of proving motive. In 1967, the factor of age was added to the list, first of those from age 40 to age 65, then, after 1986, of any age above 40. Outside the context of employment law cases, the issue of motive is rarely raised. This volume probes the complexities of age discrimination litigation, whether in matters of hiring, promotion, monetary compensation, employee benefit programs, exit incentives and early retirement programs, mandatory retirement, reductions if force, harassment, constructive discharge, discharge, and special issues for unions and apprenticeship programs. It also considers age discrimination in the form of disparate treatment through the introduction of circumstantial evidence, as well as the adverse impact model of proof when it is alleged that a practice has a foreseeably and statistically significant adverse impact on a members of a protected class, absent some employer justification based on business necessity to ensure normal operations and for which there is no alternative with a less discriminatory impact. The authors also outline the jurisdiction and procedures governing age discrimination actions and the various aspects of ADEA litigation from discovery, evidence and statistical evidence to summary judgment, jury trials, expert witnesses, defenses, EEOC litigation, public employee litigation and collective actions by certain classes of employees. They also examine alternative forms of conflict resolution, alternative avenues of relief, and resolution, including remedies, attorneys' fees and costs, and tax treatment of awards and settlements. The Appendices include the text of the ADEA, the text of 21 U.S. Supreme Court decisions on age discrimination, EEOC regulations and guidelines, the Government Employee Rights Act of 1991, sample release forms, and revenue rulings, a table of cases, and a useful table of ADEA (and Amendments) provisions which directs users to their discussion in the text. **Barbara T. Lindemann** is formerly Of Counsel at Seyfarth Shaw and co-author of Bloomberg BNA's **Employment Discrimination Law** and **Workplace Harassment Law**. David D. Kadue is a partner in Seyfarth Shaw, Los Angeles, author of **Preventing Sexual Harassment and Other Workplace Harassment: A Fact Sheet for Employees** and co-author of **Workplace Harassment Law**. They are joined by fifty contributing authors, with extensive experience in varied aspects of age and employment discrimination matters, who contributed chapters or parts of chapters. This book represents a monumental achievement in the field of age discrimination in employment and an indispensable resource to any attorney practicing in the field.

Lindemann, Barbara and Paul Grossman. **Employment Discrimination Law.** 5th ed. Washington, DC: Bloomberg BNA Books, 2012-date. 2 vols. (3,476 pp.). Supplementation to previous editions has been irregular.
Cost: $685; no supplementation to date; 4th ed.: 2008: $195; 2009: $245; 2010: $265; 2011: 0; 2012: new ed.; 3d ed.: 2000: $210; 2001: 0; 2002: $235; 2003-2006: 0; 2007: new edition.
Produced by a team of authors from the ABA Section of Labor and Employment Law, this scholarly examination of employment discrimination issues includes a discussion of disparate treatment, adverse impact, effects of past discrimination, reasonable accommodation, sexual harassment, comparable worth, wrongful discharge, union relations, and statistical proof. Includes the full text of selected U.S. Supreme Court decisions as well as excerpts from Title VII of the Civil Rights of 1964 prohibiting gender discrimination. Extensively footnoted with citations to cases, statutes and regulations. Chapters cover determination of appropriate bargaining units, collective bargaining, arbitration, strikes, picketing, lockouts, secondary boycotts, union security, union members «Bill of Rights,» union trusteeships, employment discrimination, civil rights statutes, equal pay, age discrimination,

reverse discrimination and affirmative action, employment at will, regulation of employee benefit plans, and much more. The third edition has new chapters on the law of sexual harassment and sexual orientation and provides expanded coverage of disability law. The Appendices include the full text of all major labor laws, including the Americans with Disabilities Act. This is an indispensable resource for the labor law specialist. The text is thorough and supported by exhaustive citations and notes.

Lindemann, Barbara and David D. Kadue. **Workplace Harassment Law**. Washington, DC: Bloomberg BNA Books, 2011-date. 1 vol. (1,150 pp.) or ebook.
Cost: $485; no supplementation to date; previous edition: 1997: $75; 1998: $135; 1999: $140; 2000-2010: 0.
With charges of sexual harassment ranging from the corporate office to the White House, and EEOC claims skyrocketing, this work provides timely analysis of one of the most explosive areas of contemporary law. The authors explore the various theories of liability under Title VII, including hostile environment, third party claims, harassment by supervisors, constructive discharge and retaliation. They also examine other sources of legal protection under both federal statutes, the common law, and collective bargaining agreements, and various forms of preventative, investigative and remedial action. Also addressed are many of the procedural and strategic issues which arise in such cases, including evidence, discovery, asserted defenses, injunctive and affirmative relief, monetary relief, attorneys' fees, costs, and settlement. The Appendices include a variety of relevant statutes and EEOC guidelines and policies, as well as a table of cases and index. Barbara Lindemann is of counsel to the Los Angeles law firm of Seyfarth, Shaw, Fairweather & Geraldson, a former police commissioner, and former staff attorney with the EEOC. David Kadue is a partner with the same firm where he specializes in employment law counseling and litigation. The 1997 supplement was edited by Christine Cooper, Professor of Law at Loyola University Chicago School of Law, who teaches employment and labor law.

Lipsig, Ethan, Mary C. Dollarhide, and Brit K. Seifert. **Reductions in Force in Employment Law**. 2d ed. Arlington, VA: Bloomberg BNA Books, 2011. 1 vol. (1,370 pp.). Hardbound.
Cost: $475.00; no supplementation to date (2014).
This book is a product of efforts to grapple with the kinds of work force reductions brought about by the economic challenges and dislocations that take place in a free market economy, or with what Austrian-American economist, Joseph Schumpeter, termed the "creative destruction," hastened by economic and technological innovation. First published in 1966 under the title "Downsizing," and under this title in 2007, this book analyzes the leading employment-related issues that arise in the context of work force reductions, including planning and preparation, implementation, and steps taken in the days and weeks following the announcement and rollout of such business restructurings. The analysis is necessarily limited to those labor and employment issues that arise within the context of work force reductions, and does not cover other types of business restructuring events, such as acquisitions or asset sales, except as they involve work force reductions. Following an introductory chapter which examines reductions in force (RIF) plans and alternatives, the authors address the topics of layoffs, exit incentives RIF benefits, releases, financial considerations for employers, outplacement, communications about work force reductions, retention and terminal leave programs, the WARN Act and similar state laws, ADEA impact of RIF program design, ERISA, tax code-related RIF program design considerations, Golden parachute penalties taxation of RIF benefits, amendment or termination of RIF benefit plans, RIF benefits litigation, collective bargaining issues, and wage/hour implications of reducing work time and pay. The authors provide exhaustive citations to supporting caselaw, statutes, regulations, and secondary sources. Ethan is a senior partner in the Los Angeles office of Paul Hastings LLP, while his co-authors are partner and staff attorney at the firm's San Diego office. This is an essential reference for any business engaged in work force reductions, or law firm involved in their representation.

Lopatka, Kenneth T. **NLRA Rights in the Nonunion Workplace**. Arlington, VA: Bloomberg BNA Books, 2010. 1 vol. (350 pp.). Paperbound.
Cost: $145.00 (2014).
Between 1954 and 2009, the percentage of private sector wage and salaried workers who are members of labor unions declined dramatically, from 34.8% to 7.2%. This decline has shifted the focus of workplace regulation from union organizing campaigns and elections, collective bargaining and arbitration to the enactment of a variety of federal and state minimum labor standards, antidiscrimination and antiretaliation statutes, and to the development of common law causes of action for wrongful discharge. In addition, the core right provided by the NLRA applies equally to employees who want to form a union to engage in collective bargaining and those who attempt to improve their employment situation without a union. These legal protections, combined with the negative aspects of forced unionization and dues collection (much of which is used for non-collective bargaining purposes, including electioneering) have sharply reduced the potential pool of union members. Organized labor has responded to these developments by pushing for the enactment of the so-called Employee Freedom of Choice Act (EFCA), which, ironically, calls for the elimination of the secret ballot in union organizing elections and the substitution of the "card-check" system which allows union certification after a majority of workers sign authorization cards. In the absence of the EFCA or union representation, however, employees in nonunion workplaces have a variety of rights under the National Labor Relations Act (NLRA). This volume explains how the NLRA applies to the great bulk of the private sector workforce that is not organized. Essentially, since the NLRA extends to employees and employers in their relations "affecting commerce," the National Labor Relations Board has the same purview. In other words, the reach of the statute is co-extensive with the powers of Congress under the Constitution to regulate commerce. The author of this volume addresses the scope of federal labor law, the overview of the core right and basic prohibitions at the nonunion workplace, concerted activity, concerted activity for other mutual aid or protection, prohibited concerted activity, workplace rules vulnerable to challenge for overbreadth or chilling-effect grounds, denial of access to outsiders, screening of applicants to identify union "salts," employee participation programs, and investigatory

pitfalls. The book is designed primarily for those who do not practice traditional labor law, on either the employee or employer sides. A graduate of Harvard Law School, the author is a former Chief Counsel to the Chairman of the NLRB, partner at several leading law firms, with extensive litigation experience in labor law matters.

Malsberger, Brian M. **Covenants Not to Compete: A State-by-State Survey**. 9th ed. Arlington, VA: Bloomberg BNA Books, 2013-date. 3 vols. (6,000 pp.).
Cost: $705; no supplementation to date; 7th ed.: 2011: $225.
A covenant not to compete, or a non-compete clause, is an agreement in which one party agrees not to work for the other party's direct competition in a specified area for a certain amount of time. While generally applied to employment contracts, such covenants may also be found in contracts involving the sale of a business. In a competitive, service-driven business environment, businesses have a vital interest in protecting their investments in human capital, customer relationships and confidential business information. To protect these interests, particularly in an era of high employee mobility, businesses have increasingly relied upon post-employment agreements. This resource provides exhaustive coverage of state statutory and case law on every aspect of these non-compete agreements as an aid to understanding the limits of the enforceability of restrictive covenants, and as a tool for attorneys in the drafting and counseling process. Each state section follows a uniform outline of fourteen general questions which encompass leading issues in the covenant-not-to-compete context. Volume one also contains a finding list by questions by state, providing the user which quick access to applicable state law on each of the questions. The set also cites relevant law review articles, Restatements, state professional conduct rules, and other authorities. The coverage of the three bound volumes extends to the end of 2009, with the 2011 supplement current through December 2010. The author is a senior editor at BNA, working in coordination with associate editors at the ABA's Section of Labor and Employment Law. This exhaustive reference is an essential resource for any attorney representing clients in covenants-not-to-compete issues.

Malsberger, Brian M. **Employee Duty of Loyalty: A State-by-State Survey**. 5th ed. Arlington, VA: Bloomberg BNA Books, 2013-date. 2 vols. with current supplement.
Cost: $600.00; no supplementation to date; 4th ed. 2011: $235; 2012: $240.
Employees' duty of loyalty to their employers finds its source in the common law, under which an employee has a duty to act solely for the benefit of the employer when engaging in any conduct that relates to his or her employment. Produced in conjunction with the Employment Rights and Responsibilities Committee of the ABA's Section of Labor and Employment Law, this two-volume reference provides a detailed examination of the manner in which state courts have applied the employee duty of loyalty. Reflecting the rapid expansion of litigation concerning the application of the employee duty of loyalty, courts have, in recent years, fleshed out the general agency principles which undergird this duty. This resource looks at conduct at odds with this duty, the existence of an independent cause of action for its breach, statutory authority for such actions, defenses, and relief. Breaches of the duty of loyalty, both real and alleged, are fact-sensitive and so varied as to preclude the application of mechanical rules, hence the need for access to a wide variety of specific court decisions. The introductory chapter provides an overview of the topics affecting duty of loyalty throughout the country, including, questions of first impression and other general issues. The remaining core content of this resource provide state-by-state summaries of cases involving various aspects of the employee duty of loyalty for the period from 1994 to date, with each state section following a common topical outline. The coverage of the two bound volumes extends to the end of 2008, with the 2011 supplement current through December 2010. The author is senior editor at BNA, working in coordination with associate editors at the ABA's Section of Labor and Employment Law. This massive reference is an essential resource for any attorney representing clients in breach of employee loyalty cases.

McKnight, Robert E. **Representing Plaintiffs in Title VII Actions**. 3d ed. New York: Wolters Kluwer Law & Business, 2010. 2 vols. (2,980 pp.). Looseleaf format. Annual supplementation.
Cost: $575; supplementation: 2011: $229; 2012: $249; 2013: $269; 2d ed.: 2006: $159; 2007: $179; 2008: $199; 2009: $215; 2010: $215; 2d edition: 1999; $185; 2000: $145; 2001: $105.
Title VII of the Civil Rights Act of 1964 (42 **U.S.C.** § 2000e et seq.) established a number of protected classifications afforded protection from discrimination, including race, color, national origin, gender, and religion. In this comprehensive treatise and practice guide, Robert McKnight provides coverage of the basic legal theories which undergird the plaintiffs' position in antidiscrimination actions, including those based on intent and those based on disparate impact and testing. His coverage takes the user through the entire Title VII action, including case screening and intake, proving the case, discriminatory practices, class actions, dispositions, and remedies. The third edition of this work provides expanded coverage of such matters as summary judgment, jury trials, religious discrimination, race and national origin, and choice of forum. It also addresses the use of statistical evidence to support the plaintiff's case, including the use of the defendant's electronic records. Robert McKnight is of counsel to Marek, Griggin & Knaupp in Victoria, TX, where he practices in the fields of labor and employment law, employee law and benefits, wage and hour, and civil rights, and is editor of *Fifth Circuit Civil News*.

Modern Workers Compensation. St. Paul, MN: Thomson Reuters West (Clark Boardman Callaghan), 1993-date. 4 vols. Looseleaf pamphlet format. Supplemented quarterly.
Cost: $1,798; supplementation: 1994: $200; 1995: $114; 1996: $244; 1997: $260; 1998: $276; 1999: $306; 2000: $316; 2001: $370; 2002: $425.50; 2003: $464; 2004: $545; 2005: $570; 2006: $676; 2007: $708; 2008: $788; 2009: $888; 2010: $990; 2011: $1,044; 2012: $1,138; 2013: $1,240; **Monthly Assured Print Price (APP):** $131/$1,572.
This practitioner-oriented reference tool reflects the statutory basis of much modern workers compensation law. This work integrates both statutory and case law into a concise discussion and analysis of a field which has been subject to considerable

overhaul in recent years. The textual discussion includes citations to relevant state statutory codes and court decisions enabling the user to quickly locate the law of his or her state. The set is organized in three binders: (1) compensability, (2) benefits, and (3) procedure (both administrative and judicial). Chapters cover the following topics: general construction and validity, compulsory and elective coverage, remedies against employer, remedies against third persons, governing law, covered employers, covered employees, dependents, accidents and injuries, diseases, employment connection in general, travel and commuting, off-duty injuries, weather injuries, assaults or firearms, employee misconduct, subsequent injuries, basis for compensation, earnings, medical benefits, vocal rehabilitation, compensation agreements, payment, administrative proceedings in general, time limitations, parties, notice & claim & pleadings, medical examinations, burden of proof and presumptions, admissibility of evidence, weight and sufficiency of evidence, hearing, award, administrative review, retaliation, nature of judicial proceedings, jurisdiction and venue, parties, scope of review, hearing and determination, and costs, fees and expenses. Volume three also includes a Table of Jurisdictions and Index. There are cross references to both West digests and Larson, **Law of Workmen's Compensation** at the end of each chapter.

While this work is obviously not on the same scholarly level as **Larson**, it is a convenient and quick resource for answering most workers compensation questions at lower cost. Citations are representative, not exhaustive, but do provide the user with entry points into the digests and Larson. The pamphlet format allows for fast updating and less opportunity for misfiled pages.

Modjeska, Lee M. **Federal Labor Law: NLRB Practice.** St. Paul, MN: Thomson Reuters West (Clark Boardman Callaghan), 1994-date. 2 vols. (1,253 pp.). Twice annual free-standing volumes or ProView eBook.
Cost: 2014-1: $374 ($748 annually); 2013-1 Edition: $344; 2013-2: $344; supplementation: 1994: $55; 1995: $55; 1996: $60; 1997: $103.80; 1998: $106.50; 1999: $113; 2000: $120; 2001: $141; 2002: $100.50; 2003: $184.50; 2004: $206.75; 2005: $223; 2006: $255; 2007: $315; 2008: $316; 2009: $137; 2010: $390; 2011: $427.50; 2012: $621; 2013: $688; **Monthly Assured Print Price (APP):** $48/$576.
Authored by a practicing attorney and former Assistant General Counsel of the National Labor Relations Board, this volume addresses the authority of the National Labor Relations Board. Included are a discussion of the board's structure, jurisdiction and method of review as well as the protection of organizational and representational rights, the selection of bargaining representatives, the collective bargaining process, strikes, boycotts and picketing, and internal union affairs. The Appendix includes the full text of relevant statutes and rules and regulations.

Cost-Saving Tip: Avoid the standing order and re-purchase as necessary. These twice annual replacement volumes are nothing more than attempts to milk subscriber lists.

National Lawyers Guild. **Employee and Union Member Guide to Labor Law: A Manual for Attorneys Representing the Labor Movement.** St. Paul, MN: West (Clark Boardman Callaghan), 1992-date. 2 vols. Looseleaf format or ProView eBook. Supplemented twice annually.
Cost: $1,052; ProView eBook: $966; supplementation: 1994: $125; 1995: $156; 1996: $200; 1997: $216.95; 1998: $124; 1999: $226; 2000: $119; 2001: $276; 2002: $305; 2003: $314; 2004: $313.50; 2005: $329; 2006: $368; 2007: $456; 2008: $456; 2009: $510; 2010: $597; 2011: $649; 2012: $709; 2013: $773; **Monthly Assured Print Price (APP):** $77/$924.
A practical analysis of labor law written by members of the National Labor Committee of the National Lawyers Guild with contributions from related groups sympathetic to the interests of organized labor. It attempts to grapple with the maze of state and federal statutes, case law, and regulations, administrative edicts, and contract rules which provide the legal basis for most union activity in the United States. The three-volume set is organized into 14 chapters covering the following topics: organizing the unorganized, opposing discriminatory discharges, protecting the right to strike, stopping runaway shops, fighting for a safe and healthy workplace, obtaining benefits for the disabled worker. rank and file rights in the shop, rights of union members in their unions, internal union elections, protecting the right to a pension, the duty to bargain collectively, representing employees in a bankruptcy court, employee stock ownership plans, and defending the rights of construction workers. This is a well organized and lucidly written treatise amply supported with citations to primary and secondary authorities. The perspective is decidedly pro-labor, as might expect from something sponsored by the National Lawyers Guild, but it can provide management attorneys with valuable insights into labor tactics and strategies.

Norris, Megan P. and James B. Thelen. **Family and Medical Leave and the Law**. New York: Law Journal Press, 2012. 1 vol. (various pagings), online & ebook.
Cost: print: $450 (print, online & ebook); ebook & online: $415 (2014).
The Family & Medical Leave Act of 1993 (FMLA) (Pub. L. No. 93-3, 107 Stat. 6, 29 U.S.C. §§ 2601 et seq.) was enacted to address problems created by the increased number of single-parent households and households with both parents working, and the lack of job security for working parents and employees temporarily unable to work due to serious health conditions. It provides unpaid leave in order that covered employees may attend the birth of a child or care for a family member. All private employers with fifty or more employees are covered by the Act, as are all public employees without regard to the number of employees. An employee is eligible if he or she has worked for the employer at least one year, has worked 1,250 hours in the previous 12 months and there at least fifty employees within 75 miles of the employers work site. This work is designed to assist employers, workers, labor unions, and their respective legal counsel understand their rights and obligations under the Act and its associated federal regulations. Among the topics covered by this volume are the legislative history and background of the Act, the nature of the covered employers, employees and conditions, the FMLA leave process, the certification process for medical conditions, its relationship to active military service, the amount of FMLA leave available, additional leave rights, special issues for federal and school employees, FMLA recordkeeping,

and complaints, remedies and enforcement. The appendices include Department of Labor posters and forms. The volume includes extensive citations to applicable federal statutory provisions, regulations, and case law. Megan P. Norris is a senior principal and managing director with the law firm of Miller, Canfield, Paddock and Stone, P.L.C. in Detroit, Michigan and is chair of the firm's Labor and Employment Law Group. James B. Thelen practiced labor, employment and higher education law with the same firm for 16 years before becoming Associate Dean for Legal Affairs and General Counsel at Thomas M. Cooley Law School.

Occupational Safety and Health Law Handbook. 3d ed. Rockville, MD: Government Institutes, Inc., 2014. 1 vol. (390 pp.). Hardbound.
Cost: $99 (hardcover), $97.99 (ebook) (2014).
This practical collection of articles regarding occupational safety and health laws, regulations and issues provides informed guidance for managers, engineers, and other professionals charged with supervision of workplace safety. With lucid interpretations of the key provisions of the Occupational Safety and Health Act, the fifteen contributing authors review regulations and standards governing employee safety and protection, and provide practical suggestions for ensuring workplace compliance and dealing with regulatory authorities. Chapters include: the Occupational Safety and Health Act, OSHA: the rulemaking process, the duty to comply with standards, the general duty clause, recordkeeping, employers' and employees' rights, refusal to work and whistleblower protection, hazard communication, voluntary safety and health self-audits, inspections and investigations, understanding and contesting OSHA citations, criminal enforcement of violations, judicial review of enforcement actions, imminent danger inspections, and OSHA-approved state plans. The contributors are all attorneys with extensive experience in the field.

Olshan, Regina and Erica F. Schohn. **Section 409A Handbook**. Arlington, VA: Bloomberg BNA Books, 2010-date. 1 vol. (1,124 pp.)
Cost: $345; supplementation: 2011: $145; 2012-2013: 0.
When Congress enacted the American Jobs Creation Act (Pub. Law No. 108-357, 118 Stat. 1418) in 2004, it included among its many provisions Section 885 which added Section 409A to the *Internal Revenue Code*. Section 409A provided that all amounts deferred under a nonqualified deferred compensation plan for all taxable years are currently includible in gross income to the extent not subject to a substantial risk of forfeiture and not previously included in gross income, unless certain requirements are met. The enactment of Section 409A, augmented by nearly 1,000 pages of federal regulations and guidance, has forced executive compensation experts and more general benefits practitioners to design and/or modify compensation arrangements to comply with its provisions. This volume provides the comprehensive guidance necessary to interpret and comply with the complex rules of Section 409A. The book's 32 chapters and numerous appendices address the full range of topics and issues regarding the enactment, coverage, specific provisions and issues involved in Section 409A compliance, as well as analysis and advice on many still unresolved issues. Among the issues covered are the substantial risk of forfeiture, plan aggregation, short-term deferrals, separation pay arrangements, disability, reimbursement arrangements, partnerships, plans of tax-exempt entities, foreign plans, funding arrangements, penalties, and more. The text is supported by numerous citations to IRS Code provisions, IRS and Treasury Regulations, IRS Notices, Revenue Rulings, and federal and tax court decisions. The lead authors/editors are joined by more than 26 contributing authors with expertise in the various aspects of 409A compliance.

Oncidi, Anthony J. **Employment Discrimination Depositions**. Huntington, NY: Juris Publishing, 2011. 1 vol. Looseleaf format. Updated annually or as needed.
Cost: $195; supplementation: 2013: $75.00 (2014).
Employment discrimination is discrimination in hiring, promotion, job assignment, termination, and compensation, as well as various forms of retaliation or harassment. It may be based on race, sex, religion, national origin, physical disability, age, or sexual orientation. The main body of employment discrimination laws consists of federal and state statutes. Employment discrimination lawsuits are becoming increasingly common in our litigious society. Since employment discrimination lawsuits are not generally document intensive, depositions are the primary method of garnering information critical to proving the case. This volume explains each step in the deposition process, from the decision of whether a person should be deposed to the actual questioning of the witness. It provides a discussion of effective deposition strategies and techniques as well as form questions that can be employed in specific cases. Sections are devoted to the purpose of the deposition, who should be deposed, the scheduling of the deposition, whether the deposition serves the best needs of the client, preparing to take a deposition, general deposition techniques, retaining control of the deposition, videotaping, preparing to defend a deposition, preparing the witness for a deposition, beginning the deposition, common topics relevant to the discrimination case, specific types of discrimination claims, and damages. The supporting text and sample questions are accompanied by explanatory notes and citations to relevant cases, and other primary and secondary authorities. A graduate of the University of Chicago School of Law, the author is a partner in the Los Angeles office of Proskauer Rose LLP where he serves as chair of the labor and employment group, and an Adjunct Professor of Law at the University of Southern California.

Orrick, Herrington & Sutcliffe. Employment Law Department. **Employment Law Yearbook**. New York: Practising Law Institute, 2001-date. Annual.
Cost: 2013 Edition: $295; 2010: $235; 2011: $235; 2012: $235 (2014).
The increasingly complex world of employment law receives comprehensive treatment in this annual, year-end review of current developments in the field. Fifteen chapters address such topics as wage and hour issues, wrongful termination, compensation and benefits, class and collective actions, equal employment opportunity, workplace privacy, sexual harassment, the ADA, age discrimination, race and religious discrimination, alternative dispute resolution, trade secrets, Office of Federal Contract Compliance programs, and employment law in the global era. The Employment Law Department of Orrick, Herrington & Sutcliffe is in the forefront of law firms representing

both private and public sector employers in all areas of labor and employment law. Designed for use by employers, human resources professionals, corporate counsel, and employment law practitioners, this annual volume provides practical guidance in achieving compliance under the law and avoiding costly litigation.

Paetkau, Tyler M. **Hiring and Firing**. Irvine, CA: Entrepreneur Press, 2007.
1 viol. (270 pp.).
Cost: $32.95; from $1.86 on amazon.com (2014).
As the author explains, the most treacherous parts of an employment relationship are the beginning and the end. Both are subject to numerous state and federal laws and the potential for litigation. In managing employment relationships, employers should use common sense, closely monitor the relationship from beginning to end, and reflect back to their own prior subordinate employment relationships with managers and supervisors. This review of employment practices discusses such critical topics as the decision of whether you want an employee or independent contractor, interview, the application, illegal questions and inquiries, liability in the recruitment and interview process, offer letters and required documents, background checks, privacy and workplace communications issues, keeping company trade secrets, motivating and keeping great employees, required and voluntary time off. The author also addresses the termination of the employment relationship (whether by firing, retirement, layoff, voluntary decision), and the related issues of severance pay, unemployment claims and benefits, return of company property, and the 60-day WARN Act requirements. A good general introduction to the topic for a non-legally trained business owner who wishes to manage his employment practices from a sound legal and practical basis. A number of sample form and documents are contained on a companion CD-ROM. The author is a partner in the firm of Winston & Strawn LLP in San Francisco and a specialist in labor and employment law.

Pension & Benefits Advisor on Checkpoint. New York: Research Institute of America.
Cost: $3,545 per year (10% discount to new customers) (2014).
This Internet-based service provides guidance on a broad range of pension and benefits matters, including health care, welfare benefits, pension and qualified plans, executive and international compensation. Content includes laws, analysis, forms, checklists and policies.

Perritt, Henry H. **Civil Rights in the Workplace.** 3d ed. New York: Wolters Kluwer Law & Business, 2000-date. 2 vols. Annual supplementation. (Employment Law Library)
Cost: $395; supplementation: 2001: 0; 2002: $115; 2003: $129; 2004: $149; 2005: $159; 2006: $175; 2007: $189; 2008: $205; 2009: $225; 2010: $239; 2011: $265; 2012: $285; 2013: $315; 2d edition: 1996: $70; 1997: $76; 1998: $86; 1999: $89.
A discussion and analysis of the Civil Rights Act of 1991 and its impact on employment law written by Henry H. Perritt, Jr., Professor of Law at Villanova University School of Law, former head labor lawyer for the Consolidated Rail Corp. and deputy Undersecretary of labor in the Ford administration. Professor Perritt is the author of six books and more than 30 articles in the field of labor, employment and disability law. This treatise includes a useful overview of the Civil Rights Act of 1991 including a discussion of the events leading to its adoption, both judicial and legislative. The author treats discrimination under civil rights statutes as well as that falling under the Age Discrimination in Employment Act and the Americans with Disabilities Act. There are chapters devoted to Section 1981 of Title 42 (which authorizes damages for intentional race discrimination), jury trials, compensatory and punitive damages, proof of disparate impact. proof of disparate treatment, statutes of limitations, attorneys' fees and costs, intervention and preclusive effect, and age discrimination. Appendices include the full text of the Civil Rights Act of 1991 and changes to existing law. There are also tables of cases and federal statutes contained in the **United States Code** and an Index. The author provides a clear and concise explanation of the law which is adequately supported by references to both primary and secondary sources, including cases, statutes, and legislative history documents.

Perritt, Henry H., Jr. **Employee Dismissal: Law and Practice**. 5th ed. New York: Wolters Kluwer Law & Business, 2006-date. 1 vol. Looseleaf format.
Cost: $425; supplementation: 2007: $189; 2008: $199; 2009: $219; 2010: $240; 2011: $269; 2012: $289; 2013: $309; 2014: $319; 4th ed.: 1998: $79; 1999: $79; 2000: $89; 2001: $105; 2002-2005: 0.
A comprehensive guide to the law of employee dismissal by the Dean and Professor of Law at Chicago-Kent College of Law, Illinois Institute of Technology. This work examines both the theoretical and practical sides of employee dismissal law, including employment-at-will, statutory protection, downsizing, employment termination under the ADA, arbitration, contract theories, tort theories, special problems related to public employment, proof and procedure, employer's personnel policies, wrongful dismissal legislation, pre-complaint investigation, discovery, trial tactics, jury instructions, and alternative dispute resolution. The Appendix also contains the Uniform Law Commissioners' Model Employment Termination Act. Comes with a more than 250 forms on 3 IBM-compatible disks, formatted for WordPerfect 5.1.

Pinheiro, Brian M. et al. **Employer's Guide to Health Care Reform**. New York: Wolters Kluwer Law & Business, 2014. 1 vol. (various pagings). Paperbound. Annual.
Cost: $309.00; from $252.47 on amazon.com (2014).
The Patient Protection and Affordable Care Act of 2010, otherwise known as the Affordable Care Act (ACA) or "Obamacare" (P.L. 111-148, 124 Stat. 119-1025) is the most significant regulatory overhaul of the U.S. healthcare system since the passage of Medicare and Medicaid in 1965. Despite the President's oft repeated statements that "if you like your current insurance, you can keep your current insurance" and "if you like your doctor, you will be able to keep your doctor," the reality is far different. The authors posit that "although the Affordable Care Act does not force individuals to drop or change their coverage, it remains to seen whether employers, through which many individuals currently have health insurance coverage, decide to continue to provide the same type of coverage in light of the health care reform changes." In the meantime, the response by employers will depend on a variety of factors, including the

size of the workforce, the average income level of employees, the level of unionization, whether the employer provides coverage to pre- and/or post-Medicare retirees (in addition to active employees) the types of group health plans provided to employees, whether the costs incurred under those plans are self-funded by the employer out of its operating assets or are funded through insurance (or a combination of both), the design of the employer's group health plan and the terms and conditions of coverage, whether the employer is profit or non-profit, and the degree to which health benefits continue to be viewed as an important benefit for the recruitment and retention of employees in the employer's industry.

This volume provides a comprehensive overview of the Affordable Care Act and the issues it raises for employers attempting to adapt to its complex network of laws, regulations, administrative directives, and exemptions. Following a review of the evolution of health care reform and the legal challenges to health care reform, they examine health care reform exemptions, the issues of quality, affordability and accessibility, the preservation and expansion of immediate access to coverage, coverage improvements during the transition period, the improvements effective January 1, 2014, issues of transparency and accountability, mandates of exchanges, operational changes for health plans, new taxes and other revenue raisers. Finally, they analyze the impact of health care reform going forward on both small and large employers. Half the volume consists of applicable regulations from the Federal Register and other official government sources. This is an essential resource for any small or large business or corporation grappling with the intricacies of the new health care law and its implementation. Three of the authors are members of the Employee Benefits and Executive Compensation Group at the law firm of Ballard Spahr LPP. Jean Hemphill is a partner in the Business and Finance Department of Ballard Spahr.

Rassas, Lori B. **Employment Law: A Guide to Hiring, Managing, and Firing for Employers and Employees**. 2d ed. New York: Wolters Kluwer Law & Business, 2011. 1 vol. (506 pp.). Paperbound. Includes four months free Loislaw online access.

Cost: $109.95; from $39.73 on amazon.com (2014).

This textbook provides a comprehensive and lucid overview of employment law basics designed for undergraduate students in business administration and paralegal studies. From the workplace discrimination provision of Title VII of the Civil Rights Act of 1964 (42 U.S.C. § 2000e et seq.), which prohibited discrimination based on race, color, national origin, religion, sex, pregnancy, age and disability, the author examines the legal ramifications of the hiring process, including employees versus independent contractors, the recruitment of a diverse applicant pool, the application and interview process, and pre-employment testing. Management issues addressed include compensation and benefits, paid and unpaid leave, performance management, workplace harassment, workplace privacy and personal expression, and regulation of off-duty conduct. The volume concludes with a consideration of the firing process, including employment at will, ending the employment relationship, and severance and post-employment obligations. The volume includes discussion of applicable constitutional, statutory and common law provisions, and each chapter includes endnotes to legal authorities, and sample discussion questions. A complimentary four-month student subscription to Loislaw online provides access to all applicable statutes and case citations. A graduate of George Washington University Law School, the author has spent two decades experience in employment and labor issues.

Repa, Barbara Kate. **Your Rights in the Workplace: An Employee's Guide to Fair Treatment**. 10th ed. Berkeley, CA: Nolo, 2014. 1 vol. (560 pp.). Paperbound.

Cost: $29.99; from $13.42 on amazon.com; kindle ed.: $16.49 (2014).

Employees have a variety of workplace protections under federal law, many of these amplified by similar state laws. These laws involve discrimination, wages and hours, health insurance, family and medical leave, privacy rights, health and safety, sexual harassment and a host of other issues. This book provides detailed and substantive information about the various statutory protections afforded individuals in the workplace and suggests procedures and strategies for resolving legal or personal issues in the workplace, short of litigation. The author also provides counsel on such matters as losing or leaving a job, steps to follow after a job loss, unemployment, workers' compensation, Social Security disability insurance, retirement plans, dealing with labor unions, and immigration issues. The discussion of many of the state-related legal issues is accompanied by charts detailing the law in each of the fifty states, such as laws that control the issuance of final paychecks. Well organized and clearly written, this volume can serve as a invaluable resource for both employees and employers interested in understanding their respective rights and responsibilities under the law. The author, a journalist, mediator, and consultant on workplace discrimination, is the other of several Nolo books.

Richey, Charles R. **Manual on Employment Discrimination and Civil Rights Actions in the Federal Courts**. 2d ed. St. Paul, MN: Thomson Reuters West (Clark Boardman Callaghan), 1994-date. 2 vols. Looseleaf format or ProView eBook.

Cost: $1,015; ProView eBook: $932; supplementation: 1996: $60; 1997: $70; 1998: $74.50; 1999: $90; 2000: $135; 2001: $156; 2002: $90; 2003: $224.50; 2004: $232; 2005: $252; 2006: $360; 2007: $445; 2008: $445.50; 2009: $496.50; 2010: $593; 2011: $417; 2012: $454; 2013: $497; **Monthly Assured Print Price (APP):** $74/$888.

A comprehensive examination of the types of discrimination which employees may assert in actions against employers. The author, a distinguished federal district court judge, provides a thorough analysis of such topics as AIDS in the workplace, chemical testing of employees to detect drug abuse, the application of the Equal Access to Justice Act, and the major common law claims which employees may employ despite an at will employment relationship. Judge Richey is also notable as the judge originally assigned to rule on the proposed final judgment in the merger of the Thomson Corporation and West Publishing Company, but who withdrew when the attorney for Hyperlaw, Inc. brought to his attention the fact that his own book was published by one of the Thomson-owned companies (CBC), forcing his recusal.

Rothstein, Mark A. et al. **Employment Law.** 4th ed. St. Paul: Thomson Reuters West, 2009-date. 2 vols. Irregular supplementation. Practitioner Treatise Series.
Cost: $268; supplementation: 2013: $49; 3d ed.: 2005: $34; 2006: $35; 2007: $46; 2008: $46; 2009: new edition; 2d ed.: 2000: 0; 2001: $31; 2002: 0; 2003: $45; 2004: new edition; **Monthly Assured Print Price (APP):** $8/$96.
This two-volume treatise covers all phases of employment law for the practicing attorney. The authors provide an in-depth treatment of Title VII of the Civil Rights Act of 1964, which outlawed employment discrimination and brought civil rights law into the workplace. They also address the Age Discrimination in Employment Act of 1967, the Americans With Disabilities Act of 1990, and many other state and federal laws prohibiting discrimination in employment. The work also includes discussion of the growing exceptions to the employment at will doctrine and such tort claims as defamation, invasion property and intentional infliction of emotional distress. Federal legislation regulating workplace conditions and employment relationships is also discussed, including the Occupational Safety & Health Act, Employee Retirement Income Security Act, Immigration Reform & Control Act. Additional chapters cover workers' compensation, covenants not to compete, discharge, bankruptcy, plant closings, unemployment compensation, and retirement. The Appendix includes a valuable guide to Researching Employment Law on Westlaw, although the Publisher's «Westlaw Overview» appears to suggest that updating the treatise can performed primarily by going on-line.

Rothstein, Mark A. **Occupational Safety and Health Law.** St. Paul, MN: Thomson Reuters West, 2006-date. 1 vol. Annual editions. Softcover.
Cost: 2014 Edition: $211; prior annual editions: 2006: $94; 2007: $107; 2008: $116; 2009: $103.50; 2010: $150; 2011: $164; 2012: $178; 2013: $194; **Monthly Assured Print Price (APP):** $16/$192.
Written by the Law Foundation Professor of Law at the University of Houston, this volume in West's Handbook Series covers the full range of issues involving workplace health and safety, particularly as they relate to the Occupational Safety and Health Act enacted in 1970. Chapters address the history and scope of the act, duties under the act, enforcement, adjudication, and OSHA-related litigation. The Appendices include a glossary of abbreviations and acronyms, the full text of the act, the Occupational Safety and Health Review Commission Rules of Procedure, the Commission Freedom of Information Act Regulations, and Commission Rules Implementing the Equal Access to Justice Act. There are tables of federal and state statutes, a table of cases, and index.

Ruzicho, Andrew J. and Louis A. Jacobs. **Employment Law Checklists and Forms**. St. Paul, MN: Thomson Reuters West, 1991-date. 2 vols. Looseleaf format.
Cost: $1,103; supplementation: 1995: $130; 1996: $130; 1997: $136.50; 1998: $144.50; 1999: $156; 2000: $168.50; 2001: $199; 2002: $234; 2003: $267; 2004: $287; 2005: $312; 2006: $334; 2007: $442.50; 2008: $462.50; 2009: $459; 2010: $554; 2011: $604; 2012: $658; 2013: $738; **Monthly Assured Print Price (APP):** $78/$936.
An ideal resource for the attorney advising clients on employment policies or in employment litigation. It covers management policies, discrimination, sexual harassment, wrongful termination, health and safety, wage and hour laws. and other employment-related issues. The forms and accompanying checklists take note of recent cases and statutes, including the Drug Free Workplace Act of 1988, the Americans with Disabilities Act of 1990, the Civil Rights Act of 1991, the Equal Pay Act, and the Family Medical Leave Act, among others. Andrew Ruzicho is an attorney specializing in equal employment opportunity law with extensive Justice Department experience in the field. Louis Jacobs is a Professor of Law at Ohio State University College of Law.

Schneider, Paul J. and Brian M. Pinheiro, eds. **ERISA: A Comprehensive Guide**. 4th ed. Frederick, MD: Wolters Kluwer Law & Business, 2011-date. 1 vol. Looseleaf. (1,102 pp.)
Cost: $385; supplementation: 2012: 0; 2013: $310.
The Employee Retirement Security Act of 1974 (ERISA) was the first piece of federal legislation designed to protect the rights of American workers who earn pension benefits. Among its aims, RISHA set standards for pension plan participation, vesting, and funding. It also created an insurance system to protect pension plans and provide express statutory authority and full disclosure requirements to protect against abuses of the $135 billion pool of virtually unregulated assets of 34,000 private pension plans. ERISA is designed to shore up one of the ingredients of a successful retirement saving program, the other two being Social Security and personal savings. Qualified retirement plans provide distinct tax advantages to both employees and employees since contributions are exempt from taxation until they are distributed to the employee. This resource provide an in-depth analysis of ERISA and the subsequent amendments to the Internal Revenue Code that address employee benefits. The bulk of the text is devoted to an explanation of the Titles I and IV of the Act, including the reporting and disclosure requirements for plans covered by ERISA, qualified retirement plans, coverage and nondiscrimination requirements, IRS and DOL correction procedures, ERISA's fiduciary responsibility provisions, prohibited transaction provisions, civil enforcement, ERISA preemption, single-employer pension plan terminations and insurance, withdrawal liability, continuing health care coverage, employee benefits in mergers and acquisitions, employee benefits and the unionized workforce, employee benefits in bankruptcy, executive compensation, and the impact of other employment laws on ERISA. The text is accompanied by citations to relevant sections of the law and court decisions. The editors are joined by a team of 24 contributing authors, each of whom is an expert in the field of employment benefits, labor law, or taxation.

Secunda, Paul M. and Jeffrey M. Hirsch. **Mastering Employment Discrimination Law**. Durham, NC: Carolina Academic Press, 2010. 1 vol. (224 pp.). Paperbound.
Cost: $27.00; from $14.35 on amazon.com; kindle ed.: $19.99 (2014).
The substance of employment discrimination law is found primarily in federal and state statutes and local ordinances, but also in the U.S. and state constitutions, and the common

law. This student handbook looks primarily at employment discrimination under Title VII of the Civil Rights Act of 1964. Distinguishing employment discrimination law from labor law, employment law, and employee benefits law, the authors focus on unfair employment practices in the workplace that subject some groups to adverse employment actions based on race, color, religion, sex, national origin, age, disability, and other personal characteristics dependent on the state or municipality involved. Such actions may be classified on the basis of: (1) circumstantial vs. direct evidence cases; (2) individual vs. group cases; (3) disparate treatment vs. impact cases (i.e. intentional vs. nonintentional discrimination). Following an overview of employment discrimination law, the authors examine coverage, administrative procedural issues, procedural issues in litigation, employment discrimination remedies, settlement and tax, Title VII individual disparate treatment claims, systemic disparate treatment claims, disparate impact claims, sexual and other forms of harassment, retaliation, disability discrimination, age discrimination, other civil rights protections, and the Equal Pay Act and other compensation issues. A part of the Carolina Academic Press Mastering Series, this title aims to provide students with the key substantive and procedural concepts and issues in the field. Paul Secunda is a professor at Marquette University Law School. Jeffrey Hirsch is a professor at University of Tennessee College of Law.

Seymour, Richard T. and Barbara Berish Brown. **Equal Employment Law Update**. Washington, DC: Bloomberg BNA Books, 2007-date. 1 vol.
Cost: 2007 Edition: $240 (2014).
A topically arranged compilation of summaries of appellate cases on equal employment, with expert commentary from both the plaintiff and defense perspectives. Sixty-two chapters are organized under the following parts: the scope of civil rights protections: coverage, construction and remedies; theories and proof; employment litigation; remedies; and special issues. A Table of Cases also allows the user to quick locate discussion of desired cases. Richard T. Seymour is director of the Employment Discrimination Project for the Lawyers Committee for Civil Rights Under Law. Barbara Berish Brown is a partner in the New York law firm of Paul, Hastings, Janofsky & Walker LLP. The 2007 edition contains appellate case analyses from 2005 through September 2007, with analysis of all Supreme Court decisions through June 2007.

Sprague, Robert, ed. **Workplace Data Law and Litigation**. Arlington, VA: Bloomberg BNA, 2013. 1 vol. (various pagings).
Cost: $350.00; from $308.75 on amazon.com (2014).
Published in partnership with the ABA's Section of Labor and Employment Law, this volume provides an overview of the legal issues which have arisen with regard to employment-related electronically stored information (ESI). In a world in which over 98% of all stored information is now digital, it provides users with a comprehensive overview of the various forms in which digital data can be created, stored and produced, the discovery issues and challenges of dealing with digital data, a detailed statute-by-statute analysis of data retention requirements in federal workplace-related laws, a review of emerging workplace social media and other technology-related issues and a guide to data protection privacy laws in North America, Europe, Asia and Oceania, and the ever-expanding globalization of business and increasing inter-country transfer of employee personal data. Labor and employment lawyers, in particular, will find the discussion and analysis of significant value as they navigate the various forms of employee records, including those related to date of hire, pay rate, recorded absences, performance evaluations, as well as LinkedIn contacts, Facebook, YouTube, Twitter and Instagram postings, and the uses to which such data may be employed. The sixteen chapters address workplace data in general, e-discovery challenges, data retention statutes, emerging issues related to workplace data, and international workplace data issues. Chapter 10 provides a detailed tabular summary of workplace data retention requirements for twenty-one federal statutes, including the recently enacted Equal Pay Act (EPA) and the Patient Protection and Affordable Care Act (PPACA). This is an essential resource for any labor, employment or corporate attorney engaged in record retention or e-discovery issues or representing employees impacted by the retention or use of employment data. The book was written and edited by Robert Sprague of the Department of Management and Marketing, University of Wyoming College of Business and more than sixty contributing authors.

Steingold, Fred S. **The Employer's Legal Handbook: Manage Your Employees & Workplace Effectively**. 11th ed. Berkeley, CA: Nolo, 2013. 1 vol. (496 pp.). Paperbound.
Cost: $49.99; from $29.29 on amazon.com; kindle ed.: $26.96 (2014).
The employment relationship is governed by a variety of state and federal statutes and court decisions. Failure to have a basic understanding of employment law and its legal pitfalls can be a source of considerable cost, both emotional and financial. The author's aim is to provide essential advice to small businesses that cannot afford outside counsel when hiring and other critical employment law decisions are made. This handbook provides a solid grounding in the basics of the employment law for managers, employees, and business owners, attorneys, and students. Each of the fourteen chapters provides a variety of special features that illuminate the text, including cautions, related topics, resources, and state statutory charts, The coverage ranges from hiring and personnel practices to wages and hours, employee benefits, taxes, family and medical leave, health and safety, illegal discrimination, workers with disabilities, termination, employee privacy, independent contractors, unions, and lawyers and legal research. The appendices include a directory of labor departments and agencies, and charts for state laws in eleven critical areas of employment law. The author is a private practitioner in Ann Arbor Michigan, where he advises small businesses, and the the author of such Nolo titles as **Hiring Your First Employee**, **Legal Guide for Starting and Running a Small Business**, and **The Complete Guide to Buying a Business**, and author of the monthly column **The Legal Advisor**.

Stellman, Jeanne Mager. **Encyclopedia of Occupational Health and Safety**. 4th ed. Washington, DC: International Labor Office, 1998. 4 vols. (4,000 pp.). Also available on CD-ROM. Distribution office located in Waldorf, MD. (301) 638-3152. Available at: http://www.ilocis.org/en/default.html

Cost: $120.00; from $119.98 on amazon.com (2014).
A massive collection of articles on all aspects of health and safety in the workplace written by more than 1,000 internationally recognized experts. The contributions represent virtually every professional organization and major academic, governmental and nonprofit institution involved in occupational safety and health. More than 100 articles are organized into the following parts: the body, health care, management and policy, tools and approaches, psychological and organizational factors, general hazards, the environment, accidents and safety management, chemicals, industries based on biological resources, industries based on natural resources, chemical industries, manufacturing industries, textile and apparel industries, transport industries, construction, and services and trade. Volume four contains guides, indexes, and a directory of experts. The editor is a Professor at Columbia University's Joseph L. Mailman School of Public Health in New York City and the author of numerous books and articles on occupational health and safety.

Strecker, David E. **Labor Law: A Basic Guide to the National Labor Relations Act**. New York: CRC Press, 2011. 1 vol. (197 pp.). Hardbound.
Cost: $87.95; Kindle: $63.96; from $27.71 on amazon.com (2014).
A useful overview of the U.S. labor and employment law under the National Labor Relations Act intended for employers and employees, labor lawyers, union officials, students, and the general public. Following an introduction and history of labor and employment law, the author devotes attention to the subject of dealing with labor unions under the NLRA, living with a union, the collective bargaining agreement, grievances, labor arbitration, unfair labor practice proceedings, and strikes and lockouts. The useful appendices include a list of right-to-work states, web sites of labor and employment law sources, a sample management rights clause, a sample no strikes/no lockouts clause, a sample zipper clause, a sample union authorization card (used in card check organizing campaigns), a sample NLRB petition, a sample unfair labor practice charge, and tips for witnesses in arbitration hearings. The author has practiced labor and employment law for over thirty years, and teaches labor relations at Oklahoma State University, and negotiation and management skills at the University of Tulsa.

Summers, Clyde W., Kenneth G. Dau-Schmidt and Alan Hyde. **Legal Rights and Interests in the Workplace**. Durham, NC: Carolina Academic Press, 2007. 1 vol. (984 pp.).
Cost: $95; statutory supplementation and materials: 2007: $25; (2014).
This caseBook had its genesis in a course on labor and employment law at the University of Pennsylvania taught by Professor Clyde Summers, a course merging two areas of labor law—collective labor law and individual employment law. In contrast to the traditional approach to the teaching of labor law, which has generally focused on collective labor law, this new approach is a response to the fact that only 9% of employment relationships are now covered by collective bargaining agreements, and individual employment law has probably become the more important. The materials in this volume represent an attempt to interrelate these two bodies of law into a common framework. Its premise is that, historically and functionally, the predominant purpose of labor law has been to protect workers from market forces in the individual labor market, and that individual bargaining in the labor market will lead to socially undesirable results and that the law should come to the aid of the weaker party. This may be accomplished in two ways: employees may be protected by direct regulation of terms and conditions of employment with laws regulating the minimum wage, employee health and safety, and prohibitions against discrimination; or employees may obtain a measure of protection by restructuring the labor market by replacing individual bargaining with collective bargaining in the belief that the collective labor market will produce more acceptable social results. Clyde W. Summers is a professor emeritus at the University of Pennsylvania Law School. Kenneth G. Dau-Schmidt is Associate Dean for Research and the Willard and Margaret Carr Professor of Labor and Employment Law at Indiana University School of Law. Alan Hyde is the Sidney Reitman Scholar and professor of law at Rutgers School of Law, Newark.

Tauber, Yale D. and Donald R. Levy, eds. **Executive Compensation**. Washington, DC: Bloomberg BNA Books, 2002-date. 1 vol. (780 pp.). Irregular supplementation.
Cost: OUT-OF-PRINT; was $295; from $14.00 on amazon.com (2014).
A comprehensive examination of the legal aspects of executive compensation and the design of the executive compensation package. The book's chapters are divided into three parts. Those in Part I address negotiation of employment contracts, incentives, deferred compensation, equity compensation, insurance, and the implications of mergers and securities regulations. Part 2 covers entities requiring special consideration and embraces the topics of executive compensation in the nonprofit sector, compensation, tax equalization techniques for internationally mobile executives, special issues pertaining to startup companies, including the evaluation of equity compensation offerings in early stage start-up companies. Part III covers the areas of settlement, arbitration and litigation and includes chapters on devising effective severance agreements, the advantages and disadvantages of arbitration instead of litigation in contractual disputes. The book's appendices include a sample equity allocation agreement, a sample non-qualified deferred compensation agreement, a flexible perquisites policy, and other sample documents. Yale D. Tauber is principal of Independent Compensation Committee Advisor, LLC. Donald Levy, a corporate lawyer based in New York City, has written or edited numerous books on the topics of financial and tax planning. More than 25 authors contributed chapters to this major undertaking.

Westman, Daniel P. and Nancy M. Modesitt. **Whistleblowing: The Law of Retaliatory Discharge**. 2d ed. Washington, DC: Bloomberg BNA Books, 2004-date. 1 vol. (427 pp.). Annual supplementation.
Cost: $295; supplementation: 2006: $135; $2007: $145; 2008: $165; 2009: $175; 2010: $180; 2011: $185; 2012: $190; 2013: $195.
Whistleblowing generally occurs when an employee's sense of civic or ethical responsibility overrides the duties he might owe to his employer. Often, whistleblowing results from a ethical,

criminal, financial or legal failure on the part of a corporation or governmental entity. Employees have variously been protected by the False Claims Act of 1863, provisions of the National Labor Relations Act (in so far as it protects employees from engaging in peaceful collective bargaining activities), and the common law of many jurisdictions where employers are implicated in criminal conduct. They are also protected by a variety of federal statues in the areas of civil rights, workplace safety, public health, environmental pollution, and consumer protection. However, it was the enactment of the Sarbanes-Oxley Act of 2002, a response to some widely publicized corporate scandals, which dramatically increased protections for corporate whistleblowers. This volume examines the history and evolution of whistleblower protections, the analytical framework balancing workplace responsibilities and conscience, protections in the public sector, statutory protections in the private sector, common law protection and the public policy doctrine, the Sarbanes-Oxley Whistleblower provisions, protections of general application under civil rights laws and the False Claims Act, preemption and related issues, litigating whistleblower cases, and avoiding whistleblower litigation. The appendices contain the text of significant state statutes for public and private sector employees, federal statutes protecting employees, common law public policy protections for whistleblowers, and relevant provisions of Sarbanes-Oxley. The text is heavily annotated with citations to applicable cases and states. There is also a table of cases and index. Daniel P. Westman is a litigation partner with the law firm of Shaw Pitman LLP where he has represented cases in whistleblower cases since 1982. Nancy M. Modesitt professor of law at American University where she teaches employment law and legal rhetoric.

Additional titles in the field of Labor and Employment Law are available from the following publishers: AFL-CIO Human Resources Development Institute, American Bankers Association, American Chamber of Commerce Publications, Wolters Kluwer Law & Business, Association for Union Democracy, Matthew Bender, Business & Legal Reports, Cornell University Press, CUPA-HR, Delmar Publishers, Employment Policy Foundation (EPF), Federal Bar Association, Foundation Press, Gaunt, Government Institutes, Greenwood Publishing Group, James Publishing, Kluwer Academic Press, Kluwer Law International, International Labor Office, LexisNexis, Libraries Unlimited, LRP Publications, McGraw-Hill Professional Book Group, National Employment Law Institute, Practising Law Institute, Prentice-Hall, M. Lee Smith, Publishers, Thomson Reuters West, Warren, Gorham & Lamont, West Academic. See Appendix B for addresses and telephone numbers.

Legal Forms

American Jurisprudence Legal Forms 2d. Eagan, MN: West (Lawyers Cooperative), 1966-date. 62 vols. Annual pocket parts and periodic revised volumes.
Cost: $8,499; supplementation: 1993: $445; 1994: $670; 1995: $1,028; 1996: $1,074; 1997: $1,060; 1998: $1,219.50; 1999: $1,432; 2000: $1,630; 2001: $1,663; 2002: $1,875; 2003: $1,429; 2004: $1,724; 2005: $2,009; 2006: $2,240; 2007: $2,775.50; 2008: $2,775.50; 2009: $3,718; 2010: $3,220.50; 2011: $4,313; 2012: $4,445.50; 2013: $4,845; current vols: $468/$585 (subscriber/list); **Monthly Assured Print Price (APP):** $460/$5,200; as WestlawNext add-on: $1,272.00 (1 user) (2014).
A collection of thousands of general legal forms covering personal, business, state and federal matters. The forms are grouped into 268 topical areas and published in 55 bound volumes, two paperbound general index volumes, and a two-volume looseleaf **Federal Tax Guide to Am. Jur. Legal Forms**. These forms are designed as aids to the practitioner in the preparation of «office practice» documents required for clients' business and personal affairs, as opposed to those forms used in court proceedings.

Each chapter includes the following sections: Scope of Chapter, Treated Elsewhere, Federal Tax References, Federal Research References, **ALR** System References, and Practice Aids. There are also introductory comments to each chapter, Annotation References to **ALR** and **L. Ed.**, and Checklists. Each form is accompanied by Notes on Use which key the user into substantive discussion in **Am. Jur. 2d.** The form drafting guide provides a checklists of matters which should be considered in drafting the forms. This is one of several competing legal forms sets on the market. The breadth of coverage and collateral references to other West products make this an excellent choice for the practitioner.

Cost Saving Tips: Westlaw has become the preferred format given the dramatic increases in the initial and ongoing cost of the print set. If you also want it in print, buy it used and forego the aupplements. Avoid the **Monthly Assured Print Price**, which only locks you in to high supplementation costs.

Am. Jur. Legal Forms 2d on WestlawNext PRO. Eagan, MN: West, 1994-date.
Cost: $1,272.00 (1 user) (2014).
Contains the full text of forms in the print **American Jurisprudence Legal Forms** with hypertext links to **American Jurisprudence 2d**.

Cost Saving Tip: From a cost perspective, Westlaw is clearly preferable to the print format. Given the price differential, print should now be obsolete. The best bargain is the **All Am Jur Library** on WestlawNext PRO.

American Jurisprudence Pleading and Practice Forms Annotated. Eagan, MN: West (Lawyers Cooperative), 1966-date. 79 vols. Annual pocket parts and periodic revised volumes.
Cost: $9,639; supplementation: 1992: $418; 1993: $498; 1994: $679; 1995: $844; 1996: $1,376; 1997: $952; 1998: $1,830; 1999: $1,543.50; 2000: $1,834; 2001: $2,402; 2002: $2,199; 2003: $2,108; 2004: $2,182; 2005: $3,108.50; 2006: $2,365; 2007: $3,182; 2008: $3,180; 2009: $4,149.50; 2010: $4,348; 2011: $5,571; 2012: $5,764; 2013: $6,347; Current volumes: $468/$585 (subscriber/list); **Monthly Assured Print Price (APP):** $595/$7,140; as WestlawNext add-on: $1,272.00 (1 user) (2014).

This is the only major set of general pleading and practice forms on the market. More than 30,000 forms covering all types and phases of court proceedings are organized under 363 main legal topics and published in 67 bound volumes. Access is by an annually revised two-volume General Index. Includes pre-trial, trial and post-trial forms, including orders, writs, notices, and jury instructions. Most of the forms have been taken from the files and court records of practitioners in every state and federal jurisdiction to which have been added references to applicable state statutes and court rules. Each of the topical chapters into which these forms have been organized contains a variety of features of value to the practitioner, including cross references, collateral references to the **American Law Reports** and **Federal Procedure**, Trial Aids to **Am. Jur. Trials**, relevant Annotations, an Introduction to the topic with citations to applicable section of **Am. Jur. 2d**, and form drafting checklists. A brief review of Governing Principles summarizes the more complete coverage available in **Am. Jur. 2d.** There also are Notes to each form keying the user into Am. Jur 2d. for further explanation of the legal principles involved. This set is a valuable addition to the library of any attorney. The references to other products in the West's Total Client-Service Library are a particularly useful feature.

Cost Saving Tips: Dramatic increases in the cost of this print set seem reflect the publisher's desire to push customers to the online version. If your intent is to acquire this set and keep it current, Westlaw has been a far more economical alternative. The best bargain is the **All Am Jur Library** on WestlawNext PRO.

Am. Jur. Pleading and Practice Forms on LawDesk on WestlawNext. Eagan, MN: Thomson Reuters West, 1995-date. Contains 30,000 forms.
Cost: $1,272.00 (1 user) (2014).
Contains the full text of all the forms in the print set, fully searchable, with hypertext links to other products in the same product family.

Cost Saving Tips: Dramatic increases in both the initial and subscription costs for this set make it an obvous acquisition on Westlaw. A print subscription will now cost you more than $8,000 in the first year and more than $5,000 per year thereafter. Acquiring it on WestlawNext will save you about $7,000 in the first year and $4,500 per year thereafter. If you still prefer print, buy it used and do not supplement. Update only on Westlaw. The CD-ROM is a costly waste of money in comparison to acquiring it on WestlawNext.

Bender's Federal Practice Forms. Compiled by Louis R. Frumer and Marvin Waxner. New York: Matthew Bender & Co., 1951-date. 20 vols. Looseleaf format. Also available on CD-ROM and the Internet.
Cost: $7,273 (includes annual subscription); annual renewal: 1995: $1588 (price frozen since 1992); 1996: $1,587.50; 1997: $1,587.50; 1998: $1,670; 1999: $1,750; 2000: $1,850; 2001: $1,980; 2002: $2,119; 2003: $2,225; 2004: $2,336; 2005: $2,453; 2006: $2,625; 2007: $2,835; 2008: $3,402; 2009: $3,674; 2010: $4,006; 2011: $4,246; 2012: $4,543; 2013: $4,861; 2014: $5,305; CD-ROM: $7,448; annual renewal: 1998: $1,675; 1999: $1,750; 2000: $1,850; 2001: $1,980; 2002: $2,119; 2003: $2,225; 2004: $2,336; 2005: $2,453; 2006: $2,625; 2007: $2,835; 2008: $3,434; 2009: $3,709; 2010: $4,005; 2011: $4,246; 2012: $4,585; 2013: $4,906; 2014: $5,461.08; e-book: $6,612; renewal: 2014: $5,305.
A companion to **Moore's Federal Practice**, this set provides the full text of all federal rules, notes to amendments, Advisory Committee Notes, as well as hundreds of relevant forms. Included are the Rules of Civil Procedure, Rules of Criminal Procedure, Federal Rules of Evidence, United States Magistrates, Federal Rules of Appellate Procedure, U.S. Supreme Court Rules, U.S. Tax Court Rules, Bankruptcy Rules, etc. followed by the forms applicable to each rule. Footnotes provide citations to relevant federal decisions. Includes cross-references to **Moore's Federal Practice** as an aid to more in-depth research.

Cost Saving Tips: Used sets are available in the range of $400-$500. The purchaser may them choose to purchase another used set at some later date, employing a current edition of the Federal Rules to keep up with any actual changes. The annual paperback editions of the rules are available from numerous sources, including West and Matthew Bender. The CD-ROM, once supplied at no additional charge to print subscribers, is now priced at the same level as the print, both initially and for supplementation. The CD-ROM purchaser, however, cannot allow the product to lapse without completely losing access to the text which will time expire.

Bender's Forms of Discovery. New York: Matthew Bender & Co., 1963-date. 34 vols. Looseleaf format. Supplemented periodically. Also available on CD-ROM and the Internet.
Cost: $6,383 (includes annual subscription); renewal: 1995: $1,495 (price frozen since 1992); 1996: $1,568; 1997: $1,568; 1998: $1,650; 1999: $1,715; 2000: $1,840; 2001: $1,969; 2002: $2,107; 2003: $2,213; 2004: $2,324; 2005: $2,440; 2006: $2,611; 2007: $2,820; 2008: $3,046; 2009: $3,290; 2010: $3,454; 2011: $3,730; 2012: $4,066; 2013: $4,351; 2014: $4,749; CD-ROM: $7,001 (with annual subscription); renewal: 1998: $1,570; 1999: $1,715; 2000: $1,840; 2001: $1,969; 2002: $2,107; 2003: $2,213; 2004: $2,324; 2005: $2,440; 2006: $2,611; 2007: $2,820; 2008: $3,415; 2009: $3,688; 2010: $3,873; 2011: $4,183; 2012: $4,559; 2013: $4,878; 2014: $5,430.48; eBook: $5,803; renewal: 2014: $4,749.
Contains a variety of trial practice forms, including information on interrogatories, depositions, privilege, production, requests for admission, inspections, Freedom of Information Act requests, medical discovery, and criminal discovery. This set can be used as both a pre-trial discovery tool and a trial testimony guide. Contains checklists for client interviews and a reference for expert witnesses. The Appendices contain charts comparing the discovery rules of the 50 states with the federal discovery rules, as well as the text of the discovery rules at variance with the federal rules. A unique and indispensable resource for the trial attorney. With the exception of some specialized trial practice discovery guides, this is the only major set of its kind on the market.

Cost Saving Tips: If a used set is not available, buy this set new and then let it lapse after the one-year subscription has expired. Unlike works of substantive law, this set can be used effectively in a lapsed state for a number of years before updating becomes necessary, saving the purchaser nearly $3,500 annually in supplementation costs. Simply buy another new or current used set at some future date. The prospective purchaser should be aware that Interrogatories subset also appears as a part of the **Personal Injury Library** on CD-ROM or the Internet.

Contemporary Corporation Forms. 2d ed. New York: Wolters Kluwer Law & Business, 1990-date. 4 vols. Looseleaf format. Supplemented annually.
Cost: $1,749; supplementation: 1993: $145; 1994: $275; 1995: $234; 1996: $482; 1997: $320; 1998: $375; 1999: $368; 2000: $393; 2001: $410; 2002: $690; 2003: $855; 2004: $882; 2005: $900; 2006: $920; 2007: $990; 2008: $1,062; 2009: $1,137; 2010: $1,218; 2011: $1,302; 2012: $1,405; 2013: $1,524.
A collection of corporate forms drawn from some of the country's leading law firms which are keyed to the substantive text in the publisher's 8-volume **Corporation: A Service**. The forms are accompanied by text and commentary with valuable citations to applicable state statutes.

Federal Procedural Forms. Lawyers Edition. St. Paul, MN: West (Lawyers Cooperative Publishing Co.), 1975-date. 35 vols. Annual pocket parts.
Cost: $6.335; supplementation: 1991: $433; 1992; $335; 1993: $491.50; 1994: $479.50; 1995: $604.10; 1996: $726.50; 1997: $574; 1998: $680; 1999: $872; 2000: $942; 2001: $1,109.50; 2002: $1,255.50; 2003: $1,222; 2004: $1,418; 2005: $1,489.50; 2006: $1,826; 2007: $2,033; 2008: $2,053; 2009: $2,542.50; 2010: $3,125; 2011: $3,512; 2012: $4,142; 2013: $4,815; **Monthly Assured Print Price (APP):** $348/$4,176.
This comprehensive set provides the practitioner with civil, criminal, and administrative forms organized into more than 60 chapters. Each chapter includes a scope note, a listing of matters treated elsewhere in the set, and collateral references to other Lawyers Cooperative publications, including **Am. Jur. 2d**., **Federal Procedure**, **ALR**, **Am. Jur. P.O.F.**, **Am. Jur. Trials**, **Lawyers Edition Digest**, **Federal Rules Digest: Findex**, and **Federal Rules of Evidence Digest: Findex.** The forms themselves are accompanied by General References to the relevant federal rules and valuable reminders to ensure that your research is complete and up-to-date. Research References refer the use to pertinent sections of other West sources to consult when drafting and using the specific forms. Annotation References refer to both **ALR** and **L. Ed**. annotations which discuss the legal issues addressed by the forms. Finally, Procedural Guides provide the attorney with specific advice regarding the drafting and use of the forms and textual analysis of applicable statutes, rules, regulations and case law as they apply to the forms' language. Categories of forms include: notices, jury instructions, complaints, motions, affidavits, judgments, summonses, stipulations, answers, counterclaims, subpoenas, cross claims, orders, interrogatories, and writs. An excellent and exhaustive set of forms. The editorial notes and references provide clear and thorough guidance to the practitioner involved in drafting.

Cost Saving Tips: If you want the set in print, but buy a used one for $600.00. Note that the cost of supplementation in one year is just slightly less than the cost of a new set. Buy for the bolier plate, but avoid the supplementation, particularly the **Monthly Assured Print Price** program which just locks you in to high supplementation costs for which Thomson Reuters West is famous.

Fletcher Corporation Forms Annotated. 4th ed. By Lenore M. Zajdel. St. Paul, MN: West (Clark Boardman Callaghan), 1980-date. 21 vols. Annual pocket parts and periodic revised volumes.
Cost: $5,220; supplementation: 1993: $429; 1994: $528; 1995: $511; 1996: $519; 1997: $599.70; 1998: $750; 1999: $918.40; 2000: $1,097; 2001: $1,302; 2002: $1,052; 2003: $1,152.50; 2004: $1,291; 2005: $2,531.50; 2006: $2,027.50; 2007: $1,575; 2008: $2,909; 2009: $2,432; 2010: $2,638.50; 2011: $2,793; 2012: $3,072; 2013: $3,728; **Monthly Assured Print Price (APP):** $292/$3,504.
This exhaustive collection of corporate forms which is cross-referenced to **Fletcher Cyclopedia of Corporations**. Includes actual forms used by attorneys, official state and federal forms, and unofficial model forms. Each chapter of forms is preceded by explanatory text which lays out the scope of the chapter and explains where to find the law. There are forms for preincorporation contracts and articles of incorporation, bylaws of incorporation, corporate organization, stock and capital, contracts and arrangements, corporate bonds, acknowledgments, affidavits and certificates, consolidations and mergers, foreign corporations, nonprofit corporations, and more.

Cost Saving Tips: Buy the set used for $500.00. Additional savings can be achieved by going two or more years between pocket parts. The incremental value of each year's pocket parts is hardly worth the recent cost of supplementing this set. If one does aim to bring the set up-to-date periodically, one must be sure to acquire those bound volumes revised in the interim. In the last analysis, there is plenty of boiler-plate language in this set to provide a sound basis for drafting your own forms regardless of its currency, provided you are attuned to statutory changes which may impact their use.

Nichols Cyclopedia of Legal Forms Annotated. St. Paul, MN: Thomson Reuters West (Clark Boardman Callaghan), 1983-date. 39 vols. Annual pocket parts and periodic revised volumes. Also available in CD-ROM version.
Cost: $8,570; supplementation: 1992: $546; 1993: $542; 1994: $722; 1995: $842; 1996: $893; 1997: $968.60; 1998: $968.60; 1999: $1,127; 2000: $1,340; 2001: $1,711.50; 2002: $1,921; 2003: $1,403; 2004: $1,571.50; 2005: $1,993; 2006: $2,373; 2007: $2,640.50; 2008: $2,620; 2009: $3,589.50; 2010: $3,847.50; 2011: $5,417.50; 2012: $5,959; 2013: $5,471; **Monthly Assured Print Price (APP):** $493/$5,916. Combination print/CD-ROM discount may be available.
A comprehensive resource for the practicing attorney, this set contains thousands of legal forms grouped alphabetically into 225 topics. The introduction to each chapter contains «Suggestions» which outline the law and provide references to related topics. Where appropriate, each topic also includes a «Tax Introduction» which analyzes the tax issues bearing upon the area of the law, and «Checklists» to ensure that the forms the

attorney drafts are in conformity with the Internal Revenue Code, tax regulations, and other applicable authorities. Contains forms for both personal and business transactions prepared by the publisher's editorial staff.

Cost Saving Tips: Used sets have been advertised for $300.00-$400.00 depending on their currency. Buy the set used and forego supplementation which is nothing but a cash cow for the publisher. Please note, however, that the annual supplementation cost clearly exceeds the cost of a used set, making it financially advantageous to purchase a fairly current used set every few years rather than maintaining a standing order, if you really feel it necessary. It's best to view these sets as collections of amendable boiler-plate and avoid the costly supplements which add little real value except to the publisher's bottom line.

Rabkin, Jacob and Mark H. Johnson. **Current Legal Forms with Tax Analysis.** New York: Matthew Bender & Co., 1948-date. 33 vols. Looseleaf format and eBook. Supplemented several times annually.
Cost: $3,910 (includes annual subscription); annual renewal: 1995: $1,195; 1996: $1,195; 1997: $1,195; 1998: $1,255; 1999: $1,305; 2000: $1,400; 2001: $1,498; 2002: $1,603; 2003: $1,684; 2004: $1,768; 2005: $1,874; 2006: $1,893; 2007: $1,931; 2008: $2,047; 2009: $2,170; 2010: $2,235; 2011: $2,302; 2012: $2,371; 2013: $2,561; 2014: $2,795; eBook: $3,555; renewal: 2014: $2,795.
This is one of the most respected collections of non-litigation legal forms on the market. Contains forms designed to address all types of personal and business transactions, including real estate, corporations, copyrights, partnerships, domestic relations, estate planning, credit and finance, and much more. The forms themselves are accompanied by practical legal advice regarding the nature of the transactions, tax ramifications, alternatives, and other legal requirements. Addresses the tax advantages and disadvantages and cites to relevant cases, statutes, and regulations. Includes drafting and tax compliance checklists, a synoptic Table of Contents and a master index volume.

Cost Saving Tips: Forms sets are an ideal candidate for purchase on the used lawbook market, this one selling for about $800. Buy another used set at some future date when you feel it necessary to do so. Or buy a new set and avoid the supplementation trap. In the interim, you will save thousands in supplementation costs.

Warren, Oscar L., et al. **Warren's Forms of Agreement.** New York: Matthew Bender & Co., 1954-date. 7 vols. Looseleaf format. Supplemented periodically. Also available in CD-ROM version and eBook.
Cost: $2,368 (includes annual subscription); annual renewal: 1995: $601.50; 1996: $631; 1997: $631; 1998: $665; 1999: $685; 2000: $730; 2001: $781; 2002: $804; 2003: $845; 2004: $887; 2005: $958; 2006: $997; 2007: $1,057; 2008: $1,142; 2009: $1,233; 2010: $1,296; 2011: $1,361; 2012: $1,443; 2013: $1,544; 2014: $1,685; CD-ROM: $2,414; annual renewal: 1998: $635; 1999: $655; 2000: $700; 2001: $749.00; 2002: $771; 2003: $810; 2004: $851; 2005: $911; 2006: $948; 2007: $1,024; 2008: $1,106; 2009: $1,195; 2010: $1,255; 2011: $1,318; 2012: $1,397; 2013: $1,495; 2014: $1,664.64; eBook: $2,153; renewal: 2014: $1,685.
A collection of business contracts and alternate clauses for common business transaction. The contracts have been drafted to comply with the provisions of the Uniform Commercial Code, Federal Trade Commission guidelines, Truth-in-Landing Act and other applicable state and federal laws. Each chapter is preceded by a practical commentary providing an overview of the law as well as the benefits and disadvantages of various types of contracts. The four-volumes are divided into 11 parts, including Introductory overview of general drafting considerations, organization of firm, dispositions of businesses, dispositions of personal property, dispositions of real property, credit and financing, personal services, dispute resolution, protection of parties, miscellaneous contracts, and computer contracts.

Cost Saving Tips: Forms sets are an ideal candidate for purchase on the used lawbook market, this one selling for about $300. Buy another used set at some future date when you feel it necessary to do so. Or buy new and avoid the supplementation trap.

West's Federal Forms. St. Paul, MN: West, 1951-date. 19 vols. Annual pocket parts and periodic revised volumes.
Cost: $2,422; supplementation: 1994: $304.25; 1995: $149; 1996: $149; 1997: $273; 1998: $346; 1999: $195; 2000: $391.50; 2001: $372; 2002: $645.25; 2003: $540; 2004: $604.75; 2005: $530; 2006: $747.50; 2007: $831.50; 2008: $494.50; 2009: $1,133; 2010: $626; 2011: $707.50; 2012: $1,472.50; 2013: $1,766; **Monthly Assured Print Price (APP):** $168/$2,016;
A companion to West's **Federal Practice and Procedure,** this set arranges the forms in order by federal rule number for practice before the U.S. District Courts, Courts of Appeals, and United States Supreme Court. There are also separate volumes containing forms for use in both admiralty and bankruptcy actions. The forms are accompanied by explanatory notes and supporting references to primary authority.

Cost Saving Tips: Used sets may be available at a substantial discoun, but avoid the standing order for supplementation from the publisher. If you are looking for boiler-plate language, this may be just what you require.

West's Legal Forms. 3d-5th eds. St. Paul, MN: West, 1981-date. 58 vols. Annual pocket parts.
Cost: $5,124; supp.: 1995: $256; 1996: $741; 1997: $594; 1998: $562.50; 1999: $622; 2000: $884.50; 2001: $679.75; 2002: $1,221; 2003: $1,575.50; 2004: $1,268; 2005: $1,480; 2006: $1,603; 2007: $1,800.50; 2008: $2,654; 2009: $2,047; 2010: $1,248; 2011: $1,410; 2012: $3,044; 2013: $5,705; **Monthly Assured Print Price (APP):** $358/$4,296.
This 36-volume set includes thousands of legal forms organized into fourteen individual components: Business Organizations (vols. 1-5); Employee Benefit Plans (vols. 6-6A); Domestic Relations (vol. 7); Retirement Plans (vol. 8); Debtor and Debtor Relations--Bankruptcy (vols. 9-9A); Debtor and Creditor Relations--Non-Bankruptcy Rights and Remedies (vols. 10-11);

Commercial Transactions (vols. 12-15); Estate Planning (vols. 16-18): Elderlaw (vol. 18A); Real Estate Transactions (vols. 19-23); Employment --Agency--Service Agreements (vol. 24); Patents--Trademarks--Copyrights (vol. 25); Specialized Forms (vols. 26-29); and Tax Update. The Specialized Forms in volumes 26-29 include a collection of state specific acknowledgments; affidavits and certificates; agreements; arbitration; assignments; auctions; aviation and airline services; banks, banking and financial services, bonds; building agreements; cemeteries and funeral services; computer contracts; franchise agreements; gifts, subscriptions and political contributions; guaranties and sureties; health care; indemnities; information requests; insurance; labor agreements; minerals, oil and gas; motor vehicles and transportation services; nonprofit corporations and associations; powers of attorney; receipts and acknowledgments; releases; rental and lease of goods; schools, colleges and universities; shipping and boating; theaters; and tickets. There are Tables of Statutes, Rules, and Regulations and Rulings. An annually revised paperbound volume contains a General Index and a detailed guide to each section in the entire set. The forms in this set are accompanied by expert commentary, tax considerations, notes, comments, and caveats. These provide the practicing attorney with more than boiler-plate form language, but also the technical information necessary to properly use these forms in light of current law and practice. The topical arrangement allows for ease of use with each separate component containing its own index.

Cost Saving Tips: Used sets have been offered for sale at $795.00, although you may be able to locate a better deal locally. After buying it used, forego the supplementation from the publisher if you wish to avoid the steeply rising supplementation costs. West's supplementation costs for this set were once quite reasonable, but haven risen sharply in recent years under Thomson Reuters.

Additional sources of Legal Forms are available from the following publishers: Allworth Press, American Bar Association, American Law Institute, American Medical Association (AMA), Atlantic Law Book Company, Matthew Bender, Data Trace Publishing, Gould, Institute of Government, Juris Publishing, Law-Arts Association, Lawyers & Judges Publishing Co., Lega Books, LexisNexis, LexisNexis, New York State Bar Association, Nolo Press, Oceana Publications, Inc., RIA Group, SourceBooks, Thomson Reuters West. See Appendix B for addresses and telephone numbers.

Legal Profession

Aaron, Deborah and Deborah Guyol. **The Complete Guide to Contract Lawyering**. 3d ed. Seattle, WA: Lawyer Avenue, 2003. 1 vol. (288 pp.).
Available from www.lawyeravenue.com
Cost: $29.95; from $.01 on amazon.com (2014).
The recent trend towards greater use of temporary, or contract, lawyers raises numerous questions for practicing lawyers, recent law school graduates, and law firm administrators. This volume examines a number of issues related to the use of contract lawyers, including the larger forces in the economy and business world which have driven a wider use of temporaries, the concerns of the attorney interested in working as a contract lawyer, the needs of those charged with hiring contract lawyers, and the complex ethical and business issues which affect the relationship between contract lawyers and hiring lawyers, including conflict of interest and client notification, independent contractor status, malpractice liability and coverage, written agreements and the involvement of contract lawyer placement agencies. The appendices include a variety of useful articles, ethics opinions, and a list of contract lawyer placement agencies. A former civil litigator, Deborah Aaron is the author of two books on legal career development. Deborah Guyol, formerly with Davis, Polk & Wardwell, is coordinator of the Oregon Women Lawyers Contract Lawyers Referral Service.

Aaron, Marjorie Corman. **Client Science: Advice for Lawyers on Counseling Clients through Bad News and Other Legal Realities**. New York: Oxford University Press, 2012. 1 vol. (242 pp.). Paperbound.
Cost: $39.95; from $13.05 on amazon.com; kindle: $16.19 (2014).
Client counseling and communication often requires deft diplomacy, particularly when the attorney has something to share that is not pleasing to the client. Lawyers have a professional responsibility to provide expert advice and counseling to a client regardless of how that advice may be received. Clients are fully informed only when they understand and accept the legal realities, opportunities, risk and consequences of the law and process as it applies to their circumstances. Communicating these realities must often contend with client emotion and psychology, which may resist the ramifications of their attorney's advice. In the author's view, "the only "fully informed" client is "one who can step back, seeing what his lawyer sees and understands what his lawyer knows—a client who has fully integrated the lawyer's information, explanation, and advice." The aim of this book is help the lawyer meet the highest level of practice in client counseling through understanding of client psychology and motivations that may conflict with acceptance of a rationally based settlement. Attorneys must understand, for example, that clients are often motivated by moral or principled considerations that transcend mere economic self-interest. Drawing upon a wealth of social science research, the author probes the intricacies of client communication in instances in which what the attorney must recommend is in conflict with what the client wants to hear, and will accept. Marjorie Corman Aaron is Professor of Practice and Director of the Center for Practice at the University of Cincinnati College of Law, where she teaches courses in client counseling, negotiation, mediation, mediation advocacy, and decision analysis. She has more than 20 years' experience in mediation, arbitration, and negotiation and dispute resolution training.

Abel, Richard L. **Lawyers in the Dock: Learning from Attorney Disciplinary Proceedings**. New York: Oxford University Press, 2008. 1 vol. (573 pp.). Paperbound.
Cost: $48; from $27.25 on amazon.com; kindle: $29.24 (2014).
While Americans rely on lawyers for a host of personal and business reasons, they also mistrust them. Most lawyers are trustworthy most of the time. Despite professional codes of

ethics and attempts to instill standards of ethical conduct through legal education and bar examinations, however, some lawyers continue to violate rules of professional conduct and compromise the interests of their clients. This volume examines the current state of legal ethics, with detailed attention to six cases in which New York lawyers were disciplined for overcharging, neglect, and excessive zeal. An introductory chapter provides an excellent overview of the current state of lawyer trust and betrayal. Richard Abel has been studying the legal profession since 1973, when he was hired by UCLA Law school to teach professional responsibility under the new ABA mandate following the Watergate scandal. He is the author of eight books on the legal profession.

Abrams, Lisa L. **The Official Guide to Legal Specialties: An Insider's Guide to Every Major Practice Area**. Chicago: Harcourt Legal & Professional Publications, 2000. 1 vol. (475 pp.). Paperbound.
Cost: $21.95; from $.56 on amazon.com (2014)
Selecting the specific legal specialty best suited to one's interests, skills, and temperament can be a laborious and haphazard affair. Both recent law graduates as well as experienced attorneys contemplating a career shift often lack adequate information to properly evaluate the dozens of options available to them. A project of the National Association for Law Placement, this volume explores 30 major legal specialties with the aid of experienced subject specialists. Each chapter follows a uniform format, beginning with an overview of the area, and addressing such questions as where attorneys in the practice specialty work, the type of cases and clients encountered, the daily activities involved in that practice, the rewards of such practice, the common path of entry, the skills most of important for success in that field, and the types of law school classes and experiences recommended. The author is a graduate of the University of Illinois College of Law and served as both Assistant Dean and Director of Career Services at the Chicago-Kent College of Law. She is currently a career planning consultant and teaches classes in career development, leadership, and adult learning strategies at Roosevelt University in Chicago.

Altman, Mary Ann and Robert I. Weil. **How to Manage Your Law Office.** New York: Matthew Bender & Co., 1973-date. 2 vols. Looseleaf format and eBook. Updated annually.
Cost: $416; supplementation: 1995: $145; 1996: $145; 1997: $145; 1998: $155; 1999: $162; 2000: $175; 2001: $187; 2002: $201; 2003: $212; 2004: $223; 2005: $239; 2006: $249;, 2007: $263; 2008: $279; 2009: $296; 2010: $322; 2011: $314; 2012: $336; 2013: $347; 2014: $360; eBook: $416; 2014: $360; from $293.07 on amazon.com
For more than 25 years, this manual has provided lawyers with expert advice on the principles and practices essential to efficient law office management. The authors, partners in the firm of Altman Weil & Pensa, Inc., have extensive experience as consultants to law firms. Coverage includes management principles for lawyers, the organization of private law firms, the organization of corporate legal and patent departments, legal fees, compensation and profit distribution, growth, mergers and branch offices, planning and marketing legal services, total quality management (TQM), law firm retreats, associate hiring, training and promotion, agreements for partnerships and professional corporations, personnel administration of staff employees, administrative systems and procedures, accounting and timekeeping, managing computers, office automation, law office design, nonlawyer staff, and the changing practice of law. The appendices contain a number of sample agreements and letters.

Cost Saving Tips: This is the type of title which can survive quite well without supplementation. Drop the standing order after the one year's service has run out and buy it again in when you feel you need a more recent edition.

Altman Weil Pensa's Introduction to Law Practice Management. By Marjorie A. Miller. 3d ed. New York: Matthew Bender & Co., 1993. 1 vol. (334 pp.). No supplementation.
Cost: OUT-OF-PRINT, from $1.72 on amazon.com (2014).
An excellent basic resource on the business aspects of the legal profession by members of one of the leading law office management consulting firms. Includes a discussion of management principles, the organization of various types of law firms, fee-setting and collection, building and maintaining a law practice, law office management, administration, technology, the use of legal assistants, and attorney recruitment, hiring and compensation. Designed as a law school text, this is a less costly alternative to the more detailed practitioner-oriented texts.

American Bar Association. **2013 Legal Technology Survey Report: Law Office Technology**. Chicago: American Bar Association, Legal Technology Resource Center, 2013 (May). 1 vol. (131 pp.). Paperbound. New editions published annually. Also available as pdf through the ABA web store.
Cost: $350 ($300 to ABA members); the complete set of six reports is available at a cost of $1,800 ($1,550 for ABA members).
Since 1990, the American Bar Association has conducted comprehensive surveys on law firm technology use. The 2013 results, drawing exclusively upon lawyer respondents, are segmented into six reports: Technology Basics; Law Office Technology; Litigation and Courtroom Technology; Web and Communication Technology; Online Research; and Mobile Lawyers. According to the Executive Summary, the reports are based on the results of responses to a 218-question survey which was divided into six separate survey questionnaires drawn from a random selection of 12,500 ABA lawyer members. The responses to the Law Office Technology survey are based on 818 Law Office Technology questionnaires, represented a cross-section of law firm sizes. Among the respondents, 41.7% are partners, 22.4% are solo practitioners, 12% are managing partners, 5.4% are of counsel, and 3.9% are other or do not practice in a law firm. Years of admission to the bar: 0-4 years: 10.9%; 5-9 years: 10.4%; 10-19 years: 18.4%; 20-29 years: 23.7%; and 30 or more years: 36.6%. Men represented 71.2% of the respondents, women 28.8%. The most common practice areas based on billing were litigation with 36.5%, corporate with 22.5%, wills and trusts with 19.5%, real estate with 19.1%, contracts with 19%; estates, commercial with 16.1%, employment/labor with 12.5%, general practice with 12.3%, intellectual property with 11.5%, family law 10.3%, tax with 8.8%, personal injury with 8.6%,and baning and finance with 8.2%. A variety of other specialities followed. The

respondents also indicated that the average percentage of their fees were 73.7% hourly, 12.5% fixed, 7.9% contingent, 4.4% retainer, and 1.5% other.

Each volume includes a Trend Report which describes the Legal Technology Survey Reports generally, and the individual report specifically. The Law Office Technology Report is devoted to survey findings regarding computer hardware and software usage, including primary computers, computers/personal digital assistants, printers, scanners, storage, hardware use, product brand names, communicatons, documents, general office software, scanning, legal-specific software, sccurity, software use, product brand names, online service providers, and networks/private portals/intranets/extranets.

The 2013 survey results revealed that laptops have gained ground since the 2007 survey, with 77.6% of respondents reporting laptops as their primary computer, up from 29% in 2007. Desktop computers were used by 71.1% of respondents. The availability of mobile/cell phones jumped to 88.3% in 2013, up from 71% in the 2006 survey. Computer software usage is also tallied, including software for the following functions: accounting, database, docket/calendaring—not rule-based, calendaring, anti-spam, anti-virus, conflict checking, contracts, electronic billing, integrated desktop, presentation, case management, project management, spreadsheets, time and billing, time entry, word processing, and variety of other office functions. The survey results are reported in the form of data tables, and bar charts.

The Legal Technology Survey Reports represent a significant contribution to the profession by the ABA's Legal Technology Resource Center and an invaluable tool for law firms evaluating their uses of technology or contemplating the purchase and implementation of new technology hardware or software.

American Bar Association. **2013 Legal Technology Survey Report: Online Research**. Chicago: American Bar Association, Legal Technology Resource Center, 2013. 1 vol. (104 pp.). Paperbound. New editions published annually. Also available as pdf from ABA web store.
Cost: $350 ($300 to ABA members); the complete set of five reports is available at a cost of $1,800 ($1,550 for ABA members).
Since 1990, the American Bar Association has conducted comprehensive surveys on law firm technology use. The 2013 results, drawing exclusively upon lawyer respondents, are segmented into six reports:Technology Basics; Law Office Technology; Litigation and Courtroom Technology; Web and Communication Technology; Online Research; and Mobile Lawyers. According to the Executive Summary, the reports are based on the results of responses to a 218-question survey which was divided into six separate survey questionnaires drawn from a random selection of 12,500 ABA lawyer members. The 906 responses to the Online Research survey represented a cross-section of the profession: 41.5% partners; 22.1% solo practitioners, 17% associates; 10.2% managing partners; 5.8% of counsel; and 3.4% other.

The Online Research survey covered Demographics; Demographics: Practice Areas; Demographics: Location; Legal Research: Generally; Legal Research: Locations; Legal Research: Formats; Legal Research; Online Legal Research Resources; Use of Free Online Legal Research Resources; Use of Fee-Based Online Legal Research; Legal Research Away from the Office Current Awareness; Knowledge Management; Knowledge Management: Product Brand Names; and Continuing Legal Education (CLE).

The 2013 survey findings reveal that the mean percentage of time spent conducting legal research is 17.7%, with little difference bewteen solo practitioners (19.5%) and attorneys in firms of 500 more (18.9%). Of all respondents, 6.7% conduct legal research regularly; 29.9% occasionally; 36.7% seldom; and 26.7% never. As to formats, 40.9% use print regularly; 39.5% occasionally; 16.5% seldom; and 3.1% never. CD-ROM, or other moveable media, is used regularly by just 5.5% of respondents and occasionally by another 18.9%, but seldom by 40.3% and never by 35.3%. Free Internet or online services are utilized by 88.3% of respondents (59.6% regularly; 28.7% occasionally), while 9.3% rarely use these services, and 2.4% never. As to online legal research, fully 95.9% report conducting such research online. Among this group, 92.9% of respondents report doing such research using free online legal resources; and 85.6% report using fee-based online legal research resources. The use of laptop computers to conduct research away from the office has risen significantly. Fully 60.1% of respondents now report regularly conducting such research using a laptop computer, with another 21.0% doing so occasionally. Legal research utilizing a Smartphone or Blackberry has also risen, with 25% conducting such research regularly and 22.7% occasionally. For current awareness, 97.8% now use the Internet.

But the findings of greatest interest are those which identify the fee-based online legal research providers utilized most often by the respondents. WestlawNext and Westlaw classic alone account for 28.1% and 25.7% respecttively of the responses (53.8% in all). Coming in a distant second are Lexis at 24.1% and Lexis Advance at 5.2% (29.3% in all). No other service garners as much as 3% of the respondents' votes. RIA Checkpoint and Fastcase are each cited by 2.8% of respondents, BNA by 2.1%, Loislaw by 1.8%, Practical Law Company (PLC) (also West) by 1.2%, CCH by 0.9%, Casemaker by 0.9%. Bloomberg Law, which was lavished with such rich financial resources and heralded with such fanfare comes in at a dismal 0.7%, showing how difficult it is to break the dominance of the Westlaw and Lexis duopoly over the high-end online legal research market. The survey also probes the degree to which have firms have a Knowledge Management initiative, with just 14.1% answering in the affirmative, 53.3% in the negative, and 32.4% not knowing.

The Online Survey Report reveals some interesting statistics regarding the relative use of online fee-based formats, online free formats, and print sources for various types of legal materials. For federal case law, for example the figures are: 61.3%/27.1%/2.7%; for federal legislation and statutes: 46.7%/40.6%/4.0%; federal administrative, regulatory and executive materials: 28.1%/$47.7%/2.5%; law reviews/ legal periodicals: 47.1%/28.5%/13.7%; legal citators: 50.9%/18.4%/3.2%; legal forms: and legal treatises: legal forms: 25.4%/38.6%/14.1%; public records: 20.9%/72.1%/1.6%, and legal treatises/secondary materials: 50.1%/21.9%/22.0%. The figures expose the degree to which attorneys have embraced online formats to the exclusion of print, with legal treatises, legal forms, and law reviews/periodicals being three notable exceptions. The fact that law firms have universally jettisoned their collections of print reporters is reflected in the fact than less than 3% of respondents report using federal decisions in print format. In general, the figures reflect the steady drift away from print in favor of online formats, a development exacerbated by the steady and onerous increases in the costs of print materials.

Of the five reports in this series, the report on **Online Research** offers the richest and most useful content for law librarians and other firm members responsible for the selection of legal information resources. The full report provides detailed evidence of lawyer research preferences and habits as a basis for law firm decision-making in this vital area.

American Bar Association. **2013 Compendium of Professional Responsibility Rules and Standards**. Chicago: American Bar Association, Center for Professional Responsibility, 2013. 1 vol. (686 pp.). Paperbound and ebook.
Cost: 2013 Edition: $39.95 ($29.95 to members; $19.95 to students) (2014).
A useful collection of rules and standards governing professional conduct by lawyers and judges. Includes the following: ABA Model Rules of Professional Conduct, ABA Model Code of Professional Responsibility, ABA Model Code of Judicial Conduct, ABA Canons of Professional Ethics, ABA Standards for Imposing Lawyer Sanctions, ABA Model Rules Related to Multijurisdictional Practice, Model Rules for Client Protection (Selected), ABA Professionalism Codes and Creeds, and ABA Practice Guidelines. Also included are SEC Standards Part 205) of Professional Conduct for Attorneys Appearing and Practicing Before the Commission in the Representation of an Insurer, IRS Regulations (Circular N. 230) Governing the Practice of Attorneys, CPAs, Enrolled Agents, Enrolled Actuaries, and Appraisers Before the IRS, Selected Federal Rules of Civil Procedure, Federal Rules of Appellate Procedure, and Federal Rules of Evidence regarding various aspects of attorney conduct, and Selected ABA Formal Ethics Opinions regarding various aspects of attorney and professional conduct. Produced under the auspices of the ABA's Center for Professional Responsibility and its Publications Board.

ABA/BNA Lawyers' Manual on Professional Conduct. Washington, DC: American Bar Association and Bloomberg BNA, 1984-date. 2 vols. Looseleaf format. Biweekly supplements. Available in print and on the Internet.
Cost: Full service: $1,935 per year; Internet: $2,198 per year (1 user) (2014).
An authoritative and practical guide to the resolution of ethical problems encountered by members of the legal profession. Volume one includes full text of the ABA Model Rules of Professional Conduct and other professional standards. The service is topically arranged around specific ethical issues, including qualifications, lawyer-client relationship, fees, client trust funds and property, conflicts of interest, confidentiality, trial conduct, obligations to third persons, advertising and solicitation, types of practice, misconduct and discipline, regulation of bar, and malpractice. There is a detailed subject index and table of cases. The remainder of volume one consists of full text of recent ABA ethics opinions and digests of state and local ethics opinions. Volume two is reserved for Current Reports which contain articles on court decisions, ethics opinions, disciplinary proceedings, bar association activities and legislative action. Subscription also includes transfer binders for back issues of Current Reports.

American Bar Foundation. **Analyzing Law's Reach: Empirical Research on Law and Society**. Edited by John P. Heinz. Chicago: American Bar Foundation, 2008. 1 vol. (910 pp.). Hardbound.
Cost: $89.95; from $7.14 on amazon.com (2014).
The law, legal processes, and legal institutions have been subjected to a enormous body of empirical research by scholars. Since its founding in 1952, the American Bar Foundation has been the leading research institute for the study of law. This collection of articles assembles some of the best research conducted under ABF auspices over the past twenty years as initially published in a variety of the leading scholarly journals in law, economics, and sociology, as well as the monographic literature. The articles fall under the six major areas of scholarly inquiry: criminal justice, discrimination and social justice, legal decision-making, legal history, the legal profession, and globalization. Specific articles examine such fascinating subjects as the economic analysis of a drug-selling gang's finances, juror reactions to attorneys at trial, detecting discrimination, the impact of taxes on Internet commerce, victim impact testimony, observations on the transformation of urban law practice, and the role of inside counsel in large corporations. Each section includes a bibliography of selected references. Particularly valuable to lawyers whose practices make use of empirical research or those involved in policy debates.

Anders, Kelly Lynn. **The Organized Lawyer**. Durham, NC: Carolina Academic Press, 2009. 1 vol. (155 pp.).
Cost: $22.00; from $10.99 on amazon.com; kindle: $15.99 (2014).
While lawyers are regularly sanctioned for a variety of misdeeds, including inaccessibility to clients, commingling of funds, and failure to produce records to opposing counsel, to name just a few, these failings may be generally attributed to a lack of organization. This succinct volume provides specific guidance on the mostly mundane organizational details that must be addressed by the successful lawyer. Beginning with an consideration of the attorney's organizational type, it proceeds to address such topics as office layouts, desk arrangements, paper and electronic files, financial recordkeeping, planners and electronic organizers, organization of the home office, alternative work areas, home and office libraries, personal services, marketing and entertaining, the professional wardrobe, and keeping on track. While a useful overview, some of the topics are treated with superficiality, particularly that dealing with home and office libraries. The author is Associate Dean for Student Affairs at Washburn University School of Law, director of its Externship and Pro Bono programs, and teaches Art Law.

Annotated Model Rules of Professional Conduct. 7th ed. Chicago: American Bar Association, Center for Professional Responsibility, 2011. 1 vol. (693 pp.).
Cost: $159.95 ($143.95 to ABA members; $119.95 to Section members) (2014).
As the American Bar Association's definitive resource on lawyer ethics, this volume incorporates all of the amendments made to the Model Rules of Professional Conduct through 2007, incorporating the work of the Ethics Committee, the Commission of Multijurisdictional Practice, and the Standing Committee on Ethics and Professional Responsibility. Each chapter contains the text of a rule and its comment, a detailed discussion of the rule's meaning, application and interpretation, with citations to more than 4,000 cases and ethics opinions, hundreds of law review articles, and relevant sections of the **Restatement of the Law (Third) Governing Lawyers**. First adopted in 1983, the Model Rules of Professional Conduct have been adopted in most jurisdictions. Since the ABA's adoption of wholesale changes to the Model Rules in 2002, most jurisdictions have amended their rules in response to these Model Rules amendments. Consequently, this is the first edition of the AMR to provide analysis of the major body of ethics opinions and case law interpreting these new rules. The unnanoated **Model Rules of Professional Conduct** (2014) is also available from the ABA.

Avery, Michael and Danielle McLaughlin. **The Federalist Society: How Conservatives Took the Law Back from Liberals**. Nashville, TN: Vanderbilt University Press, 2013. 1 vol. (294 pp.).
Cost: $35.00; from $11.43 on amazon.com; kindle: $10.00 (2014).
The Federalist Society for Law and Public Policy Studies was founded by three conservative law students: Steven Calabresi at Yale, and Lee Liberman and David McIntosh at the University of Chicago, assisted by such prominent conservative legal scholars as Robert Bork, Richard Posner, Antonin Scalia, Richard Epstein, and Frank Easterbrook. Its first major event was a symposium on federalism held in April 1982 and co-sponsored by the Yale and University of Chicago law school groups, the *Harvard Journal of Law and Public Policy*, and the Stanford Foundation for Law and Economic Policy. The Federalist Society was founded on the principles that the "state exists to preserve freedom, that the separation of governmental powers is central to our Constitution, and that it is emphatically the province and duty of the judiciary to say what the law is, not what it should be." It champions a "reordering of priorities within the legal system to place a premium on individual liberty, traditional values, and the rule of law." The organization quickly became a home for conservative and libertarian law students across the country who had previously felt isolated by the liberal orthodoxy of their academic institutions. Today, the organization claims that over 45,000 conservative lawyers and law students are involved in its activities, 13,000 of them dues-paying members. Four Supreme Court Justices—Samuel Alito, Clarence Thomas, Antonin Scalia and John Roberts--are current or former members, as are many members of the federal judiciary, and, during the Bush years, a number of lawyers in the Justice Department and other federal agencies. This book represents a decidedly left-of-center critique of the Federalist Society, which examines its beliefs, funding, and policy positions, with particular attention to its positions on issues of private property regulation, race and gender discrimination, personal sexual autonomy, American exceptionalism, sovereignty, and International law. Beyond its basic policy disagreements with the Federal Society and its supporters, the book inaccurately portrays the success of the Federal Society as some kind of stealth, untoward, or nefarious influence in the legal culture, rather than as an organization grounded in a fundamentally different set of philosophical presuppositions, rooted in liberty, limited government, and free markets. To the authors' revealing question: "How did this group of conservatives succeed in moving their theories into the mainstream of legal thought?" one can only reply that they were never outside the mainstream, but fundamental to the very fabric of the American experience in ordered liberty and the principle of limited government enshrined in the U.S. Constitution. Nor is there anything particularly surprising about the success of Federalist Society members once they move beyond the intellectually conformist and politically correct world of academia, where Progressive ideas are regnant, and into the broader culture where they are not. A modest incubator can, under the circumstances, produce exceptional results in the wider legal and political culture. Moreover, the authors' portrait of the dominance of Federalist Society members among federal court or agency appointments is already out-of-date with the ascendancy of the Obama administration, even if it had any validity within the scope of the vast federal bureaucracy. Also, to read the authors analysis is to get the impression that the Federalist Society has come to dominate the political life of their law schools, an assessment that is not even remotely factual, as Walter Olson details in **Schools for Misrule: Legal Academia and an Overlawyered America** (see below). Voter registration data clearly demonstrate that law school faculties, like academics generally, are dominated by registered Democrats; and a cursory examination of law school web sites reveal that most student groups or legal clinics are clearly Progressive or race- and gender-based in their political orientation. Ironically, and despite its scholarly trappings, this book is chiefly useful as a window into Progressive thinking about the Federalist Society, rather than as an objective and unbiased analysis of the organization's positions. Michael Avery is a Professor of Law at Suffolk University Law School where he teaches constitutional law and evidence, and is a past president of the National Lawyers Guild, a hard left legal organization which, according to its web site is "dedicated to the need for basic change in the structure of our political and economic system," and has been outside the mainstream of legal thought throughout its history, as well as an echo chamber for Soviet foreign policy, according to historian Guenter Lewy (see **The Cause that Failed**, pp. 283-287). Danielle McLaughlin is an Associate in the Boston office of Nixon Peabody LLP and served as editor-in-chief of the *Journal of High Technology Law* at Suffolk University Law School.

Baldwin, Ben G. **The Lawyer's Guide to Insurance: Professional Insurance Coverage for Professionals and Their Clients**. Chicago: American Bar Association, 1999. 1 vol. (317 pp.) Softbound.
Cost: OUT-OF-PRINT; was $89.95 ($79.95 to members of the Senior Lawyers Division or the Section of Real Property, Probate and Tort Law) (2014).
This reference is intended to provide lawyers and their clients

with guidance on a variety of insurance-related matters, including disability insurance, long-term care, medical insurance, homeowner's insurance, vehicle insurance, personal and professional liability insurance, variable universal life, and annuities. The author also address such topics as insurance company solvency, life insurance definitions and purposes, types of life insurance contracts, and managing life insurance. He also examines critical tax and financial planning considerations. Ben G. Baldwin is president and owner of Baldwin Financial Systems, Inc., an investment advisory firm involved in financial consulting and planning for individual and corporate clients. He is also a consultant to the industry, an author, and speaker.

Basri, Carole and Irving Kagan. **Corporate Legal Departments**. 4th ed. New York: Practising Law Institute, 2011-date. 1 vol. (approx. 430 pp.). Looseleaf format. Periodic supplementation.
Cost: $365; supplementation: 2012: $326; 2013: $340; 3d ed.: 2005: $174; 2006: $101; 2007: $236; 2008: $248; 2009: $136; 2010: $152; 2011: $310 (new ed.).
The practice of law in corporate America has become increasingly complex and demanding. The role of in-house counsel demands an intimate knowledge of corporate affairs and a variety of new skills. This volume takes an in-depth look at such issues as ethics in the corporate environment, possible conflicts of interest between officers and the corporation, the attorney-client privilege, malpractice, confidentiality, whistleblowing, internal investigations, corporate governance, recruitment of legal staff, the use of outsourcing and non-legal staff to boost productivity, time and cost accountability, use of outside counsel, and the use of such cutting-edge techniques as re-engineering and benchmarking. The volume includes hundreds of case studies and techniques for improving productivity. Carole Basri, formerly assistant general counsel at Maidenform, Inc. and now consultant to Deloitte & Touche and Executive Director of the Greater New York Chapter of the American Corporate Counsel Association, is an adjunct professor of law at NYU School of Law. Irving Kagan is a partner and counsel to Madison Partners, L.L.C., an investment and management-consulting group based in New York City.

Batman, Jean L. **Advising the Small Business: Forms and Advice for the Legal Practitioner**. 2d ed. Chicago: American Bar Association, 2011. 1 vol. (843 pp.).
Cost: $159.95; from $91.88 on amazon.com (2014).
Designed for general practitioners, small firm attorneys, and lawyers engaged in providing legal advice to small businesses, this volume provides advice and forms in a number of areas central to small business activity. The chapters cover representation of small businesses, the protection of intellectual property, business plans, contracts for small businesses, legal structures fort small businesses, organizing and cleaning up a corporation, organizing and cleaning up an LLC, organizing and cleaning up a partnership, founders and advisors, raising money through private placements, seed financing and angel investors, venture capital, hiring employees, providing equity incentives to employees, and liquidity events. The boilerplate forms, on a companion CD-ROM, can be easily adapted to individual circumstances. An ideal desktop companion for any attorney representing small business entities. Formerly a partner in the San Francisco firm of Duane Morris LLP, the author founded Legal Venture Counsel, Inc. in 2004 for the purpose of providing outside general counsel services to investors, entrepreneurs, and small businesses.

Blomquist, Robert F. **Lawyerly Virtues**. Lake Mary, FL: Vandeplas Publishing, 2008. 1 vol. (242 pp.). Paperbound.
Cost: $39.95; from $1.45 on amazon.com (2014).
The process of legal education is typically dominated by the acquisition of specific bodies of knowledge and professional skills. Ethical, spiritual and personal virtues are often lost in the course of preparing for or earning a living in the day-to-day practice of law. In this warm and wise book, Professor Robert Blomquist offers a thoughtful exposition of the vital virtues which should characterize American public lawyers. This book is his response to the low esteem with which members of the bar are held by the general public, as well as to the dissatisfaction many lawyers have with their own profession, particularly their perceived inability to contribute to the public good. His response is a discussion of the primary virtues which should be part of both a law school education and the legal profession generally, among them balance, integrity, idealism, compassion, courage, creativity, energy, justice, discipline, and perseverance. A Professor of Law at Valparaiso University since 1986, Robert Blomquist draws upon more than thirty years experience as a litigator, legal consultant, public servant, and law professor. His observations and advice should be an essential ingredient of every lawyer's professional training.

Bouchoux, Deborah E. **A Concise Guide to Legal Research and Writing**. 2d ed. New York: Wolters Kluwer & Business, 2013. 1 vol. (512 pp.). Paperbound.
Cost: $109.95; from $100.45 on amazon.com; 1st ed.: $6.10 (2014).
Legal professionals are expected to perform legal research both competently and cost-effectively. Intended as a textbook for courses in legal research and writing, this well-organized and clearly written guide provides an excellent introduction to the mechanics of legal research and the most common forms of legal writing. Following an introduction to the process of legal research, the author directs her attention to the federal and state court systems, statutory law, case law and judicial opinions, the process of locating cases through digests and annotated law report, and secondary authorities. A chapter on Special Research Issues examines legislative history, executive materials, administrative law, international law, and municipal law. Digital resources, including Westlaw, LexisNexis, non-print research tools, and Internet research are also addressed. She also discusses legal citation form, the process of updating and validating your research, and putting it all together. The chapters on legal writing examine the basics of legal writing, strategies for effective writing, legal correspondence, legal memoranda, legal briefs, and proofreading and document design. The text includes numerous features to enhance learning outcomes, including chapter overviews, key terms, practice tips, ethics alerts, help lines (telephone numbers and web sites), and cyber sites, research assignments, Internet assignments, and citation form. There is also a companion web site which contains student study aids, instructor resources, and links to helpful web

sites and updates. The book also comes with a free four-month student subscription to Loislaw Online.

Brickman, Lester. **Lawyers Barons: What Their Contingency Fees Really Cost America**. New York: Cambridge University Press, 2011. 1 vol. (556 pp.). Paperbound.
Cost: $28.99; from $8.95 on amazon.com; rent kindle ed.: $15.49 (2014).
This latest salvo in the ongoing debate over tort reform aims its barrel at contingency fee arrangements that unjustly enrich lawyers at the expense of both their clients and society at large. More generally, the book is an inquiry into how contingency fees distort the civil justice system, influence the political system, and endanger democratic governance. On the one hand, contingency fees are the way personal injury lawyers are able to finance access to the courts for those wrongfully injured. And although the general public senses that lawyers manipulate the legal system to serve their own ends, few are aware of the high costs that come with contingency fees. This volume provides a window into the seamy side of contingency fees that are protected and supported by the bench and bar. The author takes issue with the broad academic consensus, to argue that the financial incentives for lawyers to litigate are so inordinately high that they perversely impact our civil justice system and impose other unconscionable costs. In doing so, he presents a well-reasoned and exhaustively researched intellectual defense of tort reform efforts. With an introduction by Professor Richard Epstein, the author addresses such questions as the reasonableness of contingency fee profits, the degree to which tort lawyers have increased their profits by restraining competition, why the market has failed to correct the absence of price competition, the impediments posed by the bar, the litigation explosion, class actions, punitive damages, and other critical topics. This is an essential read for anyone interested in the tort reform and the role of contingency fees in that debate. Lester Brickman is professor law and former dean at Benjamin Cardozo School of Law at Yeshiva University, and a leading authority on the topics of legal ethics and contingency fees.

Bronsteen, John. **Writing a Legal Memo**. New York, NY: Foundation Press, Inc., 2006. 1 vol. (150 pp.). Softbound. Available from West Academic.
Cost: $18; from $14.80 on amazon.com; kindle ed.: $17.60 (2014).
This brief little volume provides a succinct introduction to the basic principles and practices of writing a legal memo, including guidelines for writing clear sentences, organization, research, substantive rules for writing, including analysis of cases and statutes, **Blue Book** citation style, and a writing checklist. John Bronsteen is Assistant Professor, Loyola University Chicago School of Law.

Butler, Sarina, and Richard G. Paszkiet, eds. **The Lawyer's Guide to Buying, Selling, Merging, and Closing a Law Practice**. Chicago: American Bar Association, Senior Lawyers Division, 2007. 1 vol. (215 pp.).
Cost: OUT-OF-PRINT; was $99.95 ($79.95 to members) (2014).
Building a law practice is usually a lifetime career endeavor, requiring intense and sustained activity over a period of many years. The various aspects of law firm and career management are regularly addressed in a variety of texts, manuals, seminars and CLE programs. Less considered are topics which confront the attorney at the end of his or her career, when the task of closing, selling, or merging a law practice is being contemplated; or the younger practitioner considering the acquisition of an existing practice and its client base. While there are numerous advantages to buying an existing law practice, the potential buyer must be conscious of the many factors involved before contemplating such a move, including the ethical aspects of acquiring a law practice, the valuation of a law firm, the tax consequences of «retiring» a partner's interest in a law firm taxed as a partnership, or selling a niche practice. The contributing authors also consider such topics as the business responsibilities in closing a law practice, the ethical aspects of winding down a law practice, file preservation, and the termination of client and employee relationships. This guide also includes checklists, forms, sample agreements, and sample letters as well as a material from the **ABA's Model Rules of Professional Conduct**. Due for a second edition. Believe ot or not, vultures on amazon.com are selling this title for prices ranging from $899.95 to $2,877.00.

Cain, George H. **Law Partnership: Its Rights and Responsibilities**. 2d ed. Chicago: American Bar Association, 1999. 1 vol. (362 pp.). Paperbound.
Cost: $89.95 ($79.95 to Senior Lawyer Division members); from $24.95 on amazon.com (2014).
An in-depth analysis of the law governing relations among partners and between partners and their firms and employees. Based on his analysis of more than 200 recent cases, the author outlines the mechanics of drafting a workable partnership agreement and provides guidance in the relationships between partners and associates. The author also examines the different classes of partners and their levels of authority, voting requirements and restrictions for various partner classes, meeting notifications, instances when substance may be disclosed or omitted, shares and the procedures to ensure fairness and a right of appeal, The second edition also adds a chapter on non-competition and forfeiture-for-competition clauses, including a discussion of Model Rule 5.6, defenses to the application of the rule, and prohibitions on advertising and exceptions in law practice sales. The author is a graduate of Harvard Law School with more than fifty years experience in corporate law and business litigation. He is currently Of Counsel to the New England firm of Day, Berry & Howard.

Cain, George H. **Turning Points: New Paths and Second Careers for Lawyers**. 2d ed. Chicago: American Bar Association, Senior Lawyers Division, 2010. 1 vol. (163 pp.). Paper.
Cost: $29.95 ($24.95 to members of the Senior Lawyers Division); from $4.84 on amazon.com (2014).
Disillusionment with the practice of law has affected growing numbers of lawyers, both young and not so young. Many find the life of the lawyer too demanding of their time and energies, leaving them with little opportunity to enjoy the fruits of their financial success. This volume examines the factors to be

considered when contemplating a major career move, as well as a number of the alternative career paths for which those with legal training may be suited. The author looks at the decision itself, the process of looking for new opportunities, financial considerations, and the psychological factors involved in a career change. He examines the possibilities of remaining in the practice of law, but under different circumstances. Finally he presents a number of alternative careers, including alternative dispute resolution, government service, law librarianship, teaching, and community service. The author has worked as a corporate attorney for more than fifty years and is currently Of Counsel to the Hartford firm of Day, Berry & Howard.

Calloway, James M. and Mark A. Robertson, eds. **Winning Alternatives to the Billable Hour: Strategies That Work**. 3d ed. Chicago: American Bar Association, Law Practice Management Section, 2008. 1 vol. (287 pp.). Softbound. Includes CD-ROM.
Cost: $99.95 ($74.95 to Section Members); from $59.79 on amazon.com (2014).
Law firm billing practices are among the most hotly debated issues among lawyers, CEOs, and law firm management committees. This volume, which builds on two previous ABA titles: **Beyond the Billable Hour** (1989) and **Win-Win Billing Strategies** (1992), describes the underpinnings of law firm billing and its relationship to client value. The authors of this volume analyze fifteen methods by which law firms currently bill for legal services and discuss the alternative billing methods which are available, as well as the advantages and disadvantages of each. They provide suggestions for implementing alternative billing practices and communicating these to clients, as well as the process of evaluating implemented systems and the adjustments which can be made along the way. Based on real-life experiences, this volume provides the reader with detailed information about billing practices and how to handle problems which may arise. The volume also includes a diskette containing sample forms, proposals and templates for use in implementing alternative billing systems.

Coffey, Kendall. **Spinning the Law: Trying Cases in the Court of Public Opinion**. Amherst, NY: Prometheus Books, 2010. 1 vol. (404 pp.). Hardbound.
Cost: $26.00; from $.01 on amazon.com (2014).
In many high profile cases, clients, whether civil or criminal, are tried not only before a judge and jury, but before the court of public opinion. For the media savvy attorney, shaping a client's public persona involves the skillful manipulation of a media establishment hungry for copy in a world of twenty-four hour news cycles. The author of this volume explains why a lawyer should be concerned about more than just winning a successful verdict in a court of law, but winning in the court of public opinion as well. For high-profile clients, the task of protecting reputations is critical, and one not usually addressed by a law school education. To accomplish this, the attorney must deflect the collateral damage which may accrue from the evidence introduced at trial. In this fascinating look at a number of celebrated trials, both ancient and contemporary, the author examines the techniques and machinations by which trial lawyers have attempted to shape the way in which their clients have been portrayed in the media and, through it, viewed by the public at large. He begins by focusing his attention on the historic trials of Socrates, Joan of Arc, Levi Weeks and Aaron Burr, Oscar Wilde, and Lindbergh kidnapper, Bruno Hauptmann. He then examines such celebrated modern trials as those involving O.J. Simpson, Elian Gonzalez, Illinois Governor Rod Blagojovich, Michael Jackson, the Duke lacrosse players. Michael Vick, and Martha Stewart, as well as the 2000 Florida recount. The author provides a unique perspective on an often neglected area of trial work, namely, massaging the media. A former U.S. attorney who headed the country's largest federal prosecutor's office, Kendall Coffey was personally involved in the 2000 Florida recount and Elian Gonzalez cases, and has served as a frequent commentator on hundreds of nationally televised programs.

Cohan, Lloyd D. and Debra Hart Cohen. **Being Prepared: A Lawyer's Guide for Dealing with Disability or Unexpected Events**. Chicago: American Bar Association, General Practice, Solo & Small Firm Division, 2008. 1 vol. (220 pp.). With CD-ROM.
Cost: $104.95; $79.95 for Section members; from $62.68 on amazon.com (2014).
Many lawyers, particularly those with a solo or small firm practice, have probably not contemplated to any serious degree the possibility of an accident or other unexpected event which might disrupt or destroy their legal practice. This volume provides step-by-step guidance in preparing for such unfortunate events, and protecting the interests of the firm, its clients, and the lawyer's family. In one sense, it attempts to preserve an institutional memory where one might not exist for reasons of staff turnover and an over-reliance on technology. Chapter one provides a template for the recording of the firm's institutional memory and the formation of legal relationships that will provide an emergency plan. Chapter two lays out a detailed roadmap for the helpers in the event of an unexpected event, from the steps to be taken in the first five minutes to the first forty-eight hours. Chapter three provides an overview of the law firm, with the forms necessary for recording all its essential information and data. The remaining chapters address protection of clients, avoidance of malpractice actions and ethical lapses, financial issues, and a variety of management issues. An accompanying CD-ROM provides a variety of useful forms, checklists, questionnaires, sample agreements, blog and website links to aid the attorney in implementation of the action plan. Lloyd Cohen is a practicing attorney with nearly thirty years experience in the fields of estate planning, business law, and bankruptcy. His wife, Debra Hart Cohen, brings a background in administrative support and consulting to this project, including extensive experience in the death care field.

Collins, Gary H. and David Z. Seide. **Warning the Witness: A Guide to Internal Investigations and the Attorney-Client Privilege**. Chicago: American Bar Association, 2010. 1 vol. (130 pp.). Paperbound.
Cost: $59.95 ($49.95 to members) (2014).
The attorney-client privilege is the oldest privilege under the common law for
confidential communications. It rests on the need for the attorney to know everything relating to the client's reasons for seeking legal representation if he is to carry out his professional

mission. But what if the attorney represents a corporation and, during the course of that representation, or pursuant to an internal investigation to protect the client corporation, finds it necessary to interview the corporation's individual constituents (employees, officers, directors)? Can the constituents claim the privilege? While the law is clear that the privilege extends only to the client and not to constituents, the Supreme Court case of *Upjohn Co. v. United States* (449 U.S. 383 (1981)) provides that constituents be provided with *Upjohn* warnings to establish appropriate expectations between the constituent and the corporation. These warnings are intended to (1) inform the constituent that the corporation, not the constituent, is the client for the purposes of privilege; (2) that the corporation's counsel is not bound to keep information from the constituent confidential, and (3) that the corporation alone may reveal to outside parties the content of the communications between counsel and the constituent. This succinct volume provides counsel representing corporations with guidance in striking a balance between proper representation of the corporate client and respecting the interests and expectations of the corporation's constituents who may entertain some expectation that their testimony is in some way privileged. Following a brief introduction, the author discusses the attorney-client privilege, the Upjohn case and its impact on attorney-client privilege, formalizing witness warnings, current witness warning practices, and recommended best practices. Appendices include relevant sections of the ABA Model Rules of Professional Conduct, and selected memoranda of law, table of cases, and index. Gary Collins, formerly a partner in Day Pitney's government investigations practice group, is now Managing Director and Chief Compliance Officer at GE Energy Financial Services in Stamford, CT. David Seide is a partner in the Washington, DC office of Curtis, Mallet-Prevost, Colt & Mosle LLP where he represents companies and individuals who are or may become subjects of government investigations.

Cornick, Matthew S. **Using Computers in the Law Office**. 7th ed. Florence, KY, Delmar Cengage Learning, 2014. 1 vol. (800 pp.).
Cost: $229.95; from $73.66 on amazon.com (2014).
Written for the paralegal, this volume provides a useful introduction to computers and the application of computer technology to the law office. The author introduces basic computer concepts, hardware issues, leading software applications, including Word and Excel, and computer applications for such law office activities as electronic discovery, Internet legal and factual research, timekeeping and billing, litigation support, and case management, and docket control. Mobile computing, ethics, document management, security, PDF file creation, e-filing, document assembly, the operation of the electronic courthouse and other topics are also discussed. The volume also contains more than ten hands-on tutorials which allow students the opportunity to practice the skills outlined in the text. The two CD-ROMs contain demonstration software.

Cotterman, James D., ed. **Compensation Plans for Law Firms**. 5th ed. Chicago: American Bar Association, 2010. 1 vol. (165 pp.). Paperbound.
Cost: $99.95 ($74.95 to members); from $64.11 on amazon.com (2014).
Compensation represents a tangible expression of an individual's perceived value and the most commonly accepted means of measuring one's success. Compensation decisions must reflect not only the competitive marketplace, but an internal meritocracy that corresponds with the organization's strategy and culture. Free agency in the legal profession has created competition for the best lawyers and rainmakers. Compensation systems for law firms must distinguish compensation programs for active owners from compensation systems for nonowner employees. Following an introduction that examines compensation theory, the art and science of compensation, size and compensation, payroll and draw cycles and survey date, chapters are devoted to a consideration of compensation for partners and shareholders, of counsel, associates, paraprofessionals, and staff. Compensation for partners and shareholders is examined in detail, with attention to compensation criteria, classes of partners, administration of the compensation process, measurement of a partner's value, the theoretical value of service providers and rainmakers, the allocation of large success or premium fees, rewarding the stars, and other owner compensation issues. Attention is also given to the compensation specifics for other classes of firm members. For staff members, setting wage scales, salary increases, and bonuses are considered. The Appendices include one firm's rules for allocation of client production credit, contemporary issues on capital, a retirement primer, exempt employees, benefits, and a concluding article on deciding who's right and who's wrong for your law firm. Citations to auxiliary sources provide information for further research. The book can support a current compensation system, or help a firm reevaluate current methods of compensation. Careful advance consideration is essential to the success of your compensation plan. Using the information contained in this reference, a firm can develop a compensation plan that strikes the perfect balance of fairness, simplicity, and flexibility. The book was written primarily by lead author James Cotterman in association with the leading legal consulting firm of Altman Weil, Inc.

Cunningham, George C. and John C. Montana. **The Lawyer's Guide to Records Management and Retention**. Chicago: American Bar Association, 2006. 1 vol. (291 pp.) with CD-ROM. Paperbound.
Cost: $99.95 ($89.95 to Law Practice Section members); from $35.99 on amazon.com (2014).
Records management has become one of the latest hot topics in the field of law office practice. Records management is much more than efficiency and organization, but an essential tool in the pursuit of improved client service, legal and corporate compliance, risk management, cost control, and attorney support. The need for effective records management rises exponentially as a law office becomes larger, its client base more extensive, and its case load more complex. There is an inevitable nexus between records management and legal ethics because those records have a critical legal, ethical and compliance dimension. This overview of records management and retention provides lawyers with the necessary knowledge and tools to address both the practical and strategic issues associated with the task of controlling the mass of documents they produce and for which they are responsible. Following a brief review of the role of records in the law office, the authors tackle such issues as the rationale and benefits of records

management, ethics compliance and risk management, records retention schedules, records retention and disposal, indexing, filing and records maintenance, filing and managing electronic documents, systems and technology, staffing and training, and record management program implementation. Several useful appendices include a sample records management department charter, policy statement, reading list, list associations and organizations, list of software vendors, a destruction certification memorandum, client files review and documentation procedures, and other relevant documents, all of which are contained on the accompanying CD-ROM. The authors are principals in the Pelli Group, and experienced consultants in the field of information and records management.

Cuticchia, A. Jamie. **Genetics: A Handbook for Lawyers**. Chicago: American Bar Association, 2009. 1 vol. (217 pp.). Paperbound.
Cost: $74.95; $59.95 to members; from $44.33 on amazon.com (2014).
This third title in the ABA's Legal Fundamental Series provides lawyers with a basic grounding in the science of genetics and its significance in a variety of specific legal contexts, from the history of genetics, genetic variation and mapping, to DNA fingerprinting for paternity testing, DNA forensics, genetics and health, genetic rights, and how to communicate with a jury about genetics. The text is augmented with real life examples from trials and the laboratory. Each chapter includes citations to primary and secondary authorities, including the scientific and forensic literature. It concludes with a useful glossary of scientific terms. With 20 years experience in the field of biomedical research, Dr. Cuticchia has served on the faculties of the Johns Hopkins and the University of Toronto Schools of Medicine, and is best known for his work on the Human Genome Project. This book, which brings clarity to complex scientific subject matter, will be of value to attorneys involved in any genetics-related issues, including, but not limited to, DNA fingerprinting in criminal trials, health and patent issues, and family law.

Darmstadter, Howard. **Hereof, Thereof, and Everywhereof: A Contrarian Guide to Legal Drafting**. 2d ed. Chicago: American Bar Association, Section of Business Law, 2008. 1 vol. (239 pp.). Paperbound.
Cost: $79.95; $59.95 to Business Law Section members; from $37.99 on amazon.com (2014).
A refreshingly candid and clear-headed guide to legal drafting, which the author describes as more of a companion than a textbook on the subject. In contrast to more traditional guides, which reinforce the often parodied, jargon-laden language employed by most lawyers, Howard Darmstadter characterizes his approach as more in keeping with the "plain language" school. While not eschewing technical language appropriate to the audience, his aim is to simplify legal documents whenever possible. He considers the details of word selection, sentence construction, the look of legal documents, the drafting of particular documents, agreements, boilerplate language, the securities prospectus, and more. The author has been practicing business law in New York City since 1977. He received his Ph.D. from Princeton University and J.D. from Harvard Law School. From 1966 to 1974, he taught philosophy at several universities.

Darrow-Kleinhaus, Suzanne. **The Bar Exam in a Nutshell**. 2d ed. St. Paul, MN: Thomson/West, 2009. 1 vol. (430 pp.). Paperbound. Available from West Academic.
Cost: $41 (2014).
Designed as a companion to a bar review course, this volume provides guidance in exam preparation and the test process with attention to the types of skills which are tested. The author provides advice regarding each component of the exam and suggests how to prepare for each type of question using examples and analysis of sample answers.

Denning, Brannon, Marcia McCormick, and Jeff Lipshaw. **Becoming a Law Professor: A Candidate's Guide**. Chicago: American Bar Association, 2010. 1 vol. (180 pp.). Paperbound.
Cost: $99.95; member price: $79.95; from $42.48 on amazon.com (2014).
This book might appear to be offering advice on a career decision in the face of a strong countervailing head-wind. In recent years, law school applications and enrollments are down, and many graduates are finding it difficult to find full- or even part-time work in the profession. And, while there are ominous signs in higher education generally, the bubble has yet to burst. In this environment, securing a teaching appointment to one of the nation's accredited, or even non-accredited, law schools may seem like a questionable proposition, particularly if other would-be lawyers decide to pursue the same escape route from law practice. Nevertheless, for those desirous of an academic career, this guide can serve as invaluable roadmap to the steps necessary to land that appointment, including the AALS hiring conference, on-campus interviews, preparation for the first semester of teaching, and the publication process that will help ensure continued employment and promotion. Drawing upon the authors' personal experiences, this book also contains an annotated bibliography on the hiring process, as well as a primer on the law review submissions process, as well as timelines and checklists to help the novice law professor stay organized. Brannon Denning is associate professor of law and director of faculty development at the Cumberland School of Law in Birmingham, AL. Marcia McCormick is associate professor of law at St. Louis University School of Law. Jeff Lipshaw is associate professor of law at Suffolk University Law School.

Derfner, Mary Francis and Arthur D. Wolf. **Court Awarded Attorney Fees.** New York: Matthew Bender & Co., 1983-date. 3 vols. Looseleaf format. Supplemented twice yearly.
Cost: $2,150 (includes annual subscription); annual renewal: 1995: $513 (price frozen since 1992); 1996: $538; 1997: $538; 1998: $565; 1999: $585; 2000: $630; 2001: $634; 2002: $674; 2003: $708; 2004: $725; 2005: $761; 2006: $815; 2007: $880; 2008: $959; 2009: $1,036; 2010: $1,088; 2011: $1,142; 2012: $1,245; 2013: $1,332; 2014: $1,454; CD-ROM: $2,172; renewal: 1998: $540; 1999: $585; 2000: $630; 2001: $674; 2002: $674; 2003: $708; 2004: $725; 2005: $761; 2006: $815; 2007: $880; 2008: $959; 2009: $1,036; 2010: $1,088; 2011: $1,175; 2012: $1,281; 2013: $1,371; 2014: $1,497.36; eBook: $1,955; renewal: 2014: $1,454.
Over the past twenty years, Congress has dramatically expanded the number of attorney fee provisions contained in federal statutes to more than 200, causing an explosion in the number

of attorney fee cases in all areas of federal law. These attorney fee statutes provide greater opportunities for fee recovery than existed in the past--moving beyond such areas as antitrust and securities law to such fields as environmental protection, civil rights, consumer safety, income tax, and energy law. These volumes closely examine the law and procedure governing the awarding of attorney fees in federal courts as well as the application of federal statutes in specific subject areas. This is an exhaustive scholarly work replete with citations to relevant primary and secondary authorities.

Cost Saving Tips: Buy this set on the used lawbook market, if possible. If a used set is unavailable, buy the treatise new and then drop the subscription after the initial one-year subscription expires.

Dimitriou, Demetrios. **Law Office Procedures Manual for Solos and Small Firms**. 3d ed. Chicago: American Bar Association, 2005. 1 vol. (152 pp.).
Cost: $79.95 ($69.95 to ABA members) (2014).
A step-by-step guide to establishing a structure for law office operations, including staffing, drafting a procedures manual, implementing standards of confidentiality, ethical conduct, billing and record keeping, formatting of documents and correspondence, and personnel policies. An accompanying CD-ROM contains the complete text of the manual with a template for drafting a law office policies and procedures manual. The author has over thirty years experience as a practicing attorney, arbitrator and a judge pro tem for the San Francisco Superior Court. An active member of the ABA's Law Practice Management Section, he has extensive experience on matters of professional responsibility, ethics, and fee disputes.

Documenting the Attorney-Client Relationship: Law Firm Policies on Engagement, Termination, and Declination. Chicago: American Bar Association, 1999. 1 vol. (69 pp.). Paperback with disc.
Cost: $44.95 ($35.95 to ABA Section members); from $4.25 on amazon.com (2014).
This small, but extremely useful volume is the product of a study conducted by the ABA's Section of Business Law's Committee on Law Firms which examined the procedures employed by law firms in taking on new clients and maintaining existing client relationships. The Committee solicited input from law firms on the use and content of engagement letters and the process by which they terminated clients or declined to represent them in the first place. An accompanying disc includes 10 sample policies and form letters.

Downey, Michael. **Introduction to Law Firm Practice**. Chicago: American Bar Association, 2010. 1 vol. 248 pp.). Paperbound and ebook.
Cost: $79.95 ($47.95 to LPM Section members); from $40.00 on amazon.com (2014).
Most law school graduates have an imperfect and often amorphous comprehension of how law firms operate in the real world. This book is written with the intent of filling that gap and providing recent law school graduates with the knowledge to maximize their chances for advancement in the firm environment. Forty-one chapters address everything from the forms of a law firm, office-sharing arrangements, governance, the career lattice, non-partner lawyers, partnership, nonlawyers, organizational structures, interactions with nonlawyer staff, the market for legal services, types of law practices, assessment of fees, law firm profitability, client and matter profitability, law firm compensation, client matter intake, time-billing, managing client work, pro bono, business development, client relationship management, marketing, firm culture, professional liability insurance, dealing with mistakes, diversity, mentoring, and supervision and risk management, among others. An ideal first read for any new law firm associate anxious to understand the law firm culture. The author is partner at Hinshaw & Culbertson LLP and an adjunct professor of legal ethics and law firm practice at Washington University School of Law in St. Louis.

Drogin, Eric York, ed. **Science for Lawyers**. Chicago: American Bar Association, 2008. 1 vol. (347 pp.). Paperbound.
Cost: $129.95; $119.95 to Science & Technology Law Section members; from $42.44 on amazon.com (2014).
Trial lawyers are often called upon to familiarize themselves with technical subjects of which they may have limited direct knowledge or experience. Navigating this intersection of law and science requires the ability to absorb enough science to defend, proceed against, examine, cross-examine, or consult a scientist or technical expert. This collection of essays explains thirteen applied scientific fields in jargon-free language accessible to most lawyers and educated laypersons. The essays are written by individuals with advanced training and experience in the fields of ballistics, medicine, physics, statistics, linguistics, genetics, chemistry, biology, dentistry, computer forensics, engineering, psychology, and environmental science. The book also includes dozens of photos, figures, graphics and artwork to illustrate the topics under discussion. A fascinating read for anyone who wants to gain a basic understanding of a variety of scientific subjects which may be applied in a legal context. Sadly, the author of the chapter on Environmental Science gives unwarranted praise to Rachel Carson and ***Silent Spring***, a book replete with scientific inaccuracies, misstatements, and omissions. Carson naively and unwittingly unleashed an irrational crusade by environmentalists against DDT and other pesticides which ultimately caused the death of an estimated 60 million people in the Third World. As the noted biologist Bruce N. Ames of UC Berkeley has documented, Americans ingest roughly 5,000 to 10,000 different natural pesticides and their breakdown products, and eat about 1,500 mg of natural pesticides per person per day, which is about 10,000 times more than the 0.09 mg they consume of synthetic pesticide residues. Under such circumstances, banning DDT, the most effective weapon against malaria, was a scientifically unfounded and, ultimately, deadly course of action, an action only belatedly being rectified by the WHO. The editor, who has doctoral degrees in both law and psychology, is a former President of the American Board of Forensic Psychology and has taught as an adjunct faculty member at the Franklin Pierce Law Center, and an Instructor in the Harvard Law School Trial Advocacy Workshop, among others.

Dunnewold, Mary L., Beth A. Honetschlager, and Brenda L. Tofte. **Judicial Clerkships: A Practical Guide**. Durham, NC:

Carolina Academic Press, 2010. 1 vol. (318 pp.). Paperbound.
Cost: $37.00; from $31.16 on amazon.com; kindle ed.: $27.99 (2014).
One of the best career enhancing opportunities available to recent law school graduates is the judicial clerkship. While a judicial clerkship will delay career advancement in the "real world," it will also provide a number of life and career changing benefits that will reap rewards over a lifetime. Law clerks who work for trial and appellate court judges in state and federal courts gain immeasurably by becoming intimately familiar with the judicial process, honing research, writing and analytical skills, developing lifelong professional contacts, and gaining an understanding of law firms and lawyers. This guide provides an overview of the application process and role of the judicial law clerk, as well as the substantive skills and responsibilities required of the law clerk, including legal research and writing, citation practice, drafting bench memoranda and trial court documents, drafting appellate court opinions, drafting correspondence and other documents, reviewing the work of colleagues, and observing standards of ethical and professional conduct. The concluding chapter addresses career advancement once the judicial clerkship is concluded. This is an essential handbook for any law student contemplating applying for a judicial clerkship, or for a law clerk interested in gaining a better understanding of his or her role in the judicial system. The authors are all legal research and writing instructors at Hamline University School of Law in St. Paul, MN.

Duranske, Benjamin Tyson. **Virtual Law: Navigating the Legal Landscape of Virtual Worlds**. Chicago: American Bar Association, 2008. 1 vol. (461 pp.). Paperbound.
Cost: $49.95; amazon.com kindle ed.: $39.96 (2014).
A virtual world may be defined as a computer-based simulated environment intended for its users to inhabit and in which they interact via avatars, generally depicted as textual, two-dimensional, or three-dimensional graphical representations. These virtual worlds allow for communication between users, offer persistence of user-created content, and many offer functional economies. Virtual law is much like Internet law to the degree that it references a body of preexisting law that is applied in a new context. Virtual law is the statutory and case law that impacts these various virtual worlds. Because virtual worlds attempt to replicate the real world, the law impacting them embrace aspects of criminal, tort, constitutional, property, copyright, trademark, tax, securities, and privacy law, among others. The bulk of the book's chapters address the impact of these areas of law upon the virtual environment. The author also discusses the process of establishing a professional virtual world presence. The volume concludes with a variety of virtual world resources, including a terms of use agreement, memoranda, and complaints. The author is a writer and intellectual property lawyer who edits **virtuallyblind.com**, a website that tracks virtual law issues.

Espenschied, Lenné Eidson. **The Grammar and Writing Handbook for Lawyers**. Chicago: American Bar Association, 2011. 1 vol. (300 pp.). Paperbound.
Cost: $74.95; from $42.12 on amazon.com (2014).
In an age suffering from declining standards of English usage and an educational system that fails to adequately inculcate the rules of grammar and correct forms of expression, this handbook provides a useful corrective. Lawyers, above all, depend upon the use of accurate, clear and precise language in the wide variety of legal documents they prepare in the course of their profession. The author begins by tracing the origins of the English language, while lamenting the current state of English language instruction in both public and private schools and colleges. In 1994, the National Council of Teachers of English declined to include the study of correct English usage as an objective of the subject. According to the author, "law school graduates from 2009 forward who matriculate without a gap have virtually no traditional training in correct English usage through middle school, high school, or college." This phenomenon has been exacerbated by new technologically based forms of communication like texting, FaceBook and Twitter, that encourage brevity and novel forms of spelling. In an effort to correct these educational deficiencies, the author provides users with a useful review of the basic building blocks of language, including parts of speech, verb properties, singular vs. plural, punctuation and mechanics, word usage, agreement, sentence composition, variety in sentence composition. She also applies these rules to the construction of a well-written legal memorandum, while addressing such critical elements as analysis and reasoning, and cautioning against various forms logical fallacy. Nor does she neglect the various faux pas that infect language, including split infinitives, double negatives, dangling modifiers, clichés, and the like, all of which compromise the accuracy and credibility of the legal drafter. The author is a corporate lawyer with more than 20 years experience in transactional corporate and business law, and the author of **Legal Drafting** (ABA, 2010). In 2005, she began Legalese Seminars for the purpose of providing instructional public and private seminars on legal drafting to firms and corporate law departments.

Evans, Daniel B. **Wills, Trusts, and Technology: An Estate Lawyer's Guide to Automation**. 2d ed. Chicago: American Bar Association, 2004. 1 vol. (235 pp.).
Cost: $99.95 ($89.95 to LPM and RP members); from $34.90 on amazon.com (2014).
This volume treats the selection and use of computer software to perform a variety of functions related to estate planning, fiduciary administration, tax planning, and information management. The author, the Probate-Technology editor for **Probate & Property** magazine, also provides basic information on hardware, software, spreadsheets and databases. A product of the American Bar Association's Section of Real Property, Probate and Trust Law of the Law Practice Management Section.

Ewalt, Henry W. and Andrew W. Ewalt. **Through the Client's Eyes: New Approaches to Get Clients to Hire You Again and Again**. 3d ed. Chicago: American Bar Association, 2008. 1 vol. (367 pp.).
Cost: $89.95 ($59.95 to LPM Section members); 2d ed. from $20.80 on amazon.com (2014).
Rainmaking, or the cultivation of clients, though not part of the law school curriculum, is one of the most important tasks with which the lawyer should become adept. This volume is intended to serve as a lawyer's manual on client relations. In the view of the authors, clients relations should consume no less than

two hours per week and, preferably, an average of ten hours per week if the lawyer is going to develop a new practice, achieve career advancement, or increase his or her level of compensation. But it is not just a question of hours. This time must be expended wisely if it is to achieve success. The authors contend that lawyers have "unintentionally de-emphasized the reason for the profession to exist: to satisfactorily resolve the problems of people and organizations." The authors candidly assess the negative aspects of legal practice, including the less than flattering opinion with which it is held by the general public, the fear of high fees, and the lawyers' own disillusionment with a profession beset by heavy client demands, law firm hourly requirements, and financial demands. These perceptive introductory observations are complemented by chapters considering a range of client relationships and issues, including client perceptions, the initial reception, client appreciation and understanding, involvement in the decision-making process, billing, alliances, clients' opinions, public relations, community involvement, and the impact of technology. They also offer one particularly valuable piece of advice: "treat every client like a relative." The authors also examine how these issues are played out in a variety of environments, from the solo/small practice to the corporate setting. This is one of those law practice management books whose insights should be absorbed by every attorney before opening a law practice. Henry W. Ewalt is a graduate of the University of Michigan School of Law and a solo practitioner in Pittsburgh, PA. In this third edition, he is joined by his son, Andrew, a graduate of Widener University School of Law who maintains a solo estate and trust practice in Hartford, CT.

Fischer, Judith. **Pleasing the Court: Writing Ethical and Effective Briefs**. 2d ed. Durham, NC: Carolina Academic Press, 2011. 1 vol. (129 pp.). Paperbound.
Cost: $19.00; from $13.00 on amazon.com; kindle: $13.99 (2014).
Drafting accurate, well-researched, and well-written briefs is an essential skill for any lawyer who wishes to do justice to his client and provide the court with an accurate representation of the law as a basis for its making a just decision. Stating the law accurately in representations to the court is also an ethical duty of competent representation which has its basis in the ABA's Model Rules of Professional Conduct and the Federal Rules of Civil Procedure. This modest volume is a guide to drafting effective briefs which meet high legal and ethical standards. Well-written briefs must state the law and facts accurately, provide cogent analysis for the court, utilize clear writing, avoid wordiness or legalese, avoid errors of grammar, spelling , punctuation and typography, and provide accurate citations to relevant legal authorities. In addition, the brief must observe court rules for style and form, avoid plagiarism, and aim for civility in its dealings with opposing counsel. To make her points, the author cites numerous examples of poor writing, drawn from a variety of real-life examples, which have elicited comment or criticism from the court. The appendices provides guidelines and exercises for students, and others, who wish to improve their legal writing. The author is an associate professor law at the University of Louisville, Louis D. Brandeis School of Law.

Flamm, Richard. **Lawyer Disqualification: Conflicts of Interest and Other Bases**. 2d ed. Berkeley, CA: Banks and Jordan Law Publishing Co., 2013-date. 1 vol. (1,340 pp.). Periodic supplementation.
Cost: $249; no supplementation to date; 1st ed.: 2005: $55; 2006: 0; 2007: $69; 2008-2009: 0; 2010: $99.50; 2011-2012: 0.
An exhaustive discussion and analysis of lawyer disqualification based on the author's review of more than 2,500 cases from every state and federal jurisdiction. The book consists of thirty-six chapters divided into ten parts: introductory materials, multiple representation conflicts, conflicts involving former clients, attorney-client relationships, other bases for disqualification, defenses to disqualification, deciding disqualification motions, vicarious disqualification, disqualification in special types of situations, and appellate remedies. This is the most comprehensive work of its kind in print and an essential resource for any lawyer or judge involved with disqualification proceedings. The author, a graduate of Rutgers Law School, is a nationally recognized expert in the field of legal ethics who specializes in providing representation, advice and expert witness testimony on matters of legal and judicial ethics, legal malpractice, and breach of fiduciary duties.

Flannery, William J. **The Lawyer's Field Guide to Effective Business Development**. Chicago: American Bar Association, 2007. 1 vol. (149 pp).
Cost: $59.95 ($49.95 to LPM Section members); from $27.95 on amazon.com (2014).
This compact volume provides practical business advice to lawyers, with a focus on practical ideas for business growth and relationship improvement. The author brings his experience of training more than 10,000 lawyers from around the world in client relationship management, business development and effective communication skills to the subject. The book is designed for both experienced lawyers who wish to improve their business development skills and younger lawyers who want to design successful and profitable practices. William J. Flannery is a ex-IBM executive, attorney, and pioneer in the field of business development. His enthusiastic and animated speaking and writing skills have inspired thousands of lawyers to new levels of business success.

Folberg, Jay and Dwight Golann. **Lawyer Negotiation: Theory, Practice, and Law**. 2d ed. New York: Wolters Kluwer Law & Business, 2010. 1 vol. (448 pp.). No supplementation except in the form of new editions.
Cost: $97; from $43.92 on amazon.com (2014).
This law school text focuses on the types of legal negotiations in which the disputants are represented by attorneys. It combines theoretical commentary, a well selected collection of timely writings on negotiation to illustrate the text, and questions for class discussion. The chapters include: negotiation and conflict; perception fairness and settlement psychology; competitive and cooperative negotiation; a combined approach and choosing a style; negotiation step by step—the beginning, the middle, the end; telephone and cyber negotiation; gender, culture and race; negotiation ethics; the law of negotiation; obstacles to agreement and negotiation assistance; mediating for negotiation advantage; and negotiated settlement policy and limits. The appendices are entirely web-based; however, the print edition includes an extensive Bibliography and References, table of

cases, and subject index. Jay Folberg Professor Emeritus and former Dean of the University of San Francisco School of Law. Dwight Golann is Professor of Law at Suffolk University Law School in Boston, where he teaches dispute resolution, and is one of the most respected neutrals in the United States, having successfully mediated and arbitrated hundreds of legal disputes involving business contract, partnership, real estate, insurance, employment, construction, intellectual property, franchise, personal injury, class action, securities and other issues.

Foonberg, Jay G. **The ABA Guide to Lawyer Trust Accounts**. Chicago: American Bar Association, 1996. 1 vol. (179 pp.).
Cost: $79.95 ($69.95 to LPM Section members) (2014).
A practical guide to the practices and procedures which attorneys must follow when managing client funds and in order to ensure compliance with state rules and avoid ethical violations. Jay Foonberg, one of the nation's leading authorities on law office management, discusses the history of rules applicable to the management of client funds, the pitfalls which could lead to rules violations, the risks of the IOLTA requirements, and the best ways of working with bankers and accountants to ensure compliance. The book also includes sample forms which can be adapted to a particular law office, Foonberg's «10 rules of good trust account procedures,» and «10 steps to good trust account records,» which can be adapted to local rules requirements.

Foonberg, Jay G. **How to Get and Keep Good Clients.** Global 3d ed. Las Vegas, NV: National Academy of Law, Ethics & Management, Inc., 2007. 1 vol. (620 pp.). Available from American Bar Association, or go to: http://foonberglaw.com/
Cost: $179.95 (hardcover); $99 (softcover); ebook: $24.95 ($19.95 to members) (2014)
Jay Foonberg is one this country's leading experts on the subject of law practice development and marketing. Nominated by the American Bar Association as the most outstanding post-law school legal educator in the United States, he has gained a wide following through law practice seminars and publishing activities. His book **How to Start and Build a Law Practice** is the best selling book ever published by the ABA's Law Practice Management Section. This volume is crammed with valuable advice and techniques for developing a law practice. His chapters cover such topics as the lawyer in my office, the lawyer out of the office, addressing the needs of clients and potential clients, getting business from others in the office and out of the office, using ethics to create opportunities to get clients, getting work from large or publicly held companies, office procedures as a factor in keeping clients, bombarding your clients with paper, your invoice--a factor in satisfying or angering clients, getting paid for what you do, big firm techniques that can work for a small firm, and assorted marketing tips This volume will undoubtedly pay for itself many times over. Incidentally, Foonberg recommends that you show off your law books: «Make sure your clients and prospective clients know you have these tools of the trade,» he says.

Foonberg, Jay G. **How to Start & Build a Law Practice**. 5th ed. Chicago: American Bar Association, Law Practice Management Section, Law Student Division, 2004. 1 vol. (607 pp.).
Cost: $69.95 (LPM Section members: $57.95; Law Student Division members: $27.95); from $66.43 on amazon.com (2014). Also available at: http://foonberglaw.com/
A comprehensive handbook of law practice management techniques written for both beginning and seasoned attorneys. The 128 chapters, organized into ten sections, cover such topics as getting started, getting located, getting equipped, getting clients, setting fees, managing the law office, ethics and professional responsibility, resources and advice, the Foonberg management checklist, and quality of life. The fourth edition contains 30 new chapters, including Foonberg's checklist of 554 questions which can be used to measure and improve processes, efficiency and productivity. Foonberg is the leading authority on law practice management and a veteran of the lecture circuit. His books, tapes, and lectures have influenced thousands of both young and experienced lawyers in setting up and maintaining their practices.

Fox, Elyse. **Legal Research Q & A: 401 Flashcards with Companion Book.** Charlotte, NC: Legal Information Services, 2011. 1 vol. (looseleaf format) with 401 flashcards.
Cost: $80.00 (2014).
This invaluable pedagogical tool provides law students, law librarians, lawyers, and summer associates with an effective means of mastering the basics of legal research and legal bibliography. The flashcards ask three types of questions: fill-in-the-blank, true/false, and multiple choice. The questions cover the following types of publications or topical areas: legal research generally, authority, court reports, statutes, legislative history, administrative law, court rules, attorney general opinions, digests, citation, citators, and law books. The questions and answers are replicated in the pages of the looseleaf binder. The flashcards are printed on heavy card stock with a storage bag and companion looseleaf book. Elyse Fox received her B.A. in 1972 from the University of Michigan, her J.D. in 1975 from the University of Michigan Law School, and her M.S.L.S. in 1981 from Simmons College Graduate School of Library and Information Science. She is the editor of the **Legal Information Management Index, Law Librarian's Bulletin Board**, and author of **How to File Looseleaf Services, The Legal Research Dictionary**, and the **Jury Instructions Drafting Manual and Resource Guide**.

Fox, Elyse H., compiler. **Resources in Third-Party Legal Opinion Letters**. Charlotte, NC: Legal Information Services, 2014. 1 vol. (97 pp.). Paperbound.
Cost: $95.00 (2014).
An opinion letter is a formal expression of a judgment or advice based on an expert's special knowledge. The term commonly refers to a document containing a lawyer's understanding of the law as it applies in a particular case. Attorneys issue opinion letters to their own clients and to non-clients. Those opinions letters issued to non-clients at the request of the client or another entity (often a lending institution) are referred to as third-party legal opinion letters. As stated in the introduction, this book is a (selected) bibliography of treatises, articles (online and print), bar association reports and statements, and CLE materials on the subject of legal opinion letters to non-clients (so-called "third-party opinion letters"). Excluded are opinions letters from an attorney to his or her own clients, and third-part intellectual property opinions, fairness opinions, and attorney responses

to auditor requests. As the author explains, the movement to bring some order to third-party opinion letters began in the 1970s and has been aided by state and local bar associations in the form of guidelines and the publication of forms of opinions. She follows with a brief explanation of the legal and ethical duties lawyers owe to third-party recipients, opinion liability, and law firm opinion practice. The bibliographical entries include subject-specific sources, those issued by legal and bar organizations, legal treatises, online and print articles, CLE program materials, and law school curriculum materials. Although there are legal treatises (notably **Glazer and FitzGibbon on Legal Opinion Letters**) which treat the subject in depth, this volume fills a significant gap in the bibliographical literature relating to third-party opinion letters.

Freedman, Monroe H. and Abbe Smith. **Understanding Lawyers' Ethics**. 4th ed. Newark, NJ: LexisNexis, 2010. 1 vol. (various pagings).
Cost: $45; ebook: $36; from $8.40 on amazon.com; kindle ed.: $28.44 (2014).
A lucid explanation of lawyer ethics by one of the nation's leading authorities in the field. Designed as a law school textbook, the author's discussion parallels the American Bar Association's Model Code of Professional Responsibility and Model Rules of Professional Conduct. This volume updates and expands upon Monroe Freedman's earlier **Lawyers' Ethics in an Adversary System**, published in 1975. This is one of more than 30 titles in the LexisNexis/Matthew Bender Understanding Series. Monroe H. Freedman is the Howard Lichtenstein Distinguished Professor of Legal Ethics, Hofstra University School of Law and the recipient of the American Bar Association's highest award for professionalism, in recognition of «a lifetime of original and influential scholarship in the field of lawyers' ethics.» Abbe Smith is Professor of Law, Georgetown University Law Center.

Furi-Perry, Ursula. **Fifty Legal Careers for Non-Lawyers**. Chicago: American Bar Association, 2008. 1 vol. (218 pp.).
Cost: $19.95 ($17.95 to members); from $.95 on amazon.com; kindle ed.: $9.99 (2014).
A law degree is not a sina qua non to employment in the legal field. Indeed, there are dozens of careers avenues available in the legal field to people without law degrees. The author describes these various career alternatives which exist for non-lawyers and helps the reader select a law career best suited to his or her interests, training, and aptitude. Each of the fifty careers profiled in the book features interviews with people employed, sample responsibilities, typical education and skills necessary, as well as resources to assist the potential job seeker. Ursula Frui-Perry is a nationally published free-lance writer and college instructor in Massachusetts.

Furi-Perry, Ursula. **Fifty Unique Legal Paths: How to Find the Right Job**. Chicago: American Bar Association, 2008. 1 vol. (137 pp.). Paperbound.
Cost: $59.95 ($44.95 to members); from $35.69 on amazon.com (2014).
Despite all the talk about new lawyers leaving the profession or choosing non-legal careers, a full 70% of new JDs practice in law in a private law firm setting. This small volume contains a wealth of information regarding both traditional and non-traditional career paths for both new lawyers and those interested in making midlife career changes. The author covers growing practice areas for new JDs, nonprofit and public interest careers, growing government careers, careers in academia and education, law office management and administration, the business and corporate world, and self-employment options. Additional chapters provide tips from career service professionals and advice to job applicants evaluating employment opportunities. The volume is laced with "break-in tips" for prospective job applicants in various fields, lists of subspecialties, and web resources. The author, for example, also provides insightful advice on law library careers based on consultation with practicing law librarians. The author is a graduate and adjunct professor of writing and legal reasoning at the Massachusetts School of Law, and a widely published legal writer.

Furi-Perry, Ursula, ed. **The 2013 Legal Assistant's Complete Desk Reference: A Handbook for Paralegals and Assistants**. Chicago: American Bar Association, 2013. 1 vol. (492 pp.). with companion CD-ROM. Paperbound.
Cost: $199.95 ($149.95 to members); from $125.97 on amazon.com (2014).
According to the ABA, "a legal assistant or paralegal is a person qualified by education, training or work experience who is employed or trained by a lawyer, law office, corporation, governmental agency or other entity who performs specifically designated substantive legal work for which a lawyer is responsible." The type of tasks which a paralegal may perform is limited only by statutory or court authority or by a supervising attorney's determination. In addition to generalized support tasks, paralegals have expanded their practice into a variety of highly technical and specialized subject areas. This comprehensive text provides paralegals with an overview of the most common areas of legal practice in which they operate and the career opportunities open to them. Opening with a look at a typical day in the life of a legal assistant, the author examines court systems and procedures; the preparation of legal instruments, documents and court filings; legal research and writing; trial preparation; and summaries of some of the leading areas of practice in which paralegals are likely to be involved, including bankruptcy and collections, corporate and business law, labor and employment, estate planning, family law, real estate, and intellectual property. The volume also includes a CD-ROM of sample forms and letters, a state-by-state listing of online resources, a glossary of legal terms, and subject index. This book is an essential primer for any person contemplating or beginning a career as a paralegal or legal assistant. Attorney Ursula Furi-Perry is author of eight books and over 300 articles on various aspects of legal practice.

Gallacher, Ian. **A Form and Style Manual for Paralegals**. Durham, NC: Carolina Academic Press, 2007. 1 vol. (218 pp.).
Cost: $25.00; from $17.00 on amazon.com (2014).
Designed for paralegals and paralegal students, this brief manual guides users through all stages of the writing process, from preparing to write to completing a finished draft. It uses easy to understand and jargon-free language to provide practical suggestions on grammar, punctuation, usage, document

formatting, editing and proofreading. It is designed to provide paralegals with a concise overview of the mechanics of writing lucid, technically accurate, and effective legal documents. Ian Gallacher is a Professor of Law and Director of Legal Research and Writing program at Syracuse University College of Law and formerly a partner at the law firm Goodell, DeVries, Leech and Dann in Baltimore.

Garwin, Arthur. **The Legal Assistant's Guide to Professional Responsibility**. 2d ed. Chicago: American Bar Association, Center for Professional Responsibility, 2005. 1 vol. (210 pp.). Spiralbound.
Cost: $39.95 ($29.95 to members); from $3.89 on amazon.com (2014).
A practical reference on the basics of professional conduct for legal assistants, this volume was prepared with the aid of the American Association for Paralegal Education, the National Association of Legal Assistants and the National Federation of Paralegal Associations. Topics discussed include the law of professional responsibility, the role of the legal assistant, legal ethics research, unauthorized practice of law, the legal services delivery team, confidentiality, conflicts of interest, client funds and property, advertising, legal fees and employee compensation. It also includes a number of valuable appendices, including model codes of ethics, legal research sources, and ABA model rules.

George, Tracey E. and Suzanna Sherry. **What Every Law Student Really Needs to Know: An Introduction to the Study of Law**. New York: Wolters Kluwer Law & Business, 2009. 1 vol. (214 pp.).
Cost: $32.95; from $3.05 on amazon.com; kindle ed.: $21.49 (2014).
Written in an engaging and informal style, this useful guide provides a succinct overview of what to expect in the first year of law school. The authors discuss reading assignments, teaching methods, courses taught in the first year, the process of becoming a lawyer, and preparation for law school. They also provide an overview of the tools, techniques, and information for understanding the first-year substantive law curriculum, including an overview of the American legal system and court structure, a concise review of basic civics and sources of law, and an introductions to analytic tools and methods of reasoning. They also address basic legal concepts, such as standards of review and burdens of proof, the goals of a legal education, and the life, duties, and responsibilities of being a lawyer. The volume also includes a short primer on American history and a theoretical framework of legal philosophy and its leading schools of thought. A companion website includes PowerPoint slides, problems, quizzes, additional in-class exercises, and teaching notes that explain how to use this complete teaching package to best advantage.

Gibson, K. William, ed. **Flying Solo: A Survival Guide for the Solo and Small Firm Lawyer**. 4th ed. Chicago: American Bar Association, 2005. 1 vol. (679 pp.).
Cost: $99.95 ($79.95 to ABA members); $78.00 on amazon.com (2014).
An essential resource for any attorney opening a practice for the first time or seeking to improve law office operations and productivity. A perennial ABA best-seller, this volume is based on information gathered from a wide range of contributors, including law school professors, management consultants, successful solo practitioners, and state and local bar associations. It provides a step-by-step guide through the process of opening an office and choosing a practice focus and offers advice on a range of practical issues, including law office finance, banking, billing, staffing, selecting an office location, design considerations, technology, marketing, and client relations. Fifty-seven chapters provide essential guidance in all areas of law practice operations and management. The author is a solo practitioner who specializes in arbitration, mediation, and personal injury matters, and a past chair of the ABA Law Practice Management Section.

Gibson, K. William. **How to Build and Manage a Personal Injury Practice**. 3d ed. Chicago: American Bar Association, Law Practice Management Section, 2006 1 vol. (185 pp.) with CD-ROM. Paperbound.
Cost: $69.95 ($41.95 to Law Practice Management Section members); eBook: $69.95 ($41.95 to Law Practice Section members); from $43.21 on amazon.com (2014).
Starting a personal practice is not for the faint of heart. Unlike practitioners in other fields, personal injury (PI) attorneys, operating under a contingent fee arrangement, often invest substantial time and money in a case before being paid. A successful resolution may require substantial investment in research, exhibits, doctors, engineers, and other experts, and the discovery process. Yet failure to spend the necessary funds on these ingredients to a successful case may result in legal and/or financial failure. K. William Gibson, editor of the ABA's **Flying Solo: A Survival Guide for Solo and Small Firm Lawyers**, brings more than 20 years experience in the field of personal injury law to this and other critical issues, from the decision to open a solo practice or partnership; planning for a new practice; office space and equipment; marketing; the new client; keeping clients happy; working with employees, contractors and other professionals; managing the workload; software for case/practice management, document management, and trial presentation; and preparing for settlement, arbitration, and trial. Like other entries in the ABA Law Practice Management Section's Practice-Building Series, this volume combines both nut-and-bolts and practical advice on how to establish a successful personal injury practice. A variety of relevant documents, including forms, checklists, sample letters, and questionnaires are contained both in the Appendices and on an accompanying CD-ROM. K. William Gibson is a solo practitioner in Portland, Oregon, a regular columnist for the ABA's **Law Practice** magazine, and founder of De Novo Systems, Inc., a company that publishes De Novo CaseMgr, a case and practice management software system.

Glazer, Donald W., Scott Fitzgibbon, and Steven O. Weise. **Glazer and Fitzgibbon on Legal Opinions**. 3d ed. New York: Wolters Kluwer Law & Business, 2008-date. 1 vol. (536 pp. + appendices).
Cost: $395; supplementation: 2009: $285; 2010: $183; 2011: $225; 2012: $247; 2013: $269; 1st edition: 1999: $110; 2000: 0; 2001: 0; 2d ed.: 2003: $145; 2004: $178; 2005: 0; 2006: $190; 2007: 2008: new edition.

Third-party closing opinions are opinions drafted by legal counsel to one party to a financial transaction to the party on the other side. Such opinions are routinely prepared by either inside or outside counsel as a means of determining if a corporate transaction works from a legal standpoint. The intent of this volume is " to provide practicing lawyers with guidance on the form and meaning of legal opinions and the work required to support them." Following an explanation of the opinion framework, the authors examine unqualified, qualified, and reasoned opinions, the establishment of a factual basis for the opinion, and the responsibility of principal for opinions of other counsel. They then address the standard opinion clauses, including company's status as a corporation, its qualifications to do business and its good standing in jurisdictions other than the state of incorporation. Also considered are matters of corporate power, the enforceability opinion, validity of stock issues, secondary sales of stock, security interests in personal property, no violation of law opinions, and compliance with court and administrative orders, and more. Twenty-six appendices reproduce a number of bar association reports which attempt to reflect a consensus about standard opinion language and the work required to support commonly-rendered opinions. These reports reflect a growing consensus toward uniformity, propelled, in large part, by the **ABA's 1998 Legal Opinion Principles** and the **TriBar Opinion Committee's 1998 Report**. The volume also includes a table of cases, select bibliography, and index. Additional bar association are included on an accompanying CD-ROM. Donald Glazer is an attorney with the Boston firm of Goodwin Proctor; Scott Fitzgibbon is professor law at Boston College Law School; Steven Weise is an attorney with the Los Angeles firm of Heller, Ehrman, White & McAuliffe. This is an essential resource for a firm which prepares closing opinions.

Hadden, Sally E. and Alfred L. Brophy, eds. **A Companion to American Legal History**. Malden, MA: Wiley-Blackwell, 2013. 1 vol. (582 pp.).
Cost: $200.95; from $147.80 on amazon.com (2014).
This collection of historiographical essays tracks recent scholarship on American legal history from the 17th century to the present day. The first six essays in Part I are chronological in nature, covering the 17th century, 1700-1775, 1775-1815; the Antebellum era through the Civil War, 1865-1920, and 1920-1970. The seven essays in Part II address various individual and groups, beginning with Native Americans, and continuing through African-Americans, women, families, immigrants, and the legal profession. Part III looks at a number of significant subject areas, from various aspects of law and the economy to law and labor, legal history and poverty, taxes, law and the administrative state, law and religion, legal history and the military, criminal law and justice, and intellectual property. Part IV examines legal thought, including law and literature, legal thought from Blackstone to Kent to Story, American jurisprudence in the 19th and early 20th centuries, critical legal studies, and the international context. Each essay is accompanied by a list of references. This is a significant contribution to the area of legal history and an indispensable resource and springboard to any scholar working in the field. Sally E. Hadden is Associate Professor History at Western Michigan University. Alfred L. Brophy is the Judge John J. Parker Distinguished Professor of Law at the University of North Carolina.

Hall, John Wesley, Jr. **Professional Responsibility in Criminal Defense Practice.** 3d ed. St. Paul, MN: Thomson Reuters West, 2005-date. 1 vol. (1,644 pp.). Annual cumulative supplement.
Cost: $302; supplementation: 2006: $30; 2007: $34; 2008: $37.50; 2009: $43; 2010: $51; 2011: $56; 2012: $62; 2013: $62.50; **Monthly Assured Print Price (APP):** $11/$132.
A discussion and analysis of the myriad ethical dilemmas faced by criminal lawyers in the course of their practices which involve the intermingling of constitutional law, criminal law and procedure, laws of evidence, ethical codes and personal moral codes. The chapters encompass an introduction to the law of professional responsibility of the criminal lawyer, the sixth amendment right to counsel, the lawyer's duties of fairness, honesty and candor, the lawyer-client relationship, the organization as a client, ethical duties among lawyers and within law firms, attorneys' fees, currency transaction reports, ethical duties of the defense counsel, ineffective assistance of counsel, representing the mentally ill or impaired, extrajudicial statements, conflicts of interest, ethical duties in plea discussions, duties in relations with witnesses, communications wityh persons represented by other lawyersor the unrepresented, ethical duties toward judge and jurors, ethical duties and the trial process, obstruction of justice in general, grounds for disciplinary action, client perjury, tampering with evidence, malpractice, attorney contempt, and more. Replaces the author's **Professional Responsibility of the Criminal Lawyer.**

Hamadeh, H. S. and Mark Oldman. **The Vault Guide to the Top 100 Law Firms.** 16th ed. Vault Reports, Inc., 2013. 1 vol. (768 pp.).
Cost: 2014 Edition (pdf): $39.95 (2014).
An intimate look inside 100 of the country's most prestigious law firms. The authors surveyed several thousand lawyers to determine what they thought about their own and other leading firms. The results are reflected in prestige rankings and insider information on salaries, perks, working hours, selectivity, firm culture, dress code, summer associate programs, diversity, and interviews. For example, you will read about a firm that pays its associates as much as $100,00 more than associates at comparable firms, but which requires them to bill 3,000 hours per year. The surveys provide the prospective job seeker with candid appraisals of these high profile firms, including both positive and negative aspects of each firm's culture. The publisher also sells in depth analyses of the individual firms included in this survey.

Harper, Steven J. **The Lawyer Bubble: A Profession in Crisis**. New York: Basic Books, 2013. 1 vol. 251 pp.).
Cost: $26.00; from $10.77 on amazon.com (2014).
Beneath the outward glitter of prestigious law firms and top-ranked law schools lies a profession in crisis. The phenomenon is not a new one, having been identified as early as 1993 by Dean Anthony Kronman of the Yale Law School who lamented the growing commercialism of the legal profession and the diminution of the lawyer-statesman ideal. Law firms have focused on short-term profits just as law schools have become preoccupied with the dubious rankings published by *U.S. News and World Report.* The bubble Harper speaks of is reflected in failing law firms consumed by greed, the overproduction of new lawyers, the lack of employment opportunities for graduates of the nation's law schools, mounting levels of debt that cannot be

repaid by most graduates, and greater incidence of depression, alcoholism, and substance abuse by those in the profession. Six of ten lawyers who have been practicing for more than ten years advise young people to avoid law school altogether. Harper views this as a largely self-inflicted crisis that afflicts other professions once considered to be callings, including medicine and journalism, but one that has worsened as a result of the Great Recession. His focus is on two segments of the legal profession: law schools, because they're points of entry for every prospective lawyer, and big law firms, because their special combination of power, prestige and wealth gives them a special role, and an influence far beyond the 15% of practicing lawyers they represent. In recent years, institutional loyalty and job satisfaction have evaporated as senior partners with large client billings move for promises of more money elsewhere, causing destabilization and the disappearance firms of long-standing whose profits are increasingly unable to sustain the mounting pension obligation to partners and equity holders. And the ABA, which one would expect to address the growing crisis, particularly in light of its role in the accreditation of law schools, have become the victim of regulatory capture by those it is supposed to oversee. Prospective law students have gotten the message. The numbers taking the LSAT declined by 18% between 2010 and 2011 alone, and the number of applicants by 10%. And although 70,000 applicant apply for 50,000 law school openings, less than half of these graduates find full-time employment requiring a legal degree. Harper also draws attention to the preoccupation of law schools with the *U.S. News &World Report* rankings and the incentives to boost them through the manipulation of factors that may provide little genuine benefit for law students, or are ethically deceptive, such as job placement rates. Indeed, the publication of inaccurate or misleading job placement statistics have prompted some graduates to sue their law schools. Job placement is, naturally, of critical importance to the 85% of graduates in 2011 facing an average debt of more than $100,000, a figure that exceeded $120,000 at fifty law schools. And while Harper touches only tangentially on law school costs for Westlaw and LexisNexis subscriptions, it is obvious that legal publishers bask in the culture of greed that infects the legal profession as a whole, with operating profit margins of 21-28%. While Harper's detailed observations will be of great interest to those already in the profession, they will be of even greater value to those contemplating a legal career who may be able to avoid the financial devastation and emotional anguish by looking elsewhere for professional gratification. This is a superbly written, cogently argued, and carefully documented expose of the crisis undermining a once proud profession. Stephen Harper Steven J. Harper is an adjunct professor at Northwestern University School of Law who retired after 30 years as a litigator with the Chicago firm of Kirkland & Ellis LLP.

Hatoff, Howard I. and Robert C. Wert. **Law Office Policy and Procedures Manual**. 6th ed. revised. Chicago: American Bar Association, Law Practice Management Section, 2011. 1 vol. (376 pp.). With text on CD-ROM.

Cost: $179.95 ($109.95 to LPM Section members); $107.97 on amazon.com (2014).

Law office policy and procedures manuals are essential tools for the proper and efficient management of any law firm. They inform legal and administrative personal of their responsibilities to the firm and its clients as well the firm's responsibilities to its employees and clients. Formerly titled the **Law Office Staff Manual**, this volume provides substantive content, which can be adapted to the needs of any law firm. The various sections address the following areas of law firm operations: department and committees; organization, management and administration; support personnel and their function; office policies; personnel policies and benefits; preparation of correspondence, memoranda, and legal documents; office security and emergency procedures; financial management; file system; technology; communication systems; duplication services; equipment, maintenance, and supplies; library; travel; and miscellaneous guidelines. An accompanying CD-ROM contains the manual's full text in Microsoft Word for Windows, allowing the law firm to create its own manual using and adapting the standard boilerplate language provided. Employee manuals have been held to be enforceable employment contracts by various state courts. Howard Hatoff is a retired partner in the Philadelphia firm of Blank Rome LLP. Robert West has been Executive Director of Blank Rome since 1986.

Hazard, Geoffrey C., Jr. and W. William Hodes. **The Law of Lawyering: A Handbook on the Model Rules of Professional Conduct.** 3d ed. New York: Wolters Kluwer Law & Business, 2001-date. 2 vols. (1868 pp.). Looseleaf format. Supplemented annually.

Cost: $699; supplementation: 2002: $225; 2003: $225; 2004: $253; 2005: $145; 2006: $265; 2007: $282; 2008: $302; 2009: $329; 2010: $352; 2011: $375; 2012: $550; 2013: $550; 2d ed.: 1993: $95; 1994: $95; 1995: $95; 1996: $95; 1997: $95; 1998: 1999: 0; $96; 2000: 0.

This detailed examination of the American Bar Association's Model Rules of Professional Conduct is intended primarily as guide for practicing attorneys facing immediate ethical dilemmas, however, it can also be of great value to those attorneys who wish to avoid the future possibility of ethical difficulties. The two volumes follow the order of the Model Rules, with the full text of each rule accompanied by the authors' commentary. Includes illustrative cases scattered throughout the text. One of the Appendices treats the state variations in the Rules. A well organized and useful tool for the practicing attorney. Wolters Kluwer Law & Business (formerly Prentice-Hall Law & Business) publications are, as a rule, reasonably priced given their size and coverage; and supplementation costs are reasonable as well.

Hermann, Richard L. **The Lawyer's Guide to Job Security: How to Keep Your Job—and Make the Most of It—In Good Times and Bad**. New York: Kaplan Publishing, 2010. 1 vol. (226 pp.).

Cost: $19.95; from $1.14 on amazon.com; kindle: $7.99 (2014).

According to recent statistics, attorneys are losing their jobs at the greatest rate and in the largest numbers since such statistics were first compiled. In the first six weeks of 2009 alone, more than 2,500 attorneys at top-tier law firms lost their jobs. And this does not include those losing their jobs through "stealth layoffs," entire law firm collapses, downsizing of firms not considered top-tier, and corporate, government and nonprofit layoffs. This has resulted in a significant percentage of lawyers suffering from job anxiety. The goal of this guide is to provide attorneys with some simple and commonsense workplace principles to combat possible job loss. Broadly speaking, these principles include security, success, survival, and satisfaction. Ironically, while the lawyer's goal should be to achieve indispensability, one of the cardinal rules of job security is to never assume that you are indispensable. The 230 principles outlined in this volume are organized into seven chapters: (1) staring out on the right foot; (2) building your value to the organization; (3) securing your status; (4) major workplace "don'ts"; (5) personal growth - professional growth; (6) the legal manager's corner; and (7) dispensable... in spite of yourself. For example, the author advises lawyers to read constantly, but particularly history, biography, books on self-improvement, and forward looking publications, such as **The Economist, Wired**, **Science News**, **The American Scholar**, and the **New York Review of Books**. The author, a graduate of Yale University and Cornell Law School, is currently a professor at Concord Law School, where he specializes in legal career management. He is also the founder and president of Federal Reports, Inc., co-founder of AttorneyJobs.com, and author of **The Lawyer's Guide to Finding Success in Any Job Market**.

Hillman, Robert W. **Hillman on Lawyer Mobility: The Law and Ethics of Partner Withdrawals and Law Firm Breakups.** 2d ed. New York: Wolters Kluwer Law & Business, 1998-date. 1 vol. Looseleaf format. Annual supplements.
Cost: $375; supplementation: 1999: $94; 2000: $112; 2001: $126; 2002: $135; 2003: $147; 2004: $161; 2005: $169; 2006: $178; 2007: $190; 2008: $203; 2009: $225; 2010: $218; 2011: $230; 2012: $246; 2013: $265; 1st ed.: 1995: $25; 1996: $40; 1997: $83.
The settled world of law firms, if it ever existed, has rapidly disappeared in the highly competitive environment of recent years. Firms, whether recently organized or long established, suffer downsizing, breakups, or receivership. In this fragile environment, Robert Hillman examines the ethical and legal issues involved in lawyer mobility, including tort and agency law questions, the law firm partnership , downsizing, and professional corporations and limited liability companies as alternatives to partnership. The Appendices include the Uniform Partnership Act, selected provisions from the Model Rules of Professional Conduct, and Model Code of Professional Responsibility, and selected ethics opinions.

Howard, Charles L. **The Organizational Ombudsman: Origins, Roles, and Operations -- A Legal Guide**. Chicago: American Bar Association, 2010. 1 vol. (643 pp.). Paperbound.
Cost: $89.95 (member prices range from $53.97 to $76.95 depending on Section membership); from $41.60 on amazon.com (2014).
The position of ombudsman originated in 18th century Sweden under the reign of King Charles II. As a person of legal ability and outstanding integrity, the ombudsman's role was to supervise the observance of laws and statutes. He could not only investigate allegations of official misconduct, but also prosecute officials who committed unlawful acts or neglected to perform duties properly. As the office expanded beyond the borders of Sweden, it often assumed more of an investigative, rather than a prosecutorial, function, chiefly in Finland (1933) Norway (1952), and Denmark (1955). The idea of the ombudsman spread internationally in the 1960s and 1970s, including through the Canadian provinces and states in the United States. The model of the ombudsman was refined in the United States by law professors Kenneth Culp Davis and Walter Gellhorn who, working through the ABA, developed a 1969 resolution identifying 12 essential characteristics of the office. Over time, the office developed as a agent of government who supervised and prosecuted wrongdoing, protected citizens against arbitrary or unreasonable governmental agency actions, and exhibited the traits of independence, expertise, impartiality, accessibility, and powers of persuasion rather than control. From governmental entitles, the idea of the ombudsman migrated to the universities and corporations. In this exhaustive treatment of the role of the organizational ombudsman, the author traces the origins and development of the role, the justifications for organizations to create an ombuds program, the methods of protecting the ombudsman's' confidentiality, and the information, skills and skills that are helpful to the role of the ombudsman. The Appendices consist of a variety of organizational resolutions, ethical codes, standards of practice, and best practices applicable to the role of ombudsman in various organizational capacities. Author Charles Shipman is a partner with the Connecticut law firm of Shipman & Goodwin LLP, where he was chair of the litigation department and served as independent counsel for ombudsman offices at major corporations, universities, research facilities, and other organizations.

Howarth, David. **Law as Engineering: Thinking About What Lawyers Do**. Northampton, MA: Edward Elgar Publishing, 2013. 1 vol. (237 pp.).
Cost: 39.95; from $36.13 on amazon.com (2014).
In this original and thought-provoking book, David Howarth draws an analogy between the profession of law and engineering, positing that both are fundamentally concerned with design rather than with litigation. He contends that lawyers in the transactional and legislative realm design and build social structures in much the same way that engineers build physical structures.
And while academic lawyers may draw a distinction between public and private law, legislative drafters and transactional lawyers, even though they deal with different subject matter, both make a product to satisfy their clients, both use processes of conflict-blocking designed to anticipate future problems and resolve them in coordination with the client, and both are concerned about the future impact of their efforts. Though written from a UK perspective, the author's analysis raises important sociological and evaluative questions about the nature of the functions that lawyers perform, and the good that they do, that can be applied to the profession regardless of its geographical locus, particularly in the field of legal education, and professional ethics. David Howarth is a Reader in Law and Land Economy at Cambridge University, and former member of Parliament.

Iezzi, John G. **Results-Oriented Financial Management: A Step-by-Step Guide to Law Firm Profitability**. 2d Edition. Chicago: American Bar Association, Law Practice Management Section, 2003. 1 vol. (272 pp.). Paperbound.
Cost: $99.95 ($89.95 to Law Practice Management Section members) (2014).
Law firm profitability can often depend more on sound business management skills than legal acumen. This guide provides lawyers with the knowledge to get a handle on a firm's entire financial management process, including personnel costs,

billing practices, and budget analysis. The author is a certified public accountant with extensive experience in law firm financial management.

The In-House Counsel's Essential Toolkit. Chicago: American Bar Association, 2007. 7 vols. In boxed set (1,342 pp.).
Cost: OUT-OF-PRINT; was $62.99; $44.99 to Business Law Section members; from $47.23 on amazon.com (2014).
This seven-volume boxed set provides in-house counsel with quick access to essential policies, forms and practice tips in the following areas likely to be encountered in the course of daily practice: general business contracts, corporate governance, corporate compliance, employment law, intellectual property, litigation, and training outside counsel. The analysis and practice tips are detailed enough to satisfy both the novice in-house counsel as well as the more experienced practitioner, and provide sufficient background information to allow the in-house counsel to direct the right questions to outside counsel. This essential desk reference provides a convenient and economical resource for those employed as in-house counsel. An accompanying CD-ROM provides related forms and policies that can be adapted to specific transactions. Prepared by the ABA's Committee on Corporate Counsel.

Johns, Margaret Z. and Rex R. Perschbacher. **The United States Legal System: an Introduction**. 3d ed. Durham, NC: Carolina Academic Press, 2012. 1 vol. (288 pp.).
Cost: $32; from $10.05 on amazon.com; kindle: $25.99 (2014).
Designed for incoming law students and undergraduates contemplating the study of law, this text provides a concise introductory overview of the American legal system, the legal profession, and the nature of legal education. The authors address the political institutions of both the state and national government within the federal system, the legislative branches, the operation of the court system, and the way in which laws are interpreted as they weave their way through the judicial process. Using the California Supreme Court decision in Lockyer v. San Francisco, the authors provide extensive analysis of the operation of the rule of law and the separation of powers. Margaret Z. Johns is Director, King Hall Civil Rights Clinic and Director, Legal Writing Program at the University of California at Davis School of Law. Rex R. Perschbacher is the Dean of the School of Law at the University of California at Davis School of Law.

Johnson, Creola. **Is a Law Degree Still Worth the Price? It Depends on the What the Law School Has to Offer You**. Durham, NC: Carolina Academic Press, 2014. 1 vol. (358 pp.). Paperbound.
Cost: $30.00; from $28.50 on amazon.com (2014).
Legal education is in a state of crisis. But more importantly, increasing numbers of law students and recent graduates are in a state of personal and financial crisis due to the misleading information disseminated by their law schools regarding job prospects and salaries. In recent years, graduates of at least 15 law school have filed lawsuits alleging, among other things, deceptive practices, bait-and-switch, misrepresentation of accreditation status, negligence in enrollment practices, and unlawful dismissal for unsatisfactory academic performance. At the heart of these allegation, however, are charges that law schools have misrepresented the percentages of recent graduates who are employed in the legal profession and the salaries they are being paid, charges that call into the question the time and money devoted to earning a law degree. Professor Creola Johnson, a specialist in consumer law, takes aim at this problem by focusing on the allegedly deceptive employment and salary data law schools use to induce prospective students to make poorly informed career decisions, leaving many without jobs in the legal field, insurmountable debt and a lack of sufficient income to pay it back. Her data-driven analysis reveals, among other things, that while law schools typically report post-graduation employment rates of 90% or greater, the reality is far different, with many falling below 50%. Using ABA statistics for 2012 graduates, the author reveals that dozens of law schools have less than half of their graduating classes employed in attorney positions, as well as high attrition rates, and substantially low bar passage rates. Other schools bait their students with generous scholarships that many lose due a failure meet high GPA requirements. She also casts her net over deceptive *US News'* law school rankings that give inordinate attention to unimportant factors while ignoring such important criteria as job placement. She also examines other issues of great concern to both prospective and current law students, including ABA disclosure standards, financial aid and repayment plans, adequacy of skills training, the job market, the risks associated with attending an unaccredited law school, and debt burdens which can be a life sentence for some students. Professor Johnson's yeoman work in this field follows in the wake of her Ohio State colleague Brian Tamanaha's groundbreaking book, **Failing Law Schools**, which lifted the lid from the deceptive world of law school admissions, law school ratings, and promised job prospects. Professor Johnson's message is one that should reach every undergraduate contemplating a legal career and before they make career and life decisions that may cripple them professionally and financially for years to come. It has been said that student debt has become the new mortgage for many young people. That aphorism is particularly applicable for those pursuing professional education and taking on levels of debt that can exceed $100,000-$150,000. Whether Professor Johnson's research and analysis will get into their hands in time to do some good will depend on attentive faculty advisors, guidance and financial counselors capable of spreading the word about the perils of legal education.

Jones, Nancy Byerly. **Easy Self-Audits for the Busy Law Office**. Chicago: American Bar Association, Law Practice Management Section, 1999. 1 vol. (334 pp.).
Cost: OUT-OF-PRINT; was $99.95 ($84.95 to Law Practice Management Section members); from $203.80 on amazon.com (2014).
For lawyers, balancing the needs of clients with sound law office management practices is essential if malpractice suits and/or disciplinary action are to be avoided. This volume provides the lawyer with the tools needed to conduct self-audits in various areas of law office management. These self-audits cover such areas as client interactions, individual assessment and planning, support staff management, office management systems and procedures, time and stress management, and ethics. It also provides charts to monitor monthly progress. The appendices

provide forms in the areas of confidentiality, work routing, conference recording, and stress management health checkups. Additional articles and checklists cover client feedback, lawyer behavior and habits: danger signals, staff behavior and signals, and telephone behavior.

Kennedy, Dennis and Tom Mighell. **The Lawyer's Guide to Collaboration Tools and Technologies**. Chicago: American Bar Association, Law Practice Management Section, 2008. 1 vol. (289 pp.). Paperbound.
Cost: $89.95 ($59.95 to members); from $17.99 on amazon.com; kindle ed.: $54.99 (2014).
Modern law firms are on a perpetual quest for new technologies and law office efficiencies, not that these, ironically, have increased leisure time or provided an enhanced quality of life. Many of these tools do provide more sophisticated means of communication and collaboration, both inside and outside the office, on a variety of documents (online and off), cases, transactions, and projects. The most commonly used collaboration platforms, the development of a collaboration strategy, and various practical issues, tips and techniques consume a significant portion of the volume. From Skype to conference calls, instant messaging and simple screen sharing, Extranets and simple project management tools like Basecamp, the authors review many of the most useful law office technologies. The audience for this book is a varied one, consisting of practicing lawyers, paralegals, secretaries, librarians, legal professionals who work with lawyers, office managers and executive directors of law firms, IT directors, clients and software vendors. The useful appendices include a glossary of technology terms, collaboration resources (including both print materials and online sources), a checklist of tools by category, and index. Dennis Kennedy is an information technology lawyer and technologist practicing in St. Louis. Tom Mighell is Senior Counsel and Litigation Technology Support Coordinator at Cowles & Thompson in Dallas.

Kimbro, Stephanie L. **Virtual Law Practice: How to Deliver Legal Services Online**. Chicago: American Bar Association, 2010. 1 vol. (213 pp.). Paperbound.
Cost: $79.95 ($47.95 to LPM members); from $43 on amazon.com (2014).
For many years now, lawyers and law firms have been using technology to deliver legal services to clients and communicate with other legal professionals. In recent years, however, there has been an increasing demand by the general public for the delivery of legal services over the Internet. This practical volume provides a useful overview of virtual law practice basics as well details on how to establish and deliver legal services electronically. The author provides information on how to choose a structure for the virtual law practice, select appropriate technologies, set-up the virtual law office, create a web presence, manage and market the virtual law practice, and deal with ethics and malpractice issues. Appendices include a glossary of Internet and technology-related terms, a sample process for legal services delivered online in flow-chart format, sample virtual law practice terms and conditions for a completely web-based virtual law practice providing unbundled legal services online, state bar ethics and advisory opinions, and index. The volume also includes useful case studies of individual virtual law practices. This is an essential resource for any attorney contemplating establishing a virtual law practice or enhancing an existing Internet presence. Stephanie Kimbro operates a web-based virtual law practice in North Carolina since 2006 and is the recipient of the 2009 ABA Keane Award for Excellence in eLawyering.

Kuhne, Cecil C., III. **Building Your Best Argument**. Chicago: American Bar Association, 2010. 1 vol. (265 pp.). Paperbound.
Cost: $79.95 ($69.95 to members); from $39.83 on amazon.com (2014).
The volume of litigation facing the courts at all levels, combined with the fact that many decisions are made without the benefit of oral arguments, makes judges increasingly dependent on well-written, well-reasoned, and concise written arguments. This volume guides the attorney step-by-step through the drafting of effective written arguments, with particular attention to the basics of persuasion, clarity, the strong introduction, the significance of the overview, background facts,
the use of short bursts for the diminishing attention span, the history of the case, the importance of statutory construction, the determination of Congressional intent, discussion of relevant case law, challenges to the opponent's arguments, policy considerations, organization, and the use of stellar examples. The text is accompanied by numerous examples that illustrate these characteristics of the effective written argument. As a member of the litigation team at Fulbright & Jaworski's since 1993, Cecil Kuhne has represented clients in federal and state court proceedings involving complex commercial disputes, business torts, and product liability.

Lauritsen, Marc. **The Lawyer's Guide to Working Smarter with Knowledge Tools**. Chicago: American Bar Association. 2010. 1 vol. (223 pp.). Paperbound.
Cost: $79.95 ($47.95 to Section members); from $49.13 on amazon.com (2014).
There are three kinds of knowledge tools that are available in the world of computer technology: (1) those that store and transport knowledge; (2) those that extend the human mind; and (3) those that perform autonomous knowledge work. This guide to law office knowledge systems is designed to assist lawyers and other legal professionals with software that support key aspects of law office and legal activity. The author's primary focus is on software tools for performing distinctly legal work in law offices and other legal environments, including corporations, government, and nonprofit organizations. In discussing knowledge tools, he refers to software with significant knowledge content that either does something or applies and processes knowledge, as opposed to just moving or storing knowledge. This is not a book for technologists, but for those for whom knowledge systems are a means to an end. Its goal is help legal professionals select and employ knowledge systems to improve workflow and efficiency, and work smarter. Among these knowledge systems are those that enhance work product retrieval, speed document assembly, and facilitate the use of interactive checklists. Rather than serving as strictly a "how to" manual, the author's intent is to provide a conceptual understanding of knowledge tools and assist with the process of choosing, obtaining, and using knowledge tools in order to improve law office efficiency. A graduate of M.I.T. and Harvard Law School, the author is founder of Systematics, and

has published and lectured widely on the subject of law and technology.

Law Practice Resources Library on LoislawConnect. New York: Wolters Kluwer Law & Busines.
Cost: $540.00 per year (solo practitioner) (2014).
This package of law practice management tiles includes the **Lawyer's Desk Book, The Law of Lawyering, The Lawyer's Almanac, Hillman on Lawyer Mobility, Just Memos, The Leadership Matrix,** and **Mastering the Art and Skill of Listening: A Guide to Negotiation.** The online package provides savings over buying the individual titles in print. **The Lawyers Competitive Edge: The Journal of Law Office Economics and Management**. Rochester, NY: West, 1999-date. Monthly.
Cost: $1,160 per year (2014).
Keeping abreast of developments in the field of law practice management requires constant attention from office managers and managing partners. This 20-page, monthly newsletter provides an ideal means of keeping current in a wide range of practice-related areas, including law office technology, legal research, personnel management, communications, client attraction and retention, leadership, image, advertising, continuing education, litigation support, and more. A subscription also includes the annual **Legal Software Directory**, a 56-page (1999) compilation of reviews of the leading legal professional software packages organized in seventeen subject categories, from bankruptcy and docket control to law office finance, timekeeping/billing, and trust management. **The Lawyers Competitive Edge** replaces the quarterly Law **Office Economics and Management Journal**, formerly published by Callaghan & Company (later CBC) and taken over by the West in 1996. The cost of this monthly subscription has skyrocketed over the past few years, including a jump from $356 to $1,035 (190%) between 2005 and 2013.

Litan, Robert E., ed. **Handbook on Law, Innovation and Growth**. Northampton, MA: Edward Elgar, 2011. 1 vol. (332 pp.).
Cost: $195.00; from $170.97 on amazon.com (2014).
This collection of essays provides a fascinating look at the relationship between innovation, growth, and the legal system. In his introductory essay entitled "Is the law dynamically efficient," Robert Litan discusses the role economic modes of analysis have had on legal scholarship over the past 40 years, from the initial static efficiency model to the dynamic efficiency model currently in favor that advances the central importance of maintaining economic growth that delivers continued improvements in standards of living. This volume represents an attempt by the Ewing Marion Kauffman Foundation, with which Robert Litan is associated, to embark on a long-term effort to promote scholarship among lawyers and economists and other relevant professionals to investigate the links between the law and key dynamic outcomes, specifically, innovation and growth. The essays that follow examine the relationship between law and economics in a number of key areas affecting innovation and economic growth, including the role of the entrepreneur in economic growth; integrity and innovation in public capital markets; securities litigation and innovation; incentives for innovation: bankruptcy, corporate governance and compensation systems; intellectual property rights and economic progress; torts and innovation; the role of patents; why do entrepreneurs patent?; national technology transfer mechanisms; the centrality of private ordering arrangements for innovators and entrepreneurs; and the value of lawyers as members of entrepreneurial teams. These essays direct attention to the connection between innovation, growth and the legal system, with the goal of helping policymakers better understand and implement the law in an effort to advance economic welfare through changes in the legal and regulatory system. Robert E. Litan is Vice President for Research and Policy at the Ewing Marion Kauffman Foundation, USA.

Levitt, Carole A. **The Cybersleuth's Guide to the Internet**. 12th ed. Chicago: American Bar Association, 2012. 1 vol. (450 pp.).
Cost: $64.95 (2014).
Formerly titled **Internet for Legal & Investigative Research: A Guide for Legal Professionals**, this volume provides legal researchers and investigators with tools and techniques for conducting low-cost research on the Internet, including sources for locating missing persons, personal information, phone numbers, public records, property records, birth and death records, social security numbers, employers, aliases, and negative information to attack a person's credibility, much of it available on free Internet sources. The author also provides sources for conducting free legal research on the Internet, including sources of caselaw, federal state and local primary law, secondary sources, and legal practice materials. The author is a nationally recognized author and speaker on Internet legal research, with over twenty years of experience in the legal field as a law librarian, professor of law, attorney and Internet trainer. She is President and founder of Internet For Lawyers.

Lubet, Steven. **The Importance of Being Honest: How Lying, Secrecy, and Hypocrisy Collide with Truth in Law**. New York: New York University Press, 2008. 1 vol. (269 pp.).
Cost: $35; from $33.25 on amazon.com; kindle ed.: $16.06 (2014).
Honesty in the legal system and judicial process is an often illusive commodity. Yet, as the author of this volume states, "without basic honesty, our entire judicial system—with its structure of rights, autonomy, due process, and the rule of law—would collapse because we could not rely on the good faith of the human beings who administer it." Lawyers, judges and law professors who fall short of high standards of honesty can do great damage to individuals, institutions, and the pursuit of truth and justice generally. Nor is it just the out-and out-liar who creates problems for the legal system. There are many other ways, both bold and subtle, in which lawyers and judges can fall short of the standards we should expect of them, including obfuscation, exaggeration, guile, concealment, misrepresentation, trickery, and omission. In this fascinating look at the issue of honesty in the legal system, Steven Lubet directs his attention to five areas of inquiry: clients, lawyers, judges, academics, and the medical practice. With an evenhanded and balanced perspective, despite an admittedly left-of-center legal philosophy, he paints a series of careful and fair-minded portraits of a number of individuals and incidents across the legal spectrum that illustrate instances

in which the law or justice were not served, or were served in manner which cast the system in a poor light. He is as willing to criticize Justice Scalia for his failure to recuse himself in the Dick Cheney case as he is Senate Democrats for filibustering the nomination of Court of Appeals nominee Priscilla Owens. This is an essential read for any judge, lawyer or academic who wishes to consider the place of honesty in the legal system, or individual who wants to rethink how we feel about candor and honesty in our daily lives. The author is a professor of law at Northwestern University, the author of a dozen books (including **Nothing But the Truth**), and columnist for the **American Lawyer** magazine.

Luneburg, William V. and Thomas M. Susman. **The Lobbying Manual: A Complete Guide to Federal Law Governing Lawyers and Lobbyists**. 4th ed.
with 2011 supplement. Chicago: American Bar Association, 2012. 1 vol. (577 pp.). Includes a CD-ROM of Appendix materials.
Cost: $199.95 ($179.00 to members); supplement: 2011: $59.95 ($44.95 to Admin. Law Section members) (2014).
The number of paid lobbyists in Washington has more than doubled since 2000, growing to more than 35,000. As a profession, lobbying attracts nearly half of all lawmakers who return to the private sector. Lobbyists represent corporations, industry associations, labor unions, and a broad range of private advocacy groups, all attempting to influence government policy in some way. Lobbying has also grown in tandem with the rise of the modern regulatory state and the growth of government generally. Indeed, as more decision-making is socialized in the state, the more various interest groups will be forced to fight over the outcome, or the division of the pie. This volume examines the ways in which the Congress has attempted to regulate lobbying activity, particularly in the form of the Lobbying Disclosure Act of 1995, which established criteria for determining whether an organization or firm should register their employees as lobbyists. Lobbyists register with the Secretary of the Senate Office of Public Records, which makes these registrations available for public inspection. This book provides lobbyists, whether lawyers or private advocates, with the information they need to comply with federal law and ethical guidelines, including federal laws and applicable registration forms. Author William V. Luneburg is professor of law at the University of Pittsburgh School of Law where he specializes in the fields of legislation, administrative law, civil procedure, and environmental law. Thomas M. Susman is a partner in the Washington office of Ropes & Gray, LLP and coordinates the firm's regulatory and legislative practice.

MacDonagh, Catherine Alman and Beth Marie Cuzzone. **The Law Firm Associate's Guide to Personal Marketing and Selling Skills**. Chicago: American Bar Association, 2007. 1 vol. (160 pp.).
Cost: $49.95 ($39.95 to members); from $9.71 on amazon.com (2014).
Success in the legal profession requires as much attention to personal marketing skills as it does to legal knowledge and advocacy skills. This first volume in ABA's Law Firm Associates Development Series is designed to instill in associates the skills and habits of mind necessary to professional success in their law firms or individual practices, skills which were probably not imparted in the law school curriculum. Nor will such skills be imparted in the law firm environment where new associates are expected to hit the ground running. The personal marketing and sales skills covered in this volume include the creation of a personal marketing plan, the identification of people within one's target market, professional visibility through speaking, events and publishing, preparation for client meetings, the process of «asking» for business, realizing marketing opportunities, keeping clients, staying in touch with your network inside and outside the firm, and other critical topics. A concluding chapter outlines best practices in one minute. A Trainer's Manual is a guide to facilitating group training sessions. This is an essential tool for both novice and experienced practitioners, and law firm trainers charged with imparting such skills to associates.

Magat, Joan Ames. **The Lawyer's Editing Manual**. Durham, NC: Carolina Academic Press, 2008. 1 vol. (125 pp.). Spiral-bound.
Cost: $20; from $10.63 on amazon.com (2014).
This is a lawyer's guide to the conventions that underlie effective formal prose, including grammar and punctuation, the effective use of quotations, and usage and style. It is not a legal citation manual. While outlining the most universally accepted conventions, the author also states their exceptions and, when possible, the logic for each. In the interest of effective communication with the reader, the author promotes not only the use of correct prose, but the effective use of stylistic conventions. She also advises writers on unambiguous word choice and modifier placement, conciseness, sentence and paragraph structure, and effective transitions. The manual concludes with conventions guided less by consensus than by the reader's reliance on consistency, such as whether and what to capitalize or how to treat abbreviations, symbols, and lists. The aim is less what the writer or editor chooses to do than that the choice be consistently applied for the benefit of the reader. Joan Magat is a professor at Duke University School of Law.

Mallen, Ronald E. and Jeffrey M. Smith. **Legal Malpractice**. Eagan, MN: Thomson Reuters West, 2008-date. 5 vols. Replaced annually.
Cost: 2014 Edition: $670; ProView eBook: $670; supplementation to previous (5th) ed.: 2000: $38; 2001: $148; 2002: $122; 2003: $139; 2004: 0; 2005: $200; 2006: $204; 2010: $445; 2011: $515; 2012: $560; 2013: $610; 4th edition: 1997: $65.00; 1998: $63.00; 1999: $90.00; **Monthly Assured Print Price (APP):** $51/$612.
A comprehensive guide to the professional liability of the lawyer. The authors examine such topics as prevention of malpractice, vicarious liability, liability to a non-client, theories of liability, fiduciary obligations, judgmental liability, standard of care, damages, defenses, statutes of limitations. A number of substantive areas of the law are covered, including corporate, partnership and business law, criminal law, family law, insurance counsel, litigation attorney, property law, wills, estates and trusts, litigation of the malpractice action, attorneys' professional liability insurance, and more. Includes a table of cases and index. Ronald Mallen is a partner in the San Francisco firm of Hinshaw and Culbertson and a past chair of the ABA Standing Committee on Lawyers' Professional Liability, with a practice devoted largely to professional liability defense, principally lawyers' malpractice and related insurance coverage issues. Jeffrey Smith is associated with the Atlanta office of Greenberg Traurig, specializing in ethics, legal and accounting malpractice and

securities litigation. He is also a past chair of the ABA Standing Committee on Lawyers' Professional Liability. Beginning in 2005, the work was converted to an annually revised paperbound set at lower initial cost, but higher annual maintenance cost.

Mathis, Laura. **Acting Skills for Lawyers**. Chicago: American Bar Association, 2011. 1 vol. (145 pp.).
Cost: $59.95; from $35.49 on amazon.com (2014).
Research and writing is only half the battle for the modern attorney. To bear fruit, the ideas and arguments expressed in written form must be argued persuasively to the judge or jury. The communication delivered by the body is often more significant to the achievement of a successful result than that conveyed through written expression. The lawyer is a storyteller who must use public speaking and acting skills with sufficient energy and passion to convince clients, judges and juries. This succinct volume guides the attorney through every aspect of the physical presentation, including the art of presence, vocal variety and the benefit of keeping the jury awake, how to determine your character by knowing your audience, being in your body, taking depositions/being a talk show host, improvisation, the role of the acting coach in preparation of your witness, delivering closing arguments as monologues, and how to take a great photo. The book is laced with useful photographs, illustrations, examples, quick tips, and exercises. The author is a working actress with over seventeen years experience in theatre, film and television, as an actor, director and writer, and the owner of Spotlight Legal, a firm specializing in helping lawyers apply the skills and training used in the acting profession. This is an excellent overview of the often overlooked physical aspects of the legal profession.

McAlinn, Gerald Paul, Dan Rosen, and John P. Stern. **An Introduction to American Law**. 2d ed. Durham, NC: Carolina Academic Press, 2010. 1 vol. (453 pp.).
Cost: $67.00; from $27.61 on amazon.com; kindle ed.: $39.20 (2014).
Written for undergraduates in pre-law programs, students of American law outside the United States, paralegal professionals handling American law materials, and graduate students in majors other than American law, this textbook provides an excellent overview of the American legal system. Following a consideration of the basic principles of American law, the jury system, and the legal profession, there are chapters devoted to ten substantive areas of law, including individual rights under the Constitution, civil procedure and the federal courts, contracts, torts and products liability, property, criminal law and procedure, business law, marriage and family law, and administrative law. Each chapter discusses the key concepts and doctrines central to that substantive area of law, analyzes recurring, current and developing trends, highlights areas of contemporary debate, includes excerpts of significant court decisions, provides topics for further discussion, and concludes with a list of key terms and concepts for review. The clearly written narrative assumes no previous knowledge of the American legal system The second edition of this book reflects significant developments in case law, as well as other important changes in American law, during the last five years. The authors are all professors at Japanese law schools.

McKinney, Ruth Ann. **Reading Like a Lawyer: Time-Saving Strategies for Reading Law Like an Expert.** 2nd ed. Durham, NC: Carolina Academic Press, 2012. 1 vol. (328 pp.).
Cost: $35.00; from $14.47 on amazon.com (2014).
The premise of this volume is that excellent law students and excellent lawyers are also exceptional readers, able to read hundreds or even thousands of pages of dense and complicated material efficiently. Accordingly , the author lays out strategies and techniques for honing reading skills to enhance academic and professional success. She advises reading purposefully with the idea of grasping the main idea. She addresses the task of building a strong foundation for reading in law school, with attention to briefing, advanced thinking, and advanced and expert reading. She applies these techniques to the mastery of reading a law school caseBook, reading statutes, reading cases outside of the caseBook, and reading on a computer screen. She concludes with appendices that allow the reader to test reading speed, the art of getting in a good reading groove, an advanced reading checklist, and resources for further reading. Ruth Ann McKinney is an Emeritus Clinical Professor of Law at the University of North Carolina School of Law where she also served as Director of Legal Writing & Academic Success from 1991–2008 and as the Assistant Dean for Legal Writing & Academic Success from 2008-2011. This is an essential read before embarking on a law school and a career in the law.

McMurtry-Chubb, Teri A. **Legal Writing in the Disciplines: a Guide to Legal Writing Mastery**. Durham, NC: Carolina Academic Press, 2012. 1 vol. (174 pp.). Paperbound. Includes CD-ROM.
Cost: $25.00; from $23.75 on amazon.com (2014).
This aim of this guide to legal writing is to reconceptualize law in its disciplinary contexts by communicating legal analysis and writing to pre-law and new law students using the language of their undergraduate disciplines. In so doing, the author seeks to eliminate the disconnect that exists when undergraduates are thrust into the legal discipline without adequate understanding of how their undergraduate education relates to their legal education. The author begins by examining all the aspects of the processes used to create practical legal writing, including case briefs, notes, outlines and MindMaps, legal memos, legal briefs, exam outlines, and examination answers. Additional chapters are devoted to five broad disciplinary categories: science, social science, arts, humanities, and business, each of which provides discipline-specific instruction on creating different types of legal writing. The goal, in each case, is to lead the reader to the resolution of legal problems through legal writing and provide answers for self-assessment with discipline specific explanations. The author an Associate Professor of Law at Mercer University Walter F. George School of Law in Macon, GA She brings her background in history, political science, and international relations to this multi-disciplinary project.

Meiselman, David J. **Attorney Malpractice: Law and Procedure.** St. Paul, MN: West (Clark Boardman Callaghan), 1980-date. 1 vol. (516 pp.) Annual pocket supplement.
Cost: $517; supp.: 1994: $65; 1995: $76; 1996: $86; 1997: $60; 1998: 0; 1999: $70; 2000: $74; 2001: $88; 2002: $97; 2003: $110.50; 2004: $136; 2005: $152; 2006: $212; 2007: $189; 2008: $210; 2009: $247; 2010: $272.50; 2011: $300; 2012: $351;

2013: $379; **Monthly Assured Print Price (APP):** $38/$456. This is a preventative guide for the attorney who wishes to avoid the possibility of being sued for malpractice. It provides documented analysis of the attorney-client relationship, standards of care, proximate cause in legal malpractice, damages, the statute of limitations, liability to third parties, other defenses to legal malpractice actions, pleadings, and expert testimony. Additional chapters address the specific problems faced by attorneys in the following specialties: litigation, securities, wills, trusts and estates, real property, domestic relations, appellate practice, criminal defense, and tax, corporate and contract law. Finally, the author examines the issues of vicarious liability, conflict of interest, malicious prosecution, malpractice insurance, and the prevention of legal malpractice. The Appendix includes the Code of Professional Responsibility as well as a Table of Cases and Index.

Alert: Base volume is long overdue for revision. Supplement cost is clearly excessive for a title published in 1980.

Miller, Nelson. **Teaching Law: A Framework for Instructional Mastery**. Getzville, NY: Bridge Publishing Group LLC, 2010. 1 vol. (174 pp.). Includes CD-ROM. Order from publisher at: www.bridgepublishinggroup.com/
Cost: $49.95; from $29.62 on amazon.com (2014).
This comprehensive, thoughtful and practical guide to the pedagogy of law school instruction draws upon the scholarly, empirical and practical literature to assist legal educators in designing and implementing an effective program of law school instruction. The book's 14 chapters discuss theories of educational pedagogy, course objectives, syllabi, lectures, the Socratic method, differentiating instruction (to accommodate different learning styles), integrating instruction, classroom displays, diversity, student assessment, multiple-choice questions, essay questions, grading, vision. Includes a bibliography of sources as several valuable appendices, including Bloom's taxonomy of educational objectives, syllabus checklist, exam-format checklist, grading checklist, common language of instruction, and glossary of pedagogical terms. The author effectively balances the theoretical and practical consideration of instruction to fashion a manual which can be of considerable value to both novice and experienced instructors. A companion CD-ROM contains the complete text of the book and a variety of instructional modules in PowerPoint format to complement the text.

Munneke, Gary A. **The Legal Career Guide: From Law Student to Lawyer**. 5th ed. Chicago: American Bar Association, 2009. 1 vol. (328 pp.). Paperbound.
Cost: $54.95 ($34.95 to LPM Section members); from $1.01 on amazon.com (2014).
With more than one million lawyers in the United States, staking out a career path in an increasingly competitive marketplace requires thought, preparation, and effort. This book guides the prospective lawyer through the entire career choice process, from analysis of one's skills and assessment of the marketplace through the job search. Individual chapters are devoted to a discussion of task of choosing a career vs. finding a job, the law school experience, the career-choice process, identifying skills, evaluating the market, establishing priorities, lawyers and the practice of law today, private practice, organizational practice, judicial clerkships, academic law teaching, public-interest law, law-related and nonlegal professional services, substantive practice areas, geographic practice areas, the hiring process, the future of the law practice, the job search, and renewing your options. Ideally, a book of this type should be read prior to beginning law school. It is also a book that those already in the profession can recommend to those about to begin the journey. Gary A. Munneke is Professor of Law at Pace Law School and the author or editor of numerous books and articles in the areas of law practice management, professional responsibility, legal careers, and lawyer training.

National Directory of Legal Employers. 2011-2012 Edition. Chicago: National Association for Law Placement, 2011-date. 1 vol. (1,900+ pp.). New online directory released in May 2012.
Cost: No cost; went online in 2012; 2011-2012 print ed. was $85; searchable directory also available on NALP web site: www.nalp.org (2014).
A massive compendium of detailed job-related information for law students and legal professionals. It contains essential information on the hiring needs and employment plans of over 1,700 law firms, government agencies, corporations, and public interest organizations. Information and data are presented in a series of uniform, one-page reports containing an organization's demographics, primary practice areas, employment information, salaries, benefits, minority recruitment efforts, non-discrimination policy, partnership data, other offices, and campus inter-view sites. Each entry also includes a narrative statement summarizing the organization's history, structure, and job climate. Preceding this 1297-page section of firm listings is a series of «Fast Find Indexes» which list law firms and corporations alphabetically and by state; and public interest organizations and government agencies alphabetically and by state. It also lists all employers by practice area and by office size. Produced under the auspices of the National Association for Law Placement, the **National Directory of Legal Employers** also features useful introductory suggestions for the job applicant and the Principles and Standards for Law Placement and Recruitment Activities.

Nelson, Sharon D, John W. Simek, and Michael C. Maschke. **The 2010 Solo and Small Firm Legal Technology Guide: Critical Decisions Make Simple**. Chicago: American Bar Association, 2011. 1 vol. (292 pp.). Paperbound.
Cost: $89.95 ($54.95 to LPM Section members) from $8.47 on amazon.com (2014).
Making technology decisions for a small law office can be a daunting task for those without a grounding in technology issues and their application to a law office setting. This annual guide was written to assist solo and small firm lawyers find the best technology for their dollar. It features the most current information and recommendations on computers, servers, networking equipment, legal software, printers, security products, smartphones, the iPad and other items of technology for the law office. Written in easily comprehensible language, it is designed to assist the small law office lawyer in implementing his own technology solutions, or provide the knowledge necessary to communicate with an IT professional. The authors review current legal technology products, provide step-by-step

instructions for making intelligent technology decisions, and provide information for selecting the right operating system and software for the lawyer's law office environment, including case management applications, billing systems, and document management solutions. They also cover such critical matters as the equipment necessary to go wireless, protecting the firm from security threats (e.g. viruses, spyware, and spam), the legal implications of social networking, and other applications.

Nerison, Rebecca. **Dealing with the Stresses of the Legal Profession**. Chicago: American Bar Association, 2010. 1 vol. (211 pp.). Paperbound.
Cost: $59.95 ($49.95 to members); from $34.64 on amazon.com (2014).
The law is a stressful profession. Long hours, potentially angry and disgruntled clients, demanding bosses, financial demands, scheduling problems, the incessant requirement of finding new clients, and a myriad of business-related demands create multiple levels of stress for the practicing attorney. Lawyers also operate in an adversarial system that can solve problems, but can also create more problems than it solves, while consuming time, money and emotional energy. The author points out, for example, that Type-A males are twice as likely to experience heart attacks as Type-B males. The aim of this book is to aid the attorney in managing stress by paying close attention to situations that provoke anxiety and anger. But it can also prove useful to those who live or work with an attorney, are in law school, or are contemplating a legal career. She discusses the psychology of stress, stress and anxiety, the faces of anger, meeting challenges inherent in the legal industry, happiness and success through the stages of a legal career, getting and staying happily employed, putting stress in context (is it "normal" or a problem?), strategies for addressing stress, anger and anxiety, working or living with a stressed-out lawyer, and resources for further exploration. Dr. Rebecca Nerison is a psychologist with a doctorate in counseling psychology who has been helping lawyers improve their lives and workplaces since 1997, including a decade with the Washington State Bar Association's Lawyers Assistance Program.

Olson, Walter. **Schools for Misrule: Legal Academia and Overlawyered America**. New York: Encounter Books, 2011. 1 vol. (284 pp.). Hardbound.
Cost: $25.95; from $.01 on amazon.com; kindle ed.: $12.99 (2014).
An illuminating expose of the ideologically slanted culture that pervades most American law schools by one the country's leading critics of the American legal system. Olson, whose previous books--**The Litigation Explosion** and **The Rule of Lawyers**—paint a less than flattering portrait of the litigation and class action-obsessed legal profession, now directs his attention to the legal education culture that is its breeding ground. In the author's view, with a few notable exceptions, such as the conservative and libertarian Federalist Society, the political culture of most American law schools is decidedly left-of-center, an irrefutable fact revealed by examining faculty voter registration records, opinions expressed from the professorial lectern, the leanings of student legal clinics, and, as Judge Richard Posner has observed, the frequently bizarre and tendentious titles of law review articles. In contrast to the real world of practical law, Olson argues that this culture is informed by an obsession with legal theory (e.g. critical race theory, feminist jurisprudence, critical legal studies, deconstructionism, identity politics, etc.), its associated inscrutable jargon, intellectual conformity, and political agendas advancing claims of victimization. Ideas that would be considered extreme and over-the-top among the population at large, are likely to find acceptance in the rarefied and hermetically sealed halls of the legal academy. Olson attributes this culture to three kinds of pressure: the ABA accreditation process and its associated pressures for "diversity," fear of litigation, and donors with ideological agendas. Drawing upon critiques from both inside and outside the academy, Olson points out that the elite schools are often the ones where a student is least likely to learn the practical side of the law. Nor does Olson neglect the pervasive influence of such law professors as William Prosser, whose seminal hornbook, **Prosser on Torts,** was instrumental in ushering in the trend towards strict liability for defective products, and the accompanying wave of class action litigation. And with the fruits of the multi-million dollar verdicts garnered in class action lawsuits, successful litigators have purchased the naming rights for law school buildings, classrooms and libraries, or supported clinical programs likely to advance the boundaries of future litigation. Moreover, the culture of the modern law school is predisposed to pressure government to expand in an effort to satisfy the full panoply of interest groups and special pleaders who seek governmental largesse, and with barely a thought as to the ultimate and unsustainable costs to the society as a whole. Olson's book will appeal to those concerned with the state of legal education in the United States today, including law students interested in learning the law, fair-minded individuals interested in the restoration of a modicum of intellectual balance to the academy, and taxpayers and businesses concerned about the astronomical costs of litigation and their deleterious effects upon the economy. Walter Olson is a senior fellow at the libertarian Cato Institute, where he is a frequent contributor to the Wall Street Journal and other publications, and author of the blog Overlawyered.com.

Painter, Mark. **The Legal Writer: 40 Rules for the Art of Legal Writing**. 3d ed. Cincinnati, OH: Jarndyce & Jarndyce, Division of PSA Consulting, 2005. 1 vol. (168 pp.). Paperbound.
Cost: $28.95; from $17.76 on amazon.com (2014).
Good writing skills are essential for any practicing attorney or judge. Sadly, the legal profession abounds in examples poor, abstruse, legalistic, and jargon-laden language which fails to provide the level of clarity which the law requires. The author's 40 rules promote plain language legal writing, clarity of thought, succinctness, and persuasiveness. Among the topics addressed are grammar, quotations, citations, use of Latin terms, factual presentation, form, use of short paragraphs, and more. Since 1994, the author has served as a judge on the Ohio Court of Appeals. He is an adjunct professor at the University of Cincinnati School of Law and a widely respected speaker and writer.

Pallais, Don M. **Audits and Other Accountants' Services**. Chicago: American Bar Association, 2010. 1 vol. (234 pp.). Paperbound.
Cost: $64.95 ($59.95 to members); from $44.14 on amazon.com (2014).
This volume provides lawyers and other professionals with a

working knowledge of the different kinds of services provided by accountants and the tools for comprehending the vocabulary and rules used by the accounting profession. Its basic goal is to explain the nature of the audit and the basic rules necessary to help lawyers interpret the assurance it provides. It is not intended as a comprehensive guide to the audit or auditing practice. Instead, it discusses the context of the audit, what an auditor tests, how an auditor tests, assuring the quality of the audit, what the auditor's report means, alternatives to audits (including other accountants' services), and a glossary of auditing terms. The Appendices include a review of common audit tests, sample reports, the availability of common services, and auditor workpapers, and index. Don Pellais is a CPA and Certified Fraud Examiner (CFA) with his own national practice in Richmond, VA, with 25 years experience setting professional standards on the technical staff of the American Institute of Certified Public Accountants (AICPA).

Peoples, Lee E. **Legal Ethics: A Legal Research Guide**. 2d ed. Buffalo, NY: William S. Hein & Co., Inc., 2006. 1 vol. (89 pp.).
Cost: $53 (2014).
This guide to research in the field of legal ethics includes a discussion of research strategy, secondary sources, Internet resources, primary sources, , the multijurisdictional practice of law, and the Sarbanes-Oxley Act. The author's annotations and research tips address such specific sources as ABA Model Code and Rules, state ethics codes, disciplinary proceedings, ABA ethics opinions, state ethics opinions, monographs and treatises, symposium articles and conference proceedings, CLE materials, WTO research guides and documents, electronic databases, web sites, electronic newsletters, blawgs, ethical rules for judges and lawyers, and standards for specialized areas of practice. A useful starting point for anyone conducting research in legal ethics. The author is adjunct professor of Law and Associate Director for Faculty, Research and Instructional Services, Oklahoma City University School of Law Library.

Powell, Sarah. **BIGLAW: How to Survive the First Two Years of Practice in a Mega-Firm, or, the Art of Doc Review**. Durham, NC: Carolina Academic Press, 2013. 1 vol. (184 pp.). Paperbound.
Cost: $22.00 from $20.00 on amazon.com; kindle: $10.99 (2014).
Despite the outward glamour associated with elite law firms, the reality is far different, particularly for associates in their early years of employment. In the author's view, the system is "inhumane, corrupt, broken, makes life hell for many young associates, and leaves too many bitter and jaded ex-lawyers in its wake." It is a world filled with anxiety, depression, drudgery, a sense of hopelessness, emotional abuse, and lack of professional satisfaction. Drawing upon the personal stories of friends and colleagues, the author relates the complaints of those too harried for a personal life who spend their working days performing such routine clerical chores as quality checking witness preparation binders, supervising contract attorneys, and other chores that do not even remotely resemble the practice of law. The picture she paints is of young professionals trapped in an environment that they cannot escape, often because of oppressive law school debt burdens, and fears of the risks of solo practice, and older senior associates who cannot imagine how they have become the "typical, micromanaging, obsessive, senior associate they once hated, but have no idea how to change the pattern." Ironically, the author does not regret becoming part of Biglaw, but wishes she had the information distilled in this volume during the early years she spent confused, anxious, indignant, bitter, and in fear of being fired. The topics range from life in the fast lane to reputation and trust, knowing your place in the hierarchy, document production and its discontents, compensation, judgment, prudence, precision, diligence, professionalism and the billable hour, email etiquette, information mastery and preparation, mistakes, and having a life. She asserts that success very much depends on who you now, and how you navigate your place in your work environment. While the author claims to have written the book for entry level associates caught in a tangled web of frustration and hopelessness, it is, perhaps, better read by undergraduates contemplating a legal career, or Biglaw practice, in the first place. This a refreshingly candid account by someone who experienced the negative side of Biglaw practice firsthand, but survived. This is cautionary tale, and one laced with the cold realities of big firm practice. Sarah Powell teaches Legal Analysis, Research, and Writing at Duke University School of Law. Before joining the faculty, Ms. Powell was a litigator and senior associate with Covington & Burling LLP, focusing on complex civil litigation and white collar criminal defense.

Pratt, Shannon and Alina V. Niculita. **The Lawyer's Business Valuation Handbook: Understanding Financial Statements, Appraisal Reports, and Expert Testimony**. 2d ed. Chicago: American Bar Association, 2010. 1 vol. (625 pp.). Paperbound.
Cost: $149.95 ($124.95 to members) (2014).
The valuation of a business entity is of critical importance from a variety of specific perspectives, including tax, family law, and corporate law, among others. Determining value is a relative matter, depending on the purposes for which the valuation is being conducted. Value may be a reflection of fair market value, fair value under state statutes, fair value for financial reporting, investment value, and intrinsic or fundamental value, or be calculated by such other determinants as acquisition value, book value, going concern value, enterprise value, liquidation value, strategic value, or transaction value. Various sources of authority may be employed to determine value, among them: federal and state statutory law, legally binding rules and regulations, contractual definitions of value, non-legally binding administrative rulings, precedential court decisions, direction from the court, direction from the lawyer, the use of IRS authority in non-tax situations, and opinions of other lawyers and appraisers. Sorting through these various determinants of value and their use in specific factual and legal contexts is the subject of this authoritative treatise and practice guide. The authors examine the levels and premises of value and provide an overview of business valuation approaches, methods and procedures. They consider financial disclosure terminology, and the major approaches to business valuation: the income approach, the market approach, the asset-based approach, and the excess earnings method. They also examine rules of thumb which may be used, not as primary appraisal methods, but to provide "ballpark" estimates of value. They also consider such topics as personal versus enterprise goodwill, reasonable compensation, financial statement adjustments, comparative

financial statement analysis, economic and industry analysis, discounts and premiums, and valuations for federal tax matters. Attention is also devoted to valuations in the context of shareholder and partner disputes, and marital dissolution; as well as to employee stock ownership plans, and the valuation of professional practices and small service businesses. They also discuss valuation reports from both a methodological and procedural perspective. Finally, they examine valuation from a litigation perspective, including the admissibility and impact of expert business valuation evidence, discovery and the business valuation expert, alternative dispute resolution, business valuation standards and credentials, and the cross-examination of a business valuation expert. The text is accompanied by more than 70 exhibits that explain and illustrate determinations of value and other financial calculations. The volume also includes an extensive bibliography of sources, table of cases and index. Shannon Pratt, Chairman and CEO of Shannon Pratt Valuations, is widely considered to be a leading business valuation guru, with more than 40 years experience in the field. Alina Niculita is President and COO of Shannon Pratt Valuations, and a widely published author in the field of business valuation.

Randall, Kerry. **Effective Yellow Pages Advertising for Lawyers: The Complete Guide to Creating Winning Ads**. 2d ed. Chicago: American Bar Association, Law Practice Management Section, 2005. 1 vol. (200 pp.). Paperbound.
Cost: $69.95 ($54.95 for section members); 1st ed. from $4.99 on amazon.com (2014).
This workbook is designed to assist lawyers in creating influential, call-generating Yellow Pages advertising. Each of the book's four parts examines a different part of the advertising process: learning how Yellow Pages advertising differs from other types of advertising, creating the best ad, fine-tuning the ad, and choosing the best placement and price for the ad. The volume includes workbook exercises, sample ads, and the author's advertising tips, called "Yellow Pages Pearls." Also included are four appendices dealing with the legal and ethical model and the state rules on lawyer advertising. Kerry Randall, the founder of Kennedy Greene Associates, is a leading marketing executive and expert on Yellow Pages advertising.

Rhode, Deborah L. **Pro Bono in Principle and in Practice**. Stanford, CA: Stanford University Press, 2005. 1 vol. (244 pp.). Paperbound.
Cost: $55 (cloth); $22.95 (paper); from $9.99 on amazon.com (2014).
This scholarly examination of pro bono legal services contrasts the high aspirational ideals espoused by the American legal profession against the actual amount of services provided. Indeed, despite the profession's lofty promises made regarding pro bono publico services, the average lawyer in American donates less a half hour a week and less than 50 cents a day. This is the first full scale examination of pro bono work and is based on a review of prior research and an empirical survey drawn from more than 3,000 attorneys. The author examines the bar's pro bono responsibilities, the rationale for pro bono responsibilities, altruistic behavior, public service in comparative perspective (against the medical, engineering, and business professions), pro bono services in an international context, an empirical analysis of pro bono service among American lawyers, an empirical analysis of law school pro bono programs, and an agenda for reform. Appendices include the survey questionnaire, and endnotes, and index. The author is the Ernest W. McFarland Professor of Law and Director of the Stanford Center on Ethics at Stanford University. She is one of the nation's leading authorities on legal ethics and recipient of the ABA's Pro Bono Publico Award for expanding public service opportunities in law schools.

Rice, Paul R. **Attorney-Client Privilege in the United States**. 2d ed. St. Paul, MN: Thomson Reuters West, 1999-date. 2 vols. Paperbound.
Cost: 2013-2014 Edition: $650; ProView eBook: $650; supplementation: 2000: $75; 2001: $85; 2002: $98; 2003: $111.50; 2004: $125; 2005: $159; 2006: $180; 2007: $99; 2008: $328. 2009: $334; 2010: $372; 2011: $444; 2012: $598; 2013: $598; **Monthly Assured Print Price (APP):** $54/$648
Protecting the privileged attorney-client relationship is an essential ingredient in ensuring open communication between attorneys and their clients. This resource provides detailed and exhaustive examination and analysis of all the issues related to the attorney client privilege in a variety of contexts and forms. The subjects addressed include the history of attorney-client privilege, general principles, the attorney and the various roles in which he or she may operate, clients, types of communications, confidentiality, legal advice or assistance, exceptions to the privilege, waivers, constitutional and evidentiary issues, procedures, and choice of law. Each subject area is discussed in great detail and in all its contexts. For example, the author devotes considerable attention to the subject of whose communications are privileged, from direct to derivative protection and involving a variety of parties, from agents to third parties. In addition to providing access to the history, theory, and purpose of the privilege, the author provides a comprehensive examination of leading court decisions and addresses procedures for asserting, establishing, resolving, and appealing privilege matters. Paul R. Rice has been a professor of law at the American University, Washington College of Law for thirty years where he has taught courses in evidence, criminal procedure, and civil procedure. He has published eight books and over one hundred articles on evidence, civil procedure, and judicial management of complex litigation. This is the most comprehensive treatment of the subject in print.

Risius, Jeffrey M. **Business Valuation: A Primer for the Legal Professional**. Chicago: American Bar Association, Section of Business Law, 2007. 1 vol. (196 pp.).
Cost: $89.95; from $53.54 on amazon.com (2014).
This volume provides an introduction to business valuation for attorneys with a minimal background in economics and finance. Calculation of business value may be required for a variety of reasons, from the structuring of a buy-sell agreement, the consideration of a purchase offer, shareholder litigation, or a divorce. In such situations, the attorney is often charged with securing a valuation professional, or assembling a team of professionals that can handle the legal, tax, and valuation aspects of a business agreement. The author leads with a discussion of the keys to working successfully with business valuation professionals, the tools for understanding business operations, analysis of a company's historical and prospective

financial performance, the impact of economic and industry analysis on valuation, the basic steps to a business valuation engagement, and an analysis of business enterprise value. The significant theories of business evaluation are examined in detail, including the income, market, and asset approaches. The text is accompanied by numerous financial charts and graphs to illustrate the basic concepts of business valuation. The author is Managing Director of the Valuation & Financial Opinions Group at Stout Risius Ross, Inc. A CPA, he earned his MBA in Finance at Indiana University and has extensive experience in all aspects of business evaluations, mergers and acquisition.

Romantz, David S. and Kathleen Elliott Vinson. **Legal Analysis: The Fundamental Skill**. 2d ed. Durham, NC: Carolina Academic Press, 2009. 1 vol. (158 pp.).
Cost: $23; from $1.01 on amazon.com (2014).
In an increasingly complex society subject to a dizzying array of statutes, regulations, court decisions, ordinances and rules, lawyers must apply the law to a potentially infinite number of specific factual situations. Fashioning effective legal arguments in the face of this complex body of law is one of the most critical skills a lawyer must possess. In this succinct volume, the authors explain to law students the various ways in which lawyers analyze the law, and how they can formulate arguments that will impress a judge or jury. The basis for this skill is an understanding of the foundations of legal analysis and the principles lawyers use to devise legal arguments, and predict legal outcomes. Following an overview of the rules used to analyze statutes and cases, and the role of precedent, the doctrine of stare decisis, the court hierarchy, jurisdiction, and types of authority, the authors provide the tools for identifying legal rules whether in the form of enacted rules (statutes) or case law rules, and whether those rules are implied or express. Additional chapters are devoted to an analysis of inductive analysis and analogical reasoning, deductive analysis and rule-based reasoning, statutory analysis, policy-based reasoning and other considerations, and the communication of the legal argument. The volume concludes with a glossary of terms. The second edition includes new examples and student exercises. David Romantz is the Associate Dean of Academic Affairs and former Director of Legal Methods at the Cecil C. Humphreys School of Law at the University of Memphis. Kathleen Vinson is a Professor of Legal Writing at Suffolk University Law School.

Roschwalb, Susanne A. and Richard A. Stack. **Litigation Public Relations: Courting Public Opinion**. Littleton, CO: Fred B. Rothman & Co., 1995. 1 vol. (240 pp.). Now available from William S. Hein & Co. (800) 828-7571).
Cost: $48 (2014).
A compilation of articles which explore the role of public relations in the litigation process. Written by lawyers, journalists, trial consultants and judges, the articles address the theoretical, strategic, and tactical aspects of using communications and public relations as tools to influence public opinion. Although public relations techniques are employed chiefly by wealthy litigants, a knowledge of such strategies can help level the playing field both inside the courtroom and out.

Rose, Jennifer J., ed. **Effectively Staffing Your Law Firm**. Chicago: American Bar Association, General Practice, and Small Firm Division, 2009. 1 vol. (220 pp.).
Cost: $89.95; $75.95 to members; from $35.89 on amazon.com (2014).
The modern law office reflects a variety of staffing patterns, from those populated by numerous support staff to those in which the solo practitioner goes it alone with the aid of computers, e-mail, Blackberries, and other technological gadgets. This compact volume examines a number of staffing issues and practices and offers practical and cost-efficient solutions. The book's 22 chapters cover the broad topics of going it alone, finding the right fit for law office staff, your staff/your team, paralegal and legal assistants, the rules of engagement, and knowledge of employment law. The 21 contributing authors bring a wealth of personal experiences to the subject matter, from those operating as solos, in small firms, large firms, and bar associations. They consider rented staff, support staff, recruitment, marketing with staff, care and feeding of law office staff, leadership and attorney-staff relations, motivating lawyers and employees in the small law office, paralegals, personal issues, computer policies, legal staff evaluations, workplace security, discrimination in the solo and small firm, and firing. Their practical advice is worthy of serious attention by lawyers anxious to reduce costs and increase efficiency. Editor Jennifer Rose has served as the author or editor of several ABA titles, including **How to Capture and Keep Clients**, and, from 1995 to 2007, was editor of **GP/Solo**, the flagship magazine of the ABA's General Practice, Solo and Small Firm Division.

Rotunda, Ronald D. and John S. Dzienkowski. **Legal Ethics: The Lawyer's Deskbook on Professional Responsibility.** 2013-2014 Edition. St. Paul, MN: Thomson Reuters West, 2013. 1 vol. (2,178 pp.). Annual replacement volumes. . Paperbound.
Cost: 2013-2014 Edition: $183; from $172.95 on amazon.com (2014).
This volume addresses the often appalling lack of knowledge among lawyers of the ethical guidelines which govern their profession. Organized around the ABA's Model Rules of Professional Conduct and the ABA's Model Code of Judicial Conduct, this volume presents a wide-ranging discussion of the ethical issues most likely to confront the practicing attorney. The author addresses such topics as competence, fees, scope of representation, confidentiality, conflicts of interest, meritorious claims and contentions, fairness to the opposing party, voluntary pro bono publico service, advertising, reporting professional misconduct, and much more. Produced as a joint project of the ABA Center for Professional Responsibility and the West, this volume is authored by the Albert E. Jenner, Jr. Professor of Law, University of Illinois College of Law.

Rusanow, Gretta. **Knowledge Management and the Smarter Lawyer**. New York: ALM Publishing, 2003. 1 vol. (484 pp.).
Cost: $49.95; from $12.47 on amazon.com (2014).
Knowledge Management (KM) is a term applied to the techniques used to systematically collect, transfer, preserve and manage information within organizations, as well as the systems designed to utilize that knowledge. Knowledge Management is the process of harnessing the collective wisdom and experience of organizations and utilizing it to enhance productivity and

profitability. It lies on the cutting edge of law firm management, providing attorneys with the ability to tap the collective wisdom and experience of their colleagues to promote successful outcomes for clients and the business objectives of the firm. The concept recognizes that knowledge is a continuum that proceeds from data to information to knowledge to wisdom. Without on-demand access to managed knowledge, every situation is addressed based on what an individual or group brings to a given situation. With on-demand access to managed knowledge, every situation is addressed with the sum total of everything anyone in the organization has ever learned about a situation of a similar nature. This book was the first attempt to bring the concept of Knowledge Management to the law office environment. The author explains how the application of KM theory to law office practice can greatly enhance firm productivity and client satisfaction by taping he wellsprings of knowledge which already exist in the firm. Based in New York City and Australia, the author advises U. S., Australian, and European law firms and corporations on knowledge management, e-business, legal management, and technology strategies. This is an essential read for anyone involved in law firm management.

Saltz, Sidney G. **From Handshake to Closing: The Role of the Commercial Real Estate Lawyer**. Chicago: American Bar Association, Section of Real Property, Trust & Estate Law, 2011. 1 vol. (152 pp.).
Cost: $49.95; from $29.45 on amazon.com (2014).
This brief guide provides an overview of the steps involved in handling commercial real estate transactions. It includes a discussion of the role of the broker, letters of intent, the problems involved in documenting deals, document review, communication, negotiation, due diligence, preparation of closing, and the conduct of the closing. The author brings more than 40 years experience in the field of general real estate law. A useful overview for the novice in the field of real estate transactions.

Sapp, John R. **Making Partner: A Guide for Law Firm Associates**. 3d ed. Chicago: American Bar Association, Law Practice Management Section, 2006.
1 vol. (104 pp.). Paperbound.
Cost: $59.95 ($49.95 to Law Practice Management Section members); from $3.34 on amazon.com (2014)
A fascinating inside look at the professional and personal qualities, practices, and conduct most likely to advance your career in a law firm environment. John Sapp, who authored the 1st edition of this book in 1992, and four new contributing authors examine how to achieve the status of partner. Following a brief overview of the law firm as business and the task of choosing a firm, the book's 12 chapters examine the following ingredients toward achieving that goal: be well-informed, keep learning, word hard, produce a superior work product, be ethical, watch your flanks, behave yourself, put the client first, get involved, market, and relax. Each chapter is replete with valuable career-enhancing insights and tips, including the need for humility, and respect for support staff. John Sapp is managing partner of Michael Best Friedrich LLP, a firm based in Milwaukee, WI.

Schiess, Wayne. **Preparing Legal Documents Nonlawyers Can Read and Understand**. Chicago: American Bar Association, 2008. 1 vol., (127 pp.). Paperbound.
Cost: $69.95; from $35.65 on amazon.com (2014).
A brief guide to drafting plain language legal documents accessible to the average layperson. In the author's view, "too many legal documents intended for nonlawyers are dense, archaic, and unnecessarily complex…filled with traditional legalese, jargon, terms of art, long sentences and complicated syntax." He contends that such documents may contain mistakes of syntax and substantive law, both of which are hidden by the convoluted language. He suggests picturing the audience for plain legal writing and aiming for a 10th grade audience. The chapters provide insight into forms and the plain-drafting process, the design of plain legal documents, modern drafting conventions, organization and signposting, plain letters and e-mails, advice for plain court documents, testing plain drafts, words, sentences, and using readability tests. Appendix A consists of a number of before-and after-texts that demonstrate how awkward legal documents can be simplified. The author, Director of Legal Writing at the University of Texas, hosts Legalwriting.net, a blog devoted to legal drafting.

Schmedemann, Deborah A. **Thorns & Roses: Lawyers Tell Their Pro Bono Stories**. Durham, NC: Carolina Academic Press, 2010. 1 vol. (183 pp.). Paperbound.
Cost: $24.00; from $15.31 on amazon.com (2014).
Pro bono, a shortened form of *pro bono publico*, is a term derived from the Latin meaning *public good*. It is generally used to describe professional work undertaken voluntarily and without payment as a public service. Most common among the legal profession, it is increasingly seen in other professional fields in which volunteers use the specific skills to provide services to those who are unable to afford them. These stories relate the specific pro bono legal services provided by lawyers in situations ranging from a aid to a death row inmate, addressing sexual violence in Indian country, assisting people in transitional housing facilities, providing litigation services in a products liability claim, counseling of small businesses, trying a police brutality case, and appealing the denial of disability benefits, among others. The author is a faculty member at William Mitchell College of Law. This book is the culmination of a five-year study of why lawyers perform pro bono services.

Schneider, Deborah and Gary Belsky. **Should You Really Be a Lawyer?: The Guide to Smart Career Choices Before, During and After Law School**. Seattle, WA: Lawyer Avenue Press, 2013. 1 vol. (286 pp.). Available from Lawyer Avenue Press at www.lawyeravenue.com;
Cost: $25; from $23.75 on amazon.com (2014).
Most law students have no prior knowledge about the legal profession before embarking on the most important career choice of their life. Their knowledge is often based more on television drama than on any appreciation of the day-to-day work performed by most lawyers, which can be both tedious and stressful. This ignorance results in disappointed and disillusioned law school graduates and lawyers, 40,000 of whom leave the profession each year for other pursuits. Others feel financially and emotionally trapped and are unable to escape. The authors suggest that such disappointment can be reduced or eliminated

by honest self-assessment and through real world experiences which will provide an understanding and appreciation of legal practice prior to attending law school. This book is recommended for those contemplating a legal career as well as those looking for alternatives to practicing law. Deborah Schneider is a lecturer and consultant who speaks regularly on the subject of how to make smart career choices, and other career issues. Gary Belsky is executive editor at ESPN The Magazine. Previously, he was a writer at Money magazine, covering all aspects of personal finance.

Sex-Based Harassment: **Workplace Policies for the Legal Profession**. 2nd ed. Chicago: American Bar Association, 2007. 1 vol. (49 pp.).
Cost: $34.95 ($29.95 to members); from $2.79 on amazon.com (2014).
While sexual harassment in the workplace has received widespread attention since the ABA Commission on Women in the Profession was founded in 1987, resulting in the implementation of policies and programs in the vast majority of law firms, harassment and abuse remains a serious problem in the workplace. Employees continue to complain of emotional and physical abuse whose consequences result in emotional trauma, the deterioration of social interaction, reduced productivity, lost wages, and increased employee turnover, as well as the increased likelihood of employer liability and litigation costs. Moreover, the legal profession cannot hope to maintain credibility and public confidence if it fails to comply with accepted legal standards towards its own employees. This succinct manual provides an overview of sex-based harassment and its essential elements, and outlines how employers can formulate and implement harassment policies, respond to sexual harassment complaints and how to effectuate their resolution. The appendices include a sample sex-based harassment policy and a selective bibliography.

Shapo, Helen S., Marilyn R. Walter and Elizabeth Fajans. **Writing and Analysis in the Law**. 6th ed. St. Paul, MN: Foundation Press, 2013. 1 vol. (630 pp.). Paperbound. Available from West Academic.
Cost: $109.00; from $60.31 on amazon.com (2014).
Writing is an essential skill that every lawyer must master, although it is rarely a reason why people choose to enter the legal profession. Both writing and legal analysis are employed in a variety of practical circumstances. Lawyers write to clients, adversaries, judges, third parties, courts, and prepare legal memoranda and briefs to advance their clients' case. Good writing must reflect a clear sense of audience, purpose, organization, and paragraph and sentence structure. This law school text provides an excellent introduction to the legal system, the sources of legal authority, and the wide variety of legal documents that a lawyers typically prepares in the course of his or her profession. The authors explain the organization of a legal discussion, both large-scale and small-scale, with close attention to such factors as the thesis paragraph, the writing process, effective paragraphs, sentence structure, and the types of legal arguments used in resolving questions of law. The drafting of specific types of legal documents is addressed, including the legal memorandum, opinion or advice letters, the trial brief, the appellate brief, and oral argument, as well as such critical skills as client interviewing and counseling. Each type of legal document, or stage in the writing process, is accompanied by illustrative examples and exercises to drive home essential points. This highly admirable text is characterized by effective organization, thoroughness of content, clarity of expression, and pedagogical soundness. Helene S Shapo is Professor of Law, now emeritus, at Northwestern e School of Law where she was Director of the legal writing program for 21 years. Elizabeth Fajans has an M.A. and Ph D. in English Literature and is an Associate Professor of Legal Writing and Writing Specialist at Brooklyn Law School. And Walter is Professor of Law and Director of the Writing Program at Brooklyn Law School.

Siemer, Deanne C. Franklin D. Rothschild, and Anthony J. Bocchino, et al. **Effective Use of Courtroom Technology: A Lawyer's Guide to Pretrial and Trial**. Notre Dame, IN: National Institute for Trial Advocacy, 2002. 1 vol. (417 pp.). Paperbound.
Cost: OUT-OF-PRINT; was $75; from $6.29 on amazon.com (2014).
Effective courtroom presentations require mastery of a host of technological aids unavailable a few years ago. Recent surveys have found that the vast majority of state and federal judges have had experience with the use of technology in their courtrooms. This five-part guide is designed to introduce both attorneys and judges to these technologies and help them consider the implications, costs, and possible objections presented by their use. Part one provides an overview of three levels of technology. Part two discusses the implications of employing technology, including the costs during discovery and the need for the parties to reach voluntary agreement regarding their use. Part three addresses uses of technology at the pre-trial stage, including the issue of what technologies will be provided by the courts. Part four covers the use of technology at trial, including such matters as inspection, testing, reliability, and positioning. Part five provides detailed information regarding the most common forms of equipment used in the courtroom, including evidence cameras, color video printers, electronic whiteboards, projectors and screens, annotation tools, audio systems, videoconferencing, laptop computers and presentation software, real-time reporting, monitors for jurors, virtual reality display units and holograms. The authors are experienced trial lawyers and law professors teaching in the fields of trial advocacy and evidence. The volume also includes a CD-ROM containing sample computer-generated exhibits. The Appendices a listing of federal courts with courtroom technology, applicable federal evidence rules, sample pretrial order provisions, and a directory of helpful resources.

Siemer, Deanne C. and Frank D. Rothschild. **PowerPoint 2002 for Litigators**. Notre Dame, IN: National Institute for Trial Advocacy, 2002. 1 vol. (704 pp.). Softcover with CD-ROM.
Cost: OUT-OF-PRINT; was $65; from $26.07 on amazon.com (2014).
The National Institute for Trial Advocacy has produced a number of useful titles which address both the substantive and technical aspects of courtroom presentations. This volume provides detailed information on the creation and use of electronic presentations utilizing the most current PowerPoint software which comes bundled with Microsoft's Windows XP. The authors address both the basic needs of the computer or PowerPoint

novice and the specific needs of those who already some expertise in their use. Chapters are devoted to such topics as setting up to use PowerPoint, the demonstration case file, basic moves in PowerPoint, with additional chapters devoted to text slides, photo slides, document slides, diagram, table, timeline and chart slides, argument slides, slides with video and audio elements, and slides with presentation features. The authors also address collaboration issues with colleagues and setting up a computer for using slides at trial. The accompanying CD-ROM contains a number of sample electronic exhibits, including photographs, diagrams, transcripts, video clips and other documents. It also contains a PowerPoint slide show with examples of the types of slides you will learn to create by using the book. Deanne Siemer, managing director of Wilsie Co., is nationally recognized for her handling of complex litigation cases over a career spanning more than 28 years and the author of numerous books and articles. Frank D. Rothschild is an experienced jurist.

Simpson, Reagan William and Mary R. Vasaly. **The Amicus Brief: How to Write It and Use It Effectively.** 3d ed. Chicago: American Bar Association, 2010. 1 vol. (276 pp.). Paperback.
Cost: $129.95 ($110 to Tort and Insurance Practice Section members); from $69.90 on amazon.com (2014).
This unique work provides a comprehensive look at the essential elements, mechanics, and drafting of the successful amicus brief together with excerpts of several successful briefs, including those written by Laurence Tribe, Robert Raines, Pamela Stanton Barron, Roger Townsend, Regan Simpson and Karen Grundy.

Siskind, Gregory H., Deborah McMurray, and Richard P. Klau. **The Lawyer's Guide to Marketing on the Internet.** 3d ed. Chicago: American Bar Association, Law Practice Management Section, 2007. 1 vol. (192 pp.).
Cost: $84.95 ($74.95 to members); from $50.25 on amazon.com (2014).
A guide and tutorial to integrating a web presence and a comprehensive marketing strategy by an experienced immigration lawyer who developed the first immigration practice web site. The books chapters address such topic as developing an Internet marketing plan, web site design issues, promotional content, informational content, navigational tools, interactive tools, choosing your web consultants, e-mail marketing, weblogs and podcasts, web seminar and social networking sites, advertising and search engine optimization, measuring the results of your Internet efforts, and the ethics of client development through technology. The authors' also maintain a valuable weblog on law firm marketing which provides updates to the book and other useful information on marketing techniques and strategies. See: http://www.bookblogs.com/lawmarketing

Snape, John and Gary Watt. **How to Moot: A Student Guide to Mooting**. 2d ed. New York: Oxford University Press, 2010. 1 vol. (244 pp.). Paperbound.
Cost: $47.00; from $11.50 on amazon.com (2014).
By definition, a moot is "the argument of the legal issues raised by a hypothetical case which takes place in the imaginary setting of court of law." This volume, written for an English audience, was originally published under the title of **The Cavendish Guide to Mooting**. Although the history of mooting in England and Wales may be traced back more than 500 years, this was the first book devoted to the instruction and inspiration of mooters. The methods of argumentation employed in a moot court setting follow the conventions employed in a real court of law. A typical moot in the English experience consists of five participants, including two students representing one party in the case, two students representing the other party, and the judge, who is generally a more experienced lawyer, member of the faculty, practitioner, or real judge. The ten chapters in this volume lay out, in logical sequence, the preliminaries, preparation, performance, and principles and practice of the typical moot court experience. The chapters address the nature and attraction of mooting, the participants and their parts, production of persuasive presentation, the choice and use of authorities, performance—the basics, professional practice, style, judge and judgment, authorities—advanced considerations, and competitions. The question and answer format takes the student mooter through each stage of the moot court process. The appendices consist of a sample moot transcript, sample moot problems, sample student moot problem, a judge's score sheet, a specimen moot assessment sheet, a Latin and Law-French glossary, bibliography of references, and index.

Soled, Jay. **Estate Planning Strategies: A Lawyer's Guide to Retirement and Lifetime Planning.** 4th ed. Chicago: American Bar Association, 2002. 1 vol. (315 pp.). Paperbound.
Cost: $89.95 ($79.95 to Senior Lawyers Division members); from $19.50 on amazon.com (2014).
A comprehensive guide to estate planning in light of the changes brought by the Economic Growth and Tax Relief Reconciliation Act of 2001 (EGTRRA), which fundamentally altered the nation's transfer tax system and estate planning. The author benefited from the contributions of many of the nation's top estate-planning experts and practitioners.

Stack, Richard A. **Courts, Counselors & Correspondents: A Media Relations Analysis of the Legal System**. Littleton, CO: Fred B. Rothman & Co., 1998. 1 vol. (233 pp.). Now available from William S. Hein & Co. (800) 828-7571).
Cost: $63; from $59.95 on amazon.com (2014).
A media relations manual designed to guide the attorney through the process of dealing with the press in the routine legal environment. The author addresses the constitutional right to fair trial, the ethical responsibilities of litigants, and examines the views of judges, prosecutors and defense attorneys regarding the media. The author also provides advice on how to deal with the press, whether or not that attention is sought.

Staudenmaier, Heidi McNeil, ed. **Changing Jobs: Handbook for Lawyers in the New Millennium**. 3d ed. Chicago: American Bar Association, 2003. 1 vol. (376 pp.)
Cost: OUT-OF-PRINT; was $49.95; from $.10 on amazon.com (2014).
A collection of 32 essays which examine the variety of career opportunities open to lawyers. Produced under the auspices of the Career Issues Committee of the ABA, the volume's essays are grouped into four sections: Career Planning Strategies, Career Identification, Getting the Offer, and Career Options. This is an ideal resource for the attorney engaged in his or her

initial job search, pondering a career move, or contemplating leaving the practice of law entirely. Individual essays provide the reader with the tools by which to measure his or her current job against jobs nationwide, conduct a career self-assessment, conduct a career search, draft an effective resume, and negotiate salary and benefits. One chapter is devoted to examination of the job market in various geographic areas. The final eleven chapters examine career opportunities in law firms, corporations, government agencies, U.S. Attorney's offices, the judicial branch, legal aid, legal services and public interest organizations, teaching, part-time, temporary and contract employment, as well as in a number of non-traditional careers.

Stein, Jacob A. And Andrew M. Beato. **The Law of Law Firms**. 2d ed. St. Paul, MN: Thomson Reuters West (Clark Boardman Callaghan), 2008-date. 1 vol. Annual replacement volumes.

Cost: 2013 Edition: $115; supplementation: 2009: $25; 2010: $44; 2011: $75.50; 2012: 1st annual replacement vol.: $71; ; 1st ed.: 1996: $75; 1997: $82.50; 1998: $86; 1999: $93; 2000: $99; 2001: $119; 2002: $129; 2003: $147; 2004: $164.50; 2005: $211.50; 2006: $250.50; 2007: $223; 2008: new edition; **Monthly Assured Print Price (APP):** $7/$84.

Since law firms are subject to different laws and guidelines than those applicable to individual attorneys, they must be treated differently than regular business corporations. This book is a comprehensive guide to the law governing the operation of law firms, with a discussion of such topics as the formation of the law firm, the law governing professional corporations, selection of the firm name, solicitation, operations, professional liability, dissolution, resignation, and retirement. The author also examines the principles governing disqualification, including by disqualification by current personnel, incoming personnel, outgoing personnel, as well disqualification in bankruptcy and criminal cases. He also addresses such specific issues as the ability of departing members to take clients with them, law firm liability for partner defalcations, and the necessity of multi-state law firms having local partners to practice in a state. The author is one of the country's leading authorities on the law of damages.

Stern, Duke Nordlinger and Jo Ann Felix-Retzke. **A Practical Guide to Preventing Legal Malpractice.** St. Paul, MN: Thomson Reuters West (Clark Boardman Callaghan), 1983-date. 1 vol. (425 pp.). Annual pocket supplement.

Cost: $556; supplementation: 1995: $55; 1996: $60; 1997: $72; 1998: $75; 1999: $81; 2000: $88; 2001: $102; 2002: $119.50; 2003: $136; 2004: $149; 2005: $161; 2006: $181; 2007: $182; 2008: $225; 2009: $269.50; 2010: $315; 2011: $344; 2012: $376; 2013: $408; **Monthly Assured Print Price (APP):** $41/$492.

A practical discussion of the causes of legal malpractice and the steps which should be taken to prevent being sued for malpractice. The author discusses how to analyze a law firm's malpractice exposure through a self-audit of firm procedures and systems. He addresses the substantive causes of legal practice in various legal specialties. Attention is also given to maintaining effective client relations and docket control systems, avoiding conflicts of interest, effective filing systems, professional liability insurance, and other types of law firm insurance coverages. Formerly published by Shepard's/McGraw-Hill, this title was purchased by the Thomson Corporation in 1995.

Cost-Saving Tip: Forego the overpriced supplementation which adds little to the discussion beyond some additional case summaries that can be obtained by a WestlawNext search.

Stropus, Ruta K. and Charlotte D. Taylor. **Bridging the Gap Between College and Law School: Strategies for Success**. 3d ed. Durham, NC: Carolina Academic Press, 2014. 1 vol. (183 pp.).

Cost: $29; 2d ed. from $2.84 on amazon.com; kindle ed.: $21.99 (2014).

The first year of law school is usually the most difficult because many students must learn to adjust to new ways of learning that they did not encounter in their undergraduate experience. The aim of this volume is to aid the undergraduate student in navigating the transition to law school and the peculiar pedagogical standards that govern legal education. It does so by outlining the context, process and problem solving that are unique to law school. The authors accomplish this first by describing the law school environment, which they describe as one that is both formal and hierarchical, and designed to develop independent thought and analytical skills. They discuss the process of reading and briefing law school cases, effective notetaking, synthesizing cases, the role of the law school outline, flowcharting, exam preparation, time management, additional strategies for success, bridging the gap as a 2L or 3L, and the importance of gaining legal experience. The authors, both former law school professors, bring a wealth of experience and educational and practical savvy to the task. Ruta Stropus is Director of Attorney Recruitment and Professional Development at the Illinois Attorney General's Office and a former Assistant Dean and law professor. Charlotte Taylor is Assistant Dean for Multicultural Affairs and Student Support at DePaul University College of Law.

Tamanaha, Brian Z. **Failing Law Schools**. Chicago: University of Chicago Press, 2012. 1 vol. (235 pp.) Paperbound. (Chicago series in law and society).

Cost: $25.00; from $12.56 on amazon.com; kindle ed.: $9.90 (2014).

Based on a number of key indicators, law schools, at least on the surface, appear to be thriving. Enrollments are on the rise at many institutions, finances appear to be healthy, graduates lavish them with new buildings and programs, and law professors are highly paid and play significant roles as public intellectuals, commentators, public officials, and consultants. But the reality is far different, as recent stories reporting falsification of LSAT and GPA scores, misleading placement reports, and the fundamental failure to prepare graduates to enter the profession testify. Today, it not uncommon for law students to pay more than $200,000 out-of-pocket in tuition and rack up total debt of more than $100,000 after their three-year experience, only to face the worst job market in years. With limited or non-existent job prospects, many face unimaginable levels of debt that will haunt them for years to come, much of it fueled by federal education funds that have only managed to pour fire on the inflationary blaze. Clearly, the rising debt burdens assumed by law students have substituted anguish where once hope resided. Indeed, law school education suffers from many of the same symptoms that plague higher education generally, only on steroids. Yet, as recently as 2009 and 2010, law schools continued to increase enrollments in the face of the worsening law market that will leave graduates facing an even bleaker future three years hence. In the view of Brian Tamanaha, the fundamental economic model of legal education is broken. If normal economic signals were in operation, law students would stop enrolling, or would enroll in smaller numbers. Encouraged by misleading information on job prospects from the law schools themselves, however, students continue to make poor decisions as the federal government bankrolls their foolishness. It is the author's intent to expose the disconnect that exists between the promises of a law school education and its economic returns. The winners of this charade are often the law faculty whose salaries have risen significantly while their work loads have not. Once hired, no one tells the faculty what to do, and firing the incompetent or unproductive is a rare event. Yet, for all this, the hapless students pay handsomely to be lectured by faculty who teach, on average, two classes per semester, and are often absent from their offices. The author, who served as interim dean at St. John's University School of Law, draws upon his experience in confronting a law school that, at the time of his appointment, was "in a state of dysfunction," one that served the needs of the faculty, but not the students it purported to educate. This highly readable and honest account of the inner workings of his institution, and law schools generally, exposes the ugly underbelly of legal education in the United States today. It examines the complex network of factors that combine to undermine legal education, including the regulation of law schools by the ABA; the work environment of the faculty; competitive pressures on the law schools to increase their rankings, enrollments and income; the limited information available to prospective students, and the manner in which law school is financed by federal loans, among other factors. The narrative of this no-holds-barred expose is enhanced by personal experience, hard data, and incisive commentary. The author concludes with warning signs for law students, alarms for law schools, and recommendations for steps law schools can take to improve the current state of affairs. This is an essential read for any prospective law student, particularly those enrolling in schools not in the top tier. Brian Tamanaha is the William Gardiner Hammond Professor of Law at Washington School of Law in St. Louis, a renowned scholar in the field of jurisprudence, and the author of eight books and numerous scholarly articles, including **Beyond the Formalist–Realist Divide: The Role of Politics in Judging**.

Walkowiak, Vincent S., ed. **The Attorney-Client Privilege in Civil Litigation: Protecting and Defending Confidentiality**. 5th ed. Chicago: American Bar Association, 2013. 1 vol. (770 pp.). Paperbound.
Cost: $109.95 ($94.95 to Tort section members); from $83.15 on amazon.com (2014).
The attorney-client privilege is one of the oldest and most venerated evidentiary privileges under the American legal system. It is grounded upon the principal that in order for there to be an uninhibited flow of information between attorneys and their clients, those clients, whether individuals or corporations, must be free of the fear that the details of their communications will be disclosed. In recent years, that privilege has come under stress, as evidenced by a 2003 memo issued by the Deputy Attorney General which offered special plea treatment for corporations willing to waive the attorney-client privilege and work product doctrine at the urging of prosecutors. Despite the heated controversy that accompanied this memo. It had no impact on the substantive law protecting the attorney-client privilege. This volume examines the first principles of the attorney-client privilege as well as its application in a host of specific circumstances. Twenty-four chapters provide detailed analysis of these circumstances, such as when the client is a corporation, a corporate counsel, confidentiality and its relationship to the privilege, the hidden danger of exceptions to the privilege, the self-defense exception to the attorney's ethical obligation, protection of the privilege in the E-Discovery era, putting attorneys on the witness stand, application to U.S. patent litigation, the loss of attorney-client privilege through inadvertent disclosure of privileged documents, and more. Thirty attorneys contributed the chapters contained in this volume under the general editorship of Vincent Walkowiak, senior partner in the Dallas office of Fulbright & Jaworski.

Weise, Richard H. **Representing the Corporation: Strategies for Legal Counsel.** 2d ed. New York: Wolters Kluwer Law & Business, 2001-date. 2 vols. Looseleaf format.
Cost: $695; supplementation: 1997: 0; 1998: $88; 1999: $190; 2000: $190; 2001: $294; 2002: $316; 2003: $218; 2004: $218; 2005: $290; 2006: $275; 2007: $308; 2008: $330; 2009: $364; 2010: $390; 2011: $420; 2012: $450; 2013: $500.
This two-volume guide to corporate law department management began as an outgrowth of the author's experience as Senior Vice President, General Counsel & Secretary of Motorola, Inc. and a participant in that company's quality improvement program in the late 1970's. Weise lays a detailed strategy for streamlining and improving the quality of law department management. He addresses quality criteria, designing management systems for corporate counsel, full client utilization, annual client operations reviews, knowledge reuse through automation, automated management systems, outside counsel relationships, transactions in a corporate law department, securities practice in a law department, government contract practice, corporate compliance, lawyers and integrity, and more. Each chapter is accompanied by a chapter of valuable exhibits drawn from leading corporate law departments. The author provides some particularly candid advice regarding attorney recruitment, development, and dismissal. Originally published in 1991 under the title Representing the Corporate Client: Designs for Quality.

Weishar, Hollis Hatfield. **Marketing Success Stories: Conversations with Leading Lawyers**. 2d ed. Chicago: American Bar Association, Center for Continuing Education, 2004. 1 vol. (272 pp.).
Cost: $74.95 ($64.95 to LPM Section members); from $17.13 on amazon.com (2014).
This is a collection of interviews with a number of the country's most renowned and successful attorneys, all of whom share a common interest and talent in marketing their legal practices. Conducted by legal consultant Hollis Weishar, the interviews are organized into four sections: Developing Your Approach; Enhancing Your Image; Implementing Marketing Strategies and Maintaining Your Program, and address such topics as the building of relationships, the development of marketing programs, niche marketing, the enhancement of client services, and the encouragement of referrals. The practical advice offered in these individual stories can be used to enhance any lawyer or

law firm. While these success stories will be of greatest value to young lawyers, they can serve to enhance the practices of seasoned attorneys as well. The appendices include a primer on market research and research methodologies that support the marketing of legal services. The accompanying CD-ROM contains a number of invaluable checklists, plans, sample reports, questionnaires, and templates.

Additional titles addressing all facets of the Legal Profession are available from the following publishers: American Bar Association, Wolters Kluwer Law & Business, Matthew Bender, Carolina Academic Press, Cornell University Press, Delmar Publishers, Gordon Press, Greenwood Publishing Group, Gordon Press, Harvard University Press, Lawyers & Judges Publishing Co., LexisNexis, NALP: The Association for Legal Career Professionals, National Institute for Trial Advocacy, Niche Press, Thomson Reuters West, Vault Reports, Inc., West Academic. See Appendix B for addresses and telephone numbers.

Medical Jurisprudence

Attorneys' Textbook of Medicine. 3d ed. New York: Matthew Bender & Co., 1934-date. 23 vols. Looseleaf format. Supplemented several times per year.
Cost: $6,970 (includes annual subscription); annual renewal: 1997: $1,767.00 (price frozen since 1992); 1998: $1,830; 1999: $1,900; 2000: $2,030; 2001: $2,172; 2002: $2,325; 2003: $2,399; 2004: $2,519; 2005: $2,670; 2006: $2,858; 2007: $3,086; 2008: $3,302; 2009: $3,599; 2010: $3,816; 2011: $4,045; 2012: $4,328; 2013: $4,631; 2014: $4,960; CD-ROM: $7,972; annual renewal: 1998: $1,830; 1999: $1900; 2000: $2,030; 2001: $2,172; 2002: $2,325; 2003: $2,442; 2004: $2,564; 2005: $2,744; 2006: $3,074; 2007: $3,320; 2008: $3,619; 2009: $3,908; 2010: $4,339; 2011: $4,686; 2012: $5,108; 2013: $5,466; 2014: $6,198; eBook: $6,337; renewal: 2014: $4,960; CD-ROM also part of the **Personal Injury Library** (see entry below).
This exhaustive guide to medical information is written in a style comprehensible to the layperson. In over 300 chapters, the more than sixty authors provide detailed coverage of every imaginable medical problem and condition together with various treatments. It provides information useful to the litigator in preparing the complex case, evaluating injuries, presenting evidence to the jury, and in examining and cross-examining expert witnesses. Each chapter includes Medico-Legal Annotations to cases involving the same medical conditions, with description, diagnosis, prognosis, extent of disability and monetary awards. The set also includes three volumes of color transparencies which can be used with overhead projectors in court. Chapters include extensive bibliographies with citations to the specialized medical literature.

Cost Saving Tips: Matthew Bender has made an effort to price its Personal Injury Library (see entry below) at a level certain to attract the personal injury lawyer or law firm. Priced individually, the works in this Library would total more than four times the cost of this special package. Those interested in saving on supplementation costs should cancel the subscription at the end of the initial subscription period.

Ausman, Robert K. and Dean E. Snyder. **Ausman & Snyder's Medical Library.** St. Paul, MN: Thomson Reuters West (Lawyers Cooperative), 1988-date. 13 vols. Annual pocket parts.
Cost: $2,136; supplementation: 1994: $117; 1996: $167; 1997: $200; 1998: $225; 1999: $245.00; 2000: $265; 2001: $292; 2002: $343; 2003: $390; 2004: $437; 2005: $472; 2006: $667; 2007: $594; 2008: $662; 2009: $755.50; 2010: $831; 2011: $906; 2012: $996; 2013: $1,145; **Monthly Assured Print Price (APP):** $126/$1,512.
A multi-volume guide to most of the medical issues the practicing attorney is likely to encounter in the course of his or her practice, written in non-technical language. Chapters cover gynecology, obstetrics, anesthesia, orthopedics, pediatrics, neurology, neurological surgery, psychiatry, cardiology, gastroenterology, allergy/ immunology, endocrinology, hematology, pulmonary diseases, dermatology, nephrology, infectious diseases, oncology, rheumatology, surgery, ophthalmology, otolaryngology, radiology, nuclear medicine, radiation therapy, emergency medicine, clinical pathology, rehabilitation, podiatry, chiropractic and dentistry. While written for lawyers, this is primarily a medical reference and lacks the kind of citations one finds in most legal texts. There are Total Client-Service Library References following each of thirty chapters, however, including citations to **Am. Jur. Proof of Facts**, **ALR** Annotations, other West titles, and selective citations to medical journals and texts.

Blinder, Martin. **Psychiatry in the Everyday Practice of Law.** 4th revised ed. St. Paul, MN: Thomson Reuters West (Clark Boardman Callaghan), 2008-date. 1 vol. Annual pocket part.
Cost: $284; supplementation: 2007: $55; 2008: $60.50; 2009: $69; 2010: $81; 2011: $89; 2012: $98; 2013: $105; 4th ed.: 2004: $39; 2005: $49; 2006: new ed.; 3d ed.: 1993: $55; 1994: $62; 1995: $65; 1996: $77; 1997: $85; 1998: $90; 1999: $97; 2000: $105; 2001: $125; 2002: $125; 2003: new edition; **Monthly Assured Print Price (APP):** $13/$156.
Based on the author's lectures in the clinical program at the University of California, Hastings College of Law, this one-volume work is intended as both a textbook and a reference manual. It is written to provide practicing attorneys with a more complete understanding of the issues they are likely to face in representing clients in criminal, personal injury, commercial, workers compensation, family law or competency matters. The author covers neurological and psychological concepts, psychiatric concepts, components of the psychiatric examination, mental competence in civil proceedings and commercial litigation, psychic trauma, emotional distress, psychodynamics of criminal behavior, criminal responsibility, the criminal trial, obscenity and pornography, marital dissolution and child custody, interpersonal communication, negotiations, picking juries, psychiatric malpractice, direct examination of the psychiatric witness, and cross-examination of the psychiatric witness. Includes appendices, glossary, and index. Also includes Total Client-Service Library References to the full panoply of former Lawyers Cooperative publications now part of the West.

Brophy, Michael D. **Medical Malpractice Depositions**. Huntington, NY: Juris Publishing, 2004-date. 1 vol. (994 pp.). Looseleaf format or eBook. Updated annually or when needed.
Cost: $225; supplementation: 2010: $75; 2011: $75; 2012: $50; 2013: $50; (2014).

The process of gathering, eliciting, preserving and presenting evidence from potential witnesses in medical malpractice actions is probably the most important ingredient in a successful trial. This well-crafted volume provides both plaintiff and defendant counsel with the analytical and strategic framework for conducting the medical malpractice action as well as sample depositions drawn from a variety of specific malpractice cases. Together, these tools not only address many of the issues common to all medical malpractice actions, but those which apply to specific forms of malpractice. Providing the reader with a combination of useful commentary and sample depositions, the author takes the first half of the volume to address such topics as preparation for the deposition; conducting the deposition; the plaintiff's inquiry into the defendant doctor's background, training and experience; examination of codefendants; examination of experts; examination of office records; examination of hospitals and institutions; the plaintiff's medical history; critical events in the course of medical treatment; conversations; and post-malpractice medical treatment. The second half of the volume is devoted a variety of specific areas of medicine, including anesthesiology, general (internal and family) medicine, general surgery, neurosurgery, obstetrics and gynecology, orthopedics, pediatrics, thoracic surgery, urology, and nephrology, each of which includes a summary of the primary areas in which malpractice occurs and sample depositions (forms) for interviewing key witnesses. The author practices law with the Philadelphia firm of Harvey, Pennington, Cabot, Griffith & Renneisen, primarily in the defense of healthcare providers, and is a contributing editor to the Medical Malpractice: Law and Strategy Newsletter (published by American Lawyer Media).

Courtroom Medicine Series. New York: Matthew Bender & Co., 1962-date. 34 vols. Looseleaf format or eBook. Sold individually. Available in print or ebook.

Cost: Complete set: $23,077; renewal: 2014: approx. $18,000; Cancer: $2,190; renewal: 2014: $1,640; Chest, Heart & Lungs: $1,822; renewal: 2014: $1,402; Death: $2,658; renewal: 2014: $2,049; Head and Brain: $2,588; renewal: 2014: $2,007; Hip & Thigh: $1,153; renewal: 2014: $820; Knee and Related Structures: $1,822; renewal: 2014: $1,402; Low Back: $2,553; renewal: 2014: $1,941; Neck: $2,195; renewal: 2014: $1,712; Pain & Suffering: $2,705; renewal: 2014: $2,087; Psychic Injuries: $2,116; renewal: 2014: $1,619; The Eye: $1,275; renewal: 2014: $1,025. Sold individually.

This massive set examines all major medical problems and injuries which may become the subject of litigation. Includes information on diagnosis, treatment, trial preparation, examination of expert witnesses, disability evaluation, case annotations, and specific damage awards. Chapters include bibliographies of medical literature. The series consists of the following components: The Low Back (vols. 1,1A. 1B); the Neck (vols. 2, 2A, 2B); Death (vols. 3, 3A, 3B); Pain and Suffering (vols. 4, 4A, 4B, 4C); Shoulder and Elbow (vols. 5, 5A); Hip and Thigh (vols. 7, 7A); Head and Brain (vols. 8, 8A, 8B); Knee and Related Structures (vols. 9 9A); Abdominal Injuries (vols. 10, 10A); Chest, Heart and Lungs (vols. 11, 11A); Psychic Injuries (vols. 12, 12A); Cancer (vols. 13, 13A, 13B); and the Eye (vols. 14, 14A). The volumes covering the Skin (6, 6A, 6B) are now out-of-print. This is an ideal basic medical resource for the personal injury lawyer.

Cost Saving Tips: This exhaustive, but costly, resource should be consulted in a law library if at all possible to save the onerous cost. Your research in this set should be updated by consulting the medical literature or your medical experts. Don't forget that the various components of this series are also available individually should you not require the whole series.

Dorland's Illustrated Medical Dictionary. 32nd ed. Philadelphia, PA: W.B. Saunders Co., 2011. 1 vol. (2,088 pp.). Hardbound. Available from Elsevier. Also available online at: http://www.dorlands.com/wsearch.jsp

Cost: $50.95; from $22.50 on amazon.com (2014).

The first edition of this medical dictionary was compiled by William Alexander Newman Dorland (1864-1956) in 1900. The latest edition contains thousands of medical terms reflecting the current state of scientific knowledge in the medical fields. It has been updated to reflect the current terminology in such fields as immunology, bacteriology, infectious diseases, enzymology, endocrinology, dermatology, tropical medicine, psychiatry and psychology, as well as surgery, genetics, genetic diseases, dentistry, mathematics, and statistics.

Iyer, Patricia and Barbara J. Levin. **Medical Legal Aspects of Medical Records**. 2d ed. Tucson, AZ: Lawyers & Judges Publishing Co., 2010. 2 vols. (393, 650 pp.).

Cost: Vol. 1: Foundations of Medical Records: $89.00; Vol. 2: Clinical Specialty Records: $129.00; Vol. 1: from $62.88 on amazon.com; kindle: $63.53 (2014).

Medical records are confidential, patient-identifiable documents that record the medical history of a patient during the course of their treatment by a hospital, medical facility, or health care provider. Medical records are an often crucial element in the evidentiary record of cases ranging from personal injury, healthcare, workers' compensation, medical malpractice, criminal, and even probate actions (to establish competency or lack thereof). In the legal arena, it is essential to establish the veracity and reliability of the medical record being introduced into evidence. Rules and regulations which govern the use of medical records, and which are designed to ensure their unimpeachability, vary by type of facility and jurisdiction. Since no one series of protocols governs the formal care and maintenance of medical records, their utilization in each legal proceeding is unique. This invaluable resource provides the attorney or medical facility with comprehensive guidance regarding the preservation and utilization of medical records in a variety of circumstances. Each of the 45 chapters in two volumes is authored by experts in the medical and legal fields, providing unique insights into the complex world of medical record keeping, preservation, and utilization. Volume one provides a general view of many aspects of medical records that apply across all specialties, including such topics as generating and preserving medical records, the legal aspects of charting, obtaining and organizing medical records, analyzing medical records, computerization of records, preparation for E-discovery of electronic medical record information, and autopsy reports. Volume two provides a more in-depth examination of medical records in specific clinical specialties, ranging from complimentary and alternative medicine, dental records, home care, ophthalmology, surgical, diagnostic testing, medication records, the nursing process, pain assessment, psychiatric, physical therapy, and skin trauma, among others. The text is accompanied by hundreds of illustrative charts, photographs, and drawings, as well as practice tips, and endnotes to sources. The Appendices in volume two include a guide to medical terminology, abbreviations, acronyms, and symbols; Internet resources, and textbook references, and glossary of medical terms and medical-related terms. Co-editor Patricia Iyer received her Bachelor of Science in Nursing and Masters of Science in Nursing from the University of Pennsylvania. An educator and widely published author, she is president of Med League Support Services, Inc., a legal nurse consulting company in Flemington, NJ. And Patient Safety Now, a firm that provides education about medical records to hundreds of attorneys, physicians, nurses, and paralegals. Her co-editor, Barbara J. Levin, received her B.S. in Nursing from Boston University and has more than 25 years experience in clinical nursing, writing, speaking, and consulting. This invaluable resource should be acquired by any attorney or medical professional whose practice involves the use of medical records.

Jesson, Lucinda E. and Stacey A. Tavino. **Complementary and Alternative Medicine and the Law**. Durham, NC: Carolina Academic Press, 2010. 1 vol. (295 pp.). Paperbound.
Cost: $42.00; from $27.00 on amazon.com (2014).
Americans are increasingly turning to a variety of alternative medical therapies commonly referred to as Complementary and Alternative Medicine (CAM). The most common of these alternative therapies are relaxation techniques, herbal medicine, massage therapy, and chiropractic care. As the name suggests, these alterative therapies may be used in combination with or in place of traditional medical treatments. This volume examines this phenomenon primarily from a legal perspective, but also examines the history of CAM and the cultural and social implications of its increasing role in health care. The authors' central theme is the tension that exists between the government's responsibility to protect the population from "quackery" and the individual's freedom to choose therapies appropriate to his or her own needs. Following an insightful introduction to the field of complementary and alternative medicine, the authors discuss the role of medical licensure, the scope of practice, malpractice, informed consent, regulation of dietary supplements, antitrust issues, and innovations in CAM regulation. The text is supported with numerous citations to both the medical literature and primary and secondary legal authorities. The chapters include excerpts of case studies, trial court arguments, appellate court decisions, and recent state attorney general scope of practice formal opinions, as well as sample problems and questions. The book is written not only for law students, but also for a variety of health professionals, including health care providers and administrators, consumers of complementary and alternative medicine, and attorneys. Lucinda Jessen is a professor of law and Founding Director of the Health Law Institute at Hamline University School of Law. In 2011, she was appointed Commissioner of the Minnesota Department of Human Services by Governor Mark Dayton. Stacey Tovino is a professor of law at the William S. Boyd School of Law, University of Nevada, Las Vegas.

Kitaeff, Jack. **Malingering, Lies, and Junk Science Courtroom**. Youngstown, NY: Cambria Press, 2007. 1 vol. (624 pp.).
Cost: $139.95; also $130.48 on amazon.com; Kindle price: $34.99 (2014).
How does a lawyer, a judge, or a jury distinguish between a genuine psychological or psychiatric disorder and forms of malingering designed to achieve a financial gain through litigation, or avoid criminal or civil responsibility? This scholarly examination subjects some of the most common psychiatric disorders, psychological syndromes, trauma disorders, addictions, and emotional injury claims to a solid theoretical review from several noted psychologists, psychiatrists, and lawyers. In doing so, it provides the reader with the tools for evaluating such claims from a clinical perspective. The book also examines the kind of unreliable and unsubstantiated treatment and assessment methods used by the mental health industry which may find their way into the courtroom. It also provides the latest psychological research findings as they relate to these questionable disorders and methods, drawing upon both real-life experiences in the courtroom, and relevant case law. Designed for practicing attorneys, psychologists and psychiatrists, law students, and students in mental health and criminal justice, this book will provide a means of evaluating "syndrome" evidence, its uses and abuses, malingering, and the practices by which patients, clients, and defendants (as well as psychiatrists, psychologists, and lawyers) abuse the mental health and legal systems in order to escape criminal culpability, obtain benefits, or make a case. Dr. Jack Kitaeff is a licensed clinical psychologist in Virginia specializing in forensic and police psychology. He graduated from the City University of New York. His psychology education includes an MS degree in experimental psychology from the State University of New York and a PhD from the University of Mississippi. He received his JD degree from the George Mason University School of Law. His private practice concentrates on consulting with police and sheriff departments conducting pre-employment psychological screening of law enforcement applicants, fitness-for-duty evaluations, and psychological profiling.

Lane, Fred and David A. Birnbaum. **Lane Medical Litigation Guide.** St. Paul, MN: Thomson Reuters West (Clark Boardman Callaghan), 1981-date. 5 vols. Looseleaf format. Supplemented twice annually.
Cost: $2,405; supplementation: 1993: $213; 1994: $285; 1995: $150; 1996: $475; 1997: $510; 1998: $500; 1999: $297; 2000: $321; 2001: $378; 2002: $886; 2003: $600; 2004: $672; 2005: $726; 2006: $513; 2007: $914; 2008: $1,019; 2009: $1,164; 2010: $1,280; 2011: $1,395; 2012: $1,521; 2013: $1,658; **Monthly Assured Print Price (APP):** $175/$2,100.
This fairly comprehensive overview of medico-legal issues was authored by a trial lawyer with more than 30 years experience, most of it involving medical matters. As a co-author of **Goldstein Trial Technique** and an editor of **Medical Trial Technique Quarterly,** Fred Lane has assembled a useful collection of information to guide the practicing attorney through the complete litigation process, from the client interview through the trial itself. The set is organized into five main subdivisions reflecting the questions that arise most frequently in the course of a legal practice: hospital and health care personnel; medical evidence; medical techniques and special procedures; sections of the body and their disorders; and human systems, systemic disorders

and traumatic injuries. The set also includes illustrations of trial techniques and representative awards and settlements arranged by type of injury or medical problem. The medical information is kept current by members of the publisher's Medical Advisory Board consisting of more than twenty members of the medical profession. Additional features include a glossary of medical terms, cross-references to **Goldstein Trial Technique**, a bibliography, table of anatomical drawings, and index. Heavily documented with citations to cases and statutes from all jurisdictions. An excellent, concise reference tool for the attorney engaged in a variety of legal matters involving medical issues.

Lawyers' Medical Cyclopedia of Personal Injuries and Allied Specialties. Edited by Richard M. Patterson, 5th ed. Newark, NJ: LexisNexis, 2002-date. 10 vols. Hardbound with annual pocket supplementation.
Cost: $1,022; supplementation: 2003: $465; 2004: $478; 2005: $512; 2006: $538; 2007: $202: 2008: $330; 2009: $500; 2010: $563; 2011: $191; 2012: $393; 2013: $432.
A comprehensive and authoritative reference tool for attorneys involved in personal injury, medical malpractice, workers' compensation, social security, disability income, and health insurance cases. The text is the product of dozens of specialists in medicine and the law providing in-depth information on hundreds of medical, surgical and medical treatment topics combined with references to applicable case law. The topics range from accident proneness and allergies to arthritis, burn injuries, cancer, dentistry, gynecology, pediatrics, radiology and whiplash injuries, to name just a few. Extensive bibliographical references include relevant medical journal articles, state and federal court decisions, and the **American Law Reports**. There is an emphasis on those medical conditions and injuries most likely to be the subject of litigation. Originally published by the Allen Smith Company of Indianapolis, Indiana in 1959, this work was acquired by LexisNexis and is now in its 5th edition.

Legal Medicine. American College of Legal Medicine Textbook Committee, S. Sandy Sanbar et al. 7th ed. St. Louis, MO: Mosby, 2007. 1 vol. (768 pp.). ebook.
Cost: ebook: $229.95; from $139.97 on amazon.com; kindle: $229 (2014).
This volume is a product of the American College of Legal Medicine, an organization devoted to furthering knowledge and education in the fields of medical jurisprudence and forensic medicine, and addressing problems that exist at the interface of law and medicine. This text addresses those areas of professional activity which present potential risk of legal liability. The book's fifty chapters discuss a wide range of medico-legal topics, combining discussion of substantive medical conditions and issues with a consideration of the legal ramifications of such activities. Topics include legal medicine and health law education, contracts, agency and partnership, competency and capacity, education and licensure, medical staff peer review, physician as defendant in medical malpractice, medical testimony and the expert witness, medical product liability, health insurance and professional liability insurance, risk management, fetal interests, medical records and disclosure about patients, forensic pathology, human experimentation and research, and many more. Endnotes to each chapter include references to relevant cases, statutes, and medical literature. The authors include more than fifty scholars in the fields of law and medicine, many of these with degrees in both disciplines. An excellent one-volume resource for law, medical, and academic libraries, and practitioners in both fields.

Louisell, David W., Harold Williams and Charles Kramer. **Medical Malpractice.** New York: Matthew Bender & Co., 1960-date. 7 vols. Looseleaf format, CD-ROM, or eBook. Supplemented approximately twice annually.
Cost: $2,445 (includes annual subscription); annual renewal: 1995: $578 (price frozen since 1992); 1996: $606; 1997: $606; 1998: $640; 1999: $665; 2000: $710; 2001: $760; 2002: $814; 2003: $855; 2004: $898; 2005: $961; 2006: $1,029; 2007: $1,111; 2008: $1,222; 2009: $1,320; 2010: $1,425; 2011: $1,469; 2012: $1,557; 2013: $1,666; 2014: $1,818; CD-ROM: $2,734; renewal: 1998: $580; 1999: $625; 2000; $670; 2001: $717; 2002: $768; 2003: $807; 2004: $847; 2005: $906; 2006: $970; 2007: $1,048; 2008: $1,142; 2009: $1,233; 2010: $1,369; 2011: $1,479; 2012: $1,557; 2013: $1,666; 2014: $1,955.34; eBook: $2,222; renewal: 2014: $1,818. Also available as part of the **Personal Injury Library** (see entry below)
This is a combination treatise and practice guide written for the attorney either bringing or defending against a medical malpractice claim. Lead authors David Louisell, the Elizabeth Josselyn Boalt Professor of Law at the University of California at Berkeley and Harold Williams, a practicing attorney and member of the California and Kansas bars, are joined by sixteen legal scholars and practicing attorneys in assembling a work which addresses both the theoretical and practical sides of malpractice law. This is the most thorough work of its kind on the market. The exhaustively documented text encompasses background discussion regarding the practice of medicine, its fields, and the causes of malpractice suits. Chapter also cover theories of liability, defense of malpractice cases, settling the case, handling the case of the defendant, statutes of limitation, vicarious liability, emergency room negligence, and malpractice in such specialties as psychiatry, dentistry, podiatry, radiology, obstetrics, and gynecology. Additional chapters are devoted to the subjects of damages, recent trends and new causes of action, death and the withdrawing of life support, malpractice insurance, good Samaritan statutes and consent to treatment. Coverage of procedural aspects includes discovery techniques, jury selection, opening statements, the direct case, cross examination, summation, and the court's charge. The law regarding use of expert witnesses is discussed as is the law regarding use of medical records. Illustrative damage awards are highlighted in chapter 40. The Appendices include a Medical Malpractice Case Reference Table containing a listing of cases organized by disease or medical condition and then by jurisdiction, Sources of Information in medical and related fields, a Table of Cases, and Subject Index. This is an impressive work of scholarship which should be essential resource to any attorney handling medical malpractice cases.

Cost Saving Tips: The presence of this set in **Bender's Personal Injury Law Library** on CD-ROM makes it a logical acquisition for the personal injury lawyer. This and seven other titles are available on CD-ROM for only $8,813, with renewal of $5,345.

McCormick, Harvey L. **Medicare and Medicaid Claims and Procedures.** 4th ed. St. Paul, MN: Thomson Reuters West, 2005-date. 2 vols. Irregular pocket parts.
Cost: $416; supplementation: 2006: $42; 2007: $48; 2008: $56; 2009: $69; 2010: $81; 2011: $83; 2012: $87; 2013: $92; 3d ed.: 2002: $53; 2003: $60; 2004: $72; supplementation to 2d ed.: 1993: $30.50; 1995: $41; 1996: $40; 1997: $44; 1998: $50; 1999: $55; 2000: $61; **Monthly Assured Print Price (APP)**: $14/$168.
This two-volume treatise does an admirable job of simplifying the vast body of statutes, case law, and regulations which comprise the Medicare and Medicaid laws. Authored by Harvey L. McCormick of the Missouri and Wisconsin bars, it both describes the most common portions of the laws themselves and then organizes the law into a coherent form to be of benefit to those individuals who handle Medicare and Medicaid claims and the appeals from the denial of those claims. The Medicare text covers such matters as eligibility, providers of services, inpatient hospital services, extended care services, home health services, coverages and benefits, administrative procedures and hearings, evidence, judicial review, attorneys fees. The Medicaid chapters examine general provisions, state plan requirements, fair hearing requirements, penalties and judicial review. The Appendices include Directory of Peer Review Organizations, application and administrative procedure forms, Medicaid State Agencies, and a Prospective Payment Plan for Medicare Patients. There are tables of statutes, rules, regulations, and subject indexes.

Medical Group Practice: **Legal and Administrative Guide**. Gaithersberg, MD: Wolters Kluwer Law & Business, 1998-date. 1 vol. Looseleaf format. Supplemented twice annually.
Cost: $449; supplementation: 2004: $310; 2005: $0; 2006: $354; 2007: $159; 2008: $338; 2009: $368; 2010: $460; 2011: $245; 2012: $269; 2013: $325.
As health care has become more complex, physicians and other medical professional have increasingly turned to group medical practices as vehicles for the delivery of health care services in the United States. Such organizations provide a means of attending to the complex administrative and legal requirements and procedures involved, while allowing medical professionals to focus on their specialties and patient care. This one-volume work provides practical guidance in the professional management of group health practices as a means of streamlining procedures and reducing potential risks and liabilities. Chapters are devoted to group practice formation, physician compensation, managed care contracting, credentialing and peer review, personnel and human resources, environmental compliance, reimbursement issues, billing and collections, patient care records, patient care liability, insurance, marketing and group practice, corporate compliance programs for group practices, and computers and data management. An excellent desk reference for medical group practices and the law firms which represent them. Produced by the Aspen Health Law & Compliance Center of Wolters Kluwer Law & Business.

Medical Malpractice: Guide to Medical Issues. New York: Matthew Bender & Co., 1986-date. 7 vols. Looseleaf format and eBook. No CD-ROM.
Cost: $3,015 (print) (includes annual subscription); renewal: 1997: $220 (price frozen since 1992); 1998: $780; 1999: $810; 2000: $870; 2001: $931; 2002: $997; 2003: $1,047; 2004: $1,099; 2005: $1,176; 2006: $1,259; 2007: $1,360; 2008: $1,482; 2009: $1,615; 2010: $1,713; 2011: $1,799; 2012: $1,907; 2013: $2,040; 2014: $2,227; ebook: $2,662; renewal: 2014: $2,227.
This work combines detailed medical information with complete case studies in those areas of medicine in which malpractice suits are most often brought. Includes the fields of emergency medicine, anesthesiology, general surgery, orthopedics, neurology and neurosurgery, obstetrics and gynecology, neonatology, plastic surgery, and oncology. Includes a discussion of the potential causes of medical malpractice and the ways in which doctors depart from accepted standards of care. Also distinguishes between malpractice and errors of judgment. The case studies include a detailed overview of the discovery process including a review of relevant medical records, depositions, and opinions of expert witnesses. Also includes checklists, annotations to relevant cases with amounts of damage awards, a glossary of terms, and index.

Medicare and Medicaid Guide. Riverwoods, IL: CCH Inc., 1969-date. 5 vols. Looseleaf service. Updated weekly. Also available on Internet (see below).
Cost: $2,962 per year (2014).
This five-volume looseleaf service provides detailed coverage of the programs created by Titles XVIIII (Medicare) and XIX (Medicaid) of the Social Security Act. The coverage is primarily devoted to federal laws, although State Medicaid laws are covered in more superficial fashion. Material includes federal laws, regulations, federal agency publications, federal court decisions, administrative agency rulings, and reports to Congress issued by the General Accounting Office (GAO) and the Health and Human Services Office of the Inspector General.

Medicare and Medicaid Guide [Internet]. Riverwoods, IL: CCH Inc. Internet Updated daily. Available for Windows. Search Engine: Proprietary. Includes toll-free product support.
Cost: $2,962 per year (2014).
Contains the full text of the print service with full text searching and hypertext linking. This version also includes the optional HCFA Manuals. An optional archive CD-ROM disc contains opinions, decisions, administrative rulings and other documents issued since the beginning of Medicare in 1966.

The Merck Manual of Diagnosis and Therapy of Diseases. 19th ed. Rahway, NJ: Merck & Co., 2011. 1 vol. (3,754 pp.). No supplementation between editions.
Merck Manuals are available free online at: www.merckmanuals.com.
Cost: $79.95 (2014)
Written by more than 300 experts in all fields of medicine, this classic one-volume reference provides information regarding a wide variety of medical disorders, ranging from the common to the obscure. The disease-oriented compendium includes descriptions, symptoms, diagnosis, clinical procedures, laboratory tests, laboratory and technological procedures, therapy and clinical pharmacology, complex equipment, and prophylaxis. The seventeenth edition includes a variety of new topics, including smoking cessation, Gulf War syndrome, chronic fatigue syndrome, multiple chemical sensitivity syndrome, rehabilitation, and drug therapy in the elderly. Merck also

provides the content of these Merck Manuals on the web for free at: www.merckmanuals.com.

Pegalis, Steven E. and H. F. Wachsman. **American Law of Medical Malpractice.** 3d ed. St. Paul, MN: Thomson Reuters West (Clark Boardman Callaghan), 2005-date. 3 vols. Annual pocket parts.
Cost: $610; supplementation: 2006: $150; 2007: $166; 2008: $186; 2009: $211; 2010: $231; 2011: $253.50; 2012: $279; 2013: $300; 2d ed.: 1993: $175; 1994: $191; 1995: $100; 1996: $140; 1997: $155; 1998: $163.00; 1999: $176; 2000: $191.00; 2001: $225; 2002: $264; 2003: $345; 2004: $345; 2005: new edition ($450); **Monthly Assured Print Price (APP):** $36/$432.
Both authors of this three-volume treatise are associates of the American College of Legal Medicine, one a trial attorney and the other a neurosurgeon and trial attorney. This guide to medical malpractice law was designed for use by both plaintiffs and defense counsel as a aid to understanding the issues and concepts of a malpractice action, including the determination of whether liability exists in a dispute between a patient and health care provider. It aims to provide the practitioner with an understanding of both substantive and procedural legal issues as well as basic medical information. The chapters encompass physicians and physician liability, hospitals and hospital liability, obstetrics and obstetrical malpractice, the trial of an obstetrical malpractice case, defense of medical malpractice actions, neurology and neurological malpractice, anesthesiology, pharmacology, autopsy, expert witnesses, trial of a complex malpractice case, surgery, cancer, internal medicine, pediatrics, ophthalmology, psychiatry, and malpractice panels and statutes. Includes selective case citations and a subject index.

Personal Injury Library with Interrogatories [CD-ROM]. Newark, NJ: LexisNexis Matthew Bender. One disc. Updated periodically.
Cost: Package with Interrogatories: CD-ROM: $9.365; renewal: 2014: $6,362.
A comprehensive package of Matthew Bender personal injury treatises, including the **Attorneys' Dictionary of Medicine**, **Attorneys' Textbook of Medicine**, **Damages in Tort Actions**, **Defense of Drunk Driving Cases: Criminal – Civil**, **Medical Malpractice**, **Personal Injury: Actions, Defenses, Damages**, **Premises Liability Law and Practice**, and **Proving Medical Diagnosis and Prognosis**. Purchased individually, these treatises would cost many times the price of this package.
Personal Injury Law Library [CD-ROM and Internet]. Newark, NJ: LexisNexis Matthew Bender. One disc. Updated periodically.
Cost: CD-ROM: $8,813; renewal: 2014: $5,825; Package with Interrogatories: CD-ROM: $9.365; renewal: 2014: $6,362
A comprehensive package of Matthew Bender personal injury treatises, including the **Attorneys' Dictionary of Medicine**, **Attorneys' Textbook of Medicine**, **Damages in Tort Actions**, **Defense of Drunk Driving Cases: Criminal – Civil**, **Medical Malpractice**, **Personal Injury: Actions, Defenses, Damages**, **Premises Liability Law and Practice**, and **Proving Medical Diagnosis and Prognosis**. Purchased individually, these treatises would cost many times the price of this package.

Pharmaceutical Law: Regulation of Research, Development, and Marketing. Edited by Michael E. Clark, Washington, DC, Bloomberg BNA Books, 2007. 1 vol. (900 pp.).
Cost: $535; supplementation: 2008: $215; 2009: $220; 2010: $225; 2011: $230; 2012: $235; 2013: $250.
While the pharmaceutical industry has had an enormously positive impact on the health and well being of millions of people, it has also come under increased scrutiny on a variety of fronts, not the least of which are lawsuits resulting from negative reactions to drugs. Indeed, there is an entire cottage industry among the trial bar which specializes in bringing lawsuits for negative drug reactions, VIOXX being just one notable example. Also, the pharmaceutical industry operates in a complex environment of regulatory scrutiny which presents wide-ranging opportunities to attorneys representing drug and medical device companies. This volume covers a comprehensive range of pharmaceutical law issues, including the entire drug regulatory process, the fraud-and-abuse risks in marketing and promoting drugs, off-label marketing, HIPAA's privacy regulations, the protection of clinical research subjects, the potential for antitrust, securities law, and other compliance violations, the new Medicare Part D drug benefit, and drug reimbursement methodologies.

Physician's Desk Reference. 66th ed. Montvale, N.J.: PDR Network/Thomson, 2011. 1 vol. (3,250 pp.). Available free at: http://www.pdr.net/resources/pdr-ebook/
Cost: 2014 Edition: $97.95; 2013 ed. from $4.51 on amazon.com (2014).
Published in cooperation with participating drug manufacturers, the Physician's Desk Reference (PDR) contains product information on more than 2,500 specific pharmaceutical products. Entries include product description, clinical pharmacology, indications and usage, contraindications, warning precautions, adverse reactions, dosage an administration, how supplied, clinical studies, references, etc. The volume contains a brand and generic name index, product category index, product identification guide, and product information. A diagnostic product information section contains a directory of poison control centers, discontinued products, U.S. Food and Drug Administration telephone directory, a key to controlled substance categories, a key to FDA Use-in-Pregnancy ratings, drug information centers, and adverse event report forms. This volume is relied upon by practically every American physician for FDA-approved prescribing information. Each product description is prepared by the manufacturer and edited and approved by the manufacturer's medical department, medical director, and/or medical consultant. An essential resource for the attorney involved in medical or products liability litigation. The **Physician's Desk Reference** is now owned by Thomson Reuters.

Russ, Lee, Bruce Freeman and J, Stanley McQuade. **Attorney's Medical Advisor/Atlas**. St. Paul, MN: Thomson Reuters West (Clark Boardman Callaghan), 1994-date. 14 vols. Looseleaf format. Periodic updates.
Cost: $4,627; supplementation: 1995: $450; 1996: $644.38; 1997: $537.50; 1998: $567; 1999: $662; 2000: $728; 2001: $1,251.50; 2002: $880; 2003: $1,052; 2004: $561.50; 2005: $1,122; 2006: $1,647.75; 2007: $1,826; 2008: $2,035; 2009:

$1,641; 2010: $1,564; 2011: $1,343; 2012: $1,870; 2013: $2,038;
Monthly Assured Print Price (APP): $271/$3,252
A comprehensive practitioners guide to medical conditions, injuries, diseases, impairments, diagnoses, tests, biopsies, and treatments. The service provides complete information on normal anatomy and physiology of the human body with full color atlas illustrations. Includes information about factors which may complicate a medical condition and affect long-term prognosis, as well as advice for weighing the potential value of a lawsuit.

Cost Saving Tips: Leave it to Thomson Reuters to turn a medical reference work that could perform quite adquately with periodically revised editions into a supplemented work costing several thousand dollarsd annually. Given both the high initial and supplementation costs of this set, an acquisition on the used lawbook market is definitely recommended, after which the purchaser is advied to forego supplementation. The purchaser can simply rely on the more current and specific information supplied by the expert medical witness or local medical library.

Sims, Dorothy Clay. **Exposing Deceptive Defense Doctors**. Costa Mesa, CA: James Publishing, 2009. 1 vol. (various pagings).
Cost: $99; supplementation: 2010-2014: $69.99.
Many inexperienced plaintiff's attorneys are likely to encounter defense medical experts (DMEs) who have been hired to ridicule and challenge the merits of the plaintiff's case. The frequency with which plaintiffs' attorneys encounter such behavior from DMEs is a direct consequence of a system which rewards defense experts who are willing to do the bidding of insurance carriers, even to the point of lying to protect the interests of insurers. The skilled and emphatic doctor who is willing to reach a conclusion contrary to the interests of the insurance company is simply excluded from consideration as a defense expert and the handsome fees which accompany such work. In the author's estimation, there is a pattern to this behavior which often emanates from three distinct personality disorders: obsessive compulsive disorder, sociopathic disorder, or narcissistic disorder. The savvy lawyer, however, can predict and modify the behavior of these doctors based on an understanding of these traits. This handbook provides invaluable expert guidance through the forbidding thicket posed by these hostile DMEs and their potentially damaging testimony. It provides a step-by-step roadmap through the process of deposing DMEs in both the mental health and medical fields. The specific chapters address a number of the most significant psychiatric and neurological conditions, including traumatic brain injury, depression, post-traumatic stress syndrome, and somatoform disorder, among others, and provide the tools for attacking the potentially damaging claims and assertions made by defense experts. The author also provides similar guidance when addressing the testimony of medical experts in the fields of neurology, orthopedics, PMR, radiology, and neuroradiology, vocational rehabilitation, and other fields. This reference is replete with insightful forms, checklists, practice pointers, and sample questions. Despite its practical focus, the book includes numerous citations to the medical literature, as well as tables of statutes and cases, and a detailed index. It also concludes with an invaluable chapter on technology, outsourcing and cross-examination in the practice of law. The law office practice pointers in this chapter alone will save the average attorney many times the modest cost of this volume. The entire text and many sample forms are replicated on a companion CD-ROM. The author maintained a workers' compensation and Social Security disability law practice in Florida, where she was the first woman to Chair the Workers' Compensation Section of the Florida Bar. She has lectured and consulted widely on matters related to psychological testing, and the cross-examination of medical and vocational experts. This is just one of many excellent, but modestly-priced, practice tools from James Publishing.

Sloan, Frank A. and Lindsey M. Chepke. Medical Malpractice. Cambridge, MA: MIT Press, 2008. Parerback: 2010. 1 vol. (458 pp.).
Cost: $42.00; $21 (paper); from $8.95 on amazon.com; kindle: $14.54 (2014).
This empirical and scholarly examination of medical malpractice in the United States draws upon a number of overlapping areas of research to provide an objective assessment of how this complex system really operates. That complexity is a result of the interaction of four discrete markets that determine the outcomes of individual cases: legal, medical malpractice insurance, medical care, and government activity. The authors contend that there is little fundamental disagreement among active researchers about the nature and extent of the problem and its proposed solutions. They agree that the current system is ill-suited to deterring injuries and compensating injury victims in an efficient manner, and that policy responses to previous crises (e.g. responding to high insurance premiums) have not changed the fundamental incentives of the participants in the care, claiming, claims resolutions, and insurance processes. The authors contend that the views of the various parties in the medical malpractice debate each bring a different perspective based on personal experience rather than methods of information gathering and analysis generally accepted in the scientific community. This is an admirable attempt to bring intellectual and empirical rigor to a field too often influenced by anecdote. These anecdotes advance a number of myths of medical malpractice, including (1 that there are too many medical malpractice claims; (2) only good doctors are sued; (3) dispute resolution of such cases is a lottery; (4) claimants are overcompensated for their losses; and (5) medical care is costly because of medical malpractice. The authors address both the positive and negative aspects of the current system and offer some modest achievable reforms. This is an invaluable examination of a complex field, which is of particular value to trial lawyers and other participants in the resolution of medical malpractice claims. Frank Sloan is a Professor of Health Policy and Management, and Professor of Economics, at Duke University. Lindsey Chepke is an attorney and Research Associate at the Center for Health Policy at Duke University.

Stedman's Medical Dictionary. 28th ed. Baltimore, MD: Lippincott Williams & Wilkins, 2005. 1 vol. (2,098 pp.).
Cost: $50.99 (print); $54.99 (online); from $5.91 (paper) on amazon.com (2014).
First published in 1833, this classic medical dictionary now contains more than 100,000 entries of general and specialized medical terms. Compiled by 38 editors representing the full range of medical specialties.

Additional titles on Medical Jurisprudence are available from the following publishers: ABBE Publications Assoc., American Assoc. of Medical Assistants, American College of Legal Medicine Foundation, American Health Lawyers Assoc., Ashgate Publishing Co., AMS Press, Matthew Bender, CRC Press, Delmar Publishers, Gordon Press, Gordon & Breach Publishing Group, Greenwood Publishing Group, Lega Books, LexisNexis, Medical Group Management Assoc., National Center for State Courts, National Clearinghouse for Legal Services, Mosby, Inc., C.C. Thomas Publishing Co., Thomson Reuters West, Wolters Kluwer Law & Business. See Appendix B for addresses and telephone numbers.

Military Law and National Security

Abbott, Ernest B. and Otto J. Hetzel. **A Legal Guide to Homeland Security and Emergency Management for State and Local Government**. 2d ed. Chicago: American Bar Association, 2010. 1 vol. (300 pp.).
Cost: $94.95; $75.95 to Section members (2014).
This guide to the basic structure of homeland security law and the emergency management system is designed to provide legal counsel and government administrators with the tools to meet their respective responsibilities under the law. Among the areas addressed are the application procedure for federal funds, negotiation of intergovernmental agreements, application for disaster assistance, and the management of catastrophic events. An essential reference for legal counsel or government officials involved in homeland security or emergency preparedness issues. Ernest Abbott is one of the nation's leading authorities on the legal aspects of federal disaster relief, flood, and emergency management programs and a former General Counsel for the Federal Emergency Management Agency (FEMA). Otto J. Hetzel practices law in Washington, D.C. and is a Professor of Law Emeritus at Wayne State University Law School in Michigan. He now advises local governments and private sector contractors in dealing with federal agencies and complying with federal legislation, agency regulations, Office of Management and Budget Circulars, and Federal Acquisition Requirements (FAR). He speaks frequently on homeland security issues and has published extensively in the field.

Addicott, Jeffrey F. **Terrorism Law: Materials, Cases, Comments**. 6th ed. Tucson, AZ: Lawyers & Judges Publishing Co., 2010. 1 vol. (576 pp.).
Cost: $99.00; from $39.99 on amazon.com (2014).
This law school caseBook is characterized by remarkably well-written and balanced commentary, illustrated by representative court decisions, on the many sides of terrorism and its legal and policy implications. The author draws a distinction between developing law-based responses to terrorism while at the same time promoting democracy as a long-term solution to the environment which produces terrorists. Chapters include: (1) what is terrorism; (2) the war on terror; (3) expanding the war on terror; (4)civil liberties and the war on terror; (5) necessity and rationale for the law of war—lessons from My Lai; (6) interrogation techniques; (7) contractors on the battlefield; (8) cyberterrorism; (9) a new paradigm for was and terrorism avoidance; (10) leading the way—Pax Americana or the rule of law; (11) civil litigation; and (12) responses to bioterrorism and the legal ramifications. Each chapter includes questions for discussion, and a selected bibliography. Appendices include a number of critical documents, such as U.N. Security Council Resolutions, international covenants, treaties, the U.S. War Powers Resolution, a Department of Defense Directive on detainee treatment policy, and the Kellogg-Briand Pact. The author is professor of law and Director of the Center for Terrorism Law, St. Mary's U. School of Law.

Alperen, Martin J. **Foundations of Homeland Security: Law and Policy**. Hoboken, NJ: John Wiley & Sons, 2011. 1 vol. (365 pp.). Hardbound.
Cost: $93.95; from $16.10 on amazon.com (2014).
Homeland security is an umbrella term that encompasses security efforts to protect the United States against terrorist activity, reduce America's vulnerability to terrorism, and minimize the damage and recover from attacks that do occur. The term arose following a reorganization of many U.S. government agencies in 2003 to form the United States Department of Homeland Security, a response to the September 11 attacks, The Homeland Security Act, which was created from an assortment of new and existing laws, sets policy for confronting terrorism within the United States with legislation designed to prevent attacks as well as manage crisis in the aftermath of a successful attempt. Its authority also establishes legal domain over a multitude of additional public safety matters, including natural disasters. Topically-arranged, the chapters in this volume assemble the most significant documents in the field. Following an invaluable overview of homeland security, each subsequent chapter includes a useful introduction, list of sources, the documents themselves, endnotes, and a bibliography of additional resources. The chapter coverage reflects the full range of homeland security concerns, including the strategic environment, the Homeland Security Council, intelligence gathering, the Department of Homeland Security, the Federal Emergency Management Agency (FEMA), the National Security Strategy of the U.S., border security, critical infrastructure protection, cyber security, agriculture and food, transportation security, weapons of mass destruction, and more. The volume offers important legal guidance to students, law enforcement officers, lawyers, and other related professionals who need to accurately interpret and apply homeland security law. The author, a practicing attorney and trial lawyer since 1985, received a master of arts in security studies (Homeland Security and Defense) from the Naval Postgraduate School's Center for Homeland Defense and Security and has professional first responder experience as a police officer, an EMT, and a search and rescue member.

Baker, James E. **In the Common Defense: National Security Law for Perilous Times**. Port Chester, NY, Cambridge University Press, 2014. 1 vol. (420 pp.). Paperbound.
Cost: $34.99; from $31.49 on amazon.com (2014).
The major challenge in a post 9/11 world is how to protect the American people from the genuine threat of terrorism while simultaneously protecting them from the overreach of government power and honoring the tenets of the U.S. Constitution. It is this balancing act that has confronted the United States in all previous major conflicts, from the Civil War through the

Vietnam War—how to reconcile civil liberties concerns in the face of threats to the republic and its citizens. In this timely and important book, the author argues that preserving security does not require a curtailing individual liberties, and that the rule of law is not just about liberty, but also about our moral authority, which an essential element of our national security. Chapters include (1) Perilous times - describing the threat; (2) The meaning of national security; (3) The role of national security law; (4) Constitutional law; (5) Electronic surveillance: law applied; (6) National security process; (7) Intelligence; (8) The use of military force; (9) Homeland security; (10) The national security lawyer. Glossary; Attachments. A cum laude graduate of Yale Law School, Judge James Baker was appointed to the United States Court of Appeals for the Armed Forces in 2000. He is a former Special Assistant to the President and Legal Adviser to the National Security Council. As an attorney adviser in the Office of the Legal Advisor, Department of State, he provided advice on law enforcement, intelligence, and counter-terrorism, and served as a legislative aide and acting Chief of Staff to Senator Daniel Moynihan. Judge Baker is the co-author of Regulating Covert Action (Yale Univ. Press, 1992), as well as numerous articles on national security and criminal law. He teaches national security law at the University of Iowa College of Law and Georgetown University Law Center.

Butler, Joseph and Brian Clauss, eds. **Military Service and the Law**. Chicago: American Bar Association, in association with the Illinois Institute for Continuing Legal Education, 2010. 1 vol. (209 pp.). Paperbound. Includes a companion 3-DVD set (390 min.).
Cost: $399.95 ($379.95 to ABA members) (2014).
Designed to prepare lawyers to assist veterans with the variety of legal issues common to their situation, this CLE program combines a print manual with a 390 minutes of lectures on DVD, providing 6.5 hours of CLE credit in the government practice area, and content that meets the attorney accreditation requirements for lawyers who wish to represent veterans before the U.S. Department of Veterans Affairs (VA). The aim of the course of instruction is to provide attorneys with an understanding of the intricacies of the veteran compensation and appeals system as well as the culture and values unique to the military. The program is designed to provide expert guidance to attorneys and others who wish to assist veterans with such issues as divorce and custody matters, veterans' benefits, employment and reemployment rights. In addition it provides an overview of each branch of the armed forces and its unique legal system, a resource guide and more. Although produced as a CLE program for the legal profession, is also a excellent resource for veterans' service and charitable organizations that are charged with meeting the increasing demand for assistance from veterans and active duty service members attempting to navigate the often complex and confusing system of benefits and rights. The author/presenters include lawyers who are active duty members of the military and those with extensive experience working in the military justice system or dealing with veterans' issues.

Casavant, David. **Emergency Preparedness for Facilities: A Guide to Safety Planning for the Business Continuity**. Rockville, MD: Government Institutes, 2003. 1 vol. (360 pp.). Softcover.
Cost: $138.00; from $76.54 on amazon.com (2014).
Any business or law firm concerned with ensuring its survival in the face of natural or non-natural disasters should have an organizational emergency management plan in place. This comprehensive guide provides step-by-step instructions for devising prevention and response plans to deal with potential or real disasters which threaten the existence or continuity of a business enterprise. Among the disasters addressed in this volume are power outages, chemical spills, bomb threats, riots or demonstrations, workplace violence, fire, drought, blizzard, and flood. Discussion of each emergency event is accompanied by two case studies which illustrate the importance of preparedness planning and by instructions for confronting such emergencies if they do occur. The author is president of a consulting firm specializing in emergency planning and recovery for public and private industry.

Court Martial Reports [CD-ROM]. Eagen, MN: Thomson Reuters West.
One disc. Updated quarterly. Available for Windows, and Macintosh. Search Engine: PREMISE.
Cost: $990.00 (single user) (2014).
This archival product contains decisions prior to those recorded in the **Military Justice Reporter** (pre-1975), *including* the full text of decisions from the United States Court of Military Appeals (CMA), United States Air Force Court of Military Review (AFCMR), United States Army Court of Military Review (ACMR), United States Coast Guard Court of Military Review (CGCMR),and the U.S. Navy Court of Military Review.

Dycus, Stephen, William C. Banks and Peter Raven-Hansen. **Counterterrorism Law**. 2nd ed. New York: Wolters Kluwer Law & Business, 2012. 1 vol. (872 pp.).
Cost: $189; from $91.93 on amazon.com (2014).
The law of counterterrorism began to shape long before the events of 9/11 and the attacks on the World Trade Center. In 1937, the League of Nations adopted a convention for the prevention and punishment of terrorism. After World War II, as the world experienced a variety of domestic terrorist attacks, the United Nations, beginning in 1963, approved a number of conventions to address international terrorist threats. In the United States, terrorist acts and fears of future attacks led to a number of extraordinary countermeasures, including military detention of terrorist suspects who formerly would have subject to criminal statutes, sharply increased foreign intelligence surveillance, coercive interrogation of terrorist suspects, a the revival of military commissions, and an expanded use of classified evidence in criminal cases. These efforts have been accompanied by presidential orders, legislation, and a variety of court challenges. This law school caseBook is an introduction to the body of law governing counterterrorism activities and the Supreme Court decisions that have addressed them. It provides a pedagogical framework for understanding the tension which exists between the necessity of protecting national security while simultaneously protecting civil rights and liberties guaranteed by the U.S. Constitution. Following an introduction to the nature of terrorism and counterterrorism, the book's 26 chapters examine the following broad topical areas: authorities and limits in the war on terrorists, detecting terrorist threats, detaining terrorist

suspects, interrogating terrorist suspects, prosecuting threats to national security, and homeland security, and noncriminal sanctions against terrorists and their supporters. Among the related issues addressed are data-mining, screening, continuity of government, civil liability, profiling of suspected terrorists, targeted killing, sanctions and the interactions of the branches of government in making and enforcing terrorism law and policy. The book also addresses the significant question of whether terrorism should be treated as a crime or, as a species of war, some combination of the two, or as a unique phenomenon deserving of separate legal controls. Stephen Dycus is a professor of law at Vermont Law School and an authority on national security and the law, water rights, and wills and trusts. Materials supplementary to this textbook are available at: www.aspenlawschool.com/dycus_counterterrorism

Dycus, Stephen, Arthur L. Berney, William C. Banks, and Peter Raven-Hansen. **National Security Law**. 5th ed. Frederick, MD: Wolters Kluwer Law & Business, 2011. 1 vol. (1,142 pp.).
Cost: $213.00; from $59.15 on amazon.com (2014).
Balancing the twin concerns of security and liberty, particularly in the post-9/11 era, has often resulted in serious conflicts between the Executive and Congress over their respective prerogatives under the U.S. Constitution. But these concerns and their attendant conflicts have characterized the American body politic since its inception. This law school caseBook assembles many of the significant legal and political documents (court decisions, statutes, congressional documents, etc.) that characterize domestic legal issues that arise in providing for the national defense. These documents (with commentary) have defined the parameters of this historic tension, from its origins in the pre-constitutional history and political theory in Europe to the present conflicts over the conduct of the Iraq War and War on Terror. The 37 shorter, but more thematically integrated, chapters of this edition are grouped into five parts: (I) Framework; (II) Using Force Abroad; (III) Conducting Intelligence Operations Abroad; (IV) Fighting Terrorism; and (V) Obtaining and Protecting National Security Information. Individual chapters address topics as far ranging as covert actions, screening for security, Congressional authority for national security surveillance, military detention, secret evidence, managing a WMD attack, interrogating terrorist suspects, the domestic role of the armed forces, and restraints on publication of national security information. In typical caseBook fashion, each chapter includes numerous illustrative documents accompanied by editorial commentary, and Notes and Questions.

Cost-Saving Tip: Excessively priced for a lawschool textbook. Acquire a used copy on amazon.com, or elsewhere.

Enemy Combatants, Terrorism, and Armed Conflict: a Guide to the Issues. Edited by David K. Linnan, Westport, CT: Praeger Security International General Interest, 2008. 1 vol. (408 pp.).
Cost: $85; from $22.50 on amazon.com (2014).
Striking the balance between national security on the one hand and civil liberties concerns and the rule of law on the other is the topic of this guide to the issue of enemy combatants and terrorism. The author evaluates the overlap between religion, ethics, armed conflict, and law within the context of the post 9/11 war on terror, as well as such topics as intelligence gathering, the realities of dealing with terrorist threat, the permissible bounds of interrogation, treatment of prisoners and the laws governing armed conflict under domestic and international law. In the authors' view, the current war has challenged long-standing legal interpretations because traditional wars between nation states are no longer the rule. These wars have been replaced by asymmetric warfare against terrorists operating outside the boundaries of nation states, warfare characterized by intense intelligence gathering and preventative action. Editor David K. Linnan is Associate Professor of Law, University of South Carolina with a special interest in the law of armed conflict.

Farber, Daniel and Michael G. Faure, eds. **Disaster Law**. Williston, VT: Edward Elgar Publishing, 2010. 1 vol.
Cost: $340.00 (online purchase: $306.00) (2014).
Natural and man-made disasters have plagued mankind since humans first walked on the earth. In the 21st century alone, Hurricane Katrina, the European heat wave, and the Southeast Asian tsunami, and the Japanese earthquakes have caused untold death and destruction. Although relatively new as a field of study, the international legal community is beginning to formulate legal and policy responses that address the prevention, response and management of disasters under the rubric of disaster law. The goal is address the shortcomings of legal systems facing such disasters. This collection of previously published articles places its particular emphasis on economic analysis in the areas of disaster prevention and mitigation, disaster response, insurance, and government-provided compensation. Among the issues discussed in the 27 articles are policy for natural hazards, disaster mitigation through land use strategies, the precautionary principle, emergency actions plans, disaster relief and its prevention, the problem of catastrophic loss, mitigating disaster losses through insurance, the role of government in compensating disaster victims, and catastrophic responses to catastrophic risks, among others. The editors include Daniel A. Farber, Professor of Law and Chair of the Energy and Resources Group, University of California, Berkeley; and Michael G. Faure, Professor of Comparative and International Environmental Law, Maastricht University, The Netherlands.

Federal Veterans Laws, Rules and Regulations. 2013 Edition. Charlottesville, VA: LexisNexis, 2012. 1 vol. Softbound. Annual editions.
Cost: 2013 Edition: $65.00; combination price with **Veterans Benefits Manual:** $186 (2014).
This is a compendium of all the federal laws and regulations related to veterans extracted from Title 38 of the **United States Code Service** and **Code of Federal Regulations.** It also contains relevant court rules, including Rules of Practice and Procedure of the U.S. Court of Appeals for Veterans Claims.
Fidell, Eugene R. and Dwight H. Sullivan. **Evolving Military Justice**. Annapolis, MD: Naval Institute Press, 2002. 1 vol. (362 pp.).
Cost: $49.95 (non-members); $23.54 (members); from $8.75 on amazon.com (2014).
A critical evaluation of the American system of military justice and its administration. The articles in this anthology address such topics as the fundamental principles of the Supreme Court's jurisprudence in military cases, judicial independence, judicial review of the **Manual for Courts-Martial**, the culture of change

in military law, military commissions and terrorists, a worldwide perspective on change in military justice, fair and public trial, among others. The authors are attorneys in private practice and veteran military lawyers.

Fidler, David P. and Sarah Jane Hughes. **Responding to National Security Letters: A Practical Guide for Legal Counsel**. Chicago: American Bar Association, Section of Business Law, 2009. 1 vol. (149 pp.).
Cost: $79.95; $59.95 to members; from $33.38 on amazon.com (2014).
Authorized by several federal statutes, national security letters require private parties, including banks, telecommunications companies, and others who possess third-party information, to provide the government with access to that information within their control, but without disclosing the demand to the owners of the information, or the general public. Recent statutory amendments perrnit recipients of such letters to disclose receipt to legal counsel and to challenge them in court.
Intended for company officials and legal professionals, this volume is an introductory primer to national security letters and the legal and practical characteristics of instruments that have become a far more prevalent form of administrative subpoena. National security letters stand in contrast to the trend since the 1970s toward greater privacy protections because they abrogate the terms of underlying contractual relationships between service providers and their customers by turning the trusted service provider into a private auxiliary of the government's national security authorities. The chapters in this volume explain the need for a practical guide for legal counsel on responding to national security letters, as well as understanding, receiving, reviewing and responding to national security letters. Two concluding chapters address national security letters and international issues, and monitoring the law on national security letters. The text is accompanied by citations to federal statutes, case law, and federal administrative documents. The authors are professors of law at Indiana University Maurer School of Law.

Forensic Aspects of Chemical and Biological Terrorism. Edited by Cyril H. Wecht. Tucson, AZ: Lawyers & Judges Publishing Co., 2004. 1 vol. (503 pp.).
Cost: $79; from $20.02 on amazon.com (2014).
Heightened concerns about global terrorism, including its chemical and biological manifestations, are the basis for this detailed scientific examination by a team of doctors and scientific experts. Led by Dr. Cyril Wecht (M.D., J.D.), one of the nation's leading forensic pathologists, the authors provide in-depth analysis on the scientific and technical aspects of chemical and biological weapons and the medical and public health consequences of their use. The authors discuss the effects of such chemical/biological (CBW) agents as sarin, salmonella, anthrax ricin, and smallpox. Other chapters discuss the effect of terrorist bombings, injury diagnosis and treatment, chemical warfare and terrorism agents, analytical methods, the role of medical systems, the public health aspects and preventive measures, the role of the medical examiner and coroner in the investigation of terrorism, scene investigation, psychopathy, media and psychology at the root of terrorism, threats to aviation and transportation security, bioterrorism and the law, and the truth about bioterrorism. The twenty highly qualified authors include those with medical, legal, and forensic training. A useful companion to the publisher's **Forensic Investigation and Management of Mass Disasters.**

Forensic Investigation and Management of Mass Disasters. Compiled and edited by Matthias L. Okoye and Cyril H. Wecht. Tucson, AZ: Lawyers & Judges Publishing Co., 2007. 1 vol. (458 pp.).
Cost: $99; from $60.00 on amazon.com; kindle ed.: $71.83 (2014).
Mass disasters, whether of natural or human origin, have caused tremendous loss of life and property damage. Hurricanes, tornadoes, earthquakes, floods, transportation accidents, building collapses, and environmental catastrophes have collectively produced a multidisciplinary response to the management of mass disasters and the development of mass disaster plans. Mass disasters have also fueled new developments in the fields of medicine and forensic sciences. This collection of scholarly articles addresses a host of medical and forensic topics related to various types of mass disasters. Responding to the threat of Islamic terrorism, contributor Dr. Henry Lee, and others, discuss the role of law enforcement and forensic scientists in scene investigation following bioterrorism and mass disasters. A total of 21 contributing authors examine such subjects as mass casualty identification, identification of human remains, the role of the coroner/medical examiner, mass disaster litigation in the United States, human identification of mass graves, public health aspects and preventive measures, and more. Dr. Matthias L. Okoye is a practicing physician and lawyer and Director of the Nebraska Institute of Forensic Sciences. Dr. Cyril H. Wecht is a former coroner of Allegheny County and one of the leading experts in forensic pathology.

Gill, Terry D. and Dieter Fleck, eds. **The Handbook of the International Law of Military Operations**. New York: Oxford University Press, 2010. 1 vol. (xxviii, 657 pp.). Paperbound.
Cost: $80; from $32.17 on amazon.com (2014).
This is a comprehensive guide to the many areas of international law which are relevant to the planning and execution of contemporary military operations. These include such traditional areas of international law as the law governing the use of force (*jus ad bellum*), international humanitarian law (the law of armed conflict), the law of the sea, military use of airspace, and the various types of national law of any given country involved in military operations, such as military criminal justice and disciplinary regulations. It has also come to embrace hybrid areas of the law and regulations such as the rules of engagement drawn up for a particular operation, and status-of-forces arrangements for troops deployed on another State's territory, whether in the form of formal treaties or informal ad hoc arrangements combining areas of international and national law and regulations. From these various aspects of international law, the authors attempt to identify those most relevant to military operations. The book's 32 chapters address general issues regarding international law and its application to military operations, military operations within the context of the UN collective security system, military operations within the context of the right of self defense and other possible legal bases for the use of force, capita selecta of international military operational law, and a synthesis and conclusion. The chapters follow in an order which corresponds to

the order of the black letter rules comprising the Manual found at the back of the volume, which constitutes a form of 'restatement' of the fundamental legal rules and as a best practices guide. Commentaries to the black letter rules may be found in the text of the chapters. In addition to those written by the book's editors, the individual chapters were written by 20 contributing authors with expertise in various aspects of military and international law. The "Annex" consists of The Manual on International Law of Military Operations, a glossary of terms, and index. Terry D. Gill is Professor of Law at the University of Amsterdam and the Netherlands Defense Academy and Associate Professor Public International Law at Utrecht University. Dieter Fleck is former director for International Agreements and Policy for the German Ministry of Defense. This impressive collaborative effort is an essential resource for any lawyer, government or military official concerned with the legal ramifications of international conflict.

Gilligan, Francis A. and Fredric I. Lederer. **Court-Martial Procedure**. 3d ed. Charlottesville, VA: LexisNexis, 2007-date. 3 vols. Annual cumulative supplements.
Cost: $329; supplementation: 2008: $112; 2009: $128; 2010: $134; 2011: $140; 2012: $150; 2013: $155; 2d ed.: 2000: $70; 2001: $93; 2002: $96; 2003: $100; 2004: $105; 2005: $110; 2006: $115; 1st edition: 1993: $60; 1994: $60; 1995: $60; 1996: 0; 1997: 0; 1998: $70.
A thorough examination of the criminal procedural aspects of the military court-martial, from the initial charge to conviction. The set also contains the complete text of the **Uniform Code of Military Justice, Rules for Court-Martial** and the **Manual for Courts-Martial**. The text includes extensive citations to applicable case and statutory law.

Glennon, Michael J. and Serge Sur, eds. **Terrorism and International Law**. Leiden/Boston: Martinus Nijhoff Publishers, 2008. 1 vol. (813 pp.).
Cost: $420; from $318.26 on amazon.com (2014).
Terrorism, while a term of considerable polemical impact, has limited juridical utility because no consensus exists as to its meaning. In the view of Michael Glennon, there are significant disagreements over whether specific types of conduct constitute terrorism. The aim of this report is to evaluate the impact which this definitional vacuum has had on the international legal order. Toward that end, the Hague Academy of International Law's Research Center assembled a team of 24 scholars (12 Anglophone, 12 Francophone) to assemble for four weeks of discussion, research, and writing. This collection of essays addressing the topic of "Terrorism and International Law" is the final product of this program of activities. A major issue dominating this discussion is whether there can be a comprehensive definition of terrorism under international law or whether the term can only be applied pragmatically to the individual acts and circumstances which characterize the activities of terrorists. Yet, without a comprehensive definition of terrorism under international law, discussion on an international level will have no significance, thereby precluding that acts of terrorism can exist at an international level as a matter of law. Ultimately, the authors contend, regulation of the use of force on an international scale remains primarily a political rather than a legal matter. International norms based upon dogma, doctrine or morality are not irrelevant, but they are outweighed by a number of practical concerns, including the quality of a State's leadership, the power of its domestic constituencies, the structure of the international system, and cost-benefit analysis of various courses of conduct. Also, in the absence of an international treaty on terrorism, international law has yet to construct a definition of terrorism that exists in a legally enforceable way. Among the major impediments to a comprehensive treaty on terrorism, for example, is the question of State terrorism and the relationship between freedom fighters and terrorists. While acts of terrorism are usually carried out by non-State actors, responses to State-sponsored acts of terrorism are often circumscribed by such pragmatic concerns as the State's ability to control terrorist acts or actors, and economic concerns which outweigh the political, as in the case of oil-rich Saudi Arabia, the country from which 15 of the19 September 11th terrorists originated. Commencing with the introductory Reports of the Directors of Studies, 13 essays address the following broad subject areas: Definition of Terrorism, International Responsibility and Liability, Terrorism and Armed Force, Security Council against Terrorism, Interstate Co-operation against Terrorism, and National Policies and International Law. The individual essays address such specific topics as the debate between legal positivism and pragmatism, the rules of State responsibility, wars of national liberation, the interstate transfer of terrorist suspects without human rights limits, racial profiling, and proportionality, among others. The essays, half of which are in French, are characterized by their carefully nuanced argumentation and intellectual sophistication. They are accompanied by an 84-page selective bibliography, analytical index, and table of legal instruments. Serge Sur is Director of Studies of the French Language Section of the Hague Academy of International Law's Research Center and Professor at the Universite Pantheon Assas (Paris II). Michael J. Glennon is Director of Studies of the Center's English-speaking section, and Professor of International Law, Fletcher School of Law and Diplomacy, Tufts University.

Guide to Homeland Security. 2013 Edition. Eagan, MN: West, 2013. 2 vols. (808 pp.).
Cost: $352; **Monthly Assured Print Price (APP)**: $29/$348 (2014).
A useful compilation of all the significant federal statutes, regulations, and Presidential documents falling under the umbrella of homeland security, including the Homeland Security Act of 2002, USA Patriot Act, Aviation and Transportation Security Act, Enhanced Border Security and Visa Entry Reform Act, Public Health Security and Bioterrorism Preparedness and Response Act, Terrorism Bombing Convention Implementation Act, and Terrorism Risk Insurance Act, and the Executive Orders which established the new Department of Homeland Security. The section-by-section analysis of the Homeland Security Act includes references to the Act's legislative history, and other legislative and regulatory authorities and secondary sources. The volume also includes a bibliography of materials available on Westlaw.

Gurule, Jimmy. **Unfunding Terror: The Legal Response to the Financing of Global Terrorism**. Cheltenham, UK; Northampton, MA: Edward Elgar, 2008. 1 vol. (425 pp.).

Cost: hardbound: $218 (online price: $196.20); paper: $63 (online price: $50.40); from $78.84 on amazon.com (paper) (2014).

The number and severity of terrorist attacks are heavily dependent upon their sources of financing. Prior to 9/11/2001, neither the United States nor the international community had taken steps to freeze or interdict the funds necessary to finance the recruitment, training, weapons, bribes, travel and equipment used to carry out terrorist operations. Even after the 1993 World Trade Center bombing, as well as those at the U.S. embassies in Kenya and Tanzania, Justice Department officials were primarily concerned with prosecuting the perpetrators, and stopping money laundering, rather than targeting the terrorists' financial sponsors. Even the actions of the United Nations were half-hearted and ineffectual, and the efforts of member States largely noncompliant with its resolutions. This volume provides an intensive examination of the nature of terrorist financing and the steps necessary to suppress it on a global scale. After laying out the legal framework by which to deprive Al Qaeda of funding, the author explains why steps to deprive them of funding are necessary, the financing of global jihad, the development of a global framework to combat terrorist financing, and the effectiveness of those legal responses. The author, a professor of law at Notre Dame Law School, is a former Under Secretary for Enforcement in the U.S. Dept. of the Treasury (2001-2003) and Assistant Attorney General (1990-1992). He is also the author of **The Law of Asset Forfeiture** (Lexis) and other books on international criminal law.

Hackerott, Cynthia L., Kathleen Kapusta, and Ronald Miller. **When Duty Calls: Military Leave and Veterans' Rights**. Chicago: CCH, Inc., 2003. 1 vol. (232 pp.). Paperbound.

Cost: OUT-OF-PRINT; from $6.95 on amazon.com (2014).

The rights of active military personnel (including reservists) and veterans are governed by both federal and state laws, including the Uniformed Services Employment and Reemployment Rights Act (USERRA). While federal law does not preempt state laws providing greater or additional rights, it does overrule state laws that do not provide the same level of protection. Useful for both military personnel, and their employers, this volume covers such topics as military leave and reemployment obligations, military leave and reemployment eligibility, rights and benefits during military leave, reemployment rights, reemployment obligations of federal government employers, rights and benefits after military service, protection from discrimination and retaliation, and military leave and reemployment obligations under state law. The authors are all attorneys in the field of employment law. Cynthia Hackerott has written several books in the field of employment law, employee investigations, and whistleblowing.

Homeland Securities Law Handbook: A Guide to the Legal and Regulatory Framework. Rockville, MD: ABS Consulting/ Government Institutes, 2003. 1 vol. (360 pp.). Available on amazon.com.

Cost: $98; from $1.00 on amazon.com; kindle: $69.82 (2014).

A comprehensive overview of the field of homeland security which combines a discussion and analysis of significant legislative enactments and the current bureaucratic framework, with practical guidance on how to address security concerns in business, industry and government. The work is divided into three parts: Part I: The Scope of Homeland Security; Part II: Major Issues in Homeland Security; Part III: Organizational Structure of the Homeland Security Department. Among the laws addressed are the Aviation and Transportation Security Act of 2001, the Enhanced Border Security and Visa Entry Reform Act of 2002, the Homeland Security Act of 2002, the Maritime Transportation Security Act of 2002, the Public Health Security and Bioterrorism Preparedness and Response Act of 2002, Terrorism Risk Insurance Act of 2002, and the USA Patriot Act of 2002, among others. Among the issues addressed are aviation, transportation and port security; chemical security; air, food and water supply contamination; privacy, immigration, information and cyberspace security, appropriations, grants and contracts; insurance, liability and risk, and information and disclosure issues in security audits. The authors are attorneys with several leading law firms, including Bracewell & Patterson, Blank Rome, Reed Smith, and Powell Frazer & Murphy.

Homeland Security Deskbook: Private Sector Impacts of the Defense Against Terrorism. By the attorneys of Venable LLP; general editor & coauthor, James T. O'Reilly. New York, NJ: LexisNexis (Matthew Bender), 2004. 1 vol. Looseleaf format.

Cost: OUT-OF-PRINT; supplementation: 2009: $186; from $325.00 on amazon.com (2014).

A comprehensive one-volume guide to the post-9/11 world of homeland security and the legal issues posed to attorneys practicing in this new legal environment. Impressive in both its scope and substantive detail, this volume draws on the expertise of over 20 lawyers with the leading Washington, DC form of Venable LLP under the general editorship of James O'Reilly, each of whom brings to this project a wealth of special knowledge and experience. Chapter 1: the Homeland Security Challenges for the Practicing Attorney, provides an excellent overview of the legal environment created to address the new terrorist threats. Chapter 2 describes in detail the Organization of Homeland Security Functions, including the new Department of Homeland Security, the Directorate of Border and Transportation Security, as well as the other new and restructured government departments and agencies. Additional chapters include (3) Background and Brief History of Homeland Security, (4) Critical Infrastructure, (5) Business Liability, (6) Communication and Cyber Security, (7) Local Government Preparation & Prevention Roles, (8) Government Contracting and Homeland Security, (9) Immigration Issues, (10) Trade and Transportation, (11) Environmental Aspects of Homeland Security, (12) Cooperation with Law Enforcement Agencies, (13) Disclosure, Confidentiality, and Privacy Issues, (14) the Terrorism Risk Insurance Act, (5) Science, Technology, and Intellectual Property, and (16) Food and Drug Protective Measures, and (17) Conclusions. Appendices include a chart of the Department's organization, a table of rules by category, selected state laws on Homeland Security, a table of Homeland Security Act sections, and an index. The descriptive and analytical text provides essential information to lawyers, government officials, corporations, and others operating in this new environment of heightened security concerns. This is easily the best single-volume work of its kind on the market.

Maxwell, Bruce, ed. **Homeland Security: A Documentary History**. Washington, DC: CQ Press, 2004. 1 vol. (512 pp.).
Cost: $145; from $4.83 on amazon.com (2014).
Although the United States government has responded to a variety of security threats and concerns throughout its history, beginning with the passage of the Alien and Sedition Acts of 1798, the creation of the Homeland Security Department in 2002 involved the largest restructuring of the federal government in over forty years. This volume examines the manner in which the United States has responded to homeland security threats through government reports, budget proposals, speeches, public information campaigns and press releases, testimony, and other primary sources. While the primary focus is on the post 9/11 world of homeland security, this volume also includes selected documents related to historical security concerns. Among the general themes addressed in this volume are homeland security issues and responses, the process for creating a new executive department and restructuring institutions and bureaucracies, the steps and events leading up to the creation of the Department of Homeland Security, the impact on governmental institutions and employees (including Congress, its committees and structure, federal and state bureaucracies, and civil servants), budgetary implications at the federal and state levels, challenges and ramifications for citizens and civil liberties, and missions and goals, including aviation and border security, crisis planning, and citizen preparedness. The book also includes a chronology of significant events, a list of print and web resources, and index. Bruce Maxwell is an author, investigative journalist, and newsletter publisher. A useful reference tool for anyone involved in homeland security matters or research who requires access its legislative history and historical background.

McDermott, Patrice. **Who Needs To Know? The State of Public Access to Federal Government Information**. Lanham, MD: Bernan Essential Reference Publications, 2007. 1 vol. (304 pp.). Paperbound.
Cost: $19.95; from $9.98 on amazon.com (2014).
This important study examines the current state of the public's ability to locate, obtain and use federal government information in a post 9/11 world. A major portion of the author's inquiry relates to the availability of information in an era in which national security or homeland security concerns are of paramount importance. But while the author is critical of recent efforts to limit access on national security grounds, she also addresses limitations on public access to information in non-security related areas, which directly impact the ability of members of the general public to affect public policy and hold policy makers accountable. The author is Director of OpenTheGovernment.org, and an advocate for open access to government information.

Melissen, Jan and Anna Mar Fernandez, eds. **Consular Affairs and Diplomacy**. Boston: Martinus Nijhoff, 2011. 1 vol. (333 pp.).
Cost: $172.00; from $106.00 on amazon.com (2014).
The role of consular offices and consuls may be properly understood in the context of the history of international trade, for which consular officials have served as guardians of their country's economic interests. While consular officials perform a variety of functions, including basic administrative services, urgent jobs and assignments during emergency situations, and humanitarian tasks, their practical duties in the national economic interest have generally taken precedence. For more than two centuries, the consular service has served as the most important intermediary between trading communities, and as protectors of ordinary citizens as they work, travel and marry in an increasingly globalized world. While greater political and scholarly attention has been accorded to diplomatic, rather than consular, affairs, it is the latter that have had the greater impact upon the lives of individual citizens. This estimable volume of essays brings a new level understanding to the critical dimensions of the consular service and how it has evolved over the centuries, from its early judicial functions and facilitation of trading operations, to the aid and assistance it has provided to individual nationals living and working overseas in any capacity. It also examines the manner in which diplomatic and consular affairs have merged, with overlapping areas of responsibility within foreign ministries, while acknowledging the consular offices' predominant preoccupation with practical matters. A third component of this collection is reflected in its attention to emerging transnational, rather than merely intra-state, relations, with a perspective that calls attention to the societal dimension of world politics and diplomacy. And, finally, its addresses the rise in the role of consular work as a consequence of the accelerated transnationalization of world politics and the globalization of economic affairs in the late 20th century. In addressing these concerns, the essays track three broad areas of investigation: (1) the nature of contemporary consular affairs; (2) the consular services of the Great Powers: the United States, Russia, and China; and (3) the history of the consular institution, with particular attention to the consular services of Spain, Holland and France. Together, these historical and contemporary perspectives weave a rich and illuminating tapestry of the nature of consular affairs and their place within the world of diplomacy. Jan Melissen is Head of the Diplomatic Studies Programme at the Netherlands Institute of International relations. His co-editor, Ana Mar Fernandez, is Senior Lecturer in Politics at the Autonomous University of Barcelona. They are joined by 14 experts in the field of consular and diplomatic affairs drawn from the fields of academia and diplomatic affairs.

The National Commission on Terrorist Attacks Upon the United States. **The 9/11 Commission Report**. New York: W.W. Norton & Company, 2004. 1 vol. (516 pp.).
Cost: $19.95; from $.01 on amazon.com; kindle ed.: $7.62 (2014); also available as a free download at: http://www.9-11commission.gov/report/index.htm
The National Commission on Terrorist Attacks Upon the United States (also known as the 9-11 Commission), an independent, bipartisan commission created by congressional legislation and the signature of President George W. Bush in late 2002, was chartered to prepare a full and complete account of the circumstances surrounding the September 11, 2001 terrorist attacks, including preparedness for and the immediate response to the attacks. Chaired by former New Jersey Governor Thomas Kean, the Commission was also mandated to provide recommendations designed to guard against future attacks. The report's chapters include "We Have Some Planes," the Foundation of the New Terrorism, Counterterrorism Evolves, Responses to Al Qaeda's Initial Assaults, Al Qaeda Aims at the American Homeland, From Threat To Threat, The Attack Looms, «The System Was Blinking Red," Heroism and Horror, Wartime,

Foresight--and Hindsight, What To Do? A Global Strategy, How To Do It? A Different Way of Organizing the Government, Appendices, and Notes. The Commission's final report is available from a variety of sources, including the Government Printing Office, commercial publishers and as a free pdf download from the Commission's web site.

Pohlman, H. L. **Terrorism and the Constitution: The Post-9/11 Cases**. Lanham, MD: Rowman & Littlefield Publishers, 2008. 1 vol. (321 pp.). Paperbound
Cost: $32.95 (paper); from $6.23 on amazon.com (2014).
The war on terrorism, which, unlike any other war in American history, is being waged against non-state actors motivated by a fanatical strain of Islamic fundamentalism. Led by al Qaeda and related terrorists groups willing to employ weapons of mass destruction, independent and quasi-independent jihadist cells have arisen in many western nations, posing a threat to innocent civilian populations. Confronting this terrorist threat has generated considerable reflection and debate regarding the proper balance between the exigencies of national security and the protection of individual civil liberties. In this environment, the courts have been called upon to rule on a number of significant constitutional issues. Chief among these are (1) the question of whether the war on terrorism is the type of war that requires a shift in the balance between national security and individual rights; (2) if so, what is the nature of that new balance; (3) should traditional civil liberties be limited because Al Qaeda operates by means of stealth, surprise and deception; and (4) what is the proper role of the three branches of government in this dangerous environment. This volume considers five major post-9/11 cases, each of which grapples with issues posed by the terrorist threat. These include (1) *In re Sealed Case* involving the impact of the USA Patriot Act on traditional Fourth Amendment protections against unreasonable searches; (2) *Hamdi v. Rumsfeld* and *Rumsfeld v. Padilla*, involving the detention of enemy combatants; (3) *Rasul v. Bush*, involving aliens being detained abroad (i.e. the Guantanamo detainees); (4) *U.S. v. Maussaoui*, involving the civilian trials of high profile terrorists and whether they can be fairly prosecuted in civilian courts; and (5) *Hamdan v. Rumsfeld*, regarding the legitimacy and procedures employed by military tribunals when terrorist suspects are tried. This volume assembles a number of relevant documents, including appellate briefs, oral arguments, and excerpts of decisions, together with the author's balanced analysis, to provide the reader with the tools for making informed judgments about the cases in question.

Rogers, A. P. V. **Law on the Battlefield**. 3d ed. Manchester, UK: Manchester University Press 2012. 1 vol. (384 pp.). Softbound.
Cost: $50; from $31.60 on amazon.com; kindle: $45.12 (2014).
International humanitarian law should be an essential ingredient of military planning and doctrine, imposing civilizing restraint upon international conflicts.
Indeed, the idea that war should be subject to legal restraints has its origins in the Age of Chivalry, when rules were developed for the treatment of prisoners and civilian populations following sieges. Centuries earlier, the civilizations of Egypt and India addressed the question of practices designed to alleviate suffering during times of war; and the Saracens adopted what is believed to be the first systematic code of war, based on the Koran. By the 19th century, efforts to impose limits on warfare were driven by the increasing destructiveness of continental warfare and took the form of international treaties, beginning with the Geneva Convention of 1864. In recent years, however, armed conflicts have often taken the form of civil wars, characterized by anarchy, hatred and revenge, making them far less subject to the civilized rules of warfare generally conducted by organized states. This volume focuses attention on a number of critical issues related to the conduct of war, including the concepts of military necessity, humanity, rules of distinction between civilians and combatants, the rule of proportionality, indiscriminate attacks and the distinction between customary law and treaty law. Chapters are devoted to the subjects of enemy armed forces, military objectives, precautions in attack, precautions against the effects of attacks, cultural property, environmental protection, command responsibility, the conduct of hostilities in internal armed conflicts, and the military lawyers' perspective. Major General A. P. V. Rogers is Yorke Distinguished Fellow, Faculty of Law. University of Cambridge, Fellow of the Lauterpacht Research Centre for International Law, University of Cambridge, Fellow of the Human Rights Centre, University of Essex, and a member of the International Fact-Finding Commission. Until 1997, he was Director of Legal Services for the British Army. This is an essential addition to any military law collection.

Saltzburg, Stephan A., Lee D. Schinasi, and David A. Schlueter. **Military Rules of Evidence Manual**. 7th ed. Charlottesville, VA: LexisNexis, 2006-date. 2 vols. (1,237 pp.) Print or eBook. Annual pocket supplements.
Cost: $241 (print or eBook); supplementation: 2008: $63; 2009: $74; 2010: $76; 2011: $79; 2012: $84; 2013: $87; 5th ed.: 2004: $50; 2005: $53; 2006: new edition; 2007: 0; 4th ed.: 1998: $42.50; 1999: $47.50; 2000: $50; 2001: $52.50; 2002: $57; 3d ed.: 1994: $35; 1995: $40; 1996: $48.25.
Designed for military lawyers and judges, this copiously annotated handbook to the Military Rules of Evidence features editorial comments, drafters' analysis, annotated cases, and annotated bibliographies to relevant secondary sources. Includes an extensive table of cases and subject index. According to Senior Judge Robinson O. Everett, this is the only comprehensive treatment of the Military Rules of Evidence in print. The authors include Stephen Saltzburg, the Howrey Professor of Trial Advocacy, Litigation and Professional Responsibility at George Washington University's National Law Center, Lee Schinasi, Director of the Center for Continuing Legal Education, University of Miami School of Law, and David A. Schlueter, Professor of Law at St. Mary's University.

Scheinin, Martin, ed. **Terrorism and Human Rights**. Northampton, MA: Edward Elgar Publishing, 2013. 1 vol. (835 pp.)
Cost: $399.95 (online price: $359.95); from $389.72 on amazon.com (2014).
The rise of Islamic radicalism and religiously-inspired terrorism around the globe, particularly in the wake of the events of September 11, 2001, together with the response of governments to continued threats of terrorist acts, has prompted a host of measures that simultaneously compromise human rights, privacy, and freedom of expression. Drawing on works that were originally published in the academic literature between 2002 and 2011, this collection of articles covers a variety of topics, including

detention and extraordinary rendition, targeted killings, freedom of expression, privacy and terrorist listings. The editor uses the metaphor of the pyramid to explain the impact upon human rights of post-9/11 counter-terrorism measures, with "the most visible and deeply intrusive human rights violations committed by states in the name of countering terrorism, starting with the violation of the absolute prohibition against torture" at its apex. At the base of the pyramid are those measures which, while representing an erosion of everyone's human rights, are of a tolerable enough level, reflecting a democratically-determined tradeoff between freedom and security. Somewhere halfway up the pyramid are such threats to human rights as non-discrimination, freedom of religion, and freedom of expression that may be negatively impacted for ever larger numbers of people. The premise of this collection is that counter-terrorism measures have impacted everyone's human rights, but that not all have been impacted equally. The twenty-two articles in this collection have been drawn from a variety of academic journals and address these issues in all their complexity. Beginning with four articles which provide a general framework of the status of human rights in the war on terror, the remaining articles address the topics of torture, detention and extraordinary rendition, targeted killings, freedom of expression, profiling, privacy, terrorist listings, and economic, social, and cultural rights, gender aspects and causes of terrorism. Editor Martin Scheinin is Professor of International Law and Human Rights, European University Institute, Italy.

Schlueter, David A. **Military Criminal Justice: Practice and Procedure**. 8th ed. Charlottesville, VA: LexisNexis, 2013-date. 1 vol. (1,429 pp.) Annual pocket supplement.
Cost: $213; supplementation: 2013: $76; 6th ed.: 2004: $46; 2005: $52; 2006: $56; 7th ed,: 2008: $127 (new ed.); 2009: $64; 2010: $67; 2011: $70; 2012: $75; 5th ed.: 2000: $30; 2001: $39; 2002: $43; 2003: 0; 4th edition: 1997: $32.50; 1998: $35.
An impressive analytical exposition of the subject of military criminal justice by a Professor of Law at St. Mary's University with more than 25 years experience in the field. The coverage encompasses both substantive and procedural aspects of the law and is designed for the active practitioner as well as the law student. The chapters cover the military criminal justice system, military crimes, nonjudicial punishment, jurisdiction, investigations, plea bargaining, motions practice, sentencing, and much more. Includes a number of valuable appendices, including forms, table of cases, and subject index. The text is exhaustively footnoted with references to cases, statutes and secondary sources.

Schlueter, David A. et al. **Military Evidentiary Foundations**. 5th ed. Charlottesville, VA: LexisNexis, 2013-date. 1 vol. (740 pp.). Print and eBook.
Cost: $162; no supplementation to date; 2d ed.: 2001: 0; 2002: $55; 2003-2006: 0; 1st ed: 1995: $25; 1996: $30; 1997: $35; 1998: $40; 1999: $55.
A lucid and practical examination of the rules governing the admission of evidence in military trials by some of the country's leading authorities in military law. Provides specific lines of questioning and courtroom-tested trial techniques.

Shanor, Charles A. and L. Lynn Hogue. **National Security and Military Law in a Nutshell**. 3d ed. St. Paul, MN: Thomson Reuters West, 2003. 1 vol. (469 pp.). Available fro West Academic.
Cost: $41; from $13.80 on amazon.com (2014).
An introductory overview of the laws governing national security, the military, rights of service members, the military criminal justice system, the law of armed conflict, and discharge and administrative separation from military service. Designed primarily for law students, this text can also be used by practitioners, cadets at military academies, college ROTC programs, and lawyers employed by the military branches. An updating of the authors' **Military Law in a Nutshell**.

Shields, Christopher A. **American Terrorism Trials: Prosecutorial and Defense Strategies**. El Paso, TX: LFB Scholarly Publishing, 2012. 1 vol. (170 pp.).
Cost: $67.00; from $44.89 on amazon.com (2014).
An outgrowth of the American Terrorism Study housed in Fulbright College at the University of Arkansas, this book focuses on the effectiveness of the Department of Justice placing terrorism trials squarely under the lens of public scrutiny. The discussion, which had previously focused on conviction rates and prison sentences, has produced little consensus. After the passage of the USA Patriot Act, however, the housing of terrorist suspects at Guantanamo, and the planned military tribunals, there was increased public attention on the manner in which suspected terrorists were investigated, detained and prosecuted. Moreover, the first three years after 9/11 witnessed an increase in terrorist suspects who were tried in the federal courts. Using data from the American Terrorism Study, this project involved the examination of federal court case records arising from FBI investigations conducted from 1980 to 2004 where an "official" terrorism investigation was conducted under the auspices of the Attorney General's Guidelines for terrorism investigations. The author finds that when prosecutors relied less heavily on highly politicized prosecution strategies, conviction rates increased. His findings also indicate that the more prosecutors politicize a case, the more likely the case goes to trial, increasing the odds of acquittal. Indeed, of all the prosecution strategies, explicit politicality produced the lowest conviction rates. With policy changes after 9/11, prosecutors relied less heavily on highly politicized prosecution strategies and filed fewer event-linked cases, with the result that plea bargain and conviction rates increased, despite the finding that the average count severity was only slightly lower than it was in the prior era. The author draws upon extensive data assembled by the American Terrorism Study and related studies. Christopher Shields is currently a visiting assistant professor in the Department of Sociology and Criminal Justice at the University of Arkansas, and a project manager for the Terrorism Research Center in Fulbright College. Before joining academia in 2003, Shields worked as a criminal defense attorney and rule XV prosecutor. This volume provides an invaluable empirical basis for formulating prosecution and defense strategies in terrorism trials.

State Open Government Law and Practice in a Post-9/11 World. Edited by Jeffrey F. Addicott, et al. Tucson, AZ: Lawyers & Judges Publishing Co., 2007.
1 vol. (385 pp.).

Cost: $80; amazon.com; kindle ed.: $9.99 (2014).
State public information laws typically provide exemptions to the general presumption of the public's right of access to information. This volume provides state-by-state summaries of these exemptions which have been enacted into state law in the wake of the terrorist attacks on September 11, 2001. These statutory categories include (1) critical infrastructure; (2) cyber security; (3) first response; (4) political structure; (5) public health; and (6) terror investigation. Part I also includes state-by-state cross references of the statutes concerning public information and terrorism and security laws enacted in the aftermath of 9/11, links to online sources of state laws, and other Freedom of Information (FOI) resources. Part II contains surveys of national open government laws from several countries facing increased terrorist threats, including Columbia, France, Israel and the United Kingdom. This guide was a joint production of the Center for Terrorism Law, St. Mary's University Law School, and the Reporters Committee for Freedom of the Press, a voluntary, unincorporated association of reporters and editors that works in defense of the First Amendment and freedom of information interests of the news media. Jeffrey Addicott is professor of law and Director of the Center for Terrorism Law, St. Mary's University Law School.

Stichman, Barton F., Ronald B. Abrams, and David Addlestone, eds. **Veterans Benefits Manual**. 2013 Edition. Charlottesville, VA: LexisNexis, 2013. 1 vol. (1,060 pp.). Periodic softbound editions.
Cost: $150; $186 combination price for this and **Federal Veterans Law, Rules and Regulations**. Also on combo CD-ROM: $220; print and CD-ROM combo: $300 (2014).
This volume is an exhaustive, practical manual designed to assist advocates in representing veterans and their dependents in obtaining benefits from the Department of Veterans Affairs. The book's six parts and nineteen chapters provide information and guidance on disability benefits for veterans, VA benefits for non-veterans, rules affecting the amount of benefits paid, health care and other VA benefits, the VA claims adjudication process, advocacy on behalf of VA claimants, and correction of military records. The book also includes sample forms and briefs, flow-charts, checklists, citations to legal authorities, and other sample documents relevant to the claims process. The text is written by lawyers with the National Veterans Legal Services Program, an independent nonprofit public interest law firm that provides national support center services to advocates in the field of veterans law. Barton Stichman and David Addlestone and co-directors of the NVLSP. Ronald Abrams is the NVLSP's director of legal publications and training and editor of **The Veterans Advocate**. First published by the NVLSP in 1991, the book has been taken over by LexisNexis in 1999, with annual editions planned. Also available from LEXIS Law Publishing: **Federal Veterans Laws, Rules and Regulations**, 2013 Edition (see above entry).

Terry, James P. **The War on Terror: The Legal Dimension**. Lanham, MD: Rowman & Littlefield Publishers, 2013. 1 vol. (241 pp.).
Cost: $60.00; from $45.17 on amazon.com; kindle: $47.39 (2014).
The terror threat posed, in large part, by radical Islam and its adherents has become the dominant security threat in the world today. The war on terror has raised significant legal questions regarding engagement with, and treatment of, non-State combatants who target both military and civilian targets and populations. To its credit, the United States has been in the forefront of efforts to promote legal regimes governing both the initiation of hostilities and the conduct of wars once begun. Indeed, the "Lieber Code," issued in 1863 by President Lincoln as General Order 100, was the first attempt to codify the "law of war," otherwise referred to as the "law of armed conflict" (LOAC). This document provided a substantive basis for later U.S. efforts to promote both the Hague (1899 and 1907) and Geneva (1949) Conventions that attempt to regulate the conduct of war and protect innocent civilians and military personnel in time of war. The U.S. response to the attacks of 9/11, however, raised legal questions not addressed by previous international agreements, most particularly in the way non-State combatants are treated upon capture. In this examination of the legal dimensions of the war on terror, Retired Marine Colonel James P. Terry brings a wealth of knowledge and experience derived from over forty years distinguished service as, among others, a Marine Judge Advocate and Legal Counsel to the Chairman of the Joint Chiefs of Staff, the highest legal position to which a military lawyer can aspire. These terror-related issues include the legal requirements for unconventional warfare, the international political context of state-sponsored terrorism, the law of self-defense as applied to the terrorist threat, the development of rules of engagement, the defensive uses of force short of war by the President, covert action, habeas corpus and detention of enemy combatants, torture and the interrogation of defendants, high seas terror and the elimination of piracy, environmental terrorism, war powers in the age of terror, the war on terror and media access, and future perspectives in addressing terror violence, among others. The author's analysis draws upon a host of scholarly articles, governmental reports and documents, court decisions, and relevant statutes.. This is an essential read for anyone who wishes to understand the legal complexities of the war on terror and the goal of both protecting the population against terrorism and upholding the rule of law. A senior fellow at the Center for National Security Law at the University of Virginia, Col. Terry received his undergraduate degrees from the University of Virginia, law degree from Mercer University, and Masters of Law and Doctor of Juridical Science degrees from George Washington University.

The U.S. Intelligence Community Law SourceBook: A Compendium of National Security Related Laws and Policy Documents. Andrew M. Borene, ed. 2012 Edition. Chicago: American Bar Association, 2013. 1 vol. (1,508 pp.). Annual. Paperbound.
Cost: $249.95 ($199.95 to members); from $149.87 on amazon.com (2014).
A massive compilation of national security related laws and policy documents, including federal statutes, public laws, rules of procedure for Senate and House Select Committees on Intelligence, executive orders, key intelligence community directives, detention and interrogation policy documents, military orders, presidential memoranda, cybersecurity policy documents, significant proposed legislation in 2011. Federal statutes include

the National Security Act of 1947, the Intelligence Reform and Terrorism Prevention Act of 2004, Foreign Intelligence Surveillance Act, Protect America Act of 2007, the Freedom of Information Act, and the Homeland Security Act of 2002, among others. The documents are preceded by four insightful review essays covering the topics of cybersecurity; counterintelligence; homeland security and domestic intelligence; and national security investigations and the private sector. Andrew M. Borene is Director and Assistant General Counsel for Government & Industry Affairs at ReconRobotics, and a graduate of the University of Minnesota School of Law. This is a cost-effective alternative to the various primary law source documents that embrace this field of law and policy.

Veterans Benefits Manual and Related Laws and Regulations on CD-ROM. Charlottesville, VA: LexisNexis, 2001-date. One disc. Folio. Updated annually.
Cost: $220; $300 for the complete package including CD-ROM and two print volumes (2014).
This CD-ROM product contains the complete text of the **Veterans Benefits Manual** and **Federal Veterans Laws, Rules and Regulations** (see above entries). It also includes annotations of relevant cases and hypertext links from the text of the **Veterans Benefits Manual** to the **USCS**, **CFR**, Court Rules, and adjudication manuals.

Whitley, Joe D. and Lynne K. Zusman, eds. **Homeland Security: Legal and Policy Issues**. Chicago: American Bar Association, Section of Administrative Law and Regulatory Practice, 2009. 1 vol. (284 pp.). Paperbound.
Cost: $99.95 ($89.95 to members); from $53.99 on amazon.com (2014).
In the wake of the terrorist attacks on New York City and Washington, DC in 2001, the Department of Homeland Security has emerged as a major component of the largest reorganization of the federal government since the creation of the Department of Defense in 1947. And, as a consequence of devastation wrought by Hurricane Katrina, the government's efforts have been extended to natural as well as man-made disasters. This volume provides a succinct overview of the history, organizational structure and functions of the homeland security operations of the United States government and the legal responsibilities of the various government agencies in the implementation of measures to protect homeland security and respond to these threats and disasters. Twenty authors contributed chapters that consider such topics as the history and future of homeland security, state and federal emergency powers, the role of the Northern Command in the defense of the homeland, the USA Patriot Act and the federal anti-money-laundering regime,
Information security, information protection, increased worksite enforcement, succession planning and business continuity, the Safety Act, security-based reregulation of transportation, maritime security developments, chemical facility anti-terrorism standards, international trade, CFIUS and foreign investment, and export control enforcement developments. The text includes citations to relevant state and federal laws and regulations, court decisions, and scholarly articles. The volume was produced under the auspices of the ABA's Administrative Law and Regulatory Practice Section. Editor Joe Whitley, a shareholder with the firm of Greenberg Traurig LLP, was the first General Counsel of the U.S. Department of Homeland Security. His co-editor, Lynne Zusman, is a solo practitioner in Washington, DC, an experienced litigator and negotiator, and former attorney with the Justice Department.

Wilcox, William A., Jr. **The Modern Military and the Environment: the Laws of Peace and War**. Rockville, MD, Government Institutes, Inc., 2007. 1 vol. (188 pp.).
Cost: $72 (paperbound); from $44.90 on amazon.com (2014).
What responsibilities do military officials have to respect environmental concerns during wartime and peacetime? Despite the realities of war, and military operations generally, there are environmental statutes, regulations and executive orders which govern the activities of the military. These legal authorities govern water rights, military munitions, hazardous waste disposal, military development, testing, and training operations, environmental protection and planning overseas, military land withdrawals, base realignments and closures, international environmental law, and other environmental concerns. The author describes the tension which exists between environmentalists and regulators, who are concerned with the damages inflicted on the environment by military leaders dedicated to using actual field conditions to prepare soldiers for war. The book addresses the need for greater accountability from the military, particularly on such practices as dumping spilling, stockpiling, and launching harmful chemicals. He addresses the impact of environmental laws on the military, including the National Environmental Policy Act and the Resource Conservation and Recovery Act, as well as providing an overview of the laws governing access to information concerning the military's impact on the environment. William Wilcox is an attorney in the Washington, D.C., office of Pillsbury Winthrop Shaw Pittman LLP and a lieutenant colonel in the U.S. Army Reserve has fifteen years experience as an active duty military and civilian attorney, specializing in environmental law to federal agencies.

Wittes, Benjamin, ed. **Legislating the War on Terror: An Agenda for Reform**. Washington, DC: Brookings Institution Press, 2009. 1 vol. (420 pp.).
Cost: $34.95; from $7.05 on amazon.com; kindle: $19.22 (2014).
The Executive Branch of the Federal government responded forcefully to the terrorist attacks of September 11, but it also acted without sufficient legal restraint in an effort to maximize its ability to respond to the threat of future attacks. It was often more concerned with the exercise of power in the name of security than with its legal or constitutional legitimacy. Within a few years, however, its actions were challenged by Congress and the courts, reflecting society's diminishing support for unrestrained executive branch leadership to confront the country's security challenges. Supreme Court decisions applied new restrictions on the detention of terror suspects, and Congress placed limits on interrogation practices. This volume advances the discussion to a new phase which seeks to synthesize the experience of the initial response and the reaction to it in order to construct a more durable legal framework for confronting the terrorist threat. That synthesis is based on the understanding that global counterterrorism is neither pure law enforcement nor pure warfare, but draws upon the key elements, authorities, and limits of both. As a collaboration of the Brookings Institution, the Hoover Institution, and the Georgetown Center on National

Security and the Law, a team of scholars, representing a broad spectrum of political opinion, was assembled to formulate a new architecture of U.S. counterterrorism operations. Accordingly, the chapters in this volume grapple with such topics as detention, surveillance and interrogation, administrative detention, long-term terrorist detention, optimizing criminal prosecution as a counterterrorism tool, better rules for terrorism trials, refining the immigration law's role in counterterrorism, modernizing the Foreign Intelligence Surveillance Act, national security issues in civil litigation, refining U.S. interrogation law, and targeted killing in U.S. counterterrorism strategy and law. Editor Benjamin Wittes is a senior fellow and research director at the Brookings Institution and a member of the Hoover Institution's Task Force on National Security and the Law.

Zusman, Lynne, ed. **The Fundamentals of Counterterrorism Law**. Chicago: American Bar Association, 2014. 1 vol. (399 pp.). Paperbound.
Cost: $99.95 ($79.95 to members); from $75.58 on amazon.com (2014).
The 17th century Dutch jurist, Hugo Grotius (1583-1645), was responsible for developing a workable legal framework for the conduct of war, warning that belligerents must "not believe that either nothing is allowable or that everything is." In attempting to mediate these two extremes, Grotius developed a middle ground in which recognized the necessity and legality of "just wars," while proscribing certain aspects of military conduct. As observers prognosticate about the future of warfare, a fault line seems to have developed between those who argue that the asymmetrical warfare between state actors and non-state armed groups is likely to be the norm, and those who believe that conventional warfare between national armed forces is the more likely prospect. Others suggest that between these two extremes is likely to be a hybrid strain that is neither purely asymmetrical nor purely conventional. This collection of eighteen articles deals with a wide range of timely issues involving the rules and norms of international law, including FBI and Foreign Counterterrorism Operations, Terrorism's Threat to Cities Large and Small, Lawyers, Courts and Military Commissions, Presidential Usurpation or Congressional Abdication, a Legal Ethics Primer for National Security Lawyers, and a Broad Overview of the Law of Armed Conflict in the Age of Terror. Additional chapters examine Privatizing the War on terror, Demystifying Terrorist Finance, Cyberterrorism, the Advent of Preventative War, Counterterrorism Operations, International Law and the Use of Lethal Force, among others. The team of authors, which includes those in government, military, academic, and private security-related capacities, bring a depth of knowledge and experience to the challenges posed by modern warfare and terrorism.

Zusman, Lynne K. **The Law of Counterterrorism.** Chicago: American Bar Association, 2011. 1 vol. (320 pp.). Paperbound
Cost: $99.95; from $53.06 on amazon.com (2014).
In a world plagued by terrorists, particularly those of the Islamo-fascist variety currently at war with modernity, this volume is a timely and invaluable resource. Counterterrorism is defined as «offensive measures taken to prevent, deter, pre-empt, and respond to terrorism.» By contrast, anti-terrorism is defined as «Defensive measures used to reduce the vulnerability to terrorist acts». The war on transnational terror has, nevertheless, required a careful balancing of national security concerns with the need to protect civil liberties. Among the areas examined in detail by this volume are the war in Afghanistan, the Taliban and Al-Qaeda; the DOJ torture memo; the philosophy of terrorism; war crimes jurisdiction; the 9/11 Commission; current and future national security principles; the National Security Act and IC reform; the National Counterterrorism Center; the organization and structure of the intelligence community; the National Security Council system; communications surveillance; military commissions, and the the PATRIOT Act, among others. Of particular interest to those on the front lines of combating terrorism is the chapter entitled "Updating the Counterterrorism Toolkit: A Brief Sampling of Post-9/11 Surveillance Laws," by Philip Bridwell and Jamil N. Jaffer. This is an essential resource for anyone involved in the war on terror, whether behind the scenes or on the front lines. Lynne Zusman, is a solo practitioner in Washington, DC, an experienced litigator and negotiator, former attorney with the Justice Department, and co-editor of **Homeland Security: Legal and Policy Issues**, also published by the ABA.

Additional titles on Military Law are available from the following publishers: American Bar Association, Ayer Co., Baird-Hedges Publishing Co., Central Committee for Conscientious Objectors, Government Institutes, Greenwood Publishing Group, William S. Hein & Co., LexisNexis, Naval Institute Press, Naval War College, State Mutual Book & Periodical Service, Thomson Reuters West, Transaction Publication, West Academic. See Appendix B for addresses and telephone numbers.

Municipal Corporations

Abbey, Buck. **U.S. Landscape Ordinances: An Annotated Reference Handbook**. New York: John Wiley & Sons, 1998. 1 vol. (408 pp.).
Cost: $125; from $94.05 on amazon.com (2014)
A comprehensive state-by-state reference to the planning ordinances that govern the landscapes of more than 300 American cities. The author examines the ordinances that regulate such matters as landscape buffers, parking lots, vehicular use areas, open space design, land clearing and building sites, irrigation, and tree plantings. A useful guide for attorneys involved with zoning and planning issues, as well as professionals in landscape design and municipal planning, students, municipal legislators, and community activists. The product of ten years of research and analysis. Buck Abbey, ASLA, is Associate Professor of Landscape Architecture at Louisiana State University and a recognized authority on municipal landscape ordinances.

Antieau, Chester James. **Antieau on Local Government Law.** 2d ed. New York: Matthew Bender & Co., 1998-date. 7 vols. Looseleaf format. Supplemented three times annually. Not available on CD-ROM.
Cost: $2,619 (print) (includes annual subscription); renewal: 1995: $687.00 (price frozen since 1992); 1996: $721; 1997: $721; 1998: $740; 1999: $770; 2000: $820; 2001: $877; 2002: $939.00; 2003: $986; 2004: $1,035; 2005: $1,096; 2006: $1,186.00; 2007: $1,280; 2008: $1,370; 2009: $1,466; 2010:

$1,495; 2011: $1,570; 2012: $1,664; 2013: $1,780; 2014: $1,943; eBook: $2,381; renewal: 2014: $1,943. This seven-volume encyclopedic treatment of local government law, written by one of the nation's leading experts on governmental law and civil rights, is undergoing a complete revision scheduled to be completed by the end of 1998. The new edition will be organized under a topic-based scheme designed to better reflect the structure of the law today. The topics covered include Organization, Relationship with Federal, State & Other Local Governments, General Powers, Exercise of Powers, Land Use Planning & Control, Contracts & Contractual Liability, Tort Liability, Finances, Elections and Referendums, Actions By & Against Local Governments, Services & Assistance, Education, Officers & Employees, and Local Authorities, Districts & Public Corporations. The coverage is similar in many respects to that provided by McQuillan, **Law of Municipal Corporations,** although this set does provide greater and more centralized coverage in such areas as home rule. They both include exhaustive citations to case and statutory law. The looseleaf supplementation to Antieau is provided three times yearly as opposed to the annual pocket parts to the McQuillan. While the attorney considering the purchase of a multi-volume treatise in this field should take the time to examine both sets in his or her public law library, this set is certainly a worthy alternative to McQuillan.

Ballard, Frederic L., Jr. **ABCs of Arbitrage: Tax Rules for Investment of Bond Proceeds by Municipalities**. 2011 ed. Chicago: American Bar Association, 2011. 1 vol. (340 pp.)
Cost: $149.95 ($134.95 to ABA members); from $87.95 on amazon.com (2014).
Designed for use by bond attorneys, municipal lawyers, and public finance officials, this volume explains both the basic rules governing municipal bond arbitrage and the more complicated issues applicable to various fund models, including project funds, reserve funds, revenue funds, and debt service funds. The author avoids the standard IRS code and regulation format adopted by most works in this area and instead focuses on the substantive issues and problems. Chapters include: introduction to arbitrage, initial disposition of proceeds, small issuers, revenues and proceeds, nonpurpose investments, expenditures, loans of proceeds, refundings, substance versus form, yield and rebate computations, and fitting the issue into the regulations. The author is a partner in the law firm of Ballard, Spahr, Andrews & Ingersoll and a specialist in the field of municipal bond financing and taxation.

Bodensteiner, Ivan E. and Rosalie Berger Levinson. **State & Local Government Civil Rights Liability.** 2d ed. St. Paul, MN: West (Clark Boardman Callaghan), 2011-date. 5 vols. Looseleaf format. Annual supplementation.
Cost: $1,144; ProView eBook: $1,049; supplementation: 1993: $60; 1994: $67; 1995: $45; 1996: $87; 1997: 0; 1998: $96; 1999: $173.75; 2000: $194; 2001: $225.25; 2002: $247.75; 2003: $325; 2004: $320; 2005: $335; 2006: $391; 2007: $435; 2008: $484.50; 2009: $553.50; 2010: $294; 2011: $1,027; 2012: $724; 2013: $840; **Monthly Assured Print Price (APP)**: $83/$996.
This two-volume treatise examines the grounds upon which state and local governments are subject to suit under federal civil rights acts. It provides attorneys and local governments with guidance on how to defend against civil rights actions and how to prevent liability in the first place. Outlines strategies and tactics used by plaintiffs in such cases. Provides advice on such matters as jurisdiction, procedure, defenses, immunities, enforcement, remedies, types of conduct regulated, proof of claims and attorneys fees. Also discusses the protection of Federal rights under §1983, employment discrimination, the Age Discrimination in Employment Act, and litigating Federal claims in state courts.

Fontana, Vincent R. **Municipal Liability: Law and Practice**. 3rd ed. New York: Wolters Kluwer Law & Business, 2007-date. 2 vols. Looseleaf format. Annual supplementation.
Cost: $465; supplementation: 2008-2009: 0; 2010: $219; 2011: $250; 2012: $285; 2013: $299.
With the withering away of the doctrine of sovereign immunity, municipal corporations are faced with an increasing level and variety of potential liabilities, particularly in such areas as employment, age and educational discrimination, housing, police misconduct, sexual harassment, zoning, and voting rights. This comprehensive and well-annotated text provides detailed discussion of the law regarding specific areas of municipal liability, guidance to those defending municipal departments and agencies, as well as those bringing actions against such entities. Chapters include: (1) the Civil Rights Act of 1964: Title VII; (2) Civil Rights Act of 1991; (3) Americans with Disabilities Act of 1990; (4) Age Discrimination in Employment Act; (5) Sexual Harassment in the Workplace Under Title VII; (6) Analysis of Various State Antidiscrimination in Employment Laws; (7) Property Rights; (8) Police Misconduct; (9) the Civil Rights Act of 1871; (10) First Amendment; (11) the Right to Vote; (12) Attorneys' Fees; (13) Defenses; (14) Zoning; (15) Relief—Damages; (16) Jury Instructions; (17) Discovery; (18) Legality and Privacy Issues of E-Mail in the Workplace; (19) State Freedom of Information Law; ad (20) Open Meetings Law. The text is supplemented with numerous jury instructions and, sample complaint, pleading and discovery forms in specific areas of municipal liability, as well as a table of cases and index. Vincent R. Fontana is a founding partner in the law firm of Fontana & Broderick, LLP in Garden City, New York, where he specializes in labor and employment, civil rights, constitutional law, and negligence and tort liability. He attended College of the Holy Cross and Fordham Law School, has published widely in the areas of labor and employment, and municipal liability, and is a frequent lecturer at IMLA conferences.

Griffith, Benjamin E., ed. **America Votes!: A Guide to Modern Election Law and Voting Rights**. 2d ed. Chicago: American Bar Association, Section of State and Local Government Law, 2013. 1 vol. (375 pp.). Paperbound.
Cost: $109.95 ($89.95 to ABA and Section members) from $58.75 on amazon.com (2014).
Election law and procedure, and voting rights, have become increasingly contentious subjects of debate in recent years, fueled by a number of extremely close and disputed election results, of which the 2000 presidential election is the most obvious example. This collection of articles tackles a variety of important and contentious issues, from the lessons of the 2000 and 2004 presidential elections, to language assistance provisions of the

Voting Rights Act, voter protection on election day, election day registration, felon disenfranchisement, Section 5 and the Voting Rights Act, the role of demographic and statistical experts in election law disputes, government-issued photo identification and proof of citizenship requirements, voting technology and the law, the growth of early and non-precinct place balloting, election challenges involving candidates for federal office, bailout (exemption) under the Voting Rights Act, and the origins and impact of the Help America Vote Act of 2000. Twenty-six scholars and litigators, all with significant experience in the field of voting rights and election law, contributed to the seventeen chapters in this volume. While at least half of the authors bring a nonpartisan or neutral scholarly perspective to the task, those with a left-of-center partisan background outnumber those on the right by a factor of about five to one. Each of the articles is supported with citations to relevant authorities, including cases, statutes, and scholarly articles. The editor, who is chair of the ABA Section of State and Local Government Law, brings extensive experience as a litigator on behalf of state and local government entities and officials in actions involving the Voting Rights Act, election law, civil rights actions 42 U.S.C. Section §1983, public sector insurance coverage, and environmental law. In addition to wide-ranging professional activities, he has written and edited numerous publications in his areas of expertise.

Krane, Dale, Platon N. Rigos, and Melvin B. Hill, Jr., eds. **Home Rule in America: A Fifty-State Handbook**. Washington, DC: CQ Press, 2000. 1 vol. (497 pp.).
Cost: $225; from $118 on amazon.com (2014).
Local governments are often called creatures of the state because the legal system of each state determines the powers that cities may exercise. This collection of essays addresses the relationships which exist between states and local governments. Following a legal and historical overview of home rule in America, the volume includes scholarly essays written by 81 authors which describe the particular status of state-local relations in each of the fifty states. The appendices include a variety of tables which present significant facts and figures on home rule in the states, and a glossary of terms.

Martinez, John, C. Dallas Sands, and Michael E. Libonati. **Local Government Law.** St. Paul, MN: Thomson Reuters West (Clark Boardman Callaghan), 1981-date. 4 vols. Looseleaf format. Supplemented annually.
Cost: $2,289; ProView eBook: $2,222; supplementation: 1993: $183; 1994: $208; 1995: $260; 1996: $286; 1997: $259.45; 1998: $318; 1999: $332.50; 2000: $358; 2001: $419; 2002; $484; 2003: $550.50; 2004: $608; 2005: $620; 2006: $742.50; 2007: $826.50; 2008: $926.50; 2009: $280; 2010: $1,147.50; 2011: $1,253.50; 2012: $1,375.50; 2013: $1,206; **Monthly Assured Print Price (APP):** $142/$1,704.
This four-volume treatise was written by the late C. Dallas Sands of the University of Alabama School of Law, Michael Libonati, the Carnell Professor of Law, Temple University and John Martinez, Professor of Law, University of Utah College of Law. The authors provide discussion and analysis of the place of local government in the scheme of American law, the organization and processes of local government, the powers of local government, and the accountability of local governments including both tort liability and other obligations. Their coverage of local government organization and processes extends to such areas as personnel matters, processes of governance, records, nature and scope of powers, regulatory powers, licensing, land development regulation, streets and public ways, provision of public services, welfare services, education, property, contracts, taxation, special assessments, borrowing, budget controls and fiscal administration. Includes extensive citations to primary and secondary authorities. Annual cumulative supplements provide revisions to text and recent authorities. Ideally suited as a reference for the municipal attorney, elected official, town manager, department head, or the practicing attorney specializing in municipal law.

McCarthy, David J., Jr. and Lorie Reynoids. **Local Government Law in a Nutshell.** 5th ed. St. Paul, MN: West, 2003. 1 vol. (472 pp.). Available from West Academic.
Cost: $41; from $30.96 on amazon.com (2014).
A brief overview of the scope local government authority, its sources, limitations, role in a federal system. Coverage also includes the formation of local government, statutory or alteration procedures, boundary changes, organization and operation, officers and employees, delegation of functions elections and referenda, regulation of conduct, land use, police power, acquisition, limitations on use, and disposition of goods, services and property. Also includes discussion of sources of revenue, taxation, borrowing, citizen tort claims, standing, and claims under federal civil rights law. Good introduction, but lacks citations to case or statutory law.

McQuillan, Eugene. **The Law of Municipal Corporations.** 3d ed. St. Paul, MN: Thomson Reuters West (Clark Boardman Callaghan), 2004-date. 30 vols. Annual pocket supplements.
Cost: $5,928; supplementation: 1993: $628; 1994: $706; 1995: $768; 1996: $929; 1997: $804.75; 1998: $957; 1999: $758.25; 2000: $1,114; 2001: $1,290; 2002: $1,432; 2003: $1,630; 2004: $1,662.50; 2005: $1,327.50; 2006: $2,006; 2007: $2,232; 2008: $2,584; 2009: $2,009; 2010: $3,157.50; 2011: $3,443; 2012: $3,785; 2013: $4,352; **Monthly Assured Print Price (APP):** $432/$5,184. Also available on WestlawNext: $684 per year (single user) (2014).
Published continuously since 1904, this is the definitive work in the field of municipal corporation law. It addresses every aspect of local government law from the nature and kinds of municipal corporations through the myriad functions performed at the local level. Specific chapters are devoted to such topics as legislative control of municipal corporations, elections, offices and officers, employees, meetings and proceedings of council or governing legislative body, municipal ordinances, police powers, zoning, licenses and permits, corporate property, eminent domain, municipal enterprises, public improvements, financial powers, municipal bonds, taxation, fire and police departments, public education, mandamus, and municipal liability, among others. The text is supported by numerous citations to case law and to other relevant West titles such as Sands, **Local Government Law** and Fletcher, **Cyclopedia of Corporations.** The attorney specializing in municipal law cannot afford to be without this set unless he or she has ready access to one in a public law library. It is also a basic reference for both elective and appointive

officials, city and town solicitors, etc.

Cost Saving Tips: The most cost-effective way of acquiring this title is as an add-on to a Westlaw **Municipal Law Practitioner** subscriptions. Annual cost for a single user was only $684 per year in 2013, as opposed to the $4,352 annually to maintain it in print. Print subscribers should also beware of the rising cost of supplementation for this set, including Revised volumes priced at $680 ($544 to subscribers). An excellent alternative to acquiring and maintaining the entire set in either print ot via WerstlawNext is to purchase individual chapters (now priced at $42.00 ea.) over the Thomsoin Reuters "Legal Solutions" web site. As with any of the large reference sets, most of the material is rarely, if ever, consulted.

Matthews, Thomas and Byron Matthews. **Matthews Municipal Ordinances.** 2d ed. St. Paul, MN: West (Clark Boardman Callaghan), 1994-date. 12 vols. Annual pocket supplements and periodic revised volumes.
Cost: $2,082; supp.: 1993: $226; 1994: $319; 1995: $169; 1996: $302.50; 1997: $313.33; 1998: $337; 1999: $457.50; 2000: $495; 2001: $429.50; 2002: $639; 2003: $727.50; 2004: $592.50; 2005: $653; 2006: $723.50; 2007: $841; 2008: $635; 2009: $818; 2010: $1,129.50; 2011: $1,199; 2012: $1,319; 2013: $1,455; **Monthly Assured Print Price (APP):** $154/$1,848; also available via a **Municipal Law Practitioner** subscription on WestlawNext.
This is the only multi-volume guide to the law and drafting of municipal ordinances. The authors explain how ordinances should be worded and what formal requirements must be satisfied to ensure their surviving court challenges. The seven volumes are divided into two parts: Part one contains a discussion of the substantive law and procedure regarding the role of ordinances and their preparation, drafting and construction. Part two, encompassing six of the seven volumes, contains forms of ordinances in specific areas of municipal activity, including administrative ordinances, elections, city planning, bond ordinances, environmental protection, traffic and vehicles, animals, crime and offenses, firearms, immoral conduct, nuisances and litter control, and more. An indispensable reference for the municipal attorney or city solicitor's office.

Cost Saving Tips: Considering the substantial cost of updating this 12-volume set, you may wish to drop the standing order to supplementation and update every two or three years. Only marginal value is added by the pocket parts, considering the volume of forms already in the bound volumes. If you practice regularly in the field of municipal law, the **Municipal Law Practitioner** subscription on WestlawNext may be the best value given the variety of materials available on that platform.

Mintz, Joel A., Ronald H. Rosenberg, and Larry A. Bakken. **Fundamentals of Municipal Finance**. Chicago: American Bar Association, 2010. 1 vol. (170 pp.). Paperbound.
Cost: $89.95 ($71.95 to members) (2014).
In the post-World War II era, the state and local government sector in the United States has expanded tremendously, and responded to pressures to finance an increased variety of projects and initiatives. Since the 1960s, these pressures have been exacerbated by the growth of public sector unions and cost of financing their wage and benefit demands. With state and local tax revenues failing to keep pace with these demands, local governments have increasingly had to borrow funds to finance both traditional and nontraditional expenditures, including low- and moderate-income housing projects, wastewater treatment plants, student loans, and economic development projects. There has been an increasing tendency by various subnational entities to satisfy current demands for services by transferring debt to future generations. As of September, 2007, the par amount of outstanding U.S. municipal bonds stood at a record $2,570.6 billion. This volume was written to provide nonspecialist attorneys with an introduction to the often intricate process of financing local capital projects through the issuance of municipal bonds. Toward that end, it considers the chief borrowing instruments, the key players in the issuance of municipal bonds, rating agencies, state limitations on local government borrowing, the regulation of municipal securities, federal taxation of municipal debt, and issues and procedures in municipal finance litigation. The text is supported with citations to applicable primary and secondary authorities, and includes an index. Joel A. Mintz is professor of law at Nova Southeastern University Law Center. Ronald H. Rosenberg is the Chancellor Professor of Law and the associate dean for academic affairs at William and Mary School of Law. Larry Bakken is a professor of law at Hamline University School of Law.

Municipal Legal Forms. St. Paul, MN: Thomson Reuters West (Clark Boardman Callaghan), 1994-date. 18 vols. Annual pocket supplements.
Cost: $2,147; supp.: 1993: $288; 1994: $239; 1995: $188.50; 1996: $298.50; 1997: $313.43; 1998: $332; 1999: $452.25; 2000: $386; 2001: $551; 2002: $627.50; 2003: $714; 2004: $595; 2005: $738; 2006: $726.50; 2007: $1,011; 2008: $1,125; 2009: $1,252; 2010: $964.50; 2011: $1,090; 2012: $1.221; 2013: $1,319; **Monthly Assured Print Price (APP)**: $113/$1,356;
Prepared by the publisher's editorial staff, this comprehensive collection contains over 2,400 municipal forms suitable for use in a wide variety of local government contexts. The forms are organized into 78 chapters, each of which is preceded by commentary entitled Suggestions and Reminders which lays out the scope of the chapter and provides general advice and considerations for the illumination of the user. The Suggestions and Reminders also provide citations to relevant primary and secondary sources including the appropriate sections of McQuillan, **Law of Municipal Corporations**, Sands and Libonati, **Local Government Law** and other works. Chapter coverage encompasses every imaginable topic from abutting owners and boundaries to zoning. This is the only work of its kind in print and an indispensable component of any complete municipal law collection.

Cost Saving Tips: Since most of your needs for municipal legal forms will be addressed by the bound volumes in this set, there is only a marginal necessity to keeping these volumes up-to-date if cost is a consideration. Use the set as a starting point and obtain additional forms at your public law library or draft your own using these as models. Investigate the cost on Westlaw. If you practice regularly in the field of municipal law, the **Municipal Law Practitioner** subscription on WestlawNext may be the best value given the variety of materials available on that platform. The pocket parts to the print set are just a cash cow for the publisher designed to ensnare the unwary consumer.

Reynolds, Osborne M., Jr. **Handbook of Local Government Law.** 3d ed. St. Paul, MN: West, 2009. 1 vol. (860 pp.) Availablew from West Academic.
Cost: $103; supplementation: 2013: $16.00 (2014).
An introductory student text covering the full range of issues relative to the form, powers, and operations of local governmental bodies. Includes discussion and analysis of such topics as units of local government, limits on state control of municipalities, relationship to federal government, powers, delegation of powers, municipal legislation, public officers, public employees, finances, control over utilities, local control over use of property, eminent domain, urban renewal and public housing, local planning, local regulations on trade and business, and more. The text is heavily documented with citations to cases, statutes, and a variety of secondary sources, including books and law review articles. Includes an extensive table of cases and index. Unlike most West Hornbooks, this one has been supplemented since its initial publication. Cost of both book and supplementation are reasonably priced since they are aimed at a broad law student market.

Special alert: Most West hornbooks and nutshells were sold by Thomson Reuters in 2013 to West Academic, a new entity that acquired those product lines directed at the academic market, including those of Foundation Press and Gilbert Law Summaries.

Rynard, Thomas W. **Insurance and Risk Management for State and Local Governments**. New York: Matthew Bender & Co., 1991-date. 1 vol. Looseleaf format or eBook.
Cost: $323 (print or eBook); supplementation: 1999: $107; 2000: $115; 2001: $123; 2002: $132; 2003: $139; 2004: $146; 2005: $155; 2006: $166; 2007: $179; 2008: $195; 2009: $211; 2010: $224; 2011: $233; 2012: $246; 2013: $263; 2014: $285.
Internet: 2004: $146; 2005: $155; 2006: $166; 2007: $179; 2008: $195; 2009: $211; 2010: $224; 2011: $233; 2012: $246; 2013: $263; 2014: $285.
Designed for the attorney who advises public entities on legal issues pertaining to risk management. Part I introduces the concepts of risk and risk management; Part II discusses the hazards and perils involving public entities, particularly governmental tort liability; and Part III examines insurance policies and risk management alternatives other than commercial insurance. There are specific chapters devoted to such topics as liability for civil rights violations, liability for law enforcement activities, fire protection activities, and liability for schools. The author also discusses the public official bond, risk sharing, and claims administration. Thomas Rynard is an attorney with the Jefferson City, Missouri office of Craft, Fridkin & Rhyne, practicing in the areas of administrative law, governmental legal issues (including tort defense), environmental law, and insurance regulatory practice. He is the author of numerous articles and other publications in the area of risk management for local government.

Varone, J. Curtis. **Legal Considerations for Fire and Emergency Services**. 2d ed. Clinton Park, NY: Thomson Delmar Learning, 2011. 1 vol. (647 pp.).
Cost: $105.95; paper: $84.49; from $59.75 on amazon.com (2014).
Designed primarily as a college level text on the law for fire and emergency service professionals, this volume may also serve as an invaluable guide to legal issues in the fire service, and a legal reference book for firefighters. Beginning with a lucid explanation of the American legal system and its sources of law, the author goes on to describe the types of fire departments and their basis in law. Attention is also given to administrative agencies (particularly OSHA), criminal procedure, civil liability issues, negligence, immunity from liability, contract law and employment issues, labor law and collective bargaining, employee rights and discrimination, sexual harassment and other forms of employment discrimination, fair labor, family medical leave, residency, drug testing, and public accountability laws. Each chapter includes excerpts of relevant case law and a variety of useful educational features, including sidebars, examples, learning objectives, review questions, and discussion questions. Appendices include the text of the U.S. Constitution, and materials in support of the substantive chapters, including relevant state fire and related laws, glossary, and index. The author is an attorney and Deputy Assistant Fire Chief for the City of Providence, RI. He teaches fire law at Providence College and lectures on a variety of fire and fire law related issues.

Zizka, Michael A., Timothy S. Hollister, Marcella Larsen, and Patricia E. Curtin. **State & Local Government Land Use Liability**. St. Paul, MN: Thomson Reuters West, 1997-date. 1 vol. Looseleaf format.
Cost: $247; supplementation: 1999: $40; 2000: $43.50; 2001: $51.50; 2002: $138; 2003: $69; 2004: $70; 2005: $74; 2006: $94; 2007: $99; 2008: $110; 2009: $119; 2010: $139; 2011: $152; 2012: $165; 2013: $346; **Monthly Assured Print Price (APP)**: $18/$216.
Designed for use by attorneys employed by municipalities and public agencies, this reference work addresses the complex web of laws and regulations which govern how local governmental entities handle land use questions. It examines how regulations are created, amended, and administered, how the municipality's regulatory authority is enforced, and identifies potential areas of liability. It also explains how to create programs to limit liability and how to successfully defend a land use case. The authors are all practicing attorneys in Hartford, CT who practice in the field of municipal law.

Additional titles in the field of Municipal Corporations are available from the following publishers: AMS Press, Matthew Bender, Press, William S. Hein & Co., Lewis Publications, Massachusetts Continuing Legal Education, Municipal Finance Officers Association of U.S. & Canada, Municipal Research & Services Center of Washington, New York State Bar Association, Practising Law Institute, State University of New York Press, Thomson Reuters West, West Academic. See Appendix B for addresses and telephone numbers.

Natural Resources and Energy Law

American Law of Mining. 2d ed. Edited by the Rocky Mountain Mineral Law Foundation. New York: Matthew Bender & Co., 1984-date. 6 vols. Looseleaf format. Annual supplementation.
Cost: $1,342; supplementation: 2000: $255; 2001: $273; 2002: $293; 2003: $308; 2004: $335; 2005: $359; 2006: $385; 2007: $416; 2008: $453; 2009: $492; 2010: $531; 2011: $499; 2012: $529; 2013: $566; 2014: $656; CD-ROM: $1,700; renewal: 2014: $643.62; eBook; $1,342; renewal: 2014: $656.
This is an exhaustive discussion and analysis of all aspects of mining law, except for oil and gas, covering such topics as federal lands and mineral leases, mining claims, Indian and state mineral interests, creation and transfer of mineral interests and title examination, ancillary use and water rights, organization and financing of mining operations, mine closings, private leases and acquisitions, joint exploration and development, income and production taxation, environmental regulation, administrative practice, mining and milling operations, and Canadian mining law. First published in 1961 under the auspices of the Rocky Mountain Mineral Law Foundation, the second edition was prepared under the editorship of mining lawyer Cheryl Outerbridge. Dozens of subject specialists, recruited from law schools, corporations, and private practice, were involved in the preparation of this work. The work provides extensive discussion of the historical evolution of mining laws, as well as the more recent influence of environmental laws and regulations. The authors provide citations to cases, statutes, regulations, and a wide variety of secondary authorities, including government publications and law review articles.

Beck, Robert E. **Water and Water Rights.** 3d ed. Charlottesville, VA: LexisNexis (Michie), 2009-date. 8 vols. Annual pocket parts.
Cost: $1,298; supplementation: 1993: $180; 1994: $315 (incl. one rev. vol.); 1995: $210; 1996: $356;1997: $245; 1998: $255; 1999: $270; 2000; $280; 2001: $728; 2002; $461; 2003: $163; 2004: $170; 2005: $536; 2006: $557; 2007: $618; 2008: $667; 2009: $998; 2010: $1,028; 2011: $1,058; 2012: $1,100; 2013: $1,166.
This multi-volume treatise is a complete revision of the first edition originally edited by Robert Emmett Clark between 1967 and 1976 which has been recognized as the leading work in the field. Edited by Robert Beck, Professor at the Southern Illinois University School of Law, this edition is written by a team of thirteen legal scholars and practicing attorneys. It provides the environmental attorney with a thorough and rigorous analysis of the law governing water, water rights, riparianism, prior appropriation, quantitative groundwater law, the public right to use water in place, federal and Indian rights, powers and activities, interstate water allocation, international waters, environmental controls, water pollution and water quality control, drainage, flooding and wetlands preservation, and planning. Volume six includes surveys of the laws of the fifty states and major river basins written by local experts as well as a glossary of relevant terms. Volume seven includes Cumulative Tables of Cases, Statutes and Index. This work not only addresses the statutory and common law bases of water law, but also provides an integrated and thoroughly documented background discussion of substantive topics and issues of interest to the environmental attorney. The authors provide the user with exhaustive citations to applicable state and federal cases and statutes, as well as significant secondary sources such as law review articles and leading governmental and professional studies. There is no other work in the field which matches this one in terms of coverage and scholarly analysis. For the attorney specializing in water and environmental issues, this work should be an essential purchase. Supplementation costs are not unreasonable given the size and scope of the set.

Energy Law and Transactions. Edited by David J. Muchow and William A. Mogel. New York: Matthew Bender & Co., 1990-date. 6 vols. Looseleaf format and eBook. Supplemented twice annually.
Cost: $1,878; supplementation: 2005: $673; 2006: $754; 2007: $848; 2008: $920; 2009: $998; 2010: $1,054; 2011: $1,107; 2012: $1,173; 2013: $1,255; 2014: $1,370; CD-ROM: $1,460; renewal: 2004: $620; 2005: $663; 2006: $743; 2007: $802; 2008: $890; 2009: $998; 2010: $1,054; 2011: $1,120; 2012: $1,187; 2013: $1,255; 2014: $1,370; eBook: $1,708; renewal: 2014: $1,370.
This wide-ranging work addresses the legal and business-related aspects of a variety of energy sources, including oil, gas, electricity, coal, hydroelectricity, solar, nuclear, biomass, and cogeneration. The discussion examines every aspect of these energy sources, from exploration and production through transmission, distribution, and consumption. More than 100 energy law experts contributed sections of this work, which covers such areas as basic energy law facts and principles, energy transactions and business planning, energy financing, energy taxation, conventional energy sources: production, transmission, distribution, and end uses, new energy technologies, transportation of energy, antitrust, energy and the environment, practice and procedure unique to energy transactions, and international energy transactions. The work gives appropriate attention to the highly volatile regulatory environment in which energy law operates. In addition to the inclusion of numerous citations to cases, statutes, regulations, and other regulatory issuances, the authors provide a variety of model forms, tariffs, checklists, and illustrations to aid the practitioner. The work is edited by David Muchow, an energy consultant and attorney practicing in Arlington, VA, and William Mogel, a partner at Squire, Sanders & Dempsey, a law firm with a global energy practice. The contributors are drawn from a variety of law firms, law schools, energy firms, and governmental agencies. The scope of this work makes it an ideal candidate for the library of any law firm specializing in energy law questions.

Glicksman, Robert L. and George C. Coggins. **Public Natural Resources Law**. St. Paul, MN: Thomson Reuters West (Clark Boardman Callaghan), 1990-date. 3 vols. Annual supplementation. Also on ProView eBook.
Cost: $2,360; supplementation: 1996: $330; 1997: $350.50; 1998: $372; 1999: $402; 2000: $426; 2001: $504.50; 2002: $716; 2003: $612; 2004: 685.50; 2005: $762; 2006: $837; 2007: $1,122.50; 2008: $1,286; 2009: $1,519; 2010: $1,377; 2011: $1,369.50; 2012: $1,768; 2013: $1,733; **Monthly Assured Print Price (APP)**: $172/$2,064.
As increasing amounts of land are brought under federal

control, the management of these lands and their resources is becoming a more significant and contentious issue. This treatise examines the constitutional framework within which the federal government exercises control over these lands, the legal issues involved in federal land management, federal monetary liability, the overlay doctrines and mechanisms, environmental issues, federal land use and resource preservation, public water resources management, public mineral resources management, and other related issues. The authors also address such issues as multiple use, sustained yield management of public surface resources, federal reclamation projects, public onshore oil and gas resources, and multiple mineral development. Robert L. Glicksman is Wagstaff Professor of Law, University of Kansas and a widely published authority on matters of public lands and natural resources law. George Coggins is Tyler Professor of Law, University of Kansas, and a frequent co-author with Professor Glicksman.

Hemingway, Richard W., et al. **Hemingway Oil and Gas Law and Taxation**. 4th ed. St. Paul, MN: West, 2004-date. 1 vol. (832 pp.). Hornbook Series. Available from West Academic.
Cost: $103.00; no supplementation between editions (2014).
This student textbook provides a general intriduction to the law governing oil and gas, from the definition of a mineral estate to the creation of interests in the oil and gas mineral estate by the landowner, the conveyances, partititon and adverse possession of the mineral estate, trespass. surface and sub-surface, and third-party claims, oil and gas leases, royalties, transfer of interests, federal taxation of oil and gas interests and transactions, and development costs. The text is supported by extensive references to applicable law governing oil and gas interests. The volume also includes a table of cases and index. The lead author is the Eugene O. Kuntz Professor of Oil and Gas and Natural Resources Law, Emeritus, University of Oklahoma.

Law of Federal Oil and Gas Leases. Edited by the Rocky Mountain Mineral Law Foundation. New York: Matthew Bender & Co., 1964-date. 2 vols. Looseleaf format or eBook. Annual supplementation.
Cost: $954; supplementation: 2000: $240; 2001: $251; 2002: $269; 2003: $283; 2004: $299; 2005: $320; 2006: $359; 2007: $404; 2008: $440; 2009: $477; 2010: $515; 2011: $529; 2012: $560; 2013: $628; 2014: $652.
This treatise on the law of oil and gas leases on federal lands was prepared under the auspices of the Rocky Mountain Mineral Law Foundation. The chapter coverage includes discussion of leasing legislation, options and rights to acquire, bonds, federal land records, title examinations, outer continental shelf leases, leasing in Alaska, lessee and transferee qualification, con-competitive leases, right-of-way leasing, royalties, surface management, Indian leasing, exploration, drilling, producing, and operating regulations, assignments and transfers of interests, administrative remedies and judicial review, and state and local regulation. Volume two includes a table of acronyms, definitions and abbreviations. First published in 1964, the work is the product of numerous scholars and experts in the field.

Lowe, John S. **Lowe's Oil and Gas Law in a Nutshell**. 5th ed. St. Paul, MN: West, 2009. 1 vol. (474 pp.). Paperbound. Available from West Academic.
Cost: $41; amazon.com: $29.99; kindle: $20.84 (2014).
This West Nutshell addresses the law governing the development of privately owned mineral rights. While the focus is on privately owned mineral rights, the text also addresses the impact of federal ownership of lands and the rules governing utilization of minerals on those lands. John S. Lowe is Professor of Law, Southern Methodist University, past chair of the ABA's Natural Resources, Energy and Environmental Law Section, and Trustee of the Rocky Mountain Mineral Law Foundation.

Martin, Patrick and Bruce M. Kramer. **Oil and Gas Law**. Abridged 5th Edition. New York: Matthew Bender & Co., 2013. 1 vol. (678 pp.). Softbound or eBook. Annual.
Cost: $205.00 (2014).
This abridgement of the more comprehensive treatise on oil and gas law contains the basic and more significant elements, while eliminating the more detailed discussion and footnotes of the full work. Included are discussions of the scientific and engineering background of oil and gas law, the nature of interests in oil and gas, oil and gas conveyancing, grants and reservations affecting working interest, concurrent and successive interests, the oil and gas lease--express provisions, division orders, transfer orders, gas purchase contracts, implied covenants, and pooling and unitization. This work contains the table of contents to the complete, eight-volume treatise, with bold headings indicating which sections are covered in the abridgement. The original authors devoted the bulk of their professional and professorial lives to research and writing in the field of oil and gas law. The work was originally authored by Howard Williams, professor emeritus at Stanford University School of Law and the late Charles Myers, who was, for nearly fifty years, a student, colleague, co-author, and friend of Howard Williams, as well as dean of Stanford Law School. The second abridged edition is authored by Patrick Martin, the Campanile Professor of Mineral Law who has taught at the Louisiana State University Law Center since 1977 and Professor Bruce M. Kramer, the Maddox Professor of Law at Texas Tech University School of Law. Professor Kramer is the co-author of a four-volume treatise entitled **The Law of Pooling and Unitization** and the co-author of Williams & Meyers **Oil and Gas Law**.

Maxfield, Peter C., James L. Houghton, and Robert M. Allen. **Taxation of Mining Operations**. New York: Matthew Bender & Co., 1981-date. 1 vol. Looseleaf format. Annual supplementation.
Cost: $456; supplementation: 2000: $175; 2001: $187; 2002: $201; 2003: $212; 2004: $223; 2005: $268; 2006: $279; 2007: $287; 2008: $310; 2009: $335; 2010: $365; 2011: $355; 2012: $376; 2013: $432; 2014: $445; eBook: $456; renewal: 2014: $445.
A review and analysis of federal income taxation as it applies to the mining of minerals other than oil and gas. Among the topics discussed are prerequisites to the depletion deduction, computation of the depletion deduction, lease payments unrelated to production, mineral properties and aggregations, exploration and development expenses, cost recovery, credits and losses, the alternative minimum tax, production payments, sales and leases, exchanges of mineral property, sharing arrangements, partnerships and corporations, operations on American Indian lands, foreign operations, Canadian income taxation, and

Mexican income taxation. The text provides extensive citations to relevant federal statutes, regulations, revenue rulings, and court decisions. Peter Maxfield is professor of law, emeritus, University of Wyoming College of Law. James L. Houghton is a retired partner with Ernst & Young, Tulsa, OK. Robert M. Allen, C. P.A., is a partner with Ernst & Young in Cleveland, OH.

McGrew, James H. **FERC: Federal Energy Regulatory Commission**. 2d ed. Chicago: American Bar Association, Section of Environment, Energy, and Resources, 2009. 1 vol. (294 pp.). Paperbound. Basic Practice Series.
Cost: $89.95 ($79.95 to members); from $44.14 on amazon.com (2014).
The Federal Energy Regulatory Commission came to life in 1920 as the Federal Power Commission (FPC), charged with regulating only the licensing of nonfederal hydroelectric projects. Its authority was subsequently expanded by the Federal Power Act of 1935 and the Natural Gas Act of 1938, both of which extended the federal government's role in regulating sales for resale and transmission or transportation of electricity and natural gas in interstate commerce. In 1977, Congress passed the Department of Energy Organization Act creating the Department of Energy, abolishing the FPC, and substituting the Federal Energy Regulatory Commission (FERC) in its place. In addition to the areas of regulation already under its purview, Congress also delegated to the FERC the regulation of oil pipelines under the Interstate Commerce Act, a responsibility previously exercised under the Interstate Commerce Commission. Since 1977, FERC has had responsibility for four major energy industries: hydroelectric, electric utility, natural gas pipelines, and oil pipelines industries. These regulatory duties are exercised primarily by promulgating regulations and adjudicating disputes on a case-by-case basis. The deregulation initiated by the FERC is best described as restructuring, a process which has, for example, transformed the natural gas industry and its pipelines into common carriers, providing open access transportation primarily to third parties. Following an historical overview of the FERC and its current structure, this volume directs its primary attention to the regulation of the natural gas and electric utility industries, those areas that receive the greatest share of its regulatory attention. The appendices include frequently asked questions, brief summaries of key cases, a glossary of terms, bibliography, table of authorities, and index. The author, a graduate of Harvard Law School and a partner at Bruder, Gentile and Marcoux LLP in Washington, DC, represents electric utilities and natural gas companies before the Federal Energy Regulatory Commission.

Oil and Gas Library [CD-ROM]. New York: Matthew Bender & Co. One disc. Updated quarterly. Available for Windows. Search Engine: Folio. Includes toll-free support. Also available on Internet.
Cost: $4,642 per year (annual subscription); renewal: 2000: $1,280; 2001: $1,370; 2002: $1,466; 2003: $1540; 2004: $1,617; 2005: $1,730; 2006: $1,852; 2007: $2,000; 2008: $2,220; 2009: $2,398; 2010: $2,518; 2011: $2,644; 2012: $2,803; 2013: $2,999; 2014: $3,338.46.
Contains the text of the following Matthew Bender treatises: **Law of Federal Oil and Gas Leases**, **Oil and Gas Law**, **50th Annual Institute on Oil and Gas Law and Taxation**, **The Law of Pooling and Unitization**, and the **Law of Oil and Gas Leases**. Subscription must be maintained or product will time expire. Internet subscriptions may also be specially packaged to meet the specific needs of the subscriber (see sales representative for details).

Regulation of the Gas Industry. Edited by the American Gas Association. New York: Matthew Bender & Co., 1981-date. 5 vols. Looseleaf format or eBook. Annual supplementation.
Cost: $2,874 (print); supplementation: 2000: $730; 2001: $781; 2002: $836; 2003: $878; 2004: $922; 2005: $987; 2006: $1,106; 2007: $1,244; 2008: $1,356; 2009: $1,471; 2010: $1,553; 2011: $1,631; 2012: $1,729; 2013: $1,850; 2014: $2,019; eBook: $2,613; renewal: 2014: $2,019.
A comprehensive examination of the gas industry from a legal perspective, this work provides a thorough discussion of the gas industry and the regulatory framework in which it operates, both historical and current. Additional chapters discuss pipeline organizations and operations, distributor organizations and operations, wellhead price regulations, costs and revenues (including utility rates, operating expenses, taxes, and rate of return), pipeline rates, tariffs, and schedules, distributor rates, tariffs and schedules, and administrative law and judicial review. The set also includes agency information. a glossary of gas terms, and the full text of numerous statutes and regulations applicable to the gas industry. While the work lacks the unified perspective of a single author, it benefits greatly from the varied expertise of its many contributors. Produced under the auspices and editorial leadership of the American Gas Association, Regulation of the Gas Industry was originally conceived by David J. Muchow, its General Counsel and Corporate Secretary. Individual author with experience in their respective areas were selected by the Board of Editors. An essential work for any attorney representing gas companies or dealing with the gas industry.

Schroeder, Lauren E. **Oil and Gas Law: A Legal Research Guide**. Buffalo, NY: William S. Hein & Co., Inc., 2012. 1 vol. (93 pp.). Hardbound.
Cost: $60.00; from $57.00 on amazon.com (2014).
Oil and gas law consists of statutes, regulations and case law at both the national and state levels, as well as the associated primary, secondary and online sources useful to research in this field. This annotated research guide explains the evolution of oil and gas law, following the discovery of these substances in the United States during the 19th century. The author provides an annotated listing of the major sources of oil and gas law, including the Mineral Leasing Act of 1920, the Natural Gas Act of 1938, the Natural Gas Policy Act of 1978, and the Outer Continental Shelf Lands Act of 1953, among others. She also lists those federal agencies with oversight over oil and gas exploration, extraction, and transportation, and the sources for their decisions, and lists the Congressional committees with oversight over oil and gas and related issues. The guide also lists the state statutes governing oil and gas, and the state agencies with responsibility in the field. She also provides an annotated bibliography of secondary sources, including nutshells, dictionaries, hornbooks, periodicals, Institutes, continuing legal education materials, and treatises. Additional chapters are devoted to online sources (both subscription-based and free Internet sources), international

oil and gas law, online sources of for international oil and gas law research, and research on oil spills and oil pollution at both the national and state levels. The author is Reference/Research Librarian at the University of Houston O'Quinn Law Library.

Summers, Walter Lee. **The Law of Oil and Gas**. 3d ed. Permanent edition. St. Paul, MN: Thomson Reuters West, 1954-date. 8 vols. in 10. Annual pocket parts.
Cost: $1,101; supplementation: 1996: $159; 1997: $174; 1998: $183; 1999: $198; 2000: $214; 2001: $238; 2002: $269; 2003: $307; 2004: $453; 2005: $298; 2006: $342; 2007: $380; 2008: $721.50; 2009: $758; 2010: $500; 2011: $512; 2012: $564; 2013: $655; **Monthly Assured Print Price (APP)**: $70/$840.
Originally authored by the late Walter Lee Summers (1888-1963), this comprehensive treatise examines the full range of topics related the law of oil and gas, including physical and economic facts, landowner's rights, privileges, duties, powers, and liabilities, legal interests created by oil and gas leases, the Habendum clause, drilling, rental and surrender clauses, construction of oil and gas leases, express and implied covenants of the lessee restricting development, remedies of the lessor for nondevelopment, divisibility of covenants in oil and gas leases, termination of lease by surrender, assignment of interests, rents and royalties, drilling contracts, mechanic's liens, mining partnerships, pipe lines, taxation, and leasing and production of oil and gas from state, federal, and Indian lands. Volumes 5-8 contain statutes regulating the production and transportation of oil and gas, forms on leasing, production, and transportation, table of cases, and index. Current pocket supplements are prepared by Jerome Kahnke.

Tarlock, A. Daniel. **Law of Water Rights and Resources**. St. Paul, MN: Thomson Reuters West (Clark Boardman Callaghan), 1988-date. Annual replacement volumes.
Cost: 2013 Edition: $798; 2012 Edition: $732; supplementation: 1996: $108; 1997: $113.40; 1998: $120; 1999: $152; 2000: $164; 2001: $161; 2002: $189.50; 2003: $216; 2004: $242; 2005: $257; 2006: $298.50; 2007: $332; 2007: $332; 2008: $370; 2009: $413.50; 2010: $484; 2011: $496; 2012: $550.50 (1st annual replacement vol.); **Monthly Assured Print Price (APP)**: $67/$804.
The administration and regulation of water rights as well as the allocation and distribution of water is a major source of concern throughout the United States, but particularly in the Western states where the pressures of development and requirements of irrigation (90% of current usage) press upon limited supplies. This volume in the publisher's Environmental Law Series addresses a variety of environmental and regulatory issues to ensure compliance with federal, state, and local laws and regulations. The volume's coverage includes an overview of water law, the hydrologic cycle, the common law of riparian rights, the law of groundwater allocation, the prior appropriation doctrine, appropriation of groundwater, adjudication of water rights, public water use rights, federal allocation and regulation of water, interstate allocation, and international water allocation. A. Daniel Tarlock is Distinguished Professor of Law and Director of the Program in Environmental and Energy Law at the Chicago-Kent School of Law and an internationally recognized expert in environmental law and the law of land and water use.

Tomain, Joseph P. **Tomain's Energy Resource Law in a Nutshell**. 2d ed. St. Paul, MN: West, 2011. 1 vol. (540 pp.). Available from West Academic.
Cost: $41; from $24.44 on amazon.com (2014).
A useful overview of the primary issues and topics involved in the areas of energy and natural resources law. Energy law encompasses all the component parts of the energy fuel cycle, as well as the market processes and governmental policies that interact with this cycle. Natural resources law encompasses the topics of public lands and resources law, environmental law and assessment, minerals law, timber law, and water law. The chapters also address such topics as economics and natural resources markets, resource management and protection, environmental law, environmental assessment and NEPA, federal energy policy, developing energy resources, and energy conversion and distribution. Jan Laitos is the John A. Carver, Jr. Professor of Law and Director, Natural Resources and Environmental Law Program, University of Denver College of Law and has written extensively on issues related to public lands and private property. Joseph Tomain is Dean and Nippert Professor of Law, University of Cincinnati College of Law.

Williams, Howard R., and Charles J. Meyers. **Oil and Gas Law**. New York: Matthew Bender & Co., 1959-date. 8 vols. Looseleaf format. Annual supplementation. Also available on CD-ROM and eBook.
Cost: $2,428; supplementation: 2000: $375; 2001: $401; 2002: $430; 2003: $452; 2004: $479; 2005: $513; 2006: $549; 2007: $593; 2008: $640; 2009: $694; 2010: $733; 2011: $770; 2012: $820; 2013: $877; 2014: $958; eBook: $2,207; renewal: 2014: $958.
Since the appearance of the initial two volumes in 1959, this now classic treatise on the law of oil and gas has grown to eight volumes and become the most authoritative source for detailed discussion and analysis of the topic. Frequently cited by the courts, the authors' discussion embraces such topics as conveyancing, oil and gas leases, implied covenants, pooling and unitization, division and transfer orders, gas purchase contracts, as well as taxation, accounting techniques, drafting instruments, title examinations, estate administration, and the preparation of wills and trusts. Volumes 1-6 contain the substantive discussion; volume 7 contains forms, a table of cases, and index. Volume 8, the Manual of Oil & Gas Terms Annotated, contains definitions of more than 5,000 legal, engineering, industrial, and tax terms, with references to relevant cases, law review articles, and industry and professional publications. This work was originally the product of one of the most successful collaborative partnerships by two legal scholars. Currently the Robert E. Paradise Professor of Natural Resources Law, Emeritus, Stanford University, Howard R. Williams has been immersed in the subject of oil and gas law since joining the faculty of the University of Texas School of Law in 1946. The late Charles Myers was, for roughly forty years, a student, colleague, co-author, and friend of Howard Williams, as well the dean of Stanford Law School. The work is now updated and revised by Bruce M. Kramer, Maddox Professor of Law at Texas Tech University School of Law, and Patrick H. Martin, Campanile Professor of Mineral Law at Louisiana State University Law Center, both experts in the field.

Additional titles in the fields of Natural Resources and Energy Law are available from the following publishers: American Bar Association, Matthew Bender, Foundation Press, Government Institutes, Island Press, Kluwer Academic Press, Kluwer Law International, LexisNexis, National Conference of State Legislatures, Oxford University Press, RIA Group, Thomson Reuters West, United Nations Publications, West Academic. See Appendix B for addresses and telephone numbers.

Nonprofit Corporations

Blazek, Jody. **Tax Planning and Compliance for Tax-Exempt Organizations: Forms, Checklists, Procedures**. 5th ed. New York: John Wiley & Sons, 2012-date. 1 vol. (896 pp.). Annual supplementation.
Cost: $262; e-book: $209.99; supplementation: 2013: $150; 4th ed.: 2005: 0; 2006: $70; 2007: $75; 2008: $85; 2009: $95; 2010: $105; 3d ed.: 2000: $60; 2001: $65; 2002: $70; 2003: $78; 2004: new edition.
This book is designed to remind nonprofit organizations of their privileges and responsibilities under the Internal Revenue Code and to aid them in meeting the public disclosure requirements under the law. The author discusses the process of qualifying for exemption and the types of organizations which are eligible for §501(c)(3) status, including religious, charitable, educational, scientific, and labor organizations, and social clubs and public charities. She also examines the status of private foundations, IRS recognition, maintaining tax exempt status, and the process of communicating with the IRS. The text is fully supported with references to relevant cases, statutes, regulations, Revenue Rulings, and secondary sources. The author is a partner in Blazek & Vetterling, a Houston CPA firm specializing in tax and financial planning for exempt organizations. This volume is part of the Wiley Nonprofit Law, Finance, and Management Series.

Cafardi, Nicholas P. and Jaclyn Fabean Cherry. **Understanding Nonprofit and Tax Exempt Organizations**. 2nd ed. New York: LexisNexis, 2012. 1 vol. (450 pp.) Paperbound.
Cost: $45; eBook: $36; from $16.15 on amazon.com (2014).
This volume in the publisher's *Understanding* series is intended as an introductory law school text for courses in the law of nonprofit and tax-exempt organizations. The authors examine four types of organizations: nonprofits, tax exempt organizations, charitable organizations, and private foundations. In addition to an examination of the laws governing nonprofits, the authors direct their attention to the rules, regulations, and tests that must be followed in order to obtain and retain tax-exempt status. Of primary significance in this regard are those various organizations falling under the IRC 501 (c)(3) status, including charitable, educational, scientific, religious, healthcare, and arts organizations, each of which is given chapter coverage. Political organizations under IRC Sec. 527 are also discussed, as are the issues of unrelated business income tax, charitable contributions, fundraising, and the process of securing and maintaining tax-exempt status. Selective citations to relevant IRC sections and court decisions augment the text. Appendices include relevant IRS forms, a table of cases, and a table of statutes. Nicholas Cafardi is Dean Emeritus and Professor of Law at Duquesne University. Jaclyn Fabean Cherry is Professor of Law at the University of South Carolina and a nationally recognized expert in the field of nonprofit and tax-exempt field for over twenty years.

Desiderio, Robert J. **Planning Tax-Exempt Organizations**. Newark, NJ: LexisNexis (Matthew Bender), 1983-date. 1 vol. Looseleaf format or eBook. Annual supplementation.
Cost: $315 (print or eBook); supplementation: 2010: $147; 2011: $156; 2012: $165; 2013: $172; 2014: $177; eBook: $315.
Section 501 of the Internal Revenue Code provides for the organization of various educational, cultural and charitable institutions, religious organizations, private foundations, community foundations and business leagues as tax-exempt entities. This reference work provides guidance in the process of planning a non-profit tax-exempt organization and satisfying IRS requirements to achieve and retain status as a tax-exempt entity. Among the topics discussed are the organizational and operational tests required of such organizations, their application to the various types of tax-exempt entities, disqualified persons, the taxation of unrelated business income, excise tax on investment income, self dealing, failure to distribute income, application requirements, handling IRS audits, and more. The author is Dean and Professor of Law at the University of New Mexico School of Law and a former staff member of the Legislative and Regulations Division of the Internal Revenue Service.

Fox, Richard. **Charitable Giving: Taxation, Planning and and Strategies** (formerly **Charitable Giving and Solicitation)**. Valhalla, NY: Warren, Gorham & Lamont, 1992-date. 1 vol. Looseleaf format.
Cost: print or online: $1,005 per year (2014).
This service provides comprehensive and in-depth analytical coverage of the laws and practices governing charitable contributions and deductions and planned and deferred giving programs. The chapters address the subjects of development and professional fund-raising ideas, regulation of charitable solicitations, allowance of deductions, special limitations, estate, gift and trusts rules, property gifts, jointly held and community property, gift planning, charitable remainder trusts, pooled income funds, charitable lead trusts, charitable gift annuities, bargain sales, and community and private foundations. Additional features include discussion of special tax situations, forms, worksheets and tables. There are also sample IRS approved formats for the design of tax-advantages giving programs and case histories of effective fund raising campaigns and techniques. The text is illuminated by practical tips and warnings that illustrate the substantive discussion, as well as monthly reports that alert the user to the latest charitable giving laws, cases, rulings, and IRS requirements. This product is specially designed for professionals involved in advising nonprofit and charitable organizations and clients making donations or bequests to such organizations. Richard L. Fox is a partner in the tax department of Dilworth Paxton where his practice involves a broad range of tax areas, including nonprofit organizations, corporations, partnerships and individuals, as well as trusts and estates. He received his law degree from Temple University School of Law and LL.M. in Taxation from New York University.

Cost Saving Tip: While this work has much to recommend it, it is also an example of the phenomenon by which legal publishers have turned monographic titles into serials with high annual supplementation costs. If you have other sources for current tax information, consider dropping the standing order and simply re-purchasing this work every few years. Even subscribing in alternate years will reduce your annual cost by more than $500.00, while providing annual supplementation.

Hill, Frances R. and Douglas M. Mancino. **Taxation of Exempt Organizations**. Valhalla, NY: Warren, Gorham & Lamont of RIA, 2002-date. 1 vol. Looseleaf format. Also available online. Updated as needed.
Cost: print: $385; online: $600 per year (2014).
A comprehensive guide to the law governing 501(c)(3) and other organizations recognized as tax-exempt by the federal government. The work provides in-depth coverage of the tax issues governing such organizations, including exempt activities, operating for a public benefit and the private doctrines, lobbying, political activities, public policy requirements, and the public charity status of. 501(c)(3)'s. The author also discusses a variety of other exempt organizations, including social welfare organizations, business leagues, agricultural and labor organizations, social and fraternal organizations, and title holding companies. There is also discussion of matters related to unrelated business income, special rules for social clubs, special structures and transactions, and procedural requirements, compliance, and audits, and foreign organizations and operations abroad. The text includes citations to most relevant cases, statutes, regulations, revenue rulings, important private letter rulings, technical advice memoranda, and continuing professional education materials. Frances R. Hill is a Professor of Law and Director of the Graduate Program in Taxation at the University of Miami School of Law. Douglas M. Mancino is a partner in the law firm McDermott, Will & Emery, and a Past Chair of the Exempt Organizations Committee of the ABA Section of Taxation.

Hopkins, Bruce R. **Fundraising Law Made Easy**. Hoboken, NJ: John Wiley & Sons, 2009. 1 vol. (362 pp.).
Cost: $45; eBook: $29.99; from $24.34 on amazon.com (2014).
Designed as a resource for board members of nonprofit organizations, this volume provides, in layman's language, a discussion of the basic legal and financial principles and practices governing the operation of such organizations. Following an introduction to the law of fundraising for charity, the remaining chapters include a fundraiser's law primer, state regulation of charitable fundraising, public charities and private foundations, federal annual reporting requirements, charitable giving rules, unrelated business rules, other federal tax law regulation of fundraising, fundraising and constitutional law, fundraising and governance, fundraising and IRS audits, and perspectives and commentaries. An invaluable resource for the novice in matters of fundraising law as well as a useful review for legal professionals with limited responsibility for nonprofits, particularly as it relates to IRS requirements. Bruce R. Hopkins is a senior partner in the Kansas City firm of Polsinelli, Shughart PC where he specializes in the representation of charitable and other nonprofit organizations. He is nation's most prolific author on the law of nonprofit, tax-exempt and charitable organizations and the editor of Wiley's Nonprofit Law, Finance, and Management Series.

Hopkins, Bruce R. **The Law of Tax-Exempt Organizations.** 10th ed. New York: John Wiley & Sons, 2011-date. 1 vol. (1,296 pp.) Supplemented annually.
Cost: $315; e-book: $299.99; supplementation: 2013: $225; 2014: $225; 9th ed.: 2008: $80; 2009: $85; 2010: $105; 8th ed.: 2005: $90; 2006: $95; 7th edition: 1999: $75; 2000: $80; 2001: $94; 2002: $90; 2003: $85; 2004: new edition; 6th ed.: 1993: $50; 1994: $55; 1995: $60; 1996: $65; 1997: $75; 1998: new edition. Also available on WestlawNext.
This scholarly treatise examines in depth what has variously been termed the «third sector,» the «voluntary sector,» the «private sector,» or the «independent sector,» of American society. It is an outgrowth of the author's course in tax-exempt organizations given at George Washington University's National Law Center since 1973. Its intended audience consists of lawyers, accountants, managers, fundraising executives, and volunteers interested in furthering the objectives of various nonprofit organizations. The author's discussion includes an introduction to tax-exempt organizations, an examination of various types of charitable organizations, other tax-exempt organizations, private foundations, qualification of exempt organizations, feeder organizations and unrelated income taxation, inter-organizational structures and operational forms. The Appendices include a listing of IRS Code Sections governing nonprofits, and tables of cases, IRS Rulings and Revenue Procedures, Private Letter Rulings, IRS Private Letter Rulings Cited in text, IRS Key District Offices, and a subject index. The author provides citations to relevant IRS Code Sections, cases, statutes, and regulations, as well as secondary sources. An essential reference for the attorney representing nonprofits or individuals involved in their management. Formerly published by Wiley Law Publications.

Hopkins, Bruce R. and Jody Blazak. **The Legal Answer Book for Private Foundations**. New York: John Wiley & Sons, 2001. 1 vol. (384 pp.). Paperbound.
Cost: $95; from $16.30 on amazon.com (2014).
This volume is one in a series that addresses the federal and state laws governing nonprofit organizations. This entry provides a basic overview of issues related to the law and governance of private foundations in a question and answer format that will appeal particularly to non-lawyers, including foundation board members, staff, accountants, and family members. The questions and answers are organized into 17 chapters, including basic legal definitions, self dealing, mandatory payout requirements, excess business holdings, jeopardizing investments, taxable expenditures, unrelated business activities, public charities, termination of private foundation statutes, types of foundations, alternatives to private foundations, the tax exemption recognition process, and the charitable contribution deductions. The authors are leading experts and authors in the field.

Hopkins, Bruce R. **Legal Responsibilities of Nonprofit Boards**. 2d ed. Washington, DC: BoardSource, 2009. 1 vol. (37 pp.). Paperbound.
Cost: $19 (members); $29 (non-members); from $24.49 on amazon.com (2014).

This brief pamphlet by the country's leading expert on nonprofit law and governance provides board members of nonprofit organizations with a brief introduction to their legal and ethical responsibilities and liabilities. It is the author's aim to provide sufficient information in non-technical language to enable board members to protect themselves and their organizations from mistakes and liabilities.

Hopkins, Bruce R. and Jody Blazak. **Private Foundations: Tax Law and Compliance**. 4th ed. New York: John Wiley & Sons, 2014-date. 1 vol. Also available as an E-book.
Cost: $300.00; e-book: $209.99; no supplementation to date; 3d ed.: 2010: $85; 2011: $95; 2012: $150; 2013: $150.00; 2d ed.: 2004: $65; 2005: $70; 2006: $75; 2007: $80; 1st edition: 2000: $60; 2001: $65; 2002: $70.
An excellent overview of the tax rules and regulations applicable to private foundations co-authored by a lawyer and a tax accountant. The authors provide detailed suggestions for tax compliance with line-by-line instructions for sample IRS forms and citations to relevant laws and regulations.

Hopkins, Bruce R. **The Second Legal Answer Book for Nonprofit Organizations**. New York: John Wiley & Sons, 1998. 1 vol. (303 pp.). Paperbound. No supplementation between editions
Cost: $145 (2014).
Designed for use by nonprofit executives, board members, fundraising professionals, lawyers and accountants, this volume provides an overview of the law governing nonprofit corporations in an easy to use question and answer format. Chapters cover intermediate sanctions, competition and commerciality, partnerships and joint ventures, acquiring tax-exempt status, membership associations, social welfare organizations, social clubs, political organizations, private foundation rules, ownership of interests in business enterprises, annual return preparation--in general, annual return preparation--special considerations, and disclosure and distribution rules. Endnotes provide citations to relevant cases, statutes, regulations, proposed regulations, and revenue rulings. The author is one America's leading authorities on the subject of nonprofit organizations, a lawyer with the law firm of Polsinelli, White, Vardeman, and Shalton, and the author of eleven books on nonprofit and tax-exempt organizations.

Hopkins, Bruce R. **Starting and Managing a Nonprofit Organization: A Legal Guide.** 6th ed. New York: John Wiley & Sons, 2013. 1 vol. (384 pp.). Paperbound. No supplementation between editions. Also available as an E-Book.
Cost: $60; eBook: $39.99; from $31.25 on amazon.com (2014).
A basic guide to planning, forming and operating a nonprofit organization with attention to changing statutes, rules and regulations. The procedures are illustrated using a fictitious organization. Includes checklists and a glossary.

Hopkins, Bruce R. **The Tax Law of Charitable Giving.** 5th ed. New York: John Wiley & Sons, 2014-date. 1 vol. (968 pp.) Annual supplementation.
Cost: $300; no supplementation to date; 4th ed,: 2011: $70; 2012: $125; 2013: $150; 3d ed.: 2006: $65; 2007: $70; 2008: $75; 2009: $80; 2d ed.: 2001: $60; 2002: $65; 2003: $70; 2004: $80; 1st ed.: 1994: $45; 1995: $50; 1996: $55; 1997: $67.50; 1998: $85; 1999: 0; from $153.78 on amazon.com; kindle ed.: $188.80.
A close examination of the law and regulations governing charitable giving in the United States. It examines the various forms taken by charitable gifts, including real estate and art. The author also explains the procedure of establishing and maintaining a program of charitable giving. Additional chapters cover such topics as limitations on charitable giving, estate and tax considerations, special gift situations, gifts to charitable remainder and lead trusts, gifts to pooled income trusts, charitable gift annuities, the administration of charitable giving, disclosure rules, and special events, among others. Formerly published by Wiley Law Publications.

Hyatt, Thomas K. **Nonprofit Legal Landscape**. Washington, DC: BoardSource. 2005. 1 vol. (137 pp.). Paperbound.
Cost: Out-of-print; was $27 (members); $40 (non-members); from $30.12 on amazon.com (2014).
This brief guide was written to educate board members of nonprofit corporations about the key legal issues which impact nonprofit governance. The work is a collaborative effort of attorneys, headed by Thomas K. Hyatt, with the Nonprofits Practice Group of the Baltimore firm of Ober Kaler. BoardSource, formerly the National Center for Nonprofit Boards, publishes a number of books and videos designed to educate nonprofit board members in their duties and responsibilities.

Kirschten, Barbara L. **Nonprofit Corporation Forms Handbook**. St. Paul, MN: Thomson Reuters West, 1996-date. 1 vol. (1,578 pp.). Paperbound. Annual.
Cost: 2013 Edition: $1,039; 2012 Edition: $953; 2011 Edition: $874; 2010: $802; from $99.99 on amazon.com; **Monthly Assured Print Price (APP)**: $83/$996 (2014)
A collection of all the forms likely to be required by those representing nonprofit organizations, together with step-by-step guidance in completely them accurately. Includes copies of relevant IRS publications, state and federal forms, and review of state and local tax requirements. Contains statutory provisions applicable in California, Delaware, District of Columbia, Illinois, Maryland, New York, and Virginia. Contains the application to the IRS for recognition of exemption from federal income tax, and the registration and reporting requirements for corporate and tax purposes.

Cost Saving Tip: Purchase a used copy on amazon.com or consult at a local law library.

Model Nonprofit Corporation Act. 3d ed. Chicago: American Bar Association, Section of Business Law, 2009. 1 vol. (various pagings). Paperbound.
Cost: $199.95; $169.95 to members; from $74.89 on amazon.com (2014).
The original Model Nonprofit Corporation Act (MNCA) was first promulgated in 1952 by the ABA's Committee on Corporate Laws of the Section of Corporation, Banking and Business Law.

Designed as a companion to the Model Business Corporation Act (MBCA), it followed the MBCA's organization, style and procedures. In 1979, the Committee on Nonprofit Corporations of the Business Law Section was appointed to revise the MNCA, a task that was completed in 1987 and published in 1988 by Prentice Hall Law and Business as the **Revised Model Nonprofit Corporation Act**. The Revised MNCA classified non-profit corporations into public benefit corporations, mutual benefit corporations, and public benefit corporations. Later, following the enactment of California's nonprofit corporation statute, a new classification system was adopted and nonprofits were divided into three classes: Public Benefit, Mutual Benefit, and Religious. The Revised MNCA essentially adopted this classification scheme. The third edition of the MCNA was adopted at the ABA's Annual Meeting in 2008. Its intent was to follow the Model Business Corporation Act as much as possible (acknowledging the obvious differences between nonprofit and profit corporations), and eliminate the classification scheme of the **Revised MCNA**. The third edition contains the following chapters: general provisions, incorporation, purposes and powers, name, registered office and agent, memberships and financial provisions, member meetings, directors and officers, domestication and conversion, amendment of articles of incorporation and bylaws, mergers and membership exchanges, disposition of assets, derivative proceedings, dissolution, foreign corporations, records and reports, and transition provisions. The text of each section is accompanied by cross-references and official comments.

Nonprofit Resources: a Companion to Nonprofit Governance. 2nd ed. Edited by Victor Futter, Lisa Runquist, and Victoria B. Bjorklund. Chicago: American Bar Association, 2007. 1 vol. (149pp.).
Cost: $19.95 ($17.95 to members); from $0.87 on amazon.com (2014).
First published in 2002, this comprehensive updated bibliography, arranged by topic, provides entries for hundreds of books, handbooks, professional journals, government publications, foundation reports, case and statutory cites, and Internet sites dealing with nonprofit entities.

Additional titles on the subject of Nonprofit Corporations are available from the following publishers: American Law Institute-American Bar Association, American Society of Association Executives, BoardSource, Foundation Press, Free Press, Gaunt, Greenwood Publishing Group, John Wiley & Sons, Lega Books, Moyer Bell, Nonprofit Risk Management Center, Practising Law Institute, Prentice-Hall, Thomson Reuters West, Volunteer Lawyers for the Arts. See Appendix B for addresses and telephone numbers.

Partnership

Bromberg, Alan R. and Larry E. Ribstein. **Bromberg and Ribstein on Partnership**. New York: Wolters Kluwer Law & Business, 1988-date. 4 vols. (1,904 pp.). Looseleaf format. Supplemented twice annually.
Cost: $2,325; supplementation: 1998: $590; 1999: $600; 2000: $625; 2001: $670; 2002: $785; 2003: $395; 2004: $466; 2005: $998; 2006: $1,070; 2007: $1,140; 2008: $1.231; 2009: $1,279; 2010: $1,363; 2011: $1,508; 2012: $2,418; 2013: $2,586.
If any work of legal scholarship could be described as «definitive» it would be this treatise by Alan Bromberg and Larry Ribstein. Alan Bromberg is the greatest living authority on partnership law and author of the first limited liability partnership (LLP) act which became the model for all other states. A University Distinguished Professor of Law at Southern Methodist University and Counsel to the law firm of Jenkens & Gilchrist in Dallas, he has authored more than 100 articles on securities, corporate, partnership, commodities and tax law, in addition to the multi-volume treatise **Securities Fraud and Commodities Fraud**. In this comprehensive treatise, the authors examine in depth both general and limited partnerships, including their nature and formation, partnership property, power of partners to bind partnership, and the enforcement of partnership rights and obligations. They also consider rights and duties among the partnership, and dissociation, dissolution and winding up. Larry Ribstein, the Foundation Professor of Law at George Mason University, assisted in the drafting of the ABA Model LLP Act and is author or co-author of more than 75 articles on partnership, corporate law, securities law as well as co-author of **Ribstein & Keatinge on Limited Liability Companies**.

Cain, George H. **Law Partnership: Its Rights and Responsibilities**. 2d ed. Chicago: American Bar Association, 1999. 1 vol. (362 pp.). Paperbound.
Cost: $89.95 ($79.95 to Senior Lawyer Division members); from $24.99 on amazon.com (2014).
An in-depth analysis of the law governing relations among partners and between partners and their firms and employees. Based on his analysis of more than 200 recent cases, the author outlines the mechanics of drafting a workable partnership agreement and provides guidance in the relationships between partners and associates. The author also examines the different classes of partners and their levels of authority, voting requirements and restrictions for various partner classes, meeting notifications, instances when substance may be disclosed or omitted, shares and the procedures to ensure fairness and a right of appeal, The second edition also adds a chapter on non-competition and forfeiture-for-competition clauses, including a discussion of Model Rule 5.6, defenses to the application of the rule, and prohibitions on advertising and exceptions in law practice sales. The author is a graduate of Harvard Law School with more than fifty years experience in corporate law and business litigation. He is currently Of Counsel to the New England firm of Day, Berry & Howard.

Friedland, Jerold A. **Tax Planning for Partners, Partnerships, and LLCs**. New York: Matthew Bender & Co., 1998. 1 vol.
Cost: $937; supplementation: 1999: $305; 2000: $305; 2001: $326; 2002: $349; 2003: $367; 2004: $385; 2005: $412; 2006: $441; 2007: $469; 2008: $507; 2009: $527; 2010: $528; 2011: $533; 2012: $554; 2013: $593; 2014: $647; eBook: $819; renewal: 2013: $593; 2014: $608.
A comprehensive guide to the tax aspects of partnership and

limited liability companies. The author explains in clear detail the provisions of the Internal Revenue Code which apply to partnership and LLCs and examines related IRS regulations, rulings, and court decisions. The discussion of the law is amplified by the introduction if numerous computational illustrations, practice tips, and cautions. The author discusses the issues involved in the tax classification of economic relationships, the tax accounting rules for partnerships and LLCs, how taxes are computed when distributions are made to partners or LLC members, the tax consequences of a death of a partner, and the special rules for family partnerships/LLCs.

Willis, Arthur B. John S. Pennell, and Philip F. Postlewaite. **Partnership Taxation.** 7th ed. Boston, MA: Warren, Gorham & Lamont, 2013-date. 2 vols. Looseleaf format and online. Quarterly supplementation.
Cost: $1,060 per year; Online: $1,140 per year (2014).
An excellent practitioner-oriented treatise covering all manner of tax issues relating to partnerships. The treatment is organized around the life cycle of the typical partnership and illustrated with numerous practical examples. The substantive portion of the text includes analysis of international partnerships, passive activity loss rules, special allocation regulations under section 704 (b), termination of the partnership, limited liability companies, at risk rules, and depreciation and recapture. The more than 7,000 pages of text include more than 200 pages of forms as well as the text of the partnership sections of the **IRS Code**. The late Arthur B. Willis was the member of an Los Angeles law firm, faculty member at the University of Southern California, and an active member of the ABA Tax Section. John S. Pennell is Of Counsel to McDermott, Will & Emery and a past chairman of the ABA Section of Taxation. Philip F. Postlewaite is a professor of law at Northwestern University and author of a dozen books. Originally published by Shepard's/McGraw-Hill, this title was sold to the Thomson Company in December, 1995. It is now published Warren, Gorham & Lamont under the RIA Group.

Cost Saving Tips: Subscribe in alternate years to cut supplementation cost in half.

Additional titles on the subject of Partnership are available from the following publishers: Matthew Bender, CCH, Inc., Delmar Publishers, Foundation Press, Greenwood Publishing Group, Harcourt Legal, Kluwer Academic Publications, LexisNexis, Nolo Press, Practising Law Institute, RIA Group, State Mutual Book & Periodical Service, Thomson Reuters West. See Appendix B for addresses and telephone numbers.

Patents, Trademarks & Intellectual Property

Aisenberg, Irwin M. **Modern Patent Law Precedent: Dictionary of Key Terms and Concepts.** 14th ed. St. Paul, MN: Thomson Reuters West, 2013. 1 vol. (1,455 pp.). Includes CD-ROM & Online access.
Cost: $788; **Monthly Assured Print Price (APP)**: $58/$696 (2014).
This book is similar in concept to West's **Words and Phrases**. It is organized alphabetically by word and phrase with summaries of leading cases of precedential value. The language of the summaries is largely drawn form the decisions themselves. The words and phrases are drawn from key terms in the **U.S. Code**, terms that have raised problems in claims challenged by the Patent and Trademark Office, terms of art, and general legal concepts as they apply to patent law. Citations are to the various federal reporters or to the **U.S. Patent Quarterly**.

Cost-saving tip: Excessively priced for a dictionary. In the hands of West, what should be a modestly-priced reference book becomes a high-priced serial tile with either frequent supplements or too frequent new editions. Check out amazon.com for more modestly priced earlier editions.

ABA Section of Intellectual Property Law. **Careers in IP Law: Avenues and Opportunities**. Chicago: American Bar Association, 2013. 1 vol. (90 pp.).
Cost: $24.95 ($16.95 to IP Section members);
The field of IP law draws upon practitioners from a wide variety of professional backgrounds, not limited to scientific or engineering specialties. The volume provides an invaluable introduction to the field for those contemplating a career in IP law and its subspecialties, including patent, trademark, copyright, trade secret, and new media, with a focus on employment opportunities. Lists of career-related resources and relevant publications are included. Additional chapters provide advice from the trenches and suggestions for getting involved with the ABA's Section of IP Law, and additional sources of information, including law schools, patent bar exam, patent bar exam courses, national IP organizations, publications, and notable intellectual property blogs.

Anatomy of a Patent Case. 2d ed. Prepared by the Complex Litigation Committee of the American College of Trial Lawyers. Arlington, VA: Bloomberg BNA Books, 2012. 1 vol. (288 pp.). Paperbound.
Cost: $175 (2014).
This concise yet substantial narrative summary covers all steps required to bring a patent case to trial and examines the key elements that make such litigation unique. It addresses the often complex technical, procedural, and legal issues that distinguish a patent lawsuit from other types of civil litigation. Beginning with a brief overview of a hypothetical patent lawsuit for those new to the process, then proceeds through the various of the litigation process, from the initial complaint to the Federal Circuit, the venue to which patent appeals are taken regardless of jurisdiction. Other chapters cover the motion to dismiss, to transfer, to strike, answer and counterclaims, preliminary injunction motions, the case-management conference, discovery issues unique to patent cases, claim construction, summary judgment motions, pretrial issues and motions in limine, trial, post-trial proceedings, the appeal, and the trial of a patent case in Canada. The volume includes numerous citations to federal patent decisions, as well as insights from leading judges and lawyers. The book is a project of the Complex Litigation Committee of the American College of Trial Lawyers. This is an excellent introductory overview for those new to patent litigation, or those who wish a

quick review of its basic principles and procedures.

Anawalt, Howard C. **Idea Rights: A Guide to Intellectual Property**. Durham, NC: Carolina Academic Press, 2011. 1 vol. (290 pp.). Paperbound.
Cost: $39.00; from $26.19 on amazon.com (2014).
Intellectual property (IP) refers to creations of the mind, including inventions, literary and artistic works, and symbols, names, images, and designs used in commerce. Intellectual property is divided into two categories: Industrial property, which includes inventions (patents), trademarks, industrial designs, and geographic indications of source; and copyright, which includes literary and artistic works such as novels, poems and plays, films, musical works, artistic works such as drawings, paintings, photographs and sculptures, and architectural designs. The fabric of intellectual property law in the United States was fashioned to serve the public interest, fostering a healthy environment for innovation and efficient commercial and industrial practices. In this accessible overview of the law of intellectual property aimed at the layperson, the author provides a lucid examination of intellectual property generally, patents, copyrights, trademarks, trade secrets, other legal theories and remedies, and policy. The Appendix contains an illustrative Internet case study: Case 10 v. Google. Each chapter contains numerous line drawings, diagrams, and photographs illustrating specific forms of intellectual property. The author is Professor Emeritus at Santa Clara University School of Law where he has taught, practiced and written about intellectual issues for more than 30 years.

Arena, Christopher M and Eduardo M. Carreras. **The Business of Intellectual Property**. New York: Oxford University Press, 2013. 1 vol. (412 pp.).
Cost: $225.00; from $185.25 on amazon.com; kindle: $156.00 (2014).
This volume represents an expertly crafted synthesis of intellectual property law and a consideration of the strategic management of intellectual property assets in a business environment. Intended for use by both lawyers and business managers, it explains how IP assets can be employed for maximum competitive advantage and profitability. With attention to the intersection of legal principles and business practices, the authors explain the statutory framework, case law, and the business and legal principles of accounting and valuation. Their aim is to help companies coordinate their business and innovation models to gain maximum advantage from the intellectual resources under their control. The authors argue that the United States is no longer a capitalist country as once defined by Karl Marx, but a country in which knowledge and Intellectual property are now the driving forces of value. The book's 17 chapters examine a host of issues central to the strategic exploitation of intellectual property in the business environment, beginning with a chapter entitled "Short Stories," which describes a number of real-world examples of how businesses have employed various forms of intellectual property to extract value. Additional chapters address the intellectual property economy, intellectual property as the new form of capital, business strategies, extracting the value of information assets and intellectual property, and creating and capturing value: the goals of an intellectual property strategy. It concludes with a number of valuable appendices, including a crash course in intellectual property law for business owners, a series of key questions that a business must answer, an information audit questionnaire, an intellectual property program self assessment tool, and an overview of international considerations. Formerly the Chief Patent Counsel at BellSouth, Christopher Arena is a partner with Woodcock Washburn LLP, a national intellectual property firm located in Atlanta. Eduardo Carreras, the former Chief Intellectual Property Counsel at Coca Cola, is of counsel at Woodcock Washburn.

Bonner, Kimberly M. ed. **The Center for Intellectual Property Handbook**. New York: Neal-Schuman, 2006. 1 vol. (257 pp.). Paperbound.
Cost: $90; from $20.00 on amazon.com (2014).
The digital distribution of copyrighted materials in an academic environment has become a more significant issue as more faculty and institutions have begun providing educational content online, increasing the risk of copyright infringement. This collection of articles examines a variety of intellectual property and copyright issues whose importance has been magnified by this changing legal and technological landscape. It also examines such critical questions as what rights college faculty hold to works produced in the course of their employment. The contributing authors address such topics as copyright basics, copyright ownership of instructional materials and "works for hire" at universities, fair use and licensing, electronic reserves and copyright, the TEACH (Technology, Education and Copyright Harmonization) Act, the Digital Millennium Copyright Act and the university campus, digital rights management, and higher education, copyright education programs, and copyright law, intellectual property policy and academic culture. This volume is a product of the Center for Intellectual Property at the University of Maryland University College under the editorship of its Executive Director, Kimberly M. Bonner, and the Center's staff. The contributing authors include scholars representing the fields of law librarianship, education, and information technology.

Brinckerhoff, Courtenay C. et al. **American Invents Act: Law and Analysis, 2013 Edition**. New York: Wolters Kluwer Law & Business, 2012. 1 vol. (372 pp.). Paperbound.
Cost: $228.00; from 0.49 on amazon.com (2014).
The Leahy-Smith America Invents Act (AIA) (125 Stat. 284) is the first major change to the U.S. Patent System since 1952, whose central provisions went into effect on March 16, 2013. Among its major revisions, the Act changes the U.S. patent system from a «first to invent» to a «first inventor to file» system, eliminates interference proceedings, and develops a post-grant review process. This 2013 edition dissects and analyzes the major provisions of the Act for the benefit of patent practitioners. Compiled by patent experts with the leading IP firm of Foley & Lardner, this volume provides detailed critique of the first to file provisions, derivation and derivation proceedings, changes impacting patent prosecution, the transnational program for covered business methods, *Inter Partes* Review and Post-Grant Review, provisions related to litigation, and other components of the AIA. The Appendices include the text of the Act, the Patent Act Redline Version, a Side-By-Side Comparison of Old and New Patent Act Sections, and other useful examinations of the

changes to the law. The text is heavily annotated with citations to federal statutes, regulations, and case law.

Callmann, Rudolf and Malla Pollack. **The Law of Unfair Competition, Trademarks and Monopolies.** 4th ed. St. Paul, MN: Thomson Reuters West (Clark Boardman Callaghan), 2003-date. 10 vols. Looseleaf format. Periodic supplementation.
Cost: $4,697; supplementation: 1993: $440; 1994: $504; 1995: $335; 1996: $653; 1997: $675.65; 1998: $716; 1999: $754; 2000: $834.25; 2001: $937; 2002: $1,045; 2003: $1,193; 2004: $1,332; 2005: $1,459.50; 2006: $1,638.50; 2007: $1,824; 2008: $2,537; 2009: $2,599; 2010: $2,501.50; 2011: $1669.50; 2012: $4,029.50; 2013: $3,531; **Monthly Assured Print Price (APP):** $342/$4,104.
This multi-volume treatise is the most complete exposition of the law of unfair competition on the market, combining a broad theoretical foundation of the law with an integration of antitrust law. The author treats the basic concepts of protection against unfair competition, government and business competition, and competition and monopolies. He also examines unfair advertising and pricing, unfair interference with a competitor's business relations, misappropriation of a competitor's values, the unlawful conduct of business, the law of trademarks and product simulation, parties, defenses, remedies and procedure and international protection. There is also discussion and analysis of the jurisdiction of the courts, and the jurisdiction and procedure of the Federal Trade Commission. The exhaustive footnotes often dominate the substantive text. The supplementary references are keyed to the text in the body of the set. The Appendices include federal antitrust statutes, guidelines and regulations, and a variety of relevant federal; statutes governing the areas of trade secrets, privacy, commercial bribery, unfair trade practices, control of advertising, trademark statutes, forms and treaties.

Chisum, Donald S. **Patents: A Treatise on the Law of Patentability, Validity and Infringement.** New York: Matthew Bender & Co., 1978-date. 13 vols. Looseleaf format or CD-ROM. Supplemented four times annually. CD-ROM features relevant case law and LEXIS-NEXIS online connection at no extra charge.
Cost: $5,864 (includes annual subscription); annual renewal: 1995: $1,085 (price frozen since 1992); 1996: $1,139; 1997: $1,139; 1998: $1,200; 1999: $1,255; 2000: $1,380; 2001: $1,518; 2002: $1,625; 2003: $1,707; 2004: $1,792; 2005: $1,935; 2006: $2,071; 2007: $2,634; 2008: $2,845; 2009: $3,073; 2010: $3,288; 2011: $3,518; 2012: $3,764; 2013: $4,027; 2014: $4,437; CD-ROM: $5,864; renewal: 1998: $1,145; 1999: $1,255; 2000: $1,340; 2001: $1,474; 2002: $1,578; 2003: $1657; 2004: $1,740; 2005: $1,879; 2006: $2,011; 2007: $2,558; 2008: $2,788; 2009: $3,011; 2010: $3,223; 2011: $3,449; 2012: $3,690; 2013: $3,949; 2014: $4,525.64; eBook: $5,331; renewal: 2014: $4,437.
Written by a Professor of Law at the University of Washington, this is probably the most widely respected treatise on the law of patents. The author provides a detailed examination of the issue of what subject matter is eligible for patent protection and the grounds upon which patents are granted. The text encompasses the principles and doctrines of patent law as well as the rules governing patentability, validity, and infringement. While the coverage is generally very thorough, the author acknowledges the omission of interference practice and procedure, the licensing and assignment of patent rights, and jurisdiction, procedure and remedies in patent litigation as well as tax matters. The substantive text, which is preceded by a glossary of major patent terms, also covers nonobviousness, statutory bars, adequate disclosure, claims, double patenting, priority, Patent and Trademark Office procedures, restriction, continuation applications, priority by foreign filing, reissue, direct infringement, contributory infringement, defenses, remedies, jurisdiction in patent litigation, and ownership and transfer. The Appendices include the full text of all applicable patent laws, treaties and legislative reports. An additional volume contains a cumulative guide to abstracts of all major patent-related decisions of the Court of Appeals for the Federal Circuit organized within a topical outline.

Cost Saving Tips: Any of the Matthew Bender treatises can be used as excellent starting points for legal research provided you have a system for updating your research in the primary sources. Remember that even the information in a «current» set is several months old by the time you receive it. As a cost-saving alternative, you can buy a used set, if available, or buy a new set and let it lapse after the initial year's subscription has expired.

Clarida, Robert W. **Copyright Law Deskbook**. Arlington, VA: BNA Books, 2009. 1 vol. with Case Digest CD-ROM and 2012 Cumulative Supplement.
Cost: $505; supplementation: 2012: $210; 2013: $215.
This impressive reference work aims to describe the law of copyright as it has been applied by the courts in a variety of specific factual circumstances. Accordingly, each chapter, or sub-chapter, begins with a description of applicable sections(s) of the copyright law and follows this with a discussion of the cases in order of greatest interest to the practitioner. It aims to summarize the applicable standard and then consider whether that standard has or has not been satisfied. Chapter one on Jurisdiction and Procedure, for example, examines subject matter jurisdiction, personal jurisdiction, standing, pleadings, jury trial, and declaratory judgment, and the manner in which the courts have ruled in each area. Subsequent chapters cover the issues of copyrightability, ownership, formalities, infringement, fair use, other disputes, remedies, preemption, the Digital Millennium Copyright Act, international issues, and tax, insurance, antitrust and bankruptcy. As the author himself describes it, the result is not so much a treatise or hornbook, but a professional reference that seeks to be useful to the practitioner rather than monumental. In other words, his aim is to describe the law as it is instead of what it ought to be. Indeed, it is the clarity of expression in discussing the applicable cases that the practitioner will find most valuable. The companion CD-ROM provides a 2009 cumulative Case Digest of decisions form 1993-2008. A graduate of Columbia University Law School, the author is member of the New York firm of Reitler, Kailas & Rosenblatt LLC. He is widely recognized for his wide-ranging expertise in the field of intellectual property law.

Davidow, Joel. **Patent-Related Misconduct Issues in U.S. Litigation**. New York: LexisNexis, 2013. 1 vol. (263 pp.).
Cost: $200; amazon.com kindle: $159.20 (2014).

This is the first book to specifically address misconduct claims and defenses in patent litigation, with a focus on existing case law and litigation strategies. These claims may include inequitable conduct or misuse of patent claims, reckless or sham litigation, antitrust violations, defamation or tortious interference. This misconduct may involve a misuse of the patenting process, including patents that the patentee did not invent as claimed, and inequitable conduct claims, including a failure to properly cite material references and false and misleading declarations. The author also addresses claims based on the abuse of the litigation process, including baseless and bad-purpose suits, and claims based on the misuse of the competitive and licensing processes. He also examines the issue of fees which, under normal circumstances are born by each side, but which can be shifted in cases where the defendant can show that the plaintiff should have known that the patent was invalid, unenforceable or not infringed. The volume's 12 chapters cover the broad topics of patent prosecution misconduct, patent litigation misconduct, and patent misuse and antitrust misconduct. The author also discusses cases where courts are called upon to define subtle gradations of fault and apply sanctions accordingly, or not, as the facts may dictate. A concluding chapter addresses litigation strategies. Appendices include excerpts from the Manual of Patent Examiner Practice, U.S. Patent Law (Title 35 of the U.S. Code), Antitrust Guidelines for the Licensing of Intellectual Property, a bibliography, table of cases and index. The author is a senior partner at Kile Goekjian Reed & McManus in Washington, DC with extensive experience in various sections of the Antitrust Division of the Department of Justice, and a faculty member at George Washington School. This is an essential and invaluable resource for the patent litigator.

Davies, Mark Simon. **Patent Appeals: The Elements of Effective Advocacy in the Federal Circuit**. New York: Oxford University Press, 2008. 1 vol. (297 pp.). Spiralbound.
Cost: $119; from $2.99 on amazon.com (2014).
In recent years, the U.S. Supreme Court has exercised a higher level of scrutiny over the patent decisions of the Federal Circuit and granted review in ten cases, twice its historic average. In 90% of those cases, it not only overturned the Federal Circuit's ruling, but also criticized the Federal Circuit for "fundamental misunderstandings," including inventing formalistic rules, using jargon, and failing to harmonize patent law with other areas of law. With the aim of improving the overall process of appellate review in the Federal Circuit, this volume attempts to improve the quality of Federal Circuit briefing by bringing it up to the standards of the appellate briefing received by the Supreme Court. This volume provide a step-by-step guide to the brief writing process, addressing such topics as appellate writing, preparation of a "shell," the introduction, the jurisdictional statement, statement of the issues, statement of the case, statement of facts: statutory background, statement of facts: factual background, statement of facts: prior proceedings, summary of argument, the argument, other briefs, filing the brief and the joint appendix, oral argument, and panel rehearing and rehearing en banc. The appendices include sample opening brief, sample reply brief, sample amicus brief, sample 28 (j) letters, etc. There is also a list of the top ten reasons formal briefs are rejected. The author is a counsel in the Washington, DC office of O'Melveny & Myers where he specializes in appellate and intellectual property issues.

Dinwoodie, Graeme E. and Mark D. Janis., eds. **Trademark and Unfair Competition Law**. Northampton, MA: Edward Elgar Publishing, 2014 2 vols.
Cost: $815 (online price $733.50) (2014).
Federal trademark law, in theory, provides protection and incentives for firms to make investments aimed at gaining consumer confidence in their marks, thereby lowering consumer search costs, and promoting the efficient functioning of the marketplace. The common law of unfair competition both predates trademark law and continues to exist side-by-side with it by protecting marks from imitation only to the extent that its use in the market actually identifies the goods and services of a particular firm. This two-volume set provides a rich offering of writings by scholars, lawyers and judges on the law and policy of trademark law, reflecting both American and British perspectives. The editorial aim has been to select the classic articles in the field which address the (1) themes and theories that have persisted in policy discussions, and (2) the doctrinal structure of the field that transcends particular legal systems. Although the articles generally reflect Anglo-American perspectives over the past century, they also embrace European Union perspectives since British trademark law has mirrored European Union law for the past twenty-five years. The articles in Volume I: Themes and Theories examine the history of trademark law; the justifications for protection; the development of the tort of passing off; the role of principles of unfair competition; the evolution in the function of marks; and the use of the consumer and other metrics in the shaping of trademark law. The articles in Volume II: Doctrinal Debates examine registration statutes; subject and validity of trademarks; functionality; calibrating trademark infringement; dilution; permitted uses and speech; and international issues, specifically with regard to developing countries. The editors admit a bias against what they term the "resolutely modernist conception of scholarly progress in the field" with "no linear progression of thought pointing ineluctably towards ideal solutions." Rather, they suggest, "the intellectual history of trademark scholarship demonstrates a good deal of reframing and recursion" as the best minds grapple with fundamental issues over time and national boundaries. The collection includes articles by such noteworthy scholars as Richard A. Posner, Rudolf Callahan, Alex Kozinski, and William M. Landes. While the collection provides convenient access to specialists in the field, it duplicates what already exists in the legal periodical collections of most academic law libraries, either directly or through HeinOnline.

Donner, Irah H. **Constructing and Deconstructing Patents**. Arlington, VA: Bloomberg BNA Books, 2010. 1 vol. (618 pp.).
Cost: $255.00; no supplementation to date (2014).
Each year, the Patent and Trademark Office (PTO) issues over 150,000 patents. For businesses, the protection of intellectual property (IP) assets is critical to strengthening their competitive advantages, but those patents must be properly constructed to ensure their continuing value. This volume serves as a step-by-step guide to the mechanics of patent application drafting. Original, continuation, continuation-in-part, divisional, and provisional patent applications are covered in the text, with examples taken from the invention types or technologies most regularly filed with the PTO, including mechanical, electrical, and chemical patents. The author also addresses the major areas of patent law that can affect the strength and vitality of

a patent years later. By deconstructing the major elements of a patent, and assessing its strengths and weaknesses, litigators, patent attorneys and agents are better able to prepare patent applications that can withstand legal scrutiny. The book's 17 chapters are organized around three broad topical areas: (1) an overview of patent construction; (2) constructing a patent application; and (3) deconstructing a patent. The text includes numerous rules, practice tips, and practical examples, as well as citations to statutes, regulations, and court decisions. Appendices include several real-life patent applications, glossary of terms, table of cases, and index. A companion CD-ROM contains a sample patentability opinion, selected regulations, and PTO publications. Irah H. Donner is a partner in the Intellectual Property Department of Stroock & Stroock & Lavan LLP in New York City, where he concentrates on the counseling, acquisition and enforcement of all forms of intellectual property rights, and is the author of the classic treatise **Patent Prosecution: Law, Practice, and Procedure**, also published by Bloomberg BNA Books.

Donner, Irah H. **Patent Prosecution: Law, Practice, and Procedure**. 8th ed. Arlington, VA: Bloomberg BNA Books, 2013. 3 vols. (5,248 pp.).
Cost: $600; no supplementation to date; 7th ed.: 2012: $255; 6th ed.: 2010: $225; 6th ed. from $85 on amazon.com (2014).
This is an exhaustive examination of patent prosecution, the process by which lawyers advance claims of patentability before the United States Patent Office. The protections afforded patents are limited to any "new and useful process, machine, manufacture, or composition of matter, or any new and useful improvement thereof." In consideration for the grant of a patent, the inventor must disclose to the public the invention through the published patent in order to promote the progress of science and the useful arts. This process provides the public with the knowledge to develop products around the patented invention, or to wait until the expiration of the patent to exploit the invention. Patents are public franchises rather than legal monopolies and are conveyed for a limited duration. A complete patent application includes a specification, a drawing if necessary, a claim defining the metes and bounds of the invention, a declaration, and a filing fee. It is not necessary that a working prototype actually be constructed before a patent will be granted. Patent prosecution is that process whereby the applicant or his representatives, interact with the patent office with regard to a patent, or an application for a patent. The process may be divided into pre-grant prosecution, which involves negotiation with a patent office for the grant of a patent, and post-grant prosecution, which involves other issues, such as post-grant amendment and opposition. Patent prosecution is distinct from patent litigation, which consists of legal actions relating to the patent infringement. This two-volume resource describes and explains in painstaking detail the entire process by which patents are prosecuted on behalf of clients. It includes exhaustive citations to primary law and secondary authorities. A companion CD-ROM contains the complete Appendices, including forms, and a fully searchable cumulative case digest. The author is partner in the Intellectual Property Department at Wilmer Cutler Pickering Hale and Dorr LLP, with a prior career as a control engineer. He is also an Adjunct Professor of Law at the American University Washington College of Law. The 6th edition of this estimable work incorporates the substantive changes in the law as enunciated by recent decisions of the Court of Appeals for the Federal Circuit and the U.S. Supreme Court.

Durham, Alan L. **Patent Law Essentials: A Concise Guide**. 4th ed. Santa Barbara, CA: Praeger, 2013. 1 vol. (277 pp.).
Cost: $75.00; from $66.99 on amazon.com (2014).
The granting of patents to investors is a practice that made its way from 17th century England to the American colonies. Prior to 1624 and the Statute of Monopolies, however, patents were often nothing more than Crown-sanctioned monopolies that were granted to reward loyal subjects or raise revenues for the government. Not surprisingly, such monopolies allowed patent holders to sell in greater volume and at higher prices because they were free from competition. While the Statute of Monopolies ended this unjust favoritism, it exempted patents and allowed exclusive rights to their inventors. The U.S. Constitution enshrined the practice of granting patents in Art. I, Section 8, which granted Congress the power to "promote the Progress of Science and the useful Arts, by securing for limited Times to Authors and Inventors the exclusive Right to their respective Writings and Discoveries," thereby providing the basis for both patents and copyright law in the United States. In 1836, Congress established the Patent and Trademark Office within the Department of Commerce. To the novice, mastering the intricacies of patent law and procedure can be a daunting exercise. The author's aim in this volume is to fashion just the right balance of sophistication and simplicity which can serve the needs of both the non-lawyer and those already acquainted with the field. Chapter one provides a useful roadmap to the book's content, including summaries of its twelve chapters, a brief review of the sources of law, including the Patent Act, found in Title 35 of the **U.S. Code**, federal regulations, found in Title 37 of the **Code of Federal Regulations**, and the **Manual of Patent Examining Procedure**. The final determination of the vast majority of patent cases, except when accepted on Appeal to the U.S. Supreme Court, generally rests with the Federal Circuit Courts Appeals, established in 1982. The author covers such subjects as patents distinguished from other rights, reading a patent, patentable subject matter, patent prosecution, ownership and other rights, interpreting patent claims, conditions of patentability, enforceability defenses, infringement, patent litigation, and special topics (including design patents and plant patents). The Appendices include sample utility and design patents. **Patent Law Essentials** is probably the most succinct and clearly written single-volume introduction to the subject of patents currently on the market, with citations to the most significant federal cases in support of the text. The author is a graduate of the law school at UC Berkeley and is currently the Judge Robert S. Vance Professor of Law at the University of Alabama. Before accepting his academic post, he practiced high-technology patent litigation in California's Silicon Valley.

Epstein, Michael A. **Epstein on Intellectual Property**. 5th ed. New York: Wolters Kluwer Law & Business, 2005-date. 1 vol. (1,014 pp.). Infrequent supplementation.
Cost: $435; supplementation: 2006: $160; 2007: $171; 2008: $182; 2009: $199; 2010: $212; 2011: $225; 2012: $240; 2013: $269; 4th ed.: 2003: $130; 2004: $149; 2005: new edition.

Authored by one of the world's leading authorities on the law of intellectual property, this work covers the whole range of issues that an attorney must understand in order to protect a client's intellectual property from a variety of business-world threats, including industrial espionage, misappropriation, infringement, piracy, counterfeiting, and the aggressive hiring of the client's employees by competitors. A partner in the New York firm of Weil, Gotshal & Manges, Michael Epstein brings extensive experience litigating intellectual property cases worldwide to such issues as trade secrets, copyright, patents, trademarks, noncompetition agreements, protection of computer software, Internet and multimedia law, ownership of employee inventions, licensing of intellectual property, and the design of information protection systems. The appendices include a number of agreements, forms, patents, checklists, and court decisions.

Federal Intellectual Property Laws and Regulations. 2014 Edition. St. Paul, MN: West, 2013. Annual. 1 vol. (approx. 1,236 pp.). Annual. Paperbound.
Cost: 2014 Edition: $269; 2013 Edition: $239; 2012 Edition: $227; **Monthly Assured Print Price (APP):** $22/$264.
A desktop compilation of the most commonly used federal intellectual property statutes, regulations, and inter-national agreements; published on an annual basis.

Fleming, David S. and John T. Gabrielides. **Trademark Litigation Practice**. Arlington, VA: Bloomberg BNA Books, 2010-date. 1 vol. (766 pp.).
Cost: $500; supplementation: 2011: $245; 2012: $250; 2013: $260.
The Lanham Act, found in Title 15 of the **U.S. Code**, contains the principle federal statutes governing trademark law in the United States. U.S. trademark law is also governed by the common law and by state statutes. Trademark cases brought pursuant to the Lanham Act are generally referred to as Lanham Act cases. This treatise provides detailed practical guidance through the intricacies of Lanham Act litigation, from both a substantive and procedural perspective. Coverage extends to every aspect of Lanham Act cases, from pre-filing, disclosures and discovery, to motion practice, trial, and post-trial proceedings. The authors also analyze the kinds of alternative proceedings that may be used in trademark cases, including oppositions and cancellations in the Trademark Trial and Appeal Board (TTAB); the Uniform Domain-Name Dispute-Resolution Policy (UDRP) proceedings for domain names; International Trade Commission (ITC) investigations; and alternative dispute resolution tools. Many of the practical litigation topics are presented in a convenient circuit-by-circuit format. The authors also cover the use of expert witnesses in trademark cases, injunctive and monetary relief in trademark and false advertising cases, discovery and initial disclosures (including discovery of electronically stored information), and ethics in litigation. Also included are an index, and table of cases. In keeping with the high standards of other Bloomberg BNA Books, this volume provides the user with extensive citations to both primary and secondary authorities as an aid to further research. The authors are partners in the intellectual property firm of Brinks Hofer Gilson & Linne, Chicago, IL, with extensive litigation experience in trademark and intellectual property issues before the federal courts.

Flinn, Patrick J. **Handbook of Intellectual Property Claims and Remedies**. New York: Wolters Kluwer Law & Business, 2000-date. 1 vol. (approx.850 pp.). Looseleaf format. Annual supplementation.
Cost: $389; supplementation: 2001: $120; 2002: $135; 2003: $160; 2004: $170; 2005: $170; 2006: $179; 2007: $191; 2008: $205; 2009: $224; 2010: $239; 2011: $255; 2012: $272; 2013: $291.
A guide to the substantive law, legal remedies, and procedural steps involved in intellectual property disputes, including those involving patents, copyright, trade secrets, and trademarks. The author discusses such subjects as whether or not to bring an intellectual property lawsuit, the types of intellectual property, the identification of intellectual property claims and remedies, preparing and responding to claims, remedial concepts, and the remedies available in patent , copyright, trademark, and trade secret cases. The appendices include selected provisions of the applicable Federal acts, as well as Title 28 of the U.S. Code. The author is a partner in the Intellectual Property Group of the Atlanta firm of Alston & Bird, and a respected authority in the field of intellectual property law.

Gilson, Jerome and Anne Gilson LaLonde. **Trademark Protection and Practice**. New York: Matthew Bender & Co., 2007-date. 10 vols. Looseleaf format. Updated periodically. Authority CD-ROM subscription includes no-cost online updating via LEXIS-NEXIS.
Cost: $2,579 (print or eBook) (annual subscription); renewal: 1998: $775; 1999: $810; 2000: $870; 2001: $870; 2002: $931; 2003: $978; 2004: $1,027; 2005: $1,099; 2006: $1,143; 2007: $1,212; 2008: $1,321; 2009: $1,362; 2010: $1,430; 2011: $1,502; 2012: $1,577; 2013: $1,656; 2014: $1,807; CD-ROM: $2,860; renewal: 1998: $770; 1999: $810; 2000: $870; 2001: $870; 2002: $931; 2003: $978; 2004: $1,027; 2005: $1,109; 2006: $1,187; 2007: $1,282; 2008: $1,397; 2009: $1,509; 2010: $1,584; 2011: $1,663; 2012: $1,763; 2013: $1,886; 2014: $2,060.40; eBook: $2,344; renewal: 2014: $1,807.
A comprehensive analysis of trademark law and practice in the United States, this work provides step-by-state instructions for registering a new trademark or enforcing it in a federal trademark infringement action. It also includes more than 450 trademark practice forms with drafting guides and references to PTO filing requirements. The author also examines such subjects as Internet trademark law, trademark dilution, and federal unfair competition law. The set also includes the text of the Trademark Manual of Examining Procedure, the Acceptable Identification of Goods and Services Manual, and the Trademark Trial and Appeal Board Manual of Procedure. Jerome Gilson, a partner in the Chicago intellectual property firm of Brinks, Hofer, Gilson & Lione, is a past chair of a number of committees of the International Trademark Association.

Cost Saving Tips: Drop the standing order once the initial year's subscription has expired and buy another new set at some future date. For example, buying a new set every three years will result in savings of more than $3,000 every three-year cycle.

Goldstein, Paul. **Copyright: Principles, Law and Practice.** 3d ed. Riverwoods, IL: CCH, Inc., 2005-date. 4 vols. (3,425 pp.). Looseleaf format and Internet. Annual updates.

Cost: $861; supplementation: 2006: $395; 2007: $421; 2008: $451; 2009: $483; 2010: $516; 2011: $550; 2012: $588; 2013: $631; 2d ed.: 1996: $225; 1997: $225; 1998: $238; 1999: $265; 2000: $325; 2001: $310; 2002: $326; 2003: $395; 2004: $395; 2005: new edition; Internet: Inquire.
Paul Goldstein, the Stella W. and Ira S. Lillick Professor of Law at Stanford University School of Law, has written a detailed and scholarly treatise for lawyers, judges, legal researchers and public policymakers. Its discussion and analysis of copyright doctrine under the 1976 Copyright Act is accompanied by discussion of such related issues as contract protection for ideas, unfair competition, trade secrets and the right of publicity. It also treats the courts' role in shaping copyright law, particularly as it involves such unresolved questions as what constitutes original authorship qualifying for protection, where should the line be drawn between a work's unprotectible ideas and its protectible expression, and what constitutes infringement? He also examines the role of the Copyright Office which shapes the law by providing advice to Congress and to the many artists, writers and composers who seek protection for their works. The set's 13 chapters address the topography of copyright; subject matter; publication and formalities, title, term and termination of transfers; exclusive rights in copyrighted works; contributory infringement and vicarious liability, the elements of infringement; infringement of rights in literary, visual, musical, factual and functional works; legal and equitable defenses; fair use; injunctions, ancillary and declaratory relief, criminal proceedings; monetary awards; jurisdiction, venue, etc. The Appendices nclude relevant statutes, legislative reports and regulations, copyright conventions, and forms. Includes tables of cases and statutes and an index. There are extensive citations to primary and secondary authorities, including cases, statutes, regulations, legislative history documents, and books and articles. An excellent and well-written work which can be used with equal utility by the novice and the specialist. Originally published by Little, Brown, this title was purchased in 1996 by Wolters Kluwer and merged with th Aspen (now Wolters Kluwer Law & Business) product line. Also available in an Internet version which includes every case, statute, and point of legal analysis cited in the text.

Graham, Joshua P. and Thomas G. Marlow. **U.S. Patent Prosecutor's Desk Reference**. 2012 ed. New York: Oxford University Press, 2013. 1 vol. (300 pp.).
Cost: $225; from $166.14 on amazon.com (2014).
A patent prosecutor is a patent attorney who assists a client in developing an intellectual property protection strategy, including the preparation and filing of a patent application. Patent prosecution lawyers must both be licensed to practice law as well as licensed to practice in front of the patent office. The aim of the U.S. Patent Prosecutor's Desk Reference is to assist patent prosecutors in responding to Office Actions issued by the U.S. Patent and Trademark Office (USPTO) rejecting patent application claims. Decisions of the USPTO are made on the basis of five primary bases of authority: (1) federal statutes (Title 35 of the U.S. Code); (2) the Manual of Patent Examining Procedure; (3) the Board of Patent Appeals and Interferences; (4) the U.S. Court of Customs and Patent Appeals, and (5) the U.S. Court of Appeals for the Federal Circuit. The content consists of representative rejections and responses to patent applications organized by sections of Title 25 of the U.S. Code. Each example includes citations to the authorities by which such rejection was made. Joshua P. Graham was Patent Counsel for Research in Motion, where he was a patent prosecutor and portfolio manager for the Advanced Technology group. Thomas G. Marlow is Intellectual Property Counsel and Director at Fairchild Semiconductor.

Grossman, Barry. **Patent Litigation Strategies Handbook**. 3d ed. Arlington, VA: BNA Books, 2010. 1 vol. (1,655 pp.) with 2012 supplement.
Cost: $510; supplementation: 2012: $215; 2013: $225.
Since its first enactment in 1790, United States patent law has been replaced or amended numerous times, including the Patent Act of 1793, the Patent Act of 1836, and over sixty amendments between 1837 and 1952. The Patent Act of 1952 codified existing law and simplified and clarified its language. With some notable changes and additions, the Patent Act of 1952 remains the current law. And in the last ten years alone, the Supreme Court has ruled in twelve significant patent cases. This work provides expert strategic guidance in the field of patent litigation, whose purpose is to resolve a business dispute over a property right. Acknowledging that patent litigation is a costly business, usually involving expenses of a million or more dollars for each side, the authors have approached the process with the aim of achieving the desired business goals efficiently and effectively and without unnecessary expense. They address litigation from the unique perspective of patent litigation, rather than general trial practice, and from both the patent owner's and the challenger's perspective. The contributing authors, who number more than fifty, address every stage in the litigation process, from pre-litigation considerations and strategies to the appellate process. Along the way, they address such important topics as settlement, the use of ASDR, the complaint, the discovery plan, protective orders, interrogatories, electronic discovery, patent depositions, motion practice, the trial, proving infringement, willful infringement, patent defenses, expert witnesses, evidence, and damages. The third edition adds an insightful chapter on patent litigation from the judge's viewpoint, provided by James F. Holderman, Chief Judge of the U.S. District Court, Northern District of Illinois. The contributing authors bring a depth of scholarly analysis, erudition, and professional experience to their respective chapters, together with exhaustive citations to relevant federal case law, statutes and secondary sources.

Halpern, Sheldon W., Craig Allen Nard, and Kenneth L. Port. **Fundamentals of United States Intellectual Property Law: Copyright, Patent, Trademark**. 4th ed. Frederick, MD: Wolters Kluwer Law & Business, 2013. 1 vol. (428 pp.). Paperbound,
Cost: $175.00; from $159.98 on amazon.com (2014).
This text embraces the three central areas of intellectual property law: copyright, patents and trademarks. In each case, the authors present the fundamental concepts, accompanied by supporting authority, but without the exhaustive analysis of more comprehensive treatises, like **Nimmer on Copyright**, **Moy's Walker on Patents**, or **McCarthy on Trademarks and Unfair Competition**. Each subject is distinct in its own way. Copyright requires an act of original authorship which crosses a threshold of creativity. Patent law is based on novelty of invention, with creativity and originality insufficient grounds for protection,

Trademark protection, on the other hand, is a common law concept that exists outside of any statute, and does not depend on any novelty, invention, discovery, or other work of the brain, but merely requires priority of appropriation. The coverage of each of these intellectual property fields examines the legal basis for protection, the subject matter of protection, formalities, ownership and transfer, infringement, and remedies. Intended for intellectual property practitioners, law professors, law students, and librarians, this work is sufficiently comprehensive in scope to meet the needs of the sophisticated user, while being understandable to the novice. The coverage is current to the latest computer and technological innovations deserving of protection. Sheldon Halpern is the Harald R. Tyler Chair in Law and Technology, Albany Law School. His co-authors are professors of law at Case Western Reserve University Law School and William Mitchell College of Law.

Hildreth, Ronald B. **Patent Law: A Practitioner's Guide.** 4th ed. New York: Practising Law Institute, 2012-date. 1 vol. Revised as necessary.
Cost: $295; supplementation: 2013: $175; 3d ed.: 1999: $58.50; 2000: 0; 2001: $73; 2002: $82; 2003: $87; 2004: $97; 2005: $107; 2006: $98; 2007: $112; 2008: 0; 2009: $160; 2010: $166; 2011: $170; 2012: new edition.
A practical resource designed to guide the patent attorney through the often complex process of filing a patent application and conducting patent litigation. The author, a practicing attorney with the New York firm of Brumbaugh, Graves, Donohue & Raymond, addresses such topics as patent office prosecution, patentability in general, statutory bars under Section 102, unobviousness, interference, infringement, the doctrine of equivalents, third party liability, preparation of an opinion letter, preparation of a specification for a patent application, preparation of patent claims for a patent application, preparation of an information disclosure statement, preparation of an appeal brief, and more.

Holland, Catherine J., et al. **Intellectual Property: Patents, Trademarks, Copyrights and Trade Secrets**. Irvine, CA: Entrepreneur Press, 2007. 1 vol. (402 pp.). Includes essential legal forms and documents on CD-ROM.
Cost: $32.95; from $21.89 on amazon.com (2014).
Intellectual property (IP) consists of creations of the mind which may take the form of inventions, literary works, art, music, designs, photographs, slogans, or names. Intellectual property rights may take the form of patents, trademarks, copyrights, trade secrets, or other government-granted rights. The protection of these rights is an essential ingredient to any successful business operation. This well-organized and lucidly-written guide to intellectual property law provides detailed coverage of trademarks, patents, trade secrets, copyrights, their registration, protecting the business from infringing upon the IP rights of others, and the nature and costs of IP litigation. The text includes numerous real life examples, strategy tips, and warnings, appendices, and a glossary. Like most Entrepreneur Press titles, this volume is accompanied by a CD-ROM containing numerous essential legal forms. The contributing authors are all attorneys at Knobbe, Martens, Olson & Bear, LLP, one the country's leading IP law firms.

Intellectual Property Law for Business Lawyers. By Kinney & Lange, P.A. St. Paul, MN: West, 2010-date. 1 vol. (768 pp.). Annual repalacement volumes.
Cost: 2013-2014: $194; 2012-2013 Edition: $178; 2011-2012 Edition: $163; 2010-2011 Edition: $148; supplementation: 1998: $10; 1999: $11; 2000: $12; 2001: $15.50; 2002: $18.50; 2003: $21; 2004 [1st annual edition]: $55; 2008-2009: $105; 2009-2010: $127; **Monthly Assured Print Price (APP):** $165/$192.
A basic guide to the law of intellectual property designed for use by corporate counsel and business and general practice lawyers. Prepared by the firm of Kinney & Lange, this volume addresses such topics as patent law, obtaining a patent, patent litigation, principles of copyright law, registering a copyright, principles of trademark law, registering trademarks, trademark and unfair competition litigation, trademark dilution, trade secrets, advertising law, right of publicity, transferring, licensing and securing intellectual property rights, intellectual property rights in foreign countries, and advising a business about its intellectual property. The appendices include examples of patents, copyright and trademark forms, complaints, confidentiality and employment agreements, citations to state statutes governing deceptive trade practices, unfair business practices, advertising, and the right of publicity. Also includes a table of statutes and cases, and index.

Intellectual Property Primary Law SourceBook. Newark, NJ: LexisNexis (Matthew Bender), 1998-date. 1 vol. Annual. Paperbound.
Cost: 2014 Edition: $175.
A compilation of all the significant federal statutes and regulations in the fields of copyright, patent, and trademark, including the full text of **U.S. Code** Titles 7, 15,17, 19 and 35, **Code of Federal Regulations** Titles 19 and 37, the Patent Cooperation Treaty, and regulations under the Patent Cooperation Treaty. An excellent cost-saving alternative to acquiring the complete **U.S. Code** and **Code of Federal Regulations** for the intellectual property attorney.

Intellectual Property Library [CD-ROM]. New York: Matthew Bender & Co. One disc. Updated quarterly. Available for Windows. Search Engine: Folio.
Cost: CD-ROM: $26,772 (includes annual subscription); renewal: 1998: $7,835; 1999: $8,565.00; 9,220; 2001: $9,220; 2002: $9,866; 2003: $10,360; 2004: $10,878; 2005: $11,748; 2006: $12,571; 2007: $13,577; 2008: $14,799; 2009: $15,983; 2010: $16,942; 2011: $18,275; 2012: $19,554; 2013: $20,923; 2014: $23,291.70.
Matthew Bender's Authority products are a sophisticated combination of analytical treatises and relevant primary law designed for the practitioner. This complete CD-ROM product contains the full text of the following Matthew Bender titles: Nimmer on Copyright, Chisum on Patents, Trademark Protection and Practice, Milgrim on Trade Secrets, World Patent Law & Practice, Computer Law, Court of Appeals for the Federal Circuit: Review of Patent and Trademark Cases, International Computer Law, Intellectual Property Counseling & Litigation, World Trademark Law and Practice, Patent Licensing Transactions, Entertainment Industry Contracts, Patent Office Rules and Practice, and Patent Litigation: Procedure & Tactics. Copyright, Trademark and Unfair Competition Cases, and Patent Cases

are optional selections. Lesser combinations of titles may be selected by the subscriber. The subscription also includes the LexisNexis Online Connection to recent case law.

Intellectual Property Law Resource Center [Internet]. Washington, DC: Bloomberg BNA. Updated continuously.
Cost: $4,435 (2014).
The **Intellectual Property Law Resource Center** provides comprehensive access to Bloomberg BNA's collection of intellectual property news, extensive case law (including USPQ case law), statutes, regulations, analysis, and practice tools. The platform covers all areas of IP law categorized into four practice areas: Patent Law, Trademark & Unfair Trade Practice Law, Copyright Law, and Judicial Practice & Procedure. Includes **World Intellectual Property Report** e-mail updates sent out continually, **BNA's Patent, Trademark & Copyright Journal** e-mail updates (daily), plus e-mails regarding breaking news developments.

Intellecual Property Law Treatise Library on LoisLawConnect. New Yotk: Wolters Kluwer Law & Business.
Cost: $540.00 per year (solo practitioner) (2014).
This practice library is designed to assist the attorney in navigating a variety of Intellectual property disputes. Titles include: **Trademark and Copyright Disputes: Litigation Forms & Analysis**, **Epstein on Intellectual Property**, **Guide to TTAB Practice**, **Trademark Law: Protection, Enforcement and Licensing**, **Guide to Registering Trademarks**, **Handbook on Intellectual Property Claims and Remedies**, and **US Trademark Trial & Appeal Board Database**. A cost-effective alternative to acquiring the titles in print format.

IP Analytical [WestlawNext]. Eagan, MN: Thomson Reuters West.
Cost: $2,400 per year (2014)
This authoritative collection of intellectual property treatises embraces the fields of patents, trademarks, copyrights, arts, entertainment, science, and technology. The IP Analytical collection includes such titles as: **McCarthy on Trademarks**, **Matthews' Annotated Patent Digest**, **Moy's Walker on Patents**, **Patent Law Fundamentals**, **Patry on Copyright**, **Eckstrom's Licensing in Foreign and Domestic Operations**, and hundreds of relevant law review, journal, and newsletter articles.
Cost-Saving Tip: For the IP practitioner, this library on WestlawNext is a far better value than any of the West print or former CD-ROM products. By contrast, the cost of the print version of **McCarthy on Trademarks** alone is $4,182.00 initially with supplementation of $2,508.00 in 2013 versus $2,400.00 annually for the entire **IP Analytical** library.

Kohn, Al and Bob Kohn. **Kohn on Music Licensing**. 4th ed. New York: Wolters Kluwer Law & Business, 2009-date. 1 vol. (1,803 pp.). Includes sample forms on CD-ROM. Irregular supplementation.
Cost: $419; supplementation: 2010-2013: 0; 2d ed,: 1999: $64; 2000: $78; 2001: new edition; 2002-2008: 0; 2009: new edition.
A comprehensive guide to negotiating, drafting, interpreting, and enforcing musical licensing agreements, whether in the form of publishing, recording, or performance. The authors explain the essential components of a music license, as well as critical issues involved in negotiating the eleven types of music licenses, including print licenses, mechanical licenses, electrical transcription licenses, synchronization licenses, licenses for commercial advertising, videogram licenses, musical product licenses, licenses for software, multimedia, and the Internet, performance licenses, dramatic adaptation licenses, and grand performance licenses. The volume includes more than 60 model licensing agreements on a 3.5" disc. Al Kohn is a 50-year veteran of the music industry, both as composer and arranger, and as industry executive. He was, until his recent retirement, Vice-President, Licensing, for Warner/Chappell Music, Inc. Bob Kohn is Chairman of the Board of GoodNoise, the Internet Record Company, and, formerly, Vice President of Business Development for Pretty Good Privacy, Inc., the world's leading developer of Internet encryption and security software. He is adjunct professor of law at Monterey College of Law.

Leavens, Thomas R. **Music Law for the General Practitioner**. Chicago: American Bar Association, 2013. 1 vol. (257 pp.). Paperbound.
Cost: $79.95 ($65.95 to members); from $53.89 on amazon.com (2014).
Music law consists of that amalgam of laws and business practices that affect those who make, market, distribute, and use music in all its forms. Substantively, it draws upon the law in a number of specialty areas, including copyright, trademark, contracts, identity rights, First Amendment rights of expression, and data protection. This volume is intended as an introductory exposition of the subject for the general practitioner who represents a musician, a producer, or consumer. Drawing upon the his broad experience as general counsel representing a publically-traded record company, a digital music company, and a media development and brand development company, among many others, the author paints a broad landscape of the legal issues involved in the music business. These issues encompass such matters as how value in musical properties is created, music publishing, how bands are organized and financed, and plans made for their eventual brakeup, how record companies and produces work, the world of personal representatives, personal appearances, distribution, tax considerations, the musician's estate, music and the general business client, and representing the musician. The author practices entertainment and media law with the Chicago-based firm of Leavens, Strand, Glover & Adler, LLC. and has taught Music Law at Northwestern University School of Law. I could not recommend a better "first stop" on the road to an understanding of music or media law.

Licensing Law Treatise Library on LoislawConnect. New York: Wolters Kluwer Law & Business.
Cost: $540.00 per year (solo practitioner) (2014).
A library of titles providing expert guidance in negotiating, drafting, and litigating licensing agreements, with forms and checklists. Titles include **Licensing Update**, **Drafting License Agreements**, **Licensing Agreements: Forms & Checklists**, **Licensing Royalty Rates**, **The Licensing Journal**, and the **Licensing Desk Book.**

McCarthy, J. Thomas. **McCarthy on Trademarks and Unfair Competition.** 4th ed. St. Paul, MN: West (Clark Boardman Callaghan), 1992-date. 7 vols. Looseleaf format.
Cost: $4,557; supplementation: 1993: $125; 1994: $267.50; 1995: $415; 1996: $665; 1997: $653.75; 1998: $694; 1999: $764; 2000: $810; 2001: $707; 2002: $1,052; 2003: $1,196; 2004: $1,316; 2005: $1,677; 2006: $2,020; 2007: $2,248; 2008: $2,503; 2009: $2,785; 2010: $2,428; 2011: $2,646; 2012: $2,884; 2013: $2,508; **Monthly Assured Print Price (APP)**: $332/$3,984.
Written by a Professor of Law at the University of San Francisco School of Law with a specialty in the field of trademarks and unfair competition, this treatise provides a detailed examination of commercial symbols and the law governing them. The author has been involved in the writing of this treatise since the first edition appeared in 1972 and as the field has entered the mainstream of commercial law. This edition encompasses the significant changes in federal trademark law which took place with the implementation of the 1988 Trademark Law Revision Act on November 16, 1989. The chapters discuss and analyze the basic principles of unfair competition, and trademark protection, the function of trademarks, the terminology of the field, the historical basis of trademarks, and trademarks compared with patents and copyrights. All discussed are generic terms, personal names as trademarks, geographic term marks, secondary meaning, acquisition and priority of trademark rights, loss of trademark rights, assignment and licensing, federal registration, proceedings in the Patent and Trademark Office, and appeals from decisions on trademark registration, infringement, the Lanham Act and false advertising, and much more. The Appendices include the text of relevant statutes, rules of practice and legislative history, tables of cases and statutes, and index. An exceptionally well-organized reference tool with extensive citations and illustrations.

Cost-Saving Tip: The supplementation cost for this set has clearly become excessive, reflecting the shameless milking of the publisher's subscriber list. The wise consumer should, at the very least, repurchase the set no more than every two years, bringing the annual maintenance cost to about $1,250. Buying it every three years will reduce the annual cost to about $800. Avoid the Monthly Assured Print Price, which is just the publisher's method of locking in these high supplementation costs. For the IP practitioner, **IP Analytical** library on WestlawNext is a far better value than any of the West print or former CD-ROM products. For example, the cost of the print version of **McCarthy on Trademarks** alone is $4,182.00 initially with supplementation of $2,508.00 in 2013 versus $2,400.00 annually for the entire **IP Analytical** library.

McCarthy, J. Thomas. **McCarthy's Desk Encyclopedia of Intellectual Property**. 3d ed. Washington, DC: Bloomberg BNA Books, 2004. 1 vol. (556 pp.).
Cost: $155; no supplementation to date (2014).
This practitioner's reference tool provides definitions of over 800 words used in the field of intellectual property, including phrases, statutes, and conventions on patent, trademark, copyright, trade secret, entertainment, and computer law, and uses them in context. Applying a three-level treatment to each term, the author provides (1) a concise and simple definition, (2) a more complicated and detailed explanation, and (3) a contextualized use of the term by courts, Congress and other bodies. The Encyclopedia also analyzes relevant cases and statutes and provides citations to more cases and IP treatises for additional research. The third level of information includes citations for further research in leading intellectual property treatises, cases, and other legal resources, as well as providing references to relevant web sites. It also includes a table of cases, appendices that list the treatises used by the authors, historical lists of all patent and trademark directors, commissioners, registers of copyrights, and historical data on patent grants and trademark registrations. The third edition includes information on the Digital Millennium Copyright Act, the Anti-Cybersquatting Act, digital performance rights, the Markman Hearing, First Inventor Defense, business method, the new technological anti-circumvention rights, and the Uniform Domain Name Dispute Resolution Policy. Previous editions were published in 1991 and 1995. J. Thomas McCarthy has served on the faculty at the University of San Francisco for over 35 years. An intellectual property law pioneer, he is recognized as a pre-eminent expert in the field. In 1999, the American Intellectual Property Law Association named Professor McCarthy the most influential trademark expert of the 20th Century. The J. Thomas McCarthy Institute for Intellectual Property and Technology Law Property and Cyberlaw at the University of San Francisco was named in his honor.

Milgrim, Roger M. **Milgrim on Trade Secrets.** New York: Matthew Bender & Co., 1967-date. 4 vols. Looseleaf format. Supplemented about 3 times yearly. CD-ROM features relevant case law and LEXIS-NEXIS online connection at no extra charge.
Cost: $2,691 (includes annual subscription); annual renewal: 1995: $648 (frozen since 1992); 1996: $680; 1997: $680; 1998: $715; 1999: $750; 2000: $800; 2001: $856; 2002: $916; 2003: $962; 2004: $1,010; 2005: $1,091; 2006: $1,168; 2007: $1,261; 2008: $1,362; 2009: $1,471; 2010: $1,530; 2011: $1,606; 2012: $1,702; 2013: $1,821; 2014: $1,988; CD-ROM: $2,741; renewal: 1998: $685; 1999: $750; 2000: $800; 2001: $856; 2002: $916; 2003: $962; 2004: $1,010; 2005: $1,091; 2006: $1,168; 2007: $1,261; 2008: $1,374; 2009: $1,484; 2010: $1,558; 2011: $1,636; 2012: $1,734; 2013: $1,855; 2014: $2,064.48; eBook: $2,446; renewal: 2014: $1,988. Also available as a part of the 17-title **Intellectual Property Library** on CD-ROM for $26.772; renewal: 2014: $22,387.
This is an exhaustive guide to the law and practice governing the protection and use of trade secrets and other intangible property. The author, a partner in the New York firm of Paul Hastings, Janofsky & Walker, discusses and analyzes the licensing of trade secrets and other industrial property, contractual and legal protections afforded trade secrets, criminal, antitrust and administrative applications, litigation, tax matters, and the relationship of trade secrets to copyright and patent law and the Freedom of Information Act. Extensive appendices contain laws, regulations, reports, and articles. The text is supported by extensive case annotations and citations. The set also includes a detailed table of cases and subject index.

Miller, Arthur and Michael H. Davis. **Intellectual Property: Patents, Trademarks, and Copyright in a Nutshell**. 5th ed. St. Paul, MN: West, 2012. 1 vol. (511 pp.).
Available from West Academic.
Cost: $41; $21.36 on amazon.com (2014).

This brief, student-oriented text was authored by the Harvard law professor and television personality Arthur Miller and Michael Davis, Associate Professor of Law at Cleveland State University's Cleveland-Marshall College of Law. Together, they provide a succinct overview of all three fields with limited citations to relevant case law.

Mills, John Gladstone, III, Donald Cress Reilly, III, and Robert Clare Highly. **Patent Law Fundamentals.** 2d ed. St. Paul, MN: West (Clark Boardman Callaghan), 1980-date. 3 vols. Looseleaf format. Supplemented between 3-4 times annually.
Cost: $3,953; supplementation: 1993: $334.50; 1994: $389; 1995: $440; 1996: $490; 1997: $514; 1998: $546; 1999: $590; 2000: $645; 2001: $729; 2002: $800; 2003: $855; 2004: $977; 2005: $1,301; 2006: $1,168.50; 2007: $1,300.50; 2008: $1,447.50; 2009: $1,930; 2010: $1,120; 2011: $2,294; 2012: $1,250; 2013: $2,899; **Monthly Assured Print Price (APP)**: $288/$3,456.
In the author's excellent Introduction, he describes this work as «more in the nature of a sketch, in which enough detail appears to make patent all significant features, with just enough highlighting to permit identification of salient traits and trends.» While this work lacks the detail of Chisum or Lipscomb, it provides the practicing attorney with a well-rounded overview of the chief concepts and issues in the field, with enough citations to lead the researcher to additional primary and secondary resources. The chapters cover the basic principles of patent protection, a comparison and contrast of trade secrets, trademarks, and copyrights with patents. Volume two examines the substantive requisites of a valid patent, competing rights to the same patent, and the process of obtaining patent protection. Volume three covers the exploiting of patent rights, and patents in a global context. The Appendices include the format of various types of patent documents, a table of cases, table of statutes and rules, and subject index. The author, a lawyer with a background in chemical engineering, is a primary examiner in the U.S. Patent and Trademark Office.

Cost Saving Tips: For the IP practitioner, **IP Analytical** library on WestlawNext is a far better value than any of the West print or former CD-ROM products. For example, the cost of the print version of **Mills, Patent Law Fundamentals** alone is $3,626.00 initially with supplementation of $2,899.00 in 2013 versus $2,400.00 annually for the entire **IP Analytical** library.

Model Jury Instructions: Copyright, Trademark and Trade Dress Litigation. Todd S. Holbrook and Alan Nathan Harris, eds. Chicago: American Bar Association, Section of Litigation, 2008. 1 vol. (301 pp.). Paperbound.
Cost: $120 ($95 to members); from $45.98 on amazon.com (2014).
A part of the ABA's Model Jury Instructions series, these model jury instructions are designed to serve as balanced, impartial and accurate statements of the law in copyright, trademark and trade litigation cases. The jury instructions in the area of copyright consider such issues as authorship, ownership and licensing, the scope of protection, infringement, defenses, damages, and the Digital Millennium Copyright Act, and definitions. The trademark chapter covers definitions, the acquisition of trademark rights, infringement, defenses, trademark dilution, the Anti-Cybersquatting Consumer Protection Act, and damages and monetary relief. The chapter on trade dress embraces the acquisition of trade dress rights, infringement, trade dress dilution, affirmative defenses, and damages. Each jury instruction is accompanied a list of authorities and comments. The volume also includes a table of cases and index. The text of the jury instructions is also contained on a companion CD-ROM.

Mossoff, Adam, ed. **Intellectual Property and Property Rights**. Northampton, MA: Edward Elgar Publishing, 2013. 1 vol. (895 pp.).
Cost: $465.99 (online price: $418.50) (2014).
This collection of scholarly articles explores the relationship between intellectual property rights and property rights generally. A legal right identified as 'intellectual property,' would seem to be, by definition, a type of 'property.' Indeed, copyright, patents, and trade secrets, and related legal doctrines are defined in the law s property rights. However, these legal definitions do not fully explain or justify why IP rights should be characterized as property rights from a conceptual, normative, or historical perspective. Intended for lawyers, scholars, judges, policy makers, and students, this volume explores both the theory and practice of what it means to secure IP rights as property rights. The topic takes on an even greater urgency in the calls for the extension of IP protections to rapidly burgeoning world of digital and biotech creativity. The authors of these articles attempt to address the question of whether IP is really property by looking at the issue from three analytical frameworks: (1) conceptual; (2) normative; and (3) historical. The seventeen articles Descriptive and Normative Accounts of 'Intellectual Property' as Property; Copyright; Patents; Trademarks; Trade Secrets; and the Property-Based Critique of Intellectual Property. Includes articles by such leading scholars as Richard Epstein, Frank H. Easterbrook, Justin Hushes, Wendy J. Gordon, and Adam Mossoff. The articles are reprinted from a number of leading law reviews.

Moy, R. Carl. **Moy's Walker on Patents.** 4th ed. St. Paul, MN: West (Clark Boardman Callaghan), 2003-date. 13 vols. Annual supplementation. Looseleaf format.
Cost: $1,591; supplementation: 1993: $185; 1994: $265; 1995: $181.50; 1996: $199; 1997: $209; 1998: $222; 1999: $265; 2000: $259; 2001: $307; 2002: $360; 2003: $558; 2004: $229; 2005: $218; 2006: $568.50; 2007: $366; 2008: $417.50; 2009: $586; 2010: $643; 2011: $703; 2012: $771; 2013: $856; **Monthly Assured Print Price (APP):** $111/$1,332.
Originally published by Lawyers Cooperative Publishing Company, this is a complete and thorough analysis of patent law written by a member of the New York and South Carolina bars. **Walker on Patents,** written by Albert Henry Walker, was first published in 1885 and updated, successively, by Anthony William Deller, Ernest Bainbridge Lipscomb, and R. Carl Moy. This edition attempts to retain the best of the prior work while providing the researcher with an up-to-date analysis of recent case law under the Patent Act of 1952. The author provides the user with a history of common law monopolies and patent grants for inventions and a review of the constitutional and statutory basis for U.S. patent law. The remainder of the chapters cover persons entitled to patents, novelty, utility, patentable inventions, statutory bars, nature of letters patent, the patent application,

specification, claims, patent office procedures, interferences, reissue, reexamination. designs, plants, disclaimers, title, licenses, construction and validity, infringement, courts, causes and parties, declaratory judgments, injunctions, defenses, damages, patent antitrust, and trial and appellate procedure.

The Appendices include the complete historical text of all the patent law enactments, rules of practice, and the classic Notes of Justice Joseph Story. Volume 10 contains the **Manual of Patent Examining Procedure** (MPEP), a reprint of the Government Printing Office edition. A Table of Cases and Index are contained in Volume 11. The text is supported with extensive citations to applicable court decisions. Each chapter also includes Total Client-Service Library References to other former Lawyers Cooperative titles, including **ALR**, **Federal Procedures L.Ed.**, and the **USCS**. The annual pocket parts contain revisions to text as well as notes and annotations to recent court decisions and regulatory developments. A highly recommended reference tool for the patent attorney. The set is currently in transition

Cost Saving Tips: For the IP practitioner, the **IP Analytical** library on WestlawNext is a far better value than any of the West print or former CD-ROM products. For example, the cost of the print version of **Moy's Walker o Patents** alone is $1,545 initially and was $856 in 2013 to supplement versus $2,400.00 annually for the entire **IP Analytical** library. This is a graphic example of how Thomson Reuters is driving customers to WestlawNext instead of print.

Nimmer, Melville and Nimmer, David. **Nimmer on Copyright: A Treatise on the Law of Literary, Musical and Artistic Property, and the Protection of Ideas.** New York: Matthew Bender & Co., 1963-date. 10 vols. Looseleaf format. Also available on CD-ROM and the Internet. Supplemented approximately twice a year. CD-ROM features relevant case law and LEXIS-NEXIS online connection at no extra charge.
Cost: $3,087 (includes annual subscription); renewal: 1995: $600 (price frozen since 1992); 1996: $800; 1997: $800; 1998: $840; 1999: $880; 2000: $940; 2001: $1,006; 2002: $1,077; 2003: $1,131; 2004: $1,188; 2005: $1,283; 2006: $1,373; 2007: $1,483; 2008: $1,602; 2009: $1,730; 2010: $1,818; 2011: $1,909; 2012: $2,024; 2013: $2,166; 2014: $2,364; CD-ROM: $3,121; annual renewal: 1998: $840; 1999: $880; 2000: $940; 2001: $1,006; 2002: $1,077; 2003: $1,131; 2004: $1,188; 2005: $1,283; 2006: $1,373; 2007: $1,483; 2008: $1,616; 2009: $1,745; 2010: $1,833; 2011: $1,925; 2012: $2,041; 2013: $2,155; 2014: $2,431.68; eBook: $2,807; renewal: 2014: $2,364.
Originally authored by Melville Nimmer (1923-1985), late Professor of Law at UCLA and carried on by his son David Nimmer, currently associated with the Los Angeles firm of Irell & Manella, this is considered to be the most authoritative work in the area of copyright law and the most heavily cited by the courts. The text is lucidly written and well documented throughout and employs a type face which is easy on the eye. The analysis encompasses the constitutioal, statutory and common law aspects of copyright and applies these to transactions in various creative fields. The work embraces both the substantive and the procedural aspects of copyright including the application process, infringement actions, criminal actions, the enforcement and litigating of copyright claims, trial procedure and appeals. The set includes the full text of relevant laws, regulations, international conventions, and legislative reports, as well as applicable forms and njury instructions. The text is exhaustively documented with citations to primary and secondary authorities, including cases, statutes, and legislative history documents. Although originally written in 1963, the set was completely revised in 1978. This is a first-rate work of scholarship designed for the copyright and intellectual property specialist.

Cost Saving Tips: Investigate the availability of used sets to reduce your initial outlay and do not subscribe to the updates. If you buy new, cancel the standing order at the conclusion of the initial year's subscription. Them buy a replacement at some future date. In the interim, you must devise your own method of updating your research, however, by consulting the applicable primary sources, online services, West digests, Shepard's citators, etc. Those opting for the CD-ROM or Internet versions, however, must be prepared to lose access to the text if the subscription is not maintained. As an alternative, consider the **IP Analytical** on WestlawNext which will provide a complete library of IP titles instead of just one title for about the same price as Nimmer.

O'Connor, Edward F. **Intellectual Property Law and Litigation: Practical and Irreverent Insights.** Chicago, IL: American Bar Association, Tort, Trial and Insurance Practice Section, 2010. 1 vol. (333 pp.).
Cost: $119.95 ($84.95 to Section members); from $15.80 on amazon.com (2014).
This basic overview of intellectual property law uses humor with a particular emphasis on patent litigation. The book's five main sections consider antitrust law, patents, trademarks, copyrights, the International Trade Commission, and miscellaneous issues. The author consideration patent litigation embraces such considerations as attorney-client privilege, court versus jury: who decides what, expert witnesses, infringement, the doctrine of equivalents, claim interpretation, file wrapper estoppel, reissues, inequitable conduct, and more. He also explains how to prepare and present a complex intellectual property case to a jury and coordinate an effective discovery process. With clarity of expression and a deft use of anecdotes, the author makes a complex subject understandable.

Peterson, Gale R. and Derrick A. Pizarro. **2013 Federal Circuit Yearbook: Patent Law Developments in the Federal Circuit**. New York: Practising Law Institute, 2013. 1 vol. (517 pp.).
Cost: $295.00; from $175.48 on amazon.com (2014).
The United States Court of Appeals for the Federal Circuit was established under Article III of the Constitution on October 1, 1982, and was the result of a merger of the United States Court of Customs and Patent Appeals and the appellate division of the United States Court of Claims. The Federal Circuit is unique among the thirteen Circuit Courts of Appeals in that It has nationwide jurisdiction in a variety of subject areas, including international trade, government contracts, patents, trademarks, certain money claims against the United States government, federal personnel, veterans' benefits, and public safety officers' benefits claims. The published decisions of the Federal Circuit are controlling precedent on patent issues and provide a principal source for analyzing patent law developments in the United States. The **2013 Federal Circuit Yearbook** provides a summary

of all patent decisions published by the U.S. Court of Appeals for the Federal Circuit in 2012. The case summaries are grouped under the following chapters: utility and inventions patentable; novelty and statutory bars; nonobviousness; specification and claims; interference and priority of invention; claim construction; infringement; prosecution history estoppel; inequitable conduct; remedies; PTO practice and procedure; District Court jurisdiction and procedure; appellate court jurisdiction and practice; ownership agreements and inventorship; design patents ;and miscellaneous decisions. The concise case synopses focus on the prime issues of each case and provide the reader with an informed summary of the applicable facts and law of the key rulings in the field. This annual publication is an essential resource for any patent or intellectual property attorney who wants to keep abreast of the latest decisions in the field, as well as a useful reference for corporate attorneys and inventors. Gale R. (Pete) Peterson is senior shareholder in the intellectual property law department of the San Antonia firm of Cox Smith Matthew Incorporated, and a former examiner with the Patent and Trademark Office. Derrick A. Pizzaro is also a shareholder in the intellectual property law department of the Cox Smith Matthew.

Pinckney, Francis M. and David R. Higgins. **Products Comparison Manual for Trademark Users**. 3d ed. Arlington, VA: Bloomberg BNA Books, 2013-date. 1 vol. (2,000 pp.). Includes CD-ROM. Periodic supplementation.

Cost: $475; no supplementation to date; 2d ed.: 2009: $195; 2010: $205; 2011: $215; 2012: $225; 2013: new edition.

For those involved in trademark law and litigation, distinguishing between various marks that might be confusingly similar is a matter of no small importance. Whether prosecuting trademark applications in the Patent and Trademark Office (PTO) or litigating trademark rights before the Trademark Trial and Appeals Board (TTAB) and the federal courts, trademark attorneys must have access to the decisions which can be of guidance in making such distinctions between similar marks. This handy reference volume indexes more than 50,000 TTAB and court decisions since 1929, with citations to the decisions appearing in BNA's **U.S. Patent Quarterly**. As an aid to practitioners, the authors have analyzed the findings of the TTAB and courts in order to impose editorial uniformity on the descriptions of products listed in the cases and have assigned U.S. Class numbers to each product. The products are then aggregated by Class number so that users can more easily find synonymous product terms and closely similar products. A companion CD-ROM contains all the product comparisons contained in this volume, allowing the researcher to search these comparisons electronically and link, in most cases, to the full text decisions either on the USPTO's TTAB Decisions Web page or, for those with Bloomberg BNA subscriptions, to BNA's IP Library on the Web.

Pressman, David. **Patent It Yourself: Your Step-by-Step Guide to Filing at the U.S. Patent Office**. 16th ed. Berkeley, CA: Nolo, 2012. 1 vol. (624 pp.).

Cost: $49.99; from $28.39 on amazon.com; kindle: $28.97 (2014).

A patent *is a* right granted by the national government to anyone who invents or discovers any new and useful process, machine, article of manufacture, or composition of matter, or any new and useful improvement thereof. A patent for an invention is the grant of a property right to the inventor, issued by the United States Patent and Trademark Office (USPTO) and effective only within the United States, U.S. territories, and U.S. possessions. Generally, the term of a new patent is 20 years from the date on which the application for the patent was filed in the United States or, in special cases, from the date an earlier related application was filed, subject to the payment of maintenance fees. There are three types of patents: utility patents, design patents, and plant patents. In this well-written and comprehensive volume, attorney David Pressman provides a step-by-step guide to the patent process, from an introduction to patents and other forms of intellectual property to the specific steps necessary for an inventor to patent and commercially exploit an invention without the assistance of an attorney. To that end, he covers such critical topics as the science and magic of inventing, documentation and the Provisional Patent Application, the issue of salability, patentability, the patentability search, the drafting of specifications and drawings, claims, the completion and mailing of the application, marketing, filing abroad, getting the PTO to deliver, patent extensions, use, maintenance and infringement, and the ownership, assignment and licensing of inventions. The text is supplemented with numerous illustrations, charts, sample letters, and examples. The Appendices include a variety of useful features, fee schedules, and forms. First published in 1985, this volume has become the best selling and most widely used patent book. The author, a former patent examiner with the U.S. Patent and Trademark Office, and author of many patent-related books, has over 40 years experience as a patent attorney. Unlike other commercial publishers who charge exorbitantly for updates, Nolo provides free legal updates on its web site.

Schwartz, Herbert F. and Robert J. Goldman. **Patent Law and Practice**. 7th ed. Arlington, VA: Bloomberg BNA Books, 2011. 1 vol. (394 pp.). Paperbound.

Cost: $175; ebook: $169.99; no supplementation; from $118.83 on amazon.com (2014).

The United States Constitution grants Congress the power to promote the progress of the useful arts by securing for inventors the exclusive right to their discoveries for a limited period of time. That power was first exercised in 1790 when Congress authorized the issuance of U.S. Letters Patent to inventors. Pursuant to that authority, Congress also established a procedure for examining all patent applications; and patents were only issued when an examining board determined that the invention was sufficiently useful and important. Following an historical introduction to U.S. patent law, the authors provide an overview of proceedings in the Patent and Trademark Office, proceedings in the federal courts, patentability, claim construction, infringement, equitable defense, remedies, and jury trials. The volume also includes an annotated bibliography of works on patent law, a table of cases, and subject index. The text includes detailed citations to relevant primary and secondary authorities. The primary goal in publishing this work for the first time was to draft a primer focused exclusively on patent law, and on the leading issues that federal judges confront in the field. The 6th edition was driven by a need to review the state of the law in view of several recent U.S. Supreme Court decisions and the continuing evolution of the jurisprudence in the Federal Circuit in such areas as willful infringement, claim construction and inequitable conduct. Herbert Schwartz has specialized in intellectual property law since 1964 and is a former partner and, now, currently of counsel to the firm of Ropes & Gray LLP. He received his B.S. in Electrical Engineering from M.I.T., and both his M.A. in Applied Economics and LL.B. from the University of Pennsylvania. Robert Goldman, who also practices with Ropes and Gray where he specializes in intellectual property trials, received both his B.A. in Engineering and LL.B. from Columbia University. He won the largest litigated patent damages award against the Eastman Kodak Company in the amount of $873 million.

Scott, Michael D. **Scott on Multimedia: Law**. 3d ed. New York: Wolters Kluwer Law & Business, 2008-date. 1 vol. (1,600 pp.). Looseleaf format. Annual supplementation. Includes two discs of forms.
Cost: $525; supplementation: 2009: $155; 2010: $165; 2011: $175; 2012: $374; 2013: $200; 2d ed.: 1999-2001: 0; 2002: $143; 2003: $195; 2004: $235; 2005: $250; 2006: $255; 2007: $272; 2008: new edition.
A one-volume guide to the entire multimedia industry by an attorney with wide-ranging experience in the computer and intellectual property fields, including 19 years as a computer law practitioner. Michael Scott is currently counsel to the San Francisco law firm of Steinhart & Falconer and was formerly Vice President of Wildwood Interactive, a firm providing services and financing to the interactive multimedia industry. He is also the author of **Scott on Computers** and is the founder of both the **Computer Law Journal** and **Software Law Journal**. This volume addresses such issues as patent requirements, ownership rights, privacy issues, government regulation, rights to pre-existing works and the process of creating rights to new products. It provides an overview of the entire multimedia industry, including legal, business and technical issues, discussion of the source materials used in multimedia works, expert guidance on the legal aspects of creating and distributing multimedia works, including intellectual property law, torts, licensing, contracts and government regulation. The work also provides advice on how to deal with unions, guilds, licensing societies and other organizations on questions of rights to source materials. There are model agreements and sample contract clauses. Finally, the volume provides access to source materials, citations to relevant statutes, a resources directory, glossary of terms, bibliography, etc. Supplementation cost is reasonably priced given the depth and variety of materials. A standing order is recommended for the attorney specializing in this area.

Seiter, Bill. **The Creative Artist's Legal Guide: Copyright, Trademark, and Contracts and Film and Digital Media Production**. New Haven, CT: Yale University Press, 2012. 1 vol. (244 pp.). Paperbound.
Cost: $20.00; from $8.68 on amazon.com; kindle ed.: $11.49 (2014).
The law of intellectual property has been brought to life in this illuminating and entertaining overview by Bill and Ellen Seiter. They address the subjects of copyrights, trademarks, terms and conditions, contracts, the rights of privacy and publicity, and the Internet and new media with a level of clarity and wit rarely found in law-related texts. Each subject is illustrated with numerous real-world examples from court decisions and the intellectual property literature. Each chapter also includes one or more bibliographic essays on recommended books for further reading. Highly recommended to anyone interested in an entertaining introduction to intellectual property law. Ellen Seiter is professor and Stephen K. Nenno Endowed Chair in Critical Studies, School of Cinematic Arts, University of Southern California. She is also a filmmaker, media artist, and widely published critic. Bill Seiter is managing attorney, Seiter Legal Studio of Santa Monica and an expert on intellectual property topics.

Selz, Thomas D., Melvin Simensky and Patricia Nassif Acton. **Entertainment Law: Legal Concepts and Business Practices.** 3d ed. St. Paul, MN: West (Clark Boardman Callaghan), 2006-date. 5 vols. (approx. 3,662 pp.) Looseleaf format. Supplemented annually.
Cost: $1,157; supplementation: 1993: $80; 1994: $85; 1995: $90; 1996: $98; 1997: $103; 1998: $109; 1999: $229; 2000: $240; 2001: $284; 2002: $350; 2003: $187.50; 2004: $187.50; 2005: $191.25; 2006: $401; 2007: $231; 2008: $624; 2009: $189; 2010: $247; 2011: $416; 2012: $226.50; 2013; $245; **Monthly Assured Print Price (APP)**: $46/$552.
The authors of this four-volume treatise include Thomas D. Selz and Melvin Simensky, both practicing attorneys and Adjunct Professors of Law at New York University School of Law, and Patricia Acton, Clinical Professor of Law, University of Iowa College of Law. Unlike Lindey, this is a treatise with greater attention to the discussion and analysis of the legal issues involved in entertainment law. Sample forms are concentrated in volume four. The treatise component provides analysis of industry structure, investments, risk, power of distributors, credit, billing, contracts, unfair competition, right of publicity, defamation, remedies in credit disputes, artistic control, grant of rights, representations, warranties and indemnities, and compensation. There is also a glossary of industry and entertainment terms, tables of cases, statutes and authorities, and a subject index. Volume four contains a variety of sample entertainment industry forms. This is an excellent alternative to Lindey, particularly if you have a greater interest in the substantive discussion and analysis of entertainment law issues but still require sample forms. The cost for annual supplements is also considerably less than that of Lindey.

Sheldon, Jeffrey G. **How to Write a Patent Application.** 2d ed. New York: Practicing Law Institute, 2009-date. 1 vol. Looseleaf format. Supplemented annually.
Cost: $365; supplementation: 2010: $300 (2); 2011: $318 (2); 2012: $335 (2); 2013: $372; 1st ed.: 1994: $78.50; 1998: $97.25; 1999: 0; 2000: 0; 2001: $120; 2002: $270; 2003: $270; 2004: 0; 2006: $120; 2007: $254; 2008: $268; 2009: new edition.
A complete guide to the process of writing a patent application by an attorney with the Los Angeles firm of Sheldon & Mak. This step-by-step guide explains and illustrates all the basic concepts and principles involved in the application process, explains how to work with inventors, and how to conduct the novelty search. Chapters cover writing specifications, preparing information disclosure statements, and the design patent application. There is specific coverage of applications for plant patents, electrical patents, computer software, chemical inventions, and biotechnology patents. The substantive text is accompanied by sample forms, statutes, regulations, and checklists. Designed to assist the patent attorney in writing applications that survive litigation and licensing negotiations.

Slusky, Ronald D. **Invention Analysis and Claiming: A Patent Lawyer's Guide**. 2d ed. Chicago: American Bar Association, 2012. 1 vol. (375 pp.).
Cost: $139.95 ($125.95 to members); from $82.45 on amazon.com (2014).
This invaluable guide for the novice patent attorney provides the conceptual tools for analyzing inventions and identifying the "inventive concepts" necessary before claim drafting can commence. The author employs what he calls the "problem-solution paradigm" to identify the "inventive concept" prior to capturing it in a sophisticated set of patent claims. The book's teachings are grounded in "old school" principles of patent practice formerly learned only on the job from mentors and supervisors. The author systematically works through this approach in chapters which address such topics as invention concepts, the problem solution statement, fallback features and the planned retreat, problems-solution-based independent claims, inventive-departure-based independent claims, intermediate and narrow-scope claims, assembling the dependent claims, invention settings and direct infringers, statutory claim types, claim diversity, claims review with enforcement in mind, writing the background and summary, writing the description, claim rejections, claim amendments, and working with the inventor. The novice patent attorney will also appreciate the author's inventor interview technique called "self-directed learning." The book will also serve as a valuable overview of critical conceptual and practical approaches for the experienced patent attorney.

Sung, Lawrence M. **Patent Infringement Remedies**. Washington, DC: Bloomberg BNA Books, 2004. 1 vol. (756 pp.). Annual supplementation.
Cost. $425; supplementation: 2006: $195; 2007: $195; 2008: $210; 2009: $225; 2010: $230; 2011: $240; 2012: $245; 2013: 0.
Liability from patent infringement can implicate a defendant whose conduct involves a product or process that infringes one or more claims of a U.S. patent.
A successful defense to such claims of infringement may involve a challenge to the validity of the patent claims or the enforceability of those claims. The specific remedial goals include prevention of harm, restoration of the status quo ante, compensation for proximate detriment, and punishment and deterrence. In this in-depth examination of patent infringement remedies, the author addresses such topics as direct and indirect infringement liability, the determination of patent infringement, specific infringement liability, compensatory damages, lost profits, reasonable royalty, non-compensatory damages, injunctive relief, other statutory remedies, opinions of counsel, valuation models, contracting around liability, collateral concerns, case presentation, and alternative dispute resolution, remedies for infringement, patent portfolio management considerations, and litigation matters. Appendices include a sample complaint, sample jury instructions, a patent valuation model, and an audit checklist. The volume also includes a table of cases and index. The text is buttressed by extensive citations to and excerpts from relevant patent decisions decided in the federal courts. The author is an attorney with the Technology and Intellectual Property Group of the Washington, DC firm of Nixon Peabody and a professor of law at the University of Maryland School of Law.

Torremans, Paul, ed. **Copyright Law: A Handbook of Contemporary Research**. Northampton, MA: Edward Elgar, 2008. 1 vol. (544 pp.). Hardbound.
Cost: $248 (online discount: $223.50); softbound: $94 (online: $75.20); from $72.41 on amazon.com (2014).
This collection of articles on contemporary copyright issues is the product of research by more than twenty noted international copyright scholars. Each of the articles addresses a cutting edge legal issue, or the impact of technology on traditional copyright principles. While the most of the articles have an American, Canadian, British, European or trans-national focus, the development of copyright law in Asia and the pressing issue of copyright piracy is also addressed. Among the topics considered are the role of originality in copyright, legal issues pertaining to the restoration of manuscripts, sheet music, paintings and films for marketing purposes, database protection, database copyright, public domain, multimedia works, protection of folklore, individual and collective management of copyright in a digital environment, copyright law and scientific research, copyright law and freedom of expression in Sweden, on-line teaching and copyright, copyright piracy in Asia, alternative dispute resolution, questioning the principles of territoriality, and a broadcasters' treaty. The contributors are all notable legal scholars at American, Canadian, European or international academic institutions.

U.S. Patents Quarterly. Washington, DC: Bloomberg BNA. CD-ROM. Also bundled as part of the publisher's **Intellectual Property Law Resource Center**.
Cost: $3,661 per year; Internet: not sold separately (see Intellectual Property Resource Center) (2014).
A comprehensive and authoritative service providing access to thousands of intellectual property decisions decided by the U.S. Supreme Court, U.S. Court of Appeals (including the Federal Circuit), U.S. Court of Federal Claims (and its predecessor, U.S. Claims Court), U.S. District Courts, Commissioner of Patents and Trademarks, U.S. Patent and Trademark Office, Trademark Trial and Appeal Board, U.S. Tax Court, state courts, and various special courts, with headnotes written by BNA editors. Print service utilizes BNA's unique classification system for case retrieval. Electronic service uses a special search template.

West's Legal Forms. Vol. 25-25A: Patents--Trademarks--Copyrights. 3d ed. St. Paul, MN: West, 2001-date. 2 vols. Annual pocket parts.
Cost: $353; supplementation: 1999: $12.50; 2000: $12.50; 2001: $27; 2002: $30; 2003: $34; 2004: $34; 2005: $40; 2006: $43; 2007: $45; 2008: $33.50; 2009: $37; 2010: $41; 2011: $41; 2012: $43; 2013: $53.50.
This one volume from **West's Legal Forms 2d** contains a broad collection of patent, trademark and copyright forms in a reduced format. Includes a brief overview of patent law followed by hundreds of annotated forms. May be purchased separately from the remainder of the set. The publisher will also establish a standing order for these volumes only. Supplementation cost is a rare bargain in today's world of aggressive pricing.

Wright, Bradley C., editor-in-chief. **Drafting Patents for Litigation and Licensing**. 2d ed. Arlington, VA: Bloomberg BNA Books, in cooperation with the Section of Intellectual Property Law, American Bar Association, 2013-date. 1 vol. (776 pp.).
Cost: $445; no supplementation to date; 1st ed.: 2009: $195; 2010: $195; 2011: $200; 2012: $205.
In the words of former U.S. Supreme Court Justice Henry Billings Brown, "the specifications and claims of a patent, particularly if the invention be at all complicated, constitute one of the most difficult legal instruments to draw with accuracy" and "frequently fail to describe with requisite certainty the exact invention of the patentee." Rather than a guide to the mechanics of patent drafting, this volume examines in depth the court decisions, particularly those of the U.S. Court of Appeals for the Federal Circuit, in which specific patents were interpreted, enforced or licensed to the benefit or detriment of the patent owner. Patents are not only litigated, but often licensed, either under threat of litigation or pursuant to a need to obtain intellectual property rights that may provide competitive advantage in the marketplace. The scope and strength of a patent that is the subject of a license can have enormous consequences in the form of licensing revenues. This volume is designed to help patent attorneys draft the broadest possible patents that can sustain a validity challenge. The chapters provide an in-depth examination of a number of specific legal issues and commercial environments in which patent applications have been applied and interpreted by the courts. The first four chapters address the state of the law of claim construction and infringement, the pitfalls of patent drafting, the drafting of a winning patent, and the continued prosecution of the patent. Other chapters probe the specific fields of mechanical patents; electrical patents; software, E-commerce, Internet and business method patents; chemical and pharmaceutical patents; biotechnology patents; and design patents. The concluding chapters analyze the combining of prosecution with other forms of prosecution, and the drafting U.S. patents with a view towards Europe. Each chapter is accompanied by numerous citations to federal case law. Editor and author Bradley Wright, a seasoned patent attorney with the Washington, DC firm of Banner & Witcoff, brings to this effort a background in both electrical engineering (M.I.T.) and law (George Mason). He is joined by fifteen contributing authors whose backgrounds combine legal and specific technological expertise. This is an indispensable resource to any patent attorney who wants to understand the broader legal context in which his patent instruments are likely to be applied.

Additional titles on the topics of Patents, Trademarks and Intellectual Property are available from the following publishers: Allworth Press, American Bar Association, American Intellectual Property Law Assoc. (AIPLA) American Law Institute, Aspen Publishing, Matthew Bender, Bloomberg BNA Books, Carolina Academic Press, CRC Press, Foundation Press, Gordon Press, Greenwood Publishing Group, Harvard University Press, William S. Hein & Co., Inventions Co., Kluwer Academic Publications, Kluwer Law International, Lewis Publications, LexisNexis, Nolo Press, Panel Publishers, Thomson Reuters West, West Academic. See Appendix B for addresses and telephone numbers.

Products Liability

American Law Institute**. Restatement of the Law Third. Torts: Products Liability**. St. Paul, MN: American Law Institute, 1998-date. 2 vols. (382 pp.). Annual pocket parts.
Cost: $179; supplementation: 2000: $21; 2001: $21; 2002: $26; 2003: $29; 2004: $29; 2005: $25; 2006: $28; 2007: $28; 2008: $29.50; 2009: $32; 2010: $32; 2011: $32; 2012: $33; 2013: $39.
The Restatement of the Law Third, Torts: Products Liability encompasses that aspect of tort law which deals with the liability of commercial product sellers and distributors for harm caused by their products. This volume represents the first installment in the American Law Institute's effort to completely revise and update the **Restatement Second of Torts**. It supersedes Section 402A of the **Restatement Second** promulgated 35 years ago and addresses products liability issues which were not under consideration when the earlier provision was adopted in 1964.

American Law of Products Liability. 3d ed. St. Paul, MN: West (Clark Boardman Callaghan), 1987-date. 18 vols. Looseleaf pamphlet format. Supplemented quarterly. Includes newsletter at no additional charge.
Cost: $5,408; supplementation: 1993: $581.50; 1994: $680; 1995: $810; 1996: $900; 1997: $970; 1998: $1,016; 1999: $1,096; 2000: $1,268; 2001: $1,312.50; 2002: $1,495; 2003: $1,485; 2004: $1,630; 2005: $1,894; 2006: $2,083; 2007: $2,132; 2008: $1,792.49; 2009: $2,850; 2010: $3,101; 2011: $3,254; 2012: $3,532; 2013: $3,920.50; **Monthly Assured Print Price (APP):** $327/$3,924. **Products Liability Advisory** newsletter alone: $861.96 (up from $687 in 2012). Also available on Westlaw **Products Liability Analytical Library** at approx. $1,272 per year (single user).
This set is the major competition to Frumer and Friedman's **Products Liability.** What it lacks in depth and historical analysis, it more than makes up for in terms of breadth and practical guidance for the practitioner. The topical coverage encompasses all the theories of products liability law, warnings, defenses, procedure, damages and fees. More than 40 chapters, each of which is in pamphlet form for easy replacement (and, unfortunately, theft), cover specific product groups. The text is thoroughly annotated and buttressed with references to other Lawyers Cooperative titles, including **Am Jur Proof of Facts, Am Jur Trials, American Law Reports,** etc. Where appropriate, there are citations to the laws of each state. The text is also laced with Observations, Practice Pointers, Comments, Notes, and Cautions, Illustrations, and Law Review Commentaries throughout. An extremely well-organized reference tool for the specialist. Kept current with cumulative quarterly supplementary pamphlets to each binder as well as periodic replacement of individual chapter pamphlets in body of set.

Cost Saving Tips: If you specialize in the products liability field, you may wish to consider subscribing to the **Products Liability Analytical Library** on Westlaw which provides access to a variety of products liability texts and related materials from other West publications. This is a far better value than maintaining standing orders to the same titles in print. If you purchase this print set, drop the standing order and update the basic text periodically in consultation with your sales representative. Quarterly supplementation may be excessive if you are using the set correctly to get an overview of the topic and locate representative cases on point, and not as the last step in the research process.

Bass, Lewis P. E. **Products Liability: Design and Manufacturing Defects.** 2d ed. St. Paul, MN: West (Clark Boardman Callaghan), 2011-date. 1 vol. Annual replacement volumes.
Cost: 2013-2014: $177; 2012-2013 Edition: $162; supplementation to previous editions: 2002: $37; 2003: $43; 2004: $50; 2005: $54; 2006: $61.50; 2007: $69; 2008: $76; 2009: $132; 2010: $101; 2011: $112; 2011-2012: $149; 1st ed: 1995: $40; 1996: $60; 1997: $75; 1998: $75; 1999: $81; 2000: $92; 2001: $130 (new edition); **Monthly Assured Print Price (APP)**: $15/$180.
This one-volume treatise is designed to serve the needs of the litigator in products liability actions as well as engineers and managers responsible for safe product design. Its author is a lawyer and mechanical and safety engineer with the University of Southern California's Institute of Safety and Systems Management. Attention is given to the liability of manufacturers and the entire design process, including regulatory and voluntary standards, evaluation of product design, system safety engineering, warnings, concepts, testing, the manufacturing process, industrial accidents, packaging, and use in the field. Additional chapters are devoted to product liability litigation, damages, organizing for product safety, the safety and liability audit, insurance, and risk engineering. Includes citations to cases, statutes, and regulations.

Daller, Morton F., ed. **Tort Law Desk Reference: A Fifty State Compendium**. New York: Wolters Kluwer Law & Business, 2008-date. 1 vol. Annual editions. Paperbound.
Cost: 2013 Edition: $297; prior editions: 2003: $176.00; 2004: $170.00; 2005: $175; 2006: $180; 2007: $192; 2008: $205; 2009: $230; 2010: $245; 2011: $260; 2012: $297.
This volume provides concise summaries of the products liability laws of all fifty states written by leading local practitioners. Drawing upon both state statutes and case law, these summaries cover such areas as strict liability, negligence, compensatory and punitive damages, statutes of limitations, breach of warranty, wrongful death, contribution and indemnity, and misrepresentation. An ideal tool for the products liability litigator who wishes to assess the strengths and weaknesses of his or her case across jurisdictions. Morton Daller is a trial lawyer, partner in the Fort Washington, PA firm of Daller Greenberg & Dietrich, and former President of the Philadelphia Association of Defense Counsel. Originally titled **Product Liability Desk Reference**.

Frumer, Louis R. and Melvin I. Friedman. **Products Liability.** New York: Matthew Bender & Co., 1960-date. 11 vols. Looseleaf format, CD-ROM, or eBook. Supplemented 3 times per year.
Cost: $5,992 (includes annual subscription); renewal: 1995: $1,518 (price frozen since 1992); 1996: $1,592; 1997: $1,592; 1998: $1,675; 1999: $1,750; 2000: $1,870; 2001: $2,001; 2002: $2,142; 2003: $2,250; 2004: $2,363; 2005: $2,528; 2006: $2,630; 2007: $2,840; 2008: $3,067; 2009: $3,312; 2010: $3,545; 2011: $3,651; 2012: $3,797; 2013: $4,063; 2014: $4,434; CD-ROM: $7,496; renewal: 1998: $1,595; 1999: $1,655; 2000; $1,770; 2001: $1,894; 2002: $2,027; 2003: $2,129; 2004: $2,235; 2005: $2,392; 2006: $2,560; 2007: $2,765; 2008: $3,014; 2009: $3,255; 2010: $3,614; 2011: $3,975; 2012: $4,412; 2013: $4,721; 2014: $5,352.96; eBook: $5,447; renewal: 2014: $4,434.
If you are looking for a thorough treatment of the law of products liability, this ten-volume treatise by Frumer and Friedman is the most complete on the market. Every aspect of the topic is covered in rich detail and exhaustively supported with annotated citations to both primary and secondary sources. The authors, members of the New York and Michigan bars, and the publisher's editorial staff, provide in-depth coverage of the history and of products liability law as it has evolved from a minor subfield of commercial and negligence litigation to a significant field in its own right. They trace the expansion of the legal protections offered as the common law has moved from the privity of contract doctrine to the strict liability doctrine as enunciated in Section 402A of the **Restatement (Second) of Torts**. The substance of the set consists of 100 chapters and 15 appendices with coverage of all products liability doctrines, including strict liability, breach of warranty and negligence, as well as a consideration of the issues of damages, manufacturing and design defects, evidence, specific products, product safety management, and much more. The Appendices include state and federal products liability legislation, uniform acts, ABA Recommendations, etc. The type face adopted in the more recent supplements is also easy on the eye. Volume 5 includes a valuable Table of Cases by Product.

Cost Saving Tips: Substantively, this is a first-class work of scholarship and an essential tool for the product liability specialist. The only negative aspect of this set may be the high initial and supplementation cost for some practitioners. The wise law book consumer will first seek out in his or her local law library or its availability on the used law book market where it sells for a fraction of the new set price. Or, alternatively, you can subscribe for a year, then drop the standing order. You must, however, update your research by using the primary sources, Shepardizing cases, etc. The disadvantage of the CD-ROM and Internet formats is that you cannot take advantage of the cyclical reordering strategy available with print.

Goodman, Richard M. and Center for Auto Safety. **Automobile Design Liability**. 3d ed. St. Paul, MN: West (CBC), 1991-date. 6 vols. Looseleaf format. Annual supplementation.
Cost: $1,351; supplementation: 1999: $244; 2000: $258; 2001: $300; 2002: $325; 2003: $365.50; 2004: $415; 2005: $389; 2006: $507; 2007: $733.50; 2008: $593.50; 2009: $660.50; 2010: $735; 2011: $816; 2012: $905; 2013: $1,004; **Monthly Assured Print Price (APP):** $100/$1,200.
This three-volume reference guide is designed to serve the needs of trial attorneys involved in litigating automobile products liability actions. Volume one contains a summary of automobile products liability law, a guide to cases by product defect, and the text of federal, state, and private safety standards, including applicable references to the U.S. Code and Code of Federal Regulations. Volume two contains summaries of major automobile product recalls organized by manufacturer and component. Volume three provides a comprehensive guide to

sources of information on auto defects, listings of government safety investigations, and lists of experts and consultants in the field of automobile safety, cross-referenced by area of expertise and state. It concludes with a detailed technical bibliography. The volumes include extensive citations to primary law and secondary sources, including references to other West (formerly Lawyers Cooperative) Total Client-Service Library products. Richard M. Goodman is a practicing attorney and member of the California and Michigan bars. Generous assistance was provided the staff of the Center for Auto Safety.

Madden, M. Stuart, David G. Owen, and Mary J. Davies-Scott. **Products Liability**. 3d ed. St. Paul, MN: West, 2000-date. 3 vols. Annual supplementation.
Cost: $439; supplementation: 2001: $75; 2002: $84; 2003: $96; 2004: $115.50; 2005: $124; 2006: $141; 2007: $158.50; 2008: $175; 2009: $195; 2010: $228; 2011: $249; 2012: $271; 2013: $295; 2d ed.: 1994: $42; 1995: $42; 1996: 0; 1997: 0; 1998: $95; 1999: $96; **Monthly Assured Print Price (APP)**: $30/$360.
This three-volume treatise is a worthy and economical alternative for the attorney who requires a scholarly overview of both the theories and practical application of products liability law without all the detail, product specifics, or high cost associated with either **Frumer and Friedman** or the **American Law of Products Liability**. The authors compares the various theories under which products liability actions are brought, including negligence, breach of warranty, strict liability in tort, and deceit and misrepresentation. Liability for defective design, manufacturing assembly, testing, inspection, and the duty to warn are discussed as well as liability for activities involving particularly dangerous products. Additional legal issues covered include affirmative defenses, causation, joint liability, post-manufacturing obligations, contribution and indemnity, limitation of actions, jurisdiction, conflict of laws, multiple litigation, and damages. There is a discussion of specific liability for drug products and medical devices, instruments and equipment as well as products liability insurance. The text is thoroughly supported with citations to cases, statutes, books, treatises, and articles.

Owen, David G. **Products Liability in a Nutshell.** 8th ed. St. Paul, MN: West, 2009. 1 vol. (595 pp.). Available from West Academic.
Cost: $41; from $23.00 on amazon.com (2014).
This brief, student-oriented overview in the publisher's Nutshell Series aims to state the established rules of products liability and how those rules are applied in various factual contexts, the reasons behind the rules, and how they are distinguished from other closely related rules. Chapters include: definition and scope; causes of action and damages; the parties; factors affecting choice of remedies, jurisdiction and procedure; production and design defects; inadequate warnings and instructions, and misrepresentations; and problems of proof. Case citations are selective as one might expect in a work of this kind.

Product Liability Law Treatise Library on LoisLawConnect. New York: Wolters Kluwer Law & Business.
Cost: $540.00 per year (solo practitioner) (2014).
This library addresses all aspects of products liability and personal injury litigation from first client interview to settlement, including statutes of limitations, the standards of proof, breach of warranty, negligence, strict liability and the standard of care. Titles include: **The Preparation of a Product Liabiliy Case, Product Liability Case Digest**, **Product Liability Desk Reference, Product Warnings, Defects and Hazards, Scientific Evidence and Experts Handbook, Malingering and Deception in Litigation, and Smart Charts**, together withforms and checklists drawn from the above.

Products Liability Reporter. Riverwoods, IL: Wolters Kluwer Law & Business (CCH), 1953-date. 2 vols. Looseleaf service. Also available on the Internet. Print updated biweekly, Internet biweekly.
Cost: print: $2,225 per year; Internet: contact sales representative (2014).
This two-volume looseleaf service provides comprehensive and timely coverage of products liability issues, including court decisions and rules on liability for product-related injuries. There is discussion of such topics as strict liability, breach of warranty, negligence, defense, insurance, and the Uniform Commerce Commercial Code. Includes the text of relevant products liability statutes for every jurisdiction, as well as useful charts and tables. The thoroughly annotated text also provides a summary of cases by damage awards.

Additional titles on Products Liability are available from the following publishers: American Bar Association, American Law Institute, Wolters Kluwer Law & Business, Matthew Bender, CCH, Defense Research Institute, Delacorte Press, Harvard University Press, William S. Hein & Co., Kluwer Academic Publications, Knowles Publishing, New York Law Publishing, Practising Law Institute, Roscoe Pound Institute, Thomson Reuters West, Warren, Gorham & Lamont, West Academic. See Appendix B for addresses and telephone numbers.

Public Utilities

Bonbright, James C., Albert L. Danielsen, and David R. Kamerschen. **Principles of Public Utility Rates**. 2d ed. Vienna, VA: Public Utilities Reports, Inc., 1988. 1 vol. (700 pp.).
Cost: $139.00 (2014).
This book is the classic exposition of the foundational principles underlying public utility pricing theories and policies, and the economic concepts which provide the basis for rate designs. First issued in 1961, this work is a standard reference for those involved in the analysis and implementation of fair and reasonable utility rates. The book's twenty-two chapters are grouped under the following headings: scope and general paradigm issues, the paradigm of public utility regulation, the rate base and rate of return, the rate structure, and criticism of and alternatives to traditional public utility regulation. The analysis is applied particularly to the telecommunications, electric, and gas industries. It includes a list of references, as well as author,

subject, and public law and case indices. The late James C. Bonbright (1891-1985) was an American economist and political scientist, and a pioneer in the field of public utility regulation.

Corssmit, C. W., ed. **Water Rates, Fees, and the Legal Environment**. 2d ed. Denver, CO: American Water Works Association, 2010. 1 vol. (190 pp.). Paperbound
Cost: $105.00; from $94.08 on amazon.com (2014).
Water utilities in the United States are subject to various legal environments that
Influence the management of this precious resource and govern equitable rate practices, an increasing number of which are designed to encourage conservation. Although various regulatory agencies, environmental groups, agricultural organizations, industrial trade associations, and other water-oriented institutions play a significant part in protecting water resources, most of the nation's water supply is managed by a water utility under state regulation. State enabling legislation provides the legislative basis for how these utilities are organized and the type of revenue sources they may use to collect the funds to support the water services they provide. It was in response to these concerns that the American Water Works Association (AWWA) sponsored a 2002 preconference workshop titled "Water Rates. Fees and the Legal Environment," from which this collection of articles is derived. The introductory chapter reviews the legal authority for water utilities, the history of water rate lawsuits, the methodologies employed for setting water rates, and the legal principles involved in rate design. Additional chapters consider water rate conflict resolution in the legal system, the avoidance of lawsuits, how to react to lawsuits: real of imagined, technical rate analysis and arbitration caveats. Three case studies address fee disputes in Billings, Montana; Breckinridge, Colorado; and California, while a fourth provides a confidential case study involving revenue bond compliance. The editor is vice president of Malcolm Pirnie, Inc., where he specializes in water and wastewater utility financial planning, cost-of-service analysis and rate design. He is a past chair of the AWWA Rate's and Charges Committee. The other contributors are consultants, experts, lawyers or managers with expertise in the water utility industry. This volume updates the first edition issued in 2005.

Enholm, Gregory B. and J. Robert Malko. **Reinventing Electric Utility Regulation**. Vienna, VA: Public Utilities Reports, Inc., 1995. 1 vol. (502 pp.). No supplementation except in the form of new editions.
Cost: $69; from $7.50 on amazon.com (2014).
This collection of articles examines many of the leading issues which have impacted regulation of the electrical industry in recent years. Written by utility executives, state regulators, federal regulatory commissioners, and representatives of utilities, the financial community, and producers of independent and public power, they address changes and regulation in the industry.

Ferrey, Steven. **Law of Independent Power: Development, Cogeneration, Utility Regulation**. St. Paul, MN: West (Clark Boardman), 1989-date. 3 vols. Looseleaf format. Annual supplementation.
Cost: $1,817; ProView eBook: $1,817; supplementation: 2001: $375; 2002: $412; 2003: $375; 2004: $393; 2005: $420; 2006: $718.50; 2007: $718.50; 2008: $799; 2009: $889.50; 2010: $688; 2011: $1,156; 2012: $1,271; 2013: $1,334; **Monthly Assured Print Price (APP):** $133/$1,596.
The rise of independent power production in the United States is an outgrowth of Congressional concerns regarding the use of foreign oil for the production of electricity in the resulting from the oil embargoes of the early 1970s. In an effort to reduce reliance on foreign oil, Congress sought to lessen the use of oil for generation of electricity and to encourage the use of alternative fuels, including waste, wood, biomass, wind, solar, and geothermal. In 1978, it passed the Public Utility Regulatory Policies Act (PURPA), which forced the franchised electrical utility monopolies to allow nonutility generators to connect to the transmission system and forced the utilities to buy the power generated by the nonutility generation stations for a price that equaled the cost of power that the utility would have incurred if it had built the generating station itself. This work is designed to help independent power producers, developers, financiers, energy marketers, and their attorneys understand the legal and regulatory issues involved in independent energy production. Following an overview of field, the author addresses the subject of generation technologies, the successful projects: the power market, economics, tax aspects and development strategy of independent power and demand side management, the regulation of qualifying facility (QF) power, federal regulation of independent power production and non-qualifying facilities, avoided cost, wheeling power, power auctions and bidding, and deregulation of power. Appendices (vols. 2-3) include information on state standby and backup, as well as terms, tariffs, a glossary, table of cases, and index. Steven Ferrey is a professor of law at Suffolk University Law School, a former senior counsel to the National Consumer Law Center, and a widely published author in the fields of energy and environmental law and public utilities.

Goodman, Leonard Saul. **The Process of Ratemaking**. Vienna, VA: Public Utilities Reports, Inc., 1998. 2 vols. No supplementation except in the form of new editions.
Cost: $299 (2014).
This comprehensive resource is designed to assist regulators in making rates for utilities and other regulated industries. It eschews theory for practical strategies and data which can be translated into ratemaking. The author provides a highly readable introduction of the history of regulation and rate making. He also examines such topics as the rate proceeding, discretion and judgment, revenue, cost of service (basic and advanced), depreciation, operating ratio and profit margin methods, rate of return on rate base, return of total capitalization, income taxes, the rate base, honest, economic and efficient management, prudent management, value of service and differential pricing, pricing, rate design, and rate structure rate discounts, incentives, and distributions, contract rates and other agreed charges, sliding scale and automatic adjustment clauses, statutory rate prescriptions, charters, and franchises. With 1,200 pages of text, 6,800 footnotes and 300 charts, tables and formulas, this is the definitive work on the subject and an essential acquisition for any attorney involved in regulatory issues. Leonard Saul Goodman is a member of the District of Columbia Bar with more than 40 years of practice in the administrative law of ratemaking. He currently serves as a rate consultant to government agencies and departments, and law firms.

Gutierrez, Jay M. and Alex S. Polonsky. **Fundamentals of Nuclear Regulation in the United States**. 2d ed. Vienna, VA: Public Utilities Reports, Inc., 2007. 1 vol. (345 pp.). Softbound.
Cost: OUT-OF-PRINT; was $139; 1st edition from $40 on amazon.com (2014).
As countries seeks to develop alternative sources of energy to meet increasing worldwide demand, nuclear power is becoming a more serious option across the globe. For the United States, nuclear power is an indispensable ingredient in the goal of achieving energy independence. This introductory text considers the full range of issues involved in nuclear regulation, including the role of the Niclear Regulatory Commission (NRC), and the rulemaking, licensing, hearing, inspection, and enforcement processes. It also addresses a number of current regulatory issues. An index and detailed glossary are also included to guide the reader through the terminology unique to the nuclear industry.The book is co-authored by Jay M. Gutierrez, a partner in the law firm of Morgan Lewis and former Nuclear Regulatory Commission (NRC) Regional Counsel, and nuclear regulatory lawyer, Alex Polonsky.

Harak, Charles, Olivia Bae Wein and Gillian Feiner. **Guide to the Rights of Utility Consumers**. Boston, MA: National Consumer Law Center, 2006. 1 vol. (190 pp.).
Cost: $15.00; from $1.61 on amazon.com (2014).
This book is a product of the experiences of the National Consumer Law Center, one of the nation's largest consumer advocacy organizations, in providing advice to individual consumers about their utility service. That advice has been even more critical as utility costs have rtisen 50-100% over the past five years. Moreover, had cap and trade trade legislation passed Congress in 2009, the average family would have looking at future increased energy costs of about $1,750 annually, according to the Obama administration's Treasury Department, much of which woud have been in the form of home heating and electric costs. That advocacy embraces such issues as making payment plans and avoiding utility service terminations, as well as broader issues of rate hikes, adoption of low-income discount rates, and the design of programs to make it easier for low income individuals to afford their utility bills. Designed for both consumers and those in front-line positions who provide advice to individuals with various consumer, financial, and family problems, this practical guide focuses primarily on gas and electric service issues. Following an overview of utility service and regulation, the authors discuss such practical issues as obtaining service, deposits, prior bills, and bills of others. Subsequent chapters discuss ways consumers can get help in paying or lowering their bills, restrictions on termination of service, late and reconnect charges, asserting consumer rights before the Public Utilities Commission (PUC) and elsewhere. Additional chapters discuss the basics of telephone and water services, and unregulated deliverable fuels (including home heating oil, propane, and kerosene). The Appendices include a state-by-state guide to utility terminations, selected utility regulations, utility contact information, serious illness certification, state utility regulations, federal poverty guidelines, a Consumer's Guide to Intervening ion State Public Utility Proceedings, a bibliography of other relevant NCLC publications, and subject index. Charles Harak and Olivia Bae Wein are NCLC staff attorneys focusing on low-income energy and utility issues. Gillian Feiner is a consumer fellow at the NCLC and an attorney with the Boston firm of Klein, Roddy & Ryan. This is just one of dozens of high-quality consumer law books published by NCLC.

Hyman, Leonard S., Richard Toole, and Edward di Napoli. **The New Telecommunications Industry: Meeting the Competition**. Vienna, VA: Public Utilities Reports, Inc., 1995. 1 vol. (480 p.). Paperbound. No supplementation except in the form of new editions.
Cost: $90; from $2.98 on amazon.com (2014).
A comprehensive overview of the telecommunications industry, including its history, organization, financing, and technology. Designed for both veterans and neophytes, this volume examines the history of the industry, the operations o the system, the competitive forces involved, the regulatory foundations of the industry, the rise of competition, the rate structure, the financial structure, financial analysis, and the international market place. The appendices include discussion of the Internet, a telecommunications chronology, bibliography, and historical statistics. There is also subject, figure, and tables indices. An excellent and clearly written introduction to the complicated world of telecommunications.

Hyman, Leonard S., ed. **The Privatization of Public Utilities**. Vienna, VA: Public Utilities Reports, Inc., 1995. 1 vol. (473 p.). No supplementation except in the form of new editions.
Cost: $119; from $3.50 on amazon.com (2014).
A comprehensive overview of the process by which privatization of public utilities is effectuated, including such issues as making deals, industry restructuring, after-sale issues, regulation, investment banking, stock market analysis, accounting, and more. The articles in this volume were written by a number of internationally known utility industry executives, financiers, and consultants. Includes privatization case studies from around the globe.

Hyman, Leonard S. **The Water Business: Understanding the Water Supply and Wastewater Industry**. Vienna, VA: Public Utilities Reports, Inc., 1998. 1 vol. (400 pp.).
Cost: $89; from $3.48 on amazon.com (2014).
Providing safe driking water to the populations of the United States and the woold is one of the major resource and environmental challenges facing mankind. Much of that water is delivered by both state-sponsored utilities and private water companies, some of them international in scope. This volume provides an illuminating review of the water supply and wastewater industry and the political and regulatory climate in which they operates. The author addresses water basics, operations, developmnt and structure of the industry, regulation and economics, financial structure, and international issues. A useful tool for regulators, operators, supervisors, investors, and academics.

Lesser, Jonathan A. and Leonardo R. Giacchino. **Fundamentals of Energy Regulation**. Vienna, VA: Public Utilities Reports, Inc., 2007. 1 vol.
Cost: $139; from $93.97 on amazon.com (2014).
This work is designed to provide an introductory overview

of energy regulation for a broad range of practitioners in the field, including lawyers, managers, regulators, and investors. The authors explain the regulatory framework in which energy companies operate, as well as significant economic and regulatory concepts. The text includes numerous case studies and examples. The book also reviews the practical side of some of the newer regulatory structures, including estimation of productivity and inflation factors as ingredients in price and revenue cap regulation. The authors are partners in Bates White, a national consulting firm offering services in economics, finance, and business analytics to leading law firms.

Phillips, Charles F., Jr. **The Regulation of Public Utilities**. 3d ed. Vienna, VA: Public Utilities Reports, Inc., 1993. 1 vol. (1,025 pp.). No supplementation except in the form of new editions.
Cost: $139; from $3.73 on amazon.com (2014).
A comprehensive treatise on the nature of public utility regulation in an age of deregulation. The author lucidly explains the basic concepts of the regulatory process, and provides an introductory overview of public utilities in the American economy. He also addresses the economic, legal and administrative concepts of public utility regulation and examines those issues currently facing public utility regulators. His consideration of the theory of public utility regulation includes chapters on the goals, procedures and theories of public utility regulation, accounting and finance, operating expenses, depreciation and taxes, the rate base, the rate of return, the rate structure, and service, safety and management efficiency. Finally, he devotes four chapters to a consideration of four specific industries: electric power, natural gas, telecommunications, and water. The book concludes with an appraisal of regulation. The book also includes a comprehensive index of subjects, names, and cases. A highly recommended reference work for regulators and attorneys representing utilities. Charles Phillips is the Robert G. Brown Professor of Economics at Washington and Lee University.

Pierce, Richard J. and Ernest Gellhorn. **Regulated Industries in a Nutshell.** 4th ed. St. Paul, MN: West, 1999. 1 vol. (412 pp.). Nutshell Series. Available from West Academic.
Cost: $41; from $25.67 on amazon.com (2014).
A succinct overview of the public utilities industry and the regulatory framework which governs it. This volume is primarily intended for a law school audience, but also serves as a useful overview for practicing attorneys, judges and regulators with a limited background in the law and economics of regulation. The authors discuss the reasons for regulating, the legal basis of regulation, rate regulation, maximum price regulation, rates to customers, regulation of service level and quality, minimum rate regulation, restrictions on energy, rationing restricted resources, alternatives to cost of service rate regulation, antitrust and regulation, primary jurisdiction, and regulatory failure, deregulation, and regulatory reform. Richard J. Pierce, Jr. is the Paul J. Kellner Professor of Law at Columbia University, and the author/editor of the second edition of Kenneth Culp Davis's **Administrative Law Treatise**. Ernest Gellhorn, the former T. Munford Boyd Professor of Law, University of Virginia and Dean, Case Western Reserve University, is now in private practice with the law firm of Jones, Day, Reavis & Pogue.

Public Utilities Fortnightly. Vienna, VA: Public Utilities Reports, Inc., 1929-date. 26 issues per year.
Cost: $287 for one year; $459 for two years ($317 and $519 to international subscribers). Full text of all issues from January 1, 1995 to 2010 also available online at no additional charge to print subscribers (2014).
The leading periodical in the field of public utilities. It provides a comprehensive, objective, and independent overview of the energy services industries together with timely analysis of such issues as electrical industry restructuring, nuclear decommissioning, retail wheeling, and industry mergers, and more. The best current awareness tool in the field for regulators, staff, public utility practitioners, and others interested in public utility issues.

Public Utilities Reports. **PUR Analysis of the Nation's Largest Investor-Owned Electric and Gas Utilities**. Vienna, VA: Public Utilities Reports, Inc., 2001. 1 vol. (450 pp.).
Cost: OUT-OF-PRINT; Was $199; from $150 on amazon.com (2014).
First published in 1982, this volume provides users with an overview of the finances and operations of the major investor-owned utilities in the United States and the factors that influenced their performance. This new edition reflects a number of changes in the industry, including its consolidation, the formation of holding companies and diversified investment portfolios, the impact of industry restructuring, rising energy costs, and the California energy crisis. The 2001 edition also provides insight into the major factors affecting individual company performance. Each report summarizes the company's management discussion and analysis, and highlights information to allow evaluation of the condition of individual companies, as well as a standardized view of the industry. Each individual company's performance over a three-year period includes operating data, market information, management contacts, financial indicators, revenues and other key data. This volume includes important indices covering utility subsidiary cross-references, company rankings by revenue and return on equity, and company performance by regulatory jurisdiction. Includes a companion CD-Rom (DB-IV format for Windows).

Public Utilities Reports Guide. Vienna, VA: Public Utilities Reports, Inc., 2008.
9 vols. (576 pp.). New Online Platform available December 2011. Details and options available at: http://www.pur.com/books/12.cfm
Cost: Thee pricing options for Online Platform: Gold package: $750.00; Basic Package with Print Option: $645.00; Basic Package: $595.00; from $427.45 on amazon.com (2014).
This collection of materials on utility industry operations and management has served as one of the standard educational tools for utility industry employees over the past 50 fifty years. The nine individual books in the series address the following topics: public utilities (an industry overview), regulation, delivery of service, rates and rate making, accounting, finance, organization and management, marketing and competition, and references. The series includes mid-program and final examinations to measure mastery of the material for which a Certificate of Accomplishment is provided. Completion of the

course of study also makes candidates eligible for Continuing Professional Education credits.

Schmidt, Michael R. **Performance-Based Ratemaking: Theory and Practice**. Vienna, VA: Public Utilities Reports, Inc., 2000. 1 vol. (324 pp.). Softbound. No supplementation except in the form of new editions.
Cost: $89; from $41.99 on amazon.com (2014).
With the advent of utility restructuring and competition, performance-based ratemaking (PBR) has become an increasingly attractive alternative to the old cost-based system of ratemaking. Performance-based ratemaking has numerous advantages, including the reduction of regulatory oversight and lengthy case filings, while providing incentives for efficient operations, better customer service, and allowances for inflation and productivity improvements. This volume is designed to aid utilities and regulators in making he transition to PBR by providing a discussion of both its theoretical underpinnings and real world applications. Dr. Michael Schmidt is Regulatory Policy Leader at Sempra Energy in San Diego, where he is responsible for monitoring electric and gas industry restructuring and other regulatory activities across the country. As an industry professional, he helped introduce PBR in California. He also serves as an adjunct professor of business administration at the University of Phoenix-San Diego.

Utilities Law Reporter. Chicago: Wolters Kluwer Law & Business (CCH, Inc.), 1928-date. 3 vols. Looseleaf format. Semi-monthly updates; semi-monthly report letters. Print only.
Cost: $5,545 per year (2014).
This looseleaf service provides up-to-date coverage of federal laws and regulations governing gas and electric public utilities, as well as federal and state court decisions. Two of the set's three volumes are devoted to coverage of federal laws and regulations, FERC opinions and federal court cases. The full text of leading federal statutes, including the Federal Power Act and the Natural Gas Act, is broken down section-by-section and accompanied by annotations and historical comments. Related sections of the Natural Gas Policy Act, the Public Utility Regulatory Policies Act, the Public Utility Holding Company Act, other related statutes are also covered. Volume three provides coverage of the full text of current state court decisions.

Additional titles in the field of Public Utilities are available from the following publishers: American Bar Association, American Water Works Association, CCH, Inc., Greenwood Publishing Group, Hart Publications, Kluwer Academic Publications, National Association of Regulatory Utility Commissioners, National Conference of State Legislatures, National Consumer Law Center, Oxford University Press, Practising Law Institute, Public Utilities Reports, Inc., Rowman & Littlefield Publications, Inc., Thomson Reuters West. West Academic. See Appendix B for addresses and telephone numbers.

Real Property (see also Zoning and Planning Law)

Abbott, Damien. **Encyclopedia of Real Estate Terms**. 3d ed. Washington, DC: Delta Alpha Publishing, 2008. 1 vol. (1472 pp.). A CD-ROM version and The **Shorter Encyclopedia of Real Estate Terms** are also available
Cost: $140 (ordered online: $115); from $104.75 on amazon.com; book and CD-ROM combination: $165 ($135 ordered online); Shorter version (paper): $55 (ordered online: $22.50); Shorter version plus CD-ROM: $80 ($50 ordered online) (2014);
The most comprehensive single-volume reference book of real estate terminology in print. International in its scope, the book's more than 9,000 entries cover every aspect of real estate, including appraisal, economics, finance, insurance, investment, law, taxation, taxation, urban planning, and real estate management. While weighted toward customs and practices in North American jurisdictions, it also draws upon real estate practices in Great Britain, Europe generally, Australia, New Zealand, Hong Kong, and India. Combining the features of a dictionary, thesaurus, and an encyclopedia, the **Encyclopedia of Real Estate Terms** includes more than 11,000 references, including over 6,000 cases, 2,100 statutory or code references and 5,000 bibliographical references. The appendices include a 65-page bibliography of more than 900 books on all aspects of real estate, summaries of leading English and American statutes, national and international real estate organizations and professional associations, a table of measurements, financial formulae, and real estate acronyms. The product of over 25 years research. The previous editions were published in 1987 and 2000.

American Bar Association Guide to Home Ownership: **The Complete and Easy Guide to All the Law Every Home Owner Should Know**. New York: Random House, 1995. 1 vol. (193 pp.).
Cost: from $.01 on amazon.com (2014).
A wide-ranging layperson's guide to the myriad issues associated with home purchase and ownership, including property rights and restrictions, disputes with neighbors, faulty repairs, owner's liability for injury to a house guest, title insurance, mortgage refinancing, titles of ownership, shared ownership, home security concerns, environmental hazards, lowering your taxes, cooperatives, planned communities, and much more. An authoritative and easy to comprehend reference for a general audience.

American Law Institute. **Restatement of the Law Second. Property: Landlord and Tenant.** St. Paul, MN: American Law Institute, 1977-date. 2 vols. Annual pocket parts.
Cost: $127; supplementation: 1995: $32; 1996: $34; 1997: $36; 1998: $38; 1999: $40; 2000: $42; 2001: $42; 2002: $45.50; 2003: $50; 2004: $50; 2005: $50; 2006: $50; 2007: $56; 2008: $59; 2009: $64; 2010: $64; 2011: $64; 2012: $66; 2013: $78.
Those portions of the law of Property dealing with Landlord Tenant law were the first sections completed by the team of legal scholars and judges under the leadership of Reporter A. James Casner of Harvard University Law School. They were

adopted and promulgated at Washington, D.C., on May 21, 1976 and published in 1977. Case annotations appear in the annual pocket parts.

American Law Institute. **Restatement of the Law Third. Property: Mortgages.** St. Paul, MN: American Law Institute, 1997-date. 1 vol. (743 pp.).
Cost: $85 (hardbound); $37.50 (paperbound); supplementation: 1998: $9.50; 1999: $20; 2000: $20; 2001: $21; 2002: $22.75; 2003: $25; 2004: $25; 2005: $25; 2006: $25; 2007: $28; 2008: $29.50; 2009: $32; 2010: $32; 2011: $33; 2012: $33; 2013: $39.
The promulgation of the this Restatement is a response to the nationalization of the mortgage lending market in the United States, with the goal of unifying the law of real property security throughout the country. While lenders in the United States have utilized a variety of real estate security instruments, the Restatement proceeds on the premise that only one real property security device, the mortgage, is needed. Professors Grant S. Nelson of the UCLA School of Law and Dale A. Whitman of the J. Reuben Clark Law School of Brigham Young University served as the Reporters.

American Law Institute. **Restatement of the Law Third. Property: Servitudes.** St. Paul, MN: American Law Institute, 1998-date. 2 vols. (1,349 pp.).
Cost: $195; supplementation: 2001: $42; 2002: $45.50; 2003; $50; 2004: $50; 2005: $50; 2006: $50; 2007: $56; 2008: $59; 2009: $32; 2010: $32; 2011: $64; 2012: $66; 2013: $78.
According to the American Law Institute, this project returns to the subject of servitudes law which was addressed in Volume 5 of the first **Restatement of Property**, adopted and promulgated in 1944. In the intervening years, enormous changes have taken place in the American real estate market. The use of servitudes has increased dramatically, and the arrangements implemented by servitudes have become increasingly complex. These changes, in turn, have produced changes in development practices and in the law. The new Restatement is designed to restate the law of servitudes for the future by integrating the definition and classification of servitudes in functional terms.

American Law Institute. **Restatement of the Law Third. Property: Wills and Other Donative Transfers.** St. Paul, MN: American Law Institute, 2011-date. 4 vols. Annual pocket parts.
Cost: $324; supplementation: 1995: $48; 1996: $51; 1997: $54; 1998: $57; 1999: $60; 2000: $63; 2001: $68.25; 2002: $68.25; 2003: $75; 2004: $75; 2005: $75; 2006: $75; 2007: $84; 2008: $88.50; 2009: $96; 2010: $96; 2011: $99; 2012: $99; 2013: $117.
The **Restatement of the Law Third, Property: Wills and Other Donative Transfers** is the product of a twenty year project to update the law of wills and succession. This Restatement presents a comprehensive treatment of the American law of wills, will substitutes, intestacy, gifts, powers of appointment, present and future interests, and the construction of donative documents. The coverage includes subjects treated in the Restatement of Property and the Restatement Second of Property (Donative Transfers), both of which are now superseded, as well as subjects not previously covered in those Restatements. Volume 1 addresses the law of probate transfers through wills and intestacy, including intestate distribution, the execution and revocation of wills, and post-execution events affecting wills. Volume 2 discusses nonprobate transfers (gifts and will substitutes), protective doctrines, and the construction of donative documents. Volume 3 provides a comprehensive and detailed account of the rules governing class gifts, powers of appointment, future interests, and perpetuities. The volumes are updated by cumulative annual pocket parts, the first of which were issued in 2011. The monumental effort was completed largely through the efforts of Reporter Lawrence W. Waggoner, University of Michigan Law School, and Associate Reporter, John H. Langbein, Yale Law School.

Backman, James H. and David A. Thomas. **A Practical Guide to Disputes Between Adjoining Landowners--Easements**. New York: Matthew Bender & Co., 1989-date. 1 vol. Looseleaf format. Annual supplementation. No CD-ROM.
Cost: $364 (print or eBook) (includes annual subscription); renewal: 1996: $108; 1997: $108; 1998: $115; 1999: $122; 2000: $130; 2001: $139; 2002: $149; 2003: $160; 2004: $168; 2005: $180; 2006: $193; 2007: $208; 2008: $225; 2009: $243; 2010: $262; 2011: $258; 2012: $331; 2013: $331; 2014: $316.
Property disputes between neighbors may involve one or more of a host of substantive or procedural issues. The authors, professors of law at Brigham Young University Law School, provide procedural guidance for litigating a variety of substantive legal issues, including express easements, real covenants, adverse possession, licenses, private nuisances, boundaries, trespass, zoning, water-related property rights, environmental issues, etc. They also address such procedural issues as burden of proof, the rights and responsibilities of the respective parties, the kinds of conduct which are remediable in court, possible defenses, and the types of damages which are compensable. A chapter on alternate dispute resolution considers negotiation and mediation, conciliation, fact-finding, and compromise and settlement. The text is accompanied by detailed chapter synopses, scope notes, checklists, sample forms, chapter bibliographies, statute and case references organized by state, and a detailed subject index.

Bernhardt, Roger and Ann Bernhardt. **Real Property in a Nutshell**. 6th ed. St. Paul, MN: West, 2010. 1 vol. (503 pp.). Available from West Academic.
Cost: $41; from $31.31 on amazon.com; kindle ed.: $21.64 (2014).
This brief volume in the publisher's Nutshell Series covers all the major rules in the field of real property law which are covered in the standard textbooks. Contains only a representative sampling of citations to case law.

Bloomfield, Micah and Theodore S Lynn. Real Estate Investment Trusts Handbook. St. Paul, MN: West, 1994-date. 1 vol. Looseleaf format. Annual supplementation. Volumes 29 and 29A of Securities Law Series.
Cost: 2013-2014: $977; 2012-2013 Edition: $896; ProView eBook: $977; supplementation: 2003: $210; 2004: $210; 2005: $215; 2006: $240.50; 2007: $267.50; 2008: $298.50; 2009: $359; 2010: $387; 2011: $402; 2012: $548; **Monthly Assured**

Print Price (APP): $81/$972.
Real Estate Investment Trusts (REITs) are an efficient way for many investors to invest in commercial and residential real estate businesses. As an investment, REITs combine the best features of real estate and stocks. They give an investor a practical and effective means to include professionally managed real estate in a diversified investment portfolio. This work, a part of the publisher's Securities Law Series, provides advice from noted specialists on all legal and business aspects of real estate investment trusts, from initial REIT qualification and organization to filing, taxation, record keeping, and the process of taking the investment public. The authors also provide a state-by-state summary of REIT-related tax laws, and examine investment rules. Following an overview and history of REITs, the authors discuss the process of organizing and qualifying as a REIT, taxation of a REIT, investor considerations, types and uses of REITs, records and reporting, umbrella partnership REITs, securities laws applicable to REITs, environmental regulation and liabilities of real estate investment trusts, and corporate governance of REITs. Finally, the is an examination of the benefits of REITs v. other investment options and the impact of REITs on pension funds and other tax-exempt investments.

Burke, Barlow. **Real Estate Transactions: Examples and Explanations**. 5th ed. New York: Wolters Kluwer Law & Business, 2011. 1 vol. (578 pp.). Softbound.
Cost: $49.95; from $19 on amazon.com (2014).
As part of the publisher's Explanations and Explanations Series, this volume is designed as a supplementary text for courses in real estate conveyancing and transactions, mortgages and finance, business planning, and real property investment. Its chapters include an introduction to American conveyancing, real estate brokers, contract risk of loss, the statute of frauds in real property transactions, contract of sale conditions, remedies for breach of a contract of sale, closings: deeds and escrows, deed descriptions, recording acts, title searches, abstracts and title insurance, marketable title acts and curative statutes, the Torrens system, mortgage lenders and markets, mortgages, junior liens, transfers of the mortgage, pre-foreclosure remedies, foreclosures, real estate in trouble, installment land contracts, real property owners and the Internal Revenue Code, real; estate planning: investment strategy, tax events, partnership and limited liability companies, real property transfer taxes, construction agreement and finance, environmental concerns in real estate transactions, and commercial leases. The text of each chapter is accompanied by numerous examples and explanations which provide practical application of the topic under consideration and illustrative statutes and documents. Also useful as a reference for real estate attorneys and investors. Barlow Burke is professor of law at American University.

Cozen, Stephen A., ed. **Insuring Real Property.** New York: Matthew Bender & Co., 1989-date. 3 vols. Looseleaf format or eBook.
Cost: $940 (print) (includes one year subscription); annual renewal: 1995: $183.50; 1996: $192; 1997: $192; 1998: $205; 1999: $215; 2000: $230; 2001: $246; 2002: $264; 2003: $278; 2004: $292; 2006: $334; 2007: $361; 2008: $390; 2009: $421; 2010: $435; 2011: $448; 2012: $475; 2013: $508; 2014: $554; ebook: $855; renewal: 2014: $554.
An extended discussion and analysis of all types of real property insurance contracts, including fire and extended coverage, business interruption coverage, homeowners insurance, condominium and cooperative insurance. Includes discussion of the process of insuring real property, applications, binders, premiums, and insurable interests, claims adjustment, proof of loss, contract enforcement provisions, appraisals, declaratory judgments, intervention, interpleader, policy cancellation, non-renewal suspension, rescission. Coverage also encompasses a variety of special considerations including arson, waiver and estoppel, subrogation, insurer insolvency, hazardous waste coverage. Includes extensive citations to case and statutory law, sample insurance policies, forms, and checklists.

Cross, Frank B. **Federal Environmental Regulation of Real Estate**. St. Paul, MN: West, 1993-date. 1 vol. Looseleaf format. Supplemented twice annually.
Cost: 2013-2: $387 ($774.00 per year); 2012-2 Edition: $387; supplementation: 2000: $152; 2001: $178; 2002: $184; 2003: $2003: $210; 2004: $204; 2005: $145; 2006: $279; 2007: $393; 2008: $283.50; 2009: $346; 2010: $378; 2011: $421; 2012: $619; **Monthly Assured Print Price (APP)**: $57/$684.
An examination of every major federal environmental law and regulation which affects real estate ownership, development and acquisition, including environmental cleanup standards under the Comprehensive Environmental Response, Compensation, and Liability Act (CERCLA or "Superfund"), development restrictions involving wetlands and endangered species habitats, compliance with hazardous waste regulations, and implementation of storm water run-off rules governing industrial and construction activities. Also addressed are such topics as underground storage tanks, the Resource Conservation and Recovery Act (RCRA), state-related legislation, and state voluntary cleanup programs. Frank B. Cross is the Herbert D. Kelleher Professor of Business Law at the University of Texas at Austin and the author of eight books and over 40 articles on environmental law and law and economics. His seminal work on the perils of the precautionary principle have addressed the perverse side effects that undermine the intended benefits of environmental regulation as well as the health risks of political resource misallocation.

Deems, Nyal A. and N. Stevenson Jennette III. **A Practical Guide to Winning Land Use Approvals and Permits.** New York: Matthew Bender and Co., 1990-date. 1 vol. Looseleaf format and eBook. Supplemented annually.
Cost: $371 (includes annual subscription); annual renewal: 1995: $106 (price frozen since 1992); 1996: $111; 1997: $111; 1998: $120; 1999: $127; 2000: $135; 2001: $144; 2002: $155; 2003: $163; 2004: $169; 2005: $181; 2006: $194; 2007: $209; 2008: $228; 2009: $249; 2010: $271; 2011: $264; 2012: $337; 2013: $337; 2014: $321; eBook: $371; renewal: 2014: $321; CD-ROM available as part of the **Environmental Law Library**.
Co-authored by partners in the Michigan law firm of Varnum, Riddering, Schmidt & Howlett with extensive experience in land use permitting, this volume combines a succinct yet through coverage of substantive zoning law with practical guidance and strategies in obtaining land use approvals and permits. Citations to cases and statutes are selective in order to accommodate

more substantive text. Includes coverage of procedures before administrative bodies as well as appeals to the courts. A sample court challenge to land use regulation is included together with litigation forms. Includes a table of cases and detailed index. A well organized and invaluable tool for the attorney specializing in land development and zoning law and permitting matters.

Eades, Ronald W. **Jury Instructions in Real Estate Litigation.** 2d ed. Charlottesville, VA: LexisNexis, 2006-date. 1 vol. Looseleaf format. Periodic supplemetation.
Cost: $174; supplementation: 2009: $85; 2010: $88; 2011: $93; 2012: $96; 2013: $103; 1st ed.: 1993: $25; 1995: $35; 2000: $35; 2001-2005; 2006: new edition.
Provides the litigator and judge with over 250 instructions on those issues which are likely to arise in the course of real estate litigation.

Friedman, Milton R. **Friedman on Contracts and Conveyances of Real Property**. 7th ed. New York: Practising Law Institute, 2005. 2 vols.
Cost: $535; supplementation: 2006: $276; 2007: $296; 2008: $322; 2009: $348; 2010: $376; 2011: $398; 2012: $410; 2013: $480; 6th ed.: 1999: $63.50; 2000: $96.50; 2001: $112; 2002: $260; 2003: $130; 2004: $240.
This is a classic work on the law of real property law. First published in 1954, it is the product of a lifetime dedication to the subject by a highly respected real estate attorney, legal scholar and author. Milton R. Friedman, who passed away in 1997 at the age of 93, worked on this sixth edition until just before his death. The set's thirteen chapters include: contracts of sale, assignment of contracts of sale, examination of title, marketable title, possession, mortgages, the deed, closing adjustments, adjournment or delay in closing, medium of payment, the closing, breach of contract, and easements implied on severance of commonly owned property.

Goldberg, David M. **Real Estate for the General Practitioner**. Charlottesville, VA: LexisNexis, 1997-date. 1 vol. Annual supplementation.
Cost: $149; supplementation: 1999: $35; 2000: $45; 2001: $55; 2002: $55; 2003: $58; 2004: $65; 2005: $90; 2006: $95; 2007: $103; 2008: $112; 2009: $117; 2010: $121; 2011: $128; 2012: $137; 2013: $142.
An excellent one-volume reference guide to real estate law written by an experienced New York practitioner. The author addresses such topics as buying and selling, commercial leasing, mortgages, guaranties, escrow agreements, brokerage, construction contracting, toxic conditions, covenants and other restrictions, title insurance, land use regulation, casualty and liability insurance, bankruptcy, stock deals, tax matters, litigation, checks, the Uniform Commercial Code, and more. Supplementation is reasonably priced.

Hill, David S. **Landlord and Tenant Law in a Nutshell**. 5th ed. St. Paul, MN: West, 2010. 1 vol. (326 pp.). Paperbound. Available from West Academic.
Cost: $41; from $29.44 on amazon.com; kindle ed,: $23.08 (2014).
A succinct overview of the law and rules governing relationship between landlords and their tenants written for law students. The author discusses the creation, duration and termination of several types of tenancies, termination of the lease other than by expiration of its term, possession and use of the demised premises, repairs and improvements, transfers by the landlord and tenant, extensions, renewals and options to purchase, rent and security, rent control, and insurance and taxes. The author is professor of law at the University of Colorado where he teaches property, corporate and oil and gas law.

Hovenkamp, Herbert and Sheldon F. Kurtz. **Principles of Property Law**. 6th ed. St. Paul, MN: West, 2005. 1 vol. (681 pp.). Concise Hornbook Series. Paperbound. Available from West Academic.
Cost: $48; from $19.94 on amazon.com; kindle: $30.40 (2014)
A one-volume student Hornbook, each chapter of which provides a good basic discussion of the applicable law together with questions and answers to common real property questions. The chapters examine personal property, bailments, gifts, rights of possessors, adverse possession, estates and future interests, construction of deeds, landlord and tenant law, servitudes, nuisance, legislative control over land use, cooperatives, condominiums, vendor and purchaser, modern deeds, conveyancing, assurance of title, and real estate finance. The Appendix includes a guide to Real Property Research on Westlaw, a Table of Cases, and Index. This volume is a revision of the authors' **The Law of Property: An Introductory Survey**, 5th ed.

Jordan, Cora and Emily Doskow. **Neighbor Law: Fences, Trees, Boundaries & Noise**. 7th ed. Berkeley, CA: Nolo, 2011. 1 vol. (403 pp.). Paperbound.
Cost: $29.99; from $1.04 on amazon.com; kindle ed.: $16.19 (2014).
Most legal matters affecting adjoining property owners are governed by local ordinances, but the maintenance of good personal relationships with neighbors can be just as important. This volume address the types of practical legal issues that can effect relationships between neighbors, including issues of noise, trees, unsound limbs and trees, boundary trees, ownership of fruit and nuts, obstruction of views, boundary lines, trespass and easements, fences, spite fences, dangers to children, attractive nuisances, rural neighbors and the right to farm, water, and neighboring businesses. The authors also grapple with some of the more distressing issues involving neighbors, including blighted property, weeds and rubbish, drug dealers, registered sex offenders, animal problems, and secondhand smoke. They also discuss legal research on such issues and the most common vehicles for their resolution, including mediation and small claims court. The text also features charts explaining the laws of the fifty states on selected laws affecting neighbors. Both Cora Jordan and Emily Doscow are attorneys with years of experience in mediation.

Korngold, Gerald. **Private Land Use Arrangements: Easements, Real Covenants and Equitable Servitudes**. 2d ed. Huntington, NY: Juris Publishing, 2004-date. 1 vol. (624 pp.). Print and electronic formats.
Cost: $165; supplementation: 2005-2007: 0; 2008: $25; 2009:

$30; 2010: $35; 2011: $40; 2012: $45; 2013: $45.
Easements, real covenants and equitable servitudes are legal instruments used to allocate non-possessory rights in the land of another. Legal scholarship in recent years has called for the unification of these three instruments under the umbrella of servitudes, a position also adopted in the **Restatement (Third) of Property—Servitudes**. With an increase in land development during the 20th century, these various legal instruments have come to play an increasingly important role in the application of more complex zoning, development and land use arrangements. This treatise provides an in-depth examination of the legal basis of these legal instruments and their application. It includes a discussion of easements; the creation of easements; the scope and protection of easements; succession and transfer of easements; termination of easements, licenses, real covenants and equitable servitudes; elements of covenants at law in equity; the validity, construction, operation, and enforcement of covenants; and the duration, termination, defenses, and amendment of covenants. It is designed to assist the attorney in all phases of easement and covenant issues and in the drafting easement and covenant documents. The text is richly supported with citations to statutes and court decisions. Restatements, and secondary sources. The volume also includes an 85-page Table of Cases and Statutes includes and a detailed subject index. The author is professor of law at Case Western Reserve University School of Law.

Laitos, Jam G. **Law of Property Rights Protection: Limitations on Governmental Powers**. Gaithersburg, MD: Wolters Kluwer Law & Business, 1998-date. 1 vol. Looseleaf format. Annual supplementation.
Cost: $365; supplementation: 2000: $95; 2001: $240; 2002: $120; 2003: $125; 2004: $132; 2005: $139; 2006: $146; 2007: $155; 2008: $166; 2009: $178; 2010: $190; 2011: $210; 2012: $240; 2013: $269.
The relationship which exists between private property rights and government regulation through the exercise of the police power is one which has generated considerable litigation at the end of the 20th century. The rise of the regulatory state, much of it driven by a zealous promotion of an environmental ethos, has generated a renewed interest in constitutionally protected property rights as the bedrock of a free society. This book is designed as a source for all parties who address, or experience, the clash between property rights and governmental powers. Its 19 chapters are divided into six parts: private property and the police power, the primary property-protective tools: constitutional and extra-constitutional sources, private property, the takings clause, retroactivity, and remedies. Jan Laitos is the John A. Carver Professor of Law and Director of the Natural Resources and Environmental Law Program at the University of Denver.

Levine, Mark Lee. **Real Estate Transactions: Tax Planning and Consequences**. St. Paul, MN: West, 2010-date. Annual replacement volume. 1 vol. (1,454 pp.). Softbound.
Cost: 2014 Edition: $331; 2013: $303; 2012: $279; 2011: $255; **Monthly Assured Print Price (APP)**: $24/$288 (2014).
First published in 1973, this work provides a single source reference work to serve the needs of real estate consultants, lawyers, accountants, real estate owners, brokers, investors, appraisers, students, and others concerned with tax planning as it involves real estate transactions. Among the topics treated by the author are basic real property principles, introductory tax concepts, expenses, non-fee ownership tax areas, accounting concepts, tax deferred transactions, subdivisions, construction and development, entities for ownership--tax characteristics, and non-income tax aspects. The appendices include a number of practical features, including federal tax rates, social security and Futa rates, installment sales analysis, Foreign Investors Real Property Tax Act, and forms. It also includes tables of abbreviations, statutes, rulings and regulations, cases, secondary authorities, and index. The 1999 edition encompasses the changes brought by the enactment of the Internal Revenue Service Restructuring Act of 1998 and the Omnibus Act of 1998. The author is Professor and Director, Burns School of Real Estate and Construction Management and Chairman, Legal Studies at University of Denver.

McAndrews, James P. **Commercial Real Estate: Law Practice Manual with Forms**. 2d ed. Chicago: American Bar Association, General Practice, Solo, and Small Law Firm Section, 2009. 1 vol. (367 pp.). Paperbound.
Cost: $189.95 ($149.95 to members); from $116.11 on amazon.com (2014).
The law school curriculum is devoted to the study of basic legal principles that can applied in a variety of circumstances. The specific and practical aspects of a field like commercial real estate law must be learned on the job, through hands-on experience. That is where a manual like this has great value. It is less an all-inclusive treatise, however, than a handy reference guide to the most frequently encountered aspects of a commercial real estate practice. Accordingly, it covers such subjects as brokers, options, contracts of purchase and sale, property interests, deed, and miscellaneous closing documents, easements and licenses, leases, title insurance and survey, and the various aspects of mortgage financing. It also includes a table of cases and an index. Citations are primarily to Ohio cases and statutes. A collection of forms for commercial real estate transactions is contained on a companion CD-ROM. The author has wide-ranging experience with private law forms and organizations handling a variety of real estate transactions, financing, and construction projects. He has also exercised leadership roles with numerous state and national legal, real estate, and title organizations, presented programs at various bar and trade associations, and taught business and business organizations at Lakeland Community College (OH).

Merriam, Dwight M. and Mary Massaron Ross. **Eminent Domain Use and Abuse: Kelso in Context**. Chicago: American Bar Association, 2005. 1 vol. (350 pp.). Softbound.
Cost: $114.95 ($89.95 to ABA members); from $19.94 on amazon.com (2014).
The U.S. Supreme Court decision in Kelso v. City of New London (545 U.S. 469 (2005)) was one of the most controversial and hotly contested property rights and eminent domain cases to come before the court in many years. At issue was the question of whether a governmental entity has the power to take private property for a purpose not related to a public use,

such as school, park or public utility right-of-way, but for the purpose of promoting private economic development. In ruling in favor of the city, the Supreme Court aroused the animus of property rights advocates across the country who demanded action from Congress and state legislatures to prevent future assaults on the rights of private homeowners. This collection of articles represents a cross-section of views on the subject, from academics and practitioners in the field of eminent domain to those representing municipalities and property owners. An accompanying CD-ROM contains the merits briefs, amicus briefs, and other materials related to the case. This volume and CD-ROM provide an excellent in-depth case study useful to both practitioners and students in the areas of property law and eminent domain. Dwight H. Merriam is the founding member and senior partner of the Land Group at the Hartford firm of Robinson & Cole. He represents developers, governments, landowners, and advocacy groups in land development and conservation issues. Mary Massaron Ross is head of the Appellate Practice Group of the Bloomfield Hills, Michigan law firm of Plunkett & Cooney.

Mezzullo, Louis A. **An Estate Planner's Guide to Buy-Sell Agreements for the Closely Held Business**. 2d ed. Chicago: American Bar Association, Section of Real Property, Probate and Trust Law, 2007. 1 vol. (134 pp.). Paperbound.
Cost: $139.95 ($119.95 to ABA members); from $82.23 on amazon.com (2014).
A buy-sell agreement is an agreement between owners of a business, or among the owners of the business and an outside entity, to purchase and sell their interest in the business at a price set under the agreement upon certain future events. These future events may include the death or disability of the owner, an offer from an outside party to purchase an owner's interest, or termination of employment. This guide is designed to assist the attorney advising the owners of a closely held business in structuring a buy-sell agreement which may or may not coincide with the owner's termination of employment in the business. Most of the considerations involved in the structure of a buy-sell agreement are the same regardless of whether the business entity operates as a corporation, a partnership or a limited liability company, however, there some differences, as this text explains. The author addresses the objectives of a buy-sell agreement, the planning considerations, the establishment of business value for estate tax purposes, and special considerations for the S corporation, partnership, professional corporation, closely held and family-owned business. Sample buy-sell agreements are contained on a companion CD-ROM. The author is a partner in the Rancho Santa Fe, CA office of Luce, Forward, Hamilton & Scripps LLP whose practice specializes in taxation, estate and business planning, and employee benefits.

Moynihan, Cornelius J., Sheldon F. Kurtz, and William H. Francis. **Introduction to the Law of Real Property: an Historical Background of the Common Law of Real Property and its Modern Application**. 5th ed. St. Paul, MN: West, 2011. 1 vol. (336 pp.). Available from West Academic.
Cost: $48; from $16.95 on amazon.com (2014).
First published in 1940, this classic introductory textbook on the law of real property reflects its author's view that "the study of real property law is, in large part, the study of legal history. In no branch of the law is the imprint of the past more discernible in the present." Chapters include freehold estates, nonfreehold estates, seisin and its significance, common law type of future interests, the Rule in Shelley's Case and the Doctrine of Worthier Title, common law methods of conveyancing, uses and the statute of uses, the effect of the statutes of uses, concurrent ownership. The late Cornelius J. Moynihan was Professor of Law, Suffolk University Law School and judge of the Superior Court of Massachusetts. Sheldon F. Kurtz is Professor of Law, University of Iowa.

Nichols, Philip. **Nichols on Eminent Domain**. 3d ed. by Julius Sackman et al. New York: Matthew Bender Co., 1956-date. 18 vols. Looseleaf format. Supplemented several times annually. Authority CD-ROM includes no-cost online updating via LEXIS-NEXIS.
Cost: $6,265 (includes annual subscription); annual renewal: 1995: $1,707.50 (frozen since 1992); 1996: $1,791; 1997: $1,791; 1998: $1,880; 1999: $1,960; 2000: $2,060; 2001: $2,204; 2002: $2,315; 2003: $2,431; 2004: $2,559; 2005: $2,661; 2006: $2,848; 2007: $3,033; 2008: $3,276; 2009: $3,538; 2010: $3,610; 2011: $3,646; 2012: $3,865; 2013: $4,136; 2014: $4,513; CD-ROM: $6,395; renewal: 1998: $1,795; 1999: $1,870; 2000: $2,000; 2001: $2,140; 2002: $2,290; 2003: $2,405; 2004: $2,525; 2005: $2,762; 2006: $2,892; 2007: $3,080; 2008: $3,326; 2009: $3,592; 2010: $3,701; 2011: $3,812; 2012: $3,812; 2013: $4,079; 2014: $4,540.02; eBook: $5,696; renewal: 2014 $4,513. Also available as part of the 7-title **Real Estate Law Library** on CD-ROM: $18,167; renewal: 2014: $15.141.90.
The definitive guide to the law of eminent domain. An complete examination of every aspect of the law regarding eminent domain and property valuation, including condemnation practice and procedure, evidence, discovery, expert witnesses, jury instructions, regulatory takings, police power, and compensability. Exhaustive citations and annotations to case law arranged alphabetically by state.

Cost Saving Tips: This set is obviously designed with the specialist in mind. Unless you expect to consult this work with some frequency, you would be better off utilizing the set in your local public law library prior to making such a major capital investment. If you do wish to purchase your own set, first investigate its availability on the used lawbook market. If you acquire a new set from the publisher, drop the standing order after the initial one-year subscription has expired and update using primary sources and Shepardizing relevant cases and statutes. Buy another new, or current used, set when you feel it necessary to update the base text. Unlike print, which can provide ongoing utility after cancellation, the CD-ROM and Internet subscriptions must be maintained.

Olejarski, Amanda M. **Administrative Discretion in Action: A Narrative of Eminent Domain**. Lanham, MD: Lexington Books, 2013. 1 vol. (142 pp.).
Cost: $55.00; from $38,85 on amazon.com; kindle: $31.99 (2014).
The U.S. Supreme Court's decision in Kelo et al. v. City of New London et al (545 U.S. 469, 2005) ignited broad public discussion about what "public use" entails under the strictures of the U.S. Constitution. Indeed, the focus on the Fifth Amendment's

"nor shall private property be taken for public use, without just compensation," language has focused more on the monetary compensation for said taking rather than on the issue of whether the taking was a "public use" in the first place. In the case of the Kelo property, the taking was for the benefit of a private-public development corporation to facilitate the construction of a plant by the Pfizer Corporation, a project that was, ironically, ultimately abandoned. What this study involves is a consideration of the two conflicting high-stakes rights involved in eminent domain decisions: the right of private property and the governmental right to advance to public good through eminent domain. It is the author's intention to focus attention on the issues involved and, thereby, to facilitate a dialogue between governmental officials and the community members actually impacted by eminent domain. Post-Kelo, state legislatures around the country reacted by enacting laws limiting municipal powers over such takings. The author, whose research included consultation and interviews with officials and community members in New London, looks at eminent domain in action, the problems presented to public administrators, the low standards of the high court, the narrative of eminent domain (whether procedural or constitutional), interests involved in saving the neighborhood, administrative discretion in action, and administrators' search for guidance. Her concluding chapter seeks to educate the interested parties about the responsible management of eminent domain, as well as practitioners, scholars, community members and students. This estimable volume should be required reading by anyone involved in local eminent domain issues, or in the broader administrative and constitutional issues that it raises. Amanda M. Olejarski is an assistant professor of public administration at Shippensburg University.

Patton, Rufford G. and Carroll G. Patton. **Patton and Palomar on Land Titles**. 3d ed. St. Paul, MN: West, 2003-date. 4 vols. Updated annually.
Cost: $533; supplementation: 2003: $255; 2004: $72; 2005: $77; 2006: $88; 2007: $98; 2008: $109; 2009: $123; 2010: $144; 2011: $158; 2012: $174; 2013: $188; 2d ed.: 2002: $132.50; **Monthly Assured Print Price (APP)**: $24/$288.
A thorough review of the law and practice governing proof and examination of land titles. In volumes 1-2, the authors discuss such topics as proof of title by public records, abstracts, examinations and opinions, sufficiency in general of title records, construction—description and boundaries, construction—grants and limitations, inception of private title, deeds of private grant, special classes of private conveyances, official conveyances and antecedent records, title by decree, devise, descent, entry, etc., incumbrances, and examination of registered titles. Volume 3 contains a table of cases, table of statutes, and index. The work contains extensive citations to cases and statutes. Rufford G. Patton was Past-Chairman of the ABA's Real Property Section. Carroll G. Patton was Examiner of Titles, Minnesota District Court, 4th Judicial District. They were aided by a team of state reviewers. Current pocket supplements are prepared by Joyce Palomar. Volume 3 is in 3d edition. Judge Haskell A. Holloman Professor of Law and Presidential Professor, University of Oklahoma College of Law.

Poliakoff, Gary A. **The Law of Condominium Operations**. St. Paul, MN: West (Clark Boardman Callaghan), 1988-date. 2 vols. Looseleaf format. Supplemented annually.
Cost: $798; supplementation: 1993: $56.50; 1994: $65; 1995: $85; 1996: $97; 1997: $102; 1998: $108; 1999: $117; 2000; $127; 2001: $150; 2002: $175.50; 2003: $195; 2004: $218.50; 2005: $236; 2006: $269.50; 2007: $300; 2008: $334; 2009: $466; 2010: $425; 2011: $463.50; 2012: $505; 2013: $550; **Monthly Assured Print Price (APP):** $58/696.
This two-volume treatise and practice guide was written by a team of practitioners with extensive, first-hand experience representing more than 2,000 condominium associations over a 15-year period. Substantively, such representation involves the application of a variety of legal areas, including contracts, insurance, property, torts, employment, and constitutional law. The authors examine the origins of the condominium concept, the State condominium acts, the structure and function of condominium associations, the associations' power to act, statutory powers, financial management, regulation of common elements, title issues, insurance, restraints on alienation, board liability, fiscal planning, promulgation of rules and regulations, enforcement of covenants and restrictions, protection of owner and property, resignation and removal of directors, conducting association meetings, covenants, assessments, liens, protecting hr association from risks and liabilities, transition, residual rights, warranties, taxation of association revenues, amending condominium documents, compliance with federal and state laws and regulations, specialty condominiums, association attorneys, and unit owners' responsibilities. Also included are more than 90 condominium forms. Includes citations to applicable state statutes and case law.

Portman, Janet and Marcia Stewart. **Every Tenant's Legal Guide**. 7th ed. Berkeley, CA: Nolo, 2012. 1 vol. (440 pp.). Paperbound.
Cost: $34.99; online purchase: $27.99; e-book: $20.99; from $17.41 on amazon.com; kindle: $19.24 (2014).
This comprehensive guide to landlord-tenant law for the layperson addresses all the common, and many of the less common, issues that may arise in the context of such a relationship. The authors take the view that the tenant's position is enhanced if he or she is both a responsible tenant and legally knowledgeable, while recognizing that an amicable resolution of disagreements may not always be possible. Among the subjects covered by this book are finding a place to rent, leases and rental agreements, basic rent rules, security deposits, discrimination, inspecting the rental unit and moving in, roommates, major repairs and maintenance, minor repairs and maintenance, making improvements and alterations, the right to privacy, premises liability, environmental hazards, crime on the premises, how tenancies end or change, moving out and getting your security deposit back, termination notices, evictions, and resolving problems without a lawyer, and lawyers and legal research. The appendices are chiefly comprised of state landlord-tenant law charts, and a dozen tear-out forms. Like all Nolo self-help legal books, this title is noteworthy for its clarity, comprehensiveness, and reasonable cost. Uncharacteristically for the industry, legal updates are provides free of charge on the Nolo.com web site. Since 1971, Nolo has been providing books, software and online services designed to level the legal playing field and assist laypersons in solving their legal problems.

Portman, Janet and Marcia Stewart. **Renters' Rights: The Basics**. 7th ed. Berkeley, CA: Nolo, 2012. 1 vol. (296 pp.).
Cost: $24.99; online purchase: $19.99; e-book: $24.99; online purchase: $14.99; from $12.44 on amazon.com; kindle ed.: $15.99 (2014).
Dealing with the American legal system can by a daunting experience for the uninitiated, particularly those without legal training or the financial resources to hire a lawyer. In this well-written and accessible guide, the authors provide valuable guidance to laypersons grappling with landlord-tenant issues. Among the topics discussed are securing an apartment, leases and rental agreements, rent rules, security deposits, discrimination, roommates, repairs and maintenance, tenants' rights to privacy, how tenancies change and end, getting your deposit back, landlord retaliation, rent control, and getting help with your dispute. Appendices include a brief guide to local, state and federal laws, and tables detailing the relevant laws in all fifty states and the District of Columbia. Legal updates are provides free of charge on the Nolo.com web site. Since 1971, Nolo has been providing books, software and online services designed to level the legal playing field and assist laypersons in solving their legal problems.

Powell, Richard R. and Patrick J. Rohan. **Powell on Real Property.** New York: Matthew Bender & Co., 1949-date. 17 vols. Looseleaf format, CD-ROM, or eBook. Supplemented approximately four times per year.
Cost: $4,952 (includes annual subscription); annual renewal: 1995: $1,456 (price frozen since 1992); 1996: $1,527; 1997: $1,527; 1998: $1,605; 1999: $1,665; 2000: $1,750; 2001: $1,873; 2002: $1,947; 2003: $2,057; 2004: $2,099; 2005: $2,225; 2006: $2,314; 2007: $2,453; 2008: $2,600; 2009: $2,756; 2010: $2,811; 2011: $2,895; 2012: $3,062; 2013: $3,284; 2014: $3,618; CD-ROM: $5.528; renewal: 1998: $1,530; 1999: $1,595; 2000: $1,710; 2001: $1,830; 2002: $1,959; 2003: $1,990; 2004: $2,160; 2005: $2,311; 2006: $2,404; 2007: $2,548; 2008: $2,777; 2009: $2,999; 2010: $3,090; 2011: $3,183; 2012: $3,374; 2013: $3,610; 2014: $4,018.80; eBook: $4,501; renewal: 2014: $3,618.
Richard R. Powell, the original author of this treatise, was for many years the Reporter on the Law of Property for the American Law Institute and the person chiefly responsible for **Restatement of Property.** As a Professor of Law at Columbia University, Professor Powell spent the major portion of his professional life dedicated to the preparation and revision of this major treatise on the law of real property. This is an exhaustive and scholarly work which fully examines the historical origins of the law of real property as well as its current manifestations. Its historical analysis encompasses both the European antecedents of American property law and the experience of the individual states. The major portion of the fifteen volumes in this set includes a discussion and analysis of the various permissible interests in land. Discussion also extends to such matters as the capacity to hold and to deal with interests in land, relations between the owners of permissible interests in land, relations between the owner of a permissible interest in land and the community, acquisition and transfer of interests in land. The author's analysis includes attempts to integrate the various strands of law which run through the field of real property. While it draws upon the vast common law roots of the subject matter, it gives thorough attention to modern issues and the broad role which statutory law has had in its more recent evolution. The set includes 13 substantive volumes, an index volume and a two-volume table of cases. The text is exhaustively supported with citations to case and statutory law from all fifty states. Cost aside, this is a highly recommended research tool for the practitioner in the field of real property law.

Cost Saving Tips: Powell may be available on the used lawbook market at a fraction of the cost of a new set. If you acquire a new set from the publisher, drop the standing order after the initial one-year subscription has expired and update using primary sources and Shepardizing relevant cases and statutes. Buy another new, or more current used set when you feel it necessary to update the base text. The CD-ROM and Internet versions are recommended only if you plan to maintain a current subscription.

Real Estate Law Treatise Library on LoisLawConnect. New York: Wolters Kluwer Law & Business.
Cost: $540.00 per year (solo practitioner) (2014).
This library address the full range of real estate issues from commercial transactions and lease agreements to disputes arising between brokers and buyers and sellers of residential real estate. Titles include: **Commercial Real Estate Transactions Handbook, Commercial Real Estate Leases, State-by-State Guide to Commercial Real Estate Leases, Law of Title Insurance, Law of Real Estate Brokers, Environmental Liability & RealProperty Transactions,** and forms and checklists culled from the above.
A cost-effective alternative to acquiring the above titles in print format.

Robillard, Walter G. and Lane J. Bouman. **Clark on Surveying and Boundaries.** 7th ed. Charlottesville, VA: LexisNexis, 1997-date. 1 vol. Annual supplement.
Cost: $158; supplementation: 1998: $35; 1999: $45; 2000: $53; 2001: $65; 2002: $66; 2003: $68; 2004: $75; 2005: $85; 2006: $91; 2007: $97; 2008: $106; 2009: $122; 2010: $125; 2011: $135; 2012: $141; 2013: $146; 6th ed.: 1993: $25; 1994: $30; 1995: $40; 1996: $45.
First published by the late Frank Emerson Clark in 1922, this now classic guide to the law of boundaries and surveying has been updated to reflect recent case law, statutes and regulations. An essential resource for the real estate attorney involved in property and boundary issues.

Rohan, Patrick J. **Zoning and Land Use Controls**. New York: Matthew Bender & Co., 1978-date. 10 vols. Available in ooseleaf format and eBook. Supplemented about three times yearly.
Cost: $3,542 (includes annual subscription); annual renewal: 1995: $955.50 (price frozen since 1992); 1996: $1,002; 1997: $1,002; 1998: $1,005; 1999: $1,050; 2000: $1,050; 2001: $1,124; 2002: $1,203; 2003: $1,264; 2004: $1,327; 2005: $1,420; 2006: $1,520; 2007: $1,619; 2008: $1,749; 2009: $1,889; 2010: $1,946; 2011: $2,004; 2012: $2,124; 2013: $2,273; 2014: $2,480; eBook: $3,220; renewal: 2014: $2,480; also available as part of the **Real Estate Law Library** on the Internet at: $18,167 A comprehensive guide to both the law and

procedure of zoning and land use planning by Patrick J. Rohan, the Dean and Professor of Law, St. John's University School of Law and author of **Powell on Real Property** (revised edition), as well as a number of legal scholars. This treatise is typical of many Matthew Bender titles both in its exhaustive coverage of the subject matter and frequent supplementation. In 57 chapters, the authors discuss zoning in all its manifestations, from exclusionary and inclusionary zoning to landmark, historic zoning and industrial zoning. Additional chapters are devoted to space zoning, builder exactions, adult entertainment zoning, cluster zoning, aesthetic zoning, sign regulation, floodplains, environmental regulation, environmental impact requirements, municipal comprehensive planning, objectives of zoning, subdivision controls, building permits, zoning procedure, land use arbitration, and judicial review. There are extensive forms and documents, both governmental and litigation, as well as citations to cases and statutes from all jurisdictions. This set combines first-rate scholarship with all the relevant practical aids necessary for the attorney specializing in zoning and planning matters.

Cost Saving Tips: **Rohan** may be available on the used lawbook market at a fraction of the cost of a new set. If you acquire a new set from the publisher, drop the standing order after the initial one-year subscription has expired and update using primary sources and Shepardizing relevant cases and statutes. Buy another new, or more current used set when you feel it necessary to update the base text. The CD-ROM and Internet version are recommended only if you plan to maintain a current subscription.

Saltz, Sidney G. **From Handshake to Closing: The Role of the Commercial Real Estate Lawyer**. 2d ed. Chicago: American Bar Association, 2010. 1 vol. (134 pp.). Paperbound
Cost: $49.95; from $29.37 on amazon.com (2014).
This succinct guide to the commercial real estate transaction was written for existing real estate practitioners and law students studying property law who need to understand the nitty gritty details of commercial real estate practice. Accordingly, it addresses the role of the real estate broker, pre-documentation documents, documenting the transaction, reviewing and analyzing documents, negotiating, finishing up, title, survey and searches, other due diligence issues, preparation for the closing, the closing, and concluding issues. The volume also includes a due diligence checklist bibliography, and index. The advice offered by this book is informed by the author's more than 40 year's experience in conducting commercial real estate transactions, both simple and complex. He is a graduate of Yale Law School.

Stein, Gregory M., Morton P. Fisher, Jr., and Marjorie P. Fisher. **A Practical Guide to Commercial Real Estate Transactions: From Contract to Closing**. 2d ed. Chicago: American Bar Association, Section of Real Property, Trust & Estate Law, 2008. 1 vol. (508 pp.). Paperbound.
Cost: $159.95; $139.95 to ABA members; from $84.35 on amazon.com (2014).
One of the primary deficiencies of a traditional law school education is its failure to provide graduates with the practical training and skills necessary for a real life legal career. Nowhere is this so apparent as in the field of real estate law, which requires an understanding of a host of practical legal issues and documents. Moreover, most legal treatises on the law of real property have focused their attention on its common law roots. This practical handbook fills a gaping hole in the literature on commercial real estate transactions. It's aim to is provide guidance through each step of the commercial real estate transaction, from the preparation and signing of the contract of sale to the closing. Each chapter provides a detailed checklist of the various elements, both legal and practical, which must be addressed, or at least considered, by the parties to the transaction, including every detail of contract preparation and financing, post-contract due diligence, the loan commitment, post-loan commitment due diligence, loan documents, preparing for the closing, running the closing, and post-closing matters. The appendices include eighteen of the most important forms of a commercial real estate transaction, each of which is reproduced on a companion CD-ROM. Each chapter includes notes to cited legal authorities, and comments and cautions are sprinkled throughout the text. A must have reference tool for any attorney, novice or experienced, whose practice involves the handling of commercial real estate transactions.

Thompson on Real Property. Thomas Edition. Charlottesville, VA: LexisNexis, 1994-date. 15 vols. Annual pocket parts.
Cost: $1,993; supplementation: 1995: $350; 1996: $425; 1997: $450; 1998: $470; 1999: $490; 2000: $525; 2001: $588; 2002: $699; 2003: $733; 2004: $755; 2005: $810; 2006: $855; 2007: $927; 2008: $983; 2009: $1,075; 2010: $1,175; 2011: $1,299; 2012: $1,498; 2013: $1,284.
For more than a dozen years following the death of its lead author, this major treatise on real property law languished without the benefit of supplementation. In 1994, the Michie Company released a total revision prepared under the editorial supervision of David Thomas, Professor of Law at the Brigham Young University School of Law. The authorship of its 104 chapters was carried out by a total of 31 legal scholars with special expertise in the individual sub-specialties of real property law. Substantively, this multi-volume treatise examines the historical antecedents of American property law, the role of the Restatements of Property, fee simple, life estates, marital and homestead interests, remainders, rules against perpetuities, future interests, types of tenancies, marital property, partition, rights and duties of landlords and tenants, agricultural and farm land, water rights, airspace, public lands, Indian lands, servitudes, trespass, taxation of real property, regulatory takings, donative transfers, adverse possession, marketable title, title insurance, conveyancing, mortgages, mechanics liens, and much more. The substantive text is contained in volumes 1-13. Volumes 14 and 15 contain cumulative tables and index. The text is thoroughly buttressed with citations to primary and secondary sources, though not to the same extent as **Powell.**

Cost Saving Tips: While used sets may be difficult to locate, the cost conscious attorney should not neglect this as a possible source of cost savings. Supplementation costs, while reasonable in comparison with **Powell**, can be reduced even further by buying the cumulative annual pocket parts in alternate years, and remembering, as always, to update in the primary sources.

Williams, Norman, Jr. and John Taylor. **American Land Planning Law: Land Use and the Police Power.** St. Paul, MN: West (Clark Boardman Callaghan), 1974-date. 8 vols. Annual pocket supplements.

Cost: $1,058; supplementation: 1993: $175; 1994: $210; 1995: $250; 1996: $284; 1997: $596; 1998: $316; 1999: $341; 2000: $369; 2001: $429; 2002: $502.50; 2003: $627; 2004: $280; 2005: $303; 2006: $345; 2007: $384; 2008: $428; 2009: $480; 2010: $561; 2011: $575.50; 2012: $628; 2013: $682; **Monthly Assured Print Price (APP)**: $75/$900.

A comprehensive examination of land use planning and the fundamental changes which have enveloped the field over the past thirty years. The authors closely analyze the relationship between governmental authority and private development as it has manifest itself in the resolution of environmental concerns, exclusionary zoning practices. The authors discuss and analyze over 15,000 cases in all fifty states. The contents encompass such topics as land use planning and controls, comprehensive plans, residential zoning, conflicts between residential and nonresidential land use, nonconforming uses, administrative aspects of zoning, variances, special permits, techniques to implement community design, preservation of open space, state and regional land use controls, and future trends. Volume six contains appendices, illustrations, tables of cases, and index. One of the upshots of Thomson Legal Publishing's recent acquisitions is that the West is now the publisher of three multi-volume treatises in the field of zoning and planning law--treatises formerly published independently by Lawyers Cooperative, Clark Boardman, and Callaghan and Company. All three have their strengths. Williams leans more heavily toward the planning side of the field, while Rathkopf and Anderson cover zoning law with greater specificity. Like the other two, Williams features extensive citations to both case and statutory law, and zoning ordinances.

Wilson, Donald A. **Easements Relating to Land Surveying and Title Examination**. Hoboken, NJ: John Wiley & Sons, 2013. 1 vol. (285 pp.).

Cost: $95.00; from $69.87 on amazon.com; kindle: $54.49 (2014).

An easement is the right to use another person's land for a stated purpose, and it can involve a general or specific portion of the property. A right-of-way, for example, is a type of easement that gives someone the right to travel across property owned by another person. Easements constitute one of the most complex areas of real property law and among the most frequently litigated. Easements are not real property but are often treated as such by the initiated. However, only some easements are a matter of public record, a fact which complicates the job of researchers. This treatment of easements, with examples, was designed primarily for the benefit of land surveyors and those in the title field, as well as the holders and buyers of easements such as utility companies and highway departments. It covers easements in general, easement terminology, types of easements, creation of easements, termination of easements, easements and descriptions, problem easements, the process of reversion, reversion of easements, reversion relating to highways, rules of locating and defining easements, and easements and the land surveyor, and easements and the title examiner. It also includes eighteen case studies with maps and diagrams that provide examples of some of the most common problems relating to easements. The volume concludes with a list of references, ALR references, glossary of terms, and subject index. The volume includes selective citations to primary and secondary authorities. This is an essential reference for any lawyer, surveyor or title professional who encounters easements in the course of their work. Donald A. Wilson is President of Land & Boundary Consultants, Inc. in Newfields, NH.

Ziegler, Edward H., Jr. **Rathkopf's The Law of Zoning and Planning.** 4th ed. St. Paul, MN: West (Clark Boardman Callaghan), 2001-date. 5 vols. Looseleaf format. Supplemented twice annually. An optional annual **Zoning and Planning Law Handbook** is included with the subscription, but may be declined.

Cost: $2,825; ProView eBook: $2,591; supplementation: 2005: $976.00; 4th ed.: 1993: $452.50; 1994: $404.50; 1995: $457.00; 1996: $522.00; 1997: $488.25; 1998: $519.00; 1999: $561.00; 2000: $596.00; 2001: $699.50; 2002: $784.00; 2003: $880.00; 2004: $920; 2005: $1,000; 2006: $1,200; 2007: $1.200; 2008: $1,533; 2009: $1,705; 2010: $1,501; 2011: $1,640; 2012: $1,788; 2013: $1.657; **Monthly Assured Print Price (APP):** $206/$2,472.

Originally authored by Charles Rathkopf, this classic work has been revised and updated by Edward H. Ziegler, Professor of Law at the University of Denver. This exhaustive work encompasses 57 chapters on all aspects of zoning and planning law, including all types and manners of zoning, zoning controls, judicial review of administrative zoning decisions, regulation of occupancy, developments, subdivisions, building permits, nonconforming uses, standing, and much more. The text is supported with extensive citations to cases, statutes, regulations and a variety of secondary sources.

Cost Saving Tips: The high annual supplementation cost for this set may induce you to drop the standing order and purchase a new set at periodic intervals. Supplements are not cumulative, however, and must be interfiled, making it more difficult and costly to bring the lapsed subscription up-to-date. A new set can be purchased at a future date once significant savings have been achieved. Also, dropping the annual **Zoning and Planning Handbook** will provide additional savings without compromising the treatise itself. The **Handbook** consists of both original and reprinted articles and is not essential to maintaining the currency of the set.

Alert: In 2005, West issued both a new edition (at a cost of $1,100) and supplementation which exceeded the cost of prior years ($976), bringing the total cost for subscribers in that year alone to nearly $2,100. This is a clear example of the publisher's taking advantage of its loyal standing order subscribers to fatten its bottom line. All the more reason to purchase new sets at periodic intervals and avoid the standing order.

Additional titles in the field of Real Property are available from the following publishers: American Bar Association, American College of Trusts & Estates, American Law Institute, Matthew Bender, CCH, Inc., Commonwealth Publishing, Delmar Publishers, Delta Alpha Publishing, Gaunt, LexisNexis, Mortgage Bankers Assoc. of America, Nolo Press, Panel Publishers, Prentice-Hall, Thomson Reuters West, Urban Land Institute, West Academic. See Appendix B for addresses and telephone numbers.

Religion and the Law

Barron, Jerome A. and C. Thomas Dienes. **First Amendment Law in a Nutshell**. 4th ed. St. Paul, MN: West, 2008. 1 vol. (576 pp.). Paperbound. Available from West Academic.
Cost: $41; from $18 on amazon.com (2014).
A concise overview of the philosophical underpinnings and case law which define the current state of First Amendment law, including the constitutional guarantees of freedom of speech, press, and religion. While intended chiefly as introductory students texts, the volumes in the Nutshell Series provide ideal overviews for practicing attorneys who wish a quick explication of new or unfamiliar topics without all the burdensome footnotes. Jerome Barron is the Lyle T. Alverson Professor of Law, George Washington University Law School. C. Thomas Dienes is the Patricia Roberts Harris Research Professor of Law at the same institution.

Bassett, William W. **Religious Organizations and the Law**. St. Paul: Thomson Reuters West, 2012-date. 4 vols. Looseleaf format.
Cost: $748; supplementation: 2013: $184.80; 1st ed.: 2004: $137; 2005: $151; 2006: $181.50; 2007: $202.50; 2008: $324; 2009: $265; 2010: $384; 2011: $0; 2012: new edition: $512; **Monthly Assured Print Price (APP)**: $39/$468.
Arguably the most comprehensive work on the law governing religious organizations, the book provides an in-depth examination of court decisions, statutes, ordinances, and regulations which affect the operations of religious bodies. Sections are devoted to religious organizations; the freedom of churches; the first freedom; corporate choices and organizational structures of religious organizations; formation, control, and security of religious organizations; management and financial accountability; employment standards and policies; the churches in court; fundamentals of litigation; education, health care, and social service; and religious liberty and public constraint. More than 3,000 footnotes to cases organized alphabetically by state. Also includes a detailed index, tables of statutes and cases. William W. Bassett is a professor of law at the University of San Francisco and has practiced family law, estate planning, and real estate law since 1978. He received his J.C.D. from the Gregorian University, in Rome in 1965, and his J.D. in 1972 from the Catholic University of America. He has been Professor of Law at the Catholic University of America, a Visiting Scholar at the Ludwig-Maximilans Universitat at the Monumenta Germaniae Historica, Bayerische.

Cost-saving Tip: The initial price of this set increased from $512 to $724 between 2012 and 2013, a 41% increase. What should have been an inexpensive monograph becomes a costly and heavily supplemented serial title in the hands of Thomson Reuters West which views standing order subscribers as easy marks to dispense costly supplements. Buy when a discount promotion is in effect and cancel supplementation. Update using less costly sources.

Berg, Thomas C. **The State and Religion in a Nutshell**. 2d ed. St. Paul, MN: West, 2004. 1 vol. (336 pp.). Paperbound. Available from West Academic.
Cost: $41; from $24.11 on amazon.com (2014).
A brief overview of the constitutional issues of freedom of religion, separation of church and state, equality of treatment under the law and the U.S. Supreme Court decisions which have addressed these subjects over the past 15 years. The author, a Professor of Law at Stanford University, also examines statutory enactments which treat religious matters.

Couser, Richard B. **Ministry and the American Legal System: A Guide for Clergy, Law Workers, and Congregations**. Minneapolis, MN: Fortress Press, 1993. 1 vol. (356 pp.).
Cost: $42; from $.67 on amazon.com; kindle: $24.96 (2014).
This practical guide, written primarily for clergy, church congregations and church lay leaders, provides an overview of the history and structure of the American legal system as it applies to religious bodies and professionals. It also provides discussion of various areas of law which are likely to have as direct bearing on the life of a religious body and a consideration of "risk management" strategies which can help congregations avoid legal difficulties. The author, a graduate of Yale University and Stanford School of Law, is a practicing attorney, director of the Concord, NH firm of Orr and Reno, and a member of the Christian Legal Society.

Finkelman, Paul, ed. **Religion and American Law: An Encyclopedia**. New York: Garland Publishing, 1999. 1 vol. (624 pp.).
Cost: OUT-OF-PRINT; was $315; from $80.00 on amazon.com; kindle: $216.89 (2014).
The first encyclopedic reference work covering the interplay between religion and law in American political and social life. The hundreds of concise and well-written entries include summaries all major Supreme Court cases dealing with church and state issues, biographies of Justices whose decisions have had a significant impact in the field, and a variety of topical, historical and theoretical essays on subjects of interest in the field. Edited by a leading scholar of constitutional law and history, the entries were written by more than ninety law professors, historians, and practicing attorneys. Each entry includes a list of leading cases and a selective bibliography. An essential reference tool for scholars, professionals and students.

Gaustad, Edwin S. **Proclaim Liberty Throughout the Land: A History of Church and State in America**. New York: Oxford University Press, 2003. 1 vol. (157 pp.).
Cost: $14.99; from $1.32 on amazon.com; kindle ed.: $12.82 (2014).

One of America's leading religious historians provides a concise and objective overview of the relationship of church and state in America from the colonial era to the present day. His attention is directed to most of the hotly contested issues which have divided schools, communities, and governmental entities, including witchcraft, school prayer, the teaching of evolution, polygamy, and church taxation. Edwin S. Gaustad is Professor Emeritus, University of California-Riverside.

Gey, Stephen G. **Religion and the State**. 2d ed. New York: Matthew Bender & Co., 2006. 1 vol. 900 pp.).
Cost: $169; from $54.97 on amazon.com (2014).
This law school caseBook brings together four categories of material related to the role of religion in a modern, pluralistic society: U.S. Supreme Court decisions, lower court decisions, scholarly articles, and statutes. The materials address such issues as activities which may constitute a governmental symbolic endorsement of religion, the funding of religious activities, and efforts by the courts to accommodate non-traditional or idiosyncratic religious practices. The editor is the Fonvielle and Hinkle Professor of Litigation, Florida State University College of Law.

Greenwalt, Kent. **Religion and the Constitution:** Volume 1: **Free Exercise and Fairness**. Volume 2: **Establishment and Fairness.** Princeton, NJ: Princeton University Press, 2006. 2 vols.
Cost: Vol.: 1: $31.95 (softbound); from $10.23 on amazon.com; Kindle: $17.25; Vol 2 (softbound): $31.95; from $10.23 on amazon.com; Kindle: $17.25 (2014).
In this first of two-volumes on the intersection of religious and constitutional issues, author Kent Greenwalt examines the Free Exercise clause of the U.S. Constitution and considers it in the context of a system, which attempts to balance the often competing interests of fairness, liberty and constitutional validity. He examines the history of the Free Exercise clause and the leading Supreme Court decisions which bear upon freedom of religion. Chapters are devoted to some of the important issues and controversies with a religious component, including conscientious objection to military service, confidential communications with clergy, religious exemptions and drug use, Sunday closing laws, land development and regulation, employment relations, child custody, rights of religious association, and medical procedures, among others. He concludes that religion should be taken more seriously as a force in people's lives and argues in favor of the maximum expression of religious conviction consistent with a commitment to fairness and the public welfare. In volume two, the author discusses the Constitution's Establishment Clause, which, he contends, forbids government from favoring one religion over another, or from favoring religion over secularism. The author is University Professor at Columbia University where he teaches in the law school, and former Deputy Solicitor General of the United States. He is the other several books on religion in American political life, including **Does God Belong in Public Schools?, Fighting Words**, **Conflicts of Law and Morality**, and **Religious Convictions and Political Choice**.

Guide to Representing Religious Organizations. Edited by Lisa A. Runquist and Jeannie Carmedelle Frey. Chicago: American Bar association, Section of Business Law, 2009. 1 vol. (321 pp.). Paperbound.
Cost: $89.95; $69.95 to ABA members; from $53.82 on amazon.com (2014).
Religious organizations face many of the same legal issues and concerns as other non-profit, or tax-exempt, organizations. In other cases, they may be subject to special consideration under the law. This practical guide is intended not only for those called upon to provide legal representation to religious organizations, but also for those in leadership positions who require a basic understanding of the legal environment in which religious organizations operate. The chapters discuss such matters as the constitutional rights of religious organizations, the definition of a church under IRS regulations, their formation and governance structure, tax exemption and taxation, fundraising, general employment requirements, unlawful employment discrimination, special tax and other considerations of ministers and other employees, tort liability, copyright issues, performing rights licensing, construction issues, religious land use, and the Institutionalized Persons Act of 2000. Twelve attorneys with experience representing religious organizations, or with specific subject expertise, contributed the eleven chapters in this volume. Written in a style comprehensible to the educated layperson, this introductory text provides an excellent overview of the primary legal issues likely to face religious organizations, their employees, and leadership. The volume also contains a glossary of selected terms and selective citations to primary authorities. The book is a product of the Religious Organizations Subcommittee of the Nonprofit Organizations Committee of the ABA's Business Law Section.

Hamburger, Philip. **Separation of Church and State**. Cambridge, MA: Harvard University Press, 2002. 1 vol. (528 pp.).
Cost: $28 (paperbound); from $8.23 on amazon.com; Kindle: $14.85 (2014).
A scholarly analysis of the doctrine of separation of church and state in the United States. The author argues that there is no historical foundation for the doctrine of separation of church and state in the First Amendment's guarantee of religious freedom. He assembles detailed evidence to demonstrate that the principle was almost never invoked by 18th century Americans. He argues that Thomas Jefferson, and others, retrospectively applied the doctrine to the First Amendment out of hostility to the Federalist clergy of New England; and that it was later advanced by a combination of nativist Protestants anxious to limit the role of Catholics in American life, and theologically liberal anti-Christian secularists who wished to limit the influence of Christianity and all other distinct religions. The author's detaled analysis exposes the tenuous grounds upon which the arguments of the ACLU and other radical secularists are based. The author is the John P. Wilson Professor of Law at the University of Chicago. A valuable addition to the literature addressing the continuing debate on this controversial issue.

Hitchcock, James. **The Supreme Court and Religion in American Life**. Volume 1: **The Odyssey of the Religion Clauses**; Volume 2: **From "Higher Law" to "Sectarian Scruples."** Princeton, NJ: Princeton University Press, 2004. 2 vols. (471 pp.).
Cost: Vol.1: $52.50; from $25.66 on amazon.com; kindle ed.: $31.50; Vol. 2: $52.50; from $28.74 on amazon.com; kindle ed.: $31.50 (2014).
Volume one of this two-volume history of the role of the Supreme Court in American religious life provides a scholarly examination of the decisions which have variously interpreted the Constitution's religious clauses over the course of nearly 200 years. The decisions issued by the court prior to World War II, while few in number, reinforced an accommodationist view of the religion clauses and reflected the view that it is proper for government to support religion provided that it does so in ways that do not infringe religious liberties. Since World War II, the court has enunciated a view which has narrowed the permissible scope of religion in public life, while at the same time expanding the religious liberty to embrace practices which were probably not intended by the framers. Chapters include The Kingdom of this World, Belief and Action, The Phantom Wall, Clouds of Witnesses, Expansion, Contraction, and Religious Education and Public Support. Volume two provides a close examination of the role of religion in public life, particularly in the post World War II era. Cooperation between government and religion, which was assumed from the founding until 1940, was changed radically after the war by justices who believed that they had the freedom to apply the constitution in new ways. The author suggests that the personal histories of these justices reveals that a nucleus of the court consisted of men who were alienated from their own faith and who looked upon religion as irrational, divisive, and potentially dangerous. Chapters include: Original Intent, Patterns of Establishment, Pillars of a Wall, the Faiths of the Justices, and a Fragile Wall. Historian and legal scholar James Hitchcock is professor history at St. Louis University and the author of six books, including **Catholicism and Modernity**.

Lynn, Barry W., Marc D. Stern and Oliver S. Tomas. **The Right To Religious Liberty: The Basic ACLU Guide to Religious Rights**. 2d ed. Carbondale: Southern Illinois University Press, 1995. 1 vol. 128 pp.). Paperback.
Cost: $19.95; from $.01 on amazon.com (2014).
One in a series of ACLU Guides, this volume provides a basic introduction to a number of religious rights issues from a civil libertarian perspective. The authors address such topics as the establishment of religion and the free exercise clauses of the Constitution, religion and public education, government aid to religious organizations, religious displays, the role of chaplains, religion and family law, accommodation of religion, church autonomy, conscientious objection, refusal of medical treatment for religious reasons, zoning and religious institutions, clergy confidentiality, religion in the workplace, prisoners' rights, the Religious Freedom Restoration Act, and deprogramming. Barry Lynn, an ordained minister and attorney, is Executive Director of Americans United for Separation of Church and State and a former legislative counsel for the ACLU in Washington, DC. Marc D. Stern is Co-director of the Commission on Law and Action of the American Jewish Congress. Oliver S. Thomas is an ordained minister and special counsel to the National Council of Churches of Christ in the United States.

Murray, Bruce T. **Religious Liberty in America: The First Amendment in Historical Contemporary Perspective**. Amherst, MA: University of Massachusetts Press, 2008. 1 vol. (213 pp.). Paperbound.
Cost: $19.95; from $4.52 on amazon.com (2014).
According to the language of the First Amendment, "Congress shall make no law respecting an establishment of religion, or prohibiting the free exercise thereof."
The interpretation of this language by the U.S. Supreme Court has engendered some of the most hotly contested and publicized controversies in modern American life. Beginning with the Supreme Court's decision in the case of *Everson v. Board of Education* (330 U.S. 1 (1947)), which enunciated the "wall of separation" metaphor, the court has attempted to articulate positions which uphold religious liberty while, at the same time, constraining religion's role in the public square. In this thoughtful and balanced account of the role of religion and the First Amendment's religion clauses, the author provides a useful summary of the nature of religious faith in United States, the nature of civil religion, religious liberty in public schools, and faith-based initiatives. He concludes with a historical overview of the Supreme Court's decision-making in religion cases over the past sixty years. Bruce T. Murray is a journalist and former editor with the *Los Angeles Times* and the *Orange County Register*.

Patrick, John J. and Gerald P. Long, eds. **Constitutional Debates on Freedom of Religion: A Documentary History**. Westport, CT: Greenwood Press, 1999. 1 vol. (360 pp.).
Cost: $65; from $7.94 on amazon.com; kindle ed.: $52 (2014).
A collection of over 70 primary documents detailing the history of religious liberty and freedom of religion in the United States. Following a chronology of key events, the editors present a variety of relevant documents in five chapters: Colonial Roots of Religious Liberty, 1606-1776; Religious Liberty in the Founding of the United States, 1776-1791; The Constitutional Right to Free Exercise of Religion, 1791-1991; The Constitutional Prohibition of an Establishment of Religion, 1791-1991; and Constitutional Issues on Freedom of Religion, 1991-1998. The assembled documents include colonial Acts and Charters, statements of leading figures and religious leaders, statements of delegates to the Constitutional Convention, and the text of leading U.S. Supreme Court decisions. A valuable addition to any collection of materials on constitutional law and issues.

Schutt, Michael P. **Redeeming Law: Christian Calling and the Legal Profession**. Downers Grove, IL: InterVarsity Press, 2007. 1 vol. (290 pp.).
Cost: $24.00; from $2.33 on amazon.com (2014).
This book is directed at Christian lawyers and law students who wish to integrate their Christian faith and their profession. The author points out that, until recently, law schools assumed that Christian virtue was a prerequisite to true success as lawyer, and that conflicts over substantive legal issues were essentially fights about proper biblical perspective on the subject. In our increasingly secularized society, however, such assumptions can no loner be taken for granted and the integration of faith and profession is more problematic. The author contends that because there is no teaching of vocational duty within the legal educational experience, some Christian lawyers may fall into the prevailing identity of the lawyer as "hired gun: or social

engineer. In the author's view, law practice should be a ministry of good works to those in the community. His exposition of the subject is grounded in an analysis of the historical roots of the religious basis for the practice of law, from St. Thomas Aquinas and Edward Coke to William Blackstone and American legal educator David Hoffman, whose 1846 *Course of Legal Study* contained a clear theological perspective. He contrasts this historical, religious and moral tradition with the forms of legal thought which have emerged in the 20th century, including the instrumentalism of Oliver Wendell Holmes and the pragmatic theory of Richard Posner. The Christian lawyer's goal, therefore, should be to cut through the pragmatic suppositions of modern legal education to formulate a specifically Christian calling in the practice of law. In this book's 12 chapters, the author addresses such subjects as the condition of the lost lawyer, American legal education, vocation and the local church, integrity, community, professional identity, lawyers' vice and virtues, and law and truth. He provides a thoughtful exposition and analysis of the moral and religious dimensions of the law for the Christian lawyer. The appendices provide several examples of how religious faith and the practice of law can be integrated. The author is a graduate of the University of Texas School of Law, associate professor of law at Regent University School of Law, and Director of the Institute for Christian Legal Studies.

Shaughnessy, Mary Angela. **Ministry and the Law: What You Need to Know**. Mahwah, NJ: Paulist Press, 1998. 1 vol. (128 pp.). Paperbound.
Cost: $9.95; from $3.98 on amazon.com (2014).
Written primarily as a resource for ministers who serve in the Catholic religious tradition, this volume provides a brief overview of the relationship of civil law to ministry, and discusses the role of the U.S. Constitution, due process, statutory law, common law, and most significant legal issues likely to confront the church, including the negligence, malpractice, child/vulnerable adult abuse, defamation of character, and discrimination. Also discussed are the issues of confidentiality, employment, sexual misconduct, and church finances. The author, a Sister of Charity of Nazareth, is professor of education and university legal counsel at Spalding University in Louisville, KY. She holds a law degree from the University of Louisville and a Ph.D. in education from Boston University.

Restatements of the Law

The **Restatements of the Law** represent the most significant attempt by the American legal community to draft statements of basic legal principles in those areas of the law dominated by the common law. The common law principles enunciated in the **Restatements** are based an analysis and distillation of the vast body of published appellate court decisions appearing in the various reporter series. Drafted and published under the auspices of the American Law Institute, the **Restatements of the Law** reflect the combined efforts of a committee of distinguished legal scholars and jurists. **Restatements** have been published in the areas of **Agency**, **Conflict of Laws**, **Contracts**, **Foreign Relations**, **Judgments**, **Property**, **Surety and Guaranty**, **Torts**, **Trusts**, **and Unfair Competition**. Each **Restatement** is published only after a lengthy and painstaking process involving the issuance of Tentative Drafts and their subsequent review by members of the Institute at its Annual Meeting. Published by the West for the American Law Institute, they are also available on CD-ROM, on Westlaw and LexisNexis. Discounts may apply to current print subscribers.

Complete **Restatements of the Law** (including 2d and 3d Series to date, plus **Principles of Corporate Governance)**. Philadelphia, PA: American Law Institute or St. Paul, MN: Thomson Reuters West, 1958-date. 87 vols.
Cost: $5,613 (but available at steep discount of as much as 65% from ALI); supplementation: 1994: $579.50;1995: $489.60; 1996: $489.60; 1997: $417.50; 1998: $533.50; 1999: $768. 2000: $445; 2001: $430.75; 2002: $518.50; 2003: $589.25; 2004: $625; 2005: $720; 2006: $750; 2007: $780; 2008: $1092.50; 2009: $1,135; 2010: $1,135; 2011: $1,172; 2012: 1,299; 2013: $1,283; CD-ROM being phased out (2014).

American Law Institute. **Restatement of the Law Third. Agency.** St. Paul, MN: American Law Institute, 2006-date. 3 vols. (994 pp.). Periodic Appendix volumes published. Pocket part appears in the back of the most recent Appendix volume only. Also available on CD-ROM.
Cost: $196 for complete set ($75 paperbound); no supplementation to date; 2d: 1995: $16; 1996: $17; 1997: $18; 1998: $19; 1999: $23; 2000: $74; 2001: $21; 2002: $22.75; 2003: $25; 2004: $25; 2005: $25; 2006: $25; 2007: $34; 2008: $36; 2009: $39; 2010: $39; 2011: $39; 2012: $40; 2013: $135.
Work on the second edition of the **Restatement of the Law of Agency** was begun in 1952 and the first volume was published in 1958. The main body of the work is contained in volumes one and two, while Appendices, containing Reporter's Notes and Annotations of court decisions, appear in volumes three through seven. In 2006, the Institute published Volumes 1 and 2 of **Restatement of the Law Third, Agency**. The new **Restatement** completely replaces the **Restatement Second of Agency** and addresses the changes that have developed in the field in the half-century since **Agency Second** was published in 1958.

American Law Institute. **Restatement of the Law Second. Conflict of Laws.** St. Paul, MN: American Law Institute,1971/1996-date. 7 vols. Annual pocket parts. Periodic Appendix volumes.
Cost: $473.50 for complete set; vols. 1-2 (base volumes): $127; vols. 3-5 (Appendices): $346.50; supplementation: 1997: $18; 1998: $19; 1999: $20; 2000: $21; 2001: $21; 2002: $26; 2003: $29; 2004: $29; 2005: $25.50; 2006: $25.50; 2007: $28; 2008: $29.50; 2009: $32; 2010: $32; 2011: $39; 2012: $40; 2013: $59.
Adopted and promulgated by the American Law Institute at Washington, D.C. on May 23, 1969, the base volumes of the **Restatement of the Law Second** of **Conflict of Laws** were published in 1971. The project was supervised by Reporter Willis L. M. Reese and Associate Reporter Austin W. Scott. The three Appendices volumes were published in 1971, 1980, and 1988.

American Law Institute. **Restatement of the Law Second. Contracts.** St. Paul, MN: American Law Institute, 1981-date. 12 vols. Annual pocket parts. Periodic Appendix volumes published. Pocket part appears in the back of the most recent Appendix volume only.

Cost: $823.50; vols. 1-3 (base vols.) only: $190.50 ($46.00 in softcover); vols. 4-11 (Appendices) only: $633; supplementation: 1995: $19.00; 1996: $19; 1997: $72; 1998: $19; 1999: $20; 2000: $21; 2001: $21; 2002: $22.75; 2003: $25; 2004: $25; 2005: $25; 2006: $29; 2007: $30.00; 2008: $114.50; 2009: $32.00; 2010: $32.00; 2011: $32; 2012: $40; 2013: $59.

The **Restatements** represent the most significant attempt by the American legal community to draft common law principles based upon the vast body of published appellate court decisions which appear in the various reporter series. Drafted and published under the auspices of the American Law Institute, the **Restatements** reflect the combined efforts of a committee of distinguished legal scholars and jurists. Work on the **Restatement (Second) of the Law of Contracts** was begun in 1962 and first volume was published in 1981. The main body of the work is contained in volumes one through three, while the Appendices, containing Reporter's Notes and Annotations of court decisions, appear in volumes four through nine. Supplementation is published only for certain Appendix volumes.

American Law Institute. **Restatement of the Law Third. Foreign Relations of the United States**. St. Paul, MN: American Law Institute, 1987-date. 2 vols. Annual pocket parts.

Cost: $173; supplementation: 1995: $19; 1996: $20; 1997: $21; 1998: $22; 1999: $23; 2000: $24.50; 2001: $24.50; 2002: $26; 2003: $29; 2004: $29; 2005: $29; 2006: $29; 2007: $34; 2008: $36; 2009: $32; 2010: $32; 2011: $39; 2012: $40; 2013: $59.

This constitutes a complete revision and expansion of the 1965 Restatement, which is no longer available. It addresses international law as it applies to the United States, and domestic law that has a substantial impact on the foreign relations of the United States or has other important consequences.

American Law Institute. **Restatement of the Law Second. Judgments**. St. Paul, MN: American Law Institute, 1982-1988-date. 6 vols. Annual pocket parts. Periodic Appendix volumes published. Pocket part appears in the back of the most recent Appendix volume only.

Cost: $410 for complete set; vols. 1-2 (base vols.) only: $127; vols. 3-6 (Appendixes) only: $283; supplementation (annual pamphlet): 1996: $59; 1997: $18; 1998: $19; 1999: $20; 2000: $21; 2001: $21; 2002: $26; 2003: $29; 2004: $84 (vol. 6); 2005: $25; 2006: $25; 2007: $28; 2008: $29.50; 2009: $32; 2010: $32; 2011: $32; 2012: $40; 2013: $59.

The two base volumes, covering **the Restatement of Judgments** as adopted and promulgated by the American Law Institute at Washington, D.C. on June 12, 1980, were published in 1982. The six Appendix volumes cover citations to subsequent court decisions.

American Law Institute. **Restatement of the Law Third. The Law Governing Lawyers**. St. Paul, MN: American Law Institute, 2000-date. 2 vols. (1,278 pp.).

Cost: $195; supplementation: 2001: $46; 2002: $45.50; 2003: $50; 2004: $50; 2005: $50; 2006: $50; 2007: $56; 2008: $59; 2009: $64; 2010: $64; 2011: $64; 2012: $66; 2013: $78.

These volumes clarify and synthesize the common law applicable to the legal profession. They reexamine and develop the themes historically treated by **the Restatements of Contracts**, **Torts**, and, particularly, **Agency** in the context of lawyering. There are chapters on the regulation of the legal profession, the lawyer-client relationship, client and lawyer, the financial and property relationship, lawyer civil liability, confidential client information, representing clients—in general, representing clients in litigation, and conflict of interest. The Reporter is Charles Wolfram, Cornell Law School.

American Law Institute. **Restatement of the Law Second. Property: Landlord and Tenant.** St. Paul, MN: American Law Institute, 1977-date. 2 vols. Annual pocket parts.

Cost: $127; supplementation: 1995: $32; 1996: $34; 1997: $36; 1998: $38; 1999: $40; 2000: $42; 2001: $42; 2002: $45.50; 2003: $50; 2004: $50; 2005: $50; 2006: $50; 2007: $56; 2008: $59; 2009: $64; 2010: $64; 2011: $64; 2012: $99; 2013: $78.

Those portions of the law of Property dealing with Landlord Tenant law were the first sections completed by the team of legal scholars and judges under the leadership of Reporter A. James Casner of Harvard University Law School. They were adopted and promulgated at Washington, D.C., on May 21, 1976 and published in 1977. Case annotations appear in the annual pocket parts.

American Law Institute. **Restatement of the Law Third. Property: Mortgages.** St. Paul, MN: American Law Institute, 1997-date. 1 vol. (743 pp.).

Cost: $85 (hardbound); $37.50 (paperbound); supplementation: 1998: $9.50; 1999: $20; 2000: $20; 2001: $21; 2002: $22.75; 2003: $25; 2004: $25; 2005: $25; 2006: $25; 2007: $28; 2008: $29.50; 2009: $32; 2010: $32; 2011: $32; 2012: $33; 2013: $39.

The promulgation of the this Restatement is a response to the nationalization of the mortgage lending market in the United States, with the goal of unifying the law of real property security throughout the country. While lenders in the United States have utilized a variety of real estate security instruments, the Restatement proceeds on the premise that only one real property security device, the mortgage, is needed. Professors Grant S. Nelson of the UCLA School of Law and Dale A. Whitman of the J. Reuben Clark Law School of Brigham Young University served as the Reporters.

American Law Institute. **Restatement of the Law Third. Property: Servitudes.** St. Paul, MN: American Law Institute, 1998-date. 2 vols. (1,349 pp.).

Cost: $195; supplementation: 2001: $42; 2002: $45.50; 2003; $50; 2004: $50; 2005: $50; 2006: $50; 2007: $56; 2008: $59; 2009: $64; 2010: $64; 2011: $64; 2012: $66; 2013: $78.

According to the American Law Institute, this project returns to the subject of servitudes law which was addressed in Volume 5 of the first **Restatement of Property**, adopted and promulgated in 1944. In the intervening years, enormous changes have taken place in the American real estate market. The use of servitudes has increased dramatically, and the arrangements implemented by servitudes have become increasingly complex. These changes, in turn, have produced changes in development practices and in the law. The new Restatement is designed to restate the law of servitudes for the future by integrating the definition and classification of servitudes in functional terms.

American Law Institute. **Restatement of the Law Third. Property: Wills and Other Donative Transfers.** St. Paul, MN: American Law Institute, 1999-2003-date. 2 vols. Annual pocket parts.
Cost: $324; supplementation: 2003: $123 (includes vol. 2); 2004: $50; 2005: $50; 2006: $50; 2007: $56; 2008: $59; 2009: $64; 2010: $64; 2011: $64; 2012: $99; 2013: $117.
The **Restatement of the Law Third, Property: Wills and Other Donative Transfers** offers a comprehensive treatment of the law of probate transfers and is intended to eventually replace Restatement Second, Property (Donative Transfers). This volume presents a complete treatment of the American law of wills, will substitutes, intestacy, gifts, present and future interests, the construction of donative documents, and other related matters. The coverage embraces subjects covered in the Restatement of Property and Restatement Second of Property (Donative Transfers), as well as subjects not previously covered in those Restatements.

American Law Institute. **Restatement of the Law Third. Suretyship and Guaranty.** St. Paul, MN: American Law Institute, 1996-date. 1 vol. (361 pp.).
Cost: $72; supplementation: 1997: $18; 1998: $19; 1999: $20; 2000: $21; 2001: $21; 2002: $22.75; 2003: $25; 2004: $25; 2005: $25; 2006: $25; 2007: $28; 2008: $29.50; 2009: $32; 2010: $32; 2011: $32; 2012: $33; 2013: $39.
Suretyship law governs the relationships created when a "secondary obligor" assumes liability for performing a duty of the primary obligor. Although the law is largely uncodified and often escapes attention, it has become more critical in modern business practices. This volume is the first comprehensive reformulation of suretyship law in more than 50 years, completely replacing Division II of the Restatement of Security (1941), the American Law Institute's previous coverage of the subject. It expands upon modern contract theory and those principles embodied in the Uniform Commercial Code.

American Law Institute. **Restatement of the Law Second. Torts.** St. Paul, MN: American Law Institute, 1965-79-date. 29 vols. Annual pocket parts. Periodic Appendix volumes published. Pocket part appears in the back of the most recent Appendix volume only.
Cost: $2,196.50 for complete set; vols. 1-4 (base vols.): $254; vols. 5-25 (Appendices): $1,942.50; supplementation: 1995: $96; 1996: $139; 1997: $150; 1998: $158; 1999: $337; 2000: $150.50; 2001: $152.50; 2002; $187; 2004: $158; 2005: $162; 2006: $187; 2007: $214; 2008: $154; 2009: $231; 2010: $231; 2011: $231; 2012: $238; 2013: $273.
The first portion of the **Restatement of Torts, Second**, was adopted and promulgated by the American Law Institute at Washington, D.C. on May 25, 1963, and May 22, 1964. The first two volumes, covering Sections 1-503 were published in 1965. Two additional base volumes, covering sections 504-951, appeared in 1977 and 1979. The Appendices contain the Reporter's Notes, Citations to court decisions, and cross references to the West Digest key numbers and **American Law Reports** Annotations are contained in the 21 volumes, the most recent of which are supplemented with annual pocket parts.

American Law Institute. **Restatement of the Law Third. Torts: Apportionment of Liability**. St. Paul, MN: American Law Institute, 2000-date. 1 vol. (401 pp.). Annual pocket parts.
Cost: $97.50; supplementation: 2002: $22.75; 2003: $25; 2004: $25; 2005: $25; 2006: $25; 2007: $28; 2008: $29.50; 2009: $32; 2010: $32; 2011: $32; 2012: $33; 2013: $39.
The **Restatement of the Law Third, Torts: Apportionment of Liability** constitutes the second portion to be published of the American Law Institute's **Restatement Third of Torts** (the first portion being Products Liability), superseding and expanding upon the comparable provisions of Restatement Second which were completed in 1979. As such, it presents clear principles of law governing apportionment of liability in cases when account must be taken of conduct by more actors than a single plaintiff and a single defendant. It also deals with different degrees of blameworthiness, of the effect on parties with derivative claims, or different tort claims (such as strict liability, negligence, and intent) against different defendants in the same case. As courts and legislatures have abolished the defense of contributory negligence as a bar to tortfeasor liability and replaced it with the doctrine of comparative responsibility, apportionment of liability has become a far more complicated and pertinent issue today. This Restatement addresses many of the issues which have not been fully examined in court decisions or academic literature and for which there is not yet an accepted legal doctrine. This volume consists of five Topics, including Basic Rules of Comparative Responsibility, Liability of Multiple Tortfeasors for Indivisible Harm, Contribution and Indemnity, Settlement, and Apportionment of Liability When Damages Can Be Divided by Causation. It follows the typical Restatement pattern of providing clear black-letter provisions with explanatory comments. It is enhanced by the addition of citations to cases, statutes, parallel tables an cross references to the West Digest System, **ALR** Annotations, and an index. The Reporters for this volume were William C. Powers of the University of Texas, and Michael D. Green of the University of Iowa.

American Law Institute**. Restatement of the Law Third. Torts: Products Liability**. St. Paul, MN: American Law Institute, 1998-date. 2 vols. (382 pp.). Annual pocket parts.
Cost: $263; supplementation: 2000: $21; 2001: $21; 2002: $26; 2003: $29; 2004: $29; 2005: $25; 2006: $28; 2007: $28; 2008: $29.50; 2009: $32; 2010: $32; 2011: $32; 2012: $33; 2013: $39.
The Restatement of the Law Third, Torts: Products Liability encompasses that aspect of tort law which deals with the liability of commercial product sellers and distributors for harm caused by their products. This volume represents the first installment in the American Law Institute's effort to completely revise and update the **Restatement Second of Torts**. It supersedes Section 402A of the **Restatement Second** promulgated 35 years ago and addresses products liability issues which were

not under consideration when the earlier provision was adopted in 1964.

American Law Institute. **Restatement of the Law Second. Trusts.** St. Paul, MN: American Law Institute, 1959-date. 5 vols. Annual pocket parts.
Cost: $432 for complete set; supplementation: 1995: $32; 1996: $34; 1997: $36; 1998: $38; 1999: $40; 2000: $42; 2001: $42; 2002: $45.50; 2003: $50; 2004: $50; 2005: $50; 2006: $50; 2007: $56; 2008: $59; 2009: $64; 2010: $64; 2011: $78.
The Restatement of Trusts 2d was adopted and promulgated by the American Law Institute at Washington, D.C. on May 23, 1957, and first published in 1959. The person most responsible for the preparation of the Second Edition was Professor Austin W. Scott of Harvard Law School who served as the Reporter. The Appendices, containing Reporter's Notes, Court Citations to both the first and Second Restatements, and cross references to West Key Number and **American Law Reports** annotations, keep the volumes current. **Restatement of the Law Third, Trusts** was introduced in 2003, with volune four released in 2012. It is updated by annual pocket parts (see below).

American Law Institute. **Restatement of the Law Third. Trusts.** St. Paul, MN: American Law Institute, 2003-date. 4 vols. Annual pocket parts.
Cost: $432 (vols. 1-4); supplementation: 2004: $50; 2005: $50; 2007: $189; 2008: $88.50; 2009: $96; 2010: $96; 2011: $96; 2012: $171 (incl. v. 4); 2013: $59.
The **Restatement Third of Trusts** began with a revision of the Prudent Investor portions of the **Second Restatement**, which was completed and published in a single volume in 1992. In 2003, the Institute published Volumes 1 and 2 of **Restatement Third**, which cover the nature, creation, and elements of trusts; interests and rights of beneficiaries; and trust modification and termination. Published in 2007, Volume 3 deals with trustee powers and duties and incorporates an updated version of the earlier **Prudent Investor** volume. The fourth and final volume, published in 2012, covers trust administration, particularly breaches of trust and the appropriate legal remedies.

American Law Institute. **Restatement of the Law Third. Unfair Competition 3d.** St. Paul, MN: American Law Institute, 1995-date. 1 vol. (683 pp.).
Cost: $85 (hardcover); $31.25 (softbound); supplementation: 1997: $18; 1998: $19; 1999: $20; 2000: $21; 2001: $22.75; 2002: $22.75; 2003: $25; 2004: $25; 2005: $25; 2006: $25; 2007: $28; 2008: $29.50; 2009: $32; 2010: $32; 2011: $32; 2012: $33.00; 2013: $39.
The common law action for unfair competition evolved originally to afford relief against a competitor's misrepresentation of the source of goods or services. The term "unfair competition" now describes an array of legal actions addressing methods of competition that improperly interfere with the legitimate commercial interests of other sellers in the marketplace. The **Restatement of Unfair Competition** represents the first time that the American Law Institute has addressed the subject since publication of the original **Restatement of Torts** more than 50 years ago. Since that time, the field has been transformed by a variety of legislative enactments, including the Unfair Trade Practice and Consumer Protection Act, the Lanham Act, state antidilution acts, as well as analogous common law developments.

All Restatements of the Law are published by Thomson Reuters West for the American Law Institute.

Securities Law

American Law Institute. **Federal Securities Code.** Philadelphia: American Law Institute, 1980. 2 vols. Last supplemented in 1981.
Cost: $40 (includes 1981 supplement); 1981 supplement: $10 (2014).
Adopted by the American Law Institute on May 19, 1978, the Federal Securities Code represents the American Law Institute's attempt to achieve a unifying integration of the separate federal statutes governing the field of securities law. According to the introduction, the Code has three principal aims: (1) simplification of an inevitably complex body of law in light of a half-century of administration and litigation; (2) elimination (so far as possible) of duplicate regulation; and (3) reexamination of the entire scheme of investor protection with a view to increasing its efficiency and doing so, in President Roosevelt's words, «with the least possible interference to honest business.» The text of the Code is accompanied by Reporter's comments. Not supplemented since 1981.

Bader, W. Reece. **Securities Arbitration: Practice and Forms.** Huntington, NY: JurisNet, LLC, 2007-date. 1 vol. (various pagings). Looseleaf format and electronic format. Includes pleadings and forms on a companion CD-ROM.
Cost: $175; supplementation: 2009: $75.00; 2010: 0; 2011: $85.00; 2012-2013: 0 (2014).
Arbitration has rapidly emerged as the preferred method for resolving securities disputes, replacing civil court litigation in many instances, and endorsed by recent U.S. Supreme Court decisions. Practice and procedure in securities arbitration matters is more relaxed than that of civil litigation. There is limited pretrial discovery, a less formal hearing process, decisions are less likely to follow strict legal precedent, and arbitration awards are usually final, subject to only limited judicial review. This volume provides the various participants with a complete guide to the entire securities arbitration process. The chapters are devoted to of the regulatory framework of securities arbitration, jurisdiction, the arbitration agreement, determining whether to arbitrate or litigate, compelling or resisting arbitration, commencement of an arbitration proceeding, pre-hearing matters, the conduct of the hearing, remedies and damages, awards, and enforcing or appealing an arbitral award. Lead author and editor W. Reece Bader is a partner in the firm of Orrick, Herrington & Sutcliffe and a former member of the National Arbitration and Mediation Committee of the NASDR, and past co-chair of the ABA's Alternative Dispute Resolution Committee. He is joined by eleven contributing authors.

Bainbridge, Stephen M., ed. **Insider Trading**. Northampton, MA: Edward Elgar Publishing Co., 2011. 1 vol. (740 pp.).
Cost: $365; from $336.75 on amazon.com (2014).
Insider trading refers generally to buying or selling a security in breach of a fiduciary duty or other relationship of trust and confidence, while in possession of material, nonpublic information about the security. Insider trading violations may also include "tipping" such information, securities trading by the person "tipped," and securities trading by those who misappropriate such information. Insider trading law is one way in which society allocates the property rights to information produced by a firm. Under early United States common law, insiders were permitted to trade in a firm's stock without disclosure of inside information. Over the last three decades, however, federal prohibitions of insider trading have become a central feature of modern securities regulation. Belatedly, other countries have begun to emulate the American model. Insider trading cases have been brought by the Securities and Exchange Commission against corporate officers, directors and employees; friends, business associates of such officers; employees of law, banking, brokerage and printing firms; and government employees or politicians who gained such information because of their government positions. The fifteen articles in this volume explore the following topics: (1) origins and development of insider trading law; (2) the Supreme Court's decisions in Chiarella and Dirks; (3) the misappropriation theory emerges; (4) insider trading statutes; (5) insider trading policy: the Manne debate; and (6) Insider trading policy: the post-Manne debate. The authors include some the leading experts on insider trading and securities law, including Henry G. Manne, Larry Ribstein, and Jonathan Macey, among others. The editor is the William D. Warren Professor of Law, UCLA School of Law.

Bloomenthal, Harold S. **Securities Law Handbook**. St. Paul, MN: West (Clark Boardman), 1978-date. 2 vols. Annual. Paperbound.
Cost: 2014 Edition: $886; 2013 Edition: $886; 2012 Edition: $812; 2011 Edition: $746; **Monthly Assured Print Price (APP)**: $68/$816 (2014).
This practical two-volume handbook provides the securities law specialist with in-depth coverage of basic and more specialized securities issues, including the registration of securities, the plain-English prospectus, underwriting and selling groups, annual and periodic reports, small-company offerings, exempt offerings, the Trust Indenture Act, Rule 144A and the PORTAL Market, municipal securities, shareholder proposals, Blue Sky compliance, securities law violations, EDGAR, the integrated disclosure system, private express remedies, SEC enforcement, practice before the Commission, and professional responsibility. Appendix A includes a table of Sarbanes-Oxley key provisions and SEC Implementing Rules. Updated annually, this work provides the busy securities law specialist with convenient and current coverage of the most significant securities law issues and procedures. One of the nation's leading securities law practitioners and counsel to the Denver firm of Holme, Roberts & Owen, Harold Bloomenthal has practiced securities for more than 25 years, served on the faculty of several law schools, and authored numerous books and articles in the field.

Blue Sky Law Reporter. Riverwoods, IL: Wolters Kluwer Law & Business (CCH Inc.), 1964-date. 6 vols. Looseleaf service. Semi-monthly. Also available on Internet. Print updated monthly, Internet semi-monthly.
Cost: $2,645 per year (print and Internet) (2014).
This five-volume guide provides timely coverage of state and federal regulations governing the securities industry and securities issues, including corporate securities, bonds, investment contracts, and stocks. The service provides the history and application of blue sky laws, a digest of state and federal court decrees and Attorney General opinions interpreting both blue sky laws and related statutes. It also includes the North American Securities Administrators Association (NASAA) statement of policy adoptions, limited offerings, shelf registration, standard manuals exemptions, commodities regulation, RICO laws, summaries of blue sky laws, regulations, and policy statements/orders. The state blue sky materials comprise more than four of the five volumes.

Bostelman, John T., et al. **Public Company Deskbook: Sarbanes-Oxley and Federal Governance Requirements.** 2d ed. New York: Practising Law Institute, 2009. 2 vols. (2,951 pp.). Looseleaf format. Supplemented twice annually.
Cost: $475; supplementation: 2010: $510; 2011: $530; 2012: $525; 2013: $620; 1st ed.: 2004: $319; 2005: $480; 2006: $560; 2007: $435; 2008: $405; 2009: new edition.
The Sarbanes-Oxley Act of 2002 is the most significant piece of legislation affecting corporate governance, financial disclosure and the practice of public accounting to emerge from Congress since the enactment of the securities laws in the early 1930s. A response to the corporate scandals affecting Enron, WorldCom and other publicly traded companies, the Sarbanes-Oxley Act tightened reporting practices in an effort to improve the reliability of corporate disclosures and restore public confidence in the securities industry. This two-volume reference work provides corporate directors, attorneys and accountants with a clause-by-clause discussion and analysis of the new requirements imposed by the Act and attendant rules, as well as guidance on how to meet all new governance reporting, and disclosure standards. The text also highlights the new civil and criminal penalties for violations of the Act. Regular updates track new legislation and emerging SEC rules. The author is coordinator of the Securities Law Division at the New York firm of Sullivan & Cromwell and chair of the Securities Registration Subcommittee of the ABA Committee on Federal regulation of Securities.
Cost Saving Tip: The purchase of a new copy every two years at $475 will save you over $500 every two years over the cost of maintaining a standing order to the semi-annual supplementation which cost $525 in 2008.

Brown, Gary M. **Securities Law and Practice Deskbook**. 6th ed. New York: Practicing Law Institute, 2012-date. 1 vol. Looseleaf format. Supplemented twice annually (April & Oct.).
Cost: $335; supplementation: 2013: $349 (2); 5th edition: 2007: $222; 2008: $236; 2009: $251; 2010: $271; 2011: $159; 2012: new edition; 3d ed.: 1994: $57.50; 1995: $63.75; 1996: $68.75; 1997: $73.25; 1998: $77.25; 1999: $85.75; 2000: $90.75; 2001: $98; 2002: $108; 2003: 0; 2004: 0; 2005: new edition.
When Larry Soderquist, now a Professor of Law at Vanderbilt

University, began practicing securities law, he was forced to learn by the process of trial and error, without a fundamental guide to speed the learning process. This one-volume treatise is the author's attempt to remedy the situation which he found when he began to practice. More than an overview, Soderquist's treatment strives to «convey a way of thinking about securities questions that is authentically a securities lawyer's.» Soderquist's lucid style is carried on throughout this text as he makes the complex seem manageable. The coverage examines the major Securities Acts, the registration process, the regulation of proxy solicitations and tender offers, fraud, and liability, among other topics. The volume also includes a table of authorities and index.

Federal Securities Law Reporter. Riverwoods, IL: Wolters Kluwer Law & Business (CCH), 1964-date. 8 vols. Looseleaf service. Also available on the Internet. Print and Internet updated weekly.
Cost: Print: $4,200 per year; Internet: $4,200 per year (2014). Toll-free support: (800) 835-0105.
The Federal Securities Law Reporter provides detailed coverage of federal securities laws and regulations under such statutes as the Securities Act of 1933, the Securities and Exchange Act of 1934, the Public Utility Holding Act of 1935, the Trust Indenture Act of 1939, the Investment Company Act of 1940, and the Investment Advisers Act of 1940, as well as the Securities Investor Protection Act of 1970. The service tracks developments under these laws, including the amendments, regulations, and court decisions which have followed them. The full text of all applicable laws and regulations accompanied by interpretative releases, court decisions, and releases containing rulings and rulemaking of the Securities and Exchange Commission as well as significant no-action and interpretative letters. The service also features appropriate editorial commentaries, annotations of court decisions and agency rulings, and correlators which review significant points contained within each division of the service. Includes periodic Special Reports regarding Congressional bills with explanatory Committee Reports, and new laws with explanation. This is the most comprehensive and authoritative commercial tracking service in the field of federal securities law. It is a virtual necessity for the attorney or law firm with a substantial securities practice.

Federal Securities Regulation Integrated Library [Internet]. Riverwoods, IL: Wolters Kluwer Law & Business (CCH). Online. Semi-monthly updates.. Search Engine: Proprietary. Toll-free support: (800) 835-0105.
Cost: approx. $10,000, but call for current pricing (2014).
A comprehensive Internet library of federal securities law resources including the following CCH titles: **Federal Securities Law Reporter**, **U.S. Securities Cases Archive**, **SEC No Action Letters**, **SEC Telephone Interpretations Manual**, **SEC Docket**, and **Blue Sky Laws and Regulations;** the following Aspen titles: **Securities Regulation**, **Regulation of Securities: SEC Answer Book**, **Sarbanes-Oxley Act of 2002: Analysis and Commentary**, **Securities Regulation in Cyberspace**, **Corporate Finance and the Securities Laws**, **Raising Capital: Private Placement Forms and Techniques**, and **U.S. Regulation of the International Securities and Derivatives Markets**. The service also includes the **Securities Compliance Tracker** and **SECnet** (links only; a subscription must be purchased separately). A sophisticated package designed for the securities law specialist.

Franklin, Talcott J. and Thomas F. Nealon III. **Mortgage and Asset Backed Securities Litigation Handbook**. Eagan, MN: West, 2009-date. 1 vol. (various pagings). Looseleaf format.
Cost: $525; supplementation: 2010: $211; 2011: $249; 2012: $276; 2013: $306.
Mortgage-backed securities (MBS) are asset-backed securities or debt obligations that represent a claim on the cash flows from mortgage loans, most commonly those on residential properties. Mortgage loans are purchased from banks, mortgage companies, and other originators, then assembled into pools by government agencies, government-sponsored enterprises (such as Fannie Mae and Freddie Mac), and private entities. One of the advantages of these securities is that they, at least theoretically, contain features to mitigate the risks of default associated with these mortgages. Mortgage-backed securities represent claims on the principal and payments on the loans in the pool, through a process known as securitization. These securities are usually sold as bonds, but financial innovation has created a variety of securities that derive their ultimate value from mortgage pools. The securitization of residential loans originated in the 1970s; however, commercial loans also became the subject of securitization programs in the early 1990s. While mortgage-backed securities existed in relative obscurity until recently, the subprime mortgage crisis in the period since 2008 exposed their vulnerabilities to the wider public and brought them into the litigation mainstream. This volume provides a comprehensive overview of this rapidly evolving area of law and litigation. Its chapters provide coverage of the industry generally, an overview of securitization litigation, securitization claims, borrower litigation, rating agency claims, bankruptcy considerations, trends in the industry, taxation, suits against the United States government, suits by municipalities, credit default swaps, covered bonds and accounting issues related to securitization. The Appendix contains a glossary of both commercial- and residential-backed securities (CMBS and RMBS), a table of cases and index. Under the general authorship and editorship of Talcott J. Franklin, formerly of Patton Boggs LLP in Dallas, and Thomas P. Nealon, Group General Counsel and Director of Training, Real Estate Finance and Servicing Group, LNR Partners in Miami Beach, FL, this volume's contributors includes several dozen attorney expert in the fields of real estate, securitization, and securities law. A particularly timely addition to the literature on mortgages and securitization issues.

Going Public Handbook. By Harold S. Bloomenthal, Cannon Y. Harvey, and Samuel E. Wing. St. Paul, MN: West (Clark Boardman Callaghan), 1985-date. 2 vols. Annual. West's Securities Law handbook Series.
Cost: 2013 Edition: $912; ProView eBook: $912; 2012 Edition: $836; 2011 Edition: $766.
A comprehensive guide to public financing from the initiation of the underwriting process through the closing, all within the guidelines imposed by the federal Securities Acts. Includes a variety of critical forms and other sample documents.

Goodman, Amy L. and John F. Olson, eds. **A Practical Guide to SEC Proxy and Compensation Rules**. 5th ed. New York: Wolters Kluwer Law & Business, 2011-date. 1 vol. Looseleaf format. Annual supplementation.

Cost: $389; supplementation: 2012: $210; 2013: $245; 4th ed.: 2008: $170; 2009: $199; 2010: $177; 3d ed.: 2003: new edition; 2004: $187; 2005: $193; 2006: 0; 2007: new edition; 2d ed.: 2001: $98

Recent scandals in the securities industry have prompted a higher level of scrutiny by both Congress and federal regulatory authorities. This work provides detailed coverage of the proxy process and executive compensation matters to ensure compliance with SEC rules. The discussion of corporate disclosure requirements includes the preparation of executive compensation tables, the requirements necessary to ensure the tax deductibility of executive compensation under IRC Section 162(m), and the disclosure requirements for a company seeking shareholder approval of certain employee benefit plans, The discussion of company responses to SEC regulations is accompanied by numerous examples and the full text of seven company reports. Appendices include applicable SEC rules, regulations, and releases. Amy L. Goodman is Of Counsel to the Washington, DC firm of Gibson, Dunn & Crutcher and a member of the firm's Securities Regulation and Corporate Transactions groups where she specializes in corporate governance, securities law disclosure and regulatory issues. A former staff attorney with the SEC and free-lance author, she has published widely in the field. John F. Olson is a partner with Gibson, Dunn & Crutcher who has been rated one of the "Ten Top Securities Attorneys in the D.C. Area," by Legal Times.

Hazen, Thomas Lee. **Federal Securities Law**. 2d ed. Washington, D.C.: Federal Judicial Center, 2003. 1 vol. (172 pp.).

Cost: Free-of-charge; available from FJC either in print or via its web site (2013).

The economic collapse of the 1930s led to the passage by Congress of seven federal statutes providing consumer protection in the area of federal securities, including the Securities Act of 1933, the Securities Exchange Act of 1934, the Public Utility Holding Company Act of 1935, the Trust Indenture Act of 1939, the Investment Company Act of 1940, the Investment Advisers Act of 1940, and, much later, the Securities Investor Protection Act of 1970. This monograph is an introduction and overview of some of the more complex legal issues likely to arise in the course of litigation under these federal statutes, particularly those involving securities registration, disclosure and the antifraud provisions. The text is supported by citations to the relevant statutes, regulations, and caselaw. The author, a leading expert and author in the field of securities law, is the Cary C. Boshamer Distinguished Professor of Law at the University of North Carolina at Chapel Hill School of Law. This is one of many excellent monographs and studies provided to the public at no charge by the Federal Judicial Center.

Hazen's Securities Regulation: Selected Statutes, Rules and Forms. Selected and edited by Jennings, Marsh, Coffee, and Seligman. St. Paul, MN: West, 1982-date. Annual editions. 1 vol. (1,937 pp.). Softbound.

Cost: 2014 Online Edition: $63.00; 2012 Edition: $79.00; 2010 Edition: $53.50 (2014).

An ideal compilation of securities laws, rules and forms in a handy format for the securities practitioner. Includes the full text of the Securities Acts of 1933 and 1934, the Investment Company Act of 1940, Investment Advisers Act of 1940, SEC Procedural Rules, and more. Also includes the full text of related federal statutes including the Mail and Wire Fraud statutes and the Commodity Exchange Act. An excellent alternative to lugging around numerous volumes of the **United States Code**, and at a reasonable price.

Hazen, Thomas Lee. **Treatise on the Law of Securities Regulation**. 6th ed. St. Paul, MN: West, 2009-date. 7 vols. Annual pocket parts. Practitioner's Edition.

Cost: $794; supplementation: 2010: $109; 2011: $119; 2012: $131; 2013: $145; 5th ed.: 2005: $46; 2006: $55; 2007: $68; 2008: $76; 4th ed.: 2002: $45; 2003: $55; 2004: new edition; 3d edition: 1997: $29; 1998: $32; 1999: $35; 2000: $38.50; 2001: new edition; **Monthly Assured Print Price (APP):** $26/$312.

The author, the Cary C. Boshamer Distinguished Professor of Law at the University of North Carolina at Chapel Hill, has attempted to strike a balance between the limitations of space and the demands of a complex subject area in writing this two-volume treatise. Consequently, this Practitioner's Edition, is more than the cursory overview one would normally expect in the student version of the West Hornbooks. Hazen provides detailed and well-documented coverage of both the basic and the more complex areas of the field of securities law, including market manipulation, insider trading, shareholder suffrage, and implied private remedies, among other topics. A worthy alternative to Loss and Seligman's Fundamentals of Securities Regulation, with more reasonable supplementation costs.

Holt, Michael F. **The Sarbanes-Oxley Act: Costs, Benefits and Business Impacts**. Woburn, MA, Butterworth-Heinemann, 2007. Paperbound.

Cost: $76.95; from $73.35 on amazon.com; kindle ed.: $61.56 (2014).

The Sarbanes-Oxley Act of 2002 (Pub. L. No. 107-204, 116 Stat. 745), also known as the Public Company Accounting Reform and Investor Protection Act of 2002, was a Congressional response to some egregious corporate scandals which called into question the accounting practices of American corporations. The Sarbanes-Oxley Act (SOX) is a mandatory requirement for all listed corporations, both domestic and foreign. This book goes beyond the implementation phase of the Act and looks at the resulting costs, benefits and business impacts. Designed for senior managers in the business and financial/accounting communities, this volume presents a comprehensive review of the impact that Sarbanes-Oxley legislation has had on business, the financial community, governments, large corporations, small corporations, accountants and auditors, and the public since its passage in 2002. Indeed, while acknowledging the positive benefits of SOX, the author questions whether the more than trillion dollar cost might be considered too high a price to pay for the gains. Michael Holt is also author of **The Sarbanes-Oxley Act: Overview and Implementation Procedures**, also from Butterworth-Heinemann.

Kirsch, Clifford E., ed. **Financial Product Fundamentals: Law, Business, Compliance**. 2d ed. New York: Practising law Institute, 2012-date. 1 vol. (various pagings). Looseleaf format.
Cost: $335; supplementation: 2013; $376; 1st ed.: 2003: $90; 2004: 0; 2005: $95; 2006: $95; 2007: $105; 2008: $120; 2009: $132; 2010: $273; 2011: $290; 2012: new edition.
This volume provides a basic introduction to a variety of financial instruments, both new and traditional, with which attorneys must deal in servicing their clients. These instruments include products that are offered in capital markets that help companies in their growth and expansion, as well as specific collective investment vehicles. The authors also consider the legal and regulatory regimens imposed on them, their advantages and drawbacks, and the means by which they are priced, distributed and marketed. The volume is enhanced by the addition of a number of sample forms, charts, tables and graphs. More than fifteen attorneys contributed chapters. The editor is Chief Counsel, Variable Products, for the Prudential Insurance Company of America and a former Assistant Director of the SEC's Division of Investment Management.

Levy, Steven Mark. **Corporate Financial Disclosure Answer Book**. Austin, TX: Wolters Kluwer Law & Business, 2009. 1 vol. Looseleaf format.
Cost: $359; from $70 on amazon.com (2014).
Companies that issue securities are required by federal law to disclose significant corporate information and financial results to the public. This information may be disclosed in the company's prospectus (assuming it is making a public offering) or in its annual or quarterly reports, prepared in accordance with general accepted accounting principles (GAAP). This information should include a description of the company's business and financial condition, sufficient financial data to provide trend analysis, and other financial statements to aid the prospective purchaser in making an informed decision whether or not to acquire the company's shares. Those central to the financial reporting process include company management, an independent auditor, an audit committee, and regulatory and law enforcement agencies. This volume provides an exhaustive guide to the financial reporting process, organized in a logical and clearly-written question-answer format. The introduction provides a complete listing of all the questions answered in the course of the book's 29 chapters. These questions address everything from the details of the regulatory framework and agencies to the nature of financial reporting, financial statement audits, international standards, electronic filing, SEC requirements, stock exchange requirements, and Public Company Accounting Oversight Board (PCAOB) standards under the Sarbanes-Oxley Act of 2002. The answers reference the appropriate federal statutes, regulations, SEC Rules of Practice, and other relevant sources. An ideal desktop reference book for any attorney or financial officer charged with the financial reporting process. Steven Mark Levy is a former senior partner in the Los Angeles firm of Lewis Brisbois Bisgaard & Smith whose practice consists of counseling public companies, financial institutions, securities professionals, and others, on regulatory and compliance issues. He has written two books and numerous articles in the field of securities regulation and money laundering.

Loss, Louis, Joel Seligman, and Tony Paredes. **Fundamentals of Securities Regulation.** 6th ed. New York: Wolters Kluwer Law & Business, 2011-date. 2 vols. (approx. 2,244 pp.) Annual supplementation.
Cost: $399; supplementation: 2012: $245; 2013: $285; 5th ed.: 2004: $122; 2005: $138; 2006: $150; 2007: $159; 2008: $170; 2009: $199; 2010: $212; 4th ed.: 2001: 0; 2002: $74; 2003: $105; 3d ed.: 1995: $35; 1996: $35; 1997: $45; 1998: $45; 1999: $58; Internet version available from CCH; from $270 on amazon.com (2013).
This is an economical, single-volume condensation of the exhaustive 11-volume treatise by the same authors. It covers all the important topics addressed in the larger work, but in far less detail, while providing citations to the larger work as an aid to further research. It also follows its chapter arrangement. A highly regarded and scholarly work. The text is current to January 2011. Highly recommended as an alternative to **Securities Regulation.**

Loss, Louis, Joel Seligman, and Tony Paredes. **Securities Regulation.** 3d ed. New York: Wolters Kluwer Law & Business, 1989-date. 11 vols. Annual bound supplementary volume.
Cost: $2,925; supplementation: 1992: $95; 1993: $195; 1994: $350; 1995: $385; 1996: $490; 1998: $563; 1999: $603.50; 2000: $373; 2001: $390; 2002: $740; 2003: $545; 2004: $563; 2005: $888; 2006: $925; 2007: $985; 2008: $1,061; 2009: $1,128; 2010: $1,205; 2011: $1,700; 2012: $1,775; 2013: $1,025; Internet version available from CCH: approx. $2,684 per year.
Louis Loss has been associated with this now classic treatise since its first appearance in 1951. For the third edition, he has been joined by Joel Seligman, Professor of Law at the University of Michigan. This edition reflects the major changes which have taken place in the law of securities regulation from legislative, administrative, and judicial perspectives, including the passage of the Securities Investor Protection Act, amendments to the Investment Company and Investment Adviser Acts, and amendments to the «Williams Act» sections of the Securities and Exchange Act. It also reflects the near doubling of the Securities and Exchange Act in 1975 by increasing the provisions regulating the clearance and settlement processes and municipal securities. The text also reflects administrative changes in the SEC's integrated disclosure program and «shelf» registration rule. Finally, the treatise has been updated to reflect the roughly sixty securities cases decided by the United States Supreme court during the period 1968-1987. The chapter coverage of this exhaustive work encompasses the background of the SEC Statutes, Federal regulation of the distribution of securities, coverage of the Securities Act of 1933: definitions and exemptions, protective committee reform: the Trust Indenture Act of 1939 and the SEC functions under the Bankruptcy Code, control concepts under the SEC statutes, registration and post-registration provisions of the 1934 Act, regulation of securities markets, regulation of brokers, dealers, and investment advisers, fraud, manipulation, civil liability, government litigation, SEC administrative law, and conflict of laws, procedural aspects and globalization. Volume 11 contains SEC statutes and regulations, and tables of cases for No-Action and Interpretative Letters, SEC Releases, statutes, rule citations, and form citations. This is an essential purchase for the active securities lawyer or law department, even though supplementation costs have risen significantly, from $195 in 1994 to $1,700 in 2011.

Cost Saving Tips: If annual supplementation costs are a concern, you can purchase the annual bound volume, which supplements the entire set, in alternate years. This will save you over $1,900 every other year (based on 2013 costs). This is a decision you must make based on your degree of usage and comfort level with a slightly dated supplement. Obviously, you must check the primary law, digests, and Shepardize or KeyCite relevant cases and statutes. It is recommended that you purchase any revised volumes, however, since these must be acquired eventually to maintain the integrity of the set.

Phillips, Richard M., ed. **The Securities Enforcement Manual: Tactics and Strategies.** 2d ed. Chicago: American Bar Association, Section of Business Law, 2007. 1 vol. (533 pp.).
Cost: $199.95 ($169.95 for Business Law Members); from $119.95 on amazon.com (2014).
This practical manual is designed for use by attorneys representing parties confronting securities enforcement matters. The emphasis is on the practical, rather than theoretical, aspects of securities enforcement, including inspections, investigations, and enforcement actions. It can be used as both a training manual for young attorneys and as a guide for more seasoned securities lawyers and litigators. The contributing authors include fifteen lawyers with the law firm of Kirkpatrick & Lockhart LLP who, collectively, bring more than 150 years experience in the field of securities enforcement. Individual chapters address the multilayered securities enforcement system, SEC inspections, SEC investigations, sanctions and collateral consequences, settlements, litigating SEC injunctive actions, litigating administrative proceedings, criminal enforcement, enforcement of self-regulatory organizations, Blue Sky enforcement, common ethical issues, and international enforcement.

Poser, Norman S. and James A. Fanto. **Broker-Dealer Law and Regulation**. 4th ed. New York: Wolters Kluwer Law & Business, 2007-date. 2 vol. (2,188 pp.). Looseleaf format.
Cost: $589; supplementation: 2008: $195; 2009: $205; 2010: $173; 2011: $183; 2012: $240; 2013: $212.
Dealers and brokers in the securities industry help create and maintain markets for stocks, bonds, and other securities by directing clients, at least theoretically, to investments which make best use of capital in complex and dynamic markets. Unfortunately, many broker-dealer firms and individual brokers have taken advantage of their knowledge of markets and securities instruments to engage in fraudulent or imprudent activities to the detriment of their clients and, ultimately, their firms, while violating their fiduciary responsibilities. The mortgage derivatives and subprime markets with which many securities firms were involved, have, for example, been at the center of the current economic recession. This two-volume set provides exhaustive analytical and practical guidance to attorneys representing clients on their rights, duties and liabilities under the complex body of laws and regulations governing the securities industry. The fourth edition, in particular, provides valuable insights into wave of technological advances that have affected the way securities are traded, how corporate and market information is disseminated, the new types of securities that have been created, and the process by which barriers between broker-dealer firms and other financial institutions were lowered. It is designed primarily for lawyers who advise broker-dealers, their employees, and their customers. The comprehensive coverage includes a consideration of the economics and structure of the securities industry, broker-dealers within financial conglomerates, the securities markets, the regulatory system, broker registration and exemptions, broker recordkeeping and reporting, privacy and anti-money laundering, the duty to supervise, compensation in the securities industry, electronic trading, regulation of broker-dealers, broker-dealers in public offerings, private rights of action, securities fraud, churning, conflicts of interest, unauthorized trading, market manipulation, damages, arbitration and mediation, and more. Norman S.Poser, professor emeritus at Brooklyn Law School, brings extensive experience in the securities industry and relevant government posts. James A. Fanto is a professor of law at Brooklyn Law School where he teaches courses on banking, corporate, and securities law, and corporate finance, with extensive experience in private practice with the firm of Davis, Polk and Wardwell, and as a consultant on business and securities matters. The text includes extensive citations to relevant statutes, regulations and court decisions. An essential tool for any attorney representing broker-dealers, their employees and clients.

Ratner, David L. and Thomas Lee Hazen. **Securities Regulation in a Nutshell**. 10th ed. St. Paul, MN: West, 2009. 1 vol. (415 pp.). Available from West Academic.
Cost: $41; from $26.18 on amazon.com; kindle ed.: $16.13 (2014).
This is a brief and basic overview of securities law written for law students, but also useful to practitioners. Detail and citations to cases and statutes are held to a minimum. Topical coverage includes regulation of public offerings, regulation of publicly held companies, antifraud provisions, regulation of the securities business, regulation of investment companies, sanctions for violations, civil liabilities, extraterritorial application, and state regulation.

Cost Saving Tip: An interesting phenomenon has emerged on amazon.com. Used book dealers are, not infrequently, selling books above the list cost of a new volume from the publisher. In the case of this title, nine used book dealers are offering copies at prices ranging from $53.36 to $79.96.

Robbins, David E. **Securities Arbitration Procedure Manual**. 5th ed. Charlottesville, VA: LexisNexis, 2000-date. 2 vols. Looseleaf format.
Cost: $241; supplementation: 2001: 0; 2002: $92; 2003: $97; 2004: $102; 2005: $109; 2006: $116; 2007: $123; 2008: $135; 2009: $149; 2010: $157; 2011: $163; 2012: $174; 2013: $180.
A systematic overview of the primary issues that arise in the course of a securities arbitration dispute, as well as a discussion of case evaluation, and the preparation and presentation of cases before arbitration panels. Chapters include: arbitration versus litigation, the arbitration agreement, a review of the law, arbitrability of securities disputes, case evaluation, attorneys, experts and pre-filing issues, commencing arbitration, responsive pleadings and motions, discovery at the SRO and the AAA, arbitrator at the SROs and AAA, hearing rules explained, hearing presentation techniques, deliberation and

award, available relief and effect of awards, industry arbitration, and securities arbitration. The appendices contain a number of state and federal arbitration statutes, private rules of procedure, and arbitrators guides and manuals.

SEC Compliance Expert Library [Online]. Boston, MA: Warren, Gorham & Lamont. Online. Updated regularly. Toll-free support (800-950-1216).
Cost: small – medium-sized corporations or solos: $3,460 per year (2014).
Contains the full text of the six-volume **SEC Compliance: Filing and Reporting**, including sample filing, practice aids, checklists, SEC regulations, Staff Accounting Bulletins, Industry Guides, and financial reporting releases. This is the basic product. Additional components also available.

Securities Industry Fact Book. New York: Securities Industry and Financial Markets Association, 1993-date. 1 vol. Annual.
Cost: 2013 Edition: Flash Drive (USB): $150; print: $75 (members), $125 (non-member) (2014) (212) 313-1000.
This annual statistical guide contains decades of data covering domestic and global capital markets and the securities industry in general. The 2013 edition (with historical data through 2012 provides over 100 pages of tables, charts and editorial on various aspects of the securities industry, including: underwriting, private placements, M&A activity; securities industry revenue, costs, profits and employment; stock prices and trading volume; individual investor participation; global equity market capitalization; economic trends, and much more. The Securities Industry and Financial Markets Association (SIFMA) is the leading securities industry trade group, representing securities firms, banks, and asset management companies in the United States, Europe, and Asia. It was formed on November 1, 2006, from the merger of The Bond Market Association and the Securities Industry Association.

Securities Law Techniques. A. A. Sommer, Editor-in-Chief. New York: Matthew Bender & Co., 1985-date. 7 vols. Available in looseleaf format, and eBook. Updated three times per year.
Cost: $3,072 (includes annual subscription); renewal: 1998: $755; 1999: $790; 2000: $850; 2001: $910; 2002: $974; 2003: $1,023; 2004: $1,074.00; 2005: $1,160; 2006: $1,242; 2007: $1,365; 2008: $1,502; 2009: $1,622; 2010: $1,728; 2011: $1,840; 2012: $1,978; 2013: $2,116; 2014: $2,310; eBook: $2,793; renewal: 2014: $2,310.
This work provides wide-ranging coverage of issues related to the representation of clients in securities litigation. Topics range from registration and the issues involved in an initial public offering through subsequent offerings; the conduct of a public company, including the annual meeting, reporting and proxy regulation; going private; insider trading; SEC and SRO proceedings; and private litigation. More than sixty authors under the General Editorship of A.A. Sommers contributed to the completion of this work. A first-rate practice guide for the securities law specialist.

Securities Regulation Law Library. New York: Matthew Bender & Co., 1996-date. eBook. Updated three times a year.
Cost: $5,276 (includes annual subscription); renewal: 1998: $1,515; 1999: $1,575; 2000: $1,690; 2001: $1,808; 2002: $1,808; 2003: $1,899; 2004: $1,994; 2005: $2,134; 2006: $2,284; 2007: $2,467; 2008: $2,664; 2009: $2,877; 2010: $3,022; 2011: $3,173; 2012: $3,363; 2013: $3,598; 2014: $4,005.54.
This package includes three Matthew Bender titles: **Federal Securities Act of 1933** (2 vols.), **Federal Securities Exchange Act of 1934** (2 vols.), and the **Securities Primary Law SourceBook** (5 vols.). The **Federal Securities Act of 1933** title includes two volumes of expert commentary on issues relating to the 1933 Act, including definitions, exemptions, restricted and control securities, registration, enforcement and liabilities, and discussion of the Trust Indenture Act of 1939 and the Investment Company Act of 1940. The **Federal Securities Exchange Act of 1934** includes a comprehensive examination of the 1934 Act, including such issues as registration and reporting requirements, the regulation of markets, credit and brokers and dealers, insider trading, proxy regulation, enforcement, and liabilities of attorneys, accountants, and broker-dealers. Each of the two-volume treatises is edited by A. A. Sommer, with prominent practitioners authoring each chapter. The five volume **Securities Primary Law SourceBook** includes a compilation of statutes, rules and regulations, forms, selected legislative history and SEC releases and other miscellaneous materials designed to provide supporting authority for the analytical material contained in the treatises.

Sheehan, Margaret A., Rockwell Metcalf, and Sara F. Burstein. **Practical Guide to NASD Regulation**. Chicago: Wolters Kluwer Financial Services, 2009. 1 vol. (430 pp.). Available from CCH.
Cost: Out-of-Print: was $95 (paper) (2014).
The National Association of Securities Dealers (NASD), currently known as Financial Industry Regulatory Authority (FINRA), is an industry organization representing persons and companies involved in the securities industry in the United States. A self-regulatory organization, the NASD is responsible for the regulation of the securities industry, with oversight from the Securities and Exchange Commission (SEC). It writes rules to govern the behavior of its more than 5,100 brokerage firms, 173,000 branch offices, and 676,000 registered securities representatives. This guide reorganizes the NASD rules as they relate to seven key functional area of securities firms, including (1): Relationships with Customers; (2) Relationships with Associated Persons; (3) Relationships with Regulators; (4) Relationships with other Members and Non-Member Entities; (5) Recordkeeping and Regulatory Reporting; (6) Rules Regarding Specific Products; and (7) Rules Regarding Securities Underwritings. This soft-cover volume also includes cross-references to information memos and other related documents to assist securities attorneys, compliance personnel, and branch managers. An online version provides hyperlinks to referenced Rules, Interpretive Letters and Information Memos. The authors, Margaret A. Sheehan, a partner at Alston and Bird LLP who heads the firm's Investment Products and Services Group; Sara F. Burstein, an associate at Alston and Bird LLP in the Financial Services and Products Group; and Rockwell C. Metcalf, vice-president and group counsel of Ameriprise Financial, Inc. A reference designed to be used in conjunction with the **NASD Manual**.

Spangler, Timothy, ed. **Investment Management: Law and Practice**. New York: Oxford University Press, 2010. 1 vol. (1,417 pp.).
Cost: $645.00; from $229.47 on amazon.com (2014).
The modern investment management industry is international in scope, but its legal environment is governed by the laws of the particular nations in which it operates. Thus, while this volume provides an international perspective and advances certain principles that can be applied to investment operations generally, it also attempts to address the law of investment management from a trans-Atlantic perspective, with particular attention to law and practice in the United States and the United Kingdom. Divided into three parts, it examines (1) the legal and regulatory framework in which investment managers must operate; (2) several key topics that arise regularly to trouble and perplex investment managers; and (3) the key client groups that investment managers frequently serve. Among its 30 chapters are those which provide critical information regarding the legal basis for investment management, the regulation of investment managers in the UK and United States, the standard of care, contractual duties, fiduciary duties, advertising and marketing, proxy voting, best execution, soft commissions, data protection and privacy, market abuse and insider trading, derivatives, stockholder and ownership disclosure, taxation, outsourcing, industry best practices and guidelines, and those which consider the types of clients served by the industry, from US mutual funds and ERISA plans to high net worth individuals and hedge funds, among others. Destined to become a standard reference work for practicing lawyers in the industry, whether in-house at a financial services firm or in private practice, or among financial advisers and businesspersons whose role involves an intimate familiarity with these issues. Extensively annotated with references to caselaw, securities and other related statutes, it also includes tables of cases and legislation with citations to the law of both the U.S. and UK, and a detailed subject index. Edited and with an introductory chapter by Timothy Spangler of Kaye Scholer LLP, it includes contributions from several dozen experts in various aspect of investment management law and practice.

Steinberg, Marc I. **Understanding Securities Law**. 5th ed. New York: Matthew Bender, 2009. 1 vol. (416 pp.). Legal Text Series. No supplementation.
Cost: $45; eBook: $36; from $27.00 on amazon.com; kindle ed.: $20.99 (2014).
One of a series of reasonably-priced scholarly monographs in the publisher's Legal Text Series, this volume provides a general overview of the issues likely to be covered in a basic securities regulation course. The author, the Radford Professor of Law at the Southern Methodist University School of Law, is the author of numerous treatises and law review articles on securities issues. The text's coverage encompasses the Securities Act of 1933, the Securities Exchange Act of 1934, and State securities statutes. Individual chapters are devoted to the definition of a security, issuer exemptions from registration, the registration process, resales and reorganizations, due diligence and securities act liability, section 10(b) and related issues, alternative remedies, secondary liability, issuer affirmative disclosure, insider trading, broker-dealer regulation, corporate control acquisitions and contests, and SEC enforcement. The appendices include a glossary of terms, the text of relevant acts and SEC rules, and tables of cases, statutes, rules, regulations, and releases.

Wang, William K. S. and Marc I. Steinberg. **Insider Trading**. 3d ed. New York: Oxford University Press, 2010. 1 vol. (1,147 pp.).
Cost: $275.00; from $174.23 on amazon.com (2014).
Insider trading is generally considered to be the trading of a corporation's stock or other securities, including bonds or stock options, by individuals with potential access to nonpublic information about the company. Insider trading may be legal or illegal, depending upon whether the trading was based upon nonpublic information to which the insider had access. The legal variety of insider trading takes place when corporate insiders—officers, directors, and employees—buy and sell stock in their own companies, using information available to the general public, and report these transactions to the Securities and Exchange Commission (SEC). Insider trading is illegal, however, when such trades are made pursuant to privileged, nonpublic, information available only to corporate insiders and obtained during the performance of their duties at the corporation. Similarly, illegal insider trading obtains when an insider breaches a fiduciary or other relationship of trust and confidence, where the nonpublic information was misappropriated from the company, or when relatives, friends or associates trade in securities based upon information provided to them by the corporate insider. The authors of this exhaustive treatise use the term "insider trading" in its illegal sense of trading by anyone (inside or outside of the issuer) on any type of material nonpublic information about the issuer or about the market for the security. They examine the intricacies of insider trading, its impact on society, the issuer, and the insider trader's employer, the harm to investors from a specific insider trade, the basic elements of insider trading liability under Section 10(b) of the Securities and Exchange Act and **CFR** Rule 10b-5, the activities of those who violate these provisions, actions by private plaintiffs under Rule 10b-5 against insider traders for damages, government enforcement, the ALI's **Federal Securities Code**, Rule 14e-3 regarding insider trading or tipping in the tender offer context, the Federal mail and wire fraud statutes, black-out periods, compliance programs, insider trading under Section 16 of the Securities and Exchange Act, and state common law and state law claims by the issuer. The text is supported by extensive citations to primary and secondary authorities, including federal and state case law, statutes, regulatory provisions, and the scholarly literature. William K. S. Wang is professor of law at the University of California, Hastings College of Law and a leading authority on securities and corporate law. Marc I. Steinberg is the Rupert and Lillian Radford Professor of Law and senior associate dean for research at Southern Methodist University Dedman School of Law.

Additional titles in the field of Securities Law are available from the following publishers: American Bar Association, American Law Institute, American Society of Corporate Secretaries, Wolters Kluwer Law & Business, Matthew Bender Bowne Publishing, Bloomberg BNA, CCH, Inc., Dearborn Financial Publishing, Harcourt Legal, Kluwer Academic Publications, LexisNexis, Panel Publishers, Practising Law Institute, Thomson Reuters West, Transnational Publishers, Warren, Gorham & Lamont, West Academic. See Appendix B for addresses and telephone numbers.

Social Security Law

Bush, Thomas E. **Social Security Disability Practice.** 2d ed. Costa Mesa, CA: James Publishing, 1992-date. 2 vols. Looseleaf format. Supplemented annually.
Cost: $149; supplementation: 1994: $49.89; 1995: $55.87; 1996: $54.99; 1997: $65.99; 1998: $69.99; 1999-2014: $89.99 per year.
This is a practical, working manual to Social Security disability practice which guides the user through the entire representation process, from the initial client interview through possible federal court review. The coverage includes prehearing procedure, the hearing itself, actions following the favorable decision, the Appeals Council, federal court review, and attorneys fees. While there are some citations to statutes and regulations contained within the text, these are far less extensive than those found in similar works. Citations to case law are rare. This is primarily a procedural guide and manual containing extensive forms, checklists and sample letters.

Elder Practitioner Pension & Retirement on WestlawNext PRO. Eagan, MN: West.
Cost: $1,080.00 (single user) (2014).
A comprehensive collection of resources needed when dealing with issues pertaining to pension and retirement. It includes valuable treatises, forms, handbooks plus news releases and other types of announcements to help keep you current on new developments. The library includes a variety of national and state treatises and other resources, covering topics such as federal pensions, distributions from retirement plans, and Social Security, Including the Social Security Administration Programs Operations Manual (POMS), Social Security Claims and Procedures, Social Security Handbook, Social Security Law and Practice, and Social Security Official Forms.

Federal Social Security Laws, Selected Statutes & Regulations. St. Paul, MN: West. 1 vol. Softbound. Annual.
Cost: 2013 Edition: $248; ProView eBook: $248 (2014).
A convenient one-volume source for the Social Security laws, statutes, and regulations you're most likely to need when dealing with old age, survivors benefits, and disability benefits issues. Also includes laws and regulations dealing with SSI for the aged, blind, and disabled, Equal Access to Justice Act, disclosure of official records and information, and organization and procedures of the Social Security Administration. A cost-saving alterative to the primary for the Social Security law specialist.

McCormick, Harvey L. **Medicare and Medicaid Claims and Procedures.** 4th ed. St. Paul, MN: Thomson Reuters West, 2005-date. 2 vols. Irregular pocket parts.
Cost: $416; supplementation: 2006: $40; 2007: $48; 2008: $56; 2009: $69; 2010: $76; 2011: $89; 2012: 0; 2013: 0; 3d ed.: 2002: $53; 2003: $69; 2004: $72; 2d edition: 1995: $36; 1996: $40; 1997: $44; 1998: $50; 1999: $55; 2000: $61; **Monthly Assured Print Price (APP)**: $14/$168.
This two-volume treatise does an admirable job of simplifying the vast body of statutes, case law, and regulations which comprise the Medicare and Medicaid laws. Authored by Harvey L. McCormick of the Missouri and Wisconsin bars, it both describes the most common portions of the laws themselves and then organizes the law into a coherent form to be of benefit to those individuals who handle Medicare and Medicaid claims and the appeals from the denial of those claims. The Medicare text covers such matters as eligibility, providers of services, inpatient hospital services, extended care services, home health services, coverages and benefits, administrative procedures and hearings, evidence, judicial review, attorneys fees. The Medicaid chapters examine general provisions, state plan requirements, fair hearing requirements, penalties and judicial review. The Appendices include Directory of Peer Review Organizations, application and administrative procedure forms, Medicaid State Agencies, and a Prospective Payment Plan for Medicare Patients. There are tables of statutes, rules, regulations, and subject indexes.

McCormick, Harvey L. **Social Security Claims and Procedures.** 6th ed. St. Paul, MN: West, 2009-date. 2 vols. Annual pocket parts.
Cost: $348; supplementation: 2010: $50; 2011: $55; 2012: $65; 2013: $70.50; 5th ed.: 1999: $50; 2000: $56; 2001: $65; 2002: $76; 2003: $86; 2004: $96.50; 2005: $104; 2006: $118; 2007: $131; 2008: $73.50; 2009: new edition; 4th edition: 1995: $31; 1996: $32; 1997: $36; **Monthly Assured Print Price (APP)**: $12/$144.
An excellent overview of the various rights, benefits and procedures under Title II of the Social Security Act, including retirement, survivorship, disability, and lump-sum benefits and Supplemental Security Income under Title XVI. Additional chapter coverage encompasses definitions, coverages, wages, family relationships, application for benefits, initial consideration of benefit entitlement, administrative hearing and appeal, evidence, commencing judicial review, procedures on judicial review, and remand. The discussion of SSI benefits includes basic eligibility, family relationships, benefit categories, limitations on benefits, administrative procedures, and evidence. The Appendices include a Listing of Prescribed Social Security and Supplemental Security Income Forms, Table of Statutes, table of Rules and Regulations, and Index. Includes adequate citations to primary and secondary sources. An excellent choice for the attorney who handles only the occasional Social Security case. Provides good basic coverage without all the detail found in the multi-volume works from Matthew Bender and the West. Annual pocket parts also keep supplementation costs reasonable.

Pratt, David A., and Sean K. Hornbeck. **Social Security and Medicare Answer Book**. 5th ed. New York: Wolters Kluwer Law & Business, 2013. 1 vol. (544 pp.). Includes periodic new editions.
Cost: $375; 4th ed.: 2012: $265; 3d ed.: 2010: $209; 1st ed.: 2000: $89; 2002: $110; 2d ed.: 2006: $225.
This volumes provides essential information on over 1,000 Social Security and Medicare issues in a easily comprehensible question/answer format. Topics covered include coverage under the Social Security Act, Social Security taxes and earnings, benefits programs, application for benefits and proof of entitlement, entitlement for disability, payment of benefits, administrative review process, loss of benefits, introduction to Medicare, eligibility for Medicare, Medicare secondary payer

rules, Medicare claims and appeals, Medicare financing, benefits under Medicare Part A, benefits under Medicare Part B, Medicare exclusions, Medicare (Medigap) supplemental , and new Medicare options under the Balanced Budget Act of 1997. The text is laced with illustrative examples, citations to primary authorities, in-depth tables, and extensive cross-references. David Pratt is an Associate Professor of Law at Albany Law School where he teaches courses in Federal income taxation, employee benefits and elder law. Sean Hornbeck is a litigation associate with the Wilmington, Delaware affiliate of Skadden, Arps, Slate, Meagher & Flom LLP.

Samuels, Barbara. **Social Security Disability Claims: Practice and Procedure.** 2d ed. St. Paul, MN: Thomson Reuters West, 1994-date. 4 vols. Looseleaf format.
Cost: $1,499; ProView eBook: $1,375; supplementation: 1995: $150; 1996: $195; 1997: $200; 1998: $170; 1999: $195; 2000: $219; 2001: $276; 2002: $275; 2003: $341.50; 2004: $414.75; 2005: $573; 2006: $506; 2007: $617; 2008: $266; 2009: $727; 2010: $734; 2011: $800.50; 2012: $872.50; 2013: $567; **Monthly Assured Print Price (APP)**: $108/$1,296.
This three-volume practice guide is authored by the citywide coordinator of Social Security and Supplemental Security Income for Legal Services for New York City who, since 1986, has written the supplements and replacement chapters to the first edition of the this work. This work provides a complete overview of the Social Security System with attention to all aspects of procedure before both administrative tribunals and courts. Volume two provides detailed coverage of disability evaluation, including medical evidence, consultative examinations, non-medical evidence, hearings, post-entitlement issues, benefit terminations, continuing disability review, and overpayments and underpayments. Volume three contains a number of Appendices, including the listings of medical disabilities, Social Security Rulings and Acquiescence Rulings, and Tables of cases, statutes, rulings manuals, and a subject index. In addition to extensive citations to cases, statutes and regulations, the set includes Research References to leading secondary sources including **Social Security Law and Practice**, and **American Law Reports.** As with other West titles, this set provides Practice Tips and Illustrations.

Social Security Law and Practice. St. Paul, MN: West (Clark Boardman Callaghan), 1983-date. 11 vols. Looseleaf format. Quarterly supplements.
Cost: $5,341; supplementation: 1993: $508.50; 1994: $617; 1995: $846; 1996: $949; 1997: $1,192; 1998: $950; 1999: $952; 2000: $1,080; 2001: $1,228.50; 2002: $1,642; 2003: $1,585; 2004: $1,709; 2005: $1,733; 2006: $2,052; 2007: $2,195.50; 2008: $2,396.50; 2009: $2,846; 2010: $2,846; 2011: $3,163; 2012: $3,511; 2013: $3,897; **Monthly Assured Print Price (APP)**: $314/$3,768.
This is a complete practitioner-oriented treatise and practice guide to Social Security and Medicare issues. It includes both analytical discussion of the law and practical guidance on how to handle specific problems. Volumes one to five contain an in-depth analysis of Social Security and Medicare law, including a discussion of covered employment, covered earnings, benefit programs, benefit computation, applications and payments, showing disability, representation, administrative proceedings, judicial proceedings, Medicare, and taxes. Volumes 6 and 7 contain the full text of the pertinent sections of the Social Security Act and Internal Revenue Code and regulations. Proposed legislation and regulations, a citator, and newsletter are contained in volume 8. Volume 9 contains the Subject Index and Tables which allow the user to locate those sections of the text where specific cases, statutes, regulations, and administrative handbooks are discussed. This service is distinguished by its coherent organization and easy to use format. Each of the 73 chapters is self-contained in a handy pamphlet format allowing for easy access and removal. The text is heavily supported by citations to cases, statutes, regulations, and policy manuals. Each chapter includes a brief scope note, citations to related discussion in other sections of the work, and collateral references to works in the former West Total Client-Service Library. The substantive text is supported with Recommendations, Observations, Illustrations, Cautions, all of which make this set an extremely practical working tool. The set is supplemented with cumulative quarterly updates filed under a red guide card, and by a monthly newsletter, entitled **Social Security Practice Advisory**, filed in volume 8. The monthly newsletter provides news of recent development as well as annotations to both legislative and judicial developments keyed to specific chapter and section numbers in the base text.

Cost Saving Tips: This service is generally designed for the attorney who specializes in Social Security and Medicare issues, given its frequency of supplementation. It is possible to buy the set and then not subscribe to the quarterly supplements; however, some type of newsletter is recommended to keep abreast of current developments. As usual, you must be certain to update your research in the appropriate primary sources, Shepard's citations, etc. Cost of supplementation has risen 667% since 1993.

Social Security Practice Guide. New York: Matthew Bender & Co., 1984-date. 5 vols. Looseleaf format. Supplemented twice annually.
Cost: $1,839 (includes annual subscription); renewal: 1995: $556 (frozen since 1992); 1996: $584; 1997: $584; 1998: $610; 1999: $635; 2000: $680; 2001: $728; 2002: $750; 2003: $788; 2004: $827; 2005: $868; 2005: $877; 2006: $903; 2007: $957; 2009: $1,014; 2010: $1,045; 2011: $1,076; 2012: $1,119; 2013: $1,175; 2014: $1,294; CD-ROM: $2,143; annual renewal: 1998: $585; 1999: $635; 2000: $680; 2001: $728; 2002: $750; 2003: $788; 2004: $827; 2005: $885; 2006: $921; 2007: $949; 2008: $1,015; 2009: $1,096; 2010: $1,152; 2011: $1,244; 2012: $1,319; 2013: $1,411; 2014: $1,542.24; eBook: $1,672; renewal: 2014: $1,294.
This practice manual provides a comprehensive analysis of all aspects of the Social Security system, including retirement and survivors programs, disability programs, and supplemental security income for the aged, blind and disabled.
It was written by nineteen authors, most of whom are members of the National Organization of Social Security Claimants Representatives (NOSSCR), including sixteen attorneys specializing in social security matters and three law professors. There is extensive coverage of the presentation of disability cases which comprise 90% of all the cases handled by the

Social Security Administration. The four volumes are divided into eight Parts, including coverage, retirement and survivor's benefits, disability, supplemental security income, Medicare, fees, selected regulations, and medical aspects of disability. The detailed text liberally supported with citations to cases, statutes and regulations, and is accompanied by numerous forms, tables, and interim circulars. Chapter 4 is largely devoted to a consideration of the medical aspects of various disabilities. Like the **Social Security Law and Practice**, this four-volume treatise is aimed at the specialist who requires detailed coverage and frequent supplementation. Unlike the former, however, It provides more detailed examination of the medical aspects of disability claims.

Cost Saving Tips: Investigate the availability of a used set before buying this work new. If you do purchase it new, drop the supplementation after the initial year's subscription has expired and update using primary sources, digests, and **Shepard's Citations** or **KeyCite**. Buy another new, or more current used set when you feel it necessary to update the base text. The CD-ROM and eBook versions are recommended only if you plan to maintain a current subscription.

Additional titles in the field of Social Security Law are available from the following publishers: American Bar Association, Wolters Kluwer Law & Business, Matthew Bender, Bernan Associates, CCH, Inc., Gordon Press, William S. Hein & Co., James Publishing, Kluwer Law International, Lawyers & Judges Publishing Co., Nolo Press, Practising Law Institute, Thomson Reuters West. See Appendix B for addresses and telephone numbers.

Statutory Construction

Brown, Ronald Benton and Sharon Jacobs Brown. **Statutory Interpretation: The Search for Legislative Intent**. Notre Dame, IN: National Institute for Trial Advocacy, 2002. 1 vol. (192 pp.). Paperbound.
Cost: $20; from $.01 on amazon.com (2014).
An excellent introduction to the often complex field of statutory construction. This concise and lucid overview of the subject explains the rules governing statutory construction and summarizes the strengths and weaknesses of the major schools of thought regarding the interpretation of legislative language. The authors explain the established canons of linguistic interpretation and provide guidance in grappling with the ambiguities and inconsistencies which often plague statutory language. A valuable litigation tool for attorneys who wish to evaluate the various arguments likely to be advanced by their opponents. Also useful for trial and intermediate appellate court judges who must consider the rules for statutory construction in their jurisdiction, whether these take the form of high court decisions, constitutional provisions, or statutes that mandate particular interpretative rules. For the practicing attorney, this is a low-cost alternative to the far more exhaustive **Sutherland on Statutory Construction**. Ronald Benton Brown is Professor of Law at Nova Southeastern University Shepard Broad Law Center. Sharon Jacobs Brown, a former practicing attorney, is currently a certified mediator and consultant.

Elhauge, Einer. **Statutory Default Rules: How to Interpret Unclear Legislation**. Cambridge, MA: Harvard University Press, 2008. 1 vol. (400 pp.).
Cost: $68.50; from $12.55 on amazon.com (2014).
The steady growth of statutory (and regulatory) law in the American legal system has progressively increased the importance of statutory interpretation as a tool to be employed by judges. Unlike other books which discuss the rules which should guide judges in interpreting statutes, however, this author argues that judges can, and should, use statutory default rules that are "designed to maximize the satisfaction of enactable political preferences" whenever interpretive inquiry fails to resolve the statutory meaning. In other words, judges should favor the political preferences of the polity that are shared by enough elected officials that they would be enacted into law if the issue were on the legislative agenda. He contends that such default rules explain a number of recent high-profile cases, including the Guantánamo detainees case, the decision denying the FDA authority to regulate cigarettes, the sentencing guidelines case, and the case that refused to allow the attorney general to criminalize drugs used in physician-assisted suicide. A fascinating and provocative take on the subject of statutory interpretation. Einer Elhauge is Professor of Law at Harvard Law School.

Filson, Lawrence E. and Sandra L. Strokoff. **The Legislative Drafter's Desk Reference**. 2d ed. Washington, DC: CQ Press, 2007. 1 vol. (583 pp.).
Cost: $130 (2014).
A conceptual and procedural guide to the drafting of legislative bills and administrative regulations intended for use by legislative staff, lobbyists, legal professionals and students. This step-by-step guide to bill drafting, which updates the 1992 edition, reflects the impact of the Internet and word processing technology on the legislative process. Its parts include: general overview; the first stage: preparing to put pen to paper; writing the bill: preliminary considerations; writing the provisions of a prototypical bills; writing Amendatory provisions; style, form and usage generally; the role of the courts; the uniquely federal forms and styles; and state and regulatory drafting considerations. A useful summary of the rules of statutory construction appears in chapter 8. The volume concludes with a "Quick Guide to **The Legislative Drafter's Desk Reference**," in outline form.

Gerken, Joseph L. **What Good is Legislative History?: Justice Scalia in the Federal Courts of Appeals**. Buffalo, NY, William S. Hein & Co., Inc., 2007. 1 vol. (351 pp.).
Cost: $82; from $7.46 on amazon.com (2014).
As the leading exponent of Textualism as an interpretive critique for construing statutes, Justice Anthony Scalia has also become the most vocal critic of legislative history as tool of statutory construction, whose opinions have framed the debate over its use. However, most of Justice Scalia's criticisms of legislative history appear in concurring or dissenting opinions, not majority opinions. In light of the fact that federal appellate decisions are one hundred times more numerous than those

of the U.S. Supreme Court, this study examines the impact of Justice Scalia's views upon the federal court of appeals' use of legislative history. The author's analysis is directed specifically to approximately 200 federal court of appeals opinions which discuss Justice Scalia's critique of legislative history. While these courts have often cited Justice Scalia in this regard, their rulings provide no simple answer to the question of whether or not they have adopted his criticism of legislative history. Indeed, it is clear that the courts do not accept legislative history sources uncritically, but instead have a sophisticated sense of when and how it constitutes credible evidence of Congressional intent. Following a brief history of legislative history, the author discusses the Supreme Court's treatment of legislative history prior to Justice Scalia, Justice Scalia's opinions on legislative history, general criticism of legislative history in the courts of appeals, specific applications of legislative history, legislative history cases that cite Justice Scalia, and concludes with his own observations. The appendices include an overview of the author's research methodology and a bibliography. A table of cases, which follows the table of contents, includes citations to Justice Scalia's Supreme Court opinions, non-Scalia Supreme Court decisions, and court of appeals decisions that cite Justice Scalia on the issue of legislative history. This is a thoughtful and well-researched analysis of one Justice's impact on the legislative history controversy and a significant contribution to the field. The author is senior assistant librarian at the University of Buffalo Law School Library.

Greenawalt, Kent. **Legislation: Statutory Interpretation: 20 Questions**. New York: Foundation Press, 1999. 1 vol. (316 pp.). University CaseBook Series (Turning Point Series). ASvailable from West Academic.
Cost: Online: $20; from $2.30 on amazon.com (2014).
This introductory student text on statutory construction follows a question-answer format. Includes excerpts of cases with analysis.

Jellum, Linda D. and David Charles Hrick. **Modern Statutory Interpretation: Problems, Theories, and Lawyering Strategies**. Durham, NC: Carolina Academic Press, 2009. 1 vol. (596 pp.). Paperbound.
Cost: $65.00; from $20.38 on amazon.com (2014).
Statutory interpretation is an essential component of the judicial function. Statutes are subject to the imprecise nature of language itself, legislative mistakes in the drafting process, and unforeseen circumstances not contemplated by legislators. The application of statutes to real life cases requires that judges expound and interpret statutory language. Their role is an extension of the fundamental principle, enunciated in the case of Marbury v. Madison, that "it is emphatically the province and duty of the judicial department to say what the law is." This law school textbook provides an excellent introduction to the science of statutory interpretation. The author presents an excellent overview of the often complex issues and challenges involved in interpreting statutes, including an overview of the legislative process, the rules for determining the meaning of the text through evaluation of words, punctuation and grammar, common approaches to statutory interpretation, the role of components, the textual canons, legislative history, finding and using purpose, statutes and the common law, conflicting statutes, the impact on meaning of post-interpretation legislative silence, the impact of constitutions on interpretation, and the impact of agency interpretation, and other issues. Each chapter includes concise statements of core concepts, extensive case excerpts, together with notes and questions. Appendices include Karl Llewellyn's Canons of Construction, as excerpted from his "Remarks on the Theory of Appellate Decision and the Rules of Cannon About How Statutes are to be Construed." 3 Vand. L. Rev. 395 (1949).

Mammen, Christian E. **Using Legislative History in American Statutory Interpretation**. New York: Springer, 2002. 1 vol. (199 pp.).
Cost: $135; from $112.95 on amazon.com (2014).
This book examines the use of legislative history in statutory interpretation by the United States Supreme Court. The author isolates the theoretical issues which emerge from the Court's use of legislative history and then examines those issues in the context of the thought of several leading constitutional theorists. He argues that the use of legislative history often follows the Court's determination that the statutory text is ambiguous or produces absurd results, leading the court to determine what Congress intended. However, Mammen contends that trying to ascertain Congress's intentions leads to a theoretical thicket of issues about whether a corporate body is capable of holding intentions, whether such intentions are actually discoverable, and what relationship legislative history has to legislative intentions. The author agrees with Joseph Raz that the only legislative intentions that may be identified and deemed legally authoritative as a matter of general theory are minimal intentions relating to the enactment of a particular text as a legally authoritative statute within a particular legal system. A valuable contribution to an intellectual understanding of the philosophical issues involved in the application of legislative history in the interpretation of statutes.

Martineau, Robert J. and Robert J. Martineau, Jr. **Plain English for Drafting Statutes and Rules**. New Providence, NJ: LexisNexis, 2012. 1 vol. (141 pp.). Paperbound.
Cost: $56; from $34 on amazon.com; kindle: $32.99 (2014).
This concise manual for drafting statutes and administrative rules is premised on the authors' observation that lawyers and law professors do not write well, but think they do. In making this harsh judgment, they assign blame chiefly to the educational system, both pre-legal and legal. In law school, research and writing classes give inadequate attention to writing skills, a problem that persists throughout the curriculum. For most students, 8-10 hours of classroom instruction is all they are going to get during their three-year law school experience. The authors express a decided preference for the Plain English standard of writing with the aim of making every statute or administrative rule as clear and understandable as possible to the general public, employing only words in common usage. With that background, they consider how statutes get made in a legislative body, federal administrative and court rulemaking, state rulemaking, statutes and rules in the courts, constitutional and legislative rules governing structure of a bill, mandatory form and language, arrangement of bill sections, the effect of structure and style on substance, the drafting process, plain English

principles and word choice, ambiguous and other troublesome words, plain English principles and rules on drafting a sentence, and rules on drafting specific provisions or words. The Appendix includes examples of bills and ordinances. Robert J. Martineau is Distinguished Research Professor Emeritus of Law, University of Cincinnati College of Law and a noted scholar and teacher in the field of appellate practice, oral argument, and brief writing. He is joined by his son, Robert J. Martineau, Jr., Commissioner of the Tennessee Department of Environment and Conservation. Together, they bring over 70 years experience in drafting constitutional, statutory, and administrative language.

Mikva, Abner J. and Eric Lane. **An Introduction to Statutory Interpretation and the Legislative Process**. New York: Wolters Kluwer Law & Business, 1997. 1 vol. (202 pp.).
Cost: $53 (paper); from $32.45 on amazon.com (2014).
A brief introduction to the legislative process and statutory construction. Addresses the interpretation of statutes, the legislative process, the enactment of a statute, anatomy of a statute, and the publication of statutes. The authors use sample statutes, interpretive cases to illustrate their analysis. Provides unique insights into the publication process, including a discussion of enrolled bills, slip laws, session laws, and statutory codes, among other topics. A professor of law at the University of Chicago, Abner Mikva is a former Chief Judge of the U.S. Court of Appeals, five-term congressman and Counsel to the President during the Clinton administration. Eric Lane is a professor of law at Hofstra University with experience in both state and local legislative bodies.

Popkin, William D. **A Dictionary of Statutory Interpretation**. Durham, NC: Carolina Academic Press, 2007. 1 vol. (364 pp.).
Cost: $45; from $11.44 on amazon.com (2014).
A useful reference guide to the most significant terms and ideas in the field of statutory construction. Chapter one includes definitions of over 100 terms, including legislative intent, legislative history, textualism, ambiguity, and Law and Economics, together with an extended explanation of the relevance of the term, ideas for statutory interpretation, a history of its use, and a brief consideration of the term in the context of contemporary legal issues. Chapter two includes over 35 famous quotations dealing with the interpretation of statutory construction, along with historical and critical commentary, by such legal luminaries as Learned Hand, Oliver Wendell Holmes, Guido Calabresi, Richard Posner, Roscoe Pound, and William Blackstone. A useful introduction to the modern debate regarding the interpretation of statutes and its ramifications, which reflects the author's skepticism of textualism. William D. Popkin is the Walter W. Foskett Professor Emeritus of Law at the Indiana University School of Law at Bloomington.

Popkin, William D. **Statutes in Court: The History and Theory of Statutory Interpretation**. Durham, N.C.: Duke University Press, 1999. 1 vol. (340 pp.).
Cost: $74.95; from $24.29 on amazon.com; Kindle: $30.36 (2014).
Judicial interpretation of statutory language has been a contentious issue from the beginnings of the Republic because it implicates the balance of power between the legislative and judicial braches of government. In this historical examination of the American statutory construction, William Popkin analyzes the evolution of statutory interpretation from its English and colonial origins to the present day. The chapters in Part I include: English history, the United States from the Revolution to the Founding, the 19th century, and the period from 1900 to 1960. Part II examines contemporary statutory interpretation in chapters entitled: Giving Judges as Little to Do as Possible: The Rise of Modern Textualism; Giving Judges Something To Do: Republicanism and Substantive Canons; and Ordinary Judging. This volume is intended to provide judges with a framework for their particular approach to statutory construction as well as a vocabulary to be used in explaining it. An excellent overview of the topic for judges, law professors, law students, and students of the judicial and legislative process.

Rynearson, Arthur J. **Legislative Drafting Step-By-Step**. Durham, NC: Carolina Academic Press, 2013. 1 vol. (235 pp.). Paperbound.
Cost: $45.00 (10% Internet discount) (2014).
Professional legislative drafting is a way of writing legislation in a systematic, almost scientific manner that may be applied to all legislation regardless of content. First applied on a trial basis to federal legislation in the early 1900s, it led to the creation of the nonpartisan Legislative Drafting Service, of which the current Senate and House Legislative Counsel offices are the direct descendent. Today, these offices draft most of the bills introduced in Congress. The author identifies five key steps in the legislative drafting process: (1) legalize: to achieve the desired legal effect; (2) formalize: to choose the right legislative vehicle; (3) integrate: relating new law to existing law; (4) organize: organizing the legislative text; (5) clarify: achieving clarity of expression. Legislative drafting is the process of establishing all these relationships--law, form, and words--in the form of a written document. This manual is designed to guide the beginning or intermediate drafter through this five-step framework for analysis together with simple to comprehend rules. The framework may be applied to a variety legislative vehicles, including bills, joint resolutions, concurrent resolutions, and simple resolutions. And the rules may be applied to any democratic legal system. Written primarily for legislators and their staffs, it is also designed for all who participate in the legislative process. And while learning the craft of legislative drafting is a critical preliminary step, becoming a master drafter requires a lot of practice. In addition to a detailed exposition of the five steps in effective drafting, the author also looks ahead to the process of statutory interpretation which will be applied by those attempting to make sense of legislative language, or by the courts in making a judicial determination as to its meaning. The volume also includes more than 150 examples of draft legislative language, nineteen charts and tables illustrating the text, nine drafting exercises (with answers), a description of the United States legislative process, and sixteen House and Senate bill, resolution, and amendment forms. The former Deputy Legislative Counsel of the United States Senate, Arthur J. Rynearson has drafted thousands of bills, resolutions and amendments, as an attorney-drafter in the nonpartisan Senate Legislative Counsel's Office, and has taught legislative drafting to hundreds of law students, legislators and legislative staff both in the United States and abroad.

Singer, Norman J. **Sutherland Statutory Construction.** 6th ed. St. Paul, MN: West (Clark Boardman Callaghan), 2000-date. 9 vols. Annual pocket parts.
Cost: $2,170; supplementation: 1993: $346.00 (incl. 2 rev. vols.) 1994: $367.00 (incl. 2 rev. vols.); 1995: $125.00; 1996: $185.00; 1997: $225.00; 1998: $238.00; 1999; $257.00; 2000: $407.00; 2001: $774.00; 2002: $606.00; 2003: $565.00; 2004: $417.50; 2005: $962.50; 2006: $1,011; 2007: $1,062; 2008; $1,258; 2009: $1,321; 2010: $1,288.50; 2011: $1,169.50; 2012: $1,274.50; 2013: $1,173; **Monthly Assured Print Price (APP)**: $152/$1,824.
Originally published in 1891 by Jabez Sutherland, this treatise has a well-deserved reputation as the "bible" in the field of statutory interpretation. The task of preparing the 5th edition has been assumed by Professor Norman Singer, Professor of Law at the University of Alabama. The work provides expert guidance in evaluating statutes, ordinances and regulations by providing detailed analysis of the choices between legislative intent and manifest meaning. Five major topical areas are encompassed by the eight volumes, including legislative power, legislative organization and procedure, legislative form and mode, legislative applicability, and statutory construction. Each topical section, or Part, is accompanied by Legal Commentaries written by leading statutory and constitutional scholars. The text is both lucid and detailed and is exhaustively supported with citations to cases and statutory authorities. The supplementation cost should ease a bit now that the 5th edition nears completion. Highly recommended to any attorney or law firm which deals with matters of legislative intent and interpretation.

Cost Saving Tips: Since this work is chiefly valuable for its core discussion, the cost-conscious purchaser may choose to purchase the cumulative pocket supplements every 2-3 years as a means of restraining overall law library costs. Relevant cases should obviously be Shepardized and primary law sources checked for substantive changes in the law.

Solan, Lawrence M. **The Language of Statutes: Laws and Their Interpretation**. Chicago: University of Chicago Press, 2010. 1 vol. (288 pp.). Hardbound.
Cost: $50.00; eBook: $40; from $32.00 on amazon.com (2014).
This is a book about the judicial interpretation of statutes in an age in which much of the law is a product of legislative bodies, when it ist is not amended by Executive fiat. Unlike an earlier era in which common law precedent held sway, and judges exercised the last word about how the facts of a case fit into the earlier body of precedent, the modern age is increasingly dominated by statutes and judicial interpretations of statutes. Some jurists, including Antonin Scalia, are critical of the tendency of some judges to place their own gloss and values on statutes, rather than interpreting them in the manner in which the legislature drafted them. Others, including Guido Calabresi, in his **A Common Law for the Age of Statutes**, believe that judges' need to "do justice" should continue to be driven by the common law tradition, even in an age when much of the law is statutory. It is Solon's contention that judges continue to sound like common law judges even when they are interpreting laws. For although they profess to defer to legislative intent, they make their own decisions about what pieces of legislative history and other social facts surrounding the statute's passage tell us about what the legislature really had in mind. Moreover, they adhere to common law principles of precedent so that an earlier interpretation of statute continues to have binding effect on all future cases. While both sides to the debate share a commitment to legislative primacy as a core value, they differ as to how a court should accomplish what they agree should be accomplished. In any event, judicial discretion is unavoidable when the language of the law leaves uncertainty. This important contribution to the literature of statutory interpretation offers thoughtful observations about the need to interpret statutes, about definitions, ordinary meaning, respect for the legislature, the intent of the legislature, the tension between stability, dynamism and other values, who should interpret statutes, jurors as statutory interpreters. Lawrence Solon is professor of Law at Brooklyn Law School and the author of **Language of Judges** and **Speaking of Crime: The Language of Criminal Justice**.

Additional titles in the field of Statutory Construction are available from the following publishers: Dartmouth Publishing, Duke University Press, Foundation Press, Juta & Co., LexisNexis, Thomson Reuters West. See Appendix B for addresses and telephone numbers.

Taxation
(see also Trusts and Estates)

The taxation products in this bibliography represent just a sampling of the many products in the field of taxation and estate planning. The publishers represented here publish a wealth of products and product combinations too detailed and complex to be adequately addressed by a selective bibliography. Readers are urged to visit, among others, the (1) the Thomson/RIA web site for further information on the full range of products available from Research Institute of America RIA, Warren, Gorham & Lamont (WG&L), Checkpoint, GoSystem Tax, E-Form RS, and InSource; (2) the CCH Online store for complete information on the CCH line of tax products (including former Aspen Publishing titles now published under the CCH banner); (3) Bloomberg BNA web site for complete information on the Bloomberg BNA Tax and Accounting product line, and (4) the Tax Analysts web site for information regarding the Tax Analysts product line.

Axelrod, Lawrence M. **Consolidated Tax Returns.** 4th ed. St. Paul, MN: West (Clark Boardman Callaghan), 2012-date. 2 vols. Looseleaf format.
Cost: 2013-2014 Edition: $1,292.94 (with one year's service); supplementation: 1993: $177; 1994: $177; 1995: $177; 1996: $235.20; 1997: $235.20; 1998: $235; 1999: $260; 2000: $276; 2001: $320; 2002: $171.25; 2003: $382; 2004: $431.50; 2004: $477; 2006: $592; 2007: $591; 2008: $733.44; 2009: $799; 2010: $799.56; 2011: $871.56; 2012/13 (1st replacement volume): $1,185.48;
The consolidated income tax return is a federal income tax return that reports the aggregate income and deductions of a parent corporation and its subsidiaries and the resulting taxable income of the group of corporations. This three-volume treatise

and practice guide explains how to prepare such returns and analyzes the advantages of filing consolidated returns in various kinds of situations. The substantive text is supported by numerous examples and IRS Letter Rulings. The author outlines the cost-saving strategies which can be employed in preparing such returns. The chapters include a history of the consolidated return, the affiliated group, the role of regulations, consolidated computations, consolidated deductions, capital and Section 1231 gains and losses, consolidated investment losses, and intercompany transactions. A well-written and complete text without the exhaustive citations to sources one finds in the WG&L and Matthew Bender treatises. The author is a member of Arkansas, District of Columbia and Kentucky bars.

Bittker, Boris I., Martin J. McMahon, and Lawrence A. Zelenack. **Federal Income Taxation of Individuals.** 3d ed. Boston: RIA Group, 2002-date. 1 vol. Looseleaf format. Two cumulative supplements annually. Also available Online.
Cost: $405 per year; online: $630 per year (single user) (2014).
A thorough and scholarly analysis of the law of federal income taxation as it applies to individuals. This work reflects the same in-depth analysis one finds in all works with which the name of Boris Bittker has been associated. The text is clearly written and heavily supported with relevant primary and secondary authorities. The chapters examine determination of gross income, business operating income and deductions, capital expenses, tax accounting problems of sole proprietorships, partnerships and corporations, as well the alternative minimum tax, and passive loss rules, among other topics.

Cost Saving Tips: To cut your cost in half, simply drop the standing order and purchse anew every other year, thereby going one year between supplements.

Bittker, Boris I. and Lawrence Lokken. **Federal Taxation of Income, Estates and Gifts.** 3d ed. Boston: Warren, Gorham & Lamont, 1993-date. 5 vols. Looseleaf format. Updated three times annually.. Also available Online.
Cost: $1,855 per year; Online: $1,560 per year (2014).
This massive five-volume treatise ranks among the leading works on taxation published in the United States. Bittker and Lokken have written an exhaustive work which provides an in-depth examination of taxation as it relates to individuals, corporations, partnerships, estates and gifts. The topical coverage includes: history, constitutionality and structural principles; exclusions from gross income; business and profit-oriented deductions and credits; personal exemptions, deductions and credits; sales and other dispositions of property; capital gains and losses; time value of money; deferred compensation; foreign income and foreign taxpayers; assignments of income and other transactions between related taxpayers; trusts and estates; partners and partnerships; corporations and shareholders; tax-exempt organizations; accounting methods and periods; tax practice and procedure; taxes on transmission of wealth; the gift tax; the estate tax; and tax on generation-skipping transfers. The text is supported by extensive citations to primary and secondary authorities. The five bound volumes were published between the years 1989 and 1993 (one per year) and supplemented quarterly and, now, triennially, since that time.

Cost Saving Tips: In 1997, the publisher changed this to a service publication, effectively precluding the customer from purchasing the cumulative supplements on an as-needed basis. For customers wise enough to have purchased only one of the four supplements per year, this marketing decision raised the annual supplementation cost from $125 to $1,855 ($1,560 on the web) per year. Under the current policy, the only alternative for the cost-conscious consumer is to subscribe to this annual subscription product in alternate years and, thereby, cut the average annual cost to about $927 (i.e. one-half of $1,855). Under this strategy, the customer will receive four quarterly supplements during the first year, no supplements in the second year, and four supplements in the third year, and so forth. This plan guarantees that the subscription is updated on an annual basis, as before. Naturally, the user will be on his own to monitor developments in the iterim.

Bittker, Boris I. and James Eustice. **Federal Income Taxation of Corporations and Shareholders.** 7th ed. Boston: RIA Group, 2005-date. 2 vols. Looseleaf format. Three cumulative supplements annually. Also available on the Internet.
Cost: $830 per year; online: $885 per year (2014).
Boris Bittker has earned an esteemed reputation as one of this country's experts in multiple areas of federal tax law. The sixth edition of this treatise reflects the significant changes in the Subchapter C which have taken place since the Tax Reform Act of 1986, including the Revenue Acts of 1987, 1988, 1990 and 1993 and the even more encompassing regulatory activity over that time span. While the 6th edition contains 300 pages more than the 5th edition, the authors suggest retaining the prior edition because some sections were condensed to keep the work's size under control. Professor Bittker, the Sterling Professor of Law Emeritus at Yale University and James S. Eustice, the Gerald L. Wallace Professor of Taxation at New York University examine the full range of federal tax issues, including corporate organization, capital structure, corporate income tax, corporate elections under Subchapter S, penalty taxes, dividends and other liquidating distributions of cash, stock redemptions, complete liquidations, corporate divisions, reorganizations, affiliated corporations, corporate tax attributes, and foreign corporations and foreign source income. There are thorough citations to all types of primary and secondary sources, with accompanying tables to facilitate easy access to the authors' analysis. A first class work of scholarship by authorities of the first rank.

Cost Saving Tips: Apply the strategy in the previous entry.

Burke, Karen C. **Federal Income Taxation of Partners and Partnerships in a Nutshell.** 4th ed. St. Paul, MN: West, 2013. 1 vol. (480 pp.). Available from West Academic.
Cost: $41; from $38.95 on amazon.com (2014).
Written by an Associate Professor of Law at the University of Minnesota, this student Nutshell provides both lawyers and law students with a basic introduction and conceptual framework to the law governing federal income taxation of partners and partnerships. The coverage encompasses changes in the law through the end of 1991. The chapters include an introduction of partnership taxation, the organization of a partnership, partnership tax accounting, partnership allocations, partnership liabilities, partner-partnership transactions, transfers of

partnership interests, partnership distributions, and the death or retirement of a partner. Includes illustrative examples.

Burke, J. Martin and Michael K. Friel. **Understanding Federal Income Taxation**. 4th ed. Newark , NJ: LexisNexis, 2013. 1 vol. (744 pp.). Paperbound.
Cost: $41; eBook: $36; from $30.05 on amazon.com; kindle ed.: $28.44 (2014).
Intended as a law school text to supplement caseBooks, such as the authors' **Taxation of Individual Income**, this entry in the Understanding Series provides a clearly written introduction to all major aspects of the federal income code as it is applied to the taxation of individuals and businesses. The text includes selective citations to a variety of federal tax code provisions and regulations, revenue rulings, tax court memoranda, and federal court decisions. The authors are professors at the University of Montana School of Law and the University of Florida College of Law, respectively.

Cantrell, W. Patrick. **Federal Tax Procedure for Attorneys**. Chicago: American Bar Association, General Practice, Solo & Small Firm Section, 2008. 1 vol. (448 pp.).
Cost: $89.95; $74.95 to Section members; from $27.90 on amazon.com (2014).
In the author's view, the power of the Internal Revenue Service rivals the power of the most despotic governments in history. The disparity of power between IRS employees and the average taxpayer is what motivates this approach to federal tax procedure. While the Internal Revenue Code is enormously complex, the author avoids any discussion of the substantive tax law rules. Instead, he focuses on the procedural rules contained in Code sections 6000 to 9000. Designed for use by tax attorneys, general practitioners with a casual tax practice, and scholars, this practical, hands-on manual is directed toward dealing with the federal tax code as it is, rather than what is should be. The manual is primarily a step-by-step guide through the various levels of federal tax procedure, from the examination and audit through administrative appeals, and civil tax litigation. The author addresses such particulars as the application of statutes of limitations in tax cases, penalties and interest, collection enforcement, collection defenses and remedies, fraud, and ethical considerations. A graduate of the University of Houston Bates School of Law, the author began his career with the IRS before founding Cantrell & Company, and merging with Briggs and Veselka in 2000.

Cavitch, Zolman. **Business Organizations with Tax Planning.** New York: Matthew Bender and Co., 1963-date. 16 vols. Looseleaf format or eBook. Authority CD-ROM includes no-cost online updating via LEXIS-NEXIS.
Cost: $6,433 (print) (includes annual subscription); renewal: 1995: $1,644 (price frozen since 1992); 1996: $1,725; 1997: $1,725; 1998: $1,810; 1999: $1880; 2000: $2,010; 2001: $2,151.00; 2002: $2,151; 2003: $2,259; 2004: $2,372; 2005: $2,538; 2006: $2,640.00; 2007: $2,851; 2008: $3,065; 2009: $3,310; 2010: $3,399; 2011: $3,569; 2012: $3,747; 2013: $4,009; 2014: $4,375; ebook: $5,849; renewal: 2014: $4,849; also available on the publisher's **Business Law Library** on CD-ROM: $37,053; renewal: 2014: $32,948.04.
A complete and exhaustive treatise and practice guide to the law of business organizations. Contains full discussion and analysis of every aspect of corporate law with attention to relevant areas of federal taxation. Includes a discussion of federal corporate taxation, limited partnerships, antitrust law, securities law, employment discrimination, environmental law, bankruptcy, products liability, copyright, franchising, state taxation and federal contracting. Features citations to statutes and case law from all jurisdictions, as well as relevant law review articles and legal treatises. Written by Zolman Cavitch and the Matthew Bender editorial staff. A first-rate work of scholarship loaded with numerous practice aids. Highly recommended except for the high supplementation cost.

Cost Saving Tips: The high cost of supplementation makes this an ideal candidate for purchase on the used lawbook market. If you do purchase it new, drop the standing order and buy another new or current used set when you feel it necessary to update the base text. As long as you update your research in the primary law and Shepardize relevant cases and statutes, you can obtain great utility out of a lapsed set. Remember that this is a secondary source and only the first stage in the legal research process.

Daily, Frederick W. **Stand Up to the IRS**. 11th ed. Berkeley, CA: Nolo, 2012. 1 vol. (376 pp.).
Cost: $34.99; online purchase: $20.99; from $18.00 on amazon.com (2014).
Dealing with the Internal Revenue Service is a prospect dreaded by most Americans, particularly if it involves an audit or the threat of civil or criminal penalties. In this clearly written guide, tax attorney Frederick W. Daily explains the intricacies of dealing with the IRS and the audit process. He explains the inside workings of the IRS, the filing of tax returns, winning your audit, appealing your audit, going to tax court, keeping the tax collector at bay, IRS enforced collection through liens and levies, the taxpayer advocate; family, friends, heirs and the IRS; fraud and tax crimes, issues of small business and the self-employed, penalties and interest, dealing with tax professionals, state income tax obligations, the Taxpayer Bill of Rights, and the 25 most frequently asked questions. The volume also includes a glossary of tax terms and index. The text provides an invaluable inside look at IRS practices and tactics and candid advice on how to deal with them, including confidential forms used by IRS agents during collection interviews and audits. Frederick W. Daily, who has practiced tax law for more than 35 years, is the author of **Tax Savvy for Small Business** and **Surviving an IRS Audit**, both published by Nolo. He is also a frequent guest on a television news programs.

Estate Planning Law Library on LoislawConnect. New York: Wolters Kluwer Law & Business, 2002-date.
Cost: $540 per year (2014).
A library of estate planning materials combining analytical works, forms, worksheets, and sample documents with hypertext links to primary law.
Formerly entitled: **Aspen's Estate Planning Law Library Online**. One of several subject specific treatise libraries on the Loislaw platform.

Federal Tax Coordinator 2d. New York: Research Institute of America, 1977-date. 38 vols. Looseleaf service or online. Print updated weekly. Internet Analysis updated twice weekly; primary source materials daily. Includes weekly newsletter.
Cost: $4,380 per year; Internet: $3,160; Tax Bundle: $3,360 (2014).
A detailed subject-oriented federal tax service which provides in-depth analysis of federal tax questions as they arise in practice. Coverage includes income, FICA, FUTA, estate, gift and excise taxes. The service provides expert analysis of the rules governing specific issues, with citations to controlling authorities. Features expert commentary by RIA's professional tax editors, including observations, cautions, illustrations, and recommendations. It includes the full text of the Internal Revenue Code, final, temporary and proposed regulations, tax treaties, tax court rules, as well as statements, filled-in forms, and blank forms. The lucid organization of the service makes it particularly useful to the non-tax specialist.

Cost-Saving Tip: The Tax Bundle, which includes more thn 20 tax titles, provides over $9,500 worth of content for just $200.00 more than the Federal Tax Coordinator alone.

Federal Tax Coordinator Library/State Combo with All States Tax Guide [Checkpoint Online]. New York: Research Institute of America. Updated regularly
Cost: $3,860 per year; other options also available (2014).
This product contains the full text of the **Federal Tax Coordinator 2d**, **U.S. Tax Reporter**, **Internal Revenue Code and Regulations**, **RIA's Federal Tax Handbook**, the state combination with All States Tax Guide, a state tax guide for your choice of a selected state. the current 52-week archive to the **Weekly Alert**, **Internal Revenue Bulletins** for the current year, and access to the publisher's online bulletin board. Product may be customized to include other federal tax products.

Fink, Robert S. **Tax Controversies--Audits, Investigations, Trials.** New York: Matthew Bender & Co., 1980-date. 2 vols. Looseleaf format and eBook. Annual supplementation.
Cost: $885 (with annual subscription); annual renewal: 1995: $263.50 (price frozen since 1992); 1996: $276; 1997: $276; 1998: $290; 1999: $305; 2000: $325; 2001: $348; 2002: $373; 2003: $392; 2004: $412. 2005: $494; 2006: $529; 2007: $563; 2008: $605; 2009: $641; 2010: $680; 2011: $667; 2012: $707; 2013: $756; 2014: $811; eBook: $885; renewal: 2014: $811.
Written by Robert S. Fink, a partner in the New York firm of Kostelanetz, Ritholz, Tigue & Fink, this two-volume treatise provides the user with a complete overview of the federal tax collection process, including tax examinations, fraud investigations, and prosecutions. This set is written primarily for the tax practitioner or accountant who is charged with rendering professional advice to those subject to scrutiny or prosecution by the Internal Revenue Service. The chapters include: tax examinations, appellate and tax court procedure, assessments and collection, tax preparers and practitioners, criminal investigations, criminal administrative review, summons power, the grand jury, search and seizure, the right against self-incrimination, privileged communications, use of the Freedom of Information Act in tax litigation, criminal tax issues relating to the corporation, voluntary disclosure, civil penalties, criminal charges, methods of proof, defenses, and collateral consequences of a criminal tax conviction. The Appendices include applicable IRS Code sections and regulations, IRS Manual excerpts, IRS forms, and government and defense litigation forms. A clearly written and heavily documented reference source. There are Tables of cases, statutes and regulations, IRS Administrative Pronouncements, and an Index.

Fishman, Stephen. **Working For Yourself: Law & Taxes for Independent Contractors, Freelancers & Consultants**. 8th ed. Berkeley, CA, Nolo, 2011. 1 vol. Paperbound.
Cost: $39.99; from $17.38 on amazon.com; kindle ed.: $22.99 (2014).
This is a guide for the self-employed, whether characterized as business owners, independent contractors, freelancers, or consultants. The freedom of self-employment carries with it both benefits and drawbacks. This handbook provides guidance on the range of legal and tax issues involved in running a small business or being self-employed. Although self-employment provides independence, the opportunity for higher earnings, and certain tax benefits, it also carries with it a number of negative consequences, including lack of job security, no free benefits, no unemployment insurance, no workers compensation, no free office space of equipment, few or no labor law protections, double social security tax, personal liability for debts, and the curse of dealing with deadbeat clients. The author examines the manner of choosing the legal form for a business, choosing and protecting the business name, the decision to work at home or at an outside office, obtaining licenses, permits and identification numbers, insurance, pricing one's services, reducing income taxes, dealing with the self-employment tax, paying estimated taxes, taxes for workers you hire, record keeping and accounting, safeguarding your self-employed status, retirement options, copyrights, trademarks and trade secrets, using written client agreements, drafting of your own client agreements, and reviewing a client's agreement. Like most Nolo books, the text is augmented with helpful charts, forms, resource citations, cautions, and sample agreements. The Appendices include a sample asset log, expense journal, income journal, and invoice. Stephen Fishman is a San Francisco-based attorney who has authored numerous Nolo self-help titles.

Hamill, Susan Pace. **As Certain as Death: A Fifty-State Survey of State and Local Tax Laws**. Durham, NC: Carolina Academic Press, 2006. 1 vol. (602 pp.).
Cost: $63; from $33.94 on amazon.com (2014).
A generalized survey of income, property, corporate income, general and selective sales and other tax laws for the fifty states, with a consideration of how the tax burden is allocated among the poor, middle, and upper classes. The book provides an overview of each state's tax structure and revenue sources, as well as its public school funding, population, race, religious affiliation, family income and poverty statistics, and major industries. Drawing upon these statistics, the author highlights the strengths and weaknesses of each state's tax structure. This study provides the tools for a cross-jurisdictional analysis of tax policies, particularly from a fairness perspective. Susan Pace Hamill is a professor of law at the University of Alabama School of Law where she teaches tax and business law.

Hardy, Peter D. **Criminal Tax, Money Laundering, and Bank Secrecy Act Litigation**. Arlington, VA: Bloomberg BNA Books, 2010. 1 vol. (1,669 pp.).
Cost: $525.00; supplementation: 2011: $295; 2012: $300; 2013: 0 (2014).
The Internal Revenue Service is the only investigatory agency with jurisdiction over federal criminal tax offenses. Its role has expanded in recent years with the growth of sophisticated criminal activity involving money laundering operations, offshore bank accounts, tax evasion by individuals and corporations, and violations of the Bank Secrecy Act (BSA). The average criminal IRS case is more likely to involve complex fact patterns, technical law, legal privileges, logistical challenges, and difficult questions regarding what constitutes a criminal mental state. Enforcement of the tax code can increase the litigation exposure of corporations, and involve attorney-client privilege, parallel civil and criminal proceedings, deferred prosecution agreements, evidence and conduct in foreign jurisdictions, and the difficulties involved in drawing a line between civil and criminal violations. Moreover, the IRS is now using the Bank Secrecy Act to pursue not only traditional currency reporting offenses, but to step up enforcement of offshore reporting requirements, and to require and enforce anti-money-laundering requirements for financial institutions. The monumental scope of this volume is a reflection of the complexity of the criminal cases now handled by the IRS and federal prosecutors at the Justice Department. It addresses not only current law and procedure, but offers expert practical guidance in handling a federal criminal case from beginning to end, including the full range of complex legal, factual, logistical, and tactical issues which accompany such litigation. While its primary focus is on criminal cases handled by the IRS, this volume also explores the important legal issues that may exist in a complex white-collar practice, including offshore accounts, tax shelter prosecutions, corporate prosecutions, sentencing in white collar cases, and the Supreme Court's recent interpretation of the money laundering statutes. Following an illuminating overview of the nature of IRS criminal enforcement, chapters are devoted to the consideration of the criminal tax statutes, money laundering, the Bank Secrecy Act, the investigation and review process, special issues, pleas agreements, pretrial practice, trial, and sentencing. The text is heavily supported with citations to relevant primary and secondary authorities, including IRS code sections and regulations, and federal court decisions. Designed for use by both prosecutors and defense counsel, this volume will also serve as an essential reference tool for corporate counsel, financial institutions, business and tax professionals, and federal government agencies. The Appendices include a variety relevant federal documents, including a currency transaction report, depository institution suspicious activity report, and a sample agreements involving deferred prosecution of a financial audit, tax and advisory services firm, among others. Peter D. Hardy is a principal in the Philadelphia firm of Post & Schell's national White Collar Defense, Compliance & Risk Management Practice Group. A former federal prosecutor, his practice focuses on the counseling and defense of corporations, directors, officers, managers, professionals and others who may face allegations of business-related or other misconduct.

Hellerstein, Jerome R. and Walter. **State Taxation.** 3d ed. Boston: Warren, Gorham & Lamont, 1998-date. 2 vols. One cumulative supplement annually.
A service publication. Also available on CD-ROM and the Internet.
Cost: $785 per year; Internet: $800 per year (2014).
This leading treatise on the subject of state taxation is divided into two parts: I: Corporate Income and Franchise Taxes, and II: Sales and Use, Personal Income, and Death and Gift Taxes. Volume 1 examines the development of the American state and local tax system, constitutional uniformity and equality safeguards, constitutional restrictions on state taxation affecting interstate and foreign commerce, and corporate franchise, net income and capital stock taxes. Volume two examines sales and use taxes, personal income, death, and gift taxes, and intergovernmental immunities. The well written text is heavily supported with references to state and federal tax statutes and court decisions, charts and tables.

Hoops, Frederick K. and Frederick H. Hoops III. **Family Estate Planning Guide.** 4th ed. St. Paul, MN: West (Clark Boardman Callaghan), 1995-date. 2 vols. Looseleaf pamphlet format.
Cost: $1,269; supplementation: 1996: $142; 1997: $170; 1998: $378; 1999: $195; 2000: $207; 2001: $265; 2002: $427; 2003: $284.50; 2004: $338.75; 2005: $362.50; 2006: $416; 2007: $367; 2008: $409; 2009: $550; 2010: $520; 2011: $587.50; 2012: $657; 2013: $729; 3d ed.: 1993: $65; 1994: $65; 1995: $125; **Monthly Assured Print Price (APP):** $89/$1,068
A detailed and well-organized practice guide to family estate planning. This work is distinguished by its clear language explaining all aspects of family estate planning from the tools available to the planner and initial interview to the use of various trusts arrangements to meet family objectives. Each of the twenty-nine chapters in this two-volume work includes research references to Lawyers Cooperative and other Thomson Legal Publishing products, including **ALR** Annotations, **Am. Jur 2d**, and other secondary sources. Includes citations to relevant primary and secondary sources, including cases, IRS Code Sections, Restatements, treatises, law review articles, and legislative history documents. The Appendices include sample questionnaires, letters, forms, wills, trusts, as well as IRS forms. Individual chapters can be removed and placed in one's briefcase.

Hopkins, Bruce R. **The Law of Tax-Exempt Organizations.** 10th ed. New York: John Wiley & Sons, 2011-date. 1 vol. (1,296 pp.) Supplemented annually.
Cost: $315; e-book: $299.99; supplementation: 2013: $225; 2014: $225; 9th ed.: 2008: $80; 2009: $85; 2010: $105; 8th ed.: 2005: $90; 2006: $95; 7th edition: 1999: $75; 2000: $80; 2001: $94; 2002: $90; 2003: $85; 2004: new edition; 6th ed.: 1993: $50; 1994: $55; 1995: $60; 1996: $65; 1997: $75; 1998: new edition. Also available on WESTLAW.
This scholarly treatise examines in depth what has variously been termed the «third sector,» the «voluntary sector,» the «private sector,» or the «independent sector,» of American society. It is an outgrowth of the author's course in tax-exempt organizations given at George Washington University's National Law Center since 1973. Its intended audience consists of lawyers, accountants, managers, fundraising executives, and volunteers interested in furthering the objectives of various nonprofit organizations. The author's discussion includes an introduction to tax-exempt organizations, an examination of various types of

charitable organizations, other tax-exempt organizations, private foundations, qualification of exempt organizations, feeder organizations and unrelated income taxation, inter-organizational structures and operational forms. The Appendices include a listing of IRS Code Sections governing nonprofits, and tables of cases, IRS Rulings and Revenue Procedures, Private Letter Rulings, IRS Private Letter Rulings Cited in text, IRS Key District Offices, and a subject index. The author provides citations to relevant IRS Code Sections, cases, statutes, and regulations, as well as secondary sources. An essential reference for the attorney representing nonprofits or individuals involved in their management. Formerly published by Wiley Law Publications.

Hopkins, Bruce R. **The Tax Law of Charitable Giving.** 5th ed. New York: John Wiley & Sons, 2014 (June)-date. 1 vol. (758 pp.) Annual supplementation.
Cost: $300; 4th ed. supplementation: 2011: $70; 2012: $125; 2013: $150; 3d ed.: 2006: $65; 2007: $70; 2008: $75; 2009: $80; 2d ed.: 2001: $60; 2002: $65; 2003: $70; 2004: $80; 1st ed.: 1994: $45; 1995: $50; 1996: $55; 1997: $67.50; 1998: $85; 1999: 0; from $248.90 on amazon.com (pre-order)
A close examination of the law and regulations governing charitable giving in the United States. It examines the various forms taken by charitable gifts, including real estate and art. The author also explains the procedure of establishing and maintaining a program of charitable giving. Additional chapters cover such topics as limitations on charitable giving, estate and tax considerations, special gift situations, gifts to charitable remainder and lead trusts, gifts to pooled income trusts, charitable gift annuities, the administration of charitable giving, disclosure rules, and special events, among others. Formerly published by Wiley Law Publications.

Internal Revenue Manual – Audit & Administration. Riverwoods, IL: CCH, a Wolters Kluwer business, 1977-date. 10 vols. or one disc. Updated quarterly. Available for Windows. Search Engine: Proprietary. Includes toll-free support.
Cost: Print: $2,509 per year; CD-ROM: approx. $2,299 per year; Internet: $2,224 per year (2014); Internet price is discounted to customers with other Internet products.
Contains the full searchable text of the official Internal Revenue Service operational policies and instructions.

IRS Publications [Print]. Riverwoods, IL: CCH, a Wolters Kluwer Business, 1977-date. 3 vols. Quarterly updates, or as needed.
Cost: Print: $868 per year (2014).
The full text of the official IRS Publications designed for use in the preparation of federal tax returns.

Kahn, Douglas A., et al. **Corporate Income Taxation**. 6th ed. St. Paul, MN: West, 2009. 1 vol. (774 pp.). Available from West Academic.
Cost: $103; from $59.64 on amazon.com (2014).
As a fictional entity, the corporation has an existence separate and apart from its owners. The owners of a corporation are those who own shares of stock and are referred to as shareholders. Their interests in its assets are, therefore, indirect. Creditors also have an interest in the assets of the corporation, but theirs is an interest of a different sort. The federal tax system treats corporations as distinct entities from their shareholders and taxes them on the corporation's income. The income earned by shareholders is also taxed, resulting in double taxation of the corporation's income. All corporations that are not classified as S corporations are referred to a C corporations. This Hornbook is intended as a student textbook for a basic or advanced course in corporate taxation or business planning. Its organizational structure begins with an examination of the tax consequences of a corporation's making distributions to its shareholders (§301 distributions), either on account of, or in redemption of, their stock. Other chapters address the complete liquidation of a corporation and taxable sales of a corporation's business, the distribution of stock and stock rights and Section 306 stock, S corporations, the organization of a corporation, corporate divisions, reorganizations, acquisition or retention of tax attributes, and consolidated returns. The authors' aim in doing this is provide the reader with an understanding of how the tax law treats an existing corporation and its shareholders before explaining the basics of the tax treatment of organizing or reorganizing a corporation. They seek to introduce the basic rules of corporate taxation and their exceptions, while avoiding the more complex and intricate rules. Which might conflict with student mastery of the subject matter. The book brings together four experts on corporate taxation from the worlds of academia and private practice.

Kove, Myron and James M. Kosakow. **Handling Federal Estate and Gift Taxes.** 6th ed. St. Paul, MN: Thomson Reuters West (Clark Boardman Callaghan), 2000-date. 2 vols. Annual pocket parts.
Cost: $400; ProView eBook: $400; supplementation: 2001: $161; 2002: $180; 2003; $205; 2004: $229.50; 2005: $274; 2006: $280; 2007: $312; 2008: $348; 2009: $421; 2010: $421; 2011: $463; 2012: $509; 2013: $560; 5th ed.: 1996: $130; 1997: 0; 1998: $127; 1999: $138; **Monthly Assured Print Price (APP)**: $58/$696.
This treatise was written in response to both the growing complexity of the law and regulations governing federal estate taxes and the enactment of the Federal gift tax statute. This is a practical tool designed to aid the practicing attorney in handling estate and gift tax matters. The author has assumed that the user has little or no knowledge of the applicable law and, therefore, provides step-by-step guidance through the tax proceeding. The text is supported by citations to leading cases, as well as applicable statutes, IRS code sections and regulations. The 5th edition was written by Jonathan M. Forster and Gregory J. Rupert.

Larson, Joni and Dan Sheaffer. **Federal Tax Research**. 2d ed. Durham, NC: Carolina Academic, 2011. 1 vol. (369 pp.). Hardbound.
Cost: $57.00; from $20.88 on amazon.com (2014).
Federal tax research is similar in many ways with other types of legal research. These commonalities include the need to gather the relevant facts, isolate the legal issue(s) involved, ascertain what law applies to the resolution of the issue, determine how

the issue is resolved when the law is applied to the relevant facts, and communicate the results of the research. Federal tax law may be found in a variety of sources, including the Internal Revenue Code (Title 26 of the United States Code), tax regulations, federal court decisions, legislative history, and both public and taxpayer specific guidance from the Office of Chief Counsel of the Internal Revenue Service (IRS). Forms of Public Guidance include Revenue Rulings, Revenue Procedures, Notices and Announcements, Actions on Decisions, and IRS Publications. These and other federal tax documents are published in the Internal Revenue Bulletin. Taxpayer specific guidance may take the form of Private Letter Rulings, Determination Letters, Information Letters, and Technical Advice Memoranda. In addition, there is a wealth of documents generated by the Office of Chief Counsel for Internal Use, including Field Service Advice, Technical Assistance, Service Center Advice, General Counsel Memoranda, Legal Memoranda, and more. In addition to a thorough exposition of all the relevant sources for federal tax research, the authors also discuss the research process; international tax research, cite checking, law reviews, journals and other publications; and the process of organizing the research into a finished product. The volume also includes a useful chart indicating sources for judicial opinions, both official and commercial. As a law school textbook, each chapter includes citations to related articles for further reading, and multiple choice problems for student use. The authors are professors of law, Thomas M. Cooley Law School.

Lederman, Leandra. **Understanding Corporate Taxation**. 2d ed. Newark, NJ: LexisNexis, 2010. 1 vol. (504 pp.).
Cost: $45; eBook: $36; from $25.49 on amazon.com; kindle ed.: $28.44 (2014).
This law school text on corporate taxation serves as a introductory overview for law students and a concise refresher for practitioners. The author addresses corporate taxation from incorporation through liquidation, including such topics as corporate taxation and its double taxation system, the capital structure of a corporation, redemptions of stock, stock dividends, the pass-through regime of Subchapter S, acquisitive reorganizations, corporate divisions, carryover of tax attributes, anti-abuse measures, and the integration of corporate-level and shareholder-level taxes. Included tables of cases and statutes, and index. Leandra Lederman is Professor of Law, George Mason University School of Law.

Lieuallen, Gwendolyn Griffith. **Basic Federal Income Tax**. 4th ed. New York: Wolters Kluwer Law & Business, 2012. 1 vol. (256 pp.). Paperbound.
Cost: $34.95; from $15.85 on amazon.com; kindle: $21.49 (2014).
A volume in the Emanuel CrunchTime series, this law school review text provides an invaluable exam preparation tool for courses on federal income taxation. The volume includes flow charts detailing the nature of various tax events, including analysis of income, personal deductions, trade of business losses, and capital recovery. The capsule summary addresses all the major aspects of the federal income taxation, including the identification of gross income, specific inclusions, deductions, transactions in property, tax rates and credits, and more. A series of exam tips are geared to specific aspects of federal taxation. The volume also includes sample short-answer questions and answers, and essay exam questions and answers, a glossary of terms, a table of cases, table of IRS regulations, and subject index. The author is partner in the firm of Tonkon Torp LLP, Portland, OR.

Lipton, Richard M. et al. **Partnership Taxation**. 3d ed. Newark, NJ: LexisNexis, 2012. 1 vol. (324 pp.).
Cost: $179; eBook: $107; from $170.05 on amazon.com; kindle ed.: $60.99 (2014).
This law school text provides an introductory to the Internal Revenue Code as it applies to business partnerships. Among the topics covered are the definition of the partnership and partners for tax purposes, the formation of the partnership, the outside basis and allocation of liabilities, operation of the partnership, calculation of partnership taxable income, allocation of partnership income and losses, disposition of partnership interests, partnership distributions, transactions, partnership options and amortization of intangibles, foreign partnerships, and anti-abuse provisions. The text is accompanied by readings questions and problems, as well tables of cases, statutes, and secondary sources. The volume forms part of the publisher's Graduate Tax Series.

McNulty, John K. **Federal Income Taxation of Individuals in a Nutshell**. 8th ed. St. Paul, MN: West, 2011. 1 vol. (627 pp.). Paperbound. Available from West Academic.
Cost: $41; from $26.20 on amazon.com; kindle: $23.84 (2014).
This introduction to the law of federal income taxation of individuals is intended as a supplementary student text or a review of basic principles for the practitioner. The author has attempted to set forth the general principles which emerge from the complications of the federal tax code. An introduction to the nature ands role of the income tax is followed by chapters which discuss the nature of income, statutory inclusions and exclusions from gross income, deductions, mixed deductions and other allowances, personal deductions and other allowances, annual accounting: when is income taxable, to whom is income taxable, and how is income taxable. John McNulty is the Roger J. Traynor Professor of Law at the University of California, Berkeley.

Mertens, Jacob. **The Law of Federal Income Taxation.** St. Paul, MN: West (Clark Boardman Callaghan), 1954-date. 47 vols. (treatise only: 19 vols.). Supplemented several times per year.
Cost: $8,374.56 (Treatise and Rulings); Treatise alone: $6,828; supplementation: 1996: $1,398; 1997: $1,467.90; 1998: $1,468; 1999: $1,530; 2000: $1,622; 2001: $1,876; 2002: $2,063; 2003: $1,850; 2004: $2,563; 2005: $2,832; 2006: $3,514; 2007: $3,539; 2008: $3,936.52; 2009: $4,176; 2010: $4,745.52; 2011: $5,172.48; 2012: $5,637.96; 2013: $6,145.37; Treatise and Rulings each available separately.
Originally written by Jacob Mertens and published in 1942, this work has been cited by the courts more often than all other tax treatises. The chief value of this set lies in the extensive analytical commentaries of each section of the federal income tax code, including the relevant legislative history and the interpretations rendered by the Internal Revenue Service in its Revenue Rulings and Revenue Procedures. The most extensive analytical reference on federal income tax law. Topical coverage

includes rates of tax, computation of tax for individuals, standard deduction and personal exemptions, tax rates on individual estates and trusts, corporations, alternative minimum tax, adjustments applicable to all taxpayers, adjustments applicable only to non-corporate taxpayers, adjustments applicable to corporate taxpayers, credits, construction of tax statutes, annuities, rent, interest and other income, interest on state and local bonds, effect of taxable income, corporate dividends and distributions, and more. The current work is prepared and supplemented by members of the publisher's editorial staff and selected outside tax experts. Supplementation cost of treatise portion is reasonable given its size and scope.

Cost Saving Tips: The full set includes a great deal of primary material which may be eliminated if you already receive it in other forms. Purchase only the treatise portion and reduce both your initial and annual supplementation cost.

Olshan, Regina and Erica F. Schohn. **Section 409A Handbook**. Arlington, VA: Bloomberg BNA Books, 2010. 1 vol. (1,124 pp.)
Cost: $345; supplementation: 2011: $145; 2012-2013: 0 (2014).
When Congress enacted the American Jobs Creation Act (Pub. Law No. 108-357, 118 Stat. 1418) in 2004, it included among its many provisions Section 885 which added Section 409A to the *Internal Revenue Code*. Section 409A provided that all amounts deferred under a nonqualified deferred compensation plan for all taxable years are currently includible in gross income to the extent not subject to a substantial risk of forfeiture and not previously included in gross income, unless certain requirements are met. The enactment of Section 409A, augmented by nearly 1,000 pages of federal regulations and guidance, has forced executive compensation experts and more general benefits practitioners to design and/or modify compensation arrangements to comply with its provisions. This volume provides the comprehensive guidance necessary to interpret and comply with the complex rules of Section 409A. The book's 32 chapters and numerous appendices address the full range of topics and issues regarding the enactment, coverage, specific provisions and issues involved in Section 409A compliance, as well as analysis and advice on many still unresolved issues. Among the issues covered are the substantial risk of forfeiture, plan aggregation, short-term deferrals, separation pay arrangements, disability, reimbursement arrangements, partnerships, plans of tax-exempt entities, foreign plans, funding arrangements, penalties, and more. The text is supported by numerous citations to IRS Code provisions, IRS and Treasury Regulations, IRS Notices, Revenue Rulings, and federal and tax court decisions. The lead authors/editors are joined by more than 26 contributing authors with expertise in the various aspects of 409A compliance.

Omnitax. Riverwoods, IL: CCH Inc. Online service. Updated monthly. Search Engine: Proprietary.
Cost: approx. $22,260 per year (2014). Contact sales representative for exact pricing.
Designed for law firms and corporations with comprehensive research requirements, this online service contains unlimited access to CCH's federal and state tax libraries, plus an integrated daily tax news service and a variety of other productivity tools and practice aids. Among the services included in this online package are the **Standard Federal Tax Reporter**, **Federal Estate & Gift Tax Reporter**, **Federal Excise Tax Reporter**, **CCH Federal Tax Service**, **Tax Treaties Reporter**, **U.S. Master Tax Guide**, Tax Archive Materials, **Internal Revenue Code**, federal tax regulations, full-text of federal administrative rulings and documents (including Revenue Rulings, Revenue Procedures, Treasury Decisions, Notices of Proposed Rulemaking, IRS Announcements), Letter Rulings & IRS Positions, Tax Cases, legislative documents, treaties, IRS publications, **Internal Revenue Manual**, the CCH state tax reporters for all fifty states and D.C., **CCH State Tax Guide**, **CCH Multistate Corporate Income Tax Guide**, **CCH Multistate Sales Tax Guide**, **CCH Multistate Property Tax Guide**, **California** and **New York Tax Analysis**, **CCH perform plus** II (interactive federal and state tax forms and instructions delivered over the Internet), **CCH® Tax Tracker News**, **TAXES – The Tax Magazine**, **Current Legislative Development**, **State Tax Review**, and the **Journal of Retirement Plann**ing. Consumers should contact their local sales representative for details regarding the other combinations of tax services available.

Pennell, Jeffrey N. **Estate Planning.** 8th ed. Riverwoods, IL: CCH, Inc., 1998-date. 2 vols. Print or eBook. Annual replacement volume.
Cost: $465; supplementation: 2000: $250; 2001: $165; 2002: $225; 2003: $255; 2004: $269; 2005: $279; 2006: $299; 2007: $625; 2008: $625; 2009: $365; 2010: 0; 2011: 0; 2012: $443; 2013: $465; 5th ed.: 1992: $175; 1993: $195; 1994: $295; 1995: $295; 1996: $310; 1997: $322; 1998-99: not available.
This two-volume treatise, replacing the three-volume 6th edition, provides complete coverage of the various arrangements which can be made to effectuate the devolution of an individual's wealth. While many estate plans involve the drawing up of a will, many others are based on a variety of inter vivos arrangements, including outright gifts, joint ownership, irrevocable inter vivos trusts, revocable inter vivos trusts, legal present and future interests created inter vivos, and settlements involving the distribution of life insurance proceeds. The authors' discussion is devoted largely to matters involving large estates, but also encompasses small estates. Naturally, a great preponderance of material is concerned with tax issues as they relate to various estate planning mechanisms. Professor Casner, the late Austin Wakeman Scott Professor of Law, Emeritus, Harvard Law School published his first edition of this work in 1953. Jeffrey N. Pennell, the Richard Clark Professor of Law at Emory University School of Law, has assumed the task of preparing the sixth and seventh editions following the death of Professor Casner in 1990. The chapters cover the estate plan created by the operation of law (intestate succession), wills, income taxation of estates, revocable inter vivos trusts, family annuities, non-trust gifts, life insurance, employee benefits, social security, concurrent interests in community property, future interests in an estate plan, generation-skipping transfer tax, powers of appointment, the marital deduction, the charitable deduction, planning for the payment of death costs, estate plans that cross state or national borders. Volume five contains a hypothetical proposed estate plan for Mr. and Mrs. Richard Harry Black III. Volume six contains tables of cases, IRS Code sections, Treasury regulations, Internal Revenue rulings, Internal Revenue Bulletin rulings, Letter rulings, Revenue Procedures, Technical Advice Memoranda,

state statutes, Uniform and Model Acts, **Restatements**, and secondary authorities. In 2004, responsibility for the publication and distribution of **Estate Planning** was assumed by Wolters Kluwer's sister company, CCH.

Posin, Daniel Q. and Donald B. Tobin. **Principles of Federal Income Taxation.** 7th ed. St. Paul, MN: West, 2005. 1 vol. (775 pp.) Supplemented with periodic new editions. Concise Hornbook Series. Available from West Academic.
Cost: $48.00; from $5,43 on amazon.com (2014).
A student Hornbook presenting an overview of the law governing federal income taxation. A well written and economical alternative to the more expensive works written for the practicing attorney.

Rabkin, Jacob and Mark H. Johnson. **Federal Income, Gift and Estate Taxation.** New York: Matthew Bender & Co., 1942-date. 11 vols. Looseleaf format. Not available on CD-ROM or Internet.
Cost: $3,016 (includes annual subscription); annual renewal: 1995: $730 (price frozen since 1992); 1996: $766; 1997: $766; 1998: $805; 1999: $840; 2000: $840; 2001: $840; 2002: $899; 2003: $944; 2004: $1,024. 2005: $1,229; 2006: $1,279; 2007: $1,317; 2008: $1,409; 2009: $1,522; 2010: $1628; 2011: $1,726; 2012: $1,795; 2013: $1,921; 2014: $2,214; Volumes 1-5 also available separately.
One of Matthew Bender's best selling titles, this 11-volume treatise provides the active practitioner with exhaustive scholarly discussion and analysis of federal taxation of income, gifts and estates. Originally written in 1942 by Jacob Rabkin and Mark H. Johnson, the work is currently updated by the publisher's editorial staff. In addition to a thorough, annotated analysis of the law, the text is supplemented with a variety of practical features such as rate tables, checklists of deductions, audit triggers, and tax calendars. The set also includes Congressional Committee Reports, planning aids and tax court rules. Impressive in both its scope and practical utility.

Cost Saving Tips: If you need to reduce your expenditure for this set, investigate its availability on the used law book market where it is deeply discounted (depending on currency). The periodic re-purchase of a current used or new set will sharply reduce your annual financial outlay for this title.

Rounds, Charles E., Jr. and Charles E. Rounds, III. **Loring and Rounds: A Trustees Handbook**. New York: Wolters Kluwer Law & Business, 2014. 1 vol. (1,896 pp.). Annual.
Cost: 2014 Edition $319.
First published in 1898 by Augustus Peabody Loring, **A Trustee's Handbook** has since achieved a reputation as the leading reference guide in the field of trust administration. The fifth and sixth editions were prepared by Mayo Adams Shattuck and James F. Farr, respectively. Professor Charles Rounds assumed responsibility for the seventh (1994) and successive editions. Intended as a reference guide rather than a treatise, the 2014 edition provides valuable insight into the nature of trusts and the role of the trustee, who holds title to property for the benefit of another. Professor Rounds examines the rights, duties and obligations of the parties once the trustee takes title to the trust property. Chapters include: the Property Requirement, the Trustee's Office, Interests Remaining with the Settlor, the Beneficiary, the Trustee's Duties, the Trustee's Liabilities, Miscellaneous Topics of General Interest to the Trustee, Special Types of Trusts, and the Income Taxation of Trusts. Professor Rounds is professor of Law at Suffolk University Law School. The 2014 edition provides a number of substantive updates to the 2013 edition, including a discussion of impressing a trust upon difital assets, constructive trusts, restitution of consequential gains, the concept of apportionment, unjust enrichment, and much more.

Saltzman, Michael I. **IRS Practice and Procedure.** 3d ed. Boston: Thomson Reuters Checkpoint, 1999-date. 1 vol. Looseleaf format. Three cumulative supplements annually. Also available Online.
Cost: Print: $790 per year; Online: $760 per year (2014).
The author explains and analyzes the procedures followed by the Internal Revenue Service to ensure tax compliance and to prosecute those in violation of tax laws, from drafting a ruling request to preparation for a tax appeal. The text also looks at the rules governing the preparation of income tax returns, the statutes of limitation, the administrative appeals process, and the means for obtaining the best settlement. The authors also explain how the IRS goes about obtaining information regarding a taxpayer and the rules and defenses governing these practices. The text is accompanied by references to IRS Code section, regulations, policy manuals, and other relevant authorities.

Cost Saving Tips: In 1997, the publisher changed this to a service publication, effectively precluding the customer from purchasing the cumulative supplements on an as-needed basis. For customers wise enough to have purchased only one of the four supplements per year, this marketing decision raised the annual supplementation cost from approx. $95.00 to $675 per year. Under the current policy, the only alternative for the cost-conscious consumer is to subscribe in alternate years and, thereby, cut the average annual cost to about $337 (i.e. one-half of $675). Under this strategy, the customer will receive three supplements per year during the first year, no supplements in the second year, and three supplements in the third year, and so forth. This plan guarantees that the subscription is updated on an annual basis, as before.

Standard Federal Tax Reporter. Riverwoods, IL: CCH, a Wolters Kluwer business (CCH), 1945-date. 25 vols. Looseleaf service. Weekly. Also available on Intelliconnect platform. Print and Internet updated weekly. Toll-free support (800-835-0105).
Cost: Print: $4,407 per year; Intelliconnect: contact sales representative (2014).
Published since 1913, this 22-volume looseleaf service provides full coverage of federal laws, regulations, administrative materials, court and agency decisions in the field federal taxation

State Tax Guide. Riverwoods, IL: CCH, a Wolters Kluwer business, 1960-date. 2 vols. Also available on the Internet. Search Engine: Proprietary. Toll-free support (800-835-0105). Print updated biweekly, CD-ROM and Internet monthly.
Cost: approx. $2,527 per year; Internet: approx. $2,200 per year (2014).
An encyclopedic guide to the taxes levied in each of the fifty

states and the District of Columbia, including taxes on alcoholic beverages, banks, financial companies, chain stores, cigarettes, tobacco, corporate Income, franchise, gasoline, motor fuels, inheritance, estate and gift, initial fees and taxes, insurance companies, licenses, motor vehicles, personal Income, property, sales, use, gross receipts, severance, production, stock transfer, document recording, and utilities. Includes an extensive compilation of quick-reference charts that list tax rates, due dates, tax treatments and more for each state.

Stephens, Richard B. et al. **Federal Estate and Gift Taxation.** 7th ed. Boston: Thomson Reuters Checkpoint, 1996-date. 1 vol. Three cumulative supplements annually. Also available online.
Cost: Print: $710 per year; Online: $575 per year (2014).
A detailed analysis of the law regarding federal estate and gift taxation which generally follows the outline presented by the Internal Revenue Code. Originally written as a student text, the current edition of this work provides the kind of detail useful to the experienced estate lawyer. In their effort to clarify the meaning of complex provisions of the Internal Revenue Code, the authors heavily upon Treasury regulations, legislative history, and decisions of both state and federal courts. The work is divided into four major parts: Overview, the Estate Tax, the Gift Tax, and Generation Skipping Transfers. There are tables of cases, IRS Code Sections, Treasury Regulations, Revenue Rulings and other IRS Releases.

Cost Saving Tips: The publisher's decision to convert this to a subscription publication precludes the customer from buying one of the three supplements per year. To counteract this move, subscribe in alternate years. This will allow you to maintain your annual supplementation and save over $545 every other year.

Tax Management Portfolios Plus [Print and Internet]. Washington, DC: Bloomberg BNA. Toll-free support (800-372-1033).
Cost: Print: $9,830 (2014).
A comprehensive collection of over 300 portfolios on a variety of specific tax issues. Individual portfolios are updated or replaced as necessary. Individual portfolios are written by leading tax practitioners and include in-depth analysis, information, practice documents, sample calculations, and discussion of the unwritten law. Contains the full text of the complete collection of Tax Management Portfolios, including U.S. Income (print: $4,834; Internet: $4,907); Estates, Gifts & Trusts (print: $2,339; Internet: $2,707); Foreign Income (Internet: $3,287); Tax Practice Series; journals and reports; and BNA Software spreadsheets. Includes hypertext links to tax laws and regulations; and state forms. Various components availale on Internet.

Townsend, John A., et al. **Tax Crimes**. Newark, NJ: LexisNexis, 2008. 1 vol. (534 pp.).
Cost: $179; eBook: $107; from $76.00 on amazon.com; kindle ed.: $85.60 (2014).
This law school text is devoted to a overview of the criminal tax system and various crimes under the Internal Revenue Code, including tax evasion, tax perjury, aiding and assisting false returns, corruptly impeding tax administration, conspiracy, aiding and abetting, money laundering, financial reporting crimes, mail fraud and wire fraud. The author also considers of a number of procedural issues regarding the investigation and prosecution of tax crimes, including modes of proof, prosecution policies and affirmative defenses, government information gathering, trial issues, trial and post-trial, sentencing, ethical issues in criminal tax practices, major collateral issues, and civil tax considerations. The text is accompanied by selected tax decisions, student problems, sample indictments, a glossary of acronyms and initialisms, tables of cases, statutes and secondary sources, and index. John A. Townsend is a practicing tax attorney with the firm of Townsend & Jones. Updates to the text are located online at: www.lexisnexis.com/lawschool

U.S. Master Tax Guide. **2014**. 92nd Edition. Riverwoods, IL: CCH, Inc., 1935-date. 1 vol. Paperbound.
Cost: 2014 Edition: $93.50; discounts for larger quantities (2014).
The leading desktop guide to federal taxes in the industry. Each edition provides quick answers to questions involving personal and business taxes. The text contains numerous cross-references to the Internal Revenue Code, income tax regulations, and the **CCH Standard Federal Tax Reporter**. It also includes numerous examples, checklists, rate tables, and depreciation tables.

United States Tax Reporter/State Combo with All States Tax Guide [Checkpoint]. New YorkThomson Reuters Checkpoint, 1990-date. Online. Updated daily.
Cost: $3,935 per year (2014).
A comprehensive online code-organized guide to federal tax law, regulations, committee reports, cases, rulings and explanations. It contains a complete compilation of the Internal Revenue Code and Treasury Regulations for speedy reference and concise summaries of taxes levied on every state: Includes Code Language, Committee Reports, Regulations, Proposed Regulations, Explanations, and Annotations. The subscription also includes special reports and the **RIA Federal Tax Handbook**. This is a user-friendly service in a complex field which demands well-organized research materials. The annual subscription cost is substantially less than the comparable service from Commerce Clearing House.

U.S. Tax Reporter: Estate & Gift. New York:Thomson Reuters Checkpoint. 2 vols. Looseleaf format.
Cost: $1,035 per year (2014).
Provides primary law and analysis of every aspect of estate, gift and generation-skipping taxes and related issues of planning, procedure and administration. Includes in-depth analysis with citations to controlling authorities, covering the full spectrum of estate and gift taxation. Includes a number of practice aids, including tax rates and tables for individual income, estate and trust income, and estate and gift taxes, IRS valuation tables for computation of present value of annuities, life and remainder estates, terms for years and charitable interests. Includes finding aids to Code, regulations, rulings, releases, cases and current matter. Service also includes biweekly updates.

Willis, Arthur B., John S. Pennell, and Philip F. Postlewaite. **Partnership Taxation.** 7th ed. Boston, MA: Thomson Reuters, 2012-date. 2 vols. Looseleaf format. Annual subscription. Quarterly supplementation. Also available Online.
Cost: Print: $1,060 per year; Internet: $1,140 per year (2014).
An excellent practitioner-oriented treatise covering all manner of tax issues relating to partnerships. The treatment is organized around the life cycle of the typical partnership and illustrated with numerous practical examples. The substantive portion of the text includes analysis of international partnerships, passive activity loss rules, special allocation regulations under section 704 (b), termination of the partnership, limited liability companies, at risk rules, and depreciation and recapture. The more than 7,000 pages of text include more than 200 pages of forms as well as the text of the partnership sections of the **IRS Code**. The late Arthur B. Willis was the member of a Los Angeles law firm, faculty member at the University of Southern California, and an active member of the ABA Tax Section. John S. Pennell is Of Counsel to McDermott, Will & Emery and a past chairman of the ABA Section of Taxation. Philip F. Postlewaite is a professor of law at Northwestern University and author of a dozen books. Originally published by Shepard's/McGraw-Hill, this title was sold to the Thomson Company in December, 1995. It is now published Warren, Gorham & Lamont under the RIA Group.

Cost Saving Tips: Subscribe to print version in alternate years to cut supplementation cost in half.

Zaritsky, Howard M. **Tax Planning for Family Wealth Transfers: Analysis with Forms**. 3d ed. Valhalla, NY: Thomson Reuters, 1999-date. 1 vol. Looseleaf format; with discs. Also available Online.
Cost: $375 per year; Online: $575 per year (2014).
Designed for the tax attorney, accountant, and financial planner, this guide lays out the tax planning techniques and specific transfers best suited to preserve family wealth with a minimum of tax liability. Among the transfer techniques discussed are grantor retained annuity trusts, split purchases of a residence, corporate and partnership freezes, gifts to minors, transferring assets to a disabled family member, charitable transfers benefiting family members, transfers of interest in Family Partnerships and LLCs, gifts under a durable power of attorney, Crummey trusts, installment sales to family members, and life insurance trusts. Integrated into the author's discussion is the impact of federal laws, regulations, and tax rulings upon tax planning for wealth transfers. All forms in the printed text are also available on disc at no additional charge. Howard Zaritsky is a retired partner in the law firm of Zaritsky & Zaritsky in Fairfax, VA and the author of numerous books and articles on tax and financial planning, including **Federal Income Taxation of Estates and Trusts**.

Additional titles in the field of Taxation are available from the following publishers: American Bar Association, Wolters Kluwer Law & Business, Carolina Academic Press, Matthew Bender, Bloomberg BNA, Dearborn Financial Publishing, Federal Bar Association, Greenwood Publishing Group, William S. Hein & Co., IPG Chicago, Kluwer Academic Publications, LexisNexis, MIT Press, National Conference of State Legislatures, Nolo Press, Panel Publishers, Practising Law Institute, RIA, S & S Trade Paperbacks, State Mutual Book & Periodical Service, Thomson Reuters West, Warren, Gorham & Lamont, West Academic. See Appendix B for addresses and telephone numbers.

Telecommunications Law

Brenner, Daniel L., Monroe E. Price, and Michael I. Meyerson. **Cable Television and Other Nonbroadcast Video: Law and Policy**. St. Paul, MN: West, 1986-date. 2 vols. Looseleaf format. Annual supplementation.
Cost: $861; supplementation: 1996: $244; 1997: $141; 1998: $149; 1999: $161; 2000: $171; 2001: $197; 2002: $217; 2003: $247; 2004: $247; 2005: $252; 2006: $299; 2007: $352; 2008: $373.50; 2009: $454; 2010: $458.50; 2011: $500; 2012: $545; 2013: $632; **Monthly Assured Print Price (APP)**: $63/$756.
With the passage of the Cable Communications Policy Act in 1984, Congress ushered in a new era of federal and local regulation of television. This was followed by the Cable Television Consumer Protection and Competition Act of 1992, and the Telecommunications Act of 1996. Until the introduction of cable, almost all communications policy was national in character. Now, local jurisdictions increasingly assert control through their franchising powers. This treatise is designed to assist lawyers and non-lawyers involved in communications planning and in the operation of cable systems, microwave distribution facilities, satellite services, and telephone companies. The authors of this work address a variety of issues related to cable systems, including cable technology, competition to regulate, the franchise, ownership of cable systems, cable operations, regulation of cable content, regulation of subscriber rates, franchise renewal, cable and copyright, franchise fees and taxes, cable television and telephone companies, privacy, satellite master antenna television systems, satellite video delivery, direct broadcast satellites, microwave video services, pay per view services, and Internet and cable. The relevant federal acts are reprinted in full in the appendices. Daniel Brenner is vice president for law and regulatory policy at the National Cable Television Association and a former law school professor. Monroe Price is professor of law and director of the Squadron Program in Law, Media and Society at Yeshiva University's Benjamin N. Cardozo School of Law. Michael Meyerson is a professor of law at the University of Baltimore School of Law and an author of numerous law review articles on cable television and the law.

Carter, T. Barton, Juliet Lushbough Dee, Martin J. Gaynes and Harvey L. Zuckman. **Mass Communications Law in a Nutshell**. 6th ed. St. Paul, MN: West, 2007. 1 vol. (695 pp.). Available from West Academic.
Cost: $41; from $12.75 on amazon.com (2014).

This introductory text in communications law is suitable for students in the fields of law, journalism, and communications. Coverage is balanced between a discussion of the First Amendment and mass communications, and the regulation of electronic mass media. The latter discussion includes a consideration of the Federal Communications Commission, FCC control of broadcasting, and cable and new technologies.

Ferris, Charles D., Frank W. Lloyd, and Thomas J. Casey. **Telecommunications Regulation: Cable, Broadcasting, Satellite, and the Internet.** New York: Matthew Bender & Co., 1983-date. 2 vols. Available in looseleaf format and eBook. Updated 2-3 times annually. No longer available on CD-ROM.
Cost: $1,747; (includes annual subscription); renewal: 1997: $490; 1998: $490; 1999: $505; 2000: $540; 2001: $578 2002: $619; 2003: $650.00; 2004: $683; 2005: $731; 2006: $783; 2007: $846; 2008: $914; 2009: $987; 2010: $998; 2011: $1,048; 2012: $1,111; 2013: $1,167; 2014: $1,273; eBook: $1,588; renewal: 2014: $1,273.
This treatise provides detailed coverage of the substantive, procedural, and strategic aspects of the law governing the cable television industry, and video technologies, with a special emphasis on the Telecommunications Act of 1996. The authors explore such topics as franchising of cable television systems, local and federal regulation of cable television, copyright issues, antitrust, defamation, securities and tax issues, international developments, and the regulation of such new technologies as the Internet, high definition television (HDTV), subscription television (STV), multi-point distribution service (MDS), direct broadcast satellite (DBS), satellite master antenna television (SMATV), and electronic publishing. The work includes the text of relevant federal statutes and regulations as well as sample FCC, Copyright Office, and state forms. The authors are associated with the Washington, D.C-based law firm of Mintz, Levin, Cohn, Ferris, Glovsky and Popeo, P.C. Formerly entitled **Cable Television Law: A Video Communications Practice Guide**.

Huber, Peter W., John Thorne, and Michael K. Kellogg. **Federal Telecommunications Law.** 2d ed. New York: Wolters Kluwer Law & Business, 1999-date. 1 vol. (1,518 pp.). Annual supplementation.
Cost: $319; supplementation: 2000: $105; 2001: $105; 2002: $135; 2003: $135; 2004: $173; 2005: $145; 2006: $170; 2007: $198; 2008: $212; 2009: $229; 2010: $245; 2011: $260; 2012: $556; 2013: $606.
This is a comprehensive overview of the legal and regulatory framework of the telecommunications industry. For most of the 20th century, the telecommunications industry has been viewed as a natural monopoly and its elaborate body of regulations has been viewed as a means by which a private monopoly could be reconciled with the public good. The authors all have intimate knowledge of the industry: one as an employee of a Bell company, another as an attorney who regularly represents all seven BOCs in consent decree proceedings, and the third as a Senior Fellow at the Manhattan Institute and Of Counsel at Mayer, Brown & Platt. Following an overview of the industry, the authors discuss the powers of the FCC, antitrust issues, the restructuring of the Bell System, equal access under the divestiture decree, the line of business restrictions, interpreting, enforcing, and modifying the divestiture decree, the GTE decree, pricing, telecommunications equipment, enhanced services, long-distance service, mobile telephony, telephony and cable television, international issues, and privacy. The text is heavily supported with citations to both primary law and a variety of secondary authorities.

Internet Law Resource Center [formerly Pike & Fischer's Internet Law & Regulation] [Internet]. Washington, DC: BNA, 2010-date. Internet subscription includes regular "ILR Alerts" via E-mail.
Cost: $1,943 (2014).
The most comprehensive resource for practitioners in Internet law, with an extensive archive of full-text case law, pleadings, statutes, regulations and expert insight, including full-text judicial, administrative, and arbitrator opinions and rulings. The internet and e-commerce law content is organized by practice area and presented in easy-to-navigate topical tabs, allowing users to search news and analysis at the same time. Using the Resource Center's topic pages. Researchers have access to the full-text of all U.S. court and federal agency decisions affecting the internet (including decisions by the FCC, FTC, Copyright Office), with headnotes prepared by BNA legal editors. The ***Electronic Commerce and Law Report*** offers national and global perspectives on the digital economy with objective, vital news of trends and developments insights, and legal expertise. The service also includes key legal developments, legislative activity, and trends with the *BNA Insights* series of articles and videos from expert practitioners. A People on the Move section allows you to track your competitors in the news, and find out about law firm changes. The Internet Law resource Center also provides complimentary access to *BNAInfoDash*™ on Domain Names: a targeted dashboard of content pulled from thousands of premium news sources.

Lyall, Francis and Paul B. Larsen. **Space Law: A Treatise**. Burlington, VT: Ashgate Publishing Co., 2009. 1 vol. (596 pp.).
Cost: $144.95; online price: $130.46; from $118.47 on amazon.com; Kindle: $101.49 (2014).
Space law comprises all the law that may govern or apply to outer space and activities in and relating to outer space. As the authors suggest, space law is different from the law of contracts or torts where the law elaborates a series of concepts within a single phylum. It is more akin to family or environmental law where many different laws are denoted by reference to the material with which they deal rather than being derived from the pure rational development of a single legal concept. As such, it may involve many traditional fields of law, from insurance and contracts to international, telecommunications, and torts law. It is also a field of law that is recent in origin, with regulatory and legal structures driven by advances in technology. The authors tackle a number of topics which define and comprise the evolving field of space law, from actors, history and institutions to sources of space law, the Outer Space Treaty of 1967, space objects, astronauts, the air-space boundary question, the moon and other celestial bodies, radio and the International Telecommunications Union, orbits, direct broadcasting and solar power, environmental regulation, telecommunications organizations, global navigation satellite systems, remote sensing, space activities and

international trade law, commercial activities, the military use of outer space, the search for extraterrestrial intelligence, and the future. The authors' discussion and analysis draws upon a wide and impressive range of scientific and scholarly literature, international treaties, conventions, agreements, and protocols, impacting both public and private law. Francis Lyall is professor of law at the University of Aberdeen, Scotland. Paul B. Larsen is a professor law at the Georgetown University Law Center. Since their days at the Institute of Air and Space Law at McGill University in Montreal, in 1963-64, their respective careers and collaboration, which span a period of 45 years, have taken them to numerous appointments in government and academia. They both currently teach Space law at their respective institutions.

Newton, Harry. **Newton's Telecom Dictionary**. 27th ed. New York, NY: Flatiron Publishing, 2013. 1 vol. (1,344 pp.). Softbound.
Cost: $39.95; from $18.90 on amazon.com (2014).
An indispensable and highly regarded resource for those involved in the field of telecommunications, whether legal or otherwise. Editor Harry Newton has assembled more than 12,000 definitions covering every aspect of the field, including the latest jargon in telecommunications, voice processing, computer telephony, and networking. Definitions have been contributed by AT&T, GTE, MCI, Sprint, Northern Telecom, NYNEX, Rockwell, and BellSouth. This dictionary not only defines terms in clear, non-technical language, but explains how the item works, how to use it, and how it fits into the greater scheme of things. The entries also add a bit of history and humor, making it fascinating to browse.

Perritt, Henry H., Jr. **Digital Communications Law**. Gaithersburg, MD: Wolters Kluwer Law & Business, 2010-date. 1 vol. (488 pp.). Looseleaf format. Annual supplementation.
Cost: $429; supplementation: 2011: $130; 2012: $139; 2013: $199; supplementation to predecessor title: 2001: $105; 2002: $130; 2003: $182; 2004: $193; 2005: $203; 2006: $216; 2007: $230; 2008: $247; 2009: $269; 2010: new edition; 1st edition: 1997: $57; 1998: $64; 1999: $76.
Rapid changes in information technology have raised a host of legal issues which must be addressed by either the government, the market, or the legal system, including property rights, contract and commercial issues, adjudication of competing claims for access to distribution channels for information, and the rights to obtain and sell government information. Moreover, the worldwide production and distribution of information raises jurisdictional and other questions which transcend the boundaries of sovereign nations and their individual legal traditions. Inevitably, responses by the legal system lag behind these developments in the technological sphere, increasing the likelihood of conflict. Henry Perritt has been at the forefront of these issues for a number of years, both as a widely published professor of law at Villanova University School of Law and as an advisor to numerous national and international commissions. Chairman of the ABA Section on Administrative Law and Regulatory Practice, Perritt brings a unique combination of computer expertise and legal knowledge to bear on many of these highly technical issues. The chapters in this volume examine the National Information Infrastructure as a source of legal issues, access to networks and facilities, privacy, liability for harmful communications, liability for service failures, constitutional considerations, regulation, interoperability and compatibility, electronic commerce, contracting, intellectual property, public information, civil dispute resolution and procedure, criminal law, and international law and trade. The 1998 supplement examines the efforts to reform the Internet's domain name system and the potential for private international self-regulation, among other issues. This book is an essential reference for the attorney actively involved in computer and information technology issues. When Wiley Law Publications was acquired by Wolters Kluwer in 1997, this title was assigned to Wolters Kluwer Law & Business.

Telemarketing Law Guide. Riverwoods, IL: Wolters Kluwer Law & Business, Inc., 2002-date. 1 vol. Looseleaf format. Updated quarterly.
Cost: $1,270 per year (2014).
The rapid growth of telemarketing as a tool of commerce has engendered a varied statutory and regulatory response. This looseleaf service brings together federal laws and regulations, state laws and regulations, proposed federal regulations, federal and state administrative decisions, and expert analysis and commentary. Both the federal and state sections include an introductory overview for the novice. Each state section includes an overview of that state's laws and provides answers to a uniform set of questions: who is covered under the law, whether registration is required, how registration is accomplished, time and frequency of call restrictions, and what procedures are available to prevent unwanted calls, whether automatic dial/announcing devices (ADAD) and FAX solicitation are regulated. Relevant statutes and regulations for that state, including available forms, follow these overviews. A chart of statutory and regulatory citations is also provided. Current reports provide the text of federal and state court decisions and federal state administrative decisions.

Wright, Benjamin and Jane K. Winn. **The Law of Electronic Commerce**. 4th ed. New York: Wolters Kluwer Law & Business, 2000-date. 1 vol. Looseleaf format
Cost: $535; supplementation: 2001: 0; 2002: $115; 2003: $115; 2004: $127; 2005: $268; 2006: $284; 2007: $304; 2008: $326; 2009: $353; 2010: $372; 2011: $390; 2012: $416; 2013: $462.
The rapid acceptance of commerce over the Internet has raised a number of legal and technological questions. Chief among these is the issue of security for electronic transactions involving the use of credit cards. Although millions of dollars have been invested in the development of the Secure Electronic Transaction (SET) protocol to protect credit card numbers, this protocol is having no impact upon the growth of electronic merchandising. In practice, credit card numbers are being protected by the automatic Secure Socket Layer (SSL), security built into Web browsers. This volume addresses security and other issues driven by commerce in an increasingly electronic environment. Its 21 chapters are grouped into five Parts: the Context of Electronic Commerce, Legal Proof Issues, Recordkeeping and Internal Control, Electronic Issues, and Network Service Providers and Customers. The appendices contain a number of model agreements and other documents useful in an electronic commerce context. Also included are a glossary, table of cases, table of statutes and related sources, and index.

Zuckman, Garvey L., Robert L. Corn-Revere, Robert M. Frieden and Charles H. Kennedy. **Modern Communications Law**. St. Paul, MN: West, 1999. 1 vol. (1,409 pp.). Hornbook Series. Available from West Academic.
Cost: $95; from $34.50 on amazon.com (2014).
A comprehensive treatise on the law of communications written for an Information Age audience. While written primarily for a law students, this work provides sufficient depth of discussion and analysis to serve as a useful background reference for the practitioner. The authors provide a valuable discussion of the laws and policies relating to new media, the Internet, Direct Broadcasting Satellite, and the Telecommunications Act of 1996. They also provide an overview of the leading constitutional, statutory, and administrative provisions governing communications in the United States. This is a more succinct presentation of the author's three-volume Practitioner's Treatise Series work described below.

Zuckman, Harvey L., Robert L. Corn-Revere, Robert M. Frieden, and Charles H. Kennedy. **Modern Communications Law**. St. Paul, MN: West Academic, 1999. 3 vols. Annual supplementation. Practitioner Treatise Series.
Cost: $285; supplementation: 1999: 0; 2000: $35; 2001: $39; 2002: $45; 2003: $60; 2004: $96; 2005: $77; 2006: $94.50; 2007-2012: 0; 2013: $99.
As we enter a new millennium, the formerly separate disciplines of common carrier law, cable and broadcasting law, computer law, and the First Amendment as its relates to these areas, have converged in the modern world of media and communications. This work provides a comprehensive overview of the current state of communications law in light of advances in communication technology. In sixteen chapters, the authors examine communications law and its relationship to the First Amendment, First Amendment traditions and new communications technology, the commercial speech doctrine and control of advertising by private civil actions and public regulation, privacy and the media, the new media law of defamation, the suppression or control of obscene, indecent and violent expression, newspersons' rights and responsibilities, free press and fair trial, the Telecommunications Act of 1996, the Federal Communications Commission: its jurisdiction, structure and procedures, computer communications law, regulation and deregulation of communications common carriers, regulation of cable television, regulation of broadcasting, management of the radio spectrum, and organization and regulation of international telecommunications. The appendices include a glossary of terminology, definitions, abbreviations and acronyms, a Westlaw research guide, tables of cases and authorities, and subject index. The work is suitable as both a student text and a practitioner's reference.

Additional titles in the field of Telecommunications Law are available from the following publishers not cited above: American Bar Association, Artech House, Wolters Kluwer Law & Business, Matthew Bender, Bloomberg BNA Books, Carolina Academic Press, Gaunt, Greenwood Publishing Group, Harcourt Legal, Harper Collins, Law Journal Seminars-Press, Oxford University Press, Pike & Fischer, Practising Law Institute, Thomson Reuters West, Wadsworth Publishing Co., West Academic. See Appendix B for addresses and telephone numbers.

Tort Law
(see also Products Liability)

American Law Institute. **Restatement of the Law Second. Torts.** St. Paul, MN: American Law Institute, 1965-date. 29 vols. Annual pocket parts. Periodic Appendix volumes published. Pocket part appears in the back of the most recent Appendix volume only.
Cost: $2,196.50 for complete set; vols. 1-4 (base vols.): $254; vols. 5-25 (Appendices): $1,942.50; supplementation: 1995: $96; 1996: $139; 1997: $150; 1998: $158; 1999: $337; 2000: $150.50; 2001: $152.50; 2002; $187; 2004: $158; 2005: $162; 2006: $187; 2007: $214; 2008: $154; 2009: $231; 2010: $231; 2011: $238; 2012: $238; 2013: $293.
The first portion of the **Restatement of Torts, Second**, was adopted and promulgated by the American Law Institute at Washington, D.C. on May 25, 1963, and May 22, 1964. The first two volumes, covering Sections 1-503 were published in 1965. Two additional base volumes, covering sections 504-951, appeared in 1977 and 1979. The Appendices contain the Reporter's Notes, Citations to court decisions, and cross references to the West Digest key numbers and **American Law Reports** Annotations are contained in the 21 volumes, the most recent of which are supplemented with annual pocket parts.

American Law Institute. **Restatement of the Law Third. Torts: Apportionment of Liability**. St. Paul, MN: American Law Institute, 2000-date. 1 vol. (401 pp.). Annual pocket parts.
Cost: $97.50; supplementation: 2002: $22.75; 2003: $25; 2004: $25; 2005: $25; 2006: $25; 2007: $28; 2008: $29.50; 2009: $32; 2010: $32; 2011: $32; 2012: $33; 2013: $39.
The **Restatement of the Law Third, Torts: Apportionment of Liability** constitutes the second portion to be published of the American Law Institute's **Restatement Third of Torts** (the first portion being Products Liability), superseding and expanding upon the comparable provisions of Restatement Second which were completed in 1979. As such, it presents clear principles of law governing apportionment of liability in cases when account must be taken of conduct by more actors than a single plaintiff and a single defendant. It also deals with different degrees of blameworthiness, of the effect on parties with derivative claims, or different tort claims (such as strict liability, negligence, and intent) against different defendants in the same case. As courts and legislatures have abolished the defense of contributory negligence as a bar to tortfeasor liability and replaced it with the doctrine of comparative responsibility, apportionment of liability

has become a far more complicated and pertinent issue today. This Restatement addresses many of the issues which have not been fully examined in court decisions or academic literature and for which there is not yet an accepted legal doctrine. This volume consists of five Topics, including Basic Rules of Comparative Responsibility, Liability of Multiple Tortfeasors for Indivisible Harm, Contribution and Indemnity, Settlement, and Apportionment of Liability When Damages Can Be Divided by Causation. It follows the typical Restatement pattern of providing clear black-letter provisions with explanatory comments. It is enhanced by the addition of citations to cases, statutes, parallel tables an cross references to the West Digest System, **ALR** Annotations, and an index. The Reporters for this volume were William C. Powers of the University of Texas, and Michael D. Green of the University of Iowa.

American Law Institute. **Restatement of the Law Third. Torts: Products Liability**. St. Paul, MN: American Law Institute, 1998-date. 2 vols. (382 pp.). Annual pocket parts.
Cost: $263; supplementation: 2000: $21; 2001: $21; 2002: $26; 2003: $29; 2004: $29; 2005: $25; 2006: $28; 2007: $28; 2008: $29.50; 2009: $32; 2010: $32; 2011: $32; 2012: $33; 2013: $39.
The Restatement of the Law Third, Torts: Products Liability encompasses that aspect of tort law which deals with the liability of commercial product sellers and distributors for harm caused by their products. This volume represents the first installment in the American Law Institute's effort to completely revise and update the **Restatement Second of Torts**. It supersedes Section 402A of the **Restatement Second** promulgated 35 years ago and addresses products liability issues which were not under consideration when the earlier provision was adopted in 1964.

Arlen, Jennifer, ed. **Research Handbook on the Economics of Torts**. Northampton, MA: Edward Elgar Publishing, Inc., 2013. 1 vol. (657 pp.).
Cost: $285.00 (online price: $256.50); from $241.98 on amazon.com (2014).
Torts are civil wrongs for which the law provides a remedy, primarily through the state courts. The primary purpose of tort actions is to provide relief in the form of damages for the injury received and to deter others from committing the same harms. These damages may provide compensation for pain and suffering, loss of earning capacity, and reasonable medical expenses, both present and future. Torts may be intentional, negligent, or involve strict liability for defective products. The world of tort liability is an effective legal mechanism for encouraging optimal investments in care by both insurers and victims. When liability is needed to internalize costs, the mere threat of negligence liability is usually sufficient to induce due care. When the relatively "new" field of economic analysis of law emerged in the 1960s, it began, not surprisingly, with an analysis of tort law. It gave attention to such questions as when the law needs to intervene to internalize externalities, when intervention should occur through liability rules, and what is the optimal structure of liability. Such analysis led to the formulation of economic models of torts that could provide an economic framework for an analysis of accidents that could be applied generally. One of the aims of this analysis of optimum negligence liability was to effectuate an equilibrium in which insurers and victims both take precautions and tort litigation is unnecessary. One of the central limitations of such economic analysis is that of imperfect information that precludes an understanding of the incentive effects of liability or the expected outcome of the litigation. As scholars have moved away from generalized economic models of accidents, however, they have gravitated toward the development of economic models that are more specific to the area in question. Models that may apply to industrial accidents, for example, may be inappropriate in cases of medical malpractice or products liability litigation. With the benefit this analysis, scholars have also developed a more sophisticated understanding of the litigation process In such areas as joint and several liability, vicarious liability, settlement, class actions, rules of evidence, the damage rules, and the role of the decision maker. It also provides policy makers with an empirically-informed basis for effectuating reforms of the tort system, which is often subject to anecdotally driven policy prescriptions.

This book and its twenty-one chapters are grouped into six parts: (1) Overview of Tort Litigation; (2) Economic Analysis of Liability; (3) Economic Analysis of Multi-Party Litigation; (4) The Litigation Process; (5) Damages; and (6) Reform of, and Alternatives to, the Tort System. Each of the chapters is written by a leading scholar or scholars in the field, representing a variety of empirical and doctrinal perspectives on the economic analysis of tort law, and embracing topics of both theoretical and practical significance. The lead essay, appropriately, addresses the competing perceptions of civil litigation in the United States and the fault line that divides those who criticize the tort system because of its excess litigation, inefficiencies and unpredictability from those whose problem with the American tort system stems from too few successful tort actions. Not surprisingly, he lays out a case that the successful resolution to the divide necessarily begins in a careful examination of the data and accompanying empirical analysis to help sort out these competing perspectives. This volume represents a major contribution to the field of tort law and economic analysis of the law generally. Each of these intellectually rich, heavily sourced, and empirically driven essays provides penetrating insights for anyone interested in the economic analysis of tort law, or involved in litigating tort cases. Jennifer Arlen is the Norma Z. Paige Professor of Law and Director, Center for Law, Economics, and Organization, New York University School of Law.

Barth, Stephen C. **Hospitality Law: Managing Legal Issues in the Hospitality Industry.** 4th ed. New York: Hoboken, NJ: John Wiley & Sons, Inc., 2012. 1 vol. (486 pp.).
Cost: $105.95; ebook: $69.50; from $42.79 on amazon.com; kindle: $59.50 (2014).
Hospitality managers on a daily basis confront a variety of legal issues involving their operations and services. Many of these are issues that can and should be resolved without the intervention of an attorney, provided the manger has a basic grasp of the law impacting the facilities he manages. This volume was written to instruct students in the field of hospitality on what need to know to manage a facility legally, safely and securely. The author approaches this goal by advocating the STEM process in hospitality management: Select, Teach, Educate, and Manage. These involve: (1) Selecting the right employees for the right job;

(2) Teaching proper training methods; (3) Educating managers In order that they may pass on that knowledge to employees; and (4) Manage effectively and consistently to reduce chances for mistakes and litigation. Management has been defined as consisting of four functions: planning, organizing, controlling and motivating, all of which have legal implications. The STEM process focuses almost exclusively on the motivating function. The author does this by providing readers with a basic understanding of the legal process, the legal environment of the hospitality manager, and an overview of ethics and the law. He also reviews the government agencies that impact the hospitality industry, hospitality business structures, the basics of contract law, significant hospitality contracts, legal property management, the process of legally selecting employees, legally managing employees, responsibilities as a hospitality manager, legal responsibilities of managers to guests, responsibilities to guests' property, responsibilities when serving food and beverages, responsibilities in travel and tourism, safety and security issues, and managing insurance. The text is laced with real world examples, policy statements, sample documents, class-oriented activities, case studies, situational analyses, and chapter reviews. The volume also features a glossary of industry terms and subject index. This is an excellent introduction to the subject for both students and those working in the hospitality field. The author is an attorney and professor of Hospitality Law and Leadership at the Conrad N. Hilton College of Hotel and Restaurant Management at the University of Houston. He is also the founder of HospitalityLawyer.com, the Hospitality Law Conference Series, and the Global Congress on Legal, Safety, and Security Solutions in Travel.

Berg, David. **The Trial Lawyer: What It Takes To Win**. Chicago: American Bar Association, 2003. 1 vol. (307 pp.).
Cost: $110 ($95 to Litigation Section members); $75 (paperbound) ($65 to Litigation Section members); from $49,90 on amazon (2014).
In our contemporary legal environment, many litigators are trapped in a culture of settlement in which their energies are primarily limited to the taking of depositions and the arguing of motions. Under an economic model that favors discovery and settlement, jury trials have become a gamble to be avoided. David Berg, a seasoned and highly regarded litigator, argues that a litigator's life should be primarily devoted to trial work, not only for the professional development and personal satisfaction they provide, but for the ultimate benefit of clients and the cause of justice. Drawing upon his experiences in hundreds of civil and criminal trials, he brings a sophisticated, yet humanistic, perspective to the entire trial process, from discovery to closing argument. Central to the author's approach to trial work are what he calls "The Constants of Persuasion," rules applicable in any type of case. Among these are the ability to use every available technique and bit of evidence to persuade jurors (what he calls thinking "inside the box"), the ability to tell a compelling story, humanize clients and key witnesses, warm up the courtroom, earn the jurors' trust, set the agenda, prove that standards have been violated, avoid running from your weaknesses, undermine adversaries with impeachment and admissions, and make the jury mad (at the other side). He argues that careful pretrial preparation and the discovery process are crucial to winning at trial. Similarly, he brings his experience and wisdom to bear on the subjects of jury studies and graphics, voir dire, the opening argument, cross examination, preparing and presenting witnesses, and closing arguments. This is a book to be read and re-read by both novice and experienced litigators. The author is a founding partner of the Houston/New York firm of Berg & Androphy, and has been named to The National Law Journal's list of the nation's top ten civil trial lawyers.

Bogus, Cart T. **Why Lawsuits are Good for America: Disciplined Democracy, Big Business, and the Common Law**. New York: New York University Press, 2001. 1 vol. (272 pp.).
Cost: $79 (hardcover); $24 (paperbound); new and used copies available on amazon.com from $0.99 (2014).
Unlike critics of the current tort system, Carl Bogus argues that lawsuits and the common law are an essential element of American democracy, providing ordinary citizens without money or political influence with a mechanism to challenge far more powerful interests on an almost level playing field. The contingent fee system, he argues, allows ordinary individuals to engage first-rate legal talent and seek redress from large corporations. Bogus focuses his attention primarily upon the law of products liability, a subfield of tort law under which individuals injured by unreasonably dangerous products can seek damages in a court of law. In fact, Bogus contends that the judicial system performs an important regulatory function through its decision-making in products liability cases because it creates incentives for businesses to improve their products. The chapters of this book address the war on the common law, the third branch of government, disciplined democracy and the American jury system, the American common law tradition, the three revolutions in products liability, and the future of common law. This book is an important contribution to the debate on tort reform. The author is Associate Professor of Law at Roger Williams University School of Law in Rhode Island. For an opposing view on tort reform, see Walter Olson, **The Rule of Lawyers** (below).

Brookshire, Michael L., Frank Slesnick, and John O. Ward. **The Plaintiff and Defense Attorney's Guide to Understanding Economic Damages**. Tucson, AZ: Lawyers & Judges Publishing Co., 2007. 1 vol. (193 pp.).
Cost: $39; from $37.05 on amazon.com; kindle: $35.20 (2014)
The calculation of damages is a critical element in personal injury/wrongful death actions to both plaintiff and defense attorneys and their clients. Understanding the nature of economic evidence and the role of expert testimony is often an important part of securing a desired result at trial or mediation. This book assembles a number of experts in forensic economics representing various views and perspectives on the use of economic experts and damage calculations. Its intent is to combine the interests of both forensic economists and personal injury attorneys, and to provide the latter with the tools for comprehending the nature of the economic damage analysis and the process of using experts to present or defend their case. Chapter one, on understanding experts on damage calculations, presents an essential read for any attorney engaging in personal injury litigation for the first time. The other articles provide important perspectives on such vital issues as the estimation of wage and salary losses, fringe benefit losses, the vocational/rehabilitation expert, wrongful death cases and personal consumption deductions, punitive

damages, the mediation process, structured settlements, the plaintiff attorney's perspective on economic damages at trial, and the defense trial lawyer on damage issues at deposition and trial. A companion CD-ROM provides links to such essential supporting materials as Internet sources to supplement the text, definitions of technical terms, sample direct and cross-examination questions and strategies, case studies, sample reports, and references and recommended readings. Each of the editors has served as a university professor and past president of the National Association of Forensic Economics. The fourteen contributing authors bring expertise in the fields of law, economics, vocational evaluation and life care planning, as well as practical experience in personal and death litigation.

Causes of Action. Eagan, MN: West (Shepards/Lawyers Cooperative), 1983-date. 88 vols. Annual pocket parts and three new bound volumes per year. **COA** includes 30 volumes; **COA 2d** includes 60 volumes as of February 15, 2013; 1st series may only be sold to COA 2d subscribers or obtained used. Also available on Westlaw.

Cost: 1st series: Out-of-Print, was $1,962; 2d series: $4,708; supplementation: 2d series: 1993: $725; 1994: $725; 1995: $725; 1996: $550; 1997: $700; 1998: $530; 1999: $769; 2000: $863; 2001: $1,010.50; 2002: $671; 2003: $1,038.50; 2004: $1,658.50; 2005: $1,827.50; 2006: $2,075.50; 2007: $2.310.50 (1st series: $977; 2d series: $1,333.50); 2008: $2,731.20 (1st: $1,124; 2d: $1607.20); 2009: $3,439 (1st series: $1,265 + 2d series: $2,174); 2010: $3,619.50 (1st : $1,478; 2d: $2,141.50); 2011: 2d: $2,346; 2012: 2d: $2,931; 2013: 2d: $3,505; **Monthly Assured Print Price (APP)**: 1st series: $113/$1,356; 2d series: $266/$3,192.

Although not strictly speaking a work on tort law, the articles in this series predominantly encompass a wide variety of tort matters from products liability actions to negligence and malpractice cases. Each of the 10 or more articles in each volume takes the practitioner through the steps necessary to determine whether a cause of action exists for a specific set of facts or circumstances. The articles analyze the elements of the cause of action and explain the procedure for proving these elements. The articles guide the attorney through the trial process, providing both analysis of substantive law and procedural issues. Each article also includes a COA Action Guide, an outline of contents, subject index, Practice Guides, forms, Research Guide to secondary sources and practice aids, table of cases. An extremely valuable set for the litigator. This set can be of invaluable assistance to those practitioners who have cases addressed in these articles. This title was sold to the Thomson Corporation in December, 1995 and is now part of the West.

Cost Saving Tips: This is one of those reference tools best used at your local public law library. Each new bound volume will cost you $540.00 (or $432 with subscriber discount). There were five in 2013, costing $2,160, plus another $1,296 for pocket parts for the whole set. If you decide to acquire this set new or, preferably, used, forego the supplementation given its high cost. **Causes of Action** is similar to the **American Law Reports** in the sense that the newly published volumes contain randomly selected topics which do not significantly augment the usefulness of the existing volumes. Use **Causes of Action** as a launching pad for research and update, if necessary, at your local public law library. If you buy pocket parts, do so in alternate years or less often. A Westlaw add-on is to be preferred over a standing order to the print for those interested in the entire set. Better yet, buy a pdf of the specific chapter you need on an ad hoc basis at a cost ranging from $34 to $42 in lieu of acquiring and updating the whole set.

Current Award Trends in Personal Injury. 50th ed. Thomson Reuters West (LRP), 2012. 1 vol. (52 pp.). Annual. Downloadable pdf.

Cost: 2013 Edition: $63.96; 2012: $63.96; 2011 Edition: $63.00; 2010 Edition: $45.75 (2014).

This low-cost alternative to the **JVR Personal Injury Valuation Handbooks** provides an invaluable summary of nationwide jury verdict statistics for the past seven years. The data is drawn from the nationwide database of more than 250,000 plaintiff and defense verdicts and settlements compiled by Jury Verdict Research. Included are verdicts by specific injury and liability, the median compensatory and punitive damage awards by state, million dollar and large awards for the most frequently occurring injuries, and plaintiff recovery probabilities. An essential tool for evaluating personal injury actions and probable damage amounts. Now available as downloadable pdf since its acquisition by Thomson Reuters.

Daller, Morton F., ed. **Tort Law Desk Reference: A Fifty State Compendium**. New York: Wolters Kluwer Law & Business, 2011. 1 vol. Annual. Paperbound.

Cost: 2013 Edition: $297; 2012 Edition: $297; prior editions: 2003: $176; 2004: $185; 2005: $175; 2006: $180; 2007: $192; 2008: $205; 2009: $230; 2010: $245; 2011: $260.

This volume provides concise summaries of the products liability laws of all fifty states written by leading local practitioners. Drawing upon both state statutes and case law, these summaries cover such areas as strict liability, negligence, compensatory and punitive damages, statutes of limitations, breach of warranty, wrongful death, contribution and indemnity, and misrepresentation. An ideal tool for the products liability litigator who wishes to assess the strengths and weaknesses of his or her case across jurisdictions. Morton Daller is a trial lawyer, partner in the Fort Washington, PA firm of Daller Greenberg & Dietrich, and former President of the Philadelphia Association of Defense Counsel. Originally titled **Product Liability Desk Reference**.

Diamond, John L., Lawrence C. Levine, and M. Stuart Madden. **Understanding Torts.** 5th ed. New York: Matthew Bender & Co., 2013. 1 vol. (428 pp.). Legal Text Series.

Cost: $45; eBook: $36; from $38.73 on amazon.com; kindle ed.: $30.49 (2014).

A lucid, student-oriented text which examines the basic principles of common law torts. The authors, professors of law at the University of California Hastings College of the Law; the University of the Pacific McGeorge School of Law; and Pace University School of Law, have organized the text to reflect the typical structure of law school torts classes. Coverage encompasses intentional torts and privileges, negligence, general concepts, liability without fault, products liability, nuisance, economic torts, misuse of legal processes, defamation, and invasion of privacy. The text is timely enough to consider a number of cutting-edge legal issues, including gender bias. The text includes numerous citations to both primary and secondary authorities. An inexpensive alternative to some of the practitioner-oriented treatises.

Dobbs, Dan B. **The Law of Torts**. 2d ed. St. Paul, MN: Thomson Reuters West, 2011-date. 4 vols. (3,574 pp.). Practitioner Series.
Cost: $450; supplementation: 2013: $150; 1st ed.: 2003: $65; 2004: $70; 2005: $64; 2005: $64; 2006: $68; 2007: $85; 2008: $94.50; 2009: $109; 2010: $128; 2011: new edition. Also available as one-volume Hornbook: $113 (2014).
This monumental, single-volume treatise traces its origins back through the lineage of, arguably, the most influential of 20th century law school textbooks, **Prosser on Torts**. First published in 1941, **Prosser on Torts**, had a major influence on several generations of law students and scholars, an influence which continued right up through the publication of **Prosser and Keeton on Torts** in 1984. However, rather than updating **Prosser and Keeton on Torts**, Professor Dobbs, who authored supplementation to the 1984 edition, decided that the enormous changes in tort law warranted a wholly new work. Accordingly, except for a quotation or two, this work contains not a word of **Prosser** or **Prosser and Keeton** text. The book's thirty-six chapters cover the full range of tort law issues, however, including the various aspects of interference with persons or property, the operation and alteration of the tort system in personal injury cases, and economic and dignitary injury. Professor Dobbs delineates the growing invocation of immunities by courts and legislatures, the federal preemption of state law which immunizes defendants and displaces tort law, and the increase in tort reform legislation which has limited damage awards, abolished joint and several liability, and erected barriers to full compensation. He also describes the reversal of the doctrine of strict liability as expressed in the new **Restatement of Products Liability**. The organizational structure of Dobbs' text roughly follows that of Prosser, although the latter's discussion of the contract-tort connection has been dispersed throughout this work. Dobbs also attempts to separate purely economic torts and economic/dignity torts that involve no personal harm, from personal injury/property damage torts. Dobbs limits his citation of court decisions to those of more recent vintage. He also includes far more text subdivisions than did Prosser (492 v. 140), enabling the reader to locate desired discussion more easily. On measures of both quality and cost, this work is destined to become an essential resource to any attorney involved in tort actions.

Eades, Ronald W. **Jury Instructions on Damages in Tort Actions.** 5th ed. Newark, NJ: LexisNexis, 2003-date. 1 vol. Looseleaf format. Annual pocket part.
Cost: $163; supplementation: 2004: $48; 2005: $51; 2006: $54; 2007: $58; 2008: $63; 2009: $72; 2010: $78; 2011: $84; 2012: $90; 2013: $92; 4th ed.: 1999: $30; 2000: $35; 2001: $39; 2002: $49; 3d edition: 1994: $15; 1995: $25; 1996: $29.75; 1997: $35.
Provides the litigator and judge with over 200 instructions on the kinds of issues which are likely to arise in the course of tort actions. Each instruction is supported by case law, **ALR** annotations, and law review articles. Written in language comprehensible to the layperson. Also available as a part of Michie's four-volume **Jury Instructions for Personal Injury and Tort Cases** library which sells for $260, a savings of $60 over the single volume prices.

Genson, Laura Ruhl and Anita M. Kerezman, eds. **Truck Accident Litigation.** 3d ed. Chicago: American Bar Association, Tort Trial and Insurance Law Section, 2013. 1 vol. (412 pp.). Paperbound.
Cost: $149.95 ($135.95 to Tort Trial and Insurance Practice Section members); from $79.95 on amazon.com (2014).
Have you ever wondered what rules govern those behemoth semi-trailers and their drivers as they zip by you on the highway, drive on your tail. or nearly blow you off the road? This invaluable collection of articles addresses a variety of topics regarding the trucking industry, and the applicable standards for motor carriers and drivers as they relate to their legal liability and other matters. More than forty authors contributed a total of 34 chapters bearing on such topics as an overview of trucking, commercial driver's license requirements, records retention, Federal Motor Carrier Safety Regulations, the truck accident investigation, data collection, spoliation of evidence, the truck driver, special driving situations—hazardous materials, truck driver fatigue, hours of service regulations, cargo securement, on-board electronics, tires and wheels, brakes inspection, the safety rating process, the trial, and much more. Laura Ruhl Genson is general counsel to Ruhl Forensic, Inc and a specialist in vehicle litigation. Anita Kerezman is a professional truck driver and a truck driving and training specialist.

Gibson, K. William. **How to Build and Manage a Personal Injury Practice.** 3d **ed.** Chicago: American Bar Association, 2012 1 vol. (200 pp.) with CD-ROM. Paperbound. Also available on ebok.
Cost: $69.95 ($41.95 to Law Practice Management Section members) (print or eBook); from $41.69 on amazon.com (2014).
Starting a personal practice is not for the faint of heart. Unlike practitioners in other fields, personal injury (PI) attorneys, operating under a contingent fee arrangement, often invest substantial time and money in a case before being paid. A successful resolution may require substantial investment in research, exhibits, doctors, engineers, and other experts, and the discovery process. Yet failure to spend the necessary funds on these ingredients to a successful case may result in legal and/or financial failure. K. William Gibson, editor of the ABA's **Flying Solo: A Survival Guide for Solo and Small Firm Lawyers**, brings more than 20 years experience in the field of personal injury law to this and other critical issues, from the decision to open a solo practice or partnership; planning for a new practice; office space and equipment; marketing; the new client; keeping clients happy; working with employees, contractors and other professionals; managing the workload; software for case/practice management, document management, and trial presentation; and preparing for settlement, arbitration, and trial. Like other entries in the ABA Law Practice Management Section's Practice-Building Series, this volume combines both nut-and-bolts and practical advice on how to establish a successful personal injury practice. A variety of relevant documents, including forms, checklists, sample letters, and questionnaires are contained

both in the Appendices and on an accompanying CD-ROM. K. William Gibson is a solo practitioner in Portland, Oregon, a regular columnist for the ABA's **Law Practice** magazine, and founder of De Novo Systems, Inc., a company that publishes De Novo CaseMgr, a case and practice management software system.

Hammesfahr, Robert W. and Lori S. Nugent. **Punitive Damages: A State-By-State Guide to Law and Practice**. St Paul, MN: West, 2011. 1 vol. (883+ pp.) Paperbound.
Cost: 2012-2013 Edition: $266; 2011 Edition: $244 (2014).
Punitive damages are monetary compensation awarded to an injured party that goes beyond that which is necessary to compensate a party for losses and that is intended to punish the wrongdoer. Also known as exemplary damages, punitive damages may be awarded by the trier of fact (a jury or a judge) in addition to actual damages, and are a means of punishing the defendant in a civil lawsuit. They are based on the theory that the interests of society and the individual harmed can be met by imposing additional damages on the defendant, thereby sending a warning to other's in the defendant's position from engaging in similar conduct. This comprehensive volume examines the law on punitive damages in the fifty states, first through an in-depth examination of the constitutionality of punitive damages, their recovery, the insurability of punitive damages, reinsurance of punitive damages, and conflict of law principles. Chapter seven provides state-by-state summaries of the relevant laws governing the aforementioned issues regarding punitive damages, with extensive citations to the state statutes and appellate court decisions which define the application of punitive damages in each jurisdiction. The Appendices include an extensive bibliography of punitive damage authorities, consisting of law review articles, comments and notes, and organized by 55 sub-topics; a guide to the organization of the United States civil courts, a state-by-state guide to published jury instructions, a U.S. Supreme Court decision on the constitutionality of punitive damages, tables of law and rules, cases, and subject index. Robert W. Hammesfahr is Executive Claims Expert and Managing Director at Swiss Reinsurance Company with extensive experience in claims involving the World Trade Center, subprime and liquidity crisis, asbestos, pollution, and other matters. Lori S. Nugent is partner in a major law firm with extensive experience in punitive damage work in multiple U.S. jurisdictions.

Harper, Fowler V., Fleming James, Jr., and Oscar S. Gray. **Harper, James, & Gray on Torts.** 3d ed. New York: Wolters Kluwer Law & Business, 2006-date. 6 vols. Twice annual supplements.
Cost: $1,599; supplementation: 2006 (including vols. 1-3 of new edition): $864; 2007 (including vols. 4-6 of new edition): $766; 2008: $348; 2009: $260; 2010: $296; 2011: $363; 2012: $493; 2013: $528; 2d ed.: 1993: $120; 1994: $140; 1995: $485; 1996: $350; 1997: $182; 1998: $182; 1999: $390; 2000: $396; 2001: $490; 2002: $574; 2003: $305; 2004: $370; 2005: $778; Prior to the publication of the Speiser and Minzer sets, this treatise on tort law clearly dominated the field. Drawing upon the earlier work of Fowler Harper whose **Harper on Torts** appeared in 1933, the first edition of this treatise added the work of Fleming James on the subject of accidents. It still retains its reputation as one of the preeminent works of legal scholarship. This edition draws upon the significant changes which have taken place in the law of torts over the past thirty years, providing due attention to such topics as products liability, defamation, liability for prenatal injury, privacy, domestic torts, comparative negligence, governmental liability, malicious prosecution, and abuse of process. A work of high scholarship, buttressed with extensive citations to leading cases, statutes, **Restatements**, and secondary authorities. The Tables volume (vol. 6) also contains extensive chapter by chapter bibliographies.

Jain, Sarah S. Lochlann. **Injury**: **The Politics of Product Design and Safety Law in the United States**. Princeton, NJ: Princeton University Press, 2006. 1 vol. (214 pp.). Paperbound.
Cost: $30.95 (paper); from $4.98 on amazon.com (2014).
In this broadly theoretical examination of product design and safety from an anthropological perspective, the author posits that tort law can only be understood as a part of American injury culture or within the context the broad swath of injury production in the United States, operating with a complex web of economic interests. The author contends that tort law does far more than recognize, measure and compensate for injuries, but does the social and political work of determining what will count as an injury and, ultimately, how it will be distributed in the form of product design and safety. Society has addressed the issue of injuries from product defect by both the collective model reflected by the workers compensation system and the private, individual model represented by tort law. Both systems are fraught with defects which provide imperfect levels of monetary compensation for consumer or workers injury and inadequate feedback to product designers and manufacturers. The bulk of this monograph is devoted to an in-depth analysis of several specific objects, injustices and legal struggles, including the short-handle rake used by Mexican farm workers, keyboard design and the resulting litigation wave, and the tobacco industry's marketing of cigarettes to the African-American youth. While the author alludes to the litigiousness of the American culture, and its spread to Canada and Europe, she fails to address the broad monetary costs to society of this phenomenon, estimated at $2,884 every year for a family of four. Nor does she correctly assess the root causes of rising health care costs and the growing ranks of the uninsured: a system which encourages individuals to purchase low-deductible health insurance through employers, and a tax system which does not allow for the full deductibility of out-of-pocket medical expenses. This is, nevertheless, an interesting, often illuminating, and sometimes provocative look at the nature of injury and products liability in the United States. The author is Assistant Professor of Cultural Anthropology at Stanford University.

Karp, Leonard and Cheryl L. Karp. **Domestic Torts: Family Violence, Conflict and Sexual Abuse.** Revised ed. St. Paul, MN: West (Shepard's), 2005-date. 1 vol. (759 pp.). Annual pocket part.
Cost: $258; supplementation: 2006: $80; 2007: $89; 2008: $99; 2009: $113; 2010: $131; 2011: $144; 2012: $157; 2013: $171; 1st ed.: 1995: $59; 1996: $59; 1997: $65; 1998: $68; 1999: $73; 2000: $79; 2001: $92; 2002: $101; 2003: $115; 2004: $129; 2005: new edition; **Monthly Assured Print Price (APP)**: $18/$216.
An examination of domestic torts from both the legal and psychological perspectives co-authored by a practicing attorney

and psychologist. Subject coverage includes spousal and child abuse, marital rape, sexual exploitation of children, child snatching, sexually transmitted diseases, infliction of emotional distress, third party liability, insurance matters, and civil rights issues. Excellent analytical coverage of a variety of sensitive legal issues.

Kionka, Edward J. **Torts in a Nutshell**. 5th ed. St. Paul, MN: West, 2010. 1 vol. (513 pp.). Available from West Academic.
Cost: $41; from $27.73 on amazon.com; kindle ed.: $21.80 (2014).
This is an introductory student text or review for the practitioner. Like most titles in the Nutshell series, this volume attempts to set forth the basic principles of tort law with sufficient citations to primary and secondary authority to satisfy those with a deeper interest in the subject. Following a chapter which sets forth the origins, objectives and provides an overview of the concept of tort liability, the author examines cause in fact, strict liability, liability for negligent conduct, defenses to negligent liability, liability for intentional misconduct, defenses to liability for intentional misconduct, special liability rules for particular activities (including products liability), tort and contract, immunities, survival and wrongful death, defamation, privacy, misrepresentation and nondisclosure. Edward Kionka is Professor of Law, Southern Illinois University School of Law.

Koenig, Thomas H. and Michael L. Rustad. **In Defense of Tort Law**. New York: New York University Press, 2001. 1 vol. (320 pp.).
Cost: $25 (paperbound); from $3.83 on amazon.com; kindle ed.: $17.78 (2014).
A well-argued and meticulously researched examination of the tort reform debate that considers its social, legal, and policy dimensions. The authors challenge the common misperceptions about some of the most widely publicized "frivolous" lawsuits with empirical data, and argue that tort law plays an important role in protecting consumers from dangerous products and hazards. They address such important policy questions as the wisdom of capping damage awards. They also argue that the legal system contains a number of serious gender inequities since women are, for example, disproportionately injured by defective medical products. Thomas H. Koenig is Professor of Sociology and a founding member of the Law, Policy, and Society doctoral program at Northeastern University in Boston. Michael L. Rustad is Professor of Law and Director of the High Technology Law Program at Suffolk University Law School in Boston.

Lee, J. D. and Barry A. Lindahl. **Modern Tort Law: Liability & Litigation.** 2d ed. St. Paul, MN: West (Clark Boardman Callaghan), 1990-date. 5 vols. Looseleaf format. Annual supplements.
Cost: $780; supp.: 1993: $153; 1994: $193; 1995: $200; 1996: $240; 1997: $280; 1998: $296; 1999: $320; 2000: $346; 2001: $402.50; 2002: $470; 2003: $100; 2004: $112; 2005: $122; 2006: $138; 2007: $154; 2008: $171; 2009: $96; 2010: $211; 2011: $232; 2012: $253; 2013: $147; **Monthly Assured Print Price (APP)**: $37/$444.
This treatise was originally authored by James A. Dooley, former President of the Association of Trial Lawyers of America and Justice of the Illinois Supreme Court who lectured widely on the subject of tort law. This revised edition was authored by J.D. Lee, Past President of the National Board of Trial Advocacy and the Association of Trial Lawyers of America; and Barry Lindahl, Adjunct Professor of Law, University of Iowa College of Law. This edition reflects a number of changes which have taken place in the law of torts, including the widespread adoption of comparative negligence by the both state legislatures and courts, the development in the field of governmental and official immunity, products liability, malpractice, and more. The forty-eight chapters encompass the full range of tort issues, all adequately supported with citations to case and statutory law, and the **Restatements of the Law of Torts**. The annual supplements provide the user with textual revisions as well as citations to more recent authorities. As excellent alternative for the attorney who does not require the exhaustive treatment afforded by the Speiser or Minzer sets.

Marshall, Kevin and Thomas Ireland, eds. **Measuring Loss in Catastrophic Injury Cases**. Tucson, AZ: Lawyers & Judges Publishing Co., 2005. 1 vol.
Cost: $39; from $27.21 on amazon.com (2014).
This volume addresses a number of the critical and complex issues involved in the process of measuring loss in cases of severe or catastrophic injury, including the interdisciplinary nature of measuring loss, the role of the forensic economist, the roles of vocational and rehabilitation experts, an overview of life care planning, the impact of reduced life expectancy, annuity contracts, structured settlements, periodic payment judgments, and the process of building an expert damages team. Designed as a practical tool for the practicing attorney involved in catastrophic personal injury cases. An Assistant Professor of Law at La Verne College of Law, Dr. Kevin S. Marshall received his law degree from Emery School of Law, Master of Public Affairs from the University of Texas at Dallas, and Doctor of Philosophy in Political Economy from the University of Texas, Dallas. He is certified in Quantitative Methods and Economic Analysis by the University of Texas at Dallas' School of Social Sciences for his academic achievement and coursework in Descriptive and Inferential Statistics, Costs-Benefits Analysis, Social Science Research Methods, Regression Analysis, Advanced Regression Analysis, and Econometrics. Thomas Ireland is professor emeritus of economics at the University of Missouri, St. Louis. He has written, co-written or co-edited twelve books, 120 papers, comments or book reviews in professional journals.

Martin, Gerald D. and Ted Vavoulis. **Determining Economic Damages**. Revised ed. Santa Ana, CA: James Publishing Inc., 2006-date. 1 vol. Looseleaf format. Annual supplementation.
Cost: $99; supplementation: 1997: $59.99; 1998: $64.99; 1999-2014: $69.99 per year.
This comprehensive work provides detailed guidance to attorneys who must calculate economic damages in personal injury, wrongful death, wrongful birth, and wrongful termination cases, whether from the plaintiff's or defendant's side. The contents include discussion of the role of the forensic economist, an overview of the data needed by the economist, past and future earnings, life and worklife expectancy, using reports of medical and rehabilitation experts, interest rates and present value, a sampling of methods to calculate losses, tactics and strategy,

structured settlements, Internet and computer programs, and much more. The authors are both economists with extensive experience as professors of economics, expert witnesses, and consultants to law firms.

Cost Saving Tip: The books in the James Publishing catalog are, without question, the best values in the world of legal publishing. Revised in 2006, this title is actually priced less than the previous edition—down from $119 to $99. Moreover, the cost of supplements does not change from year-to-year, a remarkable accomplishment in an environment of steadily rising supplementation costs. James Publishing also offers a consumer-friendly option for those not on standing order. For the cost of the most recent supplement plus a premium of $10, a previous purchaser can receive all new contents to any James Publishing title.

Minzer, Marilyn K. et al. **Damages in Tort Actions.** New York: Matthew Bender & Co., 1982-date. 11 vols. Looseleaf format or eBook. Supplemented 2-3 times per year. Authority CD-ROM includes no-cost online updating via LEXIS-NEXIS.
Cost: $3,670 (includes annual subscription); renewal: 1997: $860 (price frozen since 1992); 1998: $905; 1999: $940; 2000: $1,010; 2001: $1,081; 2002: $1,157; 2003: $1,215; 2004: $1,276; 2005: $1,365; 2006: $1,461; 2007: $1,577; 2008: $1,719; 2009: $1,874; 2010: $1,986; 2011: $2,085; 2012: $2,210; 2013: $2,365; 2014: $2,581; CD-ROM: $4,255 (annual subscription); renewal: 1998: $905; 1999: $940; 2000: $1,010; 2001: $1,081; 2002: $1,157; 2003: $1,215; 2004: $1,276; 2005: $1,365; 2006: $1,461; 2007: $1,577; 2008: $1,719; 2009: $1,857; 2010: $2,062; 2011: $2,268; 2012: $2,517; 2013: $2,693; 2014: $3,053.88; eBook: $3,336; renewal: 2014: $2,581.
This is probably the most thorough tort law treatise on the market today. Written by nearly twenty-five individual authors, comprising the publisher's editorial staff and outside contributors, this set consists of nearly 150 chapters covering every aspect of tort law and procedure. Specific chapters are devoted to coverage of damages, pain and suffering, loss of enjoyment of life, cost of medical treatment, aggravation of injury, spoilation of evidence, punitive damages, invasion of privacy, jury instructions, illustrative awards and settlements, initiation of the suit, discovery, settlement techniques, expert and lay witnesses, life expectancy in catastrophic disability, courtroom techniques, and structured settlements, and much more. The text is heavily supplemented with citations to relevant primary and secondary authorities, case annotations, and Practice Commentaries. Bibliographies provide the user with access to other relevant legal and medical sources.

Cost Saving Tips: Buy this set used and update periodically by buying another used set, or buy new and let the initial year's subscription to lapse. You can obtain a great deal from this work even in a lapsed state. Just be sure to update the cases and statutes cited by using the appropriate primary sources and by Shepardizing. A secondary source like this is just the first stage in the legal research process and should not be expected to be perform the entire task.

Mueller, Frederick O. and Robert C. Cantu. **Football Fatalities and Catastrophic Injuries, 1931-2008**. Durham, NC: Carolina Academic Press, 2011. 1 vol. (263 pp.). Paperbound.
Cost: $30.00; from $27.00 on amazon.com (2014).
Since the first football game was played between Rutgers and Princeton in 1869, injuries and deaths have plagued the game of football. In 1896, the death of a football player in Georgia almost brought an end to the sport in that state. And when the *Chicago Tribune* reported 18 fatalities and 159 serious injuries from football during the 1905 season, politicians and other authorities took steps to address what they perceived to be the brutal aspects of the game and eliminate its dangerous elements. Since that time, the number of reported concussions and other football-related injuries has continued to rise at the high school, collegiate and professional levels; and more lawsuits are being filed against coaches and trainers for failing to meet the appropriate standards of care, and against equipment manufacturers for defective products. This book provides a fascinating data-driven examination of the nature, causes, implications, and solutions for football fatalities and injuries in the period 1931-2008. In addition to a decade-by-decade analysis of the fatalities and catastrophic injuries over this period, the authors take a serious look at the medical aspects of football brain and spine injuries, the history of the National Operating Committee on Standards for Athletic Equipment from 1969-2008, and the prevention of catastrophic head and spine injuries. This book will be of particular value to attorneys bringing tort actions on behalf of injured players or their families, as well as educators, and those who wish to gain a deeper understanding of the dangers posed by the game. Dr. Frederick Mueller is a professor and former Department Chair of Exercise Science at the University of North Carolina at Chapel Hill where he has taught for 40 years. He is currently director of the National Center for Catastrophic Sports Injury Research and Research Director for the National Operating Committee on Standards for Athletic Equipment. Dr. Robert Cantu is a founding member and chairman of the Sports Legacy Institute Medical Advisory Board and an adjunct professor of exercise and sports science and medical director of the National Center for Catastrophic Sports Injury Research.

Nichols, John F., Sr. and Joe Phillips. **Personal Injury Depositions**. Huntington, NY: Juris Publishing, 2007-date. 1 vol. (various pagings). Looseleaf format or downloadable electronic product.
Cost: $225; supplementation: 2008: $75; 2009: $85; 2010: $75; 2011: $80; 2012: $85; 2013: $95.
This massive collection of sample depositions with supporting commentary is designed to provide guidance in the preparation, planning and strategy of personal injury cases. The introductory material provides a basic overview of the basic elements of personal injury law and the steps to be followed in preparing for a deposition, including the joint discovery plan, written discovery, the deposition and subpoena. There is also a review of substantive tort principles, including causation, defenses, vicarious liability, damages and evidence; the preparation of the deponent, the deposition itself, a checklist for the deposition examination; and common elements in personal injury depositions. The bulk of the volume consists of sample deposition questions and answers in more than sixty specific personal injury actions, from motor

vehicles and premises liability actions, to such miscellaneous torts as false imprisonment, infliction of emotional distress, invasion of privacy, abuse of process, stalking, municipal liability, transmission of venereal disease, aircraft, and ships. A graduate of the University of Houston College of Law, John F. Nichols is a highly respected litigator with a specialization in personal injury law. He has authored over 100 articles and spoken widely on topics related to trial preparation. Joe Phillips is a graduate of Berkeley's Boalt Hall School of Law and litigator who represents clients in a variety of tort actions, including products liability, class actions, maritime/aviation law and insurance bad faith claims.

Olson, Walter. **The Rule of Lawyers**. New York: St. Martin's Press, 2003. 1 vol. (358 pp.). Paperbound and Kindle.
Cost: $18.99; from $2.64 in paperback or $7.59 on Kindle on amazon.com (2014).
A well-documented and impassioned polemic regarding the abuse of the American legal system by trial lawyers who use class actions to extract massive verdicts and settlements from big business. Olson focuses his attentions upon lawsuits against producers of such products as automobiles, pharmaceuticals, tobacco, asbestos and guns, arguing that such class action suits attempt to achieve in the courtroom what various political interests are unable to achieve through the legislative process. As he demonstrates, most class action lawsuits enrich lawyers at the expense of consumers and society as a whole. His is one of numerous attacks on trial lawyers that have appeared in recent years from such figures as Peter Huber, Michael Fumento, and commentators John Stossel and Catherine Crier, which provide the intellectual and political basis for tort and products liability reform. His Web site Overlawyered.com chronicles some of the more egregious examples of tort excess. Walter Olson is a Senior Fellow at the Manhattan Institute, a New York-based think tank that advocates market-oriented solutions to public policy questions. For an opposing view on tort reform see: Bogus, Carl T., **Why Lawsuits are Good for America,** and Koenig, Thomas H., **In Defense of Tort Law** (above).

Personal Injury Law Library [CD-ROM]. New York: Matthew Bender & Co. One disc. Updated quarterly. Available Windows. Search Engine: Folio.
Cost: CD-ROM: $8,813 (annual subscription); renewal: 1998: $1,865.00; 1999: $1,940.00; 2000: $2,000.00; 2001: $2,140.00; 2002: $2,205.00; 2003: $2,316.00; 2004: $2,795.00; 2005: $2,602.00; 2006: $2,785.00; 2007: $3,008; 2008: $3,279; 2009: $3,541; 2010: $3,931; 2011: $4,324; 2012: $4,880; 2013: $5,221; 2014: $5,825.22.
Matthew Bender's Authority products are a sophisticated combination of analytical treatises and relevant primary law designed for the practitioner. This complete CD-ROM product contains the full text of the following Matthew Bender titles: **Personal Injury - Actions, Defenses, Damages**, **Proving Medical Diagnosis and Prognosis, Premises Liability-Law and Practice**, **Attorneys' Dictionary of Medicine**, **Attorneys' Textbook of Medicine, Damages in Tort Actions**, **Medical Malpractice**, **Defense of Drunk Driving Cases: Criminal**, **Civil. Bender's Forms of Discovery: Interrogatories** is an optional selection. Lesser combinations of titles may be selected by the subscriber. The subscription also includes the LEXIS-NEXIS Online Connection to recent case law.

Personal Injury Law Treatise Library on LoisLawConnect. New York: Wolters Kluwer Law & Business.
Cost: $540.00 per year (solo practitioner) (2014).
This invaluable collection addresses tort law in all fifty states, as well as personal injury pre-trial and litigation forms, sample demand letters, interrogatories, motions, complaints and cross-examination guides. Titles include: **Tort Law Desk Reference: A Fifty-State Compendium, Personal Injury: Forms and Procedures, Understanding the AMA Guides in Workers' Compensation, Malingering and Deception in Litigation, Medical Records Review, Expert Witness Update,** as well as forms and checklists culled from the above.

Personal Injury Valuation Handbooks. St Paul, Thomson Reuters West (LRP), 1964-date. 9 vols. Looseleaf format. Individual pamphlets replaced as necessary.
Cost: $1,175.04 per year; **Monthly Assured Print Price (APP):** $97.92/$1,175.04 (2014).
This service provides up-to-date coverage of personal injury verdicts organized by part of the anatomy. Individual entries summarize the case and provide the following data: court, attorneys, final demand, final offer, total verdict, compensatory damages, past medical expense claimed, filing date, and trial date. There are also pamphlets covering current award trends, and pamphlets for individual states which can be purchased as an add-ons. The most complete service of its kind for tracking jury verdicts by injury. The cost of this publication increased substantially when it was acquired by Thomson Treuters in 2011, from $755 per year to $1,049.04 between 2010 and 2011, a 39% increase.

Proving and Defending Damage Claims: A Fifty-State Guide. Edited by James J. Brown and Wendy Fleishman, New York, NY, Wolters Kluwer Law & Business, 2007-date. 1 vol. Looseleaf format.
Cost: $329; supplementation: 2008: $140; 2009: $155; 2010: $165; 2011: $175; 2012: $187; 2013: $200.
The manner in which damages are assessed in tort actions varies significantly from one state to the next. In recent years, tort reform and the codification of damage claims in such areas as medical malpractice, products liability, wrongful death and consumer rights has had a major impact on the assessment of such damages. This volume provides a unique cross-jurisdictional perspective on damage claims, from the specific legal theories involved, to the drafting or defending of a complaint, and the arguing of damages at trial. The eight chapters address the following tort areas: (1) medical malpractice damages: causes of action in tort and contract; (2) products liability actions; (3) economic damages in personal injury and wrongful death; (4) recovery for property loss; (5) damages in environmental torts; (6) remedies for actions in equity; (7) state consumer protection statutory remedies; (8) and punitive damages. Each chapter provides, in either tabular or narrative form, a state-by-state breakdown of the statutes or common law relevant to that variety of tort, as well as analysis unique to each specific area of law to assist in the handling of such cases and the calculation of recoverable damages. The volume also includes a table of cases and index. Each chapter is authored by a specialist in the field.

Remedies Law Library on LoisLawConnect. New York: Wolters Kluwer Law & Business.
Cost: $540.00 per year (solo practitioner) (2014).
The titles in this library address the collection and enforcement of judgments, and the assessment of damages at the state and topical level, including **Judgment Enforcement, Proving and Defending Damage Claims: A Fifty State Guide**, and a **Remedies Smart Chart**

Shahnasarian, Michael S. **Assessment of Earning Capacity**. 3d ed. Tucson, AZ: Lawyers & Judges Publishing Co., 2011. 1 vol. (304 pp.).
Cost: $85.00; from $58.88 on amazon.com; kindle: $55.94 (2014).
The assessment of lost earning capacity is often a critical ingredient in many personal injury and wrongful death cases. These cases and resulting damage awards can involve complex economic determinations regarding earning capacity and loss of income. This volume aims to provide a systematic means of conducting vocational evaluations and determining a client's earning capacity. Among the topics discussed are vocational expert consultation, assessing the value of earning capacity claims, investigating the integrity of vocational expert assessments, career development potential, transferable skills, rehabilitation psychology, and examining the validity of opposing experts' opinions. The volume also includes sample forms, interviews, and deposition questions. An invaluable and practical guide for those engaged in personal injury practice. The author is the founder and president of Career Consultants of America, Inc. with a doctorate in counseling psychology from Florida State University.

Sherry, John E. H. **The Law of Innkeepers: For Hotels, Motels, Restaurants, and Clubs**. 3d ed. Ithaca, NY: Cornell University Press, 1993. 1 vol. (924 pp.).
Cost: $69.95; from $26.94 on amazon.com (2014).
Traditionally, the field of hospitality law was governed by the common law which created a mutual relationship of reciprocal obligations and duties between owners and patrons or guests. Owners have a duty to furnish proper accommodations, and to exercise proper care for the safety and tranquility of guests, while guests are expected to exercise due care with respect to the owner's property and to refrain from boisterous, disruptful, or offensive conduct. In more recent years, these common law rules have been either replaced or supplemented by state and federal statutes and regulations. Both restaurants and inns are subject to regulation under the police power of the state in the form of state administrative bodies or local licensing authorities. In addition, federal law prohibits owners from refusing to accommodate or entertain persons on account of race, color, religion, or national origin. While most of the law governing hospitality law resides in case law, hotels and restaurant services are also governed by Article 2 of the Uniform Commercial Code, chiefly the express and implied warranties applied to both hotel rooms and food items served in restaurants.

In this exhaustive guide to the law governing innkeepers, hotels, motels, restaurants and clubs, Professor John Sherry traces the historical evolution of the law regarding innkeeping from its common law origins to the modern mix of common law, federal and state statutory law and regulation (including Uniform Commercial Code provisions), and local police power. His discussion addresses a wide range of legal issues, including the nature of innkeeper's duties under common law and statute, the relationship between innkeeper and guest, legal excuses for failure to receive a guest, the right to eject, duty to provide safe premises, franchise agreements, duties to non-guests, regulations governing the sale of food and beverages, the innkeeper's lien, crimes against innkeepers, employment law, environmental law and land use, catastrophic risk liability, and much more. John E.H. Sherry is Professor Emeritus at Cornell University.

Speiser, Stuart M., Charles F. Krause, and Alfred W. Gans. **The American Law of Torts**. St. Paul, MN: West (Clark Boardman Callaghan), 1992-date. 16 vols. Annual pocket parts.
Cost: $2,651; supplementation: 1993: $20; 1994: $150; 1995: $290; 1996: $325; 1997: 0; 1998: $362; 1999: $391; 2000: $415; 2001: $477; 2002: $478.50; 2003: $1,069.50; 2004: $610; 2005: $622; 2006: $745; 2007: $829; 2008; $1,037.50; 2009: $1,591; 2010: $1,606; 2011: $1,536.50; 2012: $1,678.50; 2013: $1,989; **Monthly Assured Print Price (APP):** $201/$2,412.
This is one of several outstanding multi-volume treatises on the law of torts. Originally published by the Lawyers Cooperative Publishing, the production was transferred to Clark Boardman Callaghan following the former's purchase in 1989, and is now part of the West. The authors have adopted a broad-based philosophy in mapping out their coverage of the field, acknowledging that the field of tort law may often involves a number of overlapping legal questions, including conflict of laws, jurisdictional, and limitation of actions issues as well as multiple defendants, joint several liability, apportionment, contribution and indemnity, defenses of justification, contractual issues, etc. The chapters encompass everything from negligence and damages to causation, contributory negligence, premises liability, products liability, nuisances, trespass, conversion, assault and battery, false imprisonment, defamation, fraud and deceit, disparagement of goods and slander of title. The authors discuss all leading tort cases from the colonial period to the present and include all cases from all jurisdictions decided in the period after 1975. There are citations to all relevant **ALR** annotations and **Am Jur 2d** discussions. There are Total Client-Service Library References and citations to all leading periodical articles, and the appropriate **Restatements of the Law**. The substantive coverage is exhaustive as are the citations to primary and secondary sources. A well-written, exhaustive and scholarly work which addresses both substantive and procedural issues.

Stein, Jacob A. **Stein on Personal Injury Damages.** 3d ed. St. Paul, MN: West (Clark Boardman Callaghan), 1997-date. 5 vols. Annual pocket parts.
Cost: $1,913; supp.: 1993: $239.75; 1994: $250; 1995: $185; 1996: $335; 1997: $520; 1998: $360; 1999: $360; 2000: $333; 2001: $390; 2002: $430; 2003: $490; 2004: $549; 2005: $601; 2006: $838; 2007: $933; 2008: $1,045; 2009: $1,163; 2010: $1,019; 2011: $1,111; 2012: $1,211; 2013: $1,331; **Monthly Assured Print Price (APP)**: $140/$1,680.
The objective of compensatory damages is to put the plaintiff

in the same position, so far as money can do it, as the plaintiff would have been if the contract had been performed or the tort not committed. According to Jacob Stein, this objective has not changed in the 80-odd years since that definition was first expressed by Sedgwick in 1912. What has changed has been the accumulation of thousands of cases decided since that time which have applied damages to a myriad of factual situations and novel circumstances. This five-volume treatise on the subject of personal injury damages, unlike the multi-volume tort sets, focuses its attention upon the law governing the awarding of damages in a variety of circumstances, including pain and suffering, mental anguish, impairment of earning capacity, permanent injuries, aggravation of preexisting injuries, loss of consortium, wrongful death, survival actions, and prenatal and child injuries. The author also discusses a number of procedural questions including medical expenses, mitigation, apportionment among multiple tortfeasors, compensation from a collateral source, reduction to present value, nominal and punitive damages, and pleading damages. The text contains citations to case law from all jurisdictions and each chapter includes references to leading secondary authorities. Volumes 3-5 are a companion to the text volumes. Organized in a looseleaf format, these three volumes take an in-depth look at the issues addressed in the basic text. These In-Depth Studies provide detailed coverage of specific injuries and discussion of actual damage awards, all heavily supported by case annotations and research references. Includes discussion of cases in which the evidence was held sufficient and those in which the evidence was held to be insufficient. An excellent resource for the personal injury attorney.

Towers-Romero, Sandi. **Law and the Hospitality Industry**. Durham, NC: Carolina Academic Press, 2013. 1 vol. (277 pp.). Paperbound.
Cost: $40.00; from $38.00 on amazon.com (2014).
This a practically-oriented, accessible overview of the many-faceted hospitality industry designed for paralegal students, hospitality professionals, lawyers, and others interested in the operations of the industry. The introductory chapter provides a useful overview of the hospitality industry, including travel agents and agencies, transportation, airlines, trains, issues, car rentals, lodging, admiralty law, tour operators, food services, attractions and entertainments, liability of amusement venues, gambling, Internet gambling, the economic impact of the hospitality industry, and the Internet and travel planning. Additional chapters address business structures, the system and the hospitality industry, contracts, torts/crimes, property, how to select employees, trade name, trademark, service mark, and trade dress, safety and security of guests and their property, merchant obligations as to food beverages and alcohol, crisis management/ethics, and insurance. The author is professor of hospitality law at Edison State College in Fort Myers, Florida. She received her law degree from Western State University and has more than forty years experience in the hospitality field. This is a unique and practical contribution to the legal literature that can be of tremendous value to anyone interested in the legal environment in which the hospitality operates.

Toxic Tort Litigation. Edited by D. Alan Rudlin, Chicago: American Bar Association, 2007. 1 vol. (492 pp.).
Cost: $149.95 ($129.95 to members); from $79.89 on amazon.com (2014).
Toxic tort cases usually involve a complex combination of plaintiffs and defendants, multiple jurisdictions and lawsuits, litigation procedures, and complex scientific proofs to establish causation. This volume examines the various theories of liability and damages as well as the procedural and substantive defenses to toxic tort claims. Subsequent chapters address scientific and medical evidence and causation, including the opinions of expert witnesses, case strategy, trial management, and settlement considerations. The volume also includes expert commentary from attorneys with experience in several specific areas of toxic tort litigation, including mold, lead, asbestos, silica, food products, drugs, and the gasoline additive MBTBE. Editor D. Alan Rudlin is a partner with the Product Liability and Mass Tort Practice Group at Hunton & Williams LLP in Richmond, Virginia, where he has specialized in complex and mass tort litigation, including products liability, pharmaceuticals, class actions, and toxic torts, for more than 30 years.

United States Life Tables. Hyattsville, MD, National Center for Health Statistics. 1 vol. (39 pp.). Issued annually.
Cost: Available from Lawyers & Judges Publishing at a cost of $15.00 or via free pdf download at:
http://www.cdc.gov/nchs/data/nvsr/nvsr61/nvsr61_03.pdf
Also available from Lawyers & Judges Publishing:

U.S. Historical Life Expectancy Tables, 1901-Present.
Cost: $49.00 (2014).
Essential tools for use in personal injury or wrongful death actions in which calculation of lost earnings is an issue. These tables provide the latest statistics regarding life expectancy by age, sex and race, and are admissible in court by judicial notice.

Weaver, Russell L., et al. **Mastering Tort Law**. Durham, NC: Carolina Academic Press, 2009. 1 vol. (346 pp.).
Cost: $35; from $28.00 on amazon.com; kindle ed.: $27.99 (2014).
With roots in the ancient common law, tort law evolved as a system for compensating those who suffer injury as a result of wrongful or negligent conduct of another. This succinct, yet sufficiently detailed, volume provides an excellent overview of the basic concepts and claims subsumed under the rubric of tort law. While the origins of tort law have some association with the criminal law, tort law exists primarily to provide remedies, usually in the form of monetary damages, for violation of such rights as personal security, reputation, privacy, emotional tranquility, and economic rights, such as those in property. Tort liability can arise from three primary forms of conduct: intentional tort, negligent conduct, and strict liability. This volume addresses these three primary forms of tortious conduct, as well as such doctrines as nuisance, defamation, privacy, and such economic torts as unfair competition and misrepresentation. Additional chapters address intentional interference with person or property, defenses to intentional torts, cause in fact, proximate cause, multiple tortfeasors, compensatory and punitive damages, limited duty, premises liability, wrongful death and survival, defenses to

negligence, vicarious liability, common law strict liability, products liability, civil rights, misuse of legal process, misrepresentation, and business torts. The text includes selective references to relevant cases and statutes. Each chapter includes a preliminary Roadmap of its coverage, and concludes with Checkpoints which review key concepts. The volume concludes with a Mastering Tort Law Checklist. Inaugurated in 2008, the volumes in the Carolina Academic Press Mastering Series are intended to provide law students with a basic understanding of substance and content of courses in the law school curriculum. Priced comparable to, or below, the cost of the West Nutshell series, these volumes are superior in most respects to their competitors. The volume was written by a team of six law school professors, including Russell L. Weaver, Edward C. Martin, Andrew R. Klein, Paul J. Zwier, II, Ronald W. Eades, and John H. Bauman, representing five academic institutions.

What's It Worth: A Guide to Personal Injury Awards and Settlements. Compiled by Heidi Thorson. Charlottesville, VA: LexisNexis, 1985-date. Annual. 1 vol. Paperbound or eBook.
Cost: 2013 Edition: $297; 2012 Edition: $270 (print or eBook); 2011 Edition: $257 (2014).
This is one of those reference works that personal injury attorneys reach for as soon as they have a client with an injury. **What's It Worth** will give them hard numbers regarding personal injury verdicts and/or settlements. It is also useful for defense attorneys anxious to estimate the extent of their client's potential exposure. The book's twenty-eight chapters are organized alphabetically according to type of injury. Wrongful death verdicts and settlements are also included. Each chapter is divided into four sections: (1) settlements, (2) adequate verdicts, (3) inadequate verdicts, and (4) excessive verdicts. The case descriptions are arranged alphabetically by state with the highest award of settlement listed first.

Additional titles in the field of Tort Law are available from the following publishers: American Bar Association, American Enterprise Institute, American Law Institute, Ashgate Publishing Co., Wolters Kluwer Law & Business, Matthew Bender, Carolina Academic Press, Cato Institute, Cornell University Press, Delmar Publishers, Gaunt, HarperCollins Publications, Harvard University Press, James Publishing, Kluwer Academic Publications, LexisNexis, LRP Publications, Lupus Publications, Oxford University Press, Panel Publishers, Pearson Publications, Practising Law Institute, Thomson Reuters West, University Press of America, West Academic, Yale University Press. See Appendix B for addresses and telephone numbers.

Trial Practice
(see also Evidence)

American Jurisprudence Pleading and Practice Forms Annotated. Eagan, MN: West (Lawyers Cooperative), 1966-date. 85 vols. Annual pocket parts and periodic revised volumes. **Cost:** $9,639; supplementation: 1992: $418; 1993: $498; 1994: $679; 1995: $844; 1996: $1,376; 1997: $952; 1998: $1,830; 1999: $1,543.50; 2000: $1,834; 2001: $2,402; 2002: $2,199; 2003: $2,108; 2004: $2,182; 2005: $3,108.50; 2006: $3,108; 2007: $3,182; 2008: $3,180; 2009: $4,149.50; 2010: $4,348; 2011: $4,824; 2012: $5,477; 2013: $6,973; **Monthly Assured Print Price (APP)**: $595/$7,140.
The only major set of general pleading and practice forms on the market. More than 30,000 forms covering all types and phases of court proceedings are organized under 363 main legal topics and published in 48 bound volumes. Access is by an annually revised two-volume General Index. Includes pre-trial, trial and post-trial forms, including orders, writs, notices and jury instructions. Most of the forms have been taken from the files and court records of practitioners in every state and federal jurisdiction to which have been added references to applicable state statutes and court rules. Each of the topical chapters into which these forms have been organized contains a variety of features of value to the practitioner, including cross references, collateral references to the **American Law Reports** and **Federal Procedure**, Trial Aids to **Am. Jur. Trials**, relevant Annotations, an Introduction to the topic with citations to applicable section of **Am. Jur. 2d**, and Checklist for drafting forms in that area of the law. A brief review of Governing Principles summarizes the more complete coverage available in **Am. Jur. 2d.** There also are Notes to each form keying the user into Am. Jur 2d. for further explanation of the legal principles involved. This set is a valuable addition to the library of any attorney. The references to other products in Lawyers Cooperative's Total Client-Service Library are a particularly useful feature.

Cost Saving Tips: The cost of used sets stands in stark contrast to the new set price. Depending on their currency, the prices of used sets range from $150.00 to $750.00. Buy a used set and then enter a standing order with the publisher (assuming you wish to keep it current). Better yet, buy used and forego the supplements altogether. A ten-year standing order will cost you more than $60,000 to support a set chiefly useful for its boiler-plate form language which still must adapted to suit your local needs. An outdated set can serve you nearly as well in this regard. If you wish to bring your set up-to-date periodically, simply buy another more current used set at periodic intervals, or even another new set. Employing this strategy, you can save yourself at least $40,000 over a ten-year period in comparison with what you would have spent on standing order supplementation. If currency is what you want, acquire it as a Westlaw add-on.
If you wish to maintain standing orders, the CD-ROM or Westlaw formats are far better values. If you haven't already gathered, however, supplementation to law books is a cleverly disguised racket, sort of like a license to print money. Avoid the Monthly Assured Print Price option which will only lock you in to high supplementation costs.

Am. Jur. Pleading and Practice Forms on WestlawNext. Eagan, MN: West, 1995-date.
Cost: On Westlaw: $1,272 per year (1 user).
Contains the full text of all the forms in the print set, fully searchable, with hypertext links to other products in the same product family.

Cost Saving Tips: The prices of many West's CD-ROM products have risen significantly in recent years, with this title having risen 30% since 2012 prior to its discontinuance. For those interested in the electronic format, a Westlaw add-on is the preferred option, priced at only $1,272 per year (in 2014), or less than one-seventh the cost of the CD-ROM or print formats. Indeed, a solo practitoonber can acquire the entire **American Jurisprudence 2d Library** on WestlawNext for only $2,832 per year as opposed to the nearly $50,000 cost of maintaining the same titles in print.. Those interested in cutting costs to the bone, can acquire this set on the used lawbook market and use the boiler plate forms without subscribing to the costly annual supplementation.

American Jurisprudence. Proof of Facts. 1st - 3rd. St. Paul, MN: West (Lawyers Cooperative), 1959-date. 208 vols.; **POF** [1st]: 30 volumes; **POF 2d**: 50 volumes; **POF 3d**: 128 vols.; 3 vol. Index. **POF 3d** growing at the rate of 5-6 volumes per year. **POF** [1st] not supplemented since 2006].
Total Cost: $10,569; purchased separately: 1st: $667; 2d: $1,568; 3d: $9,001; total supplementation cost: 1994: $1,144.00; 1995: $1,210.00; 1996: $1,339.55; 1997: $1,474.00; 1998: $1,553.00; 1999: $1,717.50; 2000; $1,669.00; 2001: $2,057.25; 2002: $2,004.50; 2003: $1,989.50; 2004: $2,440.00; 2005: $3,543.00; 2006: $3,845.50; 2007: $2,814.50; 2008: $3,380.50; 2009: $5,333; 2010: $5,797; 2011: $5,722; 2012: $6,686; 2013: $6,926; **Monthly Assured Print Price (APP)**: All 3 series: $656/$7,872.
One of the components of Lawyers Cooperative's (now West's) Total Client-Service Library System, **Proof of Facts** contains articles which "explain and illustrate how to prove the particular facts essential to a cause of action or a defense." The editorial bias is towards the plaintiff's side, since that is where the burden of proof lies. However, each article includes defense considerations which can be of specific value to the defense. The majority of the articles also deal with civil, rather than criminal issues. While earlier volumes in the series were written by in-house lawyer/editors as well as outside authors, the current volumes are all being written by outside (contract) authors. Each volume contains an average of twelve articles. Half of these are devoted to personal injury and related topics. The remainder are devoted to a variety of topics from civil rights and employment termination to intellectual property and bankruptcy matters, among many others. The criminal articles generally emphasize the proof of specific defenses or deal with forensic issues. About two-thirds of the articles in **Proof of Facts** [1st] have been replaced by articles in the 2d and 3d series. The typical article includes background information on the applicable law and legal issues, technical background, evidence considerations, defense considerations, elements of damages, model discovery, elements of proof, illustrative proofs, illustrative forms, jury instructions, artwork and illustrations, and bibliographies. The Total Client-Service Library References includes citations to other Lawyers Cooperative (now West) titles. This series is a valuable complement to **Am Jur Trials** in the practicing attorney's library.

Cost Saving Tips: All **Proof of Facts** series are readily available on the used law book market at prices far below the new set prices (you may wish to omit **Proof of Facts** [1st] since two-thirds of these articles have been revised). **Proof of Facts 2d** and **3rd** are available for $395 and $595 respectively, or less than $13.00 per volume. By contrast the current volumes are currently priced at $577 each (2014 list price). The cost-conscious attorney who wishes to keep the sets current can buy only the annual pocket parts and forego the purchase of the new bound volumes which are of only marginal benefit to the existing 163 volumes in all three series. The three-volume index will alert you to the existence of critical articles in later volumes. Or, you may wish to buy pocket parts every 2-3 years for even greater savings. This set is a cash cow for the publisher, but you don't have to get milked at every available opportunity. For example, buying just the pocket parts and revised indexes to all three series cost more than $3,600 in 2013. If you are not careful, the annual supplementation cost of **Proof of Facts 3d** can quickly exceed what you paid for the used set. If you wish to keep it current, a WestlawNext add-on is the preferred option at only $1,272 per year (1 user); or $2,832 as part of the **Am Jur Library (which includes Am. Jur 2d, American Law Reports, POF, Trials, and Am Jur Legal Forms).**

See your Westlaw sales representative for current deals and promotions. If you desire this publication, ask them to throw it in to seal the deal. Better yet, buy the pdfs of desired proofs at a cost of only $42 and spare yourself the cost of supplementing the entire set. Whatever you do, avoid the print set and its exorbitant ongoing costs.

Am Jur Proof of Facts on LawDesk on WestlawNext. St. Paul, MN: West (Lawyers Cooperative).
Cost: $1,272 per year on WestlawNext, or $2,832 for entire **American Jurisprudence 2d Library**.
A fully searchable database of the full text of **Am. Jur. Proof of Facts**, with hypertext links to other titles in the same product family.

Cost Saving Tips: Buying a used print set is the best option if you wish to avoid supplementation costs; however, if you do wish to keep it current, the Westlaw add-on at $1,272 per year is a much better value. Alternatively, buy pdfs of only the chapters (proofs) you need.

American Jurisprudence Trials. St. Paul, MN: West (Lawyers Cooperative), 1964-date. 128 vols. & 3 vol. index. Annual pocket parts. Set is growing at the rate of 5-6 new volumes per year.
Cost: $7,304; supplementation: 1994: $578.50; 1995: $835; 1996: $871; 1997: $962; 1998: $1,009.50; 1999: $1,089.25; 2000: $1,167; 2001: $1,308.50; 2002: $1,661; 2003: $1,697; 2004: $1,901; 2005: $1,561; 2006: $2,200; 2007: $2,692; 2008: $2,694; 2009: $2,955; 2010: $3,517.50; 2011: $3,837.50; 2012: $4,622; 2013: $5,590; **Monthly Assured Print Price (APP)**: $406/$4,872; as Westlaw add-on: $1,272 per year (1 user).
This is one of the most useful legal reference sets on the market.

The first six volumes, comprising nearly 6,000 pages, provide the practitioner with general coverage of complete trial procedure, both civil and criminal, from client interview through instructing the jury and predicting personal injury verdicts and damages. The succeeding volumes, entitled **Model Trials**, include articles covering topics of both general and specific interest written by nearly 200 lawyer/editors and practitioners. Volume 52, for example, contains chapters devoted to an overview of civil litigation, alternative dispute resolution in the construction industry, medical malpractice involving a brain-damaged infant, and the use of toxic experts. Although the emphasis is upon trial practice in specific areas, the set's main stated purpose is to assist in the resolution of cases without going to trial. The average specialized article includes material encompassing general theories of law, initial case intake, review of evidence, expert witnesses, pleadings and discovery, settlement, and trial considerations. Each chapter includes references to the Total Client-Service Library, including related **Am Jur Trials** and **Proof of Facts** articles, Collateral References to treatises and texts, Practice Aids, **American Law Reports** annotations, and periodical literature. There is an index to each article. The articles also include applications to specific fact patterns, forms, illustrations, maps, charts, and tables. The discussion of applicable court rules alerts the practitioner to possible exceptions. The attorney who is going to trial will be greatly assisted if the subject of the action is addressed by an article in **Am Jur Trials**. This is just one of the Total Client-Service Library sets which can make a valuable addition to the library of any attorney.

Cost Saving Tips: Acquiring **Am Jur Trials** on WestlawNext (see entry below) not only saves the initial cost cost of acquiring the set ($6,702, exclusive of discount, in 2013), but reduces the annual supplementation cost by about 75%%. This is also an ideal candidate for purchase on the used law book market if you are not interested in keeping it current. Complete used sets of can be purchased for approximately $600, or less than $12.00 a volume. While you may wish to enter a standing order for the annual pocket parts, be wary of including in your subscription the succeeding bound volumes, which are now selling for $638 each (list price). With 128 volumes already in the set, these new volumes will add only marginally to the utility of the set. Your annual index supplements, if you choose to receive these, will alert you to the existence of new articles which may be of particular interest and which you can obtain at your local public law library. Thus, your continuing financial outlay will only involve the periodic purchase of the annual pocket parts (once every three years is sufficient). The publisher has increased the frequency with which the bound volumes are being issued. While an average of only two volumes was published annually in the period 1965-1993, 5-6 have been published annually since 1994. The annual cost of supplementing this set is more than four times the $600 cost of most used sets. If you wish to keep it current, a Westlaw add-on is the preferred alternative at only $1,272 for a solo practitioner, or less than half the cost of a print subscription. Alternatively, you can purchase pdfs of desired chapters for $42.00 each.

Am Jur Trials on Westlaw. St. Paul, MN: West (Lawyers Cooperative), 1995-date.

Cost: $1,272 per year (1 user); $1,668 (2 users); $2,172 (3 users).
A fully searchable database of hundreds of articles with hypertext linking capability (see prior entry for full description). The CD-ROM version has now been abandoned in favor of Westlaw access. With West anxious to make deals on Westlaw subscriptions, the savvy consumer will ask for this set to be through in to the deal.

Baldwin, Scott. **Art of Advocacy: Direct Examination**. New York: Matthew Bender & Co., 1981-date. 1 vol. Looseleaf format or eBook.
Cost: $406; supplementation: 1997: $103 (annual cost frozen since 1993); 1998: $110; 1999: $117; 2000: $125; 2001: $134; 2002: $144; 2003: $152; 2004: $152; 2005: $164; 2005: $184; 2007: $207; 2008: $230; 2009: $255; 2010: $284; 2011: $295; 2012: $328; 2013: $338; 2014: $372.
A detailed and practical guide to the direct examination of witnesses in personal injury cases. Following the model of other volumes in this series, **Direct Examination** includes two introductory chapters which provide an overview of the subject and the legal principles which govern it. The remaining 31 chapters offer practical guidance on direct examination in various types of personal cases, all with sample questions and commentary. An additional chapter provides the trial lawyer with Models of Direct Examination. Also includes a bibliography and subject index.

Cost Savings Tips: Trial practice titles like this can be used effectively without subscribing to the updates. Forego the standing order and simply re-purchase it when you feel you would like a more current version.

Baum, David B. **Art of Advocacy: Preparation of the Case**. New York: Matthew Bender & Co., 1981-date. 1 vol. Looseleaf format or eBook.
Cost: $430 (print or eBook); supplementation: 1997: $103 (annual cost frozen since 1993); 1998: $110; 1999: $117; 2000: $125; 2001: $134; 2002: $144; 2003: $152; 2004: $152; 2005: $164; 2006: $184; 2007: $207; 2008: $230; 2009: $255; 2010: $284; 2011: $295; 2012: $328; 2013: $328; 2014; $328.
This is the kind of work most lawyers wished they had read prior to beginning the practice of law since case preparation is a subject rarely taught in law school. This one-volume treatise and practice guide covers every stage of case preparation, including the client interview, mechanics of beginning, investigation, organization, gathering of evidence, mining the sources, handling complex litigation, initiating the lawsuit, the middle stages, expert witnesses, preparing demonstrative evidence, the final one hundred days, and preparation and the law. The text is accompanied by many relevant forms and sample documents. There are also chapters offering advice to the client and to the expert witness. It also includes a bibliography and detailed subject index. This clearly written and well organized work belongs in the library of any trial lawyer handling personal injury cases. A graduate of the University of Wisconsin and Northwestern University Law School, David Baum is one of California's leading trial attorneys with extensive experience as a speaker and authority on trial practice.

Cost Savings Tips: Trial practice titles like this can be used effectively without subscribing to the updates. Forego the standing order and simply re-purchase it when you feel you would like a more current version.

Bender's Forms of Discovery. New York: Matthew Bender & Co., 1963-date. 34 vols. Looseleaf format. Supplemented periodically. Also available on CD-ROM and the Internet.
Cost: $6,383 (includes annual subscription); renewal: 1995: $1,495 (price frozen since 1992); 1996: $1,568; 1997: $1,568; 1998: $1,650; 1999: $1,715; 2000: $1,840; 2001: $1,969; 2002: $2,107; 2003: $2,213; 2004: $2,324; 2005: $2,440; 2006: $2,611; 2007: $2,820; 2008: $3,046; 2009: $3,290; 2010: $3,454; 2011: $3,730; 2012: $$4,066; 2013: $4,351; 2014: $4,749; CD-ROM: $7,001 (with annual subscription); renewal: 1998: $1,570; 1999: $1,715; 2000: $1,840; 2001: $1,969; 2002: $2,107; 2003: $2,213; 2004: $2,324; 2005: $2,440; 2006: $2,611; 2007: $2,820; 2008: $3,415; 2009: $3,688; 2010: $3,873; 2011: $4,183; 2012: $4,559; 2013: $4,878; 2014: $5,430.48; eBook: $5,803; renewal: 2014: $4.749. Also available in two subsets: **Interrogatories** (vols. 1-11); and **Related Discovery and Inspection** (vols. 12-16). This set is also available as a part of the **Authority Personal Injury** and **Federal Practice Libraries.**
Contains a variety of trial practice forms, including information on interrogatories, depositions, privilege, production, requests for admission, inspections, Freedom of Information Act requests, medical discovery, and criminal discovery. This set can be used as both a pre-trial discovery tool and a trial testimony guide. Contains checklists for client interviews and references for expert witnesses. The Appendices contain the discovery statutes of all fifty states. A unique and indispensable resource for the trial attorney. With the partial exception of some specialized trial practice discovery guides, this is the only major set of its kind on the market. Volumes 1-10 (11 vols.) contain interrogatories alphabetically arranged by subject. Volumes 11-20 (7 vols.) contain a variety of materials regarding the law and practice of discovery, including depositions, interrogatories, production of documents, physical and mental examination of persons, requests for admissions, subpoenas for taking depositions, appellate review of discovery orders, discovery in complex litigation, and Freedom of Information law and discovery. This is easily the most exhaustive work of its kind available.

Cost Saving Tips: For the attorney with an active personal injury practice, this set is best acquired as part of the Personal Injury Library, a reference package which is priced far below the total of its eight individual components. Ask your sales representative about current pricing.

Bensen, Eric E. and Rebecca Kelder Myers. **Bensen & Myers on Litigation Management**. Newark, NJ: LexisNexis, 2009. 1 vol. (various pagings). Paperbound. No supplementation.
Cost: $199; from $94.50 on amazon.com (2014).
This well-organized, step-by-step, guide to litigation management covers everything from the initial case evaluation to the trial. Among the topics considered are budgeting for litigation, the initial decision to bring suit, deciding whether to settle, the efficient management of the litigation team, management of the discovery process, motion preparation, preparation for trial, management principles and techniques, and trial checklists. Each section includes valuable illustrative examples, including a case evaluation worksheet, settlement worksheet, a project status summary, factual development summary, legal research summary, plaintiff v. defendant names list, document management folder, contact list, document request summary, a sample defendant's pretrial memorandum, and much more. Appendices include a quick reference guide to cutting costs and improving quality, a checklist to allow in-house counsel to determine if there is sufficient information about the management of the case, and an evaluation of the strengths and weaknesses of litigation guidelines. A specialist in intellectual property law, Eric Bensen is the co-author of **Milgrim on Trade Secrets** and **Milgrim on Licensing**. He was in private practice for more than 12 years with Paul, Hastings Janofsky & Walker LLP and Dewey Ballantine LLP and has taught as a Visiting Assistant Professor Law at Hofstra University School of Law. Rebecca Myers is an attorney at Paul, Hastings Janofsky & Walker LLP in New York where she concentrates on intellectual property law and commercial litigation.

Berg, David. **The Trial Lawyer: What It Takes To Win**. Chicago: American Bar Association, 2006. 1 vol. (307 pp.).
Cost: $110 ($96 to Litigation Section members); $75 (paperbound) ($65 to Litigation Section members); from $41.85 on amazon.com (2014)
In our contemporary legal environment, many litigators are trapped in a culture of settlement in which their energies are primarily limited to the taking of depositions and the arguing of motions. Under an economic model that favors discovery and settlement, jury trials have become a gamble to be avoided. David Berg, a seasoned and highly regarded litigator, argues that a litigator's life should be primarily devoted to trial work, not only for the professional development and personal satisfaction they provide, but for the ultimate benefit of clients and the cause of justice. Drawing upon his experiences in hundreds of civil and criminal trials, he brings a sophisticated, yet humanistic, perspective to the entire trial process, from discovery to closing argument. Central to the author's approach to trial work are what he calls "The Constants of Persuasion," rules applicable in any type of case. Among these are the ability to use every available technique and bit of evidence to persuade jurors (what he calls thinking "inside the box"), the ability to tell a compelling story, humanize clients and key witnesses, warm up the courtroom, earn the jurors' trust, set the agenda, prove that standards have been violated, avoid running from your weaknesses, undermine adversaries with impeachment and admissions, and make the jury mad (at the other side). He argues that careful pretrial preparation and the discovery process are crucial to winning at trial. Similarly, he brings his experience and wisdom to bear on the subjects of jury studies and graphics, voir dire, the opening argument, cross examination, preparing and presenting witnesses, and closing arguments. This is a book to be read and re-read by both novice and experienced litigators. The author is a founding partner of the Houston/New York firm of Berg & Androphy, and has been named to The National Law Journal's list of the nation's top ten civil trial lawyers.

Bergman, Paul and Albert Moore. **Nolo's Deposition Handbook: The Essential Guide for Anyone Facing or Conducting a Deposition**. 5th ed. Berkeley, CA: Nolo Press, 2010. 1 vol. (368 pp.). Paperbound.
Cost: $34.99; from $20.54 on amazon.com (2014).
Depositions are one of several methods of investigating the facts before trial that constitutes formal discovery. Depositions provide a mechanism of enabling the parties to a lawsuit to question each other and other potential witnesses under oath, but outside the courtroom and without a judge or jury present. Unlike written discovery requests, witnesses must answer deposition questions immediately. Information uncovered in the course of a deposition is often key to the resolution of a case, and are usually the most expensive discovery tool, since they involved attorney and stenographer costs. This volume is written primarily for the benefit of deponents, and for those taking and defending depositions. They follow the rules and procedures laid out in the **Federal Rules of Civil Procedure** (FRCP), which are used not only in all federal district (trial) courts, but also serve as the basis for the discovery practices of all states. Part I provides an overview of deposition procedures, the use of depositions in a lawsuit, preparation for depositions testimony, the response to questions, the usual admonitions, background questions, questions the deponent can refuse to answer, and expert witness deponents. Part II discusses such topics as the lay of the discovery landscape, defending a deposition, deposing a hostile witness, responding to a defending attorney's roadblocks, deposing a friendly witness, and visually recorded depositions. The volume also includes a glossary of relevant legal terms, excerpts of the **Federal Rules of Civil Procedure**, state discovery and deposition rules, sample forms, and an index. The authors are law professors at the UCLA School of Law and author of **Trial Advocacy: Inferences, Arguments and Techniques** (West). Paul Bergman is also co-author of Nolo's **Represent Yourself in Court** and **The Criminal Law Handbook**.

Bosanac, Paul. **Litigation Logic: A Practical Guide to Effective Argument**. Chicago: American Bar Association, 2009. 1 vol. (486 pp.).
Cost: $129.95; member price: $99.95; from $79.64 on amazon.com (2014).
The framing of logical and effective legal arguments is essential to winning the case. Recognizing, understanding, and utilizing the patterns of effective argumentation are the keys to success both inside and outside of the courtroom. This estimable volume addresses the subject of legal logic primarily through an analysis of the various informal fallacies which are commonly employed in a legal context. Among the more than 30 informal fallacies discussed are the ad hominem attack, poisoning the well, the appeal to authority, shifts in meaning, hypostatization: expressing abstractions, appealing to ignorance, appealing to sympathy, hurling epithets, humor and ridicule, appealing to the mob, the slippery slope, reductio ad absurdum, begging the question, the complex question, red herrings, the straw man argument, hasty generalizations, lies, damn les and statistics, and more. The author's analysis draws heavily upon real-world examples from politics and the courtroom, many of them from actual court decisions that are guilty of these informal fallacies. Unlike other books on logic, this one draws its examples exclusively from the legal world. The volume also includes a legal logic flow chart, a discussion of the rules of legal logic, and prohibited arguments. An essential acquisition for the litigator who wishes to master the art of logical argumentation and reasoning and employ it in a courtroom setting. The author has been employed by the National Labor Relations Board for more than 30 years and taught at Marquette University's Certificate in Labor Relations Program.

Bronstein, Daniel A. **Law for the Expert Witness**. 4th ed. Boca Raton, FL: CRC Press LLC, 2011. 1 vol. (252 pp).
Cost: $89.95; e-book: $89.95; from $81.25 on amazon.com (2014).
An overview of law and legal procedure governing the role and conduct of expert witnesses in the litigation process. The volume covers the procedural issues faced by the expert witness before the start of trial, the legal paperwork, evidence, disclosures, depositions, discovery, and the penalties to which the expert witness would be subject for failure to comply with the rules. The volume reflects amendments to the Federal Rules of Civil Procedure regarding required disclosures early in the litigation process, as well as the disclosure of electronic information. Using pictures and diagrams, the author also addresses the physical layout of the courtroom and its influence on the use of exhibits and demonstrations at trial. These principles are illustrated by the use of recent case studies and court decisions. The author also offers advice regarding the organization and presentation of direct narrative testimony and methods of withstanding cross- examination. Appendices include recent amendments to the Federal Rules of Civil Procedure and the Federal Rules of Evidence. Designed as an introduction to courtroom procedure for chemists, medical professionals, civil engineers, environmental toxicologists, and other professional experts called to testify, as well as a guide for attorneys preparing such experts. The author is a former trial lawyer, now professor of law.

Brophy, Michael D. **Medical Malpractice Depositions**. Huntington, NY: Juris Publishing, 2004-date. 1 vol. (994 pp.). Looseleaf format. Updated annually or when needed.
Cost: $225; supplementation: 2011: $50; 2012: $50; 2013: $50.00.
The process of gathering, eliciting, preserving and presenting evidence from potential witnesses in medical malpractice actions is probably the most important ingredient in a successful trial. This well-crafted volume provides both plaintiff and defendant counsel with the analytical and strategic framework for conducting the medical malpractice action as well as sample depositions drawn from a variety of specific malpractice cases. Together, these tools not only address many of the issues common to all medical malpractice actions, but those which apply to specific forms of malpractice. Providing the reader with a combination of useful commentary and sample depositions, the author takes the first half of the volume to address such topics as preparation for the deposition; conducting the deposition; the plaintiff's inquiry into the defendant doctor's background, training and experience; examination of codefendants; examination of experts; examination of office records; examination of hospitals and institutions; the plaintiff's medical history; critical events in the course of medical treatment; conversations; and post-

malpractice medical treatment. The second half of the volume is devoted a variety of specific areas of medicine, including anesthesiology, general (internal and family) medicine, general surgery, neurosurgery, obstetrics and gynecology, orthopedics, pediatrics, thoracic surgery, urology, and nephrology, each of which includes a summary of the primary areas in which malpractice occurs and sample depositions (forms) for interviewing key witnesses. The author practices law with the Philadelphia firm of Harvey, Pennington, Cabot, Griffith & Renneisen, primarily in the defense of healthcare providers, and is a contributing editor to the Medical Malpractice: Law and Strategy Newsletter (published by American Lawyer Media).

Brown, James J. **Judgment Enforcement Practice and Litigation**. 3d ed. New York: Wolters Kluwer Law & Business, 2009-date. 1 vol. (364 pp.).
Cost: $332; supplementation: 2010: $135; 2011: $145; 2012: $155; 2013: $166; 2d ed. 2000: $90; 2001: $126; 2002: $195; 2003: $171; 2004: $171; 2005: $178; 2006: $187; 2007: $199; 2008: $205; 2009: $265; 1st ed.: 1997: $73; 1998: $80.
This is a useful guide to the practical aspects of judgment enforcement, with special attention to federal judgment enforcement practice in the federal courts. The author brings more than 20 years litigation experience with the U.S. Justice Department and in private practice to bear upon the collection of debts. Individual chapters are devoted to a discussion of the law as it relates to the basic aspects of judgment enforcement, the judgment debtor, the use of discovery to find the debtor's assets, methods of implementation of discovery to trace assets, executing on the judgment, new litigation to enforce judgments, and receivership as a collection device. With the lack of judgment-related texts on the market, this volume is a unique contribution to the trial practice literature.

Campbell, James F., et al. **Defense of Speeding, Reckless Driving and Vehicular Homicide**. New York: Matthew Bender, 1984-date. 4 vols. Looseleaf format.
Cost: $1,208 (annual subscription); annual renewal: 1995: $293 (cost frozen since 1992); 1996: $307; 1997: $307; 1998: $320; 1999: $335; 2000: $360; 2001: $385; 2002: $412; 2003: $433; 2004: $455; 2005: $487; 2006: $522; 2007: $564; 2008: $609; 2009: $658; 2010: $691; 2011: $726; 2012: $770; 2013: $824; 2014: $899; e-book: $1,098; renewal: 2014: $899.
A comprehensive treatise and practice guide on the defense of speeding, reckless driving and vehicular homicide cases. Contains detailed, well-documented analysis of legal and technical matters combined with relevant litigation techniques. Chapters discuss legal elements of speeding offenses, speed enforcement and measurement, radar equipment, and trial of speeding, reckless driving and homicide cases.

Cost Saving Tip: Matthew Bender treatises now come with one year's service. Prior to Bender's reorganization, each release (beyond the first three months) was accompanied by an invoice. Under the current arrangement, however, the customer knows up-front what the annual charges will be. Does your practice involve a sufficient number of cases of this variety to justify maintaining a two-volume set at these prices, or do you handle only an occasional case? If your usage is likely to be infrequent, and you are unwilling to pay the $791.00, or more, required to keep this set on a current status, simply cancel the supplementation and purchase a new set several years later as the need arises. You will probably gain sufficient value from the core treatise without buying all the supplements as long as you have your own system of keeping up with local cases and statutes.

Casad, Robert C. **Jurisdiction in Civil Actions**. 3d ed. Charlottesville, VA: LexisNexis, 1998-date. 2 vols.
Cost: $337; supplementation: 1999: $35; 2000: $79; 2001: $92; 2002: $80; 2003: $81; 2004: $85; 2005: $86; 2006: $91; 2007: $97; 2008: $113; 2009: $130; 2010: $139; 2011; $138; 2012: $157; 2013: $163.
This work provides a detailed examination of civil jurisdictional issues for the practitioner, including fundamental concepts and terminology, constitutional limitations on the exercise of state court jurisdiction, statutory requirements for the exercise of jurisdiction, the long-arm statutes, the invocation of federal court jurisdiction, challenging jurisdiction, and long-arm jurisdiction in tort, contract and other actions. The author is the John H. and John M. Kane Professor of Law at the University of Kansas School of Law where he teaches civil procedure, conflict of laws, and federal courts.

Causes of Action. Eagan, MN: West (Shepards/Lawyers Cooperative), 1983-date. 88 vols. Annual pocket parts and three new bound volumes per year. **COA** includes 30 volumes; **COA 2d** includes 61 volumes as of April 1, 2014; 1st series may only be sold to COA 2d subscribers or obtained used. Also available on CD-ROM and Westlaw.
Cost: 1st series: $1,962; 2d series: $4,708; supplementation: 2d series: 1993: $725; 1994: $725; 1995: $725; 1996: $550; 1997: $700; 1998: $530; 1999: $769; 2000: $863; 2001: $1,010.50; 2002: $671; 2003: $1,038.50; 2004: $1,658.50; 2005: $1,827.50; 2006: $2,075.50; 2007: $2.310.50 (1st series: $977; 2d series: $1,333.50); 2008: $2,731.20 (1st: $1,124; 2d: $1607.20); 2009: $3,439 (1st series: $1,265 + 2d series: $2,174); 2010: $3,795 (1st : $1,478; 2d: $2,317); 2011: 2d: $2,346; 2012: $2,931; 2013: $3,267; **Monthly Assured Print Price (APP)**: 1st series: $113/$1,356; 2d series: $266/$3,192.
Although not strictly speaking a work on tort law, the articles in this series predominantly encompass a wide variety of tort matters from products liability actions to negligence and malpractice cases. Each of the 10 or more articles in each volume takes the practitioner through the steps necessary to determine whether a cause of action exists for a specific set of facts or circumstances. The articles analyze the elements of the cause of action and explain the procedure for proving these elements. The articles guide the attorney through the trial process, providing both analysis of substantive law and procedural issues. Each article also includes a COA Action Guide, an outline of contents, subject index, Practice Guides, forms, Research Guide to secondary sources and practice aids, table of cases. An extremely valuable set for the litigator. This set can be of invaluable assistance to those practitioners who have cases addressed in these articles. This title was sold to the Thomson Corporation in December, 1995 and is now part of the West.

Cost Saving Tips: This is one of those reference tools best used at your local public law library. If you decide to acquire this set new or, preferably, used, forego the supplementation given its high cost. **Causes of Action** is similar to the **American Law Reports** in the sense that the newly published volumes contain randomly selected topics which do not significantly augment the usefulness of the existing volumes. Use **Causes of Action** as a launching pad for research and update, if necessary, at your local public law library. If you buy pocket parts, do so in alternate years or less often.

Clary, Bradley G., Sharon Reich Paulsen, and Michael J. Vanselow. **Successful First Depositions**. 3d ed. St. Paul, MN: West, 2011. 1 vol. (430 pp.). Online book.
Cost: online book: $53; from $46.03 on amazon.com (2014).
Depositions are sworn pretrial testimony given by a witness in response to oral or written questions and cross-examination. The deposition is transcribed and may be used for further pretrial investigation, and may be presented at the trial if the witness cannot be present. This handbook on depositions is designed for use by law students and new attorneys preparing to take and defend their first depositions. It provides a step-by-step roadmap through the process and pitfalls of taking a deposition, preparing the deponent, representing the deponent, problem witnesses and attorneys, expert depositions, the uses of depositions, miscellaneous deposition issues, and deposition rules and procedures. The authors provide an illuminating examination of various types of problem witnesses, including the forgetful witness, the evasive witness, the belligerent witness, the rambling witness, the lying witness and the wacko witness. Attorneys can also prove problematic, ranging from the coach, the testifier (who supplants the role of the witness), the objector, the intimidator, the professor, the repeater and the timekeeper. The discussion is illustrated with numerous examples. The appendices include a variety of useful documents, including a deposition notice, subpoena duces tecum, and three illustrative case records. The authors are professors of law at the University of Minnesota Law School.

Criminal Defense Techniques. Edited by Michael Michelle A. Zeppetello and Ann W. Latner. New York: Matthew Bender & Co., 1969-date. 10 vols. Looseleaf format and eBook. Supplemented periodically. No CD-ROM.
Cost: $4,559 (print or eBook) (includes annual subscription); annual renewal: 1995: $1237.50 (price frozen since 1992); 1996: $1,298; 1997: $1,298; 1998: $1,360; 1999: $1,415; 2000: $1,490; 2001: $1,594; 2002: $1,706; 2003: $1,792; 2004: $1,882; 2005: $1,976; 2006: $2,115; 2007: $2,284; 2008: $2,467; 2009: $2,664; 2010: $2,798; 2011: $2,882; 2012: $2,997; 2013: $3,087; 2014: $3,369; eBook: $4,144; renewal: 2014: $3,369.
This set provides detailed guidance to the criminal lawyer on all aspects of criminal defense. Individual chapters are authored by a team of more than 130 experts. **Criminal Defense Techniques** covers all phases of the criminal process from pre-trial motion tactics and techniques to criminal appeals. Included are such topics as bail and pre-trial release, search and seizure, wiretapping, discovery, evidence, direct and cross-examination, opening and closing statements, probation and parole, homicide, obscenity, military proceedings, use of forensic pathology, psychological evidence, behavior modification, the ABA criminal justice standards, and many more. One of the most exhaustive works of its kind in print.

Cost Saving Tips: For substantial savings, consider purchasing a fairly current set on the used lawbook market, where Bender publications sell at deep discounts when available. After purchase, simply avoid purchasing supplements for as long as you are able and based upon changes in the law. When you feel uncomfortable with the currency of the text, purchase another used set. While this set is aimed at techniques, the substance of this work is clearly impacted by the current state of the law as reflected in the statutes and cases. If you understand that this set should be used as the first stage of the research process, you can update the relevant cases and statutes using primary sources, Shepard's Citations, KeyCite, etc. It can also be supplemented by a less exhaustive treatise, or practice, text with annual supplementation. If you do buy the set new, drop the supplementation after the initial year's supplementation has expired and update as stated above. Remember, this is a secondary source and, as such, should not be used as the last word on a given subject. The editorial lag time can be anywhere from 6-8 months by the time you receive a supplement. Even a "current" used set must be used with caution and will not reflect the most recent rulings of the U.S. Supreme Court and lower courts.

Criminal Law Advocacy. Written by Mark J. Kadish et al. with revisions by Matthew Bender editorial staff. New York: Matthew Bender & Co., 1982-date. 7 vols. Looseleaf format or eBook. Periodic supplementation. No CD-ROM or Internet.
Cost: $2.924 (print) (includes annual subscription); renewal: 1995: $792 (price frozen since 1992); 1996: $831; 1997: $831; 1998: $875; 1999: $910; 2000: $910; 2001: $974; 2002: $1,043; 2003: $1,096; 2004: $1,151; 2005: $1,232; 2006: $1,319; 2007: $1,425; 2008: $1,539; 2009: $1,662; 2010: $1,746; 2011: $1,798; 2012: $1,870; 2013: $2,001; 2014: $2,184; eBook: $2,581; renewal: 2014: $2,184.
This seven-volume work is a detailed practitioner's guide to criminal law and practice. Individual volumes deal with: Trial Investigation and Preparation, Guilty Pleas, Trial Proof, Witness Examination (vols. 4 & 5), Argument to the Jury and Jury Selection. It addresses both substantive and procedural aspects of criminal law with examples of testimony, forms, and checklists. Volume one has particularly valuable and detailed discussion of the steps in the criminal process, including a chapter on case management. Other chapters examine discovery techniques, suppression of evidence, motion practice, plea bargaining, constitutional standards for accepting pleas, real evidence, elements of guilt, privileges, objections, operation of the rules of evidence, direct and cross-examination, perjury, successful opening and closing statements, eyewitness identification. Includes examples of arguments for real trials.

Cost Saving Tips: If available, this is an ideal candidate for used purchase given both the substantial purchase and supplementation costs. As with my recommendation on most Matthew Bender sets, you must determine your comfort level with an "outdated" treatise. If you can gain substantial use from the core treatise, regardless of its relative currency, you are in a position to save thousands of dollars on supplementation costs over the life of your legal career. Just make sure you have your own method of updating the material you find in a secondary source such as this. For example, you make like the broader coverage of this set, but use a treatise with annual pocket parts for currency. Also, what other materials do you have in your library which you can use to update the cases or statutes you find relevant on a given issue? If your state and federal annotated statutes are current and you use Shepard's, do you really require the analysis of the secondary source for all recent material? If your aim is to keep this set current, there is no point in buying the used set since it is sold with an annual subscription included. If you do buy it new, let it lapse after the initial subscription period has expired. While both the substantive and procedural aspects of the law are reflected in the periodic supplements, this set has much material which will remain useful regardless of the currency of the set. Print or eBook pricing is identical.

Decof, Leonard. **Art of Advocacy: Opening Statement**. New York: Matthew Bender & Co., 1981-date. 1 vol. Looseleaf format. Also available in paperback edition.
Cost: $430; supplementation: 1997: $103.00 (annual cost frozen since 1993); 1998: $110; 1999: $117; 2000: $125; 2001: $134; 2002: $144; 2003: $152; 2004: $152; 2005: $164l 2006: $184; 2007: $207; 2008: $230; 2009: $255; 2010: $284; 2011: $295; 2012: $330; 2013: $340; 2014: $340.
This comprehensive, one-volume guide provides both novice and experienced trial attorneys with the information necessary to formulate effective opening statements in a variety of personal injury actions. Following the format of other volumes in the Art of Advocacy series, the first two chapters provide an overview of general principles and the law of opening statements. The remainder of the text is devoted to opening statements in over fifty specific types of cases, each accompanied by the author's introduction and expert commentary. Noting that the advocate's approach to openings, and trial advocacy in general, is highly subjective, the author does not hesitate to criticize some of the openings selected for inclusion in this volume. The volume concludes with a collection of capsule opening statements.

The late Leonard Decof was one of this country's leading trial lawyers, with a passion for trial advocacy. A graduate of Yale University and Harvard Law School, he is a former Dean of the International Academy of Trial Lawyers, faculty member at the National Institute for Trial Advocacy, and frequent lecturer at continuing legal education seminars, including those of the Practicing Law Institute, Association of Trial Lawyers of America, and the American Law Institute. He has written extensively on various aspects of trial advocacy, damages, medical malpractice and wrongful death. He is joined by 40 contributing authors who have contributed sample opening statements.

Cost Savings Tips: Trial practice titles like this can be used effectively without subscribing to the updates. Forego the standing order and simply re-purchase it when you feel you would like a more current version.

Derfner, Mary Francis and Arthur D. Wolf. **Court Awarded Attorney Fees.** New York: Matthew Bender & Co., 1983-date. 3 vols. Looseleaf format. Supplemented twice yearly.
Cost: $2,150 (includes annual subscription); annual renewal: 1995: $513 (price frozen since 1992); 1996: $538; 1997: $538; 1998: $565; 1999: $585; 2000: $630; 2001: $674; 2002: $674; 2003: $708; 2004: $725; 2005: $761; 2006: $815; 2007: $880; 2008: $959; 2009: $1,036; 2010: $1,088; 2011: $1,142; 2012: $1,245; 2013: $1,332; 2014: $1,454; CD-ROM: $2,172 (annual subscription); renewal: 1998: $540;1999: $585; 2000: $630; 2001: $674; 2002: $674; 2003: $708; 2004: $725; 2005: $761; 2006: $815; 2007: $880; 2008: $959; 2009: $1,036; 2010: $1,088; 2011: $1,175; 2012: $1,281; 2013: $1,371; 2014: $1,497.36; eBook: $1,955; renewal: 2014: $1,454.
Over the past twenty years, Congress has dramatically expanded the number of attorney fee provisions contained in federal statutes to more than 200, causing an explosion in the number of attorney fee cases in all areas of federal law. These attorney fee statutes provide far greater opportunities for fee recovery than existed in the past--moving beyond such areas as antitrust and securities law to such fields as environmental protection, civil rights, consumer safety, income tax, and energy law. These volumes closely examine the law and procedure governing the awarding of attorney fees in federal courts as well as the application of federal statutes in specific subject areas. This is an exhaustive scholarly work replete with citations to relevant primary and secondary authorities.

Cost Saving Tips: Buy a used set, if available, or buy a new set and let it lapse after the first year.

Easton, Stephen D. **Attacking Adverse Experts**. Chicago: American Bar Association, 2008. 1 vol. (770 pp.). Paperbound.
Cost: $165; $135 to members; from $65.02 on amazon.com (2014).
This is a systematic guide to attacking the credibility of adverse witnesses in civil cases. In the author's view, such witnesses are often not only wrong, and unworthy of respect, but "potentially very dangerous in a system designed to be a search for the truth." His strong views are the product of 15 years of full time practice as a trial attorney and a decade of teaching, researching and writing about the law, with a scholarly focus on expert witnesses. At heart is the tendency of expert witnesses to shape their testimony to please the attorneys who retain them. The 22 chapters in this volume provide a methodology for gathering relevant information, deposing the adverse expert, moving to disqualify the adverse expert, launching he attack, crossing the adverse expert, and finishing the job. In addition to citations to relevant primary and secondary authorities, the text also features checklists, cautions, sample cross-examination questions and answers. Appendices, contained on a companion CD-ROM, include checklists and outlines, charts (of the law of multiple jurisdictions), and outlines (of the law for attorneys in specified jurisdictions). The author is a trial attorney with wide-ranging experience in expert-dominated cases, a law professor, and former U.S. Attorney for the District of North Dakota. In 2006, he received the Richard S. Jacobson Award for excellence in teaching trial advocacy from the Pound Civil Justice Institute.

Erwin, Richard E., et al. **Defense of Drunk Driving Cases: Criminal - Civil**. 3d ed. New York: Matthew Bender, 1971-date. 4 vols. Looseleaf format and eBook.
Cost: $1,950 (includes annual subscription); annual renewal: 1995: $568 (cost frozen since 1992); 1996: $596; 1997: $596; 1998: $630; 1999: $655; 2000: $655; 2001: $701; 2002: $751; 2003: $789; 2004: $828; 2005: $886; 2006: $949; 2007: $1,011; 2008: $1,072; 2009: $1,136; 2010: $1,171; 2011: $1,206; 2012: $1,254; 2013: $1,383; 2014: $1,420; eBook: $1,773; renewal:

2014: $1.383.
An in-depth analysis of the law governing drunk driving and related offenses. Chapters cover double jeopardy, preliminary hearings, penalties, case evaluation, trial procedures and techniques, jury selection, field sobriety tests, examining physicians, physician-patient privilege, chemical tests, blood analysis, the intoximeter and other testing devices, chain of evidence, affirmative defenses, refusal to submit, constitutional objections, implied consent legislation, expert and character witnesses, jury instructions, etc. Also includes a bibliography, index and table of cases. This work is also heavily laced with citations to primary authority, forms and interrogatories. Statutory appendix includes citations and descriptions of drunk driving offenses for all fifty states.

Cost Saving Tip: Buy a used set, if available, or buy a new set and allow it lapse after the first year.

Federal Procedure. Lawyers Edition. St. Paul, MN: West Group (Lawyers Cooperative Publishing Co.), 1981-date. 76 vols. Annual cumulative supplements with periodic revised (recompiled) volumes.
Cost: $10,381; supplementation: 1991: $482; 1992: $491; 1993: $451.50; 1994: $830.80; 1995: $830.80; 1996: $1,081.50; 1997: $858; 1998: $973; 1999: $1,300; 2000: $1,390; 2001: $1,634; 2002: $2,181; 2003: $2,331; 2004: $2,295; 2005: $3,293; 2006: $2,995; 2007: $3,784.50; 2008: $1,396; 2009: $4,190.50; 2010: $4,652; 2011: $4,957.50; 2012: $6,969.50; 2013: $7,414; current volumes: $499 (list). **Monthly Assured Print Price (APP)** (includes new set): $576/$6,912 (2014). Best acquired as a WestlawNext add-on.
An encyclopedic reference which treats all three parts of the federal adjudicatory system: traditional courts, specialized courts, and administrative agencies and their tribunals, in 80 individual chapters contained in 33 volumes. The 80 chapters are divided into two types of coverage; core coverage encompassing general principles of procedure in all three levels of the federal court system; and topical coverage encompassing the application of general and specific procedural rules in specific types of actions or proceedings, e.g., banking and financing, bankruptcy, civil rights, environmental protection, and employment discrimination. The topical chapters cover the specialized courts and administrative agencies to which the specific action applies. This set includes a variety of practice aids, practice pointers, checklists, and law review commentary as well as collateral references to other relevant titles in the Total Client-Service Library, such as **Am. Jur. 2d**, the **ALR** series, **Am. Jur Trials**, **Am. Jur. Proof of Facts**, etc. An excellent choice for the firm heavily involved in practice before federal administrative agencies and courts. However, while the supplementation cost was initially less expensive than that for the competing set from Matthew Bender (**Mezines**), it now exceeds the cost of the Bender set by more than $1,000 per year.

Cost Saving Tip: If you are interested in the base text and do not require supplementation, buy a used set at considerable savings. If this is a set you wish to maintain, however, you are far better off acquiring it as a part of the **Federal Procedure Library** on Westlaw.

Fine, Ralph Adam. **The How-To-Win Trial Manual: Winning Trial Advocacy in a Nutshell**. Rev. 5th ed. Huntington, NY: Juris Publishing, Inc., 2010. 1 vol. (700 pp.). Purchase also includes online access.
Cost: $95; from $80.29 on amazon.com (2014).
According to Ralph Adam Fine, there is no ascertainable and verifiable truth in cases that actually make it to trial, whether civil or criminal. If there were, these cases would either not be brought or would be tossed out on a motion to dismiss or a motion for summary judgment. The same holds true for criminal cases that have not been plea-bargained. Thus, both civil and criminal cases that make it to trial can be won by either side. This volume presents the techniques honed over any years by one of the nation's leading trial advocates and teachers. Its twenty-four chapters provide hundreds of valuable insights into the keys of effective trial advocacy, from the devising of a winning theme, to the tools of persuasion, effective opening arguments, establishing empathy with the jury, the three rules of direct examination, the three rules of cross-examination, the closing argument, and successful voir dire. The author's rules for effective direct and cross-examination are illustrated with examples of testimony drawn from actual civil and criminal cases. Ralph Adam Fine has taught trial advocacy, evidence, and appellate advocacy at more than 100 continuing legal education programs around the country and conducted in-house trial advocacy programs to many law firm litigation departments. Currently a judge on the Wisconsin Court of Appeals, he presided over more than 350 jury trials during his tenure on the Wisconsin circuit court from 1979 to 1988.

Frumer, Louis R. and Melvin I. Friedman. **Personal Injury: Actions, Defenses, Damages.** New York: Matthew Bender & Co., 1957-date. 25 vols. Looseleaf format , CD-ROM and eBook. Supplemented approximately four times annually. Authority CD-ROM includes no-cost online updating via LEXIS-NEXIS.
Cost: $6,857 (includes annual subscription); renewal: 1995: $1,721.50 (price frozen since 1992); 1996: $1,806; 1997: $1806; 1998: $1,805; 1999: $1,880; 2000: $2,120; 2001: $2,268; 2002: $2,427; 2003: $2,549; 2004: $2,676; 2005: $2,863; 2006: $2,078; 2007: $3,216; 2008: $3,505; 2009: $3,785; 2010: $4,220; 2011: $4,172; 2012: $4,339; 2013: $4,643; 2014: $5,068; CD-ROM: $8,195 (annual subscription); renewal: 1998: $1,710; 1999: $1,880; 2000: $2,010; 2001: $2,151; 2002: $2,302; 2003: $2,549; 2004: $2,539; 2005: $2,717; 2006: $2,908; 2007: $3.141; 2008: $3,424; 2009: $3,698; 2010: $4,105; 2011: $4,433; 2012: $4,832; 2013: $5,170; 2014: $5,863.98; eBook: $6,234; renewal: 2014: $5,068.
One of the most impressive titles in Matthew Bender's catalog, this set is a virtual gold mine for the personal injury lawyer. Each of the more than 200 topics treated in this set includes detailed examination of the applicable theories of law together with relevant pleading forms. More than thirty attorneys contributed essays to this exhaustive work and each essay contains extensive citations and annotations to relevant case law. This is one of those works which is unfortunately underutilized because many practicing attorneys, and even law librarians, fail to take full advantage of the full range of its rich resources.

Cost Saving Tips: Buy a used set, if available, or buy a new set and let it lapse after the first year. Matthew Bender also offers this set as a part of the 8-title **Personal Injury Library** at such significant savings that a standing order is recommended as long as the price holds (see your sales representative for details).

General Litigation Treatise Library on LoisLawConnect. New York: Wolters Kluwer Law & Bsuiness.
Cost: $540.00 per year (solo practitioner) (2014).
An invaluable collection of annually updated legal treatises and practice books covering all aspects of the litigation process, including **Deposition Handbook**, **Discovery Practice**, **Electronic Discovery: Law and Practice**, **Evidence: Practice Under the Rules**, **Judgment Enforcement**, **Jury Selection**, **Malingering and Deception in Litigation**, **Motion Practice**, **Sample Voir Dire Questions**, **Witness Preparation**, **Expert Witness Update**, as well as forms and checklists drawn from these titles. An excellent cost-effective alternative to buying these titles individually in print format.

Gershman, Bennett L. **Trial Error and Misconduct**. 2d ed. Charlottesville, VA: LexisNexis, 2007-date. 1 vol. 577 pp.) Annual supplementation anticipated.
Cost: $161; supplementation: 2008: $60; 2009: $70; 2010: $74; 2011: $81; 2012: $87; 2013: $90; 1st ed.: 1999: $45; 2001: $55; 2002: $68; 2003: $71; 2004: $75; 2005: $79; 2006: $83; 2007: new edition.
This volumes addresses what the author terms the "pathologies" of the criminal trial and examines the roles of four key participants in the process: judges, prosecutors, defense lawyers, and juries. Each of these key participants is capable of infecting the trial process by violating the rules of proper trial conduct. These rules of trial conduct are rooted in the Sixth Amendment and the due process clause, supported by the procedural and evidentiary codes, and buttressed by the common law, ethical rules, and individual conscience. The first four chapters provide an in-depth examination of specific actions taken by judge, prosecutor, defense counsel, and jury that may constitute either error or rise to the level of misconduct. Chapter five examines a variety of special issues arising in the context of trial error and misconduct, including permissible and impermissible bolstering of witness credibility, polygraph tests, alibi witnesses, children's testimony, eyewitnesses, spies and stool pigeons, multiple defendants, and experts. Chapter six provides a review of the various means by which error and misconduct are reviewed and remedied, and the standards to be applied by appellate courts in conducting that review. The author, a former prosecutor in the New York State Anti-Corruption Unit and special assistant to the Attorney General, is a Professor of Law, Pace University School of Law.

Gianna, Dominic J. and Alfred S. Julien. **Opening Statements, 2d: Winning in the Beginning by Winning the Beginning.** 2d ed. St. Paul, MN: West (ATLA/Clark Boardman Callaghan), 2004-date. 1 vol. Looseleaf format. Annual supplements.
Cost: 2013-2014 Edition: $127; supplementation: 1993: $57; 1994: $64; 1995: $80; 1996: $108; 1997: $95; 1998: $99.75; 1999: $108; 2000: $116; 2001: $137; 2002: $161; 2003: $161; 2004: $188; 2005: $40; 2006: $44.50; 2007: $44.50; 2008: $55; 2009: 0; 2010: 0; 2011: $107; **Monthly Assured Print Price (APP):** $10/$120.
Authored by a former president of the Association of Trial Lawyers of America and distinguished trial attorney, this guide to opening statements provides the active litigator with excellent guidance in matters related to the law and procedure of constructing and delivering opening statements. The chapters examine such matters as general principles for openings, the law of opening statements, do's and dont's, professional malpractice cases, products liability cases, defending against the criminal charge, defending against the criminal conspiracy charge, defense openings in personal injury cases, defending the target defendant in tort cases, relation of summation to opening, opening against multiple defendants, dealing with the apparently hostile judge, openings in bench trials, and more. An excellent resource for attorney or firm heavily involved in litigation.

Cost Saving Tips: However excellent, this is one of those books which can pretty much stand on its own without the benefit of regular supplementation. Simply treat it as a monograph and purchase a new edition every few years, as you feel it necessary.

Habush, Robert L. **Art of Advocacy: Cross Examination of Non-Medical Experts.** New York: Matthew Bender & Co., 1981-date. 1 vol. Looseleaf format and eBook.
Cost: $430; supplementation: 1997: $103 (annual cost frozen since 1993); 1998: $110; 1999: $117; 2000: $125; 2001: $134; 2002: $144; 2003: $152; 2004: $152; 2005: $164.00; 2006: $184; 2007: $207; 2008: $230; 2009: $255; 2010: $284; 2011: $295; 2012: $328; 2013: $338; 2014: $361.
A comprehensive guide to one of the most difficult aspects of trial advocacy. This volume concentrates its focus on the cross examination of non-medical experts in personal injury cases and includes trial transcripts, legal background, and expert commentaries. Following the format of most of the volumes in the Art of Advocacy series, the first two chapters provide a valuable introduction to the art of cross examination and the applicable law. Thirty-nine additional chapters examine cross examination in a variety of specific factual situations, or examine such general issues as bias, competency, foundation attack, and tests and experiments. The author is a practicing attorney with the Milwaukee firm of Habush, Habush and Davis and has extensive experience as trial advocate, law school teacher, and lecturer before national and state continuing legal education seminars. He is joined by 24 contributing authors.

Cost Savings Tips: Trial practice titles like this can be used effectively without subscribing to the updates. Forego the standing order and simply re-purchase it when you feel you would like a more current version.

Hecht, Henry L. **Effective Depositions**. 2d ed. Chicago: American Bar Association, 2010. 1 vol. (848 pp.). Paperbound.
Cost: $149.95 ($119.95 to members); from $84.77 on amazon.com (2014).
Since the adoption of the **Federal Rules of Civil Procedure** in 1938, and their adoption by the states, the discovery process, and depositions in particular, have been at the heart of dispute resolution. With 98% of disputes resolved prior to trial, it is not surprising that depositions occupy the more important place in the resolution of disputes. This exhaustive collection of 25 articles by Henry Hecht and 18 contributing authors provides illuminating insights into the many stages of the deposition process. The

articles address the role and importance of depositions, discovery methods and planning, securing the attendance of the witness, preparing to take or defend a deposition, meeting the witness, establishing and preserving the attorney-client and work-product privileges, procedural and substantive preparation of the witness, discoverability of documents used to refresh the recollection of the witness, special witness preparation, taking the deposition, using documents at deposition, laying the foundation for documents, defending the deposition, problem counsel and witnesses, expert witnesses, deposition perjury, and much more. The Notes to each chapter provide citations to relevant primary and secondary authorities. The Appendices include a variety of sample documents, forms and checklists designed to simplify the deposition process. The volume also includes a table of cases, and index. This second edition expands upon and updates the edition first published in 1997. Henry L. Hecht is professor of law at University of California, School of Law (Boalt Hall).

Houts, Marshall and Walter Rogosheske. **Art of Advocacy: Appeals.** New York: Matthew Bender & Co., 1987-date. 1 vol. Looseleaf format and eBook.
Cost: $430; supplementation: 1997: $103 (annual cost frozen since 1993); 1998: $110; 1999: $117; 2000: $125; 2001: $134; 2002: $144; 2003: $152; 2004: $152; 2005: $164; 2006: $184; 2007: $207; 2008: $230; 2009: $255; 2010: $284; 2011: $295; 2012: $327; 2013: $337; 2014: $361.
A comprehensive guide to appellate practice in personal injury actions. This volume provides the practicing appellate litigator with an impressive combination of substantive and practical information related to the appeals process, as well as sample briefs, motions, arguments and practice commentary. The book is organized into five major sections: the appeals process, the written argument, oral argument, deciding the case, and, finally, motions, petitions, extraordinary writs and post-decision proceedings. Judge Rogosheske's chapter entitled "How One Appellate Judge "Reads" the Briefs," including a list of "Persuasive DO's" and "Irritating DON'T's," is a must for the appellate advocate. Marshall Houts is the creator of the Trauma series, and author of numerous books on courtroom medicine and Walter Rogosheske is a former Senior Justice of the Minnesota Supreme Court, past Chairman of the ABA Committee on the Prosecution and Defense Functions, and, currently, Distinguished Lawyer in Residence, University of Minnesota Law School where he teaches trial jurisprudence and appellate jurisprudence.

Cost Savings Tips: Trial practice titles like this can be used effectively without subscribing to the updates. Forego the standing order and simply re-purchase it when you feel you would like a more current version.

Houts, Marshall. **Art of Advocacy: Cross Examination of Medical Experts.** New York: Matthew Bender & Co., 1982-date. 1 vol. Looseleaf format and eBook.
Cost: $392; supplementation: 1997: $103 (annual cost frozen since 1993); 1998: $110; 1999: $117; 2000: $125; 2001: $134; 2002: $144; 2003: $152; 2004: $152; 2005: $164; 2006: $184; 2007: $207; 2008: $226; 2009: $246; 2010: $274; 2011: $275; 2012: $307; 2013: $317; 2014: $325.
A rich and detailed compendium of valuable information prepared to assist the trial lawyer in conducting cross examination of medical experts in personal injury cases. Following chapters that orient the attorney to general principles of cross examination and the applicable law, the bulk of the volume consists of trial transcripts with sample cross examinations in 25 specific personal injury actions accompanied by the author's commentary. The concluding portion of the book is devoted to "Models of Winning Cross Examination. A valuable addition to the library of any trial advocate. Marshall Houts is the creator of the Trauma series, and author of numerous books on courtroom medicine. Walter Rogosheske is a former Senior Justice of the Minnesota Supreme Court, past Chairman of the ABA Committee on the Prosecution and Defense Functions, and, currently, Distinguished Lawyer in Residence, University of Minnesota Law School where he teaches trial jurisprudence and appellate jurisprudence.

Cost Savings Tips: Trial practice titles like this can be used effectively without subscribing to the updates. Treat them as monographs. Forego the standing order and simply re-purchase it when you feel you feel the need for a more current version.

Hunter, Robert S. **Federal Trial Handbook--Civil.** 4th ed. St. Paul, MN: Thomson West 2005-date. 2 vols. Annual replacement pamphlets or ProView eBook.
Cost: 2013 Edition: $386; 2011 Edition: $305; prior editions: 2004: $157.00; 2005: $175; 2006: $110.50; 2008: $149; 2009: $168; 3d ed.: 1994: $40.00; 1995: $44.75; 1996: $70.00; 1997: $79.00; 1998: $64.00; 1999: $69.00; 2000: $73.00; 2001: $84.00; 2002: $99.00; 2003: new edition; **Monthly Assured Print Price (APP):** $29/$348 (2013).
Unlike the exhaustive scholarly treatments of Federal law and practice, this trial practice guide is intended as a quick, yet comprehensive reference to the law on the myriad of questions that may arise in the course of a trial in Federal court. The 4th edition has been converted into separate volumes for civil and criminal practice. The author covers topics ranging from evidence and procedure, attorney conduct, motions to jury trials, burden of proof, witnesses, evidence, judicial notice and damages. The text is supported by references to supporting case and statutory law, and includes such Lawyers Cooperative features as references to relevant Annotations in ALR, trial practice aids such as Am. Jur. Trials and Proof of Facts, and practice checklists. A well-written and nicely organized practice tool, particularly when one desires a quick answer to a question involving federal practice. Formerly published as a two-volume set covering both civil and criminal motions.

Hunter, Robert S. **Federal Trial Handbook--Criminal.** 4th ed. St. Paul, MN: Thomson West, 2005-date. 2 vols. Annual replacement pamphlets and ProView eBook.
Cost: 2013-2014 Edition: $388; 2011-2012 Edition: $356; **Monthly Assured Print Price (APP):** $32/$384 (2014).
A handy courtroom reference to the federal criminal rules intended for use by both prosecutors and defense counsel. Includes guidance on motions at every stage of the trial process.

Kimberling, John F. **How To Try a Jury Case: Trial Tactics.** South Bend, IN: National Institute for Trial Advocacy, 2007. 1 vol. (224 pp.).
Cost: $65; from $45.00 on amazon.com (2014).
This brief and clearly written introduction to the process of conducting a jury trial provides expert guidance on such topics as trial preparation, commencement of the trial, voir dire, the opening statement, direct examination of witnesses, cross-examination of witnesses, rehabilitation of your witnesses, the expert witness, and the closing argument. The author, who brings more than 40 years experience in business and personal injury litigation, is a Fellow of the American College of Trial Lawyers and has taught trial tactics at Indiana University School of Law.

Lane, Fred and Irving Goldstein. **Lane Goldstein Trial Technique.** 3d ed. St. Paul, MN: West (Clark Boardman Callaghan), 1984-date. 4 vols. Looseleaf format. Annual supplementation.
Cost: $1,923; ProView eBook: $1,764; supplementation: 1993: $102; 1994: $125; 1995: $211; 1996: $220; 1997: $250; 1998: $250; 1999: $270; 2000: $293; 2001: $346; 2002: $405; 2003: $462; 2004: $517; 2005: $530; 2006: $729; 2007: $729; 2008: $812.50; 2009: $931; 2010: $1,038; 2011: $1,116; 2012: $1,216; 2013: $1,761; **Monthly Assured Print Price (APP):** $129/$1,548.
This work had its origins in Judge Irving Goldstein's long association with the Trial Technique Institute in Chicago where he taught for many years. The first edition was Judge Goldstein's attempt to provide attorneys with a practical compendium of the procedures and techniques necessary for successful litigation. Fred Lane, a practicing attorney with the firm of Lane & Munday, is Dean of the Trial Technique Institute and past-President of the Illinois Bar Association, began teaching at the Institute with Judge Goldstein in the early 1960's. Consequently, this work reflects the experience of attorneys from every jurisdiction in the country who have studied at the Institute over the years. This is a well-organized and highly readable work of a length which properly balances the need for completeness with the requirements of economy. It covers each stage of the litigation process, from trial preparation to appellate practice. The text, which addresses both substantive and procedural matters, is supplemented with pleading forms, sample trial questions, questionnaires, memoranda of law, opening and closing statements. There are adequate, but overpowering, citations to primary law and secondary sources. Where appropriate, the author cites to case law from both the U.S. courts and individual states. An excellent and highly recommended resource for the trial attorney. Purportedly, one of the best selling practice books on the market .

Cost Saving Tips: Depending upon the use you are likely to make of the supplementary material, you can cancel your standing order and buy the cumulative supplements in alternative years, or even less frequently. This depends upon whether you hope to rely on this work for the latest analysis and case citations or merely as a starting place in the research process.

Lane, Fred and David A. Birnbaum. **Lane Medical Litigation Guide.** St. Paul, MN: Thomson Reuters West (Clark Boardman Callaghan), 1981-date. 5 vols. Looseleaf format. Supplemented twice annually.
Cost: $2,405; supplementation: 1993: $213; 1994: $285; 1995: $150; 1996: $475; 1997: $510; 1998: $500; 1999: $297; 2000: $321; 2001: $378; 2002: $886; 2003: $600; 2004: $672; 2005: $726; 2006: $513; 2007: $914; 2008: $1,019; 2009: $1,164; 2010: $1,280; 2011: $1,395; 2012: $1,521; 2013: $1,658; **Monthly Assured Print Price (APP):** $175/$2,100.
This fairly comprehensive overview of medico-legal issues was authored by a trial lawyer with more than 30 years experience, most of it involving medical matters. As a co-author of **Goldstein Trial Technique** and an editor of **Medical Trial Technique Quarterly,** Fred Lane has assembled a useful collection of information to guide the practicing attorney through the complete litigation process, from the client interview through the trial itself. The set is organized into five main subdivisions reflecting the questions that arise most frequently in the course of a legal practice: hospital and health care personnel; medical evidence; medical techniques and special procedures; sections of the body and their disorders; and human systems, systemic disorders and traumatic injuries. The set also includes illustrations of trial techniques and representative awards and settlements arranged by type of injury or medical problem. The medical information is kept current by members of the publisher's Medical Advisory Board consisting of more than twenty members of the medical profession. Additional features include a glossary of medical terms, cross-references to **Goldstein Trial Technique**, a bibliography, table of anatomical drawings, and index. Heavily documented with citations to cases and statutes from all jurisdictions. An excellent, concise reference tool for the attorney engaged in a variety of legal matters involving medical issues.

Cost Saving Tip: Drop your standing order and re-purchase as needed to avoid costly and unnecessary supplementation. While this set provides useful guidance to the attorney involved in medical litigation, it does not replace the need for medical experts and access to the appropriate medical literature.

Levy, Herbert Monte. **How To Handle an Appeal**. 4th ed. New York: Practising Law Institute, 1999-date. 1 vol. Looseleaf format. Annual supplementation anticipated.
Cost: $195; supplementation: 2001: $74.25; 2002: $84.50; 2003: $94; 2004: $104; 2005: $114; 2006: $91; 2007: $109; 2008: $109; 2009: $139; 2010: $150; 2011: $154; 2012: $160; 2013: $185.
A comprehensive guide to the appellate process by an attorney experienced in both trial and appellate work. The author covers the full range of topics related to the appellate process, including the preservation of points for appeal, relations with other counsel, fees, technical problems on appeals. perfecting the appeal, the appellate brief, relations with clients and other attorneys, oral argument, the decision, and practical suggestions for practice in the U.S. Courts of Appeals and U.S. Supreme Court. The appendices include a checklist for appellate practice, **forms**, sample briefs, the Federal Rules of Appellate Procedure, the Rules of the Supreme Court of the United States, and rules on typeface, type style, and type volume. The author provides a lucid and practical approach to appellate procedure free of excessive citations to cases and statutes.

Lipson, Ashley S. **Art of Advocacy: Demonstrative Evidence**. New York: Matthew Bender & Co., 1988-date. 1 vol. Looseleaf format and eBook.
Cost: $430; supplementation: 1998: $110 (annual cost frozen since 1993); 1999: $117; 2000: $125; 2001: $134; 2002: $144; 2003: $152; 2004: $152; 2005: $164; 2006: $184; 2007: $207; 2008: $230; 2009: $255; 2010: $284; 2011; $295; 2012: $330; 2013: $340; 2014: $350.
A guide to the use of demonstrative evidence in personal injury cases. It addresses the technical and practical problems related to the obtaining and handling of demonstrative exhibits, as well as the legal principles involved
in the use, admissibility and opposition of a wide variety of demonstrative presentations. The volume includes sample testimony, arguments, charts, diagrams, and illustrations.

Cost Savings Tips: Trial practice titles like this can be used effectively without subscribing to the updates. Forego the standing order and simply re-purchase it when you feel you would like a more current version.

Lipson, Ashley S. **Art of Advocacy: Documentary Evidence**. New York Matthew Bender & Co., 1988-date. 1 vol. Looseleaf format and eBook.
Cost: $426; supplementation: 1998: $110 (annual cost frozen since 1993); 1999: $117; 2000: $125; 2001: $134; 2002: $144; 2003: $152; 2004: $152; 2005: $164; 2006: $184; 2007: $205; 2008: $228; 2009: $253; 2010: $281; 2011: $293; 2012: $333; 2013: $343; 2014: $353.
A detailed guide designed to aid the practitioner «determine, accumulate, assemble, store, use and retrieve documentary evidence,» particularly in personal injury cases. The substantive text is accompanied by numerous examples of the types of materials likely to be encountered by the trial attorney. The chapters cover the document's physical form; forged and altered documents; determining documentary requirements; retrieval from clients and third parties; retrieval from the opposition; managing, handling and storing documents; the uniform document indexing system, evidence, use of documents at trial, use at mediations and arbitrations; medical and hospital records; technical reports; documents, computers & litigation; document reduction and disposal; medical malpractice; use in automobile negligence cases; use in products liability cases, use in premises liability cases, use in workers' compensation cases. The volume also includes a bibliography, glossary of technical terms, and subject index. The author, a managing partner in the Michigan firm of Coleman, Lipson and Bradford, has written extensively on various aspects of documentary evidence.

Cost Savings Tips: Trial practice titles like this can be used effectively without subscribing to the updates. Forego the standing order and simply re-purchase it when you feel you would like a more current version.

MacCarthy, Terence. **MacCarthy on Cross-Examination**. Chicago: American Bar Association, 2007. 1 vol. (221pp.).
Cost: $129.95 ($99.95 to members); from $75.42 on amazon.com (2014).
An incisive guide to cross-examination by one the country's leading practitioners and CLE instructors. MacCarthy's contention is that lawyers are far more skilled in opening and closing arguments because they can control the story. He argues that these same story-telling skills can also be applied to cross-examination, even when the witness is not cooperating. Among these techniques are looking good, telling and story, and using short statements, techniques designed to minimize the witness's input without appearing overly controlling, extracting, or insulting. He uses many examples drawn from his 40 years as head of the Federal Defender's Office in Chicago.

Mauet, Thomas. **Trial Techniques**. 9th ed. New York: Wolters Kluwer Law & Business, 2013. 1 vol. Paperbound. No supplementation except new editions.
Cost: 2013 Edition: $132; from $91.89 on amazon.com; kindle: $105.43 (2014).
Thomas Mauet has a singular ability to effectively communicate the essential ingredients of effective trial advocacy. This comprehensive and clearly written guide operates on the assumption that effective trial advocates have both the ability to analyze and prepare cases and the technical skills necessary to present their side effectively during trial. Each stage in the process of trial preparation and advocacy is laid out clearly and succinctly, beginning with an introduction to the trial process and proceeding through jury selection, opening statements, direct examination, exhibits, cross-examination, experts, closing arguments, objections, and trial preparation and strategy. Each area under discussion is accompanied by real-life examples, exhibits, checklists, and sample questions. Although the author's discussion is aimed primarily at the presentation of a jury trial, his techniques are equally applicable to bench trials. An excellent and reasonably-priced resource for both the law student and the seasoned trial advocate. Thomas Mauet is Director of Trial Advocacy and Professor of Law, University of Arizona.

Miller, Henry G. **Art of Advocacy: Settlement**. New York: Matthew Bender & Co., 1983-date. 1 vol. Looseleaf format and eBook.
Cost: $430; supplementation: 1997: $103 (annual cost frozen since 1993); 1998: $110; 1999; $117; 2000: $125; 2001: $134; 2002: $144; 2003: $152; 2004: $152; 2005: $164; 2006: $184; 2007: $207; 2008: $230; 2009: $255; 2010: $284; 2011: $295; 2012: $330; 2013: $330; 2014: $330.
This is a comprehensive guide to the settlement of personal injury cases. The author, an experienced trial lawyer with the firm of Clark, Gigliardi & Miller of White Plains, New York is a Past President of the New York Bar Association and Director of the New York State Trial Lawyers Association. His philosophy of settlement is predicated on the notion that it takes a good trial lawyer to be a good settler. Courtroom veterans "will find you out if you only come to settle," he argues. He suggests that are no definitive rules or formulas for settlement. It is more art than science, requiring good judgment. The individual chapters are both general and specific. There are general chapters examining such topics as the wisdom of settlement, impediments, dealing with your client, evaluating the case, bargaining, dealing with insurance companies, and settlement techniques. Specific chapters cover settlement in products liability and medical malpractice cases. The chapter on structured settlement,

written by Richard G. Halpern, is laced with specific examples. The volume also examines the law of settlement, including bad faith, the attorney's role in settlement negotiations, Mary Carter agreements, the partial settlement, documents of settlement, and the ethics of settlement, concluding with the author's "Ten Commandments of Settlement." This volume is accompanied by **Present Value and Total Payout Tables,** also by Richard G. Halpern, a valuable pamphlet which explains the calculation of present values and the approximation of the present value of a future income stream, together with present value and total payout tables. These can be of significant benefit to those handling personal injury and wrongful death actions.

Cost Savings Tips: Trial practice titles like this can be used effectively without subscribing to the updates. Forego the standing order and simply re-purchase it when you feel you would like a more current version.

Miltz, Arthur Ian. **Art of Advocacy: Discovery**. New York: Matthew Bender & Co., 1982-date. 1 vol. Looseleaf format and eBook.
Cost: $430; supplementation: 1997: $103 (annual cost frozen since 1993); 1998: $110; 1999: $117; 2000: $125; 2001: $134; 2002: $144; 2003: $152; 2004: $152; 2005: $164; 2006: $184; 2007: $207; 2008: $230; 2009: $255; 2010: $284; 2011: $295; 2012: $330; 2013: $340; 2014: $364.
A comprehensive examination of what is generally the longest phases of the litigation process. This one-volume guide includes transcripts, interrogatories, requests for admission, combined discovery demands, legal background and practice commentary to aid the trial advocate in conducting discovery in personal injury actions. An overview of the discovery process and the applicable law is followed by sample depositions in more than forty specific personal injury actions, each of which is accompanied by expert commentary by the author. Arthur Miltz is a Certified Civil Trial Attorney with the Livingston, New Jersey firm of Miltz and Sklaw, an author, and frequent lecturer at bar association and other professional seminars. He is joined by 15 contributing authors.

Cost Savings Tips: Trial practice titles like this can be used effectively without subscribing to the updates. Forego the standing order and simply re-purchase it when you feel you would like a more current version.

Motions in Federal Court. 3d ed. St. Paul, MN: West (Clark Boardman Callaghan), 1996-date. 3 vols. (1,800 pp.). Supplemented with twice annual pocket parts.
Cost: $517; ProView eBook: $427; supplementation: 1997: $50; 1998: $56; 1999: $60; 2000: $64; 2001: $37.50; 2002: $82.50; 2003: $93; 2004: $103.50; 2005: $114; 2006: $126; 2007: $141; 2008: $86.50; 2009: $122; 2010: $132; 2011: $132; 2012: $146; 2013: $153; **Monthly Assured Print Price (APP):** $33/$396.
This three-volume reference tool provides discussion and analysis of 129 of the most commonly used motions under the Federal Rules of Civil Procedure. It also includes checklists to guide the practitioner through the process of drafting, serving and filing motions in the federal courts. There are also explanations of the reasons for using each motion, the best time to file the motions, the factors employed by the courts in ruling upon the motions. Also explained are the grounds upon which the court is likely to grant or deny the motions as well as their appealability. The set is enhanced by a number of practice aids, including answers to motion questions, summaries of relevant Supreme Court decisions, and Research Guides to sources for further research. Originally prepared by the editorial staff of Shepard's/ McGraw-Hill, this book was taken over by Clark Boardman Callaghan in December, 1995.

Newberg, Herbert B. and Alba Conte. **Newberg on Class Actions**. 4th-5th ed. St. Paul, MN: West Group (Shepard's/ McGraw-Hill/Lawyers Cooperative), 2002-date. 11 vols. Looseleaf (pamphlet) format. Annual supplementation.
Cost: $1,823; supplementation: 1996: $200; 1997: $130; 1998: $272; 1999: $294; 2000: $317.50; 2001: $376; 2002: 376; 2003: $274.50; 2004: $307.75; 2005: $181; 2006: $206; 2007: $417; 2008: $465; 2009: $525; 2010: $557.50; 2011: $741.50; 2012: $861.50; 2013: $657; **Monthly Assured Print Price (APP):** $100/$1,200.
Class actions are a means whereby individuals with similar claims against a defendant can be joined together to prosecute their claims in a more efficient manner. In order to initiate a class action, one of these parties, whose claims are typical of the of the other members of the class, must agree to serve as the class representative and be approved by the court. Newberg is the premier work on the law and conduct of class actions. Designed as both a theoretical and practical reference, the book's chapters are organized into three broad sections: theory and basic requirements of class actions, general application of Rule 23, and application in specific areas. The chapters examine such topics as mass tort litigation, Chapter 11 proceedings, antitrust, employment discrimination, and other types of class actions issues. Originally published by Shepard's/McGraw-Hill, this work was purchased by the Thomson Corporation in December 1995. It was added to the West Group product line following Thomson's acquisition of West Publishing in 1996.

Nolan, Kenneth P. **A Streetwise Guide to Litigation**. Chicago: American Bar Association, 2013. 1 vol. (205 pp.). Paperbound.
Cost: $59.95; from $35.36 on amazon.com (2014).
This collection of articles originally penned for **Litigation**, the organ of the ABA's Section of Litigation, reflects the author's career experiences as a litigator in matters both big and small, simple and complex, and the specific aspects of the process. His observations are the kinds of things they don't teach in the typical law school curriculum, with its overriding focus on case law analysis, and which may often be gained only after lengthy, or painful, experience. The author is a specialist in personal injury and wrong death actions, but has also litigated cases in the areas of aviation, medical malpractice, construction, the automotive industry, and contract law. Laced with insight, humor, compassion, common sense and wisdom, these articles reflect the perspective of a lawyer with a passion for litigation, despite its physical and mental and emotional demands, and the often mundane and tedious nature of the work. Revealingly, his first courtroom experience handling an eviction case demonstrated for him early on the disconnect between legal education and real life. Cases were never cited, the law rarely cited. The book is divided into three parts: (1) Opening Thoughts, with articles

on The Basics, To Young Lawyers, Getting Business, and The Courthouse; (2) Handing a Case, with articles on judge or jury, depositions, settlement negotiations, jury selection, opening statements, direct and cross examination, closing argument, my first trial, the client's suffering. 9/11 and Victim Compensation Fund; and (3) A Trial Lawyers Life, with articles exploring the practical side of litigation. This book is an entertaining and insightful examination of the varied sides of life as a trial litigator. Kenneth Nolan is a graduate of Brooklyn Law School, past editor-in-chief of **Litigation**, and, now, senior editor of its "Sidebar" columns. His has litigated many high profile aviation cases, including the Korean Air shootdown in 1983 , the TWA Flight 800 explosion in 1996, and the Colgan Air crash near Buffalo in 2009.

North, Steven E. and Francis A. C. Sevier. **Deposition Law and Strategy**. Huntington, NY: Juris Publishing, 2002. 1 vol. (various pagings).
Cost: $175; no supplementation to date (2014).
As a part of the overall discovery process, the deposition is a form of evidence in which litigants obtain information from each other under oath and recorded for use in court at a later date. The procedure for taking depositions is set forth in Rule 30 of the Federal Rules of Civil Procedure and corresponding provisions in the rules governing state courts. Part one of this volume addresses the various aspects of deposition strategy, including pre-deposition considerations, the conduct of the deposition, defending at the deposition, post-deposition strategies, and illustrative forms of deposition strategy featuring three complete depositions with commentary. Part two looks at the law governing depositions upon oral examinations, written questions, the use of depositions in court proceedings, the perpetuation of testimony by court proceedings, persons before whom depositions may be taken, stipulations regarding discovery procedure, and forms for deposition motion practice. A companion 3.5" diskette contains 99 sample forms. Steven E. North specializes in civil trial practice, particularly medical malpractice, personal injury and tort litigation, and is the author of North's Ninety-Nine Pointers on Advanced Deposition Practices,» and numerous articles relating to medical malpractice and other tort actions. He is a faculty advisor at the Cardozo School of Law in New York. Francis Sevier is highly experienced trial attorney who has served as counsel in more than 300 jury trials. Formerly an adjunct professor at the University of Miami School of Law, he has also lectured widely at conferences and medical society meetings, and continuing legal education programs.

O'Malley, Kevin E., et al. **Federal Jury Practice and Instructions--Civil and Criminal.** 5th/6th ed. St. Paul, MN: Thomson Reuters West, 1999-date. 26 vols. A full set consists of volumes 1, 1A of the 6th ed. and volumes 2, 2A, 2B, 3, 3A, 3B, 3C of the 5th edition. Annual pocket parts. Package includes 12 circuit-specific pattern jury instruction pamphlets. [formerly Devitt and Blackmar]
Cost: $1,259; supplementation: 1994: $47; 1995: $52.50; 1996: $59; 1997: $119; 1998: $75; 1999: $90.50; 2000: $81; 2001: $366; 2002: $139.50; 2003: $159; 2004: $178; 2005: $196.50; 2006: $305; 2007: $243.50; 2008: $538.50; 2009: $481; 2010: $529; 2011: $578; 2012: $1,222; 2013: $909; **Monthly Assured Print Price (APP):** $79/$948.
Judges of the federal district courts have an obligation to instruct the jury as to the law of the case and provide reasonable guidance on the accompanying facts. This of one of the most important functions performed by the trial justice. While the judge has wide discretion in instructing the jury, he or she must observe Civil Rule 51 and Criminal 30 governing jury instruction procedure. Counsel in federal cases may, under the rules, submit requests for instructions at the close of evidence or when the court directs. The court must also advise counsel of proposed action upon these requests prior to closing arguments to the jury in order to allow them to tailor their remarks to the judge's instructions. This four-volume set provides both a discussion of the federal jury practice and instructions, and specific pattern or model instructions in a wide variety of civil and criminal matters. Each pattern instruction is accompanied by a discussion of relevant case law supporting the use of the instruction with numerous specific examples from the various federal circuits. The authors includes Judge William Lee (vol. 1), Kevin E. O'Malley (vols. 1A, 2, 2A), and Jay Grenig (vols. 3, 3A). Critical terms are clearly defined, again with examples of definitions applied in the federal courts. The free-standing supplement contains tables of cases and statutes, subject index, and a WESTLAW Electronic Research Guide to jury instructions. An indispensable resource for the federal litigator.

Osowski, Beth Driscoll. **Trial Preparation Tools**. Costa Mesa, CA: James Publishing, 2009. 1 vol. (various pagings). Looseleaf format. Includes companion CD-ROM.
Cost: $99 (2014).
The focus of this trial preparation manual is on the last 120 days before trial. It presents, in a well-organized and clearly written text, the primary considerations that should engage the attorney as he or she gets ready for trial. Beginning with a review of the case file, the elements-of-proof rubric, and trial logs and checklists, the author goes on to discuss the trial noteBook, gaps in the discovery and investigation process, strategies, themes, funding, jury considerations, alternative dispute resolution and settlement, pretrial submissions and conferences, jury selection, the opening statement, testimonial and documentary evidence, demonstrative evidence and tools, the closing argument, deliberations, verdict, judgment, and post-trial activities. The volume is replete with practice tips, forms, interrogatories, checklists, charts, and illustrations. A companion CD-ROM provides the complete searchable text of the book, including all 130 forms. The author, who received her Doctorate with Distinction from the University of North Dakota School of Law, maintains a civil practice in the State of Wisconsin. She has presented many legal seminars and written dozens of outlines for continuing legal education courses. As with all James Publishing books, this title is noteworthy for its clarity of exposition, easy-to-use format, numerous practice aides, and reasonable initial and supplementation costs.

Personal Injury Valuation Handbooks. St. Paul: Thomson West (LRP), 1964-date. 9 vols. Looseleaf format. Individual pamphlets replaced as necessary.
Cost: $1,075.04 per year; **Monthly Assured Print Price (APP):** $97.92/$1,175.04 (2014).
This service up-to-date coverage of personal injury verdicts

organized by part of the anatomy. Individual entries summarize the case and provide the following data: court, attorneys, final demand, final offer, total verdict, compensatory damages, past medical expense claimed, filing date, and trial date. There are also pamphlets covering current award trends, and pamphlets for individual states which can be purchased as an add-ons. The most complete service of its kind for tracking jury verdicts by injury.

Pope, Daniel J. and Mark Dombroff. **Trial Objections**. 2d ed. Santa Ana, CA: James Publishing, 1995-date. 1 vol. (various pagings). Looseleaf format. Annual supplementation.
Cost: $99; supplementation: 2000-2013: $59.99 per year.
A briefcase-sized reference containing statements of the most common objections likely to be employed in court. Each objection is accompanied by comments, tactics, responses, , foundations, and summaries of relevant state and federal cases. The text is also spiced throughout with valuable practice tips. Originally authored by Mark A. Dombroff, Managing Partner of the Washington, DC office of Katten Muchin Zavis & Dombroff, and a former Director of the Torts Division, Civil Division of the Department of Justice. The second edition was prepared by Daniel J. Pope, a partner in the Chicago firm of Bell, Boyd & Lloyd.

Read, D. Shane. **Winning at Trial**. South Bend, IN: National Institute for Trial Advocacy, 2007. 1 vol. (425 pp.).
Cost: $75; from $58 on amazon.com (2014).
The National Institute of Trial Advocacy, a nonprofit institute dedicated to the development of a professionally responsible trial bar, provides learning-by-doing seminars and over 180 legal publications covering all phases of litigation, including pretrial preparation, discovery, evidence, ADR, courtroom technology, trials, and appeals. The aim of this book is to teach trial advocacy skills by analyzing noteworthy civil and criminal trials and incorporating the trial techniques as applied in the courtroom. This process is applied to trial strategies and basics, voir dire, opening statements, direct examination, cross-examination, closing arguments, and exhibits and objections. The text includes numerous examples drawn from real life trials, including checklists, sample voir dire, sample questions and answers, and arguments. The book includes two companion DVDs containing footage of trial techniques employed in the O. J. Simpson criminal trial. The author is a graduate of Yale University and the University of Texas School of Law. As a member of firm of Akin Gump in Dallas and the U.S. Attorney's Office, he has served as lead counsel in numerous civil and criminal trials since 1989.

Rychlak, Ronald J. **Real and Demonstrative Evidence: A Real World Practice Manual for Winning at Trial**. 3rd ed. Huntington, NY: Juris Publishing, 2013. 1 vol. (779 pp.). Print or eBook.
Cost: $125.00 (print or eBook); from $115.00 on amazon.com (2014).
This is more than a book about demonstrative evidence, but a book about effective trial technique that illustrates the effective use of demonstrative evidence and the kind of modern technologies that bring that evidence to the attention of triers of fact. The modern era of demonstrative evidence is said to have emerged with the publication of the first edition of **McCormick on Evidence** in 1940. With the passage of time, it has becaome essential for counsel to employ physical evidence and visual aids to make an effective and credible case to a judge or jury. The author effectively explains basic trial procedure and strategy, including such matters as common objections, chain of custody examples, laying the foundation, and a checklist for expert deposition. The third edition of this treatise reflects the expanding role technology has had on the presentation of demonstrative evidence in the courtroom. He also deals with real and demonstrative evidence away from trial, laying the foundation for the introduction of evidence, objections, handling exhibits in the courtroom, real evidence at trial, photographic evidence, audio recordings, diagrams, drawings, maps, charts and graphs, models, reenactments, demonstrations and experiments, animations or other computer-generated evidence, documents, new scientific evidence, working with expert witnesses, and remote sensing and satellite imaging. The text is augmented with sample testimony, checklists, and citations to relevant primary and secondary authorities. The appendices include a selected bibliography, Federal Rules of Evidence (amended to Dec. 1, 2011), examples of real and demonstrative evidence, table of cases, and index. Ronald J. Rychlak is Mississippi Defense Lawyers Association Professor of Law at the University of Mississippi where he has taught since 1987. Page for page, this is arguably the best single-volume work on demonstrative evidence on the market. It is a far better value than Lipson's **Art of Advocacy: Demonstrative Evidence**, which not only costs far more ($430.00), but is paired with costly annual supplementation ($350.00 in 2014). In a legal publishing environment dominated by mega-publishers out to extract every last dollar from customers, Juris Publishing is proof that quality legal publications can be produced at reasonable prices.

Sand, Leonard B. et al. **Modern Federal Jury Instructions.** New York: Matthew Bender & Co., 1984-date. 5 vols. Looseleaf format. Supplemented several times annually (24 times between 1984 and 1995). Also on CD-ROM and eBook.
Cost: $2,321 (with annual subscription); renewal: 1995: $633.50 (price frozen since 1992); 1996: $664; 1997: $664; 1998: $700; 1999: $730; 2000: $750; 2001: $803. 2002: $860; 2003: $903; 2004: $975; 2005: $1,034; 2006: $1,076; 2007: $1,141; 2008: 2008: $1,209; 2009: $1,306; 2010: $1,371; 2011: $1,440; 2012: $1,526; 2013: $1,633; 2014: $1,782; CD-ROM: $2,656; renewal: 1998: $665; 1999: $730; 2000: $780; 2001: $835; 2002: $860; 2003: $903; 2004: $975; 2005: $1,043.00; 2006: $1,085.00; 2007: $1,171; 2008: $1,271; 2009: $1,373; 2010: $1,469; 2011: $1,578; 2012: $1,730; 2013: $1,851; 2014: $2,060.40; eBook: $2,110; renewal: 2013: $1,633; 2014: $1,782.
Intended primarily for the use of attorneys who must prepare requests to charge a jury, and judges who must read and consider these requests, this set provides a wide variety of both criminal and civil pattern jury instructions. Borrowing heavily from other published sources, the text of each of the instructions is accompanied by relevant case authorities and a succinct commentary which is designed to inform and instruct the user in the legal issues involved. According to the authors, each recommended charge satisfies the following criteria: (1) it is an accurate statement of the law; (2) it is expressed in language

which is comprehensible to the lay juror; and (3) it is as brief as the two criteria will permit. More than just a collection of pattern jury instructions, this reference work provides practitioners with a considered statement of each element in a civil or criminal proceeding which must be proven or disproven at trial. It is also useful to attorneys who must evaluate the probable success of a given case and those who need to determine the elements of a particular cause of action which should be alleged in a particular case. The cases cited under the authority headings provide notice to those interested in tracking trends in the various federal circuits. Includes five numbered volumes (1, 1A, 2, 3, 4) and two paperbound volumes, published periodically, containing pattern jury instructions in civil and criminal matters from the 5th, 6th, 7th, 8th, 9th and 11th circuits and the Federal Judicial Center. A well-organized and lucid reference tool. The instructions are comprehensive and the commentaries clear and concise. The most thorough work of its kind on the market.

Cost Saving Tips: Buy a used set, if available, or buy a new set and let it lapse after the first year.

Sandler, Paul Mark. **Anatomy of a Trial: A Handbook for Young Lawyers**. Chicago: American Bar Association, 2011. 1 vol. (393 pp.). Paperbound.
Cost: $99.95; from $52.95 on amazon.com (2014).
A defining legal phenomenon of the past fifty years has been the dramatic decline in the percentage of cases going to trial. In the U.S. district courts, for example, the number of civil cases going to trial has dropped from 11.5% in 1962 to 1.2% in 2010. This phenomenon has made it more difficult for young attorneys to gain necessary litigation experience. Yet, handling one's first jury trial is a major rite of passage for every young lawyer. This estimable volume guides the novice attorney through each stage of the jury trial from voir dire, opening statement, direct examination, cross-examination, and closing argument. This volume moves beyond litigation theory to a detailed examination the practical aspects of trial work informed by the author's years of experience as a litigator, supplemented by incisive contributions from five seasoned trial court judges. The author addresses these areas in the context of two particular cases, including one civil case and one criminal case. The text is enhanced with numerous examples of real-life courtroom testimony and nine sample opening and closing statements in two high-profile cases: U.S. v. Rosen, and Maffei v. Smedley, M.D. Paul Mark Sandler is chair of the trial department at the Baltimore firm of Shapiro, Sher Guinot and Sandler, a fellow of the American College of Trial Lawyers, and author and co-author of numerous books on courtroom advocacy.

Sandler, Paul Mark and James K. Archibald. **Model Witness Examinations**. 3d ed. Chicago: American Bar Association, 2010. 1 vol. (297 pp.). Paperbound.
Cost: $79.95 ($63.95 to members); from $34.99 on amazon.com (2014).
The process of effectively eliciting facts from witnesses at trial is a skill generally honed over years of courtroom experience. This concise handbook streamlines the learning process with 70 model examinations that demonstrate how to offer testimony on direct examination, how to cross-examine and impeach various types of witnesses, and how to use discovery in the examination of witnesses. The time-tested model witness examinations presented here illustrate how to elicit information in a variety of circumstances or contexts. Part 1 is aimed at eliciting facts during direct examination, including those involving recollections; documents; best evidence or original document problems; demonstrative and real evidence; opinions of the lay witness; opinions of the expert; character, habit and custom; and general interest. Part 2 includes model examinations in cross-examination and re-direct, including inconsistent statement: use of textbooks; re-direct. Part 3 covers the use of discovery devices in trial, including depositions; and interrogatories. The third edition includes new model witness examinations and updated citations, a clearly defined structure for proving facts, as well as sophisticated tactics and strategies. Paul Mark Sandler is a partner in the firm of Shapiro Sher Guinot & Sandler P.A. with years of experience in both state and federal courts. James K. Archibald is a litigation partner in the Baltimore and Washington, DC offices of Venable LLP and past president of the Maryland Association of Defense Trial Counsel.

Schweitzer, Sidney C. **Cyclopedia of Trial Practice.** 3d ed. St. Paul, MN: West (Clark Boardman Callaghan), 1968-date. 13 vols. Annual pocket supplements. Consists of three individual parts: **Basic Trials and Proofs**, **Proof of Traumatic Injuries**, and **Dollar Verdicts.**
Total Cost: $3,078; total supplementation cost: 1994: $318; 1995: $364; 1996: $481; 1997: $515; 1998: $378;1999: $518; 2000: $562; 2001: $384; 2002: $284; 2003: $284; 2004: $959; 2005: $852; 2006: $761; 2007: $1,855; 2008: $1,955; 2009: $2,014; 2010: $1,636.50; 2011: $1,785.50; 2012: $1,946.50; 2013: $2,024; **Monthly Assured Print Price (APP)**: $224/$2,688; Individual components: **Basic Trials and Proofs**: $1,242; supplementation: 1993: $86; 1994: $97; 1997: $155; 1998: $163; 1999: $176; 2000: $191; 2002: $242; 2005: $270; 2007: $348; 2008: $386; 2009: $601; 2010: $704; 2011: $767; 2012: $843; 2013: $911; **Monthly Assured Print Price (APP)**: $91/$1,092; **Proof of Traumatic Injuries**: $1,516 (exclusive of discount); supplementation: 1993: $120; 1994: $132; 1997: $205; 1998: $215; 1999: $232; 2000: $251; 2001: 0; 2005: $384; 2006: $428; 2007: $474; 2008: $643; 2009: $734; 2010: $860; 2011: $936; 2012: $1,029; 2013: $1,112; **Monthly Assured Print Price (APP)**: $111/$1,332; **Dollar Verdicts:** $449; supplementation: 1994: $89; 1996: $140; 1997: $155; 1998: 0; 1999: $110; 2000: $120; 2001: $142; 2005: $102; 2007: $75; 2008: $88; 2009: $184; **Monthly Assured Print Price (APP)**: $26/$312.
Formerly published by Lawyers Cooperative, this 11-volume practice includes three separate components. The first, subtitled **Basic Trials**, guides the practicing attorney through general trial preparation and the trial of specific actions. Part two, subtitled **Proof of Traumatic Injuries**, assists the trial attorney in proving over 600 specific kinds of traumatic injuries with specific description and analysis of medical issues and sample questions to be employed at trial. It also includes general information on medical texts, terminology, diagnostic procedures, witnesses, specialists and hospital records. The third component, **Dollar Verdicts**, consists chiefly of a tabulation of dollar verdicts for specific injuries. Awards are classified as "not excessive,"

"excessive," "Adequate," "inadequate," and "damages fixed by court." Includes an introductory discussion on the rule of comparative verdicts.

Cost Saving Tips: Look for this set on the used law book market. You may also wish to buy the supplements less often than annually due to the high annual cost.

Singer, Norman J. **Sutherland Statutory Construction.** 6th ed. St. Paul, MN: West (Clark Boardman Callaghan), 2000-date. 9 vols. Annual pocket parts.
Cost: $2,170; supplementation: 1993: $346.00 (incl. 2 rev. vols.) 1994: $367.00 (incl. 2 rev. vols.); 1995: $125.00; 1996: $185.00; 1997: $225.00; 1998: $238.00; 1999; $257.00; 2000: $407.00; 2001: $774.00; 2002: $606.00; 2003: $565.00; 2004: $417.50; 2005: $462.50; 2006: $529.50; 2007: $744; 2008; $1,018; 2009: $1,277; 2010: $1,288.50; 2011: $1,169.50; 2012: $1,275; 2013: $1,402; **Monthly Assured Print Price (APP)**: $146/$1,752.
Originally published in 1891 by Jabez Sutherland, this treatise has a well-deserved reputation as the «bible» in the field of statutory interpretation. The task of preparing the 5th edition has been assumed by Professor Norman Singer, Professor of Law at the University of Alabama. The work provides expert guidance in evaluating statutes, ordinances and regulations by providing detailed analysis of the choices between legislative intent and manifest meaning. Five major topical areas are encompassed by the eight volumes, including legislative power, legislative organization and procedure, legislative form and mode, legislative applicability, and statutory construction. Each topical section, or Part, is accompanied by Legal Commentaries written by leading statutory and constitutional scholars. The text is both lucid and detailed and is exhaustively supported with citations to cases and statutory authorities. The supplementation cost should ease a bit now that the 5th edition nears completion. Highly recommended to any attorney or law firm which deals with matters of legislative intent and interpretation.

Cost Saving Tips: The initial purchase price for this set was increased from $575 to $875 in 1997 and $2,046 in 2012. Since this work is chiefly valuable for its core discussion, the cost-conscious purchaser may choose to purchase the cumulative pocket supplements every 2-3 years as a means of restraining overall law library costs. Relevant cases should obviously be Shepardized and primary law sources checked for substantive changes in the law.

Smith, Lawrence J. **Art of Advocacy: Summation**. New York: Matthew Bender & Co., 1980-date. 1 vol. Looseleaf format.
Cost: $392; supplementation: 1997: $103 (annual cost frozen since 1993); 1998: $110; 1999: $117; 2000: $125; 2001: $134; 2002: $144; 2003: $152; 2004: $152; 2005: $164; 2006: $184; 2007: $207; 2008: $226; 2009: $246; 2010: $274; 2011: $275; 2012: $299; 2013: $286; 2014: $295.
This one-volume trial practice guide is designed to assist the trial attorney in conducting an effective summation in various types of personal injury actions. Two chapters provide a general overview of summation techniques and the law of closing argument, while the remaining 34 chapters provide detailed coverage of summation techniques in specific personal injury actions, including products liability, accident, medical malpractice and wrongful death cases. The lead author is an experienced trial advocate with wide-ranging experience as lecturer seminar participant. He is joined by 28 contributing authors. This is one of the most thorough and practical guides to the art of summation.

Cost Savings Tips: Trial practice titles like this can be used effectively without subscribing to the updates. Forego the standing order and simply re-purchase it when you feel you would like a more current version.

Starr, V. Hale and Mark McCormick. **Jury Selection.** Rev. 4th ed. New York: Wolters Kluwer Law & Business, 2010-date. 1 vol. (430 pp.) Looseleaf format.
Cost: $315; supplementation: 2010: $135; 2011: $144; 2012: $154; 2013: $179; 2d ed.: 1993: $30; 1994: $50; 1995: $53; 1996: $55; 1997: $55; 1998: $57; 2000: $94; 3d ed.: 2001: $126; 2002: $138; 2003: $157; 2004: $167; 2005: $175; 2006: $184; 2007: $196; 2008: $210; 2009: 0.
This volume combines a summary of the substantive and procedural law regarding jury selection with a complete analysis of the latest scientific methodology regarding the actual selection process. V. Starr Hale, who holds a doctorate in communications, is a leading expert in the field of jury selection and a founding member of the American Society of Trial Consultants. She has more than 15 years experience as a forensic consultant to trial lawyers. Her co-author is a practicing attorney in the state of Iowa and former member of the Iowa Supreme Court. The authors' coverage includes a history of the law of juries, including the history of the right to trial by jury, the role of statutes, rules and case law in jury selection, and current issues and developments in jury law. The heart of the volume, however, is dedicated to an exhaustive examination of the process and factors involved in selecting jurors, including chapters on pre-trial investigation, the issues study and community attitude assessment, change of venue, trial simulation, demographic analysis of the jury panel, voir dire mechanics and techniques, nonverbal communications (including appearance, voice, and movement), and jury selection in the courtroom. The Afterward includes a discussion of the evaluation and use of trial consultants. The Appendices include a variety of sample documents to be used in the jury selection process including juror questionnaires, community attitude study and change-of-venue training manuals, sample affidavits, basic outlines and voir dire questions for civil and criminal matters, and basic voir dire questions for all types of cases.

Cost Saving Tips: Drop the standing order to the annual pocket part and **Sample Voir Dire Questions** and save more than $100 per year. You can also buy the cumulative pocket at less frequent intervals as a further cost saving measure.

Stein, Jacob A. **Closing Arguments: The Art and the Law.** 2d ed. St. Paul, MN: West (Clark Boardman Callaghan), 2010-date. 1 vol. Annual paperbound editions.
Cost: 2013 Edition: $142; supplementation: 2006: $50; 2007: $55.50; 2008: $62.50; 2009: 0; 2010: $109; 2011: $120; 1st ed.: 1993: $57; 1994: $89; 1995: $55; 1996: $105; 1997: $80; 1998: $87; 1999: $94; 2000: $102; 2001: $120; 2002: $150.50; 2003: $145; 2004: $215; 2005: new edition.

First published in 1969, this is one of the finest books on the art and law of the closing argument. Unlike that time when closing arguments were dominated by dramatic oratory and hyperbole, today's trials are dominated by the facts. This volumes examines the law of the closing argument, including what is permissible and what is forbidden. For example, what is the law governing the reading of law books, appellate opinions or medical texts to the jury? Stein answers questions such as this in clear language which is heavily supported with citations to case law. In part two, he examines the art and mechanics of closing argument, including such matters as speaking style, exhibits, casting reasonable doubt, and dealing with hostile judges. Part three addresses specimens of eloquence drawn from both civil and criminal trials, including legal maxims, and quotations. These provide the litigator with a sufficient variety of examples to stimulate the framing of his or her own closing arguments. Converted to an annual paperbound voilume in 2010.

Cost Saving Tips: However excellent, this is one of those books which can pretty much stand on its own without the benefit of regular supplementation. Although the law regarding closing arguments will change by degree, it can generally be stated that the rules will not change so dramatically that the trial practitioner cannot derive great benefit from this volume if it is treated as a monograph. Since the supplementation is cumulative, you can buy the latest supplement and bring your volume up-to-date after a hiatus of several years.

Stoll-DeBell, Kirstin; Nancy L. Dempsey, and Bradford E. Dempsey. **Injunctive Relief: Temporary Restraining Orders and Preliminary Injunctions**. Chicago: American Bar Association, 2009. 1 vol. (440 pp.).
Cost: $105; $85 to members; from $48.55 on amazon.com (2013).
An injunction is a form of equitable remedy, or relief, in the form of a court order, by which a party is required to perform, or to refrain from performing, certain acts. Failure to adhere to the terms of the injunction may subject the violator to civil or criminal penalties, monetary damages and/or court-imposed sanctions. Breaches of injunctions are considered serious criminal offenses that may merit arrest and a possible prison sentence. This instructive guide provides a comprehensive overview of the history, issues, and procedural aspects of the various forms of injunctive relief, from pre-filing considerations to appellate relief. Part I examines the requirements for obtaining preliminary injunctions and temporary restraining orders in each federal circuit and for each state. Part II provides a detailed review of all the issues that should be considered before deciding to file a motion for injunctive relief. Part III provides detailed guidance on all the procedural bases for filing such motions, including the specific rules for such motions in each state, guidelines on how to file for injunctive relief, notice requirements, presentation of evidence, the federal and state specific laws governing appeals. The book also includes checklists, flowcharts to help practitioners decide whether to file such motions and if so, which type to file, and statistics detailing how often these motions are granted or denied in different types of cases. Kirstin Stoll-Debell is a partner with the firm of Merchant & Gould where she specializes in complex intellectual property cases. Nancy Dempsey is special counsel to RE/MAX International, Inc. with a specialty in intellectual property protection and litigation. Bradford Dempsey is a partner with the Finance and Restructuring Group of Faegre & Benson LLP.

Shapiro, Stephen M., et al. **Supreme Court Practice**. 10th ed. Washington, DC: Bloomberg BNA, 2013-date. 1 vol. (1,450 pp.)
Cost: $495; no supplementation to date; 8th edition: 1995: $45; 1996: 0; 1997: $65 (2014).
Since 1950, this book has served as the „bible“ for anyone practicing before the United States Supreme Court, that appellation bestowed by none other than Supreme Court Associate Justice Lewis F. Powell on the occasion of Eugene Gressman's retirement in 1987. The first edition, which appeared in 1950, was co-authored by Robert Stern (1908-2000) and Eugene Gressman (1917-2010), whose collaboration would continue through numerous editions, and Eugene Gressman's through all but the present edition. Their collaboration began in 1949 when Gressman, a five-year law clerk to Justice Murphy joined with Stern, a former lawyer in the Office of Solicitor General who had argued more than sixty cases before the Supreme Court. Their first edition drew upon not only their own wide-ranging knowledge and expertise, but upon advice and counsel from the Office of the Clerk of the Supreme Court, who reviewed their draft document and made corrections and suggestions. Since that time, the book has earned a well-deserved reputation as the definitive resource for practice before the Court.
The 10th edition, which builds upon the impressive work of the previous authors, provides detailed guidance through every aspect of practice before the U.S. Supreme Court. The opening chapter provides an authoritative introduction to the Court, its history, structure and operations. This is followed by chapters detailed the Court's jurisdiction to review decisions of the federal and state courts, the factors motivating the Court's decision to exercise its Certiorari appellate jurisdiction, and he manner and procedures whereby the Court takes such jurisdiction. Additional chapters cover In forma pauperis proceedings, certified questions, original cases, extraordinary writs, the briefs on the merits, oral argument, petitions for rehearing and final disposition of cases, motions and applications, stays, injunctions and bail, capital cases, jurisdiction, standing, mootness and abatement, and admission to the bar and disbarment. The six Appendices contain the Rules of the Supreme Court of the United States, Clerk Guidelines Regarding Filing Cases, Clerk's Guidelines Regarding Cases Selected for Review, Forms, Statutes and Regulations, and Applications and Instructions for Admission to the Bar. The text is accompanied by appropriate citations to relevant Supreme Court and federal appellate court decisions, and applicable federal statutes.

The five current co-authors bring a wealth of experience and scholarly erudition to the 10th edition. Stephen M. Shapiro and Kenneth S. Geller have been co-authors since the sixth and seventh editions, respectively, both now partners with the firm of Mayer Brown, LLP. Each has extensive experience with the Supreme Court, from petitioning and briefing to oral argument. Timothy S. Bishop, also a partner in the firm of Mayer Brown, has experience as clerk to Supreme Court Justice William J. Brennan, Jr. and in briefing and arguing cases before the Court. Edward A. Harnett is the Richard Hughes Professor for Constitutional Law and Public Law and Service at Seton Hall University School of Law who brings federal clerkship experience and an impressive record of scholarly publication to this project. Dan Himmelfarb, also a partner in the appellate litigation for Mayer Brown LPP, served as law clerk to Associate Justice Clarence Thomas and assistant to the Solicitor General of the United States, with extensive experience briefing and arguing cases before the Supreme Court in both public and private capacities. As with previous editions, the 10th edition incorporates into its discussion recent rules revisions, in this case as amended and effective July 1, 2013, which are otherwise all integrated into the existing 48 rules without being highlighted or designated as new procedures. It also contains updated guidelines and checklists for docketing and processing petitions for certiorari and appeals, and for pursuing a case after review has been granted. And the text and footnotes have been revised and augmented to incorporate recent rulings of the Supreme Court and other legal developments. Nothing in the literature remotely compares to **Supreme Court Practice** as a guide to anyone planning to bring a case before the U.S. Supreme Court.

Tiger, Michael E. **Persuasion: The Litigator's Art**. Chicago: American Bar Association, 2003. 1 vol. (325 pp.). No supplementation except in the form of subsequent editions.
Cost: $110 ($95 to ABA Litigation Section members); from $69.87 on amazon.com (2013).
A learned and eloquent statement of the principles behind effective persuasion in the courtroom by an experienced litigator and professor of law. The author examines the roots of persuasion in classical rhetoric and explains how the five elements of persuasion which can be effectively utilized in the courtroom. He takes the reader through the entire process of building the case, refining the presentation, and persuading judges and jurors through the use of techniques which combine effective storytelling with the presentation of legal themes. He includes examples of classic presentations by master advocate Edward Bennett Williams and analyzes their structure and content. The chapters examine the elements of persuasion, the speaker and the hearer, elements of the opening, persuasion during trial, elements of the closing, elements of argument to judges, and persuading judges. This volume is the fourth in the Litigation Bookshelf series published by the ABA. Michael Tigar is Professor of Law and Edward A. Moore, Sr. Scholar at American University's Washington College of Law. He has been a courtroom advocate, professor, and writer for more than 30 years.

Vincenti, Leonard M. **About Your Deposition**. Tucson, AZ: Lawyers & Judges Publishing Co., 1998. DVD. Running time: 20 minutes. Also available as part of a package including 10 copies of **About Your Deposition** booklet and 10 copies of the **Medical Expense Diary-Journal**.
Cost: $99; Kit: $129 (2013).
A deposition is a form of pretrial discovery in which one party questions the other party or a witness in the case. Often conducted in an attorney's office, a deposition requires that all questions be answered under oath and be recorded by a court reporter, who creates a deposition transcript. Depositions may also be videotaped. At trial, deposition testimony can be used to cast doubt upon (impeach) a witness's contradictory testimony, or to refresh the memory of a suddenly forgetful witness. Using professional actors, this video presentation provides clients with an overview of the deposition process and tips to ensure effective testimony. It covers such subjects as dress, deportment, telling the truth, listening carefully before to the question, thinking before answering, not volunteering information, keeping answers brief, the use of the deposition in court, injuries and medical treatment, and damages claimed. An excellent tool for reducing or eliminating a client's anxiety before a deposition and ensuring that his or her testimony is confident and convincing.

Wagner, Ward, Jr. **Art of Advocacy: Jury Selection**. New York: Matthew Bender & Co., 1980-date. 1 vol. Looseleaf format.
Cost: $430; supplementation: 1997: $103 (annual cost frozen since 1993); 1998: $110; 1999: $117; 2000: $125; 2001: $134; 2002: $144; 2003: $152; 2004: $152; 2005: $164; 2006: $184; 2007: $207; 2008: $230; 2009: $255; 2010: $284; 2011: $295; 2012: $328; 2013: $338; 2014: $382.
This one-volume practice guide presents both general principles of jury selection and specific strategies to be applied in particular types of cases. Of the book's 26 chapters, two are devoted to general voir dire techniques and the law of jury selection. The remaining 24 address jury selection in a variety of personal injury actions, from medical malpractice and rape to diving injuries and construction site accidents. The lead author, President of the West Palm Beach firm of Wagner, Nugent, Johnson, Roth, Kupfer & Rossin is joined by twenty contributing authors. Each of the specific chapters contains a sample opening of the voir dire, and sample questions covering each stage of the trial proceeding, with commentaries. The volume also includes model questions, bibliography, and index.

Cost Savings Tips: Trial practice titles like this can be used effectively without subscribing to the updates. Forego the standing order and simply re-purchase it when you feel you would like a more current version.'''

Waicukauski, Ronald, Paul Mark Sandler, and JoAnne Epps. **The 12 Secrets of Persuasive Argument**. Chicago: American Bar Association, 2009. 1 vol. (241 pp.).
Cost: $99.95; $84.95 to members; from $58.87 on amazon.com (2013).
The 12 secrets of argument were first identified 2,000 years ago with Aristotle's **Rhetoric**. Other secrets were provided by Cicero, Demosthenes and other classical scholars, as well as contemporary scholars in the fields of communication and social psychology. Still others were derived from the authors' own collective experiences and those of some of America's greatest lawyers. This brief guide to effective advocacy centers on 12 secrets of the persuasive argument with a focus on arguments presented orally by lawyers to judges, jurors, mediators and other decision-makers in structured settings. However, these same arguments can be applied in almost any setting, whether formal or informal, legal or non-legal, written or oral. They include (1) a focus on the goal; (2) tailoring the argument to the decision maker; (3) cultivating ethos; (4) basing your arguments on reason; (5) building with evidence, law and policy; (6) appealing to emotion; (7) using the best medium for the message; (8) strategically arranging your arguments; (9) arguing with style; (1) using delivery to enhance communication; and (2) engaging your listener.

Whited, Flem K., III. **Drinking/Driving Litigation: Criminal and Civil**. 2d ed. St. Paul, MN: West (Clark Boardman Callaghan), 1998-date. 4 vols. Looseleaf format.
Cost: $1,324; supplementation: 1992: $184.50; 1993: $224; 1994: $270; 1995: $449.50; 1996: $509; 1997: $605; 1998: $614; 1999: $275; 2000: $405; 2001: $477; 2002: $525; 2003: $597; 2004: $630; 2005: $795; 2006: $975; 2007: $468; 2008: $825.50; 2009: $540; 2010: $594; 2011: $654; 2012: $777; 2013: $854; **Monthly Assured Print Price (APP):** $87/$1,044.
Authored by one of the most respected names in the field, this five-volume treatise is a complete practical guide to both the law and practice of drunk driving litigation. It covers such areas as pretrial motions, arrest procedures, chemical tests, effects of alcohol, breathalyzer and other measuring devices, blood and urine testing, postmortem problems, blood alcohol, roadblocks, dram shop cases, trial issues, effects of alcohol and the variables that may affect them. Also includes jury instructions and a consideration of sentencing, appeal, and other issues involved in liquor liability. Supplementation costs vary from year-to-year, depending upon the volume of changes to the text. Generally speaking, the supplements are reasonably priced given the initial purchase price. Supplementation includes both cumulative front matter and interfiled pages, which means that updating a lapsed subscription may entail considerable filing.

Cost Saving Tips: Lapsed subscribers may find it less expensive and time-consuming to purchase a new set periodically if a sufficient number of years have elapsed.

Young, John Hardin, Terri A. Zall, and Alan F. Blakley. **Written and Electronic Discovery: Theory and Practice**. 5th ed. Louisville, CO: National Institute of Trial Advocacy, 2009. 1 vol. (434 pp.).
Cost: $75.00; $14.55 on amazon.com (2014).
The goal of discovery is to streamline the litigation process by narrowing the issues for trial, discovering what the other party intends to do at trial, helping all parties to understand the litigation at hand and, by doing so, to bring them closer to pretrial settlement. The discovery process is governed by three main provisions of the Federal Rules of Civil Procedure, including those addressing mandatory disclosures, written disclosures, and in-person examinations. The discovery process was changed significantly by the December 2006 amendments to the Federal Rules of Civil Procedure which addressed the proliferation of electronic information. This volume considers each step in the discovery process, from preparation for written discovery to interrogatories, documents, electronic information, use of written discovery in depositions, admissions, subpoenas to persons not parties, managing discovery with automated litigation support, discovery sanctions, and using written discovery at trial. Chapter 11 provides extensive sample requests for discovery and other forms. Appendices include selected Rules of Civil Procedure governing discovery, ethics and professionalism in E-discovery, and index. A companion CD-ROM includes the text of the Federal Rules of Evidence, the Convention on Taking Evidence Abroad in Civil or Commercial Matters (Hague Convention), Extraterritorial Discovery, and sample forms from Chapter 11. Like other titles available from the National Institute for Trial Advocacy, this volume provides a low-cost alterative source of authoritative information on trial advocacy skills and techniques. The authors bring extensive experience in the government and private sectors, and trial consulting.

Additional titles in the field of Trial Practice are available from the following publishers: American Bar Association, American Law Institute, American Trial Lawyers Association (ATLA), Matthew Bender, Bloomberg BNA, CRC Press, Gaunt, Glasser LegalWorks, James Publishing, Lawyers & Judges Publishing Co., LexisNexis, LRP Publications, National Institute for Trial Advocacy (NITA), National Practice Institute, Oxford University Press, Practising Law Institute, Professional Education Group (PEG), Routledge, Thomson Reuters West. See Appendix B for addresses and telephone numbers.

Trusts and Estates

American Bar Association Guide to Wills and Estates: Everything You Need to Know About Wills, Estates, Trusts, and Taxes. 2d ed. New York: Random House Reference, 2004. 1 vol. (366 pp.).
Cost: $16.99; from $7.68 on amazon.com (2014).
A basic overview of estate planning written for the general audience with attention to the law of estate planning, wills, trusts, living trusts, the choice of an executor or trustee, the benefits of living gifts, insurance, property transfers, taxes, and disability issues. The inclusion of an estate planning checklist providers users with the ability to evaluate their own estate planning needs and determine what to include in an estate plan in advance of consultation with an attorney.

American Law Institute. **Restatement of the Law Third. Property: Wills and Other Donative Transfers.** St. Paul, MN: American Law Institute, 2011-date. 4 vols. Annual pocket parts.
Cost: $324; supplementation: 1995: $48; 1996: $51; 1997: $54; 1998: $57; 1999: $60; 2000: $63; 2001: $68.25; 2002: $68.25; 2003: $75; 2004: $75; 2005: $75; 2006: $75; 2007: $84; 2008: $88.50; 2009: $96; 2010: $96; 2011: $64; 2012: $99; 2013: $117.
The **Restatement of the Law Third, Property: Wills and Other Donative Transfers** offers a comprehensive treatment of the law of probate transfers and is intended to eventually replace Restatement Second, Property (Donative Transfers). This volume presents a complete treatment of the American law of wills, will substitutes, intestacy, gifts, present and future interests, the construction of donative documents, and other related matters. The coverage embraces subjects covered in the Restatement of Property and Restatement Second of Property (Donative Transfers), as well as subjects not previously covered in those Restatements.

American Law Institute. **Restatement of the Law Second. Trusts.** St. Paul, MN: American Law Institute, 1959-date. 5 vols. Annual pocket parts.
Cost: $317.50 for complete set; vols. 1-2 (base vols.): $127; vols. 3-5 (Appendices): $190.50; supplementation: 1995: $32; 1996: $34; 1997: $36; 1998: $38; 1999: $40; 2000: $42; 2001: $42; 2002: $45.50; 2003: $50; 2004: $50; 2005: $50; 2006: $50;

2007: $56; 2008: $59; 2009: $64; 2010: $64; 2011: $78; 2012: 0. **The Restatement of Trusts 2d** was adopted and promulgated by the American Law Institute at Washington, D.C. on May 23, 1957, and first published in 1959. The person most responsible for the preparation of the Second Edition was Professor Austin W. Scott of Harvard Law School who served as the Reporter. The Appendices, containing Reporter's Notes, Court Citations to both the first and Second Restatements, and cross references to West Key Number and **American Law Reports** annotations, keep the volumes current. The bound Appendices volumes are updated by annual pocket parts. Now superceded by **Restatement of the Law Third. Trusts.**

American Law Institute. **Restatement of the Law Third. Trusts.** St. Paul, MN: American Law Institute, 2003-date. 4 vols. Annual pocket parts anticipated.
Cost: $432 (vols. 1-2 also available in one paperbound vol. at $75); supplementation: 2004: $50; 2005: $50; 2007: $189; 2008: $88.50; 2009: $96; 2010: $96; 2011: $96; 2012: $171 (vol. 4 plus p.p.); 2013: $0; 2014: $147.

American Law Institute. **Restatement of the Law Third. Trusts: Prudent Investor Rule.** St. Paul, MN: American Law Institute, 1992-date. 1 vol. (307 pp.).
Cost: $98.00 (2014).
This volume is the first installment in the American Law Institute's revision of **the Restatement of the Law of Trusts**. It is intended as a comprehensive reformulation of the traditional rules governing the trustee's duty to invest and manage the assets of the trust with prudence. As such, it reflects modern portfolio theory and contemporary investment practices and techniques.
This volume is the first installment in the American Law Institute's revision of **the Restatement of the Law of Trusts**. It is intended as a comprehensive reformulation of the traditional rules governing the trustee's duty to invest and manage the assets of the trust with prudence. As such, it reflects modern portfolio theory and contemporary investment practices and techniques.

Anderson, Roger W. **Understanding Trusts and Estates**. 4th ed. New York: Matthew Bender & Co., 2009. 1 vol. (414 pp.). Legal Text Series. No supplementation.
Cost: $43; eBook: $34; from $21 on amazon.com; kindle ed.: $18.70 (2013).
This one-volume, student-oriented text provides an excellent overview of the basic principles of the law governing wills, trusts, and future interests. The author is Professor of Law at the University of Toledo who teaches in the areas of estates, property, elder law and natural resources. It contains numerous citations to relevant cases and statutes.

Averill, Lawrence H., Jr. and Mary F. Radford. **Uniform Probate Code and Uniform Trust Code in a Nutshell.** 6th ed. St. Paul, MN: West, 2010. 1 vol. (760 pp.) No supplementation between editions. Available from West Academic.
Cost: $39; e-book: $27; from $28 on amazon.com; kindle: $17.05 (2014).
This volume in West's Nutshell series is designed to provide the attorney with a basic understanding of the provisions of the **Uniform Probate Code** which was approved by the National Conference of Commissioners on the Uniform State Laws in 1969 and is, in fact, the second longest of all the uniform acts. (the UCC being the longest). This rather lengthy Nutshell provides an excellent introductory analysis of the provisions of the Code. The text is divided into seven parts: general provisions, definitions and probate jurisdiction of he court; intestate succession, wills, and donative transfers; probate of wills and administration; foreign personal representative and ancillary administration; protection of persons under disability and their property; nonprobate transfers; and trust administration. Includes citations to Code sections, selected cases, and collateral authorities, including **Restatements**, books, and law review articles. Prior edition in 2000.

Beckert, Jens. **Inherited Wealth**. Princeton, NJ: Princeton University Press, 2008. 1 vol. (382 pp.). Paperbound.
Cost: $49.95; from $31.98 on amazon.com (2014).
While practical guides on estate planning and wealth preservation abound, the subject of inherited wealth has received little attention from an historical and sociological perspective. This unique study, translated from the original German, provides a cross-cultural perspective on the subject of inherited wealth and inheritance law in France, Germany, and the United Stares. All societies that recognize individual property rights have rules that reallocate property upon the death of its owner. Codified inheritance laws prescribe the rights of the testator to dispose of his or her property by will, or, alternatively, provide rules governing the allocation of property when an individual dies without a will (intestate). The law also dictates to what extent the state may claim all or part of the property. The substance and intent of these laws differ widely between countries and has been the subject of considerable political, economic, sociological and philosophical debate over the past two centuries. The author examines the inheritance laws of these countries from four key areas of conflict: (1) the degree of testamentary freedom; (2) the legal rights of the testator's relatives, particularly the spouse and children; (3) entails (i.e. will provisions limiting inheritance to a specified line of heirs); and (4) inheritance taxation. The author applies a wide-ranging knowledge of the various strains of philosophical and economic thought to a consideration of the apparent tension between the bequeathing of wealth as a vital ingredient of family solidarity and the degree to which that attendant reproduction of social inequality conflicts with the principle of equal opportunity. Attorneys specializing in trust and estate planning, estate taxation, tax planning, and related fields will find this an enormously engrossing cross-cultural sociological perspective on the rules governing wealth transfer. The author is a director of the Max Planck Institute for the Study of Societies in Cologne, Germany.

Bogert, George Gleason and George Taylor Bogert. 2d-3rd ed. St. Paul, MN: West, 2000-date. 23 vols. Annual pocket parts.
Cost: $2,497; supplementation: 1995: $138.50; 1996: $154.50; 1997: 0; 1998: $394.50; 1999: $190; 2000: $275; 2001: $368; 2002: $295; 2003: $336.25; 2004: $376.50; 2005: $470; 2006: $592; 2007: $797; 2008: $735; 2009: $1,198; 2010: $927.50; 2011: $798; 2012: $1,769; 2013: $1,359; **Monthly Assured**

Print Price (APP): $124/$1,488.
Professor Bogert, the late James Parker Hall Professor of Law at the University of Chicago, was associated with this major work of scholarship from the appearance of the first edition in 1935 until his death more than 40 years later. His son, George Taylor Bogert, assisted his father in preparing pocket parts and revising the bound volumes for a number of years before assuming sole responsibility following the elder Bogert's death. This is without question one of the most authoritative works of legal scholarship in this or any field. The authors' analysis of the substantive aspects of the field is accompanied by practical guidance regarding argumentative techniques which can be employed in actual trials. The text provides the researcher with a thorough analysis of the various forms which trusts may take as well as the possible actions of the parties. The set consists of 59 chapters discussing all manner of trusts, including express private trusts, charitable, constructive, testamentary, revocable, irrevocable, insurance, and business trusts. Also addressed are the statute of frauds, the wills acts, trustees, taxation of trusts, restrictive property law rules, the cy pre power, investments, tort liability for trustees, sales by trustees, leases, expenses and much more. There are also two volumes of trust forms. It includes exhaustive citations and annotations to relevant case law which often dominate the text. The pocket parts include a Westlaw Electronic Research Guide.

Cost Saving Tips: Though often difficult to locate on the used law book market, this treatise offers the cost-conscious attorney a significant potential savings. You will note that the supplementation costs to this title are reasonable in comparison with many other works from this publisher. For this reason, a standing order is strongly recommended for the active probate attorney.

Bogert, George Taylor. **Trusts.** 6th ed. St. Paul, MN: West, 1987-date. 1 vol. Practitioner's Edition. Irregular pocket parts. Available from Wewst Academic
Cost: $85; Hornbook Edition is priced at $99 (2014).
This Practitioner's Edition is a distillation of the author's multi-volume treatise on trusts and trustees. It includes a discussion of intestate succession, wills, trusts, inter vivos trusts, the role of trustees, etc. Lack of regular supplementation, however, detracts from what is essentially an excellent and economical reference tool.

Buckley, Frederick J. **Probate Depositions: Law, Strategy and Sample Depositions**. Huntington, NY: Juris Publishing, 1999. 1 vol. (104 pages). Looseleaf format.
Cost: $35 (2014).
A useful of collection of sample probate depositions, including the cross-examination of an attesting witness, cross-examination of spouse of plaintiff, cross-examination of plaintiff-contestant by defendant-proponent, cross-examination of factual witness, cross-examination of practical nurse witness, guardian witness, family physician, clinical psychologist, psychiatrist, etc. Introductory material provides a brief review of such matters as scope of inquiry, time of events, dramatic deviation, the psychiatric autopsy, problems of privilege, preparation for deposition, plan of discovery, barrister and solicitor distinction, video depositions, The author is the senior partner of Buckley, Miller & Wright in Wilmington, Ohio, and has been involved in probate law since beginning his legal practice in 1950. He is the Former Chairman of the Committee on Litigation in Decedents' Estates, Litigation Section, American Bar Association and a Fellow of the American College of Trial Lawyers.

Eber, Alan R. **Asset Protection Strategies and Forms**. Santa Ana, CA: James Publishing, 2008. 1 vol. (various pagings). Looseleaf format.
Cost: $99; supplementation: 2010-2014: $69.99.
While estate planning consists of those legal instruments and techniques which provide for the disposition of one's property after death, the basic purpose of asset protection techniques is to protect assets from litigation during one's lifetime. This is achieved by deterring litigation, by providing an incentive for an early and inexpensive settlement, and by causing your opponents to work harder and get less. In our increasingly litigious society, an adverse judgment that exceeds insurance coverage is the greatest threat to assets. Assets are also at risk due to expanding theories of liability, excessive jury awards, the deep pocket syndrome, divorce, and estate taxation. This volume provides a comprehensive roadmap to the steps which can be taken to protect assets from a variety of legal actions and their resulting judgments. Following a consideration of fraudulent transfers, the author considers the following asset protection techniques: strategic planning, domestic trusts, international asset protection trusts (IAPTs), the titling of assets and family law, corporations, family limited partnerships (FLPs), family limited liability companies (LLC), and insurance. The author concludes with a brief synopsis of techniques and examples. The asset protection strategies are accompanied summaries of the relevant law, examples, caveats, cautions, diagrams, and forms. The complete text is reproduced on a companion CD-ROM. A pioneer in the asset protection field, Alan Eber specializes in the fields of foreign and domestic asset protection and estate planning, trusts, business structuring, and wealth strategies. He received his law degree from the State University of New York and L.L.M. from New York University.

Special Comment: James Publishing is noteworthy not only for the high quality of its practitioner-oriented reference books, but also for the great value that they represent. Unlike other legal publishers that increase supplementation costs substantially year after year, James has not raised its already quite reasonable initial or supplementation costs for many years.

Esperti, Robert A. and Renno L. Peterson. **Irrevocable Trusts: Analysis with Forms.** Valhalla, NY: Warren, Gorham & Lamont, 1998-date. 1 vol. Looseleaf format. Annual supplementation.
Cost: Print: $390 per year; Online: $575 per year (2014).
Transfer of wealth between generations may involve any one of a number of trusts mechanisms. This volume provides detailed analysis of one of the most efficient of these mechanisms--the irrevocable trust. The authors provided step-by-step guidance in the design and implementation of the correct irrevocable trust for each client. Also considered are the tax ramifications, including gift and estate taxation of irrevocable trust transfers, and grantor and nongrantor trusts. Coverage also extends to

generation-skipping and irrevocable trusts, demand right trusts, short-term trusts, personal residence trusts, charitable lead trusts, special irrevocable trusts, and trustee considerations in irrevocable trusts. It also includes over 35 sample trust forms in both the text and the accompanying disc. Robert Esperti and Renno Peterson are Principals at Esperti Peterson, a national estate planning law firm and co-founders of the Esperti Peterson Institute, National Network of Estate Planning Attorneys, and the National Association of Estate Planning Advisors.

Esperti, Robert A. and Renno L. Peterson. **Love, Money, Control: Reinventing Estate Planning**. Denver, CO: Quantum Press LLC, 2004. 1 vol. (543 pp.).
Cost: $43; from $0.01 on amazon.com (2014).
Simply put, estate planning is the process of planning for the management and disposition of your assets and resources when you are deceased or no longer able to manage your own affairs. For most individuals or families who fail to plan, state intestacy laws provide a default estate plan. The primary message of this guide to estate planning is that individuals should be motivated to plan out of love for family, friends, and personal causes. Indeed, estate planning is more than just tax planning, but a range of inter-related considerations, including family legacy, financial, retirement, disability, charitable, business succession, and gift planning. This manual is the end result of an editorial process involving sixty-nine estate planning attorneys and financial advisors from across the country. Utilizing an easy to comprehend question-answer format, it provides a lucid explanation of critical estate planning issues organized under the broad headings of love, money, and control. The three chapters in Part One (Love) provide an introduction to estate planning, examine the process of planning for loved ones, and planning for loved ones and charity. Part Two (Money) examines tax basics, wealth transfer techniques, and retirement planning. Part Three (Control) considers the administration of the estate, planning for disability, living trust-centered estate planning, business succession planning, asset protection planning, planning for seniors, and finding and working with professional advisors. The appendices include a variety of estate planning and professional resources, and a glossary of terms. The text is illuminated by numerous charts and financial calculations. The authors of more than 24 books in the field, Robert A. Esperti and Renno L. Peterson are nationally recognized estate planning attorneys, and co-founders of the National Network of Estate Planning Attorneys, the Esperti Peterson Institute, The Academy of Multidisciplinary Practice, and The Estate and Wealth Strategies Institute at Michigan State University. An invaluable tool for both estate planning professionals and the general public.

Estate Law Treatise Library on LoisLawConnect. New York: Wolters Kluwer Law & Business.
Cost: $540.00 per year (solo practitioner) (2014).
Estate and retirement issues are covered in depth in this treatise library, which includes the following titles: **Practical Guide to Estate Planning, Price on Contemporary Estate Planning, Multistate Guide to Estate Planning, Estate and Gift Tax Handbook, Estate and Retirement Planning Answer Book, and Title 26 – Internal Revenue Code.** A cost-effective alterbative to buying these titles individually in print format.

Estate Planning Library with 20+ WG&L Treatises [Internet] New York: Research Institute of America. Updated continually. Available for Windows, and Macintosh. Search Engine: Folio.
Cost: $6,085 per year for entire library; $3.090 w/o treatises (2014).
This all-inclusive online package includes more than 20 authoritative WG&L treatises and journals, RIA's analysis, annotations and explanations, U.S. Estate and Gift tax treaties, IRS forms, checklists, sample will and trust forms and clauses, client letters, sample IRS correspondence, planning articles and more , a complete library of research materials to plan, draft and administer an estate plan.

Evans, Daniel B. **How to Build and Manage an Estates Practice**. 2d ed. Chicago: American Bar Association, 2008. 1 vol. (196 pp.).
Cost: $64.95 ($44.95 to Law Practice Management members); from $58.95 on amazon.com (2014).
This volume provides the attorney with a basic road map through the intricacies of establishing and maintaining a small office estates practice. The author considers such subjects as defining your practice, finding clients, ethics issues, fees and fee agreements, communicating with clients, managing files and information, getting work done, and personnel. The appendices include an estate planning questionnaire, drafting instructions for estate planning documents, an estate administration checklist, and will execution instructions. The author is a Pennsylvania practitioner specializing in the areas of estate planning, estate and trust administration, and related tax planning for closely held businesses. He is also the author of **Wills, Trusts and Technology: An Estate Lawyer's Guide to Automation** (ABA) (see next entry).

Evans, Daniel B. **Wills, Trusts, and Technology: An Estate Lawyer's Guide to Automation**. 2d ed. Chicago: American Bar Association, 2004. 1 vol. (233 pp.).
Cost: $99.95; $89.95 to LPM and RP members; from $60 on amazon.com (2014).
This volume treats the selection and use of computer software to perform a variety of functions related to estate planning, fiduciary administration, tax planning, and information management. The author, the Probate-Technology editor for **Probate & Property** magazine, also provides basic information on hardware, software, spreadsheets and databases. A product of the American Bar Association's Section of Real Property, Probate and Trust Law of the Law Practice Management Section.

Federal Estate and Gift Tax Reporter [Print, Internet]. Riverwoods, IL: CCH Inc., 1983-date. 3 vols. Search Engine: Proprietary. Print and Internet service updated weekly.
Cost: Print: $1,380 per year; Internet: $1,380 (2014).
This multi-volume looseleaf reference service contains the full text of the Internal Revenue Code and IRS regulations on federal estate, gift, and generation-skipping taxes, together with applicable final, temporary and proposed regulations and related income tax provisions. It also includes the full-text of federal court decisions and IRS rulings, including selected private letter rulings, and pending legislation. The CCH Explanations explain the primary law and provide guidance on how to apply it.

Henkel, Kathryn G. **Estate Planning and Wealth Preservation: Strategies and Solutions**. Valhalla, NY: Warren, Gorham & Lamont, 1999-date. 1 vol. Supplemented twice annually.
Cost: $420 per year; Internet: $575 per year (2014).
A practice-oriented guide to estate planning with specific attention to strategies designed to preserve wealth. The author discusses estate planning fundamentals, the power of lifetime gifts, assets providing death benefits, family business and investment entities, non-charitable actuarial techniques, valuation planning, estate freezing techniques, charitable planning, planning for marriage and other family arrangements, advanced maturity, disability and serious illness, and planning for post mortem choices. A nationally recognized expert in the field and a past Chair of the ABA Section of Taxation Committee on Estate and Gift Taxes, Kathryn Henkel has twenty years experience planning for large estates.

Hoops, Frederick K. and Frederick H. Hoops III. **Family Estate Planning Guide.** 4th ed. St. Paul, MN: West (Clark Boardman Callaghan), 1995-date. 2 vols. Looseleaf pamphlet format.
Cost: $1,097; supplementation: 1996: $142; 1997: $170; 1998: $378; 1999: $195; 2000: $207; 2001: $265; 2002: $427; 2003: $284.50; 2004: $338.75; 2005: $362.50; 2006: $416; 2007: $367; 2008: $409; 2009: $550; 2010: $520; 2011: $587.50; 2012: $657; 2013: $722; 3d ed.: 1993: $65; 1994: $65; 1995: $125; **Monthly Assured Print Price (APP):** $79/$948
A detailed and well-organized practice guide to family estate planning. This work is distinguished by its clear language explaining all aspects of family estate planning from the tools available to the planner and initial interview to the use of various trusts arrangements to meet family objectives. Each of the twenty-nine chapters in this two-volume work includes research references to Lawyers Cooperative and other Thomson Legal Publishing products, including **ALR** Annotations, **Am. Jur 2d**, and other secondary sources. Includes citations to relevant primary and secondary sources., including cases, IRS Code Sections, Restatements, treatises, law review articles, and legislative history documents. The Appendices include sample questionnaires, letters, forms, wills, trusts, as well as IRS forms. Individual chapters can be removed and placed in one's briefcase.

Hunt, L. Rush. **A Lawyer's Guide to Estate Planning Fundamentals for the Legal Practitioner**. 3d ed. Chicago: American Bar Association, 2004. 1 vol. (216 pp.).
Cost: $99.95 ($89.95 to General Practice section members) (2014).
Designed for both the specialist and non-specialist, this volume provides a review of the fundamentals of estate planning. It covers a variety of issues and strategies from the initial client interview through the execution of various types of trust documents, including the marital and bypass trust, living trust, and standby trust. It also includes a number of sample forms and client questionnaires to aid in the estate planning process.

Kirsch, Clifford E., ed. **Financial Product Fundamentals: Law, Business, Compliance**. 2d ed. New York: Practising Law Institute, 2013-date. 1 vol. (1,222 pp.). Looseleaf format.
Cost: $335; supplementation: 2013; $376; 1st ed.: 2003: $90; 2004: 0; 2005: $95; 2006: $95; 2007: $105; 2008: $120; 2009: $132; 2010: $273; 2011: $290; 2012: new edition.
This volume provides a basic introduction to a variety of financial instruments, both new and traditional, with which attorneys must deal in servicing their clients. These instruments include products that are offered in capital markets that help companies in their growth and expansion, as well as specific collective investment vehicles. The authors also consider the legal and regulatory regimens imposed on them, their advantages and drawbacks, and the means by which they are priced, distributed and marketed. The volume is enhanced by the addition of a number of sample forms, charts, tables and graphs. More than fifteen attorneys contributed chapters. The editor is Chief Counsel, Variable Products, for the Prudential Insurance Company of America and a former Assistant Director of the SEC's Division of Investment Management.

Lynn, Robert J. **Introduction to Estate Planning in a Nutshell.** 5th ed. St. Paul, MN: West, 2004. 1 vol. (352 pp.). Available from West Academic.
Cost: $39; e-book: $27; from $17.99 on amazon.com (2014).
A brief overview directed at the non-specialist encompassing the subjects of wills, trusts, future interests, insurance, pensions, federal estate and gift taxation and fiduciary administration intended for the law student, lawyer, and non-lawyer with an interest in estate planning issues. The author has purposely omitted citations to cases in order not to impede the flow of the text and distract the non-specialist.

Mezzullo, Louis A. **An Estate Planner's Guide to Family Business Entities: Family Limited Partnerships, Limited Liability Companies, and More**. 3d ed.
Chicago: American Bar Association, 2010. 1 vol. (281 pp.). Includes CD-ROM.
Cost: $139.95 ($119.95 to members) (2014).
This guide is designed to assist estate planners in formulating the most appropriate ways of transferring wealth to younger family members, with attention to both tax and non-tax considerations. Considerable attention is devoted to the factors involving in choosing the proper business entity and comparing the various business entities that are available, including limited partnership, LLCs, and S and C corporations. The author also addresses the special valuation rules governing transfers of property enacted under Chapter 14 of the Omnibus Budget Reconciliation Act of 1990 (Pub.L. 101-508, 104 Stat. 1388), which was designed prevent abusive estate freezing techniques. The text includes frequent citations to applicable Internal Revenue Code and Treasury regulations. The volume also includes sample forms for limited partnership agreements, an LLC operating agreement, LLC articles of organization, deed of gift and cover letter; and IRS Entity Classification Election forms. The sample agreements and forms also included provided on a companion CD-ROM.

Mezzullo, Louis A. **An Estate Planner's Guide to Life Insurance**. 2d ed. Chicago: American Bar Association, Section of Real Property, Trust and Estate Law, 2009. 1 vol. (98 pp.). Includes the text on a companion CD-ROM.

Cost: $139.95; $119 to members (2014).
Life insurance plans a significant role in the estate planning of most adults, particularly those married and with children. Estate planning advisors should be fully informed regarding the various life insurance products and the role they play in the financial planning for their clients. This volume provides a good overview of the role of life insurance in the estate planning process, the terminology, the types of policies, employer-provided insurance, information needed for planning, income tax ramifications, transfer taxation, and the irrevocable life insurance trust, as well as sample forms. The second edition brings the book current to December, 2008. Louis A. Mezzullo is a partner in the Rancho Santa FE, CA office of Luce, Forward, Hamilton & Scripps LLP, where his practice is devoted to taxation, estate and business planning, and employee benefits. He is the author of numerous books and articles in the field of estate planning, taxation, and employee benefit issues.

Murphy, Joseph Hawley. **Murphy's Will Clauses.** New York: Matthew Bender & Co., 1960-date. 5 vols. Looseleaf format or eBook. Supplemented approximately twice annually. Internet includes no-cost updating via LEXIS-NEXIS.
Cost: $2,071 (includes annual subscription); annual renewal: 1995: $625.00 (price frozen since 1992); 1996: $656.00; 1997: $656.00; 1998: $690.00; 1999: $720.00; 2000: $770.00; 2001: $824.00; 2002: $882.00; 2003: $927.00; 2004: $973.00; 2005: $1,022.00; 2006: $1,063; 2007: $1,132; 2008: $1,200; 2009: $1,272; 2010: $1,285; 2011: $1,298; 2012: $1,337; 2013: $1,417; 2014; $1,518; eBook: $1,741; renewal: 2013: $1,417.
This exhaustive work provides a combination of legal analysis and sample clauses for use by the active estate attorney. There is a thorough discussion of wills, codicils, basic estate planning and will drafting considerations, as well as the tax ramifications of various estate planning instruments. The text is richly supported with citations to case law, state statutes, and applicable IRS Code sections and regulations. The chapters also cover such topics as non-dispositive clauses, dispositions of property, estates and interests in property, testamentary trusts, powers of appointment, powers of invasion, powers of withdrawal, the marital deduction, limitations on freedom of testation, particular beneficiaries, charitable dispositions, dispositions for care of pets and cemetery plots, conditional and deferred legacies and devises, appointment of fiduciaries, general fiduciary powers, directions on taxes, inter vivos trusts, other will-related instruments, living wills, and health care proxies. The most impressive research tool of its kind available on the market.

Cost Saving Tips: Depending on the nature of your practice, you may wish to drop the hardcopy supplementation and buy a new set at periodic intervals. If you do drop the standing order, you must be alert to changes in the tax code and take steps to obtain this information elsewhere such as in one of the major looseleaf tax services.

Page, William Herbert. **Page on the Law of Wills.** 3rd ed. revised by William J. Bowe and Douglas H. Parker. Newark, NJ: LexisNexis Matthew Bender [Anderson Publishing), 2003-date. 8 vols. with annual pocket parts. Alsom on eBook. Originally published by Anderson Company. Acquired by LexisNexis in 2002. Volumes 1-7 issued between 2000 and 2006.
Cost: $1,024; supplementation: 1992: $210; 1993: $130; 1994: $150; 1995: $165; 1996: $175; 1997: $185; 1998: $210; 1999: $225; 2000: $225; 2001: $230; 2002: $240; 2003: $353.70; 2004: $505; 2007: $179; 2008: $190; 2009: $196; 2010: $202; 2011: $210; 2012: $354; 2013: $371.
First published in 1901 by William Herbert Page, the fourth edition of this thorough analysis of the law of wills and probate includes exhaustive citations to the case law and statutes of all fifty states. Now under revision by Jeffrey A. Schoenblum, Professor of Law, Vanderbilt University School of Law, the set also discusses such topics as will construction, will contests, will substitutes, testamentary capacity, formalities of execution, amendment and revocation, living wills, durable powers and medical directives, and generation-skipping transfer provisions. The text also examines will drafting, the selection and appointment of fiduciaries, and the use of inter vivos and other forms of trusts. A volume of forms includes both whole will and trust forms as well as sample clauses covering the full range of estate planning options. This set was acquired as a part of the acquisition of the Anderson Publishing Company by LexisNexis in 2002. The fourth edition was completely revised between 2000 and 2005.

Cost Saving Tips: Buy pocket parts every 2-3 years, or as appropriate.

Pennell, Jeffrey N. **Estate Planning.** 8th ed. Riverwoods, IL: CCH, Inc., 2012-date. 2 vols. Looseleaf format or eBook. Annual revised editions.
Cost: $465 (print or eBook); supplementation: 2000: $250; 2001: $165; 2002: $225; 2003: $255; 2004: $269; 2005: $279; 2006: $299; 2007: $625; 2008: $625; 2009: $365; 2010: 0; 2011: 0; 2012: new ed.; 5th ed.: 1992: $175; 1993: $195; 1994: $295; 1995: $295; 1996: $310; 1997: $322; 1998-99: not available.
This two-volume treatise, replacing the three-volume 6th edition, provides complete coverage of the various arrangements which can be made to effectuate the devolution of an individual's wealth. While many estate plans involve the drawing up of a will, many others are based on a variety of inter vivos arrangements, including outright gifts, joint ownership, irrevocable inter vivos trusts, revocable inter vivos trusts, legal present and future interests created inter vivos, and settlements involving the distribution of life insurance proceeds. The authors' discussion is devoted largely to matters involving large estates, but also encompasses small estates. Naturally, a great preponderance of material is concerned with tax issues as they relate to various estate planning mechanisms. Professor Casner, the late Austin Wakeman Scott Professor of Law, Emeritus, Harvard Law School published his first edition of this work in 1953. Jeffrey N. Pennell, the Richard Clark Professor of Law at Emory University School of Law, has assumed the task of preparing the sixth and seventh editions following the death of Professor Casner in 1990. The chapters cover the estate plan created by the operation of law (intestate succession), wills, income taxation of estates, revocable inter vivos trusts, family annuities, non-trust gifts, life insurance, employee benefits, social security, concurrent interests in community property, future interests in an estate plan, generation-skipping transfer tax, powers of appointment, the marital deduction, the charitable deduction, planning for the

payment of death costs, estate plans that cross state or national borders. Volume five contains a hypothetical proposed estate plan for Mr. and Mrs. Richard Harry Black III. Volume six contains tables of cases, IRS Code sections, Treasury regulations, Internal Revenue rulings, Internal Revenue Bulletin rulings, Letter rulings, Revenue Procedures, Technical Advice Memoranda, state statutes, Uniform and Model Acts, **Restatements**, and secondary authorities. In 2004, responsibility for the publication and distribution of **Estate Planning** was assumed by Wolters Kluwer's sister company, CCH.

Price, John R. **Price on Contemporary Estate Planning.** 4th ed. Riverwoods, IL: CCH, Inc., 2008-date. 1 vol. (1,500 pp.). Periodic revisions.
Cost: 2013 Edition: $465; 2012 edition: $440; supplementation: 2001: $165; 2002: $180; 2004: $199; 2005: n/a; 2006: new edition; 2007: 0; 2008 edition: $215; 2009 edition: $265; 2010: $389.
A massive one-volume treatment of all aspects of estate planning from the client interview to post-mortem planning. The author, a leading expert in the field of estate planning, examines both tax and non-tax areas, including the durable power of attorney and the living will. His discussion of tax issues includes private annuities and charitable remainder trusts. It also features a variety of practice aids such as forms, worksheets, and checklists. The author provides the practitioner with invaluable practical advice. This title was sold by Wolters Kluwer Law & Business to CCH, Inc. in 2003. They are now sister companies.

Ray, Thomas J., Jr. **Charitable Gift Planning: A Practical Guide for the Estate Planner**. 2d ed. Chicago: American Bar Association, Section of Real Property, Probate and Trust Law, 2007. 1 vol. (846 pp.). Paperbound, with companion CD-ROM.
Cost: $174.95; $149.95 to members; from $90.18 on amazon.com (2014).
Charitable tax planning is a tool through which donors of both high and middle-class worth can achieve comprehensive estate planning while avoiding taxes and augmenting the amounts they are able to pass on the family and charities. For individuals with high-net-worth, these goals are achieved through (1) discount planning; (2) insurance planning; and (3) charitable giving. While all three of these measures are important parts of the estate planning process, this book addresses the charitable giving side of estate planning. Charitable planning asks three critical questions: (1) what should the client give; (2) to whom should he give it; and (3) how should the client arrange the gift. The author begins with a comprehensive review of the charitable deduction rules for gifts by individuals and their estates in light of the Pension Protection Act of 2006, arguably the most significant reform of the charitable giving tax planning since the Tax Reform Act of 1969. The bulk of the volume is devoted to the explanation and analysis of the various instruments and issues of charitable tax planning, including donor controls and private foundations, foundation substitutes, charitable remainder trusts, dangerous DIPS for charitable remainder trusts, financial and estate planning applications for charitable remainder trusts, other deferred giving arrangements, charitable lead trusts, financial and estate planning applications for charitable lead trusts, trustee issues, charitable planning with retirement plan assets, and charitable planning with business assets. Five appendices provide drafting guides for (1) private foundations; (2) charitable remainder trusts; (3) life insurance reserved agreement and gift annuities, and (4) charitable lead trusts; and (5) the ACGA Rates. The volume includes tables of cases; statutes; Treasury regulations; and letter rulings, revenue procedures and revenue rulings. The appendices are contained on a companion CD-ROM. A graduate of the Oklahoma City University School of Law, the author is an estate and tax attorney who has practiced in the St. Louis metropolitan area since 1986. He has lectured and written widely in the estate planning field, and has conducted seminars across the country for attorneys, accountants, financial advisers, donors, and development officers.

Regan, John J. **Tax, Estate & Financial Planning for the Elderly.** New York: Matthew Bender and Co., 1985-date. 1 vol. Looseleaf format and eBook.
Cost: $453 (includes annual subscription); supplementation: 1995: $158 (price frozen since 1992); 1996: $166; 1997: $166; 1998: $175; 1999: $182; 2000: $95; 2001: $102; 2002: $207; 2003: $218; 2004: $229; 2005: $238; 2006: $248; 2007: $141; 2008: $146; 2009: $282; 2010: $285; 2011: $288; 2012: $300; 2013: $315; 2014: $337; eBook: $412; renewal: 2014: $337.
This one-volume planning guide is written by the Jack and Freda Dicker Distinguished Professor of Health Care Law at Hofstra University School of Law. The author addresses all major areas likely to impact the lives and fortunes of elderly clients, including financial planning, social security benefits, public pensions, private pensions, income tax savings, access to credit, supplemental security income program, Medicare and private health insurance, Medicaid and its alternatives, food and nutrition programs, housing concerns, planning for incapacity, health care decisions, nursing homes, guardians and conservators, the federal and estate gift tax, strategies for lifetime giving, and estate planning and wills. Each of the nineteen chapters is introduced by a valuable summary of its contents. Numerous citations to primary and secondary authorities accompany the extremely well-written and lucid text. It is also interspersed with planning notes, forms, and illustrative financial calculations.

Rounds, Charles E., Jr. and Charles E. Rounds, III. **Loring and Rounds: A Trustees Handbook**. New York: Wolters Kluwer Law & Business, 2013. 1 vol. (1,063+ pp.). Annual.
Cost: 2014 Edition: $319; 2013 Edition: $299; 2012 Edition $299 (2014).
First published in 1898 by Augustus Peabody Loring, **A Trustee's Handbook** has since achieved a reputation as the leading reference guide in the field of trust administration. The fifth and sixth editions were prepared by Mayo Adams Shattuck and James F. Farr, respectively. Professor Charles Rounds assumed responsibility for the seventh (1994) and successive editions. Intended as a reference guide rather than a treatise, the eighth edition provides valuable insight into the nature of trusts and the role of the trustee, who holds title to property for the benefit of another. Professor Rounds examines the rights, duties and obligations of the parties once the trustee takes title to the trust property. Chapters include: the Property Requirement, the Trustee's Office, Interests Remaining with the Settlor, the Beneficiary, the Trustee's Duties, the Trustee's Liabilities,

Miscellaneous Topics of General Interest to the Trustee, Special Types of Trusts, and the Income Taxation of Trusts. Professor Rounds is professor of Law at Suffolk University Law School.

Scott, Austin Wakeman. William Franklin Fratcher, and Mark L. Ascher. **Scott and Ascher on Trusts.** 5th ed. New York: Wolters Kluwer Law & Business, 2006-date. 8 vols. Annual hardbound supplement to entire set.

Cost: $3,025; supplementation: 1992: $110; 1993: $120; 1994: $245; 1995: $245; 1996: $250;1997: $260; 1998: $260; 1999: $290; 2000: $310; 2001: $325; 2002: $410; 2003: $435; 2004: $456; 2005: $479; 2006: $700; 2007: $372; 2008: $399; 2009: $432; 2010: $462; 2011: $494; 2012: $528; 2013: $569.

This is the definitive work on the law of trusts, revised and updated by a scholar personally chosen by Professor Scott. Austin Wakeman Scott, the late Dane Professor of Law Emeritus at Harvard University, was generally regarded as the country's leading authority in the field. Professor Fratcher, the R.B. Price Distinguished Professor of Law Emeritus at the University of Missouri drafted the pocket parts to the 3d edition when Scott was unable to do so and undertook the preparation of the 4th edition. He has left Professor Scott's discussion of earlier landmark cases intact, while supplementing these with discussion and analysis of more recent cases. Since the death of Professor Fratcher in 1992, the preparation of the supplement and, now, the 5th edition, has been undertaken by Mark Ascher, Professor of Law at the University of Arizona. The 5th edition incorporates a number of recent developments, including the enactment of the Uniform Probate Code, the Employee Retirement Income Security Act, the decline of the doctrine that contracts entered into by persons cohabiting without marriage are illegal, the increased use of resulting and constructive trusts, the decline in the doctrine of charitable immunity from tort liability and the decline of close court supervision of trust administration, among other changes. The chapters in the 5th edition include definitions and distinctions, the creation of a trust, the trust property, the trustee, the beneficiary, transfer of interest of the beneficiary, trust administration, liabilities to third persons, liabilities of third persons, termination and modification of the trust, charitable trusts, resulting trusts, constructive trusts, trusts and the conflict of laws. Volumes VI and VIA includes tables of cases, statutes, uniform acts, **Restatements**, bibliography, and index. While this treatise is impressive in its scholarship and attention to scholarly detail, it includes features of value to the active practitioner including the alphabetical listing of annotations to state case law. The exhaustive citations to primary authority are complemented by references to relevant secondary sources.

Cost Saving Tips With a single cumulative supplement, it is possible to drop the supplementation when your usage wanes and reinstate without any loss of coverage. However, if you are a specialist in the field, you will probably wish to maintain this set on a standing order. The recent supplementation cost may appear to be high for a single volume, but it is not unreasonable when one realizes that this single-volume is in lieu of pocket parts to a n eight-volume set. The title was acquired by Wolters Kluwer Law & Business in 1996. Price increases have been modest and incremental since that time, generally about 7% annually.

Slesnick, Twila and John C. Suttle. **IRAs, 401(k)s & Other Retirement Plans: Taking Your Money Out**. Berkeley, CA: Nolo Press, 2011. 1 vol. (385 pp.). Paperbound.

Cost: $34.99; from $21 on amazon.com; kindle: $19.49 (2014).

Individuals save for a retirement through a variety of tax-deferred retirement vehicles, including IRAs, 401(k)s, Roth IRAs, and Roth 401(k)s. A number of years ago, Congress recognized the limitations of Social Security as a sole means of support during one's retirement years by establishing a number of tax-favored plans to allow individuals to save for retirement. One type can be set up by individuals, appropriately designated individual retirement accounts, or IRAs. Others may be established by employers (or by self-employed individuals), and are described as "qualified plans," falling under Section 401 of the Internal Revenue Code. This volume is designed to assist individuals with the complexities and tax ramifications of taking money out of one of these tax-favored accounts, whether this is done before the law allows (age 59-1/2) or after, and whether done voluntarily, or compulsorily (after age 70-1/2). The authors provide an overview of the various types of retirement plans, the tax implications of these retirement accounts, and grapple with such issues as early distributions, substantially equal periodic payments, required distributions, distributions to beneficiaries, Roth IRAs, and Roth 401(k) plans. The Appendices include a number of relevant IRS forms, notices and schedules, and life expectancy tables. The text is supplemented with a variety of cautions, resources, helpful terms, tips, charts, and sample worksheets. Twila Slesnick is an Enrolled Agent qualified to represent individuals before the Internal Revenue Service. and a specialist in tax and investment planning for retirees and prospective retirees. John Suttle is attorney and CPA in private practice.

Stern, W. Rod. **Estate Planning, Wills and Trusts for Business Owners and Entrepreneurs**. Irvine, CA: Entrepreneur Press, 2007. 1 vol. (320 pp.). Includes sample forms and documents on CD-ROM.

Cost: $32.95; from $.01 on amazon.com (2014).

Estate planning involves far more than the distribution of your assets after you die. It is a structured plan for managing a variety of, often, complex financial, emotional and social relationships both during your lifetime and after you die. Creating this plan is of particular importance to the business owner who, in addition to concerns about family and friends, must attend to the needs of business partners, employees, creditors, and other parties to the operations of the business. In this lucidly written guide, laced with real-world and hypothetical examples, the author provides expert guidance through a host of estate planning issues. In Part I, he does by examining various estate planning philosophies, horror stories, and estate planning and probate myths, before effectively detailing eight specific estate planning philosophies drawn from popular television programs. In Part II, he considers estate planning goals and the specific concerns faced by business owners, including estate taxes, coordinating the estate plan with retirement benefits, making changes to an estate plan, selecting an estate planning team, and the financial process. Part three outlines the primary estate planning tools, including the simple will, family trusts, the life insurance trust, will substitutes, gifts during one's lifetime, qualified persona; residence trusts, special needs trusts, family limited partnerships, and charitable trusts for personal gain. Part IV address various elements of estate planning, including medical and financial decisions, selection of trustees and guardians, the timing of distributions to beneficiaries, reducing blended-family tensions, avoidance of costly estate disputes, and the administration of trusts post-death. Free of much of the technical jargon that characterizes many books on estate planning, this book is a refreshingly easy-to-read, yet sophisticated approach to estate planning and its many permutations. A graduate of Hastings College of Law, with a master's degree in taxation from New York University, W. Rod Stern is a partner in the Irvine, CA firm of Murtaugh, Meyer, Nelson & Treglia LLP, with more than 20 years experience in business tax and estate planning.

Turner, George M. **Irrevocable Trusts.** 3d ed. St. Paul, MN: West (Clark Boardman Callaghan), 1996-date. 2 vols. Looseleaf format. Supplemented annually. CD-ROM containing selected forms also available. Also available w/o CD-ROM.
Cost: $556 (with forms CD-ROM); supplementation: 1994: $50.00; 1995: $60.00; 1996: $160.00; 1997: $120.00; 1998: $113.00; 1999: $102.00; 2000: $110.00; 2001: $141.00; 2002: $129.50; 2003: $91.00; 2004: $102.00; 2005: $110.50; 2006: $60; 2007: $138.50; 2008: $154.50; 2009: $267; 2010: $195.50; 2011: $215; 2012: $236; 2013: $258; **Monthly Assured Print Price (APP):** $37/$444.
This treatise and practice guide provides attorneys with explanation and analysis of a variety of irrevocable trusts, including children's trusts, sprinkling trusts, Crummey trusts, irrevocable trusts for stock purchase, and charitable remainder trusts. Also includes educational, testamentary, accumulation, term, insurance, Medicaid, charitable remainder and rabbi trusts. Provides in-depth discussion of such topics as choosing a trustee, valuating assets, and working with the IRS. The volume also includes sample trust documents and forms, wills, revenue rulings, cases.

Turner, George M. **Revocable Trusts.** 5th ed. St. Paul, MN: West (Clark Boardman Callaghan), 2003-date. 4 vols. Looseleaf format. Supplemented three times per year. Includes CD-ROM containing selected forms.
Cost: $1,256; ProView eBook: $989; supplementation: 1999: $195; 2000: $211; 2001: $261; 2002: $116.50; 2003: new edition; 2004: $395; 2005: $383.50; 2006: $424; 2007: $472; 2008: $569; 2009: $552; 2010: $574; 2011: $625.50; 2012: $682; 2013: $750; **Monthly Assured Print Price (APP):** $72/$864.
A detailed, practical guide to the revocable trust and its role in estate planning which allows families to avoid the probate process, avoid taxation, and maintain control over asset management. The author, an attorney in private practice in California, provides analysis and practical guidance in such areas as basic estate planning, the probate system, tax and probate problems without a trust, the value of the revocable living trust, alternative estate planning techniques, choosing trustees and methods of trusteeship, specific documents to be considered in estate planning, tax ramifications, explaining drafts to the client, transferring assets to the trust, procedure upon death of one of the spouses, and post-mortem tax planning , among others. The Appendices include numerous, trust documents and primary sources.

Uniform Laws Annotated. Volume 8 pt. 1, 8 pt. 2, 8A, 8B, 8C: Estate, Probate and Related Laws--Uniform Probate Code. St. Paul, MN: West, 1983/97-date. 5 vols. (804 pp.) Annual pocket parts.
Cost: $1,150; supplementation: 1994: $27.75; 1995: $27.75; 1996: $30; 1997: $164; 1998: $30; 1999: $30; 2000; $40; 2001: 0; 2003: $80; 2004: $100; 2005: $106; 2006: $100; 2007: $112; 2008: $124; 2009: $128; 2010: $140; 2011: $148; 2012: $164; 2013: $1,072; **Monthly Assured Print Price (APP):** $70/$840.
Volumes 8 (Pts. 1 & 2), 8A, 8B & 8C of West's thirty-volume **Uniform Laws Annotated** contain the Uniform Probate Code as adopted by the National Conference of Commissioners on Uniform State Laws in 1969. Each provision of the text is accompanied by Comments, Library References, and Notes of Decisions which have cited that provision. The volume and its pocket part also includes a Table of Jurisdictions which have adopted the Code.

Weinstock, Harold. **Planning an Estate.** 4th ed. St. Paul, MN: West (Clark Boardman Callaghan), 1995-date. 1 vol. (470 pp.) Annual pocket part.
Cost: $186; ProView eBook: $181; supplementation: 1996: $54; 1997: $120; 1998: $128; 1999: $70; 2000: $75; 2001: $88; 2002: $108.50; 2003: $45; 2004: $50.50; 2005: $54.50; 2006: $62; 2007: $69; 2008: $77; 2009: $87; 2010: $87; 2011: $95; 2012: $104; 2013: $121; **Monthly Assured Print Price (APP):** $12/$144.
An excellent overview of estate planning designed for estate planners and other professionals who require a knowledge of the field. Harold Weinstock, a member of the California Bar, has published extensively in the fields of tax, estate planning, and trusts and estates. The author examines the full range of estate planning issues, including tax principles, the small family estate, marital deductions, community property exclusions to save death taxes, bypassing the second tax, avoiding probate and using a revocable living trust. Additional chapters are devoted to discussions of gifts, nontraditional lifetime wealth transfer devices, life insurance, annuities, handling business interests, charitable gifts and tax planning the estate after the owner's death. While the author cites to Internal Revenue Code sections and regulations in the text, there are only selective citations to case law. Each chapter includes a recommended list of law review and professional articles. The Appendices include relevant tax and annuity tables, tables of cases, statutes, Treasury regulations, Revenue Rulings and Procedures, and an index.

Westfall, David and George P. Mair. **Estate Planning Law and Taxation**. 4th ed. Valhalla, NY: Warren, Gorham & Lamont, 2000-date. 1 vol. (various pagings). Looseleaf format. Supplemented twice annually. Also available on Online.
Cost: $380 per year; Online: $575 per year (2014).
This detailed guide to current law and practice governing estate planning and taxation is designed as a desktop reference for the estate and tax law specialist. The authors examine the impact of state law and federal and state taxes in estate planning, the basis and valuation of property, jointly owned property, community property and other marital interests, life insurance, qualified retirement plans, individual retirement arrangements, and other

employee benefits, business interests, lifetime transfers to save estate taxes, gifts, sales, loans and other lifetime arrangements, premarital agreements, separation agreements, post-marital agreements and alternatives in estate planning, planning for incapacity and financing long-term care, wills, probate estates and other arrangements effective upon death, arrangements to save estate taxes, the marital deduction, noncharitable trusts, powers of appointment, split-interest trusts, and the generation-skipping transfer tax. Also includes a sample of forms. Tables of IRC sections, Treasury regulations, Revenue Rulings, Revenue Procedures, a Table of Cases, and index. David Westfall is the John L. Gray and Carl E. Shipper Professor of Law at Harvard Law School. George P. Mair is a partner in the Boston law firm of Bingham Dana LLP.

Whitman, Robert and David M. English. **Fiduciary Accounting and Trust Administration Guide**. 2d ed. Philadelphia: ALI-ABA, 2002. 1 vol. (492 pp.). Paperbound and Online.
Cost: e-book: $159; from $38.90 on amazon.com (2014).
The National Fiduciary Accounting Standards Project was created to address an apparent need for a simple and uniform set of fundamental accounting principles and model uniform accounting formats which could be used in various jurisdictions. This guideBook is designed for use by professionals who settle estates. Its stated goal is to clarify the terms, concepts and procedures in fiduciary accounting in order to help practitioners determine the necessary valuations and allocations, prepare the proper schedules, make the correct distributions, and, where necessary, file a court accounting. Among several useful appendices are model executor's and trustee's accounts, a sample letter of engagement for review of fiduciary accounts, a directory of software vendors and support services., a list of available fiduciary accounting and performance presentation software, table of cases, a table of statutes, rules, and regulations, and a subject index.

Wilkins, Robert P. **Drafting Wills and Trust Agreements: A Systems Approach.** 4th ed. St. Paul, MN: West (Clark Boardman Callaghan), 2009-date. 4 vols. Looseleaf format.
Cost: $964; no supplementation to date; 3d ed.: 1997: $140; 1998: $173; 1999: $195; 2000: $195; 2001: $231; 2002: $271; 2003: $75; 2004: $308; 2005: $319; 2006: $376; 2007: $419; 2008: $466; 2009: $552; 2010: $546; 2011: $559; 2012: $610; 2013: $707; **Monthly Assured Print Price (APP):** $64/$768.
This is a two-volume drafting guide to the full range of wills and trusts instruments. Organized by a checklist system, it provides a step-by-step discussion of the law of wills and trust together with more than 500 forms and clauses as the basis for drafting an instrument appropriate to the client's needs. Volume one discusses federal tax law considerations and the drafting of revocable trust agreements, while volume two includes the law and forms necessary for drafting an estate plan employing wills. An excellent tool to help guide the practitioner through the many legal and tax requirements involved in estate planning and the drafting of wills and trusts instruments.

Additional titles in the field of Trusts and Estates are available from the following publishers: ALI-ABA, American Bar Association, Wolters Kluwer Law & Business, CCH, Inc., Crown Publishing Group, Delmar Publishers, Esperti Peterson Institute, LexisNexis, McGraw-Hill Professional Book Group, Oxford University Press, Panel Publishers, RIA, Thomson Reuters (West), Tower Publishing, Warren, Gorham & Lamont. See Appendix B for addresses and telephone numbers.

Workers Compensation Law

American Medical Association. **Guides to the Evaluation of Permanent Impairment.** 6th ed. Chicago: AMA, 2007.
Cost: $194 ($143 to members); from $115.55 on amazon.com (2014).
The **Guides** are the product of the AMA's Committee on Rating of Mental and Physical Impairment and are designed to establish a series of practical guides for the rating of physical impairment of various organ systems. Their impact upon the field of workers' compensation is reflected in their adoption by twenty-six states. In addition to chapters outlining the standards for various types of physical and mental impairments, the volume also covers the concepts of impairment evaluation, and records and reports, and includes references to the medical literature.

Babitsky, Steven and James J. Mangraviti, Jr. **Understanding the AMA Guides in Workers' Compensation.** 6th ed. New York: Wolters Kluwer Law & Business, 2008-date. 1 vol. (various pagings). Annual supplementation.
Cost: $399; supplementation: 2009: $199; 2010: $210; 2011: $329; 2012: $235; 2013: $269; 3d ed.: 2004: $159; 2005: $169; 2006: $185; 2007: $189; 2008: new edition; 2d ed.: 1998: $52; 1999: $65; 2000: $79; 2001: $96; 1st edition: 1995: $60; 1996: $62.
Adopted by more than half the states, the AMA **Guides to the Evaluation of Permanent Impairment** are designed to reduce litigation costs by eliminating the indeterminate standards for assessing the value of permanent impairments and fixing awards. This volume presents both the theoretical and practical application of the **Guides**, providing the attorney with the information necessary to evaluate their validity and interpret awards. Chapters cover historical development of the **Guides**, medical use, validity and reliability, proving permanent impairment, using the **Guides** in cross-examination, sample proofs, and judicial interpretation of the Guides. The volume includes extensive citations to primary and secondary sources, and the medical literature.

Hood, Jack B., Benjamin A. Hardy, Jr. and Harold S. Lewis. **Workers Compensation Laws and Employee Protection in a Nutshell.** 5th ed. St. Paul, MN: West, 2011. 1 vol. (564 pp.). Paperbound. Available from West Academic.
Cost: $41; from $24.93 on amazon.com; kindle: $23.08 (2014).
This detailed one-volume overview of workers' compensation law is designed for the law student, but also useful as a brief review for the practitioner. In addition to the history and theories

of workers' compensation, the authors examine its relationship to the law of torts, the employer-employee relationship, personal injuries arsing out of and in the course of employment, death, medical expenses, disabilities and benefits, administration, third-party actions,employee protection laws, wrongful discharge, and miscellaneous employee protection laws. The text is augmented with selective citations to relevant cases, statutes, and regulations. No West Hornbook exists in this area.

Larson, Arthur and Lex K. Larson. **The Law of Workmen's Compensation.** New York: Matthew Bender & Co., 1952-date. 12 vols. Looseleaf format. Supplemented approximately three times annually. Authority CD-ROM includes no-cost online updating via LEXIS-NEXIS.
Cost: $5,399 (includes annual subscription); annual renewal: 1995: $1,558.50 (price frozen since 1992); 1996: $1,635; 1997: $1,635; 1998: $1,720; 1999: $1,790; 2000: $1,920; 2001: $2,054; 2002: $2,116; 2003: $2,222; 2004: $2,333; 2005: $2,520; 2006: $2,621; 2007: 2,778; 2008: $3,000; 2009: $3,180; 2010: $3,180; 2011: $3,212; 2012: $3,324; 2013: $3,557; 2014: $3,882; CD-ROM: $6,322; annual renewal: 1998: $1,640; 1999: $1,790; 2000: $1,920; 2001: $2,054; 2002: $2,198; 2003: $2,308; 2004: $2,423; 2005: $2,593; 3006: $2,697; 2007: $2,912; 2008: $3,174; 2009: $3,428; 2010: $3,599; 2011: $3,779; 2012: $4,006; 2013: $4,286; 2014: $4,771.56; eBook: $4,587; renewal: 2014: $3,628.
Although a few competitors have appeared upon the scene, this work remains the classic and definitive work on the subject of workers' compensation. Its author, the late Arthur Larson, was the James B. Duke Professor of Law at Duke University and former Under Secretary of Labor from 1911-1933. Originally published in 1952, the work is now updated by his son Lex K. Larson, President of Employment Law Research, Inc. and a Senior Lecturer at Law at Duke University Law School. This is an exhaustive treatise on the law and practice governing workplace injuries and the rules governing the awarding of cash and medical benefits to the injured workers. The set examines the nature and historical origins of workers compensation, the nature and definition of workplace injuries, specific inclusions or exemptions, disability and personal injury benefits, dependency and death benefits, the exclusiveness of the compensation remedy, employer misconduct, third party actions, adjective law, conflict of laws, insurance, and the relation to other kinds of wage-loss protections. The text is thoroughly supported with citations to relevant cases, with indications of those decisions in which **Larson** is cited by the courts. Includes 9 volumes of substantive text and two volumes containing the Index and Table of Cases. A virtual necessity for the attorney specializing in workers compensation.

Cost Saving Tips: Buy a used set, if available, or buy a new set and let it lapse after the first year. Finally, if you don't require the exhaustive coverage of the 12-volume work, buy the 3-volume desk edition, or, alternatively, use the desk edition as your updating vehicle.

Larson, Arthur and Lex K. Larson. **The Law of Workmen's Compensation--Desk Edition.** New York: Matthew Bender & Co., 1972-date. 3 vols. Looseleaf format. Authority CD-ROM library includes no-cost online updating via LEXIS-NEXIS.
Cost: $1,443 (includes annual subscription); annual renewal: 1995: $419.00 (price frozen since 1992); 1996: $440.00; 1997: $440.00; 1998: $465.00; 1999: $485.00; 2000: $520.00; 2001: $556.00; 2002; $573.00; 2003: $602.00; 2004: $632.00; 2005: $683.00; 2006: $711.00; 2007: $754; 2008: $814; 2009: $863; 2010: $863; 2011: $872; 2012: $903; 2013: $966; 2014: $1,055; CD-ROM: $1,769 (annual subscription); renewal: 1999: $420.00; 2000: $520.00; 2001: $556.00; 2002: $595.00; 2003: $625.00; 2004: $656.00; 2005: $709.00; 2006: $738.00; 2007: $797; 2008: $853; 2009: $921; 2010: $968; 2011: $1,045; 2012: $1,139; 2013: $1,219; 2014: $1,356.60; eBook: $1,312; renewal: 2014: $1,055.
This is an abridgment of the 11-volume treatise with fewer citations to case law. However, even this abridgment has greater coverage than any competitive product.

Cost Saving Tips: A cost-effective alternative to the complete **Larson** at one-fourth the initial cost and one-fourth the annual updating cost. If you do require the fuller coverage of the complete Larson, you can use this edition as your updating medium and save over $2,000 per year in supplementation costs.

Larson, Arthur and Lex Larson. **Workers' Compensation Law: Cases, Materials and Text**. 5th ed. New York: Matthew Bender & Co., 2013. 1 vol. (1,000 pp.). Casebound, looseleaf and eBook. Legal Text Series.
Cost: book: $185; looseleaf: $148; eBook: $111 (2014).
Written by one the nation's leading experts in the field, this student-oriented text is a combination treatise and caseBook. Chapter coverage includes nature, development and exclusive nature of workers' compensation, injuries arising out of unemployment, course of employment, personal injury by accident, disease, employment status, specific inclusions or exemptions, benefits, employee and employer misconduct, third-party-actions, adjective law, conflict laws, insurance, and relation to other kinds of wage-loss protection. The volume also contains a number of problems based upon real life cases illustrated with sample cases. The author treats such evolving areas as stress claims, occupational diseases, exclusivity cases, VDT-related injuries, and passive smoking claims. Contains numerous citations to cases and statutes. An excellent and reasonably-priced alternative to most of the practitioner-oriented works on the market.

Modern Workers Compensation. St. Paul, MN: West (Clark Boardman Callaghan), 1993-date. 3 vols. Looseleaf pamphlet format. Supplemented quarterly.
Cost: $1,798; supplementation: 1994: $200; 1995: $114; 1996: $244; 1997: $260; 1998: $276; 1999: $306; 2000: $316; 2001: $370; 2002: $425.50; 2003: $464; 2004: $545; 2005: $558; 2006: $676; 2007: $708; 2008: $788; 2009: $888; 2010: $990; 2011: $958; 2012: $1,138; 2013: $1,263; **Monthly Assured Print Price (APP):** $120/$1,440.
This practitioner-oriented reference tool reflects the statutory basis of much modern workers compensation law. This work integrates both statutory and case law into a concise discussion and analysis of a field which has been subject to considerable overhaul in recent years. The textual discussion includes citations to relevant state statutory codes and court decisions

enabling the user to quickly locate the law of his or her state. The set is organized in three binders: (1) compensability, (2) benefits, and (3) procedure (both administrative and judicial). Chapters cover the following topics: general construction and validity, compulsory and elective coverage, remedies against employer, remedies against third persons, governing law, covered employers, covered employees, dependents, accidents and injuries, diseases, employment connection in general, travel and commuting, off-duty injuries, weather injuries, assaults or firearms, employee misconduct, subsequent injuries, basis for compensation, earnings, medical benefits, vocal rehabilitation, compensation agreements, payment, administrative proceedings in general, time limitations, parties, notice & claim & pleadings, medical examinations, burden of proof and presumptions, admissibility of evidence, weight and sufficiency of evidence, hearing, award, administrative review, retaliation, nature of judicial proceedings, jurisdiction and venue, parties, scope of review, hearing and determination, and costs, fees and expenses. Volume three also includes a Table of Jurisdictions and Index. There are cross references to both West digests and Larson, **Law of Workmen's Compensation** at the end of each chapter. While this work is obviously not on the same scholarly level with **Larson**, it is a convenient and quick resource for answering most workers compensation questions at lower cost. Citations are representative, not exhaustive, but do provide the user with entry points into the digests and Larson. The pamphlet format allows for fast updating and less opportunity for misfiled pages.

Norris, Martin J. and Robert Force. **The Law of Maritime Personal Injuries**. 5th ed. St. Paul, MN: West Group (Clark Boardman Callaghan), 2009/2011-date. 2 vols. Annual cumulative pocket parts.
Cost: $475; supplementation: 1993: $81; 1994: $92; 1995: $110; 1996: $135; 1997: $145; 1998: $153; 1999: $165; 2000: $179; 2001: $208; 2002: $244; 2003: $278; 2004: $311; 2005: $357.50; 2006: $56; 2007: $52.50; 2008: $104.50; 2009: $126; 2010: $139; 2011: $151.50; 2012: $166.50; 2013: $65.50; **Monthly Assured Print Price (APP):** $22/$264.
This two-volume treatise provides a comprehensive analysis of the law as it applies to harbor workers, passengers and visitors, the Longshore and Harbor Workers' Compensation Act, and the rights and responsibilities of all those involved in maritime personal injury actions. Coverage includes chapters on bringing an action, wrongful death, limitation of liability, suits against the government, negligence, products liability, practice and procedure, and indemnification. Appendices in volume two include the Longshore and Harbor Workers' Compensation Act, Federal Rules of Appellate Procedure, Federal Rules of Civil Procedure, and Forms. It also includes a table of personal Injury cases, table of cases, table of statutes, and subject index. Formerly published by Lawyers Cooperative.

Stone, Daniel J., ed. **Occupational Injuries and Illnesses**. New York: Matthew Bender & Co., 1992-date. 3 vols. Annual editions. Print and eBook.
Cost: $565; supplementation: 1999: $230; 2000: $245; 2001: $262; 2002: $281; 2003: $296; 2004: $311; 2005: $333; 2006: $357; 2007: $386; 2008: $411; 2009: $442; 2010: $480; 2011: $474; 2012: $496; 2013: $514; 2014: $560; eBook: $565; 2014: $560.
This work provides detailed medical analysis necessary to prove or refute claims of occupational injury or disease. The text outlines the factors which contribute to work-related injuries or illnesses together with the technical data required to prove whether or not they are work-related, including information on anatomy, the mechanisms of injury, epidemeology, pathogenesis, clinical manifestations, diagnostic tests, diagnosis and prognosis, treatment and rehabilitation programs, amount of disability assessed by the AMA, and related disorders. It also includes a variety of practice aids, including medical illustrations, medico-legal case annotations, bibliographic references, and more.

Wickert, Gary L. **Workers' Compensation Subrogation in All Fifty States**. 5th ed. Huntington, NY: Juris Publishing, 2012. 1 vol. (various pagings). Also available as a downloadable electronic product. Purchase also includes online access.
Cost: $225; no supplementation to date (2014).
Under the various state laws, workers' compensation benefits are the exclusive remedy available to workers injured in the course of their employment. In exchange for these guaranteed benefits, the employee gives up his or her right to pursue a tort action against the employer for negligence. Workers' compensation subrogation statutes also provide insurance carriers with the right to be subrogated (or substituted) to the rights of the employee against any third party that may have caused an employee's injury. These subrogation statutes vary widely from state to state. This volume examines workers' compensation generally, statutory subrogation rights, allocation third-party recoveries, understanding third party litigation issues, defining third parties, the borrowed servant doctrine, contractual limitations to subrogation, extra-territorial subrogation, Longshore and Harbor Workers; compensation subrogation, hiring and subrogation counsel. The remainder of the volume is devoted to individual chapters devoted to summaries of the subrogation statutes of all fifty states and the District of Columbia. The text of each chapter includes citations to relevant case law, and summaries of applicable state laws. Appendices include a table of authorities, table of cases and table of statutes. The author, a leading expert in the field of subrogation, is the founder of the Wisconsin subrogation firm of Matthiesen, Wickert & Lehrer and oversees a National Recovery Program with local counsel in all fifty states.

Workers' Compensation Library [CD-ROM]. New York: Matthew Bender & Co. One disc. Updated quarterly. Available for Windows. Search Engine: Folio.
Cost: $13,224 (annual subscription); renewal:1997: $3,650; 1998: $3,835; $3,990; 2000: $4,270; 2001: $4,569; 2002: $4,889; 2003: $5,134; 2004: $5,391; 2005: $5,768; 2006: $6,172; 2007: $6,666; 2008: $7,133; 2009: $7,704; 2010: $8,089; 2011: $8,736; 2012: $9,522; 2013: $10,189; 2014: $11,341.38.
Matthew Bender's Authority products are a sophisticated combination of analytical treatises and relevant primary law designed for the practitioner. This complete CD-ROM product contains the full text of the following Matthew Bender titles: **Larson's Workers' Compensation Law, Social Security Practice Guide, Occupational Injuries and Illnesses,**

Benefits Review Board Service--Longshore Reporter. Lesser combinations of titles may be selected by the subscriber. The subscription also includes the LEXIS-NEXIS Online Connection to recent case law.

Additional titles in the field of Workers Compensation Law are available from the following publishers: Alliance of American Insurers, American Insurance Assoc., American Medical Association, Wolters Kluwer Law & Business, Matthew Bender, Bisel Co., Bloomberg BNA Books, Capitol Publications, Cornell University Press, Greenwood Publishing Group, Huebner Foundation for Insurance Education, Institute of Government (UNC at Chapel Hill), Insurance Institute of America, Lawyers & Judges Publishing Co., LexisNexis, National Conference of State Legislatures, National Underwriter's Co., Practising Law Institute, M. Lee Smith Publishers, Standard Publishing, Thomson Reuters West, W.E. Upjohn Institute for Employment Research, Warren, Gorham & Lamont, Workers Compensation Co., Workers Compensation Research Institute. See Appendix B for addresses and telephone numbers.

Zoning and Planning Law

Abbey, Buck. **U.S. Landscape Ordinances: An Annotated Reference Handbook**. New York: John Wiley & Sons, 1998. 1 vol. (408 pp.).
Cost: $125; from $94.05 on amazon.com (2014).
A comprehensive state-by-state reference to the planning ordinances that govern the landscapes of more than 300 American cities. The author examines the ordinances that regulate such matters as landscape buffers, parking lots, vehicular use areas, open space design, land clearing and building sites, irrigation, and tree plantings. A useful guide for attorneys involved with zoning and planning issues, as well as professionals in landscape design and municipal planning, students, municipal legislators, and community activists. The product of ten years of research and analysis. Buck Abbey, ASLA, is Associate Professor of Landscape Architecture at Louisiana State University and a recognized authority on municipal landscape ordinances and site planning law.

Burke, Barlow. **Understanding the Law of Zoning and Land Use Controls**. 3d ed. Newark, NJ: LexisNexis (Matthew Bender), 2013. 1 vol. (440 pp.).
Cost: $45; eBook: $36; from $40.50 on amazon.com; kindle ed.: $20.99 (2014).
Land use is subject to a blend of constitutional, administrative and local government regulations, of which the police power and the takings clause are the most significant. The police power, broadly stated, is the power of the states and their legislative bodies to enact regulations over persons and property with the intent of prohibiting all things inimical to their citizens' health, safety, morals, and general welfare. Police power is both inherent in state legislative bodies and plenary, that is, complete and unqualified. It is also a reserved power granted to the states under the Tenth Amendment to the U.S. Constitution, a power often delegated to local governments and municipalities, and under which Congress is prohibited from exceeding its delegated powers and encroaching upon local prerogatives. This introductory textbook, intended for use in property law courses, embraces zoning, land use, and environmental regulation from a national perspective. The author examines the full range of zoning and land use issues, with a focus on administrative and legislative relief from land use controls. The chapters cover takings, zoning and land use controls, judicial review of zoning actions, wetlands and beaches, regulation of the user, and vested rights and governmental estoppel. Barlow Burke is a Professor of Law at the American University, Washington College of Law, and the author of numerous volumes in the field of real estate brokerage, title insurance, personal property, real estate transactions, land use and federal mortgage documents.

Davidson, Michael and Fay Dolnick. **Planner's Dictionary**. Chicago: American Planning Association, Planning Advisory Service, 2004. 1 vol. (261 pp.). Paperbound w/CD-ROM.
Cost: $15.00 (2014).
This glossary of more than 4,200 terms is based on a survey conducted by the staff of the APA's Planning Advisory Service of its research library's collection of zoning ordinances, state enabling legislation, plans, reference works, and other APA research products. Initially published as PAS Report 421, this new edition provides definitions of hundreds of terms, many reflecting technological changes, new laws, and concepts which have emerged since its initial publication in 1989. This is an updated and expanded version of the Planning Advisory Service's **A Glossary of Zoning, Development, and Planning Terms** (2000).

Deems, Nyal A. and N. Stevenson Jennette III. **A Practical Guide to Winning Land Use Approvals and Permits.** New York: Matthew Bender and Co., 1990-date. 1 vol. Looseleaf format and eBook. Supplemented annually.
Cost: $371 (includes annual subscription); annual renewal: 1995: $106 (price frozen since 1992); 1996: $111; 1997: $111; 1998: $120; 1999: $127; 2000: $135; 2001: $144; 2002: $155; 2003: $163; 2004: $169; 2005: $181; 2006: $194; 2007: $209; 2008: $228; 2009: $249; 2010: $271; 2011: $264; 2012: $337; 2013: $337; 2014: $321; eBook: $371; renewal: 2014: $321; CD-ROM available as part of the **Environmental Law Library**.
Co-authored by partners in the Michigan law firm of Varnum, Riddering, Schmidt & Howlett with extensive experience in land use permitting, this volume combines a succinct yet through coverage of substantive zoning law with practical guidance and strategies in obtaining land use approvals and permits. Citations to cases and statutes are selective in order to accommodate more substantive text. Includes coverage of procedures before administrative bodies as well as appeals to the courts. A sample court challenge to land use regulation is included together with litigation forms. Includes a table of cases and detailed index. A well organized and invaluable tool for the attorney specializing in land development and zoning law and permitting matters.

Kmiec, Douglas W. **Zoning and Planning Deskbook**. 2d ed. St. Paul, MN: West, 2011-date. 2 vols. Annual replacement volumes.

Cost: 2012-2013 Edition: $638; supplementation: 2004: $211.50; 2005: $221; 2006: $208; 2007: $267; 2008: $297; 2009: $691; 2010: $421; 2011: $432; 2012: $480; **Monthly Assured Print Price (APP)**: $53/636.
This practical resource provides basic discussion and guidance on the most commonly encountered land use and planning issues, including techniques for obtaining approvals and permits, public hearings, and remedies and relief from adverse decisions. Individual chapters discuss land use control in context, the typical zoning ordinance, relevant decision-making bodies, zoning objectives and methods, administrative and legislative zoning actions, zoning litigation, subdivision control, scope, structure, and objectives of subdivision control, municipal duty to provide service to new subdivisions, land use planning, planning theory, adoption of the comprehensive plan, and the legal significance of planning. The author also examines state and federal litigation on zoning matters. A less comprehensive, but more economical, alternative to Rathkopf's **The Law of Zoning and Planning**.

Kushner, James A. **Subdivision Law & Growth Management**. St. Paul, MN: West, 2001-date. 2 vols. Paperbound. Replaced twice annually.
Cost: 2013 (Nov.) Edition: $502; 2013 (May) Edition: $502; supplementation: 2003: $272; 2004: $300; 2005: $460; 2006: $372; 2007: $418.50; 2008: $466; 2009: $517; 2010: $576; 2011: $620; 2012: $656; **Monthly Assured Print Price (APP)**: $70/840.
Urban sprawl and the pace of residential development generally have focused attention upon the entire process of growth and its management. This two-volume work examines a host of issues arising in the wake of measures used to control the pace of local development. These measures include regulation of the permissible types of structures and land uses, promotion of public infrastructure to support new development, and the financing necessary to support that infrastructure. Chapters provide discussion and analysis of such topics as growth management techniques, legal limitations on growth management activities, growth management system evaluation, subdivision control generally, financing capital improvements, subdivision planning standards, subdivision administration, enforcement of subdivision controls, and vested development rights. The author also discusses legislative and judicial trends, policy choices, management strategies, denial modifications, and specific cases illustrating these developments.

Malone, Linda A. **Environmental Regulation of Land Use.** St. Paul, MN: West (Clark Boardman), 1990-date. 1 vol. Looseleaf format.
Cost: $1,049; ProView eBook: $963; supplementation: 2003: $259; 2004: 290; 2005: $313; 2006: $357; 2007: $398.50; 2008: $443; 2009: $507.50; 2010: $594; 2011: $609; 2012: $664; 2013: $770; **Monthly Assured Print Price (APP):** $77/$924.
In the context of our modern environmentally sensitive legal and regulatory climate, land use and management decisions are fraught with peril for developers and their legal representatives. In this volume, the author addresses environmental regulation in a variety of areas, with individual chapters devoted to coastal zones, wetlands, soil conservation, farmland preservation, floodplain regulation, preservation of environmental quality, water quality, groundwater, air quality, noise control, special management techniques, growth controls for environmental preservation, critical area regulations, development rights and the taking clause, and habitat conservation requirements. The author discusses the impact of federal, state, and local laws and regulations in the field, the sources of pollution, and the health and economic impacts of land use activities and decisions, and their remedies. The text includes citations to the latest statutes, regulations and court decisions. Linda A. Malone is the Marshall-Wythe Foundation Professor of Law at The College of William and Mary School of Law and author of numerous articles and the author or co-author of ten books on international law, human rights, and environmental law.

Mandelker, Daniel R. **Land Use Law.** 5th ed. Charlottesville, VA: LexisNexis, 2003-date. 1 vol. (734 pp.) Annual pocket part.
Cost: $227; supplementation: 2004: $65; 2005: $75; 2006: $85; 2007: $94; 2008: $102; 2009: $115; 2010: $119; 2011: $123; 2012: $128; 2013: $138; 4th edition: 1998: 0; 1999: $35; 2000: $45; 2001: $55; 2002: 0; 2003: $75; 3d ed.: 1995: $30; 1996: $37.50.
A well-organized, one-volume treatise on the law of land use and zoning by the Stamper Professor of Law, Washington University School of Law in St. Louis. Mandelker examines both the practical and the constitutional involved in taking law, particularly as expressed in the case of Lucas v. South Carolina Coastal Council. He provides analysis of the law controlling land use, the constitutional framework for such laws, the comprehensive plan, the zoning system. the zoning process, exclusionary zoning, residential development controls, growth management and public facility controls, aesthetic considerations, historic preservation, and environmental controls. Citations to case law and statutes are selective rather than comprehensive.

Nolon, John R. and Patricia E. Salkin. **Land Use in a Nutshell**. 5th ed. St. Paul, MN: West, 2006. 1 vol. (448 pp.). Paperbound. Available from West Academic.
Cost: $41; from $29.00 on amazon.com (2014).
A brief, student-oriented review of the law and principles of land use and urban planning. Discusses such topics as the control of land use, common law controls on the use of land, private law devices, the planning process, the master plan and the official map, regulation of land development, eminent domain and the police power, zoning, aesthetics and preservation of historical and cultural resources, natural resources, environmental controls, taxation and the control of land use, and energy and space considerations. Replaces the earlier nushell of the same title by Wright and Paust.

Robillard, Walter G. and Lane J. Bouman. **Clark on Surveying and Boundaries.** 7th ed. Charlottesville, VA: LexisNexis, 1997-date. 1 vol. Annual supplement.
Cost: $158; supplementation: 1998: $35; 1999: $45; 2000: $53; 2001: $65; 2002: $66; 2003: $68; 2004: $75; 2005: $85; 2006: $91; 2007: $97; 2008: $106; 2009: $122; 2010: $125; 2011: $135; 2012: $145; 2013: $146; 6th ed.: 1993: $25; 1994: $30; 1995: $40; 1996: $45.
First published by the late Frank Emerson Clark in 1922, this now

classic guide to the law of boundaries and surveying has been updated to reflect recent case law, statutes and regulations. An essential to the real estate attorney involved in property and boundary issues.

Robillard, Walter G. and Donald A. Wilson. **Brown's Boundary Control and Legal Principles**. 6th ed. Hoboken, NJ: John Wiley & Sons, 2009. 1 vol. (485 pp.).
Cost: $140; e-book: $119.99; from $64.93 on amazon.com; kindle: $79.99 (2014).
The history of boundaries and their location has its origins in prerecorded times and continues down to the present day. Boundaries may be created by actions, writings, and by law. Originally designated by word of mouth, boundaries were only identified with some degree of certainty with the introduction of mapping. This volume examines the legal and physical characteristics of boundaries, including, among others, the history and concept of boundaries; the creation of boundaries; the ownership, transfer, and description of real property; boundaries, law, and presumptions; creation of metes and bounds and nonsectionalized descriptions; the creation of GLO boundaries, federal and state nonsectionalized land surveys; locating easements and reversions; and riparian and littoral boundaries; resurveying and retracing sectionalized lands; the role of the surveyor, and the ethics and moral responsibilities of boundary creation and of retracements. The authors address the many principles governing the process of surveying, illustrated with a variety of maps and diagrams, and incorporating the latest technologies impacting boundary law. The volume concludes with a glossary of legal and surveying terms. The lead author is president of Walter G. Robillard & Associates. Donald A. Wilson is president of Land & Boundary Consultants, Inc. Together, they have been responsible for updating Curtis Brown's original work for the past 20 years. This is an essential reference for attorneys in real estate and land law, professional surveyors, and local officials.

Robillard, Walter G. and Donald A. Wilson. **Evidence and Procedures for Boundary Location**. 6th ed. Hoboken, NJ: John Wiley & Sons, 2011. 1 vol. (688 pp.).
Cost: $145; e-book: $119.99; from $32.98 on amazon.com; kindle: $82.99 (2014).
An essential reference for real estate and title attorneys, surveyors, and civil engineers, this, now, classic work provides detailed information on the various types of evidence required to establish legal and accurate boundaries which will survive legal scrutiny in courts of law. Includes discussion of the nature, scope and definition of evidence, verbal evidence, plats as evidence, water boundaries, historical knowledge, preservation, of evidence, procedures for locating boundaries described in writings and on maps, original surveys and platting laws, unwritten transfers of land ownership, guarantees of title and location, professional liability, professional stature, the surveyor in court, and the professional relationship between the surveyor, the law and evidence. Contains several useful appendices, including the surveyor's report, wooden evidence, the quasi-judicial function of surveyors, geodaesia, and land acts that created the pubic lands. Walter G. Robillard is an attorney at Land Consultants, Inc. of Atlanta, GA. Donald A. Wilson is with Land Boundary, Inc. in New Fields, NH.

Rohan, Patrick J. **Zoning and Land Use Controls.** New York: Matthew Bender & Co., 1978-date. 10 vols. Looseleaf format and eBook. No longer available on CD-ROM. Supplemented about three times yearly.
Cost: $3,542 (includes annual subscription); annual renewal: 1995: $955.50 (price frozen since 1992); 1996: $1,002; 1997: $1,002; 1998: $1,005; 1999: $1,050; 2000: $1,050; 2001: $1,124; 2002: $1,203; 2003: $1,347.00; 2004: $1,327; 2005: $1,420; 2006: $1,520; 2007: $1,619; 2008: $1,749; 2009: $1,889; 2010: $1,946; 2011: $2,004; 2012: $2,124; 2013: $2,273; 2014: $2,480; eBook: $3,220; renewal: 2014; $2,480.
A comprehensive guide to both the law and procedure of zoning and land use planning by Patrick J. Rohan, the Dean and Professor of Law, St. John's University School of Law and author of Powell on Real Property (revised edition), as well as a number of legal scholars. This treatise is typical of many Matthew Bender titles in its exhaustive coverage of the subject matter and frequent supplementation. In 57 chapters, the authors discuss zoning in all its manifestations, from exclusionary and inclusionary zoning to landmark, historic zoning and industrial zoning. Additional chapters are devoted to space zoning, builder exactions, adult entertainment zoning, cluster zoning, aesthetic zoning, sign regulation, floodplains, environmental regulation, environmental impact requirements, municipal comprehensive planning, objectives of zoning, subdivision controls, building permits, zoning procedure, land use arbitration, and judicial review. There are extensive forms and documents, both governmental and litigation forms. There are citations to cases and statutes from all jurisdictions. This set combines first-rate scholarship with all the relevant practical aids necessary for the attorney specializing in zoning and planning matters.

Cost Saving Tips: Buy a used set, if available, or buy a new set and let it lapse after the first year. If you choose the CD-ROM version of this work, you have no choice but to pay the $2,120.00 annual renewal charge because the information on the last disc you receive will time expire within about a month.

Salkin, Patricia E. **American Law of Zoning.** 5th ed. St. Paul, MN: West (Clark Boardman Callaghan), 2008-date. 5 vols. Annual pocket supplements.
Cost: $870; ProView eBook: $845; supplementation: 2009: $222; 2010: $259; 2011: $284; 2012: $312; 2013: $337; 4th ed.: 1996: $95; 1997: $74; 1998: $78; 1999: $84; 2000: $91; 2001: $107.50; 2002: $236; 2003: $248; 2004: $160; 2005: $175; 2006: $339; 2007: $189; **Monthly Assured Print Price (APP):** $39/$468.
This updated, five-volume treatise provides the attorney with thorough coverage of the law of zoning and its administration. Salkin examines the scope of governmental control over private land, its constitutional basis, and the legislative limitations upon the enactment, amendment and repeal of zoning ordinances. Chapters also address such issues as exclusionary zoning, growth controls, planned unit development, mobile homes, outdoor advertising, administrative relief from zoning regulations, and planning at the local level. The authors also cover judicial enforcement of zoning and planning regulations as well as the statutes, charter provisions and ordinances by which land use is controlled and regulated. Volume five includes both model zoning ordinances and forms to be used in both administrative hearings and court proceedings, as well as a Table of Cases and

Index.. The current editor, Patricia E. Salkin, is Associate Dean, Professor of Government Law, and Director of the Government Law Center of Albany Law School where she teaches courses in land use law, government ethics, housing law and policy, current legal issues in government, and NYS administrative law.
She is the author, or co-author, of numerous works in the fields of zoning and planning law.

Williams, Norman, Jr. and John Taylor. **American Land Planning Law: Land Use and the Police Power.** St. Paul, MN: West (Clark Boardman Callaghan), 1974-date. 8 vols. Annual pocket supplements.
Cost: $1,058; supplementation: 1993: $175; 1994: $210; 1995: $250; 1996: $284; 1997: $596; 1998: $316; 1999: $341; 2000: $369; 2001: $429; 2002: $502.50; 2003: $627; 2004: $280; 2005: $303; 2006: $345; 2007: $384; 2008: $427.50; 2009: $480; 2010: $528; 2011: $576.50; 2012: $628; 2013: $681; **Monthly Assured Print Price (APP):** $70/$840.
A comprehensive examination of land use planning and the fundamental changes which have enveloped the field over the past thirty years. The authors closely analyze the relationship between governmental authority and private development as it has manifest itself in the resolution of environmental concerns, exclusionary zoning practices. The authors discuss and analyze over 15,000 cases in all fifty states. The contents encompass such topics as land use planning and controls, comprehensive plans, residential zoning, conflicts between residential and nonresidential land use, nonconforming uses, administrative aspects of zoning, variances, special permits, techniques to implement community design, preservation of open space, state and regional land use controls, and future trends. Volume six contains appendices, illustrations, Tables of Cases and Index. One of the upshots of Thomson Legal Publishing's recent acquisitions is that the West is now the publisher of three multi-volume treatises in the field of zoning and planning law--treatises formerly published independently by Lawyers Cooperative, Clark Boardman, and Callaghan and Company. All three have their strengths. Williams leans more heavily toward the planning side of the field, while Rathkopf and Anderson cover zoning law with greater specificity. Like the other two, Williams features extensive citations to both case and statutory law, and zoning ordinances.

Wilson, Donald A. **Easements Relating to Land Surveying and Title Examination**. Hoboken, NJ: John Wiley & Sons, 2013. 1 vol. (285 pp.).
Cost: $95.00; from $69.87 on amazon.com; kindle: $54.49 (2014).
An easement is the right to use another person's land for a stated purpose, and it can involve a general or specific portion of the property. A right-of-way, for example, is a type of easement that gives someone the right to travel across property owned by another person. Easements constitute one of the most complex areas of real property law and among the most frequently litigated. Easements are not real property but are often treated as such by the initiated. However, only some easements are a matter of public record, a fact which complicates the job of researchers. This treatment of easements, with examples, was designed primarily for the benefit of land surveyors and those in the title field, as well as the holders and buyers of easements such as utility companies and highway departments. It covers easements in general, easement terminology, types of easements, creation of easements, termination of easements, easements and descriptions, problem easements, the process of reversion, reversion of easements, reversion relating to highways, rules of locating and defining easements, and easements and the land surveyor, and easements and the title examiner. It also includes eighteen case studies with maps and diagrams that provide examples of some of the most common problems relating to easements. The volume concludes with a list of references, ALR references, glossary of terms, and subject index. The volume includes selective citations to primary and secondary authorities. This is an essential reference for any lawyer, surveyor or title professional who encounters easements in the course of their work. Donald A. Wilson is President of Land & Boundary Consultants, Inc. in Newfields, NH.

Yokley, E. D. **Zoning Law and Practice.** 5th rev. ed. Charlottesville, VA: LexisNexis, 2001-date. 8 vols. (issued between 2001 and 2007) Twice annual pocket supplements.
Cost: $488; supplementation: 1993: $105; 1994: $110; 1995: $110; 1996: $120: 1997: 0; 1998: $170; 1999: $180; 2000: $375; 2001: $210; 2002: $201; 2003: $210; 2004: $509; 2005: $535; 2006: $558; 2007 $601; 2008: $287; 2009: $715; 2010: $750; 2011: $755; 2012: $796; 2013: $875; eBook: $488; renewal: 2014: $875.
E. D. Yokley defines zoning law as the use of police power by the local political entity to protect itself against harmful invasions of buildings and uses in a comprehensive manner. A former Director of the Law Department, Nashville, Tennessee, and Yokley labored over this treatise for more than thirty years before turning over the task of updating to James Jay Brown, Professor of Law, Stetson University College of Law. This eight-volume treatise attempts to cover the range of issues involved in land planning and zoning law in a manner to be of use of practicing attorneys, judges, and staff members of planning and zoning boards. Yokley describes the origin and early growth of zoning law, the police power under which it is exercised, esthetic considerations, the comprehensive plan, planned unit development, the context of the zoning ordinance, accessory uses, permits, enforcement, planning commissions, procedures before boards of appeals, variances, nonconforming uses, appellate procedure. injunctions, building code and ordinances, environmental considerations, and much more. There are six volumes of substantive discussion and analysis and two volumes containing a table of cases and subject index. The author cites relevant cases from every jurisdiction. The pocket supplements provide both revised text as well as more recent citations to court decisions. While not on the same scholarly plane as **Rathkopf**, this is a useful reference tool, reasonable in price with modest supplementation costs.

Cost Saving Tips: This is a useful, but over-supplemented set, with pocket parts issued twice annually. Avoid the standing order and purchase the pocket parts on an as-needed basis, but certainly no more often than once per year.

Ziegler, Edward H., Jr. **Rathkopf's The Law of Zoning and Planning.** St. Paul, MN: West (Clark Boardman Callaghan), 1956-date. 5 vols. Looseleaf format. Also available as ProView eBook. Supplemented 3-4 times annually. An optional annual **Zoning and Planning Law Handbook** is included with the subscription, but may be declined.
Cost: $2,825; ProView eBook: $2,591; supplementation: 1993: $452.50; 1994: $404.50; 1995: $457; 1996: $522; 1997: $488.25; 1998: $519; 1999: $561; 2000: $596; 2001: $699.50; 2002: $784; 2003: $264; 2004: $920; 2005: $1,000; 2006: $1,040; 2007: $1,102; 2008: $1,194; 2009: $668; 2010: $1,501; 2011: $1,640; 2012: $1,804; 2013: $1,036; **Monthly Assured Print Price (APP):** $189/$2,268.
Originally authored by Charles Rathkopf, this classic work has been revised and updated by Edward H. Ziegler, Professor of Law at the University of Denver. This exhaustive work encompasses 57 chapters on all aspects of zoning and planning law, including all types and manners of zoning, zoning controls, judicial review of administrative zoning decisions, regulation of occupancy, developments, subdivisions, building permits, nonconforming uses, standing, and much more. The text is supported with extensive citations to cases, statutes, regulations and a variety of secondary sources.

Cost Saving Tips: The high annual supplementation cost for this set may induce you to drop the standing order and purchase a new set at periodic intervals. Supplements are not cumulative, however, and must be interfiled, making it more difficult and costly to bring the lapsed subscription up-to-date. A new set can be purchased at a future date once significant savings have been achieved. Also, dropping the annual **Zoning and Planning Handbook** will provide additional savings without compromising the treatise itself. The **Handbook** consists of both original and reprinted articles and is not essential to maintaining the currency of the set.

Additional titles on Zoning and Planning Law are available from the following publishers: American Bar Association, American Planning Association, Matthew Bender, Center for Urban Policy Research, William S. Hein & Co., Institute of Government, Johns Hopkins University Press, LexisNexis, Lincoln Land Institute, Charles P. Mills, New York Planning Federation, West, John Wiley, Wolters Kluwer Law & Business. See Appendix B for addresses and telephone numbers.

Chapter 28: State Legal Publications and Information Sources

This chapter provides the practicing attorney or library with a listing of the most significant primary law publications, reference tools and information sources for each of the fifty states and the District of Columbia. The following categories of publications and information are included: (1) Codes and Session Laws; (2) Administrative Law; (3) Court Reports; (4) Court Rules; (5) Digests, Encyclopedias and Practice Books; (6) Citators; (7) CD-ROM products (single user prices only are provided); (8) State Legal Research Guides and Histories; (9) Leading Web Sites for State Legal Research; and (10) Leading Publishers of State Specific Legal Materials. Although provided here selectively, the on-line resources of Westlaw, LexisNexis, CalLaw, CaseClerk, Casemaker, Fastcase, Loislaw, TheLaw.net, and VersusLaw provide subscribers with the full text of all, or many, state statutory codes, appellate court decisions, court rules, and administrative codes. See Chapter 25 for specific costs of these online resources.

1. Codes and Session Laws: Including official and unofficial, commercial and governmental state codes, official session laws and commercial session law services (i.e. advance legislative services). Also included are Legislative Hotlines for tracking of current legislation. Coverage of primary law resources on LexisNexis and Westlaw also provided.

2. Administrative Law: Including both administrative codes and registers, both official and commercial.

3. Court Reports: Including both official and commercial reporters. Entries will indicate if official state reports have been discontinued. Entries will also provide current cost of complete set, current annual supplementation cost for last full year, per volume cost of recent volume (both subsriber and list), **Monthly Assured Print Pricing** (monthly/annual), and annual advance sheet subscription cost.

4. Court Rules: Including the most significant commercially published court rules, both official and commecial.

5. Digests, Encyclopedias, and Practice Sets: Including all West state key number digests; state legal encyclopedias, and selective major state practice sets.

6. Citators (print): Shepard's State Citations. The all-inclusive subscription prices include paper advance sheets and any bound supplements or revisions issued during the course of the year. Advance sheets are published six times per year, monthly or bi-monthly (2 per month). Only in-state pricing included. Contact sales representative for network license fees, out-of-state pricing, and discounts.

7. CD-ROM Products: Including all available commercial and governmental CD-ROM products containing state primary law, including statutes, court decisions, courts rules; and finding tools and secondary sources such as Shepard's Citations, state legal encyclopedias, practice sets, etc. Recent yers have witnessed a decided abandonment of CD-ROM products in favor of online access.

8. State Legal Research Guides.
Includes commercially published state legal research guides, AALL-sponsored state documents bibliographies, state constitution reference guides, state legal histories, and other state-specific legal bibliographies.

9. Leading Web Sites for State Legal Research. All updated for April 2013.
If you wish to access the home page for the various states, you may begin here. Click on a state to go to its home page, and from there you will be able to access most of the state government departments from that main link.

10. A list of leading publishers of state specific legal materials, including primary law, treatises, practice books and CLE publications. All publishers and their addresses may be found in Appendix B.

NOTE: Prices for legal publications are in a constant state of flux. As an aid to the prospective purchaser, every attempt has been made to obtain current and accurate pricing and supplementation cost information for each of the publications or products listed below. The initial product prices and historic subscriber supplementation costs are intended to provide the purchaser with the information necessary to make wise consumer decisions, or comparative choices from among competing titles. They may not reflect all publishers' discounts, or special promotional prices which may be in effect at any given time (West, however, typically discounts all standing order supplementation by about 20%, reporters about 25%). Nor have network or other special charges been included. All prices are also subject to change at the publishers' discretion. The author welcomes any additions or corrections to this pricing information for inclusion in subsequent annual editions. It is recommended, however, that you contact your local sales representative, or the publisher directly, for up-to-date pricing information prior to making a purchase. A listing of publishers and their telephone numbers is located in Appendix B.

*Prices listed were obtained or verified in March/April, 2014. The year (2014) in parentheses following pricing information indicates that pricing has been updated or verified as of March/April, 2014.

Special Note: Most websites are listed without the prefixes http//: and www. You may have to add them when accessing a state web site. Also, most states allow you to link to various departments and agencies directly from their home page, so typing in the entire URL may not be necessary.

Alabama

1. Codes and Session Laws.
Code of Alabama. Charlottesville, VA: LexisNexis, 1975-date. 24 vols. in 37. Annual pocket supplements and periodic revised volumes.
Cost: $384 (in-state); $489 (out-of-state); supplementation

(in-state/out-of-state): 2002: $98/$127; 2003: $197/$246; 2004: $231/250; 2005: $241/$254; 2006: $131/$141; 2007: 161/186; 2008: $256/$267; 2009: $194/$206; 2010: $310/$320; 2011: $365/$377; 2012: $201/$213; 2013: $.

Code of Alabama 1975. St. Paul, MN: Thomson West, 1975-date. 44 vols. Hardbound. Annual pocket supplements and periodic revised volumes. The official state code.
Cost: $692; annual supplementation: 1995: $79; 1996: $156; 1997: $147.19; 1998: $98.58; 1999: $176.15; 2000: $125; 2001: $136.03; 2002: $140.65; 2003: $145.05; 2004: $78.50; 2005: $183.55; 2006: $170.40; 2007: $184; 2008: $251.04; 2009: $30; 2010: $251.63; 2011: $292.94; 2012: $267.39; 2013: $239.58; **Monthly Assured Print Pricing** (**AAP**): $29/$336.

Alabama Advance Code Service. Charlottesville, VA: LexisNexis. Supplements code between annual pocket parts.
Cost: $120 (in-state) (2014).

Alabama Advance Legislative Service. Charlottesville, VA: LexisNexis. These pamphlets are published during and immediately after current legislative session and contain the text of laws in numerical chapter sequence in order of passage.
Cost: $139 (in-state) (2014).

Alabama Code Legislative Service. St. Paul, MN: Thomson West. These pamphlets are published during and immediately after current legislative session and contain the text of laws in numerical chapter sequence in order of passage.
Cost: $231 (2014)

Acts of Alabama. [session laws] Montgomery, AL: Secretary of State. Annual.
Cost: 1994: $75 (3 vols. @ $25 ea.); 1995: $75 (3 vols.); 1996: $50 (2 vols.); 1997: $75 (3 vols.); 1998-2013: $50 per year (2 vols.) (334) 242-7200.

Legislative Hotline: House: 1-800-499-3052 (in-state); (334) 242-7600 (out-of-state) Senate: 1-800-499-3051 (in-state), (334) 242-7800 (out-of-state).

2. Administrative Law.

Alabama Administrative Code. Montgomery, AL: Legislative Reference Service, 1984-date. 23 vols. in 38. Supplemented several times annually. Also available online:
http://www.alabamaadministrativecode.state.al.us/about-code.html
(334) 242-7570.
Cost: $720 (includes one year's updates); supplementation: $120 per year for quarterly updates (2014).

Alabama Administrative Monthly. Montgomery, AL: Legislative Reference Service, 1982-date. Oct. – Sept. fiscal year. Also available online.
Cost: $60 per year (2014). (334) 242-7570.

3. Court Reports.

Alabama Reports, 1840-1976. [Ceased publication with vol. 295.] 49 vols. available
Cost: out-of-print; see Used Lawbook Dealers in Appendix C.

Alabama Appeals Reports, 1910-1976. St. Paul, MN: Thomson West. [Ceased publication with vol. 57] 42 vols.
Cost: out-of-print; see Used Lawbook Dealers in Appendix C.

West's Alabama Reporter [1st] - **3d**. St. Paul, MN: Thomson West, 1976-date. [offprint of Southern Reporter 2d-designated official in 1976]. Contains decisions of the Alabama Supreme Court and Alabama Appellate Court from 1976 to date. Current volume: 121-123 **So.3d**.
Cost: 2d series: $2,961 (194 vols.); 3d series: $1,687; annual cost: 2002: $668; 2003: $680; 2004: $620; 2005: $1057.50; 2006: $654.50; 2007: $557; 2008: $713; 2009: $623; 2010: $616; 2011: $995.25; 2012: $815; 2013: $536. Current volume: $111.91 (list); **Monthly Assured Print Pricing** (APP): $126/$1,512.

Southern Reporter [1st] - **3d**. St. Paul, MN: Thomson West, 1886-date. Contains decisions of the Alabama Supreme Court from 1886 to date, and Alabama Appellate Court from 1911 to date, as well as other Southern regional appellate court decisions. Current vol.: 130 So.3d
Cost: 1st series out-of-print (see used lawbook dealers); 2d series: $14,566; 3d series: $17,639; annual cost (2013): $12,178; current vol.: $529/$706 (subscriber/list); **Monthly Assured Print Pricing** (**APP**): $1,274/$15,288. See list of used lawbook dealers in Appendix C.

Southern Reporter 2d. Advance sheets. St. Paul, MN: Thomson West. Weekly.
Cost: $2,866.56 per year (discounted to bound volume subscribers) (2014).

4. Court Rules.

Alabama Rules Annotated. Charlottesville, VA: LexisNexis. 2 vols. Updated semiannually. Replaced annually.
Cost: 2013-2014: $106 (2014).

Alabama Rules of Court, State and Federal. St. Paul, MN: Thomson West. 2 vols. Annual.
Cost: 2013 Edition: $184 (2014).

5. Digests, Encyclopedias, and Practice Sets.

Alabama Digest 2d. St. Paul, MN: Thomson West, 1993-date. 112 vols. Annual pocket parts and periodic revised volumes, and interim pamphlets.
Cost: $5,423 ; supplementation: 1995: $175; 1996: $170; 1997: $124; 1998: $188; 1999: $635; 2000: $284; 2001: $778.50; 2002: $1,100; 2003: $401.50; 2004: $654.50; 2005: $1,626.50; 2006: $1,284; 2007: $1,338.50; 2008: $651.50; 2009: $887; 2010: $2,542; 2011: $2,793.50; 2012: $3.042; 2013: $4,298; **Assured Monthly Print Price** (**APP**): $289/$3,468.

6. Citators.

Shepard's Alabama Citations. Albany, NY: Shepard's. Monthly.
Cost: $4,371 (8 bound volumes); all-inclusive subscription: $2,273 (2014).

Online: All jurisdictional Shepard's and KeyCite are no longer available as stand-alone products, but are included as part of a jurisdictional or subject library package (2014).

7. CD-ROM Products.
Alabama Reporter and Code of Alabama. Eagan, MN: Thomson West. Premise. One disc. Updated quarterly. Contains full text of decisions of Alabama Supreme Court from 1820 to date, Court of Appeals, Court of Civil Appeals, and Court of Criminal Appeals appearing in the Southern Reporter 2d, vol. 1 to date, Attorney General opinions from 1977 to date, court rules, court orders, Alabama Code, session laws. Decisions also searchable by West Topics and Key Numbers, headnotes, and synopses. Windows and Macintosh versions available. Search Engine: PREMISE. Subscription includes online Westlaw connection. Reputed to be phased out in 2015.
Cost: $8,856 per year (2014).

LexisNexis CD --Alabama Primary Law. Albany, NY: LexisNexis. One disc. Updated periodically. Contains the text of Alabama Civil Practice Forms (3d ed.), Alabama Civil Procedure, civil statutes, rules, and case citations. Available for Windows. Search Engine: Folio; LivePublish (NextPage).
Cost: $2,401 per year (2014).

8. State Legal Research Guides. Beals
Beals, Blakeley. **State Document Bibliography: Alabama**. Chicago: AALL, 2012.
Cost: $30.00. Available from William S. Hein & Co. on electronic pdf and on HeinOnline (2014).

DeLeve, Scott. Alabama Practice Materials: A Selective Bibliography in Houdek, Frank G., ed. **State Practice Materials: Annotated Bibliographies**. Buffalo, NY: William S. Hein & Co., Inc., 2002-date. 2 vols. Looseleaf format.
Cost: $195.00 (2014).

Kitchens, Lynne B. and Timothy A. Lewis. "Alabama Practice Materials: A Selective Bibliography." **Law Library Journal** 82, No. 2 (1990): 703-725.

Stewart, William H. **The Alabama State Constitution**. New York: Oxford University Press, 2011. 1 vol. (292 pp.).
Cost: $150; from $32.58 on amazon.com; kindle: $119.99 (2014).

9. Leading Web Sites for State Law Research.

Home page:	www.alabama.gov/
Administrative Code:	www.alabamaadministrativecode.state.al.us/
Agency Directory:	www.info.alabama.gov/directory.aspx?range=2
Attorney General:	www.ago.state.al.us/
Attorney Gen. Opinions:	www.ago.state.al.us/Opinions.aspx
Bar Association:	www.alabar.org/
Constitution:	http://alisondb.legislature.state.al.us/acas/ACASLogin.asp (click on Constitution tab on left side of page)http://www.legislature.state.al.us
Dept. of Archives & History:	www.archives.state.al.us/
Governor:	http://governor.alabama.gov/
Judicial Branch:	www.judicial.alabama.gov/
Law Library:	http://judicial.alabama.gov/library.cfm
Legislature:	www.legislature.state.al.us
Secretary of State:	www.sos.state.al.us/
Statutes:	http://alisondb.legislature.state.al.us/acas/ACASLoginie.asp
Supreme Court:	http://judicial.alabama.gov/supreme.cfm

10. Leading publishers of state specific treatises, practice books, and CLE publications.
Agora Publishers, Alabama State Bar Association, Alabama Bar Institute for Continuing Legal Education, Matthew Bender, Manchester Press, National Business Institute, Samford University Press, Thomson Reuters (West). See Appendix B for addresses and telephone numbers.

Alaska

1. Codes and Session Laws.
Alaska Statutes. Charlottesville, VA: LexisNexis, 2004-date. 14 vols. Softbound. Revised every other year, with supplements in odd years.
Cost: 2012 Edition: $312 (in-state); $1,122.80 (out-of-state); prior odd-year supplementation: 2005: $107.32 (in-state); $121.30 (out-of-state); 2007: $64.49/$138; 2008: $65/$141; 2009: $129/$232; 2011: $205; 2012: $312/$1,120; 2013L $236.

Alaska Advance Code Service. Charlottesville, VA: LexisNexis, 1997-date. Supplements the Alaska Statutes between annual supplements.
Cost: $46.00 (in-state); $104.00 (out-of-state) (2014).

Alaska Advance Legislative Service. Charlottesville, VA: LexisNexis. These pamphlets are published during and immediately after current legislative session and contain the text of laws in numerical chapter sequence in order of passage.
Cost: $65.00 (in-state) (2014).

Alaska Session Laws [Slip Laws subscription]. Juneau: Alaska Legislative Affairs Agency. Annual. (907) 465-3763.
Cost: $80 (mailed) (2014). Also available on the Internet at: http://www.legis.state.ak.us/

Legislative Hotline: (907) 465-4648.

2. Administrative Law.
Alaska Administrative Code. Charlottesville, VA: LexisNexis, 1988-date. 10 vols. Looeleaf format. Updated quarterly.
Cost: $534; supplementation: $534 (2014). Also available on the Alaska state Web site at: http://old-www.legis.state.ak.us/cgi-bin/folioisa.dll/aac?

Alaska Administrative Journal [Register]. Juneau, AK: AAJ Coordinator, Office of the Lieutenant Governor, 1984-date. Biweekly. [Print eliminated effective May 15, 2000, replaced by the Online Public Notice System] (907) 465-3520.

Cost: None. Now available only at:
http://www.legis.state.ak.us/cgi-bin/folioisa.dll/aac?

3. Court Reports.
Alaska Reporter [1st] – 3d. St. Paul: Thomson West,1960-date. [offprint of P.2d-3d]. Contains decisions of the Alaska Supreme Court and Alaska Court of Appeals from 1960 to date. Current volume: 44 (307-312 P.3d).
Cost: Vols. covering P.2d: $2,291 (117 vols.); vols. covering P.3d: $1,290 (40 vols.); annual cost: 2002: $525; 2003: $601.25; 2004: $285.75; 2005: $318.50; 2006: $400; 2007: $520.50; 2008: $434; 2009: $452; 2010: $339; 2011: $470.50; 2012: $490; 2013: $437; current volume: $136.75 (list).

Pacific Reporter [1st] - **3d**. St. Paul, MN: Thomson West, 1883-date. Contains decisions of the Alaska Supreme Court from 1960-date and the Alaska Court of Appeals from 1980-date, among other states. Current vol.: 314 **P. 3d**.
Cost: 1st series out-of-print (see used lawbook dealers in Appendix C); 2d series: $13,428; used sets approx. $2000; 3d series: $15,201; annual cost (2013): $11,396; individual volume: $518/$691 (subscriber/list); **Monthly Assured Print Pricing (APP):** $1,141/$11,369; used sets may be available.

Pacific Reporter 3d. Advance sheets. St. Paul, MN: Thomson West. Weekly.
Cost: $2,866.56 per year (discounted to bound volume subscribers) (2014).

4. Court Rules.
Alaska Court Rules: State and Federal. St. Paul, MN: Thomson West. 2 vols. Annual.
Cost: 2014 Edition: $120; ProView eBook: $120.

Alaska Rules of Court. Official Version. Standish, ME: Tower Publishing, 2007-date. 1 vol. (946, 81 pp.). Published annually in October; includes April supplement at no additional cost. An official comprehensive annotated compilation of rules for all Alaska state courts.
Cost: 2013-2014 Edition: $25 (2014).

5. Digests, Encyclopedias, and Practice Sets.
West's Alaska Digest 2d. St. Paul, Thomson West, 1987-date. 31 vols. Annual pocket parts, mid-year supplement, and periodic revised volumes.
Cost: $1,714 ; supplementation: 1995: $75.00; 1996: $93.00; 1997: $103.00; 1998: $113.00; 1999: $176.00; 2000: $306.00; 2001: $517.50; 2002: $951.00; 2003: $339.00; 2004: $570.00; 2005: $709.75; 2006: $260.50; 2007: $608; 2008: $429.50; 2009: $497; 2010: $546; 2011: $1,025.50; 2012: $962; 2013: $1,145; **Monthly Assured Print Pricing**: $101/$1,212.

6. Citators.
Shepard's Alaska Citations. Albany, NY: Shepard's. Six supplements per year.
Cost: $1,066 (1 bound volume); all-inclusive subscription: $1,712 per year (in-state) (2014).

Online: All jurisdictional Shepard's and KeyCite are no longer available as stand-alone products, but are included as part of a jurisdictional or subject library package (2014).

7. CD-ROM Products.
Alaska Reporter and West's Alaska Statutes. Eagan, MN: Thomson West. One disc. Updated quarterly. Contains the full text of the Alaska Statutes, Alaska Administrative Code, decisions of Alaska Supreme Court and Court of Appeals from vol. 348 Pacific Reporter 2d (1960) to date, Alaska Reports, vols. 1-17 (1884-statehood), Alaska Court Rules: State and Federal, Attorney General opinions from 1977 to date, court orders, session laws. Decisions also searchable by West Topics and Key Numbers, headnotes, and synopses. Windows, and Macintosh versions. Subscription includes online connection to WESTLAW. Search Engine: PREMISE.
Cost: $37,872 per year (2014).

LexisNexis CD - Alaska Primary Law. Albany, NY: LexisNexis. One disc. Updated quarterly. Contains the full text of the Alaska Statutes, decision of the Alaska Supreme Court from 1960 to date, Alaska Court of Appeals from 1980 to date, Attorney General Opinions, Alaska Administrative Code, Alaska Court Rules. Available for Windows. Search Engine: Folio; LivePublish (NextPage). Includes online connection to LEXIS.
Cost: $1,687 per year (2014).

8. State Legal Research Guides.
Alaska Legal Research Resources. Maintained by the staff of the Alaska Court System.
Available at: http://www.courts.alaska.gov/aklegal.htm

Lemann, Catherine. **State Documents Bibliography: Alaska**. Chicago: AALL, 2009.
Cost: $30.00. Available from William S. Hein & Co. on electronic pdf and HeinOnline. (2014).

Lemann, Catherine. Alaska Practice Materials: A Selective Bibliography in Houdek, Frank G., ed. **State Practice Materials: Annotated Bibliographies**. Buffalo, NY: William S. Hein & Co., Inc., 2008-date. 2 vols. Looseleaf format.
Cost: $195.00 (2014).

McBeath, Gerald A. **Alaska State Constitution**. New York: Oxford University Press, 2011. 1 vol. (294 pp.).
Cost: $150; from $80.03 on amazon.com;kindle: $119.99 (2014).

9. Leading Web Sites for State Legal Research.

Home Page:	www.alaska.gov/
Administrative Code:	http://w3.legis.state.ak.us/pubs/pubs.php
Agency Directory:	www.alaska.gov/akdir1.html
Attorney Gen. Opinions:	www.law.state.ak.us/doclibrary/opinions_index.html
Bar Association:	www.alaskabar.org/
Constitution:	http://w3.legis.state.ak.us/pubs/pubs.php
Court Opinions:	www.courts.alaska.gov/appcts.htm#slips
Governor:	www.gov.state.ak.us/
Judicial Branch:	www.courts.alaska.gov

Law Library:	www.courts.alaska.gov/library.htm
Legal Research Sources:	www.courts.alaska.gov/aklegal.htm
Legislature:	http://w3.legis.state.ak.us/
Statutes:	www.legis.state.ak.us/basis/folio.asp

10. Leading publishers of state specific treatises, practice books, and CLE publications.
Alaska Bar Association, National Business Institute, Thomson Reuters West.

Arizona

1. Codes and Session Laws.
Arizona Annotated Revised Statutes. Charlottesville, VA: LexisNexis, 1956-date. 14 vols. Softbound.
Cost: 2013-2014 Edition: $658 (2013).

Arizona Advance Code Service. Charlottesville, VA: LexisNexis. Supplements code between annual pocket supplements.
Cost: $71.00 (2014).

Arizona Advance Legislative Service. Charlottesville, VA: LexisNexis. Supplements code between annual pocket supplements.
Cost: no charge to code subscribers (2014).

Arizona Revised Statutes Annotated. St. Paul, MN: Thomson West, 1956-date. 18 vols. in 65. Annual pocket supplements and periodic revised volumes.
Cost: $4,059 ; annual supplementation: 1996: $538.50; 1997: $635.50; 1998: $691; 1999: $807.50; 2000: $726; 2001: $1,288; 2002: $440; 2003: $1,394; 2004: $1,344; 2005: $1,264; 2006: $1,500; 2007: $1,277.50; 2008: $$1,663.50; 2009: $2,032; 2010: $2,228.50; 2011: $2,584; 2012: $2,648.50; 2013: $3,392; **Monthly Assured Print Pricing** (**APP**): $341/$4,092.

Arizona Revised Statutes—2013 Compact Edition. St. Paul, MN: Thomson West. 6 vols. Unannotated. Updated annually with new edition.
Cost: 2013 Compact Edition: $1,032 (2014).

Arizona Legislative Service. St. Paul, MN: Thomson West. These pamphlets are published during and immediately after current legislative session and contain the text of laws in chapter sequence in order of passage.
Cost: $80.72 per year (2014).

Arizona Bound Session Laws. St. Paul, MN: Thomson West, 2004-date. 2 vols.
Cost: 2007: $162; 2008: $180; 2009: $208; 2010: $228; 2011: $248; 2012: $294; 2013: $294.

Arizona Session Laws. Phoenix: Arizona Senate Secretary's Office. Annual. (602) 926-4231 or (602) 926-3032.
Cost: 1996: $71; 1997: $75; 1998: $42 (2 vols.); 1999: $45 (2 vols.); 2000: $67.50 (3 vols.); 2001-2013: $50 per year (2 vols. each). Add shipping.

Legislative Hotline: (602) 542-4221 (House); (602) 542-3559 (Senate).

2. Administrative Law.
Arizona Administrative Code [Official compilation]. Phoenix: Secretary of State, 1975-date. 10 vols. Looseleaf format. Supplemented several times annually. (602) 542-4086.
Cost: $575 per year ($450 for basic set and $125 for 1st year's updates); supplementation cost for 2d and future years: $125 per year (2014).

Arizona Administrative Register [Official compilation]. Phoenix: Secretary of State, 1987-date. Weekly. (602) 542-4086.
Cost: $276 (2014).

3. Court Reports.
Arizona Reports. St. Paul, MN: Thomson West, 1883-date. [Published by Secretary of State,1866-1883.] Contain opinions of Arizona Supreme Court from the 1866 to date and Arizona Court of Appeals from 1976 to date. Current vol.: 229.
Cost: $2,401 (163 vols. available); annual cost: 2002: $107; 2003: $166; 2004: $175; 2005: $119.75; 2006: $145 (list); 2007: $192; 2008: $138; 2009: $213; 2010: $231; 2011: $228; 2012: $230.40; 2013: $168; current vol.: $105 (list); **Monthly Assured Print Pricing (APP):** $72/$864.

Arizona Appeals Reports. St. Paul, MN: Thomson West, 1965-1976.
vols. 1-27. Ceased publication with vol. 27.
Cost: $816.75; used sets sell for approx. $595.00; now included in **Arizona Reports**.

Pacific Reporter [1st] - **3d**. St. Paul, MN: Thomson West, 1883-date. Contains decisions of the Arizona Supreme Court from 1866-date and the Arizona Court of Appeals from 1965-date, among other states. Current vol.: 314 **P. 3d**.
Cost: 1st series out-of-print (see used lawbook dealers in Appendix C); 2d series: $13,428; used sets approx. $2000; 3d series: $15,201; annual cost (2013): $11,396; individual volume: $518/$691 (subscriber/list); **Monthly Assured Print Pricing (APP):** $1,141/$11,369; used sets may be available.

Pacific Reporter 3d. Advance sheets. St. Paul, MN: Thomson West. Weekly.
Cost: $2,866.56 per year (discounted to bound volume subscribers) (2014).

4. Court Rules.
Arizona Annotated Court Rules. Charlottesville, VA: LexisNexis. 3 vols. Also ebook format. Annual.
Cost: 2014 Edition: $87 (2014).

Arizona Rules of Court: State and Federal. St. Paul, MN: Thomson West. 2 vols. Annual. Also available as ProView eBook.
Cost: 2014 Edition: $174.

5. Digests, Encyclopedias, and Practice Sets.
Arizona Digest 2d. St. Paul, MN: Thomson West, 1991-date. 31 vols. in 58.

Annual pocket parts and periodic revised volumes.
Cost: $4,156 ; supplementation:1995: $84.17; 1996: $94.50; 1997: $108; 1998: $217; 1999: $342; 2000: $252; 2001: $985.25; 2002: $809; 2003: $298.50; 2004: $520.50; 2005: $577.25; 2006: $1,021; 2007: $1,135; 2008: $755; 2009: $1,434; 2010: $1,649.50; 2011: $1,678.50; 2012: $1,047.50; 2013: $3,707; **Monthly Assured Print Price (APP):** $205/$2,460.

6. Citators.
Shepard's Arizona Citations. Albany, NY: Shepard's. Monthly or bi-monthly.
Cost: $1,967 (4 bound volumes); all-inclusive subscription: monthly: $2,295; bi-monthly: $2,709 (2014).

Online: All jurisdictional Shepard's and KeyCite are no longer available as stand-alone products, but are included as part of a jurisdictional or subject library package (2014).

7. CD-ROM Products.
Arizona Reports, West's. Eagan, MN: Thomson West. One disc. Updated quarterly. Contains full text of Arizona Supreme Court and decisions from 1866 date, Court of Appeals, Attorney General opinions from 1977 to date. Decisions also searchable by West Topics and Key Numbers, headnotes, and synopses. Available for Windows, and Macintosh. Subscription includes online connection to WESTLAW .Search Engine: PREMISE.
Cost: $6,384 per year (2014).

Arizona Revised Statutes on CD-ROM. Phoenix, AZ: Arizona Legislative Computer Services. Two discs. Updated annually. Disc one contains the nonsearchable text of the forty-nine titles of the Arizona Revised States; disc two contains the same data in searchable form. Available for Windows.
Search Engine: Alchemy (Information Management Research). 602-926-4236.
Cost: $15 to general public; $4,000 to corporations for resale (2014).

LexisNexis CD - Arizona Primary Law. Albany, NY: LexisNexis. One disc. Updated quarterly. Contains the full text of the Arizona Statutes Annotated, decisions of the Arizona Supreme Court from 1866 to date, Arizona Court of Appeals from 1965 to date, and Arizona Attorney General opinions. Available for Windows. Search Engine: Folio; LivePublish (NextPage). Subscription includes online connection to LEXIS.
Cost: $1,777 per year (2014).

8. State Legal Research Guides.
Herrera, Tamara S. **Arizona Legal Research**. Durham, NC: Carolina Academic Press, 2008. 1 vol. (176 pp.). Paperbound.
Cost: $25.00; from $14.00 on amazon.com (2014).

Kasper, Jacquelyn Gayle. Arizona Practice Materials: A Selective Bibliography in Houdek, Frank G., ed. **State Practice Materials: Annotated Bibliographies**. Buffalo, NY: William S. Hein & Co., Inc., 2009-date. 2 vols. Looseleaf format.
Cost: $195.00 (2014).

Leshy, John D. **The Arizona State Constitution**. 2d ed. Westport, CT: Greenwood Press, 2013. 1 vol. (526 pp.).
Cost: $150; from $126.98 on amazon.com; kindle: $119.99 (2014).

Shimpock-Vieweg, Kathy and Marianne Sidorski Alcorn. **Arizona Legal Research Guide**. Buffalo, NY: William S. Hein & Co., 1992.
Cost: $52 (2014).

State Documents Bibliography: Arizona: Survey of Arizona State Legal and Law-Related Documents. Compiled by staff of Superior Court Law Library, Maricopa County. Chicago: AALL, 2006.
Cost: $30.00. Available from William S. Hein & Co. on electronic pdf and on HeinOnline (2014).

Torres, Arturo L. and Carol Elliott. Arizona Practice Materials: A Selective Annotated Bibliography." **Law Library Journal** 80, No. 4 (1988): 577-604.

9. Leading Web Sites for State Legal Research.

Home page:	www.az.gov/
Administrative Code:	www.azsos.gov/public_services/rules.htm
Agency Directory:	http://azdirect.azdoa.gov/all.aspx
Attorney General:	www.azag.gov
Attorney Gen. Opinions:	www.azag.gov/ag-opinions
Bar Association:	www.azbar.org/
Court Opinions:	www.azcourts.gov/opinions
Constitution:	www.azleg.gov/Constitution.asp
Governor:	www.governor.state.az.us/
Judicial Branch:	www.azcourts.gov/
Law and Research Library:	www.lib.az.us/is/
Legal Information:	www.azcourts.gov/publicservices/LegalInformation.aspx
Legislature:	www.azleg.gov/
Secretary of State:	www.azsos.gov/
Statues:	www.azleg.gov/ArizonaRevisedStatutes.asp

10. Leading publishers of state specific treatises, practice books, and CLE publications.
Arizona Law Institute, LexisNexis, National Business Institute, State Bar of Arizona - CLE, Thomson Reuters West. See Appendix B for addresses and telephone numbers.

Arkansas

1. Codes and Session Laws.
Arkansas Code of 1987 Annotated. Charlottesville, VA: LexisNexis, 1987-date. 29 vols. in 46. Biennial pocket parts and periodic revised volumes. Includes court rules.
Cost: $502 (in-state); $1,168 (out-of-state); supplementation (in-state/out-of-state): 2003: $106.50/$265; 2004: $118/$265; 2005: $109/$276; 2008: $223/$537; 2009: $70.00; 2010: $481/$663;

2011: $120/$318; 2012: $120/$318; 2013: $.

Arkansas Advance Code Service. Charlottesville, VA: LexisNexis. Supplements code between annual pocket parts.
Cost: $82.00 (in-state); $95 per year (out-of-state) (2013).

West's Arkansas Code Annotated. St. Paul, MN: Thomson West, 2004-date. 48 vols. Provides annotated coverage of Arkansas statutes and court rules. Updated with annual pocket supplements and periodic revised volumes.
Cost: $2,007 ; supplementation: 2005: $367; 2006: $472; 2007: $628.50; 2008: $680.50; 2009: $830; 2010: $1,673; 2011: $1,224; 2012: $584; 2013: $1,745; **Monthly Assured Print Pricing** (APP): $121/$1,452.

Arkansas Advance Legislative Service. Charlottesville, VA: LexisNexis. These pamphlets are published during and after current legislative session and contain the text of laws in numerical chapter sequence in order of passage.
Cost: $74 (2013).

General Acts of Arkansas. [session laws]. Little Rock: Secretary of State. Published biennially in odd-numbered years.
Cost: 1995: $201.25 (7 vol.); 1997: $212.72; 1999: $128.58; 2001: $102.44 (8 vols.); 2003: $20 (6 vols.); 2005: $100 (9 vols.); 2007-date: both bound volumes and CD-ROM are free upon request. (501) 682-3419.

Legislative Hotline: (501) 682-7771 (House); (501) 682-6107 (Senate).

2. Administrative Law.

Arkansas Administrative Code. Albany, NY: LexisNexis Matthew Bender [formerly Weil Publishing], 2000-date. 23 vols. Updated monthly.
Cost: $3,604; individual volumes also available; annual renewal: 2001-2004: $1,075.00; 2005: $1,130; 2006: $1,130; 2007: $1.130; 2008: $1,186; 2009: $1,415; 2010: $1,415; 2011: $1,486; 2012: $1,578; 2013: $1,685; 2014: 1,802.

Arkansas Government Register. Albany, NY: LexisNexis Matthew Bender [formerly Weil Publishing], 2000-date. Monthly.
Cost: $1,109 per year (2014).

Arkansas Register. Little Rock: Secretary of State, 1977-date. Monthly.
Cost: $40 per year (2014); 2001-date also available at no charge on the Secretary of State's web site.

3. Court Reports.

Arkansas Cases [1st] – 3rd. St. Paul, MN: Thomson West, 1886-date. [offprint of South Western Reporter 1st, 2d & 3d] . Contains decisions of the Arkansas Supreme Court from 1886 to date and Arkansas Court of Appeals from 1979 to date. Current volume: 389-403 **S.W. 3d**.
Cost: 1st series (38 vols.): out-of-print; 2d series (211 vols.): $3,237.50; 3d series (62 vols.): $4,960; annual cost: 2002: $534.50; 2003: $647.25; 2004: $487.50; 2005: $257.50; 2006: $574; 2007: $1,274; 2008: $1,243; 2009: $1,355; 2010: $1,393; 2011: $1,435; 2012: $1,237.50; 2013: $4,125; current vol: $412.50/$550 (subscriber/list); **Monthly Assured Print Pricing (APP):** $425/$5,100; used sets may be available.

Arkansas Reports. Little Rock: Administrative Office of the Courts, 1837-date. Decisions of the Arkansas Supreme Court and Court of Appeals are combined in one volume beginning with vol. 272 of the Arkansas Reports. Current and FINAL print volume is 375. Hereafter, decisions will only be delivered electronically. (501) 682-6803.
Cost: vols. 363-375: $80 ea.; vols.; 360-362: $77 ea.; vols. 238-349 available, with some gaps, at costs ranging from $5.78 to $139 each; vols.1-237 out-of-print. Closing date for final volume is Feb. 14, 2009.

Arkansas Appellate Reports. Little Rock: Administrative Office of the Courts, 1981-date. Decisions of the Arkansas Supreme Court and Court of Appeals are combined in one book beginning with vol. 272 of the Arkansas Reports. Current and FINAL print volume is 105. Hereafter, decisions will only be delivered electronically.
Cost: see listing for Arkansas reports (above). Closing date for final volume is Feb. 14, 2009.

South Western Reporter [1st] – **3d**. St. Paul, MN: Thomson West, 1886-date. Contains decisions of the Arkansas Supreme Court from 1886-date and the Arkansas Court of Appeals from 1979-date. Current vol.: 420 S.W. 3d.
Cost: 1st series: out-of-print (see used lawbook dealers in Appendix C); 2d series: $12,480; used sets sell for approx. $2,300; 3d series: $20,134; used sets sell for approx. $1,500; annual cost (2013): $15,615; current volume: $520.50/$694 (subscriber/list); **Monthly Assured Print Pricing (APP):** $1,399/$16,788. See used lawbook dealers in Appendix C.

South Western 3d. Advance sheets. St. Paul, MN: Thomson West. Weekly.
Cost: $2,799 per year (discounted to bound volume subscribers) (2014).

4. Court Rules.

Arkansas Court Rules, State and Federal. St. Paul, MN: Thomson West, 2004-date. 2 vols. Annual.
Cost: 2014 Edition: $139.

Arkansas Advance Court Rules Service. Charlottesville, VA: LexisNexis. 1 vol. Looseleaf pamphlet service. Six bi-monthly issues.
Cost: $108 (2014).

Arkansas Court Rules Annotated. Charlottesville, VA: LexisNexis. 2 vols. Updated semiannually, replaced annually. Also available as ebook.
Cost: 2013 Edition: $26.00 (in-state); $98 (out-of-state) (2014).

5. Digests, Encyclopedias, and Practice Sets.

Arkansas Digest. St. Paul, MN: Thomson West, 1937-date. 75 vols. Annual pocket parts, mid-year supplement, and periodic revised volumes. Contains all headnotes, classified according to West's® Key Number System, for Arkansas state and federal court decisions from 1820 to date.
Cost: $5,995; supplementation: 1995: $183; 1996: $208; 1997: $229;1998: $291; 1999: $495; 2000: $582; 2001: $845.50; 2002: $1,587.50; 2003: $684.85; 2004: $837.25; 2005: $1,165; 2006: $1,036; 2007: $925; 2008: $1,384.50; 2009: $1,304; 2010: $1,950.50; 2011: $1,863.50: $1,208;

Monthly Assured Print Price (APP): $178/$2,136.

6. Citators.
Shepard's Arkansas Citations. Albany, NY: Shepard's. Monthly.
Cost: $3,590 (6 bound volumes); all-inclusive subscription: $1,720 (in-state); (2014).

Online: All jurisdictional Shepard's and KeyCite are no longer available as stand-alone products, but are included as part of a jurisdictional or subject library package (2014).

7. CD-ROM Products.
LexisNexis CD - Arkansas Primary Law. Albany, NY: LexisNexis. One disc. Updated quarterly. Contains the full text of the Arkansas Code of 1987 Annotated, decisions of the Arkansas Supreme Court from 1837 to date, Arkansas Court of Appeals from 1979 to date, and Arkansas Attorney General opinions from 1977 to date. Available for Windows. Search Engine: Folio; LivePublish (NextPage). Subscription includes online connection to LEXIS.
Cost: $1,459 per year (2014).

8. State Legal Research Guides.
Ahlers, Glen Peter. "Selected List of Legal Materials of Interest to the Practicing Bar of Arkansas." **Arkansas Law Notes** (1994): 83-88.

Berger, Coleen M. **Arkansas Legal Research**. Durham, NC: Carolina Academic Press, 2007. 1 vol. (196 pp.).
Cost: $25.00; from $20 on amazon.com (2014).

Burchfield, Jessie, Melissa Serfass and Katheryn Fitzhugh. Arkansas Practice Materials: A Selective Bibliography in Houdek, Frank G., ed. **State Practice Materials: Annotated Bibliographies**. Buffalo, NY: William S. Hein & Co., Inc., 2005-date. 2 vols. Looseleaf format.
Cost: $195 (2014).

Fitzhugh, Kathryn R. «Arkansas Practice Materials: A Selective Bibliography.» **Law Library Journal** 81 (1989): 277-292.

Fitzhugh, Kathryn C. "Arkansas Practice Materials II: A Selective Annotated Bibliography." **University of Arkansas at Little Rock Law Review** 21 (1999): 363-412.

Foster, Lynn. **Arkansas. Legal Bibliography: Documents and Selected Commercial Titles**. Chicago: AALL, 1988.
Cost: $30.00. Available from William S. Hein & Co. on electronic pdf on HeinOnline (2014).

Goss, Kay Collett. **The Arkansas State Constitution.** New York: Oxford University Press, 2011. 1 vol. (296 pp.).
Cost: $150; from $9.74 on amazon.com; kindl;e: $97.49 (2014).

9. Leading Web Sites for State Legal Research.

Home page:	www.arkansas.gov
Administrative Regulations:	www.sos.arkansas.gov/rules_and_regs/index.php/rules/search/new
Agency Directory:	www.arkansas.gov/government/agencies
Attorney General:	www.ag.state.ar.us/
Attorney Gen. Opinions:	www.ag.state.ar.us/opinions/
Bar Association:	www.arkbar.com/
Constitution:	(link from Legislature below) - OR - www.arkleg.state.ar.us/assembly/Summary/ArkansasConstitution1874.pdf
Court Opinions:	http://courts.arkansas.gov/opinions-and-disciplinary-decisions
Governor:	www.governor.arkansas.gov/
Judicial Branch	www.courts.arkansas.gov
Legislature:	www.arkleg.state.ar.us/
Secretary of State:	www.sos.arkansas.gov
Statutes:	(link from Legislature above)
Supreme Court Library:	http://courts.arkansas.gov/courts/supreme-court/library

10. Leading publishers of state specific treatises, practice books, and CLE publications.
Arkansas Bar Association, Arkansas Trial Lawyers Association, LexisNexis, M & M Press, National Business Institute, Thomson Reuters (West). See Appendix B for addresses and telephone numbers.

California

1. Codes and Session Laws.
Deering's California Codes Annotated. Charlottesville, VA: LexisNexis, 1992-date. 215 vols. Annual pocket supplements and periodic revised volumes.
Cost: $5,061; annual supplementation: 2003: $685; 2004: $797; 2005: $879; 2006: $896; 2007: $964; 2008: $949; 2009: $989; 2010: $1,247; 2011: $1,107; 2012: $1,163; 2013: $1,247.
This title was sold to Reed Elsevier in January, 1997 after the Department of Justice negotiated a consent decree with the Thomson Corporation and West Publishing requiring the divestiture of 51 titles.

Deering's California Advance Legislative Service. Charlottesville, VA: LexisNexis. Print or ebook. These pamphlets are published during and immediately after each legislative session and contain the text of laws in numerical chapter sequence in order of passage.
Cost: $293 (2014).

Deering's California Codes Annotated Advance Code Service. Charlottesville, VA: LexisNexis, 1992-date. 2 vols. Paperbound. These two volumes replace the one-volume Midyear Pamphlet. The first of two pamphlets will be published in June; the second of the two is scheduled for a September release. These pamphlets are intended to update the 1999 Deering's supplement with rules, urgency legislation, and annotations that have been generated since the end of the 1998

legislative year.
Cost: $299 per year (2014).

West's Annotated California Code. St. Paul, MN: Thomson West, 1954-date. 348 vols. Annual pocket supplements and periodic revised volumes.
Cost: $10,836 ; supplementation: 1995: $720; 1996: $1,156; 1997: $1,269.50; 1998: $975.50; 1999: $1,101.75; 2000: $1,177; 2001: $1,647; 2002: $2,059.29; 2003: $2,700; 2004: $2,756.75; 2005: $3,508; 2006: 2,250; 2007: $4,109.50; 2008: $3,708; 2009: $5,011; 2010: $5,733; 2011: $6,775.50; 2012: $6,768; 2013: $8,769; **Monthly Assured Print Pricing (APP)**: $716/$8,592. Used sets may be available.

West's California Codes. Compact edition. St. Paul, MN: Thomson West, 1978-date. 25+ vols. Annual. Unannotated.
Cost: No longer sold as a set; volumes priced individually.

Statutes of California [session laws]. Sacramento: Office of State Publishing.
Cost: 1993-2012: $250-$500 per year; (916) 445-2323.
Internet: http://www.leginfo.ca.gov/calaw.html

West's California Legislative Service. St. Paul, MN: Thomson West. These pamphlets are published during and immediately after legislative session and contain the text of laws in numerical chapter sequence in order of passage.
Cost: $1,259.04 (2014).

Legislative Hotline: (916) 319-2856 (Assembly); (916) 445-4251(Senate).

2. Administrative Law.

California Code of Regulations. Sacramento: Office of Administrative Law/Thomson West, 1945-date. 38 vols. Looseleaf format. Updated by weekly **California Regulatory Notice Register**. Available from Barclays, Thomson Reuters. (800) 537-2707. [see below]. Includes looseleaf table of content and master index
Cost: $2,615 + $74.25 s & h; supplementation: 2003: $2,413; 2004: $2,558; 2005: $2,954; 2006: $2,000; 2007: $3,288; 2008: $3,469; 2009: $3,642; 2010: $3,642; 2011: $3,640; 2012: $3,825; 2013: $3,825; 2014: $3,825;

California Regulatory Notice Register. Sacramento, CA: Barclays/Thomson West, 1993-date. Weekly. published weekly by the Office of Administrative Law, 300 Capitol Mall, Suite 1250, Sacramento, CA 95814-4339 and printed by Barclays, a subsidiary of West, a Thomson Reuters Business.
Cost: $215 per year (2014). Available from Barclay's in San Francisco: http://barclaysccr.com/store/companion_products.html
1-800-888-3600

3. Court Reports.

California Reports. 1850-date. 1st-4th series. Charlottesville, VA: LexisNexis, 2004-date. 1st series: 1850-1934 (220 vols.); 2d series: 1934-1969 (71 vols.); 3d series: 1969-1992 (54 vols.); 4th series: 1992-date (50 vols.). Current vol.: 50. LexisNexis acquired state contract from West in 2004.
Cost: 3d series California Reports: $965.00; $35.42 each; 4th series (44 vols.): $959.20; annual cost: 2003: $85; 2004: $29.50; 2005: $44.75; 2006: $33.70; 2007: $36.20; 2008: $41.70; 2009: $43.60; 2010: $43.60; 2011: $43.60; 2012: $43.60 annual subcription to both California Reports and California Appellate Reports bound volumes: $271; current volumes: $21.80; advance sheets: $320; annual subcription to both California Reports bound volumes and advance sheets: $515.

California Appellate Reports, 1st-4th series. Charlottesville, VA: LexisNexis, 2004-date. West, 1905-2004. 1st series: 1905-1934 (140 vols.); 2d series: 1934-1969 (276 vols.); 3d series: 1969-1992 (235 vols.); 4th series: 1992-date (195 vols.). Current vol.: 195. LexisNexis acquired state contract from Thomson West in 2004.
Cost: 3d series: $4,195; 4th: $1,832 (vols. 1-195); annual subcription to both California Reports and California Appellate Reports bound volumes: $271.00; current volumes: $22.50 each; advance sheets: $320; annual subcription to both California Reports bound volumnes and advance sheets: $515.

California Reporter [1st] - **3d**. St. Paul, MN: Thomson West, 1959-date. Contains decisions of California Supreme Court, California Court of Appeals, and Appellate Departments of the California Superior Court, all from 1959-date. Current vol.: 146 of 3d series.
Cost: 1st series: $2,860; 2d series: $2,415; 3d series: $10,222; annual cost: 2006: $1,709.50; 2007: $1,446.50; 2008: $2,196; 2009: $1,961; 2010: $2,737; 2011: $3,744; 2012: $6,066; 2013: $7,263; recent volume: $403.50/$538 (subscriber/list); **Monthly Assured Print Pricing (APP):** $724/$8,688.

Califoria Reporter. Advance sheets. St. Paul, MN: Thomson West. Weekly.
Cost: $2,700 per year (discounted to bound volume subscribers) (2014).

Pacific Reporter [1st] - **3d**. St. Paul, MN: Thomson West, 1883-date. Contains decisions of the California Court from 1883-date and the California Court of Appeals from 1905-date, among other states. Current vol.: 314 **P. 3d**.
Cost: 1st series out-of-print (see used lawbook dealers in Appendix C); 2d series: $13,428; used sets approx. $2000; 3d series: $15,201; annual cost (2013): $11,396; individual volume: $518/$691 (subscriber/list); **Monthly Assured Print Pricing (APP):** $1,141/$11,369; used sets may be available.

Pacific Reporter 3d. Advance sheets. St. Paul, MN: Thomson West. Weekly.
Cost: $2,866.56 per year (discounted to bound volume subscribers) (2014).

California Official Reports, Advance Sheets Pamphlets. Charlottesville, VA: LexisNexis. Published every 10 days.
Cost: $320 (2014).

4. Court Rules.

California Rules of Court: State and Federal. St. Paul, MN: Thomson West. 2 vols. Annual. Also available as ProView eBook.
Cost: 2014 Edition: $82.

Deering's California Rules of Court. Charlottesville, VA: LexisNexis. 5 vols. Annual pocket supplements.
Cost: 2012 Edition: $385 (2013).

5. Digests, Encyclopedias, and Practice Sets.
California Jurisprudence 3d. St. Paul, MN: Thomson West, 1972-date. 117 vols. Annual pocket parts and periodic revised volumes.
Cost: $10,906 ; supplementation:1994: $388; 995: $682.50; 1996: $928.50; 1997: $786; 1998: $960.50; 1999: $398; 2000: $1,054; 2001: $1,465.50; 2002: $1,823.50; 2003: $2,748; 2004: $2,367; 2005: $3.047; 2006: $3,500; 2007: $3,389; 2008: $3,810; 2009: $4,285; 2010: $4,861; 2011: $5,507.50; 2012: $4.469; 2013: $8,366; **Monthly Assured Print Pricing (APP):** $642/$7,704.

West's California Digest 2d. St. Paul, MN: Thomson West, 1981-date. 167 vols. Annual pocket parts, mid-year supplement, and periodic revised volumes.
Cost: $7,378; supplementation:1996: $716.09; 1997: $574.40; 1998: $650.25; 1999: $469.50; 2000: $1,033; 2001: $1,644.50; 2002: $1,850; 2003: $2,490; 2004: $2,967.75; 2005: $1,131; 2006: $1,500; 2007: $1,367.50; 2008: $1,425; 2009: $1,751; 2010: $2,144.50; 2011: $3,358. 2012: $3,881; 2013: $5,908; **Monthly Assured Print Pricing (APP):** $389/$4,668.

Witkin, B. E. **Summary of California Law.** 10th ed. St.. Paul, MN: Thomson West, 2005-date. 15 vols. Includes annual pocket parts and periodic revised volumes.
Cost: $2,569 ; supplementation: 1996: $357; 1997: $366; 1998: $375; 1999: $388; 2000: $392; 2001: $405; 2002: $410; 2003: $481; 2004: $490; 2005: new edition + $165; 2006: $350; 2007: $183.50; 2008: $388; 2009: $228; 2010: $383; 2011: $274; 2012: $457; 2013: $537; **Monthly Assured Print Pricing (APP):** $87/$1,044; used sets may be available.

6. Citators.
Shepard's California Citations. Albany, NY: Shepard's. Monthly or bi-monthly.
Cost: $17,848 (34 bound volumes); all-inclusive subscription: monthly: $2,461; bimonthly: $2,683 (2014).

Shepard's California Reporter Citations. Albany, NY: Shepard's.
Cost: $4,018 (5 vols.); all-inclusive subscription: monthly $2,778 (2014).

Online: All jurisdictional Shepard's and KeyCite are no longer available as stand-alone products, but is included as part of a jurisdictional or subject library package (2014).

7. CD-ROM Products.
Barclays Official California Code of Regulations. San Francisco, CA: Barclay's/Thomson West. One disc. Updated quarterly. Contains the official compilation of California regulations. Available for Windows. Substantially the same as the LawDesk version at considerable savings.
Cost: $1,630 per year (single use) (2014).

CalDisc. Spring Creek, NV: AccessLaw. Four CD-ROMs, one DVD, or Online. Updated quarterly. Contain the full text of California 2d, 3d, and 4th Series cases and California slip opinions, including California Supreme Court and California Court of Appeals decisions from 1934 to date;, all 29 California State Codes, court rules, Constitution, and current session laws. Over 89,000 cases included. Available for Windows and Macintosh. Search Engine: Folio. Online updating included with subscription. Also available online.
Cost: CD-ROM, with internet access: $264; $104.95 for each update ($164 per update for those not on standing order). CalDVD Integrated Law Library: $264; $104.95 for each update ($164 per update for those not on standing order). Online: $468 per year plus $45 startup fee in first year (2014).

California Library. Albany, NY: LexisNexis. Two DVDs. Contains the full text of nearly 40 California state practice sets, including California Points and Authorities and California Forms of Pleading and Practice, as well as California code, regulations and cases, with LEXIS-NEXIS Online Connection for most recent case law. Available for Windows. Search Engine: Folio; Live Publish (NextPage).
Cost: $62,224 per year (complete); renewal: 2007: $25,753; 2008: $28,071; 2009: $30,317; 2010: $32,136; 2011: $34.064; 2012: 36,448: Internet: 2010: $32,136; 2011: $34,064; 2012: $36,448; 2013: $38,999; individual components also available.

California Reporter (West's). Eagan, MN: Thomson West. Five DVDs. Monthly updates. Contains full text of decisions of the California Supreme Court from 1850 to date, California Court of Appeals and Appellate Department of California Superior Court. Decisions also searchable by West Topics and Key Numbers, headnotes, and synopses. Available for Windows, and Macintosh. Search Engine: PREMISE.
Cost: $4,866 per year (single user) (2014).

California Official Reports on DVD. Albany, NY: LexisNexis. One disc. Updated quarterly. Contains the full text of all California cases infobases. Also available on the Web. Search Engine: Folio; LivePublish Next Page). LexisNexis became the new official publisher of the California Reports in 2004.
Cost: $1,668 per year (2014).

California Workers' Compensation Laws CD-ROM. Albany, NY: LexisNexis. One disc. Updated quarterly. Contains California Compensation Cases, California wokers' compensation laws and regulations, and **California Law of Employee Injuries and Workers' Compensation** by Hanna, a case-winning treatise with complete coverage of the substantive and procedural aspects of law. Available for Windows. Search Engine: Folio; LivePublish (NextPage).
Cost: $3,947 per year (2013).

Deering's California Codes Annotated Law on LexisNexis CD. Albany, NY: LexisNexis. One disc. Updated quarterly. Contains the full text of Deering's California Codes Annotated, California rules of court, state bar rules, and 4,000 legal forms. Available for Windows. Search Engine: Folio; LivePublish (NextPage). Subscription includes online updating through LEXIS.
Cost: $2,417 per year (2013).

FORECITE California. Costa Mesa, CA: James Publishing Co. One disc. Updated bimonthly. Contains more than 3,000 criminal jury instructions for the State of California. Available

for Windows 95 or higher. Search Engine: Alchemy Search (Information Management Research).
Cost: $295 (includes print with monthly updates) (2014).

LexisNexis CD - California Official Reports. Albany, NY: LexisNexis. One disc. Updated quarterly. LexisNexis is the official publisher of the California Reports, the official caselaw of the state of California. The California Official Reports CD-ROM features the Official Headnotes and Summaries from the 1st series to the present. It also includes California Supreme Court cases from 1850, and California Appellate Court cases from 1905.
Cost: $1,619 per year (2014).

8. State Legal Research Guides.

Dershem. Larry D. **California Legal Research Handbook**. 2d ed. Littleton, CO: Fred B. Rothman & Co. [William S. Hein & Co.], 2008-date.
Cost: $75.00 (2014).

Fischer, Janet and Steven Feller. **California State Documents: A Bibliography of Legal Publications and Related Materials**. Chicago, AALL, 2005.
Cost: $30.00. Available from William S. Hein & Co. on electronic pdf and on HeinOnline (2014).

Grodin, Joseph R., Calvin R. Massey and Richard B. Cunningham. **The California State Constitution**. New York: Oxford University Press, 2011. 1 vol. (420 pp.).
Cost: $150; from $54.21 on amazon.com; kindle: $119.99 (2014).

Hanft, John K. **Legal Research in California**. 7th ed. St. Paul, MN: Thomson West, 2011. 1 vol. (568 pp.).
Cost: $75 (2014).

Henexon, Fay, ed. **Locating the Law: A Handbook for Non-Law Librarians With an Emphasis on California Law**. 3d ed. Southern California Association of Law Libraries, 1995.

Janes, Judy C. California Practice Materials: A Selective Bibliography in Houdek, Frank G., ed. **State Practice Materials: Annotated Bibliographies**. Buffalo, NY: William S. Hein & Co., Inc., 2005-date. 2 vols. Looseleaf format.
Cost: $195.00 (2014).

Macfarlane, Hether; Aimee Dudovitz, and Suzanne E. Rowe. **California Legal Research**. 2d ed. Durham, NC: Carolina Academic Press, 2013. 1 vol. (246 pp.). Paperbound.
Cost: $28.00; from $18.98 on amazon.com (2014).

9. Leading Web Sites for State Legal Research.

Home Page:	www.ca.gov/
Administrative Code:	http://government.westlaw.com/linkedslice/default.asp?SP=CCR-1000
Administrative Manual:	www.dgs.ca.gov/dgs
Agency Directory:	www.ca.gov/Apps/Agencies.aspx
Attorney General:	http://oag.ca.gov/
Attorney Gen. Opinions:	http://oag.ca.gov/opinions
Bar Association:	www.calbar.ca.gov/
Constitution:	www.leginfo.ca.gov/const-toc.html - OR - http://leginfo.legislature.ca.gov/faces/codes.xhtml
Court Opinions:	www.courts.ca.gov/opinions.htm
Governor:	http://gov.ca.gov/
Judicial Branch:	www.courts.ca.gov/
Law Library online:	www.publiclawlibrary.org
Legislature - Senate:	http://senate.ca.gov
Legislature - State Assembly:	http://assembly.ca.gov/
Secretary of State:	www.sos.ca.gov/
Statutes:	www.leginfo.ca.gov/statute.html

10. Leading publishers of state specific treatises, practice books, and CLE publications.

Wolters Kluwer Law & Business, Matthew Bender, California Continuing Education of the Bar (CEB), CalLaw, LexisNexis, National Business Institute, Nolo Press, Thomson Reuters West. See Appendix B for addresses and telephone numbers.

Colorado

1. Codes and Session Laws.

Colorado Revised Statutes. Newark, N.J.: LexisNexis, 2003-date. 19 vols. Replaced annually. Designated the official state code by the Colorado General Assembly's Committee on Legal Services in January 2002. Also made available free-of-charge on the Internet by LexisNexis.
Cost: 2013 Edition: $298 (2014).

Colorado Revised Statutes. Denver: Bradford Publishing Co., 2004-date. 2 vols. Published annually every September. (800) 446-2831 or (303) 292-2500.
A condensed unofficial edition of **CRS** covering selective topical areas, including Family Law and Domestic Matters; Real Property Law; and Vehicles and Traffic. Both also available on CD-ROM.
Cost: 2013 Edition: Real Property and Family Law vols.: $85.00 ea.; Motor Vehicles: $24.50 (2014).

West's Colorado Revised Statutes Annotated. St. Paul, MN: Thomson West, 1989-date. 77 vols. Annual pocket supplements and periodic revised volumes.
Cost: $5,589; supplementation: 1995: $335; 1996: $608; 1997: $749; 1998: $879.20; 1999: $748; 2000: $871; 2001: $1,171; 2003: $1,614.50; 2004: $1,599.25; 2005: $2,152; 2006: $2,394.50; 2007: $2,405; 2008: $2,585; 2009: $2,564; 2010: $3,932; 2011: $3,040; 2012: $3,929; 2013: $4,912; **Monthly Assured Print Pricing (APP):** $383/$4,596.

West's Colorado Legislative Service. St. Paul, MN: Thomson West. These pamphlets are published during and immediately after each legislative session and contain the text of laws in

numerical chapter sequence in order of passage.
Cost: $856.00 per year (2014).

Colorado Session Laws. Newark, N.J.: LexisNexis, 2003-date. Annual.
Softbound or ebook. Previously published by Bradford Publishing Company.
Cost: 2006: $49.50 (3 vols.); previous issues from Bradford Publishing Co.: 1997: $61.36 (hardbound); $48.94 (softbound) (3 vols.); 1999: $67.70 (hardbound), $54.67 (softbound only; 2000: $61.09; 2001: $60.59; 2002: $78.48 (3 vols.); 2004: $29.40 (3 vols.); 2005: $29.40; 2006: $29.40; 2007: $30; 2008: $30; 2009: $30; 2010: $37; 2011: $39; 2012: $30.90/$41; 2013: $30.30 (ebook).

Legislative Hotline: (303) 866-3055, (303) 866-3521.

2. Administrative Law.
Code of Colorado Regulations. Albany, NY: LexisNexis Matthew Bender [formerly Weil Publishing], 2002-date. Looseleaf format. 12 vols. in 30. Interfiled supplements issued monthly.
Cost: $3,942 (includes one year's updates); supplementation: 2004: $712; 2005: $965; 2006: $965; 2007: $965; 2008: $1,074; 2009: $1,128; 2010: $1,128; 2011: $1,184; 2012: $1,255; 2013: $1,343; 2014: $1,437.

[Note: the Daily Journal Corporation ceased publication of the **CCR** and **CR** with the July, 2002 issue]

Colorado Register. Albany, NY: LexisNexis Matthew Bender [formerly Weil Publishing], 2002-date. Monthly.
Cost: Included in cost of CAC (2014).

3. Court Reports.
Colorado Reporter [1st] - **3d**. St. Paul, MN: Thomson West, 1883-date. [offprint of West's Pacific Reporter--official since 1980]. Contains decisions of the Colorado Supreme Court from 1883 to date, and the Colorado Court of Appeals from 1891 to date. Designated the official reporter after the termination of the Colorado Reports (v. 200) and the Colorado Appellate Reports (v. 44). Current vol. 307-312 **P. 3d**.
Cost: P. 1st series: out-of-print; P. 2d series: $2,745; P. 3d series: $1,321; annual cost: 2006: $414; 2007: $331; 2008: $780; 2009: $641; 2010: $684; 2011: $742; 2012: $783.75; 2013: $678; current volume: $169.50/$226 (subscriber/list).

Colorado Reports. Denver: Golden Bell Press, 1864-1980, vols. 1-200 [ceased publication with vol. 200.]
Cost: Out-of-print. Prices of used sets range from $1,000.00-$1,700.00.

Colorado Court of Appeals Reports. Denver: Golden Bell Press, 1891-1980, vols. 1-44. [Ceased publication with vol. 44.]
Cost: Out-of-print. Prices of used sets range from $250.00-$500.00.

Pacific Reporter [1st] - **3d**. St. Paul, MN: West, 1883-date. Contains decisions of the Colorado Supreme Court from 1883-date and the Colorado Court of Appeals from 1970-date. Current vol.: 314 **P. 3d**.
Cost: 1st series out-of-print (see used lawbook dealers in Appendix C); 2d series: $13,428; used sets approx. $2000; 3d series: $15,201; annual cost (2013): $11,396; individual volume: $518/$691 (subscriber/list); **Monthly Assured Print Pricing (APP):** $1,141/$11,369; used sets may be available.

Pacific Reporter 3d. Advance sheets. St. Paul, MN: Thomson West. Weekly.
Cost: $2,866.56 per year (discounted to bound volume subscribers) (2014).

4. Court Rules.
Colorado Rules of Court: State and Federal. St. Paul, MN: Thomson West. 2 vols. Annual.
Cost: 2014 Edition: $201; ProView eBook: $201 (2014).

Colorado Court Rules. Charlottesville, VA: LexisNexis, 2012. 2 vols. Annual.
Cost: 2013 Edition: $70 (2014).

5. Digests, Encyclopedias, and Practice Sets.
West's Colorado Digest 2d. St. Paul, MN: Thomson West, 1987-date. 78 vols. Annual pocket parts, mid-year supplement and periodic revised volumes.
Cost: $5,553 ; supplementation: 1995: $127.42; 1996: 132.50; 1997: $147.50; 1998: $295.50; 1999: $411.50; 2000: $397; 2001: $890; 2002: $946.50; 2003: $985.50; 2004: $787; 2005: $872.50; 2006: $757.50; 2007: $431; 2008: $408; 2009: $1,042; 2010: $1,480; 2011: $2,295; 2012: $2,984; 2013: $4,967; **Monthly Assured Print Pricing (APP):** $276/$3.312.

Colorado Practice Series. St. Paul, MN: Thomson West. 33 vols. Individual components available. Also available on Westlaw.
Cost: $5,421 (but priced individually); supplementation: 1995: $180; 1996: $717.50; 1997: $432.00; 1998: $306; 1999: $641.50; 2000: $516; 2001: $671.50; 2003: $1,087; 2004-date: see costs of individual components.
Best acquired as a part of **State Secondary Resources** add-on to a WestlawNext PRO subscription at considerable savings.

6. Citators.
Shepard's Colorado Citations. Colorado Springs: Shepard's. Monthly.
Cost: $2,374 (5 bound volumes); all-inclusive subscription: $2,284 (in-state) (2014).

Online: All jurisdictional Shepard's and KeyCite are no longer available as stand-alone products, but are included as part of a jurisdictional or subject library package (2013).

7. CD-ROM Products.
Bradforms 2.0. Denver, CO: Bradford Publishing. **Now only available online**. Updated regularly. Contains more than 900 forms in the following subject areas (suites): domestic relations, probate, quitclaim/warranty deeds, mechanic's liens, real estate commission forms, UCC forms, civil procedure, public trustee forms, lease and rental forms, workers' compensation, and bankruptcy. Go to: http://www.bradfordpublishing.com/Legal-Forms
Cost: Priced by the individual form (2014).

Colorado Reporter (West's). Eagan, MN: Thomson West. One disc. Updated quarterly. Contains full text of the Colorado

Supreme Court and California Court of Appeals decisions appearing in the Pacific Reporter [1st], vols. 1-300 and Pacific Reporter 2d, vols. 1-date, as well as Attorney General opinions from 1977-date. Decisions also searchable by West Topics and Key Numbers, headnotes, and synopses. Available for Windows and Macintosh. Search engine: PREMISE.
Cost: $4,077 per year (single user) (2014).

Law on Disc—Colorado. Albany, NY: LexisNexis. One disc. Updated quarterly. Contains the full text of Colorado Revised Statutes unannotated, Colorado Advance Legislative Service, decisions of the Colorado Supreme Court (1864-date), Colorado Court of Appeals decisions (1891-date), Attorney General opinions (1970-date), and court rules. Contains free caselaw update to LexisNexis datrabase. Available for Windows. Search Engine: Folio; LivePublish (NextPage).
Cost: $1,304 per year (2014).

8. State Legal Research Guides.
Fontenot, Mitch. "Colorado Practice Materials: A Selective Annotated Bibliography." **Law Library Journal** 88, No. 3 (1996): 427-455.

Fontenot, Mitch. Colorado Practice Materials: A Selective Bibliography in Houdek, Frank G., ed. **State Practice Materials: Annotated Bibliographies**. Buffalo, NY: William S. Hein & Co., Inc., 2004-date. 2 vols. Looseleaf format.
Cost: $195 (2014).

Linz, Robert Michael. **Colorado Legal Research**. Durham, NC: Carolina Academic Press, 2010. 1 vol. (222 pp.). Paperbound
Cost: $25.00; from $17.41 on amazon.com (2014).

Oesterle, Dale A. and Richard B. Collins. **The Colorado State Constitution**. New York: Oxford University Press, 2011. 1 vol. (536 pp.).
Cost: $150; from $131.35 on amazon.com; kindle: $119.99 (2014).

Richards, Robert C. and Barbara Bintliff. **Colorado Legal Resources: An Annotated Bibliography**. Chicago: American Association of Law Libraries, Government Documents SIS, 2004. 1 vol. (70 pp.).
Cost: $30. Available from William S. Hein & Co. on electronic pdf and on HeinOnline (2014).

Wilder, Mary and Cynthia Rixey Scott. "Accessible Sources for the Colorado Revised Statutes." **Colorado Lawyer** 19 (1990): 423.

9. Leading Web Sites for State Legal Research.

Home Page:	www.colorado.gov/
Administrative Code:	www.sos.state.co.us/CCR/Welcome.do
Agency Directory:	www.colorado.gov/government/government/state-agencies.html
Attorney General:	www.coloradoattorneygeneral.gov/
Attorney Gen. Opinions:	www.coloradoattorneygeneral.gov/ag_opinions/index
Bar Association:	www.cobar.org/
Constitution:	(link from Legislature page below will take you to LexisNexis)
Court of Appeals Opinions:	www.courts.state.co.us/Courts/Court_Of_Appeals/Case_Announcements/
Governor:	www.colorado.gov/governor/
Judicial Branch:	www.courts.state.co.us/
Law Library of the Supreme Court:	http://cscl.colibraries.org/
Legislature:	www.leg.state.co.us
Rules & Reg.'s:	www.sos.state.co.us/CCR/Welcome.do
Secretary of State:	www.sos.state.co.us/
Statutes:	(link from Legislature page above will take you to LexisNexis)
Supreme Court Opinions:	www.courts.state.co.us/Courts/Supreme_Court/Case_Announcements/

10. Leading publishers of state specific treatises, practice books, and CLE publications.
Bradford Publishing Co., Continuing Legal Education in Colorado, LexisNexis, National Business Institute, Rocky Mountain Mineral Law Foundation, Thomson Reuters West, Wolters Kluwer Law & Business.

Connecticut

1. Codes and Sessions Laws.
Connecticut General Statutes Annotated. St. Paul, MN: Thomson West, 1960-date. 30 vols. in 62. Annual pocket parts and periodic revised volumes.
Cost: $5,963 ; supplementation: 1996: $719; 1997: $874.50; 1998: $787.50; 1999: $895; 2000: $918; 2001: $1,122; 2002: $1,328; 2003: $1,200; 2004: $1,456; 2005: $1,800; 2006: $2,300; 2007: $2,784.50; 2008: $3,129; 2009: $2,920.50; 2010: $3,350; 2011: $3,394.50; 2012: $3,907; 2013: $5,173; **Monthly Assured Print Pricing (APP):** $400/$4,800.

General Statutes of Connecticut. Hartford: Secretary of the State. Biennial paperbound edition. 16 vols. (860) 509-6000
Cost: 2013 Edition: $325 + shipping; 2011 Edition: $325 + shipping; individual volumes: $23.

Connecticut Legislative Service. St. Paul, MN: Thomson West. These pamphlets are published during and immediately after each legislative session and contain the text of laws in numerical chapter sequence in order of passage.
Cost: $1,024.08 (2014).

Connecticut Session Laws. St. Paul, MN: Thomson Reuters (West), 2008-date. Annual. 1 vol.
Cost: 2008: $179; 2009: $210; 2010: $210; 2011: $283.00; 2012: $317; 2013: $354.

Connecticut Public and Special Acts. Hartford: Secretary of the State. Annual. 3 vols. per year.
Cost: 1995: $94.87; 1996: $94.87; 1997: $94.87; 1998: $94.87; 1999: $94.87; 2000: $85; 2001: $85; 2002: $85; 2003: $85.00; 2004: $90.10 (2 vols.); 2005: $85; 2006: $85; 2007: $85; 2008:

$85; 2009: $85; 2010: $85; 2011: $85; 2012: $90; 2013: $90.

Legislative Hotline: (860) 566-5736.

2. Administrative Law.

Regulations of Connecticut State Agencies. Enfield: Commission on Official Legal Publications, 1962-date (July 1 – June 30). 18 vols. Looseleaf format. (860) 741-3027.
Cost: $714; text material only: $455; binders: $19 ea.; subscription (July 1-June 30): 1997: $64; 1998: $68; 1999: $68; 2000: $75; 2001: $75; 2002: $75; 2003: $75; 2004-2010: $83; 2011: $87; 2012: $87; 2013: $87; 2014: $87.

Connecticut Law Journal. Hartford: Commission on Official Legal Publications, 1986-date. Weekly. Updates Regulations of Connecticut State Agencies, court reports, etc.
Cost: $225 ($8 ea.) per year (July 1 – June 30) (2014).

Connecticut Government Register. Albany, NY: LexisNexis Matthew Bender [formerly Weil Publishing]. Monthly.
Cost: $1,109 (2014).

3. Court Reports.

Connecticut Law Journal. Enfield: Commission on Official Legal Publications, 1935-date. Weekly.
The official legal periodical. Published every Tuesday throughout the year, including holidays. The first source of Supreme and Appellate Court opinions, with pagination corresponding to the eventual bound volume versions. Also, proposed and adopted amendments to the Practice Book and to the Regulations of Connecticut State Agencies, public hearing notices, opinions of the state ethics commission, attorney discipline information and personnel notices.
Cost: $225 per year (July 1-June 30) (2014).

Connecticut Reports. Enfield: Commission on Official Legal Publications, 1814-date. Beginning with vol. 186, the official citations appear in the **Connecticut Law Journal**. Current vol.: 289
Cost: $4,160 (vols. 180-285); $40 per volume (2014); also available on CD-ROM (see below). Used sets may be available.

Connecticut Reporter. [1st] - **3d**. St. Paul, MN: Thomson West, 1887-date. [offprint of the Atlantic Reporter]. Contains decisions of the Connecticut Supreme Court from 1885 to date, Connecticut Appellate Court from 1983 to date, and Connecticut Supplement from 1935 to date. Recent volume: 77-78 **A.3d**.
Cost: Covering A. [1st series]: out-of-print; A.2d: $3,924; 3d series: $8,140; annual supplementation: 2002: $1,020; 2003: $1,221; 2004: $1,211.50; 2005: $1040; 2006: $1,353; 2007: $1,347; 2008: $1,843; 2009: $1,629; 2010: $2,474.50; 2011: $2,950; 2012: $3,114; 2013: $5,593; current volume: $508.50/$678 (subscriber/list); **Monthly Assured Print Pricing (APP):** $521/$6,252. See list of used lawbook dealers in Appendix C.

Connecticut Appellate Reports. Hartford: Commission on Official Legal Publications, 1983-date. Current decisions appear in the weekly Connecticut Law Journal. Current vol.: 117
Cost: $4,680 (vols. 1-117); $40 per volume (2014).

Connecticut Supplement. Enfield: Commission on Official Legal Publications, 1935-date. Current decisions appear in the weekly Conn. Law Journal. Current vol.: 51
Cost: $1,240 (vols. 21-51 available); $40 per volume (2014).

Connecticut Circuit Court Reports. Enfield: Commission on Official Legal Publications, 1961-74.
6 vols. Contains selected opinions from the former Connecticut Circuit Court.
Cost: Out-of-print.

Kirby's Reports: Reports of Cases Adjudged in the Superior Court of th4 State of Connecticut from the Year 1785 to May 1788. Waterbury, CT: Dissell Pub. Co., 1789. Reprintedby the State of Connecticut, 1962.
Cost: Out-of-print. See list of used lawbook dealers in Appendix C or Connecticut Reports Archives CD-ROM (below).

Root's Reports: Reports of Cases Adjudged in the Superior Court and Supreme Court of Errors, from July A.D. 1789 to June A.D. 1793. Reprinted by the State of Connecticut, 1962.
Cost: Out-of-print. See list of used lawbook dealers in Appendix C or Connecticut Reports Archives CD-ROM (below).

Day's Reports: Reports of Cases, Argued and Determined in the Supreme Court of Errors, of the State of Connecticut in the Years 1802 [-1813]. Hartford, CT: Hudson and Goodwin, 1806-1823. Reprinted by the State of Connecticut.
Cost: Out-of-print. See list of used lawbook dealers in Appendix C or Connecticut Reports Archives CD-ROM (below).

Atlantic Reporter [1st] - **2d**. St. Paul, MN: Thomson West, 1886-date. Contains decisions of the Connecticut Supreme Court from 1886 to date, Connecticut Appellate Court from 1983 to date. Current volume: 85 **A.3d**.
Cost: 1st series out-of-print (see used lawbook dealers in Appendix C); 2d series: $14,434; 3d series: $15,080; annual cost (2013): $11,151; recent vol.: $531/$708 (subscriber/list); **Monthly Assured Print Pricing (APP):** $1,163/$13,956. See list of used lawbook dealers in Appendix C.

Atlantic Reporter 2d. Advance sheets. St. Paul, MN: Thomson West. Weekly.
Cost: $2,866.56 per year (discounted to bound volume subscribers) (2014).

4. Court Rules.

Connecticut Practice Book. Enfield, CT: Commission on Official Legal Publications, 1998-date. 1 vols. Annual edition. Looseleaf. Contains rules of practice, judicial and professional code, and forms. Also available at no charge at: http://www.jud.ct.gov/publications/PracticeBook/PB.pdf
Cost: 2014 Edition: $38.

Connecticut Rules of Court: State and Federal. St. Paul, MN: Thomson West. 2 vols. Annual. Also available on ProView eBook.
Cost: 2014 Edition: $214; ProView eBook: $214.

5. Digests, Encyclopedias, and Practice Sets.

Connecticut Digest (West's). St. Paul, MN: Thomson West, 1950-date. 83 vols.
Cost: $7,191 (up 29% from 2013); supplementation: 1996: $431.50; 1997: $215; 1998: $235.00; 1999: $665; 2000: $635;

2001: $1,226.75; 2002: $1,741; 2003: $883; 2004: $1,214; 2005: $942.50; 2006: $867; 2007: $1,651; 2008: $1,719; 2009: $1,605; 2010: $2,002; 2011: $3,051.50; 2012: $2,960; 2013: $5,299; **Monthly Assured Print Pricing (APP):** $332/$3,984.

Connecticut Digest. Enfield, CT: Commission on Official Legal Publications. 4 vols. The authoritative cumulative index to the Connecticut Reports, the Connecticut Appellate Reports, the Connecticut Supplement. and the Connecticut Circuit Court Reports.
Cost: Available on **Connecticut Reports Archives CD-ROM Volume II** (see below).

Connecticut Practice Series. 2d ed. St. Paul, MN: Thomson West, 1979-date. 19 vols. Annual pocket supplements and periodic revised volumes. Contains Code of Professional Responsibility, Code of Judicial Conduct, Superior Court Civil Rules, forms, criminal jury instructions, and Connecticut trial practice, family law, and land use law.
Cost: $4,810 (but priced individually); supplementation: 1997: $231.00; 1998: $96.00; 1999: $698; 2000: $259.00; 2001: $552.50; 2003: $649.00; 2004: inquire regarding costs of individual components. Best acquired as a part of **State Secondary Resources** add-on to a WestlawNext PRO subscription at considerable savings.

6. Citators.

Shepard's Connecticut Citations. Albany, NY: Shepard's. Monthly
Cost: $2,100 (4 bound volumes); all-inclusive subscription: $2,284 (in-state) (2014).

Online: All jurisdictional Shepard's and KeyCite are no longer available as stand-alone products, but are included as part of a jurisdictional or subject library package (2014).

7. CD-ROM Products.

Connecticut Reporter and West's General Statutes Unannotated, PREMISE CD-ROM. Eagan, MN: Thomson West. One disc. Updated2-4 times annually. Contains full text of the Connecticut General Statutes Annotated, Connecticut Constitution, and all editorial features included in hardcopy set. Available in Windows and Macintosh versions. Search Engine: PREMISE; LawDesk. Subscription includes online updating via Westlaw.
Cost: $4,977 per year (2014).

Connecticut Reports Archives CD-ROM Volume II. Enfield, CT: Commission on Official Legal Publications. Eight discs. Periodic updates. Contains the full text of Connecticut Supreme Court decisions from 1785 to date, including Kirby's Reports, Root's Reports, Day's Reports, Connecticut Reports, vols. 1-179, Connecticut Supplement, vols. 1-20, Connecticut Circuit Court Reports, vols. 1-6, Digest of Decisions Connecticut (Dowling), first series (10 vol. set), and 2d series (4 vols.)Phillips Digest (3 vols.). Available for Windows. Search Engine: Alchemy Search (Information Management Research).
Cost: $300 (2014).

8. State Legal Research Guides.

Horton, Wesley W. **The Connecticut State Constitution**. 2d ed. New York: Oxford University Press, 2012. 1 vol. (216 pp.).
Cost: $150; from $130.72 on amazon.com (2014).

Hynes, Jessica G. **Connecticut Legal Research**. Durham, NC: Carolina Academic Press, 2009. 1 vol. Paperbound.
Cost: $25.00; from $17.42 on amazon.com (2014).

Saxon, Jonathan. "Connecticut Practice Materials: A Selective Annotated Bibliography." **Law Library Journal** 91, No. 1 (1999): 139-175.

Sims, Lee and Xaitlin Anderson. Connecticut Practice Materials: A Selective Bibliography in Houdek, Frank G., ed. **State Practice Materials: Annotated Bibliographies**. Buffalo, NY: William S. Hein & Co., Inc., 2005-date. 2 vols. Looseleaf format.
Cost: $195 (2014).

9. Leading Web Sites for State Law Research.

Home Page:	www.ct.gov/
Administrative Code:	www.sots.ct.gov/sots/cwp/view.asp?a=4431&q=520270
Agency Directory:	(link from home page above)
Attorney General:	www.ct.gov/ag/
Attorney Gen. Opinions:	(link from Attorney General site above)
Bar Association:	www.ctbar.org/
Constitution:	www.cga.ct.gov/asp/Content/constitutions/CTConstitution.htm
Court Opinions:	www.jud.state.ct.us/opinions.htm
Governor:	www.state.ct.us/governor/
Judicial Branch:	www.jud.state.ct.us/
Law Libraries:	www.jud.state.ct.us/LawLib/
Legal Publications (COLP):	www.jud.state.ct.us/colp/publicat.htm
Legislative Branch:	www.cga.ct.gov/
Secretary of State:	www.sots.ct.gov/
Statutes:	www.cga.ct.gov/asp/menu/Statutes.asp

10. Leading publishers of state specific treatises, practice books, and CLE publications.

Administrative Publications, Inc., Atlantic Law Book, Cambridge Institute, Commerce Clearing House, Commission on Official Legal Publications, Connecticut Bar Association, Connecticut Business and Industry Associates, Inc., Connecticut Dept. of Education, Connecticut Dept. of Labor/Office of Research, Connecticut Law Book Company, Connecticut Law Tribune, Date Trace Legal Publishers, Government Institutes, Inc., Greenwood Press, Labor Relations Publishers, Law Practice Books, LawPress, Legal Aid Society of Hartford County, LexisNexis, Lorman Education Services, National Business Institute, Office of the Probate Court Administrator, Quinnipiac School of Law, Thomson Reuters (West), University of Connecticut Law School

Foundation, University of Connecticut School of Law, Wolters Kluwer Law & Business.

Delaware

1. Codes and Session Laws.

Delaware Code Annotated. Charlottesville, VA: LexisNexis, 1974-date. 22 vols. Annual pocket supplements and periodic revised volumes.
Cost: $592.50 (in-state); $845 (out-of-state); supplementation (in-state/out-of-state): 1999: $128/$450; 2000: $74/$245; 2001: $90.50/$347; 2002: $77.50/$259; 2003: $55.40/$294; 2004: $51.50/$267; 2005: $35/$195; 2007: $41.20/$134; 2008: $57.50/$279; 2009: $63.25/$349; 2010: $172/$470; 2011: $63.25/$367; 2012: $63.25/$367; 2013: $99.75.

West's Delaware Code Annotated. St. Paul, MN: West, 2006-date. 29 vols.
Hardbound, with annual pocket supplements and revised indices.
Cost: $747; supplementation: 2008: $223.00; 2009: $282; 2010: $453; 2011: $552; 2012: $525; 2013: $611; **Monthly Assured Print Price (APP):** $47/$564.

Delaware Advance Annotation Service. Charlottesville, VA: LexisNexis. Supplements code between annual pocket supplements.
Cost: $88 (2014).

Delaware Advance Legislative Service. Charlottesville, VA: LexisNexis. These pamphlets are published during and immediately after current legislative session and contain the text of laws in numerical chapter sequence in order of passage.
Cost: $88 (2014).

Delaware Legislative Service. St. Paul, MN: West, 2009-date. These pamphlets are published during and immediately after current legislative session and contain the text of laws in numerical chapter sequence in order of passage.
Cost: $273 (2014).

Laws of Delaware. [session laws]. Dover: Legislative Library. Published biennially in odd-numbered years (covering two-year General Assembly). DE Legislative Library, P.O. 1401, Legislative Hall, Dover, DE 19903.
Cost: vol. 71 (1997-98): $80; vol. 72 (1999-2000): $80; vol. 73 (2001-2002): $80; vol. 74 (2003-2004): $80; vol 75 (2005-2006): $80; vol. 76 (2007-2008): $80; vol. 77 (2009-2010): $80; vol. 78 (2011-2012): $80.

Legislative Hotline: (302) 739-4114.

2. Administrative Law.

Code of Delaware Regulations. Albany, NY: LexisNexis Matthew Bender [formerly Weil Publishing], 1996-date. 15 vols. Updated monthly.
Cost: $3,004 (individual volumes: $135.00); annual renewal: 2001-2004: $1,250; 2005: $1,045; 2006: $1,045; 2007: $1,045; 2008: $1,475; 2009: $1,582; 2010: $1,642; 2011: $1,724; 2012: $1,827; 2013: $1,955; 2014: $2,134.

Delaware Government Register. Albany, NY: LexisNexis Matthew Bender [formerly Weil Publishing], 1996-date. Monthly.
Cost: $1,257; renewal: 2014: $1,143 (2014).

Delaware Register of Regulations. Dover: General Assembly. Weekly.
Also available online in pdf format at no cost: http://regulations.delaware.gov/register/march2014/index.shtml
Cost: $135 (2014). 1-800-282-8545.

3. Court Reports.

Delaware Reporter [1st] – 3d. St. Paul: Thomson West, 1969-date. [offprint of Atlantic Reporter 2d-3d-designated official in 1966]. Contains decisions of Delaware Supreme Court from 1966 to date. Current vol: 64-68 A. 3d.
Cost: $1,848 (87 vols.); annual cost: 2003: $292.50; 2004: $210.50; 2005: $337.50; 2006: $520; 2007: $390; 2008: $280; 2009: $592; 2010: $486; 2011: $522; 2012: $526.50; 2013: $870; individual volumes: $217.50/$290 (subscriber/list); **Monthly Assured Print Pricing (APP):** $94/$1,128; used sets may be available.

Delaware Reports. 1832-1966, vols. 1-59. [ceased publication with vol. 59].
Cost: Used sets sell for approximately $750.

Atlantic Reporter [1st] - **2d**. St. Paul, MN: Thomson West, 1886-date. Contains decisions of the Delaware Supreme Court from 1886-date, Court of Appeals from 1942-date. Current volume: 85 **A.3d**.
Cost: 1st series out-of-print (see used lawbook dealers in Appendix C); 2d series: $14,434; 3d series: $15,080; annual cost (2013): $11,151; recent vol.: $531/$708 (subscriber/list); **Monthly Assured Print Pricing (APP):** $1,163/$13,956. See list of used lawbook dealers in Appendix C.

Atlantic Reporter 2d. Advance sheets. St. Paul, MN: Thomson West. Weekly.
Cost: $2,866.56 per year (discounted to bound volume subscribers) (2014).

4. Court Rules.

Delaware Rules Annotated. Charlottesville, VA: LexisNexis. 2 vols. Updated semiannually, replaced annually.
Cost: 2014 Edition: $35 (in-state), $115 (out-of-state).

Delaware Rules of Court: State and Federal. St. Paul, MN: West. Annual.
2 vols. Paperbound. Also available on ProView eBook.
Cost: 2014 Edition: $220.

5. Digests, Encyclopedias, and Practice Sets.

No Delaware Digest (See Atlantic Digest).

6. Citators.

Shepard's Delaware Citations. Albany, NY: Shepard's. Six supplements per year.
Cost: $1,799 (2 bound volumes); all-inclusive subscription: $1,720 (2014).

Online: All jurisdictional Shepard's and KeyCite are no longer available as stand-alone products, but are now included as part of a jurisdictional or subject library package (2014).

7. CD-ROM Products.

Delaware Laws Affecting Business Entities. Wilmington, DE: Corporation Service Company. One disc. Updated semi-annually. Contains the full text of Delaware Corporation Law and other laws related to business. Also includes Delaware Chancery Court Rules. Available for Windows 3.1 or higher. Search Engine: Folio.
Cost: 2014 Edition: $94 (including print) (2014). Available in cooperation with LexisNexis.

Delaware Reporter and West's Delaware Code. Eagan, MN: Thomson West. One disc. Updated quarterly. Contains full text of decisions of Delaware Supreme Court from 1792 to date, Delaware Court of Chancery, Superior Court, Family Court Attorney General opinions from 1977 to date, and unpublished opinions from 1969 to date, Code of Delaware, State Constitution, session laws and court rules. Decisions also searchable by West Topics and Key Numbers, headnotes, and synopses. Available in Windows and Macintosh versions. Search Engine: PREMISE. Subscription includes online updating of Delaware materials via Westlaw .
Cost: $5,286 per year (2014).

LexisNexis CD - Delaware Primary Law. Albany, NY: LexisNexis. One disc. Updated quarterly. Contains full text of Delaware Code Annotated, Supreme Court decisions from 1814 to date, Superior Court decisions from 1945-date, Chancery Court decisions from 1978 to date, unreported decisions, and court rules. Available for Windows. Search Engine: Folio; LivePublish (NextPage). Includes online updating via LEXIS.
Cost: $1,624 per year (2014).

8. State Legal Research Guides.

Charles, Patrick J. and David K. King. "Delaware Practice Materials: A Selective Annotated Bibliography." **Law Library Journal** 89 (Summer 1997): 349-378.

Egler, Peter. **Selective Annotated Bibliography of Delaware State Documents and Other Resources Used in Delaware Legal Research**. Chicago: AALL, 2008.
Cost: $30.00. Available from William S. Hein & Co. on electronic pdf and on HeinOnline (2014).

Holland, Randy J. **The Delaware State Constitution**. New York: Oxford University Press, 2011. 1 vol. ((324 pp.).
Cost: $150; from $100.00 on amazon.com; kindle: $119.99 (2014).

Leading Web Sites for State Law Research.

Home Page:	www.delaware.gov/
Administrative Code:	http://regulations.delaware.gov/AdminCode/
Agency Directory:	www.delaware.gov/egov/portal.nsf/portal/agencylist_dept
Attorney General:	http://attorneygeneral.delaware.gov/
Attorney Gen. Opinions:	http://opinions.attorneygeneral.delaware.gov/
Bar Association:	www.dsba.org/
Constitution:	http://delcode.delaware.gov/constitution/index.shtml
Court Opinions:	(link from Judicial Branch below)
Governor:	http://governor.delaware.gov/
Judicial Branch:	http://courts.delaware.gov/
Legislative Branch:	http://legis.delaware.gov
Register of Regulations:	http://regulations.delaware.gov/
Secretary of State:	http://sos.delaware.gov
Statutes:	(under "Online Publications" of Legislature page above)

10. Leading publishers of state specific treatises, practice books, and CLE publications.

Matthew Bender, Delaware State Bar Association, LexisNexis, National Business Institute, Thomson Reuters West, Wolters Kluwer Law & Business. See Appendix B for addresses and telephone numbers.

District of Columbia

1. Codes and Session Laws.

District of Columbia Official Code Annotated. Charlottesville, VA: LexisNexis, 2001-date. 12 vols. in 25. Annual pocket supplements and periodic revised volumes. Now the official code. Republished in 2013 to commemorate the 40th anniversary of D.C. home rule.
Cost: $849; supplementation: 2002: $272; 2003: $275; 2004: $155; 2005: $164; 2007: $348; 2008: $438; 2009: $406; 2010: $491; 2011: $534; 2012: $1.093.

West's District of Columbia Code Annotated. St. Paul, MN: Thomson West, 2001-date. 25 vols. Annual pocket parts and periodic revised volumes. Now the official code for the District of Columbia. Updated and recodifies the 1981 edition of the District of Columbia Code Annotated. Formerly the official code.
Cost: $893; supplementation: 2002: $240; 2003: $240; 2004: $262.50; 2005: $408.50; 2006: $388.50; 2007: $368.50; 2008: $ 618.50; 2009: $550; 2010: $516; 2011: $595; 2012: $493.50; **Monthly Assured Print Pricing (APP):** $70/$840.

District of Columbia Legislative Service. St. Paul, MN: Thomson West, 2002-date. Annual. Paperbound pamplet service.
Cost: $378.96 (2013).

District of Columbia Advance Annotation Service. Charlottesville, VA: LexisNexis. Supplements code between annual pocket parts.
Cost: $150.00 per year (2014).

District of Columbia Advance Legislative Service. Charlottesville, VA: LexisNexis.
Cost: $131 per year (2014).

Legislative Hotline: (850) 488-4371.

2. Administrative Law.
Code of District of Columbia Municipal Regulations. Albany, NY: LexisNexis Matthew Bender [formerly Weil Publishing], 1999-date. 14 vols. Updated monthly.
Cost: $2,971 (includes one year's updates); annual renewal: 2001-2004: $995.00; 2005-2008: $1,045; 2009: $1,165; 2010: $1,309; 2011: $1,374; 2012: $1,456; 2013: $1,558; 2014: $1,700.

District of Columbia Municipal Regulations. Washington, D.C.: Office of Documents and Administrative Issuances, 1984-2009. 31 vols. (202) 727-5090. Now available online (see below).
Cost: Now available only online at no charge (2014).

District of Columbia Register (DCR). Washington, D.C.: Office of Documents and Administrative Issuances, 1954-date. Weekly. (202) 727-5090.
Cost: Available online only at no charge (2014).

3. Court Reports.
Atlantic Reporter [1st] - **2d**. St. Paul, MN: Thomson West, 1886-date. Contains decisions of the District of Columbia Court of Appeals (Municipal Court of Appeals before 1970) from 1942-date. Current volume: 85 **A.3d**.
Cost: 1st series out-of-print (see used lawbook dealers in Appendix C); 2d series: $14,434; 3d series: $15,080; annual cost (2013): $11,151; recent vol.: $531/$708 (subscriber/list); **Monthly Assured Print Pricing (APP):** $1,163/$13,956. See list of used lawbook dealers in Appendix C.

Atlantic Reporter 2d. Advance sheets. St. Paul, MN: Thomson West. Weekly.
Cost: $2,866.56 per year (discounted to bound volume subscribers) (2014).

4. Court Rules.
District of Columbia Court Rules Annotated. Charlottesville, VA: LexisNexis. 2 vols. Updated semiannually, replaced annually. Also available on ProView eBook.
Cost: 2013 Edition (print or eBook): $144 (2014).

District of Columbia Court Rules, District & Federal. St. Paul, MN: Thomson West. 2 vols. Annual.
Cost: 2014 Edition: $222.

5. Digests, Encyclopedias, and Practice Sets.
District of Columbia Digest. St. Paul, MN: Thomson West, 1936-date. 81 vols. Annual pocket supplements and periodic revised volumes.
Cost: $5,629 ; supplementation: 1996: $284.50; 1997: $313.50; 1998: $659; 1999: $1,055.50; 2000: $1,137.75; 2001: $966; 2002: $784; 2003: $882; 2004: $988; 2005: $1.301; 2006: $1,292; 2007: $1,370; 2008: $2,130; 2009: $1,816; 2010: $1,846; 2011: $2,471; 2012: $2,678; 2013: $3,953; **Monthly Assured Print Pricing (APP):** $313/$3,756

6. Citators.
Shepard's District of Columbia Citations. Albany, NY: Shepard's. Monthly.
Cost: $2,112 (4 bound volumes); all-inclusive subscription: $2,273 (2014).

Online: All jurisdictional Shepard's and KeyCite are no longer available as stand-alone products, but are now included as part of a jurisdictional or subject library package (2014).

7. CD-ROM Products.
LexisNexis CD - District of Columbia Primary Law. Albany, NY: LexisNexis. One disc. Updated quarterly. Contains the full text of annotated D.C. Code, Court of Appeals decisions from 1942 to date, D.C. Court Rules Annotated. Windows. Search Engine: Folio; LivePublish (NextPage). Includes an online link to Lexis.
Cost: $2,082 per year (2014).

8. State Legal Research Guides.
Chanin, Leah F., Pamela F. Gregory, and Sarah K. Wiant. **Legal Research in the District of Columbia, Maryland, and Virginia**. Buffalo, NY: William S. Hein & Co., 2000.
Cost: $68.00 (2014).

Davitt, Jennifer. **State Documents Bibliography: Washington, DC**. Chicago: AALL, 2008.
Cost: $30.00. Available from William S. Hein & Co. on electronic pdf and in Spinelli's Law Library Reference Shelf on HeinOnline (2014).

Wu, Michelle. District of Columbia Practice Materials: A Selective Bibliography in Houdek, Frank G., ed. **State Practice Materials: Annotated Bibliographies**. Buffalo, NY: William S. Hein & Co., Inc., 2002-date. 2 vols.
Cost: $195.00 (2014).

9. Leading Web Sites for State Legal Research.

Home Page:	www.dc.gov/
Agency Directory:	http://directory.dc.gov/
Bar Association:	www.dcbar.org/
Code:	(link from Council page below)
Council:	www.dccouncil.washington.dc.us/
Court of Appeals:	www.dccourts.gov
Court of Appeals Opinons:	www.dccourts.gov/internet/opinionlocator.jsf
Mayor's Office:	http://mayor.dc.gov/
Municipal Regulations:	www.dcregs.org/
Office of Documents:	(link from Secretary's Office page below)
Secretary's Office:	www.os.dc.gov/

10. Leading publishers of state specific treatises, practice books, and CLE publications.
Bar Association of the District of Columbia (the voluntary bar), The District of Columbia Bar Association (the mandatory bar), LexisNexis, National Business Institute, Thomson Reuters West. See Appendix B for addresses and telephone numbers.

Florida

1. Codes and Session Laws.
Florida Statutes. [unannotated]. Tallahassee, FL: State of Florida, Statutory Revision Department, 1963-date. Annual. 6 vols. (850) 488-2323.
Cost: 2013 Edition: $300**;** CD-ROM: $75 (2014).

LexisNexis Florida Annotated Statutes. The Florida Bar Edition. Charlottesville, VA: LexisNexis, 2011-date. 53 vols. Completely updated and reprinted biennially in even-numbered years, with a free-standing supplement in every odd-numbered year. Includes citations to The Florida Bar's CLE publications as well as LexisNexis practice guides and other primary and secondary source materials, including FL Administrative Code, A.G. opinions, etc.
Cost: $1,532 per year (2014)

West's Florida Statutes Annotated. St. Paul, MN: Thomson West, 1943-date. 35 vols. in 129. Annual pocket parts and periodic revised volumes.
Cost: $5,825 ; supplementation: 1996: $1,307; 1997: $870; 1998: $1,094; 1999: $1,037; 2000: $1,508.50; 2001: $1,865; 2002: $2,066; 2003: $2,200; 2004: $2,300; 2005: $2,450; 2006: 2,893; 2007: $2,820.50; 2008: $2,990; 2009: $3,130.50; 2010: $3,159; 2011: $3,552; 2012: $3,507; 2013: $5.044; **Monthly Assured Print Pricing:** $378/$4,536.

Laws of Florida. [session laws]. Tallahassee, FL: Law Book Distribution Office. Annual. 1 vol. Includes all local, general and special laws. (850) 488-2323
Cost: 1995: $66; 1996: $60; 1997: $48;1998: $45; 1999: $60; 2000: $75; 2001: $85; 2002: $85; 2003-2008: $90 per year; 2009: $100; 2010: $100; 2011: $100; 2012: $100; 2013: $100.

West's Florida Session Law Service. St. Paul, MN: Thomson West. These pamphlets are published during and immediately after each legislative session and contain the text of laws in numerical chapter sequence in order of passage.
Cost: $825.48 (2014).

Florida Advance Legislative Service. Charlottesville, VA: LexisNexis, 2011-date. These pamphlets or e-publications are published during and immediately after each legislative session and contain the text of laws in numerical chapter sequence in order of passage.
Cost: $335 (2014).

Legislative Hotline: (850) 488-4371

2. Administrative Law.
Florida Administrative Code Annotated. Albany, NY: LexisNexis Matthew Bender, 2004-date. 12 vols. Looseleaf format. Updated monthly.
Cost: $1,413; renewal: 2012: $1,116; 2013: $1,116; 2014: $1,216.

LexisNexis Florida Administrative Register. Albany, NY: LexisNexis, 2013-date. Electronic only. Weekly (July 1 – June 30).
Cost: $358 per year (2014).

Florida Administrative Weekly. Weekly (July 1 – June 30).
Cost: free Internet version at: https://www.flrules.org/default.asp

3. Court Reports.
Florida Cases [1st] - **3d**. St. Paul, MN: Thomson West,1941-date [offprint of Southern Reporter 2d--designated official in 1948]. Contains decisions of the Florida Supreme Court from 1941 to date and District Court of Appeal from 1957 to date. Current volume: 124-125 **So. 3d**
Cost: 1st series: out-of-print; 2d series: $5,319; 3d series: $3,412; annual cost: 2002: $1,043; 2003: $975; 2004: $1,100; 2005: $1,179; 2006: $1,165; 2007: $1,166.50; 2008: $1,764; 2009 (2d & 3d): $1,459.50; 2010: $1,691; 2011: $1,669; 2012: $1,512; 2013: $2,320; recent vol.: $136.50/$182 (subscriber/list); **Monthly Assured Print Pricing (APP**): $237/$2,844; used sets may be available.

Florida Reports. 1846-1948. [ceased publication with vol. 160].
Cost: Used sets sell for approx. $1,000.00. See used lawbook dealers in Appendix C.

Florida Supplement [1st] - **2d**. St. Paul, MN: Thomson West, 1948-1992. [ceased publication with vol. 50, 2d series (1992)] Contain decisions of various lower courts of record. 1st series: 1950-1980; 2d series: 1980-1992.
Cost: Out-of-print; see list of used lawbook dealers.

Southern Reporter [1st] - **3d**. St. Paul, MN: Thomson West, 1886-date. Contains decisions of the Florida Supreme Court from 1886 to date, and Florida district Court of Appeal from 1957 to date, as well as other Southern regional appellate court decisions.. Current vol.: 130 So.3d
Cost: 1st series out-of-print (see used lawbook dealers); 2d series: $14,566; 3d series: $17,639; annual cost (2013): $12,178; current vol.: $529/$706 (subscriber/list); **Monthly Assured Print Pricing** (**APP**): $1,274/$15,288. See list of used lawbook dealers in Appendix C.

Southern Reporter 2d. Advance sheets. St. Paul, MN: Thomson West. Weekly.
Cost: $2,866.56 per year (discounted to bound volume subscribers) (2014).

Florida Law Weekly. Tallahassee, FL: Judicial and Administrative Research Associates, Inc. 48 issues per year. Contains reports of decisions of the Florida Supreme Court and District Court of Appeals.
Cost: $420 + tax per year; Internet subscription: $390 + tax per year, or $510. for both (2014). (800) 351-0917.

Florida Law Weekly Supplement. Tallahassee, FL: Judicial and Administrative Research Associates, Inc. Monthly. Contains

reports of decision s of the Circuit, Appellate, County, and miscellaneous courts.
Cost: $250 + tax per year; Internet subscription is $250 + tax per year, or $370 for both (2014). (800) 351-0917

4. Court Rules.
Florida Rules of Court: State and Federal. St. Paul, MN: Thomson West. 2 vols. Annual. Also available on ProView eBook.
Cost: 2014 Edition: $140; ProView eBook: $136.

Florida Rules of Court: State, Federal and Local. St. Paul, MN: Thomson West. Annual. 3 vols. Paperbound. Also available on ProView eBook.
Cost: 2014 Edition: $215; ProView eBook: $209.

5. Digests, Encyclopedias, and Practice Sets.
Florida Digest 2d. St. Paul, MN: Thomson West, 1984-date. 123 vols. Annual pocket parts, mid-year supplement and periodic revised volumes.
Cost: $8,111; supplementation: 1996: $168; 1997: $380.50; 1998: $624; 1999: $781.50; 2000: $1,317.50; 2001: $1,606; 2002: $2,178; 2003: $1,400; 2004: $850; 2005: $899; 2006: 2,069.25; 2007: $2,437.50; 2008: $3,482; 2009: $5,487.50; 2010: $5,506.50; 2011: $5,748.50; 2012: $2,037; 2013: $6,907; **Monthly Assured Print Pricing (APP):** $502/$6,024.

Florida Jurisprudence 2d. St. Paul, MN: Thomson West, 1977-date. 93 vols. Annual pocket parts and periodic revised volumes.
Cost: $12,497 ; supplementation: 1996: $1,401.45; 1997: $1,825.05; 1998: $1,821.35; 1999: $2,072.70; 2000: $2,166.75; 2001: $2,208.75; 2002: $2,634; 2003: $3,200; 2004: $2,300; 2005: $4,217; 2006: $4,075; 2007: $4,536; 2008: $4,987; 2009: $6,212.50; 2010: $6,121; 2011: $7,077.50; 2012: $4,935; 2013: $8,441; **Monthly Assured Print Pricing (APP):** $738/$8,856.

6. Citators.
Shepard's Florida Citations. Albany, NY: Shepard's. Monthly or bi-monthly .
Cost: $5,616 (13 bound volumes); all-inclusive subscription: monthly: $2,453; bi-monthly: $2,729 (2014).

Online: All jurisdictional Shepard's and KeyCite are no longer available as stand-alone products, but are included as part of a jurisdictional or subject library package (2014).

7. CD-ROM Products.
Florida Cases (West). Eagan, MN: Thomson West. Three discs. Updated quarterly. Contains full text of decisions of the Florida Supreme Court from 1846 to date, and Florida Court of Appeals from 1886-date to date, and Attorney General opinions from 1977-date. Available in Windows and Macintosh versions. Search Engine: PREMISE. Subscription includes online connection to Westlaw.
Cost: $6,660 per year (2014).

Florida Criminal Cases Notebook. Costa Mesa, CA: James Publishing, Inc. One disc. Updated periodically. Contains the text of 8,000 criminal case summaries as appearing in the book by Kurt Erlenbach. Available for Windows 3.1 or higher. Search Engine: Alchemy Search (Information Management research).
Cost: $125 (including print) (2014).

Florida Law on CD-ROM. Tallahassee, FL: Law Book Services Office, 2011. One disc. Updated annually. Contains the full text of the Florida Statutes, Laws of Florida, and Florida Constitution. Runs on Windows 98/2000/ME/XP, Vista or NT systems. Folio search engine included. (850) 488-2323
Cost: 2013 Edition: $75 (2014).

Florida Library CD. Albany, NY: LexisNexis. One disc. Updated quarterly. Contains the full text more than 20 state sets in the Florida Law and Practice Library, including Southeast Transaction Guide and Florida Civil Practice Guide, as well as Florida Statutes, regulations and cases, with LEXIS-NEXIS Online Connection for most recent case law. Available for Window. Search Engine: Folio
Cost: $13,620; renewal: 2008: $8,533; 2009: $9,216.00; 2010: $9,677; 2011: $9,774; 2012: $9,969; 2013: $10,666; 2014: $11,412; individual components also available (2014).

Florida Statutes Annotated (West's). Eagan, MN: Thomson West. One disc. Updated2-4 times annually. Contains full text of Florida Constitution, Florida Statutes Annotated, Florida Rules of Court [unannotated]. Decisions also searchable by West Topics and Key Numbers, headnotes, and synopses. Available in Windows, and Macintosh versions. Search Engine: PREMISE. Subscription includes online connection to Westlaw.
Cost: Discontinued. Look for comparable materials on WestlawNext PRO (2014).

8. State Legal Research Guides.
Busharis, Barbara J. and Suzanne E. Rowe. **Florida Legal Research**. 3rd ed. Durham, NC: Carolina Academic Press, 2011. 1 vol. (240 pp.).
Cost: $25; from $4.20 on amazon.com (2014).

D'Alemberte Talbot. **The Florida State Constitution**. New York: Oxford University Press, 2011. 1 vol. (232 pp.).
Cost: $150; from $128.68 on amazon.com; kindle: $119.99 (2014).

Roehrenbeck, Carol A. **Florida Legislative Histories: A Practical Guide to Their Preparation and Use**. D & S Publishers, 1986.

Strohmeyer, Nancy L. Florida Practice Materials: A Selective Bibliography in Houdek, Frank G., ed. **State Practice Materials: Annotated Bibliographies**. Buffalo, NY: William S. Hein & Co., Inc., 2005-date. 2 vols. Looseleaf format.
Cost: $195 (2014).

Stupski, Betsy L. and Belz, Richard A. **Guide to Florida Legal Research**. 7th ed. Tallahassee, FL: The Florida Bar, CLE, 2008. 1 vol. (various pagings).

9 Leading Web Sites for State Legal Research.

Home Page:	www.myflorida.com/
Administrative Code:	www.flrules.org

Agency Directory:	www.myflorida.com/directory/
Attorney General:	www.myfloridalegal.com/
Attorney Gen. Opinions:	www.myfloridalegal.com/opinions
Bar Association:	www.floridabar.org/
Constitution:	www.leg.state.fl.us/statutes/
Court Opinions–Supreme Court:	www.floridasupremecourt.org/decisions/opinions.shtml
District Courts of Appeal:	www.flcourts.org/florida-courts/district-court-appeal.stml
Governor:	www.flgov.com/
Judicial Branch:	www.flcourts.org/
Legislature:	www.leg.state.fl.us/
Library – Supreme Court:	http://library.flcourts.org/
Secretary of State:	http://dos.myflorida.com
Statutes:	www.leg.state.fl.us/statutes/
Supreme Court:	www.floridasupremecourt.org/

10. Leading publishers of state specific treatises, practice books, and CLE publications.
Wolters Kluwer Law & Business, Matthew Bender, George T. Bisel Co., D & S Publishers, Florida Bar Continuing Legal Education Department, LexisNexis, National Business Institute, Thomson Reuters West. See Appendix B for addresses and telephone numbers.

Georgia

1. Codes and Session Laws.

Official Code of Georgia Annotated. Charlottesville, VA: LexisNexis, 1982-date. 45 vols. Annual pocket supplements and periodic revised volumes.
Cost: $378 (in- and out-of-state); supplementation (in-state/out-of-state): 2001: $202/$628; 2002: $209/ $648; 2003: $209/$648; 2004: $218/$648; 2005: $198/$616; 2006: $218/$616; 2007: $267.30/$793; 2008: $222/$616; 2009: $234/$636; 2010: $217/$588; 2011: $223.20/$741; 2012: $244/$786; 2013: $268/$864.

West's Code of Georgia Annotated. St. Paul, MN: Thomson West, 2003-date. 75 vols. Annual pocket supplements and periodic revised volumes.
Cost: $1,605 ; supplementation: 2003: $35; 2004: $160; 2005: $250; 2006: $215; 2007: $427.50; 2008: $602; 2009: $708.50; 2010: $1,043; 2011: $958; 2012: $1,068; 2013: $1,331; **Monthly Assured Print Pricing**: $104/$1,248.

Georgia Advance Annotation Service. Charlottesville, VA: LexisNexis. Supplements code 3 times per year between annual pocket parts.
Cost: $126 per year (2014).

Georgia Advance Legislative Service. Charlottesville, VA: LexisNexis. These pamphlets are published during and immediately after each legislative session and contain the text of laws in numerical chapter sequence in order of passage.
Cost: $70 per year (2014).

Georgia Legislative Service. St. Paul, MN: West, 2009-date. These pamphlets are published during and immediately after each legislative session and contain the text of laws in numerical chapter sequence in order of passage.
Cost: $351.48 per year (2014).

Georgia Laws [session laws]. Atlanta: Legislative Council. Annual. Available from Secretary of State.
Cost: 1995-2000 (per year): hardbound: $60, softbound: $50; 2001-2006: $70/$58.50; 2007: $72/$59; 2008: $71/$60; 2009: $60; 2010: $60; 2011: $60 + $30 (special session); 2012: $60; 2013: $60. Available from Darby Printing: 800-241-5292.

Legislative Hotline: (404) 656-5015 (House); (404) 656-5042 (Senate).

2. Administrative Law.

Official Compilation: Rules and Regulations of the State of Georgia. Atlanta, GA: Darby Printing Co., 2003-date. 21 vols. Looseleaf. Monthly supplementation. July 1- June 30 calendar year.
Cost: $1,509.68 (with binders and postage); annual supplementation: $952.54; government pricing also available (2014).
Also available at no charge on Internet at: http://rules.sos.state.ga.us/
The electronic version of the Rules and Regulations on the Secretary of State's website should not be regarded as the official copy.

Georgia Government Register. Newark, NJ: LexisNexis Matthew Bender, 2004-date. Monthly.
Cost: $1,257; renewal: 2014: $1,143 (2014).

3. Court Reports.

Georgia Cases [1st]– **2d** St. Paul, MN: Thomson West, 1939-date. [offprint of South Eastern Reporter 2d, 1939-date]. Contain decisions of the Georgia Supreme Court and the Georgia Court of Appeals from 1939 to date. Current vol.: 746-748 **S.E.2d**.
Cost: 2d Series (1950-date): $7,374; annual cost: 2002: $945; 2003: $866.75; 2004: $724; 2005: $1,043.25; 2006: $1,032.75; 2007: $1,119.50; 2008: $2,140; 2009: $2,438; 2010: $2,313; 2011: $2,475; 2012: $4,280; 2013: $6,162; current volumes: $474/$632 (subscriber/ist); used sets may be available; **Monthly Assured Print Price (APP)**: $620/$7,440; See list of used lawbook dealers in Appendix C.

Georgia Reports. 1846-date. Charlottesville, VA: LexisNexis, 2009-date. Current vol.: 291
Cost: Advance sheets: $271 per year (includes decisions of both Georgia Supreme Court and Georgia Court of Appeals). Bound volumes priced at $15 each; total cost in 2012: $30 (2); 2013: 15.00 (1) (2014).

Georgia Appeals Reports. 1907-date. Charlottesville, VA: LexisNexis, 2004-date. Current vol.: 321
Cost: Advance sheets: $271 per year (includes decisions of

both Georgia Supreme Court and Georgia Court of Appeals); bound volumes priced at $13.55 each: total cost in 2013: $67.75 (5).

South Eastern Reporter [1st] - **2d**. St. Paul, MN: Thomson West, 1886-date. Contains decisions of the Georgia Supreme Court from 1887-date and the Georgia Court of Appeals from 1907-date. Current vol.: 750 **S.E. 2d**.
Cost: 1st series out-of-print (see used lawbook dealers in Appendix C); 2d series: $10,480; annual cost: 2012: $7,389; 2013: $5,434; current vol.: $524/$655 (subscriber/list); **Monthly Assured Print Pricing (APP):** $846/$10,152. See list of used lawbook dealers in Appendix C.

South Eastern Reporter 2d. Advance sheets. St. Paul, MN: Thomson West. Weekly.
Cost: $2,825 (discounted to bound volume subscribers) (2014).

Official Georgia Reports. Advance Sheets. Charlottesville, VA: LexisNexis, 2004-date. Previously published by Darby Printing Co. Contain decisions of the Georgia Supreme Court and Georgia Court of Appeals. Subscription year from July 1 through June 30. LexisNexis secured the state contract in 2004.
Cost: $271 per year (2014).

4. Court Rules.

Georgia Court Rules and Procedure: State and Federal. St. Paul, MN: Thomson West. 2 vols. Annual. Also available on ProView eBook.
Cost: 2014 Edition: $255; ProView eBook: $255.

Georgia Rules of Court Annotated. Charlottesville, VA: LexisNexis. Updated semiannually, replaced annually. Also available on ebook.
Cost: 2014 Edition (print or ebook): $84 (in-state) (2014).

5. Digests, Encyclopedias, and Practice Sets.

Georgia Jurisprudence. St. Paul, MN: Thomson West, 1995-date. 26 vols. Annual pocket parts and periodic revised volumes.
Cost: $4,690 ; supplementation: 1996: $125; 1997: $175; 1998: $187.50; 1999: $750.50; 2000: $216.50; 2001: $241; 2002: $775; 2003: $321.50; 2004: $765; 2005: $851; 2006: $1,035; 2007: $964; 2008: $1,725; 2009: $1,300; 2010: $1,062; 2011: $2,323; 2012: $2,354; 2013: $3,126; **Monthly Assured Print Pricing (APP):** $326/$3,912

Georgia Procedure. St. Paul, MN: Thomson West, 1995-date. 13 vols. Annual pocket parts and periodic revised volumes.
Cost: $2,818 ; supplementation: 1996: $95; 1997: $135; 1998: $144.50; 1999: $154.50; 2000: $168.75; 2001: $431; 2002: $249; 2003: $806.50; 2004: $433; 2005: $469; 2006: $566.50; 2007: $836.50; 2008: $808; 2009: $1,120; 2010: $2,133; 2011: $818; 2012: $1,734; 2013: $1,857; **Monthly Assured Print Pricing (APP):** $170/$2,040.

West's Georgia Digest 2d. St. Paul, MN: Thomson West, 1985-date. 121 vols. Annual pocket parts, mid-year supplement and periodic revised volumes.
Cost: $7,562; supplementation: 1996: $236; 1997: $262.50; 1998: $533.50; 1999: $998.75; 2000: $1,078.25; 2001: $1,378; 2002: $1,676.50; 2003: $1,279; 2004: $1,696.25; 2005: $1,170.50; 2006: $1,325; 2007: $1,959; 2008: $1,684; 2009: $2,301; 2010: $3,281.50; 2011: $3,689; 2012: $5,884; 2013: $6,051; **Monthly Assured Print Pricing (APP):** $404/$4,848

6. Citators.

Shepard's Georgia Citations. Albany, NY: Shepard's. Monthly or semi-monthly.
Cost: $5,115 (13 bound volumes); all-inclusive subscription: monthly: $2,284 (in-state); bi-monthly: $2,709 (in-state); (2014).

Online: All jurisdictional Shepard's and KeyCite are no longer available as stand-alone products, but are now included as part of a jurisdictional or subject library package (2013).

7. CD-R0M Products.

LexisNexis CD - Georgia Primary Law. Albany, NY: LexisNexis. Two discs. Updated quarterly. Contains the full text Official Code of Georgia Annotated, Supreme Court decisions from 1846 to date, Georgia Appellate Court decisions from 1945 to date, selected federal court decisions, Attorney General opinions, and Georgia Rules of Court. Windows. Search Engine: Folio; LivePublish (NextPage). Includes online connection to LEXIS.
Cost: $1,009 per year (2014).

Michie's Georgia Civil Practice on CD-ROM. Albany, NY: LexisNexis. One disc. Updated quarterly. Contains the text of the Georgia civil statutes and rules, cases, forms, and checklists, including Georgia Civil Practice 2d, Georgia Civil procedure Forms, and Georgia Rules of Court Annotated. Available for Windows. Search Engine: Folio; LivePublish (NextPage).
Cost: $544 per year (2014).

West's Georgia Cases, Premise CD-ROM ed. Eagan, MN: Thomson West. Four discs. Updated quarterly. Contains full text of decisions of Georgia Supreme Court from1846) to date, Georgia Court of Appeals appearing in South Eastern Reporter 2d, vol. 33 (1945) to date, George Administrative Code, session laws, and Georgia Attorney General Opinions from 1977 to date. Decisions also searchable by West Topics and Key Numbers, headnotes, and synopses. Windows, and Macintosh versions available. Search engine: PREMISE; LawDesk (Folio). Subscription includes online connection to Westlaw.
Cost: $5,304 per year (single user) (2014).

8. State Legal Research Guides.

Chanin, Leah F. & Suzanne L. Cassidy. **Guide to Georgia Legal Research and Legal History**. Norcross, GA: Harrison Co. [now part of West], 1990.
Cost: OUT-OF-PRINT (2014).

Hardy, Paul T. **How to Find and Access Georgia Law**. Athens, GA: Carl Vinson Institute of Government, University of Georgia, 1993.

Hill, Melvin B., Jr. **The Georgia State Constitution**. New York: Oxford University Press, 2011. 1 vol. (312 pp.).
Cost: $150; from $135.43 on amazon.com; kindle: $119.99 (2014).

Johnson, Nancy; Elizabeth G. Adelman, Nancy J. Adams. **Georgia Legal Research**. Durham, NC: Carolina Academic

Press, 2007. 1 vol. (284 pp.).
Cost: $25.00; from $11.29 on amazon.com (2014).

Johnson, Nancy and Ronald L. Wheeler, Jr. Georgia Practice Materials: A Selective Bibliography 2d, in Houdek, Frank G., ed. **State Practice Materials: Annotated Bibliographies**. Buffalo, NY: William S. Hein & Co., Inc., 2010-date. 2 vols. Looseleaf format.
Cost: $195.00 (2014).

Johnson, Nancy P. and Nancy Adams Deel. "Researching Georgia Law." **Georgia State University Law Review** 9, No. 3 (1993): 585-646.

Stillwagon, Rebecca Simmons. **Georgia Legal Documents: An Annotated Bibliography**. Chicago, AALL, 1991.
Cost: $30.00. Available from William S. Hein & Co. on electronic pdf and on HeinOnline (2014).

9. Leading Web Sites for State Legal Research.

Home Page:	www.georgia.gov/
Administrative Regulations:	www.osah.ga.gov/documents/procedures/administrative-rules-osah.pdf ???
Agency Directory:	http://georgia.gov/agency-list
Attorney General:	www.law.ga.gov
Attorney Gen. Opinions:	http://law.ga.gov/opinions
Bar Association:	www.gabar.org/
Constitution:	http://georgiainfo.galileo.usg.edu/gacontoc.htm - OR - http://sos.ga.gov/admin/files/Constitution_2013_Final_Printed.pdf
Court of Appeals:	www.gaappeals.us/
Court of Appeals Opinions:	www.gaappeals.us/opinions.php
Governor:	www.gov.georgia.gov
Judicial Branch:	www.georgiacourts.gov/
Legislature:	www.legis.state.ga.us/
Secretary of State:	www.sos.georgia.gov/
Statutes:	(link from General Assembly page above)
Supreme Court:	www.gasupreme.us/
Supreme Court Opinions:	www.gasupreme.us/sc-op/index14.php

10. Leading publishers of state specific treatises, practice books, and CLE publications.
Carl Vinson Institute of Government, Institute of Continuing Legal Education in Georgia, LexisNexis, National Business Institute, University of Georgia Press, Thomson Reuters (West). See Appendix B for addresses and telephone numbers.

Hawaii

1. Codes and Session Laws.
Hawaii Revised Statutes. 1993 Edition. Honolulu: Published by Authority available from the Office of the Lieutenant Governor, 1995-date. 14 vols. Annual free-standing supplements. (808) 586-0255.
Cost: $375 + $28.20/$78.00 (plus postage); supplementation (exclusive of postage): 1994: $25; 1996: $40.00; 1997: $45; 1998: $45; 1999: $45; 2000: $70; 2001: $70; 2003: $65; 2004: $77; 2005: $79; 2006: $82; 2007: $87; 2008: $88; 2009: $89; 2010: $63; 2011: $120; 2012: $120; 2013: $122.40.

Hawaii Revised Statutes Annotated. Charlottesville, VA: LexisNexis, 1988-date. 20 vols. Includes 2-volume index, 2 vol. advanced legislative history, 1 vol. court rules. Annual pocket parts and periodic revised vols.
Cost: $1,036 (in-and out-of-state); supplementation (in-state/out-of-state): 2001: $521/$572; 2002: $437/ $485; 2003: $442/$490; 2004: $599/$658; 2005: $575/$633; 2006: $575/$647; 2007: $711/$763; 2008:$936/$977; 2009: $440/$464; 2010: $702/$711; 2011: $487/$513; 2012: $735/$769.

Hawaii Advance Code Service. Charlottesville, VA: LexisNexis. Supplements code between annual pocket parts. Three pamphlets per year.
Cost: $103 per year (in-state) (2014).

Hawaii Advance Legislative Service. Charlottesville, VA: LexisNexis. Supplements code between annual pocket parts.
Cost: $142 per year (2014).

Session Laws of Hawaii. Honolulu: Office of Lieutenant Governor. Annual.
Cost: 1996: $35; 1997: $35; 1998: $35; 1999: $35; 2000: $35; 2001: $35; 2003: $10; 2004: $13.50; 2005: $11; 2006: $18; 2007: $13; 2008: $13; 2009: $15; 2010: $15; 2011: $11; 2012: $21; 2013: $17.

Legislative Hotline: (808) 587-0700.

2. Administrative Law.
Hawaii Administrative Code. Albany, NY: LexisNexis Matthew Bender, 1997-date. 20 vols.
Cost: $2,971 (incl. one year's updates) + $99 postage; supplementation (see Register below): 2001: $1,295; 2002: $1,295; 2003: $1,295; 2004: $1,295; 2005: $1,360; 2006: $1,360; 2007: $1,360; 2008: $1,528; 2009: $1,959; 2010: $1,701; 2011: $1,786; 2012: $1,893; 2013: $2,026; 2014: $2,211.

Hawaii Government Register. Newark, NJ: LexisNexis Matthew Bender, 1997-date. Monthly.
Cost: $1,257; renewal: 2014; $1,143.

3. Court Reports.
Hawaii Reports. Vols. 1-75 (1847-1995) published by Authority; volumes 76-date published by West. Current volume: 129 (as of April 1, 2014).
Cost: Reprints of vols. 1-73 (Hein Co.): $2,495; vols. 74-75:

$40 ea.; vol. 76-125 (West): $1,435; annual cost: 2002: $156; 2003: $242; 2004: $255.00; 2005: $285 (list); 2006: $266; 2007: $277.50; 2008: $300; 2009: $305; 2010: $305; 2011: $330; 2012: $109.50; 2013: 219; current vol.: $109.50/$146 ea. (subscriber/list); used sets of Hawaii Reports and Hawaii Appellate Reports combined have sold for approx. $1,500.

Hawaii Appellate Reports. Honolulu: Published by Authority, 1981-1995. Vols. 1-10 continued by West's Hawaii Reports which, beginning with volume 77, contain decisions of both Hawaii Supreme Court and Hawaii Intermediate Court of Appeals. Current volume: 129 (as of April 1, 2014) (see above entry).
Cost: Reprints of vols. 1-10 (Hein Co.): $400; vols. 1-6: $47.50 each; vols. 7-10: $40 each; see above entry for cost of Hawaii Reports. Used sets of Hawaii Reports and Hawaii Appellate Reports may be available.

Pacific Reporter [1st] - **3d**. St. Paul, MN: Thomson West, 1883-date. Contains decisions of the Hawaii Supreme Court from 1959-date and the Hawaii Intermediate Court of Appeals from 1980-date. Current vol.: 314 **P. 3d**.
Cost: 1st series out-of-print (see used lawbook dealers in Appendix C); 2d series: $13,428; used sets approx. $2000; 3d series: $15,201; annual cost (2013): $11,396; individual volume: $518/$691 (subscriber/list); **Monthly Assured Print Pricing (APP):** $1,141/$11,369; used sets may be available.

Pacific Reporter 3d. Advance sheets. St. Paul, MN: Thomson West. Weekly.
Cost: $2,866.56 per year (discounted to bound volume subscribers) (2014).

4. Court Rules.

Hawaii Court Rules Annotated. Charlottesville, VA: LexisNexis. 1 vol. Updated semiannually, replaced annually. Also available on ebook.
Cost: 2014 Edition: $117 (in-state).

Hawaii Court Rules: State and Federal. St. Paul, MN: Thomson West. 2 vols. Annual. Also available on ProView eBook.
Cost: 2014 Edition: $265; ProView eBook: $465.

5. Digests, Encyclopedias, and Practice Sets.

Hawaii Digest. St. Paul, MN: Thomson West, 1939-date. 33 vols. Annual pocket parts, mid-year supplement and periodic revised volumes.
Cost: $3,047; supplementation: 1995: $160; 1996: $196; 1997: $223; 1998: $200.50; 1999: $374; 2000: $649; 2001: $1,082; 2002: $1,142; 2003: $425; 2004: $435.50; 2005: $590; 2006: $590.50; 2007: $790; 2008: $730; 2009: $947; 2010: $1,569; 2011: $1,413; 2012: $2,096; 2013: $1,760; **Monthly Assured Print Pricing (APP):** $174/$2,088.

6. Citators.

Shepard's Hawaii Citations. Albany, NY: Shepard's. Six supplements per year.
Cost: $1,178 (1 bound volume); all-inclusive subscription: $1,703 (in-state) (2014).

Online: All jurisdictional Shepard's and KeyCite are no longer available as stand-alone products, but are acquired as part of a jurisdictional or subject library package (2014).

7. CD-ROM Products.

Michie's Law on Disc for Hawaii. Albany, NY: LexisNexis. One disc. Updated quarterly. Contains full text of decisions of Hawaii Supreme Court from 1847 to date, Hawaii Intermediate Appellate Court from 1980 to date, and the complete text of the **Hawaii Revised Statutes Annotated**. Available for Windows. Search Engine: Folio. Includes online connection to LEXIS.
Cost: $1,906 per year (2014).

Hawaii Reporter and Hawaii Revised Statutes. Eagan, MN: Thomson West. One disc. Regular updates. Contains full text of decisions of Hawaii Supreme Court and Hawaii Intermediate Appellate Court from vol. 351 (1960) Pacific Reporter 2d to date, Attorney General opinions from 1977 to date, opinions of the Office of Information Practices from 1989 to date, state court rules, Hawaii Revised Statutes and Constitution, etc. Decisions also searchable by West Topics and Key Numbers, headnotes, and synopses. Available for Windows, and Macintosh. Search Engine: PREMISE.
Cost: $2,652 per year (2014).

8. State Legal Research Guides.

DuPont, Jerry and Beverly D. Keever. **The Citizens Guide: How to Use Legal Materials in Hawaii**. Honolulu, 1983.

Kahle, Richard F. **How to Research Constitutional, Legislative and Statutory History in Hawaii**. Revised ed. Honolulu: Hawaii Legislative Reference Bureau, 1997.

Lee, Anne. **The Hawaii State Constitution**. New York: Oxford University Press, 2011. 1 vol. (280 pp.).
Cost: $150; from $74.15 on amazon.com; kindle: $97.49 (2014).

Seeger, Leinaala. Hawaii Practice Materials: A Selective Bibliography in Houdek, Frank G., ed. **State Practice Materials: Annotated Bibliographies**. Buffalo, NY: William S. Hein & Co., Inc., 2004-date.
Cost: $195.00 (2014).

Seeger, Leina'ala R. **Hawaii State Documents: A Selective Bibliography of Legal Publications and Related Materials**. Chicago: AALL, 2010.
Cost: $30.00. Available from William S. Hein & Co. on electronic pdf and on HeinOnline (2014).

9. Leading Web Sites for State Legal Research.

Home Page:	www.hawaii.gov/
Administrative Code:	http://ltgov.hawaii.gov/the-office/administrative-rules/ - OR - http://ag.hawaii.gov/publications/administrative-rules/
Agency Directory:	http://portal.ehawaii.gov/government/departments-and-agencies
Attorney General:	http://ag.hawaii.gov/
Attorney Gen. Opinions:	http://ag.hawaii.gov/publications/opinions/
Bar Association:	www.hsba.org/
Constitution:	http://www.lrbhawaii.org/con

Court Opinions:	www.courts.state.hi.us/opinions_and_orders/index.html
Governor:	http://governor.hawaii.gov/
Judicial Branch:	www.courts.state.hi.us/
Law Library:	http://www.state.hi.us/jud/library
Legislative Branch:	www.capitol.hawaii.gov/
Statutes:	www.capitol.hawaii.gov/docs/HRS.htm
W.S. Richardson School of Law:	www.law.hawaii.edu/

10. Leading publishers of state specific treatises, practice books, and CLE publications.
Hawaii State Bar Association/CLE (formerly Hawaii Institute for Continuing Legal Education), Law Book Store, LexisNexis, Lorman Education Services, National Business Institute, National Center for State Courts, Pacific Law Institute, Thomson Reuters (West), Wolters Kluwer Law & Business.

Idaho

1. Codes and Session Laws.
Idaho Code Annotated. Charlottesville, VA: LexisNexis, 1947-date. 13 vols. in 25. Annual pocket parts and periodic revised volumes.
Cost: $531; supplementation (in-state/out-of-state): 2001: $234/$442.50; 2002: $322.50/$465; 2003: $356/$582; 2004: $311/$620; 2005: $294/$486; 2006: $320/630; 2007: $315/$575; 2008: $315/$575; 2009: $329/$711; 2010: $421/$766; 2011: $340/$794; 2012: $352/$841; 2013: $352/841.

Idaho Advance Code Service. Charlottesville, VA: LexisNexis. Supplements code between annual pocket parts.
Cost: $124 per year (in-state) (2014).

Idaho Advance Legislative Service. Charlottesville, VA: LexisNexis. Contains the full text of recently enacted legislation published in the order of its passage.
Cost: $109 per year (in-state) (2014).

Session Laws of Idaho. Caldwell, ID: Caxton Printers. Annual. 2 vols. (208) 459-7421
Cost: 1995: $42; 1996: $42; 1997: $42; 1998: $42; 1999: $42; 2000: $42; 2001: $53.50; 2002: $53.50; 2003: $53.50; 2004: $53.50; 2005: $59. 2006: $59; 2007: $59.50; 2008: $53.50; 2009: $53.50; 2010: $53.50; 2011: $53.50; 2012: $63.60; 2013: $63.

Legislative Hotline: (208) 334-3175.

2. Administrative Law.
Idaho Administrative Code. Boise: Office of Administrative Rules, 2010-date. CD-ROM format. Updated by Idaho Administrative Bulletin. Also available on the Internet at: http://www.state.id.us
Cost: 2014 Edition: CD-ROM: $100; (208) 332-1821

Idaho Administrative Bulletin. Boise: Office of Administrative Rules, July 1, 1993-date. Monthly CD-ROM. Also available on the Internet at: http://www.state.id.us
Cost: $100 per year (2014). (208) 332-1821

3. Court Reports.
Idaho Reports, 1866-date. St. Paul, MN: Thomson West. [vol. 94-date] Combined with Idaho Court of Appeals decisions from vol. 95 (1982)-date. Current vol.: 155.
Cost: $1,244 (vols. 67-151); annual cost of bound volumes: 2003: $124.50; 2004: $62; 2005: $124.50; 2006: $130.72; 2007: $52.28; 2008: $109.80; 2009: $137.26; 2010: $74; 2011: $148 (list); 2012: $74; 2013: $160; cost of recent vol.: $80.25/$107 (subscriber/list); **Monthly Assured Print Price (APP)**: .

Pacific Reporter [1st] - **3d**. St. Paul, MN: West, 1883-date. Contains decisions of the Idaho Supreme Court from 1883-date and the Idaho Court of Appeals from 1982-date. Current vol.: 314 **P. 3d**.
Cost: 1st series out-of-print (see used lawbook dealers in Appendix C); 2d series: $13,428; used sets approx. $2000; 3d series: $15,201; annual cost (2013): $11,396; individual volume: $518/$691 (subscriber/list); **Monthly Assured Print Pricing (APP):** $1,141/$11,369; used sets may be available.

Pacific Reporter 3d. Advance sheets. St. Paul, MN: Thomson West. Weekly.
Cost: $2,866.56 per year, or discounted with bound volume subscription (2014).

Idaho Supreme Court Report and Idaho Court of Appeals Reports. Boise, ID: Goller Publishing Corp. 26 issues per year. This advance sheet publishes Idaho appellate court opinions two weeks after issuance. Published on a calendar year basis. Print subscription ended in 2010.
Cost: Online only: $220 per year (2014). 336-4715

4. Court Rules.
Idaho Court Rules. Charlottesville, VA: LexisNexis. 2 vols. Updated semiannually, replaced annually.
Cost: 2013 Edition: $46 (in-state) (2014).

Idaho Rules of Court, State and Federal. St. Paul, MN: Thomson West. 2 vols. Annual. Also available on proView eBook.
Cost: 2013 Edition: $129; ProView eBook: $129 (2014).

5. Digests, Encyclopedias, and Practice Sets.
Idaho Digest. St. Paul, MN: Thomson West, 1938-date. 10 vols. in 47. Annual pocket parts, mid-year supplement, and periodic revised volumes.
Cost: $3,900; supplementation: 1995: $199.50; 1996: $225; 1997: $249; 1998: $673; 1999: $564; 2000: $665; 2001: $1,065.25; 2002: $979; 2003: $616; 2004: $509.50; 2005: $674; 2006: $792; 2007: $705; 2008: $1,257; 2009: $1,729; 2010: $1,389; 2011: $1,808.50; 2012: $2,287.50; 2013: $3,156;

Monthly Assured Print Price (APP): $198/$2,376.

6. Citators.
Shepard's Idaho Citations. Albany, NY: Shepard's. Six supplements per year.
Cost: $1,473 (2 bound volumes); all-inclusive subscription: $1,779 (in-state);
(2014).

Online: All jurisdictional Shepard's and KeyCite are no longer available as stand-alone products, but are acquired as part of a jurisdictional or subject library package (2014).

7. CD-ROM Products.
Idaho Administrative Code. CD-ROM Edition. Boise: Office of Administrative Rules, 1998-date. One disc. Updated by Idaho Administrative Bulletin. Also available on the Internet at: http://www.state.id.us
Cost: 2014 Edition: $100 (2014).

Idaho Bankruptcy Court Report. Boise, ID: Goller Publishing Corp. One disc. Updated annually. Contains decisions of the U.S. Bankruptcy Court for the District of Idaho from 1980 to date. Available for Windows 3.1 or higher. Search Engine: Adobe Acrobat.
Cost: $365 (initial licensing fee); annual updates: $144.69 (2014).

LexisNexis CD - Idaho Primary Law. Albany, NY: LexisNexis. One disc. Quarterly updates. Contains full text of Idaho Code Annotated, Idaho Supreme Court decision from 1866 to date, Idaho Court of Appeals decisions from 1982 to date, and Idaho Court Rules. Available for Windows. Search Engine: Folio; LivePublish (NextPage).
Cost: $1,788 per year (2014).

8. State Legal Research Guides.
Greenlee, Michael J. **Idaho State Documents: A Bibliography of Legal Publications.** Chicago: AALL, 2003.
Cost: $30.00. Available from William S. Hein & Co. on electronic pdf and on HeinOnline (2014).

Crowley, Donald and Florence Heffron. **The Idaho State Constitution**. New York: Oxford University Press, 2010. 1 vol. (336 pp.).
Cost: $150.00; from $70.12 on amazon.com; kindle: $119.99 (2014).

Fordyce-Ruff, Tenielle and Suzanne E. Rowe. **Idaho Legal Research**. Durham, NC, Carolina Academic Press, 2008. 1 vol. (225 pp.).
Cost: $25.00; from $19.75 on amazon.com (2014).

Mattimoe, Jean. Idaho Practice Materials: A Selective Bibliography in Houdek, Frank G., ed. **State Practice Materials: Annotated Bibliographies**. Buffalo, NY: William S. Hein & Co., Inc., 2009-date.
Cost: $195.00 (2014).

Seeger, Leinaala R. "Idaho Practice Materials: A Selective Bibliography," 87 **Law Library Journal** 534 (1995).

9 Leading Web Sites for State Legal Research.

Home Page:	www.idaho.gov
Administrative Code:	http://adminrules.idaho.gov/code_menu.html
Agency Directory:	http://idaho.gov/agency/agency_a.html
Attorney General:	www.ag.idaho.gov
Attorney Gen. Opinions:	www.ag.idaho.gov/publications/op-guide-cert_index.html
Bar Association:	http://isb.idaho.gov/
Constitution:	www.sos.idaho.gov/elect/publindx.htm
Court Opinions:	www.isc.idaho.gov/appeals-court/opinions
Governor:	www.gov.idaho.gov/
Judicial Branch:	www.isc.idaho.gov/
Law Library:	www.isll.idaho.gov/
Legislative Branch:	www.legislature.idaho.gov/
Secretary of State:	www.sos.idaho.gov/
Statutes:	www.legislature.idaho.gov/idstat/TOC/IDStatutesTOC.htm

10. Leading publishers of state specific treatises, practice books, and CLE publications.
Goller Publishing Corp., Idaho Law Foundation, Idaho Trial Lawyers Association, LexisNexis, National Business Institute, Ridenbaugh Press, Thomson Reuters (West), Thornton Publishing Company, University of Idaho. See Appendix B for addresses and telephone numbers.

Illinois

1. Codes and Session Laws.
Illinois Compiled Statutes Annotated. Charlottesville, VA: LexisNexis, 1993-date. 55 vols. Annual pocket parts and periodic revised volumes. Standing order includes Advance Code Service.
Cost: $1,685 (in- and out-of-state), supplementation: 2002: $585; 2003: $514; 2004: $595; 2005: $309; 2006: 346; 2007: $754; 2008: $798; 2009: $630; 2010: $780; 2011: $484; 2012: $750; 2013: $825.

Illinois Advance Code Service. Charlottesville, VA: LexisNexis. Supplements code between annual pocket parts. Included with standing order subscription to the Illinois Compiled Statutes Annotated.
Cost: $117 per year (2014).

Illinois Compiled Statutes. State Bar Edition. [unannotated]. St. Paul, MN: ThomsonWest, 1998-date. 9 vols.
Cost: 2012 Edition: $267 (2014)

West's Smith-Hurd Illinois Compiled Statutes Annotated. St. Paul, MN: Thomson West, 1993-date. 147 vols. Annual pocket

parts and periodic revised volumes.
Cost: $6,348; supplementation:1996: $303;1997: $742; 1998: $612.98; 1999: $721.50; 2000: $823; 2002: $2,101; 2003: $1,859.50; 2004: $1,889.75; 2005: n/a; 2006: $2,894; 2007: $3,352; 2008: $3,789; 2009: $3,146.50; 2010: $3,348; 2011: $4,225; 2012: $4,657.50l 2013: $5,242; **Monthly Assured Print Pricing (APP):** $412/$4,944.

Laws of Illinois [session laws]. Springfield: Secretary of State. Annual. 3 vols.
Cost: Not sold. Distributed to depository and other libraries at no charge.

Illinois Advance Legislative Service. Charlottesville, VA: LexisNexis. These pamphlets are published during and immediately after each legislative session. They contain the text of laws in numerical chapter sequence in order of passage.
Cost: $270 (2014).

Illinois Legislative Service. St. Paul, MN: Thomson West. These pamphlets are published during and immediately after each legislative session and contain the text of laws in numerical chapter sequence in order of passage.
Cost: $945.96 (2014).

Legislative Hotline: (217) 782-3944.

2. Administrative Law.

Code of Illinois Rules. Albany, NY: LexisNexis Matthew Bender, 2000-date. 22 vols. Updated monthly.
Cost: $3,359 (incl. 12 months of updates and postage); annual renewal: 2001: $910; 2002: $910; 2003: $910; 2004: $910; 2005: $960; 2006: $960; 2007: $960; 2008: $1,082; 2009: $1,082; 2010: $1,204; 2011: $1,264; 2012: $1,340; 2013: $1,434; 2014: $1,564.

Illinois Register. Springfield: Secretary of State, Administrative Code Division, 1977-date. Weekly. A Cumulative Index and the Sections Affected Index are issued quarterly. Available electronically via e-mail.
Cost: $290 per year (2014). 217-785-7538.

3. Court Reports.

Illinois Reports [1st] - **2d** series. 1819-date. St. Paul, MN: Thomson West. 1st series: 415 vols.; 2d series 242 vols. (as of Mar. 1, 2014).
Cost: $4,485; annual supplementation 2002: $142; 2003: $267; 2004: $158; 2005: $164; 2006: $143; 2007: $172; 2008: $43; 2009: $241.50; 2010: $444; 2011: $309 (list); 2012: $309; current volume: $51.50 (list); advance sheets: approx. $235 per year (or free with subscription to both bound series); used sets may be available. See used lawbook dealers in Appendix C.

Illinois Appellate Court Reports [1st] - **3d** series, 1877-date. St. Paul, MN: Thomson West. 1st series: 351 vols.; 2d series: 133 vols.; 3d series: 412 vols. (as of Mar. 1, 2014).
Cost: $9,429; upkeep: 1995: $442; $442; 1997: $472;1998: $326.50; 1999: $223.50; 2000: $173; 2002: $375.75; 2003: $267; 2004: $280.50; 2005: $291; 2006: $330.75; 2007: $466.50; 2008: $428; 2009: $219; 2010: $475; 2011: $366; 2012: $265.50; 2013: $771; current volumes: $60.50 (list); **Monthly Assured Print Price (APP):** $223/$2,676; used sets may be available; See lists of used lawbook dealers in Appendix C.

West's Illinois Decisions [1st] – **2d.** St. Paul, MN: Thomson West, 1936-date. 1st series: 174 vols.; 2d series: 375 vols. [offprint of North Eastern Reporter [1st] - 2d]. Contain decisions of the Illinois Supreme Court and Illinois Appellate Court from 1936 to date. Current volume: 375 (as of April 1, 2014).
Cost: 1st series: $1,740; 2d series: $5,839; annual upkeep: 1998: $360.50; 1999: $458; 2000: $549; 2001: $645.75; 2003: $902.50; 2004: $909; 2005: $1,107; 2006: $1,215.50; 2007: $1,233; 2008: $1,352; 2009: $1,525.50; 2010: $1,740; 2011: $2,517; 2012: $2,032; 2013: $4,818; current vol.: $438/$584 (subscriber/list); **Monthly Assured Print Price (APP)**: $377/$4,524.

Illinois Court of Claims Reports. Springfield: Court of Claims, 1889-date. Current vol.: 62 (as of April 1, 2014).
Cost: Free upon request. (217) 782-7102 Volumes 1-60 in PDF format at Secretary of State site at: www.cyberdriveillinois.com/departments/court_of_claims/volumes.html

North Eastern Reporter [1st] - **2d**. St. Paul, MN: Thomson West, 1885-date. Contains decisions of the Illinois Supreme Court from 1884-date, and the Illinois Appellate Court from 1936-date. Current volume: 999 **N.E.2d**.
Cost: 1st series: out-of-print (see used lawbook dealers in Appendix C); 2d series: $15,333; annual cost (2013): $10,146; current vol.: $534/$710 (subscriber/list); **Monthly Assured Print Pricing (APP):** $1,087/$13,044; used sets sell for approx. $2,000.00.

North Eastern Reporter 2d. Advance sheets. St. Paul, MN: Thomson West Weekly.
Cost: $2,866.56 (discounted to bound volume subscribers) (2014).

4. Court Rules.

Illinois Court Rules and Procedure: State and Federal. St. Paul, MN: Thomson West. 2 vols. Annual. Also available on ProView eBook.
Cost: 2013 Edition: $140; ProView eBook: $140 (2014).

Illinois Court Rules and Procedures: Rules of the Circuit Courts. St. Paul, MN: Thomson West. 1 vol. Annual.
Cost: 2013 Edition: $188 (2014).

Illinois Rules and Practice Handbook. 2d ed. Buffalo Grove, IL: Law Bulletin Publishing Co. 1 vol. Looseleaf format. Updated continuously.
(309) 828-7533
Cost: 2013 Edition: $139 (2014).

Illinois State Court Rules Annotated. Charlottesville, VA: LexisNexis. 2 vols. Updated semiannually, replaced annually. Paperbound or ebook.
Cost: 2014 Edition: $181 (2014).

5. Digests, Encyclopedias, and Practice Sets.

Illinois Jurisprudence. Charlottesville, VA: LexisNexis, 1992-date. 24 vols. Annual pocket supplements and periodic revised volumes.
Cost: $2,100; supplementation: 2001: $623; 2002: $819.80;

2003: $587; 2004: $454; 2005: $533; 2006: $582; 2007: $819; 2008: $845; 2009: $799; 2010: $1,016; 2011: $945; 2012: $811; 2013: $879.
This title was sold to Reed Elsevier in January, 1997 after the Department of Justice negotiated a consent decree with the Thomson Corporation and West Publishing requiring the divestiture of 51 titles.

Illinois Law and Practice. St. Paul, MN: Thomson West. 65 vols. Annual pocket supplements and periodic revised volumes.
Cost: $7,964; supplementation: 1995: $218.90; 1996: $307.50; 1997: $324; 1998: $504; 1999: $632; 2000: $872; 2001: $1,155.75; 2002: $1,750; 2003: $1,816.50; 2004: $1,746.50; 2005: $2,258; 2006: $2,516.50; 2007: $2,590; 2008: $2,873.50; 2009: $3,338.50; 2010: $3,773; 2011: $4,263; 2012: $4,719; 2013: $5,691; **Monthly Assured Print Pricing (APP)**: $557/$6,684.

Illinois Practice Series. St. Paul, MN: Thomson West, 1967-date. 30 vols. Annual pocket supplements and periodic revised volumes.
Cost: $4,748 (but priced individually); supplementation: 1998: $221.50; 1999: $273.50; 2000: $390.00; 2001: $296.00; 2003: $399.00; 2004-date: inquire regarding cost of individual components. Best acquired as a part of **State Secondary Resources** add-on to a WestlawNext PRO subscription at considerable savings.

Nichols Illinois Civil Practice with Forms. St. Paul, MN: Thomson West,1940-date. 15 vols. Annual pocket supplements and periodic revised volumes.
Cost: $3,372; supplementation: 1994: $658.50; 1995: $684;1996: $684; 1997: $588; 1998: $722; 1999: $868; 2000: $544; 2001: $435; 2002: $986; 2003: $828; 2004: $1,024.50; 2005: $1,242; 2006: $1,315; 2007: $1,219.50; 2008: $1,187; 2009: $1,272; 2010: $1,789; 2011: $1,610; 2012: $2,326; 2013: $2,365; **Monthly Assured Print Pricing (APP):** $246/$2,952.

West's Illinois Digest 2d. St. Paul, MN: Thomson West, 1982-date. 67 vols. in 231. Annual pocket parts, mid-year supplement, and periodic revised volumes.
Cost: $10,522; supplementation: 1996: $754.25; 1997: $696; 1998: $866; 1999: $854; 2000: $1,720; 2001: $1,005.99; 2002: $2,085; 2003: $1,006; 2004: $1,351.50; 2005: $1,027.75; 2006: $1,318.75; 2007: $3,644; 2008: $3,737; 2009: $5,938.50; 2010: $6,728.50; 2011: $6,109; 2012: $5,585; 2013: $9,565; **Monthly Assured Print Pricing (APP):** $609/$7,308.

6. Citators.

Shepard's Illinois Citations. Albany, NY: Shepard's. Monthly or bi-monthly.
Cost: $8,040 (24 bound volumes); all-inclusive subscription: monthly: $2,430; bimonthly: $2,716 (2014).

Online: All jurisdictional Shepard's and KeyCite are no longer available as stand-alone products, but are now included with a jurisdictional or subject library package (2014).

7 CD-ROM Products.

Illinois Decisions and Illinois Compiled Statutes State Bar Association, PREMISE® CD-ROM ed. St. Paul, MN: Thomson West. Three discs. Monthly updates. Contains the full text of decisions of the Illinois Supreme Court from 1885 to date, Illinois Appellate Court Reports in **North Eastern Reporter 2d**, 1944 to date, and Illinois Attorney General opinions form 1977 to date, Contains the full unannotated text of the Illinois Constitution, statutes, session laws, etc. Decisions also searchable by West Topics and Key Numbers, headnotes, and synopses. Windows, and Macintosh versions available. Search engine: PREMISE. Subscription includes online updates via Westlaw.
Cost: $8,298 per year (2014).

LexisNexis CD – Illinois Primary Law. Albany, NY: LexisNexis. Four discs. Updated monthly. Contains the full text of the Illinois Compiled Statutes Annotated, Illinois Supreme Court decisions from 1819 to date, Illinois Appellate Court decisions from 1944 to date, state and federal court rules, and Illinois Advance Legislative Service. Available for Windows. Search Engine: Folio; LivePublish (NextPage).
Cost: $1,814 per year (2014).

8. State Legal Research Guides.

Houdek, Frank and Jean McKnight. "Survey of Illinois Law: An Annotated Bibliography of Legal Research Tools." **Southern Illinois University Law Journal** 16 (1992): 767-806.

Johnson, Phill W. Illinois Practice Materials: A Selective Bibliography in Houdek, Frank G., ed. **State Practice Materials: Annotated Bibliographies**. Buffalo, NY: William S. Hein & Co., Inc., 2006-date.
Cost: $195.00 (2014).

Lousin, Ann. **The Illinois Constitution**. New York: Oxford University Press, 2011. 1 vol. (322 pp.).
Cost: $150.00; from $103.67 on amazon.com; kindle: $119.99 (2014).

Nyberg, Cheryl R. et al. **Illinois State Documents: A Selective Annotated Bibliography for Law Librarians**. Chicago: American Association of Law Libraries, Government Documents SIS, 1986.
Cost: $30.00. Available from William S. Hein & Co. on electronic pdf and on HeinOnline (2014).

Wendt, Laurel. **Illinois Legal Research Guide**. 2d ed. Buffalo, NY: William S. Hein & Co., 2005. 1 vol.
Price: $75.00 (2014).

Wojcik, Mark E. **Illinois Legal Research**. 2d ed. Durham, NC: Carolina Academic Press, 2009. 1 vol. (282 pp.). 2010 Teacher's Manual available.
Cost: $25.00; from $19.13 on amazon.com (2014).

9. Leading Web Sites for State Legal Research.

Home Page:	www.illinois.gov/
Administrative Code:	www.ilga.gov/commission/jcar/admincode/titles.html
Agency Directory:	www.illinois.gov/SitePages/Agencies.aspx
Attorney General:	www.ag.state.il.us/
Attorney Gen. Opinions:	www.ag.state.il.us/opinions

Bar Assoc. State:	www.isba.org/
Bar Assoc. Chicago:	www.chicagobar.org/
Constitution:	www.ilga.gov/commission/lrb/conmain.htm
Court Opinions – Appellate:	www.state.il.us/court/Opinions/recent_appellate.asp
Court Opinions – Supreme Court :	www.state.il.us/court/Opinions/recent_supreme.asp
Governor:	www.illinois.gov/gov/
Judicial Branch:	www.state.il.us/court/
Legal Research Links:	www.state.il.us/court/Links/research.asp
Legislature:	www.ilga.gov/
Library – Supreme Court:	www.state.il.us/court/SupremeCourt/library.asp
Secretary of State:	www.cyberdriveillinois.com/
Statutes:	www.ilga.gov/legislation/ilcs/ilcs.asp

10. Leading publishers of state specific treatises, practice books, and CLE publications.
LexisNexis Matthew Bender, Illinois Institute for Continuing Legal Education, Illinois State Bar Association, LexisNexis, National Business Institute, Thomson Reuters West, Wolters Kluwer Law & Business. See Appendix B for addresses and telephone numbers.

Indiana

1. Codes and Session Laws.
Burns Indiana Statutes Annotated. Charlottesville, VA: LexisNexis, 1986-date. 39 vols. Annual pocket supplements and periodic revised volumes. Advance Code Service also available as mid-year supplements to pocket parts.
Cost: $1,294 (in- and out-of-state); supplementation (in state/out-of-state): 1998: $607.50/$760; 1999: $457/ $668.50; 2000: $337/$635.50; 2001: $710/$816; 2002: $551/$712; 2003: $565/$730; 2004: $636/$805; 2005: $588/$760; 2007: $977/$1,166; 2008: $1,259/$1,464; 2009: $855/$1,055; 2010: $981/$1,210; 2011: $842/$1,059; 2012: $1,017/$1,250; 2013: $1,118 (in-state).

Burns Indiana Advance Code Service. Charlottesville, VA: LexisNexis, 1986-date. Supplements code between annual pocket parts.
Cost: $140 per year; renewal: $124 (in-state) (2014).

West's Annotated Indiana Code. St. Paul, MN: Thomson West, 1981-date. 36 vols. in 87. Annual pocket parts and periodic revised volumes. Interim Annotation Service also available as mid-year supplements to pocket parts.
Cost: $5,379 ; supplementation: 1995: $280;1996: $420; 1997: $1,292; 1998: $1,205; 1999: $996; 2000: $1,139.50; 2002: $1,575; 2003: $1,692; 2004: $1,913; 2005: $1,986; 2006: $2,149.50; 2007: $2,520; 2008: $2,755.50; 2009: $2,717; 2010: $2,972.50; 2011: $3,240.50; 2012: $3,850; 2013: $4,448; **Monthly Assured Print Pricing (APP):** $347/$4,164.

West's Indiana Legislative Service. St. Paul, MN: Thomson West. These pamphlets are published during and immediately after each legislative session and contain the text of laws in numerical chapter sequence in order of passage.
Cost: $1,056 (2014).

Burns Indiana Advance Legislative Service. Charlottesville, VA: LexisNexis. These pamphlets are published during and immediately after each legislative session and contain the text of laws in numerical chapter sequence in order of passage. Paperbound or ebook.
Cost: $150 per year; renewal: $124 (in-state) (2014).

Indiana Acts [session laws]. Indianapolis, IN: Legislative Services Agency. Annual. Now on CD-ROM and Internet only.
Cost: CD-ROM only: $30; prior year's print editions: 1995: $100 (4 vols.); 1996: $66 (short session); 1997: $41; 1998: $37; 1999: $10; 2000: $29; 2001: $55; 2004: $30; 2005: $25; 2006: $25; 2007: $25; 2008-date: online only.

Legislative Hotline: (317) 232-9856.

2. Administrative Law.
Indiana Administrative Code. Indianapolis, IN: Legislative Services Agency, 1996-date. 2003-forward Internet only.
Cost: Available on Internet at: http://www.in.gov/legislative/iac/

Indiana Register. Indianapolis: Legislative Services Agency, 1978-date. Monthly (Oct. - Sept.).
Cost: Only available on Internet after June 1, 2006 at: http://www.in.gov/legislative/register/index-26.html

3. Court Reports.
Indiana Cases. St. Paul, MN: Thomson West, 1936-date. [offprint of North Eastern Reporter 2d--designated official since 1981]. Contain decisions of the Indiana Supreme Court and the Indiana Court of Appeals from 1936 to date and Indiana Tax Court from 1987 to date. Current vol.: 994-996 **N.E.2d**
Cost: $7,564; annual upkeep: 2003: $1,085.00; 2004: $1,080.50; 2005: $1,306.00; 2006: $1,438; 2007: $1,435; 2008: $1,787; 2009: $1,793.50; 2010: $2,221.50; 2011: $2,990; 2012: $4,741; 2013: $5,160; recent vol.: $516/$688 (subscriber/list); **Monthly Assured Print Price (APP):** $543/$6,516.

Indiana Reports, 1836-1981. Vols. 1-275. [Ceased publication with vol. 275].
Cost: Used sets may be available.

Indiana Court of Appeals Reports, 1890-1979. [Ceased publication with vol. 182]
Cost: Used sets may be available.

North Eastern Reporter [1st] - **2d**. St. Paul, MN: Thomson West, 1885-date. Contains Indiana Supreme Court decisions from 1885-date, Indiana Court of Appeals decisions from 1891-date. Current volume: 999 **N.E.2d**.
Cost: 1st series: out-of-print (see used lawbook dealers in Appendix C); 2d series: $15,333; annual cost (2013): $10,146; current vol.: $534/$710 (subscriber/list); **Monthly Assured**

Print Pricing (APP): $1,087/$13,044; used sets sell for approx. $2,000.00.

North Eastern Reporter 2d. Advance sheets. St. Paul, MN: Thomson West Weekly.
Cost: $2,866.56 (discounted to bound volume subscribers) (2014).

4. Court Rules.
Burns Indiana Court Rules Annotated. Charlottesville, VA: LexisNexis. 3 vols. Updated semiannually, replaced annually.
Cost: 2014 Edition: $298 (in-state).

Indiana Rules of Court: State and Federal. St. Paul, MN: Thomson West. 2 vols. Annual.
Cost: 2014 Edition: $175; Federal, State and Local: $246 (2014).

5. Digests, Encyclopedias and Practice Sets.
Indiana Digest 2d. St. Paul, MN: Thomson West, 1991-date. 119 vols. Annual pocket supplements and periodic revised volumes. Covers period 1817-date, replacing earlier **Indiana Digest**.
Cost: $7,098 ; supplementation: 1995: $114.65; 1996: $147.50; 1997: $167.00; 1998: $265; 1999: $570; 2000: $436; 2001: $855.50; 2002: $1,319; 2003: $1,100.50; 2004: $1,093.25; 2005: $1,325.50; 2006: $1,147; 2007: $885; 2008: $755; 2009: $1,302.50; 2010: $2,680.50; 2011: $3,029.50; 2012: $4,148; 2013: $4,708; **Monthly Assured Print Pricing (APP):** $343/$4,116.

Indiana Law Encyclopedia. St. Paul, MN: Thomson West, 1957-date. 45 vols.
Cost: $4,335; supplementation: 1995: $114.65; 1996: $188.00; 1997: $203.00; 1998: $345.00; 1999: $257.50; 2000: $468.00; 2002: $1,171.50; 2003: $1,276.50; 2004: $1,395.75; 2005: $1,306.50; 2006: $1,432; 2007: $1,641.50; 2008: $1,623; 2009: $1,828; 2010: $2,344.50; 2011: $2,308; 2012: $2,911.50; **Monthly Assured Print Pricing (APP):** $271/$3,252; also available as a Westlaw add-on.

Indiana Practice Series. St. Paul, MN: Thomson West, 1967-date. 42 vols.
Cost: $8,113 (but priced individually); supplementation: priced individually; inquire regarding costs for individual components; CD-ROM (see below): $1,104.00. Also available on Westlaw at far lower cost.
Set includes the following components: Rules of Procedure Annotated (1-4A); Rules on Alternative Dispute Resolution (4B); Essential Forms (5); Trial Handbook for Indiana Lawyers (6); Commercial Code (7-8A); Procedural Forms (9-11); Evidence (12-13B); Family Law (14-15A); Criminal Procedure (16-16B); Business Organizations (17-20); Civil Trial Practice (21-22A); Courtroom Handbook on Indiana Evidence (13B); Criminal Procedure (16-16B); Civil Trial Practice (21-22); Personal Injury Law & Practice (23); Appellate Procedure (24); Anderson's Probate Forms (25-25A); Anderson's Wills, Trusts and Estate Planning (26-26A); Real Property Code Annotated (27-27A); Motions in Limine (28); Workers Compensation (29), General Index.

Best acquired as a part of **State Secondary Resources** add-on to a WestlawNext PRO subscription at considerable savings.

6. Citators.
Shepard's Indiana Citations. Albany, NY: Shepard's. Monthly.
Cost: $2,716 (8 bound volumes); all-inclusive subscription: $2,273 (2014).

Online: All jurisdictional Shepard's and KeyCite are no longer available as stand-alone products, but are included as part of a jurisdictional or subject library package (2014).

7. CD-ROM Products
Indiana Cases. Eagan, MN: Thomson West. Two discs. Updated quarterly. Contains full text of decisions of Indiana Supreme Court from 1817 to date, Court of Appeals appearing in North Eastern Reporter 2d, vols. 53 to date. Windows, and Macintosh versions. Search Engine: PREMISE. Subscription includes online updating via Westlaw.
Cost: $9,681 per year (2014).

LexisNexis CD for Indiana. Albany, NY: LexisNexis. One disc. Updated quarterly. Contains the full text of Burns Indiana Statutes Annotated, Indiana Supreme Court decisions from 1817 to date, Indiana Court of Appeals decisions from 1891 to date, and Indiana Tax Court from 1987 to date. Available for Windows. Search Engine: Folio; LivePublish (NextPage). Online updates via Lexis.
Cost: $1,777 per year (2014).

Indiana Workers' Compensation Laws. Albany, NY: LexisNexis. eBook. Updated regularly. Contains the Indiana workers' compensation laws and cases. Includes print equivalent. Available for Windows. Search Engine: Folio; LivePublish (NextPage).
Cost: 2013 Edition (eBook): $55 (2014).

8. State Legal Histories and Research Guides.
Fariss, Linda K. and Keith A. Buckley. **An Introduction to Indiana State Publications for the Law Librarian**. Chicago: AALL, 1982.
Cost: $30.00. Available from William S. Hein & Co. on electronic pdf and on HeinOnline. (2014).

The History of Indiana Law. Edited by David J. Bodenhamer and Randall T. Shepard. Athens, OH: Ohio University Press, 2006. 1 vol. (391 pp.).
Cost: $49.95; from $11.99 on amazon.com; kindle: $39.20 (2014).
A collection of scholarly articles on various aspects of Indiana legal history.

Humphrey, Richard E. Indiana Practice Materials: A Selective Bibliography in Houdek, Frank G., ed. **State Practice Materials: Annotated Bibliographies**. Buffalo, NY: William S. Hein & Co., Inc., 2004-date. 2 vols. Looseleaf format.
Cost: $195.00 (2014).

McLauchlan, William P. **The Indiana State Constitution**. New York: Oxford University Press, 2011. 1 vol. (208 pp.).
Cost: $150.00; from $19.62 on amazon.com; kindle: $119.99 (2014).

9. Leading Web Sites for State Legal Research.

Home Page:	www.in.gov/
Administrative Code:	www.in.gov/legislative/iac/
Agency Directory:	www.in.gov/core/find_agency.html
Attorney General:	www.in.gov/attorneygeneral/
Attorney Gen. Opinions:	www.in.gov/attorneygeneral/2352.htm
Bar Association:	www.inbar.org/
Constitution:	www.in.gov/legislative/ic/code/const/
Court Opinions:	www.in.gov/judiciary/opinions/
Governor:	www.in.gov/gov/
Judicial Branch:	www.in.gov/judiciary/
Law Library:	www.in.gov/judiciary/library/
Legislative Branch:	www.in.gov/legislative/
Secretary of State:	www.in.gov/sos/
Statutes:	www.in.gov/legislative/ic/code/

10. specific treatises, practice books, and CLE publications.
Matthew Bender, Indiana Continuing Legal Education Forum, LexisNexis, National Business Institute, Thomson Reuters (West). See Appendix B for addresses and telephone numbers.

Iowa

1. Codes and Session Laws.
Code of Iowa. Des Moines, IA: Iowa Legislative Services Agency. Published biennially. 7 vols. plus index and CD-ROM. Current through 2012. Softbound supplement in alternate years. (515) 281-3568.
Cost: 2013 ed.: $295 (includes 2014 CD-ROM at no additional charge); 2013 CD-ROM alone: $50; 2011 paperbound supplement: $90 (2014).

Iowa Code Annotated. St. Paul, MN: Thomson West, 1949-date. 91 vols. Annual pocket supplements, legislative service, and periodic revised volumes.
Cost: $6,518 (includes one year's supplements); supplementation: 1996: $925.50; 1997: $525.50; 1998: $1,154.50; 1999: $1,256.25; 2000: $1,168.75; 2001: $1,439; 2002: $724.50; 2003: $1,826; 2004: $1,463; 2006: $1,667.50; 2007: $2,198.50; 2008: $1,724; 2009: $2,859; 2010: $3,232; 2011: $3,809.50; 2012: $4,655.50; 2013: $5,035; **Monthly Assured Print Pricing (APP):** $412/$4,944.

Acts and Joint Resolutions of Iowa. Des Moines, IA: Iowa Legislative Service Agency. Annual.
Cost: 1996: $65; 1997: $71.92; 1998: $68.50; 1999: $68; 2000: $68.50; 2002: $78; 2003: $75; 2004: $75; 2005: $80; 2006: $80; 2007: $83; 2008: $90; 2009: $90; 2010: $90; 2011: $90; 2012: $90; 2013: $90. (515) 281-3568.

Iowa Legislative Service. St. Paul, MN: Thomson West. These pamphlets are published during and immediately after each legislative session and contain text of laws in order of passage.
Cost: $775 per year (2014).

Legislative Hotline: (515) 281-5129.

2. Administrative Law.
Iowa Administrative Code. Des Moines: Iowa Legislative Services Agency, 1975-date. Went online only in 2008, at: https://www.legis.iowa.gov/IowaLaw/AdminCode/agencyDocs.aspx
(515) 281-3568.
Cost: 2010 Edition: no cost; supplementation only available via the General Assembly's web site. Archived bimonthly back to 1998.

Iowa Administrative Bulletin & Code Supplement. Des Moines: Iowa Legislative Services Agency, 1978-date. Biweekly Supplement to Iowa Administrative Code. (515) 281-3568.
Cost: No longer available in print; no cost via General Assembly's web site beginning in 2008.

3. Court Reports.
Iowa Reports.1855-1968. Vols. 1-261. [Ceased publication with vol. 261].
Cost: Out-of-print.

West's North Western Reporter [1st] - **2d**. St. Paul, MN: Thomson West. 1st series, 1878-1988. Title changed to **West's North Western Reporter 2d** with v. 414 **N.W. 2d** (1988-date). Contains decisions of Iowa Supreme from 1878-date and Iowa Court of Appeals from 1977-date, among other states. Current vol.: 844 **N.W. 2d**.
Cost: 1st series out-of-print (see used lawbook dealers in Appendix C); 2d series $10,225; used sets sell for approx. $3,795; annual cost (2013): $7,332; recent volume: $459/$611 (subscriber/list); **Monthly Assured Print Pricing (APP):** $709/$8,508.

West's North Western Reporter 2d. Advance Sheets. St. Paul, MN: Thomson West. Weekly.
Cost: $2,808 (discounted to bound volume subscribers) (2014).

4. Court Rules.
Iowa Rules of Court. St. Paul, MN: Thomson West. 2 vols. Annual. Also available on ProView eBook.
Cost: 2014 Edition: $191.

5. Digests, Encyclopedias and Practice Books.
Iowa Digest. St. Paul, MN: Thomson West, 1941-date. 90 vols. Includes annual pocket parts, mid-year supplements, and periodic revised volumes.
Cost: $4,755 ; supplementation: 1996: $411; 1997: $215; 1998: $346; 1999: $422.75; 2000: $638; 2001: $1,442; 2002: $2,814.50; 2003: $824; 2004: $1,579; 2006: $1,276; 2007: $627; 2008: $1,657; 2009: $2,164; 2010: $1,703.50; 2011: $2,798; 2012: $3,191; 2013: $4,159; **Monthly Assured Print Pricing (APP):** $284/$3,408.

The volumes in the **Iowa Practice Series** are softbound and published annually by Thomson West:

Methods of Practice (Volz). St. Paul, MN: Thomson West, 2004-date. 1 vol.
Softbound. (Vols. 1-3, Iowa Practice Series).
Cost: 2013 Edition: $603 (2014).

Criminal Law (Rigg). St. Paul, MN: Thomson West, 2002-date. 1 vol. (Vol. 4, Iowa Practice Series).
Softbound.
Cost: 2013-2014 Edition: $206 (2014).

Criminal Procedure. (Burns). St. Paul, MN: Thomson West, 2002-date. 1 vol. (Vol. 4A, Iowa Practice Series). Softbound.
Cost: 2013 Edition: $199 (2014).

Business Organizations (Dore). St. Paul, MN: Thomson West, 2002-date. 2 vols. (Vols. 5-6, Iowa Practice Series).
Softbound.
Cost: 2013-2014 Edition: $434 (2014).

Evidence (Adams and Weeg). St. Paul, MN: Thomson West, 2002.date. 1 vol. (Vol. 7, Iowa Practice Series). Softbound.
Cost: 2013-2014 Edition: $204 (2014).

Civil Litigation Handbook (Riley). St. Paul, MN: Thomson West, 2000-date. 1 vol. (Vol. 8, Iowa Practice Series). Softbound.
Cost: 2013 Edition: $209 (2014).

Civil Practice Forms (Lindahl). St. Paul, MN: Thomson West, 2004-date. 2 vols. (Vols. 9-10, Iowa Practice Series). Softbound.
Cost: 2013 Edition: $408 (2014).

Civil and Appellate Procedure (Lindahl). St. Paul, MN: Thomson West, 2002-date. 2 vols. (Vols. 11-12, Iowa Practice Series). Softbound.
Cost: 2013 Edition: $404 (2014).

Iowa Probate. (Pulkrabek and Schmit). St. Paul, MN: Thomson West, 2003-date. 2 vols. (Vols. 13-14, Iowa Practice Series). Softbound.
Cost: 2013-2014 Edition: $434 (2014).

Iowa Real Estate Law and Practice (Erickson & Talbot). St. Paul, MN: Thomson West, 2013-date. 1 vol. (Vol. 17, Iowa Practice Series). Softbound.
Cost: 2013-2014 Edition: $192 (2014).

Workers' Compensation (Lawyer and Higgs). St. Paul, MN: Thomson West, 2003-date. 1 vol. (Vol. 15, Iowa Practice Series). Softbound.
Cost: 2013-2014 Edition: $214 (2014).

Best acquired as a part of **State Secondary Resources** add-on to a WestlawNext PRO subscription at considerable savings.

6. Citators.

Shepard's Iowa Citations. Albany, NY: Shepard's. Monthly.
Cost: $2,165 (4 bound volumes); all-inclusive subscription: $2,168 (in-state) (2014).

Online: All jurisdictional Shepard's and KeyCite are no longer available as stand-alone products, but are included as part of a jurisdictional or subject library package (2014).

7. CD-ROM Products.

Iowa Law CD-ROM. Des Moines: Iowa Legislative Service Agency. One disc. Updated annually. Includes full text of the current Code of Iowa (unannotated), the Acts and Joint Resolutions of Iowa (1993-date), Iowa Court Rules, the Iowa Administrative Code, the Iowa Administrative Bulletins, and the Iowa Court Rules.. Search Engine: Folio. (515) 281-3568.
Cost: 2013 Edition: $50 (available February, 2014).

Iowa Reporter (West's). Eagan, MN: Thomson West. One disc. Regular updates. Contains full text decisions of the Iowa Supreme Court from 1839 to date, Iowa Court of Appeals from vol.1 of the North Western Reporter 2d to date, and Attorney General opinions from 1977-date. Windows, and Macintosh versions available. Search Engine: PREMISE. Subscription includes online updates via Westlaw.
Cost: $8,202 per year (2014).

8 State Legal Research Guides.

Edwards, John D., M. Sarah Lowe, Karen L. Wallace, and Melissa R. Weresh. **Iowa Legal Research.** Durham, NC: Carolina Academic Press, 2011. 1 vol. (334 pp.). Paperbound.
Cost: $30.00; from $28.50 on amazon.com (2014).

Edwards, John D. **Iowa Legal Research Guide**. Buffalo, NY: William S. Hein & Co., 2003. 1 vol. (546 pp.).
Cost: $79.95 (2014).

Secrest, Angela K. **Iowa Legal Documents Bibliography**. Chicago: AALL, 1990. Available in print or ebook from William S. Hein & Co.
Cost: $30.00 (2014).

Stark, Jack. **The Iowa State Constitution**. New York: Oxford University Press, 2011. 1 vol. (216 pp.).
Cost: $150.00; from $80.03 on amazon.com; kindle: $119.99 (2014).

9. Leading Web Sites for State Legal Research.

Home Page:	www.iowa.gov/
Administrative Code:	www.legis.iowa.gov/law/administrativeRules
Agency Directory:	www.iowa.gov/Government
Attorney General:	www.iowaattorneygeneral.org/
Attorney General Opinions:	www.iowaattorneygeneral.org/issuing_opinions
Bar Association:	www.iowabar.org/
Constitution:	www.legis.iowa.gov/law/constitution
Court Opinions:	(link from Judicial Branch below, under General Information)
Governor:	www.governor.iowa.gov/

Judicial Branch:	www.iowacourts.gov/
Legislative Branch:	www.legis.iowa.gov
Secretary of State:	www.sos.iowa.gov
Statutes:	www.legis.iowa.gov/law/statutory

10. Leading publishers of state specific treatises, practice books, and CLE publications.
Iowa State Bar Association, Iowa Trial Lawyers Association, LexisNexis, Lorman, National Business Institute, University of Iowa Continuing Legal Education, Thomson Reuters West. Appendix B has addresses and telephone numbers.

Kansas

1. Codes and Session Laws.
Kansas Statutes Annotated. Topeka: Secretary of State, 1989-date. 7 vols. in 15. Annual pocket supplements and periodic revised volumes. (785) 296-4557. The unannotated Kansas Statutes are also available at: http://www.kslegislature.org/cgi-bin/statutes/index.cgi
Cost: $555; supplementation: 2002: $110.50; 2003: $72.50; 2005: $77.50; 2006: $84.50; 2007: $88.50; 2008: $97.50; 2009: $105.50; 2010: $105.75; 2011: $107.40; 2012: $117.50; 2013: $117.50.

West's Kansas Statutes Annotated. St. Paul, MN: Thomson West, 2008-date. 45 vols. Annual pocket parts and periodic revised volumes.
Cost: $634; supplementation: 2009: $236; previous edition (Vernon's): 1997: $452.50; 1998: $484.70; 1999: $524; 2000: $599; 2001: $680.50; 2002: $665.50; 2004: $906; 2005: $850; 2006: $1,356.50; 2007: $922; 2008: $1,151; 2009: $236; 2010: $555; 2011: $259; 2012: $301; 2013: $339; **Monthly Assured Print Pricing (APP):** $31/$372.

Session Laws of Kansas. Topeka: Secretary of State. 1 vol. Annual.
Cost: 1996: $22.50; 1997: $22.50; 1999: $21.00; 2000: $24.90; 2001: $23.75; 2002: $23.75; 2003: $33.75; 2004: $33.75; 2005: $33.75; 2006: $33.75; 2007: $33.75; 2008: $41.75; 2009: $41.75; 2010: $41.75; 2011: $41.75; 2012: $41.75; 2013: $41.75. Prices including shipping. (785) 296-4564

Legislative Hotline: (785) 296-3296.

2. Administrative Law.
Kansas Administrative Regulations. Topeka: Secretary of State, 2003-date. 6 vols. + Index. Periodic recompilations.
Cost: 2009 Edition: $232.50 (2014); supplementation: 2004: $30.00. 2005: $36.25; 2006: $36.25; 2007: $36.25; 2008: $41.25; 2010: $41.25; 2011: $41.25; 2012: $41.25; 2013: $41.25.

Kansas Register. Topeka: Secretary of State, 1982-date. Weekly.
Cost: $80 per year; single copies: $2.00 each; also free online (2014).

3. Court Reports.
Kansas Reports. 1862-date. Topeka: Supreme Court Law Library. Advance sheets combine Kansas Reports and Court of Appeals Reports. Current bound vol.: 290.
Cost: $14,040 (233 vols.) (mailed); $13,108 (picked-up); current volume (with advance sheets): $60 (mailed); $56.00 (picked up); current and non-current bound volumes: $60 each (mailed); advance sheets alone: $15 per year (2014).

Kansas Cases. St. Paul, MN: Thomson West, 1977-date. [off-print of Pacific Reporter 2d]. Contain decisions of the Kansas Supreme Court from 1968 to date and Court of Appeals from 1977 to date. Current vol.: 305-308 **P.3d**.
Cost: volumes covering 2d series: $2,171; 3d series: $4,683 ; annual cost: 2002: $267; 2003: $514.75; 2004: $653; 2005: $778.50; 2006: $866; 2007: $1,131; 2008: $685; 2009: $1,753.50; 2010: $992; 2011: $1,746; 2012: $2,506; 2013: $3,010; recent volume: $501.75/$669 (subscriber/list); **Monthly Assured Print Pricing (APP):** $313/$3,756.

Kansas Court of Appeals Reports, 1st - 2d series. Topeka: Supreme Court Library. 1st series: 1895-1901 (10 vols.); 2d series: 1977-date (47 vols.). Advance sheets combine Kansas Reports and Court of Appeals Reports. Current bound vol.: 47.
Cost: $2,460 (mailed); current subscription (including advance sheets and bound volume): $65 (mailed); individual volumes: $60 each; advance sheets alone: $15 per year (2014).

Pacific Reporter [1st] - **3d**. St. Paul, MN: Thomson West, 1883-date. Contains decisions of the Kansas Supreme Court from 1883-date and the Kansas Court of Appeals from 1895-date. Current vol.: 314 **P. 3d**.
Cost: 1st series out-of-print (see used lawbook dealers in Appendix C); 2d series: $13,428; used sets approx. $2000; 3d series: $15,201; annual cost (2013): $11,396; individual volume: $518/$691 (subscriber/list); **Monthly Assured Print Pricing (APP):** $1,141/$11,369; used sets may be available.

Pacific Reporter 3d. Advance sheets. St. Paul, MN: Thomson West. Weekly.
Cost: $2,866.56 per year (discounted to bound volume subscribers) (2014).

4. Court Rules.
Kansas Court Rules and Procedure, State and Federal. St. Paul: Thomson West. Annual. Also available on ProView eBook.
Cost: 2014 Edition $208; Federal, State and Local: $258.

Rules Enacted by the Supreme Court of the State of Kansas Annotated. Topeka: Kansas Supreme Court. Annual. [current changes appear in advance sheets to Supreme Court Reports]. Also available online on Kansas Supreme Court web site.
Cost: $25 (2014) (or no charge to subscribers to Kansas Reports, Kansas Court of Appeals Reports, or advance sheets).

5. Digests, Encyclopedias, and Practice Books.
West's Kansas Digest 2d. St. Paul: Thomson West, 1994-date. 90 vols. Annual pocket parts, mid-year supplement and periodic revised volumes.
Cost: $4,261; supplementation: 1996: $73.00; 1997: $99.00; 1998: $319.00; 1999: $436.00; 2000; $237.00; 2001: $882.50;

2002: $730.50; 2003: $439.50; 2004: $945.00; 2005: $955.50; 2006: $928; 2007: $981; 2008: $2,364; 2009: $2,674.50; 2010: $2.156; 2011: $2,036; 2012: $2,867.50; 2013: $3,406; **Monthly Assured Print Pricing (APP):** $215/$2,580.

6. Citators.
Kansas Shepard's Citations. Albany, NY: Shepard's. Monthly.
Cost: $3,152 (6 bound volumes); all-inclusive subscription: $2,254 (in-state); (2014).

Online: All jurisdictional Shepard's and KeyCite are no longer available as stand-alone products, but are included as part of a jurisdictional or subject library package (2014).

7. CD-ROM Products.
Kansas Cases and Statutes (West's). Eagan, MN: Thomson West. One disc. Regular updates. Contains the full text of Kansas statutes, court rules, and decisions of the Kansas Supreme Court from 1858 to date, Kansas Court of Appeals appearing in the Pacific Reporter 2d from vol. 155 to date. Decisions also searchable by West Topics and Key Numbers, headnotes, and synopses. Windows, and Macintosh versions available. Search engine: PREMISE; LawDesk (Folio). Subscription includes online updates via Westlaw.
Cost: $12,384 per year (2014).

8. State Legal Research Guides.
Custer, Joseph A. and Christopher Steadham. **Kansas Legal Research**. Durham, NC: Carolina Academic Press, 2008. 1 vol. (231 pp.).
Cost: $25.00; from $4.72 on amazon.com (2014).

Custer, Joseph A. Kansas Practice Materials: A Selective Bibliography in Houdek, Frank G., ed. **State Practice Materials: Annotated Bibliographies**. Buffalo, NY: William S. Hein & Co., Inc., 2002-date.
Cost: $195.00 (2014).

Heller, Francis Howard. **The Kansas State Constitution.** New York: Oxford University Press, 2011. 1 vol. (180 pp.).
Cost: $150.00; from $80.03 on amazon.com; kindle: $119.99 (2014).

9. Leading Web Sites for State Legal Research.

Home Page:	www.kansas.gov
Administrative Regs.:	www.kssos.org/pubs/pubs_kar.aspx
Agency Directory:	www.kansas.gov/government/agencies-associations-listing/
Attorney General:	http://ag.ks.gov/
Attorney Gen. Opinions:	http://ksag.washburnlaw.edu/
Bar Association:	www.ksbar.org/
Constitution:	www.kslib.info/constitution/index.html
Court Opinions:	www.kscourts.org/Cases-and-Opinions
Governor:	www.governor.ks.gov/
Judicial Branch:	www.kscourts.org/
Law Library – Supreme Court:	www.kscourts.org/kansas-courts/law-library
Legislative Branch:	www.kslegislature.org/
Secretary of State:	www.kssos.org/
Statutes:	http://kslegislature.org/li/statute/

10. Leading publishers of state specific treatises, practice books, and CLE publications.
Kansas Bar Association Continuing Legal Education, National Business Institute, Thomson Reuters West. See Appendix B for addresses and telephone numbers.

Kentucky

1. Codes and Session Laws.
Baldwin's Kentucky Revised Statutes Annotated. Official Edition. 4th ed. St. Paul, MN: Thomson West [formerly published in conjunction with Banks-Baldwin], 2006-date. 38 vols. Hardbound. Designated a Certified Version by the Kentucky Legislative Research Commission.
Cost: $1,871; supplementation:1995: $336.00; 1996: $465; 1997: 597.50; 1998: $268; 1999: $510; 2000: $510; 2001: $216.75; 2002: n/a; 2003: $763; 2004: $319; 2005: $824.50; 2006: $980; 2007: $700; 2008: $748; 2009: $912; 2010: $1,001.50; 2011: $1,094; 2012: $1,336; 2013: $1,393; **Monthly Assured Print Pricing (APP):** $118/$1,416.

Kentucky Revised Statutes Annotated [Certified Version]. Charlottesville, VA: LexisNexis, 1971-date. 35 vols. Annual pocket supplements and periodic revised volumes.
Cost: $862; supplementation: 2001: $528/$649 (out-of-state); 2002: $560/$700; 2003: $393.00/$499.00; state); 2004: $506/$615; 2005: $293/$369; 2006: approx. $345/$425; 2007: $766/$932; 2008: $676/$828; 2009: $670/$824; 2010: $595/$725; 2011: $663/$820; 2012: $430/$542; 2013: $677 (in-state).

Kentucky Advance Code Service. Charlottesville, VA: LexisNexis (Michie). Published three times per year.
Cost: $127; renewal: 2014: $107 (in-state) (2014).

Kentucky Advance Legislative Service. Charlottesville, VA: LexisNexis. Supplements code between annual pocket parts.
Cost: $78.00; renewal: 2014: $62.00 (in-state) (2014).

Kentucky Acts [session laws]. Frankfort, KY: Legislative Research Commission. Annual. Kentucky adopted annual sessions in 2001.
Cost:1996: $40.00 (2 vols.);1997 extra session: $10 (1 vol.); 1998: $80 (4 vols.); 2000: $60 (3 vols.); 2001: $10 (1 vol.); 2002: $60; 2003: $80; 2004: $50; 2005: $60; 2006: $60; 2007: $90 (3 vols., including special session); 2008: $90 (3 vols.); 2009: $90; 2010: $90; 2011: $90; 2012: $100 (3 vols.); 2013: $90. Years 2000-date also available on CD-ROM for $10 per session. (502) 564-8100.

Legislative Hotline: (502) 564-8100.

2. Administrative Law.

Kentucky Administrative Regulations. Frankfort, KY: Legislative Research Commission. Annual softbound ed. 12 vols. Regulations as in effect on June 15. (502) 564-8100. Also available online (see link below).
Cost: 2013 Edition: $170; or $250 with one year subscription to Administrative Register (2014).

Administrative Register of Kentucky. Frankfort, KY: Legislative Research Commission. Monthly (July-June). Also available online (see link below).
Cost: $96; or $250 in combination with the Kentucky Administrative Regulations (2014). (502) 564-8100

3. Court Reports.

Kentucky Decisions [1st] – **3d**. St. Paul, MN: Thomson West, 1886-date. [offprint of South Western Reporter 1st - 3d—official since 1973]. Contain decisions of the Kentucky Supreme Court from 1886 to date and Court of Appeals from 1976 to date. Current vol.: 407-413 **SW 3d**.
Cost: 1st series: $610 (61 vols.); 2d series: $2,407.50 (181 vols.); 3d series: $830; annual cost: 2003: $231; 2004: $323; 2005: $337.75; 2006: $350; 2007: $270; 2008: $272.50; 2009: $469.74; 2010: $392.14; 2011: $408; 2012: $526.88; 20; 2013: $634.50; current volume: $105.75/$141 (subscriber/list); **Monthly Assured Print Pricing (APP):** $63/$756. Contact publisher for applicable discounts, or see list of used lawbook dealers in Appendix C.

Kentucky Reports, 1785-1951. [Ceased publication with vol. 314].
Cost: Out-of-print. Used sets available for approx. $1500.00.

South Western Reporter [1st] – **3d**. St. Paul, MN: Thomson West, 1886-date. Contains decisions of Kentucky Supreme Court from 1886-date and Kentucky Court of Appeals from 1976-date. Current vol.: 420 S.W. 3d.
Cost: 1st series: out-of-print (see used lawbook dealers in Appendix C); 2d series: $12,480; used sets sell for approx. $2,300; 3d series: $20,134; used sets sell for approx. $1,500; annual cost (2013): $15,615; current volume: $520.50/$694 (subscriber/list); **Monthly Assured Print Pricing (APP):** $1,399/$16,788. See used lawbook dealers in Appendix C.

South Western 3d. Advance sheets. St. Paul, MN: Thomson West. Weekly.
Cost: $2,799 per year (discounted to bound volume subscribers) (2014).

4. Court Rules.

Kentucky Court Rules Annotated. Charlottesville, VA: LexisNexis. 3 vols. Updated semiannually, replaced annually.
Cost: 2014 Edition: $106.00 (in-state).

Kentucky Rules of Court: State and Federal. St. Paul, MN: Thomson West. 2 vols. Annual. Also available on ProView eBook.
Cost: 2014 Edition: $171; Federal, State and Local: $243.

5. Digests, Encyclopedias, and Practice Sets.

Kentucky Practice Series. St. Paul, MN: Thomson West,1989-date. 24 vols.
Cost: $5,043 (sold as individual components); supplementation: 1996: $165.00; 1997: $165.00; 1998: $175.00; 1999: $184.00; 2000: $197.00; 2001: $219.00; 2002: n/a; 2003: $310.00; 2004: $310.00. Sold as individual components. Supplemented with pocket parts or annual free-standing volumes. Also available as WestlawNext PRO add-on at dramatic savings.

West's Kentucky Digest 2d. St. Paul, MN: Thomson West, 1985-date. 54 vols. Annual pocket parts, mid-year supplement and periodic revised volumes.
Cost: $3,119; supplementation: 1995: $122; 1996: $127; 1997: $139; 1998: $197; 1999: $183; 2000: $312; 2001: $904; 2003: $344; 2004: $603; 2005: $900.25; 2006: $446; 2007: $654; 2008: $416.50; 2009: $1,004; 2010: $1,303.50; 2011: $1,865.50; 2012: $2,277; 2013: $2,140; **Monthly Assured Print Pricing (APP):** $186/$2,232.

6. Citators.

Shepard's Kentucky Citations. Albany, NY: Shepard's. Monthly.
Cost: $3,801 (6 bound volumes); all-inclusive subscription: $2,284 (in-state); (2014).

Online: All jurisdictional Shepard's and KeyCite are no longer available as stand-alone products, but are incuded as part of a jurisdictional or subject library package (2014).

7. CD-ROM Products.

Kentucky Decisions (West's). Eagan, MN: Thomson West. One disc. Updated semiannually. Contains the full text of decisions of the Kentucky Supreme Court from 1785 to date, Court of Appeals form1944 to date, and Attorney General opinions from 1977 to date. Decisions also searchable by West Topics and Key Numbers, headnotes, and synopses. Windows, and Macintosh versions available. Search engine: PREMISE. Subscription includes online updating via Westlaw.
Cost: $5,742 (2014).

LexisNexis CD for Kentucky. Albany, NY: LexisNexis. One disc. Updated quarterly. Contains the full text of the Kentucky Revised Statutes Annotated, Kentucky Rules Annotated, decisions of the Kentucky Court of Appeals (formerly the court of last resort) from 1785 to 1975, the Kentucky Supreme Court (the present court of last resort) from 1976 to date, the Kentucky Court of Appeals (now the intermediate court of appeals) from 1976 to date, and opinions of the Attorney General. Available for Windows. Search Engine: Folio; LivePublish (NextPage). Includes online connection to Lexis.
Cost: $1,777 per year (2014)

8. State Legal Research Guides.

Davis, Helane E. Kentucky Practice Materials: A Selective Bibliography in Houdek, Frank G., ed. **State Practice Materials: Annotated Bibliographies**. Buffalo, NY: William S. Hein & Co., Inc., 2009-date.
Cost: $195.00 (2014).

Ireland, Robert M. **The Kentucky State Constitution.** New York: Oxford University Press, 2011. 1 vol. (308 pp.).
Cost: $150.00; on amazon.com kindle: $119.99 (2014).

Metzmeier, Kurt X., Amy Beckham Osborne, and Shaun Esposito. **Kentucky Legal Research Manual**. 2d ed. Lexington, KY, Office of Continuing Legal education, University of Kentucky, 2002.

Torres, Arturo L. "Kentucky Practice Materials: A Selective Bibliography." **Law Library Journal** 84, No. 3 (1992): 509-541.

Valentin, Ryan and Michelle Cosby. **Kentucky State Documents: A Bibliography of Legal and Law-related Material**. Chicago: AALL, 2008.
Cost: $30.00. Available from William S. Hein & Co. on electronic pdf and on HeinOnline.com (2014).

9. Leading Web Sites for State Law Research.

Home Page:	www.kentucky.gov/
Administrative Code:	www.lrc.ky.gov/kar/frntpage.htm
Agency Directory:	http://kentucky.gov/government
Attorney General:	www.ag.ky.gov/
Attorney Gen. Opinions:	http://www.ag.ky.gov/civil/opinions
Bar Association:	www.kybar.org/
Constitution:	www.lrc.ky.gov/legresou/constitu/intro.htm
Court Opinions:	http://apps.courts.ky.gov/supreme/sc_opinions.shtm
Governor:	www.governor.ky.gov/
Judicial Branch:	http://courts.ky.gov/
Law Library:	http://courts.ky.gov/aoc/statelawlibrary
Legislative Branch:	www.lrc.ky.gov/
Secretary of State:	www.sos.ky.gov/
Statutes:	www.lrc.ky.gov/statutes

10. Leading publishers of state specific treatises, practice books, and CLE publications.
Anderson Publishing, LexisNexis, National Business Institute, Thomson Reuters West. See Appendix B for addresses and telephone numbers.

Louisiana

1. Codes and Session Laws.
West's Louisiana Statutes Annotated. St. Paul, MN: Thomson West, 1951-date. 194 vols. Annual pocket supplements and periodic revised volumes. Interim Annotation Service also available.
Cost: $7,754; supplementation: 1996: $942.00; 1997: $989.00; 1998: $1,572.25; 1999: $891.25; 2000: $1,149; 2001: $1,810.50; 2002: $2,336.50; 2003: $2,614.15; 2004: $2,655; 2005: n/a; 2006: $2,949; 2007: $3,398; 2008: $2,651; 2009: $3,861.50; 2010: $4,067; 2011: $4,606; 2012: $5,539.50; 2013: $6,145; **Monthly Assured Print Pricing (APP):** $503/$6,036.

West's Louisiana Statutes, 2014 Compact Edition. St. Paul, MN: Thomson West. 9 vols. Softbound.
Cost: 2014 Edition: $1,017; **Monthly Assured Print Pricing (APP)**: $78/$936.

State of Louisiana: Acts of the Legislature. Baton Rouge: Secretary of State. 2-3 vols. Annual.
Cost: 1995: $110; (3 vols.); 1996: $60.00 (3 vols.);1997: $110.00 (1 vol.); 1998: $60 (2 vols.); 1999: $110 (3 vols.); 2000: $60 (2 vols.); 2001: $130 (3 vols.); 2002: $80 (2 vols.); 2003: $130 (3 vols.); 2004: $150 (3 vols.); 2005: $100 (2 vols.); 2006: $200; 2007: $150 (2 vols.); 2008: $142 (3 vols.); 2009: $120.00 (3 vols.); 2010: $172 (3 vols.); 2011: $160 (2 vols.); 2012: $174; (225) 922-0539

Louisiana Bound Session Laws. St. Paul, MN: Thomson West, 2001-date. 2 vols. Hardbound.
Cost: 2002: $60; 2004: $166; 2005: $166; 2006: $198; 2007: $224; 2008: $248; 2009: $298; 2010: $354; 2011: $400; 2012: $448; 2013: $448.

West's Louisiana Session Law Service. St. Paul, MN: Thomson West. These pamphlets are published during and immediately after each legislative session and contain text of laws in numerical chapter sequence in order of passage.
Cost: $865 per year (2014).

Legislative Hotline: (225) 342-2456.

2. Administrative Law.
Louisiana Administrative Code. Baton Rouge: Dept. of State Register, 1984-date. 92 vols.
Cost: $1,080 (2014); supplementation issued every two years; see **Louisiana Register** for current updating. Also available on the Web. (225) 342-5015.

Louisiana Register. Baton Rouge: Office of the State Register, 1975-date. Monthly.
Cost: $90 (2014).

3. Court Reports.
Louisiana Cases. St. Paul, MN: Thomson West, 1966-date. [offprint of **Southern Reporter 2d-3d**] Contains decisions of Louisiana Supreme Court and the Louisiana Courts of Appeal; 2d series, 1966-2009; 3d series: 2009-date. Current volume: (125-126 **So. 3d**).
Cost: 2d series: $5,183; 3d series: $14,700; annual cost: 2002: $1,537.00; 2003: $1,615.50; 2004: $1,827.25; 2005: $1,296; 2006: $2,004; 2007: $2,454.50; 2008: $1,093; 2009: $1,973; 2010: $4,590; 2011: $4,130; 2012: $5,512; 2013: $11,187; recent volume: $508.50/$678 (subscriber/list); **Monthly Assured Print Pricing (APP):** $942/$11,304. Contact West regarding applicable discounts or see used lawbook dealers in Appendix C

Louisiana Reports. 1809-1972. [ceased publication with vol. 263].
Cost: Reprint edition available from West for $1,042.50.

Southern Reporter [1st] - **3d**. St. Paul, MN: Thomson West, 1886-date. Contains decisions of the Louisiana Supreme Court from 1886 to date, and Louisiana Court of Appeals from 1926 to date, as well as other Southern regional appellate court decisions. Current vol.: 130 So.3d
Cost: 1st series out-of-print (see used lawbook dealers); 2d series: $14,566; 3d series: $17,639; annual cost (2013): $12,178; current vol.: $529/$706 (subscriber/list); **Monthly Assured Print Pricing (APP)**: $1,274/$15,288. See list of used lawbook dealers in Appendix C.

Southern Reporter 2d. Advance sheets. St. Paul, MN: Thomson West. Weekly.
Cost: $2,866.56 per year (discounted to bound volume subscribers) (2014).

4. Court Rules.
Louisiana Rules of Court: State and Federal. St. Paul, MN: Thomson West. 2 vols. Annual. Also available on ProView eBook.
Cost: 2013 Edition: $197 (2014).

5. Digests, Encyclopedias, and Practice Sets.
West's Louisiana Digest 2d. St. Paul, MN: Thomson West,1986-date. 152 vols. Annual pocket parts, mid-year supplement, and periodic revised volumes.
Cost: $8,400; supplementation: 1996: $242; 1997: $244.50; 1998: $690; 1999: $1,565; 2000: $786; 2001: $1,677; 2002: $2,415; 2003: $3,236.50; 2004: $2,543; 2005: $2,038.50; 2006: $1,128.50; 2007: $2,139; 2008: $1,983; 2009: $2,766; 2010: $3,429.50; 2011: $4,192; 2012: $4,860; 2013: $6,615; **Monthly Assured Print Pricing (APP):** $412/$4,944.

6. Citators.
Shepard's Louisiana Citations. Albany, NY: Shepard's. Monthly.
Cost: $6,379 (13 bound volumes); all-inclusive subscription: $2,158 (in-state) (2014).

Online: All jurisdictional Shepard's and KeyCite are no longer available as stand-alone products, but are included as part of a jurisdictional or subject library package (2014).

7. CD-ROM Products.
Louisiana Cases and West's Louisiana Statutes Unannotated. Eagan, MN: Thomson West. Two discs. Monthly updates. Contains the full text of decisions of the Louisiana Supreme Court from 1944 to date, Attorney General opinions from 1977 to date), unannotated statutes, Constitution, session laws, etc. Decisions also searchable by West Topics and Key Numbers, headnotes, and synopses. Windows and Macintosh versions available. Search engine: PREMISE. Subscription includes online updating via Westlaw.
Cost: $6,942 per year (2014).

8. State Legal Research Guides.
Algero, Mary Garvey. **Louisiana Legal Research**. Durham, NC: Carolina Academic Press, 2009. 1 vol. (223 pp.). Paperbound.
Cost: $25; from $8.00 on amazon.com (2014).

Cain, Charlene and Madeline Hebert. **Louisiana Legal Documents and Related Publications**. Chicago: AALL, 2001. 1 vol.
Cost: $30. Available from William S. Hein & Co. on electronic pdf and on HeinOnline (2014).

Hargrave, W. Lee. **The Louisiana State Constitution**. New York: Oxford University Press, 2011. 1 vol. (288 pp.).
Cost: $150.00; from $9.26 on amazon.com; kindle: $119.99 (2014).

Lemann, Catherine. Louisiana Practice Materials: A Selective Bibliography in Houdek, Frank G., ed. **State Practice Materials: Annotated Bibliographies**. Buffalo, NY: William S. Hein & Co., Inc., 2006-date.
Cost: $195 (2014).

Leading Web Sites for State Legal Research.

Home Page:	www.louisiana.gov/
Administrative Code:	http://doa.louisiana.gov/osr/lac/lactitle.htm
Agency Directory:	www.louisiana.gov/Government/Agency_Index/
Attorney General:	www.ag.state.la.us/
Attorney Gen. Opinions:	www.ag.state.la.us/Opinions.aspx
Bar Association:	www.lsba.org/
Constitution:	www.senate.legis.state.la.us/Documents/Constitution/
Court Opinions:	www.lasc.org/opinion_search.asp - OR - www.lasc.org/news_releases
Governor:	www.gov.louisiana.gov/
Law Library:	www.lasc.org/law_library/library_information.asp
Legislative Branch:	www.legis.state.la.us/
Secretary of State:	www.sos.la.gov/
Statutes:	www.legis.la.gov/legis/LawSearch.aspx
Supreme Court:	www.lasc.org/

10. Leading publishers of state specific treatises, practice books, and CLE publications.
Claitor's Publishing Division, Harrison Publishing, LexisNexis, Louisiana State Bar Association, National Business Institute, Thomson Reuters West. See Appendix B for addresses and telephone numbers.

Maine

1. Codes and Session Laws.

Maine Revised Statutes Annotated. St. Paul, MN: Thomson West, 1964-date. 17 vols. in 53. Annual pocket parts and periodic revised volumes. Also includes Advance Annotation Service.
Cost: $3,628 ; supplementation: 1995: $585; 1996: $601.50; 1997: $488.50; 1998: $490; 1999: $620; 2000: $675; 2001: $754; 2002: $948; 2003: $916; 2004: $1,074; 2005: $1071; 2006: $1,226.50; 2007: $1,110.50; 2008: $1,548.50; 2009: $1,467.50; 2010: $2,057.50; 2011: $2,164.50; 2012: $2,330; 2013: $3,734; **Monthly Assured Print Pricing (APP):** $215/$2,580.

Laws of Maine. [session laws]. Augusta: Law and Legislative Reference Library. Annual. Soft cover only.
Cost: Single copies are free; inquire regarding multiple copies; Index is $10.00. (207) 287-1600.

Maine Legislative Service. St. Paul, MN: Thomson West. These pamphlets are published during and immediately after each legislative session and contain the text of laws in numerical chapter sequence in order of passage.
Cost: $953 per year (2014).

Legislative Hotline: (207) 287-1692.

2. Administrative Law.

Code of Maine Rules. Albany, NY: LexisNexis Matthew Bender, 1986-date. 21 vols. Monthly updates.
Cost: $3,572 (incl. postage); supplementation: 1997: $795; 1998: $795; 1999: $795; 2000: $775; 2001: $995; 2002: $995; 2003: $995; 2004: $995; 2005: $1,045; 2006: $1,045; 2007: $1,045; 2008: $1,045; 2009: $985; 2010: $1,307; 2011: $1,372; 2012: $1,454; 2013: $1,556; 2014: $1,698.

Maine Government Register. Albany, NY: LexisNexis Matthew Bender [formerly Weil Publishing Co.], 1991-date. Monthly.
Cost: $1,257; renewal: 2014; $1,143.

3. Court Reports.

Maine Reporter. St. Paul, MN: Thomson West, 1966-date. [offprint of Atlantic Reporter 2d-3d—official since 1966]. Contains decisions of the Maine Supreme Court from 1966 to date. Current vol.: 61-77 A.3d.
Cost: 2d-3d series: $1,546; annual cost: 2002: $244.50; 2003: $138.00; 2004: $74.50; 2005: $159.50; 2006: $172; 2007: $180; 2008: $277; 2009: $152; 2010: $202; 2011: $202; 2012: $214; 2013: $106.50; recent vol.: $106.50/$142 (subscriber/list).

Maine Reports, 1820-1965. [Ceased publication with vol. 161.]
Cost: Out-of-print, but available used for approximately $1,400.00.

Atlantic Reporter [1st] - **2d**. St. Paul, MN: Thomson West, 1886-date. Contains the decisions from the Maine Supreme Court from 1886 to date. Current volume: 85 **A.3d**.
Cost: 1st series out-of-print (see used lawbook dealers in Appendix C); 2d series: $14,434; 3d series: $15,080; annual cost (2013): $11,151; recent vol.: $531/$708 (subscriber/list); **Monthly Assured Print Pricing (APP):** $1,163/$13,956. See list of used lawbook dealers in Appendix C.

Atlantic Reporter 2d. Advance sheets. St. Paul, MN: Thomson West. Weekly.
Cost: $2,866.56 per year (discounted to bound volume subscribers) (2014).

4. Court Rules.

Maine Court Rules. 2008 State Edition. Standish, ME: Tower Publishing, 2007 1 vol. (478 pp.). Annual. Official publication of the Maine Judicial Branch.
Cost: 2013 State Edition: $39; 2013 Federal Edition: $21.00 (2014).

Maine Rules of Court: State and Federal. St. Paul, MN: Thomson West. 2 vols. Annual. Also available on ProView eBook.
Cost: 2013 Edition: $94 (2014).

5. Digests, Encyclopedias, and Practice Sets.

Maine Digest. St. Paul, MN: Thomson West, 1967-date. 49 vols.
Cost: $3,677 ; annual supplementation: 1995: $151.90; 1996: $169.50; 1997: $186; 1998: $437.50; 1999: $275; 2000: $451; 2001: $976.75; 2002: $1212; 2003: $317; 2004: $535; 2005: $388.50; 2006: $482; 2007: $706; 2008: $597; 2009: $1,227; 2010: $1,655.50; 2011: $1,546; 2012: $2,266; 2013: $3,077; **Monthly Assured Print Pricing (APP):** $201/$2,412.

Alexander, Donald G. **Maine Appellate Practice**. 4th ed. Standish, ME: Tower Publishing, 2013. 1 vol. (432 pp.). Paperbound
Cost: $65.00 (2014).

Alexander, Donald G. **Maine Jury Instruction Manual**. 2013 ed. New Providence, NJ: LexisNexis/Matthew Bender, 2013-date. 1 vol.
Looseleaf format or ebook.
Cost: $146; supplementation: 2009: $122; 2011: $142; 2012: $146.

Horton, Andrew M. and Peggy McGehee. **Maine Civil Remedies**. 4th ed. Standish, ME: Tower Publishing, 2004. 1 vol. (508 pp.).
Cost: $95.00 (2014).

Mitchell, James E. **Maine Probate Procedure: A Guide to Official and Recommended Forms**. Revised by Philip C. Hunt. New York: LexisNexis, 2000. 1 vol. Looseleaf format or ebook.
Cost: $271; supplementation: 2003: $203; 2004: $214; 2005-2011: 0; 2012: $215.

Murray, Peter L. and Richard H. Field. **Maine Evidence**. 6th ed. Portland, ME: Maine Law Book Company 2007. 1 vol. (616 pp.). Acquired by Tower Publishing.
Cost: $75 (2014).

Simmons, Jack H. **Maine Tort Law**, 2004 ed. Newark, NJ: LexisNexis, 2004-date. 1 vol. Annual supplementation.
Cost: $220; supplementation: 2012: $106 (2014).

6. Citators.

Shepard's Maine Citations. Albany, NY: Shepard's. Six supple-

ments per year.
Cost: $1,098 (2 bound volumes); all-inclusive subscription: $1,712 (in-state) (2014).

Online: All jurisdictional Shepard's and KeyCite are no longer available as stand-alone products, but are included as part of a jurisdictional or subject library package (2014).

7. CD-ROM Products.
Maine Reporter. Eagan, MN: Thomson West. One disc. Updated quarterly. Contains full text of Maine Supreme Court decisions appearing in Atlantic Reporter 2d, vols. 41 (1945) to date, and Attorney General opinions from 1977 to date. Decisions also searchable by West Topics and Key Numbers, headnotes, and synopses. Windows, and Macintosh versions available. Search engine: PREMISE.
Cost: $8,166 per year (2014).

8. State Legal Research Guides.
Hepler, Christine I. and Maureen P. Quinlan. **Maine State Documents: A Bibliography of Legal and Law-Related Materials**. Chicago: AALL, 2003.
Cost: $30.00. Available from William S. Hein & Co. in electronic pdf and on HeinOnline (2014).

Tinkle, Marshall J. **The Maine State Constitution**. New York: Oxford University Press, 2013. 1 vol. ((236 pp.).
Cost: $150.00; from $126.43 on amazon.com (2014).

Wells, William W., Jr. **Maine Legal Research Guide**. Portland: Tower Publishing, 1989.

9. Leading Web Sites for State Legal Research.

Home page:	www.maine.gov/
Administrative Code:	www.maine.gov/sos/cec/rules/rules.html
Agency Directory:	www.maine.gov/portal/government/state-agencies
Attorney General:	www.maine.gov/ag/
Attorney Gen. Opinions:	www.maine.gov/ag/about/ag_opinions.html
Bar Association:	www.mainebar.org/
Constitution:	www.maine.gov/legis/const/
Court Opinions:	www.courts.maine.gov/opinions_orders
Governor:	www.maine.gov/governor
Judicial Branch:	www.courts.maine.gov/
Law & Legis. Ref. Lib.:	www.state.me.us/legis/lawlib/
Law Libraries:	www.courts.maine.gov/news_reference/libraries
Legal Research:	www.state.me.us/legis/lawlib/iresearch.htm
Legislative Branch:	www.maine.gov/legis/
Secretary of State:	www.maine.gov/sos/
Statutes:	www.mainelegislature.org/legis/statutes/

10. Leading publishers of state specific treatises, practice books, and CLE publications.
Maine State Bar Association, LexisNexis, Maine Trial Lawyers Association, National Business Institute, Tower Publishing, Thomson West. See Appendix B for addresses and telephone numbers.

Maryland

1. Codes and Session Laws.
Annotated Code of Maryland. Charlottesville, VA: LexisNexis, 1974-date. 50 vols. Annual pocket parts and periodic revised volumes. [replacing Maryland Annotated Code of 1957; new maroon set organized alphabetically by subject rather than vol. number.]
Cost: $1,596; supplementation (in-state/out-of-state): 2001: $770/$973; 2002: $713/$902; 2003: $617/$779, 2004: $841/$1,071; 2005: $307/$374; 2008: $958/$1,195; 2009: $826/$1,023; 2010: $761/$1,082; 2011: $910/$1,137;2012: $965/$1,207; 2013: $1,165; used sets may be available. See list of used lawbook dealers in Appendix C.

West's Annotated Code of Maryland. St. Paul, MN: Thomson West, 2002-date. 72 vols. Annual pocket parts and periodic revised volumes.
Cost: $2,281; supplementation: 2003: $340; 2004: $325; 2005: $377; 2006: $700; 2007: $893.50; 2008: $952.50; 2009: $1,102; 2010: $1,450; 2011: $1,407; 2012: $1,535; 2013: $1,927; **Monthly Assured Print Pricing (APP):** $148/$1,776.

Maryland Advance Code Service. Charlottesville, VA: LexisNexis. Supplements code between annual pocket parts.
Cost: $101 per year; renewal: 2014: $81 (in-state) (2014).

Maryland Advance Legislative Service. Charlottesville, VA: LexisNexis. Monthly.
These pamphlets are published during and after each legislative session and contain the full text of laws in numerical chapter sequence in the order of passage.
Cost: $134; renewal: 2014: $118 (in-state) (2014).

West's Maryland Legislative Service. St. Paul, MN: Thomson West, 2003-date. These pamphlets are published during and after each legislative session and contain the full text of laws in numerical chapter sequence in the order of passage.
Cost: $347.02 (2014)

Laws of Maryland [session laws]. Annapolis: Dept. of Legislative Services. Annual. Hardbound or softbound. Also available online.
Cost: 1997: $150; 1998: $160; 1999: $160; 2000: $160; 2001: $180; 2002: $180 (6 vols.); 2003-2013: $180/$125.

Legislative Hotline: (410) 946-5400.

2. Administrative Law.
Code of Maryland Regulations. Annapolis: MD: Division of State Documents, 1977-date. 33 vols. Sept.-Aug. calendar year.

Cost: $1,000 (includes binders, shipping & all supplements through July 1, 2011); supplementation: $500 per year (2014). Prices subject to change. Also available on the Internet at: http://www.dsd.state.md.us/comar/

Maryland Register. Annapolis: MD: Division of State Documents, 1974-date. Biweekly. E-mail, CD-ROM, and DVD formats only available.
Cost: Print: $225; eSubscription: $190 per year; archival library available at a cost of $375 for 2 DVDs covering years 1974-2003; one year for $50.00; or $100.00 for one year of the period 2004-2011. (2014). (410) 974-2486.
Also available on the Internet at: http://www.dsd.state.md.us/MDRegister/

3. Court Reports.

Maryland Reports. 1851-date. Volumes 298-date published by Thomson West. Contain decisions of the Maryland Court of Appeals from 1851 to date. Current volume: 438.
Cost: $1,725; annual cost: 2003: $534; 2004: $576; 2005: $660; 2006: $750; 2007: $820.50; 2008: $540; 2009: $692.50; 2010: $580; 2011: $745; 2012: $800; 2013: $1,120; current volume: $186.75/$249 (subscriber/list); **Monthly Assured Printing Pricing (APP)**: $111/$1,332.

Maryland Reporter. **1st – 3d**. St. Paul, MN: Thomson West,1942-date. [offprint of Atlantic Reporter 2d-3d]. Contains decisions of the Maryland Court of Appeals from 1942 to date and Court of Special Appeals from 1967 to date. Current volume: 77-78 **A.3d**.
Cost: $5,301; annual cost: 2003: $775.50; 2004: $822.25; 2005: $932.25; 2006: $710; 2007: $1,932; 2008: $1,795.50; 2009: $2,018; 2010: $3,097; 2011: $2,980; 2012: $4,342; 2013: $4,177; current volume: $417.75/$557 (subscriber/list); **Monthly Assured Print Pricing (APP):** $557/$6,684. See list of used lawbook dealers in Appendix C.

Maryland Appellate Reports. 1967-date. Published by Thomson West, 1984 to date. Decisions of the Maryland Court of Special Appeals from 1967 to date. Current vol.: 215.
Cost: $1,921; annual cost: 2003: $534; 2004: $672; 2005: $721; 2006: $850; 2007: $580.50; 2008: $540; 2009: $950.50; 2010: $812; 2011: $1,192; 2012: $1,120; 2013: $1,307; current volume: $186.75/$249 (subscriber/list); **Monthly Assured Print Pricing (APP)**: $144/$1,728.

Atlantic Reporter [1st] - **2d**. St. Paul, MN: Thomson West, 1886-date. Includes decisions of Maryland Court of Appeals from 1886-date and Maryland Court of Special Appeals from 1967-date. Current volume: 85 **A.3d**.
Cost: 1st series out-of-print (see used lawbook dealers in Appendix C); 2d series: $14,434; 3d series: $15,080; annual cost (2013): $11,151; recent vol.: $531/$708 (subscriber/list); **Monthly Assured Print Pricing (APP):** $1,163/$13,956. See list of used lawbook dealers in Appendix C.

Atlantic Reporter 2d. Advance sheets. St. Paul, MN: Thomson West. Weekly.
Cost: $2,866.56 per year (discounted to bound volume subscribers) (2014).

4. Court Rules.

Maryland Rules Annotated. Charlottesville, VA: LexisNexis. 2 vols. Updated semiannually, replaced annually. Also available on ebook.
Cost: 2014 Edition: $132.00 (in-state).

Maryland Rules of Court, State & Federal. St. Paul, MN: Thomson West. 2 vols.
Cost: 2014 Edition: $180; ProView eBook: $175.

5. Digests, Encyclopedias, and Practice Sets.

West's Maryland Digest, 2d. St. Paul, MN: Thomson West, 1993-date. 111 vols. Annual pocket parts, mid-year supplement, and periodic revised volumes.
Cost: $5,990; supplementation: 1995: approx. $250; 1996: $80; 1997: $104; 1998: $235; 1999: $437.25; 2000: $270; 2001: $315; 2003: $1,937.50; 2004: $903.50; 2005: $1,104; 2006: $1,300; 2007: $1,421; 2008: $1,998.50; 2009: $3,352.50; 2010: $3,423; 2011: $2,711; 2012: $3,037; 2013: $4,075; **Monthly Assured Print Pricing (APP):** $323/$3,876

West's Maryland Law Encyclopedia. St. Paul, MN: Thomson West, 1960-date. 32 vols. Annual pocket parts and periodic revised volumes.
Cost: $5,097 ; supplementation: 1996: $532; 1997: $357; 1998: $793.50; 1999: $1,258; 2000: $1,372.50; 2001: $1,463.50; 2003: $958.71; 2004: $823.75; 2005: $911; 2006: $1,400; 2007: $1,378.50; 2008: $902; 2009: $1,786.50; 2010: $2,882; 2011: $2,254; 2012: $2,897; 2013: $3,544; **Monthly Assured Print Pricing (APP):** $337/$4,044.

6. Citators.

Shepard's Maryland Citations. Albany, NY: Shepard's. Monthly.
Cost: $2,711 (6 bound volumes); all-inclusive subscription: $2,243 (in-state); (2014).

Online: All jurisdictional Shepard's and KeyCite are no longer available as stand-alone products, but are included as part of a jurisdictional or subject library package (2014).

7. CD-ROM Products.

LexisNexis CD – Maryland Primary Law. Albany, NY: LexisNexis. One disc. Updated quarterly. Contains full text of the Annotated Code of Maryland, decisions of the Maryland Court of Appeals from 1770 to date, the Court of Special Appeals from 1967 to date, and Maryland Rules Annotated. Available for Windows. Search Engine: Folio.
Cost: $2,283 per year (2014).

Maryland Estate Planning, Wills and Trusts Library: Forms and Practice Manual. Brooklandville, MD: Data Trace Publishing Co. One disc. Updated annually. Contains forms and clauses on estate planning in Maryland. Available for Windows 3.1 or higher. Search Engine: Word; WordPerfect.
Cost: $299.90, including print (2014).

Maryland Reports and Maryland Appellate Reports with West's Maryland Code. Eagan, MN: Thomson West. Two discs. Regular updates. Contains full text of decisions of the Maryland Court of Appeals from 1787 to date, decisions of the Maryland Court of Special Appeals from vol. 1 (1967) to date, and opinions of the Attorney General from 1977 to date. Decisions also searchable by West Topics and Key Numbers,

headnotes, and synopses. Windows, and Macintosh versions available. Search Engine: PREMISE. Subscription includes online updates via Westlaw.
Cost: $6,837 per year (2014).

8. State Legal Histories and Research Guides.
Chanin, Leah F., Pamela J. Gregory, and Sarah K. Wiant. **Legal Research in the District of Columbia, Maryland, and Virginia**. 2d ed. Buffalo, NY: William S. Hein & Co., 2000. 1 vol. (450 pp.).
Cost: OUT-OFPRINT (2014).

Colborn, Robert J. **Research Guide for Maryland Regulations**. Annapolis, MD: Office of the Secretary of State, Division of State Documents, 1992.
Available at: http://www.lawlib.state.md.us/researchtools/guides/comarresearch.pdf

Friedman, Dan. **The Maryland State Constitution**. New York: Oxford University Press, 2011. 1 vol. (464 pp.).
Cost: $150.00; from $74,12 on amazon.com; kindle: $119.99 (2014).

Postar, Adeen and Khelani Clay. Maryland Practice Materials: A Selective Bibliography in Houdek, Frank G., ed. **State Practice Materials: Annotated Bibliographies**. Buffalo, NY: William S. Hein & Co., Inc., 2002-date. 2 vols. Looseleaf format.
Cost: $195.00 (2014).

Taylor, William L. **Maryland State Publications in Law and Related Fields: A Selective Bibliography with Annotations**. Chicago: AALL, 1996. 1 vol.
Cost: $30.00. Available from William S. Hein & Co. as electronic pdf or on HeinOnline (2014).

9. Leading Web Sites for State Legal Research.

Home Page:	www.maryland.gov/
Agency Directory:	www.maryland.gov/pages/government.aspx
Attorney General:	www.oag.state.md.us/
Attorney Gen. Opinions:	www.oag.state.md.us/Opinions
Bar Association:	www.msba.org/
Code of Maryland Regulations	www.dsd.state.md.us/comar/
Constitution:	www.msa.md.gov/msa/mdmanual/43const/html/const.html
Court Opinions:	www.courts.state.md.us/opinions.html
Governor:	www.gov.state.md.us/
Judicial Branch:	www.courts.state.md.us/
Law Library:	www.lawlib.state.md.us/
Legislature:	http://mgaleg.maryland.gov
MD Daily Record (legal newspaper):	http://thedailyrecord.com/
Secretary of State:	www.sos.state.md.us/
Statutes:	(link from Legislature above)

10. Leading publishers of state specific treatises, practice books, and CLE publications.
LexisNexis, Maryland Institute for Continuing Professional Education of Lawyers (MICPEL), National Business Institute, Thomson Reuters West, Wolters Kluwer Law & Business. See Appendix B for addresses and telephone numbers.

Massachusetts

1. Codes and Session Laws.
Annotated Laws of Massachusetts. Charlottesville, VA: LexisNexis, 1932-date. 86 vols. Annual pocket supplements and periodic revised volumes. Formerly published by Lawyers Cooperative (1932-1997), this code was sold to Reed Elsevier under the terms of the consent decree which approved the purchase of West Publishing by the Thomson Corporation in 1996.
Cost: $1,097; supplementation: 2000: $751; 2001: $600; 2002: $1,135; 2003: $1,149; 2004: $1,095; 2005: $729; 2006: $919; 2007: $1,035; 2008: $1,107; 2009: $861; 2010: $1,056; 2011: $877; 2012: $939; 2013: $939.

General Laws of Massachusetts [unannotated]. Official Edition. St. Paul, MN: Thomson West. Biennial editions. 24 vols. The official codification of the General Laws of Massachusetts.
Cost: 2013 Edition: Inquire (2014)

Massachusetts General Laws Annotated. St. Paul, MN: Thomson West, 1978-date. 45 vols. in 83. Annual pocket supplements and periodic revised volumes.
Cost: $3,994 ; supplementation: 1995: $465, 1996: $635; 1997: $698.50; 1998: $680; 1999: $735; 2000: $852; 2001: $1,190; 2002: $1,468; 2003: $1,768.55; 2004: $1,646.50; 2005: $1,603.50; 2006: $1,723; 2007: $1,835.50; 2008: $1,780.50; 2009: $1,783; 2010: $2,166.50; 2011: $2,572.50; 2012: $2,584; 2013: $3,148; **Monthly Assured Print Pricing (APP):** $259/$3,108.

Acts & Resolves of Massachusetts. Boston: Secretary of State. Annual.
Cost: 1991-2013 available @ $20-$22 per year (as of April 1, 2014).
Advance Publication of Current Acts and Resolves: $75 per year. Available from State Bookstore, State House, Boston, MA 02133. (617) 727-2834

Advance Legislative Service for the Annotated Laws of Massachusetts. Charlottesville, VA: LexisNexis. These pamphlets are published during and immediately after each legislative session and contain the text of laws in numerical chapter sequence in order of passage.
Cost: $98 per year (2014); or included free with each set of ALM.

Massachusetts Legislative Service. St. Paul, MN: Thomson West. These pamphlets are published during and immediately after each legislative session and contain text of laws in numerical chapter sequence in order of passage.
Cost: $855.48 per year (2014).

Legislative Hotline: (617) 722-2356 (House); (617) 722-1276 (Senate).

\2. Administrative Law.

Code of Massachusetts Regulations. Boston: Secretary of State, 1987-date. 25 vols. in 20. Comes in paper pamphlet form without binders. A small number of binders may be available in 1997 at $10.00 per binder. (617) 727-2831
Cost: $2,255.65 (includes 25 binders and one year subscription to Mass. Register and Cumulative Table); w/o binders: $2,005.65; future supplementation: $300 per year; binders separately are $10 each. $25 per year for separate subscription to Cumulative Table reporting amendments with citations to Register. Internet subscription: $110 per year (2014). Available from State Bookstore, Room 116 State House, Boston. (617) 727-2834.

Code of Massachusetts Regulations. Albany, NY: LexisNexis Matthew Bender [formerly Weil Publishing Co.]. 28 vols. Updated 11 times per year.
Cost: $2,675 (incl. postage); supplementation: 1995: $575, 1996: $950; 1997: $950; 1998: $748; 1999: 748; 2000: $750; 2001: $750; 2002: $755; 2003: $755; 2004: $755; 2005: $825; 2006: $825; 2007: $825; 2008: $873; 2009: $985; 2010: $1,034; 2011: $1,086; 2012: $1,162; 2012: $1,232; 2013: $1,344. No Register published by LexisNexis (Weil) for Massachusetts (see official version from Secretary of State).

Massachusetts Register. Boston: Secretary of State, 1976-date. Biweekly. Updates Code of Massachusetts Regulations every two weeks.
Cost: $300 per year; $15 each; online: $225 per year (2014). Contact: State Bookstore, Room 116 State House, Boston, MA 02133. (617) 727-2834.

3. Court Reports.

Massachusetts Reports, 1867-date. St. Paul, MN: Thomson West. [Advance sheets also available.] Contain decisions of the Massachusetts Supreme Judicial Court from 1867 to date. Preceded by 96 nominative reporters (1804-1867). Current bound vol.: 466
Cost: $2,784 (for vols. 265-466 of **Massachusetts Reports** and volumes 1-82 of **Mass. Appeals Court Reports**); annual cost of bound volumes of both series: 2012: $236.39; 2013: $101.31 (list); cost of most recent vol.: $33.77/$33.77 (list); advance sheets to both **Mass. Reports** and **Mass. Appeals Court Reports**: $218.67 per year. Internet advance sheets also available for $218.67 per year (2014).

Massachusetts Decisions. St. Paul, MN: Thomson West, 1885-date. [offprint of North Eastern Reporter [1st] - 2d]. Contain decisions of both Massachusetts Supreme Judicial Court from 1886 to date, and Massachusetts Appeals Court from 1976 to date. Most recent vol.: 992-995 N.E.2d.
Cost: 1st series: $400 (40 vols.); 2d series: $4,810; annual cost: 2004: $606; 2005: $763.25; 2006: $734; 2007: $803; 2008: $843; 2009: $1,010; 2010: $1,258; 2011: $1,596; 2012: $2,560; 2013: $2,772; recent vol.: $459.75/$613 (subscriber/list); **Monthly Assured Print Pricing (APP):** $343/$4,116; used sets may be available.

Massachusetts Appeals Court Reports.1972-date. St. Paul, MN: Thomson West. [Advance sheets also available]. Current bound vol.: 81.
Cost: $2,784 (for vols. 265-466 of **Massachusetts Reports** and volumes 1-82 of **Mass. Appeals Court Reports**); annual cost of bound volumes of both series: 2012: $236.39; 2013: $101.31 (list); cost of most recent vol.: $33.77/$33.77 (list); advance sheets to both **Mass. Reports** and **Mass. Appeals Court Reports**: $218.67 per year. Internet advance sheets also available for $218.67 per year (2014).

Massachusetts Appellate Division Reports [District Court, Appellate Division], 1936-1950 [out-of-print]. Boston: Massachusetts Lawyers Weekly, 1980-date. Annual. [Advance sheets also available.] (800) 451-9998.
Cost: Special offer on 1992-2012 (21 vols.): $179 for the complete set; individual bound volumes vary in price: 2008: $70; 2009: $73; 2010: $74.95; 2011: $74.95; 2012: $74.95; inquire regarding price and availability of volumes from 1980-1991; $80 per year for monthly advance sheets. Current vol.: 34 (2014).

North Eastern Reporter [1st] - **2d**. St. Paul, MN: Thomson West, 1885-date. Contains decisions of the Massachusetts Supreme Judicial Court from 1884 to date and the Mass. Appeals Court from 1972 to date. Current volume: 999 **N.E.2d**.
Cost: 1st series: out-of-print (see used lawbook dealers in Appendix C); 2d series: $15,333; annual cost (2013): $10,146; current vol.: $534/$710 (subscriber/list); **Monthly Assured Print Pricing (APP):** $1,087/$13,044; used sets sell for approx. $2,000.00.

North Eastern Reporter 2d. Advance sheets. St. Paul, MN: Thomson West Weekly.
Cost: $2,866.56 (discounted to bound volume subscribers) (2014).

4. Court Rules.

Massachusetts Rules of Court: State and Federal. St. Paul, MN: Thomson West. 2 vols. Annual. Also available on ProView eBook.
Cost: 2014 Edition: $160.

Massachusetts Court Rules Annotated. Charlottesville, VA: Lexis Law Publishing (Michie). 2 vols. Annual. Also available on ebook.
Cost: 2013-14 Edition: $169 (2014).

5. Digests, Encyclopedias and Practice Sets.

Massachusetts Digest 2d. St. Paul, MN: Thomson West, 1986-date. 96 vols. Annual pocket parts, mid-year supplements, and periodic revised volumes.
Cost: $7,100; supplementation: 1996: $174.50; 1997: 199.50; 1998: $515; 1999: $510; 2000: $693; 2001: $1,540; 2002: $1,383; 2003: $874; 2004: $1,039.50; 2005: $1,709.50; 2006: $1,428; 2007: $1,419.50; 2008: $2,091.50; 2009: $3,550; 2010: $3,101.50; 2011: $4,398; 2012: $4,156; 2013: $4,004; **Monthly Assured Print Pricing (APP):** $433/$5,196.

Massachusetts Legal Practice Library. Charlottesville, VA: LexisNexis, 1999-date. 11 vols. Includes Landlord-Tenant Law, Domestic Relations (4th ed.), Massachusetts Corporations and Other Business Entities (3d ed.), Massachusetts Real Estate (3d ed.), Guardianship and Conservatorship in Massachusetts (2d ed.), Criminal Practice, Massachusetts Tort Damages (2d ed.). **Cost**: $1,749 (2014).

Massachusetts Practice Series. St. Paul, MN: Thomson West, 1967-date. 90+ vols. Individual components updated separately. **Cost**: $15,232 (but sold individually); supplementation: irregular (various titles updated individually); individual titles available; 1997: $1,430.00; 1998: $1,620.00; 1999: $1,795.00; 2000: $1,747.50; 2001: $2,324.50; 2002: $2,387.00; 2003: $2,230.00; 2004: $1,296.73. See costs for individual components. Also available on WestlawNext PRO at considerable savings: $1,548 for solo practitioner; $2,508 for three attorney firm.

6. Citators.

Shepard's Massachusetts Citations. Albany, NY: Shepard's. Monthly or semi-monthly option.
Cost: $3,640 (10 bound volumes); all-inclusive subscription: monthly: $2,273 (in-state); bi-monthly: $2,683 (in-state); (2014).

Online: All jurisdictional Shepard's and KeyCite are no longer available as stand-alone products, but are included as part of a jurisdictional or subject library package (2014).

7. CD-ROM Products.

LexisNexis CD - Massachusetts Forms of Pleading and Practice.
Albany, NY: LexisNexis. One disc. Updated quarterly. Contains hundreds of pleading and practice forms suitable for use in Massachusetts. Windows. Search Engines: Folio.
Cost: $1,731 per year (2014).

LexisNexis CD - Massachusetts Primary Law. Albany, NY: LexisNexis. Two discs. Updated quarterly. Contains the full text of the Annotated Laws of Massachusetts, court rules, decisions of the Massachusetts Supreme Judicial Court from 1804 to date, Massachusetts Appeals Court from 1972 to date, Annotated Laws of Massachusetts, Massachusetts Court Rules, Massachusetts Advance Legislative Service, Attorney General opinions from 1977 to 1996, workers' compensation decisions from 1987 to 1998, and an online link to the Code of Massachusetts Regulations (CMR) on Lexis. Available for Windows. Search Engines: Folio.
Cost: $2,189 per year (2014).

Massachusetts Administrative Law Library [Online]. Boston: Social Law Library. One disc. Updated quarterly. Contains the full text of the Code of Massachusetts Regulations, and decisions of various Massachusetts administrative agencies. Program can run on both Windows and Macintosh.
Search Engine: Folio.
Cost: Now available online only: $190.00 per database per year; each additional user: $100.00 per database; Full firm members may obtain access to all of the Administrative Law Databases for 5 simultaneous users from the location on the membership account at a cost of $1,900 per year (Social Law Library members only); available on the Web at: socialaw.com (2014).

Massachusetts Cases, Premise CD-ROM. Eagan, MN: Thomson West. One disc. Quarterly updates. Contains full text of decisions of Massachusetts Supreme Judicial Court from 1899 to date, Massachusetts Appeals Court from 1972 to date, District Court, Appellate Division decisions from 1990-date, slip opinions, and Attorney General opinions from 1976 to date. Decisions also searchable by West Topics and Key Numbers, headnotes, and synopses. Available for Windows or Macintosh. Search engine: LawDesk (Folio).
Cost: $4,314 per year (2014).

Massachusetts Decisions (West's). Eagan, MN: Thomson West. One disc. Quarterly updates. Contains full text of decisions of Massachusetts Supreme Judicial Court from 1804 to date, Massachusetts Appeals Court from 1972 to date, District Court, Appellate Division decisions, and Attorney General opinions from 1976 to date. Decisions also searchable by West Topics and Key Numbers, headnotes, and synopses. Available for Windows or Macintosh. Search engine: Premise.
Cost: $5,757 per year (2014).

8. State Legal Research Guides.

Blum, E. Joan. **Massachusetts Legal Research**. Durham, NC: Carolina Academic Press, 2010.
Cost: $25; from $6.65 on amazon.com (2014).

Friedman, Lawrence and Lynnea Thody. **The Massachusetts State Constitution**. New York: Oxford University Press, 2011. 1 vol. (245 pp.).
Cost: $150.00; from $84.34 on amazon.com; kindle: $119.99 (2014).

McAuliffe, Leo and Susan Z. Steinway. **Massachusetts State Documents Bibliography**. Chicago: AALL, 1985.
Cost: $30. Available from William S. Hein & Co. as electronic pdf and on HeinOnline (2014).

Neary Mary Ann et al. **Handbook of Legal Research in Massachusetts**. 3d ed. Boston: Massachusetts Continuing Legal Education, 2009. 1 vol. Includes 2012 supplement. Looseleaf format. Supplements issued every three years. Also available as ebook.
Cost: print or ebook: $165.00 (non-member); $150.00 (sponsor); both print and ebook: $247.00 (non-member); $225.00 (sponsor) (2014).

9. Leading Web Sites for State Legal Research.

Home Page:	www.mass.gov/
Administrative Code:	www.lawlib.state.ma.us/source/mass/cmr
Agency Directory:	www.mass.gov/portal/global-agency-list.html
Attorney General:	www.mass.gov/ago/
Attorney Gen. Opinions:	www.mass.gov/ago/government-resources/ags-opinions/
Bar Assoc. - Boston:	www.bostonbar.org/
Bar Assoc. - Mass.:	www.massbar.org
Constitution:	www.malegislature.gov/Laws/Constitution
Court Opinions:	www.mass.gov/courts/court-info/sjc/about/reporter-of-decisions
General Laws:	www.malegislature.gov/Laws/GeneralLaws
Governor:	www.mass.gov/governor/

Judicial Branch:	www.mass.gov/courts/
Law Libraries:	www.lawlib.state.ma.us/
Legislative Branch:	www.malegislature.gov/
Mass. Lawyers Weekly:	www.masslawyersweekly.com/
Secretary of State:	www.sec.state.ma.us/
Social Law Library:	www.socialaw.com/
Statutes:	www.lawlib.state.ma.us/source/mass/cmr

10. Leading publishers of state specific treatises, practice books, and CLE publications.
Matthew Bender, LexisNexis, Massachusetts Bar Association, Massachusetts Continuing Legal Education, Massachusetts Lawyers Weekly, National Business Institute, Office of Advanced Legal Studies of Suffolk University Law School, Professional Education Systems, Inc., Social LawLibrary, Thomson Reuters West, Wolters Kluwer Law & Business. See Appendix B for addresses and telephone numbers.

Michigan

1. Codes and Session Laws.
Michigan Compiled Laws [unannotated]. Lansing, MI: Legislative Council, 1979-date. 6 vols. [discontinued]
Cost: Official print code no longer available. Available via the Web at: www.legislature.mi.gov/

Michigan Compiled Laws Annotated. St. Paul, MN: Thomson West, 1967-date. 104 vols. Annual pocket supplements and periodic revised volumes.
Cost: $3,734; supplementation: 1995: $570; 1996: $645; 1997: $860; 1998: $930.75; 1999: $1,106; 2000: $1,083.50; 2001: $1,644.50; 2002: $1,818; 2003: $1,645; 2004: $1,622.50; 2005: $1,626; 2006: $1,694; 2007: $1,386; 2008: $1,446.50; 2009: $1,602; 2010: $1,691. 2011: $1,910.50; 2012: $2,140; 2013: $3,226; **Monthly Assured Print Pricing (APP):** $227/$2,724. See list of used lawbook dealers in Appendix C.

Michigan Bound Session Laws. St. Paul, MN: Thomson West, 2001-date. 1 vol.
Cost: 2000: $69; 2001: $76; 2003: $86; 2004: $93; 2005: $104; 2006: $126; 2007: $126; 2008: $142; 2009: $151; 2010: $169; 2011: $189; 2012: $212.

Michigan Compiled Laws Service. Charlottesville, VA: LexisNexis, 2001-date. 27 vols. in 76. Annual pocket parts and periodic revised volumes.
Cost: $1,425 (includes one year's service); supplementation: 2003: $1,084; 2004: $944; 2005: $415; 2006: $415; 2007: $950; 2008: $1,057; 2009: $522; 2010: $1,035; 2011: $824; 2012: $674; 2013: $1,417.
This title was sold to Reed Elsevier in January, 1997 after the Department of Justice negotiated a consent decree with the Thomson Corporation and West Publishing requiring the divestiture of 51 titles.

Michigan Legislative Service. St. Paul, MN: Thomson West. These pamphlets are published during and immediately after current legislative session and contain the text of laws in numerical chapter sequence in order of passage.
Cost: 2014: $1,101 per year.

Michigan Advance Legislative Service. Charlottesville, VA: LexisNexis. These pamphlets are published during and immediately after current legislative session and contain the text of laws in numerical chapter sequence in order of passage.
Cost: $104 per year (2014).

Public and Local Acts of Michigan [session laws]. Lansing, MI: Legislative Service Bureau. 2 vols. (2000-date). Annual. (517) 373-0170
Cost: 1989: $27; 1990: $36; 1991: $28; 1992: $32; 1993: $36; 1994: $40; 1995: $47; 1996-1998 [see note at end];1999: $50 (1 v.); 2000: $60 (2 vols.); 2001: $60; 2002: $75; 2003: $80; 2004: $85; 2005: $85; 2006-2007: $100 ea.; 2008-date: online. Note: 1996 ($90), 1997 ($90) & 1998 ($95) only available from Conway Green Publishing Co. at (800) 977-2665.

Legislative Hotline: (517) 373-0169.

2. Administrative Law.
Michigan Administrative Code. Lansing, MI: Office of Regulatory Reform, 2000-date. The official source for Michigan administrative rules and regulations. Since April 2000, ORR has published the state's three administrative rule periodicals: the Michigan Register, the Michigan Administrative Code, and the Annual Administrative Code Supplement. All are available on the Web, free of charge, at: http://www.michigan.gov/orr (800) 977-2665. Also available on the Web at: www.state.mi.us/orr/admincode.htm
Cost: Web only (2014).

Michigan Register. Lansing, MI: Office of Regulatory Reform, 1984-date. Twice monthly. The official monthly record of state government regulatory activity and legislative information. Each issue contains agency administrative rules and guidelines, notices of public hearings, executive orders, attorney general opinions, and new legislative tables. Since April 17, 2000, also available at no charge on the Web at: www.state.mi.us/orr
Cost: $400 per year (Jan.-Jan.) (2014); also available at no charge on the Internet. (517) 241-1671.

3. Court Reports.
West's Michigan Reporter 2d. St. Paul, MN: Thomson West, 1941-date. [offprint of North Western Reporter 2d] Contain decisions of the Michigan Supreme Court from 1941 to date and the Michigan Court of Appeals from 1965 to date. Current vol.: 836-838 N.E.2d.
Cost: $4,555; annual cost: 2003: $417.00; 2004: $372.75; 2005: $420.00; 2005: $514.75; 2006: $702; 2007: $780; 2008: $867; 2009: $971; 2010: $965; 2011: $1,386; 2012: $2,493; 2013: $3,186; recent vol.: $398.25/$531 (subscriber/list); **Monthly Assured Print Pricing (APP)**: $381/$4,572.

Michigan Reports. 1847-date. St. Paul, MN: Thomson West. Previously published by Darby Printing Co. and Lawyers Cooperative Publishing Co. West acquired state contract in

April, 2004 and reprinted volumes 1-469. Current volume: 489. **Cost**: $5,510.75 (vols. 1-494) ; 2006: $56.04; 2007: $118.03; 2008: $92.46; 2009: $33.24; 2010: $19.44; 2011: $19.44; 2012: $34.92; 2013: $113.73; volumes 1-493 are $19.44 each; vol. 494: $35.97; **Monthly Assured Print Pricing (APP)**: $129/$1,548; Advance sheet subscription also available. Used sets of both **Michigan Reports** and **Michigan Appeals Reports** may be available. See list of used lawbook dealers in Appendix C.

Michigan Appeals Reports. 1965-date. St. Paul, MN: Thomson West. Previously published by Darby Printing Co. and Lawyers Cooperative. Current vol.: 293. West acquired state contract in 2004.
Cost: $3,120 (vols. 1-302); 2006: $107.88; 2007: $147.10; 2008: $61.64; 2009: $132.96; 2010: $38.88; 2011: $54.36; 2012: $244.44; 2013: $191.49; vols 1-301: $19.44 per vol.; latest vol. (302): $35.97; **Monthly Assured Print Pricing (APP):** $85/$1,020. Available used at considerable savings. See **Michigan Reports** above and list of used lawbook dealers in Appendix C. Note that the APP vastly exceeds actual cost.

West's North Western Reporter [1st] - **2d**. St. Paul, MN: Thomson West, 1879-date. Contain decisions of the Michigan Supreme Court from 1879-date and Michigan Court of Appeals from 1965-date. Current vol.: 844 **N.W. 2d**.
Cost: 1st series out-of-print (see used lawbook dealers in Appendix C); 2d series $10,225; used sets sell for approx. $3,795; annual cost (2013): $7,332; recent volume: $459/$611 (subscriber/list); **Monthly Assured Print Pricing (APP):** $709/$8,508.

West's North Western Reporter 2d. Advance Sheets. St. Paul, MN: Thomson West. Weekly.
Cost: $2,808 (discounted to bound volume subscribers) (2014).

Michigan Court Rules Annotated. Charlottesville, VA: LexisNexis. 2 vols. Softbound. Replaced annually, revised semiannually. Also available on ebook.
Cost: 2013 Edition: $146 (2014).

Michigan Rules of Court: State and Federal. St. Paul, MN: Thomson West. 2 vols. Annual. Also available on ProView eBook.
Cost: 2014 Edition: $168.

5. Digests, Encyclopedias and Practice Sets.

Michigan Civil Jurisprudence. St. Paul, MN: Thomson West, 1957-date. 33 vols. Annual pocket parts and periodic revised volumes. Originally published by Callaghan & Company (1957-1990).
Cost: $6,471; supplementation: 1994: $692.50; 1995: $692.50; 1996: $710; 1997: $855; 1998: $967; 1999: $1,120; 2000: $1,141.50; 2001: $1,431.50; 2002: $1,728.50; 2003: $1,772; 2004: $1,802; 2005: $1,954.50; 2006: $1,893.75; 2007: $2,331; 2008: $2,350; 2009: $2,711; 2010: $3,063.50; 2011: $3,430; 2012: $3,878; 2013: $4,622; **Monthly Assured Print Pricing (APP):** $391/$4,692; **Best value**: Acquire this and other major Michigan secondary sources on WestlawNext PRO for $2,268 per year.

Michigan Digest, 2d. St. Paul, MN: Thomson West, 1989-date. 94 vols. Annual pocket parts, mid-year supplement, and periodic revised volumes. Covers period of 1932 to date.
Cost: $5,333 (includes one year's updates); supplementation: 1996: $117;1997: $129; 1998: $307.50; 1999: $629.50; 2000: $443; 2001: $1,188; 2002: $1,158.25; 2003: $622; 2004: $906; 2005: $998.50; 2006: $1,665; 2007: $1,454; 2008: $1,492.50; 2009: $2,359.99; 2010: $2,814.50; 2011: $3,641; 2012: $2,035; 2013: $3,812; **Monthly Assured Print Pricing (APP):** $317/$3,804.

Michigan Digest. Charlottesville, VA: LexisNexis [formerly Callaghan], 1941-date. 20 vols. in 44. Annual pocket parts and periodic revised volumes. This title was sold to Reed Elsevier in January, 1997 after the Department of Justice negotiated a consent decree with the Thomson Corporation and West Publishing requiring the divestiture of 51 titles.
Cost: $2,614; supplementation: 2001: $399; 2003: $944; 2004: $1,015; 2005: $779; 2006: $667; 2007: $727; 2008: $1,509; 2009: $764; 2010: $1,387; 2011: 844; 2012: $978; 2013: $1,127.

Michigan Law and Practice. 2d ed. Charlottesville, VA: LexisNexis, 1955-date. 35 vols. Hardbound or ebook.
Cost: $2,516 (includes one year's updates); supplementation: 2003: $1,182; 2004: $1,249; 2005: $342; 2006: $819; 2007: $786; 2008: $765; 2009: $271; 2010: $846; 2011: $557; 2012: $612; 2013: $637.
This title was sold to Reed Elsevier in January, 1997 after the Department of Justice negotiated a consent decree with the Thomson Corporation and West Publishing requiring the divestiture of 51 titles.

Michigan Pleading and Practice. 2d ed. St. Paul, MN: Thomson West, 1946-date. 32 vols. Annual pocket parts and periodic revised volumes.
Cost: $4,484; supplementation: 1994: $738; 1995: $778; 1996: $605; 1997: $690; 1998: $855; 1999: $625; 2000: $663; 2001: $1,106; 2002: $1,235.50; 2003: $1,216.50; 2004: $1,271.75; 2005: $1,385.75; 2006: $1,943.50; 2007: $1,941.50; 2008: $1,916; 2009: $2,186.50; 2010: $2,387; 2011: $2,603; 2012: $2,837; 2013: $3,380; **Monthly Assured Print Pricing (APP):** $327/$3,924; Best value: Acquire this and other major Michigan secondary sources on WestlawNext PRO for $2,268 per year.

6. Citators.

Shepard's Michigan Citations. Albany, NY: Shepard's. Monthly or Bi-monthly.
Cost: $4,812 (12 bound volumes); all-inclusive subscription: monthly: $2,441 (in-state); bimonthly: $2,741 (in-state) (2014).

Online: All jurisdictional Shepard's and KeyCite are no longer available as stand-alone products, but are included as part of a jurisdictional or subject library package (2014).

7. CD-ROM Products.

LexisNexis CD for Michigan. Albany, NY: LexisNexis. Two discs. Updated quarterly. Contains the full text of decisions of the Michigan Supreme Court from 1899 to date, the Michigan Court of Appeals from 1965 to date, and the Michigan Statutes Annotated. Windows. Search Engine: Folio; LivePublish (NextPage). Subscription includes online updating via LEXIS.
Cost: $1,777 per year (2014).

Michigan Reporter. Eagan, MN: Thomson West. Two discs. Regular updates. Contains the full text of decisions of the Michigan Supreme Court from 1804 to date, Michigan Court of Appeals from 1942 to date, slip opinions, and Attorney General opinions from 1977 to date. Decisions also searchable by West Topics and Key Numbers, headnotes, and synopses. Windows and Macintosh versions available. Search Engine: PREMISE. Subscription includes online updating via Westlaw.
Cost: $7,605 per year (2014).

Michigan Reporter LawDesk CD-ROM ed.. Eagan, MN: Thomson West. Two discs. Regular updates. Contains the full text of decisions of the Michigan Supreme Court from 1899 to date, Michigan Court of Appeals from 1965 to date, slip opinions, and Attorney General opinions from 1977 to date. Decisions also searchable by West Topics and Key Numbers, headnotes, and synopses. Windows and Macintosh versions available. Search Engine: LawDesk (Folio). Subscription includes online updating via Westlaw.
Cost: $4,524 per year (2014).

8. State Legal Histories and Research Guides.
Tillman-Davis, Michael W., ed. **Michigan Legal Documents: A Bibliography of Legal and Law-Related Documents**. Chicago:AALL, 2006.
Cost: $30.00. Available from William S. Hein & Co. as electronic pdf or on HeinOnline (2014).

Fino, Susan P. **The Michigan State Constitution**. New York: Oxford University Press, 2011. 1 vol. (312 pp.).
Cost: $150.00; from $94.99 on amazon.com; kindle: $119.99 (2014).

The History of Michigan Law. Edited by Paul Finkleman and Martin J. Hershock. Athens, OH: Ohio University Press, 2006. 1 vol. (290 pp.).
Cost: $49.95; from $3.96 on amazon.com (2014).
A collection of articles on various aspects of Michigan legal history.

LeBlanc, Mary Ellen. **The Internet and Technology Guide for Michigan Lawyers**. Ann Arbor, MI: The Institute of Continuing Legal Education, 1999.

Lysaght, Pamela. **Michigan Legal Research**. 2d ed. Durham, NC: Carolina Academic Press, 2011. 1 vol. (144 pp.). Paperbound.
Cost: $25.00; from $18.70 on amazon.com (2014).

9. Leading Web Sites for State Law Research

Home Page:	www.michigan.gov/
Administrative Code:	www.michigan.gov/lara/0,4601,7-154-35738_5698---,00.html - OR - (link from Licensing and Regulatory Affairs below, then click on "Office of Regulatory Reinvention")
Agency Directory:	(link from Home Page above) - OR - www.michigan.gov/som/0,1607,7-192-29701_29702_30045---,00.html
Attorney General:	www.michigan.gov/ag
Attorney General Opinions:	(link from left side of Attorney General's page above)
Bar Association:	www.michbar.org/
Compiled Laws:	www.michiganlegislature.org/mileg.asp?page=MCLBasicSearch
Constitution:	http://legislature.mi.gov/doc.aspx?chapterindex – OR – (link from Legislative Branch below)
Court Opinions:	(link from Judicial Branch below)
Governor:	www.michigan.gov/gov
Judicial Branch:	http://courts.mi.gov
Legislative Branch:	www.legislature.mi.gov/
Licensing & Regulatory Affairs:	www.michigan.gov/lara
Michigan Legal Update:	www.icle.org/
Secretary of State:	www.michigan.gov/sos
Statues:	(link from Legislative Branch above)

10. Leading publishers of state specific treatises, practice books, and CLE publications.
Matthew Bender, LexisNexis, Michigan Bar Association, Michigan Institute of Continuing Legal Education, National Business Institute, M. Lee Smith, Thomson West. See Appendix B for addresses and telephone numbers.

Minnesota

1. Codes and Session Laws.
Minnesota Statutes [unannotated]. St. Paul, MN: Office of the Revisor of Statutes. 15 vols. Biennial in even-numbered years with pocket parts in odd-numbered years. Also available on CD-ROM (see below)
Cost: 2012 edition: $235 (includes supplement shipped in odd-numbered years at no extra charge); individual volumes: $47. State Bookstore: 651-297-3000; 800-657-3757.

Minnesota Statutes Annotated. St. Paul, MN: Thomson West, 1946-date. 52 vols. in 111. Annual pocket supplements and periodic revised volumes.
Cost: $7,429 (includes one year's revised volumes, pocket parts, and session laws); supplementation: 1996: $739; 1997: $861.50; 1998: $1,097.50; 1999: $1,128; 2000: $1,179; 2001: $1,526.75; 2002: $2098.75; 2003: $2,304; 2004: $2,870; 2005: $2,909.50; 2006: $3,052; 2007: $3,473; 2008: $2,236; 2009: $3,207.50; 2010: $3,815.50; 2011: $4,225; 2012: $4,633; 2013: $5,276; **Monthly Assured Print Pricing (APP):** $410/$4,920.

Laws of Minnesota [session law]. St. Paul, MN: Office of the Revisor of Statutes Office. Annual. Hardbound.
Cost: 1995: $43 (3 vols.); 1996: $30 (2 vols.); 1997: $45 (3 vols.); 1998: $35; 1999: $45.00; 2000: $35 (2 vols.); 2001: $40 (3 vols.); 2002: $40 (2 vols.); 2003 $40 (2 vols.); 2004: $30 (1 vol.); 2005: $40 (2 vols.); 2006: $30; 2007: $40; 2008: $40; 2009: $45 (2 vols.); 2010: $47.00 (2 vols.); 2011: $48.00; 2013: $52. State Bookstore: 651-297-3000; 800-657-3757.

Minnesota Session Law Service. St. Paul, MN: Thomson West These pamphlets are published during and immediately after each legislative session and contain text of laws in numerical chapter sequence in order of passage.
Cost: $971.04 per year (2014).

Legislative Hotline: (651) 296-6646 (House); (651) 296-0504 (Senate).

2. Administrative Law.
Minnesota Rules. St. Paul, MN: Office of the Revisor of Statutes, 1983-date. 11 vols. Softcover. Biennial editions in odd-numbered years with twice annual pocket parts in even numbered years. State Bookstore: 651-297-3000
Cost: 2013 edition: $275 (includes pocket parts between editions); individual volumes: $50.00 (2014).

Mi**nnesota State Register**. St. Paul, MN: Office of the State Register, 1977-date. Online only. Weekly. Orders to: Minnesota's Bookstore, 117 University Ave., St. Paul, MN 55155. 651-297-3000
Cost: Internet delivery: $180 per year (2014).
The Minnesota State Register is available on the Web at: www.comm.media.state.mn.us/bookstore/archives.asp. Solicitation Announcements are available at: www.mmd.admin.state.mn.us/solicitations.htm

3. Court Reports.
Minnesota Reporter. St. Paul, MN: Thomson West, 1978-date. [offprint of North Western Reporter 2d—official since 1978]. Contains the full text of decisions of the Minnesota Supreme Court from 1978 to date, and the Minnesota Court of Appeals from 1983 to date taken from the Northwestern Reporter 2d. Current volume: 836-839 N.W. 2d.
Cost: $3,358; annual cost: 2002: $503.50; 2003: $566.75; 2004: $693; 2005: $590; 2006: $602; 2007: $859.50; 2008: $753; 2009: $1,392.50; 2010: $1,392.50; 2011: $1,460; 2012: $1,752; 2013: $2,688; recent vol.: $504/$672 (subscriber/list); **Monthly Assured Print Pricing (APP):** $241/$2,892.

Minnesota Reports. 1851-1977. Vols. 1-312. [ceased publication with vol. 312—see Minnesota Reporter]
Cost: Out-of-print. Used sets approx. $1,800.00. See list of used lawbook dealers in Appendix C.

West's North Western Reporter [1st] - **2d**. St. Paul, MN: Thomson West, 1879-date. Contains decisions of the Minnesota Supreme Court from 1879-date and Minnesota Court of Appeals from 1983-date. [official since 1978]. Current vol.: 844 **N.W. 2d**.
Cost: 1st series out-of-print (see used lawbook dealers in Appendix C); 2d series $10,225; used sets sell for approx. $3,795; annual cost (2013): $7,332; recent volume: $459/$611 (subscriber/list); **Monthly Assured Print Pricing (APP):** $709/$8,508.

West's North Western Reporter 2d. Advance Sheets. St. Paul, MN: Thomson West. Weekly.
Cost: $2,808 (discounted to bound volume subscribers) (2014).

4. Court Rules.
Minnesota Rules of Court: State and Federal. St. Paul, MN: Thomson West. 2 vols. Annual. Also available on proView eBook.
Cost: 2014 Edition: $156.

5. Digests, Encyclopedias, and Practice Sets.
Dunnell Minnesota Digest. Charlottesville, VA: LexisNexis, 2001-date. 57 vols. Updated annually by pocket parts and five replacement volumes. An encyclopedic digest of Minnesota statutory and case law published since 1910 organized into 350 subject areas. The substance of each summary includes extensive caselaw references, concise statements of applicable black letter law, analysis of statutory and caselaw changes and their effect on prior rulings, appropriate administrative rules, regulations and decisions, and Attorney General opinions.
Cost: $1,868 (includes one year's service and replacement volumes at no additional charge); supplementation: 1995: $265; 1996: $295; 2000: $385; 2001; $579; 2002: $703. 2003: $828; 2004: $1,237; 2005: $749; 2006: $816; 2007: $1,439; 2008: $1,341; 2009: $831; 2010: $1,632; 2011: $1,824; 2012: $1,535; 2013: $1,224.

Minnesota Practice Series. St. Paul, MN: Thomson West. 54 vols.
Cost: $9,919 (but sold individually); supplementation: 1996: $522.75; 1997: $568.50; 1998: $827.65; 1999: $689; 2000: $745.75; 2001: $1,122; 2002: $1,123; 2003: $1,986.25; 2004: individual components updated separately. Best acquired as a part of **State Secondary Resources** add-on to a WestlawNext PRO subscription at considerable savings.

West's Minnesota Digest, 2d. St. Paul, MN: Thomson West, 1988-date. 89 vols. Annual pocket supplements and periodic revised volumes.
Cost: $6,824; supplementation: 1995: $242; 1996: $256.50; 1997: $288.50; 1998: $486; 1999: $397.75; 2000: $799; 2001: $872; 2002: $1,901.50; 2003: $1,069; 2004: $1,541; 2005: $1,432; 2006: $1,185; 2007: $1,717.50; 2008: $1,658.50; 2009: $2,302.50; 2010: $3,525; 2011: $3,735; 2012: $4,707; 2013: $5,498; **Monthly Assured Print Pricing (APP):** $391/$4,692. Used sets may be available.

6. Citators.
Shepard's Minnesota Citations. Albany, NY: Shepard's. Monthly.
Cost: $3,979 (6 bound volumes); all-inclusive subscription: $2,168 (in-state) (2014).

Online: All jurisdictional Shepard's and KeyCite are no longer available as stand-alone products, but are acquired as part of a jurisdictional or subject library package (2014).

7. CD-ROM Products.
Minnesota Reporter. Eagan, MN: Thomson West. One disc. Regular updates. Contains the full text of decisions of the Minnesota Supreme Court from 1851 to date, the Minnesota Court of Appeals from 1983 to date, unpublished Court of Appeals cases from 1987 to date, Tax Court from 1965 to date, and Attorney General opinions from 1977 to date. Decisions also searchable by West Topics and Key Numbers, headnotes and synopses. Windows and Macintosh versions. Search

Engine: PREMISE.
Cost: $8,202 per year (2014).

8. State Legal Research Guides.
Hackerson, Deborah K. **A Bibliography of Minnesota Legal Documents.** Chicago: AALL, 2010.
Cost: $30.00. Available from William S. Hein & Co. as electronic pdf or on HeinOnline (2014).

Garces, Vincente E. Minnesota Practice Materials: A Selective Bibliography in Houdek, Frank G., ed. **State Practice Materials: Annotated Bibliographies**. Buffalo, NY: William S. Hein & Co., Inc., 2002-date. 2 vols. Looseleaf format.
Cost: $195.00 (2014).

Morrison, Mary Jane. **The Minnesota State Constitution**. New York: Oxford University Press, 2013. 1 vol. (376 pp.).
Cost: $150.00; pre-order on amazon.com (2014).

Tessner, John., George R. Jackson and Brenda Wolfe. **Minnesota Legal Research Guide**. 2d ed. Buffalo, NY: W.S. Hein & Co., 2002.
Cost: $82.50; from $39.98 on amazon.com (2014).

Thorpe. Suzanne. **Minnesota Legal Research**. Durham, NC: Carolina Academic Press, 2010. 1 vol. (234 pp.). Paperbound.
Cost: $25.00; from $17.69 on amazon.com (2014).

9. Leading Web Sites for State Law Research.

Home Page:	http://mn.gov
Administrative Code:	www.revisor.mn.gov/rules/
Agency Directory:	(link from home page: Government, State Government)
Attorney General:	www.ag.state.mn.us/
Attorney General Opinions:	www.ag.state.mn.us/Resources/ResourcesAttGenOpinion.asp
Bar Association:	www.mnbar.org/
Constitution:	www.revisor.leg.state.mn.us/constitution/
Court Opinions – Court of Appeals:	www.mncourts.gov/?page=433
Court Opinions – Supreme Court:	www.mncourts.gov/?page=230
Governor:	http://mn.gov/governor/
Judicial Branch:	www.mncourts.gov
Law Library:	http://mn.gov/lawlib
Legislative Branch:	www.leg.state.mn.us/
Minnesota State Bookstore:	www.comm.media.state.mn.us/bookstore/
Secretary of State:	www.sos.state.mn.us/
Statutes:	www.revisor.mn.gov/statutes/

10. Leading publishers of state specific treatises, practice books, and CLE publications.
Advanced Legal Education of Hamline Law School, LexisNexis, Minnesota State Bar Association CLE, Minnesota Institute of Legal Education, National Business Institute, Thomson Reuters West.

Mississippi

1. Statutes and Session Laws.
West's Annotated Mississippi Code. St. Paul, MN: Thomson West, 1998-date. 51 vols. Annual pocket parts and periodic revised volumes. Now an unofficial code since the state's adoption of the LEXIS code in 1998.
Cost: $2,042; supplementation: 2000: $97; 2001: $119; 2002: $131.25; 2003: $279.50; 2004: $314; 2005: $433.50; 2006: $476; 2007: $628; 2008: $654.50; 2009: $862; 2010: $1,090.50; 2011: $1,141; 2012: $1,277; 2013: $1,660; **Monthly Assured Print Pricing (APP):** $139/$1,668.

Mississippi Code of 1972 Annotated. Charlottesville, VA: LexisNexis, 1998-date. 33 vols. Annual pocket parts and periodic revised volumes. The official state code since 1998.
Cost: $613 (in-state), $918 (out-of-state); supplementation (in-state/out-of-state): 2001: $261/$532; 2002: $268/$549; 2003: $253.50/$506; 2004: $318/$634; 2005: $263/$490; 2006: $258/$431; 2007: $272/$454; 2008: $229/$372; 2009: $268/$412; 2010: $332/$546; 2011: $371.50/$687; 2012: $409/$810; 2013: $419 (in-state).

General Laws of Mississippi [session laws]. Jackson, MS: Secretary of State, Education & Publications Division. 2-3 vols. Annual. Call: (601) 359-6344
Cost: 1994: $60; 1995: $60; 1996: $90; 1997: $100; 1998: $95; 1999: $70.00; 2000: $59.85; 2001: $68.87 2002: $74.09; 2003: $61.03; 2004: $69.04; 2005: $61.32; 2006: $63.12; 2007: $63.12; 2008: $31.37; 2009: $72.48; 2010: $238.78; 2011: $196.85; 2012: $196.85.

West's Mississippi Legislative Service. St. Paul, MN: Thomson West. These pamphlets are published for legislative session and contain text of laws in order of passage.
Cost: $94.08 per year (2014), or no charge with West's Annotated Mississippi Code.

Mississippi Advance Code Service. Charlottesville, VA: LexisNexis. These pamphlets update the annual pocket parts and contain current case annotations.
Cost: $26 per year (in-state) (2014).

Mississippi Advance Legislative Service. Charlottesville, VA: LexisNexis. These pamphlets are published during and after each legislative session and contain the full text of laws in numerical chapter sequence in the order of passage. Also available in ebook.
Cost: $16 per year (in-state) (2014).

Legislative Hotline: (601) 359-3719, (601) 359-3358, (601) 359-3229.

2. Administrative Law.
Code of Mississippi Rules. Albany, NY: LexisNexis Matthew Bender [formerly Weil Publishing Co.], 1999-date. 19 vols.

Updated monthly.
Cost: $3,292 (includes 11 months of updates) ; annual renewal: 2001: $1,200; 2002: $1,200; 2003: $1,200; 2004: $1,200; 2005: $1,260; 2006: $1,260; 2007: $1,260; 2008: $1,418; 2009: $1,504; 2010: $1,579; 2011: $1,658; 2012: $1,75; 2013: $1,880; 2014: $2,052.

Mississippi Government Register. Newark, NJ: LexisNexis Matthew Bender 1997-date. Monthly.
Cost: $1,257; renewal: 2014; $1,143.

3. Court Reports.
Mississippi Cases. St. Paul, MN: Thomson West, 1966-date. [offprint of Southern Reporter 2d-3d—official since 1966]. Contains decisions of the Mississippi Supreme Court from 1966 to date. Recent vol.: 99-101 So.3d.
Cost: $2,434; 3d: $1,766; annual cost of bound volumes: 2003: $904; 2004: $797.80; 2005: $923; 2006: $996; 2007: $839; 2008: $884; 2009: $447.50; 2010: $957.50; 2011: $1,102; 2012: $1,252; 2013: $1,376; cost of recent vol.: $73.50/$98.00 (subscriber/list).

Mississippi Reports. 1818-1966 [Ceased publication with vol. 254].
Cost: Used sets available for approx. $1,600.00.

Southern Reporter [1st] - **2d**. St. Paul, MN: Thomson West, 1886-date. Contains decisions of the Mississippi Supreme Court from 1886 to date, and Mississippi Court of Appeals from 1995 to date, as well as other Southern regional appellate court decisions. Current vol.: 105 So.3d
Cost: 1st series out-of-print (see used lawbook dealers); 2d series: $14,566; 3d series: $17,639; annual cost (2013): $12,178; current vol.: $529/$706 (subscriber/list); **Monthly Assured Print Pricing** (**APP**): $1,274/$15,288. See list of used lawbook dealers in Appendix C.

Southern Reporter 2d. Advance sheets. St. Paul, MN: Thomson West. Weekly.
Cost: $2,866.56 per year (discounted to bound volume subscribers) (2014).

4. Court Rules.
Mississippi Court Rules Annotated. Charlottesville, VA: LexisNexis. 1 vol.
Cost: 2013 Edition: $38.50 (in-state) (2014).

Mississippi Rules of Court, State and Federal. St. Paul, MN: Thomson West. 2 vols. Annual.
Cost: 2013 Edition: $182 (2014).

5. Digests, Encyclopedias and Practice Sets.
Encyclopedia of Mississippi Law. St. Paul, MN: Thomson West, 2001-date. 12 vols. This 12-volume work replaces **Summary of Mississippi Law**, first published in 1969.
Cost: $977; supplementation: 2002: $220; 2003: $560; 2004: $133; 2005: $167.50; 2006: $138.50; 2007: $975; 2008: $171.50; 2009: $208; 2010: $229; 2011: $250; 2012: $274; 2013: $318; **Monthly Assured Print Pricing (APP):** $42/$504.

Mississippi Digest. St. Paul, MN: Thomson West, 1937-date. 71 vols. Annual pocket parts and periodic revised volumes.
Cost: $5,261; supplementation: 1995: $183.50; 1996: $178; 1997: $197.50; 1998: $326; 1999: $479.50; 2000: $381; 2001: $1,013.50; 2002: $1,159.50; 2003: $1,296; 2004: $884.25; 2005: $1,083.50; 2006: $839.50; 2007: $1,368; 2008: $1,815.50; 2009: $1,898; 2010: $1,465.50; 2011: $2,468.50; 2012: $3,903; 2013: $3,141; **Monthly Assured Print Pricing (APP):** $312/$3,744.

6. Citators.
Shepard's Mississippi Citations. Albany, NY: Shepard's. Monthly.
Cost: $2,690 (3 bound volumes); all-inclusive subscription: $2,168 (in-state) (2014).

Online: All jurisdictional Shepard's and KeyCite are no longer available as stand-alone products, but are included as part of a jurisdictional or subject library package from their respecxtive publishers (2014).

7. CD-ROM Products.
LexisNexis CD – Mississippi Primary Law. Charlottesville, VA: LexisNexis. One disc. Updated quarterly. Contains the full text of the Mississippi Code of 1972 Annotated, decisions of the Alabama Supreme Court from 1944-date, Court of Appeals from 1996-date, and state court rules.
Cost: $910 per year (2014).

Mississippi Cases and West's Mississippi Code. Eagan, MN: Thomson West. One disc. Regular updates. Contains the full text of the decisions of the Mississippi Supreme Court from 1886 to date, slip opinions, Mississippi Attorney General opinions from 1977-date, West's Mississippi Code, State Constitution, session laws, and court rules. Decisions also searchable by West Topics and Key Numbers, headnotes and synopses. Windows, and Macintosh versions available. Search Engine: PREMISE and LawDesk (Folio).
Cost: $10,830 per year (2014).

8. State Legal Research Guides.
Cole, Ben. **Mississippi Legal Documents and Related Publications: A Selective Bibliography**. Chicago: AALL, 1987.
Cost: $30.00. Available from William S. Hein & Co. as electronic pdf and on HeinOnline (2014).

Gilliland, Kris and Jason Derrick. **Mississippi Legal Research**. 2d ed. Durham, NC: Carolina Academic Press, 2014. 1 vol.
Cost: Forthcoming: $30.00 (2014).

Klingen, Anne M. Mississippi Practice Materials: A Selective Bibliography in Houdek, Frank G., ed. **State Practice Materials: Annotated Bibliographies**. Buffalo, NY: William S. Hein & Co., Inc., 2002-date. 2 vols. Looseleaf format.
Cost: $195.00 (2014).

Morrison, Mary Jane. **The Mississippi State Constitution**. New York: Oxford University Press, 2013. 1 vol. (212 pp.).
Cost: $150.00; from $138.76 on amazon.com (2013).

9. Leading Web Sites for State Law Research.

Home Page:	www.mississippi.gov/
Administrative Code:	www.sos.ms.gov/regulation_and_enforcement_admin_procedures3.aspx
Agency Directory:	www.ms.gov/agency_directory/default.aspx
Attorney General:	www.ago.state.ms.us/
Attorney General Opinions:	http://government.westlaw.com/msag/
Bar Association:	www.msbar.org/
Constitution:	www.sos.state.ms.us/ed_pubs/Constitution/2007/Mississippi Constitution.pdf
Court Opinions – Court of Appeals:	http://courts.ms.gov/appellate_courts/coa/coadecisions.html
Court Opinions – Supreme Court:	http://courts.ms.gov/appellate_courts/sc/scdecisions.html
Governor:	www.governorbryant.com/
Judicial Branch:	http://courts.ms.gov/
Law Library:	http://courts.ms.gov/state_library/statelibrary.html ???
Legal Forms Online:	www.formspass.com/msbar/
Legislative Branch:	www.legislature.ms.gov
Secretary of State:	www.sos.ms.gov/
Statutes:	www.michie.com/mississippi

10. Leading publishers of state specific treatises, practice books, and CLE publications.
Mississippi State Bar, National Business Institute, Thomson Reuters West, University of Mississippi Center for Continuing Legal Education. See Appendix B for addresses and telephone numbers.

Missouri

1. Codes and Session Laws.
Missouri Revised Statutes. Jefferson City, MO: Legislative Research, 1994-date. 20 vols. Hardbound. With cumulative supplements in intervening years.
New edition anticipated.
Cost: 2000 ed.: $300; cumulative supplement set: 2001: $22; 2002; $30; 2003: $40; 2004: $40; 2005: $50; 2006: $55; 2007: $75; 2008: $75.00; 2009: $75; 2010: $100; 2011: $100; 2012: $100; 2013: $100 (7 vols.); Legislative Research: (573) 751-4223.

Vernon's Annotated Missouri Statutes. St. Paul, MN: Thomson West, 1951-date. 46 vols. in 83. Annual pocket parts and periodic revised volumes.
Cost: $4,598; supplementation: 1996: $604; 1997: $538.50; 1998: $744; 1999: $745.75; 2000: $995.25; 2001: $1,335.75; 2003: $1,506; 2004: $550; 2005: $1,115; 2006: $1,205; 2007: $1687; 2008: $1,493; 2009: $1,996.50; 2010: $2,256.50; 2011: $2,690.50; 2012: $2,932.50; 2013: $3,491; **Monthly Assured Print Pricing (APP):** $359/$4,308.

Laws of Missouri [session laws]. Jefferson City, MO: Legislative Research. 1 vol. Annual. Also available online at: http://www.moga.mo.gov/
Cost: 2000: $15; 2001: $14; 2002: $16.50; 2003: $16.50; 2004: $18; 2005: $18; 2006: $18; 2007-2012: $18; 2013: $18. (573) 751-4223

Missouri Legislative Service. St. Paul, MN: Thomson West. These pamphlets are published during and immediately after current legislative session and contain the text of laws in numerical chapter order sequence in order of passage.
Cost: $683.52 per year (2014).

Legislative Hotline: (573) 751-4633.

2. Administrative Law.
Missouri Code of State Regulations Annotated. Jefferson City, MO: Administrative Rules Division, 1988-date. 14 vols. Looseleaf format. Updated monthly. (573) 751-4015.
Cost: $330 (2014) (includes all future supplements, with no additional cost as long as you own the set).
Also available at no charge on the Internet at: http://mosl.sos.state.mo.us

Missouri Register. Jefferson City, MO: Administrative Rules Division, 1976-date. Semi-monthly. (573) 751-4015
Cost: $56 per year; $5.00 for individual issues (2014).
http://www.sos.mo.gov/adrules/moreg/moreg.asp

3. Court Reports.
Missouri Cases. [1st] – **3d**. 1886-date. St. Paul, MN: Thomson West, 1902-date. [offprint of South Western Reporter—official since 1956]. Contains decisions of Missouri Supreme Court from 1886 to date and Missouri Appeals Court from 1902 to date. Current volume: 411-413 **SW 3d**.
Cost: 1st series: $999; 2d series: $5,815; 3d series: $6,710 ; annual upkeep: 2003: $611.50; 2004: $1,100; 2005: $1,211.50; 2006: $1,345; 2007: $1,692; 2008: $1,489.50; 2009: $1,702.50; 2010: $2,412.50; 2011: $2,336; 2012: $3,505; 2013: $5,535; recent vol.: $503.25/$671 (subscriber/ist); **Monthly Assured Print Pricing (APP):** $466/$5,592; used sets may be available.

Missouri Reports. 1821-1956. vols. 1-365 [ceased publication with vol. 365].
Cost: Out-of-print. See list of used lawbook dealers in Appendix C.

Missouri Appeals Reports.1876-1954. [ceased publication with vol. 241].
Cost: Out-of-print. See list of used lawbook dealers in Appendix C.

South Western Reporter [1st] – **3d**. St. Paul, MN: Thomson West, 1886-date. Contains decisions of the Missouri Supreme Court from 1886-date, and Missouri Court of Appeals from 1902-

date. [official for Missouri Supreme Court since 1956 and for Missouri Appeals Court since 1952]. Current vol.: 420 S.W. 3d.
Cost: 1st series: out-of-print (see used lawbook dealers in Appendix C); 2d series: $12,480; used sets sell for approx. $2,300; 3d series: $20,134; used sets sell for approx. $1,500; annual cost (2013): $15,615; current volume: $520.50/$694 (subscriber/list); **Monthly Assured Print Pricing (APP):** $1,399/$16,788. See used lawbook dealers in Appendix C.

South Western 3d. Advance sheets. St. Paul, MN: Thomson West. Weekly.
Cost: $2,799 per year (discounted to bound volume subscribers) (2014).

4. Court Rules.
Missouri Court Rules: State and Federal. St. Paul, MN: West. 2 vols. Annual. Paperbound. Also available on ProView eBook.
Cost: 2014 Edition: $155; with Circuit Courts: $243 (2014).

Vernon's Annotated Missouri Rules. St. Paul, MN: Thomson West. 9 vols. Annual pocket supplements.
Cost: $582; supplementation: 1996: $71; 1997: $150.50; 1998: $125.50; 1999: $247; 2000: $92.50; 2001: $106.75; 2002: $676; 2004: $151; 2005: $170; 2006: $195; 2007: $389.50; 2008: $242; 2009: $273; 2010: $312; 2011: $340; 2012: $371; 2013: $404; **Monthly Assured Print Pricing (APP)**: $43/$516.

5. Digests, Encyclopedias, and Practice Sets.
Missouri Digest 2d. St. Paul, MN: Thomson West,1983-date. 140 vols. Annual pocket supplements and periodic revised volumes.
Cost: $7,953; supplementation: 1996: $205.50; 1997: $317; 1998: $599.25; 1999: $839.25; 2000: $1,076; 2001: $1,857; 2002: $2,657; 2003: $722.50; 2004: $621; 2005: $1,401; 2006: $1,333.50; 2007: $2,896; 2008: $2,222; 2009: $2,597; 2010: $3,047.50; 2011: $3,626.50; 2012: $3,412; 2013: $6,172; **Monthly Assured Print Pricing (APP):** $397/$4,764. No longer available on CD-ROM.

Missouri Practice Series. St. Paul, MN: Thomson West, 1961-date. 57 vols. Annual pocket parts and periodic revised volumes.
Cost: $10,846 (but sold individually); supplementation: 1996: $371.50; 1997: $782; 1998: $484.50; 1999: $1,193.55; 2000: $2,052.25; 2001: $1,985; 2003: $2,254.50; 2004: see also supp. costs for individual components. Sold as a set or individually. Various titles and authors. See publisher for details. The CD-ROM version has been discontinued. Best acquired as a part of **State Secondary Resources** add-on to a WestlawNext PRO subscription at considerable savings.

6. Citators.
Shepard's Missouri Citations. Albany, NY: Shepard's. Monthly.
Cost: $4,354 (7 bound volumes); all-inclusive subscription: $2,273 (in-state) (2014).

Online: All jurisdictional Shepard's $75.00 per month ($900/yr.); All jurisdictional KeyCite on Westlaw: $70.00 per month ($840/yr.) (2013).

7. CD-ROM Products.
Missouri Cases (West's). Eagan, MN: Thomson West. Two discs. Quarterly updates. Contains the full text of decisions of the Missouri Supreme Court from 1886-date, Missouri of Appeals Court from 1944 to date, and Attorney General opinions from 1977 to date. Decisions also searchable by West Topics and Key Numbers, headnotes and synopses. Windows, and Macintosh versions available. Search Engine: PREMISE. Subscription includes online updating via Westlaw.
Cost: $10,572 per year (2014).

8. State Legal Research Guides.
Nelson, Mary Ann. **Guide to Missouri State Documents and Selected Law-Related Materials**. Chicago: AALL, 1991.
Cost: $30.00. Available from William S. Hein & Co. as electronic pdf and on HeinOnline (2014).

Temma, Wanda M. and Julie M. Cheslik. **Missouri Legal Research.** 2d ed. Durham, NC: Carolina Academic Press, 2011. 1 vol. (240 pp.).
Cost: $27.00; from $11.94 on amazon.com (2014).

9. Leading Web Sites for State Law Research.

Home Page:	www.mo.gov/
Administrative Code:	www.sos.mo.gov/adrules/
Agency Directory:	www.mo.gov/my-government/state-agencies/
Attorney General:	www.ago.mo.gov/
Attorney General Opinions:	www.ago.mo.gov/opinions/
Bar Association:	www.mobar.org/
Constitution:	www.moga.mo.gov/const/moconstn.htm
Court Opinions:	www.courts.mo.gov/page.jsp?id=1944
Governor:	www.governor.mo.gov
Judicial Branch:	www.courts.mo.gov/
Law Library – Supreme Court:	www.courts.mo.gov/page.jsp?id=218
Legal Resources:	www.courts.mo.gov/page.jsp?id=1073
Legislative Branch:	www.moga.mo.gov
Secretary of State:	www.sos.mo.gov/
Statutes:	www.moga.mo.gov/statutes/statutes.htm

10. Leading publishers of state specific treatises, practice books, and CLE publications.
LexisNexis, Missouri Bar CLE, National Business Institute, University of Missouri at Kansas City Continuing Legal Education, Thomson Reuters (West), Wolters Kluwer Law & Business. See Appendix B for addresses and telephone numbers.

Montana

1. Codes and Session Laws.
West's Montana Code Annotated. St. Paul, MN: West, 2009-date.
42 vols. Hardbound. Includes annual pocket parts and periodic revised volumes. Original hardbound volumes current through 2008; pocket parts provide coverage of 2009 legislative session.
Cost: $492; supplementation: 2009: $177 (pocket parts only); 2010: $201; 2011: $229; 2012: $254; 2013: $269; **Monthly Assured Print Pricing (APP):** $26/$312.

Montana Code Annotated. Helena: Montana Legislative Services Division, 1978-date. Republished in odd-numbered years. 12 vols. Looseleaf. (406) 444-3064.
Cost: 2013 Edition: $390 ($340 to govt. & nonprofits); $38 per volume; 2012 annotations: $400. Annotations (13 vols.) published in even-numbered years. 2013/14 CD-ROM package version also available at cost of $175 (includes the 2013 Codes and 2014 annotations) (2014).

Montana Code Annotated Annotations. Helena: Montana Legislative Services Division. CD-ROM. Updated in even years.
Cost: 2013/2014 Package of MCA & Annotations to the MCA on CD-ROM: $325; Annotations alone: $175; CD-ROM of MCSA alone: $175 (2014).

Laws of Montana. Helena: Montana Legislative Council. Published in odd-numbered years (after legislative session).
Cost: 1995: $80 (4 vols.); 1997: $60; 1999: $60; 2001: $95; 2003: $95 (3 vols.); 2005: $95 (3 vols.); 2007: $95 (3 vols.); 2009: $95.00 (3 vols.); 2011: $95.00 (3 vols.); 2013: $95 (3 vols.).

Legislative Hotline: (406) 444-4800, (406) 444-3064.

2. Administrative Law.
Administrative Rules of Montana. Helena: Secretary of State, 197?-date. 29 vols. Looseleaf format. Quarterly updates.
Cost: $500 + $300 for first year's quarterly updates; supplementation: $300 per year (2014). (406) 444-2034

Montana Administrative Register. Helena: Secretary of State, 1977-date. Bi-monthly. Published on calendar year basis.
Cost: $325 per year (2014).

3. Court Reports.
Montana Reports. Helena: State Reporter Publishing Co. [now part of LexisNexis], 1868-date. Approx. 5-6 vols. published per year. Current vol.: 372. 800-877-9345
Cost: $79 each (vols.194 to date) with discount for larger quantities; earlier volumes also available (2014).

Montana State Reporter. Helena: State Reporter Publishing Co. [part of LexisNexis], 1973-date. Biweekly. [Advance reporter for the Montana Reports].
Cost: $410 per year (2014).

Pacific Reporter [1st] - **3d**. St. Paul, MN: Thomson West, 1883-date. Contains decisions of the Montana Supreme Court from 1883-date. Current vol.: 314 **P. 3d**.
Cost: 1st series out-of-print (see used lawbook dealers in Appendix C); 2d series: $13,428; used sets approx. $2000; 3d series: $15,201; annual cost (2013): $11,396; individual volume: $518/$691 (subscriber/list); **Monthly Assured Print Pricing (APP):** $1,141/$11,369; used sets may be available.

Pacific Reporter 3d. Advance sheets. St. Paul, MN: Thomson West. Weekly.
Cost: $2,866.56 per year (discounted to bound volume subscribers) (2014).

4. Court Rules
Montana Rules of Court: State and Federal. St. Paul, MN: Thomson West. Annual. 2 vols.
Cost: 2014 Edition: $322 (2014).

5. Digests, Encyclopedias and Practice Sets.
Montana Digest. St. Paul, MN: Thomson West, 1937-date. 10 vols. in 48. Annual pocket parts and periodic revised volumes.
Cost: $3,853; supplementation: 1994: $229; 1996: $244.50; 1997: $224.50; 1998: $445; 1999: $426.50; 2000: $580; 2001: $758; 2002: $1,132; 2003: $515; 2004: $538.50; 2005: $1,019; 2006: $983; 2007: $613.50; 2008: $1,073; 2009: $780; 2010: $1,287; 2011: $2,651; 2012: $2,651; 2013: $1,821; **Monthly Assured Print Pricing (APP):** $229/$2,748.

6. Citators
Shepard's Montana Citations. Albany, NY: Shepard's. Six supplements per year.
Cost: $1,434 (3 bound volumes); all-inclusive subscription: $1,712 (in-state) (2014).

Online: All jurisdictional Shepard's and KeyCite are no longer available as stand-alone products, but are included as part of a jurisdictional or subject library package (2014).

7. CD-ROM Products.
Administrative Rules of Montana and Montana Reports Plus. Helena, MT: State Reporter Publishing Co. [part of LexisNexis] One disc. Quarterly updates. Contains the full text of the Administrative Rules of Montana and Miontana decisions from 1868 to date. Available for Windows, and Macintosh. Search Engine: Folio.
Cost: $1,688 per year (2014)

MCA on CD-ROM. Helena: Montana Legislative Services Division. One disc. Updated annually. Contains the full text of the Montana Code Annotated and Annotations; current release contains the 2011 Code with 2010 Annotations, Available for Windows only. Search Engine: Folio.
Cost: $175; 2013/2014 package: $325/$175 (2014)

Montana Reporter and Montana Code Annotated. Eagan, MN: Thomson West. One disc. Regular updates. Contains the full text of decisions of the Montana Supreme Court from 1868 to date, Attorney General opinion from 1977 to date, Montana Code Annotated, State Constitution, session laws and court rules and orders. Decisions also searchable by West Topics and Key Numbers, headnotes and synopses. Windows and Macintosh versions available. Search Engine: PREMISE.

Subscription includes online updating via Westlaw.
Cost: $7,287 per year (2014).

8. State Legal Research Guides.

Chansler, Margaret Ann. **Montana State Documents: A Bibliography of Legal and Law-Related Material**. Chicaho: American Association of Law Libraries, Government Documents SIS, 2004. 1 vol.
Cost: $30.00. Available from William S. Hein & Co. and on Hein Online (2012).

Elison, Larry M. and Fritz Snyder. **The Montana State Constitution**. New York: Oxford University Press, 2011. 1 vol. (284 pp.).
Cost: $150.00; from $80.03 on amazon.com; kindle: $119.99 (2014).

Jordan, Stephen R. "Montana Practice Materials: A Selective Annotated Bibliography." Series on State Practice Materials, **Law Library Journal** 84, No. 2 (1992): 299-313.

Whelan, Robert K., Meredity Hoffman, and Stephen R. Jordan. **A Guide to Montana Legal Research**. 8th ed. Helena: State Law Library of Montana, 2003.
Available at no cost at: http://courts.mt.gov/content/library/guides/guide.pdf

9. Leading Web Sites for State Law Research.

Home Page:	www.mt.gov/
Administrative Code:	www.mtrules.org
Agency Directory:	www.mt.gov/govt/agencylisting.asp
Attorney General:	http://doj.mt.gov/
Attorney General Opinions:	http://doj.mt.gov/agooffice/attorney-generals-opinions/
Bar Association:	www.montanabar.org/
Constitution:	http://data.opi.mt.gov/bills/mca_toc/Constition.htm ???
Court Opinions – Supreme Court:	www.searchcourts.mt.gov
Governor:	www.governor.mt.gov/
Judicial Branch:	www.courts.mt.gov
Law Library:	www.courts.mt.gov/library/
Legislative Branch:	www.leg.mt.gov/css
Secretary of State:	www.sos.mt.gov/
Statutes:	www.leg.mt.gov/css/Laws and Constitution/
Supreme Court:	www.courts.mt.gov/supreme

10. Leading publishers of state specific treatises, practice books, and CLE publications.

LexisNexis, National Business Institute, State Bar of Montana, Thomson Reuters West, University of Montana School of Law.

See Appendix B for addresses and telephone numbers

Nebraska

1. Codes and Session Laws.

Nebraska Revised Statutes. Lincoln, NE: Revisor of Statutes, 1943-date. 6 vols. in 14.
Cost: $334 + postage & shipping; supplementation & index: 2006: $50; 2007: $90; 2008: $100; 2009: $30.00; 2010: $40.00; 2011: $43; 2012: $105; 2013: $54. Available from Nebraska State Library Publications Office (402) 471-3189.

Revised Statutes of Nebraska Annotated. Charlottesville, VA: LexisNexis, 1995-date. 25 vols. Annual pocket parts and periodic revised volumes.
Cost: $1,008 (includes one year's updates); supplementation (in-state/out-of-state): 2002: $405/$451; 2003: $412/ $465; 2004: $579/$648; 2005: $423/$474; 2006: $197/$219; 2007: $637; 2008: $690/$774; 2009: $638/$717; 2010: $1,071/$1,099; 2011: $1,132; 2012: $630/$716.

West's Revised Statutes of Nebraska Annotated. St. Paul, MN: West, 2009-date. 42 vols. Annual pocket parts and periodic revised volumes.
Cost: $870; supplementation: 2009: $99.00; 2010: $281; 2011: $326; 2012: $342; 2013: $371; **Monthly Assured Print Pricing (APP):** $39/$468.

Nebraska Advance Code Service. Charlottesville, VA: LexisNexis. Supplements code between annual pocket parts.
Cost: $86 per year (2013).

Laws of Nebraska [session laws]. Lincoln, NE: State Publishing Co.
Cost: 1995-2013: $15 per year. Available from Available from Nebraska State Library Publications Office (402) 471-3189.

Legislative Hotline: (402) 471-2709, (402) 471-2271.

2. Administrative Law.

Nebraska Administrative Rules and Regulations. Lincoln, NE: Legislative Council, 1983-date. 35 vols. Looseleaf. Updated monthly. Also available online at: http://www.sos.ne.gov/rules-and-regs/regsearch/
Cost: $1000; supplementation: complete: $500 per year; major changes only: $350 per year (2014). (402) 471-2554

No Register. Updates made to **Nebraska Administrative Rules and Regulations**.

3. Court Reports.

Nebraska Reports. Lincoln, NE: Administrative Office of the Courts, 1860-date. Current vol.: 274. Available from Available from Nebraska State Library Publications Office (402) 471-3189.
Cost: $82.50 ea. (last 4 vols.); those published in last 10 years: $40 ea.; those older than 10 years: $10 ea.; advance sheets: $190 ($210 after June 30).

Nebraska Court of Appeals Decisions. Lincoln NE: Administrative Office of the Courts, 1994-date. Current vol.: 15. Available from Available from Nebraska State Library Publications Office (402) 471-3189.
Cost: $82.50 ea. (last 4 vols.); those published within last 10 years: $40 ea.; those older than 10 years: $10 ea.; advance sheets: $175 ($192 after June 30).

Nebraska Advance Sheets. Lincoln NE: Administrative Office of the Court. Published weekly from July 1 to June 30, except during recess of the court. An advance publication to the **Nebraska Reports**.
Cost: $200 per year ($220 after July 1); $365 ($420 after July 1) for combination subscription to the **Decisions of the Nebraska Court of Appeals** and the **Nebraska Advance Sheets**. (402) 471-3730.

Decisions of the Nebraska Court of Appeals [Advance sheets]. Lincoln NE: Administrative Office of the Court, 1992-date. Published weekly from July 1 to June 30, except during recess of the court. An advance publication to the **Nebraska Court of Appeals Reports**.
Cost: $220 per year ($220 after June 30); $365 ($420 after July 1) for combination subscription to the **Decisions of the Nebraska Court of Appeals** and **Nebraska Advance Sheets**. (402) 471-3730.

West's North Western Reporter [1st] - **2d**. St. Paul, MN: West, 1879-date. Contains decisions of the Nebraska Supreme Court from 1879-date and Nebraska Court of Appeals from 1992-date. Current vol.: 844 **N.W. 2d**.
Cost: 1st series out-of-print (see used lawbook dealers in Appendix C); 2d series $10,225; used sets sell for approx. $3,795; annual cost (2013): $7,332; recent volume: $459/$611 (subscriber/list); **Monthly Assured Print Pricing (APP):** $709/$8,508.

West's North Western Reporter 2d. Advance Sheets. St. Paul, MN: Thomson West. Weekly.
Cost: $2,808 (discounted to bound volume subscribers) (2014).

4. Court Rules.

Nebraska Court Rules and Procedure, State and Federal. St. Paul, MN: West Annual.
Cost: 2014 Edition: $220; ProView eBook: $213 (2014).

Nebraska Rules of Court Annotated. Charlottesville, VA: LexisNexis. 1 vol. Softbound. Updated semiannually, replaced annually.
Cost: 2014 Edition: $136.

5. Digests, Encyclopedias and Practice Sets.

West's Nebraska Digest 2d. St. Paul, MN: Thomson West, 1995-date. 71 vols. Annual pocket parts and periodic revised volumes.
Cost: $3,689 (up 27% from 2013); supplementation: 1996: $50; 1997: $69; 1998: $158; 1999: $256.50; 2000: $321.50; 2001: $94.50; 2002: $655.50; 2003: $541; 2004: $296.50; 2005: $723; 2006: $518; 2007: $577; 2008: $728; 2009: $1,081; 2010: $967; 2011: $1,405; 2012: $1,237; 2013: $2,884; **Monthly Assured Print Pricing (APP):** $172/$2,064.

6. Citators.

Shepard's Nebraska Citations. Albany, NY: Shepard's. Monthly.
Cost: $2,218 (4 bound volumes); all-inclusive subscription: $1,912 (in-state) (2014).

Online: All jurisdictional Shepard's and KeyCite are no longer available as stand-alone products, but are included as part of a jurisdictional or subject library from their respective publishers (2014).

7. CD-ROM Products.

Nebraska Reporter and Nebraska Revised Statutes. Eagan, MN: West. One disc. Regular updates. Contains the full text of decisions of the Nebraska Supreme Court from 1871 to date, Nebraska Court of Appeals from vol.1 North Western Reporter 2d, unpublished decisions from 1992 to date, Attorney General opinions from 1976 to date; also Nebraska Revised Statutes, State Constitution, session laws, court rules and orders. Decisions also searchable by West Topics and Key Numbers, headnotes and synopses. DOS, Windows, and Macintosh versions available. Search Engine: PREMISE. On-line link to Nebraska materials on Westlaw provided at no additional charge.
Cost: $6,507 per year (2014).

8. State Legal Research Guides.

Butterfield, George, Mastthew Novak, and Brian Striman. **Nebraska State Bibliography of Legal Resources Annotated: A Selective Bibliography**.
Chicago: American Association of Law Libraries, Government Documents SIS, 2012. Electronic pdf and on HeinOnline. Available from William S. Hein & Co.
Cost: $30.00. (2014).

Charles, Patrick J., Kay L. Andrus, Ana Marie Hinman, and Ann C. Kitchel. **LexisNexis's Research Guide to Nebraska Law**. Charlottesville, VA: LexisNexis, 2006. 1 vol. (143 pp.).
Cost: distributed to purchasers of the Revised Statutes of Nebraska Annotated.

Gless, Alan G., ed. **The History of Nebraska Law**. Athens, OH: Ohio University Press, 2008. 1 vol. (318 pp.).
Cost: $49.95; from $32.00 on amazon.com (2014).

Miewald, Robert D., et al. **The Nebraska State Constitution: A Reference Guide**. 2d ed. Lincoln, NE: University of Nebraska Press, 2010. 1 vol. (460 pp.).
Cost: $50.00; from $30.85 on amazon.com (2014).

Smith, Beth. Nebraska Practice Materials: A Selective Bibliography in Houdek, Frank G., ed. **State Practice Materials: Annotated Bibliographies**. Buffalo, NY: William S. Hein & Co., Inc., 2004-date. 2 vols. Looseleaf format.
Cost: $195.00 (2014).

Wise, Sally H. and Patricia A. Cervenka. "Legal Research Tools for the Nebraska Practitioner: An Annotated Bibliography."

Nebraska Law Review 70, No. 3 (1991): 519-554.

9. Leading Websites for State Legal Research.

Home Page:	www.nebraska.gov
Administrative Code:	www.sos.ne.gov/rules-and-regs/reg-search/
Agency Directory:	www.nebraska.gov/allagencies.html
Attorney General:	www.ago.ne.gov/
Attorney Gen. Opinions:	www.ago.ne.gov/agopinions/
Bar Association:	www.nebar.com/
Constitution (searchable):	http://nebraskalegislature.gov/laws/browse-constitution.php
Court Opinions – Court of Appeals:	www.supremecourt.ne.gov/coa/opinions
Court Opinions – Supreme Court:	www.supremecourt.ne.gov/sc/opinions
Governor:	www.governor.nebraska.gov/
Judicial Branch:	www.supremecourt.ne.gov/
Law Library:	www.supremecourt.ne.gov/1082/state-library
Legislative Branch:	http://nebraskalegislature.gov
Secretary of State:	www.sos.ne.gov
Statutes:	http://nebraskalegislature.gov/laws

10. Leading publishers of state specific treatises, practice books, and CLE publications.
LexisNexis, Lorman Education Services, National Business Institute, Nebraska Continuing Legal Education, Inc., West. See Appendix B for addresses and telephone numbers.

Nevada

1. Codes and Session Laws.
Michie's Nevada Revised Statutes Annotated. Charlottesville, VA: LexisNexis, 1986-date. 26 vols. Biennial pocket supplements and periodic revised volumes.
Cost: $1,124 (includes 180 days updates at no additional cost); annual supplementation (in-state/out-of-state): 2001: $539/$611; 2002: $263/$303; 2003: $385/$434; 2004: $752/$809; 2005: $385.00/$434; 2006: $190/$237; 2007: $456/$496; 2008: $714/$754; 2009: $501/$544; 2010: $525/$624; 2011: $525/$624; 2012: $428/$473; 2013: $471.

West's Nevada Revised Statutes Annotated. St. Paul, MN: West, 2000-date. 40 vols. Biennial pocket supplements and periodic revised volumes.
Cost: $1,852 ; supplementation: 2009: $300; 2010: $805; 2011: $1,088; 2012: $1,551; 2013: $1,372; **Monthly Assured Print Pricing (APP):** $113/$1,356.

Nevada Advance Service. Charlottesville, VA: LexisNexis. Supplements code between annual pocket parts.
Cost: $106.00 (2014)

Nevada Revised Statutes. Carson City, NV: Legislative Counsel Bureau. 2013 Revision. 56 vols. Looseleaf format. Reprinted with amendments biennially. Annotations.
Cost: $695 (with binders); new contents (reprint) for those who already own the binders: $395; individual volumes: $49 each; interim supplements free of charge to subscribers (2014). (775) 684-6835.

Nevada Legislative Service. St. Paul, MN: West, 2009-date. 7 softbound pamphlets. Contains laws enacted by the Nevada Legislature from the most recently completed legislative session
Cost: $225.96 per year (2014).

Statutes of Nevada [session laws]. Carson City, NV: Legislative Counsel Bureau. Biennial.
Cost: 1879-2003 full set: $1,052; 1995: 60 (3 vols.); 1997: $60 (3 vols.); 1999: $60 (3 vols.); 2001: $95 (5 vols.); 2003: $110 (6 vols.); 2005: $110 (6 vols.); 2007: $110 (7 vols.); 2009: $110.00 (7 vols.); 2011: $110 (8 vols.); 2013: $100 (8 vols.) (2014) (775) 684-6835.

Legislative Hotline: (775) 687-5545; (775) 687-6827.

2. Administrative Law.
Nevada Administrative Code. Carson City: Legislative Counsel Bureau, 1983-date. 16 vols. Updated about six times per year. (775) 684-6835
Available online at: http://www.leg.state.nv.us/law1.cfm
Cost: $350 (includes one year's updates); supplementation: $125 per year (July-June) (2014)

Nevada Administrative Code Register. Carson City: Legislative Counsel Bureau. Published monthly. (775) 684-6835
Available online at: http://www.leg.state.nv.us/NAC/
Cost: $200 per year (July 1 - June 30) (2014).

3. Court Reports.
Nevada Reports. 1865-date. Carson City, NV: Legislative Counsel Bureau. Current vol.: 125
Cost: $3,145 (125 vols.) (some consist of two books); vols. 1-108: $25 ea; vols. 109-114: $50 ea.; vol. 115: $25; vol. 116: $50 (2 books); vol. 117: $45; vol. 118: $50; 119: $25; 120-122: $50; 123: $25; 124: $50; 125: $25. Cost depends on number of books per volume (currently $25 per book) (2014).

Pacific Reporter [1st] - **3d**. St. Paul, MN: West, 1883-date. Contains decisions of f the Nevada Supreme Court from 1883-date. Current vol.: 314 **P. 3d**.
Cost: 1st series out-of-print (see used lawbook dealers in Appendix C); 2d series: $13,428; used sets approx. $2000; 3d series: $15,201; annual cost (2013): $11,396; individual volume: $518/$691 (subscriber/list); **Monthly Assured Print Pricing (APP):** $1,141/$11,369; used sets may be available.

Pacific Reporter 3d. Advance sheets. St. Paul, MN: Thomson West. Weekly.
Cost: $2,866.56 per year (discounted to bound volume subscribers) (2014).

4. Court Rules.
Nevada Court Rules Annotated. Charlottesville, VA : LexisNexis. 2 vols. Softbound. Updated semiannually, replaced annually.
Cost: 2014 Edition: $135.

Nevada Rules of Court: State and Federal. St. Paul, MN: West. 2 vols. Annual.
Cost: 2014 Edition: $200; ProView eBook: $200.

5. Digests, Encyclopedias, and Practice Sets.
No Nevada Digest. (See Pacific Digest).

6. Citators.
Shepard's Nevada Citations. Albany, NY: Shepard's. Six supplements per year.
Cost: $1,895 (3 bound volumes); all-inclusive subscription: $1,703 (in-state) (2014).

Online: All jurisdictional Shepard's and KeyCite are no longer available as stand-alone products, but are included as part of a jurisdictional or subject library from their respective publishers (2014).

7. CD-ROM Products.
LexisNexis CD - Nevada Primary Law. Albany, NY: LexisNexis. One disc. Updated quarterly. Contains the full text of Michie's Nevada Statutes Annotated, Nevada Supreme Court decisions from 1865 to date, Nevada Administrative Code, Nevada Court Rules Annotated, Attorney General opinions, and Constitution. Includes an online link to Lexis for updates. Available for Windows. Search Engine: Folio.
Cost: $1,951 per year (2014).

Nevada Reporter and Nevada Revised Statutes Annotated. Eagan, MN: West. One disc. Regular updates. Contains the full text of decisions of the Nevada Supreme Court from 1865 to date, slip opinions, Attorney General opinions from 1977 to date, Nevada Revised Statutes, State Constitution, session laws. Decisions also searchable by West Topics and Key Numbers, headnotes and synopses. Available for DOS, Windows, or Macintosh. Search Engine: PREMISE. Subscription includes online updating via Westlaw.
Cost: $4,365 per year (2014).

Official Nevada Law Library 2013 Revision. Carson City, NV: Nevada Legislative Publications. One disc. Updated every two years. Contains the full text of the Nevada Reports, Nevada Revised Statutes with Annotations, Nevada Attorney General Opinions, Nevada Administrative Code, Nevada Court Rules, Nevada and U.S. Constitutions, U.S. Court Rules for Nevada and Ninth Circuit, and Nevada City Charters. Available for Windows. Search Engine: Folio,
Cost: 2011 NRS Revision: $395 per year ($225 when purchased with the print NRS) (2014). (775) 684-6835.

8. State Legal Research Guides.
Bowers, Michael Way. **The Nevada State Constitution**. New York: Oxford University Press, 2011. 1 vol. (224 pp.).
Cost: $150.00; from $21.91 on amazon.com (2014).

Fletcher, G. LeGrande. "Nevada Practice Materials: A Selective Annotated Bibliography. " **Law Library Journal** 91, No. 2 (Spring, 1999): 313-366.

Fletcher, G. LeGrande. "Nevada Government Documents Online: An Easy-to-Use Guide. **Nevada Lawyer** 6, No. 6, (June, 1998): 20-21.

Fletcher, G. LeGrande & James Quinn. "A Definitive Primer: Nevada Legal Information on the World Wide Web," **Nevada Lawyer** 7, no. 6 (June, 1999): 223-26.

Gross, Jennifer Larriguibel and Thomas Blake Gross, eds. **Nevada Legal Research Guide**. Buffalo, NY: William S. Hein & Co., Inc., 2012. 1 vol. (235 pp.).
Cost: $75.00 (2014).

Jarrell, Ann S. & G. LeGrande Fletcher. **Nevada State Documents Bibliography: Legal Publications and Related Material**. 2d ed. Chicago: American Association of Law Libraries, Government Documents SIS, 2000.
Cost: $30.00. Available from William S. Hein & Co. on electronic pdf and on HeinOnline (2014).

9 Leading Web Pages for State Legal Research.

Home Page:	www.nv.gov/
Administrative Code:	www.leg.state.nv.us/law1.cfm
Agency Directory:	http://nv.gov/agency/department/
Attorney General:	http://ag.nv.gov
Attorney Gen. Opinions:	http://ag.nv.gov/Publications/Opinions
Bar Association:	www.nvbar.org/
Constitution:	www.leg.state.nv.us/Const/NVConst.html
Court Opinions – Supreme Court:	http://supreme.nvcourts.gov
Governor:	http://gov.nv.gov/
Judicial Branch:	www.nevadajudiciary.us/
Law Library:	http://lawlibrary.nevadajudiciary.us/
Legislative Branch:	www.leg.state.nv.us/
Secretary of State:	http://nvsos.gov/
Statutes:	www.leg.state.nv.us/law1.cfm

10. Leading publishers of state specific treatises, practice books, and CLE publications.
LexisNexis, National Business Institute, State Bar of Nevada.

New Hampshire

1. Codes and Session Laws.

New Hampshire Revised Statutes Annotated. Charlottesville, VA: LexisNexis, 1955-date. 31 vols. Annual pocket parts and periodic revised volumes. No longer the official code.
Cost: $680 (in- and out-of-state); supplementation cost: 2004: $476; 2005: $296; 2006: $605; 2007: $328; 2008: $574; 2009: $270.85; 2010: $270.85; 2012: $270.85; 2013: $351.

New Hampshire Revised Statutes Annotated. St. Paul, MN: West, 2000-date. 37 vols.
The official code for the state of New Hampshire from its initial publication in 2000. West began by supplementing the original Lexis set with pocket parts.
Cost: $517.30 ; supplementation: 2000: $259; 2001: $143.50; 2002: $259.80; 2003: $259; 2004: $274; 2005: $269.10; 2006: $270.85; 2007: $190.35; 2008: $270.85; 2009: $216.50; 2010: $270.85; 2011: $271; 2012: $270.85; 2013: $216; **Monthly Assured Print Pricing (APP):** $27/$324

West's New Hampshire Legislative Service. St. Paul, MN: West, 2000-date.
These pamphlets are published during and immediately after the current legislative session and contain the text of newly enacted laws in numerical chapter order sequence in order of passage.
Cost: $69.96 (2014).

New Hampshire Advance Code Service. Charlottesville, VA: LexisNexis. This is a series of three cumulative pamphlets published at quarterly intervals during the year between legislative sessions, providing the user with the most up-to-date judicial decisions from state and federal courts.
Cost: $88 (2014).

New Hampshire Advance Legislative Service. Charlottesville, VA: LexisNexis. These pamphlets are published during and immediately after the current legislative session and contain the text of newly enacted laws in numerical chapter order sequence in order of passage.
Cost: $69 (2014).

Laws of New Hampshire [session laws]. Concord, NH: Secretary of State. Annual. Published by West for state. Available from State Library: (603) 271-2429
Cost: 1996-2000: $25 ea. + shipping (hardbound); 2001-2002: $60 ea. (softbound); 2003-2012: $25 (hardbound); $12.50 (softbound).

Legislative Hotline: (603) 271-2239.

2. Administrative Law.

Code of New Hampshire Rules. Albany, NY: LexisNexis Matthew Bender [formerly Weil Publishing Co.], 1996-date. 15 vols. Updated monthly. Has all official rules issued by state agencies in New Hampshire, pursuant to Administrative Procedure Act.
Cost: $3,292 for one year (price includes 11 monthly updates and postage); supplementation: 1997-2004: $1,110 per year; 2005: $1,165. 2006: $1,165; 2007: $1,165; 2008: $1,165; 2009: $1,392. 2010: $1,535; 2012: $1,627; 2013: $1,741; 2014: $2,052. Individual volumes also available.

New Hampshire Rulemaking Register. Concord, NH: Office of Legislative Services, Administrative Rules. The **Register** may also be viewed on-line in PDF.
Cost: $65 per year ($5.50 per mo.) (on July 1 - June 30 fiscal year basis) (2014). (603) 271-3680

New Hampshire Government Register. Newark, NJ: LexisNexis Matthew Bender [formerly Weil Publishing Co.], 1996-date. Monthly.
Cost: $1,257; renewal: 2014; $1,143.

3. Court Reports.

New Hampshire Reports. 1976 (vol. 117) - date. Charlottesville, VA: LexisNexis. Current vol.: 164.
Cost: prices of vols. 117-164 vary from $37.50 to $66 each; volumes 1-116 available from the Administrative Office of the Courts and LexisNexis. Most are priced at $25 and $30 per volume; some early volumes are out-of-print.

Atlantic Reporter [1st] - **2d**. St. Paul, MN: West, 1886-date. Contains decisions of the New Hampshire Supreme Court from 1886-date. Current volume: 85 **A.3d**.
Cost: 1st series out-of-print (see used lawbook dealers in Appendix C); 2d series: $14,434; 3d series: $15,080; annual cost (2013): $11,151; recent vol.: $531/$708 (subscriber/list); **Monthly Assured Print Pricing (APP):** $1,163/$13,956. See list of used lawbook dealers in Appendix C.

Atlantic Reporter 2d. Advance sheets. St. Paul, MN: Thomson West. Weekly.
Cost: $2,866.56 per year (discounted to bound volume subscribers) (2014).

New Hampshire Reports Current Case Service. Charlottesville, VA: LexisNexis. Softbound pamphlet subscription; approx. four issues per year.
Cost: $53 per year (2014).

4. Court Rules.

New Hampshire Court Rules Annotated. Charlottesville, VA: LexisNexis. 1 vol. Updated annually.
Cost: 2013-2014 Edition: $150 (2014).

New Hampshire Court Rules: State and Federal. St. Paul, MN: West One vol. Annual. Paperbound or ProView eBook.
Cost: 2014 Edition: $162; ProView eBook: $162.

5. Digests, Encyclopedias and Practice Sets.

West's New Hampshire Digest. St. Paul, MN: West, 1951-date. 35 vols.
Annual pocket parts and periodic revised volumes.
Cost: $3,749; supplementation: 1995: $170.00; 1996: $181; 1997: $199; 1998: $250; 1999: $386; 2000: $341; 2001: $389; 2002: $911.50; 2003: $391.50; 2004: $608.50; 2005: $857; 2006: $510.50; 2007: $831.50; 2008: $1,246; 2009: $595.50; 2010: $1,117; 2011: $1,425; 2012: $2,736.50; 2013: $1,757;

Monthly Assured Print Pricing (APP): $194/$2,328.

New Hampshire Practice. Charlottesville, VA: LexisNexis, 1984-date. 17 vols. Softbound. With softbound index and tables volumes.
Cost: $1,418; supplementation: 2013: $1,690; or see costs of individual components which are updated separately.

6. Citators.
Shepard's New Hampshire Citations. Albany, NY: Shepard's. Six supplements per year.
Cost: $1,016 (2 bound volumes); all-inclusive subscription: $1,712 (in-state) (2014).

Online: All jurisdictional Shepard's and KeyCite are no longer available as stand-alone products, but are included as part of a jurisdictional or subject library package by their respective publishers. (2014).

7. CD-ROM Products.
LexisNexis CD - New Hampshire Primary Law. Albany, NY: LexisNexis. One disc. Quarterly updates. Contains the full text of the New Hampshire Revised Statutes Annotated, decisions of the New Hampshire Supreme Court from 1816 to date, New Hampshire Court Rules Annotated, New Hampshire Attorney General Opinions from 1977 to date, and various titles from the New Hampshire Practice series published by LexisNexis. Available for DOS or Windows. Search Engine: Folio. Includes online updating via LEXIS
Cost: $1,482 per year (2014).

New Hampshire Reporter and West's New Hampshire Statutes. Eagan, MN: West. One disc. Quarterly updates. Contains the full text of decisions of the New Hampshire Supreme Court from 1816 to date, slip opinions, Attorney General opinions from 1977 to date, New Hampshire Statutes and court rules [unannotated], State Constitution, session laws. Available for DOS, Windows, and Macintosh. Search Engine: PREMISE. Subscription includes online updating via Westlaw.
Cost: $882 per year (2014).

8. State Legal Research Guides.
Johnson, Linda B., Cynthia R. Landau and Mary Searles. **New Hampshire State Documents: A Selected Bibliography.** Chicago: American Association of Law Libraries, Government Documents SIS, 2012.
Cost: $30.00; electronic pdf: $20.00. Available from William S. Hein & Co. on electronic pdf and on HeinOnline (2014).

Marshall, Susan E. **The New Hampshire State Constitution.** New York: Oxford University Press, 2011. 1 vol. (312 pp.).
Cost: $150.00; from $33.17 on amazon.com; kindle: $119.73 (2014).

9 Leading Web Sites for State Legal Research.

Home page:	www.nh.gov/
Administrative Code:	www.gencourt.state.nh.us/rules
Agency Directory:	www.nh.gov/government/agencies.html
Attorney General:	www.doj.nh.gov/
Attorney Gen. Opinions:	www.doj.nh.gov/media-center/opinions.htm
Bar Association:	www.nhbar.org/
Constitution:	www.nh.gov/constitution/constitution.html
Court Opinions – Supreme Court:	www.courts.state.nh.us/supreme/opinions
Governor:	www.governor.nh.gov/
Judicial Branch:	www.courts.state.nh.us/
Law Library:	www.courts.state.nh.us/lawlibrary
Legislative Branch:	www.gencourt.state.nh.us/
Secretary of State:	http://sos.nh.gov/
Statutes:	www.gencourt.state.nh.us/rsa/html/indexes

10. Leading publishers of state specific treatises, practice books, and CLE publications.
LexisNexis, National Business Institute, New Hampshire Bar Association Continuing Legal Education. See Appendix B for addresses and telephone numbers.

New Jersey

1. Codes and Session Laws.
New Jersey Statutes Annotated. St. Paul, MN: West, 1939-date. 105 vols. Annual pocket supplements and periodic revised volumes.
Cost: $4,836; supplementation: 1995: $715.00; 1996: $577.50; 1997: $888.50; 1998: $607.50; 1999: $860.00; 2000: $929.00; 2001: $1,100.75; 2002: $1,121.25; 2003: $1,205.00; 2004: $1,316; 2005: $1,296; 2006: $1,401.50; 2007: $1,715.50; 2008: $2,427; 2009: $2,060; 2010: $2,316.50; 2011: $2,754.50; 2012: $3,085.50; 2013: $3,706; **Monthly Assured Print Pricing (APP):** $308/$3,696.

Chapter Laws of New Jersey [session laws]. Trenton, NJ: Office of Legislative Services. Annual.
Cost: 1995: $50.00 (2 vols.); 1996: $25 (1 vol.); 1997: $50 (2 vols.); 1998: $25 (1 vol.); 1999: $50 (2 vols.); 2000: $25 (1 vol.); 2001: $50 (2 vols.); 2002: $25 (1 vol.); 2003: $25 (1 vol.); 2003: $80 (2 vols.); 2004: $80 (2 vols.); 2005: $80 (2 vols.); 2006: $40 (1 vol.); 2007: $80.00 (2 vols.); 2008: $40.00 (1 vol.); 2009: $40.00 (1 vol.); 2010: $107.00 (2 vols.) 2011: $108 (2 vols.); 2012: $82 (2 vols.). (609) 292-4661.

New Jersey Session Law Service. St. Paul, MN: West. These pamphlets are published during and immediately after each legislative session and contain text of laws in numerical chapter sequence in order of passage.
Cost: $971.04 per year (2014).

Legislative Hotline: (609) 292-4840.

2. Administrative Law.
New Jersey Administrative Code. Albany, NY: LexisNexis

Matthew Bender, 2005-date. 38 vols. Looseleaf format.
Cost: $1,790; individual titles also available (includes one year's service); annual upkeep: 2002: $818; 2003: $1,036; 2004: $264; 2008: $1,309; 2009:$1,309; 2010: $1,309; 2011: $1,309; 2012: $1,309; 2013: $1,309; 2014: $1,309. Gov't. discounts; also available online on Lexis.

New Jersey Register. New York: LexisNexis, 2005-date. Semi-monthly.
Cost: $211 (2d class mail); also available via 1st class mail; $15 (single issue) (2014).

3. Court Reports.

New Jersey Reports. 1948-date. St. Paul, MN: West (since 1960).
[Decisions prior to 1948 are of the Court of Errors and Appeals, the predecessor body to the current Supreme Court]. Current vol.: 217.
Cost: $2,759; annual upkeep: 2004: $158; 2005: $262; 2006: $200; 2007: $225; 2008: $294; 2009: $294; 2010: $ 220.50; 2011: $220.50; 2012: $220.50; 2013: $220.50; current volume: $55/$73.50 (subscriber/list); **Monthly Assured Print Pricing (APP):** $91/$1,092; advance sheets to both New Jersey Reports and New Jersey Superior Court Reports also available; used sets may also be available.

New Jersey Superior Court Reports. St. Paul, MN: West, 1948-date. Current vol.: 435.
Cost: $5,294; annual upkeep: 2000: $372.75; 2001: $272.60; 2002: $475.80; 2003: $474; 2004: $517; 2005: $524; 2006: $465.50; 2007: $450; 2008: $514.40; 2009: $514.50; 2010: $514.50; 2011: $368; 2012: $331; 2013: $275; current volume: $55.00/$73.50 (subscriber/list); **Monthly Assured Print Pricing (APP):** $159/$1,908; advance sheets to both New Jersey Reports and New Jersey Superior Court Reports: $125 per year; used sets of New Jersey Reports and New Jersey Superior Court Reports may be available.

New Jersey Tax Court Reports. St. Paul, MN: West, 1979-date. Current vol.: 26
Cost: $837; annual upkeep: 2002: $98.25; 2003: $193.00; 2004: $96.50; 2005: $88.50; 2006: $86.75; 2007: $101.75; 2008: $101.75; 2009: $101.75; 2010: 0; 2011: $104.25; 2012: 0; 2013: $104,25 (list); current volume: $104.25 (list); **Monthly Assured Print Pricing (APP):** $27/$324.

Atlantic Reporter [1st] - **2d**. St. Paul, MN: West, 1886-date. Contains decisions of the New Jersey Supreme Court from 1885-date and the New Jersey Superior Court, Appellate Division from 1948-date. Current volume: 85 **A.3d**.
Cost: 1st series out-of-print (see used lawbook dealers in Appendix C); 2d series: $14,434; 3d series: $15,080; annual cost (2013): $11,151; recent vol.: $531/$708 (subscriber/list); **Monthly Assured Print Pricing (APP):** $1,163/$13,956. See list of used lawbook dealers in Appendix C.

Atlantic Reporter 2d. Advance sheets. St. Paul, MN: Thomson West. Weekly.
Cost: $2,866.56 per year (discounted to bound volume subscribers) (2014).

4. Court Rules.

New Jersey Rules of Court: State and Federal. St. Paul, MN: West. 2 vols. Annual. Paperbound or ProView eBook.
Cost: 2014 Edition: $182.

5. Digests, Encyclopedias, and Practice Sets.

New Jersey Transaction Guide. New York: Matthew Bender & Co., 1948-date. 14 vols. Looseleaf format. Periodic supplements. A 14-volume general form and procedural guide for the New Jersey practitioner covering civil, non-litigation-oriented subject areas and is divided into five units: Business Entities, Commercial Transactions, Real Estate Transactions, Personal Transactions, and Estate Planning.
Cost: $3,353, renewal: 2004: $1,041; 2005: $1093; 2006: $1,164; 2007: $1,203; 2008: $1,299; 2009: $1,403; 2010: $1,473; 2011: $1,547; 2012: $1,640; 2013: $1,755; 2014: $1,915; CD-ROM: $2,695, renewal: 2014: $1,149.

New Jersey Practice Series. St. Paul, MN: West. 86 vols. Supplemented individually.
Cost: $13,519 (but priced individually); annual upkeep: 1998: $688.50; 1999: $1,525; 2000: $1,791; 2001: $2,303.50; 2003: $2,325; 2004: see supp. costs of individual components. Individual volumes also available; used sets available for approx. $1,600. Best acquired as part of a New Jersey secondary law add-on to a WestlawNext PRO subscription.

West's New Jersey Digest 2d. St. Paul, MN: West, 1984-date. 86 vols. Annual pocket parts and periodic revised volumes.
Cost: $5,076; annual supplementation: 1996: $145; 1997: $342;1998: $570; 1999: $695; 2000: $539; 2001: $1,142.75; 2002: $1,123.75; 2003: $368; 2004: $695; 2005: $662; 2006: $621; 2007: $1,593; 2008: $1,194; 2009: $2,739; 2010: $1,496; 2011: $2,495; 2012: $3,478; 2013: $4,114; **Monthly Assured Print Pricing (APP):** $308/$3,696.

6. Citators.

Shepard's New Jersey Citations. Albany, NY: Shepard's. Monthly or bi-monthly.
Cost: $6,315 (13 bound volumes); all-inclusive subscription: monthly: $2,493 (in-state); bi-monthly: $2,811 (in-state) (2014).

Online: All jurisdictional Shepard's and KeyCite are no longer available as stand-alone products, but are included as part of a jurisdictional or subject library package from their respective publishers (2014).

7. CD-ROM Products.

LexisNexis CD - New Jersey Primary Law. Albany, NY: LexisNexis. Two discs. Updated quarterly. Contains the full text of the New Jersey statutes, New Jersey Advance Legislative Service, decisions of the New Jersey Supreme Court from 1790 to date, New Jersey Superior Court from 1948 to date, New Jersey Tax Court from 1979 to date, New Jersey Equity Reports from 1924-1948, and selected federal court decisions. Available for Windows. Search Engine: Folio; LivePublish (NextPage). Includes online updating via LEXIS.
Cost: $2,236 per year (2014).

New Jersey Reports/New Jersey Superior Court Reports, PREMISE® CD-ROM ed. Eagan, MN: West. Two discs. Quarterly updates. Contains the full text of decisions of the

New Jersey Supreme Court [and its predecessors] from 1790 to date, decisions from vol. 1 of the New Jersey Superior Court Reports to date, etc. Available for DOS, Windows, and Macintosh. Search Engine: PREMISE. Includes online updating via Westlaw
Cost: $6,717 per year (2014).

New Jersey Transaction Guide. Newark, NJ: LexisNexis (Matthew Bender). One disc. Updated quarterly. Also in ebook format.
Contains the full text of the publisher's 14-volume general form and procedural guide for the New Jersey practitioner covering civil, non-litigation-oriented subject areas and is divided into five units: Business Entities, Commercial Transactions, Real Estate Transactions, Personal Transactions, and Estate Planning.
Cost: $2,223; renewal: 2008: $778; 2009: $840; 2010: $883; 2011: $927; 2012: $983; 2013: $1,052; 2014: 1,149.

8. State Legal Research Guides.
Allen, Cameron. **A Guide to New Jersey Legal Bibliography and Legal History**. Littleton, CO: Fred B. Rothman & Co., 1984. Available from W.S. Hein & Co.
Cost: $75.00 (2014).

Axel-Lute, Paul. **New Jersey Legal Research Handbook**. 4th ed. New Brunswick: New Jersey Institute for Continuing Legal Education, 1998.

Hollander, David A. New Jersey Practice Materials: A Selective Bibliography in Houdek, Frank G., ed. **State Practice Materials: Annotated Bibliographies**. Buffalo, NY: William S. Hein & Co., Inc., 2008-date. 2 vols. Looseleaf format.
Cost: $195.00 (2014).

Senezak, Christina M. New Jersey Practice Materials: A Select Annotated Bibliography." Series on State Practice Materials. **Law Library Journal** 79, No. 4 (1987): 689-705.

Senezak, Christina M. **New Jersey State Publications, A Guide for Law Libraries**. Chicago: AALL, 1984.
Cost: $30.00. Available from William S. Hein & Co. on electronic pdf and on HeinOnline (2014).

Williams, Robert F. **The New Jersey State Constitution: A Reference Guide**. Piscataway, NJ: Rutgers University Press, 1997. 1 vol. (174 pp.).
Cost: $24.95; from $10.97 on amazon.com; kindle: $12.10 (2014).

Williams, Robert F. **The New Jersey State Constitution.** New York: Oxford University Press, 2012. 1 vol.
Cost: $150.00; from $127.64 on amazon.com (2014).

9 Leading Web Pages for State Legal Research.

Home Page:	www.nj.gov
Administrative Code:	www.state.nj.us/oal/rules.html
Agency Directory:	www.state.nj.us/nj/gov/deptserv/
Attorney General:	www.nj.gov/oag/
Attorney Gen. Opinions:	www.nj.gov/oag/ag-opinions.htm
Bar Association:	www.njsba.com/
Constitution:	www.njleg.state.nj.us/lawsconstitution/consearch.asp
Court Opinions:	www.judiciary.state.nj.us/opinions
Governor:	www.nj.gov/governor/
Judicial Branch:	www.judiciary.state.nj.us/
Law Library:	http://law.njstatelib.org/
Legal Resources:	www.judiciary.state.nj.us/resource.htm
Legislative Branch:	www.njleg.state.nj.us/
Secretary of State:	www.state.nj.us/state/
Statutes:	(link from Legislative page above)

10. Leading publishers of state specific treatises, practice books, and CLE publications.
LexisNexis, National Business Institute, New Jersey Institute for Continuing Legal Education, Thomson Reuters West. See Appendix B for addresses and telephone numbers.

New Mexico

1. Code and Session Laws.
New Mexico Statutes Annotated. Eagan, MN: Thomson West, 2003-date. 31 vols. Annual cumulative supplements and periodic revised volumes.
Cost: $1,248; supplementation: 2004: $345; 2005: $749; 2006: $673; 2007: $385; 2008: $319; 2009: $420; 2010: $510; 2011: $618; 2012: $685; 2013: $712; **Monthly Assured Print Pricing (APP):** $79/$948.

Michie's Annotated Statutes of New Mexico. Charlottesville, VA: LexisNexis, 1978-date. 14 vols. Looseleaf format. Annual cumulative supplements and replacement pamphlets.
Cost: $632; annual supplementation (in-state/out-of-state): 2001: $225/$353; 2002: $187.50/$353; 2004: $250/$299; 2005: $307/$358; 2006: $316/368; 2007: $283.50/$325; 2008: $479/$562; 2009: $467/$556; 2010: $482/$588; 2011: $226/$254; 2012: $610/$711; 2013: $643/$750.

New Mexico Statutes Annotated. Santa Fe: New Mexico Compilation Commission, 1978-date. 17 vols.
Cost: 2012 Edition: $535.50 (incl shipping); supplementation: 2007: $283.50; 2008: $270; 2009: $285; 2010: $285; 2011: $315; 2012: $315; 2013: $315.

New Mexico Legislative Service. St. Paul, MN: West, 2004-date. Published three times per year.
Cost: $410.04 per year (2013).

New Mexico Advance Code Service. Charlottesville, VA: LexisNexis.
Cost: $59 per year (in-state); $89 (out-of-state) (2013).

New Mexico Advance Legislative Service. New Mexico Compilation Commission. 2 vols. Annual. Paperbound.
Cost: $40 (2013).

Laws of New Mexico. Santa Fe: Secretary of State, 1912-date. 3 vols. Annual.
Cost: 1995: $50; 1996: $35; 1997: $50; 1998: $50 (2 vols.); 1999: $75 (3 vols.); 2000: $25 (1 vol.); 2001: $75 (3 vols.); 2002: $30 (1 vol.); 2003: $120 (4 vol.), 2004: $60 (2 vols.); 2005: $120 (4 vols.); 2006: $60 (2 vols.); 2007: $120 (4 vols.); 2008: $60 (2 vols.); 2009: $160 (4 vols.); 2010: $80 (2 vols.); 2011: $120 (3 vols.); 2012: $73 (1 vol.). (505) 827-3600

Legislative Hotline: (505) 986-4600.

2. Administrative Law.
Code of New Mexico Rules. Albany, NY: LexisNexis Matthew Bender [formerly Weil Publishing Co.], 2000-date. 19 vols. Updated monthly.
Also available on the Internet at: http://www.nmcpr.state.nm.us/nmac/
Cost: $2,818 (incl. 11 months of updates and postage); annual renewal: 2005: $1,100; 2006: $1,100; 2007: $1,100; 2008: $1,163; 2009: $1,314; 2010: $1,380; 2011: $1,449; 2012: $1,536; 2013: $1,644; 2014: $.

New Mexico Register. Santa Fe: State Records Center and Archives, 1990-date. Bimonthly. Also available online at: www.nmcpr.state.nm.us/nmregister/
Cost: $270 per year; single issues: $12 each (2014). (505) 827-7332

3. Court Reports.
New Mexico Reports. 1852-2012. Santa Fe: New Mexico Compilation Commission. Last vol.: 150. Replaced by **New Mexico Appellate Reports,** 2012-date (see below). (505) 827-4821.
Cost: $3,000 (vols. 1-150); current vols. $60 ea. (2014).

New Mexico Appellate Reports. 2012-date. Santa Fe: New Mexico Compilation Commission. Current vol.: 3. Decisions available online from 2000-date. Replaced **New Mexico Reports**. See also **New Mexico One Source of Law** (under CD-ROM products). (505) 827-4821.
Cost: $147 ($49.00 ea.) (2014).

Pacific Reporter [1st] - **3d**. St. Paul, MN: West, 1883-date. Contains decisions of the New Mexico Supreme Court from 1883-date. Current vol.: 314 **P. 3d**.
Cost: 1st series out-of-print (see used lawbook dealers in Appendix C); 2d series: $13,428; used sets approx. $2000; 3d series: $15,201; annual cost (2013): $11,396; individual volume: $518/$691 (subscriber/list); **Monthly Assured Print Pricing (APP):** $1,141/$11,369; used sets may be available.

Pacific Reporter 3d. Advance sheets. St. Paul, MN: Thomson West. Weekly.
Cost: $2,866.56 per year (discounted to bound volume subscribers) (2014).

4. Court Rules.
Michie's New Mexico Rules Annotated. Charlottesville, VA: LexisNexis, 1993-date. 5 vols. Annual.
Cost: 2013 Edition: $100; 2014: $107 (in-state) (2014).

New Mexico Rules of Court, State and Federal. St. Paul, MN: West 2 vols. Annual. Also available as ProView eBook.
Cost: 2014 Edition: $276.

New Mexico Rules Annotated. Cleveland, OH: Conway Greene, 2013. 3 vols. Published in cooperation with the New Mexico Compilation Commission. this official set contains all official rules of the state of New Mexico as well as official annotations, forms and official commentary.
Cost: 2013 Edition: $80 (2014).

5. Digests, Encyclopedias and Practice Sets.
West's New Mexico Digest. St. Paul, MN: West, 1948-date. 55 vols.
Updated with annual supplements, replacement volumes, and interim pamphlets.
Cost: $3,230; supplementation: 1996: $197; 1997: $217; 1998: $235; 1999: $415.75; 2000: $583; 2001: $754.50; 2002: $888; 2003: $399.50; 2004: $777.25; 2005: $1,097; 2006: $722; 2007: $570; 2008: $2,166; 2009: $1,586; 2010: $1,284.50; 2011: $1,451; 2012: $1,398.50; 2013: $2,680; **Monthly Assured Print Pricing (APP):** $168/$2,016.

6. Citators.
Shepard's New Mexico Citations. Albany, NY: Shepard's. Six supplements per year.
Cost: $886 (2 bound volumes); all-inclusive subscription: $1,712 (in-state) (2014).

Online: All jurisdictional Shepard's and KeyCite are no longer available as stand-alone products, but are included as part of a jurisdictional or subject library from their respective publishers (2014).

7. CD-ROM Products.
Michie's New Mexico Law on Disc. Albany, NY: LexisNexis. One disc. Updated quarterly. Contains the full text of the New Mexico Statutes Annotated, full text of decisions of the N.M. Supreme Court from 1852 to date, decisions of the Court of Appeals from 1966 to date, Court Rules, Attorney General Opinions from 1912 to date, New Mexico Administrative Code, and current session laws. Available for DOS and Windows. Search Engine: Folio; LivePublish (NextPage). Subscription includes online updating via LEXIS.
Cost: $1,004 per year (2014).

New Mexico One Source of Law—Online with single user DVD. Cleveland, OH: Conway Greene, 2007-date. Online with companion quarterly DVD. A revolutionary, state-of-the-art, state-sponsored database of New Mexico legal materials. Contains full text of **New Mexico Statutes Annotated**, state and federal cases, **New Mexico Administrative Code**, federal and state constitutions, etc. Search Engine: Folio.
Cost: $715 per year (single user) (2014).

New Mexico Reports and West's New Mexico Statutes. Eagan, MN: West. One disc. Regular updates. Contains the full text of decisions of the New Mexico Supreme Court from 1852 to date, Court of Appeals from vol. 155 Pacific Reporter 2d to date, New Jersey Attorney General Opinions from 1977 to date, New Mexico statutes, court rules. Available for DOS, Windows and

Macintosh. Search Engine: PREMISE.
Cost: $8,202 per year (2014).

8. State Legal Research Guides.
Smith, Charles E. **The New Mexico State Constitution.** New York: Oxford University Press, 2011. 1 vol. (260 pp.).
Cost: $150.00; from $17.40; kindle: $119.99 (2014).

Strike, Theresa. **Guide to New Mexico State Publications**. 3d ed. Chicago: AALL, 2009.
Cost: $30.00; electronic pdf: $20.00. Available from William S. Hein & Co. on electronic pdf or on HeinOnline (20134.

Weistling, Ripple L. New Mexico Practice Materials: A Selective Bibliography in Houdek, Frank G., ed. **State Practice Materials: Annotated Bibliographies**. Buffalo, NY: William S. Hein & Co., Inc., 2010-date. 2 vols. Looseleaf format.
Cost: $195.00 (2014).

Woodward, Mary A. "New Mexico Practice Materials: A Selective Annotated Bibliography." Series on State Practice Materials, **Law Library Journal** 84, no. 1 (1992): 93-112.

9 Leading Web Sites for State Legal Research.

Home Page:	www.newmexico.gov/
Administrative Code:	www.nmcpr.state.nm.us/nmac/
Agency Directory:	www.newmexico.gov/government/A_to_Z_State_Agency_Listings.aspx
Attorney General:	www.nmag.gov/
Attorney Gen. Opinions:	http://public-records.nmag.gov/opinions
Bar Association:	www.nmbar.org/
Constitution:	www.nmonesource.com/nmnxtadmin/NMPublic.aspx
Court Opinions:	www.nmcompcomm.us/nmcases/NMCases.aspx
Governor:	www.governor.state.nm.us/
Judicial Branch:	www.nmcourts.gov/
Law Library:	www.supremecourtlawlibrary.com/
Legislative Branch:	www.nmlegis.gov/lcs/
Secretary of State:	www.sos.state.nm.us/
Statutes:	www.nmonesource.com/nmnxtadmin/NMPublic.aspx
Supreme Court:	http://nmsupremecourt.nmcourts.gov/

10. Leading publishers of state specific treatises, practice books, and CLE publications.
LexisNexis, National Business Institute, New Mexico Bar Foundation Law-Related Education, State Bar of New Mexico, West. See Appendix B for addresses and telephone numbers.

New York

1. Codes and Session Laws.
McKinney's Consolidated Laws of New York Annotated. St. Paul, MN: West, 1916-date. 319 vols. Includes annual pocket parts and periodic revised volumes. Forms also available (see Section #5).
Cost: $10,017; supplementation: 1996: $753; 1997: $1,203; 1998: $728; 1999: $1,378; 2000: $1,393; 2002: $2,049.25; 2003: $2,323.50; 2004: $2,444; 2006: $2,905; 2007: $3,907; 2008: $4,480; 2009: $4,548; 2010: $5,298.50; 2011: $5,558; 2012: $6,809.50; 2013: $8,425; **Monthly Assured Print Pricing (APP):** $624/$7,488; **New York Primary Law Resources Plus Cases and Statutes on WestlawNext PRO**: $4,380/year.

McKinney's Consolidated Laws of New York. Compact edition. St. Paul, MN: West. 4 vols. Annual.
Cost: 2014 Edition: $945 (2014).
This set provides the full text of New York statutes and New York Constitution, plus New York, federal district, and bankruptcy court orders and rules. Also provides the text, credits, and necessary validity and effective date italics for the entire statutory code of New York.

New York Consolidated Laws Service. Charlottesville, VA: LexisNexis,1998-date. 46 vols. in 150. Subscription includes annual pocket parts, periodic revised volumes, Advance Legislative Service pamphlets and Midyear Case Annotation Service.
Cost: $1,616 (with annual service); supplementation: 2005: $597; 2008: $1,070; 2010: $1,119; 2011: $1,246; 2012: $1,246; 2013: $1,469; individual volumes also available. This title was sold to Reed Elsevier in January, 1997 after the Department of Justice negotiated a consent decree with the Thomson Corporation and West Publishing requiring the divestiture of 51 titles.

New York Consolidated Laws Quarterly Update Service. Charlottesville, VA: LexisNexis,1998-date.
Supplements code between annual pocket parts. Included with standing order subscription to the **New York Consolidated Laws**
Cost: $148 per year (2014); or included in cost of maintaining NCLS (see above).

Advance Legislative Service for the New York Consolidated Law Service. Charlottesville, VA: LexisNexis,1980-date. Published during and immediately after each legislative session and contain the text of laws in numerical chapter sequence in order of passage.
Cost: $175; renewal: 2014: $158 (2014); or included in cost of maintaining NCLS (see above).

McKinney's New York Session Law Service. St. Paul, MN: West 2 vols. Bound annual volumes.
Cost: 1994: $56; 1995: $61.50; 1996: $67; 1997: $68;1998: $70; 1999: $76; 2004: $148; 2005: $180; 2006: $202; 2007: $222; 2008: $256; 2009: $296; 2010: $336; 2011: $372; 2012: $414; 2013: $464.

New York Session Law Service. Advance sheets. St. Paul, MN: West Published during and immediately after each legislative session and contain the text of laws in numerical sequence in order of passage.
Cost: $985.56 (2014)

Legislative Hotline: (518) 455-7545.

2. Administrative Law.
Official Compilation of Codes, Rules and Regulations of the State of New York. Albany, Department of State. Available from the West. 85 vols. Looseleaf format. Semi-monthly updates with four quarterly indices. Also available at no charge on West site at: http://government.westlaw.com/linkedslice/default.asp?SP=nycrr-1000
Cost: $3,114.79 + postage and handling (includes one year's supplementation); supplementation: 1995: $828; 1996: $828; 1997: $565; 1998: $565; 2001: $688; 2002: $688; 2003: $688; 2004: $688; 2005: $688; 2006: $688; 2007: $688; 2008: $784.40; 2009: $846.37; 2010: $555.62; 2011: $747; 2012: $946.30; 2013: $1,057.30. Individual volumes available at a cost of $47.76 each.

New York State Register. Albany: Department of State. Weekly.
Cost: $80 (1st class); $40 (2d class) (2014) (518) 474-6947
Online at: www.dos.ny.gov/info/register.htm

3. Court Reports.
New York Reports [1st] - **3d**. 1847-date. St. Paul, MN: West. 1st series: 1847-1956 (309 vols.); 2d series (1956-2004): 100 vols.; 3d series (2004-date): 21 vols. (April 1, 2014). Contain decisions of the New York Court of Appeals.
Cost: 1st series: out of print; 2d series: $1,195; 3d series: $1,195; annual cost (2013): $74.00 (list). Subscriptions available to weekly advance sheets: $128.88, bound volumes and bimonthly cumulative index pamphlets. Current cost per volume: $25.00 (list).

New York Appellate Division Reports [1st] - **3d**. 1896-date. St. Paul, MN: West. 1st series (1896-1956): 286 vols.; 2d series (1956-2004): 309 vols.; 3d series (2004-date): 112 vols. Current vol.: 112, 3d series (April 1, 2014).
Cost: 3d series: $1,195; annual cost (2013): $275.00 (11); current cost per volume: $25.00 each. See entry for New York Reports.

New York Miscellaneous Reports [1st] - **3d**. 1892-date. St. Paul, MN: West. 1st series (1892-1956): 208 vols.; 2d series (1956-2004): 196 vols.; 3d series (2004-date): 41 vols. Current volume: 41, 3d series (March 1, 2014).
Cost: 3d series: $1,195; annual cost (2013): $100.00; current cost per volume: $25.00 each. See entry for New York Reports.

New York Supplement [1st] - **2d**. St. Paul, MN: West, 1888-date. Contains decisions of the New York Court of Appeals from 1956-date, and Supreme Court, Appellate Division from 1888-date. Current volume: 963 **N.Y. Supp. 2d** (April 1, 2014).
Cost: 1st series (300 vols.): out-of-print (see used lawbook dealers in Appendix C); 2d series: $12,968; annual cost (2013): $9,336; recent volume: $389.25/$519 (subscriber/list)., Used sets may be available; see used lawbook dealers in Appendix C.

New York Supplement 2d. Advance sheets. St. Paul, MN: West. Weekly.
Cost: $2,401.08 per year (discounted to bound volume subscribers) (2014).

North Eastern Reporter [1st] - **2d**. St. Paul, MN: West, 1885-date. Contains decisions of the New York Court of Appeals from 1885-date. Current volume: 999 **N.E.2d**.
Cost: 1st series: out-of-print (see used lawbook dealers in Appendix C); 2d series: $15,333; annual cost (2013): $10,146; current vol.: $534/$710 (subscriber/list); **Monthly Assured Print Pricing (APP):** $1,087/$13,044; used sets sell for approx. $2,000.00.

North Eastern Reporter 2d. Advance sheets. St. Paul, MN: Thomson West Weekly.
Cost: $2,866.56 (discounted to bound volume subscribers) (2014).

New York Reports Official Advance Sheets. St. Paul, MN: West. Monthly.
Cost: $128.88 per year (2014).

4. Court Rules.
McKinney's New York Court Rules: State, Federal, Bankruptcy, and Local. St. Paul, MN: West. 3 vols. Annual. Also available as ProView eBook.
Cost: 2014 Edition: $319.

New York Court Rules Annotated. Charlottesville, VA: LexisNexis. 2 vols. Also available as ebook.
Cost: 2014 Edition: $144.00.

5. Digests, Encyclopedias and Practice Sets.
West's New York Digest, 4th. St. Paul, MN: West. Coverage from 1989-date. 274 vols. Annual pocket supplements and periodic revised volumes.
Cost: $15,224; supplementation: 1997: $1,024.50; 1998: $998; 1999: $1,169; 2000: $1,168; 2001: $1,648; 2002: $2,439.50; 2003: $2,069.50; 2004: $2,081.50; 2005: $1,816; 2006: $2,238.75; 2007: $2,793.50; 2008: $5,562; 2009: $6,665.50; 2010: $6,579.50; 2011: $8,405.50; 2012: $8,014.50; 2013: $10,420; **Monthly Assured Print Pricing (APP):** $835/$10,020;

New York Jurisprudence 2d. St. Paul, MN: West, 1998-date. 167 vols. Annual pocket supplements and periodic revised volumes.
Cost: $19,963; supplementation:1994: $1,295; 1995: $1,295; 1996: $1,500; 1997: $1,650; 1998: $1,068; 1999: $1,693; 2000: $2,244; 2001: $2,671; 2003: $3,879; 2004: $4,107.50; 2005: $4,906; 2006: $5,324.25; 2007: $7,331; 2008: $6,816.50; 2009: $8,603; 2010: $11,168; 2011: $11,632.50; 2012: $13.346; 2013: $15,847; **Monthly Assured Print Price (APP)**: $1,273/$15,276.

Caution: Available on Westlaw at a fraction of the cost of maintaining the print set.

West's McKinney's Forms for New York Laws. St. Paul, MN: West, 1989-date. 81 vols. Annual pocket supplements and periodic revised volumes.
Cost: $8,759, but also priced by individual component; supplementation: 1996: $493; 1997: $447.50; 1998: $654; 1999: $785;

2000: $899; 2001: $998; 2003: $2,052; 2004: $2,209.25; 2007: $2,572.50; 2008: $3,047.50; 2009: $3,518; 2010: $4,378; 2011: $4,425; 2012: $4,887; 2013: $4,945; **Monthly Assured Print Pricing (APP)**: $591/$7,092.

Caution: Cost of print supplementation is three times that of the equivalent on Westlaw.

6. Citators.

Shepard's New York Court of Appeals Citations. Albany, NY: Shepard's. Monthly.
Cost: $7.310 (17 bound volumes); all-inclusive monthly subscription: $1,332 (in-state) (2014).

Shepard's New York Supplement Citations. Albany, NY: Shepard's. Monthly or bi-monthly.
Cost: $11,779 (24 bound volumes); all-inclusive subscription: monthly: $2,335 (in-state); bi-monthly: $2,683 (in-state) (2014).

Shepard's New York Supreme Court Appellate Division Citations. Albany, NY: Shepard's. Monthly.
Cost: $8,287 (26 bound volumes); all-inclusive subscription: $1,332 (in-state); (2014).

Shepard's New York Miscellaneous Citations. Albany, NY: Shepard's. Monthly or bi-monthly.
Cost: $5,049 (9 bound volumes); all-inclusive subscription: $1,332 (in-state) (2014).

Shepard's New York Statute Citations. Albany, NY: Shepard's. Monthly or bi-monthly .
Cost: $5,596 (10 bound volumes); all-inclusive subscription: monthly: $1,332 (in-state); bi-monthly: $1,682 (in-state) (2014).

Online: All jurisdictional Shepard's and KeyCite are no longer available as stand-alone products, but are included as part of a jurisdictional or subject library from their respective publishers (2014).

7. CD-ROM Products.

LexisNexis CD - New York Primary Law. Albany, NY: LexisNexis. 7 discs. Updated quarterly. Contains a library of New York primary law, including cases, statutes, session laws, and court rules. Available for Windows. Search Engine: Folio; LivePublish (NextPage).
Cost: $2,432 per year (2014).

New York CD Library. Albany, NY: LexisNexis/Matthew Bender. One disc. Updated quarterly. Contains a library of more than 30 New York practice titles, with supporting primary law and forms. Available for Windows. Search Engine: Folio; LivePublish (NextPage).
Cost: $44,713 for entire library; renewal: 2008: $21,808; 2009: $23,552; 2010: $24.731; 2011: $25,968; 2012: $27,526; 2013: $29,452; 2014: $32,174.88; lesser combinations also available.

Note: West is phasing out many of its CD-ROM products. In any event, WestlawNext is a far better value than anything peviously put out on CD-ROM.

8. State Legal Research Guides.

Adelman, Elizabeth. Theodora Belniak, and Suzanne E. Rowe. **New York Legal Research**. 2d ed. Durham, NC: Carolina Academic Press, 2012. 1 vol. (282 pp.). Paperbound.
Cost: $30.00; from $23.10 on amazon.com (2014).

Galie, Peter J. **The New York State Constitution**. 2d ed. New York: Oxford University Press, 2012. 1 vol. (419 pp.).
Cost: $150.00; from $86.39 on amazon.com; kindle: $119.99 (2014).

Manz, William H., and Karen L. Spencer. **Gibson's New York Legal Research Guide**. 4th ed. Buffalo, NY: William S. Hein & Co., 2014. 1 vol. (786 pp.).
Cost: $85.00; from $80.75 on amazon.com (2014).

Gray, Kevin P. **New York Legislative History Sourcebook**. Baton Rouge, LA: Sourcebook, 2004. 1 vol. (79, 40 pp.).
Cost: $75.00; available from Kevin Gray, P.O. Box 2115, Baton Rouge, LA 70894.

Manz, William. New York Practice Materials: A Selective Bibliography in Houdek, Frank G., ed. **State Practice Materials: Annotated Bibliographies**. Buffalo, NY: William S. Hein & Co., Inc., 2009-date. 2 vols. Looseleaf format.
Cost: $195.00 (2014).

New York Lawyer's Deskbook. 2d ed. Albany: New York State Bar Association, 1998-date. 2 vols. Annual cumulative supplementation (entire contents replaced).
Provides practice guidance in twenty-five subject areas of New York law.
Cost: $345 (members), $425 (non-members); supplementation (members/non-members): 2002: $85.00/$95.00; 2003: $103/$113; 2004: $118/$128; 2005: $105/$118; 2006: $118/128; 2007: $128/$138; 2008: $128/$138; 2009: $138/$168; 2010: $138/$168; 2011-12: $138/$168; 2012-13: $138/$168; 2013-14: $158/$188.

Whittemore, Gail F. **New York Legal Documents: A Selective Annotated Bibliography**. Chicago: AALL, 2007. 1 vol. (31 pp.).
Cost: $30.00. Available from William S. Hein & Co. on electronic pdf and on HeinOnline NY (2014).

9. Leading Web Sites for State Legal Research.

Home Page:	www.ny.gov/
Administrative Code:	www.dos.ny.gov/info/nycrr.html
Agency Directory:	www.nysegov.com/citGuide.cfm?superCat=102
Attorney General:	www.ag.ny.gov/
Attorney Gen. Opinions:	www.ag.ny.gov/appeals-and-opinions/numerical-index
Bar Association:	www.nysba.org/
Bar Association (NYC):	www.nycbar.org
Consolidated Laws:	http://public.leginfo.state.ny.us/menugetf.cgi?COMMONQUERY=LAWS
Constitution:	www.dos.ny.gov/info/constitution.htm

Court of Appeals:	www.courts.state.ny.us/ctapps/
Court Opinions:	www.nycourts.gov/decisions
Governor:	www.governor.ny.gov/
Judicial Branch:	www.courts.state.ny.us/
Law Libraries:	www.courts.state.ny.us/lawlibraries/
Legal Research Sites:	www.nycourts.gov/library/buffalo/legalsites.shtml
Secretary of State:	www.dos.ny.gov
Senate:	www.nysenate.gov/
State Assembly:	www.assembly.state.ny.us/

10. Leading publishers of state specific treatises, practice books, and CLE publications.
Matthew Bender, Gould Publications, LexisNexis, National Business Institute, New York State Bar Association Continuing Legal Education, Thomson Reuters West.

North Carolina

1. Codes and Session Laws.
General Statutes of North Carolina. Charlottesville, VA: LexisNexis,1999-date. 21 vols. Biennial softbound editions with interim supplements. First edition published in 1999.
Cost: 2013 paperbound edition: $595/$818 (in-state/out-of-state); 2012 supp.: $258 (2014).

North Carolina Advance Annotation Service. Charlottesville, VA: LexisNexis. These pamphlets are published during the year to update the annotations in the General Statutes.
Cost: $128 per year (in-state) (20134).

North Carolina Advance Legislative Service. Charlottesville, VA: LexisNexis. Three times per year. These pamphlets are published and immediately after each legislative session and contain text of laws in numerical chapter sequence in order of passage.
Cost: $12 (in-state); $44 (out-of-state) (2014).

Session Laws of North Carolina. Raleigh, NC: General Assembly, Legislative Services Commission. Distributed by Secretary of State. 1-2 vols. (919) 807-2000.
Cost: 1993: $30.38;1995: $28.12; 1996: $9.10;1997: $35.76;1998: $34.54; 1999: $32.97; 2000: $19.92; 2001: $43.20; 2002: $12; 2003: $24.07; 2004: $14.45; 2005: $26.16; 2006: $19.07; 2007: $31.94; 2008: $19.13; 2009: $30.94 (2 vols.); 2010: $14.60; 2011: $41.13; 2012: $16.62.

Legislative Hotline: (919) 733-7779.

2. Administrative Law.
North Carolina Administrative Code. 15th ed. St. Paul, MN: West, 1998-date. 33 vols. Quarterly supplements.
Cost: $693 (includes one year's updates); supplementation: 2004: $495; 2007: $588.10; 2008: $588.10; 2009: $636; 2010: $636; 2011: $662; 2012: $662; 2013: $662.

North Carolina Register. Raleigh, NC: Office of Administrative Hearings [available from LexisNexis], 1986-date. Biweekly.
Cost: $219 per year (2014). (919) 733-2679

3. Court Reports.
North Carolina Reports. 1778-date. Raleigh, NC: Administrative Office of the Courts [current publisher]. Current vol.: 365 (as of March 1, 2014). (919) 890-1039
Cost: Current volumes: $19.53; vols. 1-364 and Court of Appeals Reports vols. 1-196 approx. $4,800. Advance sheets are $76.67 (in-state) and $71.16 (out-of-state) per year (including Supreme Court and Court of Appeals. All prior volumes available. Used sets may also be available. Opinions from 1998-date also available online.

North Carolina Court of Appeals Reports. Raleigh, NC: Administrative Office of the Courts, 1968-date. Current vol.: 209 (March 1, 2014). (919) 890-1039
Cost: Current volumes: $19.53. All prior volumes available. Used sets may also be available. Opinions from 1998-date also available online.

North Carolina Reporter. St. Paul, MN: West,1939-date. [off-print of South Eastern Reporter 2d. Contains decisions of the North Carolina Supreme Court from 1939 to date and the North Carolina Court of Appeals from 1968 to date.
Current volume: 747-749 S.E. 2d.
Cost: $5,252; annual cost 2002: $605; 2003: $657; 2004: $595.25; 2005: $652; 2006: $864.50; 2007: $964; 2008: $1,057; 2009: $1,545.50; 2010: $1,648; 2011: $1,936; 2012: $2,905; 2013: $4,003; current volume: $417/$556 (subscriber/list); **Monthly Assured Print Pricing (APP):** $439/$5,268.

South Eastern Reporter [1st] - **2d**. St. Paul, MN: West, 1886-date. Contains decisions of the Georgia Supreme Court from 1887-date and the Georgia Court of Appeals from 1907-date. Current vol.: 750 **S.E. 2d**.
Cost: 1st series out-of-print (see used lawbook dealers in Appendix C); 2d series: $10,480; annual cost: 2012: $7,389; 2013: $5,434; current vol.: $524/$655 (subscriber/list); **Monthly Assured Print Pricing (APP):** $846/$10,152. See list of used lawbook dealers in Appendix C.

South Eastern Reporter 2d. Advance sheets. St. Paul, MN: Thomson West. Weekly.
Cost: $2,825 (discounted to bound volume subscribers) (2014).

4. Court Rules.
North Carolina Rules of Court, State and Federal. St. Paul, MN: West 2 vols. Annual. Also available as ProView eBook.
Cost: 2014 Edition: $204; Federal, State and Local: $274.

North Carolina Court Rules Annotated. Charlottesville, VA: LexisNexis. 1 vol. Paperbound. Updated semiannually, replaced annually. Published as a part of the General Statutes of North Carolina.
Cost: 2014 Edition: $42.

5. Digests, Encyclopedias and Practice Sets.
West's North Carolina Digest 2d. St. Paul, MN: West, 1990-

date. 102 vols.
Cost: $5,851 (includes one year's upkeep); supplementation:1996: $156.00; 1997: $178.50; 1998: $245; 1999: $583.25; 2000: $341; 2001: $381.50; 2002: $964; 2003: $754; 2004: $941.75; 2005: $1,126.50; 2006: $1,459.50; 2007: $1,267.50; 2008: $1,680; 2009: $2,249.50; 2010: $2,365.50; 2011: $2,848; 2012: $2,975; 2013: $4,426; **Monthly Assured Print Pricing (APP):** $284/$3,408.

Strong's North Carolina Index. 4th ed. St. Paul, MN: West, 1989-date. 58 vols. An encyclopedic index to North Carolina case law. Annual pocket parts and periodic revised volumes.
Cost: $8,882 ; supplementation: 1995 pocket parts: $431; 1996: $553; 1997: $691.30; 1998: $436; 1999: $634; 2000: $888; 2001: $1,057; 2002: $1,838; 2004: $2,073; 2005: $2,270.50; 2006: $2,275; 2007: $2,678.50; 2008: $3,215.50; 2009: $3,724; 2010: $4,819; 2011: $4,711; 2012: $5,325.50; 2013: $6,341; **Monthly Assured Print Pricing (APP):** $497/$5,964.

.

6. Citators.

Shepard's North Carolina Citations. Albany, NY: Shepard's. Monthly or bi-monthly.
Cost: $3,342 (10 bound volumes); all-inclusive subscription: monthly: $2,284; (in-state); bi-monthly: $2,709 (in-state) (2014).

Online: All jurisdictional Shepard's and KeyCite are no longer available as stand-alone products, but are included as part of a jurisdictional or subject library package (2014).

7. CD-ROM Products.

LexisNexis CD - North Carolina Primary Law. Albany, NY: LexisNexis. Two discs. Updated quarterly. Contains the full text of the General Statutes of North Carolina annotated, State Constitution, annotated court rules, North Carolina Administrative Code, decisions of the North Carolina Supreme Court from 1778 to date, North Carolina Court of Appeals from 1968 to date, selected U.S. Supreme Court, federal appeals and federal district court opinions from 1791 to date, and Attorney General opinions from 1977 to date. Available for Windows. Search Engine: Folio; LivePublish (NextPage). Subscription includes online updating via LexisNexis.
Cost: $2,075 per year (2014).

North Carolina Reporter and West's North Carolina Statutes Annotated. Eagan, MN: West. One disc. Premise. Regular updates. Contains the full text of West's North Carolina Statutes, Constitution, court rules, North Carolina Administrative Code, decisions of the North Carolina Supreme Court from 1778 to date, Court of Appeals from 1943 to date, and Attorney General opinions form 1977 to date. Decisions also searchable by West Topics and Key Numbers, headnotes and synopses. Available for DOS, Windows or Macintosh. Search Engine: PREMISE or LawDesk. Subscription includes online updating via Westlaw.
Cost: $7,359 per year (2014).

8. State Legal Research Guides.

Baer, Miriam J. and James C. Ray. **Legal Research in North Carolina**. Durham, NC: Carolina Academic Press, 2006. 1 vol. (224 pp.).
Cost: $31; from 22.09 on amazon.com (2014).

Childs, Scott. **North Carolina Legal Research**. Durham, NC: Carolina Academic Press, 2010. 1 vol. (232 pp.). Paperbound.
Cost: $25.00; from $13.64 on amazon.com (2014).

Childs, Scott and Nick Sexton. **North Carolina Legal Research Guide**. 2d ed. Buffalo, NY: William S. Hein & Co., Inc., 2009. 1 vol. (418 pp.).
Cost: $75; from $55.00 on amazon.com (2014).

Nixon, Donna, Nichelle Perry and Jason Sowards. **State Documents Bibliography: North Carolina**. Chicago: AALL, 2010.
Cost: $30.00. Available from William S. Hein & Co. on electronic pdf and on HeinOnline (2014).

Kimbrough, Julie L. North Carolina Practice Materials: A Selective Bibliography in Houdek, Frank G., ed. **State Practice Materials: Annotated Bibliographies**. Buffalo, NY: William S. Hein & Co., Inc., 2009-date. 2 vols. Looseleaf format.
Cost: $195.00 (2014).

Matzen, Constance M. "A Selected Bibliography of North Carolina Practice Materials." **Southeastern Law Librarian** 24 (Spring, 1999): 25-34.

McKnight, Jean Sinclair. **North Carolina Legal Research Guide**. 2d ed. Buffalo, NY: William S. Hein & Co., 2009. 1 vol. (418 pp.).
Cost: OUT-OF-PRINT; from $.01 on amazon.com (2014).

Orth, John V. and Paul M. Newby. **North Carolina State Constitution**. 2d ed. New York: Oxford University Press, 2013. 1 vol. (254 pp.).
Cost: $150.00; from $121.92 on amazon.com; kindle: $119.99 (2014).

Orth, John V. **North Carolina State Constitution, with History and Commentary**. Chapel Hill: University of North Carolina Press, 1995. 1 vol. (216 pp.).
Cost: OUT-OF-PRINT; from $34.99 on amazon.com (2014).

9. Leading Web Sites for State Legal Research.

Home Page:	www.nc.gov
Administrative Code:	www.secretary.state.nc.us/ucc/
Agency Directory:	www.nc.gov/government/agencies
Attorney General:	www.ncdoj.com/
Attorney Gen. Opinions:	http://www.ncdoj.gov/About-DOJ/Legal-Services.aspx
Bar Association:	www.ncbar.org/
Constitution:	www.ncleg.net/Legislation/constitution/ncconstitution.html
Court Opinions:	http://appellate.nccourts.org/opinions/
Governor:	www.governor.state.nc.us/
Judicial Branch:	www.nccourts.org/
Legislative Branch:	www.ncleg.net

Library - Supreme Court:	www.nccourts.org/Courts/Appellate/SCLibrary.asp
Secretary of State:	www.sosnc.com/
Statutes:	www.ncleg.net/gascripts/statutes/Statutes.asp

10. Leading publishers of state specific treatises, practice books, and CLE publications.
Carolina Academic Press, Harrison Company, LexisNexis, National Business Institute, North Carolina Academy of Trial Lawyers Education Foundation, Inc., North Carolina Bar Foundation, Thomson Reuters West. See Appendix B for addresses and telephone numbers.

North Dakota

1. Codes and Session Laws.
North Dakota Century Code Annotated. Charlottesville, VA: LexisNexis, 1959-date. 24 vols. Biennial pocket supplements and periodic revised volumes.
Cost: $531 (in-state), $766 (out-of-state); annual supplementation: 2001: $390/$619; 2002: $108.00/$171; 2003: $212/$338; 2004: $76/$114; 2005: $179/$290; 2006: $189/$300; 2007: $308/$498; 2008: $114/$228; 2009: $510/$625; 2010: $510/$625; 2011: $532/$657; 2012: $203/$337; 2013: $211/$345.

North Dakota Advance Code Service. Charlottesville, VA: LexisNexis. Issued between biennial pocket parts.
Cost: $91.00; renewal: 2014: $48.

North Dakota Advance Legislative Service. Charlottesville, VA: LexisNexis.
These pamphlets are published during and immediately after current legislative session and contain the text of laws in numerical chapter sequence in order of passage.
Cost: $72.00 (2014).

Laws of North Dakota [session laws]. Bismarck, ND: Secretary of State. 2 vols. Published in odd-numbered years. (701) 328-2900
Cost:1995: $50 (2 vols.); 1997: $54; 1999: $55; 2001: $54; 2003: $54; 2005: $54; 2007: $54; 2009: $97; 2011: $54; 2013: $44.

Legislative Hotline: (701) 328-2900; (701) 328-2916.

2. Administrative Law.
North Dakota Administrative Code. Bismarck, ND: Legislative Council, 1978-date. CD-ROM format only. Quarterly updates. Available from Secretary of State. (701) 328-2900
Cost: $60.00 per year (2014).

No register.

3. Court Reports.
North Dakota Reports.1890-1953. Vols. 1-79 [ceased publication with vol. 79].
Cost: Out-of print. See used lawbook dealers.

North Western Reporter [1st] - **2d**. St. Paul, MN: West, 1879-date [official since 1953]. Contains decisions of the North Dakota Supreme Court from 1890-date and Court of Appeals of North Dakota from 1987-date. Current vol.: 844 **N.W. 2d**.
Cost: 1st series out-of-print (see used lawbook dealers in Appendix C); 2d series $10,225; used sets sell for approx. $3,795; annual cost (2013): $7,332; recent volume: $459/$611 (subscriber/list); **Monthly Assured Print Pricing (APP):** $709/$8,508.

West's North Western Reporter 2d. Advance Sheets. St. Paul, MN: Thomson West. Weekly.
Cost: $2,808 (discounted to bound volume subscribers) (2014).

4. Court Rules.
North Dakota Court Rules, State and Federal. St. Paul, MN: West. 2 vols. Annual. Also available as ProView eBook.
Cost: 2014 Edition: $264.

North Dakota Century Code Annotated Court Rules, 2012-2013 Edition. Charlottesville, VA: LexisNexis. 1 vol. Annual. Part of the North Dakota Century Code Annotated. With supplement.
Cost: 2012-2013: $44.00 (in-state); $72 (out-of-state) (2014).

5. Digests, Encyclopedias and Practice Sets.
Dakota Digest. St. Paul, MN: West, 1942-date. 62 vols. Kept up to date by pocket parts, pamphlets, bound cumulative supplements, and replacement volumes. This digest covers both North and South Dakota.
Cost: $7,876; supplementation: 1995: $296; 1996: $299.50; 1997: $329; 1998: $851; 1999: $710; 2000: $851; 2001: $1,743.75; 2002: $1,184; 2003: $603.50; 2004: $743; 2005: $1,250; 2006: $1,235.75; 2007: $1,252; 2008: $1,609.50; 2009: $3,539.50; 2010: $2,530; 2011: $3,817.50; 2012: $3,875; 2013: $4,948; **Monthly Assured Print Pricing (APP):** $398/$4,776.

6. Citators.
Shepard's North Dakota Citations. Albany, NY: Shepard's. Six supplements per year.
Cost: $989 (1 bound volume); all-inclusive subscription: $1,720 (in-state) (2014).

Online: All jurisdictional Shepard's and KeyCite are no longer available as stand-alone products, but are included as part of a jurisdictional or subject library from their respective publishers (2014).

7. CD-ROM Products.
LexisNexis CD - North Dakota Primary Law. Albany, NY: LexisNexis. One disc. Updated quarterly. Contains the full text of the North Dakota Century Code, North Dakota Supreme Court decisions from 1867 to date, Court of Appeals decisions from 1987 to date, and the North Dakota Administrative Code. Available for DOS or Windows. Search Engine: Folio. Subscription includes online updating via LEXIS.
Cost: $1,638 per year (2014).

8. State Legal Research Guides.
Leahy, James E. **The North Dakota State Constitution**. New York: Oxford University Press, 2011. 1 vol. (268 pp.).
Cost: $150.00; from $72.15 on amazon.com; kindle: $119.99 (2014).

Schwartz, Rhonda R. North Dakota Practice Materials: A Selective Bibliography in Houdek, Frank G., ed. **State Practice Materials: Annotated Bibliographies**. Buffalo, NY: William S. Hein & Co., Inc., 2008-date. 2 vols. Looseleaf format.
Cost: $195.00 (2014).

Schwartz, Rhonda R. **North Dakota State Dacuments: A Selective Annotated Bibliography of Legal and Law-Related Material**. Chicago: AALL, 2009. Available from William S. Hein & Co.
Cost: $30.00; $20.00 in pdf; also on HeinOnline (2014).

9. Leading Web Sites for State Legal Research.

Home Page:	www.nd.gov/
Administrative Code:	www.legis.nd.gov/agency-rules/north-dakota-administrative-code
Agency Directory:	www.nd.gov/agency.htm
Attorney General:	www.ag.state.nd.us/
Attorney Gen. Opinions:	www.ag.state.nd.us/Opinions/Opinions.htm
Bar Association:	www.sband.org/
Constitution:	www.legis.nd.gov/constitution
Governor:	www.governor.nd.gov/
Law Library:	www.ndcourts.com/LawLib/www6.htm
Legislative Branch:	www.legis.nd.gov/
Secretary of State:	www.nd.gov/sos/
Statutes:	www.legis.nd.gov/general-information (link is at bottom of page)
Supreme Court:	www.ndcourts.gov/
Supreme Court Opinions:	www.ndcourts.gov/Search/Opinions.asp

10. Leading publishers of state specific treatises, practice books, and CLE publications.
National Business Institute, State Bar Association of North Dakota. See Appendix B for addresses and telephone numbers.

Ohio

1. Codes and Session Laws.
Baldwin's Ohio Revised Code Annotated. St. Paul, MN: West.[formerly published by Banks-Baldwin Law Publishing Co.], 1994-date. 71 vols. Annual pocket supplements and periodic revised volumes.
Cost: $2,616.48; supplementation: 1995: $717;1996: $280; 1997: $554; 1998: $600; 1999: $600; 2000: $600; 2001: $264; 2002: $690; 2003: $165; 2004: $761; 2005: $780.50; 2006: $869.50; 2007: $772; 2008: $1,194; 2009: $1,326; 2010: $1,488; 2011: $1,668; 2012: $2,088; 2013: $2,338; **Monthly Assured Print Pricing (APP):** $218.04/$2,616.48.

Baldwin's Ohio Legislative Service Annotated. St. Paul, MN: West. Monthly. Contains the text of newly enacted laws, rule amendments, and annotations.
Cost: $1,077 per year (2013).

Page's Ohio Revised Code Annotated. Cincinnati, OH: W. H. Anderson Co./LexisNexis, 1953-date. 36 vols. Annual pocket parts and periodic revised volumes.
Cost: $1,770 (includes one year's service); supplementation (in-state/out-of-state): 2009: $1,072/$1,095; 2010: $1,141; 2011: $1,192; 2012: $1,245; 2013: $1,239.

Page's Ohio Revised Code Legislative Bulletin Service. Cincinnati, OH: W. H. Anderson Co. Monthly. Contains the text of newly enacted laws, rule amendments, and annotations. Now available from LexisNexis.
Cost: Included in cost of **Page's Ohio Revised Code**.

State of Ohio: Legislative Acts [session laws]. Columbus, OH: Secretary of State. Two-year compilations published in odd-numbered years.
Cost: vol. 145 (1993-94): $357.24 (4 vols.); vol. 146 (1995-96): $325 (5 vols.); vol. 147 (1997-98): $325; vol. 148 (1999-2000): vol. 149 (2001-2002): $300 (5 vols.); vol. 150 (2003-04): $380; 151 (2005-06): $400; vol. 152 (2007-08)-date supplied electronically at: http://www.sos.state.oh.us/SOS/historicaldocuments/LawsofOhio/historical.aspx. (877) 767-3453

Legislative Hotline: 1-614-466-8842

2. Administrative Law.
Ohio Administrative Code. Approved Edition. St. Paul, MN: West [formerly Banks-Baldwin Publishing Co.], 1977-date. 29 vols. Softbound. Individual volumes also available.
Cost: $6,225; renewal: 1998: $492.50; 1999: $752; 2000: $595; 2001: $372; 2002: $866; 2003: $921; 2004: $1,121; 2005: $1,123; 2006: $732.50; 2007: $1,594.25; 2008: $1,564; 2009: $1,574; 2010: $2,660; 2011: $3,449; 2012: $3,828; 2013: $4,590; **Monthly Assured Print Pricing (APP):** $437/$5,244.

Ohio Monthly Record. St. Paul, MN: West, 1977-date. Monthly.
Cost: $2,422.56 per year (2013).

3. Court Reports.
Ohio State Reports [1st series]. Columbus, OH: [various publishers], 1852-1965. Vols. 1-177. Contain decisions of the Ohio Supreme Court.
Cost: Out-of-print. Contact used lawbook dealers for price and availability. See also CD-ROM products.

Ohio Official Reports 2d. Cincinnati, OH: W. H. Anderson Co., 1964-1982 (vols. 1-70). Contain the following reports: Ohio State Reports 2d, vols. 1-70 (1964-1982); are bound with Ohio Appellate Reports 2d, vols. 1-70 (1965-1982); and Ohio Miscellaneous Reports 1st, vols. 1-70 (1964-1982).
Cost: Out-of-print; may be available used. See also CD-ROM products.

Ohio Official Reports 3d. Cincinnati, OH: W. H. Anderson Co., 1982-1991 (vols. 1-60). Contain the following reports: **Ohio State Reports 3d**, vols. 1-60 (1982-1991); **Ohio Appellate Reports 3d**, vols. 1-60 (1982-1991); and **Ohio Miscellaneous Reports 2d**, vols. 1-60 (1982-1991). Volumes 61-197 (1991-

date) published by West. Current volume: 197 Ohio App. & 168 Ohio Misc.
Cost: Volumes 61-date: $1,431; current volume: $49.50; Vols. 1-60 may be available used.

Ohio Official Reports Advance Sheets. St. Paul, MN: West, 1994-date.
Includes **Ohio State Reports**, 3d; **Ohio Appellate Reports**, 3d; and **Ohio Miscellaneous Reports**, 2d. **Ohio Official Reports** is published in two separate bound-volume series: one for the Supreme Court and one for the lower courts.
Cost: $135.96 per year (2013).

Ohio State Reports 3d. St. Paul, MN: West, 1991 (vol. 60) - date. Vols. 1-60 (1982-1991), 3d series published by W.H. Anderson Co. Bound in **Ohio Official Reports** (see above). 1st series: 1852-1964 (177 vols.); 2d series: 1964-1982 (70 vols.); 3d series: 1991-date Current vol.: 136
Cost: Volumes 61-date: $604 (61-136): $49.50 each (list); annual cost: 2002: $128; 2003: $107.50; 2004: $112; 2005: $115.50; 2006: $115.50; 2007: $154.00; 2008: $129.00; 2009: $175.50; 2010: $111.50; 2011: $153; 2012: $143.64; 2013: $148.50; for earlier volumes, see entry for **Ohio Official Reports 2d-3d** (above); 1st series: see list of used lawbook dealers in Appendix C.

Ohio Appellate Reports 3d. West, 1982-1991 (vols. 1-60). Bound in Ohio Official Reports (see above) with Ohio Miscellaneous Reports 2d (vols. 64-133); Vols. 1-60 published by W.H. Anderson Co. 1st series: 1913-1965 (120 vols.); 2d series: 1965-1982 (70 vols.); 3d series: 1991-date (194 vols.). Current vol.: App.: 203 and Misc. 174.
Cost: $1,431; annual cost 2003: $179.75; 2004: $93; 2005: $192.50; 2006: $198.50; 2007: $198.50; 2008: $215.00; 2009: $223.75; 2010: $223.75; 2011: $239.40 (list); 2012: $239.40; 2013: $239.40; individual vols.: $47.88 ea.; also, see entry for Ohio Official Reports 2d - 3d (above); 1st series: see list of used lawbook dealers in Appendix C. 3d series, vols. 61-date: Contact West sales representative.

Ohio Cases. St. Paul, MN: West, 1935-date. [offprint of **North Eastern Reporter** [1st] and **2d**.] Contains decisions of the Ohio Supreme Court from 1933 to date and the Ohio Court of Appeals from 1943 to date. Current vol.: 994-995 N.E. 2d.
Cost: $6,759 ; annual cost 2002: $687; 2003: $685; 2004: $692; 2005: $760.50; 2006: $1,077.50; 2007: $1,186.50; 2008: $1,185; 2009: $1,646; 2010: $1,956; 2011: $2,450; 2012: $4,236; 2013: $4,222; current vol.: $352/$469 (subscriber/list); **Monthly Assured Print Pricing (APP):** $485/$5,820.

North Eastern Reporter [1st] - **2d**. St. Paul, MN: West, 1885-date. Contains decisions of the Ohio Supreme Court from 1885-date and the Ohio Court of Appeals from 1923-date. Current volume: 999 **N.E.2d**.
Cost: 1st series: out-of-print (see used lawbook dealers in Appendix C); 2d series: $15,333; annual cost (2013): $10,146; current vol.: $534/$710 (subscriber/list); **Monthly Assured Print Pricing (APP):** $1,087/$13,044; used sets sell for approx. $2,000.00.

North Eastern Reporter 2d. Advance sheets. St. Paul, MN: Thomson West Weekly.
Cost: $2,866.56 (discounted to bound volume subscribers) (2014).

4. Court Rules.

Ohio Rules of Court: State and Federal. St. Paul, MN: West. 2 vols. Annual.
Also available as ProView eBook.
Cost: 2014 Edition: $174; Federal, State and Local: $262.

LexisNexis Ohio Rules of Court Annotated. Charlottesville, VA: LexisNexis. 1 vol. Annual. Also available as ebook.
Cost: 2013-2014: Edition (print or ebook): $130 (in-state) (2014).

5. Digests, Encyclopedias and Practice Sets.

Ohio Jurisprudence 3d. St. Paul, MN: ThomsonWest, 1977-date. 116 vols. Annual pocket parts and periodic revised volumes.
Cost: $14.374 ; supplementation: 1993: $878.50;1994: $1,040; 1995: $1,040; 1996: $1,271; 1997: $1,077.25; 1998: $1,293; 1999: $1,951.50; 2000: $2,448; 2001: $2,459.50; 2002: $3,189.67; 2003: $3,573.50; 2004: $3,705; 2005: $4,299; 2006: $4,432; 2007: $5,914.50; 2008: $5,618; 2009: $7,269; 2010: $8,479; 2011: $8,480; 2012: $10,492.50; 2013: $9,248; **Monthly Assured Print Pricing (APP):** $945/$11,340.

West's Ohio Digest. St. Paul, MN: ThomsonWest,1949-date. 30 vols. in 148. Annual pocket parts, mid-year supplement, and periodic revised volumes.
Cost: $7,947; supplementation: 1996: $568.50; 1997: $253.50; 1998: $432; 1999: $621; 2000: $1,043; 2001: $1,195; 2002: $1,338; 2003: $1,050.50; 2004: $1,157; 2005: $1,283.50; 2006: $805.50; 2007: $1,280; 2008: $1,281.50; 2009: $2,968.50; 2010: $3,317; 2011: $3,724; 2012: $3,598.50; 2013: $6,377; **Monthly Assured Print Pricing (APP):** $420/$5,040.

6. Citators.

Shepard's Ohio Citations. Albany, NY: Shepard's. Monthly or bi-monthly.
Cost: $11,970 (19 bound volumes); all-inclusive subscription: monthly: $2,493 (in-state); bi-monthly: $2,864 (in-state) (2014).

Shepard's Ohio Unreported Appellate Decisions. Albany, NY: Shepard's. Monthly or bi-monthly.
Cost: $6,751 (15 bound volumes); all-inclusive subscription: $2,158 (in-state) (2014).

Online: All jurisdictional Shepard's and KeyCite are no longer available as stand-alone products, but are acquired as part of a jurisdictional or subject library package from their respective publishers (2014).

7. CD-ROM Products.

Anderson's Ohio Primary Law (CD-ROM). Cincinnati, OH: Anderson Publishing Co. Four discs. Updated quarterly. Contains the full text of Page's Ohio Revised Code Annotated, the Ohio Administrative Code, decisions from the Ohio Official Reports 1st -3d series, Ohio Opinions from 1956 to 1980, and unreported Ohio Appellate decisions from 1973 to date.

Windows 95 or higher. Search Engine: Folio.

Cost: $2,825 per year; renewal: 2010: $1,579; 2011: $1,658; 2012: $1,757; 2013: $1,880; 2014: $2,093.

Ohio Forms of Pleading and Practice on CD-ROM. Albany, NY: LexisNexis/Matthew Bender. One disc. Contains every form needed for all aspects of pleading and practice, with total coverage on the Civil Rules, Appellate Procedure, Probate Practice, selected Special Proceedings, Criminal and Juvenile Rules and the Rules of Evidence, with annotations to case law and the complete text of the Ohio Rules of Court. Available for Windows. Search Engine: Folio; LivePublish (NextPage).
Cost: $5,186; renewal: 2008: $2,595; 2009: $2,802; 2010: $2,943; 2011: $3,031; 2012: $3,152; 2013: $3,278; 2014: $3,684.

8. State Legal Histories and Research Guides.
Corcas, Christine A. **Ohio Legal and Law-Related Documents**. Chicago: American Association of Law Libraries, Government Documents SIS, 1986.
Cost: $30.00; pdf: $20.00. Available from William S. Hein & Co. on electronic pdf and on HeinOnline (2014).

Elliott, Susan. Ohio Practice Materials: A Selective Bibliography in Houdek, Frank G., ed. **State Practice Materials: Annotated Bibliographies**. Buffalo, NY: William S. Hein & Co., Inc., 2005-date. 2 vols. Looseleaf format.
Cost: $195.00 (2014).

Gold, David M. **A Guide to Legislative History in Ohio**. Columbus: Ohio Legislative Service Commission, 1986.

Hall, Katherine L. and Sara Sampson. **Ohio Legal Research**. Durham, NC: Carolina Academic Press, 2009. 1 vol. (177 pp.). Paperbound.
Cost: $25.00; from $19.19 on amazon.com (2014).

The History of Ohio Law. Edited by Michael Les Benedict and John F. Winkler. Athens: Ohio University Press, 2004. 2 vols. (952 pp.).
Cost: $75.00; from $5.00 on amazon.com (2014).
A valuable collection of scholarly articles covering the institutions of Ohio law; Ohio legal literature, Ohio and American law, litigation and procedure, growth of Ohio law, and law and society in Ohio, published under the auspices of the Ohio State Bar Foundation.

Leonard. James. "A Select Annotated Bibliography of Ohio Practice Materials." **Ohio Northern University Law Review** 17, no. 2 (1990): 265-301.

Ohio Regional Association of Law Libraries. **Ohio Legal Resources: An Annotated Bibliography and Guide**. 4th ed. Columbus: Ohio Library Council, 1996.

Putnam, Melanie K. and Susan Schaefgen. **Ohio Legal Research Guide**. 2d ed. Buffalo, NY: William S. Hein & Co., Inc., 2010. 1 vol. (371 pp.).
Cost: $65.00; from $0.13 on amazon.com (2014).

Steinglass, Steven H. and Gino Scarselli. **The Ohio State Constitution**. New York: Oxford University Press, 2011. 1 vol. (436 pp.).

Cost: $150.00; from $135.66 on amazon.com; kindle: $97.49 (2014).

9. Leading Web Sites for State Legal Research.

Home Page:	www.ohio.gov/
Administrative Code:	http://codes.ohio.gov/oac
Agency Directory:	www.ohio.gov/agencies/
Attorney General:	www.ohioattorneygeneral.gov/
Attorney Gen. Opinions:	www.ohioattorneygeneral.gov/Legal/Opinions
Bar Association:	www.ohiobar.org/
Constitution:	www.legislature.state.oh.us/constitution.cfm
Court Opinions:	www.sconet.state.oh.us/ROD/docs/
Governor:	www.governor.ohio.gov/
Law Library:	www.sconet.state.oh.us/LegalResources/LawLibrary
Legislature:	www.legislature.state.oh.us/
Ohio Revised Code:	http://codes.ohio.gov/orc
Secretary of State:	www.sos.state.oh.us/sos/
Supreme Court:	www.sconet.state.oh.us/

10. Leading publishers of state specific treatises, practice books, and CLE publications.
Matthew Bender, LexisNexis, National Business Institute, Ohio Legal Center Institute, Ohio State Bar Association Continuing Legal Education, Thomson Reuters West. See Appendix B for addresses and telephone numbers.

Oklahoma

1. Codes and Session Laws.
Oklahoma Statutes. St. Paul, MN: West, 2011. 12 vols. Updated with bound supplementary volumes. A less expensive, unannotated alternative to the full Oklahoma Statutes Annotated.
Cost: 2013 Edition: $301.99; supplementation:1995: $78;1996: $120.57; 1997: $128.62; 1998: $160; 1999: $175; 2000: $210; 2001: $210; 2002: $277; 2003: 73; 2004: $195; 2005: $160; 2006: $246.50; 2007: $240; 2008: $290; 2009: $339; 2010: $390; 2011: $280; 2012: $290; **Monthly Assured Print Pricing (APP):** $12/$144.

Oklahoma Statutes Annotated. St. Paul, MN: West, 1936-date. 90 vols. Annual pocket parts and periodic revised volumes.
Cost: $4,351 (includes first year's pocket parts); supplementation: 1994: $310.50; 1995: $470.80; 1996: $497.50; 1997: $578.50; 1998: $629.50; 1999: $786; 2000: $841; 2001: $1,110.50; 2002: $1,367.50; 2003: $1,376; 2004: $1,196; 2005: $1,912; 2006: $1,448; 2007; $1,390; 2008: $1,549.50; 2009: $1,889; 2010: $2,332; 2011: $2,545; 2012: $3,108; 2013:

$3,644; **Monthly Assured Print Pricing (APP):** $275/$3,300.

Oklahoma Session Laws. St. Paul, MN: West. Hardbound. Annual. 2 vols.
Cost: 1991: $67.50; 1991: $95.75; 1992: $80.75; 1993: $79.25; 1994: $79.25; 1995: $78.25; 1996: $74.50; 1998: $85; 1999: $88; 2000: $104.50; 2001: $124; 2002: $92; 2003: $92; 2004: $100; 2005: $110; 2006: $110; 2008: $110; 2009: $110; 2010: $176; 2011: $176; 2012: $176; 2013: $176.

Oklahoma Session Law Service. St. Paul, MN: West These pamphlets are published during and immediately after each legislative session and contain the text of laws in numerical chapter sequence in order of passage.
Cost: $924.60 (discounted to subscribers to the OSA) (2014).

Legislative Hotline: (405) 521-2733 (House); (405) 521-5642 (Senate).

2. Administrative Law.

Oklahoma Administrative Code. Oklahoma City, OK: Secretary of State, Office of Administrative Rules, 2006-date. 19 vols. Looseleaf format. Also available on the Scretary of State's web site: www.oar.state.ok.us
Cost: 2011 ed.: $1,500; supplementation: 2007: $500; 2008: $575; 2009: $625; 2012: $200; CD-ROM: $500; supplementation: 2007: $300; 2008: $300; 2009: $300; 2010: $300; 2012: $100; 2013: $275. (405) 521-4911

Oklahoma Register. Oklahoma City, OK: Secretary of State, Office of Administrative Rules, 1983-date. Both print and CD-ROM published semi-monthly. (405) 521-4911
Cost: $500 per year (1st class); CD-ROM: $300 per year (2014); also available on the Web.

3. Court Reports.

Oklahoma Decisions. St. Paul, MN: West, 1931-date. [offprint of Pacific Reporter 2d – 3d]. Contain decisions of the Oklahoma Supreme Court from 1931 to date, Court of Criminal Appeals from 1931-date, and Court of Appeals from 1969-date. Current vol.: Pac 3d 303-313. Approx. 2-3 vols. per year.
Cost: Volumes covering P.2d: $3,220; volumes covering P.3d: $887; annual upkeep: 2002: $292; 2003: $222; 2004: $258; 2005: $184; 2006: $325; 2007: $251; 2008: $259.50; 2009: $258; 2010: $297; 2011: $283; 2012: $282.50;2013: $288; current volume: $96/$128 (subscriber/list); **Monthly Assured Print Pricing (APP):** $43/$516.

Oklahoma Reports. 1890-1953. Vols. 1-208. [ceased publication with vol. 208].
Cost: Out-of-print. See used lawbook dealers in Appendix.

Pacific Reporter [1st] - **3d**. St. Paul, MN: West, 1883-date. Contains decisions of the Oklahoma Supreme Court from 1890-date and the Oklahoma Court of Appeals from 1969-date. Current vol.: 314 **P. 3d**.
Cost: 1st series out-of-print (see used lawbook dealers in Appendix C); 2d series: $13,428; used sets approx. $2000; 3d series: $15,201; annual cost (2013): $11,396; individual volume: $518/$691 (subscriber/list); **Monthly Assured Print Pricing (APP):** $1,141/$11,369; used sets may be available.

Pacific Reporter 3d. Advance sheets. St. Paul, MN: Thomson West. Weekly.
Cost: $2,866.56 per year (discounted to bound volume subscribers) (2014).

4. Court Rules.

Oklahoma Court Rules and Procedure: State and Federal. St. Paul, MN: West. Annual. 2 vols. Also available as ProView eBook.
Cost: 2014 Edition: $177.

5. Digests, Encyclopedias and Practice Sets.

West's Oklahoma Digest 2d. St. Paul, MN: West, 1987-date. 76 vols. Annual pocket parts, a mid-year supplement, and periodic revised volumes.
Cost: $4,374; supplementation: 1994: $91.50; 1995: $102.75; 1996: $124; 1997: $145; 1998: $155; 1999: $602.75; 2000: $310; 2001: $1,258.25; 2002: $1,134.75; 2003: $268; 2004: $1,770.50; 2005: $1,165; 2006: $857; 2007: $955; 2008: $2,055; 2009: $1,888; 2010: $2,756; 2011: $2,658.50; 2012: $2,299.50; 2013: $2,670; **Monthly Assured Print Pricing (APP):** $245/$2,940.

West's Oklahoma Law Finder. St. Paul, MN: West Annual. Paperbound.
Cost: 2014 Edition: $247.

6. Citators.

Shepard's Oklahoma Citations. Albany, NY: Shepard's. Monthly.
Cost: $3,696 (6 bound volumes); all-inclusive subscription: $1,839 per year (in-state) (2014).

Online: All jurisdictional Shepard's and KeyCite are no longer available as stand-alone products, but are acquired as part of a jurisdictional or subject library package from the respective publisher (2014).

7. CD-ROM Products.

Oklahoma Decisions (West's). Eagan, MN: West. One disc. Updated regularly. Contains the full text of decisions of the Oklahoma Supreme Court from 1890 to date, Court of Appeals and Court of Criminal Appeals from vol. 154 Pacific Reporter 2d to date. Decisions also searchable by West Topics and Key Numbers, headnotes and synopses. Available for Windows, or Macintosh . Search Engine: PREMISE.
Cost: $5,535 (2014).

8. State Legal Research Guides.

Adkinson, Danny Mark and Lisa McNair Palmer. **The Oklahoma State Constitution.** New York: Oxford University Press, 2011. 1 vol. (424 pp.).
Cost: $150.00; from $31.26 on amazon.com; kindle: $119.99 (2014).

Fox, Darin. **State Documents Bibliography—Oklahoma: A Guide to Legal Research in Oklahoma.** Chicago: AALL, 2009.

Available from William S. Hein & Co.
Cost: $30.00; pdf: $20.00. Also available on HeinOnline (2014).

Long, Ann Walsh. Oklahoma Practice Materials: A Selective Bibliography in Houdek, Frank G., ed. **State Practice Materials: Annotated Bibliographies**. Buffalo, NY: William S. Hein & Co., Inc., 2007-date. 2 vols. Looseleaf format.
Cost: $195.00 (2014).

9. Leading Web Sites for State Legal Research.

Home Page:	www.ok.gov/
Administrative Code:	www.sos.ok.gov/oar
Agency Directory:	www.ok.gov/portal/agency.php
Attorney General:	www.oag.ok.gov
Attorney Gen. Opinions:	www.oag.ok.gov/oagweb.nsf/opinions.html
Bar Association:	www.okbar.org/
Constitution:	www.oklegislature.gov/ok_constitution.aspx
Court Opinions:	www.oscn.net/ Decisions are near the bottom of the page.
Governor:	www.ok.gov/governor/
Judicial Branch:	www.oscn.net/
eLaw Library:	www.oscn.net/applications/oscn/start.asp?viewType=LIBRARY
Legislative Branch:	www.oklegislature.gov/
Secretary of State:	www.sos.state.ok.us/
Statutes:	www.oklegislature.gov/osStatuesTitle.aspx
Supreme Court:	www.oscn.net/oscn/schome/

10. Leading publishers of state specific treatises, practice books, and CLE publications.
LexisNexis, National Business Institute, Oklahoma Bar Association, Thomson Reuters (West).

Oregon

1. Codes and Session Laws.
Oregon Revised Statutes. Salem, OR: Legislative Counsel Committee, 2011-date. 21 vols. Published biennially in odd-numbered years. Supplemented by session law volumes. The annotation volume only is supplemented in even-numbered years. (503) 986-1243.
Cost: 2013 Edition (print): $615 (includes s & h); individual volumes $85 each; 2012 supp. was $85.00 (2014).

West's Oregon Revised Statutes Annotated. St. Paul, MN: Thomson West, 2003-date. 53 vols. Kept up to date by pocket parts, supplementary pamphlets, and revised volumes. This compilation provides access to Oregon statutes and codified court rules, as well as a variety of editorial features including historical and statutory notes, official comments, and cross references to a number of West family publications.
Cost: $1,088; supplementation: 2004: $210; 2005: $218; 2006: $229.50; 2007: $285; 2008: $446; 2009: $401; 2010: $637; 2011: $565; 2012: $713; 2013: $843; **Monthly Assured Print Pricing (APP):** $64/$768.

Oregon Laws. [session laws]. Salem, OR: Legislative Council Committee. Published in odd-numbered years and in years with special sessions. (503) 986-1243.
Cost: 1987: $60; 1989: $70; 1990 Special session: $5; 1991: $85; 1993: $95; 1995: $105; 1996 Special Session: $10; 1997: $130; 1999: $145; 2001: $150 (3 vols.); 2002: $12; 2003: $200; 2005: $200; 2007: $215; 2008: $15.00; 2009: $245; 2010 Special Session: $65; 2010: $245; 2011: $245; 2012: $245.

Legislative Hotline: (503) 986-1180.

2. Administrative Law.
Oregon Administrative Rules Compilation. Salem, OR: Secretary of State, 1997-date. Annual. 19 vols. Looseleaf format. On Internet at: arcweb.sos.state.or.us
Cost: 2014 Edition: $650 per year ($600 if purchased before Dec. 31 of prior year). Individual volumes: $45 each. Supplementation through monthly online updates to the **OARC**, or the **Oregon Bulletin** (2014).

Oregon Bulletin [continues the **Administrative Rule Bulletin**]. Salem, OR: Secretary of State, 1958-date. Monthly updates. No print version.
Cost: Now only available at no cost on the Internet at: http://arcweb.sos.state.or.us/rules/bulletin_default.html

3. Court Reports.
Oregon Reports, 1853-date. Salem, OR: State Court Administrator. Current vol.: 352 (as of April 1, 2014).
Cost: $85 per volume (volumes 56-352 available with some gaps); periodic clearance sales to reduce inventory; used sets of Oregon Reports and Oregon Court of Appeals Reports may be available. (503) 986-5656
Opinions from 1998 to date available online at: www.publications.ojd.state.or.us/Publications/OpinionsSC.page?

Oregon Court of Appeals Reports. 1969-date. Salem, OR: State Court Administrator. Current vol.: 256 (as of April 1, 2014). (503) 986-5656
Cost: $21,760; $85 per volume (all back volumes available); used sets of Oregon Reports and Oregon Court of Appeals Reports may be available.
Opinions from 1998 to date available online at: www.publications.ojd.state.or.us/Publications/OpinionsSC.page?

Oregon Tax Court Reports. Salem, OR: State Court Administrator, 1962-date. Current vol.: 18 (as of April 1, 2014). (503) 986-5656.
Cost: $1,530; $85.00 per volume (all back volumes available). December, 2008 to date also available online at: www.publications.ojd.state.or.us/Publications/OpinionsTaxReg.page?

Oregon Appellate Court Reports. Advance Sheets. Salem,

OR: State Court Administrator. Bimonthly. Contain opinions of the Oregon Supreme Court, Court of Appeals, and Tax Court.
Cost: $440 per year; $220 for six months (2014). (503) 986-5656.

Oregon Cases. St. Paul, MN: West,1967-date. [offprint of Pacific Reporter 2d]. Contains Oregon Supreme Court decisions. Current volume: 308-311 **P.3d**.
Cost: Volumes covering P.2d: $3,275; volumes covering P.3d (2000-date): $5,336; annual upkeep: 2003: $525; 2004: $590.70; 2005: $608; 2006: $707; 2007: $787; 2008: $1,098; 2009: $2,289; 2010: $1,545; 2011: $2,030; 2012: $3,344; 2013: $4,268; current vol.: $500/$667 (subscriber/list); **Monthly Assured Print Pricing (APP)**: $383/$4,596; Contact West regarding applicable discounts or see list of used lawbook dealers in Appendix C.

Pacific Reporter [1st] - **3d**. St. Paul, MN: West, 1883-date. Contains decisions of the Oregon Supreme Court from 1883-date and the Oregon Court of Appeals from 1969-date. Current vol.: 314 **P. 3d**.
Cost: 1st series out-of-print (see used lawbook dealers in Appendix C); 2d series: $13,428; used sets approx. $2000; 3d series: $15,201; annual cost (2013): $11,396; individual volume: $518/$691 (subscriber/list); **Monthly Assured Print Pricing (APP):** $1,141/$11,369; used sets may be available.

Pacific Reporter 3d. Advance sheets. St. Paul, MN: Thomson West. Weekly.
Cost: $2,866.56 per year (discounted to bound volume subscribers) (2014).

4. Court Rules.
Oregon Rules of Civil Procedure. LexisNexis. Annual. 1 vol. Also available as ebook.
Cost: 2014 Edition: $220.

Oregon Rules of Court: State and Federal. St. Paul, MN: West 1 vol. Annual. Also available as ProView eBook.
Cost: 2014 Edition: $230; Federal, State and Local: $348 (2014).

Oregon Rules of Appellate Procedure (ORAP). Salem, OR: State Court Administrator. Annual. Contains Rules of the Oregon Supreme Court and Court of Appeals.
Cost: 2013 Edition: $13 (2014); All state court rules also available on court web site:
http://www.ojd.state.or.us/web/ojdpublications.nsf/Files/2013_ORAPs.pdf/$File/2013_ORAPs.pdf

5. Digests, Legal Encyclopedias, and Practice Sets.
Oregon Law and Practice. St. Paul, MN: West, 2003-date. 5 vols. Annual pocket supplements.
Cost: $500; supplementation: 2004: $51; 2005: $280; 2006: $128; 2007: $406; 2008: $167.20; 2009: $99; 2010: $79; 2011: $112; 2012: $125; 2013: $140.

West's Oregon Digest 2d. St. Paul, MN: West, 1994-date. 78 vols. Annual pocket parts, mid-year supplement,
Cost: $4,012; supplementation: 1995: $138.75; 1996: $70; 1997: $70; 1998: $65.00; 1999: $406; 2000: $226.25; 2001: $327.75; 2002: $1,347.50; 2003: $268; 2004: $389; 2005: $589; 2006: $589.50; 2007: $536; 2008: $1,139; 2009: $1,203; 2010: $1,382; 2011: $2,402; 2012: $2,220.50; 2013: $2,730; **Monthly Assured Print Pricing (APP):** $233/$2,796.

6. Citators.
Shepard's Oregon Citations. Albany, NY: Shepard's. Monthly.
Cost: $2,769 (8 bound volumes); all-inclusive subscription: $2,284 (in-state) (2014).

Online: All jurisdictional Shepard's and KeyCite are no longer available as stand-alone products, but are included as part of a jurisdictional or subject library from their respective publishers (2014).

7. CD-ROM Products.
Oregon Cases. Eagan, MN: West Two discs. Updated monthly. Contains the full text of decisions of the Oregon Supreme Court from 1853 to date, Oregon Court of Appeals from 1969 to date, decisions of the Oregon Tax Court from 1962 to date, Opinions of the Attorney General from 1972 to date, Oregon court rules, administrative rules, workers compensation decisions from 1987 to date, session laws, etc. Available for DOS Windows and Macintosh. Search Engine: PREMISE. Subscription includes online updating via Westlaw.
Cost: $10,773 per year (2014).

OSB CLE CD-ROM Libraries. Lake Oswego, OR: Oregon State Bar CLE. One disc. Updated semiannually. Customize a collection of many Oregon State Bar CLE titles. Available for Windows 95 or higher. Search Engine: ISYS (Odyssey Development).
Cost: Titles may be ordered individually or in packages, and are priced the same as the print editions. 15% discount on 7 or more titles.

8. State Legal Research Guides.
Clayton, Mary. Oregon Practice Materials: A Selective Bibliography in Houdek, Frank G., ed. **State Practice Materials: Annotated Bibliographies**. Buffalo, NY: William S. Hein & Co., Inc., 2005-date. 2 vols. Looseleaf format.
Cost: $195.00 (2014).

Midkiff, Stephanie and Wendy Schroeder Hitchcock. **State Documents Bibliography: Oregon.** Chicago: AALL, 2009. Available from William S. Hein & Co.
Cost: $30.00; pdf: $20.00. Also available on HeinOnline (20134).

Rowe, Suzanne E. **Oregon Legal Research**. Durham, NC: Carolina Academic Press, 2003. 1 vol. (264 pp.).
Cost: $25.00; from $.09 on amazon.com (2014).

9. Leading Web Sites for State Legal Research.

Home Page:	www.oregon.gov/
Administrative Code:	http://arcweb.sos.state.or.us/pages/rules/index.html
Agency Directory:	www.oregon.gov/a_to_z_listing.shtml
Attorney General:	www.doj.state.or.us/

Attorney Gen. Opinions:	www.doj.state.or.us/agoffice/
Bar Association:	www.osbar.org/
Constitution:	www.oregonlegislature.gov/bills_laws/Pages/OrConst.aspx - OR - http://bluebook.state.or.us/state/constitution/constitution.htm
Court Opinions:	www.publications.ojd.state.or.us/
Governor:	www.oregon.gov/gov
Judicial Branch:	www.courts.oregon.gov/
Law Library:	www.oregon.gov/SOLL/
Legislative Branch:	www.leg.state.or.us/
Secretary of State:	http://sos.oregon.gov
Statutes:	www.leg.state.or.us/ors

10. Leading publishers of state specific treatises, practice books, and CLE publications.
LexisNexis, National Business Institute, Oregon Law Institute, Oregon State Bar-CLE, Thomson Reuters West. See Appendix B for addresses and telephone numbers.

Pennsylvania

1. Codes and Session Laws.
Pennsylvania Consolidated Statutes. Harrisburg, PA: Legislative Reference Bureau, 1975-date. Individual titles in 12 looseleaf binders.
Cost: approx. $386.90 + s & h (current through July 31, 2013), but sold individually; individual titles priced from $2.50 - $12 ea. (supplemented twice annually, but only revised chapters have supplements issued). Subscriptions: (717) 787-4223; Available for sale online at:
www.pabookstore.com/pennsylvania-consolidated-statutes.html
Text available at: http://government.westlaw.com/linkedslice/default.asp?SP=pac-1000

Purdon's Pennsylvania Statutes Annotated. St. Paul, MN: West,1938-date. 144 vols. Annual pocket parts and periodic revised volumes.
Cost: $6,998; supplementation:1996: $704.50; 1997: $858; 1998: $963.50; 1999: $985; 2000: $1,075; 2001: $1,306; 2002: $1,412.50; 2004: $1,376; 2005: $1,661; 2006: $1,792.50; 2007: $2,454; 2008: $2,653; 2009: $2,043; 2010: $3,264; 2011: $4,054; 2012: $4,996.50; 2013: $5,663; **Monthly Assured Print Pricing (APP):** $442/$5,304.

Purdon's Pennsylvania Statutes and Consolidated Statutes. Compact Edition. St. Paul, MN: West, 2009. 8 vols. Softbound
Cost: 2013 Edition: $688 (2014).

Laws of Pennsylvania [session laws]. Harrisburg, PA: Bureau of Publications. Annual.
Cost: 1994: $19 (2 vols.); 1995: $19; 1996: $20 (2 vols.); 1997: $10.50 (1 vol.); 1998: $20 (2 vols.); 1999: $10.50 (1 vol.); 2000: $21 (2 vols.); 2001: $12.50 (1 vol.); 2002: $37.50 (3 vols.); 2003: $13 (1 vol.); 2004: $26 (2 vols.); 2005: $13 (1 vol.); 2006: $26 (2 vols.); 2007: $16.50 (1 vol.); 2008: $33 (2 vols.); 2009: $21 (1 vol.); 2010: $42 (2 vols.); 2011: $21 (1 vol.); 2012: $42 (2 vols.).

Pennsylvania Session Laws. St. Paul, MN: West. Hardbound. Annual.
Cost: 1997: $57.50; 1998: $57.50; 1999: $57.50; 2000: $60; 2001: $69; 2002: $81; 2003: $89; 2004: $98; 2005: $119; 2006: $132; 2007: $147; 2008: $168; 2009: $201; 2010: $227; 2011: $255; 2012: $285.

Pennsylvania Legislative Service. St. Paul, MN: West These pamphlets are published during and immediately after each legislative session and contain the text of laws in numerical chapter sequence in order of passage.
Cost: $867.00 per year (2013).

Legislative Hotline: (717) 787-2342.

2. Administrative Law.
Pennsylvania Code [of regulations]. Mechanicsburg, PA: Fry Communications, Inc., 1970-date. 61 vols. Looseleaf format. Also available at no charge on the Web at: http://www.pacode.com
Cost: $809 + tax (includes one year's updates); supplementation: $850 + tax; individual titles also available at various prices (2014). Contact Fry Communications at (717) 766-0211 for details.

Pennsylvania Bulletin. Mechanicsburg, PA: Fry Communications, Inc., 1970-date. Weekly.
Cost: $82 per year; single issue: $2 (2014). State Contracts Online also available at no cost.
Available at no charge on the web at: http://www.pabulletin.com/

3. Court Reports.
Pennsylvania Reporter [1st] **- 3d**. St. Paul, MN: West, 1939-date. [offprint of **A.2d**]. Contains all Pennsylvania cases appearing in the **Atlantic Reporter** [1st] **- 3d** from 1944 to date. Current volume: 79-80 A.3d (as of March 1, 2014).
Cost: 2d series: $6,150; 3d Series: $8,913 ; annual upkeep: 2002: $1,157.50; 2003: $1,820; 2004: $1,335; 2005: $1,762; 2006: $1,810.50; 2007: $2,242; 2008: $1985; 2009: $2,605; 2010: $2,655; 2011: $3,278; 2012: $5,583.50; 2013: $7,203; current vol.: $428.50/$571 (subscriber/list); used sets may be available; **Monthly Assured Print Pricing (APP):** $654/$7,848.

Pennsylvania State Reports, 1845-date. [designated as official]. Published by West from 1976-date. Contains decisdions of the Pennsylvania Supreme Court. Current vol.: 618 (as of April 1, 2014).
Cost: $2,790; annual upkeep: 2002: $257.25; 2003: $579.00; 2004: $456.00; 2005: $465.00; 2006: $476.15; 2007: $487.50; 2008: $341; 2009: $351; 2010: $312,52; 2011: $321; 2012: $330; 2013: $354; current volume: $88.50/$118 (subscriber/list); used sets of both **Pennsylvania State Reports** and **Pennsylvania Superior Court Reports** may be available.

Pennsylvania Superior Court Reports. St. Paul, MN: West, 1895-1997. Discontinued with volume 456. West became official

publisher at volume 241 in 1976.
Cost: Out-of-print: approx. $5,668.50 used (vols. 241-456); series discontinued; used sets of both **Pennsylvania State Reports** and **Pennsylvania Superior Court Reports** may be available.

Pennsylvania Commonwealth Court Reports. Harrisburg, PA, 1970-1976. St. Paul, West Publishing, 1976-1994. Discontinued. Decisions now appear in Atlantic Reporter.
Cost: Complete sets available used for approx. $3,000.

Pennsylvania District and County Reports. 1st - 5th series. Philadelphia: The Legal Intelligencer, 1921-date. 1st series, 1921-1954 (89 vols.); 2d series, 1955-1977 (75 vols.); 3d series, 1977-1989 (50 vols.); 4th series, 1990-2008 (83 vols.); 5th series, 2008-date (29 vols.). Current vol.: 5th series, vol. 29 (as of April 1, 2014). Five volumes published per year.
Cost: $535.00 per year (5 vols.); back volumes: $120.05 ea.; advance sheets: $267.75 per year; e-mail advance sheets free with bound volume subscription. Available from American Lawyer Media (877) 256-2472. May also available on the used lawbook market.

Atlantic Reporter [1st] - **3d**. St. Paul, MN: West, 1886-date. Includes decisions of the Pennsylvania Supreme Court from 1885 to date, the Pennsylvania Superior Court from 1931 to date, and the Pennsylvania Commonwealth Court from 1970 to date. Current volume: 85 **A.3d**.
Cost: 1st series out-of-print (see used lawbook dealers in Appendix C); 2d series: $14,434; 3d series: $15,080; annual cost (2013): $11,151; recent vol.: $531/$708 (subscriber/list); **Monthly Assured Print Pricing (APP):** $1,163/$13,956. See list of used lawbook dealers in Appendix C.

Atlantic Reporter 2d. Advance sheets. St. Paul, MN: Thomson West. Weekly.
Cost: $2,866.56 per year (discounted to bound volume subscribers) (2014).

Other county and lower courts also available.

4. Court Rules.
Pennsylvania Rules of Court: State and Federal. St. Paul, MN: West. 2 vols. Annual. Also available as ProView eBook.
Cost: 2014 Edition: $209.

Pennsylvania Rules of Court—Local Central and Local Central Key Rules. St. Paul, MN: West. 1 vol. Annual. Volume IIIA.
Contains the full text of the officially adopted local rules of civil and criminal procedure for the Courts of Common Pleas in western Pennsylvania counties.
Cost: 2014 Edition: $209.

Pennsylvania Rules of Court—Local Eastern and Local Eastern Key Rules. St. Paul, MN: West. 1 vol. Annual. Volume IIIC.
Contains the full text of the officially adopted local rules of civil and criminal procedure for the Courts of Common Pleas in western Pennsylvania counties.
Cost: 2014 Edition: $209.

Pennsylvania Rules of Court—Local Western and Local Western Key Rules. St. Paul, MN: West. 1 vol. Annual. Volume IIIE.
Contains the full text of the officially adopted local rules of civil and criminal procedure for the Courts of Common Pleas in western Pennsylvania counties.
Cost: 2014 Edition: $209.

5. Digests, Encyclopedias, and Practice Sets.
Pennsylvania Appellate Practice 2d. St. Paul, MN: West, 1994-date. 3 vols. (Volumes 20, 20A and 20B of PA Practice). Paperbound. Replaced Annually. Contains revisions of the rules of appellate procedure, annotations to cases construing the rules, and applicable forms.
Cost: 2013-2014 Edition: $855 (print of ProView eBook) (2014).

Pennsylvania Law Encyclopedia. 2d ed. Charlottesville, VA: LexisNexis, 1998-date. 53 vols. Annual pocket supplements and periodic revised volumes. Originally published by West, this set was purchased by Reed-Elsevier under the terms of the 1996 consent decree which forced the divestiture of over 50 products.
Cost: $3,931; supplementation: 2001: $916; 2002: $694; 2003: n/a; 2004: $873; 2005: $401; 2008: $384; 2009: $678; 2010: $1,079; 2011: $1,155; 2012: $1,235; 2013: $1,349.

West's Pennsylvania Digest 2d. St. Paul, MN: West, 1983-date. 205 vols.
Annual pocket parts, mid-year supplement, and periodic revised volumes.
Cost: $9,130; supplementation: 1996: $188; 1997: $391; 1998: $670; 1999: $735; 2000: $1,198; 2001: $1,658.50; 2003: $3,075; 2004: $1,991; 2005: $2,532.25; 2006: $1,790; 2007: $2,207; 2008: $3,577; 2009: $5,137; 2010: $6,282; 2011: $5,932.50; 2012: $3,352.50; 2013: $5,428; **Monthly Assured Print Pricing (APP):** $480/$5,760.

West's Pennsylvania Forms. St. Paul, MN: West, 1992-date. 16 vols. & 4 CD-ROMs.
Cost: $1,351; supplementation: 1996: $336; 1997: $170.50; 1998: $226.50; 1999: $170; 2000: $632.50; 2001: $238; 2003: $615.50; 2004: $428.00; 2005: $340; 2006: $438.50; 2007: $718; 2008: $200; 2009: $881; 2010: $714.50; 2011: $779; 2012: $931.50; 2013: $996; **Monthly Assured Print Pricing (APP):** $99/$1,188.

West's Pennsylvania Practice Series. St. Paul, MN: West, 1987-date. 15 vols. Includes practice titles on evidence, criminal offenses and defenses, criminal procedure forms and commentary, advocacy, probation and parole, PA rules of the road, DWI, tort law and advocacy, discovery, and trial hansdbook.
Cost: $5,596 (but sold individually); supplementation: 1997: $113;1998: $105; 1999: $185; 2000; $114; 2001: $250.50; 2004: see costs of individual components.

6. Citators.
Shepard's Pennsylvania Citations. Albany, NY: Shepard's. Monthly or bi-monthly.
Cost: $6,500 (14 bound volumes); all-inclusive subscription:

monthly: $2,430 (in-state); bi-monthly: $2,716 (in-state) (2014).

Online: All jurisdictional Shepard's and KeyCite are no longer available as stand-alone products, but are included as part of a jurisdictional or subject library from their respective publishers (2014).

7. CD-ROM Products.

BISEL-LINK CD-ROM. Philadelphia, PA: George T. Bisel Co. One disc. Updated semiannually.
Contains the text of seven individual Pennsylvania practice titles (30 vols.), including the topics of wills, probate, estates, fiduciaries, inheritance tax, zoning, estate planning and forms, among others. Available for DOS or Windows. Search Engine: Folio.
Cost: 2013 Editions: price depends on number of titles selected, ranging from $74.50 to $500.00 (2014).

8. State Legal Research Guides.

Fishman, Joel. **Bibliography of Pennsylvania Law: Secondary Sources**. Pennsylvania Legal Resources Institute, 1992.

Fishman, Joel. Pennsylvania Practice Materials: A Selective Bibliography in Houdek, Frank G., ed. **State Practice Materials: Annotated Bibliographies**. Buffalo, NY: William S. Hein & Co., Inc., 2004-date. 2 vols. Looseleaf format.
Cost: $195.00 (2014).

Fishman, Joel. **Pennsylvania State Documents: A Bibliography of Legal and Law-Related Material**. Chicago: AALL, 2007. Available from W.S. Hein.
Cost: $30.00; pdf: $20. Also available on HeinOnline (2013).

Silverman, Marc. "A Short Guide to Pennsylvania Legal Research," **Legal Reference Services Quarterly** 12, no. 1 (1992): 107-120.

Tavares, Bonny L. and Barbara J. Busharis. **Pennsylvania Legal Research**. Durham, NC: Carolina Academic Press, 2007. 1 vol. (256 pp.).
Cost: $25.00; from $4.59 on amazon.com (2014).

9. Leading Web Sites for State Legal Research.

Home Page:	www.pa.gov
Administrative Code:	www.pacode.com/secure/browse.asp
Agency Directory:	www.pa.gov/Government
Attorney General:	www.attorneygeneral.gov/
Attorney Gen. Opinions:	www.attorneygeneral.gov/press.aspx?id=7545
Bar Association:	www.pabar.org/
Constitution:	www.legis.state.pa.us/cfdocs/legis/LI/Public/cons_index.cfm
Court Opinions:	www.pacourts.us/courts/supreme-court/court-opinions/
Governor:	www.governor.state.pa.us/
Judicial Branch:	www.pacourts.us
Legislative Branch:	www.legis.state.pa.us/
Secretary of State:	www.dos.state.pa.us
Statutes:	www.legis.state.pa.us/cfdocs/legis/LI/Public/cons_index.cfm

10. Leading publishers of state specific treatises, practice books, and CLE publications.

George T. Bisel Co., Harrison Company, Legal Communications Ltd., LexisNexis, LocalLaw Publications, National Business Institute, Pennsylvania Bar Institute, Thomson Reuters West. See Appendix B for addresses and telephone numbers.

Rhode Island

1. Codes and Session Laws.

General Laws of Rhode Island 1956. Charlottesville, VA: LexisNexis, 1956-date. 9 vols. in 30. Annual pocket supplements and periodic revised volumes. Index volumes 8 & 9 replaced annually.
Cost: $724 (in-state), $947 (out-of-state); supplementation (in-state/out-of-state): 2001: $586/$744; 2002: $586/$771; 2003: $489/$617; 2004: $536/$697; 2005: $499/$674; 2006: $499/$674; 2007: $499/$674; 2008: $596/$754; 2009: $599/$738; 2010: $524/$744; 2011: $565/$785; 2012: $617/$860; 2013: $679/$922.

West's General Laws of Rhode Island Annotated. Eagan, MN: Thomson/West, 2006-date. 30 vols. With two-volume index. Annual pocket supplements and periodic revised volumes.
Cost: $844; supplementation: 2008: $280; 2009: $321; 2010: $360; 2011: $498; 2012: $571; 2013: $718; **Monthly Assured Print Pricing (APP):** $46/$552.

Rhode Island Advance Annotation Service. Charlottesville, VA: LexisNexis. Issued three times per year between annual pocket supplements.
Cost: $114 (2014).

Rhode Island Advance Legislative Service. Charlottesville, VA: LexisNexis, 1995-date. These pamphlets are published during and after each legislative session and contain the full text of laws in numerical chapter sequence in the order of passage.
Cost: $226.56 per year (2014).

Rhode Island Advance Legislative Service. Eagan, MN: West, 2007-date. 5-6 issues per year. These pamphlets are published during and after each legislative session and contain the full text of laws in numerical chapter sequence in the order of passage. Replaced by bound public laws.
Cost: $180.00 (2013).

Rhode Island Interim Annotation Service. Eagan, MN: Thomson/West, 2007-date. Issued 1-2 times per year between

annual pocket supplements.
Cost: Inquire.

Public Laws of Rhode Island [session laws]. Providence, RI: Joint Committee on Legislative Services. Generally 4 vols. Annual. Current volumes available from LexisNexis (1997-date). Previous years available from Documents Distribution Office, State House, Providence, RI 02903.
Cost: 1993: $150; $160; 1994: $160; 1995: $150; 1996: 100; 1997: $125; 1998: $125; 1999: $125; 2000: $125; 2002: $130; 2003: $130; 2004: $130; 2005: $130; 2006: $130; 2007: $130; 2008: $145; 2009: $155; $2010: $147; 2011: $176; 2012: $167; 2013: $178. Generally available 8 months after close of session. Years 1994-date also available via the Internet on General Assembly Web site: http://www.rilin.state.ri.us/pages/legislation.aspx

Rhode Island Acts And Resolves [local and private acts]. Providence, RI: Joint Committee on Legislative Services. Annual. Available from: Documents Distribution Office, State House, Providence, RI 02903.
Cost: $32.50, or sold as [art of 4-vol. package with Public Laws (see above).

Legislative Hotline: (401) 751-8833.

2. Administrative Law.
Code of Rhode Island Rules. Albany, NY: LexisNexis Matthew Bender [formerly the Weil Publishing Co.], 1991-date. 27 vols. Updated monthly.
Cost: $3,604 (includes monthly supplements for one year); annual supplementation: 1995: $844; 1996: $869; 1997: $869; 1998: $935; 1999: $935; 2000-2004: $1,285 per year; 2005: $1,350; 2006: $1,350; 2007: $1,517; 2008: $1,497; 2009: $1,609; 2010: $1,689; 2011: $1,773; 2012: $1,879; 2013: $2,011; 2014: $2,195.

Rhode Island Register. Albany, NY: LexisNexis Matthew Bender [formerly Weil Publishing Co.], 1992-date. Monthly.
Cost: $1,257; renewal: 2014; $1,143.

3. Court Reports.
Rhode Island Reports. Providence, RI: Supreme Court, 1828-1980. [ceased publication with vol. 122, as of April 12, 1980].
Cost: Complete set priced at $3,563.90, but sell used for approximately $600. All volumes available from Secretary of State's Office at prices ranging from $5.00 to $69 each. Price list available (Call 401-277-3290). Prices have fallen dramatically since the introduction of Rhode Island Supreme Court decisions on CD-ROM and the Internet.

Rhode Island Reporter. St. Paul, MN: West, 1980-date. [off-print of **Atlantic Reporter 2d**, vols. 412-date]. Current vol.: 68-80 **A. 3d**. 48 vols. Replaced the **Rhode Island Reports** when these were discontinued as of April 12,1980.
Cost: 1,672.50 (51 vols.); annual cost: 2002: $178.25; 2003: $185; 2004: $193.50; 2005: $171.25; 2006: $201.50; 2007: $203.75; 2008: $206; 2009: $170; 2010: $216; 2011: $224; 2012: $177; 2013: $183.75; individual volumes: $91.87/$122.50 (subscriber/list).

Atlantic Reporter [1st] - **2d**. St. Paul, MN: West, 1886-date. Contains decisions of the Rhode Island Supreme Court from 1885-date. Volumes 1-14 of the official Rhode Island Reports precede the appearance of the Atlantic Reporter [1st] in 1885. Current volume: 85 **A.3d**.
Cost: 1st series out-of-print (see used lawbook dealers in Appendix C); 2d series: $14,434; 3d series: $15,080; annual cost (2013): $11,151; recent vol.: $531/$708 (subscriber/list); **Monthly Assured Print Pricing (APP):** $1,163/$13,956. See list of used lawbook dealers in Appendix C.

Atlantic Reporter 2d. Advance sheets. St. Paul, MN: Thomson West. Weekly.
Cost: $2,866.56 per year (discounted to bound volume subscribers) (2014).

4. Court Rules.
Rhode Island Court Rules Annotated. Charlottesville, VA: LexisNexis. 1 vol. Updated semiannually, replaced annually.
Cost: 2014 Edition: $82 (in-state); ebook: $77 (2014).

Rhode Island Rules of Court, State and Federal. St. Paul, MN: West, 2009-date. 2 vols. Paperbound. Revised annually. Also available as ProView eBook.
Cost: 2013 Edition: $123 (2014).

5. Digests, Encyclopedias, and Practice Sets.
Rhode Island Digest. St. Paul, MN: West, 1952-date. 10 vols. in 37. Annual pocket parts, mid-year supplement, and periodic revised volumes.
Cost: $3,368; supplementation: 1995: $175; 1996: $183; 1997: $198; 1998: $300;1999: $430; 2000: $509; 2001: $1,006; 2002: $1,272.50; 2003: $402; 2004: $450.25; 2005: $925; 2006: $551.50; 2007: $614; 2008: $1,278; 2009: $596; 2010: $1,180.50; 2011: $1,712.50; 2012: $2,202.50; 2013: $1,851; **Monthly Assured Print Pricing (APP):** $171/$2,052.

Green, Eric D. and Robert G. Flanders, Jr. **Rhode Island Evidence Manual**. Charlottesville, VA: LexisNexis, 2000-date. 1 vol.
Cost: 2005 Edition: $174 (2014).

Hirsch, Jeffrey L. and William A. Farrell. **Labor and Employment in Rhode Island: Guide to Employment Laws, Regulations & Practices**. Charlottesville, VA: LexisNexis, 2004?-date. 1 vol.
Cost: $177; supplementation: 1994: $45; 1997: $55; 1998: $60; 1999: $65; 2000: $69; 2001: $81; 2002: $84; 2003: $174; 2004: $188; 2005: $202; 2006: $212; 2010; $142; 2011: $151; 2012: $162; 2013: $167.

Kent, Robert B., et al. **Rhode Island Civil and Appellate Procedure with Commentaries**. St. Paul, MN: Thomson/West, 2004-date. 2 vols. Looseleaf format. Annual supplementation.
Cost: $275; supplementation: 2005: $149.50; 2006: $153; 2007: $158; 2008: $161; 2009: $165; 2010: $172; 2011: $177; 2012: $184.

Model Civil Jury Instructions for Rhode Island 2003. Providence: R.I. Bar Association, Superior Court Bench/Bar Committee, 2003. 1 vol. Includes disc or CD-ROM available in Word or Word Perfect format. Also available at no charge on RI

Bar Association web site to members
Cost: $50 (2014).

Resmini, Ronald J. **Rhode Island Civil Practice and Procedure**. Charlottesville, VA: LexisNexis, 1997-date.
Cost: $259; supplementation:1998: $35; 1999: $45; 2001: $52; 2002: $55; 2003: $58; 2004: $65; 2005: $72; 2006: $77; 2007: $81; 2008: $85; 2009: $95; 2010: $105; 2011: $113; 2012: $116; 2013: $124.

Resmini, Ronald J. **Rhode Island Practice: Tort Law and Personal Injury Practice**. 2d ed. Charlottesville, VA: LexisNexis, 1999-date.
Cost: $308; supplementation: 2002: $76; 2003: $80; 2004: $88; 2005: $89; 2006: $92; 2008: $111; 2009: $123; 2010: $137; 2011: $147; 2012: $157; 2013: $163; 1st edition: 1994: $37; 1995: $45; 1996: 0; 1997: $79; 1998: $84.

6. Citators.

Shepard's Rhode Island Citations. Albany, NY: Shepard's, 1991-date. 2 vols. Bimonthly.
Cost: $1,018 (2 bound volumes); all-inclusive subscription: $1,712 (in-state); (2014).

Online: All jurisdictional Shepard's and KeyCite are no longer available as stand-alone products, but are included as part of a jurisdictional or subject library from their respective publishers (2014).

7. CD-ROM Products.

ClerkBase Public Utilities Commission. CD-ROM now replaced by Internet. Pawtucket, RI: ClerkBase, Inc. Updated continuously. Contains the full text of decisions of the R.I. Division of Public Utilities and Carriers, and the Public Utilities Decisions and Orders. Available for Windows 95 or higher. Engine: ClerkBase. Now available on Web.
Cost: Free of charge. Available at: www.compbase.com Call (401) 727-1567 for further information (2014).

LexisNexis CD - Rhode Island Primary Law. Albany, NY: LexisNexis. One disc. Updated regularly. Contains the full, annotated text of the publisher's General Laws of Rhode Island, Rhode Island Court Rules Annotated, together with decisions of the Rhode Island Supreme Court from1828 to date, Rhode Island Superior Court from 1980 to date, Attorney General opinions, R.I. Advance Legislative Service materials. Includes online updating via LEXIS at no additional charge. Available for Windows. Search Engine: Folio; LivePublish (NextPage).
Cost: $1,113 per year (2013).

Rhode Island CompBase. Pawtucket, RI: CompBase, Inc. CD-ROM now replaced by online access. Updated regularly. Contains the full text of decisions of the Appellate Division, Workers Compensation Court from 1983 to date; also includes court rules and General Laws relating to workers' compensation. Available for Windows. Search Engine: ClerkBase.
Cost: Online: $350 per year; $175.00 (six months); $75.00 (one day) (single user); additional user: $10.00. Available at: www.compbase.com Call (401) 727-1567 for further information (2013).

8. State Legal Research Guides.

Conley, Patrick T., and Robert G. Flanders. **The Rhode Island State Constitution**. New York: Oxford University Press, 2011. 1 vol. (374 pp.).
Cost: $150; from $74.59 on amazon.com; kindle: $119.99 (2014).

Winson, Gail I. **State of Rhode Island and Providence Plantations: Survey of State Documents and Law-Related Materials**. Chicago: AALL, 2004.
Cost: $30.00; pdf: $20. Also available on HeinOnline (2014).

9. Leading Web Pages for State Legal Research.

Home Page:	www.ri.gov
Administrative Regulations:	www.sos.ri.gov/rules/
Agency Directory:	www.ri.gov/guide/
Attorney General:	www.riag.ri.gov
Attorney Gen. Opinions:	www.riag.ri.gov/civilcriminal/search.php
Bar Association:	www.ribar.com/
Constitution:	www.rilin.state.ri.us/RiConstitution/
General Assembly:	www.rilin.state.ri.us/
Governor:	www.governor.ri.gov
Judicial Branch:	www.courts.ri.gov/
Law Library:	www.courts.ri.gov/Courts/SupremeCourt/StateLawLibrary/default.aspx
Secretary of State:	www.sos.ri.gov/
Statutes:	www.rilin.state.ri.us/Statutes/Statutes.html
Supreme Court:	www.courts.ri.gov/courts/supremecourt/default.aspx www.courts.ri.gov/courts/supremecourt
Supreme Court Opinions:	www.courts.ri.gov/Courts/SupremeCourt/Pages/Opinions and Orders.aspx

10. Leading publishers of state specific treatises, practice books, and CLE publications.

LexisNexis, Lorman Education Services, National Business Institute, Rhode Island Bar Association - CLE, Thomson Reuters West, Tower Publishing. See Appendix B for addresses and telephone numbers.

South Carolina

1. Codes and Session Laws.

Code of Laws of South Carolina 1976 Annotated. St. Paul, MN: West, 1976-date. 27 vols. in 47. Official code of the state of South Carolina. Annual pocket supplements and periodic revised volumes.
Cost: $1,046; supplementation: 1996: $340.61; 1997: $427.69; 1998: $382.50; 1999: $375.37; 2000: $386.77; 2001: $344.85; 2002; $416.10; 2003: $401.44; 2004: $326.98; 2006: $410.60; 2007: $406.58; 2008: $397.71; 2009: $522.17; 2010: $378.99; 2011: $517.27; 2012: $300.50; 2013: $352; **Monthly Assured**

Print Pricing (APP): $39/$468.

Acts and Joint Resolutions of South Carolina. Columbia, SC: Legislative Printing and Technology. 2 vols. Annual. Also on CD-ROM (2009-date).
Cost: 1994: $69.50/$49.50 (buckram/softcover/CD); 1995: $69.50/$49.50; 1996: $105.00/$72.50 (3 vols.); 1997-2008: $102.50/$42.50 (2 vols.); 2009: $189.50/$87.50/$20.50; 2010: $189.50/$87.50/$20.50; 2011-date: online only at: www.scstatehouse.gov/newlaws.php **Legislative Hotline**: (803) 734-2060.

2. Administrative Law.
Code of Laws of South Carolina 1976 Annotated: Code of Regulations. St. Paul, MN: West, 1976-date. 8 vols. Looseleaf format. Annual replacement pamphlets. The regulations appear in volumes 23-27 of the Code of Laws.
Cost: vols. 23-27 only: $224 (8 @ $28 ea.) (2014). Also online at: www.scstatehouse.gov/coderegs/statmast.php

South Carolina State Register. Columbia, SC: Legislative Council, 1977-date. Monthly. July 1 – June 30. Print and online. Available online from 2003 at: http://www.scstatehouse.gov/state_register.php
Cost: print: $100 per year (2014). (803) 734-2145

3. Court Reports.
South Carolina Reports. 1868-date. St. Paul, MN: West, 1998-date. Offprint of South Eastern Reporter. Vols. 324-date published by West as South Carolina Reports. Current vol.: 406.
Cost: $732 (82 vols.); annual cost: 2002: $201.25; 2003: $175.50; 2004: $232.75; 2005: $244.25; 2006: $255.50; 2007: $265.50; 2008: $278; 2009: $292; 2010: $300; 2011: $310; 2012: $335; 2013: $382.50; individual volumes: $63.75/$85 (subscriber/list). Prior volumes available at a cost of $52 per volume from R. L. Bryan Co. of Columbia, SC. (803) 779-3560.

South Eastern Reporter [1st] - **2d**. St. Paul, MN: West, 1886-date. Contains decisions of the South Carolina Supreme Court from 1886-date and the South Carolina Court of Appeals from 1983-date. Current vol.: 750 **S.E. 2d**.
Cost: 1st series out-of-print (see used lawbook dealers in Appendix C); 2d series: $10,480; annual cost: 2012: $7,389; 2013: $5,434; current vol.: $524/$655 (subscriber/list); **Monthly Assured Print Pricing (APP):** $846/$10,152. See list of used lawbook dealers in Appendix C.

South Eastern Reporter 2d. Advance sheets. St. Paul, MN: Thomson West. Weekly.
Cost: $2,825 (discounted to bound volume subscribers) (2014).

4. Court Rules.
South Carolina Rules of Court: State and Federal. St. Paul, MN: West. 2 vols. Annual. Also available as ProView eBook.
Cost: 2014 Edition: $176.

5. Digests, Encyclopedias, and Practice Sets.
South Carolina Digest, 2d. St. Paul, MN: West, 1991-date. 33 vols. in 70. Annual pocket supplements, mid-year supplement, and periodic revised volumes.
Cost: $5,255; supplementation: 1996: $129; 1997: $149.50; 1998: $163; 1999: $394.50; 2000: $188.50; 2001: $333; 2002: $805; 2003: $328.75; 2004: $550; 2005: $702.50; 2006: $785; 2007: $1,342.50; 2008: $1,251; 2009: $1,120; 2010: $1,468; 2011: $3,066; 2012: $3,168; 2013: $4,202; **Monthly Assured Print Pricing (APP):** $281/$3,372.

South Carolina Jurisprudence. St. Paul, MN: West, 1991-date. 33 vols. Annual pocket parts. Analysis covers case law, statutes and regulations. Originally published by the Harrison Company for the South Carolina Bar. Sold to the Thomson Corporation in late, 1996, and assigned to West product line.
Cost: $2,863; supplementation: 1994: $175; 1997: $250; 1998: $482; 1999: $558; 2000: $415.50; 2001: $463; 2002: $845; 2003: $607.50; 2004: $680.50; 2005: $745.50; 2006: $826; 2007: $932.50; 2008: $1,039.50; 2009: $1,199; 2010: $1,442; 2011: $1,519; 2012: $1,922; 2013: $2,044; **Monthly Assured Print Pricing (APP):** $173/$2,076.

6. Citators.
Shepard's South Carolina Citations. Albany, NY: Shepard's. Updated monthly.
Cost: $1,583 (2 bound volumes); all-inclusive subscription: $2,158 (in-state) (2014).

Online: All jurisdictional Shepard's and KeyCite are no longer available as stand-alone products, but are included as part of a jurisdictional or subject library from their respective publishers (2014).

7. CD-ROM Products.
South Carolina Reporter and Code of Laws of South Carolina Laws Annotated. Eagan, MN: West. One disc. Updated quarterly. Contains the full text of decisions of the Carolina Supreme Court from 1868 to date, and Court of Appeals from vol. 33 of the South Easter Reporter 2d to date, state court rules, Attorney General Opinions form 1959 to date, South Carolina Code of Laws, South Carolina Administrative Code, and South Carolina court rules. Decisions also searchable by West Topics and Key Numbers, headnotes and synopses. Available in DOS, Windows, and Macintosh. Search Engine: PREMISE and LawDesk. Subscription includes online connection to Westlaw.
Cost: $6,846 per year (2014).

8. State Legal Research Guides.
Melton, Pamela Rogers. South Carolina Practice Materials: A Selective Bibliography in Houdek, Frank G., ed. **State Practice Materials: Annotated Bibliographies**. Buffalo, NY: William S. Hein & Co., Inc., 2008-date. 2 vols. Looseleaf format.
Cost: $195.00 (2014).

Conroy, Terrye, Stacy Etheredge and David Lehmann. **State Documents Bibliography: South Carolina**. Chicago: AALL, 2009. Available from William S. Hein & Co.
Cost: $30.00; pdf: $20; also available on HeinOnline (2014).

Graham, Cole Blease. **South Carolina State Constitution**. New York: Oxford University Press, 2011. 1 vol. (294 pp.).
Cost: $150.00; from $8.44 on amazon.com (2014).

Taylor, Karen G. "Bibliography of South Carolina Practice Materials." **Southeastern Law Librarian** 24 (Spring, 1999):

18-23.

9. Leading Web Sites for State Legal Research.

Home Page:	www.sc.gov/
Administrative Code:	www.scstatehouse.gov/coderegs/statmast.php
Agency Directory:	www.sc.gov/Pages/agencyListin-gA-Z.aspx
Attorney General:	www.scag.gov
Attorney Gen. Opinions:	www.scag.gov/opinions
Bar Association:	www.scbar.org
Constitution:	www.scstatehouse.gov/scconstitu-tion/scconst.php
Court Opinions–Court of Appeals:	www.judicial.state.sc.us/opinions/indexCOAPub.cfm
Court Opinions–Supreme Court:	www.judicial.state.sc.us/opinions/indexSCPub.cfm
Governor:	http://governor.sc.gov
Judicial Branch:	www.judicial.state.sc.us
Law Library:	www.judicial.state.sc.us/supreme/library.cfm
Legislative Branch:	www.scstatehouse.gov/
Secretary of State:	www.scsos.com/
Statutes:	www.scstatehouse.gov/code/statmast.php
USC Law Library:	http://law.sc.edu/library/

10. Leading publishers of state specific treatises, practice books, and CLE publications.
National Business Institute, South Carolina Bar Association-Continuing Legal Education Division, Thomson Reuters West. See Appendix B for addresses and telephone numbers.

South Dakota

1. Codes and Session Laws.
South Dakota Codified Laws. St. Paul, MN: West, 2004-date. 16 vols. in 39 plus index and tables vols. Annual pocket parts and periodic revised volumes. Formerly published by LexisNexis.
Cost: $386; supplementation: 2005: $229; 2006: $187; 2007: $316; 2008: $294; 2009: $200.50; 2010: $198; 2011: $259.50; 2012: $215.50; 2013: $236.50.

Laws of South Dakota. Pierre, SD: Legislative Research Council. Annual. Available from Property Management. (605) 773-4935
Cost (includes shipping): 1995: $15.00 (1 vol.); 1996: $10.00 (1 vol.); 1997: $11.00; 1998: $12.50; 1999: $6.82; 2000: $8.46; 2001: $10.97; 2002: $10.06; 2003: $12.42; 2004: $17.99; 2005: $22.30; 2006: n/a; 2007: $19.92; 2008: $26.04; 2009: $31.55; 2010: $20.49; 2011: $34.38.

Legislative Hotline: (605) 773-3251.

2. Administrative Law.
Administrative Rules of South Dakota. Pierre, SD: Legislative Research Council, 1978-date. 13 vols. Looseleaf format. (605) 773-3251.
Cost: $250 (2014); supplementation: no set price, individual articles revised as needed. Subscribers notified when supplements are issued and billed with each shipment. Also available free on the Internet at: http://legis.sd.gov/
South Dakota Register. Pierre, SD: Legislative Research Council. Weekly. Updates the Administrative Rules of South Dakota. Also available on the Web at: http://legis.sd.gov/ (605) 773-3251.
Cost: $25 per year (2014).

3. Court Reports.
South Dakota Reports.1890-1976. Pierre, SD: Bureau of Administration. [ceased with vol. 90].
Cost: Out-of-print. See used lawbook dealers in Appendix C.

West's North Western Reporter [1st] - **2d**. St. Paul, MN: West, 1879-date. Contains decisions of the South Dakota Supreme Court from 1890-date. Official reporter since 1976. Current vol.: 844 **N.W. 2d**.
Cost: 1st series out-of-print (see used lawbook dealers in Appendix C); 2d series $10,225; used sets sell for approx. $3,795; annual cost (2013): $7,332; recent volume: $459/$611 (subscriber/list); **Monthly Assured Print Pricing (APP):** $709/$8,508.

West's North Western Reporter 2d. Advance Sheets. St. Paul, MN: Thomson West. Weekly.
Cost: $2,808 (discounted to bound volume subscribers) (2014).

4. Court Rules.
South Dakota Court Rules: State and Federal. St. Paul, MN: West, 2004-date. 2 vols. Annual. Also available as ProView eBook.
Cost: 2013 Edition: $123 (2014).

South Dakota Court Rules Annotated. Charlottesville, VA: LexisNexis. 2 vols. Replaced annually.
Cost: 2013-2014 Edition: $65 (2014).

5. Digests, Encyclopedias and Practice Sets.
Dakota Digest. St. Paul, MN: West, 1942-date. 60 vols. Kept up to date by pocket parts, pamphlets, bound cumulative supplements, and replacement volumes. This digest covers both North and South Dakota.
Cost: $7,876; supplementation: 1995: $296; 1996: $299.50; 1997: $329; 1998: $851; 1999: $710; 2000: $851; 2001: $1,743.75; 2002: $1,184; 2003: $603.50; 2004: $743; 2005: $1,250; 2006: $1,235.75; 2007: $1,252; 2008: $1,609.50; 2009: $3,539.50; 2010: $2,530; 2011: $3,817.50; 2012: $3,875; **Monthly Assured Print Pricing (APP):** $398/$4,776.

6. Citators.
Shepard's South Dakota Citations. Albany, NY: Shepard's.

Bimonthly.
Cost: $989 (1 bound volume); all-inclusive subscription: $1,712 (in-state): (2014).

Online: All jurisdictional Shepard's and KeyCite are no longer available as stand-alone products, but are included as part of a jurisdictional or subject library from their respective publishers (2014).

7. CD-ROM Products.
Dakota Disc. Pierre, SD: State Bar of South Dakota. One disc. Updated quarterly. Contains the text of the South Dakota Code, Supreme Court decisions from 1940 to date, 8th Circuit opinions from South Dakota from 1994 to date, administrative rules, Attorney General opinions from 1989 to date, federal local rules, probate and guardianship forms, pattern civil and criminal jury instructions, 8th Circuit Model Jury Instructions, etc. Available for Windows and Macintosh. Search Engine: Folio. Includes member access to Fastcase.
Cost: $500 per year (single user); additional users: $75 per year (2014). 888-952-2333

8. State Legal Research Guides.
Braun, Matthew E. South Dakota Practice Materials: A Selective Bibliography in Houdek, Frank G., ed. **State Practice Materials: Annotated Bibliographies**. Buffalo, NY: William S. Hein & Co., Inc., 2008-date. 2 vols. Looseleaf format.
Cost: $195.00 (2014).

Jorgensen, Delores A. **South Dakota Legal Documents: A Selective Bibliography**. Chicago: AALL, 1988. Available from William S. Hein & Co.
Cost: $30.00; pdf; $20; also available on HeinOnline (2014).

Jorgensen, Delores A. **South Dakota Legal Research Guide**. 2d ed. Buffalo, NY: William S. Hein & Co., 1999. 1 vol. (194 pp.).
Cost: $48.50; also available on HeinOnline (2014).

9. Leading Web Sites for State Legal Research.

Home Page:	http://www.sd.gov
Administrative Code:	http://rules.sd.gov
Agency Directory:	http://sd.gov/government.aspx#stateagencies
Attorney General:	http://atg.sd.gov
Attorney Gen. Opinions:	http://atg.sd.gov/TheOffice/OfficialOpinions.aspx
Bar Association:	www.sdbar.org
Constitution:	http://legis.sd.gov/Statutes/Constitution/default.aspx
Court Opinions:	http://ujs.sd.gov/Supreme_Court/opinions.aspx
Governor:	http://sd.gov/governor
Judicial Branch:	http://ujs.sd.gov
Legislative Branch:	http://legis.sd.gov
Secretary of State:	http://www.sdsos.gov
Statutes:	http://legis.sd.gov/statutes

10. Leading publishers of state specific treatises, practice books, and CLE publications.
National Business Institute, State Bar of South Dakota Bar CLE, Thomson Reuters West.

Tennessee

1. Codes and Session Laws.
Tennessee Code Annotated. Charlottesville, VA: LexisNexis, 1956-date. 16 vols. in 34. Annual pocket parts and periodic revised volumes.
Cost: $245.70 (in-state); $844 (out-of-state); annual supplementation: (in-state/out-of-state): 2001: $213/$959; 2002: $152/$589; 2003: $154/$590; 2004: $154/$590; 2005: $158/$614; 2008: $185.70/$692; 2009: $178.30/$679; 2010: $154/$735; 2011: $162/$746; 2012: $235.45/$1013; 2013: $263.45/$1,041.

Tennessee Advance Code Service. Charlottesville, VA: LexisNexis. Supplements code between annual pocket parts.
Cost: $27 (in-state), $63 (out-of-state) per year (2014).

Tennessee Advance Legislative Service. Charlottesville, VA: LexisNexis.
These pamphlets are published during and immediately after each legislative session and contain text of laws in numerical chapter sequence in order of passage.
Cost: $27.30 (in-state), $59 (out-of-state) per year, or included in cost of updates to code (2014).

West's Tennessee Code Annotated. St. Paul, MN: Thomson West, 2002-date. 50 vols. Annual pocket supplements and periodic revised volumes. Includes Legislative Service and Interim Annotation Service.
Cost: $1,057; supplementation: 2003: $210; 2004: $210; 2005: $472.50; 2006: $403; 2007: $450; 2008: $457.50; 2009: $488.50; 2010: $549; 2011: $585; 2012: $711; 2013: $683;
Monthly Assured Print Pricing (APP): $69/$828.

West's Tennessee Legislative Service. St. Paul, MN: Thomson West, 2002-date. These pamphlets are published during and immediately after each legislative session and contain text of laws in numerical chapter sequence in order of passage.
Cost: $339 per year (2014).

Tennessee Public and Private Acts. Nashville, TN: Secretary of State. 2 vols. Annual. (615) 741-2650
Cost: 1995: $32; 1996: $32; 1997: $32; 1998: $32; 1999: $40; 2000: $40; 2001: $45; 2002: $44; 2003: $44; 2004: $46; 2005: $48; 2006: $50; 2007: $52; 2008: $130; 2009-date: only online at: http://tennessee.gov/sos/acts/index.htm

Legislative Hotline: (615) 741-3511.

2. Administrative Law.

Official Compilation: Rules and Regulations of the State of Tennessee. Nashville, TN: Secretary of State, 1978?-2003. 24 vols. No longer available in print except as printed off website. (615) 741-2650

Cost: no new sales of print Compilation; now available at no charge on the Internet at: http://state.tn.us/sos/rules/index.htm

Tennessee Administrative Register. CD-ROM. Nashville, TN: Secretary of State, 1975?-date. Monthly. (615) 741-2650.

Cost: available at no charge on the Internet at: http://state.tn.us/sos/pub/tar/index.htm

3. Court Reports.

Tennessee Decisions [1st] - **3d**. St. Paul, MN: West, 1886-date. [offprint of South Western Reporter--official since 1972]. Contain decisions of the Tennessee Supreme Court from 1886 to date, Court of Appeals from 1932 to date, and Court of Criminal Appeals from 1967 to date. Recent vol.: 402-407 **S.W. 3d** as of March 2, 2014.

Cost: 1st series: out-of-print; 2d series (180 vols.): $2,372.50; 3d series (74 vols.): $1,672; annual upkeep: 2002: $474.50; 2003: $363.50; 2004: $392; 2005: $427.25; 2006: $318; 2007: $512; 2008: $527.50; 2009: $338.50; 2010: $640; 2011: $491; 2012: $546; 2013: $738; current volume: $147.75/$197 (subscriber/list); **Monthly Assured Print Pricing (APP):** $100/$1,200.

Tennessee Reports. 1791-1972. [Ceased publication with vol. 225]

Cost: Out-of-print. See used lawbook dealers in Appendix.

South Western Reporter [1st] – **3d**. St. Paul, MN: West, 1886-date. Contains decisions of the Tennessee Supreme Court from 1886-date, the Tennessee Court of Appeals from 1932-date, and the Tennessee Court of Criminal Appeals from 1967-date. Vols.1-74 of Tennessee Reports and vols. 1-15 of Tennessee Appeals Reports precede the appearance of the South Western Reporter [1st] in 1886. Current vol.: 420 S.W. 3d.

Cost: 1st series: out-of-print (see used lawbook dealers in Appendix C); 2d series: $12,480; used sets sell for approx. $2,300; 3d series: $20,134; used sets sell for approx. $1,500; annual cost (2013): $15,615; current volume: $520.50/$694 (subscriber/list); **Monthly Assured Print Pricing (APP):** $1,399/$16,788. See used lawbook dealers in Appendix C.

South Western 3d. Advance sheets. St. Paul, MN: Thomson West. Weekly.

Cost: $2,799 per year (discounted to bound volume subscribers) (2014).

4. Court Rules.

Tennessee Court Rules Annotated. Charlottesville, VA: LexisNexis. 2 vols. Paperbound and ebook. Updated semiannually, replaced biennially.

Cost: 2012 Edition: $35.70 (in-state); $72.00 (out-of-state) (20134).

Tennessee Rules of Court: State and Federal. St. Paul, MN: West. 2 vols. Annual. Also available as ProView eBook.

Cost: 2013 Edition: $164; State, Federal and Local: $235 (2014).

5. Digests, Encyclopedias, and Practice Sets.

West's Tennessee Digest 2d. St. Paul, MN: West, 1986-date. 77 vols. Annual pocket parts, mid-year supplement, and periodic revised volumes.

Cost: $4,255; supplementation: 1996: $147; 1997: $165; 1998: $309; 1999: $509.75; 2000: $403; 2001: $969.50; 2002: $805; 2003: $382.50; 2004: $756; 2005: $1,427.25; 2006: $389.50; 2007: $1,178; 2008: $1,806.50; 2009: $2,241; 2010: $1,708.50; 2011: $2,893; 2012: $2,781.50; 2013: $3,956; **Monthly Assured Print Pricing (APP):** $257/$3,084.

Tennessee Jurisprudence: An Encyclopedia of Tennessee Law. Charlottesville, VA: LexisNexis, 1982-date. 31 vols. Annual pocket supplements and periodic revised volumes.

Cost: $2,542; supplementation: 2001: $708.50; 2002: $652; 2003: $803; 2004: $813; 2005: $517; 2006: n/a; 2007: $857; 2008: $900; 2009: $1,487; 2010: $933; 2011: $1,271; 2012: $1,367; 2013: $927.

Tennessee Practice. St. Paul, MN: West. 30 vols.
The volumes in this series cover the following subject areas: Uniform Commercial Code, rules of civil procedure, civil procedure forms, pattern jury instructions (civil and criminal), criminal practice and procedure, and legal forms.

Cost: $5,276; supplementation: 1996: $204.00; 1997: $216.00; 1998: $235.00; 1999: $108.50; 2000: $391.50; 2001: $698.25; 2002: $698.25; 2003: $501.50; 2004: inquire regarding costs for individual components. Individual volumes also available.

6. Citators.

Shepard's Tennessee Citations. Albany, NY: Shepard's. Monthly.

Cost: $3,063 (5 bound volumes); all-inclusive subscription: monthly: $2,284 (in-state); bi-monthly: $2,695 (in-state) (2014).

Online: All jurisdictional Shepard's and KeyCite are no longer available as stand-alone products, but are included as part of a jurisdictional or subject library from their respective publishers (2014).

7. CD-ROM Products.

Michie's Tennessee Forms on CD-ROM from LEXIS-NEXIS. Albany, NY: LexisNexis. One disc. Updated quarterly. Available for Windows. Search Engine: Folio; LivePublish (NextPage). Contains over 1,000 forms collected from the four-volume Tennessee Forms, and Pritchard on Wills.

Cost: $457 per year (2014).

LexisNexis CD - Tennessee Primary Law. Albany, NY: LexisNexis. One disc. Updated quarterly. Contains the full text of the Tennessee Supreme Court decisions from 1944 to date, Court of Appeals decisions from 1943 to date, Court of Criminal Appeals from 1967 to date, Tennessee unpublished opinions from 1981 to date, and Attorney General opinions from 1977 to date. Available for DOS and Windows. Search Engine: Folio.

Cost: $1,175 per year (2014).

Tennessee Decisions and West's Tennessee Code. Eagan, MN: West. One disc. Updated quarterly. Contains full text of the Tennessee Code, Tennessee Constitution, state court rules, Tennessee Public Acts, decisions of the Tennessee Supreme Court from 1811 to date, Court of Appeals and Court of Criminal

Appeals from 1944 to date, unpublished opinions from 1985 to date, and Attorney General opinions from 1977 to date. Decisions also searchable by West Topics and Key Numbers, headnotes and synopses. DOS, Windows, and Macintosh versions available. Search Engine: PREMISE. Subscription includes online updating via Westlaw.
Cost: $9,549 per year (2014).

8 State Legal Research Guides.
Brown, Toof, III. Tennessee Practice Materials: A Selective Bibliography in Houdek, Frank G., ed. **State Practice Materials: Annotated Bibliographies**. Buffalo, NY: William S. Hein & Co., Inc., 2004-date. 2 vols. Looseleaf format.
Cost: $195.00 (2014).

Laska, Lewis L. **The Tennessee State Constitution**. New York: Oxford University Press, 2011. 1 vol. (216 pp.).
Cost: $150.00; from $93.62 on amazon; kindle: $119.99 (2014).

Best, Reba A. **Tennessee State Documents: A Bibliography of State Publications and Related Materials**. Chicago: AALL, 2009. Available from William S. Hein & Co.
Cost: $30.00; pdf: $20; also available on HeinOnline (2014).

9. Leading Web Sites for State Legal Research.

Home Page:	www.tn.gov
Administrative Code:	http://state.tn.us/sos/rules
Agency Directory:	www.tn.gov/directory/
Attorney General:	www.tn.gov/attorneygeneral/
Attorney Gen. Opinions:	www.tn.gov/attorneygeneral/op/opinions.html
Bar Association:	www.tba.org
Constitution:	www.state.tn.us/sos/bluebook/05-06/46-tnconst.pdf
Court Opinions:	www.tncourts.gov/opinionsview/all
Governor:	www.tn.gov/governor/
Judicial Branch:	www.tncourts.gov/
Legislative Branch:	www.capitol.tn.gov/
Secretary of State:	www.tn.gov/sos/
Statutes:	www.lexisnexis.com/hottopics/tncode

10. Leading publishers of state specific treatises, practice books, and CLE publications.
Harrison Company, LexisNexis, National Business Institute, M. Lee Smith Publishers, Thomson Reuters West. See Appendix B for addresses and telephone numbers.

Texas

1. Codes and Session Laws.
Vernon's Annotated Texas Statutes and Codes. St. Paul, MN: West, 1925-date. 184 vols. plus 4 index vols. Annual pocket parts and periodic revised volumes.
Cost: $6,258; supplementation: 1995: $530.00; 1996: $616.00; 1997: $842.00; 1998: $708.00; 1999: $801.50; 2000: $726.50; 2001: $1,196.50; 2002: $1,564.75; 2003: $1,719.00; 2004: $1,806.00; 2005: $1,903; 2006: $2,452; 2007: $2,573; 2008: $3,755; 2009: $3,196.50; 2010: $3,291.50; 2011: $4,061.50; 2012: $4,709; 2013: $5,372; **Monthly Assured Print Pricing (APP):** $493/$5,916.

General and Special Laws of Texas. Austin, TX: Secretary of State. Biennial. 2003-date available from West; 2001 available from LexisNexis.
Cost: 1997: $275 (6 vols.); 1999: $319 (6 vols.); 2001: $351 (6 vols.); 2003: $360 (6 vols.); 2005: $360 (6 vols.); 2007: $456 (6 vols.); 2009: $546 (6 vols.).

Texas Bound Session Laws. St. Paul, MN: Thomson West, 2009-date. 6 vols. Biennial.
Cost: 2011: $660; 2013: $738 (2014).

Legislative Hotline: (512) 463-2182, (512) 463-1252.

2. Administrative Law.
Official Texas Administrative Code. St. Paul, West, 1986-date. 23 vols.
Softbound. Replaced annually. Also available online at: http://www.sos.state.tx.us/tac
Cost: $7,878 (uo 16,7% over 2013); supplementation: 2003: $2,138; 2004: 2,110.50; 2005: $3,749; 2006: $2,682; 2007: $2,761; 2008: $3,100; 2009: $3.597.50; 2010: $5,582; 2011: $3,100; 2012: $5,022.50; 2013: $6,571; **Monthly Assured Print Pricing (APP):** $572/$6,864.

Official Texas Administrative Code and Register. Austin, TX: Secretary of State. Online service available at: http://www.sos.state.tx.us/tac/index.shtml
Cost: No-cost, value-added searchable database of both Texas Register and Texas Administrative Code, including historical and graphic material. (2013).

Texas Register. New York: LexisNexis Matthew Bender, 2005-date. Issued weekly. (512) 463-5561. LexisNexis began publication in Sept., 2005.
Cost: $259 per year (2d class), $383 per year (1st class) (2014); also on the Internet at: http://www.sos.state.tx.us.
This searchable database of both Texas Register and Texas Administrative Code, including historical and graphic material is also available at a cost of $10 per month. E-mail notification for a single agency is available for an additional $5 per month (2013).

3. Court Reports.
Texas Cases [1st] **– 3d**. St. Paul, MN: West, 1886-date [offprint of **South Western Reporter** 1st - 3d]. Latest volume: 412-413 **S.W.3d**.
Cost: 1st series: $1,340; 2d series: $6,115; 3d series: $16,870; annual upkeep: 2002: $1,600; 2003: $2,000.75; 2004: $2,053; 2005: $2,986; 2006: $2,931; 2007: $2,928; 2008: $3,087.50; 2009: $5,354; 2010: $5,282; 2011: $6,115; 2013: $12,642; individual volumes: $451.50/$602 (subscriber/list); **Monthly Assured Print Pricing (APP):** $1,143/$13,716; used sets may be available.

Texas Reports.1846-1962. [Ceased publication with vol. 163].
Cost: Out-of-print. See used lawbook dealers in Appendix C.

Texas Criminal Reports, 1892-1963. Vols. 1-173 [ceased publication with vol. 173].
Cost: Out-of-print. See used lawbook dealers in Appendix C.

South Western Reporter [1st] – **3d**. St. Paul, MN: West, 1886-date. Contain decisions of the Texas Supreme Court from 1886-date, the Court of Criminal Appeals from 1886-date, and the Court of Appeals from 1892-date. Current vol.: 420 S.W. 3d.
Cost: 1st series: out-of-print (see used lawbook dealers in Appendix C); 2d series: $12,480; used sets sell for approx. $2,300; 3d series: $20,134; used sets sell for approx. $1,500; annual cost (2013): $15,615; current volume: $520.50/$694 (subscriber/list); **Monthly Assured Print Pricing (APP):** $1,399/$16,788. See used lawbook dealers in Appendix C.

South Western 3d. Advance sheets. St. Paul, MN: Thomson West. Weekly.
Cost: $2,799 per year (discounted to bound volume subscribers) (2014).

4. Court Rules.

O'Connor's Texas Rules – Civil Trials. Houston, TX: Jones McClure Publishing Inc., 1994-date. 1 vol. Annual. Annotated rules Include Texas Rules of Civil Procedure, Texas Rules of Evidence, Texas Rules of Appellate Procedure, with Commentaries.
Cost: 2014 Edition: $125.55; subscription price: $93.00.

Texas Rules of Court: State and Federal. St. Paul, MN: West. 2 vols. Annual. Also available as ProView eBook.
Cost: 2014 Edition: $162; ProView eBook: $157; with Local: $217; ProView eBook: $211 (2014).

Vernon's Texas Rules Annotated--Civil Procedure, Evidence and Appellate Procedure. St. Paul, MN: West. 14 vols. Annual supplements.
Cost: $679; supplementation: 1996: $62.50; 1997: $68.50; 1998: $83.25; 1999: $90.50; 2000: $96.25; 2002: $115; 2003: $392.50; 2004: $368; 2005: $150; 2006: $170; 2007: $236; 2008: $326; 2009: $211; 2010: $247; 2011: $269; 2012: $294; 2013: $320.

5. Digests, Encyclopedias and Practice Sets.

O'Connor's Texas Causes of Action. Houston: Jones McClure Publishing, Inc., 2001-date. 1 vol. Biennial.
Contains over 900 pages of comprehensive commentary discussing the most common causes of action pleaded by Texas attorneys, including the elements of each causes of action, the authority for each point, cross references to relevant state pattern jury charges, and law journal articles. Covers torts, contracts, negligence, and statutory causes of action. Pleadings volume also available.
Cost: 2014 Edition: $145.00 (subscription); $195.75 (non-subscription).

Texas Jurisprudence 3d. St. Paul, MN: West, 1979-date. 90 vols. Annual pocket parts and periodic revised volumes.
Cost: $12,582; supplementation: 1991: $474; 1992: $699; 1993: $775; 1994: $825; 1995: $925; 1996: $1,310; 1997: $868; 1998: $1,257; 1999: $1,360; 2000: $1,456.50; 2001: $1,656.75; 2002: $2,384.50; 2003: $2,641; 2004: $2,788; 2005: $4,553; 2006: $3,979; 2007: $4,582; 2008: $4,554.50; 2009: $5.323; 2010: $6,460; 2011: $6,412; 2012: $7,545; 2013: $8,840; **Monthly Assured Print Pricing (APP):** $751/$9,012.

Texas Jurisprudence Pleading and Practice Forms. St. Paul, MN: West, 1953-date. 13 vols. in 39. Annual pocket parts and periodic revised volumes.
Forms designed to be used in Texas courts and based upon Texas statutes, rules and case law, with accompanying explanatory material and references to various Texas publications.
Cost: $3,675; supplementation: 1992: $62; 1993: $494; 1994: $399; 1995: $384; 1996: $240; 1997: $608; 1998: $533.50; 1999: $784.75; 2000: $813.50; 2001: $808; 2002: $1,150; 2003: $621; 2004: $695; 2005: $1,054; 2006: $420; 2007: $1,036; 2008: $1,036.50; 2009: $1,700; 2010: $1,834; 2011: $1,487; 2012: $2,032; 2013: $3,209; **Monthly Assured Print Pricing (APP):** $297/$3,564.

West's Texas Digest 2d. St. Paul, MN: West, 1982-date. 230 vols. Annual pocket parts, mid-year supplement, and periodic revised volumes.
Cost: $9,358; supplementation: 1995: $189.50; 1996: $277.50; 1997: $456.50; 1998: $737; 1999: $802.50; 2000: $1,105; 2001: $1,805; 2002: $1,860.50; 2003: $1,660; 2004: $1,811.75; 2005: $3,028; 2006: $2,949; 2007: $2,170; 2008: $3,539; 2009: $4,348; 2010: $5,267.50; 2011: $4,890; 2012: $4,474.50; 2013: $7,583; **Monthly Assured Print Pricing (APP):** $528/$6,336.

6. Citators.

Shepard's Texas Citations. Albany, NY: Shepard's. Monthly or bi-monthly.
Cost: $8,265 (19 bound volumes); all-inclusive subscription: monthly: $2,284 (in-state); bi-monthly: $2,695 (in-state) (2014).

Online: All jurisdictional Shepard's and KeyCite are no longer available as stand-alone products, but are included as part of a jurisdictional or subject library from their respective publishers (2014).

7. CD-ROM Products

Texas Library. [Formerly titled **Authority Texas Law and Practice**] Albany, NY: LexisNexis. One disc. Updated quarterly. Contains the full text of Texas state practice books selected from a list consisting of Texas Litigation Guide, Texas Transaction Guide, Texas Estate Planning, Texas Family Law Reporter, Family law: Texas Practice and Procedure, Texas Torts & Remedies, Texas Probate, Estate & Trust Administration, Texas Criminal Practice Guide, Texas Torts Update, Texas Civil Trial Guide, Texas Codes and Constitution, and more. Also contains full text of cited statutes and cases. Available for Windows. Search Engine: Folio; LivePublish (NextPage).
Cost: $19,357 for complete library; renewal: 2008: $10,265; 2009: $11,086; 2010: $11,860; 2011: $12,453; 2012: $13,325; 2013: $14,258; 2014: $15,872.22.

Texas State Case Collection. Albany, NY: LexisNexis. Four discs. Updated quarterly. Contains a massive library of Texas court decisions. Available for Windows. Search Engine: Folio;

Live Publish (NextPage). Also available on the Web.
Cost: $2,678; renewal: 2014: $2,482 per year.

West's Texas Cases. Eagan, MN: West. Two discs. Updated monthly. Contains the full text of decisions of the Texas Supreme Court from 1840 to date, Court of Criminal Appeals, and Court of Appeals from vol. 180 South Western Reporter 2d, and Attorney General opinions from 1977 to date. Includes West Topics and Key Numbers, headnotes and synopses. Available for DOS, Windows or Macintosh. Search Engine: PREMISE. Subscription includes online updates via Westlaw.
Cost: $7,983 per year (2014).

8. State Legal Research Guides.

Angell, Robert H. **A Compilation and Analysis of the 1998 Texas Constitution and the Original 1876 Test**. Lewiston, NY: E. Mellen Press, 1998.

Brandt, Lydia M. V. **Texas Legal Research: An Essential Lawyering Skill**. Texas Lawyer Press, 1995.
Cost: $49.95; from $3.92 on amazon.com (2014).

Cordon, Matthew C. and Brandon D. Quarles. **Researching Texas Law.** 3d ed. Buffalo, NY: William S. Hein & Co., 2012. 1 vol. (339 pp.).
Cost: $76; from $67.50 on amazon.com (2014).

Cordon, Matthew C. and Brandon D. Quarles. **Specialized Topics in Texas Legal Research**. Buffalo, NY: William S. Hein & Co., 2005. 1 vol. (223 pp.).
Cost: $65; from $4.00 on amazon.com (2014).

Cordon, Matthew C. Texas Practice Materials: A Selective Bibliography in Houdek, Frank G., ed. **State Practice Materials: Annotated Bibliographies**. Buffalo, NY: William S. Hein & Co., Inc., 2006-date. 2 vols. Looseleaf format.
Cost: $195.00 (2014).

Gruben, Karl T. and James E. Hambleton, eds. **A Reference Guide to Texas Law and Legal History: Sources and Documentation**. 2d ed. Austin, TX: Butterworth Legal Publishers, 1987.

May, Janice C. **The Texas State Constitution**. New York: Oxford University Press, 2011. 1 vol. (504 pp.).
Cost: $150.00; from $23.87 on amazon.com; kindle: $119.99 (2014).

Parmenter, Paris & Susan F. Ratliff. **Guide to Texas Legislative History**. Austin: Legislative Reference Library, 1986.

Simons, Spencer L. **Texas Legal Research**. Revised ed. Durham, NC: Carolina Academic Press, 2012. 1 vol. (262 pp.). Paperbound.
Cost: $26.00; from $19.95 on amazon.com (2014).

Tepper, Pamela R. **Texas Legal Research**. Albany, NY: Delmar Publishers, 1997.
Cost: from $4.64 on amazon.com (2014).

9. Leading Web Sites for State Legal Research.

Home Page:	www.texas.gov/
Administrative Code:	www.sos.state.tx.us/tac
Agency Directory:	www.texas.gov/en/Discover/Pages/agency-finder.aspx
Attorney General:	www.oag.state.tx.us
Attorney General Opinions:	www.oag.state.tx.us/opin/
Bar Association:	www.texasbar.com/
Constitution:	www.constitution.legis.state.tx.us/
Court Opinions – Supreme Court:	www.supreme.courts.state.tx.us/historical/recent.asp
Ethics Commission:	www.ethics.state.tx.us
Governor:	www.governor.state.tx.us/
Judicial Branch:	www.courts.state.tx.us/
Law Library:	www.sll.state.tx.us/
Legislative Branch:	www.legis.state.tx.us/
Secretary of State:	www.sos.state.tx.us/
Statutes:	www.statutes.legis.state.tx.us/
Supreme Court:	www.supreme.courts.state.tx.us/

10. Leading publishers of state specific treatises, practice books, and CLE publications.

Matthew Bender, James Publishing, Knowles Publishing, LexisNexis, Jones McClure Publishing, Inc., National Business Institute, State Bar of Texas Professional Development Program, Texas Lawyer Press, Thomson Reuters
West. See Appendix B for addresses and telephone numbers.

Utah

1. Codes and Session Laws.

Utah Code Annotated. Charlottesville, VA: LexisNexis, 1953-date. 27 vols. Annual pocket supplements and periodic revised volumes.
Cost: $724 (in- and out-of-state); annual supplementation (in-state/out-of-state): 2001: $470/$648; 2002: $501/$683; 2003: $496.75/$665; 2004: $515.50/$697.75; 2005: $183/$237; 2006: $467/714; 2007: $626 (in-state).; 2008: $663/$890; 2009: $359/$502; 2010: $930/$1,058; 2011: $967/$1086; 2012: $424/$591; 2013: $424/$591.

Utah Code Unannotated. Charlottesville, VA: LexisNexis, 2009-date.
5 vols. Softbound. Published annually.
Cost: 2013 Edition: $304/$358 (in-state/out-of-state) (2014).

West's Utah Code Annotated. St. Paul, MN: West, 2004-date. 37 vols. Annual pocket supplements and revised volumes. Set includes court rules.

Cost: $1,509; supplementation: 2005: $205; 2007: $310; 2008: $410; 2009: $732; 2010: $629; 2011: $789; 2012: $866; 2013: $1,086; **Monthly Assured Print Pricing (APP):** $86/$1,032.

Utah Advance Code Service. Charlottesville, VA: LexisNexis, 1986-date. Three pamphlets are published between annual supplements to the Utah Code Annotated. Each pamphlet is cumulative from the latest annual supplement.
Cost: $88.00 (in-state); $111 (out-of-state) (2014).

Utah Advance Legislative Service. Charlottesville, VA: LexisNexis. Softbound. Three issues. These pamphlets are published during and immediately after current legislative session and contain the text of laws in numerical chapter sequence in order of passage.
Cost: $83.00 (in-state); $98 (out-of-state) (2014).

Utah Legislative Service. St. Paul, MN: West, 2009-date. Softbound.
These pamphlets are published during and immediately after current legislative session and contain the text of laws in numerical chapter sequence in order of passage.
Cost: $311.52 (2014).

Laws of the State of Utah. Salt Lake City, UT: Utah Office of Legislative Printing. Annual. Also available at Utah libraries through HeinOnline from 1851 to present.
Cost: 1995: $50 (2 vols.); 1996: $50 (2 vols.); 1997: $50 (1 vol.); 1998: $50 (1 vol.); 1999: $50 (1 vol.); 2000: $50 (1 vol.); 2001: $50; 2002: $50 (1 vol.); 2003: $50 (1 vol.); 2004: $50 (1 vol.); 2005: $50; 2006: $50; 2007: $50; 2008: $50 (4 vols.); 2009: $50 (2 vols.); 2010: $50 (2 vols.); 2011: $50; 2012: $50; 2013: $50. (801) 538-1103

Legislative Hotline: (801) 538-1588.

2. Administrative Law.

Utah Administrative Code Annotated. Charlottesville, VA: LexisNexis, 2004-date. 10 vols. Softbound. Vol. 10 consists of tables and index. Replaced the five-binder set published from 1995-97.
Also available at http://www.rules.state.ut.us
Cost: 2014 Edition: $675 per year (includes semi-annual upkeep); supplementation: 2013: $237 (2014).

Utah Administrative Code. Salt Lake City, UT: Division of Administrative Rules. 2010-date. Internet: http://www.rules.utah.gov/publicat/code.htm
Cost: Free on the Internet.

Utah State Bulletins. Salt Lake City, UT: Division of Administrative Rules, 1996-date. Issued on the 1st and 15th of each month. Information summarized in **Utah State Digest**. Internet: http://www.rules.utah.gov/publicat/bulletin.htm
Cost: Free over the Internet.

3. Court Reports.

Utah Reports [1st] - **2d** series, 1855-1974 [123 vols. in 1st series; ceased publication with vol. 30 of 2d series]. Various publishers.
Cost: Out-of-print. Used sets may be available.

Utah Reporter 2d – 3d. St. Paul, MN: West Publishing, 1974-date [offprint of Pacific Reporter--official since 1974]. Current vol.: 308-311 **P.3d** (March 1, 2014).
Cost: 2d series: $1,340.50 (63 vols.); 3d series: $1,117; annual upkeep: 2005: $256.50; 2006: $350; 2007: $297; 2008: $230; 2009: $313; 2010: $324; 2011: $412; 2012: $428; 2013: $630; current volume: $78.75/$105 (subscriber/list); **Monthly Assured Print Pricing (APP):** $85/$1,020

Utah Advance Reports. Orem, UT: Code-Co Law Publishers, 1985-date. Biweekly. Contains decisions of the Utah Supreme Court and Utah Court of Appeals in advance sheet format.
Cost: $240 per year (online) (2014).

Pacific Reporter [1st] - **3d**. St. Paul, MN: West, 1883-date. Contains decisions of the Utah Supreme Court from 1881-date and the Utah Court of Appeals from 1987-date. Current vol.: 314 **P. 3d**.
Cost: 1st series out-of-print (see used lawbook dealers in Appendix C); 2d series: $13,428; used sets approx. $2000; 3d series: $15,201; annual cost (2013): $11,396; individual volume: $518/$691 (subscriber/list); **Monthly Assured Print Pricing (APP):** $1,141/$11,369; used sets may be available.

Pacific Reporter 3d. Advance sheets. St. Paul, MN: Thomson West. Weekly.
Cost: $2,866.56 per year (discounted to bound volume subscribers) (2014).

4. Court Rules.

Utah Court Rules Annotated. Charlottesville, VA: LexisNexis. 1 vol. Updated semiannually, replaced annually.
Cost: 2013 Edition: $96 (in-state); $122 (out-of-state) (2014).

Utah Rules of Court: State and Federal. St. Paul,, MN: West. 2 vols. Revised annually.
Cost: 2014 Edition: $138.

5. Digests, Encyclopedias, and Practice Books.

No Utah Digest (See Pacific Digest).

Thomas, A. David. **Utah Civil Practice**. Charlottesville, VA: LexisNexis, 2008. 1 vol. Softbound or ebook.
Cost: 2013 Edition: $142 (2014).

6. Citators.

Shepard's Utah Citations. Albany, NY: Shepard's. Six supplements per year.
Cost: $1,666 (2 bound volumes); all-inclusive subscription: $1,831 (in-state); renewal: $1,701 (2014).

Online: All jurisdictional Shepard's and KeyCite are no longer available as stand-alone products, but are included as part of a jurisdictional or subject library from their respective publishers (2014).

7. CD-ROM Products.

LexisNexis CD - Utah Primary Law. Albany, NY: LexisNexis. One disc. Updated quarterly. Contains the full text of the Utah Code Annotated, Utah Court Rules Annotated, Utah Administrative Code, decisions of the Utah Supreme Court from 1861 to date, Utah Court of Appeals from 1987 to date, Attorney

General opinions, Executive Orders, selected federal decisions form 1865 to date, and session laws. Available for Windows. Search Engine: Folio; LivePublish (NextPage). Subscription includes online updating via LEXIS.
Cost: $1,777 per year (2014).

8. State Legal Research Guides.
Cheney, Mari. **Utah Legal Resources Bibliography**. Chicago: AALL, 2009.
Available from William S. Hein & Co. on electronic pdf and on HeinOnline **Cost**: $30.00; pdf: $20; also available on HeinOnline (2014).

Staheli, Kory D. **Utah Practice Materials: A Selective Annotated Bibliography**. Provo, UT: Code-Co Law Publishers, 1996.

White, Jean Bickmore. **The Utah State Constitution**. New York: Oxford University Press, 2011. 1 vol. (264 pp.).
Cost: $150.00; from $121.04 on amazon.com; kindle: $119.99 (2014).

9. Leading Web Sites for State Legal Research.

Home Page:	www.utah.gov/
Administrative Code:	www.rules.utah.gov/publicat/code.htm
Agency Directory:	www.utah.gov/government/agencylist.html
Attorney General:	http://attorneygeneral.utah.gov/
Attorney General Opinions:	http://attorneygeneral.utah.gov/options-tools-2
Bar Association:	www.utahbar.org
Constitution:	http://le.utah.gov/Documents/code_const.htm
Court Opinions:	www.utcourts.gov/opinions/
Governor:	www.utah.gov/governor
Judicial Branch:	www.utcourts.gov/
Law Library:	www.utcourts.gov/lawlibrary/
Legislative Branch:	http://le.utah.gov/
Secretary of State:	Utah has no Secretary of State. Use this link: www.utah.gov/government/secretary-of-state.html
Statutes:	http://le.utah.gov/Documents/code_const.htm

A commercial Internet service is also available from Code-Co, containing Utah Advance Reports.
Cost: Utah Advance Reports: $240 per year (2014).

10. Leading publishers of state specific treatises, practice books, and CLE publications.
Code-Co Law Publishers, LexisNexis, National Business Institute, Utah State Bar. See Appendix B for addresses and telephone numbers.

Vermont

1. Code and Session Laws.
Vermont Statutes Annotated. Charlottesville, VA: LexisNexis, 1958-date. 31 vols. Annual pocket supplements and periodic revised volumes.
Cost: $890 (includes 90 day's service); annual supplementation: 2001: $332.50; 2002: $235.50. 2003: $218; 2004: $229.50; 2005: $121; 2006: approx. $236; 2007: $121; 2008: $368; 2009: $263.00; 2010: $263; 2011: $287; 2012: $233.50; 2013: $246.

Vermont Advance Code Service. Charlottesville, VA: LexisNexis. Softbound
These pamphlets supplement the annotations appearing in the **Vermont Statutes Annotated** between annual pocket supplements.
Cost: $60 per year (2014).

Vermont Advance Legislative Service. Charlottesville, VA: LexisNexis. Softbound
These pamphlets are published during and immediately after current legislative session and contain the text of laws in numerical chapter sequence in order of passage.
Cost: $86; renewal: $73 (in-state) (20134).

Laws of Vermont [session laws]. Montpelier, VT: Secretary of State. Annual. 1 vol. Paperbound.
Cost: 1998-2007: $11 each; 2008-2013: $22.50 (hardcover), $10.00 (softcover).

Legislative Hotline: (802) 828-2231.

2. Administrative Law.
Code of Vermont Rules. Albany, NY: LexisNexis Matthew Bender [formerly Weil Publishing Co.], 1989-date. 13 vols.
Cost: $2,423 (includes monthly supplements for one year); supplementation: 1995: $384; 1996: $415; 1997: $415; 1998: $480; 1999: $48; 2000: $480; 2001-2004: $650; 2005: $685; 2006: $685; 2007: $685; 2008: $685; 2009: $819; 2010: $860; 2011: $903; 2012: $957; 2013: $1,024; 2014: $1,117.

Vermont Government Register. Albany, NY: LexisNexis Matthew Bender [formerly Weil Publishing Co.], 1991-date. Monthly.
Cost: $1,257; renewal: 2014; $1,143.

3. Court Reports.
Vermont Reports.1826-date. Charlottesville, VA: LexisNexis. Current vol.: 188 (as of April 1, 2013).
Cost: $1,697 (55 vols.); individual prices vary from $32 to $64 (vols. 167-188); current cases service: $93 (2014).

Atlantic Reporter [1st] - **2d**. St. Paul, MN: West, 1886-date. Contains decisions of the Vermont Supreme Court from 1885-date. Volumes 1-57 of the official Vermont Reports precede the appearance of the Atlantic Reporter in 1885. Current volume: 85 **A.3d**.

Cost: 1st series out-of-print (see used lawbook dealers in Appendix C); 2d series: $14,434; 3d series: $15,080; annual cost (2013): $11,151; recent vol.: $531/$708 (subscriber/list); **Monthly Assured Print Pricing (APP):** $1,163/$13,956. See list of used lawbook dealers in Appendix C.

Atlantic Reporter 2d. Advance sheets. St. Paul, MN: Thomson West. Weekly.
Cost: $2,866.56 per year (discounted to bound volume subscribers) (2014).

4. Court Rules.
Vermont Court Rules Annotated. Charlottesville, VA: LexisNexis. 2 vols. Annual. Also available as ebook.
Cost: 2013 Edition: $83 (in-state) (2014).

Vermont Rules of Court: State and Federal. St. Paul, MN: Thomson West, 2 vols. Annual Paperbound.
Cost: 2014 Edition: $142; ProView eBook: $136.

5. Digests, Encyclopedias and Practice Sets.
Vermont Key Number Digest. St. Paul, MN: West, 1968-date. 32 vols.
Cost: $1,726; supplementation: 1995: $144; 1996: $146; 1997: $161; 1998: $161; 1999: $310; 2000: $369; 2001: $462.50; 2002; $690; 2003: $240.50; 2004: $390.50; 2005: $295; 2006: $457; 2007: $598.50; 2008: $407.50; 2009: $634.50; 2010: $820; 2011: $1,039; 2012: $637.50; 2013: $808; **Monthly Assured Print Pricing (APP):** $93/$1,116.

6. Citators.
Shepard's Vermont Citations. Albany, NY: Shepard's. Bimonthly. 2 vols.
Cost: $1,539 (2 bound volumes); all-inclusive subscription: $1,831 (in-state); renewal: 2014: $1,703.

Online: All jurisdictional Shepard's and KeyCite are no longer available as stand-alone products, but are included as part of a jurisdictional or subject library from their respective publishers (2014).

7. CD-ROM Products.
LexisNexis CD - Vermont Primary Law. Albany, NY: LexisNexis. One disc. Updated quarterly. Contains the full text of the Vermont Statutes Annotated, Vermont Court Rules, decisions of the Vermont Supreme Court from 1888 to date, Environmental Board Decisions, Vermont Law Review, and Vermont jury instructions. Available for Windows. Search Engine: Folio; LivePublish (NextPage). Subscription included online updating via LEXIS.
Cost: $1,769 per year (2014).

8. State Legal Research Guides.
Hill, William C. **The Vermont State Constitution**. New York: Oxford University Press, 2011. 1 vol. (236 pp.).
Cost: $150.00; from $35.93 on amazon.com; kindle: $119.99 (2014).

Wise, Virginia. **A Bibliographic Guide to the Vermont Legal System**. 2d ed. Chicago: AALL, 1991. Available from William S. Hein & Co.
Cost: $30.00; pdf: $20; also available on HeinOnline (2014).

9. Leading Web Sites for State Legal Research.

Home Page:	www.vermont.gov/
Administrative Code:	www.lexisnexis.com/hottopics/codeofvtrules
Agency Directory:	www.vermont.gov/portal/government/atoz.php
Attorney General:	www.atg.state.vt.us
Attorney Gen. Opinions:	www.atg.state.vt.us/issues/attorney-general-opinions.php
Bar Association:	www.vtbar.org
Constitution:	www.leg.state.vt.us/statutes/const2.htm
Court Opinions:	http://libraries.vermont.gov/law/supct
Governor:	http://governor.vermont.gov/
Judicial Branch:	www.vermontjudiciary.org/
Legal Resources:	www.vermontjudiciary.org/LC - AND - http://libraries.vermont.gov/law - AND - www.vermontlaw.edu/Research_Resources.htm
Legislative Branch:	www.leg.state.vt.us/
Secretary of State:	www.sec.state.vt.us/
Statutes:	www.leg.state.vt.us/statutesMain.cfm - OR - www.lexisnexis.com/hottopics/vtstatutesconstctrules

10. Leading publishers of state specific treatises, practice books, and CLE publications.
LexisNexis, National Business Institute, Thomson Reuters West, Vermont Bar Association. See Appendix B for addresses and telephone numbers.

Virginia

1. Codes and Session Laws.
Code of Virginia 1950 Annotated. Charlottesville, VA: LexisNexis, 1950-date. 13 vols. in 29. Annual pocket supplements and periodic revised volumes.
Cost: $680/$816 (in-state/out-of-state); annual supplementation 2001: $251.50/$334; 2002: $418/$623; 2003: $373/$508; 2004: $465/$645; 2005: $156/$211; 2008: $395/$561; 2009: $192/$209; 2010: $227/$265; 2011: $245/$283; 2012: $363.50/$485; 2013: $351/$472.50.

West's Annotated Code of Virginia. St. Paul, MN: West Group, 2001-date. 58 vols. Annual pocket supplements and periodic revised volumes. Includes CD-ROM that contains the full text of **West's Annotated Code of Virginia**, current through the most recent session of the Virginia General Assembly and General Index. Includes a companion CD-ROM.
Cost: $2,077; supplementation: 2002: $225; 2003: $290; 2004: $307; 2005: $279; 2006: $360; 2007: $691.50; 2008: $988; 2009: $918.50; 2010: $1,214; 2011: $1,356; 2012: $1,325; 2013: $1,376; **Monthly Assured Print Pricing (APP):** $131/$1,572.

Virginia Advance Code Service. Charlottesville, VA: LexisNexis.
Cost: $68 (in-state); $91 (out-of-state) per year (2014).

Virginia Advance Legislative Service. Charlottesville, VA: LexisNexis. 6 issues/yr.
These pamphlets are published during and immediately after current legislative session and contain the text of laws in numerical chapter sequence in order of passage.
Cost: $78 (in-state); $85 (out-of-state) per year (2014).

Virginia Legislative Service. St. Paul, MN: Thomson West, 2004-date. These pamphlets are published during and immediately after each legislative session and contain text of laws in numerical chapter sequence in order of passage.
Cost: $523.56 per year (2014).

Acts of Assembly of Virginia [session laws]. Richmond, VA: Legislative Automated Systems. Annual. (804) 786-1895
Cost: 1995: $50 (2 vols.); 1996: $60 (3 vols.);1997: $60 (3 vols.); 1998: $78.38 (3 vols.); 1999: $78.38 (3 vols.); 2000: $83.60 (3 vols.); 2001: $60.00 (3 vols.); 2002: $75 (3 vols.); 2003: $75 (3 vols.); 2004: $80 (2 vols.); 2005: $45 (3 vols.); 2006: $60 (3 vols.); 2007: $50 (2 vols.); 2008: $75 (4 vols. including special session); 2009: $60.00 (3 vols.); 2010: $60.00 (3 vols.); 2011: $50.00.

Legislative Hotline: (804) 698-1500.

2. Administrative Law.
Virginia Administrative Code. St. Paul, MN: West, 1996-date. 25 vols.
Looseleaf format. Supplemented twice annually. The official compilation of rules and regulations for the Commonwealth of Virginia produced under the authority of the VA Code Commission and Division of Legislative Services. Also available at no charge on the Internet at: http://leg1.state.va.us/000/srr.htm
Cost: $450; supplementation: 1996: $120; 1997: $141; 1998: $130; 1999: $126.30; 2000: $122.60; 2001: $234.70; 2002: $165.58; 2003: $193.45; 2004: $238.03; 2005: $284.73; 2006: $300; 2007: $232.38; 2008: $825; 2009: $313.50; 2010: $248; 2011: $248; 2012: $277.92; 2013: $329; **Monthly Assured Print Pricing (APP):** $34/$408. Individual volumes also available; also available on CD-ROM from West (see entry below).

Virginia Register of Regulations. Albany, NY: LexisNexis Matthew Bender [formerly Weil Publishing Co.], 2003-date. Monthly.
Cost: $253; renewal: 2014: $230.

3. Court Reports.
Virginia Reports. 1790-date. Atlanta, GA: Darby Printing Co. [for the Department of Purchases and Supply] Current vol.: 286.
Cost: Combo package for bound volumes and advance sheets: $214.50; Bound volumes:$94.33 for 2 vols.; advance sheets: $130.20; call 800-241-5292 for further information. Volumes 170-183 were published by West. Used sets may be available.

Virginia Court of Appeals Reports. St. Paul, MN: West, 1985-date. Current vol.: 61 (as of March 1, 2014).
Cost: $711 (vols. 20-61); annual cost: 2002: $76.05; 2003: $77.75; 2004: $75.05; 2005: $93.75; 2006: $110; 2007: $32.25; 2008: $64.50; 2009: $96.75; 2010: $64.50; 2011: $64.50; 2012: $66.40 (list); 2013: $68.38; individual volumes: $34.19 (list); **Monthly Assured Print Pricing (APP):** $23/$276.

South Eastern Reporter [1st] - **2d**. St. Paul, MN: West, 1886-date. Contains decisions of the Virginia Supreme Court from 1887-date and the Virginia Court of Appeals from 1985-date. Current vol.: 750 **S.E. 2d**.
Cost: 1st series out-of-print (see used lawbook dealers in Appendix C); 2d series: $10,480; annual cost: 2012: $7,389; 2013: $5,434; current vol.: $524/$655 (subscriber/list); **Monthly Assured Print Pricing (APP):** $846/$10,152. See list of used lawbook dealers in Appendix C.

South Eastern Reporter 2d. Advance sheets. St. Paul, MN: Thomson West. Weekly.
Cost: $2,825 (discounted to bound volume subscribers) (2014).

Virginia Official Supreme Court Advance Sheets. Atlanta, GA: Darby Printing Co. Six per year (covering 2 bound vols. of Virginia Reports).
Cost: $130.20 per year (2014).
Call: 800-241-5292 for further information.

4. Court Rules
Virginia Court Rules and Procedure, State and Federal. St. Paul, MN: West. 2 vols. Annual. Also available as ProView eBook.
Cost: 2014 Edition: $252.

Virginia Court Rules Annotated. Charlottesville, VA: LexisNexis. 1 vol. Paperbound. Updated semiannually, replaced annually.
Cost: 2014 Edition: $98 (in-state)

Virginia Rules of Court. Charlottesville, VA: LexisNexis. Annual with mid-year supplement. Vol. 11 of the Code of Virginia.
Cost: 2014 Edition: $40 (in-state); $75 (out-of-state); or no charge with code subscription.

5. Digests, Encyclopedias and Practice Books.
Virginia and West Virginia Digest. St. Paul, MN: West, 1943-date. 110 vols.
Annual pocket parts, mid-year supplement, and periodic revised volumes.
Cost: $6,020; supplementation: 1993: $169.50; 1994: $183.65; 1996: $247; 1997: $273.50; 1998: $513.25; 1999: $721.50; 2000: $1,113.25; 2001: $1,477.50; 2002: $1,558.50; 2003: $1,862; 2004: $958.25; 2005: $1,204.25; 2006: $1,400; 2007: $1,406; 2008: $1,344; 2009: $2,225.50; 2010: $3,202; 2011: $3,056; 2012: $3,218; 2013: $5,125; **Monthly Assured Print Pricing (APP):** $334/$4,008.

Michie's Jurisprudence of Virginia and West Virginia. Charlottesville, VA: LexisNexis, 1948-date. 53 vols. Annual pocket parts and periodic revised volumes.
Cost: $1,707; supplementation: 2003: $692; 2004: $1,179; 2005: $639; 2006: $756; 2007: $816; 2008: $673; 2009: $787; 2010: $1,281; 2011: $2,282; 2012: $2,109; 2013: $811.

6. Citators.

Shepard's Virginia Citations. Albany, NY: Shepard's. Monthly.
Cost: $2,442 (3 bound volumes); all-inclusive subscription: $2,335 (in-state), (2014).

Online: All jurisdictional Shepard's and KeyCite are no longer available as stand-alone products, but are included as part of a jurisdictional or subject library from their respective publishers (2014).

7. CD-ROM Products.

Casefinder [web]. St. Cloud, MN: Geronimo Development Corp. Now on web. Updated daily. Contains the full text of Virginia Supreme Court opinions from 1925 to date, Court of Appeals decisions from 1985 to date, unpublished Court of Appeals decisions from 1994 to date, Attorney General opinions from 1967 to date, workers compensation decisions from 1993 to date, legal ethics opinions, Virginia Code (1997), state constitution, Supreme Court rules, U.S. Supreme Court decisions from 1950 to date, and 4th Circuit decisions from 1972 to date. Web version updated daily.
Cost: $529 for annual subscription; each additional user: $189 (2014).

LexisNexis CD - Virginia Primary Law. Albany, NY: LexisNexis. Two discs. Updated quarterly. Contains the full text of the annotated Code of Virginia, Virginia Rules Annotated, decisions of the Virginia Supreme Court from 1730 to date, Virginia Court of Appeals from 1985 to date, selected federal court decisions from 1793 to date, and selected unpublished decisions of the Virginia Court of Appeals from 1993 to date. LexisNexis's Jurisprudence of Virginia and West Virginia is an optional addition to disc. Available for Windows. Search Engine: Folio; LivePublish (NextPage). Updating via LEXIS.
Cost: $1,989 per year (2014).

Virginia Forms on CD-ROM. Charlottesville, VA: LexisNexis. One disc. Updated annually. Contains forms from Virginia Forms, 4th edition and Virginia Domestic Relations Handbook. Available for Windows. Search Engine: Folio; LivePublish (NextPage).
Cost: $573 per year; renewal: 2014: $531.42.

Virginia Reporter and West's Annotated Code of Virginia. Eagan, MN: West. One disc. Quarterly updates. Contains the full text of decisions of the Virginia Supreme Court from 1729 to date, Virginia Court of Appeals from vol. 125 of South Eastern Reporter [1st] to date, unpublished decisions from 1992 to date, Attorney General Opinions form 1976 to date, the West Virginia Code, Constitution, and court rules. Decisions also searchable by West Topics and Key Numbers, headnotes, and synopses. Available for DOS, Windows and Macintosh. Search engine: PREMISE. Subscription includes online updating via Westlaw.
Cost: $26,019 per year (2014).

Alert: This and other West CD-ROM products will eventually be phased out. For this overpriced product, the end could not come quicker. It is inexplicable why any customer would choose this CD-ROM over a WestlawNext subscription to access the covered titles.

8. State Legal Histories and Research Guides.

Chanin, Leah F., Pamela J. Gregory, and Sarah K. Wiant. **Legal Research in the District of Columbia, Maryland, and Virginia.** 2d ed. Buffalo, NY: William S. Hein & Co., 2000. 1 vol. (450 pp.).
Cost: OUT-OF-PRINT; from $162.24 on amazon.com (2014).

Dinan, John. **The Virginia State Constitution**. 2d ed. New York: Oxford University Press, 2014. 1 vol. (296 pp.).
Cost: $150; from $138.76 on amazon.com; kindle: $119.99 (2014).

Lee, Leslie A. Virginia Practice Materials: A Selective Bibliography in Houdek, Frank G., ed. **State Practice Materials: Annotated Bibliographies**. Buffalo, NY: William S. Hein & Co., Inc., 2002-date. 2 vols. Looseleaf format.
Cost: $195.00 (2014).

Lichtman, Jacqueline & Judy Stinson. **A Law Librarian's Introduction to Virginia State Publications**. Revised ed. Chicago: AALL, 1988.
Available from William S. Hein & Co.
Cost: $30.00; pdf: $20; also available on HeinOnline (2014).

9. Leading Web Sites for State Legal Research.

Home Page:	www.virginia.gov
Administrative Code:	http://leg1.state.va.us/cgi-bin/legp504.exe?000+men+SRR
Agency Directory:	www.agencydirectory.virginia.gov
Attorney General:	www.oag.state.va.us
Attorney Gen. Opinions:	www.oag.state.va.us/Opinions and Legal Resources
Bar Association:	www.vsb.org
Constitution:	http://constitution.legis.virginia.gov
Court Opinions:	www.courts.state.va.us/search/textopinions.html
Governor:	www.governor.virginia.gov
Judicial Branch:	www.courts.state.va.us
Law Library:	www.courts.state.va.us/courtadmin/library
Legislature:	http://virginiageneralassembly.gov
Secretary of the Commonwealth:	www.commonwealth.virginia.gov
Statutes:	http://lis.virginia.gov/000/src.htm
Supreme Court:	www.courts.state.va.us/courts/scv

10. Leading publishers of state specific treatises, practice books, and CLE publications.

LexisNexis, National Business Institute, PESI, Virginia Continuing Legal Education, Thomson Reuters (West). See Appendix B for addresses and telephone numbers.

Washington

1. Codes and Session Laws.

Annotated Revised Code of Washington. 1994 Edition. Charlottesville, VA: LexisNexis, 1994-date. Annual. 26 vols.
Cost: $1,102; supplementation (in-state/out-of-state): 2002: $180/$211; 2003: $662/$755; 2004: $796/$971; 2005: $422/$534; 2007: $441/$559; 2008: $718/$973; 2009: $514/$628; 2010: $628/$767; 2011: $675/$830; 2012: $519/$547; 2013: $651/$679.

Revised Code of Washington. Olympia, WA: Office of the Code Reviser. 9 vols. Biennial with supplementary vols. in alternate years. Softbound. (866) 650-6369
Cost: 2012 Edition: $210; 2013 supplement: $40 (2014).

Revised Code of Washington Annotated. St. Paul, MN: West, 1962-date. 122 vols. Annual pocket supplements and periodic revised volumes.
Cost: $6.612; supplementation: 1995: $446; 1996: $642; 1997: $795; 1998: $966.40; 1999: $1,045; 2000: $1,185.50; 2001: $1,593; 2002: $1,927; 2003: $2,156; 2004: $2,338.50; 2005: $2,477; 2006: $2,477.50; 2007: $2,330.50; 2008: $2,843; 2009: $2,965.50; 2010: $3,697.50; 2011: $3,975; 2012: $4,853.50; 2013: $5,672; **Monthly Assured Print Pricing (APP):** $443/$5,316.

Laws of Washington. Olympia, WA: Office of the Code Reviser. Annual. 2-4 vols. per year.
Cost: 1889-2006: $35.00 ea. (hardbound); 2007-2013: $25.00 ea. (softbound).

West's Washington Bound Session Laws. St. Paul. Thomson West, Annual.
Cost: 2010: $182; 2011: $204; 2012: $228; 2013: $256.

Washington Advance Code Service. Charlottesville, VA: LexisNexis. Annual.
Cost: $89 (2014).

West's Washington Legislative Service. St. Paul, MN: West. These pamphlets are published during and immediately after each legislative session and contain the text of laws in numerical chapter sequence in order of passage.
Cost: $1,077 per year (2014).

Legislative Hotline: (360) 786-7573.

2. Administrative Law.

Washington Administrative Code. Olympia, WA: Office of the Code Reviser, 1977-date. 12 vols. Annual. New editions were published every two years from 1995-2009, with supplements in 2010 and 2011. It began annual publication in 2012. (360)786-6671.
Cost: 2013 ed.: $550; also available on CD-ROM: $39; with RCW: $78.

Washington State Register. Olympia, WA: Office of the Code Reviser, 1978-date. Biweekly (24 issues).
Cost: Paper: $400 per year; cumulative CD-ROM: $100; electronic: $400 per year (2014). (866) 650-6369.

3. Court Reports.

Washington Reports. [1st] – 2d. 1889-date. Charlottesville, VA: Published by LexisNexis for the Supreme Court, State Law Reports Office, 2001-date. Formerly published by West for the Commission on Supreme Court Reports (vols. 1-126); 1st series: 1889-1939 (200 vols.); 2d series: 1939-date (174 vols.) Current vol.: 174, 2d series (April 1, 2014). Back volumes still available from West.
Cost: 1st series: $4,500.00 ($22.50/vol.); 2d series vols. 123-149: $349.40; vols. 123-126: $19.50 ea.; vols. 127-130: $17.00 ea.; vols. 131-134: $19.50 ea.; vols. 135-140: $20.90 ea.; vols. 141-145: $15.65 ea.; 146-148: $19.75 ea.; 149-158: $22.75 ea.;

2007: $68.25 (3); 2008: $68.25 (3); 2009: $91 (4); 2010: $45.50 (2); 2011: $67.50; 2012: $47 (2); 2013: $49 (2); $24.50 ea.

Washington Reports. Advance Sheets. Charlottesville, VA: Published by LexisNexis for the Supreme Court, State Law Reports Office, 2001-date. 26 issues per year.
Cost: $74 per year (2014).

Washington Appellate Reports. 1969-date. Charlottesville: VA: Published by LexisNexis for the Supreme Court, State Law Reports Office, 2001-date. Formerly published by West for the Commission on Supreme Court Reports (1969-2001, vols. 1-101). Back volumes still available from West. Current volume: 169 (as of April 1, 2014).
Cost: $550.90 (volumes 73-100); volumes 1-72: $22.50 per vol.; vols. 73-77: $19.50 each; vols. 78-84: $17.00 each; vols. 85-100: $20.90 each; vols. 101-110: $15.65 ea.; vols. 111-117: $19.75 ea.; vol. 118-147: $22.75 ea.; 2007: $91 (4); 2008: $91; 2009: $113.75; 2010: $159.25; 2011: $136.50 (6); 2012: $141(6); 2013: $147 (6).

Washington Appellate Reports. Advance Sheets. Charlottesville, VA: Published by LexisNexis for the Supreme Court, State Law Reports Office, 2001-date. 26 issues /yr.
Cost: $74 per year (2014).

Washington Reporter. [P.2d – P.3d]. St. Paul, MN: West, 1950-date. [offprint of Pacific Reporter 2d - 3d series containing decisions of the Washington Supreme Court and Court of Appeals]. P.2d. 194 vols. Current volume: 309-311P. 3d.
Cost: Covering P. 2d: $3,297 (194 vols.); covering P.3d: $5,368; annual upkeep: 2002: $749.75; 2003: $838.25; 2004: $670; 2005: $817.50; 2006: $947.50; 2007: $1,419; 2008: $1,376; 2009: $1,742.50; 2010: $2,170; 2011: $2,336; 2012: $2,804; 2013: $4,831; current volume: $503.25/$671 (subscriber/list); **Monthly Assured Print Pricing (APP)**: $421/$5,052.

Pacific Reporter. [1st] - **3d**. St. Paul, MN: West, 1883-date. Contains decisions of the Washington Supreme Court, 1880-date. Current vol.: 314 **P. 3d**.
Cost: 1st series out-of-print (see used lawbook dealers in Appendix C); 2d series: $13,428; used sets approx. $2000; 3d series: $15,201; annual cost (2013): $11,396; individual volume: $518/$691 (subscriber/list); **Monthly Assured Print Pricing (APP):** $1,141/$11,369; used sets may be available.

Pacific Reporter 3d. Advance sheets. St. Paul, MN: Thomson West. Weekly.
Cost: $2,866.56 per year (discounted to bound volume subscribers) (2014).

4. Court Rules.
Washington Court Rules Annotated. 2d ed. St. Paul, MN: West. Annual. 3 vols. Includes expert practice commentary.
Cost: 2013-2014 Edition: $1,269 (2014).

Washington Court Rules: State & Federal. St. Paul, MN: West. 2 vols. Annual. Also available as ProView eBook.
Cost: 2014 Edition: $220; with Local: $324.

Washington Rules of Court Annotated. Charlottesville, VA: LexisNexis [prepared by the editorial staff of the publisher]. 3 vols. State and Local rules.
Cost: 2014 Edition: $163 (in-state) (2014).

5. Digests, Encyclopedias, and Practice Books.
Washington Digest 2d. St. Paul, MN: West, 1988-date. 96 vols. Annual pocket parts, mid-year supplement, and periodic revised volumes.
Cost: $5,198; supplementation: 1995: $130; 1996: $140; 1997: $163; 1998: $296; 1999: $439; 2000: $291.50; 2001: $586.50; 2002: $867.50; 2003: $596.25; 2004: $876; 2005: $896; 2006: $896; 2007: $997; 2008: $1,619.50; 2009: $2,774.50; 2010: $3,577; 2011: $1,887; 2012: $2,113; 2013: $2,138; **Assured Monthly Print Price (APP):** $247/$2,964.

Washington Practice Series. St. Paul, MN: West. 61 vols. Various titles.
Cost: $9,072 (but priced individually); supplementation: 1997: $899.75; 1998: $757.50; 1999: $1,015.75; 2000: $1,295.50; 2001: $898.50; 2002: $898; 2003: $1,457; 2004 et seq.: inquire regarding costs for individual components. Also available for $1,560 as WestlawNext Washington Secondary Resources add-on (single user).

6. Citators.
Shepard's Washington Citations. Albany, NY: Shepard's. Monthly or bi-monthly.
Cost: $5,008 (8 bound volumes); all-inclusive subscription: monthly: $2,335 (in-state); bi-monthly: $2,778 (in-state) (2014).

Online: All jurisdictional Shepard's and KeyCite are no longer available as stand-alone products, but are included as part of a jurisdictional or subject library from their respective publishers (2014).

7. CD-ROM Products.
LexisNexis CD - Washington Primary Law. Albany, NY: LexisNexis. Two discs. Updated quarterly. Contains the full text of the Annotated Revised Code of Washington, advance legislative service, Washington administrative code, Washington court rules annotated, decisions of the Washington Supreme Court form 1898 to date, and decisions of the Washington Court of Appeals from 1959 to date. Available for Windows. Search Engine: Folio; LivePublish (NextPage). Subscription includes online updating via LexisNexis.
Cost: $1,986 per year (2014).

Revised Code of Washington/Washington Administrative Code. Olympia, WA: Office of the Code Revisor. One disc. Updated annually. Contains the full text of the unannotated Revised Code of Washington and the Washington Administrative Code. Available for Windows 95 or higher. Search Engine: Folio.
Cost: 2013 Edition: $78 per year for both RCW and WAC; or $39 each; Decisions of Supreme Court 1st and 2d: $39 each (2014). Prepayment required. (866) 650-6369.

Washington Case Law and Revised Code of Washington Unannotated. Eagan, MN: West. Two discs. Updated monthly. Contains the full text of the Revised Code of Washington (unannotated), Washington Constitution, decisions of the Washington Supreme Court from 1854 to date, and Court of Appeals appearing in vols. 1-200 of the Washington Reports [1st], vols. 1 to date of the Washington Reports 2d, vols. 1-date of the Washington Appellate Reports, Attorney General Opinions from 1977 to date, etc. Available for DOS, Windows, and Macintosh. Search Engine: PREMISE. Subscription includes online updating via WESTLAW.
Cost: $5,406 per year (2014).

Washington Practice Series. Eagan, MN: West. One disc. Updated annually. Contains the full text of 12 Washington state practice titles, with forms. Available for DOS, Windows, or Macintosh. Search Engine: PREMISE.
Cost: Discontinued. Available on Washington State Secondary Resources on WestlawNext PRO for only $1,560 per year for solo practitioner.

8. State Legal Research Guides.
Heintz-Cho, Julie, Tom Cobb, and Mary A. Hotchkiss. **Washington Legal Research**. 2d ed. Durham, NC: Carolina Academic Press, 2009. 1 vol. (230 pp.). Paperbound.
Cost: $25.00; from $16.18 on amazon.com (2014).

Jarrett, Peggy Roebuck and Cheryl Rae Nyberg. **Washington State Documents: A Bibliography of Legal and Law-Related Documents**. Chicago, American Association of Law Libraries, Government Documents Special Interest Section, 1997. 1 vol. (41 pp.). Available from William S. Hein & Co.
Cost: $30.00; pdf: $20; also available on HeinOnline. (2014).

Utter, Robert F. and Hugh D. Spitzer. **The Washington State Constitution**. 2d ed. New York: Oxford University Press, 2013. 1 vol. (328 pp.).
Cost: $150.00; from $118.80 on amazon.com (2014).

Washington Legal Researcher's Deskbook. 3d ed. Penny A. Hezelton et al. Seattle, WA: Marian Gould Gallagher Law Library, 2002. 1 vol. (300 pp.).
Cost: $65.00 (2014).

9. Leading Web Sites for State Legal Research.

Home Page:	www.access.wa.gov/
Administrative Code:	http://apps.leg.wa.gov/wac/

Agency Directory:	http://access.wa.gov/agency
Attorney General:	www.atg.wa.gov/
Attorney Gen. Opinions:	www.atg.wa.gov/AGOOpinions
Bar Association:	www.wsba.org/
Constitution:	www.leg.wa.gov/LawsAndAgencyRules/Pages/constitution.aspx
Court Opinions:	www.courts.wa.gov/opinions/
Governor:	www.governor.wa.gov/
Judicial Branch:	www.courts.wa.gov/
Law Library:	www.courts.wa.gov/library/
Legislative Branch:	www.leg.wa.gov
Secretary of State:	www.sos.wa.gov
Statutes:	http://apps.leg.wa.gov/rcw/
Supreme Court:	www.courts.wa.gov/appellate_trial_courts/SupremeCourt/

10. Leading publishers of state specific treatises, practice books, and CLE publications.
Book Publishing Company, Continuing Legal Education Department of Washington State Bar Association, LexisNexis, National Business Institute, Professional Education Systems Inc., Themis, Inc., Thomson Reuters West, Washington State Trial Lawyers Association. See Appendix B for addresses and telephone numbers.

West Virginia

1. Codes and Session Laws.
West Virginia Code Annotated. Charlottesville, VA: LexisNexis, 1966-date. 19 vols. in 29. Annual pocket supplements and periodic revised volumes.
Cost: $614; supplementation (in-state/out-of-state): 2001: $611/$757; 2002: $614/$758; 2003: $625/$771; 2004: $487/$605; 2005: $229/$286; 2006: $284/$356; 2007: $302/$378; 2008: $684/$821; 2009: $538/$652; 2010: $935/$1000; 2011: $410/$480; 2012: $635/$771; 2013: $699/$835.

West Virginia Advance Legislative Service. Charlottesville, VA: LexisNexis. Supplements code between annual pocket parts.
Cost: $116 per year (2014).

West Virginia Advance Code Service. Charlottesville, VA: LexisNexis. These pamphlets are published during and immediately after each legislative session and contain text of laws in numerical chapter sequence in order of passage.
Cost: $118 (2014).

Acts of the Legislature of West Virginia [session laws]. Charleston, WV: House of Delegates. Annual.
Cost: 1997: $145 (2 vols.); 1998: $330 (2 vols.); 1999: $330 (2 vols.); 2000: $275 (2 vols.); 2001: $375 (2 vols.); 2002-2010: $450 per year (2 vols.) (304) 340-3229.

Legislative Hotline: (304) 347-4836.

2. Administrative Law.
West Virginia Administrative Code of State Rules. Charleston, WV: Secretary of State, Administrative Law Division, 1987-date. 12 vols. Kept up-to-date with revised pages. Monthly.
Cost: $635 (incl. one year's supplementation); supplementation: $150 per year (2014). Also available on the Internet at: http://www.wvsos.com/csr/
(304) 558-6000

West Virginia Register. Charleston, WV: Secretary of State, Administrative Law Division,1983-date. Weekly. (304) 558-6000
Cost: $250 per year (2014); also available on the Internet at: http://www.wvsos.com/adlaw/register/register.htm

3. Court Reports.
West Virginia Reports. 1864-date. St. Paul, MN: West. Current vol.: 23 (as of March 1, 2014)
Cost: Vols. 170-183: $154; vols. 184-date: $1,727; annual cost: 2002: $219.50; 2003: $221; 2004: $222.50; 2005: $342.75; 2006: $290; 2007: $92; 2008: $184; 2009: $184; 2010: $92; 2011: $230; 2012: $230; 2013: $230; current vol.: $115 (list).

West Virginia Court of Claims Reports. Charleston, WV: Clerk, Court of Claims, 1942-date. Current volume: 27.
Cost: $10.00 ea. (vols. 12 and 15-27 currently available as of April 13, 2014) (304) 347-4851. Complete online archive also available at: http://www.legis.state.wv.us/Joint/Court/report_archive.cfm

South Eastern Reporter [1st] - **2d**. St. Paul, MN: West, 1886-date. Contains decisions of the West Virginia Supreme Court from 1884-date. Current vol.: 750 **S.E. 2d**.
Cost: 1st series out-of-print (see used lawbook dealers in Appendix C); 2d series: $10,480; annual cost: 2012: $7,389; 2013: $5,434; current vol.: $524/$655 (subscriber/list); **Monthly Assured Print Pricing (APP):** $846/$10,152. See list of used lawbook dealers in Appendix C.

South Eastern Reporter 2d. Advance sheets. St. Paul, MN: Thomson West. Weekly.
Cost: $2,825 (discounted to bound volume subscribers) (2014).

4. Court Rules.
Michie's West Virginia Code Annotated State and Federal Court Rules. Charlottesville, VA: LexisNexis. 2 vols. Updated semiannually, replaced annually. Also available as eBook.
Cost: 2014 Edition: $111.

West Virginia Court Rules: State and Federal. St. Paul, MN: West. 2 vols. Annual. Also available as ProView eBook.
Cost: 2014 edition: $162.

5. Digests, Encyclopedias, and Practice Books.
Virginia and West Virginia Digest. St. Paul, MN: West, 1943-date. 110 vols. Annual pocket parts, mid-year supplement, and periodic revised volumes.
Cost: $6,020; supplementation: 1993: $169.50; 1994: $183.65; 1996: $247; 1997: $273.50; 1998: $513.25; 1999: $721.50; 2000: $1,113.25; 2001: $1,477.50; 2002: $1,558.50; 2003:

$1,862; 2004: $958.25; 2005: $1,204.25; 2006: $1,400; 2007: $1,406; 2008: $1,344; 2009: $2,225.50; 2010: $3,202; 2011: $3,056; 2012: $3,218; 2013: $5,125; **Monthly Assured Print Pricing (APP):** $334/$4,008.

Michie's Jurisprudence of Virginia and West Virginia. Charlottesville, VA: LexisNexis, 1948-date. 53 vols. Annual pocket parts and periodic revised volumes.
Cost: $1,707; supplementation: 2003: $692; 2004: $1,179; 2005: $639; 2006: $756; 2007: $816; 2008: $673; 2009: $787; 2010: $1,281; 2011: $2,282; 2012: $2,109; 2013: $811.

6. Citators.
Shepard's West Virginia Citations. Albany, NY: Shepard's. Six supplements per year.
Cost: $1,424 (2 bound volumes); all-inclusive subscription: $1,703 (in-state) (2014).

Online: All jurisdictional Shepard's and KeyCite are no longer available as stand-alone products, but are included as part of a jurisdictional or subject library from their respective publishers (2014).

7. CD-ROM Products.
LexisNexis CD - West Virginia Primary Law. Albany, NY: LexisNexis. One disc. Updated quarterly. Contains the full text of the West Virginia Code Annotated, West Virginia Court Rules Annotated and decisions of the West Virginia Supreme Court of Appeals from 1864 to date. Michie's Jurisprudence for Virginia and West Virginia are optional. Available for Windows. Search Engine: Folio; LivePublish (NextPage). Includes online updating via LEXIS.
Cost: $2,373 per year (2014).

West Virginia Reports and West's West Virginia Code. Eagan, MN: West. One disc. Quarterly updates. Contains the full text of decisions of the West Virginia Supreme Court of Appeals from 1864 to date, Attorney General Opinions form 1976 to date, the West Virginia Constitution, the Laws of West Virginia, session laws, and court rules. Searchable by West Topics and Key Numbers, headnotes, and synopses. Available for DOS, Windows, and Macintosh. Search engine: PREMISE. Subscription includes online updating via Westlaw.
Cost: $4,326 per year (2014).

8. State Legal Research Guides.
Bastress, Robert M. **The West Virginia State Constitution**. New York: Oxford University Press, 2011. 1 vol. (366 pp.).
Cost: $150.00; from $18.65 on amazon.com; kindle: $119.99 (2014).

Long, Ann Walsh. West Virginia Practice Materials: A Selective Bibliography in Houdek, Frank G., ed. **State Practice Materials: Annotated Bibliographies**. Buffalo, NY: William S. Hein & Co., Inc., 2004-date. 2 vols. Looseleaf format.
Cost: $195.00 (2014).

Stemple, Sandra; Marjorie Price and June Board. **West Virginia Legal Bibliography**. Chicago: AALL, 1990. Available from William S. Hein & Co.
Cost: $30.00; pdf: $20; Also available on HeinOnline (2014).

9. Leading Web Sites for State Legal Research.

Home Page:	www.wv.gov/
Administrative Code:	www.sos.wv.gov/administrative-law
Agency Directory:	www.wv.gov/Pages/agencies.aspx
Attorney General:	www.wvago.gov/
Attorney Gen. Opinions:	www.sos.wv.gov/administrative-law/Pages/opinionsandorders.aspx
Bar Association:	www.wvbar.org/
Code of State Rules:	www.sos.wv.gov/administrative-law
Constitution:	www.legis.state.wv.us/wvcode/wv_con.Cfm
Court Opinions:	www.courtswv.gov/supreme-court/opinions.html
Governor:	www.governor.wv.gov
Judicial Branch:	www.courtswv.gov
Law Library:	www.courtswv.gov/public-resources/law-library/law-library-home.html
Legislative Branch:	www.legis.state.wv.us/
Secretary of State:	www.sos.wv.gov
Statutes:	www.legis.state.wv.us/WVCODE/Code.cfm

10. Leading publishers of state specific treatises, practice books, and CLE publications.
Commonwealth Law Publishers, LexisNexis, National Business Institute, Thomson Reuters West.

Wisconsin

1. Code and Session Laws.
West's Wisconsin Statutes Annotated. St. Paul, MN: West, 1957-date. 72 vols. Annual pocket supplements and periodic revised volumes.
Cost: $5,222; supplementation: 1995: $540; 1996: $772.50; 1997: $775.50; 1998: $857; 2001: $545; 2002: $1,462; 2003: $1,694; 2004: $1,708; 2005: $1,582; 2006: $1,790; 2007: $1,503.50; 2008: $2,052; 2009: $2,164; 2010: $2,681.50; 2011: $2,799.50; 2012: $3,511; 2013: $3,960; **Monthly Assured Print Pricing (APP):** $311/$3,732.

.

Wisconsin Statutes and Annotations. Madison, WI: Document Sales, Dept. of Administration. 6 vols. Biennial. Available in hardcover and softcover.
Cost: 2005-2006: $140/$159 (hard/softcover) (includes postage); 2007-2008: $76/$70; 2009-2010: $79/$64; 2011-2012: $86/$51 (2014). (800) 362-7253 or (608) 264-9419.
Also on Internet at: http://www.legis.state.wi.us/rsb/07_StatsNewsRel.pdf

Laws of Wisconsin [session laws]. Madison, WI: Document Sales, Dept. of Administration. Biennial. 2 vols. Published in odd-numbered years. Also available on WisLaw CD-ROM.

Document sales: 608 266 3358
Cost: 2003: $35.75 (hardover); 2005: $34.25; 2007: $32.50; 2009: $34.00; 2011: $44.15 (2014).

Legislative Hotline: (608) 266-9960.

2. Administrative Law.

Wisconsin Administrative Code. Madison, WI: Revisor of Statutes Bureau, 1978-date. 23 vols. Looseleaf format. Available from Document Sales, Dept. of Admin. (608) 266-3358.
Cost: $870 (includes one year's supps.); supplementation: $435 per year (2014); also available at no cost on the Internet at: http://www.legis.state.wi.us/rsb/code.htm

Wisconsin Administrative Register. Madison, WI: Revisor of Statutes Bureau, 1956-date. Bimonthly. Available from Document Sales, Dept. of Admin. (608) 266-3358.
Cost: $60 per year (or included in cost of WAC) (2013); also available at no cost on the Internet at: http://www.legis.state.wi.us/rsb/code.htm

3. Court Reports.

Callaghan's Official Wisconsin Reports [1st] - **2d**. 1853-date. St. Paul, MN: West. 1st series, 1853-1957 (vols. 1-275); 2d series, 1957-date (vols. 1-336). Official.
Cost: 1st series available used for approximately $950; 2d series: $4,984; annual upkeep: 2002: $438.75; 2003: $505; 2004: $525.00; 2005: $490.50; 2006: $619; 2007: $531; 2008: $533.50; 2009: $568.50; 2010: $630; 2011: $621; 2012: $432; 2013: $468; current volume: $78/$104 (subscriber/list); **Monthly Assured Print Pricing (APP):** $159/$1,908; used sets sell for approx. $1,200. Contact publisher for applicable discounts, or see list of used lawbook dealers in Appendix C.

West's Wisconsin Reporter 2d. St. Paul, MN: West, 1941-date. [Offprint of **North Western Reporter 2d**]. Co-official since 1975. Current volume: 802-805 **N.W.2d**.
Cost: $3,769; annual cost of bound vols.: 2001: $431.25; 2002: $656.25; 2003: $650; 2004: $715; 2005: $785; 2006: $870; 2007: $806; 2008: $896.50; 2009: $1,186; 2010: $1,096; 2011: $1,548; 2012: $1,857; 2013: $1,852; current volume: $370.50/$494 (subsacriber/list); **Monthly Assured Print Pricing (APP):** $302/$3,624. See list of used lawbook dealers in Appendix C.

North Western Reporter [1st] - **2d**. St. Paul, MN: West, 1879-date. Contains decisions of the Wisconsin Supreme Court from 1879-date and the Wisconsin Court of Appeals from 1978-date. [co-official since 1975]. Current vol.: 844 **N.W. 2d**.
Cost: 1st series out-of-print (see used lawbook dealers in Appendix C); 2d series $10,225; used sets sell for approx. $3,795; annual cost (2013): $7,332; recent volume: $459/$611 (subscriber/list); **Monthly Assured Print Pricing (APP):** $709/$8,508.

West's North Western Reporter 2d. Advance Sheets. St. Paul, MN: Thomson West. Weekly.
Cost: $2,808 (discounted to bound volume subscribers) (2014).

Callaghan's Official Wisconsin Reports Advance Sheets. St. Paul, MN: West. Biweekly.
Cost: $343.56 per year (2013).

4. Court Rules.

Wisconsin Court Rules and Procedure, State and Federal. St. Paul, MN: West Publishing Co. 2 vols. Annual.
Cost: 2014 Edition: $194.

5. Digests, Encyclopedias, and Practice Books.

Callaghan's Wisconsin Digest. St. Paul, MN: West, 1950-date. 20 vols. in 46. Annual pocket supplements and periodic revised volumes.
Cost: $5,567; supplementation: 1996: $725; 1997: $420; 1998: $1,188.00; 1999: $883; 2000: $656.50; 2001: $881.50; 2002: $1,454; 2003: $1,474; 2004: $2,032.50; 2005: $2.032.50; 2006: $2,267; 2007: $1,598.50; 2008: $1,694; 2009: $2,288; 2010: $2,931; 2011: $2,481; 2012: $1,513.50; 2013: $4,487; **Monthly Assured Print Pricing (APP):** $272/$3,264.

Callaghan's Wisconsin Pleading and Practice. 4th-5th ed. St. Paul, MN: West, 2004-date. 12 vols. Supplemented with annual pocket parts and periodic revised volumes. A comprehensive coverage of pleading and practice under the Wisconsin Rules of Civil Procedure.
Cost: $2,620; supplementation: 1996: $395; 1997: $516.50; 1998: $517; 1999: $512.50; 2000: $646.50; 2001: $795.25; 2002: $766.75; 2003: $718; 2004: $842; 2005: $970; 2006: $1,105; 2007: $720.50; 2008: $802.50; 2009: $1,750; 2010: $1,080; 2011: $1,451; 2012: $1,854; 2013: $882; **Monthly Assured Print Pricing (APP):** $149/$1,788.

West's Wisconsin Key Number Digest. St. Paul, MN: West, 1964-date. 93 vols. Annual pocket parts, mid-year supplement, and periodic revised volumes.
Cost: $5,094; supplementation: 1996: $192.00; 1997: $307.00; 1998: $322.00; 1999: $434.00; 2000: $600.00; 2001: $1,200.00; 2002: $1,627.75; 2003: $620.25; 2004: $663.00; 2005: $666.50; 2006: $1,161; 2007: $1,501; 2008: $3,484; 2009: $1,280; 2010: $2,630; 2011: $2,769.50; 2012: $3,520; 2013: $4,052; CD-ROM: $3,531 per year (see entry below); **Monthly Assured Print Price (APP):** $284 3,408.

Wisconsin Practice Series. St. Paul, MN: West, 1973-date. 22 vols.
Cost: $3,856 (but priced individually); supplementation: 1997: $172.50; 1998: $172.50; 1999: $460.00; 2000: $156.00; 2001: $372.25; 2002: 184.50; 2003: $506.75. Individual components also available; best obtained as a WestlawNext PRO add-on at a cost of $1,128 per year for a solo practitioner.

6. Citators.

Shepard's Wisconsin Citations. Albany, NY: Shepard's. Monthly.
Cost: $4,171 (9 bound volumes); all-inclusive subscription: $2.683 (2014).

Online: All jurisdictional Shepard's and KeyCite are no longer available as stand-alone products, but are included as part of a jurisdictional or subject library from their respective publishers (2014).

7. CD-ROM Products.

Wisconsin Statutes and Annotations and Wisconsin Administrative Code and Register on CD-ROM (WisLaw). Madison, WI: State of Wisconsin, Dept. of Administration, Revisor of Statutes Bureau. One disc. Updated on a biennial basis. Contains the full text of the Wisconsin Statutes, annotations, Wisconsin Constitution, court rules, Attorney General opinions from 1982 to date, Wisconsin Administrative Code and Register, and Wisconsin Code of Military Justice. Available for Windows. Search Engine: Folio. Also available on the Web. (608) 266-3358
Cost: 2011-2012: $99 per year (1 user); $149 (2-4 users); $199 (no more than 10 users) (2014).

8. State Legal Research Guides.

Fritschel, Barbara. **State Documents Bibliography: Wisconsin.** Chicago: AALL, 2009. Available from William S. Hein & Co.
Cost: $30.00; pdf: $20; also available on HeinOnline (2014).

Norton, Julie A. Wisconsin Practice Materials: A Selective Bibliography in Houdek, Frank G., ed. **State Practice Materials: Annotated Bibliographies**. Buffalo, NY: William S. Hein & Co., Inc., 2010-date. 2 vols. Looeleaf format.
Cost: $195.00 (2014).

Platt, Ellen J. and Mary J. Koshollek. **Wisconsin Practice Materials: A Selective, Annotated Bibliography**. Buffalo, NY: W.S. Hein & Co., 1999. 1 vol. (169 pp.).
Cost: $47.50; from $9.40 on amazon.com (2014).

Stark, Jack. **The Wisconsin State Constitution**. New York: Oxford University Press, 2011. 1 vol. (304 pp.).
Cost: $150; from $74.21 on amazon.com; kindle: $119.99 (2014).

9. Leading Web Sites for State Legal Research.

Home Page:	www.wisconsin.gov
Administrative Code:	http://legis.wisconsin.gov/rsb/code.htm
Agency Directory:	www.wisconsin.gov/state/core/agency_index.html
Attorney General:	www.doj.state.wi.us/ag/
Attorney General Opinions:	www.doj.state.wi.us/ag/attorney-general-opinions
Bar Association:	www.wisbar.org/
Constitution:	http://legis.wisconsin.gov/rsb/2wiscon.html
Court Opinions:	www.wicourts.gov/opinions
Governor:	www.wisgov.state.wi.us/
Judicial Branch:	www.wicourts.gov/
Law Library:	http://wilawlibrary.gov/
Legislature:	http://legis.wisconsin.gov/
Secretary of State:	www.sos.state.wi.us/
Statutes:	http://legis.wisconsin.gov/rsb/stats.html

10. Leading publishers of state specific treatises, practice books, and CLE publications.

LexisNexis, National Business Institute, State Bar of Wisconsin Continuing Legal Education, Thomson Reuters (West). See Appendix B for addresses and telephone numbers.

Wyoming

1. Codes and Session Laws.

Wyoming Statutes Annotated. Charlottesville, VA: LexisNexis. 2011 Edition. 12 vols. Softbound. With current supplement. A completely new set is published every odd-numbered year, with supplements in even-numbered years. Free public access provided at: http://www.lexisnexis.com/hottopics/wystatutes/
Cost: 2013 Edition: $404.50; no supplementation to date (2014)

West's Wyoming Statutes Annotated. Eagan, MN: ThomsonWest, 2007-date. 21 volumes. Kept up date with annual pocket supplements and periodic revised volumes.
Cost: $513; supplementation: 2008: $200; 2009: $234; 2010: $257; 2011: $290; 2012: $400; 2013: $377; **Monthly Assured Print Pricing (APP):** $33/$396.

Wyoming Advance Code Service. Charlottesville, VA: LexisNexis, 1996-date.
Cost: $126 per year (2014).

Wyoming Advance Annotation Service. Charlottesville, VA: LexisNexis, 1996-date.
Cost: $109 (in-state); $125 (out-of-state) (2013).

Wyoming Advance Legislative Service. Charlottesville, VA: LexisNexis, 1996-date. Print or ebook.
Cost: $124 (2014).

Wyoming Legislative Services. St. Paul, MN: West, 2007-date. Monthly.
Cost: $199.08 (2014).

Session Laws of Wyoming. Cheyenne, WY: Legislative Service Office. Annual. (307) 777-7881. Session law archive from 2001-date available at:
http://legisweb.state.wy.us/LSOWEB/SessionArchives.aspx
Cost: 1995: $22/$29 (hard/softbound); 1996: 25/$42; 1997: $25/$42; 1998: $40/60; 1999: $32/$52; 2000: $50/$28; 2001: $68/$41; 2002: $50/$25; 2003: $38 (paper); 2004: $63/$35; 2005: $81/$51; 2006: $67/$37; 2007: $55/$46; 2008: $57.25/$31.25; 2009: $60/$57; 2010: $50/$48; 2011: $51/$49; 2012: .

Legislative Hotline: (307) 777-6185, (307) 777-7881.

2. Administrative Law.

Wyoming Administrative Code. Albany, NY: LexisNexis Matthew Bender [formerly Weil Publishing Co.], 1995-date. 11 vols. Updated monthly.
Cost: $2,785 (includes monthly supplements for 11 months); annual renewal: 1996: $563; 1997: $415; 1998: $480; 1999: $695; 2000: $695; 2001-2004: $800 per year; 2005: $840; 2006: $840; 2007: $840; 2008: $887; 2009: $1002; 2010: $1,052;

2011: $1,105; 2012: $1,171; 2013: $1,253; 2014: $1,367.

Wyoming Government Register. Albany, NY: LexisNexis Matthew Bender [formerly Weil Publishing Co.], 1995-date. Monthly.
Cost: $1,257; renewal: 2014; $1,143.

3. Court Reports.
Wyoming Reports. 1870-1959. [Ceased publication with vol. 80]
Cost: Not available new; used sets available for approx. $1,000.00-$1,200.00.

Wyoming Reporter [2d] - **3d**. St. Paul, MN: West, 1959-date. [offprint of the Pacific Reporter 2d---official since 1959]. Current vol.: 301-310 P.3d.
Cost: 2d series: $1,620; 3d series: $1,542; annual cost: 2012: $219; 2013: $225; current vol.: $112.50/$150 (subscriber/list).

Pacific Reporter. [1st] - **3d**. St. Paul, MN: West, 1883-date. Contains decisions of the Wyoming Supreme Court, 1883-date. Current vol.: 314 **P. 3d**.
Cost: 1st series out-of-print (see used lawbook dealers in Appendix C); 2d series: $13,428; used sets approx. $2000; 3d series: $15,201; annual cost (2013): $11,396; individual volume: $518/$691 (subscriber/list); **Monthly Assured Print Pricing (APP):** $1,141/$11,369; used sets may be available.

Pacific Reporter 3d. Advance sheets. St. Paul, MN: Thomson West. Weekly.
Cost: $2,866.56 per year (discounted to bound volume subscribers) (2014).

4. Court Rules.
Wyoming Court Rules. Charlottesville, VA: LexisNexis. 1 vol. Softbound with CD-ROM, or ebook. Updated semiannually, replaced annually.
Cost: 2013 Edition: $100 (2014).

Wyoming Rules of Court: Federal and State. Eagan, MN: West. 2 vols. Annual.
Cost: 2013 Edition: $155 (2014).

5. Digests, Encyclopedias and Practice Books.
West's Wyoming Digest. St. Paul, MN: West, 1956-date. 28 vols.
Cost: $3,064; supplementation: 1994: $150; 1995: $155; 1996: $193; 1997: $209; 1998: $365; 1999: $490; 2000: $831; 2001: $675; 2002: $280; 2003: $518; 2004: $580; 2005: $842; 2006: $877; 2007: $923; 2008: $1,109.50; 2009: $708; 2010: $1,096; 2011: $1,398.50; 2012: $1,800; 2013: $2,352; **Monthly Assured Print Pricing (APP):** $157/$1,884.

6. Citators.
Shepard's Wyoming Citations. Albany, NY: Shepard's. Bimonthly.
Cost: $1,970 (2 bound volume); all-inclusive subscription: $1,831 (2014).

Online: All jurisdictional Shepard's and KeyCite are no longer available as stand-alone products, but are included as part of a jurisdictional or subject library from their respective publishers (2014).

7. CD-ROM/Internet Products.
LexisNexis CD – Wyoming Primary Law. Albany, NY: LexisNexis. One disc. Updated quarterly. Contains the full text of the Wyoming Statutes Annotated, Wyoming Supreme Court decisions from 1870 to date, Wyoming Court Rules Annotated, and Wyoming Constitution. Available for Windows. Search Engine: Folio; LivePublish (NextPage). Includes online updates via Lexis.
Cost: $1,804 per year (single user) (2014).

Wyoming State Statutes on CD-ROM. Cheyenne, WY: Legislative Service Office, 2001-date. 1 disc. Word 6.0 format. Available in June of each year.
Cost: 2013 Edition: $10 per year; no charge to state or local government entity (2014).

8. State Legal Research Guides.
Person, Debora A. **Wyoming State Documents: A Bibliography of State Pu8blications and Related Materials.** Chicago: AALL, 2006.
Cost: $30.00. Available from William S. Hein & Co. on electronic pdf and on HeinOnline. (2014).

Keiter, Robert B. and Tim Newcomb. **The Wyoming State Constitution.** New York: Oxford University Press, 2011. 1 vol. (352 pp.).
Cost: $150.00; from $18,19 on amazon.com; kindle: $119.99 (2014).

Sharum, Moinica A. and Paul E. Howard. Wyoming Practice Materials: A Selective Bibliography in Houdek, Frank G., ed. **State Practice Materials: Annotated Bibliographies**. Buffalo, NY: William S. Hein & Co., Inc., 2010-date. 2 vols. Looseleaf format.
Cost: $195.00 (2014).

9. Leading Web Sites for State Legal Research.

Home Page:	www.wyoming.gov/
Administrative Rules:	http://soswy.state.wy.us/rules/
Agency Directory:	www.wyoming.gov/agencies.aspx
Attorney General:	http://attorneygeneral.state.wy.us/
Attorney General Opinions:	http://attorneygeneral.state.wy.us/98forma2.htm
Bar Association:	www.wyomingbar.org/
Constitution:	http://legisweb.state.wy.us/statutes/constitution.aspx - OR - http://soswy.state.wy.us/Forms/Publications/09WYConstitution.pdf
Court Opinions–Supreme Court:	http://wyom.state.wy.us/applications/oscn/index.asp?ftdb=STWY&level=1
Governor:	http://governor.wy.gov/
Judicial Branch:	www.courts.state.wy.us/
Law Library:	www.courts.state.wy.us/LawLibrary/
Legislative Branch:	http://legisweb.state.wy.us/

Secretary of State:	http://soswy.state.wy.us/
Statutes:	http://legisweb.state.wy.us/titles/statutes.htm

10. Leading publishers of state specific treatises, practice books, and CLE publications.

LexisNexis, National Business Institute, Wyoming Jury Verdict Reports, Wyoming State Bar Continuing Legal Education, Thomson Reuters (West). See Appendix B for addresses and telephone numbers.

Appendices

Appendix A - Leading Legal Publishers

ABC-CLIO. 130 Cremona Drive, Santa Barbara, CA 93117. (800) 368-6868.
http://www.abc-clio.com/
Founded in 1955 by Inge and Eric Boehm, ABC-CLIO has become a major publisher of reference books in history, political science, current affairs, and humanities. The first of its serial bibliographies, ***Historical Abstracts***, is published at the University of Vienna's Historical Institute in 1955. It moved its operations to Santa Barbara, CA in 1960 and began publication of the **Index to Historical Abstracts**, the first computer-produced serial bibliography index. In 1964, The American Bibliographical Center (ABC) is established and the company's second serial bibliography, ***America: History and Life***, began publication. ABC-CLIO's book publishing division was established in 1967. Today, it publishes hundreds of reference works and databases in history, political science, and other fields.

Alert Publications, Inc. 65 East Scott Street, Suite 12E, Chicago, IL 60610-5277. (312)-337-1362.
www.alertpub.com
Alert Publications, Inc. was a publisher of specialty newsletters for legal and business researchers, including **Legal Information Alert**, **Business Information Alert**, and **Research Advisor**. CEASED OPERATIONS IN 2011.

American Arbitration Association. 1633 Broadway, 10th Floor, New York, NY 10019. (800) 716-5600 (212) 716-5800.
http://www.adr.org
The American Arbitration Association is the world's leading provider of conflict management and dispute resolution services and a pioneer in the alternative dispute resolution movement. The American Arbitration Association is available to resolve a wide range of disputes through mediation, arbitration, elections and other out-of-court settlement procedures. The Association's ADR resources, including panels, rules, administration, and education and training services provide cost-effective and tangible value to counsel, businesses and industry professionals and their employees, customers and business partners. In 1978 alone, it aided in the resolution of more than 78,000 cases through mediation or arbitration and less formal means of dispute resolution such as fact-finding, mini-trials, and partnering. The American Arbitration Association published a number of periodicals and other publications designed for use by parties, counsel, neutrals, public policy leaders, educators and other who want access to the latest developments in ADR as well as perspectives on the important issues.

American Bar Association, 321 North Clark St., Chicago, IL 60654-7598 (312) 988-5522 **http://www.abanet.org**
Founded in 1876, the American Bar Association has grown to become the largest legal organization in the world with over 400,000 members. The ABA also has an active publication program with hundreds of publications produced by its more than 70 Sections, Divisions, Commissions and Committees. The ABA publishes over 60 books a year and over 50 periodicals and newsletters for its various Sections. The books cover such substantive areas as antitrust, family law, intellectual property, taxation, and law practice management. A list of ABA Sections, Divisions and Forums, each of which is an excellent source for specialized publications, may be found in Chapter 19. A complete listing of ABA publications may be found on the organization's Web site.

American Civil Liberties Union. 125 Broad Street, 18th Floor, New York, N.Y. 10004. (888) 567-2258.
www.aclu.org
Since 1920, the American Civil Liberties Union has been embroiled in what it would describe as the defense of basic civil rights and constitutionally-protected liberties. Included among its activities is the publication of materials on a variety of constitutional and political issues, foremost of which are twenty-one titles in its **Rights of**... series encompassing such areas as aliens and refugees, crime victims, older persons, prisoners, public employees, racial minorities, students, and the right to privacy.

American Correctional Association. 206 North Washington Street, Suite 200, Alexandria, VA 22314. Lanham, MD 20706-4322. (703) 224-0000
www.aca.org
The largest professional organization dedicated to the improvement of corrections and the development and training of correctional professionals has more than 20,000 members. It is the leading source of materials in the field of corrections, including more than 150 print publications and videos. Its catalog also includes significant publications from other publishers. It offers both quantity and membership discounts.

American Insurance Association. 1130 Connecticut Avenue, N.W., Suite 1000, Washington, DC 20036. (202) 828-7100
http://www.aiadc.org/aiapub/
The American Insurance Association is a full-service trade organization of property and casualty insurance companies. Founded in 1866, it is one of the oldest and most respected experts in the insurance field. It currently represents more than 300 leading property and casualty insurance companies which underwrite more than $63 billion a year in direct written premiums. It publishes more than a dozen books, manuals and newsletters aimed at different segments of the insurance industry, and maintains a state-of-the-art legislative tracking service for the property-casualty insurance industry which is available on a one-year, all-inclusive subscription basis.

American Law Institute and ALI-ABA (American Law Institute and American Bar Association Committee on Continuing Professional Education). 4025 Chesnut Street, Philadelphia, PA 19104-3099. (800) 253-6397. **http://www.ali-aba.org**
The American Law Institute was established in 1923 "to promote the clarification and simplification of the law and its better adaptation to social needs, to secure the better administration of justice, and to encourage and carry on scholarly and scientific legal work." Its chief activity has been the drafting, approval, and publication of the various **Restatements of the Law**, Model Codes, and other reform proposals. The ALI's catalogs are available both in paper and on the Internet. In 1947, the American Law Institute joined with the American Bar Association in advancing the cause of continuing education of the bar through an exten-

sive program of post admission legal education, books and periodicals. Traditional courses of study continue to be an important part of ALI-ABA's offerings, but they are now supplemented by magazines, audiotapes, satellite-television broadcasts, videotapes, and floppy disks.

American Water Works Association (AWWA). 6666 W. Quincy Ave., Denver, CO 80235. (800) 926.7337
http://www.awwa.org/
Founded in 1881, the American Water Works Association (AWWA) is the oldest and largest nonprofit scientific and educational organization dedicated to safe water in North America. As the authoritative resource on safe water, with more than 59,000 members worldwide sharing knowledge on water resource development, water and wastewater treatment technology, water storage and distribution, and utility management and operations, AWWA advances public health, safety and welfare by uniting the efforts of the full spectrum of the entire water community. The AWWA Bookstore contains the world's largest collection of books, videos and training materials for water and wastewater treatment professionals.

Anderson Publishing Co. (See LexisNexis)
www.lexisnexis.com/anderson/
Established by William Harvey Anderson in 1887, this Cincinnati-based and legal publisher's first titles were **Whittaker's Ohio Civil Code** and the **Ohio Code of Civil Procedure**. In the years that followed, the company published Ohio primary law and state specific treatises and practice books for Ohio, Kentucky, and Indiana. In addition to these state specific materials, Anderson's current catalog contains a number of national legal treatises, including Kintner's **Federal Antitrust Law**, Weissenberg's **Federal Evidence** and Kuntz's **Law of Oil and Gas,** among others. It also publishes legal journals, law school textbooks, and more than eighty titles in the criminal justice field. Since 1953, Anderson has been the publisher of **Page's Ohio Revised Code Annotated**. It later added the **Ohio Official Reports**, and **Ohio Opinions.** In recent years, the company has begun issuing Ohio primary law on CD-ROM. By industry standards, both the initial and supplementation cost of Anderson titles are reasonable. Supplementation tends to be annual. Lately an employee-owned company, Anderson Publishing Company was acquired by Reed Elsevier in 2002 and its product line absorbed into that of LexisNexis.

Andrews Publications (See **Thomson Reuters).**
http://www.andrewsonline.com
Founded in 1970, Andrews Publications has provided legal specialists and risk management professionals with a wide range of publications useful in both litigation and business-related fields. It specializes in the publication of newsletters in a variety of liability-related fields, including tobacco and insurance litigation. Its Document Access Service provides access to as large database of court documents. Andrews also publishes books and A/V programs and sponsors conferences in areas ranging from trial practice techniques to insurance/reinsurance industry litigation. On April 1, 2003, Andrews Publications was acquired by Thomson West (now Thomson Reuters). Andrews newsletters are now available on Westlaw. .

Aspen Publishers (see Wolters Kluwer Law & Business). 76 Ninth Avenue, 7th Floor New York, NY 10011 Phone: (212) 771-0600 (800)-234-1660 Fax: (212) 771-0885 www.aspenpublishers.com
A Wolters Kluwer company, Aspen Publishers is a leading provider of print and electronic information for legal, business, tax, and accounting professionals. Aspen Publishers was founded in 1959 and was purchased by Wolters Kluwer in 1978. Since that time, Aspen has grown via a succession of mergers and acquisitions, many of them involving leading names in professional publishing. Aspen's parent company, Wolters Kluwer, is the third largest legal publisher in the U.S. following Thomson/West and Reed Elsevier (LexisNexis). Aspen's position in the legal publishing business was solidified by the acquisition of a number of companies including five major players, namely **Panel Publishers**, **Prentice Hall Law & Business**, **Little, Brown and Company Legal Division**, **Wiley Law Publications**, and **Loislaw**. In 1982, Wolters Kluwer merged Aspen with **Panel Publishers**, which was founded in 1967 by William Casey, former Director of the CIA in the Reagan administration, and Irving Schreiber, both of whom were associated with C.W. Post University on Long Island. Panel's line of answer books and other resources dedicated to tax, pension, benefits, and related topics are now part of the Aspen product line. Prentice Hall Law & Business was founded in the late 1970s as part of Harcourt Brace and was sold to Simon & Schuster in 1986, after which it became part of Prentice Hall. Prentice Hall Law & Business published many of the leading titles in corporate and commercial law, including, Block Barton & Radin's *The Business Judgment Rule* and Balotti & Finkelstein's *Delaware Law of Corporations and Business Organizations*, and reference directories such as the *The Directory of Corporate Counsel* and *The Almanac of the Federal Judiciary*. Aspen Publishers acquired the company in 1994.

Little, Brown and Company's Legal Division was founded in Boston in 1837. Often described as the "Tiffany" of law publishers, the company focused its efforts on publishing subject specific legal treatises and law school texts and casebooks. Among its early titles were such classics as Christopher Langdell's *Selected Cases on Contracts* (the first modern casebook), Oliver Wendell Holmes' *The Common Law*, and Wigmore's *Evidence in Trials at Common Law*, known popularly as *Wigmore on Evidence*. Later the line was expanded to include such landmark titles as *Areeda on Antitrust* and the Loss, Seligman multi-volume compendium on securities laws. Aspen acquired the company in 1996.

Wiley Law Publications (WLP) was founded in 1983. Beginning with its *Estate Valuation Handbook*, WLP went on to publish over 300 law titles, including the market leading series on all aspects of construction law. Aspen acquired most of the WLP titles in 1997. WLP's construction law "Redbooks," long regarded as the seminal construction law guides, have since been complemented by Aspen's development of the *Construction Law Handbook* and the *Construction Law Library Online.*

In 2001, Aspen Publishers acquired **Loislaw**, an online company founded in 1987 by attorney Kyle Parker. Loislaw was the first company to offer complete libraries of state and federal law on the Internet. Its URL is **http://www.loislaw.com.** Loislaw offers on-line access to all leading primary sources of law. Subscriptions are available in a variety of formats, including state products, state and federal packages, a national collection, a federal collection, and premium collections for federal district and bankruptcy courts. Integrating Loislaw's on-line databases with the rich resources of Aspen's proprietary content was a natural step, and over 20 on-line treatise libraries are now available covering topics such as: antitrust, bankruptcy, construction law, corporate law, corporate governance, drunk driving, elder law, estate planning, evidence, family law, general litigation, insurance law, internet and e-commerce law, licensing agreements, limited liability companies, partnerships, personal injury, product liability, and securities law.

Aspen's acquisition of **Emanuel Law Publishing** (2001) and **Casenotes Publishing Co.** (2002) doubled the company's student study aid offerings and further established its leading position in the law school market. In June 2002, **Kluwer Law International**, a Wolters Kluwer Company specializing in English language international law publishing, was transferred to Aspen Publishers. KLI will continue to be headquartered in The Hague with a satellite office in London.

Also acquired in October 2002 were **Bowne & Co., Inc.'s** securities publishing division, including the *Securities Act Handbook* and the *Rules and Regulations of the Securities and Exchange Commission* (the "Red Box"), both of which are recognized as leading securities law reference tools. More recent purchases have given Aspen a firm presence in the accounting market. Aspen picked up the Miller GAAP and GAAS Guides—well known as the preferred resources for accountants and financial officers—via an acquisition from **Harcourt** in 2000. Repeating its past strategy of acquiring on-line material to support and complement its print titles, Aspen acquired the foremost accounting database, **Arthur Andersen's** *Accounting Research Manager* in October 2002. Aspen's extensive product line offers legal and business professionals top quality content in a variety of print and electronic media covering an extensive range of substantive topics, practice objectives, compliance issues, and strategic concerns. The Aspen brand is now part of Wolters Kluwer Law & Business.

Austin & Winfield (see Rowan & Littlefield) (800) 462-6420
https://rowman.com/RLPublishers
Founded by Dr. Robert West in 1992, Austin & Winfield is an imprint of the Rowman & Littlefield Publishing Group. Its focus is on scholarly works in the fields of law and criminal justice. The firm has always specialized in scholarly research with an emphasis on legal history, constitutional law, justice, and problems of American legal practice.

Banks-Baldwin Law Publishing Co. (see Thomson Reuters). Founded in 1804, Banks-Baldwin is the oldest legal publisher in the United States. Originally organized as Gould, Banks and Company, the publisher had offices in both Albany and New York City. Among its early publications were volumes of the **United States Reports**, the **New York Consolidated Laws Annotated** and **Bouvier's Law Dictionary.** Following the death of the Gould brothers, the company operated for a time under the name Banks & Brothers. In 1895, it was reorganized in New York City under the name Banks Law Publishing and in Albany under the name Banks & Company. Later, it moved to Ohio and was reorganized under the name Banks-Baldwin. Banks-Baldwin was heavily invested in the publication of state specific titles for Ohio and the surrounding states, including **Baldwin's Ohio Revised Code Annotated**, the **Ohio Administrative Code**, and **Baldwin's Kentucky Revised Statutes Annotated**, over 70 state practice manuals, handbooks, compilations and newsletters. It publishes several titles under contract, including official editions of the **Indiana Code** and the **Indiana Administrative Code. Baldwin's Ohio Legislative Service** was one of the first advance session law services in the United States and the **Ohio Administrative Code** was one of the first commercially published state administrative codes. Through a relationship with Mead Data Central, **Baldwin's Ohio Revised Code Annotated** was the first state code made available online. In recent years, it has also begun issuing the Ohio statutory and administrative codes on CD-ROM. In 1994, Banks-Baldwin was sold in West Publishing and became a subsidiary of the Minnesota-based legal publishing giant. The sales operation of Banks-Baldwin was transferred to West Publishing in 1995. In 1996, Banks-Baldwin, along with West Publishing, became part of the Thomson Corporation (now Thomason Reuters) (now 7%). in the biggest merger in legal publishing history.

Matthew Bender & Company (see **LexisNexis**) (800) 223-1940.
http://bender.lexisnexis.com/bender/us/catalog?action=home
In 1887, Matthew Bender, Sr., an employee of William Gould & Sons of Albany, New York, left to form the Matthew Bender Company. In addition to selling the books of other publishers in his storefront operation, Matthew Bender published his first title, **Fiero on Special Pleadings** in 1887. Bender expanded the company in 1905 by taking his two sons into the business. In 1911, the company bought out Banks & Company and H.B. Parsons. During World War I, Matthew Bender published annotated editions of the special federal war acts, the Federal Reserve Banking Act, and the Income Tax Law. Matthew Bender was purchased by the Times Mirror Company in 1963 as part of the latter company's expansion into the world of specialized and professional publishing.

From its modest beginnings, Matthew Bender has become one of the leading publishers of legal analytical works. Its current catalog features more than 500 titles in more than 30 subject fields and subject specific treatises and practice books for fourteen states. No other publisher approaches Matthew Bender in terms of depth of coverage. Many of its titles have achieved classic status, including **Moore's Federal Practice**, **Benedict on Admiralty** and **Collier on Bankruptcy**. Matthew Bender was also one of the first legal publishers to see the potential in CD-ROM technology, and now markets many of its print titles in the form of Authority CD-ROM libraries. In 1997, it placed its Authority line of products on the Internet, making these available either as full subscriptions or as individual "Pay-Per-Slice" purchasable units. Through enlightened marketing strategies such as these, Matthew Bender has maximized consumer options as never before.

While there is no question that Bender has and continues to produce analytical works of high quality and depth, pricing continues to be matter of concern to many customers, not the least of which have been law libraries. Significant increases in the cost of supplementation, particularly in the period between 1987 and

1992, caused a significant decline in the numbers of Matthew Bender's standing order customers. As documented in the November, 1992 issue **The CRIV Sheet** (the newsletter of the American Association of Law Libraries Committee on Relations with Information Vendors) an average of 157 national Matthew Bender titles rose a total of 117.59% between 1987 and 1991. The supplementation cost for **Moore's Federal Practice**, for example, rose from $834.00 in 1987 to $2294.50 in 1991. It rose to $2,693.00 before Matthew Bender finally froze prices in 1992.

Matthew Bender responded to this crisis by implementing a complete reorganization of company operations in 1993, of which the across the board price freeze was the most dramatic step. Under the leadership of its then President and CEO Alex Sann, Bender significantly reduced its work force, consolidated its product catalog, eliminated direct mail and telemarketing operations, and instituted annual subscription pricing to give customers a clear idea of their annual outlay for Bender titles. It also increased customer options by providing package discounts for selected product libraries. In 1995, Alex Sann, was replaced by Katherine Downing, former President and CEO of Thomson Legal Publishing. Under her leadership, Bender replaced its proprietary **Search Master** search engine with **Authority**, a FOLIO platform more in line with the industry-wide standard. After 3-4 years of frozen prices, supplementation costs are rising again.

These dramatic developments at Matthew Bender have heralded a new era of responsiveness to the needs of consumers. Under Downing's leadership, Matthew Bender has taken dramatic steps to enhance product quality, expand the variety of product formats, and provide customers with a range of purchasing options appropriate to their individual financial circumstances. While Matthew Bender publications continue to be among the more costly in their specific product categories, their editorial quality and breadth are often unequaled by the competition. In addition, Matthew Bender continues to attract many of the country's leading subject specialists to serve as authors and editors.

Responding to the Thomson Corporation's acquisition of West Publishing, Matthew Bender acquired the citator division of Shepard's/McGraw-Hill in 1996 and began integrating the Shepard's product line into the overall Matthew Bender operation by the end of the year. This acquisition began as a joint venture by Times Mirror and Reed Elsevier, each of which would control a 50% interest in Shepard's. Reed Elsevier, which owns LEXIS-NEXIS, also entered into a cross-licensing agreement with Times-Mirror to offer Matthew Bender publications online through LEXIS-NEXIS and to provide primary law from the LEXIS database to Matthew Bender to incorporate into its Authority CD-ROM and online products. Following the breakdown of the proposed merger between Reed Elsevier and Wolters Kluwer in 1998, Reed Elsevier ended months of speculation by purchasing Matthew Bender from Times Mirror for the sum of $1.6 billion. Under Matthew Bender's leadership, Shepard's began offering all-inclusive pricing for its print citators as a means of providing customers with a greater degree of predictability of annual updating costs. The all-inclusive pricing model, patterned after Bender's annual subscription pricing for its treatise products, includes not only paper advance sheets, but also bound supplements and periodic bound revisions. Also, in a major development with far-reaching implications, U.S. District Judge John S. Martin, Southern District of New York, ruling in a case brought by Matthew Bender and HyperLaw, Inc., rejected West's claim that star pagination involved a degree of creative effort deserving of copyright protection. Certain to be appealed, Judge Martin's decision was the first victory on this issue by West's competitors, and the first to be decided outside of West's home Eighth Circuit. Another significant development took place on April 10, 1997, when Matthew Bender announced the release of its new Authority On-Demand Internet legal research service aimed at the practitioners in small law offices. Authority On-Demand offers instant access to more than 250 of Bender's analytical publications, including treatises and practice libraries. Matthew Bender imprints now appear under the name LexisNexis Matthew Bender.

Many of the cost saving tips which accompany the entries in **Chapter 27: Legal Treatises** are directed at ways to reduce these supplementation costs, including purchasing condensed "desk editions," dropping standing orders, and completely repurchasing titles every few years. The periodic re-purchase of used sets is another cost saving alternative.

Bernan Press. 15200 NBN Way, P.O. Box 191, Blue Ridge Summit, PA 17214 1-800-865-3457
http://www.bernan.com
Headquartered in Pennsylvania, Bernan Associates has, for nearly 60 years, served the information needs of professionals, businesses, and libraries by providing access to U.S. and other government publications.

Bisel, George T., Company. 710 S. Washington Square, Philadelphia, PA 19106. (800) 247-3526.
http://www.bisel.com
Bisel Publishing Company has been serving the Pennsylvania legal profession for 122 years. Established in 1876 by William T. Bisel, who was joined one year later by his brother George, the company first sold law blanks and stationery, pen points, ink and pencils, later branching out into used law books. From its location in downtown Philadelphia, it began issuing new Pennsylvania legal publications, including many of the predecessor volumes of what were later to become the major Pennsylvania reference and practice sets of today, including **Purdon's Pennsylvania Digest**, **Dunlap's Book of Forms**, and **Tourbat & Haly's Practice**. William Bisel died in 1881 and George in 1941. The business moved to 710 Washington Square in 1948 and purchased the building it occupies today. Continuing under family management, the George T. Bisel Company began a more ambitious program of publishing contemporary Pennsylvania practice texts, a program which continues to expand today. The company is now managed by the fourth generation of the Bisel family.

Bloomberg BNA. 1801 S. Bell Street, Arlington, VA 22202. (800) 372-1033.
www.bna.com
Founded in 1929 as a publisher of looseleaf services, the Bureau of National Affairs has established itself as a major provider of information in the fields of environmental, intellectual property, labor, securities, and tax law. It currently publishes more than forty major looseleaf services, including such leading titles as **United States Law Week**, **Labor Relations Reporter**, **Environment Reporter**, and the **Tax Management Portfolios**

series. Specialty newsletters in such fields as tax, labor and executive practice account for another segment of the business. In the late 1940's, the company added a line of casebound books which now includes more than 150 titles in such areas as human services, labor and arbitration, environmental law, intellectual property, and appellate practice. The BNA Books division adds approximately 30-40 new titles annually to its existing product line. In recent years, BNA has begun converting selected titles to CD-ROM, such as the **Tax Management Portfolios** and the state environmental coverage in its **Environment Reporter**, to name just a few. Many BNA titles are now available on the Internet.

Prices for BNA products run the gamut, from the modestly-priced case bound book to the **Daily Report for Executives** which costs over $9,000 annually on the Web. Since a major portion of its business is in the sale of looseleaf services to specialists, the prices naturally reflect the expense of providing weekly updates. The purchaser must make that critical decision as to whether or not he or she requires a publication with such frequent updating. On annual basis, the price increases for BNA's publications have been below average for the industry and roughly comparable to those of other publishers of true looseleaf publications (publishers of legal treatises in compression binders, such as Matthew Bender, are excluded from this list. On March 22, 2007, BNA and Thomson Tax and Accounting concluded an agreement to make BNA tax products available on Thomson's Checkpoint platform. Bloomberg acquired BNA, including BNA Books, in September 2011 and began integrating its full range of proprietary legal content into Bloomberg Law. Whether the addition of BNA's analytical and current awareness content will help propel Bloomberg into the front ranks of legal information providers remains to be seen, however.

Bloomberg Law. Bloomberg Tower, 731 Lexington Avenue, New York, NY 10022.
(888) 560-2529; (212) 617-6569
www.bloomberglaw.com
Bloomberg Law is a legal, regulatory, and compliance research platform, offering a suite of news, data and analytics to the legal and compliance community. It can be tailored specifically for the needs of modern professionals, providing resources for legal research, compliance, business development, sector intelligence, and other information needs. Bloomberg Law, which debuted in December, 2009, builds upon Bloomberg L.P., a service that had already established itself as a premier source of proprietary news and financial intelligence. Its chief competitors in the high-end legal research market are Westlaw and LexisNexis. Bloomberg L.P. has expended enormous capital in developing this competitive, high-end legal research service. The New York-based company, that employs more than 10,000 people in over 135 offices around the globe, is the fastest-growing real-time financial information network in the world. Whether the addition of BNA's analytical and current awareness content will help propel Bloomberg into the front ranks of legal information providers remains to be seen, however. Mounting a genuine challenge to WestlawNext and LexisNexis at this stage in the development of the industry presents a number of substantive, logistical, and marketing challenges that may be difficult to overcome.

BRB Publications, Inc. PO Box 27869, Tempe, AZ 85285. 1-800-929-3811; FAX: 1-800-929-4981; **http://www.brbpub.com/default.asp**
BRB Publications, Inc is the nation's premier publisher of sourcebooks used for locating public records. BRB's books and electronic products provide access to over 26,000 government agencies and 3,500 record vendors that maintain, search for or retrieve public records. Profiles in their products include access procedures & restrictions fees, turn around times, web addresses along with phone numbers and addresses. BRB Publications was awarded the 2000 Publisher of the Year by Quality Books and is a past winner of a Product Achievement Award from the Information Industry Association.

Carolina Academic Press. 700 Kent Street, Durham, NC 27701 (919) 489-7486; Fax: (919) 493-5668
http://www.cap-press.com/
A general scholarly publisher, Carolina Academic Press has emerged as a leading publisher of monographs in the fields of law, political science, criminal justice, history and other subject areas. Its growing law-related output includes law school casebooks and other texts, as well as a new series of state legal research guides. Among its collection of legal writing and research books are such titles as **Plain English for Lawyers** by Richard C. Wydick, Carolyn Nygren's **Starting Off Right in Law School**, Ruta Stropus and Charlotte Taylor's **Bridging the Gap Between College and Law School: Strategies for Success** and Michael Fischl and Jeremy Paul's **Getting to Maybe: How to Excel in Law School**.

Casemaker. Lawriter LLC, 444 Chiquita Center, 250 East 5th Street, Cincinnati, Ohio 45202-4119. (877) 659-0801. **http://www.casemaker.us/**
One of the alternative computer-assisted legal research services which has had an impact on computer-assisted legal research in many states is Casemaker. Developed by Cincinnati lawyer Joseph Shea and the Lawriter Corporation, an electronic legal publisher, Casemaker began as a highly popular CD-ROM product marketed to Ohio attorneys in 1988. Joining forces with the Ohio State Bar Association, Casemaker moved to the Internet in 1998, offering Ohio State Bar members access to a complete library of Ohio legal materials. Since that time, additional state bar associations have approached Casemaker to join the Casemaker consortium. As of April, 2013, 27 state and local bar associations have done so, including all six New England states, as well as Alabama, Alaska, Colorado, Idaho, Indiana, Kansas, Kentucky, Michigan, Mississippi, Nebraska, North Dakota, Ohio, Rhode Island, South Carolina, Texas, Utah, Vermont, Washington, and Wyoming.

The Casemaker database also includes decisions of the United States Supreme Court back to 1936 and more limited coverage of decisions of federal appellate courts. It has already made a significant impact in Ohio, where bar association surveys have shown it to be the most heavily user CALR service. Casemaker is only available to members of the participating bar associations. We include Casemaker among the leading alterative CALR services because it has become the default CALR service for most bar members in the above mentioned states. In fact, more than 400,000 attorneys now have access to Casemaker as a part of their bar membership, a development which is already having an impact on Westlaw PRO and LexisNexis Advantage subscription costs which have remained relatively flat for the past couple of years.

Content for each of the states currently in the consortium features the full range of primary law, including case law, applicable federal court decisions, state codes and constitutions, session laws, regulations, rules of professional conduct, attorney general opinions, workers' compensation opinions, bar journals, and more. Moreover, Casemaker's coverage is not limited to the highest appellate courts and local federal courts, but extends to the courts of appeals, and some trial courts. Content is selected in consultation with each state bar association and, as such, it reflects the specific needs and desires of the practitioners in those states. The Casemaker search engine employs an intuitive technology which includes both Boolean and natural language protocols, a Thesaurus function, and a case history citator. It is simple to navigate and allows users to conduct in each database.

Casemaker's success is a striking indication of the need for low-cost CALR by attorneys across the country. Ohio State Bar Association surveys have revealed that utilization of Casemaker now exceeds that of any other computer-assisted legal research service. And it is not difficult to understand why. Casemaker is rapidly becoming one of the most popular benefits of state bar association membership. In states with a unified (mandatory) bar, Casemaker is being made available to every bar member. In states with a voluntary bar, Casemaker has become the single greatest factor driving the enrollment of new members. With thousands of bar members using Casemaker, the real per member cost averages a mere $20.00 per year. The strength of numbers has made Casemaker into a major success story for users of computer-assisted legal research in some states.

While Casemaker has had an impact on the legal research habits of lawyers, particularly in states whose bar associations are part of the consortium, it has also attracted competition from Fastcase, Loislaw, and the aggressively priced offerings of Westlaw and LexisNexis. The major question, however, is whether Casemaker can develop a national database of primary and secondary materials and a cross-file searching capability which will make it a major player at the national level. At present, each state's database must be searched independently. Moreover, there is no one site on the Internet where comprehensive information on Casemaker's database coverage may be found. Users are dependent upon the information supplied by the individual bar association sites regarding coverage of the other state sites. While Casemaker's growth is somewhat unhurried and deliberate, it is reflective of the interest of the state bar associations and Casemaker's own desire to remain debt-free. Now that Casemaker is available to attorneys in a majority of the states, plans are underway to expand the database to full national coverage. More recently, it has added CaseCheck+, a negative citator system designed to compete with Shepard's and KeyCite; and CaseDigest, providing federal and state case summaries drafted by Casemeker editors. Casemaker is already having a significant impact on the market for computer-assisted legal research in those states whose bar associations have chosen to participate, while restricting the ability of Westlaw and LexisNexis to expand in those states. That impact will spread gradually to other states as they come on board. This will provide a healthy consumer-oriented effect on the online legal research marketplace. Casemaker also had ambitious plans for a line of print products, but this effort has, thus far, borne little fruit.

In February, 2008, Lawriter LLC, the parent company of Casemaker, was acquired by Collexis Holdings, Inc., a leading developer of high definition search and knowledge discovery software. At the time of its sale, Lawriter was the leading legal online provider to the small and medium law firm market that comprises 450,000 attorneys.

Cato Institute. 1000 Massachusetts Ave., N.W., Washington, D.C. 20001-5403. (202) 842-0200.
www.cato.org
Founded in 1977, the Cato Institute is a nonpartisan public policy research foundation headquartered in Washington, D.C. The Institute is named for Cato's Letters, libertarian pamphlets that helped lay the philosophical foundation for the American Revolution. The Cato Institute seeks to broaden the parameters of public policy debate to allow consideration of more options that are consistent with the traditional American principles of limited government, individual liberty, and peace. Toward that goal, the Institute strives to achieve greater involvement of the intelligent, concerned lay public in questions of policy and the proper role of government. The Cato Institute undertakes an extensive publications program dealing with the complete spectrum of policy issues. Books, monographs, and shorter studies are commissioned to examine the federal budget, Social Security, monetary policy, natural resource policy, military spending, regulation, NATO, international trade, and myriad other issues. Major policy conferences are held throughout the year, from which papers are published thrice yearly in the **Cato Journal.** The Institute also publishes the quarterly magazine **Regulation** and a bimonthly newsletter, **Cato Policy Report.**

CCH Incorporated, a Wolters Kluwer business. 4025 W. Peterson Avenue, Chicago, IL 60646-6085. (800) 525-3335
www.cch.com
Founded by William Kix Miller in 1913, Commerce Clearing House responded to the enactment of the first income tax by publishing a tax guide. Its chief competitor at this time was Prentice-Hall, Inc. which was organized the same year. In the 1920's, Prentice-Hall sued Commerce Clearing House for infringement in an action which, though it proved to be inconclusive, left CCH financially drained. In order to survive, KixMiller sought assistance from the Corporation Trust Company, another publisher of materials covering federal regulatory activities. A reorganized Commerce Clearing House moved its operations to Chicago, added new titles to its catalog, and bought out several competitors. During the New Deal, in particular, CCH developed looseleaf services to cover the activities of all major and many minor regulatory fields. These services provided a combination of primary materials in the field and expert analysis. In 1995, CCH was acquired by the Wolters Kluwer company. In 1997, it was reorganized into five publishing and software units, each focusing on a defined market and subject area. The Tax Compliance software unit became a separate Wolters Kluwer U.S. unit in 1999. Currently, the CCH Publishing Business is made up of the Federal and State Tax, Health and Human Resources, Business and Finance, and Small Office/ Home Office units. Currently, CCH publishes more than 200 topical looseleaf services in fields ranging from tax and finance

to labor, pensions, securities, government contracts, etc. While most of these products appear in print, most are now also available on the Internet (see **Appendix D** for a fairly complete list). CCH Publishing is the largest unit in Wolters Kluwer's worldwide holdings, with a staff of 3,400 employees, including an editorial staff of over 600.

Price increases from Commerce Clearing House have routinely come in at the 6-8% range, competitive for the looseleaf publishing segment of the industry. Of course, the consumer of legal information must decide if the looseleaf format, whether print or online, is the appropriate one for his or her practice. Due to their frequent updating, looseleaf services are inherently more expensive than other value-added legal publications with annual supplementation. The question is, will your frequency of use be sufficient to justify such frequent supplementation?

Clark Boardman Callaghan (CBC) (see **Thomson Reuters).** The former Clark Boardman Callaghan company was a short-lived product of the corporate acquisition fever which struck the legal publishing industry during the 1980's and early 1990's. It represented the merger of two separate companies and a division of another. The Callaghan Company traced its history back to 1864, when Bernard Callaghan and another clerk left Boston's Little, Brown and Company and set up their own firm in Chicago under the name of Callaghan & Cutler. After Cutler sold his interest to James Crockett who liquidated his interest to start his own New York City firm, the company's name became Callaghan & Company. The company's early publishing activities were confined to titles of regional interest, including state statutes for Iowa, Illinois and Michigan, court reports for Illinois Michigan, Utah, Wisconsin and Wyoming, and a number of state digests and practice books. Callaghan's first treatise aimed at a national audience was McQuillan's **Treatise on the Law of Municipal Corporations**, first published in 1904. The company was sold to the Cudahy family in 1916. By 1979, when it was acquired by the Thomson Corporation of Canada, Callaghan was publishing over 200 titles, many of them aimed at the national legal market.

The Clark Boardman Company came into existence in 1916 as a book distributor and sales company in the legal market. By the 1960's, it was publishing a variety of national legal specialty titles, with particular emphasis on the fields of criminal law, securities, intellectual property, and immigration. Many of its titles were published in compression looseleaf binders which permitted interfiled supplementation. Unlike Callaghan and Company, many of Clark Boardman's titles were supplemented more than once a year, often at irregular intervals. Clark Boardman prior practice was to ship related titles to owners of another title in their subject-specific "library." Clark Boardman was purchased by the Thomson Corporation in 1980.

The third component of Clark Boardman Callaghan was that portion of the Lawyers Cooperative Publishing Company which concentrated on national subject-specific legal treatises. When Thomson acquired Lawyers Cooperative (and its subsidiaries Bancroft-Whitney and Research Institute of America) in 1989 for the sum of $810 million, it immediately began a process of strategic planning to determine the best use for its acquisition. Clark Boardman Callaghan was born in 1991 when the subject specialty line of Lawyers Cooperative was added to the product lines of Callaghan and Clark Boardman. Prior to the restructuring which followed Thomson's acquisition of West Publishing in 1996, Clark Boardman Callaghan published more than 600 legal treatises and practice books in 27 subject fields, ranging from antitrust and bankruptcy to civil rights, corporations, criminal law, employment, entertainment, immigration, family law, securities real property law and others. It also developed titles in CD-ROM format which combined analysis and primary source material in the subject field.

The transformation of these three separate entities had resulted in a combined product line of greater breadth and higher quality. Clark Boardman Callaghan's stock-in-trade had been that of taking raw legal data (the primary law) and transforming it into what the publishers refer to as "value-added" legal publications. Their legal treatises and practice books feature clearly-written analysis, better indexing and more sophisticated user aids. Since 1991, the company has also significantly raised prices, both for the base titles and their supplements. In numerous instances, formerly single-volume treatises with annual pocket parts (many of them former Lawyers Cooperative titles), have been transformed into looseleaf publications of two or three volumes. Thus, while the amount of information provided has increased, the bottom line cost for the standing order customer has also risen significantly.

Also, while the product lines have been merged from a sales and operational perspective, the format of the separate product lines has tended to remain largely intact. Thus, many old Callaghan titles are still supplemented with annual pocket parts, while former Clark Boardman titles are housed in looseleaf compression binders. The one major change has been the increasing transformation of former casebound treatises of Lawyers Cooperative into the looseleaf binder format, often with non-cumulative supplements. This trend has made it more difficult to skip supplements and buy in again at a later date. Cost saving strategies often involved skipping a sufficient number of supplements to justify the purchase of a new volume or new contents. Following the merger of West Publishing Company and the Thomson Legal Publishing companies, the CBC product line has been absorbed into that of Thomson West, operating out of Eagan, Minnesota.

Collexis Holdings, Inc. (see also Casemaker). 1201 Main Street, #980, Columbia, SC 29201. (803) 727-1113
A leading developer of high definition search and knowledge discovery software, Collexis became the parent company of Lawriter and its Casemaker online legal research service in February 2008.

Continuing Education of the Bar. 2100 Franklin St., Suite 500, Oakland, CA 94612

800-232-3444 **http://ceb.com**
Chartered in 1947 by the University of California, Continuing Education of the Bar (CEB), provides a wide range of continuing education seminars and publications to the California attorneys, including publications in both print and CD-ROM formats. Its major CD-ROM offering is **CEB on CD-ROM**, a collection of four California practice libraries: Business (12 titles), Civil Litigation (13 titles), Estate Planning (12 titles), and Real Property (18

titles). It also publishes **CEB Electronic Forms**, a series of **CEB Action Guides** providing quick access in outline format to particular legal procedures, and scores of other print publications in both substantive and procedural areas of California law.

Cornell Maritime Press, Inc. (see Schiffer Publishing, Ltd.)
Cornell Maritime Press was founded by Felix Cornell in New York in 1938. Its mission was to publish textbooks to educate merchant mariners (the Merchant Marine Act of 1936 had just created the U.S. Merchant Marine Academy). The company later expanded its publishing program to serve the entire maritime industry and, in 1955, established an imprint called Tidewater Publishers to issue regional nonfiction. Current offerings for maritime lawyers include **The Law and Practice of Marine Insurance**, **The Law of Marine Collision**, and **The Law of Tug, Tow, and Pilotage**. Forthcoming is **Key Divergences in the Law of Marine Insurance Between English and American Law**. In June, 2009, it was acquired by Schiffer Publishing, Ltd., 4800 Lower Valley Road, Atglen, PA 19310.

Courthouse News Service. 30 N. Raymond, Ste. 310, Pasadena, CA 91103. (909) 483-6165; FAX: (909) 483-6165
www.courthousenews.com
Courthouse News Service is a news wire for lawyers. It is made up of a network of correspondents who provide daily comprehensive reports on new appellate rulings, new legislation and new civil cases from the federal and state courts with the most prolific and weighty litigation.

Entrepreneur Press. 2445 McCabe Way, Suite 400, Irvine, CA 92614. (800) 864-6864 or (949) 261-2325; Fax: (949) 261-7729
http://www.entrepreneurpress.com
Since 1998, Entrepreneur Press has published a variety of titles useful to small business owners, franchise owners, home-based businesses, start-ups, non-profits, and other enterprises. A division of Entrepreneur Media, Inc., Entrepreneur Press draws upon the information and editorial resources of **Entrepreneur** magazine. From publishing seven titles in its first year, the Entrepreneur Press catalog has grown to nearly 200 titles in eleven series, including those in business law, real estate, personal finance, careers, and any topic vital to business operations and success. Its Legal Guide series includes such titles as **Asset Protection**, **Bankruptcy for Businesses**, **Business Contracts**, **Business Structures**, **Estate Planning, Wills and Trusts**, **Forming a Partnership**, **Forming an LLC**, **Harassment and Discrimination**, **Hiring and Firing**, **Incorporate Your Business**, **Intellectual Property**, **Principles of Negotiation**, **Small Claims Court Guidebook**, **Tax Planning For Business**, **The Operations Manual for Corporations**, **The Operations Manual for LLCs**, and **The Small Business Legal Tool Kit**. Reasonably priced, Entrepreneur Press books are clearly written and organized for a general audience, and include numerous helpful features, including relevant forms on accompanying CD-ROMs.

Federal Judicial Center. Information Services Office. One Columbus Circle, N.E. Washington, D.C.: 20002-8003 FAX for publication requests: 202-502-4077
www.fjc.gov
The Federal Judicial Center is the education and research agency of the federal courts. It was created by Congress in 1967 to promote improvements in the judicial administration in the courts of the United States. The Center's web site contains the results of its research on federal court operations, procedure, and history, as well as selected publications designed for use by judges and court personnel. It has published nearly 200 titles on topics related to judicial administration, many of which are available free-of-charge at the Center's web site. The Center also produces training videos available for a fee through the National Technical Information Service at: http://http://www.ntis.gov/pdf/pr1000.pdf

GaleCengage Learning (formerly the Gale Group). P.O. Box 6904, Florence, KY 41022-6904 (800) 487-8488.
www.gale.cengage.com
The GaleCengage Learning, a division of Thomson Reuters, is a world leader in e-information publishing for libraries, schools and businesses. Best known for its accurate and authoritative reference content as well as its intelligent organization of full-text magazine and newspaper articles, the company creates and maintains more than 600databases that are published online, in print and in microform. Among these databases is **Legal Trac**, a CD-ROM database of more than 800 legal periodical titles. GaleCengage Learning companies include distinguished German reference publisher K.G. Saur and the U.K.-based Graham & Whiteside. The Gale Group also includes such noted library brands as Macmillan Reference USA, Charles Scribner's Sons, Primary Source Microfilm, Responsive Database Services and U X L. Large print publisher Thorndike Press and The Taft Group, which specializes in reference materials for the nonprofit sector, are also part of the GaleCengage Learning family. In addition to serving the library community, Gale also licenses its proprietary content for integration within web-based information services. Nearly 100 organizations – including Looksmart, Borders, Dow Jones, WebMD, and Thomson Financial – presently enjoy strategic business distribution partnerships with GaleCengage. GaleCengage Learning is based in Farmington Hills, Michigan, with additional offices elsewhere in the U.S. and in the U.K., Australia, Germany, Switzerland and Malaysia. Major brands include InfoTrac, Gale Virtual Reference Library — the company's eBook platform — and the unparalleled Gale Digital Collections such as Eighteenth Century Collections Online.

Geronimo Development Corporation. 606 25th Avenue South, Suite 206, St. Cloud, MN 56301. (800) 457-6045;
www.casefinder.com
Incorporated in 1989 by two Virginia attorneys and one computer programmer, the Geronimo Development Corporation was the first company to produce a stand-alone Virginia legal research system on CD-ROM. In the Spring of 1991, it introduced CaseFinder, a DOS-based product containing Virginia case law. Moving to Minnesota in the Fall of 1991, the CaseFinder system was expanded to include 100 volumes of Virginia Supreme Court decisions. A companion CodeFinder product containing Virginia statutes was added in 1993. A Windows-based version was introduced in 1994 containing both cases and statutes, followed by the inclusion of Workers' Compensation decisions, Virginia Court of Appeals and Circuit Court decisions, Attorney General opinions, and Federal Fourth Circuit decisions. A legal ethics opinions database was added in the Winter of 1995-96; and in 1996, a database of U.S. Supreme Court decisions. In 1997, Virginia Attorney General Conflict of Interest opinions were included. Geronimo also

developed a companion product called the Database Builder in 1995, allowing users to create their own databases of documents on their hard drive which are accessible as an additional CaseFinder database. CaseFinder now features a complete Virginia legal research system that combines CD-ROM reliability with World Wide Web timeliness. Over 141,000 state and federal cases and statutes are contained on two CDs, updated monthly. Built-in web access in the CaseFinder® program provides free access to a private web site with daily updates of all databases. An annual subscription, including 12 monthly discs, is priced at $589.00. Recent opinions are available on Geronimo's Web site at no additional charge. Geronimo also provides a wealth of instructional materials, including an illustrated manual, CD-ROM tutorial, Reference Card, and toll-free technical support.

Glasser LegalWorks. (see **Thomson Reuters**).
http://westlegalworks.com/
Glasser LegalWorks was founded in 1995 when Stephen A. Glasser and Lynn S. Glasser purchased the seminar division of their old company, Prentice Hall Law & Business (now Wolters Kluwer Law & Business). The Glassers were formerly co-presidents of Prentice Hall Law & Business, a division of Simon & Schuster/Viacom. They ran Prentice Hall for nine years after selling Prentice Hall Law & Business, a company they started as a joint venture with Harcourt Brace Jovanovich in 1977, to Simon & Schuster. The Glassers were also the founders of the **Legal Times of Washington**, a legal newspaper they ran for eight years before selling it to American Lawyer Media. Glasser LegalWorks now sponsors more than 60 seminars per year on various legal topics and conducts training in such specialized fields as EDGAR. It initiated its publishing operation in October, 1995 with the release of the **Fair Lending Guide**. In 1996, it released three newsletters: **Internet Law Researcher**, **The Cyberspace Lawyer**, and **Electronic Banking Law and Commerce Report**. Other titles in the Glasser LegalWorks product line include **Getting Down to Business: Marketing and Women Lawyers**, **Compliance with Lobbying Laws and Gift Rules Guide**, **Modern Reinsurance Law and Practice**, and **America's Top Trial Lawyers**, among others. Acquired by the Thomson Corporation in 2004 and renamed West Legalworks, Glasser LegalWorks is also widely known for its management events, including The Marketing Partner Forum, Law Firm Leaders Forum and Executive Director/CFO Forum; its substantive law seminars, including ERISA Litigation, Annual Proxy Statement and Disclosure Documents conference and SEC Disclosure and Accounting conference; and its newsletters, including **Wall Street Lawyer** and **M&A Lawyer**.

Gould Publications, Inc. (see **LexisNexis**).
(800) 223-5297
www.lexisnexis.com/lawenforcement/
Publisher of a wide variety of state and federal publications, including unannotated state and federal statutes, and practice books, and course books for legal and law-enforcement professionals in print, on CD-ROM, and the Internet. Gould Publications was acquired by Reed Elsevier in December, 2004 and its titles now part of LexisNexis.

Greenwood Publishing Group (see ABC-CLIO). 130 Cremona Drive, Santa Barbara, CA 93117. 800-368-6868.
http://www.abc-clio.com

Harrison Company (see **Thomson Reuters**).

The Haworth Press, Inc. 10 Alice Street, Binghamton, NY 13904. (607) 772-5857; FAX: (607) 772-6362. **www.HaworthPress.com**
The Haworth Press, Inc., established by Bill Cohen and Patrick McLoughlin in 1978, is a publisher of books and journals for scholarly and professional audiences. The subject matter of Haworth titles includes law and legal information, criminal justice, adoption and divorce, domestic and child abuse, violence and trauma, and more. Taylor & Francis Group acquired the Haworth Press journal and book list during 2007. Journal publications formerly published by Haworth Press are now listed on the **Taylor & Francis Journals website** and the content is available on our online platform, **informaworld**.

Hein, William S., & Co., Inc. 1285 Main Street, Buffalo, NY 14209-1987. (800) 828-7571; (716) 882-2600.
www.wshein.com
The William S. Hein Company is the world's largest distributor of legal periodicals, a major micropublisher of legal materials, a book and continuation agent, periodical subscription agent, a major source for out-of-print government documents, a used law book dealer, a publisher and reprinter of law and related materials, a CD-ROM publisher, and binder. Hein has been serving the legal community since the 1920's, originally under the name of Dennis & Company, a legal periodical and used law book dealer. Since that time, Hein has expanded into a variety of other legal publishing domains, including micro, CD-ROM, and online publishing. Hein publishes a number of significant archival collections in microform, including materials from the American Law Institute, American Bar Association, Council of State Governments, and National Center for State Courts, among others. Hein is also an authorized agent for the Law Library Microform Consortium and Trans-Media.

Hein publishes such leading legal reference titles as **Redden's Modern Legal Systems Cyclopedia**, **Bieber's Dictionaries of Legal Abbreviations** and **Citations**, Kavass' **United States Treaty Index** and **Guide to Treaties in Force**, **Hein's State Statutes Checklist, Quote It** and **Quote It II**, and the **U.S. Treaties Index** on CD-ROM. It offers complete sets, partial runs, and individual volumes of many secondhand law books. A complete description of Hein's publication and reprint lines may be found in its **Checklist of Publications and Reprints**. On October 15, 1998, Hein took over Fred B. Rothman & Co., a Littleton, CO-based company with a similar profile. For the near term, Hein will continue Rothman's publishing imprint and will maintain Rothman's reprint programs, including the **AALL Publications Series**. All other operations will be merged into Hein's Buffalo-based headquarters.

In 2000, Hein released **HeinOnLine**, an electronic archive of digitally-scanned American legal periodicals and other publications available over the Internet. By 2008, **HeinOnLine** had made more than 40 million pages of material available to subscribers. Besides winning the AALL award for Best New Product and the Best Commercial Website Award from the IALL, it has been added to EContent's list of 100 most important companies in the digital content industry. Today, **HeinOnline** has over 40,000,000 pages of online content. **HeinOnline** is now available in over 150 countries and over 1,000 academic universities subscribing and over 500 law firms, including hundreds of multiple offices with each firm. Pricing begins as low as $495 for a small firm.

HeinOnline's journal collection of over 1,100 journals received over 57,000,000 hits and 16,000,000 article requests in 2007. In addition, **HeinOnline** contains full coverage of the **Federal Register** 1936 to date, and, by 2008, the **Code of Federal Regulations** from 1938 to 2004. The **U.S. Reports** collection includes not only the full replica edition of the official **U.S. Reports** from volumes 1 to current, but also preliminary prints and advance sheets. **Sources of Compiled Legislative History** now has an online presence and links access not only to the legislative histories listed there, but also to the legislative histories that are included in **HeinOnline** and all the articles on those legislative histories, whether they include the legislative history or just have additional information from the law review database. Hein has also become the first company to attempt to put the full text of the **Congressional Record** online. As of 2008, coverage includes all the early editions up until the late 1920's, and those from 1978 to date. The collection of core legal classics now includes over 1,300 titles. The most recent edition to HeinOnline's offerings is Spinelli's Law Librarian's Reference Shelf, a collection of reference works and tools for law librarians, including more than 100 legal dictionaries, legal bibliographies, cataloging publications, AALL GD-SIS State Bibliographies, the AALL Publications Series, serials, GreenSlips (Archive of bibliographic entries), Library of Congress Classification Schedules and Subject Headings, Memorials of Law Librarians, Hein's Legal Research Guide Series, and more.

Incisive Media (formerly ALM and American Lawyer Media, Inc.) 120 Broadway, 5th Floor, New York, N.Y. 10271. (800) 457-9400.
www.incisivemedia.com
Founded in 1994 and headquartered in London, Incisive Media is one of the world's leading business to business information providers, serving the financial and professional services markets globally. Bringing the product provider and purchaser business communities together in print, in person or online, Incisive Media aims to deliver high quality, timely information in whatever format best suits its customers. In 2007, it acquired American Lawyers Media (ALM) from Wasserstein Perella in a $630 million deal. ALM had been created in 1997 through the merger of American Lawyer Media, LP, and National Law Publishing, under an initiative spearheaded by Wasserstein Perella. In 2009, ALM and Incisive Media were refinanced as stand-alone businesses.

Infosources Publishing. 140 Norma Road, Teaneck, NJ 07666. 201-836-7072.
www.infosourcespub.com/
Infosources Publishing was founded in 1981 was law librarian Arlene L. Eis. Infosources publishes popular basic reference tools used in most law libraries. The annually published titles include: **Legal Looseleafs in Print**, **Legal Newsletters in Print**, and **Directory of Law-Related CD-ROMs**. **The Legal Researcher's Desk Reference** is published biennially. Infosources also publishes **The Monthly Internet Guide for the Legal Researcher**, 2d ed. by Don MacLeod, and a monthly newsletter, **The Informed Librarian: Professional Reading for the Information Professional. Legal Looseleafs in Print**, **Legal Newsletters in Print**, and **Directory of Law-Related CD-ROMs** are now marketed as components of **LawTrio Law Publications Database.**

International Municipal Lawyers Association (IMLA). 7910 Woodmont Avenue, Suite 1440, Bethesda, MD 20814. (202) 466-5424.
www.imla.org
The International Municipal Lawyers Association (IMLA) is a non-profit, professional organization that has been an advocate and resource for local government attorneys since 1935. Owned solely by its members, IMLA is the legal voice for the nation's local governments. It champions the development of fair and realistic legal solutions and provides its members with information about, and solutions to, the profusion of legal issues facing its membership today. IMLA serves as a clearinghouse of local law information for its more than 1,400 members. It collects from and disseminates information to its membership across the United States and Canada and helps governmental officials prepare for litigation and develop new local laws. Every year, IMLA's legal staff provides accurate, up-to-date information and valuable counsel to more than 1,000 requests from members. IMLA also provides a variety of services, publications and programs to help members who are facing legal challenges, including **Municipal Lawyer Magazine**, the IMLA MuniFAX Service, and the IMLA Model Ordinance Service.

James Publishing. 3505 Cadillac Avenue, Suite H, Costa Mesa, CA 92626. (800) 440-4780. **www.jamespublishing.com**
Founded in 1981, James Publishing offers an alternative to the catalogs of the conglomerate law book publishers. Its well-written and reasonably-priced books, newsletters and magazines are often filled with forms, practice tips, checklists, samples, product reviews, and case summaries. James Publishing offers a growing library of over 70 titles covering such topics as litigation, personal injury, law technology, employment, civil rights, federal practice, criminal law, family law, social security, insurance, deceptive trade practices, settlement, evidence, and corporate law. Further information may be found on the James Publishing Web site listed above. In contrast to other players in the legal information marketplace, James Publishing is the only legal publisher that has not raised prices or supplementation costs for many years.

Jefren Publishing Company, Inc., A Division of ALP Publishing, LLC 990 Park Center Drive, Ste E Vista, CA 92081-8352; 1-888-264-2665
www.jefren.com
Jefren Publishing Company, Inc. was established in 1988 by attorney Howard E. Deutch, an attorney who has practiced corporate and securities law for more than 30 years as corporate counsel for various public corporations. In the early 1980s, Mr. Deutch began using proxy statements as a source of techniques and forms for his corporate practice. He reasoned that, if these few proxy statements yielded such excellent material, an organized and indexed book of the proposals, forms and disclosures contained in all the proxy statements that corporations prepare each year would be an invaluable tool, not only in his own practice, but for every attorney who practices corporate or securities law. From this concept, **Proxy Statements: Strategy and Forms** was born. It is now a 12-volume, 15,000 page looseleaf set which contains 391 specific, comprehensive strategies for

accomplishing a broad range of corporate actions, plus 832 practice-proven forms to put those strategies into effect. Jefren is now a division of ALP Publishing, LLC.

Jones McClure Publishing. 3131 Eastside St., Suite 300, Houston, TX 77098
800) 626-6667; (713) 335-8200; FAX: (713) 335-8201.
www.jonesmcclure.com
Jones McClure Publishing was founded in 1992 to publish user-friendly law books for the legal practitioner. Since the release of the first edition of O'Connor's Texas Rules * Civil Trials, Jones McClure has published a number of popular titles written in plain English and following a unique format which includes rules, annotated commentaries, practice tips, jury charges, and forms. Its Federal Litigation Series includes titles devoted to civil rules and litigation forms in both print and electronic format, including O'Connor's Federal Civil Forms, O'Connor's Federal Rules * Civil Trials, and O'Connor's Federal Pretrial Deadlines Calculator. The Texas Litigation Series includes publications on civil rules, civil appellate rules, and litigation forms in print and CD-ROM, including O'Connor's Texas Rules * Civil Trials, O'Connor's Texas Civil Forms, O'Connor's Texas Civil Appeals, and O'Connor's Texas Pretrial Deadlines Calculator. The Texas Expert Series offers titles on causes of action and the rules of evidence, including O'Connor's Family Law Handbook, Texas Rules of Evidence Handbook, O'Connor's Texas Causes of Action Pleadings, and O'Connor's Texas Causes of Action. In addition, Jones McClure publishes an Annotated Codes Plus Series, including such titles as O'Connor's Family Code Plus, O'Connor's Federal Employment Codes, O'Connor's Intellectual Property Code, O'Connor's CPRC Plus, O'Connor's Criminal Codes Plus, O'Connor's Texas Crimes & Consequences, O'Connor's Texas Crimes & Consequences, O'Connor's Business Organizations Codes Plus, O'Connor's Business & Commerce Code Plus, O'Connor's Property Code Plus, and O'Connor's Texas Employment Codes Plus. Jones McClure plans to expand its catalog of titles to those covering other states and areas of law.

Jurisearch.Com, LLC. 1467 Greenbrier Place, Charlottesville, Virginia 22901. 877-587-4732 **www.jurisearch.com**
Jurisearch.Com provides on-line access to a library of California, Florida, Massachusetts, and federal primary law, including daily decisions of the California Supreme Court, California Courts of Appeal, U.S. Supreme Court and the 9h Circuit filed the previous day, California Supreme Court decisions from the **California Reports** 2d, 3d & 4th, California Courts of Appeal decisions from **California Appellate Reports** 2d, 3d & 4th, current cases taken from Daily Opinions so they are searchable, Review Granted Cases, California Codes (all 29), Electronic Code Annotations, California Rules of Court, Local Rules for all California Counties, Interactive Judicial Council Forms, U.S. Supreme Court Cases since 1893, 9th Circuit Cases Since 1990, California Code of Regulations, recent Assembly and Senate Bills, and more. The service is priced at $39.95 per month for unlimited use. All fifty states are now available at a cost of $69.95 per month. Contact the Jurisearch Web site for further information.

Juris Publishing, Inc. 71 New Street Huntington, NY 11743. (800) 887-4064. **www.jurispub.com**
Juris Publishing is a full-service legal publisher specializing in international law, with an emphasis on international business and investment, antitrust, ADR and arbitration, commercial arbitration and litigation, banking and bankruptcy, and intellectual property. It concentrates on business and investment publications for Asia, Latin America, Eastern Europe, Russia, and the CIS. These practical publications include translations of primary source materials and most offer periodic newsletters which track current developments in their respective fields. Juris Publishing offers discounts on all books when ordered online.

Kleinrock Publishing (see **CCH).** 11200 Rockville Pike, Suite 302, Rockville, MD 20852-3030. (877) 728-9776 **www.kleinrock.com**
Kleinrock is a leading supplier of tax research solutions and products designed to aid tax professionals in responding quickly and authoritatively to their clients tax planning and compliance questions. Headquartered in Rockville, MD, it is a division of UCG, one of the nation's leading providers of business-to-business information solutions. Among its leading products are **Kleinrock's Tax Expert** and **Kleinrock's Forms Library Plus**. In 2006, ATX/Kleinrock was acquired by CCH (Wolters Kluwer), which is maintaining ATX/Kleinrock as a distinct product line within the CCH family

Lawyers and Judges Publishing Company, Inc. 917 North Swan Road, P.O. Box 30040, Tucson, AZ 85711. (520) 323-1500. **http://www.lawyersandjudges.com**
Founded in 1963, Lawyers and Judges Publishing Company has developed an extensive line of publications aimed at the trial practitioner, including more than 30 titles in the area of accident reconstruction and litigation. It also publishes titles on medical and alcohol-related matters, and a variety of forensic tools and practice aids, such as calculators for computing accident speed from skidmarks, as well as a number of anatomical models designed for courtroom use.

Lawyers Cooperative Publishing Co. (see **Thomson Reuters).**
Founded in 1882 by James E. Briggs, Lawyers Cooperative evolved into one of the leading publishers of nationally recognized legal research tools. At the time of the company's founding, Briggs took the gamble that lawyers preferred their legal information in carefully selected and edited segments which would allow them time to digest the law and still have time to practice. Relying on both outside authors and a large team of in-house editors, Lawyers Cooperative adopted as its mission the simplification of legal research. It accomplished this by annotating, analyzing, selecting, and integrating the massive amounts of raw legal information which flow out of court houses, legislative chambers and administrative offices into forms which can be effectively utilized by the members of the practicing bar.

While LCP's selective approach to legal publishing may not have achieved the early success of the comprehensive approach adopted by West Publishing, it is now an essential component of what became the Thomas Reuters empire. Its former products are now strategically positioned within the Thomson Reuters to take advantage of a marketplace which assigns a great importance to "value-added " analysis. Lawyers Cooperative's leading publications included the components of what was called the "Total Client-Service Library (TCSL)," including **American Jurisprudence 2d**, the **ALR** series, **Am Jur Trials**, **Am Jur**

Proof of Facts, **Am Jur Legal Forms**, **Am Jur Pleading and Practice Forms**, **U.S. Supreme Court Reports Lawyers' Edition**, among others. To these, it adds a number of state statutory codes, state legal encyclopedias, state practice sets and state specific legal treatises and practice books, as well as such former Callaghan titles as the **Federal Rules Service**, **Federal Rules Digest**, **Federal Rules of Evidence Service** and **Federal Rules of Evidence Digest**. The national legal treatises and practice books formerly published by Lawyers Cooperative were turned over to Clark Boardman Callaghan following LCP's purchase by Thomson in 1989 (see CBC above). In 1997, LCP's **U.S. Supreme Court Reports, Lawyers Edition** and companion **Digest** were sold to Reed Elsevier under the terms of the consent decree which allowed the acquisition of West Publishing Company by the Thomson Corporation.

Lawyers Cooperative also embraced the CD-ROM format as a vehicle for delivering both primary law and LCP's own value-added products. By late 1995, it had released all of its TCSL titles in CD-ROM, marketed under the tradename **LawDesk**. These products, which operate under DOS, Windows and Macintosh operating systems provide hypertext linking to other LawDesk products, including many of the state LawDesk titles, some of which were acquired from Law Office Information Systems (LOIS) in the early 1990's.

On another level, however, the acquisition of Lawyers Cooperative by the Thomson Corporation was not a positive development for consumers of legal information. As much the company likes to trumpet its emphasis on "value-added" products, there is no question that prices have risen significantly since 1989. For example, **American Jurisprudence 2d**, which in 1987 cost $584.05 to supplement, now costs over $9,000 by 2012. Prices of other major titles have risen dramatically as pocket parts have risen in cost and revised volumes have appeared with increasing frequency. Publishers representatives report a significant rise in cancellations, reflecting what could be characterized as a loss of trust on the part of consumers. What happened to Lawyers Cooperative under its new corporate ownership is reflective of broader trends in the marketplace. With a limited numbers of dollars to spend on legal materials, lawyers may finally be catching on to the practices of legal publishers who have heretofore viewed them as easy marks for their aggressive supplementation practices. The days of the blind standing order are gone--swept aside in the ultimately shortsighted flurry of corporate avarice. With the Thomson Corporation's acquisition of the West Publishing Company in 1996, the Lawyers Cooperative product line was brought under the umbrella of the West Group, a new corporate entity encompassing the product lines of a number of Thomson-owned companies. For current developments, see the entry for the **Thomson Reuters**.

Law Journal Press, a division of ALM, 120 Broadway, New York, NY 10271. (800) 603-6571 or (212) 457-9400
www.lawcatalog.com
The book publishing division of American Lawyer Media publishes over 130 titles in the fields of antitrust, banking, bankruptcy, business, communications, corporate, criminal, data protection, domestic relations, elder law, environmental, health and managed care, insurance, intellectual property, Internet and technology, labor and employment, law office management, litigation, personal injury, real estate, securities, tax, and trust and estates law. Under its new ownership, Law Journal Press significantly raised its prices by moving to a combined online/print pricing model.

Legal Information Services. P.O. Box 2383,
Chapel Hill, NC 27515-2383
(919) 672-3035; Fax (919) 408-0267
http://www.legalinformationservices.com
Legal Information Services publishes legal research and law library-related titles for librarians, lawyers, and legal researchers. Users consult these titles for management, reference, research, and acquisitions. The company was founded by Elyse Fox, J.D., M.S.L.S, a law librarian and former practicing attorney. Its current titles include **Legal Information Management Index**; **Law Librarian's Bulletin Board**; **How to File Looseleaf Services**: **A Filing Manual and Reference Handbook**; **The Legal Research Dictionary: from Advance Sheets to Pocket Parts**, 2nd edition; and **Current Topics in Legal Information Management and Law Librarianship**: **Practical Reports for the Library Manager, Jury Instructions Drafting Manual and Resource Guide** and **Legal Research Q & A: 401 Flashcards with Companion Book.**

LexisNexis. 125 Park Avenue, Suite 2200 New York, NY 10017.
(800) 437-8674;(212) 309-8100
www.lexisnexis.com
LexisNexis was founded as the Data Corporation in 1966 and was later purchased by The Mead Corporation in 1968. Reed Elsevier plc, which acquired LexisNexis in late 1994, is a leading world-wide publisher and information provider. The LexisNexis Group provides information to legal, corporate, government and academic markets, and publishes legal, tax and regulatory information in online, print and CD-ROM formats. The global legal and information division of Reed Elsevier plc, LexisNexis Group combines dozens of brands, including Butterworths, Martindale-Hubbell, LexisNexis Matthew Bender, Michie, and Shepard's, among others. LexisNexis employs 13,000 people worldwide. Serving customers in more than 100 countries and maintains offices in 28 American cities and dozens of foreign countries. Its sales representatives are located in 50 U.S. cities and around the world, including Amsterdam, London, Frankfurt, Paris, Singapore, Hong Kong, Tokyo, Sydney and Toronto. The company's mission is to be the preferred provider of decision support information and services to professionals in legal, business and government markets. LexisNexis is comprised of companies operating within the North American Legal Markets group and the Corporate and Federal Markets group.

LexisNexis is the global legal publishing arm of Reed Elsevier, the Anglo-Dutch world-leading publisher and information provider. Sister business units provide global science, business-to-business and education publishing services for their markets. LexisNexis Group unites strong brands, pioneering technologies and premium information for customers in the legal, corporate, government and academic markets. More than two-thirds of its revenue is generated in the North American marketplace. At the same time the Group is the market leader in the United Kingdom and the British Commonwealth and major publisher in the legal, tax and regulatory markets in Continental Europe and Latin America. The Group is divided into four main operating units: North American Legal markets, U.S. Corporate and Federal markets, Martindale-Hubbell and the International Division. The division which comprises the Group's publishing assets, is regionally organized, in Europe, Asia-pacific and Latin America. These include the market-leading Butterworths companies in the UK and British Commonwealth, Les Editions du Juris Classeur in France, and many other companies that are household names in their markets. The Group's products are available via the World Wide Web, CD-ROM and hardcopy print.

The Lexis® service, the first commercial, full-text legal information service, was unveiled in 1973 to help legal practitioners research the law more efficiently. The companion Nexis® news and business information service launched in 1979 to richen research with recent and archival news and financial information. Since that time, the service has grown to become the largest news and business online information service, including comprehensive company, country, financial, demographic, market research and industry reports. It provides access to thousands of worldwide newspapers, magazines, trade journals, industry newsletters, tax and accounting information, financial data, public records, legislative records, and data on companies and their executives.

LexisNexis™ is a division of Reed Elsevier Inc. The Federal Tax Identification (ID) assigned to Reed Elsevier Inc. is 52-1471842. All divisions of Reed Elsevier Inc. have the same federal ID number. LexisNexis™ refers to itself on all government forms as Reed Elsevier Inc. d/b/a LexisNexis™ or LexisNexis™, a division of Reed Elsevier Inc. In 2007, LexisNexis moved its corporate headquarters to 125 Park Avenue, New York City, across the street from Grand Central Terminal.

Liberty Fund Books. 8335 Allison Pointe Trail, Ste. 300, Indianapolis, IN 46250-1684. (800) 621-2736; FAX: (800) 621-8476. **www.libertyfund.org**
Liberty Fund, Inc. is a private, educational foundation established to encourage the study of the ideal of a society of free and responsible individuals. The Foundation develops, supervises, and finances its own educational activities to foster thought and encourage discourse on enduring issues pertaining to liberty. This is done through the implementation of different programs, including over 165 conferences throughout the United States, Canada, Latin America, and Europe, and the publication of as many as 20 or more books each year. These programs focus on the place individual liberty has in an intellectual heritage evident from ancient times and continuing through our own times. The programs are intended to enrich understanding and appreciation of the complex nature of a society of free and responsible individuals and to contribute to its preservation.

Loislaw (formerly Loislaw.com, formerly Law Office Information Systems). (part of Wolters Kluwer Law & Business.). 105 North 28th Street, Van Buren, AR 72956. (800) 364-2512
www.loislaw.com
Founded by Arkansas attorney Kyle Parker in 1987, Loislaw, now owned by Wolters Kluwer, is one of the leading alternative providers of computer-assisted legal research in the United States. LOIS was the original developer of the CaseBase line of CD-ROM products for the states of Arkansas, Connecticut, Georgia, Kansas, Louisiana, Massachusetts, Mississippi, North Carolina, and Rhode Island. In 1993, it sold all but the Louisiana product to the Thomson Corporation which assigned them to the Lawyers Cooperative Publishing Company. Following the expiration of covenants not to compete, LOIS began producing new CD-ROM products for many of the same states using the PITA search engine. In February, 2001, LOIS, now operating as Loislaw, was marketing primary law for all state and federal jurisdictions, as well as decisions of the U.S. Supreme Court from 1898 to date, the **United States Code**, the **Code of Federal Regulations**, and the **Federal Register**. While Loislaw is still marketing CD-ROMs, its product development, pricing, and marketing efforts have shifted dramatically to the web-based product. Loislaw provides free jurisdictional CD-ROM products to its Internet subscribers for a shipping and handling charge. A Loislaw subscription also includes access to **LOIS GlobalCite**, a citation research service, and **LOIS LawWatch**, a service which provides subscribers with notification of any new law or article that pertains to their designated areas of interest. LOIS was the first company to offer complete libraries of state and federal law on the Internet. In 1996, LOIS unveiled its Internet site (http://www.Loislaw.com) which, as of May 1, 2007, contained primary law for all 50 states, all 13 federal circuits, and the U.S. Supreme Court (see Appendix I). Loislaw's National Collection is now priced at $1,512 annually per password which can be shared by all attorneys in a firm. For a more complete list of prices, see Chapter 25, or visit the Loislaw Web site at: **www.loislaw.com**

On December 20, 2000, Wolters Kluwer nv and Loislaw.com, Inc. entered into a definitive agreement for the sale of Loislaw.com (Nasdaq: LOIS) to Wolters Kluwer nv for approximately net $95 million, or $4.3545 per share. Wolters Kluwer nv commenced with a tender offer for all outstanding shares of Loislaw.com, and that holders of approximately 67 percent of the shares, including Founder and CEO Kyle D. Parker, agreed to tender their shares. Following the completion of the sale, Loislaw became a unit of Aspen Publishers, Gaithersburg, Md., a provider of legal, business and health care information and a Wolters Kluwer North America company. While Loislaw remains a viable alterative provider of computer-assisted legal research, it has experienced increased competition from a number of other alterative CALR providers, including VersusLaw, Fastcase, Casemaker, as well as the small law office pricing plans of LexisNexis and Westlaw.

Little, Brown and Company (see **Aspen Publishing).**

LRP Publications. 747 Dresher Road (Dept. 425), Horsham, PA 19044-0980. (800) 341-7874, Ext. 245. **www.shoplrp.com**
A publisher of legal and law-related looseleaf services in the fields of arbitration, bankruptcy, disability law, education, and jury verdicts in print, CD-ROM and online formats. Founded in 1977 by Kenneth Kahn, a practicing employment law attorney, LRP (then known as Labor Relations Press) first published case reporters for the legal profession. As the company grew, it became known as LRP Publications. LRP publishes both Human Resource Executive® magazine and Risk and Insurance® magazine and more than 120 newsletters in the fields of human resources, workers compensation, education administration, law and higher education. Major web sites include Educationdaily.com, Workindex.com, cyberFeds.com, Specialedconnection.com, and HREOnline.com. In January, 2011, LRP sold its Public Employment Group and Bankruptcy/Banking Products Group to Thomson Reuters.

Mealey Publications, Inc. (see **LexisNexis**).
http://www.lexisnexis.com/mealeys/news.aspx
Mealey Publications, Inc. was founded in 1984 by Mike Mealey, a journalist whose career had included a broad range of news gathering and writing, covering everything from the legal scene to international business to the War in Vietnam. Mealey started the company with a report on asbestos at a time when that litigation was changing the face of American law. He quickly followed with a report on Iranian assets litigation in the wake of violent upheavals in that country. Mealey's third publication was devoted to environmental and toxic tort insurance coverage disputes, perhaps Mealey's best known product--Mealey's Litigation Report--Insurance. Today, with over 20 titles in the areas of toxic torts, insurance, drugs, and medical devices, intellectual property, health care and international arbitration, Mealey Publications has earned an excellent reputation for balanced reporting on fast-changing areas of the law--areas that challenge established legal precedent and present potentially enormous liabilities to companies and insurers. Mealey Publications was acquired by LexisNexis on August 3, 2000 which now offers the full line of Mealey publications on LexisNexis. .

The Michie Company (see **also LexisNexis**).
Founded in 1897, the Michie (pronounced "MICKEY" as in THE MOUSE) Company was managed by family members until 1969 when the president died and was succeeded by the first general manager who was not a member of the family. It concentrated in the publication of state and local materials, including municipal ordinances for cities in a number of states. In 1971, the company was purchased by ITT Corporation which also acquired the Bobbs-Merrill Company of Indianapolis, Indiana. ITT subsequently transferred the entire legal publishing side of the business to the Michie Company in Charlottesville. Bobbs-Merrill was significant for its publication of the **Federal Code Annotated** which it later sold to Lawyers Cooperative Publishing and under whose ownership it became the **United States Code Service**. The acquisition of Bobbs-Merrill, which had been founded in 1855, thus moved the Michie Company's date or origin back another 42 years. Michie was later acquired by the Macmillan Company, and, in 1988, by Mead Data Central, the parent company of LEXIS. During this period, Michie also acquired the Allen Smith Company and Kluwer Publishing.

During the first half of the 20th century, the Michie Company employees in charge of codifying state statutes were attorneys on the state payroll or codifiers for hire. Over time, however, the company and its editors began to acquire greater expertise in the codification of state statutes, employing a standard format still in use. The company worked to win contracts from other states to perform complete recodifications of existing statutory law. By focusing on this specialty niche, the Michie Company was able to restrain costs, condense production schedules, and beat the competition. At present, Michie produces state statutory codes for approximately 25 states and the District of Columbia. Its catalog also includes more than 400 subject specific and state specific treatises and practice books, including more than 50 law school textbooks. Michie's purchase by Mead gave it access to the vast LEXIS data base, thus providing it with the basis for assembling state specific CD-ROM products in a large number of states. Michie's titles are tend to be somewhat below industry-wide averages after some price escalation in recent years. On average, treatises are supplemented annually, although some may go several years between supplements.

When Thomson Legal Publishing and West Publishing were forced to divest a number of titles under the terms of the Department of Justice's consent decree, Reed Elsevier was the successful bidder. These print and accompanying CD-ROM titles were later absorbed, along with the Michie products, into the new LexisNexis Matthew Bender product line. The Michie name now exists only as a brand within that product line.

NILS Publishing Co. (see **Wolters Kluwer Financial Services**).
130 Turner Street, Waltham, MA 02453. (800) 481-1522.
https://insurance.wolterskluwerfs.com/default.asp
Originally a publisher of the National Insurance Law Service, NILS has expanded its offerings to include the **INSource Healthcare** and **INSource Insurance** CD-ROM products containing laws and regulations of all fifty states, and the **Insurance Periodicals Index on CD-ROM**. All use the InnerView search engine. NILS Publishing Company was acquired by CCH, Inc. in 1997 and is now part of its Business and Finance Group. In April, 2003, Uniform Information Services, Inc. and NILS Publishing were combined under the name CCH INSURANCE SERVICES; later transferred to its sister company Wolters Kluwer Financial Services. .

Oceana Publications, Inc. (see **Oxford University Press**).
198 Madison Avenue, New York, NY 10016. (800) 334-4249.
www.oceanalaw.com
Founded by Philip Cohen in 1948, Oceana was a leading publisher of international legal texts and reference works. Drawing its authors from among the leading experts in their respective fields, Oceana has been a pioneer in the development of substantive legal texts in such fields as international trade and commercial law, banking, investment and financial law, arbitration and dispute resolution, environmental law, and intellectual property. Oceana has also developed a number of leading comparative law titles in such areas as international securities regulation, customs law and administration, European Union law, money laundering, and the North American Free Trade Agreements. Its **Constitutions of the Countries of the World** has, for more than 25 years, been the leading source for international constitutional research. It publishes the **TIARA CD-ROM: Treaties and International Agreements Researchers Archive**, a collection of the full text of more than 10,000 U.S. treaties and other international agreements from 1783 to the present. It also publishes a number of important works on U.S. law, including **Brief Writing and Oral Argument** by Edward D. Re, **The Bramble Bush** by Karl Llewellyn, and DuBoff's **Deskbook of Art Law**. The company was acquired by Oxford University Press in 2005 and has now been absorbed into the Oxford University Press product line..

Oryx (see **Greenwood Publishing Group**).

Oxford University Press, 198 Madison Avenue, New York, NY 10016-4314 (866) 445-8685; FAX: (919) 677-1303.
www.oup.com/us/
Oxford University Press is the world's largest university press, with publishing centers in the United Kingdom and the United States. Its history may be traced to 1478, when the first book was printed in Oxford. In 1578, the University obtained a

decree granting it the privilege of printing books. This privilege was enhanced in 1633 when Archbishop Laud obtained the Great Charter from King Charles I, granting permission for the University to print "all manner of books." University minutes dating back to 1688 record the deliberations of the delegates, and document the development of the OUP as it exists today. OUP's international expansion began in 1896 when it opened an office in the new York City. While this office was opened initially to sell bibles published in Oxford, by the 1920s it began to produce books on its own. The first nonfiction work published by OUP USA, **The Life of Sir William Osler**, won the Pulitzer Prize in 1926. Since that time, its books have received six more Pulitzers, several National Book Awards, and over a Bancroft Prizes in American history.

OUP USA is Oxford University Press's second major publishing center, after Oxford (UK). It publishes works that further Oxford University's objective of excellence in research, scholarship, and education. OUP USA, which is by far the largest American university press, publishes at a variety of levels, for a wide range of audiences in almost every academic discipline. The main criteria in evaluating new titles are quality and contribution to the furtherance of scholarship and education. OUP USA produces approximately 500 titles each year, of which 250 are scholarly research monographs, and imports close to 800 such works from its UK and branch offices. OUP USA has 3,300 scholarly books in print and stocks another 8,700 imports from other OUP offices around the world. All publications are first vetted by OUP's Delegates, who are leading scholars at Oxford University and other leading U.S. institutions. OUP USA employs nearly 500 people in the U.S., evenly divided between its offices in New York City and North Carolina's Research Triangle. OUP's Academic Law catalog contains an extensive collection of monographs on American, English, European, and comparative law, as well as reference books, law journals, and the Oxford Companion Series. Its online products include the Oxford Reports on International Law, the Max Planck Encyclopedia of Public International Law, Oxford Scholarship Online, Investment Claims, and Constitutions of the World Online. In 2005, it acquired Oceana Publications of Dobbs Ferry, New York, together with its extensive line of works on foreign and international law.

Pike & Fischer, Inc. (see **Bloomberg BNA**). 1010 Wayne Avenue, Suite 1400, Silver Spring, MD 20910-5600. (800) 255-8131; FAX: (301) 562-1530. **http://www.pf.com/**
Founded in 1939, Pike & Fischer is the world's leading private publisher of FCC Rules materials and a leading source for information in the field of communication law and regulation, including telecommunications law and regulation. In 1948, it launched its looseleaf subscription service entitled **Radio Regulation**, which was renamed **Communications Regulation** in 1995. It also publishes reference materials in such areas as criminal law, food safety, fertilizers and pesticides, alternative dispute resolution, administrative law, and shipping regulation. The Pike & Fischer titles have now been integrated into the Bloomberg BNA product line.

Practicing Law Institute (PLI). 810 Seventh Avenue, New York, NY 10019-5818 (800) 260-4754. **www.pli.edu**
The Practicing Law Institute was established in 1933 to provide young lawyers with continuing legal education. It now conducts more than 200 seminars annually in cities across the United States and sells Course Handbooks which closely reflect the content of these seminars. In 1945, PLI 's reference book division began releasing non-seminar materials in hardcover. PLI's catalog of hardcover textbooks and guides currently numbers more than 70 supplemented titles and is growing at the rate of 14-16 titles per year. As a non-profit corporation, PLI can afford to publish specialized legal books serving the bar. The publishing division, however, is expected to be self-sustaining from revenues generated by titles which have a broad appeal in the legal community. It also publishes a number of compression-bound titles with supplementation, audio cassettes, and video cassettes. An annual **Index Course Handbooks** provides researchers with access to all PLI titles published during the year by author, title and subject. PLI also offers standing orders to all titles in specific subject or practice areas during the course of the year for one fixed price. The subject matter covered by PLI's titles includes intellectual property, business, corporate and securities, litigation, banking, international law, immigration law, taxation, real estate, estate planning, health care, bankruptcy, insurance, technology, and employment law. PLI recently acquired the CLE Group, Inc., a leader in the development of CD-ROM-based multimedia for the legal market. The complete PLI product line is available on Bloomberg Law, and some PLI treatises are also available on Westlaw.

Public Utilities Reports, Inc. 8229 Boone Blvd., Ste. 401, Vienna, VA 22182 (800) 368-5001. **www.pur.com**
Since 1915, Public Utilities Reports, Inc. has published materials covering the regulated public utility industries in the United States. **Public Utilities Reports**, now in its 4th series, is a national legal case reporter covering decisions from all state public utility commissions. An annual subscription includes both biweekly paperback advance sheets and permanent bound volumes. Decisions are reported in full text, with headnotes and indices prepared by the PUR editorial staff. The decisions reported in **PUR 4th**--plus thousands of additional decisions not included in print publications--are available on **PURbase** CD-ROM (issued quarterly) and online through WESTLAW and LEXIS/NEXIS. It also publishes digests of PUR decisions and **Public Utilities Fortnightly**, the premier management magazine for the utility industry. Its catalog features several dozen titles on regulated utilities.

Reed Elsevier plc. Group Offices: 125 Park Avenue, 23rd Floor, New York, NY 10017, Tel: (212) 309-5498; 1-3 Strand, London WC2N 5JR, UK; Tel.: 44 20 7930 7077; Radarweg 29, 1043 NX, Amsterdam, The Netherlands, Tel.: 31 20 485 2222.
www.reed-elsevier.com
One of the world's largest publishing companies, Reed Elsevier plc is an international conglomerate which combines Reed International, based in the United Kingdom, with Elsevier, based in the Netherlands. Its United States holdings include Reed Reference Publishing, Cahners Publishing, LEXIS Law Publishing, and LEXIS-NEXIS. LEXIS-NEXIS and Michie were acquired in 1994 for the sum of $1.5 billion. Founded in Rotterdam in 1880 by five publishers and booksellers, Elsevier adopted the name of the famous 16th century Dutch printing company. The Reed Company was founded in 1894 by Albert E. Reed, an English newsprint manufacturer who later expanded into such business ventures as publishing, packaging, and paint. By the 1980's. however, the company had concentrated its focus on the publishing side of the business. Following an attempted

takeover by Robert Maxwell in 1988, Elsevier effected a merger with Reed in 1993. Total sales for the combined Reed Elsevier companies exceeded $4.2 billion in 1994. Of that figure, LEXIS-NEXIS accounted for approximately $700 million.

When Reed Elsevier acquired Mead Data Central from the Mead Corporation in 1994, it changed its name to that of its primary online service, LEXIS-NEXIS. The Michie Company, owned by Mead since 1988, was also acquired as a part of this purchase. In December, 1994, Reed merged the Michie Company with Butterworth Legal Publishers. Butterworth had begun operations in 1980 as a apart of Reed Elsevier's Legal Division, and had already acquired a number of smaller regional legal publishers, including Equity of New Hampshire and the legal titles published by Tower of Maine. One consequence of this merger has been the elimination of many of the more marginal titles in the Michie catalog, many of which were contributed by the regional publishers. Reed also owns the following domestic publishers of legal or law-related information that operate under the umbrella of Reed Reference Publishing: R.R. Bowker, Bowker-Saur, Congressional Information Service (CIS), Marquis Who's Who, and Martindale-Hubbell.

In 1996, Reed Elsevier and Times Mirror jointly acquired the citator division of Shepard's (the treatise side having already been sold to Thomson in 1995). In 1997, following the merger of the Thomson Corporation and West Publishing, Reed Elsevier was the successful bidder on the package of fifty-one divested titles which the Department of Justice required as a part of its consent decree. In 1998, Reed Elsevier acquired Matthew Bender for the sum of $1.6 billion and, with it, the remaining 50% piece of Shepard's. These acquisitions place Reed Elsevier on par with the Thomson Corporation in terms of annual North American sales of legal information, which are estimated to be in the $1.3 - $1.5 billion range for both companies. The synergies unleased by the merging of LEXIS, Shepard's, and Matthew Bender have resulted in a significantly enhanced LEXIS-NEXIS and Shepard's services, now available on the Internet at: lexis.com. These services, including Search Advisor, Core Terms, Case Summaries, and a greatly enhanced online Shepard's.

Reed Elsevier now has over 32,000 employees and realized $9.270 billion in revenues in 2012, up from $9.098 billion in 2011, and reflecting an operating profit margin of 28.0%, up from 27.1% in 2011. Reed Elsevier now operates through five major divisions:

- Elsevier (the science and medical publishing division)
- LexisNexis Risk Solutions
- LexisNexis Legal & Professional
- Reed Exhibitions
- Reed Business Information (the business division)

Combined revenues in from LexisNexis Risk Solutions and LexisNexis Legal & Professional were $3.844 billion in 2012, down from $3.853 billion in 2011, These results generally reflect a stabilization of the legal industry activity.

Revenues from LexisNexis Risk Solutions were 94% from electronic sales and 6% from print; revenues in from LexisNexis Legal & Professional were 96% from electronic sales and 4% from print. Results continue to show strong demand for electronic solutions and weak print sales.

Research Institute of America (RIA) (see **Thomson Reuters RIA).** 90 Fifth Avenue, New York, NY 10011 800-950-1216
http://ria.thomsonreuters.com/
Founded in 1935 by Carl Hovgard, Research Institute of America has concentrated its attention upon those professional fields impacted by large bodies of law and regulation, particularly the field of taxation. For many years a subsidiary of Lawyers Cooperative, RIA was purchased by the Thomson Corporation in 1989 along with Lawyers Cooperative and Bancroft-Whitney for the sum of $810 million. Research Institute of American has been integrated into the RIA Group, a professional publishing organization that includes other Thomson companies, including Warren, Gorham & Lamont, Auerbach, Practitioners Publishing Company, A.S. Pratt and SCS/Compute. Unlike some of its competitors, RIA has, from its inception, pursued a publishing philosophy which aims to translate varied primary sources into a form which is understandable to the practitioner. Its product line consists of looseleaf services, CD-ROM products, Online services, bound books, and newsletters and bulletins in the fields of taxation, estate planning, pensions and benefits. If you want to know what happened to most of those Prentice-Hall services to which you may have subscribed, you will find them in the RIA catalog. When the Thomson Corporation bought Maxwell Macmillan in 1990, little more than a year after Maxwell Macmillan had purchased Prentice Hall and changed its name, it merged its product line with those of Research Institute of America and Warren, Gorham & Lamont. Some of the old Prentice Hall titles are still recognizable under the new ownership--for example, the **Tax Court Reported and Memorandum Decisions** and the **American Federal Tax Reports.** Others, like Prentice Hall's old **Federal Tax Service** have been totally overhauled into the **United States Tax Reporter.**

Research Institute of America has taken bold steps to compete effectively in the tax and legal marketplace. Many of its looseleaf services have been overhauled and priced at levels designed to earn a greater market share from the competition. It has also moved boldly into the field of electronic delivery with its On Point System, a comprehensive electronic tax research and compliance system that the customer builds himself from a variety of individual components and packages on CD-ROM and, more significantly, the Internet. Today, RIA operates as a part of Thomson Reuters Tax and Accounting business unit.

Rothman, Fred B., & Co. (see **Hein, William S.).**

Shepard's (see LexisNexis).
http://law.lexisnexis.com/shepards
In 1873, a Chicago lawbook salesman by the name of Frank Shepard devised a method of informing Illinois lawyers of every instance in which Illinois Supreme Court cases were cited by subsequent Illinois cases. His innovation, which patterned the lawyers' habit of writing subsequent citations in the margins of their case reporters, took the form of gummed labels which could be pasted in the margins of the Illinois decisions. As time passed, these gummed labels took the form of the now familiar maroon volumes and advance sheets. Shepard's citators have become the most respected and widely used tools for verifying the currency of various forms of legal authority. The company moved its headquarters to Colorado Springs in

1947. In 1966, Shepard's was acquired by McGraw-Hill under whose ownership it developed, by 1990, a line of more than 300 subject specialty legal treatises At the same time, its list of citators had grown to more than 100. In December, 1995, Shepard's/ McGraw-Hill sold its treatise line to Thomson Legal Publishing as part of a plan to re-focus attention upon its core citator business. Finally, in 1996, Shepard's/McGraw-Hill sold its citator division jointly to Matthew Bender and Reed Elsevier which began integrating the Shepard's product line into their individual product lines. The entire Shepard's citator line will brought under the control of Reed Elsevier once the Justice Department's Antitrust Division approves Reed's purchase of both Matthew Bender and Bender's 50% share of Shepard's. Included among Shepard's citator titles are those for every state, all units of the National Reporter System, all federal courts, the **United States Code**, the **Code of Federal Regulations**, federal administrative agencies, as well as a number of subject-specific citators.

Shepard's Citations is available in print and online through LexisNexis. A variety of additional updating tools provide the legal researcher with the means to update citations found in the standard Shepard's sources, including **Shepard's Daily Update**, **Shepard's preview** on WESTLAW, and **Shepard's Overnight Citations** on LEXIS. More recently, Shepard's introduced CaseFinder, a productivity tool that uses the citations relationship between cases and statutes to quickly locate on-point precedent. One of the marketing innovations introduced by Matthew Bender is all-inclusive pricing for Shepard's print citators. Subscribers selecting this pricing option receive all print advance sheets, bound supplements, and recompilations under a fixed annual cost. This program is similar in concept to the annual subscription pricing which Matthew Bender introduced with its treatise products in 1992. In addition to the all-inclusive pricing, Shepard's offers High Volume pricing for print products to federal and state government accounts, and subscribers with three or more citator subscriptions (Case Names Citators excluded). Special combination pricing also exists for those who maintain both print and CD-ROM subscriptions.

Smith, M. Lee, Publishers. P.O. Box 5094, Brentwood, TN 37024-5094. (800) 274-6774.
www.mleesmith.com
Started in 1975 with the publication of the still-successful **Tennessee Journal**, M. Lee Smith Publishers today offers more than 125 nationally-acclaimed newsletters, videos, software, books, and directories to attorneys, human resources professionals, and other business executives. Fifty state-specific law letters and compliance updates are edited by many of the nation's largest and most prestigious law firms. Videos, software, and other products for human resources professionals and business people are created in partnership with some of America's leading experts. M. Lee Smith publishes state specific newsletters in the fields of employment, health, environmental and workers' compensation law.

Strafford Publications, Inc. 590 Dutch Valley Road, NE, Postal Drawer 13729, Atlanta, GA 30324-0729.
Customer service: (800) 926-7926; (404) 881-1141; FAX: (401) 881-0074. **www.straffordpub.com/**
Founded in the early 1980's by president Richard M. Ossoff, Strafford Publications remains independent in the midst of numerous mergers and acquisitions in the world of legal publishing. The company's Legal Publications Group specializes in case digest services and litigation reporters in nine different practice areas. Among its current titles are: **Health Law Week**, **Hospital Litigation Reporter**, **Health Insurance Litigation Reporter**, **Digest of Environmental Law**, **National Financing Law Digest**, **National Property Law Digests**, **Municipal Litigation Reporter**, **Premises Liability Report**, and **Private Security Case Law Reporter**, and a number of related books. Although there is some variation in format among Strafford's specialized services, each provides concise summaries of selected appellate level cases drawn from comprehensive reviews of decisions from courts across the United States.

Tax Analysts. 400 S. Maple Avenue, Suite 400, Falls Church, VA Arlington, VA22046. (800) 955-2444.
www.tax.org
Tax Analysts is a nonprofit publisher that provides the latest and most in-depth tax information worldwide. By working for the transparency of tax rules, fostering increased dialogue between taxing authorities and taxpayers, and providing forums for education and debate, Tax Analysts encourages the creation of tax systems that are fairer, simpler, and more economically efficient. Tax Analysts publishes a variety of tax magazines, books, databases, CDs, DVDs, online products, and other information resources for tax professionals, including the **IRS Exempt Organization Master List on CD-ROM**, **IRS Letter Rulings and Technical Advice Memorandums 1980-1995**, the **Internal Revenue Manual Disc**, the **Basic Federal Research Library**, **Complete Federal Research Library**, **One Disc**, **One Disc Premium**, **Financial Reporting Watch**, **State Tax OneDisc**, **State Research Library**, State Tax Notes, **State Tax Today**, and **Worldwide Tax Treaties Disc**, and more, all using the Folio search engine. In 2006 Tax Analysts moved to a new headquarters building in Falls Church, Va.

Tax Management, Inc. (see **Bloomberg BNA**).
1231 25th Street NW, Washington, DC 20037. (800) 372-1033.
www.bna.com/
This subsidiary of BNA has issued the famous Tax Management Portfolio series on CD-ROM, including **Tax Management Tax Practice Series on CD**, **Tax Management Multistate Tax Portfolios Series on CD**, and **Tax Management Portfolios Plus**. All use the Folio search engine. On March 22, 1907, BNA and Thomson Tax and Accounting concluded an agreement to make BNA tax products available on Thomson's Checkpoint platform.

Thomson Reuters. Three Times Square. New York, NY 10036.
www.thomsonreuters.com
If the West Publishing Company was the major presence in the world of legal publishing in the United for the 100-year period from 1876 to 1976, Thomson Reuters has clearly established itself as the dominant force since that time.

On April 17, 2008, Thomson Corporation announced that it had completed its acquisition of Reuters Group PLC, forming Thomson Reuters, the world's leading source of information for businesses and professionals in the financial, legal, tax and accounting, scientific, healthcare, and media markets. Thomson Reuters has more than 50,000 employees with operations in 93 countries on six continents and 2007 pro forma revenues of approximately $12.4 billion. Of these revenues, more than 80%

was derived from electronic products, software and services; and more than 80% was derived from subscription-based products and services.

Yet the company which has come to dominate legal publishing in the United States had much humbler origins in the remote reaches of Canada's Ontario province. The story begins with Roy Thomson a bookkeeper, cordage company manager, and farm and auto parts distributor who, in 1930, accepted a franchise arrangement to sell radios in North Bay, Ontario, a town which, at the start of the Depression, suffered from poor radio reception and an inadequate broadcast transmitter. Nevertheless, Thomson was sufficiently impressed with the future of radio that he borrowed the money to start his own radio station in 1932, largely as a tool for enhancing radio sales. By 1934, Thomson had acquired additional radio stations in Kirkland Lake and Timmons, Ontario and purchased the **Timmons Press.** Taking on a partner in 1940, Thomson devoted his attentions to the newspaper business while assigning the management of the radio stations to Jack Kent Cooke. By 1944, their company owned five newspapers and eight radio stations, all of them in Ontario.

In 1949, Thomson purchased his first newspaper outside of Ontario and dissolved his partnership with Cooke. He acquired several insurance agencies in 1951 and consolidated them into the Scottish & York Group. In the early 1950's, he acquired a number of newspapers, including **The Independent** of St. Petersburg, FL and the **Scotsman**, Scotland's leading newspaper. With the purchase of the **Scotsman**, Roy Thomson moved to Scotland, delegating responsibility for his North American holdings to his son Kenneth who was then 30 years old. When commercial television broadcasting debuted in the United Kingdom in 1957, Thomson's Scottish Television Ltd. (STV) became a major financial success. The success of his Scottish newspaper and television operations provided Roy Thomson with the capital to acquire **The Sunday Times**, London's leading Sunday newspaper, and to create the International Thomson Organisation. In 1961, the company acquired the Illustrated London News Company and created Thomson Information/Publishing as a separate division to manage what has become the most profitable of its operations. After accepting British citizenship in1964, Roy Thomson, the humble radio salesman from North Bay, Ontario accepted a seat in the House of Lords as Lord Thomson of Fleet. Between1961 and 1976, Thomson's holdings expanded in the areas of publishing, travel, and oil. At the time of his death in 1976, the bulk of Thomson's profits were being garnered from the oil business.

Following his father's death, Kenneth Thomson took control of the family's expanding operations. After selling off Scottish Television for a $190 million profit, the International Thomson Organisation moved its headquarters back to Ontario and became involved in the United States oil industry. It also formed International Thomson Organisation Ltd. (ITOL) which consisted of two primary operating divisions: International Thomson Holdings Inc. and Thomson British Holdings Ltd. In 1979, the International Thomson Holdings division acquired a number of North American publishers, including Wadsworth, Inc., Van Nostrand Reinhold, Linguistics International, Thomas Nelson International, and Callaghan & Company, the first of the legal publishing acquisitions. In 1980, two additional legal publishers were acquired: Clark Boardman and Warren, Gorham & Lamont.

In 1983, the International Thomson Organisation PLC set in motion a strategy to acquire subscription-based, rather than advertising-based, publications. Its philosophy was, and is, premised on the realization that such publications, particularly those aimed at a professional market, are far more resistant to the vagaries of the economy than those aimed at the mass market. This philosophy guided Thomson through the acquisition of Associated Book Publishers, for which it paid $323 million in 1988. Included in the ABP holdings were such legal publishers as Carswell of Canada, Sweet & Maxwell of the U.K., and the Law Book Company in Australia. At the time of this acquisition, the **Financial Times of London** opined that Thomson had maintained its immaculate record of grossly overpaying for everything it wants. According to Thomson President and CEO Michael Brown, the sum is now considered a bargain price.

In 1989, Thomson paid $810 million to acquire the Lawyers Cooperative Publishing Company, one of the United States' leading legal publishers and the chief rival to the venerable West Publishing Company. Included in that acquisition were LCP subsidiaries Bancroft-Whitney and Research Institute of America, a major publisher of looseleaf reference materials in such areas as tax and employment law. Additional acquisitions have included Maxwell Macmillan, formerly Prentice-Hall (1991), Counterpoint Publishing (1994), Information Access (1994), Barclays (1995), and the Shepard's/McGraw-Hill treatises (1995). Despite these growing holdings in legal publishing, Thomson still lacked a significant ingredient to future success: a major on-line legal database with which to further develop computer-based products. Having lost out to Reed Elsevier in its attempt to acquire Lexis-Nexis in 1994, the Thomson Organisation was determined not to let a similar opportunity slip away.

That opportunity came in August, 1995 when the West Publishing Company, that crown jewel of the industry, announced to a startled legal world that it was putting itself on the auction block. With its massive WESTLAW database and major presence in the publication of both primary law and secondary analytical materials, West was exactly what the Thomson Organisation needed to advance its corporate objectives. Then, on February 28, 1996, Thomson announced its plan to purchase West for the sum of $3.425 billion, pending antitrust clearance by the Department of Justice. Industry analysts contended at the time that time that Thomson paid an excessive price for West, probably $1 billion more than its true worth based on historic sales. The purchase price of $3.425 billion was four times historic sales of $800 million and 16 times its operating profits of slightly more than $215 million. For a business increasing revenues at only 10% per year, such multiples were considered rather steep. Analysts pointed out at the time that Reed paid a lower multiple for LEXIS-NEXIS, but that it was able to cut its effective purchase price by $300 million by exploiting tax advantages not available to Thomson. They suggested that while Reed was able to increase LEXIS-NEXIS's profit margins from 11 to 16%, Thomson may be unable to improve significantly upon West's healthy 25% profit margins. Michael Brown had heard similar comments before when Thomson purchased Associated Book Publishers. In retrospect, those concerns were unfounded. Thomson effectively managed its substantial subscriber base and control of a lion's share of leading legal information products to a record 31% profit margin in its Legal & regulatory Division in 2008.

Despite some initial indications that it was going to force some major concessions from the merging parties, the Department of Justice, on June 19, ultimately accepted a watered-down consent decree which provided almost no relief to consumers troubled by the size and market power of this legal publishing behemoth. Law librarians, in particular, were troubled by the price escalation on previously acquired Thomson publications which had virtually killed the standing order for many of its secondary materials. Protests from law librarians, large and small legal publishers, and others were summarily dismissed by attorneys at the Department of Justice's Antitrust Division who solidified their position as the pusillanimous apologists for pro-monopoly antitrust policy. The person most responsible for this charade is undoubtedly Anne Bingaman who, as President Clinton's head of the Antitrust Division at the Department of Justice, set the tone for the Division's feeble enforcement of the antitrust laws. Yet, on June 26, 1996, she had the effrontery to issue what can only be characterized as one of the most absurd and self-serving of press releases. "This settlement is a victory for all of us," she said. "We are all consumers of legal advice from time to time and as citizens we rely on access to information about our nation's laws." A more apt description of the agreement was made by HyperLaw's President Alan Sugarman who said "The Department of Justice and the State Attorneys General have served up a glass that is 90% empty, and the 10% in the glass is watered down."

The consent decree specified that Thomson-West divest itself of 51 print titles and Auto-Cite, Lawyers Cooperative's electronic verification service. Included among the print titles are **United States Reports, Lawyers' Edition**, **United States Supreme Court Digest**, **Lawyers' Edition**, **United States Code Service**, **Corbin on Contracts**, **Appleman's Insurance Law and Practice**, **Deering's Annotated California Code, Illinois Jurisprudence**, the **Annotated Laws of Massachusetts**, **Callaghan's Michigan Digest**, **Michigan Statutes Annotated**, and the **New York Consolidated Laws Service**. Only six national treatises were on the list, the greatest indication that the consent decree was a hollow instrument. These six titles, in the subject areas of bankruptcy, contracts, criminal law, federal practice, and insurance law, represented only 1.1% of the major treatises selected for inclusion in this book. In each of these five subject areas, the West-Thomson control of the market ranged between 63% and 73%. Strangely, the Justice Department provided no relief in at least thirteen additional subject areas with equal or greater market concentration, including: administrative law (66.66%); admiralty and maritime law (85.71%), arts, entertainment & sports law (71.42%); civil rights (66.66%); constitutional law (83.33%); education law (66.66%); municipal corporations (80%); products liability (66.66%); social security (66.66%); taxation (63.63%); tort law (63.63%); and trusts and estates (66.66%). Prior to the merger, Thomson's overall control of the treatise market amounted to 187, or 35.08%, of the 533 treatises selected for inclusion in the first edition of this book. The purchase of West added another 96 titles, or 18.01% of the market, bringing the total to 283 titles, or 53.09%.

The Antitrust Division's second major error was in permitting Thomson-West to gain control of both systems of legal research: West's key number system, and Lawyers Cooperative's Total Client-Service Library system. The West-Thomson attorneys were able to persuade the ill-prepared Justice Department lawyers that comparing the two systems of legal information was like comparing apples and oranges. In doing so, they not only distorted the fact that both are valid and useful methods of conducting legal research, but succeeded in distancing themselves from years of Lawyers Cooperative's marketing and promotional literature which described the TCSL system as "a comprehensive legal research system covering everything from on point cases in both state and federal jurisdictions, to principles of law, statutes, procedure, model forms, trial techniques... in short, everything you need to handle almost any legal matter."

What can explain the Antitrust Division's inept performance in fashioning such a feeble consent decree? As John Morris explains in his excellent overview of the entire matter in the September, 1996 issue of the **American Lawyer** (see "How West Was Won"), the stalemate was broken three days after the Thomson-West lawyers offered to openly license West's star pagination, the page breaks in the West case reporters, to other publishers (albeit at hefty rates certain to deter all but the largest publishers). At that point, the government's lawyers, naively believing they had forced a major concession from the merging parties, were ready to sign on the dotted line. Only later, after public criticism erupted, did they realize that they had purchased "a pig in a poke." With the very legitimacy of West's claim to copyright in star pagination under heavy fire in the aftermath of the U.S. Supreme Court's Feist decision, which dismissed the "sweat of the brow" theory of copyright protection, the Justice Department's lawyers were thoroughly outmaneuvered. West's claims to copyright in its page breaks was simultaneously being challenged in the U.S. District Court for the Southern District of New York in an action brought, and ultimately won by Matthew Bender and HyperLaw, Inc.

Once the consent decree was fashioned, the merger was allowed to proceed. The only step remaining was for the final imprimatur of the U.S. District Court for the District of Columbia. Judge Paul Friedman, who was assigned to hear the case after the withdrawal of Judge Robert Richey (who, it was pointed out, was a Thomson author),held several hearings prior to issuing a 51-page opinion on December 26,1996. While Judge Friedman was severely constrained in his role by the earlier Microsoft decision which criticized another District court judge for exceeding his authority in rejecting a Justice Department consent decree, he indicated that "Like Judge Martin [Southern District of New York], this court has serious doubts about the validity of the Eighth Circuit's 1986 opinion in Mead Data in view of the subsequent decision of the Supreme Court in Feist...and it finds unpersuasive the reasoning in Oasis Publishing." He also indicated that "the court is concerned that including the star pagination license provision in the Final Judgment might be construed as an endorsement of West's dubious copyright claim." He further noted the "the weakness of West's claim and the limited market power of many of those who must pay the license fee, particularly now that the most economically powerful critic of West's position, Thomson, has lost its incentive to contest the claim and joins West in advancing it."

In addressing Judge Friedman's concerns on the pagination issue, Thomson-West proposed free "star pagination" licenses for small publishers until the legal issue is settled, or until the year 2001. The major publishers, however, defined as those with annual sales of over $25 million, would get no price break on the pagination licenses. Those publishers were identified as LEXIS, Commerce Clearing House, Matthew Bender, and the Bureau of National Affairs. As of this writing, it appears that Judge Friedman's ruling is certain to be appealed by Hyperlaw, Inc. which sought amicus status and which has fought for years for public disclosure of the documents in West's 1988 settlement pact with LEXIS. In its February 13 memo urging Judge Friedman not to view the Microsoft decision as a straightjacket, Hyperlaw argued that

Microsoft does not anticipate a three-giant controlled industry becoming a two-giant industry where, as in the case here, 100 percent of the entire online market would be shared by those contracting two entities-- and where the Justice Department simply refuses to release any of the relevant information."

Hyperlaw further argued that:

Due in part to their "copyright cartel," Westlaw and Lexis are the only real competitors in the online legal research market, and they have a deal. Together they control almost 100% of that market," and charge four times what other proprietary databases do.

Following its purchase of the 52 divested products, Reed-Elsevier, the parent company of LEXIS-NEXIS, was able to acquire 24 additional products, although the list of titles has not yet been made public.

The Thomson Legal & Regulatory market group had combined sales of $7.8 billion in 2002 and an operating profit of approximately $1 billion. Thomson Financial & Professional Publishing division serves the needs of professionals in the fields of law, tax, accounting, intellectual property, regulatory, and human services. Among its more than 4,500 products are 180 online services, 450 CD-ROM titles, 42 software packages, 470 loose-leaf services, 180 newsletters and over 2,700 books and directories. With the acquisition of West Publishing, the division will add nearly 60 million books and pamphlets, 3.5 million hours of WESTLAW usage, and the distribution of over 1 million CD-ROM products. Prior to the acquisition of West, the division had annual sales in 1995 of $1,285 billion and an operating profit of $222 million. The West acquisition added annual revenues of approximately $825 million (1995), 54% of which is derived from WESTLAW and related CD-ROM sales. Total annual sales of legal information are estimated to fall into the $1.3 - 1.5 billion range.

On February 17, 1999, the Thomson Corporation placed its legal information service subsidiaries under the Thomson Legal and Regulatory Group. Existing Thomson legal information subsidiaries retained their present names and publishing responsibilities under the new organizational structure. On January 26, 2001, the West Group announced that it has purchased FindLaw, the leading legal information portal on the Internet.

On April 17, 2008, Thomson Corporation announced that it had completed its acquisition of Reuters Group PLC, forming Thomson Reuters, the world's leading source of information for businesses and professionals in the financial, legal, tax and accounting, scientific, healthcare, and media markets. Thomson Reuters has more than 50,000 employees with operations in 93 countries on six continents and 2007 pro forma revenues of approximately $12.4 billion. Of these revenues, more than 80% was derived from electronic products, software and services; and more than 80% was derived from subscription-based products and services.

Tower Publishing. 588 Saco Road, Standish, ME 04084-6239. (800) 969-8693. **www.towerpub.com**
Founded in Concord, NH in 1772, Tower Publishing is the nation's oldest reference directory publisher. In recent years, Tower has evolved from municipal and business directories to the publishing of highly sophisticated and custom-targeted databases and CD-ROMs. Now headquartered in Standish, ME, it publishes or provides local, national and international business information on paper and disc. Tower has also recently expanded into the legal market, with such titles as the **Maine Bar Directory**, **Maine School Law**, **Maine Manual on Professional Responsibility, the Alaska Rules of Court,** and **Wills, Gifts and Trusts** in the Rhode Island Practice Series. Tower publications are pound for pound and page for page among the best values in the field of legal publishing.

U.S. Government Printing Office. (Superintendent of Documents). 732 North Capitol Street, NW, Washington, DC 20401. (202) 512-0000. **www.access.gpo.gov/**
The U.S. Government Printing Office has released a number of its print products on CD-ROM, including the **United States Code**, the **U.S. Government Manual**, the **Monthly Catalog of U.S. Government Publications**, the **EPA Toxic Release Inventory**, and the **National Criminal Justice Document Data Base.** They use a variety of search engines, including I-SEARCH, and Adobe Acrobat.

U.S. Patent & Trademark Office. (Office of Electronic Information Products). Crystal Park 3, Suite 441, Washington, DC 20231. (703) 306-2600.
www.uspto.gov
Nearly a dozen specialized CD-ROM products, covering all manner of patent and trademark publications, research tools, and records of patents and trademarks, are produced by the Office of Electronic Information Products, all using the CD Answer search software from Dataware.

Vandeplas Publishing. 801 International Parkway, 5th Floor, Lake Mary, FL 32746. (407) 562-1947; FAX (407) 562-2001.
www.vandeplaspublishing.com
Founded by Drs. Anton Van de Plas, Vandeplas Publishing has been producing law and law-related books and periodicals since 1990. Mr. Van de Plas studied law in the United States and The Netherlands and earned his law degree at Tilburg University. As a publisher, he developed an innovative way to simplify the publishing process, which is now being applied to the publications by Vandeplas Publishing. Law texts in the English language are transformed into books and available on the market within one month. Publication proposals are approved within two weeks after submission. Every law or law related text is considered for publication. Authors maintain copyright in their work and the books are marketed and sold worldwide. Its catalog includes a

wide variety of excellent legal titles, including Edward J. Bander's **Legal Anecdotes, Wit and Rejoinder** (2007), Alan Watson's **The Shame of American Legal Education** (2006), and **How to Be a Law Professor Guide: From Getting That First Job to Retirement** by Ronald W. Eades (2008).

Versus Law, Inc. 2613 151st Place N.E., Redmond, WA 98052. (888) 377-8752, Ext. 3018
www.versuslaw.com
Founded in 1985 by Joe Acton, VersusLaw was formerly known as Timeline Publishing's Lawyers Legal Research Online. In 1992, VersusLaw began working with the U.S. Supreme Court, federal circuit and state appellate courts to assemble an affordable online database of court decisions. Initially a bulletin board service (BBS), Versus Law moved to the Internet in 1995. In 1996, it changed the name of Lawyers Legal Research into **V.** (pronounced "vee"). Its database includes U.S. Supreme Court opinions back to 1930, circuit court decisions back to 1950, and state court decisions as far back as 1950. The full-text searchable archive of court decisions is updated daily. Among the computer-assisted legal research services currently on the market, VersusLaw brings the best combination of low price and substantive content.

Warren, Gorham & Lamont (See Thomson Reuters RIA).
1 Penn Plaza, New York, NY 10119 (800) 950-1216
http://ria.thomson.com/
Warren, Gorham & Lamont issued its first legal title, **Brady on Bank Checks**, in the 1960's. Its current catalog lists some 125 legal titles in the fields of bankruptcy, corporate law, general practice, criminal law, information/intellectual property, commercial law, banking and commercial law, banking compliance, bank management operations, financial and legal planning, real estate law, real estate development, real estate financial management, and securities law. The company as a whole publishes more than 400 titles, largely in the fields of banking, business, real estate, and accounting. Purchased by the Thomson Corporation in 1980, WG&L is now a division of the RIA Group, which also includes Research Institute of America, Auerbach, Practitioners Publishing Company, and SCS/Compute. Since its purchase by the Thomson organization, the product lines of Warren, Gorham & Lamont's and its sister company Research Institute of America (RIA) have been reassigned, with WG&L concentrating its attention on the fields of taxation, accounting, law, and human resources. Where its subject coverage does overlap with that of RIA, WG&L has assumed continued responsibility for the casebound and compression-bound treatises, while RIA has focused its attention upon the looseleaf services and CD-ROM products. Warren, Gorham & Lamont publishes a number of now classic treatises in tax law and other fields, of which the most significant is Bittker and Eustice's **Federal Income Taxation of Corporations and Shareholders**.

While Warren, Gorham & Lamont publishes specialized materials of high quality, its prices are high for the industry, with single volume treatises priced in the $400 range. More significantly, supplementation costs can exceed the cost of the base volume in the course of a single year. For example, the Bittker and Eustice work cited above costs $580 annually. Many WG&L titles feature 2-4 cumulative supplements per year, making these publications, volume-per-volume, among the most expensive to maintain. In 1997, many WG&L titles were transferred to the A.S. Pratt Company and West, and annual subscription pricing instituted. This has effectively precluded customers from buying one of the 3-4 cumulative supplements issued each year. The new recommended cost-saving strategy involves subscribing in alternate years, a tactic which preserves annual supplementation while cutting average annual supplementation costs in half.

WANT Publishing Co. Graybar Bldg. - Grand Central, 420 Lexington Ave., Suite #300, New York, NY 10170. (212) 687-3774.
www.wantpublishing.com
Founded in 1975, WANT Publishing Co. is a reference book publisher whose chief products are the Your Nation's Courts Series™, now in its 24th edition, and the Best of the Web Series™. Your Nation's Court Series deals with the federal and state courts and how they operate. Best of the Web Series includes quick-reference guides for librarians, students, teachers, and all those who use the Web for research and reference. WANT Publishing was founded by Robert S. Want, who currently serves as publisher and editor-in-chief.

West (see also Thomson Reuters). 610 Opperman Drive, Eagan, MN 55164-0526. (800) 328-4880
http://west.thomson.com/store/prodsvcs.aspx
When John West founded the publishing company which bears his name in 1876, he was responding to the inability of governmental entities to respond to the needs of attorneys in a timely fashion. His **Syllabi**, containing opinions of the Minnesota Supreme Court, proved so popular with the practicing bar that he and his brother Horatio soon found themselves in charge of a burgeoning national publishing business reporting appellate court decisions from across the country. Between 1879 and 1887, the West brothers had developed a national system of regional reporters which provided opinions in an identical and consistent format together with invaluable editorial features which later provided access through a sophisticated case digesting system. The National Reporter System and the American Digest System with its ingenious Key Number system were major contributions to the field of legal publication and research.

In the nearly 120 years since its founding, West Publishing has become the premier legal publisher in the United States. Not only has it achieved the dominant position as publisher of case reporters and case digests, federal and state statutes, but it has established itself as a leading publisher of legal treatises, and practice books, and law school texts. Its **Corpus Juris Secundum** is one of only two national legal encyclopedias and its **United States Code Annotated** is the most complete source of federal statutory law with annotations. It publishes state statutory codes for twenty-two states and case digests for forty-six states, as well as digests for a variety of federal reporters series. The Hornbook series, which has become the country's leading source of law school texts, was initiated by West at the beginning of the century. In 1975, West introduced WESTLAW, its computer-assisted legal research system and, in 1988, brought to market the first of its CD-ROM titles. In the past few years, West has also introduced primary law CD-ROM products for every state in the nation and for federal cases and statutes. Its sales force consists entirely of law school graduates who represent West products in every region of the country.

Over the years, West has purchased or absorbed a number of

smaller or regional legal publishers, including the American Law Book Company, the Edward Thompson Company, Boston Law Book, Foundation Press, and, very recently, Banks-Baldwin. of Cleveland, Ohio. In the case of the American Law Book Company, publishers of **Corpus Juris**, West simply absorbed the product line into its overall operation. Other companies, such as Foundation Press, have retained their separate identity, operating as wholly-owned subsidiaries.

Then, in August, 1995, West Publishing sent a shock wave through the legal community when it announced that it was putting itself up for sale, and hired an investment firm to investigate potential buyers. According to published reports, its management came to the conclusion that the time was right to sell, given the volatility of the marketplace and West's somewhat precarious position in it. West had already been facing competition from both established and smaller niche publishers in the area of CD-ROM sales. And it continues to fend off the efforts of competitors who challenge its copyright claims to star pagination, the page breaks in the West case reporters which have given West an editorial advantage over its competitors. While West continues to assert its claim to star pagination, a number of companies are selling CD-ROM products containing state and federal primary law over which West once had near hegemony. West's own initial reluctance to embrace the CD-ROM format was, in large measure, a logical business decision not compete against its own online service, WESTLAW, or print products. However, it failed to anticipate the degree to which other publishers or CD-ROM vendors would reach out to tap an enormous market anxious to control online costs with a fixed-cost medium.

After months of speculation, the **Thomson Corporation** of Canada announced its purchase of West Publishing on February 26, 1996 for the sum of $3.425 billion. This deal, approved by the Justice Department on June 19, 1996, gives Thomson control of the dominant share of the American legal publishing market, including 53% of the legal treatises selected for inclusion in this book and both the West Key Number System and Lawyers Cooperative Total Client-Service Library System. The DOJ's Proposed Final Judgment required the divestiture of only fifty-one titles, including **United States Code Service**, **U.S. Reports L.Ed.**, and **U.S. Supreme Court Digest L.Ed.**, six national treatise titles, thirty-four state specific treatises, four state codes, one state digest, and Auto-Cite. It also required West to freely license star pagination to its National Reporter System volumes, but at a price tag guaranteed to deter would-be competitors in the CD-ROM or online business. In February, 1997, U.S. District Judge Paul L. Friedman finally approved the proposed settlement after some changes in the provisions relating to the licensing of star pagination. His concerns on the star pagination issue paralleled those of U.S. District Judge John S. Martin in the Southern District of New York who, on November 22, rejected West's claim that star pagination involved any degree of creative effort deserving of copyright protection.

Judge Friedman's concerns were to lay out the conditions under which both large and smaller publishers could use star pagination until such time as the issue is ultimately settled by the courts. LEXIS-NEXIS, which had actively opposed the merger in the earlier stages, withdrew its opposition after Reed Elsevier, its parent company, won the bid the acquire the 51 divested titles from Thomson-West, as well as 21 still to be disclosed titles.

The Thomson Corporation had previously acquired Callaghan & Company (1979), Clark Boardman (1980), Warren, Gorham & Lamont (1980), Lawyers Cooperative (1989), Bancroft-Whitney (1989), Research Institute of America (1989), Maxwell Macmillan, formerly Prentice-Hall (1991), Counterpoint Publishing (1994), Information Access (1994), Barclays (1995), and the Shepard's/McGraw-Hill treatises (1995). The pattern of significant price increases which have followed other Thomson acquisitions, including lawyers Cooperative, has already surfaced in the price increases of the former Shepard's treatises now largely marketed under the Clark Boardman Callaghan imprint. Capitalizing on the venerable West name, The Thomson Corporation has combined Clark Boardman Callaghan, Lawyers Cooperative Publishing, Bancroft Whitney, and West into the **West Group**. Combined North American sales of legal information by the West Group companies are estimated at more than $1.5 billion annually.

Westlaw and, now, WestlawNext have become a significant expense at many law firms and law libraries. One can only imagine what those costs would be were it not for the presence of its chief competitor, LexisNexis and other, smaller CALR providers. While the prices for West print products have continued to escalate, its CD-ROM and Westlaw pricing have stabilized in this more competitive online marketplace.

On February 10, 1998, West Group announced its acquisition of Federal Publications, a publisher of government contracting, construction contracting, and immigration materials. And on January 26, 2001, the West Group announced that it has purchased FindLaw, the leading legal information portal on the Internet. In 2002, West acquired The Harrison Company, a 94-year-old regional legal publisher for the southeastern United States. Harrison's products included a number of regional law titles, including those for the states of Alabama, Arkansas, Florida, Georgia, Iowa, Kentucky, Mississippi, Missouri, North Carolina, Pennsylvania, South Carolina, Tennessee, Texas, and Virginia. Some of Harrison's products have been absorbed into the West product line, while others have been abandoned as duplicative of West's existing offerings. In 2003, Thomson acquired Andrews Publications, a major publisher of litigation reporters, newsletters, special reports and online services that track the progress of major court cases in more than 45 areas of practice, which are also available on Westlaw. In 2003, Thomson also acquired Elite Information Systems, a major provider of practice management, time and billing, marketing, financial, and accounting systems for law and professional services firms. In 2010, Thomson Reuters acquired Revista dos Tribunais and Canada Law Book.

In 2010, the Thomson Reuters Legal Division experienced increases from subscription offerings that were offset by lower print and non-subscription revenues, which declined 6% and 3%, respectively, due to tightened customer budgets. However, the print attrition rate slowed substantially during 2010 and is nearing historical levels. Within Legal's non-subscription businesses, revenues from trademark searches increased, a sign of continued economic recovery. However, Legal experienced double-digit declines in Westlaw ancillary revenues as customers tightly controlled spending above their base subscription contracts. Segment operating profit and the related margin decreased reflecting lower revenues from high-margin print and non-subscription products and the impact of acquisitions and investments in strategic growth initiatives, which more than offset savings from efficiency initiatives.

In 2012, 91% of Thomson Reuters revenues were derived from electronic, software and services, and only 9% from print offerings. Within its portfolio, software and services tend to be less capital intensive, have high growth rates and yield a higher return on investment than print and CD products. However, print and CD products typically have a higher incremental profit margin than software and services. In the Legal Division, 78% of 2012 revenues were derived from subscription and transaction sales and 18% from print products. Revenue from U.S. print products declined 5% in 2012 as customers continue to control discretionary spending [and respond to higher than average price increases]. Since its introduction in February, 2010, WestlawNext now comprises more than 76% of Westlaw's revenue base, representing 47,000 legal organizations. In 2012, revenues of the legal division rose 6%, to $3.286 billion, reflecting an EBITDA of 1.243 billion, and an operating profit of $964 million. In 2012, the Legal segment has achieved an underlying operating profit margin of 29.6%, up from 29.2% in 2011. This reflects a slightly downward trend from 31.5% in 2007

As of January 1, 2013, the Legal business segment was organized around four key customer segments built around end users: U.S. law firm solutions; corporate, government and academic; and global businesses. The Legal division's revenues increased 3% in 2013 due to a 4% contribution from acquisitions, notably Practical Law. Revenues from existing businesses declined 1% driven by a decline in U.S. print. Excluding U.S. print, revenues from existing businesses increased slightly. The Legal division's operating profit margin declined from 29.6% in 2012 to 26.9% in 2013. Subscription revenues increased 8% (2% from existing businesses) led by growth from the acquisition of Practical Law (formerly PLC). Transaction revenues decreased 5% (6% from existing businesses) primarily due to lower book sales in Latin America. U.S. print revenues declined 6%, as customers continued to control discretionary spending. In 2013, U.S. print revenues were approximately 16% of our total Legal segment revenues compared to 24% in 2008. The efforts to "control discretionary spending" to which Thomson Reuters refers in its 2013 Annual Report are largely a response to extraordinary price increases in the costs of its print offerings which will continue to drive customers to its online offerings, or those of its competitors.

West Academic. 444 Cedar Street, Suite 700, St. Paul, MN 55101. In 2013, Eureka Growth Capital acquired the Law School Publishing operations of Thomson Reuters, to be operated as a stand-alone business with three imprints: West Academic, Foundation Press, and Gilbert. The West imprint will transition with West-branded titles under a licensing agreement with Thomson Reuters. The agreement promises close collaboration with Thomson Reuters on key projects. The sale represents Thomson Reuter's effort to jettison those business segments with lower profitability than those whose revenues are driven by ongoing subscription sales.

Wiley Law Publications (see **Wolters Kluwer Law & Business).**
While John Wiley & Sons has been in the publishing business since 1807, its legal division did not begin operation until 1983 when the **Estate Valuation Handbook** was released. The Wiley Law Publications catalog contained nearly 300 titles, most of them casebound legal treatises in fifteen subject areas, including bankruptcy practice, business practice and litigation, civil rights law, construction law, employee benefits/human resources, employment law and litigation, environmental law, family law, intellectual property, international law, nonprofit law and finance, paralegal practice, personal injury, real estate practice, and trial tactics and techniques. The prices of Wiley titles tend to be slightly above industry averages. Supplementation is typically annual and priced close to the industry average. In recent years, Wiley began offering libraries of subject titles on CD-ROM. In 1995, Wiley acquired several of the Shepard's treatises in the subspecialties of medical malpractice. In 1997, most of the Wiley Law Publications titles were acquired by Wolters Kluwer and assigned to Aspen Law & Business. Among the titles remaining with John Wiley & Sons are Hopkins, **Law of Tax-Exempt Organizations** and **The Tax Law of Charitable Giving**.

Wolters Kluwer nv. Stadhouderskade 1, P.O. Box 818, NL-1000 AV Amsterdam, The Netherlands.
+31 (0)29-60- 70 400
www.wolters-kluwer.com
Wolters Kluwer is a multinational publishing company with activities in 22 countries, primarily in Europe, Canada, Australia, Japan and the United States. Its high quality information products are largely concentrated in the fields of law, business, medicine, tax, education, professional training, and trade publishing. Wolters Kluwer acquired Aspen Publishers in 1978 and Panel Publishers in 1982, merging the two in 1993. In 1994, it acquired Prentice Hall's Law & Business. It acquired Commerce Clearing House in 1995 and the professional publishing division of Little, Brown and Company in 1996. Wolters Kluwer had international sales of approximately $2.6 billion in 1996. Approximately $600 million of this figure consists of the combined sales of Commerce Clearing House and Aspen Law & Business. The purchase of the legal and professional publishing division of Little, Brown and Company added another $50 million in annual sales, split almost equally between legal and tax materials.

In September, 1997, Wolters Kluwer also acquired Wiley Law Publications and merged its product line with that of Aspen Law & Business. On September 29, 1998, Wolters Kluwer acquired Ovid Technologies, a major vendor of subscription-based scientific and medical electronic information services, a move which should enhance Wolters Kluwer's electronic publishing capabilities. And on October 7, 1999, Wolters Kluwer purchased Corsearch, a U.S. trade name research firm which will become part of CCH Legal Information Services, pending approval by the Federal Trade Commission. Other Wolters Kluwer acquisitions in 1999 included the Bureau of Business Practice (BBP) from Pearson Publishing and Telecommunications Reports International, which will become a subsidiary of CCH Incorporated. On December 20, 2000, Wolters Kluwer entered into an agreement to acquire Loislaw.com, a major provider of primary law on the Internet. See the above entries for Aspen Publishers, Commerce Clearing House, Loislaw.com, and Wiley

Law Publications.

Effective January 17, 2006, Wolters Kluwer aligned several of its leading U.S-based legal and compliance businesses under the new brand name and logo of Wolters Kluwer Law & Business. These include Aspen, CCH (law and business compliance products), Kluwer Law International and Loislaw, each of which will continue to exist, representing product lines offered by Wolters Kluwer Law & Business.

Wolters Kluwer had revenues of $4.630 billion in 2012. It employs approximately 19,000 people in 150 countries worldwide and maintains operations across Europe, North America and Asia Pacific. It operates through four major divisions:

- Health & Pharma Solutions
- Corporate & Financial Services
- Tax, Accounting & Legal
- Legal, Tax & Regulatory Europe

In 2011, Wolters Kluwer Corporate Legal Services acquired National Registered Agents, Inc., a Princeton, N.J.-based company with a 16-year history of providing registered agent services to small and mid-sized businesses and the legal community that supports them. It has also changed the name of its Aspen Publishers product line to that of Wolters Kluwer Law & Business. The online segment of the business has grown to 74%, with print declining to 26%. The company's operating profit margin was 21.8% in 2012, up from 21.7% in 2011. In the Legal and Regulatory division, revenues were $1.917 billion in 2012, up from $1.865 billion in 2011, reflecting an operating profit margin of 22.4%, the same as 2011.

ABC-CLIO, Inc.
P.O. Box 1911
Santa Barbara, CA 93116-1911
Editorial:
130 Cremona Drive
Santa Barbara, CA 93117
(800) 368-6868 or (805) 968-1911
Fax: (866) 270-3856
E-mail: CustomerService@abc-clio.com
www.abc-clio.com

ABS Consulting
16855 Northchase Dr.
Houston, TX 77060-2393
(281) 673-2800
Fax: (281) 673-2950
www.absconsulting.com

AccessLaw, Inc.
(See Continuing Education of the Bar)

Advanced Legal Education of Hamline Law School
1536 Hewitt Avenue
St. Paul, MN 55104
(651) 523-2800
www.hamline.edu/law/

Agricultural Law Press
127 Young Rd.
Kelso, WA 98626
360-200-5666
www.agrilawpress.com/

AJS Publications
229 Brier Court
Island Lake, IL 60042
Phone: 847-526-5027
Fax: 847-487-5229
www.ajspublications.com

Alabama State Bar Association
415 Dexter Avenue
P. O. Box 671
Montgomery, AL 36104
(334) 269-1515 or (800) 354-6154
Fax: (334) 261-6310
www.alabar.org

Alaska Bar Association
Continuing Legal Education
P. O. Box 100279
Anchorage, AK 99510-0279
(907) 272-7469
Fax: (907) 272-2932
E-mail: info@alaskabar.org
www.alaskabar.org/

Alert Publications, Inc.
(ceased operations in 2011)
47 West Division Street, #385
Chicago IL 60610-5277
312-337-1362
Fax: 312-337-1388
E-mail: info@alertpub.com
www.alertpub.com

Allworth Press/
Skyhorse Publishing, Inc.
307 W. 36th Street, 11th Floor
New York, NY 10018
(212) 643-6816
Fax: (212) 643-6819
www.allworth.com

Allyn & Bacon
(See Pearson Higher Education)

Altman Weil Pensa, Inc.
East Coast Office
3748 West Chester Pike, Suite 203
Newtown Square, PA 19073
Phone: 610.886.2000
Fax: 610.359.0467
Midwest Office
8555 West Forest Home Avenue, Suite 202
Milwaukee , WI 53228
Phone: 414.427.5400
Fax: 414.427.5300
E-mail: info@altmanweil.com
www.altmanweil.com

American Management Association
1601 Broadway, 8th Fl.
New York, NY 10019-7420
800-250-5308 or 212-586-8100
Fax: (212) 903-8168
E-mail: customerservice@amanet.org
www.amanet.org

American Arbitration Association
1633 Broadway
New York, NY 10019
212-716-5800
800-778-7879 Customer Service
Fax: 212-716-5905
www.adr.org

American Association of Law Libraries (AALL)
105 W. Adams Street, Suite 3300
Chicago, IL 60603
312-939-4764
Fax: 312-431-1097
Email: support@aall.org
www.aallnet.org

American Assoc. of Medical Assistants
20 N. Wacker Drive, Suite 1575
Chicago, IL 60606
(312) 899-1500
Fax: 312/899-1259
www.aama-ntl.org/

American Automobile Association (AAA)
1000 AAA Drive
Heathrow, FL 32746-5063
(407) 444-7000
www.aaa.com

American Bankers Association
1120 Connecticut Ave., N.W.
Washington, DC 20036
(202) 663-5221 or (800) 226-5377
www.aba.com

American Bar Association
321 N. Clark Street
Chicago, IL 60654
(800) 285-2221
(312) 988-5000
Fax: (312) 988-5568
www.abanet.org

American Bar Foundation
750 N. Lake Shore Drive
Chicago, IL 60611-4403
(312) 988-6500
www.abf-sociolegal.org/

American Civil Liberties Union
125 Broad Street, 18th Floor
New York, NY 10004
(212) 549-2500
Fax: (212) 944-9065
www.aclu.org

American College of Legal Medicine
1100 E. Woodfield Road, Suite 350
Schaumburg, IL 60173
Phone: 847-969-0283
Fax: 847-517-7229
Email: info@aclm.org
www.aclm.org

American College of Trust & Estate Counsel
901 15th Street, N.W., Suite 525
Washington, DC 20005
(202) 684-8460
Fax: (202) 684-8459
www.actec.org/

American Correctional Association
15 Mill Wharf Plaza
Scituate Mass. 02066
(617) 471-4445
Fax: (617) 770-3339
www.corrections.com/aca

American Enterprise Institute for Public Policy Research
1150 17th Street, N.W.
Washington, DC 20036-6670
(800) 862-5801
(202) 862-5800
Fax: (202) 862-7177
Book Orders
c/o National Book Network
Attn: Order Department
4501 Forbes Boulevard, Suite 200
Lanham, MD 20706
Telephone: (800) 462-6420
Fax: (800) 338-4550
E-mail: custserv@nbnbooks.com
www.aei.org

American Health Lawyers Assoc.
1620 Eye Street, NW, 6th Floor
Washington, DC 20006-4010
Phone: (202) 833-1100
Fax: (202) 833-1105
www.healthlawyers.org/

American Immigration Center
P.O. Box 45476
Rio Rancho, NM 87174
(800) 814-1555 or (505) 891-1555
Fax: (505) 891-8887
www.us-immigration.com

American Immigration Lawyers Association
1331 G Street, NW, Suite 300,
Washington, DC 20005
(202) 507-7600
Fax: (202) 783-7853
www.aila.org

American Indian Lawyer Training Program
Imprint of: The American Indian Lawyer
1025 W Vine Street
Stockton, CA 95203-1705
(510) 834-9333

American Insurance Association
2101 L Street, NW, Suite 400
Washington, DC 20037
Tel: (202) 828-7100
Fax: (202) 293-1219
www.aiadc.org

American Intellectual Property Law Assn.
241 18th Street South
Suite 700
Arlington, VA 22202
(703) 415-0780
Fax: (703) 415-0786
Email: aipla@aipla.org
http://www.aipla.org/

American Judicature Society (AJS)
The Opperman Center at Drake University
2700 University Avenue
Des Moines, Iowa 50311
(800) 626-4089 or (515) 271-2281
Fax: (515) 271-2810
www.ajs.org/

American Law Institute and ALI-ABA
4025 Chestnut Street
Philadelphia, PA 19104-3099
(800) 253-6397 or (215) 243-1600
Fax: (215) 243-1636
www.ali.org and
www.ali-cle.org

American Lawyer Media, Inc.
120 Broadway, 5th Floor
New York, N.Y. 10271
(877) 256-2472 or (800) 888-8300
Fax: (646) 822-5146
www.americanlawyer.com/

American Maritime Cases, Inc.
Meadow at Woodberry
3600 Clipper Mill Rd - Ste 208
Baltimore, MD 21211
(410) 243-2426
Fax (410) 243-2427
www.americanmaritimecases.com/

American Medical Association
515 N. State Street
Chicago, IL 60654
(800) 621-8335
(312) 464-5000
www.ama-assn.org

American Planning Association
205 N. Michigan Ave., Suite 1200
Chicago, IL 60601
(312) 431-9100
Fax: (312) 786-6700
www.planning.org
Email: customerservice@planning.org.

American Society of Assn. Executives
1575 I Street, N.W.
Washington, DC 20005
202-626-2723 or 888.950.2723 (outside of DC metro area)
Fax: 202-371-8315
E-mail: ASAEservice@asaecenter.org
www.asaenet.org

American Society of Civil Engineers
1801 Alexander Bell Drive
Reston, VA 20191-4400
(800) 548-2723 or (703) 295-6300
Fax: (703) 295-6211
www.asce.org/

American Society of Corporate Secretaries
(see Society of Corporate Secretaries and Governance Professionals)

American Society of International Law
2223 Massachusetts Avenue NW
Washington, DC 20008
(202) 939-6000
Fax: 202-797-7133
www.asil.org/

Amnesty International USA
Div. of Amnesty International
5 Penn Plaza
New York, NY 10001
(212) 807-8400
Fax: (212) 627-1451
www.amnestyusa.org/

AMS Press, Inc.
Brooklyn Navy Yard
63 Flushing Avenue, Unit #221
Brooklyn, NY 11205-1073
(212) 777-4700
Fax: 718-875-3800
E-mail: orders@amspressinc.com
www.amspressinc.com/

Anderson Publishing Company
(see LexisNexis)

Andrews Publications
(see West)

Arizona Secretary of State
Capitol Executive Tower, 7th Floor
1700 W. Washington Street
Phoenix, AZ 85007-2808
(602) 542-4285
Fax: (602) 542-1575
www.azsos.gov/

Arizona, State Bar of - CLE
4201 N. 24th Street, Suite 100
Phoenix, AZ 85016-6266
(602) 252-4804 or 866-482-9227
Fax: (602) 271-4930
www.azbar.org/CLEandMCLE

Arkansas Bar Association
2224 Cottondale Lane
Little Rock, AR 72202
(800) 609-5668 or (501) 375-4606
Fax: (501) 375-4901
www.arkbar.com

Arkansas Trial Lawyers Assoc.
1400 W. Markham Street STE 307
Little Rock, AR 72201
(800) 442-2852 or (501) 376-2852
Fax: (501) 372-0951
www.arktla.org

Arkansas Secretary of State
State Capitol, Rm. 256
Little Rock, AR 72201
(501) 682-1010
Email: general_info@sos.arkansas.gov
www.sosweb.state.ar.us/

Artech House, Inc.
Subs. Of Horizon House
685 Canton Street
Norwood, MA 02062
(800) 225-9977 or (781) 769-9750
Fax: (781) 769-6334
E-mail: artech@artechhouse.com
www.artechhouse.com/

Ashgate Publishing Co.
110 Cherry Street, Suite 3-1
Burlington, VT 05401-3818
800-535-9544 or 802 865 7641
Fax: (802) 865-7847
www.ashgate.com

Aspen Publishers
(see Wolters Kluwer Law & Business)

Associated General Contractors of America
2300 Wilson Boulevard, Suite 400
Arlington, VA 22201
(800) 242-1767 or (703) 548-3118
Fax: (703)837-5405
Email: info@agc.org
www.agc.org/

Association of American Law Schools
1201 Connecticut Ave., N.W., Suite 800
Washington, DC 20036-2717
(202) 296-8851
Fax: (202) 296-8869
E-mail: aals@aals.org
www.aals.org/

Association of National Advertisers, Inc.
708 Third Avenue, 33rd Floor
New York, NY 10017
(212) 697-5950
Fax: (212) 687-7310
E-mail: info@ana.net
www.ana.net

Association of the Bar of the City of New York
42 West 44th Street
New York, NY 10036
(212) 382-6600
www.abcny.org

Atlantic Law Book Company
Div. of Peter Kelsey Publishing, Inc.
22 Grassmere Avenue
West Hartford, CT 06110-1215
(860) 231-9300 or (800) 259-5534
E-mail: AtlanticLawBooks@aol.com
www.atlntc.com

Austin & Winfield
(See University Press of America)

BNA Books (see Bloomberg BNA)
1801 S. Bell Street
Arlington, VA 22202
800-960-1220
www.bna.com/bnabooks/

Bancroft-Whitney
(see West)

Banks-Baldwin Law Publishing Co.
(see West)

Barclays Law Publishers
(see West)

Bar Association of the District of Columbia
1016 16th Street NW
Washington, DC 20036
(202) 223-6600
Fax: (202) 293-3388
Email: info@badc.org
www.badc.org/

BARBRI (Leeds Equity Partners)
200 W. Adams St., Suite 250
Chicago, IL 60606
(312) 894-1689
Fax: (312) 288-4607
www.barbri.com

Belknap Press
(see Harvard University Press)
79 Garden Street
Cambridge, MA 02138
(800) 405-1619 or (617) 495-2600
Fax: (800) 406-9145
Email: contact_hup@harvard.edu
www.hup.harvard.edu

LexisNexis Matthew Bender
(800) 833-9844
http://bender.lexisnexis.com

Bernan Associates
15200 NBN Way
P.O. Box 191
Blue Ridge Summit, PA 17214
800-865-3457 or 301-459-7666
Fax: 800-865-3450 or 301-459-6988
E-mail: customercare@bernan.com
www.bernan.com

Biennix Corporation
2490 Black Rock Turnpike #354
Fairfield, Connecticut 06825-2400
(203) 254-1727
www.legalcareer.com

Bisel, George T., Co.
710 S. Washington Square
Philadelphia, PA 19106-3519
(800) 247-3526 or (215) 922-5760
Fax: (215) 922-2235
E-mail: gbisel@bisel.com
www.bisel.com

Bloomberg BNA
Customer Contact Center
3 Bethesda Metro Center, Suite 250
Bethesda, MD 20814-5377
(800) 372-1033
Fax: (800) 253-0332
www.bna.com

Bowker
(an affiliated business of ProQuest)
630 Central Avenue
New Providence, NJ 07974
888-269-5372 or 908-286-1090
Fax: 908-219-0195
E-mail: TechSupport@bowker.com
www.bowker.com/

Bradford Publishing Company
1743 Wazee St # 100
Denver, CO 80202
(800) 446-2831 or (303) 292-2500
Fax: (303) 298-5014
E-mail: customerservice@bradfordpub-lishing.com
www.bradfordpublishing.com/

Brookings Institution Press
1775 Massachusetts Ave., N.W.
Washington, DC 20036-2188
(800) 275-1447, (202) 797-6000
Fax: (202) 797-6004
E-mail: communications@brookings.edu
www.brookings.edu

BuilderBooks
(National Association of Home Builders)
1201 15th St., N.W.
Washington, DC 20005-2800
(800) 223-2665 or (202) 266-8588
(800) 368-5242 (NAHB)
Fax: (202) 266-8512
www.builderbooks.com

Business & Legal Reports, Inc. (BLR)
100 Winners Circle, Suite 300
Brentwood, TN 37027
(800) 727-5257
E-mail: service@blr.com
www.blr.com

Butterworths Canada Ltd.
(see LexisNexis)
123 Commerce Valley Drive East
Suite 700
Markham, ON L3T 7W8
Canada
(800) 668-6481, (905) 479-2665
Fax: (800) 461-3275
Fax: (905) 479-2826
www.butterworths.ca/

Canada Law Book Inc.
One Corporate Plaza
2075 Kennedy Road
Toronto, Ontario M1T 3V4
Canada
(800) -387-5164 or (416) 609-3800
(Toronto & Intl.)
E-mail: carswell.customerrelations@thomsonreuters.com
www.canadalawbook.ca/

Capitol Publications, Inc.
(see Wolters Kluwer Law & Business)

Carolina Academic Press
700 Kent Street
Durham, NC 27701
(919) 489-7486
Fax: (919) 493-5668
www.cap-press.com/

Carroll Publishing
4701 Sangamore Rd, Suite S-155
Bethesda, MD 20816
(800) 336-4240 or (301) 263-9800
Fax: (301) 263-9801
Email: info@carrollpub.com
www.carrollpub.com

Carswell (Thomson Reuters)
One Corporate Plaza
2075 Kennedy Road
Toronto, ON M1T 3V4
Canada
(416) 609-3800 (Toronto & Int'l)
(800) 387-5164 (Toll Free Canada & US)
Fax: (416) 298-5082
Fax: (877) 750-9041 (Toll Free Canada only)
www.carswell.com

Casenotes Publishing Co., Inc.
(see Aspen Publishers)

Cato Institute
1000 Massachusetts Ave., N.W.
Washington, D.C. 20001-5403
(202) 842-0200
Fax: (202) 842-3490
www.cato.org

CCH, a Wolters Kluwer business
2700 Lake Cook Rd.
Riverwoods, IL 60015
800-344-3734 (Subscription and Research Support)
800-248-3248 (Book Sales Support)
www.cch.com

CCH Trademark Research Corp.
(see CCH CORSEARCH)

CCH CORSEARCH
111 Eighth Avenue, 13th Floor
New York, NY 10011
(800) 732 7241
E-mail: order@corsearch.com
www.corsearch.com/

CCH Washington Service Bureau
Wolters Kluwer Law & Business
SEC Research Department
1015 15th Street, NW 10th Floor
Washington, DC 20005
(202) 842-7355 or (800) 289-1057
www.wsb.com/

Cengage Learning
10650 Toebben Drive
Independence, KY 41051
(800) 354-9706
Fax: (800) 487-8488
www.cengage.com

Center for Computer Assisted Legal Instruction (CALI)
229 19th Avenue South
Minneapolis, MN 55455
(612) 246-0042
Fax: (612) 605-0166
www.cali.org

Center for Law & Education
1875 Connecticut Ave., N.W.
Suite 510
Washington, DC 20009
(202) 986-3000
Fax: (202) 986-6648
www.cleweb.org/

Center for Urban Policy Research
Rutgers University
33 Livingston Avenue
Civic Square-Suite 400
New Brunswick, NJ 08901-1982
(848) 932-2375
Fax: (732) 932-2363
Fax: 732-932-9983 (CUPR Press Only)
www.policy.rutgers.edu/cupr

Central Committee for Conscientious Objectors (CCCO)
405 14th Street, Ste. 205
Oakland, CA 94612
E-mail: ccco@objector.org
http://objector.org/

Chartered Property Casualty Underwriters Society
Kahler Hall
PO Box 3009
720 Providence Road
Malvern, PA 19355-0709
(800) 932-2728
Fax: (610) 725-5969
E-mail: MemberResources@theinstitutes.org
www.cpcusociety.org/

Claims Providers of America
P.O. Box 270529
San Diego, CA 92198-0529
(800) 735-6660
Fax: (858) 487-7747
E-mail: info@National-Experts.com
http://national-experts.com/

Claitor's Law Books & Publishing Div
3165 S. Acadian Thrwy at Interstate 10
PO Box 2613333
Baton Rouge, LA 70826-1333
(800) 274-1403
(225) 344-0476
Fax: 225-344-0480
www.claitors.com

Clark Boardman Callaghan (CBC)
(see Thomson West)

CLE Alabama
101 Paul Bryant Drive East, Room 120
Tuscaloosa, AL 35401
Mailing address:
CLE Alabama
P.O. Box 870384
Tuscaloosa, AL 35487
800-627-6514 or 205-348-6230
Fax: 205-348-1072
E-mail: CLEAlabama@law.ua.edu
www.clealabama.com/

Code-Co Law Publishers
P.O. Box 1471
Provo, UT 84603-1471
(801) 226-6876
Fax: (801) 226-1733
E-mail: admin@code-co.com
www.code-co.com/

College Administration Publications, Inc.
P.O. Box 600430
Saint Johns, FL 32260
(800) 367-9577
(828) 277-8777
Fax: (828) 277-8735
E-mail: contact@collegepubs.com
www.collegepubs.com

College Legal Information, Inc.
2021 Richard Jones Rd. Suite 350
Nashville, TN 37215
Mailing address:
P.O. Box 150541
Nashville, Tennessee 37215-0541
(615) 383-3332
Fax: (615) 383-3480
Email: info@collegelegal.com
www.collegelegal.com/

Comerford and Boyd
1187 Wilmette Ave., Dept 290
Wilmette, IL 60091
(800) 567-5995

Commission on Official Legal Publications (COLP)
111 Phoenix Avenue
Enfield, CT 06082-4453
(860) 741-3027
Fax: (860) 745-2178
E-mail: colp@jud.ct.gov
www.jud.ct.gov/colp

CompBase, Inc.
2220 Plainfield Pike
Cranston, RI 02921
866-676-9486 or 401-727-1567
Fax: 401-694-1236
E-mail: info@clerkbase.com
www.compbase.com

Computer Law Association, Inc.
(see International Technology Law Association)

Congressional Information Service, Inc.
(see LexisNexis)

Congressional Quarterly Books
SAGE Publications
2455 Teller Road
Thousand Oaks, CA 91320
800-818-7243
Fax: 800-583-2665 or 805-375-5291
E-mail: librarysales@sagepub.com
www.cqpress.com/

Connecticut Bar Association
30 Bank Street
PO Box 350
New Britain, CT 06050-0350
(860) 223-4400
Fax: (860) 223-4488
E-mail: msc@ctbar.org
www.ctbar.org

Connecticut Law Tribune
201 Ann Street, 4th Floor
Hartford, CT 06103
(860) 527-7900
www.ctlawtribune.com

Connecticut Secretary of State
30 Trinity Street
P. O. Box 150470
Hartford, CT 06115-0470
(860) 509-6200
Fax: (860) 509-6209
www.sots.state.ct.us/

Continuing Education of the Bar - California (CEB)
2100 Franklin St., Suite 500
Oakland, CA 94612-3098
(800) 232-3444 or (510) 302-2000
E-mail: customer_service@ceb.ucla.edu
www.ceb.com

Continuing Legal Education Dept. Washington State Bar Association
1325 Fourth Ave., Ste. 600
Seattle, WA 98101-2539
800-945-9722 or 206-443-9722
206-727-8292 (CLE)
Fax: (206) 727-8319
E-mail: cle@wsba.org
www.wsba.org

Continuing Legal Education, Inc. Colorado Bar Association
1900 Grant St, 3rd Floor
Denver, CO 80203
(888) 860-2531
(303) 860-0608
Fax: (303) 894-0821
www.cobar.org/cle

Conway Greene Co.
1400 East 30th Street, Suite 402
Cleveland, OH 44114
(800) 977-2665
(216) 619-8091
Fax: (216) 622-1788
E-mail us: info@conwaygreene.com
www.conwaygreene.com

Cornell Maritime Press
(see Schiffer Publishing, Ltd.)

Cornell University Press
Box 6525
750 Cascadilla Street
Ithaca, NY 14851-6525
(607) 277-2211
Fax: (607) 277-6292
E-mail: orderbook@cupserv.org
www.cornellpress.cornell.edu/

Corwin
Sub. of Sage Publications
2455 Teller Road
Thousand Oaks, CA 91320
800-233-9936 or 805-499-9734
Fax: 800-417-2466 or 805-499-5323
E-mail: order@corwin.com
www.corwin.com

Council of State Governments
2760 Research Park Drive
P.O. Box 11910
Lexington, KY 40578-1910
(859) 244-8000
(800) 800-1910 (Sales/Publications)
Fax: (859) 244-8001
E-mail: sales@csg.org
www.csg.org

Counterpoint Publishing
(see Thomson West)

CQ Press
(see Congressional Quarterly Books)

CRC Press
6000 Broken Sound Parkway NW, Suite 300
Boca Raton, FL 33487
(800) 272-7737 or (561) 994-0555
Fax: 800-374-3401 or (561) 361-6018
E-mail: orders@crcpress.com
www.crcpress.com

Crown Publishing Group, Inc.
A Division of Random House, Inc.
1745 Broadway
New York, NY 10019
212.782.9000
E-mail: CrownMarketing@randomhouse.com
http://crownpublishing.com/

CSA
789 E Eisenhower Parkway
Ann Arbor, MI 48103
800-521-0600 or 734-761-4700
Fax: 877-337-7015 or 734-997-4222
Email: info@proquest.com
www.csa.com

College and University Professional Association for Human Resources (CUPA-HR)
1811 Commons Point Drive
Knoxville, TN 37932-1989
877-287-2474 or 865-637-7673
Fax: (865) 637-7674
www.cupahr.org

Daily Journal Corporation
915 E First Street
Los Angeles, CA 90012
(213) 229-5300
Fax: (213) 229-5481
www.dailyjournal.com/

Darby Printing Company
6215 Purdue Drive
Atlanta, GA 30336
(800) 241-5292 or (404) 344-2665
Fax: (404) 346-3332
E-mail: sales@darbyprinting.com (sales)
E-mail: subs@darbyprinting.com (legal subs.)
www.darbyprinting.com

Dartmouth Publishing
Dist. by Ashgate Publishing Co.

Data Trace Publishing Company
110 West Road
Baltimore, MD 21204
Mailing address:
P.O. Box 1239
Brooklandville, MD 21022-9978
(800) 342-0454 or (410) 494-4994
Fax: (410) 494-0515
E-Mail: info@datatrace.com
www.datatrace.com/

Dearborn Real Estate Education
332 Front Street South, Suite 501
La Crosse, WI 54601
(800) 972-2220
E-mail: reorders@dearborn.com
www.dearborn.com

Delaware State Bar Association Continuing Legal Education
405 N. King St., Suite 100
Wilmington, DE 19801
(302) 658-5279
(800) 292-7869 (Kent & Sussex Counties)
Fax: (302) 658-5212
www.dsba.org/

Delta Alpha Publishing
c/o Port City Fulfillment Services
35 Ash Drive
Kimball, MI 48074
(800) 292-5544 or 810 388-9500
Fax: (810) 388-9502
www.deltaalpha.com

Disclosure, Inc.
(see Thomson Financial)

District of Columbia Bar Association
1101 K Street NW, Suite 200
Washington DC 20005
(202) 737-4700
(202) 626-3488 (CLE)
www.dcbar.org

Dolan Company
222 South Ninth Street
Suite 2300
Minneapolis, MN 55402
(612) 317-9420
Fax: (612) 321-0563
www.thedolancompany.com/websites.htm

Duke University Press
905 W. Main St., Suite 18B
Durham, NC 27701
888-651-0122 or 919-688-5134
Fax: 888-651-0124 or 919-688-2615
www.dukeupress.edu

EBSCO Publishing
10 Estes Street
Ipswich, MA 01938
800-653-2726
Fax: 978-356-6565
Email: information@ebscohost.com
www.ebscohost.com

Education Law Association
300 College Park
Dayton, Ohio 45469-0528
(937) 229-3589
Fax: (937) 229-3845
E-mail: ela@educationlaw.org
www.educationlaw.org

Elsevier, Health Sciences Division
1600 John F. Kennedy Blvd., Suite 1800
Philadelphia, PA 19103-2899
(800) 523-1649 or (215) 239-3900
Fax: (215) 239-3990
www.us.elsevierhealth.com

Entrepreneur Press
2445 McCabe Way, Suite 400
Irvine, CA 92614
(800) 864-6864 or (949) 622-5274
Fax: (949) 261-7729
Email: press@entrepreneur.com
www.entrepreneurpress.com

Environmental Design Research Association (EDRA)
1760 Old Meadow Road, Suite 500
McLean, VA 22102
703-506-2895
Fax: 703-506-3266
E-mail: headquarters@edra.org
www.edra.org

Environmental Law Institute, Inc.
2000 L Street, NW, Suite 620
Washington, D.C. 20036
(202) 939-3800
(800) 433-5120
Fax: (202) 939-3868
Email: law@eli.org
www.eli.org/

Faulkner & Gray, Inc.
(see Thomson Media)

Federal Bar Association
220 North Fillmore St., Ste. 444
Arlington, VA 22201
(571) 481-9100
Fax: (571) 481-9090
E-mail: fba@fedbar.org
www.fedbar.org

Federal News Service, LLC
1120 G Street NW, Suite 990
Washington, DC 20005-3801
800-211-4020 or 202-347-1400
Fax: 202-393-4733
202-216-2801 (sales)
E-mail: sales@fednews.com (sales)
www.fednews.com

Federal Publications, Inc.
(see West)

FIND/SVP
(see ORC International)

Florida Bar
Continuing Legal Education Dept.
651 E. Jefferson Street
Tallahassee, FL 32399-2300
(850) 561-5600
www.flabar.org/

Forster-Long, LLC
12160 N. Abrams, #516
(214) 838-5745
Fax: (214) 838-5754
www.forster-long.com

Foundation Press, Inc.
div. of Thomson West
395 Hudson St # 3
New York, NY 10014
(212) 367-6790 (main)
(877) 888-1330 (customer service)
Email: foundation-press@thomson.com
www.fdpress.com

Fry Communications
800 West Church Road
Mechanicsburg, PA 17055-3198
(800) 334-1429
(717) 766-0211 Ext.: 340
E-mail: info@frycomm.com
www.frycomm.com/

The Gale Cengage Learning
10650 Toebben Drive
Independence, KY 41051
(800) 354-9706
Fax: (800) 487-8488
www.gale.cengage.com

Gann Law Books
One Washington Park, Suite 1300
Newark, NJ 07102
(973) 268-1200
Fax: (973) 268-1330
E-mail: sales@gannlaw.com
www.gannlaw.com

Gaunt, Inc.
3011 Gulf Drive
Holmes Beach, FL 34217-2199
(800) 942-8683 or (941) 778-5211
Fax: 941-778-5252
www.gaunt.com/

Georgia State Department of Law
40 Capitol Square S.W.
Atlanta, GA 30334-1300
(404) 656-3300
Fax: (404) 657-8733
www.ganet.org/ago/

General Code Publishers Corp.
781 Elmgrove Road
Rochester, NY 14624
(855) 436-2633 or (585) 328-1810
Fax: (585) 328-8189
Email: info@generalcode.com
www.generalcode.com/

Geronimo Development Corp.
606 25th Ave. South, Suite 201
St. Cloud, MN 56301
(800) 457-6045 or (320) 259-9805
Fax: (320) 259-9808
E-mail: info@casefinder.com
www.casefinder.com/

Glasser LegalWorks
(see Thomson West)

Goller Publishing Corp.
P.O. Box 2576
Boise, ID 83701
(208) 336-4715 (Phone & Fax)
E-mail: info@gollerpublishing.com
www.gollerpublishing.com/

Gould Publications, Inc.
A Division of LexisNexis
1333 North US Highway 17-92
Longwood, FL 32750-3724
(800) 717-7917 or (407) 695-9500
Fax: (407) 695-2906
www.gouldlaw.com

Government Finance Officers Assn. of the U.S. & Canada (GFOA)
203 N. LaSalle St., Suite 2700
Chicago, IL 60601-1210
(312) 977-9700
Fax: (312) 977-4806
www.gfoa.org/

Government Research Service
P.O. Box 2067
Topeka, Kansas 66601
(800) 346-6898
(785) 232-7720
Fax (785) 232-1615

E-mail: info@statelegislativesourcebook.com
www.statelegislativesourcebook.com

The Graduate Group
P.O. Box 370351
West Hartford, CT 06137-0351
(860) 233-2330
Fax: 860-233-2330
E-mail: graduategroup@hotmail.com
www.graduategroup.com/

Greenwood Publishing Group, Inc.
(see ABC-CLIO)

Harcourt Legal
(see West Gilbert Law Summaries, a Div. of Thomson West)

Harcourt School Publishers
Order Fulfillment Department
6277 Sea Harbor Drive
Orlando, FL 32887
(800) 225-5425
Fax: (800) 269-5232 or (407) 345-3016
www.harcourtschool.com

HarperCollins Publishers
10 East 53rd Street
New York, NY 10022-5299
(800) 242-7737 or (212) 207-7000
E-mail: orders@harpercollins.com
www.harpercollins.com

Harrison Company, The
(see Thomson West)

Hart Publications
Dist. By Northwestern Univ. Press
629 Noyes Street
Evanston, IL 60208-4210
(800) 621-2736 or (773) 568-1550
Fax: (800) 621-8476 or (773) 660-2235
www.nupress.northwestern.edu

Harvard Law Review Association
Gannett House
Attn: Business Office
1511 Massachusetts Avenue
Cambridge, MA 02138
(617) 495-4650
Fax: (617) 495-2748
www.harvardlawreview.org/

Harvard University Press
79 Garden Street
Cambridge, MA 02138
(800) 405-1619 or (401) 531-2800
Fax: (800) 406-9145 or (401) 531-2801
Email: contact_hup@harvard.edu
www.hup.harvard.edu

Hawaii Office of the Lieutenant Governor
State Capitol
Honolulu, HI 96813
(808) 586-0255
Fax: (808) 586-0231
www.ltgov.hawaii.gov

Hawaii Supreme Court Law Library
Ali'iolani Hale, Room 115
417 South King Street
Honolulu, HI 96813
(808) 539-4964
Fax: (808) 539-4974
Email: LawLibrary@courts.hawaii.gov
www.state.hi.us/jud/library

Health Administration Press
Foundation of the American College of Healthcare Executives
Order Fulfillment Center
PO Box 75145
Baltimore, MD 21275-5145
(301) 362-6905
Fax: (240) 396-5907
http://www.ache.org/hap.cfm

William S. Hein & Co., Inc.
2350 North Forest Rd.
Getzville, NY 14068
(800) 828-7571 or (716) 882-2600
Fax: (716) 883-8100
E-mail: mail@wshein.com
www.wshein.com/

Heritage Foundation
214 Massachusetts Ave NE
Washington DC 20002-4999
(202) 546-4400 (main)
(800) 544-4843 (bookstore)
Fax: (202) 546-8328
E-mail: info@heritage.org
www.heritage.org

Home Builder Press
(see Builder Books)

HoweData
1000 SW Vista Avenue, Apt. 625
Portland, OR 97205
(503)-243-1011
Fax: (503) 227-3126
www.howedata.com

Huebner Foundation
3000 Steinberg Hall - Dietrich Hall
3620 Locust Walk
Philadelphia, PA 19104-6302
(215) 898-9631
Fax: (215) 573-2218
www.huebnergeneva.org/

IHS Group
321 Inverness Drive South
Englewood, CO 80112
(800) 525-7052
(800) 447-2273 (cust. svc.)
www.ihs.com

Idaho Law Foundation, Inc.
PO Box 895
Boise, ID 83701
(208) 334-4500
Fax: (208) 334-4515 or (208) 334-2764
http://isb.idaho.gov/ilf

Illinois Institute for Continuing Legal Ed.
3161 W. White Oaks Dr., Ste. 300
Springfield, IL 62704
(800) 252-8062
(217) 787-2080
Fax: (217) 546-6096
E-mail: info@iicle.com
www.iicle.com/

Illinois Office of the Secretary of State
213 State Capitol
Springfield, IL 62756
(800) 252-8980 (within Illinois)
217-785-3000 (outside Illinois)
www.cyberdriveillinois.com

Illinois State Bar Association
424 S. Second Street
Springfield, IL 62701-1779
(800) 252-8908 or (217) 525-1760
www.isba.org

Incisive Media
Haymarket House
28-29 Haymarket
London SW1Y 4RX
United Kingdom
+44 (0)870 240 8859
Fax: +44 (0)207 484 9797
New York:
55 Broad Street, 22nd Floor
New York, NY 10004
(646) 736-1888
Fax: (646) 390-6612
Email: customerservices@incisivemedia.com
www.incisivemedia.com/

Independent Institute
100 Swan Way
Oakland, CA 94621-1428
(510) 632-1366 (main)
(800) 927-8733 or (510) 632-1366 (sales)
Fax: (510) 568-6040
www.independent.org

Independent Publishers Group
814 North Franklin Street
Chicago, IL 60610
(312) 337-0747
(800) 888-4741 (orders)
Fax: (312) 337-5985
www.ipgbook.com

IndexMaster, Inc.
36428 S Park Dr
Avon, OH 44011-3492
(800) 829-1836 or (440) 934-7090
www.indexmaster.com

Indiana Continuing Legal Education Forum
230 East Ohio Street, Suite #300
Indianapolis, IN 46204
(317) 637-9102
Fax: (317) 633-8780
E-mail: iclef@iclef.org
www.iclef.org/

Indiana University Press
Office of Scholarly Publishing
Herman B Wells Library 350
1320 E. 10th St.
Bloomington, IN 47405-3907
(800) 842-6796
(812) 855-8817
E-mail: iuporder@indiana.edu
www.iupress.indiana.edu

Information Access Company
(see The Gale Group)

Infosources Publishing
140 Norma Road
Teaneck, NJ 07666
(201) 836-7072
www.infosourcespub.com/

Institute for Court Management
(see National Center for State Courts)

Institute for Educational Leadership
4455 Connecticut Avenue, NW, Suite 310,
Washington, DC 20008
(202) 822-8405
Fax: (202) 872-4050
E-mail: iel@iel.org
www.iel.org/

Institute for the Development of Indian Law
Oklahoma City University School of Law
2501 N. Blackwelder
Oklahoma City, OK 73106
(800) 633-7242
(405) 208-5337
Fax: (405) 521-5802
Email: lawquestions@okcu.edu
http://law.okcu.edu

The Institute of Continuing Legal Education
1020 Greene Street
Ann Arbor, MI 48109-1444
(877) 229-4350 or (734) 764-0533
Fax: (877) 229-4351 or (734) 763-2412
E-mail: icle@umich.edu
www.icle.org/

Institute of Continuing Legal Education in Georgia
P.O. Box 1885
Athens, GA 30603-1885
(800) 422-0893
(706) 369-5664 (Athens Area)
(770) 466-0886 (Atlanta Area)
E-mail: icle@iclega.org
www.iclega.org/

Institute of Government
School of Government
Knapp-Sanders Building, Campus Box 3330
UNC-Chapel Hill
Chapel Hill, NC 27599-3330
(919) 966.5381
Fax: (919) 962.0654
www.sog.unc.edu/

Institute of International Banking Law & Practice
20405 Ryecroft Court
Montgomery Village, MD 20886
(301) 869-9840
Fax: (301) 926-1265
E-mail: info@IIBLP.org
www.iiblp.org/

Insurance Information Institute
110 William Street, 24th Floor
New York, NY 10038
(800) 331-9146 or (212) 346-5500
E-mail: publications@iii.org
www.iii.org/

Insurance Educational Association
725 Town and Country Road, Suite 430
Orange, CA 92868
(800) 655-4432
www.ieatraining.com

International Advertising Association
World Service Center
275 Madison Avenue, Suite 2102
New York, NY 10016
(212) 557-1133
Fax: (212) 983-0455
E-mail: iaa@iaaglobal.org
www.iaaglobal.org/

International Labour Office
General information
4 route des Morillons
CH-1211 Genève 22
Switzerland
+41 (0) 22 799 6111
Fax: +41 (0) 22 798 8685
E-mail: ilo@ilo.org
Washington Office:
1808 I Street, NW, 9th Floor
Washington, DC 20006
(202) 617-3952
Fax: (202) 617-3960
E-mail: washington@ilo.org
www.ilo.org/

International Monetary Fund
c/o Publications Department
700 19th Street, N.W.
Washington, DC 20431
(202) 623-7000 (main)
Fax: (202) 623-4661 (main)
(202) 623-7430 (publications)
Fax: (202) 623-7201 (publications)
E-mail: publications@imf.org
www.imf.org

International Municipal Lawyers Association (IMLA)
7910 Woodmont Avenue, Suite 1440
Bethesda, MD 20814
(202) 466-5424
Fax: (202) 785-0152
E-mail: info@imla.org
www.imla.org

International Risk Management Institute, Inc.
12222 Merit Drive, Suite 1450
Dallas, TX 75251-2276
(972) 960-7693
Fax: (972) 371-5120
www.irmi.com/

International Specialized Book Services, Inc.
920 NE 58th Ave. Suite 300
Portland, OR 97213
(800) 944-6190 or (503) 287-3093
Fax: (503) 280-8832
www.isbs.com

International Technology Law Association
401 Edgewater Place, Suite 600
Wakefield, MA 01880
(781) 876-8877
Fax: (781) 224-1239
E-mail: office@itechlaw.org
www.itechlaw.org

International Trademark Association
655 Third Avenue, 10th Floor
New York, NY 10017, USA
(212) 642-1700
Fax: (212) 768-7796
E-mail: info@inta.org
www.inta.org

Inventions, Patents and Trademarks Co. (IPT)
15850 McCourtney Road
Grass Valley, CA 95949
(888) 537-2836
Fax: (530) 274-1288
E-mail: support@frompatenttoprofit.com
www.frompatenttoprofit.com

Iowa Legislative Services Agency
State Capitol Building
East 12th & Grand
Des Moines, Iowa 50319
(515) 281-3566
Fax: (515) 281-8027
www.legis.iowa.gov/Agencies/LSA.aspx

Iowa State Bar Association
625 East Court Avenue
Des Moines, IA 50309
(800) 457-3729 or (515) 243-3179
Fax: (515) 243-2511
(515) 697-7874 (CLE)
E-mail: isba@iowabar.org
E-mail: cle@iowabar.org (CLE)
www.iowabar.org/

Iowa Trial Lawyers Association a.k.a. Iowa Association for Justice
505 Fifth Avenue, Suite 630
Des Moines, Iowa 50309
(515) 280-7366
Fax: 515-280-3745
Email: info@iowajustice.org
www.iowajustice.org

IPG Chicago
Independent Publishers Group
Subs. of Chicago Review Press
814 North Franklin Street
Chicago, IL 60610
(800) 888-4741 Orders
(312) 337-0747 Trade or publisher inquiries
Fax: (312) 337-5985
www.ipgbook.com

Irwin McGraw-Hill
(see McGraw-Hill Education)

Island Press
2000 M Street NW, Suite 650
Washington, DC 20036
(202) 232-7933
Fax: (202) 234-1328
Email: info@islandpress.org
www.islandpress.org

James Publishing, Inc.
P.O. Box 25202
Santa Ana, California 92799-5202
(800) 440-4780 (sales)
(800) 394-2626 or (714) 755-5450 (cust. svc.)
Fax: (714) 751-2709
Email: customer-service@jamespublishing.com
www.jamespublishing.com

Jefren Publishing Company, Inc.
A Division of ALP Publishing, LLC.
990 Park Center Drive, Suite E
Vista, CA 92081-8352
888-264-2665
www.alppublishing.com/

JIST Publishing
875 Montreal Way
St. Paul, MN 55102
800-328-1452
Fax: 800-328-4564
E-mail: educate@emcp.com
www.jist.com

Johns Hopkins University Press
2715 N. Charles St.
Baltimore, Maryland 21218-4363
410-516-6900 (main)
Fax: 410-516-6968 (main)
800-537-5487 (books)
Fax: 410-516-6998 (books)
800-548-1784 (journals)
Fax: 410-516-3866 (journals)
www.press.jhu.edu

Jones McClure Publishing, Inc.
P.O. Box 3348
Houston, TX 77253-3348
(800) 626-6667 or (713) 335-8200
Fax: (713) 335-8201
www.jonesmcclure.com

Jurisearch.com, LLC
1467 Greenbrier Place
Charlottesville, VA 22901
(877) 587-4732
Fax: (434) 220-6091
Email: custserv@jurisearch.com
www.unilegal.com/default.asp

Jurisoft
(see LexisNexis)
(800) 262-5656

Juris Publishing, Inc.
JurisNet
71 New Street
Huntington, NY 11743
(631) 351-5430 (main)
Fax: (631) 351-5712 or (631) 673-9117
(800) 887-4064 (orders)
(631) 350-2100 (cust. svc)
www.jurispub.com

Juta & Co.
Dist. By Gaunt

Kansas Bar Association Continuing Legal Education
1200 SW Harrison St.
Topeka, KS 66612-1806
(785) 234-5696
Fax: (785) 234-3813
E-mail: info@ksbar.org
www.ksbar.org/

Keller, J.J. & Associates, Inc.
P.O. Box 368
Neenah, WI 54957
(877) 564-2333
Fax: 800-727-7516
www.jjkeller.com

Kelley Blue Book
195 Technology
Irvine, CA 92618
(949) 770-7704
800-BLUE-BOOK
www.kbb.com/

Kendall-Hunt Publishing Co.
P.O. Box 1840
Dubuque, IA 52004-1840
(800) 228-0810 or (563) 589-1000
Fax: (800) 772-9165 or (563) 589-1046
E-mail: orders@kendallhunt.com
www.kendallhunt.com

Kleinrock Publishing, Inc.
(see CCH)

Kluwer Academic Publications
(See Springer)

Kluwer Law International
(see Aspen Publishers)

Knowles Publishing, Inc.
5535 Airport Freeway
Ft. Worth, TX 76117
(800) 299-0202 or (817) 838-0202
Fax: (817) 831-0019
E-mail: custsvc@knowlespublishing.com
www.knowlespublishing.com

The Lawbook Exchange, Ltd.
33 Terminal Avenue
Clark, NJ 07066-1321
(800) 422-6686
(732) 382-1800
Fax: (732) 382-1887
Email: law@lawbookexchange.com
www.lawbookexchange.com

Law Bulletin Publishing Co.
415 N. State St.
Chicago, IL 60610
(312) 644-7800
Fax: (312) 644-4255
www.lawbulletin.com

Law Journal Press
ALM
4 MetroTech, 21st Floor
Brooklyn, NY 11201-3815
877-256-2472 or (347) 227-3170
Fax: (347) 227-3620
E-mail: reprints@alm.com
www.lawcatalog.com

Law Library Microform Consortium (LLMC)
P.O. Box 1599
Kaneohe, HI 96744
45-720 Keaahala Rd
Kaneohe, HI 96744
(800) 235-4446
E-mail: llmc@llmc.com
www.llmc.com/

Law of the Sea Institute
(see Earl Warren Legal Institute)
381 Boalt Hall
University of California, Berkeley
Berkeley, CA 94720-7200
(510) 642-5125
Fax: (510) 643-2698
Email: losi@law.berkeley.edu
www.law.berkeley.edu/1962.htm

Law Office Information Systems, Inc.
(see Loislaw)

Lawpress Corporation
P.O. Box 29
Alameda, CA 94501-0329
(800) 622-1181 or (510) 748-9309
Fax: (510) 217-6600
E-mail: info@lawpresscorp.com
www.lawpresscorp.com

Lawyers & Judges Publishing Company, Inc.
917 N Swan Rd Ste 300
Tucson, AZ 85711
Orders:
PO Box 30040
Tucson, AZ 85751-0040
(520) 323-1500
Fax: (520) 323-0055
Email sales@lawyersandjudges.com
www.lawyersandjudges.com/

Lawyers Cooperative Publishing Company
(see West)

Lawyers Weekly Publications
(see Dolan Company)

Leadership Directories, Inc.
104 Fifth Avenue, 2d Floor
New York, NY 10011
(212) 627-4140
Fax: (212) 645-0931
www.leadershipdirectories.com

Legal Counsel for the Elderly (LCE)
American Association of Retired Persons (AARP)
601 E St. NW, 4th Floor
Washington, DC 20049
202-434-2120
E-mail: lce@aarp.org
www.aarp.org/states/dc/LCE

Legal Information Institute
Cornell Law School
477 Myron Taylor Hall
Ithaca, NY 14853
(607) 255-6536
Fax: (607) 225-7193
E-mail: help@liicornell.org
www.law.cornell.edu

Legal Information Services
P.O. Box 31425
Charlotte, NC 28231-1425
(980) 333-3049
E-mail: info@legalinformationservices.com
www.legalinformationservices.com

Legal Research Systems, Inc.
(see Thomson Reuters)

Legi-Tech
(see State Net)

Legistore - Florida Office of Legislative Services
111 W. Madison St.
Tallahassee, FL 32399-1400
(850) 488-2323
Fax: (850) 488-4188
E-mail: legistore@leg.state.fl.us
www.flalegistore.com

Lewis Publications
(see CRC Press)

LexisNexis
9443 Springboro Pike
Dayton, OH 45342
(888) 285 3947 (sales)
(888) 285-9341 (sales)
(800) 543-6862 (cust. Support)
www.lexisnexis.com/

LexisNexis Matthew Bender
1275 Broadway
Albany, NY 12204
(800) 833-9844
(518) 487-3000
E-mail: customer.support@lexisnexis.com
http://bender.lexisnexis.com

LexisNexis Martindale-Hubbell
121 Chanlon Road
New Providence, NJ 07974
(800) 526-4902 or (908) 771-7777
Fax: (908) 771-8704
www.martindale.com

LexisNexis Services
LexisNexis Computing & Research
601 Benjamin Drive
Springfield, OH 45502
(800) 227-9597
www.lexisnexis.com

Libel Defense Resource Center
(see Media Law Resource Center)

Liberty Fund, Inc.
8335 Allison Pointe Trail, Suite 300
Indianapolis, IN 46250-1684
(800) 866-3520
Fax: (317) 577-9067
E-mail: info@libertyfund.org
Orders:
(800) 955-8335
Fax: 708.534.7803
E-mail: orders@libertyfund.org
www.libertyfund.org

Libraries Unlimited, Inc.
(imprint of ABC-CLIO)

Lincoln Institute of Land Policy
113 Brattle Street
Cambridge, MA 02138-3400
(800) 526-3873 or (617) 661-3016
Fax: (800) 526-3944 or (617) 661-7235
Email: help@lincolninst.edu
www.lincolninst.edu

Little, Brown and Company
(see Aspen Publishers)

LocalLaw Publications, Inc.
P.O. Box 144
Merion Station, PA 19066-0144
(610) 617-8919
E-mail: rstern@locallawpub.com
www.locallawpub.com/

Loislaw
(a division of Wolters Kluwer Law & Business)
4025 W. Peterson Avenue
Chicago, IL 60646-6085
(877) 471-5632
E-mail: supportservices@loislaw.com
www.loislaw.com

Longleaf Services, Inc.
116 S. Boundary St.
Chapel Hill, NC 27514-3808
Phone: 800-848-6224
Fax: 800-272-6817
E-mail: customerservice@longleafservices.org
www.longleafservices.org

Looseleaf Law Publications, Inc.
Orders:
P.O. Box 650042
Fresh Meadows, NY 11365-0042
(800) 647-5547
Fax: (718) 539-0941
Editorial:
43-08 162nd St.
Flushing, NY 11358
E-mail: info@LooseleafLaw.com
www.looseleaflaw.com

Lorman Education Services
P.O. Box 509
Eau Claire, WI 54702-0509
(866) 352-9539
Fax: (715) 833-3944
www.lorman.com/

Los Angeles Daily Journal
(see Daily Journal Corporation)
915 E First Street
Los Angeles, CA 90012
(213) 229-5300
Fax: (213) 229-5481
www.dailyjournal.com/

Louisiana Secretary of State
Publications Division
P. O. Box 94125
Baton Rouge, LA 70804-9125
(225) 342-2083
Publications:
8585 Archives Ave.
Baton Rouge, LA 70809
(225) 922-0309
Email: publications@sos.louisiana.gov
www.sos.la.gov

Louisiana State Bar Association
601 St. Charles Avenue
New Orleans, LA 70130-3404
(800) 421-5722 or (504) 566-1600
www.lsba.org/

LRP Publications
360 Hiatt Drive,
Palm Beach Gardens, FL 33418
Mailing address:
P.O. Box 24668
West Palm Beach, FL 33416-4668
(800) 341-7874
Fax: 561-622-2423
E-mail: custserve@lrp.com
www.lrp.com

M & M Press
P.O. Box 338
Fayetteville, AR 72702-0338
(479) 582-4265
Fax: (479) 582-4265

Madison House Publications, Inc.
(see Rowman & Littlefield)

Maine Law Book Company
(see Tower Publishing)

Maine State Bar Association
124 State Street
Augusta, ME 04330
Mailing address:
PO Box 788
Augusta, ME 04332-0788
(207) 622-7523
Fax: (207) 623-0083
E-mail: info@mainebar.org
www.mainebar.org/

Manhattan Publishing Co.
(Div. of U.S. & Europe Books, Inc.)
468 Albany Post Road
Croton-on-Hudson, NY 10520
(914) 271-5194
www.manhattanpublishing.com

Marine Law Institute
Univ. of Maine School of Law
246 Deering Avenue
Portland, ME 04102
(207) 780-4474
E-mail: oclj@maine.edu
http://mainelaw.maine.edu/academics/oclj/

Martindale-Hubbell
Customer Relations Dept.
121 Chanlon Road
New Providence, NJ 07974
(800) 526-4902
Fax: (908) 771-8704 (cust. support)
www.martindale.com

Maryland State Archives
350 Rowe Boulevard
Annapolis, MD 21401
(800) 235-4045 or (410) 260-6400
msa.helpdesk@maryland.gov
http://msa.maryland.gov/

Massachusetts Bar Association
20 West Street
Boston, MA 02111-1204
(617) 338-0500 (Boston office)
(413) 731-5134 (Springfield office)
www.massbar.org

Massachusetts Continuing Legal Education
(see Massachusetts Bar Association)
www.massbar.org/cle

Massachusetts Lawyers Weekly
Lawyers Weekly Publications, Inc.
10 Milk Street, Suite 1000
Boston, MA 02108
(800) 451-9998
E-mail: subscriptions@dolanmedia.com
http://masslawyersweekly.com

Massachusetts State Bookstore
State House, Room 116
Boston, MA 02133
(617) 727-2834
Fax: (617) 973-4858
Email: bookstore@sec.state.ma.us
www.sec.state.ma.us

McFarland
P.O. Box 611
Jefferson, NC 28640
(800) 253-2187
Fax: 336-246-4403
www.mcfarlandpub.com

McGraw-Hill Education
P.O. Box 182605
Columbus, OH 43218
(800) 262-4729 or (614) 755-4151
Fax: (614) 759-3644
(800) 338-3987 (cust. svc)
Fax: (609) 308-4480 (cust. svc)
E-mail: Orders_MHE@mcgraw-hill.com (orders)
www.mheducation.com

McGraw-Hill Professional Book Group
860 Taylor Station Rd
Blacklick, Ohio 43004
(877) 833-5524
Fax: (614) 759-3823
Email: pbg.ecommerce_custserv@mcgraw-hill.com
www.mhprofessional.com/index.html

Mealey Publications, Inc.
(see LexisNexis)
www.mealeys.com/

Media Law Resource Center
520 Eighth Avenue
North Tower – 20th Floor
New York, NY 10018
(212) 337-0200
Fax (212) 337-9893
www.medialaw.org

Medical Group Management Assoc.
MGMA Store
104 Inverness Terrace East
Englewood, CO 80112-5306
(877) 275-6462 or (303) 799-1111
Fax: (303) 397-1827
E-mail: support@mgma.com (support)
E-mail: service@mgma.com (orders)
www.mgma.com/store/

The Michie Company
(see LexisNexis)

Minnesota Institute of Legal Education (MILE)
(closed)

Minnesota Revisor of Statutes
700 State Office Building
100 Martin Luther King Jr. Blvd.
St. Paul, MN 55155-1297
(651) 296-2868
Fax: (651) 296-0569
TTY: (800) 627-3529
Email: revisor@revisor.mn.gov
www.revisor.mn.gov

Mississippi Law Institute
MLI Press
151 E. Griffith Street
Jackson, MS 39201
(601) 925-7107
Fax: (601) 925-7114
http://law.mc.edu/publications

Mississippi State Bar Association Continuing Legal Education
643 North State Street
Jackson, MS 39202
(601) 948-4471
Fax: (601) 355-8635
E-mail: info@msbar.org
www.msbar.org/for-members/cle.aspx

Missouri Bar CLE
MCLE Department
The Missouri Bar
P.O. Box 2355
Jefferson City, MO 65102-2355
(573) 638-2233
Fax: (573) 635-2811
Email: mcle@mobar.org
www.mobar.org/mcle

Missouri Secretary of State
600 W. Main
Jefferson City, MO 65101
(573) 751-4936
Mailing address:
PO Box 1767
Jefferson City, MO 65102
(573) 751-4936 (main)
(573) 751-4218 (publications)
(573) 526-2970 (publ. Fax)
E-mail: publications@sos.mo.gov
www.sos.mo.gov

MIT Press
55 Hayward Street
Cambridge, MA 02142-1493
(617) 253-5646 (main)
Fax: (617) 258-6779
(800) 405-1619 (books)
(617) 253-2889 (journals)
http://mitpress.mit.edu

Montana Legislative Services Division
PO Box 201706
Room 110, State Capitol Building
1301 E. Sixth Avenue
Helena, MT 59620-1706
(406) 444-3064
Fax: (406) 444-3036
http://leg.mt.gov/css/Services%20Division

Montana Secretary of State
State Capitol Building
1301 E. 6th Avenue
Helena, MT 59601
Mailing Address:
P.O. Box 202801
Helena, MT 59620
(406) 444-2034
Fax: (406) 444-3976
TTY: (406) 444-9068
http://sos.mt.gov

Montana, State Bar of
7 West 6th Avenue, Suite 2B
Helena, MT 59601
Mailing address:
P. O. Box 577
Helena, MT 59624
(406) 442-7660
Fax: (406) 442-7763
E-mail: mailbox@montanabar.org
www.montanabar.org

Mortgage Bankers Association
1717 Rhode Island Avenue, NW
Suite 400
Washington, DC 20036
(202) 557-2700
www.mbaa.org

Mosby, Inc.
(see Elsevier, Health Sciences Division)

Municipal Code Corp.
1700 Capital Circle SW
Tallahassee, FL 32310
Mailing address:
P.O. Box 2235
Tallahassee, FL 32316
(800) 262-2633
Fax: (850) 575-8852
www.municode.com/

Municipal Finance Officers Assn. of the U.S. & Canada
(see Government Finance Officers Assoc. of the U.S. & Canada (GFOA)

Municipal Research & Services Center of Washington
2601 Fourth Ave, Suite 800
Seattle, WA 98121-1280
(800) 933-6772 or (206) 625-1300
Fax: (206) 625-1220
E-mail: mrsc@mrsc.org
www.mrsc.org/

National Association of Broadcasters
1771 N Street, N.W.
Washington, DC 20036
(800) 368-5644
(202) 429-5300
Fax: (202) 429-4199
E-mail: nab@nab.org
www.nab.org/

National Association of Insurance Commissioners
1100 Walnut Street, Suite 1500
Kansas City, MO 64106-2197
(816) 783-8300
Fax: (816) 460-7593
E-Mail: prodserv@naic.org
www.naic.org

National Association of Regulatory Utility Commissioners (NARUC)
1101 Vermont Avenue, N.W., Suite 200
Washington, DC 20005
(202) 898-2200
Fax: (202) 898-2213
E-Mail: admin@naruc.org
www.naruc.org/

National Business Institute
PO Box 3067
Eau Claire, WI 54702
800-930-6182
Fax: 715-835-1405
Email: customerservice@nbi-sems.com
www.nbi-sems.com/

National Center for State Courts
300 Newport Avenue
Williamsburg VA 23185
(800) 616-6164
Orders:
Fulfillment Department
P.O. Box 580
Williston, VT 05495-0580
(888) 228-6272 or (802) 862-0095
Fax: (802) 864-4672
E-mail: ncsc.orders@aidcvt.com
www.ncsconline.org/

National Center on Poverty Law, Inc.
50 East Washington St., Suite 500
Chicago, Illinois, 60602
(312) 263-3830
Fax: (312) 263-3846
E-mail: info@povertylaw.org
www.povertylaw.org

National Clearinghouse of Legal Services
(see National Center on Poverty Law)

National Conference of State Legislatures
7700 East First Place
Denver, CO 80230
(303) 364-7700
Fax: (303) 364-7800
www.ncsl.org

National Consumer Law Center
7 Winthrop Square
Boston, MA 02110-1245
(617) 542-8010
Fax: (617) 542-8028
E-mail: consumerlaw@nclc.org
www.consumerlaw.org/

National Contract Management Assoc. (NCMA)
21740 Beaumeade Circle, Suite 125
Ashburn, Virginia 20147
(800) 344-8096 or (571) 382-0082
Fax: (703) 448-0939
www.ncmahq.org

National Council of Juvenile & Family Court Judges
University of Nevada-Reno
Box 8970
Reno, NV 89507
(775) 784-6012
Fax: (775) 784-6628
E-mail: staff@ncjfcj.org
www.ncjfcj.org/

National Court Reporters Assn.
8224 Old Courthouse Road
Vienna, VA 22182-3808
800-272-6272 or 703-556-6272
Fax: (703) 556-6291
TTY: (703) 556-6289
E-mail: msic@ncrahq.org
www.ncra.org

National Employment Law Institute
1101 Washington Avenue
Golden, Colorado 80401
Mailing Address
P.O. Box 1189
Golden, CO 80402
(303) 861-5600
Fax: (303) 861-5665
E-mail: neli@neli.org
www.neli.org

National Fire Protection Assn.
1 Batterymarch Park
Quincy, MA 02169-7471
(617) 770-3000 (main)
Fax: (617) 770-0700
Sales/Customer Service:
(800) 344-3555 or (617) 770-3000
E-mail: custserv@nfpa.org
www.nfpa.org

National Institute for Trial Advocacy (NITA)
1685 38th Street, Suite 200
Boulder, CO 80301-2735
800.225.6482 (main)
Fax 720.890.7069
Publications:
(800) 833-9844
Fax: (518) 487-3584
E-mail: customer.support@lexisnexis.com
www.nita.org

National Judicial College, The Div. of American Bar Assoc.
Judicial College Building/MS 358
Reno, NV 89557
(800) 255-8343 or (775) 784-6747
Fax: (775) 784-1253
E-mail: info@judges.org
www.judges.org

National Practice Institute
701 4th Ave S
Minneapolis, MN 55415
(612) 337-9082

National School Boards Association
1680 Duke Street
Alexandria, VA 22314
(703) 838-6722
Fax: (703) 683-7590
E-mail: info@nsba.org
www.nsba.org

National Tax Publications
67 Ramapo Valley Road, Suite 102
Mahwah, NJ 07430
Mailing address:
P.O. Box 767
Mahwah, NJ 07430-0767
800-914-8138 or 201-684-0828
Fax: 888-814-8140 or 201-684-0829
Email: info@nattax.com
www.nattax.com

Naval Institute Press
(see U.S. Naval Institute)

Naval War College Press
Code 32, Naval War College
686 Cushing Road
Newport, RI 02841-1207
(401) 841-2236
Fax: (401) 841-1071
E-mail: press@usnwc.edu
www.usnwc.edu/press.aspx

Neal-Schuman Publishers, Inc.
(an imprint of the American Library Association)
50 E. Huron
Chicago, IL 60611
Phone 800.545.2433
Orders/Customer Service
ALA STORE
P.O. Box 932501
Atlanta, GA 31193-2501
(866) 746-7252 or (770) 280-4185
Fax: (770) 280-4155
E-mail: ala-orders@pbd.com
www.neal-schuman.com

Nebraska Clerk of the Supreme Court
Room 2413, State Capitol
1445 K Street
Lincoln, NE 68509
Mailing address:
P.O. Box 98910
Lincoln, NE 68509
(402) 471-3731
Fax: (402) 471-3480
http://www.supremecourt.ne.gov/4857/clerk-nebraska-supreme-court-and-court-appeals

Nebraska Continuing Legal Education, Inc.
Roman Hruska Law Center
635 S. 14th St., Suite 200
P. O. Box 81809
Lincoln, NE 68508
(800) 927-0117 or (402) 475-7091
FAX (402) 475-7098
www.nebar.com

Nebraska State Library Publications Office
325 State Capitol
1445 K Street
Lincoln, NE 68509
Mailing address:
State Library
P.O. Box 98931
Lincoln, NE 68509
(402) 471-3189
Fax: (402) 471-1011
E-mail: nsc.lawlibrary@nebraska.gov
www.supremecourt.ne.gov/1082/state-library

Nebraska Secretary of State
State Capitol
1445 K St., Suite 2300
Lincoln, NE 68509
Mailing address:
P.O. Box 94608
Lincoln, NE 68509-4608
(402) 471-2554
Fax: (402) 471-3237
E-mail: sos.info@nebraska.gov

www.sos.state.ne.us

Nevada, State Bar of
Continuing Legal Education
600 E. Charleston Blvd
Las Vegas, NV 89104
702-382-2200
Fax (CLE): 888-660-0060 or 702-385-2045
www.nvbar.org

New England LawPress
204 Wyassup Road
N. Stonington, CT 06359
Mailing address:
P.O. Box 331
Westerly, RI 02891
(860) 535-0362
Fax: (860) 535-0278
E-mail: orders@nelawpress.com
www.nelawpress.com

New Generation Research, Inc.
1212 Hancock Street, Suite LL-15
Quincy, MA 02169
(800) 468-3810 or (617) 573-9554
Fax: (617) 328-1419
E-mail: customersupport@bankruptcy-data.com
www.turnarounds.com

New Hampshire Bar Association CLE
2 Pillsbury Street, Suite 300,
Concord, NH 03301
(603) 224-6942
Fax: (603) 224-2910
E-mail: NHBAinfo@nhbar.org
www.nhbar.org/NHBACLE

New Jersey State Bar Association
New Jersey Law Center
One Constitution Square
New Brunswick, NJ 08901-1520
(732) 249-5000
Fax: (732) 249-2815
www.njsba.com

New Jersey Administrative Office of the Courts
Richard J. Hughes Justice Complex
25 Market Street
Trenton, NJ 08625
(609) 292-2166
Fax: (609) 943-3038
www.judiciary.state.nj.us

New Jersey Institute for Continuing Legal Ed.
One Constitution Square
New Brunswick, NJ 08901-1520
(732) 214-8500
Fax: (732) 249-0383
E-mail: CustomerService@njicle.com
www.njicle.com

New Jersey Law Journal
238 Mulberry Street
P. O. Box 20081
Newark, NJ 07101-6081
(973) 642-0075
Fax: (973) 642-0920
Fax: (877) 256-2472 (subs.)
www.law.com/jsp/nj

New Jersey Office of Administrative Law
9 Quakerbridge Plaza
Mercerville, NJ 08619
Mailing address:
P.O. Box 049
Trenton, New Jersey 08625-0049
(609) 689-4028
Fax: (609) 689 4070
www.state.nj.us/oal

New Mexico Compilation Commission
(Supreme Court publications)
4355 Center Place
Santa Fe, NM 87507-9706
Mailing address:
P.O. Box 15549
Santa Fe, NM 87592-5549
(505) 827-4821
Fax: (505) 827-4869
http://www.nmcompcomm.us/

New Mexico, State Bar of
Center for Legal Education
5121 Masthead NE
Albuquerque, NM 87109
Mailing address:
PO Box 92860
Albuquerque, NM 87199-2860
800-876-6227 or 505-797-6000
505-821-1980 (MCLE)
Fax: 505-828-3765
Email: sbnm@nmbar.org
www.nmbar.org

New York Department of State,
Division of Administrative Rules
One Commerce Plaza, Suite 650
99 Washington Avenue
Albany, NY 12231-0001
(518) 474-6957
Fax: (518) 473-9055
www.dos.state.ny.us

New York Law Journal
345 Park Avenue
New York, NY 10010
(877) 256-2472
www.newyorklawjournal.com

New York State Bar Association
Continuing Legal Education
One Elk Street
Albany, NY 12207
(800) 582.2452
Fax: (518) 463-5993.
www.nysba.org/cle

New York University Press
838 Broadway, 3rd Floor
New York, NY 10003-4812
(800) 996-6987
(212) 998-2575
Fax: (212) 995-3833
E-mail: information@nyupress.org
E-mail: orders@nyupress.org
www.nyupress.org

Niche Publishers
2917 Meadow View Road
Falls Church, VA 22042-1338
(800) 484-4948
(703) 207-0960
Fax: (703) 207-0954
www.nichepub.com

NILS Publishing Co.
(see Wolters Kluwer Financial Services)

Nolo Press
950 Parker Street
Berkeley, CA 94710
(800) 992-6656 or (800) 728-3555
(510) 704-2248
www.nolo.com

Nonprofit Risk Management Center
15 N. King St., Suite 203
Leesburg, VA 20176
(202) 785-3891
Fax: (703) 443-1990
www.nonprofitrisk.org

North Carolina Academy of Trial Lawyers
North Carolina Advocates for Justice
1312 Annapolis Drive
P.O. Box 10918
Raleigh, NC 27605
(800) 688-1413
Fax: (919) 832-6361
www.ncaj.com

North Carolina Administrative Office of the Courts
901 Corporate Center Drive
Raleigh, NC 27607
Mailing address:
P.O. Box 2448,
Raleigh, NC 27602-2448
(919) 890-1000
www.nccourts.org

North Carolina Bar Association
8000 Weston Parkway
Cary, NC 27513
Mailing address:
P.O. Box 3688
Cary, NC 27519-3688
(800) 662-7407 or (919) 677-0561
Fax: (919) 677-0761
E-mail: askCLE@ncbar.org (CLE)
www.ncbar.org

North Dakota, State Bar Association of
504 N. Washington
Bismarck, ND 58501
Mailing address:
PO Box 2136
Bismarck, ND 58502-2136
(800) 472-2685 or (701) 255-1404
Fax: (701) 224-1621
www.sband.org

Norton, W.W. & Co., Inc.
500 Fifth Avenue
New York, New York 10110
(800) 233-4830 or (212) 354-5500
Fax: (212) 869-0856
www.wwnorton.com

Oakstone Legal & Business Publishing
(see Progressive Business Publications)
www.pbp.com

Oasis Publishing
(see Jurisearch)

Oceana Publications, Inc.
(now owned by Oxford University Press)
http://www.oup.com/us/

Ohio State Bar Association
Continuing Legal Education
1700 Lake Shore Drive
Columbus, Ohio 43204
(877) 880-1335 or (614) 487-2050
www.ohiobar.org

Oklahoma Bar Association
1901 N. Lincoln Blvd.
Oklahoma City, OK 73105
(800) 522-8065 or (405) 416-7000
Fax: 405-416-7001
www.okbar.org

ORC International
902 Carnegie Center, Suite 220
Princeton, NJ 08540-6530
800-444-4672 or 609-452-5400
Fax: 609-452-5292
E-mail: answers@orcinternational.com
www.orcinternational.com

Oregon Law Institute
Gus J. Solomon Courthouse
620 SW Main Street, Suite 706
Portland, OR 97205-3037
800-222-8213 or 503-768-6580
Fax: 503-768-6585
E-mail: oli@lclark.edu
http://law.lclark.edu/continuing_education

Oregon Legislative Counsel Committee
Oregon State Capitol
900 Court St. NE
Salem, Oregon 97301
800-332-2313
503-378-8148
Fax: 503-373-1043
E-mail: help.leg@state.or.us
www.lc.state.or.us/lcc.htm

Oregon State Bar Continuing Legal Education
16037 SW Upper Boones Ferry Rd.
Tigard, OR 97224
Mailing address:
PO Box 231935
Tigard, OR 97281-1935
(503) 620-0222 (main)
(503) 431-6413 (CLE)
(800) 452-8260 (within Oregon)
Fax: (503) 684-1366
Fax: (503) 968-4456 (CLE)
E-mail: info@osbar.org
www.osbarcle.org

Oregon State Court Administrator Oregon Supreme Court
Supreme Court Building
1163 State Street
Salem OR 97301-2563
(503) 986-5500
Fax: (503) 986-5503
Email: ojd.info@ojd.state.or.us
http://courts.oregon.gov/OJD/OSCA

Ovid, a Wolters-Kluwer business
333 Seventh Avenue, 20th Floor
New York City, NY 10001
646.674.6300
800.950.2035
Fax: 646.674.6301
Email: sales@ovid.com
www.ovid.com

Oxford University Press
2001 Evans Road
Cary, NC 27513
(919) 677-0977 (main)
(800) 451-7556 (orders)
(800) 445-9714 (cust. service)
Fax: (919) 677-1303 (cust. service)
Email: custserv.us@oup.com
http://global.oup.com/?cc=us

Public Affairs Information Service (PAIS)
(see CSA)

Panel Publishers
(see Aspen Publishers)

PEG
(See Professional Education Group)

Pennsylvania Bar Institute
5080 Ritter Road
Mechanicsburg, PA 17055-6903
(800) 932-4637 or (717) 796-0804
E-mail: info@pbi.org
www.pbi.org

Pennsylvania Historical and Museum Commission
State Book Store
State Museum Building
300 North Street
Harrisburg, PA 17120
(717) 787-3362
Fax: (717) 783-9924
www.phmc.state.pa.us/

Pike & Fischer, Inc.
(see Bloomberg BNA)

Pocket Press, Inc.
PO Box 25124
Portland, OR 97298-0124
(888) 237-2110
Fax: (877) 643-3732
Email: sales@pocketpressinc.com
www.pocketpressinc.com

Potomac Publishing Co.
(see Federal News Service)
www.potomacpublishing.com

Pound Civil Justice Institute
777 Sixth Street, NW, Suite 200
Washington, DC 20001
202-944-2841
Fax: 202-298-6390
Email: info@poundinstitute.org
www.roscoepound.org

Practising Law Institute
810 Seventh Avenue, 21st Floor
New York, NY 10019
(800) 260-4754
Fax: (800) 321-0093
E-mail: info@pli.edu
www.pli.edu

Practitioners Publishing Co.
P.O. Box 966
Ft. Worth, TX 76101-0966
(800) 431-9025 or (817) 332-3709
Fax: (817) 877-3694
http://ppc.thomson.com

Praeger Publishers
(see ABC-CLIO)

A. S. Pratt & Sons
(an imprint of Sheshunoff Information Services)
805 Fifteenth Street, NW, Third Floor
Washington DC 20005-2207
800-572-2797
800-456-2340 (cust. service)
E-mail: customercare.sis@sheshunoff.com
www.aspratt.com

Professional Education Group, Inc., The
12401 Minnetonka Blvd.
Minnetonka, MN 55305-3994
(800) 229-2531 or (952) 933-9990
Fax: (952) 933-7784
E-mail: orders@proedgroup.com
www.proedgroup.com

Professional Education Systems Institute, Inc. (PESI)
CMI Education
PO Box 1000
Eau Claire, WI 54702
800-844-8260
Fax: 1-800-554-9775
www.pesi.com

Progressive Business Publications
370 Technology Drive
Malvern, PA 19355
800-220-5000
Fax: 610-647-8089
Email: customer_service@pbp.com
www.pbp.com

Public Affairs Information Service
(acquired by CSA)

Public Utilities Reports
11410 Isaac Newton Sq., Suite 220,
Reston, VA 20190
(800) 368-5001 or (703) 847-7720
Fax: (703) 847-0683
www.pur.com

Quinlan Publishing Company
(see Thomson Reuters Legal Solutions)
www.quinlan.com/

R & G Medical Legal Solutions, LLC (a.k.a. R & G Press)
(see Lawyers and Judges)
P. O. Box 5339
Peoria, Arizona 85385-5339
(888) 486-2245
Fax: (623) 566-3438
E-mail: Contact@RNGMedCons.com
www.rngmedcons.com

Rand Corporation, The
Publications Orders
P.O. Box 2138
Santa Monica, CA 90407-2138
(877) 584-8642 or (310) 451-7002
Fax: (412) 802-4981
Email: order@rand.org
www.rand.org

Random House, Inc.
Div. of Bertelsmann AG
1745 Broadway
New York, NY 10019
(212) 782-9000
Fax: (212) 302-7985
Customer Service
Random House Distribution Center
400 Hahn Road
Westminster, Maryland 21157
800-726-0600 or 800-733-3000 or 410-848-1900
Fax: 800-659-2436 or 212-572-6045
www.randomhouse.com

RGE Publishing
(See StoreLaw)

Rhode Island Bar Association-CLE
115 Cedar Street
Providence, RI 02903
(401) 421-5740
www.ribar.com

Rhode Island LawPress
(see New England LawPress)

Rhode Island Secretary of State
Documents Distribution Office
State House
Providence, RI 02903
(401) 222-2357
Fax: (401) 222-1356
http://sos.ri.gov

RIA
Thomson Reuters Tax & Accounting
2395 Midway Rd
Carrollton, TX 75006
Mailing address:
P.O. Box 966
Fort Worth, TX. 76101-0966
(800) 431-9025 or (817) 332-3709
Fax: (888) 216-1929
http://ria.thomsonreuters.com/

Ridenbaugh Press
P.O. 834
Carlton OR 97111
(503) 852-0010
www.ridenbaugh.com

RJS Publications
(see AJS Publications)
www.rjspublications.com

Rocky Mountain Mineral Law Foundation
9191 Sheridan Blvd., Suite 203
Westminster, CO 80031
(303) 321-8100
Fax: (303) 321-7657
E-mail: info@rmmlf.org
www.rmmlf.org

Roscoe Pound Institute
(see Pound Civil Justice Institute)

Rothman, Fred B., & Co.
(see William S. Hein & Co.)

Routledge
Orders:
Routledge, c/o Taylor & Francis Group LLC
7625 Empire Drive,
Florence, KY 41042-2919
(800) 634-7064
Fax: (800) 248-4724
Email: orders@taylorandfrancis.com
Editorial:
Routledge
8th Floor, 711 3rd Avenue
New York, NY 10017
(212) 216-7800
Fax: (212) 563-2269
www.routledge.com

Rowman & Littlefield Publishers, Inc.
Corporate address:
4501 Forbes Blvd., Suite 200
Lanham, MD 20706
Customer Service / Order Fulfillment:
15200 NBN Way, Bldg. C
Blue Ridge Summit, PA 17214
(800) 462-6420 or (717) 794-3800
Fax: (800) 338-4550 or (717) 794-3803
E-mail: orders@rowman.com (orders)
E-mail: customercare@rowman.com (inquiries)
www.rlpgbooks.com

R.R. Bowker Electronic Publishing
(see Bowker)

Rules Service Company
(See Pike & Fisher)

S & S Trade Pap.
(See Simon & Schuster)

SAGE Publications, Inc.
2455 Teller Road
Thousand Oaks, CA 91320-2218
(800) 818-7243
Fax: (800) 583-2665
www.sagepub.com

Samford University
Cumberland School of Law
800 Lakeshore Drive
Birmingham, AL 35229
(205) 726-2400
www.samford.edu

Saunders, W.B. Co.
(see Elsevier, Health Sciences Division)

Schiffer Publishing, Ltd.
4800 Lower Valley Road,
Atglen, PA 19310
(610) 593-1777
E-mail: info@schifferbooks.com
www.schifferbooks.com/

Scholarly Resources, Inc.
(see Gale Cengage)

Securities Industry and Financial Markets Association (SIFMA)
120 Broadway, 35th Floor
New York, N.Y. 10271
(212) 313-1200
Fax: (212) 313-1301
www.sifma.org

Shepard's
(see LexisNexis)
www.lexisnexis.com/shepards/

Silver Platter Information, Inc.
(see Ovid, a Wolters-Kluwer business)

Simon & Schuster
1230 Avenue of the Americas
New York, NY 10020
(212) 698-7000
Fax: (212) 698-7007
www.simonandschuster.com

Smith, M. Lee, Publishers
a division of BLR
P.O. Box 5094
Brentwood, TN 37024-5094
(800) 274-6774
www.mleesmith.com/

Social Law Library
John Adams Courthouse
One Pemberton Square, Suite 4100
Boston, MA 02108-1792
Phone: 617-226-1500
Fax: 617-523-2458
www.socialaw.com

Society for Human Resource Management
1800 Duke Street
Alexandria, VA 22314
(800) 283-7476 or (703) 548-3440
TTY/TDD (703) 548-6999
www.shrm.org

Society of Corporate Secretaries and Governance Professionals
240 West 35th Street, Suite 400
New York, NY 10001
(212) 681-2000
Fax: (212) 681-2005
www.ascs.org/

Solano Press Books
P.O. Box 773
Point Arena, CA 95468
(800) 931-9373 or (707) 884-4508
Fax: (707) 884-4109
E-mail: spbooks@solano.com
www.solano.com

Solutions Software Corporation
a division of RegScan, Inc.
800 West 4th Street
Williamsport, PA 17701
(877) 373-4726
(570) 323-1010 x 1411
Fax: (570) 323-8082
www.env-sol.com

Sourcebooks, Inc.
1935 Brookdale Rd., Suite 139
Naperville, IL 60563
(800) 432-7444 or (630) 961-3900
Fax: (630) 961-2168
www.sourcebooks.com

Source Media
One State Street Plaza, 27th Floor
New York, NY 10004
(212) 803-8200
E-mail: custserv@sourcemedia.com (subscribe)
(800) 221-1809 (subscribe)
www.sourcemedia.com

South Carolina Bar Continuing Legal Education
950 Taylor Street
Columbia, South Carolina 29201
(803) 799-6653
(803) 799-5578 (CLE)
Fax (803) 799-4118
E-mail: scbar-info@scbar.org
www.scbar.org/CLE.aspx

South Dakota Attorney General
1302 E Hwy 14, Suite 1
Pierre, SD 57501-8501
(605) 773-3215
TTY: (605) 773-6585
Fax: (605) 773-4106
http://atg.sd.gov/

South Dakota Secretary of State
Capitol Building
500 East Capitol Avenue
Pierre, SD 57501-5070
(605) 773-3537
Fax: (605) 773-6580
E-mail: sdsos@state.sd.us
www.sdsos.gov

South Dakota, State Bar of Continuing Legal Education
222 E Capitol Avenue #3
Pierre, SD 57501-2596
(605) 224-7554
888-952-2333 (in state)
Fax: 605-224-0282
www.sdbar.org/

Southern Illinois University Press
1915 University Press Drive
SIUC Mail Code 6806
Carbondale, IL 62901
800-621-2736
Fax: 800-621-8476
E-mail: custserv@press.uchicago.edu
www.siupress.com/

Springer Publishing Company
11 West 42nd Street, 15th Floor
New York, NY 10036
(877) 687-7476 or (212) 431-4370
Fax: (212) 941-7842
E-mail: cs@springerpub.com (orders)
E-mail: subscriptions@springerpub.com (Journal subs.)
www.springerpub.com

State Net
2101 K Street
Sacramento, CA 95816
800-726-4566 or 916-444-0840
Fax: 916-446-5369
E-mail: info@statenet.com
www.statenet.com/

State Reporter Publishing Co.
P.O. Box 749
Helena, MT 59624-0749
(406) 449-8889
Fax: (406) 449-4083

State University of New York Press
22 Corporate Woods Boulevard, 3rd Floor
Albany, NY 12211-2504
Mailing address:
PO Box 960
Herndon, VA 20172-0960
877-204-6073 or 703-661-1575
(cust. service)
Fax: 877-204-6074 or 703-996-1010
E-mail: suny@presswarehouse.com
www.sunypress.edu

Stephens-Peck, Inc.
PO Box 1724
Sandy, UT 84091-1724
(801) 562-0843
Fax (801) 568-3102
www.peckstitlebook.us

STP Specialty Technical Publishers
1750 Grant Avenue
Blaine, WA 98230
(800) 251-0381 or (604) 983-3434
Fax: (604) 983-3445
www.stpub.com

Strafford Publications, Inc.
590 Dutch Valley Road
PO Box 13729
Atlanta, GA 30324-0729
800-926-7926, ext. 10 or
404-881-1141, ext. 10
Fax: 404-881-0074
Email: customerservice@straffordpub.com
www.straffordpub.com

Suffolk University Law School
Career Development
120 Tremont Street
Boston, MA 02108-4977
(617) 573-8000
Fax: (617) 573-8706
www.law.suffolk.edu/

Sweet & Maxwell Ltd.
Cheriton House
PO Box 2000
Andover SP10 9AH England
USA:
Global Legal Products
Thomson Reuters
610 Opperman Drive
Eagan, MN 55123
800-507-9378 (main)
Fax: 651-687- 7570
800-328-9352 (sales)
651-687-7000 (cust. service)
Email: globallegalproducts@thomson.com
www.sweetandmaxwell.co.uk/

Tax Analysts
400 S. Maple Avenue, Suite 400
Falls Church, VA 22046
800-955-2444 or 800-955-3444
703-533-4400 (Washington, DC area)
Fax: 703-533-4444
E-mail: cservice@tax.org
www.tax.org

Tax Form Library
518 W Main St
Louisville, KY 40202
(800) 466-9110 or (502) 589-7466
Fax: (502) 584-9557

Tax Management, Inc.
(see Bloomberg BNA)
www.bnatax.com

Taylor & Francis Group
Taylor & Francis
8th Floor, 711 3rd Avenue
New York, NY 10017, USA
Telephone: (212) 216-7800
Fax: (212) 563-2269
Orders:
Taylor & Francis Group LLC
7625 Empire Drive, Florence, Kentucky
41042-2919, USA
(800) 634-7064
Fax: (800) 248-4724
Email: orders@taylorandfrancis.com
www.taylorandfrancis.com

Temple University Press
TASB
1852 North 10th Street
Philadelphia, PA 19122
800-621-2736 or 215-926-2140
Fax: 800-621-8476
www.temple.edu/tempress

Tennessee Secretary of State
Division of Publications
312 Rosa L. Parks Avenue
8th Floor, Snodgrass Tower
Nashville, TN 37243-1102
Phone: (615) 741-2650
Email: publications.information@tn.gov
www.state.tn.us/sos/pub

Texas, State Bar of
Professional Development Program
P. O. Box 12487
Austin, TX 78711
800-204-2222 or 512-427-1463
Fax: 512-427-4100
800-204-2222 ext. 1806 (MCLE)
Fax: 512-427-4423 (MCLE)
E-mail: MCLE@texasbar.com
www.texasbarcle.com/CLE/home.asp

Thomas, Charles C. Publishing., Ltd.
2600 South First Street
Springfield, IL 62704
Mailing address:
P.O. Box 19265
Springfield, IL 62794-9265
(800) 258-8980 or (217) 789-8980
Fax: (217) 789-9130
E-mail: books@ccthomas.com
www.ccthomas.com

Thomson Financial
311 S. Wacker Drive, 12th floor
Chicago, IL 60606
312-408-8500
877-365-1455 (sales)
http://thomsonreuters.com/products_services/financial/

Thomson Learning
(see Cengage Learning)
www.thomsonlearning.com

Thomson Reuters
Three Times Square
New York, NY 10036
(646) 223.4000
www.thomsonreuters.com/

Thomson Reuters Legal Solutions
610 Opperman Drive
Eagan, MN 55123
800-328-2209 or 888-728-7677
http://legalsolutions.thomsonreuters.com

Thomson West
610 Opperman Drive
Eagan, MN 55123
(800) 255-2549
651-687-7000 (main)
Fax: (612) 687-7302
888-728-7677
800-328-2209 (bookstores)
E-mail: bookstore@westgroup.com
www.west.thomson.com

Thompson Publishing Group
Thompson Subscription Center
P.O. Box 105109
Atlanta GA, 30348-5109
800-677-3789
Fax: 800-999-5661
Email: service@thompson.com
www.thompson.com/public

Thornton Publishing Corporation
http://thorntonpublishing.com

Tower Publishing
588 Saco Road
Standish, ME 04084
(800) 969-8693 or (207) 642.5400
Fax: (800) 264.3870
E-mail: info@towerpub.com
www.towerpub.com

Trans-Atlantic Publications, Inc.
311 Bainbridge Street
Philadelphia, PA 19147
(215) 925-5083 or (215) 925-2762
Fax: (215) 925-1912
www.transatlanticpub.com

Transaction Publications
Transaction Publishers
Rutgers—The State Univ. of NJ
35 Berrue Circle
Piscataway, NJ 08854-8042
732-445-2280
888-999-6778 or 732-445-1245 (cust. service)
Fax: 732-445-3138
E-mail: orders@transactionpub.com
www.Transactionpub.com

Transnational Publishers, Inc.
410 Saw Mill River Road
Ardsley, NY 10502
800-914-8186 or 914-693-5100
Fax: 914-693-4430
E-mail: info@transnationalpubs.com
www.transnationalpubs.com

UMI
(see Proquest)

United Nations Publications
Customer Service
c/o National Book Network
15200 NBN Way
PO Box 190
Blue Ridge Summit, PA 17214
888-254-4286
Fax: 1-800-338-4550
E-mail: unpublications@nbnbooks.com
http://unp.un.org/

U. S. Government Bookstore
Public Documents Distribution Center
710 North Capitol Street NW
Washington, DC 20401
(202) 512-0132
Mailing address:
U.S. Government Printing Office
P.O. Box 979050
St. Louis, MO 63197-9000
866-512-1800 or 202-512-1800
Fax: 202.512.2104
E-mail: ContactCenter@gpo.gov
http://bookstore.gpo.gov

U.S. Naval Institute
291 Wood Road
Annapolis, MD 21402
(410) 268-6110 (main)
(800) 233-8764 (orders)
Fax: 410-571-1703
E-mail: trade@usni.org
www.usni.org

U.S. Patent and Trademark Office
Madison Buildings (East & West)
600 Dulany Street
Alexandria, VA 22314
Mailing address:
Mail Stop USPTO Contact Center (UCC)
P.O. Box 1450
Alexandria, VA 22313-1450
800-786-9199 or 571-272-1000
TTY: 571-272-9950
Fax: 571-273-3245
E-mail: usptoinfo@uspto.gov
www.uspto.gov

University of Chicago Press
1427 East 60th Street
Chicago, IL 60637
(773) 702-7700
Fax: (773) 702-9756
Orders:
Customer Service
Chicago Distribution Center
11030 South Langley Avenue
Chicago, IL 60628
(800) 621-2736 or (773) 702-7000
Fax: (800) 621-8476 or (773) 702-7212
E-mail: orders@press.uchicago.edu
www.press.uchicago.edu

University of Georgia Press
The University of Georgia Press
Main Library, Third Floor
320 South Jackson Street
Athens, GA 30602
Fax: 706-542-2558 or 706-542-6770
Orders:
4435 Atlanta Highway
West Dock
Athens, Georgia 30602
800-266-5842 or
Fax: 706-425-3061
www.ugapress.org

University of Idaho Press
(see Longleaf Services, Inc.)

University of Kentucky Office of Continuing Legal Education
CLE Suite, Room 20 Law Building
University of Kentucky
Lexington, KY 40506-0048
(859) 257-2921
Fax: (859) 323-9790
www.ukcle.com

University of Mississippi
Center for Continuing Legal Education
P.O. Box 879
University, MS 38677-0879
662-915-7283
Fax: 662-915-5138
E-mail: outreach@olemiss.edu
www.outreach.olemiss.edu/cle

University of Montana School of Law
Missoula, MT 59812-6552
(406) 243-4311
Fax: (406) 243-2576
E-mail: UMSchoolofLaw@umontana.edu
www.umt.edu/law

University of Oklahoma Press
1005 Asp Ave.
Norman, OK 73019-6051
Fax: (405) 325-4000
Orders:
University of Oklahoma Press
Attn: Order Department
2800 Venture Drive
Norman, OK 73069-8216
800-627-7377 or 405-325-2000
Fax: 800-735-0476 or 405-364-5798
E-Mail: presscs@ou.edu
www.oupress.com

University of Texas Press
2100 Comal St. Stop E4800
Austin, TX 78712-1303
Ph: 512-471-7233 x3
Mailing address:
P.O. Box 7819
Austin, TX 78713-7819
(800) 252-3206
(512) 471-7233
Fax: (512) 232-7178
E-mail: cs@utpress.utexas.edu
http://utpress.utexas.edu/

University Press of America
(an imprint of Rowman & Littlefield)
4501 Forbes Blvd., Suite 200
Lanham, MD 20706
Phone: (301) 459-3366
Fax: (301) 429-5748
Customer Service
(800) 462-6420 or (717) 794-3800
Fax (800) 338-4550 or (717) 794-3803
E-mail: orders@rowman.com (orders)
E-mail: customercare@rowman.com (inquiries)
http://rowman.com/Imprint/UPA

University Press of Colorado
5589 Arapahoe Ave., Suite 206C
Boulder, CO 80303
(800) 621-2736 or (720) 406-8849
Fax: (720) 406-3443
www.upcolorado.com/

University Press of Florida
15 NW 15th Street
Gainesville, FL 32611
(800) 226-3822 or (352) 392-1351
Business fax: (352) 392-0590
800-226-3822 (orders)
Fax: 800-680-1955 (orders)
E-mail: press@upf.com
www.upf.com

University Press of Kansas
2502 Westbrooke Circle
Lawrence, KS 66045-4444
785-864-4154
785-864-4155 (orders)
Fax: 785-864-4586
E-mail: upress@ku.edu (inquiries)
E-mail: upkorders@ku.edu (orders)
www.kansaspress.ku.edu

Urban Institute Press
c/o HFS
P.O. Box 50370
Baltimore, MD 21211-4370
800-537-5487 or 410-516-6956
Fax: 410-516-6998
E-mail: hfscustserv@press.jhu.edu
www.urban.org/uipress

Urban Land Institute
1025 Thomas Jefferson St., N.W.
Suite 500
Washington, DC 20007
202-624-7000
Fax: 202-624-7140
Customer Service:
800-321-5011 or 410-626-7500
Fax: 410-626-7148
E-mail: customerservice@uli.org
Orders:
800-888-4741
Email: Orders@ipgbook.com
www.uli.org

Utah Legislative Printing Office
350 North State Street, Suite 10
Salt Lake City, UT 84114
801-538-1103
Fax: 801-538-1728
http://le.utah.gov/printing/index.htm

Utah State Bar
645 South 200 East
Salt Lake City, UT 84111
801-531-9077
Fax: 801-531-0660
E-mail: info@utahbar.org
www.utahbar.org

Vermont Bar Association Continuing Legal Education
PO Box 100
Montpelier, VT 05601-0100
802-223-2020
Fax: 802-223-1573
E-mail: info@vtbar.org
www.vtbar.org

VersusLaw, Inc.
2613 – 151st Place, NE
Redmond, WA 98052
Mailing address:
PO Box 1435
Bellevue, WA 98009
888-377-8752 or 425-250-0142
Fax: 425-250-0157
www.versuslaw.com

Carl Vinson Institute of Government University of Georgia
201 North Milledge Ave.
Athens, GA 30602-5482
706-542-2736
Fax: 706-542-9301
www.cviog.uga.edu

Virginia Continuing Legal Education
105 Whitewood Road
Charlottesville, VA 22901
Mailing Address:
P.O. Box 4468
Charlottesville, VA 22905
(800) 979-8253 or (434) 979-5644
Fax: (434) 979-3147
Email: vacle@vacle.org
www.vacle.org

Volunteer Lawyers for the Arts
1 East 53rd Street, Sixth Floor
New York, NY 10022
212-319-2787
Fax: 212-752-6575
E-mail: vlany@vlany.org
www.vlany.org

Wadsworth Publishing Co.
[see Cengage Learning]
www.cengage.com/wadsworth

WANT Publishing Company
Graybar Bldg. - Grand Central
420 Lexington Ave., Suite #300
New York, NY 10170
(212) 687-3774
Fax: (212) 687-3779
E-mail: Editor@NationsCourts.com
www.nationscourts.com

Warren, Gorham & Lamont
[See RIA]

W. E. Upjohn Institute for Employment Research
300 S. Westnedge Avenue
Kalamazoo, MI 49007-4686
888-227-8569 or 269-343-5541
Fax: 269-343-7310
E-mail: publications@upjohn.org
www.upjohninst.org

Weil Publishing Company, Inc.
(see LexisNexis)
www.lexisnexis.com/weilpublishing

West (see Thomson West)

West Academic
444 Cedar Street
Suite 700
St. Paul, MN 55101
877-888-1330
Email: support@westacademic.com
http://home.westacademic.com/

John Wiley & Sons, Inc.
10475 Crosspoint Blvd.
Indianapolis, IN 46256
877-762-2974
Fax: 800-597-3299
www.wiley.com

H. W. Wilson Co.
(see EBSCO Publishing)
www.ebscohost.com/wilson

Wisconsin Department of Administration Document Sales
101 E. Wilson Street
Madison, WI 53703
(608) 266-3358
E-mail: doaweb@doa.state.wi.us
www.doa.state.wi.us

Wisconsin Legislative Reference Bureau
(formerly **Revisor of Statutes Bureau)**
One East Main Street, Suite 200
Madison, WI 53703
Reference Desk: 608-266-0341
Circulation Desk: 608-266-7040
http://legis.wisconsin.gov/lrb/

Wisconsin, State Bar of
Legal Education Publishers
P. O. Box 7158
5302 Eastpark Blvd.
Madison, WI 53707-7158
(800) 728-7788 or (608) 257-3838
Fax: (608) 257-5502
E-mail: service@wisbar.org
www.wisbar.org

Wolters Kluwer Financial Services
100 South 5th Street, Suite 700
Minneapolis, MN 55402-1466
800-552-9408 or 612-656-7700
www.insurance.wolterskluwerfs.com

Wolters Kluwer Law & Business
7201 McKinney Circle
Frederick, MD 21704
800-234-1660 or 301-698-7100
www.wolterskluwerlb.com

Workers Compensation Research Institute
955 Massachusetts Ave.
Cambridge, MA 02139-0019
617-661- 9274
Fax: 617-661-9284
E-mail: wcri@wcrinet.org
www.wcrinet.org

World Bank Group, The
Orders:
P.O. Box 960
Herndon, VA 20172-0960
(800) 645-7247 or (703) 661-1580
Fax: (703) 661-1501
E-mail: books@worldbank.org
www.worldbank.org

Wyoming Secretary of State
State Capitol Building
200 West 24th Street
Cheyenne, WY 82002-0020
(307) 777-7378
http://soswy.state.wy.us/

Wyoming State Bar Continuing Legal Education
4124 Laramie Street
PO Box 109
Cheyenne WY 82003
855-445-8058 or 307-632-9061
Fax: 307-632-3737
www.wyomingbar.org

Yale University Press
Orders:
302 Temple Street
New Haven, CT 06511-8909
203-432-0960
Fax: 203-432-0948
Ordering:
TriLiteral
100 Maple Ridge Dr.
Cumberland, RI 02864-1769
800-405-1619
Fax: 800-406-9145
E-mail: customer.care@triliteral.org
http://yalepress.yale.edu/yupbooks/

Appendix C - Used Law Book Dealers

Advanced Book Exchange, Inc.
#4 – 410 Garbally Rd.
Victoria, BC V8T 2K1
CANADA
www.abebooks.com

The Lawbook Exchange, Ltd.
33 Terminal Avenue .
Clark, New Jersey 07066-1321
800-422-6686
FAX: 732-382-1887
www.lawbookexchange.com/

John R. Mara Law Books
4524 Sycamore Street
Dallas, TX 75204
(214) 821-1979, FAX: (214) 821-8043

Antiquarian Law Book Dealers

William S. Hein & Co., Inc.
1285 Main Street
Buffalo, NY 14209
(800) 828-7571, FAX: (716) 883-8100
http://www.wshein.com/

The Lawbook Exchange, Ltd.
965 Jefferson Ave.
Union, NJ 07083
(800) 422-6686, (908) 686-1998
FAX: (908) 686-3098
www.lawbookexchange.com/

David M. Lesser.
18th & 19th century Americana,
including antiquarian law books
One Bradley Road #302
Woodbridge, CT 06525-2235
www.lesserbooks.com
E-mail: dmlesser@pcnet.com

Meyer Boswell Books, Inc.
2141 Mission Street
San Francisco, CA 94110
(415) 255-6400
FAX: (415) 255-6499
www.meyerbos.com

Linda K. Montemaggi
Used, rare & scholarly books on
Law and legal history.
244 West 101st Street
New York, NY 10025
(212) 662-5712, FAX: (212) 865-2565
www.biblio.com/bookstores/montebooks.html
E-mail: montemag@earthlink.net

Robert H. Rubin
Antiquarian books on economics
and law.
P.O. Box 267
Brookline, MA 02146
(617) 277-7677
FAX: (617) 731-5941
www.rubinbooks.com

Appendix D - State and Local Legal Newspapers

Alabama

The Alabama Lawyer (bimonthly)
Alabama State Bar
415 Dexter Avenue
P.O. Box 671
Montgomery, AL 36101-4156
(800) 354-6154
(334) 269-1515
FAX: (205) 261-6310
www.alabar.org

Alabama Messenger (weekly)
706 Frank Nelson Building
205 N. 20th Street
Birmingham, AL 35203
(205) 252-3672
www.alabamamessenger.com/

Alabama Trial Lawyers Journal (quarterly)
Alabama Trial Lawyers Association
770 Washington Ave., Ste.170
Montgomery, AL 36104
(334) 262-4974
FAX: (334) 262-1452
www.atla.net/al/

Birmingham Bar Bulletin (quarterly)
Birmingham Bar Association
2021 2d Ave. North
Birmingham, AL 35203
(205) 251-8006
FAX: (205) 251-7193

Alaska

The Alaska Bar Rag (bimonthly)
Alaska Bar Association
P.O. Box 100279
550 W. 7th Street, Suite 1900
Anchorage, AK 99501-0279
(907) 272-7469
FAX: (907) 272-2932
www.alaskabar.org

Alaska Journal of Commerce (weekly)
301 Arctic Slope Ave., Ste. 350
Anchorage, AK 99518
(907) 561-4772
www.alaskajournal.com/

The Alaska Trial Lawyer (quarterly)
Alaska Academy of Trial Lawyers
813 West Third Avenue
P.O. Box 102323
Anchorage, AK 99510
(907) 258-4040
FAX: (907) 258-8751
www.alaskatriallawyers.org/ak/

Arizona

Arizona Attorney (monthly)
4201 N. 24th Street, Ste. 200
Phoenix, Arizona 85016-6288
Phone: 602-252-4804 4
FAX: (602) 271-4930
www.azbar.org/

Arizona Business Gazette (weekly)
200 E. Van Buren
Phoenix, AZ 85004
Mailing address:
P.O. Box 194
Phoenix, AZ 85001
(602) 444-7300
www.azcentral.com/abgnews/

The Daily Territorial
3280 E. Hemisphere Loop, Ste. 180
Tucson, AZ 85706
(520) 294-1200
www.azbiz.com/daily_territorial/

Maricopa Lawyer (monthly)
Maricopa County Bar Association
303 E. Palm Lane
Phoenix, AZ 85004
(602) 257-4200
FAX: (602) 257-0522
www.maricopabar.org

The Record Reporter
1505 N. Central Ave., Ste. 200
Phoenix, AZ 85004
Tel: (602) 417-9900
Fax: (602) 417-9910
www.recordreporter.com/

Arkansas

The Arkansas Lawyer (quarterly)
400 W. Markham
Little Rock, AR 72201
(501) 375-4605
FAX: (501) 375-4901
www.arkbar.com

ATLA Docket (quarterly)
225 E. Markham #200
Little Rock, AR 72201
(501) 376-2852
FAX: (501) 372-0951

The Daily Record
P.O. Box 3595
14710 Cantrell Rd. #B8
Little Rock, AR 72203
(501) 868-4400
FAX: (501) 868-4844

California

Advocate (monthly)
Consumer Attorneys Assoc. of L.A.
3435 Wilshire Blvd. #2870
Los Angeles, CA 90010
(213) 487-1212
FAX: (213) 487-1224
www.caala.org

Bar Brief (monthly)
Beverly Hills Bar Assoc.
300 S. Beverly Hills Drive #201
Beverly Hills, CA 90212-4886
(310) 601-2422
FAX: (310) 601-2423
www.bhba.org/

The Bar Bulletin (monthly)
Fresno County Bar Association
1221 Van Ness Avenue
Fresno, CA 93721-2084
(559) 264-2619
FAX: (559) 264-8726
www.fresnocountybar.org/

Beverly Hills Bar Assoc. Journal (quar.)
Beverly Hills Bar Assoc.
300 S. Beverly Hills Drive #201
Beverly Hills, CA 90212-4886
(310) 601-2422
FAX: (310) 601-2423
www.bhba.org/

The Bulletin (monthly)
405 14th Street #208
Oakland, CA 94612
415) 893-7155

The Business Journal (3/week)
1315 Van Ness Ave., Ste. 200
Fresno, CA 93721
(559) 490-3400
FAX: (559) 490-3532
www.thebusinessjournal.com

California Bar Journal (monthly)
555 Franklin Street
San Francisco, CA 94102
(415) 561-8804
FAX: (415) 561-8861

California Lawyer (monthly)
44 Montgomery Street, Suite 250
San Francisco, CA 94104
Tel: (415) 296-2400
Fax: (415) 296-2440

California Real Estate Journal
44 Montgomery Street, Suite 250
San Francisco, CA 94104
Tel: (415) 296-2400
Fax: (415) 296-2440

Contra Costa Lawyer Magazine
(monthly)
1001 Galaxy Way #102
Concord, CA 94520
(510) 686-6900

CTLA Forum (monthly)
980 9th Street #200
Sacramento, CA 95823
916) 442-6902
FAX: (916) 442-7734

The Daily Recorder
1115 H Street
Sacramento, CA 95814
(916) 444-2355
FAX: (916) 444-0636

The Docket (quarterly)
303 Bradford St. #A
Redwood City, CA 94063
(415) 363-4230
Docket (monthly)
901 H Street #101
Sacramento, CA 95814
(916) 443-3210
FAX: (916) 443-3199
In Brief (quarterly)
4 N. 2d Street #400
San Jose, CA 95113
(408) 287-2557

The Inter-City Express
Park Plaza
1939 Harrison St., Ste. 330
Oakland, CA 94612-3532
Tel: (510) 272-4747
Fax: (510) 465-1657

Los Angeles Daily Journal
915 East First Street
Los Angeles, CA 90012-4042
(213) 229-5300
FAX: (213) 680-3682
www.dailyjournal.com/

Los Angeles Lawyer (monthly)
617 S. Olive
Los Angeles, CA 90014
(213) 896-6503
FAX: (213) 623-4328

Marin County Court Reporter
(Tues. & Fri.)
124 Paul Dr. #108
San Rafael, CA 94903
(415) 479-4311
FAX: (415) 479-4314

Metropolitan News-Enterprise (daily)
210 S. Spring Street
Los Angeles, CA 90012
(213) 628-4384
FAX: (213) 687-3886

Orange County Reporter
600 W. Santa Ana Blvd., Ste. 205
Santa Ana, CA 92701
Tel: (714) 543-2027
Fax: (714) 542-6841

Recorder, The (daily)
American Lawyer Media
10 United Nations Plaza
Third Floor
San Francisco, CA 94102
(415) 749-5400
FAX: (415) 749-5449

Riverside Business Journal
4129 Main St., #209
Riverside, CA 92501
Tel: (951) 784-0111
Fax: (951) 784-6947

Riverside Lawyer (monthly)
Riverside County Bar Assoc.
4129 Main Street, Suite 100
Riverside, CA 92501
(951) 682-1015
FAX: (951) 682-0106
www.riversidecountybar.com/

San Bernardino County Bar Bulletin (monthly)
555 N. Arrowhead
San Bernardino, CA 92401
(909) 885-1986
FAX: (909) 889-0400

San Diego Commerce
2652 4th Ave., 2nd Floor
San Diego, CA 92103
Tel: (619) 232-3486
Fax: (619) 232-1159

San Diego Daily Transcript
2131 3rd Avenue
San Diego, CA 92101
(619) 232-4381
FAX: (619) 239-5716
www.sddt.com

San Francisco Attorney
(4/year)
465 California Street, Ste. 1100
San Francisco, CA 94104
(415) 982-1600
FAX: (415) 546-9223

San Francisco Daily Journal
44 Montgomery Street, Suite 250
San Francisco, CA 94104
(415) 252-2400
FAX: (415) 296-2440
www.dailyjournal.com/

San Francisco Recorder (daily)
Recorder Printing and Publishing Co.
99 South Van Ness Ave.
San Francisco, CA
(415) 621-5400

San Jose Post-Record (daily)
Daily Journal Corporation
90 North First Street
San Jose, CA 95113-1225
(408) 287-4866
FAX: (408) 287-2544

Sonoma Co. Daily Herald-Recorder
1818 Fourth Street
P. O. Box 877
Santa Rosa, CA 95402
707) 545-1166
FAX: (707) 545-6310

The Trial Lawyer (quarterly)
225 Bush Street, #357
San Francisco, CA 94104
(415) 956-6401
FAX: (415) 956-6680
www.sftla.org/sf/

Colorado

Boulder County Bar Newsletter (monthly)
1942 Broadway, Suite 205
Boulder, CO 80302
(303) 440-4758
www.boulder-bar.org

Colorado Journal (weekly)
Public Record Corp.
1666 Lafayette Street
Denver, CO 80218
(303) 832-8262

Colorado Lawyer (monthly)
1900 Grant St. #940
Denver, CO 80203-4309
(303) 860-1118
FAX: (303) 830-3990

Daily Transcript
31 E.. Platte Street, Suite 300
Colorado Springs, CO 80903
(719) 634-1048
(719) 634-0596

The Docket (monthly)
1900 Grant St., Suite 900
Denver, CO 80203-4309
(303) 824-5310
www.denbar.org/docket/

El Paso County Bar Newsletter (monthly)
19 N. Tejon Street #200
Colorado Springs, CO 80903
(719) 473-9700
FAX: (719) 473-0604
elpasocountybar.org/

Trial Talk (6/yr.)
1888 Sherman St., Suite 500
Denver, CO 80203
(303) 831-1192
FAX: (303) 831-0111
http://www.ctlanet.org/co/

Connecticut

Connecticut Bar Journal (bimonthly)
CT Bar Association
30 Bank Street
P.O. Box 350
New Britain, CT 06050-0350
(860) 223-4400
FAXL (860) 223-4488

Connecticut Law Journal (weekly)
111 Phoenix Avenue
Office of Production and Distribution
Enfield, CT 06082
(860) 741-3027
www.jud.state.ct.us

Connecticut Law Tribune (weekly)
American Lawyer Newspapers Group
1 Post Road #100
Fairfield, CT 06430
(203) 256-3600
FAX: (203) 255-3319

The Connecticut Lawyer (monthly)
CT Bar Association
30 Bank Street
P.O. Box 350
New Britain, CT 06050-0350
(860) 223-4400
FAX: (860) 223-4488

Delaware

Advocate (quarterly)
Delaware Trial Lawyers Assoc.
913 Market St., Ste. 315
Wilmington, DE 19801
(302) 421-2801
FAX: (302) 421-2803
www.dtla.org/de/

IN RE:
Delaware State Bar Association
301 North Market Street
Wilmington, DE 19801
(302) 658-5297
FAX: (302) 658-5212
http://www.dsba.org/

District of Columbia

Bar Report (bimonthly)
1250 H Street NW 6th Floor
Washington, DC 20005
(202) 737-4700
FAX: (202) 626-3471

DC Trial (quarterly)
1919 M Street., NW, Ste. 350
Washington, DC 20036
(202) 659-3532
FAX: (202) 775-9040
http://www.tla-dc.org/dc/

Daily Washington Law Reporter
Washington Law Reporter Company
1000 Connecticut Ave., N.W., Ste. 1100
Washington, D.C. 20036-5504
(202) 331-1700
FAX: (202) 785-8476
www.dwlr.com/

Legal Times (weekly)
1730 M Street, N.W., Suite 800
Washington, DC 20036
(800) 933-4317
(202) 457-0686
FAX: (202) 785-4539
www.law.com/jsp/dc

The Washington Lawyer (bimonthly)
1250 H St., NW, 6th Floor
Washington, DC 20005-5937
(202) 737-4700
FAX: (202) 626-3471
http://www.dcbar.org

Florida

The Academy of Florida Trial Lawyers Journal (monthly)
218 S. Monroe St.
Tallahassee, FL 32301
(904) 224-9403
FAX: (904) 224-4254

The Bar Bulletin (monthly)
P.O. Box 813
301 S. Monroe St.
Tallahassee, FL 32302
(904) 222-3292
FAX: (904) 487-7947

The Bulletin (monthly)
1200 Gulf Life Dr. #830
Jacksonville, FL 32207-9092
(904) 399-4486
FAX: (904) 399-4854

The Brief (monthly)
880 N. Orange Ave. #100
Orlando, FL 32801
(407) 422-4551
FAX: (407) 843-3470

Broward Daily Business Review
P.O. Box 14366
633 S. Andrew Ave.
Fort Lauderdale, FL 33301
(305) 468-2620
FAX: (305) 468-2630
www.dailybusinessreview.com

The Dade Co. Bar Assoc. Bulletin (mo.)
Daily Business Review
100 N.E. 7th St.
Miami, FL 33132
(305) 347-6659
FAX: (305) 374-8474

Financial News & Daily Record
10 N. Newnan St.
Jacksonville, FL 32202
(904) 356-2466
FAX: (904) 353-2628

The Florida Bar Journal (monthly)
650 Apalachee Parkway
Tallahassee, FL 32399—2300
(904) 561-5600
FAX: (904) 681-3859

The Florida Bar News (bimonthly)
650 Apalachee Parkway
Tallahassee, FL 32399-2300
(904) 561-5600
FAX: (904) 681-3859

Florida Law Weekly
1327 North Adams Street
Box 4284
Tallahassee, FL 32315
(904) 222-3171

Jury Trials and Tribulations (biweekly)
9100 S. Dadeland Blvd. #400
Miami, FL 33156
(305) 670-9735
FAX: (305) 670-6146

Lawyer (monthly)
315 E. Madison St. #1010
Tampa, FL 33602
(813) 221-7777
FAX: (813) 221-7778

Miami Daily Business Review
1 SE Third Avenue, Suite 900
Miami, Florida 33131
(305) 377-3721
www.dailybusinessreview.com

Palm Beach Daily Business Review
324 Datura Street, Suite 140
West Palm Beach, Florida 33401
(561) 820-2060
FAX: (561) 820-2077
http://www.dailybusinessreview.com

The Paraclete (monthly)
St. Petersburg Bar Association
2600 M.L. King St. N., Ste. 602
St. Petersburg, FL 33704
(727) 823-7474
FAX: (727) 823-8166
http://www.stpetebar.com/

Res Ipsa Loquitur (monthly)
Clearwater Bar Association
314 S. Missouri Ave. #107
Clearwater, FL 34616
(813) 461-4869
FAX: (813) 461-0063

Georgia

Fulton County Daily Report
American Lawyer Media
190 Pryor Street, S.W.
Atlanta, GA 30303
(404) 521-1227
FAX: (404) 523-5924
www.dailyreportonline.com

Georgia Bar Journal (monthly)
104 Marietta St., NW, Ste. 100
Atlanta, GA 30303
(404) 527-8700
FAX: (404) 527-8717
www.gabar.org

Verdict (quarterly)
Georgia Trial Lawyers Association
1250 The Hurt Building
50 Hurt Plaza S.E.
Atlanta, GA 30303-2916
(404) 522-8487
FAX: (404) 522-3705
www.gtla.org/about/publications.html

Hawaii

Hawaii Bar Journal (monthly)
Hawaii State Bar Association
1132 Bishop St., Ste. 906
Honolulu, HI 96813
(808) 537-1868
FAX: (808) 521-7936
http://www.hsba.hostme.com/hbj/hbj_main.htm

HTLA Law Reporter (monthly)
1088 Bishop St. #1111
Honolulu, HI 96813
(808) 599-2769
FAX: (808) 599-2859

Idaho

The Advocate (monthly)
The Law Center
525 West Jefferson Street
Boise, Idaho 83702
P.O. Box 895
Boise, ID 83701
(208) 334-4500
FAX: (208) 334-4515
http://www2.state.id.us/isb/index.htm

Journal (quarterly)
Idaho Trial Lawyers Assoc.
P.O. Box 1777
Boise, ID 83701
(208) 345-1890
FAX: (208) 345-1894
www.itla.org/id/

Illinois

Bar Briefs (monthly)
Kane County Bar Assoc.
128 James Street
P.O. Box 571
Geneva, IL 60134-0571
(708) 232-6416
FAX: (708) 232-7978
http://www.kanebar.org

CBA Record (8/yr.)
Chicago Bar Association
321 S. Plymouth Ct.
Chicago, IL 60604
(312) 554-2040
http://www.chicagobar.org/

Chicago Daily Law Bulletin
Law Bulletin Publishing Company
415 North State Street
Chicago, IL 60610-4674
(312) 644-7800
FAX: (312) 644-4255
http://www.lawbulletin.com

Chicago Lawyer (monthly)
Law Bulletin Publishing Company
415 North State Street
Chicago, IL 60610
(312) 644-7800
(312) 644-4255
http://www.lawbulletin.com

DCBA BRIEF (monthly)
DuPage County Bar Association
126 S. County Farm Road
Wheaton, IL 60187
(630) 653-7779
www.dcba.org/brief/briefhp.htm

Illinois Bar Journal (monthly)
424 S. Second Street
Springfield, IL 62701
(800) 252-8908
(217) 525-1760
FAX: (217) 525-0712
http://www.isba.org/Member/isbajournal.asp

Illinois Legal Times (monthly)
656 W. Randolph St.
Chicago, IL 60661
(312) 756-9158

ISBA Bar News (2/mo.)
424 S. Second Street
Springfield, IL 62701
(800) 252-8908
(217) 525-1760
FAX: (217) 525-0712
www.illinoisbar.org

The Lawyer (monthly)
321 W. State #300
Rockford, IL 61101
(815) 964-4992
FAX: (815) 964-9091

Indiana

Court and Commercial Record (daily)
41 E. Washington St., Ste 200
Indianapolis, IN 46204
(317) 636-0200
FAX: (317) 263-5259

Indiana Law Reporter (24/yr.)
P.O. Box 270
209 Michigan Avenue
Crystal Falls, MI 49920-1312
(906) 875-6970

The Indiana Lawyer (bimonthly)
431 N. Pennsylvania Street
Indianapolis, IN 46204
(317) 636-0200
FAX: (317) 263-5259

Res Gestae (monthly)
One Indiana Square, Ste, 530
Indianapolis, IN 46204
(317) 639-5465
FAX: (317) 266-2581
www.inbar.org

Iowa

In Brief (quarterly)
Iowa Trial Lawyers Assoc.
218 6th Avenue #526
Des Moines, IA 50309
(515) 280-7366
FAX: (515) 280-3745
http://www.iowatla.org/

The Iowa Lawyer (monthly)
521 E. Locust
Des Moines, IA 50309
(515) 243-3179
FAX: (515) 243-2511
http://www.iowabar.org

Kansas

The Barletter (monthly)
Johnson County Bar Assoc.
130 N. Cherry, Ste. 103
Olathe, KS 66061
(913) 780-5460
FAX: (913) 780-5480
www.jocobar.org

Bar-O-Meter (monthly)
Wichita Bar Association
225 N. Market, Suite 200
Wichita, KS 67202
(316) 263-2251
FAX: (316) 263-0629
www.wichitabar.org

The Johnson Co. Legal Record (weekly)
The Legal Record
213 E. Santa Fe, Ste. 2
Olathe, KS 66061
(913) 780-57909
thelegalrecord.net.

The Journal (10/yr.)
Kansas Bar Assoc.
1200 S.W. Harrison St.
P.O. Box 1037
Topeka, KS 66612
(913) 234-5696
FAX: (913) 234-3813
ksbar.org/public/journals/

Journal of the Kansas Trial Lawyers Association (bimonthly)
719 SW Van Buren
Topeka, KS 66603
(913) 232—7756
http://www.ktla.org/ks

Topeka Metro News (Wed. & Fri.)
630 S. Kansas Ave.
P. O. Box 1794
Topeka, KS 66603
(913) 232-8600
FAX: (913) 235-8707
www.topekametro.com/

Kentucky

The Advocate (bimonthly)
12700 Shelbyville Road #4101
Louisville, KY 40243
(502) 244-1320
FAX: (502) 244-1275

Bar Briefs (monthly)
707 W. Main Street
Louisville, Ky 40202
(502) 583-5314
FAX: (502) 583-4113

The Daily Record
436 S. 7th Street
Louisville, KY 40201
(502) 583-4471

Fayette Co. Bar Assoc. Bar News
(bimonthly)
106 W. Vine St. #301
Lexington, KY 40502
(606) 266-9897

Kentucky Bar News (quarterly)
514 W. Main Street
Frankfort, KY 40601-1883
(502) 564-3795
FAX: (502) 564-3225

Kentucky Bench & Bar Magazine
(quarterly)
514 W. Main Street
Frankfort, KY 40601-1883
(502) 564-3795 FAX: (502) 564-3225

Louisiana

Baton Rouge Daily News
8252 West El Cajon Drive
Baton Rouge, LA 70815
(504) 926-8882
FAX: (504) 927-2742

Caldwell Watchman (weekly)
P.O. Box 1259
Columbia, LA 71418
(318) 649-6411
FAX: (318) 649-8358

The Daily Legal News Inc.
501 Texas Street, Room M-103
Shreveport, LA 71101-5413
(318) 222-0213

Delhi Dispatch (weekly)
P.O. Box 608
Delhi, LA 71232
(318) 378-2444

Louisiana Advocates (quarterly)
442 Europe Street
Baton Rouge, LA 70802
(504) 383-5554
FAX: (504) 387-1993

Louisiana Bar Journal (bimonthly)
601 St. Charles Ave.
New Orleans, LA 70130
(504) 566-1600
FAX: (504) 566-0930

Richland Beacon News (weekly)
P.O. Box 209
Rayville, LA 71259
(318) 725-6467

Tensas Gazette (weekly)
P.O. Box 27
St. Joseph, LA 71356
(318) 766-3258
FAX: (318) 766-4273

The Trial Brief (monthly)
442 Europe Street
Baton Rouge, LA 70802
(504) 383-5554
FAX: (504) 387-1993

West Carroll Gazette (weekly)
P.O. Box 1007
Oak Grove, LA 71255
(318) 428-3207
FAX: (318) 428-2747

Maine

Maine Bar Journal (bimonthly)
P.O. Box 788
124 State Street
Augusta, ME 04332-0788
(207) 622-7523
FAX: (207) 623-0083

MTLA News (quarterly)
160 Capitol Street
P.O. Box 420
Augusta, ME 04332-0428
(207) 623-2661
FAX: (207) 621-0118

Maryland

Bar Bulletin (monthly)
520 W. Fayette St.
Baltimore, MD 21201
(410) 685-7878

The Daily Record
11 E. Saratoga Street
Baltimore, MD 21202
(410) 752-3849
FAX: (410) 332-0698

The Maryland Bar Journal
(bimonthly)
520 W. Fayette Street
Baltimore, MD 21201
(410) 685-7878

Maryland Family Law Weekly
11 E. Saratoga
Baltimore, MD 21201
(410) 752-3849
FAX: (410) 332-0698

News-Journal (monthly)
14330 Old Marlborough Pike
Upper Marlboro, MD 20772
(301) 952-1442
FAX: (301) 952-1429

Trial Reporter (quarterly)
1018 N. Charles Street
Baltimore, MD 21201
(410) 539-4336
FAX: (410) 783-5981

Massachusetts

The Boston Bar Journal
(bimonthly)
16 Beacon Street
Boston, MA 02108
(617) 742-0615

Journal of the Massachusetts Academy of Trial Lawyers (quarterly)
15 Broad Street #415
Boston, MA 02109
(617) 248-5858
FAX: (617) 248-8701

Massachusetts Bar Association Lawyer's Journal (monthly)
20 West Street
Boston, MA 02111
(617) 542-3602, Ext. 218
FAX: (617) 426-4344

Massachusetts Law Review (quarterly)
20 West Street
Boston, MA 02111
(617) 542-3602, Ext. 218
FAX: (617) 426-4344

Massachusetts Lawyers Weekly
Lawyers Weekly Publications, Inc.
41 West Street
Boston, MA 02111
(800) 451-9998
(617) 451-7300
FAX: (617) 451-7326

Michigan

ANNOTATIONS (monthly)
Kalamazoo County Bar Association
227 W. Michigan Avenue
Kalamazoo, MI 49007
(616) 384-8257
FAX: (616) 384-8258

Bar Beat (bimonthly)
100 McKinnon Bldg.
Flint, MI 48502
(810) 232-6012
FAX: (810) 232-8310

The Detroit Legal News (daily)
2001 W. Lafayette
Detroit, MI 48216
(313) 961-3949
FAX: (313) 961-7817

Flint-Genesee Co. Legal News (weekly)
111 W. Young Street
Clio, MI 48420
(810) 686-2080
FAX: (801) 686-6850

Grand Rapids Bar Newsletter (monthly)
200 Monroe #30
Grand Rapids, MI 49503
(616) 454-5550, FAX: (616) 454-7681
Grand Rapids Legal News (weekly)
840 Ottawa NW
Grand Rapids, MI 49503
(616) 454-9293

The Legal Advertiser (weekly)
18400 Woodward Ave.
Detroit, MI 48203
(313) 868-9709
FAX: (313) 868-8765

The Legal Advertiser Oakland County (weekly)
18400 Woodward Ave.
Detroit, MI 48203
(313) 868-9709
FAX: (313) 868-8765

Macomb County Legal News (weekly)
67 Cass Avenue
Mt. Clemens, MI 48043
(810) 469-4510
FAX: (810) 469-2892

Michigan Bar Journal (monthly)
306 Townsend Street
Lansing, MI 48933-2083
(517) 372-9033
FAX: (517) 482-6248

Michigan Lawyers Weekly
333 S. Washington St., Suite 300
Lansing, MI 48933
(517) 374-6200
FAX: (517) 374-6222

MTLA Advance Sheet (8/yr.)
501 South Capitol #405
Lansing, MI 48933
(517) 482-7740
FAX: (517) 482-5332

MTLA Quarterly
501 South Capitol #405
Lansing, MI 48933
(517) 482-7740
FAX: (517) 482-5332

Pontiac-Oakland County Legal News (weekly)
P.O. Box 430238
500 W. Huron #102
Pontiac, MI 48343-0238
(810) 338-4567, FAX: (810) 338-4240

Res Ipsa Loquitur (monthly)
P.O. Box 8645
Ann Arbor, MI 48107
(313) 994-4912, FAX: (313) 663-2430

Minnesota

Bench & Bar of Minnesota (11/yr.)
514 Nicollet Ave. #300
Minneapolis, MN 55402
(612) 333-1183, FAX: (612) 333-4927

Finance and Commerce (daily)
615 South 7th Street
Minneapolis, MN 55415
(612) 333-4244
FAX: (612) 333-3243

Finance and Commerce Weekly
Appellate Courts Edition
615 South 7t Street
Minneapolis, MN 55415
(612) 333-4244
FAX: (612) 333-3243

The Hennepin Lawyer (bimonthly)
Minnesota Law Center #350
514 Nicollet Mall
Minneapolis, MN 55402
(612) 340-0022
FAX: (612) 340-9518

Minnesota Trial Lawyer (quarterly)
706 2d Avenue S. #140
Minneapolis MN 55402
(612) 375-1707
FAX: (612) 375-1707

Minnesota's Journal of Law & Politics (monthly)
10 South 5th Street #415
Minneapolis, MN 55402
(612) 338-3828
FAX: (612) 338-1876

Saint Paul Legal Ledger
640 Minnesota Building
46 E. 4th Street
St. Paul, MN 55101-1163
(612) 222-0059

Mississippi

Mississippi Law Week
6069 Old Canton Rd., #757
Jackson, MS 39211
(800) 800-3615

Voir Dire (3/yr.)
P.O. Box 1192
Jackson, MS 39205
(601) 948-8631
FAX: (601) 948-8633

Missouri

Courier Post (daily)
201 N. Main Street #205
St. Charles, MO 63301
(314) 949-6928
FAX: (314) 949-6973

Daily Events
Daily Events Corp.
327 South Patton
Springfield, MO 65806
(417) 866-1401

The Daily Record and The Kansas City Daily News-Press
3611 Troost Avenue
Kansas City, MO 64109
(816) 931-2002
FAX: (816) 561-6675

Journal of the Missouri Bar (bimonthly)
326 Monroe Street
Jefferson City, MO 65101
(314) 635-4128
FAX: (314) 635-2811

Kansas City Counselor (monthly)
8525 Rosehill Road
Kansas City, MO 66215
(913) 888-1591
FAX: (913) 541-0542

Missouri Lawyers Weekly
223 Madison Street
Jefferson City, MO 65101
(314) 659-5091 or (800) 635-5297
FAX: (314) 634-2287

The Missouri Trial Attorney (bimonthly)
P.O. Box 1792
Jefferson City, MO 65102
(314) 635-5215
FAX: (314) 634-6282

St. Charles County Record (daily)
201 N. Main Street #205
St. Charles, MO 63301
(314) 949-6928, FAX: (314) 949-6973

St. Joseph Daily Courier
1014 S. 10th Street
St. Joseph, MO 64503
(800) 635-5297 or (314) 634-8300

St. Louis Bar Journal (quarterly)
Legal Communications
612 N. 2nd St., 4th Floor
St. Louis, MO 63188
(314) 421-1880, FAX: (314) 421-0436

St. Louis Countian (daily)
612 N. 2d St. 4th Floor
St. Louis, MO 63102
(314) 421-1880
FAX: (314) 421-0436

St. Louis Daily Record
612 N. 2d St. 4th Floor
St. Louis, MO 63102
(314) 421-1880
FAX: (314) 421-0436

St. Louis Lawyer (quarterly)
Legal Communications Corp.
612 N. 2nd St., 4th Floor
St. Louis, MO 63188
(314) 421-1880
FAX: (314) 421-0436

St. Louis Watchman Advocate (daily)
200 S. Benmiston
Clayton, MO 63105
(314) 725-1515

St. Peters Courier Post (daily)
P. O. Box 496
St. Peters, MO 63376
(314) 949-6973

Wentzville Union & St. Charles County Record (daily)
100 W Pearce Blvd
Wentzville, MO 63385
636.327.6279

Montana

The Montana Lawyer (11/yr.)
The Power Block
7 W. 6th Ave., Ste. B
Helena, MT 59624
(406) 442-7660
FAX: (406) 442-7763
montanabar.org/

Trial Trends (quarterly)
32 S. Ewing, Suite 312
Helena, MT 59624
(406) 443-3124
FAX: (406) 443-6943
www.monttla.com/MT/

Nebraska

The Complete Lawyer
Nebraska State Bar Assoc.
635 S. 14th St.
P.O. Box 81809
Lincoln, NE 68501
(800) 927-0117
(402) 475-7091

FAX: (402) 475-7098

The Daily Record
3323 Leavenworth Street
Omaha, NE 68105
(402) 345-1303
FAX: (402) 345-2351
omahadailyrecord.com/

Daily Reporter
Gant Publishing Company
2145 North Cottner
Lincoln, NE 68505-2921
(402) 466-8521
FAX: (402) 466-6272

Habeas Corpus (9/yr.)
Nebraska Criminal Defense Attorneys Assoc.
1327 H Street, Ste. 102
Lincoln, NE 68508
(402) 476-1253
FAX: (402) 435-8234
nebraskacriminaldefense.org/

The Prairie Barrister (quarterly)
Nebraska Assoc. of Trial Attorneys
941 O Street, Ste. 203
Lincoln, NE 68508
(402) 435-5526
(402) 435-5547
www.nebraskatrial.com/NE/

Nevada

Advocate
Nevada Trial Lawyers Assoc.
406 N. Nevada St.
Carson City, NV 89703
(702) 883-3577
FAX: (702) 883-5372
ntla.org/

Nevada Journal
430 S. 15th St.
Las Vegas, NV 89101
Tel: (702) 383-9575
Fax: (702) 383-9576

Nevada Lawyer (monthly)
3444 Golden Pedal St.
Las Vegas, NV 89129
(702) 254-8997
FAX: (702) 804-5304
nvbar.org

Nevada Legal News (quarterly)
930 S. Fourth Street
Las Vegas, NV 89101
(702) 382-2747
FAX: (702) 598-0641

New Hampshire

New Hampshire Bar Journal (quarterly)
New Hampshire Bar Assoc.
112 Pleasant Street
Concord, NH 03301
(603) 224-6942
FAX: (603) 224-2910

New Hampshire Bar News (22/yr.)
New Hampshire Bar Assoc.
112 Pleasant Street
Concord, NH 03301
(603) 224-6942
FAX: (603) 224-2910

Trial Bar News
N.H. Trial Lawyers Assoc.
280 Pleasant St.
P.O. Box 447
Concord, NH 03302
(603) 224-7077
FAX: (603) 224-3256
www.nhtla.org

New Jersey

The Docket (bimonthly)
1201 Bacharach Blvd.
Atlantic City, NJ 08401
(609) 345-3444
FAX: (609) 345-6279

The Barrister (10/yr.)
Midlantic Bank Bldg.
Broadway & Cooper Streets
Camden, NJ 08101
(609) 964-3420
FAX: (609) 964-9016

MCBA Monthly
87 Bayard Street
New Brunswick, NJ 08901
(908) 828-3433
FAX: (908) 828-5862

New Jersey Law Journal (weekly)
238 Mulberry Street
Box 20081
Newark, NJ 07101-6081
(201) 642-0075
FAX: (201) 642-0920

New Jersey Lawyer,
The Magazine (8/yr.)
485 B Route 1 #100
Iselin, NJ 08830
(908) 750-4994, FAX: (908) 636-6030

New Jersey Lawyer, The Weekly
Newspaper
485 B Route 1 #100
Iselin, NJ 08830
(908) 750-4994
FAX: (908) 636-6030

The Straight Word (monthly)
117 High Street
Mount Holly, NJ 08060
(609) 261-4542
FAX: (609) 267-1806

New Mexico

Bar Bulletin (weekly)
State Bar of New Mexico
P.O. Box 25883
Albuquerque, NM 87125
(505) 842-6132
FAX: (505) 843-8765

New Mexico Trial Lawyer (monthly)
P.O. Box 301
Albuquerque, NM 87103
(505) 243-6003
FAX: (505) 243-6003

New York

ACBA Newsletter (monthly)
Albany County Courthouse
Room 315
Albany, NY 12207
(518) 445-7691
FAX: (518) 445-7511

THE ADVOCATE (quarterly)
851 Grand Concourse, Room 124
Bronx, NY 10451
(718) 293-5600
FAX: (718) 681-0098

The Advocate (monthly)
Dutchess County Bar Assoc.
P.O. Box 4865
Poughkeepsie, NY 12602
(914) 473-2488
FAX: (914) 473-7941

The Attorney of Nassau County
(monthly)
322 Main Street
Huntington, NY 11743
(516) 427-7000
FAX: (516) 427-5820

Bar News (monthly)
Oneida County Bar Assoc.
239 Genesee Street
Utica, NY 13501
(315) 724-4901
FAX: (315) 724-6010

Bar Notes (monthly)
71 State Street
Binghamton, NY 13901
(607) 723-6331
FAX: (607) 723-3277

The Bill of Particulars (quarterly)
132 Nassau Street
New York, NY 10038
(212) 349-5890
FAX: (212) 608-2310

The Brooklyn Barrister (11/yr.)
322 Main Street
Huntington, NY 11743
(516) 427-7000
FAX: (516) 427-5820

Buffalo Law Journal (daily)
472 Delaware Avenue
Buffalo, NY 14202
(716) 852-6220
FAX: (716) 882-3020

The Bulletin (10/yr.)
1450 Statler Towers
Buffalo, NY 14202
(716) 852-8687
FAX: (716) 852—7641

Daily Bulletin [Brooklyn]
129 Montague Street
Brooklyn, NY 11201
(718) 624-0536

Daily Record
11 Centre Park
Rochester, NY 14601
(716) 232-6920
FAX: (716) 232-2740

44th Street Notes (10/yr.)
42 West 44th Street
New York, NY 10036—6690
(212) 382-6651
FAX: (212) 768-8630

Manhattan Lawyer (weekly)
AM-Law Publishing Corp.
600 Third Avenue
New York, NY 10016
(212) 973-2800

New York County Lawyer (12/yr.)
14 Vesey Street
New York, NY 10007-2992
(212) 267-6646
FAX: (212) 406-9252

New York Jury Verdict Rptr. (weekly)
128 Carlton Avenue East
Islip, NY 11730
(516) 581-1930
FAX: (516) 581-8937

New York Law Journal (daily)
New York Law Pub. Co.
345 Park Avenue South
New York, NY 10010
(212) 545-6269
FAX: (212) 481-8074

New York State Bar Journal (8/yr.)
One Elk Street
Albany, NY 12207
(518) 463-3200

The Orange County Lawyer (quarterly)
Route 17M, P.O. Box 88
Goshen, NY 10924
(914) 294-8222
FAX: (914) 294-3557

The Queens Bar Bulletin (9/yr.)
322 Main Street
Huntington, NY 11743
(516) 427-7000, FAX: (516) 427-5820

The Record (8/yr.)
42 West 44th Street
New York, NY 10036-6690
(212) 382-6651, FAX: (212) 398-6624

Rochester Business Journal
55 St. Paul Street
Rochester, NY 14604
(716) 546-8303

The Suffolk Lawyer (10/yr.)
322 Main Street
Huntington, NY 11743
(516) 427-7000
FAX: (516) 427-5820

Trial Lawyers Quarterly
132 Nassau Street
New York, NY 10038
(212) 349-5890
FAX: (212) 608-2310

Westchester Bar Journal (quar.)
300 Hamilton Ave. #400
White Plains, NY 10601
(914) 761-3707
FAX: (914) 761-9402

Westchester Law Journal (weekly)
Westchester Law Journal, Inc.
175 Main Street
White Plains, NY 10601
(914) 948-0715

North Carolina

Around the State (3/yr.)
P.O. Box 767
Raleigh, NC 27602-0767
(919) 832-1413
FAX: (919) 832-6361

Discovery (2/yr.)
P.O. Box 767
Raleigh, NC 27602-0767
(800) 688-1413
(919) 832-1413
FAX: (919) 832-6361

The Mecklenberg Times (biweekly)
906 Pecan Ave.
P.O. Box 36306
Charlotte, NC 28236
(704) 377-6221
FAX: (704) 377-6214

North Carolina Lawyer (bimonthly)
1312 Annapolis Drive
P.O. Box 12806
Raleigh, NC 27605
(919) 828-0561
FAX: (919) 821-2410

North Carolina Lawyers Weekly
107 Fayetteville Street Mall, 3rd Fl.
Lawyers Weekly Building
Raleigh, NC 27601
(919) 829-9333
FAX: (919) 829-8088

North Carolina State Bar Quarterly
208 Fayetteville Street Mall, 3rd Fl.
Raleigh, NC 27601
(919) 828-4620

Trial Briefs (quarterly)
P. O. Box 767
Raleigh, NC 27602-0767
(919) 832-1413
FAX: (919) 832-6361

Wake Bar Flyer (monthly)
P.O. Box 10625
Raleigh, NC 27605
(919) 829-9266
FAX: (919) 821-2410

North Dakota

The Gavel (bimonthly)
State Bar Assoc. of N. Dakota
P.O. Box 2136
515 1/2 E. Broadway
Bismarck, ND 58502
(701) 255-1404
FAX: (701) 224-1621
sband.org

Ohio

The Examiner (monthly)
Akron Bar Association
70 W. Bowery St.
Suite 1100
Akron, OH 44308
(216) 253-5007
FAX: (216) 253-2140
http://www.akronbar.org

Akron Legal News (daily)
60 South Summit Street
Akron, OH 44308
(330) 376-0917
FAX: (330) 376-7001
http://www.akronlegalnews.com/

CBA Report (monthly)
Cincinnati Bar Association
225 E. 6th St., 2d Floor
Cincinnati, OH 45202-3209
(513) 381-8213, FAX: (513) 381-0528

Cincinnati Court Index (daily)
Hamilton County Legal Newspaper
Cincinnati Court Index Press
119 W. Central Parkway
Cincinnati, OH 45202
(513) 241-1450

Cleveland Bar Journal (monthly)
Cleveland Bar Association
1301 E. 9th Street, 2d Level
Cleveland, OH 44114
P.O. Box 92732-C
Cleveland, OH 44101
(216) 696-3525, FAX: (216) 696-2413
clevelandbar.org

Daily Court Reporter
Dayton Legal News, Inc.
120 W. Second Street, #418
Dayton, OH 45402
(513) 222-6000

Daily Legal News
Legal News Publishing Co.
2935 Prospect Ave. E.
Cleveland, OH 44115
(216) 696-3322
FAX: (216) 696-6329

The Daily Reporter
580 S. High St.
Suite 316
Columbus, Ohio 43215
http://www.sourcenews.com

Daily Legal News
112 W. Commerce Street #1
Youngstown, OH 44503-1127
(216) 747-7777

The Daily Reporter
Daily Reporter, Inc.
329 South Front Street
Columbus, OH 43215
(614) 224-4835
FAX: (614) 224-8649

Dayton Bar Briefs (monthly)
109 N. Main Street
Dayton, OH 45402-1501
(937) 222-7902
FAX: (513) 222-1308
daybar.org

Ohio Law (monthly)
Ohio Legal Newspapers
1220 West Sixth Street, Suite 404
Cleveland, OH 44113
(216) 621-1461

The Ohio Lawyer (bimonthly)
P.O. Box 16562
1700 Lake Shore Drive
Columbus, OH 43216-6562
(614) 487-2050, FAX: (614) 487-1008

Ohio State Bar Association Report (weekly)
P.O. Box 16562
1700 Lake Shore Drive
(800) 282-6556
Columbus, OH 43204
(614) 487-2050
FAX: (614) 487-1008
ohiobar.org

Ohio Trial (quarterly)
395 E. Broad, Ste. 200
Columbus, OH 43215
(614) 341-6800
FAX: (614) 341-6810
oatlaw.org

Toledo Bar Association Newsletter (monthly)
311 N. Superior
Toledo, OH 43604
(419) 242-9363
FAX: (419) 242-3614

The Toledo Legal News (daily)
247 Gradolph Street
Toledo, OH 43612
(419) 470-8600
toledobar.org

Oklahoma

The Advocate (quarterly)
[Oklahoma Trial Lawyers Association]
323 Northeast 27th Street
Oklahoma City, OK 73105
(405) 525-8044, FAX: (415) 528-2431
otla.org

BRIEFCASE (monthly)
Oklahoma County Bar Association
119 N. Robinson
Oklahoma City, OK 73102
(405) 236-8421, FAX: (405) 232-2210

The Journal Record (daily)
Journal Record Publishing Co.
222 N. Robinson Avenue
Oklahoma City, OK 73102
(405) 278-2800; FAX: (405) 278-6907
www.journalrecord.com/

Oklahoma Bar Journal (weekly)
Oklahoma Bar Association
1901 North Lincoln Boulevard
P.O. Box 53036
Oklahoma City, OK 73105
(405) 524-2365
okbar.org/obj

Tulsa Daily Commerce & Legal News
Neighborhood Newspapers
8541 E. 41st Street
Tulsa, OK 74145
(918) 663-1414
FAX: (918) 664-8161
neighbor-newspapers.com

Tulsa Lawyer (monthly)
Tulsa County Bar Association
1446 S. Boston
Tulsa, OK 74119
(918) 584-5243
FAX: (918) 592-0208
tulsabar.com/

Oregon

Daily Journal of Commerce
2840 NW 35th Avenue
Portland, OR 97210
(503) 226-1311
FAX: (503) 224-7140
djc-or.com/

Multnomah Lawyer (10/yr.)
Multnomah Bar Association
630 S.W. 5th Ave. Ste. 1220
Portland, OR 97204-1408
(503) 222-3275
www.mbabar.org

Oregon State Bar Bulletin (10/yr.)
Otegon State Bar
5200 S.W. Meadows Road
Lake Oswego, OR 97035-0889
(800) 452-8260
(503) 620-0222
http://www.osbar.org

Trial Lawyer (quarterly)
Oregon Trial Lawyers Assoc.
1020 S.W. Taylor, Ste. 400
Portland, OR 97205
(503) 223-5587
FAX: (503) 223-4101
oregontriallawyers.org

Pennsylvania

Adams County Legal Journal
111-117 Baltimore St.
Gettsburg, PA 17325
(717) 334-6781

Armstrong County Legal Journal
Armstrong County Courthouse
Kittanning, PA 16201
(724) 543-2500

Beaver County Legal Journal
788 Turnpike Street
Beaver, PA 15009
(724) 728-7622

Bedford County Legal Journal
% R. Martin Reily, Editor
P.O. Box 440
Bedford, PA 15522

Berks County Law Journal (weekly)
Berks County Bar Association
P.O. Box 1058
Reading, PA 19601
(215) 375-4591

Blair County Legal Bulletin
% Mrs. Robei Hare, Jr., Editor
115 Logan Blvd.
Altoona, PA 16602
(814)943-1496

Bradford County Law Journal
201 W. Lockhart St.
Sayre, PA 18840
(570)888-2244

Bucks County Law Reporter
135 E. State St.
P.O. Box 300
Doylestown, PA 18901
(215) 348-9413
(800) 479-8585

Butler County Legal Journal
228 S. Main St.
Butler, PA 16001
(724) 285-1717

Cambria County Legal Journal
P.O. Box 338
Ebensburg, PA 15931
(814) 472-9530

Carbon County Law Journal
P.O. Box 6
Jim Thorpe, PA 18229
(570) 325-9419

Centre County Legal Journal
Box 57
Bellefonte, PA 16823
(814) 355-5474

Chester County Law Reporter
Chester County Bar Association
15 W. Gay St.
PO Box 3191
West Chester, PA 19380
(610) 692-1889

Crawford County Legal Journal
(weekly)
Crawford County Bar Association
Crawford County Courthouse
P.O. Box 384
Meadville, PA 16335
(814) 332-6000

Cumberland Law Journal
Roger M. Morgenthal, Esq., Editor
2 Liberty Avenue
Carlisle, PA 17013
(717) 249-3166

Dauphin County Reporter
213 N. Front St.
Harrisburg, PA 17101
(717) 232-7536

Delware County Legal Journal
Bar Association Bldg.
Front & Lemon Sts.
P.O. Box 466
Media, PA 19063
(610) 566-6625

Erie County Legal Journal (weekly)
Erie County Bar Association
302 W. 9th St.
Erie, PA 16502-1427
(814)459-3111

Fayette Legal Journal
84 E. Main St.
Uniontown, PA 15401
(724) 437-7994

Franklin County Legal Journal
14 N. Main Street
Suite 210
Chambersburg, PA 17201
(717) 263-9773

Indiana Law Journal
% Donald R. Marsh, Esq.
307 Savings & Trust Co. Bldg.
Indiana, PA 15701
(724) 465-5651

Jefferson County Legal Journal
316 Main St.
Brookville, PA 15825
(814) 849-1237

Lackawanna Jurist (weekly)
Lackawanna Bar Association
338 N Washington Ave
Floor 3
Scranton, PA 18503-9161
(570) 969-9161

Lancaster Law Review (weekly)
Lancaster Bar Association
28 E. Orange St.
Lancaster, PA 17602
(717) 393-0737

Lawyers Journal (26/yr.)
Allegheny County Bar Association
400 Koppers Building
436 Seventh Ave.
Pittsburgh, PA 15219
(412)261-6161
FAX: 412-261-3622

Lebanon County Legal Journal
Room 305 Law Library
Municipal Bldg.
Lebanon, PA 17042
(717) 274-2801 Ext. 2301

Lehigh Law Journal (weekly)
Bar Association of Lehigh County
1114 Walnut Street
Allentown, PA 18102
(610) 433-6204
FAX: (610) 770-9826

Legal Intelligencer, The (daily)
Legal Communications, Ltd.
1617 JFK Boulevard, Suite 960
Philadelphia, PA 19103
(800) 722-7670
(215) 557-2300
FAX: (215) 557-2301

Monroe Legal Reporter (weekly)
Monroe County Bar Association
729 Monroe Street
Stroudsburg, PA 18301

Luzerne Legal Register
Room 23 Courthouse
Wilkes-Barre, PA 18711
(570) 822-6029

Lycoming Reporter
Lycoming County Courthouse
Williamsport, PA 17701
(717) 327-2258

Mercer County Law Journal
Christopher J St. John
47 Clinton Street
P.O. Box 510
Greenville, PA 16125
(570) 588-4800

Monroe Legal Reporter
% Michael R. Muth, Esq.
P.O. Box 786
Stroudsburg, PA 18360
(570) 424-7288

Montgomery County Law Reporter
Montgomery Bar Association
100 West Airy Street
P.O. Box 268
Norristown, PA 19404
(215) 279-9660

Northamption County Reporter
155 S. Ninth St.
Easton, PA 18042
(610) 258-6333

Northumberland Legal Journal
P.O. Box 126
Sunbury, PA 17801
(570) 286-7777

PaTLA News
Pennsylvania Trial Lawyers Assoc.
121 South Broad Street, Suite 600
Philadelphia, PA 19107
(215) 546-6451
FAX: (215) 546-5430
patla.org

Pennsylvania Bar News (biweekly)
100 South Street
P.O. Box 186
Harrisburg, PA 17108-0186
(717) 238-6715
FAX: (717) 238-7182

Pennsylvania Law Journal-Reporter
Packard Press
1617 JFK Boulevard, 12th Floor
Philadelphia, PA 19103
(215) 236-2000

Pittsburgh Legal Journal (daily)
Allegheny County Bar Association
400 Koppers Building
436 Seventh Ave.
Pittsburgh, PA 15219
(412)261-6161
FAX: 412-261-3622

Schuylkill Legal Record
Law Library
Schuylkill County Courthouse
401 N. Second Street
Pottsville, PA 17901
(570) 628-1235

Somerset Legal Journal
P.O. Box 501
Somerset, PA 15001
(814) 445-4021

Washington Co. Reports
523 Washington Trust Bldg.
Washington, PA 15301
(724) 225-6710

Westmoreland Law Journal
129 N. Pennsylvania Ave.
Greensburg, PA 15601
(724) 834-7260

York Legal Record
137 E. Market St.
York, PA 17401
(717) 854-8755

Rhode Island

Rhode Island Bar Journal (9/yr.)
115 Cedar Street
Providence, RI 02903
(401) 421-5740, FAX: (401) 421-2703

Rhode Island Lawyers Weekly
Lawyers Weekly Publications
41 West Street
Boston, MA 02111
(800) 451-9998, (617) 451-7300
FAX: (617) 451-7326

RITLA News (3/yr.)
One Park Row
Providence, RI 02903
(401) 273-8820, FAX: (401) 751-7830

South Carolina

SC Bar News (bimonthly)
950 Taylor Street
Columbia, SC 29202
(803) 799-6653, FAX: (803) 799-4118

South Carolina Lawyer (bimonthly)
950 Taylor Street
Columbia, SC 29202
(803) 799-6653, FAX: (803) 799-4118

South Carolina Trial Lawyer Bulletin (quarterly)
P.O. Box 11557
Columbia, SC 29211
(803) 799-5097, FAX: (803) 799-1041

South Dakota

The Barrister (bimonthly)
207 E. Capitol Ave. #206
P.O. Box 1154
Pierre, SD 57501-1154
(605) 224-9292, FAX: (605) 945-1204

Tennessee

The Bar Essentials (monthly)
One Commerce Square #1190
Memphis, TN 38103-2513
(901) 527-3573, FAX: (901) 527-3582

The Daily News
193 Jefferson Avenue
Memphis, TN 38173-0663
(901) 523-1561, FAX: (901) 526-5813

The Memphis Bar Association Magazine (quarterly)
One Commerce Square #1190
Memphis, TN 38103-2513
(901) 527-3573, FAX: (901) 527-3582

The Nashville Bar Journal (monthly)
221 4th Ave. N. #400
Nashville, TN 37219-2100
(615) 242-9272, FAX: (615) 255-3026

Nashville Record (weekly)
222 Second Avenue N.
Nashville, TN 37201
(615) 256-8288, FAX: (615) 256-8288

Res Nova (monthly)
4600 Brainerd Road
Chattanooga, TN 37411
(615) 698-5306, FAX: (615) 698-5318

Tennessee Attorneys Memo (weekly)
M. Lee Smith Publishers and Printers
162 Fourth Avenue, North
Box 2678, Arcade Station
Nashville, TN 37219
(615) 242-7395

Tennessee Bar Journal (bimonthly)
3622 West End Avenue
Nashville, TN 37205-2403
(615) 383-7421, FAX: (615) 297-8058

The Tennessee Trial Lawyer (biannual)
1903 Division Street
Nashville, TN 37203
(615) 329-3000, FAX: (615) 329-8131

Texas

Austin Daily Record
503 W. 15th Street, P.O. Box 2195
Austin, TX 78768
(512) 472-8808

Austin Lawyer (quarterly)
700 Lavaca Street #602
Austin, TX 78701-3102
(512) 472-0279, FAX: (512) 473-2720

Austin Lawyer's Journal (monthly)
700 Lavaca Street #602
Austin, TX 78701-3102
(512) 472-0279, FAX: (512) 473-2720

Bar Bulletin (monthly)
El Paso Bar Association
500 E. San Antonio, L-115
El Paso, TX 79901
(915) 532-7052, FAX: (915) 532-7067

Corpus Christi Lawyer (quarterly)
400 Mann Street #700
Corpus Christi, TX 78401
(512) 883-8833, FAX: (512) 883-4329

Daily Commercial Record
Daily Commercial Record, Inc.
706 Main Street
Dallas, TX 75202
(214) 741-6366, FAX: (214) 741-6373

Daily Commercial Recorder
6222 NW International Highway 10
Suite 101
San Antonio, TX 78201
(512) 736-4450, FAX: (512) 736-5506

Daily Court Review
6807 Wynnwood
Houston, TX 77008
(713) 869-5434, FAX: (713) 869-8887

Dallas Bar Association Headnotes (semi-monthly)
Dallas Bar Association
2101 Ross Avenue
Dallas, TX 75201
(214) 969-7066, FAX: (214) 880-0807

Epigraph (weekly)
P.O. Box 557
Springtown, TX 76082
(817) 237-1184

Fort Worth Commercial Recorder (daily)
P. O. Box 11038
Fort Worth, TX 76110
(817) 926-5351, FAX: (817) 926-5377

The Houston Lawyer (bimonthly)
1300 First City Tower
1001 Fannin
Houston, TX 77002-6708
(713) 759-1133, FAX: (713) 759-1710

San Antonio Lawyer (quarterly)
400 Mann Street #700
Corpus Christi, TX 78401
(512) 883-8833, FAX: (512) 883-4329

Texas Bar Journal (monthly)
P.O. Box 12487
Austin, TX 78711
(800) 204-2222, Ext. 6001
FAX: (512) 463-1475

Texas Lawyer (weekly)
American Lawyer Media L.P.
400 South Record Street, #1400
Dallas, TX 75202
(214) 744-9300, FAX: (214) 741-2325

Trials Lawyers Forum (2/yr.)
1220 Colorado
Austin, TX 78701
(512) 476-3852, FAX: (512) 473-2411

Voice for the Defense (10/yr.)
600 W. 13th Street
Austin, TX 78701
(512) 478-2514, FAX: (512) 469-9107

Utah

The Intermountain Commercial Record/ The Salt Lake Times (weekly)
1900 W. 1500 South
Salt Lake City, UT 84104
(801) 972-5642, FAX: (801) 972-4457

Utah Bar Journal (10/yr.)
645 South 200 East #310
Salt Lake City, UT 84111
(800) 698-9077, (FAX: (801) 531-0660

The Utah Trial Journal (quarterly)
645 South 200 East #103
Salt Lake City, UT 84111
(801) 531-7514, FAX: (801) 531-1207

Vermont

The Vermont Bar Journal and Law Digest (bimonthly)
P.O. Box 100
Montpelier, VT 05602
(802) 223-2020, FAX: (202) 223-1573

VTLA Report (bimonthly)
64 Main Street
Montpelier, VT 05602
(802) 223-0501, FAX: (802) 223-4880

Virginia

Bar Bulletin (monthly)
Norfolk & Portsmouth Bar Assoc.
1330 Old Dominion Tower
999 Waterside Dr.
Norfolk, VA 23510
(804) 622-3152, FAX: (804) 622-4406

The Journal (quarterly)
700 East Main Road #1510
Richmond, VA 23219
(804) 343-1143, FAX: (804) 343-7124

Law Letter (bimonthly)
Virginia Trial Lawyers Assoc.
700 East Main Road #1510
Richmond, VA 23219
(804) 343-1143, FAX: (804) 343-7124

News and Views (10/yr.)
Virginia Bar Association
701 E. Franklin Street #1120
Richmond, VA 23219
(804) 644-0041, FAX: (804) 644-0052

Virginia Lawyer & Virginia Lawyer Profile (monthly)
Eighth & Main Building
707 East Main Street #1500
Richmond, VA 23219-2803
(804) 775-0586, FAX: (804) 775-0501

Virginia Lawyers Weekly
Lawyers Weekly Publications
801 East Main St., Ste. 701
Richmond, VA 23219
(800) 451-9998

Washington

The Bar Bulletin (monthly)
King County Bar Association
900 4th Ave., Ste. 600
Seattle, WA 98164-1060
(206) 624-9365, FAX: (206) 382-1270

Bar News (monthly)
Washington State Bar Association
2101 4th Avenue, Ste. 400
Seattle, WA 98121-2330
(206) 727-8213, FAX: (206) 727-8319

Seattle Daily Journal of Commerce
83 Columbia Street
Seattle, WA 98104
(206) 622-8272, FAX: (206) 622-8416

Tacoma Daily Index
1019 Pacific Ave., Ste.1216
Tacoma, WA 98402
(253-627-4853

Trial News (monthly)
Washington State Trial Lawyers Assoc.
1809 7th Ave. #909
Seattle, WA 98101
(206) 464-1011

West Virginia

The Advocate (3/yr.)
W. Virginia Trial Lawyers Assoc.
1018 Kanawha Boulevard East
Charleston, WV 25339
(304) 344-0692, FAX: (304) 343-7926

The West Virginia Lawyer (monthly)
West Virginia State Bar
2006 Kanawha Blvd. E.
Charleston, WV 25311
(304) 558-1044,
FAX: (304) 558-2467

Wisconsin

The Daily Reporter
Daily Reporter Publishing Company
225 E. Michigan Street #540
Milwaukee, WI 53202
(414) 276-0273,
FAX: (414) 276-8057

Wisconsin Law Reporter (24/yr.)
P.O. Box 270
209 Michigan Avenue
Crystal Falls, MI 49920-1312
(906) 875-6970

Wisconsin Lawyer (monthly)
P.O. Box 7158
Madison, WI 53707-7158
(608) 257-3838
FAX: (608) 257-5502

The Verdict (quarterly)
Wisconsin Academy of Trial Lawyers Association
44 E. Mifflin St. #103
Madison, WI 53703
(608) 257-5741
FAX: (608) 255-9285

Wyoming

The Coffee-House (quarterly)
Wyoming Trial Lawyers Association
2111 Warren Avenue
Cheyenne, WY 82001
(307) 635-0820, FAX: (307) 634-5331

The Wyoming Lawyer (bimonthly)
P.O. Box 109
Cheyenne, WY 82003-0919
(307)632-9061,
FAX: (307) 632-3737

Appendix E - Representative Used Law Book Prices

(As of April 2014)

This list is intended only as a representative sampling of approximate law book prices as of April 10, 2014, which have appeared in recent years. Actual prices will depend upon market conditions at the time of the transaction, dealer's inventory, condition of volumes, currency of volumes at time of sale and the results of negotiations between buyer and seller. Those interested in acquiring sets of hardcopy volumes should also monitor the law librarians' list serv where many such sets are now offered free for the cost of postage. Before making a purchase, consumers are also warned to calculate the total cost of acquiring a set of used law books, including the fill-up cost for sets not completely up-to-date, and the lost value of no-charge supplementation which may accompany the purchase of a new set.

As the national market for used law books has shrunk in recent years with the disappearance of several dealers, most opportunities to purchase such volumes await the alert lawyer attuned to buying opportunities at the local level. This is particularly the case with state specific law

Admin. Decisions under the Immigration & Nationality Laws (. 1-20)	$1,095.00
Alabama Appellate Court Reports, vols. 1-57 (all)	$895.00
Alabama Code (LexisNexis)	$150.00
Alabama Reporter (West) (complete)	$1,695.00
Alabama Reports, vols. 1-295 (all)	$1,995.00
Alaska Reporter (1960-date) (West)	$1,395.00
Alaska Reports, vols. 1-17 (all)	$395.00
Alaska Statutes Annotated (LexisNexis)	$395.00
American Jurisprudence 2d (West) with 1998 supps.	$695.00
Am. Jur. Legal Forms 2d, 62 vols. (thru 2003) (West)	$895.00
Am Jur Pleading and Practice Forms (West)	$595.00
Am Jur Proof of Facts [1st], vols. 1-30, with 1997 supps. (West)	$195.00
Am Jur Proof of Facts 2d, vols. 1-50, with 1999 supps. (West)	$125.00
Am Jur Proof Facts 3d, vols. 1-98, with 2007 supps. (West)	$1,295.00
Am Jur Trials, vols. 1-65 (West) with 1997 supps.	$495.00
American Law Reports [1st] (out-of-print) (West)	$995.00
American Law Reports 2d (West)	$395.00
American Law Reports 3d (West) (w/2005 supps.)	$395.00
American Law Reports 4th (90 vols.) (West) (w/2005 supps.)	$395.00
American Law Reports 5th, vols. 1-125 with 2005 supps. (West) (	$595.00
American Law Reports Federal, vols. 1-200 (w/2004 supps.) (West)	$595.00
American Law Reports Later Case Service (West)	$195.00
American Law Reports Digest to 3d, 4th, 5th & Federal (West)	$150.00
American Law Reports Index to 2d, 3d, 4th, 5th & Fed. (West	$150.00
American Law Reports, package price for all of above (West)	$3,000.00
American Maritime Cases, 1923-1999-4 (189 vols.)	$2,495.00
Annotated Code of Maryland thru Nov. 2012 (53 vols.) LexisNexis	$150.00
Appleman on Insurance (LexisNexis)	$1,650.00
Arizona Appeals Reports, vols. 1-27 (all)	$595.00
Arizona Reports, vols. 1-175 (1866-1994)	$2,995.00
Arizona Revised Statutes Annotated (Wests) (thru 2001)	$150.00
Arkansas Cases (S.W. 2d vols. 1-890) (1886-date)	$495.00
Arkansas Code (LexisNexis)	$695.00
Arkansas Digest (thru 2005) (West)	$695.00
Atlantic Digest 1st (West)	$495.00
Atlantic Digest 2d (West)	$1,695.00
Atlantic Reporter [1st] (West)	$695.00
Atlantic Reporter 2d, vols.1-883 (1938-2005) (West)	$3,795.00
Atlantic Reporter 2d, vols. 1-888 (1938-2005)	$695.00

Atlantic Reporter 2d, vols. 464-770 (1983-2000)	$595.00
Bankruptcy Citations, 4 vols. (Shepards)	$395.00
Bankruptcy Digest, Wests (thru 2004)	$495.00
Bankruptcy Reporter (Wests), vols. 1-325 (1980-2005)	$1,995.00
Bankruptcy Reporter (Wests), vols. 1-271 (1980-2002)	$1,195.00
Bankruptcy Service, Lawyers Ed. (West)	$595.00
Benders Federal Practice Forms (MB) (thru 2003)	$695.00
Benders Forms for Civil Practice (MB), vol. 1-29.	$495.00
California Appellate Reports, 1st, vols. 1-140 (all)	$995.00
California Appellate Reports 2d, vols. 1-276 (all)	$1,495.00
California Appellate Reports 3d (1969-1994)	$1,495.00
California Reporter (Wests), vols. 1-286 and 2d, vols. 1-49	$695.00
California Reports [1st], vols. 1-220	$1,495.00
California Reports 2d, vols. 1-71 (1934-69) with Cal. App. 2d, 1-276)	$995.00
California Reports 3d, vols. 1-53	$1,095.00
California Code, Wests Annotated	$895.00
California Digest 2d (West) (thru 2004)	$795.00
California Forms of Pleading & Practice , 56 vols. (MB/LexisNexis) (thru 2003)	$895.00
California Legal Forms: Transaction Guide, 36 vols. (LexisNexis) (thru 2003)	$695.00
California Points & Authorities, 24 vols. (LexisNexis/MB) (thru 2003)	$750.00
Code of Federal Regulations Citations, 2 vols. (Shepards)	$100.00
Collier Bankruptcy Practice Guide (9 vols.) (Matthew Bender)	$350.00
Collier on Bankruptcy, 15th ed. (16 vols.) (Matthew Bender)	$650.00
Colorado Court of Appeals Reports, vols. 1-44 (all)	$495.00
Colorado Digest 2d (West)	$995.00
Colorado Reporter (Wests) (1955-1993) (141 vols.)	$1,295.00
Colorado Reports, vols. 1-100 (all)	$1,695.00
Colorado Reports & Colorado Ct. of Appeals Reports	$1,995.00
Colorado Revised Statutes Annotated (West) (thru 2005)	$795.00
Connecticut Appellate Reports, vols. 1-29 (1983-1993)	$295.00
Connecticut Digest (West)	$895.00
Connecticut General Statutes Annotated (West)	$1,195.00
Connecticut Practice (9 vols.) (West)	$100.00
Connecticut Reports, vols. 1-224	$1,795.00
Corpus Juris Secundum (w/2005 supps.) (West)	$1,695.00
Couch on Insurance 2d ed. (West)	$995.00
Current Legal Forms (Rabkin & Johnson) (Matthew Bender)	$795.00
Dakota Digest (West)	$200.00
Damages in Tort Actions (Matthew Bender/LexisNexis) (thru 1997)	$295.00
Decennial Digests, 1st-10th (1897-1996)	$4,500.00
Decennial Digest, 3d (1916-1926) (West)	$395.00
Decennial Digest, 4th (1926-1936) (West)	$395.00
Decennial Digest, 5th (1936-1946)	$495.00
Decennial Digest, 6th (1946-1956)	$495.00
Decennial Digest, 8th (1967-1976)	$495.00
Decennial Digest, 9th, Part 1 (1976-1981)	$495.00
Decennial Digest, 9th, Part 2 (1982-1986)	$495.00
Decennial Digest, 10th, Part 1 (1987-1991)	$795.00
Decennial Digest, 10th, Part 2 (1991-1996)	$795.00
Delaware Reports, vols. 1-59 (all)	$750.00
District of Columbia Appeal Cases, vols. 1-302 (West)	$2,295.00

District of Columbia Code Annotated (thru 2005) (LexisNexis)	$495.00
Education Law Reporter (Wests), vols. 1-121 (1982-1998)	$495.00
Employee Benefit Cases, vols. 1-46 (1977-2009) (BNA)	$495.00
Federal Cases, 1789-1880 (reprint) (West)	$4,130.00
Federal Claims Reporter, vols. 1-32 (1983-1995)	$595.00
Federal Digest (out-of-print)	$495.00
Federal Evidence (Kirkpatrick & Mueller) (West)	$275.00
Federal Jury Practice & Instructions, 5th ed. (West)	$395.00
Federal Labor Law Citations, 14 vols. (Shepards)	$450.00
Federal Practice and Procedure (West)	$595.00
Federal Practice Digest [1st]	$395.00
Federal Practice Digest 2d (West)	$395.00
Federal Practice Digest 3d (West)	$495.00
Federal Practice Digest 4th (to 2010) (West)	$1,495.00
Federal Practice Manual (West)	$350.00
Federal Procedural Forms (West)	$595.00
Federal Procedure, L. Ed. (complete) (West)	$695.00
Federal Reporter [1st] vols.1-300 (West)	$895.00
Federal Reporter 2d, vols. 1-999 (1924-1993) (West)	$2,495.00
Federal Reporter 3d, vols. 1-620 (1993-2010) (West)	$1,995.00
Federal Rules Decisions, vols. 1-193 (West)	$995.00
Federal Supplement, vols. 1-999 (West)	$2,995.00
Federal Supplement 2d, vols. 1-276 (West)	$1,795.00
Fletcher Cyclopedia of Corporations (West)	$800.00
Florida Cases (So., 2d, vols.1-904/905) (411 books) (West)	$1,850.00
Florida Digest 2d (West)	$350.00
Florida Jurisprudence 2d (West)	$795.00
Florida Reports, vols. 1-160 (all)	$1,095.00
Florida Statutes Annotated, Wests (thru 2003)	$495.00
Florida Supplement [1st], vols. 1-50 (all)	$495.00
Georgia Appeals Reports, vols. 1-208	$1,995.00
Georgia Cases (S.E. 2d), vols. 1-414	$1,495.00
Georgia Digest 2d, vols. 1-40 (thru 2005) (West)	$695.00
Georgia Reports, vols. 1-261 and Georgia Appeals Reports, 1-203	$1,495.00
Hawaii Digest (West)	$450.00
Hawaii Reports, v.1-70 & Hawaii Appellate Reports, v. 1-7	$1,495.00
Idaho Code (LexisNexis)	$295.00
Idaho Reports, vols. 1-123	$1,895.00
Illinois Appellate Court Reports [1st], vols. 1-351 (all)	$1,095.00
Illinois Appellate Court Reports 2d, vols. 1-133 (all)	$1,195.00
Illinois Appellate Court Reports 3d, vols. 1-215 (all)	$1,995.00
Illinois Compiled Statutes Annotated, Wests Smith Hurd (West)	$595.00
Illinois Decisions (N.E. 2d), vols. 1-233 (197-1998)	$1,095.00
Illinois Digest 2d (West)	$695.00
Illinois Jurisprudence (LEXIS)	$495.00
Illinois Law and Practice (West)	$695.00
Illinois Reports [1st], vols. 1-415 (all)	$1,195.00
Illinois Reports 2d, vols. 1-144	$1,095.00
Indiana Cases (1-690)	$1,295.00
Indiana Code, Wests Annotated (thru 2004)	$495.00
Indiana Court of Appeals Reports, vols. 1-182 (all)	$995.00

Indiana Digest	$395.00
Indiana Law Encyclopedia (West)	$495.00
Indiana Reports, vols. 1-275 (all)	$1,295.00
Indiana Reports, v. 1-275 & Indiana App. Reports v. 1-182	$1,995.00
Indiana Statutes Annotated, Burns (51 vols.) thru 2010 (LexisNexis)	$95.00
Internal Revenue Service Cumulative Bulletins, 1954 to 1994-1	$995.00
Iowa Code Annotated (West)	$495.00
Iowa Digest (West)	$395.00
Iowa Practice (West)	$150.00
Iowa Reports, vols. 1-261	$595.00
Kansas Cases (444-933 P.2d)	$995.00
Kansas Court of Appeals 2d, vols. 1-15 (1977-date)	$295.00
Kansas Digest 2d (West)	$695.00
Kansas Reports, vols. 1-251	$2,295.00
Kansas Statutes Annotated, Vernons (West)	$395.00
Kentucky Digest 2d (West)	$250.00
Kentucky Reports, vols. 1-314 (all)	$1,495.00
Kentucky Revised Statutes Annotated (West)	$250.00
Law Review Citations, 2 vols.	$50.00
Labor Law Cases (CCH) , vols. 1-122 (1937-1992)	$650.00
Louisiana Digest 2d (thru 2005) (West)	$795.00
Louisiana Reports, vols. 1-262 (all)	$1,495.00
Louisiana Statutes Annotated, Wests with 2003 supps.	$295.00
Maine Digest (West)	$595.00
Maine Reporter (A. 2d), vols. 215-675 (54 books) (West)	$495.00
Maine Reports, vols. 1-161	$995.00
Maine Revised Statutes Annotated, West's with 2006 supps.	$195.00
Martindale-Hubbell Law Directory, 1999 ed. (27 vols.)	$295.00
Maryland, Annotated Code (thru 2004) (LexisNexis)	$295.00
Maryland Appellate Reports, vols. 1-97	$1,295.00
Maryland Digest 2d (West)	$495.00
Maryland Law Encyclopedia through 2012 (35 vols.) (West)	$395.00
Maryland Reporter, vol. 1-date (1934-2002) (West)	$995.00
Maryland Reports, vols. 1-331	$1,395.00
Massachusetts, Annotated Laws of (LexisNexis))	$250.00
Massachusetts Appeals Court Reports, vols.1-42	$495.00
Mass. Decisions [1st] (West)	$295.00
Massachusetts Decisions (N.E. 2d), vols. 1-686 (West)	$995.00
Massachusetts Digest 2d (West)	$495.00
Massachusetts General Laws Annotated (West)	$195.00
Massachusetts Practice (West)	$1,495.00
Massachusetts Reports, vols. 1-416	$1,195.00
Michies Jurisprudence of Virginia & West Virginia (LexisNexis)	$395.00
Michigan Appeals Reports, vols. 1-213	$695.00
Michigan Compiled Laws Annotated (West) (thru 2001)	$195.00
Michigan Digest 2d (West)	$595.00
Michigan Laws and Practice Encyclopedia, vols.1-26 (31 books) (West)	$495.00
Michigan Reporter (1942-1993) (West)	$995.00
Michigan Reports, v.1-453 and Mich. Appeals Reports, v. 1-223	$1,595.00
Michigan Statutes Annotated (LexisNexis))	$695.00
Military Justice Reporter, Wests, vols. 1-46 (1976-1997)	$1,195.00

Minnesota Citations, 3 vols. (Shepards)	$100.00
Minnesota Digest 2d (West)	$995.00
Minnesota Reports, vols. 1-312	$1,795.00
Minnesota Statutes Annotated (West)	$795.00
Mississippi Code Annotated (West)	$395.00
Mississippi Reports, vols. 1-254	$1,595.00
Missouri Appeals Reports, vols. 1-241	$995.00
Missouri Cases [1st], vols. 1-300 (1886-1937)	$195.00
Missouri Cases 2d, vols. 1-date (1937-1997)	$995.00
Missouri Digest 2d (West)	$595.00
Missouri Practice (43 vols.)	$1,495.00
Missouri Reports, vols. 1-365	$1,095.00
Missouri Reports, v. 1-365 & Missouri App. Reports, v. 1-241	$2,495.00
Missouri Statutes Annotated, Vernons (West)	$395.00
Modern Federal Jury Instructions (West) (thru 2003)	$295.00
Modern Federal Practice Digest (out-of-print) (West)	$395.00
Montana Code Annotated (1997) (Montana Legislative Council)	$100.00
Montana Reports, vols. 1-259	$2,895.00
Moores Federal Practice, 3rd edition (31 vols.) (thru 2003)	$595.00
Municipal Law (Antieau) (Matthew Bender)	$250.00
Nebraska Reports, vols. 1-241	$995.00
Nevada Reports, vols. 1-108	$995.00
Nevada Revised Statutes Annotated	$450.00
New Hampshire Digest (West)	$2,250.00
New Hampshire Reports, vols. 1-137	$2,100.00
New Hampshire Revised Statutes Annotated (LexisNexis)	$595.00
New Jersey Administrative Code	$195.00
New Jersey Digest 2d, West's (thru 2005)	$495.00
New Jersey Equity Reports, vols. 1-142 (1830-1948)	$895.00
N.J. Law Reports (all), N.J. Equity Reports (vols. 1-142), and N.J. Misc. (vols. 1-26)	$1,095.00
New Jersey Law Reports, 1-137 (all) and N.J. Equity vols. 1-142	$395.00
New Jersey Practice, vols. 1-55 (thru 2010-2011 supps.) (West)	$1,495.00
New Jersey Reports, 1-152 and N.J. Superior Ct. Reports, 1-309	$1,195.00
New Jersey Statutes Annotated (West)	$295.00
New Jersey Superior Court Reports, vols. 1-267	$2,895.00
New Jersey Tax Court Reports (1981-2002) (19 vols.)	$195.00
New Mexico Digest (West)	$550.00
New Mexico Reports, vols. 1-112	$2,295.00
New Mexico Statutes Annotated (LexisNexis)	$395.00
New York Appellate Division Reports [1st] , vols. 1-286	$1,095.00
New York Appellate Division Reports 2d , vols. 1-189	$1,195.00
New York, McKinneys Consolidated Laws Annotated(West)	$595.00
New York, McKinneys Forms (West)	$495.00
New York Digest 3d (West)	$195.00
New York Digest 4th (West)	$795.00
New York Forms, McKinneys (West)	$750.00
New York Jurisprudence 2d, (thru 2005) (West)	$1,495.00
New York Miscellaneous Reports [1st] vols. 1-208 (all)	$1,095.00
New York Miscellaneous Reports 2d, vols. 1-156 (1956-1994)	$1,195.00
New York Official Reports, 2d series (New York Reports 2d, App. Division, App. Division, Misc. Reports)	$1,295.00
New York Practice with Forms, Carmody-Wait (LexisNexis)	$695.00

New York Reports [1st] , vols. 1-309 (1847-1956)	$1,095.00
New York Reports 2d, vols. 1-80	$1,095.00
New York Supplement [1st] vols. 1-300 (out-of-print)	$695.00
New York Supplement 2d, vols. 1-678	$1,495.00
New York Supplement Citations, 12 vols.	$495.00
Nichols Cyclopedia of Legal Forms (West)	$495.00
North Carolina Court of Appeals Report, vols. 1-110	$795.00
North Carolina, General Statutes of	$350.00
North Carolina Reports, vols. 1-333	$1,495.00
North Dakota Century Code Annotated	$200.00
North Dakota Reports, vols. 1-79 (all)	$795.00
North Eastern Reporter [1st] vols. 1-200 (out-of-print) (West)	$695.00
North Eastern Reporter 2d, vols. 1-833 (1936-2005) (West)	$3,795.00
North Eastern Reporter Citations, 11 vols.	$150.00
North Western Digest 2d (West)	$1,695.00
North Western Reporter [1st] vols. 1-300 (West)	$695.00
North Western Reporter 2d, vols. 1-649 (West) (1941-1999)	$1,295.00
Ohio Appellate Reports [1st] , vols. 1-120 (all)	$795.00
Ohio Appellate Reports 2d, vols. 1-70 (all)	$695.00
Ohio Digest 2d (West)	$795.00
Ohio Jurisprudence 3d (West)	$1,895.00
Ohio Miscellaneous Reports, vols. 1-70 (1964-1982)	$495.00
Ohio Official Reports 2d, vols. 1-70 (Anderson)	$895.00
Ohio Official Reports 3d, vols. 1-70 (Anderson)	$795.00
Ohio, Pages Ohio Revised Code Annotated (Anderson)	$350.00
Ohio State Reports 2d, vols. 1-70 (all)	$795.00
Oklahoma Criminal Reports, vols. 1-97	$895.00
Oklahoma Decisions, vols. 1-877	$595.00
Oklahoma Digest 2d (West)	$395.00
Oklahoma Reports, vols. 1-208 (all)	$495.00
Oklahoma Statutes Annotated (West) (thru 2003)	$495.00
Oregon Court of Appeals Reports, vols. 1-121	$995.00
Oregon Reports, vols. 1-316 and Oregon Ct. of Appeals Rpts., vols. 1-121	$1,295.00
Oregon Revised Statutes (official) (Legislative Counsel Committee)	$195.00
Pacific Digest (covering P.2d vols. 1-100) (West)	$250.00
Pacific Digest (covering P.2d vols. 101-366) (West)	$595.00
Pacific Digest (covering P.2d vols. 367-584) (West)	$595.00
Pacific Digest (covering vols. 585 to date) (West)	$1,495.00
Pacific Reporter [1st] vols. 1-300 (out-of-print) (West)	$995.00
Pacific Reporter 2d, vols. 1-999 ((West)	$1,995.00
Pacific Reporter 2d, vols. 70-966 (1937-1997)	$895.00
Pennsylvania Commonwealth Court Reports, vols. 1-118	$295.00
Pennsylvania Commonwealth Court Reports, vols. 1-152	$1,995.00
Pennsylvania Digest 2d (thru 2005) (West)	$795.00
Pennsylvania District & County Reports [1st] vols. 1-89	$250.00
Pennsylvania District & County Reports, 2d vols. 1-75 (1955-77)	$250.00
Pennsylvania District & County Reports, 3d vols. 1-50 (1977-89)	$495.00
Pennsylvania District & County Reports, 4th vols. 1-14 (1989-	$695.00
Pennsylvania Law Encyclopedia, 54 vols. (LexisNexis)	$395.00
Pennsylvania Reporter (A.2d vols. 1-885) (1938-2005)	$1,795.00
Pennsylvania State Reports, vols. 1-535 & Superior Rpts, vols. 1-429	$1,995.00

Products Liability (Frumer & Friedman) (thru 2005) (Matthew Bender)	$695.00
Purdons Pennsylvania Statutes Annotated (West)	$650.00
Restatement of the Law of Agency 2d, 7 vols. (ALI)	$295.00
Restatement of Conflict of Laws 2d, 5 vols. (ALI)	$295.00
Restatement of the Law of Contracts 2d	$395.00
Restatement of the Law of Judgments 2d, 4 vols.	$245.00
Restatement of the Law of Property, 1st, 2d, 3d	$500.00
Restatement of the Law of Restitution, 1st & Appendix	$135.00
Restatement of the Law of Torts 2d, 23 vols.	$995.00
Restatement of the Law of Trusts 2d & 3d, 6 vols.	$285.00
Rhode Island Digest (West)	$450.00
Rhode Island General Laws (w/2004 supps.) (LexisNexis)	$100.00
Rhode Island Reports, vols. 1-122 (1828-1980) (all)	$800.00
South Carolina Code (LexisNexis)	$450.00
South Carolina Digest 2d (West)	$895.00
South Carolina Reports, vols. 1-305	$2,495.00
South Dakota Codified Laws (LexisNexis)	$250.00
South Dakota Reports, vols. 1-90 (all)	$795.00
South Eastern Digest 2d (West)	$695.00
South Eastern Reporter [1st] vols. 1-200 (West)	$995.00
South Eastern Reporter 2d, vols. 1-488 (West)	$1,695.00
South Eastern Reporter Citations, 6 vols. (Shepards)	$200.00
South Western Reporter [1st] vols. 1-300 (West)	$995.00
South Western Reporter 2d, vols. 1-999 (West)	$1,995.00
South Western Reporter 2d, vols. 1-999 & 3d, 1-49 (West)	$1,995.00
South Western Reporter Citations, 8 vols. (Shepards)	$450.00
Southern Reporter [1st] vols. 1-200) (West)	$795.00
Southern Reporter 2d, vols. 1-703 (1941-1998) (West)	$1,695.00
Southern Reporter 2d, vols. 1-822 (1941-2002) (West)	$1,795.00
Southern Reporter Citations, 13 vols. (Shepards)	$450.00
Summary of Pennsylvania Jurisprudence (West)	$695.00
Supreme Court Reporter, vols. 1-122B (West)	$1,895.00
Tax Court Reports, 102 vols. (1942-1994) (G.P.O.)	$995.00
Tennessee Appeals Reports, vols. 1-63 (all)	$950.00
Tennessee Decisions (S.W.2d), vols. 1-955	$995.00
Tennessee Digest 2d (West)	$650.00
Tennessee Reports, vols. 1-225 (all)	$1,895.00
Texas Cases [1st] , vols. 1-300 (all) (West)	$595.00
Texas Cases (S.W. 2d), vols. 1-999, and 3d , 1-24 (1928-2000) (West)	$1,695.00
Texas Criminal Appeals Reports, vols. 1-172 (all)	$1,495.00
Texas Digest 2d (West) (thru 2005)	$795.00
Texas Jurisprudence 3d, vols. 1-77 (West) (thru 2006)	1,095.00
Texas Litigation Guide, 26 vols. (West)	$295.00
Texas Reports, vols. 1-163 (all)	$1,095.00
Texas Statutes Annotated, Vernons (West)	$295.00
Texas Transaction Guide, 24 vols.	$295.00
Uniform Law Annotated, 30 vols. (West)	$695.00
United States Administrative Citations, 5 vols. (Shepards)	$100.00
U.S. Claims Reporter, vols. 1-27 (West)	$850.00
U.S. Code Annotated (w/2011 supps.) (West)	$1,295.00
U.S. Code Congressional & Administrative News, 1941-2003	$1,295.00

U.S. Code Service (complete) (LexisNexis)	$695.00
U.S. Court of Claims Reports, vols. 1-231 (G.P.O.)	$1,495.00
U.S. Reports, vols. 1-542	$5,495.00
U.S. Supreme Court Digest (West)	$895.00
U.S. Supreme Court Digest L. Ed. (LexisNexis)	$495.00
U.S. Supreme Court Reports, L. Ed. [1st] (LexisNexis)	$795.00
U.S. Supreme Court Reports, L. Ed. 2d, vols. 1-163 (LexisNexis)	$995.00
U.S. Tax Cases , 1913 - 1992-2, 114 vols. (CCH)	$595.00
United States Reports, official edition, vols. 1-301	$1,495.00
United States Reports, official edition, vols. 257-533 (277 books)	$2,995.00
Utah Code Annotated (LexisNexis) (thru 2003)	$295.00
Utah Reporter (1974-1993) (West)	$895.00
Utah Reports [1st] , vols. 1-123 (all)	$995.00
Utah Reports 2d, vols. 1-30 (all)	$595.00
Vermont Digest (West)	$695.00
Vermont Reports, vols. 1-157	$2,895.00
Vermont Statutes Annotated (LexisNexis) (to 1996)	$150.00
Virginia, Code of (LexisNexis)	$350.00
Virginia Court of Appeals Reports, vols. 1-44	$295.00
Virginia Reports, vols. 1-251	$1,695.00
Virginia & West Virginia Digest (thru 2004) (West)	$495.00
Warrens Forms of Agreements (Matthew Bender)	$250.00
Washington Appellate Reports, vols. 1-66	$895.00
Washington Citations, 4 vols. (Shepards)	$150.00
Washington Digest 2d (West)	$1,095.00
Washington Reports [1st] , vols. 1-200 (all)	$995.00
Washington Reports 2d, vols. 1-119 (1939-1964)	$1,195.00
Washington, Wests Revised Code of	$1,195.00
Weinsteins Federal Evidence 2d ed. (Matthew Bender) (thru 2003)	$395.00
Wests Federal Forms	$395.00
Wests Legal Forms (thru 2002)	$695.00
West Virginia Code Annotated (LexisNexis)	$250.00
West Virginia reports, vols. 1-187	$2,495.00
Williston on Contracts 3d ed.	$350.00
Wisconsin Citations, 3 vols.	$100.00
Wisconsin Digest (West)	$750.00
Wisconsin Reports, 1st, vols. 1-275 (1853-1957)	$795.00
Wisconsin Reports 2d, vols. 1-178 (1957-date)	$495.00
Wisconsin Statutes Annotated (West)	$995.00
Words and Phrases (West) (w/2005 supps.)	$995.00
Wyoming Reporter, vol. 1-date (1961-date) (West)	$1,295.00
Wyoming Reports, vols. 1-80 (all)	$995.00
Wyoming Statutes Annotated (LexisNexis)	$395.00

Appendix F - Guide to Fair Business Practices for Legal Publishers

American Association of Law Libraries
Guide to Fair Business Practices for Legal Publishers

Approved by the Executive Board November 2002;
Second Edition approved July 2006;
Revised Second Edition approved April 2008.
Third Edition approved November 2012

A Brief History

The original *AALL Guide to Fair Business Practices for Legal Publishers was approved by the AALL Executive Board* in November 2002. It was a response to the rescission of the *Federal Trade Commission's Guides for the Law Book Industry*, and the FTC's explicit encouragement that AALL or other interested groups develop standards to address member concerns. The AALL Guide describes standards for the business practices of publishers that most directly affect law librarians, attorneys , procurement officers and other consumers of legal information. It consists of five general principles, each of which is accompanied by subprinciples and examples. It sets forth principled business practices that will promote fair and appropriate treatment for customers.

The AALL Guide was revised in 2008, and that revision incorporated additional examples of practices that are consistent with the AALL Guide and practices to avoid. This 2012 revision follows the earlier ones, but responds to new developments in legal publishing and the marketplace. AALL is under no illusion that the simple promulgation of a guide will solve all problems associated with the business practices of legal publishers. However, AALL believes that a good faith effort on the part of the legal publishing community to implement the provisions of the AALL Guide, coupled with consistent reference to the principles by customers will facilitate effective business relationships and minimize problems.

The AALL Guide represents the cumulative efforts of many dedicated AALL members, from the original Special Committee (Frank Houdek, Chair, Kathy Carlson, Chris Graesser, Kay Todd and Michelle Wu), the 2005-2006 Task Force (Kay Todd, Chair, Rita Dermody, Kamla King Hedges, and Richard Vaughan), and the 2011-2012 Task Force (Kay Todd, Chair, Michael Bernier, Kathy Coon, Margaret Maes, Jean Mattimoe, and Adeen Postar). Member input has throughout ensured that the Guide reflects contemporary practices. The 2011-2012 Task Force wishes to thank AALL President, Jean Wenger, AALL Past President, Darcy Kirk, and members of the Executive Board for their support of this revision.

Introduction

1. The American Association of Law Libraries Guide to Fair Business Practices for Legal Publishers ("AALL Guide") is premised on the belief that good customer service and positive customer relations benefit legal publishers as well as customers. Equally fundamental is the understanding that the relationship between publishers and customers must be built on mutual respect and trust.

2. The AALL Guide provides guidelines for legal publishers doing business with librarians, attorneys, procurement officers and other consumers of legal information, and covers the full range of their interactions, from advertising and solicitation to purchases and customer support. The best practices identified by the AALL Guide are designed to facilitate effective and productive relationships.

3. By following the provisions of the AALL Guide, legal publishers can significantly contribute to effective self-regulation in the public interest and help establish the AALL Guide as the accepted standard in the industry. AALL urges legal publishers to comply with the AALL Guide and to implement the requisite internal procedures and infrastructure to support compliance.
The AALL Guide offers practical guidelines, with examples of practices either to follow or to avoid that are intended to help explain these guidelines. The AALL Guide does not explicitly cover publishers' internal operations, understanding that the publisher is in the best position to fully implement the guidelines in a manner suitable to its business plan. The AALL Guide is designed to allow legal publishers to take advantage of evolving technology and to foster innovation while adhering to fair business practices.

4. The AALL Guide uses the term "should" in recognition that this is a voluntary code. All provisions are strongly recommended for implementation by the legal publishing community. Law librarians and consumers of legal information are encouraged to regard the AALL Guide as a minimum basis for fair business practices by legal publishers and to reference these principles in their interactions with publishers.

5. The legal information and publishing environment is rapidly evolving and AALL recognizes that the AALL Guide may need to be modified to keep pace with developing technology, new business models and practices, and the needs of customers. AALL is committed to regularly reviewing the AALL Guide and updating it as needed.

6. AALL has a longstanding interest in vendor relations, as evidenced by the work of the AALL Vendor Liaison, the Committee on Relations with Information Vendors, the Principles for Licensing Electronic Resources, and previous editions of this Guide. For further information, users of the AALL Guide should consult additional resources on the AALL website.

Definitions

Unless the context otherwise requires, words or phrases defined in this section have the meanings stated.

beta testing The final stage in the testing of a new electronic product before its commercial release, conducted by testers other than its developers.

communication Any transmission or exchange of written, oral, or electronic information between publisher representatives and customers.

customer Any individual or institution, including an employee or representative of a library, who has business dealings with a publisher.

customer service Assistance provided by a publisher to enable a customer to receive the best possible value for the product by minimizing the amount of time the customer needs to spend in answering any questions about or resolving problems concerning the product.

electronic product Information that is sold or delivered in an electronic format, or a product that relates to the management of information in an electronic format.

fair dealing The conduct of business with full disclosure.

material information Information that would be important in making a decision about a transaction.

product A tangible item, not limited to a print publication, that is distributed commercially for use or consumption.

publisher Any corporation, partnership, government entity, or person that is in the business of providing legal information for sale. This includes those who act as agents or representatives of a publisher. Whenever the term "publisher" is used it is intended to include publishers of print and electronic products.

standing order An authorization to make automatic regular or periodic shipments of new issues, new editions, or supplementary content for a specified product.

supplementation Material or information provided to update the information content of an existing product.

transaction An action involving two parties; usually an exchange or transfer of goods, services, or funds.

Principles for Fair Business Practices of Legal Publishers

The AALL Guide is based on five major principles. These principles should be considered together with their sub-principles and supporting comments and examples.

Principle 1: Truthful and Accurate Communication.
Publishers of print and electric products should engage in truthful and accurate communication with their customers or potential customers.

Principle 2: Disclosure.
Publishers should provide full disclosure about their products, services, retail prices, and terms in order to enable customers to make informed purchasing decisions.

Principle 3: Fair Dealing.
Publishers should engage in fair dealings with their customers in all aspects of the business relationship.

Principle 4: Customer Satisfaction.
Publishers should seek to ensure customer satisfaction by training customer service employees, honoring representations, answering questions, and resolving complaints and disputes in a timely and responsive manner.

Principle 5: Product Quality.
Publishers should create products that are capable of withstanding reasonable use by customers.

Principle 1: Truthful and Accurate Communication.
Publishers should engage in truthful and accurate communication with their customers or potential customers.

1.1 Publishers should engage in truthful advertising of their products and services. Their advertising and marketing should not make deceptive or misleading representations or fail to include material facts.

1.1(a) Publishers should be able to substantiate any express or reasonably implied factual claims made in their advertising or marketing. Reasonable substantiation should exist prior to disseminating any claim.

1.1(a) PRACTICE TO AVOID: Beta testing on an electronic product is not completed prior to an assertion in an advertisement that the product has undergone successful consumer testing and is ready for general distribution.

1.1(b) Publishers should not mislead customers by creating a false impression of sponsorship, endorsement, popularity, trustworthiness, or product quality through the misuse of hyperlinks, "seals," or other means.

1.1(b) PRACTICE TO FOLLOW: A statement extolling the quality of a product, used in an advertisement, should indicate if a relationship exists between the source of the statement and the publisher of the product.

1.2 Advertising and marketing materials should clearly indicate that they represent only an offer or encouragement to purchase.

1.2 PRACTICE TO AVOID 1: Material information in an advertisement is presented in such a way

as to make it difficult to distinguish between editorial content and advertising.

1.2 PRACTICE TO AVOID 2: Promotional material is presented in a form sufficiently resembling an invoice as to make it likely that a customer will be confused or misled.

1.3 Electronic methods of communication that market products should accurately describe the nature and content of the products, consistent with the information provided in print advertising for the same products.

1.3(a) Hyperlinks should not be used to indicate a different or expanded content from the actual content of the product or to materially mislead the consumer as to the product.

1.3(a) PRACTICE TO AVOID: A publisher's promotional literature for a specific product, sold separately, links to a description of "bundled" services offered at additional cost.

1.3(b) Electronic advertisers may use hyperlinks to add to or supplement information about goods or services but should not misleadingly use hyperlinks or information provided via a hyperlink to:

i. contradict or substantially change the meaning of any material statement or claim

ii. create the false impression of affiliation

iii. create the false impression that the content, merchandise, or service of another entity or business is its own

Principle 2: Disclosure. Publishers should provide full disclosure about their products, services, retail prices, and transactions in order to enable library professionals to make informed acquisitions decisions.

2.1 All information about products, services, prices, and transactions provided by publishers to customers should be clear, accurate, and easy to find.

2.1 PRACTICE TO AVOID: A publisher's invoice uses such an abbreviated title for the item being billed that it is difficult for customers to identify the item.

2.1 PRACTICE TO FOLLOW 1: A publisher's Web site minimizes the number of links the customer must follow to obtain cost data.

2.1 PRACTICE TO FOLLOW 2: A publisher makes a description of standard discounts and variable pricing options for all products and services readily available.

2.2 The content of information that appears in both print and non print advertising and marketing sources should be consistent.

2.2 PRACTICE TO AVOID: A print advertisement lists a product's price, but an electronic advertisement does not.

2.3 Prior to confirming a purchase, publishers should provide all material information necessary for a customer to make an informed decision about products and services, including but not limited to:

2.3(a) Full title, author(s) or editor(s), ISBN or ISSN, and brand/publisher

2.3(b) Actual copyright date of the book or edition, prominently displayed in all communications, including marketing material

2.3(b) PRACTICE TO AVOID: An advertisement for a previously published product that has not been updated does not disclose the copyright date, thereby implying that the product is either new or newly revised.

2.3(c) For electronic products, the system requirements for receiving or accessing the product and any known system incompatibilities, prominently displayed in all communications, including marketing material

2.3(d) Notice as to whether the product is a revision, recompilation, condensation, reprint, or otherwise taken from another source

2.3(d) PRACTICE TO AVOID: A product that is created solely by extracting material from existing publications is billed as a new product.

2.3(d) PRACTICE TO FOLLOW: A publisher clearly identifies the original source of a product that is a revision, recompilation, or condensation of an existing publication.

2.3(e) Expected publication date of next edition if known to be within the next six months.

2.3(f) Complete physical description, including whether publication is a loose-leaf or bound volume, or contains a disk or CD.

2.3(g) Cost, including (1) itemization of all components, (2) estimate of any shipping and handling charges, (3) anticipated supplementation costs, (4) applicable discounts, and (5) any other advantageous purchasing options

2.3(g) PRACTICE TO AVOID 1: The price supplied prior to purchase does not contain all elements for which the customer will be responsible, such as shipping and handling costs.
2.3(g) PRACTICE TO AVOID 2: The price supplied for anticipated supplementation includes a

charge for annual pocket parts but no estimated cost for revised volumes.

2.3(g) PRACTICE TO FOLLOW: Where the cost of shipping a CD will be $25, the publisher discloses this charge prior to purchase.

2.3(h) If offered in multiple formats, a full description of each available format, including any differences in scope, price breakdown, updating, and license restrictions

2.3(h) PRACTICE TO FOLLOW: Review the Principles for Licensing Electronic Resources. The Principles that provide guidance to library staff in working with others in the institution and with licensors to create agreements that respect the rights and obligations of both parties. http://www.aallnet.org/committee/reports/icensingPrinciplesElecResources.pdf

2.3(i) Information on supplementation

i. Expected extent, content, and format of supplementation

ii. Expected frequency of supplementation or schedule of issues

iii. Whether cost of supplementation is included in the flat rate subscription or separately charged by shipment or some other arrangement

iv. Where possible, historic data on the cost of supplementation for the product

2.4 Publishers should provide, in a way that is easily understood by the customer, all the terms of a particular transaction, including but not limited to:

2.4(a) Price or license fee to be charged

2.4(b) Any offered terms or limitations, including special offers

2.4(c) Expected shipping and handling charges

2.4(d) Titles to be shipped as part of a subscription or standing order but charged separately as an additional cost

2.4(e) Billing information

2.4(f) Return, refund and cancellation policies

2.4 PRACTICE TO FOLLOW: Publisher places the "terms of transaction" in a sidebar or text-box, clearly setout from the rest of any promotional literature.

Principle 3: Fair Dealing. Publishers should engage in fair dealings with their customers.

3.1 **Customer consent.** Publishers should obtain the customer's consent prior to making a shipment or initiating a transaction, unless such shipment is part of a standing order or subscription to which the customer has previously consented.

3.1 PRACTICE TO AVOID 1: Without prior customer consent, a publisher mass mails a new product to customers who have previously purchased an existing product.

3.1 PRACTICE TO AVOID 2: Without prior customer consent, a publisher ships a free unsolicited newsletter to a customer and then later sends an invoice for the title to the customer.

3.1(a) Where the content of a new product or supplement that is published as part of an existing subscription or standing order bears no direct relationship to the content of the standing order or represents a substantial expansion of the topic or purpose of the original subscription or product, the publisher should seek customer consent prior to shipment.

3.1(a) PRACTICE TO AVOID: Without prior customer consent, the publisher of a subscription service ships to subscribers of the service a pamphlet that includes content that has not previously been supplied as part of the subscription, where that content is not specific or closely related to the topic of the service, and charges customers for the pamphlet.

3.1(b) Where a new product or supplement is published as an addition to more than one existing title or subscription, the publisher should seek customer consent prior to shipment.

3.1(b) PRACTICE TO FOLLOW: When planning to ship identical pamphlets as part of several different subscription services, the publisher gives customers prior notice and the option to receive more or fewer copies of the pamphlet according to the needs of the customer.

3.1(c) Where a new product or supplement published as part of an existing title is substantially redundant of material already contained in that title, the publisher should seek customer consent prior to shipment.

3.1(c) PRACTICE TO AVOID: Without prior customer consent, a publisher ships a recompilation of session laws to customers who have already received the material in the same publisher's advance legislative service to which they subscribe, where recompilations have not previously occurred or been shipped as part of that subscription.

3.1(d) Publishers should seek customer consent prior to shipping materials that fundamentally alter, enhance, or augment a product or subscription. Unsolicited merchandise may be disposed of without permission, without an attempt to return, and without payment, pursuant to federal statute (39 U.S.C. § 3009). In all cases, publishers should offer a simple procedure for returning products and canceling subscriptions.

3.1(d) PRACTICE TO AVOID: A publisher requires that a customer pay postage when returning an unsolicited product.

3.1(e) Subscriptions to legal information products are traditionally "until forbid" or standing orders. However, where a substantial change in the nature, format, or scope of a product results in a significant cost increase, publishers should give customers advance notice before shipping the product.

3.1(f) Publishers should provide reasonable advance notice of new editions or recompilations that will incur a single large upkeep cost.

3.2 **Fair negotiations.** Publishers should engage in open and fair negotiations with customers regarding licensing agreements and other contracts.

3.2 PRACTICE TO FOLLOW: Review the Principles for Licensing Electronic Resources. The Principles that provide guidance to library staff in working with others in the institution and with licensors to create agreements that respect the rights and obligations of both parties. http://www.aallnet.org/committee/reports/LicensingPrinciplesElecResources.pdf

3.2(a) Publishers should not bind their customers to a non-disclose clause as a non-negotiable requirement of doing business.

3.2(b) Publishers should always provide an opportunity for their customers to negotiate contract terms. "Shrink wrap," "click-on," and other attempts to create agreements that do not provide customers with a fair opportunity to negotiate should not be required.

3.2(c) Publishers should adhere to the Principles for Licensing Electronic Resources, written collaboratively by the American Association of Law Libraries, American Library Association, Association of Academic Health Sciences Libraries, Association of Research Libraries, Medical Library Association, and Special Libraries Association and revised and adopted by the American Association of Law Libraries in 2004. http://www.aallnet.org/committee/reports/LicensingPrinciplesElecResources.pdf

3.3 **Substantive supplementation**. Product supplementation should be issued only when a significant change in the law has taken place, or when substantial additional content is provided.

3.3(a) Customers should be provided with a complete and detailed description of the supplement's contents.

3.3(b) Customers should be provided with filing/replacement instructions that are sufficiently detailed to ensure accurate updating.

3.3(c) Customers should be fully advised of the term of a subscription and what is included in it at the time of purchase. This advisement should describe the expected supplementation, including whether at the publisher's discretion no supplementation may be provided over the term of the subscription.

3.3(c) PRACTICE TO AVOID: Publisher provides a subscription invoice that does not clearly indicate to the customer what is included in the subscription.

3.4 **Unsolicited communication**. Publishers should respect reasonable requests by the customer regarding methods of contact such as telemarketing, telefax, or e-mail advertisements.

3.4 PRACTICE TO FOLLOW: A publisher honors the request of a customer to be removed from a telemarketing list, even if the publisher contracts with a third party for telemarketing services.

3.5 **Timing.** Publishers should mail out renewal notices at periods related to the date of subscription, and the notice should provide the expiration date of the current subscription.

3.5 PRACTICE TO AVOID: A publisher sends a renewal notice for a publication more than six months prior to the expiration of the subscription.

3.6 **Forthcoming Edition or Substantial Revision**. Publishers should advise customers about a forthcoming edition or substantial revision of a publication when they place an order for the publication or make an inquiry that may lead to its purchase if: (1) it is known that the new edition or revision is scheduled for publication within the next six months, and (2) the pricing structure is such that the customer will need to make a comparable investment during the year to maintain a current subscription or title.

3.6 PRACTICE TO FOLLOW: Invoices for purchase of a new title should clearly indicate the period for which supplementation will be provided at no additional charge.

Principle 4: Customer Satisfaction. Publishers should seek to ensure customer satisfaction by honoring representations, answering questions, and resolving complaints and disputes in a timely and responsive manner.

4.1 Publishers should work collaboratively with customers to resolve problems and improve products and service.

4.1 PRACTICE TO AVOID: A publisher turns an outstanding invoice over to a collection agency prior to contacting the library in question.

4.1 PRACTICE TO FOLLOW: Customers should carefully document contacts with publisher identifying date and time the contact took place, name of person in customer service, description of the problem and potential resolution.

4.2 Publishers should provide customers with ready and convenient access to information through a variety of channels.

4.2(a) Customer Service Provided by Telephone

i. Customer service should be provided on a schedule that meets the needs of the majority of the customer base.

4.2(a)(i) PRACTICE TO AVOID: Providing customer service by telephone only between the hours of 8:00 a.m. and 5:00 p.m. EST, Monday through Friday.

ii. Auto menus should provide clear options, should not have more than two levels, and should provide direct access to an employee for problems that do not fit into the options provided.

iii. Publishers should strive to provide sufficient staff to handle the expected level of calls without leaving callers on hold for extended periods of time, and should consider offering a call back option to customers who are "on hold" longer than a standard, reasonable period of time.

4.2(b) Publishers should provide as many alternative electronic options for asking questions as is possible with currently available technology, such as e mail, fax, and the Internet, and should ensure that all contact information disseminated in electronic format is kept current.

4.2(c) Technical Support should be provided on a schedule that meets the needs of the majority of the customer base.

4.3 Publishers should ensure that employees responsible for customer service duties are adequately prepared.

4.3(a) Customer service employees should have good oral and written communication skills.

4.3(b) Customer service employees should have a complete understanding of the basic products and services.

i. Customer service employees should receive adequate training before beginning communications with customers.

4.3(b)(i)PRACTICE TO AVOID: A publisher's customer service representatives are not familiar with the company's billing system and how payments are applied, and are unable to quickly and accurately identify and price any of the publisher's titles.

ii. Customer service employees should be provided timely information about all new products and special promotions.

iii. Customer service employees should have ready access to basic product and promotional reference materials.

4.3(c) Customer service employees dealing directly with customer questions should have access to basic information regarding customer accounts. An effort should be made to see that customers are able to get assistance at first link and do not have to be transferred multiple times or have to repeat their questions more than once.

4.3(d) Customer service employees should be sufficiently empowered to resolve basic problems.

4.3(e) Customers should be provided with a direct channel for making complaints or commendations, not just a generic address or e-mail address.

4.4 Publishers should respond to all inquiries in a manner that is timely for the communication medium used by the customer.

4.4(a) Publishers should confirm the receipt of all electronic inquiries.

4.4(b) Regardless of the medium used by the customer, the publisher should use the most expedient medium to make first contact with the customer, whether it be e-mail, telephone, or fax.

4.4(c) In situations where a request requires time or research, customers should be regularly updated on the progress and given an expected response time.

4.5 Publishers should ensure that their promises to resolve problems are fulfilled in a timely manner.

Principle 5: Product Quality. Publishers should create products that are capable of withstanding reasonable use by customers.

5.1 **Hardcover Materials.** Since it can be reasonably concluded that hardcover books are purchased for long-term use and may eventually be archived, publishers should meet the following standards in the production of hardcover materials.

5.1(a) ANSI/NISO Z39.48-1992 (R1997) regarding

Permanence of Paper for Publications and Documents in Libraries and Archives.

5.1(b) ANSI/NISO/LBI Z39.78-2000 regarding Library Binding.

5.2 **Softcover Materials.**

5.2(a) For softcover materials that are anticipated to remain on library shelves longer than two years, or which may logically be retained by a library for archival purposes (e.g., state codes), publishers should meet the following standards:

i. ANSI/NISO Z39.48-1992 (R1997) regarding Permanence of Paper for Publications and Documents in Libraries and Archives.

ii. Binding which will withstand reasonable use and which is designed to provide sufficient margins so that a library may easily have the item professionally bound in hardcover should it so desire.

5.2(b) Softcover materials and supplements that are replaced annually should have paper and binding strong enough to withstand reasonable use.

5.3 **Loose-Leaf Materials.**

5.3(a) Binders should be heavy-duty and easy to operate.

5.3(a) PRACTICE TO AVOID: A binder provided for a loose-leaf service loses its alignment within a few months of reasonable use by a customer.

5.3(b) When the number of pages exceeds binder capacity, the publisher should take the necessary steps to relieve the overcrowding in a timely manner.

5.3(c) Paper in publications where changes are made to individual pages on an irregular basis should meet the ANSI/NISO Z39.48-1992 (R1997) standard regarding Permanence of Paper for Publications and Documents in Libraries and Archives.

5.4 **Microforms.** Since it is known that libraries tend to purchase microforms for archival purposes, microform producers should follow the standards established by the National Archives and Records Administration ("NARA") in 36 C.F.R. Part 1230.12(d) and 36 C.F.R. Part 1230.14 (b-d).

5.4 PRACTICE TO FOLLOW: Promotional literature and advertisements for microform products should indicate that the product meets NARA standards.

5.5 **Electronic Publications.**

5.5 PRACTICE TO FOLLOW: Publishers should adhere to the Principles for Licensing Electronic Resources, written collaboratively by the American Association of Law Libraries, American Library Association, Association of Academic Health Sciences Libraries, Association of Research Libraries, Medical Library Association, and Special Libraries Association and revised and adopted by the American Association of Law Libraries in 2004. http://www.aallnet.org/committee/reports/LicensingPrinciplesElecResources.pdf

5.5(a) Electronic products should not be placed into the market until tested by a group of users that are representative of their actual anticipated customers.

5.5(b) Uninstall should be an included feature. Where possible, the uninstall feature should delete all added files. If a standard operating file has been modified by the program, the uninstall feature should return the file to the original properties or provide a message that the file needs to be reinstalled to reset the original properties.

5.5(c) Instructions and documentation should be easy to understand.

5.5(d) Statements describing the scope of information provided by electronic products should be included in the documentation for the products.

5.5(e) Products should clearly indicate their expiration date so that the publisher can be contacted if an update has not been received to try to ensure the ongoing availability of the resource.

5.5(f) Information as to the date and/or the number of the release should be included within the electronic text.

5.5(f) PRACTICE TO AVOID: Information as to the currency of the publication is provided solely on the physical disks or in product documentation that is unavailable to the user who typically accesses the publication off a server or via an intranet.

5.6 MICROFORMS. Microform producers should follow the standards established by the National Archives and Records Administration ("NARA") in 36 C.F.R. Part 1230.12(d) and 36 C.F.R. Part 1230.14 (b-d).

5.6 PRACTICE TO FOLLOW: Promotional literature and advertisements for microform products should indicate that the product meets NARA standards.

5.7 AUDIO/VISUAL MATERIALS. Audio/video materials should be playable on any audio/video equipment that meets industry standards.

5.7 PRACTICE TO FOLLOW: Promotional literature and advertisements for A/V materials should indicate any non-industry standard equipment needed.

5.8 REPLACEMENTS.

5.8(a) Customers should be able to obtain replacements for missing or damaged parts of a product for a low or reasonable cost. Defective parts should be promptly replaced at no cost.
5.8(b) The policies and process for requesting replacements should be widely publicized to customers.
5.8(b) PRACTICE TO FOLLOW: Replacement policies and instructions are clearly posted on publisher websites.

Appendix G: A Selective List of Looseleaf Services

(Including Print, CD, and Internet)

The following lists include products from Bureau of National Affairs (BNA), Commerce Clearing House (CCH), LRP Publications, Pike & Fischer, and Research Institute of America (RIA). While initially based on looseleaf services in print, it has been expanded to include products on CD-ROM and Internet (Web) formats, many of which are available in multiple formats. The complexity of current bundled offerings and pricing makes it imperative that the prospective purchaser consult with his or her sales representative to obtain exact product specifications and pricing. Pricing for a selective number of these products appears in Chapter 27 an Appendix I nder their respective subject areas.

Key: 1= web notification, 2= E-mail summaries, 3= print

Bureau of National Affairs (BNA)

ABA/BNA Lawyers' Manual on Professional Conduct (complete service) (3/Web)
Affirmative Action Compliance Manual for Federal Contractors (3)
Air Pollution Control Guide (part of BNA's Environment & Safety Library) (Web)
Americans with Disabilities Act Manual (complete service) (3)
Antitrust & Trade Regulation Daily (1, 2)
Antitrust & Trade Regulation Report (1, 2, & 3)
Banking Daily (1, 2)
Banking Report (1, 2, & 3)
Bankruptcy Law Daily (1, 2)
Bankruptcy Law Reporter (1, 2, & 3)
Benefits & Compensation Management Update (3 notification)
Benefits Practice Center (CD-ROM/Web)
BioTech Watch (1, 2)
BNA/ACCA Compliance Manual: Prevention of Corporate Liability (3 & 3 notification)
Broker/Dealer Compliance Report (1, 2)
Bulletin to Management (1, 2)
Canadian Environment & Safety Library (CD-ROM)
Chemical Regulation Daily (1, 2)
Chemical Regulation Reporter (complete service) (3/Web/CD-ROM)
Class Action Litigation Report (3 & 1, 2)
Collective Bargaining Negotiations and Contracts (3 reference and notification)
Compensation & Benefits Library 1, 3, CD-ROM)
Computer Technology Law Report (3 &1)
Construction Labor Report (1 & 3)
Corporate Accountability & Fraud Daily (1, 2)
Corporate Accountability Report (1, 2)
Corporate Compliance Library (1, 3)
Corporate Counsel Library (Web, 2)
Corporate Counsel Weekly (1, 2, & 3)
Corporate Governance Library (1, 2, & 3)
Corporate Law Daily (Web, 2)
Corporate Practice Library (1, 2, and 3)
Criminal Law Reporter (1, 2, & 3)
Daily Environment Report (1, 2)
Daily Labor Report (3 & 1, 2)
Daily Report for Executives (3 & 1, 2)
Daily Tax Report (3 & 1, 2)
E-Commerce Law Daily (1, 2)
E-Commerce Tax Report 1, 2)
EEOC Compliance Manual (3 reference & notification)
EHS Assist (Web reference)
EHS Global Alert (Web-mail)
EHS Legislative Alert (2)
Electronic Commerce & Law Report (1, 2, & 3)
Employee Benefits Cases (3)
Employment Attorney's Clint Advisor (Web)
Employment Discrimination Report (1, 2, & 3)
Employment Discrimination Verdicts and Settlements (Web reference)
Employment Guide (3 & Web reference, 3 notification)
Employment Law Library on CD
Energy Legislation Wire (1)
Environment Health & Safety Benchmarks 2004 (3 annual)
Environment & Safety Library (CD-ROM &Web reference)
Environment Library on CD
Environment Reporter (complete service) (1, 2, & 3)
Environmental Compliance Bulletin (3 & 1, 2)
Environmental Due Diligence Guide (1, 2, & 3)
Expert Evidence Report (1, 2, & 3)
Export Reference Guide (Web & CD-ROM reference)
Family Law Reporter (3 reference & notification, 1, 2)
Federal Contracts Report (1, 2, & 3)
Federal Environment & Safety Regulatory Monitoring Report (3 & 1, 2)
Global EHS Library (1, 2)
Global HR Report (Web reference & notification)
Government Employee Relations Report (3 & 1)
HazMat Transportation News (1, 2)
Health Care Compliance Library (3 & Web reference)
Health Care Daily Report (1, 2)
Health Care Fraud Report (3 & 1, 2)
Health Care Policy Report (3 & 1, 2)
Health Care Program Compliance Guide (3 reference)
Health Law & Business Library (3, CD-ROM & Web portfolios)
Health Law Reporter (3 & 1, 2)
Health Plan & Provider report (3 & 1, 2)
Homeland Security Briefing (3 & 1, 2)
HR Corporate Suite I (Web news, notification, and reference)
HR Corporate Suite II (Web news, notification, and reference)
HR Corporate Suite III (Web news, notification, and reference)
Human Resources Library (3 notification, Web & CD-ROM reference)
Human Resources Report (3 & 1, 2)
Intellectual Property Library (3 decisions, Web & CD-ROM reference)
International Business & Finance Daily (1, 2)
International Environment Daily (1, 2)
International Environment Reporter (3 reference &

notification, 1, 2)
International Tax Monitor (1, 2)
International Trade Daily (1, 2)
International Trade Reporter (reference & notification, Web notification, 2)
Job Safety and Health (3 reference & notification, Web notification, 2)
Labor & Employment Law Library (3 reference & notification, Web & CD-ROM reference)
Labor Relations Reporter (3 reference & notification, Web & CD-ROM reference)
Labor Relations Week (3 & 1, 2)
Media Law Reporter (3 decisions & notification)
Medical Research Law & Policy Report (1 & 2, E-mail summaries)
Medicare Drug Watch (Web, E-mail issued daily)
Medicare Report (3 & 1, 2)
Mergers & Acquisitions Law Report (3 & 1, E-mail summaries)
Money and Politics Report (1, 2)
Occupational Safety & Health Daily (1, 2)
Occupational Safety & Health Reporter (1, 2, & 3, CD)
Patent, Trademark & Copyright Daily (1, 2)
Patent, Trademark & Copyright Journal (1, 2, & 3)
Payroll Administration Guide (print & Web reference & notification, CD-ROM reference)
Payroll & Tax Practice Suite (Web news, notification, and reference material)
Payroll Library (3 & Web reference & notification, CD-ROM reference)
Pension & Benefits Daily (1 and 2)
Pension & Benefits Reporter (1, 2, & 3)
Pharmaceutical Law & Industry Report (1, 2, & 3)
Privacy Law Watch (1, 2)
Privacy & Security Law Report (1, 2, & 3)
Product Liability Daily (1, 2)
Product Safety & Liability Reporter (1, 2, & 3)
Right-to-Know Planning Guide (1, 2, & 3)
safety.bna.com (Web reference material)
Safety Library (1,2, CD)
SafetyNet (1, 2, & 3)
Securities Law Daily (1, 2)
Securities Regulation & Law Report 1, 2, & 3)
State Environment & Safety Regulatory Monitoring Report (1, 2, & 3)
State Environment Daily (1, 2)
State Health Care Regulatory Developments (2,3)
TaxCore (Web)
Tax Management Library (Web)
Tax Management Library: Estates, Gifts & Trusts (Web)
Tax Management Library: Foreign Income (Web)
Tax Management Library: State Tax (Web)
Tax Management Library: Tax Practice (Web)
Tax Management Library: U.S. Income (Web)
Tax Management Weekly Report (Web)
Tax Planning International Asia-Pacific Focus (1,2)
Tax Planning International European-Union Focus (3 & Web notification, 2)
Tax Planning International Indirect Taxes (1, 2, & 3)
Tax Planning International Review & Forum 1, 2, & 3)
Tax Planning International Transfer Pricing (1, 2, & 3)
Telecommunications Monitor (1, 2)
Toxics Law Daily (1, 2)
Toxics Law Reporter (3 & 1, 2)
Transportation Watch (1, 2)
U.S. Law Week (1, 2)
U.S. Patents Quarterly (1, 2, & 3, CD-ROM)
Union Labor Report Newsletter (1, 2, & 3)
Waste Management Guide (component of BNA's Environment & Safety Library)
Water Pollution Control Guide (component of BNA's Environment & Safety Library)
Workforce Strategies (3, PDF)
Workplace Law Report (3 & Web)
World Intellectual Property Report (1, 2, & 3)
World Securities Law Report (1, 2, & 3)
WTO Reporter (1, 2)

Commerce Clearing House (CCH)

Accommodating Disabilities Business Management Guide
Accountancy Law Reports
Accountants SEC Practice Manual
Accounting Articles
AICPA Audit and Accounting Guides
AICPA Audit and Accounting Manual
AICPA Financial Statement Reporting Manual
AICPA Quality Review Program Manual
AICPA Technical Practice Aids
American Stock Exchange Guide
Automobile Law Reports
Aviation Law Reports
Bankruptcy Law Reports
Blue Sky Law Reports (3/CD-ROM)
Board of Tax Appeals Regulars and Memoranda (CD-ROM)
Boston Stock Exchange Guide
Business Franchise Guide
Business Strategies
California and New York Tax Analysis (CD-ROM/Interr
California Eligible Securities List
California Medi-Cal Guide
Canadian Tax Reporter (3/CD-ROM/Internet)
Capital Changes Reports (3/CD-ROM)
CCH Business Owner's ToolKit Tax Guide (Internet)
CCH Corporate OmniTax Online Library (Internet)
CCH Entity Plus on CD-ROM
CCH Federal Tax Service (3/Internet)
CCH Federal Tax Service (3/Internet)
CCH Franchise Law Library on CD-ROM
CCH Health Care Fraud and Abuse Guide on CD-RON
CCH Managed Care Explained Plus (3/CD-ROM)
CCH Mexican Tax Library (3/Internet)
CCH Pension and Welfare Benefits Library (3/CD-ROI Internet)
CCH Perform Plus on CD-ROM
CCH Secured Transactions Guide (3/CD-ROM/Internet
CCH Smart Tax (CD-ROM/Internet)
CCH Smart Tax (CD-ROM/Internet)
CCH SmartPlanner (CD-ROM/Internet)
CCH SmartPLANNER on CD-ROM

CCH State Employment Laws on CD-ROM
CCH State SourceDocs
CCH Tax Day News and Documents (2/Internet)
CCH Tax Day News and Documents (Internet)
CCH Tax News Direct (Internet only)
CCH Tax News Direct (Internet only)
Chicago Board Options Exchange Guide
Code and Regulations (3/Internet)
Code and Regulations (3/Internet)
Commodity Futures Law Reports
CompleteTax.com (Internet)
CompleteTax Pro (Internet)
Compliance Guide for Plan Administrators on CD-ROM (3/CD-ROM/Internet)
Congressional Index
Congressional Legislative Reporting Service
Consumer Credit Guide (3/CD-ROM/Internet)
Consumer Product Safety Guide
Contract Appeals Decisions on CD-ROM (3/CD-ROM)
Copyright Law reports
Corporate Secretary's Guide
Cost Accounting Standards Guide
Creit Union Library (CD-ROM/Internet)
EEOC Compliance Manual
Employee Benefits Management (3/CD-ROM)
Employment Practices Guide
Employment Safety and Health Guide
Employment Tax Forms
Energy Management and Federal Energy Guidelines
Energy Resources Tax Reports
Exchange Guides Library on CD-ROM (3/CD-ROM)
Exempt Organizations Reports (3/CD-ROM)
Exempt Organizations Reports (3/CD-ROM)
Family Law Tax Guide
FAR Archival Information on CD-ROM
Federal Audit Guides
Federal Banking Law Reports
Federal Carriers Reports
Federal Election Campaign Financing Guide
Federal Energy Regulatory Commission Reports
Federal Estate & Gift Tax Reports (3/CD-ROM/Internet)
Federal Excise and Gift Taxation
Federal Excise Tax Reports (3/CD-ROM/Internet)
Federal Excise Tax Reports (3/CD-ROM/Internet)
Federal Securities Law Reports
Federal Securities Law; Regulations—Forms
Federal Tax Advisor
Federal Tax Articles
Federal Tax Forms
Federal Tax Guide (3/Internet)
Federal Tax Guide (3/Internet)
Federal Tax Manual with Monthly Reports
Federal Tax SourceDocs by CCH (CD-ROM/Internet)
Fiduciary Tax Guide
Financial and Estate Planning
Food Drug Cosmetic Law Reports
Fringe Benefits Tax Guide
FTG Edge (CD-ROM)
FTG Edge (CD-ROM)
Government Contracts Reports (3/CD-ROM)
Guide to Computer Law
Guide to Government Contracting
HCFA Manuals on CCH CD-ROM (3/CD-ROM)
Health Care Facility Management
Health Care Law and Management Guide on CD
Human Resources Management (3/CD-ROM)
Individual Retirement Plans Guide
Information Returns Guide
Inheritance Estate & Gift Tax Reports
Insurance Law Reports
Insurance Laws & Regulations for Financial Institutions (Internet)
Internal Revue Manual (3/CD-ROM/Internet)
International Transfer Pricing Laws: Text and Commentary (3/Internet)
IRS Code and Regulations
IRS Letter Rulings Reporter (3/CD-ROM/Internet)
IRS Letter Rulings Reporter (3/CD-ROM/Internet)
IRS Positions (3/CD-ROM/Internet)
IRS Publications (3/CD-ROM/Internet)
Labor Arbitration Awards
Labor Law Reports
Liquor Control Law Reports
Medical Devices Reports
Medicare-Medicaid Guide
Midwest Stock Exchange Guide
Multistate Corporate Income Tax Guide (CD-ROM/Internet)
Multistate Corporate Income Tax Guide (3/CD-ROM/Internet)
Multistate Part-Year Resident Return Guide
Multistate Sales Tax Guide (3/CD-ROM/Internet)
Municipal Securities Rulemaking Board
Mutual Funds Guide
National Association of Securities Dealers (NASD) Manual
New York Estates-Wills-Trusts
New York Futures Exchange Guide
New York Mercantile Exchange Guide
New York or California Tax Analysis (3/CD-ROM/Internet)
New York Stock Exchange Guide
NLRB Case Handling Manual
North American Securities Administrators Association (NASAA) Reports
OFCCP Federal Contract Compliance Manual
Pacific Stock Exchange Guide
Partnership Tax Planning and Practice (3/Internet)
Partnership Tax Reports
Payroll Management Guide (3/CD-ROM/Internet)
Pension Plan Guide (3/CD-ROM/Internet)
Pensions and Deferred Compensation
Philadelphia Stock Exchange Guide
Physicians' Medicare Guide
Products Liability Reports
Puerto Rico Tax Reporter
Revenue Rulings and Revenue Procedures on CD-ROM (CD-ROM/Internet)
RICA Business Disputes Guide
S Corporations Guide (3/Internet)
SEC Accounting Rules
SEC Docket (3/CD-ROM/Internet)
SEC No-Action Letters 1971 - Present on CD-ROM

(CD-ROM/Internet)
SEC No-Action Letters Full Text on CD-ROM (CD-ROM/Internet)
Securities Compliance Tracker™ (Internet)
Secured Transactions Guide
Securities Transfer Guide
Standard Federal Tax Reports (3/CD-ROM/Internet)
Standard Federal Tax Reports (3/CD-ROM/Internet)
State Corporate Income Tax Forms
State Legislative Reporting Service
State Motor Carrier Guide
State Personal Income Tax Forms
State Tax Cases Reporter (3/Internet)
State Tax Cases Reports
State Tax Guide (3/CD-ROM/Internet)
State Tax Reporters (all 50 states and D.C.) (CD-ROM/Internet)
State Tax Reports (available for all 50 states) (3/CD-ROM/Internet)
State Tax Review (3/Internet)
State Tax SourceDocs by CCH (CD-ROM/Internet)
Tax Court Memoranda on CD-ROM (3/CD-ROM/Internet)
Tax Court Regulars on CD-ROM (3/CD/Internet)
Tax Court Reports (3/CD-ROM/Internet)
Tax Court Reports (3/CD-ROM/Internet)
Tax Day Report
Tax Planning Review
Tax Transactions Library
Tax Treaties (3/CD-ROM/Internet)
Taxes on Parade
Trade Regulation Reports
U.S. Master Finance Guide (3)
U.S. Master Tax Guide (3/Internet)
U.S. Supreme Court Bulletin
U.S. Tax Cases on CD-ROM
U.S. Transfer Pricing Guide: Practice and Policy (3/Internet)
U.S. Transfer Pricing Guide: Practice and Policy (3/Internet)
Unemployment Insurance Reports
Utilities Law Reports
When Duty Calls: Military Leave and Veterans' Rights (3)
Workers' Compensation Law Reports

LRP Publications

Chapter 11 Theory and Practice: A Guide to Reorganization (3)
cyberFEDS Complete Library on CD-ROM
cyberFEDS Complete Library on the Web
cyberFEDS Mentor (Internet)
cyberFEDS Workers' Compensation Library (Internet)
Disability Law on CD-ROM
Early Childhood Law and Policy Reporter (3)
Federal Equal Opportunity Reporter (3/CD-ROM)
Federal Labor Relations Reporter (3/CD-ROM)
Federal Merit Systems Reporter (3/CD-ROM)
Federal Pay and Benefits Reporter (3/CD-ROM)
Individuals with Disabilities Education Law Report (3)
LRP's Bankruptcy Law on CD-ROM
National Disability Law Reporter (3)
Public Employee Reporters (9 states available) (3)
Special Education Law on CD-ROM
Workers' Compensation Law Reporters (5 states available) (3)

Pike & Fischer

AdLaw Bulletin (3, monthly)
Administrative Law, Third Series (3)
Broadcast Regulation (3, CD-ROM, Web)
Cable TV Regulation (3, CD-ROM, Web)
Communications Regulation (3, CD-ROM, Web)
Internet Law & Regulation (3 & Web)
Private Radio Rules Service (looseleaf 3 with Web)
Shipping Regulation (3)
Wireless Telecommunications Regulation (CD-ROM & Web)

Research Institute of America (RIA)

Academic Advantage Core Library
Academic Advantage Essentials Library
All States Tax Guide
American Federal Tax Reports
American Federal Tax Reports 1st Series
American Federal Tax Reports 2nd Series
Analysis of Federal Taxes: Income
Benefits Coordinator
BNA's Daily Tax Report
Business Entities
Business Entities - WEB/3 Bundle
Business Entity Treatises Library
Charitable Giving and Solicitation
Complete Tax Library
Complete WG&L Treatise Library
Compliance and Benefits Advisor for Windows
Core Federal Research & Planning Library
Core Federal Research Library for Corporate Tax Practitioners
Core Tax Library
Core Tax Library with Complete Transfer Pricing
Core Tax Library with Estate Planning Complete
Core Tax Library with Pension & Benefits Expert Complete
Core Treatise Library
Corporate Taxation - WEB/3 Bundle
Divorce Taxation
Employee Benefits Compliance Coordinator
Estate Planning & Taxation Coordinator
Estate Planning System
Federal & State Tax Guide on Checkpoint
Federal Analytical Reporter Library
Federal Income Taxation of Banks & Financial Institutions
Federal Income Taxation of Corporations & Sharehold
Federal Income Taxation of Corporations & Sharehold and Forms Library
Federal Income Taxation of Corporations & Shareholders: Forms
Federal Income Taxation of Individuals

Federal Income Taxation of Intellectual Properties & Intangible Assets
Federal Income Taxation of Passive Activities
Federal Income Taxation of Real Estate
Federal Income Taxation of S Corporations
Federal Tax Accounting
Federal Tax Collections, Liens & Levies
Federal Tax Coordinator 2d
Federal Tax Coordinator Library
Federal Tax Coordinator Library A
Federal Tax Coordinator Library Combo
Federal Tax Coordinator Library/State Combo with All States Tax Guide
Federal Tax Coordinator Library/State Combo with TAPS #2
Federal Taxation of Financial Instruments & Transactions
Federal Taxation of Income, Estates & Gifts
Federal Taxation of Partnerships & Partners
Federal Taxes Weekly Alert
IRS Letter Rulings and Memoranda
IRS Practice
IRS Practice & Procedure
IRS Procedural Forms & Analysis
Journal of Taxation - WEB/3 Bundle
Official IRS Publications
OnPoint System 1
OnPoint System 1 Combo
OnPoint System 1 with e-Form--Complete
OnPoint System 1 with e-Form-- Federal
OnPoint System 1 with e-Form-- State
OnPoint System 3
OnPoint System 3 Combo
OnPoint System 3 with e-Form--Complete
OnPoint System 3 with e-Form--Federal
OnPoint System 3 with e-Form--State
OnPoint System 4
OnPoint System 4 Combo
OnPoint System 5
Partnership Taxation
Partnership Taxation Library
Partnership/LLC Taxation Library
Pass-Through Entity Tax Digest, Second Edition
Pass-Through Taxation Library
Pending & Enacted Legislation
Pension & Profit Sharing
Pension Coordinator
PPC Federal Tax Compliance Library
Practical Tax Strategies
Real Estate Coordinator
Subchapter S Taxation
Tax Advisors Planning System
Tax Alerts *on Checkpoint
Tax Court Reported & Memorandum Decisions
Tax Desk (with State & Local Reporter)
Tax Desk
Tax Desk w/e-Form: Complete on CD
Tax Desk (Web Package 1)
Tax Desk (Web Package 2)
Tax Desk (Web Package with e-Form: Complete on CD)
Tax Desk (with State & Local Reporter and e-Form:) Complete
Tax Desk (with State & Local Reporter on Checkpoint)
Tax Desk (with TAPS #2 and e-Form RS: Complete)
Tax Desk without Federal & State Forms
Tax Guide on Checkpoint
Tax Guide with e-Form: Complete
Tax Guide with e-Form: Federal
Tax Guide with e-Form: State
Tax Guide with Elections & Compliance Statements
Tax Planning for Transfers of Business Interests
Taxation of Exempt Organizations
Taxation of Exempts
Taxation of Exempts - WEB/3 Bundle
Taxation of Regulated Investment Companies & Their Shareholders
The Alternative Minimum Tax: Compliance & Planning
The Bank Income Tax Return Manual
The Consolidated Tax Return
U.S. Tax Reporter Library
U.S. Tax Reporter Library w/Citator 2nd, e-Form RS: Complete, ECS
U.S. Tax Reporter Library w/Public Domain Library, ECS
U.S. Tax Reporter: Estate & Gift
U.S. Tax Reporter: Excise
U.S. Tax Reporter: Income
Unified Audit & Litigation Procedures for Pass-Through Entities
United States Tax Reporter Library/State Combo with All States Tax Guide
U.S Tax Reporter Library/State Combo with TAPS #2
Valuation Strategies - WEB/3 Bundle
WEB3/State Combo w/e-Form RS: Complete

Appendix H - Costs of Legal Treatises

and Other Specialty Materials

Unlike prior years, this edition includes only those titles which are supplemented.
Monographs appear only in Chapter 27.

Author/Title (Publisher)	Edition	No. of Vols	Cost	2010	2011	2012	2013	2014
ADMINISTRATIVE LAW - 7 Titles								
Federal Procedure (West)	1981-	76	$10,381.00	$4,652.00	$4,957.50	$6,969.50	$7,414.00	
Koch. Administrative Law & Practice (West)	3d ed./2010-	5	$591.00	$400.00	$60.00	$114.00	$128.00	
O'Reilly. Administrative Rulemaking (West)	2013	1	$371.00	$215.00	$235.00	$272.00	$297.00	
Pierce. Administrative Law Treatise(Wolters Kluwer)	5th ed./2009-	3	$959.00	$0.00	$172.00	$184.00	$210.00	
Stein. Administrative Law (MB)	1977-	6	$3,578.00	$2,074.00	$2,136.00	$2,264.00	$2,561.00	$2,644.00
Stein. Administrative Law [CD-ROM or web] (MB)	1977-	1 CD	$3,136.00	$1,762.00	$1,868.00	$1,999.00	$2,139.00	$2,381.70
West's Federal Admin. Practice (West)	3d-4th ed./1999-	9	$1,290.00	$604.00	$659.50	$720.00	$780.00	
ADMIRALTY AND MARITIME LAW - 7 Titles								
American Maritime Cases on DVD (AMC)	1923-	1 DVD	$1,125.00					
Benedict on Admiralty (MB)	7th ed./1958-	31	$6,273.00	$3,638.00	$3,747.00	$3,972.00	$4,434.00	$4,682.00
Benedict on Admiralty [eBook] (MB)	7th ed./1958-	eBook	$5,702.00	$4,073.00	$4,399.00	$4,795.00	$5,130.00	$4,778.70
Norris. The Law of Maritime Personal Injuries (West)	5th ed./2009/2011-	2	$475.00	$139.00	$151.50	$166.50	$65.00	
Norris. The Law of Seamen (West)	5th ed./2003-	3	$590.00	$221.50	$241.50	$265.50	$65.00	
Schoenbaum. Admiralty and Maritime Law (West)	5th ed./2011-	1	$113.00	$23.00	new ed.	0	$70.40	
Schoenbaum. Admiralty and Maritime Law (West)	5th ed./2011-	3	$291.00	$80.00	$240.00	0	$35.00	
ADVERTISING LAW - 5 Titles								
Brody. Advertising and Commercial Speech (PLI)	2d ed./2004-	1	$335.00	$140.00	$165.00	$168.00	$173.00	
Rosden. The Law of Advertisng (MB)	1973-	4	$2,672.00	$1,541.00	$1,618.00	$1,715.00	$1,962.00	$1,966.00
AGENCY LAW - 2 Titles								
ALI. Restatement of the Law of Agency 3d (ALI)	3d ed./2006-	2	$196.00	$39.00	$39.00	$40.00	$135.00	
Jordan. Durable Powers of Attorney (West)	4th ed./2004-	2	$362.00	$132.00	$121.00	$129.00	$153.00	
ANTITRUST LAW - 20 Titles								
Antitrust and Trade Regulation Resource Center (Bloomberg BNA)		Online	$2,584.00					
Antitrust Law Developments (ABA)	7th ed./2012-	2	$475.00	$0.00	$0.00	new ed.	$169.00	
Axinn. Acquisitions Under Hart-Scott-Rodino (LJP)	3d ed./2008-	3	$995.00	$419.00	$309.00	$949.00	$995.00	
Callman. Law of Unfair Competition (West)	4th ed./2003-	10	$4,697.00	$2,501.50	$1,669.50	$2,972.00	$3,531.00	
Ginsburg. Mergers, Acquisitions & Buyouts (Wolters Kluwer)	Annual	4	$589.00	$1,030.00	$1,100.00	$1,100.00	$1,178.00	
Ginsburg. Mergers, Acquis. & Buyouts [CD-ROM] (Wolters Kluwer)	Annual	1 CD	$605.00	$1,060.00	$1,130.00	$1,130.00	$1,210.00	
Hovenkamp & Areeda. Antitrust: An Analysis of Antitrust Prin. (Wolters Kluwer)	5th ed./1978-	21	$3,925.00	$754.00	$914.00	$1,874.00	$2,005.00	
Hovenkamp & Areeda. Antitrust Library [web] (Wolters Kluwer) [see CCH]		Online	$1,944.00					
Kintner. Federal Antitrust Law (Lexis)	1980-	13	$3,127.00	$755.00	$869.00	$930.00	$1,033.00	$1,063.00

Author/Title (Publisher)	Edition	No. of Vols	Cost	2010	2011	2012	2013	2014
Lifland. State Antitrust Law (LJP)	1984-	1	$313.00	$260.00	$175.00	$149.00	$313.00	
Miles. Health Care & Antitrust Law (West)	1992-	4	$2,837.00	$1,513.50	$1,650.00	$1,800.00	$2,083.00	
Scher. Antitrust Advisor (West)	4th ed/1995-	2	$249.00	$0.00	$195.00	0	0	
Trade Regulation Reporter (CCH)	1914-	7	$5,280.00					
Trade Regulation Reporter on Internet (CCH)		1 CD	$4,935.00					
Vakerics. Antitrust Basics (LJP)	1985-	1	$535.00	$330.00	$492.00	$492.00	$535.00	
Von Kalinowski. Antitrust Counseling & Litigation Tech. (MB)	1984-	5	$2,236.00	$1,275.00	$1,339.00	$1,419.00	$1,612.00	$1,657.00
Von Kalinowski. Antitrust Counseling & Litigation Tech. (MB)	1984-	5	$2,236.00	$1,275.00	$1,339.00	$1,419.00	$1,612.00	$1,657.00
Von Kalinowski. Antitrust Laws & Trade Regulation (MB)	2d ed./1997-	10	$4,661.00	$2,564.00	$2,854.00	$2,854.00	$3,054.00	$3,333.00
Von Kalinowski. Antitrust Laws & Trade Reg. (MB)		ebook	$4,237.00	$2,457.00	$2,580.00	$2,734.00	$3,054.00	$3,333.00
Von Kalinowski. Antitrust Laws & Trade Reg. Desk Ed. (MB)	2d ed./1997-	2	$1,999.00	$964.00	$1,060.00	$1,177.00	$1,259.00	$1,375.00
APPELLATE PRACTICE - 8 Titles								
Childress. Federal Standards of Review (Lexis)	4th ed./2010-	3	$439.00	new ed.	$370.00	$398.00	$426.00	
Houts. Art of Advocacy: Appeals (MB)	1987-	1	$430.00	$284.00	$295.00	$327.00	$337.00	$361.00
Knibb. Federal Court of Appeals Manual (West)	6th ed./2013-	1	$197.00	$42.00	$45.00	$49.00	new ed.	
Levy. How to Handle an Appeal (PLI)	4th ed./1999-	1	$335.00	$150.00	$154.00	$160.00	$185.00	
Supreme Court Practice (Bloomberg BNA Books)	10th ed./2013-	1	$495.00	0	$0.00	0	new ed.	
Tigar. Federal Appeals: Jurisdiction & Practice (West)	3d ed./1999-	1	$186.00	$95.00	$105.00	$116.00	$125.00	
U.S. Law Week (Bloomberg BNA)	1933-	2	$2,070.00					
U.S. Law Week (Bloomberg BNA)	1933-	Online	$3,735.00					
ARBITRATION - 5 Titles								
Domke. Domke on Commercial Arbitration (West)	3d ed./1994-	2	$591.00	$309.50	$296.50	$209.00	$227.00	
Elkouri. How Arbitration Works (Bloomberg BNA Books)	7th ed./2012-	1	$325.00	$205.00	$82.00	new ed.	0	
Miller. Art of Advocacy: Settlement (MB)	1983-	1	$430.00	$284.00	$295.00	$330.00	$330.00	$330.00
Oehmke. Commercial Arbitration (West)	3d ed./2008--	5	$1,781.00	$1,203.00	$791.00	$1,345.00	$1,339.00	
Robbins. Securities Arbitration Procedure Manual (Lexis)	5th ed./2001-	2	$241.00	$157.00	$163.00	$174.00	$180.00	
ARTS, ENTERTAINMENT AND SPORTS LAW - 24 Titles								
Champion. Fundamentals of Sports Law (West)	2d ed./2004-	1	$255.00	$100.00	$110.00	$130.00	$139.00	
Darraby. Art, Artifact & Architecture Law (West)	2013-2014	2	$824.00	$646.00	$824.00	$824.00	$824.00	
Dienes. Newsgathering and the Law (Lexis)	3d ed./2005-	1	$199.00	$0.00	$188.00	0	$58.00	
DuBoff. The Deskbook of Art Law (Oxford)	2d ed./1993-	2	$644.00	$460.00	$490.00	$240.00	$247.00	
Farber. Entertainment Industry Contracts (MB)	1986-	10	$2,341.00	$1,341.00	$1,408.00	$1,565.00	$1,716.00	$1,741.00
Farber. Entertainment Industry Contracts [CD-ROM or web] (MB)	1986-	eBook	$2,128.00	$1,406.00	$1,476.00	$1,565.00	$1,674.00	$1,742.00
Ferris. Telecommunications Regulation (MB)	1983-	4	$1,747.00	$998.00	$1,048.00	$1,111.00	$1,167.00	$1,273.00
Ferris. Telecommunications Regulation [CD-ROM or web] (MB)	1983-	eBook	$1,588.00	$1,075.00	$1,129.00	$1,208.00	$1,167.00	$1,273.00

Author/Title (Publisher)	Edition	No. of Vols	Cost	2010	2011	2012	2013	2014
Fischer. Perle & Williams on Publishing Law (Wolters Kluwer)	4th ed./2013-	2	$535.00	$348.00	$372.00	$398.00	$426.00	
Fremlin. Entertainment Law (West)	Rev. ed./2007-	1	$321.00	$104.00	$114.50	$126.00	$136.00	
Greenberg. Sports Law Practice (Lexis)	3d ed./2009-	2	$370.00	$106.00	$112.00	$120.00	$124.00	
Heinke. Media Law (Bloomberg BNA Books)	1994-	1	$275.00	$0.00	$0.00	0	0	
Lindey. Lindey on Entertainment, Pub. & the Arts (West)	3d ed./2004-	9	$2,294.00	$1,087.50	$1,228.50	$1,375.00	$1,639.00	
McCarthy. Rights of Publicity and Privacy (West)	2d ed./2010--	2	$1,166.00	$677.00	$738.00	$1,070.00	$932.00	
Media Law Reporter (Bloomberg BNA)	1977-	1	$2,753.00					
Media Law Reporter (Bloomberg BNA)		Online	$3,025.00					
Rosden. The Law of Advertising (MB)	1973-	4	$2,672.00	$1,541.00	$1,618.00	$1,715.00	$1,962.00	$1,966.00
Rosden. The Law of Advertising [eBook] (MB)	1973-	eBook	$2,429.00	$1,493.00	$1,568.00	$1,662.00	$1,778.00	$1,966.00
Sack on Defamation: Libel, Slander, and Related Problems (PLI)	4th ed./2010-	2	$395.00	new ed.	$175.00	$190.00	$196.00	
Scott. Scott on Multimedia Law (Wolters Kluwer)	3d ed./2008-	1	$525.00	$165.00	$195.00	$374.00	$200.00	
Selz. Entertainment Law (West)	3d ed./2006-	4	$1,157.00	$0.00	$416.00	$453.00	$245.00	
Shanker. Entertainment Law & Business (Juris)	3d ed./2009-	1	$150.00		$90.00	$90.00	$90.00	
Smolla. Law of Defamation (West)	2d ed./1999-	1	$1,116.00	$595.00	$649.00	$770.00	$819.20	
Uberstein. Law of Professional and Amateur Sports (West)	1988-	3	$907.00	$483.00	$526.50	$677.00	$665.00	
AUTOMOBILE LAW AND PRACTICE - 20 Titles								
Bartell. Attacking & Defending Drunk Driving Tests (James)	2007-	1	$119.00	$69.99	$69.99	$69.99	$69.99	
Blashfield. Automobile Law and Practice (West)	3d ed./1965-	17	$2,986.00	$1,472.50	$1,611.50	$2,200.00	$2,414.20	
Campbell. Defense of Speeding, Reckless Driving (MB)	1984-	4	$1,208.00	$691.00	$726.00	$770.00	$824.00	$899.00
Cohen. Apprehending & Prosecuting the Drunk Driver (MB)	1992-	1	$361.00	$141.00	$137.00	$146.00	$165.00	$170.00
Disbrow. No-Fault & Uninsured Motorist Auto Cov. (MB)	1984-	4	$2,439.00	$1,309.00	$1,401.00	$1,485.00	$1,692.00	$1,734.00
Eades. Jury Instructions in Auto. Actions (Lexis)	4th ed./2004	1	$145.00	$86.00	$116.00	$124.00	$128.00	
Erwin. Defense of Drunk Driving Cases (MB)	3d ed./1971-	4	$1,950.00	$1,171.00	$1,206.00	$1,254.00	$1,383.00	$1,420.00
Erwin. Defense of Drunk Driving Cases [eBook] (MB)		eBook	$1,773.00					$1,383.00
Fitzgerald. Intoxication Test Evidence (West)	2d ed./1995-	3	$777.00	$531.00	$585.00	$562.40	$562.40	
Goodman. Automobile Design Liability (West)	3d ed./1991-	6	$1,351.00	$735.00	$819.00	$905.00	$995.00	
Kenworthy. Killer Roads: From Crash to Verdict (Lexis)	2d ed./1999-	1	$198.00	$84.00	$91.00	$97.00	$101.00	
Kenworthy. Transportation Safety & Insurance Law (Lexis)	3d ed./2004-	2	$348.00	$117.00	$124.00	$133.00	$136.00	
Limpert. Motor Vehicle Accident Reconstruction (Lexis)	7th ed./2012-	1	$218.00	$0.00	$96.00	new ed.	$100.00	
Nissenberg. The Law of Commercial Trucking (Lexis)	3d ed./2005-	2	$235.00	$96.00	$101.00	$108.00	$116.00	
Reiff. Drunk Driving & Related Vehicular Offenses (MB)	5th ed./2010-	1	$195.00	new ed.	$60.00	0	$0.00	
Schermer. Automobile Liability Insurance (West)	4th ed./2008/09-	5	$751.00	$370.00	$326.00	$118.00	$94.40	
Sheldon. Automobile Fraud: Odom. Tampering… (Nat. Con. Law Ctr.)	4th ed./2011-	1	$140.00	$52.00	new ed.	0	$52.00	
Taylor. Drunk Driving Defense (Wolters Kluwer)	7th ed./2010-	1	$365.00	new ed.	$115.00	$125.00	$135.00	

Author/Title (Publisher)	Edition	No. of Vols	Cost	2010	2011	2012	2013	2014
Vehicular Crimes Library [CD-ROM or web] (MB)	2001-	1 CD	$1,543.00	$855.00	$906.00	$998.00	$1,068.00	$1,176.00
Whited. Drinking/Driving Litigation (West)	2d ed./1998-	4	$1,324.00	$594.00	$654.00	$777.00	$870.00	
BANKING LAW - 30 Titles								
Bailey. Brady on Bank Checks (LexisNexis/Pratt)	8th ed./1997-	1	$623.00					
Baker. The Law of Electronic Fund Transfer Systems (LexisNexis/Pratt)	3d ed./1995-	1	$623.00					
Bank Compliance Guide (CCH)		2	$967.00					
Banking & Commercial Law Library [CD-ROM] (MB)		1 CD	$21,406.00	$12,214.00	$12,825.00	$13,595.00	$14,546.00	$16,194.54
Banking Law (MB)	1981-	20	$5,195.00	$2,937.00	$3,099.00	$3,330.00	$3,531.00	$3,854.00
Banking Law [CD-ROM] (MB)		1 CD	$4,351.00	$3,009.00	$3,159.00	$3,349.00	$3,583.00	$3,989.00
Banking Laws & Regulations (Wolters Kluwer)	2010-	3	$725.00	new ed.				
Banking Report (Bloomberg BNA)	1965-	2	$2,575.00					
Banking Report [web] (Bloomberg BNA)		Online	$2,877.00					
Beckford. Bank Holding Company Compliance Manual (MB)	2d ed./1986-	1	$734.00	$467.00	$488.00	$515.00	$551.00	$589.00
Cappello. Lender Liability (Juris)	4th ed./2009	1	$195.00	$0.00	$0.00	0	0	
Clark. Law of Bank Deposits, Coll. & Credit Cards (LexisNexis/Pratt)	4th ed./1995-	1	$623.00					
Federal Banking Law Reporter (CCH)	1945-	8	$3,756.00					
Federal Banking Law Reporter [web] (CCH)		Online	$3,766.00					
Fein. Securities Activities of Banks (Wolters Kluwer)	4th ed./2012-	1	$389.00				$199.00	
Franklin. Mortgage & Asset Backed Securities Lit Hndbk (West)	2009	1	$525.00	$422.00	$0.00	$276.00	$280.00	
Geva. Law of Electronic Fund Transfers (MB)	1992-	1	$338.00	$193.00	$186.00	$202.00	$216.00	$395.00
Hardy. Criminal Tax, Money Laundering & Bank Secrecy Act Lit. (BNA Bks)	2010-	1	$525.00		$295.00	$300.00	0	
Kirsch. Financial Product Fundamentals (PLI)	2d ed./2012-	1	$335.00	$273.00	$290.00	new ed.	$376.00	
Lapine. Consumer Credit: Law, Transactions & Forms (MB)	1984-	4	$1,740.00	$981.00	$1,015.00	$1,081.00	$1,157.00	$1,238.00
Malloy. Banking Law and Regulation (Wolters Kluwer)	2d ed./2005-	3	$1,749.00	$1,232.00	$1,350.00	$734.00	$809.00	
McCoy. Banking Law Manual (MB)	2d ed./2000-	1	$437.00	$244.00	$252.00	$281.00	$301.00	$309.00
Michie on Banks and Banking (Lexis)	1995-	14	$848.00	$651.00	$690.00	$837.00	$774.00	
Norton. Commercial Loan Documentation Guide (MB)	1989-	2	$485.00	$224.00	$237.00	$251.00	$288.00	$297.00
Pollard. Banking Law in the United States (Juris Publishing)	2011-	2	$395.00			$95.00	$95.00	
The State Banking Law Reporter [web] (CCH)		Online	$3,505.00					
Tatge. American Factoring Law (Bloomberg BNA Books)	2009-	1	$465.00		$200.00	$210.00	$215.00	
Villa. Banking Crimes: Fraud, Money Laundering.(West).	1987-	2	$528.00	$44.00	$162.00	$179.00	$193.60	
Weisblatt. Checks, Drafts and Notes (MB)	1984-	3	$593.00	$339.00	$351.00	$374.00	$400.00	$436.00
Zisman. Banks and Thrifts (MB)	1991-	1	$412.00	$184.00	$186.00	$205.00	$230.00	$236.00
BANKRUPTCY LAW - 19 Titles								
Bankruptcy Code and Rules (West)	2014 Ed.	1	$168.00					

Author/Title (Publisher)	Edition	No. of Vols	Cost	2010	2011	2012	2013	2014
Bankruptcy Court Decisions (West)	2011-	2	$2,400.60	$1,195.00	$1,315.00	$1,914.00	$2,143.00	
Bankruptcy Desk Guide (West)	1990-	5	$2,560.00	$1,366.50	$1,490.00	$1,622.00	$1,816.00	
Bankruptcy Law Reporter (CCH)	1979-	3	$2,822.00					
Bankruptcy Service. Lawyers Edition (West)	1979-	23	$10,092.00	$5,546.00	$5,700.00	$6,121.00	$6,855.00	
Collier Bankruptcy Case Update (MB)		Weekly	$899.00			$693.00		
Collier Bankruptcy Cases (MB)	1979-	42+	$3,060.00	$1,805.00	$1,895.00	$2,009.00	$2,150.00	$2,242.00
Collier Bankruptcy Library [CD-ROM] (MB)		1 CD	$14,246.00	$7,053.00	$7,794.00	$8,262.00	$8,840.00	$9,840.00
Collier Bankruptcy Manual (MB)	4th ed./2011-	3	$1,338.00	$770.00	$770.00	$770.00	$824.00	$899.00
Collier Bankruptcy Manual {web] (MB)		Online	$1,217.00	$841.00	$900.00	$972.00	$824.00	$899.00
Collier Bankruptcy Practice Guide (MB)	1981-	8	$3,808.00	$2,148.00	$2,309.00	$2,344.00	$2,508.00	$2,737.00
Collier Bankruptcy Practice Guide [CD-ROM] (MB)		1 CD	$4,154.00	$2,174.00	$2,337.00	$2,536.00	$2,713.00	$2,957.00
Collier Consumer Bankruptcy Prac. Guide with Forms (MB)	1997-	3	$1,265.00	$599.00	$620.00	$733.00	$693.00	$756.00
Collier on Bankruptcy (MB)	15th ed./1985-	27	$9,415.00	$4,647.00	$5,088.00	$5,088.00	$5,444.00	$5,942.00
Collier on Bankruptcy [web] (MB)		Online	$7,999.00	$4,857.00	$5,318.00	$5,637.00	$4,011.00	$5,553.00
Drake. Bankruptcy Practice for the General Prac. (West)	3d ed./1995-	1	$223.00	$182.00	$200.00	$289.00	$223.00	
Ginsburg. Ginsburg & Martin on Bankruptcy (Wolters Kluwer)	5th ed/2010-	4	$879.00	new ed.	$825.00	$885.00	$1,077.00	
Norton. Norton Bankruptcy Law & Practice (West)	3d ed./1994-	12	$4,608.00	$2,608.50	$2,843.52	$3,099.00	$3,682.00	
Norton Bankruptcy on Westlaw (West)		Online	$1,596.00					
CIVIL RIGHTS - 15 Titles								
Bodensteiner. State & Local Govern. Civil Rights Liability (West)	2d ed./2011-	4	$1,144.00	$617.00	$808.00	$889.00	$840.00	
Cook. Civil Rights Actions (MB)	1983-	7	$2,492.00	$1,439.00	$1,511.00	$1,602.00	$1,714.00	$1,870.00
Cook. Civil Rights Actions [eBook] (MB)	1983-	ebook	$2,265.00	$1,535.00	$1,658.00	$1,807.00	$1,714.00	$1,870.00
Employment Discrimination Coordinator (West)		8 vols.	$2,160.00					
Employment Discrimination Coordinator on Westlaw (West)		Online	$2,160.00					
Freeman. Privacy Law in Marketing (Wolters Kluwer)	2007-	2	$1,004.00			$939.00		
Lee. Handbook of Section 1983 Litigation (Wolters Kluwer)	Annual	1	$384.00	$315.00	$345.00	$384.00		
Nahmod. Civil Rights and Civil Liberties Litigation (West)	4th ed./2008-	2	$467.00	$252.00	$274.50	$324.00	$343.20	
Perritt. Civil Rights in the Workplace (Wolters Kluwer)	3d ed./2000-	2	$395.00	$225.00	$265.00	$285.00	$315.00	
Rosenstock. Section 1983 Civil Rights Digest (James)	1997-	1	$99.00	$79.99	$79.99	$79.99	$79.99	$79.99
Schwartz. Section 1983 Litigation (Wolters Kluwer)	3d ed./1997-	6	$1,369.00	$1,195.00	$1,569.00	$1,469.00	$1,796.00	
Section 1983 Litigation Library on LoislawConnect (Wolters Kluwer)		Online	$540.00					
Smolla. Federal Civil Rights Acts (West)	3d ed./1994-	2	$1,190.00	$451.50	$994.00	$1,440.00	$2,380.00	
Steinglass. Section 1983 Litigation in State Courts (West)	1987-	2	$675.00	$270.00	$294.50	$400.00	$448.00	
Wang. Hate Crimes Law (West)	1993-	1	$284.00	$186.00	$239.00	$239.00	$261.00	

Author/Title (Publisher)	Edition	No. of Vols	Cost	2010	2011	2012	2013	2014
CLASS ACTIONS - 3 Titles								
Dickerson. Class Actions: The Law of 50 States (LJP)	1988-	1	$555.00	$165.00	$517.00	$517.00	$530.00	
Newberg. Newberg on Class Actions (West)	4th/5th ed./2002-	11	$1,823.00	$577.50	$741.50	$861.50	$657.00	
Rossman. Consumer Class Actions (Nat. Consumer Law Center)	8th ed./2013-	1	$210.00				new ed.	
COMMERCIAL LAW - 44 Titles								
Alces. Uniform Commercial Code Transaction Guide (West)	1988-	4	$1,475.00	$832.00	$907.00	$1,100.00	$1,232.00	
A.L.I. Restatmt. of the Law 3d. Suretyship & Guaranty (ALI)	3d ed./1996-	1	$72.00	$32.00	$32.00	$33.00	$39.00	
A.L.I. Restatmt. of the Law 2d. Unfair Competition 3d (ALI)	3d ed./1995-	1	$85.00	$32.00	$32.00	$33.00	$39.00	
A.L.I. Uniform. Comm. Code, 2013-2014 Edition (West)	2013-2014	1	$146.00	$96.00	$112.00	$123.00	$132.00	
Bailey. Brady on Bank Checks (LexisNexis/Pratt)	8th ed./1997-	1	$623.00					
Banking & Commer. Law Library [CD-ROM] (MB)		1 CD	$21,406.00	$12,214.00	$12,825.00	$13,595.00	$14,546.00	$16,194.54
Betsos. Modern UCC Litigation Forms (MB)	1969-	3	$1,257.00	$726.00	$759.00	$805.00	$861.00	$941.00
Business Law Library [CD-ROM] (MB)		1 CD	$37,053.00	$24,852.00	$26,095.00	$27,661.00	$29,597.00	$32,948.00
Business Practice Law Library on LoisLawConnect (Wolters Kluwer)		Online	$525.00					
Business Torts Library. (Wolters Kluwer)		Online	$525.00					
Clark. Law of Bank Deposits, Coll. & Credit Cards (LexisNexis/Pratt)	4th ed./1995-	1	$623.00					
Commercial Finance Guide (MB)]print or ebook]	1997-	2	$523.00	$251.00	$252.00	$264.00	$282.00	$307.00
Commercial Loan Documentation Guide (MB)	1988-	2	$485.00	$207.00	$237.00	$269.00	$288.00	$297.00
Consumer Credit Guide (CCH)	2004-	8	$3,204.00					
Consumer Credit Guide [web] (CCH)		Online	$3,440.00					
Consumer Finance Law Library on LoislawConnect (Wolters Kluwer)		Online	$540.00					
Duesenberg. Sales and Bulk Transfers Under the UCC (MB)	1966-	2	$1,224.00	$700.00	$732.00	$776.00	$830.00	$906.00
Eisenberg. Debtor-Creditor Law (MB)	1982-	10	$4,290.00	$2,566.00	$2,643.00	$2,749.00	$2,941.00	$3,210.00
Eisenberg. Debtor-Creditor Law [eBook] (MB)		eBook	$3,645.00					$3,210.00
Fonseca. .The Law of Modern Commercial Practices (West)	2d rev./1998-Ann.	3	$462.00	$279.00	$312.00	$453.00		
Fonseca. Williston on Sales (West)	5th ed./1994-	4	$647.00	$97.50	$106.50	$150.00	$132.00	
Haig. Business & Comm. Litigation in Fed. Courts (West)	3rd ed./2011-12	12	$1,434.00	$242.00	new ed.	$264.00	$296.00	
Hart. Forms and Procedures Under the UCC (MB)	1963-	8	$3,087.00	$1,743.00	$1,830.00	$1,940.00	$2,076.00	$2,265.00
Hawkland. Uniform Commercial Code Series (West)	1982-	20	$3,171.00	$1,714.50	$1,466.50	$2,187.00	$1,706.00	
Knapp. Commercial Damages (MB)	1986-	3	$1,688.00	$975.00	$1,014.00	$1,075.00	$1,150.00	$1,255.00
Knapp. Commercial Damages [eBook) (MB)		eBook	$1,534.00					$1,255.00
Lapine. Consumer Credit: Law, Transactions & Forms (MB)	1984-	6	$1,740.00	$981.00	$1,015.00	$1,081.00	$1,157.00	$1,263.00
Lawrence's Anderson on the Uniform Commercial Code (West)	3d ed./1983-	11	$4,667.00	$2,460.00	$961.00	$2,600.00	$2,847.00	
Limited Liab. Co. Law Treatise Library on LoisLawConnect (WK)		Online	$540.00					

Author/Title (Publisher)	Edition	No. of Vols	Cost	2010	2011	2012	2013	2014
Loonin. Student Loan Law (Nat. Consumer Law Ctr.)	4th ed./2010-	1	$130.00				$72.00	
McDonnell. Secured Transactions Under the UCC (MB)	1963-	5	$2,812.00	$1,605.00	$1,685.00	$1,786.00	$1,911.00	$2,085.00
McDonnell. Secured Transactions Under the UCC [CD-ROM] (MB)		CD-ROM	$2,880.00	$1,642.00	$1,758.00	$1,827.00	$1,955.00	$2,176.00
McDonnell. Secured Transactions Under the UCC [eBook] (MB)		eBook	$2,556.00	$1,674.00	$1,758.00	$1,863.00	$1,911.00	$2,085.00
Renuart. Truth in Lending with CD-ROM (Nat. Consumer Law Ctr)	8th ed./2012-	2	$240.00	new ed.	$50.00	new ed.	0	
Rossman. Consumer Class Actions (Nat. Consumer Law Center)	8th ed./2013-	1	$210.00				new ed.	
Secured Transactions Guide (CCH)	1969-	5	$3,113.00					
Spires. Doing Business in the United States (MB)	1978-	6	$2,920.00	$1,658.00	$1,708.00	$1,845.00	$1,974.00	$2,155.00
Spires. Doing Business in the United States [eBook] (MB)		eBook	$2,578.00					$2,112.00
Uniform Commercial Code Case Digest (West)	1976-	52+	$9,686.00	$4,388.00	$4,914.00	$6,400.00	$4,057.00	
Uniform Commercial Code Reporter-Digest (MB)	1965-	24+	$4,692.00	$2,776.00	$2,859.00	$2,973.00	$3,181.00	$3,472.00
Uniform Commercial Code Reporter-Digest [eBook] (MB)		Online	$4,265.00	$2,399.00	$2,519.00	$2,620.00	$2,803.00	$3,472.00
Uniform Commercial Code Reporting Service 2d (West)	1965-	67+	$15,387.60	$5,937.48	$7,125.00	$10,500.00	$12,822.95	
White. Uniform Commercial Code (West)	6th ed./2005-	5	$827.00	$155.00	$169.00	$184.00	$310.00	
Wright. The Law of Electronic Commerce (Wolters Kluwer)	4th ed./2000-	1	$535.00	$372.00	$390.00	$416.00	$462.00	
COMPUTER LAW - 16 Titles								
Battersby. Drafting Internet Agreements (Wolters Kluwer)	2d ed./2010-	1	$359.00	new ed.	$150.00	$160.00	$199.00	
Bender. Computer Law (MB)	1978-	4	$1,510.00	$865.00	$908.00	$962.00	$1,010.00	$1,102.00
Bender. Computer Law [eBook] (MB)		eBook	$1,373.00	$830.00	$872.00	$924.00	$1,010.00	$1,102.00
Campbell. The Internet: Laws and Regulatory Regimes (Juris)	2d ed./2010-	1	$175.00			$65.00	$70.00	
Delta. Law of the Internet (Wolters Kluwer)	3d ed/2008-	1	$545.00	$330.00	$350.00	$374.00	$415.00	
Guide to Computer Law (CCH)	1989-	2	$1,461.00					
Internet and e-Commerce Law Treatise Library on LoisLawConnect (WK)		Online	$540.00					
Internet Law Resource Center [web] (Bloomberg BNA)	1999-	Online	$2,720.00					
Lundberg. Electronic and Software Patents (BNA Books)	3d ed./2011-	1	$495.00			$210.00	$220.00	
Nimmer. Law of Computer Technology (West)	4th ed./2007-	1	$945.00	$275.00	$321.00	$350.00	$382.00	
Perritt. Digital Communications Law (Wolters Kluwer)	2010-	1	$429.00	new ed.	$130.00	$139.00	$199.00	
Scott. Computer & Intellectual Property Crime (Bloomberg BNA Books)	2001-	1	$340.00	0	$0.00	0	0	
Stobbs. Software Patents (Wolters Kluwer)	3d ed./2012-	1	$409.00	$272.00	$290.00	new ed.	$311.00	
Street. Law of the Internet (Lexis)	3d ed./2001-	1	$290.00	$211.00	$224.00	$240.00	$248.00	
Stuckey. Internet and Online Law (LJP)	1996-	1	$540.00	$500.00	$477.00	$477.00	$540.00	
Wright. The Law of Electronic Commerce (Wolters Kluwer)	4th ed./2001-	1	$535.00	$372.00	$390.00	$416.00	$462.00	
CONSTITUTIONAL LAW - 8 Titles								
Antieau. Modern Constitutional Law (West)	3d ed./2010-	3	$392.00	$270.00	$345.00	$379.00	$96.00	
Chandler. Constitutional Law Deskbook: Individual Rights (West)	2d ed./2008-	1	$297.00	$171.00	$188.00	$232.00	$238.00	

Author/Title (Publisher)	Edition	No. of Vols	Cost	2010	2011	2012	2013	2014
Constitution of the U.S.--Analysis & Interpretation (LC)	2004	2	$290.00	$30.00	$0.00	0	0	
Rotunda. Treatise on Constitutional Law (West)	5th ed./2012-	6	$927.00	$60.50	$66.00	new ed.	$74.00	
Supreme Court Practice (Bloomberg BNA Books)	10th ed./2013-	1	$495.00	0	$0.00	0	0	
The Supreme Court Yearbook [web] (CQ Press)	1989-	Online	$500.00					
U.S. Law Week (Bloomberg BNA)	1933-	2	$2,070.00					
U.S. Law Week [web] (Bloomberg BNA)	1933-	Online	$3,735.00					
CONSTRUCTION LAW - 19 Titles								
Acret. Construction Arbitration Handbook (West)	2d ed./2006-	1	$112.00	$68.00	$100.00	$88.00	$112.00	
Allen. Construction Law Handbook (Wolters Kluwer)	2d ed/2008-	2	$485.00	$105.00	$120.00	$120.00	$159.00	
Bruner. Bruner & O'Connor on Construction Law (West)	2002-	7	$1,187.00	$391.50	$380.00	$415.00	$454.00	
Callahan. Discovery in Construction Litigation (Lexis)	4th ed./2003-	1	$248.00	$135.00	$144.00	$154.00	$149.00	
C.F.M.A. Financial Mgmt. & Accting for Construction Industry (MB)	1988-	2	$395.00	$253.00	$261.00	$378.00	$153.00	$313.00
Construction Law Library on LoislawConnect (Wolters Kluwer)		Online	$660.00		$660.00			
Cushman. Construction Litigation (Wolters Kluwer)	2d ed./1994-	2	$315.00	$200.00	$214.00	$257.00	$279.00	
Cushman. Fifty State Construction Lien & Bond Law (Wolters Kluwer)	3d ed./2013-	3	$599.00	$288.00	$305.00	$349.00	$373.00	
Dib. Forms and Agreements for Architects, etc. (West)	Rev. ed/2008/09-	5	$4,299.00	$1,558.50	$1,870.50	$3,242.00	$3,232.00	
Driscoll. Construction Scheduling (Wolters Kluwer)	3d ed./2009-	1	$315.00	$245.00	$107.00	$125.00	$135.00	
Joy. Alt. Clauses to Stand. Construc. Contracts (Wolters Kluwer)	4th ed./2013-	1	$349.00	$135.00	$144.00	$154.00	new ed.	
Kelleher. Construction Disputes: Prac. Gde w/Forms (Wolters Kluwer)	2d ed./1994-	2	$575.00	$172.00	$164.00	$197.00	$209.00	
Sabo. Legal Guide to AIA Documents (Wolters Kluwer)	5th ed/2008-	1	$325.00	$127.00	$135.00	$144.00	$154.00	
Schwartzkopf. Calculating Construction Damages (Wolters Kluwer)	2d ed/2000-	1	$315.00	$180.00	$182.00	$194.00	$219.00	
Stein. American Institute of Architects Legal Citator (MB)	Annual/1996-	1	$319.00	$257.00	$267.00	$276.00	$290.00	$319.00
Stein. Construction Law (MB)	1986-	6	$1,844.00	$1,069.00	$1,080.00	$1,112.00	$1,213.00	$1,299.00
Stein. Construction Law [eBook] (MB)	1986-	eBook	$1,677.00	$1,165.00	$1,177.00	$1,212.00	$1,190.00	$1,299.00
Sweet on Construc. Indus. Contracts: Major AIA Docs.(Wolters Kluwer)	5th ed/2008-	2	$499.00	$118.00	$126.00	$135.00	$145.00	
Walker. State-By-State Gde to Arch, Engin. & Contractor Lic. (Wolters Kluwer)	2d ed./2012-	2	$524.00	$266.00	$285.00	$524.00	$560.00	
CONTRACT LAW - 18 Titles								
ALI. Restatement of the Law 2d. Contracts (ALI)	1981-	12	$823.50	$32.00	$32.00	$40.00	$59.00	
Contract Appeals Decisions (CCH)	1965-	1	$2,825.00					
Contract Appeals Decision [Online] (CCH)		Online	$2,947.00					
Corbin on Contracts (Lexis)	Rev. ed./1993-	15	$1,720.00	$725.00	$826.00	$884.00	$689.00	
Farnsworth on Contracts (Wolters Kluwer)	3d ed./2004-	3	$845.00	$266.00	$295.00	$710.00	$698.00	
Feldman. Drafting Effective Contracts: A Prac. Guide (Wolters Kluwer)	2d ed./1999-	1	$409.00	$272.00	$291.00	$305.00	$349.00	
Feldman. Government Contract Awards (West)	1994-	3	$855.00	$496.50	$660.00	$720.00		
Filipp. Covenants Not To Compete (Wolters Kluwer)	3d ed./2005-	2	$489.00	$215.00	$239.00	$255.00	$285.00	

Author/Title (Publisher)	Edition	No. of Vols	Cost	2010	2011	2012	2013	2014
Government Contracts Reporter [CD-ROM] (CCH)	2003-	1 CD	$5,153.00					
Government Contracts Reporter [Online] (CCH)	2003-	Online	$5,153.00					
Hunter. Modern Law of Contracts (West)	1993- Annual	2	$550.00	$289.00	$319.00	$462.00	$504.00	
Malmsberger. Covenants Not To Compete (Bloomberg BNA Books)	9th ed./2013-	3	$705.00	new ed.	$225.00	$0.00	new ed.	
McKenna. Government Contract Disputes (West)	2010-	1	$225.00		$36.00	$37.00	$32.00	
Murray. Corbin on Contracts (LexisNexis)	2013- Annual	1	$371.00			$349.00		
Nash & Cibinic eSeries [Online] (CCH)	2003-	Online	$1,180.00					
Nash. The Government Contracts Reference Book (CCH)	2013-	1	$80.00					
Williston/Lord. Treatise on the Law of Contracts (West)	4th ed./1990-	41	$4,606.00	$2,017.50	$2,203.00	$2,600.00	$3,082.00	
Yorio. Contract Enforcement (Wolters Kluwer)	2d ed./2011-	1	$339.00	$253.00	new ed.	$160.00	$171.00	
COPYRIGHT LAW - 8 Titles								
Clarida. Copyright Law Deskbook (Bloomberg BNA)	2009-	1	$505.00			$210.00	$215.00	
Goldstein on Copyright (Wolters Kluwer)	3d ed./2005	4	$985.00	$516.00	$550.00	$1,180.00	$589.00	
Goldstein on Copyright [Online] (Wolters Kluwer)		Online	Call					
Hawes. Copyright Registration Practice (West)	2d ed./1999-	1	$1,233.00	$657.00	$761.00	$415.00	$904.00	
Keller. Copyright Law: A Practitioner's Guide (PLI)	5th ed./2004-	1	$295.00	$158.00	$175.00	0	0	
Nimmer on Copyright (MB)	1963-	10	$3,087.00	$1,818.00	$1,909.00	$2,024.00	$2,166.00	$2,364.00
Nimmer on Copyright [CD-ROM] (MB)	1963-	1 CD	$3,121.00	$1,833.00	$1,925.00	$2,041.00	$2,184.00	$2,431.68
Nimmer on Copyright [Online] (MB)	1963-	Online	$2,807.00	$1,833.00	$1,925.00	$2,041.00	$2,184.00	$2,364.00
CORPORATIONS - 30 Titles								
Adams. Corporate Counselor's Business Handbook (Wolters Kluwer)	2011-	1	$299.00		$199.00	$229.00	$265.00	
ALI. Principles of Corporate Governance (ALI)	1994-	2	$153.00	$68.00	$68.00	$68.00	$78.00	
Basri. Corporate Legal Departments (PLI)	4th ed.,2011-	1	$365.00	$152.00	new ed.	$326.00	$340.00	
Block. The Business Judgment Rule (Wolters Kluwer)	6th ed./2009-	4	$785.00	0	$0.00	$450.00	0	
Block. The Corporate Counsellor's Deskbook (Wolters Kluwer)	5th ed./1999-	1	$489.00	$284.00	$498.00	$558.00	$577.00	
Blumberg on Corporate Groups (Wolters Kluwer)	2d ed./2005-	5	$739.00	$216.00	$230.00	$502.00	$560.00	
Brodsky. Law of Corporate Officers & Directors: Rights, Duties (West)	1984-	1	$760.00	$324.00	$600.00	$602.00	$760.00	
Brown. The Regulation of Corporate Disclosure (Wolters Kluwer)	3d ed./1999-	1	$699.00	$490.00	$525.00	$558.00	$620.00	
Business Law Monographs (MB)	1984-	36	$3,645.00	$1,699.00	$1,784.00	$1,927.00	$2,062.00	$2,250.00
Cavitch. Business Organizations with Tax Planning (MB)	1963-	16	$6,433.00	$3,399.00	$3,569.00	$3,747.00	$4,009.00	$4,375.00
Contemporary Corporation Forms (Wolters Kluwer)	2d ed./1998-	5	$1,749.00	$1,218.00	$1,302.00	$1,405.00	$1,524.00	
Corporation: A Service (Wolters Kluwer)	1964-	8	$2,875.00					
Corporation Governance Integrated Library [Online] (CCH)		Online	$2,600.00					
Fletcher Corporation Forms Annotated (West)	4th ed./1980-	21	$5,220.00	$2,638.50	$2,793.00	$3,503.00	$2,728.00	
Fletcher Cyclopedia of the Law of Private Corps (West)	1971-	36	$7,534.00	$4,007.00	$4,367.00	$5,198.00	$5,529.00	

Author/Title (Publisher)	Edition	No. of Vols	Cost	2010	2011	2012	2013	2014
Glazer. Glazer & Fitzgibbon on Legal Opinions (Wolters Kluwer)	3d ed/2008-	1	$395.00	$193.00	$225.00	$247.00	$269.00	
Goodman. Corporate Governance: Law & Prac. (MB)	2004-	2	$601.00	$317.00	$326.00	$336.00	$360.00	$393.00
Gross. Corporate Political Activities Deskbook (PLI)	2012-	1	$335.00			new ed.	$95.00	
Jelsma. The Limited Liability Company (James)	2012-	1	$99.00			new ed.	$69.99	$69.99
Knepper. Liability of Corp. Officers and Directors (Lexis)	8th ed./2009-	2	$514.00	$218.00	$231.00	$247.00	$315.00	
Levy. Corporate Financial Disclosure Answer Book (Wolters Kluwer)	2009-	1	$359.00	$330.00	$177.00	$189.00	$210.00	
Macey on Corporation Laws (Wolters Kluwer)	2d ed./2010-	2	$819.00	new ed.	$550.00	$894.00	$956.00	
Model Business Corporation Act Annotated (ABA)	4th ed./2008-	4	$685.95	$0.00	$249.95	0	$249.95	
Olson. Publicly Traded Corporations (West)	3d ed./2010--	2	$348.00	$400.00	$292.00	$512.00	$696.00	
O'Neal & Thompson's Close Corporations & LLCs (West)	Rev. 3d ed./2004-	2	$876.00	$532.50	$441.00	$400.00	$448.00	
Overton. Executive Compansation Answer Book (Wolters Kluwer)	8th ed./2012-	1	$385.00			$249.00	$285.00	
Presser. Piercing the Corporate Veil (West)	1991-	1	$548.00	$312.00	$347.00	$505.00	$548.00	
Smiddy. Soderquist on Corporate Law & Practice (PLI)	4th ed./2012-	1	$295.00	$304.00	$159.00	new ed.	$186.00	
Villa. Corporate Counsel Guidelines (West)	1999-	2	$313.00	$142.00	$165.00	$181.00	$196.80	
Weise. Representing the Corporation (Wolters Kluwer)	2d ed./2001-	2	$695.00	$390.00	$420.00	$450.00	$500.00	
CRIMINAL LAW - 52 Titles								
Adams. Prosecutor's Manual for Arrest, Search & Seizure (Lexis)	2d ed./2004-	1	$186.00	$74.00	$81.00	$87.00	$90.00	
Androphy. White Collar Crime (West)	2d ed./2001-	4	$671.00	$354.00	$389.50	$428.50	$480.00	
Bailey. Crimes of Violence: Homocide & Assault (West)	1973-	1	$835.00	$445.00	$485.00	$528.00	$613.00	
Bailey. Crimes of Violence: Rape & Other Sex Crimes (West)	1973-	1	$835.00	$445.00	$485.00	$528.00	$613.00	
Bailey. Handling Misdemeanor Cases (West)	2d ed./1993-	1	$686.00	$365.00	$398.00	$434.00	$473.00	
Batista. Civil RICO Practice Manual (WKL&B)	3d ed/2008-	1	$365.00	$146.00	$160.00	$182.00	$209.00	
Beale. Grand Jury Law and Practice (West)	2d ed./1997-	2	$340.00	$116.00	$126.50	$138.00	$63.00	
Brenner. Federal Grand Jury: A Guide to Law & Prac. (West)	2d ed./2006-	2	$262.00	$96.00	$85.00	$92.50	$100.50	
Business Crime: Crim. Liability of the Bus. Community (MB)	1981-	8	$3,347.00	$1,975.00	$2,034.00	$2,115.00	$2,221.00	$2,424.00
Carr. The Law of Electronic Surveillance (West)	2d ed./1986	2	$720.00	$753.00	$836.00	$928.00	$720.00	
Cassella. Asset Forfeiture Law in the US (JurisNet)	2d ed./2013-	1	$165.00	$75.00	$0.00	0	new ed.	
Cohen. Apprehending & Prosecuting Drunk Driver (MB)	1992-	1	$361.00	$141.00	$137.00	$156.00	$165.00	$170.00
Cook. Constitutional Rights of the Accused (West)	3d ed./1996-	3	$992.00	$558.50	$609.00	$883.00	$989.00	
Criminal Defense Techniques (MB)	1969-	10	$4,559.00	$2,798.00	$2,882.00	$2,997.00	$3,087.00	$3,369.00
Criminal Law Advocacy (MB)	1982-	7	$2,924.00	$1,746.00	$1,798.00	$1,870.00	$2,001.00	$2,184.00
Department of Justice Manual (Wolters Kluwer)	3d ed./2012-	8	$2,569.00	$1,607.00	$1,808.00	$3,684.00	$2,076.00	
DerOhannesian. Sexual Assault Trials (Lexis)	3d ed./2006-	2	$220.00	$74.00	$77.00	$81.00	$81.00	
Erwin. Defense of Drunk Driving Cases: Civil & Crim. (MB)	3d ed./1971-	4	$1,950.00	$1,171.00	$1,206.00	$1,254.00	$1,383.00	$1,437.00
Farrell. Criminal Defense Tools and Techniques (James)	2008-	1	$149.00		$69.99	$69.99	$69.99	$89.00

Author/Title (Publisher)	Edition	No. of Vols	Cost	2010	2011	2012	2013	2014
Fishman. Wiretapping and Eavesdropping (West)	3d ed./2008-	4	$845.00	$244.00	$268.00	$295.00	$337.00	
Gershman. Prosecutorial Misconduct (West)	Annual/2002-	1	$481.00	$371.00	$371.00	$404.00	$441.00	
Gershman. Trial Error and Misconduct (Lexis)	2d ed./2007-	1	$161.00	$74.00	$81.00	$87.00	$90.00	
Hardy. Criminal Tax, Money Laundering & Bank Secrecy (Bloomberg BNA)	2010-	1	$525.00	new ed.	$295.00	$300.00	0	
Hertz. Federal Habeas Corpus Practice and Procedure (MB)	7th ed./2011-	2	$481.00		new ed.	0	0	
Hutchison. Federal Sentencing Law & Practice (West)	Annual/1997-	1	$303.00	$233.00	$255.00	$255.00	$277.00	
Imwinkelried. Courtroom Criminal Evidence (Lexis)	5th ed./2005-	2	$230.00	$55.00	$45.00	$48.00	$51.00	
Imwinkelried. Criminal Evidentiary Foundations (Lexis)	2d ed./2007-	1	$137.00	$52.00	$55.00	$58.00	$61.00	
Imwinkelried. Exculpatory Evidence (Lexis)	3d ed./2012-	1	$194.00	$134.00	$138.00	$148.00	$153.00	
LaFave. Criminal Procedure (West)	5th ed./2009-	1	$92.00	$0.00	$0.00	0	0	
LaFave. Criminal Procedure (Prac. Ed.) (West)	3d ed./2007-	7	$874.00	$180.00	$158.00	$175.00	$192.50	
LaFave. Search and Seizure (West)	5th ed./2012-	6	$1,028.00	$213.00	$250.00	new ed.	$160.00	
LaFave. Substantive Criminal Law (West)	2d ed./1986-	3	$478.00	$120.00	$132.00	$154.00	$180.00	
Lane. Lane's Goldstein Trial Technique (West)	3d ed./1984-	3	$1,923.00	$1,024.00	$1,116.00	$1,227.00	$516.00	
Lawless. Prosecutorial Misconduct: Law, Proc. & Forms (MB)	4th ed/2008-	1	$215.00	$46.00	$48.00	$51.00	$54.00	
Levy. Federal Money Laundering Regulation (Wolters Kluwer)	2d ed/2008-	1	$359.00	$199.00	$210.00	$225.00	$241.00	
Loftus. Eyewitness Testimony: Civil and Criminal (Lexis)	5th ed./2013-	1	$190.00	$77.00	$84.00	$85.00	new ed.	
Mahoney. Relentless Criminal Cross-Examination (James)	2008-	1	$99.00	$69.99	$69.99	$69.99	$69.99	
Marcus. The Entrapment Defense (Lexis)	4th ed./2009	1	$192.00	$42.00	$45.00	$45.00	$50.00	
Mauriello. Criminal Investigation Handbook (MB)	1990-	1	$327.00	$186.00	$195.00	$189.00	$208.00	
Morosco. The Prosecution and Defense of Sex Crimes (MB)	1976-	1	$665.00	$394.00	$414.00	$439.00	$470.00	$512.00
Ringel. Searches & Seizures, Arrests & Confessions (West)	2d ed./2003/09-	3	$2,572.00	$1,369.50	$1,492.50	$787.00	$1,889.00	
Robinson. Criminal Law Defenses (West)	1984-	2	$357.00	$199.00	$219.00	$241.00	$259.00	
Rudenstein. Criminal Constitutional Law (MB)	1990-	3	$926.00	$281.00	$281.00	$293.00	$308.00	$317.00
Scott. Computer & Intellectual Property Crime (Bloomberg BNA Books)	2001-	1	$340.00	$0.00	$0.00	0	0	
Silver. Police Civil Liability (MB)	1986-	2	$963.00	$422.00	$422.00	$842.00	$874.00	$891.00
Torcia. Wharton's Criminal Law (West)	15th ed/1993-	4	$1,480.00	$788.00	$859.00	$1,021.00	$1,086.00	
Welling. Federal Sentencing Guidelines Manual (West)	Annual/ 1998-	1	$123.00	$128.00	$137.00	$114.00	$123.00	
Wharton's Criminal Evidence (West)	15th ed/1997-	8	$1,014.00	$505.50	$551.00	$799.00	$697.00	
Wharton's Criminal Procedure (West)	14th ed/2002-	8	$949.00	$512.00	$334.00	$444.00	$160.00	
Whited. Drinking/Driving Litigation (West)	2d ed/1985-	5	$1,324.00	$594.00	$654.00	$777.00	$866.00	
Wolfe. Hate Crimes Law (West)	Annual/1993-	1	$284.00	$217.00	$239.00	$261.00	$284.00	
DISABILITIES LAW - 11 Titles								
Americans with Disabilities Act (MB)	1992-	2	$359.00	$265.00	$296.00	$316.00	$326.00	$349.00
Americans with Disabilities Act Manual (complete) (Bloomberg BNA)	1992-	2	$1,931.00					

Author/Title (Publisher)	Edition	No. of Vols	Cost	2010	2011	2012	2013	2014
Americans with Disabilities: Prac. & Compl. Manual (West)	1992-	6	$3,195.00	$1,678.00	$1,709.00	$2,144.50	$2,380.00	
Blanck. Legal Rights of Persons with Disabilities (LRP)	2d ed./2013-	1	$365.00	$152.75	$0.00	$0.00	new ed.	
Coleman. Disability Discrimination in Employment (West)	1991-	1	$631.00	$356.00	$388.00	$450.00	$459.00	
Individuals with Disabilities Education Law Report (LRP)	1978-	2	$1,350.00					
Labor & Employ. Law Library: Disabilities Law (Bloomberg BNA)		Online	$1,825.00					
Marx. Disability Law Compliance Manual (West)	2007/09-	2	$1,071.00	$706.00	$308.00	$342.00	$379.00	
National Disability Law Reporter (LRP)	1990-	4	$925.00					
Perritt. Americans with Disabilities Act Handbook (Wolters Kluwer)	4th ed./2002-	4	$839.00	$550.00	$604.00	$670.00	$741.00	
Rothstein. Disabilities and the Law (West)	4th ed./2009-	1	$190.00	$31.50	$40.00	$160.00	$139.00	
EDUCATION LAW - 8 Titles								
Deskbook Ency. of American School Law (Center for Ed. & Employ.)	Annual/1981-	1	$279.00	$154.95	$279.00	$279.00	$279.00	
Harding. Tax Law of Colleges & Univ. (Wiley)	3d ed./2007	1	$230.00	$0.00	$0.00	0	0	
Individuals with Disabilities Education Law Report (LRP)	1978-	2	$1,350.00					
Kaplin. The Law of Higher Education	5th ed./2013-	2	$250.00	$0.00	$0.00	0	new ed.	
Lentz. Lentz School Security (West)	Annual/1993-	1	$268.00			$224.00	$268.00	
Rapp. Education Law (MB)	1984-	7	$1,883.00	$1,088.00	$1,142.00	$1,199.00	$1,283.00	$1,408.00
United States School Laws and Rules (West)	Annual	2	$266.00	$218.00	$218.00	$240.00	$266.00	
Weber. Special Education Law and Litigation Treatise (LRP)	3d ed./2008-	1	$295.00	$98.25	$0.00	0	0	
ELDER LAW - 22 Titles								
Begley. Representing the Elderly Client (Wolters Kluwer)	1999-	2	$545.00	$205.00	$215.00	$476.00	$492.00	
Brown. Mental Capacity (West)	2d ed./1994-	1	$394.00	$202.00	$215.00	$236.00	$265.00	
Carlson. Long-Term Care Advocacy (MB)	1999-	1	$220.00	$155.00	$167.00	$132.00	$137.00	$145.00
Elder Law Library on LoisLawConnect (Wolters Kluwer)	2006-	Online	$539.00					
English. Tax, Estate & Financial Plan. for the Elderly (MB)	1985-	1	$453.00	$302.00	$288.00	$300.00	$315.00	$337.00
English. Tax, Estate & Financial Plan. for Eld: Fms & Prac.(MB)	1991-	2	$510.00	$204.00	$608.00	$192.00	$205.00	$219.00
Estate Planning Library with 20+ WGL treatises [web] (RIA)	1995-	Online	$6,335.00					
Estate Planning Library without WGL treatises [web] (RIA)	1995-	Online	$3,220.00					
Frolik. Advising the Elderly or Disabled Client (RIA)	2d ed./1992-	1	$360.00	$285.00				
Frolik. Advising the Elderly or Disabled Client (RIA)		Online	$575.00					
Jordan. Dur. Powers of Attor. and Health Care Directives (West)	4th ed./2004-	2	$362.00	$132.00	$121.00	$129.00	$138.00	
Krauskopf. Elderlaw: Advocacy for the Aging (West)	2d ed./1993-	2	$436.00	$230.00	$253.00	$278.00	$320.00	
Lindeman. Age Discrimination in Edmployment Law (Bloomberg BNA Books)	2003-	1	$410.00				$210.00	
Margolis. Elder Law Forms Manual (Wolters Kluwer)	1999-	2	$435.00	$412.00	$430.00	$460.00	$505.00	
Margolis. Elder Law Portfolio Series (Wolters Kluwer)	1993-	2	$389.00	$416.00	$440.00	$721.00	$753.00	
Mezzullo. Advising the Elderly Client (West)	1992-	3	$1,271.00	$594.00	$647.50	$706.00	$819.00	

Author/Title (Publisher)	Edition	No. of Vols	Cost	2010	2011	2012	2013	2014
Pennell. Estate Planning (CCH)	8th ed./2012-	2	$465.00	$0.00	new ed.	new ed.	0	
Pension and Benefits Advisor on Checkpoint [Online] (RIA)		Online	$3,545.00					
Pension and Benefits Expert on Checkpoint (RIA)		Online	$5,010.00					
Pension Plan Guide (CCH)	1979-	10	$2,615.00					
Pension Plan Guide [CD-ROM or Online] (CCH)		1 CD or web	$2,615.00					
Price on Contemporary Estate Planning (CCH)	4th ed./2008-	1	$495.95	$389.00	$415.00	$415.00	$450.00	
ENVIRONMENTAL LAW - 25 Titles								
Beck. Water and Water Rights (Lexis)	3d ed./1991-	8	$1,298.00	$1,028.00	$1,058.00	$1,100.00	$1,177.00	
Conrad. Environmental Science Deskbook (West)	1998-	1	$482.00	$270.00	$297.00	$326.00	$353.00	
Cooke. Law of Hazardous Waste (MB)	1987-	4	$1,994.00	$1,139.00	$1,196.00	$1,236.00	$1,357.00	$1,481.00
Cooke. Law of Hazardous Waste [eBook] (MB)	1987-	eBook	$1,813.00	$1,140.00	$1,197.00	$1,269.00	$1,357.00	$1,481.00
Cross. Fed. Environmental Regulation of Real Estate (West)	Annual/1993-	1	$774.00	$346.00	$421.00	$774.00		
Dore. The Law of Toxic Torts (West)	1987-	4	$3,362.00	$1,791.00	$1,951.50	$2,319.00	$2,467.00	
Dwyer & Bergsund Federal Environmental Laws Ann. (West)	Annual/1994-	1	$371.00	$284.00	$313.00	$340.00		
Environment & Safety Resource Center (Bloomberg BNA)		Online	$23,583.00					
Environment Reporter (Bloomberg BNA)	1970-	14	$4,995.00					
Environmental Law Handbook (Govt Institutes)	Annual/1982-	1	$105.00	$0.00	$105.00	$105.00		
Environmental Law Library [CD-ROM] (MB)		1 CD	$10,096.00	$4,439.00	$4,661.00	$4,941.00	$5,287.00	$5,657.00
Environmental Law Reporter (ELI) [online]	1971-	Online	$1,995.00					
Federal Environmental Laws (West)	Annual	1	$238.00	$200.00	$200.00	$218.00		
Gaba. Law of Solid Waste, Pollution, etc. (West)	1992-	2	$822.00	$463.50	$505.00	$555.00	$585.00	
Grad. Treatise on Environmental Law (MB)	1973-	8	$2,796.00	$1,570.00	$1,617.00	$1,714.00	$1,382.10	$2,021.00
Grad. Treatise on Environmental Law [CD-ROM] (MB)		1 CD	$2,696.00	$1,639.00	$1,688.00	$1,688.00	$1,834.00	$1,989.00
Lathrop. Insurance Coverage for Environ. Claims (MB)	1992-	2	$299.00	$181.00	$179.00	$197.00	$211.00	$227.00
Malone. Environmental Regulation of Land Use (West)	1990-	1	$1,049.00	$594.50	$648.00	$706.00	$770.00	
Novick. Law of Environmental Protection (West)	1987-	3	$1,650.00	$936.00	$1,032.00	$1,650.00	$1,650.00	
Rodgers. Environmental Law. Prac. Ed. (West)	1986-	4	$972.00	$514.00	$565.00	$621.50	$713.00	
Rohan. Zoning and Land Use Controls (MB)	1978-	10	$3,542.00	$2,089.00	$2,004.00	$2,124.00	$2,273.00	$2,480.00
Safety Resource Center (base product) (Bloomberg BNA)	2002-	Online	$952.00					
Stever. Law of Chemical Regulation & Hazard. Waste (West)	1986-	4	$2,957.00	$1,575.00	$1,716.00	$1,990.00	$2,169.00	
Tarlock. Law of Water Rights and Resources (West)	1988-	1	$798.00	$484.00	$672.00	$600.00	$732.00	
Williams. American Land Planning Law (West)	1985-	8	$1,068.00	$561.00	$613.00	$628.00	$881.00	
EQUITY JURISPRUDENCE (No supplemented titles)								

Author/Title (Publisher)	Edition	No. of Vols	Cost	2010	2011	2012	2013	2014
EVIDENCE - 28 Titles								
Cohen. Electronic Discovery: Law & Practice (Wolters Kluwer)	2d ed./2011-	1	$475.00	$222.00	new ed.	$272.00	$289.00	
Cotchett. Federal Courtroom Evidence (Lexis)	5th ed./2003-	1	$261.00	$128.00	$143.00	$153.00	$157.00	
Evidence Law Treatise Library on LoisLawConnect (Wolters Kluwer)		Online	$540.00					
Faigman. Modern Scientific Evidence (West)	Annual/2005-	3	$390.00	$300.00	$330.00	$330.00	$360.00	
Forensic Sciences (MB)	1981-	5	$1,856.00	$1,090.00	$1,123.00	$1,168.00	$1,250.00	$1,364.00
Giannelli. Scientific Evidence (Lexis)	5th ed./2012-	2	$350.00	$91.00	$95.00	new ed.	$105.00	
Graham. Handbook of Federal Evidence (West)	7th ed./2011-	6	$803.00	$154.50	new ed.	0	$184.00	
Imwinkelried. Courtroom Criminal Evidence (Lexis)	5th ed./2011-	2	$230.00	$57.00	$45.00	$48.00	$51.00	
Imwinkelried. Criminal Evidentiary Foundations (Lexis)	8th ed./2011	1	$137.00	$0.00	$52.00	$55.00	$59.00	$64.00
Imwinkelried. Exculpatory Evidence (Lexis)	3d ed./2004-	1	$194.00	$134.00	$138.00	$148.00	$153.00	
Imwinkelried. Federal Evidence Tactics (MB)	1997-	1	$541.00	$211.00	$228.00	$244.00	$290.00	$298.00
Jones on Evidence, Criminal and Civil (West)	7th ed./1992-	6	$1,467.00	$1,497.00	$853.00	$997.00	$979.00	
Leonard. The New Wigmore (Wolters Kluwer)	2002-	5	$1,469.00	$520.00	$795.00	$900.00	$940.00	
Lipson. Is It Admissable? (James)	1998-	1	$89.98	$69.99	$69.99	$69.99	$69.99	$68.99
Loftus. Eyewitness Testimony (Lexis)	5th ed./2008-	1	$173.00	$77.00	$84.00	$85.00	new ed.	$85.00
Longo. Electronic Discovery Prac. Under Fed. Rules (Bloomberg BNA Books)	Annual/2011-	1	$160.00					
McCormick. McCormick on Evid.: Prac. Ed. (West)	7th ed./2013-	2	$358.00	$0.00	$0.00	0	0	
Michie's Fed. Rules of Evidence Manual on CD-ROM (Lexis)	1995-	1 CD	$789.00					
Mueller. Federal Evidence (West)	4th ed./2013-	6	$944.00	$183.50	$202.00	$224.00	new ed.	
Mueller. Evidence Practice Under the Rules (Wolters Kluwer)	4th ed./2012-	1	$359.00	$135.00	$144.00	new ed. $337.00	$155.00	
Saltzburg. Federal Rules of Evidence Manual (Lexis)	10th ed./2011-	5	$830.00	$179.00	$192.00	$205.00	$212.00	
Tarantino. Trial Evidence Foundations (James)	1986-	1	$99.00	$59.99	$59.99	$59.99	$59.99	$59.99
Torcia. Wharton's Criminal Evidence (West)	15th ed/1997-	4	$1,014.00	$537.00	$586.00	$799.00	$697.00	
Weinstein's Evidence Manual (MB)	2d ed./1995-	1	$487.00	$317.00	$306.00	$375.00	$401.00	$413.00
Weinstein's Federal Evidence (MB)	2d ed./1997-	6	$4,735.00	$2,313.00	$2,429.00	$2,990.00	$3,199.00	$3,491.00
Weinstein's Federal Evidence [CD-ROM] (MB)	2d ed./1997-	1 CD	$5,138.00	$2,773.00	$2,995.00	$3,265.00	$3,493.00	$3,888.24
Weissenberger. Federal Evidence (MB)	7th ed./2011-	1	$226.00		new ed.	$58.00	$65.00	
Wigmore. Evidence in Trials at Common Law (Wolters Kluwer)	4th ed./1961-	13	$2,950.00	$1,196.00	$1,280.00	$2,102.00	$2,232.00	
FAMILY LAW - 23 Titles								
Altschuler. Value of Pensions in Divorce (Wolters Kluwer)	5th ed./2013-	1	$399.00	$219.00	$239.00	$275.00	new ed.	
ALI. Principles of the Law of Family Dissolution (ALI)	2002	1	$196.00	$32.00	$32.00	$33.00	$39.00	
ALI. Uniform Laws Ann.: Family Laws vols. (West)	1968-	10	$1,391.00	$294.00	$296.00	$325.00	$360.00	
Atkinson. Modern Child Custody Practice (Lexis)	2d ed./2000-	2	$353.00	$233.00	$247.00	$264.00	$272.00	
Dundee. Quialified Domestic Rel. Order Answer Book (Wolters Kluwer)	5th ed./2011-	1	$385.00	$309.00	$329.00	$259.00	$355.00	

Author/Title (Publisher)	Edition	No. of Vols	Cost	2010	2011	2012	2013	2014
Family Law Reporter (Bloomberg BNA)	1974-	2	$1,423.00					
Family Law Treatise Library on LoisLawConnect (Wolters Kluwer)		Online	$540.00					
Feder. Valuation Strategies in Divorce (Wolters Kluwer)	4th ed./2012-	2	$289.00	$278.00	$210.00	new ed. $289.00	$269.00	
Felder. Encyclopedia of Matrimonial Clauses (LJP)	1990-	1	$570.00	$0.00	$499.00	$515.00		
Goldberg. Valuation of Divorce Assets (West)	Rev. ed./2005-	2	$408.00	$230.00	$252.00	$276.00	$300.00	
Haralambie. Hand. Child Cust., Abuse & Adop. Cases (West)	3d ed./2009-	3	$675.00	$135.00	$148.50	$163.50	$187.00	
Hollinger. Adoption Law and Practice (MB)	1988-	2	$536.00	$348.00	$349.00	$373.00	$399.00	$427.00
Karp. Dom. Torts: Fam. Viol., Conflict & Sexual Abuse (West)	Rev. ed/2005-	1	$258.00	$124.00	$136.00	$158.00	$171.00	
Kramer. Legal Rights of Children (West)	Rev. 2d ed./2005-	3	$538.00	$268.50	$295.50	$345.00	$364.00	
Lindey & Parley on Separation Agree. & Antenuptial Contr. (MB)	2d ed./2000-	2	$860.00	$453.00	$476.00	$505.00	$540.00	$590.00
McCahey. Child Custody & Visitation Law and Practice (MB)	1983-	4	$2,167.00	$1,265.00	$1,328.00	$1,394.00	$1,492.00	$1,627.00
Myers. Myers on Evidence of Interpersonal Violence (Wolters Kluwer)	2011-	1	$453.00		new ed.	$145.00	$155.00	
Nichols. Family Law Depositions (Juris)	2010-	1	$225.00		$70.00	$80.00	$95.00	
Rutkin. Family Law and Practice (MB)	1985-	4	$2,005.00	$1,175.00	$1,234.00	$1,308.00	$1,400.00	$1,528.00
Rutkin. Valuation & Distribution of Marital Property (MB)	1984-	3	$1,569.00	$926.00	$972.00	$1,011.00	$1,062.00	$1,159.00
Shulman. Qualified Dom. Relations Order Handbook. (Wolters Kluwer)	3d./2007	1	$385.00	$219.00	$448.00	$259.00	$295.00	
Soler. Representing the Child Client (MB)	1987-	1	$623.00	$395.00	$407.00	$423.00	$453.00	$494.00
Turner. Equitable Distribution of Property (West)	3d ed/2005-	3	$380.00	$141.00	$156.00	$171.00	$185.00	
FEDERAL PRACTICE AND PROCEDURE- 29 Titles								
Bender's Federal Practice Forms (MB)	1951-	20	$7,273.00	$4,006.00	$4,246.00	$4,543.00	$4,861.00	$5,305.00
Bender's Federal Practice Forms [CD-ROM] (MB)		1 CD	$7,448.00	$3,878.00	$4,110.00	$4,585.00	$4,906.00	$5,461.08
Brunet. Summary Judgment: Fed. Law & Practice (West)	Annual./2006-	1	$145.00	$49.00	$53.00	$58.00	$145.00	
Childress. Federal Standards of Review (Lexis)	4th ed./2010-	2	$439.00	new ed.	$398.00	$426.00	$151.00	
Department of Justice Manual (Wolters Kluwer)	3d ed./2012-	8	$2,569.00	$1,507.00	$1,808.00	new ed. $3,684.00	$2,076.00	
Federal Practice Library [CD-ROM] (MB)		CD-ROM	$51,212.00	$30,040.00	$33,523.00	$36,540.00	$39,098.00	$46,592.58
Federal Procedural Forms (West)	1975-	43	$6,335.00	$3,125.00	$3,512.00	$4,142.00	$4,815.00	
Federal Procedure Lawyers Edition (West)	1981-	76	$10,381.00	$4,652.00	$4,957.50	$6,969.50	$7,130.00	
Gensler. Federal Rules of Civil Procedure (West)	Annual/2010-	2	$344.00	$209.00	$209.00	$289.00	$316.00	
Graham. Handbook of Federal Evidence (West)	7th ed./2011-	8	$803.00	$132.00	new ed.	0	$184.00	
Grenig. Handbk of Fed. Civil Discovery & Disclosure (West)	3d ed./2010-	1	$276.00	new ed.	$97.00	$106.00	$118.00	
Herr. Annotated Manual for Complex Litigation (West)	Annual/2001-	1	$178.00	$138.00	$138.00	$150.00	$164.00	
Hunter. Federal Trial Handbook: Civil & Criminal (West)	4th ed.2003-	2	$742.00	$391.50	$244.00	$661.00	$742.00	
Hutchinson. Federal Sentencing Law and Practice (West)	Annual/1999-	1	$303.00	$233.00	$233.00	$255.00	$277.00	
Joseph. Sanctions: Federal Law of Litigation Abuse (Lexis)	5th ed./2013-	1	$242.00	$65.00	$68.00	$72.00	new ed.	
Knibb. Federal Court of Appeals Manual (West)	6th ed./2011-	1	$197.00	$39.00	$42.00	0	new ed.	

Author/Title (Publisher)	Edition	No. of Vols	Cost	2010	2011	2012	2013	2014
Moore's Federal Practice (MB)	3d ed./1997-	31	$7,421.00	$4,234.00	$4,376.00	$4,362.00	$4,667.00	$5,094.00
Moore's Manual--Federal Practice and Procedure (MB)	1962-	3	$1,584.00	$982.00	$1,033.00	$997.00	$1,067.00	$1,220.00
Motions in Federal Court (West)	3d ed./1996-	3	$517.00	$264.00	$132.00	$145.00	$157.00	$170.00
O'Malley. Federal Jury Practice & Instructions (West)	5th/6th ed/1999-	9	$1,259.00	$529.00	$578.00	$1,222.00	$909.00	
Saltzburg. Federal Rules of Evidence Manual (Lexis)	10th ed./2011-	5	$830.00	$179.00	$192.00	$205.00	$212.00	
Sand. Modern Federal Jury Instructions (MB)	1984-	5	$2,321.00	$1,371.00	$1,440.00	$1,526.00	$1,633.00	$1,782.00
Sinclair. Practice Before Federal Magistrates (MB)	1985-	1	$557.00	$214.00	$213.00	$252.00	$272.00	$281.00
Supreme Court Practice (Bloomberg BNA Books)	10th ed./2013-	1	$495.00	$0.00	$0.00	0	new ed.	0
Tigar. Federal Appeals: Jurisdiction & Practice (West)	3d ed./1999-	1	$186.00	$95.00	$105.00	$115.00	$125.00	
Weinstein's Evidence--United States Rules (MB)	2d ed./1991-	6	$4,735.00	$2,313.00	$2,429.00	$2,990.00	$3,491.00	
West's Federal Administrative Practice (West)	3d/4th ed./1996-	9	$1,290.00	$604.00	$659.50	$720.00	$780.00	
West's Federal Forms (West)	1951-	23	$2,422.00	$626.00	$707.50	$1,472.50	$1,766.00	
Wright. Federal Practice and Procedure (West)	Rev ed./1971-	55	$4,118.00	$2,455.00	$2,537.50	$3,031.50	$3,389.00	
GAMBLING LAW (No supplemented titles under this category)								
HEALTH AND HOSPITAL LAW - 26 Titles								
Baumann. Health Care Fraud & Abuse (ABA/BNA)	3d ed./2013-	1	$415.00	$205.00	$210.00	$220.00	new ed.	
Becker. Health Care Law: A Practical Guide ((MB)	2d ed./1998-	1	$492.00	$343.00	$362.00	$381.00	$418.00	$431.00
Beers. Generic and Innovator Drugs (Wolters Kluwer)	8th ed./2013-	1	$535.00				new ed.	
Buckley. ERISA Law Answer Book (Wolters Kluwer)	8th ed./2013-	1	$399.00	$230.00	new ed.	$249.00	new ed.	
Cacioppo. Health Care Fraud & Abuse (West)	1991-	5	$1,338.00	$800.50	$775.00	$515.00	$982.00	
Fox. Health Care Financial Transactions Manual (West)	1993-	1	$1,340.00	$763.00	$885.00	$1,228.00	$1,340.00	
Gantt. E-Health, Privacy, and Security Law (Bloomberg BNA Books)	2d ed./2011-	1	$480.00		new ed.	$220.00	$225.00	
HCFA's Laws, Regulations, Manualson CD-ROM (GPO)	Annual	1 CD	$250.00					
Health Care Compliance Portfolio Deluxe [Online] (CCH)		Online	$1,930.00					
Health Care Compliance Professional's Manual (CCH)	1999-	1	$399.00					
Health Law & Business Library [Online] (Bloomberg BNA)	1997-	Online	$3,001.00					
Health Law Practice Guide (West)	2d ed./1993-	5	$2,875.00	$1,781.50	$1,669.50	$1,836.00	$2,109.00	
Hospital Law Manual (Wolters Kluwer)	1983-	5	$2,310.00					
Hospital Law Manual [Online] (CCH)		Online	$2,310.00					
Jordan. Durable Powers of Atty & Health Care Directives (West)	4th ed./2004-	2	$362.00	$123.00	$129.00	$129.00	$153.00	
Legal Medicine [eBook] (Mosby)	7th ed./2007-	1	$229.00	$193.00	$199.00	$218.00	$229.00	
Loucks. Prosecuting & Def, Health Care Fraud Cases (BNA Books)	2d ed./2010-	1	$500.00	new ed.	$0.00	$0.00	$225.00	
Medicare and Medicaid Guide (CCH)	1969-	6	$2,859.00					
Medicare and Medicaid Guide (CCH)		Online	$2,859.00					
Miles. Health Care & Antitrust Law (West)	1992-	4	$2,837.00	$1,513.50	$1,650.00	$1,830.00	$2,083.00	

Author/Title (Publisher)	Edition	No. of Vols	Cost	2010	2011	2012	2013	2014
Nelson. Health and Welfare Benefit Plans (Juris)	3d ed./2009	1	$175.00	$20.00	$25.00	$25.00	$25.00	
Obade. Patient Care Decision Making (West)	Annual/2011-	1	$758.00	$459.50	$666.00	$696.00	$758.00	
O'Reilly. Food and Drug Administration (West)	3d ed./2007-	2	$1,250.00	$666.00	$742.00	$828.00	$919.00	
Treatise on Health Care Law (MB)	1991-	4	$1,717.00	$569.00	$586.00	$609.00	$652.00	$712.00
Wigder. Standards of Care in Emergency Medicine (Wolters Kluwer)	1998-	1	$449.00	$255.00	$279.00	$305.00	$359.00	
Zanglein. ERISA Litigation (Bloomberg BNA Books)	4th ed./2011-	1	$480.00	$190.00	new ed.	$195.00	$195.00	
IMMIGRATION LAW - 19 Titles								
AILA Link (AILA)		1 CD	$1,025.00	(non-members)				
Divine. Immigration Practice (Juris)	4th ed./2012-	1						
Fragomen. Immigration Employment Compliance Hbook.(West)	Annual/1987-	1	$853.00	$495.00	$658.00		$853.00	
Fragomen. Immigration Law and Business (West)	2d ed./2011-	2	$759.00	$621.00	$727.50	$213.00	$232.00	
Fragomen. Immigration Procedures Handbook (West)	Annual/1985-	3	$984.00	$660.00	$788.00	$828.00	$904.00	
Gordon. Immigration Law and Procedure (MB)	1960-	20	$3,446.00	$1,972.00	$2,071.00	$2,133.00	$2,282.00	$2,491.00
Gordon. Immigration Law and Procedure [CD-ROM] (MB)	1960-	1 CD	$3,218.00	$1,496.00	$1,616.00	$1,881.00	$2,013.00	$1,964.52
Ignatius. Immigration Law and the Family (West)	1995-	1	$471.00	$268.50	$298.00	$397.00	$432.00	
Imigration & Nationality Law Handbook	1991-	1						
Immigration Case Reporter (MB)	1985-	3	$1,627.00	$1,106.00	$1,172.00	$1,242.00	$1,342.00	$1,479.00
Immigration Law and Defense (West)	3d ed./1988-	2	$1,072.00	$561.00	$611.00	$787.00		
Immigration Law and Procedure. Desk Ed. (MB)	1980-	1	$559.00	$328.00	$338.00	$352.00	$377.00	$411.00
Immigration Law Library [CD-ROM] (MB)		1 CD	$3,218.00	$1,539.00	$1,571.00	$1,881.00	$2,013.00	$1,964.52
Immigration Law Service 2d (West)	1985-	11	$2,474.00	$1,276.00	$1,440.00	$1,708.00	$1,912.00	
Immigration Law Sourcebook (ABA)	2013-	1						
Interpreter Releases (West)	1923-	2	$1,939.00	$1,232.04	$1,545.00	$1,731.00		
Kesselbrenner. Immigration Law and Crimes (West)	1984-	1	$852.00	$561.00	$611.00	$630.00	$852.00	
Kurzban's Immigration Law Sourcebook (AILA)	14th ed./2014	1	$599.00	$399.00	$599.00	$599.00		$599.00
Steel on Immigration (West)	2d ed./2004-	1	$287.00	$163.00	$241.00	$263.00	$287.00	
INDIAN LAW - 1 Title								
COWAG. American Indian Law Deskbook (U. Pr. of CO)	4th ed./2008-	1	$90.00	$21.95	$21.95	0	0	
INSURANCE LAW - 22 Titles								
Appleman. New Appleman on Insurance Law Library Edition (Lexis)	2d ed./1996-	69	$3,529.00	$544.00	$550.00	$731.00	$2,593.00	
Ashley. Bad Faith Actions (West)	2d ed./1998-	1	$390.00	$210.00	$233.00	$256.00	$287.00	
Couch on Insurance t (West)	3d ed./1995-	19	$6,038.00	$1,647.00	$3,372.50	$4,165.00	$4,623.00	
Couch on Insurance, LawDesk [WestlawNext PRO] (West)		Online	$1,728.00					
Disbrow. No-Fault & Uninsured Motorist Auto. Cov. (MB)	1984-	4	$2,439.00	$1,309.00	$1,401.00	$1,485.00	$1,589.00	$1,734.00
Frangiamore. How Insurance Companies Settle Cases (James)	1989-	1	$99.00	$59.99	$59.99	$59.99	$59.99	$59.99

Author/Title (Publisher)	Edition	No. of Vols	Cost	2010	2011	2012	2013	2014
Harnett. The Law of Life and Health Insurance (MB)	1988-	6	$1,617.00	$755.00	$778.00	$809.00	$866.00	$945.00
Harnett. Responsibilities of Ins. Agents & Brokers (MB)	1974-	4	$2,220.00	$1,270.00	$1,308.00	$1,386.00	$1,483.00	$1,619.00
Insurance Law Treatise Library on LoisLawConnect (Wolters Kluwer)		Online	$540.00					
Kalis. Policyholder's Guide to Law of Insurance Cov. (Wolters Kluwer)	1997-	2	$435.00	$255.00	$270.00	$309.00	$339.00	
Leitner. Law & Practice of Insurance Coverage Lit. (West)	2000-	5	$671.00	$124.00	$136.00	$150.00	$166.00	
Magarick. Excess Liability (West)	4th ed./1999-	2	$350.00	$198.50	$221.00	$320.00	$350.00	
Miller. Miller's Standard Insurance Policies Ann. (West)	5th ed./2009-	7	$1,831.00	$948.00	$1,050.00	$1,221.00	$1,488.00	
New Appleman Insurance Bad Faith Litigation (MB)	2d ed./1984-	1	$565.00	$401.00	$411.00	$427.00	$457.00	$499.00
The New Appleman Law of Liability Insurance (MB)	1966-	5	$3,529.00	$2,145.00	$2,145.00	$2,220.00	$2,375.00	$2,593.00
New Appleman Insurance Law Practice Guide (Lexis)	Annual/2012-	3	$665.00	$502.00	$527.00		$665.00	
Pierce. Defending the Insured (Wolters Kluwer)	2005	1	$299.00	$159.00	$170.00	$182.00	$299.00	
Quinley. Insurance Settlements (James)	1990-	2	$129.00	$69.99	$69.99	$69.99	$69.99	$69.99
Rynard. Insurance & Risk Mgt. for State & Local Govs. (MB)	1991-	1	$323.00	$224.00	$233.00	$294.00	$314.00	$285.00
Schermer. Automobile Liability Insurance (West)	4th ed./2004-	5	$751.00	$370.00	$326.00	$359.00	$394.00	
Windt. Insurance Claims and Disputes (West)	6th ed./2013-	3	$510.00	$88.00	$98.00	$109.00	new ed.	
Zulkey. Litigating Insurance Disputes (Juris)	2011-	1	$175.00	$75.00	new ed.	0	$75.00	
JUDGES AND JUDICIAL CONDUCT - 2 Titles								
Flamm. Judicial Disqualification (Banks & Jordan)	2d ed./2007-	1	$299.00	$0.00	$0.00	0	0	
Judicial Conduct Reporter (AJS)	1979-	4/yr.	$40.00					
JURIES AND JURY INSTRUCTIONS - 16 Titles								
Beale. Grand Jury Law and Practice (West)	2d ed./1997-	2	$340.00	$116.00	$126.50	$138.00	$63.00	
Brenner. Federal Grand Jury (West)	2d ed./2006-	2	$262.00	$96.00	$85.00	$94.00	$101.00	
Eades. Jury Instructions in Automobile Actions (Lexis)	4th ed./2004-	1	$145.00	$102.00	$116.00	$116.00	$128.00	
Eades. Jury Instructions in Commercial Litigation (Lexis)	1996-	1	$178.00	$95.00	$103.00	$110.00	$113.00	
Eades. Jury Instructions in Real Estate Lit. (Lexis)	2d ed./2006-	1	$174.00	$88.00	$93.00	$96.00	$102.00	
Eades. Jury Instructions on Damages in Tort Actions (Lexis)	5th ed./2003-	1	$163.00	$75.00	$84.00	$90.00	$92.00	
Eades. Jury Instructions on Medical Issues (Lexis)	6th ed./2004-	1	$144.00	$74.00	$86.00	$92.00	$95.00	
Eades. Jury Instructions on Products Liability (Lexis)	4th ed./2006-	1	$162.00	$69.00	$75.00	$80.00	$83.00	
Michie's Jury Instructions on CD-ROM (Lexis)		1 CD	$758.00					
O'Malley. Federal Jury Practice & Instructions (West)	5th/6th ed./1999-	9	$1,259.00	$529.00	$578.00	$1,222.00	$909.00	
Personal Injury Valuation Handbooks (LRP)	1964-	9	$1,175.04					
Representation of Witnesses Before Fed. Grand Juries (West)	4th ed./1999-	2	$1,599.00	$753.00	$821.00	$895.00	$1,038.00	
Sand. Modern Federal Jury Instructions (MB)	1984-	5+	$2,321.00	$1,410.00	$1,536.00	$1,526.00	$1,633.00	$1,782.00
Singer. Trials & Deliberations Inside the Jury Room (West)	Rev. ed/1999-	5	$975.00		$670.50	$737.50	$818.00	
Starr. Jury Selection (Wolters Kluwer)	4th ed./2010-	1	$335.00	$135.00	$144.00	$154.00	$179.00	

Author/Title (Publisher)	Edition	No. of Vols	Cost	2010	2011	2012	2013	2014
Wagner. Art of Advocacy: Jury Selection (MB)	1980-	1	$430.00	$284.00	$295.00	$328.00	$351.00	$382.00
LABOR AND EMPLOYMENT LAW - 62 Titles								
Bornstein. Labor and Employment Arbitration (MB)	1988-	2	$1,252.00	$559.00	$587.00	$628.00	$672.00	$733.00
Buckley. ERISA Law Answer Book (Wolters Kluwer)	8th ed./2013	1	$399.00	$230.00	new ed.	$249.00	new ed. 329.00	
Compensation and Benefits Library (Bloomberg BNA)		Online	$1,817.00					
cyberFEDS Complete Library on the Web (LRP)	2002-	Online	$2,100.00					
Eglit. Age Discrimination (West)	2d ed./1993-	3	$775.00	$414.00	$446.00	$486.00	$389.00	
Elkouri. How Arbitration Works (Bloomberg BNA Books)	7th ed./2012-	1	$325.00	$205.00	$0.00	new ed.	0	
Employment Coordinator (West)	1984-	17	$5,279.04	$3,006.00	$3,297.96	$4,713.00	$5,213.00	
Employment Discrimination Coordinator (West)	1993-	8	$4,232.01	$2,614.00	$2,849.52	$3,852.48	$4,275.00	
Employment Guide (Bloomberg BNA)		1	$1,205.00					
Employment Guide [Onlinet] (Bloomberg BNA)		Online	$1,178.00					
Employment Law Deskbook (MB)	1989-	1	$474.00	$183.00	$181.00	$206.00	$220.00	$227.00
Employment Law Library [CD-ROM] (MB)		1 CD	$6,158.00	$4,747.00	$4,014.00	$4,245.00	$4,553.00	$5,068.38
Employment Law Treatise Library on LoisLawConnect (Wolters Kluwer)		Online	$540.00					
The Family and Medical Leave Act (Bloomberg BNA Books)	2006-	1	$515.00		$225.00	$0.00	$245.00	
Federal Equal Opportunity Reporter (LRP)	1979-	3	$1,575.00					
Federal Labor Laws Pamphlet (West)	Annual/1974-	1	$192.00	$156.00	$172.00	$188.00		
Federal Merit Systems Reporter (LRP)	1979-	3	$1,475.00					
Finkin. Privacy in Employment Law (Bloomberg BNA Books)	4th ed./2013-	1	$445.00	$165.00	$175.00	$185.00	new ed.	
Franckiewicz. Winning at the NLRB (Bloomberg BNA Books)	2d ed/2009-	1	$315.00	0	$0.00	0	0	
Garren. How to Take a Case Before the NLRB (Bloomberg BNA Books)	8th ed./2008-	1	$565.00	$0.00	$245.00	0	0	
Hardin. The Developing Labor Law (Bloomberg BNA Books)	6th ed./2012-	2	$710.00	$200.00	$205.00	new ed.	$210.00	
Hogan. Occupational Safety and Health Act (MB)	1977-	3	$1,299.00	$731.00	$768.00	$814.00	$871.00	$950.00
Human Resources Library [Online] (Bloomberg BNA)		Online	$2,353.00			new ed.		
Kahn. Legal Guide to Human Resources (West)	1995-	1	$1,170.00	$688.00	$679.00	$747.00	$859.00	
Kearns. The Fair Labor Standards Act (Bloomberg BNA Books)	2d ed./2010-	2	$755.00	new ed.	$0.00	$265.00	$270.00	
Labor Relations Reporter (Bloomberg BNA)	1937-	19	$9,122.00					
Labor and Employment Law Resource Center [Online] (Bloomberg BNA)		Online	$4,585.00					
Labor Relations Law Library [web] (Bloomberg BNA)		Online	$4,367.00					
Labor Law Library (CCH) [priced individually]	1934-	19	Inquire					
Lareau. Labor and Employment Law (MB)	2003-	11	$3,054.00	$1,527.00	$1,603.00	$1,715.00	$1,835.00	$2,003.00
Larson. The Law of Workmen's Compensation (MB)	1952-	12	$5,399.00	$3,180.00	$3,212.00	$3,324.00	$3,557.00	$3,882.00
Larson. The Law of Workmen's Compensation [CD-ROM] (MB)	1952-	1 CD	$6,322.00	$3,599.00	$3,779.00	$4,006.00	$4,286.00	$4,771.00
Larson. The Law of Workmen's Compensation [eBook] (MB)	1952-	eBook	$4,587.00	$3,599.00	$3,779.00	$4,006.00	$3,324.00	$3,628.00

Author/Title (Publisher)	Edition	No. of Vols	Cost	2010	2011	2012	2013	2014
Larson. Law of Workmen's Comp.-Desk Edition (MB)	1972-	3	$1,443.00	$968.00	$1,045.00	$903.00	$903.00	$1,055.00
Larson. Law of Workmen's Comp.-Desk Ed. [CD-ROM] (MB)	1972-	1 CD	$1,769.00	$968.00	$1,045.00	$1,139.00	$1,219.00	$1,356.00
Larson. Law of Workmen's Comp.-Desk Ed. [eBook] (MB)	1972-	eBook	$1,312.00	$968.00	$1,045.00	$1,139.00	$1,219.00	$1,055.00
Larson. Employment Discrimination (MB)	2d ed./1994-	10	$3,328.00	$1,986.00	$2,029.00	$2,151.00	$2,302.00	$2,538.78
Larson. Employment Discrimination [CD-ROM] (MB)	2d ed./1994-	1 CD	$3,390.00	$1,843.00	$1,946.00	$2,063.00	$2,207.00	$2,458.00
Larson. Employment Discrimination [eBook] (MB)	2d ed./1994-	eBook	$3,025.00	$1,843.00	$1,946.00	$2,063.00	$2,302.00	
Lazar. Restrictive Covenants and Trade Secrets... (Bloomberg BNA Books)	2010-	2	$800.00		$175.00	$259.00	$390.00	
Lindemann. Age Discrimination in Employment Law (Bloomberg BNA Books)	2003-	1	$410.00				$210.00	
Lindemann. Employment Discrimination Law (Bloomberg BNA Books)	5th ed./2012-	2	$685.00	$265.00	$0.00	new ed.	0	
Lindemann. Workplace Harrassment in Law (Bloomberg BNA Books)	2011-	1	$485.00	$0.00	new ed.	0	0	
Malmsberger. Covenants Not to Compete (Bloomberg BNA Books)	9th ed./2013-	3	$705.00		$225.00	new ed.	0	
Malmsberger. Employee Duty of Loyalty (Bloomberg BNA Books)	5th ed./2013-	2	$595.00		$235.00	$240.00	new ed.	
McKnight. Representing Plaintiffs in Title VII Actions (Wolters Kluwer)	3d ed./2010-	2	$575.00	new ed.	$229.00	$249.00	$269.00	
Modern Workers Compensation (West)	1993-	3	$1,798.00	$990.00	$1,044.00	$1,138.00	$1,240.00	
Modjeska. Federal Labor Law: NLRB Practice (West)	1994-	2	$748.00	$390.00	$427.50	$621.00	$688.00	
NLG. Employee & Labor Union Mem. Gde to Labor Law (West)	1992-	2	$1,052.00	$597.00	$649.00	$709.00	$773.00	
Olshan. Section 409A Handbook (Bloomberg BNA Books)	2010-	1	$345.00		$145.00	0	0	
Oncidi. Employment Discrimination Depositions(Juris)	2011-	1	$195.00		new ed.	0	$75.00	
Orrick, Herrington & Sutcliffe. Employment Law Yearbook (PLI)	Annual/2001-	1	$295.00	$235.00	$235.00	$235.00	$295.00	
Pension & Benefits Advisor on Checkpoint [Online] (RIA)		Online	$3,545.00					
Perritt. Civil Rights in the Workplace (Wolters Kluwer)	3d ed./2000-	2	$395.00	$239.00	$265.00	$285.00	$315.00	
Perritt. Employee Dismissal Law & Practice (Wolters Kluwer)	5th ed./2006-	1	$425.00	$240.00	$269.00	$289.00	$309.00	
Richey. Man. on Employ. Discrim. & Civil Rights... (West)	2d ed./1994-	2	$1,015.00	$593.00	$417.00	$454.00	$497.00	
Rothstein. Employment Law (West)	4th ed./2009	2	$268.00	$0.00	$0.00	0	$49.00	
Rothstein. Occupational Safety & Health (West)	Annual/2006-	1	$211.00	$150.00	$164.00	$178.00	$194.00	$211.00
Ruzicho. Employment Law Checklists & Forms (West)	1991-	2	$1,103.00	$554.00	$604.00	$658.00	$738.00	
Schneider. ERISA: A Comprehensive Guide (Wolters Kluwer)	4th ed./2011-	1	$385.00		new ed.		$310.00	
Sprague. Workplace Data Law & Litigation (Bloomberg BNA Books)	2013-	1	$350.00				new ed.	
Westman. Whistleblowing: Law of Retal. Discharge (Bloomberg BNA Books)	2d ed./2004-	1	$295.00	$180.00	$185.00	$190.00	$195.00	
LEGAL FORMS - 20 Titles								
American Jurisprudence Legal Forms 2d (West)	2d ed./1966-	62	$8,499.00	$3,220.50	$4,313.00	$4,445.50	$4,845.00	
Am Jur Legal Forms 2d on WestlawNext (West)		Westlaw	$1,272.00					
Am Jur Pleading and Practice Forms Annotated (West)	1966-	79	$9,639.00	$4,348.00	$5,571.00	$5,764.00	$6,347.00	
Am Jur Pleading and Practice Forms on WestlawNext (West)		Westlaw	$1,272.00					
Bender's Federal Practice Forms (MB)	1951-	20	$7,273.00	$4,006.00	$4,246.00	$4,543.00	$4,861.00	$5,305.00

Author/Title (Publisher)	Edition	No. of Vols	Cost	2010	2011	2012	2013	2014
Bender's Federal Practice Forms [CD-ROM] (MB)	1951-	1 CD	$6,144.00	$4,005.00	$4,246.00	$4,585.00	$4,906.00	$5,461.08
Bender's Federal Practice Forms [eBook] (MB)	1951-	eBook	$6,612.00					$5,305.00
Bender's Forms of Discovery (MB)	1963-	34	$6,383.00	$3,454.00	$3,730.00	$4,066.00	$4,351.00	$4,759.00
Bender's Forms of Discovery [CD-ROM] (MB)	1963-	1 CD	$7,001.00	$3,873.00	$4,183.00	$4,559.00	$4,878.00	$5,430.00
Bender's Forms of Discovery [eBook] (MB)	1963-	eBook	$5,803.00					$4,749.00
Contemporary Corporation Forms (Wolters Kluwer)	2d ed./1990-	4	$1,749.00	$1,218.00	$1,302.00	$1,405.00	$1,524.00	
Federal Procedural Forms (West)	1975-	35	$6,335.00	$3,125.00	$3,512.00	$4,142.00	$4,815.00	
Fletcher Corporation Forms Annotated (West)	4th ed./1980-	21	$5,220.00	$2,638.50	$2,793.00	$3,072.00	$3,728.00	
Nichols Cyclopedia of Legal Forms (West)	1983-	39	$8,570.00	$3,847.50	$5,417.50	$5,959.00	$5,471.00	
Rabkin. Current Legal Forms w/Tax Analysis (MB)	1948-	33	$3,910.00	$2,235.00	$2,302.00	$2,371.00	$2,561.00	$2,795.00
Warren's Forms of Agreement (MB)	1954-	7	$2,368.00	$1,296.00	$1,361.00	$1,443.00	$1,544.00	$1,685.00
Warren's Forms of Agreement [CD-ROM] (MB)	1954-	1 CD	$2,414.00	$1,255.00	$1,318.00	$1,397.00	$1,495.00	$1,684.00
Warren's Forms of Agreement [eBook] (MB)	1954-	eBook	$2,153.00					$1,685.00
West's Federal Forms (West)	1951-	19	$2,422.00	$626.00	$707.50	$1,472.50	$1,766.00	
West's Legal Forms 3d (West)	5th ed./1981-	58	$5,705.00	$1,248.00	$1,410.00	$1,584.00	$5,705.00	
LEGAL PROFESSION - 22 Titles								
Altman. How to Manage Your Law Office (MB)	1973-	2	$416.00	$322.00	$314.00	$336.00	$347.00	$360.00
ABA. 2013 Legal Tech. Survey Report: Law Office Tech. (ABA)	Annual/1990-	1	$350.00	$350.00	$350.00	$350.00	$350.00	
ABA. 2013 Legal Technology Survey Report: Online Research.(ABA)	Annual/2013-	1	$350.00	$350.00	$350.00	$350.00	$350.00	
ABA/BNA Lawyers' Manual on Professional Conduct (Bloomberg BNA)	1984-	2	$1,935.00					
ABA/BNA Lawyers' Manual on Professional Conduct [web] (Bloomberg BNA)	1984-	Online	$2,198.00					
Basri. Corporate Legal Departments (PLI)	4th ed./2011-	1	$365.00	$152.00	new ed.: 310.00	$326.00	$340.00	
Derfner. Court Awarded Attorney Fees (MB)	1983-	3	$2,150.00	$1,088.00	$1,142.00	$1,245.00	$1,332.00	$1,454.00
Flamm. Lawyer Disqualification (Banks & Jordan)	2d ed./2013-	1	$249.00	$99.50	$0.00	0	new ed.	
Glazer & Fitzgibbon on Legal Opinions (Wolters Kluwer)	3d ed/2008-	1	$395.00	$183.00	$225.00	$247.00	$269.00	
Hall. Professional Responsibility in Criminal Defense Prac. (West)	3d ed./2005-	1	$302.00	$51.00	$56.00	$62.00	$62.50	
Hamadeh. Vault Guide to the Top 100 Law Firms (Vault Rpts) annual	Annual/2012-	1	$39.95	$39.95	$39.95	$39.95	$39.95	$39.95
Hazard. The Law of Lawyering (Wolters Kluwer)	3d ed./2001-	2	$699.00	$352.00	$375.00	$550.00	$550.00	
Hillman on Lawyer Mobility (Wolters Kluwer)	2d ed./1998-	1	$375.00	$218.00	$230.00	$246.00	$265.00	
Law Practice Resources Library on LoislawConnect (Wolters Kluwer)		Online	$540.00					
The Lawyers Competitive Edge (West)	1999-	12/yr	$1,160.00	$737.04	$825.00	$924.48	$1,035.48	$1,160.00
Mallen. Legal Malpractice (West)	Annual/2008-	5	$670.00	$445.00	$515.00	$560.00	$610.00	$670.00
Meiselman. Attorney Malpractice: Law & Procedure (West)	1980-	1	$517.00	$272.50	$300.00	$351.00	$379.00	
Rice. Attorney-Client Privilege in the United States (West)	2d ed./1999-	2	$650.00	$372.00	$444.00	$548.00	$598.00	
Rotunda. Legal Ethics (West)	Annual	1	$183.00	$121.00		$168.00	$183.00	

Author/Title (Publisher)	Edition	No. of Vols	Cost	2010	2011	2012	2013	2014
Stein. The Law of Law Firms (West)	2d ed/Annual	1	$115.00	$44.00	$75.50	$83.00	$115.00	
Stern. Practical Guide to Preventing Legal Malprac. (West)	1983-	1	$556.00	$315.00	$344.00	$376.00	$408.00	
Weise. Representing the Corp. (Wolters Kluwer)	2d ed./2001-	2	$695.00	$390.00	$420.00	$450.00	$500.00	
MEDICAL JURISPRUDENCE - 22 Titles								
Attorneys' Textbook of Medicine (MB)	3d ed./1934-	23	$6,970.00	$3,816.00	$4,045.00	$4,328.00	$4,631.00	$4,960.00
Attorneys' Textbook of Medicine [CD-ROM] (MB)		1 CD	$7,972.00	$4,339.00	$4,686.00	$5,108.00	$5,466.00	$6,198.00
Attorneys' Textbook of Medicine [eBook] (MB)		eBook	$6,337.00	$4,339.00	$4,686.00	$5,108.00	$4,631.00	$4,960.00
Ausman & Snyder's Medical Library (West)	1988-	13	$2,136.00	$831.00	$906.00	$996.00	$1,145.00	
Blinder. Psychiatry in Everyday Practice of Law (West)	4th ed./2008-	1	$284.00	$81.00	$89.00	$98.00	$105.00	
Brophy. Medical Malpractice Depositions (Juris)	2004-	1	$225.00	$75.00	$75.00	$50.00	$50.00	
Courtroom Medicine Series (MB)	1962-	34	$23,077.00	$12,491.00	$14,766.00	$15,787.00	$16,286.00	$18,000.00
Lane Medical Litigation Guide (West)	1981-	5	$2,405.00	$1,280.00	$1,395.00	$1,520.00	$1,658.00	
Lawyers' Medical Cyclopedia of Personal Injuries (Lexis)	5th ed./2002-	10	$1,022.00	$563.00	$191.00	$393.00	$432.00	
Louisell. Medical Malpractice (MB)	1960-	7	$2,445.00	$1,425.00	$1,469.00	$1,557.00	$1,666.00	$1,818.00
McCormick. Medicare & Medicaid Claims & Proced. (West)	4th ed./2005-	2	$416.00	$76.00	$83.00	$87.00	$92.00	
Medical Group Practice: Legal & Admin. Guide (Wolters Kluwer)	1998-	1	$425.00	$449.00	$245.00	$269.00	$325.00	
Medical Malpractice: Guide to Medical Issues (MB)	1986-	7	$3,015.00	$1,713.00	$1,799.00	$1,907.00	$2,040.00	$2,227.00
Medicare and Medicaid Guide (CCH)	1969-	5	$2,962.00					
Medicare and Medicaid Guide [web] (CCH)		Online	$2,962.00					
Pegalis. American Law of Medical Malpractice (West)	3d ed./2005-	3	$610.00	$231.00	$253.50	$279.00	$300.00	
Personal Injury Library w/Interrogatories [CD-ROM] (MB)		1 CD	$9,365.00	$4,455.00	$4,811.00	$5,244.00	$5,611.00	$6,362.00
Personal Injury Library [CD-ROM] (MB)		1 CD	$8,813.00	$3,931.00	$4,811.00			$5,825.00
Pharmaceutical Law: Regulation of Research... (Bloomberg BNA Books)	2007	1	$535.00	$225.00	$230.00	$235.00	$250.00	
PDR Electronic Library on CD-ROM (Thomson Healthcare)	Annual/2011	1 CD	$97.95					
Russ. Attorney's Medical Advisor/Atlas (West)	1994-	14	$4,627.00	$1,564.00	$1,343.00	$1,870.00	$2,038.00	
Sims. Exposing Deceptive Defense Doctors (James)	2009-	1	$99.00	$69.99	$69.99	$69.00	$69.00	$69.99
MILITARY LAW and NATIONAL SECURITY - 8 Titles								
Court Martial Reports [CD-ROM] (West)		1 CD	$990.00					
Federal Veterans Laws, Rules and Regulations (Lexis)	Annual/2013	$65.00					$65.00	
Gilligan. Court-Martial Procedure (Lexis)	3d ed./2007-	3	$329.00	$134.00	$140.00	$150.00	$155.00	
Guide to Homeland Security (West)	Annual/2013	2	$352.00	$188.00	$282.00	$316.00	$352.00	
Saltzburg. Military Rules of Evidence Manual (Lexis)	7th ed./2006-	2	$241.00	$76.00	$79.00	$84.00	$87.00	
Schlueter. Military Criminal Justice (Lexis)	8th ed./2013-	1	$213.00	$67.00	$70.00		$76.00	
Schlueter. Military Evidentiary Foundations (Lexis)	5th ed./2013-	1	$162.00	$0.00	$0.00	0	new ed.	
Veterans Benefits Man. & Related Laws & Regs. [CD-ROM] (Lexis)	Annual/2001-	1 CD	$220.00					

Author/Title (Publisher)	Edition	No. of Vols	Cost	2010	2011	2012	2013	2014
MUNICIPAL CORPORATIONS - 9 Titles								
Antieau on Local Government Law (MB)	2d ed./1998-	7	$2,619.00	$1,495.00	$1,570.00	$1,664.00	$1,780.00	$1,943.00
Bodensteiner. State & Local Govt Civil Rights Liab. (West)	2d ed./2011-	5	$1,144.00	$294.00	$1,027.00	$724.00	$840.00	
Fontana. Municipal Liability: Law and Practice (Wolters Kluwer)	3d ed./2007	2	$465.00	$219.00	$250.00	$285.00	$299.00	
Martinez. Local Government Law (West)	1981-	4	$2,289.00	$1,147.50	$1,253.50	$1,375.50	$1,206.00	
McQuillan. Law of Municipal Corporations (West)	3d ed./2004-	30	$5,928.00	$3,157.50	$3,443.00	$3,785.00	$4,352.00	
Matthews Municipal Ordinances (West)	2d ed./1994-	10	$2,082.00	$1,129.50	$1,199.00	$1,319.00	$1,455.00	
Municipal Legal Forms (West)	1994-	18	$2,147.00	$964.50	$1,090.00	$1,188.50	$1,319.00	
Rynard. Insur. & Risk Manage. for State & Local Govts (MB)	1991-	1	$323.00	$224.00	$233.00	$246.00	$263.00	$285.00
Zizka. State & Local Government Land Use Liability (West)	1997-	1	$247.00	$131.00	$152.00	$167.00	$346.00	
NATURAL RESOURCES AND ENERGY LAW - 11 Titles								
American Law of Mining (MB)	2d ed./1984-	6	$1,342.00	$531.00	$499.00	$529.00	$566.00	$656.00
Beck. Water and Water Rights (Lexis)	3d ed./2009-	8	$1,298.00	$1,028.00	$1,058.00	$1,100.00	$1,166.00	
Energy Law and Transactions (MB)	1990-	6	$1,878.00	$1,054.00	$1,061.00	$1,187.00	$1,255.00	$1,370.00
Glicksman. Public Natural Resources Law (West)	1990-	3	$2,360.00	$1,377.00	$1,369.50	$1,768.00	$1,733.00	
Law of Federal Oil and Gas Leases (MB)	1964-	2	$954.00	$515.00	$529.00	$560.00	$628.00	$652.00
Maxfield. Taxation of Mining Operations (MB)	1981-	1	$456.00	$365.00	$355.00	$376.00	$432.00	$445.00
Oil and Gas Library [CD-ROM] (MB)		1 CD	$4,642.00	$2,518.00	$2,795.00	$2,803.00	$2,999.00	$3,338.00
Regulation of the Gas Industry (MB)	1981-	5	$2,874.00	$1,553.00	$1,631.00	$1,729.00	$1,850.00	$2,019.00
Summers. The Law of Oil and Gas (West)	3d ed./1954-	10	$1,101.00	$470.00	$512.00	$564.00	$655.00	
Tarlock. Law of Water Rights and Resources (West)	Annual/1988-	1	$798.00	$455.00	$496.00	$732.00	$798.00	
Williams. Oil and Gas Law (MB)	1959-	8	$2,428.00	$740.00	$777.00	$820.00	$882.00	$958.00
NONPROFIT CORPORATIONS - 10 Titles								
Blazek. Tax Planning & Compliance for Tax-Exempt Orgs (Wiley)	5th ed./2012-	1	$262.00	$105.00	$0.00	new ed.	$150.00	
Desiderio. Planning Tax-Exempt Organizations (MB)	1983-	1	$289.00	$147.00	$156.00	$165.00	$172.00	$177.00
Fox. Charitable Giving and Solicitation (WG&L)	1992-	1	$1,005.00					
Fox. Charitable Giving and Solicitation [online] (WG&L)	1992-	Online	$1,005.00					
Hill. Taxation of Exempt Organizations (WG&L)	2002-	1	$365.00					
Hill. Taxation of Exempt Organizations [online] (WG&L)	2002-	Online	$600.00					
Hopkins. The Law of Tax-Exempt Organzations (Wiley)	10th ed./2011-	1	$315.00	$105.00	new ed.	0	$225.00	$225.00
Hopkins. Private Foundations: Tax Law & Compliance (Wiley)	4th ed./2014-	1	$300.00	$85.00	$95.00	$150.00	0	new ed.
Hopkins. The Tax Law of Charitable Giving (Wiley)	5th ed./2014-	1	$300.00	new ed.	$70.00	$125.00	$150.00	new ed.
Kirschten. Nonprofit Corporation Forms Handbook (West)	Annual/1996-	1	$953.00	$603.00	$874.00	$953.00		
PARTNERSHIP - 3 Titles								
Bromberg. Bromberg & Ribstein on Partnership (Wolters Kluwer)	1988-	4	$2,325.00	$1,363.00	$1,508.00	$2,418.00	$2,586.00	

Author/Title (Publisher)	Edition	No. of Vols	Cost	2010	2011	2012	2013	2014
Friedland. Tax Plng. for Partners, Partenrships & LLCs (MB)	1998	1	$937.00	$528.00	$533.00	$554.00	$593.00	$647.00
Willis. Partnership Taxation (WG&L)	7th ed./2013-	2	$1,060.00	$905.00	$955.00	$1,005.00	$1,060.00	
PATENTS, TRADEMARKS & INTELLECTUAL PROPERTY - 39 Titles								
Callman. Law of Unfair Competition, Trademarks & Monop. (West)	4th ed./2003-	10	$4,697.00	$2,501.50	$1,669.50	$4,029.50	$3,531.00	
Chisum. Patents (MB)	1978-	13	$5,864.00	$3,288.00	$3,518.00	$3,764.00	$4,027.00	$4,437.00
Clarida. Copyright Law Deskbook (Bloomberg BNA Books)	2009-	1	$505.00	$0.00	$0.00	$210.00	$215.00	
Donner. Patent Prosecution: Law, Prac. & Proc. (Bloomberg BNA Books)	8th ed./2013-	3	$600.00	$225.00	$0.00	$255.00	new ed.	
Epstein on Intellectual Property (Wolters Kluwer)	5th ed./2005-	1	$435.00	$212.00	$225.00	$240.00	$269.00	
Federal Intellectual Property Laws and Regulations (West)	Annual/2012-	1	$269.00	$206.00	$227.00	$227.00	$269.00	
Fleming. Trademark Litigation Practice (Bloomberg BNA Books)	2010	1	$500.00	new ed.	$245.00	$250.00	$260.00	
Flinn. Handbook of Intellectual Prop. Claims & Remedies (Wolters Kluwer)	2000-	1	$389.00	$239.00	$255.00	$272.00	$291.00	
Gilson. Trademark Protection and Practice (MB)	2007-	10	$2,579.00	$1,430.00	$1,502.00	$1,577.00	$1,656.00	$1,807.00
Gilson. Trademark Protection and Practice CD-ROM (MB)	2007-	1 CD	$2,860.00	$1,584.00	$1,663.00	$1,763.00	$1,886.00	$2,060.00
Gilson. Trademark Protection and Practice [eBook] (MB)	2007-	eBook	$2,344.00					$1,807.00
Goldstein. Copyright: Principles, Law and Practice (CCH)	3d ed./2005-	4	$861.00	$516.00	$550.00	$588.00	$631.00	
Grossman. Patent Litigation Strategies (Bloomberg BNA Books)	3d ed./2010-	1	$510.00	new ed.	$0.00	$215.00	$225.00	
Hildreth. Patent Law: A Practitioner's Guide (PLI)	4th ed./2012-	1	$295.00	$166.00	$170.00	new ed.	$175.00	
Intellectual Property Law for Business Lawyers (West)	Annual/2010-	1	$194.00	$148.00	$163.00	$178.00	$194.00	
Intellectual Property Primary Law Sourcebook (MB)	Annual/1998-	1	$175.00	$144.00	$151.00	$151.00	$159.00	$175.00
Intellectual Property Library [CD-ROM] (MB)		1 CD	$26,772.00	$16,942.00	$18,275.00	$19,554.00	$20,923.00	$23,291.00
Intellectual Property Law Resource Center [Internet] (Bloomberg BNA)		Online	$4,435.00					
Intellecual Property Law Treatise Library on LoisLawConnect (WK)		Online	$540.00					
IP Analytical on WestlawNext)WEST)		Online	$2,400.00					
Licensing Agreements Library on LoislawConnect (Wolters Kluwer)	1999-	Online	$540.00					
McCarthy on Trademarks and Unfair Competition (West)	4th ed./1992-	7	$4,557.00	$2,428.00	$2,646.00	$2,884.00	$2,508.00	
Milgrim on Trade Secrets (MB)	1967-	4	$2,681.00	$1,530.00	$1,606.00	$1,702.00	$1,821.00	$1,988.00
Milgrim on Trade Secrets [CD-ROM] (MB)	1967-	1 CD	$2,741.00	$1,558.00	$1,636.00	$1,734.00	$1,855.00	$2,064.00
Milgrim on Trade Secrets [eBook] (MB)	1967-	eBook	$2,446.00	$1,558.00	$1,636.00	$1,734.00	$1,821.00	$1,988.00
Mills. Patent Law Fundamentals (West)	2d ed./1980-	3	$3,953.00	$1,120.00	$2,294.00	$1,250.00	$2,899.00	
Moy's Walker on Patents (West)	4th ed./2003-	13	$1,591.00	$643.00	$703.00	$771.00	$856.00	
Nimmer on Copyright (MB)	1963-	10	$3,087.00	$1,818.00	$1,909.00	$2,024.00	$2,166.00	$2,364.00
Nimmer on Copyright [CD-ROM] (MB)	1963-	1 CD	$3,121.00	$1,833.00	$1,925.00	$2,041.00	$2,155.00	$2,431.00
Nimmer on Copyright [eBook] (MB)	1963-	eBook	$2,807.00	$1,833.00	$1,925.00	$2,041.00	$2,166.00	$2,364.00
Peterson. 2013 Federal Circuit Yearbook (PLI)	Annual	1	$295.00			$275.00	$295.00	
Pinckney. Products Comparison Man. for Trademark (Bloomberg BNA Books)	3d ed./2013-	1	$475.00	$205.00	$215.00	$225.00	new ed.	

Author/Title (Publisher)	Edition	No. of Vols	Cost	2010	2011	2012	2013	2014
Scott. Multimedia: Law & Practice (Wolters Kluwer)	3d ed./2008-	1	$525.00	$165.00	$175.00	$374.00	$200.00	
Selz. Entertainment Law (West)	3d ed./2006-	5	$1,157.00	$247.00	$416.00	$226.50	$245.00	
Sheldon. How to Write a Patent Application (PLI)	2d ed./2009-	1	$365.00	$300.00	$318.00	$335.00	$372.00	
Sung. Patent Infringement Remedies (Bloomberg BNA Books)	2004-	1	$425.00	$230.00	$240.00	$245.00	0	
U.S. Patents Quarterly (Bloomberg BNA)		1	$3,661.00			$3,352.00		
West's Legal Forms: Vol. 25 (West)	3d ed./2001-	3	$353.00	$41.00	$41.00	$43.00	$53.50	
Wright. Drafting Patents for Litigation & Licensing (Bloomberg BNA Books)	2d ed./2013-	1	$445.00	$195.00	$200.00	$205.00	new ed.	
PRODUCTS LIABILITY - 12 Titles								
Restatement of the Law Third. Torts: Products Liability (ALI)	3d ed./1998-	2	$179.00	$32.00	$32.00	$33.00	$39.00	
American Law of Products Liability (West)	3d ed./1987-	18	$5,138.00	$3,101.00	$3,254.00	$3,532.00	$3,920.50	
Bass. Products Liability: Design and Manufac. Defects (West)	Annual/2011-	1	$177.00	$101.00	$112.00	$149.00	$162.00	
Daller. Tort Law Desk Reference: A 50 State Compendium (Wolters Kluwer)	Annual/2008-	1	$297.00	$245.00	$260.00	$297.00	$297.00	
Frumer. Products Liability (MB)	1960-	11	$5,992.00	$3,545.00	$3,651.00	$3,797.00	$4,063.00	$4,434.00
Frumer. Products Liability [CD-ROM] (MB)	1960-	1 CD	$7,496.00	$3,614.00	$3,975.00	$4,412.00	$4,721.00	$5,352.00
Frumer. Products Liability [eBook] (MB)	1960-	eBook	$5,447.00	$3,614.00	$3,975.00	$4,412.00	$4,063.00	$4,434.00
Goodman. Automobile Design Liability (West)	3d ed./1991-	3	$1,351.00	$735.00	$819.00	$905.00	$1,004.00	
Madden. Products Liability (West)	3d ed./2000-	3	$439.00	$228.00	$249.00	$271.00	$295.00	
Product Liability Law Treatise Library on LoisLawConnect (Wolters Kluwer)		Online	$540.00					
Products Liability Reporter (CCH)	1953-	2	$2,225.00					
Products Liability Reporter [Online] (CCH)	1953-	Online	$2,365.00					
PUBLIC UTILITIES - 3 Titles								
Ferrey. Law of Independent Power (West)	1989-	3	$1,817.00	$688.00	$1,156.00	$1,271.00	$1,334.00	
Public Utilities Fortnightly (PUR)	1929-	26/year	$287.00					
Utilities Law Reporter (CCH)	1928-	3	$5,545.00					
REAL PROPERTY - 30 Titles								
A.L.I. Restate. of the Law 2d. Property: Landlord & Tenant (ALI)	2d ed./1977-	2	$127.00	$64.00	$66.00	$66.00	$78.00	
A.L.I. Restate. of the Law 3d. Property: Mortgages (ALI)	3d ed./1997-	1	$85.00	$32.00	$33.00	$33.00	$39.00	
A.L.I. Restate. of the Law 3d. Property: Servitudes (ALI)	3d ed./1998-	2	$195.00	$64.00	$66.00	$66.00	$78.00	
A.L.I. Restate. of the Law 3d. Property: Wills & Other Donative Trans.	3d ed./2011-	4	$324.00	$96.00	$99.00	$99.00	$117.00	
Backman. Prac. Guide to Disp. Btwn Adj. Landowners (MB)	1989-	1	$331.00	$262.00	$258.00	$331.00	$331.00	$316.00
Bloomfield. Real Estate Investment Trusts (West)	Annual/1994-	1	$977.00	$387.00	$402.00	$548.00	$896.00	$977.00
Cozen. Insuring Real Property (MB)	1989-	3	$940.00	$435.00	$448.00	$475.00	$508.00	$554.00
Cross. Federal Environmental Regulation of Real Estate (West)	1993-	1	$774.00	$378.00	$421.00	$619.00	$774.00	$774.00
Deems. Prac. Guide to Winning Land Use Approvals & Permits (MB)	1990-	1	$371.00	$271.00	$264.00	$337.00	$337.00	$321.00
Eades. Jury Instructions in Real Estate Lit. (Lexis)	2d ed./2006-	1	$174.00	$88.00	$93.00	$96.00	$103.00	

Author/Title (Publisher)	Edition	No. of Vols	Cost	2010	2011	2012	2013	2014
Friedman on Contracts & Conveyances of Real Property (PLI)	7th ed./2005-	2	$535.00	$376.00	$398.00	$410.00	$480.00	
Goldberg. Real Estate for the General Practitioner (Lexis)	1997-	1	$149.00	$121.00	$128.00	$137.00	$142.00	
Korngold. Private Land Use Arrangements (Juris)	2d ed./2004	1	$165.00	$35.00	$40.00	$45.00	$45.00	
Laitos. Law of Property Rights Protection (Wolters Kluwer)	1998-	1	$365.00	$190.00	$210.00	$240.00	$269.00	
Levine. Real Estate Transactions: Tax Plan. & Conseq. (West)	Annual/2010-	1	$331.00		$255.00	$279.00	$303.00	
Nichols on Eminent Domain (MB)	3d ed./1956-	18	$6,265.00	$3,610.00	$3,646.00	$3,865.00	$4,136.00	$4,513.00
Nichols on Eminent Domain [CD-ROM] (MB)	3d ed./1956-	1 CD	$6,395.00	$3,701.00	$3,812.00	$3,812.00	$4,079.00	$4,540.00
Nichols on Eminent Domain [eBook]]	3d ed./1956-	eBook	$5,696.00	$3,701.00	$3,812.00	$3,812.00	$4,136.00	$4,513.00
Patton and Palomar on Land Titles (West)	3d ed./2003-	4	$533.00	$144.00	$158.00	$174.00	$188.00	
Poliakoff. The Law of Condominium Operations (West)	1988-	2	$798.00	$425.00	$463.50	$505.00	$550.00	
Powell on Real Property (MB)	1949-	17	$4,952.00	$2,811.00	$2,895.00	$3,062.00	$3,284.00	$3,618.00
Powell on Real Property [CD-ROM] (MB)	1949-	1 CD	$5,528.00	$3,090.00	$3,183.00	$3,374.00	$3,610.00	$4,018.00
Powell on Real Property [eBook] (MB)	1949-	eBook	$4,501.00	$3,090.00	$3,183.00	$3,374.00	$3,284.00	$3,618.00
Real Estate Law Treatise Library on LoisLawConnect (Wolters Kluwer)		Online	$540.00					
Robillard. Clark on Surveying & Boundaries (Lexis)	7th ed./1997-	1	$158.00	$125.00	$135.00	$145.00	$146.00	
Rohan. Zoning and Land Use Controls (MB)	1978-	10	$3,542.00	$1,946.00	$2,004.00	$2,124.00	$2,273.00	$2,480.00
Rohan. Zoning and Land Use Controls [eBook] (MB)	1978-	eBook	$3,220.00	$2,091.00	$2,154.00	$2,283.00	$2,273.00	$2,480.00
Thompson on Real Property (Lexis)	2d ed./1994-	15	$1,993.00	$1,175.00	$1,299.00	$1,498.00	$1,284.00	
Williams. American Land Planning Law (West)	1974-	8	$1,058.00	$528.00	$576.50	$628.00	$682.00	
Ziegler. Rathkopf's The Law of Zoning & Planning (West)	4th ed./2001-	5	$2,825.00	$1,501.00	$1,640.00	$1,804.00	$1,657.00	
RELIGION AND THE LAW - 1 Title								
Bassett. Religious Organizations and the Law (West)	2012-	2	$748.00	$384.00	$0.00	new ed.	$184.00	
RESTATEMENTS OF THE LAW - 17 Titles								
A.L.I. Restatements of the Law 2d -3d [complete] (ALI)	1958-	87	$5,613.00	$1,135.00	$1,172.00	$1,299.00	$1,283.00	
Agency 3d (ALI)	3d ed./2006-	3	$196.00	$39.00	$39.00	$40.00	$135.00	
Conflict of Laws 2d (ALI)	2d ed./1971/96--	7	$473.50	$32.00	$39.00	$40.00	$59.00	
Contracts 2d (ALI)	2d ed./1981-	12	$823.50	$32.00	$39.00	$40.00	$59.00	
Foreign Relations 3d (ALI)	3d ed./1987-	2	$173.00	$32.00	$39.00	$40.00	$59.00	
Judgments 2d (ALI)	2d ed./1982/88-	6	$410.00	$32.00	$39.00	$40.00	$59.00	
The Law Governing Lawyers (ALI)	3d ed./2000-	2	$195.00	$64.00	$64.00	$66.00	$78.00	
Property 2d: Landlord and Tenant (ALI)	2d ed./1977-	2	$127.00	$64.00	$64.00	$66.00	$78.00	
Property 3d: Mortgages (ALI)	3d ed./1997-	1	$85.00	$32.00	$32.00	$33.00	$39.00	
Property 3d: Servitudes (ALI)	3d ed./1998-	2	$195.00	$64.00	$64.00	$66.00	$78.00	
Property 3d. Wills & Other Donative Transfers (ALI)	3d ed./1999/2003-	2	$324.00	$64.00	$64.00	$99.00	$117.00	
Suretyship and Guaranty 3d (ALI)	3d ed./1996-	1	$72.00	$32.00	$32.00	$33.00	$39.00	

Author/Title (Publisher)	Edition	No. of Vols	Cost	2010	2011	2012	2013	2014
Torts 2d (ALI)	2d ed./1965/79-	29	$2,196.50	$231.00	$231.00	$238.00	$273.00	
Torts 3d: Apportionment of Liability (ALI)	3d ed,/2000-	1	$97.50	$32.00	$32.00	$33.00	$39.00	
Torts 3d: Products Liability (ALI)	3d ed./1998-	2	$263.00	$32.00	$32.00	$33.00	$39.00	
Trusts 3d (ALI)	3d ed./2003-	4	$432.00	$96.00	$39.00	$40.00	$59.00	
Unfair Competition 3d (ALI)	3d ed./1995-	1	$85.00	$32.00	$32.00	$33.00	$39.00	
SECURITIES LAW - 25 Titles								
Bader. Securities Arbitration (Juris)	2007-	1	$175.00	$0.00	$85.00	0	0	
Bloomenthal. Securities Law Handbook (West)	Annual/1978-	2	$886.00	$644.00	$746.00	$812.00	$886.00	$886.00
Blue Sky Law Reporter (CCH)	1964-	6	$2,645.00					
Blue Sky Law Reporter [Online] (CCH)		Online	$2,654.00					
Bostelman. The Sarbanes-Oxley Deskbook (PLI)	2d ed./2009-	2	$475.00	$510.00	$530.00	$525.00	$620.00	
Brown. Securities Law & Practice Deskbook (PLI)	6th ed./2012-	1	$335.00	$271.00	$159.00	new ed.	$349.00	
Federal Securities Law Reporter (CCH)	1964-	8	$4,200.00					
Federal Securities Law Reporter [web] (CCH)	1964-	Online	$4,214.00					
Federal Securities Regulation Integrated Library (CCH)		Online	$10,000.00					
Franklin. Mortgage & Asset Backed Securities Lit. Handbook (West)	2009	1	$525.00	$211.00	$249.00	$276.00	$306.00	
Going Public Handbook (West)	Annual/1985-	2	$912.00		$766.00	$836.00	$912.00	
Goodman. Practical Guide to SEC Proxy & Comp. Rules (Wolters Kluwer)	5th ed./2011-	1	$389.00	$177.00	new ed.	$210.00	$245.00	
Hazen's Securities Regulation: Sel. Statutes, Rules & Forms (West)	1982-	1	$63.00	$53.50		$79.00		
Hazen. Treatise on the Law of Securities Regulation (West)	6th ed./2009-	7	$794.00	$109.00	$119.00	$131.00	$145.00	
Kirsch. Financial Product Fundamentals (PLI)	2d ed./2012-	1	$335.00	$273.00	$290.00	new ed.	$376.00	
Loss. Fundamentals of Securities Regulation (Wolters Kluwer)	6th ed./2011-	2	$399.00	$212.00	new ed.	$245.00	$285.00	
Loss. Securities Regulation (Wolters Kluwer)	3d ed./1989-	11	$2,925.00	$1,205.00	$1,700.00	$1,775.00	$1,025.00	
Loss. Securities Regulation [web] (CCH)		Online	$2,684.00					
Poser. Broker-Dealer Law and Regulation (Wolters Kluwer)	4th ed./2007-	1	$589.00	$173.00	$183.00	$240.00	$212.00	
Robbins. Securities Arbitration Procedure Manual (Lexis)	5th ed./2000-	2	$241.00	$157.00	$163.00	$174.00	$180.00	
SEC Compliance Expert Library (WG&L)		Online	$3,460.00					
Securities Industry Fact Book (SIFA)	Annual/1993-	1	$75.00					
Securities Law Techniques (MB)	1985-	7	$3,072.00	$1,728.00	$1,840.00	$1,978.00	$2,116.00	$2,310.00
Securities Law Techniques [eBook] (MB)	1985-	eBook	$2,793.00	$1,704.00	$1,789.00	$1,896.00	$2,116.00	$2,310.00
Securities Regulation Law Library [CD-ROM] (MB)	1996-	2 CDs	$5,276.00	$3,022.00	$3,173.00	$3,363.00	$3,598.00	$4,005.00
SOCIAL SECURITY LAW - 11 Titles								
Bush. Social Security Disability Practice (James)	2d ed./1992-	2	$149.00	$89.99	$89.99	$89.99	$89.99	$89.99
Elder Practitioner Pension & Retirement on WestlawNext PRO		Online	$1,080.00					

Author/Title (Publisher)	Edition	No. of Vols	Cost	2010	2011	2012	2013	2014
Federal Social Security Laws, Selected Statutes & Regs.(West)	Annual	1	$248.00	$190.00	$209.00	$227.00	$248.00	
McCormick. Medicare and Medicaid Clms. & Procdrs (West)	4th ed./2005-	2	$416.00	$81.00	$89.00	$0.00	0	
McCormick. Social Security Claims & Procedures (West)	6th ed./2009	2	$348.00	$50.00	$55.00	$65.00	$70.50	
Pratt. Social Security and Medicare Answer Book (Wolters Kluwer)	5th ed./2013-	1	$375.00	$209.00	new ed.	$265.00		
Samuels. Social Security Disability Claims (West)	2d ed./1994-	4	$1,499.00	$734.00	$800.50	$872.50	$567.00	
Social Security Law and Practice (West)	1983-	11	$5,341.00	$2,846.00	$3,163.00	$3,511.00	$3,897.00	
Social Security Practice Guide (MB)	1984-	5	$1,839.00	$1,045.00	$1,076.00	$1,175.00	$1,294.00	
Social Security Practice Guide [CD-ROM] (MB)	1984-	1 CD	$2,143.00	$1,152.00	$1,244.00	$1,319.00	$1,411.00	$1,542.00
Social Security Practice Guide [Online] (MB)	1984-	eBook	$1,672.00					$1,294.00
STATUTORY CONSTRUCTION - 1 Title								
Singer. Sutherland Statutory Construction (West)	6th ed./2000-	9	$2,170.00	$1,288.50	$1,165.50	$1,275.00	$1,173.00	
TAXATION - 46 Titles								
Axelrod. Consolidated Tax Returns (West)	4th ed./2012-	3	$1,292.94	$799.56	$871.56	$1,185.48	$1,292.94	
Bittker. Federal Income Taxation of Individuals (WG&L)	3d ed./2002-	1	$405.00					
Bittker. Federal Income Taxation of Individuals [online] (WG&L)		Online	$630.00					
Bittker. Federal Taxation of Income, Estates & Gifts (WG&L)	3d ed./1993-	5	$1,855.00					
Bittker. Federal Taxation of Income, Estates & Gifts [online] (WG&L)	3d ed./1993-	Online	$1,560.00					
Bittker. Federal Taxation of Corps. and Shareholdeers (RIA)	7th ed./2005-	2	$830.00					
Bittker. Federal Taxation of Corps. and Shareholdeers [web] (RIA)	7th ed./2002-	Online	$885.00					
Cavitch. Business Organizations with Tax Planning (MB)	1963-	16	$6,433.00	$3,399.00	$3,569.00	$3,747.00	$4,009.00	$4,375.00
Estate Planning Law Library on LoislawConnect (Wolters Kluwer)	2002-	Online	$540.00					
Federal Tax Coordinator 2d (RIA)	1977-	38	$4,380.00					
Fed. Tax Coordinator Lib./State Combo [Checkpoint Online] (RIA)		Online	$3,860.00					
Fink. Tax Controversies-Audits, Investigations, Prosecutions (MB)	1980-	2	$885.00	$680.00	$667.00	$707.00	$756.00	$811.00
Hardy. Criminal Tax, Money Laundering & Bank Secrecay (Bloomberg BNA)	2010-	1	$525.00		$295.00	$300.00	$0.00	
Hellerstein. State Taxation (WG&L)	3d ed./1998-	2	$785.00					
Hellerstein. State Taxation [Online] (WG&L)	3d ed./1998-	Online	$800.00					
Hoops. Family Estate Planning Guide (West)	4th ed./1995-	2	$1,269.00	$613.00	$674.50	$657.00	$729.00	
Hopkins. Law of Tax-Exempt Organizations (Wiley)	10th ed./2011-	1	$315.00	$105.00	new ed.	0	$225.00	$225.00
Hopkins. The Tax Law of Charitable Giving (Wiley)	5th ed./2014-	1	$300.00	new ed.	&0.00	$125.00	$150.00	
Internal Revneue Manual -Audit & Administration (CCH)	1977-	10	$2,693.00					
Internal Revenue Manual -Audit & Administration [CD-ROM] (CCH)	1977-	1 CD	$2,299.00					
Internal Revenue Manual -Audit & Administration [web] (CCH)	1977-	Online	$2,224.00					
IRS Publications (CCH)	1977-	3	$868.00					
Kove. Handling Federal Estate and Gift Taxes (West)	6th ed./2000-	2	$400.00	$421.00	$463.00	$509.00	$560.00	

Author/Title (Publisher)	Edition	No. of Vols	Cost	2010	2011	2012	2013	2014
Mertens. Law of Federal Income Taxation (West)	1954-	47	$8,374.00	$4,745.52	$5,172.48	$5,638.96	$6,145.00	
Olshan. Section 409A Handbook (Bloomberg BNA Books)	2010-	1	$345.00		$145.00	0	0	
Omnitax [web] (CCH)		Online	$22,260.00	(approx.)				
OneDisc Premium DVD (Tax Analysts)		DVD	$359.00					
Pennell. Estate Planning (CCH)	8th ed./1998-	2	$465.00	$0.00	$0.00	new ed.	$443.00	$465.00
Rabkin. Federal Income, Gift & Estate Taxation (MB)	1942-	11	$3,016.00	$1,628.00	$1,726.00	$1,795.00	$1,921.00	$2,214.00
Rounds. Loring: A Trustees Handbook (Wolters Kluwer)	Annual	1	$319.00	$265.00	$280.00	$299.00	$320.00	
Saltzman. IRS Practice and Procedure (RIA)	3d ed./1999-	1	$790.00					
Saltzman. IRS Practice and Procedure [web] (RIA)	3d ed./1999-	Online	$760.00					
Standard Federal Tax Reporter (CCH)	1945-	25	$4,730.00					
Standard Federal Tax Reporter [Intelliconnect] (CCH)	1945-	Online	Inquire					
State Tax Guide (CCH)	1960-	2	$2,527.00					
State Tax Guide [web] (CCH)	1960-	Online	$2,200.00					
Stephens. Federal Estate and Gift Taxation (WG&L)	7th ed./1996-	1	$710.00					
Stephens. Federal Estate and Gift Taxation [web] (WG&L)	7th ed./1996-	Online	$575.00					
Tax Management Portfolios Plus (Bloomberg BNA)		300+	$9,830.00					
U.S. Master Tax Guide (CCH)	Annual	1	$93.50	$84.00	$88.50		$90.50	
U.S. Tax Reporter/State Combo [RIA]	1990-	Online	$3,935.00					
U.S. Tax Reporter: Estate & Gift (RIA)	1990-	2	$1,035.00					
Willis. Partnership Taxation (WG&L)	7th ed./2012-	2	$1,060.00					
Willis. Partnership Taxation [online] (WG&L)	7th ed./2012-	Online	$1,140.00					
Zaritsky. Tax Planning for Family Wealth Transfers (WG&L)	3d ed./1999-	1	$375.00					
Zaritsky. Tax Planning for Family Wealth Transfers [web] (WG&L)	3d ed./1999-	Online	$575.00					

TELECOMMUNICATIONS LAW - 8 Titles

Author/Title (Publisher)	Edition	No. of Vols	Cost	2010	2011	2012	2013	2014
Brenner. Cable Televisn. & Other Nonbroadcast Video (West)	1986-	2	$861.00	$458.50	$500.00	$545.00	$632.00	
Ferris. Telecommunications Regulation (MB)	1983-	2	$1,747.00	$998.00	$1,048.00	$1,111.00	$1,167.00	$1,273.00
Huber. Federal Telecommunications Law (Wolters Kluwer)	2d ed./1999-	1	$319.00	$245.00	$260.00	$556.00	$606.00	
Internet Law Resource Center [online] (BNA/P&F)	2010-	Online	$1,943.00					
Perritt. Digital Communications Law (Wolters Kluwer)	Rev. ed./2010-	1	$429.00	new ed.	$130.00	$139.00	$199.00	
Telemarketing Law Guide (CCH)	2002-	1	$1,270.00	$969.00	$1,027.00	$1,109.00	$1,198.00	
Wright. Law of Electronic Commerce (Wolters Kluwer)	4th ed./2000-	1	$535.00	$372.00	$390.00	$416.00	$462.00	
Zuckman. Modern Communications Law (West)	1999-	3	$285.00	$0.00	$0.00	0	$99.00	

TORT LAW - 25 Titles

Author/Title (Publisher)	Edition	No. of Vols	Cost	2010	2011	2012	2013	2014
ALI. Restate.of Law 2d. Torts 2d (ALI)	2d ed./1965-	29	$2,196.50	$231.00	$238.00	$238.00	$293.00	

Author/Title (Publisher)	Edition	No. of Vols	Cost	2010	2011	2012	2013	2014
ALI. Restate of Law 3d, Torts: Appor. of Lia. (ALI)	3d ed./2000-	1	$97.50	$32.00	$33.00	$33.00	$39.00	
ALI. Restate. of Law 3d. Torts: Prod. Lia (ALI)	3d ed./1998-	2	$263.00	$32.00	$33.00	$33.00	$39.00	
Causes of Action 2d (West)	1983-	60	$4,708.00	$2,141.50	$2,346.50	$2,931.00	$3,505.00	
Current Award Trends in Personal Injury (LRP)	50th ed./2011-	1	$63.96	$45.75	$63.00	$63.00	$63.96	
Daller. Tort Law Desk Reference (Wolters Kluwer)	Annual	1	$297.00	$245.00	$260.00	$297.00	$297.00	
Dobbs. The Law of Torts, Practitioner's Edition (West)	2d ed./2011	4	$450.00	$128.00	new ed.	0	$150.00	
Eades. Jury Instructions on Damages in Tort Actions (Lexis)	5th ed./2003-	1	$163.00	$79.00	$84.00	$90.00	$92.00	
Hammesfahr. Punitive Damages (West)	2011-	1	$266.00		$244.00	$244.00		
Harper, James, and Gray on Torts (Wolters Kluwer)	3d ed./2006-	6	$1,599.00	$296.00	$363.00	$493.00	$528.00	
Karp. Domestic Torts (West)	Rev. ed/2005-	1	$258.00	$131.00	$144.00	$157.00	$171.00	
Lee. Modern Tort Law: Liability & Litigation (West)	2d ed./1990-	5	$780.00	$211.00	$232.00	$255.00	$147.00	
Martin. Determining Economic Damages (James)	Rev. ed/2006-	1	$99.00	$69.99	$69.99	$69.99	$69.99	$69.99
Minzer. Damages in Tort Actions (MB)	1982-	11	$3,670.00	$1,986.00	$2,085.00	$2,210.00	$2,365.00	$2,581.00
Minzer. Damages in Tort Actions [CD-ROM] (MB)	1982-	1 CD	$4,255.00	$2,062.00	$2,268.00	$2,517.00	$2,693.00	$3,053.00
Minzer. Damages in Tort Actions [web] (MB)	1982-	eBook	$3,336.00	$2,062.00	$2,268.00	$2,517.00	$2,365.00	$2,581.00
Nichols. Personal Injury Depositions (Juris)	2007-	1	$225.00	$75.00	$75.00	$85.00	$95.00	
Personal Injury Library [CD-ROM] (MB)		1 CD	$8,813.00	$3,931.00	$4,324.00	$4,880.00	$5,221.00	$5,825.00
Personal Injury Law Treatise Library on LoisLawConnect (Wolters Kluwer)		Online	$540.00					
Personal Injury Valuation Handbooks (LRP)	1964-	9	$1,175.04					
Proving and Defending Damage Claims: A 50-State Guide (Wolters Kluwer)	2007	1	$329.00	$165.00	$175.00	$187.00	$200.00	
Remedies Law Library on LoisLawConnect (Wolters Kluwer)		Online	$540.00					
Speiser. The American Law of Torts (West)	1992-	16	$2,651.00	$1,606.00	$1,536.50	$1,678.50	$1,989.00	
Stein on Personal Injury Damages (West)	3d ed./1997-	5	$1,913.00	$1,019.00	$1,111.00	$1,210.50	$1,331.00	
What's It Worth (Lexis)	Annual/1985-	1	$297.00		$257.00	$270.00		
TRIAL PRACTICE - 59 Titles								
Am. Jur. Plead. & Prac. Forms Ann. (West)	1966-	85	$9,639.00	$4,373.00	$5,211.50	$5,477.00	$6,973.00	
Am Jur. Plead. & Prac. Forms on WestlawNext (West)	1966-	Online	$1,272.00					
Am Jur Proof of Facts 1st - 3rd (West)	1959-	208	$10,569.00	$5,797.00	$5,722.00	$6,686.00	$6,926.00	
Am Jur Proof of Facts on WestlawNext (West)	1959-	Online	$1,272.00					
American Jurisprudence Trials (West)	1964-	131	$7,304.00	$3,517.50	$3,837.50	$4,622.00	$5,590.00	
Am Jur Trials on WestlawNext (West)	1964-	Online	$1,272.00					
Baldwin. Art of Advocacy: Direct Examination (MB)	1981-	1	$406.00	$284.00	$295.00	$328.00	$338.00	$372.00
Baum. Art of Advocacy: Preparation of the Case (MB)	1981-	1	$430.00	$284.00	$295.00	$328.00	$338.00	$328.00
Bender's Forms of Discovery (MB)	1963-	34	$6,383.00	$3,454.00	$3,730.00	$4,066.00	$4,351.00	$4,749.00

Author/Title (Publisher)	Edition	No. of Vols	Cost	2010	2011	2012	2013	2014
Bender's Forms of Discovery [CD-ROM] (MB)	1963-	1 CD	$7,001.00	$3,873.00	$4,183.00	$4,559.00	$4,878.00	$5,430.00
Bender's Forms of Discovery [web] (MB)	1963-	web	$5,803.00					$4,749.00
Brophy. Medical Malpractice Depositions (Juris)	2004-	1	$225.00		$50.00	$50.00	$50.00	
Brown. Judgement Enforcement Practice and Lit. (Wolters Kluwer)	3d ed./2009-	1	$332.00	$135.00	$145.00	$155.00	$166.00	
Campbell. Defense of Speeding, Reckless Driving... (MB)	1984-	4	$1,208.00	$691.00	$726.00	$770.00	$824.00	$899.00
Casad. Jurisdiction in Civil Actions (Lexis)	3d ed./1998-	2	$337.00	$139.00	$147.00	$157.00	$163.00	
Causes of Action 2d (West)	1983-	61	$4,708.00	$2,141.50	$2,346.50	$2,931.00	$3,267.00	
Criminal Defense Techniques (MB)	1969-	10	$4,559.00	$2,798.00	$2,882.00	$2,997.00	$3,087.00	$3,369.00
Criminal Law Advocacy (MB)	1982-	7	$2,924.00	$1,746.00	$1,798.00	$1,870.00	$2,001.00	$2,184.00
Decof. Art of Advocacy: Opening Statement (MB)	1981-	1	$430.00	$284.00	$295.00	$330.00	$340.00	$340.00
Derfner. Court Awarded Attorney Fees (MB)	1983-	3	$2,150.00	$1,088.00	$1,142.00	$1,245.00	$1,332.00	$1,454.00
Derfner. Court Awarded Attorney Fees [CD-ROM] (MB)	1983-	1 CD	$2,172.00	$1,088.00	$1,175.00	$1,281.00	$1,371.00	$1,497.00
Derfner. Court Awarded Attorney Fees [online] (MB)	1983-	Online	$1,955.00					$1,454.00
Erwin. Defense of Drunk Driving Cases: Crim.-Civil (MB)	3d ed./1971-	4	$1,950.00	$1,171.00	$1,206.00	$1,254.00	$1,383.00	$1,420.00
Erwin. Defense of Drunk Driving Cases: Crim.-Civil [eBook] (MB)		eBook	$1,773.00	$1,336.00	$1,403.00	$1,501.00	$1,317.00	$1,383.00
Federal Procedure. Lawyers Edition (West)	1981-	76	$10,381.00	$4,949.00	$5,211.50	$6,969.50	$7,414.00	
Frumer. Personal Injury: Actions, Defenses, Damages (MB)	1957-	25	$6,857.00	$4,220.00	$4,172.00	$4,339.00	$4,643.00	$5,068.00
Frumer. Personal Injury: Actions, Defenses, Damages [CD-ROM] (MB)	1957-	1 CD	$8,195.00	$4,105.00	$4,433.00	$4,832.00	$5,170.00	$5,863.00
Frumer. Personal Injury: Actions, Defenses, Damages [eBook] (MB)	1957-	eBook	$6,234.00					$5,068.00
General Litigation Treatise Library on LoisLawConnect (Wolters Kluwer)		Online	$540.00					
Gershman. Trial Error and Misconduct (Lexis)	2d ed/2007-	1	$161.00	$74.00	$81.00	$87.00	$90.00	
Gianna. Opening Statements (West)	2d ed./2004-	1	$127.00	$0.00	$107.00		$127.00	
Habush. Art of Advoc.: Cross Exam. Non-Med. Experts (MB)	1981-	1	$430.00	$284.00	$295.00	$328.00	$338.00	$361.00
Houts. Art of Advocacy: Appeals (MB)	1987-	1	$430.00	$284.00	$295.00	$327.00	$337.00	$361.00
Houts. Art of Advocacy: Cross-Exam. of Med. Experts (MB)	1982-	1	$392.00	$274.00	$295.00	$307.00	$317.00	$325.00
Hunter. Federal Trial Handbook--Civil (West)	Annual/2005-	1	$386.00	$196.00	$305.00	$354.00	$386.00	
Hunter. Federal Trial Handbook--Criminal (West)	Annual/2005-	1	$388.00	$324.00	$356.00	$388.00	$388.00	
Lane Goldstein Trial Technique (West)	3d ed./1984-	4	$1,923.00	$1,024.00	$1,116.00	$1,216.00	$1,761.00	
Lane Medical Litigation Guide (West)	1981-	5	$2,405.00	$1,280.00	$1,395.00	$1,521.00	$1,658.00	
Levy. How to Handle an Appeal (PLI)	4th ed./1999-	1	$195.00	$150.00	$154.00	$160.00	$185.00	
Lipson. Art of Advocacy: Demonstrative Evidence (MB)	1988-	1	$430.00	$284.00	$295.00	$330.00	$340.00	$350.00
Lipson. Art of Advocacy: Documentary Evidence (MB)	1988-	1	$426.00	$281.00	$293.00	$333.00	$343.00	$353.00
Miller. Art of Advocacy: Settlment (MB)	1983-	1	$430.00	$284.00	$295.00	$330.00	$340.00	$330.00
Miltz. Art of Avocacy: Discovery (MB)	1982-	1	$430.00	$284.00	$295.00	$330.00	$340.00	$364.00

Author/Title (Publisher)	Edition	No. of Vols	Cost	2010	2011	2012	2013	2014
Motions in Federal Court (West)	3d ed./1996-	3	$517.00	$132.00	$132.00	$146.00	$153.00	
Newberg on Class Actions (West)	5th ed./2002-	11	$1,823.00	$557.50	$741.50	$861.50	$657.00	
O'Malley. Federal Jury Practice & Instructions (West)	6th ed./2000-	26	$1,259.00	$529.00	$578.00	$1,222.00	$909.00	
Personal Injury Valuation Handbooks (West)	1964-	9	$1,075.04	$755.00	$1,049.04	$1,075.04	$1,075.04	
Pope. Trial Objections (James)	2d ed./1995-	1	$99.00	$59.95	$59.95	$59.99	$59.99	$59.99
Sand. Modern Federal Jury Instructions (MB)	1984-	5	$2,321.00	$1,371.00	$1,440.00	$1,526.00	$1,633.00	$1,782.00
Sand. Modern Federal Jury Instructions [CD-ROM] (MB)	1984-	1 CD	$2,656.00	$1,469.00	$1,578.00	$1,730.00	$1,851.00	$2,060.00
Sand. Modern Federal Jury Instructions [web] (MB)	1984-	Online	$2,110.00	$1,442.00	$1,557.00	$1,697.00	$1,633.00	$1,782.00
Schweitzer. Cyclopedia of Trial Practice (West)	3d ed./1968-	13	$3,078.00	$1,636.50	$1,785.50	$1,946.50	$2,024.00	
Singer. Sutherland Statutory Construction (West)	6th ed./2000-	9	$2,170.00	$1,288.50	$1,169.50	$1,275.00	$1,402.00	
Smith. Art of Advocacy: Summation (MB)	1980-	1	$416.00	$274.00	$275.00	$299.00	$286.00	$295.00
Starr. Jury Selection (Wolters Kluwer)	Rev. 4th ed./2010-	1	$315.00	$135.00	$144.00	$154.00	$179.00	
Stein. Closing Argument : The Art and the Law (West)	Annual, 2010-	1	$142.00	$109.00	$120.00	$130.00	$142.00	
Supreme Court Practice (Bloomberg BNA)	10th ed./2013-	1	$495.00	$0.00	$0.00	0	new ed.	
Wagner. Art of Advocacy: Jury Selection (MB)	1980-	1	$406.00	$284.00	$295.00	$328.00	$338.00	$361.00
Whited. Drinking/Driving Litigation: Crim & Civil (West)	2d ed./1998-	4	$1,285.00	$232.00	$237.00	$777.00	$854.00	
TRUSTS AND ESTATES - 30 Titles								
ALI. Restatement of the Law 3d. Property: Wills & Donative Transfers (ALI)	2011-	4	$324.00	$64.00	$64.00	$99.00	$117.00	
ALI. Restatement of the Law 2d. Trusts (ALI)	1959-	5	$317.50	$64.00	$78.00	0	0	
ALI. Restatement of the Law 3d. Trusts (ALI)	2003-	4	$301.00	$96.00	$96.00	$171.00	0	$147.00
Bogert. The Law of Trusts and Trustees (West)	3rd ed./2000-	23	$2,424.00	$927.50	$798.00	$1,769.00	$1,359.00	
Eber. Asset Protection Strategies and Forms (James)	2008-	1	$99.00	$69.99	$69.99	$69.99	$69.99	$69.99
Esperti. Irrevocable Trusts: Analysis with Forms (WG&L)	1998-	1	$390.00					
Esperti. Irrevocable Trusts: Analysis with Forms [online] (WG&L)		Online	$575.00					
Estate Law Treatise Library on LoisLawConnect (Wolters Kluwer)		Online	$540.00					
Estate Planning Library w/20+ WG&L treatises [CD-ROM] (RIA)		Online	$6,085.00					
Estate Planning Library w/o treatises [CD-ROM] (RIA)		Online	$3,090.00					
Federal Estate & Gift Tax Reporter (CCH)	1983-	3	$1,380.00					
Federal Estate & Gift Tax Reporter [web] (CCH)	1983-	Online	$1,380.00					
Henkel. Estate Planning & Wealth Preservation (WG&L)	1999-	1	$420.00					
Henkel. Estate Planning & Wealth Preservation [web] (WG&L)	1999-	Online	$575.00					
Hoops. Family Estate Planning Guide (West)	4th ed./1995-	2	$1,097.00	$520.00	$587.50	$657.00	$722.00	
Kirsch. Financial Product Fundamentals (PLI)	2d ed./2013-	1	$335.00	$273.00	$290.00	$295.00	$376.00	
Murphy's Will Clauses (MB)	1960-	5	$2,071.00	$1,285.00	$1,298.00	$1,337.00	$1,417.00	$1,518.00

Author/Title (Publisher)	Edition	No. of Vols	Cost	2010	2011	2012	2013	2014
Page on the Law of Wills (Lexis)	3rd ed./2003-	8	$1,024.00	$202.00	$210.00	$354.00	$371.00	
Pennell. Estate Planning (CCH)	8th ed./2012-	3	$465.00	$725.00	$0.00	new ed.		
Price on Contemporary Estate Planning (CCH)	4th ed./2008-	1	$465.00	$389.00	$440.00	$465.00		
Regan. Tax, Estate & Financial Planning for the Elderly (MB)	1985-	1	$453.00	$285.00	$288.00	$300.00	$315.00	$337.00
Rounds. Loring: A Trustee's Handbook (Wolters Kluwer)	Annual	1	$319.00		$280.00	$299.00	$320.00	$319.00
Scott. The Law of Trusts (Wolters Kluwer)	5th ed,/2006-	8	$3,025.00	$462.00	$494.00	$528.00	$569.00	
Turner. Irrevocable Trusts (West)	3d ed./1996-	2	$556.00	$195.50	$215.00	$236.00	$258.00	
Turner. Revocable Trusts (West)	5th ed./2003-	4	$1,256.00	$574.00	$625.50	$682.00	$750.00	
Unif. Laws Ann., Estate, Probate, & Related Laws (West)	1983/1997--	5	$1,150.00	$140.00	$148.00	$164.00	$1,072.00	
Weinstock. Planning an Estate (West)	4th ed./1995-	1	$186.00	$87.00	$95.00	$104.00	$121.00	
Westfall. Estate Planning Law & Taxation (WG&L)	4th ed./2000-	1	$380.00					
Westfall. Estate Planning Law & Taxation [Online] (WG&L)	4th ed./2000-	Online	$575.00					
Wilkins. Drafting Wills and Trust Agreements (West)	4th ed./2009-	4	$964.00	$546.00	$559.00	$610.00	$707.00	
WORKERS COMPENSATION LAW - 9 Titles								
Babitsky. Understand. AMA Guides in Workers' Comp. (Wolters Kluwer)	6th ed./2008-	1	$399.00	$210.00	$329.00	$235.00	$269.00	
Larson. The Law of Workmen's Compensation (MB)	1952-	12	$5,399.00	$3,180.00	$3,212.00	$3,324.00	$3,557.00	$3,882.00
Larson. The Law of Workmen's Compensation [CD-ROM] (MB)	1952-	1 CD	$6,322.00	$3,599.00	$3,779.00	$4,006.00	$4,286.00	$4,771.00
Larson. The Law of Workmen's Compensation [web] (MB)	1952-	eBook	$4,587.00	$3,599.00	$3,779.00	$4,006.00	$3,324.00	$3,628.00
Larson. The Law of Workmen's Comp.-Desk Ed (MB)	1972-	3	$1,443.00	$863.00	$872.00	$903.00	$966.00	$1,055.00
Modern Workers Compensation (West)	1993-	3	$1,798.00	$990.00	$958.00	$1,138.00	$1,263.00	
Norris. The Law of Maritime Personal Injuries (West)	5th ed./2009/2011-	2	$475.00	$139.00	$151.50	$166.50	$183.00	
Stone. Occupational Injuries and Illnesses (MB)	1992-	3	$585.00	$480.00	$474.00	$496.00	$514.00	$560.00
Workers' Compnsation Library [CD-ROM] (MB)		1 CD	$13,224.00	$8,089.00	$8,736.00	$9,522.00	$10,189.00	$11,341.00
ZONING AND PLANNING LAW - 12 Titles								
Deems. A Practical Guide to Winning Land Use Approvals (MB)	1990-	1	$371.00	$271.00	$264.00	$337.00	$337.00	$321.00
Kmiec. Zoning and Planning Deskbook (West)	Annual/2011-	2	$638.00	$421.00	$432.00	$638.00	$638.00	
Kushner. Subdivision Law & Growth Management (West)	2001-	2	$1,004.00	$576.00	$620.00	$656.00	$1,004.00	
Malone. Environmental Regulation of Land Use (West)	1990-	1	$1,049.00	$594.00	$609.00	$664.00	$770.00	
Mandelker. Land Use Law (Lexis)	5th ed./2003-	1	$227.00	$119.00	$123.00	$128.00	$138.00	
Robillard. Clark on Surveying and Boundaries (Lexis)	7th ed./1997-	1	$158.00	$125.00	$135.00	$145.00	$146.00	
Rohan. Zoning and Land Use Controls (MB)	1978-	10	$3,542.00	$1,946.00	$2,004.00	$2,124.00	$2,273.00	$2,480.00
Rohan. Zoning and Land Use Controls [eBook] (MB)	1978-	eBook	$3,220.00	$2,091.00	$2,154.00	$2,283.00	$2,273.00	$2,480.00
Salkin. American Law of Zoning (West)	5th ed./2008-	5	$870.00	$259.00	$284.00	$312.00	$337.00	
Williams. American Land Planning Law... (West)	1974-	8	$1,027.00	$561.00	$575.50	$628.00	$681.00	

Author/Title (Publisher)	Edition	No. of Vols	Cost	2010	2011	2012	2013	2014
Yokley. Zoning Law and Practice (Lexis)	5th ed./2001-	8	$488.00	$750.00	$755.00	$796.00	$875.00	
Ziegler. Rathkopf's The Law of Zoning and Planning (West)	1956-	5	$2,825.00	$1,501.00	$1,640.00	$1,804.00	$1,036.00	

Appendix I - State Statutory Codes by Publisher

	West	Lexis Nexis	Official	Other
Alabama	📖	📖		
Alaska		📖		
Arizona	📖	📖		
Arkansas	📖	📖		
California	📖	📖		
Colorado	📖	📖		Bradford (partial)
Connecticut	📖		📖	
Delaware	📖	📖		
District of Columbia	📖	📖		
Florida	📖		📖	
Georgia	📖	📖		
Hawaii		📖	📖	
Idaho		📖	📖	
Illinois	📖	📖		
Indiana	📖	📖		
Iowa	📖		📖	
Kansas	📖		📖	
Kentucky	📖	📖		
Louisiana	📖			Compact ed. (West)
Maine	📖			
Maryland	📖	📖		
Massachusetts	📖	📖	📖 (West)	
Michigan	📖	📖		
Minnesota	📖		📖	
Mississippi	📖	📖		
Missouri	📖		📖	

	West	Lexis Nexis	Official	Other
Montana	📖		📖	
Nebraska	📖	📖	📖	
Nevada	📖	📖	📖	
New Hampshire	📖	📖		
New Jersey	📖			
New Mexico	📖	📖	📖	
New York	📖	📖		Gould's unannotated
North Carolina		📖		
North Dakota		📖		
Ohio	📖	📖		
Oklahoma	📖			Unannotated (West)
Oregon	📖		📖	
Pennsylvania	📖		📖	Compact ed. (West)
Rhode Island	📖	📖		
South Carolina	📖			
South Dakota	📖			
Tennessee	📖	📖		
Texas	📖			
Utah	📖	📖		
Vermont		📖		
Virginia	📖	📖		
Washington	📖	📖	📖	
West Virginia	📖			
Wisconsin	📖			
Wyoming	📖	📖		
Totals	45	33	16	5

Appendix J - Historical Coverage of Federal and State Appellate Court Decisions on Commercial Computer-Assisted Legal Research Services

	Westlaw	Lexis-Nexis	Bloomberg Law	CaseClerk	Casemaker	Fastcase	Loislaw	TheLaw.net America	VersusLaw	Google Scholar	FindLaw	Official site*
U.S. Supreme Court	1790-	1790-	1789-	1900-	1754-	1754-	1790	1900-	1900-	1791-	1893-	1991-
1st Circuit	1891-	1912-	1891-	1930-	1950-	1950-	1924-	1930-	1930-	1923-	1995-	2000-
2d Circuit	1891-	1912-	1891-	1930-	1950-	1924-	1924-	1930-	1930-	1923-	1995-	30 days
3d Circuit	1891-	1912-	1891-	1930-	1950-	1950-	1924-	1930-	1930-	1923-	1994-	1994-
4th Circuit	1891-	1912-	1891-	1930-	1950-	1950-	1924-	1930-	1930-	1923-	1995-	1996-
5th Circuit	1891-	1912-	1891-	1930-	1950-	1950-	1924-	1930-	1930-	1923-	1996-	1992-
6th Circuit	1891-	1912-	1891-	1930-	1950-	1950-	1924-	1930-	1930-	1923-	1995-	1999-
7th Circuit	1891-	1912-	1891-	1930-	1950-	1950-	1924-	1930-	1930-	1923-	1995-	30 days
8th Circuit	1891-	1912-	1891-	1930-	1950-	1950-	1924-	1930-	1930-	1923-	1995-	1995-
9th Circuit	1891-	1912-	1891-	1941-	1950-	1950-	1924-	1941-	1941-	1923-	1996-	1995-
10th Circuit	1929-	1912-	1929-	1930-	1950-	1950-	1924-	1930-	1930-	1923-	1997-	1995-
11th Circuit	1891-	1912-	1980-	1981-	1981-	1981-	1981-	1981-	1981-	1981-	1995-	1995-
D.C. Circuit	1919-	1919-	1893-	1950-	1950-	1950-	1922-	1950-	1950-	1923-	1997-	1997-
Federal Circuit	1856-	1982-	1982-	1982-	1982-	1982-	1929-	1982-	1982-	1982-	1997-	2004-
Alabama	1820-	1820-	1840-	1955-	1939-	1950-	1916-	1955-	1955-	1950-	1998-	1994-
Alaska	1959-	1960-	1960-	1960-	1950-	1950-	1923-	1960-	1960-	1950-	1991-	1991-
Arizona	1866-	1866-	1866-	1930-	1950-	1950-	1925-	1930-	1930-	1950-	1997-	1998-
Arkansas	1837-	1837-	1837-	1957-	1950-	1950-	1924-	1957-	1957-	1950-	1996-	1996-
California	1850-	1850-	1850-	1930-	1950-	1950-	1899-	1930-	1930-	1950-	1934-	1996-
Colorado	1864-	1864-	1864-	1930-	1856-	1950-	1924-	1930-	1930-	1950-	1998-	1996-
Connecticut	1785-	1785-	j1814-	1950-	1900-	1950-	1899-	1950-	1950-	1950-	2000-	2000-
Delaware	1792-	1814-	1790-	1950-	1950-	1950-	1949-	1950-	1950-	1950-	1998-	2000-
D.C.	1942-	1942-	2004-	1945-	1950-	1950-	1942-	1945-	1945-	1950-	1998-	1998-
Florida	1846-	1846-	1846-	1950-	1950-	1950-	1925-	1950-	1950-	1950-	1995-	1985-
Georgia	1846-	1846-	1846-	1940-	1939-	1950-	1939-	1940-	1940-	1950-	2006-	2008-
Hawaii	1847-	1847-	1847-	1930-	1950-	1950-	1924-	1930-	1930-	1950-	1998-	1998-
Idaho	1866-	1866-	1866-	1965-	1890-	1950-	1922-	1965-	1965-	1950-	1998-	2006-
Illinois	1819-	1819-	1819-	1985-	1950-	1950-	1925-	1985-	1985-	1950-	1996-	1996-
Indiana	1817-	1817-	1817-	1940-	1925-	1950-	1923-	1940-	1940-	1950-	1998-	1999-
Iowa	1839-	1855-	1839-	1995-	1950-	1950-	1923-	1995-	1995-	1950-	1998-	1998-
Kansas	1858-	1858-	1858-	1982-	1945-	1950-	1949-	1982-	1982-	1950-	1997-	1997-

Kentucky	1785-	1785-	1785-	1945-	1925-	1950-	1924-	1945-	1945-	1950-	1997-	1999-
Louisiana	1813-	1809-	1809-	1980-	1950-	1950-	1921-	1980-	1980-	1950-	1996-	1996-
Maine	1820-	1820-	1820-	1996-	1849-	1950-	1923-	1996-	1996-	1950-	1997-	1997-
Maryland	1787-	1770-	1851-	1950-	1950-	1950-	1899-	1950-	1950-	1950-	1995-	1995-
Massachusetts	1804-	1804-	1804-	1930-	1929-	1950-	1899-	1930-	1930-	1950-	1998-	Recent
Michigan	1805-	1843-	1847-	1930-	1942-	1950-	1923-	1930-	1930-	1950-	1995-	1942-
Minnesota	1851-	1851-	1851-	1930-	1950-	1950-	1924-	1930-	1930-	1950-	1986-	Recent
Mississippi	1818-	1818-	1818-	1954-	1919-	1950-	1924-	1954-	1954-	1950-	1985-	1996-
Missouri	1821-	1821-	1821-	1960-	1930-	1950-	1919-	1960-	1960-	1950-	1997-	1997-
Montana	1868-	1868-	1868-	1993-	1950-	1950-	1924-	1993-	1993-	1950-	1997-	1988-
Nebraska	1871-	1871-	1860-	1965-	1929-	1950-	1919-	1965-	1965-	1950-	1997-	last 90 days
Nevada	1865-	1865-	1865-	1950-	1950-	1950-	1924-	1950-	1950-	1950-	1998-	last 90 days
New Hampshire	1816-	1816-	1816-	1930-	1872-	1950-	1874-	1930-	1930-	1950-	1995-	1996-
New Jersey	1790-	1790-	1790-	1930-	1950-	1950-	1948-	1930-	1930-	1950-	1999-	1994-
New Mexico	1852-	1852-	1883-	1930-	1950-	1950-	1921-	1930-	1930-	1950-	1998-	2001-
New York	1799-	1794-	1796-	1955-	1950-	1950-	1924-	1955-	1955-	1950-	1992-	1990-
N. Carolina	1778-	1778-	1778-	1945-	1939-	1950-	1778-	1945-	1945-	1950-	1994-	1997-
N. Dakota	1867-	1867-	1890-	1930-	1950-	1950-	1924-	1930-	1930-	1950-	1996-	1971-
Ohio	1821-	1821-	1852-	1950-	1914-	1950-	1923-	1950-	1950-	1950-	1997-	1992-
Oklahoma	1890-	1890-	1890-	1954-	1890-	1950-	1934-	1954-	1954-	1950-	1934-	1909-
Oregon	1853-	1847-	1853-	1950-	1939-	1950-	1924-	1950-	1950-	1950-	1998-	1998-
Pennsylvania	1754-	1791-	1845-	1950-	1950-	1950-	1924-	1950-	1950-	1950-	1997-	1996-
Rhode Island	1828-	1828-	1828-	1950-	1828-	1950-	1828-	1950-	1950-	1950-	1997-	1999-
S. Carolina	1868-	1868-	1868-	1996-	1899-	1950-	1900-	1996-	1996-	1950-	1998-	1997-
S. Dakota	1867-	1867-	1890-	1965-	1950-	1950-	1949-	1965-	1965-	1950-	1996-	1996-
Tennessee	1811-	1791-	1791-	1950-	1950-	1950-	1925-	1950-	1950-	1950-	1995-	1995-
Texas	1840-	1840-	1846-	1950-	1924-	1950-	1890-	1950-	1950-	1950-	1998-	1998-
Utah	1861-	1861-	1873-	1950-	1939-	1950-	1923-	1950-	1950-	1950-	1996-	1996-
Vermont	1789-	1826-	1826-	1930-	1929-	1950-	1924-	1930-	1930-	1950-	1997-	1994-
Virginia	1729-	1730-	1790-	1930-	1950-	1950-	1931-	1930-	1930-	1950-	1995-	1995-
Washington	1854-	1854-	1889-	1935-	1854-	1950-	1925-	1935-	1935-	1950-	1997-	last 90 days
West Virginia	1864-	1864-	1864-	1991-	1864-	1950-	1923-	1991-	1991-	1950-	1991-	1991-
Wisconsin	1839-	1839-	1839-	1945-	1950-	1950-	1939-	1945-	1945-	1950-	1995-	1995-
Wyoming	1870-	1870-	1870-	1993-	1950-	1950-	1924-	1993-	1993-	1950-	1996-	1990-

*Official sites may be hosted either by the appropriate court or by a law school working in conjunction with the court.

Appendix K - Cost Saving Tips

Send your suggestions to:
ksvengalis@nelawpress.com

1. Consider the distance to your local public law library before leasing office space.

2. In an age of escalating prices for legal publications, wise initial selection is imperative. Be sure to investigate all available options for appropriate depth of coverage, price, and supplementation cost, among other factors. Don't buy less than you require or more than you need, and don't be caught in the supplementation trap.

3. When entering a subscription to a print legal product, be sure to determine what add-ons may be included in the subscription (e.g. advance annotation service, session laws, law finder, tax volumes, desk book, etc.) or if "related" volumes may be shipped.

4. Be sure you know how often a legal publication is supplemented before making a purchase. Supplementation is a profit-driven enterprise. The sooner you realize that, the sooner you will be able to control your legal information costs.

5. Avoid standing orders to secondary publications unless you intend to consult them frequently or they are in your area of specialization. They should be viewed as starting points for research, not tools for ascertaining the current state of the law. Use your primary law materials and citators to accomplish this.

6. Place supplementation to secondary publications on a notification before shipment basis. If necessary, order latest supplement on a "Rush" basis.

7. If a standing order is dropped, determine in advance how you will update the publication (use library copy, Shepard's, KeyCite, annotated code, case digest, legal newspaper, CD, online service, or combination of these). Remember that you will still be using many of these tools to update the treatise which is on standing order.

8. Avoid telemarketers. If one gets through to you, do not buy anything from them unless you want to end up on the publisher's list of hot prospects. Request a flyer or a link to a web site if you are at all interested. Finally, ask to be taken off of the publisher's telemarketing list.

9. Consider alternatives to a complete set (abridged editions, selected volumes, statutory subject compilations, etc.).

10. Share library and expenses with other firms in your building, or use your public or membership law library.

11. Exercise strict controls over the purchase of duplicate copies. Force lawyers who desire personal copies of items already in the library to purchase them at their own expense.

12. Check amazon.com for discounted law books (e.g. ABA titles).

13. Subscribe to "lawlib" listserv to obtain books for the cost of postage.

14. Buy used books whenever feasible, but be sure to determine fill-up cost and compare with new purchase and accompanying no-charge supplementation. Establish standing orders for supplementation with publisher when appropriate. Be aware, however, that the cost updating a used set can easily exceed your initial expenditure, e,g, National Reporter System volumes from West.

15. Law firms without librarians should assign one staff member responsibility for the library.

16. Evaluate shipments before accessioning or stamping. Be prepared to return if unsolicited and/or unnecessary. If unsolicited, request return label or claim at no cost under terms of U.S. Postal law (39 U.S.C. §3009).

17. Place library subscriptions on spreadsheet and determine appropriate frequency of supplementation for each title. Make sure your standing orders with publishers reflect these determinations.

18. Conduct annual inventory of collection and the expense incurred. Re-evaluate subscriptions based on usage patterns and cost.

19. Set Internet browser to FindLaw or other legal site.

20. Determine which public and commercial Web sites are of greatest value to a practitioner in your jurisdiction and practice areas and bookmark these.

21. Resist publisher demands to purchase more user licenses to CD or online products than absolutely necessary.

22. Determine ways to control your online research expense through fixed online pricing (e.g. WestlawNext PRO, Lexis Advantage, VersusLaw, Loislaw.com, Fastcase, etc.).

23. Consider establishing a VersusLaw account for $9.95 per month ($34.95 per month for the Professional Plan). At the very least, consider it as a back-up to a Lexis or Westlaw subscription for primary law outside of your own jurisdiction.

24. If yours is a state whose bar association is part of the Casemaker consortium, or has a Fastcase program for members, encourage attorneys to use these as their default computer-assisted legal research options, with Lexis or Westlaw as back-up when necessary. As a benefit of bar membership, Casemaker or Fastcase will involve no additional cost to you or your firm.

25. Consider a cyclical re-ordering of supplementation to secondary publications (every 2-5 years based on your usage patterns). Rush order supplementation to specific titles as needed.

26. Read fine print and contract terms. In particular, watch out for open-ended supplementation terms which may allow the publisher to ship related titles on approval. West currently has a message on its web site to encourage you to sign up for automatic supplementation on the grounds that you will "Save Money." The truth is, you will save NO money. You will only give West access to your wallet on a continuing basis. Automatic supplementation is a trap for the unwary. Unless you have a librarian to monitor your library, you are better off making purchases on an ad hoc basis when necessary,

27. Avoid broader forays into WestlawNext or Lexis Advantage from the jurisdiction(s) included in your fixed-rate contract. Consider alternatives (e.g. VersusLaw, Loislaw.com, Fastcase or Casemaker).

28. Evaluate print products, CD, and online services in a publicly accessible law library before making a purchase.

29. Avoid on-approval purchases unless you are fairly certain you will keep the material. Don't agree to an on-approval purchase at suggestion of telemarketer unless you want to wind up on more telemarketing lists.

30. Determine recent history of supplementation costs before agreeing to a purchase. Publishers should provide recent supplementation cost history in their marketing materials. (this was specified in the former FTC Guides for the Law Book Industry, but often violated in practice). Check spreadsheet of initial and supplementation costs in latest edition of Legal Information Buyer's Guide and Reference Manual, or call the publisher for this information. Remember that, beyond your initial purchase, supplementation will account for practically all your expenditures in you are on standing order.

31. Inquire about combination or institutional (e.g. library) discounts for larger purchases, or periodic sales promotions.

32. If you have a lapsed subscription, make sure your local sales representative alerts you to special fill-up promotions with no-cost supplementation for a certain period of time. Allow subscription to lapse again at end of free supplementation.

33. Use Westlaw or Lexis research attorneys before conducting complicated search in both fixed and non-fixed-cost databases.

34. Consider dropping standing orders to serial volumes in such sets as **ALR, Am Jur Trials, Am Jur Proof of Facts, Causes of Action, Am Jur Legal Forms, Am Jur Pleading and Practice Forms**, and acquire them on WestlawNext instead.

35. If you keep **Am Jur 2d** on standing order, drop annual Federal Taxation volumes, annual index volumes, and purchase pocket parts every 2-3 years. For even greater savings, purchase a current used set every 3-4 years, or acquire as a supplement to your WestlawNext or Lexis Advantage subscription.

36. Given the 20% annual increases in the cost of West National Reporter System advance sheets, drop them in favor of online access, preferably to your official state supreme court web site, Casemaker, or other low-cost CALR alternative. But be aware that, given the current annual cost of NRS advance sheets, that savings alone can pay for a basic WestlawNext Pro primary law subscription.

37. Beware of solicitations disguised as invoices which follow trial subscriptions. The tactic is based on the assumption that you are more likely to renew a subscription to which you already subscribe (even though you never actually subscribed by conscious decision).

38. Determine if the frequency with which a publication is supplemented corresponds to the frequency with which you expect consult it. If you are uncertain, be sure to reevaluate at the end of the subscription period. Don't subscribe to a weekly looseleaf service if a treatise with annual pocket part will do.

39. Don't be lulled into thinking that a fixed-rate online contract with Westlaw or Lexis can spare you from concerns about usage. The terms of your next contract will be driven by your higher usage patterns. Cost-effective searching is always a good idea.

40. If you have a fixed-rate Westlaw or Lexis contract, consider pairing it with a subscription to VersusLaw or Casemaker to keep usage, and future costs, under control. If not for your firm, do it for your clients. At the very least, encourage your users to use VersusLaw or Casemaker as their default online option to develop a basic understanding of a legal issue and its terminology before going on to one of the higher priced online services.

41. Consider becoming a member of an ABA section in your area of specialization. Take advantage of special discounts and offers.

42. If you are a Westlaw or Lexis subscriber, don't read materials while online if it will increase the costs of your future CALR contract. Print lists of citations and read in hard copy, or, if print is unavailable, offline print desired cases, statutes, etc. and then sign-off.

43. One cost-saving tip many small firms overlook is the benefit of LexisNexis and Westlaw. Many firms buy CDs that duplicate the content they already have access to online (many even have at least one flat-rate contract and continue to purchase CDs). CDs require a lot more costs than just the subscription - possibly a CD tower, server, and all the maintenance costs associated with updating. Another aspect that small firms tend to overlook is the ability to bill back time (or recover the cost) spent on CDs vs. Online. Online services are relatively easy to determine, while CDs have so many hidden costs that the time feature built in to many CDs does not accurately account for the total cost. Aside from the costs, you really can't beat those free 1-800 numbers with knowledgeable attorneys! (Ann Walsh Long)

44. Negotiate hard with LexisNexis and Westlaw to get the best deal for your firm; play one against the other to get the best deal from either (as one might with two car dealerships offering similar car models). (Luis Acosta)

45. Remember that obtaining information for "free" on the Internet may not be the most cost-efficient solution when a proprietary service can deliver the information more quickly.

46. Pay in cash to avoid shipping and handling charges or obtain publisher's cash discount.

47. Don't neglect to evaluate the usage and cost of even some of your long-standing subscriptions, particularly those available free on the Internet, such as state session laws, current case law, unannotated state statutes, etc . With advances in technology, some publications may no longer receive the level of usage to justify their cost. For example, **West's Federal Case News**, now priced at more than $700.00 per year, has been largely left behind by online services and other current awareness tools.

48. Have a strict firm policy to refer all publication telemarketers to the library staff. (Mary Margaret Serpento)

49. Never volunteer attorney names to telemarketers when asked for practitioners in a particular area. (Mary Margaret Serpento)

50. Have a strict policy that nothing may be charged to a firm library budget account without prior review and approval by librarian/library committee. (Mary Margaret Serpento)

51. Have a mandatory client file identification template for Westlaw and Lexis sessions. Review statements and contact researchers about firm-expense charges to see if they might be client-chargeable. (Mary Margaret Serpento)

52. If you maintain dual format (print/CD) subscriptions to titles for which a discount was promised on the print version, be sure to verify that the discount is being correctly applied.

53. If you are forced into making budget cuts, deflect possible negative feedback by enlisting your firm's practice groups to make the evaluations and cuts. (John Hoffman)

54. Take full advantage of your local sales representatives, particularly when considering multiple purchases. He or she can alert you to special or promotional discounts for which you would not qualify if you contacted the company directly. Sales representatives have the discretion to offer significant discounts over prices available through publisher web sites.

55. The rapid and steep increases in the costs of National Reporter System reporters and advance sheets make these an unwise acquisition in print. Get used to obtaining these current decisions off your state court web site or by periodically doing a date restricted search for current decisions on your preferred low-cost CALR service (e.g. Casemaker, VersusLaw).

56. Determine in advance what state government web sites now provide to which you now subscribe in print. For example, the availability of current legislative enactments on state legislative sites now makes the purchase of state legislative services in print unnecessary.

57. Law libraries and law firms with significant numbers of supplemented West print titles should evaluate the potential cost savings which can be achieved by subscribing to a Library Maintenance Agreement, or other package plan. While multi-year contracts offer the greatest discounts, they do not preclude taking advantage of these plans on some cyclical basis (e.g. once every three years) for even greater savings.

58. If your state bar association is not currently a member of the Casemaker consortium, urge it to join. This will provide you and your fellow bar members with a low-cost alternative to the higher-priced CALR services.

59. Have a set of collection priorities to guide your acquisition/cancellation policy.

60. Have a sense of how much you want/need to spend with each of your vendors. Don't allow high price increases from one vendor to cannibalize your expenditures with other vendors.

61. Don't get locked into one online vendor. Doing so will help guarantee steadily rising CALR costs (i.e. cost of existing contract plus percentage increase). Wipe the slate clean periodically by switching to a rival online vendor if feasible. Leave yourself escape and negotiating room.

62. Make your law firm management aware of your negotiating efforts as a means of adding credibility to your budgetary requests.

63. Library Maintenance Agreements (LMAs) with Thomson/West can provide significant cost savings to eligible libraries, with annual supplementation cost increases of about 8% instead of the 13+% for those not operating under such agreements. However, resist the demand to sign a non-competitive confidentiality agreement which will prevent you from sharing the terms of your agreement with other consumers. Also, cancel all marginal titles before entering into such an agreement.

64. Ironically, West sales representatives are telling potential LMA subscribers that supplementation costs will rise 15-16% unless they sign the LMA agreement to reduce them to 8%. In reality, West supplementation costs are rising at a rate of 10-12% annually (excluding print digests), a figure they are unlikely to achieve uniformly if customers cancel lesser-used titles. Thus, West is overstating its own supplementation cost increases to induce customers to adopt an LMA. They hope that if customers leave all titles on standing order under an LMA, they will be able to stabilize, if not increase, annual supplementation revenues at a minimum of 8%.

65. Join your local membership law library, if one exists in your area. These include such institutions as the Social Law Library in Boston, the New York Law Institute, and the Jenkins Law Library in Philadelphia, and the Cleveland Law Library, among others. Your local law school may also offer a membership subscription to area attorneys. With the high cost of legal materials and their supplementation, a membership will save you countless dollars over the course of your legal career. (Ralph Monaco)

66. As an alternative to purchasing such Thomson Reuters sets as **Am Jur Trials**, **Proof of Facts**, etc., buy desired articles over the Thomson Reuters web site at a cost of about $34 each, thereby saving thousands in acquisition and supplementation costs.

66. Don't buy books or other legal information products without first checking to see if any discounts currently apply. West often offers 20-30% discounts on orders over $250.00, and 15% on smaller orders. If a discount is not currently in effect, ask your sales representative to alert you when one is coming before buying.

67. Drop all, or most, print reporters, advance sheets, session laws, state and federal statutes, citators, and major reference tools in favor of their online equivalents to avoid the high acquisition and maintenance costs. American Jurisprudence Library titles are a good example. For example the entire Am Jur Library costs $2,832 annual on WestlawNext versus more than $50,000 annually to supplement these titles in print.

Books

AALL Guide to Fair Business Practices for Legal Publishers. Chicago: American Association of Law Libraries, 2003.

American Bar Association. **2003 Legal Technology Survey Report**: Online Research. Chicago: American Bar Association, 2004.

American Bar Association. **2003 Legal Technology Survey Report**: Law Office Technology. Chicago: American Bar Association, 2004.

American Bar Association. **2006 Legal Technology Survey Report: Law Office Technology**. Chicago: American Bar Association, Legal Technology Resource Center, 2006.

American Bar Association. **2006 Legal Technology Survey Report: Online Research**. Chicago: American Bar Association, Legal Technology Resource Center, 2006.

American Bar Association. **2007 Legal Technology Survey Report: Law Office Technology**. Chicago: American Bar Association, Legal Technology Resource Center, 2007.

American Bar Association. **2007 Legal Technology Survey Report: Online Research**. Chicago: American Bar Association, Legal Technology Resource Center, 2007.

American Bar Association. **2008 Legal Technology Survey Report: Law Office Technology**. Chicago: American Bar Association, Legal Technology Resource Center, 2008.

American Bar Association. **2008 Legal Technology Survey Report: Online Research**. Chicago: American Bar Association, Legal Technology Resource Center, 2008.

American Bar Association. Legal Technology Resource Center. **Survey of Automation in Smaller Law Firms**: 1994 Survey Report. Chicago: American Bar Association, 1994.

Bander, Edward C. **Legal Research and Education Abridgment**. Cambridge, MA: Ballinger Publishing Co., 1978.

Berring, Robert C. and Elizabeth A. Edinger. **Finding the Law**. 11th ed. St. Paul, MN: West Group,1999.

Blackman, Josh. **How to Use the Internet for Legal Research**. New York: FIND/SVP, 1996.

The Bluebook: **A Uniform System of Citation**. 18th ed. Cambridge, MA : Harvard Law Review Association, 2005.

Botluk, Diana. **The Legal List: Research on the Internet.** St. Paul, MN: Thomson/West, 1993-date. Annual.

Chiorazzi, Michael and Gordon Russell, eds. **Law Library Collection Development in the Digital Age**. New York: Haworth Press, 2002.

Cohen, Morris L., Robert C. Berring, and Kent C. Olson. **How to Find the Law**. 9th ed. St. Paul, MN: West Publishing Co., 1989.

Danner, Richard A. and Jules Winterton, eds. **International Handbook of Legal Information Management.** Farnham, Surrey, England; Burlington, VT: Ashgate, 2011.

Directory of Law-Related CD-ROMs. Compiled and edited by Arlene L. Eis. Teaneck, NJ: Infosources Publishing. Annual.

Doyle, Francis R., Frank S. Bae, Joel Fishman, and Leverett L. Preble, III. **Searching the Law.** 2d ed. Ardsley, NY: Transnational Publishers, Inc., 1999.

Doyle, Francis R. **Searching the Law: The States**. A Selective Bibliography of State Practice Materials in the 50 States. 3d ed. Ardsley, NY: Transnational Publishers, Inc., 2000.

Encyclopedia of Legal Information Sources. 2d ed. Edited by Brian L. Baker and Patrick J. Petit. Detroit, MI: Gale Research Inc., 1993.

Fox, Elyse H. **How to File Looseleaf Services**: A Filing Manual and Reference Handbook. Chapel Hill, NC: Legal Information Services, 2004.

Halvorson, T.R. **Law of the Super Searchers**. Edited by Reva Basch. Medford, NJ: CyberAge Books, 1999.

Hazelton, Penny A., ed. **Specialized Legal Research**. New York: Aspen Publishers,1986-date.

Hein Checklist of Statutes (State and Territorial). 65th ed. Buffalo, NY: William S. Hein & Co., Inc., 2012.

Hoover's Guide to the Book Business. 2d ed. Austin, TX: Reference Press, 1995.

Jacobstein, J. Myron, Roy M. Mersky, and Donald J. Dunn. **Fundamentals of Legal Research**. 8th ed. Mineola, NY: Foundation Press, 2002.

Kunz, Christina L. et al. **The Process of Legal Research**: Successful Strategies. 5th ed. New York: Aspen Publishers, 2000.

Law and Legal Information Directory. 15th ed. Steven Wasserman, Jacqueline Wasserman O'Brien, and Bonnie Shaw Pfaff, eds. 11th ed. Detroit, MI: Gale Group, 2004.

The Law Library Budget and Expenditure Report. 1999 Edition. New York: Primary Research Group, 1999.

Legal Looseleafs in Print. Compiled and edited by Arlene L. Eis. Teaneck, NJ: Infosources Publishing. Annual.

Legal Newsletters in Print. Compiled and edited by Arlene L. Eis. Teaneck, NJ: Infosources Publishing. Annual.

McDermott, James A. **Recommended Law Books**. 2d ed. Chicago, IL: American Bar Association, Section of Corporation, Banking and Business Law, 1986.

Marke, Julius J. and Richard Sloane. **Legal Research and Law Library Management**. Revised ed. New York: Law Journal Seminars-Press, Inc., 1990-2005.

Marke, Julius J., Richard Sloane, and Linda M. Ryan. **Legal Research and Law Library Management**. 2d ed. New York: Law Journal Press, Inc., 2006-date.

Matthews, Elizabeth W. **The Law Library Reference Shelf**: An **Annotated Subject Guide**. 5th ed. Buffalo, NY: Hein & Co., 2003.

Miller, Oscar J. and Mortimer D. Schwartz. **Recommended Publications for Legal Research**. Littleton, CO: Fred B. Rothman Publications, a Division of William S. Hein & Co. Annual.

Nathan's Legal Markets: **The Definitive Resource for Marketing to the Legal Profession**. Edited by Sylvia M. Dolan. 3d ed. Houston, TX: Nathan Technologies, 1996. [Now online only]

Olson, Kent C. **Legal Information: How to Find It, How to Use It**. Phoenix, AZ: Oryx Press, 1999.

Reback, Gary L. **Free the Market!: Why Only Government Can Keep the Marketplace Competitive**. Portfolio, 2009. 1 vol. (432 pp.).
Cost: $26.95; from $17.79 on amazon.com (2009).

Singer, S. Fred and Dennis Avery. **Unstoppable Global Warming: Every 1,500 Years**. New York: Rowman & Littlefield Publishers, 2007.

Surrency. Erwin C. **A History of American Law Publishing**. New York: Oceana Publications, Inc., 1990.

Woxland, Thomas A. and Patti J. Ogden. **Landmarks in American Legal Publishing**: An Exhibit Catalog. St. Paul, MN: West Publishing Co., n.d.

Wren, Christopher G. and Jill Robinson Wren. **The Legal Research Manual**: A Game Plan for Legal Research and Analysis. 2d ed. Madison, WI: Adams & Ambrose Publishing , 1988.

Wren, Christopher G. and Jill Robinson Wren. **Using Computers in Legal Research**: A Guide to LEXIS and WESTLAW. Madison, WI: Adams & Ambrose Publishing, 1994.

Articles

Aarons, Anthony. "The Battle for Your Online Dollars" **Law Office Computing** 5 (June/July, 1995):59-61.

Aarons, Anthony. "Cite-Fight: The War on West." **Law Office Computing** 5 (April/May, 1995):46-51.

Aarons, Anthony. "The Summer of New Content" **Law Office Computing** 7 (Oct./Nov., 1997): 20, 22. West unveils KeyCite.

Adkins, Andrew Z. "First CD-ROM Brief Filed in Federal Court" **Law Office Computing** 7 (Oct./Nov., 1997): 13, 26-27.

Adkins, Andrew Z. "Standing Tall Amongst Giants" **Law Office Computing** 8 (April/May ,1998): 48-53.

Ambrogi, Robert J. "Bloomberg Law: Can It Be a Contender?" **Robert Ambrogi's Law Sites,** Feb. 27, 2010 [http://www.lawsitesblog.com/2010/02/bloomberg-law-can-it-be-contender.html].

Ambrogi, Robert J. "A First Look at WestlawNext." **Robert Ambrogi's Law Sites,** Jan. 6, 2010 [http://www.lawsitesblog.com/2010/01/first-look-at-westlawnext.html].

Ambrogi, Robert J. "Meet the New, Old West." **AmLaw Tech** (August, 1999): 9-10.

Arado, Therese A. Clarke. "Loislaw and VersusLaw: Database Alternatives to Consider. **The CRIV Sheet** 29 (February 2007): 9-10.

Axelroth, Joan L. "The Media Choice: Print, Online, and CD-ROM Products." **Legal Information Alert** 14 (June, 1995): 1 (4).

Axtmann, Margaret Maes. " AALL and the Pricing of Legal Publications" **AALL Spectrum** 4, No. 9 (June, 2000): 4.

Barstain, Fred and Susan De Maio. "Profile: Interviews with Selected Legal Publishers" **Legal Publishing Review** 2 (May/June, 1990): 77-90.

Bast, Carol M. and Susan Harrell. "Has the Bluebook Met Its Match? The ALWD Citation Manual" **Law Library Journal** 92, No. 3 (Summer, 2000): 337-352.

Bauman, Norman. "The Illusions and Realities of Full-Text Searching." **Law Office Computing** 4 (June/July, 1994): 44-52.

Bauman, Norman. "Seven Rules for Using Lexis and Westlaw More Effectively" **Law Office Computing** 2 (April/May, 1992): 46-56.

Baxter, William F., et al. "No Place for Trust Busters" **House Counsel** 2 (Summer, 1997): 26-31.

Bayer, Barry D. and Benjamin H. Cohen. "The appeal of Appeals on CD-ROM." **Legal Times** 16 (July 26, 1993): 45.

Bayer, Barry D. and Benjamin H. Cohen. "At 30 Dollars, This CD-ROM disk is a Steal." **Legal Times** 15 (Jan. 18, 1993): 47.

Bayer, Barry D. and Benjamin H. Cohen. "Case Research on CD-ROM Has Arrived." **Legal Times** 15 (Dec. 28, 1992): 27.

Bayer, Barry D. and Benjamin H. Cohen. " A Cheap Way to Keep Up with the CFR." **New Jersey Law Journal** 141 (July 17, 1995): 30.

Bayer, Barry D. and Benjamin H. Cohen. "Code of Federal Regulations on Inexpensive CD-ROM." **Chicago Daily Law Bulletin** 141 (July 19, 1995): 2.

Bayer, Barry D. and Benjamin H. Cohen. "Spinning Out the Federal Code." **Legal Times** 18 (July 10, 1995): 34.

Bayer, Barry D. and Benjamin H. Cohen. "United States Code Annotated on CD-ROM." **Chicago Daily Law Bulletin** 139 (Aug., 4, 1993): 2.

Benioff, Jeanne and Kathleen Vanden Heuvel. "American Jurisprudence 2d." **Legal Reference Services Quarterly** 2 (Spring, 1982): 37-53.

Bernier, Michael G. "BNA's Law School Program: An Update." **The CRIV Sheet** (May, 2003): 5-6.

Bernstein, Paul. "What's All the Hype About CD-ROM?" **Res Gestae** 38 (July, 1992): 42.

Berring. Robert C. "American Law Book Publishing," in **The Guide to American Law**. St. Paul, MN: West Publishing Co., 1983: pp. 220-25.

Berring, Robert C. and Valerie Wedin. "Corpus Juris Secundum." **Legal Reference Services Quarterly** 1 (Spring, 1981): 67-82.

Biberman, Caren J. "Interview with Mark Schiff, Vice President of Product Marketing at Thomson Reuters regarding Launch of WestlawNext, **The CRIV Sheet** 32 (May, 2010): 3-4.

BiMonthly Review of Law Books. Edited by Edward J. Bander and Michael Rustad. Concord, MA.

Bintliff, Barbara A. "Introducing CD-ROMs into a Law Library: Administrative Issues and Concerns." **Law Library Journal** 84 (Fall 1992): 725-740.

Blackman, Josh. "Fighting Back Against Junk E-Mail." **Law Office Computing** 7 (Oct./Nov., 1997): 16, 24.

Bohls, Dawn. "Book Review: Legal Information Buyer's Guide & Reference Manual, 2009 by Kendall Svengalis (N. Stonington, CT: Rhode Island LawPress, 2009," **The CRIV Sheet** (May, 2010): 8 [reprinted from **Law Library Lights** (vol. 53, # 1, Fall, 2009].

Brink, Robert J. "New Attitude Toward Cyberspace, 'Cyberians' Needed." **Massachusetts Lawyers Weekly** 27 (Sept. 21, 1998): B4, B10.

Brown, Cynthia L. "Online Legal Research Billing Policies." **Legal Information Alert** 24 (January, 2005): 1, 4, 6, 15.

Browne, Kelly. "Does the Law Governing Public Access to Judicial Opinions Mandate Citation Reform? It Depends." **Legal Reference Services Quarterly** 17, Nos. 1/2 (1999): 75-144.

Busby, Lorraine. "Teaching Vendor Relations in the LIS Curriculum." **The CRIV Sheet** 29 (February 2007): 3-4.

Cordova, Dan. "Unbundling Online Legal Materials: One State Government Law Library Perspective," **The CRIV Sheet** 36 (February 2014): 3-5..

Coopee, Todd. "How to Climb the Search Engine Rankings." **Infoworld** (June 12, 2000): 61, 64.

Dabirashtiani, Sima. "Changing Views of the Internet—Survey of Law Librarians: Have You Been Stuck in an Information-Superhighway Traffic Jam?" **Trends in Law Library Management and Technology**, 11, No. 2 (June, 2000): 1-4.

Dabny, Dan. "Another Response to Taylor's Comparison of KeyCite and Shepard's." **Law Library Journal** 92, No. 3 (Summer, 2000): 381-385.

D'Agostino, Clare; Loretta F. Orndorff; Scott B. Schwartz; and Connie Smith. "Program H-1: Getting to Yes For Your Library: Negotiating Vendor Contracts in Your Favor." **The CRIV Sheet** 34 (November, 2011): 6.

DeWitt, Adrienne. "Happy Birthday, Treatise! A celebration of longevity comparing Moore's Federal Practice and Procedure with Wright and Miller's Federal Practice and Procedure. **AALL Spectrum** 18, No. 4 (December 2013): 19-20.

DiFelice, Beth. Boston 2004—Educational Program Summaries: Program B-2: CRIV Hot Topic: Trends in Legal Publishing [speaker: David Jastrow, Simba Information, Inc.]." **The CRIV Sheet** 27 (November, 2004): 3-4.

Eaton, Amy. "Interview with Darrell Huntsman, Vice President of New Products at LexisNexis, regarding the Launch of Lexis for Microsoft Office," **The CRIV Sheet** 32 (May, 2010): 5.

Finet, Scott. "On the Road to the Emerald City: Reducing the Cost of Living in the New Legal Information Landscape." **Legal Reference Services Quarterly** 17, Nos. 1/2 (1999): 7-12.

Gaylord, Tom. Boston 2004—Educational Program Summaries: Program F-2: Let's Make a Deal: Strategies to Avoid Paying List Price [speakers: Linda Will, Greg Lambert and Diane Frake]." **The CRIV Sheet** 27 (November, 2004): 3-4.

Gerken, Joe. "The Invention of Hein Online: The Story of Haein's dramatic transformation in response to the coming of the electronic age." **AALL Spectrum** 18, No. 4 (February 2014): 17-20, 31.

Giangrande, Mark. "Testing Google Scholar for Legal Research," **Law Librarian Blog**, Nov. 18, 2009 [http://lawprofessors.typepad.com/law_librarian_blog/2009/11/testing-google-scholar-for-legal-research.html].

Ginsborg, Michael. "Point / Counterpoint: Ending our conflicts of interest to protect consumers of legal publication," **AALL Spectrum** 15, No. 4 (February, 2011): 28, 30.

Gordon, Stacey L. "Football and Internet Research." **Legal Information Alert** 23 (October, 2004): 1, 3-4, 6, 14.

Gordon, Stacey L. "Update XX: What's New on LexisNexis, Westlaw, Loislaw, and Versuslaw." **Legal Information Alert** 22 (Nov./Dec., 2003): 1, 3-4, 6-10.

Gordon, Stacey L. "Update XXI: What's New on LexisNexis, Westlaw, Loislaw, and Versuslaw." **Legal Information Alert** 22 (Nov./Dec., 2004): 1, 3-6, 14-15.

Gordon-Brown, Andrew. "Industry update: US legal publishing industry: A growth story?" London: JPMorgan, 2002.

Graesser, Christine L.; Lesley Ellen Harris; Katherine Lowry; Tracy L. Thompson-Przylucki. "Program G-4: Anatomy of a License Agreement," **The CRIV Sheet** 34 (November, 2011): 7-8.

Graesser, Chris. "Are We Branded? Examining the Nature of Librarians' Relationships with Publishers." **AALL Spectrum** [CRIV Notes] 5, No. 2 (October, 2000): 22.

Griffith, Cary. "On the Edge of Chaos: Michael Wilens, West Group's New Chief Technology Officer." **Law Office Computing** 7 (Oct./Nov., 1997): 44-49.

Griffith, Cary. "Selecting the Right Tools for Your Firm." **Law Office Computing** 8 (April/May, 1998): 54-58.

Gullen, Ismael. "YBP Library Services: A Tour." **The CRIV Sheet** 27 (November, 2004): 10-12.

Halvorsen, T.R. "Evaluating an Online Information Service for Management: A Fastcase Review," **LLRX.com**™, August 1, 2002. [http://www.llrx.com/features/fastcase.htm]

Halvorson, T.R. "Eastlaw: A View Through the Southern California Online Users Group Rating Scale Lenses," **LLRX.com** ™, January 2, 2001. [http://www.llrx.com/features/eastlaw.htm]

Halvorson, T.R. "The LOIS Law Library: A View Through the Southern California Online Users Group Rating Scale Lenses," **LLRX.com** ™, March 1, 1999. [http://www.llrx.com/features/lois2.htm]

Halvorson, T.R. "National Law Library: A View Through the Southern California Online Users Group Rating Scale Lenses," **LLRX.com** ™, May 1, 2000. [http://www.llrx.com/features/nll.htm]

Halvorson, T.R. "Quicklaw America: A View Through the Southern California Online Users Group Rating Scale Lenses," **LLRX.com** ™, October 2, 2000. [http://www.llrx.com/features/quicklaw.htm]

Halvorson, T.R. "VersusLaw's V.: A View Through the Southern California Online Users Group Rating Scale Lenses," **LLRX.com** ™, March 15, 1999. [http://www.llrx.com/features/v.htm]

Halvorson, T.R. "What's Standing in Jurisline's Road: Barriers Erected by Lexis or Its Own Necessary Effort and Expense," **LLRX.com** ™, April 17, 2000. [http://www.llrx.com/features/jurisline7.htm]

Hane, Paula J. "Thomson Reuters Launches WestlawNext—The Next Chapter in Legal Research," **Information Today, Inc.**, Feb. 4, 2010 [http://newsbreaks.infotoday.com/NewsBreaks/Thomson-Reuters-Launches-WestlawNextThe-Next-Chapter-in-Legal-Research-60975.asp].

Hamburger, Tom and Sharon Schmickle, "High stakes and hot competition: In face of change, West Publishing fights to maintain its lead in legal publishing," **Star Tribune** [Minneapolis Edition], March 6, 1995, pp. 1A, 6A-8A.

Harrington, Ryan. "Review: WestlawNext," **AALL Spectrum Blog**, April 23, 2010 [http://aallspectrum.wordpress.com/2010/04/23/review-westlaw-next/].

Hart, Edward T. "MACRIV: A State CRIV for Massachusetts." **The CRIV Sheet** 26 (February, 2004): 6-7.

Heroy, Donna Tuke. "Shepard's Exclusive to Lexis-Nexis." **Legal Information Alert**18 (January, 1999): 6-7.

Heroy, Donna Tuke. "E-mail: Is it still serving you?." **Legal Information Alert** 23 (March, 2004): 8.

Heroy, Donna Tuke. "Legal Research on the Brink of the Millennium." **Research Adviser** 17 (October, 1999): 1-3, 7.

Heroy, Donna Tuke. "Meet KeyCite: West's New Online Citator." **Research Advisor** 11 (September/October, 1997): 1-3.

Heroy, Donna Tuke. "Shepard's Exclusive to Lexis-Nexis." **Legal Information Alert**18 (January, 1999): 6-7.

Heroy, Donna Tuke. "Ten-UP: 20 Innovations and Services We n Didn't Know About Ten Years Ago." **Legal Information Alert** 23 (September, 2004): 1, 3-4, 6, 14-15.

Hoffman, John. "Wielding the Budget Axe Without Winging Yourself." **AALL Spectrum** 5, No. 3 (November, 2000): 16-17, 26.

Houdek, Frank. "Best Practices [CCH Site Viisit]," **AALL Spectrum** [CRIV Notes] 4 (July, 2000): 18.

Houdek, Frank. "Dealing with the New World of Legal Publishing: How AALL Can Help: CRIV Online," **AALL Spectrum** 3 (July, 1999): 21.

Houdek, Frank. "Dealing with the New World of Legal Publishing: How AALL Can Help: Publisher Log Keeps Inquiries On Track," **AALL Spectrum** 3 (July, 1999): 21.

Houdek, Frank. "Dealing with the New World of Legal Publishing: How AALL Can Help: What the CRIV Does For You," **AALL Spectrum** 3 (July, 1999): 21.

Humphries, LaJean. "Cheaper Online? Our firm library's gradual move to all electronic." **AALL Spectrum** 17, No. 5 (March 2013): 17-19.

Jensen, Mary Brandt. "CD-ROM Licenses: What's in the Fine Or Nonexistent Print May Surprise You." **The CRIV Sheet** 15 (March, 1993). [Reprinted from the March, 1991 CD-ROM Professional]

Joergensen, John P. "Are Non-Profit Internet Publishers the Future of Legal Information?" **Legal Information Services Quarterly** 17, Nos. 1/2 (1999): 33-42.

Joergensen, John P. "West Library Maintenance Agreements: Deal or No Deal? Are LMAs really in the best interest of law librarians," **AALL Spectrum** 15 (March, 2011): 13, 17.

Johnson, Kenneth E. and Richard J. Krzyminski. "1999 Top 50 Legal Research Web Sites." **Law Office Computing** 9 (April/ May, 1999): 58-66.

Keefe, Thomas. Change at LexisNexis Flies Under the Radar Screen. **The CRIV Sheet** 29 (February 2007): 6-7.

Keefe, Thomas R. "ResultsPlus: The Perfect Marriage Between Technology and Tradition." **Legal Information Alert** 24 (March, 2004): 1 3-4, 6.

Kodner, Ross L. "The Internet is Not Just the Web: Legal Technology Listservs Visited." **Law Practice Management** (October, 1997): 44-49.

Krikorian, Rosanne. "CCH Account Management." **AALL Spectrum** [CRIV Notes] 4 (July, 2000): 16-17.

Krikorian, Rosanne and Brendan Starkey. "CRIV Tool — Dealing With Telemarketers." **The CRIV Sheet** (February, 1999): 9.

Kristakis, Michele. "View from the Booth," **The CRIV Sheet** 32 (May, 2010): 7.

Kuhlmann, Kristina. "Program Report: Legal Periodicals: Past and Future." **The CRIV Sheet** 20 (November, 1997): 9-10.

Laska, Meghan S. "Electronic Research Now Dominant: Time and Cost Benefits Help Technology Overtake Books As The Primary Research Tool in Massachusetts." **Massachusetts Lawyers Weekly**, Sept. 21, 1998: B1, B12-13.

Lemann, Catherine. "West's Library Maintenance Agreement." **The CRIV Sheet** 29 (May 2007).

Leiserson, Anna Belle. "The Thomson Corporation: The Birth of a Law Book Megapublisher." **The CRIV Sheet** 14 (November, 1991): 12-13.

Leiter, Richard A. "Backwards Into Future." **Legal Information Alert** 25 (October 2006): 8-9.

Leiter, Richard A. "The Internet Effect." **Legal Information Alert** 18 (February, 1999): 8, 19.

Leiter, Richard A. "Lexis-Nexis Courts End Users." **Legal Information Alert** 18 (March, 1999): 7, 14.

Leiter, Richard A. "The New Shepard's." **Legal Information Alert** 18 (July/August, 1999): 8-9.

Leiter, Richard A. "News from the Land O' Lakes." **Legal Information Alert** 18 (May, 1999): 6-7, 14.

Leiter, Richard A. "The Sky Is Falling: Two Short Tales to Ruin Your Day." **Legal Information Alert** 25 (June 2006): 8-9.

Lenz, Connie. "Enhancing Collection Development Through Reference Participation." **The CRIV Sheet** 26 (February, 2004): 5-6.

Lileks, James. "Backfence: Outsourcing? Try outsourcing this! " **Star Tribune** [Minneapolis Edition], January 20, 2004.

Lomio, Paul. Bloomberg Law, LexisNexis, Westlaw—New, Improved," **New York Times** (Jan. 25, 2010): p. 85.

Lutkenhaus, Rebecca. "Jobbers 101." **The CRIV Sheet** 23 (November, 2000): 5-6.

Lutkenhaus, Rebecca. "Publisher Profile: Anderson Publishing Company." **AALL Spectrum** [CRIV Notes] 5, No. 4 (December, 2000): 17.

Lyman, Lovisa. "Beginning Glossary of Publishing Terms for New Acquisitions/Collection Development Law Librarians." **The CRIV Sheet** 21 (February, 1999): 7-8.

Lyman, Lovisa. "Program Report: The 1997 CRIV Publishers' Open Forum." **The CRIV Sheet** 20 (November, 1997): 5-7.

McCabe, Mark J. "The Impact of Publisher Mergers on Journal Prices: An Update." **Against the Grain** 11, No. 4 (September, 1999): 58-61.

McKenzie, Elizabeth M. "Comparing KeyCite to Shepard's Online." **Legal Reference Services Quarterly** 17: 3 (1999): 85-99.

McKenzie, Elizabeth M. "New Kid on the Block: KeyCite Compared to Shepard's." **AALL Spectrum** 3 (October, 1998): 8-9, 29.

Melnick, Tedd. "Program E1: Off the Page and Beyond the Book: New Models for Buying and Selling Legal Information." **The CRIV Sheet** (November 2013): 8-9.

Miles, Kevin. "Library on a Credenza: Well-annotated deskbooks as the new center of the private law library." **AALL**

Spectrum 16 (December 2011): 17-19.

Morgan, Barbara D. and Mary O. DeSantis. "The Alert 50: The Most Useful Reference Sources for Law Librarians." **Legal Information Alert** 18 (April, 1999): 1 (5).

Morris, Jane W. "A Response to Taylor's Comparison of Shepard's and KeyCite." **Law Library Journal** 92, No. 2 (Spring, 2000): 143-157.

Moss, Lucy. "HeinOnline in the Law Firm Environment: The CRIV Sheet Interview." **The CRIV Sheet** 26 (February, 2004): 7-9.

Myers, Anne and Mike Beaird. "Aspen Organizational Structure." **The CRIV Sheet** 22, No. 3 (May, 2000): 4-5.

Neary, Mary Ann. "State Government Procurement of Electronic Legal Services." **Legal Reference Services Quarterly** 17, Nos. 1/2 (1999): 43-58.

O'Connor, Gayle. "LOIS and Versuslaw: Two Good Products on the Web." **Legal Information Alert** XVI, No. 8 (September, 1997): 1-2, 4.

O'Grady, Jean P.; Denise A. Pugh; Lisa A. Spar; and Victoria J. Szymczak. "Program K-6: The New Generation of Legal Research Databases: Eighteen Months Later," **The CRIV Sheet** 34 (November 2011): 8-10.

Pacifici, Sabrina I. "lexisONE: The New Internet Resource for Small Firm Attorneys and Solos," **LLRX.com** ™, July 6, 2000. [http://www.llrx.com/extras /lexisone.htm]

Parks, Ann. "Bloomberg Law releases new computer tool to provide in-depth legal," **The Daily Record** (Baltimore) [on BNET], March 25, 2005 [http://findarticles.com/p/articles/mi_qn4183/is_20050325/ai_n13470343/].

Pennington, Catherine. "The Best of Times, The Worst of Times: A CD-ROM Update." **The CRIV Sheet** 16 (May, 1994) 12-14.

"Principles for Licensing Electronic Resources, Final Draft, July 15, 1997." **AALL Spectrum** 2 (November, 1997): 16-17.

Rees, Warren. "A New Legal Citation Manual: What Will It Mean for Law Librarians?" **AALL Spectrum** 5, No. 1 (September, 2000): 8.

Reinke, Janet. "The Informed Law Librarian." **Legal Information Alert** 18 (March, 1999): 1-5, 14

Reinke, Janet. "West's Key Cite: What Is It and Will It Really Be Used?" **The CRIV Sheet** 20 (November, 1997): 7-8.

Rich, Rebecca. "Program A7: It's All About the Money: Rethinking the Way We Teach Cost-Effective Legal Research." **The CRIV Sheet** (November 2013): 5-7.

Richards, Rob. "The Political Economy of Legal Information: The New Landscape: A Legal Publisher's List: Librarians Cooperate to Discern the Corporate Affiliations of U.S. Legal Publishers." **Legal Reference Services Quarterly** 17, Nos. 1/2 (1999): 23-31.

Richards, Robert. "The Shape of Legal Publishing Today." **The CRIV Sheet** 20 (November, 1997): 11-12.

Rodney, Marcia J. "Collection Development: Decision-Making Authority in the For-Profit Culture," **Trends in Law Library Management and Technology** 10: 2 (June, 1999): 4-8.

Sadow, Sandy. "Collection Development: Electronic Archives of Law Reviews: An Idea on the Horizon." **Technical Services Law Librarian** 24: 3 (March, 1999): 13.

Schwartz, April. "Rothman, Hein, and AALL: A Short History of a Long-Standing Publishing Relationship." **AALL Spectrum** 5, No. 2 (October, 2000): 1, 30.

Seeger, Paula. "Finding Hope in the Funding Shortfalls." **AALL Spectrum** 12, No. 6 (April 2008): 22-25.

Shapiro, Fred R. "KeyCite and Shepard's—Coverage and Currency of Citations To Recent Cases: A Comparative Study." **Legal Information Alert** XVII, No. 4 (April, 1998): 1-3, 14.

Shapiro, Fred R. "The Most-Cited Law Reviews: Another Tool for Law Library Collection Development." **Legal Information Alert** 22 (April., 2003): 1, 3-4, 6.

Shapiro, Fred B. "The Most Cited Legal Books: A New Tool for Law Library Collection Development." **Legal Information Alert** 18 (September, 1999): 1-6.

"Shepard's Response to the Shapiro Comparative Study of Shepard's and KeyCite." **Legal Information Alert** XVII, No. 4 (April, 1998): 4-5, 14.

Snyder, Fritz. Update XV: "What's New on Lexis and Westlaw." **Legal Information Alert** 17 (November/December, 1998): 1-4, 18.

Snyder, Fritz and Stacey Gordon. "Update XVII: What's New on LEXIS, Westlaw, Loislaw, and VersusLaw." **Legal Information Alert** 19 (November/December, 2000): 1-5,6.

Solomon, Lisa. "WestlawNext Preview: Product and Pricing," **Legal Research & Writing Pro**, Jan. 27, 2010 [http://legalresearchandwritingpro.com/blog/2010/01/27/westlawnext-preview-product-and-pricing/].

Stephens, Joe K. "Cancellations Librarian." **AALL Spectrum** 2 (November, 1997): 32.

Stephens, Joe. "The Political Economy of Legal Information: The New Landscape: The Merger: What Will It Cost Law Libraries?" **Legal Reference Services Quarterly** 17, Nos. 1/2 (1999): 13-21.

Sullivan, Kathie J. "Budget and Acquisition Selection Tools for the Private Law Library: CAPLL Recommendations for PLL Vital Reading [Consumer Advisory for Private Law Librarians, bibliography],” **The CRIV Shee**t 21: (February, 1999): 9-11.

Svengalis, Kendall F. “Cost -Effective Acquisitions: An Overview,” in **The Spirit of Law Librarianship**, ed. Roy M. Mersky and Richard A. Leiter, 197-217. Littleton, CO: Fred B. Rothman & Co., 1991.

Svengalis, Kendall F. “Cutting Deals: Controlling Costs with Vendors and Dealers,” in **Managing the Private Law Library 1992: Trends, Ideas, and Solutions**, 133-145. New York: Practising Law Institute, 1992.

Svengalis, Kendall F. “Legal Publishing on the Eve of the Millennium.” **AALL Spectrum** 3 (July,1999): 19, 22.

Svengalis, Kendall F. “Legal Publishing 2000: An Interview with Kendall F. Svengalis.” **Legal Information Alert** 19, No. 4 (April, 2000): 1-4.

Svengalis, Kendall F. “Matthew Bender and Write-for-Order Revisited.” **The CRIV Sheet** 11 (June, 1989): 7-8.

Svengalis, Kendall F. “Matthew Bender Hosts ‘No Holds Barred’ Law Librarian Forum.” **The CRIV Sheet** 15 (June, 1993): 8-10.

Svengalis, Kendall F. “Matthew Bender Prices Increase 117% Between 1987 and 1991.” **The CRIV Sheet** 15 (November, 1992): 12-13.

Svengalis, Kendall F. “Shepard’s Strikes Again: Or, Buried Under the Financial Weight of Recompiled Citators.” **The CRIV Sheet** 14 (November, 1991): 10-11.

Tang, Lorna. “Vendor Profiles: Carswell.” **The CRIV Sheet** (May, 2003): 6-7.

Taylor, William L. “Comparing KeyCite and Shepard’s for Completeness, Currency, and Accuracy.” **Law Library Journal** 92, No. 2 (Spring, 2000): 127-

Thomson, Randy. “Program Report: Coping With Vendor Change.” **The CRIV Sheet** 20 (November, 1997): 10-11.

Tung, Genevieve Blake. “Academic Law Libraries and the Crisis in Legal Education.” **Law Library Journal** 105, No. 3 (Summer, 2013): 275-303.

Vaughan, Richard. “Using Technology (and Other Tricks) to Manage Legal Publishers.” **AALL Spectrum** 5, No. 1 (September, 2000): 34.

Wendt, Nina. “Looking at Legal Publishing: An Interview with Kendall F. Svengalis.” **Legal Information Alert** 17 (July/ August, 1998): 1-2. 4-5.

Wheeler, Ronald E. “Does WestlawNext Really Change Everything?” **Law Library Journal** 103, No. 3 (Summer, 2011): 359-377.

Whiteman, Michael. “Book Burning in the Twenty-First Century: ABA Standard 606 and the Future of Academic Law Libraries as the Smoke Clears.” **Law Library Journal** 106, No. 1 (Winter. 2014): 11-46.

Will, Linda and Jim Pancero. “Defending the Realm: Buying Skills for Law Librarians.” **Legal Information Alert** 27 (July/ August, 1998): 1, 4, 6, 14.

Will, Linda. “Diary of a Mad Cybrarian Or . . . Two Weeks on the Bleeding Edge.” **Legal Information Alert** 18 (February, 1999): 1-5, 18

Will, Linda. “Reflections of a Mad Cybrarian: The State of Our Profession.” **Legal Information Alert** 26 (January 2007): 1, 4, 6.

Will, Linda. “Stormy Weather: More Products, Higher Prices.” **Legal Information Alert** 26 (November/December 2007): 1, 3-4.

Yoder, Susan M. “The Rise of the Small: The Effects of Industry Consolidation on Small Legal Publishers.” **Legal Reference Services Quarterly** 17, Nos. 1/2 (1999): 59-74.

Web Sites

AALL Tools for Success in Today’s Economy: http://aallnet.pbwiki.com/

CRIVPage: http://www.aallnet.org/committee/criv/

CRIV Sheet: http://www.aallnet.org/committee/criv/news/criv-sheet.htm
Contains text of issues from May, 1999-date.

Index

A

Acquisitions toolbox 133-140
Administrative law 180-187
Admiralty and maritime law 187-190
Advertising law 190-191
Agency law 192
Alabama 637-639
Alaska 639-641
American Digest System 81-83
American Jurisprudence 2d 94-96
American Law Reports 77-78
Antitrust law 192-202
Appellate court reports, buying 26-27
Appellate practice 202-209
Arbitration and Alternative Dispute Resolution 209-216
Arizona 641-642
Arkansas 623-625
Arts, entertainment and sports law 216-224
Automobile law and practice 225-229

B

Banking and finance law 230-240
Bankruptcy law 240-245
Bibliography 867-873
Bloomberg BNA 728-729
Buying Law-Related CD-ROMs 141-148
Bloomberg Law 154-155

C

California 644-647
CALR (Computer-assisted legal research) 151-167
CaseClerk.com 166
Casemaker 163
CD-ROM 141-148
Civil rights 245-250
Class actions 250-253
Colorado 647-649
Commercial law 253-264
Computer-assisted legal research 151-167
Computer law 264-270
Connecticut 649-652
Constitutional law 270-281
Construction law 287-293
Contract law 287-293
Copyright law 293-296
Core collection 25-28
Corporations 296-308
Corpus Juris Secundum (C.J.S.) 91-92
Cost-saving tips 863-866
Criminal law 308-327

D

Delaware 652-653
Disabilities law 327-330
District of Columbia 653-655

E

Education law 370-381
Elder law 337-345
Environmental law 345-358
Equity jurisprudence 358-359
Evaluating legal materials 33-35
Evidence 359-369

F

Family law 370-381
Fastcase 163-164
Federal practice and procedure 381-390
Federal Register 61-64
Federal regulations 61-64
Federal statutes 57-60
Fixed-rate online contracts 153-154
Florida 655-657

G

Gambling law 390-394
Georgia 657-659
Guide to Fair Business Practices For Legal Publishers 798-805
Google Scholar 167

H

Hawaii 659-661
Health and hospital law 394-405
HeinOnline 104
HyperLaw 10-12

I

Idaho 661-662
Illinois 662-665
Immigration law 405-411
IndexMaster 179-180
Indian law 411-415
Indiana 665-667
Insurance law 415-423
Iowa 667-669

J

Judges, Courts and judicial conduct 423-429
Juries and jury instructions 430-434

K

Kansas 669-670
Kentucky 670-672
KeyCite 89-91, 161

L

Labor and employment law 434-456
Leading legal publishers 725-748
Legal forms 456-460
Legal profession 460-494
Legal publishers and distributors 749-771
Legal publishing, history of 7-17
LexisNexis 155-157
Loislaw.com 164-165
Looseleaf services 99-100, 819-823
Louisiana 672-673

M

Maine 674-675
Maryland 675-677
Massachusetts 677-680
Medical jurisprudence 494-501
Michigan 680-682
Military Law and National Security 501-512
Minnesota 682-684
Mississippi 684-686

Missouri 686-687
Montana 688-689
Municipal Corporations 512-516
Municipal ordinances 65-67

N

National legal newspapers 107
Natural Resources and Energy law 517-521
Nebraska 689-691
Nevada 691-692
New Hampshire 693-694
New Jersey 694-696
New Mexico 696-698
New York 698-701
Nonprofit corporations 521-524
North Carolina 701-703
North Dakota 703-704

O

Official state reporters 69-70
Ohio 704-706
Oklahoma 706-708
Oregon 708-710

P

Partnership Law 524-525
Patents, trademarks and Intellectual property 525-540
Pennsylvania 710-712
Products liability 540-542
Public utilities 542-546

R

Real property 546-556
Reed Elsevier 9-10, 12-13, 15-16
Reference titles 111-132
Regional digests 83-84
Religion and the law 556-559
Restatements of the Law 5559-562
Rhode Island 712-714

S

Search engines 142
Securities law 562-569
Shepard's Citations 87-91
Social Security law 570-572
South Carolina 714-716
South Dakota 7716-717
Specialized digests 84-85
State administrative regulations 64
State and Federal court rules 27
State legal encyclopedias 96-97
State practice books 27
State statutes 53-55
Statutory construction 572-575
Supplementation costs 37-43

T

Taxation 575-585
Telecommunications law 585-588
Tennessee 717-719
Texas 7719-721
TheLaw.net 166
Tort law 588-599
Transactional pricing 156
Trial practice 599-619
Trusts and estates 619-628

U

United States Code 57-60
Unsolicited shipments 44-45
Used law books 47-50
Used lawbook dealers 47-50. 771
Utah 721-723

V

Vermont 723-724
Versuslaw 165-166, 745
Virginia 724-726

W

Washington 727-729
West 3-9, 13-19, 745-747
West off-print reporters 70
West regional reporters 70
West Virginia 729-730
Westlaw 158-162
Wisconsin 730-732
Wolters Kluwer 10, 12-15, 747-748
Workers compensation law 628-631
Wyoming 719-720

Z

Zoning and planning law 631-635

About the Author

Kendall F. Svengalis is President of New England LawPress and retired Adjunct Professor of Library and Information Studies at the University of Rhode Island where he taught law librarianship. Born in Gary, Indiana in 1947, he received his B.A. in English literature (1970) and M.A. in American history (1973) from Purdue University. In 1975, he received an M.L.S. from the University of Rhode Island's Graduate School of Library and Information Studies. He has done additional work in American history at Brown University. In 1976, he joined the staff of the Rhode Island State Law Library as Assistant Law Librarian. In 1982, he was appointed State Law Librarian by a unanimous decision of the Rhode Island Supreme Court. During his twenty-year tenure, he ushered in an unprecedented era of growth and expansion in state law library services, marked by the introduction of computer technology to library operations and services, the dramatic growth in library collections, the professionalization of library staff, and the modernization of library facilities. He also succeeded in bringing the state's county law libraries under centralized operational and budgetary control and brought an end to the role of patronage in the hiring of library staff. The innovative techniques he pioneered in bringing law library costs under control have served as a model for law libraries across the country.

A past president of the Law Librarians of New England and the New England Law Library Consortium, he has also served on the Board of Directors of the State, Court and County Law Libraries Special Interest Section of the American Association of Law Libraries (AALL). From 1988 to 1994, he was editor of The CRIV Sheet, the Newsletter of AALL's Committee on Relations with Information Vendors, where he was able to bring his innovative ideas regarding cost-effective law library acquisitions to a national audience. In 1993, these efforts were recognized by the State, Court and County Special Interest Section of AALL which selected him as the first recipient of the Connie Bolden Significant Publications Award.

In March, 1996, one month after the announcement of the Thomson Corporation's purchase of the West Publishing Company, the first edition of his **Legal Information Buyer's Guide & Reference Manual** was published by Rhode Island LawPress, the company Ken founded in 1995. This resulted in his being retained as an expert witness by the Justice Department in its review of the proposed merger and his book being used as a part of the Justice Department's merger analysis. In 1998, the **Legal Information Buyer's Guide and Reference Manual**, 1997-98 received the Joseph L. Andrews Bibliographical Award, the highest honor bestowed by the American Association of Law Libraries on works of legal bibliography. In 1999, Ken again received the Connie E. Bolden Significant Publications Award from the State, Court, and County Law Libraries Special Interest Section of AALL for publishing three successive editions of the **Legal Information Buyer's Guide** and for aiding "law librarians nationwide in their pursuit of a cost effective and efficient avenue to collection development." Since that time, the Legal Information Buyer's Guide & Reference Manual has received numerous accolades from the legal and law library communities and has become a standard reference work and acquisitions tool in law libraries and law firms across the country.

Ken has written numerous articles on the subject of cost-effective acquisitions and the legal publishing industry for a variety of legal and law library publications and has spoken before both national and regional law librarian associations. Most recently, he has given presentations on cost-effective acquisitions to federal court librarians under the auspices of the Administrative Office of the United States Courts and spoken on the subject of the legal publishing industry at investment conferences organized by JPMorgan. He has been honored by inclusion in numerous editions of Who's Who in America and Who's Who in American Law. In 2006, he published **Gary Indiana: A Centennial Celebration**, in commemoration of the 100th annivesary of his hometown.

Ken and his wife Ellen reside in the rolling hills of eastern Connecticut and spend their leisure time as a vocal and instrumental duo performing Swedish folk music at Swedish and Scandinavian folk festivals in Connecticut, Rhode Island, New Jersey and New York. Ken is also President of the Rhode Island Swedish Heritage Association, and Vice-President of the Jussi Björling Society-USA, which honors the career and legacy of the 20th century's greatest operatic tenor.